The College Blue Book®

25th Edition

Narrative Descriptions

The College Blue Book®

25th Edition

Narrative Descriptions

Macmillan Library Reference USA
Simon & Schuster Macmillan
New York

Prentice Hall International
London   Mexico City   New Delhi
Singapore   Sydney   Toronto

Macmillan Library Reference USA
Simon & Schuster Macmillan
866 Third Avenue, New York, N.Y. 10022

ISSN: 1082-7064
ISBN: 0-02-895026-7 (Volume 1)
ISBN: 0-02-895147-6 (5-volume set)

Printed in the United States of America

printing number

2 3 4 5 6 7 8 9 10

The paper meets the minimum requirements of ANSI/NISO Z39.48-1992
(Permanence of Paper).

CONTENTS

The College Blue Book® 25th Edition

Narrative Descriptions

Almost 3,000 colleges in the United States and Canada are fully described. Procedures are given for filing admission applications. Campus facilities and costs are described. A map of each state and province is included.

Tabular Data

Colleges are listed alphabetically by state or province. Information about costs, accreditation, enrollment figures, faculty, and names of the chief administrative officer or registrar are given for each school.

Degrees Offered by College and Subject

In Part I, under the name of each college listed alphabetically by state or province, appears a list of the subject areas for which degrees are offered. Part II includes an alphabetical listing of subject areas for which degrees are granted by one or more institutions of higher education.

PREFACE

The College Blue Book® has been a standard, professional reference on higher education since it was first published in 1923. New features have been added during the intervening years to keep pace with the changing needs for information about our educational facilities. The information, especially in the areas of tuition, room and board, enrollments, library holdings, is constantly changing. It is difficult to maintain up-to-date figures in these areas, especially since our data is gathered early in the year of publication. Many schools change tuition and related costs in May and later months when our books are already on the printing presses. We therefore urge our readers to check directly with the schools for the most current cost information.

The staff of *The College Blue Book®* wishes to express its thanks to the college and university officials for the assistance and cooperation necessary to collect and prepare the data for this publication. These officials have requests for data from many sources and we sincerely appreciate the time and effort they put into completing our questionnaires. We are always open to suggestions and recommendations for improvement of *The College Blue Book®* from our readers and from the educational professions.

INTRODUCTION

The decision to continue education beyond high school years, the selection of a collegiate institution, and the area of study to be pursued are some of the essential experiences necessary for students to determine their futures. Alternatives of choice institutions, work selection, job opportunities, professional training, or even discontinuing any further education are all selective decisions open to the students

Nearly all students today have opportunities to continue education beyond high school. There are more schools accepting wider ranges of student ability and interest than ever before. This means more effort, more planning, and more personal study in making the college choice.

Self Appraisal

The best place to begin is with oneself. An appraisal with objective, honest answers is necessary. What are the personal potentials as a student? Where has the best performance been? What are the probabilities for improvement? What are the reasons for really wanting to go to college; is it for intellectual development, vocational preparation, or simply to satisfy a desire for status? What are the personal ideas of college? What is expected from the college experience? Have career plans been made? Where are the academic abilities? What subjects are preferred? What is the quality of performance in the preferred areas of study? What is the overall grade average? What is the class rank in high school? In what subject areas is there the greatest interest? What is the quality of work in these areas? Are interests and performance generally consistent? Are the expressed and recorded interests truly and accurately reflecting the inward wishes? What was liked best about the high school experience. Has the college preparatory program been followed in high school? What were the social and cultural experiences during high school years

that were most meaningful? What was considered, if anything, to be lacking?

Well-thought-out answers to these and similar questions are helpful. Discussions of such topics with counselors, parents, and teachers increases the probability of success in college selection, attendance, and completion.

The counselor today is an extremely valued resource person available to assist the student. When an effective working team of counselor-student-parent actually exists, the probabilities for the student making selective choices that prove to be the "right" ones are unquestionably the greatest. The better the student and the counselor know one another, the more effective the guidance and counseling program will be. For this to occur, the opportunity for face-to-face student-counselor discussion needs to start in the latter elementary school years and continue through high school and college.

College Appraisals

Research is continuing in the areas of college admissions and student success. The identification and understanding of causes of success and failure need professional study. However, one thing is apparent: the more careful the preparations and planning by the student, the better the chances of college admission and success.

Systemized planning should begin early. The more self-understanding and knowledge about available colleges one has, the better one can plan with corresponding success. Certainly, early in the high school career, students should be reviewing detailed information on colleges and universities with the counselor, noting academic requirements such as scholastic performance, course requirements, costs and other particular qualities of individual collegiate institutions. There is no single one-and-only college for the student. Colleges have personalities just as the students do. There are always several colleges with academic and social climates compatible and acceptable to each student.

Entrance requirements, courses available, costs, size of student body, academic pressure, special programs, geographical location, and specialty schools are some of the considerations of every student in appraising available colleges.

The College Blue Book® is dedicated to providing detailed information regarding collegiate institutions throughout the United States. Students and counselors should browse through *The College Blue Book*® and become familiar with the colleges of our country and neighboring Canada. As interest sharpens and narrows, a more selective and in-depth study of institutions should be made.

Where feasible, students should plan visits to college campuses. Campus visiting may begin during the summer between the sophomore and junior years of high school. The best time to be on a college campus, however, is during the regular term with a carefully planned visit in the spring semester of the junior year. Preparatory plans should be made with the high school counselor, reviewing discussions of earlier personal conferences. Advance arrangements should be made with admission officers of the colleges the student expects to visit. The admission officer's name and telephone number will be found in most instances in *The College Blue Book*® volume entitled *Tabular Data*. The admissions officer in many cases will want to know whether the student has actually applied for admission and probably the areas the student may plan to major in or other special interests the student has in the particular institution. The student should have prepared a summary of personal data. If possible, high school students should also talk to students of the colleges they wish to attend.

The growth of community colleges has opened up another avenue for students, especially those of limited finances or those who have not decided on their ultimate educational goals. Students will find many of these community colleges offer an excellent opportunity to gain a solid college background. Then one can choose a four-year institution to complete an undergraduate degree.

Any regular high school graduate can find a school that will accept him. Many students need to be encouraged to consider the smaller, private and public colleges of good standing.

Students entering professional training such as engineering or law might consider small schools that have cooperative programs with major universities. A knowledgeable student, through planning and guidance, can avoid unnecessary disappointment. A college career can be quite beneficial to the student who spends three to four years on a small campus and one, two, or three additional years of graduate work on another, larger campus.

xii

Costs

Costs are continuing to rise. Tuition charges as listed herein should be only be used as a guide. It would be wise to check with the institution of interest to be sure of having the most up-to-date information available.

Should the need for financial aid be a factor in selecting a college, a college-bound student should be aware that the best single source of financial assistance and information is the financial aid officer or admission director at the college. It is most important for the student to contact the finance office as early as possible during the student's senior year in high school. A principal source of financial assistance is the major federal undergraduate aid programs. Applications can be obtained from the college. Most colleges and universities also offer financial assistance in several forms including academic and general scholarships, grants-in-aid, student loans, and part-time work. For more information, see the companion volume to *The College Blue Book*®: *Scholarships, Fellowships, Grants, and Loans*.

Two-Year Colleges

Two-year colleges, referred to as junior colleges or community colleges, both public and private, offer programs that prepare students for technical and semiprofessional careers in business and industrial fields, and for transfer to senior colleges. There are hundreds of two-year colleges providing comprehensive programs meeting the lower division requirements of virtually all four-year colleges and universities.

There are decided advantages for some students to enroll in a two-year college. Some of these are: less cost, home residence, availability of highly specialized programs, opportunity for the student to mature, a smaller student body, and generally a closer relationship to the faculty. The development of two-year colleges across the nation is one of the most vital forces in education today. The two-year college is neither an extension of high school, nor a little senior college. It has its own identity, sphere of service, and contribution to make to American education. The comprehensive community college is considered one of the best means of accommodating the demands of higher education, embracing the increasing variety of abilities of students graduating from high schools, preparing students in the technological and semiprofessional occupations, and all in an economical manner.

One very important caution need to be heeded by students enrolling in two-year colleges who are planning to continue their work through a bachelor's program. Students expecting to transfer should very carefully study the requirements of the institution they ultimately plan to attend. In conference with the junior college counselor, a careful review of the planned program should be made to be sure the contemplated courses at the junior college will satisfy the requirements of the senior institution. Students who may depart from prescribed courses stated by the senior institution or fail in any of these courses will experience interference with admission or normal progress toward the bachelor degree.

Liberal Arts Colleges

The liberal arts colleges offer four years of college and award the Bachelor of Arts and the Bachelor of Science degrees. The curriculum for the first two years is usually broad with an emphasis in the humanities, natural sciences, and cultural history of our society. The last two years may provide a concentration of specific programs such as premedicine or prelaw leading to graduate professional training.

Students considering professional training at the graduate level should keep this in mind as they plan their work at the liberal arts college. Graduate schools in some cases have strict preparatory requirements. Familiarity with these requirements can greatly assist in making the transfer to graduate level without loss of credit or time.

Specialized Institutions

Four-year institutions of technology are examples of the more specialized schools where concentration in a specialty is intensively pursued throughout the college career. Most of these institutions are quite selective in admission practice and may require more high school mathematics and science than most other schools for entrance. These programs lead to engineering degrees in many fields emphasizing technology and science. Recently there has been a broadening of the program of the first two years, but in general, such a program is not nearly as comprehensive and varied as the liberal arts college. The demand for engineers and scientists with specially developed skills creates great competition for entrance into schools of technology.

There are other specialized institutions such as conservatories of music, seminaries, medical and law schools, institutions specializing in teacher training, or schools of the fine arts, most of which require specialized preparation for entrance.

Universities

The university is generally composed of a number of degree-granting colleges and schools where both bachelor and graduate degrees are grouped under one administrative head. Bachelor degrees at the university may be earned in liberal arts of one of the professions such as engineering or the physical sciences. The university, to some extent, combines what is available at the liberal arts college with the specialized institution. Complete professional training in such areas as law, medicine, and science is available on the university campus.

As a rule, universities have much larger student bodies than colleges. In order to meet the demand, most state universities have established several campuses. Many state universities are very selective in admitting students. This is particularly true for a student who is applying for admission from out-of-state.

Entrance Examinations

There are more applicants than there is room for students on many campuses. As this demand increases, colleges and universities attempt to identify those applicants who are most likely to succeed on their campuses. A quality scholastic record has more influence on acceptance and admission than any other single factor. High school grades predict with better accuracy than any other single measurement what college grades and success will be. The more selective colleges and universities may choose students who come out highest on quantitative criteria, that is, high school scholastic averages combined with test scores. Some institutions have far more applicants than they can accept whose scholastic records and test scores are of a maximum quality. In such cases, applicants are sometimes screened and accepted on the basis of categories according to residence in the state or region, special talents, minority groups, or relationship to alumni. Such procedures are used in an attempt to influence the makeup of the enrollment.

When investigating several schools, one of the most accurate ways for evaluation of an institution is to consider test scores and the high school rank order of the students actually on campus. In many instances this is more informative than the announced admission policies.

College testing is required by many colleges and universities for entering students; some have developed their own tests and over the years have established norms for such tests. Most institutions requiring tests for entrance, however, now use either the test of the American College Testing Program (ACT) or the examinations of the College Entrance Examination Board. The College Entrance Examination Board offers the Preliminary Scholastic Aptitude Test/National Merit Scholarship Qualifying Test (PSAT/NMSQT), the Scholastic Aptitude Test I: Reasoning Test, and the SAT II: Subject Tests.

Coaching, tutoring, drill, and memorization of facts can do little to improve the scores of the standardized examinations. It is recommended that students not invest time and money in cramming in hopes of improving test scores. Students can do their best preparation in general reading, completing their school assignments well, and

arriving on the proper day of the test rested and re-
freshed.

American College Testing Program (ACT)

The ACT Assessment provided by the American College Testing Program covers four subject areas: English, mathematics, reading, and science reasoning. The
ACT test is scored on a range of 1 to 36. The ACT is
administered at various test sites in the United States
and other countries on specified dates throughout the
year. Many colleges and universities recommend that
prospective students take the examination early in the
senior year.

The tests provide estimates of the students' current
level of educational development in knowledge skill
areas often required in college work. The ACT college
testing program was founded in 1959. It is a nonprofit
educational service offering programs in testing and financial need analysis.

Scholastic Aptitude Test (SAT)

The Scholastic Aptitude Test I: Reasoning Test is an
examination to measure the verbal and mathematics
abilities students have developed both in and out of
school. The Scholastic Aptitude Test II: Subject Tests,
which some colleges require for admission or placement
purposes are one-hour tests in 17 specific subjects. Un-
like the SAT I, which measures more general abilities,
the SAT II tests measure the students' knowledge. Because of this, students should try to take a SAT II Test as
soon as possible after completion of their last course in
that subject.

The SAT I and II tests are given on certain dates
throughout the year at various test centers in the United
States and foreign countries. The combination of the
student's academic record and the SAT scores, along
with other pertinent secondary information enables admissions officers to estimate how well the student will
perform on a particular college campus. The SAT is
scored on a scale of 200 minimum to 800 maximum.

Admission Policies

One of the most important considerations in planning
is to note when colleges and universities request applications, and to be sure that the applications are complete
and forwarded during the appropriate periods. Failure in
any way in this procedure will usually automatically dis-
qualify a student from acceptance.

Counselors can provide students with freshman pro-
files on many of the institutions. Studying *The College
Blue Book®*, particularly the volume *Tabular Data*, provides a great amount of information on the kind of student bodies found on the campuses of American

institutions. There are four general classifications of admission policies. An understanding of these provides
valuable guidelines in identifying colleges for consideration.

Most selective: One hundred or so institutions probably fall within this classification. Many more students
apply who meet the announced admission requirements
than the college could possibly accept. In addition to requiring outstanding academic records, personal recommendations are required from the high school, and
identification of any special qualities of the student
should be made known. In this regard, the high school
recommendation made to the collegiate institution requires special attention. Many times, particularly at selective institutions, the high school recommendation
actually provides the necessary edge for admission. The
recommendation should be on time, carefully providing
all information called for, and, finally, be precise and detailed in citing personal qualities of the applicant.

All these qualities, however, do not guarantee acceptance. It is strongly recommended that qualified students
apply to more than one institution of this type, and that
not all applicants should be made to the same type of institution.

Very Selective: There are more than 400 colleges and
universities in this classification. Colleges having a very
selective procedure in accepting students require ACT
scores of 23 or over, or an SAT I score of 600 or more.
Students should rank in the top 10 to 12 percent of their
high school graduating classes. In addition, strong recommendations stressing particular talents and achievements are necessary. Applications should be made to
several institutions of this type.

Selective: An ACT of 20 or over, or an SAT I score of
550 or more is generally necessary. Applications for admission to selective colleges and universities are usually
called for in the spring prior to fall entry. In many situations, applications may be submitted in the fall of the senior year with final confirmation to be made after all
grades are recorded and confirmed upon graduation
from high school.

Least Selective: The fourth classification represents
those institutions that will accept students with a C average on their high school work. In certain unusual instances, and under special situations, even the selective
institutions may accept students who are in this category, particularly if the scores on the ACT are in the
mid-20's or are in excess of 500 on the SAT I. Generally, for acceptance in the less selective schools, students
should have an ACT composite score of 17 or and SAT I
score of 450.

Entrance examinations may or may not be required.
Occasionally, if examinations are required, the results
are used for student placement rather than admission.
Most high school graduates can meet the requirements
for entry and will be accepted. It should be pointed out,

however, that in some cases an institution may be liberal in acceptance but carefully screens candidates for graduation. In such an institution, a high attrition rate may occur.

Open Enrollment Policy: This is becoming more common, particularly with the public junior colleges. Many students will find this privilege most helpful in continuing their formal education beyond high school. Such a policy enables those students to have a second chance who have failed to perform up to their ability during their high school years. Enrollment and attendance may enable the student to complete a most rewarding vocational program or to later transfer and complete the Bachelor degree, which otherwise might not have been possible because of the deficiency in the high school scholastic record.

A number of colleges and universities, particularly the publicly supported ones, have adopted the open enrollment policy. In response to a feeling of community responsibility, they accept any student who has a diploma (or G.E.D. equivalency certificate) from an accredited high school. This procedure allows students from disadvantaged and minority backgrounds, who might otherwise be denied such an opportunity, to acquire a college education and prepare for a meaningful occupation. These institutions have not lowered their graduation requirements; they have, instead, created opportunities for more students to satisfy these requirements.

Do not assume the erroneous generality that the tougher it is to get into an institution, the better the quality; or the easier to enter, the poorer the school. In fact, there is research evidence available indicating that it may be wise to re-examine some of our traditional no-

tions and attitudes regarding admissions. Not all degree programs on any particular campus are equally outstanding. Every institution has its particular strengths in programs available. Certain institutions are excellent places for some kinds of students in some kinds of programs, but no institution is the one most suited for everyone.

Summary

Perhaps a summary of some of the major reasons students continue to drop from college attendance may offer assistance in college selection and more particularly in successfully completing the work for Bachelor degrees once admitted. Some of the major dropout cases are (1) lack of maturity - unable to organize and manage their own lives; simply cannot do work on their own; (2) inability to read - referring both to speed and comprehension; (3) do not know how to study or to take meaningful notes and properly use the library; (4) lack of motivation - no clear-cut personal objective or reason for being in college; and (5) poor college selection - too large or too small, too hard or too easy, too confusing or too dull.

College is designed to provide average occupation preparation to be accomplished by students of average college availability and preparation. Above-average students should expect to get better than average occupation preparation, reduce the time required to graduate, or both. Below-average students must achieve at least average occupation preparation which usually requires extra effort and/or extra time.

NARRATIVE DESCRIPTIONS

Almost 3,000 institutions of higher education, in the United States and Canada, are described in this volume of *The College Blue Book*®, including universities, senior colleges, two-year colleges, and specialized institutions. The data has been gathered by direct contact with all institutions as well as by inspection of the most current college catalogues available. The arrangement of information is alphabetical by state and by college within each state.

No judgements or evaluations have been made in these entries, but many applicable facts have been presented to assist the reader in making his own.

This edition includes state or regional maps, placing the appropriate map at the beginning of each state section; each college title has the map coordinates listed in parenthesis beside it.

To assist the user of this volume in making a valid evaluation and comparison of schools, information on each school has been standardized as follows: privately or publicly supported or church-related; level: university, college, graduate school; for whom: men, women, co-educational, church-related; type: liberal arts, technological, theological, teacher education, professional; names of degrees granted; fields of specialization, schools, or departments; term system: semester, quarter, trimester; enrollment; size of faculty and faculty-student ratio; regional accreditation; number of volumes in library; cooperative education (work-study) program availability; existence of a ROTC program; entrance requirements; admission procedure; costs per year; collegiate environment; community environment.

Within the narrative descriptions are listed the degrees granted, and abbreviations designated by a school. To clarify their meaning there follows an explanation of some of the more widely used degree abbreviations:

A.A.	Associate of Arts
A.S.	Associate of Science
A.A.A.	Associate of Applied Arts
A.A.S.	Associate of Applied Science
A.B.	Bachelor of Arts
B.A.	Bachelor of Arts
B.D.	Bachelor of Divinity
B.S.	Bachelor of Science
B.Ed.	Bachelor of Education
B.F.A.	Bachelor of Fine Arts
B.Mus.	Bachelor of Music
B.Th.	Bachelor of Theology
B.B.A.	Bachelor of Business Administration
B.Arch.	Bachelor of Architecture
LL.B.	Bachelor of Laws
M.A.	Master of Arts
M.S.	Master of Science
M.Th.	Master of Theology
M.F.A.	Master of Fine Arts
M.S.Ed.	Master of Science Education
M.Mus.	Master of Music
M.B.A.	Master of Business Administration
M.P.A.	Master of Public Administration
M.S.Eng.	Master of Science in Engineering
M.L.S.	Master of Library Science
M.Ed.	Master of Education
Sp.Ed	Specialist in Education
J.D.	Doctor of Jurisprudence (Law)
Ed.D.	Doctor of Education
D.Ed.	Doctor of Education
D.B.A.	Doctor of Business Administration
D.Mus.	Doctor of Music
D.Th.	Doctor of Theology
M.D.	Doctor of Medicine
D.Vet.M.	Doctor of Veterinary Medicine
Ph.D.	Doctor of Philosophy

There are six regional accrediting commissions covering the United States that evaluate colleges and schools. Generally, these regional agencies grant accreditation to an entire institution of higher learning. They are as follows: Middle States Association of Colleges and Schools, New England Association of Schools and Colleges, North Central Association of Colleges and Schools, Northwest Association of Schools and Colleges, Southern Association of Colleges and Schools, and Western Association of Schools and Colleges.

An important consideration should be mentioned again, one which *The College Blue Book*® stresses at several points; the "right" college for Student A may not be the "right" college for Student B. A large enrollment, a small teacher-student ratio, an enormous library and exacting entrance requirements do not necessarily mean that this is the best school. Consider all the factors available: is it in a small, rural college town or a huge, vibrating metropolis; does the student need readily available transportation; does this school have specific programs he's interested in; if seeking a profession, does it have on-campus dormitories, or must the student seek other housing arrangements; do expenses fall within the student's budget; can the entrance requirements be met; if accepted, what are the chances of graduating; if the student is not sure just exactly what is wanted in the way of a career, will this school provide opportunities to find out? This revised edition of *The College Blue Book*® has been designed to assist in answering these questions and others that the college-bound student may have.

U.S. Colleges

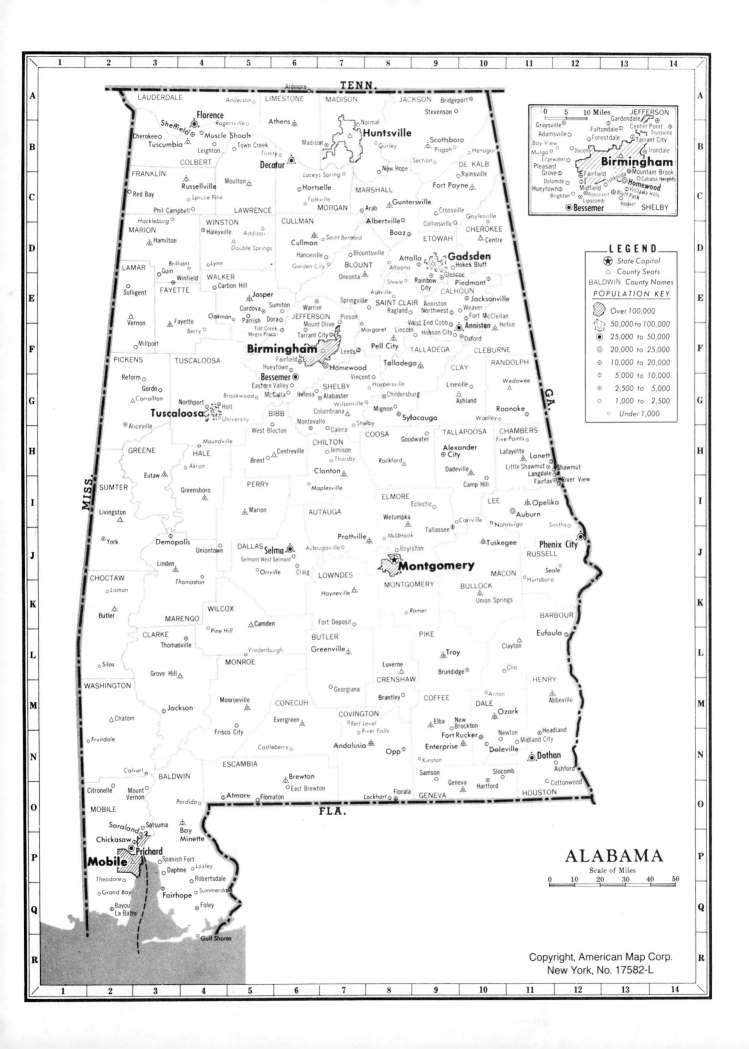

ALABAMA

Scale of Miles

0 10 20 30 40 50

LEGEND

⊛ State Capital
⊙ County Seats
BALDWIN County Names

POPULATION KEY

Over 100,000
50,000 to 100,000
25,000 to 50,000
20,000 to 25,000
10,000 to 20,000
5,000 to 10,000
2,500 to 5,000
1,000 to 2,500
Under 1,000

ALABAMA

ALABAMA AGRICULTURAL AND MECHANICAL UNIVERSITY   (B-7)
P.O. Box 908
Normal, Alabama 35762
Tel: (205) 851-5000; Admissions: (205) 851-5245; Fax: (205) 851-5249

Description: This publicly supported coeducational land-grant university is accredited by the Southern Association of Colleges and Schools. The school opened in 1875 as the Huntsville Normal School with an enrollment of 61 pupils and 2 teachers. In 1919, the institution became a junior college and its name was changed to The State Agricultural and Mechanical Institute for Negroes. By authority of the State Board of Education, the institution was permitted to offer work on the senior college level in 1939. On June 26, 1969, the Alabama State Board of Education, the governing body of the University, adopted a resolution changing the name of the institution to Alabama Agricultural and Mechanical University. The University grants a Bachelor, Masters, Educational Specialist, and Doctorate of Philosophy degree in its schools of: Agriculture, Arts and Sciences, Business, Education, and Engineering and Technology. Army R.O.T.C. is required for 1 year. Programs for certification in elementary and secondary teaching are offered. It operates on the semester system and offers one summer session. Enrollment includes 4,019 full-time, 381 part-time, and 1,200 graduate students. A faculty of 281 full-time and 76 part-time gives an undergraduate faculty student ratio of 1-15.

Entrance Requirements: Accredited high school graduates with a C average accepted; ACT or SAT required; application fee $10; advanced placement plan available.

Costs Per Year: $1,700 tuition; $3,400-out-of-state tuition; $2,550 room and board.

Collegiate Environment: The campus is comprised of 82 buildings located on 2,001 acres. The Learning Resources Center seats 1,000 students and contains over 375,000 volumes. 62% of students applying for admission meet the requirements and 90% of these are accepted, including midyear students. Special financial aid is available for economically disadvantaged students. 87% of students receive some form of financial aid.

Community Environment: Population 180,000. Located in the northern part of the state, within the city limits of Huntsville, on U.S. Highways 231 and 431, which pass through the business section of the city. Huntsville may be reached by the Greyhound bus, and United, Northwest, American, Delta, and Transair airlines. Taxi service is available to the community from all transportation centers. (See also University of Alabama - Huntsville).

ALABAMA AVIATION AND TECHNICAL COLLEGE   (M-10)
231 Highway South
PO Box 1209
Ozark, Alabama 36361-1209
Tel: (205) 774-5113; (800) 624-3468; Fax: (205) 774-5113

Description: The publicly supported, coeducational technical college was founded in 1960. It was operated by the City School System until 1962 when it was absorbed into the State Vocational Education System. The institute is accredited by the Southern Association of Colleges and Schools. The college grants the Associate degree. It operates on the quarter system and offers one summer session. Enrollment includes 500 full-time students. A faculty of 30 full-time gives a faculty-student ratio of 1-17.

Entrance Requirements: Open enrollment policy; high school graduation or GED acceptable; non-high school graduates are considered; early admission, early decision, and rolling admission plans are available.

Costs Per Year: $1,500 state resident fees and tuition; $2,460 nonresident tuition; $285 room per quarter.

Collegiate Environment: The institute is designed specifically for training in aviation maintenance and technology. The college library contains 4,335 volumes and numerous audiovisual materials. Dormitory facilities accommodate 70 men and women. Approximately 99% of the students applying for admission are accepted. 150 scholarships are available. 80% of the students receive some form of assistance.

Community Environment: Ozark's population is approximately 15,000. The college is located about 90 miles from Gulf Coast beaches.

ALABAMA SOUTHERN COMMUNITY COLLEGE   (M-5)
P.O. Box 2000
Monroeville, Alabama 36461
Tel: (205) 575-3156

Description: This publicly supported coeducational junior college is one of 12 junior colleges established by the State Legislature in 1963. It began its first classes in September, 1965. It was accredited by the Southern Association of Colleges and Schools in 1970. The school provides university parallel courses as well as occupational and short term programs. Enrollment is 1,073 full-time and 605 part-time students. A faculty of 24 full-time, 33 part-time gives a faculty-student ratio of 1-15. The quarter system is used with 2 summer sessions offered. The college grants the Associate degree. Continuing education courses are offered and cooperative education programs are available.

Entrance Requirements: Accredited high school graduation or equivalent with completion of 22 units; open enrollment policy; early admission, rolling admission, early decision and advanced placement plans available.

Costs Per Year: $1,119 resident tuition; $1,958 nonresident.

Collegiate Environment: The campus has six buildings on 100 acres. The library contains 39,006 volumes. All students qualifying for admission are accepted, including midyear students. Limited financial aid is available.

Community Environment: The campus is located in a rural area with a mild climate. The average temperature is 60 degrees. It is an excellent area for hunting and fishing. Part-time employment is available for students.

ALABAMA STATE UNIVERSITY   (J-8)
915 South Jackson Street
Montgomery, Alabama 36195
Tel: (205) 293-4473; Fax: (205) 240-6856

Description: The publicly supported university is accredited by the Southern Association of Colleges and Schools and operates on the semester system with one summer session. For years, the college has been devoted to the training of public school teachers. Once called the Alabama Colored People's University, the college opened in 1887; graduate degrees were offered first in 1940. Recent enrollment included 4,697 full-time, 418 part-time, and 373 graduate students. A faculty of 219 full-time and 90 part-time members provides a faculty-student ratio of 1:20. The school awards Associate, Bachelor, Master's, and Education Specialist degrees. ROTC Air Force program is available.

Entrance Requirements: High school graduation with 12 units including 4 units of English, and the rest distributed among mathematics, foreign language, science and social science; under certain conditions non-high school graduates are considered for admission; ACT or SAT required; TOEFL required for international students; GRE required for graduate students; early admission, early decision, rolling admission, delayed admission, midyear admission, open admission, and advanced placement plans available; also CLEP.

Costs Per Year: $1,608 resident tuition; nonresident tuition $3,108; room and board $2,010.

Collegiate Environment: The campus is situated on a 138-acre site. There are 48 buildings, including comfortable dormitory facilities for 920 men and 1,085 women. The air-conditioned library houses 204,118 volumes, 755 periodicals, and 10,490 microforms, 75% of the applicants are accepted. Financial aid is available for economically handicapped students.

Community Environment: Population approximately 200,000. Capital of Alabama. A city known for its stately homes, many of which belong to the antebellum days. The city is also known for its magnolia trees, its southern traditions and culture, and its southern hospitality. Excellent air and highway connections. Montgomery is the home of the Alabama State Capitol Building, the first capital of the Confederacy, the Department of Archives and History, the new Montgomery Public Library, Maxwell Air Force Base and Gunter Field, the Air University, and the very large Garrett Coliseum. The South Alabama State Fair, Southern Horse Show, an annual rodeo, an annual indoor track tournament, and other similar functions are held in the Garrett Coliseum. Located here is the First White House of the Confederacy, the home of the Jefferson Davis when Montgomery was the Confederate Capital.

ATHENS STATE COLLEGE   *(B-6)*
Athens, Alabama 35611
Tel: (205) 233-8100; Fax: (205) 233-8164

Description: Athens State College is a two-year degree granting institution accredited by the Southern Association of Colleges and Schools. The college is intended primarily as the Upper Division institution for support of Junior Colleges and Technical Junior College graduates. Three degree programs are offered including the Bachelor of Science, Bachelor of Arts and Bachelor of Science in Education. It operates on the quarter system with credits given in quarter hours. Enrollment is 2,470 students and a faculty of 80 full-time and 81 part-time members.

Entrance Requirements: Graduates of junior colleges are admitted as Juniors with no loss of credit; other students are admitted with accrued credits of 96 quarter hours; early admission and rolling admission plans available.

Costs Per Year: $1,650 state resident tuition; $3,300 nonresident tuition; $2,800 approximate room and board.

Collegiate Environment: The campus, located off I-65, lies in the foothills of the Cumberland Mountains. An Upper Division College, providing the community college transfer student an opportunity to experience total campus life for the last two years of his or her education. The college has fraternities, sororities and an intercollegiate program for men and women.

Community Environment: Located in the Tennessee Valley, Athens (population 16,901) is in Limestone County which has an overall population of 54,135. The town is noted for its fine antebellum homes, including the large Founders Hall, built in 1843. With an average temperature of 60 degrees and convenient to air (Huntsville), rail, and within two hours of Nashville and Birmingham, this is a rich, rapidly growing area for farming and industry. State Parks at Wheeler, Wilson Lakes, and Guntersville Reservoir provide for swimming, boating, fishing, and camping.

AUBURN UNIVERSITY   *(I-11)*
Auburn University, Alabama 36849
Tel: (334) 826-4000; Admissions: (334) 844-4080; Fax: (334) 844-6176

Description: The publicly supported university is accredited by the Southern Association of Colleges and Schools and operates on the quarter system. The university grants Bachelor, Master and Doctorate degrees in over 160 fields of study. Cooperative education programs are offered in some of the schools of the university. The university was chartered in 1856 by the Methodist Church, and became a public institution in 1872. It operates on the quarter system and offers one summer session. Enrollment includes 16,468 full-time and 1,638 part-

time undergraduates and 3,120 graduate students. A faculty of 1,172 full-time and 116 part-time gives a faculty-student ratio of 1-16.

Entrance Requirements: Accredited high school graduation or equivalent with minimum C average; units should include 4 English, 3 mathematics, 3 social studies, 2 science, 1 foreign language and an additional year each of science and social studies are recommended; ACT or SAT required; non-high school graduates considered; early admission, delayed admission, midyear admission, rolling admission and advanced placement plans available; $25 application fee.

Costs Per Year: $2,100 tuition for state residents; $6,300 nonresidents tuition; $3,933 room and board; $1,377 additional expenses.

Collegiate Environment: The campus includes 83 major buildings on 1,871 acres. 18 women's dormitories (capacity 1,957 students), 4 men's dormitories (capacity 349 students), 398 apartments for single undergraduates, and 124 apartments for married students and graduate single students. (Total apartment capacity is 1,234 students.) The library contains 1,067,176 hardbound volumes, numerous periodicals 2,859,260 microform volumes. 90% of the applicants are accepted, and students may enroll at mid-year as well as in September. The average SAT scores of the current freshman class were 509 verbal and 579 math; average composite ACT, 24.7. Financial aid is available, and 35% of the current student body receive some form of aid. The university also grants Doctor of Veterinary Medicine and Doctor of Pharmacy degrees.

Community Environment: Auburn (population 32,000) is located on U.S. 29 and Interstate 85, 55 miles east of Montgomery, 120 miles southeast of Birmingham, and 120 miles southwest of Atlanta, Georgia. Auburn University is the pride of the city. With the many churches in the area there is a cultural atmosphere which makes for pleasant living. Chewacla State Park is nearby for swimming and picnicking. The city has two well-equipped parks, a country club and 2 public courses for golf, a stadium for athletic games and many facilities for intramural sports including fields, swimming pools, racquetball and tennis courts, and a student activities building. Azaleas and camellias may be seen on the grounds of the university and many of the beautiful homes.

AUBURN UNIVERSITY AT MONTGOMERY   *(J-8)*
Montgomery, Alabama 36193
Tel: (205) 271-9300

Description: This publicly supported university is accredited by the Southern Association of Colleges and Schools. It is organized into five academic schools: Liberal Arts, Sciences, Education, Nursing, and Business. All, except Nursing, offer graduate level courses. An Air University Graduate Program is set up in cooperation with Maxwell AFB, offering master's degrees in Political Science and Public Administration. The university operates on the quarter system. Enrollment includes 6,500 students. AUM blends the traditional view of the University as a community of scholars with the contemporary view of the University as an integral part of the surrounding community.

Entrance Requirements: High school graduate or GED; ACT required for state residents; either ACT or SAT for nonresidents; early admission, deferred admission, midyear admission, rolling admission and advanced placement plans available. $25 application fee.

Costs Per Year: $1,905 ($635 per quarter) resident tuition; $5,715 ($1,905 per quarter) nonresident; $1,725 ($575 per quarter) housing.

Collegiate Environment: The campus comprises five classroom buildings, the library, the University Center, a physical education and athletic complex, and a student housing area. The University Center houses the cafeteria, the bookstore, the Counseling Center, a recreation room, lounges, and the university theater. The library contains 190,407 titles and 1,864 periodicals. On-campus efficiency apartments provide housing for 576 students.

Community Environment: See Alabama State University.

BEVILL STATE COMMUNITY COLLEGE   *(F-3)*
P.O. Box 800
Sumiton, Alabama 35148
Tel: (205) 648-3271; Fax: (205) 932-3294

Description: The publicly supported junior college is accredited by the Southern Association of Colleges and Schools and is part of the state system of community, junior, and technical colleges. It operates on the quarter system with 2 summer sessions. The college offers university parallel studies, occupational programs, and continuing education programs leading to an Associate degree or a Certificate of completion. Enrollment includes 2,400 full-time and 1,800 part-time students with a faculty of 75 full-time and 118 part-time members.

Entrance Requirements: Accredited high school graduation or equivalent; open enrollment policy; school-administered entrance exam required; nonhigh school graduates considered; early admission, early decision, rolling admissions, midyear admission, and advanced placement available.

Costs Per Year: Tuition is $26 per quarter hour.

Collegiate Environment: The college recently completed or renovated a number of buildings including the new Tom Bevill Business and Industry Building on the Walker Campus. The library contains over 85,000 volumes, 188 periodicals, 75,989 microfilms and 2,421 audiovisual materials. Dormitories accomodate 110 students. All students applying for admission are accepted, including midyear students. Various forms of financial assistance are offered, and 68% of the current students receive financial aid.

Community Environment: The Walker campus is an urban area. The Hamilton and Brewer campuses are in small town areas.

Branch Campuses: Brewer Campus, Fayette, AL; Hamilton Campus, Hamilton, AL.

BIRMINGHAM-SOUTHERN COLLEGE   *(F-7)*
800 Eighth Avenue, West
Box A-2
Birmingham, Alabama 35254
Tel: (205) 226-4600; (800) 523-5793; Admissions: (205) 226-4686;
Fax: (205) 226-3064

Description: The privately supported liberal arts college operates under the auspices of the Alabama-West Florida and North Alabama Conferences of the United Methodist Church. The college is accredited by the Southern Association of Colleges and Schools. The 4-1-4 system is employed and two summer sessions are offered. The college awards a Baccalaureate degree. This institution was opened with an enrollment of 50 students in October 1856. The campus was almost destroyed during the war between the states. Then called Southern University, it was later merged with Birmingham College in 1918 and given its present name. Continuing education courses offered; special programs include: Contract Learning Internships, Interdisciplinary Majors, Individualized Majors, Masters in Public and Private Management. 2 years of work must be completed at BSC for degree. Enrollment includes 1,583 full-time, 168 part-time and 353 evening program undergraduates and 98 graduate students. A faculty of 98 full-time and 37 part-time gives a faculty-student ratio of 1-13.

Entrance Requirements: Satisfactory grades or minimum SAT 400V, 400M or ACT 21; high school C average and completion of 16 units, including 4 English, 2 foreign language, and 8 units chosen from science, mathematics, foreign language, and social science; early admission, advanced placement, and early decision plans available; admission notification dates January 6th, and rolling up to May 1, 1995; $25 application fee.

Costs Per Year: $11,660 tuition; $4,325 room and board.

Collegiate Environment: The campus occupies 185 acres of rolling and wooded property. The Robert R. Meyer Planetarium was completed in 1964 and the College Theater in 1968. The total dormitory capacity is 460 men and 525 women. Fraternity housing is available for 87. The Franklin W. Olin Computer Science/Mathematics Facility was opened in October 1985, at a cost of $2.7 million. The Center contains a Hewlett Packard 9000 and a Digital Equipment Company AX11/750. Also, 36 IBM Personal Computers are available for use by faculty and students. Software capabilities include six new computer languages and programs. The Center is open 24 hours a day. In 1987, the College opened the Marguerite Herbert Building at a cost of more than $5 million. The facility includes a computer classroom, a computer laboratory, an education laboratory, a 98-seat conference center, and a behavorial and social science research center with both human performance and animal labs. The College completed a new entrance to the campus in the Summer of 1987 at a cost of $1.7 million dollars. The library houses 190,922 volumes. There are 6 national fraternities and 6 sororities found on campus. Ecumenical and denominational

services are held at various times during the week. About 73% of the applicants are accepted. Financial aid is available.

Community Environment: See University of Alabama - Birmingham.

BISHOP STATE COMMUNITY COLLEGE   *(P-3)*
351 North Broad Street
Mobile, Alabama 36690
Tel: (205) 690-6416

Description: This publicly supported community college has an enrollment of 2,054 students attending classes on the quarter system with one summer session. The college was begun in 1936 with a two-year college curriculum. A faculty of 49 full-time and 11 part-time gives a faculty-student ratio of 1-31. The school provides university-parallel program as well as those leading to immediate employment in business, industry, and semi-professional areas. It also provides a Development Program to meet the needs of beginning students who indicate insufficient skills for enrollment in basic college courses. A Cooperative Education program is available. The college is accredited by the Southern Association of Colleges and Schools and grants the Associate Degree. Special programs include: Special Services Program; Associate Degree in Nursing; and Career Placement; Word Processing Technology; Deaf Interpreters Training Program; Academic Advisement Program; and Cooperative Allied Health Program.

Entrance Requirements: High school graduation; C average, open enrollment; completion of 20 units; non-high school graduates considered with Equivalency Certificate; no application fee.

Costs Per Year: $1,026 tuition and fees; $1,795 nonresident tuition, based on 15 hours credit for three quarters.

Collegiate Environment: The campus has 12 buildings on 15 acres. The library contains 75,000 volumes. There are no dormitories.

Community Environment: See University of South Alabama.

CENTRAL ALABAMA COMMUNITY COLLEGE   *(H-9)*
P.O. Box 699
Alexander City, Alabama 35010
Tel: (205) 234-6346; (800) 643-2657; Fax: (205) 234-0384

Description: The publicly supported, cooeducational community college is accredited by the Southern Association of Colleges and Schools. The State Legislature's approval of Act No. 93 on May 3, 1963, established Alexander City State Junior College (ACSJC) and Nunnelley State Technical College (NSTC) in Childersburg. Central Alabama Community College was created by action of the Alabama State Board of Education on February 23, 1989, which act consolidated the two colleges. The colleges moved to their permanent locations in 1966. The college offers general, vocational-technical, senior college transfer, adult education, and training programs for the community's industrial and business needs. It awards the Associate degree. It operates on the quarter system and offers two summer sessions. Enrollment includes 1,098 full-time and 1,220 part-time students. There are 1,148 non-credit students in the Training for Business program. A faculty of 53 full-time and 60 part-time gives a faculty-student ratio of 1-20.

Entrance Requirements: High school graduation or certificate of high school equivalency; applicants who do not possess a diploma or its equivalent certificate may be admitted with 19 units from an accredited high school; rolling admission and advanced placement plans available.

Costs Per Year: $1,215 ($405 per quarter) state resident tuition; $1,957.50 ($652.50 per quarter) nonresident tuition; calculated for 15 hours per quarter.

Collegiate Environment: Central Alabama Community College consists of two main campuses with several off-site location. Presently, the College's service area spans all or parts of some twelve counties in east central Alabama. The Alexander City campus is comprised of 7 buildings located on a 90-acre campus overlooking a three-acre lake. The library is a three-story building with approximately 34,000 square feet of floor space and contains 35,000 volumes. There are no dormitories. Financial aid is available. 22% of students receive some form of financial assistance.

Community Environment: Alexander City (population 13,145) is recognized as a city with great civic pride and a sound business climate. It is a pivotal point of transportation: 78 miles southeast of Birmingham, 55 miles northeast of Montgomery, 123 miles southwest of Atlanta, and 70 miles northwest of Columbus, GA. Childersburg is strategically located on Highway 280, 35 miles southeast of Birmingham, 76 miles north of Montgomery, and 42 miles southwest od Anniston. Both campuses are located in one of the South's principal industrial areas. Industries are diversified yet bolstered by the large payrolls of two leading textile corporations and a leading paper products company. Electrical energy, various foundries, emerging high tech companies, and many small businesses comprise the economic base of the College's service area. Both cities are favored with a mild climate year round, with outstanding recreational and sports facilities. In Alexander City, Lake Martin is the focus of boating, swimming, fishing, and camping. In Childersburg, Logan Martin Lake and Lay Lake allow for sports and recreational activities.

CONCORDIA COLLEGE   *(J-6)*
1804 Green Street
Selma, Alabama 36701
Tel: (205) 874-5700; Fax: (205) 875-5755

Description: The privately supported junior college has an enrollment of approximately 399 students. It is an educational institute of the Lutheran Church-Missouri Synod. The semester system is employed with one summer session. In 1922, the college was begun by pioneer Lutheran missionaries to educate young men and women preparing for Lutheran pastoral and teaching ministries. The Junior College, grants an Associate Degree. The college is accredited with the Southern Association of Colleges and Schools. A faculty of 13 full-time and 7 part-time members gives a faculty-student ratio of 1-20.

Entrance Requirements: Accredited high school graduation or GED, C average or equivalent; open enrollment policy; completion of 20 units including 4 English, 1 mathematics, 1 science and 3 social science; early admission plan available; $5 application fee.

Costs Per Year: Tuition $1,470 per semester, room $500-$650, board $800, fees $218.

Collegiate Environment: The eighteen-acre campus includes seven major buildings with a library housing 19,875 volumes, 100 pamphlets, 98 periodicals and 776 audiovisual materials. Dormitory space is available for 60 men and 50 women. 90% of students applying for admission are accepted, including midyear students. Financial assistance is available and 98% of the current students receive some aid.

Community Environment: See Selma University.

ENTERPRISE STATE JUNIOR COLLEGE   *(N-10)*
U.S. 84 East
P.O. Box 1300
Enterprise, Alabama 36331
Tel: (205) 347-2623

Description: The publicly supported junior college is accredited by the Southern Association of Colleges and Schools. The college was conceived during a Special Education Session called in 1963 by Governor George C. Wallace. The community of Enterprise raised funds to purchase the campus site. Groundbreaking ceremonies were held in 1965 and operations moved from temporary facilities to the new campus in 1966. The college grants an Associate in Applied Science degree in its occupational program and the Associate degree in its university parallel programs. It operates on the quarter system and offers two summer sessions. Enrollment is 932 men and 1,270 women. A faculty of 53 full-time and 68 part-time gives a faculty-student ratio of 1-18.

Entrance Requirements: High school graduation or equivalent (GED); open enrollment policy; early admission, rolling admission, and advanced placement plans available.

Costs Per Year: $1,293 ($22 per credit) state resident tuition; $2,085 nonresident tuition.

Collegiate Environment: The campus consists of 7 modern, fully-equipped and air-conditioned buildings. The library contains 42,800 volumes. Financial aid is available in the form of academic, performing arts and athletic scholarships. 50% of students receive some form of financial assistance.

Community Environment: Population 20,000, Enterprise has a cosmopolitan atmosphere. Due to its proximity to Fort Rucker, approximately 35% of its populace hail from all states in the union and many foreign countries. It enjoys a mild climate. Bus, railroad and a local airport serve the area. There is excellent shopping downtown, plus three shopping centers in the area. The college has a summer work program arranged with the city and local firms; part-time jobs are also available at Fort Rucker, six miles from Enterprise. The community contains many churches, a community center, and most major social, civic, and service groups as well as many city-sponsored programs for recreation.

Branch Campuses: A branch campus is located at Ft. Rucker, AL, with offices and classroom facilities.

FAULKNER UNIVERSITY   *(J-8)*
5345 Atlanta Highway
Montgomery, Alabama 36109-3398
Tel: (334) 260-6200; (800) 879-9816; Admissions: (334) 620-6200; Fax: (334) 260-6137

Description: The privately supported liberal arts coeducational university is accredited by the Southern Association of Colleges and Schools. The school is affiliated with the Church of Christ. It was founded in 1942 in order to establish a college in which the Word of God would be taught and the Christian character developed in addition to the teaching of the usual academic program. The college grants an Associate degree. It operates on the semester system and offers one summer session. Enrollment includes 647 students. A faculty of 49 full-time and 36 part-time gives a faculty-student ratio of 1-15.

Entrance Requirements: Accredited high school graduation or equivalent with completion of 15 units, including 3 English, 9 total in lab science, language, and social studies, 3 electives; open enrollment policy; ACT or SAT and placement exam required; early admission, early decision, midyear admission, rolling admission and advanced placement plans available; $25 application fee.

Costs Per Year: $5,850 tuition; $3,300 room and board, $150 student fees.

Collegiate Environment: Ten buildings on 92 acres comprise the campus. Dormitory facilities are provided for 201 men and 199 women. The library contains 80,000 volumes. All students are required to attend chapel and to enroll in a Bible class each term. 95% of the students applying for admission are accepted, including midyear students. 75 scholarships are and 85% of the current students receive some form of financial aid.

Community Environment: See Alabama State University.

GADSDEN STATE COMMUNITY COLLEGE   *(D-9)*
P.O. Box 227
Gadsden, Alabama 35902-0227
Tel: (205) 549-8210; (800) 226-5563; Fax: (205) 549-8444

Description: This publicly supported community college operates on the quarter system with one summer session. It is one of 12 colleges created by the State Legislature in 1963. The college offers university parallel and occupational-vocational programs leading to an Associate degree or a Diploma. It is accredited by the Southern Association of Colleges and Schools. Recent enrollment included approximately 6,400 students. A faculty of 150 full time and 106 part time gives a faculty-student ratio of 1-10. Correspondent credit allowed; continuing education courses offered; cooperative education programs available in engineering; vocational; technical; and construction trades.

Entrance Requirements: Accredited high school graduation C average or equivalent; open enrollment policy; non-high school graduates considered; no application fee; early admission, early decision, rolling admission, delayed admission and advanced placement plans available.

Costs Per Year: $1,437 resident tuition; $2,337 non-resident; $2,250 room and board.

Collegiate Environment: The Wallace Drive campus consists of eight modern air-conditioned buildings on 245 acres. Dormitory space is available for 112 students. The library contains 90,000 volumes and numerous pamphlets, periodicals, microforms and sound recordings. All students applying for admission are accepted, including midyear students. Financial aid is available, and of the 295 scholarships available, 60% are for freshmen.

Community Environment: Gadsden (population 53,928) is the county seat, and is the 6th largest in Alabama. Buses and railroads serve the area. Noccalula Falls is located in the City. Industry includes steel, rubber, farm machinery, and cotton mills.

Branch Campuses: East Broad Campus; Valley Street; Anniston Center; Fort McClellan; Talladega.

GEORGE CORLEY WALLACE STATE COMMUNITY COLLEGE   *(J-6)*
P.O. Drawer 1049
Selma, Alabama 36702
Tel: (334) 875-2634; Admissions: (334) 875-2634 x199; Fax: (334) 875-2634

Description: This publicly supported, coeducational, community college is accredited by the Southern Association of Colleges and Schools. Vocational degrees offered include A.A. and A.S. in liberal arts subjects, and Diplomas in over 15 vocational-technical professions. It operates on the quarter system and offers two summer sessions. Enrollment includes 1,100 full-time and 575 part-time students. A faculty of 48 full-time and 43 part-time gives a faculty-student ratio of 1-18.

Entrance Requirements: Open enrollment policy; high school graduation for college-parallel programs; age 16 or over for vocational-technical programs; early admission, early decision, and rolling admission plans available.

Costs Per Year: $1,062.50 ($25 per credit hour 1st 12; $12.50 thereafter) state resident tuition.

Collegiate Environment: The campus, in an urban area, has 13 buildings including a library of 28,000 volumes. College buildings are ultramodern and completely air-conditioned. All students applying for admission are accepted. Scholarships are available and 65% of students receive some form of financial assistance.

Community Environment: Selma, population 35,000 enjoys a temperate climate. Railroad, bus and air service is available for the area. There are many churches in the city, as well as hospitals, a library, and theaters. Gulf beaches are only 180 miles away. Part-time employment is available. Major civic, fraternal and veteran's organizations are represented. A traditional Market Day is held in October.

HUNTINGDON COLLEGE   *(J-8)*
1500 East Fairview Avenue
Montgomery, Alabama 36106-2148
Tel: (205) 334-3300; (800) 763-0313; Fax: (205) 334-2951

Description: The privately supported, coeducational United Methodist liberal arts college is accredited by the Southern Association of Colleges and Schools. In 1854 the governor of Alabama signed the law that became the charter of the Tuskegee Female College. The college opened in 1856, and moved from Tuskegee to Montgomery in 1909. The establishment of the college was a result of concerted action of the Methodist Episcopal Church, South. Men were admitted for the first time in 1932. The college grants a Baccalaureate degree. Cooperative education programs in various fields are available. Army and Air Force ROTC are also available. The college operates on a 4-1-4 system with two sumemr sessions. A two-week January term is offered. Enrollment includes 576 full-time and 93 part-time students. A faculty of 43 full-time and 22 part-time gives a faculty-student ratio of 1-13.

Entrance Requirements: Accredited high school graduation or equivalent with completion of 16 units; recommended units include 4 English, 3 mathematics, 2 science, 3 social studies, and 2 humanities or foreign language; in exceptional cases adults may be admitted by examination; SAT or ACT required; early admission, rolling admission, and advanced placement plans available; $25 application fee.

Costs Per Year: $8,645 tuition; $4,165 room and board; $120 fees.

Collegiate Environment: The school is located on a 58-acre campus in Cloverdale, easily accessible to shopping areas and other points of interest. 89% of those who apply for admission are accepted, including midyear students. The college welcomes a geographically diverse student body. The average scores of entering freshmen were SAT 480 verbal, 440 math, ACT 20 composite. The library contains 94,000 volumes and numerous periodicals, microforms and sound recordings. Residence halls provide housing for 400 men and women. Financial

aid is available and 90% of the current student body receives some form of assistance.

Community Environment: See Alabama State University.

JACKSONVILLE STATE UNIVERSITY   *(E-10)*
Jacksonville, Alabama 36265
Tel: (205) 782-5781; (800) 231-5291; Admissions: (205) 782-5400

Description: The state supported, coeducational institution is accredited by the Southern Association of Colleges and Schools. It operates on the semester system and offers three summer sessions. Enrollment includes 5,205 full-time and 1,353 part-time undergraduate and 995 graduate students. A faculty of 281 gives an undergraduate faculty-student ratio of 1-23. The university grants Bachelor, Masters, and Educational Specialist degrees. Twelve semester hours correspondent credit allowed; cooperative education programs available. Army ROTC is offered.

Entrance Requirements: High school graduate from approved high school; ACT or SAT required; application fee $20; rolling admission, early admission, and advanced placement available. GED accepted.

Costs Per Year: $1,740 tuition for residents, $2,610 nonresidents; room $920-$1,330; board $960-$1,250.

Collegiate Environment: The student body consists primarily of citizens from northeast Alabama. However, there are students from almost all states (15% out-of-state) and many foreign countries (1% foreign). Approximately 70% of the freshman class return for the second year. The campus has 73 buildings on 341 acres located in the northern edge of the city. The library contains 476,655 volumes, 1,524 periodicals, 119,871 microforms, and 8,496 audiovisual materials. Ten dormitories provide space for 2,095 students. The university nursery school furnishes students and parents opportunity for observing responses of children in various activities.

Community Environment: Population 9,868. Jacksonville is relatively small and free from the many disctractions of a large city. The community is easily accessible by good roads and is 6 miles from Fort McClellan (military installation), 12 miles from Anniston, 22 miles from Gadsden, 75 miles from Birmingham, and 100 miles from Atlanta, GA. The climate is pleasant.

JAMES H. FAULKNER STATE JUNIOR COLLEGE   *(O-4)*
Hammond Circle
Bay Minette, Alabama 36507
Tel: (205) 580-2100; Fax: (205) 937-3404

Description: The publicly supported junior college operates on the quarter system with 1 summer session. The college provides university-parallel programs and technical professional programs leading to an Associate degree. It is accredited by the Southern Association of Colleges and Schools. The college enrolls 3,108 students. A faculty of 143 gives a faculty-student ratio of 1:22.

Entrance Requirements: Accredited high school graduation or equivalent; non-high school graduates considered; open enrollment policy; early admission, early decision, rolling admission, CLEP and delayed admission plans available; application fee $5.

Costs Per Year: $600 tuition; room and board $1,725.

Collegiate Environment: Faulkner State is noted for its handsome exotic campus. Palm-lined streets, contemporary buildings, and modern facilities create a relaxed atmosphere for student enrichment. On-campus housing is available in modern residence halls which accommodate 121 men and 154 women. The college library contains 39,700 volumes. 99% of the students who apply for admission are accepted, including mid-year students.

Community Environment: Bay Minette is the County Seat of the largest county in Alabama, touched on three sides by colorful beaches and the cities of Mobile and Pensacola, Florida. Students not only can enjoy the sun-drenched beaches of the Gulf of Mexico, but can visit several nearby historical sites and adventure trials. The city has a mild climate all year.

Branch Campuses: Fairhope; Foley.

JEFFERSON DAVIS STATE JUNIOR COLLEGE   *(O-6)*
Alco Drive
Brewton, Alabama 36426
Tel: (205) 867-4832; Fax: (205) 867-7399

Description: The publicly supported junior college with a recent enrollment of 1,053 full-time and part-time men and women is one of 12 junior colleges created by the State Legislature in 1963. The college began classes in September 1965 in a building of the First Methodist Church of Brewton and moved into the college's first new building in May 1966. The quarter system is employed with one summer session offered. The college and Schools. The college grants an Associate degree. and Schools. The college grants an Associate degree. A full-time faculty of 24 gives a faculty-student ratio of 43-1.

Entrance Requirements: Accredited high school graduation; open enrollment policy; early admission and rolling admission plan available.

Costs Per Year: $600 tuition in state, $1,050 nonresident.

Collegiate Environment: The 100-acre campus consists of 8 buildings. The library contains 27,649 volumes. There are no housing facilities on campus. The students usually commute and live in a nearby area. All those who apply for admission are accepted, including midyear students. About 50% of the students receive some form of financial aid. Scholarships are available.

Community Environment: Brewton (population 6,309) is located in extreme South Alabama, 105 miles southeast of Montgomery, 80 miles northeast of Mobile and 60 miles north of Pensacola. Escambia is the County Seat. Area is served by railroad, bus, and airline service to Pensacola. The community has a mild climate year-round with major rainfall in February and July. Approximately three-fourths of the area in the county is devoted to forestry, making Brewton a center of the wood industry. The city is large enough to provide the advantages of a large city, yet small enough to maintain the community spirit that characterizes all progressive southern towns.

JEFFERSON STATE COMMUNITY COLLEGE   *(F-7)*
2601 Carson Road
Birmingham, Alabama 35215
Tel: (205) 853-1200; Fax: (205) 853-0340

Description: This publicly supported community college is accredited by the Southern Association of Colleges and Schools. The College undertakes to make the opportunity for higher education physically and economically available to all who wish to seek it and accepts the responsbility to serve those whom it admits. The College offers both university-parallel programs and career preparation programs leading to either an Associate in Arts degree, an Associate in Science degree, an Associate in Applied Science degree, or to a Certificate of Completion. Continuing Education and Community Services courses are offered. Classes and programs are offered during the day and evening on the main campus and at off-campus locations. It operates on the quarter system and offers two summer sessions. Enrollment includes 7,313. A faculty of 144 full-time and 210 part-time gives a faculty-student ratio of 1-46.

Entrance Requirements: High School graduation or equivalent; open admission, rolling admission, midyear admission, and advanced placement plans available; no application fee.

Costs Per Year: $550 ($22 per credit hour) resident tuition; $962.50 ($38.50 per credit hour) nonresident tuition.

Collegiate Environment: The campus has 13 modern, fully air-conditioned buildings on 234 acres. The libraray contains 67,490 volumes, 306 periodical subscriptions, 6,465 titles on microforms, 3,295 records and tapes, and 26,677 government document titles. There is no housing available on campus. All applicants are accepted, including midyear students. Financial aid is available.

Community Environment: See University of Alabama - Birmingham.

JUDSON COLLEGE   *(I-5)*
P.O. Box 120
Marion, Alabama 36756
Tel: (205) 683-6161; (800) 447-9472

Description: This privately supported Baptist liberal arts college for women, founded in 1838, is owned and operated by the Alabama Baptist Convention. It is fully accredited by Southern Association of Colleges and Schools. The college, which offers liberal arts programs, is part of a 1,000-student college complex with neighboring Marion Military Institute. Courses on both campuses are available to M.I. and Judson students. Judson offers a Bachelor of Arts or Bachelor of Science degree under a four-year or two-year and ten-month program. Course and degree requirements are the same under both plans. Overseas study programs and cooperative education programs are available. Enrollment is 405 women. A faculty of 41 gives a faculty-student ratio of 1-12. The college operates on the semester system.

Entrance Requirements: Accredited high school graduation or equivalent; completion of 15 units, including 3 English; ACT required for state residents; out-of-state applicants may substitute SAT; early admission, early decision, rolling admission, delayed admission and advanced placement plans available; $20 application fee.

Costs Per Year: $5,178 tuition; $3,125 room and board.

Collegiate Environment: The campus is located on 100 acres of land. The school's facilities include a well-equipped language laboratory, a library that contains over 78,000 volumes, dormitory space for 405 women, a swimming pool, and stables. The college accepts 72% of applicants, including midyear students. Financial aid is available.

Community Environment: Marion (population 4,000) is 80 miles from Montgomery, 75 miles from Birmingham, and 100 miles from Meridian, Mississippi. The city is rich in antebellum tradition and is within easy driving distance of major cities of the Southeast. The climate is mild, and is good for outdoor sports. Excellent bus service between Marion, Selma, Montgomery, Mobile, Meridian, Tuscaloosa, Brent and Birmingham is available. Beautiful southern homes, excellent schools and several churches are located in the community.

LAWSON STATE COMMUNITY COLLEGE   *(F-7)*
3060 Wilson Road
Birmingham, Alabama 35221
Tel: (205) 925-2515; Admissions: (205) 929-6309; Fax: (205) 929-6316

Description: The publicly supported coeducational community college operates on the quarter system and offers one summer session. It is accredited by the Southern Association of Colleges and Schools. A cooperative program with the University of Alabama in Birmingham is available. Lawson offers the Associate degree and Certificate of Completion. Reading Enrichment Program is offered as well as continuing education courses. Enrollment is 1,489 full-time and 431 part-time students. A faculty of 51 full-time and 38 part-time gives a faculty-student ratio of 1-23.

Entrance Requirements: High school graduation with C average or GED; completion of 16 units, including 4 English, 1 mathematics, 1 science, and 3 social science; entrance examination; SAT and ACT optional; open enrollment; rolling admission and early decision plans available; no application fee.

Costs Per Year: $792 tuition; $1,386 nonresident tuition.

Collegiate Environment: The campus has 5 buildings on 30 acres. The library contains 28,471 volumes, 200 periodicals, 147 microforms, and 1,184 sound recordings. Financial aid is available.

Community Environment: See University of Alabama - Birmingham.

LIVINGSTON UNIVERSITY   *(I-2)*
Livingston, Alabama 35470
Tel: (205) 652-9661; (800) 621-8014; Fax: (205) 652-4065

Description: The publicly supported liberal arts university is accredited by the Southern Association of Colleges and Schools. The college was founded in 1835 when seventy citizens contributed to a fund establishing the construction of a school building. It was incorporated in 1840 as a female academy, and the first diploma was granted in 1843. In 1883 it was incorporated into the first state-supported female academy in the South. It is now a coeducational university, comprised of 4 colleges: General Studies, Business and Commerce, Education, Graduate Studies. The university grants the Associate, Bachelor, Master, and Educational Specialist degrees. 48

quarter hours of correspondence credit are allowed and continuing education classes are offered. It operates on the quarter system and offers one summer session. Enrollment includes 1,646 full-time, 140 part-time undergraduate, and 200 graduate students. A faculty of 104 gives a faculty student ratio of 1-18. Air Force and Army ROTC programs are available.

Entrance Requirements: Accredited high school graduation or equivalent; non high school graduates considered; completion of 15 units including 4 English, 2 mathematics, 2 science, 2 social science; SAT or ACT required; GRE required for graduate school; early admission, early decision, midyear admission, rolling admission, and advanced placement plans available; $15 application fee.

Costs Per Year: $1,740 tuition; $2,223 room and board; $255 student fees.

Collegiate Environment: The university is large enough to offer the advantages of a large school, yet small enough to insure attention to each individual. The campus occupies 585 acres, and facilities include a library of more than 108,000 volumes, 678 periodicals, 345,381 microforms and housing for 400 men, 340 women, and 72 families. About 85% of the students applying for admission are accepted, including midyear students. The average freshman score was ACT 18.6. 175 scholarships are available and 85% of students receive some form of financial assistance.

Community Environment: Livingston (population 3,500) is the Sumter County Seat, and is located on Interstate 59/20 and Alabama Highway 28. It is 116 miles southwest of Birmingham, 130 miles west of Montgomery, and 37 miles east of Meridian, Mississippi. Livingston is served by the Alabama Great Southern Railroad, two bus lines, and by airline service. The climate is mild. Fishing and hunting are excellent.

LURLEEN B. WALLACE STATE JUNIOR COLLEGE (N-8)
P.O. Drawer 1418
Andalusia, Alabama 36420
Tel: (334) 222-6591; Admissions: (334) 222-6591; Fax: (334) 222-6567

Description: The publicly supported, junior college opened its doors in September 1969. In May 1970 the school moved to a new campus. Accredited by the Southern Association of Colleges and Schools, the college offers university-parallel courses and technical-vocational programs for immediate employment. The college grants Certificates and the Associate degree. Correspondent credit allowed; continuing education courses offered; cooperative education programs offered in agriculture, art, business, education, engineering, health, secretarial science, computer, and humanities. It operates on the quarter system and offers two summer sessions. Enrollment includes 791 full-time, 368 part-time, and 437 evening students. A faculty of 24 full-time and 40 part-time gives a faculty-student ratio of 1-20.

Entrance Requirements: Open enrollment C average policy; non-high school graduates considered; rolling admission; early admission, early decision, midyear admission, and advanced placement plans available.

Costs Per Year: $1,125 ($375 per quarter) state resident tuition, $1,968 ($656 per quarter) nonresident tuition.

Collegiate Environment: The campus has four buildings on 152 acres. The library contains 24,000 volumes, 150 periodicals, 556 microforms and 5,000 audiovisual materials. All students applying for admission are accepted. Approximately 65% of the students receive financial aid.

Community Environment: Ponce de Leon and De Soto reached the Andalusia area in their 16th and 17th century explorations. A settlement was established on the Conecuh River and then, due to flooding, moved to the present site of Andalusia (population 12,500). The city is 85 miles from Montgomery, 125 miles from Mobile, and 180 miles from Birmingham. Major industries in Andalusia are textile mills, nut-shelling, oil plants, a box factory, a cold storage plant and a meat-packing plant. Community facilities include a number of churches, a library, two hospitals, parks, and swimming pools. The community also has an excellent public school system. Several lakes in the area provide facilities for swimming, water skiing, and fishing. The Conecuh National Forest near the city provides outdoor activities, including a game preserve providing regular hunts.

MARION MILITARY INSTITUTE (I-5)
Washington St.
Marion, Alabama 36756
Tel: (205) 683-2306; (800) 664-1842; Fax: (205) 683-2380

Description: Marion Military Institute was founded in 1842. It is a private, independent, coeducational, four-year preparatory school and two-year college. The institute is accredited by the Southern Association of Colleges and Schools. The typical MMI student usually enrolls at Marion for one of the following reasons: to develop educational potential in a structured environment that includes personal attention and discipline; to obtain a sound education in preparation for transfer to a four-year college; to prepare for West Point, Annapolis, or the Air Force or Coast Guard Academies; or to enter the ROTC two-year Early Commissioning Program and receive upon graduation a lieutenant's commission in the Army. Each cadet must pursue a challenging curriculum, including athletics and Army ROTC, and participate fully in the other activities of the Cadet Corps. The institute grants the Associate degree. The junior college operates on the semester system and offers two summer sessions. Enrollment includes 189 students. A faculty of 24 gives a faculty-student ratio of 1-8.

Entrance Requirements: Accredited high school graduation or equivalent; completion of 24 units including 4 English, 3 mathematics, and 3 social science; non-high school graduates considered; all high school applicants must take entrance tests prior to acceptance, and are encouraged to visit the campus for a formal interview; midyear admission and rolling admission plans available; $100 application fee.

Costs Per Year: $5,896 tuition; $3,300 room and board.

Collegiate Environment: The campus is comprised of 26 buildings on 124 acres. Dormitory facilities accommodate 500 men and 50 women. The library contains 32,000 volumes and numerous pamphlets, periodicals, audiovisual aids and recordings. Approximately 85% of the students applying for admission are accepted, including midyear students. Financial aid is available, and approximately 180 scholarships are offered. 95% of the current student body receives some form of financial assistance.

Community Environment: See Judson College.

MILES COLLEGE (F-7)
P.O. Box 3800
Birmingham, Alabama 35208
Tel: (205) 923-2771; (800) 445-0708; Admissions: (205) 923-2771 x226; Fax: (205) 923-9292

Description: The privately supported, liberal arts college operates under the auspices of the Christian Methodist Episcopal Church. The college is the result of early efforts put forth by the colored Methodist Episcopal Church (1907). It is accredited by the Southern Association of Colleges and Schools. It grants the Bachelor degree. The college operates on the semester system and offers one summer session. Enrollment includes 601 men and women. A faculty of 33 full-time and 20 part-time gives a faculty-student ratio of 1-12.

Entrance Requirements: Open enrollment policy; completion of 15 units including 4 English, 2 mathematics, 1 foreign language, 2 science and 2 social science, ACT required; midyear admission, and rolling admission plan available; $25 application fee.

Costs Per Year: $7,050 tuition; $2,700 room and board, $350 student fee.

Collegiate Environment: All students are required to attend chapel services. The student body is evenly divided between Baptists and Methodists with a creditable number representing other religious societies. The campus has 21 buildings on 36 acres including dormitory facilities for 150 men and 150 women. The library contains 80,000 volumes, 2,354 pamphlets, 394 periodicals, 850 microforms and 1,173 recordings. Approximately 95% of the students applying for admission are accepted. Financial assistance is available and 93% of the students receive assistance.

Community Environment: See University of Alabama - Birmingham.

MOBILE COLLEGE   *(P-3)*
P.O. Box 13220
Mobile, Alabama 36613
Tel: (205) 675-5990

Description: The privately supported college is affiliated with the Alabama Baptist State Convention and is accredited by the Southern Association of Colleges and Schools. The college offers a liberal arts and sciences program, and seeks to be a college with a human touch. Chartered in 1961, it was the first senior college to be established in the state of Alabama during the last 57 years. Enrollment includes 1,320 students attending classes on the semester system with three summer sessions. The college grants the Bachelor of Science and Arts degrees, the Associate degree in Nursing, the Master of Arts in Education, Master of Business Administration, Master of Religious Studies and Master of Science in Nursing.

Entrance Requirements: High school graduation; completion of 13 units including 4 English, 3 mathematics, 2 science, 2 social studies; ACT 15 or over required; early admission, and rolling admission plans are available; $25 application fee. Financial aid is available.

Costs Per Year: $4,650 tuition; $2,980 room and board.

Collegiate Environment: The 700-acre campus is located about ten miles from downtown Mobile. Dormitories accommodate 119 men and 132 women. The library contains 112,000 volumes. The campus site continues to be developed and all buildings are air-conditioned. Academic excellence, modern facilities, highly qualified faculty, and a Christian atmosphere are the hallmarks of a Mobile College education. Approximately 90% of the students applying for admission are accepted.

Community Environment: See University of South Alabama.

NORTHEAST ALABAMA STATE COMMUNITY COLLEGE
(C-9)
Box 159
Rainsville, Alabama 35986
Tel: (205) 228-6001; Admissions: (205) 228-6001 x22; Fax: (205) 228-4350

Description: This state-supported junior college, one of 21 created by the State Legislature in 1963, started classes in 1965. It is accredited by the Southern Association of Colleges and Schools. The college offers university parallel and terminal career education programs. It grants the Associate degree. The quarter system is used and offers one summer session. Enrollment includes 1,200 full-time and 500 part-time students. A faculty of 40 full-time and 15 part-time gives a faculty-student ratio of 1-30.

Entrance Requirements: High school graduation or Certificate of Equivalancy; open enrollment; early admission, early decision, deferred admission, rolling admission, midyear admission, and advanced placement plans available.

Costs Per Year: $1,025 state resident tuition; $1,700 nonresident tuition.

Collegiate Environment: The campus has 13 buildings on 105 acres, including a library containing 43,000 volumes. There are no dormitories. Social fraternities and sororities are prohibited on campus but there are 12 organizations in which students may become involved. Scholarships are available and 70% of students receive some form of financial assistance.

Community Environment: Rainsville, population 1,500, is in a mountainous area with a very pleasant temperate climate. The town is 58 miles from commercial airline service, six miles from Interstate 59, and eight miles from rail service. Protestant churches, and hospitals in Fort Payne and Scottsboro service the community. Recreational activities include good fishing, boating, camping, and hiking at nearby state parks.

OAKWOOD COLLEGE   *(B-7)*
Oakwood Road, N.W.
Huntsville, Alabama 35896
Tel: (205) 726-7000; Fax: (205) 726-7409

Description: The privately supported liberal arts college is accredited by the Southern Association of Colleges and Schools and owned by the general conference of Seventh-Day Adventist. It operates on the quarter system and one summer session is offered. Founded in 1896 as an industrial and manual training school, it became a junior college in 1917 and a senior college in 1934. In 1964 the college joined United Negro College Fund. The Oakwood Academy, a four-year high school, is operated in connection with the college. Current enrollment includes 498 men, 727 women full-time and 48 men and 61 women part-time. A faculty of 75 full-time and 46 part-time gives a faculty-student ratio of 1-15. The college grants the Associate and Bachelor degrees. Cooperative programs with other institutions are available.

Entrance Requirements: Accredited high school graduation or equivalent; completion of 18 units including 3 English, 2 mathematics, 2 science and 1 social science; ACT or SAT required; applicants not meeting all requirements may be admitted as special students; early admission, early decision, rolling admission, midyear admission, delayed admission and advanced placement plans available; $10 application fee.

Costs Per Year: $6,384 tuition; $3,846 room and board; $135 student fees.

Collegiate Environment: The campus consists of 988 acres, 20 of which comprise the main campus. Dormitory facilities accommodate 388 men and 471 women and 25 families. The library contains over 71,000 volumes. Financial aid is available to economically handicapped students. Scholarships are available.

Community Environment: See University of Alabama - Huntsville.

SAMFORD UNIVERSITY   *(F-7)*
800 Lakeshore Drive
Birmingham, Alabama 35229
Tel: (205) 870-2011; (800) 888-7218; Admissions: (205) 870-2901; Fax: (205) 870-2171

Description: The privately supported university is accredited by the Southern Association of Colleges and Schools. Enrollment includes 1,228 men, 2,008 women, and 1,065 graduate students full-time and 144 men and 126 women part-time. A faculty of 256 full-time and 85 part-time gives a faculty-student ratio of 1-14. The 4-1-4 system is used and two summer sessions are offered. Air Force ROTC is available. An academic cooperative plan with Auburn University, Georgia Tech, Mercer University, University of Southern California, and Washington University in St. Louis is available for engineering students. A cooperative plan with Duke University provides a degree in forestry. The college grants Bachelor, Master and Professional degrees.

Entrance Requirements: Accredited high school graduation or equivalent; completion of 18 units including 4 English and 12 in math, science, language, and social studies; ACT 21 or SAT combined 1000 required; non-high school graduates considered; early admission, early decision, advanced placement, and rolling admission plans available; $25 application fee.

Costs Per Year: $8,648 tuition; $3,844 room and board.

Collegiate Environment: The campus consists of 280 acres with 56 college buildings featuring Georgian colonial architecture. The library uses the open-stack system and contains 632,000 titles, and numerous periodicals, microforms and recordings. Dormitory facilities accommodate 1,860 men and women, fraternities accommodate 50 men, and 45 apartments are available for married students. The college hopes to provide a broad and academically sound education in a positive Christian environment. Approximately 84% of the students applying for admission are accepted, including midyear students. 83% of the current students receive some form of financial aid.

Community Environment: See University of Alabama - Birmingham.

SELMA UNIVERSITY   *(J-6)*
1501 Lapsley Street
Selma, Alabama 36702
Tel: (205) 872-2533

Description: The privately supported university was founded in 1878 and is supported by the Alabama Baptist Convention with much emphasis placed upon Christian Education. In 1881 it was incorporated as the Alabama Baptist Normal and Theological Seminary. In 1955 the college discontinued all work below the college level, and now offers two years of standard collegiate work, leading to an Associate Degree and Bachelor of Divinity. In addition, the School of Religion grants the Bachelor of Theology or Bachelor of Religious Education Degree. Enrollment is 258 students with a faculty of 25. The semester system is used and one summer session is offered.

Entrance Requirements: Accredited high school graduation or equivalent; completion of 22 units including 3 English, 1 mathematics, 2 science and 3 social studies; ACT required; rolling admission plan available; $10 application fee.

Costs Per Year: $3,100 ($1,550 per semester) tuition, $2,140 ($1,070 per semester) room and board.

Collegiate Environment: The campus consists of 22 acres; the most recent buildings are a gymnasium and two dormitories increasing housing capacity to 137 men and 118 women. Emphasis is on liberal arts, teacher preparation, and business education presented in an atmosphere of Christian fellowship. Certain courses in religion and Chapel Services three times per week are required. 95% of the students who apply for admission are accepted. The college offers a special program enabling low-mark, culturally disadvantaged students to attend. Financial aid is available, and 97% of the current student body receive some form of assistance. A new science building is under construction and Dinkins Administration building is being completely renovated.

Community Environment: An industrial city with a population of 26,684, it is located on the Alabama River about 45 miles west of Montgomery, the capital of Alabama.

SNEAD STATE COMMUNITY COLLEGE   *(D-8)*
P.O. Drawer D
Boaz, Alabama 35957
Tel: (205) 593-7180

Description: The publicly supported community college is accredited by the Southern Association of Colleges and Schools and grants the Associate degree. Founded and controlled for 32 years by the Methodist Church, Snead became part of the state system in 1967. The quarter system is used and 1 summer session is offered. Recent enrollment included 1,112 full-time and 493 part-time students. The faculty consists of 31 full-time and 45 part-time members providing a student-faculty ratio of 32:1.

Entrance Requirements: Accredited high school graduation or equivalent required; open enrollment policy; early decision, midyear admission, rolling admission, early admission and advanced placement plans available; no application fee.

Costs Per Year: $909; $1,473 nonresident; $2,480 semi-private room and board (3 quarters).

Collegiate Environment: The 42-acre campus has 16 buildings, including a library of approximately 31,900 volumes. Dormitory facilities accommodate 74 men and women. The college accepts 95% of the students who apply for admission, and students may enroll at midyear as well as in September. 602 scholarships are offered including 108 athletic. 30% of students receive some form of financial aid.

Community Environment: Boaz (population 6,500) is located 60 miles north of Birmingham, and has an average temperature of 65 degrees. Employment is available in industry and business. Churches, civic and social organizations are located in the city. Guntersville Lake is ten miles from Boaz. The town is a clothing outlet center, one of the largest in the U.S.

SOUTHEASTERN BIBLE COLLEGE   *(F-7)*
3001 Highway 280 East
Birmingham, Alabama 35243
Tel: (205) 969-0080

Description: The privately supported college The college is accredited by the American Association of Bible Colleges and grants a Bachelor and Master degree. Its Teacher Education program is ACSI-approved for certification. The semester system is used and one summer sessions are offered. Six hours of correspondent credits allowed; continuing education courses offered; 2-year missionary program for nurses available; must complete a minimum of 30 semester hours in residence for graduation. Enrollment includes 78 men and 35 women full-time and 25 men and 15 women part-time. A faculty of 12 full-time and 8 part-time gives a faculty-student ratio of 1-13.

Entrance Requirements: Accredited high school graduation or equivalent, with recommended completion of 11 units, including 4 English, 2 mathematics, 1 science, 2 foreign language and 2 social science; ACT minimum score 19 required; early decision, rolling admission and advanced placement plans available; $20 application fee.

Costs Per Year: $4,300 tuition; $2,900 room and board; $150 student fees; books average $150; additional personal expenses.

Collegiate Environment: The campus is situated on 10 acres in a suburb of Birmingham. The library contains 31,000 volumes. There are dormitory facilities for 40 men and 40 women. Unmarried, full-time students are required to live on campus unless living with family or over 21 years of age; college helps locate apartments for married students and also has married housing. Approximately 90% of the students applying for admission are accepted, including midyear students. 72 scholarships, including 31 for freshmen are available. Pell Grants and other financial aid are available.

Community Environment: See University of Alabama - Birmingham.

SOUTHERN UNION STATE COMMUNITY COLLEGE
(G-10)
Wadley, Alabama 36276
Tel: (205) 395-2211; Admissions: (205) 395-2211 X 5157; Fax: (205) 395-2205

Description: Publicly-supported coeducational, community junior college is accredited by the Southern Association of Colleges and Schools. Founded by Southern Christian Convention in 1922, the college became a part of the State Junior College system in 1964. The college grants the Associate degree. The college offers university-parallel and Occupation Education programs and a developmental program for students with inadequate preparation for college level work. It operates on the quarter system and offers one summer session. Enrollment includes 2,538 full-time and 2,113 part-time students.

Entrance Requirements: High school graduation with a C average or GED certificate; early decision, early admission, rolling admission plans available. No application fee.

Costs Per Year: $1,000 state resident tuition; $1,575 non-resident tuition, $1,950 room and board.

Collegiate Environment: The main campus has 10 buildings on 70 acres and is located in Wadley, Alabama. The library is a two-story, air-conditioned building containing 80,000 volumes. Dormitory facilities accommodate 206 men and women. Students enjoy a 15-acre lake located on the campus. The student body consists primarily of residents from the communities of East Central Alabama; 80% of freshman class returned for second year. Scholarships are available and 60% of students receive some form of financial aid. Extension campuses with day and evening class offerings are located in Valley and Opelika.

Community Environment: Population 746. Located in East Central Alabama approximately 90 miles southwest of Atlanta, and the same distance southeast of Birmingham. Wadley is on Alabama State Highways 22 and 77. Gently rolling farm and woodland, healthful country atmosphere. Easy access to neighboring cities for shopping and recreation. Hospital in Roanoke.

Branch Campuses: Valley, Wadley, and Opelika, AL.

SPARKS STATE TECHNICAL COLLEGE   *(L-12)*
P.O. Drawer 580
Eufaula, Alabama 36072
Tel: (205) 687-3543; (800) 543-2426; Fax: (205) 687-0255

Description: The publicly supported, coeducational technical college is accredited by the Southern Association of Colleges and Schools and grants Associate degrees in applied technology. It operates on the quarter system and offers one summer session. Enrollment includes 471 full-time and 83 part-time students. A faculty of 24 full-time and 14 part-time gives a faculty-student ratio of 1-15.

Entrance Requirements: Open enrollment policy; high school graduation or equivalent required for college parallel courses; pre-entrance testing required for nursing program (LPN); rolling admission plan available.

Costs Per Year: $1,035 ($345 per quarter) state resident tuition; $1,551 ($517 per quarter) nonresident tuition.

Collegiate Environment: The campus is 4 miles south of Eufaula, overlooking scenic Lake Eufaula, and contains 9 modern, air-conditioned buildings. 95% of students applying for admission are accepted, including midyear students. Approximately 90% of the students receive financial aid.

Community Environment: This city has the unique distinction of being the home of 6 Governors of Alabama, one in whose honor the school is named. The city is rich in heritage and progressive in business and civic affairs. It offers many recreational activities and job opportunities.

SPRING HILL COLLEGE   *(P-3)*
4000 Dauphin St.
Mobile, Alabama 36608
Tel: (334) 380-3030; (800) 742-6704; Fax: (334) 460-2186

Description: The privately supported liberal arts college is owned and operated by Jesuits and accredited by the Southern Association of Colleges and Schools. The first students began instruction in 1830. The college became coeducational in 1952. The college intends to give its students a deep appreciation of the human condition through its love for intellectual knowledge and truth. Enrollment includes 887 full-time and 230 part-time undergraduate and 245 graduate students. A faculty of 59 full-time and 47 part-time professors gives an undergraduate faculty-student ratio of 1-14. Army and Air Force ROTC is available. The early semester system is used, and one summer session and two mini-course sessions are offered. The college grants Bachelor degrees and six Master degrees.

Entrance Requirements: High school graduation or equivalent with rank in upper 50% of graduating class with completion of 16 units including 4 English, 2 mathematics, 2 social science, 2 natural science, 2 in academic subjects; SAT or ACT required; minimum score of 20 on ACT or 850 on SAT required; early admission, delayed admission, rolling admission and advanced placement plans available; $25 application fee; non-high school graduates considered.

Costs Per Year: $12,123 tuition and fees; $4,788 room and board.

Collegiate Environment: The campus occupies approximately 500 acres. Dormitories accommodate 758 men and women (all air-conditioned). The library houses more than 150,000 volumes with numerous pamphlets, periodicals and microforms. Students of faiths other than Catholic regularly constitute a large minority of the student body. Approximately 85% of the students applying for admission are accepted, including midyear students. Financial aid is available and 82% of students receive some form of financial aid. The middle 50% range of enrolled freshmen scores: SAT 900-1100 combined; ACT 22-26 composite. A comparable, recalculated high school grade point average is 2.7-3.6 on a scale of 4.

Community Environment: See University of South Alabama.

STILLMAN COLLEGE   *(G-4)*
3600 15th Street
Tuscaloosa, Alabama 35403
Tel: (205) 349-4240; (800) 523-6331; Admissions: (205) 349-4240; Fax: (205) 349-4252

Description: The privately supported liberal arts college is accredited by the Southern Association of Colleges and Schools to award the Bachelor of Science and Bachelor of Arts degrees. It is affiliated with the Presbyterian Church U.S.A. In 1876 the General Assembly of the Presbyterian Church in the U.S. authorized the opening of a training school for Negro ministers. Throughout the years this school has grown in size and expanded its academic program, raising its educational sights to concentrate on Christian education rather than training for the ministry, responding to the stiffening requirements for state teaching certificates and the increase in employment opportunities for African Americans in the South and the nation. A cooperative degree programs exist with colleges and universities in Alabama, Tennessee, New York, Michigan, Ohio and Washington. Army ROTC is available as an elective. It operates on the semester system and offers one summer session. Enrollment includes 905 full-time and 8 part-time students. A faculty of 56 full-time and 15 part-time gives a faculty-student ratio of 1-12.

Entrance Requirements: High school graduation with a C average; completion of 16 units including 4 English, 4 mathematics, 4 science and 4 social science; non-high school graduates considered; ACT accepted; midyear admission, rolling admission plan available; $25 application fee.

Costs Per Year: Tuition $5,200, $3,100 room and board.

Collegiate Environment: The campus has 23 buildings on 133 acres. Dormitory facilities accommodate 607 students. The library contains 92,584 volumes, 500 pamphlets, 366 periodicals, 1,200 microforms, 575 audiovisual materials and 324 recordings. 75% of applicants are accepted. Financial aid is available and approximately 90% receive assistance.

Community Environment: See University of Alabama.

TALLADEGA COLLEGE   *(F-9)*
627 West Battle Street
Talladega, Alabama 35160
Tel: (205) 761-6253; (800) 633-2440; Fax: (205) 761-6359

Description: The privately supported liberal arts college is affiliated with the United Church of Christ and the American Missionary Association. The college is accredited by the Southern Association of Colleges and Schools and grants the Bachelor degree. A colonial brick building served the first classes held in 1867. The first college in Alabama that opened its doors to Negroes was then a primary school. The first class graduated with Bachelor degrees in 1895. Enrollment includes 1,027 students with a faculty of 81, giving a student-faculty ratio of 13:1. The semester system is used. Degree exchange programs with other higher education institutions in the state are available. This latter program allows advanced students to transfer without penalty from their home college to the institution that offers a degree in one of several areas including engineering, physics, nursing, veterinary medicine, geology and law.

Entrance Requirements: High school graduation or GED; acceptable scores on ACT or SAT; 16 units of high school work.

Costs Per Year: $5,666 tuition; $3,382 room and board.

Collegiate Environment: The campus occupies 16 buildings on 130 acres. Dormitory facilities accommodate 205 men and 450 women. The library houses 86,450 volumes. 209 scholarships are available and 92% of students receive some form of financial aid.

Community Environment: Population 19,165. Talladega is at the heart of a fertile valley in the foothills of the Blue Ridge Mountains. Its elevation gives it a healthful climate. Highest point in Alabama, Cheaha Mountain is 17 miles north in Talladega National Forest. Fifty-five miles to Birmingham. Annual rainfall 54.3 inches; average temperature 63.3. Home of the Alabama School for Blind, and Alabama School for Deaf. Bus service is available. Closest airline is in Anniston. Supervised playgrounds, parks, theaters, hunting, fishing, and hiking facilities. Rich agricultural region, diversified industries, two daily newspapers, as well as three radio stations in the city.

TROY STATE UNIVERSITY   *(L-9)*
University Avenue
Troy, Alabama 36082
Tel: (205) 670-3000; (800) 551-9716; Admissions: (205) 670-3179; Fax: (205) 670-3774

Description: The publicly supported university is accredited by the Southern Association of Colleges and Schools. It grants the Associate, Bachelor, Master, and Education Specialist degrees. The past history of the University shows an institutional purpose dedicated to teacher education with a companion dedication to the Arts and Sciences, Applied Sciences, Business and Nursing. The university has grown from a normal school in 1887 to a four-year college in 1929 and attained university status in 1967. The university operates on the quarter system and offers one summer session and a two-week interim term in August and December. Enrollment includes 4,497 full-time and 571 part-time undergraduates and 412 graduate students. A faculty of 202 gives an undergraduate faculty-student ratio of 1-23. Troy State University system has independently accredited units at Dothan and Montgomery. Both grant B.A., B.S., M.S., and Ed.S. degrees. These independent sites provide programs in continuing education, serving a student body whose pursuit of education is supplementary to their at-present functional role in society. Military and civilian facilities are used and classes are conducted during after-duty hours. The Dothan-Ft. Rucker site serves approximately 2,633 students; the Montgomery site enrolls 3,408 students.

Entrance Requirements: High school graduation or equivalent; completion of 15 units, including 3 English; minimum score 18 ACT required; graduate student applicants must submit one of three test (GMAT, GRE, MAT) scores; non-high school graduates considered; early admission, early decision, advanced placement and rolling admission plans available; applicants not meeting all requirements considered as special students; $15 application fee. CLEP credit given.

Costs Per Year: $1,800 state resident tuition; $3,210 nonresident fee; $2,895 room and board.

Collegiate Environment: The campus is situated a mile from the heart of the city, occupying 460 acres. Unmarried freshmen under 21 are required to live in college housing; dormitories accomodate 689 men, 851 women and 140 married students. The library is housed in the Lurleen BiWallace Hall, designed to accommodate the many forms of printed and non-printed materials. There are 333,793 volumes in this library. 77% of applicants are accepted. Approximately 75% of freshman class returned for second year. Financial aid is available, and 70% of the current undergraduate student body receive some form of assistance.

Community Environment: Population 15,000. Troy is located at the junction of U.S. Highways 231 and 29. It is 50 miles from the state capital, Montgomery. Greyhound and Trailways bus lines provide regular bus service. The citizens take great interest in the University, and extend a cordial welcome to students. There are numerous social, church, civic and school organizations which provide cultural enrichment for the citizens and for the students of the University. Recreational facilities include parks for swimming, tennis courts, state lake for fishing, and two golf courses.

TROY STATE UNIVERSITY AT DOTHAN   *(N-11)*
P.O. Box 8368
Dothan, Alabama 36304
Tel: (334) 983-6556; Fax: (334) 983-6322

Description: This publicly supported coeducational state university is accredited by the Southern Association of Colleges and Schools. Predominantly an upper-level and graduate school, TSUD offers associate, bachelor's, master's, and education specialist degrees. Degree programs are offered in the School of Business, the School of Education, and the College of Arts and Sciences. It operates on the quarter system and offers one summer session. Enrollment includes 973 full-time and 1,393 part-time undergraduates and 659 graduate students. With a faculty of 59 full-time and 70 part-time, there is a faculty-student ratio of 1-22. 88% of the faculty hold an earned doctorate.

Entrance Requirements: Admits first year freshmen who have a minimum score of ACT 19 composite or SAT 790 combined and a minimum 2.0 (4.0 scale) high school G.P.A.; for unconditional admission of transfer students, a student is eligible if in good standing at the last college attended, and if possessing an overall grade point average of at least 2.0 on all college/university work. Rolling admission; $15 application fee.

Costs Per Year: $1,920 tuition; $3,456 nonresidents.

Collegiate Environment: On the 250-acre TSUD campus are two modern buildings designed in the Williamsburg style of architecture and occupied for the first time in 1990. Named for Wallace D. Malone, Jr., president pro tempore of the Troy State University Board of Trustees, Malone Hall houses the administration, School of Business, computer center, and classrooms. The College of Arts and Sciences, School of Education, library, and student center occupy Adams Hall, which is named for Dr. Ralph W. Adams, Chancellor Emeritus of the Troy State University System. The University Library contains 80,000 volumes, 844 periodicals, 107,219 microforms, 6,147 audiovisual materials, and 948 other items.

Community Environment: TSUD is located in Dothan, a city of approximately 55,000 in the southeastern corner of Alabama. Shopping malls and restaurants are within five minutes of the campus.

Branch Campuses: Fort Rucker, AL.

TROY STATE UNIVERSITY IN MONTGOMERY   *(J-8)*
P.O. Drawer 4419
Montgomery, Alabama 36103-4419
Tel: (334) 834-1400; (800) 355-8786; Admissions: (334) 241-9506; Fax: (334) 241-9714

Description: The Montgomery campus of Troy State University system provides academic programs serving a student body whose pursuit of education is supplementary to their present functional roles in society. The school offers the B.A., B.S., M.S., and Ed.S. degrees. The quarter system is used with one summer session. Classes, conducted primarily after work hours, are held in both civilian and military facilities. TSUM's enrollment is 3,408 men and women with a faculty of 178. It is accredited by the Southern Association of Colleges and Schools.

Entrance Requirements: High school graduation with at least eleven units; high school graduates with a C average accepted; GRE; early admission, early decision, rolling admission, delayed admission, and advanced placement plans available; $15 application fee.

Costs Per Year: $1,800 undergradute, in-state tuition.

Collegiate Environment: The university library contains 20,000 volumes, 305 periodicals, 5,696 microforms, and 1,444 audiovisual materials.

Community Environment: See Alabama State University.

TUSKEGEE UNIVERSITY   *(J-10)*
Tuskegee, Alabama 36088
Tel: (334) 727-8500; (800) 622-6531; Fax: (334) 724-4402

Description: The privately supported university is accredited by the Southern Association of Colleges and Schools. The institution was founded by Booker T. Washington in 1881 as Alabama's first normal school for the training of Negro teachers. The next year he contracted to purchase a 100-acre abandoned plantation, which became the nucleus of Tuskegee's present campus. He began a program of self-help that permitted students to live on the campus and earn all or part of their expenses. The University has a college of Arts and Sciences and Schools of Agriculture and Home Economics; Engineering and Agriculture; Business; Education; Nursing and Allied Health; and Veterinary Medicine. The University grants the Bachelor, Master and Professional degrees. Extensive cooperative education programs are available. It operates on the semester system and offers one summer session. Enrollment includes 3,309 full-time, and 289 part-time undergraduate, and 195 graduate students. A faculty of 264 gives a faculty-student ratio of 1-13.

Entrance Requirements: High school graduation or equivalent with rank in upper 50% of the graduating class; completion of 15 units including 3 English, 3 mathematics, 2 science and 3 social science; SAT or ACT required, but used for placement purposes only; early admission, rolling admission, early decision and advanced placement plans available; $25 application fee, $35 foreign application fee.

Costs Per Year: $7,070 tuition; $3,620 room and board.

Collegiate Environment: The campus has more than 150 major buildings on 4,500 acres. The library contains 216,000 volumes. Dormitory facilities accommodate 576 men, 1,746 women and 96 married students. Approximately 80% of the students applying for admission are accepted, including midyear students.

Community Environment: Tuskegee, population 12,000, is a small town with a moderate climate that is very warm in the summer. Bus and taxi service is available and airlines are nearby. Churches of all major denominations, a library and a museum contribute to the cultural atmosphere of the town. Motels and hotels are located in the area. The town also has various fraternal, civic, and veteran's organizations.

UNIVERSITY OF ALABAMA   *(G-4)*
P.O. Box 870132
Tuscaloosa, Alabama 35487-0132
Tel: (205) 348-5666

Description: The University of Alabama opened on April 12, 1831, in response to the State Legislature's declaration to establish a seminary of learning. On April 4, 1865, Federal troops burned all but four buildings, and the campus lay dormant until 1871 when determined alumni revived the institution and set its future course. Today the University of Alabama is a thriving 900-acre campus that is a pleasing blend of historic nostalgia and contemporary exuberance. This publicly supported university is accredited by the Southern Association of Colleges and Schools. Enrollment includes 19,366 students. A faculty of 1,066 provides a faculty-student ratio of 1:18. Its 127 buildings include extensive, modern facilities for classroom teaching and research, 15 residence halls, a modern health center, an art gallery and museum, various athletic facilities, and a recently completed modern student center complex. Correspondent credit is allowed; continuing education and cooperative education courses are offered; prior learning credits are available. An overseas program is also available.

Entrance Requirements: Admission at the freshman level is based on the probability of success as determined by high school GPA used in combination with scores on the ACT; 16 high school units, 12 of which should be academic, are required; specific units are also required by the various schools or colleges of the university; $20 application fee; early admission, early decision, delayed admission, rolling admission, and advanced placement plans are available; the university allows students to obtain degree credit through participation in the College Entrance Examination Board/College Level Examination Program (CLEP), and ACT/PEP Program; application deadline is August 1st.

Costs Per Year: $2,260 state-resident tuition; $5,642 out-of-state; $3,500 approximate room and board.

Collegiate Environment: The university offers its students a choice of over 150 different academic majors in the following schools and colleges: College of Arts and Sciences, College of Commerce and Business Administration, College of Community Health Science, College of Education, College of Engineering, Division of Continuing Education, Graduate School, Graduate School of Library Service, The New College, School of Communication, School of Home Economics, School of Law, School of Nursing, and the School of Social Work. Additionally, programs are offered through the Summer School and Division of Extended Services. A student must earn 1/4 of hours required for degree at school including 9 of the final 18 hours. The libraries contain 1,902,000 volumes, 2.4 million titles on microfilm, 17,603 periodical subscriptions and 15,317 records and tapes. About 43% of the students receive financial aid, and 890 different types scholarships are offered. Residence halls are available for 1,867 male students, and 2,621 for female students. Additionally, 210 apartment units are available for unmarried students.

Community Environment: The University of Alabama is part of the Tuscaloosa community, but there is a separate post office on the University campus. Tuscaloosa, with a population of 77,759 is the fifth largest city in Alabama. The city is located 50 miles southwest of Birmingham, and 100 miles northwest of Montgomery, the state capital. The community is served by major bus, rail, and airline services. Modern shopping and service facilities are accessible in the immediate area of the university campus.

UNIVERSITY OF ALABAMA - BIRMINGHAM   (E-7)
UAB Station
Birmingham, Alabama 35294
Tel: (205) 934-8221; (800) 421-8743

Description: The publicly supported university is one of three independent campuses of the University of Alabama System and was accredited as a separate institution in 1969 by the Southern Association of Colleges and Schools. The school operates on the quarter system and awards semester hours. It offers one summer session. The University is composed of the Academic Health Center which includes the Schools of Dentistry, Health Related Professions, Medicine, Nursing, Optometry, and Public Health; the Academic Affairs unit which includes the Schools of Arts and Humanitites, Business, Education, Engineering, Natural Sciences and Mathematics, and Social and Behavioral Sciences; and the Graduate School. Continuing education and cooperative education opportunities are available. Enrollment includes 6,590 full-time and 4,215 part-time undergraduates. Graduate enrollment is 3,016 full-time and 1,541 part-time students. There are 1,719 full-time and 144 part-time faculty.

Entrance Requirements: ACT; high school graduation with 16 units, including 4 English, 2 mathematics, 2 social science and 2 natural science. For entrance requirements for UAB professional schools write individual school registrar or dean of admissions. Early admis-

sion, early decision, rolling admission and midyear admission plans available. $20 application fee.

Costs Per Year: Tuition for full-time undergraduates, $2,220; out-of-state tuition $4,440; $291 student fees.

Collegiate Environment: Annual operating budget is approximately $973 million. UAB occupies an urban campus with more than 150 buildings including those still under construction. The Medical Center complex established in 1945 includes such major facilities as the 908-bed University Hospital, Rehabilitation Center, the Center for Developmental and Learning Disorders, and affiliated hospitals and agencies such as The Children's Hospital and the Birmingham Veterans Administration Hospital. The four-year University graduated its first class in 1970. To accommodate its diverse student body, UAB offers classes from 8 a.m. to 10 p.m. as well as 6 a.m. and weekend classes. Baccalaureate and certificate programs are offered in 59 majors. The Graduate School, made an autonomous unit in 1970, offers Master's Degree programs in 46 areas and 30 Ph.D. programs. Library holdings include 1,476,168 volumes. Residence halls and dormitories can accommodate 1,600 students. 310 scholarshops are available and 42% of students receive some form of financial aid.

Community Environment: Population 1 million. Cosmopolitan industrial center at start of Appalachian Mountain Range. Combines many of the traditions, graces and ways of the Old South with a forward look and modern approach to the challenge of today. Fine parks, churches of all denominations, library, art gallery, civic music association lend themselves to the cultural atmosphere of the city. Employment is available through the factories, businesses, and professional people. Water sports, golfing, fishing and hunting are available in the area.

UNIVERSITY OF ALABAMA - HUNTSVILLE   (B-7)
301 Sparkman Drive
Huntsville, Alabama 35899
Tel: (205) 895-6120; (800) 824-2255; Admissions: (205) 895-6070; Fax: (205) 895-6073

Description: The publicly supported university is accredited by the Southern Association of Colleges and Schools. The college serves commuting students from Lawrence, Madison, Morgan, Jackson, Marshall, Limestone, Cullman Counties, the lower Tennessee state area and residential students from all 50 states and 20 foreign countries. The University of Alabama, Huntsville is an autonomous member of the University of Alabama and grants Bachelor, Master and Doctorate degrees. Correspondent credit allowed; continuing education courses offered; cooperative education programs available in engineering, math, computer science, biology, physics, accounting, management and economics. Air Force and Army ROTC programs are available. The university operates on the semester system and offers three summer sessions. Enrollment includes 2,667 full-time and 2,845 part-time undergraduates and 1,929 graduate students. A faculty of 291 full-time and 168 part-time gives a faculty-student ratio of 1-10.

Entrance Requirements: Accredited high school graduation or equivalent, with completion of 20 units including 4 English, 2 mathematics, 3 social studies; ACT required; GRE required for graduate programs; GMAT required for graduate administrative science programs; MAT required for graduate English, Nursing and Public Affairs programs; TOEFL required for foreign applicants; early admission, rolling admission, midyear admission and advanced placement plans available; $20 application fee.

Costs Per Year: $1,996 resident; $3,992 nonresident.

Collegiate Environment: This university administers an Undergraduate Program, Graduate Program, and Research Institute where research is conducted for aerospace and missile-related sciences and engineering. The 337-acre campus includes 20 buildings, all of which have been constructed since 1960, exemplifying modern functional design and containing modern equipment. The library contains 426,344 volumes and numerous pamphlets, periodicals, microforms, and sound recordings. 69% of those who apply for admission are accepted, including midyear students. 33% of students receive some form of financial aid.

Community Environment: Huntsville (population 166,000) is located in the Tennessee Valley area and has an average temperature of 60 degrees. Railroads, buses, and airlines serve the area. Three U.S. highways converge at Huntsville. There are churches of all denominations, hospitals and a health center. Part time employment is available for students. Facilities for fishing, boating, golfing and hunting are in the area. Many civic and fraternal organizations serve the community.

UNIVERSITY OF MONTEVALLO   (H-6)
Palmer Hall Station 6030
Montevallo, Alabama 35115
Tel: (205) 665-6030; (800) 292-4349; Admissions: (205) 665-6030;
Fax: (205) 665-6032

Description: A public, comprehensive university accredited by Southern Association of Colleges and Schools. It grants the Bachelor and Master degrees. The college opened its doors in 1896; it became coeducational in 1956. It operates on the semester system and offers one summer session of two five-week terms. Enrollment includes 3,282 students. A faculty of 131 gives faculty-student ratio of 1-25.

Entrance Requirements: Accredited high school graduation or equivalent; completion of 16 units, including 4 English, 2 mathematics, 2 science, 4 social studies; non-high school graduates considered, GED required; ACT or SAT required; GRE required for graduate school; early admission, early decision and rolling admission plans available; $15 application fee.

Costs Per Year: $2,340 state resident tuition; $4,680 out-of-state tuition, $3,170 room and board; $200 student fees.

Collegiate Environment: The campus consists of 106 acres and more than 30 buildings. The library is a three-story building containing 261,935 volumes. The modern, indoor-outdoor natatorium allows for year-round swimming. There are 7 residence halls which provide housing for 650 men and 1,000 women. Students enjoy the university golf course, 28-acre lake and one of the best-equipped theatres in the South, all located on the campus. The university accepts 80% of the students who apply for admission, including midyear students. Financial aid is available, and 45% of the current enrollment receives some form of assistance.

Community Environment: Montevallo (population 4,000) is near the center of the state, and is accessible by automobile. Montevallo is 32 miles south of Birmingham and 68 miles north of Montgomery, and has a mild year-round climate. There are a library, golf course, municipal park, and many churches in the city. Recreational activities include hunting, lake and stream fishing, boating and water skiing on nearby lakes. Students belonging to church denominations that are not represented in Montevallo hold services in the Religious Association Room of the Student Union Building.

UNIVERSITY OF NORTH ALABAMA   (B-4)
Wesleyan Avenue
Florence, Alabama 35632
Tel: (205) 760-4100; (800) 825-5862; Admissions: (205) 760-4608;
Fax: (205) 760-4329

Description: A publicly supported university offering bachelor's and master's degrees, and accredited by the Southern Association of Colleges and Schools. The University was established in 1872. It operates on the semester system and offers one 8-weeks summer session. Enrollment is 3,808 full-time undergraduates, and 585 men and 975 women part-time undergraduates. There are 523 graduate students. A faculty of 196 full-time and 53 part-time gives a faculty-student ratio of 1-23. Undergraduate degree programs include liberal arts and sciences, business, nursing, education; graduate programs include business, education, and criminal justice. 33 hours of correspondent credit allowed; continuing education courses offered and cooperative education programs available in chemistry. Participates in Marine Environmental Science Consortium at Dauphin Island, Mobile; Senior Army ROTC.

Entrance Requirements: High school graduation or equivalent; rolling admissions; ACT required of entering freshmen for placement purposes; advanced placement available. $25 application fee.

Costs Per Year: $1,704 tuition; $2,970 nonresident; $2,808 room and board; some laboratory fees.

Collegiate Environment: Campus has 37 buildings on more than 100 acres, with dormitory capacity for 430 men and 550 women and student apartments for 50 married couples. Libraries include 294,360 volumes. Campus is located in residential section of Florence in the Tennessee River Valley. About 40% of the students receive financial

assistance; about 73% of the freshmen return for the second year. Effective fall 1991, the University no longer accepts students under an open admission policy. The average score of the entering freshman class was ACT 20 composite. About 73% of the freshmen graduated in the upper half of their high school class; 37% in the top quarter. There were 725 degrees granted recently.

Community Environment: Population 38,000. Florence is contiguous to the towns of Sheffield, Tuscumbia, and Muscle Shoals City; it is part of an urban center with a population of 134,000. Area lakes and camping sites attract vacationists and sportsmen from all over the nation. Florence is served by buses and airlines; has excellent public schools, churches, libraries, recreation facilities, cultural centers; several radio stations and a television station.

UNIVERSITY OF SOUTH ALABAMA   (P-3)
308 University Boulevard
Mobile, Alabama 36688
Tel: (205) 460-6447

Description: This comprehensive, coeducational, state-assisted university is accredited by the Southern Association of Colleges and Schools. It was founded in 1963. The university is comprised of the College of Arts and Sciences, College of Business and Management Studies, College of Education, School of Continuing Education and Special Programs, College of Engineering, College of Medicine, College of Allied Health Professions, College of Nursing, School of Computer and Information Sciences, and the Graduate School. Enrollment includes 10,366 undergraduates and 2,020 graduate students and is comprised of 3,793 men and 4,676 women full-time, and 1,577 men and 2,340 women part-time. A faculty of 724 full-time and 170 part-time gives a faculty-student ratio of 1-16. The university operates on the quarter system; each quarter is approximately 10 weeks. The university grants Bachelor degrees in 59 areas of study; Master degrees in 33 areas; educational specialist degrees in 3 areas; Ph.D degrees in Basic Medical Sciences, Communication Sciences and Disorders, Instructional Development, and Marine Sciences; and the professional M.D. degree. Preprofessional programs are offered in predentistry, premedicine, preoptometry, prepharmacy, pre-veterinary medicine, and prelaw.

Entrance Requirements: Official high school transcript and ACT or SAT (ACT preferred) required; students with combined ACT scores of less than 19 or combined SAT scores of less than 800 may be considered for admission to the Developmental Studies program; no fixed requirements for high school courses, but recommended completion of 16 units, including 4 English, 2 algebra, 1 geometry, 2 natural science, 1 U.S. history, 1 world history, 2 foreign language, social studies, natural science, or mathematics, and 3 nonvocational electives; official transcript of all courses taken at other colleges or universities required for transfer applicants; transfer applicants with less than 40 quarter hours of college work must also submit high school transcript and ACT or SAT scores; rolling admission, midyear admission, early admission, early decision, and advanced placement plans available. $20 application fee.

Costs Per Year: $2,541 undergraduate tuition and fees for state residents and residents of the university's service areas in Mississippi and Florida; $3,591 out-of-state; $3,192 approximate room and board.

Collegiate Environment: The campus is comprised of 86 major buildings on 1,200 acres in the western section of Mobile. Additional facilities include the Brookley Complex on Mobile Bay, three university-owned hospitals, and the USA Baldwin County campus in Fairhope, AL, which is located on the eastern shore of Mobile Bay. The Baldwin County campus offers undergraduate and graduate courses in education, and undergraduate courses in arts and sciences, business and management studies, adult personalized studies, allied health professions, and computer and information sciences. Dormitory and apartment housing is available on the main campus for approximately 2,100 students. The university also owns and operates 756 two- and three-bedroom houses that are rented to students and faculty. The library houses 437,451 bound volumes. 91% of applicants are accepted. Scholarships and financial aid are available and 60% of the students receive some form of financial aid.

Community Environment: Mobile (population 476,000 in greater metropolitan area) has a temperate climate. In July and August the average high temperature is 91 degrees, and the average low temperature is 71. Airlines, buses and railroads serve the area. Part-time work is available. The city has libraries, churches of all major denominations, theaters, and museums. Excellent facilities for boating, fishing, and swimming are available. Mobile hosts the annual Senior Bowl, Alabama Deep Sea Fishing Rodeo, Azalea Trail Run, and the oldest Mardi Gras celebration in the country.

WALKER COLLEGE *(E-5)*
1411 Indiana Avenue
Jasper, Alabama 35501
Tel: (205) 387-0511; (800) 777-0372; Fax: (205) 387-5175

Description: Walker College, a two-year division of the University of Alabama at Birmingham, is a small, public, coeducational two-year college established in 1938 and accredited by the Southern Association of Colleges and Schools. It offers academic and community service programs designed to provide quality education to both traditional and nontraditional students at moderate cost to both commuting and residential students in an environment supportive of the needs of the individual student. Through its affiliation with UAB, the college will make facilities available for UAB to offer upper division and graduate courses to students in the area. The associate degree is offered in fine arts, engineering, science, liberal arts, business, and other preprofessional programs on a standard sufficient for preparation and transfer to accredited four-year colleges. Seven certificate programs prepare students for immediate employment. It operates on the quarter on the quarter system and offers two summer sessions. Enrollment includes 580 full-time and 281 part-time students. A faculty of 23 full-time and 34 part-time gives a faculty-student ratio of 1-23.

Entrance Requirements: High school graduation or equivalent with completion of 22 academic units including 4 English, 2 mathematics, 2 science and 3 social science, open enrollment policy; early admission, rolling admission, midyear admission and advanced placement plans available. $20 application fee.

Costs Per Year: $1,539 tuition; $2,010 room and board; $170 student fees; additional expenses average $2,500.

Collegiate Environment: The campus occupies 60 acres and 21 buildings. The college seeks to serve Walker County. The Nicholsom library contains 20,496 volumes, 240 periodicals, 8,871 microforms, and 750 media items. Dormitory facilities accommodate 152 students. The college accepts 99% of those who apply for admission, including midyear students. 160 scholarships are available, including 90 for freshmen, and 61% of the current students receive some form of assistance.

Community Environment: Population 14,000. Mild climate. Airport facilites. City has an excellent library, large movie theater and many beautiful churches. There are parks, swimming pools, lake-fishing, and water sports for recreational activities. Employment opportunities for students are limited. Easy communting to Birmingham (40 miles).

WALLACE COMMUNITY COLLEGE *(D-7)*
Hanceville, Alabama 35077
Tel: (205) 352-6403; Admissions: (205) 352-6403; Fax: (205) 352-6400

Description: A publicly supported, coeducational community college, founded in 1966. It is accredited by the Southern Association of Colleges and Schools. Programs of study lead to the Associate degree in primarily career related areas. The college operates on the quarter system and offers one summer session. Enrollment is 5,410 students. A faculty of 224 gives a faculty-student ratio of 1-24.

Entrance Requirements: High school graduation or equivalent; open enrollment; ACT required for health programs; advanced placement available.

Costs Per Year: $1,080 tuition; $1,890 out-of-state; $1,050 room.

Collegiate Environment: The 225-acre campus is located in rural Hanceville. The library contains more than 20,000 volumes with additional microform and audiovisual holdings. Residence halls accomodate 105 students. Midyear students are accepted. Scholarships and financial aid are available. 50% of students receive some form of financial aid.

Community Environment: Hanceville is a rural community with a population of approximately 2,300, situated midway between Birmingham and Decatur. It is located on state highway 31 with easy access to I-65, both of which connect Decatur and Birmingham.

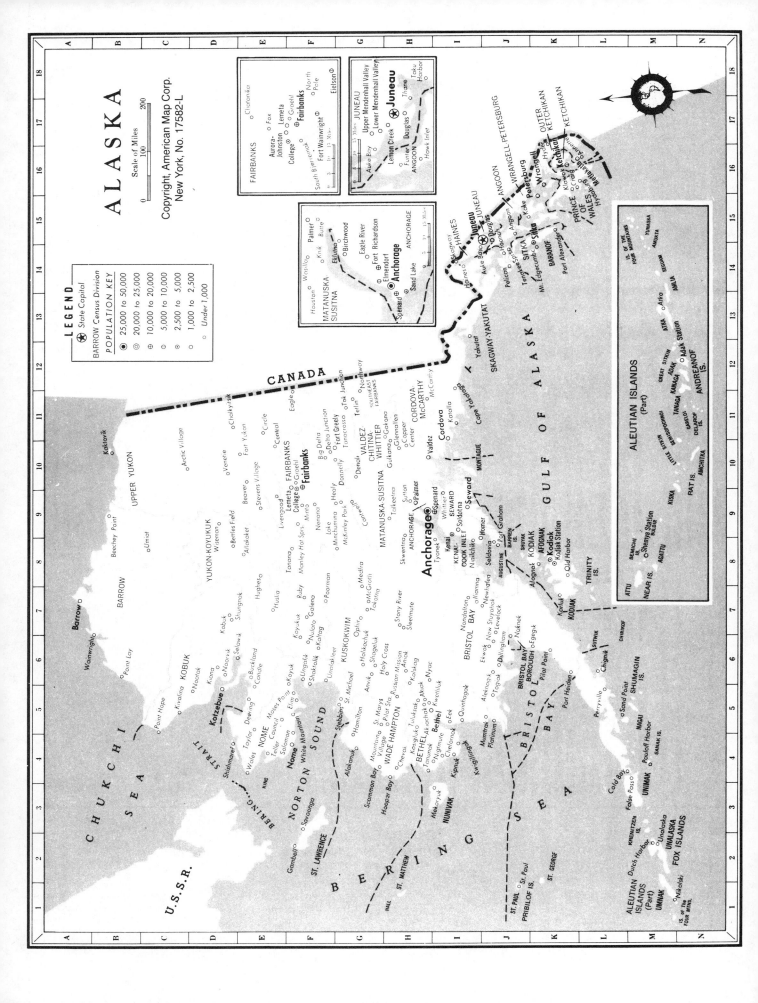

ALASKA

Scale of Miles

Copyright, American Map Corp.
New York, No. 17582-L

LEGEND
☆ State Capital
BARROW Census Division
POPULATION KEY
◉ 25,000 to 50,000
◎ 20,000 to 25,000
⊕ 10,000 to 20,000
⊕ 5,000 to 10,000
⊙ 2,500 to 5,000
○ 1,000 to 2,500
○ Under 1,000

FAIRBANKS
○ Chatanika
Aurora- ○ Fox
Johnston ○ Lemeta
College ◎ ○ Graehl
⊕ **Fairbanks** ○ North
Pole
South Brierwood ○ Eielson
Fort Wainwright

JUNEAU
Upper Mendenhall Valley
Lower Mendenhall Valley
○ Auke Bay ☆ **Juneau**
Lemon Creek
Funter ○ Douglas ○ Thane
ANGOON Hawk Inlet
Toku
Harbor

Wasilla ○ ○ Palmer
Houston ○ Knik ○ Butte
○ Birchwood
Eklutna ○ Eagle River
⊕ Fort Richardson
Elmendorf
Anchorage ANCHORAGE
Sand Lake
MATANUSKA-
SUSITNA
Spenard

CANADA

AULETIAN ISLANDS
(Part)

IS. OF THE
FOUR MOUNTAINS
YUNASKA
AMUKTA
SEGUAM ○
SEGULA ATKA ○ ○ Atka AMLIA
GREAT SITKIN ○ ADAK
SITKIN ○ SEMISOPOCHNOI KANAGA ○ Adak Station
TANAGA ○ ANDREANOF IS.
KISKA LITTLE SITKIN GARELOI
○ DELAROF IS.
RAT IS. AMCHITKA

SEMICHI IS.
Shemya Station
BULDIR
ATTU ○ AGATTU
NEAR IS.

GULF OF ALASKA

BERING SEA

CHUKCHI
SEA

BARROW
Barrow
Wainwright ○
Point Lay ○
○ Kaktovik
Beechey Point
Umiat ○

UPPER YUKON
○ Arctic Village
Venetie ○
Fort Yukon ○
Chalkyitsik ○
Circle ○
Central ○
Eagle ○
SOUTHEAST
FAIRBANKS
Northway ○
Tetlin ○
Tok Junction ○
Tanacross ○

YUKON-KOYUKUK
Wiseman ○
Bettles Field ○
Allakaket ○
Beaver ○
Stevens Village ○
Livengood ○ Lemeta
Hughes ○ College ○ ○ Graehl
Husila ○ ⊕ **Fairbanks**
Tanana ○ Manley Hot Sprs. Minto ○
Ruby ○ Nenana ○
Kobuk ○ Koyukuk ○ Nulato ○ Galena ○ Lake ○
Shungnak ○ Kaltag ○ Minchumina
Candle ○ ○ Medfra ○ Healy
Noorvik ○ Buckland ○ ○ McGrath Denali ○
Selawik ○ Ungalik ○ Takotna ○ Cantwell ○
Kotzebue Elim ○ Shaktolik ○ McKinley Park ○
Deering ○ Moses Point ○ Ophir ○ Talkeetna ○
Taylor ○ Council ○ St. Michael ○ Stony River ○ Sutton ○
Solomon ○ Anvik ○ Holy Cross ○ Skwentna ○
Nome White Mountain ○ Shageluk ○ Sleetmute ○ **MATANUSKA-SUSITNA**
Teller ○ **NOME** Unalakleet ○ ○ Aniak ○ Nyac ○ **ANCHORAGE** ○ Palmer
Wales ○ Pilot Sta. ○ Kalskag ○ Kwethluk ○ **Anchorage** ◉
KING ○ Stebbins ○ Russian Mission ○ Akiak ○ Kwethluk ○ Tyonek ○ Whittier
Shishmaref ○ Hamilton ○ St. Marys ○ Tuluksak ○ Napaskiak ○ Kenai ○ Soldotna ○
Gambell ○ Alakanuk ○ Kasigluk ○ Nightmute ○ COOK INLET ○
Savoonga ○ Mountain Village ○ **Bethel** Ninilchik ○ **Seward**
ST. LAWRENCE Chevak ○ **BETHEL** ○ Eek Homer ○ ○ Pt. Graham
Scammon Bay ○ **WADE HAMPTON** Kipnuk ○ Iliamna ○ ○ Newhalen Seldovia ○ ○ BARREN
Hooper Bay ○ Kwigillingok ○ Ekwok ○ Nondalton ○ Nakalilok IS.
Mekoryuk ○ Quinhagak ○ Nushagak ○ Koliganek ○ **KODIAK** SHUYAK
NUNIVAK Goodnews ○ Platinum ○ Togiak ○ **BRISTOL BAY** Levelock ○ Dillingham ○ Afognak ○ **AFOGNAK**
Togiak ○ Aleknagik ○ Naknek ○ Egegik ○ Kodiak Station ○ **KODIAK**
○ Mumtrak Pilot Point ○ ○ Old Harbor
BRISTOL Port Heiden ○ Karluk ○ **KODIAK**
BAY Perryville ○ **TRINITY**
BOROUGH Chignik ○ SUTWIK IS.
Sand Point ○ CHIRIKOF
Naga IS. ○ **SHUMAGIN**
Pauloff Harbor ○ **IS.**
Cold Bay ○ ○ Sanak IS.
False Pass ○ **UNIMAK**
St. Paul ○ Krenitzen IS.
PRIBILOF IS. St. George ○ Dutch Harbor ○ **UNALASKA**
ALEUTIAN UNALASKA **FOX ISLANDS**
ISLANDS Nikolski ○
(Part)
UMNAK IS. OF THE
FOUR MTNS.

U.S.S.R.

BERING STRAIT

NORTON SOUND

KOBUK

KUSKOKWIM

BRISTOL BAY

SKAGWAY-YAKUTAT
Yakutat ○
Cape Yakataga ○
MONTAGUE
Katalla ○
Cordova
CORDOVA
McCarthy ○
McCARTHY
Valdez ○
VALDEZ-
CHITINA-
WHITTIER
Glennallen ○
Copper ○
Center Gulkana ○ Gakona ○
Chitina ○
Tonsina ○
Big Delta ○
Delta Junction ○
Fort Greely
Donnelly ○

HAINES
Haines ○
Skagway ○
Hoonah ○
Tenakee Spgs. ○ Angoon ○
Pelican ○
Mt. Edgecumbe ○ **SITKA**
Sitka ○ **BARANOF**
Port Alexander ○
WRANGELL-PETERSBURG
Wrangell
Hyder ○
Kake ○
Klawock ○
Craig ○ Metlakatla ○ **KETCHIKAN**
Ketchikan ⊕
PRINCE
OF
WALES
KETCHIKAN
Hydaburg ○
OUTER
KETCHIKAN
ANGOON
PETERSBURG

SCALE OF MILES

ALASKA

ALASKA BIBLE COLLEGE   *(H-10)*
P.O. Box 289
Glennallen, Alaska 99588
Tel: (907) 822-3201; (800) 478-7884; Fax: (907) 822-5027

Description: Privately supported, four-year, nondenominational, coeducational Bible College that is accredited by the Association of Bible Colleges. Owned and operated by SEND International of Alaska, the college was founded in September, 1966 and offers a Bible Education major, with second majors in Pastoral Studies, Christian Education, Christian Camping and Missions. A one-year Bible Certificate, a two-year Associate of Arts Degree, and a four-year Bachelor of Arts Degree are offered. It operates on the semester system. Enrollment is 15 full-time and 28 part-time students. A faculty of 4 full-time and 7 part-time gives a faculty-student ratio of 1-4.

Entrance Requirements: General form with biographical sketch; two references; high school graduation with C average or GED; health form; ACT or SAT recommended; $25 application fee.

Costs Per Year: $3,300 tuition (flat fee for 12-18 credits) (otherwise $110 per credit hour); $3,400 room and board; $500 average additional expenses

Collegiate Environment: The college is designed for Christian students preparing for fields of Christian service. Dormitory facilities are available for 16 men and 16 women. Limited married student housing is available. The library currently houses 25,356 titles, 260 periodicals, 82 microforms (books), and 3,113 audiovisual materials. 90% of students receive some form of financial assistance.

Community Environment: Glennallen is a rural community that has developed on the crossroads between Anchorage, Fairbanks, and Valdez. The original impetus for the community's growth was the construction of the Alcan Highway for communication during the war years. The climate of Glennallen area runs to extremes with the temperature falling to 50 degrees or more below zero for short periods in midwinter, and rising to 70 degrees or more above zero by the close of the school year in May. Sports such as hunting, fishing, hiking, rafting, and cross country skiing are common recreational activities.

ALASKA PACIFIC UNIVERSITY   *(I-10)*
4101 University Drive
Anchorage, Alaska 99508
Tel: (907) 564-8248

Description: Alaska Pacific University is intimate, innovative, and private, founded in the Methodist tradition in 1959, the same year Alaska became a state. Alaska Methodist University opened its doors to students and was operative and fully accredited in 1964. Then, 16 years later, in June 1976, Board action closed the school for an "institutional sabbatical" to study, reassess and determine new directions. In September 1977, a little over a year later, the institution re-opened as Alaska Pacific University, with a new vision and mission. In 1981 it was again fully accredited by the Northwest Association of Schools and Colleges. APU offers undergraduate, graduate, and associate degree programs. The school is ecumenical and nonsectarian, yet it is supported by the United Methodist Church, as are seven other major universities - American, Boston, Duke, Denver, Emory, SMU and Syracuse. Current students come to APU from 18 countries and 19 states. The school is proud of its international and intercultural student body. Men and women from all parts of the globe and all regions of Alaska live in residence halls in the campus center complex, a national historic site, where the Alaska Native Claims Settlement Act was signed and designed by world famous architect Edward Durrell Stone, who also designed the Kennedy Center for the Performing Arts in Washington, D.C. The academic program at APU is based on the philosophy that education should be integrative not fragmented, and should link learning with life. The focus is on wedding liberal learn-

ing with the world of work and career options for now and the twenty-first century. Recent enrollment included 307 undergraduate and 218 graduate students. The faculty consists of 24 full-time and 50 part-time members which provides a student-faculty ratio of 11:1.

Entrance Requirements: High school graduation or equivalent with 2.5 average or better; ACT or SAT required; non-high school graduates with the GED considered; early admission, early decision, rolling admission, delayed admission and advanced placement plans available.

Costs Per Year: Tuition for full-time students $7,650, part-time students $315 per credit hour, room and board $4,150, student fees $30 - 130.

Collegiate Environment: The campus is located near the base of the Chugach Mountain Range in the center of Anchorage. The wooded campus of 300 acres has trails for skiing and running, tennis courts, swimming pool, gym, and a small lake. Residence halls for 140 students and food service are available on campus. Alaska Pacific University has dormitory living on campus. The consortium library with more than 350,000 titles and 3,900 periodicals is located within walking distance. Alaska Pacific University maintains, on-campus, an Alaskana Reference Room which has many rare and valuable historical materials. There is also a PLATO computer learning center and the public radio station is located on campus. A faculty of 51 provides the 765 students with a faculty-student ratio of 1:15.

Community Environment: Alaska Pacific University is located in Anchorage, a modern, dynamic city with half the population of Alaska. To the west is Cook Inlet, named for the famous English explorer, while mountains rise to the south, east, and north, creating a mild climate. The drive south leads to the ski resort at Alyeska, the glacier at Portage and the famous fishing of the Kenai. To the north lie the Alaska Range and Mount McKinley. Anchorage is a young city on the move. Anchorage's per capita income is twice the national average. Anchorage is lively. Dog teams race down Fourth Avenue during the winter Fur Rendezvous while opera, symphony, theater and a steady stream of rock stars, dance troupes, and artists provide cultural events for every taste. Winters are moderated by the warm Japanese current while summers are blessed with a sun that never sets. Daily intercontinental flights link Anchorage to Hawaii, Tokyo, Beijing, Moscow, Stockholm, London, and New York.

SHELDON JACKSON COLLEGE   *(K-15)*
801 Lincoln
Sitka, Alaska 99835
Tel: (907) 747-5221; (800) 478-4556; Fax: (907) 747-5212

Description: Privately supported college affiliated with the Presbyterian Church (U.S.A.). It is accredited by the Northwest Association of Schools and Colleges. The college operates on the 4-1-4 calendar system. Enrollment includes 152 men and 147 women. A faculty of 17 full-time and 8 part-time gives a faculty-student ratio of 1-12. The college grants Associate and Bachelor degrees. Approximately twenty-eight percent of the students are Alaskan natives. Some forty-five percent come from states other than Alaska and a few come from foreign countries.

Entrance Requirements: Open admissions policy; high school diploma or GED required. Placement tests are given to all entering students. The results are used to help plan their programs. Students having academic deficiencies are required to make them up before entering courses requiring college-level performance. Early decision, midyear admission, and rolling admission plans available; $25 application fee.

Costs Per Year: $9,000 tuition; $4,800 room and board; $380 student fees; additional expenses average $500.

Collegiate Environment: The campus consists of 345 acres over-looking the Pacific Ocean and located one-half mile from downtown Sitka. Library contains 89,000 volumes. College has its own salmon hatchery which provides on-the-job training for fisheries students. Residence Hall facilities are provided for single students living away from home. A limited number of accommodations are available for married students. Other campus facilities include ceramics studio, computer science laboratory with microcomputers, auditorium for theater productions, gym, raquetball courts, indoor swimming pool, and weight room. Outdoor activities include scheduled hikes, campouts, hunting, fishing, bicycling, kayaking, and cross-country skiing.

Community Environment: Campus is located in Sitka on Baranof Island, Part of Tongass National Forest in Southeast Alaska. A mild marine climate keeps Sitka cool in summer and warm in the winter. Rainfall is slightly less than 100 inches per year. Sitka is Alaska's fifth largest city with a population of about 9,000 people. It supports a sizable business community including clothing stores, sporting goods, record stores, movie theater, convention center, four museums, two radio stations, local TV station, and a number of excellent restaurants. Access is by jet, plane, or ferry.

UNIVERSITY OF ALASKA ANCHORAGE   *(I-10)*
3211 Providence Drive
Anchorage, Alaska 99508
Tel: (907) 786-1587; Admissions: (907) 786-1480

Description: Part of Alaska's state university system, the University of Alaska at Anchorage is publicly supported, coeducational, offers undergraduate and graduate degrees, and operates on the semester system with two summer sessions. Enrollment includes 4,913 full-time, 7,056 part-time, and 624 graduate students. 373 full-time and part-time faculty provide a faculty-student ratio of 1:14. Accredited by the Northwest Association of Schools and Colleges, the university is comprised of the College of Arts and Sciences, College of Community and Continuing Education, College of Career and Vocational Education, School of Engineering, School of Education, School of Business, School of Health Sciences, and School of Public Affairs.

Entrance Requirements: General admission: application, high school diploma or equivalent, 18 years of age or is a member of high school class that has graduated. Baccalaureate degree admission: SAT or ACT for placement, official transcripts of all high school and college credits with GPA of at least 2.0. 100% of applicants are accepted. There is an open enrollment policy; early admission; early decision; rolling admission; delayed admissions; and advanced placement.

Costs Per Year: Lower division undergraduate state residents $69 per credit hour; nonresident $207. Upper division undergraduate $75 per credit hour, nonresident $225. Graduate residents $150 per credit hour, nonresidents $300.

Collegiate Environment: The school has an attractive wooded campus. The library contains 552,495 bound volumes and government documents with a special collection on Alaska and the Polar Region. There are limited apartment style dorms that accommodate 400 students, but no facilities for married students. There are extension campuses at Kodiak, Kenai, and Matanuska-Susitna; extension sites at Chugiak-Eagle River; military programs at Adak/Shemya, Elmendorf Air Force Base, and Fort Richardson; and the affiliated Prince William Sound Community College.

Community Environment: Anchorage, population 250,000, is a friendly, modern progressive city and the largest in Alaska. Summertime temperatures range between 60 and 70 degrees. The winters are less severe in Anchorage than in many U.S. cities. Anchorage is the major stopover point for most international transpolar flights. Living costs are higher than in the continental U.S., with an average living cost (plus tuition) of approximately $11,000 to $14,000 per year. The city bustles with growth and activity; cultural interests are wide range and include a symphony orchestra, museums, a theater group and a dance company. Recreation facilities include theaters, golf courses, bowling alleys, swimming pools, public beaches, skating rinks, ball parks, and several excellent ski areas. Hunting and fishing are easily accessible. There are several hospitals within the city which is near Ft. Richardson Army Post and Elmendorf AFB.

Branch Campuses: Kenai Peninsula College; Kodiak College; Matanuska-Susitna College.

UNIVERSITY OF ALASKA ANCHORAGE - KENAI PENINSULA COLLEGE   *(I-9)*
34820 College Drive
Soldotna, Alaska 99669-9798
Tel: (907) 262-5801; Admissions: (907) 262-0380; Fax: (907) 262-9280

Description: A publicly supported coeducational community college operating on the semester system as an extension of the University of Alaska. The college serves the entire Kenai Peninsula, which is the size of the state of West Virginia. The college is accredited by the Northwest Association of Schools and Colleges. Associate degree in liberal arts and technology is available, as well as Certificate programs. Enrollment is 350 full-time and 1,700 part-time students. A faculty of 91 gives a faculty-student ratio of 1-15.

Entrance Requirements: Open admission policy that allows any person over 18 years of age to enter whether high school graduate or not. $35 application fee.

Costs Per Year: $1,742 resident tuition; $5,226 nonresident.

Collegiate Environment: Semesters begin in September and January. The library contains 16,000 volumes, 200 periodicals. Some financial aid is available. 75% of full-time students receive some form of aid (20% of total student population).

Community Environment: Population 15,760. The town is located on the coast and enjoys a cool climate during the spring and summer months. Public transportation in and out of Kenai is by air and highway; some bus service available. The city has a library, many churches, museum, and a full-service hospital. Part-time employment is available. Recreation includes hunting, fishing, boating, water sports and clam digging. Annual Kenai days around the middle of July is a traditional event.

Branch Campuses: Kachemak Bay Branch, Homer, AK 99603.

UNIVERSITY OF ALASKA ANCHORAGE - KODIAK COLLEGE   *(K-8)*
117 Benny Benson Street
Kodiak, Alaska 99615
Tel: (907) 486-4161

Description: Publicly supported junior college offers a liberal arts program and awards Associate in Arts and Associate in Applied Science Degrees. Accredited by the Northwest Association of Schools and Colleges, the college is an extension center of the University of Alaska. The college offers university-parallel or vocational programs, some graduate-level courses and Adult Basic Education courses for those with less than a high school education. The semester system is used and both afternoon and evening classes are held. Current enrollment includes 7 men, 24 women full-time, 163 men, and 416 women part-time. The faculty consists of 9 full-time and 52 part-time members which provides a student-faculty ratio of 12:1.

Entrance Requirements: Open enrollment policy; non-high school graduates admitted.

Costs Per Year: $51 per credit hour.

Collegiate Environment: Most classes meeting in the evening. College is located on a 60-acre campus two miles northeast of the city of Kodiak.

Community Environment: Population 8,200. Kodiak, located in the Gulf of Alaska on Kodiak Island, was once a Russian settlement. It has always looked to the sea for its livelihood and in 1968 became the largest fishing port in dollar volume in the United States. Transportation to Kodiak is an interesting trip by automobile. The Alaska Marine Highway ferry, Tustumena, serves Kodiak regularly. There is direct flight service from Anchorage. The city of Kodiak is the largest town in the Kodiak Island group and is the oldest permanent settlement in Alaska. The city is situated on the northeastern corner of Kodiak Island nestled at the foot of the 1,400 foot Pillar Mountain, overlooking the island-studded harbor of St. Paul. This northerly section of the City of Kodiak was rebuilt following the Good Friday earthquake and tidal wave of 1964. The average temperature in January is 30 degrees and in August, 55 degrees. The annual rainfall is 60 inches spread throughout the year. A number of churches, and service organizations are found in the city.

UNIVERSITY OF ALASKA ANCHORAGE - MATANUSKA - SUSITNA COLLEGE   *(H-9)*
P.O. Box 2889
Palmer, Alaska 99645
Tel: (907) 745-9774; Admissions: (907) 745-9774; Fax: (907) 745-9747

Description: The publicly supported, two-year college is accredited by the Northwest Association of Schools and Colleges through the University of Alaska - Anchorage. Founded in 1961, the college grants the Associate degree, operates on a semester system, and offers one summer session. Enrollment includes 379 full-time and 1,116 part-time students. A faculty of 14 full-time and 110 part-time gives a student-faculty ratio of 22:1.

Entrance Requirements: High school graduates or mature individuals 18 years or older may apply for admission; $35 application fee.

Costs Per Year: $1,742 tuition; $5,226 nonresident tuition.

Collegiate Environment: Semesters begin in September and January. The library consists of 40,000 volumes and 225 periodicals. Financial aid is available through scholarships such as the University of Alaska Foundation, Medical, student government, and the Native Alaska State Student Scholarship Loan.

Community Environment: Population 47,000. Palmer is a rural town with sub-arctic climate. A branch of the Alaska Railroad and bus service to Anchorage serve this area. There are churches, library, museum, hospital, and a health center in the town. Recreational activities include fishing, boating, ice skating and some swimming. There are good shopping facilities available. Palmer has the usual civic organizations found in most U.S. cities. The Alaska State Fair is the fourth weekend of August through Labor Day weekend each year.

UNIVERSITY OF ALASKA FAIRBANKS   *(F-9)*
Fairbanks, Alaska 99775
Tel: (907) 474-7821; (800) 478-1823; Fax: (907) 474-5379

Description: This pblicly supported, coeducational undergraduate and graduate university operates on the semester system and offers four summer sessions. The university was founded in 1917 as the Alaska Agricultural College and School of Mines. It became the University of Alaska by an act of the Territorial Legislature in July 1935. The university is accredited by the Northwest Association of Schools and Colleges and belongs to the Association of American Colleges. The University of Alaska Fairbanks has branch campuses in Bethel, Kotzebue, Billingham and Nome. It is comprised of the following academic colleges and schools: College of Liberal Arts, College of Rural Alaska, College of Natural Sciences, School of Agriculture and Land Resources Management, Tanana Valley Campus, School of Engineering, School of Fisheries and Ocean Sciences, School of Management, and School of Mineral Engineering. The 4-year curricula in mining engineering, geological engineering, and electrical engineering are accredited by the Board for Engineering and Technology. Army ROTC is offered as an elective. Enrollment includes 3,889 full-time and 4,550 part-time undergraduates and 839 graduate students. A faculty of 483 full-time and 211 part-time gives a faculty-student ratio of 1-15. Professional Accreditations include ABET, ACEJMC, AACSB, ACS, CSWE, NASM, American Association of Museums, Computing Sciences Accreditation Board, and NCATE.

Entrance Requirements: High school graduate with academic average of C or higher; those whose high school grades average less than C will be considered for admission based on ACT; total 16 required high school courses: English 4 units; math 3 units, natural/physical sciences 3 units, social sciences 3 units, and 3 other college-prep units; students deficient in specific subjects will be considered; $35 application fee; application deadlines are August 1 and December 1.

Costs Per Year: $2,070 resident tuition; $6,210 nonresident; $330 university fees; $3,690 room and board.

Collegiate Environment: The campus is located four miles from Fairbanks on a 2,250-acre site. Fairbanks is served by major airlines from all main points in Alaska and the lower 49 states. The University library includes 1.5 million volumes, 6,218 periodicals, 882,765 microforms and 8,667 audiovisual materials. Housing facilities for over 1,655 single students and 266 families are available.

Community Environment: Population of nearby Fairbanks is 35,000. Fairbanks is located 100 miles south of the Arctic Circle. The campus of the University of Alaska Fairbanks is four miles from the center of Fairbanks, where there is a continental climate. The normal rainfall is 11.92 inches per year. Fairbanks has many churches, a museum, theater, medical centers, and many civic and fraternal organizations. This is the area for river boating, cross-country and downhill skiing, ice hockey, snowshoeing and trapping. The annual North American Sled Dog Championship Races are held here.

UNIVERSITY OF ALASKA FAIRBANKS - NORTHWEST CAMPUS   *(F-4)*
Pouch 400
Nome, Alaska 99762
Tel: (907) 443-2201; (800) 478-2202; Admissions: (907) 443-2201; Fax: (907) 443-5602

Description: The school was established in 1974 as a community college. It became a branch of U.A.F. in 1988. It is accredited by the Northwest Association of Schools and Colleges. The Northwest Campus provides educational opportunities in the Bering Strait Region and other communities throughout rural Alaska by distance-delivered audioconference courses. It operates on the semester system. Enrollment is 300 evening students with a faculty of 10 full-time and 4 part-time. It grants the Baccalaureate degree in Rural Development, Social Work, and Teacher Education. Associate degrees in Applied Science and Arts are granted. Many certificate programs are offered.

Entrance Requirements: Any person who is 18 years of age or older who has earned a high school diploma or its equivalent is eligible for admission to Northwest Community College. A specific grade point average (GPA) in previous high school or college work is not required.

Costs Per Year: $2,100 resident tuition.

Collegiate Environment: Besides serving the people of Nome, Northwest Campus serves 16 outlying villages. Over half of the students attending the College are Native American (Eskimo) students. Financial aid is available. Classes begin in September and continue through May.

Community Environment: Northwest Campus is located in the city of Nome with a population of approximately 3,000 people. Located on the Norton Sound about 500 miles west of Fairbanks, Nome is the trading center for the Seward Peninsula, an area that embraces 157,600 square miles. There are medical and dental facilities available in town. In addition to 2 radio stations, there is a cable television station which operates 3 channels. There is a local newspaper, a library, 7 churches, 1 bank, several gift shops and a handful of fraternal and civic groups. Utility services include water, sewer, electricity, and telephone. Nome is the terminus of the famed 1,049 mile Anchorage-to-Nome Iditarod Sled Dog Race which is held annually. The city is the center of the reindeer industry, with some 100,000 reindeer in the area. Nome is accessible only by air, although some supplies are received by barge service in the summer. Temperatures range from a high of 86 degrees to a low of -47 degrees.

UNIVERSITY OF ALASKA SOUTHEAST   *(J-15)*
11120 Glacier Highway
Juneau, Alaska 99801
Tel: (907) 465-6462; Admissions: (907) 465-6462; Fax: (907) 465-6365

Description: This state supported, coeducational university was reorganized in 1986 to form one of three schools and two branch campuses of the University of Alaska statewide system. UAS is accredited by the Northwest Association of Schools and Colleges. It is composed of the School of Business and Public Administration, the School of Education, Arts and Sciences, and the School of Career Education. Programs of all the School of Career Education. Programs of all three Schools are available at the Juneau, Ketchikan and Sitka campuses. General education in the liberal arts forms the core of the educational program. The university offers certificate, associate of arts, associate of applied science, baccalaureate, professional, and master's degree programs in the applied areas of business, liberal arts, science, public administration, and teacher education. UAS's two-year and certificate programs in vocational-technical education meet the needs of industry and business in its service area. UAS promotes and supports research which strengthens its academic programs. UAS has a major commitment to outreach education. A variety of delivery methods extend educational opportunities to the people of the region. UAS responds to life-long educational, cultural, and other needs of its service area through continuing education, public service and arts and humanities activities and programs. It shares in the overall mission of the University of Alaska. Special programs include correspondence credit toward degrees, continuing education courses, and credit for certain courses by prior examination. UAS is a small, friendly university with an enrollment of 600 full-time students and 4,500 part-time students. Classes are generally small and a faculty of 63 full-time and 120 part-time provides a faculty-student ratio of 1:10.

Entrance Requirements: High school graduation or equivalent. The following units are recommended: English 4, mathematics 2, social studies 3, and natural or physical sciences 2. The school offers rolling admission and midyear admission. ACT or SAT are required. There is an open enrollment policy.

Costs Per Year: Tuition $1,914, nonresident $5,700; room $2,175-$2,500; student fees $35.

Collegiate Environment: A popular additon to the Juneau campus is an exciting and unique student housing community. Modern apartment type units, for both single students and students with families are available. Seven buildings provide homes in 50 apartments for at least 150 single students and up to 50 students with families. Residents of student housing share a community center providing a lounge/recreation room, meeting rooms, study room, exercise and game rooms in addition to laundry facilities. The library has holdings of 86,924 titles, 1,516 periodicals, 436,429 microforms, and 1,836 audiovisual materials. 80% of applicants are accepted. Scholarships are available and 70% of the students receive some form of financial aid.

Community Environment: Situated on the shores of scenic Auke Lake and with the famous Mendenhall Glacier in clear sight, the main campus is only a few miles from the heart of downtown Juneau, the capital of Alaska. Nestled between 4,000 foot snow-capped peaks on one side and the sparkling water of Gastineau Channel on the other, Juneau was the first Alaskan city founded after the American purchase of Alaska in 1867. The city is centrally located in the Tongass National Forest, the nation's largest. The combined city and borough encompass 3,108 square miles of land, ranging from tundra to moss-draped forests to wind-blown mountain peaks. Juneau's population is approximately 29,000 and as the state's capital city, provides numerous cultural, academic, and professional opportunities.

UNIVERSITY OF ALASKA SOUTHEAST - KETCHIKAN CAMPUS *(K-16)*
2600 Seventh Avenue
Ketchikan, Alaska 99901-5798
Tel: (907) 225-6177; Admissions: (907) 225-6177 x2213; Fax: (907) 225-3624

Description: Publicly supported two-year college with a coeducational enrollment of 70 full-time and 600 part-time. A faculty of 8 full-time and 50 part-time gives a faculty-student ratio of 1-12. The college is a campus of the University of Alaska Southeast. Accredited by the Northwest Association of Schools and Colleges, the college was founded in 1954. The semester system is used. The college offers university programs as well as career education programs.

Entrance Requirements: Open enrollment policy; high school and GED graduates 18 years of age or over. $30 application fee.

Costs Per Year: $1,800 tuition; $5,300 nonresident tuition.

Collegiate Environment: The campus consists of two locations, a career education building on the waterfront in downtown Ketchikan and a 42 acre campus on the hillside in the Western part of the city. The library contains over 41,000 volumes and 150 periodicals. Dormitory housing consists of 18 units.

Community Environment: Population 14,000. Located on the Revillagigedo Island 600 miles northwest of Seattle; climate is very wet - 13 feet of rain per year. Airlines and water transportation serves the area. Extensive access to the Tongass National Forest and inter-coastal waterways.

UNIVERSITY OF ALASKA SOUTHEAST - SITKA CAMPUS *(K-15)*
1332 Seward Avenue
Sitka, Alaska 99835-9498
Tel: (907) 747-6653; Fax: (907) 747-3552

Description: A branch campus of the University of Alaska Southeast and part of the University of Alaska statewide system. Accredited by the Northwest Association of Schools and Colleges. Associate degrees and certicates are offered. The school operates on the semester system and offers one summer session. Enrollment includes 100 full-time and 1,400 part-time students. A faculty of 9 full-time and 60 part-time gives a faculty-student ratio of 1-21.

Entrance Requirements: Open and midyear admission plans. $30 application fee.

Costs Per Year: Tuition is $1,700 per year for residents and $5,300 for nonresidents.

Collegiate Environment: Both day and evening classes, with a predominant part-time student enrollment. The campus is located on Japonski Island, fronting the water and within walking distance (via bridge) of the downtown area. A large newly renovated facility includes classrooms, student lounge, IBM and MacIntosh computer labs, art studio, welding/shop facilities, and a large hangar for construction and other vocational education projects. The campus is shared with a State-operated boarding high school with predominantly Native enrollment; the school serves as a lab school for various UAS Sitka campus programs. The library contains over 62,000 volumes, 360 periodicals, and 172 sound records; on-line services link this library to Alaskan and western state university holdings. Dormitory housing is available. Semesters begin in early September and late January. Scholarships are available. 100% of those applying for admission are accepted.

Community Environment: Population 8,300. Sitka is the original capital of Russian-America and was the site of the transfer of Alaska from Russia to the United States in 1867. Many historic sites and museums convey these historic origins, as well as the strong Northwest Coast Native heritage of the region. The rainy climate is mild and comparable to that of Seattle or Portland. Located on Baranof Island, adjacent to the mainland coast of the Southeast Alaskan panhandle, Sitka is surrounded by the heavily forested mountains of the Tongass National Forest. It is served by daily jet service, as well as small regional air carriers. The Alaska Marine Highway System provides weekly passenger and vehicle transportation from the southern terminal of Bellingham, Washington, and the northern terminal of Haines, Alaska. A regional center for health services, business, and education, Sitka has two hospitals, several small but important museums, two colleges, and a State-operated boarding high school.

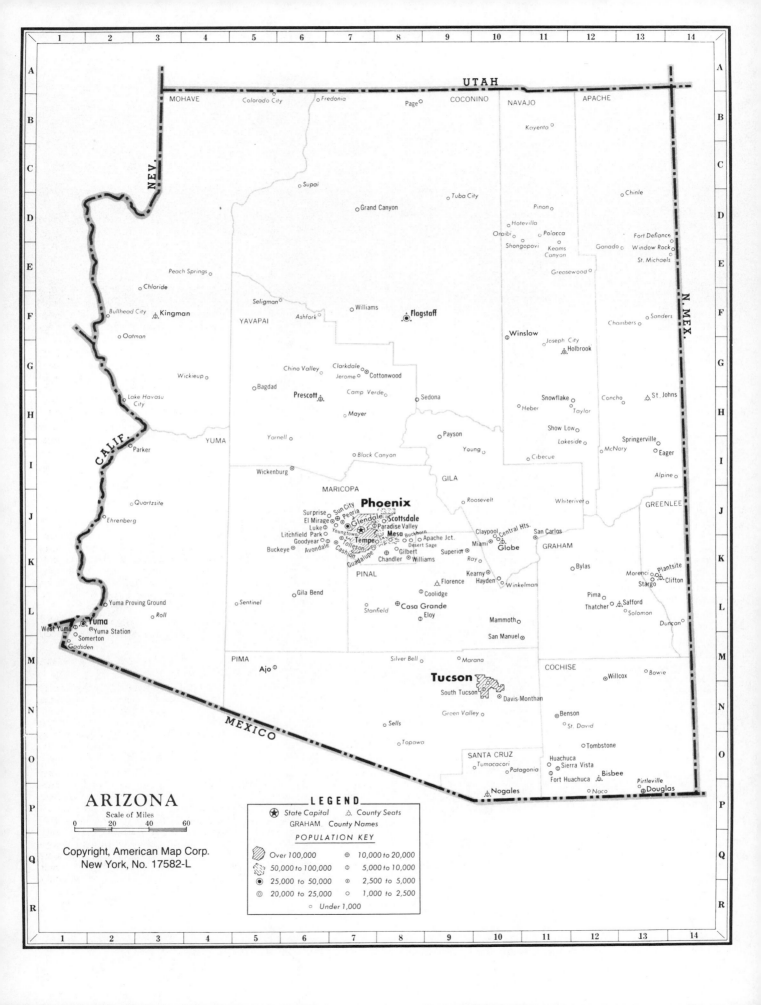

ARIZONA

Scale of Miles

0   20   40   60

Copyright, American Map Corp.
New York, No. 17582-L

L E G E N D

★ State Capital   ⚬̇ County Seats
GRAHAM County Names

POPULATION KEY

Over 100,000   ⊕ 10,000 to 20,000
50,000 to 100,000   ⊙ 5,000 to 10,000
◉ 25,000 to 50,000   ⊙ 2,500 to 5,000
◎ 20,000 to 25,000   ⚬ 1,000 to 2,500
              ⚬ Under 1,000

UTAH
NEV.
CALIF.
N. MEX.
MEXICO

MOHAVE
COCONINO
NAVAJO
APACHE
YAVAPAI
YUMA
MARICOPA
GILA
GREENLEE
PINAL
GRAHAM
PIMA
COCHISE
SANTA CRUZ

Colorado City
Fredonia
Page
Kayenta
Supai
Tuba City
Chinle
Grand Canyon
Pinon
Hotevilla
Oraibi
Polacca
Shongopovi
Keams Canyon
Ganado
Fort Defiance
Window Rock
St. Michaels
Greasewood
Peach Springs
Chloride
Bullhead City
Kingman
Oatman
Seligman
Ashfork
Williams
Flagstaff
Winslow
Joseph City
Holbrook
Chambers
Sanders
Chino Valley
Clarkdale
Jerome
Cottonwood
Wickieup
Bagdad
Prescott
Camp Verde
Sedona
Snowflake
Concho
St. Johns
Lake Havasu City
Yarnell
Mayer
Payson
Heber
Taylor
Show Low
Springerville
Parker
Young
Lakeside
Cibecue
McNary
Eager
Wickenburg
Black Canyon
Alpine
Surprise
Sun City
Peoria
Roosevelt
Whiteriver
El Mirage
Glendale
Scottsdale
Luke
Youngtown
Paradise Valley
Litchfield Park
Tolleson
Tempe
Mesa
Buckhorn
Apache Jct.
Claypool
Central Hts.
San Carlos
Goodyear
Cashion
Desert Sage
Miami
Globe
Buckeye
Avondale
Guadalupe
Gilbert
Superior
Ray
GRAHAM
Chandler
Williams
Kearny
Hayden
Bylas
Morenci
Plantsite
Quartzsite
Florence
Winkelman
Stargo
Clifton
Ehrenberg
Coolidge
Pima
Thatcher
Safford
Solomon
Yuma Proving Ground
Roll
Sentinel
Gila Bend
Stanfield
Casa Grande
Eloy
Mammoth
Duncan
Yuma
West Yuma
Yuma Station
San Manuel
Somerton
Gadsden
Silver Bell
Marana
Ajo
Tucson
South Tucson
Davis-Monthan
Willcox
Bowie
Sells
Green Valley
Benson
St. David
Topawa
Tombstone
Tumacacori
Huachuca
Patagonia
Sierra Vista
Bisbee
Pirtleville
Fort Huachuca
Naco
Douglas
Nogales

ARIZONA

AMERICAN GRADUATE SCHOOL OF INTERNATIONAL MANAGEMENT   *(J-7)*
Thunderbird Campus
59th Avenue & Greenway Road
Glendale, Arizona 85306
Tel: (602) 978-7200; (800) 848-9084; Admissions: (602) 978-7100; Fax: (602) 439-5432

Description: Informally known as "Thunderbird," this privately supported graduate school is accredited by the North Central Association of Colleges and Schools and the American Assembly of Collegiate Schools of Business. It is the only graduate school in the U.S. devoted exclusively to training for international business, languages, and interdisciplinary area studies designed to equip college graduates for international managerial careers. Degree granted: Master of International Management. Departments of Study: World Business, International Studies, Modern Languages. Enrollment is 1,500 students. A faculty of 100 gives a faculty-student ratio of 1-15. The school operates on the semester system and one summer session is offered. Overseas programs are offered in more than 12 countries.

Entrance Requirements: College and university graduates are eligible; GMAT required; TOEFL for foreign students. Careful consideration of applicant's former academic preparation and scholastic achievement; $50 application fee; "modified" rolling admissions, January 31st deadline for summer and fall applicants; July 31st for spring.

Costs Per Year: $17,050 tuition; $840-$1,110 room; $1,315 board; $75 student fees.

Collegiate Environment: The campus includes 160 acres located 16 miles northwest of Phoenix. Library houses over 90,000 books, periodicals and audiovisual materials, and features large amounts of material from foreign governments. Housing facilities accommodate 470 students. 70% of the current student body receives financial aid.

Community Environment: Glendale is a suburb of Phoenix. See Phoenix College.

Branch Campuses: Branch campuses are in Europe and Japan.

ARIZONA STATE UNIVERSITY   *(K-8)*
Box 871203
Tempe, Arizona 85287-1203
Tel: (602) 965-9011; (800) 252-2781; Admissions: (602) 965-7788

Description: This publicly supported university was founded in 1885. It is accredited by the North Central Association of Colleges and Schools and operates on the semester system with three summer sessions. The following colleges compose the university: Liberal Arts and Sciences, Architecture and Environmental Design, Business, Education, Engineering and Applied Sciences (Engineering, Agribusiness and Environmental Resources, Construction, Technology), Fine Arts, Law, Nursing, Honors, Graduate, School of Social Work, Public Programs, and Extended Education. Correspondence credit allowed; continuing and cooperative education courses offered; overseas programs available. Current enrollment includes 23,637 full-time and 7,561 part-time undergraduates and 10,991 graduate students. A faculty of 1,697 full-time and 98 part-time gives a faculty-student ratio of 1-17. Army and Air Force ROTC programs are available on an elective basis.

Entrance Requirements: High school graduation with rank in upper 50% in-state, upper 25% out-of-state; completion of 11 units including 4 English, 3 mathematics, 2 science, 2 social studies 2 foreign language recommended; SAT (if used) 930 minimum, 1,010 out-of-state; ACT minimum of 21 required in-state, 23 out-of-state; GMAT, GRE, or MAT required for graduate students; GED accepted in place of high school diploma; rolling admission, midyear admission, advanced placement plans available; $35 application fee for out-of-state applicants.

Costs Per Year: $1,828 state-resident tuition; $4,690 room and board; $7,434 out-of-state tuition; $66 fees.

Collegiate Environment: Located near metropolitan Phoenix, Arizona State University Main is situated on 600 acre site. The library contains over 3,000,000 volumes, 32,800 periodicals, 4,200,000 microforms 29,300 records/tapes/CDs; 41 CD-ROMs; 9 local databases, 8 commercial databases, and 75,000 audiovisual materials. Dormitory facilities accommodate 4,780 men and women. Fraternities house 680 men, sororities 564 women. There are 5,800 scholarships offered. 55% of the students receive financial aid. 80% of applicants are accepted.

Community Environment: The population of Tempe is 150,615. Tempe is a surburan community located 9 miles southeast of the center of Phoenix, and 7 miles west of Mesa. Tempe is in the metropolitan area of Phoenix. The climate is dry and mostly sunny. Buses and airlines serve the area. Tempe is a rapidly growing and friendly city, with many restaurants, shops and clubs located in its downtown area.

Branch Campuses: Arizona State University West in northwest Phoenix. Arizona State University West offers upper-division courses, baccalaureate, and master's programs.

ARIZONA WESTERN COLLEGE   *(L-1)*
P.O. Box 929
Yuma, Arizona 85366-0929
Tel: (602) 726-1000; Fax: (602) 344-7730

Description: This publicly supported coeducational community college was established in 1962 and is accredited by the North Central Association of Colleges and Schools. The college provides both university-parallel and vocational-technical programs. The semester system is used and 1 summer session is offered. Enrollment includes 1,496 full-time and 4,203 part-time students. A faculty of 81 full-time and 253 part-time gives a faculty-student ratio of 1-16.

Entrance Requirements: Open enrollment; non-high school graduates admitted; rolling admission, midyear admission and advanced placement plans available.

Costs Per Year: $780 state-resident tuition and fees per year; $5,100 out-of-state; $2,800 room and board.

Collegiate Environment: The college is located on 640 acres 7 miles from the heart of the city of Yuma. The library is one of 29 buildings and contains 53,000 volumes and numerous pamphlets, periodicals, microforms and recordings. Dormitory facilities are available for 356 single students and 30 married students. 99% of the students applying for admission are accepted, including midyear students. Scholarships are available and 60% of students receive some form of financial aid.

Community Environment: Population 50,000. This is a metropolitan area with a warm, dry climate. Rail, air, and all other modes of transportation are available. Yuma is located on the bank of the Colorado River, midway between Phoenix and San Diego. There are over 50 churches of major denominations, a public library, historic Yuma Territorial Prison and Museum, Yuma Fine Arts Association, Community Concert Association, and the St. Thomas Mission. Part-time employment is available. The city has many civic, fraternal and veteran's organizations. Recreational activities include boating, fishing, water skiing and hunting. The Silver Spur Rodeo is in February; the County Fair is in April.

CENTRAL ARIZONA COLLEGE   *(L-8)*
8470 N. Overfield Road
Coolidge, Arizona 85228
Tel: (602) 426-4260; Fax: (602) 426-4234

Description: The public community college first opened its campus in 1969 to 1736 students. Enrollment is 3,052 students. The college operates on a semester basis with two summer terms, and is fully accredited by the North Central Association of Colleges and Schools. A faculty of 211 gives a faculty-student ratio of 1-18. Continuing education courses offered; credit allowed for certain courses by prior examination; cooperative education programs available.

Entrance Requirements: Open enrollment policy; non-high school graduates considered; early admission, early decision, midyear admission, advanced placement plans available.

Costs Per Year: Resident tuition $660; nonresidents $4,005, based on 12 credit hour semesters; room and board $2,750.

Collegiate Environment: The college is comprised of three sites in Pinal County: Signal Peak Campus (Coolidge), Aravalpa Campus (Winkelman), and Apache Junction Center (Apache Junction). The Signal Peak Campus is the largest and is comprised of twelve buildings located on 400 acres on a rural site. Additional facilities include an Olympic-size swimming pool, an air strip and a rodeo arena. The college library contains 83,000 volumes and 16,326 microforms. On-campus housing is available in dormitories for 340. Financial aid is available for economically disadvantaged students with 20% of all students receive financial assistance.

Community Environment: Population 7,000. Coolidge is located in Pinal County near the intersection of two major interstate freeways that serve the areas of Southern California and Arizona's two principal cities, Phoenix and Tucson. One can be in the heart of either city within an hour. There are four Native American Reservations in the county. The area is rich in history of mining, cattle and agriculture. Few places on earth have more hours of sunshine a year than south-central Pinal County, which averages approximately 4,000 hours per year according to U.S. Weather Bureau records.

COCHISE COLLEGE   *(P-13)*
Route 1, Box 100
Douglas, Arizona 85607
Tel: (602) 364-7943; (800) 966-7943; Fax: (602) 364-0236

Description: The publicly supported community college is accredited by the North Central Association of Colleges and Schools. It offers courses equivalent to the first two years of university studies and provides technical training. It offers programs in aviation (pilot and mechanics), business, computer science, technology (including electronics and pre-engineering), nursing, and courses in the sciences and liberal arts. It operates on the semester system and offers two summer sessions. Enrollment includes 5,600 students. A faculty of 288 gives a faculty-student ratio of 1-18.

Entrance Requirements: High school graduation, GED, or 18 years of age; open enrollment policy; non high school graduates considered; early admission, midyear admission, and rolling admission plans available.

Costs Per Year: $800 ($25 per unit) state resident tuition; $4,864 ($152 per unit) nonresident tuition; $3,006 room and board.

Collegiate Environment: The Douglas campus is comprised of 15 buildings, including the library containing 80,000 hardbound volumes as well as periodical subscriptions, microforms, and audiovisual materials. Residence halls can accommodate 264 students. 256 scholarships are available, and 65% of students receive some form of financial assistance.

Community Environment: Douglas, population 17,000, located in Cochise County, has a dry climate with average yearly temperatures of 79.2 degrees high and 46.3 degrees low. The area is scenically beautiful and rich in historical lore. Hotels, motels, churches, a library, hospital, medical center, and civic and service organizations are available. There are recreational facilities for golf, tennis, football, baseball, basketball, and swimming. The Cochise County Fair is the last weekend in September. Part-time work is available for students.

Branch Campuses: Willcox Center, AZ.

DEVRY INSTITUTE OF TECHNOLOGY   *(J-7)*
2149 W. Dunlap Avenue
Phoenix, Arizona 85021-2995
Tel: (602) 870-9222; (800) 528-0250; Admissions: (602) 870-9201; Fax: (602) 870-1209

Description: The school is a private coeducational college offering programs in Electronics Engineering Technology, Accounting, Computer Information Systems, and Business Operations. Programs are developed and updated regularly with input from business and industry leaders. The Phoenix campus was established in 1967 and is accredited by the Commission on Institutions of Higher Education of the North Central Association of Colleges and Schools. It operates on the semester system, has one summer session, and grants associate and bachelor's degrees. Enrollment includes 1,711 men and 382 women full-time, 441 men and 103 women part-time. A faculty of 62 full-time and 18 part-time gives a faculty-student ratio of 1-37.

Entrance Requirements: High school graduation or GED is required. The school requires prospective students to take its own exam or submit acceptable ACT/SAT/WPCT scores. Rolling admission and delayed admission plans are available, and a proficiency exam (or CLEP) is given to students seeking advanced standing. The application fee is $25.

Costs Per Year: $6,335 tuition.

Collegiate Environment: The structure of the building is open and provides multipurpose spaces for guest lectures, exhibits and student projects; laboratories are fully equipped with modern, sophisticated electronics instruments. The library has 13,605 books, 210 periodicals and audiovisual materials. 93% of applicants are accepted; new students and transfers are accepted at midyear. Scholarships are available and 78% of the students receive some form of financial aid.

Community Environment: Fortune Magazine calls Phoenix a boom town - one of the country's strongest business centers. Many large companies have gravitated to the city, lured in part, by the made-to-order weather. The result is expanding highway systems, a growing housing market and a thriving metropolitan area. Phoenix is home to professional sports teams, year-round golf, a world-famous zoo and botanical gardens. It has a yearly average temperature of 70.3 degrees and unusually sunny skies, according to the United States Weather Bureau.

EASTERN ARIZONA COLLEGE   *(L-12)*
Thatcher, Arizona 85552-0769
Tel: (520) 428-8322; (800) 678-3808; Fax: (520) 428-8462

Description: This publicly supported community college is accredited by the North Central Association of Colleges and Schools. The college offers university-parallel programs and vocational-technical courses. It operates on the semester system and offers two 5-week summer sessions. Enrollment includes 1,189 full-time and 3,598 part-time students. A faculty of 53 full-time and 195 part-time gives a faculty-student ratio of 1-19.

Entrance Requirements: Open enrollment policy; early admission, rolling admission, delayed admission and advance placement plans available; non-high graduates considered; $5 application fee for out-of-state applicants.

Costs Per Year: $628 state-resident tuition; $4,040 out-of-state; $3,200 room and board; $900 average additional expenses.

Collegiate Environment: The campus consists of 39 acres and 34 buildings. Dormitory facilities accommodate 135 men and 135 women. The library contains 42,800 volumes, 250 periodicals, 40 microforms and 3,000 audiovisual items. Most students applying for admission are accepted and 44% of the freshmen return for the second year. The college offers 315 scholarships. 44% of students receive some form of financial aid.

Community Environment: Population 3,000. Thatcher is located in the broad valley of the Gila River. It is on Highway 70 about 75 miles east of the junction of Highways 60 and 70 at Globe, about 165 miles east of Phoenix, and 250 miles west of El Paso. Nearby Safford, with a population of over 8,000, is the county seat of government for Graham County. In addition, it serves as the hotel and shopping center for the upper Gila Valley. The area enjoys an invigorating climate with sunshine 90% of the year; rainfall is approximately nine inches during the year. The valley is flanked by the 10,000-foot Graham Mountains, Gila Mountain Range, Indian Hot Springs, Red Knolls Desert Theatre, Coolidge Dam, and the Great Surface copper mines. All are within easy driving distance. Elevation: 3,000.

EMBRY-RIDDLE AERONAUTICAL UNIVERSITY *(E-11)*
3200 Willow Creek Road
Prescott, Arizona 86301-3720
Tel: (602) 776-3728; (800) 442-3728

Description: Embry-Riddle Aeronautical University (ERAU) operates with two campuses, one in Prescott, Arizona, and one in Daytona Beach, Florida. The College of Continuing Education operates on selected military sites and aviation centers worldwide. ERAU is accredited by the Southern Association of Colleges and Schools and is professionally accredited in selected programs by respective addrediting organizations. The University offers a Bachelor of Science, Associate of Science, and Masters degrees in twenty areas. The school operates on a semester calendar and offers two summer terms offered at the residential campuses. Air Force and Army ROTC programs are available. At the Prescott campus, enrollment includes 1,240 full-time and 138 part-time students. A faculty of 56 full-time and 29 part-time gives a faculty-student ratio of 1-16. The College of Continuing Education enrolls approximately 12,000 students, primarily on a part-time basis, at over 91 resident centers.

Entrance Requirements: High school graduation (or equivalent); entrance requirements vary according to degree program selected. Rolling admission. SAT or ACT required. $30 application fee.

Costs Per Year: $7,990 tuition; $7,840 nonengineering tuition; $3,322 room and board.

Collegiate Environment: The Prescott campus is located just outside the city of Prescott, just minutes from the flight line at Ernest A. Love Field. Situated on 510 acres, the campus includes classrooms, a library, dormitories, laboratories, wind tunnels, and computer labs. Dormitory and housing facilities accommodate 720 men and women with additional housing close to campus. The library on the Prescott campus has over 180,869 volumes, plus additional microfilm and other resources. 77% of applicants are accepted. Scholarships are available and 71% of the full-time students receive some form of financial aid.

Community Environment: The Prescott area is one of the most colorful areas of the Bradshaw Mountains and has an approximate population of 50,000. The campus is surrounded by a national forest, rolling ranchlands, hiking trails, and wilderness areas. The city of Phoenix is approximately 90 miles away.

Branch Campuses: Daytona Beach, FL 32114-3900, tel: (904) 226-6100 or 1-800-222-3728.

GLENDALE COMMUNITY COLLEGE *(J-7)*
6000 West Olive Avenue
Glendale, Arizona 85302
Tel: (602) 435-3000; Fax: (602) 435-3329

Description: The publicly supported junior college is accredited by the North Central Association of Colleges and Schools. Professional accreditations include the National League for Nursing and the Accrediting Bureau for Engineering Technology. It provides university-parallel programs, educational programs for terminal training, and Certificate programs. It operates on the semester system and offers three summer sessions. Enrollment includes 4,675 full-time, 13,358 part-time, and 7,982 evening students. A faculty of 220 full-time and 467 part-time gives a faculty-student ratio of 1-22.

Entrance Requirements: Open enrollment policy; non-high school graduates admitted; advanced placement plan available.

Costs Per Year: $1,024 county resident tuition; $4,448 state resident tuition; $5,024 nonresident tuition.

Collegiate Environment: The college is located on 160 acres in western Maricopa County. The mild climate enables students to enjoy informal outdoor social and study areas and large open spaces between buildings. Palm tree-lined walkways extend between structures of contemporary southwestern architecture that blend with the natural landscape. The 29 buildings of the campus include an Instructional Materials Center, Student Center, High Tech Center and Fitness Center, in addition to those housing well-equipped laboratories and facilities for biology, chemistry, physics, electronics, automotives, and agriculture. A Performing Arts Center offers a colorful setting for intimate theater productions and lectures. The library contains 75,467 volumes.

Community Environment: Glendale is a suburb of Phoenix.

GRAND CANYON UNIVERSITY *(J-7)*
3300 West Camelback Road
P.O. Box 11097
Phoenix, Arizona 85061
Tel: (602) 249-3300

Description: Privately supported liberal arts college is accredited by the North Central Association of Colleges and Schools. The college was founded and is supported by the Arizona Southern Baptist Convention. The college offers a liberal arts/teacher training program in a Christian atmosphere. All requirements for elementary or secondary teaching certificate may be met. The 4-1-4 system is used plus two summer sessions. The college enrolls 1,846 students. A faculty of 60 full-time, 78 part-time gives a faculty-student ratio of 1:17.

Entrance Requirements: High school graduation with rank in upper half of graduating class; completion of 16 units including 4 English, 2 mathematics, 2 science, and 2 social science; non-high school graduates considered; ACT or SAT is required; Early admission; early decision, delayed admission, rolling admission and advanced placement plans available; $15 application fee.

Costs Per Year: $4,560 tuition; $2,800 room and board, $440 student fees.

Collegiate Environment: Continuous emphasis on Christian growth is stressed. All students taking nine or more semester hours are required to attend Chapel. The campus has 70 acres and dormitory facilities and apartment style housing for men and women. The library houses 93,721 volumes. There is also a listening room in the Fleming Memorial Library containing over 6,000 recordings of masterworks. The college accepts 95% of those who apply for admission. Financial aid is available, and 80% of the current student body receives some form of assistance.

Community Environment: See Phoenix College

MESA COMMUNITY COLLEGE *(K-8)*
1833 West Southern Avenue
Mesa, Arizona 85202
Tel: (602) 461-7600

Description: Publicly-supported junior college accredited by the North Central Association of Colleges and Schools. The college offers university-parallel programs as well as vocational, technical, and professional courses. The college grants the Associate degree. It operates on the semester system and offers two summer sessions. Enrollment includes 21,454 students. There is a faculty of 229 full-time and 550 part-time members.

Entrance Requirements: Open enrollment policy; ACT required; non-high school graduates considered; rolling admission, midyear admission and advanced placement plans available.

Costs Per Year: $1,024 ($32/cr) resident; $4,424 ($57/cr for 1-6 hours + $157/cr for 7 and more hours) nonresident.

Collegiate Environment: The campus buildings are constructed in a Spanish-Indian architecture style. The library now contains over 53,000 volumes and 300 periodicals. 100% of the students applying for admission are accepted. Scholarships are available and 25% of students receive some form of aid.

Community Environment: Population 375,000, Arizonia's third largest city, located 16 miles east of Phoenix, adjacent to Tempe, and near the Superstition Mountains. The average yearly temperature is 68.3 degrees, low humidity and 86 percent of the daylight hours are sunny. Mesa is a beautiful and friendly city; there are part-time jobs available for the college students. Most kinds of sports and recreation facilities available, plus many cultural activities.

Branch Campuses: Chandler Extension, Chandler, AZ 85227, (602) 461-7407.

MOHAVE COMMUNITY COLLEGE *(F-3)*
1971 Jagerson Avenue
Kingman, Arizona 86401
Tel: (520) 757-4331; Admissions: (520) 757-0847; Fax: (520) 757-0808

Description: The college is a publicly supported, coeducational, two-year school. Founded in 1971, it first offered programs in technical studies. In 1974, the school became part of the state system of community colleges and now has liberal arts studies as well. It is accredited by the North Central Association of Colleges and Schools. The college awards Certificates and the Associate degree. It operates on the semester system with one summer session. Enrollment is 660 full-time and 4,556 part-time students. A faculty of 41 full-time and 160 part-time gives a faculty-student ratio of 1-14.

Entrance Requirements: High school graduation is preferred but not required; open enrollment; $5 application fee.

Costs Per Year: $580 district/county resident tuition; $3,480 state/nonresident tuition.

Collegiate Environment: The college has several sites for instruction: Kingman, Lake Havasu City, Mohave Valley and high schools in those areas. Personnel are readily available for guidance, counseling, placement, and testing. The college library has 29,500 volumes, 371 periodicals and 760 microforms. All applicants are accepted. Students are admitted at midyear, and financial aid is available.

Community Environment: The Kingman campus is accessible by all forms of transportation: bus, rail and air. The area is a rapidly expanding one, offering a variety of year-round activities due to its arid climate. Lake Havasu City boasts the famous London Bridge and English Village. Both areas provide opportunities for hunting, fishing, camping and water sports.

NAVAJO COMMUNITY COLLEGE   *(D-13)*
P.O. Box 67
Tsaila, Arizona 86556
Tel: (602) 724-3311; Fax: (602) 724-3327

Description: This publicly supported coeducational junior college is the nation's first institution of higher learning that is owned and operated by Native Americans. The school is fully accredited by the North Central Association of Colleges and Schools. The policy direction and guidance is Navajo Indian with members of the Board of Regents selected by the Navajo Tribal Government. In addition to the usual liberal arts courses, the college offers Navajo studies, career opportunities, university-parallel programs and secretarial training. It operates on the semester system and offers two summer sessions. Enrollment includes 904 full-time and 1,115 part-time students. A faculty of 57 full-time and 99 part-time gives a faculty student ratio of 1-13.

Entrance Requirements: Open enrollment; high school diploma, GED, or letter of recommendation from principal; students admitted in following order of priority; (1) those who live on the reservation (Navajo and non-Navajo), (2) other Indians, (3) non-Indians from outside the reservation; early admission, early decision, midyear admission, and rolling admission plans available.

Costs Per Year: $600 tuition; $2,740 room and board; $10 student fees.

Collegiate Environment: College facilities include the library containing more than 35,000 volumes, 490 periodicals, 11,457 microforms, and 2,100 audiovisual materials, and dormitories that accommodate 285 full-time students. Food service is available to both residents and nonresidents of the dormitories. Adult Basic Education programs that have been established for those unable to participate in on-campus programs include oral English, reading English, basic arithmetic, and special electives such as personal health, and agriculture. These classes are located in fifteen communities on the reservation. Approximately 100% of applicants are admitted, including midyear students. Financial aid is available, and 90% of students receive some form of financial assistance.

Community Environment: The campus is located on the Navajo reservation in northeastern Arizona, at Tsaile, Chinle, Arizona, 150 miles northeast of Flagstaff. Nearby towns provide facilities for shopping and recreation. The nearest town is 25 miles away.

NORTHERN ARIZONA UNIVERSITY   *(F-8)*
NAU Box 4084
Flagstaff, Arizona 86011
Tel: (602) 523-9011; (800) 345-1987 in AZ; Admissions: (602) 523-5511; Fax: (602) 523-6023

Description: The publicly supported university is accredited by the North Central Association of Colleges and Schools. In 1899, plans for the Northern Arizona Normal School were completed, leading to the

graduation in 1901 of four women. The institution became a four-year college in 1925, gained the right to confer Master degrees (Education) in 1937 and attained university status in 1966. Colleges include Arts and Science, Creative and Communication Arts, Education, Foresty, Business Administation, Engineering, Hotel and Restaurant Management, Health Professions, and Social and Behavorial Sciences. A cooperative education program is available in the College of Engineering. It operates on the semester system and offers two summer sessions. Enrollment includes 5,335 men and 6,134 women fulltime and 1,147 men and 1,440 women part-time undergraduate, and 4,353 graduate students. A faculty of 607 full-time and 263 part-time gives a faculty-student ratio of 1-23. Air Force and Army ROTC are available.

Entrance Requirements: High school graduation with rank in upper 50%; completion of 16 academic units including 4 English, 3 mathematics, 2 laboratory science, and 2 social science; minimum ACT 22 (state resident), 24 (nonresident), or SAT 930 (state resident), 1010 (nonresident) required; rolling admission, midyear, and advanced placement plans available; $35 nonresident application fee.

Costs Per Year: $1,896 state resident tuition; $6,746 nonresident tuition; $3,000 room and board.

Collegiate Environment: The 719-acre campus includes the library containing 1,363,000 volumes, three dining halls, eight Research Centers and four Activity Centers. Residence halls and apartments accommodate 2,567 men, 3,026 women and 397 families. Approximately 82% of applicants are accepted, including midyear students. Numerous scholarships are offered and 60% of students receive some form of financial assistance.

Community Environment: Flagstaff, population 50,000, is a city of Seven Wonders in the heart of the Coconino National Forest located at the foot of the San Francisco Peaks. Mountain slopes, canyons, buttes, Indian ruins, forests, and deserts mingle in a setting forever challenging in its appeal. The elevation, the protection provided by the forest, and the Arizona sunshine give Flagstaff unsurpassed year round climate. Recreational activities include hiking, bicycling, boating, fishing, and hunting. Skiing is nearby as are the Grand Canyon, the Petrified forest, numerous Indian villages, and national monuments.

NORTHLAND PIONEER COLLEGE   *(G-11)*
103 First Avenue at Hopi
P.O. Box 610
Holbrook, Arizona 86025
Tel: (602) 524-1993

Description: Northland Pioneer College opened its doors in the fall of 1974 as a multicampus college with the mission of providing educational services directly to many communities of Navajo County in Northeastern Arizona. By intergovernmental agreement, the College serves several communities in Apache County as well. With district offices in Holbrook, Arizona, the College provides full-service campuses in Winslow (Little Colorado Campus), Holbrook (Painted Desert Campus), Snowflake/Taylor (Silver Creek Campus), and Show Low (White Mountain Campus). Satellite centers with full-time personnel and some controlled facilities can be found at the Arizona Department of Corrections Winslow Unit, Kykotsmovi (Hopi), Whiteriver (Apache), Kayenta, St. Johns, Springerville/Eagar, and Heber. In addition, limited services are provided at numerous other extension units. The service area of 21,000 square miles includes many unique geographical areas such as Monument Valley, the Painted Desert, the Petrified Forest, and the White Mountains. The Grand Canyon is less than a day's drive from the college.

Entrance Requirements: Open enrollment. New students taking basic skills, English, math, or nine credits are required to take a placement test prior to completing registration process.

Costs Per Year: $20 per credit to Arizona residents, $75 for out-of-state residents. Registration fee $20.

Collegiate Environment: The four main campuses are located in small communities within the college district and vary from high desert vistas to forested mountainous areas. The residence halls are at the Painted Desert Campus in Holbrook and house 70 students. Learning resource centers are located at the four main campuses and at five centers. Financial aid is available. Approximately 60% of students receive some form of financial aid. Northland has pioneered numerous unique delivery systems and adaptions to make educational opportunities available to its rural and remote communities.

Community Environment: The service area of 21,000 square miles has a population of approximately 130,000 people. The largest communbity has fewer than 10,000 persons living within the city limits. The service area includes parts of three Indian reservations. The economy is based primarily on agriculture, tourism, and the lumber industry.

PHOENIX COLLEGE   *(J-7)*
1202 W. Thomas Road
Phoenix, Arizona 85013
Tel: (602) 264-2492; Admissions: (602) 285-7500; Fax: (602) 285-7813

Description: The publicly supported, coeducational junior college is accredited by the North Central Association of Colleges and Schools. The college offers university parallel and occupational programs. It operates on the semester system and offers two summer sessions. Enrollment includes 12,500 students. The faculty-student ratio is 1-22. Army and Air Force ROTC programs are available as electives.

Entrance Requirements: Accredited high school graduation or GED certification.

Costs Per Year: $960 county resident tuition; $4,470 state resident tuition; $4,870 nonresident tuition.

Collegiate Environment: Fifteen buildings located on 47 acres comprise the campus but no housing accommodations are provided. The library contains 75,501 volumes. Scholarships are available.

Community Environment: Phoenix, population 824,230, is a thriving industrial and agricultural city. Easily accessible, served by railroads, buses and airlines, the city has many churches, libraries, museums, and theatres, as well as numerous fine restaurants, hotels, and motels. It is located in proximity to many scenic and historical places of interest including the Grand Canyon, the Petrified Forest, Montezuma Castle, and Oak Creek Canyon. It is one of the outstanding winter resorts of America with The Valley of the Sun nearby.

PIMA COMMUNITY COLLEGE   *(N-10)*
4905 East Broadway
Tucson, Arizona 85709-1120
Tel: (520) 748-4500; (800) 860-7462; Admissions: (520) 748-4640; Fax: (520) 748-4790

Description: Publicly supported multi-campus junior college is comprised of five campuses and was established in 1970. The college is fully accredited by the North Central Association of Colleges and Schools. The college offers university-parallel and equivalent programs and technical and skill-improvement courses. Air Force, Army and Navy ROTC programs are available. The college operates on the semester system and offers three summer sessions. Enrollment is 7,256 full-time and 20,704 part-time students. A faculty of 314 full-time and 1,222 part-time gives a faculty-student ratio of 1-19.

Entrance Requirements: Open enrollment; non-high school graduates under age 18 must have written approval of parents and written release from principal of last high school attended; international students with an F-1 visa must have completed an equivalent academic program to an American secondary school; rolling admission and midyear admission plans available; $15 application fee for out-of-state applicants.

Costs Per Year: $724 district-resident and state-resident tuition; $4,354 out-of-state.

Collegiate Environment: West Campus is comprised of 14 buildings on 260 acres. The college also has a Downtown Campus located on 14 acres in downtown Tucson, an East Campus located on 58 acres on the eastside of Tucson and a Desert Vista Campus located on 51 acres on the southside of Tucson. Additionally, Pima Community College offers courses and programs in 70 off-campus locations throughout Pima County. Located in an area where history has for generations reflected the interaction of people from varied ethnic and cultural backgrounds, the college is committed to the concept of a pluralistic society. 99% of those who apply for admission are accepted. 3,100 scholarships are available, including 2,300 athletic. 30% of students receive some form of financial aid. Campus libraries contain 185,988 print and nonprint titles, 1,454 subscriptions and a large microfilm collection.

Community Environment: See University of Arizona.

PRESCOTT COLLEGE   *(H-6)*
220 Grove Avenue
Prescott, Arizona 86301
Tel: (602) 778-2090; Fax: (602) 776-5137

Description: This privately supported coeducational liberal arts college is fully accredited by the North Central Association of Colleges and Schools and was founded in 1966. It grants the Bachelor's degree and operates on the 1-3-1-3-1 system. Current enrollment is 400 full-time. A faculty of 40 full-time and 60 part-time provides a student-faculty ratio of 9-1. Through small classes, extensive field work, and innovative educational philosophy, students work toward degrees in Environmental Studies, Human Development, Humanities, Outdoor Action and many others.

Entrance Requirements: High school graduation or G.E.D. accepted and students can be admitted at midyear. Approximately 59% of the applicants are accepted. Early admission, midyear admission and delayed admission plans are available. $25 application fee.

Costs Per Year: Tuition $9,800, student fees $510

Collegiate Environment: Library holdings include 17,000 titles, 380 periodicals, and 900 audiovisual items. There is no student housing. About 70% of the students receive financial aid.

Community Environment: Located a mile high in the forested mountains of central Arizona, Prescott has a moderate climate and four seasons. Described by "Arizona Highways" magazine as "Everybody's Hometown," the community of Prescott is known for its friendly atmosphere and small town charm. Prescott was the capital of the Territory of Arizona back in the 1800's and the old governor's mansion still stands today. The town is rich in local history including gold-mining lore, cowboys, and the historic Roughriders. Classic Victorian homes and tall cottonwoods line the streets. With clean air, abundant sunshine, and natual beauty in every direction, the Prescott area is truly an enjoyable place to live.

SCOTTSDALE COMMUNITY COLLEGE   *(J-7)*
9000 E. Chaparral Road
Scottsdale, Arizona 85250
Tel: (602) 423-6000; Admissions: (602) 423-6100; Fax: (602) 423-6200

Description: The publicly supported coeducational community college opened in September 1970 as part of the Maricopa County Community College system. The college is accredited by the North Central Association of Colleges and Schools and provides university-parallel and occupational programs all leading to the Associate degree. The semester system is used and three summer sessions are offered. Academic cooperative plans are available with Arizona State University. Enrollment includes 2,500 full-time and 7,500 part-time students. A faculty of 140 full-time and 260 part-tiem gives a faculty-student ratio of 1-33.

Entrance Requirements: Open enrollment policy; non-high school graduates over age 18 admitted; ACT or SAT not required; early admission, early decision, midyear admission, rolling admission and advanced placement plans available.

Costs Per Year: $1,024 ($32/cr) district tuition; $3,936 ($32/cr) out-of-district; $4,274 ($32/cr) out-of-state

Collegiate Environment: The library contains over 32,000 volumes, 2,000 pamphlets, 546 periodicals, 6,622 microforms and 2,000 recordings. All students applying for admission are accepted, including midyear applicants. Financial aid is available for economically handicapped students.

Community Environment: Scottsdale is a suburb of Phoenix; see Phoenix College.

SOUTH MOUNTAIN COMMUNITY COLLEGE   *(J-7)*
7050 South 24th Street
Phoenix, Arizona 85040
Tel: (602) 243-8000; Fax: (602) 243-8329

Description: Founded in 1979, the publicly supported community college is accredited by the North Central Association of Colleges and Schools. It operates on the semester system and has two summer sessions. The college is coeducational and offers an associate degree. Enrollment includes 730 full-time and 1,688 part-time students. A faculty of 43 full-time and 150 part-time gives a faculty-student ratio of 1-18.

Entrance Requirements: High school graduate or equivalent; open enrollment; early admission, early decision, rolling admission, delayed admission and advanced placement available; life experience credits and CLEP accepted.

Costs Per Year: $1,024 tuition; $5,024 for out-of-state residents.

Collegiate Environment: Contemporary single-story buildings house classrooms and labs. Computer labs on campus feature Apple, IBM, and Digital equipment. Athletic facilities include playing fields, tennis and racquetball courts, and fitness center. A professionally staffed child care center is available on campus for students and employees with children from 2-7 years. The library has 26,231 volumes, 475 periodicals, 107,013 microform units, and 2,783 audiovisual units. Financial aid is available and approximately 350 scholarships are awarded. 30% of students receive some form of aid.

Community Environment: Located near both downtown Phoenix and Tempe, the college is just minutes from I-10 and Superstition freeways and Arizona State University. Ample parking is available. The college is served by the Phoenix Transit Bus System. Affordable housing, shopping, and services are within easy commuting distance. The campus is located in the shadow of South Mountain Park, the largest municipal park in the United States.

SOUTHWESTERN COLLEGE *(J-7)*
2625 East Cactus Road
Phoenix, Arizona 85032
Tel: (602) 992-6101

Description: Located in sunny Phoenix, Arizona, this Conservative Baptist Bible college serves students from many evangelical denominations. Southwestern offers a Bachelor's degree in Elementary Education, Christian Ministries, and Biblical Studies. Courses are available in Youth Ministries, Missions, Counseling, and Music. The college is accredited by the North Central Association of Colleges and Schools and by the Accrediting Association of Bible Colleges. The college operates on the semester system and offers one summer session. Enrollment includes 160 full-time students. The faculty includes 9 full-time and 9 part-time members.

Entrance Requirements: High school graduation; completion of 20 units, including 3 English, 1 mathematics, 2 foreign language, 1 science and 2 social science; ACT required; non-high school graduates considered; rolling admission and advanced placement available; $25 application fee.

Costs Per Year: $5,600 tuition; $2,450 room and board; $240 student fees; additional expenses average $150.

Collegiate Environment: The campus includes 19 acres and nine buildings cooled by refrigeration in the summer. There are dormitories and apartments accommodating 60 men, 50 women and 6 married students. The library contains 50,000 volumes, 105 periodicals, 19,430 microforms, and 928 sets of audiovisual materials. Financial aid is available and 60% of the current student body receives financial assistance. 95% of the applicants are accepted.

Community Environment: See Phoenix College.

UNIVERSITY OF ARIZONA *(N-10)*
Tucson, Arizona 85721
Tel: (602) 621-3237

Description: Founded in 1885, this state-supported university is accredited by the North Central Association of Colleges and Schools. Enrollment includes 21,597 full-time and 4,871 part-time undergraduates and 8,838 graduate students. A faculty of 1,489 full-time and 614 part-time gives a faculty-student ratio of 1-20. 96% of the faculty have doctorates. The university operates on the early semester calendar system and offers two summer sessions. The university was founded in 1885 and is accredited by the North Central Association of Colleges and Schools. Colleges and Schools of the University: Agriculture, Architecture, Arts and Sciences (with a Faculty of Fine Arts),

Business and Public Administration, Education, Engineering and Mines, Law, Medicine, Nursing, Pharmacy, School of Family and Consumer Resources, School of Health Related Professions, and the School of Renewable Natural Resources. The Honors Center has a rich variety of offerings available to students, including: interdisciplinary seminars, honors projects, colloquia, faculty-student dialogues, and an Honors Semester Abroad program in England. There is an extensive Cooperative Education program available to those with satisfactory academic standing. Army, Navy and Air Force ROTC programs are available on elective basis. Sixty semester hours correspondence credits allowed; credit allowed for certain courses by prior examination. Study Abroad Programs include summer and semester programs in Brazil, England, Italy, Spain, and Mexico. Numerous international academic programs include formal faculty exchanges between the University and institutions in France, Austria, Britain, and Mexico.

Entrance Requirements: State residents ACT minimum 22 (24 for nonresidents) or SAT minimum 930 (1010 for nonresidents) required, or minimum overall grade-point of 3.0, or rank in upper 25% of graduating class; completion of 16 units including 4 English, 3 mathematics, 2 laboratory sciences, 2 social sciences, and 5 electives; high school graduation required; early decision, rolling admission, delayed admission, midyear admission and advanced placement plans available; $35 application fee.

Costs Per Year: $1,894 general university fee; $7,500 ($5,606 and $1,894 fee) nonresident tuition; $4,230 room and board.

Collegiate Environment: Located in the city of Tucson, the University of Arizona is comprised of more than 135 buildings on an attractively landscaped 343-acre campus. The library system contains more than 4,125,669 volumes, 4,624,724 microforms and 33,900 recordings. Residence hall facilities accommodate approximately 5,200 men and women. Fraternities house 700 men and sororities house 700 women. There are more than 13,000 scholarships and grants available. Approximately 84% of the students applying for admission are accepted. 78% of the freshman class returned for sophomore year. About 35% of the senior class continued on to graduate school. The diverse student body is comprised of residents from all 50 states as well as more than 116 different countries. The university participates in NCAA Division I athletics. Affiliated with the Pacific 10 Athletic Conference (PAC 10), University of Arizona athletes compete in nine intercollegiate sports for men and eleven intercollegiate sports for women.

Community Environment: Tucson is in a valley of the Sonoran Desert, and is surrounded by mountain ranges. Just north of the city are ski slopes and ponderosa pines as well as canyons and grassy meadows, which are popular with hikers and climbers. Yet Tucson has mild winters (average yearly temperature is 85 degrees) and attracts golf, tennis and other sports enthusiasts year-round. The city has a professional symphony orchestra, opera company, theater company, and ballet, in addition to outstanding medical facilities. Located sixty miles north of Mexico, the community reflects the cultures of its Native American, Spanish, Mexican and other pioneer forefathers. Approximately 700,000 reside in the metropolitan area.

UNIVERSITY OF PHOENIX *(J-7)*
4615 East Elwood Street
Phoenix, Arizona 85040
Tel: (602) 966-9577; Fax: (602) 894-1758

Description: This privately supported undergraduate and graduate school is accredited by the North Central Association of Colleges and Schools. It grants the Bachelor's and Master's degrees. UOP has 34 campuses and learning centers located in Arizona, California, Colorado, Hawaii, Nevada, New Mexico, Utah and Puerto Rico. UOP also offers its educational programs worldwide through Online, its computer distance education system. The school offers credit at the undergraduate level for prior learning, which may be earned as a result of professional training or experience. Classes are held year-round, and a qualified student may begin a degree program in virtually any month of the year, The university currently enrolls 20,843 working adult students, and there is a faculty of 2,300.

Entrance Requirements: High school graduate or GED; current employment or minimum of 3 years work experience; rolling admission and delayed admission plans available; $50 application fee.

Costs Per Year: $6,500 average tuition; $100 student fees. Costs vary by program and geographical area.

Collegiate Environment: 80% of applicants are accepted. Scholarships are available and 55% of students receive some form of financial aid. There are no dormitory facilties. UOP's teaching/learning model is designed for working adults and is structured to enable students who are employed full-time to earn their degrees and still meet their personal and professional responsibilities. Students attend weekly classes, averaging 15 students in size, and also meet weekly as part of a three to five person study group. Courses are designed to facilitate the application of knowledge and skills to the workplace and are taught by faculty members who possess advanced degrees and have an average of 15 years of experience in business, industry, government and the professions. Currently, approximately 80% of UOP's students receive some level of tuition reimbursement from their employers.

Community Environment: UOP is one of very few universities that operates in multiple states. This allows students who relocate to another state to continue their program at the UOP location in that state (where applicable) or through one of UOP's distance education delivery systems.

Branch Campuses: The University has facilities in California, Colorado, Hawaii, Nevada, Utah, New Mexico, and Puerto Rico. Not all programs are available at all locations.

YAVAPAI COLLEGE   *(H-6)*
1100 East Sheldon Street
Prescott, Arizona 86301
Tel: (602) 445-7300; Fax: (602) 445-2193

Description: The publicly supported coeducational community college, founded in 1966, is accredited by the North Central Association of Colleges and Schools. It provides university-parallel programs as well as occupational, general, and continuing education. It operates on the semester system and offers two summer sessions. Enrollment is 1,268 full-time and 4,712 part-time students. A faculty of 82 full-time and 282 part-time gives a faculty-student ratio of 1-27.

Entrance Requirements: High school graduation or GED Equivalency Certificate; open enrollment policy; advanced placement plan available; $10 out-of-state application fee.

Costs Per Year: $656 fees and tuition; $4,680 out-of-state; $2,720 state-resident room and board.

Collegiate Environment: The 100-acre campus overlooks the city of Prescott as well as Granite Mountain and Thumb Butte, two of the state's geographical landmarks. All buildings have been erected since 1969 and are air-conditioned. Space is available in residence halls for 400 men and women. Library holdings include 64,000 volumes, 441 periodicals, 4,030 microforms and 3,150 audiovisual materials. The Yavapai College Verde Valley branch campus was opened in 1975. It is located 41 miles southwest of Prescott in the pleasant community of Clarkdale. The historic gold mining town of Jerome is nearby, and the magnificent red sandstone scenery of Sedona is a short drive away. The campus is coeducational, with regular enrollment of more than 1,400 students. Campus facilities are modern and complete, and host a variety of course offerings in university transfer programs as well as in occupational and general interest areas.

Community Environment: Population 30,000. The city of Prescott is imbued with thoroughly Western informality. The city is easily reached from all parts of the United States by regularly scheduled airlines and bus service. Climate is ideal, embracing four seasons, but without the extremes of heat, cold, dryness, or dampness. Employment opportunities are average for a community of this size. Prescott has a community concert program, and an active interest in the arts provides cultural atmosphere. Prescott Frontier Days are held during the July Fourth weekend; this is the original cowboy rodeo of America. The Yavapai County Fair is held during September. There is horse racing at Prescott Downs on weekends from Memorial Day through Labor Day.

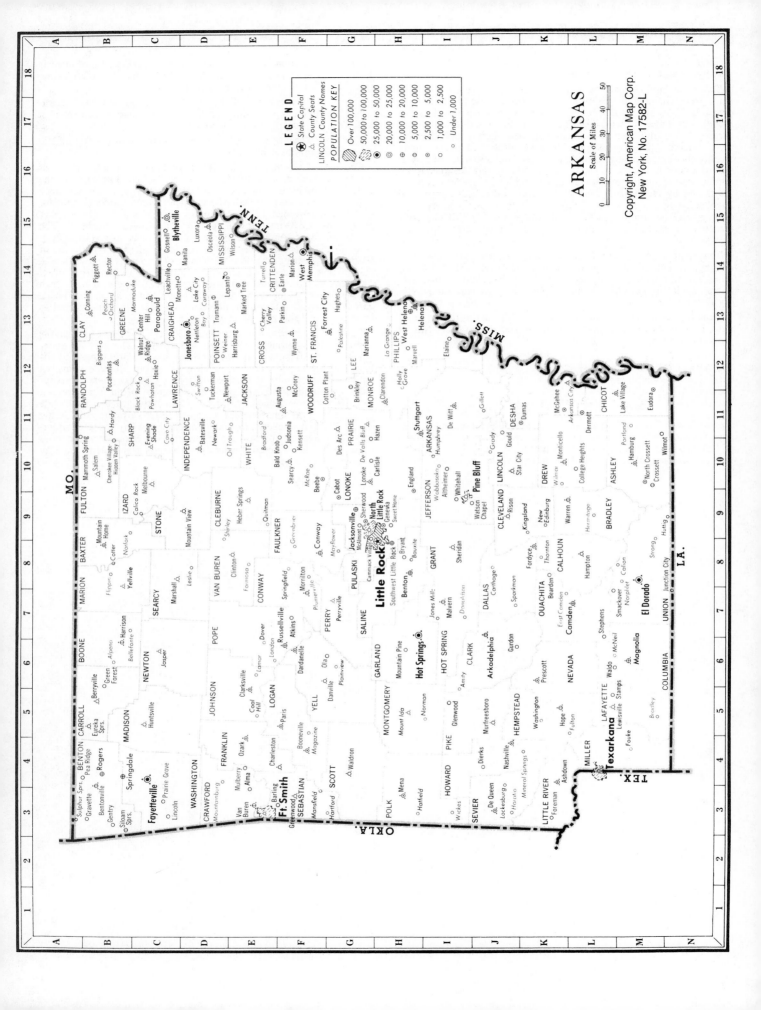

ARKANSAS

Scale of Miles

Copyright, American Map Corp.
New York, No. 17582-L

ARKANSAS

ARKANSAS STATE UNIVERSITY (D-13)
P.O. Box 1630
State University, Arkansas 72467
Tel: (501) 972-2031

Description: This state-controlled university is accredited by the North Central Association of Colleges and Schools. It operates on the semester system with 2 summer terms. The university developed from one of the four two-year state agricultural schools established in 1909 by an act of the Arkansas General Assembly. The school was reorganized and granted its first Baccalaureate degrees in 1931. At present, the school also offers the Masters degree, a Doctoral degree, and the Specialist degree. Continuing education courses are available. Cooperative education is available in agriculture economics, accounting, business administration and business education. Professional accreditations are ABET, ACEJMC, AACSB, CAHEA, CRE, CSWE, NASM, NCATE and NLN. Enrollment includes 7,003 full-time, 1,654 part-time, and 974 graduate students. A faculty of 394 full-time and 52 part-time gives an undergraduate faculty-student ratio of 1-19.

Entrance Requirements: Accredited high school graduate or GED; ACT scores of 19 or better; required grade average of C or better with the recommended following units: 4 English, 3 mathematics (including algebra I, algebra II and geometry), 3 natural science, and social science (including American history or civics or American government and world history); early admission available with 15 units high school credit and B average; early decision, rolling admission, midyear admission, and advanced placement plans available.

Costs Per Year: $1,800 tuition; $3,720 out-of-state; $2,580 room and board; $130 student fees.

Collegiate Environment: The campus consists of 38 buildings on 675 acres. Dormitory facilities accomodate 2,400 students. The library holds a total of 1,317,800 volumes, periodicals and microforms. About 72% of the applicants are accepted. About 62% of the freshmen returned for the second year. 1,908 scholarships are available and 60% of the students receive some form of financial aid.

Community Environment: Jonesboro is located on Crowley's Ridge, bordering the rich Mississippi Delta Agricultural and Industrial Center. Buses, railroads and airlines service the area. Jonesboro is 65 miles from Memphis, 133 miles from Little Rock, and 261 miles from St. Louis. The mean temperature is 60 degrees, and the average annual rainfall is 48.21 inches. There are 77 active clubs, and organizations, theaters, a Community Center, and several city parks in the city. Lake Frierson and Craighead Forest Park and lake are nearby.

ARKANSAS STATE UNIVERSITY - BEEBE BRANCH (F-10)
P.O. Drawer H
Beebe, Arkansas 72012
Tel: (501) 882-6452; Admissions: (501) 882-6452; Fax: (501) 882-8370

Description: This state-controlled college is accredited by the North Central Association of Colleges and Schools. The semester system is employed, with two summer sessions. This branch campus was added to the State University by an act of the State General Assembly in 1955 and offers only Associate degree programs. Enrollment includes 1,820 full-time students. A faculty of 78 gives a faculty-student ratio of 1-19.

Entrance Requirements: Graduation from high school, non-high school graduates considered; rolling admission, early decision, early admission, and midyear admission plans available.

Costs Per Year: $984 tuition; $1,544 out-of-state; $1,780 room and board.

Collegiate Environment: The campus has 20 buildings on 350 acres. The library contains 48,300 volumes, 300 periodicals, 3,200 microforms and 1,000 bound recordings. There is dormitory space available for 100 men and 56 women. 40 scholarships are available for freshmen and about 60% of the students receive some form of financial assistance.

Community Environment: Beebe is 35 miles from Little Rock, the State Capitol.

ARKANSAS TECH UNIVERSITY (F-6)
Russellville, Arkansas 72801
Tel: (501) 968-0389

Description: This state-supported, coeducational university is accredited by the North Central Association of Colleges and Schools. It operates on the semester system and offers two summer sessions. The institution was created by an act of the Arkansas General Assembly in 1909 as one of four Agricultural School Districts offering the first two years of college work. In 1950, the first baccalaureate degrees were awarded, and a graduate program leading to the Master of Education degree was established in 1976. In accordance with an act of the General Assembly and by the authority of the State of Arkansas Board of Higher Education, the name of Arkansas Polytechnic College was changed to Arkansas Tech University, effective July 9, 1976. Arkansas Tech University purposes to provide high quality educational programs within its five broad areas of emphasis: business and industry, teacher preparation, liberal education in the arts, preparation in the physical and life sciences, and information technology and systems. Although two of the university's five schools are vocationally oriented, the basic need for a broad development of the student's knowledge is clearly recognized in the general education program required of all students. Enrollment includes 1,617 men, 1,917 women full-time, 394 men, 828 women part-time, and 196 graduate students. The faculty consists of 180 full-time and 50 part-time members providing a student-faculty ratio of 19:1.

Entrance Requirements: Completion of high school graduation requirements; participation in ACT or SAT for admission, advising and placement; and cumulative high school grade point of 2.50 or better on a 4.00 scale.

Costs Per Year: $1,500 in-state; $3,000 out-of-state; $2,370 room and board; $60 student activity fee.

Collegiate Environment: The campus consists of 475 acres and 56 major buildings. Library contains 190,695 volumes, 9,000 pamphlets, 1,170 periodicals, and 544,097 microforms. Housing is provided for approximately 80% of student body. There are 4 male dorms, 4 female dorms, and 76 campus apartments for married students. About 99% of the applicants are accepted. Various forms of financial assistance are available.

Community Environment: Russellville, the crossroads for State Highways 7, 22, 124, and 64, is located equidistant from Little Rock, Hot Springs, Harrison, and Fort Smith. Interstate 40 passes just north of Russellville, a city of 18,000. A 36,600 acre lake, formed by a lock and dam on the navigable Arkansas River, lies southwest of the city. The area, served by airplane, rail, and bus lines, is experiencing vigorous industrial development, which includes the construction of the first nuclear power plant in the Southwest. Recreational facilities in the area include lakes, picnic areas, city parks, swimming pools, tennis courts, and private country clubs. There are the usual civic organizations of a city. Part-time employment is available in stores and on campus.

CENTRAL BAPTIST COLLEGE (F-8)
1501 College - CBC Station
Conway, Arkansas 72032
Tel: (501) 329-6872; Fax: (501) 329-2941

Description: The private, liberal arts college is controlled by the Baptist Missionary Association of Arkansas. It operates on the semester system and offers one summer session. Enrollment includes 183 men and 114 women. A faculty of 13 full-time and 9 part-time gives a faculty-student ratio of 1-18. The college accepts students as a divine trust and seeks to provide a wholesale consciousness of our cultural heritage in music, art, literature and science as well as basic Christian training. The college was started in 1952 as a junior college, and a Baccalaureate program was subsequently added. It currently offers Bachelor's degree programs in Bible and religious education, and grants Associate degrees.

Entrance Requirements: High school graduation with a C average and 15 units, 3 of which must be English, 2 mathematics, 2 science and 2 social science; score of 16 or over on ACT; non-high school graduates considered; student may be required to present evidence of good moral character; $25 application fee.

Costs Per Year: $3,244 tuition; $2,606 room and board; $50 student fees; ministers, ministers' wives and ministers' children under the age of 21 pay one-half of normal tuition fee.

Collegiate Environment: The student body is required to take 3 semester hours of Bible and to attend chapel. The campus is located in the heart of Conway, a city of colleges. The grounds constitute 11 acres. The library contains approximately 32,428 titles, 311 periodicals, 860 microforms, and 1,987 audiovisual materials. About 95% of the applicants are accepted. Various types of scholarships are offered and approximately 78% of the students receive some form of aid. Dormitories are available for 106 men and 80 women.

Community Environment: See University of Central Arkansas.

CROWLEY'S RIDGE COLLEGE   (C-13)
100 College Drive
Paragould, Arkansas 72450
Tel: (501) 236-6901

Description: A private, nonsectarian junior college directed by members of the Church of Christ requires all students to enroll in Bible class and attend chapel. The college was founded in 1953 as the Crowley Ridge Academy, offering the first 12 years of a child's education. In 1964, the junior college level was added and the present name was adopted. The college is a member of the American Association of Junior Colleges and is presently a correspondent in the North Central Association of College and Schools. Recent enrollment was 161 students and a faculty of 6 full-time and 7 part-time members. The 4-year Bible Institute offers Bachelor's of Biblical Literature degree. 16 correspondent credits allowed.

Entrance Requirements: High school diploma required; nongraduates with 15 acceptable units including 3 units in English; $10 room reservation fee required with application. Early admission, rolling admission, advance placement plans available.

Costs Per Year: $1,650 tuition per semester; $1,200 room and board(semester); student fees $120.

Collegiate Environment: Five buildings on 120 acres serve a capacity of 200 students. The library contains 11,887 volumes, 250 pamphlets, 64 periodicals, and 568 AV materials. Ninety- five percent of all applicants are accepted. Eighty percent of the freshman class returned for their second year. Student housing accommodates 60 men and 120 women. Various forms of financial assistance are available, including a work-study program.

Community Environment: Paragould, the county seat of Greene County is strategically located on main routes to Memphis and St. Louis. The climate is temperate. This city serves the agricultural area of northeast Arkansas and supports diversified industries. Reynold's Park, which is on the north edge of the city, has facilities for swimming, camping, picnicking, boating and fishing. Crowley's Ridge State Park is 12 miles from Paragould.

EAST ARKANSAS COMMUNITY COLLEGE   (G-13)
Newcastle Road
Forrest City, Arkansas 72335
Tel: (501) 633-4480

Description: Classes began in August 1974 in this public school and occupancy of the new campus began in 1975. It is accredited by the North Central Association of Colleges and Schools. The college

offers the Associate of Art and Associate of Applied Science degrees. All Arkansas colleges and universities accept credits from this school. Some credit is given for correspondence courses and certain other courses by prior examination. Cooperative education programs are available for all majors. It operates on the semester system and offers one summer session and evening courses. Enrollment includes 740 full-time and 563 part-time students. A faculty of 50 full-time and 24 part-time gives a faculty-student ratio of 1-20.

Entrance Requirements: C Average; open enrollment policy or GED; nongraduates 18 years or older considered; early admission, rolling admission, delayed admission and early decision plans available.

Costs Per Year: $720 county resident tuition; $888 state resident tuition; $1,092 nonresident tuition

Collegiate Environment: 16 buildings constitute the campus, which is in its first phase of development. The campus adjoins the campus of Crowley's Ridge Vocational Technical School. Plans for future development include four new buildings. The library contains 20,000 hardbound volumes. 95% of applicants are accepted, including students at midyear. 30 scholarships, 20 for freshmen, are available. 650 students (44%) receive some form of financial assistance.

Community Environment: Forrest City, with a population of 13,803, is the county seat of St. Francis County.

HARDING UNIVERSITY   (F-10)
Searcy, Arkansas 72143
Tel: (501) 279-4407; (800) 477-4407; Fax: (501) 275-4865

Description: Private coeducational, liberal arts college affiliated with the Church of Christ and accredited by the North Central Association of Colleges and Schools. Harding became a senior college in 1924 and moved to Searcy in 1934. Academic cooperative plans with the University of Arkansas are available for students majoring in engineering. The college grants both Bachelor's and Master's degrees. Army ROTC is available. It operates on the early semester system and offers three summer sessions. Enrollment is 3,817 students. A faculty of 200 gives a faculty-student ratio of 1-19.

Entrance Requirements: High school graduation with a C average; completion of 15 units, including 4 English, 4 math, 3 social studies and 3 natural sciences recommended; ACT or SAT required; early admission, rolling admission, delayed admission, and advanced placement plans available; $25 application fee.

Costs Per Year: $5,160 tuition; $952.50 student fees; $3,528 room and board; $700 average additional expenses.

Collegiate Environment: The campus consists of 200 acres close to the town's business section. The 44 buildings are well equipped and efficiently furnished. The library contains 342,000 volumes, 32,083 periodicals, 71,615 microforms and 3,217 recordings. Dormitory facilities accommodate 939 men, 1,076 women and 124 married students. Average scores for the freshman class, ACT 24. 80% of the freshman class returned to this campus for the second year. Financial aid is available for qualified students.

Community Environment: This is a rural area 50 miles from Little Rock. The climate is temperate. A public library, churches, and a hospitals all serve the area. This is an excellent medical community with two 100-bed hospitals and more than 40 physicians in a city of 16,000. There are a river and several lakes in the area providing recreational facilities. Harding owns a 1,200-acre camp in the Ozarks for student use.

Branch Campuses: Florence, Italy; London, England; Athens, Greece.

HENDERSON STATE UNIVERSITY   (J-7)
Box 7560
1100 Henderson Street
Arkadelphia, Arkansas 71999
Tel: (501) 246-5511; (800) 228-7333; Admissions: (501) 230-5028; Fax: (501) 230-5144

Description: This public college was established in 1890 and is accredited by the North Central Association of Colleges and Schools. A Graduate Studies program was inaugurated in 1955. The university grants the Bachelor's and Master's degrees. Up to 30 hours of correspondent credit is allowed. Continuing education courses are offered.

The college operates on the semester system and offers two summer sessions. Enrollment includes 3,796 students. A faculty of 162 full-time and 56 part-time gives a faculty-student ratio of 1-18.

Entrance Requirements: Somewhat competitive enrollment policy; completion of 15 units including 4 English, 2 mathematics, 2 science and 2 social science; ACT required; non-high school graduates considered; early admission, early decision, rolling admission, midyear admission and advanced placement plans available.

Costs Per Year: $1,728 tuition; $3,456 nonresident; $2,520 room and board; additional expenses average $700 per year.

Collegiate Environment: The campus is located in a residential area and includes 25 major buildings on 127 acres. The air-conditioned library contains 200,000 volumes. Dormitory facilities accommodate 1,347 men and women. 95% of applicants are accepted. 65% of the freshman class return for the sophomore year. The average score of the entering freshman class is ACT 20.8 composite. 446 scholarships are available, including 317 for freshmen and 71 athletic. Financial assistance is also available. About 30% of the senior class continued on to graduate school.

Community Environment: Arkadelphia is 55 miles southwest of Little Rock, and 35 miles south of Hot Springs, America's oldest national park. Arkadelphia is a modern, progressive city, and a well-known educational center. The Missouri Pacific Railroad, U.S. Interstate 30, U.S. Highway 67, and state highways make this city easily accessible from all parts of the state.

HENDRIX COLLEGE *(F-8)*
1601 Harkrider Street
Conway, Arkansas 72032-3080
Tel: (501) 329-6811; (800) 277-9017; Admissions: (501) 450-1362; Fax: (501) 450-1200

Description: Private coeducational, liberal arts college affiliated with the United Methodist Church and accredited by the North Central Association of Schools. The college grants the Bachelor degree. The 3-3 semester plan is used in which students attend three eleven-week terms and take three courses per term. Academic cooperative plans are available with Columbia University, Vanderbilt University, and Washington University for engineering students and American University for students majoring in political science. Army ROTC is available as an elective. Enrollment includes 941 students. A faculty of 70 full-time and 12 part-time gives a faculty-student ratio of 1-14.

Entrance Requirements: High school graduation; SAT or ACT required; non-high school graduates considered; early admission, delayed admission, midyear admission and advanced placement plans available; $25 application fee.

Costs Per Year: $2,534 tuition (semester); $965 room and board; additional books and personal expenses average $1,000.

Collegiate Environment: The college has been in continuous operation for a century. 80% of the students live on campus in dormitory facilities accommodating 749 students. The library contains 156,563 volumes, 598 periodical subscriptions, and 76,808 microform materials. The college accepts a geographically diverse student body and admits midyear students. 90% of applicants are accepted. About 80% of the freshman class return for the sophomore year. Approximately 200 scholarships are available and 81% of the current student body receives some form of financial aid.

Community Environment: See University of Central Arkansas

JOHN BROWN UNIVERSITY *(B-3)*
200 W. University Street
Siloam Springs, Arkansas 72761
Tel: (501) 524-7150; (800) 634-6969; Fax: (501) 524-4196

Description: Private, Christian university accredited by the North Central Association of Colleges and Schools. From its beginning in 1919, the university has been coeducational and not a regional institution, drawing students from all over the country. It operates on the semester system. Enrollment is 1,018 students. A faculty of 70 gives a faculty-student ratio of 1-15. Academic cooperative plans are available for students majoring in medical technology. The college grants Associate and Bachelor's degrees. Thirty of the final 45 hours must be taken in residence.

Entrance Requirements: ACT or SAT required; high school graduates rank in upper 50% of the graduating class; non-high school graduates considered; completion of 16 units including 4 English, 4 mathematics, 2 social science, 2 laboratory sciences, and 2 foreign language; rolling admissions, early admission, advance placement, delayed admission and early decision plans are available; $25 application fee.

Costs Per Year: $6,390 tuition; $3,360 room and board; $130 activities fee; additional expenses average $1,200.

Collegiate Environment: The campus includes 200 acres located in a picturesque foothill region of the Ozark Mountains; there are 43 buildings, including housing units for married students as well as dormitory facilities for 354 men and 338 women. Student life has been greatly enhanced by the recreational center, which includes a large swimming pool, spacious recreational center, 4 racquetball courts, fitness center, indoor elevated track, theater, snack shop, a lighted field, tennis courts and picnic ground with outdoor fireplaces. The library contains 93,000 volumes, 515 periodicals, 125 microforms and 2,035 audiovisual materials. Average high school standings of a recent freshman class: 50% in the top quarter; 24% in the second quarter; 19% in the third quarter; ACT 23. The college offers 452 scholarships and 78% of the current student body receives financial aid. Midyear students are accepted. Approximately 20% of the senior class continued on to graduate school.

Community Environment: Located in the Benton County foothills of the beautiful Ozarks. The town is easily accessible from all parts of the state. The seasons are delightfully mild. Siloam Springs is far enough south to insure mild winters, and the summer nights are pleasantly cool. Northwest Arkansas is considered a very healthful location, and is noted as a summer retreat for many tourists from all sections of the United States.

LYON COLLEGE *(D-10)*
P.O. Box 2317
Batesville, Arkansas 72503
Tel: (501) 793-9813

Description: The private, coeducational college is affiliated with the Presbyterian Church, U.S.A., and is accredited by the North Central Association of Colleges and Schools. Founded in 1872, the college is an institution which offers a liberal arts program leading to Baccalaureate degrees in arts and sciences. Operations of the college were moved in 1954 to a new 136-acre site. Recent enrollment included 701 students and the faculty consists of 44 full-time and 29 part-time members. The 4-1-4 system is employed, with one summer session.

Entrance Requirements: High school graduation with a 2.50 GPA and 15 units recommended-4 English, 3 mathematics, 3 science, 3 social studies, and 1-2 foreign language; high school graduate or GED required. ACT or SAT required; application fee $15.00 by August 15 for the Fall term; rolling admission and advanced placement available.

Costs Per Year: $7,600 tuition; $3,300 room and board.

Collegiate Environment: The campus includes 22 buildings on 136 acres. The student body represents a cross section of many denominations coming from 15 states and 2 foreign countries. Approximately 87% of the student body graduated in the top 50% of high school class; 67% in the top quarter, 63% of the freshman class returned for second year. About 76% of the applicants are accepted. The average high school grade point average at the freshman class was 3.4, with a composite ACT between 20-25. The library contains 91,000 volumes, 800 periodicals, 3,000 microforms and AV material. 313 students reside in a variety of housing options. Financial aid is offered and about 95% of the current student body received assistance. Special programs include Nichols Travel Program, Outdoor Experiences, Mentor Program, Student Research. Many student organizations enhance the primarily residential campus.

Community Environment: Batesville is located on the banks of the White River, in the foothills of the Ozarks 90 miles north of Little Rock, and 120 miles northwest of Memphis. The climate is mild, summer mean is 78 degrees and the winter mean is 40 degrees. Average annual rainfall is 48 inches. There are many churches in the area, a fine city library, hospitals, and 4 radio stations and cable TV.

MISSISSIPPI COUNTY COMMUNITY COLLEGE   (C-15)
P. O. Box 1109
Blytheville, Arkansas 72316
Tel: (501) 762-1020

Description: This state-supported, junior college was founded in 1974, and is accredited by the North Central Association of Colleges and Schools. It operates on a semester system with two summer sessions. The school awards a certificate and Associate degrees. Enrollment includes 1,680 students. A faculty of 98 gives a faculty-student ratio of 1-16.

Entrance Requirements: High school graduation or GED on an open door policy; early admission, early decision, midyear admission, advanced placement, dual enrollment (high school and college) and rolling admission plans.

Costs Per Year: $720 tuition county resident; $864 out-of-county; $1,920 out-of-state or international.

Collegiate Environment: There are 40 scholarships of which approximately 70% are for freshmen. Currently 70% of the students receive financial aid. One hundred percent of applicants eligible for enrollment are accepted. The library houses 85,000 volumes, 342 pamphlets, 350 periodicals and 1,100 audiovisual materials.

Community Environment: Rural - Population 24,000.

OUACHITA BAPTIST UNIVERSITY   (J-7)
P.O. Box 3754
Arkadelphia, Arkansas 71998
Tel: (501) 245-5000; (800) 342-5628; Admissions: (501) 245-5110; Fax: (501) 245-5500

Description: Private, coeducational university founded in 1886 by the Arkansas Baptist State Convention. It is accredited by the North Central Association of Colleges and Schools. Academic cooperative plans are available with Vanderbilt, University of Arkansas and the University of Southern California for students majoring in engineering, pre-med, and medical technology. The university grants the Bachelor degree. It operates on the semester system and offers two summer sessions. Enrollment includes 1,392 full-time and 48 part-time students. A faculty of 94 full-time and 29 part-time gives a faculty-student ratio of 1-13.

Entrance Requirements: Traditional enrollment policy; 2.5 GPA; completion of 16 units including 4 English, 2 mathematics, 2 science, 3 social science; ACT minimum score 19 required; non-high school graduates on basis of entrance and intelligence tests; rolling admission, early admission, early decision, midyear admission and advanced placement plans available; $25 application fee sent to Admissions Counselor by August 15 for fall term.

Costs Per Year: $6,970 tuition; $2,900 room and board; $100 student fees; $400 average additional expenses.

Collegiate Environment: Attendance at chapel is required of all students. The library contains over 280,000 volumes and government documents, 1,100 periodicals, 370,000 nonbook items, and 8,000 media items. Dormitory facilities accommodate 1,215 men and women. 84% of applicants are accepted. Scholarships are available and 90% of the students receive some form of financial aid.

Community Environment: Ouachita Baptist University is located in Arkadelphia, Arkansas, about 70 miles southwest of Little Rock on I-30 and 35 miles south of Hot Springs. There is frequent Amtrak service service to and from the city. Facilities for air transportation are available both in Hot Springs and Little Rock. Arkadelphia has a population of more than 10,000, including the students of Ouachita and Henderson State University.

PHILANDER SMITH COLLEGE   (H-9)
Little Rock, Arkansas 72203
Tel: (501) 375-9845

Description: This private liberal arts college is affiliated with the Methodist Church. It is accredited by the North Central Association of Colleges and Schools. Founded in 1877, the four-year college operates on the semester system and offers one summer session. Recent enrollment included 800 students. The college grants the Bachelor's degree.

Entrance Requirements: High school graduation with a C average or above; completion of 16 units including 3 English and 2 mathematics; ACT required; advanced placement plan available; non-high school graduates considered; $5 application fee.

Costs Per Year: $2,375 tuition; $2,300 room and board.

Collegiate Environment: The campus is located on 12 city blocks in the heart of the capital of Arkansas and contains a library of 70,000 volumes.

Community Environment: See University of Arkansas - Little Rock.

PHILLIPS COUNTY COMMUNITY COLLEGE   (H-13)
Post Office Box 785
Helena, Arkansas 72342
Tel: (501) 338-6474; Fax: (501) 338-7542

Description: Founded in 1965, the district-governed junior college is accredited by the North Central Association of Colleges and Schools. The college grants Certificates and the Associate degree. Correspondence credit allowed; continuing education courses offered; cooperative education programs available in business and social studies departments. The semester system is used and one summer session is offered. Enrollment includes 685 full-time and 835 part-time students with a faculty of 66 giving a faculty-student ratio of 1:23

Entrance Requirements: College employs an open door admissions policy; SAT or ACT accepted; early admissions and advanced placement plans are available.

Costs Per Year: $840 district resident, $1,056 nondistrict, $1,968 nonresident

Collegiate Environment: The campus consists of 12 buildings on 80 acres. The library contains 35,000 volumes, 327 periodicals and 1,400 microforms. Sixty-one percent of the freshman class returned to this campus for their second year.

Community Environment: Helena is in a suburban area, and blessed with a mild, warm climate. There are churches of major denominations, libraries and a museum. Helena has an accredited general hospital and major civic and service organizations.

SHORTER COLLEGE   (G-9)
604 Locust Street
North Little Rock, Arkansas 72114
Tel: (501) 374-6305; Fax: (501) 374-9333

Description: This private two-year college is sponsored by the African-Methodist Episcopal Church. The college is accredited by the North Central Association of Colleges and Schools and the Arkansas Council of Independent Colleges and Universities. It grants the Associate degree. The college operates on the semester system and offers two summer sessions. Enrollment is 309 students. A faculty of 103 gives a faculty-student ratio 1-15.

Entrance Requirements: ACT or SAT required; open enrollment policy; 4 English, 2 mathematics, 2 science, and 2 social science units required; non-high school graduates considered; early admission, midyear admission, and rolling admission plans available; $8 application fee.

Costs Per Year: $1,200 tuition; $1,200 room and board.

Collegiate Environment: Facilities of the college include a library with 11,746 hardbound volumes, and dormitory housing which accommodates 60 students. 90% of applicants are accepted. Financial aid is available for economically disadvantaged students and 90% of students receive some form of financial assistance.

Community Environment: North Little Rock is a separate municipality across the Arkansas River from Little Rock. The climate is mild. It has the largest municipal park in the state, which totals 1,575 acres, and is the social and cultural center of the state with the finest residential area in the Central South. Hot Springs is a one-hour drive away. Off-campus student housing is available.

SOUTH ARKANSAS COMMUNITY COLLEGE   (M-8)
P.O. Box 7010
300 South West Avenue
El Dorado, Arkansas 71731-7010
Tel: (501) 862-8131

Description: The publicly supported, coeducational two-year college was a branch campus of Southern Arkansas University. It was established in 1975 by an act of the State General Assembly and is accredited by the North Central Association of Colleges and Schools. The college operates on the semester system with three summer terms. Enrollment includes 561 men and 473 women full-time and 631 men and 727 women part-time. The faculty includes 46 full-time and 30 part-time members. Students in the college receive the Associate of Arts degree and those in two-year occupational programs receive the Associate of Applied Science degree or certificate.

Entrance Requirements: High school graduation or equivalent. Open enrollment, early admission, and rolling admission. Degree seeking students must take the ACT, SAT or ASSET Test; early admission, midyear admission, and rolling admission plans available.

Costs Per Year: $930 ($31/cr) tuition for district resident; $1,100 ($37/cr) out-of-district; $1,560 ($52/cr) out-of-state resident.

Collegiate Environment: The college is located on a downtown site of approximately five acres near the heart of El Dorado, the largest city in South Central Arkansas. The three college buildings include an administrative building, a classroom building, and a gymnasium. The library holds 21,939 volumes, 225 periodicals, 53,899 microforms and 967 audiovisuals. No on-campus housing is available and all students commute. All students applying for admission who meet the requirements are accepted. 80 scholarships are available and 50% of the current full-time students receive some form of financial aid. Application for financial aid is made with CSX, Arkansas Application for Federal and State Student Aid.

Community Environment: El Dorado is the seat of Union County, lying 117 miles south of Little Rock. Passenger bus and air service is available. Community services include a public library, two hospitals, several churches, an arts center, and good shopping facilities. There is good hunting and fishing in the general area, and water sports on nearby lakes and rivers. Important industries are timber, poultry, oil, and chemicals.

SOUTHERN ARKANSAS UNIVERSITY   (M-6)
Magnolia, Arkansas 71753
Tel: (501) 235-4000; (800) 332-7286; Fax: (501) 235-5005

Description: The four-year college is accredited by the North Central Association of Colleges and Schools. The semester system is used and two summer sessions are offered. The college grants Associate, Bachelor's, and Master's degrees. Correspondent credit allowed; continuing education courses offered. Enrollment includes 2,122 full-time and 365 part-time undergraduates and 127 graduate students. A faculty of 126 full-time and 6 part-time gives a faculty-student ratio of 1-19.

Entrance Requirements: Accredited high school graduation; a 15+ ACT composite or rank in the upper half of high school graduating class; minimum of 20 units including 4 English, 3 social science, 3 mathematics, 3 science, 7 electives (no more than 4 units in vocational subjects); ACT required; 21-year-old students with GED equivalency or adequate scores on college entrance exams accepted.

Costs Per Year: $1,632 tuition; $2,544 nonresidents; $2,410 room and board.

Collegiate Environment: The campus is situated on 120 acres, with an additional 540 acres used by the Agriculture Department as a laboratory for its students. The library houses over 140,016 volumes, 1,200 pamphlets, 13,243 periodicals, 725,649 microforms, 6,214 audiovisuals and 5,765 sound recordings and has seating facilities for 1,338 students. 200 scholarships including 100 for freshmen, are available. Financial aid is available. 62% of students receive some form of financial aid. Dormitory facilities available for 618 men, 446 women and for 72 married students.

Community Environment: Magnolia has a wonderful climate; 225 days of the year are considered the growing season. Business men of the city are very interested in their city, which makes for a fine community. The Louisiana and Northwest Railroad runs through Magnolia, as well as the Southwestern Greyhound Bus Lines and the Continental Trailways. Magnolia is the center of the oil industry of Arkansas, and contains a number of industrial plants. There are churches, libraries, and a city hospital. The recreational activities include fishing, hunting, swimming, baseball, football and golfing.

SOUTHERN ARKANSAS UNIVERSITY TECH   (L-7)
One Tech Boulevard - Tech Station
Camden, Arkansas 71701
Tel: (501) 574-4500; Fax: (501) 574-4520

Description: The only technical/junior college in the state, the college is a leader in computer-aided technologies. It serves students seeking Associate degrees identified with specific career goals and those preferring college transfer. A one-semester high-tech prep program is offered for those needing to upgrade skills for entrance into high-tech degree programs in CAD/CAM, CIM, robotics, and computer science. It is accredited by North Central Association of College and Secondary Schools. It operates on the semester system and offers two summer terms. Enrollment is 387 full-time and 810 part-time students. A faculty of 50 gives a faculty-student ratio of 1-22.

Entrance Requirements: High school graduation or GED; open enrollment; rolling admission plan available.

Costs Per Year: $1,032 tuition; $1,548 nonresident; $1,950 room and board.

Collegiate Environment: Excellent facilities were made available by the Brown Foundation of Houston, Texas, in a gift to the State of Arkansas when the Institute was created in 1967. The administrative area, comprised of 6 buildings and 70 acres of land of the former Shumaker Naval Ammunition Depot, was renovated in early 1968 for use by the Institute. Financing of the renovation and equipping the facility was done with the aid of a grant from the Economic Development Administration. The library houses 19,000 hard-bound volumes. There is student housing for 122 students. Midyear students are accepted.

Community Environment: The Camden area is an active commercial center in South Arkansas. A large manufacturing sector, including high tech defense production, gives the community an economic vitality that complements its natural assets of hills, forests, lakes and rivers. Outdoor recreational opportunities abound. Full retail, restaurant and professional services are available.

UNIVERSITY OF ARKANSAS - FAYETTEVILLE   (C-4)
Fayetteville, Arkansas 72701
Tel: (501) 575-2000; (800) 377-8632; Admissions: (501) 575-5346;
Fax: (501) 575-7515

Description: The state-controlled, coeducational university was founded in 1871, is accredited by the North Central Association of Colleges and Schools, and grants undergraduate and graduate degrees. The university operates on the semester system and offers three summer terms. Total enrollment includes 6,340 men and 5,286 women full-time and 1,452 men and 1,414 women part-time. Enrollment components are 10,224 full-time and 1,620 part-time undergraduates and 2,648 graduate students. A faculty of 796 full-time and 79 part-time provides a faculty-student ratio of 1:16. Air Force and Army ROTC programs are offered.

Entrance Requirements: Graduation from an accredited high school, completion of core courses and a minimum GPA of 2.25; non-high school graduates considered on basis of G.E.D. ACT or SAT and SAT2 writing are required for scholarship and academic advising. Midyear admission, rolling admission, and advanced placement available. $15 application fee.

Costs Per Year: $1,728 state-resident tuition, $2,880 nonresident; student fees $80, $3,225 room and board.

Collegiate Environment: The main campus is located on 357 acres and includes 130 buildings. 85% percent of those who apply for admission are accepted. Dormitory space is provided for 1,408 men and 1,276 women, and 334 apartments for married students are available. Fraternities and sororities house an additional 1,150 men and women. The university library contains 1,423,667 volumes, over 16,332 periodicals, 1,402,865 microforms and 16,613 audiovisual materials. 2,611 scholarships are available, and approximately 62% of the current students receive some form of assistance.

Community Environment: Population of Fayetteville is 45,000. The climate is temperate. All modes of transportation except trains serve the area. There are a number of churches, a library, three hospitals and several theaters in the area. Part-time employment is available. There are fishing and water sports at nearby lakes and backpacking, hiking, camping and spelunking in surrounding mountains and forests. The city has major civic, veteran's and fraternal organizations.

UNIVERSITY OF ARKANSAS - LITTLE ROCK   (H-9)
2801 South University
Little Rock, Arkansas 72204
Tel: (501) 569-3000

Description: This publicly supported, coeducational university is accredited by the North Central Association of Colleges and Schools. The school grants an Associate degree, Bachelors degree, Masters degree, Doctoral degree, and Juris Doctor degree. Begun in 1927 as a junior college, it became a four-year school in 1957 and took the name Little Rock University. The present organization and name were incorporated in 1969 with the mergers of Little Rock University and the University of Arkansas. It operates on the semester system and offers three summer sessions. Enrollment includes 2,745 men, 3,471 women full-time, 2,040 men, 3,252 women part-time, 1,676 graduate students and 5,992 evening students. A faculty of 479 full-time and 261 part-time gives a faculty-student ratio of 1-16.

Entrance Requirements: High school graduation with a 2.5 average; non-high school graduates considered; completion of 15 units, including 4 English, 3 mathematics and other electives; ACT or SAT required, $15 application fee; minimum scores: ACT composite 21, SAT composite 800 for unconditional admission; conditional admission; early admission, early decision, rolling admission, delayed admission and advanced placement plans available.

Costs Per Year: $2,302 undergraduate tuition and fees; $5,518 nonresident undergraduate; $3,022 resident graduate; $6,216 nonresident graduate.

Collegiate Environment: Located on 150 acres, the campus has 30 buildings. A residence hall is available with a capacity of 306 students. The newly constructed library contains 394,780 volumes, 2,626 periodicals, and 691,612 titles on microforms. The law library contains 215,000 volumes. 59% of the students receive some form of financial assistance. The average ACT composite score of the current freshman class was 19.4. Midyear students are admitted. There were 155 Associate, 831 Bachelor, 371 Master, 99 Juris Doctor, and 8 Doctoral degrees granted recently.

Community Environment: Little Rock is the state capital and county seat. The average summer temperature is 80 degrees, and the winter average is 42 degrees. The city has many churches, libraries, symphony, little theatre, fine arts center, and museum, and a natural history museum. Broadway Road Shows and the Arkansas State Opera also enrich the cultural atmosphere of Little Rock. All modes of transportation are available. Student employment is plentiful. Sports include tennis, hunting, fishing and horseback riding. There are living quarters available in all parts of the city.

UNIVERSITY OF ARKANSAS - MONTICELLO   (K-10)
P.O. Box 3596
Monticello, Arkansas 71655
Tel: (501) 367-6811; Admissions: (501) 460-1026

Description: The state-controlled college is accredited by the North Central Association of Colleges and Schools and operates on the semester system with two summer sessions. The college was created in 1909 by an act of the State General Assembly in a community noted for its fine churches and rich cultural tradition. In 1971, the Arkansas Agricultural and Mechanical College became part of the University of Arkansas. The enrollment includes 2,080 full-time and 278 part-time undergraduate students and 36 graduate students. A faculty of 107 full-time and gives a faculty-student ratio of 1-20. 15 hrs. correspondent credit allowed; continuing education offered; cooperative education available in Forestry.

Entrance Requirements: Completion of 20 units including 3 English, 2 units mathematics. A certificate of High School Attendance will not entitle the applicant to admission. Early decision and rolling admission plans available; midyear students accepted.

Costs Per Year: $1,704 tuition; $3,720 out-of-state tuition; $2,240 room and board; $108 student fees.

Collegiate Environment: The campus includes 790 acres with 64 buildings. There are four college dormitories equipped with the most modern furniture. The library contains 123,511 volumes, 869 periodi-

cals, and 7,200 microforms. About 98% of the applicants are accepted and 73% of the student body receive some form of financial aid. Approximately 50% of the current freshman class returned for their second year.

Community Environment: Monticello is the Drew County Seat. This is a center of Southeast Arkansas located 94 miles from Little Rock; 115 miles from Hot Springs; 70 miles from Greenville, Mississippi; 85 miles from Monroe, Louisiana. The average mean temperature is 65 degrees. Railroads and buses serve the area. The farming area is a rich agricultural region and the city has a number of industrial plants manufacturing carpeting, boats, and timber. Monticello is considered a "growing family" community. There are three city parks, and excellent hunting and fishing in the county.

UNIVERSITY OF ARKANSAS - PINE BLUFF   (I-9)
Pine Bluff, Arkansas 71601
Tel: (501) 543-8000; (800) 264-8272; Admissions: (501) 543-8492; Fax: (501) 542-8014

Description: This state-supported Land Grant Institution is accredited by the North Central Association of Colleges and Schools. UAPB is the second oldest public institution in the state, and the oldest with a black heritage. It was founded in 1873 as Branch Normal College, a branch of the University of Arkansas. It opened to students on September 27, 1875. In 1927, it became Arkansas Agricultural, Mechanical & Normal College (Arkansas AM&N, also knowm as Arkansas State College) and merged with the University of Arkansas system in 1972. Today, known as the University of Arkansas at Pine Bluff, it has five areas of emphasis: the School of Liberal and Fine Arts, the School of Business and Management, the School of Education, the School of Agriculture and Home Economics and the School of Science and Technology. It offers 42 Associate, Bachelor and Master degree programs, with more than 700 courses. The Division of Military Science offers the ROTC program which allows an individual to compete for a commission as a Second Lieutenant in the Army, Army National Guard or the Army Reserve while attending college. The university operates on the semester system and offers two summer sessions. Enrollment includes 2,947 full-time and 749 part-time undergraduates, and 127 graduate students. A faculty of 193 full-time and 36 part-time gives a fauclty-student ratio of 1-21.

Entrance Requirements: High school graduates averaging C grades or better; completion of at least 21 units, including 4 English, 3 math, 3 science, and 3 social studies, 2 foreign language, 5 health and safety, 5 fine arts, 4 electives; ACT required; students from unaccredited high schools must take qualifying tests; rolling admission, midyear admission, early admission, early decision and advanced placement plans available.

Costs Per Year: $1,536 tuition; $3,552 nonresident tuition; $180 student fees; 2,484 room and board.

Collegiate Environment: Located in Southeast Pine Bluff, the vast campus is a scenic blend of oak and pine trees which comprise 318 acres of 41 major buildings and 235 acres of agricultural and aquacultural research farms. The 83-acre main campus includes five new buildings of recent construction, including a new student housing complex which accommodates 1,050 students. The Kenneth L. Johnson Health, Physical Education and Recreation complex features raquetball and tennis courts, a swimming pool, a gymnastics gymnasium, a basketball arena and lecture hall. UAPB is a member of the National Association of Intercollegiate Athletics (NAIA) and is a corresponding member of the National Collegiate Athletics Association (NCAA). The library contains 208,000 volumes, approximately 22,228 government documents, 829 periodicals, 410,159 microforms, 1,000 audiovisual materials, and 3 computerized retrieval systems. Dormitory housing is available for 1,050 students. About 85% of the applicants are accepted. The average ACT composite score of the current freshmen was 16.

Community Environment: The university is located on the Arkansas River, 45 miles south of Little Rock. Pine Bluff is the second oldest city in the state. The average temperature is 63 degrees, average rainfall is 50 inches, and average snowfall is 5.4 inches. Pine Bluff is noted for diversified industry. The two most important are the manufacturing of lumber, and electric transformer. The Leisure Group-Ben Pearson Archery, Inc., is one of the world's largest bow and arrow manufacturers, and is located in Pine Bluff. There are churches of all denominations, a YWCA, radio station, theaters, hotels and motels.

The recreational facilities include tennis courts, swimming pools, golf course, bowling, a five hundred-acre lake downtown, plus twenty-two lakes in Jefferson County. Recreational resources include fishing, boating, swimming and camping. Pine Bluff is the scene of what many believe is the location of the first shot of the Civil War. Some of the homes on West Barraque, which is the oldest street in Jefferson County, date from the Civil War.

UNIVERSITY OF ARKANSAS, MEDICAL SCIENCES CAMPUS   (H-9)
4301 West Markham
Slot 601
Little Rock, Arkansas 72205
Tel: (501) 686-5454

Description: The present Medical Sciences Campus evolved from the original School of Medicine of the University of Arkansas in 1879. It is accredited by the North Central Association of Colleges and Schools. It is comprised of the College of Medicine, College of Nursing, College of Pharmacy, College of Health Related Professions and the Graduate School. The school operates on the semester system and offers one summer session. Enrollment includes 1,475 full-time and 389 part-time undergraduates and 412 graduate students. The faculty of 509 is supported by some part-time and volunteer members.

Entrance Requirements: Requirements vary within each program. Contact Director of Admissions in specific college for details.

Costs Per Year: Tuition ranges from $1,908 to $6,996 per year for in-state students, depending upon the program selected, and about double those amounts for out-of-staters. General living expenses are approximately $6,000-$9,000 per academic year. Fees in each school vary.

Collegiate Environment: Located in the center of Little Rock, the Medical Sciences Campus utilizes two nine-story buildings for its classrooms and laboratory facilities. The University Hospital and the Barton Institute of Medical Research are located nearby and afford the students the opportunity of utilizing these facilities. Also nearby are the Arkansas State Hospital, the 500-bed McClellan VA Hospital, and the Child Study Center. All single students attending any of the Medical Center schools are required to live in the Residence Hall. Space is provided for about 422 single students and 102 married students on the first five floors of the Residence Hall. Various forms of financial assistance are available. The library holds 177,319 volumes, 1,757 periodicals, and 2,560 audiovisual materials.

Community Environment: See University of Arkansas - Little Rock

UNIVERSITY OF CENTRAL ARKANSAS   (F-8)
Donaghey at Bruce
Conway, Arkansas 72035
Tel: (501) 450-3128; Fax: (501) 450-5228

Description: The University of Central Arkansas is a public, coeducational institution accredited by the North Central Association of Colleges and Schools. Established in 1907 with emphasis on teacher education, the character of the University has changed to the multipurpose nature of its current varied and complex curricula. The University is now organized into a School of Health Sciences, the Graduate School, and five colleges: Business Administration, Education, Arts and Letters, Natural Science and Mathematics, and Health and Applied Sciences. Special honors curricula include the Honors College that offers optional programs of accelerated education for gifted undergraduates, as well as departmental honors programs. Internships in public administration and business; co-curricular activities in broadcasting, drama, speech and journalism; and study abroad in Spanish are available. Despite its growth, the University hopes to preserve the informality and friendliness of a small school. It awards Bachelor and Master degrees and offers sixth-year programs leading to the Specialist's Degree in Education in School Counseling and Educational Leadership. The semester system is employed, with two summer sessions offered. Enrollment includes 7,577 full-time and 1,615 part-time undergraduate, and 1,035 graduate students. A faculty of 360 full-time gives a faculty-student ratio of 1-21. Army ROTC program available.

Entrance Requirements: ACT or SAT scores; high school GPA; rank in high school graduating class; high school coursework; recommendation from teachers and/or counselors; special talents; admission

is competitive for 2,000 freshmen class spaces; early admission, early decision, midyear admission, and advanced placement plans are available.

Costs Per Year: $1,586 stae resident tuition; $3,172 nonresident tuition; $2,600 room and board; $414 student fees.

Collegiate Environment: The 220-acre campus is located in central Arkansas on the southwestern edge of Conway which is thirty miles from the State Capital (Little Rock). In Main Hall, students of the Speech Department operate radio station KUCA-FM. Meadors Hall houses the ROTC program (which is available as an elective), and contains a firing range. There is coeducational housing on campus including four dormitories for men (capacity 710) and seven for women (capacity 1,271). The UCA Library houses 292,898 volumes, 2,400 periodicals and 546,000 microforms and online is the Interlibrary Loan Service. It is the only computerized library in the State of Arkansas. Over $50 milloin has been spent over the last five years constructing new dormitories, academic buildings, and on library renovation and additions. A new student center is under construction. Athletic facilities on campus include a stadium seating approximately 7,000; an athletic dormitory, track facilities; a lighted basketball facility accommodating 6,000; a lighted baseball field, and an olympic swimming pool. The average score of the entering freshman class was ACT 21.8 composite. Financial aid is available and 70% of students receive some form of financial assistance.

Community Environment: Conway is a growing center (population 26,328) served by major highways, the Union Pacific Railway, and Little Rock National Airport (30 miles away). It is within a few miles of the geographic center of the state. Lake Conway, which covers approximately 6500 acres, between Conway and Little Rock, is one of the principal resorts of the state. The Arkansas River, the largest to cross the state, is less than ten miles from Conway. Conway is a city of colleges and is the government seat of Faulkner County. Many beautiful residences, churches, businesses, and public buildings are found here.

UNIVERSITY OF THE OZARKS   (E-5)
415 College Avenue
Clarksville, Arkansas 72830
Tel: (501) 754-3839

Description: Privately supported Presbyterian liberal arts university owned and operated by a 33 member board of trustees and accredited by the North Central Association of Colleges and Schools and the National Council for the Accreditation of Teacher Education. Recent enrollment included 712 full-time students and 67 part-time students. The faculty has 41 full-time and 15 part-time members. The semester system is used. The college grants the Bachelor and Master of Education degrees.

Entrance Requirements: High school graduation from state or N.C.A. accredited institution; GED accepted; ACT required with minimum score of 18, early admission and rolling admission plans.

Costs Per Year: $4,920 tuition and activity fees per year; $2,850 room and board.

Collegiate Environment: An excellent view of the Ozark mountains is seen from the 37-acre campus. Students under 21 must live in dormitories unless living with relatives. Dormitory facilities accommodate 168 men and 228 women. There are 12 apartments for married students. The library houses 65,000 volumes, 11,000 pamphlets, 412 periodicals, 1,958 microforms and 1,900 recordings. The Memorial Chapel is the center of religious life on campus. 218 scholarships are available and 85% of the current student body receive financial aid. About 20% of the senior class continued on to graduate school.

Community Environment: Clarksville is the county seat of Johnson County. The town lies 105 miles northwest of Little Rock on Interstate 40, & is 65 miles east of Fort Smith. The Continental bus line serves this area. Primarily an agricultural community, it also has some manufacturing. There are motel accommodations, and a hospital. A swimming pool, athletic fields, baseball park, football field, tennis courts, and all the outdoor sports are available. Annual events include the Peach Festival.

WESTARK COMMUNITY COLLEGE   *(F-3)*
P.O. Box 3649
Fort Smith, Arkansas 72913
Tel: (501) 785-7100; Fax: (501) 785-7105

Description: Publicly supported, community junior college founded in 1928. Enrollment is 2,372 full-time and 3,100 part-time students. A faculty of 114 full-time and 120 part-time gives a faculty-student ratio of 1-24. The semester system is used and three summer sessions are offered. The college is accredited by the North Central Association of Colleges and Schools and grants both Certificate and Associate degrees. Correspondence credit allowed 30; cooperative education programs available.

Entrance Requirements: Open enrollment policy; ACT or SAT accepted; early decision, rolling admission, delayed admission plans available; non-high school graduates considered.

Costs Per Year: $778 district tuition; $1,018 out-of-district; $1,810 out-of-state; additional expenses average $400.

Collegiate Environment: The college is located to serve Sebastian County and a number of neighboring communities in Western Arkansas and Eastern Oklahoma on a seventy-five acre campus in a residential section of the city. The library contains 50,295 volumes, 595 periodicals, 41,343 microforms and 2,645 audiovisual materials. Nearly all of the students applying for admission are accepted. 35% of the financial aid is available through scholarships, and 67% of the students receive financial aid.

Community Environment: Westark is located in Fort Smith, Arkansas, on the Arkansas-Oklahoma border. Fort Smith, with a population of approximately 71,384, is the trade center for a four-county area of more than 200,000 persons. With more than 200 manufacturing plants that represent a variety of products, Fort Smith is the leading manufacturing center in western Arkansas. Other major economic factors in the area are agriculture, health care, and tourism. Fort Smith is located in the Arkansas River Valley between the Ozark and Ouachita Mountain Ranges.

WILLIAMS BAPTIST COLLEGE   *(C-12)*
Walnut Ridge, Arkansas 72476
Tel: (501) 886-6741; (800) 722-4434; Fax: (501) 886-3924

Description: This private, four-year college is accredited by the North Central Association of Colleges and Schools and supported by the Arkansas State Baptist Convention. The college offers the Associate and Bachelor's degrees. It offers cooperative education programs with vocational-technical schools. Army ROTC is available. The college operates on the semester system and offers two summer sessions. Enrollment includes 519 full-time and 93 part-time students. A faculty of 28 full-time and 12 part-time gives a faculty-student ratio of 1-17.

Entrance Requirements: Score on ACT, high school graduation with a 2.0 GPA; 16 units including 4 English, 3 math, 3 social science, and 2 science; nonhigh school graduates considered; $20 application fee.

Costs Per Year: $4,400 tuition; $2,522 room and board; $75 student fees.

Collegiate Environment: The campus of 177 acres with 75 buildings including the library which contains 75,000 volumes. Residence halls accomodate 241 students, including families. The college offers special programs enabling low-mark, culturally disadvantaged students to attend. 95% of the students receive financial aid. All students are required to take courses in Bible History and Interpretation.

Community Environment: Walnut Ridge is a rural area with a temperate climate. Railroads serve the area as well as a city airport. There are churches of major denominations, a public library, and a hospital. Part-time employment opportunities are limited. Recreational activities include boating and water sports. The city has a Lions and Kiwanis organization. An annual county fair is held.

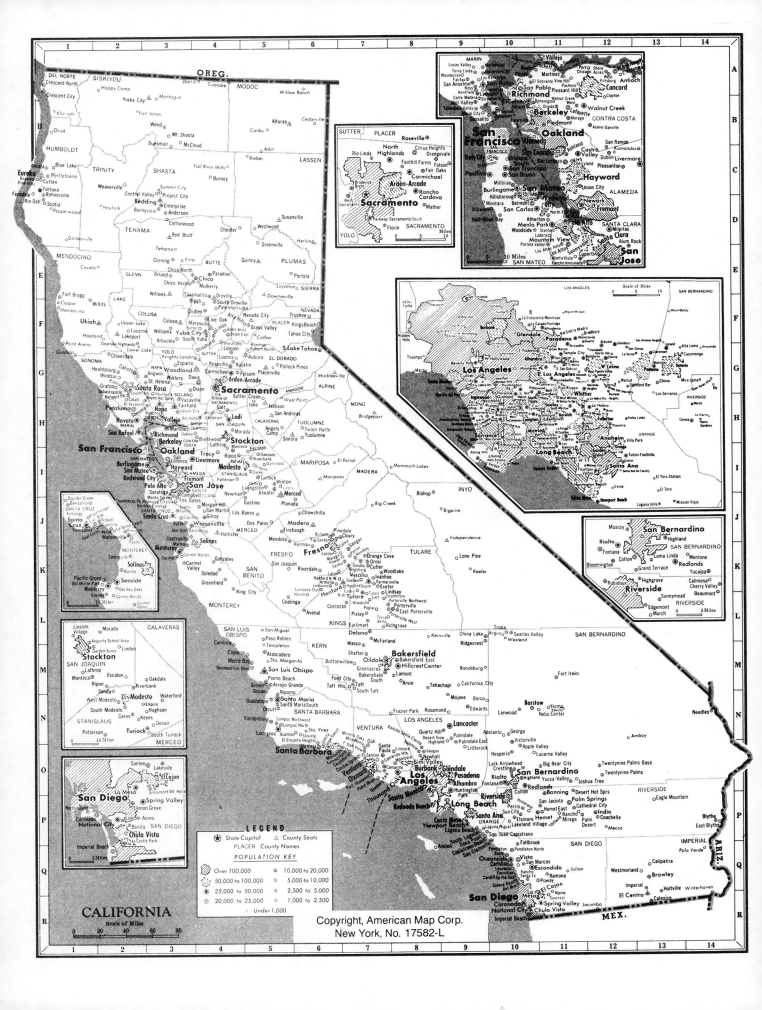

CALIFORNIA

ACADEMY OF ART COLLEGE *(I-3)*
79 New Montgomery Street
San Francisco, California 94105
Tel: (415) 274-2200; (800) 544-2787; Admissions: (415) 274-2200;
Fax: (415) 546-9737

Description: Privately supported, coeducational, professional college was established in 1929, and teaches advertising and graphic design, illustration, fine arts, photography, fashion design and illustration, computer arts, interior design, motion pictures and video, and product and industrial design. It operates on the semester system and offers one summer session. Enrollment includes 2,600 full-time and 550 part-time undergraduates and 300 graduate students. A faculty of 45 full-time, 120 part-time and 25 evening members gives an undergraduate faculty-student ratio of 1-19. Students may participate in cooperative programs with the University of San Francisco.

Entrance Requirements: A B.F.A. degree candidate must be a graduate of an approved secondary school or have high school equivalency certificate; open enrollment, rolling admission, early decision, early admission, and advanced placement plans available; undergraduate application fee $50, graduate application fee $25.

Costs Per Year: Undergraduates $300 per unit; graduates $350 per unit; room $4,950; $40 student fees.

Collegiate Environment: The Academy is located in seven buildings in downtown San Francisco. The central location of the Academy allows the student to participate directly with the San Francisco art world and many of the cultural activities for which San Francisco is justly famous. Buildings have large studio areas with natural and supplemental lighting to allow for constant usage at all times of the day and evening. Photography lab equipped for both black and white and color printing is available to all students. Film rooms, lecture rooms, large drawing and painting studios, pottery wheels, woodworking and metal equipment are also available to all students. The library contains 7,000 volumes and 3,500 periodicals. Dormitory facilities house an unspecified number of students. 30% of students receive financial aid. Approximately 93% of undergraduates applying are accepted; about 70% of those applying to graduate school are admitted.

Community Environment: Lining the street between the Powell and Sutter buildings are several of San Francisco's finest art galleries. The area provides an ideal environment for studying and developing as an artist.

ALLAN HANCOCK COLLEGE *(N-5)*
800 South College Drive
Santa Maria, California 93454
Tel: (805) 922-6966; Admissions: (805) 922-6966 X 3248; Fax: (805) 928-7905

Description: This publicly supported, coeducational community college is accredited by the Western Association of Schools and Colleges. University-parallel, occupational, and general education programs are offered that lead to a Certificate or an Associate degree. The college operates on the semester system for both day and evening classes, and offers one summer term. Enrollment includes 2,218 full-time and 5,352 part-time students. A faculty of 210 full-time and 350 part-time gives an overall faculty-student ratio of 1-21.

Entrance Requirements: All applicants are accepted if high school graduate or at least 18 years of age. Open admission, midyear admission and advanced placement plans available.

Costs Per Year: $390 ($13/unit) resident; $1,500 ($50/unit) resident with $3,420 ($114/unit) nonresident.

Collegiate Environment: This college serves students who reside in the Allan Hancock college district or within a California high school district that does not maintain a junior college. The 100-acre campus has 27 buildings including a new Learning Development Center that contains over 47,500 volumes, 5,000 pamphlets, 5,000 periodicals, 7,000 microforms and 2,628 sound recordings. There is also a new Humanities Complex and Consumer Education Building. Scholarships are available. 34% of students receive some form of financial aid.

Community Environment: Population 82,572. Santa Maria is located in the Central Coast region on United States Highway 101, 175 miles north of Los Angeles and 262 miles south of San Francisco. Average temperature ranges from 45 degrees minimum to 68.2 degrees maximum. Greyhound Bus, Delta-Sky West and United Airlines serve the area. Santa Maria has two hospitals, churches, a library, and a number of manufacturing firms. A municipal swimming pool, golf courses, parks and playgrounds provide facilities for sports. Hunting and fishing opportunities are good.

Branch Campuses: Two off-campus centers serve students in the Lompoc and Vandenberg Air Force Base communities. Five eight-week terms are offered at the VAFB center.

AMERICAN RIVER COLLEGE *(G-4)*
4700 College Oak Drive
Sacramento, California 95841
Tel: (916) 484-8011; Fax: (916) 484-8674

Description: The publicly supported, coeducational, junior college is accredited by the Western Association of Schools and Colleges. The college offers university transfer programs, general and vocational programs and Certificate programs to assist those already employed. The Associate in Arts and Associate in Science degrees are offered for day and evening classes. It operates on the semester system and offers one summer session. Enrollment includes 4,607 full-time and 15,088 part-time students. A faculty of 315 full-time and 460 part-time gives a faculty-student ratio of 1-25.

Entrance Requirements: High school graduation or equivalent; or Adults over 18 years of age; open enrollment policy; non-high school graduates are considered; ACT or SAT for placement, not acceptance purposes; early admission, early decision, rolling admission and advanced placement plans available.

Costs Per Year: $403 ($13 per unit) state resident tuition; $1,550 ($50 per unit) state resident with BA tuition; $3,720 ($120 per unit) nonresident tuition.

Collegiate Environment: Located on a 153-acre site, the college has steadily expanded its facilities since its beginning in 1955. The library contains 70,000 volumes, 600 periodicals, 1,700 sound recordings and 4,856 microforms. The student body consists of legal residents of the Los Rios Community College District or of a district not served by a junior college. Students live off campus, as there are no dormitories. All those applying for admission are accepted, as well as midyear students. Financial aid is available in the form of employment, grants, loans or scholarships.

Community Environment: See California State University - Sacramento.

ANTELOPE VALLEY COLLEGE *(N-9)*
3041 West Avenue K
Lancaster, California 93536
Tel: (805) 943-3241

Description: The publicly supported, coeducational, community college is accredited by the Western Association of Schools and Colleges and operates on the semester system with one summer term. Day and evening classes offered. Programs offered include occupational education, university-parallel, and general education leading to an Associate in Arts or Science degree. With a recent enrollment of 9,833 men and women full-time and part-time and a faculty of 346.

Entrance Requirements: All high school graduates admitted; non-high school graduates over 18 may be admitted at discretion of the college; SAT, ACT or local assessment tests for placement purposes.

Costs Per Year: $5 per unit to a maximum of $50 for California residents; $104 additional per unit for nonresidents.

Collegiate Environment: The campus consists of 23 buildings on 160 acres. The library contains over 41,820 volumes, 225 periodicals and 4,184 microforms.

Community Environment: Population 75,000. Lancaster is located in the center of the Antelope Valley in a semi-desert region. Lancaster has over 350 days of sunshine a year and the climate is the reason that the United States Air Force and almost every manufacturer of aircraft build and maintain establishments in this area. There has been a great increase in population and excellent employment opportunities have developed in proportion to the growth.

ARMSTRONG UNIVERSITY   *(H-3)*
2222 Harold Way
Berkeley, California 94704
Tel: (510) 848-2500; Fax: (510) 848-9438

Description: This privately supported school of business with an enrollment of 150 men and women is accredited by the Accrediting Commission of Independent Colleges and Schools of the Career College Association. The school operates on the quarter system and offers one summer session. The university awards an Associate degree, Bachelor's degree and Master degree in business subjects. A faculty of 20 gives faculty-student ratio of 1-8. Armstrong's Center For Lanaguage & Intercultural Communication (CLIC) offers an intensive, high-quality English language program for international students.

Entrance Requirements: High school graduation or passing GED with minimum 2.0 GPA (C average); open enrollment; college preparatory course required; early admission, rolling admission and advanced placement plans available; $35 application fee; $50 foreign students.

Costs Per Year: $5,940 tuition; $40 student fees.

Collegiate Environment: The college emphasizes education of students for careers in business and for positions of leadership. Located in the business district of Berkeley, the modern building offers classrooms, study areas and a library containing over 12,000 volumes. About 90% of the applicants are accepted. Students may enroll midyear as well as in the fall.

Community Environment: See University of California - Berkeley.

ART CENTER COLLEGE OF DESIGN   *(O-9)*
1700 Lida Street
Pasadena, California 91103
Tel: (818) 396-2322; Admissions: (818) 396-2322; Fax: (818) 405-9104

Description: This privately supported, nonprofit, coeducational art college is accredited by Western Association of Schools and Colleges and by the National Association of Schools of Art and Design. It operates on the trimester system and offers one summer session. The Bachelor of Fine Arts is granted in fine arts, advertising, graphic/packaging design, illustration, photography and film. The Bachelor of Science is conferred in industrial design. The Master of Fine Arts or Master of Science degree is offered in all subjects. Enrollment includes 1,200 full-time and 400 part-time non-degree students. A faculty of 58 full-time and 254 part-time gives a faculty-student ratio of 1-9.

Entrance Requirements: Evidence of art intelligence, imagination, and studio skills in the applicant's portfolio; B average students accepted; high school graduation with rank in upper half of graduating class; $45 application fee; SAT or ACT required for students currently in high school; rolling admission, advanced placement plans available; personal interview recommended; portfolio should include at least 12 samples of original work, specific to one major.

Costs Per Year: $14,600 tuition; $3,000-$4,000 expendable art major supplies, $3,000-5,000 expendable photograph major supplies.

Collegiate Environment: The Art Center occupies a dramatic steel and glass building on a 175-acre secluded hillside atop the San Rafael hills. The campus is easily reached by freeways from all surrounding southern California areas. The library contains 40,000 volumes, 400 periodicals, 35,000 slides, 126 films, and 415 videos. The average student age is 23; only about 5% of the students enter directly after high school. 95% of students enroll after 1-4 years of college. The average high school standing of the freshman class was in the upper 30%. Scholarships are available for new students. 87% of students receive some form of financial aid.

Community Environment: See California Institute of Technology.

AZUSA PACIFIC UNIVERSITY   *(G-12)*
901 E. Alosta Ave.
P.O. Box 7000
Azusa, California 91702
Tel: (818) 815-6000; (800) 825-5278; Admissions: (818) 812-3014; Fax: (818) 969-7180

Description: The privately supported, Christian, liberal arts university is accredited by the Western Association of Schools and Colleges. The university awards a Bachelor degree and a Master degree. Army ROTC is available. A 4-4-1 calendar system is used with two summer sessions. Current enrollment includes 2,183 full-time and 100 part-time undergraduate students, and 1,948 graduate students. A faculty of 162 full-time and part-time gives an overall faculty-student ratio of 16-1.

Entrance Requirements: High school graduation or equivalent with a GPA of 2.5 or better; 15 units recommended including 4 English, 2 mathematics, 2 foreign language, 1 science, and 3 social science; high moral character; those who cannot meet the regular requirements may petition the committee on admissions; ACT or SAT; rolling admission, midyear admission and advanced placement plans available. $45 application fee.

Costs Per Year: $11,636 tuition; $3,860 room and board.

Collegiate Environment: The 50-building, 70-acre campus is located near the center of town with a view of the nearby foothills. The library contains 110,000 books, periodicals, microforms and sound recordings. Dormitories accommodate 1,364 students. 82% of applicants are accepted. The average scores of the entering freshman class were SAT 897 combined, ACT 23 composite. 728 scholarships are available, and 82% of the students receive some form of financial aid.

Community Environment: Azusa is a suburban area 30 miles east of Los Angeles with a temperate climate. Bus service, air and rail facilities are nearby. The city has a public library, churches of major denominations, hospitals and clinics within a 10-mile radius. Mountains and the beaches are within easy driving distance and Azusa is close to the cultural and recreational advantages of Los Angeles County.

BAKERSFIELD COLLEGE   *(M-7)*
1801 Panorama Drive
Bakersfield, California 93305
Tel: (805) 395-4301; Fax: (805) 395-4241

Description: The publicly supported junior college is accredited by the Western Association of Schools and Colleges. University-parallel programs, credit and noncredit courses in educational, technical, vocational areas are offered. The college awards Certificates and the Associate degree. It operates on the semester system and offers one summer session. Enrollment includes 12,434 full-time and part-time students with a faculty of 450.

Entrance Requirements: High school graduation and residence in Kern Community College district; non-high school graduates over 18 may be admitted; placement tests are required; open enrollment; rolling admission, early admission, early decision, midyear admission, and advanced placement plans available; Aug. 15 application deadline.

Costs Per Year: $403 ($13 per unit) state resident tuition; $1,550 ($50 per unit) state resident with BA tuition; $3,534 ($114 per unit) nonresident tuition; $3,800 room and board; $5 student fees.

Collegiate Environment: The college is located in the seat of Kern County, which is noted for its rich agricultural and petroleum industries. The 150-acre campus includes about 18 buildings. The library is located in the center of the campus and includes 54,886 volumes, 221 periodicals and 11,000 pamphlets. There is housing on campus for 63 men and women. All applicants are accepted.

Community Environment: See California State University - Bakersfield.

Branch Campuses: Located in Delano and Ridgecrest (Cerro Coso Community College).

BARSTOW COLLEGE   *(N-10)*
2700 Barstow Road
Barstow, California 92311
Tel: (714) 252-2411

Description: The publicly supported, coeducational community college is accredited by the Western Association of Colleges and Schools. University-parallel, vocational, and general education programs are offered leading to an Associate degree. The semester system is used with one summer session. The enrollment totals 3,200 with a full-time faculty of 28.

Entrance Requirements: Any high school graduate or person 18 or older residing within the boundaries of the Barstow Junior College District; nonresidents may also qualify under certain circumstances.

Costs Per Year: $100 tuition for California residents; $96 per unit for nonresident, $50 student fees.

Collegiate Environment: 8 buildings on 200 acres comprise the campus and the library contains over 32,000 volumes. 50% of full-time students receive financial aid.

Community Environment: This is a desert community with a dry, warm climate. The Santa Fe and Union Pacific Railroads meet here. Greyhound and Orange Belt bus service is also available. The city has a county library, hospital, many churches, including numerous Protestant Churches, an Episcopal Church, a Roman Catholic Church, a Jewish Synagogue. There is a Community Players Association, which presents locally produced programs. Lectures and concerts are presented throughout the year. Part-time employment is available. Barstow has 4 parks and swimming pools for recreation. There are 82 civic, fraternal, and veterans organizations.

BETHANY BIBLE COLLEGE   *(J-3)*
800 Bethany Drive
Scotts Valley, California 95066
Tel: (408) 438-3800

Description: The privately-supported, coeducational college was founded in 1919 and is accredited by the Western Association of Schools and Colleges. Essentially a Bible College associated with the Assemblies of God, it does, however, provide various other academic majors. The 4-4-1 term system is used. Enrollment during a recent school year was 470 men and women full-time and part-time. The college awards a Bachelor of Arts degree. A three-year Diploma program is available in the areas of religious education; ministerial and music. An A.A. degree is offered in General Business or Office Administration.

Entrance Requirements: Experience of Christian conversion; high school graduation with 15 units and scholastic average of C; ACT and placement tests in Bible and English required; application fee $35; two references (pastor, educator or employer) required; early admission, early decision and rolling admission plans available.

Costs Per Year: $5,880 tuition; $3,000 room and board.

Collegiate Environment: The 19-building, 165-acre campus is located in the heart of California redwoods on slopes of Santa Cruz mountains, seven miles from the Pacific Ocean. The library contains 45,718 volumes, 500 pamphlets, 257 periodicals, and 302 microforms. Housing facilities are available for 200 men and 280 women. There are scholarships available; 70% of the students receive financial aid. Ninety-four percent of applicants are accepted. Religious courses and chapel attendance are required for graduation.

Community Environment: See University of California - Santa Cruz

BIOLA UNIVERSITY   *(H-11)*
13800 Biola Avenue
La Mirada, California 90639
Tel: (310) 903-6000; (800) 652-4652; Admissions: (310) 903-4752; Fax: (310) 470-9

Description: The privately supported, interdenominational Christian university is accredited by the Western Association of Schools and Colleges and has several professional accreditations. Biola requires a minimum of 30 units of biblical studies and theology of all students regardless of major. The 4-1-4 calendar system is employed with two summer sessions. Undergraduate enrollment during a recent school year was 812 men and 1,237 women full-time; graduate enrollment was 847. Faculty consists of 142 full-time and 81 part-time. The university awards a Bachelor of Arts, Bachelor of Music or Science degree (24 majors in all). Master' and Doctoral degrees are awarded through three on-campus graduate schools: Talbot School of Theology, the School of Intercultural Studies, and Rosemead School of Psychology.

Entrance Requirements: High school graduation or equivalent; completion of 16 units including 3 English, 2 math, 2 social sciences, 2 foreign language, 1 science, and 6 electives; non-high school graduates considered; SAT (400V, 400M) or ACT (16); GRE required for graduate school; application fee $35; two references (pastor and school or employer) required; early admission, early decision, delayed admission, advanced placement and rolling admission plans available. Applicant should have been a Christian for one year.

Costs Per Year: $12,652 tuition; $1,236 room and $1,094 board per semester. Graduate program tuition varies.

Collegiate Environment: The campus is located 22 miles southeast of Los Angeles and has 40 buildings on 95 acres. The library contains 206,000 volumes, 1,146 periodicals, and 4,550 microforms. Student housing is available for 1,466 men and women. Numerous scholarships are available and 68% of the students receive financial aid. Approximately 70% of the applicants are accepted; 70% of applicants to the graduate division are accepted.

Community Environment: Population 40,000. La Mirada is a suburban area less thatn one hour from the Los Angeles International Airport. The Santa Fe Railroad and buses serve the area as does the Santa Ana Freeway. There are libraries, churches, and a hospital. Part-time employment is available. The beaches are 20 miles away and the mountains are an hour and half drive with Knott's Berry Farm and Disneyland is a few minutes from campus. Annual festivals are the La Mirada Arts and Culture and the La Mirada Gras.

BROOKS COLLEGE   *(P-9)*
4825 E. Pacific Coast Highway
Long Beach, California 90804
Tel: (310) 597-6611; (800) 554-2449

Description: This privately supported two-year, coeducational fashion college is an accredited member of the Western Association of Schools and Colleges. The school operates on a trimester system with one summer session. Enrollment includes 785 students with a faculty of 12 full-time and 40 part-time. Two-year programs leading to the Associate degree are offered in Fashion Merchandising, Fashion Design and Interior Design.

Entrance Requirements: High school graduation or equivalent; open enrollment policy; early admission, early decision, delayed admission, midyear admission and advanced placement plans available; $250 non-refundable application fee, if accepted.

Costs Per Year: $7,810 tuition; $4,780 room and board; $130 student fees.

Collegiate Environment: The college provides dormitory space for 650 students. Library holdings include 12,000 books and periodicals. Approximately 70% of applicants are accepted, including midyear students. Classes start in September and January. 15 scholarships are offered and 70% of the students receive some form of financial aid.

Community Environment: See California State University - Long Beach.

BROOKS INSTITUTE   *(O-6)*
801 Alston Road
Santa Barbara, California 93108
Tel: (805) 966-3888; Admissions: (805) 966-3888 x217; Fax: (805) 565-1386

Description: Brooks Institute is a private specialized college that offers a four-year Bachelor of Arts Degree in Professional Photography in three years, and a Master of Science Degree. The Institute is accredited by the Accrediting Commission for Independent Colleges and Schools (ACICS). The school is in session year-round (trimester); it enrolls a new class each half trimester. Enrollment includes 450 undergraduate and 20 graduate students. A faculty of 21 full-time and 13 part-time gives an undergraduate faculty-student ratio of 1-17. The Bachelor degree program combines professional schooling and business courses received at Brooks Institute with liberal arts education, part of which must be acquired prior to admission from another accredited junior or senior college. Photographic majors are offered in seven professional areas: illustration/advertising, media, industrial/scientific, portraiture, commercial, color technology and motion picture production. Independent study and graduate study may be pursued as well. Other programs offered are undersea phototechnology, photojournalism, multimedia and video presentations, and digital imaging.

Entrance Requirements: High School diploma or equivalent and completion of 9 of the 15 semester credits in general education (including English Composition) from another accredited college; rolling admission with six entrance dates per year in January, March, April, July, September, and November; application may be made upon graduation from high school; $25 application fee; SAT/ACT not required; completion of college transfer credits required before acceptance; portfolio required only for advanced placement in photography sequence with previous 4x5 view camera experience.

Costs Per Year: $12,900 annual tuition (three trimesters); $4,000 per year average materials and supply costs.

Collegiate Environment: The spacious facilities provide numerous kinds of laboratories, studios, work locations, and classrooms all equipped with the most professional photographic equipment. The Photographic Library contains 6,342 volumes, 2,920 papers and pamphlets, 450 periodical volumes and 133 periodical subscriptions. There is no housing on campus. 75% of all applicants are accepted. 60% of the students receive financial aid.

Community Environment: See University of California - Santa Barbara.

BUTTE COLLEGE   *(E-4)*
3536 Butte Campus Dr.
Oroville, California 95965
Tel: (916) 895-2511; Fax: (916) 895-2411

Description: The publicly-supported, coeducational junior college is accredited by the Western Association of Colleges and Schools. Operating on the semester system, the college offers career education, general education and university-parallel programs leading to a Certificate or Associate degree. Enrollment is approximately 3,315 full-time and 6,847 part-time students with a faculty of 153 full-time and 500 part-time.

Entrance Requirements: All high school graduates and certain non-high school graduates are accepted; achievement tests are required for placement purposes; early admission, early decision, rolling admission, delayed admission and advanced placement plans available.

Costs Per Year: Tuition is $13/unit for California residents; $125/unit nonresident; and $77 service fee per semester.

Collegiate Environment: A new campus has just been completed and is situated on 900 acres in a country setting. The library contains 57,000 volumes. Approximately 75% of the freshman class returned for the sophomore year; 95% of the students applying for admission meet the requirements and are accepted.

Community Environment: Butte College is located in the geographical center of Butte County, population 121,400, at the edge of the Sierra Foothills. The county's amenities include a clean environment, moderate climate, ready access to necessities and luxuries and proximity to recreational areas, including the huge Lake Oroville.

CABRILLO COLLEGE   *(J-3)*
6500 Soquel Drive
Aptos, California 95003
Tel: (408) 479-6100

Description: State-controlled community college accredited by the Western Association of Schools and Colleges was founded in 1959 and offers day, evening, and off-campus classes. The college operates on the semester system with summer sessions. Enrollment includes

5,691 men and 7,838 women with a faculty of 224 full-time and 352 part-time. The college offers university-transfer programs, general education programs, occupational programs. and technical training. A Certificate or Associate degree is granted.

Entrance Requirements: Any person 18 years of age or having a high school diploma, GED or certificate of proficiency may attend. Open enrollment and rolling admission plans available. Three weeks should be allowed for Admissions and Records to process new applications.

Costs Per Year: 12 semester units: $120 for California residents; $1,272 nonresident. Fees: $47 for full-time students; $29.50 for part-time students.

Collegiate Environment: The campus consists of 134 acres with 20 major buildings. The library contains 68,000 volumes. Of the 237 scholarships available, 16 of 273 are for entering freshmen. Approximately sixty percent of the freshman class returned to this campus for their second year.

Community Environment: Aptos is a suburban area nine miles from Santa Cruz, with a temperate climate. There is a municipal library, churches of major denominations within a ten mile area, and 2 hospitals in the county. Excellent water sports area for swimming, surfing and deep sea fishing. Fine shopping facilities are available. The University of California at Santa Cruz is nearby.

Branch Campuses: Watsonville Center, 18 West Lake Avenue, Watsonville, CA 95076.

CALIFORNIA BAPTIST COLLEGE   *(P-10)*
8432 Magnolia Avenue
Riverside, California 92504
Tel: (909) 689-5771; (800) 782-3382; Fax: (909) 351-1808

Description: Privately supported, coeducational liberal arts college is owned and operated by the Southern Baptist Convention. It is accredited by the Western Association of Schools and Colleges. Religion courses are required. The college divisions include Fine Arts, Humanities, Business Administration, Natural Sciences, Religion and Professional Services. The college grants an Associate degree, the Bachelor of Arts or Science degrees, and Master's degrees. The graduate programs are Marriage and Family Counseling, and Education. The college operates on the 4-1-4 system and offers one summer session. Enrollment is 900 students. A faculty of 73 gives a faculty-student ratio of 1-12.

Entrance Requirements: High school graduation or equivalent, with completion of 4 units in English and 2 each in math, science, foreign language, and social studies; score of 19 or over on ACT, 400M, 400V or over on SAT; two letters of recommendation (one educator and one pastor or other); evidence of good moral character; early admission, early decision, rolling admission, delayed admission, mid-year admission and advanced placement plans available; $30 application fee.

Costs Per Year: $7,800 ($3,900/semester for 13-18 units) tuition; $4,494 room and board per year.

Collegiate Environment: The campus includes seven main buildings on 77 acres located 50 miles east of Los Angeles. The library contains 105,000 volumes. Student housing is available for 200 men, 260 women and 96 married students. About 85% of the students receive financial aid. More than 500 scholarships are available, all of which are open to freshmen as well as upperclassmen. Approximately 85% of the applicants are accepted, including midyear students.

Community Environment: See University of California - Riverside.

CALIFORNIA COLLEGE OF ARTS AND CRAFTS   *(I-3)*
5212 Broadway
Oakland, California 94618
Tel: (510) 653-6522; (800) 447-1278; Fax: (510) 547-5379

Description: The privately supported coeducational college is accredited by the Western Association of Schools and Colleges. Founded in 1907, it educates students in art and design. The college operates on the semester system with one six-week summer session. The Bachelor and Masters of Fine Arts and the Bachelor of Architecture degrees are awarded by the college. Enrollment includes 879 full-time and 171 part-time undergraduates and 83 graduate students. A faculty of 36 full-time and 215 part-time gives a faculty-student ratio of 1-12.

Entrance Requirements: Accredited high school graduation or equivalent with a minimum C average; SAT or ACT recommended; $30 application fee; advanced placement and rolling admission plans available.

Costs Per Year: $14,410 tuition; $2,500 room; $100 student fees.

Collegiate Environment: The college has two campuses, one in North Oakland on 4 acres and one in the south-of-market area of San Francisco. Dormitory space is provided for 60 students. The library contains more than 30,000 volumes. Financial aid is available, and 60% of the current student body receives some form of assistance. Students are admitted at midyear as well as in the fall.

Community Environment: See Laney College.

CALIFORNIA COLLEGE OF PODIATRIC MEDICINE *(I-3)*
1210 Scott Street
San Francisco, California 94115
Tel: (415) 292-0407; (800) 443-2276 in CA; Fax: (415) 292-0439

Description: This privately supported college is accredited by the Western Association of Schools and Colleges and the Council on Podiatric Medical Education of the American Podiatric Medical Association. The college was founded in 1914 in order to create an educational institution on the highest plane that would prepare young men and women to devote their lives effectively to podiatric medicine. It operates on the semester system. Enrollment includes 400 men and women.

Entrance Requirements: Successful completion of three full academic years at an approved college; 6 semester hours of English, 8 biological sciences, 8 inorganic chemistry, 8 organic chemistry, 8 physics, 8 mathematics and 12 humanities and social sciences; MCAT required; letters of recommendation from college pre-professional committee and from podiatric physician; $90 application fee.

Costs Per Year: $17,000 tuition; $1,100 student fees.

Collegiate Environment: The college is an adjuct to the Pacific Coast Hospital, a modern, fully equipped general hospital. There are three buildings on campus. The library contains 25,000 volumes. The facilities of the University of California Medical Library are also available to students. Housing is available through a cooperative program with the University of San Francisco. About 55% of applicants are accepted; 98% of the students receive financial aid. 98% of the freshman class returned for the sophomore year.

Community Environment: See San Francisco State University.

CALIFORNIA INSTITUTE OF INTEGRAL STUDIES *(A-2)*
765 Ashbury Street
San Francisco, California 94117
Tel: (415) 753-6100; Fax: (415) 753-1169

Description: This private graduate school founded in 1968 offers interdisciplinary programs which concentrate on the concepts of human development presented in Eastern and Western psychologies, philosophies, religions, cultures and literatures. The Institute is engaged in exploring the significant bridge areas where East and West meet; instead of offering a fragmented or exclusive approach, the Institute's curriculum is based on a broader, multidimensional program and education defined as integral education. The Institute is accredited by the Western Association of Schools and Colleges. The quarter system is used with one summer session. Recent enrollment was 1,000 students with a faculty of 750 full time and 40 part time. The institute has recently added a B.A. completion program.

Entrance Requirements: A Bachelor's degree from an accredited institution; departmental requirements; $60 application fee.

Costs Per Year: $270-$345 per unit.

Collegiate Environment: In Fall 1985, the Institute moved to its present location at 765 Ashbury Street, in San Francisco's Haight-Ashbury district, near Golden Gate Park. Classrooms and offices for student services are easily accessible on the first floor; a cafeteria-student lounge, as well as a bookstore, are located on the lower level. Faculty and administrative offices are housed on the second floor, with the Institute library and meditation room on the third. The library is particularly strong in the fields of Asian area studies, comparative philosophy, comparative religion, psychology, counseling and psychotherapy; it contains 30,000 hard bound volumes, periodicals, and additional materials. The majority of applicants is accepted, and students may be admitted at mid-year.

Community Environment: See San Francisco State University

CALIFORNIA INSTITUTE OF TECHNOLOGY *(O-9)*
1201 East California Boulevard
Pasadena, California 91125
Tel: (818) 395-6811; (800) 568-8324; Admissions: (818) 395-6341; Fax: (818) 683-3026

Description: This privately supported university of science and engineering is accredited by the Western Association of Schools and Colleges. It operates on the quarter system. The California Institute of Technology was founded in 1891 as Throop Institute. Its early officers and trustees envisioned the development of a distinguished institution of engineering and scientific research, emphasizing the humanities or liberal arts as an important part of the education of every scientist and engineer. In recognition of this change in direction, in 1921 the name was changed to California Institute of Technology. Today the institute has over 18,060 alumni (ten of whom have received Nobel prizes). Enrollment is 1,944 students. A faculty of 731 full-time and 25 part-time gives a faculty-student ratio of 1-3. The institute offers 4-year undergraduate courses with options available in various fields of science, engineering, applied science, and certain humanities subjects leading to the degree of Bachelor of Science. In the graduate section, the one-year program leads to a Master of Science degree; a two-year program leads to the Engineers degree; the Doctor of Philosophy degree is also awarded, generally following three to five years of graduate work.

Entrance Requirements: SAT, SAT II and 3 Subject Tests required; two of which must be math level IIC and Writing, and one of the following: physics, chemistry, or biology; completion of 15 high school units including 3 English, 4 mathematics, 1 chemistry, 1 physics, and 1 social science; the institute has an early action plan (such candidates must have taken the required college board test by November); $40 application fee; early admission and deferred admission plans available.

Costs Per Year: $17,370 tuition; $5,195 room and board; $216 student fees.

Collegiate Environment: Off-campus facilities include the Palomar Observatory and the 200-inch Hale telescope, which were dedicated in 1948, Jet Propulsion Laboratory, Kerckhoff Marine Laboratory, and the Owens Valley Radio Observatory. The libraries collectively subscribe to about 6,500 journals and contain 520,733 volumes. Housing is available for 800 undergraduate and 560 graduate students. There are 7 undergraduate student houses and freshmen live on campus. Nearly all of the student body graduated in the top decile of the high school class; 96% of the freshman class returned for the next year. About 26% of the applicants are accepted. The average SAT scores of a recent freshman class were 650V, 750M math, and the average high school standing was in the top 10% of the class. Approximately 70% of the students receive some form of financial assistance.

Community Environment: Population 135,000. Pasadena is located at the foot of the San Gabriel Mountains, the center of a large metropolitan area with ideal climate throughout the year. The famous Huntington Library, located in nearby San Marino, is open to the public and makes available its rich resources for scholarly research work in numerous fields. Pasadena has many cultural activities in the fields of art, music, and literature. The finest talent in America can be seen and heard in Pasadena and Los Angeles. Exhibits of famous artists and art instruction are provided by the community. The annual New Year's Day Tournament of Roses is held in the winter, and nearby is the Rose Bowl that seats 104,000 people.

CALIFORNIA INSTITUTE OF THE ARTS *(O-8)*
24700 McBean Parkway
Valencia, California 91355
Tel: (805) 255-1050; (800) 292-2787; Fax: (805) 254-8352

Description: The privately supported coeducational art institute, composed of the Schools of Art, Dance, Film and Video, Music and Theater is accredited by the Western Association of Schools and Colleges. Recent enrollment was 659 undergraduates and 383 graduate students. A faculty of 149 gives a faculty-student ratio of 1-7. The semester system is used. The Institute grants a Bachelor and Master of Fine Arts degree. Founded in 1961 with the merger of Chouinard Art Instutute and the Los Angeles Conservatory of Music, the Institute is a community of the arts.

Entrance Requirements: High school graduation or equivalent; portfolio or audition required. Evidence of talent in a particular area of concentration outweighs results of tests and transcripts. The student will be expected to furnish such evidence; application should be made to specific school and they will outline specific requirements. Early decision, rolling admission, early admission and advanced placement plans available. $50 application fee.

Costs Per Year: $15,450 tuition; $5,500 room and board; $60 fees.

Collegiate Environment: The campus is situated on 60 acres of rolling hills 35 miles north of Los Angeles. One five-level building houses the classrooms, offices and laboratories and the other, a student residence, accommodates 450. Various forms of financial aid are available and 80% of students receive financial aid. The library has 65,000 volumes, 12,000 microforms, and 550 periodicals. Forty five percent of the applicants are accepted.

Community Environment: Valencia is located on the Golden State Freeway (Interstate 5) 35 miles miles north of Los Angeles, and historically has been devoted to agriculture and cattle ranching. The area, encompassing the towns of Newhall, Saugus, Valencia and Castaic, is surrounded by the Tehachapi Mountains to the North, the San Gabriel to the east and the Santa Susana to the west. In the last 10 years light industry and numerous housing developments have contributed to the city's growth.

CALIFORNIA LUTHERAN UNIVERSITY   *(O-8)*
60 Olson Road
Thousand Oaks, California 91360
Tel: (805) 492-2411; (800) 252-5884; Fax: (805) 493-3114

Description: Privately supported, coeducational, liberal arts university is accredited by the Western Association of Schools and Colleges and is affiliated with the Evangelical Lutheran Church in America. It grants the Bachelor of Arts and Bachelor of Science degrees through the College of Arts and Sciences and School of Business and School of Education. In addition, the university offers Masters degrees in education, business, public administration, and marriage and family counseling. The college operates on the semester system and offers two summer sessions. Undergraduate enrollment recently was 659 men and 713 women full-time and 175 men and 220 women part-time.

Entrance Requirements: SAT or ACT, high school graduation with rank in upper half of graduating class, one academic recommendation, and a B average; completion of 4 units of English, 3 mathematics, 2 foreign language, 2 science, and 2 social science; rolling admission, midyear admission and advanced placement plans available; personal interview encouraged. $35 application fee.

Costs Per Year: $12,950 annual tuition; $5,300 room & board; $180 fees.

Collegiate Environment: The campus includes 40 buildings on 285 acres in an area known for its moderate climate. The dormitory capacity is 450 men and 450 women. The library contains 100,760 volumes and numerous periodicals and sound recordings. Scholarships are available, and 80% of the current student body receives financial assistance. Seventy-five percent of those who apply for admission are accepted. Students may enroll at mid-year.

Community Environment: Located in the Conejo Valley, Thousand Oaks has a mild pleasant climate with temperatures ranging from a mean low of 57 degrees in winter to a mean high of 77 degrees in summer. Average rainfall is 14 inches, the rainy season being between October and April. Buses, trains and airlines serve the area. Principal industries are electronics, aerospace, research, insurance and manufacturing. There are numerous shopping areas in Thousand Oaks. Recreational facilities include the community center, theatres, championship golf courses, Lake Sherwood, and the marinas in Oxnard and Ventura. Pacific Ocean Beaches are thirty minutes from The Campus.

CALIFORNIA MARITIME ACADEMY   *(H-3)*
Post Office Box 1392
Vallejo, California 94590
Tel: (707) 648-4222

Description: The publicly supported maritime college for men and women is a specialized institution for the education and training of prospective officers for the American Merchant Marine. Enrollment is 475 students. A faculty of 27 full-time and 8 part-time gives a faculty-student ratio of 1-15. The academy is fully accredited by the Western Association of Schools and Colleges. The Academy operates on the semester system. It awards a Bachelor of Science degree in Marine Transportation, Business Administration, Mechnical Engineering, or Marine Engineering Technology. Midshipmen, as the students are called, meeting the physical and educational requirements of the U.S. Coast Guard are licensed as third mates, or third assistant engineers, and qualify in this capacity to serve aboard any American Flag Ship at graduation, or to work in nearby related industries.

Entrance Requirements: Good moral character; high school graduation with a C average; SAT or ACT required; completion of 15 high school units including 4 English and 2 mathematics; medical exam required; rolling admission and advanced placement plans available; application deadline for fall term is March 15th. $55 application fee.

Costs Per Year: $1,658 tuition; $6,090 out-of-state; $4,770 room and board; $2,700 student fees.

Collegiate Environment: Located on the north shore of the Carquinez Strait, the Academy includes 13 buildings on a 67-acre campus. The training ship "Golden Bear" is used for the annual 2 1/2 month sea training cruise. The library contains approximately 21,000 volumes. Dormitories accommodate 460 students. 70% of applicants are accepted. Scholarships are available and 70% of the student body receives some form of financial aid.

Community Environment: Vallejo has a population of 103,000 and is located on the north shore of the Carquinez Strait, adjacent to San Pablo Bay.

CALIFORNIA POLYTECHNIC STATE UNIVERSITY - SAN LUIS OBISPO   *(M-5)*
San Luis Obispo, California 93407
Tel: (805) 756-2311

Description: The publicly supported, coeducational technological university is accredited by the Western Association of Schools and Colleges. The university awards the Bachelor and Master degrees in many areas, and is composed of the Schools of Agriculture, Architecture and Environmental Design, Business, Liberal Arts, Engineering, Professional Studies, Science, and Mathematics as well as the Center for Teacher Education. The university offers a learn-by-doing philosophy with emphasis on occupational and career training. There is a cooperative education program available for all majors. Army ROTC is also available. The university operates on the quarter system and offers one summer session. Enrollment includes 12,091 full-time and 1,311 part-time undergraduates and 1,148 graduate students. A faculty of 603 full-time gives a faculty-student ratio of 1-19. The quarter system is employed.

Entrance Requirements: First time freshman eligibility is determined by high school grade point average, scores on either the ACT or SAT tests, whether the applicant is a resident of California, and whether four year of college preparatory English, three years of college preparatory mathematics, one year U.S. history, one year lab science, 2 years foreign language and one year visual and performing arts have been completed. Transfer students accepted. Application fee is $55.

Costs Per Year: $454 for less than 6 units and $676 for 6 or more units; $7,626 ($164/unit) nonresidents.

Collegiate Environment: The school recognizes local and national social fraternities and sororities. Campus organizations cover all departments and activities. Library holdings include 864,000 volumes, 3,385 subscriptions and 1,560,000 microforms. Dormitories accommodate 2,739 students. 55% of applicants are accepted. Scholarships are available and 53% of the students receive some form of financial aid.

Community Environment: San Luis Obispo, located midway between San Francisco and Los Angeles, is 12 miles from the Pacific

Ocean. The average high winter temperature is in the 60's, and the summer high average is in the 70's. Buses, trains and airlines serve the area. There are 3 hospitals and a student health center. Student housing is available in campus dormitories and college approved housing in the city. Part time work is available in the community. Recreation includes surfing, fishing, clamming, golfing, hunting, boating and swimming. The Mission San Luis Obispo de Tolosa was founded in 1772, named for the Bishop of Toulouse, an Italian saint of the 13th century.

CALIFORNIA SCHOOL OF PROFESSIONAL PSYCHOLOGY - LOS ANGELES   (O-8)
1000 South Fremont Ave.
Alhambra, California 91803-1360
Tel: (818) 284-2777; (800) 457-1273; Fax: (818) 284-0550

Description: CSPP, a private, nonprofit, graduate school and the first autonomous school of professional psychology, was founded in 1969 and opened the Los Angeles campus in 1970. It is fully accredited by the Western Association of Schools and Colleges. The Doctoral Clinical Programs are accredited by the American Psychological Association. CSPP-LA awards Doctoral degrees in Clinical and Organizational Psychology. Students participate in practica or internships during their years in the program. It operates on the semester system and offers one summer session. Enrollment is 550 students. A faculty of 80 gives a faculty-student ratio of 1-7.

Entrance Requirements: Baccalaureate degree in psychology from an accredited institution or completed coursework in statistics, tests and measurements, abnormal, experimental, physiological or learning theory, or score 80% on GRE advanced psychology subtest; 3.0 GPA.

Costs Per Year: $14,900 tuition.

Collegiate Environment: Located in Alhambra, 8 miles east of downtown Los Angeles, it is accessible from I-10 (the San Bernardino Freeway) and I-710 (the Long Beach Freeway). The campus is located in a 38-acre shared complex and has 14 classrooms, a library, a computer laboratory, faculty and administrative offices, and an Organizational Development Center. The library contains 20,000 volumes. There is also a cafeteria and a 175-seat auditorium on site. 30% of all applicants are accepted. 92% of the students receive some form financial aid.

Community Environment: Los Angeles is the largest city in California and the second largest in the nation. A population of over seven million people is contained in LA county's more than four thousand square miles. The peoples of Los Angeles embrace a rare diversity of cultures, environments, and lifestyles. Southern California is known for its ocean beaches and year-round mild climate. Mountains and deserts are readily accessible. The concentration of cultural, educational, and recreational resources around Los Angeles is among the most extensive in the United States.

Branch Campuses: 1350 M. St., Fresno, CA 93721; 1005 Atlantic Ave., Alameda, CA 94704; 6212 Ferris Square, San Diego, CA 92121-3205.

CALIFORNIA STATE POLYTECHNIC UNIVERSITY - POMONA   (G-13)
3801 West Temple Avenue
Pomona, California 91768
Tel: (909) 869-2000

Description: Cal Poly Pomona is fully accredited by the Western Association of Schools and Colleges. Founded in 1938 on the site of the former Voorhis School for Boys in San Dimas, the university moved in 1956 to its present Kellogg Campus (the former W.K. Kellogg Ranch) on the western edge of Pomona. In 1966 it became part of what is now the California State University, and was accorded full university status in 1972. The university's educational philosophy places emphasis on career-oriented curriculum to prepare both undergraduate and graduate students for professional and occupational roles in the community. Students may participate in a variety of special programs including Army ROTC and CSU approved international programs in sixteen countries. Enrollment includes 10,611 full-time and 4,161 part-time undergraduates and 294 full-time and 1,238 part-time graduate students. A faculty of 920 gives an overall faculty-student ratio of 1:18.

Entrance Requirements: High school graduation; SAT or ACT required; California high school graduates among upper one-third; early admission, midyear admission, early decision, rolling admission, and advanced placement plans available. $55 application fee.

Costs Per Year: $1,584 tuition and fees, $8,964 nonresident; room and board $4,724, student fees $136.

Collegiate Environment: The 1,400-acre campus is one of the largest of the statewide CSU system. The library contains 529,433 volumes, 2,964 periodicals, 2,003,847 microforms and 4,349 records and tapes. Six coed resident halls provide on campus housing for 1,184 students. Apartments provide coed housing for 800 students. There are 11 intercollegiate sports programs, six for women and five for men. The Arabian Horse Center, with one of the largest and well known stables of Arabian horses in America, continues the tradition of monthly Sunday horse shows begun by W.K. Kellogg in 1926. Cal Poly Pomona and Cal Poly San Luis Obispo students join in entering a float in the Tournament of Roses Parade each year. They contribute more than 25,000 volunteer hours and gain worldwide attention for their humorous and animated floats, the only entry in the Rose Parade that is totally a student effort. 61% of applicants are accepted. Scholarships are available and 38% of students receive some form of financial aid.

Community Environment: The university is located in a suburban area approximately 30 miles east of downtown Los Angeles, served by freeways, buses, railroads, and Ontario International Airport approximately 12 miles from the campus. The Pomona Valley and adjacent San Gabriel Valley offer community facilities, major service organizations, and opportunity for housing and part-time employment.

CALIFORNIA STATE UNIVERSITY - BAKERSFIELD   (M-7)
9001 Stockdale Highway
Bakersfield, California 93309-1099
Tel: (805) 664-2136

Description: The publicly supported liberal arts university opened for instruction in September, 1970; it is one of the 20 campuses of the California State University system. The university operates on the quarter system with two summer sessions and is accredited by the Western Association of Schools and Colleges. Eighteen Bachelor Arts, 11 Bachelor of Science, and 11 Masters degrees are offered. Recent enrollment was 5,462 students; 60% of the students are women. A faculty of 223 full-time, and 100 part-time gives an overall faculty-student ratio of 1-16.

Entrance Requirements: High school graduation; high school equivalency considered; SAT or ACT required; requires 4 years college prep English, 3 years college prep mathematics, 1 year U.S. History and Gov't, 1 yr. science with lab, 2 yrs. foreign language, 1 yr. visual and performing arts and 3 yrs. of approved electives. California resident must have grade point average and test scores placing them in upper third of California graduates; nonresidents must rank in upper one-sixth of high school class; application fee $55; advanced placement, early admission, and early decision plans available. GRE or GMAT required for graduate programs; applicants to graduate division must have minimum 2.50 GPA (higher for certain programs) in last 90 quarter hours or 60 semester hours and a degree from an accredited institution.

Costs Per Year: No tuition for California residents; $6,165 tuition for nonresidents; $3,475 room and board (19 meal plan); $915 student fees.

Collegiate Environment: The 375-acre campus is located just outside the metropolitian city of Bakersfield, population 161,750. Thirty buildings comprise the campus. Recent facilities include the 500-Seat Dore Fine Arts Theatre, a nine-lane artificial surface track, baseball diamond, the Todd Madigan Art Gallery, an Olympic size pool and aquatic complex, John Antonio Sport Center and a 4,000 seat gymnasium. Construction will soon begin on the Walter W. Stiern Library, a $2.2 million, 150,000 square foot facility. The campus dormitory contains six three-story residence halls capable of housing 300 students in a living-learning residential environment. The library contains 315,000 bound volumes, 453,448 titles on microform and 2,700 periodicals. Various forms of financial aid are available, and 40% of the current student body is receiving financial assistance. Approximately 74% of first time freshman who apply for admission are accepted; 68% of those accepted enroll.

Community Environment: Bakersfield is the county seat of Kern County which is noted for its rich agriculture, petroleum and light industries. The city is located 112 miles north of Los Angeles and 295 miles south of San Francisco. Airlines, buses and transcontinental Railroads and Amtrak passenger services are available in the area. Bakersfield is considered the trading center of Southern San Joaquin Valley. Part-time employment is available. Central California beaches are located approximately 100 miles west of the campus. Shirley Meadow ski area is located 51 miles northeast of Bakersfield, 20 minutes from Lake Isebella. The county is home of the world-famous Edwards Air Force Base.

CALIFORNIA STATE UNIVERSITY - CHICO   *(E-4)*
Chico, California 95929-0720
Tel: (916) 895-6116; (800) 542-4426; Fax: (916) 898-4359

Description: The state-supported, coeducational, liberal arts, and teacher education university is accredited by the Western Association of Schools and Colleges. The semester system is employed with a special, optional session during January, and four summer sessions. Undergraduate enrollment is 11,419 full-time and 1,288 part-time students. There are 1,525 graduate students. A faculty of 630 full-time and 205 part-time gives a faculty-student ratio of 1-21. The 7 academic divisions of the university grant Bachelor and Master degrees.

Entrance Requirements: Combined high school GPA and either ACT or SAT test scores will be evaluated to determine eligibility; required completion of 15 units including 4 English, 3 math, 1 U.S. history, 1 lab science, 2 language, 1 visual/performing arts, and 3 academic electives; Non-high school graduates with GED considered; early admission, rolling admission, and advanced placement plans are available. Requirements for master's status: GPA of at least 2.75 in last 60 units and at least 3.0 in last 30 units; completion of GRE may be required; acceptance by the appropriate department or division; $55 application fee.

Costs Per Year: Tuition free for state residents plus $2,006 for student fees; $246/unit nonresident tuition; $4,632 room and board.

Collegiate Environment: Originally established in 1887 on eight acres of cherry orchards along the Big Chico creek and donated to the city by General John Bidwell, the campus now includes 66 buildings on 130 acres. The University also maintains a nearby agricultural farm of 1,218 acres. Six on-campus resident halls provide housing for 1,480 students. The library houses 1,436,072 volumes including government documents. 77% of first-time freshmen who apply for admission are accepted. More than 50% of the current undergraduate students receive financial assistance. Students are admitted at midyear as well as in the fall.

Community Environment: Chico is located close to the northern end of the Sacramento Valley and is one of the oldest communities in the state. Chico was started in the early 1840s on a 2,200-acre parcel of land south of Big Chico creek known as Potter's Half League. In 1860, John Potter sold the Half League to General Bidwell, who is considered the city's founder. Today Chico has a population of 46,750 (87,000 in the Greater Chico area) and Butte county has a population of 201,000. Chico is considered the business center for a large agricultural area, which produces an abundance of rice, grains, nuts and fruits. Winters are mild and summers are hot, averaging 95-110 degrees. Regional airlines connect Chico with adjacent cities, including San Francisco and San Jose. Greyhound Bus service is available. Part-time employment is available but scarce. Chico is the home of Bidwell Park, one of the largest and most beautiful municipal parks in the nation. Lower Bidwell Park starts near the campus and extends 10 miles east along the Big Chico creek. The park offers swimming in the creek, hiking, a municipal golf course, horseback riding, archery, a children's park, picnic areas, and a shooting range among its recreational facilities. Biking is a favorite (and practical) means of transportation. Skiing facilities are only two hours away. Bidwell Mansion, located on campus, is now a historical site maintained by the Department of Parks and Recreation.

CALIFORNIA STATE UNIVERSITY - DOMINGUEZ HILLS
(H-10)
1000 East Victoria Street
Carson, California 90747
Tel: (310) 516-3532

Description: The publicly supported, coeducational university operates on the semester system with two summer sessions and is accredited by the Western Association of Schools and Colleges. The degrees granted within the Schools of Humanities and Fine Arts, Sciences, Mathematics and Technology Management, Social and Behavioral Sciences, Education and University College include the Baccalaureate and Masters level degrees. Enrollment is approximately 4,273 full-time and 2,633 part-time undergraduates with 853 full-time and 1,806 part-time graduate students. A faculty of 318 gives a faculty-student ratio of 1-19.

Entrance Requirements: SAT or ACT required; high school graduates with 3.0 grade-point average eligible with any score; high school diploma with combined grade point-average and test score placement in upper third of California high school graduates (nonresidents - upper sixth); completion of 15 college-preparatory units required, including 4 English and 3 mathematics; non-high school graduates 21 years or older with GED equivalency considered; application fee $55; advanced placement, early admission, early decision and rolling admission plans available.

Costs Per Year: $792 per semester state resident fees; $246 per credit additional for nonresident; $2,598 room and board.

Collegiate Environment: The college stands amid the countryside of historic Rancho San Pedro and is easily accessible from Southwest Los Angeles County. The average high school standing of the freshman class was in the upper 60%. 26% of the current student body receives some form of financial aid. The library contains 400,000 volumes, 4,739 periodicals and 569,634 microforms.

Community Environment: This is a metropolitan area in Los Angeles County with a Mediterranean climate. Trains, buses and airlines serve the area. Carson is surrounded by freeways, which makes the larger nearby cities easy to reach. The city has churches, hospitals, a new YMCA building and library. The State Department of Employment, which is located in Torrance, has established a program designed to aid students in finding employment.

CALIFORNIA STATE UNIVERSITY - FRESNO   *(K-6)*
5150 N. Maple Avenue
Fresno, California 93740-0057
Tel: (209) 278-2261

Description: The publicly supported liberal arts university is accredited by the Western Association of Schools and Colleges. The semester system is employed with three summer sessions. The university grants a Baccalaureate degree and a Master degree. Founded in 1911, the college has grown to include special arrangements for use of facilties in Visalia for the Visalia Center. The Schools of the college are Technology, Agricultural Sciences, Business and Administrative Sciences, Education, Human Development, Engineering, Natural Sciences, Arts and Humanities, Health and Social Work, Social Sciences, and Graduate Studies and Research. Enrollment includes 14,750 full-time, 2,527 part-time, and 2,994 graduate students. A faculty of 594 full-time gives an overall faculty-student ratio of approximately 1-18. An extensive overseas study program is offered.

Entrance Requirements: High school graduation in upper one third of class; SAT or ACT required, if high school GPA is 2.99 or less; high school graduation required; nonresident high school graduation in upper one sixth of class; 30 semester units of college preparatory subjects required. Application fee $55; early admission, rolling admission, midyear admission, early decision and advanced placement plans available; GRE required for graduate school in most departments.

Costs Per Year: Tuition $1,802 for state residents; $7,706 out-of-state residents; room and board $4,398.

Collegiate Environment: The university is located on a 1,410-acre site in the northeast section of the city of Fresno. The library contains over 866,211 volumes and 2,928 periodicals and 1,055,684 microforms. Dormitory space is provided for 850 students, and fraternities and sororities house an additional 500 students. There are over 318 scholarships available and 38% of the current student body receives some form of financial assistance. 78% of the students applying for admission meet the requirements and are accepted. Students are admitted at midyear as well as in the fall.

Community Environment: Fresno (population 510,00) is located in the heart of the San Joaquin Valley, at the center of the state. The climate is mild all year. All modes of transportation serve the area. Fresno is in an agricultural area producing figs, grapes and cotton. Roma Winery and several other wineries are located here; other industries include processing and packing of fruit, the manufacture of cottonseed oil, livestock and poultry feed, agricultural equipment and aircraft parts. There are facilities in the area for swimming, fishing, sailing, water skiing, horseback riding, hiking, rock climbing and all the winter sports. Three national parks and two national forests are nearby.

CALIFORNIA STATE UNIVERSITY - FULLERTON   *(H-12)*
Fullerton, California 92634
Tel: (714) 773-2370

Description: The publicly supported coeducational university is accredited by the Western Association of Schools and Colleges. Founded in 1957 and operating on the early semester system, the college offers two six-week summer sessions as well as continuing education courses and services. The college awards Bachelor and Masters degrees to its graduates. Enrollment includes 12,944 full-time and 9,153 part-time undergraduates and 3,751 graduate students. A faculty of 623 full-time and 477 part-time gives an overall faculty-student ratio of 1-22.

Entrance Requirements: SAT or ACT required; high school graduates with 3.0 grade point average eligible with any score; high school diploma with combined grade-point average and test score placement in upper third of California high school graduates (nonresidents - upper 6th); under certain circumstances non-high school graduates considered; college preparatory courses are recommended; GRE required for some graduate programs; early admission, early decision, midyear admission and advanced placement plans available; $55 application fee.

Costs Per Year: $7,380 out-of-state tuition; no tuition for California residents; $3,476 room; $1,800 student fees.

Collegiate Environment: Located in Orange County, one of the fastest growing counties in the nation, the campus is situated on 225 acres. The library contains 690,337 volumes, 4,497 periodicals and 838,165 microforms. Special programs for the culturally disadvantaged are offered. Dormitories for 396 students are available. 78% of the applicants are accepted, and students are admitted at midyear as well as in the fall. Scholarships are available and 13% of the students receive some form of financial assistance.

Community Environment: Fullerton is in a metropolitan area with a temperate climate. Airlines, buses and trains serve the area. Freeways make all neighboring cities easily accessible. Fullerton is an area of many cultural interests, in art, music and theatre. The city is near Disneyland and the California Angel Stadium; 35 miles from Hollywood and Los Angeles. Recreational facilities include the beaches and the mountains which are both within easy driving distance. Part-time work is available. The major service clubs are represented in the city.

Branch Campuses: Satellite campus of CSU - Fullerton on a section of the campus of Saddleback College in Mission Viejo. Course offerings are at the upper division and graduate levels. These courses and programs are intended to provide a more convenient location for those students who live and work in southern Orange County.

CALIFORNIA STATE UNIVERSITY - HAYWARD   *(C-11)*
Hayward, California 94542
Tel: (415) 881-3811

Description: The publicly supported university with a coeducational student body is accredited by the Western Association of Schools and Colleges, and operates on the 4-quarter system. The university opened its doors in 1959. The undergraduate enrollment is 2,693 men and 3,954 women full-time, 1,145 men and 1,819 women part-time. Graduate enrollment is 1,248 men and 2,154 women. A faculty of 652 gives a faculty-student ratio of 1-19. The university is divided into the Schools of: Arts, Letters, and Social Sciences; Science; Business and Economics; Education. The unversity grants the Bachelor and Master degree. The Moss Landing Marine Lab offers studies in marine sciences in conjunction with other California State Universities.

Entrance Requirements: SAT or ACT required; high school graduation or equivalent with a minimum C average; California residents in

upper third of all California high school graduates (non-residents in upper sixth); GRE or GMAT required for some graduate programs; application fee $55; advanced placement plan available.

Costs Per Year: $6,576 tuition for out-of-state residents; California residents tuition free; $1,076 student fees for three quarters; $1,434 for four quarters

Collegiate Environment: Education and excellence for a diverse student population university, but emphasis is also placed on enriching a student's life outside the classroom. The campus includes 354 acres in rolling hills which command a view of the San Francisco Bay area. California Teaching, Supervision and Service Credentials are available through the fifth year credential program. The library contains over 750,000 books and periodicals, 515,516 microforms and 16,805 sound recordings, over 15,000 maps and over 130,000 federal, State and instructional documents. Approximately 70% of the applicants meet the requirements and are accepted.

Community Environment: Population 110,000 in a metropolitan area of 5 1/2 million. Hayward is a suburban area near Oakland, Berkeley, San Francisco and San Jose. The climate is mild. All modes of transportation serve the area. The university's proximity to all major Bay Area cities provides access to museums, art galleries, plays, concerts, and libraries as well as to the recreational opportunities of the bay. The climate makes outdoor recreation a year-round activity. Its nearness to ocean and mountain areas offer recreational diversity.

CALIFORNIA STATE UNIVERSITY - LONG BEACH   *(P-9)*
1250 Bellflower Blvd.
Long Beach, California 90840
Tel: (213) 985-4111

Description: The publicly supported, coeducational university, is accredited by the Western Association of Schools and Colleges and professionally by numerous respective accrediting institutions. Established in 1949, the University grants the Bachelor's and Master's degrees in over 50 majors. The college was the birthplace of the First International Sculpture symposium ever to be held in the United States and was the first college or university in the world to sponsor such an event. Enrollment includes 16,359 full-time and 9,740 part-time undergraduates and 5,183 graduate students. A faculty of 784 full-time and 508 part-time gives an overall faculty-student ratio of 1-33.

Entrance Requirements: Accredited high school graduation; SAT or ACT; required pattern of high school courses, top 1/3 of the state graduates; non-high school graduates considered; advanced placement and early decision plans available; $55 application fee.

Costs Per Year: $1,751 tuition for legal residents of California; $9,623 ($246/unit for 32 units plus $1,751) nonresidents; $5,300 room and board.

Collegiate Environment: The 322-acre campus has a total of 62 building complexes including a library which contains 1,045,216 volumes. The campus residence hall complex has a capacity of housing 1,448 men and women. About 90% of the applicants are accepted. Scholarships are available and 35% of students receive some form of financial aid.

Community Environment: Long Beach is approximately 20 miles south of Los Angeles and has a mediterranean climate. The eight mile beach area provides the finest and safest public bathing on the Pacific Coast. All modes of transportation serve the area. There are 25 city parks which provide facilities for golf, tennis, baseball, swimming, shuffleboard, lawn bowling and others. Long Beach can boast of having the largest protected harbor in North America. The city has a sports arena and a municipal auditorium.

CALIFORNIA STATE UNIVERSITY - LOS ANGELES   *(O-8)*
5151 State College Drive
Los Angeles, California 90032
Tel: (213) 343-3000

Description: The publicly supported, coeducational liberal arts college, accredited by the Western Association of Schools and colleges. The quarter system is used with one summer session. This college is one of the West's major urban centers of higher education and has been in existence for 40 years. The degrees granted include the Bachelor degree, Master degree and a Ph.D in Special Education, all offered through the six major divisions: Schools of Business and Economics, Education, Engineering and Technology, Natural and Social Sciences, and Arts and Letters. Cooperative education program is offered by 13 departments, providing alternating quarters of work and school. The college offers special outreach programs for veterans, parolees and handicapped students as well as an educational opportunity program for disadvantaged students. The enrollment is 21,596 students. A faculty of 670 full-time and 600 part-time provides a faculty-student ratio of 1:17.

Entrance Requirements: High school graduation with a rank in upper third of class (nonresidents sixth); non-high school graduates considered upon completion of GED requirements; SAT or ACT required. GMAT required for Business; GRE required for several graduate programs; application fee $55; rolling admission and advanced placement plans available.

Costs Per Year: No tuition for California residents; $137 per unit for nonresidents; $913 student fees.

Collegiate Environment: The campus has 13 buildings on 173 acres. The facilities are of contemporary character, and the campus is planned in such a way that it will retain a spacious, open atmosphere, created by landscaped plazas and courts integrated with contemporary concrete, brick, and glass buildings. Extensively planted surrounding hillsides and parking areas. The academic community is committed to strong educational programs, research, and creative and community service activities. The University's close proximity to the civic, cultural, multicultural, and economic centers of the Greater Los Angeles Basin enables it to foster strong cooperative relationships with community, business, educational, cultural, and political institutions. The campus is the site of the Los Angeles County High School for the Arts. The University supports an effective library that contains 791,997 volumes and subscribes to 3,458 periodicals. The University also supports the use of new technologies to enhance and enrich the instructional process and prepares students to understand cultural diversity and to serve the changing needs of a global society. Students have access to various computing facilities including terminal and microcomputer labs, digital labs, electronic classrooms, and advanced workstations labs. The University has international programs in Austrlia, Brazil, Canada, Denmark, France, Germany, Great Britain, Israel, Italy, Japan, Mexico, New Zealand, Peru, Spain, and Sweden. 46% of the undergraduates receive financial aid.

Community Environment: See University of California - Los Angeles.

CALIFORNIA STATE UNIVERSITY - NORTHRIDGE (F-9)
18111 Nordhoff Street
Northridge, California 91330
Tel: (818) 885-3700; (800) 885-3700; Fax: (818) 885-3766

Description: Formerly called San Fernando Valley State College, this publicly supported, coeducational university is accredited by the Western Association of Schools and Colleges. A faculty of 1,808 gives a student-faculty ratio of 19-1. The university awards the Bachelor and Master degrees. Campus services are offered for the deaf and disabled in tutorial and supportive areas. Programs are available for the educationally disadvantaged. The university operates on the semester system and offers two summer sessions. Enrollment includes 14,498 full-time and 9,812 part-time undergraduates and 4,926 graduate students. A faculty of 973 full-time and 835 part-time gives a faculty-student ratio of 1-17.

Entrance Requirements: High school graduation with a composite scholastic average and ACT or SAT score in the upper third of California H.S. graduates; upper sixth for non-California residents; early decision, midyear admission, rolling admission and advanced placement plans available. $55 application fee.

Costs Per Year: No tuition for state residents; $4,836 ($189/unit) nonresidents; $958 student fees; $5,500 room and board.

Collegiate Environment: The campus consists of 350 acres with 18 major buildings, including housing facilities for 2,200. The library has an open-shelf arrangement with 1,000,342 volumes and 4,000 periodicals. Financial aid is available, and 24% of the current student body receives some form of assistance. About 75% of the applicants are accepted, including midyear students.

Community Environment: Located north of Los Angeles and part of the Los Angeles metropolitan area. Climate is mild; all modes of transportation available in the Los Angeles area. The community facilities include churches, library, hospitals and all the service organizations are represented. Part-time employment available in this center for electronic and space research and development; about three-quarters of the students work. Northridge enjoys the cultural and recreational advantages of Los Angeles; is 20 miles from the Pacific Ocean and near the mountain areas for winter sports.

CALIFORNIA STATE UNIVERSITY - SACRAMENTO (G-4)
6000 J Street
Sacramento, California 95819
Tel: (916) 278-6011; Admissions: (916) 278-5603; Fax: (916) 278-5603

Description: The publicly supported, coeducational university is accredited by the Western Association of Schools and Colleges. The university was the result of a Bill passed by State Legislature in 1947. Classes were conducted at Sacramento Junior College until 1953 when the present campus was established. Formerly Sacramento State College, the present name was adopted June 1, 1972. The university grants the Bachelor, Master and Professional degrees. Educational Opportunity Programs are available for low income, minorities and educationally disadvantaged. The university operates on the semester system and offers five summer sessions. Enrollment includes 14,682 full-time and 8,106 part-time students. There are 4,640 graduate students. A faculty of 793 full-time and 450 part-time gives a faculty-student ratio of 1-21.

Entrance Requirements: High school graduates with a composite scholastic average and SAT or ACT score placing the student in upper third of California H.S. graduates; for non-California residents, upper sixth; rolling admission, midyear admission and advanced placement plans available; $55 application fee.

Costs Per Year: $7,626 ($246/unit) nonresident tuition; $4,600 room and board; $2,000 student fees.

Collegiate Environment: Residence hall capacity is 500 men and 500 women. Off campus housing is available to students. Library contains 916,869 volumes, 144,317 periodicals, 104,779 microforms and 106,602 audiovisual materials. About 80% of the applicants are accepted, including midyear students. 35% of the students receive financial aid.

Community Environment: Sacramento, the capital of California, is the gateway to historic Gold Rush country and the High Sierra vacation regions. All modes of transportation serve the area; San Francisco is a two-hour drive on the freeway. The cultural center of Northern California, Sacramento has the historic Crocker Art Gallery, symphony orchestra, summer theater series, state library, a state museum, a state railroad museum and the Sacramento History Center. Numerous part time jobs on campus and in the city are available through the Student Placement Office and the California Department of Employment. There are many post-college vocational opportunities with defense industries, two air bases, state and local government and other growing industrial and high-tech firms. Off campus housing is available to students. There are many points of interest and a great number of recreational facilities in the Sacramento area; parks, zoo, golf courses, boating and fishing on the American and Sacramento Rivers. Squaw Valley, 100 miles away, was the home of the 1960 Olympics for winter sports. There are good health facilities and a wide range of fraternal and civic organizations.

CALIFORNIA STATE UNIVERSITY - SAN BERNARDINO (O-11)
5500 University Parkway
San Bernardino, California 92407
Tel: (714) 880-5200

Description: The state assisted coeducational liberal arts college operates on the quarter system with five summer sessions. Founded in 1965, the college has adopted a three-course, three-term academic program which extends from September to June. A full load is three academic courses per quarter. 186 quarter units including six quarter units in physical education are required for graduation. Accredited by the Western Association of Schools and Colleges, the college awards the Bachelor and Master degrees. The enrollment was 11,927 including part-time students. A faculty of 642 including part- time faculty gives an overall faculty-student ratio of 1-18. Programs for the educationally disadvantaged are offered.

Entrance Requirements: SAT or ACT required; high school diploma with combined grade-point average and test score placement in upper third of California high school class (nonresidents-upper sixth); high school graduates with 3.21 grade average eligible with any score; application $55 fee; early admission, early decision, rolling admission and advanced placement plans available.

Costs Per Year: Tuition free for state residents; student fees $933 resident; $5,865 nonresident; $4,015 room and board.

Collegiate Environment: The campus is located on 430 acres. The library contains 480,000 volumes, pamphlets, 3,200 periodicals, 385,000 microforms and 9,278 records and tapes. Student housing is available for 430 students. Financial aid is available, and 20% of the current student body receives some form of assistance. New federal funding for middle income families is being increased and more than one half of the undergraduate students may be eligible for financial aid. Of the 55 scholarships offered, 16 are for freshmen. Eighty-five percent of the students who apply for admission are accepted, including midyear students. The average SAT scores for the freshman class were V450, M430 and average ACT composite score was 18.

Community Environment: Population 104,000. San Bernardino is located 58 miles east of Los Angeles at the foot of the San Bernardino Mountains. Climate is ideal with 312 days of sunshine a year. Citrus groves surround the city. Greyhound and Trailways bus lines and Santa Fe Railroad serve the area. The nearest airport is Ontario International. San Bernardino has art galleries, Swing Auditorium, theaters, many churches, and a library. Pacific Ocean beaches provide water sports. Resort areas of Lake Arrowhead and Big Bear Lake in the mountains have facilities for water sports and winter sports. Cajon Pass offers a scenic drive through the mountains into the Mojave Desert; City Creek Highway connects with the Rim of the World Drive at Running Springs.

CALIFORNIA STATE UNIVERSITY - STANISLAUS   *(I-5)*
801 West Monte Vista Avenue
Turlock, California 95380
Tel: (209) 667-3122; Fax: (209) 667-3788

Description: The publicly-supported, coeducational liberal arts college was formerly known as Stanislaus State College. It is accredited by the Western Association of Schools and Colleges. The college opened in 1957 and limited its first years to juniors and seniors; its first freshman class was admitted in 1965 when operations began on the new campus. It operates on the 4-1-4 system and offers 2 summer sessions. The college offers degrees in the arts and humanities, social sciences, natural sciences, and in professional areas such as business administration, education, physical education, nursing, and vocational education. Enrollment includes 4,369 full-time and 1,508 part-time undergraduate students, and 1,140 graduate students. A faculty of 247 full-time and 88 part-time gives a faculty-student ratio of 1-18.

Entrance Requirements: High school graduation with a composite scholastic average and SAT or ACT score placing the applicant in the upper third of California high school graduates; for non-California residents upper sixth; Non-high school graduates considered; high school students may be considered for advanced placement program if recommended by principal; completion of units 4 English, 3 math, 1 laboratory science, 2 foreign language, 1 visual/performing arts, and 1 American history; $55 application fee; college preparatory courses recommended; early decision, early admission, rolling admission, delayed admission and advanced placement plans available.

Costs Per Year: $246 per unit nonresident tuition; $4,737 room and board; $1,434 student fees.

Collegiate Environment: The campus has 11 buildings on 200 acres. Yosemite Hall is a college-owned coeducational dormitory for students at the college with a capacity for 280 students. Approximately 60% of the student body graduated in the top quarter of the high school class. The master plan for the campus was designed for an eventual enrollment of 12,000 students. The library contains 280,000 volumes, 3,882 periodicals and 700,000 microforms. About 85% of the applicants are accepted. 51% of students receive some form of financial aid.

Community Environment: Population 37,160. This is a growing and prosperous residential community in a rural area of central California. Dairying is of major importance; turkeys, melons, grapes and peaches are the chief products. The area is served by bus and railroad. Two general hospitals, one clinic, many churches, three libraries and most all of the major fraternal and civic organizations are represented in Turlock. Part-time employment opportunities are average. Special events are the Stanislaus County Fair and the Annual Chamber of Commerce Roundup Week in the fall. A summer concert series is held at the university.

CALIFORNIA WESTERN SCHOOL OF LAW   *(R-10)*
225 Cedar Street
San Diego, California 92101
Tel: (619) 525-1401; (800) 255-4252 x1401; Fax: (619) 696-9999

Description: California Western School of Law is an innovative, privately supported law school that offers practical training with the academic curriculum. The school has been fully accredited by the American Bar Association since 1962 and has been a member of the Association of American Law Schools since 1967. Enrollment is 808 full-time students. A faculty of 46 full-time and 26 part-time gives a faculty-student ratio of 1-18. The school operates on a trimester system, which offers students the option to graduate in two years; there are two entering classes per year (August and January).

Entrance Requirements: A baccalaureate or equivalent is required; LSAT required. Admission is competitive. Rolling admission.

Costs Per Year: $18,250 tuition for 2 trimesters; $70 student fee for 2 trimesters.

Collegiate Environment: California Western offers specialty courses in Telecommunications, Sports Law, International Law, Entertainment Law and Biotechnology. 42% of applicants are accepted. At least 80% of the students participate in the clinical internship program. Students enrich their education by participating in Law Review/International Law Journal, appellate advocacy teams, advocacy honors board, moot court competitions, legal fraternities, and various academic and social student organizations. The library contains 219,840 volumes. Scholarship programs are available, and approximately 80% of the student body receives financial aid.

Community Environment: California Western is located in downtown San Diego, near the center of the legal community. Besides having 325 days of sunshine a year, 70 miles of accessible beaches, near mountains for hiking and skiing, and the desert for spectacular scenery and backpacking, San Diego offers a large variety of cultural opportunities. Balboa Park, the site of numerous museums and theaters, is just a five-minute drive from the campus. The world-famous San Diego Zoo is also nearby. Sports fans can watch major league baseball, football, hockey and indoor soccer or take advantage of more than 50 public golf courses, miles of jogging and biking paths, the beaches and Mission bay for sailing and surfing.

CANADA COLLEGE   *(I-3)*
4200 Farm Hill Boulevard
Redwood City, California 94061
Tel: (415) 364-1212; Admissions: (415) 306-3226; Fax: (415) 306-3457

Description: The publicly supported, coeducational community college, in the San Mateo County Community College District, is accredited by the Western Association of Schools and Colleges. The college offers both day and evening classes, and operates on the semester system with one summer session. Enrollment includes 1,941 men and 3,735 women. The faculty conists of 107 full-time and 151 part-time members. The school provides university-parallel programs as well as programs for improvement of skills in business and industry. It grants Associate of Arts and Associate of Science degrees and certificates.

Entrance Requirements: High school graduation or equivalent; non-high school graduates over 18 years of age may also be admitted; open enrollment policy; early admission, rolling admission and delayed admission plans available.

Costs Per Year: $403 ($13/unit) state residents; $3,503 ($113/unit) out-of-state residents.

Collegiate Environment: Canada College is comprised of nine buildings on a 131 acre site in the western foothills of Redwood City.

To the east it overlooks San Francisco Bay and to the west the Pacific Coast foothills. All applicants who complete admission procedures and residence requirements are accepted, including mid-year students. The library contains 48,300 volumes, 3,000 pamphlets, 170 periodicals, 3,000 microforms and 5,600 sound recordings. Financial aid is available.

Community Environment: Redwood City is noted for its municipally owned deepwater harbor on the San Francisco Bay. It is the seat of San Mateo County. This is a rapid growing residential and manufacturing center and is also one of the best known chrysanthemum growing centers in the country. Recreation facilities include parks, bay and the beaches for swimming, fishing and boating. The mountains are within reasonable distance for winter sports.

CERRITOS COLLEGE   *(H-11)*
11110 Alondra Boulevard
Norwalk, California 90650
Tel: (310) 467-5005; Fax: (310) 860-9680

Description: The publicly supported, coeducational community college is accredited by the Western Association of Schools and Colleges. It operates on the semester system and offers two summer terms. Enrollment includes 3,000 full-time and 18,000 part-time students. A faculty of 222 full-time and 606 part-time gives a faculty-student ratio of 1-49. The college provides university-parallel programs, preparation for immediate employment in business and industry, and general education. It grants the Associate in Arts degree and Certificates on completion of vocational programs.

Entrance Requirements: Non-high school graduates are considered; open enrollment; midyear admission and rolling admission plans available.

Costs Per Year: $403 ($13/unit) resident; $1,550 ($50/unit) resident with B.A. degree; $3,534 ($14/unit) nonresident; $3,906 ($126/unit) international.

Collegiate Environment: The campus consists of 140 acres and 19 buildings located in the center of the school district. The library is a modern, air-conditioned building that contains 74,249 volumes. Various forms of financial assistance are available to those students requiring aid. 41% of students receive aid. All applicants are accepted, and students are admitted at midyear as well as in the fall.

Community Environment: Norwalk is an urban area 17 miles from Los Angeles. The climate is sub-tropical. There is bus and rail service to Los Angeles, where other major transportation facilities are located. The city has many community facilities, industrial firms and retail outlets. Part-time work is available.

CHABOT COLLEGE   *(C-11)*
25555 Hesperian Boulevard
Hayward, California 94545
Tel: (415) 786-6600

Description: This publicly supported, coeducational community college is accredited by the Western Association of Schools and Colleges. Opening with an overflow enrollment on a temporary campus of seven and one-half acres in San Leandro in 1961, the college later moved to a 96-acre site in Hayward. A branch campus in the Livermore-Amador Valley was opened in 1975. It provides university-parallel programs as well as vocational-technical and general educational studies. A Certificate and an Associate in Arts degree are granted. Air Force and Army ROTC programs are available. The college operates on the quarter system and offers three summer sessions. Enrollment includes 4,293 full-time and 10,411 part-time students. A faculty of 850 provides a faculty-student ratio of 1-18.

Entrance Requirements: Open enrollment policy; high school graduation; non-high school graduates 18 years of age or over admitted; ACT suggested for counseling and placement purposes; nonresidents must have high school graduation with a C average; early admission, early decision, and advanced placement plans available.

Costs Per Year: No tuition for California residents; $34 student fees per quarter hour; $70 per quarter hour for nonresidents.

Collegiate Environment: The Hayward campus, consisting of 30 buildings, is one of California's most modern educational centers. Its design, featuring Mediterranean West architecture, has attracted much attention. The focal point of the campus is the two-story library,

which houses more than 115,000 volumes. The Livermore-Amador Valley campus is comprised of 8 buildings including a new Technical-Vocational Center. Both branches of the college offer a wide range of programs for transfer students seeking the Baccalaureate degree as well as a complete two-year program. Special programs are available for physically handicapped and learning-disabled students. Various forms of financial aid are available, and approximately 20% of the current students receive some assistance. All those who apply for admission are accepted. Students may enroll at midyear as well as in the fall.

Community Environment: See California State University - Hayward.

Branch Campuses: Livermore-Amador Valley Campus.

CHAFFEY COMMUNITY COLLEGE   *(G-14)*
5885 Haven Avenue
Rancho Cucamonga, California 91737
Tel: (909) 987-1737; Fax: (909) 941-2783

Description: Chaffey College, one of the first colleges established in California, is a two-year public community college. It is accredited by the Western Association of Schools and Colleges. Chaffey Junior College of Agriculture, a department of Chaffey Union High School, was founded in 1883 and has been publicly funded since 1916. The college has six administrative units that provide an extensive range of the highest quality transfer and occupational classes: Arts and Humanities; Business and Applied Technology; Physical, Life and Health Sciences; Social and Behavioral Sciences; Student and Support Services; and Instructional and Institutional Services. The college has lower-division courses, occupational courses, and general education courses. In addition, Learning Centers located both on campus and off campus provide the community with resource centers for the development of basic skills needed for academic and vocational pursuits. It operates on the semester system and offers one summer session. Enrollment includes 16,500 students. A faculty of 190 full-time and 350 part-time gives a faculty-student ratio of 1-30.

Entrance Requirements: Non-high school graduates 18 years of age admitted; high school students who are 16 years of age or who have completed 10th grade may be admitted to an Educational Enrichment program if properly recommended; midyear admission, rolling admission, and advanced placement plans available.

Costs Per Year: $403 ($13 per credit) state resident tuition; $1,550 ($50 per credit) resident with Baccalaureate degree or higher tuition; $3,720 ($120 per credit) nonresident tuition.

Collegiate Environment: The campus has 16 buildings on 200 acres of rolling lawns and native foliage in the foothills of the San Gabriel mountains. The library contains 72,000 volumes, 9,100 pamphlets, 254 periodicals, 7,194 microforms and 3,276 audiovisual materials. The college has no dormitory facilities, the Student Activities office maintains information on available nearby housing. The Campus Center serves as a dining room and for other student activities. Chaffey College is a member of the football conference and offers intercollegiate athletic competition. The gymnasium, seating capacity 2,000, also has a dance room, and weight room. Additionally there are 8 tennis courts, a 4,200-seat stadium with a football field and track, a baseball field, playing courts, two other fields, and diving and swimming pools. 100% of applicants are accepted, including midyear students. 50% of freshmen return for their sophomore year.

Community Environment: Rancho Cucamonga is a suburban community 44 miles east of Los Angeles. With the west end of San Bernadino County the area has a population of 475,000. It has dry climate conditions, with temperatures ranging from 25 to 112 degrees during the year. Farming, namely citrus and grapes, is the main economy. Rail, bus, and air (Ontario International Airport) serve the area. There are four hospitals nearby.

CHAPMAN UNIVERSITY   *(I-12)*
333 N. Glassell Street
Orange, California 92666
Tel: (714) 997-6711

Description: This privately supported, coeducational liberal arts college was founded by members of the Christian Churches (Disciples of Christ) and is accredited by the Western Association of Schools and Colleges. It operates on the 4-1-4 calendar system and offers three summer sessions. The college offers 36 Bachelor and pre-professional programs, and grants the Bachelor and Master degrees. It conducts degree-oriented programs in academic centers throughout the United States. These academic programs are carefully coordinated with the home campus and are an integral part of the total Chapman University program. air Force and Army ROTC programs are available. Enrollment includes 1,908 full-time and 233 part-time undergraduates and 1,144 graduate students. A faculty of 134 full-time and 176 part-time gives a faculty-student ratio of 1-12.

Entrance Requirements: High school graduation or equivalent with a C+ average; ACT or SAT required, minimum scores SAT 800 combined, ACT 19 composite; non-high school graduates considered for admission; each applicant is treated individually; early admission, early decision, rolling admission, midyear admission and advanced placement plans available; March 1 priority application deadline; $30 application fee.

Costs Per Year: $17,372 tuition; $6,220 room and board.

Collegiate Environment: The university is located on a 40-acre campus in the city of Orange, 32 miles southeast of Los Angeles. Residence halls can accommodate 858 students in dormitories and 268 in apartments. The library contains 190,000 volumes, 1,806 periodicals, 8,092 microforms and numerous audiovisual materials. 76% of applicants are accepted. The average score of the entering freshman class was SAT 976 combined. Scholarships are available, and 66% of the current student body receives some form of assistance.

Community Environment: Orange is located 32 miles southeast of Los Angeles and 94 miles north of San Diego. Its climate is mild with a very low rainfall. It is accessible by car, bus or train and plane. Orange County Airport is a short distance away, and Los Angeles International Airport is a 45-minute drive away. As the name implies, Orange lies in a vast citrus belt; avocados are also grown here. All the necessary facilities of a city are available as well as many recreational facilities for swimming, golf, surfing, skiing, fishing, hunting, and boating. Beaches and mountain resorts are nearby.

CHRISTIAN HERITAGE COLLEGE *(R-10)*
2100 Greenfield Drive
El Cajon, California 92021
Tel: (619) 588-7747; (800) 676-2242; Fax: (619) 440-0902

Description: The school is a privately supported, coeducational college that provides a nondenominational but Christian approach to education. It was founded in 1970 as a center where all curricula and studies could be developed around the concept of Biblical creationism. The college operates on the semester system and offers 2 summer sessions. The college is fully accredited by the Western Association of Schools and Colleges, and awards the Bachelor degree. Enrollment includes 310 full-time and 19 part-time and 121 evening students. The faculty-student ratio is 1-15.

Entrance Requirements: High school graduation or GED is required; SAT; early decision, advanced placement and rolling admission plans available; $25 application fee.

Costs Per Year: $8,636 tuition; $4,120 room and board.

Collegiate Environment: The campus consists of 30 acres with 16 buildings. Facilities include a church, dormitories, and dining hall as well as classroom buildings. Outdoor facilities include tennis, basketball, volleyball courts, soccer, baseball fields, and a swimming pool. Dormitory space can accomodate 226 students. The library has 75,000 volumes. There are many scholarships available, and more than 90% of the students receive financial assistance. 75% of applicants are accepted, including students at midyear.

Community Environment: The campus is two miles from the center of El Cajon, a suburb of San Diego. The location of the college affords short travel distances to nearby mountain, desert and beach resorts.

CHURCH DIVINITY SCHOOL OF THE PACIFIC *(H-3)*
2451 Ridge Road
Berkeley, California 94709
Tel: (510) 204-0700; Fax: (510) 644-0712

Description: Privately supported, coeducational theological seminary of the Episcopal Church is accredited by the Western Association of Schools and Colleges and by the Association of Theological

Schools. The school is an affiliate of the Graduate Theological Union, Berkeley, California. The college has changed its residence twice since it was founded in 1893 and is open to all wishing to prepare for the ministry and other forms of church work. It grants the Master of Divinity Degree, Master of Theological Studies, and in cooperation with the Graduate Theological Union grants the Master of Arts and Doctoral degrees. It operates on the semester system and offers one summer session. Enrollment is 98 students. A faculty of 10 gives a faculty-student ratio of 1-9.

Entrance Requirements: BA degree or its equivalent from an accredited college or university; GRE required; preseminary studies are recommended; rolling admission plan available; $30 application fee.

Costs Per Year: $7,526 tuition; $3,816 room and board.

Collegiate Environment: The school is located one block north of the North Gate of the University of California, one of the nation's leading centers of scholarship and research, and is adjacent to other seminaries in the area. Many facilities of these institutions are shared by all, as well as the cultural advantages of the university community. The libraries have also been combined and result in a collection of over 509,000 volumes. Housing facilities are available for 52 single students and 23 families.

Community Environment: See University of California - Berkeley

CITRUS COLLEGE *(G-12)*
1000 West Foothill
Glendora, California 91740
Tel: (818) 914-8511

Description: The publicly-supported, coeducational community college is accredited by the Western Association of Schools and Colleges. Founded in 1915, this was the first community college in Los Angeles County and the fifth in California. The college now serves the residents of the Azusa, Bradbury, Glendora, Duarte, Monrovia, and Claremont communities School Districts. It provides university-parallel programs and two-year vocational and occupational courses in both the day and evening sessions. The college grants a Certificate and an Associate degree. It operates on the semester system and offers one summer session. Enrollment includes 2,916 full-time and 7,573 part-time students. A faculty of 129 full-time and 260 part-time members provides a faculty-student ratio of 1-27.

Entrance Requirements: 100% of applicants accepted. High school graduate or over 18 years of age required; ACT or SAT or ASSET necessary for placement purposes; rolling admission plan available; midyear students are accepted.

Costs Per Year: $100 per unit ($2,400) nonresident tuition; no tuition for California residents; student fees, $13 per unit.

Collegiate Environment: The college occupies a modern 104-acre campus in the foothills of the beautiful San Gabriel Mountains. The newest addition to the campus, a $1.5 million building which houses a child development center and student support services, was completed in 1978, bringing the number of major buildings to 25 plus athletic facilities. There are no dormitories. 30% of freshman class returned for second year. Of 165 scholarships offered by the college 125 are available to freshmen.

Community Environment: See Azusa Pacific University

CITY COLLEGE OF SAN FRANCISCO *(I-3)*
50 Phelan Ave.
San Francisco, California 94112
Tel: (415) 239-3000; Admissions: (415) 239-3285; Fax: (415) 239-3936

Description: The publicly supported, coeducational community college is accredited by the Western Association of Schools and Colleges. The City College of San Francisco was established in 1935 as an integral part of the San Francisco Unified School District. Day and evening classes are offered. It operates on the semester system and offers one summer session. The college grants the Certificate and the Associate degree. Enrollment is approximately 30,000with a faculty of 1,764, giving a faculty-student ratio of 1:17.

Entrance Requirements: High school graduation or 18 yrs old.

Costs Per Year: $100 resident tuition; $3,000 nonresident.

Collegiate Environment: College houses 82,219 volumes in the library. The college offers many advantages, but it can offer none more important than the interest of instructors and counselors in those whom they teach and advise. It is this quality from which students at the college benefit most. A wide choice of majors and courses are available. Students may complete the first two years of training for a profession, satisfy freshman and sophomore requirements in the liberal arts, prepare for employment at the end of two years of training, take evening courses, remove high school deficiences, or get other special preparation. Included among program offerings are Afro-American studies, Chinese studies, Latin-American studies, Philippine studies, and Women's studies. 99% of all applicants are accepted. 36% of the students receive some form of financial aid.

Community Environment: See San Francisco State University

THE CLAREMONT GRADUATE SCHOOL *(G-13)*
160 East 10th Street
Claremont, California 91711
Tel: (909) 621-8069

Description: The privately supported graduate school is accredited by the Western Association of Schools and Colleges. Established in 1925, it currently offers advanced programs in humanities, botany, mathematics, social sciences, management, fine arts, education, and information science that lead to the Master degree and the Doctorate. Preparation for elementary and secondary school teaching is also offered. Enrollment is 2,000 students. A faculty of 75 gives a faculty-student ratio of 1-12. The school operates on the semester system and offers a summer session.

Entrance Requirements: Bachelor's degree from recognized institution; excellent undergraduate record; confidential letters of recommendation from teachers or employers; GRE required (before January for fall registration); GMAT required for MBA applicants; $40 application fee.

Costs Per Year: $17,750 tuition; $130 student fees.

Collegiate Environment: The 16 buildings of the Graduate School and the facilities of the five undergraduate colleges comprise an expanded campus for graduate education. In addition to buildings owned and operated by the Graduate School, graduate students may also use the art and music studios, science laboratories, multiple libraries and athletic facilities of the Claremont Colleges. (See Claremont University Center for further information.) The campus library contains 2,000,000 volumes, 5,300 periodicals and 12,000 microforms. Housing for 100 students is available. Approximately 60% of the applicants are accepted. Financial aid is available, and 40% of the current student body receives assistance.

Community Environment: Population 21,500. Claremont is located at the foot of Sierra Madres, 35 miles east of Los Angeles on Highway 66. It is best known as a college community and it is said this city has more trees on its streets than citizens. The climate is warm, and not too dry nor humid. There are churches of many denominations, civic organizations, theaters and libraries. For those who are interested in the outdoor sports, there is skiing in nearby mountain areas, hiking, swimming, tennis and golf. Beach areas are nearby for swimming and boating.

CLAREMONT MCKENNA COLLEGE *(G-13)*
890 Columbia Avenue
Claremont, California 91711
Tel: (909) 621-8088; Fax: (909) 621-8516

Description: This private coeducational college is accredited by the Western Association of Schools and Colleges and offers a liberal arts program with emphasis on public affairs, economics, government, international relations, pre-law, and pre-business. It operates on the semester system. Qualified students may study for a semester in a foreign country, in Washington, DC, or at Haverford or Colby colleges. CMC was founded in 1946. Enrollment is 877 students. A faculty of 103 full-time and 12 part-time gives a faculty-student ratio of 1-9. The college grants the Bachelor degree and is one of the six Claremont Colleges.

Entrance Requirements: Both academic and nonacademic criteria will be evaluated; high school graduation with B average minimum; completion of college preparatory course including 4 units in English, 3 mathematics, 2 foreign language, 3 science, and history; SAT or ACT required; $40 application fee; 2 personal references required; interview urged; early decision, deferred admission, midyear admission, and advanced placement plans available.

Costs Per Year: $17,000 tuition; $140 student fees; $2,850 room; $3,160 board.

Collegiate Environment: The campus (25 buildings on 50 acres) is located in a residential, college community of 37,000, 35 miles east of Los Angeles. Recreational areas are close at hand (a one-hour drive to the mountains, beaches or desert). The college shares several buildings with other Claremont colleges, including libraries containing 1,905,102 volumes. Dormitories and student apartments accommodate 850 students on campus. Approximately 94% of the student body graduated in top 25% of the high school class. 92% of the freshman class returned for sophomore year. About 40% of the applicants are accepted, including students at midyear. 70% of the current freshman class receives some form of financial aid.

Community Environment: See Claremont Graduate School.

CLAREMONT UNIVERSITY CENTER *(G-13)*
160 East 10th Street
Claremont, California 91711
Tel: (909) 621-8026; Fax: (909) 621-8517

Description: Claremont University Center is the central coordinating agency for The Claremont Colleges -- a group of six adjacent, autonomous institutions: The Claremont Graduate School, Claremont McKenna College, Harvey Mudd College, Pitzer College, Pomona College and Scripps College. These colleges form a consortium of prestigious educational insitutions that is unique in American higher education. Total enrollment of all the Colleges is about 5,500 with about 4,000 undergraduates. Full cross-registration is permitted. The Claremont University Center administers all the central programs and services that serve all the Colleges and is active in promoting intercollegiate cooperation. Among the major common facilities are the Libraries of The Claremont Colleges (1,700,000 volumes), Bridges Auditorium (2,500 seats), Huntley Bookstore, Monsour Counseling Center, and Baxter Student Health Services, and the McAlister Chaplains Center.

Costs Per Year: $17,750 tuition; $130 fees.

COGSWELL COLLEGE *(I-3)*
1175 Bordeaux Drive
Sunnyvale, California 94089
Tel: (408) 541-0100; Fax: (408) 747-0764

Description: The privately supported college was organized in 1887. Its programs include electronics, mechanical, computer, music engineering technology, and computer graphics. Upper division evening programs are available in electrical engineering and quality engineering. The college is accredited by the Western Association of Schools and Colleges. The electronics and mechanical programs are accredited by the Accrediting Board for Engineering and Technology. The trimester system is used. The college presently grants the following degrees; B.S. in Engineering Technology, B.S. degrees in Electrical Engineering and Software Engineering, and a B.A. in Computer and Video Imaging. Enrollment includes 284 men and 65 women. There are 12 full-time and 36 part-time faculty members. The faculty-student ratio is 1-9.

Entrance Requirements: High school graduation; units including 4 English, 4 mathematics, and 2 science. A solid background in high school mathematics, and science is important. The BA program requires strong English and arts skills. Freshman Placement Test; SAT or ACT accepted but not required; rolling admission, advanced placement and delayed admission plans available; non-high school graduates are considered under certain circumstances (G.E.D., P.E.P.)

Costs Per Year: $3,480 per trimester tuition.

Collegiate Environment: The college occupies a one-story building on 4 acres in the heart of Silicon Valley. Cogswell has 8 technology laboratories, including a software engineering lab, a computer-aided-design (CAD) lab, musical-digital interface (MIDI) studios, two computer imaging labs, and two video labs. There are also a computer lab furnished with the lastest equipment, and a physics/chemistry lab. The library contains 12,000 volumes and 400 periodicals.

Community Environment: Population of the district 174,000; within an hour's drive from the San Francisco Bay area. Buses and trains serve the area and the San Jose Municipal Airport is nearby. There are parks, playgrounds, and nearby beaches for recreation plus all the cultural advantages of the San Francisco Bay area.

COLLEGE OF ALAMEDA *(I-3)*
555 Atlantic Avenue
Alameda, California 94501
Tel: (510) 522-7221; Fax: (510) 769-6019

Description: This publicly supported coeducational community college has an enrollment of 1,661 full-time, 4,301 part-time and 1,959 evening students. A faculty of 100 full-time and 96 part-time gives a faculty-student ratio of 1-30. The college is accredited by Western Association of Schools and Colleges. One of four colleges in Oakland's Peralta Community College District, classes began sessions in September 1968. The degrees granted are an Associate of Arts or Science in university-parallel and Certificates in certain occupational programs. The college operates on the quarter system and offers one six-week summer term.

Entrance Requirements: High school graduates or 18 years of age; open enrollment policy.

Costs Per Year: $10 per unit; $50 per unit resident with BA degree or higher; $110 per unit nonresident.

Collegiate Environment: A new 62-acre campus in the city of Alameda was dedicated in October 1970. The Aeronautics program is conducted on a 2 1/2 acre site near Oakland Airport. There are no housing facilities on campus. All applicants are accepted. About 60% of the freshman class returned for the sophomore year. A library of 31,000 volumes, 6,000 pamphlets, 198 periodicals, 22,688 microforms and 850 sound recordings supports the educational curriculum.

Community Environment: See Laney College.

COLLEGE OF MARIN *(A-9)*
835 College Avenue
Kentfield, California 94904
Tel: (415) 457-8811; Admissions: (415) 485-9412

Description: The publicly supported, coeducational junior college is accredited by the Western Association of Schools and Colleges. Founded in 1926, the college was renamed in 1989. The college grants an Associate in Arts or Science degree in its college transfer, vocational and technical, and general education programs. It operates on the semester system and offers one summer session. Enrollment includes 9,817 students.

Entrance Requirements: High school graduation or 18 years old; ACT and college entrance examinations required; midyear admission and advanced placement plans available.

Costs Per Year: $390 ($13/unit) resident tuition; $1,500 ($50/unit) resident with B.A. degree or higher; $4,230 ($141/unit) nonresident.

Collegiate Environment: The campus is comprised of 20 buildings situated on 76 acres. The library holds over 38,000 volumes. All students applying for admission who meet requirements are accepted as well as midyear students. Various forms of financial assistance are available. Indian Valley compus is 12 miles norht of Kentfield.

Community Environment: Kentfield is suburban community in a beautiful countryside across the Golden Gate from San Francisco. Located on a peninsula with the Pacific Ocean on one side and San Francisco on the other. A mild climate averaging 70 degrees; average rainfall 36 inches per year. The Greyhound bus line serves the area. Entertainment and recreational facilities are close by and shopping facilities are good. Good opportunities for part-time employment.

COLLEGE OF NOTRE DAME *(D-10)*
1500 Ralston Ave.
Belmont, California 94002
Tel: (415) 593-1601; Fax: (415) 508-3607

Description: This privately supported, Roman Catholic College is accredited by the Western Association of Schools and Colleges. Founded by the Sisters of Notre Dame de Namur, the liberal arts college was granted its charter in 1868 and offered a 2-year program until 1951, when a 4-year program was initiated. Three coeducational

fifth-year graduate programs were initiated for preparing teachers for elementary (1963), secondary (1967), and Montessori, pre-school levels (1967). The college operates on the semester system and offers two summer sessions. It grants Bachelor and Master degrees. Air Force ROTC is available. Enrollment includes 768 full-time and 345 part-time undergraduates and 254 full-time and 516 part-time graduate students. A faculty of 168 gives a faculty-student ratio of 1-10, which allows for individual attention and personal direction.

Entrance Requirements: High school diploma or equivalent; completion of 13 high school units including 4 English, 2 mathematics, 2 foreign language, 1 science and 2 social science; SAT or ACT; transfer students must have attained a C average in all college courses undertaken; midyear admission, rolling admission, and advanced placement plans available; $35 application fee.

Costs Per Year: $13,500 tuition; $6,100 room and board.

Collegiate Environment: Located in Belmont, a residential suburb, the campus has 19 buildings on 80 acres. There are modern classrooms, efficient laboratories, a library containing 100,000 titles, a well-equipped dining hall, tennis courts, and a swimming pool. Dormitories and student apartments accommodate 328 men and women. 70% of the applicants are accepted. The middle 50% range of entering freshmen scores was SAT 760-1000 combined, ACT 17-26 composite. 85 scholarships are available, including 62 for freshmen. 67% of the students receive some form of financial aid.

Community Environment: Population 27,000. This city is located 25 miles south of San Francisco, and has the advantages of a suburban location. The climate is ideal. The average high is 69.5 degrees, and the low is 47 degrees; the average rainfall is 19.8. Belmont is on the main line of Southern Pacific Railroad. San Francisco International Airport is 12 miles away. Students attending Notre Dame are close enough to San Francisco to enjoy all the cultural and recreational benefits such as major drama, music and opera productions, the theater, rock group performances and professional and collegiate sports. The beaches of the Pacific Ocean are 12 miles away. Two hours to the north is the wine country, and a few hours' drive east are the historic gold country, Lake Tahoe, and the Sierra Nevada Range with famous facilities for skiing and other winter sports.

COLLEGE OF SAN MATEO *(A-10)*
1700 West Hillsdale Boulevard
San Mateo, California 94402
Tel: (415) 574-6161

Description: The publicly supported, coeducational junior college is accredited by the Western Association of Schools and Colleges. This is one of three colleges within the San Mateo Junior College District which was established in 1922. The enrollment was 1,300. The semester system is used and one summer session is offered. There is a cooperative education program which allows either part time work and part time classes, or 6 months full time work, 6 months full time classes. Programs lead to the Associate degree.

Entrance Requirements: High school graduation; non-graduate 18 years or age or over admitted.

Costs Per Year: $10 per unit, $113 per unit for non-California residents.

Collegiate Environment: The beautiful $20,000,000 campus overlooking the city has 28 buildings on 153 acres. The library contains over 80,000 volumes, 850 periodicals and 2,500 microfilms. All students applying for admission are accepted.

Community Environment: San Mateo, located on picturesque El Camino Real, is an attractive residential suburb, 19 miles south of San Francisco. Climate is moderate and the city claims to have an average of 258 days of sunshine each year. San Mateo has access to all major forms of transportation and has a municipal transit system. There are many churches, hospitals, and libraries. An outstanding retail shopping center is found on the Peninsula. Recreational facilities include golf courses, yacht harbor, public beach, public parks and the Bay Meadows Race Track.

COLLEGE OF THE CANYONS *(O-8)*
26455 North Rockwell Canyon Road
Valencia, California 91355
Tel: (805) 259-7800

Description: This publicly supported, coeducational community college held its first classes in September 1969. The college is accredited by the Western Association of Schools and Colleges and offers university-parallel programs and occupational and general educational courses. The early semester system is used and one summer session is offered. The college grants the Certificate and the Associate degree. Enrollment includes 1,799 full-time and 4,305 part-time students. A faculty of 65 full-time and 163 part-time gives a faculty-student ratio of 1-30.

Entrance Requirements: High school graduates, or non-graduates over 18 years of age; residents of Santa Clarita District; placement examinations required; advanced placement, early admission and rolling admission plans are available.

Costs Per Year: $403 ($13/credit) resident; $1,550 ($50/credit) resident with BA or higher degree; $3,162 ($102/credit) nonresident.

Collegiate Environment: The college is housed in the rolling hills of Valencia. There are many new buildings on campus, including a Child Development Center Laboratory, an Instructional Resource Center and a student center/humanities building. The library contains 42,685 volumes, 6,794 pamphlets, 232 periodicals, 56,892 microforms, and 2,322 audiovisual materials. All students applying for admission are accepted including students at midyear, and 50% return for the sophomore year. Many scholarships are available and 15% of students receive some form of financial aid.

Community Environment: The Valencia-Newhall-Saugus Canyon Country communities comprise an unincorporated area 32 miles northwest of Los Angeles near the San Fernando Valley. The average mean temperature is 65 degrees. Community facilities include hospitals, churches, a library, newspapers and banks. Recreational facilities include theaters, parks, a riding stable and golf courses. Desert area and many secluded canyons are nearby. The Castaic Reservoir water recreation area opened in 1970.

COLLEGE OF THE DESERT   *(P-11)*
43500 Monterey Ave.
Palm Desert, California 92260
Tel: (619) 346-8041

Description: Publicly-supported, coeducational junior college accredited by the Western Association of Schools and Colleges. Recent enrollment included 11,029 students with a faculty of 373. The semester system is used. The college's first students were received in the fall of 1962. The college grants a Certificate and the Associate degree. Programs are college parallel, occupational training, and general education.

Entrance Requirements: Open enrollment policy; high school graduation; non-high school graduates over 18; advanced placement plan available.

Costs Per Year: $10 per unit for residents; $102 per unit for non-California residents.

Collegiate Environment: Twenty buildings on 160 acres comprise the campus. One hundred percent of students applying for admission are accepted. Financial aid is available for economically handicapped students. The library contains over 48,000 volumes. Special programs are offered for the culturally disadvantaged.

Community Environment: Palm Desert is a resort area with a population of 12,000, where the climate is temperate. Buses and planes serve the area; Highway 111 goes through town. There are churches of major denominations, civic and service groups, and hospitals are nearby. Indio and Palm Springs have such recreational activities as boating, fishing, water skiing, and hiking. There are nearby mountains for winter sports. The area is a major center for golf and tennis tournaments.

Branch Campuses: Cooper Mountain Campus, P.O. Box 1398, 6162 Rotary Way, Joshua Tree, CA 92252, (619) 365-0614.

COLLEGE OF THE REDWOODS   *(C-1)*
Tompkins Hill Road
Eureka, California 95501-9302
Tel: (707) 445-6717

Description: The publicly-supported, coeducational community college is accredited by the Western Association of Schools and Colleges and operates on the semester system with one summer session.

Founded in 1964, the college moved to its permanent campus in 1967. The college enrolls 7,033 students. A faculty of 412 gives a student-faculty ratio of 17-1. The college grants Certificates and Associate of Arts and Science degrees.

Entrance Requirements: Residence in the Redwoods Community College District or in an area which does not maintain a junior college or if in another junior college district, permission from that district; ACT recommended; early admission, rolling admission and advanced placement plans available; open enrollment policy.

Costs Per Year: California residents $13 per unit to a maximum of $50; nonresidents $121 additional per unit; $3,684-$3,897 room and board.

Collegiate Environment: The Main Campus in Eureka of gently sloping lands eight miles south of the Humboldt County Courthouse and 10 miles north of Fortuna, rising to the northeast of Highway 101. Dormitories and a student center were completed in 1968 with a capacity for 80 men and 80 women. Approximately 90% of the applicants are accepted. Financial aid is available to all economically handicapped students.

Community Environment: Eureka is located on the north coast of Humboldt Bay, 283 miles north of San Francisco; the climate is cool and humid. Buses and railroads serve the area, airlines to connecting flights in San Francisco, Oakland, Sacramento and Portland are available. Community facilities include two hospitals, a medical center, churches, libraries, and a good downtown shopping area. The city provides a park, a community recreation building and a 18 hole golf course. Fishing and hunting are excellent; mountain area very near. In Summer, salmon fishing is good in Humboldt and Trinidad Bay north of the city; in early fall, steelhead and salmon are caught in the Eel Mud, and Trinity Rivers nearby. Eureka sponsors an annual Rhododendron Festival and two fairs each year.

Branch Campuses: There are also 2 Education Centers, one located in Del Norte county, north of the Main Campus and the other at Ft. Bragg, over 120 miles south of the main campus.

COLLEGE OF THE SEQUOIAS   *(K-7)*
915 South Mooney Boulevard
Visalia, California 93291
Tel: (209) 730-3700; Fax: (209) 730-3894

Description: This publicly supported, coeducational junior college is accredited by the Western Association of Schools and Colleges. It offered the first post-high school instruction to students of this area in 1925. In 1940, the college moved to its 55-acre campus where new buildings had been completed. It offers programs that lead to the Certificate and Associate degree. The college operates on the semester system and offers one summer session. Enrollment includes 3,719 full-time and 5,780 part-time students. A faculty of 162 full-time and 317 part-time gives an overall faculty-student ratio of 1-26.

Entrance Requirements: High school graduation; non-high school graduates over 18 years of age considered; rolling admission and mid-year admission.

Costs Per Year: $403 ($13/unit) resident; $1,550 ($50/unit) resident with BA degree; $3,937 ($127/unit) nonresident; $25 student fees.

Collegiate Environment: There are no dormitories on the campus. The 30 buildings are modern and well equipped. The library contains 70,000 titles, 5,000 periodicals, and 6,000 microforms. 99% of all applicants are accepted. 484 scholarships are available and 15% of students receive some form of financial aid.

Community Environment: Visalia is 42 miles southeast of Fresno. It is the Tulare County seat and is situated in the fertile San Joaquin Valley. Visalia ranks highest in the world in agricultural production of citrus fruits, dairy products, olives, cotton and walnuts. Buses, planes and railroads serve the area. A number of manufacturers and industrial plants are located here as well as churches, hospitals, and more. Tulare County Park provides recreational facilities for picnicking, water sports, and the High Sierra mountain wonderland in the Sierra National Forest. Also located here are a symphony orchestra, ballet and theater groups. There are 20 city parks, 5 golf courses, 8 theaters and 2 hospitals.

Branch Campuses: There are 9 off-campus locations within the district. The COS farm provides each agriculture student with hands-on education in a wide range of skills. The laboratory consists of a 70-cow registered Holstein herd that is one of the top herds in the area of milk production. A complete horticultural facility and related work sites allow students to learn practical, current landscape techniques. A 120-acre laboratory provides students with worksites in the areas of animal science, horse production, dairy, ornamental horticulture, floriculture, turf culture, crop production, vegetable gardening and soils.

COLLEGE OF THE SISKIYOUS   *(B-3)*
800 College Avenue
Weed, California 96094
Tel: (916) 938-4461; Admissions: (916) 938-5215; Fax: (916) 938-5367

Description: The publicly supported, coeducational community college is accredited by the Western Association of Schools and Colleges. The program for the education for adults was initiated in 1957 when the Siskiyous Joint Junior College District was formed. The new facilities on the present campus were initiated in 1959. The college grants the Associate degree. It operates on the semester system and offers one summer session. Enrollment includes 779 full-time and 2,082 part-time students. A faculty of 54 full-time and 75 part-time gives an overall faculty-student ratio of 1-25.

Entrance Requirements: High school graduation or over age 18; early decision, rolling admission, midyear admission and advanced placement plans available.

Costs Per Year: $450 ($15/unit) resident tuition; $1,500 ($50/unit) resident with B.A. degree or higher; $3,420 ($114/unit) nonresident; $3,910 room and board.

Collegiate Environment: The highly supportive, personalized learning environment is enhanced by the presence of two modern, well-equipped residence halls that accommodate 146 students. In addition, off-campus housing is available in the nearby community. The tree-studded campus has a magnificent view of Mt. Shasta. The library contains 37,800 volumes, 3,509 pamphlets, 250 periodicals, 10,000 microforms and 10,478 audiovisual materials. 99% of students applying for admission are accepted, and 45% return for the sophomore year.

Community Environment: Centrally located in Siskiyou County, just off Interstate 5, the historic lumber town of Weed lies nestled at the base of majestic 14,162-foot Mt. Shasta. At the mid-point between two major population centers - Medford, Oregon, to the north and Redding to the south - Weed is easily accessible by airline, train and bus services. The climate features four distinct seasons with an average snowfall of 24 inches. Outdoor enthusiasts will delight in the spectacular alpine environment of this rural northern California region, which provides for a wide variety of recreational activities including downhill and cross-country skiing, hunting, fishing, hiking, rock climbing, wind surfing, and more.

Branch Campuses: In response to the needs of Northern Siskiyou County residents, COS opened a branch campus in Yreka in the spring of 1990. Yreka is located approximately 30 miles north of the main campus.

COLUMBIA COLLEGE   *(H-6)*
11600 Columbia College Drive
Sonora, California 95370
Tel: (209) 533-5100; Admissions: (209) 533-5231; Fax: (209) 533-5104

Description: The state-supported, coeducational community college is accredited by the Western Association of Schools and Colleges. The Yosemite Community College District Board of Trustees authorized the formation of Columbia College and scheduled its opening for September 1968. Enrollment includes 651 full-time and 1,638 part-time students. A faculty of 40 full-time and 50 part-time gives a faculty-student ratio of 1-24. The semester system is used and one summer session is offered. The school grants the Associate degree, and provides occupational, general educational, and university-parallel programs.

Entrance Requirements: Graduates of accredited high schools or persons 18 years of age or older are eligible for admission; rolling admission, midyear admission, early admission and early decision plans available.

Costs Per Year: $390 ($13 per credit) resident; $1,550 ($50 per credit) resident with BA degree; $3,930 ($131 per credit) nonresident; $2,000 room.

Collegiate Environment: The college is located on 244 acres of forest land adjacent to Columbia State Historic Park in Tuolumne County. Fourteen campus buildings are situated around San Diego Reservoir, from which wooded foothills join the rugged majesty of the Sierra Nevada. The library currently holds 31,989 volumes, 6,508 pamphlets, 305 periodicals, 190 microforms and 4500 recordings. All students applying for admission are accepted. 81 scholarships are available, including 47 for freshmen. 31% of the current student body receives financial assistance. On-campus student apartments for 200 are available.

Community Environment: Columbia is located in the foothills of the Sierra Nevadas, and was once one of the largest and most important mining areas ever found. Columbia State Historic Park is located in the downtown area.

COLUMBIA COLLEGE - HOLLYWOOD   *(O-8)*
925 North La Brea Avenue
Los Angeles, California 90038
Tel: (213) 851-0550; Fax: (213) 851-6401

Description: This privately-supported, coeducational college offers a four-year program of professional courses in television and motion picture arts and sciences. Courses are designed to afford a realistic and practical education in television and motion picture production. The college grants the Associate and Bachelor degrees. It operates on the quarter system and offers one summer session. All classes are held in the evening. Enrollment includes 200 men and women full-time and part-time. A part time faculty of 41 gives a faculty-student ratio of 1-25.

Entrance Requirements: Open enrollment policy; rolling admission and admission plans available; $100 registration fee if applicant receives acceptance.

Costs Per Year: $5,520 tuition; $250 student fees.

Collegiate Environment: The campus has one building of 25,000 sq. feet which houses a complete color television studio and fully equipped motion picture sound stage. Campus facilities include editing rooms, videotape editing facilities, study hall and bookstore, make-up room, sound mixing room, projection theatre, and all other professional facilities required of the television or film major. The library holdings include 800 volumes.

Community Environment: The college is located close to freeways, public transportation, housing, and major recreational areas in Southern California.

COMPTON COMMUNITY COLLEGE   *(P-9)*
1111 East Artesia Boulevard
Compton, California 90221
Tel: (213) 637-2660; Fax: (310) 639-8260

Description: The publicly-supported, coeducational community college was founded in 1927 and is accredited by the Western Association of Schools and Colleges. It operates on the semester system offering day and evening classes. Enrollment includes 5,400 students. A faculty of 170 gives a faculty-student ratio of 1:24. The college grants A.A., A.S. Degrees, and Certificate of Achievement and provides university-parallel and general education programs.

Entrance Requirements: High school graduation or over 18 years of age. Early admission early decision plans available; students admitted at mid-year.

Costs Per Year: $390 ($13/cr) resident; $1,550 ($50/cr) resident with B.A. degree; $3,390 ($113/cr) nonresident.

Collegiate Environment: The 83-acre campus was first occupied in 1953 and serves the communities of Compton, Enterprise, Lynwood, Paramount and Willowbrook. Ninety-eight percent of students applying for admission are accepted. The college library contains more than 40,000 volumes. No dormitories or on campus housing available. Approximately 5% of the student body graduated in top 10% of high school class; 45% of the freshman class returned to this campus for the sophomore year.

Community Environment: Located between the cities of Los Angeles and Long Beach in the center of a large residential area. The population of the general area surrounding the city is now about 200,000, and is increasing each year. The city offers a mild climate and many days of sun. Mountains and the beaches are both nearby which provide a wealth of recreational activities. Work for room and board in private homes may be secured, part-time employment is also available.

CONTRA COSTA COLLEGE   *(H-2)*
2600 Mission Bell Drive
San Pablo, California 94806
Tel: (510) 235-7800; Admissions: (510) 235-7800 x210; Fax: (510) 236-6768

Description: The publicly supported, coeducational junior college was founded in 1948 and is accredited by Western Association of Schools and Colleges. Students may attend day or evening classes. The college offers university-parallel and vocational programs and awards the Certificate and Associate degrees. It operates on the semester system and offers one summer session. Enrollment includes 1,894 full-time, 6,299 part-time and 2,174 evening students. There are 117 full-time and 105 part-time faculty members.

Entrance Requirements: High school graduation; non-graduates over 18 years of age admitted if residents of district; rolling admission, advanced placement plans available.

Costs Per Year: $390 ($13/unit) resident; $1,368 ($45.60/unit) nonresident; $3,990 ($133/unit: $13 enrollment fee & $114 tuition fee & $6 facilities use) foreign students; $114 student fee.

Collegiate Environment: The college is located on eighty acres in the cities of San Pablo and Richmond and serves one of the largest college districts in California. All students applying for admission are accepted. The library houses 60,000 volumes. There are 17 buildings on the campus. 8% of students receive financial aid.

Community Environment: San Pablo is located on San Francisco Bay north of Richmond and Oakland on Highway 40. Buses and railroads serve the area. The city has 70 major industries; skilled and unskilled labor opportunities are available. San Pablo community facilities include churches, library and hospitals. Recreational facilities are provided by the beaches nearby and the mountain resort area for winter sports, which are approximately a three hour drive.

COSUMNES RIVER COLLEGE   *(G-4)*
8401 Center Parkway
Sacramento, California 95823-5799
Tel: (916) 688-7410; Admissions: (916) 688-7410; Fax: (916) 688-7467

Description: This coeducational community college was founded in 1970 and has a projected on campus capacity for 12,000 students. Enrollment is 8,361 with a faculty of 137 full-time and 257 part-time members. Students may attend day or evening class on the semester system and one summer session is offered. The college is accredited by the Western Association of Schools and Colleges and grants the Certificate and the Associate degree. In additional to main campus the college supports services and instruction at the Folsom Lake and the El Dorado Centers. Combined enrollment for all three sites is 12,220 and a full-time faculty of 137.

Entrance Requirements: High school graduates or those over 18 years of age. Rolling admission, delayed admission and advanced placement plans available.

Costs Per Year: $390 for residents with less than B.A.; $4,140 for nonresidents; $4,410 for international students.

Collegiate Environment: New buildings, still being constructed, attempt to recall earth forms and vegetation structures natural to Sacramento Valley. The library which is the major structure on campus sets the general architectural style and tone for other buildings. Currently two new buildings are under construction: the Fine Arts Complex and the Spectator Gymnasium. The library presently contains 50,000 volumes. All students applying for admission are accepted.

Community Environment: See California State University - Sacramento.

CRAFTON HILLS COLLEGE   *(O-10)*
11711 Sand Canyon Road
Yucaipa, California 92399
Tel: (909) 794-2161; Fax: (909) 794-0423

Description: The publicly supported, co-educational community college opened with its first class in 1972. The school is accredited by the Western Association of Schools and Colleges. Students may attend day or evening classes on a semester system calendar. One summer session is offered in day college and one in evening college. It grants Certificates in some occupational fields and an Associate degree. Recent enrollment includes 2,299 men and 2,925 women with a faculty of 52 full-time and 90 part-time.

Entrance Requirements: Open enrollment policy; high school graduation or 18 years of age or older. Midyear admission, rolling admission, advanced placement plans available.

Costs Per Year: $403 ($10/credit) resident tuition; $1,550 ($50/credit) resident with BA degree; $3,317 ($107/credit) nonresident.

Collegiate Environment: The 518 acre campus is located in a softly rolling hill area and along with San Bernardino Valley College serves the San Bernardino community college district. The library contains 54,000 volumes. Financial aid is available, and 10% of the current student body receives some form of assistance. 99% of the applicants are accepted including midyear students.

Community Environment: See California State University - San Bernardino

CUESTA COLLEGE   *(M-5)*
P.O. Box 8106
San Luis Obispo, California 93403-8106
Tel: (805) 546-3140; Fax: (805) 546-3904

Description: This publicly supported coeducational community college had a recent enrollment of 7,966 students. A faculty of 194 gives a faculty-student ratio of 1-33. Objectives are to provide university-parallel programs, occupational training, general education. The college operates on the semester system and offers one summer session. It is accredited by the Western Association of Colleges and Schools and grants the Certificate and Associate degree.

Entrance Requirements: High school graduates or over 18 years of age; early admission, early decision, rolling admission, and advanced placement plans available.

Costs Per Year: $130 state-resident tuition; $2,850 nonresidents; $15 student fees.

Collegiate Environment: The campus has 26 buildings on 160 acres, including a library of 44,073 volumes. All students applying for admission are accepted. Financial aid is available.

Community Environment: See California Polytechnic State University - San Luis Obispo.

CYPRESS COLLEGE   *(H-11)*
9200 Valley View
Cypress, California 90630
Tel: (714) 826-2220; Fax: (714) 527-8238

Description: This publicly supported, coeducational junior college is accredited by the Western Association of Schools and Colleges. The college received national attention as the "Instant Campus" because 19 temporary, relocateable, modular buildings were erected in 74 days in the summer of 1966. Students may attend day or evening classes. The college operates on the semester system and offers one summer session. It grants the Associate degree. Enrollment includes 4,546 full-time and 8,719 part-time students. A faculty of 250 full-time and 300 part-time gives a faculty-student ratio of 1-29.

Entrance Requirements: Open door policy; graduation from high school or equivalent; nongraduates over 18 years may be admitted on basis of ability to benefit; out-of-state applicants must be high school graduates and supply evidence of abilities; ACT or SAT accepted but not required; rolling admissions, midyear admission plans available.

Costs Per Year: $390 ($13/unit) resident; $1,500 ($50/unit) resident with B.A. degree or higher; $3,420 ($114/unit) nonresident.

Collegiate Environment: Located on 107 acres in Orange County, the college is near a variety of recreational and resort facilities. Nineteen buildings comprise the campus, and the library houses over 100,000 volumes. Special programs are offered for the culturally disadvantaged that enable low-mark disadvantaged students to attend. All students applying for admission are accepted, including students at midyear.

Community Environment: Cypress is a rapidly growing suburban city, 20 miles east of Los Angeles. The climate is dry and mild. Buses, trains, freeway system and the Los Angeles International Airport 20 miles away all serve the area. The city has three private hospitals, twelve churches, a library, and an amphitheater. There are city parks, a golf course, swimming pool and a gymnasium for those interested in sports. Anaheim Stadium is seven miles away, Disneyland five and one-half miles, Knotts Berry Farm and Movieland Wax Museum two and one-half miles. Beaches and mountain areas provide additional recreational facilities and are within easy driving distance. Many universities and colleges are nearby.

DE ANZA COLLEGE   *(E-11)*
21250 Stevens Creek Boulevard
Cupertino, California 95014
Tel: (408) 996-4419

Description: Publicly supported, coeducational community college primarily serving Cupertino and Sunnyvale in the Foothill College District. Enrollment is approximately 24,000 men and women attending day and evening classes. A faculty of 800 gives a faculty-student ratio of 1:30. The quarter system is used. The college is accredited by the Western Association of Colleges and Schools and grants the Certificate and the Associate Degree. U.S. Army and Air Force R.O.T.C. unit at nearby Santa Clara University available for De Anza students.

Entrance Requirements: High school graduation or over 18 years of age and not disqualified from another college; ACT or SAT accepted but not required; application fee $18.

Costs Per Year: $585 tuition for California residents; $3,375 nonresident tuition; $40 student fees.

Collegiate Environment: Unique features of the campus include the 80,000-volume library, olympic aquatic complex, an advanced technology center with student labs housing more than 400 work stations, and a planetarium (all buildings air-conditioned). No dormitories. All students applying for admission are accepted.

Community Environment: Population of the district 174,000; within an hour's drive from the San Francisco Bay area. Buses and trains serve the area, the San Jose Municipal Airport is nearby for air transportation. There are parks, playgrounds and nearby beaches for recreational activities; plus other cultural advantages of the San Francisco Bay Area.

DEEP SPRINGS COLLEGE   *(J-9)*
mail via HC72 Box 45001
Dyer, NV 89010-9803
Deep Springs, California
Tel: (619) 872-2000

Description: This liberal arts college for men is supported by a trust fund established by Mr. L. L. Nunn in 1917. The students participate directly in governing the school and in the physical maintenance of the campus and facilities. Deep Springs owns and operates a large ranch and alfalfa farm; students are required to work on the ranch approximately 4 hours per day. They are also responsible for operations of the dairy, library, post office and other college and ranch facilities. The student body is limited to 26. A faculty of 6 full-time and 5 part-time gives a faculty-student ratio of 1-3. The college is accredited by the Western Association of Schools and Colleges and offers the Associate of Arts degree. The trimester system is used. Students normally transfer as juniors after 2 or 3 years to schools such as Harvard, Yale, Berkeley, and Cornell.

Entrance Requirements: High school graduation with rank usually in upper 10% of the graduating class; non-high school graduates considered under certain circumstances; SAT required.

Costs Per Year: All students receive scholarships covering all costs; estimated value of annual scholarship is $29,000.

Collegiate Environment: All campus buildings (19) are situated in Deep Springs Valley, a semi-arid region east of the Sierra Nevada. The library contains over 22,000 volumes. The student body prohibits social ties outside the community; rarely do students leave the valley. Excellent academic records are maintained by all students. Relations between teachers and students are close and informal. Dormitory facilities accommodate 25 men. Average scores of the class are SAT 720V, 690M. Approximately 25% of those who apply are accepted.

Community Environment: Population 50. Deep Springs is located in a small valley equidistant from Reno and Los Angeles, east of the main crest of the Sierra Nevada in California and just a few miles from the Nevada border. The nearest town is Big Pine, 28 miles from the school. The climate is semi-arid, typical of the desert - clear, dry, and invigorating with as much daily variation as 30 degrees. The extremes in temperature are not noticeable because of the dryness of the area.

DEVRY INSTITUTE OF TECHNOLOGY   *(O-8)*
901 Corporate Center
Pomona, California 91768-2642
Tel: (909) 622-8866; (800) 243-3660; Admissions: (909) 622-9800; Fax: (909) 623-5666

Description: The Los Angeles campus of this proprietary, coeducational school was established in 1983 and is accredited by the North Central Association of Colleges and Schools. Programs are developed and updated regularly with direct input from business and industry leaders. It operates on the semester system, has one summer session, and grants associate and bachelor degrees. Enrollment includes 1,872 men and 517 women full-time, and 353 men and 102 women part-time. A faculty of 46 full-time and 94 part-time gives a faculty-student ratio of 1-24.

Entrance Requirements: High school diploma or GED certification; minimum of 17 years of age; must pass DeVry entrance examination or submit acceptable ACT/SAT/WPCT scores; accepts foreign students if requirements are met. Rolling admission, advanced placement. $25 application fee.

Costs Per Year: $6,335 tuition.

Collegiate Environment: The school is housed in a building of 87,000 square feet standing on 11.8 acres. Classrooms and laboratories are large and two skylighted atria welcome students and visitors. The location provides direct access to the Southern California freeway system and is conveniently located near a wide variety of shopping, recreational, and health care facilities. The library houses 14,353 bound volumes, 181 periodicals, and 55 mircofilms. Clubs and intramural sports are available. 91% of applicants are accepted. Scholarships are available and 81% of the students receive some form of financial assistance.

Community Environment: As the nation's second largest city, the greater Los Angeles area continues to flourish on the forefront of commerce, entertainment, recreation, communications, education, and the arts. Its spectacular Pacific beaches range from isolated inlets to 10-mile stretches. Nearby mountains, lakes, and rivers offer opportunities for skiing, hiking, and camping. Professional sports teams include the Rams, Raiders, Dodgers, Angels, Kings, and Lakers. Movies, plays, comedy acts, and musicals abound. Some of the country's finest art collections are housed in L.A.'s J. Paul Getty, Norton Simon, and the L.A. County Museums.

DIABLO VALLEY COLLEGE   *(A-11)*
Pleasant Hill, California 94523
Tel: (510) 685-1230

Description: This publicly supported, coeducational community college is accredited by Western Association of Colleges and Schools. Enrollment includes 23,196 students. A faculty of 546 gives a faculty-student ratio of 1-42. This is one of three institutions operated by the Contra Costa community college district, and was established in 1948. The college grants the Certificate and Associate degrees and offers university-parallel, general and vocational education programs. It operates on the early semester system and offers one summer session.

Entrance Requirements: High school graduation or 18 years of age; non-high school graduates considered.

Costs Per Year: $3,600 nonresident tuition, no tuition for California residents.

Collegiate Environment: The campus includes 25 buildings on 100 acres of gently rolling hills near Mt. Diablo, a famous northern California landmark. The library contains 72,000 volumes. All students applying for admission are accepted and 30% receive financial aid.

Community Environment: Population 31,000. Pleasant Hill is a suburban residential community that has an average winter temperature of 46.4 degrees and summer temperature of 71.8 degrees. It is located 22 miles from San Francisco. All transportation facilities are available nearby. Churches representing 14 denominations, a hospital and excellent shopping facilities comprise the town. Employment opportunities are available. Pleasant Hill enjoys the cultural atmosphere of the San Francisco Bay Area. A nearby beach area provides recreational facilities; the mountain area for winter sports is accessible for a weekend trip.

DOMINICAN COLLEGE OF SAN RAFAEL   *(H-2)*
50 Acacia Avenue
San Rafael, California 94901-8008
Tel: (415) 485-3204; (800) 788-3522; Fax: (415) 485-3214

Description: The privately supported, coeducational Roman Catholic liberal arts college is independently owned and operated by a board of trustees. The college is accredited by the Western Association of Schools and Colleges and grants the Bachelor's and Master's degree. Founded in 1890, the first Bachelor's degree was granted in 1917, and the first Master's degree was granted in 1951. The college operates on the semester system and offers one summer session. The college also operates its facilities as a conference center during the summer. Enrollment includes 551 full-time and 124 part-time traditional undergraduate and 313 graduate students. In addition, there are 261 evening students. A faculty of 45 full-time and 109 part-time gives a traditional undergraduate faculty-student ratio of 1-14.

Entrance Requirements: High school graduation or equivalent with completion of 15 units, including 4 English, 2 mathematics, 2 foreign language, 1 science, and 1 social science; non-high school graduates considerd; SAT or ACT required; GRE required for graduate level; early admission, early decision, rolling admission, delayed admission and advanced placement plans available; March 2 priority application deadline; $35 application fee.

Costs Per Year: $13,620 tuition; $6,090 room and board; $270 student fees; additional expenses average $2,700 for books, supplies, etc.

Collegiate Environment: The campus consists of 20 buildings on 80 acres surrounded by the hills which rim Magnolia Valley. There is seclusion for those who wish it or a half hour away there is the city of San Francisco and the Berkeley campus of the University of California. There are more than 91,000 volumes in the library. Dormitory space is provided for 250 students. Approximately 80% of the students applying for admission are accepted and 80% of the freshmen return for the sophomore year. Financial aid is available and 73% of the student body receives some form of financial assistance.

Community Environment: Located in the hills of Marin County 25 minutes from San Francisco across the Golden Gate Bridge, Dominican is close enough to permit easy access to the city's diverse cultural attractions - the opera, symphony, theaters and playhouses. The campus adjoins San Rafael (pop. 51,000), which boasts a climate rated as one of the six most ideal in the world, in addition to a wide variety of libraries, museums and churches. The nearby cities of Mill Valley, Bolinas, and Sausalito harbour a large community of writers, painters and other artists, and a diverse collection of shops, restaurants and galleries. Five state parks and beaches lie within easy reach, including Muir Woods, the Golden Gate National Recreational Area, and the Point Reyes National Seashore.

DOMINICAN SCHOOL OF PHILOSOPHY AND THEOLOGY
(I-3)
2401 Ridge Road
Berkeley, California 94709
Tel: (510) 849-2030; Fax: (510) 849-1372

Description: The privately supported, coeducational theological seminary (Roman Catholic) was established for candidates for the priesthood in the Dominican Order, and now welcomes lay students in all its degree programs. The college grants Bachelor and Master degrees in Philosophy and Master degrees in Theology and Divinity. Dominican School is a member institution of the Graduate Theological Union (GTU). Some of the graduate degrees are granted jointly by the school and GTU. Enrollment includes 69 full-time and 17 part-time students. A faculty of 10 full-time and 23 part-time provides a faculty-student ratio of 1-4.

Entrance Requirements: Applicants for the Bachelor's program must have completed two years of college and be in upper-division standing; 2.5 GPA is required; applicants to Master's programs in Philosophy or Theology must have Bachelor's degree and maintained an undergraduate 3.0 GPA (B average); GRE required; applicants for the Master in Divinity program must have a Bachelor or equivalent and an undergraduate GPA of 2.5; GRE not required for this program; $30 application fee.

Costs Per Year: $6,000 undergraduate and graduate tuition; $30 student fees.

Collegiate Environment: Located at the Graduate Theological Union in Berkeley, California, the Dominican School is one of nine separate schools that have formed an ecumenical and interreligious consortium. Cross-registration among the different schools in the consortium and the University of California, Berkeley, allows for maximum use of faculty and curriculum offerings for theology students.

Community Environment: Berkeley campus, see UC Berkeley; Oakland campus, see Laney College.

EL CAMINO COLLEGE   *(H-10)*
16007 Crenshaw Boulevard
Torrance, California 90506
Tel: (310) 715-3111

Description: Publicly supported coeducational community college accredited by the Western Association of Schools and Colleges. The semester system is used with one summer session. Founded in 1946, the college takes its name from the old King's Highway or El Camino Real, as it was known in the early Spanish days. The college offers programs in general education, occupational education, and university-parallel courses and grants the Associate degree. Recent enrollment included 2,699 men, 3194 women full-time, 8,445 men and 9,994 women part-time students. The faculty consists of 319 full-time and 424 part-time members.

Entrance Requirements: High school graduation; non-high school graduates over 18 years and able to profit from instruction.

Costs Per Year: $135 California resident tuition; $3,750 nonresident tuition; $7.50 student fee.

Collegiate Environment: The college is located in southwest Los Angeles County between the Redondo Beach and Manhattan Beach Boulevards. The college now occupies a 126-acre campus with 22 modern brick and concrete buildings. The library contains 94,000 volumes. Financial aid is available for economically handicapped students.

Community Environment: Torrance, situated in southwest Los Angeles County, is a suburb of Los Angeles and does enjoy the advantages of the city's cultural and recreational facilities. All forms of commercial transportation are convenient. Outstanding shopping centers are in the city as well as all the other usual community facilities. Climate is normally sunny and mild. Beaches and mountains are within easy driving distance for recreation.

EVERGREEN VALLEY COLLEGE   *(I-3)*
3095 Yerba Buena Road
San Jose, California 95135
Tel: (408) 274-7900

Description: One of two colleges that comprise the San Jose/Evergreen Community College District, the college was established in 1975. It provides a flexible, varied educational environment of traditional and nontraditional learning modes. Built by the community, the college's design combines a philosophical, organizational and physical environment supportive of optimum individual development. The college is fully accredited by the Western Association of Schools and Colleges. It operates on the early semester system and offers one summer session. Enrollment includes 1,813 full-time students and 7,986 part-time students. A faculty of 140 full-time and 158 part-time members gives a faculty-student ratio of 1-33.

Entrance Requirements: Open enrollment; high school graduation is not required; entrance exam required. Rolling admission, early admission, early decision plans are available.

Costs Per Year: $13 per unit and $6 mandatory fee per unit for state residents; $136 per unit nonresident tuition; $221 student fees.

Collegiate Environment: The college is organized into mini-colleges called clusters. Each cluster is divided into educational centers. General support facilities, such as the library and audiovisual aids center, service all clusters, while lounge areas, study spaces and food services are conveniently situated in each cluster. The library houses 42,782 titles, 368 periodicals, 115 microforms and 5,652 audiovisual materials. All students applying for admission are accepted. Approximately 14% of the current student body receives some form of financial assistance.

Community Environment: See San Jose State University.

FEATHER RIVER COLLEGE   *(E-5)*
Post Office Box 11110
Quincy, California 95971
Tel: (916) 283-0202; (800) 442-9799; Admissions: (916) 283-0202 X 276; Fax: (916) 283-3757

Description: Publicly supported, coeducational community college is now its own Community College District. The college has been granted accreditation by the Western Association of Schools and Colleges. The college offers general education, vocational-career education, university-parallel programs and grants the Associate degree. It operates on the semester system and offers one summer session. Enrollment includes 400 full-time and 800 part-time students. A faculty of 25 full-time and 70 part-time gives a faculty-student ratio of 1-25.

Entrance Requirements: High school graduation; non-high school graduates over 18 years of age considered; early admission, early decision, midyear admission, advanced placement and rolling admission plans available.

Costs Per Year: $360 resident tuition; $3,360 per unit nonresidents.

Collegiate Environment: As a rural college, Feather River strives to develop and offer programs and services responsive to needs of the diverse geographical area served by it; surrounded by hills and pine trees, it is rural in setting as in service. One mile north of the town of Quincy, it is just west of State Highway 70. Still erecting its buildings and facilities, the new library presently contains 16,000 volumes. Specialty programs include natural resources (forestry), wildlife and fish hatchery management, horse management and recreation leadership.

Community Environment: Quincy is located in the Feather River vacation area and is the center of the California pine industry with headquarters of Plumas National Forest. Quincy is the county seat. The area is known for excellent hunting and fishing and winter sports.

FOOTHILL COLLEGE   *(D-11)*
12345 El Monte Road
Los Altos Hills, California 94022-4599
Tel: (415) 949-7777; Admissions: (415) 949-7325; Fax: (415) 949-7375

Description: The publicly supported, coeducational community college is accredited by the Western Association of Schools and Colleges. The quarter system is used and one summer session is offered. This college serves northern Santa Clara County and was formed in 1957. Recent enrollment included approximately 15,000 full-time and part-time students. The faculty consists of 197 full-time and 350 part-time members. Foothill grants the Certificate and the Associate degree. The college emphasizes transfer to California Universities and career programs in Electronics, the Health Sciences and Business. Programs in creative writing, drama, music, literature, math, science, and pre-law are especially strong.

Entrance Requirements: Open enrollment; residence in the state of California; high school graduation or equivalent; non-high school graduates considered; advanced placement, early admission and midyear admission plans available.

Costs Per Year: $390 ($13/cr) resident; $1,550 ($50/unit) resident with B.A. degree; $3,390 ($113/unit) nonresident tuition; $66 student fees.

Collegiate Environment: The 121-acre campus is located in the Los Altos Hills. On-campus parking accommodates 3,000 cars. Special features of the campus include a planetarium and observatory, an FM radio station, a college theatre which seats 970, an olympic-size swimming pool and a football stadium. The library contains 85,000 volumes, an extensive pamphlet file, 500 periodicals, 5,000 microforms, 6,000 recordings and has an extensive Audiovisual Services Department. All students applying for admission are accepted, and students may enroll at midyear. Limited financial aid is available.

Community Environment: This is a suburban area with temperate climate averaging 50 to 80 degrees. Los Altos Hills is strictly residential but all recreational and commercial facilities and services may be found in the neighboring cities of Palo Alto, Los Altos, Mountain View and Sunnyvale.

FRANCISCAN SCHOOL OF THEOLOGY   *(H-3)*
1712 Euclid Avenue
Berkeley, California 94709
Tel: (510) 848-5232; Fax: (510) 549-9466

Description: The privately supported Roman Catholic graduate seminary is accredited by the Western Association of Schools and Colleges and Association of Theological Schools. It was formerly called the Old Mission Theological Seminary, previously located in Santa Barbara. The school grants the Master of Arts, Master of Theological Studies, and Masters of Divinity degrees and is a member of Graduate Theological Union, through which Th.D., Ph.D. degrees are granted. It operates on the semester system. Enrollment includes 75 full-time and 26 part-time graduate students. A faculty of 8 full-time and 3 part-time gives a faculty-student ration of 1-9.

Entrance Requirements: Bachelor's degree. April 1 and Sept. 1 are preferred application deadlines; application fee $20.

Costs Per Year: $6,000 tuition.

Collegiate Environment: The school is one of nine within the Graduate Theological Union. Housing facilities are limited to 12 apartment units. The school shares a common library with participating seminaries, with access to over 400,000 volumes and 3,000 periodicals. 95% of applicants are accepted. 31% receive financial aid.

Community Environment: See University of California - Berkeley

FRESNO CITY COLLEGE   *(K-6)*
1101 East University Avenue
Fresno, California 93741
Tel: (209) 442-4600

Description: Publicly supported, coeducational, junior college is accredited by the Western Association of Schools and Colleges. Established in 1910 this was the first junior college in California. In 1950, plans were made for the community college to acquire the University Avenue Campus. The trustees of 17 high school districts approved committee recommendations to join Fresno City and Reedley Colleges to form the State Center Community College District which assumed operation of Fresno City College in 1964. Enrollment includes 2,716 men and 3,279 women full-time, 5,415 men and 6,539 women part-time. A total faculty of 852 gives an overall faculty-student ratio of 1:22. The early semester system is used and four summer terms are offered. The college offers university-parallel, occupational, and general educational programs and grants the Associate degree. ROTC/Army and Air Force programs available.

Entrance Requirements: High school graduation or over 18 years of age; open enrollment policy; early admission, early decision, rolling admission, delayed admission and advanced placement plans available; CLEP accepted.

Costs Per Year: $100 student fees for California residents; $102 per unit nonresident tuition; additional expenses average $7,000; $15 health services fee.

Collegiate Environment: The campus consists of 102 acres. The library contains over 54,547 volumes. 98% of students applying for admission are accepted. Of 132 scholarships offered, 3 are available for freshmen.

Community Environment: See California State University - Fresno.

FRESNO PACIFIC COLLEGE   (K-6)
1717 South Chestnut Avenue
Fresno, California 93702
Tel: (209) 251-7194; (800) 660-6089; Admissions: (209) 453-2039;
Fax: (209) 453-2007

Description: The privately supported, coeducational college is a church-related liberal arts college sponsored by the Mennonite Brethren Church. Accredited by the Western Association of Schools and Colleges, it operates on the semester system with 2 summer sessions. The college grants a Baccalaureate degree, offers courses in education qualifying for teaching credentials and offers a Master's degree in Education. Enrollment includes 739 full-time and 35 part-time undergraduates and 874 graduate students. A faculty of 56 full-time and 99 part-time gives a faculty-student ratio of 1-15.

Entrance Requirements: High school graduation or equivalent; non-high school graduates with exceptional academic qualifications considered; completion of 15 high school units including 4 English, 3 mathematics, 2 foreign lang., 1 laboratory science and 2 social science; SAT, minimum 400V, 400M, or ACT, minimum 19, required; application fee $30; early admission, early decision, rolling admission, delayed admission and advanced placement plans available.

Costs Per Year: $10,500 tuition; $1,500 room and $1,270-$2,380 board.

Collegiate Environment: The campus has a total of 11 buildings on 23 acres in Fresno. College housing is provided for 114 men and 122 women; there are apartments for 12 married students. The library contains 92,000 volumes, 3,000 microforms and 2,000 sound recordings. About 95% of the students receive some form of financial assistance. Approximately 85% of all applicants are accepted and 85% of the freshmen returned for their second year.

Community Environment: See California State University - Fresno.

FULLER THEOLOGICAL SEMINARY   (O-9)
135 North Oakland Avenue
Pasadena, California 91182
Tel: (818) 584-5200; (800) 235-2222x5400; Fax: (818) 584-5449

Description: Privately supported, coeducational, multi-denominational graduate theological institution accredited by the Western Association of Schools and Colleges. In 1947, 39 students enrolled in the first entering class, held in the building of the Lake Avenue Congregational Church of Pasadena. The Seminary moved to its present location in 1953, then having a student body of 250. Enrollment has reached 1,600; a faculty of 70 provides an overall faculty-student ratio of approximately 1-22. The quarter system is used and five summer sessions are offered. The seminary grants the Master and Doctorate degrees.

Entrance Requirements: Baccalaureate degree from an accredited institution; a good working knowledge of the English language are strongly desired; $25 application fee.

Costs Per Year: $171.25 per unit; room $350-$850.

Collegiate Environment: The campus occupies six acres with 22 buildings including a library containing 126,000 volumes, 744 current periodicals, 2,000 microforms and 150 recordings.

Community Environment: See California Institute of Technology

FULLERTON COLLEGE   (H-12)
321 East Chapman Avenue
Fullerton, California 92634
Tel: (714) 871-8000; Admissions: (714) 992-7568; Fax: (714) 870-7751

Description: The publicly supported, coeducational community college is accredited by the Western Association of Schools and Colleges. The college was first established as a department of the Fullerton Union High School in 1913 and reorganized as a district junior college in 1922. The college offers vocational programs, general educational and university-parallel programs and grants the Certificate and Associate degrees. It operates on the semester system and offers one summer term. Enrollment includes 5,955 full-time and 12,753 part-time students. A faculty of 268 full-time and 280 part-time provides a faculty-student ratio of 1-34.

Entrance Requirements: Open enrollment policy; non-high school graduates considered; entrance examination, SAT or ACT accepted; additional testing for skills placement. Rolling admission, early decision and advanced placement plans available.

Costs Per Year: $390 ($13/unit) resident; $1,500 ($50/unit) resident with B.A. degree; $3,420 ($114/unit) nonresident, U.S. citizen; $3,510 ($117/unit) international student; $10 mandatory health fee.

Collegiate Environment: The campus has 16 buildings on 76 acres including the library housing 92,288 volumes, 12,845 pamphlets, 687 periodicals, 153,390 microforms and 3,169 audio visual materials. Campus housing is not available. All students applying for admission are accepted and 60% of the freshman class returned for the sophomore year. Financial assistance is available.

Community Environment: See California State University - Fullerton

GAVILAN COLLEGE   (J-4)
5055 Santa Teresa Boulevard
Gilroy, California 95020
Tel: (408) 847-1400; Admissions: (408) 848-4735; Fax: (408) 848-4801

Description: This publicly supported, coeducational community college is accredited by the Western Association of Schools and Colleges. This is a community college with a varied program of activities serving the citizens of Southern Santa Clara and San Benito Counties. Enrollment includes 4,700 students with a faculty of 76 full-time and 106 part-time. The college offers university-parallel, general education, vocational and technical programs. The semester system is used with one summer session. The college grants the Certificate and Associate degrees.

Entrance Requirements: High school graduation or over 18 years of age; non-high school graduates admitted under certain circumstances; rolling admission and delayed admission plans available; students are admitted at midyear.

Costs Per Year: $390 ($13 per credit) resident; $1,550 ($50 per credit) resident with BA degree; $3,930 ($131 per credit) nonresident; $4,170 ($139 per credit) foreign national.

Collegiate Environment: The 150-acre campus is located against hills with many live oaks and a series of ponds and waterfalls which have been developed to provide an outdoor "way of life." The library contains 45,000 volumes, 4,800 pamphlets, 2,000 microforms and 2,154 recordings. Financial aid is available.

Community Environment: Gilroy has a population of 30,000 and is located 77 miles south of San Francisco; served by buses and railroads. There are churches, a hospital, a library, and radio station. Gilroy has theatres, parks, civic organizations, and a public swimming pool for recreational activities; nearby are beaches and five state parks.

GLENDALE COMMUNITY COLLEGE   (O-9)
1500 N. Verdugo Rd.
Glendale, California 91208
Tel: (818) 240-1000; Admissions: (818) 240-1000 x5300; Fax: (818) 549-9436

Description: The publicly supported, coeducational community college was founded in 1927. It operates on the semester system with one summer session. Recent enrollment included 2,871 full-time and 10,768 part-time students. The school is accredited by the Western Association of Schools and Colleges and grants the Certificate and the Associate degree.

Entrance Requirements: High school graduation; non-high school graduates over 18 years may be admitted; placement examinations are required prior to registration as well as a counselor interview.

Costs Per Year: $360 tuition for California residents; $3,200 non-resident tuition.

Collegiate Environment: Located on the slopes of the San Rafael mountains, the campus overlooks the valley of the Glendale area. The library contains over 67,000 volumes. Midyear students are accepted and financial aid is available.

Community Environment: Glendale is located in the Greater Los Angeles area. The climate is mild; average temperature in summer is

71 degrees, in winter 60 degrees. There are many churches and libraries. A symphony orchestra and an art association contribute to the cultural atmosphere of the city. Buses and railroads serve the area; the Los Angeles International Airport is within easy driving distance. Beaches and mountains are nearby and provide all sports activities during both winter and summer. There are city parks, country clubs, the Verdugo Swim Stadium and the Casey Stengel Field.

GOLDEN GATE BAPTIST THEOLOGICAL SEMINARY
(B-9)
Strawberry Point
Mill Valley, California 94941-3197
Tel: (415) 388-8080; (800) 735-5060; Admissions: (415) 388-8080 x251; Fax: (415) 383-0723

Description: This privately supported, coeducational theological seminary is affiliated with Southern Baptist Convention. Founded in 1944, it is accredited by the Western Association of Schools and Colleges, the Association of Theological Schools in the United States and Canada, and the National Association of Schools of Music. The seminary has three divisions: Theology, Christian Education, and Church Music. It grants the Diploma, Master, and Doctorate degrees. The seminary operates on the semester system and offers one summer session. Enrollment is 710 students. A faculty of 24 full-time and 46 part-time gives a student-faculty ratio of 1-18.

Entrance Requirements: All students who are properly recommended by their churches and meet other requirements specified in the catalog are accepted; $25 application fee.

Costs Per Year: $1,600 per year Southern Baptists; $4,000 others.

Collegiate Environment: The seminary's library holds 132,000 volumes. Student housing includes dormitories for 260 men and women as well as housing facilities for married students. There is a child-care program to assist students attending seminary classes. Some financial assistance is available.

Community Environment: Population 13,250. Mill Valley is a suburban area near San Francisco, eight miles north of the Golden Gate Bridge. The climate is temperate. All means of public transportation are available. Churches of most denominations are located here, and there are hospitals in nearby areas. Recreational facilities are unlimited. The shopping areas are 5-10 minutes away.

Branch Campuses: Golden Gate Seminary has branch campuses in Southern California, Pacific Northwest, New Mexico, and Arizona. All are commuter campuses, and matriculation fees are equal to the cost of the Mill Valley campus.

GOLDEN GATE UNIVERSITY   *(I-3)*
536 Mission Street
San Francisco, California 94105-2968
Tel: (415) 442-7000; (800) 448-4968; Admissions: (415) 442-7200; Fax: (415) 495-2671

Description: The privately supported, nonsectarian, coeducational university was founded in 1901 and is accredited by the Western Association of Schools and Colleges. The university annually awards some 1,800 degrees, more than three-fourths of which are graduate level. The university is organized into the school of Arts & Sciences, the School of Business, the School of Public Service and International Studies, the School of Taxation, the School of Technology and Industry, and the School of Law. The School of Law is approved by the American Bar Association and accredited by the State Bar of California and by the Association of America Law Schools. In addition to conducting Bachelor's, Master's and Doctoral degree programs on its San Francisco campus, the university operates satellite campuses in Rohnert Park, Los Altos, Walnut Creek, Sacramento, Monterey, Los Angeles, and Seattle. The Cooperative Education Program assists students in finding employment whereby they may work full-time in alternate trimesters, or part-time concurrently with their studies. The university operates on the trimester calendar system and offers one summer session. Enrollment includes 497 full-time and 1,404 part-time undergraduates and 4,712 graduate and professional students. A faculty of 90 full-time and 531 part-time gives a faculty-student ratio of 1-16.

Entrance Requirements: Applicants for admission to the undergraduate programs must have a high school GPA of 3.0 or better. The minimum requirement for admission to the Graduate program is a

Bachelor's or higher degree from an accredited college. M.B.A. applicants must take the GMAT. M.S. applicants must have an undergraduate GPA of 2.5 or better. Other requirements vary by department. Early decision, rolling admission and advanced placement plans available; students may be admitted at mid-year. Undergraduate application fee $40, graduate fee $50, international fee $60.

Costs Per Year: $7,800 ($260/unit) undergraduate tuition; $11,100 ($370/unit) graduate; $190 fees.

Collegiate Environment: The university is located in the downtown business district of San Francisco. An accelerated program of three full semesters is offered during the calendar year. The library contains over 325,000 volumes. Financial aid is available and approximately 30% of the students receives some form of assistance.

Community Environment: See San Francisco State University

GOLDEN WEST COLLEGE   *(I-11)*
15744 Golden West Street
Huntington Beach, California 92647-0592
Tel: (714) 895-8130; Fax: (714) 895-8690

Description: The publicly supported, coeducational community college is accredited by the Western Association of Schools and Colleges. This college opened in 1966 with a first semester enrollment of 2,000 regular day students. The faculty and administration have accepted the challenge to provide an environment in which students are motivated toward standards of excellence in human affairs through responsible experimentation and innovation. Programs provided include university-parallel, general education, occupational and skill education. The college grants the Certificate and the Associate degree. It operates on the semester system and offers one summer session. Enrollment includes 4,940 full-time and 8,154 part-time students. A full-time faculty of 641 gives a faculty-student ratio of 1-30.

Entrance Requirements: High school graduation or over 18 years of age; under certain circumstances non-high school graduates considered; early decision, early admission, advanced placement, midyear admission, and rolling admission plans available.

Costs Per Year: $13 per credit tuition for California residents; $107 per credit nonresident; student fees $20.

Collegiate Environment: The campus consists of 18 buildings on 122 acres (no dormitories). The Library/Media center has a collection of over 93,000 books, 450 periodical titles, and 9,800 non-print materials. The college's computer services center provides Computer Assisted Instruction programs as part of the regular curriculum.

Community Environment: Huntington Beach is located in the northern coastal region of Orange County, which is 35 miles southeast of Los Angeles. The climate is moderate with a mean yearly temperature of 70 degrees. All major transportation facilities available. Eight miles of the finest, safest beach in California is located here. The city has three public golf courses and parks for recreational activities. This is one of the fastest growing cities in the west.

GRADUATE THEOLOGICAL UNION   *(H-3)*
2400 Ridge Road
Berkeley, California 94709
Tel: (415) 649-2400; Admissions: (415) 649-2460

Description: This privately supported graduate school of theology and religious studies is accredited by the Western Association of Schools and Colleges and by the Association of Theological Schools of the United States and Canada. The semester system is used. Recent enrollment included 254 Doctoral and 100 Masters students. The Union has nine participating theological schools and a number of affiliated centers. Its faculty is drawn largely from the combined faculties of the participating schools, with a total of approximately 63 members. The Union grants the Ph.D. and the Th.D. degrees and the M.A. jointly with its participating schools. Each of the participating seminaries grants the Master of Divinity, Doctor of Ministry and other professional degrees. Close cooperation exists between GTU and the University of California at Berkeley. Joint Ph.D Degree programs in Near Eastern Religions and Jewish studies are offered by the two institutions. The GTU and its member schools have reciprocal library privileges with the University. The GTU library system contains over 630,000 volumes. The member schools of the Union are: the American Baptist Seminary of the West, the Church Divinity School of the

Pacific (Episcopal), the Franciscan School of Theology, the Jesuit School of Theology at Berkeley, the Pacific Lutheran Theological Seminary, the Pacific School of Religion (Interdenominational), the Dominican School of Philosophy and Theology the San Francisco Theological Seminary (Presbyterian), Starr King School for the Ministry (Unitarian/Universalist). The affiliated centers are: Center for Jewish Studies, School of Applied Theology, Center for Women and Religion, Center for Ethics and Social Policy, St. John the Divine Orthodox Divinity Institute, Center for Hermeneutical Studies, Center for Theology and the Natural Sciences, and the Institute for Cross Cultural Education.

Entrance Requirements: Bachelors degree from an accredited institution; applicants should have a distinguished undergraduate record; graduate level work in religious studies; GRE required.

Costs Per Year: $6,000 tuition for Masters level and $10,150 for doctoral level for each year of the two years required residency.

Collegiate Environment: Composed of six Protestant and three Roman Catholic institutions, the GTU draws upon the religious communities which created it and works cooperatively with the University of California, Berkeley. About 40% of the students applying for admission are accepted.

Community Environment: See University of California - Berkeley

GROSSMONT COLLEGE   *(R-11)*
8800 Grossmont College Drive
El Cajon, California 92020
Tel: (619) 465-1700; Admissions: (619) 589-0808; Fax: (619) 461-3396

Description: The publicly supported, coeducational community college is accredited by the Western Association of Schools and Colleges. The first college classes convened in 1961 on a high school campus. A 35-acre site was purchased and in 1964 the campus was officially dedicated. The enrollment is approximately 15,000. The semester system is used and one summer session is offered. The college grants the Certificate and Associate degree and provides university-parallel, general educational, and career vocational programs.

Entrance Requirements: High school graduation or 18 years of age; placement examination required.

Costs Per Year: $2,900 nonresident tuition; no tuition for California residents; $332 student fees.

Collegiate Environment: The campus occupies 136 acres with seven buildings including a library containing 106,047 volumes. All students applying for admission are accepted and financial aid is available. There are 73 different Associate degree programs.

Community Environment: El Cajon is situated east of San Diego in a suburban community with a Mediterranean climate. Gillespie Airport and buses serve the area. The County Branch Library is located here; there are churches of all denominations. Employment is available through the California Department of Employment which is located on the Grossmont college campus. There are recreational facilities at both the beaches and in the nearby mountain area. Annual festivities include the "Mother Goose Parade."

HARTNELL COLLEGE   *(K-4)*
156 Homestead Ave.
Salinas, California 93901
Tel: (408) 758-8211

Description: Publicly supported, coeducational community college, accredited by the Western Association of Schools and Colleges. Formerly known as Salinas Junior College, which was founded in 1920, the school was renamed Hartnell College in 1948 and honors William Edward Petty Hartnell, who founded the first school in this locality in 1834. Enrollment includes 7,469 students attending classes in day and evening sessions. A faculty of 346 gives a faculty-student ratio of 1:21. The semester system is used and two summer sessions are offered. The college provides university-transfer, vocational, and general educational programs and grants the Certificate and Associate degree.

Entrance Requirements: High school graduation; non-high school graduates over 18 years may be admitted to special status; open enrollment; students are admitted at midyear

Costs Per Year: No tuition for California residents; $2,900 nonresident tuition; student fees $100.

Collegiate Environment: Hartnell Community College District has two campuses. The Hartnell College campus is on 50 acres located a few blocks from downtown Salinas. The East Campus, only a few miles from the original Hartnell site, has 140 acres of fertile land and is the center for courses in agriculture and mechanics. Buildings on the two campuses are valued at more than $35,000,000 and the library houses over 69,000 volumes. No dormitories.

Community Environment: Population 78,000. Salinas is the county seat of Monterey County, 106 miles south of San Francisco on Highway 101. Southern Pacific Railroad, Greyhound bus and United Airlines serve the area. The Santa Lucia Mountains are to the west of Salinas and the Gabilan foothills to the east. Agriculture is the chief factor of economy in Salinas with new industries designed to take advantage of the abundant harvest. The climate is comfortable, the average temperature being 57 degrees. Salinas has a great number of churches, YMCA, theatres, community concert association, Monterey County symphony, a variety of civic, fraternal and veteran's organizations. John Steinbeck was born here. Part-time employment opportunities for students available in nearby recreational areas, agriculture, industrial and commercial firms. The recreational facilities include nine municipal recreation centers, a municipal golf course, private country clubs, the Monterey Peninsula playland area, the famous white sandy beaches of Carmel, a 20-minute drive away, flying clubs, a ski club, and many hobby clubs. This is the location of the oldest and largest four-day California Rodeo.

HARVEY MUDD COLLEGE   *(G-13)*
Claremont, California 91711
Tel: (909) 621-8000; Admissions: (909) 621-8011; Fax: (909) 621-8360

Description: Privately supported, coeducational college of engineering and physical science accredited by the Western Association of Schools and Colleges. The fifth of the Claremont Colleges, it was founded in 1955 and opened its doors to its first freshman class in 1957. The school operates on the semester system. Enrollment is 635 full-time undergraduates and 8 graduate students. A faculty of 70 full-time and 29 part-time gives a faculty-student ratio of 1-8. The college grants the Bachelor of Science and the Master of Science degree. Army and Air Force ROTC are available.

Entrance Requirements: High school graduation with courses consisting of 4 English, 4 mathematics, 2 science, 2 language, and 1 history; SAT and 3 Achievement Tests required including Math Level 2; non-high school graduates may be admitted on special conditions; early decision plan available; $40 application fee; $60 application fee for foreign residents.

Costs Per Year: $18,100 tuition; $466 student fees; $6,920 room and board; $1,600 average additional expenses.

Collegiate Environment: Located at the foot of the San Gabriel Mountains, the campus is in the City of Claremont, which is a residential college community with a population of 30,000. There is dormitory capacity for 632 students. Shared library facilities house over 1,900,000 volumes. Approximately 42% of the students applying for admission are accepted and all students graduated in the top quarter of their high school class. The middle 50% range of scores for the entering freshman class were SAT 600-700 verbal, 710-770 math. Over 95% of the freshman class returned for the sophomore year. Scholarships are available and 75% of the students receive some form of financial aid. Midyear students are rarely admitted.

Community Environment: See Claremont Graduate School.

HASTINGS COLLEGE OF LAW   *(I-3)*
200 McAllister Street
San Francisco, California 94102
Tel: (415) 565-4623

Description: A publicly supported, coeducational, graduate law school of the University of California. The college is approved by the American Bar Association and is a charter member of the Association of American Law Schools. Original plans called for a location at Berkeley but from the first class in 1878 the institution has remained in San Francisco. The enrollment of 1,253 students and a faculty of 53 full-time and 25 part-time provides a faculty-student ratio of 1-23.

The semester system is used. The college grants the Juris Doctor degree.

Entrance Requirements: Bachelor's degree or equivalent foreign degree from a college or university of approved standing; Law School Admission Test required; $40 application fee.

Costs Per Year: $3,965 California resident tuition; $11,664 nonresident tuition.

Collegiate Environment: The college is located less than a block from the Supreme Court, the District Court of Appeals for the Appellate District, the Public Utilities Commission, and the Industrial Accident Commission. The offices of other State Boards and Commissions are located in the nearby State Building. Students have a unique opportunity to observe law in practice, law in operation and law in the making. All students are admitted on a full-time basis and only at the beginning of the fall term. No part-time or evening program is offered. Library contains over 520,000 volumes. 70% of the students receive financial aid.

Community Environment: See San Francisco State University.

HEBREW UNION COLLEGE - JEWISH INSTITUTE OF RELIGION *(O-8)*
3077 University Mall
Los Angeles, California 90007
Tel: (213) 749-3424; Fax: (213) 747-6128

Description: The privately supported, coeducational college-institute is accredited by the Western Association of Schools and Colleges. An arrangement exists between the Hebrew Union College and the University of Southern California whereby students may enroll simultaneously in both institutions with reciprocal course credits. The campus has five schools, a School of Rabbinic Studies, School of Graduate Studies, School of Education, School of Judaic Studies, and a School of Jewish Communal Service. The institute offers programs leading to the Bachelor, Master and Doctoral degrees. It operates on the semester system. Enrollment includes 65 students. A faculty of 25 gives a faculty-student ratio of 1-3.

Entrance Requirements: SAT and GRE required; $60 application fee.

Costs Per Year: $7,000 tuition.

Collegiate Environment: The Los Angeles School occupies a 5-acre site in the center of the city, adjacent to the University of Southern California. Housed within the two-winged building are the Mae Swig Educational Center, the Anna Grancell Student Center, the Frances-Henry Library, the Joseph Periodical Reading Room, the Walter S. Hilborn Chapel, the Tartak Learning Center, the Jacob Sonderling Conference Room, the Martin Gang Lecture Hall, the Gustine and John Weber Grand Hall, a Faculty Center, and administrative offices. The library contains more than 80,000 volumes as well as periodicals, microfilms, records, and tapes covering every aspect of Jewish intellectual endeavor. The library also houses the Joseph H. Rosenberg Branch of the American Jewish Archives and a branch of the American Jewish Periodical Center. The Hebrew Union College Skirball Museum is one of the foremost Jewish museums. Its collection, consisting of approximately 20,000 items, includes archaeological artifacts, paintings, sculpture, photographs, manuscripts, decorative arts, prints, drawings, and folk art related to 4,000 years of Jewish history and culture. 75% of all applicants accepted. 96% receive financial aid.

Community Environment: See University of California - Los Angeles.

Branch Campuses: 3101 Clifton Avenue, Cincinnati, OH 45220-2488; 13 King David Street, Jerusalem, Israel 94101; Brookdale Center, 1 West 4th St., New York, NY 10012-1186.

HOLY NAMES COLLEGE *(I-3)*
3500 Mountain Boulevard
Oakland, California 94619-1699
Tel: (510) 436-1321; (800) 430-1321; Fax: (510) 436-1325

Description: HNC is a privately supported, Catholic liberal arts college accredited by the Western Association of Schools and Colleges. The primary goal of the College is the preparation of students for life in the contemporary world. Total enrollment is 966; undergraduate enrollment is 282 full-time and 308 part-time students. There are 376 graduate students. A faculty of 51 full-time and 117 part-time professors gives an overall faculty-student ratio of 1-10. The school operates on the trimester system and offers one summer session. Weekend College employs the trimester system. Programs lead to Bachelor's and Master's degrees and exchange classes are available with Mills College, Oakland; St. Mary's College, Moraga; U.C. Berkeley; California College of Arts and Crafts, Oakland; California State University, Hayward; Graduate Theological Union, Berkeley; and the Peralta Colleges. Air Force and Army ROTC programs are available.

Entrance Requirements: High school graduation; completion of a minimum of 15 units including 4 English, 3 mathematics, 2 foreign language, 1 science, and 1 social science; non-high school graduates are considered; SAT or ACT required; rolling admission, delayed admission, midyear admission and advanced placement plans available; $35 application fee.

Costs Per Year: $11,480 tuition; $290 student fees; $5,280 room and board; additional expenses average $1,500.

Collegiate Environment: Rooms in the residence halls are assigned by the Director of Residence; facilities accommodate 187 men and 200 women. The library contains 109,000 volumes, 44,500 microforms, 4,249 records/tapes, and 448 periodicals in addition to items in the music department library. Scholarships are available and 82% of the current student body receives financial aid.

Community Environment: The College is located in the Oakland hills, overlooking San Francisco Bay and San Francisco itself. The campus is within 15-45 minutes of all the rich cultural, recreational, and sports activities of San Francisco, Berkeley and Oakland. Easy day trips can be made to the wine country, beaches, ski areas and National Parks.

HUMBOLDT STATE UNIVERSITY *(C-1)*
Arcata, California 95521
Tel: (707) 826-4402; Admissions: (707) 826-4402; Fax: (707) 826-6194

Description: The publicly supported, coeducational university has an enrollment of 7,049 students; a faculty of 345 full-time and 166 part-time gives a faculty-student ratio of 1-28. Accredited by the Western Association of Schools and Colleges, the college operates on the semester system with summer sessions. Colleges of the University include Behavioral and Social Sciences; Arts and Humanities; Natural Resources and Sciences; Professional Studies. The university grants the Bachelor and Master degrees and various teaching and administrative credentials.

Entrance Requirements: Eligibility Index which places the student in the upper third of class (nonresidents upper sixth); high school equivalency non-high school graduates considered; SAT or ACT required; completion of 15 unit subject area requirement; application fee $55; advanced placement, early decision and rolling admission plans available.

Costs Per Year: $9,202 for nonresident tuition; California residents $1,822; $4,933 room and board.

Collegiate Environment: The campus provides modern educational facilities, an activity program and a congenial dormitory life. It boasts a Forest Service Laboratory, a Marine Laboratory maintained a seagoing research vessel, a 360-acre demonstration forest, a 280-acre dune preserve, wildlife game pens, and a fish hatchery maintained on campus. The library contains over 470,536 volumes, receives 2,291 periodicals. Approximately 40% of the student body graduated in the top 10% of their high school class, 80% in the top quarter and 100% in the top half. About 68% of the undergraduate applicants are accepted, and students may enroll at midyear as well as in the fall. On-campus housing is available for 1,352 men and women. Financial aid is awarded on the basis of need, and approximately 49% of the current students receive some form of assistance.

Community Environment: Population 13,000. The city is located on the north shore of Humboldt Bay in northwestern California near the mountains and redwoods. Arcata has an unrestricted panorama of mountains, bay, dairy and farm lands, sand dunes and the Pacific Ocean. Buses and airlines serve the area. Arcata is eight miles north of Eureka, and 275 miles north of San Francisco. Industry includes lumbering, manufacturing of wood products, tourism and dairy products. Humboldt Bay region climate is moist, but stimulating, with no extremes of heat or cold. Summer and fall are considered particularly delightful seasons. The city has a library, churches and the usual service clubs. The recreational opportunities include hunting, trout fishing in mountain streams, salmon fishing in Humboldt Bay and Trinidad Bay, and deep sea fishing. There is an Azalea Reserve, three miles north.

HUMPHREYS COLLEGE *(H-4)*
6650 Inglewood Avenue
Stockton, California 95207
Tel: (209) 478-0800; Fax: (209) 478-8721

Description: Founded in 1896, Humphreys College is dedicated to educating students in the areas of business and law. It is accredited by the Western Association of Schools and Colleges. The college is a member of the Association of Independent California Colleges and Universities, and prides itself on providing a highly personalized education. Students can earn either an Associate in Science, Associate in Arts, or Bachelor of Science degree, or go on to further their education to earn a Juris Doctor from Humphreys College School of Law. The college operates on the quarter system and offers one summer session. Enrollment includes 428 full-time and 364 part-time undergraduates and 101 graduate students. A faculty of 19 full-time and 44 part-time gives an undergraduate faculty-student ratio of 1-11.

Entrance Requirements: High school graduation; entrance and placement examinations; early decision, rolling admission, delayed admission and advanced placement plans available; $20 application fee.

Costs Per Year: $5,460 tuition; $4,660 room and board.

Collegiate Environment: Humphreys College is located on a 10-acre suburban campus in northern California. It is within walking distance from a city library and several shopping areas. On campus is a swimming pool, basketball court, and tennis court. Located 10 miles from the school is the San Joaquin Delta, which provides an excellent place for all types of water sports. San Francisco is only a 90-minute drive away, and the state capital is located 40 miles north. 74% of the students receive financial aid. Special programs are offered for the culturally disadvantaged. The library contains 20,500 titles and 600 microforms. 90% of applicants are accepted, and 62% of last year's freshman class returned for the sophomore year.

Community Environment: See University of the Pacific.

IMPERIAL VALLEY COLLEGE *(Q-13)*
380 E. Aten Road
P.O. Box 158
Imperial, California 92251
Tel: (619) 352-8320; Fax: (619) 355-2663

Description: This publicly supported, coeducational community college is accredited by the Western Association of Schools and Colleges. The college has served residents of the Imperial Valley for 73 years. The Associate degree was first conferred in 1934. The Certificate and Associate degree are granted. The college operates on the semester system. Enrollment is 5,226 students. A faculty of 224 gives a faculty-student ratio of 1-23.

Entrance Requirements: High school graduation; non-high school graduates considered. Midyear admission available.

Costs Per Year: $403 ($13/unit) fees, resident; $1,550 ($50/unit) resident with B.A. degree or higher; $3,600 ($120/unit) nonresident; $400 average additional expenses.

Collegiate Environment: 165-acre campus is located in one of the richest, productive agricultural regions in the country. In 1959, a ground-breaking service was held for the new campus. There are now 12 buildings. The library contains 51,726 volumes and a variety of audiovisual materials. All students applying for admission are accepted, including midyear students. 63% of the freshman class returned to this campus for the second year. The college has a special program that enables low-mark, culturally disadvantaged students to attend. The average high school standing of the freshman class was in the top 70%. Four hundred scholarships are available, and 60% of the freshman class receives financial aid.

Community Environment: Imperial is in the southern desert area of California known as the Imperial Valley. It has a very dry climate. The Chocolate Mountains are separated from Imperial by a ribbon of sand dunes. Buses and airlines serve the area. The surrounding Imperial Valley is a large and abundant agricultural area. There are six

small cities in surrounding area that provide additional employment opportunities. The annual midwinter fair and the Christmas Parade are here at Imperial.

JESUIT SCHOOL OF THEOLOGY AT BERKELEY *(H-3)*
1735 Le Roy Avenue
Berkeley, California 94709
Tel: (415) 841-8804; (800) 824-0122; Fax: (510) 841-8536

Description: The Jesuit School of Theology at Berkeley (JSTB) is both a professional theological school and a Pontifical Faculty of theology. It is one of two Jesuit centres in the United States that provide the theological, professional and personal preparation of men and women for ordained and nonordained leadership in the Christian community. The student community is a mix of lay men and women. The school is accredited by the Western Association of Schools and Colleges. The semester system is used. Current enrollment is 232 students. A faculty of 35 gives a faculty-student ratio of 1-7. Formerly named Alma College of the University of Santa Clara, the school moved to Berkeley and the Graduate Theological Union in October 1969. Programs lead to a Master of Arts degree, Master of Divinity, Master of Theology, Master of Sacred Theology, a Licentiate in Sacred Theology, and Doctor of Sacred Theology.

Entrance Requirements: GRE required; Master of Divinity or equivalent required for Advanced Master degrees.

Costs Per Year: $7,400 ($3,700 per semester) tuition.

Collegiate Environment: See Graduate Theological Union, Berkeley, California.

Community Environment: See University of California - Berkeley.

JOHN F. KENNEDY UNIVERSITY *(H-3)*
12 Altarinda Road
Orinda, California 94563
Tel: (510) 254-0200; Admissions: (510) 253-2211; Fax: (510) 254-6964

Description: The privately supported coeducational evening university is a four-year university offering classes at the undergraduate and graduate levels. It is accredited by the Western Association of Schools and Colleges. Programs lead to the Bachelor, Master, and Professional degrees in law. The university operates on the quarter system and three summer session are offered. Enrollment includes 481 men and 1,319 women with a faculty of 24 full-time and 650 part-time members.

Entrance Requirements: Interview, personal ststement, high graduation of equivalent for undergraduate programs; Bachelor's degree for graduate programs; rolling admissions; $50 application fee.

Costs Per Year: $237 per unit; $28 fee.

Collegiate Environment: The library contains 64,800 volumes and 600 periodicals. Approximately 88% of applicants are accepted. Financial aid is available, and 35% of students receive some form of financial assistance.

Community Environment: Orinda, population 15,000, is located just east of the Oakland-Berkeley Hills, California. Oakland, 10 miles away, and San Francisco, 20 miles, are easily accessed. Climate is mild the year round, with the average temperature 65-70 degrees. Hunting, fishing, boating, camping and winter sports are nearby.

Branch Campuses: Walnut Creek, CA: School of Law, School of Management; Campbell, CA: Graduate School of Professional Psychology (second campus).

KINGS RIVER COMMUNITY COLLEGE *(K-7)*
995 North Reed Avenue
Reedley, California 93654
Tel: (209) 638-3641; Admissions: (209) 638-3641; Fax: (209) 638-5040

Description: The publicly supported, coeducational community college is accredited by the Western Association of Schools and Colleges. The college opened in 1926 and moved to the present campus in 1956. The college grants a certificate and the Associat degree. It operates on the early semester calendar system and offers one summer session. Enrollment includes 5,117 students. A faculty of 80 full-time and 153 part-time gives a faculty-student ratio of 1:22.

Entrance Requirements: High school graduation or 18 years of age; open enrollment policy; rolling admission plan available.

Costs Per Year: $390 ($13/unit) resident; $1,550 ($50/unit) resident with B.A. degree or higher; $3,420 ($114/unit) nonresident; $2,140 room and board; $120 student fees.

Collegiate Environment: The 382-acre campus is in a rural area and services 17 high school districts. The library is centrally located on campus and contains 29,000 volumes, 800 pamphlets, 170 periodicals, 16,800 microforms and 1,820 sound recordings. Of the 137 scholarships are available, including 81 are for freshmen. 33% of students receive some form of financial aid. Dormitory capacity is 102 men and 102 women. One hundred percent of the applicants are accepted.

Community Environment: Population 15,200. Reedley is in a rural area southeast of Fresno with a temperate climate. The rich farmlands around Reedley produce a diversity of crops, including citrus fruits, plums, peaches, grapes, tomatoes, celery and walnuts. The community has 19 packing houses, two wineries, and a sawmill. There are a number of churches, a public library and a hospital. Part-time employment is available. Reedley is near Kings Canyon and Sequoia National Parks which provide recreational activities. Major civic, fraternal and veteran's organizations are part of the town.

L.I.F.E. BIBLE COLLEGE   *(O-8)*
1100 Covina Blvd.
San Dimas, California 91773
Tel: (714) 981-1759

Description: This privately supported, coeducational Bible college is controlled by International Church of the Foursquare Gospel and is accredited by the American Association of Bible Colleges. The semester system is used with one summer session, and students may attend day or evening classes. Since its founding in 1925, the college has graduated more than 7,000 students, most of whom went on to serve in the Christian ministry. Degrees granted: B.A., B.Th., Teacher Training Diploma, Standard Ministerial Diploma, A.A. Enrollment includes 279 full-time and 93 part-time students. A faculty of 11 full-time and 12 part-time gives a faculty-student ratio of 1-19.

Entrance Requirements: Evidence of an approved Christian character (at least one year's Christian experience); should have received or be seeking the baptism and leading a life separated from the world; SAT or ACT required; high school transcript or GED; midyear admission and rolling admission plans available; $35 application fee.

Costs Per Year: $4,320 tuition; $2,660 residence fees; $300 student fees.

Collegiate Environment: There is student housing for 168 students. The library contains over 32,511 volumes. The new campus is located in the San Gabriel Valley community of San Dimas. Aproximately 92% of all applicants are accepted, including students at midyear. 75% of the students receive financial aid.

Community Environment: See University of California - Los Angeles.

LA SIERRA UNIVERSITY   *(P-10)*
4700 Pierce Street
Riverside, California 92515
Tel: (714) 785-2000; (800) 874-5587

Description: The privately supported, coeducational university is accredited by the Western Association of Schools and Colleges and owned by the Seventh-day Adventist Church. The institution began as La Sierra Academy in 1922, became a junior college, and later La Sierra College, a four-year liberal arts college. From 1967 to 1990 the institution was the Liberal Arts campus of Loma Linda University, after which it became the independent campus of La Sierra University. La Sierra University is comprised of five academic units: the College of Arts and Sciences, the Schools of Business and Management, Education, and Religion, and the Center for Lifelong Learning. Curricula in liberal arts and sciences and preprofessional health-related fields are offered by the College of Arts and Sciences through undergraduate and graduate programs; professional education programs are offered through the School of Education in conjunction

with the College of Arts and Sciences; the School of Business and Management and the School of Religion offer both undergraduate and graduate degrees. The Center for Lifelong Learning offers classes for adults from all four schools, though it only offers degree programs through the College of Arts and Sciences and the School of Business and Management. The University grants Associate Bachelor, Master, Education Specialist, and Doctoral degrees. It operates on the quarter system and offers two summer sessions. Enrollment includes 1,300 full-time and 300 part-time and 150 graduate students. A faculty of 97 full-time and 11 part-time members which provides a student-faculty ratio of 13-1.

Entrance Requirements: High school graduation with a C average; completion of 16 units including 4 English, 2 math, 2 social science, 2 history, 2 science; ACT or SAT required; early admission and rolling admission plans available. $30 application fee.

Costs Per Year: $12,180 tuition; $3,885 room and board; $145 fees.

Collegiate Environment: La Sierra University has 30 buildings on a 400-acre site. The library has 525,214 volumes. Residence halls accommodate 650 students. 75% of the applicants are accepted and 80% receive some form of financial aid.

Community Environment: See University of California - Riverside.

LANEY COLLEGE   *(I-3)*
900 Fallon Street
Oakland, California 94607
Tel: (415) 834-5740

Description: Publicly supported, coeducational junior college maintained by the Peralta Community College District of Northern Alameda County. Accredited by the Western Association of Schools and Colleges, the college operates on the semester system and offers one summer session. It grants the Associate degree and the Certificate for vocational programs. Enrollment includes 2,589 full-time and 7,844 part-time and 3,653 evening students. A faculty of 291 gives a faculty-student ratio of 1-48.

Entrance Requirements: High school graduates or non-high school graduates 18 years of age or older; open enrollment; midyear admission and rolling admission plans available.

Costs Per Year: $390 ($13/unit) resident tuition; $1,550 ($50/unit) resident with B.A. degree; $4,050 ($135/unit) nonresident tuition.

Collegiate Environment: Laney is adjacent to the Oakland Museum, a ten- minute walk from the heart of downtown Oakland. The library houses over 77,000 volumes.

Community Environment: Oakland is the fourth largest city in the state. Located on the mainland side of San Francisco Bay; adjoined on the north by Berkeley; on the south by Alameda and San Leandro. Climate is mild and the average temperature is 65.9 degrees. All modes of transportation are available; the Oakland Airport is a 12-minute drive. Oakland has all the advantages of a large metropolitan area, being a part of the San Francisco Bay Area. Numerous churches, museums, libraries, hospitals, service groups, and organizations are in the city. Oakland has many tourist attractions and recreational facilities. Lake Merritt, a 160-acre body of salt water, is the only tidal lake in the heart of any American city. There are parks, golf courses, swimming pools within a short distance.

LASSEN COLLEGE   *(D-5)*
P.O. Box 3000
Susanville, California 96130
Tel: (916) 257-6181; Fax: (916) 257-8964

Description: The publicly supported, coeducational community college is accredited by the Western Association of Schools and Colleges. In 1941 a garage on Main Street was rebuilt and converted to house four classrooms (the college's first separate building). The Lassen Community College District was formed in 1965. In 1973 the college moved to a new 14 million dollar campus located one mile from Susanville. The college operates on the semester system and offers three summer sessions. It grants the Certificate and Associate degree, offering vocational specialization in a variety of programs. With a recent enrollment of 1,945 and a faculty of 185, the faculty-student ratio was 1-15.

Entrance Requirements: High school graduation; open enrollment policy; non-high school graduates considered; early admission, and rolling admission, and plans available.

Costs Per Year: $403 ($13/unit) state resident tuition; $4,464 ($144/unit) out-of-state; $3,416 room and board.

Collegiate Environment: The campus consists of 12 buildings on 240 acres and includes a library containing 20,000 volumes. Approximately 30% of the current student body receive financial aid. The college offers a wide variety of vocational programs plus courses acceptable for transfer to all four-year colleges and universities in California. The college has developed a self-paced open entry/exit concept to meet the individual needs of students. The college has dormitory facilities for 100 students.

Community Environment: Population 7,000. Located in northern California on Highways 36, 395 and 139, Susanville is situated in a valley surrounded by high mountains, streams and Eagle Lake. Average mean temperature is 49.8 degrees with average rainfall of 18 inches. Besides the shopping facilities, Susanville has 14 churches, a theater, a radio station, fraternal and civic organizations. Recreational facilities include tennis courts, bowling alley, and hunting, fishing, and skiing in the mountain areas. Housing is available in dormitories, apartments and boarding houses. The Lassen County Fair is held each year in August.

LINCOLN UNIVERSITY   *(I-3)*
281 Masonic Avenue
San Francisco, California 94118
Tel: (415) 221-1212; Fax: (415) 387-9730

Description: Privately supported coeducational university founded in 1919 and composed of an International College of Undergraduate and Graduate Studies. It is accredited by the Accrediting Commission for Independent Colleges and Schools. Programs of study lead to the Bachelor and Master degrees. The university operates on the semester system and offers one summer session. Enrollment includes 350 undergraduates and 166 graduate students. A faculty of 8 full-time and 28 part-time gives a faculty-student ratio of 1-14.

Entrance Requirements: College of Undergraduate and Graduate Studies: high school graduation or its equivalent for undergraduate; for graduate program undergraduate degree is needed; $50 application fee.

Costs Per Year: Undergraduate: $6,045 ($195/unit) tuition and fees; Graduate: $6,820 ($220/unit) tuition and fees.

Collegiate Environment: The main campus is located at Masonic and Turk, close to the Center of San Francisco. The libraries contain 54,534 volumes. Financial assistance is available and 40 students currently receive financial aid. Special international programs are offered in Business Administration and in English as a second language. Midyear students are accepted in the College Division.

Community Environment: See San Francisco State University.

LOMA LINDA UNIVERSITY   *(O-10)*
Loma Linda, California 92350
Tel: (909) 824-4300; (800) 422-4558; Fax: (909) 824-4879

Description: This privately supported, coeducational university is owned by the Seventh-day Adventist Church. The land and buildings for the university were acquired at Loma Linda in 1905, and the state charter was granted in 1909. Professional curricula are offered by the Schools of Medicine, Dentistry, Public Health, Nursing, and Allied Health Professions. Graduate programs of the departments of the schools are offered through the graduate school. The university is accredited by the Western Association of Schools and Colleges, and the professional schools are accredited by their respective professional organizations. Enrollment includes 3,041 students. The quarter system is used, and three summer sessions are offered. The university grants the Associate, Bachelor, Master, and Doctorate degrees.

Entrance Requirements: Prerequisites, application fees, and admission tests vary from school to school; all undergraduate programs require one to two years of college course work prior to entry.

Costs Per Year: $12,000 undergraduate tuition; $1,635 room; $13,250 graduate tuition.

Collegiate Environment: Loma Linda has 36 buildings on 100 acres. The library contains over 275,000 volumes. Dormitories accommodate 315 women and there are apartments for 180 men and women. Financial aid is available.

Community Environment: Loma Linda is located 56 miles east of Los Angeles, between Redlands, San Bernardino, and Riverside. The climate is pleasant and mild. Loma Linda is a medical center that has three hospitals, including the 515-bed University Medical Center and the 500-bed Jerry L. Pettis Memorial Veterans Hospital. Pacific ocean beaches, ski slopes, and lakes for boating and water skiing are all within a one-hour drive. Part-time and full-time work is available.

LOS ANGELES CITY COLLEGE   *(O-8)*
855 North Vermont Avenue
Los Angeles, California 90029
Tel: (213) 953-4000; Admissions: (213) 953-4385; Fax: (213) 953-4536

Description: The publicly supported, coeducational community college was founded in 1929 and is accredited by the Western Association of Schools and Colleges. Enrollment includes 3,600 full-time and 9,750 part-time students. A faculty of 500 full-time and 400 part-time gives an faculty-student ratio of 1-15. The semester system is used and one summer session is offered. The college grants the Certificate and Associate degree. Special programs include Electronics, Office Administration, and Business. A radio - TV theatre - film faculty trains technical personnel for the local performing arts industry. In addition, the college provides lower division courses for all four-year degree majors.

Entrance Requirements: Open enrollment policy; high school graduation required for applicants under 18 years of age; early admission, midyear admission and rolling admission plans available; Aug. 15 application deadline.

Costs Per Year: $390 ($13/unit) resident; $1,500 ($50/unit) resident with Bachelor's degree or higher; $3,960 ($132/unit) out-of-state; $4,110 ($137/unit) foreign; $8.50 mandatory fees.

Collegiate Environment: The campus consists of more than 40 acres easily accessible from all parts of the city. Classes are held in 13 buildings of modern design and 25 classrooms and special-purpose bungalows. The library contains 125,000 volumes, 130 periodicals and 4000 microforms. Financial aid is available, and 51% of the current student body receives some form of assistance. 100% of those applying for admission are accepted. Students may enroll at midyear as well as in the fall.

Community Environment: See University of California - Los Angeles

LOS ANGELES COLLEGE OF CHIROPRACTIC   *(O-9)*
16200 E. Amber Valley Drive
P.O. Box 1166
Whittier, California 90609-1166
Tel: (310) 947-8755; (800) 221-5222; Fax: (310) 947-5724

Description: Privately supported, coeducational professional college with professional accreditation. The charter was applied for by Doctor Charles A. Cale and received in 1911. The college is accredited by the Western Association of Colleges and Schools. It is professionally accredited by the Council on Chiropractic Education. Programs of study lead to the Doctor of Chiropractic degree. The college operates on the trimester system and offers one summer session. The program may be completed in 10 trimesters. Enrollment includes 728 full-time and 21 part-time students. A faculty of 49 full-time and 33 part-time provides a faculty-student ratio of 1-13.

Entrance Requirements: Prechiropractic college work (not less than 75 semester hours) to include a minimum of 6 semester units in biological sciences with related laboratories, 12 semester units in general and organic chemistry with related laboratories, 6 semester units in physics with related laboratories, 6 semester units in English/Communications, 3 semester units in psychology, and 15 semester units in social sciences/humanities. $50 application fee; students are admitted in September and January of each year.

Costs Per Year: $9,416 tuition, including fees.

Collegiate Environment: The college is located in a peaceful, residential neighborhood within minutes of downtown Whittier. Its 38-

acre campus is a harmony of nature and contemporary architecture. 22 builings are located on the campus with 172,000 square feet of usable floor space. The Learning Resource Center and spacious classroms are equipped with state-of-the-art audiovisual, video and computer-assisted learning resources to enhance modern educational teaching methods. These facilities are complimented by contemporary laboratories and furnished with equipment made especially for such disciplines as x-ray, biochemistry, pathology, histology, and dissection. The library, tailored to chiropractic education, holds 19,225 volumes. Beyond the traditional academic facilities, the campus boasts an athletic complex including a gymnasium, weight rooms, tennis, volleyball and basketball courts, a quarter-mile track and baseball diamonds. There is also a performing arts complex, a bookstore and attractive, quiet garden areas. Parking is provided on campus. In mid-1982 the college opened the Whittier Chiropractic Health Center on campus. Additionally, LACC maintains outpatient clinics in the cities of Glendale and Pasadena, as well as satellite clinics within the facilities of the Salvation Army Adult Rehabilitation Centers in Los Angeles and Pasadena, and the Center of Achievement for the Physically Disabled at California State University, Northridge. Aproximately 35% of applicants are admitted and 85% of first term students normally continue the program.

Community Environment: Nestled on the southern slope of the beautiful La Puente hills, Whittier, California, boasts a rich and proud heritage dating back to the 1880's. Named for the Quaker poet, John Greenleaf Whittier, the city has grown steadily to approximately 78,000 residents. The city is 14 miles from downtown Los Angeles. Within a one- or two-hour drive are desert spas, snowy mountain slopes, inland lakes, national parks, ocean beaches, deep sea fishing, major amusement centers, professional sports activities, the opera and theater.

LOS ANGELES HARBOR COLLEGE   *(I-10)*

1111 Figueroa Place
Wilmington, California 90744
Tel: (310) 522-8200; Admissions: (310) 522-8216; Fax: (310) 834-1882

Description: One of nine colleges of the Los Angeles Community College District, Los Angeles Harbor College is a public-supported, coeducational, two-year institution. Founded in 1949, it is accredited by the Western Association of Schools and Colleges. Harbor has a technical division, a business division, nursing division, and an academic or general education division. Programs lead to the Certificate and to the Associate in Arts degree. The college operates on the semester system and offers one summer session. Enrollment includes 2,640 full-time and 5,360 part-time students. A faculty of 145 full-time and 140 part-time gives a faculty-student ratio of 1-22.

Entrance Requirements: Open enrollment policy; high school graduates and non-high school graduates 18 years or older admitted; early decision, rolling admission, and advanced placement plans available; CLEP (subject tests only) and credit by examination are accepted; early application is strongly urged.

Costs Per Year: $13 per unit; $50 per unit resident with BA degree or higher; $132 per unit nonresident; $27.50 student fees.

Collegiate Environment: The college is located near the Port of Los Angeles, the West Coast's busiest harbor. The campus is four miles from downtown San Pedro, six miles from Long Beach and 17 miles from the Los Angeles Civic Center. The 85-acre campus is adjacent to Harbor Park, which features a lagoon, swimming pool, golf course, and other recreational facilities operated by the city. Most of Harbor's 17 buildings are single-story, providing easy access for the physically handicapped. New structures include a nursing learning laboratory and a 22,000-square-foot music building. The Library/Learning Resource Center, which contains 75,000 volumes, has been enlarged to 25,000 square feet. 99% of all applicants are accepted. 30% of students receive some form of financial aid.

Community Environment: The Harbor College service area encompasses a multicultural population of 369,907 persons who live in the communities of San Pedro, Wilmington, Carson, Gardena, Lomita, Harbor City, and on the Palos Verdes Peninsula and parts of South Los Angeles. A business, industrial, shipping and civic center of the Port of Los Angeles, Wilmington is located in the heart of the Southern California oil refining district. Points of interest are Marineland, the Queen Mary, Ports O' Call Village, and a Korean Liberty Bell, all within easy driving distance.

LOS ANGELES PIERCE COLLEGE   *(F-8)*

6201 Winnetka Avenue
Woodland Hills, California 91371
Tel: (818) 347-0551; Fax: (818) 710-9844

Description: Los Angeles Pierce College is one of 9 publicly supported, coeducational Los Angeles community colleges. It is accredited by the Western Association of Schools and Colleges. Pierce opened in 1947 as an agricultural college. In 1951 the college widened its offerings and also became coeducational. Today Pierce features the first 2 years of college academics along with over 50 vocational programs including agriculture. It operates on the early semester system and offers a summer session. Enrollment includes 5,492 full-time, 12,822 part-time, and 5,501 evening students. A faculty of 288 full-time and 231 part-time gives a faculty-student ratio of 1-45.

Entrance Requirements: Open enrollment policy; non-high school graduates considered; early decision, rolling admission, advanced placement, and early admission plan for high school seniors available.

Costs Per Year: $390 ($13/unit) resident; $1,500 ($50/unit) resident with BA degree or higher; $4,080 ($123/unit + $13/unit fee) nonresident; $15 per year health fees.

Collegiate Environment: Located on 427 acres, the college is developing a program to bring additional numbers of minority students to the campus. The library contains 100,000 volumes, 23,174 pamphlets, 506 periodicals, 5,123 microfilms and 979 recordings. Approximately 99% of the students applying for admission are accepted. Financial aid is available.

Community Environment: Woodland Hills is a suburban area of Los Angeles with a subtropical climate. Buses serve the area. Woodland Hills has major civic and service organizations, a library, churches and a hospital. Part-time employment is available. It is known for its beautiful residential area. Beaches are within easy driving distance for water sports; a public park with swimming pool and theaters are in the area. There are outstanding shopping centers nearby.

LOS ANGELES SOUTHWEST COLLEGE   *(O-8)*

1600 West Imperial Highway
Los Angeles, California 90047
Tel: (213) 744-5000

Description: Publicly supported, coeducational junior college accredited by the Western Association of Schools and Colleges. Students may attend day or evening classes. Programs lead to the Associate degree. The college operates on the semester system and offers one summer session. Enrollment includes 6,035 students. A faculty of 350 gives a faculty-student ratio of 1-17.

Entrance Requirements: Open enrollment policy; non-high school graduates of 18 years old admitted; early admission, midyear admission and rolling admission plans available.

Costs Per Year: $390 ($13/unit) resident tuition; $1,500 ($50/unit) resident with B.A. degree or higher; $3,750 ($125/unit) nonresident; $150 approximate additional expenses.

Collegiate Environment: The campus is close to the neighboring communities of Gardena, Inglewood, and Hawthorne. Forty-one buildings on 67 acres comprise the campus and the library houses 63,191 volumes. About 99% of the students applying for admission meet the requirements. Special programs for the culturally disadvantaged are offered as well as courses in American Negro history.

Community Environment: See University of California - Los Angeles

LOS ANGELES TRADE-TECHNICAL COLLEGE   *(O-8)*

400 West Washington Boulevard
Los Angeles, California 90015
Tel: (213) 744-5000; Fax: (213) 748-7334

Description: The publicly supported, coeducational community college is accredited by the Western Association of Schools and Colleges. Formerly known as the Frank Wiggins Trade School, this vocational institution has served the Los Angeles area for over a quarter of a century. Enrollment is 8,512 full-time and 8,717 part-time. A faculty of 605 gives an overall faculty-student ratio of 1-26. The college operates on the semester system and grants the Certificate and Associate degree.

Entrance Requirements: Open enrollment policy; non-high school graduates over 18 years of age admitted; early admission and rolling admission plans available.

Costs Per Year: $39 ($13/cr) resident; $1,550 ($50/cr) resident with B.A. degree; $4,110 ($137/cr) nonresident.

Collegiate Environment: The main campus is located in the heart of downtown Los Angeles. The library contains 75,000 volumes and numerous pamphlets, microforms and recordings. The college offers business, trade, and technical education, as well as general education and college transfer courses. Special programs are offered for the culturally disadvantaged as well as work incentive programs for the hardcore unemployed. All applicants are accepted; students may enroll at midyear as well as in the fall. Financial aid is available, and approximately 35% of the current students receive some form of assistance.

Community Environment: See University of California - Los Angeles.

LOS ANGELES VALLEY COLLEGE   (F-9)
5800 Fulton Avenue
Van Nuys, California 91401
Tel: (818) 781-1200

Description: This publicly supported, coeducational community college is accredited by the Western Association of Schools and Colleges. A cooperative education program is available whereby students are accredited for work during school semesters. Enrollment is 16,001 students. A faculty of 255 full-time and 300 part-time gives an overall faculty-student ratio of 1-34. The college operates on the semester system and offers one summer session. Programs lead to the Associate degree and to the Certificate.

Entrance Requirements: Open enrollment policy; non-high school graduates admitted; students under age 18 who have passed the proficiency test or have a special student permit signed by high school principal may be accepted; midyear admission, early admission and early decision plans available.

Costs Per Year: $390 ($13/unit) resident; $1,550 ($50/unit) resident with BA degree or higher; $3,990 ($133/unit) nonresident.

Collegiate Environment: The campus is located on 105 acres in the heart of the San Fernando Valley. The library contains more than 120,000 volumes. All students applying for admission are accepted, including midyear students. Limited financial aid is available.

Community Environment: Van Nuys is an urban area and part of Los Angeles where many major missile and space industries have plant sites. Bus service is available. The city has libraries, a YMCA, churches of nearly all denominations, hospitals, shopping areas, and many civic, fraternal and veterans organizations. Van Nuys is the center of the San Fernando Valley, making it a financial, industrial, professional, and administrative center.

LOYOLA MARYMOUNT UNIVERSITY   (O-8)
Loyola Blvd. at West 80th St.
Los Angeles, California 90045
Tel: (310) 338-2700; (800) 568-4636; Admissions: (310) 338-2750;
Fax: (310) 338-2797

Description: Loyola Marymount is an independent University, affiliated with the Roman Catholic Church through its association with the Society of Jesus (Jesuits), the Religious of the Sacred Heart of Mary and the Sisters of St. Joseph of Orange. The University includes the Colleges of Business, Communications and Fine Arts, Liberal Arts, Science and Engineering and Loyola Law School. Preparation for teaching credentials is offered within the College of Liberal Arts and the Department of Education. Enrollment was 3,972 undergraduates, 1,195 graduate students and 1,379 law students. The undergraduate student faculty ratio is 14:1. A faculty of 266 full-time and 237 part-time are associated with the graduate and undergraduate program. The law students are served by 45 full-time and 42 part-time faculty. The semester system is used and two summer sessions are offered. Special

programs include internships, study abroad and a Washington Semester. LMU grants Bachelor and Master degrees and the Juris Doctorate.

Entrance Requirements: High school graduation or equivalent with completion of 16 units including 4 English, 3 mathematics, 3 foreign language, 2 science (some majors require more) and 3 social science; SAT or ACT required; GRE required for graduate school; advanced placement; early admission, early decision, delayed admission and rolling admission plans are available; $35 application fee.

Costs Per Year: $14,640 tuition; $6,190 room and board; $183 mandatory fees; additional expenses average $2,000.

Collegiate Environment: All colleges and divisions of the University except the School of Law are located on the Westchester campus, a 130-acre mesa overlooking the Pacific Ocean; the School of Law is located on the downtown campus at 1440 W. 9th St. in Los Angeles. The main campus library contains 244,229 volumes and the Law School library contains 202,816 volumes. Housing facilities are 168 apartments which accommodate 1,684 students. Approximately 72% of the students applying for admission are accepted, including midyear students. Financial aid is available and 58% of the current student body receives some form of financial assistance. Air Force ROTC is available.

Community Environment: See University of California - Los Angeles

MARYMOUNT COLLEGE   (L-9)
30800 Palos Verdes Drive East
Rancho Palos Verdes, California 90275-6299
Tel: (310) 377-5501; Fax: (310) 377-6223

Description: Established by the Religious of the Sacred Heart of Mary, Marymount College has a philosophy rooted in Christian tradition. While it is a Catholic College, students of all denominations are accepted. It is coeducational, offering the Associate in Arts degree, and is fully accredited by the Western Association of Schools and Colleges. The school operates on the semester system and offers one summer session. Enrollment includes 733 full-time and 34 part-time and 258 evening students. A faculty of 52 full-time and 28 part-time gives a faculty-student ratio of 1-14. Air Force ROTC is available.

Entrance Requirements: High school graduation or equivalent; SAT or ACT recommended for placement purposes and advising, not for admission selection; rolling admissions, delayed admission, early admission, midyear admission and advanced placement plans available; $35 application fee.

Costs Per Year: $12,190 tuition; $160 student fees; $6,156 room and board.

Collegiate Environment: There are 9 buildings on this 26-acre campus, which is located on the Palos Verdes Peninsula overlooking the Pacific Ocean. The college encourages young men and women from all over the world to travel and discover the resources offered by other cultures. 80% of the applicants are accepted, and students are admitted at midyear as well as in the fall. 45% of the students are from out of state. The library contains over 35,000 volumes and numerous pamphlets, periodicals, microform titles, and audiovisual materials. 310 students live in college apartments located about seven minutes from the campus. Scholarships are available and 45% of the current student body receives some form of assistance.

Community Environment: Population 68,000. Palos Verdes Peninsula includes Palos Verdes Estates, Rolling Hills, Rolling Hills Estates and Rancho Palos Verdes. The area is mainly residential and has a temperate climate (no smog). Bus service is available to Los Angeles. Shopping facilities are nearby. Part-time employment is available, especially during the summer.

MASTER'S COLLEGE   (O-8)
21726 Placerita Canyon Road
Santa Clarita, California 91321-1200
Tel: (805) 259-3540; Fax: (805) 254-1998

Description: The privately supported, nondenominational, coeducational Christian college of arts and sciences was founded in 1927 to meet the need for an Evangelical Baptist School on the West Coast. It is accredited by the Western Association of Schools and Colleges. Enrollment is 367 men and 386 women full-time; 34 men and 32 women part-time. A faculty of 44 full-time and 41 part-time gives a faculty-student ratio of approximately 1-19. The semester system is used.

Entrance Requirements: High school graduation; non-high school graduates considered; high school graduates with a C average accepted; SAT required; advanced placement, and rolling admission plans available; $25 application fee.

Costs Per Year: $7,890 tuition; $4,226 room and board; $420 student fees.

Collegiate Environment: The campus has 22 buildings on 110 acres, including housing facilities for 275 men and 318 women. The library contain approximately 150,000 titles, 452 periodicals and 3,500 microforms. Married students can easily locate apartments in Newhall and nearby communities. Financial aid is available and 77% of the current student body receives financial assistance. There are a total of 419 scholarships available. 86% of the applicants are accepted, and students may enroll at midyear as well as in the fall.

Community Environment: See College of the Canyons.

MENDOCINO COLLEGE *(F-2)*
Box 3000
Ukiah, California 95482
Tel: (707) 468-3103

Description: This public college of the Lake Mendocino Community College District was founded in 1972. The school is accredited by the Western Association of Schools and Colleges. It offes liberal arts and technological courses. Full transfer credit is given by the California State College and University System as well as other accredited colleges and universities. The college offers extension classes, summer programs, work experience education and, as a member of the Bay Area Television Consortium for Community College Television, offers college credit courses via television. It operates on the semester system and offers one summer session. Enrollment includes 1,000 full-time and 2,400 part-time students. A faculty of 49 full-time and 170 part-time provides a faculty-student ratio of 1-20.

Entrance Requirements: High school graduation; open enrollment; GED acceptable; nongraduates over 18 years may be considered; early admission, early decision, midyear admission, rolling admission and advanced placement plans are available; no application fee.

Costs Per Year: $312 tuition maximum for state residents; $3,600 nonresident tuition.

Collegiate Environment: The college has a brand new campus. The library contains 100,000 volumes. All applicants are accepted, and students are admitted at midyear as well as in the fall. Financial aid is available, and 20% of current students receive some form of assistance. The campus serves the school districts of Anderson Valley, Round Valley, Ukiah, Willits Unified, Upper Lake Union, Kelseyville Unified, and Lakeport Unified.

MENLO COLLEGE *(D-11)*
Atherton, California 94027-4301
Tel: (415) 688-3753; (800) 556-3656; Admissions: (415) 688-3753;
Fax: (415) 324-2347

Description: The privately supported, coeducational college is accredited by the Western Association of Schools and Colleges. It operates on the semester system and offers several summer sessions. Enrollment includes 564 students. A faculty of 40 gives a faculty-student ratio of 1-26. Army ROTC program is available.

Entrance Requirements: Accredited high school graduation or equivalent with completion of 12 units; high school graduates with a C average sometimes accepted; SAT or ACT required; a personal recommendation necessary from educators; early decision, midyear admission, rolling admission, and advanced placement plans available; $40 application fee.

Costs Per Year: $14,815 tuition; $6,200 room and board; $200 student fees.

Collegiate Environment: The tree lined campus, a few minutes drive from Palo Alto and Stanford University, includes a library containing 62,000 volumes, and 5 residence halls with a capacity of 474. All unmarried students under the age of 21, unless living with parents, must reside on campus. There are also 2 academic buildings, 4 athletic fields, 2 pools, the student union, and a dining hall. Average

freshmen scores were SAT Verbal 398, Math 460. About 87% of applicants are accepted. Some financial aid is available and about 57% of students receive some form of financial assistance.

Community Environment: This is a residential community 30 miles south of San Francisco and 20 miles north of San Jose. The climate is moderate. The Southern Pacific Railroad, and Pacific Greyhound Bus serve the area with San Francisco International Airport 16 miles north. Activities are planned for all ages at the recreation center and many parks and playgrounds.

MENNONITE BRETHREN BIBLICAL SEMINARY *(K-6)*
4824 East Butler Avenue
Fresno, California 93727-5097
Tel: (209) 251-8628; Fax: (209) 251-7212

Description: The privately supported, coeducational graduate seminary is accredited by the Western Association of Schools and Colleges and professionally by the Association of Theological Schools. Affiliated with the Mennonite Brethren Church, the seminary was founded in 1955 to fill the need for a theological institution at the graduate level that trains Christian workers for the Church and community. The seminary awards a post-graduate diploma in Christian Studies and Masters degrees. It operates on the 4-1-4 calendar system and offers one summer session. Enrollment is 91 men and 38 women. A faculty of 11 full-time and 20 part-time gives an overall faculty-student ratio of 1-9.

Entrance Requirements: All students are accepted who are of evangelical faith and in sympathy with the principles of the seminary; courses are designed for students who have completed a B.A. degree or equivalent; GRE, TOEFL required; rolling admission and midyear admission plans are available. $25 application fee.

Costs Per Year: $5,640 ($188/credit).

Collegiate Environment: The campus is located in a quiet residential section of Fresno, approximately three miles from downtown district. There are three national parks within easy driving distance, which contain some of the most scenic areas of the West. The campus has four buildings and a library of 143,150 volumes, 1,080 periodicals, and 180,000 microforms. There are no campus dormitories; however, there are 10 apartments for married students on campus. Other housing is available near the campus. 95% of applicants are accepted. Approximately 90% of the students receive some form of financial aid.

Community Environment: See California State University - Fresno.

MERCED COLLEGE *(D-11)*
3600 M Street
Merced, California 95348
Tel: (209) 384-6000

Description: This publicly supported coeducational community college is accredited by the Western Association of Schools and Colleges. The college operates on the semester system and offers two summer sessions. It offers university transfer programs and vocational-technical courses that lead to a Certificate of Completion or an Associate degree. Enrollment includes 2,948 full-time and 3,636 part-time students. A faculty of 126 full-time and 300 part-time gives a faculty-student ratio of 1-18.

Entrance Requirements: High school graduation and residence in district; non-high school graduates 18 years of age or older may be admitted; high school seniors in top 10% of class may take part-time classes at the college if written permission is obtained from high school principal; college placement tests are required; rolling admission and midyear admission plans available.

Costs Per Year: $390 ($13/unit) resident tuition; $1,500 ($50/unit) rsident with B.A. degree or higher; $3,420 ($114/unit) nonresident.

Collegiate Environment: The campus consists of 15 buildings on 143 acres; 110 acres were donated to the college by the CHM Company and the Yosemite Land and Cattle Company. The library contains over 30,000 volumes and 350 periodicals. There are no dormitory residences on campus. All applicants are accepted, and students are admitted at midyear as well as in the fall. 200 scholarships are available and 35% of the students receive some form of financial aid.

Community Environment: Merced is a rural suburban area with a dry temperate climate. All forms of transportation serve the area. Merced has a library, churches, theaters, symphony, and two general hospitals. Job opportunities are good during the summer. Merced is located at the foot of the Sierra Nevada Mountains and near Yosemite National Park, which provides recreational facilities for camping, hiking, fishing, and skiing, the major winter sport. All national service clubs are represented here.

MERRITT COLLEGE *(I-3)*
12500 Campus Drive
Oakland, California 94619
Tel: (415) 531-4911

Description: The publicly supported, coeducational junior college is maintained by the Peralta Community College District. The college operates on the semester system with one summer session and is accredited by the Western Association of Schools and Colleges. University parallel, technical-vocational and general education programs are offered in both day and evening programs; all lead to a Certificate or Associate degree. Enrollment includes 1,128 full-time and 4,641 part-time and 1,783 evening students. A faculty of 335 gives a faculty-student ratio of 1-35.

Entrance Requirements: High school graduation or equivalent; nongraduates over 18 years of age considered; classification tests required; health examinations are required in certain programs; open enrollment; early admission, early decision, midyear admission, advanced placement and rolling admission plan available.

Costs Per Year: $390 ($13/unit) resident tuition; $1,550 ($50/unit) resident with B.A. degree; $4,050 ($135/unit) nonresident.

Collegiate Environment: The central campus is currently located in Oakland, a short distance from the dividing line of Berkeley and Oakland. All students who apply for admission and meet the requirements are accepted. 26 scholarships are offered, including 19 for freshmen and 36% of the current student body receives some form of financial assistance. The college library contains over 56,000 volumes.

Community Environment: See Laney College

MILLS COLLEGE *(I-3)*
5000 MacArthur Blvd.
Oakland, California 94613
Tel: (510) 430-2135; (800) 876-4557; Admissions: (510) 430-2135; Fax: (510) 430-3314

Description: The privately supported, residential, liberal arts college is for women but admits men in the graduate school. It is accredited by the Western Association of Schools and Colleges. Founded in 1852, the campus moved to its present site in 1871, and the first baccalaureate degrees were granted in 1889. The college grants a Baccalaureate and Master degree and offers courses leading toward California teaching credentials. Air Force, Army and Navy ROTC programs are available. It operates on the early semester calendar system. Enrollment includes 803 full-time and 60 part-time undergraduates and 309 graduate students. A faculty of 73 full-time and 68 part-time gives a faculty-student ratio of 1-12.

Entrance Requirements: Accredited high school graduation and recommendation for admission by high school. College preparatory courses recommended, including 4 English, 3 mathematics, 2 foreign language, 2 science and 2 social science; SAT I required. SAT II: subject tests highly recommended. Application fee $35; rolling admissions, except for International and Merit Scholarship applicants who must apply by February 15 for fall entrance.

Costs Per Year: $14,530 tuition; $6,180 room and board; $854 student fees.

Collegiate Environment: The 135-acre campus is set among hills and tall stands of eucalyptus and pine. It is surrounded by the city of Oakland, and within 20-30 minutes of the downtown centers of both Oakland and San Francisco. There are more than 40 buildings on campus, and the library contains 210,802 volumes, 8,032 microfilms and 3,503 sound recordings. Seventy percent of the student body graduated in the top 30% of the high school class. 83% of the students applying for admission are accepted. Scholarships are available and 75% of undergraduates receive some form of financial aid. Dormitory space is available for all women students. Residence halls accommo-

date 504 women. In addition to the traditional liberal arts curriculum, Mills offers a pre-medical sequence, majors in Political, Legal and Economic Analysis, Business Economics, Communication, Ethnic Studies, Women's Studies, and the opportunity to create one's own major.

Community Environment: See Laney College

MIRACOSTA COMMUNITY COLLEGE *(Q-10)*
1 Barnard Drive
Oceanside, California 92056
Tel: (619) 757-2121

Description: This publicly supported, coeducational community college is accredited by the Western Association of Schools and Colleges. It operates on the semester system and offers one summer session. This college was one of the first community colleges in San Diego County, established in 1934. In 1964, the college moved to a new campus located four miles from the ocean. Enrollment includes 2,381 full-time and 6,052 part-time students. A faculty of 91 full-time and 283 part-time gives an overall faculty-student ratio of 1-25. The college offers university transfer, vocational-technical and general education courses. It grants a Certificate and an Associate degree.

Entrance Requirements: Legal residence in Mira Costa Community College District or an area not served by a community college or a district that grants written permission to attend; open enrollment policy; high school graduation or equivalent; nongraduates in their junior year of high school considered; rolling admission, early admission and advanced placement plans available.

Costs Per Year: $403 ($13/unit) resident; $1,550 ($50/unit) resident with BA degree or higher; $3,534 ($114/unit) nonresident; $40 student fees.

Collegiate Environment: Both campuses and a center consist of 225 acres of rolling hills that command a panoramic view. The library contains 53,227 volumes, 163,774 periodicals, microforms and sound recordings. 83 scholarships are available, and approximately 15% of the current students receive financial assistance. All applicants are accepted.

Community Environment: Oceanside is located in Southern California, 40 miles north of San Diego, adjacent to the San Diego Freeway. Buses and trains serve the area. There are many churches and hospitals in the city. Some opportunity exists for part-time employment for students. Oceanside is a resort with a four-mile beach area and a 1,900-foot pleasure pier; a fleet of fishing boats operates from Oceanside's harbor. There are no dormitories for students; however, suitable rooms may be found within cities of Carlsbad and Oceanside. Many wild birds may be seen here in the marshes and lagoons. Mission San Luis Rey is four miles east. San Elijo center is located 22 miles north of San Diego adjacent to San Elijo Lagoon and the San Diego Freeway.

MODESTO JUNIOR COLLEGE *(I-5)*
435 College Avenue
Modesto, California 95350-9977
Tel: (209) 575-6470; Fax: (209) 575-6630

Description: The publicly supported coeducational junior college is accredited by the Western Association of Schools and Colleges. The college was organized in October 1921 as the first state junior college established under an Act of the California State Legislature. The college operates on the semester system and offers one summer session. Enrollment is 12,166, with a faculty of 263, giving a faculty-student ratio of 1-46. Transfer, vocational-technical, business and general education programs lead to a Certificate, Diploma or an Associate degree.

Entrance Requirements: Accredited high school graduation; non-high school graduates over 18 years of age may be admitted as provisional students; early admission, early decision, rolling admission, delayed admission, and advanced placement plans are available.

Costs Per Year: $403 ($13/unit) state-resident tuition; $3,472 ($112/unit) nonresidents; $50/unit for students with B.A. degree or higher; $10 health fee; $4/semester student fee.

Collegiate Environment: The campus is located on two sites totalling 125 acres, and consists of 25 buildings. The library contains more than 63,600 volumes. All students meeting admission requirements are accepted. Various forms of financial assistance are available. Students may enroll at midyear.

Community Environment: Modesto is located in the heart of the San Joaquin Valley and is the access point for the Sonora Pass vacationland in the Stanislaus National Forest, Mother Lode Country and the Big Oak Flat route to Yosemite. Modesto is the county seat of Stanislaus County. Churches of all denominations, a library, hospitals, plus the usual businesses make up the city of Modesto. There are 20 parks, playgrounds, golf courses, tennis courts, swimming pools for recreational facilities plus areas where there is boating, fishing, hunting and skiing. Part-time employment is available.

MONTEREY INSTITUTE OF INTERNATIONAL STUDIES
(K-3)
425 Van Buren Street
Monterey, California 93940
Tel: (408) 647-4123

Description: The privately supported, liberal arts college is accredited by the Western Association of Schools and Colleges and was founded in 1955. The focus of the Institute is preparing students for international careers in private, public, nonprofit, and educational sectors. Its students come from over 50 countries. Its programs are interdisciplinary, combining crosscultural perspectives with the opportunity to refine foreign language skills in Arabic, Chinese, English, French, German, Italian, Japanese, Russian, or Spanish. Operating on the semester system with one summer term, it offers Bachelor's and Masters's degrees. Enrollment includes 655 full-time and 89 part-time undergraduate and 678 graduate students. A faculty of 67 full-time and 70 part-time members gives an undergraduate faculty-student ratio of 1-11.

Entrance Requirements: Admission to undergraduate upper-division requires completion of 2 years of college with a miniumum B average; admission to graduate division requires a minimum B average and a Bachelor's degree or equivalent from an accredited institution; application fee $50; TOEFL required for non-native English speaking students; rolling admission, delayed admission and advanced placement plans available; midyear students are accepted in some majors.

Costs Per Year: $15,200 tuition.

Collegiate Environment: The Institute is located on the Monterey Peninsula about 130 miles south of San Francisco. The campus is located near downtown Monterey. The library contains 64,200 volumes and 500 periodicals, with a state-of-the-art integrated computer system and CD-ROM work stations. 78% of students applying for admission are accepted. 60% of the students receive financial assistance and approximately 60 scholarships are available.

Community Environment: See Monterey Peninsula College

MONTEREY PENINSULA COLLEGE   *(K-3)*
980 Fremont Street
Monterey, California 93940-1799
Tel: (408) 646-4000; Admissions: (408) 646-4002; Fax: (408) 655-2627

Description: The publicly supported, coeducational community college uses the semester system with one summer session and is accredited by the Western Association of Schools and Colleges. The college commenced its operation in 1947 on an evening basis only but has expanded to include a day program. Faculty of 350 and enrollment of approximately 8,300 students gives faculty-student ratio of 1-25. Offering university transfer, technical-vocational and general education programs, the college awards Certificates and Associate degrees.

Entrance Requirements: High school graduation or 18 years old; open enrollment.

Costs Per Year: $13 per unit (about $400) in fees for California residents; additional $110 per unit nonresident tuition.

Collegiate Environment: 19 buildings on 87 acres comprise the campus; the library contains 64,000 volumes. All students applying for admission are accepted including midyear students.

Community Environment: Monterey Peninsula's poulation is approximately 150,000 including the cities of Carmel, Carmel Valley, Marina, Monterey, Pacific Grove, Pebble Beach, and Seaside. Monterey is a good two hour drive south of San Francisco on Highway 1. Airlines and buses serve the area. The climate is pleasing; average

summer temperature is 60 and winter average is 51 degrees. This is the home of the Bach Festival, Golf Tournaments, Sports Car Races, the Monterey Jazz Festival, and the County Fair. Artists, photographers, and writers enjoy Monterey for its beautiful scenery and good weather. Little theatre groups, music groups, art council and symphony guilds make up the cultural atmosphere of the city. Monterey Peninsula is a popular playground with several golf courses, facilities for fishing, boating, hunting and tennis. There are twelve championship golf courses in the area.

MOORPARK COLLEGE   *(O-8)*
7075 Campus Road
Moorpark, California 93021
Tel: (805) 378-1400; Admissions: (805) 378-1429; Fax: (805) 378-1499

Description: The publicly supported, coeducational community college is accredited by the Western Association of Colleges and Schools. The college was established in 1967 to serve the communities of eastern Ventura County. The college offers university transfer, vocational-technical and general education programs leading to a Certificate of Achievement and an Associate degree to its day and evening students. It operates on the early semester calendar system and offers one summer session. Enrollment includes 10,605 students. A faculty of 400 gives a faculty-student ratio of 1-27.

Entrance Requirements: Meet California residence requirement; high school graduation or 18 years of age; rolling admission, midyear admission and advanced placement plans available.

Costs Per Year: $390 ($13/unit) resident tuition; $1,500 ($50/unit) resident with B.A. or higher degree; $3,420 ($114/unit) nonresident.

Collegiate Environment: The campus consists of ten buildings on 134 acres, located in eastern Ventura County on a hillside between Simi and Moorpark. The library contains 55,000 volumes and numerous periodicals and microforms. All applicants are accepted. 15% of the students receive financial aid.

Community Environment: See California Lutheran University

MOUNT SAINT MARY'S COLLEGE   *(O-8)*
12001 Chalon Road
Los Angeles, California 90049
Tel: (213) 471-9516; (800) 999-9893; Fax: (310) 440-3258

Description: The privately supported, liberal arts Roman Catholic college for women allows men to participate in undergraduate music, nursing program, extended day, and graduate division programs. It is accredited by the Western Association of Schools and Colleges. This college was founded and received its official charter in 1925 by the Sisters of St. Joseph of Carondelet. There are 2 campuses: The Main Campus (Chalon Road) offers four-year courses of study leading to a Baccalaureate degree; The Doheny Campus (Chester Place) offers two-year courses of study leading to the Associate degree, and the graduate division granting a Master's degree. The semester system is used, with a limited summer session. Enrollment includes 1,351 undergraduate students. A faculty of 68 full-time and 107 part-time gives a faculty-student ratio of 1-12.

Entrance Requirements: Graduation from an accredited high school with B average; 16 high school units recommended, including 4 English, 3 mathematics, 2 foreign language, 2 science, and 2 social science; SAT or ACT required; students applying for the Associate degree program at the Doheny campus are accepted with a C average in high school; under certain circumstances non-high school graduates are considered for admission to the Associate degree program; G.E.D. is acceptable; GRE is required for the graduate program; rolling admission, midyear admission, and advanced placement plans available; $30 application fee.

Costs Per Year: $12,914 tuition; $5,500 room and board; $300 student fees.

Collegiate Environment: The campus is located on a 56-acre tract in Brentwood Hills, Los Angeles with buildings of Spanish colonial architecture. The library contains 140,000 volumes, 687 periodicals, 4,760,881 microforms and 1,400 sound recordings. Dormitory space is available for 520 women. Approximately 43% of the students applying are accepted. 77% receive financial assistance.

Community Environment: See University of California - Los Angeles.

MOUNT SAN ANTONIO COLLEGE   *(G-12)*
1100 North Grand Avenue
Walnut, California 91789
Tel: (909) 594-5611

Description: The publicly supported community college operates on the semester system with two summer sessions and is accredited by the Western Association of Schools and Colleges. Founded in 1946, this college offers a diversified program designed to develop qualities essential for citizens in a democratic society. Offering day, weekend and evening classes, the enrollment includes 17,562 men and 19,803 women. A faculty of 315 full-time and 380 part-time gives a faculty-student ratio of 1:30. The college awards a Certificate of Completion, Diploma or an Associate degree.

Entrance Requirements: High school graduation; open enrollment policy; nongraduates 18 years of age or over admitted.

Costs Per Year: $190 tuition; $3,000 out-of-state tuition; $50 maximum student fee.

Collegiate Environment: Situated in the rolling San Jose hills, the 421-acre campus has a rural setting removed from the noise and confusion of city life. There are 63 buildings; no dormitories. Library houses 76,153 volumes, 1,318 periodicals, 20,308 microforms and 9,585 sound recordings. Financial assistance is available. Students may enroll at midyear.

Community Environment: Walnut is close to recreational areas such as Disneyland, beaches, Mt. Baldy Park, Lake Arrowhead, Palm Springs, and Hollywood.

MOUNT SAN JACINTO COLLEGE   *(P-11)*
1499 N. State St.
San Jacinto, California 92583
Tel: (909) 487-6752; Fax: (909) 654-6738

Description: Publicly supported, coeducational community college is accredited by the Western Association of Schools and Colleges. It operates on the semester system and offers one summer session. Enrollment is 1,654 full-time and 5,356 part-time students. A faculty of 200 gives a faculty-student ratio of 1-35. Founded in 1961 to fulfill the need for a community college in Riverside County, the first class began in 1963. The college offers occupational training, general education, transfer, and adult education programs leading to a Certificate of Achievement or an Associate degree.

Entrance Requirements: High school graduation; non-high school graduates over 18 years may be admitted on probation; early admission and advanced placement plans available; open enrollment policy.

Costs Per Year: $403 ($13/unit) resident; $1,550 ($50/unit) resident with B.A. degree; $3,503 ($113/unit) nonresident.

Collegiate Environment: The campus is located on 160 acres in an area that has clear, dry desert and mountain air. The library contains more than 35,000 volumes. Financial aid is available, and 90% of the current students receive some form of assistance. All those who apply for admission are accepted, and students may enroll at midyear as well as in the fall.

Community Environment: Population 120,000. The college serves several communities varying in elevation from 1,500 feet to 4,500 feet, including Banning, Beaumont, Elsinore, Hemet, Idyllwild, Perris, Sun City, Canyon Lake, Murrieta, Temecula, Aguanga, Anza, and San Jacinto. Citrus fruits, walnuts, olives, cherries, watermelon, apples, and potatoes are some of the area's products. The largest single industry is the light, smokeless manufacture of mobile homes and travel trailers. The pleasant climate attracts retirees from throughout the nation. It is an easy drive to the mountains, the deserts, and the beaches.

Branch Campuses: Menifee Valley Campus, 28237 La Piedra Road, Menifee, CA, (714) 672-6752.

NAPA VALLEY COLLEGE   *(H-3)*
Napa, California 94558
Tel: (707) 253-3000; Fax: (707) 253-3064

Description: This publicly supported, coeducational community college was one of the first three junior colleges to be accredited by the Western Association of Schools and Colleges. Founded in 1947, the school operates on the early semester system and offers one summer session for both day and evening classes. The college awards Associate of Arts and Associate of Science degrees and vocational certificates. Enrollment is 1,799 full-time and 5,303 part-time students. A faculty of 97 full-time and 200 part-time gives an overall faculty-student ratio of 1-18.

Entrance Requirements: High school graduation or equivalent; non-high school graduates over 18 years able to profit from instruction admitted; TOEFL for foreign students; open enrollment; rolling admission, early admission, delayed admission and advanced placement plans available.

Costs Per Year: $403 ($13/credit) resident; $1,550 ($50/credit) resident with BA degree or higher; $3,720 ($120/credit) nonresident.

Collegiate Environment: The campus is located in the city of Napa, the gateway to one of the finest agricultural areas of the state. As a part of the San Francisco Bay area, Napa enjoys the cultural and recreational advantage of this large metropolitan region. The library contains more than 42,000 volumes. Midyear students are accepted. Financial assistance is available.

Community Environment: Population 58,000. The town of Napa, in the southern wine district, is the center of a fruit and nut raising region as well as the southeastern entrance to the Redwood Empire. Located in the Napa Valley area, there are numerous wineries, most of which are open to the public for tours. The climate is delightful. Buses and trains serve the area. Napa has churches of all denominations, hospitals, clinics, and libraries. Recreation includes parks, picnic grounds, swimming pools, and golf courses.

Branch Campuses: Located in St. Helena.

NATIONAL UNIVERSITY   *(Q-10)*
4025 Camino del Rio South
San Diego, California 92108
Tel: (714) 563-7100

Description: Established in 1972 and fully accredited by the Western Association of Schools and Colleges, the university specializes in offering higher education opportunities to career oriented adults. Classes leading to associate, bachelor, master, and professional degrees are offered in an intensive one-course-per-month format. Faculty consists primarily of respected professionals with years of career experience who bring both academic and contemporary expertise in their chosen field to the classroom. Enrollment is approximately 10,000 students, with a teacher-student ratio of 1-16.

Entrance Requirements: High school graduation or GED; admissions interview; $60 application fee.

Costs Per Year: $5,535 undergraduate tuition; $5,625 graduate.

Collegiate Environment: The central university is located in San Diego's beautiful Mission Valley, easily accessible from all major San Diego freeways. The library houses 116,000 hardbound volumes. A number of scholarships are available. There is no student housing on campus. Qualified applicants may begin classes any month of the year.

Community Environment: See University of California - San Diego

NAVAL POSTGRADUATE SCHOOL   *(K-3)*
Monterey, California 93943
Tel: (408) 656-3093; Fax: (408) 656-2891

Description: This publicly supported, technological graduate school serves officers of the U.S. Navy, U.S. Armed Forces and other Armed Forces; civilian employees of the United States Government are also eligible to attend. Accredited by the Western Association of Schools and Colleges, the school operates on the quarter system with 1 summer session and grants Master's, Engineer's, and Doctoral degrees. Established in 1909 in Annapolis, the only curriculum offered was marine engineering. The present campus opened in 1951 and currently has extensive program offerings in scientific, engineering and administrative subject areas. Enrollment is 1,725 graduate students. A faculty of 346 gives a faculty-student ratio of 1-5.

Entrance Requirements: Bachelor's degree required; applicants should apply through their respective branches of the Armed Forces; requirements vary with each program; GRE required for doctoral programs only, TOEFL 540 minimum; open only to members of U.S. and other forces and civilian employees of the U.S. government.

Costs Per Year: Only charge is for textbooks and related supplies.

Collegiate Environment: The school is located in the city of Monterey. The campus covers about 600 acres and includes a 1,000,000-volume library and a beach area used for research and recreation. School housing accommodates 877 students. Extensive recreational facilities offered for students and their spouses include sailing, swimming, golf, tennis and competitive team sports.

Community Environment: See Monterey Peninsula College.

OCCIDENTAL COLLEGE   *(O-8)*
1600 Campus Road
Los Angeles, California 90041
Tel: (213) 259-2700

Description: The privately supported, coeducational, liberal arts college has an enrollment of 1,600 and a faculty of 123 full-time providing a faculty-student ratio of 1:13. Accredited by the Western Association of Schools and Colleges, it operates on the trimester system and offers two summer sessions. The college grants Bachelor and Master degrees. Occidental College was founded in 1887 by a group of Presbyterian ministers and laymen but is no longer church-affiliated. The first Baccalaureate degree was conferred in 1893. More than one-half of each year's graduating seniors continues on to graduate and professional schools. The college has occupied its present campus since 1914. Overseas programs in China, Japan, Mexico, Peru, England, France, Germany and Spain.

Entrance Requirements: High school graduation or equivalent; SAT or ACT required; achievement tests recommended; non-high school graduates are sometimes admitted if mature; GRE required for graduate school; early admission, delayed admission and advanced placement plans available; application fee $30; teacher and counselor recommendations required. Fundamental aim of admission policy is to enroll a high ability, well prepared, diversified student body in terms of economic, social, ethnic, religious and geographic criteria.

Costs Per Year: $13,695 tuition; $5,100 room and board; $483 fees.

Collegiate Environment: The college, located in a residential part of Eagle Rock, a section of northeast Los Angeles, is comprised of 33 buildings on 120 acres. Residence halls have a capacity of 1,253. There is a coeducational complex with two sections, communal facilities including a lounge, recreational room, library and three seminar rooms. The library contains 478,507 volumes. About 55% of the applicants are accepted. Financial aid is available, and 63% of the current student body receives some form of assistance.

Community Environment: See University of California - Los Angeles

OHLONE COLLEGE   *(D-12)*
43600 Mission Boulevard
Fremont, California 94539
Tel: (510) 659-6000; Admissions: (510) 659-6100; Fax: (510) 659-6057

Description: This publicly supported, coeducational community college was officially named Ohlone College in 1967. It honors the early Indians who inhabited the Fremont-Newark Area. Enrollment is 2,803 full-time and 7,024 part-time students. A faculty of 141 full-time and 300 part-time gives an overall faculty-student ratio of 1-22. The college operates on the semester system and offers 1 summer session. It is accredited by the Western Association of Schools and Colleges. The college started classes in 1967 at a temporary campus site; a new $25 million campus was opened in 1974. The college offers university transfer, vocational-technical and general education courses leading to a Certificate of Achievement or an Associate degree. Army ROTC is available. Classes are held during the day and in the evening.

Entrance Requirements: High school graduation or equivalent; open enrollment policy; non-high school graduates over 18 years may be admitted; assessment testing required; early admission, midyear admission, and rolling admission plans available.

Costs Per Year: $390 ($13/unit) resident; $1,500 ($50/unit) resident with BA degree or higher; $3,240 ($114/unit) nonresident; $3,525 ($117.50/unit) foreign citizen.

Collegiate Environment: Designed as an "Educational village," the campus is nestled in the Mission San Jose foothills on a 534-acre site. The library contains 60,000 titles, 25,000 periodicals, 15,000 microforms and 12,000 audiovisual materials. Various forms of financial aid are available. All students applying for admission are accepted.

Community Environment: The Fremont area is one of the faster growing areas of California. Mild climate is enjoyed in this city located on the San Francisco Bay. Fremont is within easy driving distance of San Francisco, Berkeley, Oakland and Palo Alto, and enjoys the cultural advantages of those cities. Beaches are nearby for swimming, boating and fishing. There are numerous golf courses and parks for recreational facilities. Shopping facilities are good.

ORANGE COAST COLLEGE   *(P-9)*
2701 Fairview Road
P.O. Box 5005
Costa Mesa, California 92628-5005
Tel: (714) 432-5773

Description: The publicly supported, coeducational community college was founded in 1947 to serve the people of the Orange Coast area. It is accredited by the Western Association of Schools and Colleges. The semester system is used with two summer sessions. Enrollment includes 8,465 men, 8,142 women full-time, 3,994 men, and 4,022 women part-time. A faculty of 363 full-time and 450 part-time gives a faculty-student ratio 1:30. The college offers career programs, college transfer, and general education leading to certificate of achievement and the Associate of Arts degree and opportunities for retraining and life-long learning.

Entrance Requirements: Applicants are accepted provided residence requirements are met; must be over 18 years of age if not a high school graduate; out-of-state applicants can be accepted on recommendation of Dean of Admissions; rolling admission plan available.

Costs Per Year: $403 ($13 per unit) California resident tuition; $3,317 ($107 per unit) out-of-state tuition; $40-$60 student fees.

Collegiate Environment: There are 55 buildings on the 210-acre campus. No dormitories are provided. The library contains 97,000 volumes. The college offers 55 different career and certificate programs and encompasses 157 disciplines. The campus is located near the beautiful Pacific with lovely beaches offering unlimited boating and swimming. Orange Coast is considered one of the finest two-year colleges of the west.

Community Environment: Costa Mesa is three miles inland from the Pacific Ocean and Highway 101-A. It can be reached by the freeway system in Orange County and Highway 55. The city has a moderate climate - mild winters, and cool summer breezes from the ocean. The Los Angeles Museum, Pasadena Art Gallery, and the Los Angeles Griffith Park Planetarium are 50 miles from Costa Mesa. The mountains and the desert are an easy two hour drive. Costa Mesa is at the edge of Newport Beach and offers all recreational activities with its beaches, canals, and waterways for those who enjoy boating and fishing. Also Orange County's employment outlook is even better then the nation's because it is particularly strong in the area of defense, electronics, housing, and business sciences, as well as tourism. The area is productive in agriculture, electronics and light industry, offering part-time employment for students. Excellent shopping centers in and around the area. Costa Mesa is near some of the west's most beautiful cities, yet away from the noise of downtown traffic. The campus is located within 15 minutes of the new Orange County Performing Arts Center; Irvine Industrial Center (home of many high-tech industries); South Coast Plaza (one of the nation's largest shopping malls); and the University of California at Irvine (a major educational and research institution).

OXNARD COLLEGE   *(O-7)*
4000 South Rose Ave.
Oxnard, California 93033
Tel: (805) 488-0911

Description: The school is a publicly supported, coeducational community college. It was founded in 1975 as part of the Ventura County Community College District. The college is fully accredited by the Western Association of Schools and Colleges. It operates on an early semester basis with one summer session. Enrollment includes 2,989 men and 3,111 women. A faculty of 85 full-time and 200 part-time faculty provides a faculty-student ratio of 1:25. The college grants Associate degrees.

Entrance Requirements: High school graduation is not required; early admission, advanced placement, early decision, rolling admission, and delayed admission plans available.

Costs Per Year: $135 district resident tuition; $3,300 nonresident tuition; $50 student fees.

Collegiate Environment: The first permanent buildings on the college's land were opened for classes in the fall of 1979. A three-college library system is available; library holdings include 26,000 volumes and numerous audiovisual materials. Students activities include intercollegiate sports, musical and dramatic organizations, school publications and other recreational activities. Financial aid in the form of grants, loans and part-time employment opportunities are available to students requiring assistance; approximately 10% of the student body receive some form of financial assistance. In addition to a full range of academic programs, Oxnard College has its own color television studio, cable television station, and classes in telecommunications, as well as a college newspaper produced by the journalism students. The Hotel and Restaurant Management program has its own fully equipped kitchen on campus as well as a dining room where students gain practical experience. There are intercollegiate teams for soccer (football), baseball, basketball, cross country, and track. Most of these sports have both women's and men's teams.

Community Environment: The city of Oxnard has a population of approximately 128,000 people, and is located on the Gold Coast of California, situated about 45 miles south of Santa Barbara and 60 miles north of Los Angeles. The climate has been described as Mediterranean. Oxnard has seven miles of shoreline with wide, uncrowded beaches. It is a paradise for people who love to boat, surf and sportfish. There are many museums and points of historical interest. Some of the major annual events include the California Strawberry Festival in May, Fiestas Patrias Celebration in September, and the Parade of Lights in December.

PACIFIC CHRISTIAN COLLEGE   *(H-12)*
2500 E. Nutwood Avenue
Fullerton, California 92631
Tel: (714) 879-3901; (800) 762-1294; Fax: (714) 526-0231

Description: The privately supported, coeducational, Christian college is affiliated with the Churches of Christ and Christian churches. Operating on the 4-1-4 academic calendar with one summer session, the college enrolls 897 including part-time and evening students. A faculty of 55 gives and overall faculty-student ratio of 1-16. Pacific Christian College is accredited by the Western Association of Schools and Colleges. The college grants the Associate in Arts degree, the Bachelor of Arts degree and the Master of Arts degree.

Entrance Requirements: Accredited high school graduation or equivalent with completion of 15 units; SAT or ACT required; early admission, early decision, rolling admission, delayed admission and advanced placement plans available; $30 application fee.

Costs Per Year: $7,600 tuition; $3,115 room and board; $210 student fees.

Collegiate Environment: The college is located across the street from California State University, Fullerton, in Orange County, which is one of California's fastest growing communities. The college is located on 11 acres and the library houses over 55,000 volumes. Dormitory space is available for 196 men and 232 women. 85% of those who apply for admission are accepted, including mid-year students. Financial aid is available and 85% of the current students receive some form of assistance.

Community Environment: See California State University - Fullerton.

PACIFIC COAST UNIVERSITY   *(P-9)*
440 Redondo Boulevard, #203
Long Beach, California 90814
Tel: (310) 439-7346

Description: The privately supported, coeducational law school operates on the quarter system and offers evening classes only. The school was founded in 1927 and has been in continuous operation since that date. The enrollment is 80 students. The faculty is composed of members of the California bench and the bar and class size is limited to 45 or fewer students. The four-year program leads to the Juris Doctor degree.

Entrance Requirements: Two years college work acceptable to the California State Bar Office; the typical student is over 25 years of age with self and family support experience and several years experience in law occupations; candidates may take the College Level Examination Program (CLEP) in lieu of the two years of college.

Costs Per Year: $995 tuition.

Collegiate Environment: The school is located in downtown Long Beach convenient to many communities because of the extensive California freeway system. The library contains over 8,000 volumes. Other universities in the area offer courses in the same building, providing the law school student with the opportunity to pursue a subject of particular interest to him.

Community Environment: See California State University - Long Beach

PACIFIC LUTHERAN THEOLOGICAL SEMINARY   *(H-3)*
2770 Marin Avenue
Berkeley, California 94708
Tel: (510) 524-5264; (800) 235-7587; Fax: (510) 524-2408

Description: The privately supported, coeducational, graduate theological institution with an enrollment of 120 is a member of the Graduate Theological Union. A full-time faculty of 14 gives an overall faculty-student ratio of 1-9. Accredited by the Association of Theological Schools, the seminary operates on the 4-1-4 system with one summer session. It was founded in 1950 and presently serves the Evangelical Lutheran Church in America. The seminary grants a Master of Arts in Theology degree, a Master of Divinity degree, and a Master of Theology degree. The main purpose of the Seminary is to train men and women for competent pastoral ministry, especially in the Lutheran Church. PLTS has an extension program in Los Angeles through the School of Theology at Claremont.

Entrance Requirements: College and university graduates; one year of Greek required; approval of the appropriate church body is required for admission to candidacy for ordained ministry; $30 application fee.

Costs Per Year: $5,400 tuition; room and board available.

Collegiate Environment: The campus includes six buildings on nine acres located in the Berkeley hills area of the town. Two miles down the hill from the campus are located other facilities of the Graduate Theological Union. Most of the facilities of the G.T.U., including the 600,000-volume library, are shared by all the member schools. The campus library contains 355,000 volumes. The seminary has dormitory capacity of 20-30 and a 42-unit apartment building. About 90% of the students receive financial assistance.

Community Environment: See University of California - Berkeley.

PACIFIC OAKS COLLEGE   *(O-9)*
5 Westmoreland Place
Pasadena, California 91103
Tel: (818) 397-1351

Description: The privately supported, coeducational upper-division college and graduate school is accredited by the Western Association of Schools and Colleges and operates on the semester system with 2 summer sessions. The college was founded by seven Quaker families in 1945. The college seeks to contribute knowledge about human development and to foster conditions which promote the development of children and adults as competent, confident, and thoughtful individuals, capable of contributing to a peaceful society. Programs in early childhood and parent education, elementary teaching, college teaching and administration, marriage and family therapy and human development are offered. Enrollment includes 10 men, 64 women full-time, 13 men, 83 women part-time, and 393 graduate students. A faculty of 18 full-time and 44 part-time provides a faculty-student ratio of 1:12.

Entrance Requirements: Completion of 60 college units required including English composition, psychology, sociology or anthropology.

Rolling admission and delayed admission plans available. Application fee $50; personal interview recommended.

Costs Per Year: Tuition $375 per credit; student activity fee $25. No housing on campus.

Collegiate Environment: Pacific Oaks has two campuses located in a quiet residential section of Pasadena. At the California Blvd. campus there are three large converted residences and two smaller buildings. Within the confines of the one and half acre campus, the college operates a Children's School with programs for children from infancy through the third grade. The second campus, approximately 1 mile away, consists of two large and beautiful old houses on Westmoreland Place adjacent to the historic Gamble House. Classrooms are informal. In keeping with the educational goals of the college, direct experience with the children is the essential focus of the programs. Parent education is a major focus in the Children's School, thus enabling students to develop their experience in relation to parent education. The library includes over 30,224 volumes and periodicals. About 95% of the applicants are accepted.

Community Environment: See California Institute of Technology

Branch Campuses: Outreach classes toward the B.A. and M.A. in Human Development are offered in San Diego, CA; Phoenix, AZ; the San Francisco Bay Area; Portland, OR; and Seattle, WA. An elementary teacher credentialing program is offered on a branch campus in Seattle.

PACIFIC SCHOOL OF RELIGION   (H-3)
1798 Scenic Avenue
Berkeley, California 94709
Tel: (510) 848-0528; (800) 999-0528; Admissions: (510) 848-0528; Fax: (510) 845-8948

Description: The privately supported, interdenominational, coeducational graduate theological institution is accredited by the Western Association of Schools and Colleges and the Association of Theological Schools. From its founding in 1866, this school of religion has offered theological education with high academic standards relevant to the needs of our day. The school is a member of the Graduate Theological Union, located in Berkeley, California, sharing the facilities including the 351,270-volume library. The school grants a Master, Doctor and Advanced Professional degree as well as a Certificate of Special Studies. The school operates on the semester system and offers one summer session. Enrolllment is 192 students. With a faculty of 12 and an additional 80 in GTU schools, the faculty-student ratio is 1-13.

Entrance Requirements: Bachelor's degree from an approved college; evidence of the possibility of a fruitful ministry; B average; $50 application fee.

Costs Per Year: $6,500 tuition; $3,000 room and board; $50 student fees.

Collegiate Environment: Located in the San Francisco Bay Area, the campus has 16 buildings on eight acres. Students can use the various facilities of the Graduate Theological Union. The campus library contains 351,270 volumes and 165,902 microforms. School housing accommodates 62 single and 67 married students. 83% of applicants are accepted. Financial assistance is available to Master degree candidates only; approximately 65% of these students receive some form of aid.

Community Environment: See University of California - Berkeley.

PACIFIC UNION COLLEGE   (G-3)
Angwin, California 94508
Tel: (707) 965-6336; (800) 862-7080; Fax: (707) 965-6432

Description: This privately supported, coeducational, liberal arts, Seventh-Day Adventist college is accredited by the Western Association of Schools and Colleges. Founded in 1882, the school was formerly known as Healdsburg College and moved to its present site in 1909. It operates on the quarter system and offers one summer session. Enrollment includes 1,404 full-time, 141 part-time undergraduate, and 33 graduate students. A faculty of 112 full-time and 9 part-time gives a faculty-student ratio of 1-12. The college awards the Associate, Bachelor and Master degrees, and offers preparation for the California Registered Nurse examination.

Entrance Requirements: High school graduation or equivalent with C average; ACT required; GRE required for graduate school; $30 application fee; early admission, early decision, rolling admission, midyear admission, and advanced placement plans available.

Costs Per Year: $12,360 tuition; $3,945 room and board; $600 books and supplies.

Collegiate Environment: The campus is located on Howell Mountain eight miles from St. Helena at an elevation of 1,700 feet. The college owns 2,000 acres of mountainous woodland, but only 200 acres are used for buildings and recreational facilities. The library contains 250,000 volumes, 1,200 periodicals and numerous audiovisual materials. Dormitory space is available for 1,400 students. 71% of students applying for admission meet the requirements and are accepted. Financial aid is available, and 87% of the current student body receives some form of assistance. Students may enroll at midyear as well as in the fall.

Community Environment: This is a rural incorporated area on Howell Mountain, an extinct volcano, 80 miles from San Francisco. The climate is not extreme, although it is not unusual to have as much as 60 inches of rain in the winter. Bus service is available in St. Helena; railroads and airlines serve the San Francisco Bay area. Freeways are nearby. A hospital is located five miles from Angwin. Employment is available for students.

PALO VERDE COLLEGE   (P-14)
811 West Chanslorway
Blythe, California 92225
Tel: (619) 922-6168; Fax: (619) 922-0230

Description: Publicly supported, coeducational, community college accredited by the Western Association of Schools and Colleges. Founded in 1947, the college moved to its new location on its 20th anniversary. The college grants an Associate degree. It operates on the semester system and offers two summer sessions. Enrollment includes 250 full-time and 950 part-time and 650 evening students. A faculty of 19 full-time and 40 part-time gives a faculty-student ratio of 1-30.

Entrance Requirements: High school graduation or capable individuals 18 years or older; open enrollment policy; out-of-district residents must obtain permits and certificates of health; advanced placement, midyear admission, and rolling admission plans available.

Costs Per Year: $390 ($13/unit) state resident tuition; $1,500 ($50/unit) resident with B.A. degree or higher; $3,210 ($107/unit) nonresident.

Collegiate Environment: The campus is located near the Colorado River and is 165 miles west of Phoenix, Arizona, and 225 east of Los Angeles. All students meeting the requirements are accepted, including midyear students. Special programs are offered for the culturally disadvantaged. Financial aid is available, and 40% of the current students receive some form of assistance. The college library contains 18,000 items.

Community Environment: Blythe is in the Palo Verde Valley, which is mainly an agricultural region. The climate is dry and temperate. Greyhound Bus serves the area. Blythe is located on Interstate 10 between Los Angeles and Phoenix. There is a public library, a hospital, 30 churches and 2 clinics. Blythe is considered a 365-day farming area. There are good part-time employment opportunities. The city has the usual civic organizations. Recreation includes hunting, boating, and fishing on the Colorado River.

PALOMAR COMMUNITY COLLEGE   (Q-10)
1140 West Mission Road
San Marcos, California 92069
Tel: (619) 744-1150; Admissions: (619) 744-1150 x2171; Fax: (619) 744-2932

Description: The publicly supported, coeducational community college uses the semester system with 2 summer sessions and is accredited by the Western Association of Schools and Colleges. Founded in 1946, the campus moved to its present site in 1950. The college grants an Associate Degree and Certificates. Enrollment is 23,707; a faculty of 1,033 gives a faculty-student ratio of 1-23.

Entrance Requirements: High school graduation or 18 years of age; open enrollment; early admission, early decision and rolling admission plans are available; students are admitted at midyear.

Costs Per Year: $13 per unit up to $300 per year for California residents; $107 per unit nonresidents.

Collegiate Environment: The campus is located in northern San Diego County, approximately one-half mile west of San Marcos and about 40 miles north of San Diego. The library contains 150,000 volumes. All students applying for admission are accepted. Special programs for the culturally disadvantaged are offered. Scholarships and financial aid are available.

Community Environment: Located in the northern San Diego County, 40 miles northeast of San Diego. San Marcos lies in the "perfect climate belt" of Southern California. The beaches are 15 miles distant and provide the recreational facilities for water sports. Palomar Mountain, the home of the famed Observatory, is 45 miles away.

PASADENA CITY COLLEGE *(O-9)*
1570 East Colorado Boulevard
Pasadena, California 91106
Tel: (213) 578-7123; Admissions: (818) 585-7394; Fax: (818) 585-7915

Description: The publicly supported, coeducational community college is accredited by the Western Association of Schools and Colleges, and operates on the semester system with two summer sessions. The present college is the product of the development of junior college level work in Pasadena since 1924. The college serves the Pasadena Area Community College District, which includes the school districts of Arcadia, La Canada, Flintridge, Pasadena, Rosemead, San Marino, South Pasadena and Temple City. Offering general education, occupational education, college transfer and continuing education programs, the college grants an Associate degree. Enrollment is 22,000 including part-time students. A faculty of 1,019 gives a faculty-student ratio of 1-23.

Entrance Requirements: High school graduation or 19 years or older; early admission, early decision, rolling admission and advanced placement plans available.

Costs Per Year: $13/unit state-resident tuition; $117/unit nonresident; $250 approximate book fees.

Collegiate Environment: Thirty-three buildings on 55 acres comprise the campus, which is centrally located in Pasadena. The library contains approximately 100,000 volumes. No campus housing is provided. Special programs are offered for the culturally disadvantaged as well as courses in American Indian, Asian-American, Chicano, and Pan-African studies. 99% of those who apply are admitted, and midyear students are accepted. Financial aid is available, and 20% of the current student body receives some assistance.

Community Environment: See California Institute of Technology.

PATTEN COLLEGE *(B-11)*
2433 Coolidge Avenue
Oakland, California 94601
Tel: (510) 533-8300; Fax: (510) 534-4344

Description: The privately supported, coeducational college is accredited by the Western Association of Schools and Colleges. Founded in 1944 as the Oakland Bible Institute, it is affiliated with the Christian Evangelical Churches of America, Inc. Its present location and name were adopted in 1960. Associate and Bachelor degrees are awarded. The college operates on the semester system. Enrollment includes 180 full-time and 636 part-time students. A faculty of 12 full-time and 14 part-time gives a faculty-student ratio of 1-12.

Entrance Requirements: High school graduation or GED required; completion of 22 units as follows: 4 English, 2 mathematics, 2 laboratory science, 1 foreign language, 4 social science, 1 history, and 8 electives; SAT or ACT recommended; early admission, early decision, midyear admission, rolling admission, and advanced placement plans available; July 15 and Dec. 15 application deadlines; $30 application fee.

Costs Per Year: $4,620 tuition; $4,580 room and board; $160 student fees.

Collegiate Environment: The campus consists of 5 acres in the midst of a residential community. It includes classrooms, dormitories, a student center, and chapel situated around a landscaped plaza. The library has 30,000 volumes, and enrolled students have access to Bay Area theological libraries. Housing is available for 40 students. The

college requires that students complete an assignment in Christian service each semester. In addition to its program of worship and religious growth, the school has athletic, social and musical activities. 95% of applicants are accepted, and new and transfer students are admitted at midyear. Scholarships are available, and 90% of students receive some form of financial aid.

Community Environment: The Oakland Bay Area is beautiful and there is easy access to San Francisco, Lake Merritt, and the Regional Park System. There is a variety of cultural, sporting, religious, and recreational activity available.

PEPPERDINE UNIVERSITY *(O-8)*
24255 Pacific Coast Highway
Malibu, California 90263
Tel: (310) 456-4392; Fax: (310) 456-4861

Description: This privately supported, coeducational liberal arts university is accredited by the Western Association of Schools and Colleges. Founded in 1937, it emphasizes the standards and concerns of the Christian faith. The university includes the Seaver College of Letters, Arts and Sciences; the School of Business and Management; the Graduate School of Education and Psychology; and the School of Law. It grants the Bachelor, Master, Doctor of Education, and Juris Doctor degrees. Since 1963, the college has maintained an annual program of study abroad and maintains its own facilities in Heidelberg, the site of Germany's oldest university, as well as in Florence, London, and the newest, in Japan. The university operates on the semester system and offers two summer sessions. Enrollment includes 2,661 full-time, 149 part-time undergraduate, and 4,454 graduate students. A faculty of 150 full-time and 149 part-time gives a faculty-student ratio of 1-13.

Entrance Requirements: High school graduation with a B+ average; SAT or ACT; letters of recommendation; early action, and midyear admission plans available; $45 application fee.

Costs Per Year: $18,200 tuition; $6,770 room and board; $70 student fees.

Collegiate Environment: Pepperdine University is located in Malibu, within greater Los Angeles, the largest metropolitan area in the United States. It is a short drive to the mountains, and the desert. The library has holdings of 330,240 titles, 2,139 subscriptions, and 104,914 microforms. Residence halls accommodate 1,800 students. Approximately 53% of the applicants are accepted, including midyear students. The middle 50% of scores for entering freshmen were ACT 24 composite, SAT 1000-1100 combined. Various forms of financial assistance are offered and 73% of a recent freshman class received aid. 81% of the freshman class returned for the sophomore year.

Community Environment: See University of California - Los Angeles.

PITZER COLLEGE *(G-13)*
1050 North Mills Ave.
Claremont, California 91711
Tel: (909) 621-8129; Fax: (909) 621-8521

Description: The privately supported, coeducational liberal arts college operates on the semester system. It is accredited by the Western Association of Schools and Colleges. The sixth and newest member of the Claremont Colleges, the institution was founded in 1963 as a women's college. It became coeducational in 1970 and now makes every effort to admit students of diverse ethnic, cultural, geographical, and socioeconomic backgrounds; the excitement of experimentation has spread among the students, faculty and administration. The college grants a Bachelor degree. Enrollment is 750 full-time students. A full-time faculty of 85 gives a faculty-student ratio of 1-10.

Entrance Requirements: Accredited high school graduation in upper quarter of high school class; college preparatory courses recommended: 4 English, 2 foreign language, 2 science, 3 social science and 3 mathematics; 3 references required; personal interview recommended; early admission, midyear admission, and advanced placement plans available; Feb. 1 application deadline; $40 application fee.

Costs Per Year: $17,688 tuition; $5,900 room and board; $1,548 student fees.

Collegiate Environment: The campus is located at the base of the San Gabriel mountains in eastern Los Angeles County, 35 miles from

Los Angeles. As a member of the Claremont Colleges, the institution shares in the academic life of the larger community through courses offered in adjacent colleges and through joint extracurruicular activities. The Honnold Library of the Claremont Colleges contains more than 2 million volumes, plus numerous periodicals, microforms and audiovisual materials. Housing on campus accommodates 600 men and women. 50% of students applying for admission meet the requirements and are accepted, including midyear students. Special programs are offered for minority students as well as courses in American Black history and Chicano Studies. Financial aid is available, and 40% of the current student body receives some form of assistance.

Community Environment: See Claremont Graduate School.

POINT LOMA NAZARENE COLLEGE   (R-10)
3900 Lomaland Drive
San Diego, California 92106
Tel: (619) 221-2200; Admissions: (619) 221-2273; Fax: (619) 221-2579

Description: This privately supported, coeducational, liberal arts college is affiliated with the Church of the Nazarene. It is accredited by the Western Association of Schools and Colleges. Formerly called Pasadena College, the purpose of the college is to prepare students for service and leadership in an environment of vital Christianity. Founded in Los Angeles in 1902, the college moved to Pasadena in 1910. The college has been in its present location in Point Loma since 1973 and still maintains a branch campus in Pasadena. The Bachelor of Arts degree is offered in 44 major fields of study along with a Bachelor of Science in Nursing. A Master of Arts degree is offered in Education or Religion. A Master of Ministry degree is also offered. Army, Navy and Air Force ROTC programs are available. The college operates on the early semester system and offers three summer sessions. Enrollment includes 2,051 full-time and 340 part-time undergraduates and 389 graduate students. A faculty of 122 full-time and 24 part-time gives a faculty-student ratio of 1-15.

Entrance Requirements: High school graduation from an accredited school with a 2.5 GPA; equivalency diploma accepted; SAT or ACT required; GRE required for graduate school; importance given to moral character; deferred admission, early decision, early admission and rolling admission plans available; $20 application fee.

Costs Per Year: $10,880 tuition; $4,480 room and board; $140 student fees.

Collegiate Environment: The college occupies 87 acres in a beautifully landscaped setting overlooking the Pacific. Campus housing is available for 1,200 students. The library contains 135,993 volumes and 15,270 periodicals. 84% of those applying for admission are accepted, at midyear as well as in the fall. Numerous scholarships are offered, and 83% of current students receive financial assistance.

Community Environment: Point Loma Nazarene College enjoys many advantages from its location in Southern California. San Diego is an area of matchless climate and spectacular scenery. Neighboring institutions afford advantages in library, cultural, and scientific resources. They involve the University of California, San Diego; San Diego State University; University of San Diego; San Diego Symphony; San Diego Opera; Scripps Institute of Oceanography; Palomar Observatory; and Balboa Park with its world famous Zoo, Natural History Museum, Fine Arts Gallery, Old Globe Theatre, Museum of Man, Photographic Arts Museum, Aerospace Museum, Starlight Opera, and Reuben H. Fleet Space Theatre and Museum. The College is located on the Point Loma peninsula overlooking the Pacific Ocean only fifteen minutes from the center of metropolitan San Diego. Los Angeles is two and one-half hours driving time to the north and Mexico thirty minutes to the south. The ocean is immediately to the west and San Diego Bay and the Laguna Mountains are to the east.

POMONA COLLEGE   (G-13)
333 N. College Way
Claremont, California 91711
Tel: (909) 621-8134

Description: Pomona College is a highly selective, coeducational, national liberal arts and sciences college with an enrollment of 1,375 students. A faculty of 153 provides a faculty-student ratio of less than 1 to 10, and the average class size is 14. Founded in 1887, the college is accredited by the Accrediting Commission for Senior Colleges and Universities of the Western Association of Schools and Colleges. It grants the Bachelor of Arts degree.

Entrance Requirements: Accredited high school graduation with superior academic grades and outstanding personal qualifications; a small percentage of students either leave high school after junior year, or obtain a GED; college-preparatory courses recommended, including 4 units English, 3 mathematics, 2 lab science, 3 foreign language, and 2 social science; SAT or ACT required; SAT II highly recommended; application fee $50; early decision and advanced placement plans available.

Costs Per Year: $17,720 tuition and fees; $7,220 room and board; $180 student fees.

Collegiate Environment: The college is the founding member of the Claremont Colleges and shares with the other colleges the facilities of the Honnold Library, which contains more than 1,800,000 volumes, 6,700 periodicals, 1,100,000 microforms and sound recordings. Students may enroll in the other colleges one third of their time. One hundred percent of the student body graduated in the top quarter of their high school class. Dormitory facilities are guaranteed for four years and accommodate all students who want to live on campus. The college is highly selective; only 35% of applicants are accepted. The average SAT scores of a recent freshman class were 640V and 710M. 52% of the student body receives some form of financial assistance.

Community Environment: See Claremont Graduate School.

PORTERVILLE COLLEGE   (L-7)
100 East College Avenue
Porterville, California 93257
Tel: (209) 781-3130; Fax: (209) 784-4779

Description: The publicly supported, coeducational junior college is accredited by the Western Association of Schools and Colleges. The college was established in 1927 and moved to its present campus in 1955. Offering both day and evening programs, the college grants an Associate degree. It operates on the semester system and offers one summer session. Enrollment includes 427 men, 634 women full-time and 645 men and 1,072 women part-time. A faculty of 58 full-time and 70 part-time provides a faculty-student ratio of 1:23.

Entrance Requirements: High school graduation or 18 years of age; open enrollment policy; early admission, early decision, midyear admission, rolling admission plans available.

Costs Per Year: $403 ($13/cr) state residents; $1,550 ($50/cr) resident with B.A. degree; $3,503 ($113/cr) out-of-state; $35 student fees; $900 additional expenses.

Collegiate Environment: The campus is located at the foot of the scenic High Sierra mountains. The campus has 16 buildings on 54 acres; library contains 29,000 volumes, 300 current periodicals, 1,358 audiovisual materials and 13,900 microforms. One hundred percent of the applicants is accepted; students may enroll at mid year as well as in the fall. Financial aid is available, and 20% of the current student body receives assistance.

Community Environment: Population 30,000. Porterville is located at the foot of the High Sierra wonderland in southeastern Tulare County and is in a vast olive, grape, peach, walnut, cotton and citrus growing area. The annual rainfall is 11.47 inches with an annual mean temperature of 62.8 degrees. The community has many churches, library, auditorium, and an excellent shopping center with several new shopping centers in outlying areas. Porterville has a community concert and theatre series each year. Employment opportunities are good. Bus transportation is available to the airlines and to railroad passenger stations. Porterville is a 1 1/2 hour drive from Sequoia National Park; 2 1/2 hours from Kings Canyon National Park, and 3 hours from Yosemite National Park; Sequoia National Forest has giant redwoods and aspen. Recreational activities include skiing, fishing, camping, hunting in season, golf, boating, and tennis. No campus housing is provided; however, students can find some housing in the community.

RANCHO SANTIAGO COLLEGE   (P-9)
1530 West 17th Street
Santa Ana, California 92706
Tel: (714) 564-6000

Description: Publicly-supported, coeducational junior college accredited by the Western Association of Schools and Colleges.

Founded in 1915; current campus site dedicated in 1947. The semester system is used and two summer sessions are offered. Programs lead to the Certificate and Associate degree. Enrollment includes 4,801 full-time and 21,036 part-time with a faculty of 264 full-time and 400 part-time.

Entrance Requirements: High school graduation or over 18 years of age. Placement tests required. Rolling admission and advanced placement plans available.

Costs Per Year: $10 per unit resident, $104 per unit nonresident tuition; $50 student fees; approximate additional expenses $250.

Collegiate Environment: There are 6 separate divisions with complete facilities. The library contains 87,000 volumes and 950 periodicals. Offers educational television, visual aids equipment, films and a classical music library. The planetarium was completed in 1957 and is a multi-story structure which provides 65,000 square feet of classroom and laboratory space. The observatory is located next to the administration building and has an eight-inch refracting telescope. 52% of the freshman class returned for their next year. The college offers 150 different Associate degree programs and 75 programs leading to a Certificate. Thirty-two scholarships are for freshman and a total of 75 scholarships are available. 25% receive financial assistance.

Community Environment: Population 400,000. Santa Ana is the county seat of Orange County, and is located 35 miles south of Los Angeles. Orange County is considered one of the richest agricultural and industrial areas in the state. City facilities include many churches of major denominations, libraries, very fine shopping centers, and hospitals. The Charles W. Bowers Memorial Museum, which has an outstanding collection of Indian and early California relics, is located here. Recreational facilities include beaches ten miles away for all water sports, the mountain areas for major winter sports, and the desert area which is within easy driving distance. Part-time employment is available, room and board may be secured in private homes; apartments are available in all price ranges.

Branch Campuses: Orange Campus, 8045 E. Chapman, Orange, CA 92669 Garden Grove Center, 13162 Newhope, Garden Grove, CA 92643

RIO HONDO COLLEGE   (G-11)
3600 Workman Mill Road
Whittier, California 90608
Tel: (213) 692-0921

Description: The publicly supported, coeducational community college enrolls 13,500 day and evening students with a faculty of 873. Operating on a semester system with one summer session, the school is accredited by the Western Association of Schools and Colleges. In 1963, the college opened its first classes for 1,800 part-time students and has since moved to new facilities. The college grants an Associate degree in both its day and evening programs and certificate in certain occupational fields.

Entrance Requirements: High school graduates or 18 years of age; open enrollment policy; early admission and early decision plans available;

Costs Per Year: $10 per unit for California residents; $99 per unit for nonresidents; $57 student fees.

Collegiate Environment: The campus is located two miles north of Whittier on a beautiful 120-acre site. The library contains over 72,958 volumes. Ninety-eight percent of those who apply for admission are accepted, including midyear students.

Community Environment: Small ex-urban community, 23 miles from downtown Los Angeles. District population of approximately 350,000. Small business and manufacturing predominate.

RIVERSIDE COMMUNITY COLLEGE   (P-10)
4800 Magnolia Avenue
Riverside, California 92506
Tel: (714) 684-3240

Description: The publicly supported, coeducational, community college is accredited by the Western Association of Schools and Colleges. Programs of study are primarily vocational and lead to Certificates and the Associate degree. The college operates on the semester system and offers one summer session. Enrollment includes 20,500

full-time and part-time students. A faculty of 800 gives a faculty-student ratio of 1-26.

Entrance Requirements: High school graduation or 18 years of age or older; open enrollment policy; release permits required for out-of-district residents; early admission, midyear admission, early decision, and advanced placement plans available.

Costs Per Year: $403 ($13 per credit) resident tuition; $1,550 ($50 per credit) resident with BA tuition; $3,317 ($107 per credit) nonresident tuition.

Collegiate Environment: The college, located in the city of Riverside, occupies several blocks. Some of the college's facilities are available for use by the local residents creating close ties with the community. The library, with a seating capacity of 800, contains over 75,000 volumes. Students are admitted at midyear as well as in the fall.

Community Environment: See University of California - Riverside.

Branch Campuses: Norco Campus, 2001 3rd Street, Norco, CA; Moreno Valley Campus, 16130 Lasselle, Moreno Valley, CA.

SADDLEBACK COLLEGE   (P-10)
28000 Marguerite Parkway
Mission Viejo, California 92692
Tel: (714) 582-4500; Admissions: (714) 582-4555

Description: The publicly supported coeducational junior college is accredited by the Western Association of Schools and Colleges. It grants the Associate degree with a recent enrollment of 23,316 students and a faculty of 222 full-time and 311 part-time. The school operates on the early semester system and offers one summer session. Enrollment includes 21,000 students. Faculty includes 222 full-time and 311 part-time members.

Entrance Requirements: High school graduates or 18 years of age.

Costs Per Year: $403 ($13/unit) resident tuition; $3,720 ($120/unit nonresident; $10 health fee.

Collegiate Environment: Campus is located in the hills of Mission Viejo, a twenty minute drive from the beach. The campus eventually will consist of a complex on 200 acres. Library contains 100,000 volumes. Various forms of financial aid are available.

Community Environment: Mission Viejo is largely a residential community located in the rolling hills midway between Los Angeles and San Diego off the San Diego freeway. This is one of Orange County's fast growing areas, with a dry temperate climate. Good shopping facilities are available with most major department stores. Buses serve the area, Orange County Airport is a short drive from Mission Viejo. Beach resorts are located nearby for all water sports. The mountains are approximately a two hour drive for winter sports. Ski slopes abound in the Big Bear area.

SAINT JOHN'S COLLEGE   (M-7)
5118 East Seminary Road
Camarillo, California 93010
Tel: (805) 482-4697

Description: The privately supported liberal arts college for men is accredited by the Western Association of Schools and Colleges. Operating on the semester system, the institution contains a four-year college granting a Bachelor degree. Founded in 1927, it is composed mainly of young men studying for the Catholic Priesthood in the Roman Catholic Church. Enrollment is 100 students. A faculty of 25 gives a faculty-student ratio of 1-4.

Entrance Requirements: Applicants must be suitable candidates for the priesthood in the Catholic Church and must have the ability to succeed in the four-year liberal arts curriculum and following post-graduate requirements; College Entrance Examinations and high school diploma or GRE required; advanced placement plan available; certificate of baptism and confirmation; letter of recommendation from pastor required.

Costs Per Year: $6,000 tuition; $1,100 room and board; $35 student body fees; $55 room and key deposit; $30 enrollment fee.

Collegiate Environment: The college campus of 150 acres is located two miles east of the city of Camarillo, 60 miles northwest of Los Angeles. Library contains 130,000 volumes for both the graduate and undergraduate divisions of the college and about 39,000 periodicals and pamphlets.

Community Environment: This is a rural, suburban area located on Highway 101 midway between Los Angeles and Santa Barbara. The average temperature is 72 degrees; average annual rainfall is 15.4 inches. Southern Pacific Railroad goes through Camarillo, and the Golden West airlines serves the Oxnard area, which is ten miles west. There are churches of all denominations, four hospitals within a ten-mile radius, as well as excellent shopping facilities. Part-time employment is available. The Point Mugu State Park is nearby. Pacific Ocean beaches are ten miles west, and county parks are available for those who enjoy fishing, camping and hiking. The Ranchero Days, Camarillo Fiesta, and the Christmas Pageant are held annually.

SAINT MARY'S COLLEGE OF CALIFORNIA   (I-3)
Moraga, California 94575
Tel: (510) 631-4224; Fax: (510) 376-7193

Description: This privately supported, coeducational, Roman Catholic liberal arts college is accredited by the Western Association of Schools and Colleges. It operates on the 4-1-4 system. Three schools comprise the College: Liberal Arts, Economics and Business Administration, and Science. All three schools grant the Bachelor and Master degree. The faculty is composed of both secular instructors and Brothers of the Christian Schools. This is the largest religious organization in the Catholic Church devoted exclusively to teaching. Enrollment recently was 4,000 students. A faculty of 141 full-time and 90 part-time gives a faculty-student ratio of 1-16.

Entrance Requirements: High school graduation or equivalent with better than a B average; high school courses totalling 16 units: 4 English, 3 mathematics, 2 foreign language, 2 laboratory science and 2 social science; SAT or ACT required; minimum scores depend on grade point averages; GRE required for graduate school; $35 application fee; early admission, rolling admission, delayed admission and advanced placement plans available.

Costs Per Year: $13,332 tuition; $6,300 room and board.

Collegiate Environment: The campus consists of more than 420 acres in a valley surrounded by rolling hills. San Francisco is 21 miles away. The library contains 179,485 volumes, 4,200 pamphlets, 1,084 periodicals, 177,756 reels and fiche and 3,461 sound recordings. Dormitory space is available for 1,400 students. About 65% of the applicants are accepted. Financial aid is available, and 67% of the current student body receives some form of assistance. The college granted 685 Bachelor degrees and 193 Master degrees to a recent graduating class (including undergraduate external degrees). Average high school standing of the freshman class was in the upper 20%; average SAT scores of the freshman class were 483V, 546M. Students may enroll at midyear as well as in the fall.

Community Environment: See Diablo Valley College.

SAINT PATRICK'S SEMINARY   (D-11)
320 Middlefield Road
Menlo Park, California 94025
Tel: (415) 325-5621; Admissions: (415) 325-5621; Fax: (415) 322-0997

Description: A private seminary incorporated in 1891 with construction of the present main building beginning in 1894; four years later the seminary opened to receive its first students. The preparation of men for the priestly ministry is carried on under the direction of the Archbishop of San Francisco and the priests of the Society of St. Sulpice and in accordance with the directives of the Second Vatican Council, the Sacred Congregation of Catholic Education and the Bishops' Committee on Priestly Formation. St. Patrick's Seminary is fully accredited by the Association of Theological Schools in the United States and Canada and the Western Association of Schools and Colleges. Degrees conference are Master of divinity and Master of Arts in Theology. The Bachelor of Sacred Theology is offered in affiliation with St. Mary's Seminary and University in Baltimore, Maryland. The seminary operates on the semester system and offers no summer sessions. Enrollment includes 52 full-time and 2 part-time students. A faculty of 15 full-time and 15 part-time gives a faculty-student ratio of 1-2.

Entrance Requirements: Bachelor degree from an accredited college or equivalent and acceptance for a diocese by the Bishop; GRE

or MAT required; TOEFL required for foreign students; July 31 application deadline; $200 application fee.

Costs Per Year: $6,250 tuition; 6,250 room and board; $260 student fees.

Collegiate Environment: The library contains 94,979 hard bound volumes. There are dormitory facilities for 96 students. Scholarships of $500 per year are available to residents of San Francisco; 20% of the students receive financial aid.

Community Environment: This is a residential community 30 miles south of San Francisco and 20 miles north of San Jose. The climate is moderate. There are buses and trains to the area, and the San Francisco International Airport is 16 miles north.

SAN BERNARDINO VALLEY COLLEGE   (O-10)
701 South Mount Vernon Avenue
San Bernardino, California 92410
Tel: (909) 888-6511; Admissions: (909) 888-6511 X 1143; Fax: (909) 889-4988

Description: The publicly supported coeducational junior college, founded in 1926, is the first of two junior colleges to be created by the San Bernardino Junior College District. It is fully accredited by the Western Association of Schools and Colleges. The college grants a certificate and the Associate degree. It operates on the semester system one summer session. Enrollment includes 275 men, 238 women full-time, 652 men, and 735 women part-time with a faculty of 160 full-time, 205 part-time members.

Entrance Requirements: The college admits without examination the graduates of any high school and such other candidates 18 years of age or more that may be recommended by the President of the college. Any man or woman who has served in the Armed Forces of the United States is eligible for admission. Request for information should be forwarded to the Director of Admissions; early admission, early decision, rolling admission and advanced placement plans are available.

Costs Per Year: $450 ($15/unit) resident; $1,500 ($50/unit) resident with B.A. degree; $3,870 ($129/unit) nonresident.

Collegiate Environment: The campus is located in the residential area of San Bernardino. Nineteen buildings are grouped conveniently around the central quadrangle of the campus. The outer areas of the campus contain a small and superbly equipped auditorium, an art gallery, Planetarium, two gymnasiums, two competition-size swimming pools, playing fields, and tennis and handball courts. The college library contains 100,000 books, periodicals, pamphlets, film strips, microfilm and recordings.

Community Environment: See California State University - San Bernardino

SAN DIEGO CITY COLLEGE   (R-10)
1313 Twelfth Avenue
San Diego, California 92110
Tel: (619) 230-2475

Description: This publicly supported coeducational community college is accredited by the Western Association of Colleges and Schools. It is a member of the San Diego Community College district, which created in 1970 and is composed of four institutions: San Diego City College, San Diego Mesa College, and San Diego Miramar College. Air Force and Army ROTC programs are available through San Diego State University. The college grants the Certificate and the Associate degree, and prepares students for transfer to state colleges and universities. It operates on the semester system and offers one summer session. Enrollment includes 13,943 full-time and part-time students. A faculty of 300 provides a faculty-student ratio of 1-24.

Entrance Requirements: High school graduation or age 18 and over; advanced placement, delayed admission, and rolling admission plans available.

Costs Per Year: $10 per unit; $50 per unit resident students with BA or higher degree; $106 per unit nonresidents; $10 fees nonresidents.

Collegiate Environment: The campus has eight buildings on 35 acres including the library containing over 92,000 volumes, and numerous periodicals and microforms. Midyear students admitted and approximately 99% of the students applying for admission are accepted. Scholarships are available and 23% of students receive financial aid. The college is in the heart of San Diego adjacent to rental housing, transportation, and recreational areas such as the bay, ocean, Mexico and mountain skiing.

Community Environment: See University of California - San Diego.

SAN DIEGO MESA COLLEGE   (R-10)
7250 Mesa College Drive
San Diego, California 92111
Tel: (619) 627-2600; Fax: (619) 627-2960

Description: This publicly supported coeducational junior college is accredited by the Western Association of Schools and Colleges. Completed in 1964, the campus provides facilities for arts and sciences, business education, medical and dental assisting and technical areas. The college operates on the semester system and offers one summer session. It grants the Certificate and Associate degree. Enrollment includes 25,000 students. A faculty of 241 full-time and 600 part-time provides a faculty-student ratio of 1-40.

Entrance Requirements: High school graduation; nongraduates 18 years of age or older admitted.

Costs Per Year: $403 ($13 per unit) resident; $1,550 ($50 per unit) resident with BA degree or higher; $3,689 ($119 per unit) nonresident.

Collegiate Environment: The library provides more than 83,000 volumes, 1,314 periodicals and 712 audiovisual materials for student use. Financial aid is available for economically handicapped students.

Community Environment: San Diego lies along and around one of the world's ten most beautiful protected natural harbors, and has a very special "sea-washed, air-conditioned climate." The maximum average temperature of 70.8 degrees and a minimum of 55.4 degrees does make the climate very special. The Santa Fe Railroad, buses, and numerous airlines serve the area. The city is a manufacturing and shipping center, with its main industries being tourism, fishing, fish packing, and the construction of aircraft parts, missiles, and boats. San Diego County is the country's largest producer of avocados. San Diego has a public library with 30 branches, nine general hospitals, museums, galleries, and churches. There are numerous golf courses, all aquatic sports, hiking, mountain climbing, horseback riding, skiing and other and other snow sports, fishing, and hunting. This is the home of the San Diego Chargers, the professional football team, and the San Diego Padres, the professional baseball team. Known as a winter playground, San Diego has 19 miles of Pacific Ocean shores with beautiful beaches. The population of San Diego is 1,200,900 with a greater metropolitan area population of 2,166,200.

SAN DIEGO STATE UNIVERSITY   (R-10)
5300 Campanile Drive
San Diego, California 92182-8080.
Tel: (619) 594-6871

Description: A publicly supported liberal arts and sciences university, San Diego State is one of 20 coeducational campuses of the California State University System. San Diego State is fully accredited by the Western Association of Schools and Colleges. The early semester system is used and five summer sessions are offered. Current enrollment includes 27,787 full-time, 6,411 part-time, 5,547 graduate students. A faculty of 909 full-time and 1,327 part-time provides a faculty-student ratio of 1-13. The university provides a program of instruction for undergraduate and graduate studies through the Bachelor and Master degrees in the Liberal Arts and Sciences, in applied fields and in the professions, including the teaching profession. Doctoral degrees are awarded jointly with the University of California and Claremont Graduate School. ROTC available.

Entrance Requirements: High school graduation with a composite scholastic average and ACT or SAT score in upper third of California H.S. graduates; higher score for non-California residents; satisfactory completion of a college preparatory core program of 15 credits to include: 4 years English, 3 years math, 2 years foreign language, 1 year natural science with lab, 1 year U. S. history/government, 1 year visual performing arts, 3 years electives from above; rolling admission and advanced placement plans available; $55 application fee.

Costs Per Year: $1,902 resident tuition; $9,282 nonresident tuition; $6,000 room and board, $55 student fees.

Collegiate Environment: Accommodations for 3,019 students are available in 8 residence halls on campus, and fraternities and sororities house an additional 590. The library has more than 1,095,581 volumes, 2.8 million microforms, seats 3,000 readers, and provides typing rooms, group study rooms, microfilm reading rooms, listening facilities, exhibit areas and individual study areas. The university makes every effort to see that students who wish to attend are not prevented from doing so because of inadequate financial resources. Twenty-two percent of the current student body receives some form of financial aid. Imperial Valley campus, located at Calexico, is a division of San Diego State University. The curriculum at Calexico includes the recommended upper division and postgraduate program of courses leading to a Bachelor's degree and the Standard Teaching Credential.

Community Environment: San Diego lies along and around one of the world's ten most beautiful protected natural harbors, and has a very special "sea-washed, air-conditioned climate." The maximum average temperature of 70.8 degrees and a minimum of 55.4 degrees does make the climate very special. The Santa Fe Railroad, buses, and numerous airlines serve the area. The city is a manufacturing and shipping center, with its main industries being tourism, fishing, fish packing, and the construction of aircraft parts, missiles, and boats. San Diego County is the country's largest producer of avocados. San Diego has a public library with 30 branches, nine general hospitals, museums, galleries, and churches. There are numerous golf courses, all aquatic sports, hiking, mountain climbing, horseback riding, skiing and other snow sports, fishing, and hunting. This is the home of the San Diego Chargers, the professional football team, and the San Diego Padres professional baseball team. Known as a winter playground, it has 19 miles of Pacific Ocean shores with beautiful beaches. The population of San Diego is 1,200,900 with a greater metropolitan area population of 2,166,200.

SAN FRANCISCO ART INSTITUTE   (I-3)
800 Chestnut Street
San Francisco, California 94133
Tel: (415) 771-7020

Description: Privately supported coeducational art college is accredited by the Western Association of Schools and Colleges. The institute was established in 1871 with a dual goal of exhibition and education. It operates on the semester system and offers two summer sessions. Enrollment is 662 students. A faculty of 64 full-time and 50 part-time gives a faculty-student ratio of 1-9. The institute grants the Bachelor and Master degrees.

Entrance Requirements: Rolling admission, midyear admission and advanced placement plans available; $50 application fee.

Costs Per Year: $15,486 tuition; additional expenses average $4,000.

Collegiate Environment: The library contains 25,500 specialized volumes; college maintains no dormitories. 75% of applicants are accepted. Financial aid is available, and 68% of the current student body receives assistance.

Community Environment: See San Francisco State University.

SAN FRANCISCO COLLEGE OF MORTUARY SCIENCE
(I-3)
1598 Dolores Street
San Francisco, California 94110
Tel: (415) 824-1313; Fax: (415) 824-1390

Description: The privately supported professional college is accredited by the Western Association of Schools and Colleges and was established in 1930 by a number of funeral directors. The semester system is used with one summer session. The enrollment includes 52 men and 23 women. A faculty of 2 full-time and 4 part-time gives a faculty-student ratio of 1:13. The college grants the Diploma, and Associate degree.

Entrance Requirements: High school graduation or equivalent; open enrollment policy; rolling admission and early admission plans available; $25 application fee.

Costs Per Year: $8,400 tuition; $125 lab fees; $650 books.

Collegiate Environment: The campus is located in the heart of San Francisco. The library contains 750 volumes. Most students applying for admission are accepted, including mid-year students. 90% receive financial assistance.

Community Environment: See San Francisco State University

SAN FRANCISCO CONSERVATORY OF MUSIC   *(I-3)*
1201 Ortega Street
San Francisco, California 94122
Tel: (415) 759-3431; Fax: (415) 759-3499

Description: A privately supported coeducational music college, the San Francisco Conservatory of Music was founded in 1917 and offers training in all instruments and related music subjects at the Preparatory, Junior Conservatory, Adult Extension and Collegiate levels. The conservatory is accredited by the Western Association of Schools and Colleges. It operates on the semester system. Enrollment includes 252 full-time and 21 part-time undergraduates and 122 graduate students. A faculty of 23 full-time and 35 part-time gives an overall faculty-student ratio of 1-7. The college grants the Bachelor, Master and Specialist degrees. The faculty includes most of the first chair players of the San Francisco Symphony, artists and staff of the San Francisco Opera and other outstanding Bay Area musicians.

Entrance Requirements: High school graduation or equivalent; ACT or SAT required; entrance exam required; early admission, early decision, rolling admission, midyear admission and advanced placement plans available; musical proficiency required. $60 application fee.

Costs Per Year: $13,000 tuition; $250 student fees; $8,770 additonal expenses (including estimate for room and board).

Collegiate Environment: The San Francisco Conservatory of Music is situated in the Sunset District of the City of San Francisco. The library contains 39,000 volumes and 7,000 recordings. Approximately 55% of the students applying for admission are accepted, including midyear students, and 80% return for the sophomore year. The average scores for the recent freshman class were SAT 468 verbal, 463 math. Of 100 scholarships offered, 15 are available for freshmen; 75% of the current student body receives financial aid.

Community Environment: See San Francisco State University.

SAN FRANCISCO LAW SCHOOL   *(I-3)*
20 Haight Street
San Francisco, California 94102
Tel: (415) 626-5550; Admissions: (415) 626-5550; Fax: (415) 626-5584

Description: The privately supported coeducational evening law school was organized in 1906 and in 1909 became the first night law school to be chartered under the laws of California; it is accredited by the Committee of Bar Examiners of the State Bar of California. The semester system is used and the college grants the Juris Doctor degree after completion of at least 20 units per year for four years. Enrollment includes 107 men and 68 women. A faculty of 29 gives a faculty-student ratio of 1-6.

Entrance Requirements: Bachelor degree or a minimum of 60 units of college work; completion of the law school admission test; applicants not meeting all requirements may be considered for special status; early admission and midyear admission; $40 application fee; application deadlines June 1 and Nov. 15.

Costs Per Year: $3,800 tuition.

Collegiate Environment: The library contains approximately 22,225 volumes. The purpose of the school is to prepare men and women for the professional practice of law, to train advisors to the legal aspects of business; and to train students in the legal nature of public affairs.

Community Environment: See San Francisco State University.

SAN FRANCISCO STATE UNIVERSITY   *(I-3)*
1600 Holloway Avenue
San Francisco, California 94132
Tel: (415) 338-2164

Description: The publicly supported, coeducational liberal arts university is accredited by the Western Association of Schools and Colleges. The semester system is used and varying summer sessions are offered. The college was established in 1899 with a primary function of training elementary school teachers. The state gave the college the right to grant Bachelor's degrees in 1923; five-year program for a credential and Master's degree in 1949. Recent enrollment included 11,036 men and 15,494 women. A faculty of 971 gives a student-faculty ratio of 19:1. The college grants the Bachelor, Master and Doctorate degrees.

Entrance Requirements: High school graduation with scholastic average in the upper third of California H.S. graduates, higher score for non-California residents; SAT or ACT required; application fee $55; and advanced placement plans available.

Costs Per Year: Tuition free for California residents; nonresident tuition $7,380; room and board $4,840-5,116; apartment only $3,900; fees $757 full-time students; $481 part-time students.

Collegiate Environment: The Lake Merced campus houses a complete and modern educational community. Residence halls provide room and board for 1,500 students and the library contains approximately 770,000 volumes, 4,500 periodicals, and 800,000 microforms. Midyear students are accepted.

Community Environment: San Francisco is one of the most cosmopolitan cities in the United States. It is the financial center of the west, and an important industrial city. A great port, it serves as the terminus for Trans-Pacific and coastwise steamship lines and airlines. The city is located on hills at the end of a narrow peninsula with the Pacific Ocean on one side and the San Francisco Bay on the other. The annual temperature averages 57 degrees. San Francisco Bay is the largest land-locked harbor in the world, and is the home of the beautiful Golden Gate Bridge. All modes of transportation serve the area. A large civic center includes the city hall, public library, civic auditorium, state building, federal office building, health center, opera house and war memorial building. The opera house is the only municipally owned opera house in America. Job opportunities vary considerably but are available. San Francisco has 438 churches, 52 public parks, and 100 theaters. Recreational facilities are numerous for all water sports, hiking, and fishing. Mountain resort areas are approximately a three hour drive. Famous Chinatown is located here, as is the picturesque Fisherman's Wharf.

SAN FRANCISCO THEOLOGICAL SEMINARY   *(A-9)*
2 Kensington Road
San Anselmo, California 94960
Tel: (415) 258-6500; (800) 447-8820; Admissions: (415) 258-6532; Fax: (415) 258-1608

Description: This privately supported, coeducational graduate theological school of the Presbyterian Church (USA) was established for the education and training of ministers and unordained leaders in the educational, evangelistic, missionary and musical responsibilities of the Church. It is fully accredited by the American Association of Theological Schools and the Western Association of Schools and Colleges. The Seminary operates on a 4-1-4 system and offers one summer session. Enrollment includes 800 students. There are 23 faculty members. A member of the Graduate Theological Union of Berkeley, the school grants the Master of Divinity, Master of Arts in Theological Studies, and Doctorate degrees to its members. A branch campus is located in southern California on the campus of Claremont School of Theology at the Butler Ecumenical Center. The MATS and much of the M.Div. degree program requirements may be completed here, allowing students who live and work in southern California to remain in their communitites of faith and support. Contact branch, listed below.

Entrance Requirements: Seminary is open to qualified students of all denominations of Christians; Bachelor of Arts degree required, based upon four years of work beyond secondary education; May 1 application deadline; $35 application fee.

Costs Per Year: $5,600 tuition; tuition for advanced degrees may differ.

Collegiate Environment: The San Francisco Theological Seminary since 1964-65 has engaged in doctoral work at the Th.D., and Ph.D. levels, and work at the Masters level through participation in the Graduate Theological Union. The Graduate Theological Union offers doctoral programs in religion with a faculty appointed from the American Baptist Seminary of the West, Pacific School of Religion, San Francisco Theological Seminary, the Church Divinity School of the

Pacific, the Pacific Lutheran Theological Seminary, Starr King School for the Ministry, St. Albert's College, Jesuit School of Theology of Berkeley, and the Franciscan School of Theology, and with the cooperation of the faculty of the Graduate Division of the University of California at Berkeley and with Stanford. See listing for G.T.U. for further information. Members of G.T.U. share the common library of over 600,000 volumes. Campus housing is not required but is available for single as well as married students. Financial aid is available for M.Div students.

Community Environment: Population 15,000, San Anselmo is a suburban city located two miles west of San Rafael, the county seat of Marin County, and 20 miles north of San Francisco. The climate is mild, with an average minimum temperature of 45 degrees and a maximum temperature of 75 degrees. The rainfall averages 40 inches during the rainy season in the winter and spring months. Golden Gate Transit Bus service is provided to San Rafael and San Francisco. Shopping areas are composed primarily of small and medium-size businesses with friendly, courteous service. All types of recreation and entertainment facilities are available in or near San Anselmo, including those of San Francisco, which is 40 minutes away.

Branch Campuses: SFTS/SC, 1325 N. College Avenue, Claremont, CA, 91711; phone: (909) 621-9885, fax: (909) 626-3265.

SAN JOAQUIN DELTA COLLEGE   *(H-4)*
5151 Pacific Avenue
Stockton, California 95207
Tel: (209) 474-5635; Fax: (209) 474-5649

Description: This publicly supported coeducational junior college is accredited by the Western Association of Schools and Colleges. This college was first established as Stockton Junior College in 1935. Its present name and operations commenced in 1963. Enrollment is 15,438 students. A faculty of 579 gives an overall faculty-student ratio of approximately 1-30. The college operates on the semester system and offers one summer session. Liberal Arts and Technological programs lead to the Certificate and Associate degree.

Entrance Requirements: Open enrollment policy; high school graduation not required; advanced placement and rolling admission plans available.

Costs Per Year: $13 per unit; $50 per unit resident with BA degree or higher.

Collegiate Environment: San Joaquin Delta is a cluster college with five learning centers on 165 acres including a library containing 80,000 volumes. All students applying for admission are accepted, including students at midyear. Approximately 50% of students receive financial aid.

Community Environment: See University of the Pacific.

SAN JOSE CHRISTIAN COLLEGE   *(I-3)*
790 South Twelfth Street
San Jose, California 95112
Tel: (408) 293-9058; Fax: (408) 293-7352

Description: This privately supported theological institution is accredited by the Accrediting Association of Bible Colleges. Enrollment includes 138 full-time and 121 part-time students. A faculty of 39 gives a faculty-student ratio of 1-12. The college is supported by individuals and congregations of independent evangelical churches. It operates on the quarter system and offers one summer session. This college was established in 1939 near the San Jose State University campus. The present campus was established in 1951. The school grants the Bachelor of Religious Education Degree; Christian Arts Certificate; and the Bachelor of Arts and Science in Pastoral, Missions, Christian Education, Youth Ministry and Christian Counseling.

Entrance Requirements: High school graduate with a C average accepted; ACT or SAT required; evidence of Christian character and motivation; non-high school graduates considered; rolling admission, delayed admission, early decision, early admission and advanced placement plans available; $30 application fee.

Costs Per Year: $6,000 ($125/cr) tuition, $3,240 room and board; $300 student fees.

Collegiate Environment: There are two student residences on campus (capacity 35 men, 40 women, and 8 married couples). The campus has eight buildings on eight and a half acres. The library contains 31,502 titles, 1,880 periodicals, 40 microforms and 2,120 audiovisual materials. Approximately 15% of the student body graduated in the top 10% of the high school class, and 40% ranked in top quarter. 60% of the freshman class returned for second year. 95% of the applicants are accepted. Students may enroll at midyear. Scholarships are available, and 60% of the current student body receives financial assistance.

Community Environment: See San Jose State University.

SAN JOSE CITY COLLEGE   *(I-3)*
2100 Moorpark Avenue
San Jose, California 95128-2798
Tel: (408) 298-2181

Description: Publicly-supported coeducational junior college accredited by the Western Association of Schools and Colleges. Classes began in 1921 on San Jose State University campus. In 1953, the San Jose Unified School District took over complete operation and moved the campus to its present location. Recent enrollment was 11,423. Student faculty ratio is 17:1. The semester system is used and one summer session is offered. The college grants the Certificate and the Associate degree.

Entrance Requirements: High school graduation or 18 years of age; early admission, rolling admission plan available; open enrollment. Placement tests required.

Costs Per Year: $5 per unit to a maximum of $50; nonresidents $109 additional per unit.

Collegiate Environment: The campus has 33 buildings on 58 acres. The library contains 66,776 volumes, 6,538 pamphlets and 1,139 microforms, 409 periodicals, and 2,940 recordings. All students applying for admission are accepted.

Community Environment: See San Jose State University

SAN JOSE STATE UNIVERSITY   *(I-3)*
1 Washington Sq.
San Jose, California 95192
Tel: (408) 924-2000; Fax: (408) 924-2050

Description: A publicly supported, coeducational liberal arts university, San Jose State is the oldest of the California State system of colleges, dating back to 1857. The university is fully accredited by the Western Association of Schools and Colleges. The university grants the Bachelor's and Master's degrees. A Cooperative Education work-study program is available to students desiring to complement their education with work experience gained by alternating school periods with work periods in industry. The university operates on the semester calendar system and offers a January session and three summer sessions. Enrollment includes 28,000 students. A faculty of 860 full-time and 915 part-time gives a faculty-student ratio of 1-20.

Entrance Requirements: High school graduation with a composite scholastic average and ACT or SAT score placing him in upper third of California H.S. graduates; higher score for non-California residents; GRE required for graduate school; $55 application fee; rolling admission, early admission, early decision and advanced placement plans available.

Costs Per Year: Resident fees and room and board $7,936; nonresident $14,286.

Collegiate Environment: The library has approximately 700,000 volumes, 11,000 periodicals, 650,000 microforms, and 25,000 AV materials. Seven residence halls accommodate 2,000 students and 148 apartments are available for married students. The university offers both a six week and two three week summer sessions and a three week session in January. The middle 50% range of scores for the entering freshman class were SAT 423-428 verbal, 479-538 math, ACT 19-22 composite.

Community Environment: Population 686,178. 15th largest city in U.S. Located in the Santa Clara Valley, known world-wide as "Silicon Valley". 50 miles south of San Francisco, and 30 miles from the Pacific Ocean. The Mount Hamilton Range rises to 4,209 feet on the east, and the Santa Cruz Range provides the western view. San Jose was the first capital of California. Recreational facilities are numerous, including Alum Rock Park, six miles away which includes a museum, picnic grounds, active mineral springs, a large swimming pool, mineral baths, and several miles of marked trails. Mountain resort areas are within easy driving distance for the major winter sports. Points of interest are Lick Observatory on the summit of Mount Hamilton, Rosicrucian Egyptian Temple, Oriental Museum, Winchester Mystery House.

SANTA BARBARA CITY COLLEGE   *(O-6)*
721 Cliff Drive
Santa Barbara, California 93109-2394
Tel: (805) 965-0581; Admissions: (805) 965-0581 X 2220; Fax: (805) 963-7222

Description: This publicly supported, coeducational two-year college is accredited by the Western Association of Schools and Colleges. Founded in 1911, this was the second junior college established in California. The college moved to its present location in 1959. Enrollment includes 4,910 full-time and 6,344 part-time students. A faculty of 201 full-time and 275 part-time gives an overall faculty-student ratio of approximately 1-35. The semester system is used, and one summer session is offered. Liberal Arts and Technological programs lead to the Certificate and Associate Degree.

Entrance Requirements: High school graduation, GED, or 18 years of age; SAT or ACT accepted; open admission, early admission, rolling admission, early decision and open admission plans available.

Costs Per Year: $390 ($13/unit) resident enrollment fee; $3,210 ($107/unit) out-of-state; $3,540 ($118/unit) foreign applicants; $1,000 approximate additional expenses.

Collegiate Environment: The campus is located on a site immediately above and overlooking the ocean. There are 13 buildings, including a library containing 88,000 volumes, 419 periodicals and 191 microforms. 320 scholarships are available ranging from $50 to $8,000, and 1,300 of the current students receive financial aid. Approximately 100% of the students applying for admission are accepted.

Community Environment: See University of California - Santa Barbara.

SANTA CLARA UNIVERSITY   *(E-12)*
500 El Camino Real
Santa Clara, California 95053
Tel: (408) 554-4700; Fax: (408) 554-5255

Description: Founded in 1851 at the site of one of California's 21 missions, Santa Clara became the first institution of higher learning in the state. The Mission Church remains the signature building on campus, a reminder of the university's roots and its commitment to the community in which it is located. Santa Clara is a Jesuit University accredited by the Western Association of Schools and Colleges. Army ROTC is available on campus; Air Force ROTC is offered through a cooperating school. Undergraduate programs are offered in the College of Arts and Sciences, School of Business, and School of Engineering. Graduate programs are offered in: Graduate School of Business, School of Engineering, School of Law, the Graduate Division of Counseling, Psychology and Education, and the Department of Pastoral Ministries. It operates on the quarter system and offers one summer session. Enrollment includes 3,909 full-time and 109 part-time undergraduates and 3,500 graduate and first professional students. A faculty of 353 full-time and 229 part-time gives an undergraduate faculty-student ratio of 1-14.

Entrance Requirements: High school graduation with completion of 16 units including 4 English, 3 mathematics, 1 science, 3 foreign language, 1 social science, and 4 additional courses from these listed subject areas; SAT required; rolling admission and advanced placement plans available; $40 application fee.

Costs Per Year: $13,584 tuition; $5,904 room and board.

Collegiate Environment: The Santa Clara University campus has grown dramatically along with its enrollment. Varied buildings cover its 104 acres, but the campus has lost none of the serenity or charm with which it was originally endowed well over a century ago. The campus is set with immense redwoods, spruces, sycamores and olive trees, and is lined with tall date palms. The library contains 593,593 volumes, 5,703 periodicals, 576,121 microforms, 486,697 government documents, and 6,200 audiovisual materials. Dormitory facilities accommodate 1,931. Approximately 66% of the students applying

for admission are accepted and 90% return for the sophomore year. Approximately 64% of the current student body receives financial aid.

Community Environment: Population 90,000. Santa Clara is known as the "Mission City." It has an ideal climate, with a mean temperature of 71 degrees. Buses, trains and airlines serve the area. Community facilities include churches, a community symphony orchestra and an art gallery. Santa Clara is in the heart of "Silicon Valley," a dynamic center of high technology and progressive businesses. There are numerous part-time work opportunities. Recreational facilities include miles of beaches within a 30-minute drive of the university. San Francisco is 50 miles to the north.

SANTA MONICA COLLEGE   *(O-8)*
1900 Pico Blvd.
Santa Monica, California 90405
Tel: (310) 450-5150

Description: The publicly supported, coeducational, community college is accredited by the Western Association of Schools and Colleges. Classes were first held in 1929 with a move to the present campus in 1952. The college grants Certificates and the Associate degree. It operates on the semester system and one summer session is offered. Enrollment includes 5,604 full-time and 16,487 part-time students. A faculty of 694 gives an overall faculty-student ratio of 1-27.

Entrance Requirements: High school graduation; non-graduates 18 years of age or over admitted; SAT or ACT accepted but not required; rolling admission, midyear admission, and advanced placement plans available.

Costs Per Year: $403 ($13 per unit) state resident tuition; $3,875 ($125 per unit) nonresident tuition; $20 student fees

Collegiate Environment: The campus has 23 buildings on 45 acres. The library contains 103,495 volumes, 500 periodicals, 18,915 microforms and 5,250 recordings. Radio station KCRW-FM is located on campus. Students may enroll at midyear as well as in the fall.

Community Environment: A residential city and beach resort, Santa Monica is part of the Los Angeles metropolitan area. The temperature averages 64.2 degrees. All forms of major transportation serve the area. Excellent shopping facilities are in the city. Part-time employment is available. Beach area includes Ocean Park, Malibu Beach, and Will Rogers State Beach, providing recreational activities in addition to the city facilities for outdoor sports.

SANTA ROSA JUNIOR COLLEGE   *(G-2)*
1501 Mendocino Avenue
Santa Rosa, California 95401
Tel: (707) 527-4685; Admissions: (707) 527-4685; Fax: (707) 527-4685

Description: The publicly supported, coeducational junior college is accredited by the Western Association of Schools and Colleges. The college was established in 1918 and given its present campus in 1929. The first building was completed in 1931 and began the development of the campus which is presently valued in excess of $25,000,000. Programs of study are career oriented. The college grants the certificate and Associate degrees. It operates on the semester system and offers one summer session. Enrollment includes 4,838 full-time and 16,854 part-time students. A faculty of 276 full-time and 696 part-time gives a faculty-student ratio of 1-29.

Entrance Requirements: High school graduation; non-high school graduates 18 years of age or over considered for admission; midyear admission and rolling admission plans available.

Costs Per Year: $406 tuition for California residents; $4,046 nonresident tuition; $1,750 room only.

Collegiate Environment: The campus has 25 buildings on 97 acres. The campus nursery school accommodates 48 children who are observed by students of the schools of Nursing, Economics and Psychology. The library contains 112,590 volumes, 2,000 pamphlets, 639 periodicals, and 2,125 microforms and recordings. Coeducational dormitories accommodate 72 men and women. All students applying for admission are accepted. 1,400 scholarships are available, including 900 for freshmen. 40% of students receive some form of financial aid.

Community Environment: A suburban area, 55 miles north of San Francisco, with temperate climate, Santa Rosa is the major commercial center for Northern Coastal California. Public Library, churches of major denominations, hospitals, and shopping facilities make up the city. The community sponsors a symphony chorus, actor's workshop, community theater, as well as having major service organizations. Part-time employment is available. The Luther Burbank Home and Gardens are located here.

SCHOOL OF THEOLOGY AT CLAREMONT   (G-13)
1325 North College Avenue
Claremont, California 91711
Tel: (909) 626-3521; (800) 626-7824; Fax: (909) 626-7062

Description: The privately supported theological seminary is affiliated with the United Methodist Church, Disciples of Christ Presbyterian Church, and Episcopal Church. Founded in 1885 by Methodists, the School of Theology at Claremont is fully accredited by the Western Association of Schools and Colleges. The enrollment is 450 including part-time students; a faculty of 26 full-time and 24 part-time gives a faculty-student ratio of 1-10. The college grants degrees on the Master and Doctor level. It operates on the early semester system and offers a summer session featuring two-week intensive courses.

Entrance Requirements: Bachelor of Arts with a grade point average of at least 2.75; applicants not meeting all requirements may be admitted on a provisional basis; GRE and entrance exam required for doctoral level; $30 application fee; rolling admission and delayed admission plans available.

Costs Per Year: $6,825 tuition; $4,600 room and board; $130 student fees.

Collegiate Environment: The school works closely with the six educational institutions known as The Claremont Colleges. The library has 140,000 volumes, 670 periodicals, and 1,000 microforms; it also shares in the use of The Claremont Colleges' main library of more than 1,500,000 volumes, in addition to sharing other facilities. Spouses of degree students may enroll as auditors with the approval of the instructors and payment of a $25 registration fee. Residence hall facilities accommodate 164 students. New apartments were constructed in 1993. Approximately 70% of the students applying for admission are accepted.

Community Environment: See Claremont Graduate School.

SCRIPPS COLLEGE   (G-13)
1030 Columbia Avenue
Claremont, California 91711
Tel: (909) 621-8149; Fax: (909) 621-8323

Description: Founded in 1936, this private liberal arts college for women is located at the foot of the San Gabriel Mountains in Claremont, California. A member of the The Claremont Colleges group, it is accredited by the Western Association of Schools and Colleges. The enrollment is 613 women. A faculty of 58 full-time and 34 part-time gives a faculty-student ratio of 1-9. The semester system is used. The college grants the baccalaureate degree.

Entrance Requirements: High school graduation with rank in upper 20% of the graduating class; SAT or ACT required, completion of 17 units including 4 English, 4 mathematics, 3 foreign language, 3 social science, and 3 science; early decision, midyear admission, and advanced placement plans available; $40 application fee.

Costs Per Year: $17,238 tuition; $7,350 room and board; $112 fees.

Collegiate Environment: Scripps is a college whose purpose is to educate women to live successfully and confidently in a changing world. At Scripps, students can take advantage of the personalized atmosphere of a small college and the diversity of a coeducational university setting. Scripps is located at the foot of the San Gabriel Mountains. The library system of the Claremont Colleges contains 1,905,102 volumes, 6,800 periodicals and 1,125,000 microforms. All freshmen reside in residence halls, which accomodate 552 women. 78% of the applicants are accepted. The middle 50% range of scores for the entering freshman class is SAT 500-610 verbal, 520-640 math. The average ACT score is 25 composite. Scholarships are available and 50% of the current student body receives some form of financial aid.

Community Environment: See Claremont Graduate School.

SHASTA COLLEGE   (D-3)
11555 Old Oregon Trail
P.O. Box 496006
Redding, California 96049-6006
Tel: (916) 225-4600; Admissions: (916) 225-4841; Fax: (916) 225-4995

Description: The publicly supported two-year college is accredited by the Western Association of Schools and Colleges. The enrollment is approximately 11,000. The semester system is used. Programs of study lead to the Certificate and Associate degree.

Entrance Requirements: High school graduation; non-graduates 18 years of age or over admitted.

Costs Per Year: No costs to California residents; $2,855 non-resident tuition; board and room available; $125 student fees.

Collegiate Environment: Dormitory facilities accommodate 120 students. Ninety-eight percent of the students applying for admission meet the requirements and are accepted. Students are admitted at midyear as well as in September. Financial assistance is available. The library provides more than 62,560 volumes for student use.

Community Environment: Redding is located at the northern end of the Sacramento Valley and is served by buses, railroads and airlines. The city provides unlimited recreational opportunities; Shasta National Forest, Sacramento Canyon, Mount Shasta, Shasta Dam which is the second largest concrete dam in the world and Shasta Lake which encompasses 30,000 acres. Excellent fishing, camping, picnicking and swimming in the area. Redding is a trade center with good shopping facilities.

SIERRA COLLEGE   (G-4)
5000 Rocklin Road
Rocklin, California 95677
Tel: (916) 624-3333; Admissions: (916) 781-0430; Fax: (916) 781-0403

Description: Publicly supported, coeducational community college accredited by the Western Association of Schools and Colleges. The college was established in 1914, but events of World War I caused its discontinuance after only a few years. It was reestablished in 1936 and in 1961 the college moved to a new $10,000,000 campus. Day and evening classes are available. Programs of study lead to the Certificate and Associate degrees. The college operates on the early semester system and offers one summer session. Enrollment includes 3,945 full-time and 9,874 part-time students. A faculty of 125 full-time and 360 part-time gives a faculty-student ratio of 1-28.

Entrance Requirements: High school graduation or 18 years of age; open enrollment, early admission, early decision, and rolling admission plans available.

Costs Per Year: $312 state-resident enrollment fee; $2,880 ($120 per unit) nonresident tuition; $3,568 room and board; $15 health fee; $650 estimated additional expenses.

Collegiate Environment: The campus has 14 buildings on 170 acres. The library contains 61,100 volumes. There is dormitory capacity for 154 men and women. Approximately 98% of the students applying for admission are accepted including midyear students.

Community Environment: Population 9,820. Rocklin is located on Interstate 80 in the Loomis Basin, 23 miles northeast of Sacramento; the center of a large deciduous fruit-raising area. All forms of transportation available at nearby cities of Auburn and Roseville. Rocklin has libraries, hospitals, clinics, a health department, churches, and civic, fraternal, and veteran's organizations. Industry includes three lumber mills and a granite quarry. Recreational activities include swimming, picnicking, skiing, fishing and hunting. Seasonal and part-time employment is available.

SIMPSON COLLEGE   (I-3)
2211 College View Drive
Redding, California 96003-8606
Tel: (916) 224-5600; (800) 598-2493; Admissions: (916) 224-5606; Fax: (916) 224-5627

Description: The privately-supported, coeducational Christian College of liberal arts and professional studies is the western regional campus of The Christian and Missionary Alliance. The college is accredited by the Western Association of Schools and Colleges. Objectives of the college are to provide education for the Christian in ministry and in selected professions; to engender growth in all areas of the Christian life: academic, spiritual, social and physical. It operates on the semester system and offers four summer sessions. Enrollment includes 352 full-time, 7 part-time, and 262 evening undergraduates and 199 graduate students. A faculty of 24 full-time and 25 part-time provides an undergraduate faculty-student ratio of 1-16. Programs lead to the Associate, Bachelor and Master degrees.

Entrance Requirements: High school graduation or equivalent; completion of 16 units recommended; SAT or ACT required; rolling admission, midyear admission, and advanced placement plans available; $20 application fee.

Costs Per Year: $7,200 tuition; $3,690 room and board; $550 student fees.

Collegiate Environment: The new campus has five brand-new buildings on sixty acres; the master plan forecasts fifteen. The library contains 54,574 volumes, 269 periodicals, 70,570 microforms and 1,072 audiovisual materials. Dormitory facilities for 288 are available and all unmarried students under 23 years of age must reside on campus. Approximately 75% of the students applying for admission are accepted and 70% return for the sophomore year. Average score of a recent freshman class ACT was 21.6 and 45% graduated in the top fifth of their high school class. Financial aid is available and 85% of the current student body receive financial assistance.

Community Environment: See Shasta College.

SKYLINE COLLEGE   *(C-10)*
3300 College Drive
San Bruno, California 94066
Tel: (415) 355-7000; Admissions: (415) 738-4251

Description: The publicly supported, coeducational community college is one of three colleges in the San Mateo County Community and College District. It opened in the fall of 1969. Accredited by the Western Association of Schools and Colleges, Skyline grants the Associate degree and a Certificate. It operates on the semester system and offers one summer session. Enrollment includes 8,172 full-time and 5,913 part-time students and 3,514 evening students. A faculty of 302 gives a faculty-student ratio of 1-47.

Entrance Requirements: High school graduate or over 18 years of age; placement tests required; may be SAT, ACT, Skyline placement test.

Costs Per Year: $820 ($410 per semester) for California residents; $3,800 nonresident tuition; fees $113.

Collegiate Environment: The newest of three community colleges in San Mateo County Community College District is located on a 111-acre site, represents a $10 million investment, and plans to continue expansion. The library contains 49,000 volumes and 300 periodicals. 65% of a recent freshman class returned for sophomore year.

Community Environment: Population 50,000. San Bruno, located 12 miles south of San Francisco, is known as "The Airport City." The climate is temperate all year long, with cool, often foggy summers. All modes of transportation serve the area. This is a residential community with regional shopping centers, churches, library, and hospitals in nearby cities. Cultural advantages of San Francisco are appreciated by the people in San Bruno since it is so near.

SOLANO COMMUNITY COLLEGE   *(H-3)*
4000 Suisun Valley Road
Suisun, California 94585
Tel: (707) 864-7000; Admissions: (707) 864-7171; Fax: (707) 864-7157

Description: Publicly-supported, coeducational community college accredited by the Western Association of Schools and Colleges. The campus, opened in February 1971, provides permanent facilities for all disciplines. Enrollment is 10,000; a faculty of 340 gives a faculty-student ratio of 1:35. The semester system is used with one summer sessions. Programs of study lead to the Certificate and Associate Degree.

Entrance Requirements: High school graduation, GED, or 18 years of age; open enrollment, advanced placement and midyear admission plans available.

Costs Per Year: $3,000 nonresident tuition; $13/unit for California residents.

Collegiate Environment: Established in 1945 as Vallejo Junior College, Solano Community College functioned as part of the Vallejo Unified School District until the College became a countywide institution in 1967. As part of California's public community college system, Solano College serves the cities of Vallejo, Benicia, Fairfield, Suisun, Vacaville, Dixon and Winters, as well as two military installations: the Mare Island Naval Shipyard and Travis Air Force Base. Many graduates of the area's fifteen public high schools and three private schools choose to take advantage of the educational offerings at SCC. The library contains 36,000 volumes. 25% of the students receive financial aid.

Community Environment: Solano county is one of California's most rapidly growing counties. Suisun is located just off Interstate 80, halfway between San Francisco and Sacramento. The area is well known for its production of fruits, vegetables and wine grapes. Numerous businesses and industries are located in surrounding communities.

SONOMA STATE UNIVERSITY   *(G-2)*
1801 East Cotati Avenue
Rohnert Park, California 94928
Tel: (707) 664-2778; Admissions: (707) 664-2778; Fax: (707) 664-2060

Description: The publicly-supported, coeducational liberal arts university is accredited by the Western Association of Schools and Colleges. Created in 1960, construction of the first permanent building commenced in 1962. The move to the permanent campus occurred in 1966. The first degrees were offered in elementary education and the general elementary credential. During the second year of operation these programs were expanded while freshmen were beginning a general program of liberal arts. The college grants the Bachelor and Master's degrees and awards teacher certification. It operates on the semester system and offers three summer sessions. Enrollment includes 1,820 men, 2,774 women full-time, 705 men, and 1,310 women part-time. A faculty of 230 full-time and 169 part-time gives a faculty-student ratio of 1:21.

Entrance Requirements: High school graduation with a composite scholastic average and SAT or ACT score placing in the upper third of California H.S. graduates; for non-California residents, upper sixth; application fee $55; midyear acceptance; early admission, early decision and rolling admission plans available.

Costs Per Year: $7,974 nonresident tuition, $2,070 resident, $5,328 room & board.

Collegiate Environment: Campus environment has variety of social, recreational, cultural and intellectual activities. Student government is directly involved in student affairs. Student organizations include clubs, recreational groups, preprofessional associations, honor societies as well as religious and political groups. The Student Union provides focal point for many activities and services and houses student government. Athletic facilities include weight-gymnastics, dance studio, tennis courts, outdoor racquet courts, large gym, swimming pool and several athletic fields. Media facilities include photographic, campus radio station, newspaper and magazine publications. Cultural events include concerts, theatrical and dance productions and art exhibits. Residence halls for 900 students are available. Library contains 453,462 volumes, 32,123 pamphlets, 1,596 periodicals, 1,380,049 microforms and 14,590 sound recordings.

Community Environment: Population 50,000. Rohnert Park is a rapidly growing suburban community with temperate climate. Located near Santa Rosa (pop. 108,000) in Sonoma County. Buses and airlines serve the area. Community facilities include many shopping centers, civic and sports clubs. Recreational facilities include swimming pools, baseball parks, a community park, golf courses and others within a 20 mile radius. Rohnert Park has the annual Founders Day Parade. There are five hospitals within a 10 mile radius. The Valley of the Moon, San Francisco, the Russian River recreation areas, Redwood National Park and Lake Tahoe are all within driving range from an hour to a half day. Sonoma county produces premium wine and is the location of many famous wineries.

SOUTHERN CALIFORNIA COLLEGE   *(P-9)*
55 Fair Drive
Costa Mesa, California 92626
Tel: (714) 556-3610; (800) 722-6279; Fax: (714) 668-6194

Description: Privately supported, coeducational liberal arts college controlled by the Assemblies of God. The college is accredited by the Western Association of Schools and Colleges. Founded in 1920 as a training institute for ministers, the college began offering a liberal arts curriculum in 1959. The college has six divisions: Humanities and Fine Arts; Natural Science and Mathematics; Religion; Social Sciences; Business; and Professional Studies; offering a total of 29 different majors. It awards the Bachelor and Master degrees. The college operates on the semester system and offers three summer sessions. Enrollment includes 857 full-time, 82 part-time undergraduate, 108 graduate, and 49 evening students. A faculty of 45 full-time and 75 part-time gives an undergraduate faculty-student ratio of 1-18.

Entrance Requirements: Evidence of sound moral character; high school graduation with a 2.5 GPA and rank in upper 50% of graduating class; ACT or SAT required; early decision, midyear admission, rolling admission, and advanced placement plans available; July application deadline; $30 application fee.

Costs Per Year: $9,220 tuition; $4,124 room and board; $300 student fees.

Collegiate Environment: Student must have a 2.0 GPA for the previous semester in order to participate in extracurricular activities. Chapel attendance is required of all students. The library contains 115,000 volumes. The 40-acre campus has 4 residence halls as well as apartments for married students, with a total capacity of 650 students. 80% of applicants are accepted. 80% of students receive some form of financial assistance.

Community Environment: The college is adjacent to Newport Beach, the pleasure boat harbor of the West. See Orange Coast College.

SOUTHERN CALIFORNIA COLLEGE OF OPTOMETRY   *(H-12)*
2575 Yorba Linda Blvd.
Fullerton, California 92631
Tel: (714) 449-7444; (800) 829-9949; Fax: (714) 879-9834

Description: The privately supported coeducational college was founded in 1904 and is accredited by the Western Association of Schools and Colleges. This was the first college to bring optometric education to California. It operates on the quarter system and offers one summer session. Recent enrollment included 155 men and 228 women. A faculty of 86 gives a faculty-student ratio of 1-8. The College grants the Doctor of Optometry (O.D.) degree. In addition, students who have not earned a baccalaureate degree prior to enrollment may earn a Bachelor of Science in Visual Science (B.S.) degree at the conclusion of the second professional year, provided the student has successfully completed the first two years of the optometry curriculum and has fulfilled all additional requirements.

Entrance Requirements: High school graduation; Optometry Admission Test (OAT) required; 90 semester units or 135 quarter units of college-level work for the Doctor of Optometry degrees; B.A. required for admission beginning the Fall of 1997; $50 application fee.

Costs Per Year: $14,550 tuition; $90 student fees.

Collegiate Environment: Situated on a seven-acre site, the College is adjacent to California State University, Fullerton. The campus and all its facilities are entirely new, having been completed in 1973; the College owns and operates the Optometric Center of Fullerton, a major clinic on campus; the Optometric Center of Los Angeles, a major clinic, located at 3916 South Broadway in Los Angeles. The library contains 15,000 volumes and journals. The College operates the most extensive off-campus optometric clinical program in the world. Senior students may select from nearly 80 outreach clinical sites in 18 states. Approximately 25% of the students applying for admission are accepted and 88% receive some form of financial aid. Midyear students are not accepted.

Community Environment: See California State University - Fullerton.

SOUTHWESTERN COLLEGE   *(R-10)*
900 Otay Lakes Road
Chula Vista, California 92010
Tel: (619) 421-6700; Admissions: (619) 482-6550; Fax: (619) 482-6413

Description: The publicly supported, coeducational community college is accredited by the Western Association of Schools and Colleges. The semester system is used and one summer session is offered. The Southwestern Community College District was voted into existence in 1960. Recent enrollment included 7,125 men and 8,302 women. The faculty consists of 204 full-time and 400 part-time members. The college grants Certificates and the Associate degree.

Entrance Requirements: Open enrollment policy; high school graduation; non-graduates over 18 years of age admitted; college administered test required.

Costs Per Year: $390 tuition, $3,630 nonresident tuition, $28.75 student fees.

Collegiate Environment: No housing facilities are available on campus. The library contains 66,496 volumes and regularly receives 696 periodicals. College has a special program enabling low-mark, culturally disadvantaged students to attend. All students applying for admission are accepted. Students are admitted at mid-year. 73% of the students receive financial aid.

Community Environment: Chula Vista is a suburban area near San Diego with wonderfully mild climate. This area is served by the San Diego Transit System. The city has a recreation department and shopping center. Chula Vista has the usual civic organizations.

Branch Campuses: Southwestern College Education Center at San Ysidro

SOUTHWESTERN UNIVERSITY SCHOOL OF LAW   *(U-8)*
675 South Westmoreland Avenue
Los Angeles, California 90005
Tel: (213) 738-6700; Admissions: (213) 738-6717

Description: The independent, nonprofit, nonsectarian, coeducational law school has an enrollment of 1,150 with a faculty of 80, giving an overall faculty-student ratio of 1:13. It was organized as an independent college in 1911. Approved by the American Bar Association and a member of the Association of American Law Schools, it grants the Juris Doctor Degree (J.D.) Classes are offered in both full-time and part-time divisions. The full-time day division takes three years to complete; part-time evening students may complete their course of studies in four years. A special four year part-time day division, PLEAS (Part-time Legal Education Alternative at Southwestern) accommodates students who have child-care responsibilities. A special 2 year program leading to the J.D. degree was instituted in 1974 as an alternative approach to the study of law. This program, SCALE (Southwestern's Conceptual Approach to Legal Education), combines a study of the sources of law in history, philosophy, and economics with a pragmatic, problem-solving approach to the acquistion of substantive knowledge and lawyering skills. The semester system is used and one summer session is offered in the evening only. Southwestern's faculty currently includes 49 full-time members and a pool of 50 adjunct members. Students participate in an award-winning Moot Court Honors Program, Law Review, Journal of Law and Trade in the Americas, Trial Advocacy Competitions, and more than 30 law fraternities and student organizations. Southwestern's Student Bar Association was named "best in the region" five times in recent years by the ABA/Law Student Division. The law school also offers an extensive externship program where students are placed in public law offices and government agencies under the supervision of attorneys.

Entrance Requirements: A Bachelor's degree from an approved college or university; Law School Admission Test required; $50 application fee. First year students are admitted at the beginning of the fall term only.

Costs Per Year: $575 per semester unit; $7,515 per SCALE period (3 times per year)

Collegiate Environment: The law school campus consists of a seven story building and a student commons plaza. Southwestern's comprehensive law library contains over 360,000 volumes and subscribes to the LEXIS, WESTLAW, RLIN, Wilsonline, and Legal Trac computerized legal research systems. It also houses one of the most extensive multi-media legal collections in southern California. Special collections include environmental law, entertainment law, constitutional law, international law, and taxation. 87% percent receive financial aid.

Community Environment: Located half-way between downtown and the Pacific Ocean, in the Wilshire Center district of Los Angeles. With the second largest concentration of employment, income, business, industry, and finance in the country, Los Angeles is quickly emerging as the cultural and financial center of the Pacific Rim countries and holds a major key to the future of the world market. Less than a block from Wilshire Boulevard, the city's main thoroughfare, Southwestern is in the midst of major law firms and corporate headquarters and is just a short distance from the courts and government offices in the civic center. This metropolitan venue provides a stimulating atmosphere for legal study and affords a wide range of career opportunities for students and graduates.

STANFORD UNIVERSITY   *(I-3)*
Stanford, California 94305-3005
Tel: (415) 723-2091; Admissions: (415) 723-2091; Fax: (415) 725-2846

Description: The privately supported coeducational university was established under an 1885 Founding grant by Leland and Jane Stanford in memory of their only son, Leland Stanford, Jr., who died at age 15. The Stanford gift, the greatest in the history of American Education, totaled more than $20,000,000. The Stanfords felt the Palo Alto Farm was an ideal place for the University because of the climate and proximity to a major city, San Francisco. They patterned the institution after the great European universities rather than the colleges of the eastern United States of the time. Undergraduate enrollment is 6,561 students. There are 7,470 graduate students. An undergraduate and graduate faculty of 1,428 gives an overall faculty-student ratio of 1-10. The University is world renowned and is fully accredited by Western Association of Schools and Colleges and most professional accrediting agencies. It operates on a quarter system and offers one summer session. Degrees granted: Bachelor, Master and Doctorate. Schools of the University: Business (Graduate), Earth Science, Education, Engineering, Humanities and Sciences, Law, Medicine. Within the School of Humanities and Sciences is the Division of Marine Biology and Oceanography, located in the Hopkins Marine Station in Pacific Grove, California, on the south side of Monterey Bay, 90 miles from the main University Campus at Palo Alto. Stanford operates overseas campuses in Berlin, Florence, Kyoto, Moscow, Oxford, Paris, Rome, and Santiago. More than a quarter of each graduating class has studied overseas at some time during undergraduate years.

Entrance Requirements: High school graduation or equivalent; completion of the four-year college preparatory course; SAT or ACT required; CEEB Achievement Tests in English composition and any two others are strongly recommended; graduation in upper 10% of high school class recommended; GRE required for graduate school; application fee $50; advanced placement plan available. Dec. 15 application deadline, Nov. 1 early decision.

Costs Per Year: $18,669 tuition; $6,796 room and board.

Collegiate Environment: Stanford University seeks a diverse student body. Admission is highly competitive, and only 21% of the students applying for admission are accepted. Stanford University has campuses abroad in England, Germany, Austria, Italy and France. Approximately 63% of the Stanford student body receives some form of financial aid. Libraries contain over 6.4 million volumes, 900,000 manuscripts and 4.2 million microforms. Predominantly a residential college, Stanford houses approximately 90% of its undergraduates. Stanford offers student service centers, 75 undergraduate student residences, a nondenominational church, a hospital and health center, a student union, an art museum, a radio station, a bookstore, a post office, fire and police departments, a shopping center, multiple auditoriums, 4 swimming pools, 26 tennis courts, a sports center, a stadium, an athletic pavilion, and an 18-hole golf course.

Community Environment: Stanford is an unincorporated campus adjacent to Palo Alto. Palo Alto with a population of 60,000 is located 30 miles south of San Francisco with an ideal climate, the summer average being 70 degrees and the winter average 55 degrees. The average rainfall is 15.5 inches. The city is served by all modes of transportation, the San Francisco Airport being 18 miles north. Palo

Alto has three libraries, a museum, art gallery, hotels, hospitals, and churches. The Silicon Valley, in large part an offspring of Stanford, begins at campus edge. The cultural and recreation opportunities of San Francisco and San Jose are added to the many of the Stanford campus and the surrounding area. The Pacific Ocean is 32 miles to the west; the Monterey peninsula is 75 miles to the south. The Sierra Nevada, 160 miles away and the site of several national parks, are a popular resort area for camping, hiking, and skiing.

STARR KING SCHOOL FOR THE MINISTRY   *(H-3)*
2441 Le Conte Avenue
Berkeley, California 94709
Tel: (415) 845-6232

Description: The privately supported coeducational theological graduate school enrolled 43 students. The college is the Pacific Coast Educational Center for the Unitarian Universalist denomination. The semester system is used, and one summer session is occaisionally offered. The college is a member of the Graduate Theological Union, with whom it grants some Master and Doctoral degrees, and is accredited by the Association of Theological Schools. Starr King awards the Master of Divinity Degree. Educational standards require that the school keep a small format of no more than 44 students. A faculty of 14 gives a faculty-student ratio of 1-3.

Entrance Requirements: Undergraduate degree with a B average; highest personal and academic integrity; $65 application fee.

Costs Per Year: $6,100 tuition.

Collegiate Environment: As a member of the Graduate Theological Union, the school shares the joint library facilities of over 400,000 volumes. The campus is located in the midst of a university and seminary community, two blocks from the University of California campus. Admission is highly selective and one applicant in three is accepted. The school has no dormitories. 40% of the students receive financial aid.

Community Environment: See University of California - Berkeley

TAFT COLLEGE   *(M-7)*
29 Emmons Park Drive
Taft, California 93268
Tel: (805) 763-4282; Fax: (805) 763-1038

Description: The publicly supported, coeducational junior college is accredited by the Western Association of Colleges and Schools. It operates on the early semester system and offers one summer session. The college was established in 1922; new campus and facilities were first occupied in 1956. Programs of study lead to the Certificate and to the Associate degree. Enrollment includes 319 full-time and 690 part-time students. A faculty of 59 provides a faculty-student ratio of 1:17.

Entrance Requirements: Open enrollment policy; non-high school graduates considered; early admission, early decision, rolling admission, midyear admission, advanced placement plans available.

Costs Per Year: No tuition for California residents; $3,420 nonresident tuition; $390 enrollment fee; $2,600 room and board; $170 student fees; $10 parking fee; $60 textbook rental; additional expenses average $500.

Collegiate Environment: The campus has seven buildings on 20 acres including residence halls for 48 women and 128 men. The library contains 25,788 volumes, 148 periodicals, 585 microforms and 1,005 recordings. Most students applying for admission are accepted, and students may enroll at midyear as well as in the fall. 90 scholarships are available, including 54 for freshmen and 33% of the current student body receives some form of financial aid.

Community Environment: The population of the Taft area is 18,500. Centrally located two and one-half hours north of Los Angeles, Taft has a mild climate with hot summers. The city, surrounded by oilfields, is an important supply point for field equipment. Churches of all denominations, hospital, library, a local radio station, and shopping facilities make up the town. Part-time employment is available. Recreational facilities include a theatre, bowling alley, golf course, and more. Apartments are available.

THOMAS AQUINAS COLLEGE   *(O-7)*
10000 North Ojai Road
Santa Paula, California 93060
Tel: (805) 525-4417

Description: The school is a privately supported, coeducational college affiliated with the Roman Catholic Church. It operates on the semester system. Founded in 1971, it offers a four-year required program of reading and discussion of Great Books: the greatest writings in mathematics, science, literature, history, theology and philosophy. All classes are seminars and tutorials. Enrollment is 221 students. A faculty of 22 gives a faculty-student ratio of 1-10. The college is fully accredited by the Western Association of Schools and Colleges, and grants the Bachelor of Arts degree.

Entrance Requirements: High school graduation or GED; 4 units of English, 4 social studies, 3 mathematics, 2 laboratory science and 2 foreign language required; SAT or ACT required; early admission, rolling admission and admission plans available.

Costs Per Year: $13,400 tuition; $5,200 room and board.

Collegiate Environment: The college is located on a lovely 175-acre campus 15 miles from the California coast. The facilities include classrooms, a library of 36,000 volumes, a chapel, swimming pool and athletic fields. The school has dormitory facilities for 231 students. Students enrolled come from various religious and social backgrounds, but share the desire to live a life of serious scholarship. 57% of applicants are accepted. The average scores of the entering freshman class were SAT 1175 combined, ACT 27 composite. 86% are accepted. 75% of the student body receives some form of financial aid.

Community Environment: The college is located in a rural setting 60 miles from Los Angeles and 45 miles from Santa Barbara. It is bordered on three sides by Los Padres National Forest.

UNITED STATES INTERNATIONAL UNIVERSITY   *(R-10)*
10455 Pomerado Road
San Diego, California 92131
Tel: (619) 635-4772; Fax: (619) 693-8562

Description: Founded in 1952 as California Western University, the school became United States International University in 1966. The privately supported, coeducational university is accredited by the Western Association of Schools and Colleges and grants the Associate, Bachelor, Master and Doctorate degrees. In addition to the undergraduate program, graduate programs are offered through the College of Business Administration, Department of Education, Department of Liberal and Interdisciplinary Studies, and Department of Psychology and Family Studies. Two associated campuses abroad (Kenya, Mexico) also offers degree programs. The university operates on the quarter system and offers two summer sessions and a Fall-Winter Intensive session. Enrollment includes 791 full-time and 490 part-time undergraduates and 1,024 graduate students. A faculty of 51 full-time and 61 part-time provides a faculty-stuent ratio of 1-13. 93% of the faculty hold doctoral degrees. Class size averages 15 to 20 students.

Entrance Requirements: Accredited high school graduation, minimum of 16 academic units in last three years of high school; SAT or ACT required; GRE, MAT or GMAT required for various graduate divisions; early admission, rolling admission, delayed admission, advanced placement plans available; $30 application fee; autobiographical statement; recommmendations required.

Costs Per Year: Undergraduate: $10,290 full-time tuition; Graduate: $220-$400 per unit; $4,435 room and board.

Collegiate Environment: Campus occupies 160 acres of wooded land in the city of San Diego, a quiet natural setting of seclusion and beauty only fifteen minutes from downtown San Diego. Approximately 60% of the students applying for admission are accepted, including midyear students. The university seeks a geographically diverse student body. Merit scholarships are offered which provide 24% to 30% of tuition for undergraduates entering with a 3.0 GPA or higher. 75% of the current student body receives some form of assistance. All facilities have been designed to bring faculty and students together in an environment conducive to learning. Apartment complexes, each with its own swimming pool, are located well away from classroom areas and accommodate 300 men and 300 women. The library contains 250,000 volumes and numerous pamphlets, periodicals, microforms and recordings.

Community Environment: See University of California - San Diego

UNIVERSITY OF CALIFORNIA - ADMINISTRATION   *(H-3)*
317 University Hall
Berkeley, California 94720
Tel: (415) 642-5860

Description: A tradition of excellence in teaching and research has guided the University of California for over 100 years. It began as the College of California in Oakland and was moved to Berkeley in 1873. As the Berkeley campus grew, other campuses were added throughout California. The nine-campus University of California is now one of the largest in the world and includes the Berkeley, Los Angeles, Davis, Irvine, Riverside, San Diego, San Francisco, Santa Barbara, and Santa Cruz campuses. All of the University's campuses have uniform admission requirements, highly qualified faculty, high academic standards, and excellent libraries. Each campus, however, is distinctive and each has its own character and style. The University also has 16 campuses abroad in various parts of the world.

Entrance Requirements: To be eligible for admission to the University as a freshman, candidates must meet the Subject Requirement, the Scholarship Requirement, and the Examination Requirement. A nonresident of California must also meet certain additional requirements and must show exceptional academic promise.

UNIVERSITY OF CALIFORNIA - BERKELEY   *(H-3)*
Berkeley, California 94720
Tel: (415) 642-6000

Description: A publicly supported coeducational university, this oldest and largest of the University of California campuses is accredited by the Western Association of Schools and Colleges and its individual colleges are also accredited by respective professional organizations. Enrollment is 16,824 men and 13,798 women in undergraduate study. The semester system is employed, and 1 summer term is offered. Founded in 1868, this state university has grown to include a distinguished faculty of 1,786. Recent enrollment included 8,781 graduate students. The 25 academic subdivisions of the University award undergraduate and graduate degrees. A Cooperative Education program is available for Engineering students. ROTC Program available in Army, Navy, Air Force, Marines, on an elective basis.

Entrance Requirements: See University of California - Administration.

Costs Per Year: Tuition $2,904; $7,699 nonresident; $5,730 room and board.

Collegiate Environment: An area of 1,282 acres, big, exciting, and beautiful. Groves of oak, redwood, and eucalyptus, meandering Strawberry Creek, hiking and running trails, and spacious lawns ideal for strolling or quiet study. Berkeley is more than a campus; it is a community, a place to grow. The recently completed Recreational Sports Facility has facilities for handball, squash, weight lifting, swimming, and a host of other sports. The library contains 7,600,000 volumes. The Daily Californian, the independent student newspaper, publishes notices of movies, lectures, concerts, exhibits, and sports events. More than 250 student organizations flourish, covering a wide range of interests - the Associated Students, forensics, the KALX Radio Station, the Cal Band, political action groups, sports clubs, ethnic associations, and humor and literary magazines, to name just a few. Berkeley has a wide range of housing choices and is able to accomodate all freshmen who apply within the stated deadlines. There is campus-provided housing such as residence halls, co-op housing, and International House for 5,000 single students and 1,022 families. There is also private housing in sororities and fraternities, in boarding houses, in apartments, and in houses to share. 38% of applicants are accepted. 50% receive financial aid.

Community Environment: The City of Berkeley (population 106,500) has a long history as one of America's most lively, culturally diverse, and politically adventurous cities. The surrounding San Francisco Bay Area offers culture, entertainment, and natural beauty without rival, much of it within easy reach by BART (Bay Area Rapid Transit).

UNIVERSITY OF CALIFORNIA - DAVIS   (G-4)
175 Mrak Hall
Davis, California 95616
Tel: (916) 752-1011; Admissions: (916) 752-2971; Fax: (916) 752-6363

Description: The publicly supported, coeducational university was originally known as the University Farm in 1909, when the student body consisted of 18 young men studying for careers in agriculture. The student body has grown to include 22,444 students. A faculty of 1,262 full-time and 250 part-time gives a faculty-student ratio of 1:19. Accredited by the Western Association of Schools and Colleges, this research university's undergraduate colleges, professional schools, and graduate division are accredited by respective professional organizations. The quarter system is used with two summer terms. Hundreds of academic internship are available through the Internship and Career Center. Army ROTC available on voluntary basis. Offers Bachelor, Master, Doctorate Degrees from the College of Agricultural and Environmental Sciences, College of Engineering, College of Letters and Science, Division of Biological Sciences, School of Law, School of Medicine, School of Veterinary Medicine and Graduate Division and Graduate School of Management.

Entrance Requirements: See University of California - Administration.

Costs Per Year: $7,699 nonresident tuition; $5,285 room and board, $4,099 student fees.

Collegiate Environment: The university is located on a 5,146 acre campus 13 miles west of Sacramento and 72 miles northeast of San Francisco in the Central Valley. The library contains 2.7 million volumes, 601,813 pamphlets, 49,098 periodicals, 3.3 million microforms, 13,882 sound recordings, and 35,000 rare books. 1,579 undergraduates received scholarships. The university provides housing for 3,850 undergraduates in a variety of residence halls on- and off-campus. 14 national fraternities and 9 national sororities provide living quarters for 398 undergraduate members and pledges. 69% of students applying for admission are accepted and 93% of the freshman class returned to the campus for the second year. 69% undergraduates received some form of financial aid; financial and tutorial assistance is provided for minority students who are recruited and admitted to the university under the Educational Opportunity Program.

Community Environment: Population 50,000. Located in the center of the Sacramento Valley, the climate is typical of the Great Central Valley of California - cool in the winter and warm in the long dry summer season. January average temperatures range from a low of 37 to a high of 54 degrees; July average temperatures range 57 to 97 degrees. The average annual rainfall is 17 inches. The agricultural region surrounding Davis produces numerous crops including tomatoes, alfalfa, wheat and corn. Berkeley and San Francisco are within one hour by train, bus or car. Part-time employment is available either on or off campus. Davis is only 2-3 hours from the Lake Tahoe vacation area in the Sierra Nevada Mountains.

UNIVERSITY OF CALIFORNIA - IRVINE   (P-9)
Irvine, California 92717
Tel: (714) 856-5011

Description: This is the University of California's youngest campus. Irvine opened classes in 1965. The Irvine campus was planned from the beginning with the intention that five fundamental Schools would represent five fundamental areas of knowledge, as well as provide an academic structure for related studies. The five Schools are Biological Sciences, Fine Arts, Humanities, Physical Sciences, and Social Sciences. Areas of knowledge which cross these major school boundaries are represented by the Program in Social Ecology, the Program in Comparative Culture, and the Department of Information and Computer Science. In addition to the basic Schools and the associated cross-disciplinary Programs and Departments, there are three Schools with primarily professional orientation: Management, Engineering and Medicine. The remaining academic units consist of the Office of Teacher Education and the Department of Physical Education. Navy and Air Force ROTC are available on campus. The university is fully accredited by the Western Association of Schools and Colleges. Enrollment includes 13,597 undergraduate students and 3,495 graduate students. A faculty of 811 gives a faculty-student ratio of 1-16. The university operates on the quarter system with 2 summer sessions.

The eight schools and many divisions of the University grant Bachelor, Master, Doctor and teaching accreditation degrees.

Entrance Requirements: See University of California - Administration.

Costs Per Year: Resident: $4,049 undergraduate, $4,807 graduate; nonresidents add $7,699.

Collegiate Environment: The campus is about five miles from the Pacific Ocean and the City of Newport Beach and is connected by a modern freeway system to the city of Los Angeles. The university currently has residence halls and dining facilities at Mesa Court and Middle Earth for 2,330 single students, and 200 two-bedroom apartments house 800 single undergraduates. Additionally, 862 one-, two-, and three bedroom apartments are available for full-time registered students who are married, or graduate students, or are over 25 years of age. Finally, the campus boasts a trailer park with 80 trailer spaces available. The library contains more than 1,500,000 volumes, holds 19,618 active serial subscriptions, and is a member of the University of California Library system, with access to more than 14 million volumes. 67% of students applying for admission meet requirements and are accepted. The mean SAT scores of the freshmen were 459V, 569M. 40% of the students receive financial aid.

Community Environment: UCI's location offers the cultural and economic resources of an urban area along with access to the scenic, recreational areas of Southern California. Located 40 miles south of Los Angeles, five miles from the Pacific Ocean, and nestled in 1,489 acres of coastal foothills near Newport Beach, UCI lies amid rapidly growing residential communities and a dynamic national and multinational business and industrial complex that affords many employment opportunities. The campus itself remains an oasis of green, a natural arboretum planted with trees and shrubs from all over the world.

UNIVERSITY OF CALIFORNIA - LOS ANGELES   (O-8)
405 Hilgard Avenue
Los Angeles, California 90024
Tel: (213) 825-3101

Description: This publicly supported, coeducational university is academically ranked among the leading universities in the United States. It has attracted distinguished scholars from all over the world. Operating on the quarter system with two summer sessions, the university is accredited by the Western Association of Schools and Colleges and its individual colleges are accredited by respective professional organizations. The 11 schools and 1 college that comprise the University grant Bachelor, Master, Doctorate degrees as well as Teacher Certification Credentials, M.D. degree, the Juris Doctor degree and the D.D.S. degree. Beginning with 250 students in 1919, the student body enrollment has risen to 35,110 (Fall 1994). Enrollment includes 23,619 undergraduates and 11,491 graduate students. A faculty and teaching staff of 3,210 gives an overall faculty-student ratio of 1-17. ROTC is available on voluntary basis for Army, Navy (including Marines), and Air Force.

Entrance Requirements: See University of California - Administrationn.

Costs Per Year: No tuition for state residents; $7,699 nonresident tuition; $5,410-$6,425 room and board; $3,893.50 student fees.

Collegiate Environment: The campus lies at the foot of the Santa Monica mountains in the residential community of Westwood, five miles from the Pacific Ocean and 30 minutes from the center of Los Angeles. 220 buildings on 419 acres comprise the campus; the library contains 6,247,320 volumes, 94,156 periodicals, 6,377,470 microforms and 200,174 sound recordings. The residence hall capacity is 5,700; apartments are available for 1,009 families. The total membership in Greek fraternities and sororities is 3,342 students. 1,600 students live in fraternity and sorority houses. Other off-campus accommodations are listed at the Office of Housing Services. 42% of high school students applying for admission are offered admission. Special programs for the culturally disadvantaged enabling low-mark disadvantaged students to attend are offered. Financial aid is available, and 40% of the undergraduates receive some form of assistance.

Community Environment: Los Angeles is a major metropolitan center with a semi-arid climate. There are very fine museums and libraries in the city, and a music center, which contribute to the cultural atmosphere of the city. Los Angeles has many points of interest, and is near enough to the beaches and to the mountains for all sports. There are excellent metropolitan shopping centers.

UNIVERSITY OF CALIFORNIA - RIVERSIDE *(P-10)*
900 University Avenue
Riverside, California 92521
Tel: (909) 787-1012; Admissions: (909) 787-3411

Description: The publicly supported, coeducational university opened its doors to undergraduates in 1954 after serving the University as a major center of research for nearly 50 years. UCR offers the quality and rigor of a major research institution, while still assuring its undergraduates personal attention and a sense of community. It grants Bachelor, Master and Doctorate degrees and is accredited by the Western Association of Schools and Colleges and by the American Chemical Society. The University operates on the quarter system and offers 2 summer sessions. Enrollment is 8,700 students. A faculty of 584 full-time and 155 part-time gives a faculty-student ratio of approximately 1-14.

Entrance Requirements: See University of California - Administration.

Costs Per Year: $4,093 student fees; $7,699 nonresident tuition; California residents tuition free; $5,430 room and board.

Collegiate Environment: The campus is located two miles east of downtown Riverside and is within one hour's drive of Los Angeles, Palm Springs, Lake Arrowhead, and the Pacific Ocean. Residence halls can accommodate 2,500 students and 268 apartments are available for married students with 317 additional university-owned apartments. 74% of students applying for admission are accepted, including midyear students. The library contains 1,507,000 volumes. Financial aid is available, and 50% of the current students receive assistance.

Community Environment: Population 250,000. A suburban area 60 miles east of Los Angeles with a temperate climate, Riverside is an important residential and commercial center in Riverside County. This city launched the navel orange industry in southern California. Major transportation facilities are available. Riverside has churches of the major denominations, a library, hospitals and all public health services. Recreational activities include all water sports. Beaches, desert and mountain/ski resort areas are nearby.

UNIVERSITY OF CALIFORNIA - SAN DIEGO *(Q-10)*
Student Outreach and Recruitment, 0337
9500 Gilman Drive
La Jolla, California 92093
Tel: (619) 534-2230; Fax: (619) 534-5723

Description: The publicly supported, coeducational university has its origins in the closing years of the nineteenth century when La Jolla was selected as the site for a marine research field station of the Pacific. This project became the Scripps Institution of Oceanography and was made a part of the University of California in 1912. The university is accredited by the Western Association of Schools and Colleges and by numerous professional accrediting institutions. The university consists of Scripps Institution of Oceanography and five undergraduate colleges: Revelle College, John Muir College, Thurgood Marshall College, Earl Warren College, Eleanor Roosevelt College, the School of Medicine and the graduate division, granting Bachelor, Master, and Doctor degrees. The five undergraduate colleges offer five distinct philosophies which prepare students for any major offered: Revelle College offers a broad curriculum with a Renaissance perspective including mathematics, natural sciences, social sciences, humanities, foreign language and fine arts; John Muir College is designed to guide students toward a broad and liberal education while allowing them a substantial choice in the development of that education; Thurgood Marshall College has an academic focus on understanding the factors which determine social change and development and also has a special commitment to the establishment of a multiracial, multicultural community; Earl Warren College asks students to link their studies to personal and professional goals, giving the student the opportunity to plan a program suited to the student's own interests and incorporates at least three major disciplinary fields (social sciences, humanities and fine arts, science and quantitative studies); UCSD's newest college is Eleanor Roosevelt College, which provides an international focus to an undergraduate education. An emphasis is placed on interdisciplinary, cross-cultural studies and foreign language. Roosevelt's students are encouraged to study abroad. Scripps Institution of Oceanography offers oceanographic programs at the graduate level only.

Entrance Requirements: High school graduation or equivalent; completion of 4 units of English, 3 math, 2 science, 2 foreign language, 2 social studies, 2 units of College Preparatory electives; SAT or ACT required; 3 CEEB Achievement tests, English composition, math, and social science or foreign language or English literature or science, required; early admission and advanced placement plans available; $40 application fee.

Costs Per Year: $4,263 resident, $11,898 nonresident tuition; $6,411 room and board.

Collegiate Environment: The 1,200-acre campus is located on a mesa overlooking the Pacific, adjacent to the residential community of La Jolla and 12 miles from downtown San Diego. 63% of applicants are accepted. Special programs for the culturally and economically disadvantaged are offered. The library contains 2.2 million bound volumes, 2 million titles on microfilm, 48,212 records, tapes, and CD's, and 24,414 periodical subscriptions. Housing facilities are provided for 4,676 students and guaranteed for freshmen for two years and transfer students for one year who meet all deadlines. The average SAT scores of the current freshman class were 504 verbal and 604 math. Financial aid is available, and approximately 46% of the current student body receives some form of assistance.

Community Environment: La Jolla is within the corporate limits of San Diego and is a popular resort with a rocky coast and fine beaches. San Diego lies along and around one of the world's ten most beautiful protected natural harbors, and has a very special seawashed, air-conditioned climate. The maximum average temperature of 70.8 degrees and a minimum of 55.4 degrees makes the climate very special. Amtrak, buses and major airlines all serve the area. The city is a manufacturing and shipping center, with its main industries being fishing, fish packing and the construction of aircraft parts, missiles and boats. San Diego County is the country's largest producer of avocados. San Diego has a large public library, hospitals, museums, galleries and churches. There are numerous golf courses, all aquatic sports, hiking, mountain climbing, horseback riding, skiing and other snow sports, fishing and hunting. Sea World, the world-famous San Diego Zoo and Wild Animal Park and Balboa Park also provide recreational opportunities. This is the home of the 1994 AFC Champion San Diego Chargers, the professional football team, and the San Diego Padres professional baseball team. Known as a winter playground, it has 70 miles of beautiful beaches. Population of San Diego is 1,118,279 with a greater metropolitan area population of 2,509,919.

UNIVERSITY OF CALIFORNIA - SAN FRANCISCO *(I-3)*
MU-200 Box 0244
San Francisco, California 94143
Tel: (415) 476-9000

Description: The publicly supported medical university that offers only professional training in the health sciences at the upper division and graduate level, enrolls 3,739 students. Founded in 1864, it operates on the quarter system.

Entrance Requirements: Upper-division college status; college courses; Dentistry - 90 semester units, including 6 English and 28 science; 6 social science; Dental Hygiene - 60 units, including 6 English, 18 science and 9 social science; Medicine - 90 units, including 6 English, 32 science; Physical Therapy - 90 units, including 6 English, 20 science and 12 social science; Nursing - 58 units, including 6 English, 18 science and 18 social science; Pharmacy - 60 units, including 6 English, 6 mathematics and 26 science. Students who enter as undergraduates with a Bachelor's degree must have a minimum GPA of 2.00 in all academic work attempted. Additional requirements must be met depending on student's major; application fee $40.

Costs Per Year: $1,545 per quarter for California residents; $4,000 per quarter for nonresidents.

Collegiate Environment: The University of California, San Francisco is located in the center of the city and commands an impressive view of San Francisco Bay. The clinical teaching facilities include the Joseph M. Long and the Herbert C. Moffitt Hospitals, Medical Sciences Building, Clinical Sciences Building, Health Science Research Buildings and the Langley Porter Psychiatric Institute. Other buildings include Ambulatory Care Clinics Building and Parking Structure,

School of Nursing Building, School of Dentistry Building and the Central Campus Court and student union. Residence halls for 172 single students and apartments for 165 married students and their families are available. The library contains 627,956 volumes. Special services are offered for qualified culturally disadvantaged students.

Community Environment: See San Francisco State University

UNIVERSITY OF CALIFORNIA - SANTA BARBARA   *(O-6)*
Santa Barbara, California 93106
Tel: (805) 893-8000; Admissions: (805) 893-2485

Description: The publicly supported, coeducational university operates on the quarter system and offers one summer session. Enrollment is 17,834 students. A faculty of 950 gives a faculty-student ratio of 1-18. The university is accredited by the Western Association of Schools and Colleges. In 1968 UCSB celebrated its 25th year as a campus of the University of California. The first Master of Arts programs were initiated in 1954 when the move to the present campus was undertaken. The four schools and colleges of the University grant Bachelor, Master and Doctor degrees. National research centers include the Institute for Theoretical Physics, Optoelectronics Technology Center, Materials Research Laboratory, Center for Ecological Analysis & Synthesis, the Center for Quantized Electronic Structures and the David Simonett Center for Spatial Analysis. Organized research units include Center for Chicano Studies, Marine Science Institute, Institute for Interdisciplinary Applications of Algebra and Combinations, Institute for Crustal Studies, Neuroscience Research Institute, Institute for Polymers and Organic Solids, Institute for Computational Earth Systems Science, Community and Organizations Research Institute and Quantum Institute. Army ROTC is available on voluntary basis.

Entrance Requirements: See University of California - Administration.

Costs Per Year: $4,098 annual tuition and fees; $7,699 nonresident; $5,901 room and board.

Collegiate Environment: The campus is located on the Pacific Seashore nine miles from the city of Santa Barbara. Forty-one major buildings have been completed and others are under construction. The library contains over 2 million volumes. There are 550 university-operated apartments for married students and dormitory capacity for 2,700 single students. 84% of the student body lives within a mile of the campus center. Approximately 90% of the freshman class had a high school GPA above 3.0. Average SAT scores of the freshman class were 455V and 544M. Special programs are offered for the culturally disadvantaged and also for disabled students. 83% of all applicants are accepted. 49% of undergraduates receive financial aid.

Community Environment: The University is located in Goleta, a suburb of Santa Barbara. Santa Barbara is a county seat, the largest city between Los Angeles and San Francisco, and is known as the "Riviera of the Pacific." The city lies at the foot of the Santa Ynez Mountains, facing the Pacific Ocean. The climate is moderate, and the temperature varies only 7 degrees in summer and winter. All modes of transportation serve the area, and hotel and motel accommodations are numerous. Santa Barbara has all the community facilities plus many points of interest, a planetarium, botanic garden, natural history, art, historical museums, and more. The annual horse show, Old Spanish Days, August Fiesta, Semana Nautica (Marine sports week), and flower shows are the highlights of the year. Active music organizations and the Symphony Orchestra are an important part of the cultural life of the city. Recreational facilities include golf courses, tennis courts, water sports at the beach, and many other activities.

UNIVERSITY OF CALIFORNIA - SANTA CRUZ   *(J-3)*
Office of Admissions
Santa Cruz, California 95064
Tel: (408) 459-4008

Description: This publicly supported, coeducational university was established in 1965. It is accredited by the Western Association of Schools and Colleges and operates on the quarter system with two summer sessions. Each undergraduate is affiliated with one of the eight small, residential colleges of liberal arts and sciences, but is entitled to participate in courses campus-wide. Thus students enjoy the advantages of both the small college atmosphere and the extensive resources of the entire university community. Undergraduate degree programs are offered in the full range of traditional disciplines and a number of interdisciplinary areas. Students may also follow individually designed majors. Doctoral programs are offered in seventeen fields. Current enrollment includes 9,857 full-time and 260 part-time undergraduates and 1,018 graduate students. A faculty of 379 full-time and 155 part-time gives a faculty-student ratio of 1-19.

Entrance Requirements: See University of California - Administration.

Costs Per Year: $7,699 nonresident tuition; $6,081 room and board; $4,384 student fees (resident and nonresident); $1,665 miscellaneous.

Collegiate Environment: The Santa Cruz campus overlooks the northern end of Monterey Bay and occupies 2,000 acres of rolling meadows and redwood forest. Each college has its own classrooms, faculty and administrative offices, residence houses, dining commons, and recreation areas, and the central facilities include the 1,096,962 volume library, science laboratories, a performing-arts complex, computer center, and athletic areas. About half of the students live on campus. Dormitories accommodate 4,000 students, and 199 apartments are available for married couples. Academic and personal counseling are available in the colleges for both resident and commuting students. The campus's Educational Opportunity Program and other special programs facilitate the admission and support of minority and low-income students. 78% of applicants are accepted. Over half the current student body receives some form of financial aid. Santa Cruz students have an exceptional record of admission to graduate and professional schools and awards for financial support.

Community Environment: The City of Santa Cruz, population 47,000, and other nearby communities are easily accessible from the campus via the local bus system. The Santa Cruz area has long been a popular resort because of its recreational facilities, which include 10 miles of beaches, a widely varied coastal zone, and the densely wooded Santa Cruz Mountains. The temperate climate is characterized by sunny summer days with foggy mornings and rain in the winter. Many of the city's Victorian houses have been restored in recent years, and its main shopping street has been revitalized. For its size, Santa Cruz has a remarkable variety of outstanding restaurants in all price ranges. Numerous cultural activities are sponsored by the University, the local junior college, and community organizations.

UNIVERSITY OF JUDAISM   *(O-8)*
15600 Mulholland Dr.
Los Angeles, California 90077
Tel: (310) 476-9777; Fax: (310) 471-1278

Description: Privately supported, coeducational school specializes in Jewish studies and Liberal Arts, and attempts to meet the professional needs of Jewish life in America as well as provide professional preparation for careers in a variety of fields. Operating on the semester system, the college is accredited by the Western Association of Schools and Colleges. Enrollment includes 175 full-time and 13 part-time undergraduates and 86 graduate students. A faculty of 11 full-time and 34 part-time gives a faculty-student ratio of 1-6. Divisions: Fingerhut School of Education and Lieber School of Graduate Studies; Lee College; and Ziegler School of Rabbinic Studies. Degrees granted: B.Lit., Master of Arts in Education, Master in Business Administration, B.A., Master of Arts in Jewish Studies, and Master of Hebrew Letters.

Entrance Requirements: High school graduation; SAT or ACT required; GRE required for graduate studies; early decision, rolling admission, advanced placement and delayed admission plans available; $25 application fee.

Costs Per Year: $10,938 ($440/unit) tuition; $6,100 room and board.

Collegiate Environment: The university was founded in 1947. The central location of the new Familian campus offers many advantages, including a joint undergraduate program with Mt. Saint Mary's. The library contains more than 170,000 volumes. Financial assistance is available, and 75% of the current enrollment receives some form of financial aid. The Ziegler School of Rabbinic Studies offers a joint program with the Jewish Theological Seminary of America, by which students can be admitted to both schools simultaneously and fulfill the requirements of the preparatory and first years of the seminary's rabbinical school, through the MHL program.

Community Environment: Los Angeles enjoys a mild and delightful climate. The city is served by all modes of transportation and freeways. The Hollywood Bowl has special summer-long programs of music and the lively arts. There are many theaters, both movie and stage, the Griffith Park Zoo, Planetarium, museum, and art shows, all offering broad cultural and recreational activities. Within the city are excellent world-famous restaurants, night clubs and fine hotels and motels providing outstanding accommodations and service. Employment is usually available on full- or part-time basis.

UNIVERSITY OF LA VERNE   *(G-13)*
1950 Third Street
La Verne, California 91750
Tel: (909) 593-3511

Description: The University of La Verne is an independent university emphasizing the liberal arts, the sciences, and career preparation. Founded in 1891 by members of the Church of the Brethren, the University proudly acknowledges the importance of its Christian heritage. Faculty and students are drawn from all segments of life. The 45-member Board of Trustees if fully reflective of the pluralistic nature of contemporary society. The current undergraduate enrollment is about 1,100 with a faculty of 200 full-time and 50 part-time. La Verne students are encouraged to think seriously about the world and its people and are assisted in forming values that promote a commitment to what is best for all people. The University also offers study through a graduate and professional studies program, the School of Continuing Education, and the College of Law. It is accredited by the Western Association of Schools and Colleges and the 4-1-4 system is used. Programs of study lead to the Bachelor, Master, Juris Doctor, Doctor of Educational Management, and Doctor of Public Administration.

Entrance Requirements: High school graduation; SAT or ACT; high school and/or college transcripts required; interview recommended; early decision, rolling admission and advanced placement plans available; $20 application fee.

Costs Per Year: $60 per credit; $1,000-1215 room and board.

Collegiate Environment: One of the special qualities of La Verne is the vitality one finds on its 26-acre campus-a-place of contrasts. Buildings that have stood for years are found next to buildings of contemporary architectural design. The campus has two focal points. One is Founders Hall, built in 1926, which houses classrooms and administrative offices, including the office of the president. The other is the Student Center and Dailey Theater, called "supertents" by the students. This facility is a huge building in which student life shapes itself; among the structured activities that take place are athletic events, plays, concerts, and movies. Students are also involved in theater; the campus newspaper, magazine, yearbook, and literary magazines; the campus radio station; and television productions. La Verne teams participate in ten intercollegiate men's sports and seven intercollegiate women's sports. Men's sports are baseball, basketball, golf, soccer, cross-country, football, volleyball, tennis, track and field. Women's sports are basketball, softball, cross-country, tennis, track and field, volleyball, and soccer. There are more than 150,000 volumes housed in the library. Approximately one-half of the full-time students reside in dormitories on campus (dormitory capacity is 105 men and 138 women). 80% of the students applying for admission are accepted. Financial assistance is available. There are a total of 870 scholarships.

Community Environment: La Verne is a suburban area approximately 35 miles east of Los Angeles, Pasadena, Beverly Hills and Hollywood. The Santa Fe, Union Pacific and the Southern Pacific railroads serve the area as well as the Metropolitan Bus Lines out of Los Angeles. La Verne is overshadowed on the north by the snow-capped San Gabriel Mountains, which rise to a height of 10,000 feet. La Verne is within easy driving distance of the beaches and mountains which provide both summer and winter recreational activities.

UNIVERSITY OF LAVERNE COLLEGE OF LAW, SAN FERNANDO VALLEY CAMPUS   *(F-9)*
21300 Oxnard Street
Woodland Hills, California 91367
Tel: (818) 883-0529; Fax: (818) 883-8142

Description: Formerly known as the University of San Fernando Valley the privately supported professional law school was chartered in 1962; the school moved to its present location in 1995. The college operates on the semester system and offers both a 3-year full-time program and a 4-year part-time program that includes summer sessions. Enrollment is 300 with a faculty of 20 giving a student-faculty ration of 14-1.

Entrance Requirements: Preferably Bachelor or equivalent degree. A minimum of 60 semester hours of college work. LSAT $30 application fee.

Costs Per Year: $390 per semester unit.

Collegiate Environment: Classes are held in a modern, two-story structure of 32,000 square feet, including a courtroom, seminar rooms, student lounges. The library contains over 70,000 volumes.

Community Environment: Woodland Hills is a suburb of Los Angeles, located in the San Fernando Valley and has a mild climate. The annual mean temperature is 63 degrees with an annual rainfall average of 18.6. All modes of transportation serve the area; the Los Angeles International Airport is within easy driving distance; the Southern Pacific Railroad and Santa Fe Railroad both provide excellent service. The school is within easy driving distance of the many Cultural and social activities of the Los Angeles metropolitan area and provides easy access to the mountains and beaches of Southern California.

UNIVERSITY OF REDLANDS   *(O-10)*
1200 East Colton Avenue
P.O. Box 3080
Redlands, California 92373-0999
Tel: (909) 793-2121; Admissions: (909) 335-4074; Fax: (909) 335-4089

Description: The University of Redlands is an independent, coeducational liberal arts university. It is fully accredited by the Western Association of Schools and Colleges. It operates on the 4-1-4 calendar system. The university's main divisions are: the College of Arts and Sciences, the Johnston Center for Individualized Learning, the School of Music, and the Alfred North Whitehead Center for Lifelong Learning. More than 30 Bachelor's and 4 Master's degrees are offered. The Arts and Sciences Program offers more than 30 majors in traditional liberal arts, as well as programs of study in professional and preprofessional fields. The Johnston center allows students to combine classes from existing majors and to negotiate course contracts with professors for an individualized course of study. Johnston students live in residence halls where classrooms and professors' offices are located, in order to foster a continuous sense of academic exploration. The Whitehead Center allows working adults to receive degrees in business by attending classes during evenings and weekends. Whitehead students attend classes at regional centers throughout southern California. University enrollment is includes 1,508 full-time and 3,000 evening students. A faculty of 156, 82% of whom hold doctorates or terminal degrees, gives a faculty-student ratio of 1-13. Most students live on campus. Students may choose from more than 50 study-abroad options in Europe, Asia, Australia, Africa, and South America. Air Force and Army ROTC programs are available at nearby state schools.

Entrance Requirements: High school graduation with B+ average; SAT or ACT required; two recommendations and personal essay required; rolling admission processing begins December 1; students may defer admission for up to one year; $40 application fee.

Costs Per Year: $16,530 tuition; $6,205 room and board; $825 student fees and books.

Collegiate Environment: The 130-acre campus is located one mile from downtown Redlands and is surrounded by residences, orange groves and palm trees that are set against the San Bernardino Mountains. There are 44 buildings, including the Armacost Library and the new Hunsaker University Center that provide the academic and social focus of the campus. There are twelve residence halls that house 55 to 180 students each, 2 sets of university-operated apartments, 4 honor houses, and 10 fraternity and sorority houses that are mostly nonresidential. In total, the residence halls and apartments accomodate 1,390 students. 15%-20% of students are members of local fraternities and sororities. Students are also highly active in student government and community service, and there are more than 60 clubs and organizations. The university offers intramural athletics and 19 intercollegiate sports in NCAA Division III. 80% of the freshmen return for the second year. 80% of the applicants are accepted. Scholarships are available and 75% of the students receive some form of financial aid. 65% of the students graduate within four years.

Community Environment: Redlands is located halfway between Los Angeles and Palm Springs. It has a mild climate. The average yearly temperature is 65 degrees, and the average rainfall 14.45 inches. Once a principal center for navel oranges, the city has developed a more diversified economy in recent years. There are 60 churches, a community hospital and satellite clinics, a city library, fraternal and social service organizations, and museums. Buses serve the area, and the Ontario International Airport is 30 minutes from the campus. Through the Office of Community Service Learning and other organizations, students at the university have many opportunities to interact with community members.

UNIVERSITY OF SAN DIEGO   *(R-10)*
5998 Alcala Park
San Diego, California 92110-2492
Tel: (619) 260-4506; (800) 248-4873; Fax: (619) 260-6836

Description: The Catholic University which bears the city's name was chartered in 1949. Today the University of San Diego includes the College of Arts and Sciences, School of Business Administration, School of Education, School of Law, and Hahn School of Nursing. The University is fully accredited by the Western Association of Schools and Colleges. The university grants the Bachelor, Master, Doctoral and Professional degrees. It operates on the 4-1-4 calendar system and offers three summer sessions. The enrollment includes 6,000 students. A faculty of 275 full-time and 246 part-time gives a faculty-student ratio of 1-18.

Entrance Requirements: Average college prepatory GPA of 3.0-3.6; Recommend 4 or more academic courses per semester including 4 years of English, 3-4 years of mathematics, 3-4 years of science, 3-4 years of foreign language, and 3-4 years of social science; SAT or ACT required, GRE required for graduate school; early action; $45 application fee.

Costs Per Year: $14,220 tuition per year; $6,800 room and board per year; $100 student fees per year; additional expenses average $1,000 per academic year.

Collegiate Environment: The University of San Diego seeks to acquaint every student with the intellectual, cultural and ethical values of our civilization while providing the opportunity to develop career centered competency. Residence Hall housing is guaranteed for all students and required for all freshmen not living with relatives in San Diego. Combined libraries contain 488,000 volumes and numerous periodicals, pamphlets, microforms and audio-visual materials. 70% of applicants are accepted. The middle 50% range of scores of the entering freshman class was 410-520 verbal, 470-600 math. 945 scholarshops are available and 60% of the students receive some form of financial aid.

Community Environment: Known for many reasons as "America's Finest City," San Diego has an almost perfect climate with warm, sunny days and cool evenings. Throughout the year, students can take advantage of San Diego's many outdoor recreational and cultural opportunities. The museums of Balboa Park, the Old Globe Theatre, the Zoo, Sea World, the beaches, the opera, and downtown San Diego and La Jolla are only minutes away. The rapidly developing economy of Greater San Diego provides varied employment opportunities for the USD graduate.

UNIVERSITY OF SAN FRANCISCO   *(I-3)*
2130 Fulton St., Ignation Heights
San Francisco, California 94117-1080
Tel: (415) 666-6563; (800) 225-5873; Fax: (415) 666-2217

Description: USF is private, coeducational, Jesuit, and Roman Catholic. The University was founded in 1855 by members of the Society of Jesus. It is San Francisco's first university. USF is accredited by the Western Association of Schools and Colleges, the American Assembly of Collegiate Schools of Business, the National League for Nursing, the American Bar Association, and the California State Commission on Teacher Credentialing. Enrollment is 7,328 students. A faculty of 424 gives a faculty-student ratio of approximately 1-17. USF is comprised of the College of Liberal Arts and Sciences, the McLaren College of Business, the School of Nursing, the School of Education, The School of Law, and the College of Professional Studies. The University offers certificate, credential, baccalaureate, masters degree, and doctoral programs.

Entrance Requirements: High school graduation with a B average; completion of 16 academic units; SAT or ACT required; advanced placement and CLEP accepted; transfer students accepted; early decision and honors acceptance plans available; $35 application fee.

Costs Per Year: $14,008 full-time undergraduate tuition; $6,670 room and board; $100 student association fees; $2,000 average personal, travel, and book expenses.

Collegiate Environment: The campus has 15 buildings on 52 acres, located one block from Golden Gate Park in a residental area of San Francisco. The Gleeson Library contains 494,000 volumes, 2,318 periodicals, 415,000 microforms, and 3,000 recordings; there are listening channels, microform readers and a variety of research data bases available as well. Harney Science Center houses the Computer Center, the Institute for Chemical Biology, the Physics Research Laboratories, and the Fire Safety Research Laboratories. Modern residence halls provide comfortable facilities for 488 men and 627 women; all freshmen and sophomore undergraduate students under age 21, who do not live at home, reside on campus. 70% of all applicants are accepted. Financial aid is available, and approximately 70% of the current student body receives financial assistance. Approximately 60% of the senior class continues onto graduate school. Approximately 65% of the student body graduates in the top 20% of the high school class and 76% ranks in the top 40%. USF offers 8 certificate programs, 49 baccalaureate degree majors, 31 masters degree programs, 7 doctoral degree programs, and 7 educational credential programs.

Community Environment: The University of San Francisco is located on 52 wooded acres in the heart of one the world's most dynamic and diverse cities. USF is just minutes from downtown and the Pacific Ocean. The University enjoys all the advantages of an urban campus, while still maintaining the serenity of a more suburban campus, as it sits on its own hill overlooking the City and the San Francisco Bay. San Francisco's diversity and geographical compactness afford students opportunities for community involvement and employment experiences that few other cities can match.

UNIVERSITY OF SOUTHERN CALIFORNIA   *(O-8)*
University Park
Los Angeles, California 90089-0911
Tel: (213) 740-1111; Fax: (213) 740-6364

Description: The privately supported, coeducational university is one of the major universities of the country. The university is fully accredited by the Western Association of Schools and Colleges and by the major professional accrediting bodies of the United States covering the following divisions of the University: the School of Architecture; School of Business Administration; School of Dentistry; School of Education; School of Engineering; School of Medicine; The Law Center; School of Journalism; Division of Health Related Professions; School of Music; School of Pharmacy; and the School of Social Work. Programs of study lead to the Bachelor, Master, Professional and Doctorate degrees. Army, Navy, and Air Force ROTC programs are available. It operates on the semester system and offers three summer sessions. Undergraduate enrollment includes 13,682 full-time and 1,236 part-time students. A faculty of 1,236 part-time students. A faculty of 1,634 full-time and 987 part-time gives and undergraduate faculty-student ratio of 1-14. There are 12,946 graduate students.

Entrance Requirements: High school graduation or equivalent; minimum of 20 yearlong courses in the following subjects: English, mathematics, social studies, laboratory science, foreign language and additional year-long courses - electives. Students intending to major in architecture, business, engineering, mathematics, and the sciences should concentrate additional attention on mathematics and science courses. SAT or ACT required; early admission, early decision, mid-year admission, and advanced placement plans available. $50 application fee for paper applications; $35 for computer disk applications.

Costs Per Year: $17,230 tuition, $6,482 room and board; $330 student fees.

Collegiate Environment: The university includes the general library and 17 specialized subject departmental libraries housing 3,200,000 bound volumes, numerous periodicals, pamphlets, microforms and audio-visual materials. Computer laboratories at the university have modern high speed computers and there are now micro-computer labs in many areas around campus. The university has units in Air Force, Army, and Naval ROTC. Along with typical engineering curriculum, the School of Engineering offers a formal 5-year baccalaureate Cooperative Education Program providing alternate semesters of work in industry and studies at USC Dormitories and apartments accommodate 6,000 men and women; fraternities and sororities house approximately 2,000 more students. Approximately 72% of undergraduate students applying for admission are accepted; 40% of applicants to graduate school are accepted. Students may be admitted at midyear in some programs. Financial aid is available, and 61% of the under graduates are receiving some form of financial assistance. University of Southern California has study abroad programs in 17 countries throughout Great Britain, Europe, Africa, Asia and the Middle East.

Community Environment: See University of California - Los Angeles

UNIVERSITY OF THE PACIFIC   *(H-4)*
3601 Pacific Avenue
Stockton, California 95211
Tel: (209) 946-2211; (800) 959-2867; Fax: (209) 946-2689

Description: The privately supported coeducational university is accredited by the Western Association of Schools and Colleges. The university grants the Bachelor, Master, Professional and Doctorate degrees. The university is California's first chartered institution of higher education and is comprised of the following liberal arts colleges and professional schools: College of the Pacific, offering over 60 different majors; Conservatory of Music; School of Education; School of Engineering; School of International Studies; School of Pharmacy; School of Dentistry (located in San Francisco); McGeorge School of Law (located in Sacramento); School of Business and Public Administration; University College (re-entry program) and the Graduate School. Emphasis is placed on the personal approach to higher education, featuring close working relationships between students and faculty members. The university operates on the early semester system and offers three summer sessions. Enrollment includes 3,255 full-time and 264 part-time undergraduates and 621 graduate students. A faculty of 247 full-time and 75 part-time gives a faculty-student ratio of 1-15.

Entrance Requirements: High school graduation or equivalent with strong college-preparatory program and B average or better; SAT or ACT accepted; counselor's recommendation required; GRE required for graduate school; early admission, early action, rolling admission, midyear admission and advanced placement plans available; $50 application fee.

Costs Per Year: $17,550 tuition and fees; $5,326 room and board (required for freshmen and sophomores).

Collegiate Environment: The main campus of 175 acres is located in the northwest section of Stockton. Athletic facilities, student residence halls, a student center and library are all located on campus. The library contains 990,000 volumes, and numerous pamphlets, periodicals, microforms and recordings. Residence halls, university-operated apartment complexes, fraternities and sororities house 1,700 students. Approximately 80% of the students applying for admission are accepted, including midyear students. Financial assistance is available, and 65% of the current student body receives financial aid. Students come from throughout the United States and 40 foreign countries.

Community Environment: Stockton, population 230,000, is located 80 miles east of San Francisco and 40 miles south of Sacramento. The city is located in a rich agricultural region. All major forms of transportation serve the area. Stockton has 110 churches, general hospitals, a library, museum, and fine shopping facilities. Recreational facilities include theaters, parks, playgrounds, stadiums, a large events center, and a baseball stadium. The city is only a short drive away from facilities for water skiing, sailing, and golf, and the Sierra Nevada mountain range is also nearby.

UNIVERSITY OF WEST LOS ANGELES   *(G-9)*
1155 West Arbor Vitae Sreet
Inglewood, California 90301-2902
Tel: (310) 215-3339

Description: This privately supported, coeducational law school was founded in 1966. Enrollment includes 600 law and 250 paralegal students. A faculty of 50 gives a faculty-student ratio of 1-14. In 1971 the university established the School of Paralegal Studies. The law school operates on the semester system. The school of Paralegal Stud-

ies operates on the trimester system. The university grants the Bachelor and Juris Doctor degrees and certificates.

Entrance Requirements: For Paralegal Studies: Associate degree or equivalent for Bachelor of Science, Bachelor of Art or Science with 2.5 GPA for certificate program; rolling admission; $20 application fee; for law studies: Bachelor's degree or 60 units.

Costs Per Year: $3,600 tuition and fees (Paralegal); $7,500 (Law).

Collegiate Environment: The new School of Law building is located near both San Diego and Santa Monica freeways. The library contains 40,000 volumes. 90% of all applicants are accepted. Midyear students are admitted for Paralegal Studies. 75% of the students receive financial aid.

Community Environment: See West Los Angeles College.

VENTURA COLLEGE   *(O-7)*
4667 Telegraph Road
Ventura, California 93003
Tel: (805) 654-6400

Description: The publicly supported, coeducational, community college serves all the communities of Ventura County. Curriculum enables students to elect programs either to parallel the first two years of the four-year institution of their choice or to prepare themselves for skilled employment at the termination of a two-year course. The College makes a special effort to provide classes small enough to promote close relationships between students and teachers and to assure the student of special individual attention as may be required. The enrollment includes 11,000 students with a faculty of 190 full-time and 280 part-time. The semester system is used and one summer session is offered. Programs of study lead to the Certificate and Associate degree. The college is accredited by the Western Association of Schools and Colleges.

Entrance Requirements: Open enrollment policy; early admission, early decision, advanced placement, delayed admission and rolling admission plans available.

Costs Per Year: $403 (13/unit) resident; $1,550 ($50/unit) resident with B.A degree; $3,410 ($110/unit) nonresident; $10/unit health fees.

Collegiate Environment: The college is located on 103 acres of hillside land with some of the finest community college facilities in Southern California. Its striking buildings and equipment provide facilities for an excellent community college instructional program. The library has a collection of 72,270 volumes, 366 periodicals, 6,222 microforms and 2,815 audiovisual materials. A modern Student Center incorporates a college bookstore, a student lounge and offices for the student activities office and for the student government. All students applying for admission are accepted, and students may enroll at midyear as well as in the fall. Some financial aid is available; 15% of the current student body receives assistance.

Community Environment: Population 86,000. Ventura is the county seat of Ventura County as well as one of the oldest settlements on the coast. The climate is pleasant all year, rain during a few months in the winter and spring; atmosphere is smog free. City is located in the South Central Coast Region, 63 miles northwest of Los Angeles and is served by the Southern Pacific Railroad, Greyhound Bus and Pacific Airlines. Community facilities include hospitals, libraries, churches, and many civic and service clubs. Other facilities include recreation centers, a golf course, and the county fair grounds. An extensive ocean coastline, forest reserves, mountains and wildlife all combine to make the area ideal for recreation.

VICTOR VALLEY COLLEGE   *(N-10)*
18422 Bear Valley Road
Victorville, California 92392
Tel: (619) 245-4271; Fax: (619) 245-9745

Description: This publicly supported, coeducational community college is accredited by the Western Association of Schools and Colleges. The district was created in 1960 and includes the communities of Adelanto, Apple Valley, Cedar Springs, Helendale, Hesperia, Lucerne Valley, Oro Grande, Phelan, Wrightwood, Los Flores and Victorville. Enrollment is 6,600 full-time and 1,300 part-time students. A faculty of 88 full-time and 285 part-time gives a faculty-student ratio of 1-21. The college operates on the early semester system and offers one summer session. Programs of study lead to the Certificate and Associate degree.

Entrance Requirements: High school graduate or over 18 years of age; open enrollment policy.

Costs Per Year: $10 per unit; $50 per unit resident with BA degree or higher; $97 per unit nonresident; $30 student fees; $250 average additional expenses.

Collegiate Environment: The campus has 12 buildings on 230 acres. No dormitories are available. The library contains 50,372 volumes, 3,350 pamphlets, 603 periodicals and 2,640 recordings. All students applying for admission are accepted, and 50% return for the second year.

Community Environment: Victorville is a suburban area with a dry temperate climate. Amtrak, Santa Fe and Union Pacific Railroads, and Greyhound bus lines serve the area. The town has a library, churches of major denominations, hospitals, major civic organizations, and shopping facilities. Part-time employment opportunities are good. Victorville is the distributing point for an irrigated agricultural area. The San Bernardino County Fair is held here each year around Labor Day.

WEST COAST UNIVERSITY   (O-8)
440 Shatto Place
Los Angeles, California 90020-1765
Tel: (213) 427-4400; (800) 248-4928; Fax: (213) 380-4362

Description: The privately supported, coeducational, evening university, established in 1909, has an enrollment of 1,000 men and 600 women. The college is accredited by the Western Association of Schools and Colleges. WCU offers programs in engineering, technology, computer science, business, and management leading to the Associate, Bachelor and Master degrees. The university has branch divisions in San Diego, Camarillo, Orange, and Vandenberg Air Force Base, California. Six 8-week semesters are used. A faculty of 150 gives a faculty-student ratio of 1-10.

Entrance Requirements: High school graduation or equivalent; open enrollment policy; entrance exam may be required; rolling admission; $35 application fee.

Costs Per Year: $340 per unit.

Collegiate Environment: The university operates five centers. The library contains more than 15,000 volumes, with a full range of microforms and audiovisual materials. Approximately 80% of the students applying for admission are accepted, and students may enroll throughout the year. Limited financial aid is available.

Community Environment: See University of California - Los Angeles.

Branch Campuses: Orange County Center, 500 S. Main St., Orange, CA 92668-4593, (714) 953-2700, (800) 282-2WCU, fax: (714) 543-2757; San Diego County Center, 9682 Via Excelencia, San Diego, CA 92126-4556; (619) 695-2844, (800) 252-5WCU, fax: (619) 695-0641; Santa Barbara County Center, Vandenberg Air Force Base, CA 93439, (805) 734-8232, (800) 242-6WCU, fax: (805) 734-0233; Ventura County Center, 400 Mobil Ave., Camarillo, CA 93010-6313, (805) 987-5199, fax: (805) 987-3701.

WEST HILLS COMMUNITY COLLEGE   (L-5)
300 Cherry Lane
Coalinga, California 93210
Tel: (209) 935-0801; (800) 266-1114; Admissions: (209) 935-0801 x218; Fax: (209) 935-5655

Description: The publicly supported, coeducational, community college is accredited by the Western Association of Schools and Colleges. The college was established in 1932 as an Extension Center of Fresno State College; it became an independent unit in 1941 and constructed a new campus in 1955. It was known as Coalinga College until 1969. Occupational preparation, community service, and university-parallel programs lead to the Certificate and Associate degree. The school operates on the semester system and offers one summer session. Enrollment includes 454 full-time and 2,226 part-time students. A faculty of 47 full-time and 74 part-time gives a faculty-student ratio of 1-22.

Entrance Requirements: Open enrollment policy; non-high school graduates accepted; rolling admission plan available.

Costs Per Year: $403 ($13/credit) state resident tuition; $1,550 ($50/credit) resident with BA degree; $3,720 ($120/credit) nonresident; $3,973 ($128/credit) foreign student; $2,732 room and board; $30 student fees.

Collegiate Environment: The campus has 18 buildings, including residences that accommodate 99 men and 22 women. The agriculture program is conducted on a 153-acre farm equipped with classrooms, a laboratory, shops and a Grade-A dairy barn. All students applying for admission are accepted, and students are admitted at midyear as well as in the fall. The library contains 35,000 volumes. Financial aid is available, and 75% of the current students receive some form of assistance.

Community Environment: Coalinga is surrounded by oil derricks and acres of irrigated farm land on the western side of San Joaquin Valley midway between San Francisco and Los Angeles. The summers are warm; the remainder of the year the climate is moderate. The average mean temperature is 62.2 degrees. A library, hospital, churches, museum and theatres are in the area. Recreational facilities include a golf course, swimming pool, good hunting, football, baseball and softball. Part-time employment is available for students. Housing is available in private homes and dormitories. Coalinga has an annual Veterans Day Celebration, and the Horned Toad Derby.

WEST LOS ANGELES COLLEGE   (G-9)
4800 Freshman Drive
Culver City, California 90230
Tel: (310) 287-4200

Description: The publicly supported community college opened its doors to students for the first time in February of 1969. Recent enrollment was 9,500. A faculty of 436 gives a faculty-student ratio of 1-24. The college operates on a semester system, and one summer session is offered. One- and two-year career programs and a complete range of transfer-preparation programs are available. A satellite campus located in Marina del Rey provides outreach classes at 23 community locations. The Los Angeles Airport College Center became part of this school in 1978. The college is accredited by the Western Association of Schools and Colleges and grants the Certificate and Associate degree.

Entrance Requirements: Open enrollment policy; high school graduation; non-graduates 18 years of age or older admitted; early admission, rolling admission and advanced placement plans available.

Costs Per Year: $5 per unit; $112 per unit nonresidents.

Collegiate Environment: Ninety-eight percent of those who apply for admission are accepted, and students may enroll at midyear as well as in the fall. The college library contains 50,000 titles and numerous periodicals and microforms. Financial aid is available, and 20% of the students are receiving some form of assistance.

Community Environment: Culver City is an industrial and residential city located near Los Angeles. The world's largest motion picture studio, Metro-Goldwyn-Mayer, was located here, as well as the Desilu Studios. All forms of transportation serve the area; Los Angeles International Airport is near. Churches of all major denominations are in the area; there are excellent shopping facilities available.

WEST VALLEY COLLEGE   (I-3)
14000 Fruitvale Avenue
Saratoga, California 95070
Tel: (408) 867-2200 ·

Description: This publicly supported college is accredited by the Western Association of Schools and Colleges. The college opened its doors for classes in temporary quarters on September 14, 1964. Enrollment includes 13,000 full-time and part-time students. A faculty of 473 gives a faculty-student ratio of 1-28. Programs of study lead to the Certificate and Associate degree. The college operates on the semester system and offers one summer session.

Entrance Requirements: High school graduation; non-graduates 18 years of age or over admitted.

Costs Per Year: $13 per unit; $50 per unit resident with BA degree or higher; $120 per unit nonresident.

Collegiate Environment: The library contains 82,959 volumes, 491 periodicals and 18,275 microforms. The college offers 37 Associate degree programs. 2% of the students receive financial aid.

Community Environment: See San Jose State University.

Branch Campuses: Mission College, 3000 Mission College Blvd., Santa Clara, CA 95054, (408) 988-2200.

WESTERN STATE UNIVERSITY COLLEGE OF LAW OF ORANGE COUNTY   *(H-12)*
1111 North State College Boulevard
Fullerton, California 92631
Tel: (714) 738-1000

Description: Privately-supported, coeducational law college, offers both full- and part-time law study programs. The B.S.L. degree (non-professional) program may be completed in 2 years; the J.D. program may be completed in from 2 1/2 to 4 years of full-time, part-time or combination, law study. Recent enrollment was approximately 1,150 students. A faculty of 52 gives a faculty-student ratio of 1-29. The semester system is used and summer session is offered. The college is fully accredited by the Western Association of Schools and Colleges.

Entrance Requirements: At least two years of college (most applicants have baccalaureate); LSAT required; applicants not meeting normal pre-legal education requirements may be admitted as Special Students; $25 application fee; rolling admission plan available.

Costs Per Year: $298 per unit, $200 miscellaneous fees, $350 books. year for 3 year program; $300 books.

Collegiate Environment: The college has a fully-equipped law library, with 63,179 volumes. Approximately 75% of the students applying for admission are accepted, and students may be admitted at midyear. There are 94 scholarships available, and 44% of the current student body receives financial aid. Dormitories are available in cooperative arrangement with adjacent Pacific Christian College. This school is part of a five-institution postsecondary educational community.

Community Environment: See California State University - Fullerton.

WESTERN STATE UNIVERSITY COLLEGE OF LAW OF SAN DIEGO   *(R-10)*
2121 San Diego Ave.
San Diego, California 92110
Tel: (619) 297-9700; Fax: (619) 294-4713

Description: The privately supported, coeducational, law college is accredited by the Western Association of Schools and Colleges. Courses are conducted both during the day and in the evenings. It operates on the semester system and offers one summer session. Enrollment includes 634 students. A faculty of 18 gives a faculty-student ratio of 1-35.

Entrance Requirements: Two years of college or the equivalent as determined by Law School; admission test (LSAT); $35 application fee; rolling admission plan available.

Costs Per Year: $12,144 ($414/unit).

Collegiate Environment: The college maintains a law library of approximately 41,000 volumes. 56% of applicants are accepted. Financial assistance is available.

Community Environment: See University of California - San Diego.

WESTMONT COLLEGE   *(O-6)*
955 La Paz Road
Santa Barbara, California 93108
Tel: (805) 565-6000; (800) 777-9011; Admissions: (805) 565-6200; Fax: (805) 565-6234

Description: This privately supported, coeducational evangelical Christian college of arts and sciences is accredited by the Western Association of Schools and Colleges and grants the Bachelor degree. The college was founded in Los Angeles in 1940; moved to Santa Barbara in 1945. It operates on the semester system and offers one summer session. Enrollment includes 1,271 full-time and 9 part-time students. A faculty of 77 full-time and 39 part-time gives a faculty-student ratio of 1-16.

Entrance Requirements: High school graduation with a 'B' average recommended; 16 units including 4 English, 3 mathematics (2 algebra and 1 geometry), 2 physical and 1 biological science, 2 foreign language, 2 social studies and 2 History recommended; SAT or ACT required; Feb. 15 application; $30 application fee.

Costs Per Year: $15,420 tuition; $5,580 room and board, $910 fees.

Collegiate Environment: Dormitories house 998 men and women and off campus housing is available. There are five modern residence hall facilities. The library contains 150,000 volumes, 710 periodicals, 20,687 microforms and 5,300 recordings. The 133 acre campus is nestled between the Santa Ynez Mountains and Pacific Ocean. 83% of the freshman class returned for the sophomore year. The average scores of the entering freshman class were SAT 500 verbal, 560 math. Scholarships are available and 80% percent of the current student body receives some form of financial aid. Religious courses are required for graduation and Chapel attendance is required. Army ROTC is available in conjunction with University of California at Santa Barbara.

Community Environment: See University of California - Santa Barbara

WHITTIER COLLEGE   *(G-11)*
13406 East Philadelphia
Whittier, California 90608
Tel: (310) 907-4238; Admissions: (310) 907-4238; Fax: (310) 907-4870

Description: The privately supported, coeducational liberal arts college was chartered by the state of California in 1901 and is controlled by an independent and self-perpetuating board of trustees. It is accredited by the Western Association of Schools and Colleges. Divisions of the College are: Humanities and Fine Arts, Social Sciences, Natural Sciences, and Teacher Education. Programs of study lead to the Bachelor and Master degrees, and the J.D. Study abroad programs in Copenhagen, South India and 18 other countries through a consortium agreement with the University of Miami. The college operates on the 4-1-4 system and offers two summer sessions. Enrollment includes 1,289 full-time and 26 part-time undergraduate and 800 graduate students. A faculty of 88 full-time and 34 part-time gives a faculty-student ratio of 1-14.

Entrance Requirements: High school graduation; completion of 3 English, 2 mathematics, 2 foreign language, 1 science, 1 social science; SAT or ACT required; early decision, early admission, rolling admission, midyear admission, and advanced placement plans available; $35 application fee.

Costs Per Year: $16,899 tuition; $5,813 room and board; $288 student fees.

Collegiate Environment: The campus occupies a hillside tract of 95 acres. The Whittier Campus library contains more than 325,000 volumes and 800 periodicals. The Law Library contains 72,000 volumes and 1,400 periodicals. Residence halls house 754 men and women. The amphitheatre has a seating capacity of 3,000 and the Shannon Center for the Performing Arts houses a 400 seat theatre and a smaller studio theatre. Approximately 71% of the students applying for admission are accepted. There are a total of 765 scholarships, 257 for freshmen.

Community Environment: Whittier enjoys a beautiful setting at the foot of the Puente Hills, in a suburban area in southeast Los Angeles County. The climate is pleasant with a minimum temperature of 53 degrees, a maximum temperature of 73 degrees, and an average rainfall of 15 inches. Buses and railroads serve the area with connection to the Los Angeles International Airport via helicopter, and to the metropolitan area via the freeway system. Modern shopping facilities are available in addition to many manufacturing plants. Recreational facilities include parks, theaters, nearby Disneyland, beaches, and mountains less than one hour away. The Whittier College School of Law is located on a 4-acre campus in the Hancock Park section of Los Angeles.

WOODBURY UNIVERSITY   *(O-8)*
7500 Glenoaks Boulevard
P.O. Box 7846
Burbank, California 91510-7846
Tel: (818) 767-0888; Fax: (818) 504-9320

Description: Founded in 1884, Woodbury University is a nonprofit, independent, coeducational, nonsectarian university accredited by the Western Association of Schools and Colleges located twenty minutes from downtown Los Angeles. Known as a professional school in the design and business fields, the university offers bachelor's degrees from the schools of Architecture and Design, Business and Management, and Arts and Sciences. The Master of Business Administration is also offered. The interior design program is professionally accredited by the Foundation for Interior Design Education Research (FIDER) and the architecture program is accredited by the National Architectural Accrediting Board. The university operates on the quarter system and offers one summer session. Evening and weekend programs are also available. Enrollment includes 734 full-time and 211 part-time and 33 evening undergraduates and 117 graduate students. A faculty of 30 full-time and 140 part-time gives a faculty-student ratio of 1-18.

Entrance Requirements: High school graduation or equivalent with a C average or better; SAT or ACT required; letters of recommendation, writing sample required; interview recommended; transfer students with 30 semester units or more must demonstrate satisfactory progress at the college level; additional requirements for international applicants; $30 application fee; $50 for international applicants.

Costs Per Year: $12,180 tuition Bachelor of Science progams; $12,660 tuition Bachelor of Architecture (five-year) program; $5,490 room and board.

Collegiate Environment: Woodbury is on a 22-acre campus in the foothills of Burbank. Woodbury students learn from professional educators and working professionals in both design and business fields. Additional staff provide counseling, job placement, student activities, and other services on a personal basis. The campus library houses 68,738 volumes in addition to periodical subscriptions, microforms and audiovisual materials. Residence halls are available. Approximately 20% of the students live on campus. Numerous clubs and organizations, including fraternities and sororities, are offered. The university does not participate in any intercollegiate sport programs. 87% of applicants meet criteria and are accepted. Scholarships and financial aid are available. 57% of students receive some form of financial aid.

Community Environment: Southern California is famous for the variety of terrain it offers and the array of activities available to its residents. Valleys, mountains, beaches, and deserts enable Woodbury students to escape to practically any climate they wish. Woodbury is surrounded by a residential neighborhood in a city known as the heart of the entertainment industry. Students are just minutes away from the many benefits of southern California: historical and cultural events and museums, world-class entertainment, professional sporting events, and vast beaches, deserts, mountains, and valleys for recreational leisure.

WRIGHT INSTITUTE   *(H-3)*
2728 Durant Avenue
Berkeley, California 94704
Tel: (510) 841-9230

Description: Privately-supported coeducational graduate school, it is accredited by the Western Association of Schools and Colleges and the American Psycological Association. The institute grants the Doctorate degree only in clinical psychology. It operates on the semester system and offers one summer session. A recent enrollment of 208 students and a faculty of 35 give a faculty-student ratio of 1-6.

Entrance Requirements: Bachelor degree or equivalent; GRE; $25 application fee.

Costs Per Year: $12,500 tuition.

Collegiate Environment: The library contains 8,500 volumes and 60 periodicals and journals. A limited amount of financial aid is available. 30% of all applicants are accepted. 80% receive financial aid.

Community Environment: See University of California - Berkeley.

YUBA COLLEGE   *(F-4)*
2088 N. Beale Rd.
Marysville, California 95901
Tel: (916) 741-6700; Admissions: (916) 741-6720; Fax: (916) 741-3541

Description: This publicly supported, coeducational junior college is accredited by the Western Association of Schools and Colleges. The college operates on a semester system with one summer session. Evening classes and one summer session are offered. The college grants A.A. and A.S. degrees, and Certificates of Completion. Enrollment includes 2,650 full-time and 7,500 part-time undergraduates. A faculty of 138 full-time and 128 part-time gives a faculty-student ratio of 1-45.

Entrance Requirements: High school graduation; non-high school graduates 18 years of age or over may be accepted; ACT, SAT or APS encouraged for placement.

Costs Per Year: $390 ($13/cr) resident tuition; $1,550 ($50/cr) resident with B.A.; $3,750 ($125/cr) nonresident; $3,400 room & board.

Collegiate Environment: Students at the college include graduates or non-high school graduates at least 18 years of age who want two rather than four years of higher education in the Arts and Sciences or technical, vocational, and semi-professional training; many students are also bound for a four-year college or university, most of whom live at home; adults who have not graduated from high school or who through part-time study hope eventually to earn a college diploma; and senior citizens seeking through education to develop new interests. The library contains 61,000 volumes. Residence halls accomodate 198 students.

Community Environment: Marysville is 50 miles north of Sacramento, has a moderate climate, and is the center of a rich agricultural area. Amtrak serves the area. The city has a hospital, churches, shopping center, and civic organizations. Excellent boating, hunting and fishing facilities are available.

Branch Campuses: Woodland Campus; Lake County Campus; Colusa Center; Beale AFB Center.

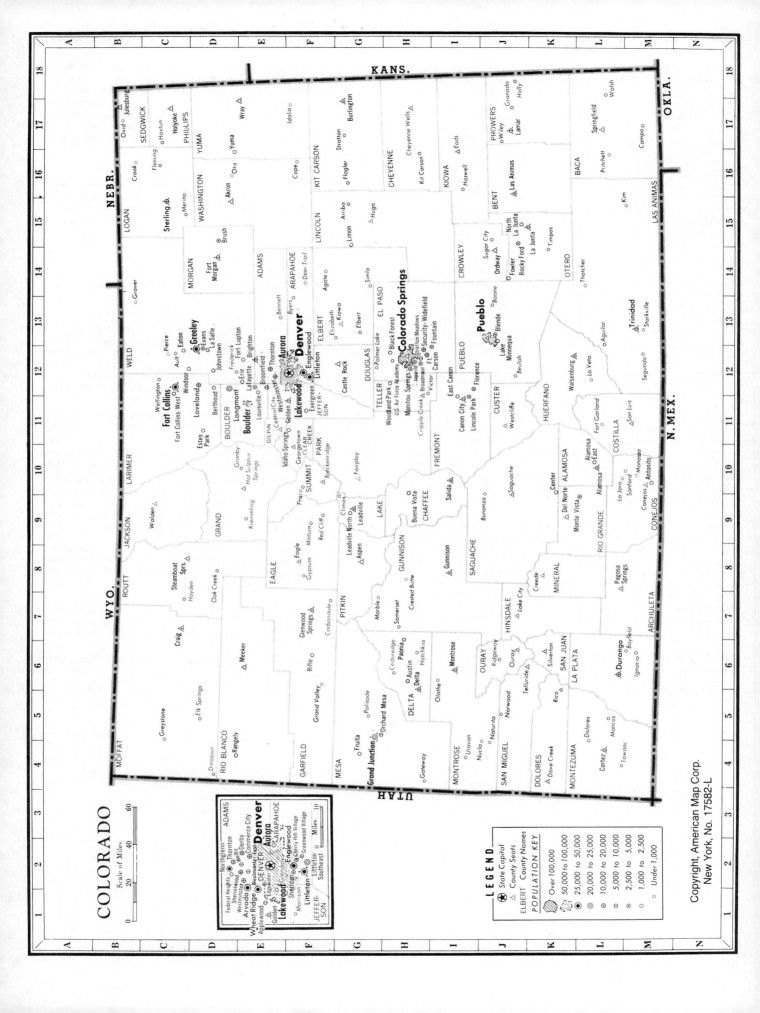

COLORADO

ADAMS STATE COLLEGE   (L-10)
Alamosa, Colorado 81102
Tel: (719) 589-7712; (800) 824-6494; Admissions: (719) 589-7712;
Fax: (719) 589-7522

Description: This state-controlled college is accredited by the North Central Association of Colleges and Schools. The college opened in 1921 offering a four-year program leading to a Bachelor degree and a life certificate to teach in Colorado public schools. Although teacher education ranks foremost and was the original purpose of the college, the program has been broadened to include the liberal arts, preprofessional and vocational programs and now grants Associate, Bachelor, and Masters degrees. The college operates on the semester system and offers one summer session. Enrollment includes 1,913 full-time and 192 part-time undergraduates and 357 graduate students. A faculty of 132 full-time and 20 part-time gives a faculty-student ratio of 1-20.

Entrance Requirements: High school graduates must rank in upper two-thirds of graduating class; high school graduates ranking in lower one-third of their high school class are considered on an individual basis for admission to the Associate of Arts programs; non-high school graduates considered with a satisfactory GED; 15 high school units required, including 3 English; 2 mathematics, 2 science, 2 social studies, and 4 general; completion of ACT examination with minimum of 21 is required; early decision, early admission, midyear admission, rolling admission and advanced placement plans available; $15 application fee.

Costs Per Year: $1,386 resident tuition; $4,816 nonresident tuition; $3,751 room and board; $339 student fees; $1,824 approximate additional expenses.

Collegiate Environment: There is an observatory-planetarium on campus, and there are residence halls for 824 students. The library contains 204,509 volumes, 586,000 microforms, and 54,543 bound periodicals. There are 941 scholarships offered including 320 for freshmen and 120 athletic. Over 80% of all students receive some type of financial aid. 92% of the applicants are accepted.

Community Environment: Located in the center of San Luis Valley, an extensive grazing and farming area larger than the state of Connecticut, Alamosa is completely surrounded by mountain ranges. It has an ideal climate, with an average yearly temperature of 65 degrees. A commuter airline and a bus line serve the area. Alamosa has churches, radio stations, libraries, hotels and motels, a hospital and a number of civic, social, cultural, fraternal and veterans organizations.

AIMS COMMUNITY COLLEGE   (D-12)
5401 West 20th Street
Greeley, Colorado 80631
Tel: (303) 330-8008; Admissions: (303) 330-8008; Fax: (303) 339-6664

Description: This public two-year college is accredited by the North Central Association of Colleges and Schools. It is located in the county seat of Weld County and began operations in 1967. The philosophy of Aims College has been developed around the belief that each individual should be allowed an opportunity to succeed. Pre-baccalaureate programs designed for students interested in transferring to a four-year institution as well as vocational, technical programs designed for employment at certain industrial and commercial enterprises are part of the curriculum. The primary purpose is to serve the people of North Central Colorado with quality educational programs. Enrollment includes 963 men and 1,143 women full-time, and 1,757 men and 3,104 women part-time. A faculty of 121 full-time and 320 part-time gives a faculty-student ratio of 1-16. The college operates on the quarter system and offers two summer sessions.

Entrance Requirements: Open enrollment policy; non-high school graduates or persons who have successfully completed the GED may apply for admission to a degree program.

Costs Per Year: $1,012.50 tuition; $1,800 out-of-district; $5,490 out-of-state.

Collegiate Environment: A campus of approximately 185 acres was purchased in 1969. In addition to the main campus there are two satellite campuses; Ft. Lupton and Loveland. There are no dormitories available. The library contains approximately 40,000 volumes. All students applying for admission are accepted, including students at midyear. Financial aid is available to economically handicapped students.

Community Environment: See University of Northern Colorado.

ARAPAHOE COMMUNITY COLLEGE   (F-12)
2500 West College Drive
Littleton, Colorado 80160-9002
Tel: (303) 797-5621; Fax: (303) 797-5970

Description: Arapahoe Community College opened in 1966 and is accredited by the North Central Association of Colleges and Schools. It operates on the semester system and offers one summer session with the option for two five-week sessions. The college offers pre-Baccalaureate transfer programs, and career programs in health, business, and technical occupations. It operates on the semester system and offers one summer session with option for two five-week sessions. Enrollment includes 1,857 full-time and 5,489 part-time students. A faculty of 96 full-time and 278 part-time gives a faculty-student ratio of 1-19.

Entrance Requirements: Open enrollment policy; high school graduate, or GED; non high school graduate 16-18 years or older and not enrolled in secondary school; midyear admission, rolling admission, and advanced placement plans available.

Costs Per Year: $1,292 state resident tuition; $5,489 nonresident tuition.

Collegiate Environment: The campus is situated on 50 acres. The main campus building was completed in 1974, the annex in 1977. The library contains 41,443 volumes, 2,200 periodicals, 5,600 microforms, and 6,022 audiovisual materials. Recreational facilities include a gymnasium, swimming pool, Fitness Center, and tennis courts. Financial aid is available and 18% of students receive some form of financial assistance.

Community Environment: Littleton is a surburban area 10 miles from Denver with seasonal variations in temperature. There are churches of all denominations, shopping centers, and medical clinics, with all forms of transportation available. Community facilities include parks with playground equipment, public swimming pools, indoor tennis courts, fairgrounds, golf courses and an ice rink. Skiing in the nearby mountains is excellent. Part-time employment is available.

BELLEVIEW COLLEGE   (F-12)
P.O. Box 1340
5455 W. 83rd Avenue
Westminster, Colorado 80030
Tel: (303) 427-5461; Fax: (303) 429-0910

Description: The private Bible and liberal arts college was founded in 1920 and is affiliated with Pillar of Fire Church. The semester system is employed, with one summer session. Belleview College grants a Bachelor of Arts or Science degree and also the Bachelor of Theology degree. The campus also includes the Bible Seminary and a preparatory school. Enrollment includes 15 part-time students. There are 8 part-time faculty members.

Entrance Requirements: High school graduation with a C average; completion of 16 units including 4 English, 2 mathematics, 2 science, 2 foreign language and 2 social science; non-high school students may be considered by special examinations.

Costs Per Year: $2,700 tuition; $2,800 room and board; $38 student fees.

Collegiate Environment: Campus has eight buildings on 600 acres. The library contains 15,000 volumes. Financial assistance is available and about half of a recent class received some form of aid. The college maintains a radio station dedicated to religious, patriotic, public service, and educational programs.

Community Environment: Belleview College is located on a scenic promotory in Westminster, Colorado, some eight miles from the center of Denver, to the northwest.

BLAIR JUNIOR COLLEGE   *(H-12)*
828 Wooten Road
Colorado Springs, Colorado 80915
Tel: (719) 574-1082; Fax: (719) 574-4493

Description: The private, two-year, coeducational institution was established in 1897. It is accredited by the North Central Association of Colleges and Schools and by the Association of Independent Colleges. The college aims to prepare students to enter the business world with day and evening programs, offering a diploma for 12-15 month programs and granting the Associate degree. It operates on the quarter system and offers one summer session. Enrollment includes 321 full-time and 17 part-time students with a faculty of 5 full-time and 25 part-time members.

Entrance Requirements: High school graduation or equivalent; entrance exam required; early admission, early decision, rolling admission, and advanced placement plans available; $25 fee required.

Costs Per Year: $11,400

Collegiate Environment: Located on the eastern edge of Colorado Springs, the college has a new and modern building. There are fully equipped facilities as well as a library holding 5,000 volumes in addition to other reference materials. Financial assistance is available as well as work-study programs.

Community Environment: See Colorado College

COLORADO CHRISTIAN UNIVERSITY   *(F-12)*
180 South Garrison
Lakewood, Colorado 80226
Tel: (303) 202-0100; Admissions: (303) 202-0100 x165; Fax: (303) 274-7560

Description: This private, Christian, interdenominational college of the Bible, arts and sciences and career education is the result of a 1989 merger between Colorado Christian College and Colorado Baptist University. The purpose of the school is to train students for effective Christian service in whatever career field they choose. Accreditation is with the North Central Association of Colleges and Schools and the American Association of Bible Colleges. The school operates on a two-semester system and there are six two-week summer sessions. Enrollment includes 678 full-time and 51 part-time undergraduates and 240 graduate students. There are also 914 evening students. A full-time faculty of 41 gives a faculty-student ratio of 1-23. Army ROTC is offered.

Entrance Requirements: High school graduation with a C average or GED; ACT or SAT required; $35 application fee; advanced placement plan available.

Costs Per Year: $6,720 tuition; $3,480 room and board; $500 student fees.

Collegiate Environment: The campus has 9 buildings on 25 acres. The library contains 40,000 volumes and 300 periodicals. 267 students are housed on campus in two-bedroom, fully furnished, carpeted apartments. 80% of applicants are accepted. The college is approved for most federal aid programs, and offers various scholarships for entering students. 75% of students receive some form of aid.

Community Environment: See University of Denver.

Branch Campuses: Undergraduate extension courses are available in Colorado Springs, CO, and Grand Junction, CO; for more information, call (303) 234-1478.

COLORADO COLLEGE   *(H-12)*
14 E. Cache La Poudre
Colorado Springs, Colorado 80903
Tel: (719) 389-6000

Description: This private, coeducational college, founded in 1874, is accredited by the North Central Association of Colleges and Schools. A distinctive feature of the College's program is the Block Plan, instituted in 1970, a curricular format which divides the academic year into eight three and one-half week segments, or "blocks," and permits a student to concentrate on one course at a time. The college has an enrollment of 906 men and 998 women, comprising 1,856 full-time and 19 part-time undergraduates and 29 graduate students. A full-time faculty of 155 and a part-time faculty of 48 gives a faculty-student ratio of 1-12, permitting small, personal classes. The college offers a Baccalaureate degree and a Master of Arts in Teaching as well as cooperative programs in engineering with Columbia University, Rensselaer Polytechnic Institute, the University of Southern California, and Washington University in St. Louis, Missouri, and a cooperative program with Rush University in which a student may transfer into Rush's medical technology or nursing programs after two years at Colorado College. Students may take advantage of programs with the University of Regensburg, Germany, Kansai Guidai, Japan, the University of Gottingen, Germany. Co-operative programs are offered in Fosestry with Duke University, a Washington semester at American University or semester programs in Perignan, France; Guanajato, Mexico and Luneberg, Germany. Colorado College has joined with twelve other independent liberal arts colleges in a consortium known as the Associated Colleges of the Midwest (ACM). The group includes Coe, Cornell, and Grinnell in Iowa; Carleton, Macalester, and St. Olaf in Minnesota; Knox, Lake Forest, and Monmouth in Illinois; and Beloit, Lawrence and Ripon in Wisconsin and the University of Chicago undergraduate school. Through the ACM, Colorado College students may participate in a variety of programs in the United States and abroad including studies in India, China, Costa Rica, Japan, Latin America, London, the University of Manchester, Florence, Czech Republic, and Russia.

Entrance Requirements: Completion of ACT or SAT; high school graduation and 18 recommended academic units; nonhigh school graduates considered; $40 application fee. Advanced placement is available. Colorado College participates in the Common Form process, which allows an applicant to complete one form for application to Colorado College or any of about 85 other leading colleges and universities.

Costs Per Year: $17,142 tuition; $4,310 room and board.

Collegiate Environment: The campus has over 40 buildings on 90 acres including a new student center and 73,000 square feet of new science facilities. Students. below the rank of senior are required to live in residence halls and to dine on campus unless they are 24 years of age, veterans, married, or living with immediate relatives. There are four residence halls in which French, German, Russian, or Spanish are spoken exclusively. The library contains over 535,000 volumes including government documents and access to computerized data bases, and subscribes to 1,530 periodicals. Various forms of financial assistance are available and the average award for a recent freshman was $13,000. About 55% of the students receive some form of aid.

Community Environment: Colorado Springs is located 70 miles south of Denver at the foot of Pikes Peak. It is known for its healthful climate and spectacular scenery. Colorado Springs averages more than 310 days of sunshine each year, has clean air, low humidity, cool summer nights, and mild winters. Buses, airlines, and good highways serve the area. There are numerous fine hotels and motels. The city has a fine arts center, museums, art galleries, opera, symphony, and theater. Areas for skiing, hunting, fishing, backpacking, and camping are nearby.

COLORADO MOUNTAIN COLLEGE - ALPINE CAMPUS
(C-8)
1330 Bob Adams Drive, Dept. RP
Steamboat Springs, Colorado 80487
Tel: (303) 870-4417; (800) 621-8559; Fax: (303) 945-7279

Description: The public, coeducational junior college was established in 1965 to serve the remote and sparsely populated central part of Western Colorado. The college is fully accredited by the North Central Association of Colleges and Schools and operates on the semester system. Enrollment includes 368 full-time and 475 part-time students. A faculty of 14 full-time and 100 part-time gives a faculty-student ratio of 1-14. The college maintains other campuses in Leadville and Glenwood Springs. The college offers an academic cooperative plan in the field of liberal arts with the University of North Colorado, Adams State College, University of Colorado, Boulder, Metropolitan State College, Western State College, Colorado State University, Fort Lewis College, and other Colorado colleges whereby students receive an Associate in Arts degree from Colorado Mountain College and the Bachelor's degree from the other school.

Entrance Requirements: High school graduation; open admission; non-high school graduates considered; ACT or SAT accepted; mid-year admission, deferred admission, and rolling admission plans available.

Costs Per Year: $930 tuition in-district; $1,800 state resident, $5,550 out-of-state tuition; $3,700 room and board; $130 student fees; $400 books.

Collegiate Environment: Situated just above the downtown area, the campus features magnificent views of the town and the Steamboat ski area. Campus facilities include a library and learning resource center with 22,000 titles and 180 periodicals, photography and computer laboratories, dormitories with space for 120 students, a cafeteria, and classroom area. A new academic building with 45,000 sq. ft. was completed for Fall 1992. 145 scholarships are available and 60% of the students receive financial aid. Continuing education courses are offered and life experience credits are given. The student government coordinates campus clubs and activities.

Community Environment: Steamboat Springs is 175 miles northwest of Denver. A permanent population of 6,000 swells to over 25,000 on Christmas Eve, largely due to the attraction of the town's famous champagne powder. The town flourishes with the contrasting influences of working cattle ranches and a world-class ski resort. The surrounding area offers unlimited opportunities for downhill and cross-country skiing, and hunting. Students learn additional outdoor skills through college-sponsored activities such as winter survival, desert camping, and orienteering.

COLORADO MOUNTAIN COLLEGE - SPRING VALLEY CAMPUS   *(F-7)*
Dept. RP, 3000 C.R. 114
Glenwood Springs, Colorado 81601
Tel: (303) 945-7481; (800) 621-8559; Fax: (303) 945-7279

Description: The public, coeducational junior college was established in 1965 to serve the remote and sparsely populated central part of Western Colorado (i.e. Eagle, Lake and Pitkin Counties) and a major portion of Garfield and Summit Counties, plus a small portion of Routt County. The college is fully accredited by the North Central Association of Colleges and Schools and grants the Associate degree. The college maintains other campuses in Leadville and Steamboat Springs. The college offers an academic cooperative plan in the field of liberal arts with the University of Northern Colorado, Adams State College, University of Colorado, Boulder, Colorado State University, Metropolitan State College, Fort Lewis College, and other Colorado colleges whereby students receive an Associate in Arts degree from Colorado Mountain College and the Bachelor's degree from the other school. The college operates on the semester system and offers limited summer classes. Enrollment includes 247 full-time and 329 part-time students. A faculty of 23 full-time and 30 part-time gives a faculty-student ratio of 1-11.

Entrance Requirements: High school graduation; non-high school graduates considered; ACT or SAT accepted; open admission; mid-year students accepted; early admission, early decision, rolling admission, delayed admission and advanced placement.

Costs Per Year: $930 district tuition; $1,800 state residents; $5,550 out-of-state tuition; $3,700 room and board; $130 student fees.

Collegiate Environment: The mountain campus is located in the heart of summer and winter recreational areas. There is excellent skiing near the campus. There is dormitory capacity for 140 students. The library contains 33,900 volumes, 165 periodical subscriptions, 131,000 microforms and 3,400 sound recordings. 240 scholarships are available, including 111 for freshmen. 60% of the students receive some form of financial aid.

Community Environment: Glenwood Springs is an urban area with a moderate climate; a beautiful place to live. Railroads and buses serve the area and charter air service is available. Glenwood Springs is the county seat of Garfield County, and has the best shopping facilities in the county. The city has churches of all major denominations, library, museum, theatres, hospital and many of the civic clubs. Hot mineral springs have made Glenwood Springs a popular resort. Seven miles above the town is the Shoshone Hydroelectric Plant. The Colorado employment office is located here; several businesses hire part-time workers. Over 1,000 miles of fishing streams and more than 100 lakes are accessible from Glenwood Springs. The Sunlight Ski area is located nine miles south of the town; it has a 7,000 foot double chair lift. Aspen and Snowmass are 45 miles away. Other recreational activities include fishing, hiking, hunting and tennis. Strawberry day is an annual event in June.

COLORADO MOUNTAIN COLLEGE - TIMBERLINE CAMPUS   *(G-9)*
901 S. Highway 24, Dept. RP
Leadville, Colorado 80461
Tel: (719) 486-2015; (800) 621-8559; Fax: (303) 945-7279

Description: The public, coeducational junior college was established in 1965 to serve the sparsely populated central part of Western Colorado (i.e. Eagle, Lake and Summit Counties) plus a small portion of Routt County. The college is fully accredited by the North Central Association of Colleges and Schools and grants an Associate degree. It operates on the semester system and offers limited summer sessions. The enrollment includes 328 full-time and 406 part-time students. A faculty of 54 gives a faculty-student ratio of 1-16. The college maintains other campuses in Glenwood Springs and Steamboat Springs.

Entrance Requirements: High school graduation; non-high school graduates considered; SAT or ACT; open admission; mid-year students accepted; early admission, early decision, rolling admission, delayed admission and advanced placement plans available.

Costs Per Year: $930 tuition in district; $1,800 state resident; $5,550 out-of-state tuition; $3,700 room and board; $130 student fees; $400 books.

Collegiate Environment: The 300-acre mountain campus is located in the heart of summer and winter recreational areas. There is excellent skiing near the campus. Timberline campus has a housing capacity of 171 students. The library contains over 22,000 volumes. Scholarships are available and about 60% of the current freshman class received some form of financial assistance. The school offers 3 transfer programs, 4 non-transfer occupational degree programs, and 3 certificate programs.

Community Environment: Leadville, situated at an altitude of 10,000 feet, is a rural community with a dry climate. Leadville has been the center of a famous mining district since the Placer Mines were opened in 1860. It became the silver capital and one of Colorado's greatest mining camps. Mining and tourism are major industries at the present. The city has a library, branch museum of the Colorado State Historical Society, churches, medical clinic and a hospital. Part-time work opportunities are available nearby. Recreation activities are numerous and include ice skating, golfing, tennis, fishing, soccer, bowling, swimming. There is skiing at Ski Cooper on the top of Tennessee Pass 12 miles north of Leadville and at nearby Copper Mountain, Vail, Keystone, Breckenridge and A-Basin. The World's Championship Pack Burro Race is an annual event the first weekend in August.

COLORADO NORTHWESTERN COMMUNITY COLLEGE   *(D-4)*
500 Kennedy Drive
Box 298
Rangely, Colorado 81648
Tel: (303) 675-2261; (800) 562-1105; Admissions: (303) 675-3220; Fax: (303) 675-3343

Description: This district-supported, two-year community college on the western slope of Colorado is accredited by the North Central Association of Colleges and Schools. The college was established in 1960 and the present campus opened in 1962. It operates on the semester system and offers one summer session. Enrollment includes

448 full-time and 1,247 part-time students. A faculty of 43 full-time and 149 part-time gives a faculty-student ratio of 1-10. The college offers transfer, general education, and vocational programs. A wide range of intercollegiate athletics is available to men and women. Evening classes serve a three-county area.

Entrance Requirements: Open admissions; ACT recommended; non-high school graduates considered; rolling admissions, early admission, midyear admission and advanced placement plans avaialble; $10 application fee.

Costs Per Year: No tuition for district residents; $950 in-state; $3,500 out-of-state; $3,410 room and board; $450 student fees.

Collegiate Environment: 150-acre rural campus located on the western slope of Colorado, 300 miles northwest of Denver and 130 miles west of Steamboat Springs. All courses are taught by qualified and experienced faculty. Average class size is 13. The library contains more than 31,000 volumes. There is a Learning Assistance Center, and a Counseling and Job Placement Center. Federal, state, and institutional financial aid is available, including grants, loans, work-study, and 123 scholarships for freshmen. Dormitory accommodations for 300 men and women are available. There is a range of intercollegiate sports for men and women, and a large intramural athletic program; there are also social, service, and professional clubs, including the ski club, the student senate, and others.

Community Environment: Rangely is a rural community (population 2,500) located on the western slope of Colorado, 300 miles northwest of Denver and 130 miles west of Steamboat Springs. It is a friendly community that offers a sharp change of pace from the urban areas. Excellent area for cross-country skiing, backpacking, river rafting, fishing and hunting. Close to Dinosaur National Monument and Flaming Gorge Dam and Reservoir. The area is two hours from downhill skiing at Steamboat Springs, Powder Horn and Sunlight Mountain. Community recreation facilities include: The Taylor Draw Dam Reservoir, a nine-hole golf course, tennis courts, a fitness trail, an ice skating rink, an indoor olympic-size swimming pool, racquetball courts, and a dance and aerobics room. Bus and airport facilities are nearby.

COLORADO SCHOOL OF MINES   *(F-11)*
1500 Illinois
Golden, Colorado 80401
Tel: (303) 273-3220

Description: The state-supported engineering institution is accredited by the North Central Association of Colleges and Schools, the American Chemical Society and the Accreditation Board of Engineering and Technology. It operates on the semester system and offers one summer session. Founded in 1874, this is the oldest institution in the United States devoted exclusively to the education of mineral engineers. Recent enrollment included 2,051 men and 591 women full-time, and 391 men and 113 women part-time. A faculty of 175 full-time and 25 part-time gives a faculty-student ratio of 1-14.

Entrance Requirements: High school graduation with a B+ average; completion of 16 units including 4 English, 4 mathematics, 3 science and 2 social science; SAT or ACT required; $25 application fee all students; rolling admission, delayed admission, early admission, early decision, midyear admission, and advanced placement plans available.

Costs Per Year: $4,326 tuition; $13,064 out-of-state; $4,200 room and board; $434 student fees.

Collegiate Environment: The campus is situated in the heart of the great mineral-producing area of the Rocky Mountains. The students benefit from an environment of geological activity, field production and mineral explorations. The campus has five modern residence halls for 460 men and 115 women, and 50 apartments for married students are maintained. The library was completed in 1954 and provides a fitting structure for one of the largest and most complete specialized libraries in the West. It contains 310,000 volumes, 2,100 pamphlets, 2,500 periodicals and 1,000 sound recordings. The geology museum includes exhibition room and space for reference material and a collection of invertebrate fossils. Financial aid is available and about 85% of the the students receive aid of one kind or another.

Community Environment: CSM is located in Golden, only 15 miles west of Denver's downtown business district. Golden is a community of 15,000 people nestled in the foothills of the Rocky Mountains.

Maintaining a distinct identity from the other Denver suburbs, Golden is also home to the National Earthquake Center and the National Renewable Energy Laboratory. Many CSM students enjoy the outdoors, and favorite summer activities include hiking, jogging, camping, and bicycling. During the winter months, skiing is the major activity with some of the world's best slopes virtually in CSM's backyard. With a population of over two million people, nearby Denver offers all the attractions of a major metropolitan area. As a commercial, transportation, and financial center for the Rocky Mountain region, Denver is home to many government agencies, colleges and universities, and business involved in natural resources, computers, and biotechnology.

COLORADO STATE UNIVERSITY   *(C-12)*
Fort Collins, Colorado 80523
Tel: (303) 491-6909; Fax: (303) 491-7799

Description: Colorado State University is located in Fort Collins, Colorado, a community of 92,000 situated at the foot of the Rocky Mountains with an excellent climate and beautiful mountains creating an ideal college setting about 65 miles north of Denver. The state-supported university operates on the semester system and offers three summer terms. Colorado State University is accredited by the North Central Association of Colleges and Secondary Schools. Enrollment is 15,740 full-time and 2,060 part-time undergraduates, and 3,661 graduate students. The faculty numbers 1,576.

Entrance Requirements: Admission decision is based on secondary school grades, aptitude test scores, class rank, pattern of high school academic units, trend in quality of high school performance, and personal essay; letters of recommendation are encouraged; most significant factor is scholastic achievement during high school; $30 application fee; rolling admission plan available.

Costs Per Year: $2,124 tuition; $8,412 out-of-state; $4,062-$5,084 room and board; $584.54 mandatory fees; $1,500 average additional expenses.

Collegiate Environment: The main campus is located on 666 acres with 100 buildings. There is also a 30,000-seat athletic stadium. Morgan Library was completed in 1965 and houses collections totaling over 3 million items including periodicals, manuscripts, microfilms, and recordings with reading areas for over 1,500 students. Ten residence halls provide space for more than 4,500 students. On-campus apartment housing is provided for more than 800 families and single, nontraditional-age and graduate and international students. Fraternity and sorority houses provide additional living facilities. Approximately 65% of the student body receives some form of aid. 78% of the applicants are accepted and 81% return to this campus for the second year. 90% graduated in the upper half of their high school class, 60% in the top quarter. The average SAT scores of the current freshmen were 476V, 543M; composite ACT score average was 24.7.

Community Environment: Fort Collins has many churches, a local airport, hotels, motels, hospital, and is the shopping center of Northern Colorado; part-time employment is available for students and some full-time employment is available for graduates.

COLORADO TECH   *(H-12)*
4435 N. Chestnut
Colorado Springs, Colorado 80907
Tel: (719) 598-0200; Admissions: (719) 598-3740; Fax: (719) 598-3740

Description: The private, coeducational university was founded in 1965. The school is accredited by the North Central Association of Colleges and Schools. Telecommunications and Engineering Technology and Electrical Engineering programs are accredited by the Accreditation Board for Engineering and Technology. It operates on the quarter system and offers one summer session. Enrollment includes 550 full-time and 800 part-time undergraduates and 300 graduate students. A faculty of 28 full-time and 60 part-time gives a faculty-student ratio 1-14.

Entrance Requirements: High school graduation or GED required; SAT, minimum 1000 with 550M; ACT 24; early admission, delayed admission, midyear admission and rolling admission plans available; advanced placement is possible from previous course work, CLEP and the Advanced Placement Program of the CEEB; $50 application fee.

Costs Per Year: $4,680 undergraduate tuition; $5,160 Master's program tuition; $8,160 Doctoral program tuition; $250 student fees.

Collegiate Environment: Located in Colorado Springs, the college is found in a blend of residential, business and academic environments. Many reasonable apartments and houses in the immediate area are available for rentals. New students and transfers are admitted quarterly; 60% of applicants are accepted. Financial aid is available for students demonstrating need. 190 scholarships are available. 60% of enrolled students receive financial aid. The library holdings include 12,000 hardbound volumes. The campus provides state-of-the-art computer and engineering labs.

Community Environment: Colorado Tech is located at the foot of beautiful Pikes Peak. This ideal location provides convenient access to Colorado's magnificent outdoor recreational facilities: skiing, camping, hunting, fishing, and backpacking. Beautiful Colorado Springs and its environs constitute a progressive, growing city of approximately 400,000.

COMMUNITY COLLEGE OF DENVER   *(F-12)*
Campus Box 201
1111 West Colfax Avenue
Denver, Colorado 80204
Tel: (303) 556-2430

Description: The publicly supported community college was founded in 1969 and is accredited by the North Central Association of Colleges and Schools. The school operates on the semester system and has one summer session. It offers an associate degree and provides both correspondence and continuing education courses. The current enrollment of 5,929 has 4,122 part-time students, and includes a faculty of 93 full-time and 255 part-time.

Entrance Requirements: Open enrollment policy; rolling admission, delayed admission, and advanced placement. CLEP accepted.

Costs Per Year: $1,098 tuition; $3,924 tuition for out-of-state residents.

Collegiate Environment: The campus is in Denver and is conveniently located. Financial aid is available and approximately 40% of the student body receives some support.

Community Environment: See University of Denver.

DENVER CONSERVATIVE BAPTIST SEMINARY   *(F-12)*
P.O. Box 10000
University Park Station
Denver, Colorado 80250
Tel: (303) 761-2482; (800) 922-3040; Admissions: (303) 761-2482 x223; Fax: (303) 761-8060

Description: The seminary is accredited by the North Central Association of Colleges and Schools and by the Association of Theological Schools. It was organized by a group of Conservative Baptist leaders in the spring of 1950. Operating on the quarter system, with five two-week summer sessions, the seminary grants Master of Arts, Master of Divinity, and Doctor of Ministry degrees. The seminary cooperates with Fuller Theological Smeinary in Colorado Springs offering the Master of Divinity. Through the Dayspring Center for Christian Studies it offers the Master of Arts in Philosophy of Religion. The seminary enrolls 650 students, with 110 Doctoral students and approximately 80 enrolled as weekend students. A faculty of 21 full-time and 24 part-time gives a faculty-student ratio of 1-14.

Entrance Requirements: Bachelor's degree; commitment to Christian faith; references; recommendation from local church; scores on aptitude section of GRE; GRE 1500 combined recommended; rolling admission; $25 application fee.

Costs Per Year: $6,120 total for three quarters; $4,260 one-bedroom rental apartment.

Collegiate Environment: The seminary consists of 9 buildings including 80 units of apartments for married and single students. The library contains 135,000 volumes, 2,285 microforms and 580 periodicals. Approximately 80% of those who apply for admission are accepted. Financial aid is available on a limited basis.

Community Environment: See University of Denver.

FORT LEWIS COLLEGE   *(L-6)*
1000 Rim Drive
Durango, Colorado 81301
Tel: (970) 247-7184; Fax: (970) 247-7179

Description: This state-controlled liberal arts college is accredited by the North Central Association of Colleges and Schools. It operates on the trimester system with 3 summer sessions. Enrollment includes 2,187 men and 1,922 women. A faculty of 250 gives a faculty-student ratio of 1-20. The college grants an Associate degree and a Baccalaureate degree.

Entrance Requirements: High school graduation with a C or better average; ACT minimum of 20 required; SAT accepted; grade point average considered; GED accepted with scores of 50 or better (ACT/SAT required); transfers accepted with C or better average; $20 application fee; rolling admission, early decision, advanced placement, early admission, and delayed admission plans available.

Costs Per Year: $1,558 state-resident tuition; $7,118 nonresident; $3,778 room and board; $378 student fees.

Collegiate Environment: The campus has 37 buildings on 267 acres. The library contains 180,000 volumes, 925 periodicals, 45,000 microforms, 4,000 sound recordings, and many other audiovisual materials. Financial assistance is available, and 40% of the current student body receives some type of federal or state aid. 90% of the applicants are accepted, including students at midyear. 75% of the students graduated in the upper 2/3 of their graduating class. 64% of the student body returns the following year. 45 states and 14 foreign countries are represented in the student body.

Community Environment: Durango is located in the Four-Corners region where the states of Colorado, Utah, Arizona, and New Mexico come to a common point. Durango has magnificent mountain landscapes and glistening sunshine at an elevation of 6,700 feet. A modern jet port serves the area. Near Durango nestled in the spruce of the high country gleam thousands of mountain lakes, including two of the larger, Lemon and Vallecito. A few miles south is Navajo Lake, which extends into New Mexico. Agriculture and tourism are an integral part of the economy, as is retailing education, medicine, and law. La Plata County is home to over 27,000 people, and Durango has a population of over 13,000. Purgatory ski area offers complete ski resort facilities.

FRONT RANGE COMMUNITY COLLEGE   *(F-12)*
3645 W. 112th Ave.
Westminster, Colorado 80030
Tel: (303) 466-8811; Admissions: (303) 466-8811 x471; Fax: (303) 466-1623

Description: The two-year, public college was founded in 1968. It is accredited by the North Central Association of Colleges and Schools. The college offers certificates and degrees in both transfer and vocational technical programs. Air Force and Army ROTC programs are available. The college operates on the semester system and offers one summer session. Enrollment includes 3,066 full-time and 7,676 part-time students. A faculty of 149 full-time provides a faculty-student ratio of 1-30.

Entrance Requirements: Open enrollment policy; early admission, early rolling admission and advanced placement plans available.

Costs Per Year: $1,312.80 tuition; $5,464.80 out-of-state tuition; $88.80 student fees.

Collegiate Environment: Located near Broomfield 10 miles from the downtown Denver area. The library contains 42,032 volumes, 360 periodicals, 13,790 microforms, 1,483 audio tapes and 1,422 video tapes. All students of 18 years or older applying for admission are accepted.

Community Environment: See University of Denver

ILIFF SCHOOL OF THEOLOGY   *(F-12)*
2201 South University Boulevard
Denver, Colorado 80210
Tel: (303) 744-1287; (800) 678-3360; Fax: (303) 777-3387

Description: Established in 1892, the private graduate school is an official seminary of the United Methodist Church and is accredited by the Association of Theological Schools and the North Central Association of Colleges and Schools. The purpose of the school is to prepare men and women for Christian ministry and other forms of religious and academic leadership. Iliff offers four graduate degrees and no undergraduate degrees. It offers the Master of Divinity, the Master of Arts in Religion, and the Master of Arts degrees. Iliff grants the Ph.D. in Religious and Theological Studies. Iliff also offers cooperative degrees with the Graduate School of Social Work and the University of Denver. It operates on the quarter system with several summer sessions. Enrollment is 330 graduate students. The faculty consists of 23 full-time and 22 part-time members.

Entrance Requirements: For Master's degrees: Bachelor degree from an accredited college; personal recommendations and a personal statement required; 2.5/4.0 overall G.P.A.; $25 application fee. Ph.D. and M.A. require 3.0/4.0 overall G.P.A. and writing sample. Ph.D. requires master's degree as well.

Costs Per Year: $8,280 master's degree tuition; $8,160 Ph.D. tuition; room and board available.

Collegiate Environment: The campus joins the University of Denver campus and these two institutions enjoy friendly relations and academic cooperation. There are five buildings on seven acres. The library contains 175,761 volumes. There are 67 self-contained apartment units for single, married, or married students with families. Various forms of financial assistance are available. The school accepts about 80% of its applicants at the master's level.

Community Environment: See University of Denver.

LAMAR COMMUNITY COLLEGE   *(J-17)*
2401 South Main Street
Lamar, Colorado 81052
Tel: (719) 336-2248; Fax: (719) 336-2448

Description: The state-controlled two-year college is accredited by the North Central Association of Colleges and Schools and operates on the semester system with 2 summer sessions. The college was organized in 1937 with a desire to provide at least two years of education beyond high school for residents within a 50-mile circle. Enrollment is 500 full-time and 600 part-time students. A faculty of 23 full-time and 53 part-time gives a faculty-student ratio of 1-18.

Entrance Requirements: Open door policy; early admission, early decision, rolling admission, delayed admission, midyear admission and advanced placement plans available.

Costs Per Year: $3,264 ($102/credit) tuition; $10,736 ($335.50/credit) out-of-state; $3,620 room and board; $248 student fees; $500 books.

Collegiate Environment: The campus has seven buildings on 115 acres located in the city of Lamar, the center of an area of modern farming and ranching industries. The campus buildings are ultramodern and beautifully furnished. Dormitory capacity is available for 110 men and 91 women. Library contains 30,000 volumes, 2,000 pamphlets, 151 periodicals, 804 microforms and 2,000 sound recordings. 70% of freshman class returned for sophomore year. Financial assistance is available for students requiring aid and about 80% of the student body received aid.

Community Environment: Lamar is an All-America City located at the junction of U.S. Highways 50, 287, and 385 with a dry climate and a population of 9,000. Livestock and poultry are primary concerns in this extensively irrigated area for which Lamar is a trading center. Airlines, railroads and buses serve the area. The community facilities include churches, a hospital and clinics, a library and various civic clubs. Part-time employment is available. The recreational activities include hunting, fishing, boating, golfing, swimming, and baseball.

MESA STATE COLLEGE   *(G-5)*
P.O. Box 2647
Grand Junction, Colorado 81502
Tel: (303) 248-1376; (800) 982-6372; Fax: (303) 248-1973

Description: Founded in 1925 as a junior college, Mesa State College became a four-year state college in 1974 offering Bachelor of Arts, Bachelor of Science, Bachelor of Science in Nursing, Bachelor of Business Administration and Associate degrees. Mesa is governed by the board of trustees of the State Colleges in Colorado and is accredited by the North Central Association of Colleges and Schools.

The college operates on the semester system and offers three summer sessions. Enrollment includes 3,747 full-time and 891 part-time students. A faculty of 159 full-time and 17 part-time gives a faculty-student ratio of 1-21.

Entrance Requirements: High school graduation; open enrollment policy for 2-year programs, moderately selective entrance requirements for 4-year programs; non-high school graduates considered; ACT or SAT required; early admission, early decision, rolling admission, midyear admission and advanced placement plans available. $30 application fee.

Costs Per Year: $1,434 tuition; $5,016 nonresident; $3,798 room and board (five-day meal plan); $380 student fees.

Collegiate Environment: The library contains 200,000 volumes and 951 periodicals. The campus has 22 buildings on 45 acres. Dormitories house 718 men and women; four apartment buildings provide residence facilities for 70 men and 70 women. Students participate in a variety of financial aid programs. Both traditional academic and vocational-technical programs are offered in numerous preprofessional, professional, and career-oriented programs. Activity programs in business, drama, music, sciences, athletics, forensics, journalism, radio, scholarship, government, and other subject-related fields are offered. Financial aid is available, and 75% of the current student body receives some form of assistance. Applicants are admitted at the beginning of any term.

Community Environment: Grand Junction is located in an irrigated valley in the heart of a vast vacationland that is also rich in energy-related natural resources. The climate is invigorating, sunny, and mild. Many college activities involve physical features of the region, including agriculture, biology, geology, and engineering field trips; skiing; backpacking; river rafting; and Outing Program. The community has churches of many denominations, excellent public schools, library facilities, cultural programs, city parks, golf courses, tennis courts, four hospitals, and good transportation services including three major airlines. Recreational activities in the nearby mountains and deserts include hiking, camping, boating, fishing, hunting, cross-country and downhill skiing, and more. Employment opportunities have been above average in the area during recent years.

METROPOLITAN STATE COLLEGE OF DENVER   *(F-12)*
P.O. Box 173362
Denver, Colorado 80217-3362
Tel: (303) 556-3058; Fax: (303) 556-6345

Description: The state-controlled college is accredited by the North Central Association of Colleges and Schools. The college was founded in 1963 to provide a multipurpose urban-type college dedicated to excellence in teaching and service to the community. It operates on the semester system and offers two summer sessions. Enrollment includes 9,361 full-time and 8,100 part-time undergraduate students. A faculty of 371 full-time and 547 part-time gives a faculty-student ratio of 1-19. The college grants a Bachelor degree.

Entrance Requirements: High school graduation with 15 units completed; rank in upper 2/3 of graduating class; high school students less than 20 years of age must submit ACT or SAT test scores, high school grade point average and class rank; a sliding scale using test scores and high school performance is used to determine admission; non-high school graduates considered with GED; $25 application fee; early admission, early decision, deferred admission, rolling admission and advanced placement plans available.

Costs Per Year: $1,564 tuition; $6,544 out-of-state; $284 student fees.

Collegiate Environment: The college is located in the Auraria Higher Education Center in downtown Denver. Upper-division education majors tutor at certain junior and senior high schools. There is a special financial-aid program available that enables low-mark, disadvantaged students to attend. The library contains 731,000 volumes, 2,389 periodicals, and 11,525 microforms. No dormitories are provided on campus. 88% of the applicants are accepted. 66% of students receive some form of financial aid.

Community Environment: See University of Denver.

Branch Campuses: Metro North: 11990 Grant St., Suite 102, Northglenn, CO, 80233; Metro South: 5660 Greenwood PLAZA Blvd., Suite L100, Englewood, CO 80111; Metro on the Mall: 1554 California St., Suite 200, Denver, CO 80202

MORGAN COMMUNITY COLLEGE   (D-14)
17800 Road 20
Fort Morgan, Colorado 80701
Tel: (303) 867-3081; (800) 622-0216; Admissions: (303) 867-3081
x109; Fax: (303) 867-6608

Description: The state supported, coeducational, two-year college began operations in 1970. It is fully accredited by the North Central Association of Colleges and Schools and offers courses in liberal arts and vocational training leading to Associate degrees and Certificates of completion. The school operates on the semester system with two summer sessions. Enrollment includes 213 full-time and 616 part-time students. A faculty of 25 full-time and 80 part-time gives a faculty-student ratio of 1:8.

Entrance Requirements: Open enrollment policy; high school diploma is not required for admission; mid-year admission, rolling admission, early admission, delayed admission and early decision plans available.

Costs Per Year: $1,302 tuition; $5,454 out-of-state tuition; $78 student fees.

Collegiate Environment: Morgan Community College is situated on a 10 acre tract of land with four halls; Willow Annex, Cottonwood Hall, Aspen Hall, and Spruce Hall. Cottonwood Hall was completed in 1980, with Aspen and Spruce Halls being completed in 1985. In addition, the college makes use of public schools and other facilities when necessary. library contains 13,803 bound volumes, 88 periodicals and 1,632 audio-visual materials. Financial assistance is available; more than 65% of the student population receives such assistance.

Community Environment: The Morgan County area has an abundant supply of recreational facilities for spare time enjoyment. In addition to the athletic activities close at hand, the student has access to the metropolitan offerings in Denver, an hour drive away on Interstate highways, and the beautiful Rocky Mountains, a two hour drive on Interstate highways.

NAZARENE BIBLE COLLEGE   (H-12)
1111 Chapman Drive - Box 15749
Colorado Springs, Colorado 80935
Tel: (719) 596-5110; (800) 878-3873; Admissions: (719) 596-5110 X
166; Fax: (719) 550-9437

Description: The private, coeducational Bible college opened in the fall of 1967 and is affiliated with the Church of the Nazarene. The college is accredited by Accrediting Association of Bible Colleges. It grants the Associate and Bachelor degrees. There is also a one-year Diploma Program in piano pedagogy and an 18-hour (3-year) diploma program in hymn playing. There is a Lay Ministries Diploma for 48 quarter hours of work (one year), a Women's Studies Diploma (20 quarter hours) and a Women's Studies Certificate (10 quarter hours). The ABS meets the educational requirements for ordination in the Church of the Nazarene. It operates on the quarter system and offers two summer sessions. Enrollment is 436 full-time students. A faculty of 14 full-time and 15 part-time gives a faculty-student ratio of 1-24.

Entrance Requirements: High school graduation or GED; open enrollment policy; non-high school graduates may be considered; mid-year admission and rolling admission plans available. $20 application fee.

Costs Per Year: $3,840 tuition; $105 student fees.

Collegiate Environment: The 65-acre campus includes 6 buildings. The rapidly growing library collection contains 50,000 volumes, 236 periodicals, 2,165 microforms, and 3,210 sound recordings. 98% of the applicants are accepted. 95% of the students receive some form of financial aid.

Community Environment: See Colorado College.

NORTHEASTERN JUNIOR COLLEGE   (C-15)
100 College Drive
Sterling, Colorado 80751
Tel: (303) 522-6600; (800) 626-4637; Admissions: (303) 522-6600
x651; Fax: (303) 522-4945

Description: The county-government controlled junior college is accredited by the North Central Association of Colleges and Schools.

The college was organized in 1941 and the committee purchased the present college site in 1945. Programs of study are primarily vocational and lead to the Associate degree. The college operates on the semester system and offers one summer session. Enrollment includes 944 full-time and 3,000 part-time students. A faculty of 72 full-time and 25 part-time gives a faculty-student ratio of 1-35.

Entrance Requirements: High school graduation; open enrollment policy; non-high school graduates considered if they have completed the GED; ACT required for some programs; early admission, early decision, midyear admission, and advanced placement plans available; $15 application fee.

Costs Per Year: $1,745 state resident tuition; $4,565 nonresident tuition; $3,720 room and board.

Collegiate Environment: The campus has 18 buildings on 36 acres. Residence halls provide a total living-learning experience for the students with a capacity for 409 men and women. The library contains 65,000 volumes, 5,900 periodicals, 6,600 microforms and 3,500 audio-visual materials. 95% of applicants are accepted. Various forms of financial assistance are available and 50% of the student body receives some form of aid.

Community Environment: Sterling, population 15,000, in northeastern Colorado on the South Platte River, has a mild climate. Trains and buses serve the area. Community facilities include churches, hospitals, libraries, a health center, and museum. Recreational activities include golf, tennis, swimming, bowling, roller skating, and boating. Rooming houses and private homes are available for student housing. The County Fair and Overland Trail Roundup are annual events. Part-time work is available.

OTERO JUNIOR COLLEGE   (J-15)
18th and Colorado Avenue
La Junta, Colorado 81050
Tel: (719) 384-6831; Fax: (719) 384-6880

Description: The state controlled junior college is accredited by the North Central Association of Colleges and Schools and operates on the semester system with one summer session. The College was opened in 1941 and offered a continuation school program. The college officially became a two-year college in 1968. Enrollment includes 714 full-time and 382 part-time students. A faculty of 35 full-time and 35 part-time gives a faculty-student ratio of 1-16.

Entrance Requirements: Open enrollment policy. Rolling admissions.

Costs Per Year: $1,224 resident tuition; $4,026 out-of-state tuition; $3,690 room and board; $84 student fees.

Collegiate Environment: The campus has 13 buildings on 50 acres. The library was opened in 1961 and contains 33,000 volumes. The most unusual building is the Koshare Kiva completed in 1949 through the efforts of the Koshare Indian Dancers and patrons of this world-famous Boy Scout troop. Dormitories have a capacity for 100 men and 60 women. Of the 100 scholarships offered, 70 are for freshmen. All applicants are accepted. 75% of students receive financial aid.

Community Environment: La Junta is located in the rich agricultural and stock-raising territory of the Arkansas River Valley with a mild year-round climate; the average mean temperature being 54.1 degrees, and the average yearly precipitation, 13.61 inches. The community facilities include a library, churches, many shopping facilities, hotels, motels, hospital and the community sponsored concert association. La Junta has many of the civic and service organizations. Industries include canning, manufacture of copper tubings and the renovation of railroad cars. The Kid's Rodeo is held here each year in August.

PARKS JUNIOR COLLEGE   (F-12)
9065 Grant Street
Denver, Colorado 80229
Tel: (303) 457-2757; Fax: (303) 457-4030

Description: The private, coeducational junior college was founded in 1895 and offers specialized training for occupations in business and industry. The school is accredited by the Association of Independent Colleges and Schools and confers associate of applied science degrees upon completion of the program. Day and evening programs of varying duration are available. The enrollment is 1,577 students.

Entrance Requirements: High school graduation or equivalent; all programs require entrance tests. Students may enter if they demonstrate an ability to benefit from the programs. Rolling admissions, early decision, midyear admissions and advanced placement available; $25 application fee.

Costs Per Year: $11,400, all books included.

Collegiate Environment: Located in metropolitan Denver, the school building is fully equipped with all modern equipment, and handicapped accessible. The school will assist students in locating appropriate housing nearby. A placement service is provided at no charge to the graduates. Various forms of financial assistance are available.

Community Environment: See University of Denver

PIKES PEAK COMMUNITY COLLEGE   (H-12)
5675 S. Academy Blvd.
Colorado Springs, Colorado 80906
Tel: (303) 576-7711

Description: Pikes Peak Community College, located at the foot of Pikes Peak is a two-year institution of higher education offering a broad program in transfer, occupational, and preparatory subjects emphasizing student and community needs. It is fully accredited by the North Central Association. The college grants the Associate degree. It operates on the semester system and offers limited summer classes. Present enrollment for day and evening classes is over 6,000 students.

Entrance Requirements: Open door admissions policy; all high school graduates and other persons with comparable qualifications are admitted as regular students. Other individuals who are at least 16 years old may be admitted if they can reasonably be expected to successfully complete the courses in which they enroll.

Costs Per Year: $942 tuition; $3,768 out-of-state tuition.

Collegiate Environment: The library contains 37,387 volumes, 341 periodicals, 15,536 microforms and 4,761 audio visual materials. No dormitories are available on campus. Scholarships available. 100 percent of applicants are accepted. 46 percent of the freshmen returned to this campus for the second year. The campus, completed in 1978, is one of the most modern and best equipped in the state of Colorado. It is located on a 212 acre site on the southwest edge of Colorado Springs near the intersection of Interstate 25 and South Academy Boulevard. At present, the facilities include three buildings which house 82 classrooms and laboratories, a library, a theatre, a gymnasium, a day care center, dining facilities, a student center, and a bookstore.

Community Environment: Pikes Peak Community College is located in Colorado Springs a community of approx. 278,000 people situated 70 miles south of Denver. The dry, temperate climate and 310 days of sunshine annually make it a highly desirable place to live year-round. Skiing, hiking, fishing, hunting, backpacking and camping can be enjoyed within a one-half hour to one hour drive from Colorado Springs. Many high technology industries are located in Colorado Springs. Housing is readily available and buses serve the campus from all parts of the city.

PUEBLO COMMUNITY COLLEGE   (J-13)
900 West Orman Avenue
Pueblo, Colorado 81004
Tel: (719) 549-3200; Admissions: (719) 549-3010; Fax: (719) 543-7566

Description: The publicly supported community college traces its history to 1933 when it was a junior college. The name was officially changed to Pueblo Community College in 1982. Its current mission is to provide educational programs to fill the occupational needs of students in technical and vocational fields, to provide two-year transfer programs, and to provide a broad range of programs in personal and vocational education for adults. The college operates on the semester system with one summer session and it is accredited by the North Central Association of Colleges and Schools. Enrollment includes 1,604 students full-time, 2,375 part-time, and 881 evening with a faculty of 90 providing a faculty-student ratio of 1-28.

Entrance Requirements: High school graduate or equivalent. Open enrollment.

Costs Per Year: $942 tuition; $3,768 tuition for out-of-state residents; $88 student fees.

Collegiate Environment: The college is located on 35 acres and contains eight buildings, including a learning resources center of over 33,000 volumes. Interlibrary loan services are available. Approximately 80% of the students receive financial aid. There are campuses in Canon City, Cortez, and Durango.

Community Environment: Pueblo (population 126,000) is 42 miles south of Colorado Springs and 112 miles south of Denver on I-25. The site of Pueblo was a crossroad for Indians, Spanish troops, friars, fur trappers, and explorers. A trading post was built in 1842 and served travelers on their way to California. Pueblo's location as the focal point for travel to the Rocky Mountain Empire continues to serve business and industry in the area. Puebloans enjoy clean air, uncrowded highways, and nearby water and mountain recreation set in the warm pleasant atmosphere of the Southwest. Pueblo boasts a fine community college, a university, symphony orchestra, chorale, ballet, theatrical groups, and a beautiful new arts center.

RED ROCKS COMMUNITY COLLEGE   (F-11)
12600 West 6th Avenue
Golden, Colorado 80401
Tel: (303) 988-6160

Description: The publicly supported comprehensive, coeducational, community college was founded in 1969. As a stand alone college, it offers transfer and vocational programs. Accredited by the North Central Association of Colleges and Schools, the college grants the Certificate and Associate degree. The semester system is used and one summer session is offered. Enrollment is approximately 6,500 students, with a faculty of 79 full time and 59 part time.

Entrance Requirements: Open enrollment; non-high school graduates admitted; early admission, delayed admission, advanced placement plans available; no application fee.

Costs Per Year: $1,024 tuition; $3,850 nonresident tuition; $108 student fees; additional expenses average $100 per semester.

Collegiate Environment: The college is a commuter school and no dormitory facilities are provided. The library contains 42,904 volumes, 550 pamphlets, 357 periodicals, 20,211 microforms, and 22,801 recordings. All students applying for admission are accepted including mid-year. Financial aid is available; scholarships are awarded and 21% of the students receive financial assistance. Programs for the educationally disadvantaged are offered.

Community Environment: See Colorado School of Mines

REGIS UNIVERSITY   (F-12)
3333 Regis Boulevard
Denver, Colorado 80221-1099
Tel: (303) 458-4900; (800) 388-2366; Fax: (303) 964-5534

Description: The Jesuit liberal arts university is accredited by the North Central Association of Colleges and Schools and is controlled by the Roman Catholic Church. The university was founded in the New Mexico territory in 1877 by a group of Jesuits. It operates on the semester system and offers 3 summer sessions. Enrollment includes 1,170 full-time and 64 part-time students. A faculty of 62 full-time and 25 part-time gives a faculty-student ratio of 1-16.

Entrance Requirements: High school graduation with a C+ average and completion of 15 units including 4 English and 2 mathematics; SAT or ACT required; application fee $40; rolling admission, early admission, and advanced placement plans available.

Costs Per Year: $12,700 tuition; $5,880 room and board; $450 student fees.

Collegiate Environment: The campus has 11 buildings on 90 acres. The library contains 262,637 volumes and also holds periodicals and audiovisual materials. Residence halls accommodate 600 students. Approximately 90% of the applicants are accepted. Recent average SAT scores were 480 Math, 492 Verbal. The average ACT score was 22. Scholarships are available. 79% of the students receive some form of financial aid. Students have the opportunity to attend Loyola University-Rome or Gonzaga-Florence for one year.

Community Environment: See University of Denver.

TRINIDAD STATE JUNIOR COLLEGE   *(M-13)*
600 Prospect Street
Trinidad, Colorado 81082
Tel: (719) 846-5621

Description: The state-controlled, coeducational junior college is accredited by the North Central Association of Colleges and Schools. The college was established in 1925 and was operated in conjunction with Trinidad High School. It relocated to its present site in 1935. 48 different programs, primarily vocational-technical, are offered. The college grants the Associate degree. It operates on the semester system and offers one summer session. Enrollment is 1,211 students. A faculty of 115 gives a faculty-student ratio of 1-12.

Entrance Requirements: High school graduation or GED; ACT required; rolling admission plans available; $10 registration deposit.

Costs Per Year: $1,224 state resident tuition; $4,026 nonresident tuition; $3,614 room board; $262 student fees.

Collegiate Environment: The campus is located a few blocks from the central section of town on a hill overlooking the city. There are four dormitories for 320 men and 96 women. The library contains 69,000 volumes, 2,200 pamphlets, 355 periodicals, 1,150 microforms and 700 sound recordings. 97% of the applicants are accepted. Financial aid is available for eligible students.

Community Environment: Located in South Central Colorado, Trinidad is the County Seat of Las Animas County and was a trading post on the Old Santa Fe Trail. Good highways, busses, and the railroad serve the area. Leading industries are coal production, farming, and ranching. The area offers Monument Lake, a 1,200-acre city owned park with fishing, boating and camping; Trinidad Lake, located 36 miles west of Trinidad in scenic Stonewall Valley, with water skiing, fishing, boating, camping, hiking and a recreation area; Cuchara Ski Area, located 50 miles west of Trinidad in scenic Cuchara valley.

UNITED STATES AIR FORCE ACADEMY   *(H-12)*
Colorado Springs, Colorado 80840-5651
Tel: (719) 472-2520; (800) 443-9266; Fax: (719) 472-3647

Description: The service institution with a special mission of producing Air Force career officers is controlled by the federal government and accredited by the North Central Association of Colleges and Schools. The Academy has been educating professional officers since 1955. Enrollment is open to men and women. Graduates receive a commission as second lieutenants in the U.S. Air Force and are obligated to serve as officers for six years. Graduates who then complete Pilot or Navigator Flight training must serve a longer committment determined by Air Force policy in effect at that time. It operates on the semester system and offers three summer sessions. Enrollment is 4,000 cadets. A faculty of 517 officers gives a faculty-student ratio of 1-8. The Academy offers a one-semester exchange program with Ecole de l'Air, the French Air Force Academy.

Entrance Requirements: The Cadet Wing strength is stabilized at 4,000. Admission is controlled by law, permitting young men and women who are U.S. citizens to be appointed each year. (New class enters in early July for Basic Cadet Training.) Citizens of foreign countries are admitted in limited numbers. Applicants must be at least 17 and not yet 22 years of age on July 1 of the year in which they desire to be admitted. They must be unmarried, have no dependents of any kind, and have a good moral character and physical health. To apply, return the completed application by December 31 of senior year in high school. Students must obtain a nomination from one of a variety of sources. These include Presidential, Vice-Presidential, Congressional nominations, Medal of Honor nominations, and Deceased or Disabled Veteran nominations. A detailed information booklet, "Instructions for Applications" is sent with admissions forms. To enter the Academy upon graduation from high school, a student is advised to apply during the spring of the junior year. If a student is considered competitive for an Academy appointment, he or she will be required to take a candidate fitness test, a medical exam, and either the SAT or the ACT. Competitive mid-range SAT scores are 520-610V, 620-710M; competitive ACT scores are Math 27-31, Sci. Reasoning 26-31, English 26-29, and Reading 26-31. The Academy does not offer graduate degree programs, but top students can vie for a variety of postgraduate scholarships.

Costs Per Year: Paid by U.S. government; appointee must deposit $2,500 before entrance to Academy.

Collegiate Environment: The Air Force Academy is situated on the northern boundary of the city of Colorado Springs, which has a metropolitan population of more than 350,000 people. Approximately 50 miles to the north is Denver, the state capital, which has a population of more than 1 million. The Academy site covers 18,000 acres and sits at the base of the Rampart Range of the Rocky Mountains. The average elevation of the Academy is 7,000 feet above sea level. Cadets may visit any and all cities in the state when they have off-base privileges. 20% of applicants are accepted.

Community Environment: See Colorado College.

UNIVERSITY OF COLORADO - BOULDER   *(E-11)*
Boulder, Colorado 80309
Tel: (303) 492-1411; Admissions: (303) 492-6301; Fax: (303) 492-7115

Description: The University of Colorado was established in Boulder by the State Constitution in 1876. It is a coeducational university operating on a semester system with 2 summer sessions. A recent enrolllment included 24,548 men and women. The University is accredited by the North Central Association of Colleges and Schools and by respective professional agencies.

Entrance Requirements: Units vary from college to college within UCB; SAT or ACT required; $40 application fee; rolling admission and advanced placement plans available. Admission is selective and is based on evaluation of many criterea including a general level of academic performance before admission to the University as indicated by the evaluation of work taken at other educational institutions; evidence of scholarly ability and accomplishment as indicated by scores on standardized tests of scholastic aptitude; motivation and potential for academic growth and ability to work in an academic community, as indicated by trends in the student's record, by letters of recommendation from teacher's and others qualified to evaluate the student, by accomplishments outside academic work, and other relevent evidence.

Costs Per Year: $2,769 resident; $13,845 nonresident; room and board $4,123.

Collegiate Environment: The 600-acre campus includes more than 150 buildings surrounded by green lawns and tall native trees. Approximately 70-75% of the freshmen and transfer students applying for admissions are accepted. The University seeks a diverse student body and through its five colleges and five professional school offers more than 2,500 courses in over 150 fields of study. Financial aid is available. The university provides housing for approximately 1/4 of student body. Family housing is also available. The library contains 2.28 million volumes.

Community Environment: Boulder is 30 miles northwest of Denver at an altitude of over 5,000 feet with a temperate climate. There is an average of over 300 days of sunshine each year. The population of Boulder is approx. 90,000. Bus lines serve the area; municipal airport is nearby. Boulder is known for its beautiful setting and for its healthful climate. Scientific research and development is the major industry. Many of the vital parts for spacecraft have come from the laboratories of Boulder. Besides the cultural events, many of which are associated with the University, there are a great number of recreational opportunities. These include golf, tennis, swimming, boating, hunting, fishing, and skiing. Boulder has several fraternal, civic, and veterans organizations.

UNIVERSITY OF COLORADO - COLORADO SPRINGS
(H-12)
Austin Bluffs Pkwy.
P.O. Box 7150
Colorado Springs, Colorado 80933-7150
Tel: (719) 593-3000; (800) 990-8227; Admissions: (719) 593-3383; Fax: (719) 593-3316

Description: A gift of the Cragmor Foundation, the Colorado Springs campus, then 80 acres, was opened to classes in September 1965. The state-supported university is accredited by the North Central Association of Colleges and Schools. It operates on the semester system and offers one summer session. Enrollment is 2,587 full-time and 1,547 part-time undergraduate students, and 1,676 graduate students. A faculty of 177 full-time and 184 part-time gives a faculty-student ratio of 1-15.

Entrance Requirements: High school graduation or GED; SAT 500V and 500M or ACT 24; GRE required for graduate school; completion of 15 units including 4 English, 3 mathematics, 2 laboratory scinece, 2 foreign language, 1 social science, 1 history, 1 science; rolling admission, early decision, delayed admission, midyear admission and advanced placement plans available; application deadline for fall term is July 1; $40 application fee for undergraduate, $40 for MBA (all other graduate programs-$30), $50 for foreign students (undergraduate and graduate).

Costs Per Year: $1,160 tuition; $4,292 nonresident; $179 student fees.

Collegiate Environment: UCCS is one of the four campuses of the University of Colorado system. It has six colleges: the College of Business and Administration and the Graduate School of Business Administration; the School of Education; the College of Engineering and Applied Science; the College of Letters, Arts and Sciences; the Graduate School of Public Affairs and the Graduate School. Graduate programs, except for Business and Public Affairs, are coordinated by the Graduate School, which is part of the systemwide Graduate School. 74% of applicants are admitted, including students at mid-year. Approximately 35% of students receive some financial aid. The library has more than 400,000 holdings. On-campus student housing is planned for Fall 1996.

Community Environment: See Colorado College.

UNIVERSITY OF COLORADO - DENVER   *(F-12)*
P.O. Box 173364
Denver, Colorado 80202
Tel: (303) 556-3287; Fax: (303) 556-4838

Description: The urban campus of the University of Colorado was founded in 1912 as an extension division, and given status as a separate campus in 1972. It is a publicly supported, coeducational university offering programs in 30 undergraduate fields and 45 graduate areas in the liberal arts, and professional degree programs. The school operates on a semester basis with one summer sessions and is fully accredited by the North Central Association of Colleges and Secondary Schools. There are 10,475 students enrolled; a faculty of 319 full-time and 250 part-time gives a faculty-student ratio of 1-16. The university grants Master, Bachelor, Ph.D. and Ed.S degrees.

Entrance Requirements: High school graduation or GED is required. SAT with a combined score of 1070; or ACT with a minimum score of 26; GRE required. Graduate must be in top 15% of class with business and English students higher. Early decision plan, early admission, rolling admission, delayed admission, and advanced placement is possible, as well as obtaining credit from correspondence courses and CLEP. The application fee is $30.

Costs Per Year: $1,865 tuition; $9,614 out-of-state tuition; $218 student fees.

Collegiate Environment: The university shares the new 169 acre Auraria Campus located next to the Denver Center for the Performing Arts. As part of the Auraria Higher Education Center, facilities are shared with Metropolitan State College of Denver, and the Community College of Denver. The Auraria library has 600,000 volumes. Of those applying, 84% are accepted; new students and transfers are accepted at mid-year. Scholarships are limited to in-state students and 14% of the student body receives financial aid.

Community Environment: See University of Denver

UNIVERSITY OF DENVER   *(F-12)*
University Park
MRB 107
Denver, Colorado 80208
Tel: (303) 871-2000; (800) 525-9495; Admissions: (303) 871-2036; Fax: (303) 871-3301

Description: The private university, founded in 1864, is accredited by the North Central Association of Colleges and Schools. The quarter system is used, with one summer session. Approximately 8,522 students are enrolled with a faculty of 399.

Entrance Requirements: High school graduation; completion of 15 units, including 4 English, 3 mathematics, 3 science, 3 social science, and 2 foreign language; ACT or SAT required; no minimum GPA specified. Average GPA of incoming freshmen is 3.1. Average scores:

SAT 1007, ACT 24. Students accepted at midyear; early admission, delayed admission, advanced placement, and rolling admission plans available. $30 application fee.

Costs Per Year: $15,192 tuition; room and board $5,064.

Collegiate Environment: The campus has 60 buildings on 125 acres. Residence halls accommodate 1,600 students. The Chamberlin Observatory includes a 20-inch reflector and a large astronomical library. The Child Study Center is operated by the university psychology department. The university library system contains over 1,835,000 titles, 5,102 periodicals and 879,528 microforms. Museums in Denver afford excellent opportunity for study. The campus is located in a residential area seven miles from downtown. The Park Hill Campus houses the Lamont School of Music, the College of Law, and The Women's College. The College offers a scholar's program which affords unusual opportunities for students with outstanding academic talent. The Junior Year Abroad program allows for study including England, Spain, Italy, Denmark, France, and Germany. 70% of the applicants are accepted.

52% of the students receive financial aid and 28% participate in work-study programs.

Community Environment: Denver is a metropolitan area, capital of Colorado, situated at the foot of the Rocky Mountains. The climate is temperate and considered healthful. The State Museum, Art Museum, Museum of Natural History, many public and private hospitals, churches, and the fine shopping areas make up the city. Part-time employment opportunities are good. Denver is the gateway to the playgrounds of the mountains; the city's mountain parks of 20,000 acres include the Genesee Mountain with its game preserve. There are lakes in the area for water sports and fishing. Denver has become a great center for snow sports activities, with several of the best known ski areas located 55 to 85 miles from Denver in the Arapaho National Forest. The annual National Western Stock Show is in January.

UNIVERSITY OF NORTHERN COLORADO   *(D-12)*
Greeley, Colorado 80639
Tel: (303) 351-1890; Fax: (303) 351-2984

Description: Founded in 1889, it is accredited by the North Central Association of Colleges and Schools. UNC maintains its historic role as a leader in the field of teacher education while offering more than 100 degree programs through its colleges: Arts and Sciences, Business Administration, Education, Health and Human Sciences, Performing and Visual Arts; and its Graduate School. The University operates on the semester system and offers three summer sessions. Enrollment includes 8,969 full-time, and 1,457 part-time undergraduate and 1,595 graduate students. A faculty of 421 full-time and 116 part-time gives a faculty-student ratio of 1-21.

Entrance Requirements: Each applicant is evaluated on an individual basis, but in general new freshmen are admitted with an ACT score of 22 or SAT of 900; cumulative GPA of 2.8; accredited high school graduation required with a minimum of 15 secondary school units, including 4 English, 2 science, 2 social science, and 3 years of college-prep mathematics; the School of Music requires auditions of applicants; GRE is required for doctoral admission; TOEFL or Michigan Test of English Language is required for foreign students; $30 application fee.

Costs Per Year: Undergraduate: $1,829 state resident tuition, $7,731 nonresident tuition; Graduate: $2,163 state resident tuition, $8,228 nonresident tuition; $4,128 room and board; $398 student fees.

Collegiate Environment: The 236-acre campus is located in a residential section of Greeley. Two main campuses connect at a recently renovated University Center. Campus halls, suite-style housing, graduate houses, and apartments house 2,848 students. The James A. Michener Library has holdings of 2,000,000 volumes, microforms, and other reference materials. The Career Services Center offers a co-op education internship program. Students may study at other campuses in the United States or abroad through the National Student Exchange and the Study Abroad Program. Campus life at UNC offers a variety of activities including participation in the student newspaper, student government, theatre, radio productions; and membership in academic, international, religious, and cultural groups. 76% of freshman applicants, 87% of transfers, and 57% of graduate students were recently accepted. Scholarships are available and 63% of undergraduates receive some form of financial aid.

Community Environment: Located one hour north of Denver and one hour east of Rocky Mountain National Park, the city of Greeley has a population of more than 60,000. It has a symphony, rock and jazz concerts, community theatre, and the largest 4th of July rodeo in the country. The dry, desert climate produces sunny days and cool nights. There is some snow and very little rain.

UNIVERSITY OF SOUTHERN COLORADO   *(J-13)*
2200 Bonforte Blvd.
Pueblo, Colorado 81001
Tel: (719) 549-2100; (800) 872-4769; Admissions: (719) 549-2461; Fax: (719) 549-2419

Description: The publicly supported polytechnic, regional coeducational university is accredited by the North Central Association of Colleges and Schools. It operates on the semester system and offers one summer session. The university has a unique role and mission in Colorado by emphasizing career-oriented, technological and applied programs in addition to a strong liberal arts curriculum. Established in 1933, the institution recieved university status in 1975. Enrollment includes 3,543 full-time and 957 part-time students. A faculty of 278 provides a student-faculty ratio of 1-18. The university offers selected bachelor's degree programs in Colorado Springs and at Peterson Air Force Base (Colorado), the United States Air Force Academy (Colorado), Altus Air Force Base (Oklahoma), and McGuire Air Force Base (New Jersey) through its Division of Continuing Education. The Division also offers an external degree completion program in social sciences. For more information, please call 1-800-388-6154.

Entrance Requirements: First-time applicants are eligible for admission if they achieve a CCHE admission index score of 79. This score can be achieved by various combinations high school grade-point averages and ACT or SAT combined score. Students with non-traditional backgrounds are encouraged to apply. Application fee $15.

Costs Per Year: $1,644 state resident; $7,100 nonresident; $3,836 room and board; $324 student fees.

Collegiate Environment: The campus has 14 buildings on 800 acres. The library contains 195,000 volumes, 1,300 periodicals, and 6,500 microforms. Dormitory space for 525 men and women is provided. 91% of those applying for admission are accepted. Scholarships are available and about 71% of the freshman class receive some form of financial assistance.

Community Environment: Pueblo is a city of approximately 100,000 people located on the Arkansas River on the eastern slope of the Rocky Mountains. The city is a manufacturing and retail center for southeastern Colorado with a mild and semi-arid climate. Recreational activities including skiing, hiking, camping, boating, fishing, and swimming are available in Pueblo and its immediate vicinity. The city and the university cooperate to provide cultural activities including a symphony and theatrical productions.

WESTERN STATE COLLEGE OF COLORADO   *(I-8)*
Gunnison, Colorado 81230
Tel: (303) 943-2119; (800) 876-5309; Fax: (303) 943-7069

Description: Western State College of Colorado is the state's oldest institution of higher learning west of the Continental Divide. It was established in 1911 as a two-year institution and in 1923 was authorized to confer the bachelor's degree. A major effort is now underway to concentrate the college's resources on providing "an exemplary liberal arts undergraduate education," combining the arts and sciences with professional preparation. Academic majors are available in 22 different disciplines. The calendar system is comprised of alternating 12-week and 8-week sessions. The first session begins in mid-September. Benefits include: flexibilty in scheduling classes, more concentrated and in-depth studies, opportunity to use innovative teaching methods, and opportunity to finish course of study in three years by attending classes year-round. Students who wish to finish in four years would attend two 12-week seesions and one 8-week session per year. Western State College is accredited by the North Central Association of Colleges and Schools, the National Council for Accreditation of Teacher Education, the Colorado State Board of Accountancy, the Colorado Department of Education, and the National Association of Schools of Music. Enrollment includes 2,500 full-time and 150 part-time students. A faculty of 140 provides a faculty-student ratio of 1-20.

Entrance Requirements: High school graduates with 2.5 GPA or rank in the upper two-thirds of the graduating class; ACT minimum score 20 or SAT 820; majority of high school units should be chosen from the academic fields of English, foreign languages, mathematics, science, and social studies; early application advised; CLEP and other competency tests available; April 15 is equal consideration date; admissions decisions are made on a rolling basis until April 15; $25 application fee.

Costs Per Year: $1,915 tuition; $6,435 out-of-state; $4,088 room and board; $537 student fees.

Collegiate Environment: Located in the heart of Colorado's Rocky Mountains at an elevation of 7,735 feet above sea level, the campus includes 42 buildings on 132 landscaped acres, plus 280 adjoining undeveloped acres and the 1,200 acres of "W" Mountain located across the valley. The library contains 250,000 volumes, in addition to more than one-half million government documents, microforms, and audio-visual materials and 825 carefully selected periodicals. Computerized access to all local and regional holdings is available. Although upper-class students are free to find housing in the community residence halls accomodate 1,556 students. Students come from 48 states and about 12 other countries, with about 65% from Colorado. 82% of applicants are accepted. Almost all the students are full-time residents. Intercollegiate and intramural sports and about 60 clubs and organizations offer activities for all interests. Campus media operated by the students include a newspaper, a yearbook, a literary magazine, an FM radio station and a student-run radio station.

Community Environment: Gunnison is a community with a population of about 7,000. Western State students are welcome to participate in all kinds of cultural, recreational, and religious activities offered by the community. The summer climate and the natural beauties of the region annually attract millions of tourists. Winter sports enthusiasts enjoy unexcelled skiing at Crested Butte Mountain Resort and Monarch Ski Area and ice fishing on Colorado's Blue Mesa Resevoir, which is located just 9 miles from the campus.

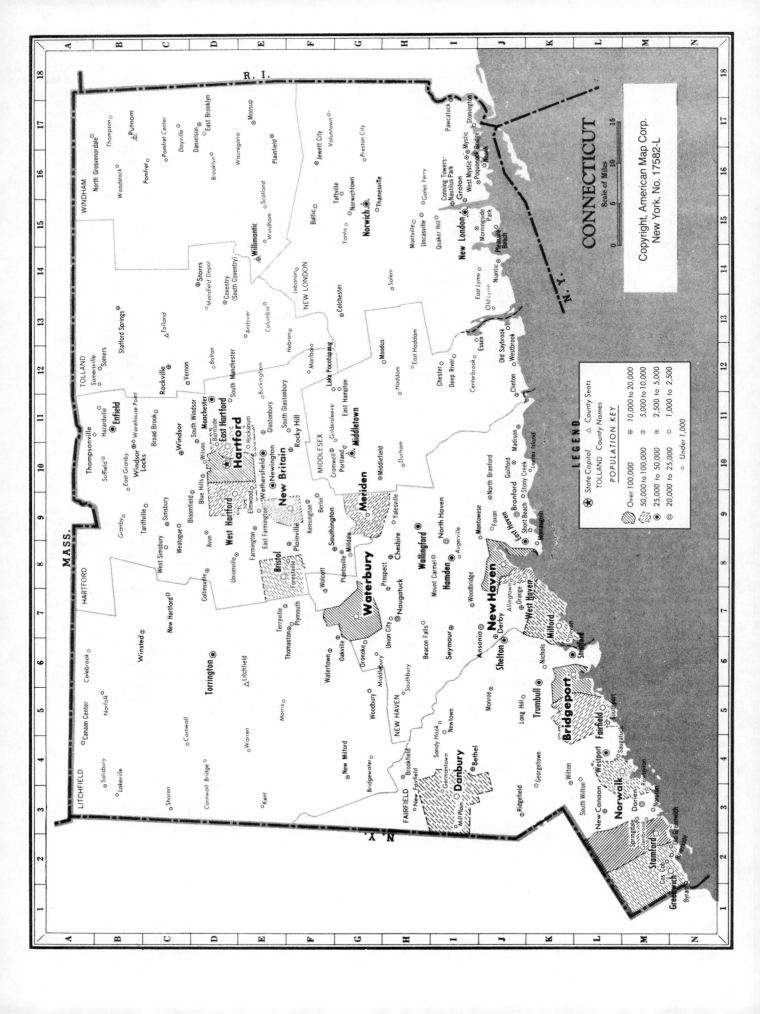

CONNECTICUT

ALBERTUS MAGNUS COLLEGE *(J-8)*
700 Prospect Street
New Haven, Connecticut 06511-1189
Tel: (203) 773-8501; (800) 578-9160; Admissions: (203) 773-8501;
Fax: (203) 773-9539

Description: This privately supported liberal arts college was established in New England under Roman Catholic, Dominican auspices. It was founded in 1925 by the Dominican Sisters of Saint Mary of the Springs and is accredited by the New England Association of Schools and Colleges. The school operates on the trimester calendar system. Enrollment is 50 full-time and 30 part-time and 600 evening students. A faculty of 68 full-time and 35 part-time provides a faculty-student ratio of 1-12. The college grants the Bachelor of Arts, Bachelor of Fine Arts, Associate of Arts degrees, Bachelor of Science, and Master of Arts in Liberal Studies.

Entrance Requirements: Accredited high school graduation with 16 units including 4 English, 3 mathematics, 2 laboratory science, 2 foreign language, 2 social science, (1 U.S. History), and 3 electives; SAT or ACT required; two recommendations from 1 counselor and 1 teacher required; early admission, rolling admission, delayed admission, midyear admission and advanced placement plans available; $35 application fee.

Costs Per Year: $11,980 tuition; $5,500 room and board, $150 student fees.

Collegiate Environment: The college is located on Prospect Hill on the outskirts of New Haven and has both an urban and suburban setting. The 55-acre campus encompasses several former private estates, and dormitory facilities are available for 400 women and men. The library contains 100,000 volumes, 410 periodicals, and numerous microforms and sound recordings. 80% of those who apply for admission are accepted, including midyear students. 45% of the freshmen graduated in the top fifth of their high school class; 50% ranked in the top quarter. The average SAT scores of the entering freshman class were 460 verbal and 440 math. Scholarships are available and 90% of the student body receives some form of financial aid. The college awarded 120 Bachelor degrees, 3 Bachelor of Fine Arts, and 23 Associate degrees to the recent graduating class.

Community Environment: See Yale University.

CAPITAL COMMUNITY TECHNICAL COLLEGE *(D-10)*
61 Woodland Street
Hartford, Connecticut 06105
Tel: (203) 520-7800

Description: This community-technical college is the result of the 1992 merger between Greater Hartford Community College and Hartford State Technical College. Enrollment includes 2,965 full-time and part-time students. The semester system is used with two summer sessions and programs of study include liberal arts, early childhood education, nursing, secretarial science, social services, business administration; many courses are designed for transfer to 4-year colleges. The school is accredited by the New England Association of Schools and Colleges and grants Certificates and Associate degrees. The faculty consists of 180 full-time and approximately 50 part-time instructors.

Entrance Requirements: Open enrollment policy; accredited high school graduation or equivalent; rolling admission. $10 application fee.

Costs Per Year: $47 per credit hour, $29 student fees.

Collegiate Environment: The college serves the large metropolitan area of the state's capital city. The library contains 45,000 volumes, 1,000 pamphlets, and 275 periodicals. 98% of the applicants are accepted, including midyear students. Approximately 47% of the current student body receive some form of financial assistance.

Community Environment: See Trinity College

CENTRAL CONNECTICUT STATE UNIVERSITY *(F-9)*
1615 Stanley Street
New Britain, Connecticut 06050
Tel: (203) 832-3200; Admissions: (203) 832-2278; Fax: (203) 832-2522

Description: This university was founded in 1849 as New Britain Normal School, and is the oldest of Connecticut's publicly supported institutions of higher learning. In 1947, it became the first teachers college in New England to be accredited by the New England Association of Schools and Colleges. It operates on the semester system and offers two summer sessions. Enrollment includes 6,415 full-time and 5,544 part-time undergraduates, and 2,307 graduate students. A faculty of 381 full-time and 353 part-time provides an faculty-student ratio of 1-17.

Entrance Requirements: Accredited high school graduation or equivalency certificate with completion of 16 units including 4 English, 3 mathematics, 2 science, 2 foreign language, and 2 social science; SAT scores range from 900-1100; $20 application fee; rolling admission and advanced placement plans available.

Costs Per Year: $3,270 tuition and fees; $8,362 out-of-state; $4,872 room and board.

Collegiate Environment: Thirty-six buildings on 176 acres comprise the campus. The library contains 534,224 volumes and 430,567 microforms. Coed dormitory facilities are available for 1,813 students. 63% of students applying for admission are accepted, including midyear students. Financial assistance is available and more than 40% of the current students receive aid.

Community Environment: Population 75,000. Known as the "Hardware City of the World," New Britain is located nine miles southwest of Hartford. Sleigh bells were the first items manufactured here. Now there are 250 manufacturing establishments and over 600 retail outlets. Access to New York City is by train, and there is commercial air service nearby. New Britain has 44 churches of major denominations, outstanding hospital facilities and is now undertaking urban renewal projects. Points of interest are the New Britain Institute and Art Museum, memorial monuments, municipal golf course and the parks.

CONNECTICUT COLLEGE *(I-15)*
Mohegan Avenue
New London, Connecticut 06320
Tel: (203) 447-1911; Admissions: (203) 439-2200; Fax: (203) 439-4301

Description: Connecticut College is a coeducational institution committed to the liberal arts. It is accredited by the New England Association of Schools and Colleges. Committed to fostering an independent student body, students participate in institutional governance and in the strong honor code. Rigorous academic standards, close working relationships with faculty, and the opportunity to do in-depth study in a broad range of disciplines and activities challenge students to achieve their full intellectual potential. The college operates on the semester system. Enrollment includes 1,604 full-time and 205 part-time undergraduates and 54 graduate students. A faculty of 156 full-time and 13 adjunct provides a faculty-student ratio of 1-11.

Entrance Requirements: Accredited high school graduation; completion of a college-preparatory program including 4 English, 3 foreign language (or 2 years each of 2 foreign languages), 3 mathematics, 2 science, 2 social science; SAT I optional; three Achievement Tests or ACT required; GRE for graduate students; $35 application fee; early admission, early decision and advanced placement plans available; $45 application fee.

Costs Per Year: $18,740 tuition; room and board $6,300.

Collegiate Environment: The 702-acre campus, with 89 buildings, is located in a setting of great natural beauty. Dormitory facilities are available for all undergraduates, and the library contains 456,700 volumes, 293,293 pamphlets, 2,161 periodicals, 259,101 microforms and 15,868 sound recordings.

Community Environment: On the west bank of the Thames River, three miles from Long Island Sound, known historically as "The Whaling City." New London is an maritime center located midway between Boston and New York. It is a popular summer resort. Ocean Beach Park, a fifty-acre tract, borders a half-mile-long beach and provides recreational facilities. New London is the location of the annual Yale-Harvard Crew Races held each June.

EASTERN CONNECTICUT STATE UNIVERSITY   *(E-14)*
Hurley Hall
Willimantic, Connecticut 06226
Tel: (203) 465-5286; Fax: (203) 465-4382

Description: The publicly supported, coeducational university for liberal arts and sciences and professional studies is accredited by the New England Association of Schools and Colleges. The University was founded in 1889 for the education of elementary school teachers and now offers strong programs in the liberal arts and sciences, as well as professional programs in business administration, communications, and teacher education. All programs provide practicums and internships. The university operates on the semester system and offers three summer sessions. Enrollment includes 2,811 full-time and 1,480 part-time students. A faculty of 128 full-time and 156 part-time gives a faculty-student ratio of 1-19. Programs of study lead to the Associate, Bachelor, or Master degree. Academic cooperative programs are available with the University of Connecticut and Southern Connecticut State University. Army and Air Force ROTC are available at the University of Connecticut.

Entrance Requirements: Graduation from an accredited high school with rank in upper 50% or equivalency, with completion of 16 units, including 4 English, 3 mathematics, 2 science, 2 social science, and 2 foreign language; SAT required; rolling admission, early admission, delayed admission, and advanced placement plans available; $20 application fee.

Costs Per Year: $1,842 tuition; $5,962 out-of-state; $4,316 room and board; $1,242 student fees; $2,050 student fees for out-of-state residents.

Collegiate Environment: The campus is located on 174 acres in an attractive residential section of the city of Willimantic. The library contains more than 150,000 volumes; campus residence facilities are available for 1,522 students. 63% of the students applying for admission are accepted, including midyear students. Financial aid is available and approximately 60% of current students receive aid.

Community Environment: Located 28 miles from Hartford and New London and halfway between Boston and New York, Willimantic, with a population of approximately 22,000, is primarily a retail and service center for eastern Connecticut. Bus service connects the city with major transportation facilities in Hartford, Providence, and New York. Willimantic has excellent health and hospital services and recreational facilities include the Willimantic Golf Course and nearby lakes and state parks.

FAIRFIELD UNIVERSITY   *(I-5)*
North Benson Road
Fairfield, Connecticut 06430-5195
Tel: (203) 254-4100; Fax: (203) 254-4199

Description: This privately supported, coeducational Roman Catholic liberal arts college was established by the Jesuits in 1942. It welcomes all persons regardless of race, color or creed who share its vision, respect its process, and wish to participate in its community. The university is accredited by the New England Association of Schools and Colleges. It operates on the semester system and offers one summer session. Enrollment is 2,900 full-time and 1,200 part-time undergraduates, and 800 graduate students. A faculty of 200 full-time and 130 part-time gives a faculty-student ratio of 1-16.

Academic cooperative programs are available with the University of Connecticut, University of Bridgeport, Sacred Heart, and New York University Dental School.

Entrance Requirements: Accredited high school graduation with rank in upper 20%; completion of 15 units including 4 English, 1 social studies, 3 math, 2 foreign language, and 1 lab science; SAT and three Achievement Tests required; early admission, early decision, delayed admission, midyear admission, and advanced placement plans available; $40 application fee.

Costs Per Year: $15,000 tuition; $6,200 room and board; $310 student fees; $1,500 average additional expenses.

Collegiate Environment: 30 buildings on 200 acres comprise the campus, located five miles west of Bridgeport. The library contains 310,000 volumes. Dormitories accommodate 2,240 students. An average of 70% of applications are accepted. The average scores of entering freshmen were SAT 502 verbal, 562 math. 89% of the freshman class returned to the campus for a second year. Special programs are offered for the culturally disadvantaged. Financial aid is available, and 65% of the current students receive some form of assistance. The college awarded 781 Bachelor and 119 Master degrees and 19 Certificates of Advanced Study degrees during a recent academic year. About 19% of the senior class continued on to graduate schools. A special feature of the campus is the new $7.5 million Center for the Arts.

Community Environment: Population 60,000. Fairfield is a suburban area one hour north of New York City on the Long Island Sound. The climate is temperate. The Metro-North New Haven branch serves the area, as well as the Connecticut Turnpike and Merritt Parkway. Community facilities include libraries, churches and shopping areas. Part-time employment opportunities are available. Beaches are nearby for water sports; other sports include bowling and tennis. A special annual event is the Dogwood Festival.

GATEWAY COMMUNITY TECHNICAL COLLEGE   *(J-8)*
60 Sargent Drive
New Haven, Connecticut 06511
Tel: (203) 789-7043; Fax: (203) 777-8415

Description: The publicly supported coeducational community college was founded in 1968. It is accredited by the New England Association of Schools and Colleges and operates on the semester system with three limited summers sessions. The college will accept up to 45 credit hours in correspondence courses but 15 hours must be earned in residence to graduate. The college offers The Associate in Applied Sciences, and Certificates, and has a continuing education program. Enrollment includes 5,213 students. A faculty of 100 gives a faculty-student ratio of 1-52.

Entrance Requirements: High school graduate or equivalent; open enrollment; life experience credits given and CLEP accepted. $10 application fee.

Costs Per Year: $1,646 tuition; $4,622 tuition for out-of-state residents. $158 student fees.

Collegiate Environment: The Long Wharf campus is located on 5 acres in New Haven, accessible by bus, rail, and air transportation. The North Haven Campus is located in a suburban area and is also accessible by bus and shuttle. The library has holdings of 35,829 books, periodicals, microforms, and audiovisual materials. Additional facilities are available in the New Haven area.

Community Environment: See Yale University.

Branch Campuses: Long Wharf Campus, 60 Sargent Drive, New Haven, CT, 06511; North Haven Campus, 88 Bassett Road, North Haven, CT 06473, tel: (203) 234-3343.

HARTFORD GRADUATE CENTER   *(D-10)*
275 Windsor Street
Hartford, Connecticut 06120-2991
Tel: (203) 548-2400; (800) 433-4723; Admissions: (203) 548-2420; Fax: (203) 548-7823

Description: The Hartford Graduate Center, a privately supported, coeducational, graduate school was established in 1955 by the Rensselaer Polytechnic Institute of Troy, New York. In 1975, HGC became an independent, Connecticut-chartered institution which offers Rensselaer's Master's degrees in Management, Business Administration, Computer Science, Electrical Engineering, Mechanical Engineering, Engineering Science, and Metallurgy. The Center awards in its own name the Master of Science in Management, Health Care Management, and Biomedical Engineering. In recent years the Center has expanded its course offerings to include a wide range of professional development programs customized to meet the requirements of the employed professional in business and industry. These short-term, intensive programs are presented by the Professional Development Center of The Hartford Graduate Center. Courses leading to Master's degrees in Computer Science, Management, Electrical and Mechanical Engineering are also offered in Groton, Connecticut. The total enrollment at both locations is 1,333 men and 628 women. Faculty includes 32 full-time and 75 part-time members. The semester system is used with one summer session. The Center is an active participant in the Hartford Consortium for Higher Education, and offers, jointly with Trinity College a cooperative Bachelors-Master's degree in engineering. The Hartford Graduate Center is fully accredited by the New England Association of Schools and Colleges and the Board of Governors for Higher Education of the State of Connecticut.

Entrance Requirements: The Center offers a competitive admissions process. A Bachelor's degree from an accredited undergraduate institution is required. Two letters of reference, and official transcripts of all prior academic work must be presented. Degree status is awarded to college graduates if required documents indicate ability to undertake a graduate program; non-matriculated status is given to college graduates who may not meet all the requirements but clearly possess academic promise to begin graduate study on a course by course basis. Rolling admissions and midyear admission plans available; $25 application fee.

Costs Per Year: $6,375 ($425/credit) tuition.

Collegiate Environment: The Center's eight-level building includes classrooms, research laboratories, meeting rooms, administrative offices, a library of 30,000 volumes, 535 periodicals, a collection of CD-ROMs in management and the sciences, an on-line, shared regional network, and access to Internet. Attached to this structure is a three-level building designed for continuing education, containing a special lecture and management case study hall, and seminar rooms. In addition, a three-story parking garage provides enclosed parking for approximately 450 cars. 75% of applicants are accepted. Scholarships are available. 5% of the students receive some form of financial aid. The center is approved for the training of veterans.

Community Environment: See Trinity College.

Branch Campuses: Groton, Connecticut.

HOLY APOSTLES COLLEGE   (F-10)
33 Prospect Hill Road
Cromwell, Connecticut 06417
Tel: (203) 632-3000; (800) 330-7272; Admissions: (203) 632-3030; Fax: (203) 632-0176

Description: Founded in 1957, the college is a privately supported theological seminary, whose purposes include the education of mature men for the priesthood of the Roman Catholic Church, as well as preparation of lay men and women for the liberal arts degree. It is accredited by the New England Association of Schools and Colleges. The seminary grants the Associate, Bachelor, and Master's degrees. It operates on the semester system and offers two summer sessions. Enrollment includes 115 students. A faculty of 24 provides a faculty-student ratio of 1-5.

Entrance Requirements: High school graduation or equivalent with completion of 15 units; open enrollment policy; proper motivation for candidates seeking the priesthood; personal interview required; rolling admission, midyear admission plans available. $50 application fee.

Costs Per Year: $4,200 tuition; $6,150 room and board; $100 student fees.

Collegiate Environment: The institution is conducted by the Society of the Missionaries of the Holy Apostles and offers the graduates the freedom to enter any diocese, religious community or missionary society of their choice. 80% of the students who apply are accepted. Scholarships are available and 25% of the students receive some form of financial. The library contains 53,000 volumes, and living facilities are available for 120 men.

Community Environment: Population 10,400. Cromwell is located near the center of Connecticut, 10 miles south of Hartford and 3 miles north of Middletown, with super highways leading to most corners of the state; it is primarily a residential town. The greenhouse area is one of the largest in the world. Cromwell is known as Rose Town because of the large number of roses grown in the greenhouses. The cultural facilities include churches, library and homes of historical interest.

HOUSATONIC COMMUNITY TECHNICAL COLLEGE
(K-6)
510 Barnum Avenue
Bridgeport, Connecticut 06608
Tel: (203) 579-6400; Admissions: (203) 579-6475; Fax: (203) 579-6993

Description: The publicly supported coeducational community college was established in 1966 and is accredited by the New England Association of Schools and Colleges. The college offers transfer programs and career programs in technical and semi-technical professions, and grants the Associate degree. The semester system is used with three summer sessions and evening classes available. Enrollment includes 476 full-time and 2,379 part-time students. The faculty is comprised of 43 full-time and 92 part-time members.

Entrance Requirements: Open enrollment policy; placement exam required; non-high school graduates considered; midyear admission and advanced placement plans available; $10 application fee.

Costs Per Year: $1,488 tuition; $4,464 out-of-state tuition; $158 student fees.

Collegiate Environment: All students applying for admission who meet minimum requirements are accepted. The library contains 29,000 volumes, 300 periodicals, 22,000 microforms, 10,588 audiovisual materials. Financial aid is available, and 50% of the current student body receives some form of assistance. The college offers 17 different Associate degree programs.

Community Environment: See University of Bridgeport

MANCHESTER COMMUNITY TECHNICAL COLLEGE
(D-11)
60 Bidwell Street
Manchester, Connecticut 06040
Tel: (203) 647-6000

Description: This publicly supported, coeducational junior college opened in 1963 and moved to its present campus in 1967. Enrollment recently included 6,673 full-time and part-time students. The faculty consists of 102 full-time and 155 part-time members. The college offers university parallel and vocational programs and grants the Associate degree. The college is accredited by the New England Association of Schools and Colleges. The semester system is used with one summer session and a 3-week winter intersession.

Entrance Requirements: Open enrollment policy; high school graduation or equivalent; non-high school graduates considered; early admission, and advanced placement plans available; $10 application fee.

Costs Per Year: $516 per semester, nonresident $1,680 per semester tuition; $79 student fees.

Collegiate Environment: Located on 160-acres, the college facilities consist of 12 buildings. The library contains 54,000 volumes and 230 periodicals. All applicants meeting the requirements are accepted, including midyear students, except in the Allied Health programs which have selective admissions. Financial aid is available and approximately 65% of the current student body receives some form of assistance.

Community Environment: Population 48,000. A suburban community, located 8 miles away from Hartford, served by bus and highway; temperate climate. Cultural facilities include libraries, Junior Museum, many churches and YMCA; Manchester also has large shopping centers plus a downtown Main Street; a hospital with Class A rating, community health and guidance organizations, and many civic and service groups. Part time work is available for students.

MIDDLESEX COMMUNITY TECHNICAL COLLEGE
(G-10)
100 Training Hill Road
Middletown, Connecticut 06457
Tel: (203) 343-5719; Fax: (203) 344-7488

Description: This publicly supported, coeducational junior college was founded in 1966. The college operates on the semester system and offers two summer sessions. Enrollment is 761 full-time and 2,249 part-time students. The faculty consists of 50 full-time and 100 part-time instructors. The college offers university-transfer and vocational programs and grants the Associate degree. It is fully accredited by the New England Association of Schools and Colleges.

Entrance Requirements: Open enrollment policy; high school graduation or equivalent; early admission, delayed admission, rolling admission and advanced placement plans available; $10 application fee.

Costs Per Year: $1,488 tuition; $4,464 out-of-state; $158 student fees.

Collegiate Environment: The college occupies a 38-acre campus about 1 1/2 miles from downtown Middletown. The library contains more than 43,000 volumes and 300 periodicals. The college provides ample student parking and is served by the municipal bus route, which stops at the campus twice each hour. The college has also recently completed construction of an 1,800-square-foot child care facility on campus. Almost all of the students who apply are accepted. Financial aid is available, and 345% of the current student body receives some form of assistance.

Community Environment: See Wesleyan University.

MITCHELL COLLEGE   *(I-15)*
437 Pequot Avenue
New London, Connecticut 06320
Tel: (203) 443-2811; (800) 443-2811; Fax: (203) 444-1209

Description: The privately supported, coeducational junior college is accredited by the New England Association of Schools and Colleges. Founded in 1938, the college offers day, evening, and summer programs to part-time and full-time students. Recently the college enrolled 212 men and 188 women full-time and 135 men and 185 women part-time. A faculty of 25 full-time and 47 part-time gives a ratio of 1-15. The college offers university-parallel, vocational, and general programs, and grants the Associate degree. The semester system is used and one summer session is offered.

Entrance Requirements: High school graduation or equivalent; personal interview required; non-high school graduates considered; early admission, early decision, rolling admission, delayed admission, advanced placement plans available; $30 application fee.

Costs Per Year: $11,000 tuition; $5,200 room and board; $500 student fees.

Collegiate Environment: The campus lies on the west bank of the Thames River, about a quarter of a mile from Long Island Sound. Dormitory facilities are available for 260 men and 223 women and the library contains 49,100 volumes, 150 periodicals, and 1,800 recordings. Approximately 70% of the students applying for admission are accepted. Financial assistance is available. Out of 200 scholarships, 120 for freshmen; 60% of the students receive financial aid.

Community Environment: See Connecticut College

NAUGATUCK VALLEY COMMUNITY TECHNICAL COLLEGE   *(G-7)*
750 Chase Parkway
Waterbury, Connecticut 06708-3809
Tel: (203) 575-8078; Admissions: (203) 575-8078; Fax: (203) 596-8766

Description: Naugatuck Valley Community Technical College is the result of the 1992 winter merger between Mattatuck Community College and Waterbury State Technical College. It is fully accredited by the New England Association of Schools and Colleges and grants certificate and associate degrees. It operates on the semester system with one summer session. Current enrollment includes 899 men, 956 women full-time and 1,515 men and 2,297 women part-time.

Entrance Requirements: Open enrollment. High school diploma or GED required. Advanced placement plan available.

Costs Per Year: $1,368 resident tuition; $4,440 nonresident tuition, plus $152 fees.

Collegiate Environment: The campus includes a library of 35,000 volumes.

Community Environment: See Teikyo Post University.

NORTHWESTERN CONNECTICUT COMMUNITY TECHNICAL COLLEGE   *(C-7)*
Park Place
Winsted, Connecticut 06098
Tel: (203) 738-6329; Fax: (203) 379-4465

Description: This publicly supported, coeducational junior college was founded in 1965. The college is accredited by the New England Association of Schools and Colleges and offers university-parallel and professional and vocational programs. The college operates on the semester system with one summer session and grants the Associate degree. Enrollment includes 442 full-time and 1,661 part-time students. A faculty of 39 full-time and 55 part-time gives a faculty-student ratio of 1-12.

Entrance Requirements: Open enrollment policy; high school graduation or equivalent; delayed admission, rolling admission, midyear admission and advanced placement plans available; $10 application fee.

Costs Per Year: $1,488 tuition; $4,440 out-of-state; $152 student fees.

Collegiate Environment: The campus has 7 buildings on 5 acres. The library contains 50,000 volumes and 249 periodicals. All students applying for admission are accepted including midyear students. Financial aid is available. Special programs include a Center for Career Education of the Deaf, which helps to mainstream all hearing-impaired students into the school environment. This program includes all services such as interpreters, note takers, counseling, and speech therapy.

Community Environment: Population 11,400. Winsted is a suburban community with a temperate climate. It has excellent shopping areas, library, churches, and a YMCA. Airport facilities are 30 miles away, but easy to reach. Recreational facilities are good, including excellent fishing in surrounding areas, boating on Highland Lake, and winter sports at Sundown ski area about three miles southeast.

NORWALK COMMUNITY TECHNICAL COLLEGE   *(L-4)*
188 Richards Avenue
Norwalk, Connecticut 06854-1655
Tel: (203) 857-7000; Admissions: (203) 857-7060; Fax: (203) 857-3335

Description: The publicly supported, coeducational community and technical college is accredited by the New England Association of Schools and Colleges. The college offers technical, career, and liberal arts programs leading to the Associate degree and a one-year certificate program in career fields as well as preparatory programs for technologies. It operates on the semester system and offers three summer sessions. Enrollment includes 1,139 full-time and 4,105 part-time students. A faculty of 50 full-time and 34 part-time gives a faculty-student ratio of 1-22.

Entrance Requirements: College administered "no fee" placement tests in algebra, writing and reading. High school graduation; for technical programs: 3 years in academic math, 2 in algebra, 1 in geometry, 1 lab sciences (either physics or chemistry); SAT recommended; midyear admission and rolling admission plans available; $10 application fee.

Costs Per Year: $1,650 resident tuition and fees; $4,622 out-of-state.

Collegiate Environment: The campus consists of 2 buildings on 17 acres. The library contains 17,000 volumes in addition to pamphlets, 1,200 periodicals and 100 microforms. The college accepts 100% of the students who apply for admission, and students may enroll at midyear. Financial aid is available, and 40% of the current student body receives some form of assistance.

Community Environment: Norwalk is a suburban community located on Long Island Sound and is 50 minutes by rail from Grand Central Station in New York City. Community facilities include major shopping areas, libraries, churches, symphony orchestra, and the Silvermine Guild Artists.

QUINEBAUG VALLEY COMMUNITY-TECHNICAL COLLEGE   *(D-17)*
742 Upper Maple Street
Danielson, Connecticut 06239
Tel: (203) 774-1130; Fax: (203) 774-7768

Description: Founded in 1971, this state supported liberal arts and vocational college is accredited by the New England Association of Schools and Colleges. It offers career oriented and liberal arts programs. It awards certificates and the Associate degree. It operates on the semester system and offers a summer session. Enrollment includes 303 male and 863 female students. Full-time faculty members number 17, part-time faculty approximates 40, resulting in a teacher-student ratio of 1-22.

Entrance Requirements: High school graduation or equivalent; open enrollment policy; early admission, delayed admission, and advanced placement plans available; $10 application fee.

Costs Per Year: $1,488 tuition state residents; $4,464 tuition out-of-state; NEBHE tuition $2,232; $158 student fees.

Collegiate Environment: All applicants are accepted (to maximum space available). Credits allowed for certain courses by prior testing. Scholarships are available. The college is housed in a new campus building on Maple Street in Danielson. The library contains 26,000 volumes and 200 periodicals. Administered and housed by the college is the government document depository collection.

Community Environment: Population, 4,580. Located in Northeastern Connecticut, Danielson is in the midst of a semi-rural area which is supported by poultry and dairy industries. Outdoor recreational possibilities abound. The Connecticut turnpike provides easy access to New London, Old Mystic, Massachusetts and Rhode Island.

Branch Campuses: QVCTC Willimantic Center, 1320 Main St., Willimantic, CT 06226, Delia Berlin, Director

QUINNIPIAC COLLEGE   *(I-8)*
Mt. Carmel Avenue
Hamden, Connecticut 06518
Tel: (203) 281-8600; (800) 462-1944; Fax: (203) 281-8906

Description: The privately supported, coeducational professional and liberal arts college It is fully accredited by the New England Association of Schools and Colleges. Founded in 1929, the college now includes programs toward the degrees Bachelor of Arts, Bachelor of Science, Master in Professional Studies, Master of Science, Master of Business Administration, Master of Health Science, Master of Arts in Teaching, and Juris Doctor. It operates on the semester system and offers two summer sessions. Enrollment includes 3,000 full-time and 1,100 part-time undergraduates and 500 graduate students. A faculty of 208 full-time and 125 part-time gives a faculty-student ratio of 1-15. Academic cooperative plans are available with the University of New Haven and Albertus Magnus.

Entrance Requirements: High school graduation or equivalent with rank in upper 50%; completion of 16 units including 4 English, 3 mathematics, 2 sciences, 3 social studies; SAT or ACT required; SAT minimum 450V, 450M; early admission, delayed admission and advanced placement plans available; $40 application fee.

Costs Per Year: $12,030 tuition; $6,140 room and board; $590 student fees.

Collegiate Environment: 31 buildings on 180 acres comprise the campus, which is located nine miles from New Haven. The library contains 180,000 volumes, and numerous pamphlets, periodicals, microforms and recordings. Dormitory accommodations are available for 2,300 students. 65% of the applicants are accepted. Scholarships vary, and 65% of the students receive financial aid.

Community Environment: Hamden town population is 55,000. Campus is located at base of Sleeping Giant State Park.

SACRED HEART UNIVERSITY   *(L-6)*
5151 Park Avenue
Fairfield, Connecticut 06432-1000
Tel: (203) 371-7999; Admissions: (203) 371-7880; Fax: (203) 371-7889

Description: Sacred Heart University is a privately supported, Cahtolic, coeducational, liberal arts university which was founded in

1963. It is accredited by the New England Association of Schools and Colleges, the American Bar Association, the Council on Social Work Education, and the National League for Nursing. The university grants 28 Bachelor degree programs and 7 Master's degrees in the health sciences, liberal arts and sciences, business and education fields. 9 new academic programs have been added. The university operates on the semester system and offers two summer sessions. Full-time undergraduate enrollment has grown by 38% in the past five years. Enrollment includes 1,912 full-time and 1,931 part-time undergraduates and 1,610 graduate students. A faculty of 117 full-time and 241 part-time yields an overall faculty-student ratio of 1-14. The university offers courses at satellite campuses in Stamford, Connecticut; Derby, Connecticut, Lisbon, Connecticut as well as Luxembourg in Europe.

Entrance Requirements: High school graduation or equivalent; completion of 16 academic units; including 4 English, 2 mathematics, 2 social science, 1 science; SAT required; GRE required for graduate program; non-high school graduates considered; rolling admission, early admission, midyear admission and advanced placement plans available; $30 application fee; personal interview highly recommended.

Costs Per Year: $11,625 tuition; $6,065 room and board; $380 student fees.

Collegiate Environment: The 56-acre suburban campus includes six coeducational residence halls which accommodate 1,900 students and a 1.2 million synthetic-surfaced athletic field and track and six tennis courts. Classrooms, laboratories and offices have been renovated and expanded. A new University Learning Center features peer and professional tutoring in a state-of-the-art facility. The language Laboratory has been renovated into a multi-media resource area. The University Library presently holds 160,500 books, 1,311 periodicals and subscriptions, 13,845 microfilm reels and provides access to 16 CD-ROM databases and 6 on-line databases. Entering first-year students are assigned a portable computer. Students have access to local, national and international networks through classrooms, laboratories and all residence hall rooms. Sixteen new NCAA Division II athletic teams have been introduced including men's and women's varsity crew, equestrian, ice hockey, lacrosse, tennis and track and field. 83% of applicants are accepted. The average scores of the entering freshman class are SAT 440 verbal, 460 math. Scholarships are available and 70% of the students receive some form of financial aid.

Community Environment: Sacred Heart University is located in coastal Fairfield, Connecticut, one hour northeast of New York City. Numerous Fortune 500 companies are headquartered in Fairfield County providing students with unique opportunities for outside learning and hands-on experience. The campus is less than a mile from one of the state's major shopping malls. Beaches, restaurants, stores, movies, theaters and all accessible as are major transportation centers.

SAINT JOSEPH COLLEGE   *(D-9)*
1678 Asylum Avenue
West Hartford, Connecticut 06117
Tel: (203) 232-4571; Fax: (203) 233-5695

Description: Founded in 1932, Saint Joseph College is Connecticut's only four-year college for women. Sponsored by the Sisters of Mercy of Connecticut, this private, independent, nonprofit institution has an enrollment of 813 women in the traditional undergraduate college, 474 women and men in the undergraduate McAuley Weekend College, and 720 women and men in the graduate division. A faculty of 75 full-time and 80 part-time gives an undergraduate faculty-student ratio of 1-12. the College has been nationally recognized for its philosophy of bonding a strong liberal arts curriculum with professional education opportunities: internships, clinical placements, study abroad, and other practicum experiences. The traditional college offers over 30 majors; open cross registration with colleges in the Hartford Consortium for Higher Education, (Trinity College, University of Hartford, and the two-year Hartford College for Women, etc.) is available. The coeducational McAuley Weekend College Program leads to a BS in Business Adminstration (Accounting or Management) or a BA in American Studies, social work, and BS in nursing. Teacher certification is also available through the weekend college. The Center for Graduate Studies offers MA, MS, and CAGS degrees. The College operates on the semester system and offers two summer sessions.

Entrance Requirements: High school graduation; completion of 16 academic units; SAT or ACT required; letter of recommendation required; interview strongly recommended for freshmen, required for transfer students; early admission, rolling admission, early decision, and advanced placement plans available; $25 application fee.

Costs Per Year: $11,000 tuition; $4,155-$4,380 room and board.

Collegiate Environment: The campus is situated on 84 suburban acres. Residence halls accommodate 333 women; the library contains over 115,000 volumes and 736 periodicals, and provides access to 1.3 million volumes in the libraries of the the Hartford Consortium for Higher Education. Facilities include computer (VAX) and microcomputer (Apple, ATT, IBM) labs, and computer technology is integrated in many majors. There are two laboratory schools on campus: the School for Young Children and the Gengras Center for Special Education. There is an Art Study Gallery with rotating college-owned art collections. An all-weather track and tennis courts are available. 74% of applicants are accepted.

Community Environment: The campus is located in a suburban community within 5 miles of Hartford, the capital of Connecticut. Known as the Insurance City, Hartford offers multiple internship and employment possibilities and diverse attractions such as ballet, opera, theater, symphony, museums, historic landmarks, sporting events, shopping, churches, and hospitals. Many volunteer opportunities are also available.

SAINT THOMAS SEMINARY *(D-9)*
467 Bloomfield Avenue
Bloomfield, Connecticut 06002
Tel: (203) 242-5573; Fax: (203) 242-4886

Description: This privately supported, Roman Catholic resident college for men is operates on the semester system. The purpose of this college is to prepare young men for study for the Roman Catholic priesthood. The degree is awarded from one of three local universities in which the student is matriculated. The graduate of St. Thomas Seminary spends 4 years of further study in advanced or major seminaries before ordination to the priesthood. Enrollment is 10 full-time students. A faculty of 2 full-time and 3 part-time gives a ratio of 1-2.

Entrance Requirements: High school graduation with 16 college-preparatory units including 4 English, 3 mathematics, 2 science, 2 social science, 4 foreign language; SAT required, minimum score: 400M; 400V; candidates are admitted from the Archdiocese of Hartford and from the Diocese of Norwich; if space is available, men from other dioceses in the East are enrolled; rolling admission, delayed admission, early decision, early admission, midyear admission and advanced placement plans available.

Costs Per Year: $2,000 tuition; $2,600 out-of-state tuition; $700 room and board; $100 student fees.

Collegiate Environment: The campus has three buildings on 167 acres and the library contains 30,000 volumes. There are two dormitories with room for 15 men. The college accepts 60% of those who apply for admission.

Community Environment: Population 7,000. Bloomfield adjoins West Hartford. All modes of transportation serve the area. Cultural and recreational facilities are in greater Hartford. See also Trinity College for information on Hartford.

SOUTHERN CONNECTICUT STATE UNIVERSITY *(J-8)*
501 Crescent Street
New Haven, Connecticut 06515
Tel: (203) 392-5200; Admissions: (203) 392-5644

Description: This publicly supported, multipurpose university is accredited by the New England Association of Schools and Colleges, the National Council for the Accreditation of Teacher Education, and by other professional organizations. Undergraduate enrollment is 5,556 full-time and 2,410 part-time. A faculty of 324 in the day division and 337 in the evening division gives an overall faculty-student ratio of 1-19. The college operates on the semester system and offers 2 summer sessions. Founded in 1893 as the New Haven Normal School, the college has advanced to include new facilities and an expansion of its curricular offerings. Programs of study lead to the Associate, Bachelor, Master and Professional degree. Army and Air Force ROTC programs are available.

Entrance Requirements: High school graduation or equivalent with rank in upper 50% of class; completion of 16 units including 4 English, 3 mathematics, 2 foreign language, 2 science and 2 social science; SAT minimum 425M, 425V required; rolling admission,midyear admission and advanced placement plans available; $20 application fee.

Costs Per Year: $1,842 tuition; $5,962 out-of-state; $4,846 room and board; $2,269 out-of-state student fees.

Collegiate Environment: The campus is located on 165 beautiful acres overlooking the city of New Haven. The library contains over 920,000 volumes, and dormitory facilities accommodate 2,500 students. 60% of applicants are accepted. Financial assistance is available and 38% of student body receives financial aid.

Community Environment: See Yale University.

TEIKYO POST UNIVERSITY *(G-7)*
800 Country Club Road
P.O. Box 2540
Waterbury, Connecticut 06723-2540
Tel: (203) 596-4520; (800) 345-2562; Fax: (203) 756-5810

Description: Founded in 1890, Teikyo Post is a 4-year private, coeducational, residential, nondenominational, nonprofit college of business and liberal arts. It is fully accredited by the New England Association of Schools and Colleges. The semester system is used. Enrollment recently included 529 students full-time and 1,265 part-time and evening. A faculty of 28 full-time and 100 part-time gives a faculty-student ratio of 1-15.

Entrance Requirements: Accredited high school graduation or equivalent with completion of 16 units - 4 English, 2 math and 1 science preferred; SAT or ACT required; written recommendations from high school principal or counselor; personal interview recommended; early admission, early decision, rolling admission, delayed admission and advanced placement plans available; $40 application fee.

Costs Per Year: $11,700 tuition; $5,600 room and board; additional expenses average $500.

Collegiate Environment: Teikyo Post's 70-acre campus includes 4 classroom buildings that accommodate the School of Business and School of Arts and Sciences. Classroom instruction is complemented in the Programmed Audio Learning Systems Center. The college library is fully air-conditioned and contains 50,000 volumes. The Campus Center houses dining facilities, a bookstore, Eagle's Nest student lounge, recreation areas and a pool. There are five modern, attractive residence halls, which accommodate 320 men and women. University-owned off-campus housing is also available. Personal, career and academic counseling is available through the student development office. The university accepts 75% of the students who apply for admission, and students may enroll at midyear. Financial aid is available, and 80% of the current students receive some form of assistance. Army ROTC is offered.

Community Environment: Waterbury is a city of approximately 110,000, located in the northwest part of the state. There are three other colleges in the area and fifteen other institutions of higher learning within a 30-minute drive. The Greater Waterbury area offers ample opportunities for cultural, athletic, and recreational activities.

Branch Campuses: West Hartford, Meriden, Hamden, Bethel, Trumbull.

THREE RIVERS COMMUNITY TECHNICAL COLLEGE
(G-15)
Mahan Drive
Norwich, Connecticut 06360
Tel: (203) 886-1931; Fax: (203) 886-0691

Description: The publicly supported, coeducational junior college opened in 1970 and offers university-parallel and vocational programs and grants the Associate degree. The college is fully accredited by the New England Association of Schools and Colleges. The semester system is used and one summer session is offered. Enrollment includes 733 full-time and 2,523 part-time students with a faculty of 46 full-time and 88 part-time.

Entrance Requirements: Open enrollment policy; high school graduation or equivalent; non-high school graduates considered; $10 application fee.

Costs Per Year: Tuition and fees, state resident $1,396; nonresident $4,206.

Collegiate Environment: All students applying for admission are accepted, including midyear students. Financial assistance is available. The library contains 18,500 volumes, 1,136 pamphlets, 240 periodicals, 26,900 microforms and 2,900 audiovisual materials. Special programs are available for the educationally disadvantaged. There are Braille/tape library resources for sight-impaired students and all fields of study are open to students with disabilities.

Community Environment: Population 41,739. The metropolitan area has a temperate climate and an average temperature of 48 degress with an average rainfall of 41.22 inches. Norwich is located on the Connecticutt Turnpike at the headwaters of the Thames River. The city was founded in 1659 and is now an industrial city with hundreds of manufacturing plants in the area. Community facilities include shopping centers, a downtown shopping area, a hospital, and numerous civic, service, social, and professional organizations. Many points of historical interest are located here.

TRINITY COLLEGE   *(D-10)*
300 Summit Street
Hartford, Connecticut 06106
Tel: (203) 297-2180; Fax: (203) 297-2287

Description: The privately supported, coeducational liberal arts college was founded in 1823 by Epicscopalian clergy and laymen and was known as Washington College until 1845. It operates on the semester system. Enrollment includes 1,766 full-time and 225 part-time undergraduates and 185 graduate students. A faculty of 163 full-time and 74 part-time gives a faculty-student ratio of 1-10. The college is accredited by the New England Association of Schools and Colleges. The institution is open to all races and religions and grants the Bachelor and Master degrees.

Entrance Requirements: High school graduation; completion of 4 units in English, 3 mathematics, 2 foreign language, 2 laboratory science and 2 history; SAT and English Composition Achievement Test or ACT required; early admission, early decision, delayed admission and advanced placement plans available; $50 application fee.

Costs Per Year: $18,810 tuition; $5,690 room and board; $530 student fees.

Collegiate Environment: The campus is comprised of 90 acres with athletic facilities of 19 acres. Dormitory capacity is 1,700 students. The library contains 878,891 volumes, 2,150 periodicals and 200,000 microforms. The college accepts 59% of those who apply for admission. Transfer students are permitted to enroll at midyear, but freshmen are admitted only in the fall. The middle 50% ranges of scores for the entering freshman class were SAT 520-610 verbal, 570-660 math. 770 scholarships are available, including 209 for freshmen. 46% of the current student body receives some form of financial aid.

Community Environment: Hartford, the capital of the state, is a major city and port of entry. All forms of transportation serve the area along with the interstate expressways and major highways. Community and cultural facilities include more than two hundred churches, major civic, fraternal and veteran's organizations, hospitals, excellent shopping areas, the Mystic Seaport, Shakespeare Theatre, Symphony Orchestra and Opera Association. Opportunities are excellent for internships. Points of interest are the Wadsworth Atheneum, Connecticut State Library and Mark Twain's house.

TUNXIS COMMUNITY TECHNICAL COLLEGE   *(E-9)*
Farmington, Connecticut 06032
Tel: (203) 677-7701

Description: The public, community college is accredited by the New England Association of Schools and Colleges. It offers associate degrees in occupational fields, as well as in liberal arts and pre-professional programs for students wishing to go on to a four-year baccaureate program. Certificate programs are also offered. Credit courses are offered in cooperation with Connecticut Public Television. It operates on the quarter system an offers three summer sessions. Enrollment includes 1,586 full-time and 3,731 part-time students. A faculty of 46 full-time and 132 part-time gives a faculty-student ratio of 1-29.

Entrance Requirements: High school graduation or equivalent, or demonstration of ability to perform at the college level. The college has an open door admissions policy. $10 application fee.

Costs Per Year: $1,128, nonresident $3,672 per year

Collegiate Environment: Library holdings include 255,000 volumes. Financial aid including scholarships, loans, and student employment are available.

Community Environment: Farmington was settled in 1640 and incorporated in 1645. It is a suburban, residential town with a population of 2,500.

UNITED STATES COAST GUARD ACADEMY   *(I-15)*
15 Mohegan Avenue
New London, Connecticut 06320-4195
Tel: (203) 444-8444

Description: The federally supported and governed military academy is accredited by the New England Association of Schools and Colleges. It operates on the semester system with a mandatory summer term. The Academy was established in 1876 to educate and train young men and women to become career commissioned officers in the United States Coast Guard. Enrollment is approximately 738 men and 182 women. A faculty of 111 provides a faculty-student ratio of 1-8. The school grants a B.S. degree and commission as an Ensign in the U.S. Coast Guard. Subject major areas include Civil Engineering, Naval Architecture and Marine Engineering, Electrical Engineering, Mechanical Engineering, Marine Science, Management, Government, and Math and Computer Science.

Entrance Requirements: High school graduation or equivalent with completion of 15 units and high average; SAT or ACT required; applicant must be United States citizen, between 17 and 21 years of age, unmarried, with good moral character and in excellent physical condition.

Costs Per Year: The Coast Guard Academy is a Federal Service Academy where the tuition is borne by the government. In addition, each cadet is paid a monthly stipend of approximately $550 for books, uniforms, and other personal expenses.

Collegiate Environment: The campus is located in New London, Connecticut, on the western shore of the Thames River. There are 26 buildings on 120 acres and the library contains 151,694 volumes, 1,023 periodicals and 51,378 microforms. The Academy provides housing for all students. Admission is highly competitive; only 8% of those who apply for admission are accepted. Congressional nominations are not required and midyear students are not accepted. The average scores of the entering class were SAT 544 verbal, 645 math; ACT 25 English, 28 math.

Community Environment: See Connecticut College.

UNIVERSITY OF BRIDGEPORT   *(L-6)*
University Avenue
Bridgeport, Connecticut 06602
Tel: (203) 576-4000; (800) 972-9488; Fax: (203) 576-4941

Description: This privately supported, coeducational university is accredited by the New England Association of Schools and Colleges. In 1927 a number of visionary citizens obtained a charter for the newly formed junior college; it achieved four-year university status in 1947. The university operates on the semester system and offers two six-week summer sessions. Enrollment includes 737 full-time and 290 part-time undergraduates and 912 graduate students. A faculty of 91 full-time and 102 part-time gives an undergraduate faculty-student ratio of 1-8. The semester system is employed and 2 summer sessions are offered. Army ROTC is available. The university has an off-campus facility in Stamford, Connecticut which allows for accessibility from southern Connecticut and Westchester County, New York. Courses are conveniently scheduled. Graduate programs are offered in Business (MBA), Counseling and Human Resources, and Education; degree completion program (IDEAL) offered for undergraduate adult students.

Entrance Requirements: High school graduation with a C average and rank in upper half of graduating class; completion of 16 units including 4 English, 3 math, 2 foreign language, 1 lab science, 1 social science, and a minimum of 5 electives; SAT required (ACT may be substituted); 1-3 Recommended Tests required; early admission, early decision, rolling admission, delayed admission, midyear admission, and advanced placement plans available; $35 application fee.

Costs Per Year: $12,250 tuition; $6,810 room and board; $624 student fees.

Collegiate Environment: University of Bridgeport is situated on an 86-acre campus located in Southern New England, 60 miles northeast of New York City and is bordered by Long Island Sound. The campus includes 75 buildings of diverse architectural styles including newly renovated science and engineering facilities. Also located on campus are the Arnold Berhard Center with art galleries, studios, theatre, classrooms, meeting rooms, and exhibit rooms and the Wheeler Recreation Center which is a complete recreation and physical fitness facility. There are five co-ed residence halls on campus. The Magnus Wahlstrom library contains 250,000 bound volumes, 3,200 records and tapes, 900,000 microforms, and 900 periodicals and serials subscriptions. 85% of the students receive financial aid. Merit and leadership scholarships are available. The campus also has an intensive English language program on campus for students who are not native speakers of English.

Community Environment: Bridgeport is named for the first drawbridge erected over the Pequonock River and is easily accessible by auto, bus and train, automobiles using the Merrit Parkway and the Connecticut Thruway. Bridgeport is the home of P.T. Barnum. Barnum Institute of Science and History and the Museum of Art, Science and Industry is located in Bridgeport. Seaside Park, a 225-acre park stretching two and one half miles along Long Island Sound, offers opportunities for swimming, field sports, tennis and ice skating. Beardsley Park has woodland walks and drives, a large lake and a zoo. Sixty-five percent of Connecticut's largest corporations are located in Fairfield County. These companies provide students with excellent opportunities for employment, before and after graduation.

UNIVERSITY OF CONNECTICUT   (D-14)
Storrs, Connecticut 06269
Tel: (203) 486-2000; Admissions: (203) 486-3137; Fax: (203) 486-1476

Description: The publicly supported, coeducational state university is accredited by the New England Association of Schools and Colleges as well as by respective professional organizations. Founded in 1881 as the Storrs Agricultural School, the University now offers comprehensive freshman-sophomore programs at branches in Hartford, Waterbury, Avery Point, Stamford, and Torrington. Air Force and Army ROTC programs are available. The university operates on the semester system and offers two summer sessions. Enrollment includes 11,991 full-time and 2,728 part-time undergraduate students. In addition, there are 7,073 graduate students. Faculty includes 1,171 full-time and 48 part-time, giving an undergraduate faculty-student ratio of 1-17.

Entrance Requirements: High school graduation in upper range of class; completion of 16 units including 4 English, 3 mathematics, 2 science; 2 social science/history, 2 foreign language; SAT or ACT required; early admission, delayed admission and advanced placement plans available; $40 undergraduate or graduate application fee; $45 international application fee.

Costs Per Year: $3,900 tuition, $11,890 out-of-state; $2,604 residence hall; $2,520 7-day meal plan; $910 student fees.

Collegiate Environment: 383 stuctures on 4,000 acres comprise the main campus. The Homer Babbidge Library contains approximately 1,900,000 volumes. Dormitory facilities are available for 8,633 students. 65% of students applying for admission are accepted, including midyear students. Special programs for the culturally disadvantaged are offered and financial aid is available. 33% of students receive some form of financial aid. The University granted 3,082 Bachelor, 204 Professional, and 1,258 Master degrees and 246 Doctorates to the graduating class.

Community Environment: Population 12,100. A rural area 25 miles east of Hartford; temperate climate. Buses serve the area, other modes of transportation available at Hartford. Community facilities include Protestant, Catholic churches, a Jewish Synagogue, small campus shopping area and a hospital in Willimantic nine miles away. Good shopping facilities are available in Willimantic. Part-time employment opportunities are limited. The university provides countless recreational and sports facilities besides the nearby lakes and the State Parks.

UNIVERSITY OF HARTFORD   (D-9)
200 Bloomfield Avenue
West Hartford, Connecticut 06117
Tel: (203) 768-4296; (800) 947-4303; Fax: (203) 768-4961

Description: The privately supported, coeducational university is accredited by the New England Association of Schools and Colleges. The university is composed of nine schools and colleges including: College of Arts and Sciences, College of Education, Nursing and Health Professions, College of Engineering, the Barney School of Business and Public Administration, Hartford Art School, Hartt School of Music, Hartford College for Women, College of Basic Studies and Ward Technical College. Inter-collegiate registration with the Hartford Consortium is available. The university operates on the semester system and offers two summer sessions. Enrollment includes 3,891 full-time and 1,374 part-time students. A faculty of 316 full-time and 389 part-time gives a faculty-student ratio of 1-11.

Entrance Requirements: High school graduation with a rank in upper 50%; completion of 16 units, including 4 English, 2-3 1/2 mathematics, 2 science, 2 social science; SAT or ACT required; early admission, midyear admission, rolling admission, and advanced placement plans available; $35 application fee.

Costs Per Year: $14,220 tuition; $6,000 room and board; $690 student fees; $1,200 average additional expenses.

Collegiate Environment: Modern 300-acre campus. The library collection includes 643,000 hardbound volumes. Residence halls accommodate 3,415 students. 87% of applicants are accepted. Average high school standing of the 1994 freshman class: 31% in the top fifth; 20% in the second fifth; 24% in the third fifth, 25% in the bottom two fifths. The average scores of entering freshmen were SAT verbal 448, math 504. Financial aid is available, and 75% of the students receive some form of financial assistence.

Community Environment: The University is located in a suburban area of West Hartford, four miles from the center of Hartford. In addition to the many activities available on campus, the proximity to a metropolitan area affords a multitude of cultural, educational and recreational opportunities.

UNIVERSITY OF NEW HAVEN   (J-8)
300 Orange Avenue
West Haven, Connecticut 06516
Tel: (203) 932-7000; (800) 342-5864; Admissions: (203) 932-7133

Description: The private, coeducational university is accredited by New England Association of Schools and Colleges. UNH was founded by the YMCA in 1920 as a branch of Northeastern University by an Act of the State General Assembly. In 1926, the college was incorporated as an independent entity and authorized to grant Associate degrees. In 1958, authorization to offer courses leading to Bachelor degrees was granted. Divisons of the University are the school of Public Safety and Professional Studies, Graduate School, School of Arts and Sciences, School of Business, School of Engineering, and School of Hotel, Restaurant and Tourism Administration. Air Force ROTC is available. The university operates on the 4-1-4 calendar system and offers two summer sessions. Enrollment includes 2,059 full-time and 3,886 part-time undergraduates and 2,538 graduate students. A faculty of 151 full-time and 175 part-time gives a faculty-student ratio of 1-19.

Entrance Requirements: Vary slightly according to the Division or School; generally, all require high school graduation with recommended completion of 16 units, including 4 English, 3 math, 2 Science and 2 Social Science; ACT or SAT required; rolling admission, delayed admission, and midyear admission available; $25 application fee.

Costs Per Year: $10,600 tuition; $4,900 room and board; $200 student fees.

Collegiate Environment: The University is composed of 23 major buildings spread out over 73 acres of land. Dormitories are available for 493 men and 257 women. Library holdings include 339,404 hardbound volumes. 71% of applicants are accepted. The middle 50% ranges of scores for the entering freshman class were SAT 400-550 verbal, 400-600 math. Scholarships are available and 70% of the students receive some form of financial aid.

Community Environment: Located in West Haven, a town with a population of 54,000; ten minutes from downtown New Haven. Cultural attractions include the Shubert Theater, The Palace, Long Wharf Theater, Yale Repertory Theater. The university is accessible to many shopping malls and the beaches of Long Island Sound.

Branch Campuses: The University has a Southeastern Connecticut branch in Groton, CT.

WESLEYAN UNIVERSITY   *(G-10)*
High Street & Wyllys Avenue
Middletown, Connecticut 06457
Tel: (203) 347-9411

Description: The privately supported, coeducational college recently had an enrollment of approximately 1,339 men and 1,356 women. The college is accredited by the New England Association of Schools and Colleges and operates on the semester system. The college has had a tradition of educational innovation and experimentation since its founding 1831 as a school dedicated to the preparation of young men for the ministry and the professions. Long a nondenominational institution, Wesleyan first admitted women in 1872. Coeducation was discontinued in 1912, but resumed in 1969; the student body is now equally composed of women and men. The faculty consists of 282 full-time and 158 part-time members. The university grants the Bachelor, Master and Docorate degrss, a Master of Arts in Liberal Arts, and a Certificate of Advanced Study and is no longer affiliated with any religious denomination. There are academic cooperative plans available with several other colleges, including Smith, Amherst, Trinity, Dartmouth, Vassar, Mt. Holyoke, Wellesley and others.

Entrance Requirements: High school graduation or equivalent recommended units, 4 English, 4 math, 4 lab science, 4 language, 4 social studies; SAT and three Achievement Tests required; early admission, early decision, delayed admission, advanced placement plans available; personal interview required; $45 application fee.

Costs Per Year: $18,150 tuition; $5,390 room and board; $630 student fees.

Collegiate Environment: Campus has 62 buildings on 120 acres. Housing is available for 2,557 students. The library contains 1.3 million volumes. College offers study abroad in eight countries, including Italy, Japan, the USSR, Spain, Germany, France, Africa, Latin America, Israel and China. 31% of students applying for admission is accepted, including midyear students. Financial aid is available, and 44% of current students receive some form of assistance. 1,045 scholarships were recently awarded. The graduating class was awarded 650 Bachelor, 109 Master and MALS, and 23 Doctorates and CAS.

Community Environment: Population 45,000. In central Connecticut, 15 miles south of Hartford and 20 miles north of New Haven, Middletown is an important research and manufacturing center. Buses and railroads serve the area with an airline service nearby. Middletown has 21 churches of all denominations, hospital, three libraries with branches, several inns, motels, theatres and a shopping area. The various civic, fraternal and veterans organizations are active within the city. Parks, tennis courts, basketball courts, ball fields, picnic grounds and swimming pool provide facilities for recreation.

WESTERN CONNECTICUT STATE UNIVERSITY   *(I-13)*
181 White Street
Danbury, Connecticut 06810
Tel: (203) 837-9000; Fax: (203) 837-8320

Description: The publicly supported, coeducational university was established in 1903 as a normal school. Accredited by the New England Association of Schools and Colleges, the university offers four-year teacher, liberal arts, nursing, library science, criminal justice, health education, business administration, and medical technology programs as well as a two-year liberal arts program and a six-year Masters program. The college operates on the semester system and offers two summer sessions. Enrollment includes 3,016 full-time and 3,229 part-time undergraduate students. A faculty of 181 full-time and 208 part-time provides a faculty-student ratio of 1-17.

Entrance Requirements: High school graduation or equivalent in upper half of class; completion of 16 units including 4 English, 3 mathematics, 2 laboratory science, 2 social studies, 2 foreign language; SAT required; early admission, early decision, midyear admission, rolling admission, delayed admission and advanced placement plans available; $20 application fee.

Costs Per Year: $3,286 tuition; $8,388 out-of-state tuition; $4,108 room and board; $792 student fees; $1,214 out-of-state fees.

Collegiate Environment: The 28-acre main campus is near the business center of Danbury in one of the most attractive rural regions of New England. Library contains 165,000 volumes, and dormitories provide housing for a total of 900 students. 45% of students applying for admission are accepted, including midyear students. Scholarships are available and 40% of students receive some form of aid.

Community Environment: Population 60,000. Danbury is within easy commuting distance of Stamford, Waterbury, Bridgeport, New Haven and Torrington. Cultural centers in Danbury and in the surrounding cities are within easy reach. Trains and buses serve the area. Recreational facilities include nearby Candlewood Lake for swimming, boating and fishing. Part time work is available in the community.

Branch Campuses: The 315 acre Westside campus houses the Ancell School of Business, and also includes such modern facilities as the Perkin-Elmer Computing Center (open and available 24 hours a day), the Robert S. Young Business Library, a PAR fitness course, an outdoor recreational area, as well as student study areas, lounges and club offices. The Charles Ives Center for the Arts is also located on this campus, and a field house/gymnasium and additional playing fields are now under construction. Dormitories offer all-female, coeducational and apartment-style living; they are located on both campuses and provide housing for almost 30% of the undergraduates. The Housing Office will also assist in making rental arrangements in the Danbury area.

YALE UNIVERSITY   *(J-8)*
P.O. Box 1502A
Yale Station
New Haven, Connecticut 06520
Tel: (203) 432-1900; Fax: (203) 432-7329

Description: The privately supported, coeducational university is composed of 12 schools and colleges; Yale College became coeducational for the first time in its history in September 1969. It is accredited by the New England Association of Schools and Colleges. Yale was founded in 1701 and was the first university in the United States to award a Ph.D. degree. Colleges and Schools of the university: Yale College, Graduate School, School of Art, School of Architecture, School of Organization Management, School of Forestry & Environmental Studies, Schools of: Medicine, Divinity, Law, Music, Nursing, Drama. The university grants the Bachelor, Master and Doctorate degrees. It operates on the semester system and offers a summer session. Air Force and Army ROTC are available. Enrollment includes 5,166 full-time and 95 part-time undergraduates and 5,703 graduate and first professional students. The total faculty numbers 2,775, including instructing and research faculty.

Entrance Requirements: No minimum GPA required, although most successful candidates in top 10% of class; SAT and 3 Achievement Tests or ACT required; the university has far more academically qualified students that apply than it can possibly accept; therefore, a review of each qualified candidate is made to identify particular qualities and accomplishments that make the student outstanding; every effort is made on the part of the university to recognize the disadvantaged student who does show promise of being able to profit by attendance; early admission, early action, delayed admission and advanced placement plans are available; $65 application fee.

Costs Per Year: $21,000 tuition; $6,630 room and board.

Collegiate Environment: The campus is located in the city of New Haven on Long Island Sound among the scenic attractions of southern New England. It is 90 minutes from New York by train or car, and Boston is only 2 1/2 hours away. Students from 77 foreign countries and all of the United States are represented on the campus. Living accommodations are provided for 5,700 undergraduate and graduate students. The library contains more than 9 million volumes. Approximately 20% of students applying for admission are accepted; midyear students are not accepted. Financial aid is available, and more than 40% of the current student body receives some form of assistance.

Community Environment: Southern Connecticut's major city, New Haven is in many respects a college town. The average temperature is

50.7 degrees. Buses, railroads, and airlines serve the area. New Haven is engaged in one of the most successful urban renewal projects in the country, restoring and rebuilding housing, community facilities and commercial redevelopment. Points of interest are the museums and libraries. New Haven also has the usual civic organizations, hospitals, shopping centers, hotels and motels. Employment is available. The recreational facilities include theaters, swimming areas, tennis courts, archery ranges, indoor swimming pool, bowling alleys, riding stables, roller skating rinks, municipal golf course and many parks. Important manufacturing establishments are located here.

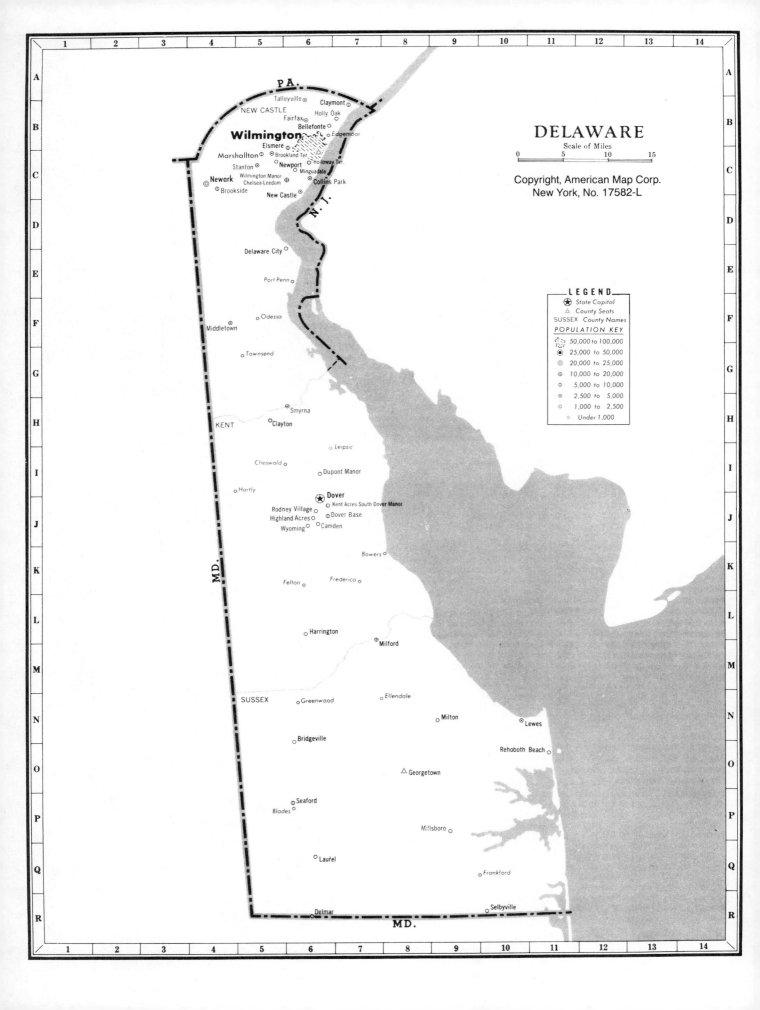

DELAWARE

DELAWARE STATE COLLEGE   *(J-6)*
North Dupont Highway
Dover, Delaware 19901
Tel: (302) 739-4917; Fax: (302) 739-5203

Description: This publicly supported, coeducational liberal arts college is accredited by the Middle State Association of Schools and Colleges. It operates on the semester system and offers three summer sessions. Enrollment totals 1,261 men and 1,674 women attending day and evening sessions, including 240 graduate students. A faculty of 166 full-time and 16 part-time gives a faculty-student ratio of 1-15. Academic cooperative plans with the University of Delaware and Delaware Technical and Community College are available.

Entrance Requirements: Accredited high school graduation with a C average and 15 units including 4 English, 2 mathematics, 2 science and 1 social science; SAT required; early admission, early decision, and rolling admission plans available; $10 application fee.

Costs Per Year: $1,678 fees; $4,346 out-of-state resident tuition; $3,464 room and board.

Collegiate Environment: The campus has 17 buildings on 400 acres. Dormitory facilities accommodate 441 men and 572 women. The library contains 161,565 volumes, 2,739 periodical titles, 73,266 microforms, and 5,549 audiovisual materials. Approximately 65% of the students applying for admission are accepted, including at midyear, and 76% of a recent freshmen class returned for the sophomore year. Of 275 scholarships offered, 120 are available for freshmen. About 68% of the student body receives some form of financial aid.

Community Environment: Dover, the capital of Delaware, is 75 miles from Philadelphia, 85 miles from Baltimore, 90 miles from Washington, DC, and 160 miles from New York City. Penn-Central Railroad, Greyhound and Trailways buses serve the area. Dover is an agricultural section noted for fruit, produce, grains and poultry. Many fine old colonial homes steeped in the traditions of the activity of the old town are found in the area. "The Green" is the center of activity of the old town and still the hub from which radiate many of the political and government activities of both the city and the state. Located 10 miles south of "The Green" is Barratt's Chapel, often called the "Cradle of Methodism in America." Each year on Dover Days, the first Saturday and Sunday in May, many historic homes are open to the public for a small fee. Dover is the home of the largest air freight terminal in the world. General Food's multimillion-dollar Jell-O plant and Playtex Corporation are also located here.

DELAWARE TECHNICAL AND COMMUNITY COLLEGE - SOUTHERN CAMPUS   *(O-8)*
P.O. Box 610
Georgetown, Delaware 19947
Tel: (302) 856-5400; Admissions: (302) 856-5400 x346; Fax: (302) 856-5428

Description: The publicly supported, coeducational college was founded in 1967. The college offers occupational-technical, pre-technology and liberal arts programs leading to the Certificate and Associate degrees. The college is accredited by the Middle States Association of Colleges and Schools and now has four campuses throughout Delaware. It operates on the semester system and offers two summer sessions. Enrollment includes 1,900 full-time and 1,685 part-time sutdents. A faculty of 75 full-time and 180 part-time members provides a facutly-student ratio of 1-15.

Entrance Requirements: SAT or ACT accepted; Placement exam; early admission, early decision, rolling admission plans available; $10 application fee.

Costs Per Year: $1,200 tuition; $3,000 out-of-state tuition; $60 student fees.

Collegiate Environment: The Southern Branch campus has three buildings on 120 acres. The library contains 35,000 volumes, 500 periodicals, 1,000 microforms and 800 audiovisual materials. All students applying for admission are accepted, and financial assistance is available. Special programs are available for the culturally disadvantaged.

Community Environment: Georgetown is the county seat of Sussex County, a rural area with a moderate climate. Buses serve the area, an airport provides service for the city and surrounding countryside. Community facilities include churches, library, three hospitals, excellent shopping and the usual civic, fraternal and veterans organizations. Deep sea fishing and surf and inland water fishing are within 23 miles. Beaches for swimming and surfing are located 18 miles away. Redden State Forest located five miles north offers facilities for picnicking and camping. The area is nationally known for the Del Mar Chicken Festival and Bi-Annual "Return Day."

DELAWARE TECHNICAL AND COMMUNITY COLLEGE - TERRY CAMPUS   *(J-6)*
1832 North Dupont Parkway
Dover, Delaware 19903
Tel: (302) 739-5321

Description: State-supported school of the four-campus Delaware Technical and Community College system, it is accredited by the Middle States Association of Colleges and Schools. Terry campus offers two-year Associate and one-year Diploma programs with transfer to other Delaware Technical campuses, and direct transfer to Delaware State College, Salisbury State College, and to approximately 40 other Baccalaureate institutions across the nation. It operates on the early semester system and offers one summer session. Enrollment includes 394 full-time and 1,187 part-time students. A faculty of 40 full-time and 58 part-time gives a faculty-student ratio of 1-15.

Entrance Requirements: Open enrollment policy; high school graduate or GED or 18 years of age and able to benefit from instruction; CGP required; placement exams in English, reading , and math; early decision, early admission, midyear admission, rolling admission, and advanced placement plans available; $10 application fee.

Costs Per Year: $1,200 state resident tuition; $3,000 nonresident tuition; $125 fees.

Collegiate Environment: A three building, modern facility situated on a 70-acre landscaped tract, the campus includes a library housing 15,969 titles, a dining area, classroom and lab space, administrative offices, and student recreational areas. There are no dormitories on campus. 100% of applicants are accepted, including midyear students. Financial aid is available, and 35% of students receive some form of financial assistance.

Community Environment: Located a few miles north of Dover. See Delaware State College.

DELAWARE TECHNICAL AND COMMUNITY COLLEGE - WILMINGTON CAMPUS   *(C-6)*
333 Shipley Street
Wilmington, Delaware 19801
Tel: (302) 888-5288; Fax: (302) 577-2548

Description: The publicly supported, coeducational, multi-campus, two-year college offers allied health technology, business technology, public and community service and career-oriented curriculum leading to Certificates and Associate degrees. The college is accredited by the Middle States Association of Colleges and Schools. It operates on the semester system and offers two summer sessions. Enrollment includes 5,000 students. A faculty of 116 full-time members gives a faculty-student ratio of approximately 1-43.

Entrance Requirements: High school graduation; open enrollment policy; non-high school graduates admitted; college-parallel program students must meet entrance requirements of the University of Delaware; early admission, early decision, rolling admission, delayed admission and advanced placement plans available; $10 application fee.

Costs Per Year: $1,200 tuition; $3,000 out-of-state tuition; $30 student activity fees.

Collegiate Environment: The campus has 2 buildings. The library contains 25,000 volumes and 500 periodicals. All students applying for admission are accepted. Financial assistance is available.

Community Environment: See Goldey-Beacom College.

Branch Campuses: Delaware Technical and Community College, Stanton Campus, 400 Stanton-Christiana Road, Newark, DE 19713

GOLDEY-BEACOM COLLEGE   (C-6)
4701 Limestone Road
Wilmington, Delaware 19808
Tel: (302) 998-8814; (800) 833-4877; Fax: (302) 998-3467

Description: Godley-Beacom College is a private, coeducational college founded in 1886 in the heart of Wilmington, Delaware. The College moved to its new suburban campus, equidistant between Newark and Wilmington, in September of 1974. The College is accredited by the Middle States Association of Colleges and Schools and awards Associate in Science degrees, Bachelor of Science degrees in business studies, and Master of Business Administration. An academic year is made up of 2 fifteen-week semesters with a winter and a summer session. Enrollment includes 852 full-time and 905 part-time undergraduates and 90 graduate students. The faculty consists of 25 full-time and 50 part-time members.

Entrance Requirements: High school graduation; early decision, rolling admission, and delayed admission plans available; advanced placement for business skills recognized; $30 application fee.

Costs Per Year: $6,120 tuition.

Collegiate Environment: The college is located on 28 acres in the rolling hills of northern Delaware. Apartment-style residence halls are available; residence facilities on campus accomodate 305 students. Student organizations, clubs, intercollegiate and intramural athletics, fraternities, and sororities play an important role in college life at Goldey-Beacom College. The library contains 27,000 volumes. 79% of the applicants are accepted. Financial aid is available and 75% of students receive some form of aid.

Community Environment: Known as the "Chemical Capital of the World," Wilmington (pop. 71,529) lies on the west bank of the Delaware River in northern Delaware. Railroads and airlines serve the area. Almost 300 industries are located in the area. A great variety of items are shipped from Wilmington, including such products as automobiles, airplanes, steel, clothing, hosiery, machinery, paper and paper products. Points of interest include Holy Trinity Church (Old Swedes), Wilmington Institute, Free Library, Brandywine Park, Fort Christian State Park, Delaware Art Center, Hagley Museum, Old Town Hall, and the Henry Francis du Pont Winterthur Museum. Nearby are Longwood Gardens and the Brandywine Museum.

Branch Campuses: A Business Training Center is located in downtown Wilmington and provides primarily skill-related certificate programs.

UNIVERSITY OF DELAWARE   (C-4)
Newark, Delaware 19716
Tel: (302) 831-8123

Description: University of Delaware is a state-assisted university accredited by Middle States Association of Colleges and Schools. It was established in 1743 and is comprised of the following colleges: Agricultural Sciences, Arts and Science, Business and Economics, Education, Engineering, Human Resources, Nursing, Physical Education, Athletics and Recreation, Marine Studies and Urban Affairs. The 4-1-4 semester system is used and two summer sessions are offered. Enrollment is 13,461 full-time, 1,409 part-time, and 4,000 evening undergraduate students. There are 3,210 graduate students. A faculty of 973 full-time and 40 part-time gives an undergraduate faculty-student ratio of 1-15. The graduate faculty-student ratio is 1-15. The university grants the Associate, Bachelor, Master and Doctorate degrees.

Entrance Requirements: High school graduation; minimum completion of 4 English units, 2 mathematics, 2 foreign language, 2 History or science, 3 social science and 3 academic electives; SAT required; non-high school graduates considered; early admission, early decision, midyear admission and advanced placement plans available; $40 application fee.

Costs Per Year: $3,690 tuition; $10,220 nonresident; $4,230 room and board; $455 student fees.

Collegiate Environment: The campus occupies 1,000 acres in Newark, which includes a 500-acre farm. The library contains 2,100,000 volumes, and dormitory facilities are provided for 7,300 students. 85% of state-resident applicants are accepted. 60% of out-of-state applicants are accepted. Approximately 25% of the student body graduated in the top 10% of the high school class. Approximately 86% of the freshman class returns for sophomore year. 2,000,000 is available for scholarships for entering freshmen and 62% of the undergraduates receive some form of financial aid.

WESLEY COLLEGE   (J-6)
Dover, Delaware 19901
Tel: (302) 736-2400

Description: Private coeducational college affiliated with the United Methodist Church and accredited by The Middle States Association of Colleges and Schools. The semester system is used with 3 summer sessions. Programs of study lead to the Certificate, Associate and Bachelor degrees. Recent enrollment included 406 men and 446 women full-time and 244 men and 259 women part-time. A faculty of 50 full-time and 45 part-time gives a faculty-student ratio of 1-17.

Entrance Requirements: High school graduation; completion of 16 units including 4 English, 2 mathematics, 1 science and 1 social science; non-high school graduates considered; SAT; early decision, early admission, rolling admission, midyear admission, advanced placement plans available; $20 application fee.

Costs Per Year: $9,890 tuition; $4,674 room and board; $405 student fees.

Collegiate Environment: The campus has 15 buildings on 12 acres in the residential heart of Dover. Dormitory facilities are available for 350 men and 350 women. Gymnasium-student center includes basketball court and an olympic size swimming pool. College Center has facilities for snack bar, dining rooms, receptions, concerts, lectures, movies, recreation, crafts, radio station, bookstore, galleries, lounges, outdoor theater. Library holdings number 55,241 in books and audiovisual materials. 75% of applicants are accepted. 150 scholarships are available and 68% of the students receive some form of finanacial aid.

Community Environment: See Delaware State College

WILMINGTON COLLEGE   (B-5)
320 Du Pont Highway
New Castle, Delaware 19720
Tel: (302) 328-9401; Admissions: (302) 328-9407; Fax: (302) 328-5902

Description: The private, career-oriented college was founded in 1967. The college is accredited by the Middle States Association of Colleges and Schools and professionally the National League for Nursing. The college grants the Bachelor's degree, the Associate's degree, and two Master's degrees. Air Force and Army ROTC programs are available. The college operates on the trimester calendar system and offers two summer sessions. Enrollment includes 4,000 students. A faculty of 160 gives a faculty-student ratio of 1-22.

Entrance Requirements: High school graduation or equivalent with a C average; non-high school graduates considered; open admission and rolling admission plans available; $25 application fee. Work experience and military schools are evaluated for credit award.

Costs Per Year: $5,400 tuition.

Collegiate Environment: 18 buildings on 20 acres comprise the campus in New Castle, which is located six miles south of Wilmington, near historic New Castle, on U.S. 13, less than a mile from exits I-95, I-495, I-295, and the Delaware Memorial Bridge. The library contains over 100,000 volumes, 5,000 periodicals volumes, 6,300 microforms, and 4,250 audio- visual materials. Admission is open to all students judged capable of contributing to and profiting from the courses of study offered. 98% of applicants are accepted. Scholarships ar limited. 20.6% of students receive some form of financial aid.

Community Environment: Situated on the west bank of the Delaware River in North Delaware, the city has many buildings dating from 1679. The Strand, a block-long cobbled street, is bordered by tree-lined brick walks and gutters. In 1823, the Great Fire burned some of the fine townhouses but a number survived; other structures were built or rebuilt immediately after the fire. Many of the historic houses are opened to the public on New Castle Day, the third Saturday in May.

Branch Campuses: Wilmington College has instructional sites in Wilmington, Dover (2), and Georgetown, Delaware.

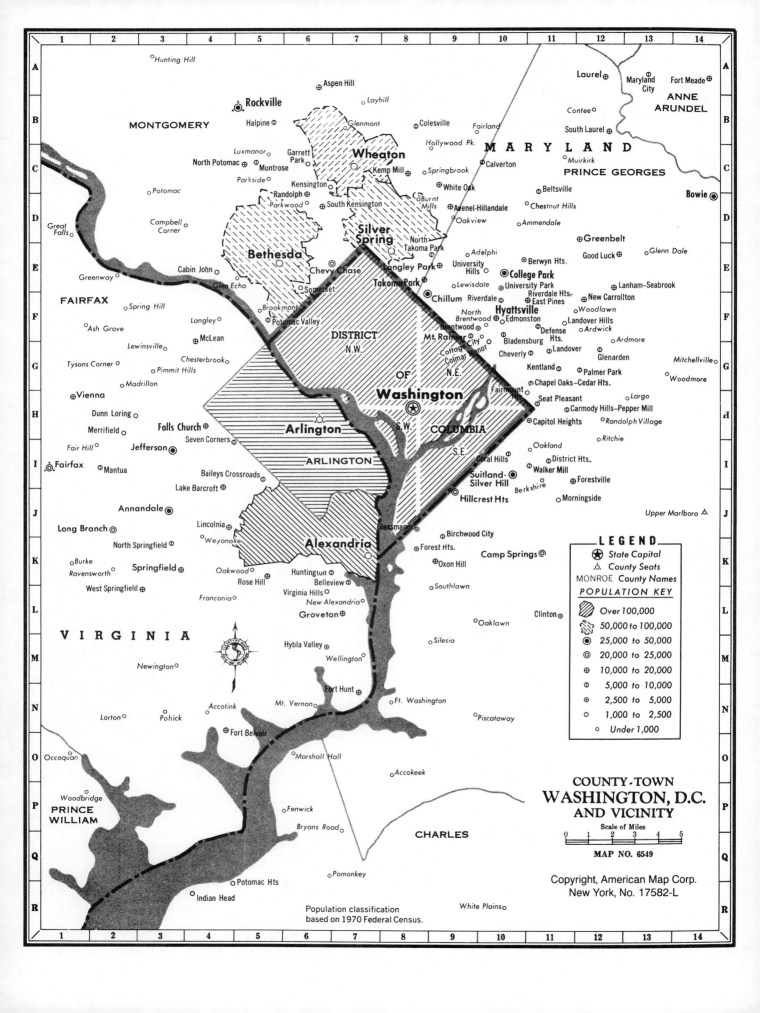

COUNTY-TOWN
WASHINGTON, D.C.
AND VICINITY

Scale of Miles

MAP NO. 6549

Copyright, American Map Corp.
New York, No. 17582-L

Population classification
based on 1970 Federal Census.

L E G E N D
- ★ State Capital
- ⊙ County Seats
- MONROE *County Names*

POPULATION KEY
- Over 100,000
- 50,000 to 100,000
- 25,000 to 50,000
- 20,000 to 25,000
- 10,000 to 20,000
- 5,000 to 10,000
- 2,500 to 5,000
- 1,000 to 2,500
- Under 1,000

DISTRICT OF COLUMBIA

AMERICAN UNIVERSITY
440 Massachusetts Avenue N.W.
Washington, District of Columbia 20016
Tel: (202) 885-1000; Admissions: (202) 885-6000; Fax: (202) 885-6014

Description: Privately supported, coeducational university affiliated with the Methodist Church and accredited by the Middle States Association of Colleges and Schools. The university was founded in 1893 and was to be a graduate school only. An undergraduate, liberal arts program was added in 1925. American University offers overseas and other special programs. ROTC available through Consortium of Universities of the Washington Metropolitan area: Army-Georgetown University, Air Force-Howard University. The university operates on the semester system and offers two summer sessions. Enrollment includes 11,708 full-time and part-time undergraduates. A faculty of 548 full-time and 450 adjunct gives a faculty-student ratio of 1-15.

Entrance Requirements: High school graduation with rank in upper 50%; completion of 16 units including 4 English, 3 mathematics, 2 social sciences, 2 natural sciences, 2 foreign language; SAT or ACT required. Early admission, early decision, delayed admission, midyear admission, and advanced placement plans available. $45 application fee.

Costs Per Year: $15,934 tuition; $6,600 room and board; $210 student fees; additional expenses average $600.

Collegiate Environment: The campus has over 30 buildings on 85 acres located in northwest Washington and the library contains 602,617 bound volumes and 770,000 microvolumes. The Broadcast Center houses radio stations WAMU-AM and WAMU-FM and studios for broadcasting and television classes. Dormitories for undergraduate men and women accommodate 3,550 students. 70% of applicants meet criteria and are accepted. Financial aid is available and 60% of students receive some form of aid.

Community Environment: Washington, the capital of the United States, is located on the Potomac River between Maryland and Virginia. It is a beautiful and historic city of tree-shaded streets, impressive buildings, and lovely residential neighborhoods. All major forms of transportation are available: North meets South at the historic Union Railroad Station, and three major airports serve Washington. Through the northwest area flows Rock Creek, lined all the way with a wooded park that is the city's largest and finest natural recreation area. Shopping facilities are excellent. Numerous points of interest are in the Capitol vicinity: United States Capitol, Senate and House office buildings, Supreme Court Building, Library of Congress, U.S. Botanic Garden, and John F. Kennedy Center for the Performing Arts. In the Mall and Constitution Avenue area are the National Gallery of Art, National Archives, Federal Bureau of Investigation, Armed Forces Institute of Pathology and Medical Museum, Smithsonian Institute and the Washington Monument. Near the White House are the U.S. Treasury and Blair House; west of the Mall are the Pan American Union, Constitution Hall, American Institute of Pharmacy, Lincoln Memorial, Potomac Park and Thomas Jefferson Memorial. Georgetown has the Dumbarton House, Dumbarton Oaks Park, and Dumbarton Oaks Research Library and Collection. Located in the northwest section are the House of the Temple, Washington Chapel, Islamic Center, Naval Observatory, Washington Cathedral, Rock Creek Park, National Zoological Park, and the National Bureau of Standards. In the northeast section are the National Shrine of the Immaculate Conception, Anacostia Park and U.S. National Arboretum. Within the southwest section are Fort Lesley J. McNair, Bolling Air Force Base and Fort Washington. Other facilities include outdoor theatres, free concerts, embassies and legations of many countries, Walter Reed Army Medical Center and the Naval Medical Center.

CATHOLIC UNIVERSITY OF AMERICA
620 Michigan Avenue, N.E.
Washington, District of Columbia 20064
Tel: (202) 319-5305; (800) 673-2772; Admissions: (202) 319-5305; Fax: (202) 319-6533

Description: This privately supported, coeducational Roman Catholic University is accredited by the Middle States Association of Colleges and Schools and by numerous professional organizations. Founded in 1887, the university was established as a graduate and research institution, but introduced undergraduate programs in 1904. The University is divided into ten schools: Arts and Sciences, Engineering, Architecture and Planning, Music, Nursing, Philosophy, Social Services, Law, Library and Information Science, and Religious Studies. Undergraduate students are admitted in the Schools of Arts and Sciences, Architecture and Planning, Engineering, Music, Nursing, and Philosophy. The schools of Social Service and Religious Studies teach undergraduate majors who receive their degrees from the School of Arts and Sciences. In addition, Metropolitan College administers the General Studies program. Its degrees are granted through Arts and Sciences. Study abroad programs are also available. Programs of study lead to the Bachelor degree. Graduate studies are offered in all the Schools and programs lead to Master's, Professional and Doctoral degrees. The college operates on the semester system and offers a summer sessions and a "mini-semester." Enrollment includes 2,179 full-time and 189 part-time undergraduates and 3,764 graduate students. Approximately 95% of the 379 faculty members have Doctoral or First Professional degrees. There are also 295 adjunct and part-time faculty members. The faculty-student ratio is 1-9.

Entrance Requirements: High school graduation with rank in upper third; recommended high school courses include 4 English, 3 college-preparatory mathematics, 2 foreign language, 4 social science, 3 laboratory science and 1 Fine Arts/Humanities; SAT or ACT required; early action, early admission, midyear admission and advanced placement plans available; $30 undergraduate and graduate application fee.

Costs Per Year: $13,712 undergraduate tuition for all schools except Engineering and Architecture; $13,830 undergraduate tuition for Engineering and Architecture; $460 fees; $6,408 room and board.

Collegiate Environment: 57 buildings on 155 acres comprise the campus, and the library contains over 1,348,162 volumes. Dormitory facilities are available for 1,588 students. Approximately 82% of undergraduate students applying for fall admission are accepted. The middle 50% range of entering freshmen scores were SAT 460-570 verbal, 510-610 math; ACT 22-27 composite. Scholarships are available and 72% of the undergraduates receive financial aid. The university also accepts transfer students and midyear students. 692 Bachelor's, 592 Master's, 354 Professional degrees and 117 Doctorates were granted to a recent graduating class.

Community Environment: See American University.

DOMINICAN HOUSE OF STUDIES
487 Michigan Avenue, N.E.
Washington, District of Columbia 20017
Tel: (202) 529-5300

Description: This Roman Catholic Seminary and graduate school in theology was founded in 1905, on its transfer from somerset, Ohio, where it had begun in 1834. As a constituent member of the Cluster of Independent Theological Schools, it is accredited by the Middle States Association of Colleges and Schools, and the Association of Theological Schools to grant the S.T.B. as a first professional degree and the S.T.L. In addition, it is accredited by the Roman Catholic Congregation of Catholic Education to grant these degrees in the name of the Holy See. Three years of post-baccalaureate study are required for the M. Div. and two additional years for the S.T.L. The present student body of 33 is taught by a faculty of 13 full-time and 4 part-time instructors. Through its membership in the Washington Theological Consortium, students may cross-register for over 300 courses in theology and pastoral studies in each semester. The school operates on the semester system with no summer sessions.

Entrance Requirements: Degree candidates are required to have earned the A.B. or equivalent. Deficiencies in philosophy can be made up in the course of graduate studies. GRE is required.

Costs Per Year: $2,000 tuition per semester, $25 application fee, $30 annual fees.

Collegiate Environment: The school is housed in a Roman Catholic Dominican priory which is located in the vicinity of the Catholic University. The school library contains 50,000 volumes and receives 264 subscriptions. In addition, students have free access to nearly one million volumes in the libraries of all theological schools in Washington.

Community Environment: Located in Northeast Washington, a short distance from unlimited resources: educational, research, artistic, cultural and political available in one of the great cities of the world.

GALLAUDET UNIVERSITY
800 Florida Ave., N.E.
Washington, District of Columbia 20002
Tel: (202) 651-5484; Admissions: (202) 651-5750/5114; Fax: (202) 651-5744

Description: This federally supported, coeducational liberal arts university is the only one in the world designed exclusively for deaf and hard of hearing students. The university is accredited by the Middle States Association of Colleges and Schools, the National Council for Accreditation of Teacher Education and the Council on Social Work Education. It was founded in 1864 to provide a liberal higher education for deaf persons who need special facilities to compensate for their hearing loss. Students are able to learn and communicate in a unique multicultural, bilingual environment. Gallaudet offers opportunities for a total education in and out of class e.g., internships, paraprofessional work experience, consortium courses at other colleges and universities, and cultural activities in the nation's capital. The university grants the Bachelor, Master and Doctorate degrees. It operates on the semester system and offers two summer sessions. Enrollment includes 2,175 full-time undergraduates and 461 graduate students. A faculty of 300 full-time and 30 part-time gives a faculty-student ratio of 1-8.

Entrance Requirements: High school graduation or equivalent; evidence of hearing loss to a degree that would make attending university of normal-hearing students difficult; satisfactory performance on our own entrance exam; Achievement and Aptitude examinations; SAT or ACT acceptables; early admission, early decision, rolling admission, midyear admission delayed admission and advanced placement plans available; $35 undergraduate application fee, $50 graduate application fee.

Costs Per Year: $5,100 undergraduate tuition; $5,600 graduate tuition; $5,700 room and board; $280 student fees; additional expenses average $380.

Collegiate Environment: The campus is located on 99 acres in northeast Washington, D.C. The library contains over 202,000 volumes and dormitory accommodations are available for 1,324 men and women. Approximately 57% of the students applying for admission are accepted and 67% return for the sophomore year. 30% of the senior class continued on to graduate school.

Community Environment: See American University

GEORGE WASHINGTON UNIVERSITY
2121 I Street, Suite 102
Washington, District of Columbia 20052
Tel: (202) 994-6040; (800) 447-3765; Admissions: (202) 994-6040; Fax: (202) 994-0958

Description: The privately supported, coeducational university had a total enrollment of 19,298 students. A faculty of 1,403 full-time and 768 part-time gives a faculty-student ratio of 14-1. The school is accredited by the Middle States Association of Colleges and Schools as well as numerous professional organizations and operates on the semester system with two summer sessions. This nonsectarian college was founded in 1821. Its founding was inspired by George

Washington's desire for the establishment of a national university in the federal city. The University has Programs of study leading to the Associate's, Bachelor's, Master's and Doctorate degrees. Degrees are offered in Law, Medicine, Arts and Sciences, Business, Education and Human Development, Engineering and International Affairs.

Entrance Requirements: High school graduation in the top 40% of the class with 15 units including 4 English, 2 mathematics, 2 foreign language, 2 science and 2 social science; SAT or ACT; English and Math Achievement Tests recommended. Transfer students should have a 2.50 average; early admission, early decision and advanced placement plans available; $50 application fee.

Costs Per Year: $18,300 tuition; $6,590 room and board; $732 student fees.

Collegiate Environment: The campus is located on approximately 45 acres in the federal section of Washington, D.C., within several blocks of the White House, State Department and Kennedy Center. University libraries contain over 1.7 million volumes. Dormitory space is available for 3,074 undergraduates. A full complement of social activities, organizations, and athletics is available. The college accepts 59% of the students who apply for admission, and freshman students are admitted at midyear as well as in fall. Financial aid is available, and 73% of the current undergraduate student body receives some form of assistance.

Community Environment: See American University

GEORGETOWN UNIVERSITY
37th & "O" Streets, N.W.
Washington, District of Columbia 20057
Tel: (202) 687-3600; Fax: (202) 687-5084

Description: This privately supported, Roman Catholic coeducational university is accredited by the Middle States Association of Colleges and Schools. Army, Navy and Air Force ROTC are available. Founded in 1789, Georgetown was the first American college to receive a university charter from the federal government. The university is composed of five undergraduate schools and three graduate and professional schools with programs leading to the Bachelor's, Master's and Professional and Doctorate degrees. The semester system is used and five summer sessions are offered. The university has graduated a remarkable number of men and women who have served in responsible positions in the United States government. Current enrollment numbers 2,966 men and 3,263 women undergraduates and 5,855 graduate students. A faculty of 500 full-time and 198 part-time gives a faculty-student ratio of 1-11.

Entrance Requirements: High School graduation; SAT or ACT required: Achievement tests recommended; general subject requirements: completion of four years of English, at least 2 years of social studies, modern language; 3 mathematics, and 1 year of natural science; additional credits required for some programs; early action, deferred enrollment and advanced placement plans available; $45 application fee.

Costs Per Year: $16,440 tuition; $13,560 graduate tuition; $6,400 room and board.

Collegiate Environment: The 110-acre campus is located on the heights above the Potomac near Key Bridge. All of the university facilities are located there, except the Law Center, which is in downtown Washington. Dormitories accommodate 80% of the student body. 29% of applicants are accepted. The middle 50% of score ranges were SAT 540-650V, 590-690M; ACT 26-32 composite. The libraries contain 1.9 million volumes, more than 24,000 periodical titles and 164,000 titles on microforms. The university offers 108 different degree programs.

Community Environment: See American University.

HOWARD UNIVERSITY
2400 Sixth Street, N.W.
Washington, District of Columbia 20059
Tel: (202) 806-2752; (800) 822-6363; Admissions: (202) 806-2752; Fax: (202) 806-4465

Description: This privately supported, coeducational university was authorized by a charter of the 39th Congress in 1897. The university is accredited by the Middle States Association of Colleges and Schools. Traditionally, Howard has maintained the largest gathering of black scholars in the world, producing approximately one-half of the nation's black physicians, pharmacists, engineers and architects. The college administers 17 schools and colleges. The School of Arts and Sciences, Pharmacy, Engineering, Business, Allied Health, Communication, Nursing, Education, and Fine Arts may be entered upon completion of high school. Previous college training is required for the graduate school and the schools of religion, law, social work, dentistry, medicine, and pharmacy. There is a new school of Continuing Education. The university operates on the semester system and offers two summer sessions. Enrollment includes 9,085 full-time and 1,847 part-time undergraduate and 2,354 graduate students. A faculty of 2,223 gives an undergraduate faculty-student ratio of 1-6.

Entrance Requirements: High school graduation; completion of 16 units including 4 English, 2 mathematics, 2 science, 2 social science, and 2 foreign language; ACT or SAT scores; other requirements vary with school and college; non-high school graduates considered; early admission, rolling admission, delayed admission and advanced placement plans available; $25 application fee.

Costs Per Year: $8,105 tuition and fees; $5,020 room and board.

Collegiate Environment: The University operates four campuses which total over 260 acres. The 89-acre main campus is just five minutes from downtown Washington, D.C. Most of the dormitories, administrative offices, classroom buildings, a teaching hospital and academic resources are here. The hilly 22-acre West Campus near Rock Creek Park contains additional administrative offices, centers, institutes and The Howard Law Center. Other campuses include the School of Divinity campus in northeast Washington and the Beltsville, Maryland facility for the study of life and physical sciences.

Community Environment: See American University.

Branch Campuses: The University operates three branch campuses including The Howard Law Center near Rock Creek Park, West Campus, the School of Divinity campus in northeast Washington and the Center for Advance Research in the Life and Physical Sciences campus in Beltsville, Maryland.

MOUNT VERNON COLLEGE
2100 Foxhall Road, N.W.
Washington, District of Columbia 20007
Tel: (202) 625-0400; (800) 682-4636; Admissions: (202) 625-4687; Fax: (202) 625-4688

Description: Mount Vernon is an undergraduate college for women accredited by the Middle States Association of Colleges and Schools. The college offers the Bachelor of Arts degree in 13 interdisciplinary programs of study. In addition, intensive periods in internship, study abroad and independent study are available. Enrollment includes 300 full-time, 40 part-time, and 90 evening program undergraduates and 90 graduate students. A faculty of 38 full-time and 30 part-time gives a faculty-student ratio of 1-13.

Entrance Requirements: High school graduation; completion of 16 units including 4 English, 2 mathematics, 2 foreign language, 1 science and 1 social science; SAT or ACT test scores. Early admission, rolling admission, advanced placement, delayed admission, midyear admission and early decision plans available; $35 application fee.

Costs Per Year: $13,780 tuition; room and board $6,915.

Collegiate Environment: The college is located on a 26 acre wooded campus in a fine residential area of northwest Washington D.C. Dormitory facilities accommodate 310 students; upper classmen may live off campus. Approximately 80% of students applying for admission are accepted. 60% of the students receive some form of financial aid.

Community Environment: See American University.

OBLATE COLLEGE
391 Michigan Avenue, N.E.
Washington, District of Columbia 20017
Tel: (202) 529-6544

Description: This privately supported seminary for men is accredited by the Middle States Association of Colleges and Schools and is a participating member of the Cluster of Independent Theological Schools, a cooperative program involving the De Sales Hall School of Theology, and the Pontifical Faculty of Theology of the Immaculate Conception. It is also a member of the Washington Theological Con-

sortium. The college was founded in 1916 and is dedicated to the education and formation of young men assigned to the Catholic priesthood, in particular, for those members of the religious community known as the Missionary Oblates of Mary Immaculate. The semester system is used. Enrollment includes 25 full-time and 9 part-time students. A faculty of 12 gives a faculty-student ratio of 1-4.

Entrance Requirements: 90 college credits, including 12 English, 6 mathematics, 6 social science, 6 foreign language, and 4 theology.

Costs Per Year: $4,500 tuition; $50 student fees.

Collegiate Environment: The campus has 2 buildings on 8 acres. The library contains 59,000 volumes.

Community Environment: See American University.

SOUTHEASTERN UNIVERSITY
501 Eye Street, S.W.
Washington, District of Columbia 20024
Tel: (202) 265-5343

Description: Founded in 1879, this private, independent, coeducational institution is chartered by the Congress of United States. Southeastern is accredited by the Council on Higher Education of the Middle States Association of Colleges and Schools and is accredited by the Accrediting Commission of the Association of Independent Colleges and Schools. Enrollment includes 450 undergraduate and graduate students. The institution is served by 10 full-time and 130 adjunct professors, emphasizing the philosophy of practical and professional experience in the classrooms. The teacher-student ratio was 1-10.

Entrance Requirements: High school graduation or equivalent. University placement tests required; rolling admission, advanced placement plans; $45 application fee.

Costs Per Year: $6,297 undergraduate tuition; $5,145 graduate; $125 student fees; room and board not available, but University will assist in finding accommodations.

Collegiate Environment: Southeastern University is located in the heart of residential, redeveloped Southwest Washington, in its own attractive contemporary campus close to the Maine Avenue waterfront, the Arena Stage Theater, and L'Enfant Plaza. It is surrounded by the Environmental Protection Agency, Capitol Hill, the Departments of Health, Education, and Welfare, Housing and Urban Development, Transportation, Agriculture, and the Federal Bureau of Investigation. It is very near the new Hirshhorn Museum, the Smithsonian Institution, the National Gallery of Art, and the National Air and Space Museum.

Community Environment: See American University.

STRAYER COLLEGE
1025 15th Street, NW
Washington, District of Columbia 20005
Tel: (202) 728-0048; (800) 765-8680; Fax: (202) 289-1831

Description: Strayer College is an independent, nonsectarian four-year college with eight campusis in the metropolitan Washington, D.C. area. It is accredited by the Middle States Association of Colleges and Schools. Its primary mission is to provide students with a business-oriented education enabling them to achieve career goals. The college grants the Associate, Bachelor, and Master's degrees. It operates on the quarter system and offers one summer session. Enrollment includes 2,403 full-time and 3,381 part-time undergraduates, and 942 graduate students. A faculty of 60 full-time and 220 part-time gives overall faculty-student ratio of 1-28.

Entrance Requirements: High school diploma or GED and Institutional Placement Test. $25 application fee.

Costs Per Year: Undergraduate: $6,750 ($150/cr) full-time, $160/cr part-time; Graduate: $5,940 ($220/cr).

Collegiate Environment: Strayer seeks students who have a desire for an education in the field of business. The College provides the educational experiences necessary for students to develop the knowledge, skills, understanding, and appreciations consistent with sound business principles and practices. Because of its favorable locations in the Wash. D.C. area, Strayer students from the Distrct of Columbia, Maryland, and Virginia and attracts international students from more than fifty countries. 98% of applicants are accepted. Scholarships are available and 28% of students receive some form of financial aid.

Community Environment: See American University

Branch Campuses: 3045 Columbia Pike, Arlington, VA 22204; 2853 PS Business Center, Woodbridge, VA 22192; 9990 Battleview Parkway, Manassas, VA 22110; 2730 Eisenhower Avenue, Alexandria, VA 22303; 45150 Russell Branch Parkway, Ashburn, VA 22011; 4500 Plank Road, Fredericksburg, VA 22407; 6830 Laurel Street, NW., Washington, DC 20012.

TRINITY COLLEGE
125 Michigan Ave., N.E.
Washington, District of Columbia 20017
Tel: (202) 939-5000; Admissions: (202) 939-5040; Fax: (202) 939-5134

Description: The privately supported liberal arts college for women is managed by the Sisters of Notre Dame de Namur. It was founded in 1897. The college is accredited by the Middle States Association of Colleges and Schools. The college is part of the Consortium of Washington Universities and grants the Bachelor and Master degrees. Enrollment includes 398 full-time and 650 part-time undergraduates and 382 graduate students. The faculty consists of 84 members.

Entrance Requirements: High school graduation; completion of 16 units; SAT or ACT; early admission, early decision, rolling admission, delayed admission, advanced placement plans available; $35 application fee.

Costs Per Year: $11,750 tuition; $6,430 room and board; $158 student fees.

Collegiate Environment: Seven buildings on 27 acres comprise the campus and the library contains 160,000 volumes, 609 periodicals, and 7,000 microforms. Dormitories provide housing for 383 students. 76% of applicants are accepted. 80% of the current student body receives some form of financial assistance.

Community Environment: See American University

UNIVERSITY OF THE DISTRICT OF COLUMBIA
4200 Connecticut Ave., N.W.
Building 39, Room A07
Washington, District of Columbia 20008
Tel: (202) 294-6071; Admissions: (202) 274-5010; Fax: (202) 274-6067

Description: The University of the District of Columbia is accredited by the Middle States Association of Colleges and Schools. This comprehensive land-grant university was created after a federal commission in 1963 found a compelling need for higher education in Washington, D.C., particularly for the District's black and poor residents. Established in 1977 as a result of a merger of the District of Columbia Teachers College, Federal City College, and the Washington Technical Institute, the campus is spread among three areas of northwest Washington. It offers programs of study that lead to associate, teacher's, and master's degrees. Double majors, independent study and internships are possible. Undergraduates may take graduate level courses. The university is a member of the consortium of Universities of the Washington Metropolitan area with American U., Gallaudet, Georgetown U, George Washington U, Howard U, South-

eastern U, Trinity College and U of Maryland. Air Force, Army and Navy ROTC programs are available. It operates on the semester system and offers one summer session. Enrollment includes 3,742 full-time and 6,857 part-time undergraduates and 595 graduate students. A faculty of 387 full-time and 196 part-time gives a faculty-student ratio of 1-14.

Entrance Requirements: High school graduation or satisfactory GED scores; a baccalaureate degree from a regionally accredited college or university completion of the appropriate entrance test (GRE, GMAT, NTE, or Miller's Analogy Test) and two letters of recommendation for graduate programs.

Costs Per Year: $1,046 tuition resident; $3,854 nonresident; $1,982 graduate; $13,854 nonresident graduate, plus $400 student fees and books.

Collegiate Environment: The campus is composed of three sites known as the Van Ness (main campus), Georgia, Harvard, and Mt. Vernon Campuses. The University is academically organized into the Colleges of Arts and Sciences and Professional Studies. The university maintains an honors program, and provides remedial courses in Math, English, and reading. Services available: Career and academic guidance and placement services, special counseling for veteran and older students, diagnostic testing, health services and facilities for the handicapped. 88% of the students are District residents and 76% are African American. Sports facilities include an athletic field and a gymnasium, which houses a swimming pool, racquetball and tennis courts, weight lifting and exercise rooms.

Community Environment: See American University

WESLEY THEOLOGICAL SEMINARY
4500 Massachusetts Avenue, N.W.
Washington, District of Columbia 20016
Tel: (202) 885-8600; (800) 882-4987; Admissions: (202) 885-8659; Fax: (202) 885-8605

Description: Privately supported graduate school affiliated with the United Methodist Church; accredited by the Association of Theological Schools in the U.S. and Canada, the Middle States Association of Colleges and Schools, and approved by the University Senate of the United Methodist Church and the Association for Clinical Pastoral Education. The seminary grants the Master's and Doctorate degrees and is a charter member of the Washington Theological Consortium. It operates on the semester system and offers one summer session. Enrollment includes 605 graduate students. A faculty of 24 full-time and 22 part-time gives a faculty-student ratio of 1-13.

Entrance Requirements: Bachelor's degree and maturity of motivation toward the Christian ministry; $35 application fee.

Costs Per Year: $8,100 ($270/cr); $4,000 room & board; $70 orientation fee; $30 student fees.

Collegiate Environment: The campus has five buildings on seven acres. The library contains 115,000 volumes. Dormitory facilities accommodate 163 students, and there are facilities for 41 married students. 75% of applicants are accepted. 50% of first-year class received financial assistance. The recent graduating class was granted 64 Master's, and 16 Doctorate degrees.

Community Environment: See American University

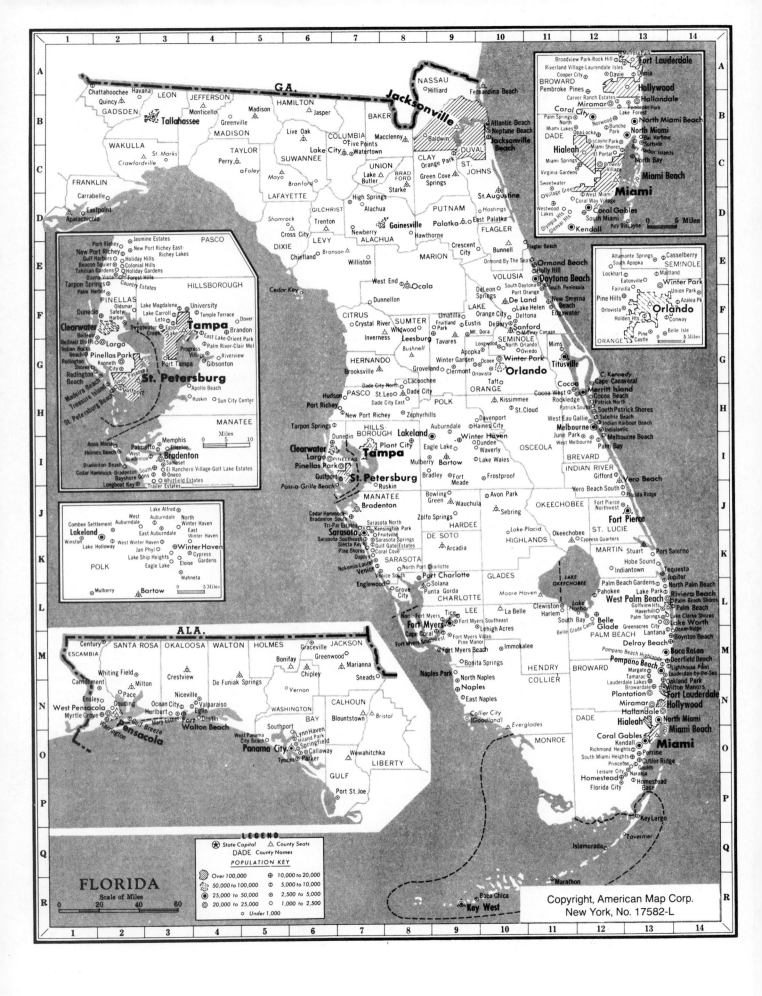

FLORIDA

Scale of Miles

0   20   40   60

LEGEND

★ State Capital   △ County Seats
DADE County Names
POPULATION KEY

Over 100,000	10,000 to 20,000
50,000 to 100,000	5,000 to 10,000
25,000 to 50,000	2,500 to 5,000
20,000 to 25,000	1,000 to 2,500
	Under 1,000

FLORIDA

BARRY UNIVERSITY   *(O-13)*
11300 Northeast Second Avenue
Miami Shores, Florida 33161-6695
Tel: (305) 899-3000; (800) 695-2279; Admissions: (305) 899-3100;
Fax: (305) 899-3104

Description: Barry University is an independent, coeducational, Catholic institution of higher education in the liberal arts and professional studies within the Judeo-Christian and Dominican traditions. The college was founded in 1940, became a university in 1981, and is accredited by the Southern Association of Colleges and Schools. The university grants the Bachelor, Master, and Doctorate degrees. Semester abroad and campus exchange programs are available. It operates on the semester system and offers two summer sessions. Enrollment includes 1,558 full-time and 2,299 part-time undergraduate, and 2,136 graduate students. A faculty of 216 full-time and 284 part-time provides a faculty-student ratio of 1-14.

Entrance Requirements: High school graduation with at least a C average and 16 units; minimum SAT verbal 504, math 458 or ACT 22 composite required; non high school graduates accepted with proof of GED and official test scores; CLEP accepted; early admission, early decision, midyear admission, and advanced placement plans available; $30 application fee.

Costs Per Year: $11,290 tuition; $5,360 room and board; $220 student fees.

Collegiate Environment: The campus has 26 buildings on 90 acres. The library contains 656,530 volumes, 2,300 periodicals, 450,000 microfilms and 4,200 audiovisual materials. Dormitory facilities accommodate 550 students. Approximately 69% of the students applying for admission are accepted. 35 scholarships are available and 77% of undergraduates receive some form of financial assistance.

Community Environment: Located only minutes from the cities of Miami and Ft. Lauderdale, Barry University offers easy access to the recreational facilities and cultural opportunities of Florida's Gold Coast area. Golf, tennis, swimming, skin and scuba diving, sailing and waterskiing are available all year long. Professional football and basketball are provided by the Miami Dolphins and the Miami Heat respectively. The Miami Beach Theater of the Performing Arts, Coconut Grove Playhouse and Miami Ballet Society provide a full season of highly acclaimed performances. Well known personalities entertain regularly in the area. The Miami/Ft. Lauderdale area provides ready access to beaches, recreational, and ecological features including the Florida Keys, the Everglades, and National, State and Marine parks.

BETHUNE-COOKMAN COLLEGE   *(E-11)*
640 Second Avenue
Daytona Beach, Florida 32015
Tel: (904) 255-1401; (800) 448-0228; Fax: (904) 257-5338

Description: Private, coeducational college affiliated with the United Methodist Church. It is accredited by the Southern Association of Schools and Colleges. The college is the result of a merger in 1923 of two Florida institutions: Cookman Institute of Jacksonville, founded in 1872 by the Reverend D.S.B. Darnell, and the Daytona Normal and Industrial Institute for Girls, founded in 1904 by Mary McLeod Bethune. Both institutions were established on Christian principles, and at the time of their founding provided much needed rudimentary training for negro boys and girls. In 1932 the school instituted a junior college program. Later the dual program of high school and junior work was discontinued and the entire emphasis placed on the two-year program. In 1941, a four-year college degree program in liberal arts and teacher training was instituted. The college operates on the semester system and offers one summer session. Enrollment is 2,233 full-time and 112 part-time students. A faculty of 124 full-time

and 60 part-time gives a faculty-student ratio of 1-18. Army and Air Force ROTC programs are available.

Entrance Requirements: High school graduates with a C average accepted; completion of 24 units including 4 English, 3 mathematics, 3 natural science and 5 social science, 9 electives; SAT/ACT recommended; 2 letters of recommendation; pre-entrance medical record; $25 application fee.

Costs Per Year: $5,615 tuition and fees per year; $3,395 room and board per year.

Collegiate Environment: The college campus and grounds consist of 52 acres of land, on which are 33 buildings. The library contains 150,494 volumes. Dormitory accommodations are available for 1,529 students. 77% of applicants are accepted. The average scores of the admitted freshmen were SAT verbal 370, math 412, and ACT 16 composite. Scholarships are available and 94% of students receive some form of financial assistance.

Community Environment: Daytona Beach is a resort area located on the Atlantic Ocean with a subtropical climate. All modes of transportation serve the area. The community facilities include two libraries, two museums, many churches, a hospital and major civic organizations. Part-time employment opportunities are available. Recreational activities include water sports, stock car racing, motor bike racing, and archery. Beach drivers almost outnumber swimmers. Spring vacation brings an influx of college students. Special events include the Antique Car Meet and car racing known as the Speed Week.

Branch Campuses: Spuds, FL

BREVARD COMMUNITY COLLEGE   *(H-12)*
1519 Clearlake Road
Cocoa, Florida 32922
Tel: (407) 632-1111; Admissions: (407) 632-1111 x62720; Fax: (407) 633-4565

Description: The community college was established in 1960 and moved to its present campus in 1963. The college is accredited by the Southern Association of Colleges and Schools and grants the Associate degree. It operates on the semester system and offers two summer sessions. Enrollment includes 14,447 full-time and part-time students. Faculty includes 242 full-time and 715 part-time.

Entrance Requirements: High school graduation; open enrollment policy; non-high school graduates considered; early admission, early decision, rolling admission, delayed admission and advanced placement plans available; $20 application fee.

Costs Per Year: $1,120 state resident tuition; $1,560 nonresident tuition.

Collegiate Environment: The campus has ten buildings on 90 acres in the heart of the "Space Capital of the Nation," encompassing Cape Canaveral and the Kennedy Space Center. The buildings are modern and air-conditioned. A complete learning center houses the library of 117,301 volumes, 12,000 pamphlets, 1,388 periodicals, 948 microforms, and 12,208 audiovisual materials. All students applying for admission are accepted. 202 scholarships are offered. 36% of students receive some form of financial assistance.

Community Environment: Cocoa, a suburban area with a subtropical climate, is the leading shipping point for the famous Indian River citrus fruits, and a resort town. Airline and bus service provide transportation for the area. Community facilities include four hospitals, two clinics and many churches. Part-time employment is limited. Recreational activities are water sports, golf, bowling and fishing.

Branch Campuses: Melbourne; Titusville; Patrick AFB; and Palm Bay.

BROWARD COMMUNITY COLLEGE   *(N-13)*
225 East Las Olas Blvd.
Fort Lauderdale, Florida 33301
Tel: (305) 761-7465; Fax: (305) 761-7466

Description: This publicly controlled junior college is accredited by Southern Association of Colleges and Schools. The college grants the Associate in Arts and Associate in Science degrees. The college was authorized by the Florida State Legislature in 1960. There are four major campus locations in Broward County. It operates on the trimester calendar system and two summer terms are offered. Enrollment is 31,000 students and there is a faculty of 750. Two-year Army ROTC is available.

Entrance Requirements: High school graduation or equivalent; non-high school graduates with GED; early admission, early decision, rolling admission and advanced placement plans available; $25 application fee.

Costs Per Year: $1,024.50 ($34.15 per credit) resident; $3,802.50 ($126.75 per credit) nonresident.

Collegiate Environment: The central campus has 10 buildings on 152 acres including a library containing over 200,000 volumes. There are articulated programs with Florida Atlantic University. The North Campus, located on 113 acres in Coconut Creek, has 15 buildings. The South Campus is located in the Hollywood area and began classes in 1977. 96% of those who apply for admission are accepted, and students may enroll at midyear. The college has a special program enabling culturally disadvantaged students with low grades to attend. Scholarships and financial aid are available and 40% of the students receive some form of financial aid.

Community Environment: Fort Lauderdale, population 150,000, is located on the Atlantic Ocean coastline, 25 miles north of Miami. The climate is subtropical and the average year-round temperature is 75 degrees.

Branch Campuses: South Campus, 7200 Hollywood Pines Blvd., Pembroke Pines, FL 33024; Central Campus, 3501 Southwest Davie Rd., Davie, FL 33314; North Campus, 1000 Coconut Creek Blvd., Coconut Creek, FL 33066; Downtown Campus and administrative offices, 225 E. Las Olas Blvd., Ft. Lauderdale, FL 33301.

CENTRAL FLORIDA COMMUNITY COLLEGE   *(E-8)*
P.O. Box 1388
Ocala, Florida 32678
Tel: (904) 237-2111 x334; Fax: (904) 237-3747

Description: Public-controlled community college is accredited by the Southern Association of Colleges and Schools. The college was established in 1957 and the permanent campus was constructed in 1968. Programs of study are vocational-technical. The college grants the certificate and the Associate degree. The college operates on the early semester system and offers summer sessions. Enrollment includes 2,500 full-time and 3,500 part-time students. A faculty of 105 gives a faculty-student ratio of 1-55. The Bronson Center in Levy County opened in 1982 on a 20-acre site east of Bronson. In 1993, this campus relocated to Chiefland to accomodate more students. The college leases space in the Providence Mall for the Levy County Campus. The Citrus County Campus at Lecanto opened as a joint use facility with the Citrus County School Board. The success of this campus led to the acquisition in early 1994 of an 88-acre site in Lecanto. Construction of a 40,000 square foot free-standing campus commenced in February, 1995.

Entrance Requirements: Open enrollment policy; non-high school graduates considered for admission, early admission, midyear admission, rolling admission and advanced placement plans available.

Costs Per Year: $923 ($38.44/credit) state resident tuition; $3,300 ($139.68/credit) nonresident tuition.

Collegiate Environment: The campus has 18 buildings on 120 acres. The library contains over 60,000 volumes and numerous pamphlets, periodicals, microforms and recordings. Approximately 99% of the students applying for admission are accepted and 60% of the freshman class returned for their second year. A full range of financial aid opportunities are available. 236 scholarships, including 48 athletic and 52 activities are available. 75% of students receive financial aid. A student residence center adjacent to the Ocala Campus was opened in 1994, featuring 1,260 square foot apartments.

Community Environment: Ocala, the county seat, is the largest city in Marion County (located in central Florida), and the hub of local economic and cultural activity. Service and light manufacturing industries provide the majority of employment opportunities, although agriculture is also important to the area. The 450 horse farms in the Ocala area rival Kentucky's as the home of the best American thoroughbreds. Ocala boasts a mild climate, beautiful countryside and proximity to major tourist and recreational facilities. Numerous lakes provide fishing and other water sports. Ocala has 16 parks and playgrounds, two municipal swimming pools, and an 18-hole public golf course. The Sunshine Christmas Parade is an annual event.

Branch Campuses: Citrus County Campus, 3820 W. Educational Path, Lecanto, FL 34461-8054

CHIPOLA JUNIOR COLLEGE   *(M-7)*
3094 Indian Circle
Marianna, Florida 32446
Tel: (904) 526-2761; Fax: (904) 526-4153

Description: Founded in 1947, this publically controlled college is accredited by the Southern Association of Colleges and Schools. Programs of study are primarily university parallel and have a career orientation. The college grants the Associate degree. It operates on the semester system and offers two summer sessions. Enrollment includes 1,002 full-time and 1,682 part-time students. A faculty of 66 full-time and 11 part-time gives a faculty-student ratio of 1-35.

Entrance Requirements: High school graduation with C average or equivalent; non high school graduates considered; early admission, early decision, midyear admission, rolling admission, and advanced placement plans available; Aug. 1 application deadline.

Costs Per Year: $1,074 resident tuition; $4,107 nonresident tuition; $1,500 room and board; $700 average additional expenses.

Collegiate Environment: The campus has 16 buildings on 105 acres. The library houses more than 44,167 volumes. There are dormitory facilities for 218 students. 47% of students receive some form of financial assistance. 70% of the freshman class returned for their second year.

Community Environment: Marianna, located in northwest Florida, has an annual average temperature of 68.1 degrees and an average rainfall of 54.51 inches. Buses serve the area along the U.S. Highway 90. Community facilities include a hospital, several motels, a library, churches, and two radio stations. The Florida Caverns State Park, three miles north, has extensive limestone caverns with guided trips available. Picnic areas, campsites, rock gardens, a museum, and golf course are located here. There are fine beaches for all water sports, and excellent hunting in the area.

CHRISTIAN FAITH COLLEGE   *(I-6)*
7100 142nd Avenue North
Largo, Florida 34641
Tel: (813) 531-4498; Fax: (813) 391-0497

Description: The private Bible college had a recent enrollment of 80. It is licensed by the State Board of Independent Colleges and Universities with the State of Florida. The semester system is used, and two summer sessions are offered. A faculty of 16 gives a faculty-student ratio of 1-3.

Entrance Requirements: Students from all churches and denominations with approved Christian character are admitted; high school graduation or equivalent with 16 units required, including 4 English, 2 mathematics, 2 science, 2 social science, and 2 language; non-graduates 18 years of age or over admitted; rolling admission and delayed admission plans available; $10 application fee.

Costs Per Year: $1,050 tuition; $1,200 room and board; $150 student fees.

Collegiate Environment: The college accepts 95% of the applicants; students are permitted to enroll at midyear. The campus has four buildings on 20 acres, and a small lake is located on the property. Single students live in dormitories with a capacity of 15 men and 15 women. The library contains 8,000 volumes.

Community Environment: See Clearwater Christian College.

CLEARWATER CHRISTIAN COLLEGE   *(I-6)*
3400 Gulf-To-Bay Boulevard
Clearwater, Florida 34619
Tel: (813) 726-1153; (800) 348-4463; Fax: (813) 726-8597

Description: Private, liberal arts college. The first students enrolled in 1966. The first building on the new campus was completed in 1966; students moved into the residence hall in 1967. The semester system is used. Recent enrollment was 455 full-time students. A faculty of 23 gives a faculty-student ratio of 1-15. Correspondence credit allowed; continuing education courses offered. Air Force and Army ROTC programs are available through a neighboring institution.

Entrance Requirements: High school graduation or equivalent with a C average; ACT or SAT recommended; rolling admission, advanced placement, early admission plans available; $25 application fee.

Costs Per Year: $4,400 tuition; $3,200 room and board.

Collegiate Environment: The campus has five buildings on 50 acres located on beautiful Tampa Bay; Clearwater beaches are within a 15 minute drive (swimming, boating, fishing, and water skiing are year-round sports). The library contains 3,900 volumes and residence halls accommodate 285 students. Approximately 90% of those who apply for admission are accepted. Financial aid is available, and 80% of the current student body receives some form of assistance.

Community Environment: Clearwater is located on Pinellas Peninsula, between Clearwater and Old Tampa Bays, 20 miles west of Tampa. The area is an all-year resort and citrus center. Amtrak, all major airlines, and buses serve the area. Airports are in St. Petersburg and Tampa. Community facilities include churches of all denominations, a library, museums, hotels, motels, two hospitals, a health center, city parks, floral gardens, a civic center, a maritime center and the usual fraternal civic and veterans organizations. Employment is available in the citrus packing and canning industries. The broad white sand beach on the gulf is the main attraction in the city. This beautiful beach provides for water sports, deep sea fishing, boating, etc. The Philadelphia Phillies baseball team comes here for spring training. The Clearwater Yacht Club and four golf courses including the Professional Golfers Association Club provide additional recreational facilities.

DAYTONA BEACH COMMUNITY COLLEGE   *(E-11)*
P.O. Box 2811
Daytona Beach, Florida 32115-2811
Tel: (904) 255-8131; Fax: (904) 947-3109

Description: This state community college is accredited by the Southern Association of Colleges and Schools. The college was authorized in 1957 by the Florida Legislature and became the state's first comprehensive community college. Programs of study are primarily vocational-technical. University parallel and continuing education courses are available. Special programs include Interactive TV courses, telecourses, cooperative education programs, and dual enrollment programs as well as an Honors Program, and an English Language Institute. The college is one of the few to offer courses in seven foreign languages. It also operates joint-use facilities with the University of Central Florida on the Daytona Beach campus. DBCC maintains articulation agreements with all Florida state universities. The college grants the Associate degree. It operates on the semester system and offers two summer sessions. Average total yearly enrollment is 36,500 students in all programs, with 17,490 students in college-credit courses. Undergraduate degree enrollment is 4,608 full-time and 6,553 part-time students. The faculty-student ratio is 1-22.

Entrance Requirements: High school graduation or equivalent; non-high school graduates considered; early admissions, dual enrollment and advanced placement plans available.

Costs Per Year: $1,040 district/state resident tuition; $3,908 nonresident tuition; additional expenses include lab fees, textbooks, and materials.

Collegiate Environment: The college operates four major campuses and a learning center in its two-county district. Each major campus consists of more than 100 acres, offers full student development and counseling services, and operates a library and a bookstore. The Daytona Beach campus consists of 19 classroom buildings and three service buildings. The library contains 80,155 volumes, 421 periodicals, 212 microforms, and 1,830 audiovisual materials. More than 70% of students currently enrolled are continuing students. Special programs

are offered to meet the needs of individuals with educational deficiencies. Financial assistance is available.

Community Environment: See Bethune-Cookman College, University of Central Florida, Embry-Riddle Aeronautical University, and Stetson University.

Branch Campuses: Flagler/Palm Coast, Palm Coast, FL; Four Townes Learning Center, Debary, Florida; South Campus, New Smyrna Beach, Florida; West Campus, Deland, Florida.

ECKERD COLLEGE   *(I-7)*
4200 - 54th Ave. South
St. Petersburg, Florida 33711
Tel: (813) 864-8331; (800) 456-9009; Fax: (813) 866-2304

Description: This private, liberal arts college is an independent institution, related to the Presbyterian Church (USA). It is accredited by the Southern Association of Colleges and Schools and the American Chemical Society. Since its founding in 1958, it has earned a reputation for creating new and better opportunities for learning, superior methods of education, and a rewarding and enriching educational experience. It pioneered the concept of Winter Term in 1962. An off-campus independent study term is now the basis of 4-1-4 systems. The Mentor program, where a specially trained student-selected faculty member guides the student during a special three-week freshmen orientation program, then through two courses, in conjunction with the Freshmen Foundations Collegium and the General Education Program, is a valuable learning resource. The student explores academic disciplines, cultural heritage and personal values clarification. Off-Campus Programs, Honors Program, Career Service Program and the Academy of Senior Professionals provide additional resources for aspiring pre-professionals. Army and Air Force ROTC programs are available through the University of South Florida, Tampa. The college operates on the 4-1-4 system and offers two summer sessions. Enrollment includes 675 men and 712 women. A faculty of 90 full-time and 34 part-time gives a faculty-student ratio of 1-12.

Entrance Requirements: High school graduation with 18 units including 4 English, 4 mathematics, 3 social science, 3 science, and 2 foreign language; SAT or ACT required; application fee $25; early admission, advanced placement, rolling admission, and deferred admission plans available.

Costs Per Year: $15,360 tuition; $4,080 room and board; $160 student fees.

Collegiate Environment: The campus has 68 modern, air conditioned buildings on 267 acres of prime waterfront property on the suncoast of Florida. The student residences, many of which overlook water, each accomodate 34-36 students, and provide accomdations for 1,080 students. Library contains 140,000 volumes. Semester abroad in London is offered in both the fall and spring at the college's own Study Center, adjacent to the University of London and only a few minutes from London's famed West End. The college assists students participating in study programs in Florence (art), Barcelona, Aix-en-Provence or Avignon, Germany (language), or Japan. Opportunities for study abroad are also available during each winter term (special four-week period of independent study for undergraduates). 77% of applicants are accepted and 80% of freshmen return for sophomore year. The student body is diverse, coming from 49 states and 50 countries. All students are members of the Organization of Students (ECOS) which develops and finances activities, projects, social events and special programs. The college is a member of NCAA (Division II) and the Sunshine State Conference. It offers a full program of intercollegiate and intramural sports, and a national award-winning waterfront program. Religious life includes regularly scheduled worship services and small group activities for study and sharing. On average, students admitted have earned "B" averages or higher in academic high school subjects, rank in the top quintile of their classes, and have an average score of SAT 1080 combined, ACT 25 composite. Financial aid and scholarships are available. 83% of freshmen receive financial aid. The average financial aid package is $12,600, a combination of grants, work, and loans.

Community Environment: St. Petersburg, known as the "Sunshine City," has a wonderful semi-tropical climate. One newspaper gives away its entire edition every day the sun fails to appear before press time. This has happened less than 5 times yearly in the past four decades. The city is the state's fourth largest, and is the most important tourist center on the west coast of Florida. The city has 33 miles of shoreline on the Gulf of Mexico and several fresh water lakes: an excellent location for all water sports. Other sports are baseball, basketball, soccer, cross country, volleyball, softball, golf, and tennis. This is the spring training area for the St. Louis Cardinals and the New York Mets. The Tampa Bay area also offers the professional football Buccaneers, the soccer Rowdies, and the hockey Lightning. Numerous points of interest include the Sunken Gardens of St. Petersburg, Fort DeSoto Park, Sunshine Skyway, the St. Petersburg Museum of Fine Arts, the Dali Museum, the Sun Dome, and the international headquarters of the Women's Tennis Association.

EDISON COMMUNITY COLLEGE   *(L-9)*
8099 College Parkway, SW
P.O. Box 60210
Fort Myers, Florida 33906-6210
Tel: (813) 489-9300; Admissions: (813) 489-9300; Fax: (813) 489-9127

Description: This state community college serves the counties of Charlotte, Collier, Lee, Hendry and Glades. It is accredited by the Southern Association of Colleges and Schools. The first students entered the college in the fall of 1962 and the first permanent campus was constructed in 1965 in Lee county. The second permanent campus was opened in Collier county in 1992. A temporary campus exists in Charlotte county. The college grants Certificates and the Associate in Arts and Associate in Science degrees. Continuing education courses are offered. The semester system is used and two summer sessions are offered. Enrollment is more than 10,000 students. There is a faculty of 93 full-time and approximately 250 part-time.

Entrance Requirements: High school diploma or GED; early admission, early decision, delayed admission, CLEP and advanced placement plans available.

Costs Per Year: $750 state resident tuition; $3,800 nonresident tuition; $5,670 room and board.

Collegiate Environment: Six buildings on 80 acres comprise the campus and the library contains over 53,242 volumes. The college does not provide room and board. Special programs are offered for the culturally disadvantaged and numerous scholarships are available. 100% of the students applying for admission are accepted including midyear students. 40% of the current students receive financial aid.

Community Environment: Edison Community College campuses are located on the sunny coast of southwest Florida, between Miami and Tampa. The climate is semitropical. The offshore islands have many attractive beaches, and majestic Royal Palms line the streets. All modes of transportation serve the area. Tourism, commercial fishing, shrimping and livestock production are important industries. The community facilities include churches of all denominations, hospitals, little theater groups, dances, and lecture halls. The salt-water bays and fresh-water lakes nearby are among the finest fishing grounds anywhere. Other sports include boating, hunting, horseback riding, golfing, bowling, tennis, shuffleboard and greyhound racing in Bonita Springs.

Branch Campuses: Charlotte County Campus, 2511 Vasco St., Punta Gorda, FL 33950, (813) 639-8322; Collier County Campus, 7007 Lely Cultural Parkway, Naples, FL 33962, (813) 732-3700.

EDWARD WATERS COLLEGE   *(B-9)*
1658 Kings Road
Jacksonville, Florida 32209
Tel: (904) 355-3030

Description: This private, coeducational, liberal arts college had a recent enrollment of 737 students. A faculty of 67 provides a student-faculty ratio of 16:1. It operates on the semester system with one summer session offered. The college was founded in 1866 when the Reverend Charles H. Pierce, the first presiding elder of the African Methodist Episcopal Church in Florida, commenced to raise funds for a school which later became the state's first institution for higher education for Negroes.

Entrance Requirements: High school graduation or equivalent; CEEB CAT required; $15 application fee.

Costs Per Year: $3,116 tuition; $3,500 room and board.

Collegiate Environment: The campus is located on six acres in the western section of Jacksonville. Dormitory accommodations are

available for 100 men and 175 women. The library contains over 120,000 titles, 240 periodicals, 499 microforms, and 1,319 audiovisual materials.

Community Environment: See Jacksonville University

EMBRY-RIDDLE AERONAUTICAL UNIVERSITY   *(E-11)*
600 South Clyde Morris Boulevard
Daytona Beach, Florida 32114-9970
Tel: (904) 226-6100; (800) 222-3728; Fax: (904) 226-7070

Description: Embry-Riddle Aeronautical University (ERAU) has two residential campuses, one in Daytona Beach, Florida, one in Prescott, Arizona, and the College of Continuing Education operating on selected military sites and aviation centers worldwide. The University has an enrollment on its two residential campuses (Florida and Arizona) of 6,000 students. With 350 full-time faculty on the two residential campuses, the faculty-to-student ratio is 1-17. The College of Continuing Education enrolls approximately 7,000 students, mostly on a part-time basis, at over 80 resident centers. ERAU offers the Bachelor of Science degree in 14 areas; the Associate of Science degree in 2; and the Master of Science in Aviation Business Administration, Aerospace Engineering, and Aeronautical Science. ERAU is accredited by the Southern Association of Colleges and Schools and has professional accreditation in selected other university programs. ERAU operates on on a semester calendar with two summer terms for the residential campuses.

Entrance Requirements: High school graduation (or equivalent); entrance requirements vary according to degree program. Rolling admission. SAT or ACT required; $30 application fee.

Costs Per Year: $8,200 tuition and fees; $3,698 room and board.

Collegiate Environment: The Daytona Beach Campus is located adjacent to the Daytona Beach Regional Airport, with 22 building on 86 acres, and excellent year-round recreational facilities. The Jack R. Hunt Memorial Library contains over 44,000 volumes plus subscriptions, microfilms and other media resources. Dormitory and housing facilities accommodate 990 men and women with additional housing close to campus. There is housing for 725 students at Prescott. 63% of applicants are accepted. The campus also has its own Flight line and Maintenance facilities on the campus property. Other facilities include classrooms, simulator labs, wind tunnels, a weather room, and computer labs. The Prescott Campus is located just outside the city of Prescott, Arizona, just minutes from the Flight Line at Ernest A. Love Field. Located on 510 acres, the campus includes classrooms, library, dormitories, laboratories, wind tunnels and computer labs. The library on the Prescott Campus has over 2,500 volumes plus additional microfilm and other resources.

Community Environment: The Daytona Beach area has a population of approximately 300,000 in the immediate vicinity, and the campus itself has approximately 4,800 students. Boasting one of the finest recreational beaches in the world, Daytona Beach is also the home of the Daytona International Speedway. Other major local attractions include Walt Disney World and Sea World near Orlando (approximately 80 miles away). The area also provides ample housing and excellent opportunities for part-time employment for ERAU students. The Prescott area is one of the more colorful areas of the old 'Wild West.' with a population in the immediate area approaching 50,000. The Prescott Campus of approximately 1,500 students is surrounded by a national forest, and close to mountains and excellent outdoor recreational areas. The city of Phoenix is about 90 miles away.

Branch Campuses: Prescott, AZ 86301, (602) 776-3728, (800) 442-3728.

FLAGLER COLLEGE   *(D-10)*
King St. P.O. Box 1027
St. Augustine, Florida 32085-1027
Tel: (904) 829-6481

Description: The private, liberal arts college was chartered in 1963 and opened to its first freshman class in the fall of 1968. The college is accredited by the Southern Association of Colleges and Schools and grants a Bachelor of Arts degree. The early semester system is used and 1 summer session is offered. Enrollment includes 1,350 full-time and 39 part-time students. A faculty of 47 full-time and 76 part-time gives a faculty-student ratio of approximately 1-21. Special programs include overseas studies and work at the Florida School for the Deaf and the Blind.

Entrance Requirements: Accredited high school graduation with minimum C+ average; completion of 16 units with recommended 4 English, 3 mathematics, 2 science, and 4 social studies; SAT or ACT required; early admission, midyear admission, delayed admission and advanced placement plans available; $20 application fee.

Costs Per Year: $5,120 tuition and fees; $3,200 room and board; $1,100 average additional expenses.

Collegiate Environment: The college is located in the heart of the historic city of St. Augustine, which by actual date of founding is the oldest city in the United States. The focal point of the campus was originally the famous Ponce de Leon Hotel, described as a masterpiece in American architecture. The Ponce de Leon is listed in the National Register of Historic Places. The dining hall room, student center, some administrative offices, and residence halls for 495 students are contained within the Ponce de Leon Hotel. Kenan Hall, a multipurpose academic facility, contains most of the College's classrooms, seminar rooms, laboratories, and faculty offices. The library and the computer center are also located in Kenan Hall. In addition, the highly centralized 37-acre campus includes other administrative buildings, classrooms, a 180-bed dormitory, a performing arts theater, a gymnasium, ten tennis courts, an intramural field, and a swimming pool. An 18-acre athletic complex that provides facilities for soccer, baseball, softball, and intramurals is located two miles from the campus. The library contains 125,000 books, 575 periodicals, 15,102 microforms, and 933 audiovisual materials. Living accommodations are available for 280 men and 415 women. Approximately 50% of students who apply for admission are accepted, and students may enroll at midyear. Financial aid is available, and 83% of the current students receive financial assistance. Approximately 27% of the senior class continued on to graduate school.

Community Environment: St. Augustine, the nation's oldest city, has a very mild climate; average high temperature is 79.9 degrees and the average low is 58.3 degrees. The city is located approximately 40 miles south of Jacksonville, near the Atlantic coast. St. Augustine is undergoing a restoration program to extend over a twenty-year period that will return the entire area to an authentic likeness of its colonial days. The leading industries are tourist trade, airplane rebuilding, aluminium extrusion, boat-building, food processing, and shrimp fishing. Recreation facilities include a championship golf course, beaches, tennis courts, and the ocean for deep sea fishing. The Matanzas River affords miles of protected waters for boating and fishing. The city has churches of all denominations, numerous hotels and motels, 2 hospitals, and a library. All the major civic and fraternal organizations are represented. Sightseeing tours are available by horse-drawn carriages and trains. There are many many points of interest, some of which are the Cathedral of St. Augustine, Lightner Museum, Marineland, Alligator Farm, Casa Del Hidalgo, Fountain of Youth, Mission of Nombre De Dios, Oldest Schoolhouse, the Zimenes House, Memorial Presbyterian Church, and the Castillo de San Marcos.

FLORIDA AGRICULTURAL AND MECHANICAL UNIVERSITY *(B-3)*
Tallahassee, Florida 32307
Tel: (904) 599-3796; Fax: (904) 561-2428

Description: This state university was founded by constitutional provision and legislative enactment in 1887 as the Colored Normal School. The institution has displayed remarkable growth and in 1957 was part of the first group of institutions operated for blacks to be admitted to full membership in the Southern Association of Secondary Schools and Colleges. It is also accredited by numerous professional organizations. The school operates on the early semester system and offers 2 summer sessions. Special programs include a Washington, DC, program in Architecture and an academic cooperative plan with Florida State University. Enrollment includes 8,704 full-time and 1,071 part-time undergraduates, and 543 graduate students. A faculty of 466 full-time and 134 part-time gives a faculty-student ratio of 1-18.

Entrance Requirements: High school graduation with at least a C average; completion of 19 units including 4 English, 3 mathematics, 3 laboratory science, 3 social science, 2 foreign language, and 4 additional from those listed; SAT composite 900 or ACT 21 required;

early admission, early decision, rolling admission, and advanced placement plans available; $20 application fee.

Costs Per Year: $1,767 tuition; $6,669 nonresidents; $2,964 room and board.

Collegiate Environment: The university is located on the highest of the seven hills of the State capital, approximately one mile from the center of the city. The library contains 372,860 volumes, 3,300 periodicals, and 62,610 audiovisual materials. Dormitory facilities are available for 2,088 students. Approximately 61% of students applying for admission are accepted as well as midyear students. Army, Air Force and Navy ROTC are available as well as courses in American history and special programs for the culturally disadvantaged. Scholarships are available.

Community Environment: Tallahassee, a community of varied interests, provides an ideal setting for a thriving comprehensive university. The community abounds in a broad range of programs and activities, including three institutions of higher education; city, county, and state government; civic and community organizations; art galleries; theater and music archives, libraries and museums; state parks and recreational facilities; tree-shaded streets and highways; and a 13,500-seat Civic Center.

FLORIDA ATLANTIC UNIVERSITY *(M-13)*
777 Glades Road
P.O. Box 3091
Boca Raton, Florida 33431-0991
Tel: (407) 367-3040; (800) 299-4328; Fax: (407) 367-2758

Description: The state-supported university enrolls 2,990 full-time undergraduate men, 3,667 full-time undergraduate women, 5,554 part-time undergraduates, and 2,337 graduate students. The university is accredited by the Southern Association of Colleges and Schools and grants the Associate, Bachelor, Master, Specialist and Doctorate degrees. The university was established in 1961. It operates on the semester system and offers 3 summer sessions. Correspondence credit is allowed; continuing education courses are offered; cooperative education programs are available; overseas programs are available. The last 30 semester hours must be taken in residence.

Entrance Requirements: Freshman admission is competitive based on SAT/ACT results, academic core GPA and completion of 19 academic units; transfer admission with fewer than 60 semester hours requires 2.0 college GPA and high school record as required for freshman admission; transfers with 60 or more semester hours must have 2.0 college GPA; GRE or GMAT required for graduate admission; early admission, rolling admission and advanced undergraduate placement plans available; $20 application fee.

Costs Per Year: $1,791 resident tuition; $6,693 nonresident tuition; $3,930 room and board.

Collegiate Environment: The university is located on a 750-acre site just a few miles west of the Atlantic Ocean. The 31 buildings include the five-story library containing 611,462 volumes, 3,997 periodicals, 2,588,873 microforms and 23,213 audiovisual materials. Dormitory facilities accommodate 500 men and 550 women. These figures will change significantly in September 1995 when an additional dormitory facility opens. Financial assistance is available. 73% of applicants are accepted. 93% of transfer applicants are accepted. The university gymnasium hosts sporting and cultural events, and has a seating capacity of 5,000.

Community Environment: A resort and suburban area located on Florida's east coast, Boca Raton is 40 miles north of Miami and 25 miles from Ft. Lauderdale and Palm Beach airports. The area enjoys a subtropical climate. Several shopping centers, a library, Catholic churches, several Protestant churches, several synagogues and two hospitals are some of the community facilities. Local industry includes large regional centers for IBM, Sensolmatic, Siemens and other high tech multinational corporations. Recreational activities include swimming, tennis, golf, surf casting, and deep-sea fishing. There are three public beaches and numerous superior golf courses nearby. Cultural recreational activities are many. Special events are the Spanish Festival and the polo matches on each Sunday from January through April. Within an hour's drive are West Palm Beach, Fort Lauderdale, and Miami, with their varied cultural and recreational activities. The Atlantic Ocean is just 3 miles away, and Everglades National Park lies to the west and south.

Branch Campuses: Florida Atlantic University is a distributed university with a residential campus in Boca Raton and academic campuses in Fort Lauderdale, Davie, Palm Beach Gardens, and Fort Pierce. Academic colleges are headquartered at individual campuses but offer programs throughout the university's system.

FLORIDA BAPTIST COLLEGE   *(F-4)*
506 South Oakwood Avenue
P.O. Box 2758
Brandon, Florida 33509-2758
Tel: (813) 684-1389; Fax: (813) 689-0544

Description: This corporation includes the Florida Baptist College, Florida Baptist Institute. The College is a member of the American Baptist Association of Theological Schools. Grants the Associate, Bachelor and Master degrees. The college operates on the semester system. Enrollment includes 50 full-time and 22 part-time undergraduate students. A faculty of 12 gives a student-faculty ratio of 1-6.

Entrance Requirements: Open enrollment; high school graduation or equivalent; non-high school graduates may be admitted; early admission, early decision, rolling admission, and advanced placement plans available; $20 appplication fee.

Costs Per Year: $600 tuition; $80 fees; $960 room.

Collegiate Environment: The campus has 7 buildings on 10 acres bordered by Oakwood Avenue to the east, Dew Bloom Road to the South and Lithia-Pinecrest Road to the West. On-campus housing is available to individuals as well as married couples. Financial aid is available and 25% of the current student body receives some form of assistance. 90% of those who apply for admission are accepted.

Community Environment: University of South Florida

FLORIDA BAPTIST THEOLOGICAL COLLEGE
1306 College Drive
Graceville, Florida 32440
Tel: (904) 263-3261; (800) 328-2660; Fax: (904) 328-2660

Description: This privately supported college offers four years of theological studies to students who are preparing for positions of leadership in Baptist and other evangelical churches. It operates on the semester system with two summer sessions. The college is owned and operated by the Florida Baptist Convention, in harmony with the objectives of the Southern Baptist Convention. Enrollment includes 421 full-time and 70 part-time students. A faculty of 14 full-time and 9 part-time gives a faculty-student ratio of 1-21.

Entrance Requirements: High school graduation or equivalent; applicants must have at least one year Christian experience and be a member in good standing with a church affiliated with the Southern Baptist Convention or other evangelical denominations; rolling admission plan available; $20 application fee.

Costs Per Year: $2,440 tuition; $1,125 room without meals; $84 student fees.

Collegiate Environment: The campus has 71 buildings on 150 acres. The library contains 50,132 volumes. Dormitory facilities accommodate 96 men and 36 women, and housing is available on campus for 64 married couples. The college accepts 95% of applicants, and students may enroll at midyear. Financial aid is available, and 73% of the current student body receives some form of assistance. The institute awards Associate and Bachelor degrees.

Community Environment: Graceville is in northwest Florida near the borders of Alabama, Florida and Georgia. 23 miles north is Dothan, Alabama, and 20 miles southeast is Marianna, Florida. Railroads and buses serve the area. One excellent shopping center is available.

FLORIDA COLLEGE   *(F-4)*
119 Glen Arven
Temple Terrace, Florida 33617
Tel: (813) 988-5131; Fax: (813) 899-6772

Description: The private liberal arts junior college emphasizes University preparatory and general education courses in a moral environment. The college is accredited by Southern Association of Colleges and Schools and grants the Associate degree. Members of Churches of Christ began the college in 1946 but the college is independent of the church. The college operates on the semester system. Enrollment includes 368 full-time and 4 part-time students. A faculty of 25 full-time and 4 part-time gives a faculty-student ratio of 1-13.

Entrance Requirements: High school graduation with 2.0 grade point average or higher; completion of 14 academic units including 4 English, 2 algebra, 2 lab science and 2 social science; ACT; non-high school graduates considered; rolling admission, early admission, early decision and advanced placement plans available; $25 application fee.

Costs Per Year: $4,800 tuition; $3,220 room and board.

Collegiate Environment: The campus has 21 buildings on 195 acres. The library contains 32,262 volumes, 304 periodicals and 916 recordings. Dormitory facilities accommodate 233 men and 204 women. Scholarships are available and 80% of students receive some form of financial aid.

Community Environment: Located near Tampa, Temple Terrace has a subtropical climate. Buses serve the area. Community facilities include a library, churches, and one community college and two universities. Part-time employment is limited. Sport activities include boating, fishing, golf, professional baseball, football and soccer. Cultural and recreational facilities, broad and varied, are also available in Tampa.

FLORIDA COMMUNITY COLLEGE AT JACKSONVILLE   *(B-9)*
501 West State Street
Jacksonville, Florida 32202
Tel: (904) 646-2136; Fax: (904) 646-2226

Description: This two-year community college is state funded and governed by a District Board of Trustees composed of local citizens appointed by the Governor. It is accredited by the Southern Association of Colleges and Schools. Enrollment includes 5,962 full-time and 13,688 part-time students. A faculty of 391 full-time and 1,142 part-time provides a faculty-student ratio of 1-22. The school operates on the semester system and offers a multiterm Spring/Cross/Summer term that lasts 6 weeks, 12 weeks, and 6 weeks, respectively. Chartered in 1963, FCCJ opened its doors to students in 1966. It grants both the Technical Certificate and Associate degrees, and offers postsecondary job training programs, adult studies, and continuing education. A European study/travel abroad program is available. In addition to the traditional campus classrooms, courses are taught via cable television, on site at business locations, on military bases, at college campuses and at area sites.

Entrance Requirements: Open door policy for college-credit programs; high school graduation or GED required; transcript from previously attended colleges or universities required for transfer students; $20 application fee; $75 application fee international students; special admissions programs available for non-high school graduates; accelerated college, early admission, midyear admission, dual enrollment, and special student plans also available.

Costs Per Year: $1,074 resident tuition; $4,026 out-of-state.

Collegiate Environment: All students applying for admission are accepted, including midyear students. Special programs are offered for the culturally disadvantaged, and scholarships are available. The Learning Resource Center Library contains 229,434 volumes, 1,893 periodicals, 1,794 microforms and 16,597 audiovisual materials.

Community Environment: The college is located in Jacksonville, Florida, which has a population of 969,038. The four college campuses, college centers and sites are conveniently located. Public transportation is available throughout the city. On-campus housing is not available.

FLORIDA INSTITUTE OF TECHNOLOGY   *(H-12)*
150 W. University Blvd.
Melbourne, Florida 32901
Tel: (407) 768-8000; (800) 888-4348; Fax: (407) 723-9468

Description: This private, independent institution is accredited by the Southern Association of Colleges and Schools. Founded in 1958, the school was formerly known as the Brevard Engineering College. The institution was founded as an evening school for those working at the Kennedy Space Center; daytime programs were established in 1962 to meet the needs of others seeking high quality education on a full-time basis. Florida Tech encompasses 5 separate schools that offer a full scope of programs in the fields of natural science, engineering, business, psychology, aviation and related disciplines. The university offers degrees at the doctoral, master and bachelor levels. Special programs include cooperative education and continuing education. Army ROTC is available. The institute operates on the semester system and offers two summer sessions. Enrollment includes 1,684 full-time, 199 part-time and 2,685 graduate students. A faculty of 222 full-time and 243 part-time gives a faculty-student ratio of 1-12.

Entrance Requirements: High school graduation or equivalent; completion of 16 units including 4 English, 4 math, 3 science; SAT 500M and 500V or ACT 26 English and 27 math usually required; early admission, rolling admission, early decision, midyear admission and advanced placement plans available; $35 application fee.

Costs Per Year: $13,700 tuition; $4,140 room and board; $750 books; $1,200 transportation; $1,500 miscellaneous.

Collegiate Environment: The campus is situated on nearly 175 acres of partially wooded land in the city of Melbourne, Brevard County, Florida. The Melbourne campus is the home of the College of Science and Liberal Arts, the College of Engineering, the School of Business, the School of Psychology and the School of Aeronautics. The Flight Operations Department for the School of Aeronautics is located at the Melbourne International Airport, 5 minutes from campus. Dormitory facilities are available for 1,000 students. 80% of students applying for admission are accepted including midyear students. 70% of the current student body receives some form of financial aid.

Community Environment: Florida Tech is located on Florida's space coast, approximately 30 miles south of Kennedy Space Center, 60 miles east of Orlando and 170 miles north of Miami, in the city of Melbourne. The university is situated on 175 acres of partially wooded and beautifully landscaped grounds. Nearly one-fifth of the acreage consists of tropical gardens, a forest of palms, water oaks, orchids and tropical vegetation. It is 5 minutes from the Melbourne International Airport, which is host to 4 major airlines. Recreation includes public swimming pools, golf courses, a tourist club with facilities for a number of sports, a harbor, and a yacht basin. Fresh and salt water fishing are available.

FLORIDA INTERNATIONAL UNIVERSITY (O-13)
University Park
Miami, Florida 33199
Tel: (305) 348-2363; Admissions: (305) 348-2363; Fax: (305) 348-3648

Description: This public supported coeducational university was established on June 22, 1965 as a member institution of the state University System of Florida. The first classes were held in 1972 for upper-division and graduate students; classes for freshmen and sophomores began in 1981. The school is accredited by the Southern Association of Colleges and Schools and operates on the semester system with two summer sessions. FIU's extensive and diversified curriculum of over 180 academic programs is aimed at producing educated and sensitive leaders. The university grants the Bachelor's, Masters, and Doctorate degrees. It is composed of the Colleges of Arts and Sciences, Business Administration, Education, Engineering and Design, Health, Urban and Public Affairs and the Schools of Accounting, Computer Science, Hospitality Management, Journalism and Mass Communications, and Nursing. Enrollment includes 21,138 undergraduates and 5,409 graduate students. A faculty of 788 full-time and 385 part-time gives a faculty-student ratio of 1-22.

Entrance Requirements: High school graduates with 19 units including 4 English 3 mathematics, 3 laboratory science, 3 social studies, and 2 foreign language. Application fee $20. Application deadline is June 1.

Costs Per Year: $1,680 ($56/cr) resident; $6,570 ($219/cr) nonresident; $80 student fees; $2,495 room.

Collegiate Environment: University Park occupies 344 acres in the western suburbs of Dade County. The campus has 13 major academic buildings, a residential apartment complex for 800 students and a new athletic arena. The North Miami campus encompasses 200 acres on Biscayne Bay, including a large natural cypress preserve. Campus facilities includes six academic buildings, an Olympic-type aquatic center, and apartment-style housing for 552 students. The two campuses are linked by a university-operated transportation system. The libraries on campus contain 1,016,699 volumes, 11,931 periodicals, 66,560 audiovisual materials and over 2.8 million microform units. 2,882

scholarships are available, including 693 for freshmen. 31% of the students receive financial aid.

Community Environment: The Greater Miami area offers cultural diversity and a dynamic economical and aesthetic climate. South Florida is a major center of higher education and stands at the forefront of international trading, finance and banking, as well as tourism and a developing high technology industry. Miami International Airport is served by more airlines than any other airport in the country. One of the most culturally diverse cities in America, Miami has many distinctive neighborhoods. Both visual and performing arts thrive in Miami. The Metro-Dade Cultural Complex in downtown Miami houses the metropolitan Library, the Museum of South Florida, and the Center for the Fine Arts. The city also maintains both an opera and three ballet companies. A wealth of galleries, libraries, and theaters are valuable resources. The greater Miami area also hosts many sports events and offers year round recreation activities such as fishing, boating, scuba diving, wind surfing, snorkeling, swimming, and deep-sea fishing.

FLORIDA KEYS COMMUNITY COLLEGE (R-9)
5901 West College Road
Key West, Florida 33040
Tel: (305) 296-9081; Fax: (305) 292-5155

Description: The public-controlled, community college is accredited by the Southern Association of Colleges and Schools. The college was authorized in 1963 and moved to Stock Island in 1968. The college grants Certificates and the Associate degree. Special programs include cooperative education and continuing education. The trimester system is used in conjunction with two six-week summer sessions. Enrollment is 1,849 full-time students. A faculty of 74 full-time gives a faculty-student ratio of 1-23.

Entrance Requirements: High school graduation or equivalent; open enrollment policy, except for limited access Nursing Program; non-high school graduates considered; early admission and advanced placement plans available; $15 application fee.

Costs Per Year: $1,035 state resident tuition; $3,870 nonresident tuition; $850 average additional expenses.

Collegiate Environment: The campus has five buildings on 126 acres. The library contains 26,000 volumes, 300 pamphlets, 300 periodicals, 9,419 microforms and 5,412 audiovisual materials. All students applying for admission are accepted. Financial aid is available and 25% of the current student body receives financial assistance.

Community Environment: Key West is the southernmost city in the continental United States. It is a tropical island 157 miles southwest of Miami with an Old-World atmosphere. The setting is a blend of Cuban, West Indian, and Bahamian. The climate is warm and the air is almost pollen free. A rich and colorful history is retained in a thriving modern city. All forms of transportation serve the area. Searstown and four shopping centers are among the nation's most unique, all having a tropical flair. Year-round outdoor recreation includes a coral reef several miles offshore and provides some of the world's finest fishing and diving. Numerous points of interest are the Audubon house, Ernest Hemingway Home and Museum, Martello Gallery and Museum, the Lighthouse and the Military Museum.

FLORIDA MEMORIAL COLLEGE (O-13)
15800 NW Florida Memorial College Ave.
Miami, Florida 33054
Tel: (305) 626-3600; (800) 822-1362; Admissions: (305) 626-3600; Fax: (305) 626-3106

Description: Florida Memorial College is a four-year coeducational, Baptist-related institution accredited by the Southern Association of Colleges and Schools and approved by the Florida State Department of Education. It is a member institution of the United Negro College Fund. The current enrollment is 1,500 men and women. The faculty is multi-racial; faculty-student ratio of 1:20. Florida Memorial offers twenty-three majors and minors and grants the Bachelor of Arts and Bachelor of Science degrees. It offers Air Force ROTC. The college operates on the semester system and offers one summer session.

Entrance Requirements: Open enrollment; completion of 16 units including 4 English, 1 mathematics, 1 science and 4 social science; high school graduation with 2.0 G.P.A.; application; official transcript; letters of recommendation; personal statement; health form;

=SAT or ACT test scores; international students must submit a notarized affidavit of support and bank statement; rolling admission, early decision and midyear plans; $15 application fee.

Costs Per Year: $4,160 tuition; $3,190 room and board; $390 student fees.

Collegiate Environment: The college's 77-acre site is situated around a lake and features 14 modern buildings, including four residence halls. The focal points of activity are the college's 100,000 volume library and the J.C. Sams Student Activity Center. The William Lehman Aviation Center is home to the college's aviation and computer science programs. This three-story complex features several laboratories, a large auditorium and three flight simulators. Four fraternities and four sororities have active chapters. The college is a member of the National Association of Intercollegiate Athletics and offers competition in basketball, cross-country indoor track and field, for both men and women. In addition, men compete in baseball and women in volleyball. 81% of applicants are accepted. Scholarships are available and 80% of the students receive some form of financial aid.

Community Environment: FMC's main campus is located in Miami, 15 miles north of downtown. The north Dade County location of the campus offers convenient access to all points in the Miami area as well as Fort Lauderdale, and provides strudents a wealth of recreational, cultural, leisure, employment and additional educational opportunities. FMC also maintains several off-campus sites through its Division of Extension & Continuing Education.

FLORIDA SOUTHERN COLLEGE   *(I-8)*
111 Lake Hollingsworth Drive
Lakeland, Florida 33801-5698
Tel: (813) 680-4100; (800) 274-4131; Admissions: (813) 680-4131;
Fax: (813) 680-4120

Description: Private, liberal arts college is affliated with the United Methodist Church and accredited by the Southern Association of Colleges and Schools. The college was founded in 1885. It grants the Bachelor's degree. Army ROTC programs are available to both men and women. The college operates on the semester system and offers two summer sessions, as well as May optional (held in England) and winter Mini-mester option. Enrollment includes 1,370 full-time and 99 part-time and 300 evening program undergraduates and 50 graduate students. A faculty of 95 full-time and 31 part-time gives a faculty-student raito of 1-15.

Entrance Requirements: High school graduation with a minimum C average and 18 units, including 4 English and 3 mathematics, 2 science, 2 foreign language and 2 social science; non-high school applicants considered; early admission, rolling admission and advanced placement plans available; $30 application fee.

Costs Per Year: $8,760 tuition; $5,100 room and board; $640 fees.

Collegiate Environment: The campus, located on a beautiful lake, is near the exact geographical center of Florida. The college is known for having the world's largest collection of Frank Lloyd Wright buildings. The library contains 158,143 volumes. The Panhellenic building houses six of the chapters of national sororities at Florida Southern; total dormitory capacity is 1,250 men and women.

Community Environment: Lakeland is located in the geographical center of Florida, 35 miles East of Tampa, 50 miles west of Orlando, 100 miles from the Atlantic Ocean, 35 miles from Disney World and 60 miles from the Gulf of Mexico. The Seaboard Coast Line Railroad serves the area. The "World's Citrus Center" is the permanent spring training headquarters of the Detroit Tigers. Excellent shopping facilities in the city; a civic center, concert association, and community theatre are part of the lively community. Recreational facilities include 12 lakes within the city for excellent fishing, golf courses, boating, hiking, and waterskiing. The annual Orange Cup Regatta Hydroplane Race is held the weekend closest to February 1st.

FLORIDA STATE UNIVERSITY   *(B-3)*
216 B WJB
Tallahassee, Florida 32306-1007
Tel: (904) 644-2525; Admissions: (904) 644-6200; Fax: (904) 644-0197

Description: The state university is accredited by the Southern Association of Colleges and Schools and numerous professional organizations. The university was authorized in 1851; it is one of Florida's oldest universities. Army, Navy and Air Force ROTC are available as electives. The university grants the Bachelor's, Master's, Advanced Master's, Specialist, Professional and Doctorate degrees. Correspondence credit is allowed. Continuing education courses are available. Overseas programs are offered in Italy, England, Costa Rica, Switzerland, Yugoslavia, Panama, Barbados, France, the Netherlands, and Russia. The university operates on the semester system and offers three summer sessions. Enrollment includes 23,650 full-time and 5,980 part-time undergraduates and 5,649 graduate students. The faculty is 1,435 full-time and 133 part-time. The faculty-student ratio varies with the level of instruction.

Entrance Requirements: High school graduate or equivalent; SAT or ACT; 19 units required including 4 English, 3 mathematics (Algebra I and higher), 2 of the same foreign language, 3 natural sciences (at least 2 lab science), 3 social studies, and 4 electives preferably from above areas; early admission, rolling admission and credit allowed for Advanced Placement, International Baccalaureate, and College Level Examination Program; $20 application fee.

Costs Per Year: $1,798 state-resident tuition and fees; $6,700 out-of-state; $2,280 room; $2,150 board; $600 books and supplies.

Collegiate Environment: The main campus is located on 405 acres and the physical plant ranges in architectural design from collegiate Gothic to ultramodern. University housing accomodates 3,979 students and consists of undergraduate, graduate, and family residences that include dormitories and apartments for full-time degree-seeking students. Also, close to campus are privately owned residence halls, sorority and fraternity houses, scholarship houses, apartments, duplexes, and rental houses. The main library facility and its branches holdings include 2,065,664 hardbound volumes, 18,436 current serials, and 3,933,253 microforms. The FSU Supercomputer Computations Research Institute has two of the world's most powerful supercomputers, and the Tandem Van de Graaff Superconducting Accelerator Laboratory has been ranked in the top four in the nation by the National Science Foundation. In addition, FSU was recently selected to house the National High Magnetic Field Laboratory. 74% of applicants are accepted. The University attracts students from all counties in the state, from all states in the country, and from 119 countries in the world. The middle 50% range of enrolled freshmen scores were SAT 460-550 verbal, 530-620 math, 990-1170 combined; ACT 22-27 composite. Numerous scholarships are available. 49% of students receive some form of financial aid.

Community Environment: Situated in north Florida, FSU is nestled in the heart of Tallahassee, the state's capital city. A classic college town, Tallahassee is not only one of Florida's oldest and fastest growing cities, it is also part of the "other Florida" with its rolling hills, canopy roads, mild climate, and southern hospitality. More than 100 state and federal agencies furnish students with opportunities for internships, research, and work-study programs that match all areas of academic interest. Part-time jobs are plentiful. In addition, Tallahassee affords a rich offering of social, cultural, and recreational activities, making it an excellent place to live, study, and grow.

Branch Campuses: FSU's Panama City campus is located on the Emerald Coast, 100 miles from Tallahassee, and provides undergraduate and graduate programs.

FORT LAUDERDALE COLLEGE   *(N-13)*
1040 Bayview Drive
Fort Lauderdale, Florida 33304
Tel: (305) 568-1600; (800) 468-0168; Admissions: (305) 568-1600;
Fax: (305) 568-2008

Description: Private, business oriented college that had its beginning in 1940 as a private business school. It is accredited by the Accrediting Council for Independent Colleges and Schools as a senior college of business. The quarter system is used and one summer term is offered. Enrollment includes 550 full-time and 50 part-time students. A faculty of 11 full-time and 29 part-time gives a faculty-student ratio of 1-20.

Entrance Requirements: Open enrollment C average policy; early admission, early decision, deferred admission, midyear admission, and advanced placement plans available; $25 application fee.

Costs Per Year: $4,140 annual tuition; $3,510 apartment; $150 fees.

Collegiate Environment: Downtown location adjacent to City park and one quarter mile from the Atlantic Ocean. The College is contractually associated with the new Broward County Library housing 500,000 volumes which is directly across from the college. Apartment living is available for 52 students. 85% of applicants are accepted. 60% of students receive some form of financial assistance.

Community Environment: See Nova University

GULF COAST COMMUNITY COLLEGE (O-6)
5230 West Highway 98
Panama City, Florida 32401
Tel: (904) 769-1551; Admissions: (904) 872-3892

Description: The public community college was authorized and opened in 1957. It has occupied its present location since 1960. The college is accredited by the Southern Association of Colleges and Schools. Programs of study lead to the Associate degree. The college operates on the semester system and offers two summer sessions. Enrollment includes 3,412 men and 4,619 women. A faculty of 103 full-time and 252 part-time gives a faculty-student ratio of 1-19.

Entrance Requirements: High school graduation or equivalent; units to include 4 English, 3 mathematics, 3 science, 3 social science; non-high school graduates considered; open admission, midyear admission, early admission, deferred admission, rolling admission, and advanced placement plans available.

Costs Per Year: $1,057 resident tuition; $4,036 out-of-state tuition.

Collegiate Environment: The campus has 20 buildings on 80 acres. The library contains nearly 69,542 volumes, and numerous periodicals, microfilms and audio-visual materials. All qualified applicants are accepted. Financial assistance is available, and 57% of the current student body receives some form of aid.

Community Environment: Panama City is an urban area with a temperate climate and is recognized as one of the most progressive industrial and resort cities in the state. A new municipal marina includes a city hall, an auditorium, a library, and berths for about 400 boats. The community facilities include libraries, churches of major denominations, two hospitals and several clinics; shopping facilities are excellent. Some part-time employment is available. The city's industries include a paper company, oil companies, wholesale fisheries, chemical production, boat manufacturing. Outdoor sports include golfing, yachting, sailing, water skiing and swimming. Panama City is a noted sport fishing center for both fresh and salt water fish.

HILLSBOROUGH COMMUNITY COLLEGE (I-7)
39 Columbia Drive
P.O. Box 31127
Tampa, Florida 33631-3127
Tel: (813) 253-7004; Fax: (813) 253-7196

Description: This public community college commenced operation in the fall of 1968. It is accredited by the Southern Association of Colleges and Schools. The college offers both college transfer and technical-occupational programs, as well as extensive counseling and guided studies programs. Continuing education courses are offered. The Associate degree is awarded. It operates on the semester system and offers two summer sessions. Enrollment includes 5,560 full-time and 13,534 part-time students. A faculty of 240 full-time and 451 part-time gives a faculty-student ratio of 1-26. Air Force ROTC is available under a cross enrollment agreement with the University of South Florida.

Entrance Requirements: Open enrollment; completion of 24 units including 4 English, 3 mathematics, 3 lab. science, 3 social science; ACT or SAT, ASSET or Placement Exams required; early admission, early decision, deferred admission, midyear admission, rolling admission, dual enrollment, and advanced placement plans available; $20 application fee.

Costs Per Year: $1,020 state resident tuition; $3,915 nonresident tuition.

Collegiate Environment: The library contains 94,677 bound volumes in addition to periodical subscriptions, microforms, and audiovisual materials. No dormitory facilities are provided. 900 scholarships are available and 39% of students receive some form of financial assistance.

Community Environment: See University of South Florida.

INDIAN RIVER COMMUNITY COLLEGE (J-13)
3209 Virginia Avenue
Fort Pierce, Florida 34981-5599
Tel: (407) 462-4700; Admissions: (407) 462-4748; Fax: (407) 462-4699

Description: The district-governed community college is accredited by the Southern Association of Colleges and Schools. The semester system is used and two summer sessions are offered. The college was authorized in 1959 and moved to its permanent campus in 1963. It has a student enrollment of 48,000 and a full-time faculty of 158.

Entrance Requirements: Graduation from an accredited high school or its equivalent; ASSET, SAT, or ACT used for placement purposes only.

Costs Per Year: $960 tuition; $3,840 nonresident.

Collegiate Environment: The campus has 26 modern buildings on 112 acres, an olympic pool complex, a library containing 60,000 volumes, a professional quality fine arts center, and a student center that provides the cafeteria, book store and student government association office and five off-campus centers. The college provides student housing.

Community Environment: A midsize city on the east coast of Florida with a subtropical climate, the area is known for citrus fruits and winter vegetables. Florida's Turnpike, I-95, Florida East Coast Railroad and the Greyhound bus line serve the area. Community facilities include a public library, YMCA, churches, hospitals, mental health centers, beaches and recreational activities. Part-time employment opportunities are moderate. Swimming from two ocean beaches, golf and sports fishing are the principal outdoor sports.

Branch Campuses: Vero Beach; Stuart; Okeechobee; Port St. Lucie.

INTERNATIONAL FINE ARTS COLLEGE (O-13)
1737 North Bayshore Drive
Miami, Florida 33132
Tel: (305) 373-4684; (800) 225-9023; Fax: (305) 374-5933

Description: The college was chartered by the State of Florida as a private junior college in 1965. It was established to educate qualified high school graduates and college transfer students in the fashion merchandising, interior design, commercial art, computer graphics, and fashion design fields. The college is fully accredited by the Commission on Colleges of the Southern Association of Colleges and Schools to confer the Associate of Arts degree. Because of the large number of semester credits students earn during their first two years at International Fine Arts College, graduates may transfer to a local university and there earn their Bachelor's degrees with approximately one additional year of study. The college operates on the semester system and offers one summer session. Enrollment is 685 students. A faculty of 10 full-time and 31 part-time gives a faculty-student ratio of 1-17.

Entrance Requirements: Accredited high school graduation; open enrollment policy; early decision, rolling admission, and midyear admission plans available; $50 application fee.

Costs Per Year: $9,975-$11,740 tuition & fees; $2,915 room.

Collegiate Environment: The college is housed within a museum-like, 55-year-old building of great beauty, located on Biscayne Bay. There are 9,250 volumes in the library. Housing is available for 191 students. 71% of those who apply for admission are accepted. Scholarships are available and 75% of the current student body receives some form of assistance. The campus is adjacent to fashionable department stores as well as cultural and recreational facilities.

Community Environment: See Barry University.

JACKSONVILLE UNIVERSITY (B-9)
2800 University Blvd. North
Jacksonville, Florida 32211
Tel: (904) 745-7000; (800) 225-2027; Admissions: (904) 745-7000; Fax: (904) 745-7012

Description: The private university is accredited by the Southern Association of Colleges and Schools. Over 50 undergraduate programs are offered in the Colleges of Arts & Sciences, Business and Fine Arts. Students from 42 states and 60 countries are enrolled at the university. The average class size is maintained at 20 students within a highly personalized and supportive learning environment. Academic cooperative plans are available with Columbia, The University of Florida, Georgia Institute of Technology, Georgia Tech, Washington University in St. Louis, Stevens Institute of Technology and the University of Miami. Navy, Marine, and Army ROTC are available. The University grants the Bachelor of Science, Bachelor of Arts, Bachelor of Fine Arts, Bachelor of Music, Bachelor of Music Education, and Bachelor of Art Education. Master's degrees are granted in Business Administration, and in Arts in Teaching. The university operates on the semester system and offers two summer sessions. Enrollment includes 1,700 full-time and 300 part-time undergraduates and 500 graduate students. The student-faculty ratio is 1-15.

Entrance Requirements: High school graduation with completion of 14 units including 4 English, 2 mathematics, 2 science, 3 social studies; SAT or ACT required; transfer applicants considered; early admission, rolling admission and advanced placement plans available; $25 application fee. August 1st application deadline for fall admission.

Costs Per Year: $9,600 tuition; $4,250 room and board.

Collegiate Environment: The campus has 29 buildings on 260 beautiful, riverfront acres; one-fifth of the campus area is forest. Residence halls accommodate 550 men and 450 women. Library holdings include 320,000 hardbound volumes. Approximately 69% of the students applying for admission are accepted including midyear. Financial aid is available and 75% of the current students receive some form of assistance.

Community Environment: Jacksonville is located on the St. John's River near the Atlantic Ocean; temperate climate characterized by short mild winters and long relatively warm summers; the average temperature being 67.8 degrees. The city functions as the financial, industrial, transportation and commercial center of Florida. Along with the usual community facilities, there are seven hospitals, churches of almost all denominations, excellent shopping facilities, civic auditorium which features the finest of concerts, plays and ballet and many little theatre groups. Part-time employment is available. Jacksonville and the surrounding area provide ample beaches and facilities for yachting, swimming, fishing and golfing. The Friendship Park on the south side of the St. Johns River contains the spectacular Friendship Fountain and marina. A sports complex consists of the Coliseum, Gator Bowl and ball park.

JONES COLLEGE   *(B-9)*
5353 Arlington Expressway
Jacksonville, Florida 32211
Tel: (800) 331-0176; Admissions: (904) 743-1122; Fax: (904) 743-1122

Description: Private business college; accredited by the Accrediting Commission of the Association of Independent Colleges and Schools as a senior college of business. It was founded in 1918 as Jones Business College. The college grants the Associate and Bachelor degrees. It operates on the trimester calendar system and offers one summer session. Enrollment includes 1,200 students. A faculty of 57 gives a faculty-student ratio of 1-21.

Entrance Requirements: Open enrollment policy; high school graduation; rolling admission, early decision, midyear admission and advanced placement plans available.

Costs Per Year: $4,350 ($145/credit) tuition per year, based on 30 credits.

Collegiate Environment: The campus has two modern, air-conditioned buildings on 3.4 acres, including a library of 38,191 volumes. Approximately 10% of the student body graduated in top 10% of high school class; 75% of the freshman class returned for second year.

Community Environment: See Jacksonville University.

Branch Campuses: 5975 Sunset Drive, Suite 100, South Miami, FL 33143, tel: (305) 669-9606.

LAKE CITY COMMUNITY COLLEGE   *(C-7)*
Route 19, Box 1030
Lake City, Florida 32025
Tel: (904) 752-1822; Fax: (904) 755-1521

Description: The state-supported community college is accredited by the Southern Association of Colleges and Schools. The college has

expanded its facilities and services since it opened in 1962 and now includes a University parallel division, a career education division and an evening division. Enrollment recently included 596 men and 450 women full-time and 374 men and 526 women part-time. A faculty of 74 full-time and 96 part-time gives a faculty-student ratio of approximately 1-15. The semester system is used and two summer sessions are offered. The college grants the Certificate and Associate degree. Continuing education courses are offered.

Entrance Requirements: High school graduation or equivalent; early admission, early decision, rolling admission, delayed admission, open enrollment and advanced placement plans available; non-high school graduates considered; ACT or other approved placement test required; $15 application fee.

Costs Per Year: $1,300 state-resident tuition; $3,915 nonresidents; $2,700 room and board; additional expenses average $500.

Collegiate Environment: Twenty-four buildings comprise the campus, including a library of 40,000 volumes, 284 periodicals, 9,096 microforms, and numerous audiovisual materials. Dormitory facilities are available for 92 men and 92 women. Financial aid is available and 40% of the current student body receives some form of financial aid. 100% of the students applying for admission are accepted and about 2/3 of the freshman class returns for the sophomore year.

Community Environment: Lake City is the county seat of Columbia County, located midway between Atlanta and Miami. It has a temperate climate. Community facilities include excellent hospital and health facilities and fine motel accommodations. Lake City is known as the Forestry Capital of the World. Annual deer and bear hunting is staged in nearby Osceola National Forest. Numerous lakes and streams are well stocked with bass, bream, and speckled perch.

LAKE-SUMTER COMMUNITY COLLEGE   *(F-9)*
Leesburg, Florida 34788
Tel: (904) 787-3747

Description: This public-controlled community college was authorized in 1961 and began operation in 1962. The college is accredited by the Southern Association of Colleges and Schools and employs the semester system. Enrollment includes 865 men and 1,658 women. The faculty consists of 41 full-time and 73 part-time members which provides a faculty-student ratio of 1-20.

Entrance Requirements: Open enrollment policy; non-high school graduates considered. Placement examination required; early admission, midyear admission, rolling admission and advanced placement plans available; $15 application fee.

Costs Per Year: $870 ($36.25/credit, 24 credit hours) tuition for residents, $3,222 ($134.25/credit for 24 credit hours) tuition for nonresidents.

Collegiate Environment: The college is located on a 110-acre site and includes modern, air-conditioned classrooms, a library of 52,000 volumes, auditorium, gymnasium, math/science building, fine arts center, multipurpose building, liberal arts building, lecture hall, and college union. The campus includes an 18-acre Nature Trail for those students seeking quiet solitude. The college grants Associate degrees in 51 different areas. All qualified students applying for admission are accepted. Six semester hours correspondent credit allowed; continuing education courses as well as cooperative education programs offered. Scholarships are available and 24% of students receive some form of financial aid.

Community Environment: Leesburg is a rapidly growing rural area with a temperate climate, located in central Florida near the shores of Lakes Griffin and Harris, within easy driving distance of metropolitan areas. Community facilities include numerous libraries, churches, general hospitals, active major civic and service groups. Part-time and full-time employment are available. Many forms of recreation are found, including fishing, swimming, golf, tennis, shuffleboard, water skiing and hunting. Lake Griffin State Park nearby provides additional recreational facilities.

LYNN UNIVERSITY   *(M-13)*
3601 North Military Trail
Boca Raton, Florida 33431-5598
Tel: (407) 994-0770; (800) 544-8035; Fax: (407) 241-3552

Description: This private institution was founded in 1962 and is accredited by the Southern Association of Colleges and Schools. The University offers Masters programs in Health Career Administration, Hospitality Administration, Sports Management, International Management and Education, Bachelor programs in Liberal Arts, Business, Hospitality and Education, and a limited number of two-year programs. Semester study abroad in Ireland, France, Sweden and Japan is available. The university operates on the semester system and offers three optional summer sessions for undergraduates; 10 week terms for graduate programs. Enrollment is 1,500 undergraduates and graduate students. A faculty of 75 gives an overall faculty-student ratio of 1-20.

Entrance Requirements: High school graduation, recommendation of guidance counselor and SAT or ACT scores are required for undergraduate applicants. Transfer students must submit an offical college transcript from prior instituions and the recommendation of the Dean of Students. Applicants for the Graduate programs must have completed a Bachelor's degree form an accredited college or university and should have a minimum "B" average in junior and senior level course work. Graduate applicants who have not met the minimum average, but do show promise and ability to do graduate level work as demonstrated throgh supporting application materials, are also considered for admission. Early admission, rolling admission, delayed admission, midyear admission and advanced placement plans available; $25 application fee.

Costs Per Year: Undergraduate: $14,850 tuition; $5,950 room and board; $800 fees. Graduate: $10,500 ($350/credit) tuition; $50 registration fee.

Collegiate Environment: The 123 acre campus is located three miles from the ocean in Boca Raton, mid-way between Palm Beach and Fort Lauderdale. Campus buildings include classrooms, a library, computer classrooms, laboratories and photography studios, as well as a learning resource center, international center, auditorium, dining room and residence halls for 700 students. All buildings are modern and completely air-conditioned. Sports facilities include a gymnasium, fitness center, weight rooms, aerobics room, pool, tennis courts, baseball diamond, soccer field and softball fields, and basketball court. Financial aid is available in the form of grants, loans and jobs and about 40% receive such aid. About 75% of applicants are accepted based largely on class rank and counselor recommendations. Students come from almost every state and 35 countries. 70% of students live on campus.

Community Environment: See Florida Atlantic University.

MANATEE COMMUNITY COLLEGE   *(J-7)*
5840 26th Street West
Bradenton, Florida 34207
Tel: (813) 755-1511

Description: The state-governed community college is accredited by the Southern Association of Colleges and Schools. It operates on the semester system with two summer terms. The college was established in 1957 to meet the vocational-professional needs of the Manatee-Sarasota community and to provide a university parallel curriculum. The college grants an Associate degree and a Certificate. Recent enrollment included 3,190 full-time and 4,771 part-time students. A faculty of 152 full-time and 164 part-time provides a faculty-student ratio of 1-25.

Entrance Requirements: High school graduation or GED; early admission, rolling admission and advanced placement plans available; $15 application fee.

Costs Per Year: $1,054 resident tuition; $3,876 out-of-state.

Collegiate Environment: The campus has 17 buildings on 100 acres located in a residential area of the city. The auditorium is an ultra-modern facility with 900 seats. The library contains 66,390 volumes and 334 periodicals. There are 41 different Associate degree programs offered. Various forms of financial assistance are available. 100% of the applicants are accepted.

Community Environment: A suburban area with a subtropical climate, Bradenton is located on the west coast and is known as "The Friendly City;" the hub of activities are in Manatee County. Air service at the Bradenton-Sarasota airport are available. Shopping centers, hospital, city parks, theaters and a modern municipal auditorium are part of the community facilities. The city is a rich agricultural area, producing, processing and shipping citrus fruits, winter vegetables and gladiola. Some part-time employment is available. Recreational facilities include beaches, a municipal pier, yacht basin, boat launching, and fishing. Points of interest are the South Florida Museum and Planetarium, and the De Soto National Memorial. The Pittsburgh Pirates baseball team trains here. A De Soto celebration is an annual event in March. Venice, Florida, is located approximately 42 miles south of the Bradenton campus.

Branch Campuses: Manatee Community College's South Campus is located in Sarasota County on Route 41, 42 miles south of the Brandenton campus. The campus occupies a 100-acre site that is easily accessible from the communities of South Sarasota, Venice, Englewood, and North Port.

MIAMI-DADE COMMUNITY COLLEGE   *(O-13)*
300 N.E. 2nd Avenue
Miami, Florida 33132
Tel: (305) 237-7478; Fax: (305) 237-7534

Description: The publicly-controlled community college is accredited by the Southern Association of Colleges and Schools. Students attending Miami-Dade may enroll in Army or Air Force ROTC at University of Miami. The college was established in 1960; it has now become the largest community college in the United States. Recent enrollment figures on all campuses included 46,432 students with a faculty of 837 full-time and 1,062 part-time. The college grants both the Certificate and Associate degrees. It operates on the semester system with two summer terms. Continuing education courses offered; cooperative education programs available.

Entrance Requirements: Open enrollment policy, high school graduation or equivalent. Early admission, delayed admission, rolling admission, and advanced placement plans available.

Costs Per Year: Florida resident $942; nonresident $3,276.

Collegiate Environment: Miami-Dade Community College has five campuses: the North, South, Mitchell Wolfson New World Center, Medical Center Campus and the Homestead Campus. The North Campus is situated on 245 acres in northern Dade County, with facilities totaling over 800,000 net assignable square feet. The 185 acre Kendall Campus, in southwest Dade County, contains seven major buildings having over 600,000 net assignable square feet. The Mitchell Wolfson New World Center Campus, located in the heart of the city, has a six-story and a new three-story and is accessible from all sections of the Greater Miami area by bus. The fourth campus is the Medical Center Campus. It is located adjacent to the Jackson Memorial Hospital complex, and contains 119,000 net assignable square feet. The newest campus is the Homestead Campus which was opened in the fall of 1990. It serves the southernmost area of Dade County. The combined libraries contain 335,932 bound volumes, 2,517 periodicals, 596,095 microforms and 22,513 audiovisual aids. All qualified applicants are accepted. Financial aid is available and 32% of the current student body receives some form of assistance.

Community Environment: See Barry University. See also Florida International University and University of Miami.

NEW COLLEGE OF THE UNIVERSITY OF SOUTH
FLORIDA   *(K-7)*
5700 North Tamiami Trail
Sarasota, Florida 34243-2197
Tel: (813) 359-4269

Description: New College is a public residential liberal arts college that provides intensive, top-quality education at low state tuition rates. Enrollment is 257 men and 284 women. The faculty-student ratio is 1-10. The school serves as an honors college for the State University System of Florida. Small classes, personal attention, and independent study characterize the school. 95% of the faculty hold earned doctorates. Graduates typically pursue professional careers and are innovators in their chosen fields. The college is accredited by the Southern Association of Colleges and Schools. It was founded 1960 as a non-sectarian private college. In 1975, it became unit of University of South Florida, but retained its private college flavor and highly selective admissions policy. Tuition and fees are similar to other Florida public colleges.

Entrance Requirements: Admission is highly selective; the college seeks students who have demonstrated above average ability, academic motivation and self-descipline; requirements include State University System application; New College Supplementary Application; high school transcript (transfers must also submit college transcripts); SAT or ACT scores; two academic recommendations; interview (for local students); $20 application fee; rolling admissions policy; deadline for priority consideration for scholarship awards is February 1; the fall class closes no later than May 1; the spring class closes no later than December 1; only students transferring from community colleges in Florida may apply for spring admission.

Costs Per Year: $2,030 state-resident tuition and fees; $7,913 out-of-state; $3,717 room and board.

Collegiate Environment: The college has a unique educational philosophy that attracts bright students of initiative and growth potential. A flexible contract system maximizes students' input into their curricula. Measurements of student progress are provided in the form of written evaluations from the faculty. Seminars, tutorials, and independent study are emphasized and there is opportunity for off-campus study. Graduation requirements include seven completed contracts (one per semester), three independent study projects, a senior thesis, and an oral baccalaureate exam. The attractive, bayside campus is located on the north edge of Sarasota in National Historic District, and contains landmark buildings. A new music and arts facility opened in 1992. The library holds 230,000 volumes. Dormitory rooms are designed to afford maximum privacy. Student life is informal. Academic life is intense, but ample recreational resources include a 25-meter outdoor pool, lighted outdoor tennis and basketball courts; and a fully equipped fitness center. Students initiate social and recreational activities with support of professional residential life staff. Approximately one-third of the class consists of transfer students. 28% of applicants are accepted. 60% of students receive some form of financial aid. The middle 50% ranges of test scores of the freshman class were 1160-1350 combined SAT and 27-31 composite ACT.

Community Environment: Located on the southwest Florida coast with a semitropical climate, Sarasota (population 51,000) is an art center and leading resort. All major airlines serve Sarasota. The Ringling Museum of Art and Asolo State Theater adjoin the campus. A major performing arts center is 2 miles away. Part-time work is available. The recreational facilities are outstanding, and there are several white sand beaches that extend along the Gulf of Mexico.

NORTH FLORIDA JUNIOR COLLEGE   *(B-5)*
1000 Turner Davis Drive
Madison, Florida 32340
Tel: (904) 973-2288; Admissions: (904) 973-2288 x120; Fax: (904) 973-2288

Description: A state junior college accredited by the Southern Association of Colleges and Schools. The first classes were organized in temporary quarters in 1958. Construction began in 1959 on permanent college buildings. The college grants Certificates and the Associate degree. It operates on the semester system and offers two summer sessions. Enrollment includes 500 full-time, 500 part-time, and 250 evening program students. A faculty of 42 full-time and 25 part-time gives a faculty-student ratio of 1-25.

Entrance Requirements: High school graduation or equivalent; open enrollment policy; early admission and advance placement plans available; $10 application fee

Costs Per Year: $810 state resident tuition $652; $3,120 nonresident tuition.

Collegiate Environment: The campus has 14 buildings on 96 acres. The library contains 38,000 volumes, 5,096 periodicals, 916 microforms, and 7,355 sound recordings. All structures are of modern design and fully climate controlled for student comfort. There are 78 scholarships, 32 for freshmen, available. 30% of the students receive some form of financial assistance. About 60% of first year students return for the second year.

Community Environment: Madison is located in a rural area with a temperate climate. Railroads and buses serve the area along with three highways. Community facilities include a public library, hospital, ten churches, and major civic and fraternal organizations. Within easy reach are large shopping and cultural centers. Part-time employment opportunities are limited. Recreational facilities include a golf course, recreation center, and many facilities for all water sports.

NOVA SOUTHEASTERN UNIVERSITY   *(N-13)*
3301 College Avenue
Fort Lauderdale, Florida 33314
Tel: (305) 475-7360; (800) 338-4723; Fax: (305) 475-7098

Description: Founded in 1964, Nova Southeastern University is today the second largest independent or non-tax-supported university in the state of Florida. Based upon annual expenditures, it is among the 100 largest independent colleges and universities in this country. Nova Southeastern University is an independent, nonsectarian, non-profit, and racially nondiscriminatory university. Bachelor of Science degrees are offered in: education, psychology, computer sciences, ocean studies, business, accounting, legal studies, life sciences (premedicine), and liberal arts (B.A.). The university also offers programs leading to the Doctor of Philosophy degree in behavioral, life, and ocean sciences. The Juris Doctor is offered in law. The Education Specialist and Master of Science degrees are offered in education both on campus and in an off-campus format. The Master of Science degree is offered in on-campus programs in various specialties of behavioral science as well as ocean sciences. The Master of Arts degree is offered in various specialities of education and life sciences. The Doctor of Education, Doctor of Business Administration, and Doctor of Public Administration degrees are offered in an-off campus format. At the masters level, the university also offers, in an off-campus format, degrees in public service, child care administration, and business management. A certificate program in education is also available. Enrollment includes 2,140 full-time and 1,535 part-time undergraduates and 9,500 graduate students. A faculty of 174 full-time and 261 part-time gives an undergraduate faculty-student ratio of 1-11.

Entrance Requirements: For undergraduate day programs: high school transcript; SAT or ACT scores required; interview recommended; for all other programs, requirements vary; $25 application fee.

Costs Per Year: $765 per 3-credit undergraduate course; $540-$1,125 per 3-credit master's course; $5,300-$7,290 per year for doctoral program depending on program; $3,390-$4,500 housing per year; $1,862 meal plan.

Collegiate Environment: The main campus has 14 permanent buildings and several temporary buildings, and utilizes various other facilities in the vicinity of the campus. Two additional buildings are in various stages of planning or construction. Four apartment buildings totaling 332 units are available.

Community Environment: Nova Southeastern University is located on a 200-acre site west of Fort Lauderdale in the town of Davie, 10 miles inland from the Atlantic Ocean and easily accessible from major U.S. and state highways including the Sunshine State Parkway. The climate is subtropical and the average year-round temperature is 75 degrees. Nova Southeastern University is situated in close proximity to Broward Community College and to the Nova complex of elementary, middle and high schools.

OKALOOSA-WALTON COMMUNITY COLLEGE   *(N-4)*
100 College Boulevard
Niceville, Florida 32578
Tel: (904) 678-5111; Admissions: (904) 729-5372; Fax: (904) 729-5215

Description: This community-governed two-year college offers college credit, adult education and vocational programs and grants the Associates of Arts and Associate of Science degrees. The college operates on the semester system with two 6-week summer terms and is accredited by the Southern Association of Colleges and Schools. Founded in 1963, the campus is now located on 264 acres of land that was formerly part of the Eglin Air Force Reservation. Enrollment is 701 men and 939 women full-time, and 2,122 men and 2,966 women part-time. A faculty of 77 full-time and 188 part-time gives a faculty-student ratio of 1-21.

Entrance Requirements: Candidates for admission to the degree programs must be high school graduates or possess high school equivalency certificates; open enrollment policy; early admission, early decision, rolling admission, midyear admission and advanced placement plans available; $15 application fee.

Costs Per Year: $874 state-resident tuition; $3,370 out-of-state.

Collegiate Environment: The campus is located at the northern boundary of Niceville between State Road 85 and State Road 285 in a beautiful wooded area. The library contains 80,432 volumes, numerous pamphlets, periodicals, microforms, and audiovisual materials. All applicants who meet the requirements are accepted. 500 scholarships are available and 25% of students receive some form of financial aid.

Community Environment: Twin cities with temperate climate, largely residential in nature. Many residents are military retirees or civil service personnel. Airlines and Greyhound and AmTrak buses serve the area. Large shopping centers are within easy driving distance. Part-time job opportunities for students are extremely limited.

Branch Campuses: Fort Walton Beach; Eglin Air Force Base; Hurlburt Field; DeFuniak Springs; and Crestview.

ORLANDO COLLEGE   (G-10)
5500 Diplomat Circle
Orlando, Florida 32810
Tel: (407) 628-5870; (800) 628-5870; Admissions: (407) 628-5870;
Fax: (407) 628-2616

Description: Private business college, accredited by The Accrediting Council of the Association of Independent Colleges and Schools as a senior college of business (formerly Jones College). The college operates on the quarter system and offers one summer session. Enrollment is 1,700 students. A full-time faculty of 61 gives a faculty-student ratio of 1-28.

Entrance Requirements: High school graduation with a C average; entrance examination required; ACT or SAT required; early admission, early decision, rolling admission, midyear admission and advanced placement plans available.

Costs Per Year: $3,928 average per academic year.

Collegiate Environment: The library include 7,713 volumes. Six scholarships are available. The college has two Orlando locations and a branch campus in Melbourne, Florida. Orlando College, part of Phillops Colleges, Inc., was established in 1953.

Community Environment: See University of Central Florida.

Branch Campuses: 2411 Sandlake Rd., Orlando, FL 32809; 2401 No. Harbor City Blvd., Melbourne, FL 32935

PALM BEACH ATLANTIC COLLEGE   (L-13)
901 S Flagler Avenue
P.O. Box 24708
West Palm Beach, Florida 33416-4708
Tel: (407) 835-4309; (800) 238-3998; Fax: (407) 835-4347

Description: The college is a comprehensive liberal arts college accredited by the Southern Association of Colleges and Schools. It was founded in 1968 by leaders of Baptist churches and continues to offer quality education with a distinctive Christian emphasis to students of all faiths. The college offers more than 40 programs of study, and grants three baccalaureate degrees and three master's degrees. A nontraditional bachelor's degree program is offered evenings and at off-campus sites. Eighty percent of the faculty have the terminal degree in their field. The college operates on the semester system and offers three summer sessions. Enrollment is 1,900 full-time students. A faculty of 40 full-time and 42 part-time gives a faculty-student ratio of 1-17.

Entrance Requirements: Accredited high school graduation with recommended 2.5 average; completion of at least 18 units including 4 English, 3 foreign language, 3 mathematics, 3 physical and 3 social sciences; ACT or SAT required; character reference and recommendation from high school teacher or counselor required; early admission, early decision, midyear admission, rolling admission and advanced placement plans available; $25 application fee.

Costs Per Year: $7,900 tuition; $3,600 room and board.

Collegiate Environment: The college is located in downtown West Palm Beach, facing Florida's Intracoastal Waterway. The 23-acre campus includes Cambridge-style buildings that combine dormitories which accomodate 711 students and classroom/office space as well as more traditional buildings. The library contains more than 80,000 volumes, 450 periodicals and 54,000 microforms. Chapel attendance is required, and students must deveote 45 hours annually to community service. 65% of applicants are accepted. Average scores of a recent freshman class were SAT 450V, 450M; ACT 21. Semesters begin in September and January, and midyear students are accepted. Scholarships are available and 90% of students receive some form of financial aid.

Community Environment: West Palm Beach is the county seat of Palm Beach County, one of the fastest-growing areas in Florida. The campus is minutes away from the Atlantic Ocean and just across the Intracoastal Waterway from Palm Beach. Cultural, athletic and recreational events abound, and a railway system offers easy access to Fort Lauderdale and Miami.

PALM BEACH COMMUNITY COLLEGE   (L-13)
4200 Congress Avenue
Lake Worth, Florida 33461
Tel: (407) 439-8000; Fax: (407) 439-8255

Description: The state-controlled junior college is accredited by the Southern Association of Colleges and Schools. The college was founded in 1933 as a community response to the depression for students who could not afford to live away from home and attend a university for four years. One million forty-seven thousand dollars was voted for erecting buildings on a permanent campus in 1956. The college operates on semester system with 2 summer sessions. Enrollment includes 2,345 men, 2,687 women full-time, 4,339 men, and 7,128 women part-time. A faculty of 181 full-time and 521 part-time gives a faculty-student ratio of 1-24. The Associate degree is awarded at the completion of the program. Fifteen semester hours correspondence credit allowed; continuing education courses offered.

Entrance Requirements: High school graduation or equivalent; open enrollment C average policy; rolling admission, and advanced placement plans available. July 27 application deadline. Application fee is $20.

Costs Per Year: $1,110 (35.80/credit) resident tuition; $4,129 ($133.20/credit) out-of-state tuition.

Collegiate Environment: The college has four campuses. The library contains 134,965 volumes, 29,634 pamphlets, 6,830 periodicals, 51,753 microforms and 2,104 sound recordings. There are no dormitories on campus.

Community Environment: Located south of West Palm Beach, Lake Worth has an annual average temperature of 75 degrees and an average rainfall of 61.72 inches. All modes of transportation serve the area. Recreational activities are golfing, shuffleboard, polo, tennis, swimming, water skiing, jai alai, deep sea and fresh water fishing. Deep sea fishing for sailfish, surf fishing for pompano and blue fish are excellent; fresh water fishing at Lake Osborne. Points of interest are the Palm Beach Speedway, Kennel Club Race Track, and art galleries.

PASCO-HERNANDO COMMUNITY COLLEGE   (O-12)
36727 Blanton Road
Dade City, Florida 33525
Tel: (904) 567-6701; Admissions: (813) 847-2727; Fax: (813) 844-7244

Description: This state supported, community/junior college is accredited by the Southern Association of Colleges and Schools and professionally by respective accrediting institutions. Founded in 1972, it offers vocational-technical programs and awards the Associate degree. It operates on the semester system and offers three summer sessions. Enrollment is 1,949 full-time and 5,771 part-time students. A faculty of 68 full-time and 187 part-time gives a faculty-student ratio of 1-30.

Entrance Requirements: High school graduation not required; open enrollment; early admission, early decision, midyear admission, rolling admission, and advanced placement plans available; $20 application fee.

Costs Per Year: $1,128.40 ($36.40/cr) resident tuition; $4,203.60 ($135.60/cr) nonresident.

Collegiate Environment: Library holdinag include 57,000 hardbound volumes. Dormitory facilities are not available. Almost all applicants are accepted. The college offers programs for the educationally disadvantaged. 250 scholarships are available and 53% of the students currently receive some form of financial assistance.

Community Environment: See Saint Leo College.

149

Branch Campuses: Brooksville, New Port Richey.

PENSACOLA JUNIOR COLLEGE   *(N-2)*
1000 College Boulevard
Pensacola, Florida 32504-8998
Tel: (904) 484-1000; Admissions: (904) 484-1600; Fax: (904) 484-1829

Description: The public junior college opened in 1948 and moved to its present campus in 1957. PJC became a true community college when the Center for Adult Studies was established in 1964. The College was accredited by the Southern Association of Colleges and Schools in 1956. A campus was opened in Milton in 1971 and moved to its present location in 1985. A campus was also opened in Warrington in 1977. The college offers college level courses for transfer, vocational employment, vocational certificate, high school, adult basic education courses as well as continuing education, lifelong learning, and recreation/leisure courses. The semester system is used with two summer terms. The college enrolls approximately 1,791 men, 2,638 women full-time, 3,024 men, and 4,503 women part-time students. The faculty includes 250 full-time and 450 part-time members which provides a faculty-student ratio of 1-20.

Entrance Requirements: Graduation from an accredited high school or equivalent; open enrollment policy; early admission, dual enrollment, and other accelerated education plans are available.

Costs Per Year: $1,035 tuition for resident students; $3,873 tuition for nonresident students.

Collegiate Environment: A comprehensive college, PJC has locations in Pensacola, Warrington, Milton, Downtown, and NAS. The College owns 344.8 acres, with more than fifty buildings located on the five locations. The combined PJC libraries contain more than 200,000 books, periodicals, and documents. While the Pensacola Campus is the oldest, with a broad range of liberal arts, science, and technology programs, the Warrington Campus is home of the nursing, dental, and allied health programs which are some of the best in the region. The Milton Campus offers a complete selection of courses to meet degree requirements with special curricula in Natural Resource Studies. PJC is an open-door institution and invites all applicants.

Community Environment: Pensacola Junior College offers courses at five locations in Escambia and Santa Rosa counties in northwest Florida. Famous for the white sand beaches of the Emerald Coast, Pensacola is the center of a growing metropolitan area of almost a quarter of a million residents. With a 28% increase in construction starts since 1985, the Florida Panhandle is booming. Pensacola is the "Cradle of Naval Aviation" and several Navy bases are located in the area, including the Pensacola Naval Air Station, Whiting Field, Corry Field, and Saufley Field. The white beaches of the Gulf of Mexico are a mecca for tourists. The area is served by the University of West Florida as well as Pensacola Junior College. In addition, the city has numerous museums, galleries, and historical areas, including Seville Quarter, a part of Pensacola dating back to the mid 1700's. Florida's First Place City continues to grow and expand.

POLK COMMUNITY COLLEGE   *(I-9)*
999 Avenue H, N.E.
Winter Haven, Florida 33881-4299
Tel: (813) 297-1000; Admissions: (813) 297-1001; Fax: (813) 297-1060

Description: The publicly controlled community college is accredited by the Southern Association of Colleges and Schools and operates on the trimester system with 2 summer sessions. The first academic year started in 1964 on a temporary campus; the college moved to its present location in 1968. Programs of study are primarily vocational-technical. The college awards an Associate degree. Correspondence credit is allowed, and there are continuing education courses available. Army ROTC is offered as an elective. Enrollment includes 945 men and 1,160 women full-time, and 1,359 men, and 2,562 women part-time. A faculty of 125 full-time and 170 part-time gives a faculty-student ratio of 1-24.

Entrance Requirements: High school graduation or equivalent; units should include 4 English, 3 mathematics, 3 laboratory science, and 3 social science; open enrollment policy; early admission, early decision, rolling admission, midyear admission, delayed admission and advanced placement plans available; $20 application fee.

Costs Per Year: $1,084 ($36.13/credit) tuition in-state; $4,064 ($135.46/credit) out-of-state.

Collegiate Environment: The main campus has seven buildings on 100 acres. A second campus in Lakeland opened in January, 1988. The library contains 82,664 volumes, 3,500 pamphlets, 474 periodicals, 11,336 microforms and 1,150 sound recordings. No dormitories are provided on campus. All high school graduates from accredited Florida schools are accepted. Financial assistance is available.

RINGLING SCHOOL OF ART AND DESIGN   *(K-7)*
2700 North Taniani Trail
Sarasota, Florida 34234
Tel: (813) 351-4614; (800) 255-7695; Fax: (813) 359-7523

Description: This private art college was founded in 1931. Ringling School of Art and Design is accredited by the Southern Association of Colleges and Schools, NASAD and FIDER. The school grants the Bachelor of Fine Arts degree in Computer Animation, Photography, Fine Arts, Graphic Design, Illustration, and Interior Design. It operates on the semster system. Enrollment includes 807 full-time students. A faculty of 94 provides a faculty-student ratio of 1-9.

Entrance Requirements: High school graduation or equivalent; portfolio; entrance exam not required; rolling admission plan available; $30 application fee.

Costs Per Year: $10,300 tuition; $5,700 room and board; $1,500 supplies.

Collegiate Environment: The library contains 13,000 volumes and 25,000 slides. A gallery with major exhibitions complements the program. Spacious new air-conditioned dorms are available and accommodate 165 students.

Community Environment: See New College of the University of South Florida.

ROLLINS COLLEGE   *(G-10)*
Hamilton Holt - Campus Box 2720
Winter Park, Florida 32792
Tel: (407) 646-2000; Admissions: (407) 646-2161; Fax: (407) 646-1502

Description: The private, liberal arts college is accredited by the Southern Association of Colleges and Schools. Founded in 1885, Rollins offered the first college level work in Florida. The college awards the Bachelor and Master's degrees, and offers continuing education programs. The college operates on the 4-1-4 calendar system and offers day and evening programs. Enrollment includes 1,422 full-time day program undergraduates, 1,229 evening program undergraduates, and 633 graduate students also in the evening program. A faculty of 145 full-time and 26 part-time gives a faculty-student ratio of 1-12.

Entrance Requirements: High school graduation with a B average with rank in upper 45% of graduating class; completion of 15 units, including 4 English, 3 mathematics, 2 social science, 2 foreign language, 2 science; SAT or ACT, CEEB in English required; early admission, early decision, delayed admission, midyear admission, CLEP (550) honors program and advanced placement plans available. $35 application fee.

Costs Per Year: $17,495 tuition; $5,555 room and board; $500 student fees.

Collegiate Environment: The campus has 57 buildings on 67 acres in a residential community adjacent to the city of Orlando. There is dormitory space available for 1,092 men and women. The library contains 263,658 volumes, 1,554 current periodicals, 37,758 microforms and 3,640 audiovisuals. Almost 60% of the applicants are accepted. The average scores of the entering freshman class were SAT 504 verbal, 564 math. 88% of the freshman class returned for sophomore year. 291 scholarships are available, including 55 athletic and 60% of the student receive some form of financial aid. Overseas programs in Australia offered; Junior Year Abroad available.

Community Environment: Within the metropolitan area of which Orlando is the center, Winter Park is a residential area of great beauty. This Florida area is popularly known as "The Lake Region." Orange groves, subtropical forest, flowering shrubs and trees are the dominant features of the landscape. Scenic boat trips may be taken through a chain of four lakes. Annual events are the Sidewalk Arts Festival and a Bach festival held on the campus of Rollins College.

SAINT JOHN VIANNEY COLLEGE SEMINARY   *(O-13)*
2900 S.W. 87th Avenue
Miami, Florida 33165
Tel: (305) 223-4561; Fax: (305) 223-0650

Description: Founded in 1959, the seminary is under the auspices of the Roman Catholic Church and is a four-year college for men preparing for the Catholic priesthood. It is fully accredited by the Southern Association of Colleges and Schools. The college operates on the semester system. Recently the seminary enrolled 47 students. The faculty consists of 9 full-time and 9 part-time members.

Entrance Requirements: Accredited high school graduation; SAT or ACT required; applicants must apply through their respective home diocese; they must present: a baptismal certificate issued within the past six months, confirmation certificate, parents' marriage certificate, and a letter of recommendation from their own pastor; rolling admission and advanced placement plans available.

Costs Per Year: $6,500 tuition per year, $4,000 room and board.

Collegiate Environment: Located in the southwest section of Greater Miami, the campus comprises 30 acres and includes 7 buildings. All students live on campus in dormitory facilities. The library contains over 52,000 volumes.

Community Environment: See Barry University

SAINT JOHNS RIVER COMMUNITY COLLEGE   *(D-9)*
5001 St. Johns Avenue
Palatka, Florida 32177-3897
Tel: (904) 312-4200; Admissions: (904) 312-4030; Fax: (904) 325-6627

Description: The publicly controlled community college with an enrollment of 1,340 full-time and 2,004 part-time is accredited by the Southern Association of Colleges and Schools and operates on the trimester system. The college was established in 1958 to serve the counties of Clay, Putnam and St. Johns. A faculty of 73 full-time, 94 part-time gives a faculty-student ratio of 1-22. Two summer sessions are offered.

Entrance Requirements: High school graduation or equivalent; open enrollment policy; application fee $20; early admission, delayed admission, advanced placement, early decision and rolling admission plans available.

Costs Per Year: $1,110 tuition for Florida residents, $4,440 for non-Florida residents. Room and board $5,188.

Collegiate Environment: The 103-acre campus includes an air-conditioned student service center, library containing 52,711 volumes, two classroom buildings, gymnasium, science building, technical building, and fine arts complex. The college does not provide housing facilities, but a private housing is available. Day and night classes are also offered at a branch campus at Orange Park (near Jacksonville) and at St. Augustine. Night classes are offered in other nearby cities. About 99% of the applicants are accepted, including midyear students. Various forms of financial assistance are available. The college is the home of the Florida School of the Arts, offering degrees in the areas of theater, dance, music, graphic arts, and Fine arts. There are 14 Associate degree programs offered.

Community Environment: A small rural area 24 miles from the Atlantic Ocean; climate is temperate. Railroads and buses serve the area. Several industries are located in the area, some of which are the manufacturing of paper and paper products, furniture, fish and meat packing, livestock and dairy products, citrus and other garden crops, and shipbuilding. A number of churches, a library, and a hospital are located here. Some part time employment is available. Recreational activities are fishing, hunting and water sports. Special events are the art shows and the Azalea Festival.

Branch Campuses: Orange Park Center, College Drive; St. Augustine Center, Hildreth Drive, St. Augustine FL.

SAINT LEO COLLEGE   *(H-8)*
Highway 52
Saint Leo, Florida 33574
Tel: (904) 588-8200; (800) 334-5532; Fax: (904) 588-8257

Description: The institution is a Catholic, coeducational liberal arts college offering a four-year program leading to the baccalaureate degree. It is accredited by the Southern Association of Colleges and Schools. The college was founded in 1889 and is the oldest Catholic College in the State of Florida. It operates on the semester system and offers one summer session. Enrollment is 1,000 full-time and part-time students. 1,000 students attend Evening and Weekend College while 7,000 students attend classes at 13 Military Bases throughout the Eastern United States. Students come to Saint Leo College from 34 states and 27 countries. A faculty of 77 (75% with doctorates) provides a faculty-student ratio of 1-15. Special programs include: continuing education, CLEP, Freshman Studies Program and a Teacher Recertification Program.

Entrance Requirements: Basic requirements are graduation from a secondary school with a satisfactory academic record, completetion of 14 high school units including 4 English, 3 math, 2 science, 1 foreign language and 2 social studies, satisfactory SAT or ACT scores, and positive recommendations from the applicant's high school guidance counselor or college; early admission, rolling admission, midyear admission and advanced placement plans available. $35 application fee.

Costs Per Year: $9,608 tuition; $2,541 room; $2,574 board; $756 student fees.

Collegiate Environment: The College proper occupies 170 acres of rolling hills and wooded grounds landscaped with a variety of tropical and semitropical plants and trees bordering spring-fed Lake Jovita. Most students reside on campus and residential facilities are available for both men and women. The newly expanded library contains 110,000 volumes, 650 current periodicals and newspapers, 207 microforms and 2,450 pieces of media software. Students of all religious beliefs are encouraged to enroll. 70% of applicants are accepted. Approximately 78% of freshmen return for the second year. 70% of students receive financial aid. Saint Leo College participates in NCAA Division II intercollegiate athletics.

Community Environment: Saint Leo is located 25 miles north of Tampa, and 38 miles from Tampa International Airport. Semi-tropical climate. Orlando and Disney World are 65 miles to the east.

SAINT PETERSBURG JUNIOR COLLEGE   *(I-7)*
P. O. Box 13489
St. Petersburg, Florida 33733
Tel: (813) 341-3600; Fax: (813) 341-4792

Description: This coeducational, public junior college was chartered by the State of Florida in 1928. The school is accredited by the Southern Association of Colleges and Schools and operates on the semester system with one summer session. The college, a multiple campus institution, had a recent enrollment of 8,344 full-time and 12,843 part-time students for all campuses. The faculty consists of 312 full-time members. An Associate degree is awarded at the completion of the two year program.

Entrance Requirements: High school graduation or equivalency certification; non-high school graduates over age 19 may be accepted; application fee $20; early admission, advanced placement, mid year admission, early decision and delayed admission plans available; credit up to 45 semester hours, may be awarded through CLEP and institutionally devised examinations; $20 application fee.

Costs Per Year: $993 tuition; $1,986 out-of-state tuition.

Collegiate Environment: The St. Petersburg campus is located on 25 acres in a residential area five miles west of downtown St. Petersburg. The Clearwater Campus is located on 77 acres in a rapidly developing urban environment 4 miles east of downtown Clearwater. The Tarpon Springs Center is located on 50 acres south of Tarpon Springs and adjacent to Innisbrook, a country club community. The college administration is located in the city of Pinellas Park, midway between the St. Petersburg and Clearwater campuses. Each campus has its own library, but students have facilities of all campuses available. The library contains 197,600 volumes, 1,351 periodicals, 242 microforms, and 9,312 audio visual items. The college is an "open-door" institution and all applicants meeting admission requirements are admitted. Some programs, particularly in health related fields, have limited access. Approximately 50% of freshmen returned for the second year. There are no dormitories on the campuses. Housing is available nearby. 859 scholarships are available and 70% of the students receive some form of financial aid.

Community Environment: See Eckerd College.

SAINT THOMAS UNIVERSITY   *(O-13)*
16400 Northwest 32nd Avenue
Miami, Florida 33054
Tel: (305) 628-6546; (800) 367-9006/9010; Admissions: (305) 628-6546; Fax: (305) 628-6510

Description: The private coeducational college is sponsored by the Archdiocese of Miami and accredited by the Southern Association of Colleges and Schools. The college grants Bachelors degree, Masters degree, and a Juris Doctorate. Continuing education courses and cooperative education programs available. The college operates on the semester system and offers two summer sessions. Recent enrollment included 408 men, 537 women full-time, 129 men, and 295 women part-time. There are 1,019 graduate students. A faculty of 73 full-time and 60 part-time gives an undergraduate faculty-student ratio of 15-1.

Entrance Requirements: High school graduation and 16 units including 4 English, 2 mathematics, 1 foreign language, 1 science and 2 social science; SAT, ACT required; $30 application fee. Early admission, early decision, delayed admission, rolling admission and advanced placement plans available. Student must fill out application, submit ACT/SAT scores, and pay $30 application fee.

Costs Per Year: $9,600 tuition; room and board, $4,600; student fees, $380.

Collegiate Environment: The campus has 12 buildings on 140 acres. The library contains 135,000 volumes. Dormitory facilities accommodate 350 men and women.

Community Environment: See Barry University

Branch Campuses: South Dade Center, Kendall

SAINT VINCENT DE PAUL REGIONAL SEMINARY   *(M-14)*
10701 S. Military Trail
Boynton Beach, Florida 33436
Tel: (407) 732-4424

Description: The graduate theologate for men is accredited by the Southern Association of Colleges and Schools, and American Association of Theological Schools. It is controlled by the Catholic Church and operates on the semester system. The seminary was opened in 1963. Student enrollment was 73. A faculty has 13 full-time members. The Seminary grants a Master's degree in Divinity, and an M.A. in Theology.

Entrance Requirements: B.A. or B.S. Degree; applicant must present certificates of Baptism, Confirmation and parents' marriage as well as letter of recommendation from pastor and rector of college previously attended.

Costs Per Year: $8,000 tuition; $5,000 room and board; $20 student fees.

Collegiate Environment: The seminary complex comprises eight buildings on 160 acres. The main chapel has a seating capacity of 400. Residence halls accommodate 120 students. The library contains 60,000 volumes.

Community Environment: A suburban area on Florida's east coast, Boynton Beach is 12 miles south of Palm Beach, has a tropical climate. Railroads, buses and airlines serve the area; Palm Beach International Airport is six miles south and the Ft. Lauderdale Airport is 30 miles south. The Florida Turnpike is close by. Shopping centers, county health services, hospital, and civic center are a part of the community facilities. Part-time employment opportunities are limited. The numerous recreational activities are golf, tennis, shuffleboard, three golf courses, boating, fishing, swimming and other water sports. A citywide recreation program is conducted.

SANTA FE COMMUNITY COLLEGE   *(D-8)*
3000 NW 83rd Street
Gainesville, Florida 32602
Tel: (904) 395-5444

Description: This publicly controlled community college was established by the Florida State Legislature in 1965 and is accredited by the Southern Association of Colleges and Schools. Total enrollment is 11,535. There are 250 faculty members. The college offers extensive academic and occupational opportunities as well as a wide variety of Community Education classes. Army and Air Force ROTC are offered.

Entrance Requirements: Open admissions; degree programs require high school graduation; early admissions, dual enrollment, advanced placement, early decision, and rolling admission plans available. $30 application fee.

Costs Per Year: $1,260 full-time resident tuition; $4,860 nonresident.

Collegiate Environment: Eighteen buildings on 115 acres comprise the main campus including a library containing 56,000 volumes, a gymnasium, tennis and raquetball facilities, a teaching zoo, classrooms, and a cafeteria. Financial aid is available in the form of grants, loans and work study programs.

Community Environment: See University of Florida.

Branch Campuses: Starke/Andrews, 209 W. Call St.; Starke, FL 32091; Downtown Center, 401 NW 6th St., Gainesville, FL 32601; Institute of Public Safety, Airport Industrial Park, Gainesville, FL 32601.

SEMINOLE COMMUNITY COLLEGE   *(F-10)*
100 Weldon Boulevard
Sanford, Florida 32773
Tel: (407) 323-1450

Description: The public community college operates on the semester system with two summer sessions. It was founded by an act of the 1965 Florida State Legislature. The college is accredited by the Southern Association of Colleges and Schools. Enrollment includes 3,016 full-time and 5,217 part-time students. A faculty of 164 full-time and 441 part-time gives a faculty-student ratio of 1-15. The college grants an Associate degree, and offers programs for continuing education and cooperative education programs in engineering, business and public service fields.

Entrance Requirements: Accredited high school graduation, non-high school graduates with GED certification; graduates of nonaccredited high schools may be admitted on a provisional basis; $25 application fee; early admission and rolling admission plans available.

Costs Per Year: $1,136 ($35.50 per credit) resident; $4,080 ($127.50 per credit) nonresident

Collegiate Environment: The campus is located on 170 acres of beautiful rolling country southwest of Sanford, convenient to recreational activities and several important centers of population. The library contains 75,918 volumes, 950 periodicals, 23,045 microforms and 7,918 audiovisual materials. All of the applicants are accepted, with the exception of transfer students that are not in good academic standing. Correspondence credit is allowed.

Community Environment: A residential city with subtropical climate. Sanford is located 20 miles northeast of Orlando. Air service is available through Orlando International Airport, and Amtrak serves the area. Part-time employment for students is available in the metropolitan Orlando Area. Lake Monroe is a recreation area nearby with a municipal zoo, picnic facilities and playground. Other sports include boating, fishing, tennis, and more. The close proximity to Orlando offers many convenient cultural and recreational activities.

SOUTH FLORIDA COMMUNITY COLLEGE   *(J-10)*
600 W. College Drive
Avon Park, Florida 33825
Tel: (813) 453-6661

Description: This public junior college is accredited by the Southern Association of Colleges and Schools. It began operation in 1966 in temporary facilities and moved to its permanent campus in 1970. Programs of study are primarily vocational-technical. The college grants an Associate degree. It operates on the semester system and offers two summer sessions. Enrollment includes 4,103 men and women full-time and part-time. A faculty of 52 provides a faculty-student ratio of approximately 1-50.

Entrance Requirements: High school graduation or equivalent; open admission, early admission and advanced placement plans available.

Costs Per Year: $1,152 ($36 per credit) resident tuition; $4,124 ($128.88 per credit) nonresident.

Collegiate Environment: The campus is an 80-acre isthmus located between Lake Lelia on the north and Lake Glenada on the south. The library holdings include 42,000 volumes. Some dormitory facilities are available. 58 scholarships are available, inlcuding 24 athletic. 26% of students receive some form of financial aid.

Community Environment: An urban area in south central Florida; semi-tropical climate and a tourist center. Trains and buses serve the area. Citrus production is the main source of income. Part time employment is limited to eating establishments and grocery stores. Recreational activities are numerous; they include golfing, bowling, tennis, shuffleboard, water sports, hunting, fishing and camping. Avon Park has many active civic organizations. The annual Halloween Carnival and Fashion Show is a special event.

SOUTHEASTERN COLLEGE   *(I-8)*
1000 Longfellow Boulevard
Lakeland, Florida 33801
Tel: (813) 665-4404

Description: The private Bible college granting a Bachelor degree was founded in 1935 and is controlled by the Assemblies of God. The college is accredited by the Southern Association of Colleges and Schools and the Accrediting Association of Bible Colleges. The semester system is employed and a summer session is offered. A student enrollment of 1,105 and a faculty of 45 gives a faculty-student ratio of 1-24.

Entrance Requirements: High school graduation with a C average and 16 units; evidence of good Christian character; at least 17 years of age; application fee $40; ACT or SAT required; rolling admission, early admission, and early decision plans available.

Costs Per Year: $4,062.50 ($125/cr) tuition; $2,866 room and board; $360 student fees.

Collegiate Environment: The campus has 31 buildings on 57 acres overlooking Lake Bonny. The buildings are modern and air conditioned. The library contains 85,000 volumes; dormitory capacity for 360 men, 385 women and 25 families. Approximately 10% of a recent class graduated in the top 10% of high school class; sixty percent of the freshman class returned for their sophomore year. About 98% of the applicants are accepted. Various forms of financial assistance are available; 70% of freshmen receive some form of aid.

Community Environment: See Florida Southern College.

STETSON UNIVERSITY   *(F-10)*
401 North Woodland Boulevard
DeLand, Florida 32720
Tel: (904) 822-7100; (800) 688-0101; Admissions: (904) 822-7100;
Fax: (904) 822-8832

Description: Stetson is a private comprehensive university and is accredited by the Southern Association of Colleges and Schools. The college of arts and sciences and schools of music and business administration are on the DeLand campus and the college of law is in St. Petersburg. The DeLand campus operates on the semester system and offers two summer sessions. Florida's oldest private university, Stetson was founded in 1883 and chartered by the State of Florida as DeLand University in 1887. The name was changed to John B. Stetson University in 1889 in honor of the Philadelphia hatmaker who became a major benefactor. The College of Law, the first in Florida, was organized in DeLand in 1900 and moved to its present location in 1953. The university also pioneered in music and business education. Graduate study leading to the Master of Arts degree has been offered since early in the century and master's degrees in business administration and accountancy also are awarded. Undergraduate enrollment is 2,000 full-time and 82 part-time students and 900 graduate students. The faculty is comprised of 183 full-time and 70 part-time members. Full year study abroad programs are available in Madrid, Spain; Moscow, Russia; Dijon, France; Freiburg, Germany; Guanajuato, Mexico; and Nottingham, England, and there are several one-semester and minimester programs at the United Nations in New York, Washington, D.C., Russia, Latin America, and other countries. Special cooperative programs in forestry and environmental studies, medical technology, and engineering are available.

Entrance Requirements: High school graduation with rank in upper 50% of graduating class; completion of 16 college-preparatory courses including 4 English, 3 mathematics, 2 science, 2 foreign language, 2 social studies. early decision, early admission, midyear admission, and advanced placement plans available. March 1 application deadline; $25 application fee.

Costs Per Year: $13,110 tuition; $4,589 board and room; $590 fees, etc.

Collegiate Environment: Shaded by century-old oaks, the 150-acre main campus of the university is within easy walking distance of downtown DeLand, a residential city of 18,000. Most of the buildings date from the late 1800s and all have been carefully restored and renovated in the last 10 years. Architecture ranges from Carpenter Gothic to Moorish to Southern Colonial. The principal administrative building, DeLand Hall, is in the National Register of Historic Places. Housed on this campus are the College of Arts and Sciences and the Schools of Music and Business Administration. The College of Law is located in St. Petersburg in the "Boom Era" Rolyat Hotel. The library collection on the main campus consists of 366,486 titles, 1,358 periodical subscriptions, and 207,947 government document titles in the state's oldest federal document depository. Residence halls are available for 1277 men and women. Also on the campus are Gillespie Museum of Minerals with the South's largest collection of rocks and minerals, and the Duncan Gallery of Art.

Community Environment: DeLand is located in Central Florida, equidistant from Daytona Beach and Orlando, in a region dotted with many lakes. The university is adjacent to the city's downtown historic district. DeLand is famous for its oak trees, planted by its founders. Average annual temperature is 72 degrees. All forms of transportation are available. Income is derived from citrus production, fern growing, light manufacturing, tourism, lumber, and cattle. Community facilities include a new public library, art museum, churches of all denominations, two hospitals, hotels, motels, and guest homes. Recreational activities are golf, tennis, boating, fishing, swimming, and water skiing. Points of interest include the Spring Garden Ranch Harness Track; DeLeon Springs, Blue Springs, and Hontoon Island State Parks; Canaveral National Seashore; and Ocala National Forest. Walt Disney World and Sea World are within a one hour drive.

TALLAHASSEE COMMUNITY COLLEGE   *(B-3)*
444 Appleyard Drive
Tallahassee, Florida 32304-2895
Tel: (904) 922-8140; Fax: (904) 488-2203

Description: This coeducational community college is controlled by the state government. It is accredited by the Southern Association of Colleges and Schools. It operates on the semester system and offers 3 summer sessions. The college was established in 1965 in Leon County to expand the educational opportunities for the citizens of Wakulla and Leon Counties. Gadsden County joined the district in July 1966. The college grants an Associate degree. Enrollment includes 4,685 full-time and 4,967 part-time students. A faculty of 135 full-time and 233 part-time gives a faculty-student ratio of 1-30.

Entrance Requirements: High school graduation or equivalent; rolling admission and advanced placement plans available; $15 application fee.

Costs Per Year: $1,050 state residents; $3,840 out-of-state.

Collegiate Environment: The campus has 33 buildings on 183 acres. The new library contains 77,984 volumes. Various forms of financial assistance are available. 20% of students receive some form of financial aid.

Community Environment: See Florida State University.

Branch Campuses: Gadsen Center, Quincy.

TAMPA COLLEGE   *(I-7)*
3319 W. Hillsborough Ave.
Tampa, Florida 33614
Tel: (813) 879-6000; Fax: (813) 871-2483

Description: The private business college was founded in 1890 and was chartered as a degree-granting school by the State of Florida in 1953. It is accredited by the Accrediting Commission of the Association of Independent Colleges and Schools as a senior college of business. The curriculum is designed to provide young men and women with a professional business education. The college grants the Associate, Bachelor, and Master degrees. It operates on the quarter system and offers one summer session. Enrollment includes 1,477 students. A faculty of 37 gives a faculty-student ratio of 1-30.

Entrance Requirements: High school graduation with a C average; entrance examination required; early admission, early decision, rolling admission, midyear admission, and advanced placement plans available; $25 application fee.

Costs Per Year: $4,320 ($90 per quarter credit hour) tuition; $4,725 room and board.

Collegiate Environment: The library contains 12,000 volumes, 200 pamphlets, 68 periodicals and 259 audiovisual materials.

Community Environment: See University of South Florida

Branch Campuses: Tampa College- Brandon, 3924 Coconut Palm Drive., Tampa, FL 33619, (813) 621-0041.

TRINITY COLLEGE OF FLORIDA   *(H-7)*
2430 Trinity Oaks Boulevard
New Port Richey, Florida 34655
Tel: (813) 376-6911; Admissions: (813) 376-6911; Fax: (813) 376-0781

Description: Trinity currently holds candidate status with the American Association of Bible Colleges and is approved by the State of Florida. It operates on the semester system and offers two summer sessions. This private school was founded in 1932 as the Florida Bible Institute and in 1946 the faculty and curriculum were enlarged and the name changed to Trinity College. The college is interdenominational in character and evangelical in nature. Students graduate with a double major. Everyone majors in Bible and then chooses from four others as their second major. Enrollment includes 50 full-time and 80 part-time students. A faculty of 6 full-time and 10 part-time gives a faculty-student ratio of 1-8.

Entrance Requirements: High School graduation or equivalent; ACT or SAT scores; sixteen years of age or over and of approved Christian character; application fee $25; references from pastor and two other Christian individuals are required; early admission, early decision, rolling admission, delayed admission, advanced placement plans available.

Costs Per Year: $95 per credit hour tuition; room and board $1,800; student fees $260.

Collegiate Environment: Approximately 95% of the applicants are accepted including midyear students. Dormitories accomodate 34 students. The library has holdings of 48,000 volumes.

Community Environment: See Clearwater Christian College.

UNIVERSITY OF CENTRAL FLORIDA   *(G-10)*
P.O. Box 160111
Orlando, Florida 32816-0111
Tel: (407) 823-2000; Admissions: (407) 823-3000

Description: The University of Central Florida is a member of the State University System of Florida. It is accredited by the Southern Association of Colleges Schools, and professionally by several accrediting institutions. The university grants the Associate, Baccalaureate, Masters, and Doctoral degrees. It operates on the semester system and offers four summer sessions. Enrollment includes 14,349 full-time and 10,289 part-time and 10,289 part-time undergraduates and 4,549 graduate students. A faculty of 604 full-time and 508 part-time gives an overall faculty-student ratio of 1-18. Air Force and Army ROTC are available as electives. Correspondence credit is allowed; continuing education courses and cooperative education programs are offered.

Entrance Requirements: The most important criterion in the admissions decision is the high school academic record: quality and level of difficulty of courses, grade point average, grade trends, consistency; and SAT or ACT test scores; early admission, rolling admission, delayed admission, early decision and advanced placement plans available; $20 application fee.

Costs Per Year: $1,810 state-resident tuition; $6,713 nonresident; $4,310 room and board; $590 average book and supplies, $1,800 average additional expenses.

Collegiate Environment: Residential units are air-conditioned and arranged on a suite plan with capacity for 1,578 men and women. The library contains 965,267 hard bound volumes, 5,486 periodical subscriptions, 1,311,617 microform titles, and 11,147 audiovisual materials. The university is geographically located within commuting distance of Orlando, Winter Park, Cape Canaveral, Cocoa, and Daytona Beach. It contains five colleges: Business Administration, Arts

and Sciences, Education, Engineering, Health and Public Affairs, and a Liberal Studies Program. Classes began in 1968 with 1,492 freshmen and junior students. Approximately 81% of the students who applied for a recent term were accepted.

Community Environment: Orlando has become a focal point for business and major industry, easily accessible by major forms of public transportation, and serves as a regional retail market for eight counties and over a million people. The area's reputation as a tourism mecca has brought a resultant surge in the hospitality industry as well. It also is an important agricultural center, noted for citrus and truck gardening. The temperate climate year-round provides ideal conditions for numerous recreational opportunities: fishing, boating, dog and horse racing, Jai-Alai, golf, tennis, and other outdoor activities. Points of interest include Walt Disney World, Epcot Center, MGM Studios, Universal Studios, Sea World, plus such seasonal attractions as the Church Street Station, Citrus Open Golf Tournament, Walt Disney World Golf Classic, Orlando Horse Show, Central Florida Fair, Orlando Magic Pro-Basketball, and Citrus Bowl. Cultural activities are widespread in the Orlando-Winter Park area, and include annual Sidewalk Art Festivals, Orlando Shakespeare Festival, the Florida Symphony Orchestra, Central Florida Civic Theatre, and the John Young Museum and Planetarium, located adjacent to the Loch Haven Art Center.

UNIVERSITY OF FLORIDA   *(D-8)*
W. University Ave. and 13th Street
Gainesville, Florida 32611
Tel: (904) 392-3261; Admissions: (904) 392-1365

Description: The University of Florida is a combined state university and land-grant college located in the northern center of the State. It operates on the semester system with two summer sessions and is accredited by the Southern Association of Colleges and Schools. While its beginnings go back to the days previous to Florida's admission to the Union in 1845, its first college, the College of Arts and Sciences, did not open until 1853. Recent enrollment included 11,9098 female and 13,329 male full-time undergraduates and 1,457 female and 1,695 male part-time undergraduates. In addition, there are 9,798 graduate and professional students. A faculty of 2,920 full-time, 190 part-time gives a faculty student ratio of 1-17. Correspondence credit allowed; continuing education courses offered; cooperative education programs available as well as overseas programs. Last 30 semester hours must be earned in residence. Army, Navy, and Air Force ROTC are available as electives.

Entrance Requirements: Accredited high school graduation with rank in upper 40%; minimum of 19 academic units; 4 English, 2 foreign language, 3 mathematics to include algebra I, geometry and algebra II, 3 science (2 must be with lab), 3 social studies, and 4 academic electives required; SAT 420V, 420M or ACT composite 19 required for consideration; admission is selective; early admission, early decision and advanced placement plans available; $20 application fee.

Costs Per Year: $1,830 tuition; $7,100 nonresident tuition; $3,950 room and board; additional expenses average $1,100; graduate tuition $9,340 for nonresidents.

Collegiate Environment: The university is located in Gainesville, a city of approximately 80,000, excluding University of Florida students. Situated in north central Florida, midway between the Atlantic Ocean and the Gulf of Mexico, the city is known as an agricultural and small industrial center. In addition to a moderate climate, recreational facilities are located nearby with university and private golf courses in easy reach of the campus and swimming and boating accommodations are available at nearby springs and rivers. Living quarters are available for 3,992 men, 4,104 women and 980 families. Of this total, fraternities and sororities house 1,000 men and 700 women. Beginning freshmen will receive housing contracts upon approval of admission; however, no student is required to live on campus. Approximately 65% of the students applying for admission are accepted including midyear students and 85-90% of the freshman class returned to the campus for a second year. The library contains 2.9 million volumes and pamphlets, 28,000 periodicals, 2.7 million microforms and 165,156 audiovisual materials. There are 2,965 scholarships offered. 30% of the current student body receives financial aid. Overseas programs are available in many countries; 2.5 GPA required to participate.

Community Environment: Gainesville is the county seat of Alachua County located on the rolling highlands of north-central Florida midway between the Gulf of Mexico and the Atlantic Ocean. The climate is subtropical with an average mean temperature of 70 degrees. Railroads, buses and airlines serve the area. Gainesville is the focal point of diversified industrial and agricultural activities. The city facilities include churches of many denominations, center for science, education and medicine, medical center with hospital, museum and numerous civic organizations. Recreational facilities include golf courses, swimming at nearby springs, boating and fresh-water fishing in surrounding lakes and rivers. Both the Atlantic Ocean and the Gulf of Mexico are within a two-hour drive. Off-campus housing is available for over 20,000 students in addition to university housing.

UNIVERSITY OF MIAMI   *(O-13)*
Coral Gables, Florida 33124
Tel: (305) 284-4323; Fax: (305) 284-2507

Description: The private, nonsectarian university was chartered in 1925 and is accredited by the Southern Association of Colleges and Schools. The university awards undergraduate and graduate level degrees. It operates on the semester system and offers two summer sessions. Enrollment includes 7,425 full-time, 945 part-time undergraduate, and 5,364 graduate students. A faculty of 956 full-time and 498 part-time provides a faculty-student ratio of 1-9. Air Force and Army ROTC are available.

Entrance Requirements: Admission is selective and is offered to applicants whose credentials are academically sound, who demonstrate personal integrity and seriousness of educational purpose; applicants must submit SAT or ACT scores, guidance counselor evaluations, class rank and an essay; early admission, early decision, and advanced placement plans available; $35 application fee.

Costs Per Year: $17,340 tuition and fees; $6,852 room and board.

Collegiate Environment: The 260-acre main campus in Coral Gables incorporates 2 colleges and 11 schools, residential halls, administration buildings and is connected to downtown Miami and the Medical School campus by Metrorail. The 16-acre Rosenstiel School of Marine and Atmospheric Sciences campus is situated on Virginia Key in Biscayne Bay with an off-campus research station on Fisher Island. The School of Medicine, located in Miami's civic center, is Florida's first medical school and forms the hub of the fourth largest health care facility in the U.S. The university's 106-acre south campus is for research and development projects and is located 12 miles southwest of the main campus. Facilities here include an experimental farm, industrial chemical laboratory, and research center. The University Conference Center is located downtown on the Miami River. The library system of the entire university contains 1.8 million volumes, 18,890 serial subscriptions, and 1 million microforms. The university art gallery serves both the university and the community. Five coed residential halls house all incoming on-campus students. About 59% of applicants are accepted. Various forms of financial assistance are available, and 80% of students receive some form of financial aid.

Community Environment: A part of the metropolitan Miami area, Coral Gables is known as "City Beautiful" with the mildest climate in the United States. The Miami International Airport is nearby. The city offers a distinguished retail shopping district, the opera, theatre, ballet, concerts, the Vizcaya Museum, and Lowe Gallery. Recreational activities are numerous including swimming, golf, tennis, boating, very good sport fishing, and snorkelling and scuba diving among the only coral reefs in the continental United States, in the Florida Keys. The Everglades National Park is a few miles away. Annually is the Orange Bowl Festival.

UNIVERSITY OF NORTH FLORIDA   *(B-9)*
4567 St. Johns Bluff Road S.
Jacksonville, Florida 32224-2645
Tel: (904) 646-2624; Fax: (904) 646-2703

Description: The publicly supported, coeducational, four year university was created by the Legislature of the State of Florida in 1965. The first classes began in 1972. Operating on the early semester system with 2 summer sessions, the school is accredited by the Southern Association of Colleges and Schools. Enrollment includes 1,694 men, 2,297 women full-time, 2,060 men, 3,214 women part-time, and

1,399 graduate students. A faculty of 346 full-time and 5 part-time gives a faculty-student ratio of 1:17. Army ROTC is available.

Entrance Requirements: Accredited junior college graduation or completion of 60 semester hours or 90 quarter hours of collegiate work for transfer students. For Freshmen, GPA of 3 or higher; SAT 1050, ACT 24, ACTE 25, completion of 4 English, 3 math, 3 science, 2 language, 3 social studies, 2 foreign language. Application fee $20; rolling admission, advanced placement and early admission plans available.

Costs Per Year: Tuition $1,732 for residents; $6,730 for nonresidents; $4,980 room and board; $25 orientation fee.

Collegiate Environment: Located on 1,000 acres, the campus presently has 15 buildings. The library contains 1,178,000 volumes, periodical titles, microforms and sound recordings. Dormitories can house 1,000 students. 60% of applicants are accepted.

Community Environment: See Jacksonville University

UNIVERSITY OF SOUTH FLORIDA   *(I-7)*
4202 Fowler Avenue, SVC 1036
Tampa, Florida 33620-6900
Tel: (813) 974-3350; Fax: (813) 974-9689

Description: This state university operates on the semester system and offers 3 summer sessions. When it was opened to a charter class of 2,000 freshmen in 1960 it became the first state university in the United States to be totally planned and initiated in this century. The university is accredited by the Southern Association of Colleges and Schools. The school grants Bachelor, Master's, and Doctorate degrees. The first doctoral program began in 1968 and each year new degree programs are being offered. Enrollment includes 14,808 full-time, 8,818 part-time undergraduates, and 6,278 graduate students. A faculty of 1,504 provides an overall faculty-student ratio of 1-22.

Entrance Requirements: High school graduation or equivalent with B average; completion of 19 units including 4 english, 3 math, 3 lab science, 2 language, 3 social studies, and 4 academic electives; SAT or ACT required; graduated with a C plus average and SAT 450V, 450M, or ACT 21 eligible for admission; application fee $20; early admission, rolling admission, delayed admission and advanced placement plans available; GRE or GMAT required for graduate programs.

Costs Per Year: $1,860 state-resident tuition; $6,760 tuition for non-Florida residents; $4,420 room and board.

Collegiate Environment: Fifty-eight major buildings on 1,672 acres comprise the Tampa campus, which is eight air miles northeast of downtown Tampa. The library contains over 1,000,000 volumes, and dormitory facilities are available for 3,300 students. 65% of the applicants are accepted. 287 scholarships are available including 187 for freshmen.

Community Environment: Tampa, located on the west coast of Florida, is the seventh largest port in the nation. It is a significant industrial and commercial center; the second largest city in the state. A fine harbor with a 34 foot channel to the Gulf of Mexico is located here. It is important in trade and travel to and from Central and South America. Annual mean temperature is 72.3 degrees, the average rainfall is 49 inches. All modes of travel serve the area. Industries include cigar manufacturing, phosphate, beer, cement, cans, wire and cable, and canned citrus fruits and vegetables. Tampa is a tourist city with many recreational facilities; yacht basin, golf courses, tennis clubs, saddle clubs, swimming pools, bowling alleys, baseball diamonds, and basketball courts. Salt water fishing is excellent. Swimming is excellent all year in Tampa Bay, and at the municipal beach on Courtney Campell Causeway. The Tampa Bay Buccaneers is the local NFL team and the Cincinnati Reds make Tampa their spring training quarters. Points of interest are the Busch Gardens, Lowry Park, Tampa Art Institute, and the Tampa Museum.

Branch Campuses: Sarasota; St. Petersburg; Fort Myers; Lakeland.

UNIVERSITY OF TAMPA   *(F-4)*
401 West Kennedy Blvd.
Tampa, Florida 33606-1480
Tel: (813) 253-6228; (800) 733-4773; Admissions: (813) 253-6228; Fax: (813) 254-4955

Description: The private, nonsectarian university is accredited by the Southern Association of Colleges and Schools and operates on the semester system with two summer terms. The university was founded in 1931 by public-spirited citizens who wanted to provide higher education for community young people who lacked finances to go away to college; today it is a residential institution with students from 48 states and 56 foreign countries. The university grants the Associate, Bachelor, and Masters degrees. Enrollment includes 708 men, 738 women full-time, 179 men, 352 women part-time, 408 graduate students, and 226 evening students. A faculty of 129 full-time and 38 part-time members provides a student-faculty ratio of 1-13. Continuing education courses are offered. One-year abroad programs are available in Mexico, Spain, The Netherlands, and France.

Entrance Requirements: High school graduation with a C+ average and 15 units, including 4 English, 2 mathematics, 2 science and 2 social science; SAT or ACT required, minimum SAT V450, M450, ACT 21; GMAT required for graduate programs; application fee $25; early admission, rolling admission, delayed admission, midyear admission and advanced placement plans available.

Costs Per Year: $12,390 tuition, $4,620 room and board; $594 student fees.

Collegiate Environment: The campus has 42 buildings on 69 acres overlooking the scenic Hillsborough River. The library contains 238,000 volumes, 1,880 periodicals, 50,000 microforms and 2,312 sound recordings. Modern air-conditioned residence halls accommodate 906 men and women. 75% of applicants are accepted. Approximately 80% of the current students receive some form of financial assistance.

Community Environment: The university is situated along the Hillsborough River adjacent to the downtown area of Tampa, Florida. The city of Tampa (population 300,000) is part of the Tampa Bay metropolitan area of 2 million. This rapidly growing area is a business and resort center featuring year-round sunshine with school year temperatures averaging 60-80 degrees Farenheit and excellent job prospects. Tampa's ultramodern international airport is just 15 minutes from campus. The city is easily accessible by interstate highway, bus or rail. Tampa is 45 minutes from the beaches of the Gulf of Mexico and 90 minutes from Central Florida's parks and amusement areas such as Walt Disney World.

UNIVERSITY OF WEST FLORIDA   *(N-2)*
Pensacola, Florida 32514-5750
Tel: (904) 474-2230

Description: One of ten state universities in Florida, this university enrolls freshmen, sophomores, juniors, seniors, and masters degree students. Enrollment includes 8,000 students. A faculty of 344 provides a faculty-student ratio of 1-23. The university operates on the semester system and offers one summer session. It is accredited by the Southern Association of Colleges and Schools. Many programs are accredited by their respective professional accrediting organizations. Correspondence credit is allowed, and cooperative education programs are available.

Entrance Requirements: Graduation from an accredited junior or community college; completion of 60 semester hours of collegiate work; GRE required for most graduate programs; rolling admission is available; $20 application fee; for freshmen and sophomores: graduation from accredited high school or equivalent; completion of 19 units including 4 English, 3 math, 3 science, 3 social science, 2 foreign language, and 4 electives; SAT or ACT required.

Costs Per Year: $1,542 state-resident tuition; $7,334 nonresidents; $4,134 room and board.

Collegiate Environment: The university's 1,000-acre main campus is located 10 miles north of downtown Pensacola. In addition, classes are taught at university centers at Eglin Air Force Base, Fort Walton Beach, and Pensacola Naval Air Station. An undeveloped 125-acre campus on Santa Rosa Island provides extensive recreational activities. The university's John C. Pace Library contains 850,000 volumes, 1,088,000 microforms and more than 6,338 periodicals. There are living accommodations for 800 students. 60% of students receive some form of financial aid.

Community Environment: Pensacola is Florida's westernmost metropolitan area, situated approximately 50 miles east of Mobile, Alabama. A mild climate and more than 200 miles of Gulf and bay shoreline combine to produce an environment perfect for outdoor recreation. Pensacola is the home of the largest naval air training facility

in the United States and of Florida's largest industrial plant. Boating, skin diving, swimming, surfing, and sailing are among the numerous water-related sports enjoyed practically year-round. More than 20 miles of Pensacola Beach are within the confines of the National Seashore, including historic Fort Pickens. Numerous museums and related facilities provide amateur historians with a wealth of exploring. The U.S. Naval Air Training museum provides a historical compendium of naval aviation in the United States. Such annual events as the Fiesta of Five Flags, the Gulf Coast Fine Arts Festival and the West Florida Music Festival draw thousands of people annually.

VALENCIA COMMUNITY COLLEGE   *(G-10)*
1800 South Kirkman Road
Orlando, Florida 32802
Tel: (407) 299-5000; Admissions: (407) 299-5000 x1507

Description: The publicly supported community college is governed by the State of Florida and an appointed board. It was founded in 1967 to serve the needs of Orange and Osceola counties. It is accredited by the Southern Association of Colleges and Schools and operates on the semester system with three summer sessions. The school enrolls 3,293 men, 3,849 women full-time, 6,143 men, and 8,809 women part-time. A faculty of 252 full-time and 600 part-time gives a faculty-student ratio of 1-25. Continuing education courses offered; cooperative education programs available. The college grants an Associate degree.

Entrance Requirements: High school graduation or GED equivalent; application fee $20; early admission, rolling admission, early decision, midyear admission and advanced placement plans available.

Costs Per Year: $1,200 tuition; $3,900 tuition for out-of-state students.

Collegiate Environment: The college moved to its permanent campus in 1971. Various forms of financial assistance are available. The library contains 73,602 volumes and special programs are offered for the culturally disadvantaged. Midyear students are accepted.

Community Environment: See University of Central Florida

WARNER SOUTHERN COLLEGE   *(I-9)*
5301 Highway 27 South
Lake Wales, Florida 33853
Tel: (813) 638-1426; (800) 949-7248; Admissions: (813) 638-2109; Fax: (813) 638-1472

Description: The coeducational Christian liberal arts college is accredited by the Southern Association of Colleges and Schools. The college was founded in 1964 and began classes in 1968. Students and faculty who emphasize spiritual values and are oriented to service occupations and church ministries are most at home at the college. It operates on the early semester calendar system and offers two summer sessions. Enrollment is 290 full-time and 91 part-time students. A faculty of 21 full-time and 46 part-time gives a faculty-student ratio of 1-14. Continuing education courses are offered.

Entrance Requirements: High school graduation with rank in upper half of graduating class; completion of 4 units of English, 2 mathematics, 2 science, 2 foreign language, and 3 social studies; minimum 18 ACT or minimum 700 composite SAT required; early admission, early decision, midyear admission, rolling admission and advanced placement plans available. $25 application fee.

Costs Per Year: $6,600 tuition; $3,500 room and board; $480 student fees.

Collegiate Environment: Located on 370 acres of land in the heart of Florida, the campus consists of 20 buildings with plans for several more in the future. The library contains 75,000 volumes, 5,500 periodicals, 6,200 microforms, and audiovisual materials. Dormitories accommodate 88 men and 121 women. Various forms of financial assistance are available and 83% of the current students receive some form of aid. 80% of the applicants are accepted. The average SAT scores of the freshmen were 404V, 409M.

Community Environment: See Webber College.

WEBBER COLLEGE   *(I-10)*
P.O. Box 96
Babson Park, Florida 33827
Tel: (813) 638-1431; (800) 741-1844; Fax: (813) 638-2823

Description: Webber College is a small coeducational institution accredited by the Southern Association of Colleges and Schools. Founded in 1927, the college is a privately endowed non-profit organization that offers Associate of Bachelor Degree Programs. It operates on the semester system and offers two summer sessions. Enrollment includes 315 full-time and 105 part-time students. A faculty of 12 full-time and 15 part-time gives a faculty-student ratio of 1-15.

Entrance Requirements: High school diploma with a minimum 2.0 Grade Point Average or GED equivalent; SAT or ACT scores, TOEFL required of applicants for whom English is a second language; early admission, early decision, rolling admission and advanced placement plans available; $35 application fee.

Costs Per Year: Tuition $6,390; room and board $3,000.

Collegiate Environment: Webber's atmosphere is enhanced by Florida's famous year-round sunshine. The college's campus is located on beautiful Lake Caloosa. With fifty-five miles of coastline, the lake affords water skiing, sailing, canoeing, swimming and fishing. Besides recreational activities, Webber offers intercollegiate and intramural athletics for men and women. The 40 acres of developed campus consist of male and female dormitories, a student center, a dining hall, a classroom building, an administration building, gymnasium, a student services building and a library. The library contains 35,000 volumes, 3,000 pamphlets, 160 periodicals, 5,700 microforms, 1,500 sound recordings, and audiovisual materials.

Community Environment: The college is located in Babson Park, Florida, a small Central Florida town about one hour from Disney World and Sea World and 30 minutes from Cypress Gardens.

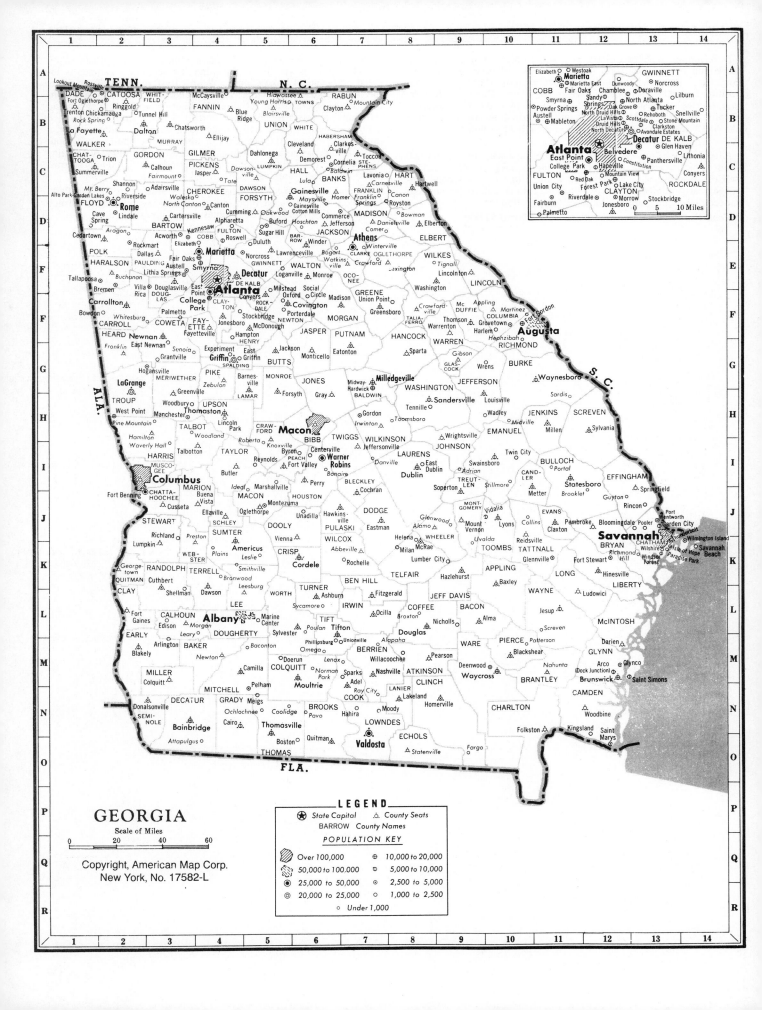

GEORGIA

Scale of Miles

0   20   40   60

Copyright, American Map Corp.
New York, No. 17582-L

LEGEND

⭐ State Capital   ⌖ County Seats
BARROW   *County Names*

POPULATION KEY

▨ Over 100,000		⊕ 10,000 to 20,000
▨ 50,000 to 100,000		⊕ 5,000 to 10,000
● 25,000 to 50,000		⊙ 2,500 to 5,000
◉ 20,000 to 25,000		○ 1,000 to 2,500
	∘ Under 1,000	

GEORGIA

ABRAHAM BALDWIN AGRICULTURAL COLLEGE *(M-6)*
ABAC Station Box 4
Tifton, Georgia 31794
Tel: (912) 386-3230; Fax: (912) 386-7006

Description: Abraham Baldwin Agricultural College is a two-year, residential, coeducational institution which offers diverse opportunities for students through a variety of programs. These programs which lead to an Associate degree include the college parallel or transfer programs, career technological programs, continuing education short courses, and special services. The multi-purpose institution is a member of the American Association of Junior Colleges, the Southern Association of Junior Colleges, and is fully accredited by the Southern Association of Colleges and schools. Located in South Central Georgia, the school was initially established in 1908 as the Second District A & M School, then became known as South Georgia A & M College in 1924, and later became Georgia State College for men in 1929. The institution became a part of the University System of Georgia in 1933 when it was renamed Abraham Baldwin Agricultural College. Abraham Baldwin was a signer of the United States Constitution and was a founder of the state-supported system of colleges and universities in Georgia. The college operates on the quarter system and offers a summer session. Enrollment includes 2,318 full-time and 433 part-time students. A faculty of 112 full-time and 15 part-time gives a faculty-student ratio of 1-25.

Entrance Requirements: High school graduation with a C average or GED scores; SAT or ACT required; early admission, rolling admission, early decision, midyear admission and advanced placement plans available; $5 application fee.

Costs Per Year: $1,254 state residents; $3,180 nonresidents; $2,250 room and board; $275 student fees.

Collegiate Environment: Thirty-eight buildings on 390 acres comprise the campus which is located in south central Georgia, 55 miles from Florida and 110 miles from Alabama. Dormitory facilities are available for 776 men and 422 women. The library contains 60,000 volumes, 1,806 periodicals, 3,894 microforms and 10,970 audiovisual materials. Ninety-nine percent of students applying for admission are accepted including midyear students. Financial aid is available for economically handicapped students, and 60% of the current student body receives some form of assistance.

Community Environment: A rural area between Macon and Valdosta having a temperate climate. All modes of transportation serve the area. Scheduled airlines are nearby at Moultrie and Albany. Tifton is an agricultural area; plants are grown here and then sent north for transplanting. Other products are tobacco, cotton, peanuts, melons, commercial grasses and livestock. Part- and full-time employment is good. Recreational activities include hunting, tennis, golf, swimming and other water sports.

AGNES SCOTT COLLEGE *(E-4)*
Decatur, Georgia 30030
Tel: (404) 638-6000; (800) 868-8602; Admissions: (404) 638-6285; Fax: (404) 638-6414

Description: Colonel George Washington Scott founded the College in 1889 to bring quality education, then found primarily in the East, to women in the South. The college is accredited by the Southern Association of Colleges and Schools. Today, academic excellence is still emphasized in a, puposely small, friendly, informal atmosphere. 85% of classes have fewer than 20 students, and there is one computer for every 5 students. The college offers a Master of Arts in Teaching Secondary English. It also offers a dual-degree program with Georgia Tech in several engineering and computer science fields, and in architecture with Washington University. Through the colleges involvement with the University Center in Georgia, students

may cross register with the 18 other colleges and universities that participate in this program. Students also have access to the millions of volumes housed at these institutions. Over 300 internships and externships are offered in Atlanta and elsewhere through the Office of Career Planning and Counseling. The Year 5 program allows graduates to return the next year (full-time or part-time) on a tuition-free basis. Study abroad is available for qualified students through the Global Awareness program with recent trips to Japan, Mexico, Russia, and South Africa. The college operates on the semester system. Enrollment includes 514 full-time, 56 part-time undergraduate, and 24 graduate students. A faculty of 142 full-time and 31 part-time gives an undergraduate faculty-student ratio of 1-8. Air Force and Navy ROTC programs available through the Georgia Institute of Technology.

Entrance Requirements: Each applicant's school record, SAT (middle range 940-1190 combined) or ACT scores, recommendations, and personal essay will be reviewed; school activities, community service and special talents are also important considerations; completion of 16 units including 4 English, 3 mathematics, 1 or more science, 1 or more social science, 2 foreign language, and additional academic electives is recommended; early admission, early decision, deferred admission, midyear admission, and advanced placement plans available; Jan. 5 scholarship application deadline, March 1 priority deadline for Fall semester; $35 application fee.

Costs Per Year: $13,800 tuition; $5,800 room and board; $135 activity fee.

Collegiate Environment: The 100-acre campus is located in Decatur. The library contains 194,000 volumes, 774 periodicals, and 24,898 microforms. Residence halls accommodate 407 students. All students live on campus unless commuting from their homes in the area. The Alston Campus Center houses student lounges, a snack bar, bookstore, racquetball courts, a studio dance area, an aerobics room and the chapel. There are approximately 40 clubs and organizations on campus including the strong Student Government Association. Approximately 80% of applicants are accepted. Financial aid is available, and through scholarships, grants, educational loans, student employment, and payment plans, 89% of students receive some form of financial assistance.

Community Environment: Downtown Atlanta, 6 miles away, is easily accessible. An international city, it offers opportunities for interaction with a variety of cultures and excellent opportunities for internships. The city also offers extensive cultural and recreational facilities including concerts, a symphony orchestra, theatrical groups, cabarets, pubs, parks, and major-league sports teams. Within two hours drive are the mountains and five hours away is the Georgia coastline. Atlanta will host the 1996 Summer Olympic Games.

ALBANY STATE COLLEGE *(L-5)*
504 College Drive
Albany, Georgia 31705
Tel: (912) 430-4646; (800) 822-7267; Fax: (912) 430-3936

Description: This public-controlled liberal arts college is accredited by the Southern Association of Colleges and Schools. The college was established in 1903 and soon offered junior college level work in teacher education, agriculture and home economics. The academic program has grown to provide instruction in business administration, teacher education, arts and sciences, and collegiate nursing. The college grants the Baccalaureate and Masters degrees. The Graduate School offers degrees in Business Administration, Criminal Justice, Education, Nursing, Public Administration, Educational Leadership, and Educational Specialist. The school operates on the quarter system and offers two summer sessions. Enrollment includes 2,664 undergraduates and 303 graduate students. A faculty of 151 gives a faculty-student ratio of 1-20.

Entrance Requirements: High school graduation or satisfactory completion of GED tests and possession of a State Department of Education High School Equivalency Certificate; completion of 16 units including 4 English, 3 mathematics, 3 science, 3 social science, and 2 foreign language; SAT scores of at least 350V, 350M; early admission and midyear admission plans available.

Costs Per Year: $1,442 ($447/quarter) state-resident tuition; $2,844 (948/quarter) out-of-state tuition; $2,859 ($953/quarter) room and board; $396 ($132/quarter) student fees.

Collegiate Environment: The campus has more than 20 buildings on 131 acres, and the campus is presently in a phase of expansion. New classrooms and dormitories have recently been completed (dormitory capacity for 360 men and 622 women). The library contains 1,500,000 volumes, 600 pamphlets, 700 periodicals and 471,000 microforms. The Office of Financial Aid makes every effort to ensure students awareness of the several types of financial resources that are available. Scholarhips, loans, grants, and employment are only a few of the available resources. 90% of the applicants are accepted.

Community Environment: The campus is situated in a progressive community that affords a variety of advantages. Albany is located on the Flint River. Air transportation is accessible at the new Southwest Georgia Regional Airport. The Marine Corps Supply Center is located here. Albany's economy is broadly based on agriculture, manufacturing, and business from the nearby military bases. The most notable industry is the production of papershell pecans; more than 700,000 pecan trees cover 60,000 acres in the vicinity. The Spanish peanut industry and other diversified businesses and farming contribute to the city's high rating in retail sales. Part-time employment is available. Radium Springs, four miles south, has the largest natural spring in the state.

ANDREW COLLEGE   *(K-3)*
College Street
Cuthbert, Georgia 31740
Tel: (912) 732-2171; Fax: (912) 732-2176

Description: The private, two-year liberal arts college is controlled by the United Methodist Church and accredited by the Southern Association of Colleges and Schools. The college operates on the quarter system and offers one summer session. The charter was granted in 1854 and is the second oldest charter in the United States giving an educational institution the right to confer degrees upon women. It operated for 63 years as a four-year college but became a two-year junior college in 1917; it became co-educational in 1956. Enrollment includes 151 men and 169 women. A faculty of 26 gives a faculty-student ratio of 1-16.

Entrance Requirements: High school graduation with a C average and a minimum of 18 units; SAT. Application fee $15 with application to Dean of Admission. Early admission, advanced placement, early decision, midyear admission, rolling admission and special programs for international students available. $15 application fee.

Costs Per Year: $5,343; room and board $4,020.

Collegiate Environment: The campus has thirteen buildings on 46 acres. The library contains 33,000 volumes, 60 periodicals, and 260 microforms and 500 audiovisual materials. There is dormitory capacity for 150 men and 150 women. 85% percent of all applicants are accepted. Merit scholarships, based on academic performance and/or leadership qualities are available. Athletic scholarships in soccer, tennis, softball and baseball are offered. 87% of the students receive some form of financial aid.

Community Environment: Cuthbert is a rural community 40 miles from Albany, and 55 miles from Columbus. Its climate is ideal. Buses serve the community. Airline services are available one hour away. Part-time employment exists for students. Community facilities include a library, churches, and good shopping. A public recreation center, two swimming pools, golf course and nearby lakes provide facilities for fishing, boating and water skiing.

ARMSTRONG STATE COLLEGE   *(J-13)*
11935 Abercorn Street
Savannah, Georgia 31419
Tel: (912) 927-5275

Description: The publicly controlled liberal arts college is coeducational and accredited by the Southern Association of Colleges and Schools. The college was founded in 1935 as a junior college and offered a four-year program and Bachelor's degree. It moved to a new campus in 1965. At present, the college offers first year pre-professional programs in forestry and veterinary medicine and the complete three-year pre-professional programs in dentistry, law, medicine and optometry as well as a Associate degree in Nursing and allied medical health fields. It operates on the quarter system and offers 4 summer sessions. Enrollment includes 3,864 full-time, 1,176 part-time, and 870 evening students. A faculty of 243 full-time and 130 part-time provides a faculty-student ratio of 1-14. ROTC Army and Navy programs are available.

Entrance Requirements: High school graduation with a recommended C average and 21 units including 4 English, 3 mathematics, 3 science, 3 social science, and 2 foreign language; score 380 or more on SAT verbal, and 380 math; application fee $10; early admission, early decision, midyear admission, and rolling admission plans available.

Costs Per Year: $1,623 tuition for resident students; $4,467 tuition for out-of-state students; $3,546 room and board (double occupancy).

Collegiate Environment: The campus has 14 buildings on 250 acres. The library is a modern, two-story building completed in 1965 and expanded in 1976, which contains 171,396 volumes and over 1,120 periodicals. Various forms of financial assistance are available and 40% of the present student body receives some form of aid.

Community Environment: The college is located on the southside of Savannah, 30 miles from the Atlantic Ocean. All modes of transportation are available. Savannah is a highly industrialized metropolitan area with only minor agricultural activities. Industrial plants number over 350. This city is considered to be one of the first planned cities in North America. The charm of the city comes from the cobblestoned riverfront, and the many squares shaded by majestic oak trees. Points of interest include Factor's Walk, Savannah riverfront shopping, Johnson Square, Pink House, Owens-Thomas House, Cathedral of St. John the Baptist, Independent Presbyterian Church, Colonial Park, and many others.

ART INSTITUTE OF ATLANTA   *(E-4)*
3376 Peachtree Road, N.E.
Atlanta, Georgia 30326
Tel: (404) 266-1341; (800) 275-4242; Admissions: (404) 266-2662; Fax: (404) 848-9551

Description: This two year coeducational institution is accredited by the Southern Association of Colleges and Schools. Its purpose is to prepare students to move directly into career opportunities. The institute grants the Associate degree and a Bachelor degree in Interior design. It operates on the quarter system and offers one summer session. Enrollment includes 1,360 students. A faculty of 38 full-time and 77 part-time gives a faculty-student ratio of 1-19.

Entrance Requirements: High school graduation or GED equivalency; application fee $50Early admission, early decision, rolling admission and advanced placement plans available. Students are admitted in mid-year. Housing available for 185 students. The Library contains 20,000 volumes.

Costs Per Year: Varies depending on curriculum.

Collegiate Environment: The classroom building is located in a major fashion and business district, across from Lenox Square. Facilities include a library of 1,000 volumes. Dormitories can accommodate 185 students. 96% of applicants are accepted. 80% receive some form of financial aid.

Community Environment: See Clark Atlanta University.

ATLANTA CHRISTIAN COLLEGE   *(E-4)*
2605 Ben Hill Road
East Point, Georgia 30344
Tel: (404) 761-8861; (800) 776-1222; Admissions: (404) 761-8861; Fax: (404) 669-2024

Description: This private Bible College is affiliated with the Christian Church and is accredited by the Southern Association of Colleges and Schools. It operates on the semester system and offers one summer session. The college grants a Baccalaureate, and an Associate degree. Degree programs are offered in early childhood education, human relations, music, business and Bible with specializations in preaching, Christian education, youth ministry, missions, and pre-seminary. Enrollment includes 132 men and 136 women. A faculty of 13 full-time and 22 part-time gives a faculty-student ratio of 1-18.

Entrance Requirements: High school graduation with a C average; SAT of 750 combined or ACT 18 composite; early admission, early decision, midyear admission, rolling admission and advanced placement plans available.

Costs Per Year: $4,495 ($145/credit) tuition; $3,030 room and board; $320 fees.

Collegiate Environment: The campus has 15 buildings on more than 50 acres. It is located just ten minutes from downtown Atlanta. The library contains 55,826 volumes, 85 periodicals, 10,647 microforms, and numerous audiovisual materials. Dormitory space is available for 85 men, 95 women and 50 families. 70% of the applicants are accepted. Various forms of financial assistance are offered. 90% of the current student body receives some form of aid.

Community Environment: A suburban area with temperate climate, East Point is served by all major forms of transportation. Along with the usual community facilities, the opportunities are excellent for part-time employment.

ATLANTA COLLEGE OF ART   *(E-4)*
1280 Peachtree Street, N.E.
Atlanta, Georgia 30309
Tel: (404) 733-7685; (800) 832-2104; Admissions: (404) 733-5100;
Fax: (404) 733-5107

Description: The Atlanta College of Art provides an educational environment for the career-minded student with a talent and passion for making art. Founded in 1928, the College is an accredited institutional member of the National Association of Schools of Art and Design and the Southern Association of Colleges and Schools. It operates on the semester system and offers one summer session. Enrollment includes 435 full-time students from thirty-one states and eleven foreign countries. The faculty consists of 23 full-time and 50 part-time members which provides a faculty-student ratio of 1-10.

Entrance Requirements: High school graduates or equivalent; completed application; $25 nonrefundable application fee; statement of purpose; official transcripts; SAT or ACT scores; portfolio of twelve to fifteen pieces of work, three of which are required to be drawings from direct observation.

Costs Per Year: $7,850 tuiton; $3,150 housing; student fees $250.

Collegiate Environment: Occupying 88,000 square feet of space in the Memorial Arts Building of the Woodruff Arts Center and the adjacent sculpture building, the Atlanta College of Art has the following well-lighted, well-ventilated studios and classrooms: two visual studies studios; three drawing studios; a photo shooting studio and two darkrooms; silkscreen, lithography, and intaglio and relief printmaking studios; papermaking and bookbinding facilities; three painting studios; five design studios; video and computer studios; a sculpture building (which includes a complete woodshop, a foundry, and working studios); and several academic classrooms. Advanced-level students in painting, design, and sculpture are allotted individual work spaces. The new, two-story college library has approximately 30,000 volumes, 70,000 slides, and 1,500 files on Georgia artists. It subscribes to over 250 periodicals and houses an exceptional collection of more than 1,000 artists' books, a collection that is nationally recognized and unparalleled in the region. The newly renovated Rich Auditorium, which seats 400, is the scene of many events, including visiting artists' lectures, performances, film series, commencement, and other College gatherings. The new Atlanta College of Art Gallery, a museum-quality space of 3,850 square feet, shows eight to ten exhibitions a year, including the annual faculty show, juried student and senior shows, contemporary exhibitons organized by the gallery, and traveling exhibitions featuring works by internationally recognized artists. Gallery 100, which offers exhibits of student work that are changed weekly, is maintained by the students themselves. The High Museum of Art is an integral part of the College's academic life; teachers often take classes to the museum, and visiting artists, critics, and curators give lectures and gallery talks there, often in conjunction with studio demonstrations, critiques of student work, and workshops at the College. Dormitory facilities accomodate 120 students. Need-based and merit-based scholarships are available.

Community Environment: Atlanta, host of the 1996 Summer Olympic Games, offers students the best of the Sun Belt: long, bright, crisp fall and spring seasons with short and mild winters in the largest cosmopolitan center in the Southeast. With one of the fastest-growing economies in the nation, Atlanta today is a city bursting with newness and enormous energy while still retaining its traditions and flavor. Home to Art Papers, the city has a flourishing "grass roots" art scene-an optimal environment for the emerging artist or designer. Atlanta has scores of galleries and alternative spaces that exhibit a broad variety of artwork; a ballet and an opera; numerous movie houses showing new releases and foreign and classic films; a growing number of theater companies, large and small; many opportunities for rock, jazz, and avant-garde music; and outdoor performances and art festivals. In addition, Atlanta has a myriad of natural areas and parks, restaurants of every description, and three professional sports teams. The Atlanta College of Art is located in midtown, the cultural heart of the city, a neighborhood where skyscrapers soar above tree-lined streets filled with restored older residences, some dating from the Victorian era. The Arts Center station of MARTA, Atlanta's clean and efficient rapid transit system, is located just across the street from the College residence hall and offers easy access to many points of interest.

ATLANTA METROPOLITAN COLLEGE   *(F-4)*
1630 Stewart Avenue, S.W.
Atlanta, Georgia 30310
Tel: (404) 756-4001; Admissions: (404) 756-4000; Fax: (404) 756-5686

Description: Formerly called Atlanta Junior College, this unit of the University System of Georgia was opened in 1974. The school provides liberal arts courses for transfer to senior institutions, general education courses and career programs designed to prepare persons for gainful employment. Cooperation with the Atlanta Area Technical School provides vocational and technical education. The college grants the Associate degree. The college operates on the quarter system and summer sessions are offered. Enrollment is 1,882 full-time students. A faculty of 60 full-time and 14 part-time gives a faculty-student ratio of 1-25.

Entrance Requirements: High school graduation or GED equivalant; completion of 4 units of English, 3 mathematics, 3 science, 3 social science, 2 foreign language; SAT required with minimum scores of 350 Verbal and 350 Math, ACT minimum scores of 16 verbal and 11 math. Students with lower scores, or who do not meet other criteria, are eligible under the Development Studies Program. Early decision and advanced placement plans available; Sep. 8 application deadline; $10 application fee.

Costs Per Year: $1,197 tuition state resident; nonresident $3,237; $40 student fees.

Collegiate Environment: The College offers a variety of services to students designed to enhance classroom learning. These are offered through the Learning Resources Center, the Business Laboratory, the Computer Science Laboratory, the Science Learning Center, and the Writing Center. The library includes 40,000 titles and 320 subscriptions. There is an Upward Bound Program for high school students with potential for college success and a Special Services Program for students facing academic hardship. Financial aid is available. 80% of the students receive some form of assistance.

Community Environment: The College, though within view of the city, is situated on a 83-acre wooded tract with several lakes on which there are proposed plans for future development. It is located next to Atlanta Area Technical College, and is convenient to major bus lines and Hartsfield International Airport, and is adjacent to Interstate 75-85 South.

AUGUSTA COLLEGE   *(F-11)*
2500 Walton Way
Augusta, Georgia 30910
Tel: (706) 737-1401; (800) 341-4373; Admissions: (706) 737-1632;
Fax: (706) 667-4355

Description: Founded in 1925, the college is a four-year, state-supported, arts and sciences college and is part of the University System of Georgia. It is accredited by the Southern Association of Colleges and Schools and is authorized to grant degrees of Bachelor of Science, Bachelor of Arts, Bachelor of Business Administration, Masters degree in Business, Education and Psychology, and Associate degrees. The school operates on the quarter system and offers two summer sessions. Army ROTC is available. Enrollment includes 2,994 full-time and 1,814 part-time undergraduates and 865 graduate students. A faculty of 187 gives an undergraduate faculty-student ratio of 1-25.

Entrance Requirements: Accredited high school graduation with completion of 16 units including 4 English, 2 foreign language, 2 mathematics, 3 science, and 3 social science; SAT or ACT required; early admission, early decision, rolling admission, delayed admission, midyear admission and advanced placement plans available; $10 application fee.

Costs Per Year: $1,542 matriculation fee; $4,224 nonresidents.

Collegiate Environment: The campus, the former plantation of an eighteenth-century Southern leader, is comprised of 30 buildings located on 72 acres surrounded by one of Augusta's finest residential areas. It is on a hill overlooking the business section of the city and the base panorama of the Savannah River Valley. In addition to the main campus, the college maintains its own 18-hole golf course that comprises over 200 acres. The library contains 465,000 volumes, 1,192 periodicals, 1,200,000 microforms and 6,558 audiovisual materials. 82% of applicants are accepted. Scholarships are available and 77% of students receive some form of financial aid.

Community Environment: Augusta, located on the Savannah River in east central Georgia, is a river port and industrial center, and is the third leading producer of clay products in the southeast. All forms of transportation are available. Recreational facilities include lakes for fishing, boating and hunting, golf courses, horseback riding, and polo. The famous Augusta National Golf Club course, home of the Masters Golf Tournament, is located here. Some of the points of interest are the Mackay Trading Post, Meadow Garden, Fort Augusta, Confederate Monument, New Savannah Bluff Lock and Dam System, churches of historic interest, and two large enclosed shopping malls.

BERRY COLLEGE   *(C-2)*
Mount Berry, Georgia 30149
Tel: (404) 232-5374

Description: The private, four-year college is accredited by the Southern Association of Colleges and Schools and operates on the quarter system, with one summer session. The forerunner of Berry College was founded by Miss Martha Berry in 1902. The corporate name of the college is Berry College, Inc. The enrollment included 1,805 men and women. A faculty of 87 gives a faculty-student ratio of 1-16. The college grants the Baccalaureate, Masters and Specialist in Education degrees.

Entrance Requirements: High school graduation with a B average and rank in upper half of graduating class; completion of 16 units including 4 English, 2 mathematics, total of 4 in science, foreign language and social studies; high school equivalent diploma accepted; SAT or ACT required; freshman applicants for whom the high school grade-point average and test scores indicate a high probability of earning at least a "C" average are admitted; non-high school graduates considered; application fee $20; early admission, early decision, rolling admission, delayed admission and advanced placement plans available.

Costs Per Year: $6,990 tuition, $3,360 room and board.

Collegiate Environment: The campus has 100 buildings on 28,000 acres. The Georgian and Gothic campus structures are nestled among forest, fields, lakes and streams, creating an atmosphere of natural charm and quiet which contributes to the educational and spiritual growth of students and faculty. Dormitory capacity is 508 men and 683 women. The library contains 123,904 volumes, 1,100 periodicals, 268,573 microforms and numerous audiovisual materials. Of 866 scholarships offered, 336 are available to freshmen; 56% of the applicants are accepted.

Community Environment: Located on Highway 27 between Chattanooga and Atlanta, Mount Berry is in the mountains of North Georgia in Floyd County, adjoining Rome. Recreation, cultural facilities and transportation are found in Rome.

BEULAH HEIGHTS BIBLE COLLEGE   *(E-4)*
892-906 Berne Street, S.E.,
P.O. Box 18145
Atlanta, Georgia 30316
Tel: (404) 627-2681; Fax: (404) 627-0702

Description: The private Bible College is controlled by the International Pentecostal Church of Christ and operates on the semester system with an 8-week summer session. The college is accredited by the Transnational Association of Christian Colleges and Schools. The college award the Associate and Baccalaureate degree. Enrollment is 125 full-time and 170 part-time students. A faculty of 4 full-time and 30 part-time gives a faculty-student ratio of 1-20.

Entrance Requirements: High school graduation with completion of 16 units; equivalency diploma accepted; evidence of high moral Christian character required; early admission, early decision, delayed admission, advanced placement and rolling admission plans available; $15 application fee; application deadline for fall term is August 25th.

Costs Per Year: $2,560 tuition; $1,300 room and board; $70 fees.

Collegiate Environment: The campus has 13 buildings on four acres. The library contains 20,000 volumes, 1,000 pamphlets, and 25 sound recordings. Dormitory space is available for 30 men and 20 women. All applicants are accepted. 45% of students receive financial aid.

Community Environment: See Clark Atlanta University.

BRENAU WOMEN'S COLLEGE   *(D-5)*
One Centennial Circle
Gainesville, Georgia 30501
Tel: (404) 534-6100; (800) 252-5119; Fax: (404) 534-6114

Description: This private, liberal arts college for women is accredited by the Southern Association of Colleges and Schools. It is a women's college with coed divisions. It operates on the semester system and offers two summer sessions. The university was founded in 1878 and offers programs in liberal arts, business, fine arts, public administration, nursing, and teacher education. Baccalaureate and Masters degrees are granted. Enrollment includes 1,048 full-time and 404 part-time undergraduates and 789 graduate students. A faculty of 95 full-time and 81 part-time gives a faculty-student ratio of 1-13.

Entrance Requirements: High school graduation with a C average and rank in upper 40% of the graduating class; completion of 20 units including 4 English, 2 mathematics, 2 foreign languages, 1 science, and 2 social science; 800 or over on SAT; application fee $30; early admission, early decision, rolling admission, delayed admission and advanced placement plans available.

Costs Per Year: $9,588 tuition; $5,883 room and board.

Collegiate Environment: Students may reside in sorority houses beginning their sophomore year. Residence halls and sorority houses each accommodate 30-80 women. Facilities are available for 440 women. The library contains 86,217 bound volumes, 486 periodical subscriptions, 131,622 titles on microfilm, 9,102 records and tapes, and 16 CD-ROM collections. 75% of the applicants are accepted. 75% of the current freshmen graduated in the upper half of their high school class; 10% ranked in the top quarter and 58% ranked in the top 40%. About 60% of the freshmen returned for the second year. 48% of the students receive financial aid.

Community Environment: Gainesville is the "Queen City of the Mountains" at the foot of the Blue Ridge Mountains, 52 miles northeast of Atlanta. The climate is generally mild and moderate. Amtrack and Trailways Bus are available. Headquarters for the Chattahoochee and Oconee National Forests. One of the world's largest producing and processing centers. Gainesville has among its industrial products, textiles, hosiery, furniture, etc. Agricultural products of the area include peaches, apples, grapes and field crops. Quinlan Art Center has exhibits featuring state and area artists. Recreational facilities are the golf course, city parks, swimming pools, tennis courts, and the 600-mile shoreline of Lake Lanier, the largest lake in Georgia. Part of Lake Lanier is within the city limits of Gainesville. All water sports may be enjoyed here. Annual horse shows are some of the special events.

BREWTON-PARKER COLLEGE   *(J-9)*
Highway 280
Mount Vernon, Georgia 30445-0197
Tel: (912) 583-2241; (800) 342-1087; Fax: (912) 583-4498

Description: This private four-year college was founded in 1904 and is accredited by the Southern Association of Colleges and Schools. The school operates on the quarter system and offers one summer session. It is controlled by the Georgia Baptist Convention. Recent enrollment inlcuded 624 men, 688 women full-time, 485 men, and 374 women part-time. A faculty of 72 full-time and 145 part-time gives a faculty-student ratio of 1-15. The college offers the Associate and Bachelor degrees.

Entrance Requirements: Accredited high school graduates, non-high school graduates over 18 years with GED equivalency; application fee $15; early admission, midyear admission, early decision and delayed admission plans available.

Costs Per Year: $4,500 tuition; $2,580 board and room; $150 student fees.

Collegiate Environment: The college is located on a spacious 280 acre campus. College buildings include residence halls for 280 men and 300 women; a student center cafeteria; and air-conditioned classrooms; a spacious library containing 60,000 volumes, 2,100 periodicals, 800 microforms and 1469 sound recordings. Recreational facilities include a beautiful five-acre lake, a fully equipped gym, and lighted tennis courts. 78% of applicants are accepted. The college offers 450 scholarships, including 50 athletic. 95% of students receive some form of financial aid.

Community Environment: The campus is located partly in Ailey and partly in Mt. Vernon, the county seat of Montgomery County. The two towns have a combined population of 2,500. The area has mild winters with adequate rainfall to support a variety of agricultural and forest products. Movies, skating, bowling, shopping and numerous other activities are available in nearby communities such as Vidalia.

BRUNSWICK COLLEGE   *(M-12)*
Altama at Fourth Street
Brunswick, Georgia 31523
Tel: (912) 264-7235; Fax: (912) 262-3072

Description: Founded in 1961, this publicly controlled two-year, community college is a member of the University System of Georgia and is accredited by the Southern Association of Colleges and Schools. It offers students university transfer programs, selected career programs, developmental and continuing education programs. The college grants a certificate and an Associate degree. It provides access to baccalaureate and master's degree programs in cooperation with other members of the University System. The college operates on the quarter system and offers three summer sessions. Enrollment includes 278 men and 583 women full-time, and 318 men and 656 women part-time. A faculty of 65 gives a faculty-student ratio of 1-27.

Entrance Requirements: High school graduation or equivalent; completion of 18 high school units; SAT score of 350V, 350M, or better; basic skills examination required if scores are below this; early admission, midyear admission rolling admission and advanced placement plans available. $5 application fee.

Costs Per Year: $1,209 ($403/quarter) state resident tuition; $3,252 ($1,084/quarter) nonresident; $20 student fee; $25 athletic fee.

Collegiate Environment: Brunswick College is located in the coastal city of Brunswick in Glynn County. The 193-acre campus has been carefully planted with trees and shrubs indigenous to the area. Paved parking lots accommodating over nine hundred automobiles are provided for student use. The 11 campus buildings include the Academic Building, the Hargett Administration Building, the Howard E. Coffin Health and Physical Education Center with heated swimming pool, the Clara Wood Gould Memorial Library, the Student Center, the Mechanical Building, Warehouse and Shop, the Science Building, Vocational-Technical Building, Allied Health Building, and the Southeast George Conference Center with a 350 seat auditorium. Its holdings include 60,000 printed volumes, 330 periodical subscriptions, and more than 94,000 unites of microfilm and microfiche. There are no dormitories on campus. Approximately 99% of the applicants are accepted. 172 scholarships are available, including 74 for

freshmen, and 45% of the current student body receives some form of assistance.

Community Environment: Brunswick is the county seat of Glynn County, which includes the historic resort islands of St. Simons, Sea Island and Jekyll Island. The climate is mild with a mean temperature of 68 degrees. Buses and railroads serve Brunswick. Besides being a tourist center, Brunswick is an industrial city. Recreational activities are unlimited; they include golfing, bowling, fresh and salt water fishing, deep sea fishing, tennis, picnicking, surfing and water skiing at excellent beaches. Numerous points of historical interest are in or near Brunswick. Kings Bay Naval Submarine Base and the Federal Law Enforcement Training Center are nearby.

CARVER BIBLE INSTITUTE AND COLLEGE   *(E-4)*
P.O. Box 4335
Atlanta, Georgia 30302
Tel: (404) 527-4520; (800) 262-4253; Admissions: (404) 527-4523; Fax: (404) 527-4526

Description: This private Bible institute was founded in 1943 as an evening school for the training of black Christians in the South. The school added a Bible college curriculum leading to the Baccalaureate degree in Bible in 1964. The college is accredited by the the Southern Accrediting Association of Bible Institutes and Bible Colleges. It grants certificates and the Bachelor degree. The college operates on the semester system and offers one summer session. Recent enrollment included 88 men and 12 women. A faculty of 7 full-time and 18 part-time gives a faculty-student ratio of 1-8. Certificate and Bachelor's degrees are awarded.

Entrance Requirements: High school graduation or equivalent; evidence of Christian living; rolling admission plan available; $10 application fee.

Costs Per Year: $1,920 ($60/cr) tuition; $952 room fees per year; $50 fees.

Collegiate Environment: The library contains 14,000 volumes, 25 periodicals, 257 recordings and tapes. There are dormitories for 38 men and 18 women, plus five apartments for married couples.

Community Environment: See Clark Atlanta University.

CLARK ATLANTA UNIVERSITY   *(E-4)*
James P. Brawley Drive at Fair Street, S
Atlanta, Georgia 30314
Tel: (404) 880-8000; (800) 688-3228; Fax: (404) 880-8222

Description: The private, liberal arts university is affiliated with the United Methodist Church. The college was founded in 1869 by the Freedmen's Aid Society of the Methodist Church and is a member of the Atlanta University Center. In 1989, Clark College merged with Atlanta University to form what is now Clark Atlanta University. It is accredited by the Southern Association of Colleges and Schools and the semester system is employed with one summer session. Recent enrollment included 1,221 men, 2,645 women full-time, 211 men and 403 women part-time. The faculty consists of 251 full-time members and 70 part-time members which provides a faculty-student ratio of 1:16. ROTC Army, Air Force, and Navy programs are available.

Entrance Requirements: High school graduation with a C average and 16 units including 4 English, 2 mathematics, 1 foreign language, 2 science, and 2 social science; combined score of 850 or more on SAT, or 13 on ACT required; character recommendations required. For graduate programs: graduation from colleges of approved standing with a record that shows promise of ability to do graduate work. Early decision, rolling admission and advanced placement plans available; $20 application fee.

Costs Per Year: $6,300 tuition; $3,752 room and board; $800 student fees.

Collegiate Environment: The campus has 11 buildings on 24 acres. The library contains 751,674 volumes (consortium library). Dormitory capacity is for 1,500 students. The college is in the process of expanding existing facilities. Approximately 27% of the student body graduated in top quarter of high school class. 69% of the applicants is accepted. Various forms of financial assistance are available, and 86% of the students receive some form of aid.

Community Environment: Atlanta, capital of Georgia, is the commercial, industrial and financial giant of the southeast. It is located in the foothills of the Blue Ridge Mountains. Atlanta's moderate climate permits year-round golf, fishing and outdoor living. All major forms of public transportation are available. Peachtree Street is experiencing one of the biggest building booms in the country. Peachtree Center includes the Atlanta Merchandise Mart, and the 22-story Regency Hyatt Hotel. Bridges 22 stories above the street connect buildings on the Peachtree Center. The city is the cultural center of the south with her symphony, art center and theaters. Atlanta is a major manufacturing and business center manufacturing over 3,500 different commodities. Excellent part-time employment opportunities are available. Recreational activities include all major sports, swimming, golfing, boating, horseback riding, tennis, and fishing. Many spectator sports events take place here in the Atlanta Stadium. Some of the many points of interest are the Georgia State Capitol, Atlanta Memorial Arts Center, Fernbank Science Center Planetarium, and the Stone Mountain Park.

CLAYTON STATE COLLEGE   (E-4)
P.O. Box 285
Morrow, Georgia 30260
Tel: (404) 961-3500; Fax: (404) 961-3700

Description: This state-supported, four-year liberal arts college is accredited by the Southern Association of Colleges and Schools. It operates on the quarter system and offers 2 summer sessions. It was opened in 1969 as the tenth junior college in the University System of Georgia, and officially became a senior college on July 1, 1986. Enrollment includes 1,778 full-time and 3,083 part-time students. A faculty of 108 full-time and 85 part-time provides a faculty-student ratio of 1-25.

Entrance Requirements: High school graduation or equivalent; SAT or ACT required; early admission, rolling admission, delayed admission and advanced placement plans available.

Costs Per Year: $1,548 resident tuition; $4,392 nonresident.

Collegiate Environment: Located on a 163-acre campus just 12 miles south of the heart of Atlanta, there are presently 10 buildings completed and a Learning Resources Center. The library contains 61,474 volumes, 484 periodicals, and 25,053 audiovisual materials. Almost all of the applicants are accepted, including students at mid-year.

Community Environment: The campus is located in suburban metropolitan Atlanta.

COLUMBIA THEOLOGICAL SEMINARY   (E-4)
701 Columbia Drive
Decatur, Georgia 30030
Tel: (404) 378-8821; Fax: (404) 377-9696

Description: This graduate seminary of the Presbyterian Church (U.S.A.) is accredited by the Association of Theological Schools and the Southern Association of Schools and Colleges. The seminary operates on the semester system with one summer session and grants 3 different Master's and 2 Doctorate degrees. Through the Atlanta Theological Association, Columbia Seminary is affiliated with the Candler School of Theology, Erskine Theological Seminary, Interdenominational Theological Center, Lutheran Theological Southern Seminary, the Georgia Association for Pastoral Care, the Atlantic Psychiatric Center and the Pastoral service of Georgia Baptist Hospital. It is also a member of the University Center in Georgia, which allows students access to the combined facilities of many of Georgia's academic institutions. Enrollment is 640 students with a faculty of 33 members.

Entrance Requirements: Four-year degree from an accredited university or its equivalent; rolling admission plan available; $30 application fee.

Costs Per Year: $5,760 tuition; $3,920 room and board.

Collegiate Environment: The campus includes 10 buildings on 60 acres. The library contains 102,766 volumes, 600 current periodical titles, 850 microforms and 2,531 audiovisual materials. Dormitory capacity is 40 single men and women, and additional housing is available for 95 couples. Approximately 70% of those who apply for admission are accepted. Financial aid is available, and about 78% of the students currently enrolled receive some form of assistance.

Community Environment: See Agnes Scott College.

COLUMBUS COLLEGE   (I-2)
Algonquin Drive
Columbus, Georgia 31993
Tel: (706) 568-2001; Admissions: (706) 568-2035; Fax: (706) 568-2462

Description: The public-controlled liberal arts college is accredited by the Southern Association of Colleges and Schools. Columbus College is the result of a community endeavor and was established in 1958 as a junior college. Construction of a permanent facility was begun in 1961 and the college was approved as a senior college in 1965. It operates on the quarter sstem and offers two summer sessions. Enrollment includes 2,979 full-time and 1,853 part-time undergraduate students and 702 graduates. A faculty of 173 full-time and 114 part-time gives an undergraduate faculty-student ratio of 1-23.

Entrance Requirements: High school graduation or satisfactory scores on the GED; total score of 350 verbal and 350 math SAT; application fee $20; mid-year students accepted. Rolling admission plan available.

Costs Per Year: $1,422 in-state tuition; $4,266 for nonresident tuition; $231 student fees.

Collegiate Environment: The campus has 18 buildings on 132 acres. The library contains 244,963 volumes, 1,397 periodicals, 504,996 microforms and 15,191 nonprint units. Dormitories house 250 students on campus. 90% of the applicants are accepted. 55% of first-time freshmen returned for second year. 67% of students receive some form of financial aid. The average SAT scores of the current freshman were 420 verbal and 440 math.

Community Environment: Columbus, Georgia's second largest city, is located in the Chattahoochee Valley, 100 miles south of Atlanta on the Georgia-Alabama border, having an annual mean temperature of 65 degrees and annual rainfall of 37 inches. All forms of transportation serve the area. Columbus is one of the South's largest textile centers, a regional retail center, and manufacturers high-tech industrial products, iron and metal goods, hosiery, processed foods, soft drinks, candy and peanut products. Cultural facilities are the churches, libraries, symphony orchestra, Museum of Arts and Sciences, Fort Benning Little Theatre, and Springer Opera House which is the State Theatre. With the completion of the dam projects on the Chattahoochee River and the Apalachicola River in Florida, Columbus became a port city. A navigable waterway extends to the Gulf of Mexico and the Intracoastal Canal. Oliver Dam provides facilities for all water sports. There are recreational facilities at community centers, golf courses, bowling alleys, and swimming pools.

COVENANT COLLEGE   (A-1)
Lookout Mountain, Georgia 30750
Tel: (706) 820-1560; (800) 637-2687; Fax: (706) 820-2165

Description: It is the desire of the college to offer its Christian educational opportunities to all who qualify for admission, regardless of individual economic circumstances, within the limits of its available funds. The college, affiliated with the Presbyterian Church in America, was founded in 1955 and is accredited by the Southern Association of Colleges and Schools. It operates on the early semester calendar system and offers a May term and one summer session. Enrollment includes 617 full-time and 47 part-time traditional undergraduates and 40 graduate students. There are 147 adults in continuing education courses. A teaching faculty of 43 full-time and 12 part-time gives a faculty-student ratio of 1-15. The college grants the Associate, Bachelor and Master in education degrees. Army ROTC is available in conjunction with the University of Tennessee in Chattanooga. Study abroad is available in France, Germany, Spain, Russia and Israel. The college offers its own semester abroad program in the Czech Republic. Covenant's QUEST program is offered for adults with a minimum of five years of work experience who have also completed a minimum of two years of college. The program includes coursework, production of a portfolio, and an applied research project. A Bachelor of Science or Arts degree is granted in Organizational Management.

Entrance Requirements: High school graduation or GED with rank in upper 50% of the graduating class; completion of 16 units including 3-4 English, 2 mathematics, 2 foreign language, 2 history or social science, 2 natural science, and 3-4 electives; 2.5 minimum GPA; minimum SAT 900 combined or ACT 21 required; TOEFL 500; midyear admission, rolling admission, delayed admission, and advanced placement plans available; $20 application fee.

Costs Per Year: $9,700 tuition; $3,800 room and board; $260 student fees; $400 average additional expenses.

Collegiate Environment: The college campus is located at the top of Lookout Mountain. The library contains 72,575 volumes, 450 periodical subscriptions, 27,000 titles on microfilm, 8,737 audiovisual materials. Dormitory facilities provide living accommodations for 540 students. 81% of the students live on campus. Approximately 80% of the students applying for admission are accepted, including midyear students. Financial aid is available for economically disadvantaged students, and 86% of the current students receive financial assistance.

Community Environment: Lookout Mountain is a suburban community that enjoys the cultural, recreational and social facilities of Chattanooga. The community has churches of all denominations, a library, various cultural opportunities, an aquarium, several hospitals, and health center at nearby Chattanooga. Part-time jobs are available.

DALTON COLLEGE *(B-2)*
213 N. College Drive
Dalton, Georgia 30720
Tel: (706) 272-4436; (800) 829-4436; Fax: (706) 272-4588

Description: This public college is accredited by the Southern Association of Colleges and Schools. The college was chartered in 1963, construction began on the first five buildings in 1966, and in September 1967, the college opened with four buildings completed. The college is the twenty-fourth unit of the University System of Georgia. It grants the Associate degree, offering primarily career oriented programs of study. The college operates on the quarter system and offers one summer session. Enrollment includes 1,371 full-time and 1,634 part-time students. A faculty of 84 full-time and 26 part-time gives a faculty-student ratio of 1-27.

Entrance Requirements: High school graduation or equivalent; completion of 16 units including 4 English, 3 mathematics, 3 science, 2 foreign language, and 3 social science; SAT minimum 350V, 350M required; early admission, rolling admission, early decision, advanced placement and midyear admission plans available.

Costs Per Year: $1,074 state residents; $2,973 out-of-state; $30 student fees.

Collegiate Environment: The campus consists of approximately 130 acres and the library contains 124,551 volumes, 851 periodicals, 87,989 microforms (including microfiche) and 3,919 cassettes. 70% of applicants are accepted. 58 scholarships are offered including 43 for freshmen. 33% of the current student body receives some form of aid.

Community Environment: Dalton is an urban area 20 miles south of the Tennessee line. The climate is mild year-round. This is known as the "Carpet Capital of the World." Railroads and buses serve the area. Commercial air transportation is available at Chattanooga, 31 miles distant. Fishing is excellent in the many surrounding lakes. Nearby mountains offer opportunities for hunting, fishing, hiking, and other sports. Recreation within the city includes a supervised recreation program at the center with swimming, football, baseball, softball, tennis, and an indoor picnic area.

DEVRY INSTITUTE OF TECHNOLOGY *(F-4)*
250 N. Arcadia Avenue
Decatur, Georgia 30030
Tel: (404) 292-7900; (800) 221-4771; Admissions: (404) 292-2645; Fax: (404) 292-2321

Description: The Atlanta campus of this proprietary, coeducational school was established in 1969 and and is accredited by the North Central Association of Colleges and Schools. Programs are developed and updated regularly with direct input from business and industry leaders. It operates on the semester system, has 1 summer session, and grants associate and bachelor degrees. Enrollment includes 1,515 men, 591 women full-time, 399 men, 205 women part-time, with a faculty of 70 full-time, 31 part-time providing a faculty-student ratio of 1-32.

Entrance Requirements: High school diploma or GED certification; minimum of 17 years of age; must pass DeVry Entrance Examination or submit acceptable ACT/SAT/WPCT scores; accepts foreign students if requirements are met as outlined in catalog; rolling admission and advanced placement available: $25 application fee.

Costs Per Year: Tuition $6,335.

Collegiate Environment: The school is currently located in a 21-acre wooded site in Decatur. The modern, 2-story building has 103,000 square feet of space. The institute is convenient for commuting. Most activities are planned by the DeVry Student Activities Organization, a group of elected representatives that sponsors dances, parties, intramural sports tournaments, outings in Atlanta, and ski and raft trips. The library has over 14,102 bound volumes, 150 periodicals, and 186 microforms. 88% of applicants are accepted. Scholarships are available and 73% of the students receive some form of financial assistance.

Community Environment: Decatur, named for U.S. naval hero Stephen Decatur, was founded in 1823, which predates the city of Atlanta. Decatur serves as the professional, governmental, and financial center of DeKalb County. The shopping district around the courthouse square offers a variety of specialty shops. In Adair Park, the Swarton House and the Mary Gay House, home of Civil War heroine Mary Gay, have been converted into museums.

EAST GEORGIA COLLEGE *(I-10)*
131 College Circle
Swainsboro, Georgia 30401
Tel: (912) 237-7831; Fax: (912) 237-5161

Description: This public junior college is accredited by the Southern Association of Colleges and Schools. Enrollment is 893 full-time and part-time students. A faculty of 24 gives a faculty-student ratio of 1-37. The college operates on the quarter system and offers one summer session. It was established in 1973 to serve Emanuel County and commuting area residents, and offers liberal arts, teacher education, and preprofessional curricula.

Entrance Requirements: High school graduation or GED equivalent; SAT required; early admission and rolling admission plans available.

Costs Per Year: $1,017 state-resident matriculation fee; $2,943 nonresident tuition for 3 quarters; $15 student fees per quarter.

Collegiate Environment: The campus of East Georgia College consists of 6 buildings and covers 207 acres. The library contains 41,300 volumes, 200 periodicals, 1,000 audiovisual materials, and 2,700 microforms. There are no dormitory facilities. Financial aid is available.

Community Environment: Swainsboro, the county seat of Emanuel County, is located in the southeast section of Georgia near the Center of the vast southern pine forest. The climate is mild with an annual mean temperature of 66 degrees; the average rainfall is 42 inches. Transportation is provided by the Georgia and Florida Raidroad and Greyhound. Community facilities include one hospital, 24 churches, restaurants, hotels, motels, and shopping areas. Industry, agriculture, and forestry are important to the economy of the area. Agricultural products include cotton, tobacco, peanuts, soybeans, corn, and potatoes. Some of the industries manufacture sprinkler system valves, furniture, dressed lumber, seed processing, playground equipment, knitwear, molded plastics, screws, rivets, and component parts. A well-staffed and budgeted recreation department offers many recreational opportunities to youth. Fish ponds are in abundance in Emanuel County. Many fresh water streams are filled with trout and bream. Quail and wild turkeys abound and there are excellent reserves for hunting. The first week in May is set aside for the annual Emanuel County Pine Tree Festival.

Branch Campuses: Dublin Residence Center, Dublin, GA.

EMMANUEL COLLEGE *(D-7)*
P.O. Box 129
Franklin Springs, Georgia 30639
Tel: (706) 245-7226; (800) 860-8800; Fax: (706) 245-4424

Description: This private college was founded in 1919 and is controlled by the Pentacostal Holiness Church. It is accredited by the Association of Southern Colleges and Schools. Programs of study lead to the Associate and Baccalaureate degrees. The college operates on the semester system and offers one summer session. Enrollment includes 489 full-time and 60 part-time students. A faculty of 33 gives a faculty-student ratio of 1-15.

165

Entrance Requirements: Accredited high school graduation or GED equivalent; SAT or ACT required; open enrollment policy; early admission, early decision, midyear admission, rolling admission and advanced placement plans available; $25 application fee.

Costs Per Year: $4,300 tuition; $3,100 room and board; $260 student fees.

Collegiate Environment: Ten buildings on 90 acres comprise the campus. The library contains 39,000 volumes and 220 periodicals. Dormitory facilities can accommodate 280 students. All students are required to attend chapel. 90% of applicants are accepted. Special financial aid is available for economically disadvantaged students, and 92% of the current student body receives some form of assistance.

Community Environment: Franklin Springs, located in northeast Georgia near the Blue Ridge Mountains, was formerly a health resort and boasts of a mild, healthful and invigorating climate. It is also the home to The Advocate Press.

EMORY UNIVERSITY   *(E-4)*
Boisfeuillet Jones Center
Atlanta, Georgia 30322
Tel: (404) 727-6036; (800) 727-6036

Description: This private university is accredited by the Southern Association of Colleges and Schools and is affiliated with the United Methodist Church. The semester system is employed with 2 summer sessions. The university includes the following schools: Emory College, Emory Business School, School of Public Health, Graduate School, School of Law, School of Medicine, School of Nursing, Candler School of Theology, and Oxford College, a 2-year Arts and Science division in Oxford, Georgia. Recent Emory College undergraduate enrollment included 2,077 men and 2,449 women, including 560 men and women on the Oxford Campus. There are 4,952 graduate students. Faculty includes 1,700 full-time and part-time instructors. The university grants undergraduate and graduate level degrees.

Entrance Requirements: High school graduation with a B average and 16 units including 4 English, 3 science, 3 mathematics, 2 social studies and 2 foreign language; high SAT or ACT score; GRE required for graduate programs; additional requirements for the various divisions and schools must be met; early admission, early decision, delayed admission and advanced placement plans available; $40 application fee.

Costs Per Year: $17,600 tuition; $6,000 room and board; $230 fees; $600 books; $925 miscellaneous expenses.

Collegiate Environment: The university has 112 buildings on 631 acres. The library contains 2,200,000 volumes, 17,000 journals, 5,600 linear feet of manuscripts and 1,800,000 microforms. Dormitory space is available for 3,470 men and women and 120 families. Scholarships are available and 57% of students receive some form of financial aid. About 49% of the applicants are accepted, and 28% of admittants matriculated during a recent year. The average scores of the entering freshman class were 585 verbal, 660 math, and ACT 29 composite.

Community Environment: Emory is located in a residential area of Atlanta, 6 miles from downtown. Atlanta, capital of Georgia, is the commercial, industrial and financial giant of the southeast. It is located in the foothills of the Blue Ridge Mountains. Atlanta is host to the 1996 Olympic Games. Atlanta's moderate climate permits year-round golf, fishing and outdoor living. All major forms of public transportation are available. Peachtree Street is experiencing one of the biggest building booms in the country. Peachtree Center includes the Atlanta Merchandise Mart, and the 22-story regency Hyatt Hotel. Bridges 22 stories above the street connect buildings on the Peachtree Center. The city is the cultural center of the South with a symphony, art center, and theaters. Atlanta is a major business and manufacturing center that produces more that 3,500 different commodities. Excellent part-time employment opportunities are available. Recreational activities include all major sports, swimming, golfing, boating, horseback riding, tennis, and fishing. Many spectator sports events take place in the Atlanta Stadium.

FLOYD COLLEGE   *(D-2)*
P.O. Box 1864
Rome, Georgia 30163
Tel: (404) 295-6339; (800) 332-2406; Fax: (706) 295-6610

Description: The state-supported, liberal arts, junior college is accredited by the Southern Association of Colleges and Schools. It operates on the quarter system and offers two summer sessions. The college was established in 1968 as a part of the University System of Georgia. Enrollment is 2,868 students. A faculty of 70 full-time and 20 part-time gives a faculty-student ratio of 1-31.

Entrance Requirements: High school graduation or equivalent; non-high school graduates may be considered; SAT required; early decision, rolling admission, delayed admission and advanced placement plans available.

Costs Per Year: $978 tuition; $2,829 nonresident tuition.

Collegiate Environment: The campus covers 226 acres, which includes a 70-acre scenic lake and four modern buildings. No dormitories are provided on campus. The library contains 44,000 volumes, 773 pamphlets, 470 periodicals, 9,145 microforms and 564 sound recordings. 99% of the applicants are accepted. 374 scholarships are available, 45 of which are for freshmen. 46% of the students receive some form of financial aid.

Community Environment: See Shorter College.

Branch Campuses: Cartersville and Acworth, GA.

FORT VALLEY STATE COLLEGE   *(I-5)*
Fort Valley, Georgia 31030
Tel: (912) 825-6211

Description: The public-controlled college, a unit of the University System of Georgia, is accredited by the Southern Association of Colleges and Schools. The college was established in 1895 and the first four-year college class graduated in 1941. Programs of study lead to the Associate, Bachelor and Master degrees. It operates on the quarter system and offers two summer sessions. Enrollment includes 2,815 students. A faculty of 155 gives a faculty-student ratio of 1-19.

Entrance Requirements: High school graduation with a C average and 15 units including 4 English, 3 mathematics, 3 science, 3 social science, and 2 foreign language; non-high school graduates considered; minimum SAT verbal 350, math 350.

Costs Per Year: $1,838 resident tuition; $4,404 nonresident tuition; $1,264 resident boarding; $2,458 nonresident boarding

Collegiate Environment: The campus has 57 buildings on 645 acres (a farm includes 300 acres). The library contains 178,927 volumes and dormitory accommodations for 300 men and 750 women are available.

Community Environment: Fort Valley is a rural area having a temperate climate. This is the main peach-growing section of the state. Miles of blooming peach orchards are a beautiful sight in the spring. Buses serve the area. Community facilities include churches of major denominations, a library, and hospital. The Blue Bird Body Company, manufacturers of school bus bodies, is located here. Part-time employment opportunities are limited. The Massee Lane Farms located five miles southwest has one of the finest collections of camellias in the country.

GAINESVILLE COLLEGE   *(D-5)*
Mundy Mill Road
P.O. Box 1358
Gainesville, Georgia 30503
Tel: (404) 535-6239; (800) 745-5922; Admissions: (404) 535-6241

Description: The public-controlled two-year college is accredited by the Southern Association of Colleges and Schools. The college was founded in 1964. It operates on the quarter system and offers two summer sessions. Enrollment includes 1,094 men and 1,548 women. A faculty of 99 gives a faculty-student ratio of 1-27. The college grants an Associate degree.

Entrance Requirements: High school graduation or equivalent; completion of 16 units including 4 English, 3 mathematics, 3 science, and 3 social science; non-high school graduates considered; SAT or ACT, Entrance Exams required; Early admission, rolling admission, midyear admission and advanced placement plans available.

Costs Per Year: $1,137; $3,180 nonresident; $63 student fees.

Collegiate Environment: The campus has 10 buildings on 229 acres. The library contains 63,848 volumes, 7,604 pamphlets, 4,790 periodicals, 38,800 microforms and 1,749 recordings. There are no dormitories provided on campus. Financial aid is available. 90% of the applicants are accepted. The average SAT scores of the freshman were 400 verbal and 420 math. 60% of the freshman returned for the second year.

Community Environment: See Brenau Women's College.

GEORGIA COLLEGE   *(G-7)*
Campus Box 023
Milledgeville, Georgia 31061
Tel: (912) 453-5004; (800) 342-0471; Fax: (912) 453-1914

Description: The public-controlled senior comprehensive college is accredited by the Southern Association of Colleges and Schools. It operates on the quarter system and offers 2 summer sessions. The college granted its first degree in 1921; the graduate program was initiated in 1958. Enrollment included 1,466 men and 2,375 women full-time, and 634 men and 1,180 women part-time. A faculty of 201 gives a faculty-student ratio of 1-23.

Entrance Requirements: High school graduation with 1.8 average GPA; completion of 16 units including 4 English, 3 mathematics, 3 science, 2 foreign language, and 3 social science; SAT or ACT required; high school students of outstanding achievement may be considered upon completion of junior year with at least 15 units; early admission, midyear admission, rolling admission and advanced placement plans available. $10 application fee.

Costs Per Year: $1,743 tuition; $4,587 out-of-state; $2,760 room and board.

Collegiate Environment: The main campus consists of 43 acres in the center of Milledgeville. Twenty-three acres provide the site for the major educational facilities and twenty acres, two blocks away, are used for student housing and the new multipurpose building. Many of the 30 buildings are red brick with Corinthian columns and limestone trim. The athletic complex, known as West Campus, is on a 642-acre site just outside the city. A few miles east of the campus, East Campus consists of Rocky Creek Park and Lake Laurel. Rocky Creek is a 100-acre recreational facility on Lake Sinclair. Lake Laurel is a teaching, conference, and recreation center with its own 15-acre lake, picnic areas, nature trails and rustic lodge. The Library contains 150,000 volumes, 4,000 periodicals, 100 microforms and 14,000 sound recordings. Facilities house 400 men and 800 women. Army ROTC is offered. 78% of applicants are accepted. Scholarships are available and 65% of the student receive some form of aid.

Community Environment: Milledgeville, the county seat for Baldwin County, is less than a dozen miles from the geographic center of Georgia, and is approximately 100 miles from Augusta, Albany, Atlanta and Columbus, and 30 miles from Macon. The town, which was the antebellum capital of Georgia, now has a population of 35,000 and is a center of history and culture. It is located on the fall line in a setting of natural beauty of rolling hills and recreational lakes.

Branch Campuses: Branch campuses that offer only junior-level and senior-level courses in a limited number of majors are located in Macon, Dublin, and Warner Robins.

GEORGIA INSTITUTE OF TECHNOLOGY   *(E-4)*
Atlanta, Georgia 30332
Tel: (404) 894-2000; Admissions: (404) 894-4154; Fax: (404) 894-9511

Description: The public-supported technological university was founded in 1885. The first class consisted of 84 students in a Mechanical Engineering program. The university now is comprised of five colleges and grants undergraduate and graduate degrees in approximately 84 major fields. It operates on the quarter system and offers one summer session. Undergraduate enrollment includes 8,600 men and 2,797 women full-time, and 1,167 men and 327 women part-time. There are 3,676 graduate students. A faculty of 714 gives an overall faculty-student ratio of 1-18. Army, Navy, and Air Force ROTC programs are available.

Entrance Requirements: High school graduation with a B average and 16 units including 4 English, 4 mathematics, 3 lab science, 3 so-

cial science, and 2 foreign language; SAT or ACT required; early admission, delayed admission, rolling admission, and advanced placement plans available; $25 application fee.

Costs Per Year: $2,277 tuition and fees; $4,455 nonresident tuition and fees; $4,404 room and board.

Collegiate Environment: Located on 330 acres in Atlanta, the Institute is constantly adding new facilities and programs. The library is of contemporary design and contains 2,473,000 volumes. Housing facilities for 5,106 student are available. There are 300 apartments for married students. 49% of applicants are accepted. The average scores of the entering freshman class are SAT 559 verbal, 673 math. 10,580 scholarships are available and 70% of the students received financial aid.

Community Environment: See Clark Atlanta University.

GEORGIA MILITARY COLLEGE   *(G-7)*
201 East Green Street
Milledgeville, Georgia 31061
Tel: (912) 454-2700; (800) 342-0413; Fax: (912) 454-2688

Description: The public (independent) military junior college is accredited by the Southern Association of Colleges and Schools. It operates on the quarter system and offers one summer session. Enrollment includes 1,300 students. A faculty of 107 gives a faculty-student ratio of 1-15. Founded in 1879 in the former State Capitol as a military preparatory school for boys, the junior college department was added in 1930 and was designated as an Honor School by the United States War Department in 1933.

Entrance Requirements: High school graduation or GED equivalency; open enrollment policy; SAT or ACT required for Army ROTC contract cadets; $25 application fee.

Costs Per Year: $3,960 ($1,320/quarter or $60/cr), 3,825 room and board.

Collegiate Environment: The school offers a four-year senior ROTC Army program as well as a two-year ROTC program. The college specializes in academic preparation and a two-year commisions program. The library contains 20,000 volumes. Dormitories accommodate 300 men and women. The institution also contains a preparatory high school. Various scholarships are available, and 89% of the student body receives some financial assistance.

Community Environment: Milledgeville, an educational center, was the state capital from 1807 to 1867. Georgia Military College occupies the old state house. Railroads and buses serve the area. Some of the industries are spinning, canning, manufacture of clay products, and mobile homes. Job opportunities are numerous in textile plants. Nearby Lake Sinclair provides boating, fishing and water skiing. The early nineteenth-century homes add atmosphere and beauty to community life.

GEORGIA SCHOOL OF PROFESSIONAL PSYCHOLOGY
(E-4)
990 Hammond Drive
Atlanta, Georgia 30328
Tel: (404) 671-1200; (800) 362-3094; Fax: (404) 671-0476

Description: The privately supported graduate school is fully accredited by the North Central Association of Colleges and Schools. It operates on a trimester system with one summer session. The school was established in 1990 to provide a setting in which extensive training could be pursued in the area of professional psychology. The Georgia School of Professional Psychology is a unit of the American Schools of Professional Psychology with professional schools in Arlington, VA; Atlanta, GA; Chicago, IL; Honolulu, HI; Minneapolis, MN; and Rolling Meadows, IL. It does not promote any one clinical psychological orientation. Currently, it offers psychoanalytic, client-centered, experiential, family systems, integrative-eclectic, behavioral, neuropsychological, and group approaches to intervention. The school grants a Masters and a Doctorate degree. Recent enrollment was 341 students with a core faculty of 13.

Entrance Requirements: Graduation from an accredited institution with a baccalaureate or more advanced degree; GRE or MAT; $55 application fee.

Costs Per Year: $13,540 tuition per year; $300-$500 approximate fees.

Collegiate Environment: A coeducational professional school, the college has a great diversity of students, ranging from recent college graduates to change-of-career students. The school maintains a curriculum support library, containing current textbooks, psychology literature, diagnostic testing materials, reference texts and commonly used journals. This library is supplemented by the Emory University Library system, where students of the school have full privileges. Financial aid is available.

Community Environment: The location provides an interesting blend of the old and new. The old Atlanta can be seen in nearby theaters and stately homes near local universities. The new is evidenced in the shops, live entertainment and the downtown business district via MARTA, the city's public transportation system. The school is accessible by MARTA and from the main interstates; parking is available in adjacent lots. (See also Atlanta University.)

GEORGIA SOUTHERN UNIVERSITY *(I-11)*
U.S. 301 South
Statesboro, Georgia 30460
Tel: (912) 681-5611

Description: The public-controlled college was established in 1906 as one of ten district agricultural and mechanical schools. It is accredited by the Southern Association of Colleges and Schools. The college grants Associate, Baccalaureate, Master's, and Education Specialist degrees, and it is Georgia's newest Regional University. Dual degrees are offered with Georgia Tech: 3 years GSU, 2 years GA Tech. The university operates on the quarter system and offers two summer sessions. Enrollment includes 14,138 students. There are 600 faculty members and a faculty-student ratio of 1-24.

Entrance Requirements: High school graduation or equivalent; Completion of 15 units including 4 English, 3 math, 3 science and 3 social science; 2 foreign language; SAT or ACT; mid-year students accepted; early admission, early decision, and advanced placement plans available; $10 application fee.

Costs Per Year: $1,721 state-resident tuition; $2,844 out-of-state; $3,270 room and board; $456 student fees.

Collegiate Environment: The campus has 95 buildings on 511.96 acres. The library contains 463,102 volumes, 3,272 periodicals, 682,024 microforms, 6,953 audiovisual materials and a computerized learning resource center. Dormitory housing is available for 3,144 students. Fraternities and sororities provide housing for additional 180 men and 36 women. Various forms of financial assistance are available and 70% of the current student body receives some form of aid.

Community Environment: Statesboro is an attractive, small town of 18,121 with theaters, restaurants, recreational and entertainment facilities, and businesses that deal primarily with students and the campus. Many students work full or part time in Statesboro and live in a variety of student apartment complexes located near the campus.

GEORGIA SOUTHWESTERN COLLEGE *(K-4)*
Glessner Street
Americus, Georgia 31709
Tel: (912) 928-1279

Description: The publicly controlled, liberal arts college is accredited by the Southern Association of Colleges and Schools. The college was founded in 1906 as an agricultural and mechanical school and began transition to a four-year college in 1964. The college grants the Associate, Bachelor's, and Master's degrees. It operates on the quarter system and offers two summer sessions. Enrollment includes 2,533 students. A faculty of 125 full-time and 30 part-time gives a faculty-student ratio of 1:17.

Entrance Requirements: High school graduation or equivalent; C average and 21 units including 4 English, 2 yrs foreign language, 3 mathematics, 3 science and 3 social science; SAT required, minimum scores are 280 verbal and 280 math for provisional admission; regular admission requires 350-V and 350-M; midyear students accepted; early admission, advanced placement and rolling admission plans available. $10 application fee.

Costs Per Year: $1,809 state resident tuition; $4,653 nonresident; $2,520 room and board; $500 books, $129 student fees.

Collegiate Environment: The campus has 24 buildings on 187 acres of wooded land including recreational areas, a spring-fed lake, and a natural lakeside theatre. The library contains 136,905 volumes, 822 periodicals, 295,640 microforms and 4,498 audiovisual materials. Dormitory space accommodates 515 men and 664 women. 80% of the applicants are accepted. Academic and athletic scholarships are available and 63% of the students receive some form of financial aid.

Community Environment: Americus is located 135 miles south of Atlanta, the climate is mild with a yearly mean temperature of 65.7 degrees, and an annual rainfall of 49 inches. Airlines serve the area. The usual community facilities include a hospital, clinics, library, daily newspaper, radio stations, and shopping centers. Manufactured products include shirts, lumber, nails, auto parts, and paper products. Kaolin and Bauxite nearby. Outdoor sports include tennis, baseball, golf and basketball. Charles Lindbergh made his first solo flight from Souther Field. Historic sites in Americus include Plains, home of President Jimmy Carter, and Andersonville National Cemetery and Civil War prison site.

GEORGIA STATE UNIVERSITY *(E-4)*
University Plaza - 519 One Park Pl. So.
Atlanta, Georgia 30303
Tel: (404) 658-2000; Admissions: (404) 651-2365

Description: The public-controlled university is accredited by the Southern Association of Colleges and Schools. The college was established in 1913 with a speciality in business. The academic program expanded in 1961. The university grants the Bachelor, Master's, and Doctoral degrees and professional certification in education. It operates on the quarter system and offers one summer session. Enrollment includes 7,906 full-time and 8,773 part-time undergraduates and 7,097 graduate students. 28% of the undergraduates and 57% of the graduate students attend evening programs. A faculty of 801 full-time and 53 part-time gives a faculty-student ratio of 1-18.

Entrance Requirements: High school graduation or equivalent; C average and 15 units including 4 English, 3 mathematics, 3 science, 3 social science, and 2 foreign language; SAT required; non-high school graduates considered on a limited basis; early admission, early decision, rolling admission, and advanced placement plans available. $10 application fee.

Costs Per Year: $2,003 state-resident tuition; $6,952.50 nonresident; $246 miscellaneous.

Collegiate Environment: Located in the hub of the rapidly growing city of Atlanta, the university is a part of the University System of Georgia. The library contains 1,535,309 volumes, 12,270 periodicals, 1,785,238 microforms and 549,785 U.S. Documents, and 36,464 annual reports of corporations. 86% of the applicants are accepted. The university assists students in locating housing. 280 scholarships are available, including 45 for freshmen and 26% of students receive some form of financial aid.

Community Environment: See Clark Atlanta University.

GORDON COLLEGE *(G-5)*
103 College Avenue
Barnesville, Georgia 30204
Tel: (404) 358-5000

Description: This state-supported two-year college is accredited by the Southern Association of Colleges and Schools. Established in 1852, Gordon is one of the oldest schools in the South. The college offers university-parallel programs leading to an Associate degree. It operates on the quarter system and offers two summer sessions. Enrollment includes 1,360 full-time and 799 part-time students. A faculty of 72 full-time and 49 part-time gives a faculty-student ratio of 1-17.

Entrance Requirements: High school graduation with a C average and 18 units, including 4 English, 3 mathematics, 3 science, and 3 social science; non-high school graduates considered; SAT or ACT required; minimum scores SAT 350V, 350M.

Costs Per Year: $1,194 tuition; $3,237 nonresident; $2,130 room and board; $120 student fees.

Collegiate Environment: The campus is 125 acres. The library contains 71,000 volumes. Dormitory facilities for 310 students are available. The college believes in small classes with constant contact between student and instructor. The college offers 44 Associate degree programs. 95% of the applicants are accepted. Scholarships are available and approximately 48% of the current student body receives some form of financial aid.

GWINNETT TECHNICAL INSTITUTE *(F-5)*
P.O. Box 1505
1250 Atkinson Road
Lawrenceville, Georgia 30246-1505
Tel: (404) 962-7580; Admissions: (404) 962-7582; Fax: (404) 962-7985

Description: The publicly supported coeducational technical college was founded in 1984 and is operated by the Gwinnett County Public Schools System. It is accredited by the Southern Association of Colleges and Schools and awards associate degees. Enrollment includes 1,063 full-time and 2,033 part-time students with a total faculty of 84, providing a faculty student ration of 1:18.

Entrance Requirements: Open enrollment policy; high school graduation or GED acceptable. ACT, ASSET, or SAT required.

Costs Per Year: $816 tuition; $1,156 out-of-state.

Collegiate Environment: The campus has two buildings totaling more than 275,000 square feet on an 89 acre campus. The library is 17,000 square feet and contains meeting rooms and personal computers in addition to its 16,000 volumes, 1,500 audiovisuals, 260 periodicals. All students qualifying for admission are accepted. Financial aid is available.

Community Environment: The campus is located in Lawrenceville, GA, 30 miles northeast of Atlanta. Located between U.S. Interstate 85 and Georgia Highway 316, the campus is easily reached by passenger transportation. This suburban Atlanta community is characterized by clean, high tech industries, which sustains the need for a skilled workforce.

INSTITUTE OF PAPER SCIENCE AND TECHNOLOGY *(F-4)*
500 10th Street, N.W.
Atlanta, Georgia 30318
Tel: (404) 853-9500; (800) 558-6611; Admissions: (404) 853-9556; Fax: (404) 853-9510

Description: The Institute is a privately supported graduate school affiliated with the Georgia Institute of Technology. It is accredited by the Southern Association of Colleges and Schools. The program is multi-disciplinary in nature, and the educational philosophy is to develop "scientific generalists" who are well versed in several disciplines within the sciences. Every student admitted to the program on a full-time basis, and who is a citizen of a North American country or possesses a permanent residence visa receives a full tuition scholarship and fellowship stipend. The curriculum is exclusively at the graduate level and involves an integrated course of study in chemistry, physics, mathematics, biology, engineering, and general studies. The Master of Science degree is awarded at the end of the second year, and the Doctor of Philosophy degree is awarded at the end of approximately 4 years. The Institute operates on the quarter system and offers one summer session. Enrollment is approximately 80 students with a faculty of 27. The faculty-student ratio is 1-3. It also offers continuing education programs as short courses for representatives of industry.

Entrance Requirements: Graduate of an accredited college or university with a B.S. degree, minimum GPA of 3.0; GRE score in the 50th percentile; students usually admitted in September. Deadline for Fall admissions April 15.

Costs Per Year: $20,000 tuition; $10,300 room and board; additional expenses average $600.

Collegiate Environment: The library has the world's major collection of scientific and technical literature concerning science underlying the manufacture, modification, and use of paper. It contains approximately 38,000 bound volumes, 820 periodicals, 2,100 microforms. Nearly all students receive a full tuition scholarship. Over 90% of first year class return for second year.

Community Environment: See Clark Atlanta University.

INTERDENOMINATIONAL THEOLOGICAL CENTER *(E-4)*
671 Beckwith Street, S.W.
Atlanta, Georgia 30314
Tel: (404) 527-7707

Description: The private theological graduate seminary is accredited by the Southern Association of Colleges and Schools and the Association of Theological Schools. It operates on the semester system. This seminary was created in 1958 through the cooperation of four schools of theology: Gammon Theological Seminary (Methodist), Morehouse School of Religion (Baptist), Phillips School of Theology (Christian), and Methodist Episcopal. Two schools have been added: Johnson C. Smith (Presbyterian), and Charles H. Mason Theological Seminary (Church of God in Christ). The seminary is also a member of the Atlanta University Center and the Atlanta Theological Association. The Center grants three Masters and two Doctorate degrees. The Center also grants three dual degrees. Enrollment includes 294 full-time and 88 part-time graduate students. There are 32 faculty members.

Entrance Requirements: Bachelor's degree from a recognized college or university; A.B. degree or its equivalent; certificate from official of Church endorsing applicant as an acceptable candidate required; midyear admission plan available. $25 application fee.

Costs Per Year: $4,000 tuition; $2,860 room; $1,500 board.

Collegiate Environment: The six-building, ten-acre campus is located in the heart of the Atlanta University area; facilities are of the most modern type. The library contains 322,258 volumes, and dormitories accommodate 103 students. Almost all students receive financial assistance.

Community Environment: See Clark Atlanta University.

KENNESAW STATE COLLEGE *(D-3)*
P.O. Box 444
Marietta, Georgia 30061
Tel: (404) 423-6300; Fax: (404) 423-6541

Description: The coeducational senior college, a unit of the University System of Georgia, was established in 1963 to provide programs of post-secondary school education to the community within commuting distance of the college. The college is fully accredited by the Southern Association of Colleges and Schools to offer the Associate degree and its Bachelor of Arts, Bachelor of Science, and Bachelor of Business Adminstration programs. The college is SACS accredited for level five (masters) degree programs. An overseas program sponsored by the University of Georgia is available to qualified students. Army ROTC is offered. The college operates on the semester system and offers three summer sessions. Enrollment includes 5,587 full-time and 5,291 part-time undergraduates and 1,037 graduate students. A faculty of 331 full-time and 107 part-time gives a faculty-student ratio of 1-27.

Entrance Requirements: High school graduation; non-high school graduates considered with GED equivalency and acceptable SAT scores; SAT or ACT required; minimum scores V430; M430; ACT 13; early admission, early decision, delayed admission, midyear admission and advanced placement plans available; provisional enrollment plans also available.

Costs Per Year: $1,341; $4,023 out-of-state, $171 student fee.

Collegiate Environment: The campus is located on 152-acre tract of land eight miles north of Marietta and features modern architecture. Twelve buildings serve the college and the library contains 300,000 volumes, 2,100 periodicals and 485,000 microforms. 63% of students applying for admission are accepted. Army ROTC is offered. Financial aid is also available and 17% of the student body receives some form of aid.

Community Environment: A suburban area seven miles from Marietta, the average January temperature is 45 degrees and the average July temperature is 80 degrees, with an average rainfall of 50 inches. Community facilities include churches, and civic organizations. Shopping areas and hospitals are in Marietta and Kennesaw. The campus is in view of Kennesaw Mountain, site of the Civil War and the "The Great Locomotive Chase." See also Marietta Cobb Area Vocational-Technical School.

LAGRANGE COLLEGE   *(G-2)*
LaGrange, Georgia 30240
Tel: (706) 882-2911; Admissions: (706) 812-7260; Fax: (706) 884-6567

Description: The private, liberal arts college is accredited by the Southern Association of Colleges and Schools and is controlled by the United Methodist Church. The college was founded in 1831 as LaGrange Female Academy; it became coeducational in 1953. It operates on the quarter system and offers one summer session. The current enrollment is 970 full-time students. A faculty of 81 full-time gives a faculty-student ratio of 15-1. The college grants an Associate, Bachelor, and Graduate Masters Degree.

Entrance Requirements: High school graduation with a C average and 15 units including 4 English, 2 mathematics, 2 science, 2 soc. sci., and score of 400 or more (verbal) and 400 or more (math) on SAT; application fee $20; early admission, early decision, rolling admission and advanced placement plans available.

Costs Per Year: $7,650 tuition; $3,585 room and board; $225 student fees.

Collegiate Environment: The college seeks to provide a Christian education for Christian living. Church attendance is not compulsory; local churches cooperate with campus leadership to promote denominational interests. The campus has 23 buildings. Dormitory space is provided for 480 men and women. The library contains 127,000 volumes. 70% of the applicants are accepted and 66% of the students receive some form of aid.

Community Environment: LaGrange is located in west central Georgia 45 miles north of Columbus, 70 miles Southwest of Atlanta. West Point Lake is accessible. It is one of the largest textile manufacturing centers in the South. Many notable ante-bellum homes and gardens may be seen here.

MACON COLLEGE   *(H-6)*
College Station Drive
Macon, Georgia 31297
Tel: (912) 471-2800; Fax: (912) 471-2846

Description: This public, coeducational two-year college offers college transfer, occupational, continuing education, developmental, and cultural programs. Accredited by the Southern Association of Colleges and Schools, the school operates on the quarter system with two summer sessions. Founded in 1968, with a charter class of 1,110 students, this college became the 25th institution of the University System of Georgia. Enrollment is 1,592 full-time and 3,495 part-time students. A faculty of 129 gives a faculty-student ratio of 1-26.

Entrance Requirements: High school graduation or GED equivalent; 15 units including 4 English, 3 mathematics, 3 science, 3 social science, 2 foreign language; SAT required; early admission, joint-enrollment, midyear admission and advanced placement plans available.

Costs Per Year: $1,200 tuition; $3,200 nonresident; $450 books/supplies.

Collegiate Environment: Thirteen buildings serve the college, and the library contains 73,520 volumes and 390 periodicals. 95% of applicants are accepted. 40% of the students receive some form of financial aid.

Community Environment: See Mercer University - Macon.

Branch Campuses: Robins Resident Center, Bldg. 905, Rm. 145, Robins AFB, GA 31098; Macon College Downtown Center, 384 Second St., Macon, GA 31210; Warner Robins campus, Advanced Technology Park, 151 Osigian Blvd., Warner Robins, GA 31088.

MEDICAL COLLEGE OF GEORGIA   *(F-11)*
1120 Fifteenth Street
Augusta, Georgia 30912
Tel: (706) 721-2725; Admissions: (706) 721-2725; Fax: (706) 721-0186

Description: The public-controlled medical college is accredited by the Southern Association of Colleges and Schools. It operates on the quarter system. Founded in 1828 as the Medical Academy, the college is the oldest school of medicine in Georgia. Enrollment is 865 men and 1,233 women including 1,177 graduate students. There are 686 full-time and 105 part-time faculty. The college grants graduate-level and undergraduate-level degrees.

Entrance Requirements: High school graduation or GED equivalency required; high school units completed: 4 English, 3 math, 3 science, 2 foreign language, 3 social studies; early admission and early decision plans available.

Costs Per Year: $1,899 tuition, $5,697 nonresident tuition, $1,008 room; $249 student fees.

Collegiate Environment: The Medical College campus is situated near the center of Augusta. Dormitory space is available for 111 men, 216 women and 100 families. The library contains 159,834 titles, 1,410 periodicals, 4,005 microforms and sound recordings. The Medical College of Georgia Hospital contributes teaching and clinical research facilities (600 beds) and is an integral part of the medical college. College schools and departments include dental hygiene, diagnostic medical sonography, health information technology, health information management, medical technology, nursing, radiography, nuclear medicine technology, occupational therapy, physical therapy, physical therapist assistant, physician's assistant, radiation therapy technology, respiratory therapy, occupational therapy assistant, and neurodiagnostic technology. Financial aid is available and 75% of the student body receives some form of aid.

Community Environment: See Augusta College.

MERCER UNIVERSITY - ATLANTA   *(E-4)*
3001 Mercer University Dr.
Atlanta, Georgia 30341
Tel: (404) 986-3000; (800) 694-2284; Admissions: (404) 986-3134; Fax: (404) 986-3135

Description: Opened in 1968 as the Atlanta Baptist College, the college merged with Mercer University on Macon in 1972 and is now known as the Cecil B. Day Campus of Mercer University in Atlanta. It is accredited by the Southern Association of Colleges and Schools. Mercer University is a church-related institution with historic Baptist roots and is dedicated to excellence and scholarly descipline in the fields of liberal learning and professional knowledge. The Cecil B. Day Campus grants bachelor's degrees in Business Administration and Computer Science and Master's degrees in Businees Administration; Health Education (Early Chilhood and Middle Grades Education); Electrical Engineering; and Engineering Management. The Southern School of Pharmacy also located on the Atlanta campus, offers the Doctor of Pharmacy; Master's and Ph.D. degree programs and operates on an early semester calendar. The Cecil B. Day campus in Atlanta operates on a quarter calendar with three summer sessions. The pharmacy program operates on a semester calendar. Enrollment includes 25 full-time, 176 part-time undergraduate, and 943 graduate students. A faculty of 130 gives a faculty-student ratio of 1-17.

Entrance Requirements: Application form & fee $35, International $50; Transcript(s); Transfer GPA: 2.3/higher, rolling admission plans.

Costs Per Year: $5,895 tuition.

Collegiate Environment: The college is located on a 335-acre campus, 11 miles from downtown Atlanta. Seventy-six percent of students applying for admission are accepted. Mid-year students are accepted. The library consists of 80,000 volumes, 700 periodicals, 19,000 microforms, and 2,000 sound recordings. No dormitories are available at present. Various forms of financial assistance are available.

Community Environment: See Clark Atlanta University.

MERCER UNIVERSITY - MACON   *(H-6)*
1400 Coleman Avenue
Macon, Georgia 31207
Tel: (912) 752-2650; (800) 342-0841; Fax: (912) 752-2828

Description: Mercer is a private, liberal arts university, founded in 1833. It is accredited by the Southern Association of Colleges and School and is composed of the College of Liberal Arts, the Stetson School of Business and Economics, the School of Engineering, the Walter F. George School of Law, the Mercer University School of Medicine, University College, the Southern School of Pharmacy, and the School of Business and Economics-Atlanta. It operates on the quarter system and offers two summer sessions. The university grants the Bachelor, Master's and Doctoral degrees. Army ROTC is available as an elective. Enrollment includes 2,173 full-time, 97 part-time, and 344 graduate students. A faculty of 166 full-time and 25 part-time provide a faculty student ratio of 1-14.

Entrance Requirements: There is flexibility in the admission requirements: high school diploma; minimum of 17 units, including 15 academic; high school record showing rank in class, scores on the SAT or ACT, a recommendation by the guidance counselor, and a list of extracurricular activities. Early admission, early decision, deferred admission, midyear admission, rolling admission, and advanced placement plans available; $25 application fee.

Costs Per Year: $11,988 undergraduate tuition; $4,122 room and board.

Collegiate Environment: The campus is located on 150 acres. Residence halls accommodate approximately 1,139 students, and freshmen are guaranteed housing. The new university library provides 95,000 feet of space, contains 24-hour study rooms, and has the capacity to house 500,000 volumes. The university's Shelley and Robert Burns collections are both considered the most extensive in the South and are probably among the largest in the United States. Approximately 84% of applicants meet requirements and are accepted. Financial assistance is available and 85% of the students receive financial aid.

Community Environment: Macon's central location allows easy access to the Georgia coast, the Florida beaches, and the north Georgia mountains. Macon, population 250,000, is 75 miles south of Atlanta and is served by two interstate highways, I-75 and I-16. The Macon airport is served by two commuter airlines. Macon is a blend of the old, with many historic mansions and sites, and the new.

MERCER UNIVERSITY SOUTHERN SCHOOL OF PHARMACY   (E-4)
3001 Mercer University Drive
Atlanta, Georgia 30312
Tel: (404) 986-3300; Admissions: (404) 986-3232; Fax: (404) 986-3315

Description: The Southern School of Pharmacy is part of the Mercer University system and controlled by the Southern Baptist Convention. Opened as an independent college in 1903, the school's objective is to prepare men and women for the practice of pharmacy. It operates on the semester system and offers two summer sessions. Enrollment is 500 students. A faculty of 40 gives a faculty-student ratio of 1-12.

Entrance Requirements: In this professional school, two years of college work and a grade average of 2.5 are required for admission with certain specific courses required; rolling admission plan; application deadline is Jan. 31; application fee, $25.

Costs Per Year: Tuition is $11,510 per year. No housing facilities are available.

Collegiate Environment: The School of Pharmacy moved to the Cecil B. Day campus at Mercer University in 1991. It is located on a superb tract of 335 beautifully wooded acres in Northeast Atlanta. Dormitory facilities are not available. 25% of applicants are accepted. Financial aid is available. 80% of the students receive some form of financial aid.

Community Environment: See Clark Atlanta University.

MIDDLE GEORGIA COLLEGE   (J-7)
Sarah Street
Cochran, Georgia 31014
Tel: (912) 934-6221

Description: The public-controlled junior college is accredited by the Southern Association of Colleges and Schools. The college was established in 1884 as New Ebenezer College and in 1927 became the Middle Georgia Agricultural and Mechanical Junior College. It operates on the quarter system and offers one summer session. Enrollment includes 999 men and 1,170 women. A faculty of 75 full-time and 25 part-time gives a faculty-student ratio of 1-27.

Entrance Requirements: High school graduation with a C average and 18 units including 4 English, 4 mathematics, 4 science, 4 social science and 2 foreign language; non-high school graduates considered; application fee $5; SAT or ACT required; early admission, roll-

ing admission, early decision and advanced placement plans available. Students are admitted at mid-year.

Costs Per Year: $1,074 resident tuition; $3,117 non-resident; room and board, $3,105, fees, $240.

Collegiate Environment: The campus has 26 buildings on 160 acres including six tennis courts and a three-acre pond. Modern residence halls accommodate 500 men and 450 women. The library contains 80,000 volumes, 500 periodicals, 100 microforms and 100 sound recordings. 95% of the applicants are accepted. The average SAT scores of the current freshman class were 400 verbal and 420 math. About 80% of the freshman returned for the second year.

Community Environment: Cochran is 40 miles south of Macon, between interstate highways 75 and 16, almost squarely in the center of the state. Both mountain and beach resorts are about three hours away.

Branch Campuses: Non-residential campus (no dormitories) in Dublin, GA, about 30 miles from main campus in Cochran. Dublin Campus offers day and evening classes. Students may alternate between campuses. Associate degree nursing program is available at both campuses.

MOREHOUSE COLLEGE   (E-4)
830 Westview Drive, S.W.
Atlanta, Georgia 30314
Tel: (404) 215-2632; (800) 851-1254; Fax: (404) 215-2711

Description: Morehouse College is an independent four-year undergraduate liberal arts college for men located about a mile west of downtown Atlanta, the cultural and economic center of the South. Dotted with a mixture of old and an increasing number of new buildings, the campus of more than 40 acres forms part of the Atlanta University Center, the largest private educational complex with a predominantly black enrollment in the world. The college operates on the semester system and offers one summer session. It is accredited by the Southern Association of Colleges and Schools. Enrollment is approximately 2,480 students from 37 states, the District of Columbia, and 15 foreign countries. The faculty includes 143 full-time and 46 part-time.

Entrance Requirements: High school graduation with a C average and 16 units including 4 English, 3 mathematics, 2 science, and 2 social science; recommended SAT composite score of 1000; advanced placement, early admission, early decision, delayed admission, midyear admission and rolling admission plans available; $35 application fee.

Costs Per Year: $7,050 tuition; $5,490 room and board; $1,420 fees.

Collegiate Environment: The campus comprises forty acres of land. Dormitories accomodate for 1,300 students. The library contains 550,000 volumes, 1,500 periodicals, 10,000 microforms and 5,000 audiovisual materials. Approximately 47% of applicants are accepted for the freshman class. 45% of the student body graduated in the top tenth of the high school class, and approximately 60% ranked in the top quarter. The average scores of the entering freshman class were SAT 480 verbal, 530 math. About 75% of the freshman class returned for the second year. Scholarships are available and 60% of the freshman class receives some form of financial assistance.

Community Environment: See Clark Atlanta University.

MORRIS BROWN COLLEGE   (E-4)
Martin Luther King Drive, N.W.
Atlanta, Georgia 30314
Tel: (404) 220-0270; Admissions: (404) 220-0152; Fax: (404) 220-0371

Description: This private, liberal arts college was founded by the African Methodist Episcopal Church. The school is accredited by the Southern Association of Colleges and Schools. The college was founded in 1881 as a preparatory school for the Christian education of black men and women. The first class graduated in 1890, and the liberal arts college was organized four years later. The college is a member of the Atlanta University Center. Army, Navy and Air Force ROTC are available. It operates on the semester system. Enrollment includes 1,992 students. There are 128 faculty members.

Entrance Requirements: High school graduation with rank in upper half of graduation class; completion of 15 units, 12 of which must be in academic subjects; SAT and GRE required; character references required; early admission and early decision available; $20 application fee.

Costs Per Year: $6,770 tuition; $4,438 room and board.

Collegiate Environment: The campus is situated in the center of Atlanta. 30% of students applying for admission are accepted, including midyear students. Dormitory facilities are available for 428 men and 456 women. The library contains 36,908 volumes.

Community Environment: See Clark Atlanta University.

NORTH GEORGIA COLLEGE   *(C-5)*
Dahlonega, Georgia 30597
Tel: (706) 864-1400; Fax: (706) 864-1756

Description: The state-controlled military college is accredited by the Southern Association of Colleges and Schools. It operates on the quarter system and offers one summer session. Enrollment is 1,022 men and 1,850 women. A faculty of 120 gives a faculty-student ratio of 1-22. Founded in 1873, the college is a part of the University System of Georgia and grants an Associate Degree, a Baccalaureate degree and a Master of Education degree. All resident male students must participate in the Army ROTC program.

Entrance Requirements: High school graduation; completion of 16 units including 4 English, 3 mathematics, 3 science, 2 foreign language and 3 social science; SAT or ACT required; some non-high school graduates considered; $10 application fee; early admission, rolling admission, delayed admission and advanced placement plans available.

Costs Per Year: $1,422 state-resident tuition; $4,266 nonresident; $2,670 room and board.

Collegiate Environment: The library contains more than 112,000 volumes, and numerous pamphlets, periodicals, microforms, and audiovisual materials. Dormitories accommodate 509 men and 693 women. Financial aid is available. Midyear students are admitted.

Community Environment: Dahlonega is located in northeastern Georgia, 20 miles from Gainesville. Atlanta is one hour away. This Georgia community was the site of the country's first gold rush in 1828 and is the southern gateway to the Chattahoochee National Forest. Outdoor activities include fishing, boating, swimming, camping and picknicking. Points of interest are the Gold Museum and a former active gold mine which visitors can tour. The Appalachian Trail is 15 miles from Dahlonega.

OGLETHORPE UNIVERSITY   *(E-4)*
4484 Peachtree Road N.E.
Atlanta, Georgia 30319-2797
Tel: (404) 261-1441

Description: Oglethorpe is a selective university of liberal arts and sciences located about 10 miles north of downtown Atlanta. Enrollment is 1,086 students. The university was founded in 1835. It is accredited by the Southern Association of College and Schools and operates on the semester system with three summer sessions. Oglethorpe has a 90-acre wooded campus featuring English gothic architecture.

Entrance Requirements: High school graduation with a B average or 2.5 GPA; units should include 4 English, 3 mathematics, 2 science, and 2 social science; high school equivalency diploma accepted; advanced placement, rolling admission, delayed admission, and early admission plans available; $25 application fee.

Costs Per Year: $10,120 tuition; $4,000 room and board.

Collegiate Environment: The college accepts 79% of those who apply for admission, including students from all sections of the country and abroad. Dormitory capacity is 415 students. The library contains 94,000 volumes. 83% of the students graduated in the top quarter of their high school class. Average scores were SAT 1171; ACT 27. Financial assistance, both need-based and merit-based, is available.

Community Environment: Oglethorpe students enjoy the scenic setting of a suburban campus combined with the opportunities of a great international city. Atlanta offers professional and amateur art and entertainment, professional and amateur sports, renowned intellectual and research activities, and world-class dining and enjoyment opportunities. It also offers small town values of friendliness, courtesy, and respect. Students can find part-time employment, internships, cultural activities, and an active job placement program, all of which are enhanced by the Atlanta location.

OXFORD COLLEGE OF EMORY UNIVERSITY   *(F-5)*
Office of Admission and Financial Aid
Oxford, Georgia 30267
Tel: (404) 784-8328; (800) 723-8328; Fax: (404) 784-8359

Description: This college offers the first two years in arts and sciences of Emory University of Atlanta. Established by the Methodist Church, the school is accredited by the Southern Association of Colleges and Schools. Chartered by the Georgia Legislature in 1836, Emory University opened Oxford College on the University's original campus in 1929. Students completing sophomore year at Oxford receive AA degree and automatically join junior class of Emory College in Atlanta. The school operates on the semester system and offers two summer sessions. Enrollment is 560 full-time students. A faculty of 41 full-time and 8 part-time gives a faculty-student ratio of 1-10.

Entrance Requirements: High school curriculum most important in the admisson decision; college-preparatory courses should include 4 English, 3 mathematics, 2 laboratory science, 2 foreign language, 2 social studies; SAT or ACT required; application fee $35; early admission, midyear admission, rolling admission, and advanced placement plans available.

Costs Per Year: $12,700 tuition, $4,400 room and board; $150 student fees.

Collegiate Environment: Dormitory facilities accommodate 517 students and the library contains 70,127 titles. 82% of students applying for admission are accepted as well as midyear students. 72% of the freshman class received some form of financial aid.

Community Environment: Oxford is two miles from Covington, and 38 miles from Atlanta. The city enjoys a mild climate-spring begins in late February, and the temperature seldom falls below 32 degrees during the winter months. Churches are in Oxford and in Covington. Recreational activities include golfing, hunting, boating, and fishing.

PAINE COLLEGE   *(F-11)*
1235-15th Street
Augusta, Georgia 30901-3182
Tel: (706) 821-8200; (800) 476-7303; Fax: (706) 821-8293

Description: The private liberal arts college is controlled by the United Methodist and the Christian Methodist Episcopal Churches. It is accredited by the Southern Association of Colleges and Schools. It operates on the semester system and offers one summer session. Enrollment is 686 full-time students. A faculty of 61 gives a faculty-student ratio of 1-12. Founded in 1882 as a preparatory school for black children, the institute was recharted as a college in 1903. However, there were no public schools for blacks at that time, and the school continued to provide secondary education for its students as well as college work. It was not until 1945 that the school discontinued its preparatory classes. The college grants a Baccalaureate degree.

Entrance Requirements: High school graduation with 2.0 GPA; completion of 15 units including 4 English, 2 mathematics, 2 science, and 2 social science; SAT required; ACT may be substituted; essay and recommendation required; $10 application fee; early admission, early decision, rolling admission, delayed admission and advanced placement plans available.

Costs Per Year: $5,200 tuition; $3,739 room and board; $268 student fees.

Collegiate Environment: The main college campus covers 54 acres and includes the administration buildings, classroom buildings, and dormitories. Dormitory facilities are available for 148 men and 256 women, and the library contains 125,000 volumes, 5,000 pamphlets, 600 periodicals, 5,504 microforms and 943 recordings. 80% of students applying for admission are accepted, including midyear students. Financial aid is available; approximately 90% of the present student body receives some form of financial assistance.

Community Environment: Augusta, located on the Savannah River in east central Georgia, is a river port and industrial center, and is the third leading producer of clay products in the southeast. All forms of transportation are available. Recreational facilities include lakes for fishing, boating and hunting, golf courses, horseback riding, and polo. The famous Augusta National Golf Club course, home of the Masters Golf Tournament, is located here. Some of the points of interest are the Mackay Trading Post, Meadow Garden, Fort Augusta, Confederate Monument, New Savannah Bluff Lock and Dam System, churches of historic interest, and two large enclosed shopping malls, one of which is the largest in Georgia.

Branch Campuses: Fort Guidon.

PIEDMONT COLLEGE   *(C-6)*
Demorest, Georgia 30535
Tel: (706) 778-3000; (800) 277-7020; Fax: (706) 776-2811

Description: The private, liberal arts college is accredited by the Southern Association of Colleges and Schools. The college is related historically to the Congregational Christian Churches of the United States. The semester system is employed. Enrollment is 321 men and 527 women. A faculty of 50 full-time and 15 part-time gives a faculty-student ratio of 1-16. Founded in 1897, the college offers B.A. and B.S. degrees.

Entrance Requirements: High school graduation or GED with a C average and rank upper half of graduating class; completion of a minimum of 16 units including 4 English, 3 mathematics, 2 science, and 2 social science; SAT or ACT required, SAT preferred; early admission, early decision, rolling admission and advanced placement plans available; $20 application fee.

Costs Per Year: $5,640 tuition; $3,620 room and board; $450 student fees.

Collegiate Environment: The campus has 16 buildings on 50 acres. The library contains 100,000 volumes, 436 periodicals and 2,100 sound recordings, and is a repository for U.S. Geological survey maps. Dormitory capacity for 160 men and 100 women, and apartments for married students are available. Students of all denominations are welcomed, and midyear students are accepted.

Community Environment: Located in Habersham County in the northeastern corner of Georgia in the foothills of the southern Blue Ridge Mountains. Climate is considered unusually healthful. Buses serve the area with the railroad serving Toccoa, eighteen miles away. Atlanta, served by the International Airport, is 85 miles southwest.

REINHARDT COLLEGE   *(D-4)*
Waleska, Georgia 30183
Tel: (404) 479-1454; Admissions: (404) 720-5526; Fax: (404) 720-5602

Description: The private, two-year college is accredited by the Southern Association of Colleges and Schools and is affiliated with the Methodist Church. The quarter system is employed. Recent enrollment included 380 men and 475 women. A faculty of 40 full-time and 25 part-time gives a faculty-student ratio of 1-17.

Entrance Requirements: High school graduation from an accredited high school; SAT or ACT required; G.E.D. Certificates acceptable; application fee $15; midyear students accepted; early admission, early decision, rolling admission and delayed admission plans available.

Costs Per Year: $4,608 ($95/cr); $4,050 room and board; $510 student fees.

Collegiate Environment: The campus has 14 buildings on 565 acres. The library contains 45,000 current volumes, 15 periodicals, 1,719 microforms and 9,335 sound recordings. Dormitory space is provided for 407 men and women. Scholarships are awarded on basis of financial need; any student qualifying for aid will be assisted. 80% of the student body receives financial aid. 85% of the applicants are accepted. 85% of the freshman returned for the second year.

Community Environment: Waleska is located on the summit of a ridge, an hour's drive from metropolitan Atlanta. The high altitude assures a crisp, dry atmosphere and a year-round climate never excelled in its healthful and invigorating qualities. The picturesque southern foothills of the Blue Ridge Mountains surround Waleska.

SAVANNAH COLLEGE OF ART AND DESIGN   *(J-13)*
P.O. Box 3146
Savannah, Georgia 31402-3146
Tel: (912) 238-2483; Fax: (912) 238-2456

Description: The Savannah College of Art and Design is a private, nonprofit, tax-exempt, degree-granting college accredited by the Southern Association of Colleges and Schools. Students benefit from the focused curriculum of a specialized college, but still enjoy the wealth of extracurricular and athletic activities usually found at a university. The college grants the Bachelor of Fine Arts and Master of Fine Arts degrees and also awards the five-year Bachelor of Architecture degree. It operates on the quarter systems and offers one summer session. All students develop a strong base in the fine arts and liberal arts, with many options in course selection outside their majors. The college has a dedicated ESL faculty to teach and advise students as they become more fluent in English as a second language. International students may study ESL and at the same time enroll in other classes while improving their English language skills. The emphasis in all programs is career preparation. Classes are available in weekday and evening sessions. During the summer months, the college sponsors three- and four-week sessions in New York City and Europe, as well as a ten-week session in Savannah. Enrollment includes 2,206 full and part-time undergraduate and 282 graduate students. A faculty of 113 full-time and 30 part-time gives an undergraduate faculty-student ratio of 1-16.

Entrance Requirements: Recommended high school graduation with 2.0 GPA or higher, with exceptional aptitude for history or the visual arts; SAT or ACT; official transcript(s) from each high school or college attended; three letters of recommendation; graduate school applicant should be college graduate with 3.0 GPA or higher and exceptional aptitude for history or the visual arts; official transcript(s) from each college attended; three letters of recommendation; portfolio of studio work; personal interview required; rolling admissions policy.

Costs Per Year: $10,800 tuition; $3,100-$3,600 room; $1,000 books and supplies.

Collegiate Environment: Located in picturesque historic Savannah, the campus includes 38 buildings. Ten art galleries feature student work throughout the year. Ancillary services include a bookstore/cafe, two diners, an art framing and supply store, and a commercial printing press. The library contains 33,000 volumes. Residence hall space is provided for 600 students. Numerous student organizations are available. 65% of applicants are accepted. 85% of the student body receives some form of financial aid.

Community Environment: The college is located in the downtown historic district of Savannah, Georgia, only minutes from Georgia's golden coast. The metropolitan area population is 160,000. Savannah is a popular tourist area, creating activities available to students throughout the year. Students enjoy new-age technology in an old-world environment. The college's authentic double-decker London buses transport students to and from classes free of charge.

SAVANNAH STATE COLLEGE   *(J-13)*
Savannah, Georgia 31404
Tel: (912) 356-2181

Description: This state college, a unit of the University System of Georgia, is an undergraduate and graduate college of arts and sciences, with a School of Business, School of Sciences and Technology, and a School of Humanities and Social Sciences. The college enrolled 1,584 men and women. A faculty of 125 gives a faculty-student ratio of 1-14. It is accredited by the Southern Association of Colleges and Schools and operates on the quarter system. Founded in 1890 to serve the educational needs of black students, today the college offers a quality education to all students. The college has an advanced computer network to serve academic computing and is in the process of completing new buildings for the School of Business and Marine Biology.

Entrance Requirements: Accredited high school graduation with a minimum combined score on the SAT of 750. The following high school units are required: 4 English, 3 science, 3 mathematics, 2 social science, and 2 foreign language. Provisional admissions are available for those students who do not meet the SAT or high school unit requirements. GED accepted; SAT or ACT required; application fee

$10; rolling admission, early admission, and advanced placement plans available.

Costs Per Year: $1,635 resident day student; $4,215 nonresident day student; $3,780 resident boarding students; $6,360 nonresident boarding students.

Collegiate Environment: The campus consists of 38 buildings on 165 acres and presents a setting of unique natural beauty highlighted by 200 year old mossdraped oaks and salt marsh estuaries. Dormitory facilities available for 1,000 students and the library contains 264,274 bound volumes, 813 periodicals and 334,000 microforms. Ninety percent of students applying for admission are offered acceptance as regular or provisional students. Financial aid is available for students with demonstrated financial need and for students of high academic ability.

Community Environment: See Armstrong State College

SCHOOL OF VISUAL ARTS   *(J-13)*
110 President Street
Savannah, Georgia 31401
Tel: (912) 651-1280; (800) 218-8090; Fax: (912) 233-8076

Description: The privately supported, coeducational college, founded in 1993, is a branch campus of the School of Visual Arts, New York. It is fully accredited by the Middle States Association of Colleges and Schools. It operates on the semester system and offers one summer session. It grants the Bachelor degree. Special programs include continuing education courses and summer workshops in Greece and Spain. Enrollment includes 21 men and 9 women full-time with a faculty of 2 full-time and 3 part-time.

Entrance Requirements: High school diploma or GED required. SAT or ACT. Freshmen and transfer students admitted at midyear. Early decision and rolling admission plans. $30 application fee.

Costs Per Year: $9,000 tuition; $3,000 room; $220 student fees.

Collegiate Environment: The library contains 1,800 volumes and 55 periodicals. Dormitories accommodate 40 students. $100,000 is available for scholarships and 90% of the students receive financial aid.

Community Environment: Located in Savannah, GA, population 250,000. Students can take advantage of the architectual and design heritage in the suburban context of this small city.

SHORTER COLLEGE   *(D-2)*
315 Shorter Avenue
Rome, Georgia 30165-4298
Tel: (706) 291-2121; (800) 868-6980; Admissions: (706) 291-2121; Fax: (706) 236-1515

Description: The private liberal arts college was established in 1873 as the Cherokee Baptist Female College; it was moved to its present location in 1910. It is accredited by the Southern Association of Colleges and Schools and is controlled by the Georgia Baptist Convention. It operates on the semester system and offers one summer session. Enrollment includes 702 full-time and 80 part-time students. A full-time teaching faculty of 58 and 15 part-time gives a faculty-student ratio of 1-12. Admission requirements include a minimum age of 23 and two years full-time work experience. Documented learning from professional schools and courses, licenses, certifications and the like may be assessed for credit. Programs offered include a Communications Component for those with no prior college credit, a General Education Component for those with 15-41 semester hours of transfer credit, and a Degree Component leading to the degrees Bachelor of Science in Business Administration and Bachelor of Science in Management.

Entrance Requirements: High school graduation with a C average and 15 units including 4 English, 3 mathematics, 2 foreign language recommended, 3 social science and 3 science; early admission, rolling admission, midyear admission and advanced placement plans available. $20 application fee.

Costs Per Year: $7,100; $3,600 room and board; $110 activity fee.

Collegiate Environment: The campus has 16 buildings on 150 acres. The library contains 177,310 volumes. Residence halls accommodate 442 students. An activities complex with gymnasium was added in 1994. 79% of the applicants are accepted. The middle 50% range of scores for the entering freshman class was SAT 390-508 ver-

bal, 440-560 math. 40% of the class had graduated in the top 25% of their high school class. Scholarships are available. Nearly 100% of the students receive some form of financial aid, due to state tuition equalization.

Community Environment: Rome is located in the foothills of northwest Georgia, 68 miles northwest of Atlanta and 65 miles south of Chattanooga. The city enjoys an average temperature of 73 degrees, and a minimum of 49 degrees. All forms of transportation are available. More than 100 industries are situated here; some of them being General Electric, Inland Container Corporation, and the Georgia Kraft Co. Besides the usual community facilities, some of the cultural advantages are the municipal auditorium, symphony orchestra, little theatre, and art association. Golf courses, swimming pools, bowling alleys, tennis courts and the spectator sports provide for recreation. Allatoona Lake is 30 miles, where one can enjoy water skiing, motor boat races, sailing, and fishing. Weiss Lake is also within a short distance of Rome.

SOUTH GEORGIA COLLEGE   *(L-8)*
South Peterson Avenue
Douglas, Georgia 31533
Tel: (912) 383-4200; (800) 342-6364; Admissions: (912) 383-4210; Fax: (912) 383-4392

Description: The public community/junior college is accredited by the Southern Association of Colleges and Schools and the National League for Nursing. In 1927, the Eleventh District A & M School became South Georgia Junior State College, the first state-supported junior college in Georgia. The high school classes were discontinued in 1933 and the present name was adopted by 1937. The college grants the Associate degree. It operates on the quarter system and offers one summer session. Enrollment includes 424 men and 843 women. A faculty of 45 full-time and 14 part-time gives a faculty-student ratio of 1-20.

Entrance Requirements: Accredited high school graduation; non-high school graduates with GED certification; SAT or ACT required; Completion of 4 English, 3 math, 3 science, 2 foreign language, 3 social studies. Application fee $5; early admission, early decision, midyear admission, rolling admission and advanced placement plans available.

Costs Per Year: $1,074 tuition; $3,117 nonresidents; $2,670 room and board; $120 student fees.

Collegiate Environment: The college is a complex of 28 buildings plus the president's home and is located on more than 250 acres of beautiful grounds. Dormitory accommodations are available for 200 men and 200 women and the library contains 81,282 titles, 388 periodicals, 13,833 microforms, 3,085 audiovisual materials. Mid-year students are accepted and 75% of the students applying for admission are accepted. 50% of the freshman class returned to this campus for a second year. Scholarships are available and 75% of the freshman class receives some form of financial aid.

Community Environment: Douglas is situated in the southern part of Georgia; having a delightful climate, winters are mild, and the summers pleasant. This community is one of the largest tobacco markets in the South. Livestock, poultry, naval stores, light industry, and the manufacture of mobile homes. Part-time employment is available for students. The community facilities include churches of all denominations, regional library, hospital, community concert association. Recreational facilities are the golf course, recreation center, tennis courts, pools, etc.

SOUTHERN COLLEGE OF TECHNOLOGY   *(D-3)*
South Marietta Parkway
Marietta, Georgia 30060
Tel: (404) 528-7281; (800) 635-3204; Fax: (404) 528-7292

Description: The public, coeducational college is a unit of the University system of Georgia. The school offers Associate transfer programs and Bachelor degrees in the areas of engineering technology, architecture, computer science, construction, environmental development, mathematics, physics, management of technology, industrial distribution, technical and professional communication, and manufacturing. Master's degrees are offered in engineering technology, computer science, technical and professional communication, and management of technology. Founded in 1948, the school operates on the quarter system and offers one summer session. It is accredited by the Southern Association of Colleges and Schools. Enrollment includes 2,131 full-time and 1,343 part-time undergraduate students. There are 485 graduate studentds in Master's programs. A faculty of 140 full-time and 60 part-time members gives a faculty-student ratio of 1-20.

Entrance Requirements: High school graduation or equivalent; college preparatory courses including 4 English, 3 mathematics and 3 science; SAT or ACT required; early admission, delayed admission, and rolling admission plans available.

Costs Per Year: $1,689 state-resident tuition, $4,533 nonresident, $3,600 room and board.

Collegiate Environment: The college is located on a 200-acre campus in Marietta, Georgia, located 15 miles northwest of Atlanta. In addition to the academic and administration buildings, the campus includes a student center, which serves as a focal point for student life, two dormitories housing approximately 500 students and a library. The library houses a collection of more than 100,000 catalogued volumes and 40,000 nonbook items, including periodicals and audiovisual materials. Day and evening studies are available, as well as a cooperative education program. 77% of those who apply for admission are accepted, including midyear students. Limited financial aid is available.

Community Environment: See Kennesaw College.

SPELMAN COLLEGE   *(E-4)*
350 Spelman Lane, S.W.
Atlanta, Georgia 30314
Tel: (404) 681-3643; (800) 241-3421; Fax: (404) 215-7788

Description: The private, liberal arts college for women is accredited by the Southern Association of Colleges and Schools. The school was founded in 1881 in the basement of the Friendship Baptist Church with 11 pupils, mainly women out of slavery. In 1883, the Atlanta Baptist Female Seminary was moved to a new location and the first college degrees were granted in 1901; the name was changed to Spelman College in 1924. Although the college is proud of its heritage as the first college for black women, today it admits women without regard to race or creed. Enrollment is 1,933 full-time and 43 part-time students. A faculty of 134 full-time and 75 part-time gives a faculty-student ratio of 1-15. The college grants a Baccalaureate degree and became a part of the Atlanta University Center in 1929. It operates on the semester system. Men may enroll in any classes offered at Spelman as exchange students from the University Center.

Entrance Requirements: High school graduation with a minimum C average; completion of 15 units including 4 English, 2 mathematics (algebra and geometry), 2 science (including at least 1 laboratory science), and 2 social science; SAT or ACT required; $35 application fee; early admission, early decision, and CLEP plans available.

Costs Per Year: $8,875 tuition and fees; $5,890 room and board.

Collegiate Environment: The college is a member of the Atlanta University Center and shares facilities and resources of five other institutions of higher education in the Atlanta area. The library contains 409,991 volumes, 2,693 periodicals, 69,750 microform titles and 1,708 audiovisual materials. Dormitory facilities are available for 1,117 women. 36% of applicants are accepted. 85% of the students receive some form of financial aid.

Community Environment: See Clark Atlanta University.

THOMAS COLLEGE   *(N-5)*
1501 Millpond Rd.
Thomasville, Georgia 31792
Tel: (912) 226-1621; Fax: (912) 226-1653

Description: Founded in 1950, this independent 2-year college is accredited by the Southern Association of Colleges and Schools. It grants the Associate and Bachelors degrees. Army ROTC is available as an elective. The school operates on the quarter system and offers one summer session. Enrollment includes 635 full-time and 11 part-time stuedents. A faculty of 70 gives a faculty-student ratio of 1-17.

Entrance Requirements: Accredited high school graduation or equivalent; Comparative Guidance and Placement exam required for applicants out of high school over 3 years or without SAT or ACT scores; open enrollment policy; early admission, early decision, roll-

ing admission, and delayed admission plans available; $25 application fee.

Costs Per Year: $3,375 tuition; $300 student fees.

Collegiate Environment: The 18-acre campus, a portion of the former Birdwood plantation, is on the outskirts of Thomasville, a modern city known as "The Rose City." The library contains 32,500 volumes. Financial aid is available.

Community Environment: Thomasville is 50 miles west of Valdosta in southwest Georgia, less than an hour's drive to the Gulf of Mexico. This town is a natural beauty spot famed for its profusion of flowers. Many old plantations and estates are in the surrounding area. The Rose Festival is an annual event. Points of interest are the Big Oak, which is estimated to be 300 years old, and the Rose Test Gardens. The city population is 20,000. The county population is 39,000.

TOCCOA FALLS COLLEGE   *(C-7)*
Toccoa Falls, Georgia 30598
Tel: (404) 886-6831; (800) 868-3257; Fax: (706) 886-6412

Description: The private Christian College with a recent enrollment of 442 men and 469 women works in full fellowship with all evangelical Christian groups. A faculty of 59 gives a faculty-student ratio of 1-18. The college was established in 1907 to prepare dedicated persons for Christian ministries, and was authorized to grant Bachelor of Arts in biblical education in 1939. It now offers also a Bachelor of Science, a Bachelor of Theology and an Associate of Arts Degree. The college is accredited by the American Association of Bible Colleges and The Southern Association of Colleges and Schools. It operates on the 4-1-4 system with two summer sessions.

Entrance Requirements: High school graduation or GED equivalent; ACT or SAT scores; evidence of sound Christian experience and character; limited number of older students without high school credentials may be admitted as special students; application fee $20; early admission, early decision, rolling admission, delayed admission and advanced placement plans available.

Costs Per Year: $6,376 tuition; $3,708 room and board.

Collegiate Environment: The famous Toccoa Falls (17 feet higher than Niagara Falls) is located on the 1100-acre campus. Dormitory capacity for 567 is available. The library contains 88,648 volumes. Approximately 35% of the student body graduated in top 20% of high school class. 80% of the freshman class returned for the sophomore year. 75% of the applicants are accepted. Various forms of financial assistance are available; 80% of the students receive some form of aid. The college offers Bachelor degrees as well as an Associate degree in General Studies.

Community Environment: Toccoa is a rural area in the foothills of the Blue Ridge Mountains. The Southern Railway and Greyhound Bus provide public transportation. Industries located here are the manufacturing of machinery, garments, furniture and thread. Mountain lakes and resorts are a short distance, providing fishing, hunting, water sports, and picknicking. Toccoa has a municipal recreation center and golf course.

TRUETT-MCCONNELL COLLEGE   *(C-6)*
Cleveland, Georgia 30528
Tel: (404) 865-2138

Description: The private, coeducational junior college sponsored by the Georgia Baptist Convention is accredited by the Southern Association of Colleges and Schools. The college operates on the quarter system and offers one summer session. Current enrollment includes 881 men and 1,111 women. A faculty of 30 full-time and 105 part-time gives a faculty-student ratio of 1-12.

Entrance Requirements: High school graduation or equivalent; completion of 16 units, including 4 English, 2 mathematics, 2 science, 2 foreign language, and 2 social science; SAT or ACT required; minimum SAT scores of 325 verbal and 325 math required; non-high school graduates considered; application fee $20; early admission, early decision, rolling admission, delayed admission and advanced placement plans available.

Costs Per Year: $3,825 tuition, $2,505 room & board; $105 student fees.

Collegiate Environment: The campus has 14 buildings. Dormitory space for 180 men and 179 women is provided. The library contains 30,000 volumes, 180 periodicals, 500 microforms, and 1,847 audiovisual materials. Approximately 50% of the current freshmen receive financial assistance. Ninety percent of the applicants are accepted.

Community Environment: Cleveland is in the mountains of north Georgia, a few miles south of the famous Vogel State Park. Bus service is available. The community, with its inspiring mountain scenery, provides a wholesome environment for young people. The Chattahoochee National Forest is 10 miles away.

UNIVERSITY OF GEORGIA *(E-7)*
Athens, Georgia 30602
Tel: (404) 542-2112

Description: Established in 1785 as a land-grant institution, The University of Georgia is the oldest chartered university in the United States. It is accredited by the Southern Association of Colleges and Schools. The University has developed its curriculum from a program of classical studies to over 170 fields of study in 13 schools and colleges: Agriculture, Arts and Sciences, Business Administration, Education, Environmental Design, Veterinary Medicine, Forest Resources Journalism, Home Economics, Law, Pharmacy, Social Work, and the Graduate School. The University has several study-abroad programs in France, Mexico, Spain, Germany, Italy, and England. It grants the Bachelor Master's and Dorctoral degrees. The university operates on the quarter system and offers three summer sessions. Enrollment includes 22,832 undergraduates and 6,637 graduate students. An instructional faculty of 1,788 full-time and 139 part-time gives an undergraduate faculty-student ratio of 1-14.

Entrance Requirements: High school graduation with a B average (3.0) and 15 units including 4 English, 3 mathematics, 3 science, and 3 social science; minimum combined SAT score of 950; high school equivalency diploma accepted; non-high school graduates considered; early admission, early decision, rolling admission, midyear admission for transfer students and advanced placement plans available; a compact with Maryland and West Virginia makes it possible for the School of Veterinary Medicine to accept applicants from those states. $25 undergraduate application fee; $30 graduate application fee.

Costs Per Year: $2,175 tuition; $5,757 out-of-state; $3,615 room and board; $1,335 miscellaneous.

Collegiate Environment: The University has 299 buildings and lies in the heart of Athens. The campus and adjacent land used by the College of Agriculture and School of Forest Resources encompass approximately 5,000 acres; in addition, the University holds about 38,000 acres of land throughout Georgia. The library contains 3,215,717 volumes, 55,954 periodicals, 4,518,130 microforms, and 36,725 audiovisual materials. Housing capacity includes dormitory space for 7,627 men and women; sorority/fraternity quarters for 1,312; and 545 units for married students. 78% of those who apply for admission are accepted. The average scores of the current freshman class were SAT 497 verbal, 548 math. About 85% of the freshmen return for the second year. A wide choice of financial assistance plans are available. 10,937 scholarships and grants are offered and 50% of the students receive some form of financial aid.

Community Environment: Athens, the largest city in the rolling Piedmont area of northeast Georgia, is 70 miles northeast of Atlanta. Many of its building exemplify Greek Revival architecture characteristic of the Old South. It enjoys a mild climate, with an annual mean temperature of 60 degrees. Recreational facilities include parks, golf courses, swimming pools, tennis courts, baseball parks, a bowling center, and skating rinks, as well as areas for hunting, fishing and boating. Athens, serviced by buses and an airline, has numerous lodging accommodations and restaurants both in town and on campus. Its manufactured products include textiles, plastics, metals, electrical equipment, dairy products, and paper goods.

VALDOSTA STATE UNIVERSITY *(N-7)*
North Patterson Street
Valdosta, Georgia 31698
Tel: (912) 333-5791; (800) 618-1878; Fax: (912) 333-5482

Description: This publically supported, four-year university is accredited by the Southern Association of Colleges and Schools. Founded in 1913 as South Georgia State Normal College for Young Ladies with a two-year program, it progressed to a four-year program in 1922, a name-change and coeducational in 1950, and was elevated to university status in 1993. Programs of study lead to the Associate, Bachelor, Master, and Doctorate degrees in liberal arts and education. Enrollment includes 6,442 full-time, 1,295 part-time undergraduate, and 1,423 graduate students. A faculty of 392 full-time and 80 part-time gives a faculty-student ratio of 1-21. Air Force ROTC is available.

Entrance Requirements: High school graduation with completion of 15 units including 4 English, 3 mathematics, 3 science, 2 foreign language and 3 social science; non high school graduates with GED certification; SAT or ACT required, minimum SAT Verbal 400, Math 400 for unconditional admission; early admission, rolling admission, midyear admission and advanced placement plans available; $10 application fee.

Costs Per Year: $1,785 state resident tuition; $4,629 nonresident tuition; $3,030 room and board; $600 student fees.

Collegiate Environment: The college is comprised of two campuses that are located less than a mile from each other and total more than 175 acres. Both campuses are recognized for their exceptional beauty and are connected by a college-owned bus service that operates regularly throughout each class day. 29 buildings serve the college including the library containing 372,960 volumes, 3,000 periodicals, 854,468 microforms, and 10,158 audiovisual materials. Dormitory facilities are available for 1,850 students. 68% of applicants are accepted, including midyear students. Of 100 scholarships offered, 75 are for freshmen, and 45% of students receive some form of financial assistance. 70% of freshmen returned for their sophomore year.

Community Environment: Valdosta, located in the south-central section of Georgia, is the largest city of the 16-county area that it serves. Buses and railroads serve the area, and airlines are available in Valdosta, Tallahassee, Jacksonville and Atlanta. Average temperature for the year is 67 degrees. Valdosta is the largest inland naval stores market in the world. Industries are tobacco, lumber, mobile homes, cotton, paper and metal goods. Part-time jobs for students are plentiful. Valdosta Entertainment Association brings outstanding cultural events to the city. The Gulf of Mexico and the Atlantic Ocean are within 125 miles. Near the city are numerous freshwater lakes that provide fishing, boating, water skiing, beaches for swimming and picnic areas. Valdosta boasts a congenial atmosphere and friendly spirit. Newcomers and visitors are welcomed.

WESLEYAN COLLEGE *(H-6)*
4760 Forsyth Road
Macon, Georgia 31297
Tel: (912) 477-1110; (800) 447-6610; Fax: (912) 757-4030

Description: The private, liberal arts college for women is accredited by the Southern Association of Colleges and Schools and is affiliated with the United Methodist Church. Wesleyan obtained the first state charter for granting degrees to women in 1836. The college operates on the early semester system. Enrollment includes 500 full-time and 58 part-time students. A faculty of 39 full-time and 19 part-time provides a faculty-student ratio of 1-10. The college grants the Baccalaureate degree.

Entrance Requirements: High school graduation with completion of 16 units including 4 English, 3 mathematics, 2 science, 3 social studies, and 4 academic electives; non-high school graduates considered; acceptable SAT or ACT scores; two recommendations, one from English teacher, and an essay; early admission, rolling admission and advanced placement plans available; $25 application fee.

Costs Per Year: $11,500 tuition; $4,500 room and board; $180 activity fee; $175 software fee; $500 estimated cost for books.

Collegiate Environment: The campus has 15 buildings on 200 acres. The library contains 136,735 volumes, 561 periodicals, 21,141 microforms and 6,354 audiovisual materials. Dormitory space is available for 550 women. 84% of the applicants are accepted. The average SAT score of entering freshmen is 1014 combined. Financial aid is available and 80% of students receive some form of aid.

Community Environment: The college is located in suburban Macon. There are 5 other coed colleges within a 60-mile radius of Macon.

WEST GEORGIA COLLEGE   *(F-2)*
Maple Street
Carrollton, Georgia 30118
Tel: (404) 836-6500

Description: The college is accredited by the Southern Association of Colleges and Schools. All programs preparing teachers through the masters level are accredited by the National Council for Accreditation Teacher Education, and by the Georgia State Department of Education. Other programs are professionally accredited by respective institutions. In 1933 the Board of Regents of the University System of Georgia established the school as a junior college member of the University System. Since becoming a senior college in 1957, the college has been among the faster growing institutions of higher education in the South. The college grants an Associate, Baccalaureate, Master's and Specialist (post-Master's) degree. Additionlly, the college offers three Ed.D. programs in cooperation with the University of Georgia. Army ROTC is also availble. The college operates on the quarter system,and offers one summmer session. Enrollment includes 4,750 full-time and 1,240 part-time undergraduates and 2,320 graduate students. A faculty of 349 gives a faculty-student ratio of 1-24.

Entrance Requirements: Applicants must have a 2.5 high school academic grade point average or a total SAT score of 700 (ACT composite 17): 18 high school units are required, including 4 English, 3 math, 2 lab science, 2 foreign language, and 3 social studies. Early admission, midyear admission, rolling admission, rolling admission, and advanced placement plans are available; $10 application fee.

Costs Per Year: $1,515 state-resident tuition; $4,356 out-of-state; $2,913 room and board; $384 student fees.

Collegiate Environment: The college is situated on 395 acres of land, much of which is wooded. The campus is noted for its exceptional beauty. Dormitory facilities are available for 995 men and 1,767 women, and the library contains 307,487 standard bound volumes, 1,511 periodicals and 951,773 microforms. 73% of students applying for admission are accepted, including midyear students. Financial assistance is available. 50% of students receive some form of aid.

Community Environment: Located in northwest Georgia, 48 miles southwest of the state capital, Atlanta, Carrollton has a mild climate with an average temperature of 63 degrees. Part-time employment is available. The benefits of this unique area include a safe, peaceful small town atmosphere, offering educational excellence in a personal environment, within 45 minutes of the cultural and social diversities of Atlanta. Private housing is available.

Branch Campuses: Dalton, GA; Newman, GA.

YOUNG HARRIS COLLEGE   *(B-6)*
P.O. Box 98
Young Harris, Georgia 30582
Tel: (706) 379-3111; (800) 241-3754; Fax: (706) 379-4306

Description: The private junior college is affiliated with the United Methodist Church and is accredited by the Southern Association of Colleges and Schools. The college was founded in 1886 as a four-year institution and became a junior college in 1912. It operates on the quarter system and offers one summer session. Enrollment includes 550 students. A faculty of 34 provides a faculty-student ratio of 1-15. The school will cover 100% of students' demonstrated financial need.

Entrance Requirements: High school graduation or equivalent; non-high school graduates considered; SAT or ACT required; early admission, early decision, advanced placement, rolling admission and delayed admission plans available; $25 application fee.

Costs Per Year: $5,360 tuition; $3,405 room and board; $540 student fees.

Collegiate Environment: The campus has 18 buildings on 35 acres. There are modern residence halls for 204 women and for 238 men. The library contains 60,383 volumes, 220 periodicals, and 10,900 microforms. The Maxwell Center for Business, Mathematics, and Science houses a 110-seat Spitz Planetarium. The gymnasium has an indoor swimming pool of six lanes. The new Goolsby Center offers large, modern classrooms and a state-of-the-art black box theatre. Extracurricular activity groups include the art students league, a theatre/drama group and a choir ensemble. There is a student newspaper and a literary magazine. A health clinic and personal counseling are available. 70% of applicants are accepted. The average scores of entering freshmen were ACT 23, SAT 910 combined. There are 75 scholarships available and 71% of students receive some form of financial aid.

Community Environment: Young Harris is situated in the Blue Ridge Mountains; the climate is moderate. Atlanta, Asheville, Chattanooga and Greenville, South Carolina, are within one hundred miles. Shopping facilities are limited. Baptist and Methodist churches, a Lions Club, a clinic, and two hospitals serve the community. Recreational activities are fishing, boating, hiking, horseback riding, picnicking, swimming, tennis, and golf. The county fair is an annual event.

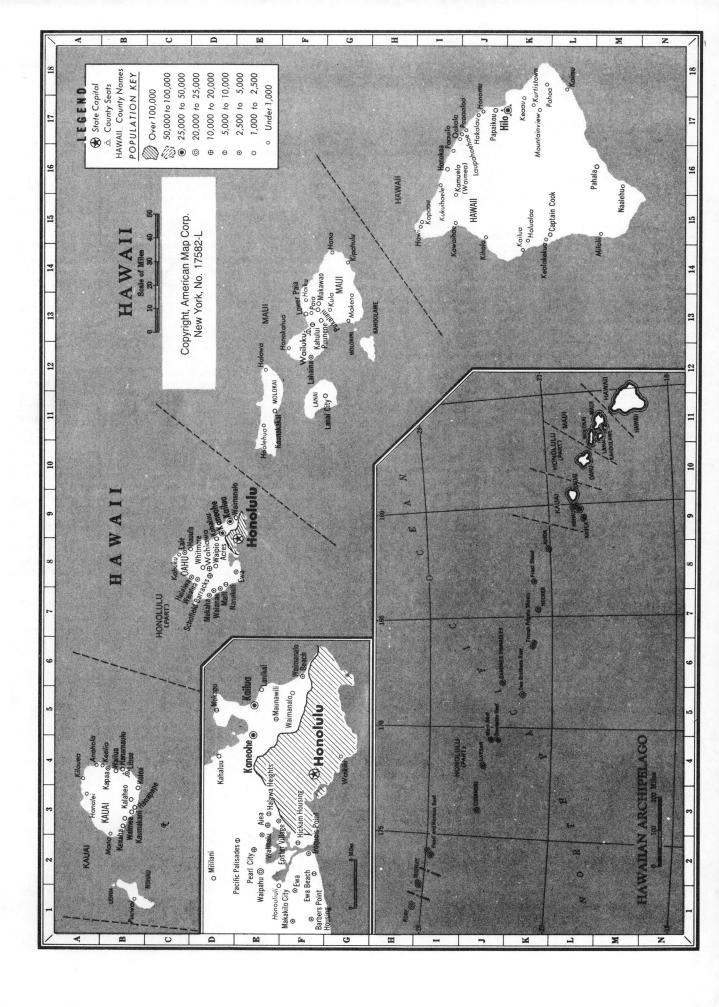

HAWAII

LEGEND

- ✪ State Capital
- ◌̇ County Seats
- HAWAII. County Names

POPULATION KEY

- ▨ Over 100,000
- ▨ 50,000 to 100,000
- ◉ 25,000 to 50,000
- ◎ 20,000 to 25,000
- ⊕ 10,000 to 20,000
- ⊖ 5,000 to 10,000
- ⊙ 2,500 to 5,000
- ○ 1,000 to 2,500
- ○ Under 1,000

Scale of Miles

HAWAII

KAUAI

MAUI

MOLOKAI

LANAI

KAHOOLAWE

HAWAII

HONOLULU (PART)

OAHU

Honolulu

Hilo

HAWAIIAN ARCHIPELAGO

NORTH PACIFIC OCEAN

HAWAII

AMERICAN SCHOOL OF PROFESSIONAL PSYCHOLOGY
(F-4)
845 22nd Avneue, Building MDLC
Honolulu, Hawaii 96816-4521
Tel: (808) 735-0109; (800) 626-5636; Fax: (808) 734-2875

Description: The privately supported graduate school is fully accredited by the North Central Association of Colleges and Schools. It operates on a trimester system with one summer session. The school was established in 1994 to provide a setting in which extensive training could be pursued in the area of professional psychology. It does not promote any one clinical psychological orientation. Currently, it offers psychoanalytic, client centered, experimental, family systems, integrative-eclectic, behavioral, neuropsychological, and group approaches to intervention. The school grants Masters and Doctorate (PsyD) degrees. Current enrollment is 79 students with faculty of 25.

Entrance Requirements: Graduation from an accredited institution with a baccalaurate or more advanced degree.

Costs Per Year: $13,540 tuition; $300-$500 fees.

Collegiate Environment: A coeducational professional school, it has a great diversity of students, ranging from recent college graduates to change-of-career students. The school maintains a learning center containing computer and research equipment, current periodicals, journals, books, and other research aids. In addition, students have borrowing privileges with the Hawaii State Library System, Sinclair and Hamilton Libraries at the University of Hawaii, and the Hawaii State Hospital Medical Library. Financial aid is available.

Community Environment: The school is located in a quiet residential area just minutes from the business district of Honolulu. Students of the Hawaii Campus enjoy convenient access to theaters, museums, art galleries, and shopping. In addition, the location offers an abundance of outdoor activities. Training sites are available in the Honolulu mentropolitan area.

Branch Campuses: Arlington, VA; Atlanta, GA; Chicago, IL; Minneapolis, MN; Rolling Measows, IL.

BRIGHAM YOUNG UNIVERSITY - HAWAII CAMPUS *(C-8)*
55-220 Kulanui Ave.
Laie, Hawaii 96762
Tel: (808) 293-3738; Fax: (808) 293-3741

Description: The private liberal arts college is accredited by the Western Association of Schools and Colleges. The college was founded in 1955 and is controlled by the Church of Jesus Christ of Latter-day Saints. More than one-fourth of its students are from foreign countries and an international atmosphere prevails at the college. Enrollment is 2,000 full-time and 100 part-time students. A faculty of 111 full-time and 40 part-time gives a faculty-student ratio of 1-19. A 4-4-2-2 term system is used and one summer session is offered.

Entrance Requirements: High school graduation with rank in upper half of graduating class; non-high school graduates over 21 considered; foreign students are required to meet college standards of English Proficiency Test; ACT recommended; $10 application fee; early admission, early decision, delayed admission, midyear admission, and advanced placement plans available.

Costs Per Year: $2,375 tuition for Latter-day Saint members; $3,565 tuition for others; $4,375 room and board.

Collegiate Environment: The college's modern campus is grouped in several clusters, with the main classroom and administration cluster serving as the focal point. Further away are classrooms, laboratories, and seminar rooms, all equipped with instructional television and other modern educational equipment. The campus is located on 60 acres of land with dormitory facilities for 416 men and 740 women. There are also 250 apartments available for married students. Army

and Air Force ROTC available. 50% of applicants are accepted. The library contains more than 160,000 volumes, 1,000 periodicals, 470,000 microforms and 4,650 audiovisual materials. Financial aid is available, and 60% of the current enrollment receives some sort of financial aid.

Community Environment: A rural community on the island of Oahu, 35 miles from Honolulu on the seashore, Laie is nestled against the Koolau Mountain range. The adjacent Mormon Temple is the "Taj-Mahal of the South Pacific." The Polynesian Culture Center is made up of seven native villages representative of those in Fiji, Tonga, New Zealand, Tahiti, Samoa, and Hawaii. Outdoor sports are surfing, fishing, and scuba diving.

CHAMINADE UNIVERSITY OF HONOLULU *(E-8)*
3140 Waialae Avenue
Honolulu, Hawaii 96816-1578
Tel: (808) 735-4711; (800) 735-3733; Admissions: (808) 735-4735; Fax: (808) 739-4647

Description: The private university is affiliated with the Roman Catholic Church and accredited by the Western Association of Schools and Colleges. Enrollment included 800 students both full and part time in day and evening sessions. The semester system is used and 2 summer sessions are offered. Programs of study lead to the Associate, Bachelor's, and Master's degrees. Enrollment includes 800 full-time and 160 part-time and 1,500 evening program undergraduates and 450 students. A faculty of 58 full-time and 100 part-time gives a faculty-student ratio of 1-16.

Entrance Requirements: High school graduation with 2.5 GPA; 16 units including 4 English, 3 mathematics, 2 science, 3 social studies, 4 electives (4 should be college prep); early admission, rolling admission, midyear admission and advanced placement plans available; SAT and ACT required. Minimum Scores SAT V450; M450; ACT:20; $50 application fee.

Costs Per Year: $10,600 tuition resident; $5,300 room and board.

Collegiate Environment: The college is located on 62 acres in the St. Louis Heights section about two miles from the Waikiki area and four miles from downtown Honolulu. The campus is shared with St. Louis, a secondary school. Dormitory facilities accommodate 232 men and women. The library contains 60,000 volumes, 550 periodicals, 3,000 microforms, and recordings. The college seeks a geographically diverse student body. 86% of the students applying for admission are accepted including midyear. Financial aid is available. Army and Air Force ROTC are also available.

Community Environment: See University of Hawaii - Manoa.

HAWAII PACIFIC UNIVERSITY *(E-8)*
1164 Bishop St.
Honolulu, Hawaii 96813
Tel: (808) 544-0200; (800) 669-4724; Admissions: (808) 544-0238; Fax: (808) 544-1136

Description: This coeducational, privately supported university and graduate school is accredited by the Western Association of Schools and Colleges and the National League for Nursing and was founded in 1965. It grants the Associate, Bachelor, and Masters degrees in 40 areas in the liberal arts and business. In addition, the school offers a 45-semester-hour MBA program, a 36-hour MSIS program, and a 45-hour Human Resource Management program. The university is nationally known for its developmental mathematics and English programs, and its ESL program. It operates on the 4-1-4 system and offers three summer sessions. Enrollment includes 4,080 full-time and 2,895 part-time undergraduate students. A faculty of 141 full-time and

351 part-time gives a faculty-student ratio of 1-18. In addition, there are 935 graduate students on campus.

Entrance Requirements: High school graduation or equivalent; ACT or SAT accepted but not required; high school students with a C+ average (2.5 GPA) are accepted; early admission, early decision, rolling admission, delayed admission, and advanced placement plans available.

Costs Per Year: $6,300 tuition and fees.

Collegiate Environment: HPU is the "Downtown University" in Honolulu, located in seven modern buildings in the heart of the business district, in close proximity to most of Hawaii's major governmental, business, and cultural institutions. The university has a residential 135-acre campus eight miles away, linked by a free shuttle bus system. Housing may be arranged for students near the college or in University dormitories. The university features a rich curricular and extracurricular program of activities and student organizations, including some 37 preprofessional, social, cultural, and honor organizations; a newspaper; a literary magazine; and theatrical productions. Students from 50 states of the Union and 80 foreign countries are in attendance. The University admits 72% of applicants, including students at midyear. It participates in all federal and Hawaii financial aid programs. 35% of students receive some form of financial aid. Library holdings include 122,000 titles, 1,750 periodicals, 207,000 microforms, and 16,650 audiovisual materials.

Community Environment: Honolulu, the travel capital of the world and nexus of the Pacific Basin, is a cosmopolitan city of some 800,000. Its leading industries are the travel industry, agriculture, and government-related services. Positions are available for HPU students in a wide variety of fields via the university's Cooperative Education Program and, for upper-division and MBA students, its Internship Program. Such cultural institutions as the Bishop Museum, the Honolulu Academy of Arts, and the Honolulu Symphony are located within two to four miles of the campus. Recreation facilities, most of them free, are widely available throughout Hawaii and are among the finest in the world; also among the world's finest are Hawaii's many major restaurants and hotels.

HEALD BUSINESS COLLEGE   *(E-8)*
1500 Kapiolani Boulevard
Honolulu, Hawaii 96814
Tel: (808) 955-1500; Fax: (808) 955-6964

Description: This private, business college was founded in 1863 and is accredited by the Accrediting Commission for Community and Junior Colleges of the Western Association of Schools and Colleges. The college offers two-year programs leading to the Associate degree in accounting, business administration and sales, medical assisting, office administration, secretarial, tourism and hotel management. The quarter system is used. Enrollment includes 350 full-time and 150 part-time and 100 evening students. A faculty of 25 full-time provides a faculty-student ratio of 1-24.

Entrance Requirements: High school graduation or equivalent; entrance exam prior to final acceptance; $50 application fee.

Costs Per Year: $6,300 ($2,100/quarter) tuition.

Collegiate Environment: The College occupies 30,000 square feet in the 1500 Kapiolani Building, which is accessible to the handicapped. The second floor is the hub of student activity, with academic and accounting department offices easily accessible. The college bookstore and snack shop are adjacent to the student lounge. The third floor focuses on a spacious resource center, modern computer center for information processing classes, office procedures classroom and medical assisting classroom.

Community Environment: Heald is conveniently located in the Ala Moana/Kapiolani Business District just one block from the huge Ala Moana shopping, hotel, and office complex. Its location offers favorable transportation factors: Kapiolani Boulevard is a primary traffic artery that provides a direct link with both downtown and Waikiki, freeway access is excellent, and Ala Moana is a focal point of the bus system providing public transportation to all parts of the island. See also University of Hawaii-Manoa.

HONOLULU COMMUNITY COLLEGE   *(E-8)*
874 Dillingham Blvd.
Honolulu, Hawaii 96817
Tel: (808) 845-9129

Description: Two-year state college is administered by the University of Hawaii. The school was established in 1920 as a territorial trade school. It is accredited by the Western Association of Schools and Colleges. Programs of study are primarily vocational-technical and lead to the certificate or Associate degree. It operates on the semester system with two summer sessions. Army ROTC is available. Enrollment includes 5,147 full-time and part-time students. A faculty of 215 gives a faculty-student ratio of 1-24.

Entrance Requirements: High school graduation or equivalent; nongraduates 18 years of age or older admitted; open enrollment; early admission, midyear admission, advanced placement and rolling admission plans available.

Costs Per Year: $500 tuition and fees; $2,940 nonresident tuition and fees.

Collegiate Environment: The campus is located one mile from the heart of downtown Honolulu. Educational programs in twenty-six trade-technical areas are offered. The library contains 52,642 books, 280 magazine titles and periodicals. Ninety-seven percent of the students applying for admission are accepted, including midyear students. Financial aid is available for economically disadvantaged students. 19% of students receive some form of financial aid.

Community Environment: See University of Hawaii - Manoa.

KAPIOLANI COMMUNITY COLLEGE   *(E-8)*
4303 Diamond Head Road
Honolulu, Hawaii 96816
Tel: (808) 734-9111; Admissions: (808) 734-9559

Description: Two-year college is administered by the University of Hawaii. This college was a established in 1957 as technical school and is accredited by the Western Association of Colleges and Schools. It grants certificates and the Associate degree. The college operates on the semester system and offers one summer session. Enrollment includes 2,627 full-time and 5,012 part-time students. A faculty of 190 full-time and 127 part-time gives a faculty-student ratio of 1-24.

Entrance Requirements: High school graduation or 18 years old; rolling admission; $10 nonresident application fee.

Costs Per Year: $500 state resident tuition and fees; $2,940 tuition for nonresidents.

Collegiate Environment: The library contains 23,000 volumes and 305 periodicals. Financial aid is available for economically disadvantaged students. The campus has 52 acres. This campus offers liberal arts, vocational-career programs and some allied health programs on one of the most scenic parts of Oahu.

Community Environment: See University of Hawaii - Manoa.

KAUAI COMMUNITY COLLEGE   *(B-4)*
3-1901 Kaumualii Highway
Lihue, Hawaii 96766
Tel: (808) 245-8311; Admissions: (808) 245-8225; Fax: (808) 246-6377

Description: The two-year state college is accredited by the Western Association of Schools and Colleges. It offers programs in liberal arts, college transfer, health service, public service, business and trade-technical subjects. This college was established in 1923 as vocational school, and in 1964 the school administration was transferred to the University of Hawaii and the college was converted to a community college. It operates on the semester system is and offers one summer session. Enrollment includes 625 full-time and 882 part-time students. A faculty of 84 full-time and 34 part-time gives a faculty-student ratio of 1-13.

Entrance Requirements: High school graduation; open enrollment policy; non-high school graduates considered; early admission.

Costs Per Year: $450 resident, $2,690 nonresident.

Collegiate Environment: The campus has 11 buildings on 100 acres. The library contains 36,000 volumes, 2,000 pamphlets, 366 periodicals, 5,746 microforms and 20,000 audiovisual materials. 95% of the students applying for admission are accepted. Financial aid is available and 20% of students receive some form of financial assistance.

Community Environment: Kauai is known as the "Garden Island," offering magnificent scenery and lush vegetation, beautiful waterfalls, the spectacular Waimea Canyon, the great "hidden" valley of Kalalau, and colorful tropical plants and flowers. Airlines and boats serve the area. Honolulu is 100 nautical miles away. Industries are sugar and tourism; oceanography research and development is conducted here. Community facilities include five public libraries and many churches of all denominations. Several county beach parks and one major state park provide recreation facilities for boating, swimming, scuba diving, deepsea and surf fishing. Wild boar, goat and pheasant hunting are favorite sports.

LEEWARD COMMUNITY COLLEGE   *(E-2)*
96-045 Ala Ike
Pearl City, Hawaii 96782
Tel: (808) 455-0217

Description: Two-year state college is administered by the University of Hawaii and accredited by the Western Association of Schools and Colleges. The college was established in 1968 on a newly developed campus. Enrollment includes 2,623 full-time and 3,821 part-time students. A faculty of 179 full-time and 286 part-time gives a faculty-student ratio of 1-23. The college operates on the semester system and offers one summer session. Army and Air Force ROTC programs are available as electives at the University of Hawaii (Manoa Campus).

Entrance Requirements: High school graduation or equivalent; open enrollment policy; non-high school graduates considered; early admission and midyear admission plans available; $10 application fee for nonresidents.

Costs Per Year: $504 state-resident tuition; $3,096 nonresident tuition; $15 student fees.

Collegiate Environment: The campus has 49.5 acres and is still being developed. The library contains 51,484 volumes, 416 periodicals, 12,523 microforms and 5,343 audiovisual materials. Scholarships are available. 10% of students receive some form of financial aid. All state residents applying for admission are accepted.

Community Environment: See University of Hawaii - Manoa.

MAUI COMMUNITY COLLEGE   *(F-13)*
310 Kaahumanu Avenue
Kahului, Hawaii 96732
Tel: (808) 244-9181; Admissions: (808) 242-1276; Fax: (808) 242-9618

Description: The two-year college is administered by the University of Hawaii. The college was established in 1965 as a vocational school. It provides occupational, transfer, liberal arts and general education programs. The college is accredited by the Western Association of Schools and Colleges. It operates on the semester system and offers one summer session. Enrollment includes 1,542 full-time and 1,897 part-time students. The faculty-student ratio averages 22-1.

Entrance Requirements: High school graduation; non-graduates 18 years of age or older admitted. Open enrollment; early admission plan available.

Costs Per Year: $504 tuition and fees; $3,096 nonresident tuition and fees; room available.

Collegiate Environment: The campus has 24 buildings on 78 acres. The library contains 24,449 volumes and 250 periodicals. Dormitory facilities accommodate 25 men and 30 women. Scholarships are available. 9% of the students receive some form of financial aid.

Community Environment: Kahului is an urban community on the Island of Maui enjoying an average temperature of 74.9 degrees. Both airlines and boats serve the area. The community facilities include churches of most denominations, hospital, clinic and shopping center. The pineapple and sugar industries provide work during the summer. Recreational activities are mainly surfing and swimming. The Island of Maui has three golf courses; the Maui Country Club, Royal Kaanapali Golf Course and the Waiehu Golf Course.

UNIVERSITY OF HAWAII - HILO   *(J-17)*
1400 Kapiolani Street
Hilo, Hawaii 96720-4091
Tel: (808) 933-3311; Fax: (808) 933-3691

Description: The University of Hawaii at Hilo is composed of the College of Arts and Sciences and the College of Agriculture. The institution is a public, residential, liberal arts university. It is accredited by the Western Association of Schools and Colleges. It operates on the semester system and offers one summer session. Enrollment includes 2,159 full-time and 711 part-time students. A faculty of 206 full-time and 75 part-time gives a faculty-student ratio of 1-13.

Entrance Requirements: High school graduation with rank in upper 50% of class; completion of 15 units including 4 English, 2 mathematics, 2 natural science, and 7 electives; high school equivalency diploma accepted; minimum SAT score of 800 combined or ACT composite 19 required; non-high school graduates considered; early admission, rolling admission, and advanced placement plans available; $10 application fee for nonresidents.

Costs Per Year: $480 state-resident tuition; $2,800 nonresident; $3,537 room and board; $50 student fees.

Collegiate Environment: The campus is located on a 115-acre site on the island of Hawaii. Dormitory facilities accommodate 690 students. The library contains 200,000 volumes and numerous pamphlets, periodicals and microforms. Other facilities include the Space Grant College, Small Business Development Center, Kalakaua Marine Education Center and an additional 110-acre agricultural farm in Panaewa. The college seeks a geographically diverse student body. Financial aid is available, and 32% of the current enrollment receives some form of assistance.

Community Environment: Hilo is a metropolitan area on Hawaii Island located 200 air miles from Honolulu. It has a semitropical climate with temperatures averaging in the 70s both summer and winter. The average rainfall is 130 inches, most of which falls at night. Both temperatures and rainfall vary due to range of elevations on the rest of the island. Aloha and Hawaiian Airlines serve the island. Agriculture and tourism are the economic bases of the island. Shopping facilities are good in Hilo. The cultural opportunities are numerous. Recreational activities are deep sea fishing, bird and game hunting, swimming and other water sports, hiking, camping, and horseback riding in the mountains. Golf courses, bowling centers, swimming pool, tennis courts, gymnasiums and ball parks are other available facilities for recreation. Hawaii Island has the only active volcano in the state. More orchids are grown here than any other place in the world. The island is rich in historical sites.

Branch Campuses: University of Hawaii - West Hawaii, Kealekekua, HI (Kona).

UNIVERSITY OF HAWAII - MANOA   *(E-8)*
2600 Campus Road, Room 001
Honolulu, Hawaii 96822
Tel: (808) 956-8975

Description: State university founded in 1907 and accredited by the Western Association of Schools and Colleges. In 1920 the College of Arts and Sciences was added, and the institution became the University of Hawaii. Geographical location generates interest in tropical agriculture, oceanography, geophysics, and marine sciences. The academic work at the university is administered by seven colleges with programs in arts and sciences, business administration, education, engineering, continuing education, health sciences and social welfare, and tropical agriculture. Four professional schools are included in the College of Health Sciences and Social Welfare: Medicine, Nursing, Public Health, and Social Work. The School of Architecture, the School of Library Studies, the School of Law and the School of Ocean, Earth Science & Technology are additional professional schools. The university operates on the semester system and offers two summer sessions. Undergraduate enrollment is 11,307 full-time and 2,188 part-time students. There are 6,720 graduate students. A faculty of 1,227 full-time and 257 part-time gives an undergraduate faculty-student ratio of 1-11. Army and Air Force ROTC programs are available.

Entrance Requirements: High school graduation with rank in upper 40%; 15 units including 4 English, 2 mathematics (including second-year algebra or geometry), 2 science, and 7 other college-preparatory courses (additional science, higher mathematics, language, and/or social studies); SAT average 438V, 538M; early admission, rolling admission, advanced placement plans available; non-high school graduates considered; application deadlines are May 1 for fall, Nov 1 for spring; $10 application fee for nonresidents.

Costs Per Year: $1,460 resident tuition; $4,460 nonresidents; $5,103 room and board, $97 student fees.

Collegiate Environment: The campus has 280 buildings on 300 acres located a ten-minute drive from Waikiki Beach. Dormitory facilities accommodate 3,183 students. Library holdings include 2,786,852 volumes and numerous periodical subscriptions, microfiche, and audiovisual media. 64% of applicants are accepted. The average SAT scores of enrolled freshmen are 438 verbal, 538 math. Financial aid and scholarships are available. 37% of students receive some form of financial aid.

Community Environment: Honolulu is on the island of Oahu, the third largest of the Hawaiian Islands, and is the home of over 750,000 persons, which is over 80% of Hawaii's population. The transportation, primarily by air throughout the islands, is excellent. The airlines offer frequent daily flights by jet to the other main islands of Hawaii. A cosmopolitan influence is seen everywhere in Hawaii's architecture, music, art, theater, dress and foods. Cultures from other lands have filtered down through the generations to produce what is called today a "typical Hawaiian atmosphere." The Bishop Museum is famous for its collections of Pacific arts and artifacts. The Honolulu Academy of Arts, Symphony Orchestra, Honolulu Community Theater, the Magic Ring Theatre, and the beautiful Neal S. Blaisdell Center are other cultural facilities. The numerous recreational activities include skin diving, swimming, spear fishing, surfing, golf, tennis, sailing, and hiking. Many beautiful and interesting sights may be seen on the island of Oahu. Excellent restaurants offer a wide variety of exotic cuisine.

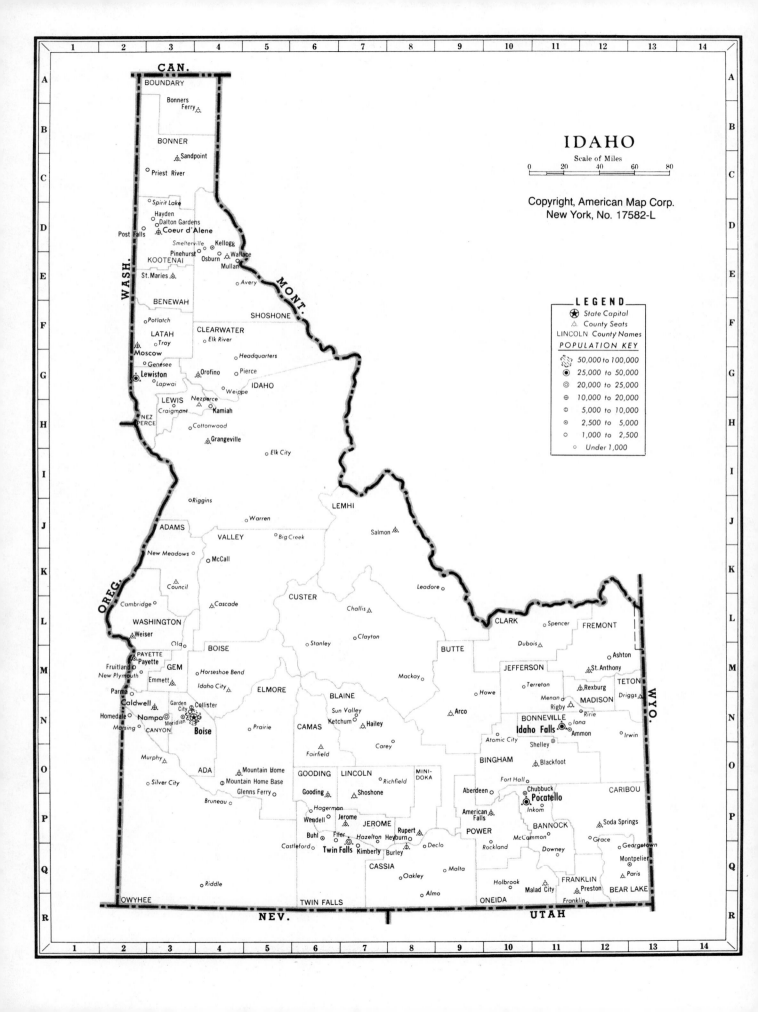

IDAHO

ALBERTSON COLLEGE   (N-3)
2112 Cleveland Boulevard
Caldwell, Idaho 83605
Tel: (208) 459-5305; Fax: (208) 454-2077

Description: This independent, private, coeducational college is accredited by the Northwest Association of Schools and Colleges. This college, established in 1891, is nonsectarian and nondiscriminatory in spirit and instruction. Two semesters of 13 weeks, divided by a 6-week winter session, comprise the regular calendar. Undergraduate enrollment includes 310 men and 336 women. A faculty of 64 full-time and 35 part-time provides a faculty-student ratio of 1-11.

Entrance Requirements: High school graduation or equivalent; recommended units include 4 years English, 3 years mathemtics, 2 years laboratory science, 3 years social science, and 2 years foreign language; SAT or ACT required; rolling admission, midyear admission, and advanced placement plans available; $25 application fee.

Costs Per Year: $14,100 tuition; $3,075 room and board; $217 student fees.

Collegiate Environment: The campus has 21 buildings on 43 acres. Dormitories have a capacity of 500 students. The library contains 161,489 bound volumes, 792 periodical subscriptions, 75,000 government documents, 45,940 microform titles and audiovisual materials. A science center provides independent research facilities for students. An activities and athletic center, outdoor amphitheater, and a $6 million fine and performing arts building (completed in 1994) is available for sports, culture, entertainment, and the arts. Approximately 87% of applicants are accepted. Financial aid is available, and 83% of the current student body receives assistance.

Community Environment: Caldwell, a town of 20,000, is located in a valley of irrigated farm land. Agriculture, food-processing and light industry are major factors in the city's economy. The state capital, Boise, is 30 miles away and offers cultural facilities and other advantages of an urban center. Within a short drive are mountains, deserts, and white-water rivers, offering a host of outdoor activities, such as skiing, rafting, and hiking. The state of Idaho has slightly more than 1 million people.

BOISE STATE UNIVERSITY   (N-3)
1910 University Drive
Boise, Idaho 83725
Tel: (208) 385-1177; (800) 632-6586; Fax: (208) 385-3765

Description: This state university is accredited by the Northwest Association of Schools and Colleges. The college was established in 1932 as a community college; it progressed into a four-year university with the first graduation in 1967, and became a part of the state system in 1969. It operates on the semester system and offers three summer sessions. Enrollment includes 8,070 full-time, 4,287 part-time, and 2,301 graduate students. A faculty of 498 full-time and 394 part-time gives a faculty-student ratio of 1-19.

Entrance Requirements: High school graduation or equivalent; SAT, ACT or TSWE required; minimum SAT combined 700; ACT 17 composite; non-high school graduates considered; requirements vary for vocational-technical students; early admission, early decision, midyear admission and advanced placement plans available; $15 application fee.

Costs Per Year: $1,876 resident fees; $6,062 out-of-state tuition and fees; $3,106 room and board.

Collegiate Environment: The campus has 29 buildings on 110 acres opposite Julia Davis Park. Residence halls accommodate 900 women and men. Apartments accomodate 170 families, and there are also houses for 12 families. Sororities and fraternities house 50 men and 32 women. The library contains 416,023 titles, 57,000 periodicals,

988,137 microforms and 16,744 recordings. Approximately 82% of the students applying for admission are accepted including midyear students. $8,628,000 is available for scholarships. 50% of the student body receives some form of financial aid.

Community Environment: Boise is the capital of Idaho and its largest city. It is located on the Boise River at the upper end of the Boise Valley. It enjoys mild winters with very little snow and temperate summers with cool nights. Community facilities include hospitals and libraries. The Idaho Concert and Artists Association features artists of national and international fame. Points of interest are the State Capitol, Ann Morrison and Julia Davis Parks, Platt Gardens, State Historical Museum, Pioneer Village, Urquides Village, Boise Heights, Idaho City and Silver City. The latter two are pioneer gold rush communities. Year-round recreational opportunities are available in and around Boise.

COLLEGE OF SOUTHERN IDAHO   (Q-7)
315 Falls Avenue
P.O. Box 1238
Twin Falls, Idaho 83303-1238
Tel: (208) 733-9554; Fax: (208) 736-3014

Description: This public junior college was founded in 1965. Accredited by the Northwest Regional Accrediting Association, the school operates on the semester system and offers one summer session. The college provides programs in general education and community services. Enrollment includes 2,218 full-time and 1,874 part-time students. A faculty of 120 full-time and 130 part-time gives a faculty-student ratio of 1-16.

Entrance Requirements: High school graduation; non-high school graduates considered; open enrollment; ASSET required; early admission, early decision, rolling admission, midyear admission, delayed admission and advanced placement plans available.

Costs Per Year: $1,000 state-resident tuition; $2,400 out-of-state; $2,900 room and board.

Collegiate Environment: Ten buildings on 240 acres comprise the campus. Almost all applicants are accepted for admission. The library contains 46,603 volumes, 324 periodicals, 28,750 microforms and 1,049 video materials. Dormitories house 250 men and women. 434 scholarships, including 124 athletic, are available. 65% of the students receive financial aid.

Community Environment: Twin Falls is a pleasant residential town with a population of 30,000. It is the county seat of Twin Falls County, which is the cultural and trade center of South Central Idaho's Magic Valley. The city is located at the junction of Transcontinental Highway 30 and International Highway 93. Buses, railroads and airlines serve the area. Due to the climate, location and natural surroundings, the area provides an unlimited variety of outdoor recreational facilities and activities. The city serves as headquarters for the Sawtooth National Forest.

IDAHO STATE UNIVERSITY   (P-10)
Pocatello, Idaho 83209
Tel: (208) 236-0211; (800) 888-4781; Admissions: (208) 236-2475; Fax: (208) 236-4000

Description: Idaho State University is accredited by the Northwest Association of Schools and Colleges. The university was founded in 1901 as the Academy of Idaho, and was established as Idaho State University in 1963. Colleges include Arts and Sciences, Business Administration, Education, Pharmacy and Health-Related Professions, School of Applied Technology, College of Engineering, and Graduate School. In addition the university's continuing education program includes three off-campus centers. The university operates on the semester system and offers two summer sessions. Enrollment includes 5,228 men and 6,649 women comprising 9,638 undergraduates and 2,239 graduate students. A faculty of 480 full-time and 179 part-time gives a faculty-student ratio of 1-17.

Entrance Requirements: High school graduation or equivalent; minimum 2.0 GPA and core units of 4 English, 3 mathematics, 2.5 social science, 3 natural science, 1 foreign language or humanities, 1.5 college prepartory electives; ACT or SAT required; GRE required for graduate programs; early decision, rolling admission, midyear admission and advanced placement plans available.

Costs Per Year: $1,500 state-resident tuition; $3,750 out-of-state tuition; $2,850-$3,140 room and board.

Collegiate Environment: The campus has 69 buildings on 792 acres. Dormitories and fraternities house 1,121 men and women with additional housing for 268 married students. A new library houses 511,579 volumes. 90% of those who apply for admission are accepted. 1,496 scholarships are available and 75% of the current students receive some form of financial aid.

Community Environment: Pocatello is located in a farming and industrial area of southeastern Idaho where the climate is dry and sunny. Planes, buses and trains provide transportation. The community facilities include many churches, two hospitals, the district health department, hotels, motels, etc. The municipal park has facilities for archery, baseball, field games, and includes a swimming pool and a zoo. Other facilities outside of Pocatello are in the intermountain region, which offers some of the best hunting and fishing in the United States. Swimming, boating, horseback riding and skiing is available for the outdoor life. Rodeos and the Indian Sun Dances are special annual events.

LEWIS-CLARK STATE COLLEGE (G-2)
8th Avenue & 6th Street
Lewiston, Idaho 83501
Tel: (208) 746-2341

Description: The publicly supported coeducational college is accredited by the Northwest Association of Schools and Colleges. The early semester system is used and two summer sessions are offered. The college was established in 1893 to train and educate teachers; it became a four-year college with a liberal arts program in 1965. The college also offers two-and four-year programs leading to the A.D.-R.N. and B.S.N. degrees. Recent enrollment includes 1,212 men and 1,817 women. A faculty of 90 full-time and 51 part-time members provides a faculty-student ratio of 1:21.

Entrance Requirements: Open enrollment policy; ACT required for students under 21 years of age at the time of college entrance; early admission, early decision, delayed admission, advanced placement, rolling admission plans available.

Costs Per Year: $1,170 state-resident tuition; $3,700 nonresident tuition; $2,714-$3,046 room and board.

Collegiate Environment: The 30-acre campus is located in an attractive residential section of the city. The library contains 132,153 book titles and 612 current periodical subscriptions. Dormitory facilities accommodate 68 men and 76 women. Most students applying for admission are accepted. Financial aid is available, and 67% of the current enrollment receives some form of assistance.

Community Environment: Lewiston is a small urban area that is a major community in the new Nez Perce National Park area; climate is temperate. It is the center of a vast lumbering, mining, farming and ranching territory. Planes, buses and trains serve the area. Community facilities include libraries, museums, YMCA, hospital, clinics, community concert series and shopping areas. Part-time employment opportunities are good. Facilities are good for boating, fishing and big game hunting. Boat trips up the Grand Canyon of the Snake River are spectacular journeys; shorter trips are available. The log drives down the Clearwater River and the Lewiston Roundup are special events.

NORTH IDAHO COLLEGE (D-3)
1000 West Garden Avenue
Coeur d'Alene, Idaho 83814
Tel: (208) 769-3311

Description: Publicly controlled junior college accredited by the Northwest Association of Schools and Colleges and the National

League for Nursing. The college was established in 1933 as a private school until 1939 when the state passed the Junior College Act. It operates on the early semester system and offers one summer session. Enrollment includes 1,928 full-time and 1,396 part-time students. A faculty of 147 gives a faculty-student ratio of 1-16.

Entrance Requirements: As a community college, North Idaho College accepts students with an "Open Door" admissions policy. All students who graduate from high school or who have completed the GED will be accepted for admission. Students in high school should plan a college prep curriculum for academic programs. Application for admission should be submitted with a $10 application fee by the application deadline.

Costs Per Year: $980 district resident tuition; Idaho residents from out-of-district must file a certificate-of-residency to qualify for in-district rates; out-of-state tuition $3,060; $3,310 room and board.

Collegiate Environment: The campus has fifteen buildings on 44 acres located on the shores of Lake Coeur d'Alene and the Spokane River with over 3,300 feet of beach front property. Residence Hall capacity is for 48 men and 48 women. The library contains 45,000 volumes. A library/computer science building was completed in 1991. Approximately 45% of the students receive financial aid.

Community Environment: Coeur d'Alene is located on the north shore of Lake Coeur d'Alene, 33 miles east of Spokane, Washington. The area is a popular resort for summer and winter events. Two major ski areas are only minutes away from downtown and the lake offers many water sports activities. Average summer high temperature is 82 degrees and average summer lows are 51 degrees, average winter high temperature is 38 degrees and the average low is 26 degrees. There is an average of 50 inches of snow each year and total average precipitation is 26 inches. Transportation facilities for the Spokeane/Coeur d'Alene area include bus, train and airline. Facilities of the community include library, hospital, county health unit and active civic clubs. The college hosts art and music programs for the community in its 1,200 seat Boswell Hall auditorium. Coeur d'Alene draws its industry from tourism, mining, forestry products and agricultural. Outdoor sports are boating, biking, hunting, fishing, golfing, water and snow skiing, sailing, windsurfing and swimming.

NORTHWEST NAZARENE COLLEGE (N-3)
Nampa, Idaho 83651
Tel: (208) 467-8011

Description: This private, liberal arts college is accredited by the Northwest Association of Schools and Colleges. It operates on the quarter system with two summer sessions. The college was started in 1913 with the organization of an elementary school; first degrees were conferred in 1917. The college is owned and operated by the Church of Nazarene. Enrollment includes 572 men and 646 women. A faculty of 80 gives a faculty-student ratio of 1-15. An academic cooperative plan with the University of Idaho is available for students majoring in engineering; credit for correspondence and by prior examination allowed toward degree.

Entrance Requirements: Open enrollment policy; ACT required; non-high school graduates considered; early admission, delayed admission, and advanced placement plans available.

Costs Per Year: $7,821 tuition; $2,590 room and board; $399 student fees.

Collegiate Environment: The college maintains a wholesome Christian environment. The campus has 18 buildings on 64 acres and includes a library containing 125,000 volumes, 11,000 periodicals, 20,831 microforms and 1,530 recordings. Housing facilities accommodate 347 men and 589 women. Ninety-five percent of students applying for admission are accepted, including midyear students. 80% of the current student body receives financial aid.

Community Environment: Nampa, located in southwestern Idaho, has a mild climate with an average mean temperature of 51 degrees and average rainfall of 13 inches. It is the agricultural, industrial and transportation center of southwest Idaho. Industries are processing and packing food, building mobile homes, feed mills, creameries, poultry and seed houses; the Carnation Can Company is located here. Community facilities include excellent library, churches representing 22 denominations, hospitals, motels and hotels. One hundred fifty civic, fraternal, and veterans organizations are active. Part-time employment is available. Recreational facilities consist of six parks, softball fields, baseball diamond, horseshoe courts, tennis courts, roller skating rink and bowling alleys; other facilities are Lake Lowell for swimming, boating, fishing and hunting. A ski run is within 35 miles. Points of interest are the Deer Flat National Wildlife Refuge, Givens' Hot Springs, Lakeview Park and Silver City and De Lamar, old mining towns. The Snake River Stampede, a rodeo, is an annual event held in July.

RICKS COLLEGE   *(M-12)*
Rexburg, Idaho 83460-4104
Tel: (208) 356-1020; Fax: (208) 356-1220

Description: This private, two-year college is accredited by the Northwest Association of Schools and Colleges. The school was established in 1888 and is owned and operated by the Church of Jesus Christ of Latter-day Saints. The semester system is employed with 3 five-week summer sessions offered. Enrollment includes 3,226 men, 4,545 women full-time, 105 men, and 113 women part-time. A faculty of 305 full-time and 80 part-time members gives a faculty-student ratio of 1-27. Credit for correspondence courses; cooperative education programs are available. Graduates of Ricks College are eligible to attend four-year colleges as matriculated juniors.

Entrance Requirements: Open enrollment policy; ACT required; non-high school graduates considered; early admission, advanced placement plans available; $15 application fee.

Costs Per Year: $1,750 tuition for members of the Church of Jesus Christ of Latter-day Saints; $2,560 nonmembers; $2,880-$3,140 room and board; miscellaneous $600.

Collegiate Environment: The campus has 35 buildings on 255 acres. Dormitory facilities are available for 460 men, 1,000 women and 60 married students. The library contains 135,471 volumes, 800 current periodicals, 120,005 microforms and 21,200 AV materials. Approximately 75% of the students applying for admission are accepted including midyear students. Average scores of the freshman class, ACT 22. 60% of undergraduates receive some form of financial aid. Army ROTC is available.

Community Environment: In Madison County, in the heart of the great Upper Snake River Valley, the city was founded by pioneers of the Church of Jesus Christ of Latter-day Saints and is a trading center. Agricultural products are potatoes, sugar barley, and dry farm wheat. Rexburg is primarily a residential town; the city has a wholesome atmosphere, and a progressive city administration maintains a clean thriving community. The descendants of the pioneers are active in church, civic, and social life, evidenced by beautiful and distinctive church buildings, housing 19 LDS Wards. The area is a sportsman's paradise, and ski enthusiasts have their choice of many fine ski areas, all within easy driving distance. The area abounds in scenic attractions, such as nearby Yellowstone National Park and Jackson Hole Wyoming. The college is an integral part of community life.

UNIVERSITY OF IDAHO   *(F-2)*
Moscow, Idaho 83843
Tel: (208) 885-6326; (800) 422-6013; Fax: (208) 885-9061

Description: The State of Idaho's land grant institution is accredited by the Northwest Association of Schools and Colleges. The university was founded in 1889 and administers nine colleges: Letters and Science, Art and Architecture, Agriculture, Engineering, Law, Mines and Earth Resources, Forestry, Wild-life and Range Sciences, Education, Business and Economics, and Graduate Programs. Enrollment includes 7,935 full-time students and 2,109 part-time students. A faculty of 659 gives a faculty-student ratio of 1-16. The school operates on the early semester system and offers one summer session. Academic cooperative plans are available for students majoring in veterinary science and medical technology. Army, Navy and Air Force ROTC are available as electives.

Entrance Requirements: Graduation from an accredited high school and completion of the following courses with at least 2.0 GPA based on ACT or SAT scores: 8 units English, 6 mathematics, 5 social science, 6 science, 2 humanitites or foreign language and 3 other college preparatory unit; ACT score betweem 15-36 composite or SAT combined score of 790-1600, depending on cumulative GPA; early admission, early decision, rolling admission, delayed admission, midyear admission, and advanced placement plans available; $25 application fee.

Costs Per Year: $1,548 state-resident tuition and fees; $5,748 non-resident; $3,540 room and board.

Collegiate Environment: The campus has 140 buildings on 1,200 acres. Dormitory housing is available for 1,217 men, 898 women, and 203 families. Fraternities and sororities provide housing for 3,709 men and women. The library contains 1,680,568 volumes, 10,694 periodicals, 113,798 microforms and 5,989 recordings. Approximately 90% students applying for admission are accepted. Average scores: SAT 458 verbal, 516 math; ACT 22.7 composite. There are 2,150 scholarships available, including 800 for freshmen, and 65% of the current student body receives some form of financial aid. About 25% of the senior class continues on to graduate school.

Community Environment: The location is rural, combining the peace, calm, and simplicity of the country with the intellectual atmosphere of a progressive college town. Moscow is in Idaho's Palouse Hill country and leads the nation in the production and processing of seed peas and lentils. Community facilities include a library, churches, clinics, hospital, hotels and motels and 2 shopping malls. Air, bus and railroads serve the area. Part-time work is available. Apartments and rooms may be rented. Eight miles away is Washington State University, the land grant institution for the state of Washington. There is an active faculty exchange, cross registration, and multiple library resources.

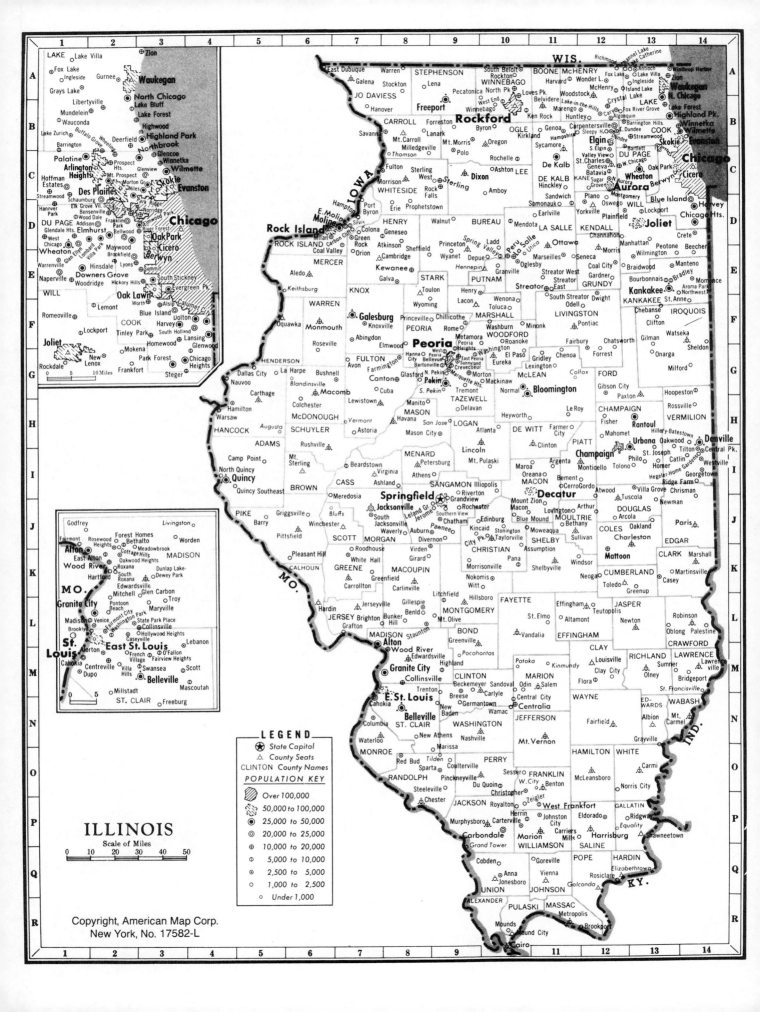

ILLINOIS

Scale of Miles

0 10 20 30 40 50

LEGEND
☆ State Capital
⚬ County Seats
CLINTON County Names
POPULATION KEY
▨ Over 100,000
▧ 50,000 to 100,000
◉ 25,000 to 50,000
◎ 20,000 to 25,000
⊕ 10,000 to 20,000
⊙ 5,000 to 10,000
⊙ 2,500 to 5,000
○ 1,000 to 2,500
○ Under 1,000

Copyright, American Map Corp.
New York, No. 17582-L

ILLINOIS

ADLER SCHOOL OF PROFESSIONAL PSYCHOLOGY
(C-14)
65 E. Wacker Place, Suite 2100
Chicago, Illinois 60601
Tel: (312) 201-5900; Fax: (312) 201-5917

Description: Founded in 1952, the Alder School of Professional Psychology is a nonsectarian, independent, not-for-profit coeducational institution. It operates on the trimester system with a summer session and is accredited by the North Central Association Commission on Institutions of Higher Education. The school grants the Doctor of Clinical Psychology (Psy.D.) degree, the M.A. degree in Counseling Psychology, the M.A. in Marriage and Family Counseling, the M.A. in Substance Abuse Counseling, the M.A. in Counseling: Art Therapy, the M.A. in Gerontology and the M.A. in classroom Psychology. The school also offers several graduate cetificate programs. Enrollment includes 143 full-time and 323 part-time students. A faculty of 17 full-time and 29 part-time gives a faculty-student ratio of 1-10.

Entrance Requirements: Baccalaureate degree from an accredited college with minimum of 12 semester credit hours of psychology for M.A. program and Graduate Certificate in Substance Abuse Counseling programs. Baccalaureate degree from an accredited college with a minimum of 18 semester credit hours of psychology for Doctor of Psychology in Clinical Psychology (Psy.D.) degree; rolling admission; $50 application fee, plus required application materials.

Costs Per Year: Tuition $260 per credit hour.

Collegiate Environment: The school's facilities include a library of over 7,000 volumes, 120 periodicals and 500 audiovisual materials. Through membership in the Illinois State Library Network and interlibrary loan agreements, students have access to other learning facilities. 70% of applicants are accepted. Students attend on a full-time or part-time basis. Evening and weekend classes are available. Financial aid is available. 40% of students receive some form of financial aid.

Community Environment: See University of Chicago.

AMERICAN ACADEMY OF ART *(C-14)*
332 S. Michigan Avenue, 3rd floor
Chicago, Illinois 60604
Tel: (312) 461-0600; Fax: (312) 294-9570

Description: The privately supported art academy which was founded in 1923 is classified as a private college by the Illinois Office of Education. The academy operates on the semester system and offers one 8 week summer session. Recent enrollment included 225 men and 169 women. A faculty of 16 full-time and 17 part-time gives a faculty-student ratio of 1-11. The American Academy of Art awards two-year Associate of Applied Science degrees in COmmercial Art of Fine Art and a two-year continuation Bachelor of Fine Arts degree.

Entrance Requirements: High School graduation or equivalent; open enrollment policy. All incoming students are required to submit portfolio for evaluation and admission approval. Rolling admission plan available; $25 application fee.

Costs Per Year: $11,280 tuition.

Collegiate Environment: All students are commuting students as there are no dormitory facilities available. All parts of the United States are represented in the student body, as well as many foreign countries. Approximately 75% of the students pursue various commercial art programs, with the remaining 25% pursuing the Fine Art programs. Three scholarships for the A.A.S. program are awarded each year to high school seniors through competitions. Ninety percent of those who apply for admissions are accepted, and students are admitted at midyear.

Community Environment: See University of Chicago

AMERICAN CONSERVATORY OF MUSIC *(C-14)*
16 North Wabash, Suite 1850
Chicago, Illinois 60602
Tel: (312) 263-4161; Fax: (312) 263-5832

Description: The privately supported conservatory was founded in 1886. The conservatory was one of the active forces in creating the National Association of Schools of Music and is a charter member of that organization. Its degree courses are organized on a collegiate basis. The conservatory offers the Bachelor, Master's and Doctorate degrees. It operates on the semester system and offers one summer session. Enrollment includes 80 full-time and 60 part-time students. A faculty of 10 full-time and 40 part-time provides a faculty-student ratio of 1-8.

Entrance Requirements: Accredited high school graduation or equivalent; completion of 15 units including 3 English, 3 mathematics, 3 social studies, and 3 natural sciences, 3 in music and art; high school graduates with C average accepted; ACT or SAT required; early decision, delayed admission, advanced placement and early admission plans available.

Costs Per Year: $8,000-$11,00 tuition; $1,000 student fees.

Collegiate Environment: School facilities include a library containing a comprehensive collection of full orchestra scores, chamber music, operas, and a 15,000-volume collection of music-related literature. 80% of students applying for admission are accepted including midyear students. Special financial aid is available for economically handicapped students, and 65% of the current student body receives some form of assistance.

Community Environment: See University of Chicago.

AUGUSTANA COLLEGE *(D-6)*
639 38th Street
Rock Island, Illinois 61201
Tel: (309) 794-7341

Description: This privately supported liberal arts college is affiliated with the Lutheran Church and operates on the three-term semester system with 3 summer sessions. Founded in 1860 as the first Scandinavian college in America, it included a theological seminary until 1948. Grants the Bachelors of Arts, Music, and Music Education degrees. Extensive overseas program offers fall term seminars in Europe, East Asia, and South America; summer language programs in Germany, France, Sweden, Peru. Offers extensive music program, nationally ranked intercollegiate athletic and debate teams, and intramural athletics. Has coordinated (B.A./B.S. or B.A./M.A., usually 3-2) degree programs with major universities in engineering, environmental management and forestry, landscape architecture, medical technology, and occupational therapy. Dental early admission with Northwestern and Iowa Universities. The college is accredited by the North Central Association of Colleges and Schools; professional accreditation: Phi Beta Kappa, American Chemical Society, National Association of Schools of Music, National Council for Accreditation of Teacher Education, and Council on Social Work Education. Degree requirements include English, literature, fine arts, philosophy, social and natural sciences, religion, foreign language, speech communications. Enrollment includes 2,002 students. A full-time faculty of 173 gives a faculty-student ratio 1-13.

Entrance Requirements: Accredited high school graduation or equivalent with rank in upper half of graduating class; college-preparatory courses including 3-4 English, 2 mathematics, 1 foreign language, 2 science, and 2 social science; under certain circumstances C average in high school accepted; SAT or ACT required; early admission (on part-time basis), early decision, rolling admission, delayed admission, midyear admission, and advanced placement plans available; $20 application fee.

Costs Per Year: $13,968 tuition; $4,257 room and board; $96 student fees.

Collegiate Environment: 22 buildings on 110 acres comprise the campus, which is located on a scenic bluff overlooking the Mississippi River Valley and the historic Rock Island Arsenal. The campus is situated in the geographic center of a metropolitan area known as the Quad-Cities. Dormitory facilities are available for 625 men and 752 women. The library contains more than 363,046 volumes. College accepts 84% of the applicants, including midyear students. Financial assistance is available, and 91% of the current student body receives financial aid.

AURORA UNIVERSITY *(C-12)*
347 South Gladstone Avenue
Aurora, Illinois 60506
Tel: (312) 892-6431

Description: This privately supported liberal arts college began in 1893 as Mendota Seminary; its parent organization was the Western Advent Christian Publication Association, but in 1899 a separate charter was procured and the college became an independent corporation. Today it is a fully accredited, four-year, senior-level college of liberal arts, non-denominaational, and accredited by the North Central Association of Colleges and Schools. Enrollment is 1,400 full-time, 300 part-time, and 500 graduate students. A faculty of 100 full-time and 10 part-time provides a faculty-student ratio of 1-18. It operates on the trimester system and offers 2 summer sessions. It offers a program for preparation of State teaching certificate. Credit is allowed for correspondence courses and for previous experience or training in certain courses. Chorus, choir, and extensive intercollegiate and intramural athletic programs are available.

Entrance Requirements: SAT or ACT required, minimum scores SAT 800 combined; ACT composite 20; high school equivalency diploma accepted; under certain circumstances non-high school graduates are accepted; rolling admission; no application fee.

Costs Per Year: $10,250 tuition; $3,850 room and board; $60 student fees.

Collegiate Environment: The college is comprised of 20 buildings that are located in a beautiful residential city, just 38 miles west of Chicago. The college is a member of the Associated Colleges of the Chicago Area for the purpose of cooperating in science education activities with the Argonne National Laboratory. The facilities at Argonne enable students to receive instruction in radiation biology, computer applications, uses of radioisotopes, spectroscopy, and uses of nuclear reactors. Dormitory facilities are available for 470 men and women. The library contains over 115,000 volumes and numerous periodicals, microforms and audiovisual materials. 75% of students applying for admission are accepted, including midyear students. Financial assistance is available, and 95% of students receive some form of financial aid.

Community Environment: Aurora is a large suburb in the Chicago metropolitan area but retains its own distinctive community life and atmosphere. The city is located in the Fox River Valley, 40 miles west of Chicago. Aurora is a city of schools, churches, libraries, and beautiful homes. Phillips Park provides facilities for tennis, swimming and golf.

BARAT COLLEGE *(B-13)*
700 East Westleigh Road
Lake Forest, Illinois 60045
Tel: (708) 295-4260; Fax: (708) 234-1084

Description: Chartered by the State of Illinois in 1919, this privately supported Catholic related coed liberal arts college is accredited by the North Central Association of Colleges and Schools. Enrollment includes 463 full-time, 266 part-time, and 402 evening students. A faculty of 40 full-time and 55 part-time gives a faculty-student ratio of 1-12. The college operates on the semester system and offers one summer session. It allows credit by prior examination for previous experience and training. It offers tutorial program at Oxford, England; also BSN degree for nurses who have an R.N. diploma. The college grants the Bachelor degree. It has cross-registration with Lake Forest College for all subjects. It also offers a strong theater and dance program and a continuing education program for community men and women.

Entrance Requirements: High school graduation or equivalent; top half of class; SAT minimum of 450 and 450V or ACT composite score of 19; early admission, rolling admission, early decision and advanced placement plans are available; $20 application fee.

Costs Per Year: $11,190 tuition; $4,680 room and board.

Collegiate Environment: The 30-acre wooded campus is located in a lake-front suburban community 30 miles north of downtown Chicago. Dormitory facilities are available for 600 students. The library contains 100,000 volumes. 73% of applicants are accepted. 402 scholarships are available, 262 of which are need-based. 73% of students receive some form of financial aid.

Community Environment: A beautiful residential suburb north of Chicago on Lake Michigan, Lake Forest is close to superhighways and rail terminals, and is a one-hour drive from major airports. Shopping is excellent at Market Square, Old Orchard, and Edens Shopping Centers. This college and residential suburb is one of the wealthiest communities in the metropolitan area. Recreational facilities include sailing, golf, skiing, tennis, bowling, and horseback riding. The nearness to Chicago provides Lake Forest with outstanding cultural opportunities.

BELLEVILLE AREA COLLEGE *(N-8)*
2500 Carlyle Road
Belleville, Illinois 62221
Tel: (618) 235-2700; (800) 222-5131; Fax: (618) 235-1578

Description: This publicly supported community college operates on the semester system with one summer session and is accredited by the North Central Association of Colleges and Schools. Professional accreditation includes Accreditation Board for Engineering and Technology for engineering technology, National League for Nursing for technical nursing, the American Medical Association for medical technology and physical and occupational therapy, and the American Chemical Society. The college offers liberal arts and technological courses. Extracurricular activities include chorus, orchestra, and intercollegiate and intramural athletics. Up to 30 credits are allowed by prior examination in certain courses for previous experience or training, and up to 16 credits are allowed for correspondent courses. U.S. Air Force ROTC is available. The college grants the Associate degree. Enrollment is 3,909 full-time and 11,798 part-time students. A faculty of 127 full-time and 650 part-time gives an overall faculty-student ratio of 1-20. Founded in 1946, the college moved to its present 150-acre campus in 1970.

Entrance Requirements: Open enrollment; high school graduation or equivalent; units including 4 English, 2 mathematics (geometry and higher), 3 social studies, 3 science; mature non-high school graduates considered for admission; early admission, early decision, rolling admission, and delayed admission plans available; entrance exam required; $10 application fee.

Costs Per Year: $1,200 district-resident tuition; $2,550 state-resident; $4,440 out-of-state.

Collegiate Environment: The community college endeavors to serve all who can benefit from education beyond the high school level. All applicants are accepted, and students are admitted at midyear as well as in the fall. The library contains 74,954 volumes. Financial aid is available, and 41% of the current students receive some form of assistance.

Community Environment: Belleville (population 42,785) is the county seat of St. Clair County, 20 miles from the heart of St. Louis, Missouri. The 2,100-square-mile Belleville Area College district blends a dichotomy of rural and urban, farming and industrial lifestyles. The campus is surrounded by acres of productive farm land. Industry in the area includes brewing, steel production, and some of the largest printing concerns in the nation. Scott Air Force Base is nearby. Because of the diversity offered to Belleville Area College students, the choice of part-time employment and/or entertainment is virtually unlimited. The college is a commuter college. Buses run every half hour except during the night. No dormitories are available; however, several excellent apartment complexes are located within walking distance of the campus.

BLACK HAWK COLLEGE - EAST CAMPUS   (E-8)
P.O. Box 489
Kewanee, Illinois 61443
Tel: (309) 852-5671; Admissions: (309) 852-5671 X 220; Fax: (309) 856-6005

Description: This state supported two-year college opened in 1967 and became the first multi-campus downstate junior college in Illinois. It is accredited by the North Central Association of Colleges and Schools. It offers both liberal arts and vocational-technical programs and grants the certificate and Associate degrees. The school operates on the semester system and offers one summer session. Inter-collegiate and intra-mural athletics are available. Enrollment is 703 students. A faculty of 23 full-time and 43 part-time gives a faculty-student ratio of 1-20.

Entrance Requirements: Open enrollment; high school graduation or equivalent; non-high school graduates may be admitted; rolling admission and midyear admission plans. Contact Director of Educational Services for information; deadline for Fall term, first day of classes. No application fee.

Costs Per Year: $1,444 tuition; $1,980 out-of-district tuition; $4,740 out-of-state tuition; $45 student fees; $550 books and supplies.

Collegiate Environment: All students applying for admission are accepted. The campus includes 5 buildings on 102 acres. The library contains over 15,819 volumes. Financial aid is available.

Community Environment: Kewanee (population 12,500), which began as an early railroad depot is surrounded by a fertile agricultural region. The city's industries produce work gloves, steel boilers, valves and varied heavy machinery. Kewanee, a rural area, is 140 miles southwest of Chicago, accessible via state and national highways. Community facilities include hospital, library and churches of many denominations.

Branch Campuses: Black Hawk College-Quad Cities Campus, 6600 34th Avenue, Moline, IL 61265, (309) 796-1311

BLACK HAWK COLLEGE - QUAD CITIES CAMPUS   (D-7)
6600 34th Avenue
Moline, Illinois 61265
Tel: (309) 796-1311

Description: This publicly supported, district-governed community college recently enrolled 2,048 full-time and 3,670 part-time men and women. With a faculty of 130 full-time and 175 part-time, the faculty-student ratio is 1-17. The school operates on the semester system with 1 summer session and is accredited by the North Central Association of Colleges and Schools. Founded in 1946, the college existed for two years as an extension center of the University of Illinois. Following a successful referendum, the college became the first area junior college district in this state in 1962, and the first multi-campus downstate junior college in 1967 with the opening of the East Campus in Kewanee. Grants Certificate, Associate degree. Offers transfer and vocational and Outreach programs.

Entrance Requirements: Open enrollment; non-high school graduates admitted; rolling admission, early admission, early decision, delayed admission and advanced placement plans available.

Costs Per Year: $1,200 for district residents; $1,980 for state residents; $4,740 for nonresidents. Fees, $45.

Collegiate Environment: Four buildings on 149 acres comprise the campus; the library contains 44,758 volumes, 10,000 bound periodicals, 13,000 microforms and 825 audiovisual materials. All students applying for admission are accepted including midyear students.

Community Environment: Moline is located 167 miles west of Chicago, enjoying a continental-type climate with average annual rainfall of 33 inches. All forms of transportation are available. Moline is part of the urban area which includes Davenport, Iowa, and Rock Island, Illinois, called the "Farm Implement Capital of America". It is the home of the John Deere Implement Company. Other products manufactured here are machine tools, elevators, office equipment, furniture, truck bodies, traffic signals, candy, and paint. Community facilities include 54 churches representing 28 denominations, four hospitals, radio and TV stations. Recreation opportunities are provided by seven parks, three swimming pools, tennis courts, golf courses and water sports on the Mississippi River.

Branch Campuses: Black Hawk College-East Campus, P.O. Box 489, Kewanee, IL 61443.

BLACKBURN COLLEGE   (K-8)
Nicolas Street
Carlinville, Illinois 62626
Tel: (217) 854-3231

Description: The college is a privately supported liberal arts university which is affiliated with the Presbyterian Church. It conducts an on-campus student Work Program whereby all students work 15 hours per week in addition to course work, and offers program for preparation of State teaching certificate. Off-campus programs include semester in Mexico, semester in Washington. Allows some correspondence credit and credit by prior examination in certain courses for previous experience or training. Offers band, chorus, choir, theatre, extensive intercollegiate and intramural athletics. Recent enrollment included 225 men and 225 women with a faculty of 38. The school grants a Bachelor degree. The school is accredited by the North Central Association of Colleges and Schools and operates on the semester system. The college was founded in 1837 by the Reverend Gideon Blackburn, a Presbyterian minister and a former president of Centre College of Kentucky.

Entrance Requirements: Accredited high school graduation with rank in top 60% of graduating class; completion 4 units of English, 2 social studies, 2 math, 2 science; SAT or ACT required; high school equivalency diploma accepted; under certain circumstances, non-HS graduates and those with C average considered. Special admission plans available: rolling admission, delayed admission, advanced placement, early admission and early decision.

Costs Per Year: $7,820 tuition; $3,000 room and board; $300 student fees.

Collegiate Environment: 16 buildings on 80 acres comprise the campus which is located on part of the original site selected by the founder in 1835. Dormitory facilities are available. The library contains 77,000 volumes. 83% of applicants accepted, including midyear students. Financial assistance is available, and 90% of the current students receive assistance.

Community Environment: Carlinville (population 6,000) is the county seat of Macoupin County, located 45 miles south of Springfield, 60 miles north of St. Louis. Trains and buses serve the area. This is a predominantly agricultural area. Local industries include packaged dairy products, gloves, truck bodies, electronic equipment, couplings, plates, and coal mining. Lake Carlinville offers boating, water skiing, swimming, fishing, and picknicking.

BRADLEY UNIVERSITY   (G-9)
1501 W. Bradley Avenue
Peoria, Illinois 61625
Tel: (309) 677-1000; (800) 447-6460; Fax: (309) 677-2797

Description: This privately supported university is comprised of 6 colleges and schools: Liberal Arts and Sciences, Education and Health Sciences, Engineering and Technology, Business and Administration, Communications and Fine Arts, and the Graduate School. Enrollment includes 4,588 full-time and 473 part-time undergraduates and 821 graduate students. A faculty of 300 gives a faculty-student ratio of 1-15. The institution operates on the semester system and offers 2 summer sessions and 2 intermissions. It is accredited by the North Central Association of Colleges and Schools, and professionally by the American Chemical Society, Accreditation Board for Engineering and Technology, National Association of Schools of Music, the National Council for Accreditation of Teacher Education, the American Assembly or Collegiate Schools of Business, and several other professional organizations and associations. It offers Cooperative Education programs (alternating work and class periods) in all areas of study. An overseas program is offered in Austria, Germany, France, Spain, Israel or England. Army ROTC is available. Band, chorus, orchestra, and very extensive intercollegiate and intramural athletics are available. Bachelor and Master degrees are granted. The university was founded in 1897 by Mrs. Lydia Moss Bradley in memory of her husband and children as a nonsectarian, nonpolitical, nonpartisan, privately endowed educational institution.

Entrance Requirements: Accredited high school graduation or equivalent with completion of 3 units in English, 2 mathematics, 1 science, and 2 social science; admission to any particular program may require additional units; SAT or ACT required; mature non-high school graduates may be considered for admission; GRE required for graduate school; rolling admission, midyear admission, advanced placement & CLEP credit granted; $35 application fee.

Costs Per Year: $10,870 tuition; $4,440 room and board; $58 student fees.

Collegiate Environment: The campus of the university is spacious yet convenient with classrooms, laboratories, and dormitories within easy walking distance of one another. 40 buildings on 65 acres comprise the campus and the library contains 531,744 volumes. Dormitory accommodations are available for 2,237 students; fraternities and sororities provide housing for an additional 450 men and 385 women. 94% of students applying for admission are accepted. The university seeks a geographically diverse student body. Average scores of the freshman class were: SAT 530V, 600M; ACT 25. 59% of the freshman class ranked in the upper quarter of the high school class, and 84% were in the upper half. 1,300 scholarships are available, including 462 for freshmen. 80% of the current student body receives financial assistance.

Community Environment: Peoria is the second largest metropolitan area in Illinois; all modes of transportation are available. It is the hub of the central area of the state for cultural, business and professional activities. Peoria is a manufacturing and shipping center located in the heart of the farm belt. Community facilities include good shopping areas and recreational opportunities and a new civic center featuring nationally known entertainment. Points of interest are Fort Creve Coeur, Indian burial mounds, Peoria Historical Society Museum, Lakeview Center for Arts and Sciences, Wildlife, Prairie Park, and the Planetarium. Total metropolitan area population is 350,000.

CARL SANDBURG COLLEGE   *(F-7)*
2232 South Lake Storey Road
Galesburg, Illinois 61401
Tel: (309) 344-2518; Fax: (309) 344-3291

Description: This publicly supported technological and liberal arts junior college operates on the semester system and opened its facilities with an enrollment of 615 students in 1967. The community college is now offering college parallel, vocational-technical, and adult education courses and recently enrolled 3,899 students. It offers band, chorus, and intercollegiate and intramural athletics. Credit allowed for correspondence courses and by prior examination in certain courses for previous experience or training. Employs semester system with one summer sessions. A faculty of 153 gives a faculty-student ratio of 1-25. Is accredited by the North Central Association of Colleges and Schools. Grants Certificate and Associate degree.

Entrance Requirements: Open admissions policy; accredited high school graduation or GED equivalent. Mature non-high school graduates may be accepted for vocational, technical, and adult education programs; ACT accepted; rolling admission, advanced placement.

Costs Per Year: $1,530 tuition; out-of-district students pay $3,398 tuition; out-of-state students pay $6,401 tuition.

Collegiate Environment: A $9,000,000 campus on Lake Storey near Galesburg, which is near the population center of the district. Granted 92 Certificates and 140 Associate degrees. Library contains 31,000 volumes and 23,800 microforms. Special financial aid is available for economically handicapped students and 30% of the current freshman class receives some form of financial aid. No student housing.

Community Environment: Galesburg (population 36,290), once selected as one of the four ideal American cities by noted editor and author, Edward Bok, is located 180 miles southwest of Chicago on the main lines of the Burlington and Santa Fe Railroads. The Carl Sandburg birthplace preserves the early home of the poet and contains interesting Sandburg and Lincoln memoirs.

CATHOLIC THEOLOGICAL UNION AT CHICAGO   *(C-14)*
5401 South Cornell Avenue
Chicago, Illinois 60615
Tel: (312) 324-8000; Admissions: (312) 324-8000; Fax: (312) 324-8490

Description: The privately supported graduate school of theology is incorporated in the state of Illinois as an institution of higher learning

and is accredited by the North Central Association of Colleges and Schools and by the Association of Theological Schools. Founded in 1967, the school provides training for the priesthood for 30 Roman Catholic orders and for the Ukrainian Catholic Church, as well as education for a variety of other ministries. It is open to all men and women wishing to study theology or prepare for ministry in the Roman Catholic tradition. Teh school grants the Master and Doctoral degrees. It operates on the quarter system and offers one summer session. The seminary recently enrolled 246 men and 119 women full-time and part-time. These figures include 200 full-time and 165 part-time graduate students. A faculty of 30 full-time and 10 part-time gives a faculty-student ratio of 1-8.

Entrance Requirements: Bachelor's degree from a recognized college or university; personal interview may be required; $35 application fee; rolling admission plan available.

Costs Per Year: $230 per credit; room and board $3,650-$5,150; student fees $3 per credit.

Collegiate Environment: The Catholic Theological Union occupies a nine-story building housing offices, a library of 115,200 volumes, classrooms, food service, lounges, some living quarters and two adjacent student resident buildings. It is located in the Hyde Park-Kenwood area of Chicago's southside, only 15 minutes by car or train from the center of the city. The University of Chicago and four schools of theology are within walking distance. The proximity of the libraries of the other theological schools and of the library of the University of Chicago, especially of the Divinity School and the Oriental Institute, affords broad and valuable possibilities for consultation and research. 80% of the applicants are accepted. Financial assistance is available.

Community Environment: See University of Chicago

CHICAGO STATE UNIVERSITY   *(C-14)*
95th Street at King Drive
Chicago, Illinois 60628
Tel: (312) 995-2513; Fax: (312) 995-3820

Description: Publicly supported state university offering liberal arts, business, allied health, nursing and teacher education programs. It is accredited by the North Central Association of Colleges and Schools and professionally by numerous accrediting organizations. It offers preparation for the state teaching certificate. It operates on the semester system with course offerings during 10-, 8- and 6-week summer sessions. Offers Cooperative Education program (alternating work and class periods) in business; Intensive Education (specialized class size and instruction); University Without Walls (nontraditional instruction); and Individualized Curriculum (individually tailored degree requirements). Army ROTC is available. Enrollment includes 3,053 men and 6,948 women. A faculty of 402 gives a faculty-student ratio of 1-22. Offers extensive music programs as well as intercollegiate and intramural athletics.

Entrance Requirements: First quartile rank in the high school class and a minimum composite ACT score of 15; or second quartile rank in the high school class and a minimum composite ACT score of 16; those ranking in the lower half of their high school class must have a composite ACT score of 17; those applicants under 25 years of age with a GED will be required to present evidence of a score of 250 and a composite ACT of 15 or a score of 225 and a composite ACT score of 17; completion of 15 academic units including 4 English, 3 math, 3 science, 3 social studies, and 2 electives; early decision, midyear admission, rolling admissiona dn advanced placement plans available.

Costs Per Year: $2,210 state-resident tuition and fees; $6,146 non-residents.

Collegiate Environment: Library contains 280,000 volumes, 1,377 periodicals, and 378,886 microforms. No student housing. 80% of students receive financial assistance. 60% of applicants are accepted.

Community Environment: See University of Chicago.

CHICAGO THEOLOGICAL SEMINARY   *(C-14)*
5757 South University Avenue
Chicago, Illinois 60637
Tel: (312) 752-5757, x229; (800) 367-2871; Fax: (312) 752-5925

Description: The privately supported graduate seminary is affiliated with the United Church of Christ. It is accredited by the North Central

Association of Colleges and Schools and by the Association of Theological Schools. Founded in 1855, the seminary today offers programs leading to the Master of Divinity, Master of Arts in Religion, Master of Sacred Theology, Doctor of Philosophy, and Doctor of Ministry degrees. It operates on the quarter system. Enrollment is 212 students. A faculty of 13 gives a faculty-student ratio of 1-16.

Entrance Requirements: B.A. degree or its equivalent with a good record from an accredited college or university; GRE required for Ph.D. students only; $50 application fee.

Costs Per Year: $7,996 tuition; $7,719 room and board, and miscellaneous

Collegiate Environment: The seminary is located approximately seven miles southeast of the downtown business district of Chicago known as the Loop. The library contains 98,000 volumes and dormitory facilities are available for 40 men, 40 women, and 61 families. Midyear students are accepted. Federal student aid is available.

Community Environment: See University of Chicago.

CHICAGO-KENT COLLEGE OF LAW OF ILLINOIS INSTITUTE OF TECHNOLOGY   *(C-14)*
565 W. Adams St.
Chicago, Illinois 60661
Tel: (312) 906-5000; Admissions: (312) 906-5020

Description: Chicago-Kent College of Law, Illinois Institute of Technology, is nationally acclaimed for its innovative approaches to traditional legal education and its specialized programs within the law shcool curriculum. The law school's unique affiliation with the Illinois Institute of Technology, one of the nation's largest scientific research centers, provides support for interdisciplinary programs including the Center for Law and Computers, the certificate program in Environmental and Energy Law and the Intellectual Property Program. The law library, one of the largest in the country, contains extensive computer facilities and the collection of the Library of International Relations, a major reference and research center for international study. Chicago-Kents's special programs include the Legal Research and Writing Program, the Program in Environmental and Energy Law, the Center for Law and Computers, the Program in International and Comparative Law, the Program in Litigation and Dispute Resolution Studies and Trial Advocacy. The law school enrollment is 895 full-time and 371 part-time students. There are 70 full-time and 73 part-time faculty members.

Entrance Requirements: 84 hours required; Bachelor's degree required except in exceptional circumstances; Law Admission Test required; Test of English as a Foreign Language (TOEFL) and the Test of Written English (TWE) are required for students for whom English is not the native language or for those who did not receive their undergraduate education at an institution which uses English as the primary language of instruction; $40 application fee.

Costs Per Year: Tuition for students entering in the 1994-95 academic year is charged at a flat rate of $17,300 for full-time students and $12,360 for part-time students.

Collegiate Environment: The College of Law is located in downtown Chicago, the heart of the city's commercial and legal communities. The new law school building, completed in 1992, is conveniently located near all forms of public transportation. An essential educational feature of the classrooms and library is the extensive computer network. Seats in selected classrooms, many library carrels and numerous locations throughout the building are tied to the computer network, enabling students with their own laptop computers to connect into the network and the many legal databases. There are three computer labortatories with more than 80 personal computers reserved for student use. The modern Marovitz Courtroom integrates design features from the best courtroom and trial advocacy training facilities in the nation. The law library currently contains 477,000 volumes, placing it among the top 15% of national law libraries. The collection contains the Library of International Relations and a wealth of material in environmental and energy law, intellectual property, international trade and labor law. The law offices of Chicago-Kent, one of the largest in-house clinical education programs in the country, offers eight clinical education programs that include civil, criminal, health, immigration, tax and transaction law, and externships with government agencies and federal judges. Merit and need-based scholarships are available. 77% of students receive some form of financial aid. Contact (312) 906-5180 for Financial Aid Office.

Community Environment: IIT Chicago-Kent is located downtown, in the heart of Chicago's legal community. Law students may also take advantage of the facilities and campus atmosphere of the main campus of IIT, located three miles south of the law school building and connected to it by a free minibus service.

CITY COLLEGES OF CHICAGO   *(C-14)*
226 W. Jackson Boulevard
Chicago, Illinois 60606
Tel: (312) 641-0808

Description: The City Colleges of Chicago, a multicollege system, incorporates 7 colleges that serve their districts on the community college level. The schools operate on the early semester system and are accredited by the North Central Association of Colleges and Schools. The Central Administration is located at 226 W. Jackson. Existing facilities include Daley, Kennedy-King, Harold Washington, Malcolm X, Olive-Harvey, Truman, and Wright. As community colleges, the City Colleges have both pre-transfer liberal arts and science programs and occupational programs in engineering and industrial technologies; business; health occupations; and public and human services. More than 250 separate programs are available. The majority are two-year Associate degree programs, although more flexible Certificate programs exist. The colleges are located throughout the city to provide convenient accessibility to every student. Approximately 80,000 fulltime and part-time students are enrolled annually in the City Colleges of Chicago. The school employs 854 full-time and 1,231 part-time faculty members. See individual listings for additional information.

Entrance Requirements: High School graduates; GED accepted; ACT scores required for placement; various admission plans are available at the different locations.

Costs Per Year: Tuition costs vary; average costs are: $988 per year city residents; $2,968 state residents; $4,061 out-of-state.

Community Environment: See University of Chicago.

CITY COLLEGES OF CHICAGO - HAROLD WASHINGTON COLLEGE   *(C-14)*
30 E. Lake Street
Chicago, Illinois 60601
Tel: (312) 553-5600; Admissions: (312) 553-6000; Fax: (312) 553-6077

Description: The public junior college serves the central portion of the Chicago Area. The school is accredited by the North Central Association of Colleges and Schools and the Council on Social Work Education. It operates on the semester system with one summer session. Enrollment is 1,083 full-time and 6,410 part-time students. A faculty of 147 full-time and 63 part-time gives a faculty-student ratio of 1-30.

Entrance Requirements: Open enrollment; accredited high school graduation; resident non-high school graduates 19 years or older may be admitted as special students; rolling admission plan available; no application fee.

Costs Per Year: $1,285 tuition city residents; $3,665 state resident; $4,508 out-of-state.

Collegiate Environment: 2 out of 3 students are part-time. 70% are over 21. The largest programs are Liberal Arts, Business Administration and Data Processing. Developmental remedial and noncredit adult education courses available; English as a second language program serves 1,000 foreign students.

Community Environment: See University of Chicago.

CITY COLLEGES OF CHICAGO - HARRY S. TRUMAN COLLEGE   *(C-14)*
1145 West Wilson Avenue
Chicago, Illinois 60640
Tel: (312) 989-6120

Description: This liberal arts community college is accredited by the North Central Association of Colleges and Schools and approved by the Illinois Community College Board and the Illinois Office of Education, Department of Adult, Vocational, and Technical Education. The medical records programs is approved by the American Medical Records Association. It operates on the semester system with one summer session of eight weeks. An enrollment of 5,618 students with a faculty of 157 provides a student-faculty of 30-1.

Entrance Requirements: High school graduation; SAT; ACT for research and placement only; high school graduates with a C average accepted; open enrollment; early admission, early decision, rolling admission, delayed admission, and advanced placement plans available.

Costs Per Year: Tuition: $800; out-of-district: $2,232; out-of-state: $3,164.

Collegiate Environment: The 18-acre campus includes a gym, swimming pool, and a theater. The library has 61,000 volumes. There is no on-campus housing. Scholarships, such as Pell and ISSC, are available as well as ones for academic achievement.

Community Environment: See University of Chicago

CITY COLLEGES OF CHICAGO - KENNEDY-KING COLLEGE   *(C-14)*
6800 S. Wentworth Ave.
Chicago, Illinois 60621
Tel: (312) 602-5000; Admissions: (312) 602-5049; Fax: (312) 602-5247

Description: This public junior college was founded in 1934. It is accredited by the North Central Association of Colleges and Schools. Programs are primarily vocational-technical, but a liberal arts curriculum is also provided. The college grants the Associate degree. It operates on the semester system and offers one summer session. Enrollment is 2,680 full-time students. A faculty of 106 gives a faculty-student ratio of 1-25.

Entrance Requirements: Open enrollment policy; accredited high school graduation or equivalent; placement entrance exam required; resident non-high school graduates 19 years or older may be admitted as special students; early admission, early decision and advanced placement plans available.

Costs Per Year: $1,225 tuition for district resident; $3,606 out-of-district; $4,449 out-of-state.

Collegiate Environment: This junior college places emphasis on vocational-technical programs. 100% of students applying for admission are accepted. The library contains approximatetly 42,000 volumes. Academic and athletic scholarships are available, and 80% of the current student body receives some form of financial aid.

Community Environment: See University of Chicago.

CITY COLLEGES OF CHICAGO - MALCOLM X COLLEGE *(C-14)*
1900 W. Van Buren Street
Chicago, Illinois 60612
Tel: (312) 850-7050; Fax: (312) 850-7092

Description: Formerly known as the Crane Campus, the public junior college was founded in 1911, when 28 students attended the first class in the Crane Technical High School Building near the west side of Chicago. This was the beginning of Chicago's present public community college system. It was later known as Herzl Junior College, and renamed Malcolm X College in 1969 at the request of local community residents. The college operates on the semester system. Crane was fully accredited by the North Central Association of Colleges and Schools in 1917. Enrollment is 1,000 full-time and 2,184 part-time students. A faculty of 88 gives an overall faculty-student ratio of 1-25.

Entrance Requirements: Accredited high school graduation with completion of 16 units; resident non-high school graduates, 19 years or older, may be admitted as special students; ACT required.

Costs Per Year: $1,200 tuition; $3,200 out-of-district; $4,500 out-of-state.

Collegiate Environment: One large building serves the college, and the library contains 24,000 volumes. Approximately 90% of students applying for admission are accepted including midyear students. 65% of students recevie some form of financial aid. Special programs are offered for the culturally disadvantaged enabling low-mark students to attend.

Community Environment: See University of Chicago.

CITY COLLEGES OF CHICAGO - OLIVE-HARVEY COLLEGE   *(C-14)*
10001 South Woodlawn Avenue
Chicago, Illinois 60628
Tel: (312) 291-6100; Admissions: (312) 291-6349; Fax: (312) 291-6304

Description: The south section of Chicago is served by this public junior college, which was founded in 1958. The former Fenger and Southeast campuses merged in 1970 to form the Olive-Harvey campus. The school operates on the semester system and is accredited by the North Central Association of Colleges and Schools. The college recently enrolled 3,306 students. It has a faculty of 98 full-time and 21 part-time members.

Entrance Requirements: Accredited high school graduation; resident non-high school graduates 19 years or older may be admitted as special students; ACT required for placement.

Costs Per Year: $1,185 district resident tuition; $3,566 out-of-district; $4,409 out-of-state.

Collegiate Environment: The library of this junior college contains 16,000 volumes. 95% of students applying for admission are accepted including midyear students. Special programs for the culturally disadvantaged are offered. Financial aid for economically disadvantaged students is available.

Community Environment: See University of Chicago.

CITY COLLEGES OF CHICAGO - RICHARD J. DALEY COLLEGE   *(C-14)*
7500 South Pulaski Road
Chicago, Illinois 60652
Tel: (312) 838-7500; Admissions: (312) 838-7599; Fax: (312) 838-7524

Description: Formerly Southwest College. Founded in 1960, this two-year community college is municipally governed and is accredited by the North Central Association of Colleges and Schools. It offers career and vocational programs of study and grants certicates and the Associates degree. The school operates on the semester system and offers one summer session. Enrollment includes 5,230 full-time and 3,501 part-time and 1,583 evening students. A faculty of 119 full-time and 30 part-time gives a faculty student ratio of 1-62.

Entrance Requirements: Admission is open to all graduates of accredited high schools and to transfer students from other colleges and universities; applicants, 19 years of age or older, who have not completed high school may be admitted as special students; ACT is required for placement; rolling admission, midyear admission, and advanced placement plans available. No application fee.

Costs Per Year: Tuition: $1,305 district; out-of-district: $3,186; out-of-state $4,228.

Collegiate Environment: The school is located in the southwest section of Chicago. Student services are provided including job placement. Approximately 95% of students applying for admission meet the requirements and are accepted. The library contains 18,000 volumes. 21% of students receive some form of financial aid.

Community Environment: See University of Chicago

CITY COLLEGES OF CHICAGO - WILBUR WRIGHT COLLEGE   *(C-14)*
3400 N. Austin Avenue
Chicago, Illinois 60634
Tel: (312) 794-3182

Description: Located in the northwest section of Chicago, this public community college enrolled 6,000 men and women recently. A faculty of 190 gives a faculty-student ratio of 1-32. The college was founded in 1934. It is accredited by the North Central Association of Colleges and Schools and it employs the early semester system with one summer session.

Entrance Requirements: Accredited high school graduation or equivalent; open enrollment; resident non-high school graduates, 18 years or older, may be admitted as special students; ACT required; rolling admission plan available.

Costs Per Year: $800 city resident tuition; $2,232 state resident tuition; $3,164 out-of-state tuition.

Collegiate Environment: The campus is comprised of one building on five acres. The library contains 62,000 volumes. 100% of students applying for admission are accepted including midyear students. Special financial aid is available for economically handicapped students, and 60% of the current students receive financial aid.

Community Environment: See University of Chicago

COLLEGE OF DUPAGE   (E-1)
22nd Street & Lambert Road
Glen Ellyn, Illinois 60137
Tel: (312) 858-2800

Description: The publicly supported community college serves the needs of District 502 in the areas of Baccalaureate degree studies, occupational-technical programs, general, and continuing education. The school operates on the quarter system with 7 overlapping summer sessions. Enrollment is 8,560 full-time and 23,065 part-time students. A faculty of 299 full-time and 1,509 part-time gives a faculty-student ratio of 1-18. Allows alternating work and study periods in occupational areas. Conducts freshman program for educationally disadvantaged. Offers band, chorus, choir; extensive intercollegiate and intramural athletics. Army ROTC is available through Wheaton College. Grants Certificates and Associate degrees. The school was founded in 1967 and is accredited by the North Central Association of Colleges and Schools.

Entrance Requirements: Accredited high school graduation; non-high school graduates over 18 years capable of profiting from instruction accepted; open enrollment; special admission plans include early admission, rolling admission, delayed admission, and advanced placement; $10 application fee.

Costs Per Year: $1,000 city- or county-resident tuition; $3,555 state residents; $4,635 out-of-state residents.

Collegiate Environment: The campus consists of ten buildings with other facilities rented as they are needed. New multimillion-dollar Art Center and Physical Education Building were recently completed. No student housing. Library contains 137,009 volumes. Seaton Computing Center, dedicated Spring 1990, has 4 classrooms, 1 CADD-CAM Lab and 2 open labs with 286 stations. All applicants are accepted, including midyear students.

Community Environment: Glen Ellyn is an attractive residential village with trees, rolling terrain, and well-landscaped dwellings; a suburban area near Wheaton, served by the Chicago and North Western Railroad, the shopping facilities are excellent. Glen Ellyn also has a library, YMCA, clinic in town, and hospitals nearby. Lake Ellyn is nearby for recreation, boating, swimming, etc.

COLLEGE OF LAKE COUNTY   (A-1)
19351 West Washington Street
Grayslake, Illinois 60030
Tel: (708) 223-6601; Fax: (708) 223-0822

Description: The publicly supported community college is accredited by the North Central Association of Colleges and Schools and the National League of Nursing. It features liberal arts and technological programs, and allows up to 30 credits for certain courses by prior examination for previous experience and training. A precollege program for the educationally disadvantaged is also offered. The college grants a Certificate and the Associate degree. It operates on the semester system and offers one summer session. Enrollment is 1,123 men and 1,615 women full-time, and 5,025 men and 7,231 women part-time. A faculty of 183 full-time gives a faculty-student ratio of 1-40.

Entrance Requirements: Accredited high school graduation or equivalent; open enrollment; non-high school graduates over 18 years of age admitted; ACT required for some applicants; early admission, rolling admission, and advanced placement plans available.

Costs Per Year: $1,320 district resident tuition; $5,387 state resident tuition; $6,701 nonresident tuition.

Collegiate Environment: The campus consists of 15 buildings on 232 acres, including a library of 107,432 volumes. All applicants are accepted, and students are admitted at midyear as well as in the fall. Scholarships are available. 25% of students receive financial aid.

Community Environment: The college has 2 campuses. The main campus centrally located in Grayslake (population 6,400), and the second campus situated in Waukegan (population 67,600). Waukegan

is situated in the northeast corner of Illinois on the scenic shores of Lake Michigan. Excellent transportation facilities are available. Waukegan is an industrial city and is part of the metropolitan area of Chicago. Two of the principal industrial products are pharmaceutical supplies and outboard motors. Community facilities include over 50 churches of various denominations and municipal libraries. Recreation and sports include fishing, swimming, skiing, and hunting in the forest preserves. There are more than 60 lakes located in the county.

COLLEGE OF SAINT FRANCIS   (D-13)
500 Wilcox Street
Joliet, Illinois 60435
Tel: (815) 740-3400; (800) 735-7500; Fax: (815) 740-4285

Description: This privately supported liberal arts college operates on the semester system and offers one summer session. It is accredited by the North Central Association of Colleges and Schools. The college is under the auspices of the Roman Catholic Church and is one of the educational institutions of the Congregation of the Third Order of Saint Francis of Mary Immaculate. Under the title of Assisi Junior College, the college was founded in 1920. With the opening of the fall term in 1930, the senior college curriculum began and the present name was adopted. It grants the Bachelor and Master degrees. Enrollment is 850 full-time and 250 part-time undergraduates, and 800 graduate students. A faculty of 52 full-time and 46 part-time gives a faculty-student ratio of 1-14.

Entrance Requirements: Accredited high school graduation with rank in upper half of graduating class; completion of 16 college-preparatory courses; ACT required; $15 application fee; rolling admission, advanced placement, early admission, early decision, and delayed admission plans available. $20 application fee.

Costs Per Year: $9,810 tuition; $4,160 room and board; $180 fees.

Collegiate Environment: The campus is located on 16 acres and contains 7 buildings including a library of 185,000 volumes and 680 current periodicals. Dormitory facilities are available for 450 men and women. 69% of students applying for admission are accepted including midyear students. Approximately 52% of the student body graduated in the top quarter of the high school class and 35% ranked in the upper tenth. 84% of the previous freshman class returned to this campus for a second year. About 85% of students receive financial aid; the average amount of assistance is $7,620. Scholarships range from $1,000 to $7,000. Awarding of scholarships is based on ACT, class rank, and extracurricular activities of the applicant.

Community Environment: Joliet is a multiethnic city of over 80,000. Situated on the Des Plaines river, I-80 and I-55, the city supports a wide range of commerce and industry. Parks, recreation and entertainment facilities are within easy reach of college and area residents. A recreation center provides racquetball courts, a nautilus center, classrooms and arena. A new auditorium/performing arts center will open in the spring of 1993.

COLUMBIA COLLEGE   (C-14)
600 South Michigan Avenue
Chicago, Illinois 60605
Tel: (312) 663-1600

Description: Founded in 1890, Columbia College is a four-year, coeducational, private college. It is accredited by the North Central Association of Colleges and Schools. Within a liberal arts framework, curriculum emphasizes visual, performing and media arts. The college awards both Bachelor and Master's degrees. It operates on the semester system and offers one summer session. Enrollment includes 4,985 full-time and 2,108 part-time undergraduates, and 527 graduate students. The faculty-student ratio is 1-8.

Entrance Requirements: Admission based on secondary school recommendation and record, class rank, SAT or ACT, character, and extracurricular involvement; students with academic difficulty reviewed individually; open admissions; delayed admission and early admission plans available.

Costs Per Year: $7,310 tuition; $4,456 housing; $450 books; $1,475 other expenses.

Collegiate Environment: The library contains 65,000 volumes and 250 periodical subscriptions. Dormitory facilities for students are available. The college offers an accelerated program, double major,

195

independent study, internships, and self-designed major. Remedial learning services are available. Financial aid is available.

Community Environment: The college is located in the dynamic South Loop neighborhood. It is within walking distance of the Art Institute of Chicago, the Shedd Aquarium, major theaters and an orchestra hall. Across the street from the campus, beautiful Grant Park and Lake Michigan are situated.

CONCORDIA UNIVERSITY   *(D-3)*
7400 Augusta
River Forest, Illinois 60305
Tel: (708) 771-8300; (800) 285-2668; Fax: (708) 209-3176

Description: This private liberal arts university is supported by The Lutheran Church-Missouri Synod and is operated for the purpose of providing Christian Education for students interested in careers within the church and/or within business and society. The university operates on the quarter system and offers two summer sessions. It is accredited by the North Central Association of Colleges and Schools, the National Council for the Accreditation of Teacher Education and the National League for Nursing. It was originally founded in 1864 to prepare teachers for service in the sponsoring church body and has since expanded its curricular offerings to include 30 majors in various professional and preprofessional programs. Summer session, correspondence study, and extension work began in 1932. Full-time graduate work during the regular school year was initiated in the 1966-67 session. Concordia attained university status in the 1989-90 academic year, and its schools and colleges include the College of Arts and Sciences, the College of Education, the West Suburban College of Nursing, the School of Graduate Studies, and the College of Continuing Education. Extensive music, intercollegiate, intramural athletics programs are available. Credit is granted by prior examination in certain courses for previous experience and training. Religious subjects required. Enrollment includes 1,128 full-time and 188 part-time undergraduates, and 958 graduate students. A faculty of 98 full-time and 103 part-time gives a faculty-student ratio of 1-17.

Entrance Requirements: High school graduation or equivalent with completion of 15 units including 3 English, 1 mathematics, 1 science, and 1 social science; ACT required; high school graduates with C average accepted; rolling admission and advanced placement plans available.

Costs Per Year: $9,888 tuition; $83 student fees; $4,452 room and board.

Collegiate Environment: Located in the beautiful residential Chicago suburb of River Forest, the campus of the university consists of 40 acres with the following facilities: administration/general classroom building, fine arts hall, laboratory science building, six residence halls, two gymnasiums, dining hall, education/communication center, swimming pool, human performance laboratory, student union, worship and performing arts center, early childhood lab school, art gallery, and a central service and heating plant. The Klinck Memorial Library houses more than 154,820 books, 654 periodicals, 335,595 microforms and 5,333 audiovisual materials. It seats 240 students in large reading rooms and study carrels. Living accommodations are provided for 300 men and 400 women. 77% of applicants are accepted. 83% of students receive financial aid, 65% based on need.

Community Environment: Concordia is located in the beautiful village of River Forest, a friendly community with tree-lined streets and stately homes. A shopping mall, restaurants, movie theater, and train station are all within four blocks of the campus. River Forest is just 10 miles from the excitement of downtown Chicago. The metropolitan Chicago area offers students a wide variety of cultural and educational activities, night-life, and entertainment.

DANVILLE AREA COMMUNITY COLLEGE   *(H-14)*
2000 East Main Street
Danville, Illinois 61832
Tel: (217) 443-1811; Admissions: (217) 443-8800; Fax: (217) 443-8560

Description: This publicly supported junior college is accredited by the North Central Association of Colleges and Schools. The college was founded in 1946 and offers general education, liberal arts and preprofessional transfer work, technological and terminal education,

and community services. Grants the Associate degree. Offers orchestra and extensive intercollegiate and intramural athletics. Allows credit for correspondence courses and by prior examination for previous experience or training. It operates on the semester system and offers two summer sessions. Enrollment includes 1,170 full-time and 1,519 part-time and 709 evening program students. A faculty of 139 gives a faculty-student ratio of 1-20.

Entrance Requirements: Open enrollment policy; high school graduation or GED; successful performance in preparatory courses for occupational programs; early admission, rolling admission, delayed admission, midyear admission and advanced placement plans available; ASSET recommended; application deadline for fall term is August 19th; no application fee.

Costs Per Year: $1,152 ($36/credit) district resident tuition; $3,853.76 ($120.43/credit) out-of-district; $5,448.96 ($170.28/credit) out-of-state.

Collegiate Environment: The college is located on its own 72-acre campus. The library contains 40,000 volumes. Scholarships are available, and 70% of the current full-time students receive financial assistance.

Community Environment: Danville (population 39,000) is the county seat of Vermillion County situated in the eastern part of the state, four miles from the Indiana border, 124 miles south of Chicago. Four railroads serve the area. The city is the site of the large radio telescope used by the University of Illinois for studying signals a billion light years away; it is in the middle of the corn belt. Community facilities include many churches, a newspaper, radio stations, a TV station, hospitals, YMCA and YWCA. Within the city are ten city parks. Nearby is Lake Vermilion for boating, swimming and fishing; Kickapoo State Park is also available for camping and fishing. Annual events are the All Breed Dog Show, boat races, and auto races.

DEPAUL UNIVERSITY   *(C-24)*
25 East Jackson Blvd.
Chicago, Illinois 60604
Tel: (312) 362-8300; (800) 433-7285; Fax: (312) 362-5749

Description: DePaul University, located in Chicago, is one of the ten largest Catholic universities in the world. The University was founded in 1898 by Vincentian Fathers, and its distinctive spirit is that of St. Vincent de Paul: the perfection of the person through purposeful involvement with other persons, communities, and institutions. The quarter system is used with two summer sessions. The following graduate degrees are offered: master's degrees in liberal arts and sciences, commerce, education, and music; the M.F.A. in theater; the J.D.; the Master of Law in taxation; and the Ph.D. in computer science, philosophy, and psychology. The University has two campuses. The Loop campus, including the Administration Center, O'Malley Place, the Blackstone Theater, and the Frank J. Lewis Center, home of the Colleges of Law and Commerce and the School for New Learning, is located in the heart of downtown Chicago. The College of Liberal Arts and Sciences, the School of Music, the School of Education, and The Theatre School are located on a 32-acre campus in the historic Lincoln Park area. Enrollment is 16,499 undergraduates, 5,612 graduate students, and 3,609 evening students. A faculty of 494 full-time and 676 part-time gives a faculty-student ratio of 1-17. In a typical year, 1,000 first-year students come from 200 high schools, with 68 percent from the greater Chicago area. Few undergraduate classes are scheduled in the afternoon, allowing time for study and part-time employment. The more than 85 student organizations offer unlimited opportunities for participation in both community and University activities. There are music performance groups, theater groups, student publications, and honor and service societies. Facilities include 2 gymnasiums, a swimming pool, handball and tennis courts, and extensive physical education equipment. Seven residence halls and off-campus housing are available at Lincoln Park. Both campuses have student centers and career counseling and placement offices.

Entrance Requirements: Accredited high school graduation or equivalent; completion of a minimum of 4 units English, 2 math, 1 science, 2 social science and additional units in college preparatory subjects recommended; SAT or ACT required, average scores SAT 1055 combined, ACT 24; GRE of GMAT required for graduate school; early admission, early decision, rolling admission, delayed admission, advanced placement plans available; $20 application fee.

Costs Per Year: $10,014 tuition and fees; $4,703 room and board.

Collegiate Environment: The Lewis Center Library, Law Library, and Lincoln Park Library contain 615,019 volumes, 16,088 periodical subscriptions, and extensive microcard and microfilm collections. Among the outstanding holdings are the Dickens, Napoleonic, Horace, and Irish collections, the Farthing Collection of Illinois Sessions and Statutes, the antiquarian treasury of St. Thomas More's works, and the Verrona Williams Derr-African/American Collections. The libraries have reciprocal borrowing agreements among several cooperative groups. Among the other academic facilities are a 140-seat lecture/recital hall, the Concert Hall with a seating capacity of 500, and the 1,400-seat Scat Blackstone Theater for theater productions. 69% of applicants are accepted. Dormitory space is available for 1,426 men and women.

Community Environment: DePaul is located in a culturally and academically rich urban environment. The downtown campus is minutes away from the Art Institute, Orchestra Hall, Lake Michigan, and the LaSalle Street business district. Because 75% of DePaul's students work to help finance their education, they find that the downtown location provides many employment opportunities. Facilities of the Colleges of Law and Commerce have undergone extensive remodeling, and further renovations are in progress, thus ensuring DePaul's continuing commitment to the growth and development of downtown Chicago. At the Lincoln Park campus, restoration of the community as paralled the expansion of University facilities. The potpourri of stores, theaters, musical groups, and events reflects the broad spectrum of interests of the people who live and work in the area. A short walk or local bus ride enables students to browse through neighborhoods of craft shops and fine old Victorian homes or visit the area's conservatory, zoo, and two museums.

Branch Campuses: Courses are offered in two off-campus facilities Northwest and West of Chicago. Foreign study programs are also available.

DEVRY INSTITUTE OF TECHNOLOGY   (C-14)
3300 North Campbell Avenue
Chicago, Illinois 60618-5994
Tel: (312) 929-8500; (800) 383-3879; Admissions: (312) 929-6550;
Fax: (312) 348-1780

Description: The Chicago campus of this proprietary, coeducational school was established in 1931 and is accredited by the North Central Association of Colleges and Schools. Programs are developed and updated regularly with direct input from business and industry leaders. It operates on the semester system, has 1 summer session and grants associate and bachelor degrees. Enrollment includes 1,362 men and 479 women full-time, 699 men and 318 women part-time, with a faculty of 54 full-time and 66 part-time providing a faculty-student ration of 1-33.

Entrance Requirements: Entrance Requirements: High school diploma or GED certification; minimum 17 years of age; must pass DeVry Entrance Examination or submit acceptable ACT/SAT/WPCT scores; accepts international students if requirements are met as outlined in catalog. Advanced placement and rolling admission plans available. $25 application fee.

Costs Per Year: $6,335 tuition.

Collegiate Environment: DeVry/Chicago occupies a contemporary, 103,000-square-foot facility and is located in a predominantly residential area on Chicago's northwest side. Soundproof, moveable partitions give the classrooms flexibility, and laboratories are equipped with sophisticated electronic instruments. The campus also includes an area for outdoor sports activities, vending machines, and parking for students, faculty and staff members. A number of restaurants are located near the campus, which is easily accessible by public transportation. 87% of applicants are accepted. Scholarships are available and 75% of the students receive some form of financial assistance.

Community Environment: Poet Carl Sandburg called Chicago the "City of the Big Shoulders." With its strategic position on the southwest shores of Lake Michigan, Chicago is the transportation center of the country. For students seeking the diversity of a large metropolis, Chicago offers a rich cultural heritage, a cosmopolitan atmosphere, scenic parks, gardens, zoos, the lakefront and world-renowned architectural masterpieces and museums.

DEVRY INSTITUTE OF TECHNOLOGY - ADDISON   (C-13)
1221 North Swift Road
Addison, Illinois 60101-6106
Tel: (708) 953-1300; (800) 346-5420; Admissions: (708) 953-2000;
Fax: (708) 953-1236

Description: The DuPage campus of this proprietary, coeducational school was established in 1982 and is accredited by the North Central Association of Colleges and Schools. Programs are developed and updated regularly with direct input from business and industry leaders. It operates on the semester system, has 1 summer term, and grants associate and bachelor degrees. Enrollment includes 1,500 men and 360 women full-time, and 782 men and 229 women part-time. A faculty of 55 full-time and 47 part-time gives a faculty-student ratio of 1-37. Army ROTC is available.

Entrance Requirements: High school diploma or GED certification; minimum 17 years of age; must pass DeVry Entrance Examination or submit acceptable ACT/SAT/WPCT scores; foreign students accepted if requirements met. Rolling admission and advanced placement plans available. $25 application Fee.

Costs Per Year: Tuition $6,335.

Collegiate Environment: The institute in now situated in a new 92,000 square foot facility with a library holding 8,120 titles, 176 periodicals and 139 microforms. 93% of applicants are accepted. Scholarships are available and 72% of the students receive some form of financial assistance.

Community Environment: Addison, just 20 miles west of downtown Chicago, offers distinct advantages. It is located outside the densely populated areas of greater Chicago, yet is accessible to the activities and advantages of a major metropolitan area. Chicago offers a rich cultural heritage, a cosmopolitan atmosphere, scenic parks, gardens, zoos, the lakefront, and world-renowned architectural masterpieces and museums.

DR. WILLIAM M. SCHOLL COLLEGE OF PODIATRIC MEDICINE   (C-14)
1001 N. Dearborn Street
Chicago, Illinois 60610
Tel: (312) 280-2940; (800) 843-3059; Fax: (312) 280-2997

Description: The privately supported, professional podiatry college enrolled 431 men and women recently. Founded in 1912, the school operates on the academic year system and is accredited by the Council on Podiatry Education of the American Podiatry Association and the North Central Association of Colleges and Schools and has a full-time faculty of 39. The school grants Doctor of Podiatric Medicine degree.

Entrance Requirements: Minimum 3 years or 90 semester hours of pre-professional college work; MCAT required; rolling admission plan. June 1 application deadline. $90 application fee.

Costs Per Year: $16,400 in-state tuition; $16,700 out-of-state tuition; $110 student fees.

Collegiate Environment: The college is located on the Near North Side of Chicago, convenient to business, residential, and recreational centers. The college is served by four buildings and the library contains 2850 volumes. 40% of those who apply for admission are accepted.

Community Environment: See University of Chicago

EAST-WEST UNIVERSITY   (C-14)
816 S. Michigan Avenue
Chicago, Illinois 60605
Tel: (312) 939-0111; Fax: (312) 939-0083

Description: The privately supported, coeducational university is accredited by the North Central Association of Colleges and Schools and was founded in 1978. It grants the Associate of Applied Science, Associate of Arts, Bachelor of Arts, and Bachelor of Science degrees. In addition, the school offers job and career related professional education geared to the service economy. It operates on the quarter system and offers one summer session. An enrollment of 129 men and 131 women full-time and 5 men and 3 women part-time with a faculty of 10 full-time and 16 part-time provides a student-faculty ratio of 11-1.

Entrance Requirements: High school graduation or equivalent with open enrollment policy. The school offers early admission, early decision, rolling admission, and advanced placement. $25 application fee.

Costs Per Year: Tuition $6,150 with an annual fee of $35.

Collegiate Environment: East-West is a commuter campus, housed in a four-storied building, which serves approximately 350 students of many different racial, national, ethnic, religious, and socio-economic backgrounds. The campus is equipped with a library/research center; student and faculty lounges; data processing, electronics, English and word processing labs; school auditorium; elevators, vending machines and other necessary conveniences. The atmosphere among students, faculty, staff, and administration is cordial and personal. Library holdings include 22,000 titles, 125 periodicals, 1,361 microforms, and 150 audiovisual materials.

Community Environment: Located in Chicago's South Loop (Burnham Park) District, East-West overlooks scenic Grant Park and is within walking distance of the Field Museum, Shedd Aquarium, Adler Planetarium, Art Institute and Buckingham Fountain. Also within walking distance of the University is the "Loop" (Chicago's main business and banking district) and the recently renovated, historic Printer's Row area. The accessibility of such cultural landmarks adds to the overall education of the students.

EASTERN ILLINOIS UNIVERSITY   *(K-13)*
Charleston, Illinois 61920
Tel: (217) 581-2223; (800) 252-5711; Fax: (217) 581-5188

Description: The publicly supported state university has been accredited by the North Central Association of Colleges and Schools since 1915; it is also accredited professionally by the National Council for Accreditation of Teacher Education, the American Assembly of Collegiate Schools of Business, American Home Economics Association, National Association of Schools of Art and Design, National Association of Schools of Music, American Speech and Hearing Association. It was established as the Eastern Illinois State Normal School in 1895 and has grown to include 35 departments. Grants Bachelor, Master, and Specialist in Education degrees. It operates on the semester system and offers three summer sessions. Enrollment includes 9,027 full-time and 842 part-time undergraduates and 1,432 graduate students. A faculty of 598 full-time and 59 part-time gives an undergraduate faculty-student ratio of 1-17. Preparation for State teaching certificate. Has academic cooperative plans in engineering with University of Illinois.

Entrance Requirements: High school graduation or GED, including completion of the following academic units: 4 English, 3 math, 3 science, 3 social studies; SAT or ACT required; class rank in upper half of class requires a minimum ACT of 18; upper 3/4 requires a minimum ACT of 22; GRE required for graduate programs; early admission, rolling admission and advanced placement plans available; deadline for application is 10 days prior to registration if no application cut off is in effect; housing is limited so students should apply early for housing.

Costs Per Year: $1,902 state-resident tuition; $5,706 out-of-state; $3,066 room and board; $782 student fees.

Collegiate Environment: The campus is comprised of 70 buildings on 320 acres. Living accommodations for 5,300 students, including 208 apartments and a Greek Court Complex. The library contains 900,000 volumes, 3,200 periodicals, 1.5 million microforms, and 12,453 sound recordings. 75% of those applying are accepted including midyear students. There are 2,000 scholarships available in addition to Federal and State awards, and 72% of the current student body receives financial aid.

Community Environment: Located in east central Illinois, 50 miles south of the University of Illinois at Champaign-Urbana, Charleston (population 20,000) is second only to Springfield in Lincoln Lore. Airline service is available at the county airport. Within the community are churches of all denominations, medical facilities, library, and motels. Part-time employment is available. Fox Ridge and Lincoln Log Cabin State Parks nearby are of historical, scenic, and recreational interest.

ELGIN COMMUNITY COLLEGE   *(B-12)*
1700 Spartan Drive
Elgin, Illinois 60123
Tel: (708) 697-1000

Description: The publicly supported junior college features liberal arts transfer programs and technical-vocational programs. The college is accredited by the North Central Association of Colleges and Schools and by the National League for Nursing for technical nursing. Founded in 1949 as a liberal arts institution, the college has developed new curricula and now includes many new courses in business subjects, data processing courses, music, astronomy, robotics, computer aided design, graphics, art, and a two-year nursing program. The college grants the Associate degree. It operates on the semester system and offers one summer session. Enrollment includes 2,151 full-time and 6,931 part-time students. A faculty of 115 full-time and 350 part-time gives a faculty-student ratio of 1-18.

Entrance Requirements: Open enrollment policy; high school graduation or GED; ACT requested for full-time students; early admission, early decision, midyear admission and rolling admission plans available; $15 application fee.

Costs Per Year: $1,264 district-resident tuition; $4,095 state-resident tuition; $5,027 out-of-state tuition; $24 student fees.

Collegiate Environment: The college is situated on a 100-acre campus which is located in the southwest area of Elgin. The library contains 50,000 volumes and astronomy classes are held at the Elgin Observatory which includes a Spitz A-3-P planetarium. All who apply for admission are accepted, and students may enroll at midyear as well as in the fall. 27% of the student body receives some form of financial assistance. No student housing is available. There are pre-college and freshman programs for educationally disadvantaged students.

Community Environment: See Judson College

ELMHURST COLLEGE   *(D-2)*
190 Prospect Avenue
Elmhurst, Illinois 60126-3296
Tel: (708) 617-3400; (800) 697-1871; Fax: (708) 617-3245

Description: The privately supported liberal arts college enrolls is accredited by North Central Association of Colleges and Schools, and by the National Council for the Accreditation of Teacher Education and the National League for Nursing. Affiliated with the United Church of Christ, the school is open to students of all faiths, color, and creeds. The college was founded in 1871 as a normal school; it then developed into a seminary. In 1924, the college was reorganized as a senior college and it became coeducational in 1930. The school operates on the 4-1-4 system with one summer session. Enrollment includes 1,711 full-time and 1,064 part-time students. A faculty of 95 full-time and 48 part-time gives a faculty-student ratio of 1-15. Offers preparation for State teaching certificate. Religious subjects required. U.S. Air Force and Army ROTC available. Allows credit for correspondence courses and for courses by prior examination for previous experience and training. Grants the Bachelor degree. Offers extensive program in music, intercollegiate and intramural athletics.

Entrance Requirements: Accredited high school graduation or equivalent with rank in top half of graduating class; completion of 16 units recommended, including 4 English, 3 mathematics, 2 foreign language, 3 science, and 3 social science; ACT or SAT at or above national averages required; under certain circumstances non-high school graduates admitted; early admission, rolling admission, delayed admission, midyear admission, and advanced placement plans available; $15 application fee.

Costs Per Year: $9,124 tuition; $4,100 room and board.

Collegiate Environment: The college buildings are situated on 38 acres located 16 miles west of Chicago. Residence Hall facilities are available for 550 men and women and the library contains 216,500 books, periodicals, microforms and audiovisual materials. Scholarships are available, and 55% of the current student population receives some form of financial aid. 84% of the applicants are accepted.

Community Environment: A beautiful residential suburb of Chicago, 16 miles west of the Loop, Elmhurst has a population of approximately 40,000. Residents enjoy the advantages of life in a small city and the resources of a large city with its social and cultural facilities.

EUREKA COLLEGE   (G-10)
300 E. College Avenue
Eureka, Illinois 61530
Tel: (309) 467-6350; (800) 322-3756

Description: The privately supported, liberal arts college was founded in 1855 by the Disciples of Christ and continues to be affiliated with that church. The college is accredited by the North Central Association of Colleges and Schools. It was the first coeducational college in Illinois and offers a liberal arts foundation for all major fields of study and preparation for the state teaching certificate. Chorus, and extensive intramural and intercollegiate athletics are offered. The college grants the Bachelor degree. It operates on the term system (4 eight-week terms in each school year) and offers one summer session. Enrollment is 480 students. A faculty of 43 gives a faculty-student ratio of 1-11.

Entrance Requirements: 12 college preparatory courses including 3 English, 2 mathematics, 2 social science, and 1 science; ACT or SAT accepted; class rank in upper 50%.

Costs Per Year: $11,630 tuition; $1,675 room; $1,975 board; $150 activity fee; $1,000 average additional expenses.

Collegiate Environment: Situated on a spacious 112-acre campus at the southeast edge of Eureka, 20 miles east of Peoria, the college consists of 31 buildings. The library contains 85,000 volumes, 3,500 pamphlets, 361 periodicals and 3,089 microforms. All students except those who reside with parents or those who commute are required to live in the college residence halls, which accommodate 384 men and women; fraternities accommodate an additional 60 men and 30 women. 75% of applicants are accepted. 150 scholarships are available, 35 for freshman. 87% of the student body receives some form of financial assistance. 80% of last year's freshman class returned for their second year.

Community Environment: A small community in central Illinois, between Bloomington and Peoria, Eureka (population 4,000) is 140 miles southwest of Chicago. The community provides a public library, churches, and a hospital. A lake more than a mile long offers boating and fishing. Part-time employment is available.

GARRETT-EVANGELICAL THEOLOGICAL SEMINARY
(B-14)
2121 Sheridan Road
Evanston, Illinois 60201
Tel: (312) 866-3900

Description: The privately supported seminary is a graduate professional school of theology of the United Methodist Church. It is accredited by the North Central Association of Colleges and Schools, the Association of Theological Schools in the United States and Canada, and approved by the University Senate of the United Methodist Church. Operating on the quarter system with 2 summer sessions, the seminary recently enrolled 230 men and 248 women for the Fall Quarter. Garrett-Evangelical's purpose is to enable men and women to engage in preparing themselves for various vocations of Christian ministry. Garrett-Evangelical offers resources to train African-American, Asian, and Hispanic ministers for service to both ethnic and white congregations; to the creation of openess and receptivity for women in the professional ministry; and to the cause of peace and world community. Although an autonomuous institution, Garrett-Evangelical functions as a graduate school of religion of Northwestern University. A faculty of 25 full-time and 4 part-time provides a faculty-student ratio of 1-15. Grants Masters and Doctorate degrees. 90% of applicants are accepted.

Entrance Requirements: Accredited college or university graduation with rank in upper third of graduating class; graduates of nonaccredited colleges may be admitted under special conditions. Rolling admission and delayed admission plans available. Contact Office of Student Affairs for information.

Costs Per Year: Tuition $5,310 for basic programs; $12,430 for advanced degree programs; $3,800 room and board; approximate $220 matriculation and student fees.

Collegiate Environment: Students normally begin their program in the Fall Quarter, although Winter and Spring admission is possible. Living accommodations are provided in the form of dormitory rooms for 140 men and 85 women and 64 apartments. The combined libraries of Garrett-Evangelical and Seabury Western Theological Seminary contain 270,000 volumes. Under a cooperative arrangement with the Graduate School of Northwestern University, qualified seminary students may do exchange work and also earn advanced degrees through the university. Garrett-Evangelical is located in the middle of Northwestern's main campus. This major university library is also open to Garrett-Evangelical students.

Community Environment: See Northwestern University

GOVERNORS STATE UNIVERSITY   (G-3)
University Park, Illinois 60466
Tel: (708) 534-5000; Admissions: (708) 534-4490; Fax: (708) 534-8951

Description: This publicly supported state university enrolls only juniors, seniors, and masters-level students and is accredited by the North Central Association of Colleges and Schools. It is organized into four colleges: Business and Public Administration; Arts and Sciences; Education; and Health Professions. The University was established in response to growing enrollments of state community and junior colleges and designed to be a dynamic, evolving opportunity for learning. Majors offered feature business, public administration, liberal arts, teacher education, biology, chemistry and allied health professions; preparation for state teaching certificate is also offered. The university operates on a trimester system of three trimesters, which also includes eight-week blocks within each trimester; three summer sessions are offered. Enrollment includes 2,610 full-time and 167 part-time undergraduates and 2,931 graduate students. A faculty of 315 gives a faculty-student ratio of 1-18. The university grants telecourses, correspondence courses, and by prior examination for previous courses and training and experience. Army and Air Force programs available. The university is accredited by the North Central Association of Colleges and Schools.

Entrance Requirements: 60 semester hours of college credit with a C or better average, or an Associate degree in Arts or Science and good standing at last institution attended; rolling admission plan available.

Costs Per Year: $1,968 state-resident tuition; $5,904 nonresident; $130 student fees; additional expenses average $1,800.

Collegiate Environment: The university accepts approximately 78% of its degree-seeking applicants, and students are permitted to enroll each trimester. Library contains 233,000 volumes, 2,600 periodicals, 600,000 microforms and 20,000 audiovisual materials. 34% of the current enrollment receives financial assistance.

Community Environment: Located in University Park, Illinois, on 750 acres, the University is in a suburban/rural setting. However, it is about 35 miles from downtown Chicago and thiry miles from Kankakee or Joliet, Illinois, in the Southern metropolitan area of Chicago. The campus is accessible via public transportation, from the city and most of the southern suburbs. Governors State University is a commuter institution. There is no student housing available.

GREENVILLE COLLEGE   (M-9)
315 East College Avenue
Greenville, Illinois 62246
Tel: (618) 664-1840

Description: The privately supported liberal arts college recently enrolled 853 students. The college is sponsored by the Free Methodist Church and is accredited by the North Central Association of Colleges and Schools and the National Council for the Accreditation of Teacher Education. Originally called Almira College, the school was founded in 1892 to provide higher education for young men and women under distinctive Christian influences. The college operates on the 4-1-4 semester system with 3 summer sessions and is open to students of any faith who seek a liberal education within Christian principles. Religious subjects and chapel attendance required. Grants the Bachelor degree. Has academic cooperative plan with Univ. of Illinois in engineering whereby 3 years of pre-engineering are given at Greenville, 2 years of engineering at U. of I.; former grants B.A., latter B.S. degrees. Allows credit for correspondence courses and for certain courses by prior examination for previous experience and training. Offers extensive music, intramural and intercollegiate athletic programs. Enrollment includes 853 full-time and 50 part-time students. A faculty of 55 full-time and 6 part-time gives a faculty-student ratio of 1-14. Offers preparation for State teaching certificate.

Entrance Requirements: Accredited high school graduation or equivalent; completion of 16 units with a recommended 4 English, 2 mathematics, 1 science, 1 social science, 2 foreign language. Under certain circumstances will accept non-HS graduates. Rolling admission, early admission, early decision, delayed admission, midyear admission and advanced placement plans available; $10 application fee.

Costs Per Year: $10,950 tuition; $4,750 room and board.

Collegiate Environment: The college campus is comprised of 20 buildings on eight acres located about 50 miles east of St. Louis. Students attend classes, chapel, church services, and athletic games in a compact group of buildings; a modern college union contains lounges, conference rooms, food and book store services. The library contains 115,000 volumes. Dormitories house 590 students. The college accepts 95% of those who apply for admission, and students may enroll at midyear as well as in the fall. Scholarships are available and 90% of the students receive some form of finanicla aid.

HEBREW THEOLOGICAL COLLEGE   (B-14)
7135 North Carpenter Road
Skokie, Illinois 60077
Tel: (312) 267-9800; Fax: (708) 674-6381

Description: This privately supported college is composed of a Liberal Arts college, Rabbinic College, advanced Hebrew studies division, teachers institute, and Talmudic Research Institute. It operates on the semester system and offers one summer session. It is approved by the Illinois State Department of Public Instruction and the U.S. Office of Education. Overseas studies in Israel are offered. Enrollment is 120 students pursuing the B.A., with an additional 100-150 at-large students enrolled in coursework each semester. Faculty-student ratio is 1-10. The college grants the Bachelor of Arts in Judaic Studies degree, Rabbinic ordination, and Certificates in Computer Science and Education.

Entrance Requirements: Accredited high school graduation with grade point average of 2.5; completion of a secondary Hebrew Day school curriculum or equivalent, and satisfactory scores on Sat (minimum combined score of 900, neither score below 400) and/or ACT (minimum score of 22). Two letters of recommendation and a personal interview.

Costs Per Year: $5,100 tuition; $4,875 room and board; $250 student fees; $1,400 average additional expenses.

Collegiate Environment: The campus is comprised of three buildings located on 13 acres. The library contains 60,000 volumes and dormitory facilities are available. Financial assistance is available, and 60% of the current enrollment receives some form of aid. The college accepts 60% of those who apply for admission, and students may enroll at midyear as well as in the fall.

Community Environment: A suburb of Chicago and adjacent to Evanston, Skokie (population 68,627) has all the usual community facilities as well as good shopping areas.

HIGHLAND COMMUNITY COLLEGE   (B-9)
Pearl City Road
Freeport, Illinois 61032
Tel: (815) 235-6121

Description: This publicly supported junior college was founded in 1962. It is accredited by the North Central Association of Colleges and Schools. It grants certificates and the Associate degree. It operates on the semester system and offers one summer session. Credit is allowed for certain courses by prior examination for previous experience and training. Precollege and freshman programs for the educationally disadvantaged are offered. Extensive music and intramural and intercollegiate athletic programs are also available. Enrollment is 898 men and 1,733 women. A faculty of 46 full-time and part-time gives an overall faculty-student ratio of 1-50.

Entrance Requirements: Open enrollment policy; high school graduation or equivalent; rolling admission, early admission, early decision and midyear admission plans available; non-high school graduates admitted under certain circumstances.

Costs Per Year: $1,140 district resident tuition; $3,480 state resident; $4,410 nonresident.

Collegiate Environment: The college has a permanent 185-acre campus on the west edge of the city. All qualified applicants are accepted and students may enroll at midyear. The library contains 38,000 volumes, 231 periodicals, 6,800 microforms and 743 audiovisual materials.

Community Environment: Freeport (population 28,000), a rural area on the Pecatonica River, is in a rich dairying and agricultural area. Industries in the city produce batteries, tires, precision switches, engines, curtain rods, and other goods. Railroads, buses, and airlines serve the area. Community facilities include a library, YMCA, YWCA, churches of major denominations, hospital, museum, community players, and a community concert series. City and state parks provide recreational facilities for major sports, including boating.

ILLINOIS BENEDICTINE COLLEGE   (E-1)
5700 College Road
Lisle, Illinois 60532-0900
Tel: (708) 960-1500

Description: Formerly known as Saint Procopius College, the privately supported Roman Catholic college of liberal arts and sciences recently enrolled 748 men and 892 women in the undergraduate division and 953 students in the graduate division. A faculty of 88 full-time and 157 part-time gives a faculty-student ratio of 1-15. The undergraduate division operates on the semester system and offers two summer session. The graduate division operates on the quarter system. Grants the Bachelor degree in Arts, Science or Music. The school is accredited by the North Central Association of Colleges and Schools and the American Chemical Society. It was founded and is supported by the Benedictine Monks of Saint Procopius Abbey. The Abbey, founded in 1885 and located across from the college campus, was named after Saint Procopius, an outstanding priest and monk of Bohemia, who established a monastery in that country in 1032. The college was founded in Chicago in 1887 and secured its charter from the State of Illinois in 1890. The monastic community decided to transfer the institution from the city to the more congenial atmosphere of the country and the present location was selected and purchased in 1901. The area is now suburban, 25 miles from Chicago.

Entrance Requirements: Accredited high school graduation or equivalent with rank in upper half of graduating class; completion of 16 college-preparatory units including 4 English, 2 mathematics, 2 foreign language, 1 science, and 1 social science; ACT with minimum score of 20 or SAT with minimum combined score of 770 required; GMAT or GRE required for Masters program; rolling admission and advanced placement plans available; $25 application fee.

Costs Per Year: $10,500 tuition; $4,520 room and board; $150 student fees.

Collegiate Environment: The college is located about 25 miles west of Chicago and lies midway between the towns of Lisle and Naperville. The college consists of ten buildings on a 108-acre site. The library contains 162,874 volumes, and dormitory facilities are available for 600 men and women. The college welcomes students of all faiths and seeks a geographically diverse student body. 89% of students applying for admission are accepted, including midyear students. 74% of the freshman class graduated in the top half of the high school class, 47% in the top quarter. The average score for the entering freshman class was ACT 23.4 composite. 90% of the current enrollment receives some form of financial aid.

Community Environment: Lisle (population 19,000) is a suburban city located in Greater Chicago between Downers Grove and Naperville; it enjoys a temperate climate. Trains and buses serve the area. Ten shopping centers are located within 10 miles of the campus. Part-time employment is available for students. Recreational activities include varsity and intramural sports. Lisle is the home of the world famous Morton Arboretum. IBC is located in DuPage county, one of the fastest growing areas in the Midwest.

ILLINOIS CENTRAL COLLEGE   (G-9)
One College Drive
East Peoria, Illinois 61635
Tel: (309) 694-5011; (800) 422-2293; Admissions: (309) 694-5235; Fax: (309) 694-5450

Description: This publicly supported community college serves a district comprised of all or parts of ten counties including Peoria, Tazewell, Woodford, Marshall, McLean, Livingston, Logan, Stark, Mason and Bureau Counties. The school operates on the semester system and offers 1 summer session. It grants Certificates and Associate degrees. It offers liberal arts transfer programs, general education programs, and career programs. The college is accredited by the North Central Association of Colleges and Schools. Enrollment is 4,033 full-time and 8,175 part-time students. A faculty of 189 full-time and 400 part-time gives a faculty-student ratio of 1-21.

Entrance Requirements: Open enrollment policy; high school graduation or equivalent; mature non-high school graduates able to benefit from instruction admitted; SAT or ACT recommended; early admission, and advanced placement plans available.

Costs Per Year: $1,200 district-resident tuition; $3,120 out-of-district; $4,200 out-of-state.

Collegiate Environment: The campus consists of 6 buildings located on 434 acres. The library contains approximately 82,000 volumes. Financial aid is available and 42% of the current student body receives some form of assistance. All applicants who meet the requirements are admitted. Midyear students are accepted.

Community Environment: Illinois Central College is located in rural Tazewell County on the outskirts of East Peoria, IL. Primarily a commuter college, adequate bus transportation is available from the city of Peoria. The large rolling campus of 434 acres provides an open feeling for attending students. With the surrounding wooded areas, the beautiful campus provides easy access to classrooms, laboratories, bookstore, cafeteria, and other student services. Illinois Central faculty and staff are committed to student learning and take pride in the large number of successful graduates. Over the 25-year history of the college, approximately 225,000 different individuals have taken classes, and more than 20,000 have received degrees and certificates. Illinois Central College offers a diverse curriculum including college transfer, career education, developmental assistance and continuing community education.

ILLINOIS COLLEGE   (J-7)
1101 West College Avenue
Jacksonville, Illinois 62650
Tel: (217) 245-3030; Fax: (217) 245-3034

Description: This privately supported liberal arts college is associated with the United Presbyterian Church and the United Church of Christ. It is accredited by the North Central Association of Colleges and Schools. Founded in 1829, it was the first college in the state to graduate a class. It allows credit for certain correspondence courses and for certain courses by prior examination for previous experience and training. Two courses in religion are required. Special programs include an academic cooperative program in engineering with the University of Illinois and Washington University of St. Louis, whereby 3 years of pre-engineering are given here, and 2 additional years at one of the universities, with Illinois College granting the B.S. degree and the latter granting the engineering degree; a 2-2 nursing program with Mennonite College of Nursing; and a 3-2 occupational therapy degree is offered in conjunction with Washington University in St. Louis. Bachelor of Arts and Bachelor of Science degrees are granted. The college operates on the semester system and offers two summer sessions. Enrollment includes 959 full-time and 27 part-time students. A faculty of 63 full-time and 31 part-time gives a faculty-student ratio of 1-15.

Entrance Requirements: Accredited high school graduation with rank in upper 50% of graduating class; completion of 15 units including 4 English, 3 mathematics, 2 science, and 2 social science; minimum ACT 20 or SAT 800 combined required; GED accepted; under certain circumstances non-high school graduates and C average students may be admitted; early admission, early decision, rolling admission, and advanced placement plans available; Aug. 15 application deadline; $10 application fee.

Costs Per Year: $7,050 tuition; $3,450 room and board.

Collegiate Environment: The college is situated on 60 acres in the west residential area of the city. A total of 20 buildings serve the college. The library contains 135,000 volumes, 600 periodicals, 4,404 microforms and 2,652 audiovisual materials. Dormitory facilities are available for 700 students. The college has a Phi Beta Kappa chapter. Extensive music, and intercollegiate and intramural athletic programs are offered. 81% of applicants are accepted, including midyear students. 90% of students receive some form of financial assistance.

Community Environment: Jacksonville (population 20,553) is located in the west-central part of Illinois. It is the home of the only ferris wheel factory in the United States. Within the city are a library, many churches, hospitals, movie theaters, golf courses and lakes for boating and fishing. Good part-time jobs are available.

ILLINOIS COLLEGE OF OPTOMETRY   (C-14)
3241 South Michigan Avenue
Chicago, Illinois 60616
Tel: (312) 225-1700; (800) 397-2424; Fax: (312) 225-3405

Description: The privately supported college is accredited by the North Central Association of Colleges and Schools and the American Optometric Association. Founded in 1872, the college has become the profession's largest, as well as its oldest, educational institution. The college awards Bachelor and Doctorate degrees. It operates on the quarter system and offers one summer session. Enrollment is 600 students. A faculty of 58 gives a faculty-student ratio of 1-11.

Entrance Requirements: Bachelors degree highly recommended; minimum of three academic years of college work at an accredited college or university; required are 2 semesters English, 1 calculus, 2 biological science, 3 chemistry, 2 physics, 1 psychology, 1 statistics, 1 microbiology; prerequisites must include evidence of 4 years accredited high school work or equivalent, college entrance examination, and Optometry Admission Test; students not admitted at midyear; rolling admission plan; $35 evaluation fee.

Costs Per Year: $18,921 tuition; $2,616 room; $1,290 board.

Collegiate Environment: ICO is committed to offering the most advanced teaching and clinic facilities. A new wing opened in 1985 housing a library, lecture facilities, gymnasium and administrative offices. The library contains 14,000 volumes, 160 periodicals, 3,000 microforms and 550 audiovisual materials. The coed dormitory, Brady Hall, can house 200 men and women. Financial aid is available for needy students and 85% of the current class receives some form of financial aid.

Community Environment: See University of Chicago

ILLINOIS INSTITUTE OF TECHNOLOGY   (C-14)
10 West 33rd Street
Chicago, Illinois 60616
Tel: (312) 567-3025; (800) 448-2329; Fax: (312) 567-6939

Description: The privately supported university was established in 1940 through the merger of two pioneer Chicago institutions of higher learning, Armour Institute of Technology (founded in 1892) and Lewis Institute (founded in 1896). The institute offers professionally oriented education programs on the undergraduate and graduate levels and is coeducational and nondenominational. Recent undergraduate enrollment included 2,271 men and 989 women full-time and 2,522 men and 910 women part-time. A faculty of 514 provides a student-faculty ratio of 1-11. It is accredited by the North Central Association of Colleges and Schools as well as by the following professional organizations: National Association of Schools of Art, Accrediting Board for Engineering and Technology (for aerospace, chemical, civil, electrical, mechanical, metallurgical and materials engineering); National Architectural Accrediting Board, American Bar Association, Association of American Law Schools, and the American Chemical Society. Offers Cooperative education program (alternating work and class periods) in engineering, business and design. Allows credit for certain courses by prior examination for previous experience and training. Offers overseas programs in a variety of academic fields, as prearranged with advisor, and academic cooperative plans in nursing and medical technology, law, business administration and public administration. College also offers an extensive intercollegiate athletic program. Grants Bachelor, Master, Professional, and Doctorate degrees. The academic organization of the university consists of the Armour College of Engineering; the Lewis College of Sciences and Letters; the College of Architecture, Planning and Design; the Stuart School of Management & Finance; the Chicago-Kent College of Law; and the Graduate School. The university operates on the semester system with one summer session and offers Navy, Army, and Air Force ROTC programs.

Entrance Requirements: Accredited high school graduation with completion of 16 units in college-preparatory work and preferred rank in upper quarter of graduating class; HS units should include 4 English, 3-4 math, 2 laboratory science, 1 social studies. ACT or SAT required. GRE required for graduate school. Midyear admission, delayed admission, advanced placement, and rolling admission plans available. $30 application fee.

Costs Per Year: $15,280 tuition; $4,620 room and board.

Collegiate Environment: The campus consists of 50 buildings on 120 acres and has been designated as one of the official architectural landmarks of the city of Chicago. The library contains 750,000 volumes. Dormitories and fraternity housing can accommodate 1,214 students; facilities are also provided for married students. Various forms of financial assistance are available, and 90% of the current students receive financial aid. The university accepts 70% of applicants to the undergraduate schools and 60% of applicants to the graduate division.

Community Environment: See University of Chicago

ILLINOIS SCHOOL OF PROFESSIONAL PSYCHOLOGY - CHICAGO CAMPUS   *(C-14)*
Two First National Plaza
20 S. Clark Street, Third Floor
Chicago, Illinois 60603
Tel: (312) 201-0200; (800) 742-0743; Admissions: (312) 201-0200; Fax: (312) 201-1907

Description: The privately supported graduate school is fully accredited by the North Central Association of Colleges and Schools, and the Psy.D. program is accredited by the American Psychological Association. It operates on a trimester system with one summer session. The school was established in 1976 to provide a setting in which extensive training could be pursued in the area of professional psychology. The Illinois School of Professional Psychology (Chicago Campus) is a unit of the American Schools of Professional Psychology, Chicago, IL, with professional schools in Atlanta, GA; Arlington, VA; Chicago, IL; Honolulu, HI; Minneapolis, MN; and Rolling Meadows, IL. It does not promote any one clinical psychological orientation. Currently, it offers psychoanalytic, client-centered, experiential, family systems, integrative-eclectic, behavioral, neuropsychological and group approaches to intervention. The school grants a Masters and a Doctorate degree. Current enrollment is 748 students with a core faculty of 33.

Entrance Requirements: Graduation from an accredited institution with a baccalaureate or more advanced degree.

Costs Per Year: $13,540 tuition per term; approximately $300-$500 fees.

Collegiate Environment: A coeducational professional school, the school has a great diversity of students, ranging from recent college graduates to change-of-career students. The school maintains a curriculum support library of 6,000 titles, containing current textbooks, diagnostic testing materials, reference texts and commonly used journals. Financial aid is available.

Community Environment: Located in downtown Chicago, students have easy access to neighboring colleges and universities, libraries, shops, restaurants, theatres, and the arts. Availability of public transportation is excellent. The Illinois School (Chicago Campus) is within walking distance of Chicago's famous lakefront parks and harbors. In addition, the location of the school permits students a centralized access to Chicago's many hospitals, schools, clinics, and other social service agencies.

ILLINOIS SCHOOL OF PROFESSIONAL PSYCHOLOGY - MEADOWS CAMPUS   *(C-2)*
One Continental Towers
1701 Golf Road, Suite 101
Rolling Meadows, Illinois 60008
Tel: (708) 290-7400; (800) 626-6771; Fax: (708) 290-8432

Description: The privately supported graduate school is fully accredited by the North Central Association of Colleges and Schools. It operates on a trimester system with one summer session. The school was established in 1994 to provide a setting in which extensive training could be pursued in the area of professional psychology. It does not promote any one clinical psychological orientation. Currently, it offers psychoanalytic, client-centered, experimental, family systems, integrative-eclectic, behavioral, neuropsychological, and group ap-

proaches to intervention. The school grants Masters and Doctorate (PsyD) degrees. Current enrollment is 190 with a faculty of 17.

Entrance Requirements: Graduation from an accredited institution with a baccalaurate or higher degree.

Costs Per Year: $13,450 tuition; $300-$500 fees.

Collegiate Environment: A coeducational professional school, it has a great diversity of students, ranging from recent college graduates to change-of-career students. The school maintains a curriculum support library containing current textbooks, diagnostic testing materials, reference texts, and commonly used journals. Financial aid is available.

Community Environment: The school is conveniently situated in Rolling Meadows, a NW suburb of Chicago, IL. Students have convenient access to Highways I-90 and 290. Shopping, health club and restaurants are located within the professional building, as well as in the surrounding suburbs. Training sites are available throughout the suburbs as well as in the city of Chicago.

Branch Campuses: Arlington, VA; Atlanta, GA; Chicago, IL; Honolulu, HI; Minneapolis, MN.

ILLINOIS STATE UNIVERSITY   *(G-10)*
North & School Streets
Normal, Illinois 61761
Tel: (309) 438-2111; (800) 366-2478; Admissions: (309) 438-2181; Fax: (309) 438-8192

Description: The publicly supported university was established by the State of Illinois in 1857, and was the first state institution of higher education in Illinois and the second school for teacher education west of the Allegheny mountains. The school operates on the semester system with one variable length summer session. It is accredited by the North Central Association of Colleges and Schools and professionally by National Association of Schools of Art and Design, American Association of Collegiate Schools of Business, Council on Social Work Education, American Speech-Language Hearing Association, National Association of Schools of Music, and the National Council for Accreditation of Teacher Education as well as others. Students come from most parts of Illinois, most other states, and from many foreign countries. Academic programs include liberal arts, business, fine arts, technology, contract major, and state teaching certificate program, as well as overseas programs at Grenoble and Angers, France; and Salzburg, Austria; and Nagoya, Japan; with others in England, Spain, Australia, Italy and Scotland. There is also an academic cooperative plan in engineering with the University of Illinois. The college allows credit for certain courses by prior examination. Programs for the educationally and economically disadvantaged, and intramural and intercollegiate athletics are available. Enrollment is 8,465 men and 10,701 women. A faculty of 799 full-time and 150 part-time gives a faculty-student ratio of 1-20. The university grants Bachelor, Master, and Doctorate degrees.

Entrance Requirements: Freshman admission is granted to accredited high school graduates based on a combination of high school class rank and ACT composite score; strong college-preparatory background recommended, with completion of 13 high school units including 4 English, 3 mathematics, 2 social science, 2 laboratory science, and 2 foreign language and/or fine arts; applicants may submit SAT scores in place of ACT; early admission, rolling admission, and advanced placement plans available.

Costs Per Year: $2,599.50 state-resident tuition; $7,798.50 nonresident; $815 student fees; $3,403 room and board; $3,142.50 average additional expenses.

Collegiate Environment: The university campus is comprised of 62 buildings on 850 acres located near the geographical center of Illinois. The library contains 1,400,000 volumes and numerous pamphlets, microforms, and sound recordings. Dormitories house 6,971 men and women; there are 292 units for families. Fraternities and sororities provide housing for an additional 504 men and 396 women. The university accepts 83% of those who apply, and students may enroll at midyear. 36% of the current freshmen graduated in the top quarter of their high school class, 78% in the top half. The average composite ACT score for freshmen was approximately 22. Financial aid is available, and 66% of the current student body receives some form of assistance.

Community Environment: Bloomington-Normal, with a combined population of 98,000, has a strong agricultural base with many business and industrial affiliations. Located at the intersection of Interstates 55 and 74, it is 125 miles from Chicago, 65 miles from Springfield, and 175 miles from St. Louis. Winters are moderately cold, summers are warm, and spring and fall are delightful. Both the twin-cities offer business districts for shopping, banking, and professional services, as well as municipal year-round recreational programs.

ILLINOIS VALLEY COMMUNITY COLLEGE (E-10)
2578 East 350th Road
Oglesby, Illinois 61348-1099
Tel: (815) 224-2720

Description: This publicly supported community college is accredited by the North Central Association of Colleges and Schools. Its technical nursing program is professionally accredited. The college grants certificates and Associate degrees. Allows up to 16 credits for certain courses by prior examination for previous experience and training. Offers band, chorus, and a variety of intercollegiate athletics. Grants Certificates and Associate degrees. The school operates on the semester system and offers three summer sessions. Enrollment includes 11,409 full-time and 1,866 part-time students. A faculty of 76 full-time and 122 part-time gives a faculty-student ratio of 1-16.

Entrance Requirements: Open enrollment policy. High school graduation or equivalent usually required for degree programs; SAT or ACT required for placement; early admission, early decision, rolling admission, midyear admission and advanced placement plans available.

Costs Per Year: $1,050 tuition, $40.50 student fee.

Collegiate Environment: The campus is comprised of 12 buildings on 420 acres and includes a library containing 36,879 volumes, 594 periodicals, 40,360 microforms and 2,864 audiovisual materials. Financial aid is available for economically disadvantaged students and 38% of the current enrollment receives some form of assistance. All students applying for admission are accepted, and students may enroll at midyear as well as in the fall.

Community Environment: Oglesby (population 4,175) is almost 75 miles southwest of Chicago, 50 miles northeast of Peoria.

ILLINOIS WESLEYAN UNIVERSITY (G-10)
P.O. Box 2900
Bloomington, Illinois 61702
Tel: (309) 556-1000; (800) 332-2498; Admissions: (309) 556-3031;
Fax: (309) 556-3411

Description: The privately supported liberal arts university operates on the 4-4-1 system and is accredited by the North Central Association of Colleges and Schools; professional accreditation includes National Association of Schools of Music and National League for Nursing. It is affiliated with the United Methodist Church. The first classes were conducted in the basement of the Methodist Church of Bloomington in 1851. Today the university is composed of a College of Liberal Arts, College of Fine Arts and a School of Nursing. It offers preparation for the state teaching certificate. It also offers an overseas program, The Institute of European Studies. The university allows credit for certain courses by prior examination for previous experience and training. Innovative internship opportunities exist. Grants Bachelor degrees. There is a very extensive music program. It offers intercollegiate and intramural athletics. Enrollment includes 1,829 full-time and 26 part-time students. A faculty of 143 full-time and 32 part-time gives a faculty-student ratio of 1-13.

Entrance Requirements: Accredited high school graduation or GED certification; cumulative grade point average of B or higher; completion of 15 college-preparatory units with minimum of 4 English, 2 mathematics, 2 foreign language, 2 science, 3 social studies; SAT or ACT required; advanced placement, early decision, early admission, rolling admission, delayed admission plans available; under certain circumstances non-high school graduates admitted.

Costs Per Year: $15,410 tuition; $4,290 room and board; $100 student fees.

Collegiate Environment: The campus is comprised of 40 buildings on 60 acres in the heart of Bloomington's north residential district. The library contains 200,000 volumes and residence halls can accommodate 1,100 men and women. All freshmen live in university residences. Fraternities and sororities maintain chapter houses for their

members with additional housing for 540 men and women. The college accepts 55% of applicants including midyear students. Scholarships are available and 85% of the students receive financial aid.

Community Environment: Illinois Wesleyan University is located in Bloomington, Illinois, which is known as a research, insurance, retail, education and business center. Siutated in a corporate community of 100,000 people, Bloomington is now one of the fastest growing communities in the country and is listed among the most desirable places to live in the nation.

JOHN A. LOGAN COLLEGE (P-10)
RR 2
Carterville, Illinois 62918
Tel: (618) 985-3741; Admissions: (618) 985-3741 x221; Fax: (618) 985-2248

Description: This public community college is accredited by the North Central Association of Colleges and Schools. The college was founded in 1968 and is organized into several educational divisions including baccalaureate-oriented education, occupation-oriented education, adult education, community services, and general studies. The school grants the Associate degree and certificates. It operates on the semester system and offers one summer session. Enrollment includes 6,250 students. A faculty of 213 gives a faculty-student ratio of 1-29.

Entrance Requirements: Accredited high school graduation or equivalent; 15 total units should include 4 English, 3 mathematics, 3 laboratory science, 3 social science, 2 electives for transfer students only; ASSET required for placement purposes; reading test required; open enrollment, non-high school graduates considered for admission; early admission, early decision, miyear admission, advanced placement, and delayed admission plans available.

Costs Per Year: $900 district-resident tuition; $2,550 state resident; $4,050 out-of-state.

Collegiate Environment: The community college graduated its first class in 1970 and moved to its present campus in 1972. The library contains 46,000 volumes, 3,000 pamphlets, 420 periodicals, 2,800 microforms, and 8,700 audiovisual materials. All those who apply for admission are accepted and students may enroll at midyear. 130 scholarships are available, and 60% of the current student body receives some form of financial aid.

Community Environment: Carterville (population 3,061) is located in the heart of southern Illinois, 200 miles south of Springfield and Champaign on Illinois-13 and Interstate 57. Buses, railroads, and air lines serve the area. Industries include manufacturing of household appliances, automotive trim, and ladies' garments. The economy has a strong coal-mining, agricultural, and service-oriented background and growth potential. Employment is available. Community facilities are numerous in the five-county area with emphasis on outdoor activities of all types, including hunting, fishing, camping, sailing and water skiing on numerous lakes. Cultural and artistic centers are found in and around the area.

JOHN MARSHALL LAW SCHOOL (C-14)
315 South Plymouth Court
Chicago, Illinois 60604
Tel: (312) 427-2737; (800) 537-4280; Admissions: (312) 987-1406;
Fax: (312) 427-2922

Description: The private law school, founded in 1899 as a nonprofit educational institution, is accredited by the American Bar Association. The school has strong intellectual property, informatics, legal writing, and advocacy programs. It grants the Juris Doctor degree. It operates on the semester system with one summer session. Enrollment includes 1,210 students with a faculty of 108 giving a faculty-student ration of 1:23.

Entrance Requirements: Bachelor's degree from accredited institution; Law School Admission Test entrance examination required; $40 application fee.

Costs Per Year: $15,750 tuition; $70 student fees.

Collegiate Environment: The school has two large buildings which include offices of administration, classrooms, courtrooms, library, and student lounges. The library has 328,344 holdings.

Community Environment: See University of Chicago.

JOHN WOOD COMMUNITY COLLEGE   (I-4)

150 S. 48th St.
Quincy, Illinois 62301
Tel: (217) 224-6500; Admissions: (214) 224-6500x4338; Fax: (217) 224-4208

Description: This state supported liberal arts and technical college was founded in 1975 and opened with an enrollment of 670. The college operates under the "common market" concept. Students are sent to area colleges and technical schools and to Project Outreach courses for instruction. Culver-Stockton College, Gem City Colleges, Hannibal-LaGrange College, Quincy College and Quincy Technical Schools are participants in this program. Grades, credits, certificates and degrees are received from John Wood Community College. The college is accredited by the North Central Association of Colleges and Schools, insuring transfer credits throughout the country. It is also a member of the American Association of Collegiate Registrars and Admissions Officers. Enrollment recently was 1,000 full-time students and 2,000 part-time students. The school operates on the semester system with 2 summer sessions and grants the Associate degree.

Entrance Requirements: High school graduation or GED required. Open enrollment policy; course placements exam required; rolling admission, and advanced placement plans are available.

Costs Per Year: $1,176 tuition, $2,780 state resident; $4,708 nonresident.

Collegiate Environment: The college accepts all those who apply for admission and students may enroll at midyear. Students have use of the combined library facilities of the "common market" schools listed above, which contain over 500,000 volumes.

Community Environment: See Quincy College

JOLIET JUNIOR COLLEGE   (D-13)

1216 Houbolt Avenue
Joliet, Illinois 60436
Tel: (815) 729-9020

Description: This publicly supported junior college was founded in 1901 and is America's oldest public junior college. The college was chartered in 1978. It is accredited by the North Central Association of Colleges and Schools and employs the semester system with two summer sessions. The school enrolls 1600 men, 1519 women full-time, 2748 men, and 4,560 women part-time. A faculty of 146 full-time and 445 part-time gives a faculty-student ratio of 1-21. It offers programs including two-year preprofessional training for degree candidates, two-year general education, one- and two-year vocational training, and adult education. Diplomas and Associate degrees are granted.

Entrance Requirements: Accredited high school graduation or equivalent; early admission, early decision, delayed admission, advanced placement plans available; open enrollment policy; non-high school graduates over 18 years of age condsidered; ASSET required.

Costs Per Year: $1,000 district-resident tuition; $3,300 nonresident; $100 student fees.

Collegiate Environment: The college occupies a newly built campus which is continuing to expand. All students applying for admission are accepted, and students may enroll at midyear. Financial aid is available for economically disadvantaged students, and special programs for the culturally disadvantaged are offered. The library contains 46,859 volumes. Intercollegiate athletic programs are available for both men and women.

Community Environment: Joliet is a leading industrial area 38 miles southwest of Chicago's Loop. Railroads and buses are accessible; Midway and O'Hare Airports serve the area. Industries are steel, petroleum products, chemicals, wallpaper, machinery, and greeting cards. Shipping is also a major industry. Community facilities include excellent libraries, churches of almost every denomination, hospitals, YMCA, hotels and private rooming houses. Outdoor sports include hunting, boating, fishing, golf, and other sports.

JUDSON COLLEGE   (B-12)

1151 North State Street
Elgin, Illinois 60120
Tel: (708) 695-2500; (800) 879-5376; Fax: (708) 695-0216

Description: The privately supported Christian liberal arts college is affiliated with the American Baptist Churches in the U.S.A., and the Illinois Baptist State Association. It operates on the 4-1-4 system. The college was chartered in 1963 and is the outgrowth, dating back to 1920, of the college division of Northern Baptist Theological Seminary of Chicago. It is accredited by the North Central Association of Colleges and Schools. The college grants credit for correspondence courses and allows credit for certain courses by prior examination. It offers first career programs in teacher education, business administration, computer information sciences, communications, human services and paraministry, four of which are offered in cooperation with other colleges. It grants the Bachelor of Arts degree, and offers preparation for State teaching certificate. Enrollment is 605 men and women. A faculty of 58 gives a faculty-student ratio of 1-14.

Entrance Requirements: Accredited high school graduation or equivalent; open enrollment policy; completion of 12 units including 3 English, 2 mathematics, 1 science, and 1 social studies; ACT required; early decision, early admission, rolling admission, delayed admission, and advanced placement plans available; $30 application fee.

Costs Per Year: $7,120 tuition; $320 student fees; $3,820 room and board.

Collegiate Environment: The campus is composed of 14 buildings located 40 miles from downtown Chicago. Single students under the age of 22 are required to live on campus unless living with their parents or guardians. Living accommodations are provided for 180 men and 180 women. Chapel attendance and religious subjects are required. Services are planned to provide Christian teaching, meaningful worship, and a broad cultural experience. 77% of students applying for admission are accepted, and students may enroll at midyear as well as in the fall. The library contains 50,000 volumes. Special financial aid is available for economically handicapped students, and 94% of the current enrollment receives some form of assistance.

Community Environment: Elgin (population 80,000) is located 40 miles west and north of the heart of Chicago in the beautiful Fox River Valley, the center of a rich, highly populated area and the home of many fine industries employing skilled craftspeople. Cultural activities include the community theater, Elgin Symphony Orchestra, Audubon Museum in Lord's Park, and the Laura Davidson Sears Academy of Fine Arts.

KANKAKEE COMMUNITY COLLEGE   (E-13)

P.O. Box 888,
River Road
Kankakee, Illinois 60901
Tel: (815) 933-0345

Description: The publicly supported junior college provides academic, occupational, and continuing education programs for both youth and adults. The school began operation in 1968. Recent enrollment included 1,090 full-time and 2,539 part-time students. The college operates on the semester system with one summer session and is fully accredited by the North Central Association of Colleges and Schools. A faculty of 51 full-time and 92 part-time gives a faculty-student ratio of 1-21. Allows correspondent credit and credit by prior examination toward degrees. Grants Certificate and Associate degree.

Entrance Requirements: Open enrollment policy. Accredited high school graduation or equivalent required for degree programs; ACT required. Special admission plans: early admission, early decision, rolling admission, advanced placement.

Costs Per Year: $1,136 district-resident tuition; $2,384 state-resident tuition; $6,308 out-of-state tuition; $80 miscellaneous.

Collegiate Environment: College is located on a 178-acre site. The library contains 40,000 volumes. All students who apply for admission are accepted, and students are admitted at midyear as well as in the fall. Financial aid is available, and 50% of the current student body receives assistance.

Community Environment: Kankakee (population 31,000), one of the fastest growing cities of Illinois and the U.S., has beautiful residential sections along the banks of the picturesque Kankakee River. Kankakee is located 60 miles southwest of Chicago and is the seat of Kankakee County. Some of the world's largest gladiolus fields are nearby. The manufacturing plants offer ample opportunity for employment. Nearby Chicago provides the cultural facilities for the outlying area. Kankakee County Fair and Championship Rodeo is an annual event in August.

KASKASKIA COLLEGE   *(N-10)*
27210 College Road
Centralia, Illinois 62801
Tel: (618) 532-1981; Fax: (618) 532-1990

Description: This publicly supported community college offers liberal arts and technological subjects, and has a freshmen program for the educationally disadvantaged. Enrollment is 1,513 full-time and 1,734 part-time students. A faculty of 64 full-time and 164 part-time gives an overall faculty-student ratio of 1-24. The college grants Certificates and the Associate in Arts, Science, and Applied Science degrees. Credit is allowed for correspondence courses and credits for certain courses by prior examination for previous experience and training. The school operates on the semester system and offers 2 summer sessions. It is accredited by the North Central Association of Colleges and Schools, the National League for Nursing and the American Dental Association. The college was founded in 1940 and was formerly known as the Centralia Junior College, which was the first college in Illinois to be created in accordance with the law that permitted a tax levee for the support of a community college.

Entrance Requirements: Accredited high school graduation or equivalent; open enrollment policy; non-high school graduates considered for certain programs; early admission, early decision, midyear admission, rolling admission and advanced placement plans available. $10 application fee.

Costs Per Year: $1,080 district-resident tuition; $2,296 state resident; $4,544 nonresident; $1.75 per credit hour student fees.

Collegiate Environment: The campus consists of nine buildings located on 195 acres. The library contains 30,000 volumes. Nearly all of the applicants are accepted. Financial aid is available.

Community Environment: Centralia, located 60 miles east of St. Louis, has mild winters and warm summers. Buses and planes serve the area. Community facilities include a hospital, library, hotels, motels, rooming houses, and a good shopping area. Three lakes are located nearby, for hunting and fishing, and there are three golf courses. The local merchants and civic organizations sponsor a Halloween Parade each year.

KENDALL COLLEGE   *(B-14)*
2408 Orrington Avenue
Evanston, Illinois 60201
Tel: (708) 866-1304; Fax: (708) 866-1320

Description: The privately supported coeducational college operates on the trimester system with summer term and accredited by the North Central Association of Colleges and Schools. Founded in 1934 as a 2-year college, the school now offers the Bachelor as well as the Associate degree in several areas of study. Although affiliated with the United Methodist Church, chapel services and religion courses are not required. The current enrollment included 508 men and women. A faculty of 30 full-time and 15 part-time members gives a faculty-student ratio of 1-10.

Entrance Requirements: Accredited high school graduation or equivalent; ACT or SAT required; rolling admission and midyear admission plans available; $30 application fee.

Costs Per Year: $8,346 tuition; $4,956 room and board; $150 student fees.

Collegiate Environment: The college is located in a pleasant residential section of Evanston, less than two blocks from the beaches of Lake Michigan. Modern dormitory facilities are available for 122 men and 124 women and the library contains 26,000 volumes. 70% of students applying for admission are accepted including midyear students. Financial aid is available, and 70% of the current student body receives some form of assistance.

Community Environment: See Northwestern University

KISHWAUKEE COLLEGE   *(C-11)*
Malta, Illinois 60150
Tel: (815) 825-2086

Description: The publicly supported junior college is accredited by the North Central Association of Colleges and Schools. The college operates on the early semester system and offers two summer terms. Programs in vocational and technical training, general education, adult education, and two-year university parallel courses are provided. Grants Certificate of Completion, Associate degree. Allows credit for correspondence courses and by prior examination toward degrees. Has Cooperative Education program (alternating work and class periods) in all career education programs. Army ROTC is available. Enrollment includes 2,407 students. Faculty numbers 205 members.

Entrance Requirements: Accredited high school graduation or equivalent; non-high school graduates considered for certain programs; ACT recommended (SAT may be substituted). Open enrollment program; rolling admission, midyear admission and advanced placement plans available. No application fee.

Costs Per Year: $1,152 ($36/cr) county residents; $4,736 ($148/cr) in-state; $5,792 ($181/cr) out-of-state, ($65/cr) foreign out-of-district; $58 student fees.

Collegiate Environment: The college is housed in five temporary buildings on the northeast corner of 120-acre site. Facilities include a library of 24,000 volumes, student center, and physical education facility. No student housing. 280 students are currently receiving financial assistance. 50% of the freshmen graduated in the top half of their high school class. The average score of the entering freshman class was ACT 18 composite. The college awarded 50 Certificates and 303 Associate degrees recently.

Community Environment: See Northern Illinois University

KNOX COLLEGE   *(F-7)*
K-Box 148
Galesburg, Illinois 61401
Tel: (309) 343-0112; (800) 678-5669; Fax: (309) 343-5276

Description: This privately supported, independent, liberal arts college was founded in 1837. It is accredited by the North Central Association of College and Schools and by the American Chemical Society. Academic cooperative programs are available in engineering with Columbia, University of Illinois, Washington, and Rensselaer; in business administration with University of Chicago, University of Iowa and Washington; in forestry and environmental management with Duke; in law with Columbia and University of Chicago; in medicine, nursing and medical technology with Rush; and in social work with the University of Chicago. Credit is allowed for certain courses by prior examination. Choir, jazz band, orchestra, theater, and extensive intercollegiate and intramural athletics are offered. It confers the Bachelor degree and offers its own overseas programs in France and Spain and consortium programs in Asia, Europe, Latin America, and the United States. The college operates on a three-term calendar. Enrollment includes 1,042 full-time and 14 part-time students. A faculty of 91 gives a faculty-student ratio 1-12.

Entrance Requirements: Accredited high school graduation or equivalent; completion of 15 college-preparatory units including 4 English, 3 math, 3 lab science, 2 foreign language, and 3 social science; SAT or ACT required; under certain circumstances non-high school early admission graduates accepted; early action, early admission, rolling admission, midyear admission, deferred admission, and advanced placement plans available; $25 application fee.

Costs Per Year: $16,497 tuition; $4,257 room and board; $195 fees.

Collegiate Environment: The campus is comprised of 28 buildings located on 70 acres within easy walking distance of the principal business area, theaters, and churches. Facilities include a 760-acre outdoor laboratory for studies in biology and geology. The college offers a three-three plan, whereby a student ordinarily studies three courses each term for three terms annually. The library contains 266,503 volumes and 732 periodicals. Housing is available for 839 students; 5 fraternities provide additional housing for 103 men. The school seeks a geographically diverse student body. 83% of those who apply for admission are accepted, and students may enroll at midyear as well as in the fall. The middle 50% range of test scores of entering freshmen were SAT verbal 490-600, math 520-660, ACT 24-29. 79% of the students receive some form of financial aid based on demonstrated need. 98% of the freshmen who applied for aid received 100% of their demonstrated need. Recently the average aid award was $15,067, and 5 Lincoln scholarships of full tuition were awarded. An additional 140 merit scholarships were awarded for academic and creative arts accomplishments.

Community Environment: Knox College is situated in the small city of Galesburg, Illinois, with a population of 33,500. It is 180 miles west of Chicago and easily accessible by Amtrak, Interstate Highway 74, and Greyhound bus lines.

LAKE FOREST COLLEGE   *(B-13)*
555 North Sheridan Road
Lake Forest, Illinois 60045
Tel: (708) 735-5000; (800) 828-4751; Fax: (708) 753-6291

Description: A privately supported liberal arts college located 30 miles north of Chicago, Illinois. Lake Forest College offers 27 majors and grants the Bachelor of Arts degree. Students are offered more than 50 extracurricular activities that range from athletics to the theater. It operates on the early semester system and offers two summer sessions. Enrollment is 1,050 students, and the faculty-student ratio is 1-11.

Entrance Requirements: High school graduation with a minimum of 15 units, including 4 English, 4 mathematics, 3 social science, 3 science, and 2 foreign language; SAT or ACT; high school graduates with a B average considered; early admission, early decision, delayed admission, and advanced placement plans available; $20 application fee; application deadlines: March 1, Jan. 1 for early decision.

Costs Per Year: $16,880 tuition; $3,970 room and board; $1,150 student fees.

Collegiate Environment: The college occupies a 107-acre campus of spacious lawns and beautiful trees; it is an integral part of the community since the town and the college were founded together over a century ago. The library contains 340,000 volumes. 1,250 periodicals, 100,000 microforms and 10,000 audiovisual materials. Eight residence halls provide accomodation for 966 students. 58% of those who apply for admission are accepted. Financial aid is available, and 64% of the current students receive some form of assistance. 88% of the previous freshman class return for a second year.

Community Environment: See Barat College.

LAKE LAND COLLEGE   *(K-12)*
South Route 45
Mattoon, Illinois 61938
Tel: (217) 234-5253; (800) 252-4121; Admissions: (217) 234-5252; Fax: (217) 234-5390

Description: This publicly supported comprehensive community college is accredited by the North Central Association of Colleges and Schools and by professional organizations including the American Dental Association for dental assisting and dental hygiene, and the National League for Nursing for technical nursing. It offers liberal arts transfer, vocational-technical, and general studies programs and awards the Associate degree. Cooperative education programs are available in child care, agriculture, and service electronics. The educationally disadvantaged may access freshman and pre-college programs. Intercollegiate and intramural athletics available. The college operates on the semester system and offers one 8-week summer session. Enrollment includes 2,118 full-time and 2,713 part-time students. A faculty of 120 full-time and 220 part-time gives a faculty-student ratio of 1-14.

Entrance Requirements: Open enrollment policy; non-high school graduates admitted; early admission and rolling admission plans available; $10 application fee.

Costs Per Year: $1,248 ($39 per credit hour) district resident tuition; $2,634 ($82.30 per credit hour) state resident tuition; $6,062 ($189.44 per credit hour) nonresident tuition.

Collegiate Environment: The college was founded in 1966 and moved to the present campus in 1970. The library contains over 50,000 volumes. All those who apply for admission are accepted, and students may enroll at midyear as well as in the fall. Financial aid is available, and 60% of the current students receive financial assistance. The college recently granted 416 Certificates and 680 Associate degrees.

Community Environment: Mattoon (population 20,000) is an agricultural, commercial, industrial, oil and transportation center with an average temperature of 53 degrees and an annual rainfall of 39 inches.

Bus, train, and air service is available. Community facilities include churches of all denominations, many civic, service, and fraternal organizations, a civic center, hospital, nursing center, clinic, and excellent shopping facilities. Part-time employment is available. Recreational facilities include golf courses, swimming pools, bowling lanes, theatres, skating rinks, and Lakes Paradise and Mattoon with swimming, boating, fishing and an amusement park. Mattoon is located in the heart of the Lincoln-Lore Lane with many historic points of interest in the area.

LEWIS AND CLARK COMMUNITY COLLEGE   *(J-1)*
5800 Godfrey Rd.
Godfrey, Illinois 62035
Tel: (618) 466-3411; (800) 642-1794; Admissions: (618) 467-2222; Fax: (618) 466-2798

Description: This publicly supported junior college is accredited by the North Central Association of Colleges and Schools. It offers university-transfer, general studies, and vocational-technical programs. The school also allows credit for correspondence courses and credit by prior examination for previous training and experience. It grants Certificate of Completion, Certificate of Proficiency, Associate degree. It operates on the semester system and offers 2 summer sessions. Enrollment includes 1,606 full-time and 3,928 part-time students. A faculty of 307 gives an overall faculty-student ratio of 1-19.

Entrance Requirements: High school graduation or equivalent; completion of 16 units; ACT or SAT required; open enrollment; non-high school graduates considered for admission; early decision plans available.

Costs Per Year: $1,184 ($37/cr) district-resident tuition; $3,611 ($112.84/cr) state resident; $6,400 ($200/cr) nonresident; $96 student fees.

Collegiate Environment: The college is located on a picturesque 275-acre campus north of the Mississippi River, ten minutes from Alton, and includes 20 buildings. The library contains 33,818 volumes. All those who apply for admission are accepted, and students are admitted at midyear as well as in the fall. Financial aid is available, and 67% of the current students receive some form of assistance.

Community Environment: Godfrey (population 1,225) is near Alton (population 40,000), an industrial city just north of St. Louis, having a glass industry, oil refineries, and manufacturing steel products, brass, bronze, and copper goods. Railroads serve the area and air service is available at St. Louis airport, approximately 17 miles away. Alton has a community concert association, civic orchestra, little theater, and other similar facilities at the nearby colleges. Part-time work is available in industrial and commercial establishments. Recreational activities are golf, water sports, tennis, and spectator sports. Hunting and fishing opportunities are outstanding.

LEWIS UNIVERSITY   *(D-13)*
Route 53
Romeoville, Illinois 60441
Tel: (815) 838-0500; Fax: (815) 838-9456

Description: The privately supported Roman Catholic University is directed by the Brothers of the Christian Schools. It operates on the semester systema nd offers one summer session. It offers a variety of clubs, organizations, fraternities and an extensive intercollegiate, NCAA-II, and intramural athletic program. Academic divisions include the College of Liberal Arts and Sciences, Aviation Maintenance, Teacher Education, College of Nursing, College of Business, and Continuing Education; preparation for State teaching Certificate is also offered. The university allows credit for certain courses by prior examination for previous experience and training. A freshman program for the educationally disadvantaged is available. The Certificate, and Associate, Bachelor and Masters degrees are granted. The school was founded in 1932 and was known as the Holy Name. It was a technical school until it was closed in 1942, when the United States Navy was given use of its facilities for training pilots. Upon reopening in 1944, the transition to a college curriculum was continued and the school became a four-year degree granting college in 1950. Today the college is accredited by the North Central Association of Colleges and Schools and the National League for Nursing. The college also holds membership in the National Education Association. Undergraduate enrollment is 2,012 full-time and 2,089 part-time students, and

724 graduate students. A faculty of 148 gives a faculty-student ratio of 1-16.

Entrance Requirements: Accredited high school graduation with rank in upper 50% of graduating class and average of C or above; completion of 15 college-preparatory units including 3 English and 12 in a combination of math, science, social science, foreign language; ACT required; early decision, early admission, rolling admission, delayed admission, and advanced placement plans available; $25 application fee.

Costs Per Year: $9,200 tuition; $4,200 room and board.

Collegiate Environment: The college occupies 125 acres of a 670-acre development located 35 miles southwest of Chicago and six miles north of Joliet. The Lewis-Lockport Airport is adjacent to the main campus and the college offers aviation maintenance management courses. The library contains 176,553 volumes and dormitory facilities are available for 900 students. 49% of the applicants are admitted, including midyear students. Financial aid is available.

Community Environment: Romeoville, located 35 miles southwest of Chicago, enjoys a seasonal climate. The Regional Transportation Authority between Chicago and Joliet serves the area, as well as Amtrak. Romeoville has the usual civic, fraternal, and veterans' organizations. Part-time employment is available.

LINCOLN CHRISTIAN COLLEGE   *(H-10)*
100 Campus View Drive
Lincoln, Illinois 62656
Tel: (217) 732-3168; Admissions: (217) 732-3168 X 2228; Fax: (217) 752-5914

Description: The privately supported Bible college is accredited by the American Association of Bible Colleges, the North Central Association of Colleges and Schools, and is a member of COPA. It is affiliated with the Church of Christ/Christian Church. The college, founded in 1944, operates on the semester system and offers one summer session. Grants Bachelor degrees. Its programs include Christian Ministries, Christian Education, Business, Missions, Sacred Music, and preparation for seminary studies. The school is sponsored by the Christian Church (Church of Christ). Allows credit for correspondence courses. Enrollment includes 441 full-time and 112 part-time students. A faculty of 15 full-time and 26 part-time gives a faculty-student ratio of 1-19.

Entrance Requirements: High school graduation or equivalent; open enrollment policy; early decision, rolling admission, and midyear admission plans available; ACT required; $20 application fee.

Costs Per Year: $4,160 tuition; $3,026 room and board.

Collegiate Environment: The college consists of nine buildings located on 227 acres. The library contains 113,000 volumes and dormitory facilities are available for 212 men, 204 women and 53 families. Approximately 85% of students applying for admission are accepted including midyear students. Special grants are available based on church membership and 92% of the student body receives some form of financial aid.

Community Environment: See Lincoln College.

LINCOLN COLLEGE   *(H-10)*
300 Keokuk Street
Lincoln, Illinois 62656
Tel: (217) 732-3155; Admissions: (217) 735-5050 X250; Fax: (217) 732-8859

Description: This privately supported junior college was founded in 1865 and is one of the oldest independent, coeducational, liberal arts colleges in American higher education. It is accredited by the North Central Association of Colleges and Schools. The school offers college transfer and terminal programs, preliminary preparation for State teaching certificate, and allows credit for certain courses by CLEP examination. Extensive supportive sources, fine arts, athletics, human sources and business programs are available. Associate degrees are granted. The college operates on the semester system and offers 3 summer sessions. Enrollment includes 450 full-time and 100 part-time students. A faculty of 50 gives a faculty-student ratio of 1-13.

Entrance Requirements: High school graduation or equivalent; ACT required, minimum score ACT 17; early decision, rolling admission, and midyear admission plans available; $25 application fee.

Costs Per Year: $8,750 tuition; $4,000 room and board; $360 student fees.

Collegiate Environment: The campus occupies 38 acres at the northern edge of Lincoln within walking distance of the town's business district. The college maintains two museums that contain historical documents of Lincoln, America, and all Presidents of the United States. The library contains approximately 35,000 volumes and dormitory facilities are available for 247 men and 162 women. Scholarships are available. 86% of the current student body receives financial aid.

Community Environment: Lincoln (population 17,582) was founded in 1852, the only one of 24 similarly named cities of the United States that was named for Abraham Lincoln before he became famous. He assisted in planning the city and performed law work necessary for its incorporation. Lincoln christened the town with the juice of a watermelon when the first lots were sold in 1853. Lincoln is midway between Chicago and St. Louis on the main line of Alton route of GM & O Railroad. Churches of many denominations are located here.

LINCOLN LAND COMMUNITY COLLEGE   *(J-9)*
Shepherd Road
Springfield, Illinois 62708
Tel: (217) 786-2200; (800) 727-4161; Admissions: (217) 786-2243; Fax: (217) 786-2492

Description: The publicly supported, district-governed community college is accredited by the North Central Association of Colleges and Schools. It offers liberal arts and technological courses. It has a Cooperative Education program (alternating work and class periods) in applied science programs, and a program for the educationally disadvantaged. Offers band, chorus, jazz band, intercollegiate athletic programs. Grants Certificate, Associate degree. It operates on the semester system and offers one summer session. Enrollment includes 2,400 full-time and 7,400 part-time

students. A faculty of 126 full-time and 300 part-time gives a faculty-student ratio of 1-25.

Entrance Requirements: Accredited high school graduation or equivalent; non-high school graduates considered for admission; open enrollment; early admission, early decision, rolling admission plans available.

Costs Per Year: $36 per credit, $99 per credit for nonresidents; $13 student fees.

Collegiate Environment: The college is comprised of six buildings located on 40 acres, including a library of 70,000 volumes. Ninety-nine percent of those who apply for admission are accepted, including midyear students. Of 120 scholarships available, 80 are for freshmen; 20% of the student body receives financial assistance.

Community Environment: See Springfield College in Illinois

LOYOLA UNIVERSITY OF CHICAGO   *(C-14)*
820 North Michigan Avenue
Chicago, Illinois 60611
Tel: (312) 915-6500; (800) 262-2373; Fax: (312) 915-6449

Description: The privately supported Roman Catholic university recently enrolled 13,806 students. It is comprised of the graduate school, undergraduate colleges, and professional schools which are accredited by the North Central Association of Colleges and Schools as well as by respective educational and professional organizations as follows: American Association of Collegiate Schools of Business, American Chemical Society, American Bar Association, Association of American Law Schools, American Medical Association, Association of American Medical Colleges, National League for Nursing, American Psychological Association, Council on Social Work Education and National Council for the Accreditation of Teacher Education. The university employs the semester system and offers two summer terms. Enrollment includes 5,236 full-time and 2,870 part-time undergraduates and 5,700 graduate students. A faculty of 606 full-time and 501 part-time gives a faculty-student ratio of 1-13. Loyola University was founded in 1870 by priests of the Society of Jesus. Its original name was Saint Ignatius College, a liberal arts college and high school on the westside of Chicago. After the present Lake Shore Campus was acquired and the School of Law established downtown, a new charter from the State of Illinois recognized and incorporated the institution under the legal title of Loyola University in 1909. Allows 24 hours credit for elective courses by CLEP examination. Offers Year Abroad program (Sophomore, Junior, or Senior year) at Loyola's Rome Center. Has program for the educationally disadvantaged, involving both freshmen and precollege students. U.S. Army ROTC available. Core curriculum, freshman experience required. Offers band, chorus, choir, and extensive intercollegiate and intramural athletic programs. Grants Certificate, Bachelor, Master, Professional, Doctorate degrees.

Entrance Requirements: Accredited high school graduation in top 50% of class; completion of 15 acceptable units of high school work including 4 English, 2 mathematics, 1 laboratory science, 1 social science, and no more than 2 units in nonacademic subjects; high school equivalency diploma accepted; rolling admission and advanced placement programs available. GRE required for graduate school. Under certain circumstances non-high school graduates and graduates with "C" average accepted. Seeks a geographically diverse student body. Students may be admitted at midyear. SAT or ACT required; average scores, SAT V and M: 1000; ACT: 24. Contact Director of Admissions for information. $25 application fee; priority date for Fall semester, April 1.

Costs Per Year: $13,000 tuition; $5,330 room and board.

Collegiate Environment: The university is composed of five campuses. The Lake Shore Campus is a 45-acre site on the shores of Lake Michigan in Chicago's Rogers Park district accommodating graduate and undergraduate students in the arts and sciences and nursing; all residence halls are located on this campus. The Water Tower Campus is Loyola's downtown campus and offers graduate and undergraduate programs in arts and sciences, business administration, education, and in the professions of law and social work. The Medical Campus includes the Loyola University Stritch School of Medicine and the Loyola University Hospital. The Mallinckrodt Campus, located in the north suburbs of Chicago, offers a limited number of courses in the arts and sciences and professional programs. The Rome Center campus is a 5-acre campus in Rome, Italy, and serves as headquarters for the university's overseas program in liberal arts. Student housing available for 1,988 students. The libraries contain 1,349,098 volumes, 20,000 periodicals, 860,000 microforms and 39,000 audiovisual materials. 75% of the current enrollment receives financial assistance. Many races, and religious denominations are represented in the student body which comes from 50 states and many countries in Europe, Asia, and Africa. The university accepts approximately 75% of those who apply to undergraduate programs. Average high school standing of current freshmen: 58% were in top quarter of graduating class, 88% in top half.

Community Environment: See University of Chicago.

Branch Campuses: Mallinckrodt Campus, 1041 Ridge Road, Wilmette, IL 60091, (708) 853-3000.

LUTHERAN SCHOOL OF THEOLOGY AT CHICAGO
(C-14)
1100 East 55th Street
Chicago, Illinois 60615
Tel: (312) 753-0700; Admissions: (312) 753-0726; Fax: (312) 753-0782

Description: This privately supported seminary and graduate school of theology traces its origin back to 1860 when the first of its predecessor institutions, Augustana Theological Seminary, was founded. The present Lutheran institution was the result of the merger of five seminaries. It is accredited by the North Central Association of Colleges and Schools and the Association of Theological Schools. It is a member of the Association of Chicago Theological Schools. The basic four-year program of graduate-professional studies leads to the Master of Divinity degree; also grants other Master and Doctorate degrees. It operates on the quarter system and offers one summer session. Enrollment includes 227 men and 158 women with a faculty of 21 members.

Entrance Requirements: Baccalaureate degree or equivalent from an accredited college or university. GRE recommended. Rolling admission, delayed admission; students may be admitted at midyear. Contact Director of Admissions for information. Seeks a geographically diverse student body. $25 application fee.

Costs Per Year: $4,200 tuition for Lutheran students, $6,480 for non-Lutheran students; $161-$500 per month room; $36 student fees.

Collegiate Environment: The academic complex houses the library, classrooms, offices for faculty and administration, chapel-auditorium, dining hall, lounges, book store, and recreation area. The buildings are three stories high and supplied with the latest in equipment and furnishings for theological education including the homiletics and interactive distance learning equipment laboratory. Housing is provided for 400 students in seminary-owned apartments located across the street from the main buildings. The library contains approximately 470,000 volumes. 90% of applicants are accepted. There are numerous scholarships available, and 65% of the current enrollment receives financial assistance.

Community Environment: See University of Chicago

MACCORMAC JUNIOR COLLEGE   (C-14)
506 S. Wabash
Chicago, Illinois 60605
Tel: (312) 922-1884

Description: The privately supported junior college had a recent enrollment of 150 men and 350 women. The business school was founded in 1904. Today the school operates on the quarter system with 1 summer session and is authorized to confer the Associate degree.

Entrance Requirements: Accredited high school graduation or equivalent; completion of 16 college-preparatory courses for transfer students; ACT required, SAT may be substituted; under certain conditions students with "C" average may be accepted; early decision, rolling admission, delayed admission, midyear admission and advanced placement plans available; application fee $20.

Costs Per Year: $7,125 tuition.

Collegiate Environment: The college building is in the very heart of Chicago's education district. The library holdings include 11,000 hardbound volumes. There is no student housing. Financial assistance is available. Suburban campus is located in Elmhurst, IL.

Community Environment: See University of Chicago

MACMURRAY COLLEGE   (J-7)
E. College at Lurton
Jacksonville, Illinois 62650
Tel: (217) 245-7000; (800) 252-7485; Fax: (217) 245-5214

Description: The privately supported liberal arts college maintains its historical alliance with the Methodist Church and is financially supported, in part, by the Central Illinois Conference of the Methodist Church. It is accredited by the North Central Association of Colleges and Schools and professionally by the National Association of Schools of Music and by the National League for Nursing. Grants Bachelor degree. The college operates on the 4-1-4 system and offers one summer session. Enrollment includes 648 full-time and 67 part-time students. A faculty of 55 full-time and 26 part-time gives a faculty-student ratio of 1-12. Allows credit for correspondence courses and credit in certain courses by prior examination for previous experience and training. Has Cooperative Education program (alternating work and class periods) in all departments. January term study tours and junior-year abroad programs are available. Academic cooperative plan in engineering with Columbia University and Washington University provides for 3 years of preengineering at MacMurray, 2 years at the other; MCM grants BA, other college grants degree in Engineering. Preparation for State teaching certificate is also offered. The institution dates its history from 1846, when a group of Methodist clergymen founded it as Illinois Conference Female Academy. The MacMurray College for Men was founded in 1955 as a coordinate college.

Entrance Requirements: Accredited high school graduation or equivalent; completion of 16 units; 4 English, 3 math, 2 science, 2 foreign language, 2 social studies; SAT or ACT recommended; ACT score of 20 with 17 minimum in English and Reading components; TOEFL for foreign students; early admission, rolling admission, midyear admission and advanced placement plans available; $10 application fee.

Costs Per Year: $9,620 tuition; $3,750 room and board.

Collegiate Environment: The campus, located in a residential section of Jacksonville, covers over 60 acres of landscaped land on which are located seven academic buildings, six residence halls, and six other structures. The library contains 140,000 volumes, 605 periodicals, 100 microforms and 956 sound recordings. The college seeks a geographically diverse student body and accepts approximately 71% of students who apply for admission, including midyear students. The middle 50% ACT score for the current freshmen was 18-23. There is housing provided for 337 men and 438 women. Special financial aid is available for economically handicapped students and 86% of the current student body receives some form of financial aid. Scholarships and financial aid awarded on the basis of talent and academic merit.

Community Environment: See Illinois College

MCCORMICK THEOLOGICAL SEMINARY   *(C-14)*

5555 South Woodlawn Avenue
Chicago, Illinois 60637
Tel: (312) 947-6300; (800) 228-4687; Admissions: (312) 947-6314; Fax: (312) 947-6273

Description: The privately supported graduate theological seminary enrolls 64 men and 71 women in its Master of Divinity program, 49 students in other master's level programs, and 361 students in its Doctor of Ministry program (an extension program for pastors). Founded in 1829, the school is related to the Presbyterian Church (U.S.A.) and is an accredited and charter member of the Association of Theological Schools in the United States and Canada. It is one of the twelve member seminaries of the Association of Chicago Theological Schools, is a member of the North Central Association of Colleges and Schools, and is associated with the University of Chicago. Through a program of individualized guided education, each student at the seminary develops, with the guidance of an advisor and a recommended distribution of courses, a pattern and program of theological studies appropriate to his or her needs and capacities. Cross registration is offered within the Association of Chicago Theological Schools (450 courses offered annually) and bi-registration, at reduced cost, with the University of Chicago. Combined degree programs in such areas as social work and law are available through other Chicago schools and universities. A coordinated Master of Divinity and Doctor of Philosophy program has been instituted with the University of Chicago.

Entrance Requirements: Baccalaureate degree or its equivalent; GRE strongly recommended; indications of valid interest in theological education; $30 application fee.

Costs Per Year: $5,265 tuition.

Collegiate Environment: The seminary is located in the Hyde Park neighborhood of Chicago, five miles south of the Loop and home of five of the ACTS seminaries and the University of Chicago. The library, combined with that of the Lutheran School of Theology at Chicago, houses 400,000 volumes. Dormitories house 84 students and there are also 22 apartments for married students. Students have access to the University of Chicago's Regenstein Library (3,000,000 volumes), as well as university health care facilities, cultural events and athletic facilities. Extensive supervised field education opportunities are available in the Chicago metropolitan area. Financial aid is available based on financial need.

Community Environment: See University of Chicago.

MCHENRY COUNTY COLLEGE   *(B-12)*

Route 14 and Lucas Road
Crystal Lake, Illinois 60012
Tel: (815) 455-3700; Admissions: (815) 455-3700 X 8530; Fax: (815) 455-3766

Description: This publicly supported community college is accredited by the North Central Association of Colleges and Schools. It operates on the semester system and offers one summer session. The School offers liberal arts and technological programs. Extracurricular activities include chorus, intercollegiate baseball, basketball, softball and volleyball. Allows up to 30 hours credit for CLEP or proficiency examinations and for military experience and training. Precollege and freshman programs for the educationally disadvantaged are available. Enrollment includes 372 men and 512 women full-time and 1,250 men and 1,906 women part-time. A faculty of 186 gives a faculty-student ratio of 1-22.

Entrance Requirements: Open enrollment policy. Non-high school graduates over 18 years of age admitted; rolling admission and advanced placement plans available.

Costs Per Year: $1,110 ($37/cr) district resident tuition; $4,202 ($140.08/cr) state resident; $5,077 ($169.22/cr) nonresident.

Collegiate Environment: The college moved to a new campus in 1976. All applicants are accepted, and may enroll at midyear as well as in the fall. The library contains 29,030 volumes, 8,300 microforms and 4,220 sound recordings. 10% of the current student body receives financial assistance.

Community Environment: Crystal Lake after which the city (population 25,500) was named, is the only natural spring-fed lake between Chicago and Wisconsin. Within the city are 27 large industrial firms and 45 smaller ones, churches, library, medical center, hospitals, and 350 apartment units ranging from small to luxury townhouses. Recreational facilities include the 400 acres of parks and beaches along the lake for all types of water sports and other recreation.

MCKENDREE COLLEGE   *(L-3)*

701 College Road
Lebanon, Illinois 62254
Tel: (618) 537-4481; (800) 232-7228; Fax: (618) 537-6259

Description: This private, small, career-oriented liberal arts college is the oldest college in the United States with continuous ties to the United Methodist Church. It is accredited by the North Central Association of Colleges and Schools. Founded in 1828, by a group of pioneer Methodists, it was first called Lebanon Seminary. The college offers professional programs including preparation for the State teaching certificate, and preprofessional programs. Internships are available in all majors and credit for certain courses is allowed by prior examination. Transfer credit is allowed for up to 70 semester hours from junior and community colleges and up to 96 semester hours from 4-year colleges and universities. The college operates on the semester system and offers five summer sessions. Other sessions are offered on a one month basis year-round. Enrollment includes 837 full-time and 795 part-time students. A faculty of 48 full-time and 115 part-time gives a faculty-student ratio of 1-12. Air Force ROTC is available.

Entrance Requirements: Accredited high school graduation or equivalent with rank in upper 50% of graduating class; recommended completion of 4 units in English, 3 mathematics, 2 science, and 2 social science; ACT or SAT required; minimum ACT 18; rolling admission, midyear admission, and advanced placement plans available; No application fee.

Costs Per Year: $8,640 ($270 per semester hour) tuition; $3,570 room and board.

Collegiate Environment: The campus is comprised of 20 buildings on 40 acres. The library contains 70,840 volumes and dormitory facilities are available for 306 students. The college offers theatre, and choir. Intercollegiate men's baseball, basketball, soccer, and softball, and women's volleyball, basketball, soccer, and softball are available as well as an extensive intramural athletic program. 72% of applicants are accepted, including midyear students. Financial aid is available based on need and merit, and 85% of students receive some form of financial assistance.

Community Environment: Lebanon, population 3,564, is 23 miles east of St. Louis. The city has the usual Mississippi Valley climate, neither too hot nor too cold but unpredictable. Scott Air Force Base is six miles from downtown. Employment is available in Belleville, 12 miles away, Fairview Heights, 12 miles away, and in St. Louis proper. Hospital facilities are in Belleville, Highland, Breese and St. Louis. Local recreational activities are tennis, hunting, fishing, golfing, picnicking, and community theater.

MEADVILLE/LOMBARD THEOLOGICAL SCHOOL   *(C-14)*

5701 South Woodlawn Avenue
Chicago, Illinois 60637
Tel: (312) 753-3178; Admissions: (312) 753-3288; Fax: (312) 753-1323

Description: The privately supported institution is a Unitarian-related, Universalist-related, coeducational, graduate school offering 2 basic professional degree programs: the Master of Divinity and the Doctor of Ministry. It is a fully accredited member of the Association of Theological Schools and is affiliated with the University of Chicago. The theological school was founded in 1844. It operates on the quarter system and offers an intensive summer session. Enrollment includes 41 full-time and 26 part-time graduate students. A faculty of 4 full-time and 4 part-time gives a faculty-student ratio of 1-8.

Entrance Requirements: Baccalaureate degree or equivalent from an accredited college or university; GRE required; rolling admission and midyear admission plans available; $35 application fee.

Costs Per Year: $13,106 tuition.

Collegiate Environment: The campus is comprised of 4 buildings on the campus of the University of Chicago, including the library, which contains 96,000 volumes. Ample housing is available for single and married students on campus. Most students receive financial assistance; the amount for each student is based on individual need.

Community Environment: See University of Chicago.

MIDSTATE COLLEGE   *(G-9)*
244 S.W. Jefferson Street
Peoria, Illinois 61602
Tel: (309) 673-6365

Description: Privately supported two-year junior college of business. Enrollment is 470 students with a faculty of 20 full-time and 40 part-time members. The school operates on the quarter system with 1 summer session and is accredited by the North Central Association of Colleges and Schools. Midstate grants an Associate degree, diploma, and certificate.

Entrance Requirements: High school graduation or GED; open enrollment; early admission, early decision, rolling admission, delayed admission plans; $25 application fee.

Costs Per Year: $4,800 tuition; $1,575 room; $105 student fee (figures based on a 9-month academic year).

Collegiate Environment: The school is fully air-conditioned and includes a library of 10,000 volumes and dormitory facilities for 82 men and women. Ninety percent of the applicants are accepted, including midyear students. 85% of the current student body receives financial assistance.

Community Environment: Peoria is the third largest city of downstate Illinois. All modes of transportation are available. It is the hub of the central area of the state for cultural, business and professional activities. Peoria is a manufacturing and shipping center located in the heart of the farm belt. Community facilities include good shopping areas and recreational opportunities. Job opportunities are good, particularly for summer work. Points of interest are Fort Creve Coer, Indian burial mounds, Peoria Historical Society Museum, Lakeview Center for Arts Sciences, the Planetarium, the Peoria Civic Center, and Wildlife Prairie Park.

MIDWESTERN UNIVERSITY   *(C-14)*
555 31st Street
Downers Grove, Illinois 60515
Tel: (800) 458-6253; Admissions: (708) 515-6472

Description: The privately supported professional college is approved by the American Osteopathic Association. Founded in 1902 as the Chicago School of Osteopathy, the original charter was revised and the present name was adopted in 1913. It grants a Professional degree. It operates on the quarter system. Enrollment includes 591 students. A faculty of 386 gives a faculty-student ratio of 1-2.

Entrance Requirements: B.S. or B.A. degrees recommended; completion of minimum 90 semester hours of credit from a regionally accredited college or university including one year of biology, organic chemistry, inorganic chemistry, physics and English required; Medical College Admissions Test required; rolling admission plan; $30 supplemental application fee.

Costs Per Year: $16,620 resident tuition; $20,200 out-of-state; $5,575 room and board; students are required to furnish own standard medical microscope, dissection kit, laboratory gowns, and prescribed textbooks; additional expenses average $4,000.

Collegiate Environment: 14 buildings on 104 acres comprise the campus and the library contains 20,500 volumes. The Chicago Osteopathic Hospital and Medical Center and the Olympia Falls Osteopathic Hospital and Medical Center are the major teaching hospitals of the college. An on-campus residence hall and apartment housing is availabe. 10% of the applicants are accepted. Approximately 85% of the current enrollment receives financial assistance.

Community Environment: See University of Chicago.

MILLIKIN UNIVERSITY   *(I-11)*
1184 West Main Street
Decatur, Illinois 62522
Tel: (217) 424-6210; (800) 373-7733; Fax: (217) 424-3993

Description: The privately supported university is affiliated with the Presbyterian Church U.S.A. and offers undergraduate degrees from the College of Arts and Sciences, Tabor School of Business, College of Fine Arts, and the School of Nursing. The university operates on the semester system and offers one summer session. Enrollment is 1,797 full-time and 95 part-time students. A faculty of 120 full-time and 67 part-time gives an overall faculty-student ratio of 1-15. The college is accredited by the North Central Association of Colleges and Schools and professionally by the National Association of Schools of Music and the National League for Nursing. Allows credit for correspondence courses (6 semester hours) and by proficiency examination in several areas. Has overseas program with Institute of European studies and offers a Washington semester and a United Nations semester. Grants Bachelor degrees. Historically, Millikin was founded in 1901 as the Decatur College and Industrial School, and together with nearby Lincoln College was known for 50 years as the James Millikin University. This corporate identity was dissolved in 1953, when the separate institutions of Lincoln College and Millikin University were designated.

Entrance Requirements: High school graduation or equivalent with rank in upper half of graduating class and completion of 15 units, including 4 English, 3 math, 2 science, 2 foreign language, and 2 social studies; SAT or ACT required; minimum ACT score of 20 composite, or SAT 900 combined; candidates with lower requirements may be accepted as conditional students; delayed admission, midyear admission, advanced placement and rolling admission plans available; auditions required for admission to School of Music; personal interviews recommended; $25 application fee.

Costs Per Year: $11,910 tuition; $4,278 room and board; $91 student fees.

Collegiate Environment: The 40-acre campus is located near one of Decatur's most attractive residential areas, one mile west of the central business district. Facilities include six classroom buildings, a library, a University Center, gymnasium, physical education center, fine arts center, and nine large residence halls. There is also an athletic complex including a football field and running track. The library contains 163,218 volumes, 1,000 periodicals and 21,809 microforms. Living accommodations are available for 1,250 students, including fraternities and sororities that house 130 men and 170 women. 81% of applicants are accepted. Financial aid is available, and 87% of the current student body receives some form of assitance.

Community Environment: Decatur is a diversified industrial community known as the "Soybean Capital of the World." Bus and air service are available. Many part-time jobs are available. A well-developed park system provides varied recreational opportunities. South of Decatur is the Lincoln Trail Homestead State Park, which marks the first homestead site of the Lincoln family in Illinois.

MONMOUTH COLLEGE   *(F-6)*
700 East Broadway
Monmouth, Illinois 61462
Tel: (309) 457-2131; (800) 747-2687; Fax: (309) 457-2141

Description: The privately supported college is an independent, residential liberal arts college that enrolled 386 men and 446 women full-time and 5 part-time students recently. There are 51 full-time and 20 part-time faculty members. The faculty-student ratio is 1-13. The college operates on the semester system and offers a summer term. It is accredited by the North Central Association of Colleges and Schools and the American Chemical Society. Founded in 1853 by Presbyterians of Scottish descent as a preparatory school for ministers of the Associated Reformed Presbyterian Church, Monmouth has retained its Scottish traditions and its affiliation with the church, now the United Presbyterian Church of the United States of America. It was one of the first colleges in the nation to operate as a coeducational institution and is the birthplace of the first two sororities in the nation, Pi Beta Phi and Kappa Kappa Gamma. It was one of the first in the Midwest to be accredited for the preparation of chemists by the

American Chemical Society. It also offers preparation for State teaching certificate, and programs in nursing, hospital administration, medical technology, and pre-engineering. A wide range of overseas programs in Europe, Asia, and sub-Asia through the Associated College of the Midwest is available. Army ROTC is available. Academic cooperative programs in engineering are offered with 3 universities, whereby 3 years are given at Monmouth, 2 at other school; Monmouth grants the BA, and the BS is granted from the other university. There is a similar program in nursing and medical technology with Rush University (2 years-2 years). Extracurricular activities include extensive music, intramural and intercollegiate athletic programs, forensics and theater.

Entrance Requirements: High school graduation or equivalent with B average and rank in upper 50% of graduating class; recommended minimum of 14 units including 4 English, 3 social science, 3 mathematics, 2 science and 2 foreign language; SAT minimum 400V, 400M or ACT 19 required; non-high school graduates considered under certain circumstances; early admission, early decision, delayed admission and advanced placement plans available; no application fee.

Costs Per Year: $13,460 tuition; $4,200 room and board.

Collegiate Environment: The campus is located in a residential section of the city and is composed of 38 buildings on 30 acres. The library contains 250,000 volumes, 61,000 microforms and 635 periodicals; living accommodations are available for 500 men and 500 women. There are 6 Greek letter fraternities and sororities. 75% of the applicants are accepted, including midyear students. Financial assistance is available and 98% of the student body receives some form of financial aid.

Community Environment: Monmouth is located about 180 miles southwest of Chicago and 180 miles north of St. Louis in the heart of the rich corn belt of the Midwest. Although agriculture is the backbone of economy in the area, numerous small businesses and light industry firms are located here. As a region noted for beef cattle feeding, Monmouth holds a 3-day Prime Beef Festival in September. Monmouth Park, a natural forest at the outskirts of the city, has playground equipment, picnic facilities and an 18-hole municipal golf course.

MONTAY COLLEGE   (C-14)
3750 West Peterson Avenue
Chicago, Illinois 60659-3115
Tel: (312) 539-1919

Description: Privately supported liberal arts junior college recently enrolled 394 students. It is conducted by the Congregation of the Sisters of Saint Felix of the Roman Catholic Church and is accredited by the North Central Association of Colleges and Schools. Holds institutional membership in the American Association of Community and Junior Colleges. The school had operated as an extention of Loyola University until 1953 when it opened formally as an independent institution. The college operates on the semester system with one summer session, and provides an adult education program of evening and Saturday classes. Allows credit for correspondence certain courses by prior examination for previous experience and training. Grants the Associate degree.

Entrance Requirements: Accredited high school graduation with rank in upper 75% of graduating class; completion of 16 units including 4 English, 2 mathematics, 2 laboratory science, 2 social science. Rolling admission, early decision and advanced placement plans available. $10 application fee; $25 for foreign students.

Costs Per Year: $4,900 tuition and $60 student fees.

Collegiate Environment: The campus in the northwest section of Chicago is beautifully landscaped and covers an area of approximately 34 acres. The library contains 67,000 volumes. 85% of those who apply for admission are accepted, and students may enroll at midyear. Seventy percent of the current enrollment receives financial assistance.

Community Environment: See University of Chicago

MOODY BIBLE INSTITUTE   (C-14)
820 North La Salle Drive
Chicago, Illinois 60610
Tel: (312) 329-4000; (800) 967-4624; Admissions: (312) 329-4266;
Fax: (312) 329-2055

Description: The privately supported Bible institute is accredited by the North Central Association of Colleges and Schools and the American Association of Bible Colleges and the National Association of Schools of Music. The institute was founded in 1886 as a training school, dedicated to teaching men and women in fundamentals of the English Bible and practical Christian work. The college grants the Bachelor degree. It operates on the semester system with various summer sessions. Offers and allows credit for correspondence courses. Offers band, collegiate choirs, intercollegiate basketball, volleyball, and soccer; intramural athletics. Enrollment includes 1,389 full-time and 66 part-time undergraduates and 77 graduate students. A faculty of 78 full-time gives a faculty-student ratio of 1-21.

Entrance Requirements: High school graduation or equivalent with a 2.5 grade point average and rank in upper half of graduating class; 12 academic subjects; ACT required. Evidence of good Christian character and membership in an evangelical Protestant church also required; early decision, deferred admission, and midyear admission plans available; $35 application fee.

Costs Per Year: No tuition; $4,100 room and board; $1,209 student fees; additional expenses average $1,100.

Collegiate Environment: The institute consists of 13 buildings, and the library contains 127,000 volumes. Living accommodations are provided for 654 men, 517 women, and 28 couples. 68% of applicants are accepted. 50% of the freshman class was in the top quarter of high school class, 79% in the top half.

Community Environment: See University of Chicago

MORAINE VALLEY COMMUNITY COLLEGE   (F-3)
10900 South 88th Avenue
Palos Hills, Illinois 60465
Tel: (708) 974-4300; Admissions: (708) 974-2110

Description: The publicly supported community college has an enrollment of 4,518 men and women full-time, and 8,755 men and women part-time. A faculty of 163 full-time and 469 part-time gives an overall faculty-student ratio of 1-21. The curriculum is designed to meet the occupational, academic, and cultural needs of the citizens of Southwest Cook County. The school was founded in 1967 and the first on-campus facilities were available for the 1969 fall semester. The school uses the semester system with 1 summer session. It is fully accredited by the North Central Association of Colleges and Schools. Offers band, chorus, intercollegiate and intramural athletics.

Entrance Requirements: High school graduation or equivalent; open enrollment policy; non-high school graduates are admitted for certain courses; special admission programs include rolling admission and advanced placement plan.

Costs Per Year: $1,232 for district residents; $3,932 for state residents; $4,532 for out-of-state residents.

Collegiate Environment: The campus is located on a 306-acre tract in the city of Palos Hills, immediately adjacent to the Cook County Forest Preserve. The campus facilities total more than 640,000 square feet. The college offers counseling and academic advising services, financial aid services, services for students with special needs, a child care center, an Adult Center, and a placement service. Students are admitted at midyear as well as in the fall. The college library contains 81,062 volumes, 564 periodicals, 648 titles on microfilm and 4,044 audiovisual materials.

Community Environment: Palos Hills is located 20 miles south of downtown Chicago near Oak Lawn, a suburban area that has access to all the cultural, educational, and recreational opportunities of Chicago. All major forms of transportation are available. The climate is seasonal. Part-time employment is available.

MORRISON INSTITUTE OF TECHNOLOGY   (C-8)
701 Portland Avenue
Morrison, Illinois 61270
Tel: (815) 772-7218; Admissions: (815) 772-7218 x11; Fax: (815) 772-7584

Description: Morrison Institute of Technology was founded in 1973, when it purchased the facilities of the Institute of Drafting and Technology and expanded all programs. It is accredited by the Accreditation Board for Engineering and Technology. In 1975 Morrison was granted two-year college status by the State of Illinois. The institute operates on the semester system. Morrison offers engineering technology programs in design and drafting, highway engineering, and building construction. Using 45 computers contributes to the rapid growth of the school as a leader in computer aided drafting (CAD) and the extensive use of Auto-CAD. Enrollment includes 190 full-time and 3 part-time students. A faculty of 14 full-time and 1 part-time provides a faculty-student ratio of 1-20.

Entrance Requirements: High school graduation or GED; high school graduates with a C average accepted; 2 college preparatory mathematics and drafting courses recommended; open enrollment; rolling admission, early admission, delayed admission, midyear admission and advanced placement plans available, $25 application fee, $25 dorm reservation.

Costs Per Year: $6,810 tuition; $1,800 room and board.

Collegiate Environment: Situated on 17 acres, Morrison's campus includes a new Engineering Technology Center, main offices, classroom complex, student recreation center, dormitories and apartments for 181 students, and a library containing 3,010 volumes. Intramural athletics are part of the yearly agenda. All qualified students applying for admission are accepted. 24 performance and 5 academic shcoalrships are available and 85% of the current enrollment receives some form of financial assistance.

Community Environment: Morrison is located 130 miles west of Chicago and 10 miles east of the Mississippi River. It is close to the Chestnut Lodge Winter Ski Area. Students are welcome in the local Theater Association and recreation leagues. Morrison also has two city parks and a state park with 1,700-acre lake. Community facilities include shopping areas, 16 churches, a public library, and two medical centers.

MORTON COLLEGE   *(C-14)*
3801 South Central Avenue
Cicero, Illinois 60650
Tel: (708) 656-8000; Admissions: (708) 656-8000 x342; Fax: (708) 656-9592

Description: This publicly supported community college operates on the semester system and offers 1 summer session. It offers liberal arts, technological, business and teaching-preparation programs. Chorus, intercollegiate and intramural athletics as well as student government, clubs and organizations are available. It is accredited by the North Central Association of Colleges and Schools, and professionally by the American Physical Therapy Association and American Dental Association for dental assistant. Enrollment includes 837 full-time and 3,519 part-time students. A faculty of 50 full-time and 202 part-time members gives an overall faculty-student ratio of 1-18.

Entrance Requirements: Accredited high school graduation or equivalent; open enrollment policy; non-high school graduates considered for certain programs; ACT recommended, TOEFL required for international students; early admission, early decision, rolling admission and advanced placement plans available; $10 application fee.

Costs Per Year: $1,350 district-resident tuition; $4,722 out-of-district; $5,675 nonresident.

Collegiate Environment: The college was founded as Morton Junior College in 1924 and became a member of the American Association of Junior Colleges in 1929. The library contains 40,759 volumes. All students applying for admission are accepted. Limited financial assistance is available; 15% of the current student body receives some form of financial aid.

Community Environment: A residential and industrial suburb on the west side in the greater Chicago area, Cicero has a population of 62,000.

NATIONAL COLLEGE OF CHIROPRACTIC   *(D-2)*
200 E. Roosevelt Road
Lombard, Illinois 60148-4583
Tel: (708) 629-2000; (800) 826-6285; Fax: (708) 268-6600

Description: The National College of Chiropractic is a five-year academic program, not-for-profit, coeducational, private, professional college with an enrollment of approximately 800 students. The college was founded in 1906 and operates on the trimester system with one summer session. Allows credit for correspondence courses from accredited colleges and by prior examination for previous training and

experience. Grants the Doctor of Chiropractic and Bachelor of Science degrees. The faculty consists of 72 full-time and 16 part-time members. The college is fully accredited by the North Central Association of Colleges and Schools, and the Council on Chiropractic Education. The college operates three public clinics and works in conjunction with two Salvation Army Clinics in surrounding areas which provide training to senior interns.

Entrance Requirements: Minimum (75 semester hours) pre-professional college work at accredited college or university; $55 application fee; Baccalaureate degree or equivalent will be required by September, 1999.

Costs Per Year: $4,421 per trimester tuition; $1,158-$2,492 per trimester room.

Collegiate Environment: The campus is composed of nine buildings located on 30 acres. The library contains 23,000 volumes and living accommodations are provided for 200 men, women, and families. 90% of the current students receive some form of financial assistance.

Community Environment: Lombard (population 49,000) is served by the Chicago-Northwestern Railway, buses, and O'Hare Field. The city enjoys a temperate climate. Excellent community facilities include the Helen Plum Library, 23 churches of all major denominations, shopping center, YMCA, and numerous civic, fraternal, business, and social organizations. A hospital is in Downers Grove, two miles distant. Six parks, swimming pool, and a year-round recreation program provide facilities for recreational activities. Special events include the annual Lilac Time Festival and Parade.

NATIONAL-LOUIS UNIVERSITY   *(B-14)*
2840 Sheridan Road
Evanston, Illinois 60201
Tel: (800) 443-5522 x5522; (800) 443-5522 x5151; Admissions: (800) 443-5522 x5151

Description: National-Louis University is a private, independent, comprehensive university. It was founded in 1886 and was known as National College of Education until 1989. The university is accredited by the North Central Association of Colleges and Schools and by the National Council for Accreditation of Teacher Education. The university is composed of a College of Arts and Sciences, a College of Management and Business, and National College of Education (which retains the historic name of the institution). The university offers undergraduate and graduate programs in liberal arts, allied health programs, accounting, business administration and management, computer information systems, human services, and teacher education, with preparation for the State teaching certificate. Allows credit for for certain courses by prior examination for previous experience and training. It operates on the quarter system and offers two summer sessions. Enrollment includes 3,800 full-time and 3,507 part-time undergraduate students and 4,084 graduate students. A faculty of 261 full-time and 400 part-time gives an undergraduate faculty-student ratio of 1-13.

Entrance Requirements: High school graduation or equivalent; recommend completion of 4 units in English, 2 math, 1 social studies, 2 science; SAT or ACT required; minimum scores: SAT 375V, 375M; ACT 19. Under certain circumstances non-HS graduates accepted. Special admission plans available: rolling admission, advanced placement. $25 application fee.

Costs Per Year: $9,540 tuition; $4,252 room and board; additional expenses average $625-$850.

Collegiate Environment: The college is located on the border between Evanston and Wilmette, lakeshore suburbs just north of Chicago. The six buildings which serve the campus include a library of 156,198 volumes and dormitory facilities for 180 men and women. 85% of the current enrollment receives financial assistance.

Community Environment: See Northwestern University

Branch Campuses: 18 South Michigan, Chicago, IL 60603; 200 Napeville Road, Wheaton, IL, 60187; 1000 Capitol Drive, Wheeling, IL, 60090

NORTH CENTRAL COLLEGE   *(E-1)*
30 North Brainard Street
Naperville, Illinois 60566
Tel: (708) 420-3414; Fax: (708) 420-4234

Description: The privately supported liberal arts college was established in 1861. It is affiliated with the United Methodist Church. The college is accredited by the North Central Association of Colleges and Schools. It offers preparation for the State teaching certificate; exceptional, funded, independent study programs; work-study and internship programs; career planning and placement services; international study; a Washington, D.C., term; and a United Nations term. It also offers band, chorus, other special musical groups; extensive intercollegiate and intramural athletic program for both men and women; theater; and an award winning (6 Marconi awards) broadcasting experience on college-owned FM-station. The college operates on a trimester or 3-3 systen and offers a midwinter term for individual research and study, and one summer session. Enrollment includes 1,377 full-time and 727 part-time undergraduat, and 340 graduate students. A faculty of 93 full-time and 78 part-time gives an undergraduate faculty-student ratio of 1-15 and an overall faculty-student ratio of 1-14. Air Force, Army and Navy ROTC programs are available.

Entrance Requirements: High school graduation with minimum of C average and rank in upper half of graduating class; recommended completion of 13 units including 3 English, 3 mathematics, 2 laboratory science, 3 social studies and 2 foreign language; minimum SAT verbal 410, math 410 or minimum ACT 20 required; high school equivalency diploma accepted; early admission, early decision, rolling admission, and advanced placement plans available; $20 application fee.

Costs Per Year: $11,718 tuition; $4,398 room and board; $120 student fees.

Collegiate Environment: The 54-acre campus is situated in the historic residential section of the city, near the central business district. The college library contains 113,647 volumes, 1,061 periodicals and 30,000 microforms. Residence halls can accommodate 865 students. The college seeks a geographically diverse student body and 78% of applicants are accepted, including midyear students. 76% of the previous freshman class returned to the campus for a second year.

Community Environment: Naperville (population 88,000) is a suburban community 29 miles west of Chicago on the Burlington Northern Railroad route. It has a moderate temperate climate. It is the site of many corporate and scientific research installations and is in the "Corporate Corridor of the Midwest." Community facilities include public and college libraries, a YMCA, hospital, many churches, motels, shopping facilities, restaurants, entertainment facilities and numerous civic organizations. Many parks and attractive natural surroundings provide for outdoor sports and recreation. Part-time employment for students is generally available.

Branch Campuses: Schaumburg, IL; St. Charles, IL.

NORTH PARK COLLEGE   (C-14)
3225 W. Foster Avenue
Chicago, Illinois 60625-4987
Tel: (312) 583-2700; (800) 888-6728; Admissions: (312) 244-5500;
Fax: (312) 244-4953

Description: The school is a private, coeducational institution affiliated with the Evangelical Covenant Church. The college is accredited by the North Central Association of Colleges and Schools. It operates on the semester system and offers four summer sessions. Enrollment includes 906 full-time and 207 part-time undergraduates and 84 evening program undergraduates and 254 graduate students. A faculty of 75 full-time and 15 part-time gives a faculty-student ratio of 1:15.

Entrance Requirements: High school graduation; high school transcripts; application form and personal statement; recommendation form; ACT or SAT I required; rolling admission, early admission, midyear admission, deferred admission, and advanced placement plans available; $20 application fee.

Costs Per Year: $12,580 tuition; $4,280 room and board; $450 per semester hour part-time tuition.

Collegiate Environment: North Park's 30 acre campus has a small-town flavor and warmth. The principal classrooms and administrative buildings are set off by spacious lawns and bordered by four residential halls, two men's and two women's. The library holdings include 217,024 volumes. Campus activities range from NCAA Division III sports for men and women, intramurals, student government, newspaper, and numerous musical performance groups to Urban Outreach, a nationally acclaimed, student-run volunteering organization. 82% of applicants meet admission criteria and are accepted. Many scholarships are available and 85% of students receive some form of financial aid.

Community Environment: See University of Chicago.

NORTH PARK THEOLOGICAL SEMINARY   (C-14)
3225 W. Foster Avenue
Chicago, Illinois 60625-4987
Tel: (312) 244-5500; (800) 964-0101; Admissions: (312) 244-5530;
Fax: (312) 244-5530

Description: Founded in 1891, the privately supported graduate seminary is affiliated with the Evangelical Covenant Church. It is accredited by the Association of Theological Schools. Courses in biblical, theological, historical, and ministerial studies lead to the Master of Divinity, Master of Arts in Theological Studies, or Master of Arts in Christian Education. It operates on the quarter system and offers two summer sessions. Enrollment includes 115 men and 47 women. A faculty of 17 full-time and 18 part-time gives a faculty-student ratio of 1-8.

Costs Per Year: $5,075 tuition; $275-$615 room per month; $405 student fees.

Collegiate Environment: The seminary is located on the same campus as North Park College. Separate seminary facilities include a library of 69,000 volumes and 75 apartments for single students and married couples with children. 95% of the applicants are accepted, including midyear students. Scholarships are available, and 70% of the current enrollment receives some form of assistance.

Community Environment: See University of Chicago.

NORTHEASTERN ILLINOIS UNIVERSITY   (C-14)
5500 North St. Louis Avenue
Chicago, Illinois 60625
Tel: (312) 794-2600; Fax: (312) 794-6246

Description: The publicly supported liberal arts college was established in 1961 and is accredited by the North Central Association of Colleges and Schools. It grants Bachelor and Master degrees in many subject areas, and offers preparation for State teaching certificate. It operates on the semester system and offers two summer sessions. Enrollment includes 3,962 full-time and 3,441 part-time undergraduates and 2,825 graduate students. A faculty of 334 full-time and 199 part-time gives a faculty-student ratio of 1-21.

Entrance Requirements: High school graduation or equivalent with rank in upper half of graduating class or ACT minimum 19 or SAT minimum 870 required; midyear admission and advanced placement plans available.

Costs Per Year: $1,902 state-resident tuition; $5,706 nonresident; $267.25 student fees.

Collegiate Environment: The college is comprised of eight buildings on 67 acres. The library contains 600,000 volumes. Approximately 73% of students applying for admission are accepted including midyear students. 30% of the students graduated in the top quarter of their high school class. The average score for the entering freshman class was ACT 17 composite. Scholarships are available and 37% of the student body receives some form of financial assistance.

Community Environment: See University of Chicago.

Branch Campuses: Inner City Studies campus, 700 Oakwood Blvd., Chicago, IL 60653; El Centro, 3119 N. Pulaski, Chicago, IL 60641; Chicago Teachers Center, 770 N. Halsted, Chicago, IL.

NORTHERN BAPTIST THEOLOGICAL SEMINARY   (E-2)
660 East Butterfield Road
Lombard, Illinois 60148
Tel: (708) 620-2105; (800) 938-6287; Admissions: (708) 620-2128;
Fax: (708) 620-2194

Description: The privately supported theological seminary has an enrollment of 270 men and women and has a faculty of 47. It is related to the American Baptist Churches, USA and operates on the quarter system. The school is fully accredited by the North Central Association of Colleges and Schools and by the Association of Theological Schools in the United States and Canada. The seminary was founded in the Second Baptist Church of Chicago in 1913. The objective of the seminary is the graduate professional training of men and women for the various ministries of Christian Church. Grants the Master of Arts in Theological Studies, Christian Education and Masters of Divinity and Doctor of Ministry degrees.

Entrance Requirements: Bachelor's degree (preferably the BA) from a regionally accredited college or university; "C" average or its equivalent during the college program; preseminary studies as recommended by the Association of Theological Schools; evidence of a vocation to the ministry. Apply to Registrar for fall entrance.

Costs Per Year: $165 per credit hour; campus apartments available, $280-$670 per month; $60 student fees.

Collegiate Environment: A new campus is located on 40 acres of rolling hills, 30 minutes from Chicago's Loop. The library facilities contain 55,000 volumes. Living accommodations are available for single students and married students; all apartments equipped with kitchens.

Community Environment: See National College of Chiropractic.

NORTHERN ILLINOIS UNIVERSITY   (C-11)
DeKalb, Illinois 60115
Tel: (815) 753-1000; (800) 892-3050 in IL; Admissions: (815) 753-0446; Fax: (815) 753-8312

Description: This publicly supported state university is accredited by the North Central Association of Colleges and Schools and professionally by the American Association of Collegiate Schools of Business, American Chemical Society, American Home Economics Association, American Council on Education for Journalism, National League for Nursing, National Council for the Accreditation of Teacher Education, American Speech and Hearing Association, American Psychological Association, National Association of Schools of Theater, American Bar Association, American Dietetic Association and the Accreditation Board of Engineering and Technology. The school was established as the Illinois State Normal School in 1895 and offered only a two-year curriculum in teacher education until 1921. It became a university in 1957 and since that time has developed into eight major divisions: the College of Liberal Arts and Sciences, College of Visual and Performing Arts, College of Professional Studies, the College of Education, the College of Business, the Graduate School, the College of Law and the College of Continuing Education. Credit is allowed for correspondence courses (up to 30 semester hours) and by prior examination for previous training and experience. Semester Abroad is available in Australia, Austria, China, Costa Rica, Denmark, Ecuador, England, France, Holland, Israel, Mexico, Russia, and Spain. It operates on the semester system and offers one summer session. Enrollment includes 16,682 full-time and 6,199 part-time undergraduate, and 6,458 graduate students. A faculty of 1,040 full-time and 193 part-time gives a faculty-student ratio of 1-17. The University offers Army ROTC.

Entrance Requirements: Accredited high school graduation with composite or rank in upper half of high school class; academic units including 4 English, 2-3 math (algebra and geometry or algebra II), 2-3 science (1 lab), 2-3 social science (1 U.S. history), 1-2 foreign language or art or music, and 3 electives from above list; ACT or SAT required; rolling admission and advanced placement plans available.

Costs Per Year: $2,772.80 state resident tuition and fees; $8,318.40 nonresident tuition; $3,346 room and board; $950.32 student fees (including $250.90 health insurance).

Collegiate Environment: The university is comprised of 56 buildings on 589 acres, located 60 miles west of Chicago. The library contains 1,493,981 volumes, more than 14,000 periodicals and 2 million microforms. Dormitory facilities are available for 7,400 students and 80 families. Numerous clubs and organizations are available as well as 22 social fraternities and 15 social sororities. Special programs for the culturally disadvantaged, and courses in black American history. ESP (Educational Services and Programs) serves a diverse student population. Minorities and other underrepresented groups are especially sought. Approximately 69% of students applying for admission

are accepted including midyear students. There are 6,500 scholarships available. 65% of students receive some form of financial aid.

Community Environment: DeKalb (population 33,000) is located 60 miles west of Chicago with buses serving the area. The Del Monte Company, the DeKalb Agricultural Association, and other industrial plants are here; barbed wire was invented and first manufactured in DeKalb.

NORTHWESTERN UNIVERSITY   (B-14)
Box 3060-1801 Hinman Avenue
Evanston, Illinois 60204-3060
Tel: (708) 491-7271

Description: This privately supported, nondenominational university was chartered in 1851 and is one of the nation's largest independent institutions of higher learning. Enrollment includes 7,561 full-time and 42 part-time undergraduates and 7,927 graduate students. A faculty of 801 gives an undergraduate faculty-student ratio of 1-11. The university operates on the quarter system and offers 2 summer sessions. It is accredited by the North Central Association of Colleges and Schools and by respective professional organizations for the following programs: business, chemistry, dentistry, engineering (chemical, civil, electrical, engineering sciences, environmental health and sanitary, general, industrial and management, mechanical, metallurgical and materials), hospital administration, journalism, law, medicine, medical technology, physical therapy, music, psychology, speech pathology and audiology, and teacher education. It has a Cooperative Education program of alternating work and class periods in engineering. Many programs feature special majors and combination Bachelor-Master degrees. Navy ROTC program is available. Air Force Reserve Officers Training Corp. (AFROTC) can be taken in Cooperation with Illinois Institute of Technology, and Army ROTC can be taken in Cooperation with Loyola University in Chicago. The university offers extensive programs in all phases of music, as well as intercollegiate and intramural athletics. The university is located on two separate campuses fronting on Lake Michigan. The Evanston Campus includes the College of Arts and Science, the Graduate School, the McCormick School of Engineering and Applied Sciences, the Schools of Education, Journalism, Music, and Speech and the Kellogg Graduate School of Management. Garrett Theological Seminary and Seabury-Western Theological Seminary are cooperating institutions that occupy leased land on the Evanston Campus. The Chicago Campus includes the School of Law, the Medical School, the Dental School, and the J.L. Kellogg Managers Program.

Entrance Requirements: High school graduation with completion of 16 college-preparatory courses including a minimum of 4 English, 3-4 mathematics, 2-4 foreign language, 2-3 science, and 2-3 social sciences, SAT or ACT required; appropriate Bachelor degree required for graduate schools; early decision, delayed admission, and advanced placement plans available; 60 superior high school students admitted to the Medical School while in senior year of high school; program leads to MD in seven years from high school graduation; 30 students admitted to each of 2 honors programs: 3-year BA programs in Integrated Sciences and a 4-year program in Mathematical Methods in the Social Sciences; apply to Undergraduate Admissions Office early in senior year of high school; $50 application fee.

Costs Per Year: $16,404 tuition; $5,520 room and board.

Collegiate Environment: The larger campus, running a mile along the shoreline and bordered on the other three sides by the suburban city of Evanston, contains 182 buildings on a 234-acre tract. Twelve miles south, on a 20-acre lakefront site one mile from Chicago's downtown Loop, is the Chicago Campus of the university. The Chicago Campus is the heart of the Northwestern University Medical Center, which coordinates the educational, research, and service facilities of the Medical School, the Dental School, and affiliated hospitals. Total library holdings include 3,600,000 volumes, 36,000 periodicals and 2.5 million microform units. Living accommodations are provided for 4,500 single men and women and 253 married graduate students. 25 fraternities and 13 sororities provide additional housing for 1,441. Need-based scholarships are available; 60% of the student body receives financial aid. The university accepts 38.7% of those who apply for admission, and permits students to enroll at midyear as well as in fall. The middle 50% ranges of test scores for current freshmen were: SAT 540-640V, 610-710M; ACT 27-31.

Community Environment: Evanston is a residential city on Lake Michigan, adjoining the north limits of the city of Chicago. With Lake Michigan forming an impressive backdrop, an abundance of oak, elm, and maple trees enhance the beauty of the community. Situated 12 miles from the center of Chicago, Evanston offers the advantages of a quiet, modern community close to a great thriving city. Excellent shopping facilities are available.

OAKTON COMMUNITY COLLEGE   *(C-2)*
1600 East Golf Road
Des Plaines, Illinois 60016
Tel: (708) 635-1600

Description: This publicly supported, coeducational, community college was established in 1969 and is accredited by the North Central Association of Colleges and Schools. The college operates on a semester system with one summer session. The school's programs are in both liberal arts and technological areas, and it awards Certificates and Associate degrees. Enrollment is currently 10,501 students with 150 full-time and 350 part-time faculty members making the teacher-student ratio 1-22. The college grants up to 45 credits in certain courses by prior examination.

Entrance Requirements: High school graduation or GED is required; ACT suggested; open enrollment policy; rolling admission, advanced placement; $15 application fee.

Costs Per Year: $990 ($33/credit hour) district resident; $3,540 ($118/credit hour) nondistrict; $3,990 ($133/credit hour) out-of-state; $15 student fees.

Collegiate Environment: In addition to its academic program, the college provides a student development program and learning resource center. The former is designed to assist students in their personal, social and educational development, and the latter provides the material, and equipment for use in study. There is a learning lab and an audiovisual center in addition to a library housing 65,000 volumes. Of those applying, 99% are accepted. Students may enroll at midyear as well as in the fall. Financial aid is available to students requiring it.

Community Environment: Des Plaines, population 53,568, is a suburban community situated about 12 miles from the center of Chicago, the third largest city in the nation. Cultural facilities of Chicago include museums which cover a wide variety of fields, art galleries, research libraries, theaters, opera, and symphony orchestra.

OLIVET NAZARENE UNIVERSITY   *(E-13)*
P.O. Box 527
Kankakee, Illinois 60901
Tel: (815) 939-5011

Description: This privately supported, coeducational, evangelical, liberal arts college is affiliated with the Church of the Nazarene. The college operates on the semester system and offers two summer terms. It is accredited by the North Central Association of Colleges and Schools, the National Council for the Accreditation of Teacher Education, and the National League for Nursing. The institution was founded in 1907. In 1909, the school added a college of liberal arts and became known as Illinois Holiness University. In 1940, a new campus was purchased and developed. Programs include preparation for State teaching certificate and freshman program for the educationally disadvantaged. Religious subjects and chapel attendance required. Offers extensive music program as well as intercollegiate and intramural athletics. Allows credit for correspondence courses (up to 30 semester hours) and by prior examination for previous training and experience (up to 30 semester hours). Enrollment includes 1,996 students with a faculty of 80 full-time and 40 part-time members.

Entrance Requirements: Accredited high school graduation with rank in top 75% of graduating class, minimum C average in 15 college preparatory units; non-high school graduates 21 years or older may be admitted by special examinations; ACT required, minimum score 16. Rolling admission, midyear admission, early decision, and advanced placement.

Costs Per Year: $9,300 tuition; $4,360 room and board; $140 student fees.

Collegiate Environment: The campus consists of 168 acres located in the historic village of Bourbonnais, 60 miles south of Chicago. The 29 buildings of the college occupy about 60 acres, the remainder serving as playing fields, parking, and sites for future development. The library contains 200,000 volumes, and living accommodations are provided for 1,300 students. Eighty percent of students applying for admission are accepted including midyear students. Financial assistance is available, and approximately 75% of the current enrollment receives some form of financial aid.

Community Environment: The campus is in the historic village of Bourbonnais (16,000) on the north edge of Kankakee, Illinois (100,000). This is the growing edge of the community, with excellent schools and small businesses. A new shopping mall and numerous stores provide shopping convenience and employment opportunities. Major industries in the area include Armour Pharmaceutical, Armstrong Tile, Quaker Oats, General Foods, and a variety of metal working plants. The proximity to the Chicago metropolitan area is a definite asset.

OLNEY CENTRAL COLLEGE   *(M-13)*
305 North West
Olney, Illinois 62450
Tel: (618) 395-4351

Description: The publicly supported community college is one several colleges which comprise the multi-campus system known as the Illinois Eastern Community Colleges. It is accredited by the North Central Association of Colleges Schools. The school recently enrolled 1500 students and has a faculty of 30 full-time and 45 part-time members. It operates on the semester system with 1 summer session. Founded in 1963, the college offers a basic foundation of educational experience in the first two years of any college program. In addition to baccalaureate-oriented programs, a wide range of vocational-technical programs are offered.

Entrance Requirements: Open enrollment policy; non-high school graduates admitted; SAT, ACT, or Asset required; entrance exam required for placement; rolling admission plans available. $10 application fee.

Costs Per Year: $864 District Students, $1,800 tuition out-of-district residents; $2,500 out-of-state residents;

Collegiate Environment: The college is located on 103 acres within walking distance of the city of Olney. The Learning Resource Center includes a library of 27,000 volumes and numerous periodicals and audio-visual materials. The college assists students in finding private housing within the city. Almost all students applying for admission are accepted, and may enroll at the beginning of any semester. Financial aid is available, and 25% of the current student body receives some form of assistance.

Community Environment: A small community accessible by major highways, Olney (population 10,000) has a public library, 26 churches, hospital, numerous civic and service organizations and industrial plants which employ over 2000 people. Recreational facilities include municipal swimming pool, 2 golf courses, bowling center, and a lake for boating and fishing.

PARKLAND COLLEGE   *(I-12)*
2400 W. Bradley Avenue
Champaign, Illinois 61821-1899
Tel: (217) 351-2200; (800) 346-8089; Fax: (217) 351-2581

Description: Parkland College is a public two-year community college that provides educational opportunities for more than 200,000 residents of East Central Illinois. Parkland's district encompasses a 2,875-square-mile area over parts of 12 counties, and serves 54 communities and 27 high school districts. It operates on the semester system and offers one summer session. Enrollment includes 3,718 full-time and 4,745 part-time students. A faculty of 142 full-time and 407 part-time gives a faculty-student ratio of 1-18. The College offers more than 80 different vocational technical career programs, 15 baccalaureate transfer areas, and programs for the educationally underprepared. Band, chorus, theater, and extensive intramural and intercollegiate athletics are some of the more than 50 extracurricular activities available. The Parkland men's basketball team won the

NJCAA Division II championship in 1986. The school is accredited by the North Central Association of Colleges and Schools and by several professional associations. Credit is granted for correspondence courses and by prior examination for previous training and experience.

Entrance Requirements: Accredited high school graduation or equivalent; non-high school graduates may be considered for certain programs; ACT required for health career programs; rolling admission plan available.

Costs Per Year: $990 district-resident tuition; $3,435 state residents; $5,098 nonresidents.

Collegiate Environment: The college moved to the present campus in 1973. The 233-acre campus, adjacent to 110 acres of park district land, contains 68 classrooms, 55 specialized labs, a library collection of more than 100,000 volumes, 1,003 periodicals and 5,016 audiovisual materials. There is also an art gallery, a dental clinic, an educational FM radio station and an experimental agricultural land laboratory. Parkland's Cultural Center, completed early in 1987, contains a performing arts theater and the second largest Planetarium in the state. 60% of the current enrollment receives financial assistance. 100% of applicants are accepted, including midyear students. The school granted 119 certificates and 762 Associate degrees during the recent school year.

Community Environment: See University of Illinois - Urbana-Champaign.

PARKS COLLEGE OF SAINT LOUIS UNIVERSITY   *(M-1)*
Cahokia, Illinois 62206
Tel: (618) 337-7575, x223; (800) 851-7878

Description: This privately supported technological college under the auspices of the Roman Catholic Church is one of four campuses within Saint Louis University, St. Louis, Mo. The college specializes in aerospace subjects. It operates on the semester system and offers one summer session. Enrollment is includes 718 men and 113 women. A faculty of 89 full-time and 30 part-time gives a faculty-student ratio of 1-8. The college is accredited by the North Central Association of Colleges and Schools. Its flight programs are accredited by the FAA. U.S. Air Force ROTC is available on campus.

Entrance Requirements: High school graduation or equivalent with minimum B average, rank in top half of high school class; 16 units required by program: 4 English, 3 mathematics, 2 natural science, 2 social sciences, 2 foreign languages, and 3 electives; SAT or ACT required for traditional students; rolling admission and advanced placement plans available; $25 application fee.

Costs Per Year: 9,700 tuition; $4,266 room and board.

Collegiate Environment: College facilities include a library of 47,269 volumes, 268 periodicals, and 56,150 microforms. 1.4 million volumes are available in the Saint Louis University Libraries. Student housing is provided for 315 students. 79% of applicants are accepted, and students are permitted to enroll at midyear. The average ACT score for current freshmen was ACT 24.0. Scholarships are available.

Community Environment: Cahokia is a suburb of the St. Louis a metropolitan area (population 1,821,700) directly across the Mississippi River from downtown St. Louis, Missouri. Buses, trains and planes serve the area.

PRAIRIE STATE COLLEGE   *(D-14)*
201 S. Halsted Street
Box 487
Chicago Heights, Illinois 60411
Tel: (312) 709-3516

Description: The publicly supported community college is accredited by the North Central Association of Colleges and Schools. The Dental Hygiene program is accredited by the American Dental Association. The college's nursing program is accredited by the National League for Nursing. Originally the college was organized by Bloom Township High School District 206 in 1958. As of 1967, the district was expanded to include the Bloom, Rich, Crete-Monee Townships and Homewood-Flossmoor areas. The college provides instruction of the first and second year college levels and all post-high school, ter-

minal, vocational, and general education for the district. It also offers a tutorial assistance program for the educationally disadvantged. The college operates on the semester system and offers one summer session. Enrollment is 5,000 students.

Entrance Requirements: Open enrollment policy; accredited high school graduation with class rank equal to that required by the public universities in Illinois for baccalaureate-oriented applicants; ACT requested for placement of all students; early admission, early decision, rolling admission, advanced placement plans available; $10 application fee.

Costs Per Year: $1,643 ($53/credit) district resident tuition; $3,875 ($125/credit) state resident; $4,185 ($135/credit) nonresident.

Collegiate Environment: The college program is operated in several locations. These include the main campus building, the Dental Bldg. on North Campus, the Beecher High School, Homewood-Flossmoor High School, Rich South High School, the Bloom Township High School Buildings, and the Saint James Hospital The Learning Center contains a selection of 40,000 carefully selected books, periodicals, pamphlets, audio-visual and other pertinent materials to serve the specific needs of the students enrolled. The evening college program includes courses in most of the departments and programs of the college and the new Weekend College is designed to meet the needs of working adults.

Community Environment: Chicago Heights is a metropolitan area located 25 miles south of the Chicago loop. Railroads and buses serve the area. Within the city are shopping centers, many churches, a library, and a hospital. For recreation, there are many parks, a community center with an educational, recreational and social service program, and a Forest Preserve of 1,350 acres.

PRINCIPIA COLLEGE   *(L-7)*
Elsah, Illinois 62028
Tel: (618) 374-5176; (800) 277-4648; Fax: (618) 374-4000

Description: The privately supported liberal arts college operates on the quarter system and is accredited by the North Central Association of Colleges and Schools. It offers preparation for State teaching certificate, and Principia Abroad travel-study programs are available. Enrollment is 550 full-time students. A faculty of 72 gives a faculty-student ratio of 1-8. The college offers choir and orchestra, and extensive intercollegiate and intramural athletic programs. Although not affiliated with the Christian Science Church, students, faculty and staff are Christian Scientists.

Entrance Requirements: Accredited high school graduation; completion of 16 units including 4 English, 3 mathematics, 2-3 foreign language, 3 natural science, and 2 social science and/or history; SAT or ACT required; rolling admission plan available; $35 application fee.

Costs Per Year: $12,816 tuition; $5,424 room and board; $231 student fees.

Collegiate Environment: The campus is located on the bluffs of the Mississippi River approximately 10 miles from Alton and 35 miles from St. Louis. The college is comprised of 50 buildings and the library contains 200,000 volumes and 1,055 periodicals. Dormitory facilities are available for all students. 75% of the current student body receives financial assistance. 82% of those who apply for admission is accepted. The average high school standing of current freshman class: 57% graduated in the top half. Average SAT scores were 507V, 560M.

Community Environment: Principia College is located on 2,600 acres of the highest and loveliest section of the Piasa Bluffs above the Mississippi River. In a setting rich in beauty and historical significance, three great rivers may be seen from the bluffs: the Mississippi below, the Missouri to the southeast, and the Illinois, which joins the Mississippi to the west several miles upstream. Mean temperatures are 28-78 degrees, and rainfall averages 35 inches. Recreation, entertainment, and shopping are found in Alton and St. Louis. Part-time student employment is available at the college.

QUINCY UNIVERSITY   *(L-4)*
1800 College Avenue
Quincy, Illinois 62301
Tel: (217) 222-8020; (800) 688-4295; Admissions: (217) 228-5210;
Fax: (217) 228-5479

Description: Quincy University, founded in 1860, is an independent, Catholic, liberal arts university conducted by the Franciscan Friars. It is accredited by the North Central Association of Colleges and Secondary Schools, the National Association of Schools of Music, and the Association of Collegiate Business Schools and Programs (ACBSP). It operates on the semester system and offers 4 summer sessions. Enrollment includes 1,023 full-time and 84 part-time undergraduates and 57 graduate students. A faculty of 71 full-time and 32 part-time gives a faculty-student ratio of 1-12. Quincy University grants the Bachelor of Arts, Bachelor of Fine Arts, Bachelor of Science, Master of Education and Master of Business Administration degrees, and also offers elementary and secondary teaching certification. Pre-professional programs include a 3-2 pre-engineering program, pre-dentistry, pre-law, pre-medicine, pre-veterinary medicine, and pre-physical therapy. Special programs include student-designed majors, honors program, interdepartment majors, independent studies, independent research, study abroad and internships. CLEP and AP credit are accepted. Optional tuition payment and guaranteed tuition plans are available.

Entrance Requirements: Each applicant for admission is evaluated individually; ACT or SAT required; completion of 16 academic units including 4 English, 3 math, 2 science, 2 foreign language and 2 social studies; rolling admission, early admission, delayed admission, midyear admission, and advanced placement plans available; early application is recommended.

Costs Per Year: $10,700 tuition; $4,260 room and board; $210 student fees.

Collegiate Environment: The University participates in the federal Pell Grant, Supplemental Educational Opportunity Grant (SEOG), Perkins Loan, College Work-Study (CWS), and Stafford Loan programs. Illinois State Scholarships are available for qualifying Illinois residents. Quincy University academic scholarships and need-based grants are also available. Financial aid programs are available for transfer students and upperclass students, as well as for incoming freshmen. Students who wish to apply for aid must complete the Free Application for Federal Student Aid (FAFSA). Notification of financial awards are made on a rolling basis. Early application is recommended. 71% of applicants are accepted. The mean ACT score of accepted students is 23. Approximately 56% of freshmen graduate in the top fifth of their high school class, and 82% rank in the top two-fifths. Quincy University is a residential campus, with 70% of students living on campus. Campus housing options include single-sex and coed residence halls, apartments, houses and married student housing. Numerous and varied campus organizations offer unlimited opportunities for students to participate in both University and community activities. A student-operated National Public Radio station, music performance groups, publications, honor and service societies, a lecture series, and concerts are a few of the many extracurricular opportunities available to students. 80% of the students participate in intramural sports. The University maintains membership in NCAA Great Lakes Valley Conference. Intercollegiate sports for men are football, basketball, cross-country, soccer, baseball, tennis, and volleyball. Women's intercollegiate sports are basketball, cross-country, volleyball, soccer, softball, and tennis. The Brenner Library houses 229,742 volumes and 154,101 microtext items, and subscribes to over 645 periodicals. Through the University's membership in the Online Computer Library Center, students have access to millions of books in libraries throughout the Midwest and the nation. The library is also equipped with a computerized reference service.

Community Environment: The University is located in a residential section of Quincy, a city of 50,000, located on the bluffs of the Mississippi River. It is within easy traveling distance of St. Louis (2 1/2 hours), Kansas City (4 hours), and Chicago (4 hours).

REND LAKE COLLEGE   *(N-11)*
Route 1, Ken Gray Parkway
Ina, Illinois 62846
Tel: (618) 437-5321

Description: The publicly supported district-governed junior college enrolls 3,462 men and women. The school operates on the semester system with 1 summer session and is accredited by the North Central Association of Colleges and Schools. In 1967, the college assumed the assets, liabilities, and responsibilities of the Mount Vernon Community College, established in 1956. The college is organized to furnish university-parallel, occupational, general, and adult education to a district comprised of parts of eight counties of southern Illinois. Offers precollege and freshman program for the educationally disadvantages. Faculty includes 57 full-time and 137 part-time.

Entrance Requirements: Accredited high school graduation or equivalent; open enrollment policy; non-HS graduates may be admitted; ACT required for placement; advanced placement plan available.

Costs Per Year: $840 tuition for district residents; $3,320 tuition for state residents; $4,620 out-of-state tuition; $32 student fees.

Collegiate Environment: The college occupies a 350-acre campus. The library contains 20,000 volumes. All students who apply for admission are accepted, including midyear students. Financial aid is available through federal aid programs; approximately 15% of the current students receive assistance.

Community Environment: School is located in a rural area with all forms of transportation available. Industries in nearby Mount Vernon (population 16,382) include the manufacture of electric equipment, radiators, women's wear, shoes, forest products, and chemicals. Oil production and agriculture are important in the surrounding areas. Cultural opportunities offered by the library, State Law Library and Museum. Community facilities include 40 churches of major denominations, hospitals, clinic, and major civic and service organizations. Recreational activities are boating, fishing, swimming, bowling, and golf. Mt. Vernon State Fair is an annual event.

RICHLAND COMMUNITY COLLEGE   *(J-10)*
One College Park
Decatur, Illinois 62521
Tel: (217) 875-7200

Description: This publicly supported liberal arts and technological community college is accredited by the North Central Association of Colleges and Schools. It grants the Associate degree. It allows credit towards degree by prior examination for previous training and also for correspondence courses. Enrollment includes 999 full-time and 2,802 part-time students. A faculty of 49 full-time and 148 part-time gives a faculty-student ratio of 1-28.

Entrance Requirements: Open enrollment; high school graduation or equivalent, including completion of 4 units English, 3 mathematics, 3 science, 3 social studies, and 2 electives; non-high school graduates considered; SAT or ACT recommended; early admission, early decision, midyear admission, rolling admission, advanced placement plans available; no application fee.

Costs Per Year: $1,185 district-resident tuition; $2,354 state-resident; $4,420 out-of-state.

Collegiate Environment: The library houses 25,000 volumes, 1,200 pamphlets, 253 periodicals, 5,689 microforms and 2,000 sound recordings. No student housing. All applicants are accepted. 40% of the previous freshman class returned to campus for sophomore year. Scholarships are available and 25% of the students receive some form of financial aid.

Community Environment: See Millikin University.

ROCK VALLEY COLLEGE   *(B-10)*
3301 North Mulford Road
Rockford, Illinois 61111
Tel: (815) 654-4250; Fax: (815) 654-5568

Description: The publicly supported, district-governed community college was established in 1965 to serve the needs of Winnebago, Boone and Ogle Counties. It operates on the semester system and offers 1 summer session. Accredited by the North Central Association of Colleges and Schools, the college offers courses in vocational-technical and liberal arts areas. Enrollment is 2,244 full-time and 6,437 part-time students. A faculty of 138 full-time and 100 part-time gives a faculty-student ratio of 1-38. The college grants Certificate and Associate degree.

Entrance Requirements: Accredited high school graduation or equivalent required for degree programs; non-high school graduates considered for admission; early admission, open decision, advanced placement, and rolling admission plans available.

Costs Per Year: $1,100 county-resident tuition; $3,800 state-resident; $6,200 out-of-state; $40 student fees.

Collegiate Environment: The campus is located on 217 acres. The ten college buildings include a library of 60,580 volumes, 477 periodicals, 247 microforms and 8,935 audiovisual materials. The college offers special programs for the culturally disadvantaged. 38% of students receive financial aid. 98% of applicants are accepted, and students may enroll at midyear.

Community Environment: See Rockford College.

ROCKFORD BUSINESS COLLEGE   *(B-10)*
730 North Church Street
Rockford, Illinois 61103
Tel: (815) 965-8616; Fax: (815) 965-0360

Description: This privately supported, two-year business college is accredited by the Association of Independent Colleges and Schools. It awards diplomas and the Associate of Applied Science degree. Credit from Rockford can be transferred to certain four-year colleges with which the school is affiliated. Similarly, students transferring to Rockford may receive credit for related courses completed successfully at their former school. It operates on the quarter system with one summer session. Enrollment includes 90 men and 270 women. A faculty of 20 provides a faculty-student ratio of 1-18.

Entrance Requirements: High school graduation or GED; open enrollment; the TABE test is given at the college; early decision, early admission, advanced placement, midyear admission and rolling admission plans available; $50 application fee.

Costs Per Year: $5,000 - $10,000 tuition.

Collegiate Environment: College classrooms are equipped with modern business machines and equipment and are fully air-conditioned. The library contains more than 3,000 volumes. 99% of the applicants are accepted, and students are permitted to enroll at midyear. Financial aid is available through State and Federal programs.

Community Environment: See Rockford College

ROCKFORD COLLEGE   *(B-10)*
5050 East State Street
Rockford, Illinois 61108-2393
Tel: (815) 226-4050; (800) 892-2984; Fax: (815) 226-4119

Description: The privately supported liberal arts college is accredited by the North Central Association of Colleges and Schools. The college, founded in 1847, is open to all students, regardless of religious affiliation. A Washington Semester and a U.N. Semester are offered. Also offered are pre-law, pre-medicine, pre-dentistry, pre-engineering, and other pre-professional programs; a five-year accelerated MBA program, and an extensive fine and performing arts program. Intercollegiate and intramural athletics are offered. Preparation for State teaching certificate is available. Army ROTC is available through Northern Illinois University in DeKalb. The college operates on the semester system and offers one summer session. Enrollment includes 907 full-time and 364 part-time undergraduates and 340 graduate students. A faculty of 84 full-time and 53 part-time gives a faculty-student ratio of 1-14.

Entrance Requirements: Accredited high school graduation with 2.5 average and rank in upper 50% of graduating class; completion of 15 units including 4 English, 2 mathematics, 2 foreign language, 2 science, and 3 social studies; SAT or ACT required; GRE or GMAT required for graduate school; early admission, rolling admission, delayed admission, midyear admission and advanced placement plans available; $35 application fee.

Costs Per Year: $12,400 tuition; $4,080 room and board.

Collegiate Environment: The college is located on a 130-acre campus of partly wooded, gently rolling terrain at the eastern edge of the

city. Twenty-six buildings serve the college and include a library of 166,000 volumes and dormitory facilities for 300 men and 300 women. The college accepts 75% of those who apply for admission, and permits students to enroll at midyear as well as in the fall. The average score of the entering freshman class was ACT 21 composite. Scholarships are available and 98% of the undergraduates receive some form of financial aid.

Community Environment: Rockford (population 147,370), the second largest city in the state, is 90 miles northwest of Chicago, situated in the historic and attractive Rock River Valley close to the Wisconsin border. Rockford is also an important industrial city that produces machine tools, textiles, furniture, hardware and automobile accessories.

ROOSEVELT UNIVERSITY   *(C-14)*
430 South Michigan Avenue
Chicago, Illinois 60605
Tel: (312) 341-3500; Fax: (312) 341-3523

Description: This privately supported university was founded in 1945. It is accredited by the North Central Association of Colleges, the Illinois State Examining Board for Teacher Education, and several other professional orgranizations. Roosevelt operates on a semester system and offers four summer sessions. The university offers an extensive music program, and intercollegiate and intramural athletics are available. A cooperative plan with Art Institute of Chicago for fine arts and liberal arts, with Spertus College of Judaica for Jewish studies, with Sherwood School of Music and with American Conservatory of Music is available. Divisions of the university include College of Arts and Sciences, Walter E. Heller College of Business Administration, Chicago Music College, University College, College of Education, Graduate Division, Labor Education Division. Certain courses accepted by examination. Recent enrollment included 1,932 full-time and 4,764 part-time students. A faculty of 158 full-time and 430 part-time provides a faculty-student ratio of 1:14.

Entrance Requirements: Accredited high school graduation with rank in upper 50% of graduating class; completion of 15 units of college-preparatory work including 4 English; students with C average and non-high school graduates considered. Composite score of 20 on the enhanced ACT. The university has an early admission program for outstanding high school juniors; early decision, rolling admission, delayed admission, midyear admission, and advanced placement plans also available. $20 application fee.

Costs Per Year: $9,000 tuition; $4,500 room and board; $60 student fees. Additional expenses average $1,000.

Collegiate Environment: The home of Roosevelt University is the historic Auditorium Building on Chicago's lakefront. Purchased by the university in 1947, this ten-story structure has been converted into an efficient educational plant with a library containing 400,000 volumes; 1,600 periodicals, numerous microforms and 16,207 recordings. Housing is provided for 360 students. Approximately 425 scholarships are available; 75% of the current student body receives financial aid. 65% of those who apply for admission are accepted, and students may enroll midyear and summer.

Community Environment: Roosevelt University's downtown location places students only blocks away from such cultural and educational resources as the Art Institute, Orchestra Hall, the Opera House, the Field Museum of Natural History, the Band Shell, the Shedd Aquarium and the Adler Planetarium. Roosevelt University is also located in the hub of the city's mercantile and financial districts - the Board of Trade, the State Street department stores, the LaSalle and Dearborn Streets banking houses, law offices, and government buildings all being in close proximity to the university.

Branch Campuses: The university has one branch campus in Arlington Heights, IL.

ROSARY COLLEGE   *(D-3)*
7900 West Division Street
River Forest, Illinois 60305
Tel: (708) 366-2490; (800) 828-8475; Admissions: (708) 524-6800; Fax: (708) 366-5360

Description: The institution is a privately supported Roman Catholic liberal arts college conducted by the Dominican Sisters of

Sinsinawa, Wisconsin. It is accredited by the North Central Association of Colleges and Schools and professionally by the American Library Association and the American Dietetic Association. The institution traces its origin to an 1848 charter granted by the State of Wisconsin to Sinsinawa Academy, a frontier school, which was incorporated as Saint Clara College in 1901, moved to River Forest and finally incorporated by the State of Illinois as Rosary College in 1918. It offers preparation for the State teaching certificate. Students who qualify may participate in the Honors Program. Overseas study includes programs in Heidelberg, London, Milan, Salamanca, and Strasbourg. It operates on the semester system and offers two summer sessions. Enrollment includes 635 full-time, 227 part-time undergraduate, and 989 graduate students. A faculty of 72 full-time and 44 part-time gives a faculty-student ratio of 1-11.

Entrance Requirements: Accredited high school graduation, completion of 16 college preparatory units including 14 from among English, mathematics, foreign language, science, and social science; SAT or ACT required; rolling admission, midyear admission, and advanced placement available; $20 application fee; $100 tuition deposit.

Costs Per Year: $11,500 tuition; $4,600 room and board; $48 student fees; $1,500 average additional expenses.

Collegiate Environment: The campus is located on 30 wooded acres, ten miles west of the Loop, the business center of Chicago. Seven buildings serve the campus and include a library of 287,000 volumes, a new College Center and residence halls. Students are also offered chorus, and intercollegiate baseball, basketball, tennis, soccer, and volleyball. Middle 50% of scores were ACT 19-24. 70% of applicants are accepted, including midyear students. Approximately 70% of students receive some form of financial assistance.

RUSH UNIVERSITY   (C-14)
1653 W. Congress Parkway
Chicago, Illinois 60612
Tel: (312) 942-5000

Description: The privately supported university is fully accredited by the North Central Association of Colleges and Schools, American Medical Association, National Accrediting Agency for Clinical Laboratory Science and also by the Americn National League for Nursing. The school is part of the Rush-Presbyterian-St. Lukes Medical Center Complex. The school recently enrolled 1,300 men and women. It operates on the quarter system with one summer session, and grants the Bachelor, Master, and Doctorate degrees in various areas of the health sciences. The faculty consists of 573 full-time and 254 part-time.

Entrance Requirements: Completion of two years (90 quarters/60 semester hours) of liberal arts and sciences at an accredited college or university. $25 application fee.

Costs Per Year: $3,130 per quarter tuition; $150 per month room.

Collegiate Environment: The university's facilities include a library of 85,000 volumes, limited athletic facilities, and living quarters for 81 men and 205 women. Sixty-two percent of those who apply to the undergraduate division are accepted. Financial aid is available, and 77% of the current student enrollment receives some form of assistance.

Community Environment: See University of Chicago

SAINT XAVIER UNIVERSITY   (C-14)
3700 West 103rd Street
Chicago, Illinois 60655
Tel: (312) 298-3000; (800) 462-9288; Fax: (312) 779-9061

Description: Founded in 1847 by the Sisters of Mercy, this privately supported Roman Catholic institution is a four-year, liberal arts university. Enrollment includes 4,454 students. A faculty of 160, which consists of laymen and women, clergymen and religious, gives a faculty-student ratio of 1-16. The university operates on the 4-1-4 semester system with summer sessions. It is accredited by the North Central Association of Colleges and Schools. U.S. Air Force ROTC is available. It offers chorus, choir, intercollegiate soccer, baseball, basketball, softball, volleyball, football, and intramural sports.

Entrance Requirements: Accredited high school graduation with C average and rank in upper half of graduating class; completion of 16

college-preparatory units including 4 English, 3 mathematics, 2 science, and 2 social science; SAT or ACT required; non-high school graduates may be accepted provisionally; rolling admission, advanced placement plans available; minimum scores required: SAT 450V, 450M; ACT 18; GMAT, MAT, or GRE required for graduate school; $25 application fee.

Costs Per Year: $10,860 tuition, $4,624 room and board; $118 student fees.

Collegiate Environment: Situated on a 47-acre campus, the nine-building complex includes a library of 143,000 volumes and dormitory facilities for 400 men and women. Dormitory facilities are all coeducational. 90% of the previous freshman class returned to the college for a second year. 80% of the current enrollment receives financial assistance. Athletic scholarships are also available; for further information contact the athletic department.

Community Environment: See University of Chicago.

Branch Campuses: 15255 South 94th Avenue, Orland Park, IL, 60462, (708) 460-1211; 20 Rue de Saint Petersbourg, 75008 Paris, France, (33) 01-42-93-13-87, (MBA only); Piazza Del Carmine, 2, 20121 Milan, Italy, (39) 02-861-647 (MBA only).

SAUK VALLEY COMMUNITY COLLEGE   (C-9)
173 Illinois Route 2
Dixon, Illinois 61021-9110
Tel: (815) 288-5511; Admissions: (815) 288-5511; Fax: (815) 288-3190

Description: The publicly supported community college was established by and for the citizens of the Public Community College District Number 506 of Illinois. The district is comprised of parts of Ogle, Lee, Whiteside, Bureau, Carroll, and Henry Counties. Enrollment includes 1,026 full-time and 1,607 part-time students. A faculty of 55 full-time and 130 part-time gives a faculty-student ratio of 1-16. The college operates on the semester system and offers 1 summer session. It is accredited by the North Central Association of Colleges and Schools. The institution was founded in 1965 and offers programs in general education, liberal arts transfer, and occupational and technical studies. It offers a Cooperative Education program (alternating work and class periods) in business; and precollege and freshman programs for the educationally disadvantaged. Chorus, choir, glee club, and intercollegiate and intramural athletics are available.

Entrance Requirements: Non-high school graduates admitted; early admission, early decision, rolling admission, advanced placement, and delayed admission plans available.

Costs Per Year: $1,200 city- and district-resident tuition; $3,302 out-of-district; $4,272 out-of-state; $500 average additional expenses.

Collegiate Environment: The campus is located along Rock River at the western edge of Lee County midway between Dixon and the twin cities of Sterling and Rock Falls. Special programs are offered for the culturally disadvantaged enabling low-mark students to attend. The library contains 48,300 volumes. All applicants are accepted, including students at midyear. 20% of recent freshmen were in the top 20% of their high school class, and 50% were in the top half. 52% of last year's freshmen returned for second year.

Community Environment: Dixon has a population of 15,701; Sterling (population 16,281) is a small industrial city, enjoying a seasonal climate. Ozark Airlines and Greyhound buses serve the area. Community facilities include public library, many churches, YMCA, YWCA, hospital, and all the major civic and service groups. Jobs are plentiful since this is a highly industrialized area. Recreational opportunities are the many city parks for swimming, tennis, picnic areas, boating and fishing, golfing, bowling, roller skating, miniature golf and go-karting.

SCHOOL OF THE ART INSTITUTE OF CHICAGO   (C-14)
37 South Wabash Avenue
Chicago, Illinois 60603
Tel: (312) 899-5100; (800) 232-7242; Admissions: (312) 899-5219; Fax: (312) 899-1840

Description: Founded in 1866, the privately supported institute is a nonprofit professional college of art, fully accredited by the North

Central Association of Colleges and Schools since 1936 and by the National Association of Schools of Art since 1948. The school operates on the semester system with a 3-week interim session and with 1 summer session. The school grants Bachelor and Master of Fine Arts degrees and Professional Certificates in Art Therapy and Art History. Enrollment is 1,337 students. The faculty consists of 104 full-time and 197 part-time members.

Entrance Requirements: Accredited high school graduation or equivalent and art portfolio. ACT or SAT recommended. Non-HS graduates considered. Early decision, early admission, delayed admission, midyear admission, rolling admission, and advanced placement plans available; $45 application fee.

Costs Per Year: $15,300 tuition; 16,680 graduate tuition.

Collegiate Environment: The institute is a professional college of art offering fully accredited undergraduate and graduate degree programs. The library contains 18,000 bound volumes and an extensive collection of films, video and slides. Residence halls accomodate 200 students. Approximately 75% of students applying for admission are accepted. 80% of the current student body receives some form of financial aid.

Community Environment: See University of Chicago

SEABURY-WESTERN THEOLOGICAL SEMINARY   *(B-14)*
2122 North Sheridan Road
Evanston, Illinois 60201
Tel: (708) 328-9300; Fax: (708) 328-9624

Description: The privately supported graduate theological seminary is fully accredited by the North Central Association of Colleges and Schools. The seminary operates on the quarter system with three summer sessions. The seminary is controlled by the Episcopal Church. Current enrollment is 64 students with a faculty of 17 giving a faculty-student ratio of 1-9.

Entrance Requirements: Bachelor's Degree for Master/Professional Programs; nongraduates may be admitted to LTH Programs; rolling admission plan available.

Costs Per Year: $9,300 tuition; $4,662 room and board.

Collegiate Environment: The seminary occupies most of a city block adjacent to the campus of Northwestern University, and a short distance from Lake Michigan. The library contains 275,000 volumes and coed living accommodations are provided for 50 students, and 35 families. 70% of the students receive financial assistance.

Community Environment: See Northwestern University

SHIMER COLLEGE   *(B-8)*
438 North Sheridan Road
P.O. Box A500
Waukegan, Illinois 60079
Tel: (708) 623-8400; (800) 215-7173; Fax: (708) 249-7171

Description: The privately supported, four-year liberal arts college is accredited by the North Central Association of Colleges and Schools. The college was founded in 1853 and was chartered as the Frances Shimer Academy of the University of Chicago in 1896. By 1958, the college had established its Bachelor degree program and legally adopted its present name. The educational approach used by the college, sometimes called the "great book approach," is based on small discussion classes, no lectures, and no textbooks; original sources are used. The college offers a year of study on Oxford to qualified students and grants the Bachelor of Arts degree. It operates on the semester calendar system. Enrollment is 120 men and women. A faculty of 19 gives a faculty-student ratio of 1-7.

Entrance Requirements: Accredited high school graduation or equivalent; non-high school graduates are considered; admissions are highly individualized; early admission, early decision, rolling admission; delayed admission and midyear admission available. $10 application fee.

Costs Per Year: $12,500 tuition; $1,650 room; $100 student fees.

Collegiate Environment: The college is located in a historic, residential section of Waukegan, IL, a midsized city midway between Milwaukee and Chicago. The campus consists of seven buildings, including a dormitory and small gymnasium. Library holdings include 35,000 volumes. The college maintains a campus abroad located in Oxford, England. 90% of applicants are admitted, including midyear students. 90% of the students receive financial aid.

Community Environment: Waukegan (population 70,000) is the county seat of Lake County on Lake Michigan. Students enjoy all the usual services of a small city, including a nearby state park. Excellent public transportation is available to Chicago.

SOUTHEASTERN ILLINOIS COLLEGE   *(P-12)*
3575 College Road
Harrisburg, Illinois 62946
Tel: (618) 252-6376; Admissions: (618) 252-6376; Fax: (618) 252-3156

Description: This publicly supported junior college is accredited by the North Central Association of Colleges and Schools. The school was founded in 1960 by the citizens of Harrisburg Township High School, District 101. It became part of the statewide junior college system in 1965 and a Class I junior college in 1967. Transitional course work is available for marginally prepared students. The college operates on the semester system and offers two summer sessions. Enrollment includes 3,400 full-time students. A faculty of 183 gives a faculty-student ratio of 1-18.

Entrance Requirements: Open enrollment policy; accredited high school graduation or GED required for degree programs; non-high school graduates may be accepted as special students; ACT or ASSET required; CLEP credit accepted; midyear admission and rolling admission plans; Aug. 15 deadline for Fall application; No application fee.

Costs Per Year: $800 district resident tuition; $4,000 out-of-district tuition; $6,000 nonresident tuition.

Collegiate Environment: The college is comprised of five buildings and the library contains 35,100 volumes. All applicants are accepted. A geographically diverse student body is welcome, and midyear students are accepted. Average freshmen scores were ACT 16. There are 90 scholarships offered, all of which are available to freshmen, and 60% of students receive some form of financial assistance.

Community Environment: Harrisburg is an important coal mining, dairying, agricultural, and commercial center. Community facilities include a library, hospital, churches, an historical museum, and TV and radio stations. Recreational facilities are unlimited with Shawnee National Forest and other federal and state recreation areas within five to ten miles. Many large lakes are in the area. The Saline County Fair is an annual event each July. Some part-time work available.

SOUTHERN ILLINOIS UNIVERSITY AT CARBONDALE
(P-10)
Carbondale, Illinois 62901-4710
Tel: (618) 453-4381; Admissions: (618) 536-4405; Fax: (618) 453-3250

Description: This publicly supported, multipurpose and diversified state university was established in 1869. It is one of two universities within the Southern Illinois University System. It is accredited by the North Central Association of Colleges and Schools, and by numerous professional organizations. The university has educational programs in operation at the Carbondale Campus; at Southern Acres, ten miles east of Carbondale, some College of Technical Careers programs; at Little Grassy Lake, ten miles southeast of Carbondale, recreation, outdoor education, classes, and workshops are held; at Southern Illinois Airport, five miles west of Carbondale, aviation programs; and at Springfield is the Medical School. It operates on the early semester system and offers one summer session. Enrollment includes 13,366 men and 9,796 women, of which 16,434 are full-time, 2,278 are part-time, and 4,450 are graduate students. A faculty of 1,543 gives a faculty-student ratio of 1-16.

Entrance Requirements: Accredited high school graduation or GED equivalent; minimum ACT 20 required; rolling admission; No application fee.

Costs Per Year: $2,318 state resident tuition and fees; $6,953 nonresident tuition; $3,256 room and board; $864 student fees.

Collegiate Environment: The 255 buildings which house SIUC's classrooms, offices, and student services are connected by a network of walkways through lawns bordered with native trees, shrubs, and flora. The library houses 2.1 million bound volumes, 12,274 periodical subscriptions, and 3 million titles on microfilm. Residence halls accommodate 5,600 students. University offerings include faculty and peer mentoring programs, accommodations for students with a disibility, numerous social clubs, sports activities, cultural presentations, and outdoor recreational activities. 63% of applicants are accepted and join the diverse body of students hailing from 47 states and 118 countries. Financial aid is available with 88% of students receiving some form of financial assistance.

Community Environment: Carbondale, an economic center of Southern Illinois, is only a few hours from Chicago, St. Louis, and Memphis. It sits amid rolling hills, farmlands, and orchards just 60 miles above the confluence of the Mississippi and Ohio Rivers. The area from Carbondale south is ruggedly scenic and suitable for a wide range of year-round outdoor activities. Within minutes are four large recreational lakes, the two great rivers, and spectacular 240,000-acre Shawnee National Forest. A large number of smaller lakes, state parks, and recreational areas are within easy driving distance.

SOUTHERN ILLINOIS UNIVERSITY AT EDWARDSVILLE
(M-8)
Box 1047
Edwardsville, Illinois 62026
Tel: (618) 692-2720

Description: The publicly supported campus of Southern Illinois University at Edwardsville includes the Edwardsville Campus, the School of Dental Medicine at Alton, and East St. Louis Center. The University is accredited by the North Central Association of Colleges and Schools and professionally by the American Assembly of Collegiate Schools of Business, American Chemical Society, American Dental Association, Council on Social Work, the Accreditation Board for Engineering and Technology, National Association of Schools of Music, National League for Nursing, National Council for Accreditation of Teacher Education, and American Speech and Hearing Association. See also SIU Carbondale Campus. The university operates on the semester system and offers one summer session. Enrollment includes 6,694 full-time and 4,251 part-time undergraduates and 2,629 graduate students. A faculty of 525 full-time and 218 part-time provides a faculty-student ratio of 1-16.

Entrance Requirements: Combination of high school class rank and ACT score; GRE, GMAT or Miller Analogy required for graduate schools, early admission, midyear admission, rolling admission, advanced placement plans available.

Costs Per Year: State residents $1,842 tuition; non-residents $5,526; room and board $3,498; student fees and books $402.

Collegiate Environment: The general administrative offices for the Edwardsville Campus are located on the center campus, which is comprised of 2,600 rolling and wooded acres along the Mississippi Bluffs. Buildings include Lovejoy Library, John Rendleman Office Building, Peck Classroom Building, Communications Building, Science Laboratory building, the University Center, classroom buildings and Vadalabene Center. Campus housing for students is provided by apartments and residence halls. It is located near beautiful Tower Lake on the campus, and is limited to 1,632 single students and 93 families. The university library holdings include 1,000,000 bound volumes, 1.2 million microform units, 6,130 periodicals, 38,845 audio-visual titles, and 1 million government and research documents. The East St. Louis Center includes laboratories, classrooms, libraries, and other facilities designed and equipped for university-level operation. 79% of students applying for admission are accepted, including midyear students. Scholarships are available and 60% of the current enrollment receives some form of financial aid. The university offers optional Air Force and Army ROTC programs and special programs for the disadvantaged. The Southern Illinois University School of Dental Medicine in Alton, Illinois, recently opened a new and expanded dental clinic with 72 patient care stations for student clinical experience. The Dental School offers students a quality, affordable education in a small-town environment 25 miles from St. Louis.

Community Environment: Edwardsville (population 14,000) is a suburban St. Louis community with a public library, many churches, museum, YMCA, and hospital facilities nearby. It is located only 30 minutes from Lambert St. Louis International Airport.

SPERTUS COLLEGE *(C-14)*
618 South Michigan Avenue
Chicago, Illinois 60605
Tel: (312) 922-9012; Admissions: (312) 322-1769; Fax: (312) 922-6406

Description: Formerly known as the College of Jewish Studies, the privately supported liberal arts college opened in 1925 to provide a basic Jewish education for high school graduates with only a rudimentary knowledge of Hebrew. It has been expanded to include programs in Bible, Hebrew, language and literature, Talmud, history, philosophy, communal service and teacher education. The college is accredited by the North Central Association of Colleges and Schools and is a post-baccalaureate institution only. It operates on the quarter system and offers one summer session. Enrollment includes 55 full-time and 135 part-time students. A faculty of 2 full-time and 21 part-time gives a faculty-student ratio of 1-8.

Entrance Requirements: Accredited bachelor's degree; rolling admission plan available; $50 application fee.

Costs Per Year: $5,400 tuition; registration fee $75.

Collegiate Environment: The college specializes in Judaic and Hebraic studies and serves as the department of Judaic and Hebraic studies for a consortium of colleges and universities in northern Illinois. The library contains 90,000 volumes. Financial assistance is available. Midyear students are accepted.

Community Environment: See University of Chicago.

SPOON RIVER COLLEGE *(G-8)*
R.R. 1
Canton, Illinois 61520
Tel: (309) 647-4645; (800) 334-7337; Fax: (309) 647-6498

Description: The publicly supported junior college is fully accredited by the North Central Association of Colleges and Schools. Formerly known as Canton Community College it offers career and vocational programs and univerity parallel curricula. It grants the Associate degree. The college operates on the early semester calendar system and offers one summer session. Enrollment includes 833 full-time and 1,500 part-time students. A faculty of 34 full-time and 90 part-time gives a faculty-student of 1-19.

Entrance Requirements: Open enrollment policy; high school graduation or GED equivalent; non-high school graduates may be admitted; early admission, early decision, rolling admission, midyear admission and advanced placement plans available.

Costs Per Year: $1,050 district-resident tuition; $1,416.45 non-district residents.

Collegiate Environment: The college consists of four buildings and contains a library of 32,251 volumes. Financial assistance is available and 75% of students receive some form of financial aid.

Community Environment: Canton is situated in an extremely fertile agricultural district with a seasonal climate. Planes and buses are available. Air service at Peoria some 30 miles distant. Industries are coal mining and the manufacture of farm implements. The city has a library, YMCA, YWCA, concert association, hospital, a downtown shopping area with over 100 retail outlets. Additional shopping facilities in Peoria. Recreational activities are boating, fishing, hunting, bowling, and golf. At least 12 retail and community-sponsored events are conducted each year.

Branch Campuses: Macomb Campus, 208 S. Johnson, Macomb, IL 61455; Havana Center, 230 W. Main, Havana, IL 62644; Rushville Center, 229 W. Washington, Rushville, IL 62681.

SPRINGFIELD COLLEGE IN ILLINOIS *(J-9)*
1500 North 5th Street
Springfield, Illinois 62702
Tel: (406) 365-3396; (800) 821-8320; Fax: (406) 365-8132

Description: The privately supported liberal arts two-year college was founded by the Ursuline Sisters and is accredited by the North Central Association of Colleges and Schools. It offers programs in liberal arts, teacher education, and career-vocational areas of study. The college grants the Associate degree and does not discriminate against applicants, students, or employees on the basis of race, color, religion, sex, handicap, or national or ethnic origin. The college operates on the semester system with 1 summer session. Enrollment includes 150 men and 260 women. A faculty of 15 full-time and 28 part-time gives a faculty-student ratio of 1-10.

Entrance Requirements: Accredited high school graduation or equivalent; completion of 16 units, including 3 English; ACT or SAT required; high school average of C accepted; early admission, delayed admission, and rolling admission plans available; $15 application fee.

Costs Per Year: $5,700 tuition; $140 student fees.

Collegiate Environment: The campus is comprised of six buildings on 12 acres and includes a library of 17,861 volumes, 211 periodicals, 24 microforms and 2,111 audiovisual materials. Dormitory facilities are provided for 32 students. The college welcomes a geographically diverse student body. 95% of the applicants are accepted. 68 scholarships are available and 89% of the students receive some form of financial aid.

Community Environment: Springfield (population 100,000), the capital of Illinois, is in one of the richest agricultural sections in America and one of the greatest coal-producing counties of Illinois. The city is also an important industrial center. Airlines, buses, and railroads serve the area. There are a number of parks and facilities for golf, boating, and many other outdoor sports. Springfield was the home of Abraham Lincoln preceding his presidency. Some of the many points of interest are Lincoln's Home, the Lincoln Tomb and Monument, museums, and more.

TRINITY CHRISTIAN COLLEGE   *(F-3)*
6601 West College Drive
Palos Heights, Illinois 60463
Tel: (708) 597-3000; (800) 748-0085; Admissions: (708) 239-4708;
Fax: (708) 385-5665

Description: The privately supported liberal arts college was established in 1959 by Reformed Christians in the Chicago area. The college operates on 4-1-4 system and is fully accredited by the North Central Association of Colleges and Schools with professional accreditation by the National League for Nursing. Semester in the Netherlands or Spain with full academic program is offered, and religious subjects required. Credit is allowed for correspondence courses and by prior examination for previous training and experience. Choir, instrumental ensemble, intercollegiate, and interscholastic athletics are available. Enrollment includes 571 full-time and 575 part-time students. A faculty of 37 full-time and 45 part-time gives a faculty-student ratio of 1-14.

Entrance Requirements: Accredited high school graduation with minimum C average, including 3-4 English, 2 mathematics, 2 science, 2 social science; non-high school G.E.D. graduates may be admitted; SAT or ACT required, minimum ACT Score: 18; early admission, rolling admission, midyear admission and advanced placement plans available; $20 application fee.

Costs Per Year: $10,700 tuition; $4,200 room and board.

Collegiate Environment: The campus grounds were formerly a country club. It is comprised of eleven buildings on 50 wooded acres and includes a library of 63,000 volumes and living accommodations for 400 men and women. 97% of the applicants are accepted. Scholarships are available and 83% of students receive some form of financial aid.

Community Environment: Palos Heights is residential area located 25 miles from downtown Chicago. See University of Chicago.

TRINITY COLLEGE   *(B-2)*
2077 Half Day Road
Deerfield, Illinois 60015
Tel: (312) 948-8980; (800) 482-3669; Admissions: (708) 317-7000;
Fax: (708) 317-7081

Description: Founded in 1897 by the Evangelical Church of America. Trinity is accredited by the North Central Association of Colleges and Secondary Schools. Trinity is a member of the Christian College Consortium, and the American Association of Colleges for Teacher Education. Students come from approximately 36 states and 13 foreign countries; 80% of the student body resides on campus. The College draws 40% of its students from the Evangelical free Church with the next largest groups of students coming from Baptist, Independent, Presbyterian, and Reformed traditions. Enrollment of 1,006 students. A faculty of 40 full-time and 26 part-time gives a faculty-student ratio of 1-16.

Entrance Requirements: Accredited high school graduation with rank in upper half of graduating class; completion of 15 units including 3 English, 8 other college-preparatory courses; ACT or SAT required; Contact Director of Admissions for information. Early admission, midyear admission, early decision, rolling admission, delayed admission plans. $20 application fee.

Costs Per Year: $10,270 tuition; $4,120 room and board; $290 student fees.

Collegiate Environment: The college is comprised of seven buildings located on 80 acres, 25 miles north of Chicago. The library contains 98,000 volumes and dormitory facilities are available for 360 men and 378 women. Approximately 70% of students applying for admission are accepted. 50% of the student body graduated in the top quarter of their high school class. 85% of the current enrollment receives some form of financial aid.

Community Environment: Located on a spacious 120 acre campus 25 miles north of Chicago and 3 miles from suburban city of Deerfield (population of 20,000)

Branch Campuses: Trinity College at Miami, 500 N.E. First Avenue, P.O. Box 019674, Miami, FL 33101-9674, tel.: (305) 577-4600.

TRINITY EVANGELICAL DIVINITY SCHOOL   *(C-2)*
2065 Half Day Road
Deerfield, Illinois 60015
Tel: (708) 317-8000; (800) 345-8337; Fax: (708) 317-8097

Description: The privately supported, graduate, theological school is affiliated with the Evangelical Free Church of America, and is accredited by the Association of Theological Schools and the North Central Association of Colleges and Schools. The school grants the Master of Divinity, Master of Religious Education, Master of Arts, Master of Arts in Religion, Master of Theology, Certificate in Bible Studies, Doctor of Ministry, Doctor of Education degrees, Ph.D. in Theological Studies, and Ph.D. in Intercultural Studies. It operates on the quarter system and offers 4 summer sessions. Enrollment is 841 full-time and 584 part-time students. A faculty of 47 full-time and 60 part-time gives a faculty-student ratio of 1-20.

Entrance Requirements: Bachelor's degree or equivalent; GRE or MAT may be required; $25 application fee.

Costs Per Year: $7,590 tuition; $3,900 room and board; $75 student fees.

Collegiate Environment: The school is located on a wooded 50-acre campus about six miles from the shores of Lake Michigan, 30 miles from the Chicago Loop area. The library contains 157,000 volumes, 1,200 periodical titles, and 105,000 microform titles. Living accommodations are provided for 99 men, 34 women, and 143 families.

Community Environment: A suburban area near Chicago.

Branch Campuses: Trinity College at Miami, P.O. Box 019674, Miami, FL, 33101, (305) 577-4600

TRITON COLLEGE   *(D-3)*
2000 Fifth Avenue, C-100A
River Grove, Illinois 60171
Tel: (708) 456-0300; Admissions: (708) 456-0300 x3130; Fax: (708) 583-3108

Description: Triton College is a publicly supported, district-governed community college which has a credit enrollment of 11,898 men and women. The school offers programs which prepare students to transfer to four-year institutions, and also provides career and technical programs which prepare students with competencies consistent with employment opportunities. The school was founded in 1964 and the campus encompasses 63 square miles in the western suburbs of Chicago. The school operates on the semester system with three summer sessions. The college is accredited by the North Central Association of Colleges and Schools and maintains professional accreditation in various health career programs. The Cooperative Education program incorporated work experience with course work. Intercollegiate and intramural athletics are available. A wide range of clubs and activities are available as well as career services, advising and counseling. financial assistance is available.

Entrance Requirements: Open enrollment policy; high school transcript; some health careers programs have special admission requirements; ACT recommended; early admission, rolling admission and advanced placement plans available.

Costs Per Year: $43 per credit hour district-resident tuition; $132.15 per credit hour state residents; $195.86 per credit hour non-residents.

Collegiate Environment: The campus is comprised of 18 buildings located on 100 acres and includes a library of 81,500 volumes. The college has a campus computer center housing over 100 computers to support all academic areas. A modern college center houses student lounges and service areas.

Community Environment: Triton college district is in the near west suburbs of Chicago. The college is approximately 15 miles from downtown Chicago.

UNIVERSITY OF CHICAGO   *(C-14)*
1116 E. 59th St.
Chicago, Illinois 60615
Tel: (312) 702-8650; Fax: (312) 702-4199

Description: The private university enrolls 6,981 men and 4,635 women. Of these, 1,922 men and 1,525 women are undergraduate students. Of the University's 1,889 faculty members, 596 teach undergraduates, providing a faculty-student ratio of 1-6. Average class size is 25. Both graduate and undergraduate students have ample opportunities to do independent study and research. The university operates on the quarter system with one summer session. It is accredited by the North Central Association of Colleges and Schools and by various regional and professional agencies. A diversity of generous donors, including the American Baptist Education Society, Marshall Field, and most notably John D. Rockefeller, made the creation of the university possible in 1891. The university is composed of the College; the four graduate Divisions of Biological Sciences, Humanities, Physical Sciences, and Social Sciences; six professional schools: the Divinity School, the Graduate School of Business, the Law School, the Graduate School of Public Policy Studies, the School of Medicine; and the School of Social Service Administration; the University Office of Continuing Education and the University of Chicago Press University Extension.

Entrance Requirements: Accredited high school graduation; recommended courses include 4 English, 4 mathematics, 4 science, 2 history, 2 social studies, 3 foreign language; SAT or ACT required; GRE required for graduate school; personal interview recommended; early admission, early notification, delayed admission, and advanced placement plans available; admission is based on overall high school record, potential for success in college, and personal interview; Jan 15 application deadline; $55 application fee.

Costs Per Year: $18,930 tuition; $6,380 room and board; $486 student fees.

Collegiate Environment: The campus has expanded from 13 buildings erected during its first five years to over 197 structures covering 190 acres on both sides of the Midway Plaisance. The library contains 6 million volumes, 46,000 periodicals, 2 million microforms, and 15,000 sound recordings. In addition, the library holds over 7 million manuscript and archival pieces, and 375,000 maps and aerial photographs. Residential halls on or near the campus house 2,273 undergraduate students. 50% of those who apply for admission are accepted. The middle 50% of enrolled freshmen had SAT scores of 560-680V and 620-720M, and between 27-31 on ACT. Approximately 92% of the student body graduated in the top 20% of the high school class, and 93% of the previous freshman class returned to the campus for a second year. The college encourages all who need help

to apply for financial aid, and provides some aid to all who demonstrate financial need. Aid packages generally consist of gift, loan and/or term time work. Approximately 70% of the students receive some form of financial aid. Army and Air Force ROTC programs are available.

Community Environment: Chicago, with a population of nearly 3 million, is the third largest city in the nation, a metropolitan area extending along the southern end of Lake Michigan. It is a leading industrial, medical, educational, and cultural center. The University's campus is located in a residential neighborhood along the lake shore fifteen minutes away from the central downtown area. Cultural facilities include museums that cover a wide variety of fields, art galleries, research libraries, public libraries, theaters, opera, and symphony orchestra. Numerous recreational activities and points of interest are available.

UNIVERSITY OF ILLINOIS - CHICAGO   *(C-14)*
801 S. Morgan (Box 4348)
Chicago, Illinois 60680
Tel: (312) 996-7000; Admissions: (312) 996-4350

Description: This publically supported state university is accredited by the North Central Association of Colleges and Schools and professionally by numerous respective accrediting organizations. UIC consists of 13 academic, undergraduate, graduate, and professional colleges. A broad classification of its programs include liberal arts and sciences, business, architecture, education, engineering, allied health, law, medicine and dentistry. UIC grants Bachelors, Masters, Doctorates, and First Professional degrees. It offers extensive cooperative education programs and internships. Academically talented students may apply to the Honors College. Air Force, Army, and Navy ROTC programs are available. Study abroad programs are available to France, Spain and Austria. UIC operates on the early semester calendar system and offers one summer session. Enrollment includes 11,766 men and 13,099 women comprising 16,206 undergraduates, 6,344 graduate and 2,315 professional degree program students. A faculty of 2,037 gives an overall faculty-student ratio of 1-11.

Entrance Requirements: Accredited high school graduation or equivalent; freshmen selected by combination of rank in graduating class and score on SAT or ACT; completion of 16 units college-preparatory work with minimum of 4 English, 2-3 math, 2 science, 2-3 social studies; early admission, midyear admission, rolling admission and advanced placement plans available. Apply early in senior year of HS. Under certain circumstances non-HS graduates accepted. Feb. 28 priority application deadline. $30 application fee.

Costs Per Year: Tuition $2,660; $7,650 for non-residents, $1,108 students fees.

Collegiate Environment: The University of Illinois at Chicago UIC is a comprehensive university consisting of 13 academic colleges. Its 71 contemporary buildings on 170 acres are located just south and west of the Loop. The library contains 1,600,000 volumes. Dormitories available for 2,100 students; The university also assists students in finding suitable housing in the Chicago area. The university offers special Honors programs. 65% of applicants are accepted. The middle 50% range of scores for the entering freshman class was ACT 18-24 composite. Scholarships are available and 57% of the undergraduates receive some form of financial aid.

Community Environment: Located just a few blocks west of Lake Michigan and downtown Chicago (The Loop), UIC is an urban institution accessible to the cultural and commercial enterprises of the city.

UNIVERSITY OF ILLINOIS - URBANA-CHAMPAIGN   *(I-13)*
506 South Wright Street
Urbana, Illinois 61801
Tel: (217) 333-1000; Admissions: (217) 333-0302

Description: The publicly supported state university is fully accredited by the North Central Association of Colleges and Schools. It is also accredited by respective professional organizations for the following subject areas: architecture, art, business, chemistry, dance, engineering of various types including agricultural, ceramic, chemical, civil electrical, industrial, mechanical, metallurgical and materials, aeronautical and astronautical, mining, and computer; forestry, journalism, landscape architecture, law, librarianship, music, psychology, social work, speech pathology and audiology, teacher education, veterinary medicine. The university grants Baccalaureate, Masters, Doctorate and Professional degrees. The university offers a Cooperative Education program (alternating work and class periods) in engineering; special programs for cross-departmental majors 23 different overseas programs. Precollege, freshman, and undergraduate programs for the educationally disadvantaged are available. Enrollment includes 14,579 male and 11,769 female undergraduates and 9,843 graduate students. A faculty of 1,932 full-time and 63 part-time gives a faculty-student ratio of 1-13.

Entrance Requirements: Accredited high school graduation or equivalent; completion of 15 units including minimum 4 English, 3 mathematics, 2 social science, 2 laboratory science, 2 foreign language; ACT or SAT accepted. There are no minimum score requirements; beginning freshmen are selected on a best-qualified basis using a combination of rank in class plus score on ACT or SAT as the selection criteria. Under certain circumstances non-HS graduates and graduates with "C" average may be accepted. GRE for graduate school required in some instances. Special admission plans available; early admission, (equal consideration period as follows: a beginning freshman application should be submitted between Sept. 15 and Nov. 15 of senior year in HS for best chance of being accepted), rolling admission, delayed admission (College of Liberal Arts & Sciences only), advanced placement. $30 application fee, $40 application for international students.

Costs Per Year: $2,760 lower division, $2,900 upper division state-resident tuition; $7,560 lower, $7,700 upper division out-of-state tuition; $4,260 room and board; $930 student fees.

Collegiate Environment: The university consists of 190 buildings located on 1,388 acres. The library contains 8,500,000 volumes, 3,200,000 titles on microform, 125,000 records and tapes, and 91,000 periodical subscriptions. Living accomodations are provided for 5,194 men, 5,128 women, and 978 families; sororities and fraternities house an additional 4,000 students. 75% of students applying for admission are accepted, including midyear students. Approximately 87% of the student body graduated in the top quarter of their high school class. There are athletic scholarships offered plus various types of gift aid available to all students from Federal, State, and Institutional programs; 85% of the current undergraduate enrollment receives financial assistance.

Community Environment: Champaign-Urbana are adjoining, making a continuous community surrounding the University of Illinois. Chicago is 128 miles north and Springfield is 87 miles west. The mean annual temperature is a pleasant 52.7 degrees and the average rainfall is 36.34 inches. Railroads, airlines, and 3 Interstate highways serve the area. The cities provide hospitals, clinics, libraries, many churches, nine radio stations, three TV stations plus cable television, and all the prominent fraternal and service organizations. Recreational activities are golfing, tennis, racquetball, boating, swimming, roller skating, ice skating. Parks and a large Forest Preserve provide additional facilities for outdoor sports.

UNIVERSITY OF ILLINOIS AT SPRINGFIELD   (J-9)
Sheperd Road
Springfield, Illinois 62794-9243
Tel: (217) 786-6600

Description: The publicly supported upper-division state university is a fully accredited by the North Central Association of Colleges and Schools. Conceived in 1967 and opened in 1970, Sangamon State University is one of Illinois' two senior institutions of higher learning; offers the final two years of baccalaureate work and also study leading to the Master of Arts degree; Master of Business Administration, and Masters of Public Administration. Graduated its first students in December, 1971. Grants the Bachelor of Arts, Bachelor of Science, Master of Business Administrations, Master of Public Admistration and Master of Arts. Enrollment includes 4,536 students. The school operates on the semester system with 1 summr session. Most undergraduates participate in an Applied Study Term. Preparation for State teaching certificate is offered. Also offers a fully accredited B.S. in Nursing and a B.S. in Medical Technology. The faculty consits of 160 members.

Entrance Requirements: AA or AS degree or 60 hours from accredited institution for undergraduates; Bachelor's degree from accredited institution for graduate school.

Costs Per Year: Tuition for state residents $75 per credit; $226 per credit for nonresident; $792 room; $84 student fees.

Collegiate Environment: Students participate in governing the university. Student housing is available through apartments for 300 students, and university keeps list of approved residences. Library contains over 528,000 volumes, 2,650 periodicals and numerous sound recordings, microforms and 104,000 Government publications. Financial aid is available. Hands on use of computers and science laboratories. NAIA National Soccer champion in 1986 and 1988.

Community Environment: Springfield has an area population of almost 190,000 and is less than 100 miles from St. Louis and less than 200 miles from Chicago. The city's major employers are city, county, state and federal governments, health care delivery systems, insurance companies and other service industries. There are 16,000 public employees in Springfield, with more than 100 State and National organizations headquartered in the immediate area.

VANDERCOOK COLLEGE OF MUSIC   (C-14)
3209 South Michigan Avenue
Chicago, Illinois 60616
Tel: (312) 225-6288; (800) 448-2655; Fax: (312) 225-5211

Description: VanderCook is a privately supported professional college. In 1909, Mr. H. A. Vandercook founded the school of music to train professional musicians, directors, and teachers. In 1928, the school was incorporated as a nonprofit teacher training institution and its curriculum was approved by the Illinois State Department of Public Instruction. The school operates on the semester system and offers one summer session. It is accredited by the North Central Association of Colleges and Schools and the National Association of Schools of Music. It offers preparation for state teaching certificates. Enrollment includes 66 undergraduates and 100 graduate students. A faculty of 7 full-time and 24 part-time gives a faculty-student ratio of 1-5.

Entrance Requirements: Open enrollment; accredited high school graduation; SAT or ACT required; special entrance examinations including audition required; rolling admission, midyear admission and early decision plans available.

Costs Per Year: $9,100 tuition; $4,700 room and board; $800 average additional expenses.

Collegiate Environment: The college has one building on South Michigan Avenue adjacent to the Illinois Institute of Technology. Dormitory-type rooms are available for 60 men and 40 women in the modern facilities of the Illinois Institute of Technology. The library contains 24,000 volumes. 80% of applicants are accepted. Academic talent based scholarships are available. 90% of students receive some form of financial aid.

Community Environment: See University of Chicago.

WABASH VALLEY COLLEGE   (N-14)
2200 College Drive
Mount Carmel, Illinois 62863
Tel: (618) 262-8641

Description: This publicly supported community college was founded in 1960. It operates on the semester system and offers two summer sessions. The college offers programs in vocational-technical and academic areas. Enrollment is 716 full-time and 1,846 part-time students. A full-time faculty of 43, plus 51 part-time instructors gives a faculty-student ratio of approximately 1-20. The college grants the Associate degree and is fully accredited by the North Central Association of Colleges and Schools. It is administered by the state as one of the Illinois Eastern Community Colleges.

Entrance Requirements: Open enrollment. Accredited high school graduation or equivalent; completion of 16 academic units including 3 English, 2 math, 1 science and 2 social studies. Non-high school graduates may be considered for certain programs; ACT required; rolling admission; $10 application fee.

Costs Per Year: $864 tuition for district residents; $3,236 state-resident tuition; $4,314 out-of-state tuition;

Collegiate Environment: The campus consists of seven buildings on 120 acres and the library contains 33,000 volumes and serves as both a federal and state depository. Financial assistance is available, and 85% of the present student body receives some aid. All applicants who meet the requirements are accepted; students may enroll at mid-year as well as in the fall.

Community Environment: Mount Carmel (population 8,900) is a rural community enjoying a temperate climate. Community facilities include a library, one Catholic church, 23 Protestant churches, a hospital, and many civic and social organizations; also has student job placement agencies. Recreational activities are swimming, golf, bowling, tennis, boating, and fishing. The city's special event is the annual Agricultural Products Promotion Days.

WAUBONSEE COMMUNITY COLLEGE *(C-12)*

Illinois Route 47
Sugar Grove, Illinois 60554
Tel: (312) 466-4811

Description: The publicly supported liberal arts and technological junior college was founded in 1966 and was named for a Pottawatomie Indian Chief who lived in the Fox River Valley during the 1800's. Recent enrollment included 648 men and 708 women full-time and 2,153 men and 3,349 women part-time. A faculty of 438 gives a faculty-student ratio of 1-16. The college is accredited by the North Central Association of Colleges and Schools. Band, chorus, choir, intercollegiate and intramural athletics are offered. The college operates on the early semester system with a summer session.

Entrance Requirements: Open enrollment policy. Non-high school graduates admitted; midyear students admitted; ACT preferred. Special admission plans: rolling admission. 100% of applicants accepted; average standing of freshman class: upper 50% of HS class. Average ACT composite score of freshman class: 19. Contact Admissions and Records for information. $10 application fee.

Costs Per Year: $1,018 district-resident tuition; $3,382 state-resident tuition; $4,360 out-of-state tuition; $28 student fees.

Collegiate Environment: The college is located on 183 acres and contains a library of 50,000 volumes, 433 periodicals, 411 microforms and 5,674 audiovisual materials. The school offers courses in American Black history. There is no student housing available. 24% of student body receive financial assistance.

Community Environment: See Aurora University.

WESTERN ILLINOIS UNIVERSITY *(G-6)*

University Circle
Macomb, Illinois 61455
Tel: (309) 295-1414; Admissions: (309) 298-3157; Fax: (309) 298-3111

Description: This publicly supported state university was originally founded in 1899 as a normal school, and teacher education remains an important purpose of the institution. However, in response to the strong demand for expanded educational opportunities in many fields, the university now includes the Colleges of: Arts and Sciences, Business and Technology, Education and Human Services, and Fine Arts and Communication, and School of Graduate and International Studies. The university operates on the semester system and offers 3 summer sessions. It is accredited by the North Central Association of Colleges and Schools and professionally by the National Council for the Accreditation of Teacher Education, the American Chemical Society, and the American Assembly of Collegiate Schools of Business. It grants the Bachelor, Master, and Specialist degrees. Enrollment includes 8,511 full-time and 1,531 part-time undergraduates, and 2,557 graduate students. A faculty of 606 full-time and 39 part-time provides an undergraduate faculty-student ratio of 1-15.

Entrance Requirements: Approved high school graduation with 22 ACT or with 18 ACT and rank in upper half of graduating class; high school equivalency diploma accepted; ACT or SAT required; minimum ACT 22, SAT 910 combined; or minimum ACT 18, SAT 720 if ranked in top 50% of high school class; GRE required for graduate school; deferred admission, midyear admission, rolling admission, and advanced placement plans available.

Costs Per Year: $1,902 state-resident tuition and fees; $5,706 non-resident; $3,193 room and board; $705 mandatory fees.

Collegiate Environment: The campus extends over 1,050 acres with 53 buildings, and is located just 40 miles east of the Mississippi River. The library contains 709,000 volumes and living accommodations are provided for 5,900 men, women, and families. Fraternities and sororities house an additional 500 men and women. The college offers Army ROTC programs. Students are permitted to enroll at midyear. The university recently accepted 73% of applicants. Scholarships are available and 73% of students receive some form of financial aid.

Community Environment: Macomb is located 240 miles southwest of Chicago and 150 miles north of St. Louis on the main line of the Burlington Railroad. Besides agriculture, Macomb's industries produce ball bearings, plastic bags, porcelain insulators, and pottery. This is a friendly, midwest community balanced by the youthfulness and creativity of the rapidly expanding university. The community facilities include a hospital, library, hotels, motels, and many clubs and organizations in the city. Recreational facilities include a swimming pool, bowling alleys, parks, and movie theaters.

Branch Campuses: Rock Island Regional Undergraduate Center.

WHEATON COLLEGE *(C-13)*

Wheaton, Illinois 60187
Tel: (708) 752-5005; (800) 222-2419; Fax: (708) 752-5245

Description: The privately supported liberal arts Christian college is interdenominational and offers courses leading to undergraduate degrees in arts, science, and music. The Graduate School offers the Master of Arts degree in seven areas of study, plus a new program leading to the Psy.D. The college is accredited by the North Central Association of Colleges and Schools and professionally by American Chemical Society, National Association of Schools of Music, and the National Council for the Accreditation of Teacher Education. It offers preparation for State teaching certificate. Overseas program includes summer sessions in France, Germany, Spain, Asia, Israel, and England; U.S. summer programs include science program at the Black Hills Science Station, leadership program, High Road program at Honey Rock Camp, Northern Wisconsin, and an art program in Colorado. Religious subjects and chapel attendance required; U.S. Army ROTC is available. An academic cooperative plan in engineering with the Illinois Institute of Technology, the University of Illinois, Washington University, and Case Western Reserve University is available; the participant receives a B.S. from Wheaton and a Professional degree from the university. There is also a 3-2 nursing program in cooperation with Emory University, Goshen Nursing Schol, Rush University, and the University of Rochester. The college operates on the semester system and offers two summer sessions. Enrollment includes 2,234 full-time and 62 part-time undergraduates, and 346 graduate students. A faculty of 160 full-time and 108 part-time gives an undergraduate faculty-student ratio of 1-15. Extensive programs in music, and intercollegiate and intramural athletics are offered.

Entrance Requirements: Accredited high school graduation with rank in upper half of graduating class; completion of 16 college-preparatory units with 15 from academic subjects; SAT or ACT required; apply to Director of Admissions by February 1 for fall entrance; advanced placement plan available; $30 application fee.

Costs Per Year: $12,300 tution; $4,370 room and board.

Collegiate Environment: The college is comprised of 35 buildings on 80 acres, located in a residential community 25 miles west of Chicago. Dormitory facilities accomodate 1,889 students. The libraries contain 995,126 volumes, periodical subscriptions, and other documents. Financial aid is available to all who demonstrate need and 61% of the current enrollment receives financial assistance. 59% of applicants are accepted. Middle 50% range of test scores for freshman class: SAT 1110-1300 combined; ACT 26-30.

Community Environment: Wheaton (population 51,000) is a small city, located 25 miles from Chicago and 18 miles from O'Hare International Airport. Excellent shopping facilities are available as well as numerous civic, fraternal, business, and social organizations, and hospitals. Parks, golf clubs, and forest preserves provide recreational facilities.

WILLIAM RAINEY HARPER COLLEGE   *(C-1)*

1200 West Algonquin Road
Palatine, Illinois 60067-7398
Tel: (708) 397-3000; Admissions: (708) 925-6206

Description: This publicly supported community college began its first classes in 1967. It is accredited by the North Central Association of Colleges and Schools, the American Dental Association for dental hygiene, the American Bar Association, the American Medical Association, the National Association of Schools of Music, and the National League for Nursing. It has a pre-college program for the educationally disadvantaged and grants a Certificate and the Associate degree. Liberal arts, technological, career, and preprofessional courses are offered as well as band, chorus, orchestra, intercollegiate and intramural athletics. The college operates on the semester system and offers one summer term. Enrollment includes 15,000 full-time and part-time credit students. A faculty of 800 gives a faculty-student ratio of 1-19.

Entrance Requirements: Accredited high school graduation or equivalent; non-high school graduates may be admitted; for transfer Associate degrees only: high school units must include 4 English, 2-3 social science, 2-3 mathematics, 2-3 science (1 lab science), 1-2 foreign language, art or music, and up to 4 additional from above or vocational education areas; SAT or ACT required for full-time students who have completed less than 12 semester hours of college level credit at a C or above level; open enrollment policy; $15 application fee.

Costs Per Year: $1,080 district resident tuition; $4,960 state resident tuition; $5,800 nonresident tuition.

Collegiate Environment: The campus is comprised of 15 buildings on 220 acres and the library contains 111,109 volumes, 831 periodicals, 448 microforms and 13,200 audiovisual materials. No student housing is available. All applicants are accepted.

Community Environment: Palatine (population 32,272) is called "A Real Home Town." It enjoys a temperate climate. Rail and bus service are available. Community facilities include churches of major denominations, a public library, and hospitals nearby. Many active organizations provide social, recreational, and cultural programs and functions.

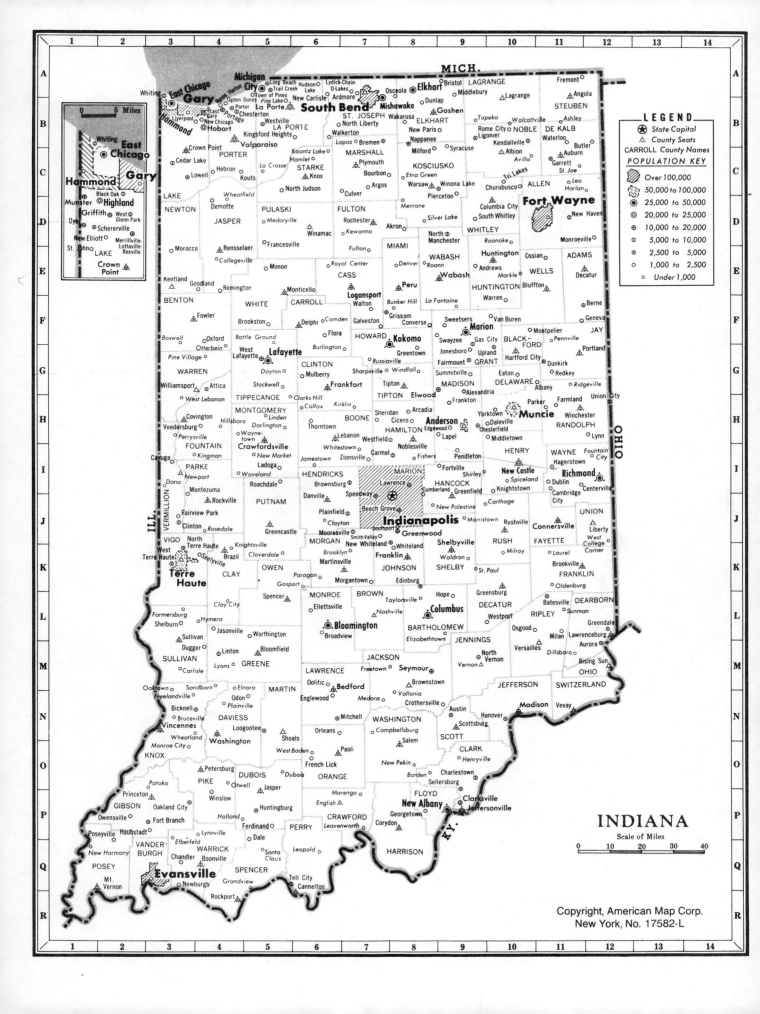

INDIANA

Scale of Miles

0   10   20   30   40

LEGEND

- State Capital
- County Seats
- CARROLL County Names

POPULATION KEY

- Over 100,000
- 50,000 to 100,000
- 25,000 to 50,000
- 20,000 to 25,000
- 10,000 to 20,000
- 5,000 to 10,000
- 2,500 to 5,000
- 1,000 to 2,500
- Under 1,000

INDIANA

ANCILLA COLLEGE   *(C-6)*
Union Road
Donaldson, Indiana 46513
Tel: (219) 936-8898; Fax: (219) 935-1773

Description: The privately supported junior college is sponsored by the Roman Catholic Church and is accredited by the North Central Association of Colleges and Schools. Established in 1937 as a teacher training institute, in 1966, men and women within commuting distance of the college were invited to participate in a program of liberal arts. The college grants the Associate degree. It operates on the semester system and offers two summer sessions. Enrollment includes 703 students. A faculty of 35 gives a faculty-student ratio of 1-20.

Entrance Requirements: High School graduation with a C average and 16 units including 3 English, 2 mathematics, 2 science, and 2 social science; minimum SAT verbal 350, math 350; $25 application fee.

Costs Per Year: $2,670 tuition; $45 fees; $400 books.

Collegiate Environment: The 60-acre campus is located in a rural area that includes Lake Gilbraith. The two-story college building was completed in 1966; the library contains 30,000 volumes. There are no dormitories. 60% of students receive some form of financial assistance.

Community Environment: Situated in a rural area with a temperate climate.

ANDERSON UNIVERSITY   *(H-9)*
1100 East 5th Street
Anderson, Indiana 46012
Tel: (317) 649-9071; (800) 428-6414; Fax: (317) 641-3851

Description: This privately supported, Christian, liberal arts college was established by the Church of God in 1917. It is accredited by the North Central Association of Colleges and Schools, the National Council for Accreditation of Teacher Education, the Association of Theological Schools, the National Association of Schools of Music, the National League for Nursing and the Association of Collegiate Business Schools and Programs. The liberal arts program was authorized in 1929 and the graduate School of Theology was established in 1950 to train pastors for the Church of God. Associate, Bachelor, and Master degrees are granted. It operates on the semester system and offers four summer sessions. Enrollment includes 1,698 full-time, 64 part-time, 134 graduate, and 262 evening students. A faculty of 160 full-time and 70 part-time gives a faculty-student ratio of 1-15.

Entrance Requirements: Contact Director of Admissions for information.

Costs Per Year: $11,400 tuition; $3,750 room and board; $100 technology fee.

Collegiate Environment: Anderson University campus has 26 buildings on 100 acres; the air-conditioned library was remodeled and enlarged in 1989 and contains 152,368 volumes. A $5 million addition and renovation to the science building was completed in 1993. All unmarried out-of-town students registered for five or more hours must reside in college-residence facilities (capacity for 525 men and 650 women). Students come from a wide variety of backgrounds and geographic locations including foreign countries. All nationalities, races and faiths are welcome. 79% of applicants are accepted. Approximately 42% of the student body graduated in the top fifth of the high school class. There are 427 scholarships, 147 for freshmen, available. 82% of the current freshman class receives financial aid. 75% of the freshman class returned for sophomore year.

Community Environment: Anderson (population 62,000) is located 35 miles northeast of Indianapolis, and is known for the automotive electrical systems and lighting equipment produced by Delco-Remy

Division America. Other industries located here manufacture recreation equipment, files, copper wire, corrugated paper boxes, dairy products and agricultural products. Railroads, buses and airports serve the area. The community has a library, churches, and hospitals. Recreational facilities include four 18-hole golf courses and 14 city parks. Mounds State Park is nearby. Employment opportunities are available.

ASSOCIATED MENNONITE BIBLICAL SEMINARY   *(A-8)*
3033 Benham Avenue
Elkhart, Indiana 46517-1999
Tel: (219) 295-3726; (800) 964-2627; Fax: (219) 295-0092

Description: This graduate theological seminary is supported by the Mennonite Church and the General Conference Mennonite Church. It is accredited by the Association of Theological Schools and the North Central Association of Colleges and Schools. The seminary grants the degrees Master of Divinity, The Master of Arts in Peace Studies, and Master of Arts in Theological Studies. It operates on the semester system with an interim term and several two-week summer sessions. Enrollment is 62 full-time and 93 part-time students. A faculty of 15 full-time and 13 part-time gives a faculty-student ratio of 1-7.

Entrance Requirements: Applicants are expected to be members in good standing of some Christian Church and, if not yet committed to the ministry, at least open-minded to a call to the ministry or to some other church vocation. Graduation from the liberal arts course of an accredited college is essential for admission. Graduates from a nonaccredited college may be accepted on probation, which can be removed by the action of the faculty after one semester in residence. Application fee $30.

Costs Per Year: Tuition $4,930; fees $28.

Collegiate Environment: All buildings erected since 1957; student housing available for single and married students. The library contains more than 101,362 hardbound volumes. The Mennonite Historical library at Goshen College contains 39,000 volumes. Financial aid is available through scholarships and jobs. 75% of students receive some form of financial aid.

Community Environment: Elkhart is a small city of about 50,000 in northern Indiana, just a half hour from South Bend (and Notre Dame University) and two hours from Chicago. Several major industries - musical instruments, pharmaceuticals, electronic components, mobile homes and recreational vehicles - provide a broad economic base. Shipshewana, a village in nearby Amish county, is Indiana's busiest tourist attraction. Cultural opportunities include symphonies, art museums, galleries, and repertory theaters; outdoor activites are available at city and county parks, many northern Indiana lakes and nearby Lake Michigan.

BALL STATE UNIVERSITY   *(H-10)*
2000 University Avenue
Muncie, Indiana 47306
Tel: (317) 285-8300; (800) 482-4278; Admissions: (317) 285-8300;
Fax: (317) 285-1632

Description: The publicly supported state university is accredited by the North Central Association of Colleges and Schools, and holds professional accreditation from the National Council for Accreditation of Teacher Education, National League for Nursing, National Architectural Accrediting Board, National Association of Schools of Music, American Chemical Society, Council on Social Work, Education, and by the American Medical Association for Medical Technology. The university was founded in 1918. The university features applied science and technology, architecture and planning, business, fine arts, sciences and humanities, and teachers' college. It offers preparation for the state teaching certificate. The school conducts correspondence courses and allows 30 quarter hours toward credit; it also allows up to 63 hours credit by prior examination in certain courses for previous experience or training. Ball State's London Center makes possible one academic quarter of studies in England. A program for the educationally disadvantaged assists provisional freshmen to qualify for regular admission. The university operates on the semester system and offers two summer sessions. Enrollment includes 8,934 men and 10,581 women comprising 17,317 undergraduates and 2,198 graduate students. A faculty of 930 full-time and 180 part-time gives a faculty-student ratio of 1-21.

Entrance Requirements: High school graduation in top 50% of class; GED considered; 800 on SAT or 19 on ACT; recommended units include 8 English, 6 math, 4 science, and 6 social science; application deadline is March 1 for fall semester and December 1 for spring semester; freshmen are admitted in four classifications-admission with honors, admission with distinction, regular admission, and admission to University College; rolling admission, midyear admission, deferred admission, and advanced placement plans available; $25 application fee.

Costs Per Year: $2,864 state-resident tuition; $7,244 nonresident; $3,608 room and board.

Collegiate Environment: The campus has 57 buildings on 955 acres. There are 31 residence halls with a capacity of approximately 6,400 students. The library contains 1,064,433 titles, 3,525 periodicals, and 288,583 microforms. 87% of the applicants are accepted, and students are permitted to enroll at midyear. There are approximately 500 scholarships available for freshmen and 70% of the students receive financial aid.

Community Environment: Muncie is the county seat and the largest city in east-central Indiana. It is located on the White River, 66 miles northeast of Indianapolis. All forms of commercial transportation are available.

BETHANY THEOLOGICAL SEMINARY   *(I-12)*
615 National Road, West
Richmond, Indiana 47374
Tel: (317) 983-1800; Admissions: (317) 983-1810; Fax: (317) 983-1840

Description: This privately supported seminary was founded in 1905. The school operates on the quarter system and is accredited by the North Central Association of Colleges and Schools and the Association of Theological Schools. Enrollment is 41 full-time and 29 part-time students with a faculty of 5 full-time and 5 part-time. It offers year long certificate program and two masters degree programs. Bethany recently relocated to Richmond, Indiana, and joined in affiliation with Earlham School of Religion.

Entrance Requirements: Bachelor's degree with emphasis on liberal arts from an accredited college or university; satisfactory grade average in undergraduate courses; adequate preseminary foundation; rolling admission plan available; $25 application fee.

Costs Per Year: $4,908 tuition.

Collegiate Environment: Bethany's new 24,000 square foot building contains a chapel, meeting rooms, classrooms, and office space. Earlham School of Religion is located next door. Students are able to cross register and take FSR classes. Students can also avail themselves of the services on the Earlham campus. The library is now housed in Earlhams's Lilly Library, which contains 350,000 volumes.

Community Environment: Richmond is located just west of Dayton, Ohio, and is easily accessible from Dayton or Indianapolis. Shopping facilities, hospitals, churches, and civic centers are nearby.

BETHEL COLLEGE   *(A-7)*
1001 West McKinley Avenue
Mishawaka, Indiana 46545
Tel: (219) 259-8511; (800) 422-4101; Fax: (219) 257-3326

Description: Privately supported liberal arts college, founded in 1947 by the Missionary Church. It operates on the semester system and offers one summer session. Accredited by the North Central Association of Colleges and Schools. Grants Associates, Bachelor, and Master's degree. Enrollment includes 756 full-time and 414 part-time

undergraduates and 30 graduate students. A faculty of 64 full-time and 47 part-time gives a faculty-student ratio of 1-18.

Entrance Requirements: High school graduation with a C average or equivalent and 16 units recommended including 4 English, 2 mathematics, 2 foreign language, 2 science, and 2 social science; ACT or SAT; application required; $25 application fee.

Costs Per Year: $9,300 tuition; $3,000 room and board; $100 fees.

Collegiate Environment: The campus has 28 buildings on 60 acres in an urban area; dormitory capacity for 430 students. The library contains 74,000 volumes, 387 periodicals and 3,759 microforms. 80% of applicants are accepted, including midyear applicants. Scholarships are available and 75% of the students receive some form of financial aid.

Community Environment: Mishawaka-South Bend is an urban environment of 250,000. (See University of Notre Dame.)

BUTLER UNIVERSITY   *(J-8)*
4600 Sunset Avenue
Indianapolis, Indiana 46208
Tel: (317) 283-8000

Description: Privately supported university accredited by North Central Association of Colleges and Schools; professional accreditation by American Chemical Society, National Association of Schools of Music, American Council on Pharmaceutical Education, National Council for the Accreditation of Teacher Education; The university operates on the semester system and offers two summer sessions. The university was founded in 1855 and is dedicated to liberal arts education of undergraduate students pursuing courses of general and professional study including business, music, dance, drama, radio-TV, pharmacy, pre-law, pre-dentistry, pre-medical, Special Education, Speech Pathology, teacher education, and preparation for state teaching certificate. Enrollment includes 2,710 full-time and 12 part-time undergraduates, and 928 graduate students. A faculty of 223 full-time and 138 part time provides a faculty-student ratio of 1-13. Army ROTC is available.

Entrance Requirements: High School graduates; SAT or ACT scores are required and with class rank are evaluated to determine acceptance; a B average is required; non-high school graduates considered if recommended by their high school as having exceptional ability and maturity; GED acceptable; Completion of 16 units including 4 English, 3 mathematics, 2 laboratory science, 2 foreign language, 2 social studies. Early admission, early decision, rolling admission, delayed admission, midyear admission and advanced placement plans available. Credit given by prior examination in certain courses for previous experience or training. Contact Dean of Admissions for information and forms. $25 application fee.

Costs Per Year: $13,130 tuition; $14,290 pharmacy tuition; $4,110-$4,420 room and board; $175-$225 student fees; $600 miscellaneous.

Collegiate Environment: The campus has 18 buildings on 290 acres located in a residential area. The observatory and planetarium house a 38-inch telescope; library contains 286,112 volumes and 2,757 periodicals. Residence halls accommodate 1,890 students. 34% of the freshmen ranked in the top 10% of their high school class, 55% ranked in the top 20%. The middle range of scores for the entering freshman class was SAT 440-560 verbal, 480-610 math. 88% of the freshman class returned for the second year. 888 need based, performance, athletic, and academic scholarships are available, ranging from $1,000 to full tuition. There is a co-op program with Dow Chemical for chemistry majors and internships are required for Radio/TV, Public & Corporate Communications.

Community Environment: Indianapolis is the capital city, located in the exact center of the state, enjoying a fine climate. All modes of transportation are available. Excellent city facilities include library with 21 branches, museum, churches of all denominations, and 17 hospitals. Recreational facilities consist of 32 parks and eight golf courses with additional facilities for auto races, boating, baseball, basketball, football, riding, swimming, roller skating, boxing, wrestling, and ice skating.

CALUMET COLLEGE OF SAINT JOSEPH   *(B-3)*
2400 New York Ave.
Whiting, Indiana 46394
Tel: (219) 473-4224; Fax: (219) 473-4259

Description: Calumet College is a privately supported, Roman Catholic liberal arts college open to all qualified men and women. The college operates on a semester system and offers three summer terms. Enrollment is 444 full-time and 642 part-time students. A faculty of 110 gives a faculty-student ratio of 1-15. The college is fully accredited by the North Central Association of Colleges and Secondary Schools. It offers program in preparation of State teaching certificate. Credit is allowed for correspondence courses and for certain courses by prior examination (CLEP) for previous experience and training. It also has a Cooperative Education program (alternating class and work periods) in many areas. Religious subjects are required. Intramural basketball, flag football and volleyball are offered. The college grants Certificates, Associate and Bachelor degrees.

Entrance Requirements: Graduation from an approved high school with a minimum of 15 units including 4 English, 3 math, 2 science, 1 foreign language and 2 social studies; under certain circumstances non-high school graduates considered; early admission, rolling admission, and delayed admission plans available; minimum SAT scores 340V, 340M; ACT 15; applications should be filed as early as possible and all credentials should be in the hands of the Director of Admissions at least three weeks before the opening of the school term; $25 application fee.

Costs Per Year: $3,690 tuition; $500 miscellaneous including books; $65 student activity fee.

Collegiate Environment: No dormitory facilities are available. The library contains 107,494 bound volumes. Midyear students are admitted. 64% of the freshmen class returned to the campus for the second year. Recently, 215 Bachelor's degrees were awarded.

Community Environment: Hammond-Whiting, facing Lake Michigan, is one of the greatest industrial regions in the world. Industries produce pig iron, rolled, forged and casted steel products, petroleum, lead and aluminum products, chemicals, railroad freight cars and building materials. Part-time employment is available.

Branch Campuses: Credit courses are available through Andrean High School.

CHRISTIAN THEOLOGICAL SEMINARY (J-8)
P.O. Box 88267
Indianapolis, Indiana 46208
Tel: (317) 924-1331; Admissions: (317) 923-2300; Fax: (317) 923-1961

Description: Christian Theological Seminary is a privately supported ecumenical graduate seminary of the Christian Church (Disciples of Christ). It is accredited by the North Central Association of Colleges and Schools and the Association of Theological Schools. The seminary operates on the semester system with two summer sessions. The basic degree in preparation for ordination is a Master of Divinity, with 70% of the seminary's graduates in parish ministry. The Master of Arts degrees in Counseling, Christian Education and Church Music and a Master of Theological Studies are also offered. Advanced degrees include the Master of Sacred Theology and the Doctor of Ministry. Enrollment includes 164 full-time and 161 part-time graduate students. A faculty of 20 full-time and 10 part-time gives a faculty-student ratio of 1-7.

Entrance Requirements: A.B. degree or equivalent. $15 application fee.

Costs Per Year: $5,670 ($189/cr) tuition; $15 fees; room and board available.

Collegiate Environment: The seminary, including a new chapel, counseling center and student housing, is located on a 40-acre campus. The library contains approximately 140,000 volumes and 866 periodicals. Commuter and full-time student housing available. 248 scholarships are available.

Community Environment: Indianapolis, Indiana, located near the population center of the United States in a rich agricultural region, is becoming the national center for amateur sports, has a world-class zoo and a metropolitan university anchored by the nation's largest medical school. Located near the campus are the Indianapolis Museum of Art, Clowes Hall for the Performing Arts, Butler University and the Children's Museum.

CONCORDIA THEOLOGICAL SEMINARY (D-11)
6600 N. Clinton Street
Fort Wayne, Indiana 46825-4996
Tel: (219) 481-2100; Admissions: (219) 481-2155; Fax: (219) 481-2121

Description: This privately supported graduate seminary is maintained by the Lutheran Church-Missouri Synod. It operates on the quarter system and offers 3 summer sessions. It is accredited by the Association of Theological Schools and North Central Association of Colleges and Schools. Founded in 1846, the seminary seeks to admit students who possess suitable personal qualifications for the Gospel Ministry and who have also demonstrated their consecration and academic ability. It grants the Master of Divinity degree. The Division of Graduate Studies offers the Master of Arts in Religion, the Master of Sacred Theology, and the Doctor of Ministry degrees. Enrollment is 259 full-time and 56 part-time students. A faculty of 28 gives a faculty-student ratio of 1-11. Choir and instrumental groups are offered. The seminary also sponsors a program of continuing education for ministers and other professional church workers.

Entrance Requirements: Bachelor's degree from accredited college or university; GRE and placement test required; preseminary courses in German, Latin, Greek, and religion are preferred but not mandatory; midyear admission and rolling admission plans; $35 application fee.

Costs Per Year: $4,950 tuition; $3,300 room and board; $255 student fees.

Collegiate Environment: The seminary is located in the northeastern part of Fort Wayne. The campus site comprises 191 acres of gently rolling land, bordered on the east by the St. Joseph River and on the west by a beautifully wooded area of 25 acres. 90% of the applicants are accepted. Approximately 95% of the previous freshman class returned to the campus for a second year. 80% of the current student body receives financial aid. The library contains 144,000 volumes, 761 periodicals, 3,493 microforms and 7,537 audiovisual materials. Student housing is available for 204 students.

Community Environment: See Indiana Institute of Technology.

DEPAUW UNIVERSITY (J-5)
313 S. Locust Street
Greencastle, Indiana 46135
Tel: (317) 658-4800; (800) 448-2495; Admissions: (317) 658-4006; Fax: (317) 658-4007

Description: Selective, independent, coeducational liberal arts university established in 1837 and is accredited by the North Central Association of Colleges and Schools, American Chemical Society, National Council for Accreditation of Teacher Education, and the National Association of Schools of Music. It is affiliated with the United Methodist Church. The university structure includes the College of Liberal Arts, and the School of Music. The university grants the Bachelor of Arts and Bachelor of Music degrees. Special academic offerings include the Honor Scholar Program the Management Fellows Program, the Science Research Fellows Program, and Media Fellows. Domestic off-campus semesters include the New York Arts Program, Newberry Library Program in Chicago, Oak Ridge Science Semester, Urban Semester in Philadelphia, Drew Semester on the United Nations, and the Washington Semester. DePauw sponsors a music program in Vienna, Austria. Through cooperative arrangements with other colleges DePauw students participate in programs in Africa, Australia, Belgium, China, Denmark, England, France, Germany, Greece, Hungary, Indonesia, Ireland, Italy, India, Japan, Latin America, Middle East, Poland, Switzerland, Thailand, Scotland, Spain, and the former Soviet Republics. 3-2 plan in engineering with Columbia, Case Western, and Georgia Institute of Technology. Its extensive music program as well as intercollegiate and intramural athletics. The university operates on the 4-1-4 calendar system. Enrollment includes 2,037 full-time and 24 part-time undergraduates. A faculty of 148 full-time and 48 part-time gives a faculty-student ratio of 1-11.

Entrance Requirements: High school graduation required; 15 units including 4 English, 3 mathematics, 2 foreign language, 3 science, and 3 social science; delayed admission, midyear admission and advanced placement plans. Application fee $25. Apply in December or February by submitting an application to Office of Admissions; non-refundable tuition deposit of $200 plus refundable room and board deposit of $50 must be made; additional requirements must be met for School of Music. All freshman women and men students must reside in a university residence hall during freshman year.

Costs Per Year: $15,175 tuition per year, $5,245 room & board; $300 fees.

Collegiate Environment: The 125 acre campus blends over $20 million in new facilities with a rich, historic past. East College, the oldest building, is entered in the National Register of Historic Monuments. An outstanding renovation of Roy O. West Library was recently completed at a cost of $5 million. A new residence hall opened in 1989, bringing the total number of dormitories to seven. 984 students live in residence halls, 523 in sororities, and 724 in fraternities. 15 fraternities and ten sororities provide additional housing for approximately 1,250 students. The F.W. Olin Biological Sciences Building opened in Fall 1993. The Olin building features more laboratories than classrooms which reflects DePauw's emphasis on student-faculty collaborative research. DePauw's Center for Contemporary Media opened in 1991. It consolidates state-of-the-art facilities for print media and broadcast media. It is a unique endeavor among American liberal arts institutions and epitomizes DePauw's tradition of producing leaders in the field of journalism. Library contains 276,470 volumes, 1,352 periodicals, 204,242 microforms, and audiovisual units. Library facilities include Media Services, Library Computer Services (including word processing lab and graphic production facilities), Archives and Special Collections, and three satellite libraries: Music, Curriculum, and Science Libraries. 83% of applicants are accepted. The middle 50% ranges of scores for the entering freshman class were SAT 490-600 verbal, 540-670 math; ACT 23-28 composite. 80% of the freshman class were in the top quarter of their high school graduating class. Scholarships are available and 73% of the undergraduates receive some form of financial aid. 90% of the freshman class returned for sophomore year. There were 461 Bachelor's degrees awarded.

Community Environment: Greencastle is located 40 miles west of Indianapolis, and within a 4-hour drive of Chicago, Cincinnati, Columbus, Louisville, and St. Louis. Community facilities include churches and a county hospital. The resort areas of Cataract Lake and Mansfield Lake are within 15 miles, provide facilities for water sports and fishing.

EARLHAM COLLEGE   *(I-12)*
National Road West
Richmond, Indiana 47374
Tel: (317) 983-1600; (800) 327-5426; Admissions: (317) 983-1600; Fax: (317) 983-1560

Description: This independent, liberal arts college is fully accredited by the North Central Association of Colleges and Schools, and professionally by the American Chemical Society. Other accreditation includes Great Lakes Colleges Association, Phi Beta Kappa, and NCAA Div. III. Earlham, founded by the Religious Society of Friends (Quakers), operates on a trimester system of three 11-week terms. Enrollment is 966 full-time and 16 part-time students. A faculty of 78 full-time and 11 part-time gives a faculty-student ratio of 1-12. Its educational tradition is respected for its academic excellence, its concern with outstanding teaching, and its commitment to the support and academic fulfillment of individual students. Earlham offers 29 departmental majors, in addition to programs in interdisciplinary areas such as Peace and Global Studies, Human Development and Social Relations, International Studies, and a nationally recognized Japanese Studies program. Extensive off-campus study programs are offered, and more than 60% of Earlham students participate in programs in the United States or in 20 foreign countries, including England, Germany/Austria, Kenya, Jerusalem, Japan and France.

Entrance Requirements: Most accepted applicants have at least a B average in their academic courses in high school; applicants should have at least 15 academic units, including 4 English, 3 mathematics, and 2 or more each in language, science and history/social studies; writing sample (either original essay or a piece of academic or creative work; recommendations from a teacher and high school counselor, high school transcript and SAT or ACT required; early decision, early action, regular decision, early admission, and delayed admission plans available; college credit is offered for all AP courses in which a grade of 4 or 5 is achieved; $30 application fee.

Costs Per Year: $21,465 inclusive expenses; 16,632 tuition; $4,305 room and board; $528 fees.

Collegiate Environment: Earlham is a residential college community. Most students live either in one of 7 residence halls or in college-owned off-campus housing. All dormitories house both first-year and upperclass students. Earlham's two libraries house more than 360,000 volumes, in addition to more than 177,921 units of microfilm, 25,000 art slides, approximately 15,000 maps and 1,408 periodicals and newspapers. In addition to the dormitories and libraries, Earlham's campus consists of four classroom buildings, a student center, a field-house, playing fields, riding stables and ring, two biological stations, a natural history museum and a planetarium. 68% of applicants are accepted. The middle 50% range of scores of enrolled freshmen is SAT 480-610 verbal, 480-620 math. More than 65% of freshmen rank in the top quarter of their high school class. Extensive financial aid is available. More than 62% of the students receive need-based financial aid.

Community Environment: The campus lies at the southwest edge of Richmond, IN, a city of 40,000 people. Richmond is 70 miles from Cincinnati, OH, and Indianapolis, IN, and 40 miles from Dayton, OH. Local activities include auctions, the city's arboretum, the pedestrian shopping mall downtown, the symphony orchestra, civic theater and opera companies, a historical museum and the art assocation. The city is served by buses. Airline service is available in Dayton, OH.

FRANKLIN COLLEGE OF INDIANA   *(K-8)*
500 East Monroe Street
Franklin, Indiana 46131
Tel: (317) 736-8441

Description: Franklin College is a small, privately supported residential college accredited by the North Central Association of Colleges and Secondary Schools and National Council for Accreditation of Teacher Education. It is a liberal arts college operating on a 4-1-4 semester system and 1 summer session. Enrollment of 400 men and 480 women. It was founded in 1834 by Baptist pioneers and today the college maintains a voluntary relationship with the American Baptist Churches, USA. Franklin College grants the Bachelor's degree and prepares students for the state teaching certificate. A faculty of 86 gives a faculty-student ratio of 1:10. Offers music, inter-collegiate, intra-mural athletics programs; junior year abroad; Washington semester; Harlaxton semester; United Nations semester.

Entrance Requirements: HS graduation with 12 units, college preparatory and include 3 English, 3 mathematics, 3 science, and 3 social science credits. Foreign language is not required. Rolling admission, advanced placement, early admission, delayed admission, early decision plans. SAT or ACT required; minimum scores of SAT Verbal 400, Math 400. Contact Director of Admissions for information. Applications should be completed as early as possible after completion of the junior year in high school. Admissions examines academic record, SAT/ACT scores, recommendations, activities and personal information supplied by the applicant.

Costs Per Year: Tuition $8,090, board and room $3,110; miscellaneous $70. Financial assistance available; institutional academic scholarships, grants and loans.

Collegiate Environment: 63% of the students applying for admission are accepted, including midyear. Approximately 95% of the current freshman class receives financial aid Approximately 86% of the student body graduated in the top half of the high school class, 57% in the top quarter. Slightly over 79% of the students returned to the campus for the second year. The library contains 105,621 volumes, 496 periodicals and 354 microforms; dormitory facilities for 229 men, 338 women, 4 fraternities provide additional housing for 75 men. Has academic cooperative plan with Duke University in forestry, with with Indiana University in ROTC, and in engineering and occupational therapy with Washington University, St. Louis, MO.

Community Environment: Franklin (population 15,000) is situated 20 miles south of Indianapolis with facilities that include a library, 15 churches representing major denominations, hospital, various service, fraternal, and veteran's organizations. Part-time job opportunities are available. Recreational activities are fishing, swimming, tennis, and bowling.

GOSHEN COLLEGE   *(B-8)*
1700 South Main Street
Goshen, Indiana 46526
Tel: (219) 535-7535; (800) 348-7422; Fax: (219) 535-7609

Description: This privately supported liberal arts college was founded by the Mennonite Church in 1894. It is accredited by the North Central Association of Colleges and Schools. Its professional accreditations include the National Council for Accreditation of Teacher Education, the National League of Nursing, and the Council of Social Work Education. Programs in nutrition are approved by the American Dietetics Association. The college operates on the semester system and offers two summer sessions. Enrollment includes 957 full-time and 143 part-time students. A faculty of 85 full-time and 40 part-time gives a faculty-student ratio of 1-13. The college offers an overseas program and alternating study and work semesters. It also allows credit for up to 12 hours of correspondence courses, and credit for courses by prior examination.

Entrance Requirements: High school graduation with a C average; upper 50% of graduating high school class; non-high school graduates considered; admission to Goshen does not imply admission to professional curriculum (teacher education and nursing programs); minimum combined SAT score of 920 or ACT 21; application deadline for fall semester is August; rolling admission, delayed admission, and advanced placement plans available; application fee $15.

Costs Per Year: $9,900 tuition; $3,760 room and board; $900 miscellaneous.

Collegiate Environment: The college offers a study-service semester abroad that yields regular college credit and costs the same as study on campus. Under the supervision of a professor, students spend seven weeks studying the host nation and the remaining seven weeks are spent in a peace-corps type of voluntary assignment. The Goshen campus has 18 buildings on 135 acres; the four-story library contains 115,000 volumes; residence halls accommodate 315 men, 439 women. The college also operates the Merry Lea Environmental Learning Center, a 900-acre tract 30 miles southeast of the college. The college has provided a modern trailer court with 25 house-trailer lots for married students. Average SAT scores of current freshmen are 470V, 524M; average rank is upper 25% of high school class. Of the scholarships available, 204 are for freshmen, and 90% of the current freshmen receive financial aid. 90% returned for the sophomore year.

Community Environment: Goshen, "The Maple City" is a diversified small industry center, situated ten miles south of the Michigan state line. Annual mean temperature is 55 degrees, and the annual rainfall is 34 inches. All forms of transportation are available, and the airport is five miles southeast. Community facilities include a public library, hospital, 24 churches and many civic, service and social organizations. Goshen is noted for its large number of Amish farmers, and hundreds of lakes are within a 40-mile radius.

GRACE COLLEGE   *(C-9)*
200 Seminary Drive
Winona Lake, Indiana 46590
Tel: (219) 372-5131; (800) 544-7223

Description: Privately-supported liberal arts college affiliated with the Fellowship of Grace Brethren Churches and is accredited by the North Central Association of Colleges and Schools. It operates on the semester system and offers 3 summer sessions. Grace College was founded in 1948 as a collegiate division of Grace Theological Seminary, founded in 1937. Grants the Bachelor's degree. Offers preparation for State teaching certificate. Conducts a French, Spanish, German and Russian Junior Year Abroad program. Religious subjects and chapel attendance are required. Extensive music and intercollegiate athletic programs. Graduate program, Grace Theological Seminary, awards the Master degree. Current enrollment includes 256 men, 344 women full-time, 39 men, and 41 women part-time. The faculty consists of 33 full-time and 28 part-time members.

Entrance Requirements: High school graduation with rank in upper half of graduating class; C average and 16 units including 4 English, 2-3 mathematics, 2-3 foreign language, 2-3 science, and 2-3 social science; score of 19 or over on ACT; SAT score of 800 or more; non-high school graduates considered; four-year college or university degree required for the seminary; early admission, early decision, rolling admission, advanced placement. Deadline for Fall term, August 1; application fee $20. For graduate program write to Grace Theological Seminary, Director of Admissions.

Costs Per Year: $8,958 tuition and fees; $3,818 room and board.

Collegiate Environment: The campus has 16 buildings on 150 acres located at Winona Lake. There are residence halls, capacity for 230

men and 304 women; library contains 147,000 volumes, 520 periodicals, 8,000 sound recordings, and 45,000 microforms. 73% of the freshman class returned for a second year. The average score for the entering freshman class was ACT 21.4 composite. The average high school standing of the class was in top 30% and 43% of the class was in the top quarter of high school class. 700 scholarships are available and 81% of the students receive some form of financial aid. 27% of the senior class continued on to graduate school.

Community Environment: One of the outstanding Christian summer resorts in America, Winona Lake, population 2,940, is situated two miles from Warsaw, Indiana, on the main line of Amtrack Railroad. This is a resort area for the entire family.

HANOVER COLLEGE   *(N-10)*
Hanover, Indiana 47243
Tel: (812) 866-7000; Admissions: (812) 866-7021; Fax: (812) 866-7098

Description: This privately-supported liberal arts college is accredited by North Central Association of Colleges and Schools and affiliated with the United Presbyterian Church. The college was founded in 1827 and is the oldest of the four-year private colleges in Indiana. It operates on a three-term calendar: four courses are taken in the first 14 weeks; four the second 14; and one the last 4 weeks. One religion course is required. The college grants the Bachelor's degree. Credit given by prior examination in certain courses for previous experience or training. Overseas program offers spring term (4 weeks) in foreign language conversation, Shakespeare in England, and more. The college has band, choir, and ensembles; extensive intercollegiate and intramural athletics are available. It offers preparation for state teaching certificate. Enrollment includes 1,096 students. A faculty of 87 provides a faculty-student ratio of 1-13.

Entrance Requirements: High school graduation in top 40% of high school class; completion of 16 units including 4 English, 2 mathematics, 2 foreign language, 2 science, and 2 social science; SAT and achievement tests in English, math, and foreign language required; minimum scores SAT 500V, 500M, ACT 20; non-high school graduates considered; $20 application fee; deadline for application is March 1 for priority consideration; early decision available for applicants with strong scholastic and personal characteristics; advanced placement, rolling admission plans available.

Costs Per Year: $8,200 tuition; $3,485 room and board; $260 student fees; $1,000 miscellaneous.

Collegiate Environment: There are 34 buildings on 600 acres; students use the most advanced educational equipment and modern facilities. The library contains 300,000 volumes, 920 periodicals, 20,000 microforms, and 2,600 sound recordings. Almost all of the faculty and students live on the campus; there is dormitory capacity for 1,050 students. There are five national fraternities and four national sororities. 80% of the freshman class returned for the sophomore year. Average high school standing of freshman class is in the top 30%; 60% are in the top quarter. The college seeks a geographically diverse student body, and students may be admitted at midyear. 75% of applicants are accepted. Extensive scholarship assistance is available, and 65% of the current freshman class receives financial aid.

Community Environment: Hanover (population 4,000) is located four and one-half miles from Madison, Indiana, overlooking the beautiful Ohio River valley from a hilltop nearly 400 feet above the river. All forms of transportation are available in Madison. Community facilities include a modern hospital. Hanover is rich in historic lore and antiques. Clifty Falls, a large and interesting State Park, well known throughout Indiana and the Middle West for its rugged scenery, serves this community.

HOLY CROSS COLLEGE   *(A-7)*
Notre Dame, Indiana 46556
Tel: (219) 233-6813; Fax: (219) 233-7427

Description: Holy Cross College is a privately supported, nonresidential junior college conducted by the Brothers of Holy Cross and affiliated with the Roman Catholic Church. It opened in the fall of 1966 with its first class limited to student Brothers. In the fall of 1968 the college became a coeducational liberal arts junior college offering a liberal arts/business transfer curriculum. Holy Cross College places emphasis on the basic academic disciplines, leaving to the senior college the task of specialization and professional preparation. The college operates on a semester system and offers summer sessions. It grants the Associate of Arts degree. Up to 15 semester hours credit are accepted for correspondence courses and up to 30 hours credit are accepted by prior examination in certain courses for previous experience or training. Six semester hours in Philosophy and/or Religious Studies are required for graduation. Enrollment is 430 students. A faculty of 32 gives a faculty-student ratio of 1-13. The school is accredited by the North Central Association of Colleges and Schools and the Indiana Department of Public Instruction. Air Force and Army ROTC programs are available.

Entrance Requirements: High school graduation with C average; minimally competitive ACT or SAT are required; 16 high school units required; early admission, early decision, rolling admission, and advanced placement plans available; application deadline for fall semester is July 1; $20 application fee.

Costs Per Year: $4,650 tuition ($150 per credit hour).

Collegiate Environment: 92% of applicants are admitted, including students at midyear. Dormoitory housing is not available. The library holdings include 12,000 volumes and a computer link to the University of Notre Dame. 42% of students receive some form of financial aid.

Community Environment: See University of Notre Dame.

HUNTINGTON COLLEGE   *(E-10)*
2303 College Avenue
Huntington, Indiana 46750
Tel: (219) 356-6000; (800) 642-6493; Admissions: (219) 356-6000 x1012; Fax: (219) 356-9448

Description: Privately supported, liberal arts college dedicated to Christian initiatives, and controlled by the Church of the United Brethern in Christ. The school is accredited by North Central Association of College and Schools. The college operates on the 4-1-4 semester system and offers two summer sessions. Enrollment includes 325 men and 313 women. A faculty of 40 full-time and 25 part-time gives a faculty-student ratio of 1-13. Grants Bachelor degree; the theological school of Huntington College grants the Master degree, also AA degree.

Entrance Requirements: High school graduation with a C+ average and 15 units including 4 English, 3 mathematics, 2 social science, and 2 science; Special admission plans: early admission, midyear admission, rolling admission, and advanced placement plans available; $20 application fee.

Costs Per Year: $9,950 tuition per year; $2,920 room and board; $250 fees.

Collegiate Environment: The campus has thirteen buildings on 110 acres; dormitory capacity for 160 men, 195 women, and 24 families; library contains 131,000 volumes 600 periodicals, 20,000 microforms. In 1966 an eight-acre lake was constructed for teaching marine biology and water sports. The botanical garden and arboretum were completed in 1935. 90% of applicants are accepted. Average scores of the entering freshman class were: SAT 935 combined, 445 verbal, 490 math; ACT 23 composite. Approximately 55% graduated in the top quarter; 72% of the freshman class returned for second year. Financial aid is available. 92% of students receive some form of aid.

Community Environment: Huntington (population 18,217) is located 24 miles southwest of Fort Wayne and is 90 miles north of Indianapolis. It is in a grain and industrial region. City facilities include museums, library, many churches, YMCA, hospital and numerous civic organizations. The retail and industrial organizations and citizens of the community appreciate the importance of the college students in the overall well being of the community. Salamonie Reservoir, six miles southwest has facilities for camping, picnicking, fishing, and boating.

INDIANA INSTITUTE OF TECHNOLOGY   *(D-11)*
1600 East Washington Boulevard
Fort Wayne, Indiana 46803
Tel: (219) 422-5561; (800) 937-2448; Admissions: (219) 422-5561 X 206; Fax: (219) 422-7696

Description: The privately supported technical institute is accredited by the North Central Association of Colleges and Schools. The school grants Associate and Bachelor of Science degrees. It offers cooperative education programs (parallel work and classes) in computer science, computer information systems, accounting and business administration is offered. All students are required to lease or own personal computers. The institute operates on the semester system and offers two summer sessions. Enrollment includes 1,175 students. A faculty of 22 full-time and 42 part-time gives a faculty-student ratio 1-20.

Entrance Requirements: High school graduation with a C average and 16 units including 4 English, 3 1/2 mathematics, 2 science; 4 social studies; rolling admission, midyear admission, and advanced placement plans available; $25 application fee.

Costs Per Year: $8,960 tuition; room and board $3,970, dormitory deposit $150; computer deposit $200; computer fee $550; activity fee $30; estimated book cost $500; miscellaneous $2,000.

Collegiate Environment: The campus is comprised of 12 buildings on 25 acres and houses 265 men and 90 women. The library contains 55,000 volumes, 6,000 periodicals and 750 microforms. 90% of applicants are accepted. 30 scholarships are available and 80% of students receive some form of financial aid.

Community Environment: Fort Wayne (population 178,000) is the hub of the great north central industrial and agricultural America and gateway to the northern Indiana Lake region. The facilities of the city include 147 churches, and a civic theater and Philharmonic Symphony. The gasoline tank and pump industry originated here. A General Motors truck plant is located here, along with electronics, automotive and agricultural industries. Points of interest are the Allen County War Memorial Coliseum, Cathedral of the Immaculate Conception, Concordia Senior College, Fort Wayne Art School and Museum, Lincoln Museum, Lincoln Tower Building, Historical Fort Wayne and many city parks.

INDIANA STATE UNIVERSITY   *(K-3)*
217 North 6th Street
Terre Haute, Indiana 47809
Tel: (812) 237-2121; (800) 742-0891; Admissions: (812) 237-2121; Fax: (812) 237-8023

Description: This publicly supported state university is accredited by the North Central Association of Colleges and Schools. It operates on the semester system and offers three summer sessions. Founded in 1865, Indiana State University is a general, multipurpose, public-supported institution of higher education offering undergraduate and graduate studies. Degree programs are offered in teacher education, the humanities, and sciences. Practical arts programs are offered to students who desire specialization in fields that may or may not lead to a degree. Preparation for state teaching certificate is available. Indiana State is characterized by small classes, many of which are of 20-35 students. Nine out of ten undergraduate classes are taught by full-time professors. Enrollment includes 10,033 undergraduates and 1,608 graduate students. A faculty of 561 full-time and 80 part-time provides a faculty-student ratio of 1-19. A cooperative education (alternating work and class periods) program is offered in all areas. Extensive music programs, business, nursing technology, physical education and recreation, and intercollegiate and intramural athletics are available. Army and Air Force ROTC programs are available.

Entrance Requirements: Freshman applicants are normally expected to be ranked in the upper 50% of their high school class; candidates who have not achieved this level are reviewed individually, with consideration given to standardized test scores, the difficulty of the student's high school curriculum, grades earned in academic subjects, and other evidence that the applicant has the potential for success in university studies; a limited number of students may be admitted conditionally if they agree to follow a prescribed course of study and advisement; $20 application fee.

Costs Per Year: $2,802 state-resident tuition; $6,892 nonresident; $3,706 room and board.

Collegiate Environment: A scholarship program of nearly $1 million dollars awarded per year is available for students who rank in the top 25% of their graduating class. The scholarships are awarded based on merit, and are very competitive. The campus, located on approximately 97 acres, allows students accessibility to all buildings and services in less than a ten minute walk. There are 176 academic majors. On-campus residence halls accomodate 4,416 students. The library holdings include 1,200,000 volumes. With more than 180 organizations at Indiana State, involvement in campus activities provides students with the opportunities to develop friendships, add to their education, and learn leadership skills. These groups include: honor societies, religious organizations, service and special interest groups, and fraternities and sororities. 87% of applicants are accepted. 50% of the current students receive some form of financial aid.

Community Environment: Indiana State is located in Terre Haute, a city of 60,000, on the banks of the Wabash River. Terre Haute is within a 500-mile radius of more than half the population of the United States. Chicago, St. Louis, Cincinnati, Louisville, and Nashville are within a half-day drive, and Indianapolis is only an hour and a half away. Terre Haute's cultural attractions include the Terre Haute Symphony Orchestra, Community Theater, the Sheldon Swope Art Museum, the Eugene V. Debs. Museum, and the Vigo County Historical Museum. The educational atmosphere of the city is enhanced by Saint Mary-of-the-Woods College, Rose-Halman Institute of Technology, and Indiana Vocational-Tech College.

INDIANA UNIVERSITY - BLOOMINGTON   (L-6)
Bloomington, Indiana 47405
Tel: (812) 855-0661; Admissions: (812) 855-0661

Description: Indiana University, founded in 1820, is the state's largest institution of higher education. It is accredited by the North Central Association of Colleges and Schools and by numreous professional accrediting organizations. The Bloomington campus, which is the flagship of the statewide Indiana University system, is a national and international center of education and research in the sciences, humanities, and the professions. Enrollment includes 16,677 men and 18,917 women. This comprises 26,182 undergraduates and 7,612 graduate students. A faculty of 1,418 full-time and 375 part-time gives a faculty-stduent ratio of 1-20. The major areas and fields of study offered at Indiana University Bloomington are organized into the specific schools and divisions: College of Arts and Sciences; the Graduate School; School of Business; School of Continuing Studies; School of Education; School of Health Physical Education, and Recreation; School of Law; School of Music; School of Library and Information Science; School of Public and Environmental Affairs; School of Optometry; and the University Division. Currently, there are 390 degree programs at Indiana University Bloomington. Extensive music and intercollegiate athletic programs are also available. Indiana University Bloomington operates throughout the year on a system of two academic semesters and two additional summer programs that vary in length.

Entrance Requirements: While the overwhelming majority of admitted students completed an average of 19 year-long academic courses and rank in the upper third of their high school class, there are always exceptions, including students from schools that do not provide rank. Each application is personally reviewed with attention focused primarily upon the number of strong college-preparatory courses, their level of difficulty, the student's willingness to accept challenge, and grade trends. "Late bloomers" with modest class rank but rising grades in challenging academic programs are encouraged to apply. Test scores for any application are rarely a factor. High school diploma or GED; completion of 4 years English, 3 mathematics, 1 laboratory science, 2 social science; Indiana residents must have total 28 semesters college preparatroy courses including the above, and 8 additional in foreign language, mathematics, laboratory science, social science, or computer science; nonresidents must complete 32 semesters including the basic requirement and 12 additional; class rank should be upper half for state residents, upper third for nonresidents; SAT or ACT required; minimum ACT 21 composite, SAT 860 combined for resident; minimum ACT 25 composite or SAT 1000 combined for nonresident; rolling admission, delayed admission, midyear admission and advanced placement plans available; apply by February 15; $35 application fee.

Costs Per Year: $3,296 state-resident tuition and fees; $10,016 out-of-state tuition and fees; $3,863 room and board.

Collegiate Environment: The campus of Indiana University-Bloomington includes nearly 100 research centers, institutes and museums. Among the notable research facilities are the Kinsey Institute for Research in Sex, Gender, and Reproduction, the 200 million volt variable particle cyclotron for atomic research, the Folklore Institute, the Indiana University Libraries which house 5,556,926 volumes, and the Lilly Library, which houses the University's collection of rare books and manuscripts. Its holdings number more than 400,000 books, a

copy of the Gutenberg Bible, 6.1 million manuscripts, and over 100,000 pieces of American sheet music. University residence halls accomodate 17,868 students. The university participates in NCAA Division I sports and has some club sports that compete intercollegiately. 82% of applicants are accepted. The average scores of the entering freshman class were SAT 467 verbal, 533 math. 3,000 scholarships are offered, including 350 academic and 334 athletic scholarships. 67% of the undergraduates receive some form of financial aid.

Community Environment: The 1,900-acre main campus is located in a community of 60,000 in southern Indiana. Indianapolis, site of the I.U. Medical Center, is 50 miles away. Places of worship are located in the immediate community for all faiths. The city is served by air and bus.

INDIANA UNIVERSITY - EAST   (I-12)
2325 Chester Blvd.
Richmond, Indiana 47374-1289
Tel: (317) 973-8208; (800) 959-3278; Fax: (317) 973-8388

Description: This publicly supported school is one of eight campuses of the state university. It is accredited by the North Central Association of Colleges and Schools. Enrollment is 1,006 full-time and 1,405 part-time students. A faculty of 64 full-time and 115 part-time gives a faculty-student ratio of 1-16.

Entrance Requirements: High school graduation or equivalent including 8 semesters of English, 6 math, 4 social studies, 2 lab science, and 8 others; SAT or ACT; rolling admission and advanced placement plans available; $25 application fee.

Costs Per Year: $1,894 state-resident tuition; $4,910 nonresidents; $96 student fees.

Collegiate Environment: The library contains 53,500 volumes. Financial aid is available. 60% of students receive some form of financial assistance.

Community Environment: The school is located on out-lying area of Richmond, which has a population of about 39,000.

INDIANA UNIVERSITY - KOKOMO   (G-8)
2300 South Washington Street
Kokomo, Indiana 46902
Tel: (317) 453-2000; Admissions: (317) 455-9389; Fax: (317) 455-9475

Description: Indiana University at Kokomo was established in 1945. It is accredited by the North Central Assocaition of Colleges and Schools. It operates on the semester system and offers two summer sessions. Enrollment includes 1,636 students. A faculty of 180 gives a faculty-student ratio of 1-15. The college grants Associate, Bachelor degree. Courses are offered toward toward a Master's degree, which is granted by IU at Indianapolis. See Indiana University at Bloomington for further information.

Entrance Requirements: High school preparatory work of 28 units should include 8 units of English and 18 additional units in mathematics, science, foreign language, and social studies. Students seeking admission to the College of Arts and Sciences or the School of Nursing should include 2 or more years of mathematics, science or a foreign language. See Indiana University at Bloomington for further information. Applications may be filed after completion of the junior year in high school. An application fee of $30 is required of each student who is new to the university. All questions concerning admission should be directed to the Admissions Office.

Costs Per Year: Undergraduate in-state tuition $1,800; undergraduate out-of-state tuition $4,500.

Community Environment: Kokomo (population 44,042) is an urban area, enjoying a temperate climate, with excellent community facilities; shopping areas, library, museum, 71 churches and two hospitals. All forms of transportation are available. The General Motors Corp. and Chrysler Corp. plants in Kokomo manufacture car radios, transistors, transmissions, and aluminum die castings. Kokomo is the home of Elwood Haynes who invented one of the first American automobiles in 1893. Part-time employment is available.

INDIANA UNIVERSITY - NORTHWEST   *(B-3)*
3400 Broadway
Gary, Indiana 46408
Tel: (219) 980-6500; (800) 437-5409; Fax: (219) 981-4219

Description: This publicly supported Indiana University Northwest
is the end result of a process of growth and change that began in 1922
when the university offered its first formal classes in Lake County.
Accredited by the North Central Association of Colleges and Schools
and the National League for Nursing, A.A.C.S.B., N.C.A.T.E., and
All Allied Health Agencies. The college operates on a semester basis
and offers two summer sessions. Enrollment is 2,614 full-time and
2,415 part-time undergraduates, and 610 graduate students. A faculty
of 181 full-time and 181 part-time gives an undergraduate faculty-student ratio of 1-16. Army ROTC is available. See also Indiana University, Bloomington Campus, for additional information.

Entrance Requirements: Based on strength of college preparatory
program, including senior year, grade trends in college preparatory
subjects, and rank in class; in-state students must be in top half of
class, out-of-state students must rank in top third; rolling admission,
delayed admission, and advanced placement plans available; apply by
February 15; $25 application fee.

Costs Per Year: $2,310 state-resident tuition; $5,781 out-of-state.

Collegiate Environment: The main campus in Gary is situated on
about 240 acres of wooded park land, which includes municipal playing fields, baseball diamonds, and golf courses. Students at Indiana
University Northwest come mostly from Lake and Porter Counties in
northwest Indiana. Most are full-time students living at home who are
working toward Bachelor's degrees in arts and sciences, education,
health field, or business. The college library holdings include 206,600
volumes, 1,100 periodical subscriptions, and 190,222 microforms.
77% of applicants are accepted.

Community Environment: Gary (population 150,000) is the second
largest city in Indiana, a metropolitan area, and is in one of the
country's outstanding steel production areas. The United States Steel
Corp. is located here on Lake Michigan. All forms of transportation
are available. Community facilities include libraries, churches, hospitals, and shopping areas. Part-time employment is available. Marquette Park nearby has a four-mile beach, a pavilion, piers, and a
picnic area.

INDIANA UNIVERSITY - PURDUE UNIVERSITY FORT WAYNE   *(D-11)*
2101 Coliseum Boulevard
Fort Wayne, Indiana 46805
Tel: (219) 481-6812

Description: Publicly-supported Indiana University at Fort Wayne
was founded as an integral part of Indiana University in 1917. In
1964, the university moved from its location on South Barr Street to
the present 412-acre campus it now shares with Purdue University.
This unique co-operation between two major universities is manifest
in their sharing of academic departments as well as physical facilities.
A joint six-building campus services over 10,000 Indiana University-
Purdue students. University courses in the credit programs at the Fort
Wayne Campus are identical with the courses at Bloomington and
West Lafayette. Accredited by the North Central Association of Colleges and Schools and other professional organizations. Indiana University-Purdue University Fort Wayne operates on a semester basis
with 2 summer terms. Enrollment includes 5,063 full-time and 6,450
part-time students. Faculty includes 329 full-time and 319 part-time
members.

Entrance Requirements: Based on strength of college preparatory
program, including senior year, grade trends in college preparatory
subjects, and rank in class. In-state students must be in top half of
class, out-of-state top third. Rolling admission, delayed admission,
and advanced placement plans available. Apply by February 15. $30
application fee.

Costs Per Year: Undergraduate residents $80.25 per credit and
graduate residents $105.20 per credit; nonresident undergraduate
$198.85 per credit and graduate $235.55 per credit; student fees $500.

Collegiate Environment: The Fort Wayne Campus has a variety of
student organizations in which all students are encouraged to participate. These include a Student Senate, the Student Union Board, an extensive music program which includes The University Singers, debate

team, film series, fraternities, sororities, student publications, and over
fifty department clubs and interest groups. The university also sponsors an active intercollegiate and intramural program that includes
baseball, cross country, tennis, football, basketball, softball, soccer,
and golf. Indiana University-Purdue University participates in various
student loan and scholarship programs. The library contains 417,815
volumes, 46,567 periodicals, 222,143 microforms and 2,700 audiovisual materials. Application blanks and detailed information may be
obtained from the Office of Scholarships and financial aids. 73% of
applicants are accepted.

Community Environment: See Indiana Institute of Technology

INDIANA UNIVERSITY - PURDUE UNIVERSITY INDIANAPOLIS   *(J-8)*
425 University Boulevard, CA 129
Indianapolis, Indiana 46202-5143
Tel: (317) 274-4591; Admissions: (317) 274-4591; Fax: (317)
274-5930

Description: Indiana University, founded in 1820, is the state's
largest institution of higher education. The Indianapolis campus,
along with the Bloomington campus, form the core campuses of this
statewide system. Classes were first offered in Indianapolis by Indiana
University in 1916. In 1968, Indiana University at Indianapolis was
created by the Indiana University Board of Trustees. Less than a year
later, in 1969, the Board of Trustees of both Indiana and Purdue Universities adopted a resolution creating Indiana University-Purdue University Indianapolis (IUPUI). Indiana University was given the
responsibility for management, including all financing and representation to the legislature for funding. Under the merger agreement, each
discipline was assigned to one of the two universities. Indiana University offers degree programs at Indianapolis in the following schools
and divisions: School of Business; School of Journalism; Graduate
School; School of Dentistry; School of Education; Herron School of
Art; School of Law, Indianapolis; School of Liberal Arts; School of
Public and Environmental Affairs; School of Medicine; School of Allied Health Sciences; School of Nursing; School of Physical Education; School of Social Work; and School of Continuing Studies. The
Purdue University School of Engineering and Technology, Indianapolis, and the Purdue University School of Science, Indianapolis, include academic programs that are the responsibility of Purdue
University. Each university is responsible for awarding degrees from
the associate through the professional and graduate levels. Currently,
there are 179 authorized degree programs at IUPUI. Notable research
facilities at IUPUI are the Krannert Institute of Cardiology, the
Regenstreif Institute of Psychiatric Research, and the Human Genetics
Research and Training Center. The university is located at the center
of one of the nation's largest and most rapidly developing cities. Recent enrollment for IUPUI was 26,766 students. The 12,051 full-time
and 14,715 part-time students include 7,283 graduate students and
6,959 evening students. A faculty of 1,350 full-time and 647 part-time
gives a faculty-student ratio of 1-16.

Entrance Requirements: High school graduation in the top 50% of
high school class for Indiana residents; top 33% for nonresidents; 14
high school units should include 4 English, 3 mathematics, 2 social
science, 1 science, and 4 electives; SAT or ACT required; students
with GED considered; rolling admission, midyear admission and advanced placement plans available; $25 application fee.

Costs Per Year: $2,766/year ($92.20/credit) state-resident undergraduate tuition; $8,490/year ($283/credit) nonresidents; $3,260 room
and board.

Collegiate Environment: The university seeks a geographically diverse student body, and midyear students are accepted. 87% of applicants are accepted. The average scores of the entering freshman class
were SAT 391 verbal, 437 math. Scholarships are available and 46%
of undergraduates receive some form of financial aid. Very limited
student housing (620 students capacity) is available. Library holdings
include 700,000 bound volumes.

Community Environment: See Butler University.

INDIANA UNIVERSITY - SOUTH BEND   *(A-7)*
1700 Mishawaka Ave.
P.O. Box 7111
South Bend, Indiana 46634
Tel: (219) 237-4872; Fax: (219) 237-4834

Description: Publicly supported Indiana University at South Bend is accredited by the North Central Association of Colleges and Schools. Associate, Bachelor, and Master degrees are granted. It operates on the semester system with two summer sessions. Enrollment includes 4,248 students. A faculty of 309 gives a faculty-student ratio of 1-14. See also information in Indiana University at Bloomington description.

Entrance Requirements: Indiana resident: graduate from accredited high school, ranks in the upper 50% of class, above average SAT score; nonresident: average of C+ or better; completion of high school units including 4 English, 9 or more from among mathematics, science, foreign language, and social science; for Arts and Sciences and Nursing, additional 2 units each of mathematics, science, and foreign language; early admission, early decision, midyear admission, rolling admission, and advanced placement plans available; Aug.1 application deadline for Fall term; $35 application fee.

Costs Per Year: $2,412 undergraduate state resident tuition; $1,668 graduate state resident tuition; $6,594 undergraduate nonresident tuition; $3,750 graduate nonresident tuition; $24 student fees.

Collegiate Environment: Located on a beautiful site adjacent to the St. Joseph River, the campus has added buildings steadily since Northside Hall, the main building, was

dedicated in 1962. Of these are the library, containing 370,204 holdings, and one of the finest equipped theaters in the state of Indiana, with a capacity of 800, it serves for programs of community interest as well as for a number of dramatic, musical, and special events produced by or for the students. The college has a variety of student organizations in which all students are encouraged to participate. These include a Student Senate, various academic departmental clubs, other student-interest organizations, and intercollegiate athletics. The campus newspaper, The Preface, and literary annual, The Analecta, are published by the students. Financial aid is available.

Community Environment: See University of Notre Dame.

INDIANA UNIVERSITY - SOUTHEAST   *(P-9)*
4201 Grant Line Road
New Albany, Indiana 47150
Tel: (812) 941-2000; (800) 852-8835; Admissions: (812) 941-2212;
Fax: (812) 941-2559

Description: Indiana University Southeast is one of eight campuses that make up Indiana University. It is accredited by the North Central Association of Colleges and Schools and operates on the semester system with two summer sessions. All IUS students are commuters and activities and student services are offered to meet the needs of the students. Current enrollment includes 1,006 men, 1,546 women full-time, 1,122 men, 1,790 women part-time. The faculty consists of 140 full-time and 200 part-time members providing a student-faculty ratio of 19-1.

Entrance Requirements: Based on strength of college preparatory program including senior year, grade trends in college preparatory subjects, and rank in class. In-state students must be in top half of class, out-of-state top third. Rolling admission, delayed admission, and advanced placement plans available. Apply by July 15. $27 application fee.

Costs Per Year: Tuition $2,499; $6,480 out-of-state.

Collegiate Environment: The library contains 210,000 volumes. The average SAT scores for freshman class: Verbal, 400; Math, 400. Average high school standing of freshman class: top 50%. The university offers a wide variety of student activities and organizations, intramural athletics and intercollegiate sports: basketball, baseball, women's basketball, and volleyball.

Community Environment: New Albany (population 38,000), a highly industrialized area, enjoys a temperate climate. It is one of the Falls Cities, the others being Louisville, Kentucky and Jeffersonville, Indiana. Buses and railroads serve the area with airlines available at Louisville, Kentucky, Airport. The American Commercial Barge Line, one of the largest, has a terminal there. Community facilities include many churches, Steamboat Museum, hospital and parks. Some part-time employment is available. Ohio River provides facilities for all water sports. Derby Week is an annual event.

INDIANA WESLEYAN UNIVERSITY   *(F-9)*
4201 South Washington Street
Marion, Indiana 46952
Tel: (317) 674-6901; (800) 332-6901; Admissions: (317) 677-2138;
Fax: (317) 677-2333

Description: Indiana Wesleyan University (formerly Marion College) is a privately supported liberal arts college. The University is accredited by the North Central Association of Colleges and Schools. It offers an Associate and Bachelor degree as well as graduate programs in Ministerial Education and Community Health Nursing. The college is affiliated with The Wesleyan Church. It offers program for State teacher certification. It operates on the 4-1-4 calendar system and offers two summer sessions. Enrollment includes 4,575 students. A faculty of 106 full-time and 44 part-time gives a student-faculty ratio of 1-16.

Entrance Requirements: High school diploma with a minimum of a C average and rank in upper half of graduating class; SAT or ACT required. Early admission, early decision, rolling admission, delayed admission and advanced placement plans available.

Costs Per Year: Tuition $9,726; room and board $3,932; fees $500; additional expenses average $800.

Collegiate Environment: The library holdings include 130,000 volumes. Housing facilities are provided for students. 67% of students applying for admission are accepted. The college seeks a geographically diverse student body. Athletic, academic and music scholarships are offered and 98% of the student body receives some form of financial aid.

Community Environment: Marion is an industrial city in a farming and fruit raising region, located 70 miles northeast of Indianapolis and 50 miles southwest of Ft. Wayne in Grant County. Bus service is available. Major industries located here are RCA, Fisher Body, Foster-Forbes Glass, General Plastics, and General Tire. Part-time employment is abundant. Mississinewa Lake and Salamonie Reservoir and Dam are nearby, providing facilities for many outdoor sports; also the city has facilities for tennis, swimming, and picnics. The Easter Pageant is an annual event.

MANCHESTER COLLEGE   *(D-9)*
1000 East Street, Apt. F
North Manchester, Indiana 46962
Tel: (219) 982-2141

Description: Manchester College is a privately supported liberal arts college. It is accredited by North Central Association of Colleges and Schools and is affiliated with the Church of the Brethren. The 4-1-4 semester system with January term and 3 summer sessions. The college was founded in 1860 and moved to North Manchester in 1889; it then merged with Mount Morris College of Illinois in 1932. A faculty of 110 gives a student-faculty ratio of 9:1. Manchester features teacher education with preparation for state teaching certificate and offers accredited bacualaurate degree in social work. The college allows courses by prior examination in certain courses. Year Abroad program Marburg/Lahn, Germany; Strasbourg, Nancy, France; Barcelona, Spain; Dalian, Peoples Republic of China; Cheltenham, England; Athens, Greece; Cuenco, Ecuador. Special programs feature Peace Studies and Environmental Studies, both interdisciplinary programs. Current enrollment includes 492 men, 526 women full-time, 10 men, 25 women part-time, and 19 graduate students. The faculty consists of 72 full-time members and 19 part-time members providing a student-faculty ratio of 9:1. The college grants the Associate, Bachelor's and Master's degrees.

Entrance Requirements: High school graduation with a C average and 38 units. Average SAT scores of Freshman class: Verbal 431; Math, 489. Average stand of freshmen in HS class: top 73%. Fifty percent of freshman class was in top quarter of HS class. Non-HS graduates considered. Seeks a geographically diverse student body. Students admitted at mid-year. Special admission plans available: rolling admission, delayed admission, advanced placement. Applications for Fall term desired by August 1. Contact the Director of Admissions for information. 72% of applicants accepted. Application fee, $10.

Costs Per Year: $8,690 tuition; $3,440 room and board; $270 student fees.

Collegiate Environment: The campus has about 35 buildings on over 200 acres. Residence Hall capacity for 550 men and 550 women; library contains 156,000 volumes. 89% of the freshman class returned for sophomore year. Extensive music program and inter-collegiate and intra-mural athletics. Financial aid is available and 90% of the current freshman class receives some form of assistance.

Community Environment: North Manchester (population 6,000) is situated in north central Indiana, 35 miles west of Ft. Wayne, and 100 miles north of Indianapolis, and two hours from Chicago, enjoying a favorable climate. Bus facilities and airlines are within 30 miles. Community facilities include a library, indoor swimming pool, churches of many denominations, a medical clinic across the street from campus and a hospital within 20 minutes.

MARIAN COLLEGE   *(J-8)*
3200 Cold Spring Road
Indianapolis, Indiana 32600
Tel: (317) 929-0321

Description: Privately supported liberal arts college which is accredited by North Central Association of Colleges and Schools and National Council for Accreditation of Teacher Education. The college operates on the semester system and offers one summer session. The college was founded in 1851 as a women's college by the Sisters of St. Francis, Oldenburg, and became coeducational in 1954. Grants Associate and Bachelor's degrees. Offers preparation for State teaching certificate. Allows up to 60 hours credit, by prior examination, for certain courses, for previous experience or training. Has special adult education programs, honors programs. Religious subjects required. Has academic cooperative plan whereby Marian conducts first two years of certain programs and cooperating institution provides last two years, as follows: nursing Indiana University; medical technology, St. Vincent's Hospital; engineering, Purdue and Notre Dame. Enrollment includes 314 men, 588 women full-time, 62 men, and 324 women part-time. A faculty of 77 full-time and 63 part-time members provides a faculty-student ratio of 1-13. Offers chorus, glee club, extensive intercollegiate and intramural athletics. ROTC Air Force and ROTC Army programs are available.

Entrance Requirements: High school graduation with standing in top 50% of HS class and 30 units, including 3 English, 2 mathematics, 2 foreign language, 1 science, 1 social science; 85% of applicants are accepted including at midyear. Average SAT scores of freshman class: Verbal, 402; Math, 450; average HS standing of freshman class is upper 20% of HS class; 47% of freshman class were in top quarter of HS class. SAT or ACT required. Contact Director of Admissions for information. Application fee $15. Deadline for Fall semester: August 15. Special admission plans available: early admission, early decision, rolling admission, delayed admission, advanced placement. Students admitted at midyear.

Costs Per Year: $8,484 tuition; $3,412 room and board; $120 fees.

Collegiate Environment: The campus has 28 buildings on 114 acres. A three-wing men's dormitory was constructed in 1966, and a library in 1970. Dormitory capacity for 250 men and 306 women; library contains 105,000 volumes. 75% of the freshman class returned for sophomore year. Financial aid is available and 75% of the student body receives some form of assistance.

Community Environment: See Butler University

OAKLAND CITY COLLEGE   *(P-3)*
100 Lucretia Street
Oakland City, Indiana 47660
Tel: (812) 749-4781

Description: The privately supported liberal arts college was granted its charter in 1885 and is controlled by General Baptist Association. It is accredited by the North Central Association of Colleges and Schools. It is professionally accredited by the National Council for Accreditation of Teacher Education. Preparation for State teaching certificate is offered. Some correspondence course credit allowed; credit also allowed by prior examination in certain courses for previous experience or training. Sponsors overseas travel seminars for credit. Offers a special program for the educationally disadvantaged. One religion subject required for graduation; major in religion offered as well as pre-ministry course. Music program includes choir, gospel teams, popular music, intercollegiate and intramural athletics pro-

grams are available. The school grants Associate and Bachelor degrees, and also offers the Master of Arts in Religion. It operates on the semester system and offers two summer sessions. Enrollment includes 382 men and 313 women full-time undergraduate students.

Entrance Requirements: Accredited high school graduation; rolling admission, early decision, early admission and delayed admission plans available; application fee $25.

Costs Per Year: $7,500 tuition; room and board $2,996; $241 student fees.

Collegiate Environment: The campus has 15 buildings on 20 acres. Five new buildings have been erected since 1956 including dormitories which have a capacity for 150 men and 115 women. Construction began in January 1995 on a new fine arts building, the Comwell-Reed Center. The library contains 65,638 volumes. 98% of the applicants are accepted, including mid-year students. Financial assistance is available and 98% of students receive some form of financial aid.

Community Environment: Oakland City is a friendly rural-suburban community with a midwest climate, temperatures ranging from a high of 98 degrees to a low of ten degrees. Average rainfall is over 40 inches annually. Community facilities include six churches, both Protestant and Catholic, numerous civic and service groups, library, individual stores, and a shopping center 15 miles away. Some part time jobs are available for students.

PURDUE UNIVERSITY - CALUMET   *(B-3)*
2233 171st St.
Hammond, Indiana 46323
Tel: (219) 989-2213; (800) 228-0799, x2400; Fax: (219) 989-2775

Description: Purdue University Calumet is a regional campus of state-supported Purdue University and is accredited by the North Central Association of Colleges and Schools. For persons who expect to obtain a liberal education that will prepare them for life or the professions, it offers studies that lead to Certificates, Associate, Baccalaureate, and Master degrees; and provides programs that meet the professional, cultural and general educational needs of the community. Purdue University Calumet is professionally accredited by the following: Accreditation Board for Engineering and Technology (ABET), American Chemical Society, Indiana State Board of Nursing Education and Registration, Indiana State Board of Vocational and Technical (ISBVTE), Indiana Teacher Training and Licensing Commission of the Indiana State Department of Public Instruction, National Council for Accreditation of Teacher Education (NCATE), National League for Nursing. Programs featured at this campus include biology, communications, English, history, engineering, computer engineering, mathematics, chemistry, French, German, physics, political science, psychology, sociology and Spanish. Career-related programs include elementary and secondary teaching, engineering, nursing, construction technology, manufacturing technology, restaurant and hotel management, supervision technology, electrical technology, industrial engineering technology, and computer technology. It also offers various types of continuing education, dramatic performances, and concerts, as well as graduate programs in teaching, art history, education, engineering, industrial management, communication, biology, nursing, English and math. Social and cultural development and leadership experience are derived through involvement in the forty-five campus organizations available for participation by students. Intramural, athletic and recreational facilities are available. The university operates on the semester system with one summer session. Enrollment includes 9,496 full-time and part-time students. The faculty-student ratio is 1-29.

Entrance Requirements: Admission requirements vary among the different schools and departments; an applicant's eligibility for consideration to the school or curriculum of his choice will depend upon many factors, among which are: subject matter requirements for the school or curriculum to which he is applying, high school class standing, College Entrance Examination Board Scholastic Aptitude Test results, high school comments and recommendations, previous college work (if any), and other personal information; open admissions, mid-year admission, rolling admission, and advanced placement plans available.

Costs Per Year: Undergraduate: $2,536 ($79.25 per credit hour) state resident tuition, $6,384 ($199.50 per credit hour) nonresident tuition; Graduate: $2,992 ($93.50 per credit hour) state resident tuition,

$8,225 ($235 per credit hour) nonresident tuition; $26.25 per contact hour laboratory fee.

Collegiate Environment: The library contains 215,830 volumes. There are no dormitory facilities. 104 scholarships are available. 39% of the students receive some form of financial assistance.

Community Environment: Purdue University Calumet primarily serves the communities located in the northwestern part of the state. This area is adjacent to metropolitan Chicago. It is situated in the southeastern section of Hammond, just off the Borman Expressway and Indianapolis Boulevard.

PURDUE UNIVERSITY - LAFAYETTE (G-5)
West Lafayette, Indiana 47907
Tel: (317) 494-4600; Fax: (317) 494-0544

Description: This publicly supported state-controlled university is accredited by North Central Association of Colleges and Schools and by all major professional agencies for the following subjects: business; chemistry; engineering: aeronautical & astronautical, agricultural, chemical, civil, electrical, industrial, mechanical, metallurgical, computer and electrical, construction engineering & management, materials, nuclear; engineering technology (electrical, mechanical); forestry; nursing; pharmacy; psychology; teacher education; veterinary medicine; speech pathology and audiology; building construction and contracting; dietetics; aviation technology; interior design; athletic training; marriage & family therapy; and landscape architecture. Army, Navy and Air Force ROTC are available. The university was established in 1869 primarily as a technical institution offering instruction in engineering and agriculture. Today the university includes Schools as follows: Science; Liberal Arts; Education; Consumer and Family Sciences; Pharmacy and Pharmacal Sciences; Technology; Veterinary Medicine; Agriculture; Graduate School; Management; Nursing; and Health Science. Schools of Engineering include the following: School of Aeronautical & Astronautical Engineering, School of Agricultural Engineering, Construction Engineering & Management Division, School of Chemical Engineering, School of Civil Engineering, School of Electrical Engineering, School of Industrial Engineering, Division of Interdisciplinary Engineering Studies, School of Mechanical Engineering, School of Materials Engineering, and School of Nuclear Engineering. The university operates on the semester system and offers one summer session. Enrollment is 26,525 full-time and 2,786 part-time undergraduates, and 6,522 graduate students. A faculty of 2,081 full-time and 90 part-time gives a faculty-student ratio of 1-16.

Entrance Requirements: High school graduation or GED; strong rank in upper half for state residents; rank in upper third for nonresidents; 15 units including 4 English, 2-3 mathematics, and 1-2 laboratory science; SAT or ACT required; early admission, rolling admission and advanced placement plans available; $30 application fee.

Costs Per Year: $2,884 resident tuition; $9,556 nonresidents; $4,200 room and board.

Collegiate Environment: The library system contains 1,900,000 volumes, 16,400 periodicals, and 1,800,000 microforms. Dormitory capacity is 12,183 students. 47 national fraternities and 25 national sororities provide housing for 5,500. 83% of applicants are accepted. Scholarships are available and 43% of the student body receives financial aid.

Community Environment: Lafayette is located 65 miles northwest of Indianapolis and 120 miles southeast of Chicago. It is located on the Wabash River, in a rich grain-growing county where livestock and dairying are principal agricultural industries. All forms of commercial transportation are available. The community facilities include libraries, churches that represent 34 denominations, Lafayette Symphony Orchestra, Civic Theatre, museums, hospitals, a TV station, and good shopping at downtown locations and 8 other shopping centers. Many hotel and motel accommodations are available for the conventions at Lafayette.

PURDUE UNIVERSITY - NORTH CENTRAL (B-5)
1401 S. U.S. Highway 421
Westville, Indiana 46391
Tel: (219) 785-5458; (800) 872-1231; Fax: (219) 785-5358

Description: North Central is a regional campus of publicly supported Purdue University. Persons who expect to obtain a Bachelor's degree may take the freshman and sophomore years in most curricula at any of the regional campuses. Five baccalaureate programs are available in Elementary Education, Supervision, Liberal Studies, English, and Mechanical Engineering Technology. The college is accredited by the North Central Association of Colleges and Schools and National League for Nursing for technical nursing. It operates on the early semester system and offers one summer term. Subjects at this campus include agriculture, nursing, management, general business, technology, engineering, liberal arts; preparation for State teaching certificate is also offered. Credit is allowed for correspondence courses and by prior examination in certain courses for previous experience or training. Pre-college and freshman programs for the educationally disadvantaged are available. The university offers intercollegiate basketball, baseball, and intramural athletics for men and women. Enrollment is 1,358 full-time and 1,998 part-time undergraduates, and 44 graduate students. A faculty of 85 full-time and 130 part-time gives a faculty-student ratio of 1-15.

Entrance Requirements: Undergraduate: $2,377.50 ($79.25) resident tuition, $5,985 ($199.50/cr) nonresident; Graduate: $3,097.50 ($103.25/cr) resident, $7,050 ($235/cr) nonresident.

Costs Per Year: Undergraduate: $2,377.50 ($79.25/cr) resident tuition, $5,985 ($199.50/cr) nonresident; Graduate: $3,097.50 ($103.25/cr) resident, $7,050 ($235/cr) nonresident.

Collegiate Environment: Most of the first two-year programs offered at Lafayette are available with a variety of certificates and Associate degree programs. No dormitories. The library contains 80,200 volumes and 358 periodicals. 91& of applicants are accepted. The average scores of the entering freshman class were ACT 21 composite, SAT 383 verbal, 423 math. 20 scholarships are available including 2 for freshmen. 38% of the undergraduates receive some form of financial aid.

Community Environment: This small community (Westville population 1,170) located 12 miles south of Lake Michigan is progressing under a town and country zoning plan. Community facilities include six major civic organizations, two churches, a library, two parks, good transportation and shopping facilities.

ROSE-HULMAN INSTITUTE OF TECHNOLOGY (K-3)
5500 Wabash Avenue
Terre Haute, Indiana 47803
Tel: (812) 877-1511; (800) 552-0725; Fax: (812) 877-3198

Description: Privately supported technological and professional engineering college for men. It is accredited by the North Central Association of Colleges and Schools and by the Accrediting Board for Engineering and Technology for its chemical, civil, electrical, and mechanical engineering programs. Credit is given by prior examination in certain courses for previous experience or training. A three-and-a-half-week summer research program for high school juniors is available. Band, glee club, and extensive intercollegiate athletics are offered. The school grants Bachelor and Master degrees. The institute operates on the quarter system. Enrollment includes 1,300 undergraduate and 90 graduate students. A faculty of 110 full-time and 9 part-time gives a faculty-student ratio of 1-14.

Entrance Requirements: High school graduation; rank in top 20% of high school class; 18 high school units, including 4 English, 4 mathematics, 3 science, and 2 social science; SAT verbal 540, math 670, or ACT required; rolling admission, early admission, early decision, delayed admission and advanced placement plans available; Mar. 1 application deadline; $35 application fee;

Costs Per Year: $14,300 tuition; $4,400 room and board; $1,800 miscellaneous.

Collegiate Environment: The campus is located on a rolling, wooded, 140-acre estate, 4 1/2 miles east of downtown Terre Haute, a community of 60,000. Residence halls accommodate 600 students. 20% of the students live in fraternity houses and 20% are married or commuters. The library contains 65,000 titles, and students also have access to Indiana State University and St. Mary of the Woods Libraries. 60% of applicants are accepted. The average scores of the enrolled freshmen were SAT verbal 540, math 670. Students are not admitted at midyear. Scholarships are available and 90% of the students receive some form of financial assistance.

Community Environment: See Indiana State University.

SAINT FRANCIS COLLEGE   *(D-11)*
2701 Spring Street
Ft. Wayne, Indiana 46808
Tel: (219) 434-3100; (800) 729-4732; Admissions: (219) 434-3279; Fax: (219) 434-3194

Description: This privately supported college in the liberal arts tradition is administered by the Sisters of Saint Francis of the Roman Catholic Church. It is accredited by North Central Association of Colleges and Schools. It operates on the semester system and offers two summer sessions. It also has a graduate school. The college was founded in 1890 as a training school for the Sisters of St. Francis of the Perpetual Adoration. The charter was granted in 1940 when the college evolved into a regular four-year women's college and began granting the Bachelor degree. The first male students were admitted in 1959, and Master degree programs were first offered in 1960. The college offers courses in preparation for State teaching certificate. Intercollegiate and intramural athletics are available. Religious subjects are required. Enrollment includes 556 full-time and 231 part-time undergraduates and 218 graduate students. A faculty of 80 gives a faculty-student ratio of 1-13.

Entrance Requirements: High school graduation, 16 units including 4 English, 2 science, 2 mathematics, and 1 social science; minimum scores of SAT 400V, 400M or ACT 19; rolling admission, early admission, and delayed admission plans available; $20 application fee.

Costs Per Year: $8,670 tuition; $3,820 room and board; $200 student fees; $450 books; $1,000 miscellaneous.

Collegiate Environment: The campus has 12 buildings on 70 acres. The library contains 85,000 volumes. Dormitory capacity is 65 men and 130 women. 92% of all applicants are accepted. 85% of the students receive financial aid.

Community Environment: Fort Wayne (population 180,000) is Indiana's second largest city, located within 160 miles of Chicago, Detroit, Toledo, Columbus, Cincinnatti and Indianapolis.

SAINT JOSEPH'S COLLEGE   *(E-4)*
Rensselaer, Indiana 47978
Tel: (219) 866-6000; (800) 447-8781; Fax: (219) 866-6122

Description: This privately supported liberal arts college is accredited by the North Central Association of Colleges and Schools and professionally by the National Council for Accreditation for Teacher Education. It is affiliated with the Roman Catholic Church. The college grants Associate, Bachlor and Master's degrees. It operates on the semester system and offers one summer session. Correspondence course credit allowed as well as credit by prior examination in certain courses for previous experience or training. Overseas program planned on an individual basis. Has academic cooperative plan with Purdue, in agriculture, whereby Saint Joseph's provides three years. Enrollment includes 813 full-time and 217 part-time undergraduate students. A faculty of 62 full-time and 24 part-time gives a faculty-student ratio of 1-14. Chorus, glee club, stage band, and intercollegiate and intramural athletics are available to both men and women.

Entrance Requirements: High school graduation with 15 units; 2 English, 2 mathematics, 2 science, 2 social science, and 2 foreign language; plus 5 additional units from any area; SAT or ACT required; early admission, early decision, rolling admission, delayed admission, and advanced placement plans available; $15 application fee.

Costs Per Year: $11,200 tuition; $4,250 room and board; $330 student fees.

Collegiate Environment: The campus has 30 buildings on 140 acres, including a library that contains 169,970 volumes, 700 periodicals, and 32,000 audiovisual items. There are 10 student residence halls with a capacity of 925 students. 76% of applicatns are accepted, including midyear students. The average scores of the entering freshmen class were SAT 421 verbal, 475 math. The average high school standing of a recent freshman class: 69% in the top half; 38% in the top quarter. Scholarships are available, and 92% of the students receive some form of financial aid. 70% of the freshman class returns for sophomore year.

Community Environment: Rensselaer (population 5,000) is a rural area with community facilities that include a library, 15 churches, a hospital and some of the civic and service groups. Part-time employment is available. Recreational facilities are a public park, swimming pool, golf course, bowling alleys, tennis courts, and recreational lake.

SAINT MARY'S COLLEGE   *(A-7)*
Notre Dame, Indiana 46556
Tel: (219) 284-4587; Admissions: (219) 284-4587; Fax: (219) 284-4716

Description: This privately supported liberal arts college for women is affiliated with Roman Catholic Church. It is accredited by North Central Association of Colleges and Schools and by respective accrediting bodies in fields of art (NASA); elementary and secondary education (NCATE); music by the National Association of Schools of Music; and Nursing by State of Indiana Board of Nurses Registration and Nursing Education and National League for Nursing. Sophomore year programs in Rome, Ireland, and India are available, as well as a student exchange program with University of Notre Dame and academic cooperation with four other colleges in the South Bend area. A cooperative degree plan in engineering with Notre Dame requires that the student spend three years at Saint Mary's, two at Notre Dame. The college awards the Bachelor's degree. It operates on the semester system. Enrollment includes 1,552 full-time and 24 part-time students. A faculty of 116 full-time and 80 part-time gives a faculty-student ratio of 1-11.

Entrance Requirements: High school graduation with 16 college preparatory units including 4 English, 3 mathematics, 2 foreign language, 1 lab science, and 2 social studies; SAT or ACT accepted; early admission, early decision, rolling admission, deferred admission, midyear admission, and advanced placement plans available; $30 application fee.

Costs Per Year: $12,730 tuition; $4,514 room and board; $836 fees.

Collegiate Environment: In addition to a large classroom facility and four residence halls accommodating 1,574 women, Saint Mary's has a fine arts center, a science building, center for modern language, athletic facility and college center on a 275-acre campus beside the St. Joseph's River. The new library contains 192,000 volumes, 1,146 periodicals, 65 microforms and 2,303 audiovisual materials. 84% of the applicants are accepted, including midyear students. Approximately 67% of the student body graduated in the top quarter of the high school class. The average scores of the entering freshman class were SAT 477 verbal, 534 math, and ACT 24 composite. 90% of the freshman class returned for sophomore year. Financial aid is available, and 57% of the current student body receives some form of assostance.

Community Environment: Saint Mary's College is located on 275 acres beside the St. Joseph's River just off the Indiana Toll Road and within easy access to the South Bend airport. The educational and cultural advantages of the neighboring University of Notre Dame, of South Bend and of Chicago are available.

SAINT MARY-OF-THE WOODS COLLEGE   *(K-3)*
St. Mary-of-the-Wood, Indiana 47876
Tel: (812) 535-5151; (800) 926-7692; Admissions: (812) 535-5106; Fax: (812) 535-5215

Description: Privately supported liberal arts college for women accredited by North Central Association of Colleges and Schools, professionally by the National Association of Schools of Music; American Association for Music Therapy; and Indiana Department of Education for Teacher Training. It is owned by members of Saint Mary-of-the-Woods College Corporation and operated by the Board of Trustees of the college. The College was founded in 1840 by the Sisters of Providence and in 1846 became the first institution to be chartered by Indiana for the higher education of women. Offers its undergraduate degrees through both a resident program and a Women's External Degree (WED) program. Students in the resident program may earn a B.A. or B.S. in any of over 30 majors. Associate degrees are offered in Gerontology, Humanities, Early Childhood Education, general business, paralegal, and equine studies. The College offers one graduate degree: a Master of Arts in Pastoral Theology. Offers teacher and other pre-professional training; preparation for teaching certification. Offers opportunities for study abroad, internships and Supplemental Learning Experiences (SLE); Also offers chorus, intramural and intercollegiate athletics, an artist/lecture series and active theatre production schedule. The school also sponsors a Peace and

Justice Committee, an award winning news magazine, literary magazine and approximately 75 clubs and organizations as well as student government. Enrollment includes 380 full-time and 760 part-time undergraduates and 80 graduate students. The faculty consists of 72 members. The faculty-student ratio is 1-12. The WED program offers women an opportunity to obtain the B.A., B.S., A.A., or A.S. degree through a learning contract method by study at home and through resources in the student's local community. Allows Life Experience Credit (LEC) for previous experience and training in selected subjects and credit for professional courses.

Entrance Requirements: High school graduation with 16 units including 4 English, 3 mathematics, 2 foreign language (recommended), 3 science, and 2 social science; score of 400 or more on SAT verbal and math; early admission, early decision, rolling admission, delayed admission, advanced placement plans available; portfolio of work may be substituted for SAT or ACT in creative arts area; application fee $30.

Costs Per Year: Resident program $11,780 tuition and fees; $4,410 room and board.

Collegiate Environment: The campus is located in a rural setting. Facilities of the campus include a library with holdings of 139,817 hardbound volumes in addition to numerous periodical subscriptions, microforms and audiovisual materials. Residence halls accomodate 700 women. Intercollegiate sports are offered. 82% of applicants are accepted. Scholarships are available and 80% of the students receive some form of financial aid.

Community Environment: St. Mary-of-the-Woods is located just outside Terre Haute (population 70,335) combining a rural setting with the cultural advantages of the nearby city. Major transportation facilities are available in Terre Haute.

SAINT MEINRAD COLLEGE   *(Q-5)*
St. Meinrad, Indiana 47577
Tel: (812) 357-6611; (800) 752-9384; Admissions: (812) 357-6575;
Fax: (812) 357-6977

Description: The privately supported liberal arts college for Catholic men was founded in 1861 and is operated by Benedictine Monks. The college is accredited by North Central Association of Colleges and Schools. The college grants the Bachelor degree with majors including Classical Languages, English, History, Natural Sciences, Philosophy, Psychology, and Spanish. Religious subjects and chapel attendance required. Credit may be allowed for correspondence courses and by prior examination in certain courses for previous experience or training. The college operates on the semester system and offers no summer sessions. Intercollegiate and intramural athletics are available. Enrollment includes 127 full-time students. A faculty of 38 full-time members gives a faculty-student ratio of 1-3.

Entrance Requirements: High school graduation with a C average; recommend 15 units including 4 English, 2 foreign language, 2 science, 2 mathematics; and 2 social science; SAT or ACT required; early admission, rolling admission, and early decision plans available.

Costs Per Year: $6,304 tuition; $4,226 room and board; $86 fees.

Collegiate Environment: The campus has 15 buildings on 250 acres. Lake Fintan provides swimming, boating, and fishing. Dormitory capacity is 170 men; library contains over 150,000 volumes and 550 periodicals. Financial aid includes scholarships, the Direct Federal Insured Student Loan Program, and the College Work-Study Program. 92% of the current enrollment receives financial aid. 75% of all applicants are accepted, including midyear students.

Community Environment: Rural location 50 miles from Evansville; St. Meinrad is in Harrison Township of Spencer County. The St. Meinrad Archabbey is one of seven archabbeys in the world. The monastery, college, and school of theology are structures of rare beauty. Complete accommodations for visitors are available on campus, as well as in surrounding communities.

ST. ELIZABETH HOSPITAL SCHOOL OF NURSING   *(G-5)*
1508 Tippecanoe Street
Lafayette, Indiana 47904
Tel: (317) 423-6400; Fax: (317) 742-7659

Description: Privately supported, the St. Elizabeth Hospital School of Nursing is conducted by the Roman Catholic Franciscan Sisters,

and offers a basic professional program of three years leading to a diploma and registration as R.N. The school operates on a semester system and offers one summer session. It is accredited by the Indiana State Board of Nursing and the National League for Nursing. Enrollment includes 236 full-time and 29 part-time students. A faculty of 25 full-time gives a faculty-student ratio of 1-10. Behavioral and physical sciences and the humanities are taught in a core design concurrently with nursing. The core design integrates the sciences to provide a general and humanistic Liberal Arts education. Students can receive up to 54 college credits from St. Joseph College in Rensselaer, IN. Graduates of St. Elizabeth Hospital School of Nursing have the option to pursue a B.S.N. degree through a completion program at Saint Joseph's in Rensselaer.

Entrance Requirements: Applications are accepted from both men and women; graduation from accredited high school with a minimum grade average of C and rank in upper 50% of graduating class; recommended preparatory work includes a minimum of 6 English, 2 math, and 2 science (biology strongly recommended); psychology, sociology, and typing also recommended; SAT minimum 400V, 400M or ACT minimum composite score of 19 required; GED applicants need average standard score of 50 or better with adequate verbal and math skills (40th percentile or better); early decision, early admission, rolling admission, delayed admission and advanced placement plans available; $25 application fee.

Costs Per Year: First year tuition $7,880; second $7,370; third $7,370; first year room and board at Rensselaer $4,250.

Collegiate Environment: The atmosphere and tone of the school is Catholic in nature. There is, however, no interference with the religious convictions of non-Catholic students. The freshman year is spent on the Saint Joseph's College campus and the remaining two years are at St. Elizabeth Hospital School of Nursing. Students develop basic skills through selected learning experiences in simulated laboratories, clinical facilities in hospital settings and community agencies. Both male and female student housing is available the first year at St. Joseph's campus. The St. Elizabeth School of Nursing, Lafayette campus does not have student housing available. Students are not required to live on campus; however, it is highly recommended during the freshman year at Saint Joseph's College. Off-campus housing is the responsibility of each student. Transitional housing is only available on St. Elizabeth for a 30-day period to allow students time to locate suitable housing in the community. 88% of the students receive financial aid.

Community Environment: See Saint Joseph's College.

TAYLOR UNIVERSITY   *(G-10)*
500 West Reade Avenue
Upland, Indiana 46989-1001
Tel: (317) 998-5134; (800) 882-3456; Fax: (317) 998-4925

Description: This privately supported, Christian, interdenominational, liberal arts college is accredited by the North Central Association of Colleges and Schools. The college was founded by the Methodist Episcopal Church. The college was organized in 1846 and continues to emphasize the objectives of world evangelism. Religious subjects and chapel attendance are required. Preprofessional and teacher education programs (for elementary and secondary levels) are available, and preparation for State teaching certificate is offered. Taylor grants the Associate, Bachelor of Arts, Bachelor of Science and Bachelor of Music degrees. It operates on the 4-1-4 calendar system and offers two summer sessions. Enrollment is 1,786 full-time and 45 part-time students. A faculty of 119 full-time and 29 part-time gives a faculty-student ratio of 1-18. Credit is allowed for correspondent courses and for CLEP subject exams. The university offers chorus and extensive intercollegiate and intramural athletics.

Entrance Requirements: High school graduation with recommended rank in top 25% of graduating class, 3.3 GPA, and SAT score of 850 combined; high school units including 4 English, 3-4 mathematics, 3-4 laboratory science and 2 social science; 2 of foreign language recommended; midyear admission, rolling admission and advanced placement plans available; $20 application fee; international student applicants must demonstrate academic competency in the English language, ability to finance education, and willingness to accept Protestant religious orientation and standards for community life.

Costs Per Year: $10,965 tuition; $4,000 room and board; $210 student fees.

Collegiate Environment: The campus has 27 buildings on 250 acres. The Randall Environmental Science Center was completed in the fall of 1992. Residence halls accomodate 1,414 students. The library contains 172,685 volumes. The property contains a 10-acre lake, a wooded picnic area, and a 65-acre arboretum. A geographically diverse student body is sought, and midyear students are admitted. 60% of applicants are accepted. Scholarships are available and 75% of students receive some form of financial aid.

Community Environment: Upland (population 3,700) has all the advantages of quiet, country life with the nearby cities for activities. It is located 14 miles southeast of Marion and 23 miles north of Muncie. Buses and trains are accessible. The communities have churches of many denominations, health services and hospitals. Recreational activities are hunting, tennis, boating, fishing, golf and other sports.

Branch Campuses: Taylor University - Fort Wayne, 1025 W. Rudisill Blvd., Fort Wayne, IN 46807.

TAYLOR UNIVERSITY - FORT WAYNE CAMPUS   *(D-11)*
1025 West Rudisill Boulevard
Ft. Wayne, Indiana 46807
Tel: (219) 456-2111; (800) 233-3922; Fax: (219) 456-2119

Description: This evangelical, interdenominational Christian liberal arts college was founded in 1846. It is accredited by the North Central Association of Colleges and Schools. Programs of study lead to the Associate and Bachelors degrees. Chapel programs, urban ministries, outreach opportunities and small fellowship groups are an integral part of academic life. Off-campus programs include the opportunity of overseas study. The Institute of Holy Land Studies in Jerusalem, Taylor University in Singapore, and Daystar University in Nairobi, Kenya are notable examples. Overseas mission projects provide opportunity for travel. The American Studies Program, in Washington, D.C., cooperative exchange programs and internships or practicums are also available. The university is affiliated with the National Christian College Athletic Association and offers 15 intramural sports programs including basketball, flag football, softball, tennis, and volleyball. The university operates on the 4-1-4 system and offers three summer sessions. Enrollment includes 301 full-time and 122 part-time students. A faculty of 34 full-time and 19 part-time provides a faculty-student ratio of 1-11.

Entrance Requirements: High school graduation with a B- average, minimum score SAT 850 combined, and top 40% high school rank; suggested high school program with 4 English grammar and composition, 3-4 mathematics, 2 social science, and 3-4 laboratory science, foreign language encouraged; midyear admission, rolling admission available; contact Director of Enrollment for information; application deadlines are August 20 for fall semester, January 20 for spring; $20 application fee.

Costs Per Year: $9,000 tuition, $3,600 room and board; $2,110 miscellaneous including books and supplies

Collegiate Environment: The college occupies a 32-acre campus in a residential area. There are 5 buildings on the north campus and 6 are on the south campus. The library contains over 63,000 volumes. Residence halls accomodate 100 men, 140 women, and 11 families. Other facilities include a gymnasium, athletic field, and the WBCL radio station. 94% of applicants are accepted, including midyear students. 30% of the freshman class was in the top quarter of high school class. The student body is geographically diverse, coming from 19 states and 5 countries, representing over 30 denominations. Scholarships and grants averaging $2,500 are available. 85% of students receive some form of financial aid.

Community Environment: Taylor Fort Wayne is located in the suburbs of Fort Wayne, a community of 200,000 in northeast Indiana. The campus, surrounded by the beautiful Southwood and Oakwood Park residential additions, is 124 miles northeast of Indianapolis, 158 miles east of Chicago and 161 miles southwest of Detroit.

TRI-STATE UNIVERSITY   *(A-11)*
Angola, Indiana 46703-0307
Tel: (219) 665-4100; (800) 347-4878; Fax: (219) 665-4292

Description: Privately supported liberal arts and professional university accredited by North Central Association of Colleges and Schools. Professional accreditations are by the Accreditation Board for Engineering Technology for aerospace, civil, electrical, chemical and mechanical engineering programs, and the Technology Accreditation Commission of the Accreditation Board for Engineering and Technology for drafting and design technology programs. The university operates on the quarter system and offers two summer sessions. It was founded in 1884 by a group of local citizens, and was part of the Alfred Holbrook normal school movement that spread throughout much of the United States during the last half of the nineteenth century. By 1902, degrees were offered in law, pharmacy, and music, and the School of Engineering was founded. In 1927, the School of Business Administration was organized; the School of Arts and Sciences began in 1967. In the fall of 1975, the college became known as Tri-State University. It offers preparation for State teaching certificate. Credit is allowed in certain courses by prior examination for previous experience and training. Cooperative Education programs (alternating work and class periods) are available in engineering, business, and technology areas. The school grants Associate and Bachelor degrees. Band, drama, glee club, and extensive intercollegiate and intramural athletics are available. Enrollment is 1,002 students. A faculty of 72 full-time and 14 part-time gives a faculty-student ratio of 1-13.

Entrance Requirements: High school graduation with a minimum of 4 years of English and 2 years of science, social studies, and mathematics; SAT or ACT required; early admission; delayed admission; and rolling admission plans are available; advanced placement credit given to applicants achieving a grade of four or five on advanced placement examination; $20 application fee.

Costs Per Year: $10,050 tuition; $4,350 room and board; $186 fees; $700 miscellaneous.

Collegiate Environment: Residence halls accommodate 480 men and 175 women; 8 fraternities provide housing for 175 additional men. The library contains 149,669 volumes, 591 serial subscriptions, and 7,503 microforms. 80% of applicants are accepted. Average SAT scores of a recent freshman class: 443V, 545M. Average high school standing was in the top 30%. 90% of the students receive financial aid through 65 types of aid programs and 4 types of loan programs.

Community Environment: Angola (population 6,000) is situated at the intersection of U.S. Highways 20, 27, I-69 and the Indiana Toll Road. The city has a small airport. Recreational facilities include three golf courses, including one located on the Tri-State campus, Pokagon State Park five miles north, and many miles of shoreline surrounding more than 100 spring-fed lakes.

UNIVERSITY OF EVANSVILLE   *(Q-3)*
1800 Lincoln Avenue
Evansville, Indiana 47722
Tel: (812) 479-2000; (800) 423-8633; Admissions: (812) 479-2468; Fax: (812) 474-4076

Description: This privately supported university is affiliated with the United Methodist Church and is accredited by North Central Association of Colleges and Schools. The University was founded in 1854 and moved to Evansville in 1919. It features liberal arts, teacher education, pre-professional, business administration, engineering, computing science, health sciences, fine arts, and various continuing education programs. It provides preparation for state teaching certificate. The semester system is used with 1 summer session. A Cooperative Education program for engineering, computing science, and physics with alternate work and class periods is available. The school grants Associate, Bachelor's and Master's degrees. The school offers extensive music and drama programs, and intercollegiate and intramural athletics. A campus in Grantham, England, provides students with an opportunity to study overseas. Enrollment includes 2,849 full-time undergraduate students. A faculty of 179 full-time and part-time gives a faculty-student ratio of 1-16.

Entrance Requirements: High school graduation with 16 units, including 4 English, 3-4 mathematics, 2-3 laboratory science, 2 foreign language, 2 social studies, SAT or ACT scores, counselor's recommendation, and recognition of high school are evaluated; early admission, early notification, rolling admission, delayed admission, and advanced placement plans available; GRE required for Graduate School; under certain circumstances non-high school graduates are considered; must be in top 50% of high school graduating class; $30 application fee.

Costs Per Year: $11,800 tuition; $4,340 room and board, $200 student fees, $700 books.

Collegiate Environment: The 75-acre suburban campus is located in Southwestern Indiana, close to the Illinois and Kentucky boarders. Served by air and bus. Residence halls accommodate 1,697 students, including 4 sorority suites; some dormitories are air-conditioned. Five fraternities also provide housing for 211 men. The library was expanded threefold in 1986 and contains 238,631 volumes, $1,162 periodicals, 317,014 microforms, and 5,446 sound recordings. 89% of applicants are accepted, including students at midyear. A geographically diverse student body is sought. Average SAT scores of the freshmen were 492V, 530M. The average scores of the entering freshman class were SAT 502 verbal, 529 math; ACT 25 composite. Approximately 81% of the student body graduated in upper 40% of high school class. There are 190 athletic and 1,860 other scholarships; of these, 59 athletic and 515 other are for freshmen. 90% of the students receive financial aid.

Community Environment: Evansville (population 136,000) is the fourth largest city in Indiana, and is the largest in Southern Indiana. Cultural activities include a philharmonic orchestra, art museum, planterium, zoo, civic and repertory theaters, and the remains of early Indian settlement.

Branch Campuses: An overseas program is conducted at Harlaxton College, Grantham, England, in most academic areas (visiting students from other schools may apply). Associate degrees are granted.

UNIVERSITY OF INDIANAPOLIS   *(J-8)*
1400 E. Hanna Avenue
Indianapolis, Indiana 46227
Tel: (317) 788-3216; (800) 232-8634; Fax: (317) 788-3300

Description: The University of Indianapolis is a private, coeducational university in Indiana's capital city. The institution is grounded in the traditional liberal arts and is accredited by the North Central Association of Colleges and Schools. It has also received accreditation from the National Council for Teacher Education, Department of Education of the State of Indiana, National Association of Schools of Music, National League for Nursing, American Physical Therapy Association and the American Occupational Therapy Association. Founded in 1902, the University of Indianapolis is one of three United Methodist Church affiliated institutions of higher education in Indiana. The university's location in Indianapolis provides students with many valuable resources, including unique internships and excellent clinical experiences. There are nearly 70 four-year programs of such to choose from, more than a dozen two-year programs, and a number of minors, teacher endorsements, and master's degrees in arts, science, and business administration. The university offers a dual degree program in Mechanical/Electrical Engineering. U of I has branch campuses on the island of Cyprus and has academic exchanges with a number of universities throughout the United States. Operating on a 4-4-1 system, the university has a spring term of varying length at the end of the second semester and two 7-week summer sessions. Enrollment includes 1,456 full-time and 1,639 part-time undergraduates and 783 graduate students. A faculty of 130 full-time and 190 part-time gives a faculty-student ratio of 1-15.

Entrance Requirements: High school graduation with a C average; rank in top 50% of high school class; 12 units college preparation subjects; rolling admission, delayed admission, and advanced placement plans available.

Costs Per Year: $11,120 tuition; $4,080 room and board.

Collegiate Environment: The campus has thirteen buildings on 60 acres. There are four residence halls with a capacity for 348 men, 458 women, and 28 families. Married students who wish accomodation in college-owned apartments should request an application for apartment accomodations. The library contains 165,000 volumes, 2,000 periodicals, 4,949 microforms and 1,628 audiovisual materials. Army ROTC is offered. 92% of applicants are admitted, including students at midyear. 85% of current freshmen receive financial aid.

Community Environment: The university is located in the southern, residential suburb of Indianapolis known as University Heights. Indianapolis is the nation's third largest capital city and is known as the "Amateur Sports Capital of the World." The metropolitan area has a population of more than one million. Recreational, cultural, and social opportunities abound. Bus, train, and airline services are within minutes of the campus. There are also numerous shops, restaurants, hotels, and a major shopping mall nearby.

UNIVERSITY OF NOTRE DAME   *(A-7)*
Notre Dame, Indiana 46556
Tel: (219) 631-7505

Description: This privately supported university is under the auspices of the Roman Catholic Church. It is accredited by North Central Association of Colleges and Schools and by respective professional accrediting associations in the following subject areas: architecture, business, chemistry, engineering (aerospace, chemical, civil, electrical, engineering sciences, mechanical, metallurgical, and materials), law, and pre-medicine. Sophomore year abroad is available to: Innsbruck, Austria; Angers, France; Nagoya, Japan; London, England; Dublin, Ireland; Fremantle, Australia; Jerusalem, Israel; Mexico City, Mexico; Toledo, Spain; Rome, Italy; and Santiago, Chile. Theology is required. An academic cooperative plan is offered with 6 colleges in engineering. The student spends 3 years at a liberal arts college and 2 years at Notre Dame; receives BA from own college, BS in Engineering from Notre Dame. Extensive intercollegiate sports program with scholarships, many intramural sports, and music programs are offered. The university operates on the semester system and offers one summer session. Undergraduate enrollment includes 5,900 men and 4,100 women. There are 2,400 graduate students. A faculty of 650 full-time and 260 part-time gives an undergraduate faculty-student ratio of 1-13.

Entrance Requirements: High school graduation in top 5% of high school class with an A average and 16 units with 4 English, 3 math, 1 laboratory science, 2 foreign language, and 2 social studies; additional for engineering or science includes 1 pre-calculus, 1 chemistry, 1 physics, SAT or ACT required; GRE for graduate school; early decision and advanced placement plans available; application deadline for fall semester is January 6; $40 application fee.

Costs Per Year: $17,050 tuition; $4,400 room and board; $2,00 average additional expenses.

Collegiate Environment: The campus has 105 buildings on 1,250 acres. Its twin lakes and wooded areas provide a setting of natural beauty. Residence halls accomodate 6,400 students. The library system holds 2,000,000 volumes, plus 16,300 periodicals, 1.2 million microforms, and 35,000 audiovisual materials. 42% of applicants meet entrance criteria and are accepted. Average SAT scores of enrolled freshmen are 570 verbal, 650 math. The average high school standing of the freshmen class is the 95th percentile. 97% of the freshmen class returned for the second year. Midyear students are not accepted. There are 1,700 academic scholarships; of these, 375 are for freshmen; 200 athletic scholarships; of these, 50 are for freshmen. 65% of the current student body receives financial aid.

Community Environment: The South Bend area has a population of over 100,000. The downtown district, located 3 miles south of the campus, has enjoyed a complete urban renewal and offers attractive services to the students. The College Football Hall of Fame recently opened there. The construction of a world-class water raceway provides excellent opportunities for challenging kayaking, tubing and canoeing. Several major shopping malls with direct bus service to campus are less than 15 minutes away.

UNIVERSITY OF SOUTHERN INDIANA   *(Q-4)*
8600 University Boulevard
Evansville, Indiana 47712
Tel: (812) 464-1765; (800) 467-1965; Fax: (812) 465-7154

Description: The University of Southern Indiana was established in 1965 as a campus of Indiana State University, and was made a seperate state university in 1985. It is accredited by the North Central Association of Colleges and Schools. More than 60 undergraduate programs are offered through the University's academic divisions. These divisions are the School of Business, School of Education and Human Services, School of Liberal Arts, School of Nursing and Health Professions, and School of Science and Engineering Technology. Selected master's degrees include: Technology, Humanities, Science and Mathematics, and Social Sciences. Selected master's degrees are offered, primarily in professional and technical studies, and in cooperation with other universities in Indiana. Associate degrees are also offered. It operates on the semester system and offers two summer sessions. Enrollment includes 4,298 full-time and 3,145 part-time undergraduates and 409 graduate students. A faculty of 184 full-time and 159 part-time gives an undergraduate faculty-student ratio of 1-20.

Entrance Requirements: High school graduate or equivalent with a C average; SAT or ACT required; GRE required for graduate school; high school units must include 4 English, 3-4 math, 2-3 lab science, 2 language, and 2 social studies; early admission and advanced placement plans available.

Costs Per Year: Undergraduate: $2,240 ($72.25/credit), $5,456 ($176/credit) nonresident; Graduate: $3,286 ($106/credit), $6,572 ($212/credit) nonresident; $1,742-$2,174 room

Collegiate Environment: Located midway between Evansville and Mt. Vernon on State Highway 62, the university consists of 300 acres of rolling countryside. Facilities include an art center, a science center, library, university center, technology center, a theater, and a physical activities center. Dormitory housing accomodates 1,450 students. The library contains 196,419 volumes and 1,536 periodicals. University scholarships are available in addition to state and federal financing, and 48% of students receive financial aid.

Community Environment: See University of Evansville.

VALPARAISO UNIVERSITY   *(B-4)*
Valparaiso, Indiana 46383-6493
Tel: (219) 464-5000; (800) 348-2611; Fax: (219) 464-5381

Description: This private, church-related (Lutheran Church-Missouri Synod) college was founded in 1859 as a pioneer in coeducational institutions. It operates within the Lutheran tradition and is accredited by North Central Association of Colleges and Schools. Professional accreditations include National Council for Accreditation of Teacher Education, National Association of Schools of Music, Council on Social Work Education, American Bar Association, Association of American Law Schools, The Accreditation Board for Engineering and Technology, the American Chemical Society, Indiana State Department of Education, Indiana State Board of Nurses' Registration and Nursing Education, and National League for Nursing. Divisions of the University; College of Arts and Sciences, College of Business Administration, Christ College, College of Engineering, College of Nursing, Graduate Division, School of Law. There are 43 Bachelors and Masters degree programs in liberal arts and elementary teaching. The Juris Doctorate is also awarded. Credit is given by prior examination in certain courses for previous experience or training. Overseas program in Cambridge, England, Reutlingen and Tubingen, Germany, Paris, France and Puebla, Mexico (these four conduct one-semester study), Hangzhou, China and Kansai Gaidai, Japan. Programs for preparation for state teaching certificate, honors or independent study, United Nations semester, Washington D.C. semester, urban studies, foreign summer tours. Offers band, chorus, choir, orchestra, extensive intercollegiate and intramural athletics. Religious subjects are required. The university operates on the semester system and offers two summer sessions. Enrollment includes 3,169 full-time and 311 part-time undergraduates and 782 graduate and professional students. A faculty of 249 full-time and 117 part-time gives an undergraduate faculty-student ratio of 1-14.

Entrance Requirements: High school graduation with HS units as follows recommended: 4 English, 3 mathematics, 3 laboratory science, 2 foreign language, 2 or 3 social studies; SAT or ACT required; graduates with "C" average and non-high school graduates sometimes considered, early admission, rolling admission, midyear admission, and advanced placement plans available. Contact Director of Admissions for information; admisssion application priority deadline Jan. 15 for scholarship consideration; application fee $30.

Costs Per Year: $11,800 tuition, $450 fees, $3,260 room and board.

Collegiate Environment: The campus has over 70 buildings on 310 acres; library contains over 259,830 standard volumes and bound periodicals, 5,400 audiovisual materials and 122,000 microforms. The University Chapel of The Resurrection was dedicated in 1958 and accommodates over 3,000 persons. Student housing available for 1,112 men, 1,416 women. 82% of applicants are accepted, including midyear students. The average high school standing of the freshmen class is the upper 12% of high school class. The middle 50% range of scores for entering freshmen: SAT 450-550 verbal, 500-650 math; ACT composite 24-30. Financial aid is available. Competitive merit awards range up to $10,000 per year. 75% of students receive some form of financial aid.

Community Environment: Valparaiso University is located 50 miles southeast of Chicago, and is located in a residential community of 27,000. For those interested in off-campus recreation and entertain-ment, it is a 20 minute drive to the Indiana Dunes National Lakeshore and less than an hour to the many theaters, museums, restaurants and athletic events of Chicago.

VINCENNES UNIVERSITY   *(N-3)*
1002 North First Street
Vincennes, Indiana 47591
Tel: (812) 885-4313; (800) 742-9198; Fax: (812) 885-5868

Description: This publicly supported junior college is accredited by the North Central Association of Colleges and Schools and the National League for Nursing (for technical nursing). Founded in 1801, this university is Indiana's oldest institution of higher learning. Programs are offered in arts, sciences, education, engineering and technology with a branch campus in Jasper, Indiana. It operates on the semester system and offers two summer sessions. Enrollment includes 4,229 men and 3,112 women. A faculty of 410 gives a faculty-student ratio of 1-18.

Entrance Requirements: High school graduation or GED; open enrollment policy; SAT and Achievement tests required for placement only, not for admission; early admission, early decision, rolling admission, delayed admission and advanced placement plans available.

Costs Per Year: $2,131.50 state resident tuition; $5,166 nonresident tuition; $3,532 room and board (15 meals), $3,756 (19 meals).

Collegiate Environment: The main campus has 50 buildings on 75 acres. The library contains 90,000 volumes, 600 periodicals, 2,400 microforms and 15,000 audiovisual materials. Dormitory capacity is available for 1,950 men and 1,050 women. Approximately 20% of the student body graduated in top quarter of high school class. 95% of applicants are accepted, including students at midyear. 65% of students receive some form of financial aid. 76% of the freshman class return for their sophomore year.

Community Environment: Vincennes (population 20,000) is the oldest city in the state and was the capital of the Old Northwest. On the banks of the Wabash River, Vincennes is the distribution point for this area, which produces peaches, apples, cantaloupes, watermelons, sweet potatoes and wheat. Points of interest are the Cathedral Library, George Rogers Clark National Historic Park, Harrison Mansion, Indiana Territory State Memorial and the Old Cathedral.

WABASH COLLEGE   *(H-5)*
Crawfordsville, Indiana 47933
Tel: (317) 364-4225; (800) 345-5385; Fax: (317) 364-4295

Description: This privately supported liberal arts college for men operates on the semester system. It is fully accredited by the North Central Association of Colleges and Schools as well as by the American Chemical Society. Wabash College was founded in 1832. It offers program of preparation for state teaching certificate. Credit is allowed by prior examination in certain courses for previous experience or training. An overseas program in conjunction with its membership in Great Lakes College Association is available. An academic cooperative plan is offered with Columbia and Washington Universities in engineering: 3 years at Wabash, 2 at Columbia and Washington (the AB is granted by Wabash, and the BS is conferred by Columbia and Washington); or 4 years at Wabash, 2 at Columbia (AB from Wabash, MS from Columbia and Washington). A 3-3 program in law with Columbia is also available. The college offers band, chamber music ensemble, glee club, and extensive intercollegiate and intramural athletics. It grants the Bachelor degree. Enrollment is 800 men. A faculty of 84 gives a faculty-student ratio of 1-10.

Entrance Requirements: Recommended high school units include 4 English, 2 of one foreign language, 3-4 mathematics, 2 science, and 2 social studies; applicants deficient in one or more requirements may be admitted by the Committee on Admissions; SAT or ACT required; interview recommended unless circumstances make it impractical; non-high school graduates may be considered; advanced placement plans available; $15 application fee.

Costs Per Year: $13,700 tuition, $4,405 room & board, $250 fees, $1,135 average additional expenses.

Collegiate Environment: The housing capacity of fraternities and dormitories is 777 men. Contents of the library are 240,482 volumes, 991 periodicals, 7,981 microforms, and 5,675 audiovisual materials. Middle 50% ranges of SAT scores of the recent freshmen were 450-

590V, 560-680M. Average high school standing of the freshman class was in the top 20%, and 75% ranked in the upper quarter. 95% of students receive financial aid. 37% of graduating class continued on to graduate school immediately after graduation.

Community Environment: Crawfordsville (population 13,500), is located 45 miles northwest of Indianapolis. It is a balanced rural/industrial community, and has many churches, a hospital, and motels. Recreational facilities include golf courses and swimming pools. Shades State Park is 14 miles away, and Turkey Run State Park is approximately 25 miles distant. Points of interest are the Lane Place Museum and Lew Wallace "Ben Hur" Museum.

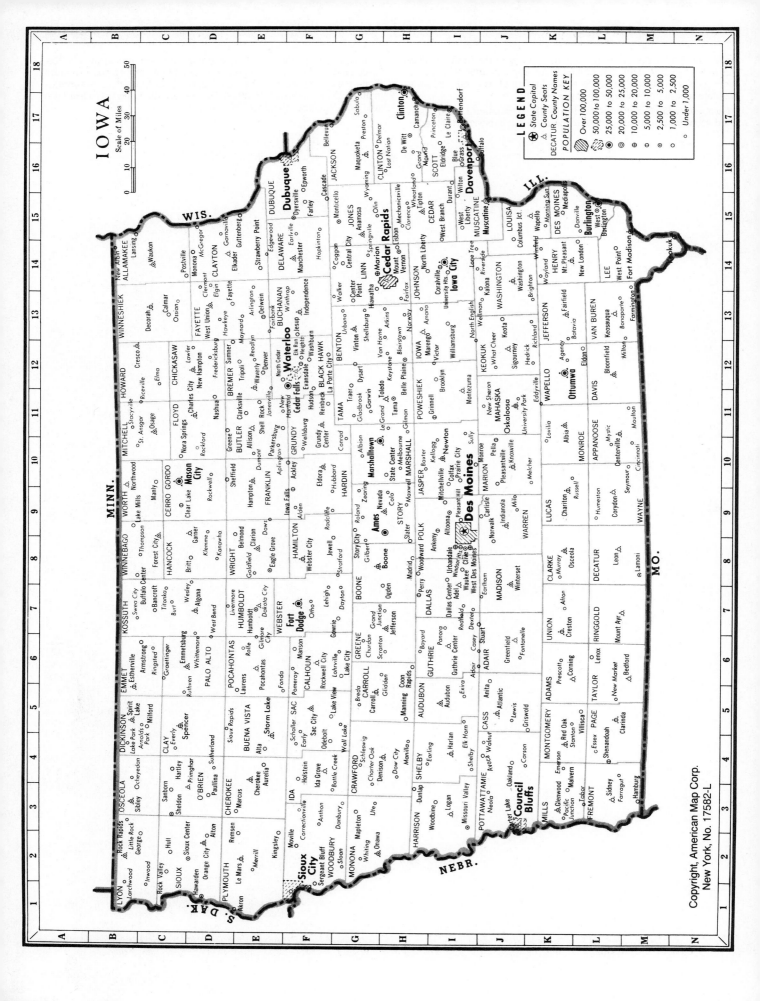

IOWA

BRIAR CLIFF COLLEGE (F-1)
3303 Rebecca Street
Sioux City, Iowa 51104-2100
Tel: (712) 279-5321; (800) 662-3303; Fax: (712) 279-5410

Description: This privately supported, coeducational, Roman Catholic, liberal arts college is fully accredited by the North Central Association of Colleges and Schools, the Council on Social Work Education, the National League for Nursing and the Iowa State Department of Public Instruction. Enrollment is 747 full-time and 410 part-time students. A faculty of 65 full-time gives a faculty-student ratio of 1-18. The school operates on the three-term system and offers two summer sessions. It offers preparation for the State teaching certificate, as well as an academic cooperative plan with Iowa State University in pre-engineering, St. Lukes Hospital in Medical Technology and the Marian Health Center in Radiologic Technology.

Entrance Requirements: Accredited high school graduation or equivalent; completion of 16 academic units; ACT or SAT required; early admission; delayed admission; advanced placement and rolling admission plans available; $20 application fee.

Costs Per Year: $10,260 tution; $3,597 room and board; $1,380 average additional expenses.

Collegiate Environment: 88% of students applying for admission are accepted. The college seeks a geographically diverse student body and will admit students at midyear. The average score of entering freshmen is ACT 22 composite. Financial assistance is available for economically disadvantaged students, and 93% of students receive some form of aid. The college library contains more than 155,402 volumes, 540 current periodicals, 28,000 microforms, and 3,000 audiovisual materials. Dormitory facilities are provided for 200 men and 354 women; computer access is available.

Community Environment: Sioux City (population 90,000) is the center of a wide trade territory on the western border of the state. It was named All-America City in 1990. The annual mean temperature is 48.4 degrees and the annual average rainfall is 29.3 inches; snow fall averages 32.5 inches. All forms of commercial transportation are available. Community facilities include 2 major hospitals, libraries, many churches of all denominations, a museum, community theatre, convention center, municipal auditorium, local symphony orchestra and an art center. The city has extensive wholesaling and shipping interests and is a great livestock, grain market, and meat-packing center. Recreational activities are hunting, fishing, golfing, and swimming. Many lakes and the Missouri River are available for boating and water skiing. Horse races, dog races, and stock-car races are held nearby from the middle of May until the middle of October. The Port of Sioux City River Cade is an annual festival marked by parades, water sports, carnivals and concerts.

BUENA VISTA COLLEGE (E-4)
College & West 4th Streets
Storm Lake, Iowa 50588
Tel: (712) 749-2235; (800) 383-9600; Fax: (712) 749-2037

Description: Buena Vista College is a privately-supported, liberal arts school. It is fully accredited by the North Central Association of Colleges and Schools and by the National Council for Accreditation of Teacher Education and offers preparation for the State teaching certificate. The college is affiliated with the Presbyterian Church in the U.S.A. but is Christian rather than denominational in its outlook. Members of the board of trustees, faculty, and the student body belong to many different faiths. The 4-1-4 semester system is employed, with two summer sessions offered. The interim term is used for innovative and conventional educational experiences including internships and travel programs. Overseas programs are currently in China, Japan, and Taiwan. Enrollment includes 520 men and 522 women full-time and 43 part-time students at its main campus at Storm Lake. At its branch campuses in Creston, Mason City, Denison, Ottumwa, Council Bluffs, Fort Dodge, Marshalltown, and Spencer an additional 1,350 students are enrolled. A faculty of 70 full-time and 22 part-time at the Storm Lake campus gives a faculty-student ratio of 1-14.

Entrance Requirements: Accredited high school graduation or equivalent with rank in upper half of class; ACT or SAT required; early admission, early decision, rolling admission, midyear admission, and advanced placement plans available; $25 application fee.

Costs Per Year: $13,306 tuition; $3,797 room and board; $500 average additional expenses

Collegiate Environment: The 60-acre campus includes 13 buildings. A renovated library houses 164,000 volumes. The Science Center has a greenhouse and a live-animal room on the roof in addition to a glass-walled ecology laboratory. The Harold Walter Siebens School of Business/Siebens Forum features the School of Business, computer center, student leadership center, and conference center. Lage Communication Center houses the mass communication department and the campus-wide telecommunication system. Housing is available for 475 men and 475 women. 79% of students applying for admission are accepted, including midyear students. The average standing of the freshman class is 47% in the top 20%, and 70% in the top third. The average score of the freshman class was ACT 24 composite. Financial aid is available, and more than 95% of the current student body receive some form of assistance.

Community Environment: Storm Lake (population 9,800) is the county seat of Buena Vista County, and is located 75 miles east of Sioux City and 160 miles northwest of Des Moines. Bus lines and nearby airport facilities provide adequate transportation. Several churches of various Christian denominations are represented in the community.

CENTRAL COLLEGE (J-10)
812 University Avenue
Pella, Iowa 50219
Tel: (515) 628-5285; (800) 458-5503; Fax: (515) 678-5316

Description: This privately supported, liberal arts college is affiliated with the Reformed Church in America. It is accredited by the North Central Association of Colleges and Secondary Schools, and the National Association of Schools of Music. It provides a four-year program of broad cultural training and grants the Bachelor degree. Special programs include overseas programs in Mexico, Paris, Vienna, Spain, London, China, The Netherlands and Wales, and urban studies programs in Chicago and Washington, D.C. The school also offers 3-2 programs in Engineering, Architecture, and Occupational Therapy and a 3-4 program in architecture with Washington University (St. Louis). The college operates on the quarter system and offers two summer sessions. Enrollment includes 1,413 full-time and 46 part-time students. A faculty of 88 full-time and 46 part-time gives a faculty-student ratio of 1-13.

Entrance Requirements: Accredited high school graduation or equivalent with rank in the upper 50% of graduating class; other students may be accepted providing they can demonstrate capability for doing college work on a standardized test of academic aptitude; ACT required (SAT may be substituted); recommended completion of 16 college-preparatory courses including 4 English, 2+ mathematics, 3 social studies, 2+ science (including a combination of biology, chemistry and/or physics) and 2+ foreign language; under certain circumstances students not meeting the requirements may be accepted. Admission plans include rolling admission, delayed admission and advanced placement; application fee $20.

Costs Per Year: $10,938 tuition, $3,660 room and board, $141 student fees.

Collegiate Environment: Housing is available for 1,307 students on the Pella campus; there are also 4 local fraternities and 2 sororities. The college library contains 178,325 volumes, 944 periodicals, 52,940 microforms, and 7,873 audiovisual materials. 87% of applicants are accepted. The middle 50% range of scores for the entering freshman class was ACT 21-28 composite. Scholarships are available and 92% of the current student body receives some form of assistance. Approximately 73% of the previous freshman class returned to the campus for their second year.

Community Environment: Pella (population 9,000), a rapidly growing agricultural and industrial community, is located 43 miles southeast of Des Moines. Active churches, libraries, and a community hospital serve the area. Pella is widely known for its attractive homes, gardens, and fine community spirit. Red Rock Dam and Lake is located four miles south. Tulip Time is an annual event here dedicated to preserving the Dutch heritage of the town.

CLARKE COLLEGE   *(F-16)*
1550 Clarke Drive
Dubuque, Iowa 52001
Tel: (319) 588-6300; (800) 383-2345; Fax: (319) 588-6789

Description: Clarke College, founded in 1843, is a coeducational, liberal arts college affiliated with the Roman Catholic Church. It is accredited by the North Central Association of Colleges and Schools and professionally by the National Council for Accreditation of Teacher Education, Council on Social Work Education, National Association of Schools of Music and National League for Nursing. The school grants the Bachelor of Arts, Bachelor of Fine Arts, Bachelor of Science, Master of Arts and Associate of Arts degrees. The curriculum offers 37 departmental majors that encompass 43 areas of study, and students can complement their studies with cooperative education internships, and off-campus or overseas study experience. A cooperative effort with two other colleges in Dubuque enables students to take classes and participate in activities on three campuses. The college operates on the semester system and offers three summer sessions. Enrollment includes 1,002 students. A faculty of 52 full-time and 39 part-time gives a faculty-studnets ratio of 1-13.

Entrance Requirements: Accredited high school graduation or equivalent with rank in upper half of class; completion of 16 units of academic work including 4 units of English, 3 history, 2 foreign language, 3 science (1 lab), and 3 mathematics: satisfactory ACT or SAT score required; 2.0 high school GPA; admission plans include early admission, rolling admission, delayed admission, and advanced placement; $20 application fee.

Costs Per Year: $10,770 tuition; $3,600 room and board.

Collegiate Environment: The picturesque campus, situated on the bluffs of the Mississippi River in Dubuque, Iowa, includes buildings that were constructed between 1879 and 1994. College residences accommodate approximately 600 students. The library contains 171,030 volumes, 522 periodicals, and 8,500 microforms. The college accepts 72% of those who apply, including midyear students. The median range of enrolled freshmen scores was ACT 22-26 composite. Financial aid is available, and 98% of the current student body receives some form of assistance.

Community Environment: The small city of Dubuque is located on the Mississippi River where Iowa, Illinois and Wisconsin meet. The oldest city in Iowa, it features rugged bluffs and Victorian architecture. Excellent air connections with Chicago's O'Hare Airport and the Minneapolis-St. Paul Airport are available. The city is the cultural, recreational and commercial center of the tristate area, and offers theater, symphony, art galleries, museums, dog racing, riverboat gambling, and concerts as well as facilities for boating, skiing, golf and tennis.

CLINTON COMMUNITY COLLEGE   *(H-18)*
1000 Lincoln Boulevard
Clinton, Iowa 52732
Tel: (319) 242-6841; (800) 462-3255; Admissions: (319) 242-6841 x349; Fax: (319) 242-7868

Description: The publicly supported, liberal arts and technological, community college was organized in 1946 as part of the Clinton Community School System. In 1966, it became a part of the Eastern Iowa Community College District. It is accredited by the North Central Association of Colleges and Schools. In addition, the college offers programs in Electronic Engineering Technology, Technical Drafting for Construction & Manufacturing, Office Education (Clerical or Secretarial), and Practical Nursing or Associate Degree Nursing. A number of academic and vocational courses are offered each semester several nights a week. It operates on the semester system and offers one summer session. Enrollment includes 1,200 students. A faculty of 36 full-time and 22 part-time gives a faculty-student ratio of 1-17. Offers intercollegiate baseball, basketball, softball, and a variety of intramural sports, a student senate, service clubs, music, student newspaper, cheerleading, ski club, business clubs and drama. Cooperative Education program (alternating work and class periods) in the Office Education program. Offers pre-college and freshman programs for the educationally disadvantaged.

Entrance Requirements: Open enrollment; any student who is a graduate of an approved high school or who has qualified for an equivalency certificate may be admitted; ACT scores are used for counseling purposes and are recommended of all academic and technical students; early admission, early decision, rolling admission, delayed admission, midyear admission and advanced placement plans available; $25 application fee.

Costs Per Year: $1,410 tuition for full-time state resident students; $2,115 tuition for out-of-state students; $165 student fees.

Collegiate Environment: The expanded college facilities and buildings are modern in every respect and provide for a quality program for the first and second year of college work. The library contains 16,000 volumes, 135 periodicals, 727 microforms, and 2,214 audiovisual materials. 98% of applicants are accepted. The average standing of freshmen: top 50% of high school class; 30% were in the top quarter, 20% in the top half. The average score of entering freshmen was ACT 19 composite. Scholarships are available and 70% of the students receive some form of financial aid. The college awarded 180 Associate degrees recently.

Community Environment: See Mount Saint Clare College

COE COLLEGE   *(H-14)*
1220 1st Avenue N. E.
Cedar Rapids, Iowa 52402
Tel: (319) 399-8500; (800) 332-8404; Admissions: (319) 399-8500; Fax: (319) 399-8816

Description: The privately supported, liberal arts college is affiliated with the United Presbyterian Church, and is approved by the Synod of Lakes and Prairies, the Church Board of Christian Education, and the General Assembly of the Presbyterian Church. It is accredited by the North Central Association of Colleges and schools and by professional accrediting institutions. The college grants the Bachelor degree. An extensive off-campus program includes programs abroad (Europe, Japan, China, Russia, Yugoslavia and Latin America) and/or work-service internship opportunies of one term working in a professional capacity. A 3/2 Program in Engineering and 3/4 Program in Architecture. The University of Chicago's Bachelor/Masters Degree Program in Social Service Administration is also available. Army ROTC is available as an elective. The college operates on the 4-1-4 system and offers two summer sessions. Enrollment includes 1,098 full-time and 206 part-time undergraduates and 39 graduate students. A faculty of 86 full-time and 38 part-time gives a faculty-student ratio of 1-12.

Entrance Requirements: Accredited high school graduation or equivalent; early decision, early admission, deferred admission, midyear admission; units should include 4 English, 3 mathematics, 3 science, 2 foreign language; SAT or ACT required; advanced placement plans are available; $25 application fee.

Costs Per Year: Tuition $13,925, board and room $4,390, student activity fee $125; additional expenses average $1,000.

Collegiate Environment: 79% of the students who apply for admission are accepted, including midyear students. Financial assistance is available, and 85% of the current students receive some form of aid. Dormitory facilities accommodate 533 men, 425 women. The library contains 203,185 volumes and subscribes to 916 periodicals. The Student Senate coordinates campus social events, and allocates funds for the "Comos' the student newspaper; "Acorn' the yearbook; and station KCOE-FM, the student radio station.

Community Environment: Cedar Rapids, a metropolitan community of 150,000 is located just 225 miles west of Chicago in east-central Iowa. All forms of commercial transportation are available. Community facilities include over 100 churches, a symphony orchestra, library, hospital, and shopping in the downtown area, plus three shopping centers. Part time employment is available. Cedar Rapids has over 59 city parks which offer a variety of recreational facilities. Points of interest are the Cedar Rapids Art Center, Iowa Masonic Library, Paramount Theater of Performing Arts, Five Seasons Civic Center, and Theatre Cedar Rapids.

CORNELL COLLEGE   *(H-14)*
Mount Vernon, Iowa 52314
Tel: (319) 895-8811; (800) 747-1112; Admissions: (319) 895-4477; Fax: (319) 895-4451

Description: This privately supported, liberal arts college is accredited by the North Central Association of Colleges and Schools, the American Chemical Society, and the National Association of Schools of Music. The college was founded in 1853 and has no restrictions regarding race or creed for students or staff members. The school maintains its relationship with the United Methodist Church although it is governed by a private Board of Trustees. Enrollment includes 1,133 full-time students. A faculty of 76 full-time, 50 part-time gives a faculty-student ratio of 1-13. A One-Course-At-A-Time calendar system is employed, and the college offers vocal and instrumental music programs, and intercollegiate and intramural athletics in addition to academic studies.

Entrance Requirements: Accredited high school graduation or equivalent with completion of 15 units including 3 English, 2 mathematics, 2 science, and 2 social studies; SAT or ACT required; early decision, delayed admission, and advanced placement plans available; $25 application fee.

Costs Per Year: $15,248 tuition; $4,323 room and board; $125 student fees.

Collegiate Environment: 85% of the students applying for admission are accepted. The college expects students to work with the administration and the faculty to establish principles and regulations for academic and social conduct. The use of motor vehicles is not prohibited, but vehicles must be registered with the college. All students, with few exceptions, live in college residence halls and board in the Commons. Housing is available for 1,020 men and women. The library contains 187,000 volumes, and numerous microforms and sound recordings. Financial assistance is available, and 80% of the current student body receives some form of aid.

Community Environment: Mount Vernon is a small town located 15 miles east of Cedar Rapids and 22 miles north of Iowa City. Bus and airline service are available in Cedar Rapids. The community and college share many facilities. Community facilities include churches and various civic, fraternal and veteran's organizations. Opportunities for student employment off campus are limited. Excellent recreational facilities are available at the Palisades State Park, MacBride State Park and Coralville Reservoir, for fishing and boating, golf, bowling, swimming, and cross-country skiing. Downhill skiing facilities are available within 70 miles.

DES MOINES AREA COMMUNITY COLLEGE - ANKENY CAMPUS   *(I-9)*
Ankeny, Iowa 50021
Tel: (515) 964-6241; (800) 362-2127; Fax: (515) 964-6391

Description: The publicly supported, junior college operates on the semester system with one summer session and is accredited by the North Central Association of Colleges and Schools. The college has an enrollment of 11,214 students. A faculty of 650 provides a faculty-student ratio of 1-17. The school offers liberal arts transfer and vocational-technical programs, and grants Certificates and Associate Degrees.

Entrance Requirements: Accredited high school graduation or equivalent; open enrollment policy; non-high school graduates may be accepted for certain programs; rolling admission, early decision, early admission, midyear admission and delayed admission plans available; ACT required for degree and college transfer programs; $10 application fee.

Costs Per Year: Tuition $1,110; out-of-state $2,220; student fees $144.

Collegiate Environment: Most vocational-technical programs require one year of study for graduation. 60% of those who apply are accepted, including midyear students. Financial aid is available for economically handicapped students. The library contains 45,000 volumes, 550 periodicals and numerous audiovisual materials.

Community Environment: Ankeny (population 22,000) is five miles from the capital city of Des Moines and its recreation centers, theatres and competitive sports. Three of the main industries are manufacturing of farming equipment, retail products, and insurance. Community facilities include a library, churches, city parks, and a public golf course.

DES MOINES AREA COMMUNITY COLLEGE - BOONE CAMPUS   *(G-8)*
1125 Hancock Drive
Boone, Iowa 50036
Tel: (515) 432-7203; (800) 362-2127; Admissions: (515) 432-7203; Fax: (515) 432-6311

Description: The publicly supported, junior college is fully accredited by the North Central Association of Colleges and Schools. The school offers liberal arts transfer and vocational-technical programs. It operates on the semester system and offers one summer session. Enrollment includes 1,100 students. A faculty of 30 full-time, 20 part-time gives an overall faculty-student ratio of 1-25. A cooperative education program (alternating work and class periods) in business courses, a freshman program for the educationally disadvantaged.

Entrance Requirements: Open enrollment policy; non-high school graduates considered; ACT required for degree programs; early admission, midyear admission and rolling admission plans available; $10 application fee.

Costs Per Year: Tuition $1,320; out-of-state tuition $2,640.

Collegiate Environment: All students applying for admission are accepted, including midyear students. Financial assistance is available, and 60% of the current students receive some form of aid. The college library includes over 14,000 volumes, 120 periodicals, 1,000 microforms, 2500 audiovisual materials.

Community Environment: Boone is an urban area with a temperate climate. The city has excellent medical facilities. Part-time employment is available. Railroads and a municipal airport serve the area. Recreational activities include swimming, golf, tennis, boating. Ledges State Park is nearby. The Holiday Parade and the Band Festival are special annual events.

DIVINE WORD COLLEGE AND SEMINARY   *(F-16)*
102 Jacoby Drive, S.W.
P.O. Box 380
Epworth, Iowa 52045
Tel: (319) 876-3353; (800) 553-3321; Fax: (319) 876-3407

Description: The privately supported, liberal arts college and seminary for men is accredited by the Association of Independent Colleges and Schools and the North Central Association of Colleges and Schools. The seminary enrolls 85 seminarians full-time. A full-time faculty of 23 and part-time faculty of 4 gives a faculty-student ratio of 1:4. The school operates on the semester system. The seminary is an integral part of the training program of the Divine Word Missionaries under the auspices of the Roman Catholic Church. Overseas programs are available in usually Japan or the Phillipines during the Junior year.

Entrance Requirements: High school graduation or equivalent with completion of 16 units of academic work including 4 units of English, 2 mathematics, 1 science and 1 social science; SAT preferred or ACT required; admission plans include rolling admission, early admission, early decision, and advanced placement; $25 application fee.

Costs Per Year: Tuition $7,000; room and board $1,200.

Collegiate Environment: The campus includes 2 buildings and occupies 35 acres. The chapel, with a seating capacity of over 400, is built along modern liturgical lines. Outdoor sports facilities and a modern indoor pool and gymnasium provide facilities for recreation. The college has dormitory space for 125 students and the library houses more than 89,464 volumes. The seminary admits both freshmen and transfer students. Scholarships are available and 98% of the current student body receive some form of assistance. The college awarded 9 Bachelor degrees recently.

Community Environment: A rural community, Epworth (population 1,600) is in a scenic area 15 miles west of Dubuque and 10 miles east of Dyersville. The climate is moderate. Dubuque can be reached by bus, train or air service. Bus service furnishes transportation to Epworth.

DORDT COLLEGE   *(C-2)*
494 4th Street N. E.
Sioux Center, Iowa 51250
Tel: (712) 722-6080; (800) 343-6738; Admissions: (712) 722-6080;
Fax: (712) 722-1967

Description: The privately supported, liberal arts college was founded in 1955 as a two-year college under the educational leadership of the Christian Reformed Churches in the Midwest. In 1965 the college became a four-year institution and the first B.A. degrees were conferred. The school operates on a semester basis and is accredited by the North Central Association of Colleges and Schools. Enrollment includes 545 men and 565 women full-time, 16 men and 32 women part-time. A faculty of 71 full-time, 15 part-time gives a faculty-student ratio of 1-13. In addition to academic subjects, the school offers vocal and instrumental music programs, and intercollegiate and intramural athletics. Religion courses are required. Preparation for the State teaching certificate is also offered.

Entrance Requirements: Accredited high school graduation or equivalent with 18 academic units including 10 units from the fields of social science, English, foreign language, natural science, or mathematics, but must include 3 English and 2 algebra/geometry; ACT required; early admission, early decision, rolling admission, and advanced placement plans available; $10 application fee.

Costs Per Year: $9,800 tuition; $2,650 room and board.

Collegiate Environment: 90% of the students applying for admission are accepted. Students are permitted to enroll at midyear as well as in September. Financial aid is available, and 95% of the current student body receives some form of assistance. The library contains more than 160,000 volumes. Housing is available for 430 men, 430 women and 20 families. The college granted 197 Bachelor degrees recently.

Community Environment: Sioux Center (population 5,100) is a rural area with a temperate climate. College transportation serves the area. A public library, hospital, churches, clinics and shopping areas are all available within the community. Part-time employment may be found. Recreational activities include swimming, golf, and fishing.

DRAKE UNIVERSITY   *(I-9)*
2507 University Avenue
Des Moines, Iowa 50311-4505
Tel: (515) 271-3181; (800) 443-7253; Fax: (515) 271-2831

Description: This independent national university is accredited by the North Central Association of Colleges and Schools and by the following professional associations: American Assembly of Collegiate Schools of Business, American Chemical Society, Accrediting Council on Education in Journalism and Mass Communication, American Bar Association, Association of American Law Schools, National Association of Schools of Music, American Council on Pharmaceutical Education, National Association of Schools of Art and Design and the National Council for Accreditation of Teacher Education. The university operates on the semester system with two summer sessions and is composed of seven individual colleges and schools which include the College of Business and Public Administration, School of Education, College of Arts and Sciences, School of Fine Arts, School of Journalism and Mass Communication, College of Pharmacy and Health Sciences and the Law School. As well as granting the Bachelor degree, the university offers Master degree programs in liberal arts, business, fine arts, education, journalism, and mass communication. The College of Pharmacy and Health Sciences offers the Doctor of Pharmacy degree. The Specialist in Education and Education Doctorate degrees are also offered. The student body, which represents every section of the United States and numerous foreign countries, consists of 2,790 men and 3,164 women. Enrollment includes 3,273 full-time and 645 part-time undergraduates and 2,036 graduate students. A faculty of 278 gives an undergraduate faculty-student ratio of 1-16. In addition

to academic subjects, the school offers extensive instrumental and vocal music programs, and intercollegiate and intramural athletics. Overseas study is available through the Center for International Programs and Services. Army and Air Force ROTC programs are available.

Entrance Requirements: Accredited high school graduation or equivalent with minimum C average; completion of 16 units and ACT or SAT required; early admission; rolling admission; delayed admission; and advanced placement plans available; International Baccalaureate; CLEP; GRE, MAT, or GMAT required for Graduate School; $25 application fee.

Costs Per Year: $13,420 tuition; $4,770 room and board.

Collegiate Environment: The school occupies a 120-acre site and includes a library of more than 580,000 titles and numerous pamphlets and 550,000 microforms. Residence halls provide living accommodations for 790 men and 958 women, and fraternities and sororities accomodate 482 additional students. 93% of students applying for admission are accepted. 38% of the entering freshmen ranked in the top 10% of the high school class, 64% ranked in the top 25%, and 87% were in the top half. Financial aid is available for economically handicapped students. Approximately 80% of freshmen receive financial aid. More than 2,000 scholarships are provided annually.

Community Environment: Des Moines is Iowa's capital city, and its metropolitan population of 300,000 is the largest in the state. The downtown area includes the Convention Center, a skywalk system linking office buildings and shops, and a major restoration and conversion of historic buildings in the former city market area. A Civic Center offers plays, concerts and other entertainment. The Art Center, in a park setting of trees and gardens, houses a permanent collection of paintings and sculpture, in addition to traveling exhibits. Major business interests include a concentration of home offices of insurance companies and the pivotal operation of a large publishing firm.

ELLSWORTH COMMUNITY COLLEGE   *(F-10)*
1100 College Avenue
Iowa Falls, Iowa 50126
Tel: (515) 648-4611; (800) 322-9235; Fax: (515) 648-3128

Description: Ellsworth Community College is a publicly supported institution under the jurisdiction of the Iowa Valley Community College District. The college is accredited by the North Central Association of Colleges and Schools and the Iowa Department of Public Instruction. It is a member of the American Association of Community and Junior Colleges and of the Iowa Association of Community Colleges and Vocational-Technical Institutes. The school grants diplomas, certificates and Associate degrees. The college operates on the early semester system and offers two summer sessions. Enrollment is 600 full-time and 150 part-time students. A faculty of 45 gives a faculty-student ratio of 1-17.

Entrance Requirements: Admission to the programs in arts and sciences requires accredited high school graduation or equivalent; vocational-technical programs require either accredited high school graduation or equivalent, or aptitude and ability to profit from vocational or technical education; ACT required; rolling admission; early admission, early decision, and advanced placement plans available; $25 application fee.

Costs Per Year: $1,800 tuition; $3,600 out-of-state; $3,000 room and board; $300 student fees.

Collegiate Environment: The library contains over 27,000 volumes and 260 periodical subscriptions. Housing is available for 200 men and 180 women. 147 scholarships are available, including 44 for freshmen and 79% of the current student body receives some form of financial assistance.

Community Environment: Iowa Falls (population 6,127) is a rural area situated on the Iowa River. Community facilities include 18 churches of all denominations, a hospital, library, motels, hotels, and various civic and service organizations. Part-time jobs are available. Recreational facilities include a theater, hunting, fishing, water skiing, swimming and two nine-hole golf courses.

EMMAUS BIBLE COLLEGE   *(F-16)*
2570 Asbury Road
Dubuque, Iowa 52001
Tel: (319) 588-8000; (800) 397-2425; Admissions: (319) 588-8000;
Fax: (319) 588-1216

Description: The privately supported, Bible school was founded in 1941 and is accredited by the Accrediting Association of Bible Colleges. The college grants certificates for one-year programs, and the Bachelor degree. It operates on the early semester calendar system. Enrollment is 222 students. A faculty of 12 gives a faculty-student ratio of 1-19.

Entrance Requirements: High school graduation or equivalent; SAT or ACT required, minimum scores 260V, 260M; Christian character with strong motivation to study scriptures required, evidence of conversion to God. Rolling admission, midyear admission and advanced placement plans available; $10 application fee.

Costs Per Year: $6,500 student fees including room and board. No tuition charge.

Collegiate Environment: 95% of applicants are accepted. Scholarships are available and 55% of the students receive some form of financial aid. The library holdings include 32,000 volumes. Dormitory facilities accommodate 210 students.

Community Environment: Emmaus Bible College is located in Dubuque, Iowa, a Mississippi River City, of 60,000 people. It serves as the metropolitan center of 300,000 residents in the tri-state trading area. It is a city of traditional values and loyalties reflecting the past with a progressive spirit toward the future. Dubuque provides many wholesome activities for the Emmaus student. The Dubuque Symphony Orchestra performs regularly at the Five Flags Center. The Spirit of Dubuque, a paddlewheeler, plies the Mississippi and provides dining en route. Fall brings out the beauty of the variety of trees and foliage along the river and its tributaries. Dubuque is also a center for education, boasting three colleges in addition to Emmaus, as well as two seminaries. Located close to Dubuque is the Northeast Iowa Technical Institute providing excellent vocational and technical training, which students may opt for while studying Bible on the Emmaus campus. This healthy environment is a suitable setting for the Emmaus education and for the community outreach of Christian service and evangelism.

FAITH BAPTIST BIBLE COLLEGE   *(I-8)*
1900 Northwest Fourth Street
Ankeny, Iowa 50021
Tel: (515) 964-0601; (800) 352-0147; Fax: (515) 964-1638

Description: The privately supported theological college operates on the semester system with two summer sessions. Enrollment is 94 men, 92 women full-time, 16 men, and 20 women part-time. A faculty of 15 full-time and 3 part-time gives a faculty-student ratio of 1-14. It is an independent educational institution approved by the General Association of Regular Baptist Churches, and is also an Accredited Member of the American Association of Bible Colleges. The college was originally established in 1921 in Omaha and in 1967 it opened for classes on the campus in Ankeny. In addition to academic subjects, the school offers vocal and instrumental music programs, and intercollegiate and intramural athletics. Special programs include missionary internship programs and apprenticeships.

Entrance Requirements: Accredited high school graduation or equivalent; open enrollment policy; ACT or SAT required; Christian character and dedication required; rolling admission, deferred admission, midyear admission and advanced placement plans available; $20 application fee.

Costs Per Year: Tuition $5,320; board and room $3,160; student fees $480; additional expenses average $500.

Collegiate Environment: 99% of the students who apply for admission are accepted, including midyear students. The library contains 55,000 volumes, 4,000 pamphlets, numerous periodicals and recordings. Housing for 96 men, and 144 women, and 48 families is provided. Financial aid is available and 80% of the students receive some form of assistance. The college seeks a geographically diverse student body.

Community Environment: See Des Moines Area Community College - Ankeny Campus.

GRACELAND COLLEGE   *(M-8)*
700 College Avenue
Lamoni, Iowa 50140
Tel: (515) 784-5000

Description: The privately supported, liberal arts college was founded in 1895 and is accredited by the North Central Association of Colleges and Schools, National Council for Accreditation of Teacher Education and by the National League for Nursing. It is sponsored by the Reorganized Church of Jesus Christ of Latter Day Saints and grants the Bachelor degree. Students of all religious affiliations are admitted. It has satellite programs in elementary education and business administration at Indian Hills Community College in Centerville, Iowa and elementary education at North Central Missouri College in Trenton, Missouri. The college operateson the 4-1-4 semester system with one summer session. Enrollment includes 450 men and 483 women full-time, 31 men and 94 women part-time. A faculty of 62 full-time and 14 part-time gives a faculty student ratio of 1-14.

Entrance Requirements: Accredited high school graduation or equivalent with rank in upper half of graduating class; completion of 15 academic units recommended including 3-4 English, 2-4 mathematics, 2 social science, 2 science; ACT or SAT required; score of 27 or over on ACT required, combined score of 840 on SAT required; early admission, early decision, rolling admission, delayed admission and advanced placement plans available; $20 application fee. $80 college deposit.

Costs Per Year: $8,335 tuition; $2,780 room and board; $85 student fees.

Collegiate Environment: The college maintains a Christian atmosphere, and convocations and assemblies are considered to be an integral part of the general education program of the college. Visiting speakers and artists augment the faculty in providing a varied program. 78% of those who apply for admission are accepted, and midyear students are admitted. About 40% of the student body graduated in the top quarter of their high school class, and 80% in the upper half. Financial aid is available, and 93% of the current student body receive some form of assistance. The campus is located on 183 acres and 30 buildings serve the college, including a library containing 109,106 volumes and 551 periodicals, 63,394 microforms and 2,483 audiovisual materials. Dormitory facilities are available for 294 men, 294 women and 9 families.

Community Environment: Lamoni (population 2,700), a picturesque town in the rolling hills of south central Iowa, is within easy driving distance of Des Moines, Omaha, Council Bluffs, and Kansas City. Bus transportation is available to these urban centers. The city has an excellent library and shopping area including several antique malls. Churches play an important part in the life of the community and a county hospital is located in neaby Leon. Citizens enjoy world-renowned artists in concert and theater productions at the college fine arts center, movies, sports, clubs, and lodges. Nine Eagles State Park (12 miles southeast), Central Park, and Foreman Park provide facilities for recreation.

GRAND VIEW COLLEGE   *(I-9)*
1200 Grandview Avenue
Des Moines, Iowa 50316
Tel: (515) 263-2800; (800) 444-6083; Fax: (515) 263-2998

Description: This privately supported four year college had a recent enrollment of 375 men and 638 women full-time, 150 men and 255 women part-time. A faculty of 73 full-time and 48 part-time gives a faculty-student ratio of 1-15. It operates on the 4-4-1 system and offers 3 summer sessions. It is affiliated with the Evangelical Lutheran Church in America. It was founded in 1896 and is accredited by North Central Association of Colleges and Schools, the National League for Nursing and approved by the State of Iowa. The college offers A.A., B.A., and B.S.N. degrees. Army ROTC is available.

Entrance Requirements: Accredited high school graduation or equivalent required; ACT required; open enrollment; rolling admission, early admission, delayed admission, and advanced placement plans available; no application fee.

Costs Per Year: $9,820 tuition; $3,360 room and board; $50 student fees.

Collegiate Environment: The campus is located on 26 acres and consists of 13 buildings including a library of over 98,000 volumes and dormitory facilities for 116 men and 130 women. 95% of those applying for admission are accepted including midyear students. 95% of the day college enrollment receives financial aid in an average amount of over $9,700 per student.

Community Environment: See Drake University.

GRINNELL COLLEGE   *(I-11)*
P.O. Box 805
Grinnell, Iowa 50112-0810
Tel: (515) 269-3600; (800) 247-0113; Fax: (515) 269-4800

Description: This privately supported, liberal arts college is accredited by the North Central Association of Colleges and Schools, and the National Council for Accreditation of Teacher Education; on the approved list of the American Chemical Society; member of the Associated Colleges of the Midwest, Phi Beta Kappa and other national and regional associations. The college operates on a semester basis. Enrollment is 579 men and 716 women full-time. A faculty of 140 full-time and 13 part-time gives a faculty-student ratio of approximately 1-10. In addition to academic subjects, the school offers vocal and instrumental music programs, and extensive intercollegiate and intramural athletics. Overseas programs include Junior Year Abroad and various other programs in 31 countries. Domestic programs include Fine Arts Program in New York, Howard University Semester, National Theatre Institute, Newberry Library Semester, Oak Ridge Science Semester, Urban Studies Program, Washington Center Semester, and Wilderness Field Station. Academic cooperative programs are available in Architecture (with Washington University), Business (with University of Chicago), Dentistry (with any recognized dental school), Engineering (with any recognized engineering school, including California Institute of Technology, Columbia University, Rensselaer Polytechnic Institute, and Washington University), Law (with Columbia University), and Medicine (with any recognized medical school, including Rush University). Interdisciplinary concentrations are available in Afro-American Studies, Gender and Women's Studies, Technology Studies, Chinese Studies, Environmental Studies, Latin American Studies, Russian and Eastern European Studies, and Western European Studies.

Entrance Requirements: Graduation from an accredited secondary school with 4 units of English, 3 units of mathematics, and 9 other elective units; satisfactory results on SAT and ACT; admission plans include early admission, early decision, delayed admission, advanced placement; $25 application fee.

Costs Per Year: $16,236 tuition; $4,782 room and board; $392 student fees.

Collegiate Environment: The 57 buildings on this 95-acre campus include Burling Library and Windsor Science Library, which contains 363,916 volumes, currently receives 2,453 periodicals, is a select depository for federal documents, and also has 14,908 recordings, 7,830 microfilm reels, and 179,400 microfiche; and dormitories that accommodate 1,084 students. 56% of the students who apply for admission are accepted, and transfer students are admitted at midyear as well as in August. The college seeks a geographically diverse student body. 87% of the current freshmen graduated in the top fifth of their secondary school class and 98% graduated in the top two-fifths. Average test scores for freshmen were: SAT 606V, 653M; ACT 29. Financial aid is available, and 70% of the current student body receives some form of assistance. 92% of the previous freshman class returned to the college for the sophomore year.

Community Environment: Grinnell (population 8,900) is located 55 miles east of Des Moines and 60 miles west of Iowa City, and is a five-hour drive from Chicago.

HAWKEYE COMMUNITY COLLEGE   *(F-12)*
Box 8015
1501 East Orange Road
Waterloo, Iowa 50704
Tel: (319) 296-2320; Fax: (319) 296-2874

Description: This school is a publicly supported community college. It operates on the early semester system with a summer session. It is fully accredited by the North Central Association of Colleges and Schools, Accreditation Board for Engineering and Technology, American Dental Association and the Committee on Allied Health Education and Accreditation. It grants the Diploma and Associate degrees in various technical and professional fields. Enrollment is 2,434 full-time and 992 part-time students. A faculty of 111 full-time and 48 part-time provides a faculty-student ratio of 1-16.

Entrance Requirements: Accredited high school graduation or equivalent; open enrollment policy; delayed admission, early admission, early decision, rolling admission and advanced placement plans available

Costs Per Year: $1,830 tuition; $3,660 out-of-state; $139 student fees.

Collegiate Environment: Approximately 98% of the students applying for admission are accepted including midyear students. The library contains 20,000 volumes. Financial aid is available to economically handicapped students and 76% of the current student body receives some form of financial assistance. Half of the courses offered at Hawkeye Institute of Technology may be completed in one year.

Community Environment: Waterloo (population 75,000), an industrial city, manufactures tractors and processes meat. The internationally famous National Dairy Cattle Congress is located here. The horse racing cart known as the Sulky is manufactured here by the Jerald Sulky Company. Highlights of interest are the Museum of History and Science and Waterloo Greyhound Park.

INDIAN HILLS COMMUNITY COLLEGE   *(K-12)*
525 Grandview
Ottumwa, Iowa 52501
Tel: (515) 683-5111; (800) 726-2585; Fax: (515) 683-5184

Description: Indian Hills Community College is an innovative two-year college located in southeastern Iowa. It was established in 1966 by state enacted legislation as one of Iowa's 15 community colleges. Indian Hills is fully accredited by the North Central Association of Colleges and Schools. Campuses are located in Ottumwa and Centerville. Indian Hills provides career options with 38 technical education training programs. The college has been a leader among two-year college technical programs, including instruction in Robotics/Automation and Laser/Electro-Optics. A variety of music, dance and performing arts subjects are available in the arts and sciences. The college awards diplomas and associate degrees. Educational offerings are provided all year. The college operates on the quarter system and offers one summer session. Enrollment includes 2,350 full-time and 900 part-time students. There are 186 faculty members.

Entrance Requirements: Accredited high school graduation or equivalent, or evidence of demonstrated interest, aptitude, and ability to profit from training; open enrollment policy; rolling admission, early decision; early admission and advanced placement plans available.

Costs Per Year: $1,320 tuition, $1,980 nonresident $1,645 room and board.

Collegiate Environment: Indian Hills Community College has an open-door policy for admission; however, some specific programs do have additional admission standards. Students may enroll at the beginning of each term. Housing is available for 497 students. 95% of all applicants accepted. 485 scholarships are available and 80% of the current student body receives some form of financial assistance. The college library contains 29,900 volumes, 4,500 audio/visual items, and 234 periodical titles. The college maintains a very active Student Senate. There is a full program of intra-murals as well as inter-collegiate programs available in basketball, baseball, softball and golf. The college also boasts an award-winning health and recreation facility offering basketball, tennis, weight lifting, racquetball, track, health spa and other activities. An innovative building featuring technology transfer capabilities has recently been constructed to house both mechanical and electrical related technologies. Administrative headquarters and facilities are located on 126 wooded acres at the northeastern edge of Ottumwa, Iowa. Opportunities for nature walks and outdoor theatre events are located on campus. The Centerville campus contains 72 acres at the northwestern edge of that city in southern Iowa. Students have access to men's and women's athletics and several college sponsored clubs. Indian Hilss also operates a child development center for children of students and staff.

Community Environment: The population of Ottumwa is 27,000. This community is located about 85 miles southwest of Des Moines.

Recreational activities are available at Lake Rathbun, about six miles northwest of Centerville.

IOWA CENTRAL COMMUNITY COLLEGE - EAGLE GROVE CENTER   *(E-8)*
Eagle Grove, Iowa 50533
Tel: (515) 448-4723

Description: The Eagle Grove Center is one of several attendance centers of the publicly supported Iowa Central Community College. The central administration is located at Fort Dodge. The Center had its origin in 1928 when it was incorporated as a Junior College and a part of the Eagle Grove Public School system. A program of college transfer courses is offered making it possible for students to complete the first two-year requirements of a typical Baccalaureate degree. Several career-option and vocational programs are also offered. The college operates on the semester system. The enrollment is 150 students.

Entrance Requirements: Open enrollment; graduates of high school will be admitted unconditionally; non-high school graduates attending high schoool may also enroll in programs for which they qualify; rolling admission, advanced placement plans. Contact Director of Admissions for information.

Costs Per Year: $800 per semester for residents; $1,100 per semester for nonresidents.

Collegiate Environment: Almost all of those applying for admission are accepted including midyear students. 8% of a recent freshman class graduated in the upper tenth of their high school class, 20% in the upper quarter, and 47% in the upper half. The college has a special concern for the individual student and provides counseling services for all those enrolled. A college placement service is available to all students.

Community Environment: A rural community, Eagle Grove (population 4,489) has a temperate climate. Railroads and highways serve the area, as well as a municipal airport. Community facilities include a new public library, churches, municipal swimming pool and golf course. Part-time work is available.

IOWA CENTRAL COMMUNITY COLLEGE - FORT DODGE CENTER   *(F-7)*
330 Avenue M
Fort Dodge, Iowa 50501
Tel: (515) 576-7201; (800) 362-2793; Admissions: (515) 576-7206; Fax: (515) 576-7206

Description: The publicly supported, community college is part of the Iowa Community College system. Other centers of the college are located in Eagle Grove, Webster City and Storm Lake. It is accredited by the North Central Association of Colleges and Schools. A full program of college transfer courses is offered, making it possible for students to complete the first two years of study toward a Baccalaureate degree. Career programs are available to provide education in the technological, business, secretarial, food marketing/management, and nursing fields. The school grants Certificates and Associate degrees. It operates on a semester system and offers one summer term. Enrollment is approximately 1,600 full-time, 600 part-time and 37,000 adult education evening students. A faculty of 96 full-time, 1 part-time in the day session provides a faculty-student ratio of 1-20. Cooperative education programs (alternating work and class periods) are available in vocational-technical subjects. The college also offers precollege and freshman programs for the educationally disadvantaged and a cooperative program in nursing with University of Iowa.

Entrance Requirements: Open enrollment policy; high school graduates admitted unconditionally; non-high school graduates attending high school may enroll in programs for which they qualify; early admission, rolling admission, and advanced placement plans available.

Costs Per Year: $1,800 state-resident tuition; $2,800 out-of-state; $125 student fees; $2,835 room and board; additional annual expenses average $1,500.

Collegiate Environment: Almost all of those applying for admission are accepted. Students may enroll at midyear. Housing is available for 220 men and 220 women. The library contains 60,687 titles and 461 periodicals.

Community Environment: Fort Dodge (population 31,000), situated in north-central Iowa, is surrounded by rich farmlands and also has a

number of industries. All forms of commercial transportation are available. Fort Dodge is one of the largest producers of gypsum products in the world. Churches, hospitals, a library, museum, art gallery, and many of the major civic, fraternal, business, and professional organizations are represented. Job opportunities are good. Student housing is available in private homes. Recreational activities are swimming, boating, hunting, and fishing.

IOWA CENTRAL COMMUNITY COLLEGE - WEBSTER CITY CAMPUS   *(F-8)*
1725 Beach Street
Webster City, Iowa 50595
Tel: (515) 832-1632

Description: A publicly supported, junior college, the Webster City Campus was originally incorporated in 1926. With the exception of three years during World War II, the college has been in continuous operation. A full program of college transfer courses is offered, making it possible for students to complete the first two years of a typical Baccalaureate degree. A nine-month Cooperative Office also is available to provide instruction for employment in that field. A two year career option in Aviation-Airport management is available. The semester system is employed with one summer term. Enrollment is 220 students. A faculty of 21 gives a faculty-student ratio of 1-15. See also Fort Dodge Campus.

Entrance Requirements: Open enrollment; graduates of high school will be admitted unconditionally; non-high school graduates attending high school may also enroll in programs for which they qualify; ACT; rolling admission, early admission, and advanced placement plans available.

Costs Per Year: $1,740 state-resident tuition; $2,610 out-of-state; $2,200 room and board; $175 student fees.

Collegiate Environment: The library contains 16,000 volumes. Almost all of the students applying for admission are accepted. Midyear students may enroll at the college. 40% of the students receive financial assistance.

Community Environment: Webster City is 20 miles west of Fort Dodge on the Boone River, located at a railroad junction. Churches of major denominations, a library, and hospital are a part of the community, along with a recreation center, golf course, two theaters, and a bowling alley.

IOWA LAKES COMMUNITY COLLEGE - EMMETSBURG CAMPUS   *(C-6)*
3200 College Drive
Emmetsburg, Iowa 50536
Tel: (712) 852-4236; (800) 346-6018; Admissions: (712) 852-3554; Fax: (712) 852-2152

Description: The publicly supported community college is a part of the area community college system of Iowa. A two-year program is offered either of a terminal nature or as preparation for a four-year college or university. The college is accredited by the North Central Association of Colleges and Schools, the Iowa State Department of Education, the Regents Committee on Educational Relations and is a member of the American Association of Junior Colleges and the Iowa Junior College Association. The college operates on the semester system and offers one summer term. Enrollment is 1,336 full-time students. A faculty of 69 full-time and 28 part-time gives a student-faculty ratio of 28:1. See also Estherville Campus.

Entrance Requirements: Open enrollment; graduation from accredited high school or equivalent; non-high school graduates are considered upon successful completion of the GED; early admission, early decision, deferred admission, midyear admission, rolling admission and advanced placement plans available.

Costs Per Year: $1,760 resident tuition; $2,848 nonresident tuition; $2,717 room and board; $300 fees.

Collegiate Environment: Campus facilities include a library of 36,000. Scholarships are available and 80% of the students receive financial aid. 95% of all applicants accepted.

Community Environment: Emmetsburg is situated on the west fork of the Des Moines River, 160 miles northwest of Des Moines, and has an average rainfall of 27 inches. Railroads and buses serve the area and a small airport is available for private planes. Community facilities provide ten churches, a hospital, and a library. Recreational facilities include a lake offering swimming, boating, fishing, and ice skating. A nine-hole golf course, city parks, and a state park provide picnic and camping facilities.

IOWA LAKES COMMUNITY COLLEGE - NORTH CAMPUS
(B-5)
300 S. 18th St.
Estherville, Iowa 51334
Tel: (712) 362-2601; (800) 521-5054; Admissions: (712) 362-2604;
Fax: (712) 362-7649

Description: The publicly supported, junior college is under the control of the Iowa Lakes Community College Merged Area III Board of Education as of July 1, 1968. It is a public institution with two principal attendance centers at Emmetsburg and Estherville, located 25 miles apart. It is accredited by the North Central Association of Colleges and Schools. It operates on the semester system and offers two summer sessions. Enrollment includes 1,336 full-time and 1,414 part-time students. A faculty of 70 full-time and 27 part-time gives a faculty-student ratio of 1-28. The college offers liberal arts transfer programs, career option programs, and vocational-technical courses. Instrumental and vocal music programs, and intercollegiate and intramural athletics are available. A Cooperative Education program (alternating work and class periods) is offered in business, agriculture, farm equipment mechanics, and nursing. Also offered are: Special Needs programs for students with social, mental, educational problems; precollege and freshman programs for the educationally disadvantaged; and high school completion programs for those without high school diplomas.

Entrance Requirements: Open enrollment; graduation from an accredited high school required for degree programs; non-high school graduates of post-high school age with satisfactory completion of GED admitted to other programs; other non-high school graduates are admitted to certain career-trade programs subject to meeting program requirements; rolling admission, early admission, early decision, delayed admission, midyear admission and advanced placement plans available.

Costs Per Year: $1,760 tuition; $2,848 out-of-state; $2,717 room and board; $300 student fees.

Collegiate Environment: The north and south campuses each house a learning resource center. Together they consist of 36,000 volumes, 3,500 pamphlets, 340 periodicals, 641 microfilms, 3,778 recordings, and 2,622 film strips. Student housing accomodates 124 men and women. About 95% of the students applying for admission are accepted. The college seeks a geographically diverse student body. 167 scholarships are available including 111 freshmen and 90% of the students receive some form of financial assistance.

Community Environment: Estherville is located on the west fork of the Des Moines River, 185 miles northwest of the city of Des Moines. The climate is moderate. The average winter temperature is 14 degrees, and the summer average is 72.9 degrees. Community facilities include a library, churches, hotel, motels, and hospital. A number of lakes in the area provide fishing, boating, and swimming. Iowa's Spirit and Okoboji Lakes are 15 miles away, and there are 11 other lakes nearby.

IOWA STATE UNIVERSITY   *(H-9)*
Alumni Hall
Ames, Iowa 50011-2010
Tel: (515) 294-5836; (800) 262-3810; Admissions: (515) 294-5836;
Fax: (515) 294-2592

Description: The publicly assisted, state university is accredited by the North Central Association of Colleges and Schools and professionally by numerous accrediting institutions. The University is organized into nine Colleges which include the Colleges of Agriculture, Business, Design, Education, Engineering, Family and Consumer Sciences, Veterinary Medicine, Liberal Arts and Sciences, and the Graduate College. As a result of the University's vital contributions in the field of energy, the United States Department of Energy operates a major research center at the University. Overseas study in Germany, France, Spain, England, Australia, Switzerland, Mexico, Scotland, Wales, New Zealand, Korea and Austria is available. Military training is offered through the Army, Navy, and Air Force ROTC programs on

an elective basis. Preparation for state teaching certification is also offered. The university operates on the early semester calendar system and offers one summer session. Enrollment includes 18,652 full-time and 1,660 part-time undergraduates and 4,416 graduate students. A facutly of 1,575 full-time and 184 part-time gives a faculty-student ratio of 1-18.

Entrance Requirements: High school graduation or equivalent with 12 units including 4 English, 3 mathematics, 3 science, 2 social science; rank in upper half of high school class; ACT or SAT I; early admission, deferred admission, midyear admission, rolling admission and advanced placement plans available; $20 application fee; $30 application fee for international students.

Costs Per Year: $2,396 state resident tuition; $8,004 tuition for out-of-state students; $3,382 room and board.

Collegiate Environment: The university is situated on 1,770 rolling acres of prairie in the northwest sector of Ames. The library contains over 1,900,000 volumes, 21,000 periodicals and 2,400,000 microforms. Living accommodations are provided for 8,129 in residence halls, 1,127 in apartments, and 2,781 in fraternities and sororities. 88% of applicants are accepted. 10,500 scholarships are available, including 350 athletic. 75% of the students receive some form of financial aid.

Community Environment: Ames is located approximately 30 miles north of Des Moines. Average annual temperature is 50 degrees, average rainfall is 31 inches, and average snowfall 30 inches. Buses and a municipal airport serve the Ames area. Community facilities include churches, libraries, and radio stations. Facilities for sports include 3 golf courses, 2 bowling alleys, 4 swimming pools and many tennis courts. Ice skating is available at the Cyclone Area Community Center and at Brookside Park and Lake LaVerne in season.

IOWA WESLEYAN COLLEGE   *(K-14)*
601 N. Main
Mount Pleasant, Iowa 52641
Tel: (319) 385-8021; (800) 582-2383; Admissions: (319) 385-6231;
Fax: (319) 385-6296

Description: The privately supported, liberal arts college was established in 1842 and is one of the oldest colleges west of the Mississippi River. The college is affiliated with the United Methodist Church and is accredited by the North Central Association of Colleges and Schools, the National Council for Accreditation of Teacher Education, and the University Senate of the United Methodist Church. The school operates on the 4-1-4 calendar system and offers two summer sessions. Enrollment includes 239 men, 275 women full-time, and 116 men, 243 women part-time. A faculty of 42 full-time and 21 part-time gives a faculty-student ratio of 1-14. The Responsible Social Involvement program (RSI) requires all graduates to have completed 160 work-service clock hours for 6 credit hours toward a degree.

Entrance Requirements: High school graduation or equivalent with completion of 15 units of high school credit; ACT or SAT required; admission plans include early admission, early decision, rolling admission, delayed admission, advanced placement. $15 application fee.

Costs Per Year: Tuition $10,400; $3,550 room and board.

Collegiate Environment: The college accepts 95% of the students who apply for admission, and students may enroll at mid-year as well as in September. The average ACT score for freshmen was 19.6. The campus includes a library of 110,000 volumes and housing facilities for 200 men and 255 women. New Student Week, Homecoming activities, Opportunities in Business, Spring Thing and the President's Reception are some of the outstanding social events of the year. Financial aid is available, and approximately 95% of the current freshman class receive some form of financial assistance. The college recently awarded 182 Bachelor degrees.

Community Environment: Mount Pleasant (population 8,000) is located at the intersection of U.S. Highways 218 and 34; railroads and a municipal airport serve the area. Community facilities include many churches, libraries, a hospital, motels, and civic and fraternal organizations. Part time employment is available. Two state parks are nearby which provide facilities for boating and fishing.

IOWA WESTERN COMMUNITY COLLEGE - CLARINDA CAMPUS   *(L-5)*
923 East Washington
Clarinda, Iowa 51632
Tel: (712) 542-5117; (800) 521-2073; Fax: (712) 542-4608

Description: A publicly supported, junior college, the Clarinda Campus was founded in 1923 and course offerings are primarily liberal arts, with roughly 35% of the enrollment in the vocational-technical division. It is accredited by the North Central Association of Schools and Colleges. Programs of study lead to the Associate degree. The college operates on the quarter system and offers one summer session. Enrollment includes 202 full-time and 170 part-time students. A faculty of 16 full-time and 18 part-time gives a faculty-student ratio of 1-17. Vocal and instrumental music programs, intercollegiate and intramural athletics are available.

Entrance Requirements: Open enrollment policy for HS graduates or equivalent; non-high school graduates may be admitted by successful completion of the GED test; nonresident student requirements are the same as those of resident students.

Costs Per Year: Resident tuition $1,470; nonresident tuition $2,250; room $1,100-$1,400; student fees $45.

Collegiate Environment: The library contains 33,632 volumes, 125 periodicals, 4,438 microforms, and 12,839 audiovisual materials. All applicants who meet the requirements are accepted, and midyear students are admitted. Financial assistance is available. The college does not seek a geographically diverse student body.

Community Environment: Clarinda is a rural community located 80 miles from Omaha, Nebraska, and 130 miles from Des Moines. The climate is seasonal. Community facilities include 17 churches, the Cardinal Canteen, designed and run by students, a hospital and an airport. Part time employment is available. Recreational activities are swimming, boating, water skiing, golf and bowling.

IOWA WESTERN COMMUNITY COLLEGE - COUNCIL BLUFFS CAMPUS   *(J-3)*
2700 College Road
Box 4-C
Council Bluffs, Iowa 51502
Tel: (712) 325-3200; (800) 432-5852; Admissions: (712) 325-3277; Fax: (712) 325-3424

Description: The publicly supported, community college was founded in 1966. It offers liberal arts and vocational-technical programs. It is fully accredited by the North Central Association of Colleges and Schools, Accreditation Board for Engineering and Technology, American Dental Association and the Committee on Allied Health Education and Accreditation. Attendance centers are located at Clarinda, Harlan, Atlantic, and Shenandoah. Army and Air Force ROTC are available. The college operates on the semester system and offers one summer session. Enrollment includes 1,781 full-time and 2,643 part-time students. A faculty of 160 full-time gives a faculty-student ratio of 1-28.

Entrance Requirements: Open enrollment policy for high school graduates; ACT recommended but not required; non-high school graduates may be admitted with GED; college-administered entrance exams required for full-time students; early admission, early decision, rolling admission, midyear admission and advanced placement plans available; $15 application fee.

Costs Per Year: Resident tuition $1,770; nonresidents $2,655; room $1,400; student fees $180; additional expenses average $70.

Collegiate Environment: 98% of students who apply for admission are accepted, including midyear students. The college seeks a geographically diverse student body. Financial aid is available, and 69% of the current student body receives assistance. The library contains 24,000 volumes, and housing facilities are provided for 512 students.

Community Environment: Council Bluffs (population 54,000) is situated on the Missouri River, opposite Omaha, Nebraska, and was for centuries the scene of Native American ceremonial powwows and many other historical events. This is principally a railroad town and farming center but has a diversity of small manufacturing and service businesses.

KIRKWOOD COMMUNITY COLLEGE   *(H-14)*
6301 Kirkwood Boulevard S.W.
Cedar Rapids, Iowa 52406
Tel: (319) 398-5517; (800) 363-2022; Admissions: (319) 398-5517; Fax: (319) 398-1244

Description: This publicly supported community college operates on the semester system and offers four summer terms. It was established in 1965 to serve the areas of Benton, Iowa, Linn, Jones, Johnson, Cedar, and Washington counties. The school is accredited by the Iowa State Department of Public Instruction the North Central Association of Colleges and Schools, the American Dental Association and the Committee on Allied Health Education and Accreditation. College parallel curricula offered in the Arts and Sciences Division have been developed to meet the transfer requirements of four-year colleges and universities in the State of Iowa. Vocational-Technical curricula are approved by the Vocational-Technical Division of the State Department of Public Instruction. The school grants the Diploma, Certificate of completion, and Associate degree. Enrollment is 5,038 full-time and 4,574 part-time students. A faculty of 190 full-time and 251 part-time gives a faculty-student ratio of 1-27.

Entrance Requirements: High school graduation or equivalent; open enrollment policy; ACT recommended for students entering the Arts and Sciences division; ASSET required for students entering the Career Education division; early admission, early decision, midyear admission, rolling admission and advanced placement plans available; no application fee.

Costs Per Year: $1,230 tuition; $2,460 out-of-state.

Collegiate Environment: Almost all students applying for admission are accepted. The college library contains 51,400 volumes, 400 periodicals, 1,300 microforms and 8,000 audiovisual materials. 330 scholarships are available. 56% of the students receive some form of financial aid.

Community Environment: Cedar Rapids/Marion is a dynamic community of 130,000, and Kirkwood students enjoy its many options for recreation, entertainment, and shopping. Located just five minutes north of the campus, downtown Cedar Rapids features a new Five Seasons Center, which holds an arena accommodating 8,000 persons for rock concerts, sports events, auto and ice shows, and more. Numerous restaurants, night spots, and movie theaters round out the entertainment scene. There are 62 parks for swimming, golfing, tennis, boating, and camping, and there is shopping in two large malls and the thriving downtown business districts of Cedar Rapids and Marion. Cultural activity centers around the Cedar Rapids Symphony, Art Museum, and Community Theater, as well as the area's four colleges. Religious activity is based in more than 125 congregations of all faiths. Apartment and condominium housing is available in all price ranges, and more new units are being built. Cedar Rapids/Marion is an attractive and stimulating place to live as well as learn. In addition to the Cedar Rapids campus, there are Kirkwood learning centers in each of the seven counties in the College's service area.

LORAS COLLEGE   *(F-16)*
1450 Alta Vista
Dubuque, Iowa 52001
Tel: (319) 588-7100

Description: This privately supported, liberal arts college is affiliated with the Roman Catholic Church and enrolls 1,624 full-time and 240 part-time students. A faculty of 156 gives an overall faculty-student ratio of 1-13. It operates on a semester basis with three summer sessions. It is accredited by the North Central Association of Colleges and Schools, the American Chemical Society, the Council on Social Work Education and by the Iowa State Department of Instruction. It is one of the three founding members of the Tri-College Consortium (Loras, Clarke and the University of Dubuque). The college is made up of 20 academic departments with 47 majors in the areas of liberal arts, and preprofessional studies. Independent study, individualized majors, and certain areas of cooperative education are available at Loras.

Entrance Requirements: Accredited high school graduation in top one half of class and recommend at least 16 units including 3 English and 2 each in mathematics, natural science and social science; score of 20 on ACT required (SAT may be accepted under certain circumstances); GRE required for graduate school; rolling admission, early admission, early decision, delayed admission and advanced placement plans plans available; $20 application fee.

Costs Per Year: $9,115 tuition; $3,470 approximate room and board.

Collegiate Environment: Approximately 78% of the students applying for admission are accepted as well as midyear students. Average ACT score of the freshman class was 21. The library contains 326,634 volumes and 1,080 periodicals. Housing is available for 500 men and 400 women. The Consortium member institutions, which include Loras, Clarke College, and the University of Dubuque, granted 450 Bachelor's and 85 Master's degrees recently. 75% of students receive some financial aid.

Community Environment: The small city of Dubuque is located on the Mississippi River where Iowa, Illinois and Wisconsin meet. The oldest city in Iowa, it features rugged bluffs and Victorian architecture. Excellent air connections with Chicago's O'Hare Airport and with the Minneapolis-St. Paul Airport are available. The city is the cultural, recreational and commercial centerof the tri-state area. It offers theater, symphony, art galleries, museums, dog racing, riverboat gambling, and concerts. Facilities are available for boating, skiing, golf and tennis.

LUTHER COLLEGE *(C-13)*
700 College Drive
Decorah, Iowa 52101
Tel: (319) 387-1287; Fax: (319) 387-2159

Description: This independent, liberal arts college operates on 4-1-4 system and offers two summer terms. It is accredited by the North Central Association of Colleges and Secondary Schools. It is also professionally accredited by the American Chemical Society, the National Association of Schools of Music, the American Association of Collegiate Schools of Business, the Council on Social Work Education, the National Council for Teacher Accreditation and the National League of Nursing. For 75 years the school admitted men only, but in 1936 it became coeducational. Luther College receives support from the American Lutheran Church. Enrollment is 929 men and 1,362 women full-time and 92 part-time students. A faculty of 156 full-time and 45 part-time gives a faculty-student ratio of 1-13. The school offers a variety of liberal arts, professional and preprofessional programs, and grants the Bachelor degree. Religion courses are required. Overseas programs in Germany, France, Austria, Malta, Spain, England, Japan, China, Hong Kong and Norway are available. The college also offers extensive vocal and instrumental music programs, and intercollegiate and intramural athletics.

Entrance Requirements: Accredited high school graduation or equivalent with rank in upper half of class; completion of 4 English, 3 mathematics, 2 lab science, and 3 social studies units; SAT or ACT required, minimum ACT 21; early admission, rolling admission, delayed admission and advanced placement plans available; $20 application fee.

Costs Per Year: $13,240 tuition; $3,560 room and board.

Collegiate Environment: Located in scenic Northeast Iowa bluff country, Luther has an expansive 800-acre campus with 24 modern buildings. The library contains more than 300,000 volumes and numerous microforms and sound recordings. 89% of the students who apply for admission are accepted including midyear students. 70% of the student body graduated in the top quarter of the high school class, and 91% graduated in the top half. Students participate in planning social and cultural programs and activities, and there is joint student-faculty community assembly. The college provides assistance to economically disadvantaged students and more than 80% of the students receive some form of financial aid. Approximately 89% of the previous freshman class returned to the campus for the second year. The college welcomes students from various geographical locations. All students are required to live on campus. College housing facilities accommodate 2,016 students.

Community Environment: Decorah (population 8,000) is on the banks of the Upper Iowa River, in an area known as Little Switzerland, in northeast Iowa. Twin Springs and Siewer Springs state fish hatcheries are nearby. Decorah has set aside more than 328 acres for recreation. Outdoor activities include golf, skiing, hiking, hunting and fishing.

MAHARISHI INTERNATIONAL UNIVERSITY *(K-13)*
Fairfield, Iowa 52557-1155
Tel: (515) 472-5031; Fax: (515) 472-1189

Description: Maharishi International University is a private, non-sectarian, coeducational institution founded in 1971 by Maharishi Mahesh Yogi. The University is accredited by the North Central Association of Colleges and Schools. MIU offers six doctoral programs, fourteen master's programs and seventeen baccalaureate programs, and an associate of arts program in the sciences, arts and humanities. Enrollment includes 440 full-time and 121 part-time undergraduates and 185 graduate students. A faculty of 71 full-time and 11 part-time gives a faculty-student ratio of 1-11. The University operates on a semester calendar system which is based on the block system. Students take one course at a time, full-time, in blocks of one week to one month. MIU students are required to practice transcendental meditation as part of their curriculum.

Entrance Requirements: Applicants are evaluated on the basis of academic achievement, academic and personal promise, motivation, dedication, and maturity. The materials required for admissions are completed application and fee, official high school transcripts, personal recommendations; SAT or ACT for all students; TOEFL for international students from non-English speaking countries; an interview on or off campus with a representative of the University is strongly recommended but not required; rolling and midyear admission plans available; $25 application fee for undergraduates and $40 for graduate students.

Costs Per Year: Undergraduate: $13,760 tuition; $3,728 room and board; $216 activity fee. Graduate: $14,984 tuition and fees

Collegiate Environment: The MIU campus covers 262 acres and has 1.2 million square feet of building space, including dormitories and dining halls, classrooms, research and teaching laboratories in the sciences, electronic engineering, computer science, mathematics, languages, visual technologies, video production, music, and human performance (physical fitness), a library with the latest computer technology and an elementary and secondary school. The Historic Campus District, registered with the National Registry of Historic Places, consists of a circle of five buildings dating from 1857-1912. The library has a collection of 147,000 bound volumes and subscribes to 1,326 periodicals, 49,000 microform units and numerous CD-ROM rference sources. There are also abundant resources for study and research, including public use Internet and work stations giving students access to library catalogues in most countries worldwide. The library is also equipped with FirstSearch, a service giving internet users anywhere on campus direct electronic access to more than 40 reference databases. Another database, WorldCat, provides direct electronic access to the world's largest library information network (18,000 libraries sharing more than 32 million books, journals and other information). MIU provides state-of-the-art technologies for rapid delivery of documents located electronically, and a campus-wide close-circuit television network with approximately 9,300 hours of videotaped and audiotaped courses, conferences, presentations, and live satellite broadcast receiving capability. The new sports complex houses four tennis courts, three basketball/volleyball courts, a running track, gymnastics area, weight room, archery range, golf driving range, and batting cages. Outdoor athletic facilities include a swimming pool, a track, a soccer stadium, and a jogging/exercise course. Both large and small dormitory facilities are spread throughout the campus and offer single and double-occupancy rooms. All dormitories are single-sex. All unmarried students under age 30 are required to reside on campus. 67% of applicants are accepted. Scholarships are available and 84% of the students receive some form of financial aid.

Community Environment: The University is located in the City of Fairfield, in the southeast corner of Iowa. A thirty percent growth in the population and the appearance of numerous new businesses in Fairfield in recent years have spurred an unprecedented level of economic and cultural growth in the community. Fairfield is viewed as one of the great success stories in Iowa, and is recognized throughout the state for its creativity in business, the arts, and education. Fairfield is located within easy access of Chicago, St. Louis, and Kansas City, and is only one hour south of Iowa City where the University of Iowa is located.

MARSHALLTOWN COMMUNITY COLLEGE (G-10)
3700 South Center Street
Marshalltown, Iowa 50158
Tel: (515) 752-7106; Fax: (515) 752-8149

Description: This publicly supported, community college is accredited by the North Central Association of Colleges and Schools and professionally by program accrediting institutions including the American Dental Association, for dental assisting. It is a member of the Iowa Valley Community College District. It operates on the semester system with one summer session. Enrollment includes 291 men, 477 women full-time, and 139 men, and 364 women part-time. A faculty of 45 full-time and 68 part-time provides a ratio of 1-15. In addition to academic subjects, it offers community-oriented and participatory instrumental music programs, and intercollegiate and intramural athletics. Pre-college and freshman programs for the disabled and educationally disadvantaged are available. Army ROTC is offered.

Entrance Requirements: Accredited high school graduation or equivalent; open enrollment; applicants for transfer programs to a four-year college or university should meet prerequisites of the particular institution; post-high school age applicants who do not have high school diplomas may apply for conditional admission; applicants not meeting all requirements will be admitted into appropriate basic skills program; early decision, deferred admission, midyear admission and rolling admission plans available; application fee $25.

Costs Per Year: $3,870 (30 credit hours/year) resident tuition; $7,740 tuition required for out-of-state or international students; $150 ($5/credit hour) student fees.

Collegiate Environment: Library contains 35,000 titles, 286 periodicals, 2,813 microforms and 4,286 audiovisual materials. 100% of applicants are accepted, and students may enroll at any time. The college accepts a geographically diverse student body. Since 1966, the college has offered a summer program and courses are determined on the basis of student needs and availability qualified faculty members. 256 scholarships are available, including 64 for freshmen.

Community Environment: Marshalltown, an industrial city in central Iowa, is an important bus and truck terminal. The community facilities include 32 churches, hospitals, a library and many civic service clubs, as well as a Chamber of Commerce. Opportunities for part time or seasonal employment are excellent. Recreational facilities include an expanding park system; three golf courses; YMCA; two swimming pools; large youth soccer, football, and Little League complexes; a five-mile in-city walk/jog/bike path with greenbelt environment; new playgrounds; two bowling alleys; and three theaters.

MORNINGSIDE COLLEGE (F-1)
1501 Morningside Ave.
Sioux City, Iowa 51106
Tel: (712) 274-5111; Fax: (712) 274-5101

Description: The privately supported, liberal arts college has an enrollment of 423 men and 542 women in the day division, 124 students in evening classes, and 129 graduate students. A faculty of 64 full-time provides a teacher-student ratio of 1-15. It was established in 1894 by the United Methodist Church and has maintained a continuous and close relationship since that time. The college is accredited by the North Central Association of Colleges and Secondary Schools, the National Council for Accreditation of Teacher Education, the Iowa Board of Nursing, the National League for Nursing, the National Association of Schools of Music, and the University Senate of the United Methodist Church. The school operates on the semester basis and offers a May Interim and two summer terms. It is authorized to grant the Bachelor and Master degrees. Exchange programs exist with Kansai Gaidai University in Japan, University of Caen in France, and Edge Hill College and Oxford University in England.

Entrance Requirements: Accredited high school graduation or equivalent with a recommended minimum of 16 units, including 4 English, 2 mathematics, 2 science, 3 social science, and 1 foreign language; SAT or ACT required; early admission, early decision, rolling admission and advanced placement available; $15 application fee.

Costs Per Year: $10,210 tuition; $3,520 room and board; $166 student fees.

Collegiate Environment: The college seeks a geographically diverse student body, and enrolls students at midyear as well as in September.

Housing facilities for 660 students include men and women residence halls, coed residence halls, married student apartments and two Greek houses. 87% of applicants accepted. Financial aid is available and 95% of students receive some form. Academic scholarships and talent grants are available to both incoming freshman and upperclass students. The college library contains 115,699 volumes, 130,079 microforms, 3,375 audio materials, 901 film and video materials, and 588 periodical subscriptions.

Community Environment: See Briar Cliff College.

MOUNT MERCY COLLEGE (H-14)
1330 Elmhurst Drive N.E.
Cedar Rapids, Iowa 52402
Tel: (319) 363-8213; (800) 248-4504; Admissions: (319) 368-6460;
Fax: (319) 363-5270

Description: This privately supported, Roman Catholic, liberal arts college is accredited by the North Central Association of Colleges and Schools. It offers a liberal arts curriculum, including preparation for the state teaching certificate. The college operates on the 4-1-4 semester system and offers two summer sessions. Enrollment includes 713 full-time and 514 part-time students. A faculty of 62 full-time and 36 part-time provides a faculty-student ratio of 1-13.

Entrance Requirements: Accredited high school graduation or equivalent with C average and rank in upper 50% of class; completion of 16 units including 4 English, 2 mathematics, 1 laboratory science, and 2 social studies; ACT required, minimum score 19; early admission, rolling admission, delayed admission and advanced placement plans available; May 1 application deadline; $20 application fee.

Costs Per Year: $10,500 tuition; $3,555 room and board; $500 average additional expenses.

Collegiate Environment: The college is situated on a 36-acre campus northeast of the business section of Cedar Rapids. The college library contains over 96,000 volumes, 658 periodicals, 1,042 microforms, and 3,474 audiovisual materials. A new recreation/athletic center was constructed in 1985 and campus housing was expanded. Two dormitories and apartment-style living accommodate 500 resident students. The college accepts 90% of the students applying for admission, and seeks a geographically diverse student body. Students may enroll at midyear as well as in September. Financial aid is available. Of 1,043 scholarships available, 107 are for freshmen. 85% of the current students receive some form of assistance.

Community Environment: See Kirkwood Community College.

MOUNT SAINT CLARE COLLEGE (H-18)
400 N. Bluff Blvd.
Clinton, Iowa 52732
Tel: (319) 242-4023; (800) 242-2003; Admissions: (319) 242-4253;
Fax: (319) 242-2003

Description: The privately supported college is conducted by the Roman Catholic Sisters of Saint Francis and is accredited by the North Central Association of Colleges and Schools. Members of other denominations are welcome as are students from various geographical locations. It is the aim of Mount Saint Clare to provide the background work for a liberal education and the student is encouraged to look upon education as a long-range process. The college also offers the Bachelor degree in Business Administration, Accounting, Computer Information Systems, Liberal Arts, Social Science, Clinical Cytotechnology, and a Bachelor of General Studies. The college grants the Associate and Bachelor degree. The school operates on the semester system and offers three summer sessions. Enrollment is 400 full-time and 100 part-time students. A faculty of 23 full-time and 24 part-time gives a faculty-student ratio of 1-11.

Entrance Requirements: Accredited high school graduation or equivalent with rank in upper 50% of class; ACT required; rolling admission, midyear admission and advanced placement plans available; $20 application fee.

Costs Per Year: $10,300 tuition; $3,800 room and board; $80 student fees.

Collegiate Environment: The library was built in 1958 and houses 75,000 volumes, with 1,200 current periodicals available in the reading room. Living accommodations are provided for 200 students. The college offers a special orientation program to entering students to give them an overview of college life, and guidance services are provided. The college brings public speakers and musicians of renown to the campus. The college also sponsors educational tours to Europe if there is sufficient interest shown by the student body. 90% of the students who apply for admission are accepted, including midyear students. The average score of the entering freshman class was ACT 20.5 composite. Financial aid is available, and 94% of the full-time students receive some form of financial assistance.

Community Environment: Mount St. Clare College is located on a wooded bluff overlooking the Mississippi River in Clinton, Iowa (population 35,000). Situated midway between Chicago and Des Moines, the city of Clinton is home to a minor league baseball team, a symphony orchestra, a pre-professional ballet company, summer stock theater, art shows, and other cultural events. Clinton is 45 minutes from the Quad Cities, three hours from Chicago, and five hours from Minneapolis. The quality of life in the city and on campus is typical of the wholesome lifestyle the Midwest is known for throughout the country.

Branch Campuses: Maquakata, IA; Sauk Valley, IL.

MUSCATINE COMMUNITY COLLEGE   *(J-15)*
152 Colorado Street
Muscatine, Iowa 52761
Tel: (319) 263-8250; (800) 462-3255; Fax: (319) 264-8341

Description: This publicly supported branch of the Eastern Iowa Community College District is accredited by the North Central Association of Colleges and Schools. The college offers programs in vocational-technical and academic areas. It grants Certificates and Associate degrees. The college operates on the semester system and offers two summer sessions. Enrollment includes 624 full-time and 633 part-time students. A faculty of 33 gives a faculty-student ratio of 1-17.

Entrance Requirements: Open enrollment policy; all high school graduates are accepted; GED also accepted; non-high school graduates are considered under special arrangements; completion of 15 units required; early admission, midyear admission, rolling admission, and advanced placement plans available; $20 application fee.

Costs Per Year: $1,504 in-state tuition; $2,256 out-of-state (based on 16 credit hours).

Collegiate Environment: The college occupies a campus adjoining Weed Park. The college has provided over 50 years of service to the Muscatine Area. All applicants are accepted. Financial assistance is available and 54% receive some form of aid. The library consists of 19,588 titles, 176 periodicals, 1,754 and audiovisual materials.

Community Environment: Muscatine, an industrial center, is located on the Mississippi River, and has an annual mean temperature of 50 degrees, and an average rainfall of 34 inches. Vegetables and melons are raised in the vicinity; over three million bushels of grain are shipped from here each year. Community facilities include many churches and a library. Parks, a golf course, a bowling alley and skating rink offer recreation. The Mississippi River and nearby Cedar and Iowa rivers provide excellent picnicking, fishing and boat launching facilities. Points of interest are the Laura Musser Art Gallery and Museum, and Weed Park.

NORTH IOWA AREA COMMUNITY COLLEGE   *(C-10)*
500 College Drive
Mason City, Iowa 50401
Tel: (515) 423-1264

Description: The publicly supported, liberal arts and technological junior college was founded in 1918 and was formerly known as Mason City Junior College. It became an area community college in 1966. It is accredited by the North Central Association of Colleges and Schools and operates on the semester system with one summer term. In addition to academic and vocational-technical subjects, the college offers vocal and instrumental music programs, intercollegiate and intramural athletics. A Cooperative Education program in business subjects is also offered. Programs for the educationally disadvantaged are available. Recent enrollment included 863 men, 950 women full-time, 403 men, and 662 women part-time with a faculty of 84 full-time members.

Entrance Requirements: Accredited high school graduation or GED equivalent; open enrollment; non-high school graduates and those not meeting all requirements may be admitted as special students; ACT and college entrance examinations required in certain programs for placement; midyear admission, early decision, rolling admission plans available.

Costs Per Year: $1,832 tuition; $2,648 tuition for out-of-state students; $5,400 room and board.

Collegiate Environment: The community college is comprised of 8 buildings on 310 acres. The library contains 36,000 volumes. Housing is provided for 440 students. 83% of the applicants are accepted, including mid-year students. 48% of the previous freshman class returned to the campus for a second year. The average score for entering freshmen was ACT 19.8 composite. Average high school standing, top 50%: 13% in top quarter, 40% in top half. 57 scholarships, including 31 for freshmen are available and 66% of the student body receives some form of aid. Courses begin in September and January and a summer term begins in June.

Community Environment: Mason City (population 30,379) is located in the north center of the state midway between Des Moines and Minneapolis - St. Paul, and has an average winter temperature of 28 degrees, summer average 63 degrees. One bus line and an airline offer transportation. The community facilities include hospitals, a library, Art Center, hotels and motels. Brick, tile and Portland cement are manufactured from the deposits of clay, limestone and sand in this area. Part-time work is available. Recreation activities include golf, water sports in summer, ice boating in winter, ice skating, pheasant and duck hunting.

NORTHEAST IOWA COMMUNITY COLLEGE   *(C-13)*
Box 400
Calmar, Iowa 52132
Tel: (319) 562-3263; (800) 788-2256

Description: Founded in 1966, this comprehensive community college serves the transfer, technical, and vocational educational needs of northeast Iowa residents, business, and industries. The school is accredited by the North Central Association of Colleges and Schools. It offers over 50 vocational and technical programs, as well as the Associate in Arts degree and general education courses. NICC offers programs leading to Associate in Arts, Associate in Science with a Career Option, or Associate in Applied Science degrees, and diplomas. Students may major in a wide variety of majors in business, health, industrial technologies, and agriculture fields. Unique areas such as Nondestructive Testing and John Deere Ag Tech are available. The school operates on the semester system and offers one summer session. Enrollment includes 1,410 full-time and 1,130 part-time students. A faculty of 150 full-time and part-time gives a faculty-student ratio of 1-20.

Entrance Requirements: High school graduation or equivalent; students will be accepted into programs in which they demonstrate reasonable potential for success; ASSET required; early admission, midyear admission, and advanced placement plans available.

Costs Per Year: $1,860 ($60 per credit) resident tuition; $3,720 ($120 per credit) nonresident; $8.25 per credit hour student fees.

Collegiate Environment: The campuses are located in one of the most beautiful areas of the Midwest. Northeast Iowa contains rolling hills, picturesque streams, wooded areas, lush farmland and natural beauty. The campuses at Calmar and Peosta and the Dubuque Downtown Center feature modern and attractive facilities. A library of 21,918 volumes, classrooms and well equipped labs are a part of the setting. Financial aid is available and 60% of students receive some form of aid.

Community Environment: Calmar is located 10 miles from Decorah, 25 miles from Cresco, 17 miles from Postville, and 24 miles from New Hampton. The town's primary business is agriculture and related fields. Two firms here manufacture furniture and truck racks. Recreational facilities are provided by Calmar Lake, Upper Iowa River, and Turkey River, which furnish great opportunity for fishing and hunting. Northeast Iowa operates a second campus at Peosta, Iowa, which is located approximately ten miles west of the city of Dubuque. The rural area of Peosta is similar to that of Calmar, except that it is close to the metropolitan area of Dubuque, which has a population of nearly 70,000. It offers a wide range of cultural and recreational activities and is situated on the Mississippi River. The popularity of Northeast

Iowa is pointed out by the growing numbers of tourists who travel to the area from all over the Midwest.

Branch Campuses: Northeast Iowa Community College, 10250 Sundown Road, Peosta, IA 52068.

NORTHWEST IOWA COMMUNITY COLLEGE (C-3)
603 West Park Street
Sheldon, Iowa 51201
Tel: (712) 324-5061; (800) 352-4907; Fax: (712) 324-4136

Description: The publicly supported, two-year community college has an enrollment of 281 men and 148 women full-time, 38 men and 107 women part-time. A faculty of 35 full-time and 20 part-time gives a faculty-student ratio of 1-12. It serves the district known officially as Merged Area IV, and consists of Lyon, O'Brien, Sioux, and Osceola counties and part of Cherokee County. The college operates on the semester system and offers one summer session. The school is accredited by the North Central Association of Colleges and Secondary Schools.

Entrance Requirements: Accredited high school graduation or equivalent; completion of following units: 3 English, 1 math, 2 social science, and 2 science; non-high school graduates 16 years of age or older who show aptitude, interest and ability to benifit by instruction also admitted; diagnostic test may be required for certain programs; rolling admission, early admission, and midyear admission plans are available; $10 application fee.

Costs Per Year: $2,080 tuition and fees; $3,120 out-of-state; $2,125 room and board.

Collegiate Environment: The school is located on a new 146-acre site, one mile west of Sheldon. It contains modern, fully equipped educational facilities. The library houses 8,904 volumes. Dormitory housing is available for 40 students. 95% of the students who apply for admission are accepted. New students may enroll at the beginning of each semester. Financial aid is available and 72% of the current student body receives some form of assistance. Scholarships are available for 22 freshmen.

Community Environment: Sheldon (population 5,100) is the trading center for a rich, five-county farmland area. Bus and train transportation are available, airline service is within 55 miles at Sioux City. Local parks and a golf club provide facilities for recreation. The Iowa Lakes Region is a 50 mile drive. Community facilities include public libraries, churches, a modern hospital, and an indoor swimming pool.

NORTHWESTERN COLLEGE (D-2)
101 College Lane
Orange City, Iowa 51041
Tel: (712) 737-7130; (800) 747-4757; Fax: (712) 737-8847

Description: The privately supported, Christian, liberal arts college is affiliated with the Reformed Church in America, accredited by the North Central Association of Colleges and Schools and by the National Council for Accreditation of Teacher Education. It offers programs leading to the Bachelor of Arts degree and an Associate of Arts degree in Office Management. It was founded in 1882 as Northwestern Academy and began its four-year program in 1957. The college operates on the semester system and offers three summer terms. Enrollment includes 1,141 full-time undergraduate students. A faculty of 50 full-time, 30 part-time gives a faculty-student ratio of 1-16. Intercollegiate, intramural athletics and extensive vocal and instrumental music programs are available. Religion courses are required.

Entrance Requirements: Accredited high school graduation or equivalent with completion of 16 units recommended including 4 English, 3 mathematics, 2 science, 2 social science; minimum score of 16 on ACT required, SAT may be substituted; applicants not meeting all requirements may be accepted with provisional status; rolling admission, delayed admission, and advanced placement plans available; August 15 application deadline; $25 application fee.

Costs Per Year: $9,900 tuition; $3,075 room and board.

Collegiate Environment: The campus of more than 40 acres is located on the south border of Orange City, a growing Dutch community situated in northwest Iowa. The library contains 131,000 volumes and dormitory facilities are provided for 340 men, 420 women and 25 families. The college holds chapel services 5 days a week and attendance is required 3 times a week. 86% of the students who apply for

admission are accepted, including midyear students. The college welcomes a geographically diverse student body. Financial aid is available for economically disadvantaged students and 91% of the current student body receive some form of financial aid. 82% of the previous freshman class returned to the college for their sophomore year.

Community Environment: Orange City (population 5,000) is a rural town enjoying a good climate. Airlines are within 45 miles. Community facilities include a public library, churches, a hospital, medical clinic, musical groups, professional concert series, and literary organizations. Tulip Time in May is an annual event.

PALMER COLLEGE OF CHIROPRACTIC (I-17)
1000 Brady Street
Davenport, Iowa 52803
Tel: (319) 326-9600; Fax: (319) 326-8409

Description: Palmer College of Chiropractic is a private graduate professional college, founded by D. D. Palmer, Father of Chiropractic. The Academic year is based on a trimester system and one summer session is offered. Enrollment is 1,998 with a faculty of 132 full-time, giving a faculty to student of ratio 1-15. Palmer College is fully accredited by the North Central Association of Colleges and Schools and the Council on Chiropractic Education, fully approved by the Iowa Department of Education, Veterans Administration, and the United States Immigration and Naturalization Service.

Entrance Requirements: The entrance requirements are sixty semester (or ninety quarter hours) of undergraduate coursework at 2.25/4.0 grade average. Prerequisites must include six semester hours each of biological science, organic chemistry, inorganic chemistry, college physics; all courses accompanied by laboratories. Also required are six semester hours in English-communication skills, fifteen semester hours in social sciences or humanities, and three semester hours of psychology. Rolling admission and delayed admission plans. Application fee is $50.

Costs Per Year: $4,290 tuition per trimester, $3,276 room and board per trimester; additional transportation and personal expenses.

Collegiate Environment: Many campus activities are available through professional organizations, fraternities, and athletic clubs (national collegiate rugby champions). Over 80 clubs are active on campus. The college has a strong student government and exceptional college newspaper, The Beacon. Library holding include 49,084 volumes. 11% of students are international. The campus community is closely knit because all students are working for the same goal. 316 scholarships are available and 95% of the student body receives financial aid.

Community Environment: Palmer College is located in Davenport, Iowa, part of the Quad-Cities on the Iowa-Illinois border, divided by the Mississippi River. Metropolitan area population about 390,000.

SAINT AMBROSE UNIVERSITY (I-17)
518 West Locust
Davenport, Iowa 52803
Tel: (319) 383-8845

Description: The privately supported, Roman Catholic, liberal arts university is accredited by the North Central Association of Colleges and Schools. Originally established for men only, it now accepts women into its liberal arts undergraduate and graduate programs. It operates on the semester system and offers one summer session. Enrollment includes 1,227 men and 1,357 women. A faculty of 105 full-time and 85 part-time gives a faculty-student ratio of 1-14.

Entrance Requirements: Accredited high school graduation with minimum 2.5 GPA and ACT 20 for full admission; 2.0 GPA and ACT 15 for subject-to-review admission; 15 units required includes 4 English, 3 math, 3 social science, 3 science, 2 foreign language; early admission, early decision, midyear admission, and rolling admission plans available; $25 application fee.

Costs Per Year: $10,500 tuition; $1,710-$2,400 room; $2,050-$2,310 board.

Collegiate Environment: The college library holdings include 150,000 bound volumes. Housing is available for 900 students. Approximately 80% of applicants are accepted, including midyear students. The university seeks a geographically diverse student body.

Financial aid is available and 92% receive some form of financial assistance.

Community Environment: Davenport, with a population of 100,000, is within a bi-state quad-city area (greater population 360,000) near the Mississippi River.

SCOTT COMMUNITY COLLEGE   *(I-17)*
500 Belmont Road
Bettendorf, Iowa 52722
Tel: (319) 359-7531

Description: The publicly supported comphrensive community college operates on the semester system and offers two summer sessions. The college is accredited by the North Central Association of Colleges and Schools and is one of three schools which are part of the Eastern Iowa Community College District. It grants certificates, diplomas, and the Associate degree. Enrollment is 4,000 students. A faculty of 77 full-time, 120 part-time gives a faculty-student ratio of 1-33.

Entrance Requirements: Open enrollment policy for students; accredited high school graduation or equivalent required; under certain conditions non-high school graduates may be admitted; rolling admission, delayed admission, early admission, early decision and advanced placement plans available; $20 application fee.

Costs Per Year: $1,570 state resident tuition; out-of-state tuition $2,775; $130 student fees.

Collegiate Environment: All of those applying for admission are accepted, including midyear students. Financial aid is available, and 50% of the current student body receive some form of assistance. The college is located on a 181-acre campus, completed in 1974. The library contains 18,549 volumes, 161 periodicals, 702 microforms and 1,712 audiovisual materials.

Community Environment: See Marycrest College

Branch Campuses: Urban Center, Career Assistant Center

SIMPSON COLLEGE   *(J-9)*
701 N. C
Indianola, Iowa 50125-1299
Tel: (515) 961-6251; (800) 362-2454; Fax: (515) 961-1498

Description: Founded in 1860, the privately supported college of liberal arts and sciences is affiliated with the United Methodist Church and is accredited by the North Central Association of Colleges and Schools, the National Association of Schools of Music, and the University Senate of the United Methodist Church. The regular academic year consists of a 14-week fall semester, a 14-week spring semester and a 3-week program during the month of May. The May term is provided for intensive study in a single academic course. The school also offers two summer sessions. Enrollment is 1,071 full-time and 542 part-time students. A faculty of 72 full-time and 97 part-time gives an overall faculty-student ratio of 1-13. Cooperative education programs (alternating work and class periods) are available in all academic departments. Overseas programs include Europe, China, Japan, Central America, and Russia. May term and summer study programs are also offered. In addition to liberal arts programs, the college offers preprofessional courses for medical technology, nursing, law, physical therapy, optometry, veterinary pharmacy, medicine, and dentistry, theology, and engineering. Extracurricular activities include instrumental and vocal music programs, intercollegiate and intramural athletics, foreign language clubs, Amnesty International, student government, Greek organizations, theater groups, academic clubs, and a religious life council.

Entrance Requirements: Accredited high school graduation in top half of class; ACT or SAT required; early admission, early decision, rolling admission, delayed admission, and advanced placement plans available.

Costs Per Year: $12,050 tuition; $3,980 room and board; additional expenses average $2,200.

Collegiate Environment: The college accepts 87% of the students who apply for admission, including midyear students and students from various geographical locations. Dormitory space is available for 574 students, and fraternities and sororities accommodate an additional 338 students. All students under 23, except those who are married or living with parents or relatives, are required to live in college residence halls, in fraternity or sorority houses, or in other college-approved housing. The library contains 145,905 volumes, 593 periodicals and 10,610 microfilms. Financial aid is available, and 90% of the current student body receives some form of assistance.

Community Environment: Indianola (population 13,000) is located 20 minutes from Des Moines, the state capital, and enjoys the advantages of both a charming small town and a metropolitan center. Major transportation facilities are found in Des Moines, including the Des Moines International Airport. While Des Moines is known as a commercial and industrial city in the heart of a great agricultural state, it is also known for its educational, cultural, philanthropic, and religious institutions.

SOUTHEASTERN COMMUNITY COLLEGE - KEOKUK
(N-15)
355 Messenger Road
Keokuk, Iowa 52632
Tel: (319) 524-3221

Description: The publicly supported, junior college is fully accredited by North Central Association of Colleges and Schools, the State Department of Public Instruction and the Iowa Committee of Secondary School and College Relations. Transfer courses have been carefully planned to correspond with the work in four-year colleges and universities in the midwest. The school operates on the semester basis with one summer session and includes a total enrollment of 600. A faculty of 24 gives a ratio of 22:1. The college has both the Arts and Science Division and a Vocational-Technical Division.

Entrance Requirements: Open enrollment; accredited high school graduation for college transfer programs; any high school graduate or post-high school age applicant may be admitted to vocational-technical programs. Rolling admission and advanced placement plans.

Costs Per Year: $532 tuition; $798 non-state residents; $36 student fees.

Collegiate Environment: Most students in attendance at the college commute and the college does not seek a geographically diverse student body but midyear students may enroll. A work-study program is offered by the school to assist economically handicapped students. The library contains 51,500 volumes, 260 periodicals, 43 microforms, 600 audiovisual materials. 85% of the student body receives financial aid.

Community Environment: An industrial city, Keokuk (population 14,631) is located in the extreme southeast tip of Iowa, overlooking Illinois and Missouri. The climate is seasonal.

SOUTHEASTERN COMMUNITY COLLEGE - WEST
BURLINGTON   *(L-15)*
1015 South Gear Avenue
P.O. Box Drawer F
West Burlington, Iowa 52655
Tel: (319) 752-2731; Fax: (319) 752-4957

Description: The publicly supported, two-year college is accredited by the Iowa State Board of Public Instruction, the Iowa State Board of Regents, and the North Central Association of Colleges and Schools. It operates on the semester system. Enrollment includes 1,264 full-time and 744 part-time students. A faculty of 75 full-time, 10 part-time gives a ratio of 1:23. The Burlington campus has an Arts and Science Division which offers courses that are readily transferable to any college or university. The Career Education (Vocational-Technical) Division offers courses in business education, health occupations, and technical, trade, and industrial curricula. Grants Diploma and Associate degrees.

Entrance Requirements: Open enrollment policy; accredited high school graduation required for college transfer programs; ASSET requested; early admission, early decision, rolling admission and delayed admission plans.

Costs Per Year: $1,400 tuition; $2,100 non-state residents; $2,400 room; $64 student fees.

Collegiate Environment: 100% of the students applying for admission are accepted and mid-year students are admitted. 40% of the previous freshman class returned to the campus for their sophomore year. The library contains 42,439 volumes, 215 periodicals, 6,425 microforms, 27,187 audiovisual materials. 45% of the students receive financial aid.

Community Environment: West Burlington, an urban area and a manufacturing and distributing point, enjoys a temperate climate. Community facilities include hospitals, health center, good shopping areas and the usual major civic, fraternal, and veterans' organizations. Part time employment is available. The recreational facilities include marinas, municipal dock, swimming pool, tennis courts, golf courses, and the facilities of Geode State Park, 11 miles from downtown.

SOUTHWESTERN COMMUNITY COLLEGE   (K-7)
1501 West Townline Road
Creston, Iowa 50801
Tel: (515) 782-7081; (800) 247-4023; Fax: (515) 782-3312

Description: The publicly supported, junior college provides a liberal arts program, vocational-technical education and adult education. It operates on the early semester system and offers two summer sessions. The school is fully accredited by the North Central Association of Colleges and Schools. Enrollment includes 800 full-time and 391 part-time students. A faculty of 101 gives a faculty-student ratio of 1-14.

Entrance Requirements: Accredited high school graduation or equivalent; open enrollment policy; non-high school graduates may enroll in programs for which they qualify; ACT recommended for those taking college parallel course; rolling admission plan available.

Costs Per Year: $1,696 tuition; $2,416 out-of-state; $2,400 room and board.

Collegiate Environment: The college accepts all applicants, and students are admitted at midyear as well as in September. The college provides dormitory space for approximately 31 women and 42 men. The library contains 19,368 volumes. All students are assigned to a faculty member who acts as their advisor. Placement service is also available. Financial aid is available, and 80% of the current student body receives some form of assistance. Approximately 55% of the previous freshman class returned to the campus for the sophomore year.

Community Environment: Creston (population 8,234) is a town in an area of both urban and rural sections. Railroad and bus service and air charter service are available. The community provides a public library, 20 churches, a hospital, medical clinic, shopping areas and a number of civic organizations. Part-time employment is available. Recreation facilities are available on three lakes for water sports. Hunting, fishing, ice skating, golf, tennis and spectator sports are all enjoyed within this community.

TEIKYO MARYCREST UNIVERSITY   (I-17)
1607 West 12th Street
Davenport, Iowa 52804
Tel: (319) 326-9512; (800) 728-9705; Admissions: (319) 326-9225; Fax: (319) 326-9250

Description: The privately supported, liberal arts college was opened in 1939 under the auspices of the Roman Catholic Church. It is accredited by the North Central Association of Colleges and Schools, the Council on Social Work Education, and the National League for Nursing. Offers preparation for state teaching certificate. Operates on semester system with various summer programs. Offers vocal music programs, inter-collegiate basketball, soccer, volley ball, cross-country, baseball, softball intra-mural athletics. Enrollment includes 1,200 students. A faculty of 81 gives a faculty-student ratio of 1-14.

Entrance Requirements: Accredited high school graduation or equivalent with "C" average and completion of 15 units; nonaccredited high school graduates may be accepted with satisfactory scores on series of examinations; rolling admission. $25 application fee.

Costs Per Year: $4,990 tuition per semester; $3,660 room and board; $168 student fees; additional expenses average $900 per year.

Collegiate Environment: The college consists of 8 buildings on a 23-acre campus which includes a library of 109,000 volumes, 16,444 pamphlets, 554 periodicals, 22,200 audio visual materials. Residence halls accommodate 230 students. Scholarships are available and 65% of students receive financial aid. Teikyo Marycrest University con-

tains a geographically diverse student body at its Davenport campus. 66% of its students were in the top quarter of their high school class.

Community Environment: Davenport (population 100,400), part of the Iowa-Illinois Quad Cities (375,000 population), is situated on the north bank of the Mississippi River, having an average temperature of 57 degrees and average rainfall of 50 inches. Commercial transportation is available. Community facilities are excellent including 91 churches, hotels, hospitals, four local radio stations, four TV stations, a public library, and numerous civic and service organizations. Some of the industries' products are brooms, clothing, food, machinery, foundry products, and aircraft instruments. The 27 city parks offer varied recreational facilities. In Vandeer Veer Park are rose gardens with approximately 2,500 species of roses.

TEIKYO WESTMAR UNIVERSITY   (E-2)
1002 3 Ave. S.E.
Le Mars, Iowa 51031
Tel: (712) 546-2070; (800) 352-4634; Fax: (712) 546-2080

Description: The privately supported, liberal arts university is accredited on probation by the North Central Association of Colleges and Schools. The college operates on the semester system and offers two summer sessions. Enrollment is 305 men and 146 women full-time, 83 men and 32 women part-time. A faculty of 30 full-time and 37 part-time provides a faculty-student ratio of 1-14. Teikyo Westmar is affiliated with Brethren Colleges Abroad, which sponsors a Junior Year in Marburg, Germany. Students may participate in HECUA-sponsored programs in Chicago and Minneapolis as well as Scandinavia and South America. International internship opportunities in nearly any field are available in Japan, England and the Netherlands. Religion courses are required. In addition to liberal arts, the university offers international business, management, marketing, and finance. Preparation for state teaching certificate is available.

Entrance Requirements: 2 of the following 3 criteria must be met: 2.3 grade point average, 20 ACT, and rank in upper half of high school class; admission plans include early admission, early decision, rolling admission, delayed admission and advanced placement; no application fee.

Costs Per Year: Tuition $9,980; room and board $3,640; student fees $280.

Collegiate Environment: The college accepts 78% of those who apply for admission. Midyear students may enroll at the college and a geographically diverse student body is welcome. The library contains 100,961 volumes, 510 periodicals, 6,373 microforms, and 1,478 audiovisual materials. Housing is available for 354 men, 200 women, and 8 families. Financial aid is available, and 60% of the current students receive some form of assistance. The college granted 67 Bachelor degrees recently.

Community Environment: LeMars (population 8,500) is 25 miles northwest of Sioux City, and has an average mean temperature of 52 degrees and average rainfall of 27 inches. Buses serve the area along with a private airport. Community facilities include 16 churches, a public library, hospital, motels, and numerous civic, service and social organizations. Some outdoor activities are ice skating, and golf. The county fair is an annual event.

UNIVERSITY OF DUBUQUE   (F-16)
2000 University Avenue
Dubuque, Iowa 52001
Tel: (319) 589-3200; (800) 722-5583; Fax: (319) 556-8633

Description: This privately supported liberal arts university has an enrollment of 1,200 graduate and undergraduate students. A faculty of 65 gives a faculty-student ratio of 1-15. In addition to regular academic subjects, the school offers environmental science, aviation flight and management programs; intercollegiate and intramural athletics; and freshman programs for the educationally disadvantaged. Preparation for state teaching certificate is available. The university operates on the semester system and offers three summer sessions. The institution is divided into four schools: Liberal Arts and Science, Applied Programs, Business and Computer Science, and Theology, which houses the UD Theological Seminary. The university is related to the General Assembly of the United Presbyterian Church. The school is accredited by the North Central Association of Colleges and Schools, the National Council for Accreditation of Teacher Education, Association of Theological Schools, and the National League for Nursing. It is approved by the Council on Social Work Education. Cooperative Education programs (alternating work and class periods) are offered in business, special education, and social services. Overseas programs include semesters in Colombia, Ecuador, Mexico, and Norway, as well as travel tours during vacation periods. The university is a member of Dubuque Tri-College program, which includes Clarke College and Loras College, through which students may enroll for credit in other school's classes, and utilize libraries and other facilities.

Entrance Requirements: Graduation or equivalent from high school with 13 units, including 4 English, 3 math, 3 science, and 3 social science; additional academic courses in fine and performing arts are considerd; minimum ACT 18 or SAT composite 740 required; early admission, rolling admission, delayed admission, and advanced placement plans available; $15 application fee.

Costs Per Year: $11,510 tuition; $4,340 room and board; $170 student fees.

Collegiate Environment: The university is located on a 56-acre campus in the residential area of Dubuque. The library contains more than 168,866 volumes, 1,200 periodicals, 20,225 microforms and 4,500 audiovisual materials. Living accommodations are provided for 256 men and 200 women. Between 70-80% of the applicants are accepted. Financial assistance is available and 80% of the students receive some form of aid.

UNIVERSITY OF IOWA   *(I-4)*
Calvin Hall
Iowa City, Iowa 52242
Tel: (319) 335-3847; (800) 553-4692; Fax: (319) 335-1535

Description: The publicly supported university was founded in 1847. It is a residential institution that consists of ten colleges and offers liberal arts programs and a broad spectrum of graduate and professional studies. It is a member institution of the Association of American Universities and a member of the Western Conference known as the "Big Ten." The university is accredited by the North Central Association of Colleges and Secondary Schools, and individual colleges and schools of the university are members of various accrediting associations in the following subject areas: business, chemistry, dentistry, dental hygiene, engineering (chemical, civil, electrical, industrial and mechanical), hospital administration, journalism, law, librarianship, medicine, medical technology, physical therapy, music, nursing, pharmacy, physicians assistant, psychology, social work, speech pathology and audiology, teacher education, counseling, dietetics, biomedical engineering, leisure studies, nuclear medical technology, diagnostic medical sonography, radiography, and clinical pastoral education. The school operates on the semester system and offers one summer session. Enrollment includes 13,296 men and 13,636 women. A faculty of 1,803 gives an overall faculty-student ratio of 1-15.

Entrance Requirements: Graduation from an accredited high school and acceptable class rank or admission index score (a combination of class rank and ACT or SAT); completion of 15 units: 4 English, 3 math, 3 science (including 2 lab science), 2 language, and 3 social studies; students not meeting these requirements may be considered for admission based on special characteristics that indicate definite promise of success; early admission, rolling admission, delayed admission, and advanced placement plans available; $20 application fee.

Costs Per Year: $2,291 state-resident tuition; $8,149 nonresident; tuition higher for graduate school and schools of dentistry, law, and medicine; $3,423 room and board; $3,066 average additional expenses.

Collegiate Environment: The 1,880-acre campus includes a library of more than 3,567,227 bound volumes and housing accomodations for 5,522 men and women and 749 families. Fraternities and sororities provide housing for an additional 1,324 men and women. Students are admitted to the university at midyear as well as in August. 86% of those applying for admission are accepted. 89% of the current freshmen graduated in the upper half of their high school classes; 22.2% were in the top tenth. Financial aid is available and 65% of the current student body receives some form of assistance.

Community Environment: Greater Iowa City (population 71,740) is located in eastern Iowa. Major transportation facilities are accessible. The university hospital and medical and scientific research depart-

ments make Iowa City an important medical center. Public and historical libraries, historical museums, churches of most denominations, hospitals, and civic, fraternal and veterans' organizations are a part of the community.

UNIVERSITY OF NORTHERN IOWA   *(F-12)*
23rd and College
Cedar Falls, Iowa 50614
Tel: (319) 273-2281; (800) 772-2037; Fax: (319) 273-6792

Description: The publicly supported state university enrolled 4,472 men and 5,943 women full-time, 871 men and 1,286 women part-time recently. (This enrollment includes 9,863 full-time and 1,369 part-time undergraduates and 1,340 graduate students.) A faculty of 630 full-time and 225 part-time gives an overall faculty-student ratio of 1-15. The institution is fully accredited by the North Central Association of Colleges and Schools and by numerous professional accrediting organizations. The instructional departments are formally grouped into six colleges: Business, Social and Behavioral Sciences, Education, Humanities and Fine Arts, Natural Sciences and Graduate College. Each college is administered by a dean. On the graduate level, the University offers a Master of Arts, Master of Arts in Education, Master of Business Administration, Master of Music, Master of Philosophy, Master of Public Policy, Specialist, Specialist in Education, Doctor of Education, Doctor of Industrial Technology. Undergraduate courses available in preparation for the state teaching certificate. The university operates on the early semester system and offers three summer sessions. Extensive vocal and instrumental music programs and intercollegiate and intramural athletics are available. A student exchange program exists with Japan, Austria, Denmark, Mexico, Spain, China, Germany, Chile, Finland, France, Nigeria, and Russia. Army ROTC program is available.

Entrance Requirements: Accredited high school graduation or equivalent rank in upper half of graduating class; completion of 15 units: 4 units of English (including 1 year of composition), 3 years of mathematics (including one year of algebra), 3 years of social studies, 3 years science (including lab), and 2 years of electives from subjects listed plus a foreign language, humanities or fine arts; ACT required for all applicants; SAT may be substituted; rolling admission, delayed admission and advanced placement plans available; $20 application fee.

Costs Per Year: $2,386 state-resident tuition; $6,462 out-of-state; additional tuition required for graduate programs; $2,930 room and board.

Collegiate Environment: The university is comprised of 56 principal buildings, which include a library of 754,934 volumes and living accommodations for 2,050 men, 2,881 women, and 365 families. There are 4 sororities and 7 fraternities on the campus in addition to numerous other student organizations. The university welcomes students from all geographical locations. Students may enter the university in the spring semester beginning in January, or at midyear. 48% of the current freshmen graduated in the top quarter of their high school class, 94% in the top half. The average score of all applicants accepted was ACT 23.1 composite. 82% of those applying for admission were accepted. Financial aid is available and 67% of all undergraduates receive some form of assistance.

Community Environment: Cedar Falls is an active industrial community on the Cedar River, situated in northeast Iowa. All forms of commercial transportation are available. Part-time work is available. Recreational facilities include many parks, Cedar River for fishing and boating, and two public golf courses.

UNIVERSITY OF OSTEOPATHIC MEDICINE AND HEALTH SCIENCES   *(I-9)*
3200 Grand Avenue
Des Moines, Iowa 50312
Tel: (515) 271-1450; (800) 240-2767; Admissions: (515) 271-1450; Fax: (515) 271-1578

Description: This private medical university operates on a continuous twelve-month basis. Enrollment is 808 men and 506 women full-time and 44 part-time students. A faculty of 68 full-time gives a faculty-student ratio of 1-11. Its primary goal is to produce academically competent osteopathic physicians, podiatric physicians, physicians' assistants, physical therapists, and health care administrators . Specific objectives are to encourage and facilitate scientific research, to provide graduate and postdoctoral continuing medical education, and to serve the community in a variety of professional affairs. The college is accredited by the American Osteopathic Association, the American Podiatry Association, the Committee on Allied Health and Accreditation, the American Physical Therapy Association and the North Central Association.

Entrance Requirements: Osteopathic Medicine: Bachelor's, any major; 8 sem. hrs. each of bio., chem., organic chem., physics, all with lab; 6 sem. hrs. of English comp., speech, or communication; new MCAT; cumulative GPA of 2.50 and C average in each prerequisite area; $50 application fee. Podiatric Medicine: minimum of 90 sem. hrs. toward Bachelor's; 8 sem. hrs. each of biology, chem., organic chem., physics, all with lab; 6 sem. hrs. of Eng. composition, speech, or communication; new MCAT, but may apply without scores if registered for test; no application fee. Physician Assistant: minimum of 60 sem. hrs. toward Bachelor's and minimum 2.75 GPA; 12 sem. hrs. biology (human biology, anatomy, physiology, microbiology, with lab); 8 sem. hrs. of chemistry (general and organic with lab) biochemistry recommended; 6 sem. hrs. of psychology (general, abnormal, human devel., marriage and family; 6 sem. hrs. Eng. comp., speech, or communication; 500 clock hrs. direct patient care experience; $35 application fee. Physical Therapy: Bachelor's degree, any major, minimum 3.0 GPA; 12 sem. hrs. biology/zoology with lab; 8 sem. hrs. each physics and chem. with lab; 6 sem. hrs. upper div. psychology including 1 of abnormal psych.; 6 sem. hrs. Eng., speech, or communications, 1 in composition; 3 sem. hrs. humanities; $35 application fee. Health Care Administrator: Bachelor's degree, any major; minimum 3.0 GPA for unconditional acceptance; GRE or GMAT may be required of applicants below 3.0; $35 application fee.

Costs Per Year: $20,000 Osteopathic; $18,900 Podiatric; $9,400 Physician Assistant; $11,025 Physical Therapist; $210/credit hour Health Care programs tuition.

Collegiate Environment: The college consists of a main campus with a library of over 24,000 volumes and 5 clinics within commuting distance. About 16% of students applying for admission are accepted. The school year begins in June or September. The college seeks a geographically diverse student body. Almost 90% of the recent entering class received some form of financial aid. Students interested in or in need of financial help should write to the Director, Student Financial Aid, of the college.

Community Environment: Des Moines, Iowa's capital city, has a population of about 340,000 including the greater metropolitan area that encompasses Polk and Warren Counties. It is known as an insurance, printing and convention city with some 396 factories producing over 500 different products ranging from cosmetics to combines with a value of $500 million annually. Higher education facilities include Drake University, Grandview College and Des Moines Area Community College serving over 17,000 full-time students. Des Moines is easily accessible by auto on Interstate Highways 35 and 80. It is also an important air center that handles more than 100 commercial planes on 5 airlines daily.

UPPER IOWA UNIVERSITY   *(D-3)*
Box 1859
Fayette, Iowa 52142
Tel: (319) 425-5281; (800) 553-4150; Fax: (319) 425-5277

Description: Upper Iowa University, located in the scenic Volga River Valley in northeast Iowa, is a private, liberal arts school. It is accredited by the North Central Association of Colleges and Schools and the Iowa Department of Public Instruction. The college operates on the semester system and provides two summer sessions. Current enrollment includes 600 resident students. A faculty of 40 provides a faculty-student ratio 1-15. The school grants the Associate and Bachelor degrees.

Entrance Requirements: Accredited high school graduation or equivalent; completion of 16 units including 4 English, 4 social science, 3 mathematics, 3 science, 2 academic electives; ACT is required; SAT may be substituted; admission plans include early admission, early decision, midyear admission, rolling admission, delayed admission and advanced placement plans available; $15 application fee.

Costs Per Year: $8,840 tuition; $3,360 board and room.

Collegiate Environment: Upper Iowa University is located on a residential campus with collegiate brick buildings. Housing is available for 440 students. The library contains 89,000 volumes. The college accepts 74% of the students who apply for admission, including midyear students. Financial aid is available to any student based on need and academic success. Currently, 93% of the student body receives some form of assistance.

Community Environment: Fayette (population 1,293) is a rural area in northeastern Iowa, 50 miles from the Mississippi River. Community facilities include five churches and hospital service in the county seat 8 miles away. The city has a Chamber of Commerce and other civic and fraternal organizations. Part-time work is available for students and families. Outdoor sports include hiking, cross-country skiing, hunting, fishing, and golf.

VENNARD COLLEGE   *(J-11)*
Box 29
University Park, Iowa 52595
Tel: (515) 673-8391; (800) 338-2407; Admissions: (800) 338-2407; Fax: (515) 673-8365

Description: This privately supported, interdenominational Bible college is accredited by the American Association of Bible Colleges. The school offers seminar studies in selected countries for students who plan on vacational mission work. Extracurricular activities include vocal and instrumental music programs and some intercollegiate athletics. It operates on the semester system with one summer session. Enrollment is 120 full-time students. A faculty of 13 gives a faculty-student ratio of 1-15.

Entrance Requirements: Accredited high school graduation or equivalent; a limited number of non-high school graduates are accepted as special students; ACT required; early decision, rolling admission, and advanced placement plans available; $10 application fee.

Costs Per Year: $5,520 tuition; $3,220 room and board; $578 student fees.

Collegiate Environment: The library holdings include 47,000 volumes and 300 periodicals. Housing is provided for 120 men, 120 women, and 16 married students. The college welcomes a geographically diverse student body and students may enroll at midyear. 95% of students who apply for admission are accepted. Financial aid is available, and 94% of the current student body receives some form of assistance.

Community Environment: See William Penn College.

WALDORF COLLEGE   *(C-9)*
Forest City, Iowa 50436
Tel: (515) 582-8112; Fax: (515) 582-8194

Description: The residential, privately supported, junior college is owned by the Evangelical Lutheran Church in America. It is accredited by the North Central Association of Colleges and Schools. The college features liberal arts and preprofessional transfer programs as well as vocational courses. Cooperative education programs (alternating work and class periods) are available in all subject areas. In addition to academic subjects, the school offers band, chorus, choir, intercollegiate and intramural athletics. Religion courses are required. It operates on the semester system. Enrollment includes 327 men and 246 women. A faculty of 48 gives a faculty-student ratio of 1-11.

Entrance Requirements: Accredited high school graduation or equivalent; ACT or SAT required; early admission, rolling admission, midyear admission and advanced placement plans available; $15 application fee.

Costs Per Year: $9,600 tuition; $3,525 room and board.

Collegiate Environment: Since 1962 the campus has nearly tripled in size. The college consists of 12 major buildings including a library containing 40,000 volumes, a music center, and a recently completed physical education facility. Housing is available for 240 men and 230 women. The college accepts 85% of the students who apply for admission, and students may enroll at midyear as well as in September. Financial aid is available, and 96% of the current student body receives some form of assistance. Of the 268 scholarships offered, 167 are available to freshmen. Approximately 73% of the previous freshmen returned to the campus for their sophomore year.

Community Environment: Forest City (population 4,500), so named for the numerous trees covering the slopes of the rolling hills surrounding the city, is in north-central Iowa on the Winnebago River, near Mason City (population 30,000) and midway between Minneapolis and Des Moines. It is also the county seat and retailing center of Winnebago County, and serves as both the manufacturing and administrative center for Winnebago Industries. A modern community hospital, civic auditorium, new schools, YMCA, and the public library are a part of the town. A few miles to the east is Pilot Knob State Park, offering hiking and winter sports.

WARTBURG COLLEGE   *(E-12)*
222 9th St., N.W.
Waverly, Iowa 50677
Tel: (319) 352-8264; (800) 772-2085; Fax: (319) 352-8579

Description: The privately supported, liberal arts college is affiliated with the Evangelical Lutheran Church in America. The college is accredited by the North Central Association of Colleges and Schools, the Council on Social Work Education and the National Association of Schools of Music. Wartburg provides over 30 programs, including Business Administration and Computer Science, in a liberal arts context, with a Christian perspective, and has a commitment to assist students in preparing for lives of leadership and service. Special programs include Urban Internship, May Term Consortium Exchange, Leadership Education, and Global and Multicultural Studies programs enhance the liberal arts curriculum. Religion subjects required. Special 2-3 year programs with other institutions in medical technology, occupational therapy, and engineering are available. Preparation for the state teaching certificate is offered. The school offers extensive vocal and instrumental music programs (including music therapy), as well as intercollegiate and intramural athletics. Overseas programs include May Term, Summer Abroad, and Junior Year Abroad, exchange programs with universities in Brazil, Germany, Indonesia, Japan, and Turkey. It operates on the 4-4-1 semester system and offers two summer sessions. Enrollment includes 1,291 full-time and 114 part-time students. A faculty of 90 full-time and 45 part-time gives a faculty-student ratio of 1-14.

Entrance Requirements: Accredited high school graduation or equivalent with rank in upper half of class; recommended units include 4 English, 3 mathematics, 3 science, 2 social science, and 2 foreign language; ACT or SAT required; non-high school graduates may be admitted on basis of GED score; rolling admission, early admission, and advanced placement plans available; $20 application fee.

Costs Per Year: $11,600 tuition; $3,610 room and board; $120 student fees; $800 average additional expenses.

Collegiate Environment: The College offers a competitive academic program, preparing students for leadership in business, education, social service, health, church, other professions, and graduate school. The 4-4-1 academic program with the May Term offers a flexible curriculum design and numerous off-campus travel and internship/field experience opportunities. The library contains 145,130 volumes, 744 periodicals, and 6,300 microforms. Housing is available for 459 men and 590 women. 87% of the applicants are accepted. Financial aid is available, and 96% of the students receive some form of assistance.

Community Environment: Waverly is a rural Iowa community (population 8,500), within 15 minutes of the Waterloo-Cedar Falls metro area (population 120,000). A variety of cultural events are available. The community provides libraries, a museum, a hospital, churches, clinics, shopping facilities and a community symphony. Part-time employment opportunities are limited.

WARTBURG THEOLOGICAL SEMINARY   *(F-16)*
333 Wartburg Place
Dubuque, Iowa 52001
Tel: (319) 589-0200; (800) 225-5987; Fax: (319) 589-0333

Description: The privately supported, graduate theological seminary, owned and operated by the Evangelical Lutheran Church in America. It is fully accredited by the North Central Association of Colleges and Schools, and the Association of Theological Schools. It operates on the 4-1-4 calendar system and offers one summer session. Enrollment includes 199 students. A faculty of 25 gives a faculty-student ratio of 1-8.

Entrance Requirements: Bachelor of Arts degree or its equivalent from an accredited college or university; college courses including 2 years of English, 2 years of Greek, 2 years of another foreign language, and 1 year each of history, social science, natural science, philosophy, and psychology; $25 application fee.

Costs Per Year: $4,200 tuition; $2,900 room and board; $107 student fees.

Collegiate Environment: The seminary is a member of the Schools of Theology in Dubuque, which consists of the University of Dubuque Theological Seminary and the School of Religion at the University of Iowa. Reciprocal registration is offered within this group. Housing for 222 students is provided. During the regular 4-month semester, the full-time student registers for 9-15 credit hours of class work. For the 1-month interim period, one unit of work on a subject of special interest is pursued.

Community Environment: See Clarke College.

WESTERN IOWA TECH COMMUNITY COLLEGE   *(F-1)*
4647 Stone Avenue
Sioux City, Iowa 51102
Tel: (712) 274-6400; (800) 352-4649; Admissions: (712) 274-6412; Fax: (712) 274-6403

Description: The institute is a publicly supported, two-year, technical school. Courses offered are approved by the Iowa State Board of Public Instruction, the Iowa Board of Nursing, the Veteran's Administration, and the U.S. Office of Education. It is a member of the Iowa Association of Community Colleges and Vocational-Technical Institutes. The college is accredited by the North Central Association of Colleges and Schools. The school operates on the semester system and has an enrollment of 1,050 full-time students, 1,600 part-time. A faculty of 77 full-time, 79 part-time provided a teacher-student ratio of 1:16.

Entrance Requirements: Open enrollment policy; requirements vary with type of program taken; technology students are required to possess the qualities and maturity of high school graduates and must have completed two years of mathematics including algebra and geometry; physics and chemistry are recommended; rolling admission plan available; $10 application fee.

Costs Per Year: $55 per credit state resident tuition; $110 per credit out-of-state tuition; $58 student fees.

Collegiate Environment: The college library contains 18,000 volumes, 470 periodicals, 4,295 microforms, 9,000 audiovisual materials.

Community Environment: See Briar Cliff College

WILLIAM PENN COLLEGE   *(J-11)*
Trueblood Avenue
Oskaloosa, Iowa 52577
Tel: (515) 673-1012; (800) 779-7366; Fax: (515) 673-1396

Description: This privately supported, liberal arts college is supported by the Iowa Yearly Meetings of Friends, the Oskaloosa community, and the alumni and former students of Penn College and Nebraska Central College. A Quaker college since its beginning in 1873, it has held a policy of equal educational opportunity for all individuals. It is fully accredited by the North Central Association of Colleges and Schools and by the National Council for Accreditation of Teacher Education. It operates on the semester system and offers one summer session and a 2-week interim session. Enrollment is 689 students. A faculty of 40 full-time and 16 part-time gives faculty-student ratio of 1-15. The college offers band, chorus, choir, and intercollegiate and intramural athletics.

Entrance Requirements: Accredited high school graduation or equivalent; completion of 15 units including 3-4 English, 2 natural science, 2 mathematics, 2 social science, 2 language, and 3-4 electives; score of 17 or over on ACT required; SAT may be substituted; C average accepted; early admission, early decision, rolling admission, delayed admission, and advanced placement plans available; $15 application fee.

Costs Per Year: $9,600; $270 student fees; $2,930 room and board; $1,400 average additional expenses.

Collegiate Environment: Known as the "Friendly College," the spirit at the school is traditional and is due to the close relationship existing between the students and faculty. Every student at the school is assigned to a faculty member for the purpose of individual guidance and each freshman is tentatively assigned to a faculty member prior to registration. The library contains 73,829 volumes. Student housing capacity is 275 men and 200 women. Almost 71% of the previous freshman class returned to the campus for the sophomore year. Average ACT score of the freshman class was 20. Average high school standing of the freshmen was in the top 40%; 25% ranked in the top quarter and 55% were in the top half. 82% of applicants are accepted. 97% of students receive some form of financial aid.

Community Environment: Oskaloosa (population 12,000) is located 60 miles southeast of Des Moines in one of the nation's richest agricultural areas. All commercial transportation is available. Community facilities include many churches and cultural activities. Swimming, golf, and other outdoor activities are available.

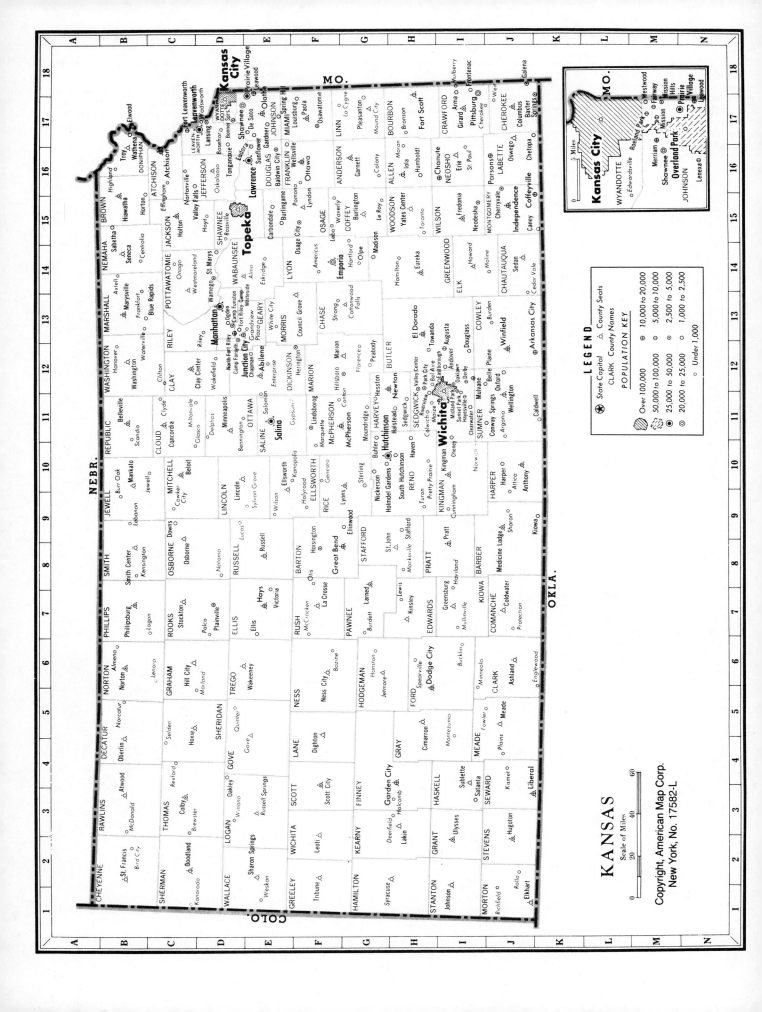

KANSAS

Scale of Miles

Copyright, American Map Corp.
New York, No. 17582-L

LEGEND

⊛ State Capital ⚬ County Seats
CLARK County Names
POPULATION KEY

⬛ Over 100,000	⊕ 10,000 to 20,000
▨ 50,000 to 100,000	⊙ 5,000 to 10,000
◉ 25,000 to 50,000	⊚ 2,500 to 5,000
⊚ 20,000 to 25,000	⚬ 1,000 to 2,500
	⚬ Under 1,000

KANSAS

ALLEN COUNTY COMMUNITY COLLEGE   (H-16)
1801 North Cottonwood
Iola, Kansas 66749
Tel: (316) 365-5116; Fax: (316) 365-3284

Description: The community college had its beginning in 1923 with the establishment of the Iola Junior College as an extension of the high school serving District 10. In 1965, the Allen County Community Junior College was created and in 1966 the voters of the county approved a $1,500,000 bond issue to construct a campus-type facility. The college is accredited by the North Central Association of Colleges and Schools. The school operates on the early semester system and offers two summer sessions. It enrolls 753 full-time and 858 part-time men and women. The faculty consists of 32-full time and 23 part-time members.

Entrance Requirements: Accredited high school graduation or equivalent for degree programs; non-high school graduates may enroll with special permission; open enrollment policy; ACT recommended; ASSET; early admission, early decision, open admission, midyear admission, advanced placement, rolling admission and delayed admission plans available.

Costs Per Year: $832 tuition Kansas residents; $2,160 tuition out-of-state resident; $2,600 room and board; $224 student fees; $160 book rental; approximate additional expenses $400.

Collegiate Environment: The college has occupied its present 88-acre campus since 1970. There is a relaxed atmosphere, with close relationships between student and faculty due to small class size. There is an active athletic and intra-mural program. The library contains 50,000 volumes and dormitory facilities are available for 154 students. Almost all of those who apply for admission are accepted, including midyear students. Special financial aid is available for economically handicapped students and special programs are offered for the culturally disadvantaged. 39% of students receive financial aid.

Community Environment: Iola is a rural area with community facilities that provide a library, hospital, many churches and a fine arts center. Part-time employment is available. Fishing, boating, golf and bowling are some of the recreational activities. The County 4-H Fair is an annual event as is the Farm-City Day Celebration.

BAKER UNIVERSITY   (E-16)
8th and High Street
Baldwin City, Kansas 66006
Tel: (913) 594-6451; (800) 873-4282; Fax: (913) 594-6721

Description: The private, liberal arts college operates on the 4-1-4 system, which includes a four-week interim in January and has two summer sessions. It is accredited by the North Central Association of Colleges and the National Council for Accreditation of Teacher Education. The Kansas-East Conference of the Methodist Church founded the school in 1858 and from that date to the present time the college record of service has been unbroken. It is the oldest four-year university in Kansas. The school attracts nearly 93% of its students from outside the community. Enrollment is 870 full-time and 12 part-time students. A faculty of 64 full-time and 13 part-time gives a faculty-student ratio of 1-12. Overseas programs include Spain, France, England, Denmark. Army and Air Force ROTC programs are available.

Entrance Requirements: Accredited high school graduation with a 2.5 grade point average; SAT or ACT required (minimum score 19 on ACT); non-high school graduates considered; early admission, early decision, rolling admission, delayed admission and advanced placement plans available; $20 application fee.

Costs Per Year: $7,350 tuition, $3,750 room and board; $200 student fees.

Collegiate Environment: The campus has 28 buildings on 54 acres. The library contains over 71,000 volumes and dormitory facilities are available for 300 men and 366 women. 79% of last year's freshman class returned for the sophomore year. Financial assistance is available. 89% of the current student body receives some form of aid.

Community Environment: A rural town located 45 miles southwest of Kansas City and 15 miles south of Lawrence. The city is 10 miles from Lone Star Lake, which provides some of the recreational facilities. Trains and buses are available for transportation. Churches of many denominations are represented here. A shopping center, a public library, and a clinic all serve the community. The larger shopping centers of Kansas City and Topeka are excellent as are the cultural advantages of these two cities, which contribute to the enjoyment of the smaller surrounding areas.

BARCLAY COLLEGE   (I-7)
607 North Kingman
Haviland, Kansas 67059
Tel: (316) 862-5252; (800) 826-0226; Fax: (316) 862-5403

Description: A four-year college program offering majors in Bible Theology, Pastoral Ministry, Christian Education, Christian Ministries and Missions and Business Administration. There is a strong Music program as well. The school operates on the 4-1-4 calendar system and offers one summer session. An enrollment of 93 full-time and 13 part-time students with a faculty of 14 full-time and part-time provides a faculty-student ratio of 1-9. The school is accredited by the American Association of Bible Colleges.

Entrance Requirements: Accredited high school graduation or equivalency diploma; SAT or ACT required; open enrollment policy; early decision, midyear admission, rolling admission and advanced placement plans available; $10 application fee.

Costs Per Year: $3,600 tuition; $2,700 room and board; $665 student fees.

Collegiate Environment: All qualified applicants are accepted, including midyear students. College facilities include living accommodations for 56 men and 52 women and a library of 50,000 volumes. Financial aid is available, with 95% of students receiving some form of assistance.

Community Environment: Haviland is a small town in a rural area with a friendly and supportive atmosphere. Especially welcoming to young families.

BARTON COUNTY COMMUNITY COLLEGE   (G-8)
Route 3 Bissell's Point Road
Great Bend, Kansas 67530
Tel: (316) 792-2701

Description: The community college was formed in 1965 as a result of an election by the people of Barton County, Kansas. The college opened in the fall of 1969 and is accredited by the North Central Association of Colleges and Schools. It operates on the semester system with two summer sessions. The college offers courses in vocational-technical and academic areas and grants the Associate degree. Enrollment includes 1,021 full-time and 5,700 part-time students. A faculty of 79 full-time and 247 part-time gives a faculty-student ratio of 1-22.

Entrance Requirements: Accredited high school graduation or equivalent; open enrollment policy; non-high school graduates over 18 may be admitted as special students; rolling admission plan available.

Costs Per Year: $1,088 ($34/cr) tuition; $2,480 ($77.50/cr) out-of-state; $2,200 room and board.

Collegiate Environment: The campus of the college is located near the center of Barton County on a 160-acre site in the Bissell Point area. The 8 buildings total more than 200,000 square feet of usuable area and are air-conditioned for year-round operation. The Shafer Memorial Art Gallery is 7,900 square feet. The library contains more than 33,000 volumes and 305 periodical titles. 100% of students applying for admission are accepted, including midyear students. Financial aid is available, and 81% of the students receive some form of assistance. Housing can accommodate 290 students.

Community Environment: An urban area, Great Bend (population 18,000) is in the wheat belt and is a large oil producing area. Thirty churches, a library, a hospital and good shopping facilities are a part of the community. Brit Spaugh Park has recreational facilities for tennis, baseball, swimming, and picnicking. Cheyenne Bottoms, nearby, is a wildlife and waterfowl refuge of more than 18,000 acres of which 15,000 acres are covered by water. All forms of commercial transportation are available.

Branch Campuses: There are associate degree nursing completion satellites in Hays and Junction City; 14 outreach sites in the service area; and a branch campus at Fort Riley Military Base.

BENEDICTINE COLLEGE   *(C-16)*
1020 North 2nd Street
Atchison, Kansas 66002
Tel: (913) 367-5340; (800) 467-5340; Fax: (913) 365-6102

Description: The Roman Catholic, coeducational, liberal arts college operates on the semester system and offers one summer session. The college is accredited by the North Central Association of Colleges and Schools, the National Association of Schools of Music, and the National Council for Accreditation of Teacher Education. Enrollment is 376 men and 359 women full-time and 11 men and 57 women part-time. A faculty of 57 full-time and 31 part-time provides a faculty-student ratio of 1-12. The college grants the Bachelor degree, Bachelor of Music and Bachelor of Music Education. Foreign language study program in France, Spain, Austria, Germany. Study abroad in England, Wales and Holland. Army ROTC program is available.

Entrance Requirements: High school graduation or equivalent in top 50% of class with 16 units required, including 4 English, 2 math, 2 social science, 1 science, 2 foreign language; under certain circumstances non-high school graduates and high school graduates with C average accepted; SAT or ACT required; early admission, early decision, rolling admission, midyear admission and advanced placement plans available. $25 application fee.

Costs Per Year: $9,550 tuition; $3,850 room and board; $110 student fees.

Collegiate Environment: The library contains 307,773 volumes, 811 periodicals, and 8,099 audiovisual materials and dormitory facilities are available for 383 men and 312 women. 85% of applicants are accepted. Financial aid is available, and 90% of the students receive some form of assistance.

Community Environment: Atchison is located on the Kansas-Missouri border, within 30-50 miles of St. Joseph and Kansas City, Missouri, and Topeka and Kansas City, Kansas.

BETHANY COLLEGE   *(F-11)*
421 North First Street
Lindsborg, Kansas 67456
Tel: (913) 227-3311; (800) 826-2281; Admissions: (913) 227-3380;
Fax: (913) 227-2860

Description: This liberal arts college was founded in 1881 and is controlled by the Evangelical Lutheran Church in America. It operates on the 4-1-4 system with one summer session. It is accredited by the North Central Association of Colleges and Schools, the Council on Social Work Education, the National Association of Schools of Music and the National Council for Accreditation of Teacher Education. As a member of the Associated Colleges of Central Kansas, it offers a variety of cooperative programs. Humanities, science, and social science compose the various divisions of the college. Enrollment includes 665 full-time and 78 part-time students. A faculty of 54 full-time and 27 part-time provides a faculty-student ratio of 1-13.

Entrance Requirements: Completion of 15 college-preparatory courses, including 4 English, 3 math, 3 social science, 2 laboratory science, 1 foreign language, and 1 physical education; ACT or SAT required; early admission, rolling admission, delayed admission, midyear admission and advanced placement plans available. $10 application fee.

Costs Per Year: $8,740 tuition; $3,225 room and board; $145 student fees.

Collegiate Environment: The college is comprised of 19 buildings located on 43 acres. The library contains 115,000 volumes and living accommodations are available for 630 students. Approximately 90% of students applying for admission are accepted including midyear students. 440 scholarships are available, including 125 for freshmen. 96% of the students receive some form of financial aid.

Community Environment: Located in the heart of fertile Smoky Hill Valley of central Kansas, Lindsborg is a village founded by Swedish pioneers and steeped in Swedish culture. Bethany College is world famous for the Messiah Festival, presented annually during Holy Week. The three-day Svensk Hyllnings Festival, held biennially in odd-numbered years, honors the pioneers from Sweden who settled in the Smoky Hill Valley in the 1860s.

BETHEL COLLEGE   *(H-12)*
North Newton, Kansas 67117
Tel: (316) 283-2500

Description: The private college was founded in 1887 by the Mennonite Church. Enrollment is 644 men and women. A faculty of 59 full-time and 24 part-time provides a teacher-student ratio of 1-11. The college operates on the 4-1-4 system and offers one summer term. The college grants the Associate and Bachelor degrees. It is accredited by the North Central Association of Colleges and Schools, the National League of Nursing and the Council on Social Work Education.

Entrance Requirements: High school graduation or equivalent with rank in upper third of graduating class; ACT score of 19 or above is required for automatic admission; SAT may be substituted with a combined score of 770 required for automatic admission; early admission, midyear admission, and rolling admission plans available; no application fee.

Costs Per Year: $8,540 tuition; $3,580 room and board; $200 student fees.

Collegiate Environment: Bethel College is the oldest Mennonite college in North America. It is located on 60 acres and consists of 13 buildings. The library contains 114,000 volumes. Three residentce halls and student apartment houses provide living accommodations for 290 men, 270 women, and 20 families. Approximately 70% of students applying for admission are accepted including midyear students; student loans and government funds are available and 97% of the current student body receives some form of financial aid. A variety of scholarships are available and many of these are for freshmen.

Community Environment: Newton and its surrounding territory constitute one of the largest Mennonite Settlements in the United States. It is a friendly suburban city 25 miles from Wichita. This is the home of flour mills and small industry. Community facilities include a library, Recreation Center and excellent shopping areas. Bowling alleys, roller skating rink, golf course and nearby lakes provide facilities for recreation. Work opportunities are good. The Bethel College Fall Festival and the college's Christmas festival are annual special events.

BUTLER COUNTY COMMUNITY COLLEGE   *(H-13)*
Havehill Road and Towanda Avenue
El Dorado, Kansas 67042
Tel: (316) 321-2222; Admissions: (316) 322-3245; Fax: (316) 322-3316

Description: This community governed, two-year college is accredited by the North Central Association of Colleges and Schools, the Kansas State Board of Education, and is a member of the American Association of Community and Junior Colleges. The college offers programs in vocational-technical and academic areas and has student guidance and placement services. The college grants the Certificate and the Associate degrees. The college maintains major regional centers located in Andover, Wichita (McConnell Air Force Base), Emporia, Eureka, Marion and Rose Hill which serve their local communities and other community locations in smaller towns such as, Douglass, Goessel and White City. Also, located in Augusta, the college has a rapidly growing entity, the BCCC Business and Industry Institute, which is meeting the training and retraining needs throughout the region. The college operates on the semester system and offers one eight-week summer session. A faculty of 113 full-time and 132 part-time provides a faculty-student ratio of 1-20.

Entrance Requirements: Accredited high school graduation or GED equivalent; open enrollment policy; non-high school graduates may be admitted; early admission, early decision, rolling admission, delayed admission, midyear admission and advanced placement plans available.

Costs Per Year: $885 tuition for state residents; $2,336 out-of-state residents; $3,000 room and board; $320 student fees.

Collegiate Environment: The college is housed on a 80-acre campus located on the southwest edge of the city. The campus contains 15 buildings including a laboratory science building, an academic building, lecture hall, three vocational-technical buildings, a library of 40,000 volumes, a fine arts complex, a physical education building, a student activity center and cafeteria. Three residence halls accomodate 260 students. The design of the buildings makes the campus one of the most unusual and modern in the State of Kansas and all of the buildings are air-conditioned for year-round use. 90% of the applicants are accepted. Scholarships are available for qualified applicants and 76% of the students receive some form of financial aid.

Community Environment: Butler County attracts visitors because of its location near the scenic Flint Hills in Kansas and the El Dorado Lake, a federal Corps of Engineers Project covering approximately 4,500 acres. Butler County has an approximate population of 50,000 persons in nine communities. Butler County communities offers good schools, numerous musical, writing and civic clubs with an emphasis toward educational and cultural opportunities. Located jsut 30 minutes east of Wichita, a city of approximately 300,000 residents, Butler County residents and BCCC students are also offered all the advantages of a major metropolitan city.

CENTRAL BAPTIST THEOLOGICAL SEMINARY   (D-18)
Seminary Heights, 31st and Minnesota
Kansas City, Kansas 66102
Tel: (913) 371-5313; (800) 677-2287; Admissions: (913) 371-5313;
Fax: (913) 371-8110

Description: The seminary is a graduate professional school of theology. It was founded in 1901 and is affiliated with the American Baptist churches in the U.S.A. The seminary welcomes American Baptist students and those of other denominations and is accredited by the Association of Theological Schools in the United States and Canada and the North Central Association of College and Schools. The school operates on the early semester system and offers one summer session. Enrollment includes 100 students taught by a core faculty of 9, giving a student-teacher ratio of 12-1. Adjunct professors also provide instruction for the Masters of Divinity and Masters of Religious Arts programs.

Entrance Requirements: Bachelor's degree or equivalent from accredited college or university. The TOEFL exam for international students is required. Submit completed application, official transcripts from all post-high school educational institutions, four satisfactory recommendations, including a pastor and a professor. Midyear admission plan. Application fee $25.

Costs Per Year: $4,500 ($150/cr) full-time student tuition; $157.50/cr part-time; $100 student fee. Full-time minority American Baptist students are eligible for a 15% reduction of tuition. Entering Masters of Divinity students are assessed a $100 fee.

Collegiate Environment: The seminary is located on a beautiful 24-acre campus with access to many churches in metropolitan Kansas City. Housing is available for 78 students. The library contains 69,254 volumes and living accommodations are provided. Chapel services are held Tuesdays, Wednesdays and Thursdays. Financial assistance is available.

Community Environment: Kansas City is the second largest city in the state. The city is an acknowledged leader in livestock marketing and meat packing, automobile assembly, soap manufacturing and flour milling. The community facilities offer excellent shopping areas, many churches, summer theater, little theater, major league sports, and numerous civic and service organizations.

CENTRAL COLLEGE   (F-11)
1200 S. Main St.
McPherson, Kansas 67460
Tel: (316) 241-0723; (800) 835-0078; Fax: (316) 241-6032

Description: In 1918, four years after its relocation in Kansas, this private, junior college was recognized and accredited by the Kansas State Department of Education. In 1975 the college was fully accredited by the North Central Association of Colleges and Schools. It is the oldest accredited junior college in the state and it operates on the 4-1-4 system. Enrollment includes 194 men, 132 women full-time, 3 men, 6 women part-time, and 115 graduate students. A faculty of 18 full-time, 7 part-time provides a teacher-student ratio of 1-16. The school is affiliated with the Free Methodist Church of North America.

Entrance Requirements: Accredited high school graduation or equivalent; ACT or SAT required. Open enrollment policy. Apply to Admissions Office early in senior year. Submit completed application; have scholastic transcripts and test scores forwarded; $50 deposit and physical examination required upon acceptance; $5 application fee.

Costs Per Year: $7,900 tuition; $3,200 room and board; $300 student fees.

Collegiate Environment: The college is located on an attractive 15-acre campus which was acquired from Walden College. The student body is composed of young people of many denominations and all students applying for admission are accepted including midyear students. The library contains 22,000 volumes, 150 periodicals, 20 microforms, 600 audiovisual materials, and living accommodations are provided for 280 students and 20 families. Special financial aid is available for economically handicapped students. 85% of students now receiving some form of financial aid. 250 scholarships are available. The college grants Associate and Bachelor degrees.

Community Environment: See McPherson College

CLOUD COUNTY COMMUNITY COLLEGE   (C-11)
2221 Campus Drive
P.O. Box 1002
Concordia, Kansas 66901
Tel: (913) 243-1435; (800) 729-5101; Admissions: (913) 243-1435
x209; Fax: (913) 243-1043

Description: The first classes of this public, junior college met in February 1965, in the Concordia High School facilities. Cloud County Community College became a member of the statewide system of junior colleges in July, 1965, which extended the boundaries of its district to include Cloud County. A new campus was provided in 1968. The school is accredited by the North Central Association of Colleges and Schools. The college operates on the semester system and offers two summer sessions. Enrollment includes 750 full-time and 324 evening students at its Concordia campus. The faculty includes 45 full-time members, giving a faculty-student ratio of 1-17. The college has an active Community Education program, which enrolls approximately 1,500 students at its 30 locations throughout its 11-county service area.

Entrance Requirements: Accredited high school graduation or equivalent for degree program; non-high school graduates may be considered for other programs; open enrollment; C average; ACT recommended; rolling admission, midyear admission and advanced placement plans available.

Costs Per Year: $1,280 state-resident tuition and fees; $2,320 out-of-state; $2,700 room and board.

Collegiate Environment: The campus is located on 40 acres and includes a library containing 17,990 volumes. Dormitory facilities are provided for 236 single students. All applicants meeting the requirements are accepted including midyear students. The College participates in the Pell and SEOG Grant programs, Work Study, National Direct Student Loans, and the Guaranteed Student Loan Program-Higher Education Loan Program. 65% of the students receive financial aid. 560 scholarships are available, 230 of which are athletic.

Community Environment: Located in the Republican River Valley, Concordia is a central shopping, industrial and medical district for the citizens of North Central Kansas. The city of approximately 7,000 is home to St. Joseph Hospital, which is operated by the Sisters of St. Joseph. The city features a large municipal swimming complex, a vigorous summer recreational program, tennis courts and spacious parks. Concordia hosts the annual North Central Kansas Rodeo and the annual Fall Fest Celebration, and is the home of the Cloud County Fair. The Brown Grand Theater, which is on the National Register of Historic Sites, features many cultural events throughout the year.

COFFEYVILLE COMMUNITY COLLEGE   (K-15)
Eleventh and Willow Streets
Coffeyville, Kansas 67337
Tel: (316) 251-7700; (800) 782-4732; Fax: (316) 252-7098

Description: Established in 1923, this public, junior college was among the first such institutions to be chartered by the state. It is accredited by the North Central Association of Colleges and Schools. Today the college is the largest two-year residential institution in southeastern Kansas. Programs of study lead to the Associate degree. The college is accredited by the North Central Association of Colleges and Schools. It operates on the semester system and offers one summer term. Enrollment includes 1,295 full-time and 1,293 part-time students. A faculty of 43 full-time and 29 part-time gives a faculty-student ratio of approximately 1-25. The Associate degree is granted.

Entrance Requirements: Accredited high school graduation or GED equivalent; open enrollment policy for state residents; nonresident graduates must rank in upper 60% of graduating class; completion of 15 units including 3 English, 1 mathematics, 1 science, 1 social science; early admission and rolling admission plans available.

Costs Per Year: $736 state residents; $2,176 out-of-state residents; $2,650 room and board.

Collegiate Environment: All applicants who meet the requirements are accepted, including midyear students. The library contains 26,000 volumes and coed dormitory facilities are available for 325 men and women. Special financial aid is available for economically disadvantaged students. Of 340 scholarships available, 180 are for freshmen. 60% of current students receive some form of financial aid. The school offers special programs for the culturally disadvantaged.

Community Environment: A town of diversified industries, Coffeyville has churches of many denominations, a hospital and numerous civic, service and social organizations. A municipal airport, railroads and bus lines provide transportation. A significant point of interest is the Coffeyville Historical Museum. Coffeyville was once the home of the famous baseball pitcher, Walter Johnson; a memorial to Johnson may be seen in Walter Johnson Park.

COLBY COMMUNITY COLLEGE   (C-3)
1255 South Range
Colby, Kansas 67701
Tel: (913) 462-3984

Description: The public, community college opened to students for the first time in the fall of 1964. It was the first community college in the state to organize a functional Endowment Association. It is accredited by the North Central Association of Colleges and Schools. The school operates on the semester system and offers two summer terms. Enrollment includes 775 full-time and 1,300 part-time students. 50 full-time faculty and 120 part-time give a faculty-student ratio of 1-12.

Entrance Requirements: Accredited high school graduation or equivalent; open enrollment policy; non-high school graduates may be considered for certain programs; early admission, early decision, delayed admission, advanced placement and rolling admission plans available; $10 application fee.

Costs Per Year: $1,088 state-resident tuition; $2,624 out-of-state; $2,650 room and board.

Collegiate Environment: College facilities include a library of 31,000 volumes, 375 periodicals, 2,200 microforms and 7,100 audiovisual materials. Dormitories provide living accommodations for 100 men and 164 women. Financial aid is available, and 80% of the current student body receives some form of assistance. College offers a variety of organizations, and activities ranging from the sponsoring of

Special Olympics, to a Ski Club that enjoys the mountains only a four-hour drive away from Colby.

Community Environment: Colby is in the state's leading wheat-producing area, the northwest corner of the state. Population 6,000. Trains and buses provide transportation. Community facilities include a fine hospital, library and churches of most faiths. Job opportunities are open with the city and community providing employment for students wherever possible.

COWLEY COUNTY COMMUNITY COLLEGE   (J-12)
125 South Second Avenue
P.O. Box 1147
Arkansas City, Kansas 67005
Tel: (316) 442-0430; (800) 593-2222; Admissions: (316) 441-5303; Fax: (316) 441-5350

Description: The district governed, junior college was established in 1922 and is accredited by the North Central Association of Colleges and Schools. The college offers both day and evening programs in vocational-technical and academic areas and grants the Associate degree. It operates on teh semester system and offers one summer term. Enrollment includes 532 men, 649 women full-time, 667 men, and 1,139 women part-time. A faculty of 50 full-time and 137 part-time members provides a faculty-student ratio of 1-18.

Entrance Requirements: Accredited high school graduation or GED equivalent required for degree programs; non-high school graduates may be admitted; early admission, early decision, rolling admission, delayed admission, midyear admission and advanced placement plans available.

Costs Per Year: $810 tuition for state residents; $2,250 tuition for out-of-state residents; room and board $2,440.

Collegiate Environment: Students who do not live at home are expected to live in quarters approved by the college and lists of rooms and apartments suitable for student housing are available at the business office. Dormitory facilities are available for 180 students. The library contains 24,250 volumes. Approximately 99% of students applying for admission are accepted including midyear students. 270 scholarships are available, including 160 for freshmen. 37% of students receive some form of financial aid.

Community Environment: Arkansas City is an important industrial city in an agricultural region, as well as an oil refining center. Rail transportation to and from the city is available. Principal industries are oil refining, milling, and meat packing. Community facilities include a large hospital, hotels, motels, and many civic clubs as well as the Chamber of Commerce. Part time employment is available. A state lake is nearby for recreation. Arkalalah, a fall celebration, attracts thousands each year.

DODGE CITY COMMUNITY COLLEGE   (H-5)
2501 North 14th Avenue
Dodge City, Kansas 67801
Tel: (316) 225-1321; (800) 262-4565

Description: The district governed, community college was established in 1935 and was housed in the Senior High School building until it later became an independent legal entity with Ford County as its legal district. It is accredited by the North Central Association of Colleges and Schools. The school operates on the semester system and offers three summer terms. Recent enrollment included 1,059 men and 1,432 women. The faculty consists of 53 full-time and 108 part-time members which provides a student-faculty ratio of 15:1.

Entrance Requirements: High school graduation or GED equivalent; non-high school graduates over 21 may be admitted as special students; ACT required; midyear admission and rolling admission plans available.

Costs Per Year: $810 tuition state residents; $2,100 tuition out-of-state residents; $2,600 room and board; $243 student fees; $600 approximate additional expenses.

Collegiate Environment: The community college library contains 27,118 volumes and dormitory facilities are available for 146 men and 154 women. All students applying for admission are accepted including midyear students. Special programs are offered for the culturally disadvantaged enabling low-mark students to attend.

Community Environment: Dodge City serves as a supply and trade center for a large agricultural area. It is located on the plains of western Kansas. All modes of transportation are accessible. Community facilities include a library, hospitals, churches of all major denominations, community concert association, and many fraternal, civic and veteran's organizations. Sports include golf, bowling, fishing, hunting and boating. Points of interest are Boot Hill, Fort Dodge and Point Rocks. Special events are Dodge City Days rodeo and the Square Dance Festival.

DONNELLY COLLEGE   *(D-18)*
608 N. 18th Street
Kansas City, Kansas 66102
Tel: (913) 621-6070; Fax: (913) 621-0354

Description: This private, liberal arts, community college offers the Associate degree and was founded in 1949. Affiliated with the Roman Catholic Church and sponsored by the Archdiocese of Kansas City in Kansas; it is accredited by the North Central Association of Colleges and Schools and several state agencies. In addition to the standard liberal arts curriculum, the college offers special programs in Intensive English, pre-college Basic Education for Life-Long Learning (B.E.L.L.), Preschool teacher preparation and Entrepreneurship. The college enrolls approximately 635 men and women; a faculty of 42 provides a faculty-student ratio of 1-16.

Entrance Requirements: High school graduation or GED; open enrollment; C average; early admission; early decision, rolling admission and advanced placement plans.

Costs Per Year: $2,570 tuition.

Collegiate Environment: The library houses 30,000 volumes, 100 periodicals and 5,000 audiovisual materials. 90% of the applicants are accepted. 80% receive financial aid.

Community Environment: See Central Baptist Theological Seminary.

EMPORIA STATE UNIVERSITY   *(F-14)*
1200 Commercial Street
Emporia, Kansas 66801
Tel: (316) 341-5465; Fax: (316) 341-5073

Description: The state university is accredited by the North Central Assocaition of Colleges and Schools and the National Council for Accreditation of Teacher Education. It has led all other colleges and universities in the certification of teachers for Kansas schools every year since 1948, when statistics were first compiled by the State Department of Public Instruction. In 1865, one teacher and 18 students began regular work in the upper room of a school building owned by the city of Emporia. The first graduating class in 1867 consisted of two young women and it was in that year that the first permanent building was completed. The university operates on the semester system and offers two summer sessions. Enrollment includes 1,888 men and 2,487 women full-time and 513 men and 1,187 women part-time. A faculty of 234 full-time and 52 part-time provide a faculty-student ratio of 1-20.

Entrance Requirements: Accredited high school graduation or GED equivalent; open enrollment policy for Kansas residents; non-high school graduates may be considered on provisional basis; ACT required; GRE required for graduate studies; early admission, early decision, rolling admission, midyear admission and advanced placement plans available. $15 application fee.

Costs Per Year: $1,729.50 tuition state residents; $5,401.50 tuition out-of-state residents; $3,145 room and board.

Collegiate Environment: The original campus of 20 acres has been enlarged to 200 acres. The library contains 427,812 titles and on-campus living accommodations are provided for 1,130 single men and women and for 90 families. More than 150 social fraternities, sororities, and other social clubs on the campus are enthusiastically supported by the college administration and provide housing for an additional 262 students. 99% of applicants are accepted are accepted. 1,100 scholarships are available and 65% of the student body receives some form of financial aid.

Community Environment: Emporia, close to the nation's geographical center, is an industrial city as well as a "university town." From this agricultural area more than 100,000 cattle are sent to market each year. The community facilities include a hospital, libraries, an auditorium and many civic, social and veteran's organizations. All forms of commercial transportation are available. Parks, golf courses, a skating rink, tennis courts, ball fields, bowling alley, and swimming pools are some of the facilities for recreation.

FORT HAYS STATE UNIVERSITY   *(E-7)*
600 Park Street
Hays, Kansas 67601-4099
Tel: (913) 628-5880

Description: The university is a state assisted, liberal and applied arts university established and maintained to serve the people of Kansas. In 1900 the federal government enacted legislation granting the land of the abandoned Fort Hays Military Reservation to the State of Kansas for a state university, an agricultural experiment station, and a state park. In 1902, the university opened with 34 students, 2 faculty members, and 19 courses. The student body enrollment now includes 3,822 full-time, 1,676 part-time, and 1230 graduate students attending classes on the semester system with one summer session. The university is fully accredited by the North Central Association of Colleges and Schools, the National Council for Accreditation of Teacher Education, National League for Nursing and numerous professional associations. The faculty consists of 239 full-time and 26 part-time members. ROTC/Army program available.

Entrance Requirements: Accredited high school graduation or equivalent; open enrollment policy; non-high school graduates may be accepted upon examination; ACT or SAT acceptable; early decision and advanced placement plans available; $25 application fee.

Costs Per Year: $1,902 tuition state residents; $6,169 out-of-state residents; $3,172 room and board.

Collegiate Environment: The campus of the university is located adjacent to and southwest of the Hays city limits on Big Creek, a wooded stream which flows through the campus. This area, consisting of about 80 acres, is a part of 7,600 acres which was once the old Fort Hays Military Reservation. The university was assigned 4,160 acres of this land. A large portion of this area is used for agricultural purposes, providing vocational projects for students, and a source of income. It is also used extensively for research by university classes. The campus and the adjacent state park furnish areas for recreation and sports. Big Creek provides fishing and skating facilities and furnishes excellent field facilities and materials for biological science research. Approximately 98% of students applying for admission are accepted including midyear students. There are numerous scholarships available. The university library contains 314,000 volumes and 1,155,000 microforms. Living accommodations are provided for 645 men and 756 women.

Community Environment: Fort Hays, a military post on the old frontier, gave this railroad town its name of Hays. Known as an agricultural, educational, and regional medical center Hays has vast interests in oil and livestock as well. Ellis county, the county in which Hays is located, is the largest oil producing county in the State of Kansas. Fort Hays Experiment Station, one of the largest dryland experiment stations in the world, is located here.

FORT SCOTT COMMUNITY COLLEGE   *(H-17)*
2108 South Horton
Fort Scott, Kansas 66701
Tel: (316) 223-2700; (800) 871-3722; Fax: (316) 223-6530

Description: Fort Scott Community College, a public, two-year college established in 1919, strives to offer the best education and opportunities for individuals of all ages. Emphasis is placed on lifelong learning, personal enrichment, marketable vocational skills and a sound academic background. Educational curriculum offered at FSCC includes approximately 45 programs of study ranging from agriculture to speech and theatre arts. FSCC offers a full two-year transfer program as well as one and two year certificate programs in various vocational fields. It is fully accredited by the Kansas State Department of Education and the North Central Association of Colleges and Schools, which makes FSCC college credit hours fully accepted and transferable to most of the colleges and universities throughout the 50 states. The college enrolls 1,694 students. A faculty of 67 provides a faculty-student ratio of 1-26. The college operates on the semester system and offers three summer sessions.

Entrance Requirements: Open enrollment; applicants must be 18 years of age or older with a high school education or equivalent; ACT recommended.

Costs Per Year: $600 tuition; $2,230 out-of-state; $2,225 room and board.

Collegiate Environment: The college's 4 multipurpose structures are located on a 135-acre campus complete with lighted tennis courts, softball fields, a baseball field, football practice field, livestock pasture, truck driving range, game field and a one-mile fitness course encircling the campus lake. The college library contains over 24,000 volumes. Dormitory facilities are provided for 165 students. Sources of funding include grants, loans, scholarships, college work-study, part-time employment, and Veteran's Benefits. 80% of the current students receive some form of financial aid.

Community Environment: FSCC is located in Fort Scott, Kansas, a thriving agricultural-industrial town at the intersection of U.S. highways 69 and 54 in southeast Kansas. About 9,000 persons live in Fort Scott and an additional 6,000 live in the surrounding Bourbon County area. Fort Scott citizens continue to value their historic background, dating from the time the town was established as a military outpost in 1842. The original army post on the Indian frontier, restored and operated by the National Park Service as the Fort Scott National Historic Site, draws thousands of tourists annually. The city is served by major highways and bus lines and has a municipal airport. Superb medical facilities, including a 164-bed hospital, provide medical services for much of southeast Kansas. Numerous cultural opportunites include an active arts council and civic symphony. Outstanding community recreational programs and facilites, 180 acres of parks and several area lakes enhance the college experience for FSCC students.

FRIENDS UNIVERSITY   *(I-12)*
2100 University Avenue
Wichita, Kansas 67213
Tel: (316) 261-5800

Description: The private, liberal arts, Christian college was founded by the Kansas Yearly Meeting of Friends, and is located on property that was formerly Garfield University. The school is accredited by the North Central Association of Colleges and Schools, the National Council for Accreditation of Teacher Education and the National Association of Schools of Music. The university is nonsectarian and embraces a student body of over 60 denominations, however, Bible courses are required in addition to the courses in the various disciplines. The university grants the Associate, Master and Bachelor degree. It operates on the semester system and offers two summer sessions. Enrollment includes 1,823 full-time undergraduates and 503 graduate students. A faculty of 54 full-time and 64 part-time gives a faculty-student ratio of 1-20.

Entrance Requirements: Accredited high school graduation or equivalent with minimum 11 units of credit: 4 units of English, 2 laboratory science, 2 social studies, 1 elective and 2 mathematics; SAT or ACT required, ACT preferred; mature non-high school graduates may be admitted as provisional students; early admission, rolling admission, midyear admission, and advanced placement plans available; $15 application fee.

Costs Per Year: $8,631 tuition; $3,130 room and board.

Collegiate Environment: The campus is located on a 54-acre tract of land approximately two miles southwest of downtown Wichita. The library contains over 89,000 volumes, and living accommodations are provided for 100 men, 120 women and 65 married students. Approximately 85% of students applying for admission are accepted including midyear students. Financial aid is available for economically handicapped students; 1,500 scholarships are available and 92% of students receive financial aid.

Community Environment: See Wichita State University

GARDEN CITY COMMUNITY COLLEGE   *(H-4)*
801 Campus Drive
Garden City, Kansas 67846
Tel: (316) 276-7611; (800) 658-1696

Description: This community college is accredited by the North Central Association of Colleges and Schools. It offers liberal arts, vocational-technical and professional courses for day and evening stu-

dents. The college was established in 1919 as part of the city school district and joined the state system in 1965. The school operates on a semester system and offers three summer sessions. Enrollment includes 1,028 full-time and 1,191 part-time students. A faculty of 92 full-time and 21 part-time gives a faculty-student ratio of 1-23.

Entrance Requirements: Accredited high school graduation or GED equivalent required for degree programs; completion of 15 units; non-high school graduates may be considered for other programs; ACT reuired.

Costs Per Year: $832 state-resident tuition; $2,240 out-of-state; $2,650 room and board; $224 student fees.

Collegiate Environment: The campus, which includes 11 buildings on 138 acres, was first occupied in the fall of 1969. The library contains 39,200 volumes and dormitory facilities are available for 172 men and 62 women. The college welcomes a geographically diverse student body and will accept midyear students. Scholarships are available and 67% of the students receive some form of financial aid.

Community Environment: Garden City is on the Arkansas River in a fertile agricultural area. Predominant crops are corn, alfalfa, wheat and grain sorgums, with beef cattle production very strong. Shopping facilities are good. Finnup Park, a large recreational development, contains a swimming pool, picnic sites, museum and zoo. Other facilities for recreation are golf courses and local parks. One of the largest buffalo herds is located at Garden City on the Buffalo Preserve. All forms of commercial transportation are available.

HASKELL INDIAN JUNIOR COLLEGE   *(E-16)*
155 Indian Avenue #1282
Lawrence, Kansas 66046
Tel: (913) 749-8454; Fax: (913) 749-8429

Description: he institute is a United States government school for Indians, operated under the administration of the Bureau of Indian Affairs, Department of the Interior. The institute was founded in 1884 and is one of the oldest government boarding schools for Indians in the United States. The school operates on the semester system with one summer session and enrolled 900 men and women students recently. A faculty of 82 provides a teacher-student ratio of 1-14. The school normally enrolls students from 90 tribes and 30 states and offers post-high school training in 24 vocations and a complete business course. Courses are organized on a practical basis with a proper balance between shop and classroom instruction and on-the-job training. The college is a Recognized Candidate for Accreditation by the North Central Association of Colleges Haskell is a federally funded educational institution for Native Americans that has an average enrollment of 900 students each semester. These students represent more than 140 tribes from 32 states. Haskell was founded in 1884 and eveolved from an elementary program to a secondary and later a post-secondary training school. In 1970, Haskell received accreditation from the North Central Association as a junior college. Today, students select programs that prepare them to transfer to a baccalaureate degree-granting institution, continue their baccalaureate program at Haskell in teacher education, or enter directly into employment. Haskell integrates Native American culture into all of its curricula. This focus, in adddition to is intertribal constituency, makes Haskell's programs unique and exciting.

Entrance Requirements: At least one-fourth degree Indian blood; approval of Agency and Area officials; high school graduation or equivalent; open enrollment policy; Student must be either an official member of a tribe eligible for BIA education benefits or at least one-fourth Indian blood descendant of an enrolled member of a tribe eligible for BIA education benefits; high school graduation or GED; ACT required; $5 application fee.

Costs Per Year: $70 fees.

Collegiate Environment: he college is situated on approximately 320 acres of land located in the geographical center of the nation. There are approximately 100 buildings of all kinds on the campus and classrooms are well furnished and shops are adequately supplied with modern tools and equipment. The library contains 17,000 volumes and living accommodations are provided for 400 men and 400 women. All students applying for admission are accepted including midyear students. Special programs are offered for the Approximately 85% of the students attending Haskell reside on the 320-acre campus. College services complement and support academic programs by providing wholesome living conditions in seven modern residence halls, appropriate social and cultural activities, and financial, social and vocational counseling. Student who live in residence halls receive meals at no charge. Off-campus students receive one meal per day at no charge each day classes meet. The library contains more than 40,000 volumes, including reference materials, and approximately 4,500 books written by or about Indians of North America. The Learning Resource Center offers professional faculty tutorial services in composition, mathematics, social sciences and other areas on request. A fully equipped microcomputer lab that contains McIntosh, Apple and IBM computers is available for student use.

Community Environment: See University of Kansas.

HESSTON COLLEGE   *(G-11)*
Box 3000
Hesston, Kansas 67062
Tel: (316) 327-4221; (800) 995-2757; Admissions: (316) 327-8222;
Fax: (316) 327-8300

Description: The private, two-year college, controlled by the Mennonite Church, opened in 1909. It is accredited by the North Central Association of Colleges and Schools and the National League for Nursing. The college operates on the 4-1-4 system and offers three summer sessions. Enrollment includes 404 full-time and 58 part-time students. A faculty of 36 full-time and 21 part-time gives a faculty-student ratio of 1-14. Course offerings are designed to meet transfer, preprofessional, and career needs.

Entrance Requirements: High school graduation or equivalent; open enrollment policy; non-high school graduates may be considered; ACT or SAT required; midyear admission, rolling admission, and advanced placement plans available; $15 application fee.

Costs Per Year: $8,100 tuition; $3,650 room and board.

Collegiate Environment: The college is comprised of 15 buildings located on 46 acres and includes living accommodations for 199 men and 173 women. Special financial aid is available for economically disadvantaged students. Currently, 90% of students receive some form of aid.

Community Environment: Hesston is a small, progressive, south central Kansas town with a population of 3,000. It is located 35 miles north of Wichita, and has ready access to air, rail, and bus transportation. Part-time employment for students is available in the area and is coordinated through the Cooperative Education office on campus. A temperate climate allows considerable outside activity. Recreational facilities located in or near Hesston include an 18-hole golf course, bike trails, tennis courts, year-round swimming pool, and numerous county and state parks and lakes.

HIGHLAND COMMUNITY COLLEGE   *(B-16)*
Main at Elmira
Highland, Kansas 66035-0068
Tel: (913) 442-6000; Admissions: (913) 442-6020; Fax: (913) 442-6100

Description: This community college is the oldest college in Kansas, having been established by the Presbyterian Church in 1858, three years before Kansas became a state. Since its establishment, it has changed from university status to a two-year college administered at one time by local control and later by county control. Enrollment includes 630 full-time and 1,850 part-time students. A faculty of 34 full-time and 181 part-time provides a faculty-student ratio of 1-14. The college is a member of the American Association of Community and Junior Colleges, and is fully accredited by the North Central Association of Colleges and Schools. It operates on the early semester system and offers three summer terms.

Entrance Requirements: Accredited high school graduation or GED equivalent; completion of 20 units including 4 English, 3 math, 2 science, and 2 social studies; non-high school graduates may be admitted as special students; ACT or SAT required; early admission, early decision, rolling admission, midyear admission and advanced placement plans available.

Costs Per Year: $780 tuition state residents; $2,100 out-of-state residents; $2,530 room and board; $300 student fees; $240 textbook rental.

Collegiate Environment: The college is located in Doniphan County, ten miles south of the Nebraska state line and 25 miles west

of St. Joseph, Missouri. 5 buildings serve the college, including a library of 32,000 volumes and dormitory facilities for 346 men and women. Approximately 88% of students applying for admission are accepted including midyear students. Financial aid is available for economically disadvantaged students, and 83% of students receive some form of aid.

Community Environment: Highland is a rural town near Kansas City. All major forms of transportation are available. A number of churches, shopping facilities and a medical clinic serve Highland. The cultural and recreational facilities of Kansas City are easily accessible to this area. Fishing is excellent on Brown County State Lake and the Missouri River.

HUTCHINSON COMMUNITY COLLEGE   *(G-10)*
1300 North Plum Street
Hutchinson, Kansas 67501
Tel: (316) 665-3500; (800) 289-3501; Admissions: (316) 665-3535;
Fax: (316) 665-3310

Description: This public, community college is accredited by the North Central Association of Colleges and Schools and the Kansas State Department of Education. The college opened its first session in the senior high school building in the fall of 1928, and a new site for the campus was acquired in 1938. In 1965, the college officially became a part of the State System of Public Junior Colleges. The school operates on the semester system and offers two summer terms. Enrollment includes 2,500 full-time and 2,539 part-time students. A faculty of 254 gives an approximate faculty-student ratio of 1-21.

Entrance Requirements: Accredited high school graduation or GED equivalent; open enrollment policy; non-high school students may be admitted as special students; ACT recommended; early admission, midyear admission, rolling admission, delayed admission and advanced placement plans available.

Costs Per Year: $1,056 ($33/cr) resident tuition and fees; $2,448 ($76.50/cr) nonresident; $2,500 room and board; $200 miscellaneous.

Collegiate Environment: The college consists of a North Campus of 47 acres and a South Campus of 425 acres on the former Hutchinson Air National Guard Base located south of the city. The library has a collection of more than 42,750 books and bound periodicals. There are dormitory facilities for 194 men and 204 women. Almost all students applying for admission who meet the requirements are accepted. The college seeks a geographically diverse student body and accepts midyear students. 260 academic scholarships are available. 57% of the previous freshman class returned to the campus for a second year.

Community Environment: Hutchinson is the location of a vast salt reserve estimated to be 4,000 square miles in area and about 325 feet thick. This is also a wheat growing area and it has an oil industry of major importance as well. The community facilities are excellent, including many fine churches, a city library, a new hospital with the latest facilities, parks, a TV station and a municipal airport. All forms of commercial transportation are available. Hutchinson is the retail and wholesale center for all of southwest Kansas. The Kansas State Fair and the National Junior College Basketball Tournament are annual events held here. The Kansas Cosmosphere and Space Discovery Center is located on the Hutchinson College campus.

INDEPENDENCE COMMUNITY COLLEGE   *(J-15)*
College Avenue at Brookside Drive
Independence, Kansas 67301
Tel: (316) 331-4100

Description: This public, two-year, community college, founded in 1925, is accredited by the North Central Association of Colleges and Schools. The school offers courses in vocational-technical and academic areas. It operates on the semester system and offers two summer session. Enrollment is 1,800 students. A faculty of 33 full-time and 106 part-time gives a faculty-student ratio of 1-15.

Entrance Requirements: Accredited high school graduation or GED equivalent; open enrollment policy; non high school graduates may be admitted on provisional basis; early admission, early decision, midyear admission, rolling admission, and advanced placement plans available.

Costs Per Year: $1,120 ($35 per credit hour) resident tuition; $2,992 ($93.50 per credit hour) nonresident tuition; $2,350 room and board.

Collegiate Environment: The college library contains 32,026 volumes. Dormitories provide housing for 124 students. 100% of students applying for admission are accepted, including midyear students. Financial aid is available for economically disadvantaged students and 75% of students receive financial assistance. 40% of freshmen return to the school for their sophomore year.

Community Environment: Independence, is in a predominately agricultural region that also produces oil. The community includes a number of churches, a hospital and numerous civic, fraternal and veteran's organizations. An airport is within a ten-minute drive. Montgomery County State Lake and the Elk City Reservoir provide facilities for all water sports. Other recreational activities are golf, tennis and bowling.

JOHNSON COUNTY COMMUNITY COLLEGE   *(N-16)*
12345 College Boulevard
Overland Park, Kansas 66210-1299
Tel: (913) 469-8500

Description: The publicly supported, community college enrolled approximately 4,678 students full-time and 4,368 men, 5,989 women part-time. It operates on the semester system and offers one summer term. A faculty of 263 full-time and 435 part-time gives a faculty-student ratio of 1-22. The college is fully accredited by the North Central Association of Colleges and Schools, the American Bar Association, the American Dental Association, Committee on Allied Health Education and Accreditation and the National League for Nursing.

Entrance Requirements: High school graduation or equivalent; open enrollment policy; applicant must be 18 years of age or older; early admission, early decision, rolling admission, midyear admission, and advanced placement plans available; $10 application fee.

Costs Per Year: $1,020 ($34 per credit) state resident tuition and fees; $3,000 ($100 per credit) out-of-state residents.

Collegiate Environment: All applicants who meet the requirements are accepted, including midyear students. The college library contains 78,708 hardbound volumes, 580 periodicals, 1,200,000 microforms and 2,300 audiovisual materials. Scholarships are available and 25% of the students receive some form of financial aid.

Community Environment: See Kansas City College and Bible School

KANSAS CITY COLLEGE AND BIBLE SCHOOL   *(N-16)*
7401 Metcalf, U.S. Highway 69
Overland Park, Kansas 66204
Tel: (913) 722-0272

Description: The College and Bible school has three departments of education: elementary, secondary, and college. The courses offered in elementary and high school departments are the same as outlined for all Kansas schools with courses in Bible added as the requirement of this school. In the college, the liberal arts course is maintained and stressed in addition to theology, missionary training and music. This private, coeducational college operates on the semester system. Enrollment is 150 men and women. A faculty of 26 gives a faculty-student ratio of 1-6. The college confers the Bachelor of Arts degree in various subjects.

Entrance Requirements: Accredited high school graduation or equivalent with completion of 24 units; open enrollment policy; applicants unable to meet requirements may be admitted as special students; entrance examinations required; $25 application fee; early admission, early decision, rolling admission and advanced placement plans available.

Costs Per Year: $2,040 tuition; $2,450 room and board; $230 student fees.

Collegiate Environment: The campus consists of 7 buildings located on 14 acres and includes a library of 14,000 volumes and living accommodations for 50 men and 50 women. Attendance at Sunday School and church services is required; all students are required to be present at all chapel services. The school seeks a geographically diverse student body and midyear students are welcome. Pell Grants and Guaranteed Student Loans are available.

Community Environment: Overland Park, a suburb of Kansas City, has excellent community facilities including shopping centers, libraries, hospitals, museums, and churches of many denominations. All major forms of transportation are available in nearby Kansas City.

KANSAS CITY KANSAS COMMUNITY COLLEGE   *(D-18)*
7250 State Avenue
Kansas City, Kansas 66112
Tel: (913) 334-1100; Fax: (913) 596-9609

Description: Founded in 1923, KCKCC is the second largest community college and the ninth largest educational institution in Kansas. Many of the students are recent high school graduates, who take their first two years of general course work at the college before transferring to a four-year institution. A variety of two-year career and occupational programs that lead to the Associate degree are also offered. The college operates on the semester system and offers one summer term. It is accredited by the North Central Association of Colleges and Secondary Schools. Recent enrollment was 1,759 full-time and 4,383 part-time students. A faculty of 388 gives a faculty-student ratio of 1-16. The college offers courses providing college transfer credit, general education, occupational education, and remedial education.

Entrance Requirements: Accredited high school graduation or equivalent; open enrollment policy; non-high school graduates may be considered for special program; out-of-state residents accepted if space available; advanced placement plan available.

Costs Per Year: $33 per credit; $81 per credit out-of-state; $300 approximate additional expenses.

Collegiate Environment: KCKCC is a community college in an urban setting. Most of the students commute to campus or live in apartment complexes within walking distance of the campus. KCKCC has no on-campus housing; students must make their own housing arrangements. The campus library has 66,906 volumes. 385 scholarships are available, 250 of which are for freshmen. 66% of the students receive some form of financial aid.

Community Environment: See Central Baptist Theological Seminary.

Branch Campuses: The Leavenworth Center, in Leavenworth, KS, is an extension of the main campus and has an enrollment of approximately 1,000 students. Individuals can complete the majority of their education requirements at the center; however, they may be required to take classes on the main campus to complete their associate degree.

KANSAS NEWMAN COLLEGE   *(I-12)*
3100 McCormick Avenue
Wichita, Kansas 67213
Tel: (316) 942-4291; (800) 736-7585; Admissions: (316) 942-4291 x144; Fax: (316) 942-4483

Description: This Catholic, liberal arts college is a privately supported institution and is accredited as a four-year college by the Kansas State Department of Public Instruction and the North Central Association of Colleges and Schools, the American Library Association, National League for Nursing, National Association for Intercollegiate Athletics and the Association of Catholic Colleges and Universities. The school was founded in 1933 as Sacred Heart College and changed to its present name in 1965. The college operates on the semester system and offers two sumemr sessions. Enrollment includes 1,030 full-time and 894 part-time undergraduate students. A faculty of 85 full-time and 150 part-time gives an undergraduate faculty-student ratio of 1-14. The college offers courses leading to the Bachelor of Arts and Bachelor of Science Degrees, Associate of Arts and Associate of Science Degrees, an Associate of Science in Nursing Degree and an Associate of Science in Health Science Degree; graduate courses in Education are also offered.

Entrance Requirements: Accredited high school graduation or equivalent; completion of 20 units including 4 English, 2 mathematics, 2 science, and 2 social science; ACT or SAT required. $15 application fee; recommendation from high school principal or counselor; early admission, rolling admission, delayed admission and advanced placement plans available.

Costs Per Year: $7,710 tuition; $3,390 room and board.

Collegiate Environment: The campus is located on 51 acres. Its 10 buildings include a library of 100,000 volumes. There are numerous student organizations on campus as well as an athletic and physical recreation program. The college welcomes a geographically diverse student body and accepts midyear students; 86% of students applying for admission are accepted. Approximately 70% of the student body graduated in the top half of their high school class. Financial aid is available. 88% of students receive some form of financial assistance. There were 200 Bachelor and 50 Associate degrees awarded recently.

Community Environment: See Wichita State University

KANSAS STATE UNIVERSITY *(D-13)*
112 Anderson Hall
Manhattan, Kansas 66506
Tel: (913) 532-6250; (800) 432-8270; Fax: (913) 532-6393

Description: The university, founded in 1863, was established under the Morrill Act, by which land-grant colleges came into being. At first the university was located on the grounds of Bluemont Central College, chartered in 1858, but in 1875 most of the university was moved to its present site. The university is accredited by the North Central Association of Colleges and Schools, Accreditation Board for Engineering and Technology, American Assembly of Collegiate Schools of Business, American Council for Construction Education, American Dietetic Association, American Home Economics Association, Council on Social Work Education, Foundation for Interior Design Education Research, National Architecture Accrediting Board and the National Council for Accreditation of Teacher Education. It operates on the semester system and offers two summer sessions. Enrollment includes 14,723 full-time and 2,269 part-time undergraduates and 3,672 graduate students. A faculty of 1,284 full-time and 230 part-time gives a faculty-student ratio of 1-16. Nine colleges and a graduate school offer a variety of courses and optional Army and Air Force ROTC programs are available. Overseas programs exist in over 100 countries.

Entrance Requirements: Accredited high school graduation or equivalent, with priority given to Kansas residents; ACT required; well-qualified graduates of accredited out-of-state high schools with high test scores and class rank in the upper 50% of their high school class may be admitted; adult non-high school graduates are sometimes admitted as special students if the high school work completed was of good quality, and if they show promise as evidenced by scores on ACT; early admission, rolling admission, delayed admission and advanced placement plans available.

Costs Per Year: $1,766 in-state tuition; $7,484 out-of-state tuition; $3,220 room and board; $1,600-$2,000 approximate additional expenses.

Collegiate Environment: The campus itself consists of 668 carefully landscaped acres on which the main buildings, most of them constructed of native limestone, are located. Beyond the campus proper there are over 4,000 acres of land belonging to the university which are used for experimental work in agriculture. In addition there are four branches of the Agricultural Experiment Station located on approx. 6,000 acres in numerous outlying experimental fields. There are 121 buildings which serve the university. The library system contains 1,330,248 volumes, 9,438 periodicals, 3,751,300 microforms and 75,264 audiovisual materials. The university provides residence hall accommodations for 4,100 single students and 1,000 married students. Others find privately owned rooms and apartments from university-approved listings and fraternities and sororities provide housing for an additional 3,200 students. 72% of applicants are accepted. Financial aid is available and 70% receive some form of aid. 3,100 scholarships are available.

Community Environment: Manhattan, a beautiful city, situated on the Blue River and Kansas River, enjoys the excellent recreational facilities of Tuttle Creek Dam. The community offers libraries, churches, hospitals, hotels, motels, rooming houses and four attractive shopping centers including Manhattan Town Center. Numerous civic, service and social organizations exist. Part-time work is available. Historic Fort Riley is eight miles away.

KANSAS STATE UNIVERSITY, SALINA COLLEGE OF TECHNOLOGY *(E-11)*
2409 Scanlan Avenue
Salina, Kansas 67401
Tel: (913) 825-0275; Admissions: (913) 532-6250

Description: The technical college is a unique state school directly under the jurisdiction of the Kansas State Board of Regents. The school was founded in 1965 and is accredited by the North Central Association of Colleges and Schools. It grants the Associate and Bachelor degrees. The college operates on the semester system with one summer term. Enrollment includes 422 full-time and 336 part-time students. A faculty of 38 gives a gives a faculty-student ratio of 1-12.

Entrance Requirements: Accredited high school graduation or equivalent with completion of college-preparatory courses including 4 English, 3 mathematics, 1 science, 1 social science; open enrollment policy; ACT required; early admission, early decision, advanced placement, rolling admission and midyear admission plans available.

Costs Per Year: $1,300 tuition state residents; $5,044 out-of-state residents; $2,500 room and board; $140 student fees.

Collegiate Environment: All students applying for admission are accepted, including midyear students. The college library contains over 22,500 volumes, 370 periodicals and 1,198 audiovisual materials and living facilities are available for 100 students.

Community Environment: Salina, situated in the central part of the state, is the fifth largest city in Kansas. The wheat that supplies Salina's large flour mill and grain storage tanks comes from one of the greatest hard wheat belts in the world. Major forms of transportation are available. Community facilities include a public library, municipal shopping center, museum, community theatre and many churches. Points of interest are the Kanapolis Lake and Rock City.

KANSAS WESLEYAN UNIVERSITY *(E-11)*
100 East Claflin
Salina, Kansas 67401
Tel: (913) 827-5541; (800) 874-1154; Admissions: (913) 827-5541 x307; Fax: (913) 827-0927

Description: The university was founded by the Methodist Episcopal Church in 1886. It is accredited by the North Central Association of Colleges and Schools, the Unviersity Senate of the United Methodist Church and the State Department of Education. This liberal arts college offers undergraduate courses which lead directly to professional and vocational opportunities as well as basic preparation for graduate and professional studies. It grants the Associate and Bachelor degrees. The university operates on the 4-1-4 calendar system and offers two summer sessions. Enrollment includes 403 full-time and 238 part-time undergraduates and 17 graduate students. A faculty of 44 full-time and 9 part-time gives a faculty-student ratio of 1-14.

Entrance Requirements: Accredited high school graduation or equivalent with 2.5 g.p.a.; ACT or SAT required; rolling admission and advanced placement plans available; $15 application fee.

Costs Per Year: $9,120 tuition; $3,300-$3,500 room and board; $420 additional expenses.

Collegiate Environment: The college is located on a beautiful 28-acre campus and consists of 12 buildings including a library of 82,000 volumes and dormitory facilities for 120 students. Numerous student organizations are represented on campus. 85% of those applying for admission are accepted including midyear students, and 70% of the previous freshman class returned for their sophomore year. Scholarships are available, and 98% of the current student body receive some form of financial assistance.

Community Environment: See Kansas State University, College of Technology.

LABETTE COMMUNITY COLLEGE *(J-13)*
200 South 14th Street
Parsons, Kansas 67357
Tel: (316) 421-6700; Fax: (316) 421-0180

Description: The community college, founded as Parsons Junior College in 1923, attained its present status as a county college district in 1965. For almost 40 years the college shared all facilities with Parsons High School, but in 1962 began to occupy its own quarters. It is fully accredited by the North Central Association of Colleges and Secondary Schools. It operates on the semester system and offers two summer terms. Enrollment includes 2,270 men and women. A faculty of 33 full-time and 155 part-time gives a faculty-student ratio of 1-13.

Entrance Requirements: Kansas accredited high school graduation, resident nonaccredited high school graduates may be admitted on provisional basis with successful completion of special entrance examinations; residents 20 years of age or older may be admitted with successful completion of GED examinations; non-Kansas accredited high school graduates with high rank in graduating class considered; early admission, early decision, rolling admission, midyear admission and advanced placement plans available.

Costs Per Year: $930 tuition state residents; $2,610 out-of-state residents; $90 student fees; $2,200 room and board.

Collegiate Environment: The college occupies 5 buildings located on 4 acres which include a library of 20,000 volumes, well-furnished classrooms, ultra-modern biological and physical science laboratories and modern shops for cooperative industrial training and police science. Almost all students applying for admission are accepted including midyear students. 99% of all applicants accepted. 1,483 scholarships are available, including 140 athletic. 65% of the students receive some form of aid. Semester begins in August and January and 58% of the previous freshman class returned to the junior college for a second year.

Community Environment: This is an agricultural and industrial area, dairying being the principal source of income. Lake Parsons, which is municipally owned, provides facilities for picnicking, fishing and boating. Camping is available at Marvel Park and the Neosho Water Fowl Management Area, 12 miles north of the city, affords fishing and hunting as well.

MANHATTAN CHRISTIAN COLLEGE   *(D-13)*
1415 Anderson
Manhattan, Kansas 66502
Tel: (913) 539-3571

Description: This private, Bible college is an accredited member of the Accrediting Association of Bible Colleges. The school was founded in 1927 and operates on the semester system. It grants the Bachelor degree. Enrollment includes 271 students. A faculty of 11 full-time and 7 part-time gives a faculty-student ratio of 1-16.

Entrance Requirements: Accredited high school graduation or equivalent; early admission, early decision, midyear admission, rolling admission amd advanced placement plans available. $20 application fee.

Costs Per Year: $4,730 tuition; $2,946 room and board; $500 student fees and additional costs.

Collegiate Environment: The college is located near Kansas State University, which complements the Bible college's academic offerings. Laboratory science is a required subject at the college that, by special arrangement, the students take at the university. The college library contains over 28,000 hardbound volumes, 170 periodicals, 1,551 microforms, and 2,815 audiovisual materials. Residence hall accomodate 177 students. 82% of students applying for admission are accepted including midyear students. 110 scholarships are available, including 52 for freshmen. Approximately 74% of the student body receives some form of financial aid.

Community Environment: See Kansas State University.

MCPHERSON COLLEGE   *(F-11)*
1600 East Euclid
McPherson, Kansas 67460
Tel: (316) 241-0731

Description: McPherson College, chartered in 1887, is an independent, liberal arts institution related to the Church of the Brethren and accredited by the North Central Association of Colleges and Schools, the American Library Association and the Association of Independent Colleges and Schools. The academic year is based on a 4-1-4 system with a limited summer session. Over fifty percent of the faculty has earned doctorates. Enrollment includes 364 full-time and 115 part-time students. A faculty of 34 full-time and 15 part-time provides a faculty-student ratio of 1:10.

Entrance Requirements: Students are admitted to McPherson College who have a high school diploma or the equivalent, and who receive corresponding, standardized test scores and appropriate personal qualities. Early admission, early decision, rolling admission, delayed

admission and advanced placement plans available. Transfer students are welcome. $15 application fee.

Costs Per Year: $7,550 tuition; $3,810 room and board, $260 student fee.

Collegiate Environment: McPherson College is housed on a 27-acre campus. Most of the buildings have been constructed since 1960, but some older structures add an historic flavor to the campus. The library contains 61,525 volumes, 1,173 periodicals and 2,899 audiovisual materials. The dormitories can house a total of 496 single students with 23 apartments for married couples. Students are primarily from the midwest, but most states are represented, as well as several foreign countries. In addition to academic pursuits, students participate in a variety of activities, including publications, drama, athletics, music, and student government. A variety of scholarships and grants are available to students, and 90% of the student body receives some form of financial aid.

Community Environment: McPherson is a small city of 12,000 located near Highway I-135. The county seat, as well as the business center for the surrounding agricultural area, McPherson's principal industries include oil refining, insulation, plastic pipe, pharmaceuticals, mobile homes, and farm equipment. The community supports many cultural activites such as a symphony, theatre guild, chorale, and art festival. Air transportation is available at nearby Wichita, Salina and Hutchinson, as well as churches, motels, and several parks.

MID-AMERICA NAZARENE COLLEGE   *(E-17)*
2030 College Way
Olathe, Kansas 66062
Tel: (913) 782-3750; Fax: (913) 791-3290

Description: The private, liberal arts college began its first year of operation in 1968. It is controlled by the Church of the Nazarene. The college is accredited by the North Central Association of Colleges and Schools and the National League for Nursing. It grants the Associate, Bachelor, and Master's degrees. Air Force and Army ROTC programs are available. Enrollment includes 1,111 full-time and 159 part-time undergraduates and 175 graduate students. A faculty of 69 full-time and 48 part-time gives a faculty-student ratio of 1-18.

Entrance Requirements: High school graduation or equivalent with completion of 15 units including 3 units in English, 2 1/2 mathematics, 2 laboratory science and 2 social studies; ACT or SAT required; rolling admission and midyear admission plans available; $15 application fee.

Costs Per Year: $7,440 tuition; $3,928 room and board; $488 student fees.

Collegiate Environment: The college is composed of 112 acres of gently rolling land on the east side of Olathe, a city of 50,000 people and the county seat of Johnson County. The library contains 80,000 volumes, 300 periodicals, 20,000 microforms. Dormitory facilities are available for 568 men and women. Admission is selective. 96% of applicants are accepted. All students and faculty members are required to attend chapel and are expected to attend Sunday services. Students from various geographical locations are admitted, as are midyear students. 87% of the student body receives some form of financial aid. Special programs are offered for the culturally disadvantaged enabling low-mark students to attend.

Community Environment: Olathe is the county seat of Johnson County. Shopping facilities are good, and there are 22 churches and a library in the community. A number of industries are located here, including Delco Batteries, General Motors, Ford Motor Company, Coca-Cola, and U.S. Rubber, all offering part-time employment. Railroads and buses serve the area. This is the only city with a full range of services in suburban Johnson County. Kansas City is 19 miles away, and Lawrence is 30 miles away.

NEOSHO COUNTY COMMUNITY COLLEGE   *(I-16)*
1000 South Allen
Chanute, Kansas 66720
Tel: (316) 431-2820; (800) SAY-NCCC; Admissions: (316) 431-2820x264; Fax: (316) 431-0082

Description: The public, Community college was originally established in 1936 as Chanute Junior College. The citizens of Neosho County provided a new campus and four buildings, which were ready for occupancy in 1968. There are 1,600 men and women full-time and part-time attending classes on the semester system. A faculty of 42 full time and 60 part time provides a teacher-student ratio of 1-17. The college offers programs that include college or university parallel, occupational training, general cultural education, refresher, and vocational courses. The college is fully accredited by the North Central Association of Colleges and Schools.

Entrance Requirements: Accredited high school graduation or equivalent required for degree programs; open enrollment policy; completion of 16 units; mature non-graduates are accepted for certain programs; early decision and advanced placement plans available.

Costs Per Year: $1,050 state-resident tuition; $2,500 out-of-state; $2,700 room and board

Collegiate Environment: All students applying for admission are accepted including midyear students. Special financial aid is available for economically handicapped students and 350 scholarships are available, 125 of which are for freshmen. Residence facilities accommodate 40 men and 40 women. The college library contains 34,000 volumes and 210 periodicals, and is housed in a separate structure of unique octagonal design on the campus.

Community Environment: An industrial city with rural and urban sections, Chanute is the girlhood home of Osa Johnson, famous African and South Seas explorer. Oil production, manufacturing and agriculture are important to the city's economy. The varied industries include a cement plant, an oil field equipment manufacturing company, a garment factory and machine shops. Some part-time employment is available. Chanute has good shopping facilities, a hospital, many churches, a theater, a skating rink, commercial family recreation, a lake and a municipal golf course. A Mexican Fiesta, the Fall Festival, and a Horse Show are special annual events.

OTTAWA UNIVERSITY   *(F-16)*
10th and Cedar
Ottawa, Kansas 66067
Tel: (913) 242-5200; (800) 755-5200; Admissions: (913) 242-5200 x5555

Description: Founded by Baptists in 1865, the university continues to serve as an integral part of the American Baptist Convention. Enrollment includes 545 students. A faculty of 46 gives a faculty-student ratio of 1-16. The school operates on the semester system and offers two summer sessions. The university is accredited by the North Central Association of Colleges and Schools and holds membership in a variety of education associations.

Entrance Requirements: High school graduates accepted with rank in upper half of graduating class; non-high school graduates may be admitted as SAT or ACT required; minimum SAT scores of 450V and 450M required; minimum ACT score of 18 required; transfers must have C average; early admission, early decision, rolling admission, delayed admission and advanced placement plans available.

Costs Per Year: $7,960 tuition; $3,570 room and board.

Collegiate Environment: A total of 27 buildings comprise the campus, which is located on 60 acres in the southeast section of Ottawa, 50 miles southwest of Kansas City. The library contains over 84,000 volumes and living accommodations are provided for 264 men, 154 women, and 5 families. Numerous student organizations are located on the campus including 14 social clubs, and the university is a member of the Kansas College Athletic Conference. About 97% of students applying for admission are accepted, including midyear students. The university enrolls a geographically diverse student body. Scholarships are available and 95% of the students receive some form of financial aid.

Community Environment: The city is named for the Indians who established a new reservation here in 1834. Pomona Dam and Reservoir, fifteen miles northwest, provides facilities for picnicking, camping, trailering, swimming, boating, fishing and hunting. Forest Park on the Marais des Cygnes River provides additional outdoor recreational facilities. Community facilities include libraries, municipal airport and trains and buses for transportation. Other cultural and recreational activities are enjoyed in Kansas City, which is an hour's drive away.

PITTSBURG STATE UNIVERSITY   *(I-18)*
1701 South Broadway
Pittsburg, Kansas 66762
Tel: (316) 231-7000; (800) 854-7488; Admissions: (800) 854-7488; Fax: (316) 232-7515

Description: The multi-purpose, state-supported university is accredited by The North Central Association of Colleges and Schools, the Accreditation Board for Engineering and Technology, the American Chemical Society, the Council on Social Work Education, the National Association of Schools of Music, the National Council for Accreditation of Teacher Education and the National League for Nursing. The university recognizes main areas of endeavor, which include general education, liberal arts and sciences, technology and applied science, specialized occupational education, teacher education, graduate education, continuing education, community services, and research. An Army ROTC program is available. The college operates on the semester system and offers one summer term. Enrollment includes 4,942 full-time and 1,435 part-time undergraduate students. A faculty of 244 full-time and 39 part-time members gives a faculty-student ratio of 1-21.

Entrance Requirements: Accredited high school graduation or equivalent; recommended units of 4 English, 3 math, 3 science, 2 foreign language, and 3 social studies; open enrollment policy for Kansas residents; non-high school graduates with rank in upper half of graduating class admitted; nonaccredited high school graduates may be considered on basis of examinations; ACT required; GRE required for graduate studies; early admission, early decision, rolling admission, delayed admission and advanced placement plans available; $15 application fee.

Costs Per Year: $1,754 state-resident tuition; $5,426 out-of-state; $3,024 room and board.

Collegiate Environment: The campus is located on 234 acres and is comprised of 41 buildings that include a library of 290,798 volumes, 1,368 periodicals, 516,718 microforms and 386 audiovisual materials. Living accommodations are provided for 731 men, 698 women, and 47 families. There are 5 chapters of national fraternities and 3 chapters of national sororities on campus in addition to numerous other student organizations. Almost 95% of students applying for admission are accepted including midyear students. Semesters begin in August and January. The university offers Associate, Bachelor and Master degrees. Financial assistance is available and 57% of current students receive some form of aid. Out of 924 scholarships, approximately 314 are for freshmen.

Community Environment: Pittsburg is the largest city in southeast Kansas. It is widely known for its fine homes, large churches, excellent schools, and many municipal facilities. Much of the coal mining in Kansas is done in this area. Some of the abandoned open pits have been flooded and stocked for fishing, swimming, boating and water skiing. Part-time employment opportunities are good. Other recreational activities within the city are bowling, tennis, golf and swimming.

PRATT COMMUNITY COLLEGE   *(I-8)*
Highway 61
Pratt, Kansas 67124
Tel: (316) 672-5641; (800) 794-3091; Fax: (316) 672-5288

Description: The coeducational publicly supported community college was founded in 1938 (although it traces its history in the community to 1891). The current main campus was completed in 1968. Pratt is accredited by the North Central Association of Colleges and Schools. It awards an associate degree in addition to a one-year certificate program. It operates on the semester system and offers two summer sessions. Recent enrollment was 1,291 students. A faculty of 80 gives a faculty-student ratio of 1-17.

Entrance Requirements: High school graduate or equivalent; open enrollment, early admission, early decision, and rolling admission. CLEP accepted.

Costs Per Year: $800 tuition; $2,272 tuition for out-of-state residents. Room and board $2,640.

Collegiate Environment: The college is located just outside of Pratt in a rural setting. Dormitory facilities are available for 119 men and for 52 women. The library holdings include 26,000 volumes. Financial aid is available.

Community Environment: Pratt (population 6,885) is the county seat of Pratt county and is approximately 75 miles due west of Wichita. This rural setting provides a vast range of recreational activities.

SAINT MARY COLLEGE   *(D-17)*
4100 South 4th Street Trafficway
Leavenworth, Kansas 66048
Tel: (913) 682-5151; (800) 752-7043; Fax: (913) 682-2406

Description: The Roman Catholic, liberal arts college was founded by the Sisters of Charity of Leavenworth as St. Mary Academy in 1858 and became a junior college in 1923. Today the college is a four-year, degree-granting institution that enrolls 1,091 students. A faculty of 40 full-time and 65 part-time gives a faculty-student ratio of 1-11. The college is accredited by the North Central Association of Colleges and Secondary Schools and by the National Council for the Accreditation of Teacher Education. The college operates on the semester system and offers one summer session.

Entrance Requirements: Accredited high school graduation or equivalent with rank in upper half of graduating class; C+ average in 16 units including 4 English, 2 mathematics, 2 foreign language, 1 science, 2 social science; ACT required; applicants not meeting all requirements may be admitted as probational students; rolling admission available; $20 application fee.

Costs Per Year: $6,600 tuition; $3,500 room and board; $250 student fees.

Collegiate Environment: Saint Mary's 240-acre hilltop campus contains a library of 118,000 volumes, 461 periodicals, 24,085 microforms and 5,674 audiovisual materials and dormitory facilities for 300 students. Students who do not live with parents or relatives while attending college live on campus. Approximately 92% of students applying for admission meet the requirements and are accepted including midyear students. Special financial aid is available for economically handicapped students and 65% of the current student body receives some form of financial aid. Almost 82% of the student body graduated in the top half of their high school class, 56% in the top quarter. There are scholarships available and many of these are offered to freshmen.

Community Environment: Leavenworth is 26 miles northwest of Kansas City, which contributes to the economic and recreational interest of the community.

SEWARD COUNTY COMMUNITY COLLEGE   *(J-3)*
Box 1137
Liberal, Kansas 67901
Tel: (316) 624-1951; (800) 373-9951; Admissions: (316) 629-2710; Fax: (316) 629-2725

Description: The two-year, liberal arts college was founded in 1967 and officially opened its doors to students in September, 1969. The college serves citizens of Seward County and the surrounding area of Western Kansas. It is accredited by the North Central Association of Colleges and Secondary Schools. Seward operates on the semester system and offers one summer session. Enrollment includes 565 full-time and 1,126 part-time students. A faculty of 47 full-time and 67 part-time provides a teacher-student ratio of 1-18.

Entrance Requirements: High school graduation or equivalent; open enrollment policy; non-high school graduates may enter as special students; ACT recommended; rolling admission, early admission, delayed admission, midyear admission and advanced placement plans available.

Costs Per Year: $864 tuition state residents; $2,176 tuition out-of-state residents; $2,800 room and board; $320 student fees.

Collegiate Environment: The new campus on the north edge of Liberal was first occupied in the fall of 1973. Dormitory facilities are available for 66 men and 66 women. The school offers a variety of sports including baseball, basketball, tennis and track and field. The college library has 33,000 hardbound volumes, 505 periodicals, 530 microforms. All students applying for admission are accepted if they meet the requirements, including midyear students, and 44% of the previous freshman class returned for their sophomore year; 252 scholarships are offered, including 120 for freshmen and 53% of the current student body receive some form of financial aid.

Community Environment: Liberal is the county seat of Seward County. Oil discoveries have added significantly to the economic importance of Liberal. Southwestern Kansas is rich in wheat, oil and gas, and growing agri-related industries such as cattle/swine feed operations and meat packing. Part time employment is available. All forms of commercial transportation are available. A golf course, parks and swimming pools are some of the recreational facilities. Shopping facilities are excellent.

SOUTHWESTERN COLLEGE   *(J-12)*
100 College Street
Winfield, Kansas 67156
Tel: (316) 221-8236; Fax: (316) 221-8344

Description: The private college was chartered in 1885 by the Methodists of Kansas and enrolled 43 students in 1886. Since that time it has expanded its enrollment to include 590 full-time and 147 part-time undergraduate and graduate students. A faculty of 43 full-time, 17 part-time provides a faculty-student ratio of 1-12. The college operates on the semester system and offers two summer sessions. The college confers the Bachelor degree in arts, music, science, business administration, and philosophy. The school is accredited by the North Central Association of Colleges and Secondary Schools, the Kansas State Board of Education, the University Senate of the United Methodist Church and by other professional associations.

Entrance Requirements: Accredited high school graduation or equivalent with C average in 18 units; SAT or ACT required; GRE required for graduate programs; early admission, early decision, midyear admission, rolling admission, delayed admission and advanced placement plans available; $15 application fee.

Costs Per Year: $7,200 tuition; $3,532 room and board; $250 student fees.

Collegiate Environment: The college is located on 70 acres and is comprised of 12 buildings that include a library of 95,000 volumes, 400 periodicals, and 10,000 microforms. Dormitories for 352 students are available. There are more than 25 social and service organizations on campus. About 70% of students applying for admission are accepted including midyear students. The college is pleased to have students come from many geographical regions and foreign countries. Financial aid is available for economically handicapped students and 85% of the current student body receives some form of financial aid.

Community Environment: Located in Winfield, Kansas, a town of 11,000 residents. There is a small town atmosphere in Winfield, but the city of Wichita is only 45 miles away.

STERLING COLLEGE   *(G-10)*
Sterling, Kansas 67579
Tel: (316) 278-2173; (800) 346-1017; Fax: (316) 278-3690

Description: As a cooperative effort between the community of Sterling and the United Presbyterian Church of the Synod of Kansas, the college was chartered in 1886 and opened in 1887. Originally the college was called Cooper Memorial College; the present name was adopted in 1920. The college is accredited by the North Central Association of Colleges and Schools and by the National Council for Accreditation of Teacher Education, and is a member of the Associated Colleges of Central Kansas. It operates on the 4-1-4 calendar system. Enrollment is 550 part-time students. A faculty of 34 full-time and 10 part-time gives a faculty-student ratio of 1-14.

Entrance Requirements: Accredited high school graduation or equivalent with rank in upper half of graduating class; completion of 17 units including 3 English, 2 mathematics, 1 science, 2 social science; ACT or SAT required; students graduating below the 50th percentile of their high school class may be admitted if test scores are sufficiently high; early decision, early admission, rolling admission, delayed admission, midyear admission and advanced placement plans available; $10 application fee.

Costs Per Year: $8,000 tuition; $3,100 room and board; $100 student fees; $600 approximate additional expenses.

Collegiate Environment: The college is located on 45 acres, and includes a library of 84,000 volumes, 420 periodicals, 1,200 microforms, and 1,000 audiovisual materials. Living accommodations are provided for 600 men and women. 94% of students applying for admission are accepted, including midyear students. 175 scholarships aare offered including 90 for freshman and 45 athletic. 90% of the student body receives some form of financial aid. The college seeks a geographically diverse student body.

Community Environment: Sterling is in a rich wheat-growing, oil producing area with community facilities that include churches, Chamber of Commerce and many businesses. Opportunities for part time work are good. Train and bus service are available as well as an airport in Hutchinson, 25 miles away. Recreational activities are baseball, fishing, picnicking, and swimming at the municipal lake and college swimming pool.

TABOR COLLEGE   *(G-12)*
400 South Jefferson
Hillsboro, Kansas 67063
Tel: (316) 947-3121; (800) 822-6799; Fax: (316) 947-2607

Description: The Christian, liberal arts college is sponsored and supported by the Mennonite Brethren and North American Baptist Churches. It was founded in the spring of 1908. The college is accredited by the North Central Association of Colleges and Secondary Schools. It grants Associate and Bachelors degrees. In addition, it operates an adult degree completion program at the Tallgrass Executive Park in Wichita, Kansas. The college operates on the 4-1-4 system. Enrollment includes 470 full-time and 33 part-time students. A faculty of 46 full-time and 26 part-time gives a faculty-student ratio of 1-16.

Entrance Requirements: High school graduation or equivalent with completion of 17 units; ACT or SAT required; applicants not meeting all requirements may be admitted conditionally; $10 application fee; early admission, rolling admission and advanced placement plans available.

Costs Per Year: $8,480 tuition; $3,410 room and board; $200 student fees.

Collegiate Environment: The campus is located on 26 acres in the southeast part of Hillsboro. The 20 buildings that serve the college include a library of 350,000 volumes, 2,700 periodicals, and living accommodations for 208 men and 160 women. Approximately 61% of students applying for admission are accepted including midyear students. Financial aid is available for economically disadvantaged students and 100% of the student body receives aid. The college welcomes a geographically diverse student body. The academic year begins in September with an interterm in January and a second semester beginning in February.

Community Environment: Situated in the wheat and dairy area of central Kansas, Hillsboro is the leading trade center of western Marion County. Community facilities include a hospital, park, swimming pool and golf course.

UNIVERSITY OF KANSAS   *(E-16)*
P.O. Box 505
Lawrence, Kansas 66045
Tel: (913) 864-2700; Admissions: (913) 864-3911; Fax: (913) 864-5221

Description: The University of Kansas was established in 1864 and its first class in 1866 had 55 students. Since then the university has steadily grown to include an enrollment of 21,868 full-time and 6,181 part-time students. A faculty of 1,723 full-time and 366 part-time gives a faculty-student ratio of 1-15. The university operates on the semester system and offers one summer session. It is accredited by the North Central Association of Colleges and Schools and by numerous relevant professional organizations. Freshmen are admitted directly to the following academic divisions of the University: the College of Liberal Arts and Sciences, the School of Architecture and Urban Design, the School of Engineering, the School of Fine Arts, and the Department of Health, Physical Education, and Recreation in the School of Education. Sophomores can enter the School of Social Welfare. A student must be a junior to enroll in the Schools of Business, Journalism and Mass Communications, Pharmacy, Nursing and in most departments of the Schools of Education and Allied Health. The university has a highly regarded Graduate School and Law School. The University of Kansas Medical Center is located in Kansas City (40 miles east of Lawrence) and has the Schools of Allied Health, Medicine, and Nursing. Study abroad programs is more than 60 countries. Programs for all 4 branches of ROTC are available.

Entrance Requirements: Any graduate of an accredited Kansas high school who has not attended another institution since graduation is admitted; graduates at accredited out-of-state high schools to be admitted to the College of Liberal Arts and Sciences must meet one of the following criteria: (1) 3.0 GPA (4.0 scale); (2) 2.0 GPA and ACT composite score of 24 or SAT score of 990; (3) 2.0 GPA and 4 years of English, 3 math, 3 social science, 3 natural science, and 2 foreign language; outstanding non-high school graduates may be admitted; ACT or SAT required; rolling admission, midyear admission and advanced placement plans available; $15 application fee.

Costs Per Year: $2,038 state-resident tuition and fees; $7,382 out-of-state; $3,384 room and board.

Collegiate Environment: The main campus in Lawrence occupies about 1,000 acres and is comprised of more than 100 main buildings that include a research library system of about 3,292,923 volumes. University residence halls provide comfortable quarters and meals for 2,588 undergraduate and 1,370 graduate students. There are also a variety of living accommodations available in scholarship halls, rooming houses, private homes, apartments, and university-owned apartments. There are 28 social fraternities and 18 sororities, most maintaining chapter houses near the campus. Membership is approximately 1,950 men and 2,150 women. 70% of applicants are accepted. $6.3 million in privately sponsored scholarships is available, and 43% of undergraduates receive some form of financial aid. The university has highly regarded museums, theater productions, concerts and a chamber music series. There are a wide range of sports (Big Eight Conference), recreational facilities and more than 300 clubs available to students.

Community Environment: Lawrence, a town about 70,000, is set among the rolling hills of northeast Kansas. The cosmopolitan quality of the campus extends to the community, making a wide variety of cultural, ethnic, and recreational opportunities available to university students. Lawrence offers shopping areas, restaurants, entertainment, and recreational facilities that are either within easy walking distance of the campus or served by the university bus service. Near Lawrence there are several lakes for boating, fishing and swimming. Metropolitan Kansas City, with its professional sports, ballet, opera, concerts, night spots, galleries, museums, festivals, and international airport, is about 40 miles east of Lawrence. Topeka, the state capital, is 30 miles west.

WASHBURN UNIVERSITY OF TOPEKA   *(D-15)*
1700 College
Topeka, Kansas 66621
Tel: (913) 231-1010; Admissions: (913) 231-1030; Fax: (913) 231-1089

Description: The university, founded in 1865 as a Congregational school called Lincoln College, is accredited by the North Central Association of Colleges and Schools and by respective professional organizations. It became a public institution in 1941 and now receives a third of its income from the tax receipts of the city of Topeka, half from tuition and an additional financial supplement from the State of Kansas. The university's programs include a liberal arts college; a law school, offering a three-year professional program; studies in elementary education, administration and psychology; continuing education; a center for social and behavioral research; and a program that emphasizes international relations and includes the nationally known "Washburn Semester at Copenhagen." It operates on the semester system and offers two summer sessions. Enrollment includes 3,021 full-time and 2,650 part-time undergraduate, and 768 graduate students. A faculty of 255 full-time amd 185 part-time gives a faculty-student ratio of 1-18. Army and Air Force ROTC programs are available.

Entrance Requirements: Accredited high school graduation or GED equivalent; open enrollment policy for state residents; ACT required; GRE required for graduate studies; early admission and rolling admission plans available.

Costs Per Year: $2,700 state resident tuition; $5,130 nonresident tuition; $3,310 room and board; $32 student fees.

Collegiate Environment: The university is located in the southwest part of the city of Topeka and is surrounded by a quiet residential district. A devastating tornado destroyed many buildings in 1966, but a new campus arose from the rubble, giving the university unique advantages of long history and tradition coupled with modern and efficient buildings and equipment. The new buildings, including a library of 500,000 volumes, 1,500 periodicals, 100,000 microforms, and 1,520 audiovisual materials, are grouped in an area that comprises approximately half the campus. The other half provides space for an athletic field, practice fields, and a baseball diamond. There are residence halls and apartments for 165 men and women and 48 families. Additional living accommodations for 240 students are provided by 4 fraternities and 4 sororities as well as by private homes off campus. 95% of students applying for admission are accepted. Midyear students are accepted as well as students from various geographical locations. Financial aid is available and 80% of the current student body receives some form of assistance.

Community Environment: Topeka, the state capital of Kansas, is situated on the edge of the wheat belt approximately 60 miles from Kansas City. The leading industries are meat packing, tire manufacturing, grain milling, printing and publishing, and the manufacture of steel products. Excellent community facilities include libraries, museums, many churches, and outstanding medical facilities. The Topeka Civic Theatre and Topeka Community Concert group provide the citizens with unusual cultural activities. Lake Shawnee is a popular recreation spot; Gage Park is a beautiful park within the city that has the finest facilities for picnicking and swimming, as well as lovely rose gardens. All major forms of commercial transportation are available. The Menninger Clinic located here is one of the world's largest psychiatric research and training centers.

WICHITA STATE UNIVERSITY *(I-12)*
1845 Fairmount Drive
Wichita, Kansas 67208-1595
Tel: (316) 689-3085; (800) 362-2594; Fax: (316) 689-3795

Description: The university traces its origin to Fairmount College, which was founded by the Congregational Church in 1895. In 1926, the citizens of Wichita approved the proposal that Fairmount College become a municipal institution. The Municipal University of Wichita was established that year. The University was added to the Kansas state system of higher education in 1963 and Wichita State University came into being in 1964. It operates on the early semester system and offers two summer sessions. Enrollment includes 7,284 full-time and 7,274 part-time undergraduate and 2,623 graduate students. A faculty of 485 full-time and 227 part-time gives an undergraduate faculty-student ratio of 1-17. The University is accredited by the North Central Association of Colleges and Secondary Schools, the National Council for the Accreditation of Teacher Education, the National Association of Schools of Music and many other professional organizations.

Entrance Requirements: Accredited high school graduation or equivalent; open enrollment for state residents; rank in upper half of graduating class for nonresidents; completion of 15 college-preparatory units recommended; including 4 English, 3 math, 3 science, 2 language, and 3 social studies; non-high school graduates may be admitted as special students; rolling admission and advanced placement plans available.

Costs Per Year: $2,159 ($69.65/credit hour) tuition state residents; $7,713 ($247.80/credit hour) tuition out-of-state residents; $2,986 room and board.

Collegiate Environment: The 320-acre campus is situated in the northeastern section of the city. Its 46 buildings house the classrooms, laboratories, shops and offices required by programs of six colleges. These academic units are: Fairmount College of Liberal Arts and Sciences, W. Frank Barton School of Business, College of Engineering, College of Education, College of Fine Arts, College of Health Professions, and Graduate School. The Division of Academic Outreach and University College provide academic support services. There is dormitory capacity of 900 and the library contains 972,116 volumes. There are 13 fraternities and 8 sororities on campus, and these provide housing for an additional 130 students. More than 2,400 scholarships are availabe and nearly 60% of the student body receives financial aid. The campus is modern and accessible and at the same time retains the flavor of the University's 98 year heritage. 53 pieces of sculpture by internationally known artists adorn the campus. "Personages Oiseaux", a colorful mural created by the great Spanish artist Joan Miro, is displayed on the wall of the Edwin A. Ulrich Museum of Art.

Community Environment: Wichita (population 400,000) is the largest city in Kansas. It is located 161 miles southeast of the center of the United States. Primary economic factors contributing to the growth and development of the city have been aircraft manufacturing (Boeing Military Airplane Company, Beech Aircraft, Inc., Cessna Airplane Co., and Gates Learjet), oil and natural gas, air conditioners, heating and lighting units as well as camping equipment (Coleman Co. Inc.), and agriculture. It is the Aviation Center of the World. Pizza Hut, Inc. is also centered in Wichita. WSU is an important resource to the Wichita area business community. The university supports research and development through programs such as the Center for Productivity Enhancement and the National Institute for Aviation Research. The corporate community utilizes programs offered by the University's Center for Management Development for continuing professional development. The Center for Entrepreneurship and Small Business Management encourages development of small businesses, while the Hugo Wall Center for Urban Studies supports local and state government activities. Nearby lakes and the Little Arkansas river provide facilities for canoeing, boating and water skiing. Several theater groups stage productions throughout the year and the Wichita Symphony (80% of the members are affiliated with WSU) has provided more than 25 years of professional music. The city's civic and cultural complex offers an outstanding library in addition to a modern convention and performing arts center.

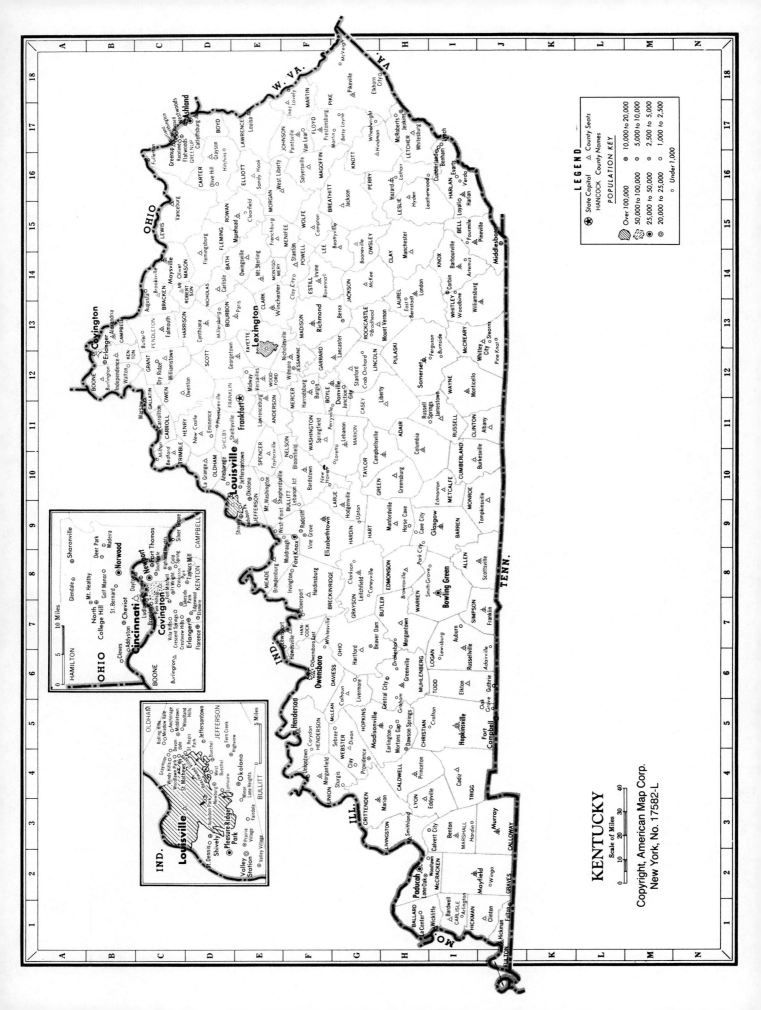

KENTUCKY

Scale of Miles

LEGEND

⊕ State Capital   ᐃ County Seats
HANCOCK County Names

POPULATION KEY

⊕ Over 100,000   ⊕ 10,000 to 20,000
⊕ 50,000 to 100,000   ⊙ 5,000 to 10,000
⊙ 25,000 to 50,000   ○ 2,500 to 5,000
◎ 20,000 to 25,000   ○ 1,000 to 2,500
                     ○ Under 1,000

KENTUCKY

ALICE LLOYD COLLEGE   (H-17)
100 Purpose Road
Pippa Passes, Kentucky 41844
Tel: (606) 368-2101; Admissions: (606) 368-2101; Fax: (606) 368-2125

Description: The private four-year liberal arts institution was founded in 1923 but traces its heritage to the establishment of the Caney Creek Community Center in 1916. The college is accredited by the Southern Association of Colleges and Schools. Each student participates in a required work program, minimum of 10 hours per week during school year. The college operates on the semester system. Enrollment includes 548 full-time and 22 part-time undergraduate students. A faculty of 30 full-time and 8 part-time gives a faculty-student ratio of 1-18.

Entrance Requirements: Accredited high school graduation; rolling admission, and advanced placement plans. ACT or SAT required.

Costs Per Year: No tuition; board and room $2,560; student fees $360.

Collegiate Environment: The campus includes some 300 acres in the lush valley on either side of Caney Creek. Many of its buildings are situated on steep hillsides, leaving the more level terrain open for recreational areas and athletic facilities. The library contains 65,000 volumes and living accommodations are provided for 158 men and 215 women. 50% of all applicants accepted. Financial aid is available for every student.

Community Environment: Located in a small, rural town, the primary industries being coal mining and farming.

ASBURY COLLEGE   (F-12)
Wilmore, Kentucky 40390
Tel: (606) 858-3511

Description: The college was founded in 1890 and is named for Bishop Francis Asbury, who aided in the organization of the first church school in Kentucky and the second oldest in America. The liberal arts college is governed by a board that is bound by a constitution to operate the college according to the doctrinal standards set up and taught by John Wesley and his immediate followers. It is interdenominational and is open to those who desire training in a Christian atmosphere. The coeducational college is accredited by the Southern Association of Colleges and Schools. It operates on the early semester system and offers two summer sessions. Enrollment is 1,157 students. A faculty of 80 full-time and 34 part-time gives a faculty-student ratio of 1-14. 70% of the full-time faculty holds the Ph.D. Study programs in France, England, and South America are available.

Entrance Requirements: Accredited high school graduation with a minimum 2.3 average and rank in upper 50% of graduating class; completion of 16 units including 4 English, 3 mathematics, 2 science, 3 social science, 2 foreign language; early admission, midyear admission, delayed admission and advanced placement plans available; $25 application fee.

Costs Per Year: $9,644 tuition; $2,890 room and board; $125 student fees.

Collegiate Environment: The college is located on 400 acres and is composed of 18 buildings that include a library of 155,000 volumes, 11,210 periodicals, 1,009 microforms and 5,554 sound recordings; and living accommodations for 446 men, 544 women, and 25 families. Chapel attendance is required. Attendance at Sunday School and church service is expected of all students at the church of their own choice. 90% of students applying for admission who meet the requirements are accepted. The average scores of the entering freshman class were ACT 24 composite, SAT 1000 combined. The college will accept mid-year students and welcomes those from various geographic locations. Classes begin in August and January, and the first summer session begins in May. Financial assistance is available. Of the 450 scholarships offered, 170 are for freshmen. The college recently awarded 275 Bachelor's degrees to its graduating class.

Community Environment: This is rural town with air and bus service available in nearby Lexington, Kentucky. There are several natural and historic points of interest located nearby: High Bridge, Shakertown, Fort Harrod, Boone's Tavern, National Cemetery at Camp Nelson, Kentucky Horse Park, world famous thoroughbred farms and Natural Bridge.

ASBURY THEOLOGICAL SEMINARY   (F-12)
204 North Lexington Avenue
Wilmore, Kentucky 40390-1199
Tel: (606) 858-3581; (800) 227-2879; Admissions: (606) 858-2211; Fax: (606) 858-2287

Description: The seminary is an interdenominational school of theology operating on the graduate level. It offers religious education within the Wesleyan-Armenian tradition in the interpretation of the Holy Scriptures. The enrollment includes a total of 985 students pursuing studies on the 4-1-4 system with two summer sessions. The faculty is 43 full-time members. The seminary was founded in 1923 and is accredited by the Association of Theological Schools in the United States and Canada and the Southern Association of Colleges and Schools. The seminary provides a cooperative program of study with the American Institute of Holy Land Studies.

Entrance Requirements: B.A. degree or its equivalent from a college accredited by a regional accrediting agency. M.Div. degree or its equivalent from an accredited seminary required for Th.M., D.Miss. D.Min. program; $25 application processing fee.

Costs Per Year: $169 per credit; $1,829 board and room.

Collegiate Environment: The seminary campus adjoins that of Asbury College, located approximately 16 miles south of Lexington. The library contains more than 169,000 volumes, 750 periodicals, 6,295 microforms, and 10,473 audiovisual materials, and living accommodations are provided for 122 men, 53 women, and 155 families. Midyear students are accepted. Special financial aid is available for economically handicapped students and the Seminary provides a $32 per hour grant to all full-time degree candidates. There were 181 Master's degrees awarded.

Community Environment: See Asbury College

ASHLAND COMMUNITY COLLEGE   (D-17)
1400 College Drive
Ashland, Kentucky 41101
Tel: (606) 329-2999; Admissions: (606) 329-2999 x458; Fax: (606) 325-8124

Description: The public, junior college is a member of the community college system of Kentucky. It was founded in 1937 and provides two years of study in most major fields offered by the University of Kentucky, the University of Louisville, regional state universities and colleges, and other senior institutions. It also offers two-year Associate degree programs designed to prepare students for immediate employment on a technical or semiprofessional level as well as continuing educational opportunities for citizens in its immediate area. The school operates on the semester system with two summer sessions and is accredited by the Southern Association of Colleges and Schools. Enrollment includes 3,061 students. A faculty of 61 full-time and 20 part-time gives a faculty-student ratio of 1:24.

Entrance Requirements: Accredited high school graduation or equivalent; open enrollment policy; ACT required; early admission;

283

early decision, rolling admission, delayed admission and advanced placement plans available; no application fee.

Costs Per Year: $1,060 tuition; $3,840 tuition for out-of-state students. One year state residency prior to enrollment.

Collegiate Environment: The junior college moved to new facilities in 1970. The library contains 33,681 volumes. Almost all students applying for admission who meet the requirements are accepted including midyear students. Financial aid is available for economically handicapped students. 80% of a recent freshman class returned to the college for a second year. Classes begin in August and January.

Community Environment: On the Ohio River, Ashland has a temperate climate with an average annual temperature of 55 degrees. This city has 25 industries including steel, oil refining, a coal and coke-processing plant, a firebrick factory and a leather plant. This is also one of the largest freight-shipping points on the Chesapeake & Ohio Railway. More than 21 million tons of barge traffic on the river passes the city annually. The Greenup Locks and Dam complex consist of two adjacent chambers which elevate 1,100 foot modern tows in 20 minutes as opposed to the six hours previously required. Transportation is provided by bus and railroad. Part time work is available. City services include a public library, churches of 15 denominations, Y's (no overnight facilities), and hospitals. Recreational facilities easily accessible are indoor theatres, several drive-ins, golf courses, boating, fishing, two state parks, bowling alleys, municipal swimming pool and private swim club, baseball, tennis, and croquet.

BELLARMINE COLLEGE   *(E-9)*
Newburg Road
Louisville, Kentucky 40205
Tel: (502) 452-8131; (800) 274-4723; Fax: (502) 456-3331

Description: The private institution is a coeducational, liberal arts college was founded in 1950 by the Catholic Archdiocese of Louisville. It became coeducational and independent in 1968. It merged with Ursuline College in 1968. The college operates on the semester system and offers three summer terms. It is accredited by the Southern Association of Colleges and Schools. Enrollment includes 1,235 full-time and 604 part-time undergraduates and 546 graduate students. The faculty consists of 87 full-time and 83 part-time members, giving a faculty-student ratio of 1-13. Six hours of correspondent credit allowed; continuing education courses offered. Graduate programs are available in Business Administration, Nursing, Education and Social Administration. Optional Air Force and Army ROTC programs are available.

Entrance Requirements: Accredited high school graduation with rank in upper half of graduating class; completion of 18 units including 4 English, 3 mathematics, 2 science, 2 social science; non-high school graduates may be admitted with acceptable GED scores; minimum score of 21 on ACT or SAT 900 combined score required; GRE required for graduate program; early admission, rolling admission, delayed admission, midyear admission and advanced placement plans available; $20 application fee.

Costs Per Year: $8,840 tuition; $2,950 room and board.

Collegiate Environment: The college is located on a beautiful 120-acre plot of rolling hills and forest within the city limits of Louisville. It consists of 18 major buildings, the oldest of which was constructed in 1950, and the library contains 117,358 volumes, 4,837 records and tapes, and 614 periodical subscriptions. Dormitory facilities are available for 400 students. 89% of students applying for admission meet the requirements and are accepted. The average score of the entering freshman class was ACT 23 composite. The college welcomes a geographically diverse student body and will accept midyear students. Scholarships are available and 90% of the current student body receives some form of assistance. Classes begin in August and 75% of the previous freshman class returned to the campus for a second year.

Community Environment: See University of Louisville.

BEREA COLLEGE   *(G-13)*
Berea, Kentucky 40404
Tel: (606) 986-9341; (800) 326-5948; Admissions: (606) 986-9341 x5083; Fax: (606) 986-7476

Description: The private, liberal arts college grew out of a nonsectarian religious community founded in 1855. The college operates on the 4-1-4 system with one summer session and is accredited by the Southern Assoiacion of Colleges and Schools. Its resources are devoted to the advancement of the people of the southern Appalachian Mountain region and 80% of its students are chosen from this area. As an integral part of the educational program, each student is expected to perform some of the labor required in maintaining the institution. Enrollment includes 1,492 full-time and 44 part-time students. A faculty of 113 full-time and 14 part-time gives a faculty-student ratio of 1:13.

Entrance Requirements: Accredited high school graduation or equivalent with rank in upper three-fifths of graduating class; SAT or ACT required; minimum required scores: ACT 17 or SAT 350 Verbal; $5 application fee; rolling admission, midyear admission, and advanced placement plans available.

Costs Per Year: No tuition charges; $2,835 room and board.

Collegiate Environment: The college campus proper, located on the Berea Ridge in the foothills of the Cumberland Mountains comprises approximately 140 acres. The college gardens, adjacent to the main campus cover 50 acres and farmlands, including the experimental farms cover 1,100 acres. Some of the campus buildings, of which there are more than 100, date from the early days (1855) of the college. The library contains 263,711 volumes, 1,603 periodicals, and numerous microforms and sound recordings. Living accommodations are provided for 570 men, 725 women, and 18 families. Approximately 32% of freshmen applying for admission are accepted for fall terms. About 75% of the freshmen returned to the college for the second year. Tuition charges for all students are covered by guaranteed scholarships. All students must work at least ten hours per week in the Student Labor Program. The Labor Program provides opportunities for students to learn by doing. There are over 100 different labor departments encompassing all operational phases of the College.

Community Environment: Nestled in the foothills of the Cumberland Mountains, Berea draws 80% of its students from the Appalachian regions of nine southern states. The Churchill Weavers, one of the largest hand-weaving companies in the country, is located here. Excellent motels are found in this community as well as the college hotel.

BRESCIA COLLEGE   *(F-6)*
717 Frederica St.
Owensboro, Kentucky 42301
Tel: (502) 686-4241; (800) 264-1234

Description: Brescia College is a private, Catholic, four-year, coeducational, liberal arts college which was established by the Ursuline Sisters of Mount St. Joseph. It is accredited by the Southern Association of Colleges and Schools. Brescia College operates on the semester system and offers two summer sessions. Founded in 1925 as a women's junior college, by 1950 it had become a four-year coeducational institution. In 1964 the College was reorganized under a lay Board of Trustees invested with ownership and control. Brescia College is committed to the concept of value-centered education and to responding in innovative ways to the needs of its students. Its mission can be summarized in four key concepts: Catholic, liberal arts, career and community service. In addition to its degree programs, Brescia offers strong preprofessional programs for law, dentistry, medicine, veterinary medicine, optimetry, pharmacy, speech pathology, audiology and engineering; acceptance rate for graduates into professional schools is over 90%. Brescia also cooperates with nearby Kentucky Wesleyan College in many educational ventures. Recent enrollment included 154 men, 287 women full-time, 87 men, and 212 women part-time. A faculty of 41 full-time and 27 part-time provides a faculty-student ratio of 1-14.

Entrance Requirements: Accredited high school graduation or equivalent. Rank in upper 50% of graduating class and completion of college preparatory curriculum including 4 English, 3 mathematics, 2 science, 2 social studies; ACT or SAT required; students not meeting requirements considered on an individual basis; $15 application fee; rolling admission and advanced placement plans available.

Costs Per Year: $7,500 tuition; $3,200 room and board.

Collegiate Environment: The Brescia College campus consists of sixteen buildings within or adjacent to a two-block area near downtown Owensboro. Its facilities include an excellent library of 128,000 hardbound volumes; a graduate center; a well-equipped science building; a speech and hearing clinic; an administration building which houses offices, classrooms, art studios, computer lab, a learning center, and a little theater; a campus center which houses a bookstore, game room, dining hall, snack bar, gymnasium, racquetball court, weight-lifting room, walking track, study pavilion, art gallery, board room, TV room, meeting room, and offices for student services and student government; and converted residences that serve as athletic building, ministry formation building, and residence halls. The library campus center, and classroom buildings are accessible to disabled persons. Residence halls provide space for approximately 175 students. Brescia offers religious studies courses in Nashville and Knoxville, Tennessee, and with appropriate enrollments, at other off-campus sites. Students from all over the U.S. and many foreign countries enrich the educational environment. About half the student body consists of older and/or part-time students; most Brescia students integrate their study with part-time employment. 65% of the students receive financial aid.

Community Environment: Brescia College is located in Owensboro, Kentucky, on the Ohio River. With a metropolitan population of 87,500, Owensboro is easily accessible from any direction and is served by both American Airlines and Northwest AirLink. The college campus is within walking distance of the revitalized downtown are, the performing arts center, the public library, and the art museum, as well as numerous restaurants, churches, and parks. Many Owensboro industries and professional organizations cooperate with Brescia in providing enriching off-campus learning opportunities for students, particularly in the areas of business, education, sociology, speech and hearing, and special education.

CAMPBELLSVILLE COLLEGE   *(H-10)*
200 College Street West
Campbellsville, Kentucky 42718
Tel: (502) 465-8158; (800) 264-6014; Admissions: (502) 789-5220;
Fax: (502) 789-5020

Description: Campbellsville College was founded in 1906 by the Russell Creek Baptist Association. It is accredited by the Southern Association of Colleges and Schools. The college is a private, four-year, coeducational college undergirded by a strong liberal arts component. Affiliated with the Kentucky Baptist Convention, Campbellsville is open to students of all denominations. Four academic extension centers are operated at various locations. It grants the Associate and Bachelor degrees. It operates on the semester system and offers one summer session. Enrollment includes 1,034 full-time and 195 part-time students. A faculty of 66 gives a faculty-student ratio of 1-16.

Entrance Requirements: Accredited high school graduation with minimum C average and rank in upper 50% of graduating class; ACT or SAT accepted; non-high school graduates with GED equivalency admitted; early admission, early decision, rolling admission, delayed admission and advanced placement plans available.

Costs Per Year: $6,060 tuition; $3,070 room and board; $600 books.

Collegiate Environment: The college is located on 50 acres in one of the most attractive parts of the city, less than one-half mile from the business center. It consists of 14 buildings that include a library of 95,000 volumes, 7,700 bound volumes, 577 periodicals, 12,700 microforms and 4,184 sound recordings. Living accommodations are provided for 160 men, 200 women, and 34 families. Chapel attendance is required of all students and they are encouraged to attend regularly the services of the church of their choice. Approximately 62% of students applying for admission who meet the requirements are accepted. The college welcomes students from various geographical locations and will accept midyear students. Approximately 90% of the students receive financial aid in the form of scholarships, grants, loans, and student employment.

Community Environment: The 50-acre Campbellsville campus is situated precisely in the center of Kentucky, one-half mile from downtown Campbellsville (population 10,500), 40 minutes southeast of Elizabethtown, one and one-half hours from Louisville and Lexington, and just over two hours from Nashville. The college is located on KY55 and can be reached from the north by way of the Bluegrass Parkway and from the south by way of the Cumberland Parkway.

CENTRE COLLEGE   *(G-12)*
College & Walnut Sts.
Danville, Kentucky 40422
Tel: (606) 236-5211; (800) 423-6236; Fax: (606) 238-5507

Description: This privately supported, coeducational, liberal arts college was founded in 1819 by the Presbyterian leaders of Kentucky. The college is independently governed. Enrollment is 955 men and women. A faculty of 83 full-time and 13 part-time gives a faculty-student ratio of 1-11. The college operates on the three-semester system, which is a modified 4-2-4 program. It is accredited by the Southern Association of Colleges and Schools. The college offers its own semester abroad programs in London, England, and Strasbourg, France. Winter-term courses in a variety of subjects are offered abroad by the college's regular faculty. Semester-length study abroad programs are available through Associated Colleges of the South in Warsaw, Poland; Dresden, Germany; and Budapest, Hungary.

Entrance Requirements: Accredited high school graduation completion of 18 units recommended including 4 English, 3 mathematics, 2 foreign language, 2 science, 2 social science, and some fine arts; $25 application fee; early action, early decision, deferred admission and advanced placement plans available.

Costs Per Year: $12,700 tuition; $4,350 room and board; $400 activity fees.

Collegiate Environment: The 100-acre campus is located in the bluegrass area of central Kentucky, 85 miles southeast of Louisville and 30 miles south of Lexington. It is comprised of 31 buildings that include a library of 200,000 volumes and living accommodations for 932 students. Approximately 80% of students applying for admission who meet the requirements are accepted. The college welcomes a geographically diverse student body and will accept midyear students. More than 55% of the current freshmen were in the top 10% of their high school class, and more than 85% were in the top fifth. The middle 50% ranges of scores of the freshmen were: ACT 25-29; SAT 470-590V, 520-640M. Financial aid is available on the basis of need. About 63% of the students receive aid. 173 competitive merit scholarships are available in each freshman class. The college awarded 198 Bachelor's degrees to its recent graduating class.

Community Environment: Danville is a prosperous community located on the southern edge of Kentucky's famous bluegrass region. The town has a rich historical heritage. It was the first seat of government west of the Alleghenies, and is also known for its early contributions in medicine, education, and government. Today, Danville is a model in Kentucky and the region as a center for light industry, with more than a dozen major employers. Midwinter days average 35 degrees; midsummer temperatures average 80 degrees. There is sunshine 60% of the time. Transporation is provided by a bus line and three main highways. Danville has fine horse farms, many churches, a library, a Regional Arts Center, bowling alley, fishing, boating, waterskiing, golf, and theaters. Part-time jobs are available.

CLEAR CREEK BAPTIST BIBLE SCHOOL   *(I-15)*
300 Clear Creek Road
Pineville, Kentucky 40977
Tel: (606) 337-3196; Fax: (606) 337-2372

Description: The privately supported, adult educational institution is maintained to meet a specific need in the program of Southern Baptist Education. It was founded in 1926 and has become a recognized member of the family of Kentucky Baptist Schools. A recent enrollment included 170 men and women. The Bible school operates on a semester system and offers three summer terms. It is accredited by the American Association of Bible Colleges.

Entrance Requirements: 21 years of age or older; good moral character; 1 year of approved Christian experience and church membership; $25 application fee.

Costs Per Year: $1,870 tuition, $2,310 non-Southern Baptist.

Collegiate Environment: The campus is located near the center of 700 acres of beautifully wooded mountain land owned by the school. There are approximately 56 buildings of various types on the campus, many of them constructed of native stone in a distinctive style of architecture. The library contains 33,000 volumes, 300 periodicals, and 1,900 audiovisual materials. The Bible school welcomes students from all geographical locations. Limited financial aid is available for economically handicapped students.

Community Environment: The campus bounds Pine Mountain State Park. Pineville, founded in 1799, is located in a rural area 16 miles north of Cumberland Gap, and is served by the Greyhound bus line. Churches, a small shopping area and some part-time employment are available.

CUMBERLAND COLLEGE   *(J-13)*
College Station
Williamsburg, Kentucky 40769
Tel: (606) 549-2200; (800) 343-1609; Admissions: (606) 539-4241;
Fax: (606) 539-4490

Description: This private liberal arts college is controlled by a Board of Trustees elected by the Kentucky Baptist Convention and was founded in 1889. It is accredited by the Southern Association of Colleges and Schools and is a member of the American Association of Colleges for Teacher Education and the American Chemical Society. The college grants the Bachelor and Master degrees. Army ROTC is available as an elective. The college operates on the semester system and offers one summer session. Enrollment includes 1,319 full-time and 151 part-time undergradautes and 80 graduate students. A faculty of 99 full-time and 5 part-time gives a faculty-student ratio of 1-15.

Entrance Requirements: High school graduation or GED equivalency, ACT or SAT, and application for admissions required; early admission, early decision, rolling admission, delayed admission, midyear admission and advanced placement plans available; $25 application fee.

Costs Per Year: $7,098 tuition; $3,526 room and board.

Collegiate Environment: The college is located in the southern part of the mountains of Kentucky. It is composed of 30 buildings that include a library of 148,448 volumes and dormitory facilities for 850 students. Approximately 72% of students applying for admission are accepted including midyear students. The average scores of the entering freshman class were ACT 20 composite, SAT 907 combined. Scholarships are available and 86% of the undergraduates receive some form of financial aid. Semesters begin in September and January. Students are welcomed from various geographical locations. The college has inter-collegiate teams in basketball, football, tennis, cross country, soccer, track, baseball, swimming and golf. It also offers a varied program of intramural activities, and both individual and team sports are available.

Community Environment: Located in the southeastern part of Kentucky, Williamsburg is accessible via railroad, bus service and interstate highway. The city offers facilities that include 14 churches of various denominations, 4 medical clinics, civic organizations and city parks. Recreation is found at Cumberland Falls State Park, Cumberland Lake, Laurel Lake, cinemas and theaters. There is adequate modern housing available and motels nearby. Part-time employment opportunities are available for students.

EASTERN KENTUCKY UNIVERSITY   *(F-13)*
Lancaster Avenue
Richmond, Kentucky 40475
Tel: (606) 622-2106

Description: Founded in 1906 by an Act of the State Legislature of Kentucky, Eastern offers a sound curriculum which includes a good general education while preparing students for careers of their choice. It is accredited by the Southern Association of Colleges and Schools, American Bar Association, American Chemical Society, American Dietetic Association, American Speech-Language-Hearing Association, Council on Social Work Education, National Association of Schools of Public Affairs and Administration, National Council for Accreditation of Teacher Education, National League for Nursing and the National Recreation and Park Association. The university has grown large enough to provide job offerings within its nine academic colleges and Graduate School. Programs offered include liberal arts, business, allied health, teacher education, law enforcement, technology, and professional as well as continuing education and cooperative education. Summer programs to England, France, and Mexico are available. It operates on the semester system and offers one summer session. Enrollment includes 11,479 full-time, and 2,675 part-time undergraduate, and 1,906 graduate students. A faculty of 529 full-time

and 326 part-time gives a faculty-student ratio of 1-19. Army and Air Force ROTC programs available.

Entrance Requirements: High school graduation (minimum of 20 credits) and Kentucky Pre-College Curriculum requirements satisfied or GED equivalent; 20 units should include 4 English, 3 mathematics, 2 science, 1 laboratory science, and 1 social science; ACT required; out-of-state graduates must rank in upper half of graduating class or score minimum ACT 21; non-high school graduates over 21 years of age may be admitted as special students; rolling admission, midyear admission, and advanced placement plans available.

Costs Per Year: $1,790 state resident tuition; $4,950 nonresident tuition; $3,126 room and board.

Collegiate Environment: The university is located on 581 acres in the heartland of Kentucky, where the famed Bluegrass region meets the foothills of the Cumberlands. The 59 buildings of the university include a library of 820,610 volumes and living accommodations for 5,882 men and women and 357 families. There are several local social fraternities and sororities as well as numerous other student organizations. Approximately 96% of students that applied for admission and met the requirements were accepted. Midyear students are accepted as well as those from various geographical locations. Classes begin in August and January. About 64% of the student body graduated in the top half of their high school class. The average score of the current freshmen was ACT 19.9 composite. Financial aid is available for economically disadvantaged students, and approximately 65% of the students receive some form of assistance. The university recently awarded 201 Associate, 1,406 Bachelor, and 297 Master degrees. About 65% of the freshmen returned to the college for their second year of studies.

Community Environment: Local industries are a miniature lamp plant and tool and die manufacturing. Richmond is located in the famous Bluegrass Region, 26 miles southeast of Lexington, and 55 miles to the State Capital of Frankfort on the Kentucky River. Recreational facilities are available at nearby parks and lakes. There are part-time work opportunities available.

ELIZABETHTOWN COMMUNITY COLLEGE   *(F-9)*
College Street Road
Elizabethtown, Kentucky 42701
Tel: (502) 769-2371

Description: The public, two-year college was founded in 1964 and is a member of the Community College System of the University of Kentucky. The community colleges provide two years of study in most major fields offered by the University of Kentucky, the University of Louisville, regional state universities and colleges, and other senior institutions. A minimum of 24 credits must be completed within the Kentucky Community College System, with at least 15 of these completed at this college. An honors program for "gifted students" and a basic studies program for students in need of remedial work are available. The facilities at Elizabethtown serve a student body in both academic and technical areas. Enrollment includes 4,297 students. A full-time faculty of 80 gives a faculty-student ratio of 1:53. The school operates on the semester system and offers one summer session. It is accredited by the Southern Association of Colleges and Schools and professionally by the National League for Nursing.

Entrance Requirements: Open enrollment policy; accredited high school graduation or equivalent required for degree programs; Kentucky non-high school graduates eligible to take GED may be admitted; ACT required; early admission, early decision, rolling admission and advanced placement plans available.

Costs Per Year: $980 tuition; $2,490 out-of-state.

Collegiate Environment: The college library contains 30,000 volumes and 273 periodicals. Financial aid is available for economically handicapped students and 74% of the current student body receives some form of assistance. 95% of students applying for admission are accepted, including midyear students.

Community Environment: Brown-Pusey Community House, formerly a stagecoach inn, has been restored and now serves as a community center and library. This is a rural area with rail and bus service, and a local airport. Elizabethtown provides recreation with two theaters, a recreational lake owned by the city, a park with olympic-size pool and a par-three golf course. Community services include the County Health Department, one hospital and 39 different organizations. A County Fair and City Festival are held annually.

GEORGETOWN COLLEGE   *(E-12)*
400 East College Street
Georgetown, Kentucky 40324
Tel: (502) 863-8009; (800) 788-9985

Description: The college was the first Baptist college west of the Alleghenies. Founded in 1829, it is the third oldest Baptist institution of higher learning in America. The college is accredited by the Southern Association of Colleges and Schools and is a member of the Association of American Colleges and the Southern Association of Baptist Colleges. The liberal arts college operates on the accelerated semester system and offers 2 summer terms. Enrollment includes 1,136 full-time undergraduate students and 269 graduate students. A faculty of 73 full-time and 36 part-time gives an undergraduate faculty-student ratio of 1-14. The college confers degrees including the Master of Arts in Education, Bachelor of Arts, Bachelor of Science, Bachelor of Science in Medical Technology, Bachelor of Music Education and the Bachelor of Science in Nursing. Army and Air Force ROTC programs are available.

Entrance Requirements: High school graduation or equivalent with rank generally in upper half of graduating class and completion of 20 units with recommended 4 English, 2 mathematics, 2 foreign language, 2 science, and 2 social science; persons over 20 years of age may be admitted with satisfactory performance on entrance examinations; ACT or SAT required; $20 application fee; early decision, midyear admission, rolling admission, and advanced placement plans available.

Costs Per Year: $8,000 state-resident tuition; $8,100 out-of-state; $3,950 room and board; $50 student fees.

Collegiate Environment: The campus is situated on a beautiful 52-acre expanse of slightly rolling terrain and is located in the heart of the Bluegrass, 12 miles north of Lexington and 75 miles east of Louisville. The 33 college buildings include a library of 125,851 volumes and living accommodations for 490 men and 538 women. About 90% of the applicants meet admission requirements and are accepted. Most undergraduates are full-time residents of the traditional college age. The college welcomes students from various geographical locations and will accept midyear students. Financial aid is available based on need as well as academic achievement. About 95% of the students receive aid. The average ACT composite score of the current freshmen was 23.8. About 70% of the freshmen returned to the college for the second year.

Community Environment: This town was the site of McClelland's Fort, a log stockade that was completed about 1776. Today the city is a residential and educational community located 12 miles north of Lexington, and can be reached by several major highways. Recently identified as one of Kentucky's two "safest cities," Georgeotown is also the site of the Toyota Corporation's new manufacturing plant. The Kentucky State Horse Park is only 5 miles south of the campus.

HAZARD COMMUNITY COLLEGE   *(H-16)*
One Community College Drive
Highway 15 S.
Hazard, Kentucky 41701
Tel: (606) 436-5721

Description: The public, community college began the first academic year in 1968-69. It is a member of the Community College System of the University of Kentucky and provides two years of study in most major fields offered by the University of Kentucky, the University of Louisville, regional state universities and colleges, and other senior institutions. The college is accredited by the Southern Association of Colleges and Schools. It operates on the semester system and offers one summer term. Enrollment includes 1,695 students. A faculty of 65 full-time and 60 part-time gives a faculty-student ratio of 1:14. The Associate Degrees in Arts and Science qualify students to transfer to the 4-year program of their choice. The Associate Degrees in Applied Science qualify students for immediate employment in Business, Nursing and Secretarial Administration.

Entrance Requirements: High school graduation or equivalent; open enrollment policy; Kentucky non-high school graduates over 21 years of age may be admitted; ACT or CCP required; early admission, roll-

ing admission, early decision, delayed admission and advanced placement plans available.

Costs Per Year: $700 tuition; $2,100 tuition for out-of-state students.

Collegiate Environment: The original college building was completed in 1968. The new Learning Resources and Technical Center was completed in 1988. Located one mile south of the center of town, the wooded campus is the focal point for most course offerings. Off-campus sites also make classes available in the four surrounding Counties served by the college. Students at HCC derive a number of benefits from the College's affiliation with the University of Kentucky, ranging from free basketball tickets to the UK Student Health Plan. The college's own dramatic productions and a first-rate Community Concert Series are also open to the students free of charge. In addition to regular classes, which are offered on weekdays, evenings and weekends, the college allows correspondent credit. Continuing education programs are also available. Almost all those who apply are accepted. Classes begin in August and January and midyear students are accepted. Financial aid is available for economically handicapped students and 50% of the students receive some form of financial aid. Scholarships are available.

Community Environment: Hazard, the County Seat of Perry County, is the retail and cultural center of southeastern Kentucky. The college serves a 5-county, all-rural area (Breathitt, Knott, Leslie, Letcher, and Perry Counties). Hazard Community College's service area is also in the heart of the state's coal country, in the Cumberland Mountains of Kentucky.

HENDERSON COMMUNITY COLLEGE   *(F-5)*
2660 S. Green Street
Henderson, Kentucky 42420
Tel: (502) 827-1867; (800) 696-9958; Admissions: (502) 830-5256; Fax: (502) 826-8391

Description: The public, junior college was founded in 1960 and is a member of the Community College System of the University of Kentucky. Enrollment includes 1,200 men and women. A faculty of 75 gives a faculty-student ratio of 1-16. The school operates on the semester system with one summer session and is accredited by the Southern Association of Colleges and Schools. It provides two years of study in most major fields offered by the University of Kentucky, the University of Louisville, regional state universities and colleges, and other senior institutions.

Entrance Requirements: High school graduation or equivalent; units must include 4 English, 3 mathematics, 2 social science, 2 science; Kentucky non-high school graduates over 21 years of age may be admitted; ACT required; rolling admission plan available.

Costs Per Year: $960 tuition; $2,880 tuition for out-of-state students.

Collegiate Environment: The college consists of 6 buildings located on 100 acres and includes a library of 24,000 volumes, 15,000 pamphlets and 126 periodicals. All applicants who meet the requirements are accepted, including midyear students. Students are welcome from geographically diverse areas. Approximately 60% of the recent student body graduated in the top half of their high school class. Financial aid is available.

Community Environment: An industrial city, Henderson is on the Ohio River in an important oil-producing and agricultural area. Principal crops are corn, soybeans and tobacco. Part-time employment is available. Transportation provided by rail and bus lines within the city and airlines located in Evansville, Indiana, nine miles away. Ellis Park Racetrack, three miles north, offers thoroughbred racing August through Labor Day and harness racing from in late May to late July. 95 organizations embrace all types of activities. There is a hospital and clinics, public library, YMCA, and 36 churches offering community service. This is the home of Audubon Museum which houses the world's finest collection of Audubon items. The city has one of the finest summer recreational programs in the state of Kentucky.

HOPKINSVILLE COMMUNITY COLLEGE   *(I-5)*
P.O. Box 2100
Hopkinsville, Kentucky 42240
Tel: (502) 886-3921

Description: This junior college is a member of the Community College System of the University of Kentucky. It is accredited by the Southern Association of Colleges and Schools. It operates on the semester system and offers one summer session. It provides two years of study in most major fields offered by the University of Kentucky, the University of Louisville, regional state universities and colleges, and other senior institutions. Extension centers are located at Cadiz, Elkton, Princeton and Fort Camphill, KY. Enrollment is 898 full-time and 1,714 part-time students. A faculty of 51 full-time and 120 part-time gives a faculty-student ratio of 1-16.

Entrance Requirements: Accredited high school graduation or equivalent; open enrollment policy; state-resident non-high school graduates may be admitted if they are eligible to take the GED; ACT required; early admission and midyear admission plans available.

Costs Per Year: $960 state-resident tuition; $2,880 out-of-state.

Collegiate Environment: The campus consists of 3 buildings located on 70 acres and the library contains 45,000 volumes. Almost all state residents who apply for admission are accepted. 75 scholarships are offered, including 50 for freshmen, and about 60% of the students receive some form of assistance. There were 171 Associate degrees awarded to the recent graduating class. Classes begin in August. The college does not seek a geographically diverse student body.

Community Environment: Hopkinsville is noted as an agricultural and industrial center with important livestock, grain, barley and dark tobacco markets. Products manufactured include shoes, clothing, hardwood flooring, lighting fixtures, industrial springs, feed and flour. The city is served by railroad, bus, and airlines at nearby Clarksville and Nashville, Tennessee.

JEFFERSON COMMUNITY COLLEGE   *(E-9)*
109 E. Broadway
Louisville, Kentucky 40202
Tel: (502) 584-0181

Description: The public, junior college was founded in 1968 and is a member of the Community College System of the University of Kentucky. The college has a coeducational capacity for over 6,500 students, operates on the semester system and offers one summer term. It provides two years of study in most major fields offered by the University of Kentucky, the University of Louisville, regional state universities and colleges, and other senior institutions. The faculty-student ratio is 1-16. The college is accredited by the Southern Association of Colleges and Schools.

Entrance Requirements: Accredited high school graduation or equivalent; open enrollment policy; Kentucky non-high school graduates over 19 years of age may be admitted; ACT required; rolling admission plan available.

Costs Per Year: $640 tuition; $1,920 tuition for out-of-state students.

Collegiate Environment: The college occupies 4 buildings located in the downtown area near business and medical centers and also operates an extension suburban campus. The library contains over 26,000 volumes. 99% of those who apply are accepted. Financial aid is available for economically handicapped students and a special program is offered for the culturally disadvantaged. Classes begin in August and midyear students are accepted.

Community Environment: See University of Louisville

KENTUCKY CHRISTIAN COLLEGE   *(D-16)*
100 Academic Parkway
Grayson, Kentucky 41143
Tel: (606) 474-3000; (800) 522-3181; Fax: (606) 474-3155

Description: The privately supported college is designed for the preparation of young men and young women who plan to enter Christian vocations. Included are those who will serve as ministers, missionaries, evangelists, Christian teachers, church secretaries, church musicians, and religious education directors. The Bible college was founded in 1919 by members of Christian Churches. It operates on the semester system and offers one summer session. It is incorporated as a nonprofit institution by the Commonwealth of Kentucky and is accredited by the American Association of Bible Colleges and the Southern Association of Colleges and Schools. Enrollment is 478 full-time and 22 part-time students. A faculty of 22 full-time and 10 part-

time gives a faculty-student ratio of 1-18. 18 correspondent credits allowed.

Entrance Requirements: High school graduation with completion of 16 units including 4 English, 2 mathematics, 2 social science; limited number of non-high school graduates over 21 years of age may be admitted; ACT required; $25 application fee; early admission, early decision and rolling admission plans available.

Costs Per Year: $9,458 tuition, room, and board.

Collegiate Environment: The campus area for the college includes 16 acres and an adjacent farm, known as the Canton Farm, which is composed of 128 acres. The 8 buildings contain a library of 95,836 volumes. Men and women who do not live in their own homes in the vicinity are required to live in the dormitories, which accommodate 156 men, 183 women, and 154 families. Chapel attendance is required. Approximately 90% of students applying for admission are accepted, including midyear students. 80% of the previous freshman class returned to the college for their second year. Financial assistance is available for economically handicapped students and about 80% of the students receive aid. The college awarded 92 Bachelor's degrees to a recent graduating class.

Community Environment: Grayson can be accessed via Greyhound Bus. It has many Protestant churches and several organizations, including the Creative Arts Club and Chamber of Commerce. Health services are provided by two clinic and two hospitals within 20 miles. Recreation available includes hunting, fishing, boating, bowling, swimming, horseback riding and miniature golf with three state parks in the area. Grayson is a friendly town with complete up-to-date modern stores comparable to a city twice its size.

KENTUCKY MOUNTAIN BIBLE COLLEGE   *(G-15)*
Box 10
Vancleve, Kentucky 41385
Tel: (606) 666-5000; (800) 879-5622; Fax: (606) 666-7744

Description: The Bible Institute was founded in 1931 under the direction and control of the Kentucky Mountain Holiness Association. The college is committed to the Wesleyan interpretation of Christian doctrine and offers a two-year Associate of Arts and a four-year Bachelor of Arts in religion. The school enrolled 76 students attending classes on the semester system. A faculty of 12 gives a faculty-student ratio of 1:6. Programs offered in Christian Education, Ministerial, Missionary, and Sacred Music programs of study.

Entrance Requirements: High school graduation with completion of 18 units and a C average in recommended courses including 3 English, 2 history, 2 science, and 2 mathematics; graduates with less than C average occasionally admitted on probationary basis; ACT required; $25 application fee; rolling admission plan available.

Costs Per Year: $2,700 tuition; $2,530 room and board; $360 student fees.

Collegiate Environment: The institute is comprised of 12 buildings which include a library of 20,000 volumes and 543 pamphlets, and dormitory facilities for 40 men and 40 women. Chapel 4 days a week is required and student prayer meetings are conducted each Sunday. The institute welcomes students from various geographical locations and will accept midyear students. Classes begin in September. About 90% of the applicants are accepted. Approximately 80% receive financial assistance.

Community Environment: Vancleve is a rural town located 7 miles northwest of Jackson on State Highway 15. Radio Station WMTC is located here. Part-time employment found on campus.

KENTUCKY STATE UNIVERSITY   *(E-12)*
East Main Street
Frankfort, Kentucky 40601
Tel: (502) 227-6349; (800) 633-9415; Fax: (502) 227-6239

Description: Kentucky State University, founded in 1886, is a State-supported liberal arts institution. It is accredited by the Southern Association of Colleges and Schools. Enrollment includes 2,564 men and women. A faculty of 136 gives a faculty-student ratio of 1:13. The semester system is employed with one summer session. Correspondent credit allowed; continuing education courses offered; cooperative education programs available in Business, Industrial Technology, Computer Science, History and Political Science, Sociology, Home Economics, Math/Pre-Engineering, Public Affairs, Biology, Criminal Justice, Psychology and Physical Education. Last 32 semester credit hours must be earned at this institution.

Entrance Requirements: A graduate of an accredited high school will be unconditionally admitted if he or she meets the Pre-College Curriculum (PCC) requirements established by the Kentucky Council on Higher Education and has an admission index of 430. The admission index is a numerical score determined by computing the cumulative grade-point average (on a 4.0 scale) times 100, and the American College Test (ACT) Composite (or converted SAT) times 10, and adding the two scores. Nontraditional applicants (25 years of age or older) may substitute results of the Career Planning and Placement test (CPP-II) for ACT or SAT results if pursuing an associate degree. $5 application fee.

Costs Per Year: All inclusive costs non-boarding in-state students $1,680; nonresident $4,840; room and board $2,896.

Collegiate Environment: The college is located on 475 acres on a beautiful hill overlooking the city of Frankfort, the capital of Kentucky. The campus consists of 33 buildings which include a library of 336,063 volumes and dormitory facilities for 447 men and 451 women. There are several fraternities and sororities located on the campus as well as numerous other student organizations. Approximately 60% of students applying for admission are accepted, including midyear students. The college welcomes out-of-state students but they are required to pay additional tuition. About 58% of the recent student body graduated in the top half of their high school class, 42% in the top quarter. Financial aid is available for economically handicapped students and 85% of the student body receives some form of financial aid.

Community Environment: Founded in 1786, Frankfort was selected as Kentucky's capital in 1792. Located at the western edge of the Bluegrass region, Frankfort, population 27,500, is home to several plants which manufacture electronic equipment, shoes, underwear, metal auto trim, precision parts and screws. There is access to rail and bus lines. The city has a public library, hospital, Y's, shopping facilities, theatres, and swimming. Organizations including major civic, fraternal, and veterans' are located in the area.

KENTUCKY WESLEYAN COLLEGE *(F-6)*
3000 Frederica Street
P.O. Box 1039
Owensboro, Kentucky 42302-1039
Tel: (502) 926-3111; (800) 999-0592; Admissions: (502) 926-3111 x144; Fax: (502) 926-3196

Description: Affiliated with the United Methodist Church, Kentucky Wesleyan is a coeducational institution accredited by the Southern Association of Colleges and Schools and the University Senate of the United Methodist Church. Founded in 1858, Wesleyan continues its tradition of development of the whole person. In recent years Wesleyan graduates have enjoyed exceptional job placement and high graduate school admission rates. The college grants the Baccalaureate degree and an Associate Nursing degree. The school operates on the semester system and offers two summer sessions. Enrollment inclues 630 full-time and 111 part-time students. A faculty of 50 full-time and 26 part-time gives a faculty-student ratio of 1-11.

Entrance Requirements: Accredited high school graduation or GED equivalent; minimum C+ average in college-preparatory units; 16 high school units should include 4 English, 2 mathematics, 1 foreign language, and 3 social science; applicants not meeting all requirements may be admitted on a probationary or special status; minimum: ACT 19 or SAT 800 combined; $20 application fee; early admission, early decision, rolling admission, midyear admission and advanced placement plans available.

Costs Per Year: $8,000 tuition; $4,150 room and board; $200 student fees.

Collegiate Environment: The campus of 70 acres lies in the south end of Owensboro, 110 miles west of Louisville and 48 miles east of Evansville, Indiana. The 27 buildings include a library of 106,964 volumes, 448 periodicals, 22,055 microforms and 3,119 audiovisual materials, and dormitory facilities for 210 men and 192 women. There are several national sororities and fraternities as well as numerous other student organizations. About 69% of students applying for admission are accepted. The college welcomes students from various geographical locations and will accept midyear students. Classes

begin in September and January and the summer session begins in June. Financial assistance is available. 95% of current students receive some form of financial aid. About half of the full-time students receive scholarships. 172 of them are for freshmen.

Community Environment: Owensboro, population 55,000, with sunshine 52-60 percent of the year is the largest city in western Kentucky. There are good commercial bus and air transportation facilities. The city has public libraries, many churches, two hospitals, three medical centers and a public health center. Recreation facilities include theaters, drive-ins, bowling alleys, golf courses as well as fishing, boating, swimming, indoor athletics and other activities.

LEES COLLEGE *(G-15)*
601 Jefferson Street
Jackson, Kentucky 41339
Tel: (606) 666-7521

Description: The privately supported college had its beginnings as Jackson Academy in 1883. Lees is accredited by the Southern Assoication of Colleges and Schools and is a member of the National Association of Colleges and Universities, and the Association of Presbyterian Colleges and Universities. It operates on the semester system and offers one summer session. Relationship to the Presbyterian Church has been continuous since 1906. The college is a Christian institution that is neither dogmatic nor sectarian. The emphasis is primarily on the liberal arts. However, the curriculum has been expanded to include two-year programs in Nursing, Business/Secretarial, and Computer Information Science. Continuing education courses are also offered. Enrollment includes 495 full-time and 159 part-time students. A faculty of 24 full-time and 28 part-time members provides a faculty-student ratio of 1:12.

Entrance Requirements: Accredited high school graduation or GED equivalent; C average in 17 completed units including 3 English, 2 science, 2 social science and 2 mathematics; mature non-high school graduates may be admitted as special students; early admission, early decision, rolling admission plans.

Costs Per Year: $4,200 tuition; $2,700 room and board.

Collegiate Environment: The 17-acre campus is located in the town of Jackson, about 85 miles southeast of Lexington. There are 5 main buildings which include dormitory facilities for 150 men and 90 women and a library of 35,000 volumes, 389 reels microforms, 11,400 pieces of microfiche, 236 periodicals and 873 sound recordings. Chapel attendance is optional for all regular students. The college welcomes students from various geographical locations and will accept midyear students. Financial aid is available for economically handicapped students. about 85% of the applications are accepted. 30 hours are required to be taken on campus. Student work is available on campus.

Community Environment: Jackson is located on the Kentucky River and can be accessed via Mountain Parkway, Kentucky State Highways 15, 30, and 52. It has a healthful climate.

LEXINGTON BAPTIST COLLEGE *(E-13)*
147 Walton Avenue
Lexington, Kentucky 40508
Tel: (606) 252-1130

Description: This privately supported, coeducational, Baptist, Bible college was founded in 1950. The college operates on the semester system and offers one summer term. Enrollment includes 60 men and 10 women. Programs of study lead to the Associate's and Bachelor's degrees.

Entrance Requirements: Accredited high school graduation or equivalent; open enrollment policy; completion of 16 units; rolling admission and midyear admission plans; $15 application fee.

Costs Per Year: $950 tuition; $50 student fees; $150 average additional expenses.

Collegiate Environment: The college consists of 1 building. The library contains approximately 16,000 volumes. Approximately 90% of students applying for admission are accepted including midyear students.

Community Environment: See University of Kentucky.

LEXINGTON COMMUNITY COLLEGE   (E-13)
Oswald Bldg., Cooper Drive
Lexington, Kentucky 40506-0235
Tel: (606) 257-4872; Admissions: (606) 257-6066; Fax: (606) 257-4339

Description: The publicly supported, coeducational, community college is a unit of the Community College System and is situated on the University of Kentucky Campus. It is accredited by the Southern Association of Colleges and Schools. It offers technical and pre-baccalaureate education in many fields leading to an Associate in Applied Science, Arts or Science degrees at the successful completion of a two-year curriculum designed to give the student a basic general education combined with technical knowledge. The school operates on the semester system and offers two summer sessions. Enrollment includes 1,347 men, 1,490 women full-time, 772 men and 1,490 women part-time. A faculty of 120 full-time and 145 part-time gives a faculty-student ratio of 1-17.

Entrance Requirements: High school graduation or equivalent; open enrollment policy for most programs; ACT required; early decision, early admission, rolling admission plans available.

Costs Per Year: $1,950 state-resident tuition; $5,190 nonresident tuition; $2,500 room and board.

Collegiate Environment: Lexington Community College students are eligible for all aspects of student activities on the University of Kentucky Campus, and may reside in the University dormitories. Full-time students will receive I.D. cards which permit them to attend sporting and cultural events. The students are afforded the health care and protection provided by the University of Kentucky for its student body. On the Lexington Campus the transfer student will take upper division work in his field of concentration or chosen profession and in related courses. 100% of the students applying for admission are accepted, including midyear students. Scholarships are available and 30% of the students receive some form of financial aid.

Community Environment: See University of Kentucky

LEXINGTON THEOLOGICAL SEMINARY   (E-13)
631 South Limestone
Lexington, Kentucky 40508
Tel: (606) 252-0361; Admissions: (606) 252-0361; Fax: (606) 281-6042

Description: The privately supported, coeducational, graduate seminary is run by the Christian Church (Disciples of Christ). The seminary operates on the 4-1-4 system with two summer sessions. Enrollment includes 195 graduant students, and a faculty of 14 provides a faculty-student ratio of 1-14. The school is accredited by the Association of Theological Schools and Southern Association of Colleges and Schools, and grants Master of Divinity, Master of Arts and Doctor of Ministry degrees.

Entrance Requirements: Rolling admission; college graduation necessary for admission; $15 application fee; apply by June 1 for fall term.

Costs Per Year: $3,750 tuition; $1,200 room; $30 student fees.

Collegiate Environment: The library contains 100,000 volumes and 1000 pamphlets. Scholarships are available and virtually all of the students receive some form of financial aid. Dormitories house 14 men, 8 women, and 52 families. Midyear students are accepted. Chapel attendance is encouraged. The seminary grants approximately 38 degrees per year.

Community Environment: See University of Kentucky.

LINDSEY WILSON COLLEGE   (H-10)
210 Lindsey Wilson Street
Columbia, Kentucky 42728
Tel: (502) 384-2126; (800) 264-0138; Fax: (502) 384-8200

Description: This privately supported, four-year college was founded in 1903. It is associated with the Kentucky and Louisville Conferences of the United Methodist Church. The college operates on the semester system and offers three summer sessions. Enrollment is 917 full-time and 174 part-time students. A faculty of 40 gives a faculty-student ratio of 1-23. Programs of study lead to the Associate, and Bachelor's degrees. An evening college designed for working students offers both Associate and Bachelor's degrees at the Columbia Campus. Lindsey Wilson is accredited by the Southern Association of Colleges and Schools, and by the University Senate of the United Methodist Church.

Entrance Requirements: Open enrollment policy; completion of 16 units including 3 English and 2 mathematics; SAT or ACT accepted; non-high school graduates considered; early admission, early decision, delayed admission, and rolling admission plans available.

Costs Per Year: $8,448 includes tuition, room and board, and fees.

Collegiate Environment: The main campus of the college, known as the A.P. White Memorial Campus, is noted for its beauty. The library contains 62,164 volumes, 1,350 periodicals, 90,148 microforms and 5,844 audiovisual materials. Dormitories are available for 350 men and women. Buildings also include a new sports building and student union. Approximately 95% of students applying for admission are accepted, including midyear students. Classes begin in August and January. Financial aid is available. There are active intercollegiate and intramural sports programs.

Community Environment: Columbia is the seat of Adair County. The climate is moderate. The city is located 8 miles from Green River Lake State Park and 20 miles from Cumberland Lake State Park, both known for their boating, fishing, water skiing and other water activities. Community services include seven churches, a modern hospital, and adequate shopping. There are several service clubs, and an excellent relationship exists between the local population and the college.

LOUISVILLE PRESBYTERIAN THEOLOGICAL SEMINARY   (E-9)
1044 Alta Vista Road
Louisville, Kentucky 40205
Tel: (502) 895-3411; (800) 264-1839; Fax: (502) 895-1096

Description: The privately supported, coeducational seminary is supported and operated by the Presbyterian Church, U.S.A. Founded in 1853 and accredited by the Southern Association of Colleges and Schools and by the Association of Theological Schools in the United States and Canada, the seminary is both a graduate and a professional school. Enrollment includes approximately 200 students attending classes on the 4-1-4 system. A faculty of 19 gives a faculty-student ratio of 1-10. Students of all denominations are welcome at the seminary, including those who seek theological education but have not reached the point of becoming official candidates for the ministry. Programs of study lead to the Master of Arts, Master of Divinity and Doctor of Ministry degrees. Academic cooperative programs are available with the University of Louisville, Bellarmine College, and other colleges and seminaries.

Entrance Requirements: Bachelor of Arts degree or academic equivalent from accredited college or university; rolling admission, delayed admission, early decision, and midyear admission plans available; $50 application fee.

Costs Per Year: $5,400 tuition; $4,000 room and board; $220 student fees.

Collegiate Environment: The campus is located on a beautiful 55-acre campus nestled among the wooded hills of Louisville's Cherokee and Seneca Parks. The 10 buildings of the seminary include a library of 110,000 volumes and living accommodations for 95 students. Only a half mile from the seminary is Southern Baptist Theological Seminary, and the two institutions cooperate closely in many ecumenical functions, including the sharing of prominent church leaders, educators, and scholars who visit their campuses. Several fine Roman Catholic colleges and seminaries are also located nearby, offering still more ecumenical contacts. Approximately 70% of the students applying for admission are accepted, including midyear students. Financial aid is available and 90% of students receive some form of aid.

Community Environment: See University of Louisville.

MADISONVILLE COMMUNITY COLLEGE   (H-5)
College Drive
Madisonville, Kentucky 42431
Tel: (502) 821-2250

Description: The publicly supported, coeducational, junior college is a member of the Community College System of the University of Kentucky. The college is accredited by the Southern Association of

Colleges and Schools. It operates on the semester system and offers one summer session. Enrollment includes 726 students. A faculty of 28 full-time and 55 part-time gives a faculty-student ratio of approximately 1-28. The college provides transfer curricula, two year career programs, and continuing education programs leading to the Associate degree. Correspondent credit is allowed; alternating program in Mining and Reclamation Technology - parallel program in Business field.

Entrance Requirements: Open enrollment policy; accredited high school graduation or equivalent; 18 units required; ACT required; early admission, early decision, rolling admission and advanced placement plans available. All Kentucky residents who have secured the GED Certificate or are eligible to take the GED.

Costs Per Year: $960 tuition; $2,880 for out-of-state students.

Collegiate Environment: The college is located on 150 acres and includes a library of 24,000 volumes, 600 pamphlets, 160 periodicals, and numerous microforms and recordings. All applicants meeting the requirements are accepted, including midyear students. Financial aid is available, and 45% of the students receive some form of assistance.

Community Environment: Centered on a plateau between the Pond and Tradewater Rivers, Madisonville is one of the principal loose leaf tobacco markets in western Kentucky. Underground coal mining operations are in the vicinity. Good shopping facilities are available. The city has several churches, a public library, and one theatre. The climate is moderate and part-time employment is available.

MAYSVILLE COMMUNITY COLLEGE   (C-14)
1755 US #68
Maysville, Kentucky 41056
Tel: (606) 759-7141; Admissions: (606) 759-7818; Fax: (606) 759-7176

Description: This publicly supported, coeducational, junior college was founded in 1966 and is a member of the Community College System of the University of Kentucky. The college is accredited by the Southern Association of Colleges and Schools. It operates on the semester system and offers one summer session. Enrollment includes 664 full-time and 745 part-time students. The college provides transfer curricula, two-year career programs, and continuing education, and grants the Associate degree. Correspondent credit is allowed. Cooperative programs are available for A.A.S. degree students.

Entrance Requirements: Open enrollment policy; accredited high school graduation or equivalent; state-resident non-high school graduates over 21 years of age admitted; ACT required; rolling admission, midyear admission and advanced placement plans available.

Costs Per Year: $780 resident tuition; $2,340 out-of-state; $200 average additional expenses.

Collegiate Environment: The college consists of 3 buildings located on 125 acres and includes a library of 31,148 volumes and 215 periodicals. Approximately 99% of the students applying for admission are accepted. 130 scholarships are available and 70% of the current student body receives some form of financial aid. Semesters begin in August and January and midyear students are accepted. A special program is offered for the culturally disadvantaged that enables students with low grades to attend.

Community Environment: From 1786 to 1789, Daniel Boone and his wife operated a tavern in Maysville, one of the first incorporated towns in Kentucky. Known as one of the largest burley tobacco markets in the world, the city has three large redrying plants and 18 loose-leaf sale warehouses. These warehouses are open daily from 10 to 2 during the tobacco sale and auction season. The manufacture of power driven pulleys, bicycle parts and the Carnation Company's condensing and canning operations are among Maysville's chief industries. Part-time employment is available. This is a metropolitan city with an average temperature of 55.3 degrees, and an average rainfall of 43.58 inches. Various civic, fraternal and veteran's organizations are available. Little Theatre, Cinema 4, boating, golf courses, and several private clubs are easily accessible for recreation. There are excellent shopping facilities and a hospital and clinic in town.

MID-CONTINENT BAPTIST BIBLE COLLEGE   (I-2)
P.O. Box 7010
Mayfield, Kentucky 42066
Tel: (502) 247-8521

Description: The privately supported, coeducational Southern Baptist college was founded in 1949. Enrollment is 60 full-time and 53 part-time students. A faculty of 16 gives an overall faculty-student ratio of approximately 1-8. The semester system is used and two summer sessions are offered. Programs of study lead to the Bachelor's degree. It is accredited by the Southern Association of Colleges and Schools.

Entrance Requirements: Open enrollment policy; high school graduation or equivalent with completion of 16 units; non-high school graduates admitted to non-degree programs; early admission, early decision and rolling admission plans available; $10 application fee.

Costs Per Year: $1,680 tuition; $1,312 room; $50 student fees.

Collegiate Environment: The college attempts to provide an atmosphere that is most conducive to reverent study and to the development of strong Christian character. Students are required to attend chapel services. All of the students applying for admission are accepted including midyear students. The library contains 32,599 volumes. A continuing expansion program has moved the school to a new, larger campus north of the town.

Community Environment: Mayfield is centrally located in the Mississippi River Valley. Transportation, commerce, industry and agriculture contribute to the prosperity of the area. Religious, medical and social facilities are available in the area.

MIDWAY COLLEGE   (E-12)
512 E. Stephens Street
Midway, Kentucky 40347
Tel: (606) 846-4221; (800) 755-0031; Admissions: (606) 846-5348; Fax: (606) 846-5349

Description: Founded in 1847, this privately supported, liberal arts, college for women, though nonsectarian, has an affiliation with the Christian Church Disciples of Christ. It is accredited by the Southern Association of Colleges and Schools, the American Bar Association and the National League for Nursing. The college offers a liberal arts education for both transfer and terminal students. It grants the Associate and Bachelor degrees with an Associate degree in Nursing offered at Danville, KY (606) 239-2461. Correspondent credit is allowed, continuing education courses are offered, and seminars and workshops in special areas. It operates on the semester system and offers two summer sessions. Enrollment includes 427 full-time and 362 part-time students. A faculty of 38 full-time and 42 part-time gives a faculty-student ratio of 1-12. Army ROTC is available.

Entrance Requirements: Accredited high school graduation; completion of 18 units including 4 English, 2 mathematics, 2 science, and 3 social science; ACT 18 minimum or SAT required; midyear admission, rolling admission, delayed admission, and advanced placement plans available; $15 application fee.

Costs Per Year: $7,300 tuition; $4,110 room and board.

Collegiate Environment: The school is located in the rolling hills of Bluegrass country less than 15 minutes from Lexington and Frankfort. The campus contains 7 permanent structures that include dormitory facilities for 225 women and a library containing 34,500 volumes, 344 periodicals, 5,769 microforms and 4,800 recordings. Approximately 81% of students applying for admission are accepted, including midyear students. Financial aid is available and 87% of the current student body receives some form of financial assistance.

Community Environment: Appropriately named, Midway is located halfway between Lexington and Frankfort in Woodford County. The climate is moderate. Midway has seven churches of various denominations and several large horse farms.

MOREHEAD STATE UNIVERSITY   (E-5)
University Boulevard
Morehead, Kentucky 40351
Tel: (606) 783-2000; (800) 585-6781; Fax: (606) 783-5038

Description: This publicly supported, coeducational university traces its history to the establishment of the Morehead State Normal School in 1922. Through the years, facilities and offerings in other fields have been developed in addition to that of training teachers and graduate work. Enrollment is 6,012 full-time and 1,037 part-time undergraduates, and 1,648 graduate students. A faculty of 341 full-time and 92 part-time gives a faculty-student ratio of 1-18. The school operates on the semester system and offers two summer sessions. Cooperative education programs, alternating work/class periods, are available through various departments in all academic areas. Academic cooperative plans with affiliated hospitals are available for medical technology students. Pre-med, pre-law, pre-vet, pre-engineering and a joint Doctorate program are offered with the University of Kentucky. The university is accredited by the Southern Association of Colleges and Schools and grants the Associate, Bachelor's, Master's and Specialist in Education degrees.

Entrance Requirements: High school graduation or GED; 20 units including 4 English, 3 math, 2 social science, and 2 science; ACT or SAT required as well as the Kentucky Pre-college curriculum; rolling admission and advanced placement plans available.

Costs Per Year: $1,900 tuition; $5,060 out-of-state; $2,900 room and board; $1,050 miscellaneous.

Collegiate Environment: The university is comprised of approximately 42 buildings that are located on 809 acres. The library contains 385,549 volumes and numerous pamphlets, periodicals, microforms and recordings. Living accommodations are provided for 3,400 students. 87% of all applicants are accepted. 70% of students receive financial aid. 1,200 scholarships are offered. Semesters begin in August and January, and midyear students are accepted.

Community Environment: The city of Morehead is located between Lexington, KY, and Huntington, WV. Community services include a hospital, several churches, five motels, several restaurants and 2 shopping centers. Area recreation includes the Daniel Boone National Forest. The campus is a 1-hour drive from several state parks, and 20 minutes from swimming, boating, fishing, and water skiing. The campus also has Eagle Lake for recreation with a golf course and horseback riding. Several annual local festivals and university-sponsored Appalachia celebrations provide further entertainment.

MURRAY STATE UNIVERSITY   *(J-13)*
Murray, Kentucky 42071
Tel: (502) 762-3741; (800) 272-4678; Fax: (502) 762-3050

Description: The publicly supported, coeducational university had its beginning when Murray State Teachers College opened in 1923. With the addition of liberal arts courses and preprofessional programs, the name was changed to Murray State University by an Act of the General Assembly in 1966. Enrollment is 6,199 full-time and 1,761 part-time undergraduates, and 1,274 graduate students. A faculty of 354 full-time and 22 part-time gives a student-faculty ratio of 1-18. The university is accredited by the Southern Association of Colleges and Schools, Accreditation Board for Engineering and Technology, Accrediting Council for Education of Journalism and Mass Communication, American Assemby of Collegiate Schools of Business, American Chemical Society, American Speech-Language-Hearing Association, American Veterinary Medical Association, Council on Social Work Education, National Association of Schools of Music, National Council for Accreditation of Teacher Education and the National League for Nursing. It operates on the early semester system and offers two summer sessions. It grants the Associate, Bachelor, Master and Specialist in Education degrees. Overseas study and exchange programs have been available in England, Yugoslavia, Germany, Costa Rica, Belize, Finland, Kenya, and other parts of Europe; a Semester at Sea is also available. An Army ROTC program is available as an elective. Correspondent credit for 32 hours is allowed; continuing education courses and cooperative education programs are also available.

Entrance Requirements: High school graduation or equivalent; out-of-state graduates must rank in upper third of graduating class; non-high school graduates considered; ACT required; test scores must predict successful academic performance; early admission, rolling admission, delayed admission and advanced placement plans available; $15 application fee.

Costs Per Year: $1,680 tuition; $5,040 out-of-state; $3,000 room and board.

Collegiate Environment: The state university is located about 45 miles south of Paducah. The university provides living accommodations for 1,500 men, 2,000 women and 144 families. The library contains 440,000 volumes. 85% of those who apply for admission are accepted. The university welcomes students from various geographical locations and will accept midyear students. There are scholarships

available and about half of them are offered to freshmen. Approximately 55% of the current student body receives financial assistance.

Community Environment: A marker on the campus of Murray State University indicates the site of the home of Nathan Stubbenfield, pioneer experimentalist in the field of wireless telephony. Many authorities credit him with the invention of the radio. Located about 45 miles south of Paducah are a hospital and several churches. Part-time employment is available. Lakes nearby provide many opportunities for recreation. The campus is 15 miles from Kentucky Lake, the largest lake created by the Tennessee Valley Authority, 20 miles from Lake Barkley, and 15 miles from Land Between Lakes, a recreation area of 177,000 acres.

NORTHERN KENTUCKY UNIVERSITY   *(B-12)*
Louie B. Nunn Drive
Highland Heights, Kentucky 41076
Tel: (606) 572-5220; (800) 637-9948; Fax: (606) 572-5566

Description: Northern Kentucky University is the youngest public institution of higher learning in Kentucky, having been founded in 1968. The university also has a graduate division and the Salmon P. Chase College of Law is affiliated with the university. Northern is accredited by the Southern Association of Colleges and Schools. It operates on the semester system and offers five summer sessions. Continuing education courses are offered as well as cooperative education programs. Air Force ROTC is available through the University of Cincinnati. Army ROTC is available through Xavier University. Enrollment includes 7,153 full-time and 3,698 part-time undergraduates and 712 graduate students. A faculty of 373 full-time and 377 part-time provides a faculty student ratio of 1-17.

Entrance Requirements: Open enrollment policy; completion of 20 units including 4 English, 3 mathematics, 2 science, 2 social science; ACT, GRE required; early admission, rolling admissions and advanced placement plans are available. Application fee is $25.

Costs Per Year: Undergraduate: $1,960 ($83/credit) in-state tuition and fees, $5,320 ($223/credit) out-of-state; Graduate: $2,120 ($116/credit) in-state, $5,800 ($320/credit) out-of-state; School of Law: $4,540 ($191/credit) in-state, $11,890 ($497/credit) out-of-state; Room and Board: $3,070 traditional housing with 19 meal plan.

Collegiate Environment: The college will accept students from various geographical locations as well as midyear students. Approximately 100% of the students who complete the application process are accepted. The library contains 289,891 volumes, 1,577 periodicals, 667,524 microforms and 2,528 recordings. 700 students reside in traditional dormitory style or apartment residences which have a capacity for 1,000 students. Of 294 scholarships awarded in the autumn of 1994, 100 went to freshmen. 48% of the undergraduate students receive financial aid.

Community Environment: Located in the largest metroplitan area of any state university in Kentucky, NKU is seven miles southeast of Cincinnati, Ohio.

PADUCAH COMMUNITY COLLEGE   *(H-2)*
P.O. Box 7380 Drive
Paducah, Kentucky 42002-7380
Tel: (502) 554-9200

Description: The state supported, coeducational, community college was founded in 1932. As a member of the Community College System of the University of Kentucky, the college provides transfer curricula, two-year career programs and continuing education. The college is accredited by the Southern Association of Colleges and Schools and grants the Associate degree. The enrollment includes 536 men, 852 women full-time, 603 men, 1,249 women part-time. A faculty of 71 full-time and 52 part-time gives a faculty-student ratio of 1:25. The semester system is used and one summer session is offered.

Entrance Requirements: Open enrollment policy; accredited high school graduation or equivalent; non-high school graduates considered; ACT required; early admission, early decision, rolling admission, advanced placement plans available.

Costs Per Year: $980 tuition; $2,880 out-of-state tuition; per semester additional expenses average $780.

Collegiate Environment: Approximately 95% of the students applying for admission are accepted and 50% the previous freshman class returned to the college for a second year of instruction. Average high school standing of the freshman class, top 40%: 20% in the top quarter, 30% in the second quarter; 30% in the third quarter; 20% in the bottom quarter; average scores, ACT 18 composite. 105 scholarships are offered including 75 for freshmen. and 45% of the current student body receive some form of financial assistance. The new campus is located on a beautiful 84-acre site which contains a library of 30,016 volumes.

Community Environment: A busy town with a leisurely atmosphere, Paducah was named for Indian Chief, Paduke, who is buried on the bank of the river. It is an important market for burley and dark tobacco. Diversified industries include boat and barge builders electronics and chemicals plants. Part-time work is available. Located at the confluence of the Tennessee and Ohio Rivers, average winter temperature is 46.2 degrees, summer, 73.4 degrees. Highways, airlines, and bus lines serve the community. A public library, many churches, two hospitals, hotels and motels and many civic organizations are available. Recreation at nearby Kentucky and Barkley Lakes and the 'Land Between Lakes' area as well as three state parks, several public parks, a swimming pool, golf courses and theatres.

PIKEVILLE COLLEGE   *(G-18)*
Pikeville, Kentucky 41501
Tel: (606) 432-9200; Fax: (606) 432-9328

Description: The privately supported, coeducational, liberal arts college traces its history to the Pikeville Collegiate Institute, which was established in 1889. It was founded by and is still affiliated with the Presbyterian Church (U.S.A.). The college is accredited by the Southern Association of Colleges and Schools and is approved for teacher education by the Kentucky Department of Education. Programs of study lead to the Bachelor or Associate degrees. It operates on the semster system and offers two summer sessions. Enrollment includes 800 full-time and 100 part-time and 100 evening students. A faculty of 60 full-time and 12 part-time gives a faculty-student ratio of 1-17.

Entrance Requirements: Accredited high school graduation; completion of 16 units including 4 English, 1 mathematics, 3 science, and 4 social studies recommended; ACT required; early admission, early decision, midyear admission, rolling admission and advanced placement plans available; $10 application fee.

Costs Per Year: $6,000 tuition; $3,000 room and board.

Collegiate Environment: The college is located on 27 acres surrounded by the foothills of the Cumberland Mountains. It consists of 12 buildings that include a library of 93,000 volumes and dormitory facilities for 120 men, 80 women, and 7 families. Approximately 99% of students applying for admission are accepted including midyear students. Semesters begin in August and January.

Community Environment: An important mining and trade center surrounded by Elkhorn coalfield. Col. James A. Garfield was sworn in as brigadier general in what is now Pikeville Park. Located in the heart of Big Sandy Valley. Surrounded by Cumberland foothills, Breaks Park, southeast of town, provides recreational facilities. Part-time employment is available.

PRESTONSBURG COMMUNITY COLLEGE   *(F-17)*
One Bert T. Combs Drive
Prestonburg, Kentucky 41653-9502
Tel: (606) 886-3863; Fax: (606) 886-6943

Description: The public, community college was founded in 1964 and is a member of the Community College System of the University of Kentucky. The college is accredited by the Southern Association of Colleges and Schools. It offers transfer curricula for those who wish to complete the first two years of a baccalaureate program, two-year Associate degree programs designed to prepare the student for immediate employment on a technical or semiprofessional level, and continuing educational opportunities for the citizens in the immediate area. The college operates on the semester system and offers one summer session. Enrollment is 2,866 students. A faculty of 83 full-time and 41 part-time gives a faculty-student ratio of 1-23.

Entrance Requirements: High school graduation or equivalent; open enrollment policy for residents; Kentucky non-high school graduates considered; ACT required; early admission, rolling admission, midyear admission, and advanced placement plans available.

Costs Per Year: $1,125 tuition; $3,045 out-of-state.

Collegiate Environment: Virtually all students applying for admission are accepted including midyear students. 70% of the students receive financial aid. College facilities include a library of 33,269 volumes, 312 periodicals and 3,058 audiovisual materials. All applicants are accepted.

Community Environment: Prestonsburg is the site of a revolutionary war battle and General Garfield's headquarters in 1862. Surrounding the city are eastern Kentucky's coal, oil and gas fields. The urban area has transportation provided by bus and car. The city has hospitals, churches of all denominations, average shopping facilities, and good opportunities for part-time employment. Recreational facilities are available at a state park with boating, fishing, swimming, water skiing, horseback riding, and high lift. Locally are a public park, bowling alley, golf course, swimming pool and tennis courts. The Kentucky Highland Folk Festival, The Jenny Wiley Festival and Horse Show are annual events.

SAINT CATHARINE COLLEGE   *(F-11)*
Highway 150
Saint Catherine, Kentucky 40061
Tel: (606) 336-9303

Description: This privately supported, coeducational, junior college was established in 1931 under the direction of the Dominican Sisters of the Congregation of Saint Catharine of Siena, the pioneer foundation of the Dominican Sisters in the United States. The Roman Catholic school is accredited by the Southern Association of Colleges and Schools. It operates on the semester system and offers one summer term. The college welcomes students of all faiths and from various geographical locations. Programs of study lead to the Associate degree. A special "nursing bridge," a two-year program, allows a licensed practical nurse to become a registered nurse. Correspondent credit is allowed; continuing education courses are offered; cooperative education program for business students are available; and credit is given for TV courses and military service. Enrollment includes 220 full-time and 133 part-time students. A faculty of 14 full-time and 27 part-time provides a faculty-student ratio of 1-12.

Entrance Requirements: Open enrollment policy; accredited high school graduation; non-high school graduates considered; GED accepted; ACT or SAT required; early admission, rolling admission and advanced placement plans available; $15 application fee.

Costs Per Year: $4,500 tuition; $2,850 room and board; $190 student fees; $400 additional book expenses.

Collegiate Environment: St. Catharine College is located on U.S. Highway 150 near Springfield. It lies amid the gently rolling hills of central Kentucky and is a one-hour drive from the major cities of Louisville and Lexington. In addition to the 10 acres of the college campus proper, students have access to most of the 643 acres of Saint Catharine grounds for hikes and picnics. The library contains approximately 25,000 volumes, and living accommodations are provided for 70 students. Students may earn a part of their college expenses by various types of work on campus. Scholarships and grants are offered each fall including academic, art and athletic scholarships. 85% of the current student body receives financial aid.

Community Environment: Located 45 minutes from Green River Lake and 30 minutes from Taylorsville Lake, Springfield has many points of interest; the County Clerk's office has the record of the marriage of Abraham Lincoln's parents and the Lincoln homestead is located five and one-half miles north of town. There is an eighteen-hole golf course.

SOMERSET COMMUNITY COLLEGE   *(H-12)*
808 Monticello Road
Somerset, Kentucky 42501
Tel: (606) 679-8501; Admissions: (606) 679-8501; Fax: (606) 679-5139

Description: The publicly supported, coeducational, junior college is a member of the Community College System of the University of Kentucky. It is accredited by the Southern Association of Colleges and Schools and the Committee on Allied Health Education and Accreditation. It operates on the semester system with two summer terms. The enrollment includes approximately 1,336 full-time and 1,190 part-time students. A faculty of 100 full-time and 100 part-time gives a faculty-student ratio of 1:21. Academic cooperative programs are available with Western Kentucky University and the University of Kentucky. Handicapped programs are available.

Entrance Requirements: Open enrollment policy; accredited high school graduation or equivalent; ACT required; early admission, early decision, midyear admission and rolling admission plans available.

Costs Per Year: $960 tuition; $2,880 out-of-state tuition.

Collegiate Environment: The college occupies 4 building located on 85 acres. The library contains 38,605 volumes, 1,309 periodicals and numerous microforms and recordings. All students applying for admission are accepted including midyear students. Special financial aid is available for economically handicapped students and 72% of the current student body receives some form of assistance.

Community Environment: Located in an urban area in south central Kentucky, railroad and bus service are available to Somerset. It has a local YMCA, library, hospital and other health services and various organizations including Rotary, Kiwanis, Jaycees, and a Chamber of Commerce. Recreation is provided with 3 theatres, drive-ins, golf, tennis, and Lake Cumberland with 1,225 miles of shoreline.

SOUTHEAST COMMUNITY COLLEGE *(I-16)*
700 College Road
Cumberland, Kentucky 40823
Tel: (606) 589-2145; Admissions: (606) 589-2145 x2107; Fax: (606) 589-5423

Description: The public, coeducational junior college was founded in 1960 and is accredited by the Southern Association of Colleges and Schools. It is a member of the Community College System of the University of Kentucky. The college operates on the semester system and offers one summer term. It provides transfer curricula, two-year career programs, and continuing education. Enrollment includes 1,751 full-time and 1,018 part-time students. A faculty of 65 full-time and 60 part-time gives a faculty-student ratio of 1-20.

Entrance Requirements: Open enrollment policy; accredited high school graduation or equivalent; state-resident non-high school graduates over 21 years of age may be admitted; ACT required; early admission, early decision, midyear admission and rolling admission plans available.

Costs Per Year: $980 tuition; $2,940 out-of-state.

Collegiate Environment: The college is located on 121 acres and consists of four buildings that include a Learning Resources Center with 30,300 bound volumes and numerous audiovisual materials. 90-95% of students applying for admission are accepted and almost 45% of the previous freshman class returned to the college for a second year. Scholarships are available, including 40 for freshmen. 68% of the current student body receives some form of financial assistance. Semesters begin in August and January.

Community Environment: Cumberland is a rural town in Harlan County of southeastern Kentucky. The city has Protestant and Catholic churches, and a community hospital and other medical services. Recreation is provided by movie theaters, fishing at Kingdom Come State Park Lake, picnic areas, a lodge and trailer park and a city park. Local merchants employ college students since the town serves an area of approximately 20,000 persons. Various civic, service, fraternal and veteran's organizations, including a Chamber of Commerce, enhance the community spirit.

Branch Campuses: Middlesboro, KY; Whitesburg, KY.

SOUTHERN BAPTIST THEOLOGICAL SEMINARY *(E-9)*
2825 Lexington Road
Louisville, Kentucky 40280
Tel: (502) 897-4011; (800) 626-5525; Fax: (502) 897-4723

Description: The major purpose of the seminary is to conduct a program of post-baccalaureate professional and graduate theological education designed to equip both men and women for effective intellectual and spiritual leadership in all aspects of the Christian ministry. The seminary began its first session in Greenville, South Carolina, in 1859, and was moved to Louisville in 1877. It is an accredited member of the American Association of Theological Schools and operates on the 4-1-4 calendar system and offers two summer terms. A recent enrollment included 3,000 students. Programs of study lead to the Master's and Doctorate degrees.

Entrance Requirements: Baccalaureate degree from a regionally accredited college for degree programs; limited number of unaccredited college graduates may be admitted on a provisional basis; applicants over 30 years of age with high school graduation or equivalent may be admitted to the diploma course with acceptable scores on seminary placement tests; midyear admission and rolling admission plans available; $35 application fee.

Costs Per Year: $1,750 ($1,000 fee plus $75/course) Southern Baptist Church member tuition; $3,500 ($2,000 fee plus $150/course) nonmember tuition; $150-$350/month for room and board.

Collegiate Environment: The campus of the seminary is situated in a beautiful residential area on gently rolling hills within easy reach of downtown Louisville. The library contains 284,982 volumes and living accommodations are provided for 165 men, 121 women, and 400 families.

Community Environment: See University of Louisville.

SPALDING UNIVERSITY *(E-9)*
851 S. 4th Street
Louisville, Kentucky 40203
Tel: (502) 585-9911; Admissions: (502) 585-7111; Fax: (502) 585-7158

Description: The University today is an independent, coeducational, urban university that has evolved from an academy established in 1814 by the Sisters of Charity of Nazareth. The University is accredited by the Southern Association of Colleges and Schools. Other accreditations include: National League for Nursing for the nursing program; American Psychological Association for the psychology progarm; Council on Social Work Education for the social work program; and American Dietetic Association for its coordinated Undergraduate Program in Dietetics. The teacher education, counseling psychology, and librarianship programs are approved by the Kentucky State Department of Education. The University operates its graduate and undergraduate programs on the semester system with three summer sessions. The University is noted for the close relationship that exists between students and faculty and for its emphasis upon learning rather than upon being taught. The enrollment includes 849 undergraduates and 369 graduate students. Of the undergraduates, 587 are full-time and 262 are part-time students. A faculty of 66 full-time and 68 part-time gives a faculty-student ratio of 1-18. At least 32 of the last 42 credits must be earned at Spalding for graduation. A Weekend College program enables students to earn a baccalaureate degree by attending classes on weekends only. Air Force and Army ROTC are available through the University of LaSalle.

Entrance Requirements: High school graduation or GED equivalent; completion of 12 units including 4 English, 2 social science, 2 foreign language, 2 mathematics, and 2 science; SAT or ACT required; $20 application fee; early admission, early decision, rolling admission, and advanced placement plans available.

Costs Per Year: $9,000 tuition; $2,800 room and board; $96 student fees.

Collegiate Environment: The University, located on 5 acres two blocks from the main business section of Louisville, is a charter member of the Kentuckiana Metroversity, a consortium of 7 institutions of higher education. The library contains 160,967 volumes, and residence hall facilities are provided for 304 students. Approximately 70% of students applying for admission are accepted including midyear students. The college welcomes all qualified students regardless of age, race, color, religion, national origin, sex or handicap. Financial aid is available for eligible students; about 90% of the full-time students receive some form of financial aid. Classes begin in August and January. Weekend College terms begin in August, November, February, and June.

Community Environment: See University of Louisville.

SUE BENNETT COLLEGE *(H-14)*
151 College Street
London, Kentucky 40741
Tel: (606) 864-2238; Admissions: (606) 864-2238 x1111

Description: The privately supported, coeducational college, founded in 1896 is under the auspices of the United Methodist Church and is accredited by the Southern Association of Colleges and

Schools. It grants the Associate and Bachelor degrees. The college operates on the semester system and offers three summer sessions. Enrollment includes 500 men and women. A faculty of 31 full-time and 2 part-time gives a faculty-student ratio of 1-15.

Entrance Requirements: Open enrollment policy; high school graduation or GED; ACT required; rolling admission, early admission, early decision and delayed admission plans available; $15 application fee.

Costs Per Year: $6,158 tuition and fees; $3,853 room and board; additional expenses average $1,300.

Collegiate Environment: The junior college campus of 70 acres is situated on a hill overlooking the town of London. There are 15 buildings which include dormitory facilities for 125 students, and a library of 50,000 volumes. Financial aid is available for economically handicapped students, and 80% of the current student body receive some form of assistance. About 80% of the students continued on to a four-year college.

Community Environment: London is located 75 miles from Lexington and 100 miles north of Knoxville, Tennessee. Transportation is provided via airlines, commercial passenger bus and rail service. Community services include nine churches, a public library, little theatre, State Area Library and a hospital. There are many civic and fraternal organizations. A Kiwanis Club project sponsors a Student Loan and Scholarship Fund for Sue Bennett students. A state park of 800 acres has pioneer relics in 5 log buildings. Good recreational facilities are found at Lake Cumberland and Laurel River Lake for water skiing, boating, fishing and camping. There is a public swimming pool, picnic grounds, natural amphitheatre, hunting, golf and 2 drive-in theatres. Part time employment is available.

THOMAS MORE COLLEGE   *(B-12)*
Crestview Hills, Kentucky 41017
Tel: (606) 341-5800; (800) 825-4557; Fax: (606) 344-3345

Description: The liberal arts college was formerly known as Villa Madonna College, founded by the Benedictine Sisters of Covington in 1921. The Catholic college offers four-year programs leading to the Bachelor of Arts, Bachelor of Science, or Bachelor of Elected Studies degree and provides a Division of Continuing Education. The college also offers a variety of two-year Associate Degrees in the Arts and Sciences. The semester system is used. The college is accredited by the Southern Association of Colleges and Schools. Enrollment includes 802 full-time and 533 part-time students. A faculty of 66 full-time and 67 part-time members provides a student-faculty ratio of 11:1. Cooperative Education Programs available in all majors. Special programs available in Experimental Learning, Career Development and Study Skills.

Entrance Requirements: Accredited high school graduation or equivalent with completion of 16 units including 4 English, 2 mathematics, 2 science, 2 foreign language, 2 social science; ACT or SAT required; early admission, Aug. 15 deadline for Nursing Program, rolling admission, advanced placement plans available; $15 application fee.

Costs Per Year: $9,964 tuition; $4,086 room and board, $150 fees.

Collegiate Environment: The 320-acre campus is situated in the rolling uplands of northern Kentucky, just eight miles from the heart of Cincinnati, Ohio. The 9 buildings include a library of 117,000 bound volumes, 60 titles on microform, 654 periodical subscriptions and 1,599 records/tapes. Living accommodations are for 275 men and women. The college offers an intercollegiate and intramural athletic program and contains numerous student organizations. About 90% of students applying for admission meet the requirements and are accepted, including midyear students. There are scholarships available and special financial aid is provided for economically handicapped students; 70% of the current student body receives financial assistance.

Community Environment: The Area-Gateway to the South on the south bank of the Ohio River and west bank of Licking River is directly across from Cincinnati, Ohio. Locally are 104 diversified industries including the manufacture of electrical equipment, automatic packaging machinery, metalworking, fruit processing and petroleum refining. Turfway Park Racetrack nearby holds meets in late summer. Three railroads and a bus line serve the city; Greater Cincinnati is close by. The town provides good shopping, recreation, entertainment

and community services. Devou Park (550 acres), golf courses, fishing, swimming pools, drive-in theaters, Kings Island, and water sports on the river are just a few of the recreational facilities.

TRANSYLVANIA UNIVERSITY   *(E-13)*
300 North Broadway
Lexington, Kentucky 40508
Tel: (606) 233-8300; (800) 872-6798; Admissions: (606) 233-8242; Fax: (606) 233-8797

Description: This privately supported, coeducational, liberal arts college was chartered in 1780 by the Virginia Legislature and has been related to the Christian Church (Disciples of Christ) since 1865. Enrollment is 816 students full-time and 29 part-time. A faculty of 65 full-time and 13 part-time gives a faculty-student ratio of 1-12. The college operates on the 4-4-1 system and offers two summer sessions. It is accredited by the Southern Association of Colleges and Schools. Army and Air Force ROTC are available. Students may study abroad during fall, winter, May and summer terms. Scholarships are available for summer study Austria, Britain, Ecuador, France, Germany, Italy, Mexico, and Spain. Special internships can be arranged in Washington, DC, and in Frankfort, Kentucky.

Entrance Requirements: Accredited high school graduation or equivalent; 12 academic units and ACT or SAT required; early admission, delayed admission and advanced placement plans available; $20 application fee; March 15 is application deadline.

Costs Per Year: $11,550 tuition; $4,630 room and board; $470 general fees.

Collegiate Environment: The college welcomes students from various geographical locations and there are no restrictions as to race, color, or creed. About 93% of students applying for admission are accepted including midyear students and 86% of the freshman class returns for the sophomore year. Average test scores of the recent freshman class were ACT composite 26.6; SAT combined 1070. 73% of the current student body receives some form of financial assistance. The library contains 125,000 volumes, and living accomodations are provided. The final 19 units must be taken at Transylvania for degree.

Community Environment: See University of Kentucky.

UNION COLLEGE   *(I-14)*
310 College Street
Barbourville, Kentucky 40906
Tel: (606) 546-4223; (800) 489-8646; Fax: (606) 546-2215

Description: The privately supported, coeducational, liberal arts college is a Methodist educational institution that offers its services to young people of all denominations. It was founded in 1879 by a group of progressive citizens of Barbourville and was purchased by the Kentucky Conference of the Methodist Episcopal Church in 1886. The school operates on the semester system with two summer sessions and is accredited by the Southern Association of Colleges Schools. Enrollment is 998 full-time students. A full-time faculty of 62 gives a faculty-student ratio of 1-16.

Entrance Requirements: Accredited high school graduation with rank in upper two-thirds of graduating class; minimum C average and completion of 20 units including 4 English, 3 mathematics, 2 science, and 2 social studies; non-high school graduates may be admitted with GED certification; ACT minimum score 17 or SAT minimum combined score 750 required; baccalaureate degree and GRE required for graduate programs; $20 application fee; early admission, delayed admission, advanced placement and rolling admission plans available.

Costs Per Year: $7,800 tuition; $2,930 room and board; $50 student fees.

Collegiate Environment: The college consists of 16 buildings located on 100 acres and includes a library of 88,958 volumes and living accommodations for 474 students and 29 families. 76% of all applicants are accepted. 110 scholarships are available, based on ACT score above 21 or SAT combined score above 900. 89% of the students receive financial aid. Continuing education courses offered; an Appalachian semester and Army ROTC are available.

Community Environment: On the famous Wilderness Road, Barbourville is one of the first settlements of southeastern Kentucky. Major industry is a garment factory. It is a rural environment and the climate is mild. Greyhound bus service is available within 25 miles of the college. State and National Parks are about 30 miles away. The city has a hospital, four churches, three service clubs, a veterans' organization and 18 civic clubs. This is the home of the annual Daniel Boone Festival held in October.

UNIVERSITY OF KENTUCKY *(E-13)*
S. Limestone
Lexington, Kentucky 40506
Tel: (606) 257-2000

Description: More than 100 years have passed since the university was established as a separate state institution. Today the university offers opportunities for specialization and the pursuit of particular interests with 17 colleges and a graduate school. The undergraduate colleges are organized into Arts and Sciences, Agriculture, Education, Engineering, Business and Economics, Nursing, Communications, Fine Arts, Library Science, Architecture, Human Environmental Sciences, Allied Health professions, and Social Work. Four professional schools in Medicine, Dentistry, Law and Pharmacy are available in addition to the University's Graduate school. The university operates on the semester system with two summer sessions. It is accredited by the Southern Association of Colleges and Schools and by numerous respective educational and professional organizations. Enrollment includes 18,748 full-time and 5,449 part-time students. The faculty consists of 1,658 full-time and 423 part-time members which provides a student-faculty ratio of 1:16. There are study abroad programs and ROTC Army and Air Force programs are offered.

Entrance Requirements: A student's high school GPA and his/her ACT composite scores are combined to determine acceptance to the university. There are those students whose GPA & ACT scores warrant an automatic acceptance; for those with lesser scores, there is a delayed consideration pool. An applicant with a high school GPA of less than 2.0 on a 4.0 scale or who has an ACT composite of 18 or less will not be accepted for admission to the university. Completion of 11 high school units is required including 4 English, 3 math, 2 laboratory science, and 2 social studies; 2 foreign language courses are also recommended. Rolling admission, midyear admission, and advanced placement plans are available. Application deadlines are

August 1 and December 1. $15 application fee for domestic students; $25 application fee for international students.

Costs Per Year: Approximate costs: $1,988 tuition; $5,264 out-of-state tuition; $2,952 room and board; $318 student fees.

Collegiate Environment: The university libraries house over 2,212,083 volumes, numerous periodicals, microforms and sound recordings, and ranks among the largest of the South and Midwest. Living accommodations are provided for 2,549 men, 2,863 women, and 360 families; with 315 single units for graduate students. 19 national fraternities and 16 national sororities maintain chapters here in addition to numerous other student organizations. The university maintains counseling and testing services as well as an international student office which assists over 1,296 international students. Financial aid is available for students with demonstrated need and/or merit and about 58% of the students receive aid. Midyear students are accepted. Semesters begin in August and January. The average composite ACT score of the current freshmen was 24.3.

Community Environment: Lexington is located in the famous Bluegrass area of Kentucky. It is centrally located with Louisville 80 miles to the west and Cincinnati 90 miles to the north. Travel is made easier with close access to Interstates 75 and 64. The Mountain Parkway connects the Bluegrass with eastern Kentucky, and the Bluegrass Parkway links the western part of the State and Interstate 65. Lexington, known throughout the world as the home of the thoroughbred, attracts thousands of horse fans and buyers each year. Keeneland, a thoroughbred race track, and the famous trotting track, the Red Mile, draw racing fans. The thoroughbred is not Lexington's only equine citizen; the standardbred, the quarterhorse, the saddle horse, and the Arabian are some of the many other breeds that live on some of the world's most famous farms in the Bluegrass. Since 1974, Lexington has been governed by an urban county form of government. The Lexington-Fayette County population is approximately 250,000, and this second largest city in Kentucky has seen steady growth in population. Lexington is very proud of its quality of life which can be attributed to the rich history of the area, and this quality is carefully monitored so that expansion and growth will enhance rather than hinder that lifestyle. Its economy is diverse in its job opportunities with the University of Kentucky and LexMark being the major employers. Employment can also be found in equine related businesses, tobacco, medicine, and retail and service industries. Among the many products manufactured in this area are electric typewriters and computer printers, peanut butter, tobacco processing and by-products, paper goods, and various equine-related products. Lexington's climate includes a mean annual termperature of 55 degrees Fahrenheit, and annual precipitation is 44 inches. The Bluegrass area has four distinct seasons with no prolonged periods of extreme temperatures or precipitation.

UNIVERSITY OF KENTUCKY - COMMUNITY COLLEGE SYSTEM *(E-13)*
Lexington, Kentucky 40506
Tel: (606) 257-8607; Fax: (606) 257-5640

Description: Community colleges in Kentucky occupy a unique position with University membership on the one hand and community orientation on the other. Each college is an integral part of the University but each college, through its local advisory board and other ties, relates itself to the needs of the community. Each of the units of the college system is accredited by the Southern Association of Colleges and Schools. The community colleges have been charged with three functions which include offering of transfer curricula for those who wish to complete the first two years of a Baccalaureate program; offering two-year Associate degree programs, designed to prepare the student for immediate employment on a technical level; and providing continuing educational opportunities for the citizens of their immediate areas. The Community College System is headed by a Chancellor; a president is responsible for general administration of each college. Students are admitted to a community college of the University of Kentucky as freshmen, as students with advanced standing from other institutions, as transient students, and as non-degree students. A minimum of 60 semester hours is required for an Associate degree. 24 semester hours must be completed in the Community College System or University of Kentucky and 15 semester hours must be completed in the college granting degree. The student should write to the admissions office of the community college in which he or she intends to enroll for an application blank, stating whether he or she is entering from high school or from another college, or applying for readmission. At the present time, there are 14 institutions which comprise the Community College System of the University of Kentucky. They operates on the semester system and offer one 8-week summer session which, in some cases, is replaced by two 6-week sessions. Enrollment includes 45,581 students and the faculty consists of 1,260 members.

Entrance Requirements: ACT required; open enrollment policy, early admissions, advanced placement, and early decision plans available.

Costs Per Year: $960 state resident tuition; $2,880 nonresident tuition.

Collegiate Environment: The combined library facilities of the college system contains over 500,000 volumes, 3,685 periodicals, 250,060 microforms and 41,573 audiovisual titles. 99% of the applicants are accepted.

Community Environment: See University of Kentucky.

UNIVERSITY OF LOUISVILLE *(E-9)*
Louisville, Kentucky 40292
Tel: (502) 852-5555; (800) 334-8635; Admissions: (502) 852-6531; Fax: (502) 852-6526

Description: This publicly supported, coeducational, liberal arts university was founded in 1798 as Jefferson Seminary. It was later known as Louisville College, and in 1846 became a university with an Academic Department, Medical School and School of Law. Enrollment includes 15, 469 undergraduate students and 5,908 graduate students. A faculty of 1,763 gives a faculty-student ratio of 1-12. The semester system is used with three summer sessions and evening classes offered. Air Force and Army ROTC is available as an elective. The university is accredited by the Southern Association of Colleges and Schools, Accreditation Board for Engineering and Technology, American Bar Association, American Dental Association, American Physical Therapy Association, Association of American Law Schools, Committee on Allied Health Education and Accreditation, Council on Social Work Education, Liason Committee on Medical Education, National Association of Schools of Music, National Council for Accreditation of Teacher Education and the National League for Nursing. It grants the Certificate, Associate, Bachelor's, Master's, Professional and Doctorate degrees. 24 correspondent credits are allowed; continuing education courses are offered; cooperative education is a basic part of the Speed Scientific School Professional Engineering Program. 7-week international exchange programs offered. Special programs include Kentuckiana Metroversity Inc., a consortium of 6 institutions, and the Minority Affairs office.

Entrance Requirements: Accredited high school graduation or equivalent with completion of 11 academic units; non-high school graduates considered; SAT minimum 450V, 450M, or ACT minimum 20 required; early admission, early decision, rolling admission and advanced placement plans available; $25 application fee.

Costs Per Year: $2,390 tuition; $6,750 nonresident; $3,800 room and board; $1,400 average additional expenses.

Collegiate Environment: The campus is located on 140 acres and consists of 90 buildings that include a library system of 1,232,945 volumes. Dormitories provide living accommodations for approximately 2,000 students. There are several national fraternities and sororities located at the campus as well as numerous other student organizations. Fraternities also provide housing. Approximately 66% of students applying for admission are accepted including midyear students. Average high school standing of the freshman class: top 30%. Average ACT score was 20. Financial aid is available for economically handicapped students and 65% of the current student body receives some form of financial aid. Special programs for the culturally disadvantaged are offered, enabling students with low grades to attend. Classes begin in August and January. The university is composed of the following schools: Arts and Sciences, Education, Business, Dentistry, Graduate, Law, Medicine, Music, Speed Scientific School, Urban & Public Affairs, Allied Health, Nursing and Medical Center-Artificial Heart Transplants and Donor Transplants.

Community Environment: Louisville is known as the Derby City for the annual running of the Kentucky Derby at Churchill Downs. The city was the base of supplies for Clark's expeditions, which culminated in the conquest of the northwest. U.S. river boats pass through the locks around 25-foot falls in the Ohio River. Louisville is an important distilling center and one of the largest tobacco product manufacturing centers in the world. There are many other local manufacturing firms in the area, and part-time employment is available. There is a communitywide fund for music, drama, and art, and the city has resident opera, ballet, orchestra, and theater companies.

WESTERN KENTUCKY UNIVERSITY   *(I-8)*
1 Big Red Way
Bowling Green, Kentucky 42101
Tel: (502) 745-0111; Admissions: (502) 745-2551

Description: The publicly supported, coeducational university was established by Act of the 1906 Legislature of Kentucky and was known as Western State Normal School. With the expansion of its programs and the additions of new colleges, it was designated as a university by the Kentucky General Assembly in 1966. A variety of programs are provided by its four colleges and community college. The university operates on the semester system with three summer sessions. It is accredited by the Southern Association of Colleges and Schools, Accreditation Board for Engineering and Technology, Accrediting Council on Education in Journalism and Mass Communications, American Assembly of Collegiale Schools of Business, American Chemical Society, American Dental Association, American Dietetic Association, Committee on Allied Health Education and Accreditation, Council on Social Work Education, National Association of Schools of Music, National Council for Accreditation of Teacher Education and the National League for Nursing. Enrollment is 9,960 full-time and 2,749 part-time undergraduates, and 2,036 graduate students. A faculty of 556 full-time and 323 part-time gives a faculty-student ratio of 1-19. The university offers overseas programs in England and France. Army and Air Force ROTC programs are available.

Entrance Requirements: High school graduation; minimum C average, college-preparatory courses in high school; non-high school graduates over 19 years of age may be admitted with GED certification; ACT required; early admission, early decision, rolling admission and advanced placement plans available.

Costs Per Year: $1,930 tuition; $5,260 nonresident; $1,556 room.

Collegiate Environment: The college, located on a hill known as College Heights, overlooks the city of Bowling Green. The library contains 794,537 volumes, 4,884 periodical titles, 2,400,000 microforms and 14,972 audiovisual materials. The residence hall provides living accommodations for 5,316 students. Western has more than 150 student organizations representing a wide range of interests including fraternities and sororities as well as departmental clubs. The university has intercollegiate athletic teams in football, basketball, soccer, volleyball baseball, golf, track, cross country, swimming and tennis. Approximately 85% of students applying for admission are accepted including midyear students. Many events are available to the university student without charge; included among these are the Rodes-Helm and University Lecture Series, university-sponsored concerts, arts exhibits, musicals, convocations, receptions, and similar events. Financial aid is available, and about 70% of the students receive financial assistance.

Community Environment: The city of Bowling Green is located on the Barrer River in Warren County in southern Kentucky. Situated 60 miles north of Nashville, and 103 miles south of Louisville, Bowling Green has about 80 churches of 26 denominations, a public library, and two hospitals. Recreation is provided by local theaters and parks, including nearby Mammoth Cave National Park.

Branch Campuses: Glasgow campus opened in 1989. Enrollment is approximately 1,000 students. Nursing, Elementary Education, and general studies programs are available.

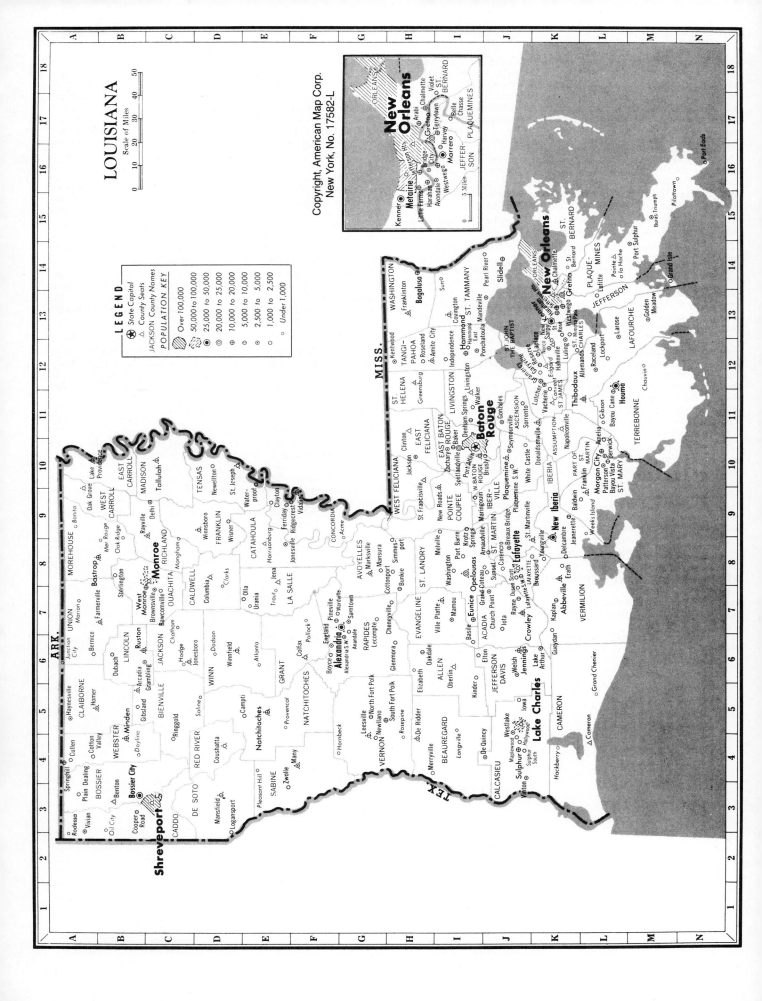

LOUISIANA

CENTENARY COLLEGE OF LOUISIANA *(C-3)*
2911 Centenary Blvd.
Shreveport, Louisiana 71104
Tel: (318) 869-5131

Description: The private, four-year college is accredited by the Southern Association of Colleges and Schools, the National Association of Schools of Music, and the American Chemical Society and is approved by the University Senate of the Methodist Church. The college traces its beginning to the founding of the College of Louisiana, the oldest institution of higher learning in the state. It offers the Bachelor of Arts, Bachelor of Science and Bachelor of Music degrees; the Master of Science in Business Administration, Elementary Education, Elementary School Administration and Supervision, and in Secondary School Administration and Supervision. The college offers academic cooperative programs in Engineering Science with Columbia University, Louisiana Tech, Texas A & M, Southern Methodist University, Washington University in St. Louis, and Case Western Reserve; and in Forestry with Duke University. It operates on the 4-4-1 system and offers two summer sessions. Enrollment includes 405 men and 609 women. A faculty of 65 full-time and 28 part-time gives a faculty-student ratio of 1-11.

Entrance Requirements: Accredited high school graduation with rank in upper 50% of graduating class; minimum 2.5 GPA and completion of 16 units including 4 English, 3 mathematics, 3 social science, 3 science, and 8 electives (should include 2 foreign language); non high school graduates admitted with satisfactory scores on GED tests; SAT or ACT required, minimum SAT Verbal 450, Math 450, ACT 21; early admission, early decision, deferred admission, rolling admission, midyear admission, and advanced placement plans available; $20 application fee.

Costs Per Year: $8,950 tuition; $3,490 room and board; $306 student fees.

Collegiate Environment: The modern campus covers 68 acres of picturesque, tree-studded land located an ideal distance from the business center of Shreveport. The 21 college buildings include a library of 167,000 volumes, 923 periodicals, 286,080 microforms, and 10,859 sound recordings, and dormitory facilities for 1,010 students. Fraternities provide housing for another 20 men. There are numerous student organizations located on the campus. About 93% of applicants are accepted. The college welcomes students from various geographical locations, including midyear students. The middle 50% of freshmen scores were ACT 21-28 composite, SAT Verbal 420-560, Math 450-600 combined. Of 211 scholarships available, 169 are open for freshmen and many have more than one recipient each year. Financial aid is awarded on the basis of need, academic excellence, and specific talents. Approximately 72% of the student body receives some form of financial aid. Almost 75% of the freshmen returned to the college for their second year.

Community Environment: See Louisiana State University - Shreveport

DELGADO COMMUNITY COLLEGE *(K-13)*
501 City Park Avenue
New Orleans, Louisiana 70119
Tel: (504) 483-4400; Admissions: (504) 483-1895; Fax: (504) 483-1895

Description: The two-year college was established as Issac Delgado Central Trades School in 1921 and has grown into a comprehensive, community college. The college is accredited by the Southern Association of Colleges and Schools. The college provides technical and vocational education; transfer programs paralleling courses of higher educational institutions; adult and continuing education programs; and comprehensive evaluation in the Rehabilitation Center for the Handicapped. It grants the Associate degree. It operates on the semester system and offers one summer session. Enrollment includes 6,289 full-time and 8,347 part-time students. A faculty of 359 fall-time and 400 part-time gives a faculty-student ratio of 1-25.

Entrance Requirements: Accredited high school graduation or GED; open admissions policy; non-high school graduates may be accepted with the Test of Adult Basic Education (TABE); applicants over 16 years of age may be admitted to certain programs; ACT for placement purposes; midyear admission, rolling admission, and advanced placement plans available; $15 application fee.

Costs Per Year: $1,116 tuition; $2,856 tuition for out-of-state students.

Collegiate Environment: Anticipating greater growth, the college acquired two branch campus sites, and in the fall of 1967 started classes on its first branch campus located on the West Bank in Algiers. Plans are in the process of development for classes and programs to be conducted on the Jackson Barracks branch campus. The main campus is located on 57 acres adjacent to City Park and contains a modern library with a book capacity of 119,000 volumes. Approximately 99% of students applying for admission are accepted, including midyear students. 495 scholarships are available and 60% of the students receive some form of financial aid. Semesters begin in September and January and a summer term is offered in June.

Community Environment: See Tulane University

Branch Campuses: West Bank Campus, Algiers

DILLARD UNIVERSITY *(K-13)*
2601 Gentilly Boulevard
New Orleans, Louisiana 70122
Tel: (504) 283-8822; Admissions: (504) 286-4670; Fax: (504) 286-4895

Description: The private institution has the distinction of being both one of the oldest and the youngest of the predominately Negro colleges. Formed by the merger of Straight College (Congregational) and New Orleans University (Methodist), both founded in 1869, the university makes no distinction as to religious belief, race, or nationality in the admission of students and the selection of faculty. The university operates on the semester system and is accredited by the Southern Association of Colleges and Schools and by the League for Nursing. The recent enrollment was 1,600 students working toward the Bachelor of Arts, Bachelor of Science, and the Bachelor of Science in Nursing degrees. The university offers a six-week summer program, and new students may enter in any term. Dillard's academic program includes a major in Japanese studies, the only one of its kind in the South. Army ROTC is available.

Entrance Requirements: Accredited high school graduation or equivalent; completion of 18 units including 4 English, 4 mathematics, 3 science, 3 social science; non-high school graduates may be admitted to certain programs; SAT or ACT required; Pre-nursing and Guidance examination required for nursing programs; $10 application fee.

Costs Per Year: $6,700 tuition: $3,650 room and board.

Collegiate Environment: The main campus consists of 19 buildings on a 48.2-acre tract, located in one of the most beautiful residential areas of the city. About 90% of students applying for admission meet the requirements and 72% of these are accepted, including midyear students. Dormitory housing accomodates 500 students. The library contains 130,000 volumes and more than 500 periodicals. Financial aid is available for economically handicapped students.

Community Environment: See Tulane University.

GRAMBLING STATE UNIVERSITY   *(B-6)*
P.O. Drawer 607
Grambling, Louisiana 71245
Tel: (318) 247-3811; (800) 381-6712; Admissions: (318) 274-2435;
Fax: (318) 274-3292

Description: This state university traces its history to the founding of an industrial school in 1901. It was made a state junior college in 1928, a four-year program was inaugurated in 1940, and a state university in 1974. It is accredited by the Southern Association of Colleges and Schools and the Louisiana State Department of Education, and by respective professional accrediting organizations. The university is organized into the College of Business, College of Education, College of Liberal Arts, College of Science and Technology, School of Nursing, School of Social Work, School of Graduate Studies, and the College of Basic Special Studies. Air Force and Army ROTC programs are available as electives. The university operates on the semester system and offers one summer session. Enrollment includes 7,600 full-time and 703 part-time undergraduates and 700 graduate students. A faculty of 400 full-time and 50 part-time gives a faculty-student ratio of 1-32.

Entrance Requirements: Accredited high school graduation with the completion of 22 units including 4 English, 3 mathematics, 3 science, 3 social science, 1 language, 1 computer literacy, 2 physical education; out-of-state accredited high school graduates must rank in upper half of graduating class; early admission, early decision, rolling admission, delayed admission, midyear admission and advanced placement plans available; ACT required, SAT accepted, GRE. $5 application fee.

Costs Per Year: $1,044 tuition state resident; $2,019 nonresident; $2,700 room and board; $175 fees plus a $60 fee for international students.

Collegiate Environment: The campus is located on 380 acres and consists of 78 buildings which include dormitory facilities for 3,798 men and women. There are four national fraternities and five national sororities located on campus in addition to numerous other student organizations. The library holdings includes 1,000,000 volumes, periodicals, microfilms and audiovisual materials. Approximately 71% of the students applying for admission are accepted including midyear students and those from various geographical locations. Half of the recent study body graduated in the top half of their high school class, 25% in the top quarter. 90% of the students receive some form of financial aid and 486 scholarships are available, including 178 for freshmen.

Community Environment: Suburban location five miles from Ruston, 35 miles from Monroe, and 70 miles from Shreveport. There is easy access to several major airlines and buses. There are theatres in nearby Ruston. Excellent hunting, fishing, boating facilities are nearby. This is the home of the annual North Louisiana Broiler Show and Fair, and an annual Housing Clinic. The City has many fraternal, athletic, social and civic organizations, including a Chamber of Commerce.

LOUISIANA COLLEGE   *(F-7)*
P.O. Box 560
Pineville, Louisiana 71359
Tel: (318) 443-5846

Description: Founded in 1906, the private, liberal arts, coeducational college is operated under the auspices of the Louisiana Baptist Convention. It is accredited by the Southern Association of Colleges and Schools. Professional accreditations include the National Association of Schools of Music and the National League for Nursing. The college features 15 academic departments. Louisiana College boasts demonstrative evidence of superior academic preparation with higher than average acceptance rates of its graduates into high ranking Medical and Law schools and the equally strong showing of its teaching and nursing graduates.It operates on the semester system and offers two summer terms. Enrollment includes 892 full-time and 134 part-time students. A faculty of 75 full-time gives a faculty-student ratio of 1-17.

Entrance Requirements: Acceptance by Louisiana College is based on one of the following criteria: minimum ACT 20 composite or SAT 800 combined, or minimum 2.0 GPA in academic subjects and rank in upper 50% of high school graduating class with an acceptable ACT

or SAT score; early admission, midyear admission, rolling admission, and advanced placement plans available; No application fee.

Costs Per Year: $4,470 (based on 15 hours per semester); $2,850 room and board; $400 fees.

Collegiate Environment: 16 major buildings on 81 wooded acres comprise the campus. The library holdings include 125,000 titles, 551 subscriptions, and 62 microforms. Freshmen must live in dormitories and the housing capacity is 215 men, 350 women, and 44 married students. Fraternities and sororities are available. Approximately 60% of the student body participates in intramural sports. The varsity sports are basketball, baseball, and cross country. Approximately 90% of the student body receives some form of financial assistance.

Community Environment: Alexandria-Pineville is in the geographic heart of the state. The urban population of 113,000 enjoys several major shopping malls, movie theaters, cultural attractions, fine restaurants, historical landmarks and churches representing nearly every denomination. The area is particularly noted for outdoor recreation opportunities, including year-round water sports and public hunting land. Part-time job opportunities in the community are numerous for college students.

LOUISIANA STATE UNIVERSITY - ALEXANDRIA   *(G-7)*
8100 Highway 71 South
Alexandria, Louisiana 71302-9633
Tel: (318) 473-6413

Description: LSU at Alexandria was established by the Louisiana Legislature in 1959 to offer a two-year basic program of college instruction. The first freshman class was admitted in 1960. It is accredited by the Southern Association of Colleges and Schools. The institution offers basic academic work that allows students to complete the first two years of various curricula leading to the Bachelor's degree. Several professional courses commonly found in the first two years of these curricula are also offered. It operates on the semester system and offers an eight-week summer session. Enrollment includes 1,056 full-time and 1,425 part-time students. A faculty of 73 full-time and 25 part-time gives a faculty-student ratio of 1-25.

Entrance Requirements: Open enrollment policy; accredited high school graduation; nonresident accredited high school graduates with high academic achievement and aptitude will be considered; Louisiana non-high school graduates over 21 years of age may be admitted by entrance examinations; ACT required; early admission, early decision, midyear admission, and advanced placement plans available; No application fee.

Costs Per Year: $1,060 state resident tuition; $2,164 nonresident tuition.

Collegiate Environment: The campus is located just south of Alexandria on a beautiful 3,114-acre tract of alluvial Red River Valley land known as Oakland Plantation. Campus development is provided by a master plan for long-range expansion and the library, constructed in 1964, contains 121,577 volumes, 550 periodicals, 17,174 microforms, and 6,782 audiovisual materials. The school accepts students from various geographical locations as well as midyear students. About 96% of applicants are accepted. 74 scholarships are offered and financial aid is available for economically disadvantaged students. 38% of students receive some form of financial aid. About 46% of freshmen return for their second year of studies.

Community Environment: On the banks of the Red River, Alexandria is in an important agricultural and lumbering area. The temperature is mild year-round. Rail, air, and bus lines serve the area. Churches of many denominations are represented here, and community groups include YWCÁ, YMCA, the Community Center, Little Theatre, Art League, and the Service League. A 100-acre city park provides for tennis, baseball, softball, golf, picnicking, swimming in the municipal pool, and a zoo. Camping, boating, swimming and picnicking are available at nearby Cotile Reservoir, and lakes nearby provide excellent fishing.

LOUISIANA STATE UNIVERSITY - EUNICE   *(0-7)*
P.O. Box 1129
Eunice, Louisiana 70535
Tel: (318) 457-7311; Fax: (318) 546-6620

Description: The two-year commuter college was authorized by the 1964 Legislature as a basic and integral part of the University System to extend additional facilities and opportunities to southwest Louisiana. It opened in 1967 and offers more than 150 freshman and sophomore courses. Approximately 100 different curricula represent the areas of agriculture, business administration, education, engineering, humanities, natural sciences, social sciences, and preprofessional preparation. It operates on the semester system and offers one summer session. Enrollment is 1,309 full-time and 1,552 part-time students. A faculty of 73 full-time and 47 part-time gives a faculty-student ratio of 1-24. The school is accredited by the Southern Association of Colleges and Schools.

Entrance Requirements: Accredited high school graduation with completion of 21 units; out-of-state accredited high school graduates must have above-average rank; ACT required; early admission, early decision, rolling admission and advanced placement plans available.

Costs Per Year: $528 per semester tuition; $1,128 per semester out-of-state.

Collegiate Environment: One of the newest divisions of the Louisiana State University System, the campus is located just southwest of Eunice on a beautiful 100-acre tract of land. The two-year division concerns itself primarily with the problems of students in their courses of study and their guidance during the period of transition from high school to the four-year college. Scholarships are available and 50% receive financial aid. The library contains 88,909 titles and 28,322 microforms. 95% of the applicants are accepted.

Community Environment: Reached by U.S. Route 190, State Route 29, and State Route 13, Eunice also has transportation via Continental Trailways and the municipal airport. The city has several Catholic and Protestant churches as well as civic, fraternal and veteran's organizations. Recreational facilities include a 120-acre park with lake, golf courses, two swimming pools, eight tennis courts, baseball diamonds, youth center, art and handicraft shops, and ping pong. Hunting and fishing are good in this region. The city has a local hospital.

LOUISIANA STATE UNIVERSITY - SHREVEPORT   *(C-3)*
One University Place
Shreveport, Louisiana 71115
Tel: (318) 797-5061

Description: Louisiana State University in Shreveport was authorized by the 1964 Louisiana Legislature and opened for classes in 1967 as a two-year commuter campus of the Louisiana State University System. In 1972, baccalaureate degree-granting authority was granted by the legislature, and the first commencement was held in May 1975. LSU in Shreveport is fully accredited by the Southern Association of Colleges and Schools. It operates on the semester system and offers three nine-week summer sessions. Enrollment is 2,323 full-time and 1,914 part-time students. A faculty of 169 full-time and 39 part-time gives a faculty-student ratio of 1-17.

Entrance Requirements: Louisiana residents must be graduates of state-approved high schools with 23 units including 4 English, 3 mathematics, 3 social science, 3 science; out-of state high school graduates must rank in upper half of class and have high academic achievement and aptitude; state residents must have high school grade point average of at least 2.3 or achieved enhanced ACT composite score of 18 or higher; Louisiana non-high school graduates over 21 years of age may be admitted by entrance examination; ACT required; GRE or GMAT required for graduate; early admission, early decision, rolling admission, midyear admission, rolling admission and advanced placement plans available. $10 application fee for U.S. citizens; $20 for international students.

Costs Per Year: $1,930 tuition; $4,630 out-of-state; $2,410 graduate tuition; $5,830 graduate nonresident.

Collegiate Environment: The campus is located on 200 acres in south Shreveport and consists of a science building, a business and education building, a liberal arts building, health and physical education building, the administration building, the University Center and a library that contains 211,379 titles, 52,487 periodicals, and 170,972 microforms. A health and physical education building has been completed. About 25% of the students receive some type of financial assistance. Late afternoon and evening classes are offered that provide university work at the same level as day classes. Approximately 99% of the applicants are accepted, including midyear students. Army ROTC is available.

Community Environment: The townsite was bought from the Caddo Indians in 1835 and incorporated as Shreveport in 1839; today the city is the third largest in the state. This area leads the state in cotton production and is important for grains, oil and gas wells, and manufacturing within a 100-mile radius. Annual average temperature is 66.1 degrees. Four rail lines, two bus lines and four airlines serve the community. The city has 15 radio stations, an abundance of churches, main and branch libraries and many other community facilities. Cultural activities are offered by Symphony Orchestra, Civic Opera, Civic Chorus and Oratorio Society, Gas Light Players, Port Players, Little Theatre, Summer Theatre, the Planetarium and the State Exhibit Museum.

LOUISIANA STATE UNIVERSITY AND AGRICULTURAL AND MECHANICAL COLLEGE   *(-10)*
Baton Rouge, Louisiana 70803
Tel: (504) 388-3202; Admissions: (504) 388-1175; Fax: (504) 388-5991

Description: The Louisiana State Agricultural and Mechanical College was established in New Orleans in 1874. Two state institutions were merged and began their first joint session in Baton Rouge in October, 1877, under the legal name of Louisiana State University and Agricultural and Mechanical College. It is the state's premier educational institution and one of the top 100 research universities in the nation. LSU offers curricula leading to bachelor's degrees in 72 major fields, master's degrees in 77 major fields, and doctoral degrees in 55 major fields. The professional D.V.M. degree is also offered through the School of Veterinary Medicine. The University contains the College of Agriculture, College of Arts and Sciences, College of Basic Sciences, College of Business Administration, College of Design, College of Education, College of Engineering, General College, Junior Division, the School of Music, and the School of Mass Communication. Post-baccalaureate and professional divisions are the Graduate School, School of Library and Information Science, School of Social Work, School of Veterinary Medicine, and Center for Wetland Resources. Optional Army and Air Force ROTC programs are available. Recent enrollment included 12,768 men and 12,549 women. The faculty consists of 1,227 full-time and 90 part-time members.

Entrance Requirements: Freshman entrance requirements for Louisiana residents are graduation from an accredited high school and the submission of SAT or ACT scores; out-of-state applicants must have an above-average academic record. Freshman applicants must have completed 17 1/2 specified high school units. GRE required for graduate admission, which is selective. Application fee $25 for U.S. residents.

Costs Per Year: $2,645 tuition and fees; $5,945 out-of-state fees and tuition; $3,310 room and board.

Collegiate Environment: LSU is located on more than a 2,000-acre tract of land--a former plantation site--in the southeastern part of Baton Rouge. The campus is bordered on the north, south, and east by business, industrial, and residential areas of the city and on the west by the Mississippi River. The University's more than 250 buildings are grouped on a 650-acre plateau that constitutes the main part of the campus. University libraries offer students and faculty strong academic support through collections containing 2,278,482 volumes. On-campus living accommodations are provided for approximately 5,861 students. Scholarships, educational opportunity grants, student loan funds, student employment, and other types of financial aid are available; approximately 60% of the current student body receives some type of financial aid. Semesters begin in August and January, and a nine-week summer term begins in June. Qualified applicants may enroll at the beginning of any term.

Community Environment: Baton Rouge, with a metropolitan-area population of more than 500,000, is the capital of Louisiana, the state's second largest port for ocean-going vessels, and the fifth largest such port in the nation. A rich mixture of French, Spanish, and English cultures reflects Baton Rouge's history. Geographically, Baton Rouge is the center of South Louisiana's main cultural and recreational attractions. New Orleans is 80 miles to the southeast; the Feliciana parishes, noted for their antebellum homes, is less than an hour's drive to the north; and to the west lies the Acadian-French country of bayous, lakes, and marshes. Baton Rouge's industry is widely diversified. It is a major petrochemical center, as well as a center for banking and financial services and a major retail center. Cultural organizations include the Baton Rouge Symphony, the Baton Rouge Opera Association, and ballet and community theater groups. Baton Rouge has 36 recreation centers, 5 golf courses, and 123 parks. Mild temperatures make outdoor activities possible throughout the year.

LOUISIANA STATE UNIVERSITY MEDICAL CENTER - NEW ORLEANS *(K-12)*
1901 Perdido Street
New Orleans, Louisiana 70112
Tel: (504) 568-4800

Description: The LSU Medical Center was founded in 1931. It is a part of the Louisiana State University System and now includes the LSU Medical School in New Orleans, LSU Medical School in Shreveport and Schools of Dentistry, Nursing, Allied Health and Graduate Study. The individual curricula in each school are accredited by the appropriate professional organizations. Enrollment includes 2,400 students enrolled in the Medical Center. A faculty of 1,180 gives a faculty-student ratio of 1-2.

Entrance Requirements: Schools of Medicine: completion of 3 full academic years at an approved college of arts and sciences; 90 semester hours credit including laboratory courses of 8 biology, 6 general inorganic chemistry, 3 quantitative analysis, 6 organic chemistry, 8 physics, and 9 English; Medical College Admissions Test required. Graduate School: baccalaureate degree from accredited college or university; GRE required. School of Dentistry: minimum of 3 full academic years at approved college of arts and sciences; completion of 90 semester hours including laboratory courses of 8 zoology, 8 general inorganic chemistry, 8 organic chemistry, 4 comparative anatomy or embryology, 8 physics, and 9 English; Dental Aptitude Test required. School of Nursing: satisfactory achievement in prescribed subjects in the first year of college work; prerequisites of accredited high school graduation and completion of college preparatory courses; evidence of good health and of personal and social fitness for professional nursing.

Costs Per Year: Each school has varying tuitions; call school for exact figures. Graduate programs have higher rates than undergraduate programs.

Collegiate Environment: The Medical Center is located on three campuses: as part of one of the world's largest medical complexes adjacent to Charity Hospital in downtown New Orleans; on a 23-acre site near City Park in New Orleans and adjacent to Confederate Memorial Hospital in Shreveport. New facilities include a modern School of Dentistry building, a Medical School facility in Shreveport, completed in 1975, a Medical Education Building and Lions Eye Research Center in New Orleans. Charity Hospital in New Orleans, Confederate Memorial in Shreveport, State hospitals in Baton Rouge, Lafayette and Lake Charles, as well as numerous other hospitals serve as clinical teaching facilities. A student center and residence hall providing housing for over 300 married and single students is located across the street from classrooms and laboratories. A broad program of student aid is administered by the Medical Center to offer needy students opportunities to defray expenses through awards, scholarships, and loans. There were 327 graduates; 8 Master of Communications Disorders, 8 Associate of Science in Dental Hygiene; 11 Associate of Science in Dental Laboratory Technology; 17 Bachelor of Science in Dental Hygiene; 1 Bachelor of Science in Dental Laboratoty Technology; 50 Doctor of Dental Surgery; 3 Master of Science and 5 Doctor of Philosophy Degrees in the Basic Sciences; 158 Doctor of Medicine; 3 Associate of Science in Nursing; 62 Bachelor of Science in Nursing; and 1 Master of Nursing.

Community Environment: See Tulane University.

LOUISIANA TECH UNIVERSITY *(F-7)*
Box 3168
Ruston, Louisiana 71272
Tel: (318) 257-0211; Admissions: (318) 257-3036; Fax: (318) 257-2499

Description: The state-supported, coeducational university was founded in 1894 as the Industrial Institute and College of Louisiana and opened with an enrollment of 202 students. Louisiana Tech is organized into the Division of Admissions, Basic and Career Studies, six colleges and four schools. The colleges are: Administration and Business, Arts and Sciences, Education, Engineering, Home Econom-

ics, and Life Sciences. The schools include: Graduate School, School of Art and Architecture, School of Forestry, and School of Professional Accountancy. It is accredited by the Southern Association of Colleges and Schools and by respective professional organizations. The University has adopted the uniform quarter system as its calendar and quarters are twelve weeks in length. An optional Air Force ROTC program is offered as well as two summer terms. A summer program is offered in Rome, Italy. The College of Engineering offers a Cooperative Education program (alternating work and study) in Agriculture. Continuing education courses offered. The enrollment includes 5,137 men and 4,886 women with a faculty of 386 full-time and 78 part-time, giving a faculty-student ratio of 1:25.

Entrance Requirements: Accredited high school graduation; ACT required; GRE, MAT, GMAT required for graduate programs; early admission, early decision, rolling admission, delayed admission and advanced placement plans available. In addition a University Credit Examination by subject is available. There is a $20 application fee.

Costs Per Year: $2,262 tuition; $3,957 out-of-state tuition; $2,325 room and board.

Collegiate Environment: The university is comprised of 110 buildings located on 1,312 acres which include a library of 968,724 volumes, 627,976 government documents, 2,506 periodicals, 990,555 microforms and 2,579 sound recordings and living accommodations for 1,978 men, 1,781 women, and 42 apartments for married student housing. Unmarried full-time undergraduate students are required to live in campus housing unless commuting from home of parents or relatives. Almost 90% of students applying for admission meet the requirements and are accepted. Students are accepted from various geographical locations as well as those that apply at midyear. Financial aid is available for economically handicapped students and 50% of the recent class received some form of financial aid. There are 2,398 scholarships available; 140 are athletic scholarships. The average ACT composite score of the current freshmen was 22.3. About 60% of the freshmen returned to the University for the second year of studies. Louisiana Tech awards approximately 187 Associate, 1,285 Bachelor, 2 Specialist, 375 Master degrees and 17 Doctorates.

Community Environment: This is an urban area with bus service available. City has a public library, several churches, its own hospital, medical clinics, and good shopping facilities. Theatres, drive-in, golf, fishing, boating, and a campus olympic swimming pool provide recreation opportunities. There is also a concert association.

LOYOLA UNIVERSITY *(K-13)*
Campus Box 18
6363 St. Charles Avenue
New Orleans, Louisiana 70118
Tel: (504) 865-3240; (800) 456-9652; Fax: (504) 865-2110

Description: In 1912, the College of the Immaculate Conception was united with Loyola College on its present campus and Loyola College was expanded to become Loyola University. The university was duly incorporated by the General Assembly of Louisiana and empowered to grant all university degrees in 1912. Today the university includes the College of Arts and Sciences, College of Business Administration, College of Music, School of Law, City College, Institute of Human Relations, and a Graduate and Evening Division. The Jesuit University is under the auspices of the Roman Catholic Church and is accredited by the Southern Association of Colleges and Schools as well as by other educational and professional organizations. It operates on the semester system and offers two summer sessions. Enrollment is 2,647 full-time and 867 part-time undergraduates. There are also 608 graduate students, and the School of Law has 703 full-time and 86 part-time students. A faculty of 486 gives an undergraduate faculty-student ratio of 1-14 and an average class size of 24-32.

Entrance Requirements: Accredited high school graduation or equivalent. ACT or SAT; standard tests required for graduate programs; $20 application fee; early admission, rolling admission, and advanced placement plans available.

Costs Per Year: $9,570 tuition; $4,910 room and board; $110 student fees.

Collegiate Environment: The university is situated in the Garden District of New Orleans and includes a library of 262,456 volumes 6,592 periodicals, 253,094 microforms, and 7,779 audiovisual materials. There are dormitory facilities for 1,069 students. The university is a member of the New Orleans Consortium, which includes Xavier

University and Notre Dame Seminary. The Consortium was established in 1967 and has made possible the sharing of curriculum, libraries, and cultural events for students of the member institutions. Loyola offers Junior Year Abroad through the Loyola Rome Center, and other study abroad opportunities in London, Greece, Mexico City, and the Republic of Georgia. Loyola offers an optional Army ROTC program, and Navy and Air Force ROTC are available cross-campus. It welcomes students from various geographical locations and will accept midyear students. Approximately 54% of students applying for admission meet the requirements and are accepted. Work-study programs, financial aid, and scholarships are available. 55% of the students receive some form of financial aid.

Community Environment: See Tulane University.

MCNEESE STATE UNIVERSITY   *(J-5)*
4100 Ryan St.
Lake Charles, Louisiana 70609
Tel: (318) 475-5000; (800) 622-3352; Fax: (318) 475-5189

Description: The college was founded in 1939 as a division of Louisiana State University offering only the first two years of higher education. It advanced to a four-year status and separated from LSU in 1950 and its administration was transferred to the State Board of Education. The state college was organized into several academic divisions: Education, Liberal Arts, Sciences, Business, and Graduate Studies. Expansion of the Division of Graduate Studies enables the college to confer a total of 8 graduate degrees, including that of Education Specialist which is a degree beyond the Master's level. The college is accredited by the Southern Association of Colleges and Schools. It operates on the semester system and offers one summer session. An Army ROTC program is available. Enrollment includes 7,724 full-time, 1,408 part-time, and 1,136 graduate students. A faculty of 297 full-time and 50 part-time provides a faculty-student ratio of 1-26.

Entrance Requirements: High school graduation or equivalent; open enrollment for residents; out-of-state accredited high school graduates must rank in upper half of graduating class; Louisiana non-high school graduates over 18 years of age may be admitted by passing entrance examinations; ACT required; GRE required for graduate admission; rolling admission; early admission, early decision, delayed admission, and advanced placement plans available, $10 application fee.

Costs Per Year: $1,934 state resident tuition; $3,484 nonresident tuition, $2,310 room and board.

Collegiate Environment: The campus is comprised of 686 acres and includes a library of 253,446 volumes, 2,064 periodicals and 463,360 microforms. Dormitories provide living accommodations for 1,335 men and women, and 116 married students. Fraternities offer housing for 216 men. Sororities offer housing for 211 women. Special Financial aid is available for economically disadvantaged students and 52% receive some form of financial aid. There were 2,625 scholarships available and 740 of them were offered to freshmen.

Community Environment: The city owes its development to the combination of Capt. J. B. Watkins, a variety of natural resources and a deepwater port. In 1887 Captain Watkins of New York moved his newspaper to Lake Charles and started an overwhelming advertising program, which, with the terminus of a railroad at New Orleans, resulted in the development of a 17-mill lumber industry. The discovery of oil in the early 1900's and a new process of mining sulphur further enriched the city. Forests are presently nearly depleted and the sulphur supply is no longer industrially profitable. This city with its vast oil companies in southwest Louisiana is a leader in the petrochemical industry. A deepwater port since 1926, it is currently the nation's leading rice port. Docks also handle general cargo, the output of chemical and petrochemical plants and products of the city's two large rice mills. Student employment is available. Transportation is provided by commercial passenger air lines, rail, and bus service. There are libraries, YMCA, a great number of churches, and three hospitals easily accessible. Recreation includes fishing, hunting, theatres, and an annual rodeo.

NEW ORLEANS BAPTIST THEOLOGICAL SEMINARY
(K-13)
3939 Gentilly Boulevard
New Orleans, Louisiana 70126
Tel: (504) 282-4455; (800) 662-8701; Admissions: (504) 282-4455; Fax: (504) 286-3591

Description: Founded in 1917, the seminary was called the Baptist Bible Institute and was the first theological institution established by the Southern Baptist Convention. The present name was adopted in 1946 and a new campus was purchased in 1947. The seminary offers programs in Theology, Religious Education, Psychology and Counseling, Biblical Studies, and Church Music. It is accredited by the Southern Association of Colleges and Schools, the Association of Theological Schools, and the National Association of Schools of Music. It grants the Master and Doctorate degrees. It operates on the semester system and offers two summer terms. Currently the seminary enrolls 5,736 students. The faculty includes 48 full-time and 79 part-time members.

Entrance Requirements: Bachelor's degree or equivalent; completion of educational prerequisites for intended course of study; minimum 20 years of age; applicants without college degree and over 35 years of age may be admitted to certain courses.

Costs Per Year: $1,300 tuition; $100-$325 per month for room.

Collegiate Environment: The 81-acre campus now has 114 buildings of French Colonial architecture. The library contains 218,000 volumes and living accommodations are provided for 264 men, 84 women, and 438 families. The seminary welcomes students from various geographical locations and will accept midyear students. Approximately 85% of those applying for admission meet the requirements and are accepted.

Community Environment: See Tulane University

NICHOLLS STATE UNIVERSITY   *(L-11)*
P.O. Box 2004
Thibodaux, Louisiana 70310
Tel: (504) 446-8111

Description: This four-year university was established originally as a junior college branch of the Louisiana State University and began its first semester in 1948. It began operations as a four-year state college in 1956. Enrollment is 5,335 full-time and 2,270 part-time students. A faculty of 265 gives a faculty-student ratio of 1-27 though the average class size is 16 students. In 1970, the name was changed from Francis T. Nicholls State College to its present name by an Act of the State Legislature. The university operates on the semester system, with one summer term, and is accredited by the Southern Association of Colleges and Schools. It offers the Associate of Science, Bachelor of General Studies, Bachelor of Arts, Bachelor of Music, Bachelor of Music Education, Bachelor of Science, Bachelor of Science in Nursing, Master of Arts, Master of Education, Specialist in School Psychology, Master of Business Administration, and Master of Science. Special programs include life experience credit, credit by prior examination, continuing education courses, and allowance of half of correspondent credit toward degrees.

Entrance Requirements: Accredited high school graduation or equivalent; ACT required for placement; early admission, midyear admission and advanced placement plans available; $10 application fee.

Costs Per Year: $1,861 tuition; $3,661 nonresident; $2,550 room and board.

Collegiate Environment: The property of the university, approximately 210 acres, was formerly a part of historic Acadia Plantation. The library contains 278,386 volumes, 803,432 microforms and approximately 1,783 periodicals. Dormitory facilities are available for 901 students including 20 units for married students. Approximately 98% of students applying for admission are accepted as well as midyear students. 1,132 scholarships are offered, 199 of which are available to freshmen. Approximately 62% of the student body receives some form of financial aid.

Community Environment: The campus is located in a sugar-belt town on the banks of picturesque Bayou Lafourche. Incorporated in 1838, this was the first trading post established between New Orleans and the country along Bayou Teche in southeastern Louisiana. There are many beautiful plantations in the vicinity. Thibodaux presents a small town atmosphere. It is a quick 45 miles from historic New Orleans. The year-round climate is mild to moderate. Transportation to Thibodaux is provided by rail and bus. The city has public library, churches representing all denominations, and a hospital. Recreation includes movies, theater, hunting, boating, fishing, golf, bowling, swimming and tennis. Student employment is available in the area and on campus.

NORTHEAST LOUISIANA UNIVERSITY   (B-8)
700 University Avenue
Monroe, Louisiana 71209
Tel: (318) 342-1000; (800) 372-5127; Fax: (318) 342-5161

Description: The university opened for its first session in 1931 and functioned as a junior college until 1950 when it became a four-year institution governed by the State Board of Education. Programs are offered by the university in the Colleges of Business Administration, Education, Liberal Arts, Pharmacy and Health Sciences, Pure and Applied Sciences, and the Graduate School. It is accredited by the Southern Association of Colleges and Schools and by respective professional organizations. The institution operates on the semester system and offers two summer terms. An optional Army ROTC program is available. Enrollment includes 9,236 full-time and 2,143 part-time undergraduates and 1,165 graduate students. A faculty of 501 full-time and 67 part-time gives a faculty-student ratio of 1-19.

Entrance Requirements: Open enrollment policy; ACT required; GRE required for graduate school; GMAT required for MBA; early admission, rolling admission, midyear admission and advanced placement plans available; $25 application fee.

Costs Per Year: $1,938 tuition; $4,086 nonresident; $2,060 room and board.

Collegiate Environment: The campus is located on 238 acres in the eastern part of the city of Monroe, situated in northeast Louisiana midway between Shreveport and Vicksburg, Mississippi. There are 66 buildings that serve the college, including a library of 1,042,421 volumes, periodicals, and microforms, and dormitory facilties for 1,474 men and 1,984 women. Average ACT score of the freshman class was 19. Financial aid is available and 67% of the current student body receives some form of financial assistance.

Community Environment: Monroe enjoys a mild climate with temperatures ranging from 28 degrees in winter to 96 degrees in the summer. Air, rail, and bus service is available. The Civic Center in downtown Monroe, Strauss Playhouse, Masur Museum, and the local parks offer cultural and popular programs, including sports events of all kinds. The beautiful Ouachita River, Bayou DeSiard, and many nearby lakes offer opportunities for fishing, boating, skiing, swimming, and picnicking.

NORTHWESTERN STATE UNIVERSITY   (E-5)
Natchitoches, Louisiana 71457
Tel: (318) 357-4503

Description: The state college was founded in 1884 as a two-year Normal School and became a four-year institution in 1918. It is accredited by the Southern Association of Colleges and Schools and by respective professional organizations. Today the college offers two-year Associate degree programs as well as degree programs in the School of Liberal Arts, School of Business, School of Education, School of Science and Technology, School of Nursing, and the Graduate School. It operates on the semester basis and offers multiple summer terms as well as an optional Army ROTC program. The university enrolls 2,276 men, 3,557 women full-time, 590 men, 1,483 women part-time, and 855 graduate students. A faculty of 277 full-time and 32 part-time members provides a faculty-student ratio of 1-27.

Entrance Requirements: Accredited high school graduation; nonaccredited high school graduates may be admitted by examination; non-high school graduates over 21 years of age may be admitted as special students; ACT required; early admission, early decision, rolling admission, delayed admission and advanced placement plans available; $5 application fee.

Costs Per Year: $1,880 tuition; $4,100 for out-of-state students; $2,216 room and board; $147 student fees.

Collegiate Environment: The college occupies 900 acres in an area of gently rolling pine hill land immediately west of Natchitoches, located 58 miles northwest of Alexandria. It contains 83 buildings which include a library of 692,959 volumes, 2,700 periodical titles and 437,500 microforms. Dormitory housing is provided for 2,422 students. About 90% of those applying for admission are accepted including midyear students. Scholarships are available. 61% of the students receive some form of financial aid.

Community Environment: City was founded as a French trading post in 1714 by Louis Juchereau de St. Denis in order to stimulate trade with the Indians and prevent Spanish occupation. Believed to be the oldest town in the Louisiana Purchase, it is chiefly an agricultural center. Interesting old homes and plantations may be seen; and during the annual tour, usually the second weekend in October, these homes are open. City has a mild, humid climate. Transportation provided by two railroads and a bus service, the chief manufactured products are gas, bricks, and lumber. Entertainment and recreation facilities include large auditorium seating 5,000 persons, one theatre, several city parks, swimming pools, bowling alley, year-round boating, hunting, and fishing on the Cane River Lake, Sibley Lake, and Chaplin Lake. Service is rendered the community by a hospital, branch libraries, and several motels and hotels.

NOTRE DAME SEMINARY GRADUATE SCHOOL OF THEOLOGY   (K-14)
2901 South Carrollton Avenue
New Orleans, Louisiana 70118
Tel: (504) 866-7426

Description: The graduate seminary was established in 1923 with its primary objectives to prepare men for entrance into the priesthood of the Roman Catholic Church; to offer training in theology to qualified religious, laymen, and laywomen; and to offer a program of continuing education to the clergy. The seminary is fully accredited by the Southern Association of Colleges and Schools and Association of Theological Schools. Master and Professional degrees are granted. It employs the semester system. Enrollment includes 97 full-time and 26 part-time students. There are 15 full-time and 8 part-time faculty members.

Entrance Requirements: Bachelor of Arts degree or its equivalent; minimum C average in 128 undergraduate college credits; GRE required; rolling admission, $10 application fee.

Costs Per Year: $5,876 tuition; $4,400 room and board; $500 student fees.

Collegiate Environment: The school of theology is comprised of two buildings that contain a library of 94,000 titles and dormitory facilities for men. Approximately 90% of those applying for admission are accepted including midyear students. Housing is available for 120 students.

Community Environment: See Tulane University.

OUR LADY OF HOLY CROSS COLLEGE   (K-13)
4123 Woodland Drive
New Orleans, Louisiana 70114-7399
Tel: (504) 394-7744; Admissions: (504) 394-7744 x126

Description: The college was established by the Marianites of Holy Cross and is now operated under a combined lay-religious Board of Regents and Administration. It was founded in 1916 and functioned as a two-year Normal School until 1938 when it became a four-year teacher institution. The college became coeducational in 1967 and is accredited by the Southern Association of Colleges and Schools. The semester system is used and one summer session is offered. Enrollment includes 168 men, 541 women full-time, 136 men, 398 women part-time undergraduates, and 75 graduate students. The faculty consists of 31 full-time and 70 part-time members. Our Lady of Holy Cross College offers majors in six divisions: Business and Economics, Education, Humanities, Natural Sciences, Nursing, and Social Sciences.

Entrance Requirements: Open enrollment policy; completion of 24 units; non-high school graduates considered; early admission, advanced placement plans available; $15 application fee.

Costs Per Year: $4,800 tuition; $415 miscellaneous.

Collegiate Environment: The college is located on 40 acres and contains two buildings which include a library of 46,548 volumes, 813 periodicals, 150,890 microforms and 13,817 audiovisual materials. All students applying for admission are accepted including midyear students and 90% of the freshman class return for the sophomore year. Financial aid is available.

Community Environment: See Tulane University

SAINT JOSEPH SEMINARY COLLEGE   *(I-13)*
Saint Benedict, Louisiana 70457-9990
Tel: (504) 892-1800; Fax: (504) 892-3723

Description: The privately supported seminary for men was established in 1891. A Bachelor of Arts degree is offered in Liberal Arts. The seminary is conducted by the Benedictine Monks of St. Joseph Abbey and is accredited by the Southern Association of Colleges and Schools. It operates on the semster system. Enrollment includes 58 full-time and 81 part-time students. A faculty of 37 part-time provides a faculty-student ratio of 1-4.

Entrance Requirements: High school graduation or equivalent; open enrollment policy; completion of 17 units including 3 English, 2 mathematics, 2 foreign language, 2 science, 1 social science; ACT required; non-high school graduates considered; early decision, rolling admission, midyear admission, advanced placement plans available; $10 application fee.

Costs Per Year: $5,550 tuition; $4,350 room and board; $130 student fees.

Collegiate Environment: The seminary is comprised of 11 buildings located on 1200 acres, one hour's drive from New Orleans. The extensive campus, with its large gymnasium, outdoor pool, and two lakes, provides adequate facilities for recreation. The library contains 63,000 titles, 170 periodicals, and 800 microforms. Dormitory facilities are provided for 125 men. Approximately 95% of the students applying for admission are accepted including midyear students. Financial aid is available, and 67% of the current student body receives some form of assistance.

Community Environment: City located four miles north of Covington and 50 miles north of New Orleans. There is bus service available to Covington from New Orleans, Baton Rouge, Hammond. Taxi service provides transportation to college from Covington.

SOUTHEASTERN LOUISIANA UNIVERSITY   *(I-12)*
P.O. SLU 752
Hammond, Louisiana 70402
Tel: (504) 549-2123; (800) 222-7358; Fax: (504) 549-5632

Description: Publicly supported, coeducational university established in 1925. It began its four-year curricula program in 1937 and is fully accredited by the Southern Association of Colleges and Schools. Today the college is organized into five colleges which include Arts & Science, Business, Education, Basic Studies, and Nursing. The university operates on the semester system and offers one summer session. Undergraduate enrollment includes 10,290 full-time and 2,333 part-time students, and graduate enrollment is 1,289. A faculty of 431 full-time and 149 part-time gives an overall faculty-student ratio of 1-32.

Entrance Requirements: High school gradation or equivalent; open enrollment policy for residents; completion of 24 units including 4 English, 3 mathematics, 3 science, 3 foreign language, 3 social science, 1 fine arts, 2 physical education; non-high school graduates considered; ACT, GMAT or GRE required; early admission, midyear admission, open admission, rolling admission, and advanced placement plans available. $10 application fee.

Costs Per Year: $1,810 state-resident tuition; $4,042 out-of-state tuition; $2,080-$3,110 room & board.

Collegiate Environment: The campus of 375 acres is situated in the northwest section of the city of Hammond. It contains 85 buildings which include a library of over 310,000 volumes, 2,200 periodical titles, 293,110 microforms and 17,000 audiovisual materials. Dormitories provide living accommodations for 2,000 students, and 80 families. Approximately 99% of the students applying for admission are accepted, including mid-year students. 676 scholarships are available and 55% of the current student body receives some form of financial aid.

Community Environment: City is located in the Southeastern section of the state. Climate is subtropical. Transportation to and from city available via Illinois Central Railroad and Greyhound Bus Co. There are five libraries, six local theatres, golf, hunting, fishing, boating at Lake Ponchartrain for recreation. Two hospitals, six motels and numerous apartments are available. Part-time employment for students is limited. There are 35 civic, fraternal, and veteran's organizations in Hammond.

SOUTHERN UNIVERSITY - NEW ORLEANS   *(K-13)*
6400 Press Drive
New Orleans, Louisiana 70126
Tel: (504) 286-5000; Admissions: (504) 286-5314; Fax: (504) 286-5320

Description: The publicly supported, coeducational liberal arts college is a branch campus of the Southern University and Agricultural and Mechanical College. It was established in 1956 and is accredited by the Southern Association of Colleges and Schools. It operates on the semester system with one summer term. Programs of study lead to the Associate and Bachelor degrees. There are 3,500 full-time students enrolled.

Entrance Requirements: Open enrollment policy; completion of 15 units including 3 English, 2 mathematics, 2 science, 2 social science; college entrance examinations required; rolling admission plan.

Costs Per Year: $1,662 state-resident tuition; $3,426 nonresident.

Collegiate Environment: The college is comprised of five buildings located on 18 acres and contains a library of 90,000 volumes. Approximately 98% of students applying for admission are accepted including midyear students.

Community Environment: See Tulane University.

SOUTHERN UNIVERSITY - SHREVEPORT   *(C-3)*
Martin L. King Jr. Dr.
Shreveport, Louisiana 71107
Tel: (318) 674-3342

Description: The publicly-supported, coeducational junior college is a branch of the Southern University and Agricultural and Mechanical College. It was established in 1967 and operates on the early semester system with one summer term. The university enrolls approximately 330 men and 770 women. A faculty of 45 full-time and 10 part-time gives a faculty-student ratio of 17-1.

Entrance Requirements: Accredited high school graduation; completion of 15 units including 3 English, 2 mathematics, 2 science, 2 social science; college entrance examinations required. Early admission, rolling admission and early decision plans,

Costs Per Year: $910 tuition and fees; $2,040 non-resident tuition and fees.

Collegiate Environment: The college is comprised of five buildings located on 101 acres. 98% of those applying for admission are accepted including midyear students and 60% of the freshman returned for their sophomore year. Semesters begin in August and January and a summer term is offered in June.

Community Environment: See Louisiana State University - Shreveport

SOUTHERN UNIVERSITY AND AGRICULTURAL AND MECHANICAL COLLEGE   *(I-10)*
P.O. Box 9253
Baton Rouge, Louisiana 70813
Tel: (504) 771-2011

Description: Publicly-supported, coeducational university founded in 1881. The university's instructional program is centered in eight colleges and schools which include agriculture, arts and sciences, business, education, engineering, home economics, law, and graduate studies. The university is accredited by the Southern Association of Colleges and Secondary Schools. It operates on the semester system with one summer term and offers an optional Army ROTC and Naval NROTC programs. The university has two branch campuses located in New Orleans and Shreveport. The university enrolls approximately 4,294 men and 5,774 women. A faculty of 482 gives a faculty-student ratio of 1-20.

Entrance Requirements: High school graduation; completion of 20 units including 3 English, 2 mathematics, 2 science, 2 social science; applicants not meeting all requirements may be admitted by special examination.

Costs Per Year: $1,988 tuition; $3,234 required for out-of-state students; $2,851 room and board, $104 miscellaneous.

Collegiate Environment: The main campus is located on 592 acres, the Shreveport branch on 101 acres, and the New Orleans branch on 18 acres. The main campus consist of 156 buildings which include a library of 260,000 volumes and living accommodations for 1,371 men, 1,637 women, and 34 families. Approximately 90% of students applying for admission are accepted including midyear students. Students are welcome from various geographical locations and 82% of the previous freshman class returned to the university for their sophomore year. Financial aid is available for economically handicapped students and 90% of the recent freshman class received some form of financial aid.

Community Environment: See Louisiana State University and Agricultural and Mechanical College.

TULANE UNIVERSITY *(K-13)*
6823 St. Charles Avenue
New Orleans, Louisiana 70118
Tel: (504) 865-5731; (800) 873-9283; Fax: (504) 862-8715

Description: The private, nonsectarian university admits students without regard to place of residence, race, religion, or national origin. It is composed of 11 schools and colleges and 11 research centers. The university operates on the semester system and offers five summer sessions. Optional Army, Navy, and Air Force ROTC programs are also offered. The undergraduate divisions are Tulane College, which admits only men; Newcomb College, which admits only women; and the School of Architecture and the School of Engineering, which admit both men and women. Special opportunities include an honors program, combined degree programs, and the Junior Year abroad program. University College conducts evening courses offering degree and certificate programs in fields such as Paralegal Studies, Computer Science, Applied Business and Real Estate. The graduate divisions of the university are the Schools of Business, Law, Medicine, Public Health and Tropical Medicine, Social Work, and the Graduate School. The university also has an intercollege Center for Teacher Education that coordinates the academic program for those who wish to become teachers, and the Summer School, which is also an intercollege activity. Total enrollment is 11,362 students. Undergraduate enrollment is 4,952 students: 1,468 men in Tulane College, 1,857 women in Newcomb, 149 men and 105 women in Architecture, and 590 men and 250 women in Engineering. A total faculty of 927 gives a faculty-student ratio of 1-13.

Entrance Requirements: Accredited high school graduation; completion of 16 units including 4 English, 4 mathematics, 3 foreign language, 2 sciences, and 2 social studies; SAT or ACT required; early entrance, early notification and Deans' Honor Scholarship admission available; $35 application fee.

Costs Per Year: $20,218 tuition and fees; $5,950 room and board.

Collegiate Environment: The 110-acre main campus is located in the city's university section directly across from Audubon Park, which has facilities for golf, tennis, canoeing, and horseback riding. The school contains 63 buildings on campus, including a library. New facilities completed since 1986 include the $7 million A.B. Freeman School of Business, the $12 million Aron Residence at Stadium Place, the $12 million Boggs Center for Energy and Biotechnology, and the $14 million Reily Student Recreation Center. Special research facilities include the Newcomb College Center for Research on Women, the Amistad Research Center, the Middle American Research Institute, the Roger Thayer Stone Center for Latin American Studies, the Murphy Institute of Political Economy, the Tulane Regional Primate Research Center, the Institute of Comparative Law, and the United States-Japan Cooperative Biomedical Research Laboratories. Institutional dormitory capacity is 3,418 including graduate, medical, and married students. There are national fraternities and nonresidential sororities at the university in addition to numerous other student organizations. 47% of the freshmen ranked in the top tenth of their graduating high school class. Average composite SAT score is 1183. The middle 50% range of enrolled freshmen composite scores are 1110-1260 Tulane; 1070-1250 Newcomb; 1110-1273 Architecture; 1101-1313 Engineering; and 1090-1260 overall. Need-based and merit-based financial aid is available, and more than half of the undergraduates receive some form of financial aid or scholarship.

Community Environment: Year-round New Orleans offers festivals and jazz bands, symphonies and operas, Broadway shows and concerts. But the City that Care Forgot also blends its unique French and Spanish heritage to offer quiet entertainment in museums, galleries, quaint restaurants or strolls through the European ambiance of the French Quarter. The 1.3 million people living in the metropolitan area succeed as well in running Louisiana's business, banking, judicial and cultural capital. Many students find the city to be as much a place of learning and intellectual challenge as the classroom. Moderate temperatures can be enjoyed year-round. New Orleans is one of the greatest distributing points in the South, and one of the largest ports in the United States; it is a marketing center for cotton, oil, salt, sulphur, natural gas, agricultural and forest products. Good transportation facilities are available. This is a paradise for those who fish or hunt. Since the city is a tourist attraction, there are many recreational facilities and community services available. Work opportunities are available for students.

UNIVERSITY OF NEW ORLEANS *(K-13)*
Lakefront
New Orleans, Louisiana 70148
Tel: (504) 286-6000; Admissions: (504) 286-6595; Fax: (504) 286-5522

Description: The University of New Orleans is a member of the Louisiana State University System and was established as the Louisiana State University, New Orleans, by the Legislature in 1956 to bring publicly supported higher education to the citizens of the state's largest urban complex. It opened in 1958 with a freshman class only and by 1961 it was operating as a full four-year, degree-granting university. In 1974 the name was changed to the University of New Orleans, but the school remains a member of the Louisiana State University System. The academic segments of the university are organized into a College of Business Administration, a College of Liberal Arts, a College of Sciences, a College of Education, a College of Engineering, a Metropolitan College, a College of Urban and Public Affairs, and a Graduate School. The university is accredited by the Southern Association of Colleges and Schools. It is professionally accredited by the American Assembly of Collegiate Schools of Business, Accreditation Board for Engineering and Technology, National Association of Schools of Music, and the National Council for Accreditation of Teacher Education. The university operates on a two-semester plan with an additional nine-week summer session and two summer minisessions of 5 and 9 weeks. A summer program is offered at Innsbruck, Austria. Enrollment includes 9,060 full-time and 6,179 part-time undergraduate and 3,567 graduate students. A faculty of 518 full-time and 180 part-time gives an undergraduate faculty-student ratio of 1-21. Army and Air Force ROTC programs are available.

Entrance Requirements: ACT score of 20; GPA 2.0; 17 1/2 units; early admission, early decision, advanced placement, special student plans available; Aug. 15 application deadline; $20 application fee.

Costs Per Year: $2,362 tuition; $5,154 out-of-state students; $3,106 room and board.

Collegiate Environment: The university occupies a 195-acre campus on the southern shores of Lake Pontchartrain in one of the finest residential areas of the city. A master plan for the development of the physical plant envisions the evolution of the most modern campus in the state. Twenty-eight buildings in this plan have now been completed and now include a library of 1,951,770 volumes and dormitory facilities for 252 men, 308 women, and housing for 40 graduate, 14 disabled and 120 married students. One-half mile from the main campus is a 100-acre tract known as the East Campus on which the 10,000 seat UNO Lakefront Arena is located. Several social fraternities and sororities are located at the campus in addition to numerous other student organizations. All Louisiana high school graduates 25 years and older applying for admission are accepted. Special financial aid is available for economically handicapped students. Of 770 scholarships, 81 are athletic. 58% of the students receive financial aid.

Community Environment: See Tulane University.

UNIVERSITY OF SOUTHWESTERN LOUISIANA *(J-8)*
East University Avenue
Box 41210
Lafayette, Louisiana 70504
Tel: (318) 482-1000; Admissions: (318) 482-6195; Fax: (318) 482-6195

Description: Publicly-supported coeducational comprehensive university accrediting by the Southern Association of Colleges and Schools and by respective professional and educational institutions. Established in 1898, the institution was originally called the Southwestern Louisiana Industrial Institution. When it became a senior college in 1921, its name was changed to the Southwestern Louisiana Institute of Liberal and Technical Learning and its present name was adopted in 1960. The university offers courses in African Americans history and Junior Year Abroad in France in addition to its other curricula. Academically, the university comprises the undergraduate, degree-granting colleges of Biological, Mathematical, and Physical Sciences; Applied Life Sciences; Engineering, Nursing, Education, Business Administration, and General Studies, the Graduate School, and the University College. Enrollment includes 12,550 full-time and 4,239 part-time undergraduates and 1,376 graduate students. A faculty of 582 full-time and 90 part-time gives a faculty-student ratio of 1-22.

Entrance Requirements: Open enrollment policy for undergraduates, non high school graduates considered; early admission, early decision, rolling admission, midyear admission, rolling admission and advanced placement plans available. There is a $5 application fee for U.S. Citizens, $15 application fee for others.

Costs Per Year: $1,885 tuition; $4,886 non-resident; $2,196 board and room; additional expenses average $500.

Collegiate Environment: The campus, including demonstration farms and recreational areas, consists of 1,436 acres. The library contains 701,598 volumes, 1,755,716 microforms and 6,716 recordings. Dormitories provide living accommodations for 1,360 men, 1,650 women and 140 married students. Numerous student organizations are located on the campus and social life is made more attractive by the existence of national and local social and professional fraternities and sororities. Approximately 99% of students applying for admission are accepted including midyear students. Financial aid is available for economically disadvantaged students, of 2,015 scholarships offered, 300-350 are for freshmen and 68% of the current student body receive some form of financial assistance. The university awarded 85 Associate, 1,696 Bachelor, 10 Education Specialists, 362 Master, and 31 Doctorate degrees between July 1, 1993 and June 30, 1994.

Community Environment: On the Vermillion River, Lafayette was founded in 1823 by the French Acadians from Nova Scotia about whom Longfellow wrote his poem "Evangeline." The city is also most attractive during the azalea season, usually from late February to late March, when a 21 mile azalea trail is marked. Industries in the city include canning, metal works, masonry products and meatpacking and refrigeration equipment. Major oil and allied companies are in Lafayette, which contribute to job opportunities. Horseracing at Evangeline Downs on U.S. Highway 167 takes place from late April to early September. The mean average temperature is a mild 68.4 degrees; rainfall averages 58 inches per year. Rail, highway, and air transportation is available. Many churches representing 14 denominations, hospitals and branch libraries are easily accessible for community services. Recreation include parks, swimming, pools, baseball, football, a lighted 18-hole golf course, dancing, shows, three TV, and six radio stations, as well as indoor athletics.

XAVIER UNIVERSITY OF LOUISIANA *(K-13)*
7325 Palmetto Street
New Orleans, Louisiana 70125
Tel: (504) 486-7411; Admissions: (504) 483-7388

Description: The private university was established by the Sisters of the Blessed Sacrament in 1925 and is now operated under a combined lay-religious Board of Trustees and Administration with a multiracial faculty. It is accredited by the Southern Association of Colleges and Schools and by respective professional organizations. The university includes the College of Arts and Sciences, the College of Pharmacy, and the Graduate School. The university offers Bachelors, Masters, and the Doctor of Pharmacy Degrees. There is a cooperative plan with Tulane University, GA Institute of Technology, University of Detroit, University of Maryland and University of New Orleans for pre-engineering students. Cooperative Education programs (alternating work and class periods) are available in Business, Natural Science, Mathematics, Computer Science, Political Science, Public Administration, and Sociology. It operates on the semester system and offers two summer sessions. Enrollment includes 3,022 full-time and 195 part-time undergraduate, and 269 graduate students. A faculty of 207 full-time and 53 part-time gives a full-time faculty-student ratio of 1-14. Army ROTC is available.

Entrance Requirements: Accredited high school graduation with rank in upper 50% of graduating class; minimum C average and completion of 16 units including 4 English, 2 foreign language, 2 mathematics, 1 science, 1 social science; achievement tests optional; non-high school graduates may be admitted with GED certificates; early decision, early admission, midyear admission, and advanced placement plans available; $25 application fee.

Costs Per Year: $6,900 tuition; $4,000 room & board; $150 student fees.

Collegiate Environment: The library specializes in Catholic and Negro collections and contains 85,000 volumes, 600 periodicals, and 193,251 microforms. Dormitories provide accommodations for 700 students. Additional housing is available in fraternities and sororities. The university accepts those from diverse geographic locations. 63% of applicants are accepted, including midyear students. Financial aid and scholarships are available for economically disadvantaged students and 85% of students receive some form of financial assistance.

Community Environment: See Tulane University

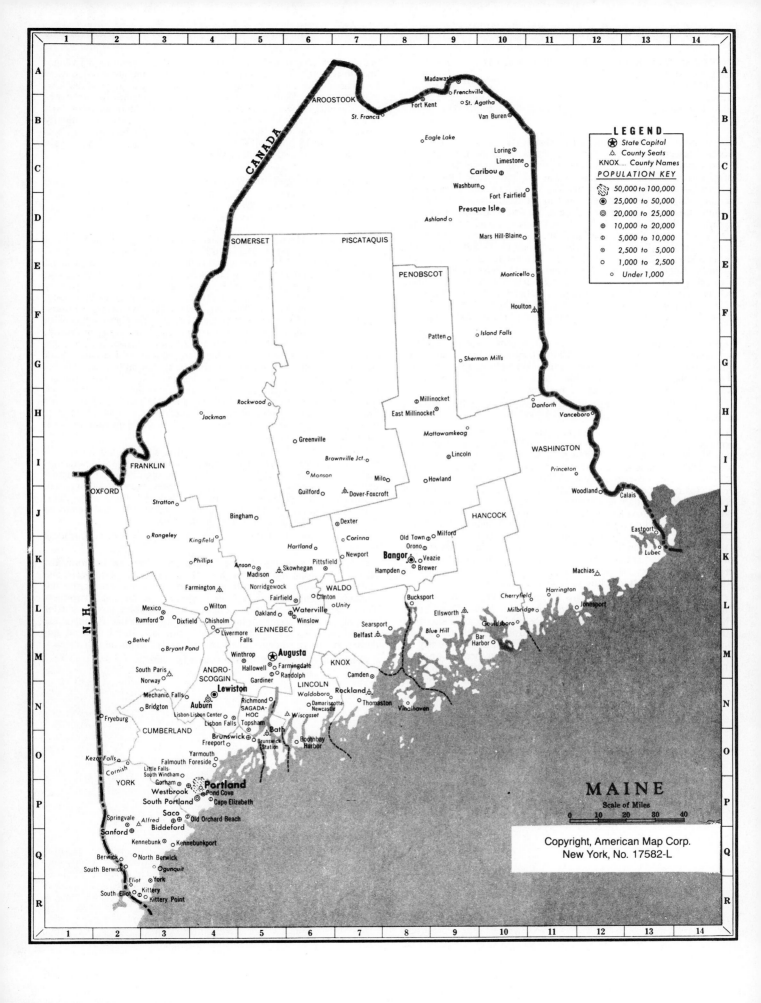

MAINE

Scale of Miles

MAINE

BANGOR THEOLOGICAL SEMINARY *(K-8)*
300 Union Street
Bangor, Maine 04401
Tel: (207) 942-6781; Admissions: (207) 942-6781 x22; Fax: (207) 990-1267

Description: The private seminary was founded in 1814 and is affiliated with the United Church of Christ. It is open to students of all races and denominations, and its primary purpose is to provide professional training for the pastoral ministry. The seminary operates on the semester system and is accredited by the Association of Theological Schools and the New England Association of Schools and Colleges. There are 209 students enrolled. Faculty of 10 full-time and 9 part-time gives a faculty-student ratio of 1-10.

Entrance Requirements: Official transcripts of academic record, four recommendations and a personal statement required in addition to a personal interview; midyear admission and rolling admission plans available; $25 application fee.

Costs Per Year: $5,800 tuition; $45 student fees.

Collegiate Environment: The seminary campus consists of more than nine acres and includes 16 buildings located eight miles from the University of Maine at Orono. The seminary libraries contain 120,000 volumes, 425 current periodical subscriptions, and 775 microfilms. Living accommodations are provided for 37 single students and 30 families. Approximately 70% of students applying for admission are accepted including midyear students and those from various geographical locations. Financial aid is available for qualified students. 75% of students are receiving financial aid. Seminary graduates are associated with the United Church of Christ, Methodist, Presbyterian, Episcopal, Baptist, Universalist-Unitarian, and other churches. About 95% of the freshmen returned to this campus for the second year.

Community Environment: At the head of tidewater and navigation on the Penobscot River, Bangor is the principal commercial city in eastern Maine. City's proximity to great timberlands made it an early center for shipyards and sawmills. Beside pulp, paper and wood products, the city produces tools, machinery, furniture, shoes, cigars, clothing and furs. Cold, dry winters with average snowfall of 72 inches; warm summers. Air and bus terminals, this is the crossroad for the main highway system of state. There is a public library, public recreation program, historical society, Symphony Orchestra and Chorus, many churches, Y's, general and two private hospitals. Recreation facilities include swimming pools, municipal auditorium seating 7,500 for ice shows, circuses, basketball and concerts. Part-time employment is available for students.

BATES COLLEGE *(N-4)*
23 Campus Avenue
Lewiston, Maine 04240
Tel: (207) 786-6000; Fax: (207) 786-6123

Description: Founded in 1855, this private liberal arts college has always been coeducational and open to students of any race, national origin or religion. The college operates on the 4-4-1 system and is accredited by the New England Association of Schools and Colleges, the Carnegie Foundation for Advancement of Teaching, and the American Chemical Society. The 4-4-1 program offers students a five-week term in April-May that enables concentrated studies and practical applications in one subject. There is an overseas program in which students can spend their junior year abroad. Enrollment is 1,515 students. A faculty of 148 full-time and 28 part-time gives a faculty-student ratio of 1-11.

Entrance Requirements: Rank in upper 20% of graduating class; $40 application fee; early admission, early decision, delayed admission and advanced placement plans available.

Costs Per Year: $22,850 comprehensive fee.

Collegiate Environment: The campus is located on 125 acres and is comprised of 59 buildings that include a library of 547,020 volumes, 1,738 periodicals, 250,994 microforms, and 19,283 audiovisual materials. Dormitory facilities are available for 725 men and 725 women. The college does not have fraternities or sororities, but all students have a share in the undergraduate program of extracurricular activities that enrich campus life. The college calendar is so arranged that students who wish to complete the degree program in three years may elect to do so; other students take the same program over a four-year period. Approximately 39% of students applying for admission meet the requirements and are accepted. The college welcomes a geographically diverse student body and midyear students are sometimes accepted. Financial aid is available for economically disadvantaged students, and approximately 37% of the current student body receives some form of aid. Classes begin in September, and 95% of the previous freshman class returned to the campus for the sophomore year.

Community Environment: The second largest city in state, Lewiston is Maine's leading textile center. It is located on the Androscoggin River at Twin Falls, directly opposite the city of Auburn. Minimum-maximum temperatures are 0-50 degrees in the winter and 50-90 degrees in the summer. Commercial transportation is available via air and bus. The city has several churches, Y's, a public library, two hospitals, several movie theaters, and hotels and motels.

BEAL COLLEGE *(K-8)*
629 Main St.
Bangor, Maine 04401
Tel: (207) 947-4591; (800) 660-7351

Description: The private business college was founded in 1891 and is recognized by the State and the Attorney General. The school operates on the modular system, and classes begin six times throughout the year. The college is accredited by the Accrediting Council for Independent Colleges and Schools. It also offers two summer sessions and an evening program. The college grants a Certificate, Diploma or Associate degree upon completion of program. Continuing education courses are offered. Enrollment is 451 students with 25 faculty members giving a faculty-student ratio of 1-15.

Entrance Requirements: High school graduation or equivalent; early decision, midyear admission, delayed admission and rolling admission plans available; $25 application fee; personal interview recommended; $25 application fee.

Costs Per Year: $3,720 tuition; $25 student fees.

Collegiate Environment: The campus is located in Bangor near center of town. The library holdings number 8,127 volumes. About 90% of students applying for admission are accepted as well as midyear students and those from various geographical locations. 77% of the students receive financial aid.

Community Environment: See Bangor Theological Seminary

BOWDOIN COLLEGE *(O-5)*
Brunswick, Maine 04011
Tel: (207) 725-3100; Fax: (207) 725-3101

Description: The private college was established by charter from the General Court of Massachusetts in 1794. The college began its active educational life with 8 students in 1802 and enrolled only men. In 1970, the college voted to enroll women undergraduates. It is accredited by the New England Association of Schools and Colleges and operates on the semester system. There are over 125 approved study abroad programs. It is also a member of 12 college exchange; 3-year liberal arts at Bowdoin, 2-year engineering programs at Columbia or Cal Tech, leading to both AB and BS; also a 3-2 year liberal arts/law program with Columbia, leading to an AB from Bowdoin, JD from Columbia. Enrollment is approximately 1,470 full-time students. A faculty of 129 gives a faculty student ratio of 1-11.

Entrance Requirements: High school graduation, completion of 20 college-preparatory (not required, recommended) courses including 4 English, 4 mathematics, 4 foreign language, 4 social science, 3 laboratory science; $50 application fee; early decision, delayed admission, and advanced placement plans available.

Costs Per Year: $20,230 tuition; $5,945 room and board; $325 student fees.

Collegiate Environment: The college is located on 110 acres and contains more than 50 buildings which include a new science library and a library of 828,000 volumes and periodicals, over 100,000 volumes in microfiche, 60,000 maps, 2,000 photographs, 400,000 manuscript items, and numerous sound recordings. First-year students are required to live on campus. Dormitory facilities are provided for 1,215 students. Eight coeducational social fraternities provide additional housing for 200 men and women. The college welcomes a geographically diverse studenty body. Mid year students are accepted by transfer only. Financial aid is available for economically handicapped students, and 40% (60% including Stafford loans and grants) of the students receive financial aid. Over 90% of students graduate within five years after matriculation.

Community Environment: Brunswick, a community of 20,500, is located within brief driving distance of several fine beaches and summer resort areas; skiing is available in winter. There are excellent highways and airline service to Portland, only 26 miles away. The area has several excellent motels. The town has a public library, Maine State Music Theatre, which features Broadway musicals each summer, and churches of many denominations, shopping centers and movie theaters; good restaurants. Recreational facilities include golf, hunting, boating, fishing, skiing, biking, backpacking, and other sports.

CASCO BAY COLLEGE   *(P-4)*
477 Congress Street
Portland, Maine 04111
Tel: (207) 772-0196

Description: The private junior college was established in 1863. The school operates on the trimester system and has two summer sessions. It is accredited by the Association of Independent Colleges and Schools. The school offers one-year college-level courses in the field of business and two-year programs leading to an Associate degree in business administration, business teacher education and secretarial sciences. Student enrollment is 380 full-time and 80 part-time. A faculty of 9 full-time and 12 part-time gives a faculty-student ratio of 1-19.

Entrance Requirements: High school graduation or equivalent; $75 application fee; rolling admission plan available.

Costs Per Year: $5,500 tuition; $100 student fees.

Collegiate Environment: The school library contains 4,000 volumes. Housing is provided in college apartments. Approximately 99% of students applying for admission are accepted as well as midyear students and those from various geographical locations. 80% of the previous freshman class returned to the business school for their second year.

Community Environment: Portland has a fine harbor and its shipping industry has been important since colonial days. It is a leading wholesale distributing point for northern New England and has over 175 manufacturing establishments. Community facilities include professional stage and dance companies, Historical Society, museums of art, Symphony Orchestra and annual series of community concerts, dramatic groups, fine library, municipal auditorium, and Sports Arena. It is a center of summer and winter recreational facilities. The 350-year-old city is rich in history and has experienced a dynamic rebirth in recent years, becoming the state's cultural and economic hub. Cosmopolitan and culturally diverse, Portland is consistently ranked among the most livable cities.

CENTRAL MAINE TECHNICAL COLLEGE   *(N-4)*
1250 Turner Street
Auburn, Maine 04210
Tel: (207) 784-2385; (800) 891-2002; Fax: (207) 777-7354

Description: Established in 1964, CMTC offers associate degree, diploma and certificate programs in 13 occupational programs, with most programs offering a cluster of employment training options. It is accredited by the New England Association of Schools and Colleges. Through its Continuing Education Division, short-term courses are offered to students enrolled on a part-time basis. The primary aim of the college is to enable students to acquire the skills and attitudes needed for obtaining employment in occupations of their choice. Enrollment is 450 full-time and 250 part-time credit students, and 669 evening students. A faculty of 46 full-time and 2 part-time gives a faculty-student ratio of 1-29.

Entrance Requirements: High school graduation or equivalency certificate; completion of specific high school courses varies with each program; personal interview required; rolling admission; $15 application fee.

Costs Per Year: $1,850 tuition; $4,100 out-of-state; $3,200 room and board.

Collegiate Environment: CMTC is located on the shore of Lake Auburn, about three miles from the center of the city. Its 110-acre campus provides a beautiful setting for this educational institution with its instructional facilities and dormitory accommodation for 104 students. Selection of students starts in September and continues until class quotas are filled. Students who are selected are notified as decisions are made. The library contains 12,000 titles, 175 periodicals, 538 microforms and 375 audiovisual materials. A full range of student services and student activities complements the educational programs, including intercollegiate athletics, and recreational and social activities.

Community Environment: See Bates College.

COLBY COLLEGE   *(L-6)*
Mayflower Hill
Waterville, Maine 04901
Tel: (207) 872-3000; (800) 723-3032; Admissions: (207) 872-3168; Fax: (207) 872-3474

Description: Colby, founded in 1813, is an independent, coeducational, residential college of liberal arts offering the Bachelor of Arts degree in 46 areas of study. It is located on Mayflower Hill overlooking the city of Waterville. It is accredited by the New England Association of Schools and Colleges. It operates on a 4-1-4 semester system. Enrollment is 748 men and 902 women full-time. A faculty of 150 provides a faculty-student ratio of 1-11. There are several study abroad programs and 75% of Colby students study abroad. Army ROTC is available through the University of Maine at Orono. Special programs include Sea Semester and exchanges with several American colleges. There are dual degree programs in engineering with Case Western, University of Rochester, and Dartmouth College.

Entrance Requirements: Completion of 16 college-preparatory units recommended, including 4 English, 3 mathematics, 3 foreign language, 2 science, and 2 social science; SAT or ACT required; early decision, advanced placement, early admission and delayed admission plans available; $45 application fee. There are two early decision rounds: ED1 due date is Nov. 15 and ED2 due date is Jan. 1. Normal application deadline is Jan. 15.

Costs Per Year: $18,930 tuition; $5,590 room and board; $900 student fees.

Collegiate Environment: There are 46 buildings on the 714-acre campus including Miller Library, which contains 488,000 volumes, 2,710 periodicals, 266,000 microforms and 79,000 audiovisual materials. 26 coeducational dormitories house 1,590 students. There are more than 80 student organizations. Student interests include drama, music, athletics, student government, and the Outing Club. The college seeks students from geographically diverse areas; also seeks a racially and ethnically diverse student population. Transfer students are admitted midyear. 42% of the freshman applicants were admitted. The middle 50% range of entering freshmen scores were SAT 540-630 verbal, 590-690 math. Financial aid is awarded on the basis of need; 32% of the students received grant aid. 65% received some form of aid. The college also offers its own Parent Loan Program. Approximately 93% of the freshman class return as sophomores. The college awards approximately 450 bachelor degrees annually to its graduating class.

Community Environment: Colby is one mile from Waterville, a regional center for industry, professional, and retail trade. Major employers in the area include Scott Paper, Hathaway Shirt, Keyes Fibre, and Mid-Maine Medical Center. Transportation from Boston is provided by bus.

COLLEGE OF THE ATLANTIC *(M-9)*
105 Eden Street
Bar Harbor, Maine 04609
Tel: (207) 288-5015; (800) 528-0025; Fax: (207) 288-4126

Description: This private, coeducational college was founded in 1969 and enrolled its first class of 30 students in the fall of 1972. The college is accredited by the New England Association of Schools and Colleges and awards the and Bachelor of Arts and Masters of Philosophy in Human Ecology: the study of people and their relationships with the natural and social environments. There are three 10-week terms. The college provides an education in social/environmental thought and action through interships, workshops, seminars and research which supplement the academic courses. International exchange programs with the Czech Republic and Uruguay are available. Enrollment includes 215 full-time and 25 part-time undergraduates and 5 graduate students. The faculty consists of 20 full-time and 12 part-time, giving an undergraduate faculty-student ratio of 1-8.

Entrance Requirements: High school graduation with rank in upper level of high school class; completion of college preparatory units including 4 English, 3 mathematics, 2 foreign language, and 2 science; written application, teacher references and personal interview carry considerable weight in the admissions process; early decision, early admission, deferred admission, midyear admission and advanced placement plans available; 2 early admissions options are: March 1 deadline for first year students, April 15 deadline for transfer students; March 1 deadline for regular admission; $40 application fee.

Costs Per Year: $15,450 tuition; $4,500 room and board; $1,021 miscellaneous.

Collegiate Environment: College of the Atlantic is located on the shores of Frenchman Bay and occupies four former estates just outside Bar Harbor. The 25-acre campus has residences for 100 students, a solar and wood heated workshop, and 1 solar greenhouse. A new library accommodates more than 32,000 volumes, 383 periodicals, 50 microforms, 664 audiovisual materials, and a collection of 235 videos. There are 42 computers on campus. Internet and First Search services are available. About 58% of applicatnts are accepted. The mean SAT scores of the entering 1994 freshmen class were 571 verbal, 568 math. Financial assistance and scholarships are available. 59% of students receive some form of financial aid. Students who wish to take courses not available at COA are encouraged to make use of the exchange between the University of Maine at Orono.

Community Environment: Bar Harbor and Mount Desert Island's natural environment provide excellent opportunities for environmental studies. Cooperative resource sharing is available with the Jackson Laboratory, Mount Desert Island Biological Laboratory, Acadia National Park and the local school system. In the summer, Bar Harbor is supported by the tourist trade. Other businesses which provide for local economy are boatbuilding, fishing and lobstering. Bar Harbor is easily accessible by Bar Harbor Airlines, Greyhound Bus or automobile via State Routes 1 and 3.

EASTERN MAINE VOCATIONAL TECHNICAL INSTITUTE
(K-8)
354 Hogan Road
Bangor, Maine 04401
Tel: (207) 941-4600; (800) 286-9357; Fax: (207) 941-4608

Description: The institute was founded in 1966 and is conducted under the authority of the Maine Technical College Board of Trustees. The state school operates on the semester system and offers one- and two-year programs in vocational-technical and academic areas. Enrollment includes 673 full-time and 277 part-time students. There are 126 faculty members. The faculty-student ratio is 1-10. It is accredited by the New England Association of Schools and Colleges-Commission on Vocational, Technical, Career Institutions.

Entrance Requirements: High school graduation or equivalent; $15 application fee; rolling admission plan available.

Costs Per Year: $1,740 tuition based on $58/credit hour; $3,810 out-of-state based on $127/credit hour; $3,200 room and board; $235 student fees.

Collegiate Environment: The institute is located on 90 acres and consists of 7 buildings that include a library of 16,000 volumes, 110 periodicals and dormitory facilities for 190 students. Approximately 41% of students applying for admission meet the requirements and are accepted. The school does not seek a geographically diverse student body; midyear students are accepted. About 50% of the recent student body graduated in the top half of their high school class and 25% in the top quarter. Financial aid is available, and 85% of students receive some form of financial aid. 71% of the previous freshmen returned to the institute for their second year.

Community Environment: See Bangor Theological Seminary.

HUSSON COLLEGE *(K-8)*
One College Circle
Bangor, Maine 04401
Tel: (207) 941-7100; (800) 448-7766; Fax: (207) 941-7988

Description: The private coeducational business college was founded in 1898 and is accredited by the New England Association of Schools and Colleges and the National League for Nursing. All courses are grouped into six departments including accounting, business administration, business education, management information systems, office management and secretarial studies, and nursing. The college offers two-year Associate degree programs, four-year Bachelor degree programs, and a Masters of Science in Business. A Cooperative Education program is available. It operates on the semester system and offers two summer sessions. Enrollment includes 918 full-time, 111 part-time, and 803 evening undergraduate, and 245 graduate students. A faculty of 44 full-time and 34 part-time gives a faculty-student ratio of 1-20. Army and Navy (for nursing only) ROTC available.

Entrance Requirements: Accredited high school graduation or equivalent; rank in upper 50% of graduating class; college-preparatory courses recommended; early admission, early decision, midyear admission, rolling admission, and advanced placement plans available; $25 application fee.

Costs Per Year: $7,800 tuition; $4,200 room and board; $100 student fees.

Collegiate Environment: The college is located on 170-acres and is comprised of six buildings including a library of 38,321 volumes, and dormitory facilities for 600 students. Approximately 88% of applicants are accepted, including midyear students. Classes begin in September and January. Financial aid is available and approximately 92% of students receive some form of financial assistance. 77% of freshman return for their sophomore year.

Community Environment: See Bangor Theological Seminary

KENNEBEC VALLEY TECHNICAL COLLEGE *(L-6)*
92 Western Avenue
Fairfield, Maine 04937
Tel: (207) 453-5000; Admissions: (207) 453-5131; Fax: (207) 453-5011

Description: Founded in 1970, this school is one of this state's seven public technical colleges. It is accredited by the New England Association of Schools and Colleges. The main function is to prepare students for entry-level positions. It offers an Associate degree and it's own diploma. The college operates on the semester system. Enrollment is 445 full-time and 750 part-time students. A faculty of 36 full-time and 105 part-time gives a faculty-student ratio of 1-12.

Entrance Requirements: Admission requirements vary by program; $20 application fee.

Costs Per Year: $1,740 state resident tuition (based on 15 credit hours per semester); $3,810 nonresident tuition; $150-$200 student fees.

Collegiate Environment: In addition to classrooms and laboratories, the college has a library containing 17,500 volumes, 150 periodicals and newspapers, and numerous microforms, records, tapes, films, pictures and audiovisual equipment. There are no dormitories. 70% of the student body receives some sort of financial aid.

Community Environment: See Colby College.

MAINE COLLEGE OF ART (P-4)
97 Spring Street
Portland, Maine 04101
Tel: (207) 775-3052; (800) 639-4808; Admissions: (207) 775-3052;
Fax: (207) 772-5069

Description: This privately supported coeducational college was founded in 1882. It operates on the semester system with one summer session and grants the Bachelor of Fine Arts degree. Enrollment is 257 full-time and 24 part-time students. A faculty of 23 full-time and 26 part-time provides a faculty-student ratio of 1-10. The school is accredited by the New England Association of Schools and Colleges and by the National Association of Schools of Art and Design.

Entrance Requirements: Accredited high school graduation or equivalency diploma; SAT and art portfolio required; early admission, early decision, delayed admission, midyear admission, advanced placement, and rolling admission plans available; $30 application fee.

Costs Per Year: $12,300 tuition; $1,360-$4720 room and board; $45-$55 student fees.

Collegiate Environment: The college accepts 72% of those who apply for admission. Freshmen must enroll at the beginning of the fall term; transfer students may be admitted at midyear. School facilities include a library of 18,000 volumes, 100 periodicals and 37,000 art slides. Scholarships are available and 95% of the current student body receives some form of financial assistance.

Community Environment: See Westbrook College.

MAINE MARITIME ACADEMY (M-8)
Battle Avenue
Castine, Maine 04420
Tel: (207) 326-4311; (800) 227-8465; Fax: (207) 326-2515

Description: The Academy is maintained by the State of Maine with the aid of the federal government. It is accredited by the New England Association of Schools and Colleges. It operates on a three-term system, including a spring term and has a limited summer session. The mission of the college is to provide an educational environment that emphasizes active student involvement in both the curricular and cocurricular educational processes. Maine Maritime provides public service to the state while perpetuating Maine's heritage of the sea. It confers a Bachelor of Science degree. The United States Coast Guard issues Third Mate or Third Assistant Engineer Licenses to qualified graduates. Navy ROTC is available. The Academy has a capacity for 650 students, and a limited number of freshmen are admitted each year. There are 650 students enrolled. A faculty of 65 gives a faculty-student ratio 1-10.

Entrance Requirements: High school graduation with rank in upper half of graduating class; minimum course requirements of 4 English, 3 mathematics, and 2 laboratory science; SAT or ACT required; physical examination required; $15 application fee; rolling admission, early decision, delayed admission, and advanced placement plans available.

Costs Per Year: $3,880 tuition; $6,930 out-of-state; $4,550 room and board; $500 student fees.

Collegiate Environment: The campus is comprised of 20 buildings located on 30 acres, including dormitory facilities for 614 men and women. The 533-foot TV State of Maine is the training ship of the Academy that provides an excellent laboratory while moored to her dock at Castine. The library contains 71,000 titles, 860 periodicals, 134,000 microforms, and 100 sound recordings. Approximately 75% of students applying for admission meet the requirements and are accepted. Classes begin in September and transfer students are accepted in fall and spring. 80% of the previous freshman class returned to the Academy for the second year. The average SAT scores of the current freshmen were 450V, 505M. Financial aid is available for economically handicapped students, and 50% of a recent freshman class received some form of aid. The Academy awarded 135 Bachelor degrees to its recent graduating class.

Community Environment: The French erected the first fort here in 1613, but the first permanent settlement was made by the English in 1760. Fort George, partially restored, is maintained as a memorial today. Castine is on south central coast of Maine, 35 miles south of Bangor.

NORTHERN MAINE TECHNICAL COLLEGE (D-10)
33 Edgemont Drive
Presque Isle, Maine 04769
Tel: (207) 768-2700; (800) 535-6682; Admissions: (207) 768-2785;
Fax: (207) 768-2831

Description: The institute was established in 1961 and offers two-year programs in vocational-technical and academic areas. It is fully accredited by the New England Association of Schools and Colleges. The semester system is employed. Enrollment totals 650 full-time and 660 part-time students. A faculty of 50 gives a teacher-student ratio of 1-26.

Entrance Requirements: High school graduation; $15 application fee; Open, rolling admissions.

Costs Per Year: $1,798 ($58/credit) resident tuition; $3,937 ($127/credit) nonresident; $3,200 room and board; $375 student fees.

Collegiate Environment: The institute contains a library of 10,000 volumes and dormitory facilities for 230 students. More than 60% of the previous freshman class returned to this campus for their second year.

Community Environment: See University of Maine - Presque Isle

SAINT JOSEPH'S COLLEGE (O-3)
Windham, Maine 04062-1198
Tel: (207) 892-6766; (800) 338-7057; Admissions: (207) 893-7746;
Fax: (207) 893-7861

Description: Saint Joseph's is a private, Catholic, coeducational liberal arts college founded in 1912 with the sponsorship of the Sisters of Mercy. Accredited by the New England Association of Schools and Colleges and the National League of Nursing, the college is rapidly expanding. Enrollment is 720 full-time and 233 part-time students. There are also more than 5,200 students enrolled in the distance education program. A faculty of 45 full-time and 46 part-time provides a faculty-student ratio of 1-16. The college operates on the semester system and offers two summer sessions. A strong advisement system affords each student a caring and supportive academic environment. Army ROTC is available.

Entrance Requirements: Applicants to the freshman class are admitted on the strength of their secondary school curriculum, class rank, grade point average, and SAT scores in relation to their intended major. 100% of last year's freshman class had at least a 2.0 grade point average in high school, 74% ranked in the top half of their class, and their median SAT verbal and mathematical scores were similar to the national averages. Counselor recommendations are required. Campus interviews are strongly encouraged, and most prospective freshmen visit the College. Transfer students are a valuable addition to the student body, and they may be admitted in either the fall or spring semester. Rolling admission, early admission, delayed admission and advanced placement available. $25 application fee.

Costs Per Year: $9,985 tuition; $5,180 room and board; $295 misc. fees.

Collegiate Environment: The college is located on the shores of Lake Sebago in the town of Standish, Maine. The 315-acre campus includes residence halls for 500 students. The library contains more than 75,250 volumes and 470 periodicals. 82% of those that apply are accepted. Financial aid is available and 85% receive some form of assistance.

Community Environment: Rural area with a temperate climate, there is no public transportation available. The college has several vans to provide transportation for students. The Greater Portland Community has many cultural, artistic, social, and recreational facilities and events.

SOUTHERN MAINE TECHNICAL COLLEGE (P-4)
Fort Road
South Portland, Maine 04106
Tel: (207) 767-9520; Fax: (207) 767-9671

Description: The public college was founded in 1946 and is accredited by the New England Association of Schools and Colleges. It offers two-year programs in vocational-technical and academic areas and grants the Associate degree. The college operates on the semester system and offers one summer session. Enrollment totals 1,200 students. A faculty of 96 gives a faculty-student ratio of 1-13.

Entrance Requirements: Accredited high school graduation or equivalent; units to include 4 English, 1 mathematics, and 1 science; SAT required for candidates for Associate degrees; $15 application fee; rolling admission, advanced placement and CLEP available.

Costs Per Year: $1,740 ($58/credit) resident tuition; $3,810 ($127/credit) nonresident; $3,150 room and board; $180 student fees.

Collegiate Environment: The college contains a library of 15,000 volumes, 330 periodicals, and 120 microforms. There are living accommodations for 110 men and 40 women. Approximately 63% of students applying for admission are accepted, and some midyear students are admitted. Need-based financial aid is available. 60% of students receive some form of financial aid. Classes begin in late August, and 80% of the previous freshman class returns to the institute for the second year.

Community Environment: See Westbrook College.

THOMAS COLLEGE   (L-6)
180 West River Road
Waterville, Maine 04901
Tel: (207) 873-0771

Description: As a pioneer in business education since 1894, this private college combines general education and specialized education for the profession of business. It is accredited by the New England Association of Schools and Colleges. The college grants Associate, Bachelor and Master degrees. It operates on the semester system. Enrollment includes 440 full-time, 440 part-time and 540 evening program undergraduates, and 100 graduate students. The faculty-student ratio is 1-21.

Entrance Requirements: Recognized high school graduation or equivalent. Rank is considered in relation to secondary school. Typically upper 50% of graduating class; completion of 18 units including 4 English, 3 mathematics, 3 science, 2 social science, 9 electives; SAT and 3 years of college prepatory mathematics and science recommended for B.S. program; $25 application fee; early admission, early decision, advanced placement, rolling admission, and delayed admission plans available.

Costs Per Year: $9,200 tuition; $4,600 room and board; $150 student fees.

Collegiate Environment: The college occupies a 70-acre campus that borders the Kennebec River. The library contains 23,500 volumes, and dormitory facilities accomodate 320 students. Financial assistance is need-based. 90% of the current student body receives some form of financial aid. Approximately 85% of the students are accepted. About 70% of the freshmen graduated in the top half of their high school class, 36% were in the top quarter. The average SAT scores of the current freshmen were 400V, 460M. 85% of the freshmen returned to this campus for the second year.

Community Environment: See Colby College.

UNITY COLLEGE   (L-7)
P.O. Box 5321
Unity, Maine 04988-0532
Tel: (207) 948-3131; Fax: (207) 948-5626

Description: This private college was founded in 1965 as an independent, nondenominational institution of higher learning with an emphasis on environmental science, natural resource management, and wilderness-based outdoor recreation. It operates on the semester system, has one summer institute, and is accreditated by the New England Association of Schools and Colleges. The college has two major divisions of study that include social sciences and environmental sciences. It also offers a terminal, two-year program in forestry and fine arts. Army ROTC is available. Enrollment is 487 full-time and 33 part-time students. A faculty of 29 provides a faculty-student ratio of 1-15.

Entrance Requirements: Official high school transcript or GED; 2 letters of recommendation; SAT recommended; early admission, midyear admission, rolling admission, and advanced placement plans available. $25 application fee.

Costs Per Year: $9,430 tuition; $9,930 out-of-state; $4,895 room and board; $365 student fees.

Collegiate Environment: The 186-acre campus is located in the very heart of Maine on the brow of Quaker Hill overlooking the village of Unity, 35 miles south of Bangor and 18 miles east of Waterville. The nine college buildings include a library of 40,000 volumes, 500 periodicals, 440 microforms, and 534 sound recordings, and dormitory facilities for 312 men and women. 85% of students applying for admission meet the requirements and are accepted. In general, first-year students are admitted in September only; however, other students are accepted at midyear. Almost 80% of the current freshman class graduated in the top 60% of their high school class, 40% in the top quarter and 20% in the third quarter. 80 scholarships are available and 92% of the students receive some form of financial aid. 75% of the previous freshman class returned to the campus for the sophomore year.

Community Environment: Located on Lake Winnecook, which is three miles long and has excellent fishing, canoeing, and sailing. The town has several small businesses, two churches, public library, and several fraternal organizations. Transportation is provided by air and bus lines. The climate is cool.

UNIVERSITY OF MAINE - AUGUSTA   (M-5)
46 University Drive
Augusta, Maine 04330
Tel: (207) 621-3000; Admissions: (207) 621-3465; Fax: (207) 621-3116

Description: By an Act of the Maine Legislature, the University of Maine at Augusta was established in 1965. It is accredited by the New England Association of Schools and Colleges, the Committee on Allied Health Education and Accreditation of the American Medical Association, and the National League for Nursing. It offers the Associate of Arts, Associate of Science, Bachelor of Music, and Bachelor of Science degrees. The semester system is employed and one summer session is offered. A wide variety of courses are offered at the undergraduate and graduate level in the evening. A Cooperative Education program is offered in Nursing, Medical Laboratory Science, Public Administration and Social Services. The Augusta campus offers live and interactive television courses to students throughout the state using the Education Network of Maine. It offers courses at centers located throughout the state. Enrollment includes 937 full-time and 4,539 part-time undergraduates and 6 graduate students. A faculty of 172 provides an undergraduate faculty-student ratio of 1-24.

Entrance Requirements: High school graduation or equivalent; with completion of 16 units; open enrollment policy; $25 application fee; open admission, deferred admission, early admission, advanced placement, early decision, midyear admission, and rolling admission plans available.

Costs Per Year: $2,460 tuition; $6,000 out-of-state tuition; $105 student fees.

Collegiate Environment: The campus in Augusta is located in the state's capital city which offers a wide variety of educational, professional, and recreational opportunities. The university in Augusta is a commuter campus. The library contains 40,000 titles, 500 periodicals, 500 microforms, and 500 audiovisual items. Financial assistance is available for economically disadvantaged students. 65% of students receive some form of aid. About 88% of the applicants are accepted. 65% of the freshmen returned to this campus for the second year.

Community Environment: Capital of the state since 1832, Augusta is located on Kennebec River. Main industries include manufacture of cotton textiles, paper products, boots and shoes, steel fabrication, printing, poultry, and food processing. There are part-time employment opportunities for students. The city offers a wide variety of professional and recreational opportunities. The climate is cool with many lakes close to city. Shopping facilities are good.

UNIVERSITY OF MAINE - FARMINGTON   (L-4)
102 Main Street
Farmington, Maine 04938
Tel: (207) 778-7000; Fax: (207) 778-8182

Description: The University of Maine at Farmington, the first state-supported college in Maine, is accredited by the New England Association of Schools and Colleges. Founded in 1863 to prepare teachers for public schools. Today, this small, selective undergraduate college offers personal attention and stimulating courses. UMF is the public alternative to a private liberal arts college, and provides a traditional New England small-college atmosphere. It is a major component of the University of Maine System, offering a variety of education and special education majors and four-year degrees in liberal arts, rehabilitation/human services and community health. With an enrollment of 1,942 full-time and 296 part-time students, the school is small enough to maintain its traditionally friendly atmosphere, and to respond to the needs of individual students. A faculty of 103 full-time and 43 part-time provides a faculty-student ratio of 1-16. There is also a comprehensive student services program that provides counseling, health care, financial aid, placement service, and social and sports activities. The university operates on the semester system and offers a May term and two five-week summer sessions.

Entrance Requirements: High school diploma or GED; high school units recommended: 4 English, 3 mathematics, 2 social studies, 2 laboratory sciences, 2 foreign languages, and 3 electives; an optional SAT or optional ACT and 2 CEEB Achievement tests; early admission, early notification, deferred admission, midyear admission, rolling admissions, and advanced placement plans available.

Costs Per Year: $2,820 tuition; $6,870 out-of-state, $3,970 room and board; $240 fees.

Collegiate Environment: The beautiful 50-acre campus consists of 35 buildings, mostly built in the last two decades. The Student Center is the hub of many campus activities. The center contains lounges, exhibit areas, snack bar, bookstore, game room, publications office, radio station, student organization offices and a central dining area. A new Health and Fitness Center provides excellent facilities for intramural sports, walking, jogging, running, weight training and swimming. A state-of-the-art academic computer center, which opened in 1991, serves individual students and faculty and entire classes in subjects ranging from calculus to music composition. The library contains 104,149 volumes, 687 periodicals and numerous microforms and audiovisual materials. Dormitories provide housing for 854 women and men. Scholarships are available, and 75% of the current student body receives some form of assistance.

Community Environment: Farmington has a population of about 7,000 people and is located in the heart of the mountains and lakes of western Maine. The area abounds in a four-seasonal recreational environment, highlighted by major ski areas located at Sugarloaf, Saddleback, and Sunday River.

UNIVERSITY OF MAINE - FORT KENT   *(B-8)*
Pleasant Street
Fort Kent, Maine 04743
Tel: (207) 834-3162

Description: This college was established in 1878 as a training school for teachers and in 1968 became a unit for the newly created university system that merged the five state colleges and the University of Maine. Today, it serves the entire state in the field of higher education. It operates on the semester system with three summer terms and is accredited by the New England Association of School and Colleges. The college offers Associate and Bachelor of Arts degrees. Credits are granted to students who study in foreign countries to acquire language proficiency and cultural familiarity. There is also a student exchange program. In addition to the regular day program, an evening division was instituted to provide the opportunity for recent high school graduates and for adults to improve their educational level. Enrollment is 610 students. A faculty of 33 gives a faculty-student ratio of 1-14.

Entrance Requirements: Accredited high school graduation or GED; 16 units including 4 English, 2 mathematics, 2 science, 2 social science; SAT required; early admission, early decision, rolling admission, midyear admission, and advanced placement plans available. $25 application fee.

Costs Per Year: $2,700 tuition; $6,600 out-of-state; $3,600 room and board.

Collegiate Environment: The college is located on the Saint John River, a few minutes from the Canadian Province of New Brunswick. Dormitory facilities are provided for 150 men and women. Library holdings include 57,173 volumes. 88% of students applying for admission are accepted including midyear students. 35 scholarships and

financial aid are available for qualified applicants. 90% of students receive some form of financial aid.

Community Environment: Separated from Canada by the St. John River, farming and lumbering are the economic mainstays of the area, but many people earn a living as guides for sports lovers. The town has a public library, churches, hospital, one theater, hunting and fishing, and a downhill ski slope. The area is excellent for outdoor winter recreational activities. Some part-time employment is available on campus.

UNIVERSITY OF MAINE - MACHIAS   *(K-12)*
9 O'Brien Avenue
Machias, Maine 04654
Tel: (207) 255-3313; Fax: (207) 255-4864

Description: The college is a state-supported member of the University of Maine and is accredited by the New England Association of Schools and Colleges. Opening as Washington State Normal School in 1909 with 43 students, the college has expanded both its curriculum and enrollment. The present name was adopted in 1970. Program offerings include a state-subsidized program for the preparation of elementary and junior high school teachers, and secondary school teachers in the field of business education; liberal arts, recreation management, business technology, and biological technology. It operates on the semester system and offers two summer sessions. Enrollment includes 635 full-time and 313 part-time students. A faculty of 40 full-time and 19 part-time gives a faculty-student ratio of 1-16.

Entrance Requirements: Accredited high school graduation; completion of 16 units including 4 English, 3 mathematics, 3 science, and 2 social science; minimum ACT 20 or SAT Verbal 450, Math 450 required; early admission, early decision, rolling admission, midyear admission, and advanced placement plans available; $25 application fee.

Costs Per Year: $2,700 state resident tuition; $6,600 nonresident tuition; $3,680 room and board; $175 student fees.

Collegiate Environment: The 42-acre campus is located on O'Brien Hill overlooking a deep gorge where the Machias River tumbles into Machias Bay. The 10 college buildings include a library of 85,000 titles and dormitory facilities for 310 students. The college welcomes students from diverse geographical locations and approximately 86% of applicants are accepted, including midyear students. Classes begin in September and January. Financial aid is available for economically disadvantaged students and 80% of students receive some form of financial assistance. 64% of freshmen return for their sophomore year.

Community Environment: Founded in 1763, Machias is the oldest town in Maine east of the Penobscot River and houses an historical museum. Principal industries include lumbering, blueberry canning, farming, and fishing. Salmon fishing is good.

UNIVERSITY OF MAINE - ORONO   *(K-8)*
Orono, Maine 04469
Tel: (207) 581-1110; Admissions: (207) 581-1572; Fax: (207) 581-1556

Description: The University of Maine is the oldest and largest campus of a statewide system that includes campuses at Augusta, Farmington, Fort Kent, Presque Isle, Machias, Orono and Portland-Gorham. It is accredited by the New England Association of Schools and Colleges. The University of Maine was established originally as the State College of Agriculture and the Mechanic Arts under provisions of the Morrill Act, approved by President Lincoln in 1862. Administrative units of the University of Maine include the College of Natural Resources Forestry and Agriculture, Business Administration, Education, College of Arts and Humanities, College of Engineering, College of Sciences, College of Behavioral and Social Sciences. The university grants the Bachelor, Master's and Doctoral degrees. The university offers optional Army and Navy ROTC programs. There are a wide range of opportunities to study abroad, preferably in the junior year at selected foreign universities. Other special programs include an Honors Program and an Onward Program. Enrollment includes 8,684 undergraduates and 2,317 graduate students. A faculty of 577 full-time and 158 part-time gives a faculty-ratio of 1-14.

Entrance Requirements: High school graduation; completion of 16 units including 4 English, the other unit requirements varying by program; SAT requird; early admission, early decision, midyear admission, rolling admission after March 1 and advanced placement plans available. $25 application fee.

Costs Per Year: $3,920 tuition and fees; $10,070 out-of-state tuition and fee; $4,680 room and board.

Collegiate Environment: The extensive campus of over 3,200 acres is situated about a mile from the business section of Orono and borders the Stillwater River. The university is approximately eight miles from Bangor, the third largest city of the state. The university libraries contain 668,000 titles, 5,400 periodicals and 555,000 microforms. Living accommodations are available for 2,150 men and 2,150 women. Additional housing is provided by numerous fraternities and sororities as well as off-campus accommodations. 82% of applicants are accepted. Almost all of the recent freshman class graduated in the top half of their high school class, 56% in the top quarter and 17% in the highest tenth. 499 scholarships are available and 75% of students receive some form of financial aid.

Community Environment: Rural area with pleasant summers and cold winters. Outdoor sports are a leading industry in the state. Bangor, the third largest city of the state, has excellent library, churches of all faiths, YMCA, YWCA, modern hospitals and many shopping centers. The community is served by buses, airlines, and excellent highways. The University of Maine is located approximately eight miles from Bangor in Orono, a town of about 10,000 population.

UNIVERSITY OF MAINE - PRESQUE ISLE   *(D-12)*
181 Main Street
Presque Isle, Maine 04769
Tel: (207) 768-9400; Admissions: (207) 768-9532

Description: This former state college, founded in 1903 and part of the University of Maine system since 1968, is a multipurpose institution, offering B.A., B.S., A.A., B.F.A., B.L.S., A.S. M.P.A., and M.A. degrees, and transfer programs with other colleges within the system. It is accredited by the New England Association of Schools and Colleges. It operates on the semester system and offers 6 summer terms. An Atlantic Community Studies Program is available. Enrollment includes 985 full-time and 379 part-time students. A faculty of 67 full-time and 37 part-time gives a faculty-student ratio of 1-15.

Entrance Requirements: Accredited high school graduation; completion of 16 units including 4 English, 3 mathematics, 2 science, 3 electives, 2 foreign language; SAT or ACT required; non-high school graduates with GED certificates may be admitted; early admission, early decision, rolling admission, midyear admission, and advanced placement plans available; $25 application fee.

Costs Per Year: $2,700 tuition; $6,600 out-of-state; $90 student fees; $3,630 room and board.

Collegiate Environment: Situated on the southern edge of Presque Isle, a small city of 12,000, in the heart of Aroostook County, the college consists of 14 buildings on almost 150 acres. The libray contains 116,700 volumes, 930 periodicals, 4,150 microforms and 460 audio-visual materials. Dormitory facilities are available for 350 students. The college will accept students from various geographical backgrounds. Approximately 82% of students applying for admission meet the requirements and are accepted. Almost 50% of the recent freshman class graduated in the top half of the high school class and 20% ranked in the top quarter. Scholarships are available and 75% of students receive some financial aid.

Community Environment: Aroostook County, in which Presque Isle is located, is largely unspoiled countryside in the heart of the potato-growing district. Presque Isle offers motels, hotels, restaurants, and shopping centers within walking distance of campus. The area features state parks, backpacking trails, mountain climbing and many streams and rivers. Airline and bus service is available.

UNIVERSITY OF NEW ENGLAND   *(P-3)*
Hills Beach Road
Biddeford, Maine 04005
Tel: (207) 283-0171

Description: This private university, which specializes in career-oriented programs, was first established as a liberal arts college in 1953 and was accredited by the New England Association of Schools and Colleges in 1966. The same year also marked the arrival on campus of

the first lay president and the admission of women students. Formerly St. Francis college, the University was created in 1978 with the opening of the University of New England College of Osteopathic Medicine (UNECOM). UNECOM welcomed its first class of 36 students in september 1978, and now accepts 70 students per year for a FTE of 280. In 1980, the University initiated physical therapy and occupational therapy programs and in 1986 established the associate degree in nursing program and two new graduate programs: the masters in health and school psychology and the masters in social work. Cooperative Education Programs, Internships, Practicums and an Individual Learning Program for the learning disabled are available. Undergraduate enrollment includes 230 men, 512 women full-time and 35 men, 115 women part-time. Graduate and first professional programs enroll another 421 students. The faculty includes 100 full-time and 30 part-time members. The university operates on the 4-1-4 system and offers 2 summer sessions.

Entrance Requirements: Accredited high school graduation; SAT or ACT required; $30 application fee; personal interview recommended, early admission, early decision, rolling admission, delayed admission, and advanced placement plans available.

Costs Per Year: $10,700 tuition; $4,850 room and board; $530 student fees.

Collegiate Environment: The campus is located in southern Maine and consists of 126 acres of land overlooking the Atlantic Ocean. The 12 college buildings include a library of 92,650 titles, 638 periodicals and 6,355 microforms, and dormitory facilities for 160 men and 280 women. About 75% of students applying for admission are accepted including midyear students and those from various geographical locations. Approximately 80% of the previous freshman class returned to the college for their sophomore year. Financial aid is available with over 90% of students receiving some form of aid. The average SAT score of the freshmen were 470 verbal and 480 math.

Community Environment: On the Saco River, the University of New England is located outside the small City of Biddeford (pop. 25,000) on the coast of Southern Maine, two hours from Boston and 25 minutes from Portland, Maine's largest city. Part-time work is available for students. Biddeford city services include hospital, churches, library, and Chamber of commerce. Recreational facilities good, with beaches of Biddeford Pool, Kennebunk, and Old Orchard; golf, fishing, swimming, skiing, are within easy reach.

UNIVERSITY OF SOUTHERN MAINE   *(P-4)*
37 College Avenue
Gorham, Maine 04038
Tel: (207) 780-4141; (800) 800-4876; Admissions: (207) 780-5670;
Fax: (207) 780-5640

Description: Gorham State Teachers College was established in 1878 and Portland Junior College was established in 1933. The two campuses were merged into the University of Southern Maine in 1973. It is a full-fledged campus of the University of Maine system, offering four-year degree programs in a number of areas of concentration, graduate programs in law, business administration, secondary education, and a more limited variety of graduate courses in other areas of concentration. Continuing education courses, and Associate degree programs in Business Administration, Therapeutic Recreation and Liberal Arts are also offered. The institution is accredited by the New England Association of Schools and Colleges. The University of Maine School of Law is located in Portland and is accredited by the American Bar Association. It is a full-time day school, offering a three-year program of law study to those who already hold a Bachelor's degree from an accredited college or university. An International Student Exchange program is available to England, Austria, Brazil, France, Holland, Japan, Soviet Union, and Ireland. Air Force ROTC is available through the University of New Hampshire. The university operates on the semester system and offers two 7-week summer sessions. Enrollment is 3,571 full-time and 4,307 part-time undergraduate students, and 1,750 graduate and law students. A faculty of 323 full-time and 213 part-time gives a faculty-student ratio of 1-15.

Entrance Requirements: High schoool graduation with rank in upper 50% of high school class; completion of 16 units including 4 English, 3 mathematics, 2 laboratory science, 2 social science, and 2 foreign language; SAT or ACT required; $25 application fee; early admission, rolling admission, CLEP, and advanced placement plans available.

Costs Per Year: $3,030 resident tuition; $8,580 out-of-state; $4,494 room and board; $250 student fees.

Collegiate Environment: USM has three campuses with a total of 126 acres. One is in Portland, another is approximately 10 miles away in the town of Gorham, and the third campus is located in Lewiston-Auburn. The libraries contain 348,952 bound volumes, 3,708 serial subscriptions, 972,746 microforms, and 4,480 audiovisual materials. Dormitories are provided on the Gorham campus for 1,100 students. 400 housing spaces are available in Portland. Financial assistance is available for economically disadvantaged students. About 75% of the freshman applicants are accepted. The middle 50% ranges of scores for the entering freshman class was SAT 840-1034 combined.

Community Environment: See Westbrook College.

WESTBROOK COLLEGE   *(P-4)*
716 Stevens Avenue
Portland, Maine 04103
Tel: (207) 797-7261; Fax: (207) 797-7225

Description: The private, four-year, residential, coeducational college was founded in 1831, making it the third oldest institution in Maine. The school operates on the semester system and is accredited by the New England Association of Schools and Colleges. Westbrook combines a liberal arts education with career-oriented majors; areas of study include: American studies, business management, dental hygiene, early childhood education, English, human development, individualized major, medical technology, nursing, pre-law, and psychology. Enrollment is 249 full-time and 138 part-time students. A faculty of 32 full-time and 138 part-time gives a faculty-student ratio of 1-10.

Entrance Requirements: High school graduation; $25 application fee; rolling admission, advanced placement, and deferred admission plans available.

Costs Per Year: $11,650 tuition; $4,650 room and board; $250 student fees.

Collegiate Environment: The college is comprised of 17 buildings located on 40 acres with dormitory facilities for 350 students. The library holdings include 50,000 volumes and 540 periodical subscriptions. About 75% of students applying for admission meet the requirements and are accepted. Classes begin in September, and mid-year students are accepted. Approximately 75% of the recent freshman class graduated in the top half of their high school class. Financial aid is available and 80% of all students receive financial assistance.

Community Environment: Portland has been destroyed three times; once by Indians, again by French and Indians, and then by a British fleet in 1775. With a fine harbor, shipping industry has been important since colonial days. It is leading wholesale distributing point for northern New England and has over 175 manufacturing establishments. Many community facilities include professional stage and dance companies, Historical Society, museums of art, Symphony Orchestra, and annual series of community concerts, dramatic groups, fine library, Municipal auditorium, and Sports Arena. It is a center of summer and winter recreational facilities for which Maine Westbrook is located just 2 miles from the center of Portland, Maine's largest city. The 350-year-old city is rich in history and has experienced a dynamic rebirth in recent years, becoming the state's cultural and economic hub. Cosmopolitan and culturally diverse, Portland is consistently ranked among the most livable cities. Westbrook students take advantage of Portland's diverse business, financial, and health care sectors, gaining on-the-job experience and academic credit by working in local businesses, hospitals, and nonprofit organizations. Many students choose to remain in Portland after graduation to pursue their professional careers.

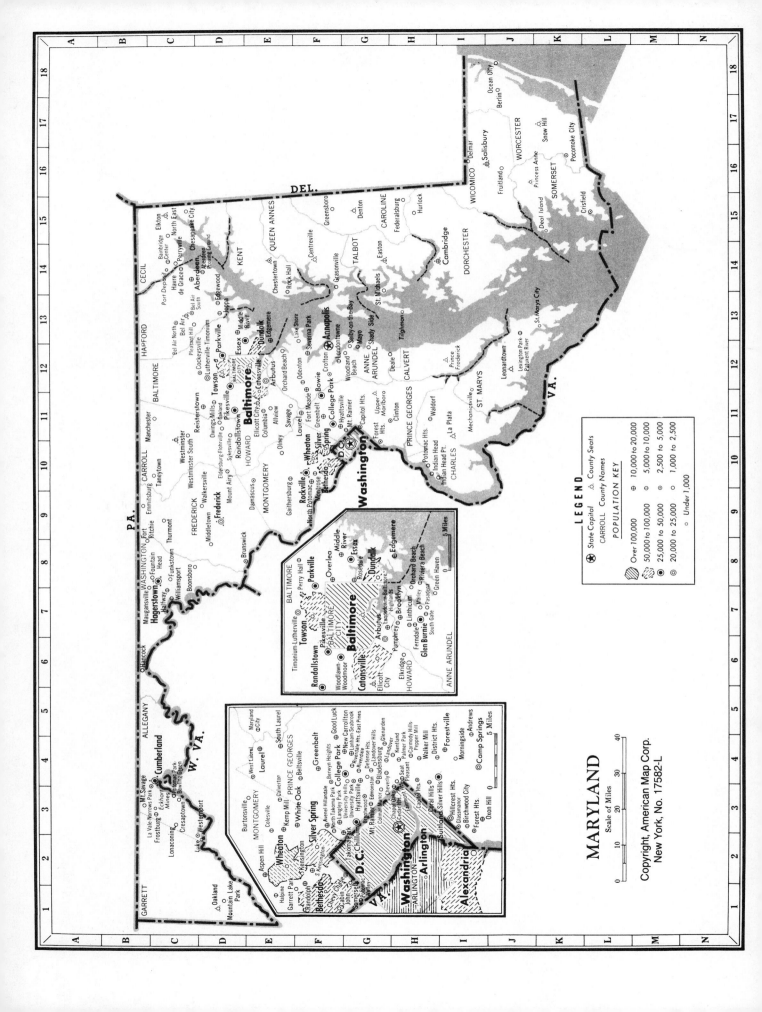

MARYLAND

Scale of Miles

Copyright, American Map Corp.
New York, No. 17582-L

LEGEND

⊛ State Capital   ⊙ County Seats
CARROLL County Names

POPULATION KEY

⊛ Over 100,000   ⊕ 10,000 to 20,000
  50,000 to 100,000   ⊙ 5,000 to 10,000
  25,000 to 50,000   ⊙ 2,500 to 5,000
⊙ 20,000 to 25,000   ○ 1,000 to 2,500
                        ○ Under 1,000

MARYLAND

ALLEGANY COMMUNITY COLLEGE   (C-4)
Willow Brook Road
Cumberland, Maryland 21502
Tel: (301) 724-7700; (800) 342-6319; Admissions: (301) 724-7700 X 202; Fax: (301) 724-6892

Description: The public, two-year college was founded in 1961 and offers both day and evening courses in vocational-technical and academic areas. It is accredited by the Middle States Association of Colleges and Schools. The school employs the semester system and offers one summer session. Enrollment includes 1,573 full-time and 1,304 part-time students. A faculty of 87 full-time and 137 part-time gives a faculty-student ratio of 1-19. The establishment of the Everett Center in Bedford and the Somerset Center are consistent with the revised ACC mission statement to provide regional service to the two Pennsylvania counties that art contiguous to Allegany County. Approval to offer degrees and certificate programs was secured from the Pennsylvania Department of Education following a comprehensive survey of residents of the two communities. 260 are enrolled at Somerset and 200 are enrolled at Everett.

Entrance Requirements: Open enrollment policy. Accredited high school graduation or equivalent required for degree programs; ACC Placement Test required for degree programs; early admission, midyear admission and advanced placement plans available; no application fee.

Costs Per Year: $2,560 tuition, in-state; $3,260 out-of-state.

Collegiate Environment: A campus located on a 370-acre site was occupied by the school in the fall of 1969. The library contains 41,988 volumes, 809 videos and films, 421 periodicals, 15,194 microforms and 2,008 recordings. All of the students applying for admission that meet the requirements are accepted including midyear students. Financial aid is available, and 65% of the current student body receive some form of financial aid.

Community Environment: An urban community, Cumberland is on the eastern edge of the Georges Creek coal region. Industries located here include: Chessie System Railroad, Westvaco, and Allegany Ballistics Laboratory. Recreational facilities include a city recreation program, golf courses, swimming pools, bowling alleys and some spectator sports.

ANNE ARUNDEL COMMUNITY COLLEGE   (F-12)
101 College Parkway
Arnold, Maryland 21012-1895
Tel: (301) 647-7100

Description: This public two-year community college was established in 1961 and is accredited by the Middle States Association of Colleges and Schools. Transfer, career, and continuing education programs are offered by the school and all courses of instruction, except those in continuing education, lead to the degree of Associate in Arts. The college operates on the semester system and offers 3 summer sessions. Enrollment is 2,822 full-time and 8,466 part-time students. A faculty of 198 gives a faculty-student ratio of 1-57.

Entrance Requirements: Open enrollment; accredited high school graduation or equivalent; SAT or ACT or placement exams; rolling admission and advanced placement plans available.

Costs Per Year: $1,740 ($58/cr) county tuition; $3,180 ($106/cr) out-of-county; $6,060 ($202/cr) out-of-state and foreign; $20 registration; $90 ($3/cr) fees.

Collegiate Environment: Anne Arundel's new campus is located on a 230-acre tract in Arnold, approximately 18 miles south of Baltimore and eight miles north of Annapolis. Student housing is not available. Facilities include the 400 seat Pascal Center for the Performing Arts, an art gallery, astronomy lab., bookstroe, cafeteria, child care center,

indoor pool and 3,000-seat athletic stadium. The library contains 115,000 volumes, 550 periodicals, 24 microforms and 2,333 audiovisual materials. Scholarships are available and 60% of the students receive some form of financial aid.

BALTIMORE HEBREW UNIVERSITY   (E-12)
5800 Park Heights Avenue
Baltimore, Maryland 21215
Tel: (410) 578-6918; Admissions: (410) 578-6917; Fax: (410) 578-6940

Description: The university offers undergraduate (BA and BHL) degrees in Judaic and Hebraic studies, a graduate degree (MA) in Judaic studies and a Ph.D. in Jewish studies. The university is accredited by the Middle States Association of Colleges and Schools. It operates on the semester system and has day and evening sessions and a summer program. Enrollment includes 26 full-time and 229 part-time undergraduates and 64 full-time graduates and doctoral students. A faculty of 11 full-time, 17 part-time provides a faculty-student ratio of 1-15.

Entrance Requirements: High school graduation; early admission, early decision, rolling admission, midyear admission, and advanced placement plans available; $20 application fee.

Costs Per Year: Undergraduate: $3,750 ($375/course) tuition; Graduate: $4,600 ($460/3-credit course).

Collegiate Environment: The college contains the Joseph Meyerhoff Library that houses more than 68,000 volumes, 200 periodical subscriptions and a collection of modern Jewish art. Financial aid is based on need.

Community Environment: The university is located in residential northwest Baltimore, the center of Jewish life in the city and county. Tree-lined streets, numerous aparmert complexes, convenient parking, public transportation and nearby shopping make the area amenable. There are orthodox, conservative, reform and reconstructionist synagogues in the area, along with kosher restaurants, delicatessens and two community centers, including one located on the campus. Affordable housing can be found near the university. Colleges and institutions that offer cooperative programs are less than 30 minutes away, and field work assignments are often within walking distance of the campus. Baltimore offers a colorful inner harbor, national aquarium, symphony orchestra, baseball and football teams, theatres, opera, and numerous museums. See university of Baltimore.

BOWIE STATE UNIVERSITY   (F-11)
Jericho Park Road
Bowie, Maryland 20715
Tel: (301) 464-3211; Admissions: (301) 464-6566; Fax: (301) 464-7521

Description: The state university offers a four-year curriculum leading to the Bachelor degree with majors in liberal arts, teacher education programs, and computer science. It is accredited by the Middle States Association of Colleges and Schools, the National Council for the Accreditation of Teacher Education and the Maryland State Department of Education. The college owes its origin to a bequest left in 1850 by Nelson Wells to be used in establishing a school to train black teachers. The school was started in 1865 and provided teacher education only until 1963; it now offers majors in 18 areas in arts and sciences and has a graduate school offering the Master of Education, the Master of Arts, a Master of Science degree. The college operates on the semester system with 1 summer session. Enrollment includes 859 men, 1,326 women full-time, 347 men, 706 women part-time, and 1,658 graduate students. A faculty of 136 full-time and 82 part-time members provides a faculty-student ratio of 1:26.

Entrance Requirements: High school graduation or equivalent; completion of 20 units, including 4 English, 3 mathematics, 2 science, 3 social studies, plus 8 electives; SAT required; non high school graduates considered; early admission, early decision, midyear admission, rolling admission, advanced placement plans available; $10 application fee.

Costs Per Year: $1,156 tuition; $2,727 out-of-state tuition; $1,198 room and board; $353.50 student fees.

Collegiate Environment: The college is comprised of 21 buildings located on 312 acres about one mile north of the town of Bowie. The library contains 119,000 volumes and dormitory facilities are provided for 864 students. 80% of students applying for admission are accepted including midyear students and those from various geographical locations. Financial aid is available for economically handicapped students and 85% of the current enrollment receives some form of financial aid. Out-of-state enrollment is limited to 15%.

Community Environment: A suburban community with good transportation facilities. Baltimore-Washington Airport at Baltimore is 14 miles. Student employment is available in many commercial establishments and private homes. Bowie is near beaches and many recreation centers.

CAPITOL COLLEGE *(F-2)*
11301 Springfield Road
Laurel, Maryland 20708
Tel: (301) 953-3200; (800) 950-1992 USA; Admissions: (410) 792-8800 Balt.; Fax: (301) 953-3876

Description: The private college of engineering, computer and engineering technology was founded in 1964. The college is fully accredited by the Middle States Association of Colleges and Schools and professionally by the Accreditation Board for Engineering and Technology. The college offers a four-year program leading to the Bachelor of Science degree. It operates on the semester system and offers one summer session. Enrollment includes 324 full-time and 355 part-time undergraduate, and 102 graduate students. A faculty of 23 full-time and 30 part-time gives a faculty-student ratio of 1-13.

Entrance Requirements: High school graduation or equivalent; completion of 4 English, 2 laboratory science, 2 social science, and 3 math (including Algebra II); SAT or ACT scores; moderately selective policy; early decision, early admission, midyear admission, and rolling admission plans available; $25 application fee.

Costs Per Year: $8,400 tuition; $2,812 room.

Collegiate Environment: The college occupies 4 buildings in a quiet, suburban setting. The library contains 10,460 volumes. There are apartment-style residences provided on campus which accomodate 100 students. Facilities include 2 electronics labs, 2 computer labs, 1 telecommunications lab, and a 340-seat auditorium. Financial aid for economically disadvantaged students, including freshmen, is available. 68% of students receive some form of financial assistance.

Community Environment: The town is in Prince George's County, a suburban area within easy reach of Washington, DC, and Baltimore, MD. Much of Washington's electronic industry is located in this area. The Capital Beltway is only four minutes from the school, providing easy access to the metropolitan area.

CATONSVILLE COMMUNITY COLLEGE *(E-12)*
800 S. Rolling Road
Catonsville, Maryland 21228
Tel: (410) 455-6050; Admissions: (410) 455-4304; Fax: (410) 455-4504

Description: This community college was established by the Baltimore County Board of Education in 1956 and is accredited by the Middle States Association of Colleges and Schools. It offers two-year programs in career and academic areas. Programs of study lead to the certificate or Associate degree. The college operates on the semester system and offers two summer sessions. There are 10,288 students enrolled.

Entrance Requirements: Open admissions policy; early admission, early decision, rolling admission plans available; $10 application fee; assessment mandatory for all full-time and/or degree seeking students.

Costs Per Year: $1,736 ($56/credit) in-county tuition; $3,069 ($91/credit) out-of-county tuition; $4,929 ($159/credit) out-of-state tuition; $2 per credit activity fee.

Collegiate Environment: The college is located on 105 acres on the Knapp Estate and existing buildings have been converted to college use. Many new structures have been added to the campus and include a library of 100,000 volumes, 10,000 pamphlets, 800 periodical titles, 35,000 microforms and 20,000 recordings and tapes. All students applying for admission are accepted including midyear students. Financial aid is available and of 15 scholarships awarded, 10 are offered to freshmen.

Community Environment: A suburban area 8 miles from Baltimore, Catonsville enjoys the transportation facilities of Baltimore, as well as the cultural and recreational advantages. Part-time employment opportunities are good. Excellent facilities for water sports.

Branch Campuses: Carroll County College, 1601 Washington Rd., Westminister, MD 21157, (401) 876-9600.

CECIL COMMUNITY COLLEGE *(C-15)*
1000 North East Rd.
North East, Maryland 21901
Tel: (410) 287-6060; (800) 282-3245; Admissions: (410) 287-1004; Fax: (410) 287-1026

Description: The community college was established in 1968 and is accredited by the Middle States Association of Colleges and Schools. It offers programs in the vocational-technical and academic areas. A newly developed Weekend College program offers classes Friday nights and Saturday. It operates on the semester system and offers one summer session. Enrollment includes 1,500 students. A faculty of 40 full-time and 60 part-time gives a faculty-student ratio of 1-15.

Entrance Requirements: Open enrollment policy; non-high school graduates admitted; early admission, early decision, midyear admission, and rolling admission plans available; $25 application fee.

Costs Per Year: $1,612 ($52 per credit) county resident tuition; $3,255 ($105 per credit) state resident tuition; $4,340 ($140 per credit) nonresident tuition; fees vary.

Collegiate Environment: The community college conducts classes on a day, evening, and Weekend College schedule. The library contains 24,000 volumes and 200 periodicals. All students applying for admission are accepted including midyear students. 40% of the current students receive financial assistance.

Community Environment: North East is approximately 5 miles west of Elkton. Elkton is nestled in the valley where the Chesapeake Bay begins and is within easy reach of all major cities on the East Coast. All forms of major commercial transportation are available. Three interchanges on the John F. Kennedy Turnpike and a super highway make New York or Washington, D.C., an easy two-hour drive. Elkton, rich in historical sites, has churches, health centers and good shopping. The area offers good hunting, fishing, camping, yachting and racing and is an ideal location for vacationing with beaches, parks, and marinas.

CHARLES COUNTY COMMUNITY COLLEGE *(I-11)*
Box 910, Mitchell Road
La Plata, Maryland 20646
Tel: (301) 934-2251; Fax: (301) 934-5255

Description: The coeducational junior college was established in 1958 and is accredited by the Middle States Association of Colleges and Schools. The college offers both transfer and terminal programs in vocational-technical and academic areas. It operates on the semester system and offers one summer session. Enrollment includes 634 men, 841 women full-time, 1,457 men and 2,978 women part-time. A faculty of 76 full-time and 279 part-time gives a faculty-student ratio of 1-21.

Entrance Requirements: Open enrollment; accredited high school graduation or equivalent; non high school graduates may be admitted after a personal interview; early admission, early decision, midyear admission, rolling admission, and advanced placement plans available; $20 application fee.

Costs Per Year: $1,798 ($58 per credit hour) state residents; $5,394 ($174 per credit hour) nonresidents; $50 student fees.

Collegiate Environment: The college is located on a 173-acre campus, four miles west of La Plata. It operates as a day and evening commuting college and does not maintain dormitory facilities. There is a library containing 44,715 volumes, 568 periodicals, 4,571 microforms and 12,500 audiovisual materials. Students are accepted at midyear. Financial aid is available. There are 146 scholarships, 100 for freshmen, available. 20% of students receive some form of financial assistance. 30% of the previous freshman class returned to the campus for their second year.

Community Environment: La Plata, a rural town, is within a short distance of Washington, D.C. Community recreational activities include bowling, hunting, swimming, boating, camping, fishing, water sports, and fox hunting. Some of the special events are the annual county fair, tobacco auctions, and the Maryland Garden Tours.

CHESAPEAKE COLLEGE   *(G-14)*
P. O. Box 8
Wye Mills, Maryland 21679
Tel: (301) 822-5400

Description: The institution functions as a public comprehensive two-year community college and is accredited by the Middle States Association of Colleges and Schools It was founded in 1965. There are 2,023 students enrolled. A faculty of 36 full-time and 94 part-time gives a faculty-student ratio of 1-20. The school operates on the early semester system with 2 summer terms and offers programs in vocational-technical and academic areas.

Entrance Requirements: Open enrollment policy; early admission, rolling admission, early decision and advanced placement plans available; credit for learning by experience.

Costs Per Year: $1,170 tuition; $2,650 out-of-district tuition, $4,650 out-of-state tuition; $69 student fees; $119 out-of-district student fees.

Collegiate Environment: The college is located on a new 170-acre campus and contains five buildings including a library of 31,000 volumes. All students applying for admission are accepted including midyear students. Financial aid is available for economically handicapped students and 181 students receive aid; academic scholarships are offered. The college offers a special program for the culturally disadvantaged enabling low-mark students to attend.

COLLEGE OF NOTRE DAME OF MARYLAND   *(E-12)*
4701 North Charles Street
Baltimore, Maryland 21210
Tel: (410) 435-0100; (800) 435-0200; Admissions: (410) 532-5330;
Fax: (410) 532-6287

Description: Founded in 1873 and chartered by the state of Maryland in 1896, the College of Notre Dame of Maryland was the first Catholic college for women in the United States to award the Bachelor of Arts degree. The college is accredited by the Middle States Association of Colleges and Schools and approved by the Maryland State Department of Education. It grants the Bachelor and Master's degree. Cooperative education programs exist with the Johns Hopkins University, Loyola College, Towson State University, Morgan State University, Goucher College, Coppin, and the Maryland Institute, College of Art. Army ROTC is available through a consortium with Loyola. The college operates on the semester system. Enrollment includes 699 full-time and 1,987 part-time undergraduates and 522 graduate students. A faculty of 74 full-time and 11 part-time gives a student-faculty ratio of 15:1.

Entrance Requirements: Accredited high school graduation with rank in upper half of graduation class; completion of 18 units including 4 English, 3 mathematics, 3 foreign language, 2 science, 2 social science, 4 electives; SAT required; early admission, early decision, rolling admission, midyear admission, and advanced placement plans available. $25 application fee.

Costs Per Year: $11,740 tuition; $5,845 room and board; $100 student activities fee.

Collegiate Environment: The college is located on a 58 acre campus in the northern suburbs of Baltimore. The 8 college buildings include a library of 290,000 volumes, 2,000 periodicals, 378,138 microforms, and 24,000 audio/visual materials. The dormitory facilities can house 435 women. Other buildings on campus provide a computer center

and a media center with a radio station and color television facility, study and lounge areas, art and photographic galleries, a bookstore, an auditorium, a chapel, a gym, a swimming pool, an exercise room, a dance studio, student activity resource center, and training center. Campus sports facilities include two playing fields and four tennis courts. 75% of applicants are accepted. The average scores of the entering freshman class were SAT 470 verbal, 494 math. Scholarships are available and 85% of the students receive some form of financial aid.

Community Environment: Like Boston, Baltimore is a college town. There are nine nearby colleges and universities and over 60,000 students in the Baltimore metropolitan area which enhances academic and social opportunities. The Notre Dame campus is located 15 minutes from the nationally known Inner Harbor area where concerts, fairs and ethnic festivals are sponsored. Both mountains and ocean are only a few hours from Notre Dame, providing opportunities for skiing in the winter and relaxing on the beach in the summer. Annapolis, home of the U. S. Naval Academy, is about 45 minutes from Notre Dame, and Washington, D. C., with all of its resources, is less than an hour's drive from the college.

COLUMBIA UNION COLLEGE   *(F-10)*
7600 Flower Avenue
Takoma Park, Maryland 20912
Tel: (301) 891-4124; (800) 835-4212; Fax: (301) 270-1618

Description: The institution is a liberal arts college granting baccalaureate degrees. It is accredited by the Middle States Association of Colleges and Schools and operates on the early semester system with two summer sessions. The college exists primarily for the purpose of providing special opportunities in higher education for the Seventh-day Adventist youth of the Columbia Union Conference, and for others who may find its program suitable to their requirements. Cooperative Education program is available. Enrollment includes 480 full-time and 499 part-time students. A faculty of 39 full-time, 7 part-time and 43 evening gives a faculty-student ratio of 1-8.

Entrance Requirements: Accredited high school graduation or equivalent; minimum C average and completion of 18 units including 4 English, 3 mathematics, 2 science, 3 social studies, 4 electives; SAT with minimum score of 400 verbal, 400 math or ACT with minimum score of 18 required; early decision, early admission, delayed admission, midyear admission, rolling admission, advanced placement plans available; $20 application fee.

Costs Per Year: $10,500 tuition; $3,850 room & board; $275 student fees; additional expenses average $300.

Collegiate Environment: The campus occupies 19 acres in a location that has the advantages of proximity to Washington, D.C. with its many educational and cultural opportunities. The 13 buildings of the college are adjoining the grounds of the Washington Adventist Hospital. The library contains 124,016 volumes and dormitory facilities are provided for 198 men and 240 women. Chapel attendance is required of all students. Approximately 81% of students applying for admission are accepted including midyear students and those from various geographical locations. About 66% of the freshman class return for the sophomore year. Financial aid is available, and 70% of the current student body receive some form of financial assistance. About 25% of the senior class continued on to graduate school.

Community Environment: A suburb of Washington, D.C., the residents of Takoma Park enjoy the cultural and recreational facilities of that city. There are many opportunities for part-time employment. Shopping facilities are excellent.

COPPIN STATE COLLEGE   *(E-12)*
2500 West North Avenue
Baltimore, Maryland 21216
Tel: (410) 383-5990; (800) 635-3674; Admissions: (410) 383-5990;
Fax: (410) 333-7094

Description: Coppin State College is a fully accredited four-year State College located in West Baltimore City. Coppin was founded in 1900 as a school for teacher education. Since its early days it has grown into a comprehensive college offering through day, evening and week-end classes 17 baccalaureate and 4 master degree programs. Coppin is accredited by the Middle States Association of Colleges and Schools. The undergraduate and graduate programs in teacher education are accredited by the National Council for the Accreditation of Teacher Education, the Council on Rehabilitation Education, and the Maryland State Department of Education. The Nursing program is accredited by the National League of Nursing and the Social Work program is accredited by the National Council on Social Work education. Army ROTC is available. The college operates on the semester system and offers two summer sessions. Enrollment includes 2,480 full-time and 800 part-time undergraduates and 211 graduate students. A faculty of 104 full-time and 128 part-time gives a ratio of 1-15.

Entrance Requirements: High School graduation or the Equivalent; completion of 20 high school units, 4 in English, 3 math, 2 science, 3 social science, 2 foreign language; SAT or ACT scores required; preditive index based on high school English and SAT scores, and high school average, determines admission status. Early admission, early decision, midyear admission, rolling admission and advanced placement plans available. $20 application fee.

Costs Per Year: $2,605 tuition; $5,177 out-of-state tuition; $677 student fees.

Collegiate Environment: The college is located on a 34 acre campus in northwest Baltimore City and has a library of 141,035 volumes, 663 periodicals and 231,573 microforms. The college now offers dormitory facilities for some students in one building. Approximately 70% of the students applying for admission are accepted, including midyear students. 50% of the students are accepted into graduate school.

Community Environment: See University of Baltimore

EASTERN CHRISTIAN COLLEGE   *(C-13)*
2410 Cresswell Road
Bel Air, Maryland 21014
Tel: (301) 734-7727

Description: The private bible college was founded in 1959 and is under the direction of the Church of Christ/Christian Church. Its programs are designed to provide training for those who plan to become local ministers, missionaries, directors of Christian education, church secretaries, and ministers of music. The college operates on the semester system. There is an enrollment of 26 full-time students. A faculty of 11 part-time gives a ratio of 1-4.

Entrance Requirements: High school graduation, completion of 16 units including 3 English, 2 mathematics, 3 science, and 3 social studies; TOEFL for foreign students; $20 application fee.

Costs Per Year: $3,450 tuition; $2,800 room and board; $600 books and supplies.

Collegiate Environment: The college is comprised of seven buildings located on 44 acres and includes a library of 14,000 volumes and dormitory facilities for 20 men and 26 women. All students applying for admission are accepted, including midyear students, according to catalog requirements.

Community Environment: Bel Air is a suburban city on the John F. Kennedy Memorial Highway. The community provides a library and churches of major denominations. The Susquehanna River and state parks provide facilities for water sports. Part-time employment is limited.

ESSEX COMMUNITY COLLEGE   *(E-12)*
7201 Rossville Blvd.
Baltimore, Maryland 21237
Tel: (410) 522-1213

Description: The public, two-year college was established in 1957 and offers transfer and career programs leading to the Associate in Arts degree. It operates on the semester system with three summer sessions offered and is accredited by the Middle States Association of College and Secondary Schools and the Maryland State Department of Education. The Medical Laboratory Technician Program, the Nuclear Medicine Program, and the Physician Assistant Program have been accredited by the American Medical Association; the Radiography Technology Program has been accredited by the American Registry of Radiologic Technologists; the Veterinary Technology Program has been accredited by the American Veterinary Association; and the Nursing Program has been accredited by the National League for Nursing and the Maryland State Board of Examiners of Nurses. The Theatre and Drama programs are fully accredited by the National As-

sociation of Schools of Theatre and the American Theatre Association and the College is a Community/Junior College member of the National Association of Schools of Music. Membership is held in the American Association of Community and Junior Colleges, the National Junior College Athletic Association -- Region XX, and the Maryland JUCO Athletic Conference. There is an enrollment of 2,834 full-time and 7,085 part-time students. A faculty of 191 full-time and 292 part-time gives a faculty-student ratio of 1-21.

Entrance Requirements: Open enrollment; high school graduation or equivalent for degree programs; SAT or ACT recommended; early admission, early decision, rolling admission, delayed admission, advanced placement plans available. $10 application fee, non-refundable one-time fee.

Costs Per Year: $974 tuition; $514 County resident; $974 State resident and $1,786 non-resident; $30 student fees.

Collegiate Environment: The college campus of approximately 140 acres is situated on high ground in a wooded setting where a panoramic view of the surrounding countryside may be enjoyed from many of the campus buildings. Eight major academic buildings approved for the campus have been completed. There is a library of 92,000 titles 900 periodicals, and 7,000 microforms. 14 scholarships are available.

Community Environment: See University of Baltimore

FREDERICK COMMUNITY COLLEGE   *(D-9)*
7932 Opossumtown Pike
Frederick, Maryland 21702
Tel: (301) 846-2430; Fax: (301) 846-2498

Description: This publicly-supported community college is accredited by the Middle States Association of Colleges and Schools. It operates on the semester system and offers three summer sessions. The college offers programs in vocational-technical and academic areas that lead to a certificate and the Associate degree. Enrollment includes 1,368 full-time and 3,000 part-time students. A faculty of 68 full-time and 200 part-time gives a faculty-student ratio of 1-17.

Entrance Requirements: Open enrollment policy; accredited high school graduation or equivalent; 20 units including 4 English, 3 mathematics, 2 science, and 2 social science; institutional placement tests required; non-high school graduates considered; rolling admission plan available; $15 application fee.

Costs Per Year: $1,662 tuition; $3,150 out-of-county; $4,806 out-of-state; $187.50 student fees ($6.25 per credit hour).

Collegiate Environment: The college occupies a new 110-acre campus. The library contains 41,000 volumes, 350 periodicals, 1,600 microforms and numerous audiovisual materials. All students applying for admission are accepted including midyear students. Financial aid is available.

Community Environment: See Hood College.

FROSTBURG STATE UNIVERSITY   *(C-3)*
Frostburg, Maryland 21532
Tel: (301) 689-4201; Admissions: (301) 689-4201; Fax: (301) 689-7074

Description: The institution was founded in 1898 and first opened as the State Normal School in 1902. Since then, the university has grown to a four-year, comprehensive institution. The semester system is used and two summer sessions are offered. It is accredited by the Middle States Association of Colleges and Schools. The arts and science program offers majors in approximately 30 areas of study including accounting, art, business administration, business education, computer social sciences, natural sciences, modern foreign languages, music, and recreation, with special programs in urban studies, departmental internships, and study abroad. Programs in pre-professional studies are available leading to admissions into dental, medical, and law schools. Students seeking a career in education can find programs in elementary, early childhood and secondary education. The university also has programs in wildlife and fisheries management. There are cooperative programs in engineering, nursing, pharmacy and physical therapy. There are graduate programs in Education, Management, Wildlife Management, Biology, Fisheries, Counseling Psychology and Modern Humanities. Army ROTC is available. Enrollment includes 4,241 full-time and 1,202 part-time students. The faculty consists of 232 full-time and 82 part-time members which provides a student-faculty ratio of 1:17.

Entrance Requirements: Accredited high school graduation or equivalent. Admission will be granted on the basis of grades, rank, scholastic aptitude test scores, and other evidence such as recommendations. Rolling admission. $25 application fee. Students who wish to transfer from other colleges or community colleges, must have a 2.0 (C) average with a minimum 25 credit hours attempted of academic course work.

Costs Per Year: $3,072 tuition; $6,548 non-resident tuition; $4,376 room and board, $602 miscellaneous.

Collegiate Environment: The campus, which is set in the mountains, contains a number of new buildings including the library, the student center, and the health and physical education complex. The College Library contains 196,637 volumes, 1,166 periodicals, and 29,463 A-V materials. Dormitory facilites are provided for 2,002 students. 67% of students applying for admission are accepted. The university will accept full-time or part-time freshmen, transfer, and graduate students at mid-year as well as those from varying geographical locations. Average high school standing of the 1988 freshman class top 50%; average SAT scores: 434 V, 482 M. Financial aid is available for qualified students and 65% of the student body receive some form of financial aid. The college awarded 437 Bachelor and 47 Master degrees to the graduating class.

Community Environment: The state university, in the City of Frostburg (population 7,327) is located in the mountains of western Maryland at an elevation of 2,200 feet. There are nearby state parks and winter sports activities including ice skating, skiing, and sleighing.

GARRETT COMMUNITY COLLEGE   *(D-2)*
Box 151
Mosses Road
McHenry, Maryland 21541
Tel: (301) 387-6666

Description: This publicly supported junior college employs the semester system with 1 summer session offered. Allows credit for certain courses by prior examination for previous training and experience. The enrollment includes 232 men and 413 women. A faculty of 15 full-time and 25 part-time gives a faculty-student ratio of 1-16. The school is fully accredited by the Middle States Association of Colleges and Schools.

Entrance Requirements: Open enrollment; high school graduation or equivalent; non-high school graduates considered for admission; early admission and rolling admission plans available.

Costs Per Year: $50 per credit for residents; $110 per credit for nonresidents.

Collegiate Environment: The library contains 24,300 volumes and, 310 periodical subscriptions. All applicants are accepted including midyear students, and 85% of the previous freshman class returned to the campus for their second year. Financial assistance is available and 48% of the current enrollment receives financial aid.

GOUCHER COLLEGE   *(D-12)*
Baltimore, Maryland 21204
Tel: (410) 337-6100; (800) 468-2437; Fax: (410) 337-6354

Description: Founded in 1885, Goucher is a private, coeducational liberal arts and sciences college. Goucher operates on the semester system and is accredited by the Middle States Association of Colleges and Schools and the American Chemical Society. The core curriculum provides a firm grounding in the liberal arts, and every student must complete an off-campus experience (internship, study abroad, or independent study). The college is also a leader in combining information technology with the liberal arts. Goucher participates in a cooperative program enabling students to take a limited number of courses at neighboring institutions, such as Johns Hopkins University and the Maryland Institute College of Art at no additional expense. Enrollment includes 968 full-time and 63 part-time undergraduates and 99 graduate students. There are 146 full and part-time faculty, and a 10:1 student to faculty ratio.

Entrance Requirements: Accredited high school graduation; completion of 14 (recommended distribution: 4 English, 3 mathematics, 2 foreign language, 2 laboratory science, 2-3 social studies; SAT re-

quired; ACT may be substituted; non- high school graduates may be admitted; early admission, early decision, midyear admission and advanced placement plans available. $40 application fee.

Costs Per Year: $15,588 tuition; $6,074 room and board; $100 student activities fees.

Collegiate Environment: The college is situated on a planned campus of over 287 acres in suburban Towson. The 17 buildings include the Julia Rogers library of 279,000 volumes, 1,100 periodicals, numerous microforms and audiovisual materials, and several special collections. Facilities include the Hoffberger Science Building, including the Advanced Technology Lab; the Decker Center for Information Technology, and the Thormann International Technoloy and Media Center; the Rosenberg Art Gallery; the Meyerhoff Arts Center, with visual art and theatre wings; the Todd Dance Studio, the new 50,000 square foot Athletic Center, with a field house, weight rooms, racquetball and squash courts; the Welsh Gymnasium, with a large pool and sundeck; and 1,000-seat Kraushaar Auditorium. The latter is noted for its fine acoustics and is the site for performances by leading social, cultural, and artistic figures. Additional athletic facilities include six well-kept tennis courts and hockey and lacrosse fields. Dormitory facilities for all students are provided. 72% of applicants are accepted. The undergraduates come from most states and several foreign countries. the recent student body graduated in the top 20% of their high school class and 85% in the top 50%. Of the previous freshman 85% returned to the college for their sophomore year. The average scores of the entering freshman class were SAT 540 verbal, 570 math. Scholarships are available, and 65% of the current enrollment receives institutional financial assistance.

Community Environment: Goucher is located on 287 wooded acres in suburban Towson, seat of Baltimore County. The college is 20 minutes away from downtown Baltimore, an hour's drive from Washington, D.C., and 25 miles from the state capital of Annapolis, on the Chesapeake Bay. There are extensive walking, riding, and running trails that help create a small college atmosphere.

HAGERSTOWN JUNIOR COLLEGE   *(C-8)*
751 Robinwood Drive
Hagerstown, Maryland 21740
Tel: (301) 790-2800; Fax: (301) 733-4229

Description: The two-year, public community college offers both transfer and career-oriented programs. It is accredited by the Middle States Association of Colleges and Schools. It operates on the semester system and offers three summer terms. Enrollment includes 1,141 full-time and 1,894 part-time students. A faculty of 59 full-time and 130 part-time gives a faculty-student ratio of 1-19. Cooperative Education programs (alternating work and class periods) are available in business and hotel-motel management.

Entrance Requirements: Open enrollment policy; ACT or SAT required; non high school graduates considered; early admission, early decision, rolling admission, rolling admission and advanced placement plans available. $10 application fee.

Costs Per Year: $1,952 tuition; $2,784 out-of-county tuition; $3,648 out-of-state tuition; $61 student fees.

Collegiate Environment: The campus is located on a 187-acre site and contains eight buildings which include a library of 45,000 volumes and 450 periodicals. 100% of the students applying for admission are accepted including midyear students. Average high school standing of a recent freshman class: 30% in the top quarter; 20% in the second quarter; 30% in the third quarter, 20% in the bottom quarter; The average scores of the entering freshman class was ACT 17 composite. Scholarships are available and 65% of the students receive some form of financial aid. The college awarded 20 Certificates and 330 Associate degrees recently.

Community Environment: In the heart of Cumberland Valley, Hagerstown is a manufacturing city, producing aircraft, pipe organs, shoes, trucks, leather and rubber goods, furniture, chemicals, toys and electrical equipment. All forms of commercial transportation are available. Recreational facilities are numerous. Points of interest are Antietam Battlefield, Old Ft. Frederick State Park, Hager House, and Washington County Museum of Fine Arts. Special events include the annual Halloween Mummer's Parade.

HARFORD COMMUNITY COLLEGE *(C-13)*
401 Thomas Run Road
Bel Air, Maryland 21014
Tel: (410) 836-4223; Fax: (410) 836-4169

Description: The publicly supported community college was established in 1957 and is accredited by the Middle States Association of Colleges and Schools. It operates on the semester system and offers four summer terms. Programs in vocational-technical and academic areas are offered. The college enrollment is 1,360 full-time and 4,033 part-time students. A faculty of 83 full-time and 301 part-time gives a faculty-student ratio of 1-21.

Entrance Requirements: Open door policy; completion of 4 English, 2 mathematics, 2 science required for some programs; non-high school graduates considered; early admission, early decision, delayed admission, advanced placement and rolling admission plans available.

Costs Per Year: $1,392 ($58/credit) in-county tuition; $2,208 ($92/credit) out-of-county; $3,240 ($135/credit) out-of-state; $139-$324 (10% of tuition) student fees.

Collegiate Environment: The college is located 30 miles north of Baltimore and three miles east of Bel Air. It is comprised of 15 buildings on 211 acres and includes a library of 54,145 volumes, 428 periodicals, 41,392 microforms and 13,410 recordings. All students applying for admission are accepted, including at midyear. 40% of students receive some form of financial aid.

Community Environment: See Eastern Christian College.

HOOD COLLEGE *(D-9)*
Frederick, Maryland 21701-9988
Tel: (301) 663-3131; (800) 922-1599; Fax: (301) 696-3819

Description: This independent liberal arts college for women was founded in 1893 and is accredited by the Middle States Association of Colleges and Schools. Hood is affiliated with the united Church of Christ and welcomes students of all religious faiths and national origin. It offers programs of study leading to the Bachelor of Arts and Bachelor of Science, and Masters. The curriculum emphasizes a combination of academic instruction in the liberal arts and career fields and off-campus opportunities for practical research and internships. The college operates on the semester system and offers one summer session. Enrollment includes 1,005 undergraduates and 900 students. A faculty of 78 full-time and 15 part-time provides a faculty-student ratio of 1-14.

Entrance Requirements: High school graduation or equivalent; completion of 16 units; SAT or ACT required; early admission, early decision, delayed admission, midyear admission and advanced placement plans available; $30 application fee.

Costs Per Year: $13,960 tuition; $6,040 room and board; $150 student fees.

Collegiate Environment: The library houses 163,000 volumes and numerous microforms, microfiches and audiovisual materials. Dormitory facilities are provided for 520 women. An estimated 79% of students applying for admission are accepted, including students at midyear. 55% of the current freshman class graduated in the top 25% of the high school class. 70% of the current enrollment receives financial aid. 80% of the freshmen returned to the college for their sophomore year.

Community Environment: Hood College is located on almost 50 acres near downtown Frederick, Maryland, a community of approximately 49,000. The campus is 45 miles west of Baltimore and an equal distance northwest of Washington D.C. The proximity of the Hood campus to these major metropliton areas increases the opportunities open to students to participate in social and cultural activities, to complete internships, and to explore prominent research facilities.

HOWARD COMMUNITY COLLEGE *(E-11)*
Little Patuxent Parkway
Columbia, Maryland 21044
Tel: (410) 992-4856/4822; Fax: (410) 992-4803

Description: Founded in 1969, this publicly supported community college is accredited by the Middle States Association of Colleges and Schools. The school offers programs leading to the associate degree or to a certificate. Competetive and selective programs include the James W. Rouse Scholars Program, the Summer Honors Program for high school students, nursing and cardiovascular technology. It is coeducational and operates on the semester system with two summer sessions and an intercession. Enrollment is 1,291 full-time and 3,700 part-time students. A faculty of 90 full-time and 230 part-time gives a faculty-student ratio of 1-20.

Entrance Requirements: Open admissions; high school diploma or equivalent required for selective programs, including nursing and cardiovascular technology; minimum SAT composite score of 1000 or ACT 24 for admission to Rouse Scholars program; advanced standing is available; August 28 application deadline; selective programs have differing application deadlines.

Costs Per Year: $2,130 county resident tuition; $2,990 tuition for out-of-county residents; $4,200 tuition for out-of-state residents; student fees are 10% of tuition bill.

Collegiate Environment: Howard Community College is situated on a wooded 120-acre campus with excellent classroom, library, laboratory, computer and athletic facilities. The college has an outdoor track, tennis and basketball courts, soccer fields, and an indoor pool. The library contains over 35,000 volumes. There are numerous student activities and clubs. Financial aid, 230 scholarships, and loan programs are available. 20% of students receive some form of financial aid. Numerous services are available for students with disabilities. Other student services available include advisory, counseling, tutoring, and job assistance.

Community Environment: Columbia, a planned city of 100,000, was designed as a community of village centers. Small lakes, parks, and bicycle paths add charm and access to the outdoors. Situated between two major cities, Baltimore and Washington, there is quick access to transportation facilities at airports and rail stations. The Columbia Mall provides major shopping facilities, and each village center complements the mall with supermarkets and convenience stores. The college serves as a cultural center in the county and hosts a variety of concerts, stage productions and cultural activities in its theatre.

JOHNS HOPKINS UNIVERSITY *(E-12)*
3400 N. Charles Street
Baltimore, Maryland 21218
Tel: (410) 516-8171; Fax: (410) 516-6025

Description: The private university was founded in 1876 and is accredited by the Middle States Association of Colleges and Schools and professionally by the American Chemical Society, Accrediting Board for Engineering and Technology, American Medical Association, American Public Health Association and the National Association of Schools of Music. The Peabody Institute, recognized as one of the leading professional schools of music in the United States became formally affiliated with Johns Hopkins in 1977. It is located one mile from campus in the Mt. Vernon section of Baltimore. Graduate-level instruction in International Studies is offered at the Paul H. Nitze School of Advanced International Studies, located in Washington D.C., and includes centers for foreign studies in Bologna, Italy, and Nanjing, China. A Cooperative Education program is available in Engineering. Matriculated students may take courses at cooperating institutions (Goucher College, Maryland Institute of Art, Loyola College, Baltimore Hebrew College, College of Notre Dame of Maryland, Towson State University, Morgan State University) at no extra expense. Army and Air Force ROTC programs are available. The university operates on the 4-1-4 calendar system and offers two summer sessions. Enrollment for the Homewood Campus includes 2,134 men and 1,270 women full-time and 79 part-time students. A faculty of 361 full-time and 109 part-time gives an overall faculty-student ratio of 1-10.

Entrance Requirements: Admission is limited and selective. High school graduates should have a "B" average or better, and recommended completion of 16 units including 4 English, 4 math, 2-3 of science, foreign language, and social studies. The high school equivalency diploma is accepted. The student is also required to submit the SAT and three Achievement Tests (1 of which must be Writing), or the ACT. Early decision, early admission, deferred admission and advanced placement plans are available. Transfer students are accepted at midyear. The application fee is $50.

Costs Per Year: $19,750 tuition, $6,955 room and board; $420 matriculation fee; $1,280 miscellaneous (books, travel expenses, spending money).

Collegiate Environment: The 140-acre campus, once a country estate known as "Homewood," is spacious, wooded, and quiet but within the busy city of Baltimore. The Homewood campuss is the site of the School of Arts and Sciences and the G.W.C. Whiting School of Engineering. The 50 buildings that comprise the Homewood campus include libraries housing 2.2 million volumes, 1.75 million volumes on microfilm, 14,500 periodicals, and 5,400 audiovisual materials. In 1992, four of the residence halls underwent 30 million dollars worth of renovatons. They currently house sophomores and some freshmen. Housing is guaranteed for all freshmen and sophomores. Other housing options include upperclassmen residencies, fraternity and sorority houses, as well as a wide variety of private housing. About 60% of the undergraduates receive some form of financial aid. 29% of applicants are accepted. The middle 50% range of scores for the enrolled freshman class was SAT 1240-1420 combined. The average score of the entering freshman class was ACT 29 composite. Most of the students applying to Hopkins have a "B" average or better.

Community Environment: See University of Baltimore

LOYOLA COLLEGE   *(E-12)*
4501 North Charles Street
Baltimore, Maryland 21210
Tel: (410) 617-2252; (800) 221-9107 x2252

Description: The private, liberal arts college is conducted in the Catholic Jesuit tradition. It is accredited by the Middle States Association of Colleges and Schools and the American Assembly of Collegiate Schools of Business It provides undergraduate and graduate programs. Junior Year Abroad, internships, and the Honors Program are available. The college operates on the 5-5 semester system and offers two summer sessions. Enrollment includes 3,247 full-time undergraduates, and 2,974 graduate students. A faculty of 220 full-time and 186 part-time gives a faculty-student ratio of 1-14. Army ROTC is available as an elective.

Entrance Requirements: Accredited high school graduation with rank in upper 50% of graduating class; completion of 16 units including 4 English, 2-3 mathematics, 2-3 foreign language, and 1-2 social science; minimum SAT Verbal 540, Math 560 required; early admission, midyear admission, and advanced placement plans available; $30 application fee.

Costs Per Year: $14,000 tuition; $6,300 room and board; $385 student fees.

Collegiate Environment: The campus is located on 65.1 acres in a residential area of northern Baltimore. The library contains 277,450 volumes, 1,983 periodicals, 378,138 microforms, and 22,510 audiovisual units. Dormitory facilities provide for 157 men, 150 women, and five apartment buildings accommodating 1,900. Approximately 65% of applicants are accepted, including midyear students. The Presidential Scholarship, an award of $5,000 to full tuition is available under certain guidelines, including an SAT 1200 combined score and a 3.5 GPA. 58% of students receive some form of financial assistance. 87% of freshmen returned for their sophomore year.

Community Environment: See University of Baltimore.

MARYLAND INSTITUTE, COLLEGE OF ART   *(E-12)*
1300 Mount Royal Avenue
Baltimore, Maryland 21217
Tel: (410) 669-9200; Admissions: (410) 225-2222; Fax: (410) 669-9206

Description: This private institute is accredited by the Middle State Association of Colleges and Schools and professionally by the National Association of Schools of Art & Design, and the Foundation for Interior Design Education Research. The Maryland Institute, College of Art is the oldest professional degree-granting art college in the country which provides a highly diversified curriculum, in studio arts and related liberal arts courses leading to the Bachelor of Fine Arts degree. The program integrates writing and liberal arts ideas and theories with studio skills, reflecting the belief that artists need to be literate and knowledgeable of cultural background. The Master of Fine Arts, Master of Arts in Teaching and a 5-year dual degree (BFA & MAT) are also offered. It allows limited credit by prior examination for previous training and experience. The college operates on the semester system and offers one summer session. Enrollment is 788 full-

time and 26 part-time students. A faculty of 66 full-time and 70 part-time gives a ratio of 1-11.

Entrance Requirements: Accredited high school graduation or equivalent; early admission, early decision, rolling admission, delayed admission and advanced placement plans available. $40 application fee.

Costs Per Year: $14,950 tuition; $5,050 room and board.

Collegiate Environment: Located in the heart of Baltimore, the college maintains twenty-two buildings. The library includes 50,000 volumes, 200 periodicals, and 80,000 slides. There is dormitory space for over 300 students. 65% of the current enrollment receives some form of financial aid.

Community Environment: See University of Baltimore

MONTGOMERY COLLEGE - GERMANTOWN CAMPUS
(F-10)
20200 Observation Drive
Germantown, Maryland 20874
Tel: (301) 353-7700; Admissions: (301) 353-7818/7823; Fax: (301) 353-7815

Description: The school is a publicly supported, coeducational community college. Montgomery College, the first community college in the state, was organized in 1946, as a higher education division of the Montgomery County school system. In 1950, the first college-owned campus was acquired in Takoma Park; in 1965 a second site in Rockville; and in 1975, a third campus was opened in Germantown. The college at Germantown is accredited by the Middle States Association of Colleges and Secondary Schools. It awards Certificates and Associate degrees. In addition, there are programs in general education preparing students for transfer to a four-year college or university. It operates on the semester system and offers 2 summer sessions. Enrollment is 642 full-time and 2,474 part-time students. A faculty of 47 full-time and 130 part-time gives a faculty-student ratio of 1-19.

Entrance Requirements: High school graduation or GED generally required; open enrollment policy; non-high school graduates may be admitted on a part-time basis; early placement, advanced placement, and rolling admission plans available; $25 application fee.

Costs Per Year: $780 maximum tuition; $1,485 maximum out-of-district; $2,0700 maximum out-of-state; consolidated fee equal to 10% of total tuition.

Collegiate Environment: Classes are offered at the campus and at several off-campus locations. The college provides counseling and placement services. All students applying for admission are accepted. New students are admitted at midyear. 25 scholarships are available, 15 of which are for freshmen. 6% of students receive financial aid.

Community Environment: See Montgomery College - Rockville Campus.

MONTGOMERY COLLEGE - ROCKVILLE CAMPUS
(F-10)
51 Mannakee Street
Rockville, Maryland 20850
Tel: (301) 279-5000

Description: The college, the first institution of its kind in the State of Maryland, was organized at Takoma Park in 1946 as the higher education division of the Montgomery County School system. It is accredited by the Middle States Association of Colleges and Schools and by the Maryland State Department of Education. In 1965, the Rockville Campus, was made a part of the Montgomery Junior College. The Germantown Campus was established in 1975 at Gaithersburg Admissions policies and academic standards of the college are identical at each campus. The college provides higher education for technical, semiprofessional careers, as well as programs for transfer to baccalaureate programs in other institutions. In addition, the college offers community services through continuing education and cultural programs. It operates on the semester system with two summer terms. Recent enrollment was 14,366 students. A faculty of 247 full-time and 363 part-time gives a faculty-student ratio of 1-23.

Entrance Requirements: Open enrollment; accredited high school graduation or equivalent generally required; non high school graduates may be admitted on a part-time basis; rolling admission, advanced placement and early placement programs available.

Costs Per Year: $1,485 tuition; $2,739 tuition for out-of-district residents; $3,762 tuition for out-of-state residents. A consolidated fee equal to 10% of total tuition is included.

Collegiate Environment: The campus is located on the western edge of Rockville. Fourteen buildings are equipped and in use at the present time. Counseling and placement services are offered and financial aid is available. All those who apply for admission are accepted, including midyear students. About 19% of the current enrollment receive some form of financial aid. The library contains 108,148 volumes, 858 periodicals, 15,768 microforms and 6,443 records and tapes.

Community Environment: Rockville, with neighboring cities of Washington, D.C., and Baltimore, is a city of industry and businesses. A great deal of printing and technical research is done within the city. This city was the All-American City in 1954 and 1961. The community provides a variety of churches, libraries, parks and playgrounds and camping areas.

MONTGOMERY COLLEGE - TAKOMA PARK CAMPUS
(F-10)
7600 Takoma Avenue
Takoma Park, Maryland 20912
Tel: (301) 650-1300; Admissions: (301) 650-1500; Fax: (301) 650-1497

Description: The College was the first institution of its kind in the State of Maryland and was established in 1946. It is accredited by the Middle States Association of Colleges and Schools and by the Maryland State Department of Education. There is an enrollment of 1,170 full-time and 3,691 part-time students. A faculty of 100 full-time and 139 part-time gives a ratio of 1-20. Admissions policies and academic standards of the college are identical for the Takoma Park Campus, the Rockville Campus and the Germantown Campus. The college provides two-year programs in vocational-technical and academic areas. It operates on the semester system with one summer term. For enrollment and faculty figures, see Rockville Campus.

Entrance Requirements: Open enrollment; accredited high school graduation or equivalent for degree programs; non high school graduates may be admitted as special students; early admission, early decision, midyear admission, rolling admission and advanced placement plans available; $25 application fee.

Costs Per Year: $1,170 tuition; $3,270 tuition for out-of-county Maryland residents; $4,590 tuition for out-of-state residents; a consolidated fee equal to 10% of total tuition.

Collegiate Environment: There are seven buildings on the campus and the library contains 58,464 volumes and 8,181 nonprint items including computer software and videotapes. Late afternoon and evening classes are still a primary function of this community college in addition to its daytime services. All students applying for admission are accepted, including midyear students. Financial aid is available with 19% of students receiving financial aid. There are 35 scholarships, 20 of them for freshmen.

Community Environment: See Columbia Union College

MORGAN STATE UNIVERSITY   *(E-12)*
Hillen Road & Coldspring Lane
Baltimore, Maryland 21239
Tel: (410) 319-3333; (800) 332-6674; Admissions: (410) 319-3000; Fax: (410) 319-3968

Description: The urban-oriented university was chartered in 1867 and was known as the Centenary Biblical Institute until 1890 and as Morgan State College until 1975 when it was granted university status. It is accredited by the Middle States Association of Colleges and Schools. The university is a comprehensive institution with programs leading to undergraduate liberal arts, pre-professional degrees and masters and doctoral degrees emphasizing teaching, research and public service. The institution consists of the College of Arts and Sciences, a School of Education and Urban Studies, a School of Engineering, a School of Business and Management, a Graduate School, and the Continuing Studies Program. The university also provides and evening school weekend university. It operates on the se-

mester system and offers one summer session. Enrollment is 5,800 students. A faculty of 240 full-time and 100 part-time gives a faculty-student ratio of 1-17. An optional Army ROTC program is offered.

Entrance Requirements: Accredited high school with rank in upper 50% of graduating class; minimum C average in 16 units including 4 English, 2 mathematics, and 1 science; SAT required; early admission, early decision, rolling admission, midyear admission, and advanced placement plans available; April 15 application deadline; $20 application fee.

Costs Per Year: $2,634 resident tuition and fees, $5,842 nonresident tuition and fees; $4,840 room and board.

Collegiate Environment: The 122-acre campus is located in the northeastern residential section of Baltimore. The 34 college buildings include a library of 300,000 volumes, 2,083 periodicals, 31,033 audiovisuals, 30,489 BVE microfilm and 56,470 BVE microforms. Dormitory facilities for 1,800 students are available. Ten national Greek-letter societies have chapters at the college, and there are numerous other student organizations. Approximately 50% of students applying for admission are accepted, including midyear students. The average high school standing of the freshman class was in the top 50%. Need-based financial aid is available, and 82% of the current student body receives some form of aid. The average high school standing of the freshman class was in the top 50%. The college awarded 435 Bachelor, 110 Master and 3 Doctorate degrees to the graduating class.

Community Environment: See University of Baltimore.

MOUNT SAINT MARY'S COLLEGE   *(B-9)*
Emmitsburg, Maryland 21727
Tel: (301) 447-5214; (800) 448-4347; Fax: (301) 447-5755

Description: The liberal arts college is the oldest independent (and second oldest overall) Catholic college in the United States and was founded in 1808. A major seminary was established at the same time. The college is fully accredited by the Middle States Association of Colleges and Schools, the Association of Theological Schools in the United States and Canada, and by the State Board for higher education in Maryland. Graduate programs in theology, business administration, and education are offered Study in Western Europe, Japan, China, Australia and elsewhere is available through accredited agencies. Army ROTC is available. Students from other beliefs are welcome to attend. Undergraduate enrollment is 667 men and 725 women. A faculty of 93 full-time and 46 part-time gives a faculty-student ratio of 1-14. Graduate enrollment is 416 students. The graduate faculty is 9 full-time and 17 part-time.

Entrance Requirements: Accredited high school graduation with preferred rank in upper half of graduating class; completion of 16 units including 4 English, 3 mathematics, 3 science, 2 foreign languages, and 3 social studies; SAT or ACT required (SAT preferred); GMAT required for graduate programs; early action, early admission, delayed admission and midyear admission placement plans available; $25 application fee.

Costs Per Year: $12,850 tuition; $6,200 room and board.

Collegiate Environment: The college is located on a campus of more than 1,400 acres and includes a library of 185,000 volumes, 935 periodicals and 12,800 microforms. Dormitory facilities are available for 524 men and 577 women. 80% of the student body graduated in the top half of the high school class. Students are welcome from various geographical locations. 87% of the applicants are accepted. The middle 50% range of scores of the entering freshmen class were SAT 410-520 verbal, 540-560 math, 860-1060 combined; Recentered Scale 490-600 verbal, 480-570 math. Scholarships are available and 73% of undergraduates receive some form of financial aid.

Community Environment: The Blue Ridge Mountains are the setting of this rural town in northwest Maryland, which is 20 miles from Westminster, 3 miles from the Mason-Dixon line, 12 miles from Gettysburg, PA, and approximately a one-and-a-half-hour drive to Downtown Baltimore or Washington, DC.

NER ISRAEL RABBINICAL COLLEGE   *(E-12)*
400 Mt. Wilson Lane
Baltimore, Maryland 21208
Tel: (410) 484-7200

Description: The rabbinical college was founded in 1933 and is accredited by the Maryland State Board of Education and is authorized to confer the degrees of Rabbi, Master of Talmudic Law, and Doctor of Talmudic Law. The purpose of the College is to provide scholastic and moral training for young men so that they may become teachers and rabbis in the Jewish Orthodox faith. The college is on the semester system and offers one summer session and cooperative programs with specific rabbinical colleges in Israel and Canada. Enrollment approaches 500 students.

Entrance Requirements: Minimum age of 17 years and of Jewish faith, high school graduation with rank in upper thirty percent of class; completion of college preparatory units including 4 English, 3 mathematics, 3 foreign language, 3 social sciences; knowledge of Bible, Talmud, Hebrew language, history, and ritual; entrance examinations required; early admission, early decision and rolling admission plans available. No application fee.

Costs Per Year: $3,400 tuition; $3,400 room and board; $100 student fees.

Collegiate Environment: The campus is comprised of eight buildings located on 57 acres which include a library system of 15,450 volumes and 125 periodicals and dormitory facilities for 275 men and 20 families. Students are admitted at mid-year and the school seeks a geographically diverse student body. Financial aid is available for economically handicapped students.

Community Environment: See University of Baltimore.

NEW COMMUNITY COLLEGE OF BALTIMORE   *(E-12)*
2901 Liberty Heights Ave.
Baltimore, Maryland 21215
Tel: (410) 333-5555

Description: The community college, formerly Baltimore Junior College, was opened in 1946 by the Department of Education of Baltimore City. It is a two-year, public junior college offering day, evening, and summer programs, and granting the Associate degree. It is accredited by the Middle States Association of Colleges and Schools and operates on the semester system with two summer sessions. Academic cooperative plans are available for students studying law enforcement. There are 5,300 students enrolled. A faculty of 148 full-time and 355 part-time gives a ratio of 1-22.

Entrance Requirements: Open enrollment policy; accredited high school graduation or equivalent; CCB placement test; early admission, early decision, rolling admission, delayed admission. $15 application fee.

Costs Per Year: $1,000 Baltimore City resident tuition; $2,000 Maryland resident tuition; $2,900 out-of-state tuition; $60 student fees.

Collegiate Environment: The college has two campuses, the Liberty Campus in Northwest Baltimore comprised of four buildings on 18 acres, and the Harbor Campus, opened in 1976, and comprised of two modern buildings on six acres in the heart of Baltimore's revitalized downtown area. Libraries on both campuses contain a total of 131,082 volumes, 19,254 pamphlets, 1,273 periodicals, 14,400 microforms and 15,388 audiovisual materials. The college owns and operates a 50,000-watt radio station, WBJC-FM. All students applying for admission are accepted including midyear students and 71% return for the second year.

Community Environment: See University of Baltimore

PRINCE GEORGE'S COMMUNITY COLLEGE   *(G-11)*
301 Largo Road
Largo, Maryland 20772
Tel: (301) 322-0819; Admissions: (301) 322-0865; Fax: (301) 808-0960

Description: The public community college first held classes in 1958, and offers a full program of two-year courses in business administration, liberal arts, engineering, and teacher education, engineering technologies, health technologies, computer sciences and public service technologies. Degree centers are located at Andrews Air Force Base and at F. Roosevelt High School. The college operates on the semester system and offers two summer sessions. It is accredited by the Maryland State Department of Education and by the Middle States Association of Colleges and Schools. Enrollment includes

2,900 full-time day and 9,300 part-time day students and 2,850 evening students. A faculty of 235 full-time and 380 part-time gives a faculty-student ratio of 1-21.

Entrance Requirements: Open enrollment; accredited high school graduation or equilvalent recommended; placement examinations required; early admission, early decision, rolling admission available.

Costs Per Year: $1,900 tuition; $3,800 out-of-county; $6,250 out-of-state; $1,000 student fees.

Collegiate Environment: The community college occupies a 150-acre campus and is comprised of eight buildings that include a library of 79,000 volumes, 2,000 pamphlets, 450 periodicals, 12,918 microforms and 14,680 sound recordings. The college offers an Associate in Arts degree in 54 curricula and one-year certificates in various areas. Financial aid is available for those students who qualify. All applicants, including midyear students, are accepted. The college awarded 24 Certificates and 1,040 Associate degrees recently.

Community Environment: Largo, within 10 miles of Washington, D.C., is in an area of rapid growth with major planned communities and shopping centers.

SAINT JOHN'S COLLEGE   *(F-12)*
P.O. Box 2800
Annapolis, Maryland 21404
Tel: (410) 263-2371; (800) 727-9238

Description: The private liberal arts college was founded as King William's School in 1696 and was chartered as Saint John's College in 1784. It is accredited by the Maryland State Department of Education and by the Middle States Association of Colleges and Schools. Students and faculty at St. John's work together in small discussion classes without lecture courses, written finals, or emphasis on grades. The program is a rigorous interdisciplinary curriculum based on great books: literature, mathematics, philosophy, theology, sciences, political theory, music, history and economics, from Homer to Freud, and Euclid to Einstein. The college operates on the semester system. Enrollment is 208 men and 187 women full-time and 3 part-time undergraduates adn 60 graduate students. A faculty of 63 full-time and 8 part-time gives a faculty-student ratio of approximately 1-8.

Entrance Requirements: Accredited high school graduation or equivalent; completion of college-preparatory courses including 4 English, 3 mathematics, 2 laboratory science, and 2 foreign language; early admission, rolling admission, midyear admission and delayed admission plans available; no application fee.

Costs Per Year: $17,430 tuition; $5,720 room and board; $100 student fees.

Collegiate Environment: The campus of 36 acres lies in the Historic District, adjoining College Creek, one block from the State House and across the street from the United States Naval Academy. The 17 buildings include 18th-century homes (now classrooms, offices, and dormitories), 19th-century Victorian structures, and 20th-century structures designed to complement the older buildings. There are six student dormitories offering single and double rooms for 300 students. The library houses 90,000 volumes, 150 periodicals, 961 microfilms, and 2,800 audiovisual materials. Freshmen are admitted at midyear (January); they are required to complete the second freshman semester during the summer session. Almost all of the recent student body graduated in the top half of their senior high school class, 60% in the top quarter and 33% in the highest tenth. 70% of applicants are accepted. The college maintains another campus in Santa Fe, New Mexico. The SAT ranges for the middle 50% of the current freshmen were 570-660 verbal and 520-650 math. 85% of the freshmen return to this campus for the second year. Of 200 scholarships available, 50 are for freshmen. 50% of the current enrollment receives financial assistance.

Community Environment: See United States Naval Academy.

SAINT MARY'S COLLEGE OF MARYLAND   *(K-13)*
Saint Mary's City, Maryland 20686
Tel: (301) 862-0292; (800) 492-7181; Admissions: (301) 862-0292; Fax: (301) 862-0906

Description: This four-year, nondenominational state college of liberal arts and sciences is accredited by the Middle States Association of Colleges and Schools. It operates on the semester system and offers one summer session. Saint Mary's was founded in 1840 and became the first junior college of the state in 1926. The transition from a junior to a senior college began in 1967. Today the college offers majors in art, dramatic arts, foreign language, mathematics, physics, philosophy, chemistry, biology, history, human development, psychology, music, natural science, political science, sociology/anthropology, student designed majors, and public policy. Current enrollment includes 588 men, 765 women full-time, and 70 men, and 142 women part-time. A faculty of 103 full-time and 54 part-time gives a faculty-student ratio of 1-13. An honors program is offered, as well as a study-abroad programs in England, France, Costa Rica, and China. A credit-earning internship program for a full semester is a highly successful program.

Entrance Requirements: Accredited high school graduation minimum C average and completion of 20 units including 4 English, 3 mathematics, 2 science, 3 social science, 2 foreign language, and 7 electives; SAT required; average GPA 3.42; average SAT is 565 verbal, 604 math; early decision, early admission, midyear admission and advanced placement plans available; $25 application fee.

Costs Per Year: $4,500 tuition; $7,800 tuition for non-Maryland students; $4,970 room and board; $935 student fees.

Collegiate Environment: The 275-acre campus is located adjacent to the Saint Mary's River. The 32 college buildings include a library of 146,126 volumes and 1,563 periodicals, 23,710 microforms and 22,261 audiovisual materials. Dormitory facilities for 1,030 students including townhouse-style residences for 311 students, are provided. About 65% of students applying for admission are accepted. 227 scholarships are available, 82 of them for freshmen. 52% of the students receive some form of financial assistance. The average combined SAT scores of the current freshmen were 1170, the highest among any of Maryland's public colleges and universities.

Community Environment: On the St. Mary's River where the Potomac River joins the Chesapeake Bay, St. Mary's City was settled in 1634 and became the first capital of Maryland. It is the third oldest English settlement in the New World and the only 17th Century settlement site remaining undisturbed. Washington, D.C., Baltimore and Annapolis are nearby. Historic points of interest are the Leonard Calvert Monument, Reconstructed State House of 1676 and Trinity Church.

SAINT MARY'S SEMINARY AND UNIVERSITY   *(D-12)*
5400 Roland Avenue
Baltimore, Maryland 21210
Tel: (410) 323-3200; Fax: (410) 323-3554

Description: The Roman Catholic institution is devoted principally, but not exclusively, to preparing young men for the Roman Catholic priesthood. It is accredited by the Middle States Association of Colleges and Schools and the Association of Theological Schools. Founded just 15 years after the United States, St. Mary's Seminary and University was opened in 1791 by the fathers of Saint Sulpice, a French society of diocesan priests dedicated to training parish priests. In 1805, the Maryland General Assembly chartered St. Mary's as a civil university. Pope Pius VII granted St. Mary's canonical recognition as an Ecclesiastical Faculty in 1822, the first such honor bestowed in the United States. St. Mary's has responded to the needs of the times throughout its history. In 1968, it became America's first Catholic seminatry to open an Ecumenical Institute, a graduate theological evening school for men and women of all religious traditions. In recent years, St. Mary's has initiated programs for the ongoing formation of diocesan priests. Construction of a separate facility adjacent to the seminary, the new St. Mary's Center for Continuing Studies, is scheduled for 1995. The Centers's signature program is an executive sabbatical where priests tend to spiritual needs, participate in theological inquiry, and explore national and international issues. The school enrolls 92 students in the School of Theology and 196 students in the Ecumenical Institute. A School of Theology faculty of 22 full-time and 10 part-time gives a faculty-student ratio of 1-4.

Entrance Requirements: Bachelor's degree or equivalent; minimum 24 credit hours in philosophy, 12 credit hours in religious studies, and 6 credit hours in humanities for seminarian applicants; recommendations from pastor, rector and chancery office required; $40 application fee.

Costs Per Year: $8,100 tuition; $6,160 room and board; $320 student fees.

Collegiate Environment: As a result of its highly successful Bicentennial Campaign, St. Mary's is an outstanding modern seminary with a refurbished main lecutre hall, library, bookstore, kitchen and dining room, community center, exercise room, and residential areas. Seminarians also use athletic facilities at several nearby institutions, including Loyola College. St. Mary's library holdings include 101,801 volumes on theology, philosophy, church history, liturgy, canon law, pastoral works, and scripture. Residence halls accomodate 177 students. 90% of applicants are accepted. Scholarships are available and 90% of students receive some form of financial aid.

Community Environment: See University of Baltimore.

SALISBURY STATE UNIVERSITY   *(J-16)*
Salisbury, Maryland 21801
Tel: (410) 543-6000; Fax: (410) 543-6068

Description: The four-year, comprehensive liberal arts college offers undergraduate programs leading to the Bachelor of Arts, Bachelor of Science degrees, and Bachelor of Social Work; and graduate programs leading to the Master of Education, Master of Science, Master of Business Administration and Master of Arts degree. The state university is accredited by the Middle States Association of Colleges and Schools. The school operates on the 4-1-4 system and offers one summer session. There are 6,000 students enrolled. Faculty numbers 350, giving a faculty-student ratio of 1-19.

Entrance Requirements: High school average of C+ or better; ACT or SAT; early admission, early decision, and advanced placement plans available; GRE required for graduate programs. $25 application fee.

Costs Per Year: $3,324 tuition, $6,436 out-of-state; $4,790 room and board.

Collegiate Environment: The college is located on 140 acres in the southern suburbs of Salisbury, 115 miles to the southwest of Baltimore and Washington, D.C. The 24 college buildings include a library of 250,000 volumes and dormitory facilities for 1,800 students. Resident freshmen are not permitted to have motor vehicles at the college. Approximately 45% of students applying for admission are accepted including midyear students and those from various geographical locations. The average scores of admitted freshmen were SAT 508 verbal and 576 math. Almost all of the recent student body graduated in the top half of their high school class, 60% in the top quarter, and 25% in the highest tenth. Financial aid is available for economically disadvantaged students. 50% of students receive some form of aid.

Community Environment: The hub of the Del-Mar-Va Peninsula, Salisbury is located with the Atlantic Ocean to the east and Chesapeake Bay to the west. Salisbury is the second largest port in the state and a major trading center of the Eastern Shore. Boat building, food processing, and the manufacture of wood products, clothing and automotive equipment are primary industries. Community facilities include a library, civic center, churches, hospitals and numerous civic and fraternal organizations. Boating and fishing are some of the outdoor activities of the community.

SOJOURNER-DOUGLASS COLLEGE   *(E-12)*
500 North Caroline Street
Baltimore, Maryland 21205
Tel: (301) 276-0306

Description: Sojourner-Douglas was formerly the Homestead-Montebello Center of Antioch University, which was established in 1972. On July 1, 1980, the Center became an independent institution and adopted its present name to honor Sojourner Truth and Frederick Douglass. The college is established to provide educational opportunities that link the world of work with the academic community. Programs are specially designed to develop and enhance knowledge and skills in the self-directed, self-motivated adult learner. The college is accredited by the Middle States Association of Colleges and Schools and approved by the Maryland State Board for Higher Education. The Bachelor of Arts degree is offered in three broad areas of concentration: Administration, Human and Social Resources, and Human Growth and Development. Enrollment is 157 men and 243 women full-time and 10 men and 31 women part-time, which gives an average class size of 20. Of the 51 faculty members, 58% hold terminal degrees. The faculty-student ratio is 1-9.

Entrance Requirements: High school graduation or equivalent with graduates having a C average accepted; open admission; early admission, rolling admission, delayed admission, and advanced placement plans available; $10 application fee.

Costs Per Year: Tuition $2,750; student fees $60.

Collegiate Environment: The primary administrative and classroom facilities are housed in Dunbar Community School Complex, which is a multipurpose, multieducational campus. The campus also houses a mayor's station, a Department of Social Security, a Department of Social Services, and several other related agencies to serve the needs of the community. The library contains 12,000 volumes, 33 periodicals, 302 microfilm items, and audiovisual materials. The college operates under admission criteria that utilize both traditional and nontraditional approaches. Approximately 70% of applicants are accepted. 75% of the students receive financial assistance.

Community Environment: The school is located in the heart of Baltimore. Baltimore, located in the center of Maryland and accessible from every major state highway, is the core of a metropolitan area extending into five adjacent counties: Baltimore, Anne Arundel, Carroll, Harford, and Howard. The metropolitan area has more than 1,000 different employers, primarily in the high technology and service industries. Recreational facilities are ample and can be found both on campus and in several public parks and indoor facilities.

TOWSON STATE UNIVERSITY   *(E-12)*
Baltimore, Maryland 21204
Tel: (410) 830-2000

Description: The institution is the oldest and largest of Maryland's public colleges and traces its history to 1866. At that time the General Assembly of Maryland established a state-wide public school system and authorized the first state teacher training institution, the Maryland State Normal School, later known as the State Teachers College at Towson, and since 1976, known under its present name. The college is accredited by the Middle States Association of Colleges and Schools and operates on the 4-1-4 system with two summer sessions. Enrollment includes 3,799 undergraduate men, 5,525 women full-time, 1,389 undergraduate men, 2,009 women part-time, and 1,829 graduate students. A faculty of 473 full-time and 780 part-time gives a faculty-student ratio of 1-17.

Entrance Requirements: High school graduation or equivalent; a minimum C+ average, 2.5 GPA or higher; 20 total units including 4 English, 3 mathematics, 2 science, 3 social science, 2 foreign language, 7 electives; SAT or ACT required; GRE required for selected graduate programs only; early admission, early decision, midyear admission, rolling admission, and advanced placement plans available; $25 application fee.

Costs Per Year: $2,454 tuition; $5,454 tuition required for out-of-state students; $4,330 room and board; $843 student fees.

Collegiate Environment: The campus of 306 acres is situated a mile and one-half from the northern border of the City of Baltimore. The 24 college buildings include a library of 545,439 volumes, 2,126 periodical subscriptions, and 708,029 microforms. It has dormitory and apartment facilities for 3,420 men and women. Approximately 64% of students applying for admission are accepted including midyear students and those from various geographical locations. The average scores of the admitted freshman class were SAT 456 verbal, 511 math. 191 scholarships are available for freshmen and 70% of the students receive some form of financial aid.

Community Environment: See University of Baltimore

UNITED STATES NAVAL ACADEMY   *(F-12)*
Annapolis, Maryland 21402
Tel: (410) 293-4361; (800) 638-9156; Fax: (410) 293-4348

Description: The U.S. Naval Academy, founded in 1845, is the undergraduate college of the U.S. Navy. It offers a four-year course leading to the Bachelor of Science degree and training of young men and women for careers as officers in the naval service. Graduates are commissioned as Ensigns in the U.S. Navy or Second Lieutenants in the U.S. Marine Corps. The Academy is accredited by the Middle States Association of Colleges and Schools and the Accreditation Board for Engineering and Technology. It operates on the calendar year of two semesters. U.S. citizens are appointed to the Academy

without regard to race, sex, creed, or national origin. Enrollment is 4,250. A faculty of 620 gives a faculty-student ratio of 1-7.

Entrance Requirements: Unmarried, between 17 and 22 years of age, good moral character, and sound physical health; accredited high school graduation or equivalent; rank in upper 40% of class recommended; completion of college-preparatory courses; SAT or ACT required; applicant must obtain a nomination from a member of Congress, the president, vice president or other authorized source; physical examination required; no application fee.

Costs Per Year: Tuition and fees are paid by United States government; $2,000 uniform deposit required upon admission; midshipmen receive pay of $545 per month.

Collegiate Environment: The Academy is comprised of 249 buildings located on 329 acres on the Severn River. The library contains 750,000 volumes; dormitory facilities are provided for 4,300 students. There are 33 varsity and 35 intramural sports available and all midshipmen participate either at the varsity or intramural level. Approximately 10% of students applying for admission are accepted. 81% of a recent entering class graduated in the top fifth of the high school class.

Community Environment: Annapolis, located on the Chesapeake Bay, is the capital of Maryland and the county seat of Anne Arundel County. It is a very popular center for boating, sailing, and fishing. The city contains some of the finest and best preserved examples of eighteenth-century architecture in the United States. It is the home of St. John's College, founded in 1696 as King William's School. Annapolis is located about 30 miles from both Baltimore and Washington, DC.

UNIVERSITY OF BALTIMORE   *(E-12)*
Charles at Mount Royal
Baltimore, Maryland 21201
Tel: (410) 837-4200; Admissions: (410) 837-4777

Description: The university was founded in 1925 and is accredited by the Middle States Association of Colleges and Schools and by the American Bar Association. It is a member of the University of Maryland System. It is composed of three main divisions which include the Gordon College of Liberal Arts, the School of Law, and the Merrick School of Business. The university grants the Bachelor and Masters degrees. It operates on the semester system and offers one summer session. Enrollment includes 2,367 men, 2,495 women full-time, 1,508 graduate students, and 1,055 law students. A faculty of 163 full-time and 137 part-time members gives a faculty-student ratio of 1-11.

Entrance Requirements: Rolling admission and midyear admission plans available; $20-$30 application fee.

Costs Per Year: $1,754 state resident, $2,342 nonresident; graduate programs vary.

Collegiate Environment: The university library contains 210,445 titles, 4,428 periodicals, 659,498 microforms. The university has no dormitories but assists non-resident students in finding acceptable living quarters. Approximately 77% of students applying for admission are accepted including midyear students and those from various geographical locations. 385 scholarships are available and 21% of the current student body receives some form of financial assistance.

Community Environment: Baltimore is an important industrial and educational center for the state of Maryland and the regional northeastern United States. The port has an active international market and foreign trade. Downtown Baltimore has become a popular tourist site; the Inner Harbor complex, including Harborplace and the National Aquarium, is recognized internationally. A new stadium to house the Baltimore Orioles has been completed at Camden Yards in downtown Baltimore. Pimlico Race Course is the home of the annual Preakness race. University of Baltimore is located in the cultural center of the city, adjacent to the Lyric Opera House, Meyerhoff Symphony Hall and the Maryland Institute of Art.

UNIVERSITY OF MARYLAND - BALTIMORE COUNTY CAMPUS   *(D-12)*
5401 Wilkens Avenue
Baltimore, Maryland 21228
Tel: (410) 455-2291; Fax: (410) 455-1094

Description: The University of Maryland Baltimore County, one of eleven institutions comprising the University of Maryland system, was founded in 1963 and is accredited by the Middle States Association of Colleges and Schools and several professional accreditations. There is an enrollment of 10,600 students. A faculty of 388 full-time and 225 part-time gives a faculty-student ratio of 1-15. It operates on a 4-1-4 calendar system and offers several summer sessions. UMBC is a public, four-year research institution emphasizing arts, humanities, and science curricula. The University offers baccalaureate degrees in twenty-seven fields, master's degrees in twenty-six fields, and doctorates in nineteen fields. Enrollments have been growing, particularly in Biological Sciences, Psychology, Social Work, Sociology, Visual Arts, Engineering, and Policy Sciences. UMBC has an extensive cooperative education program (alternating work and study).

Entrance Requirements: High school graduation or equivalent; completion of 13 units, including 4 English, 3 mathemematics, 2 science, 3 social science, and 2 foreign language; SAT or ACT required; GRE required for graduate school; rolling admission for transfer students; three decision dates for freshmen: December 1st, February 1st, and April 1st; delayed admissions and advanced placement plans available; $25 application fee.

Costs Per Year: $2,928 tuition; $7,992 out-of-state; $642 fees; $4,482 average room and board.

Collegiate Environment: UMBC, the youngest member of the University of Maryland system, is housed on 500 acres in suburban Catonsville. In addition to administrative, classroom, laboratory, and student union buildings, there is the Albin O. Kuhn Library and Gallery, which holds 503,000 volumes. More than 90% of the library's monographs are represented in an integrated on-line catalog and circulation system. As one of the major photographic archives in the nation, its Special Collections Department houses more than one million photographs and negatives. There are housing facilities for 2,227 students. Financial aid is available and 41% of current undergraduates receive some form of financial assistance. Of those applying for freshman admission, 57% are accepted; 47% of the degree-seeking graduate school applicants are accepted.

Community Environment: The ultramodern 500-acre campus is in an open-country setting in Catonsville, only minutes from the heart of Baltimore and less than an hour from the nation's capital. Baltimore, just six miles from the campus, is a rich resource for university students. Opportunities for musical, athletic, theatrical, and cultural events abound. The dynamic and dramatic Inner Harbor area features a convention center, the Maryland Science Center, Pier 7 Performing Arts Pavilion, the National Aquarium, and the lively collection of shops and restaurants called Harborplace. The Morris Mechanic Theatre brings Broadway to Baltimore, while the Baltimore Symphony Orchestra and internationally acclaimed artists perform in the striking new Meyerhoff Concert Hall. The Walters Art Gallery, the Enoch Pratt Library, and the Baltimore Orioles are also part of the city's rich tradition. Washington, only 32 miles from the campus, offers the student a wealth of academic, cultural, political, and leisure activities.

UNIVERSITY OF MARYLAND - COLLEGE PARK CAMPUS
(F-11)
College Park, Maryland 20742-5235
Tel: (301) 314-8385; Fax: (301) 314-9693

Description: Founded in 1856, College Park is part of the University of Maryland's 11-campus system. It is accredited by the Middle States Association of Colleges and Schools and various professional accrediting organizations. Thirteen colleges and schools make up the academic organization: Agriculture; Architecture; Arts and Humanities; Behavorial and Social Sciences; Business and Management; Computer, Mathematical, and Physical Sciences; Education; Engineering; Health and Human Performance; Journalism; Library and Information Services; Life Sciences; and Public Affairs. In addition there are some aspects of the Virginia-Maryland Regional College of Veterinary Medicine at College Park. Within these colleges or schools, the undergraduate may specialize in one of more than 100 majors or create a program of individual studies. Pre-professional education is offered in 11 fields. The graduate student may choose among some 78 masters or 69 doctoral academic areas. Headquartered on campus is the Maryland Agricultural Experiment Station which conducts research into all phases of agriculture and related fields. Areas of emphasis include the protection and enhancement of land and water resources, pest management, new crop development, animal nutrition, and poultry and egg production. The station operates 10 farms and research centers (encompassing more than 3,200 acres of land) at locations throughout the state. The university operates on the semester system and has two summer sessions. Enrollment includes 24,479 full-time and 8,014 part-time students. Of these, 8,769 are graduate students. A faculty of 2,208 full-time and 624 part-time gives a faculty-student ratio of 1-12.

Entrance Requirements: High school graduation or GED accepted; SAT or ACT required; GRE for graduate school; early action, early admission, midyear admission, rolling admission, and advanced placement plans are available; $30 application fee.

Costs Per Year: $3,179 state resident tuition; $9,123 nonresident tuition; $5,146 room and board; $615 required fees.

Collegiate Environment: Located between Baltimore and Washington, DC, this 1,500-acre campus encompasses 250 major buildings. The library contains 2,371,383 volumes, 18,675 periodicals, and 5,669,518 documents and microforms. There are residence hall accommodations for 7,187 men and women, fraternities and sororities house another 2,800, and there are 476 apartments for married students. 72% of applicants meet the criteria and are accepted. The middle 50% range of enrolled freshmen scores are SAT 1000-1200 combined. Numerous scholarships are available and 42% of the current student body receives financial aid.

Community Environment: Located in suburban College Park, a town of 25,000, the campus lies just nine miles from the center of the nation's capital, Washington, DC. A university shuttle bus system connects with all major public transit, including local bus routes, the metro subway system, and Amtrak, as well as National and Baltimore-Washington International airports.

UNIVERSITY OF MARYLAND - EASTERN SHORE CAMPUS
(J-16)
Princess Anne, Maryland 21853
Tel: (410) 651-2200; (800) 232-8637; Fax: (410) 651-7922

Description: Founded in 1886 as the Delaware Conference Academy, the Eastern Shore Campus later became known as Maryland State College, a division of the University of Maryland. In 1970, the Eastern Shore Campus became part of the University of Maryland's five-campus system. The historically black, land grant institution is accredited by the Middle States Association of Colleges and Schools and other professional accrediting agencies. It operates on the semester system and offers two summer sessions. Enrollment is 2,429 full-time and 262 part-time undergraduates, and 234 graduate students. A faculty of 150 full-time and 100 part-time gives a faculty-student ratio of 1-18. The campus is organized into the Schools of Arts and Sciences, Professional Studies, Agricultural Sciences and Graduate Studies and Research. In addition, an agricultural research unit and a Cooperative Extension Program are housed on the campus. The campus offers programs leading to the B.A. and B.S. degree in 33 disciplines, 8 pre-professional programs, an honors program, the M.S. degree in 6 fields, the M.D. degree, and the Ph.D. in two areas of study.

Entrance Requirements: High school graduation or GED; SAT or ACT required; GRE for graduate school; early admission, early decision, rolling admission, delayed admission and advanced placement plans available; $25 application fee.

Costs Per Year: $2,740 tuition; $7,401 out-of-state; $3,730 room and board.

Collegiate Environment: The campus is located on 600 acres of land with 24 major buildings. The campus library houses a collection of 150,000 books, bound periodicals and microfiche. Campus residences accommodate 1,457 men and women. Of those applying for admission, 90% are accepted. Approximately 90% of the students receive some form of financial assistance. 65% are accepted into graduate school.

Community Environment: The campus is located in the beautiful, historic town of Princess Anne, just 15 minutes from Salisbury and approximately 45 minutes from the popular beaches of Ocean City. The city of Salisbury serves a population in excess of 80,000 and provides a variety of social and cultural events and facilities in addition to numerous shopping centers.

UNIVERSITY OF MARYLAND - UNIVERSITY COLLEGE
(F-11)
University Boulevard at Adelphi Road
College Park, Maryland 20742-1600
Tel: (301) 985-7000

Description: Founded in 1947, University of Maryland University College (UMUC), one of the country's leading centers for lifelong education, serves as a vital statewide and worldwide campus for students who prefer to pursue higher education on a part-time basis. UMUC is accredited by the Middle States Association of Colleges and Schools. UMUC grants Bachelor of Arts, Bachelor of Science, and six Master's degrees including Master's of General Administration, as well as associate degrees and certificates to military personnel. Evening and weekend credit classes meet in College Park, at more than 30 off-campus centers in Maryland, and at approximately 160 sites overseas. UMUC operates on the semester system and offers two summer sessions. Enrollment includes 5,746 full-time and 26,409 part-time undergraduates and 4,147 graduate students. The Open Learning program of guided study - based upon the British Open University - offers rigorous interdisciplinary courses with optional class attendance for motivated adults. UMUC's Center for Professional Development offers many non-credit short courses and training programs and helps plan conferences, workshops, seminars, and classes for professional and civic groups using the modern UMUC residential conference center, at the Center of Adult Education in College Park.

Entrance Requirements: High school graduation is required; G.E.D. acceptable; advanced placement and midyear admission plans available. There is an open enrollment policy; C average. $25 application fee.

Costs Per Year: $5,220 tuition undergraduate, in-state.

Collegiate Environment: Financial aid consists of Federal, state, and institutional grants; state and institutional scholarships; Federal and private student loans; Federal and institutional student employment. Special programs consist of weekend and evening courses.

Community Environment: The administrative site is located at College Park, a small town of 25,000. Programs are offerd at more than 30 locations throughout Maryland, Northern Virginia, and the Washington, D.C. area. See also University of Maryland-College Park Campus.

UNIVERSITY OF MARYLAND AT BALTIMORE *(D-12)*
520 W. Lombard Street
Baltimore, Maryland 21201
Tel: (410) 837-4200

Description: The University of Maryland's Baltimore City Campus was founded in 1807. UMAB is accredited by the Middle States Association of Colleges and Schools and several professional accrediting institutions. There is an enrollment of 3,569 full-time and 1,158 part-time students. A faculty of 1,072 full-time and 376 part-time gives a student-faculty ratio of 1:2. It operates on a 4-1-4 calendar system with one summer session. The University of Maryland at Baltimore (UMAB) is the Campus for the Professions for the University of Maryland. It includes the professional schools, the graduate programs offered in conjunction with the professional schools, and the University of Maryland Medical System (UMMS) which includes the Maryland Institute for Emergency Medical Services Systems (MIEMSS). The seven professional schools include: Medicine, Dental, Law, Graduate, Nursing, Pharmacy, and Social Work and Community Planning. The six professional schools and the graduate school offer 62 degree programs. Also, residency programs are offered in 20 medical and three dental specialties. The University of Maryland Medical System (UMMS) consists of the 785-bed University of Maryland Hospital, the Shock Trauma Center of MIEMSS--the first major trauma program in the nation combining multi-disciplinary teaching and research with expert round-the-clock care for the critically ill and injured in the state, and the University of Maryland Cancer Center. UMMS provides health care services for more than 245,000 outpatient and inpatient visits annually. The UMAB campus is located in downtown Baltimore, a city that has become a model for urban rebirth and vitality. The Baltimore metropolitan area has nearly 2 million people, which represents almost one-half of the State of Maryland's population of 4.2 million. The total UMAB employee population numbered 2,688 for the fall quarter of 1988, including 2,014 full-time

faculty and 674 part-time faculty. In addition, UMMS employs 3,824 people.

Costs Per Year: $1,862 tuition; $5,810 out-of-state resident tuition; $1,750 for room only; $484 student fees.

Collegiate Environment: This 16-square-block, 32-acre campus in downtown Baltimore is the home of one of the nation's oldest and largest centers of professional and graduate education. The library contains 186,870 titles, 7,353 periodical subscriptions, 261,640 microforms and 3,414 audiovisual materials. There is dormitory space for 276 students. Scholarship are available and 72% of the student body receives some form of financial aid.

Community Environment: See University of Baltimore.

VILLA JULIE COLLEGE   *(F-6)*
Green Spring Valley Road
Stevenson, Maryland 21153
Tel: (410) 486-7000; Admissions: (410) 486-7001; Fax: (410) 486-3552

Description: This private coeducational college was founded as a one-year professional school in 1947, in 1952 it became a two-year college, and in 1984 a four-year college. The college is accredited by the Middle States Association of Colleges and Schools. The college offers the Associate and Bachelor degrees. It operates on the semester system and offers a summer and winter session. Enrollment includes 1,035 full-time and 631 part-time students. A faculty of 115 full-time and 73 part-time gives faculty-student ratio of 1-15.

Entrance Requirements: High school graduation; SAT preferred; personal interview, essay, and letters of recommendation are required; rolling admission, midyear admission, and advanced placement plans available; $25 application fee.

Costs Per Year: $7,490 tuition and fees.

Collegiate Environment: The college is situated on a 60-acre site in the beautiful Green Spring Valley area just northwest of Baltimore. The library contains 49,989 volumes, 442 periodical subscriptions, and 3,000 units of audiovisual materials. There are 100 computer terminals for student use. Approximately 50% of students applying for admission are accepted, including midyear students. Semesters begin in September and January. Financial aid is available with 63% of the current enrollment receiving financial assistance. 73% of the previous freshman class returned to the college for their sophomore year.

Community Environment: Located in the open countryside of Baltimore County, 20 minutes from the center of urban Baltimore, the college offers a country setting with city conveniences.

WASHINGTON BIBLE COLLEGE   *(G-10)*
6511 Princess Garden Parkway
Lanham, Maryland 20706
Tel: (301) 552-1400

Description: Washington Bible College is located on a 63-acre campus 10 miles from the nation's capital. It is accredited by the Accrediting Association of Bible Colleges and the Maryland State Board for Higher Education. Since its founding in 1938, the purpose of WBC has been to prepare students for Christian ministries or church vocations through a program which includes biblical, general and professional studies. The educational philosophy of the College is founded upon the truth of the Bible as the only adequate and complete rule of faith and practice. Implicit in this belief is the conviction that the Scriptures constitute the core of education and become the integrative force for the program of instruction - all truth being God's truth. It operates on the semester system and offers three summer sessions. Enrollment includes 140 full-time and 225 part-time undergraduates and 140 graduate students. A faculty of 12 full-time and 24 part-time gives a faculty-student ratio of 1-13.

Entrance Requirements: High school graduation or equivalent; SAT or ACT required; early admission, early decision, midyear admission, advanced placement and rolling admission plans available; $15 application fee.

Costs Per Year: $5,760 tuition; $3,600 room and board; $178 student fees.

Collegiate Environment: The campus is located on a 63-acre campus in suburban Lanham. The library contains 70,000 volumes, and dormitories are provided for 249 students. All full-time students under age 21 who do not live with parents or close relatives are required to live in the dormitory. Financial assistance is available for economically disadvantaged students. 95% of applicants are accepted, including students at midyear.

Community Environment: Lanham is within a few minutes drive of the Capitol Building in Washington, D.C. and is within two miles of the main highways leading to Baltimore and Annapolis. Public transportation, via the Capital Beltway, makes the metropolitan recreational and cultural facilities easily accessible.

WASHINGTON COLLEGE   *(E-14)*
Washington Ave.
Chestertown, Maryland 21620
Tel: (410) 778-2800; (800) 422-1782; Admissions: (410) 778-7700;
Fax: (410) 778-7287

Description: The private liberal arts college was established in 1782 and is the tenth oldest college in the United States. It operates on the semester system and is accredited by the Middle States Association of Colleges and Schools and the American Chemical Society. Special programs include a creative writing program and affiliations with Manchester College, England, and St. Andrews University, Scotland. Enrollment is 834 full-time and 47 part-time students. A faculty of 65 full-time and 19 part-time gives a faculty-student ratio of 1-12.

Entrance Requirements: Accredited high school graduation or equivalent; completion of 15 units including 4 English, 3 mathematics, 3 science, 2 foreign language, and 3 social science; SAT or ACT required; early admission, early decision, delayed admission, rolling admission, and advanced placement plans available; $35 application fee.

Costs Per Year: $16,040 tuition; $5,558 room and board.

Collegiate Environment: The campus, 112 acres not far from the broad Chester River, is located on the eastern shore of Maryland about a 90 minute drive from Baltimore, Washington, and Philadelphia. The library contains more than 200,000 volumes, 799 periodicals, 130,197 microforms and 3,737 audiovisual materials. Dormitory facilities are provided for 350 men and 350 women. Freshmen and sophomores are expected to live on campus. There are three national Greek-letter fraternities and three national sororities as well as numerous other student organizations. 75% of the students applying for admission are accepted including midyear students and those from various geographical locations. Financial aid is available for those who qualify and 75% of the current student body receives some form of financial aid. 88% of the previous freshman class returned to the campus for the sophomore year.

Community Environment: Chestertown is on the eastern shore of Maryland, 40 miles from Chesapeake Bay Bridge. The community facilities include churches and numerous civic and service organizations. Boating, fishing and hunting are some of the outdoor sports of the area.

WASHINGTON THEOLOGICAL UNION   *(F-10)*
9001 New Hampshire Avenue
Silver Spring, Maryland 20903
Tel: (301) 439-0551; (800) 334-9922; Fax: (301) 445-4929

Description: The Washington Theological Union is an independent graduate Roman Catholic school of theology, formerly known as the Washington Theological Coalition. It began in 1968 and was legally incorporated in the State of Maryland in 1969. It is authorized to grant the degrees, Master of Arts in the field of theology, Master of Divinity, and Master of Arts in Pastoral Studies. It is accredited by the the Middle States Association of Colleges and Schools and the Associa-

tion of Theological Schools in the United States and Canada. Enrollment is 124 full-time and 165 part-time students with a faculty of 25 full-time and 34 part-time teachers.

Entrance Requirements: Bachelor's degree from an accredited college with at least 90 hours in liberal arts studies; cumulative 2.5 GPA; 18 credits in philosophy; GRE; $25 application fee.

Costs Per Year: $8,500 tuition; $60 student fees.

Collegiate Environment: The central administration is located in Maryland. Classes are held there as well as several locations within the District of Columbia. On-campus housing and nearby housing for men and women are available. The Office of Student Services will assist in locating housing suited to the needs of students. Early application ensures housing preference. The library contains 55,000 volumes and 355 periodicals. Membership in the Consortium facilitates free cross-registration for the students as well as access to libraries and other resources offered.

WESTERN MARYLAND COLLEGE   *(C-10)*
Westminister, Maryland 21157
Tel: (410) 848-7000; (800) 638-5005; Admissions: (410) 857-2230;
Fax: (410) 857-2729

Description: The private college opened in 1867 and was chartered in 1868 under the auspices of the former Methodist Protestant Church. No longer affiliated with the Methodist Church, the college is accredited by the Middle States Association of Colleges and Schools and professionally by the American Chemical Society, National Council for the Accreditation of Teacher Education and Council on Social Work Education. It offers programs leading to the Bachelor of Arts, Master of Education, Master of Science, and Master of Liberal Arts degrees. The school operates on the 4-1-4 calendar system and offers two summer terms. Army ROTC program is available. Enrollment includes 1,142 full-time students and 41 men and 61 women part-time. A faculty of 89 full-time and 76 part-time gives a faculty-student ratio of approximately 1-9.

Entrance Requirements: Accredited high school graduation with minimum rank in upper 40% of graduating class; completion of 15 units including recommended courses of 4 English, 3 social studies, 2 foreign language, 3 mathematics, and 3 science; SAT or ACT required; early decision, midyear admission and advanced placement plans available; $30 application fee.

Costs Per Year: $15,300 tuition; $5,365 room and board.

Collegiate Environment: The 160-acre campus is situated on the crest of a hill in a rural area of Maryland. The 22 college buildings include a library of 160,000 volumes, 900 periodicals, 216,257 microforms and 7,958 sound recordings, and dormitory facilities for 1,300. There are five social fraternities and four sororities on the campus as well as numerous other student organizations. Approximately 64% of students applying for admission meet the requirements and are accepted. The college will accept midyear students as well as those from various geographical locations. 70% of the recent student body graduated in the top quarter of the high school class. The middle 50% range of scores for the entering freshman class was SAT 950-1050 combined. Financial aid is available on the basis of financial need and 80% of the current enrollment receives some form of financial aid. The college awarded 249 Bachelor and 135 Master degrees to the graduating class.

Community Environment: Westminister is the county seat of Carroll County. Community facilities include churches of most denominations, general hospital, health center, library, and the cultural advantages of the college. Outdoor activities include tennis, swimming, golf, ball parks, a 40-acre natural park and a 7-acre recreation area.

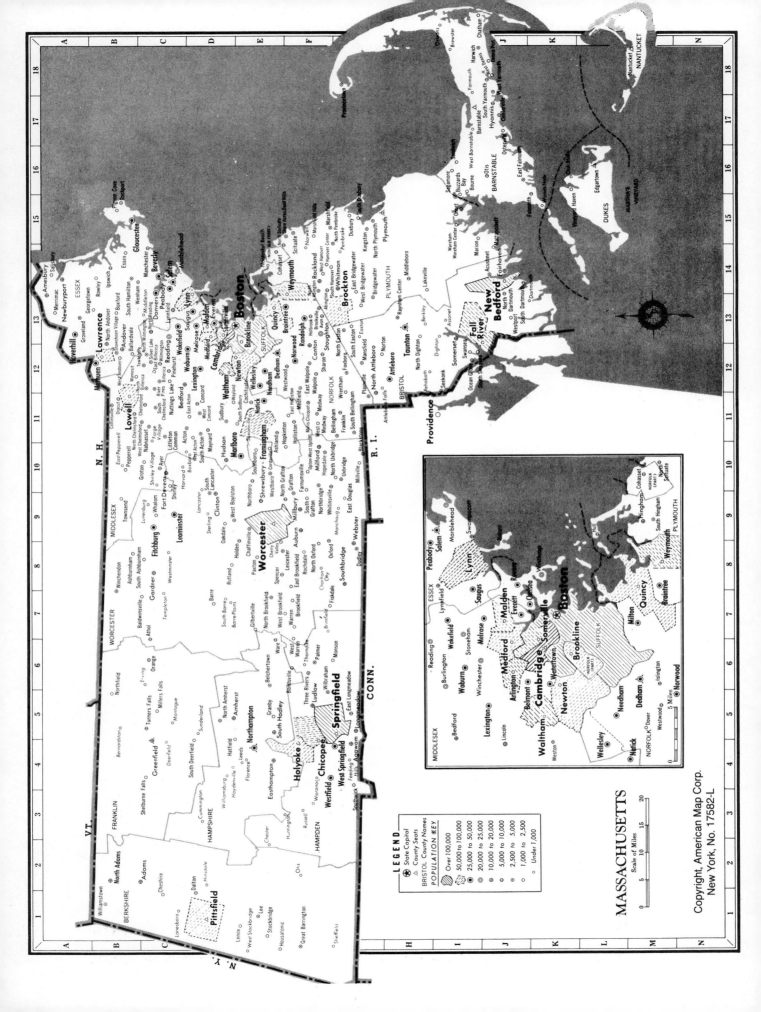

MASSACHUSETTS

Scale of Miles

0   5   10   15   20

LEGEND

⊛ State Capital
△ County Seats
BRISTOL County Names

POPULATION KEY

Over 100,000
50,000 to 100,000
25,000 to 50,000
20,000 to 25,000
10,000 to 20,000
5,000 to 10,000
2,500 to 5,000
1,000 to 2,500
Under 1,000

MASSACHUSETTS

AMERICAN INTERNATIONAL COLLEGE *(G-5)*
1000 State Street
Springfield, Massachusetts 01109
Tel: (413) 737-7000; (800) 242-3142; Fax: (413) 737-2803

Description: This private, independent college offers programs in teacher education, arts and sciences, and business administration and nursing (BSN). The semester system is used and two summer sessions are offered. The college is accredited by the New England Association of Schools and Colleges and grants the Bachelor, Master, and doctoral degrees. The institution is organized into a Day College, an Evening College, and a Summer Division. Enrollment is 675 men and 575 women full-time, and 150 men and 121 women part-time. A faculty of 83 full-time and 40 part-time gives a faculty-student ratio of 1-16.

Entrance Requirements: Accredited high school graduation or equivalent; completion of 16 units including 4 English, 2 mathematics, 2 science, 2 social sciences, 1 foreign language and 5 electives; SAT or ACT required; non-high school graduates considered; GRE required for some graduate programs; early admission, early decision, rolling admission, delayed admission, midyear admission and advanced placement plans available; $20 application fee.

Costs Per Year: $9,210 tuition; $4,880 room and board; $350 student fees.

Collegiate Environment: The campus is located on 58 acres and includes dormitory facilities for 750 men and women. It is in an urban environment; the campus is located 1-and-1/2 miles from downtown Springfield. The library contains 125,000 volumes, 625 periodicals, 4,000 microforms and 20,000 audiovisual materials. Approximately 79% of students applying for admission are accepted and 78% of the freshman class returns for the sophomore year. Midyear students are admitted as well as those from various geographical locations. Financial aid is available for economically handicapped students and 67% of the current student body receives some form of financial aid.

Community Environment: Springfield is a city of 165,000 that offers a multitude of activities for college students, including a quadrangle of museums, Stage West Theater Company, and the Springfield Civic Center.

AMHERST COLLEGE *(D-5)*
PO Box 2231
Amherst, Massachusetts 01002
Tel: (413) 542-2328

Description: The private, liberal arts college was founded in 1821 as an independent, nonsectarian institution for men, and is now coeducational. Amherst operates on the 4-0-4 system. It offers courses leading to the Bachelor of Arts degree and is accredited by the New England Association of Schools and Colleges. The college participates in a five-college cooperative program including interchange course registration with Mount Holyoke College, Smith College, Hampshire College, and the University of Massachusetts. Recent enrollment included 891 men and 717 women full-time. A faculty of 163 full-time and 2 part-time gives a faculty-student ratio of 1-10.

Entrance Requirements: Accredited high school graduation; minimum completion of college-preparatory courses including 4 English, 3 mathematics, 2 foreign language, 1 history, 1 science; SAT or ACT, and three Achievement Tests required; early decision, early admission, delayed admission programs available; non high school graduates considered; $50 application fee.

Costs Per Year: $19,760 tuition; $5,300 room and board; $292 student fees.

Collegiate Environment: The college is located on 964 acres and includes a library of 786,345 volumes, 4,530 periodicals, and 417,618

microforms. Dormitories provide housing for all students. Off campus housing is used by 1% of the students. Other physical resources include a wildlife sanctuary and a forest for the study of ecology, an observatory and planetarium, computer center, and varied equipment for scientific research. Approximately 21% of students applying for admission are accepted, virtually all as matriculating students. The college welcomes a geographically diverse student body, freshmen are admitted only at the beginning of the Fall term. The mean scores of the entering freshman class were SAT 628 verbal, 675 math. Almost all of the recent student body graduated in the top fifth of their high school class. Financial aid is available for economically disadvantaged students. 40% of students receive scholarship grants and 60% of the current student body receive some form of financial aid. There were 681 scholarships offered in a recent school year and 166 of them were available to freshmen. Approximately 28% of the senior class continue to graduate school directly after graduation.

Community Environment: Well-known American poets Emily Dickinson, Robert Frost and Eugene Field, and author Ray Stannard Baker (David Grayson) all lived in Amherst. Located on eastern edge of Connecticut Valley, the city has mean winter temperature of 25.2 degrees, and summer, 72 degrees. Annual rainfall is 43.8 inches. Rail and bus service is available. Recreation provided at Mt. Sugarloaf and Mt. Tom Reservation nearby. City has theatres, golf, tennis, fishing, and ice skating. Community opera performs annually.

ANDOVER NEWTON THEOLOGICAL SCHOOL *(D-12)*
210 Herrick Road
Newton Centre, Massachusetts 02159
Tel: (617) 964-1100; (800) 964-2687; Admissions: (617) 964-1100 X 272; Fax: (617) 965-9756

Description: The theological institution, known as Andover Newton Theological School, was founded in 1807 and is the oldest Protestant graduate school of theology in the United States. In 1931, the seminary became affiliated with the Newton Theological Institution which had been established by Baptists in 1825. Since 1967, it has been a member of the Boston Theological Institute which brings together the faculties, libraries, and resources of nine major seminaries in the Boston area of which five are Protestant, one is Greek Orthodox, and three are Roman Catholic. It operates on the semester system and is accredited by the Association of Theological Schools in the United States and Canada and the New England Association of Schools and Colleges. Enrollment includes 96 full-time and 416 part-time graduate students. A faculty of 22 full-time and over 70 part-time gives a faculty-student ratio of 1-7.

Entrance Requirements: B.A. degree or equivalent from an accredited institution; liberal arts background recommended, rolling admission plan; $15 application fee.

Costs Per Year: $7,000 ($286/cr) tuition; $3,945 board and room.

Collegiate Environment: The school's hilltop campus is 7 miles from Boston and Cambridge. Its 26 buildings include a library of 204,000 volumes, 560 periodicals, 1,111 microforms, and 10,000 pamphlets, and living accomodations for 69 men and 61 women, and 74 families. Students come from 34 states and 8 foreign countries, 40 denominations, and nearly 250 different colleges and universities. Student aid is awarded on the basis of need and merit.

Community Environment: See Boston University.

ANNA MARIA COLLEGE *(E-8)*
Sunset Lane
Paxton, Massachusetts 01612-1198
Tel: (508) 849-3360; (800) 344-4586; Fax: (508) 849-3362

Description: This liberal arts, coeducational college is accredited by the New England Association of Schools and Colleges. It was founded in 1946 by the Sisters of Saint Anne to provide a well-rounded education to students concerned with a solid foundation for their future careers. The college welcomes students of all faiths. AMC is a member of the Worcester Consortium of Colleges, allowing students to cross register for classes. The college grants the Associate, Bachelor, and Master degrees. It operates on a 4-1-4 system and offers two summer sessions. Enrollment includes 134 men and 255 women full-time, and 270 part-time students. A faculty of 138 gives a faculty-student ratio of 1-16. Air Force and Army ROTC are available.

Entrance Requirements: High school graduation; completion of 16 units including 4 English, 2 science, 2 social science, 2 foreign language, and 4 academic electives; SAT or ACT required; completed application, transcripts, and two recommendations; midyear admission, rolling admission, and advanced placement plans available; June 1 application deadline; $30 application fee.

Costs Per Year: $11,230 tuition; $5,028 room and board; $375 student fees.

Collegiate Environment: The 180-acre campus is situated eight miles from downtown Worcester and a one-hour drive from Boston and Providence. The thirteen college buildings include a library of 68,000 volumes which also houses the computer lab, and a residence hall for 290 students. Computers are also located in the residence hall, in the Moll Art Center, and in the Learning Center. The athletic program currently sponsors nine intercollegiate varsity teams. Approximately 75% of applicants are accepted. Classes begin in September and midyear students are accepted. Financial aid is available for students demonstrating need, and 85% of students receive some form of financial assistance.

Community Environment: The city is located in the geographical center of Massachusetts, eight miles northwest of Worcester. Summer and winter sports are available in the area. Excellent job opportunities for students are available in the immediate area.

AQUINAS COLLEGE AT MILTON   *(M-7)*
303 Adams Street
Milton, Massachusetts 02186
Tel: (617) 696-3100; Fax: (617) 696-8706

Description: A private, two-year college for women sponsored by the Congregation of the Sisters of Saint Joseph of Boston. The college is accredited by the New England Association of Schools and Colleges. It awards the Associate degree. The college operates on a modular schedule. Enrollment is 200 women full-time and 2 part-time. A faculty of 17 full-time and 4 part-time gives a faculty-student ratio of 1-12.

Entrance Requirements: High school graduation or GED; transcript and diploma; rolling admission plan available; $25 application fee.

Costs Per Year: $7,750 tuition; $200 student fees.

Collegiate Environment: The campus is located on 15 acres and includes a library of 11,000 volumes, 110 periodical titles, 7,700 microforms, and 409 audiovisual materials. Approximately 85% of students applying for admission meet the requirements and are accepted including midyear students. Financial aid is available and 75-78% of the current student body receives some form of financial aid.

Community Environment: See Curry College.

AQUINAS COLLEGE AT NEWTON   *(D-12)*
15 Walnut Park
Newton, Massachusetts 02158
Tel: (617) 969-4400

Description: Founded in 1961, the private junior college for women is conducted by the Congregation of the Sisters of Saint Joseph of Boston. The school offers several two year programs including: Business Administration-Accounting, Management, Early Childhood Education, General Business/Liberal Studies, Medical Assisting, and Office Administration. Each program combines a core of liberal studies with necessary job skills, and awards the Associate in Science Degree. The College also offers five one-year certificate programs that give students immediate employment skills. They are: biotechnology assistant, medical assisting technician, office administration, medical

secretary, executive secretary, legal secreaty, and office technology specialist. The college year consists of 12-week semesters in the fall and spring and a 6-week midwinter term. The school is fully accredited by the New England Association of Schools and Colleges. Recent enrollment was 250 women full-time, and 15 evening. A faculty of 20 full-time and 10 evening gives a faculty-student ratio of 1-9.

Entrance Requirements: High school graduation or equivalent; $15 application fee; early admission, rolling admission, and delayed admission plans available.

Costs Per Year: $6,800; $250 student fees.

Collegiate Environment: The 14-acre campus is located only ten miles from Boston. The buildings contain two modern electronic laboratories and a library of 14,950 volumes, 110 periodicals, and 4,000 audiovisual materials. Approximately 94% of students applying for admission are accepted. The college offers a lifetime career placement service to its graduates. Four scholarships are available, and 58% of students receive some form of financial aid.

Community Environment: See Boston University.

ASSUMPTION COLLEGE   *(E-9)*
500 Salisbury Street
Worcester, Massachusetts 01615-0005
Tel: (508) 767-7000; Admissions: (508) 767-7285; Fax: (508) 799-4412

Description: The private liberal arts college is conducted by the Assumptionist Fathers and was established in 1904. It is accredited by the New England Association of Schools and Colleges. It operates on the semester system and offers two summer terms. Recent enrollment included 672 men, 1,013 women full-time, 1 man and 3 women part-time. A faculty of 111 full-time and 51 part-time members with a faculty student ratio of 1-16. ROTC available as an elective. The college has a Junior year abroad program and an exchange program with other Worcester colleges. The college is a member of the Worcester Consortium for Higher Education.

Entrance Requirements: Accredited high school graduation with rank in upper 50% completion of 15 units including 4 English, 2 mathematics, 2 foreign language, 1 science, 1 social science; SAT or ACT required; delayed admission, midyear admission, early decision, rolling admission and advanced placement programs available; $25 application fee.

Costs Per Year: $12,000 tuition; $5,920 room and board; $125 student fees; additional expenses average $600.

Collegiate Environment: The college occupies a campus in the residential section of Worcester, approximately three miles from the center of the city. The library contains 188,837 volumes, 1,198 periodicals, 3,260 microforms. The media center handles the audiovisual needs of the college: it operates at TV studio and has listening facilities for language practice, taped lectures, and classical music, with over 3,000 recordings available. Dormitory facilities are available for 675 men and 825 women. Approximately 50% of the students applying for admission are accepted. Financial aid is available.

Community Environment: See Clark University

ATLANTIC UNION COLLEGE   *(D-9)*
P.O. Box 1000
South Lancaster, Massachusetts 01561-1000
Tel: (508) 368-2000

Description: The private, liberal arts, professional institution was founded in 1882 by the Seventh-Day Adventist denomination. It is accredited by the New England Association of Schools and Colleges, the Council on Social Work Education, the National League for Nursing and is approved for Veteran Training. Instructional departments of the college are grouped in nine divisions including applied arts, biology and chemistry, education, fine arts, language and literature, mathematics and physics, nursing, social sciences, and theology and religion. The college operates on the semester system and offers two summer sessions. Qualified students may study in France, Austria, or Spain. Special programs also include an Honors Core Program and Adult Degree Program. Recently the college enrolled 583 full-time and 169 part-time students. A faculty of 45 full-time and 31 part-time gives a faculty-student ratio of 1-11.

Entrance Requirements: High school graduation or equivalent; ACT required with a minimum score of 18; early admission, rolling admission and advanced placement plans available; $25 application fee.

Costs Per Year: $10,600 tuition; $3,600 room and board; $400 student fees.

Collegiate Environment: The college is located in central Massachusetts and contains 60 buildings including a library of over 100,000 volumes, 590 periodicals and 6,629 microforms. Dormitories house 145 men and 245 women. Regular attendance at chapel exercises and work appointments are required of all students. Freshmen are permitted to have cars on campus. The college welcomes a geographically diverse student body and will accept midyear students. Financial aid is available for economically disadvantaged students. Scholarships are available including music, athletic, merit, and need-based. 95% of students receive some form of financial aid. The college awarded 45 Associate and 93 Bachelor degrees to its graduating class.

Community Environment: This is a rural community located in the approximate center of the state. A historic town, old stone walls and New England architecture is found here. Moderate climate in spring and fall; winters are cold.

BABSON COLLEGE   *(E-12)*
Mustard Hall
Babson Park, Massachusetts 02157-0310
Tel: (617) 239-5522; (800) 488-3696; Fax: (617) 239-4006

Description: The private college is an independent, nonsectarian professional institution that offers programs of study in business management at both the undergraduate and the graduate levels. It was established in 1919 as a business school for men and became coeducational in 1968. The college is accredited by the New England Association of Schools and Colleges and also is accredited by the American Association of Collegiate Schools of Business. Enrollment is 1,047 men and 584 women at the undergraduate level, 355 graduate students in the day division, and 1,277 graduate students in the evening division. A faculty of 123 full-time and 52 part-time gives a faculty-student ratio of 1-12. The semester system is used and two summer sessions are offered. Exchange programs are available.

Entrance Requirements: Accredited high school graduation with rank in the upper half of graduating class; completion of college-preparatory courses including 4 units of English, 3 mathematics, 1 lab science, 2 social science; SAT and Math and English Achievement test required; GMAT required for graduate programs; early decision, early action, rolling admission (graduate only), and advanced placement plans available; $50 application fee; $75 international application fee.

Costs Per Year: $17,430 tuition; $7,275 room and board; $685 student fees.

Collegiate Environment: The college is situated on a 450-acre campus in Wellesley, 12 miles from Boston. The college buildings include 12 residence halls and 1,237 students. The Horn Library maintains an extensive business collection including annual reports and 10-K reports filed with the SEC by 11,000 companies. Its holdings include 110,342 volumes, 1,482 periodicals, 345,947 microforms and 1,738 audiovisual materials. Babson has a competitive NCAA Division III intercollegiate program featuring 20 varsity sports. Approximately 51% of students applying for admission are accepted including midyear students, and 88% of the freshmen return for the sophomore year. 84% graduated in the top two-fifths of high school class; 54% in the first fifth. Financial aid is available for financially needy students, and 49% of the current student body receives some form of financial assistance.

Community Environment: Breadth distinguishes Babson from other undergraduate management programs. The focus of the Babson education blends professional (40%) and liberal arts (40%) courses with campus and field experiences in a small college setting where both halves of the faculty work together to help students perform well and to grow in response to change. Babson is located 30 minutes by car from Boston.

BAY PATH COLLEGE   *(G-5)*
588 Longmeadow Street
Longmeadow, Massachusetts 01106
Tel: (413) 567-0621; (800) 782-7284; Fax: (413) 567-9324

Description: Bay Path College offers both associate and bachelor's degrees. Associate degree programs include Accounting, Arts and Sciences, Business Administration, Criminal Justice, Early Childhood Education, Entrepreneurship, Fashion Merchandising and Retail Management, Health Administration, Human Services, Interior Design, Legal Assistant (Paralegal), Marketing, and Occupational Therapy Assistant, and Travel and Hospitality Administration. Bachelor's degree programs include Business, Business/Accounting, Psychology, Psychology/Criminal Justice, Psychology/Early Childhood Education, and Legal Studies. The college's sequential degree format allows each student to earn a two-year degree, and to earn a bachelor's degree with an additional two years of study. Internships are available in most associate-level programs and in all baccalaureate-level programs. Bay Path is a member of the Cooperating Colleges of Greater Springfield, which consists of eight colleges with a combined student enrollment of more than 20,000 students. Cross registration is offered. The college is accredited by the New England Association of Schools and Colleges. It operates on the semester system. Enrollment is 550 women full-time and 101 part-time. A faculty of 28 full-time and 22 part-time gives a faculty-student ratio of 1-19.

Entrance Requirements: High school diploma or equivalent, completion of 12 high school units including 4 English, 2 mathematics, 2 social science, and 2 science; official copy of high school transcript, recommendation from guidance counselor, and interview are required; $SAT or ACT required; rolling admissions program enables the college to accept candidates soon after their credentials are received and reviewed by the admissions committee; early admission, early decision, midyear admission, deferred admission, and advanced placement programs are available. $25 application fee.

Costs Per Year: $16,425 resident student plan (tuition, room and board); $10,200 commuter student plan (tuition and lunches).

Collegiate Environment: Bay Path is located in Longmeadow, MA. Springfield, MA, is three miles to the north; Hartford, CT, is 23 miles south. Facilities include main classroom buildings, computer laboratories, a fashion and design studio, occupational therapy laboratory, and science laboratories. The Catok Art Center serves as an art and music studio and as an art gallery. The library has more than 38,000 volumes, periodicals, reference collections, and an academic support center. A Fitness and Wellness Center, tennis courts, student center, and snack bar are also available. Dormitory housing is available for 450 students. The college operates its own preschool on campus. 24-hour security is offered to students. 75% of those applying for admission are accepted. Scholarships and financial aid are available and 82% of the current student body receives some form of assistance.

Community Environment: Longmeadow is a small, residential, historic town located on the Connecticut/Massachusetts border. Its location near two major cities provides cultural and social advantages.

BAY STATE COLLEGE   *(D-13)*
122 Commonwealth Avenue
Boston, Massachusetts 02116
Tel: (617) 236-8000; Fax: (617) 536-1735

Description: The 2-year college is coed and was established in 1946 as a nondenominational institution. It is accredited by the New England Association of Schools and Colleges. The college offers career oriented programs and grants the Associated degree. The school operates on a semester system and offers one summer session. Enrollment is 700 full-time students with 200 in the evening division. A faculty of 24 full-time and 18 part-time gives a student-faculty ratio of 22-1.

Entrance Requirements: High school graduation or equivalent, recommendation and interview; rolling admission, and midyear admission plans available. $25 application fee.

Costs Per Year: $9,200 tuition; $9,600 Allied Health tuition; $6,400 room and board.

Collegiate Environment: The 2-year college utilizes six buildings in the famous Back Bay area of Boston. Dormitory facilities are provided for 250 women and 30 men. The library contains 20,000 volumes. The school offers a job placement service and part-time employment is available. Classes begin in September and January.

90% of those applying for admission are accepted and 87% of students currently receive financial aid.

Community Environment: See Boston University.

BECKER COLLEGE - LEICESTER CAMPUS *(E-8)*
3 Paxton St.
Leicester, Massachusetts 01524
Tel: (508) 791-9241; Admissions: (508) 791-9241 x445; Fax: (508) 892-0330

Description: The private college was founded in 1784 as Leicester Academy and is one of the oldest educational institutions in the nation. It offers 26 associate degree programs, and three bachelor degree programs which were initiated in September 1993. The college is accredited by the New England Association of Schools and Colleges, The American Physical Therapy Association, The American Veterinary Medical Association, The National League for Nursing, and The American Occupational Therapy Association. The college operates on the semester system and is a participating member of the Worcester Consortium for Higher Education, an association of 10 area colleges. There is an exchange program with a private junior college in Japan. Enrollment includes 450 full-time and 15 part-time students. A faculty of 23 full-time and 12 part-time gives a student-faculty ratio of 1-15.

Entrance Requirements: Accredited high school graduation or equivalent; completion of 16 units including 4 English; early admission, early decision, delayed admission, advanced placement, rolling admission; $25 application fee.

Costs Per Year: $8,290 tuition; $4,340 room and board; $150 student activity fee.

Collegiate Environment: The 75-acre campus is located within six miles of the metropolitan and cultural center of Worcester. The college library contains 30,000 volumes, 199 periodicals, 750 microforms and 1,350 audiovisual materials. Dormitory facilities are available for 500 students. The college welcomes a geographically diverse student body and will accept midyear students. Financial aid is available for economically handicapped students and 75% of current students receive some form of financial aid.

Community Environment: Located about six miles west of Worcester, the city is easily accessible by train, bus, plane, or automobile. New England climate. Many recreational facilities available including theatres, hunting in season, boating, fishing, and golf. Art Museum, Memorial Auditorium, Historical Association, Antiquarian Society, Horticultural Society, Higgins Museum, and churches of all denominations provide cultural and community service in the area.

BECKER COLLEGE - WORCESTER CAMPUS *(E-9)*
61 Sever Street
Worcester, Massachusetts 01609
Tel: (508) 791-9241

Description: The private, coeducational 2+2 junior college is accredited by the New England Association of Schools and Colleges. It is professionally accredited by the American Physical Therapy Association, the American Occupational Therapy Association and the National League for Nursing. It offers both specialized curricula in business, secretarial science, allied health, and retailing, which are aimed at developing skills, and a general educational foundation in liberal arts for a business administration degree at a four-year college. It was established in 1887 and operates on the semester system. Enrollment includes 528 full-time and 75 part-time and 500 evening students. A faculty of 30 full-time and 20 part-time gives a ratio of 1-15.

Entrance Requirements: Accredited high school graduation or equivalent; completion of 16 units; advanced placement, early admission, early decision, rolling admission, delayed admission, midyear admission and advanced placement plans available; $25 application fee.

Costs Per Year: $8,290 tuition; $4,340 room and board; $155 student fees.

Collegiate Environment: The college is comprised of 34 buildings located on ten acres in the residential section of the city. The library contains 36,000 volumes and dormitory facilities are provided for 50 men and 500 women. Students not living at home are required to reside in dormitories or homes approved by the Dean of Students. Ap-

proximately 90% of students applying for admission are accepted including midyear students. 75% of the previous freshman class returned to the college for their second year. Financial aid is available 76% of the current student body receives some form of aid.

Community Environment: See Clark University.

BENTLEY COLLEGE *(D-12)*
175 Forest Street
Waltham, Massachusetts 02154-4705
Tel: (617) 891-2244; (800) 523-2354; Fax: (617) 891-3414

Description: Founded in 1917, the college is the eighth largest independent college in Massachusetts. It is accredited by the New England Association of Schools and Colleges and professionally by the American Assembly of Collegiate Schools of Business. The college operates on the semester system and offers two summer terms. It offers both day and evening classes. Enrollment includes 3,168 full-time and 1,305 part-time undergraduates and 2,126 graduate students. A faculty of 195 full-time and 155 part-time provides an undergraduate faculty-student ratio of 1-16. The college grants Bachelor degrees in Accountancy, Business Communication, Business Economics, Computer Information Systems, Economics-Finance, Finance, Management, Marketing, Mathematical Sciences, Liberal Arts, English, History, Philosophy, and International Culture and Economy. The college also has five-year BA/MBA and BA/MSA programs for highly motivated students with high academic standing. Graduate school awards Master's degrees in the following concentrations: Accountancy, Business Communications, Business Economics, International Business Management, Finance, Management Information Systems, Marketing, Operations Management, and Taxation. Overseas programs are sponsored in Australia, France, Belgium, Japan, United Kingdom, and Mexico. Army ROTC is available through Boston University. Air Force ROTC is available through the University of Lowell.

Entrance Requirements: High school graduation; completion of 16 units including 4 English, 4 mathematics, 1 lab science, 2 social studies, 2 foreign language, and 3 additional courses; SAT or ACT or 3 Achievements required. Minimum TOEFL of 550 for foreign students. GMAT required for graduate programs; early admission, early decision, early action, deferred admission and advanced placement available; $35 application fee.

Costs Per Year: $13,800 tuition; $5,510 room & board; $65 fees.

Collegiate Environment: The college is located on 110 acres approximately nine miles west of Boston. It is comprised of more than 30 buildings which include a library of 192,566 volumes, 2,606 periodicals, 215,000 microfiche items, and 4,400 audiovisual titles. Living accommodations for 2,700 students are available. The college welcomes students from 42 states and 66 countries and will accept students at midyear. Financial aid is available for students. Need and non-need based scholarships are available including over 100 endowed scholarships. 66% of freshmen, and 70% of all undergraduates receive financial aid.

Community Environment: Bentley College, located in suburban Waltham, Massachusetts, offers students a peaceful and relaxing setting on a picturesque 110-acre campus. Nine miles away is Boston. Bentley offers a shuttle service into Cambridge at Harvard Square, and from here, the entire city of Bston is accessible through public transportation. Fraternities, sororities, sports organizations, and over 70 clubs sponsor social activities for all students. Bentley offers students transportation not only to Boston, but also to the center of Waltham, which also connects to public transportation. From here, numerous stores, restaurants, and offices are within reach, many offering employment opportunities for Bentley students.

BERKLEE COLLEGE OF MUSIC *(D-13)*
1140 Boylston Street
Boston, Massachusetts 02215
Tel: (617) 266-1400; (800) 421-0084, x222; Fax: (617) 536-2632

Description: The independent, coeducational school of music was established in 1945 and was authorized to confer the degree of Bachelor of Music in composition, music education, and applied music in 1963. In addition, the college offers majors in: Commercial Arranging; Jazz Composition; Music Education; Professional Music; Film Scoring; Music Synthesis; Music Production and Engineering; Performance; Songwriting; Music Business/Management; and a 5-year dual major. The music education program was approved for purposes of teacher certification by the Massachusetts Board of Higher Education in 1967. The school operates on the early semester system with one summer semester and a five-week performance program. Summer programs are held in Claremont, CA, and Umbria, Italy. The school is accredited by the New England Association of Schools and Colleges. Enrollment includes 2,212 men and 474 women. A faculty of 138 full-time and 142 part-time gives a faculty-student ratio of 1-8.

Entrance Requirements: Accredited high school graduation or equivalent; completion of 15 units recommended; SAT or ACT required for degree programs; minimum two years of musical study recommended; non-high school graduates considered; rolling admission, delayed admission, midyear admission, and advanced placement plans available; $50 application fee.

Costs Per Year: $11,550 tuition; $6,990 room and board; $50 student fees.

Collegiate Environment: The school is located in the heart of Boston adjacent to the Prudential Center which provides numerous facilities for the performing arts, including the Berklee Performance Center, a modern acoustically-designed major concert hall in Boston for contemporary music. The school library contains 38,000 volumes and 51 periodicals, and dormitory facilities are available for 760 students. Midyear students are accepted as well as those from various geographical locations including 75 countries. Scholarships are available and are merit-based upon submission of a Berklee is located in the heart of Boston's historic Back Bay neighborhood, near many of the nation's other leading colleges and universities, the Museum of Fine Arts, Symphony Hall, and other cultural and performing arts centers. On campus, the 1,200-seat Berklee Performance Center provides an acoustically designed venue for year-round contemporary music performances. The library contains 38,000 bound volumes, 6,000 recordings, 14,000 scores, and 51 periodical subscriptions. On-campus housing is available in three residence halls for 824 students. 78% of applicants are accepted. Students come from across the United States and from 75 foreign countries. Midyear students are accepted. Scholarships are merit-based, and are awarded through review of cassette tape submission. 61% of all students receive some form of financial aid.

Community Environment: See Boston University.

BERKSHIRE COMMUNITY COLLEGE   *(D-1)*
West Street
Pittsfield, Massachusetts 01201
Tel: (413) 499-4660

Description: The public community college, founded in 1960, was the first community college to be operated by the Commonwealth of Massachusetts. It is accredited by the New England Association of Schools and Colleges. The college offers two-year programs leading to the Associate degree. It operates on the semester system with one summer session. Enrollment includes 930 full-time and 1,514 part-time students. A faculty of 71 full-time, 35 part-time, and 61 evening gives a faculty-student ratio of 1-20.

Entrance Requirements: Accredited high school graduation; open enrollment policy; rolling admission, midyear admission, and advanced placement plans available; $10 application fee.

Costs Per Year: $1,150 state resident tuition; $5,640 nonresident tuition; $1,260 student fees.

Collegiate Environment: The college services include counseling and placement, and facilities include a library of 42,571 volumes, 1,000 pamphlets, 308 periodicals, 7,756 microforms, and 3,357 audiovisual materials. Approximately 100% of applicants are accepted, including midyear students. Semesters begin in September and January. Financial aid is available for economically disadvantaged students.

Community Environment: Set amid the rolling Berkshire hills, this attractive industrial area encompasses largest transformer plant in the world, as well as long-established textile and paper industries. The city has three libraries, numerous churches, two hospitals, a museum, YMCA, and good shopping facilities. Regular transportation is available by rail bus and air. Theatres, bowling, three golf courses, two-large lakes, many parks, and closeness to area festivals and summer attractions make this city a favorite recreation spot. Part-time employment is available.

BOSTON COLLEGE   *(D-13)*
Commonwealth Avenue
Chestnut Hill, Massachusetts 02167
Tel: (617) 552-3100; Fax: (617) 552-0798

Description: The private institution is one of 28 Jesuit colleges and universities in the United States and has the largest full-time enrollment of any Jesuit university in the nation. Enrollment is 9,079 full-time undergraduate students, 4,303 full-time graduate students, and 1,316 continuing education students, of all religious faiths. A faculty of 604 full-time and 381 part-time gives a faculty-student ratio of 1-15. The University is accredited by the New England Association of Schools and Colleges. The University is comprised of 11 divisions that include the College of Arts and Sciences, School of Management, School of Nursing, School of Education, Graduate School of Arts and Sciences, Graduate School of Education, Graduate School of Nursing, Law School, School of Social Work, Graduate School of Management and the Evening College of Arts, Sciences, and Business Administration. The University operates on the semester system and offers two summer sessions. Study abroad opportunities include Junior Year Abroad, exchange programs, and summer programs. In Ireland, students can pursue Irish studies at University College, Cork, through Junior Year Abroad or a summer theater program. Honors programs at Oxford University and Manchester College in England are available through Junior Year Abroad. Exchange programs exist with universities in France, Holland, Japan, and China. Additional special programs include an Immersion Program in French or Spanish, Scholar of the College Program, Perspectives Program, Program for the Study of Faith, Peace and Justice, an Honors Program, and the PULSE program, which offers more than 200 Boston College freshmen and sophomores the opportunity to combine supervised social service or social advocacy field work with a study of Philosophy, Theology and other disciplines.

Entrance Requirements: Completion of 18 units including 4 English, 4 mathematics, 4 foreign language, 3 lab science, 2 social studies, and academic electives; SAT or ACT and three Achievement Tests required; early decision, early admission, early action, deferred admission, midyear admission, and advanced placement plans available; $50 application fee.

Costs Per Year: $17,890 tuition; $7,270 room and board; $466 student fees.

Collegiate Environment: The main campus at Chestnut Hill is six miles from the center of Boston in an area known as University Heights. The Heights is a three-level campus of more than 200 acres punctuated by more than 80 buildings including some examples of the finest in English collegiate Gothic architecture. With the completion of two suite-style residence halls in the fall of 1993, housing will be available to all incoming students. The Newton Campus is a forty-acre tract located approximately one and a half miles from the Chestnut Hill Campus. The university doors are open to all students without regard to race, religion, age, sex, or national origin. 41% of students applying for admission are accepted. The middle 50% ranges of scores of entering freshmen are SAT 520-610 verbal, 600-690 math. $34.6 milllion in scholarships were awarded to undergraduates in 1994. Approximately 66% of undergraduate applicants receive some form of financial aid. College facilities include a library of more than 1,368,339 volumes, and living accommodations for 6,434 students.

Community Environment: Boston College considers, and the students concur, that the suburban location of the campus six miles from Boston is the ideal setting for a University. The campus boasts superior academic, residential, and recreational facilities, and the dynamic Greater Boston area offers unlimited cultural, educational, and personal opportunities for individual development within a cosmoplitan atmosphere.

BOSTON CONSERVATORY   *(D-13)*
8 The Fenway
Boston, Massachusetts 02215
Tel: (617) 536-6340; Fax: (617) 536-3176

Description: The college of music, musical theater and dance was founded in 1867 and is one of the first conservatories in the country to offer professional training in the three performing arts. The conservatory is accredited by the New England Association of Schools and Colleges and is professionally accredited by the National Association of Schools of Music. It operates on the semester system and offers one summer term. Enrollment includes 377 full-time, and 56 graduate students. A faculty of 40 full-time and 120 part-time gives a faculty-student ratio of 1-5.

Entrance Requirements: Accredited high school graduation or equivalent; SAT or ACT recommended; auditions required; Bachelor of Music degree or equivalent for graduate music program; Bachelor of Fine Arts or equivalent for graduate dance program; deferred admission, rolling admission, early admission, midyear admission, and advanced placement plans available; $60 application fee.

Costs Per Year: $12,300 tuition; $6,100 room and board; $635 student fees.

Collegiate Environment: The conservatory is comprised of six buildings, including a library of 44,000 volumes and 10,000 recordings, and residence facilities for 120 students. Approximately 65% of students applying for admission are accepted. Classes begin in September. Midyear admission possible for transfer and graduate students. Scholarships are available, and approximately 85% of the current student body receives some form of financial aid.

Community Environment: Located in an urban environment in central Boston near Symphony Hall and the Museum of Fine Arts. Public transportation, metropolitan shopping, artistic areas and fine dining are within walking distance.

BOSTON UNIVERSITY   *(D-13)*
121 Bay State Road
Boston, Massachusetts 02215
Tel: (617) 353-2300; Admissions: (617) 353-2300; Fax: (617) 353-9695

Description: This independent university dates back to 1839 when it was established as a theological seminary. By 1874, programs in law, music, oratory, liberal arts, medicine, and a graduate school of all sciences were offered. Today, students in the nonsectarian university have available to them the rich resources of 16 schools and colleges. The university is accredited by the New England Association of Schools and Colleges. The university grants the Baccalaureate, Master's, and Doctoral degrees. Air Force, Army and Navy ROTC programs are available. The university operates on the semester system and offers two summer terms. Undergraduate enrollment includes 6,509 men and 7,764 women full-time and 322 men and 323 women part-time. There are 7,472 part-time graduate students. The faculty includes 1,822 full-time and 866 part-time members. The undergraduate student-faculty ratio is 9-1.

Entrance Requirements: Accredited high school graduation; completion of 21 high school units; SAT or ACT required; CEEB achievement tests required for some programs; high school equivalency accepted; early decision, early admission, delayed admission, midyear admission and advanced placement plans available; GRE required for some graduate programs. $50 application fee.

Costs Per Year: $19,420 tuition; $7,100 room and board; $280 student fees; $475 books & supplies; $1,800 commuter board; $275-$1,975 transportation; $750 other expenses.

Collegiate Environment: The university has located its educational plant along the historic Charles River. Academic and administrative facilities, residence halls, and science laboratories are centered heare. The libraries contain over 1,950,000 volumes, 3,329,000 microform items, 71,000 audio or video tapes and discs, 28,795 periodical subscriptions, 350 CD-ROMS, and access to Internet and computer networks. Dormitory facilities are provided for 8,649 men and women. All freshmen under 21 years of age are required to live in university residence halls unless residing with parents or legal guardians. Sorority and fraternity houses with accomodations for 260 students are considered university-approved housing, but are not owned or managed by the university. The university has its own 20,000-watt radio station and a commercial television station (WABU). The Schools of Medicine and Graduate Dentistry are located in the south end of Boston adjacent to the University Hospital also located on the campus of the Medical Center. An African Study Center with primary emphasis on the social sciences, and the Human Relations Center focusing on problems of change in group and community relationships are also maintained by the university. One of the nation's largest study abroad programs is sponsored by the university. Study abroad semesters, internships and exchanges are available in many areas, including Australia, Eastern Europe, England, France, Greece, Israel, Italy, Niger, Spain, and the Soviet Union. About 63% of the students applying for

undergraduate admission meet the requirements and are accepted, including midyear students and those from various geographical locations. The middle 50% ranges of scores for the entering freshman class were SAT 500-600 verbal, 550-650 math, 1050-1250 combined, ACT 24-29 composite. 45% of applicants to graduate programs are admitted. 84% of the freshman class returns for the sophomore year. Scholarships, student loans, and work opportunities are provided, and 67% of the current freshmen receive some form of financial aid.

Community Environment: Historic capital of Massachusetts, Boston is a contrast of past and present with broad avenues disappearing into crooked, narrow streets of colonial Boston. Modern stores and buildings stand next to Revolutionary shrines. The city is the largest market of the wool, shoe and leather industries, and one of the most important fishing ports in United States. Complete intercity transportation of buses, subways, and trolleys, as well as railroad, bus lines, and air transportation to and from the area are available. Many recreational facilities are available. Part-time employment for students is also available.

BRADFORD COLLEGE   *(A-13)*
320 South Main Street
Bradford, Massachusetts 01835
Tel: (508) 372-7161; (800) 336-6448; Fax: (508) 372-5240

Description: The private 4-year college of liberal arts was founded by members of the Congregational Church in 1803 and became a junior college for women in 1932. It was the first such institution to meet the standards set by the New England Association of Schools and Colleges, and continues to be accredited by that organization. In the spring of 1971 the college opened its enrollment to both men and women and in 1972 introduced its first B.A. program. Today Bradford offers Bachelor of Art degree programs in Humanities, Creative Arts, Human Studies (the social sciences), Management and Natural Science and Mathematics. The college operates on the semester system. Enrollment is 560 full-time students. A faculty of 36 full-time and 12 part-time gives a faculty-student ratio of 1-12.

Entrance Requirements: Accredited high school graduation or equivalent; recommended completion of 16 units, including 4 English, 3 mathematics, 2 laboratory science, 3 foreign language, 2 social studies, and 2 electives; early admission, early decision, midyear admission, rolling admission, and delayed admission programs available; no application fee.

Costs Per Year: $14,080 tuition; $6,270 room and board; $300 student fees.

Collegiate Environment: The college is situated on 75 acres approximately 35 miles north of Boston. It consists of 12 major buildings, including a library of 60,000 volumes and dormitory facilities for 400 students. Approximately 78% of students applying for admission are accepted. Financial aid is available for students who demonstrate need. 70% of the students receive financial aid. There are 350 scholarships, of which 120 are for freshmen.

Community Environment: Residential neighborhood in town of Bradford located on south bank of Merrimack River and now part of the City of Haverhill, an industrial community just across the river. City has public library, churches of major denominations, and one hospital. All winter and summer sports are easily accessible. Nearby Boston provides many recreational and cultural advantages as well as good shopping facilities.

BRANDEIS UNIVERSITY   *(K-5)*
415 South Street
Waltham, Massachusetts 02254-9110
Tel: (617) 736-3500; (800) 622-0622; Fax: (617) 736-3536

Description: This private nonsectarian university was established in 1948 by members of the American Jewish community and was fully accredited by the New England Association of Schools and Colleges in 1953. Brandeis combines two important traditions in higher education: the dedication to teaching that is characteristic of a small, selective college and the facilities and renowned faculty usually associated with a large research university. It is composed of the College of Arts and Sciences, the Graduate School of Arts and Sciences, the Florence Heller Graduate School for Advanced Studies in Social Welfare and the Graduate School for International Economics and Finance. The University operates on the semester system and offers two summer sessions. Enrollment is 2,877 undergraduates and 1,000 gruaduate students. The student body represents all fifty states and 65 foreign countries. A faculty of 490 gives a faculty-student ratio of 1-8.

Entrance Requirements: Applicants should have followed a strong academic preparatory course in high school with completion of 4 years of English, at least 3 college-preparatory mathematics, 3 foreign language (including senior study when possible), and minimum 1 each of history and lab science; teacher recommendations, personal statement, and standardized test scores contribute to evaluation; SAT I and three SAT II: Subject tests, one of which should be writing, or ACT required; $50 application fee; the two-part application procedure has deadlines of January 1 and February 1.

Costs Per Year: $19,380 tuition; $6,750 room and board; $450 student fees.

Collegiate Environment: More than 90% of undergraduates live on campus in university residence halls that are situated within a few minutes' walk of classes. With more than 130 clubs and fewer than 3,000 undergraduates, students have ample opportunity to get involved in organizations and assume positions of leadership if they choose. Student-initiated and student-run clubs are chartered with relative ease to accomodate new interests and causes. Intramural sports are available and are coeducational. Brandeis does not recognize exclusive or secret societies such as social fraternities or sororities. 68% of applicants are accepted and offered admission. The middle 50% range of enrolled freshmen scores is 540-640 verbal, 590-700 math. Financial aid is based on need, as determined by information provided on the Financial Aid Form of the College Scholarship Service. Over 50 four-year merit-based scholarships are available to domestic applicants. Merit scholarships are also available to international applicants. Aid packages generally include scholarship, loan, and work-study components. 65% of the freshman class received some form of aid.

Community Environment: Waltham is a city of 58,000, ten miles west of Boston on the Charles River. It is a traditional manufacturing community that now hosts extensive high-tech industries. Good job and community service opportunities for students are available. The city is served by commuter railroad and excellent bus lines for easy access to Boston and Cambridge. The locale has two colleges, four hospitals, a wide range of religious institutions, public library, Federal Archives and Records Center, parks, and a variety of ethnic restaurants.

BRIDGEWATER STATE COLLEGE   *(G-13)*
Gates House
Bridgewater, Massachusetts 02325
Tel: (508) 697-1200; (800) 698-2006; Admissions: (508) 697-1237; Fax: (508) 697-1746

Description: The state college was established in 1840 and is accredited by the New England Association of Schools and Colleges. It operates on the semester system with two summer terms. Its professional accreditations include chemistry, speech-language-hearing, social work, and nursing. The college grants the Bachelor and Master's degrees. The enrollment of 3,278 men and 4,888 women includes 5,270 full-time and 1,592 part-time undergraduates and 1,304 graduate students. A faculty of 260 full-time and 298 part-time members provides a student-faculty ratio of 15:1. Army ROTC is offered in a cooperative program with Stonehill College. Air Force ROTC is offered on campus.

Entrance Requirements: Accredited high school graduation with rank in upper 50%; completion of 16 units recommended including 4 English, 3 mathematics, 2 foreign language, 2 lab science, 2 social science and 3 college preparatory electives. SAT required; rolling admission for transfer students, CLEP and advanced placement plans available; $10 application fee in state, $40 nonresident.

Costs Per Year: $1,408 tuition; $5,542 tuition for non-Massachusetts residents; $4,102 room and board; $4,120 student fees.

Collegiate Environment: The campus is located on 170 acres approximately 30 miles south of Boston. It is comprised of 28 buildings which contain a library of 207,383 volumes and 42,682 periodicals and dormitory facilities for 680 men and 1,208 women. Approximately 73% of students applying for admission are accepted including midyear students. The average scores of the entering freshman class were SAT 434 verbal, 480 math. The average high school standing of the freshman class, top 53%; 19% in the top quarter. 1,012 scholar-

ships are available and 47% of the undergraduates receive some form of financial aid.

Community Environment: This largely residential colonial town has among its manufactures, shoes, leatherboard, nails, and bricks. Extensive excavations by archeologists have revealed the remains of two Indian civilizations in the area. Town is mostly residential located about 30 miles southeast of Boston with all its cultural advantages.

BRISTOL COMMUNITY COLLEGE   *(J-13)*
777 Elsbree Street
Fall River, Massachusetts 02720
Tel: (508) 678-2811

Description: The state-supported junior college was established in 1965 and offers university-parallel and career programs in business, education, engineering, human services, liberal arts, and medical fields. It operates on the semester system with two summer terms. The college is accredited by the New England Association of Schools and Colleges. Enrollment includes 3,300 day students and 2,000 evening students.

Entrance Requirements: Accredited high school graduation or equivalent required for degree programs; SAT or ACT required; applicants not meeting all requirements may be admitted as provisional or special students; rolling admissions, midyear admission, early admission and early decision plans available; $10 application fee.

Costs Per Year: $2,460 tuition; $6,900 tuition for non-Massachusetts residents.

Collegiate Environment: The college is located on 110 acres in northeastern Fall River and includes a library of 47,557 volumes, 4,983 pamphlets, 325 periodicals, 9,750 microforms and 3,175 recordings. Financial aid is available and 60% of the current student body receive some form of financial assistance. Approximately 98% of the students applying for admission are accepted including midyear and 70% of the freshman class return for the sophomore year. Average high school standing of a recent freshman class, top 50%; 20% in the top quarter. The average scores of the entering freshman class were SAT 400 verbal, 400 math.

Community Environment: Located approximately 50 miles south of Boston, Massachusetts and 18 miles southeast of Providence, Rhode Island on the New England Coast, the City is easily assessible by train, bus and air. Fall River's major industries include textiles, needlecrafts, and rubber and chemicals. The City, the factory outlet capital of New England, is experiencing a revitalization in its business and residential districts. Many opportunities exist for part-time and full-time work for students.

BUNKER HILL COMMUNITY COLLEGE   *(E-13)*
250 New Rutherford Avenue
Charlestown, Massachusetts 02129-2991
Tel: (617) 228-2000; Admissions: (617) 228-2235; Fax: (617) 228-2082

Description: Founded in 1973, this liberal arts career college became the 15th of the state's community colleges. It is accredited by the New England Association of Schools and Colleges. The college grants the Associate degree and offers short-term Certificate programs. It operates on the semester system and offers two summer sessions. Enrollment is 2,414 full-time and 3,706 part-time students. A faculty of 120 full-time and 220 part-time gives a faculty-student ratio of 1-20.

Entrance Requirements: High school graduation or GED; open enrollment policy except for Allied Health programs; acceptance is on first come, first served basis; rolling admission, advanced placement plans available; $10 application fee.

Costs Per Year: $2,250 ($75 per credit) state resident tuition; $6,690 ($223 per credit) nonresident/foreign tuition.

Collegiate Environment: This commuter college provides many special programs for college students and community residents. Facilities include a library with more than 44,000 holdings. Other buildings making up the college complex are a lecture hall, art gallery, bookstore, cafeteria, auditorium, lounges, classrooms, conferences rooms and various student centers. 70% of those applying for admission are accepted. Financial aid is available. 40% of students receive some form of financial assistance.

Community Environment: The college is located on a 21-acre site in the Charlestown District of Boston. The campus is very near the Bunker Hill Monument and the U.S.S. Constitution. The school is within immediate access to Boston's bus-streetcar-subway system.

Branch Campuses: Chelsea, MA.

CAPE COD COMMUNITY COLLEGE   *(J-17)*
Route 132
West Barnstable, Massachusetts 02668
Tel: (508) 362-2131; Fax: (508) 362-3988

Description: The public college was established in 1961 and is accredited by the New England Association of Schools and Colleges. It is a member of the College Consortium for International Studies. The college offers two-year transfer, general, and occupational programs and grants the Associate degree. A Cooperative Education Program is availabe in many subjects and many study abroad choices are available. The semester system is used and three summer sessions are offered. Enrollment is 2,461 students full-time and part-time. There were an additional 3,004 students enrolled in the college's evening division. A faculty of 88 full-time, 120 part-time and 250 evening gives a faculty-student ratio of 1-13.

Entrance Requirements: High school graduation or equivalent; open enrollment policy; rolling admission, advanced placement and midyear admission plans available; $10 application fee for residents, $35 for nonresidents.

Costs Per Year: $960 state resident tuition; $4,512 nonresident tuition; $1,032 student fees.

Collegiate Environment: The campus is located on 120 acres and includes a library of 54,000 volumes, 425 different periodicals. 23,723 microforms and 1,560 audiovisual materials. Financial aid is available for students demonstrating need. 60% of these students currently receive financial aid.

Community Environment: A rural village in the town of Barnstable on Cape Cod with several museums dedicated to early Americana in the area. The community has excellent facilities for all sports, yacht races and tournaments, and many historic celebrations. Part-time employment is available with exceptional opportunities in the summer. Transportation provided by air and bus. Shopping facilities are excellent.

CLARK UNIVERSITY   *(E-9)*
950 Main Street
Worcester, Massachusetts 01610
Tel: (800) 462-5275; Admissions: (508) 793-7431; Fax: (508) 793-8821

Description: An independent liberal arts university, Clark offers undergraduate programs in the arts and sciences, graduate and postgraduate study for traditional age students as well as for adult learners. Clark was established in 1887 as a graduate school and undergraduate education was added in 1902; the undergraduate college is now the university's largest division. The university is accredited by the New England Assoiation of Schools and Colleges and operates on the semester system with two summer school programs. There is an evening division. The opportunity to study in Great Britain, Germany, France, Spain, Italy, Luxembourg and Japan is available on Clark sponsored programs. In addition, Clark students travel abroad in a variety of affiliated programs. Clark also participates in the Washington Semester program. Academic cooperative programs with the Worcester Consortium for Higher Education gives students access to nine other member institutions in the area. Enrollment includes 2,000 undergraduate and 500 graduate students. A faculty of 180 provides an undergraduate faculty-student ratio of 1:12. ROTC programs are available at Holy Cross and Worcester, Polytechnic Institute.

Entrance Requirements: Accredited high school graduation; completion of 16 units recommended/preferred; 4 English, 3 mathematics, 2 foreign language, 2 social studies, 3 science; SAT and 1 English with Composition CEEB required; two other Achievement Tests are recommended; GRE required for graduate studies; GMAT is required for MBA program; early decision, early admission, delayed admission, advanced placement plans available; non high school graduates considered; $40 application fee.

Costs Per Year: $17,600 tuition; $4,550 board and room; $400 student fees.

Collegiate Environment: The campus consists of 45 acres and is located 1 1/2 miles from the business center of Worcester and 38 miles west of Boston. The 40 college buildings include a library of 500,000 volumes, 2076 periodicals, 58,000 microforms and 800 audiovisual materials. Living accommodations for 1,520 students are provided. All single students who are not living with families are required to live in university-operated residence facilities for at least their first two years of study. Approximately 71% of students applying for admission are accepted including midyear and approximately 90% return for the sophomore year. The middle 50% range of SAT scores for entering freshmen was 460-570V, 520-640M. Approximately 60% of the current student body receives some form of financial aid.

Community Environment: An industrial center and state center for biotechnology and related research, Worcester is the second largest city in all of New England. Good transportation facilities make area easily accessible. Located 38 miles west of Boston, city has several religious groups of all denominations, as well as significant libraries, museums, parks, theatre, and music facilities and municipal recreation opportunities and recently completed centrum (seating 13,000) houses concerts, sport events, and exhibits. Many students take advantage of the city's offerings through paid and unpaid internships with area corporations and institutions.

COLLEGE OF THE HOLY CROSS   *(E-9)*
1 College Street
Worcester, Massachusetts 01610
Tel: (508) 793-2443; Fax: (508) 793-3888

Description: The coeducational liberal arts college was founded in 1843 and is directed by the Jesuits. It operates on the semester system. Air Force and Army ROTC programs are available through Worcester Consortium for Higher Education. An extensive study abroad program is offered. The college holds institutional membership in numerous professional and educational organizations and is accredited by the New England Association of Schools and Colleges. Enrollment is 1,307 men and 1,413 women. A faculty of 213 full-time, 52 part-time gives a faculty-student ratio of 1-13.

Entrance Requirements: High school graduation or equivalent; candidate should submit evidence of superior achievements within a college preparatory program. No specific units required; curriculum should emphasize study in English, mathematics, foreign language (ancient or modern), the sciences, history and social science; SAT, or ACT, and three SAT II subject tests, one of which should be writing; early decision, early admission, deferred admission and advanced placement programs available; $50 application fee.

Costs Per Year: $18,000 tuition; $6,300 room and board; $355 student fees.

Collegiate Environment: The college is comprised of 27 buildings located on 174 acres and includes a library of 501,347 volumes, 2,180 periodicals and 463 microforms and dormitory facilities for 2,128 students. Approximately 46% of students applying for admission are accepted. Financial aid is available for all accepted students with financial need. 51% of the students receive some form of financial aid.

Community Environment: See Clark University

CURRY COLLEGE   *(M-7)*
1071 Blue Hill Ave.
Milton, Massachusetts 02186
Tel: (617) 333-2210

Description: This private, four-year, nondenominational institution is a deliberately small liberal arts and professionally oriented college. Largely residential, it was founded in 1879. The college is accredited by the New England Association of Schools and Colleges. It operates on the semester system with one summer session. Curry offers eight main undergraduate programs: Nursing, Business Management, Communications, Education, Visual Arts, Sociology, Sciences, and Liberal Arts. Enrollment includes 971 full-time and 160 part-time students. A faculty of over 81 full-time and 92 part-time gives an overall faculty-student ratio of 1-12. The Perry School for teacher training has now become part of the college. Degrees awarded are the M.Ed., B.A., and B.S. Army ROTC is available with Suffolk University.

Entrance Requirements: Accredited high school graduation; completion of 16 units including 4 English, 3 Mathematics, 2 Science, 2 Foreign Language, 2 Social Sciences, and 3 Electives; SAT or ACT required; early admission, early decision, rolling admission, deferred admission and advanced placement plans available; $40 application fee.

Costs Per Year: $13,600 tuition; $5,450 room; $600 student fees.

Collegiate Environment: The campus of 120 acres is located in Milton, an affluent suburb, seven miles south of Boston. The 30 college buildings include a library of 110,000 volumes, 650 periodicals and 10,000 microforms. Dormitories provide housing accommodations for 650 students. About 67% of students applying for admission are accepted. The college welcomes students from various geographical locations and will accept midyear students. Financial aid is available. 50% of students receive financial aid.

Community Environment: Suburban location about seven miles south of Boston near the Neponset River in the town of Milton. All forms of transportation easily accessible. Shuttle bus to Boston, rapid transit. Blue Hills Reservation, a summer and winter sports center with golf course, ice rink, ski slopes, is located nearby. Job opportunities, community services, and cultural advantages will be found in neighboring Boston, as well as on campus.

DEAN COLLEGE   *(G-11)*
99 Main Street
Franklin, Massachusetts 02038-1994
Tel: (508) 528-9100; Fax: (508) 528-7846

Description: Founded by members of the Universalist Church in 1865 and known as the Dean Academy, the private institution has operated exclusively as a junior college since 1957. It is accredited by the New England Association of Schools and Colleges. It offers programs in humanities, mathematics and science, social science, physical education and athletics, visual and performing arts, and business. The college operates on the semester system and offers two summer terms. Enrollment includes 915 full-time and 1,300 part-time students. A faculty of 49 full-time, and 77 part-time and evening gives an overall faculty-student ratio of 1-18.

Entrance Requirements: Accredited high school graduation; completion of 16 units; advanced placement, rolling admission, and midyear admission plans available; $20 application fee.

Costs Per Year: $10,455 tuition; $6,000 room and board; $605 student fees.

Collegiate Environment: The campus is located on 100 acres and borders the business district of Franklin. The 35 college buildings include a library of 52,500 volumes, 330 periodicals and 23,000 microforms, and living accommodations for 875 students. All students must live on campus unless commuting from home or receiving special permisssion; resident students are permitted to have cars on campus. The college is nondenominational and welcomes students from various geographical locations. Approximately 85% of students applying for admission are accepted including midyear students, and 70% return for the sophomore year. Over 50% of the current student body receives some form of financial aid. Approximately 80% of Dean graduates transfer to four-year colleges.

Community Environment: Franklin is located 30 miles southwest of Boston. This is a rapidly growing area easily accessible by bus and rail. It is the birthplace of Horace Mann. The community has swimming pools, tennis courts, ski facilities, riding, golf, movies, bowling, and dancing. There are many shopping centers nearby. Some part-time employment is available for students.

EASTERN NAZARENE COLLEGE   *(E-13)*
23 E. Elm Avenue
Quincy, Massachusetts 02170
Tel: (617) 745-3500; (800) 883-6288; Fax: (617) 745-3470

Description: The private, four-year liberal arts college is affiliated with the Church of the Nazarene. It operates on the 4-1-4 system and offers two summer sessions. The college is accredited by the New England Association of Schools and Colleges. Enrollment is 661 full-time undergraduates and 67 graduate students. A faculty of 66 full-time and 15 part-time gives a faculty-student ratio of 1-13.

Entrance Requirements: Accredited high school graduation or equivalent; completion of 4 units of English, 1 mathematics, 1 science, 1 foreign language, and 1 social studies; SAT or ACT required; applicants not meeting all requirements may be admitted as special students; early admission, early decision, delayed admission, rolling admission, and advanced placement plans available; $20 application fee.

Costs Per Year: $9,490 tuition; $3,600 room and board; $670 student fees.

Collegiate Environment: The college is located only minutes away from Boston and is comprised of 13 buildings on 15 acres. The new library contains 122,604 volumes, 1,478 periodicals and 5,396 microforms. The college provides dormitory facilities for 268 men, 320 women and 104 married students. Students are expected to conform to the college code and voluntarily agree to abstain from the use of alcohol and tobacco. Chapel attendance is required of all resident students. Financial aid is available, including government grants, government loans, and a variety of scholarships in the categories of Academic Achievement, Activities, Family, Multicultural, Nazarene Church, and General Scholarships. 80% of the students receive some form of financial aid.

Community Environment: See Quincy College.

ELMS COLLEGE   *(F-5)*
291 Springfield Street
Chicopee, Massachusetts 01020
Tel: (413) 594-2761; (800) 255-3567; Admissions: (413) 592-3189; Fax: (413) 592-4871

Description: The private liberal arts college for women was founded by the Sisters of Saint Joseph and established in 1928. It is accredited by the New England Association of Schools and Colleges. Professional accreditations include the American Bar Association, the American Chemical Society, The National League for Nursing, and the Council on Social Work Education. The college grants the Associate, Bachelors, and Masters degrees. An overseas program is available in Ireland, France, and Spain. Air Force and Army ROTC are available. The college operates on the semester system and offers two summer sessions. Enrollment includes 600 full-time and 444 part-time undergraduates and 158 graduate studnets. A faculty of 53 full-time and 52 part-time gives an undergraduate faculty-student ratio of 1-16.

Entrance Requirements: Accredited high school graduation with rank in upper half of graduating class; completion of 17 units including 4 English, 3 mathematics, 2 foreign language, 2 science, 2 social science, SAT or ACT required; early admission, midyear admission, advanced placement and rolling admissions plans available; $25 application fee.

Costs Per Year: $11,400 tuition; $4,765 room and board; $400 student fees.

Collegiate Environment: The college is comprised of 11 buildings on 32 acres which include dormitory facilities for 363 women. Approximately 80% of students applying for admission are accepted and midyear students are admitted. The college welcomes a geographically diverse student body. Financial aid is available for economically disadvantaged students and 90% of the students receive some form of financial aid. The college library contains 98,700 volumes, 700 periodicals, 65,994 audiovisual materials The average SAT scores of the current freshmen were 450 verbal and 450 math.

Community Environment: Rural area two and one half miles from Springfield. Climate is temperate. City served by two railroads, Interstate 91, and Massachusetts Turnpike. Community has public library, several churches, and city infirmary. Some part-time employment is available. Recreation provided by local theatre and sports center. Major civic, fraternal and veterans' organizations and shopping area in town.

EMERSON COLLEGE   *(D-13)*
Beacon Street
Boston, Massachusetts 02116
Tel: (617) 578-8600

Description: Established in 1880, this private coeducational college specializes in communication and performing arts. It is accredited by the New England Association of Colleges and Schools. The semester system is used with two summer programs. Offers Bachelor Degrees, Master of Arts, Master of Fine Arts and Master of Science in Speech. Bachelor of Music degree is offered in conjunction with the Longy School of Music in Cambridge. The college has a continuing education division with day and evening programs. The college also has a campus in Holland used as a base for travel and study in many parts of Europe. Recent enrollment included 794 men, 1,130 women full-time, 65 men, 98 women part-time, 761 graduate students, and 263 evening students. A faculty of 97 full-time and 141 part-time members provides a student-faculty ratio of 11-1.

Entrance Requirements: Accredited high school graduation or equivalent; completion of 16 units including 4 English, 2 mathematics, 2 science, 2 social science; SAT or ACT required; GRE required for graduate programs; early admission, rolling admission plans available; $25 application fee.

Costs Per Year: $13,504 tuition; $7,288 room and board; $303 student fees.

Collegiate Environment: The campus is comprised of 19 buildings located on four acres and includes a library of 85,000 volumes and dormitory facilities for 775 men and women. All freshmen enrolling directly from high school under 21 years of age and not living with immediate relatives must live in college residences. The broadcasting department operates a noncommercial FM station and a TV facility for the production of live television programs. Approximately 74% of students applying for admission is accepted including midyear students and students from various geographical locations.

Community Environment: See Boston University

EMMANUEL COLLEGE *(D-13)*
400 The Fenway
Boston, Massachusetts 02115
Tel: (617) 735-9715

Description: This private liberal arts college for women was founded by the Sisters of Notre Dame of Namur in 1919 and is the first Catholic college for women in the Northeast. It is one of the only women's colleges in the East with a coed campus, and its residence halls are open year-round. It operates on the semester system and offers two summer sessions. Enrollment is 1,300 students. The faculty consists of 51 full-time and 51 part-time members. The college is accredited by the New England Association of Schools and Colleges. Cooperative programs are offered with Simmons College; a 3-2 Dual Degree Program is available with Worcester Polytechnic Institute, Columbia University and Northeastern University. An Internship Program for academic credit is available. There is a semester in Washington for political science majors and a California Semester program, as well as opportunities for students to study abroad. Emmanuel College was recently ranked as a selective liberal arts college by the Carnegie Foundation, and is the only women's college in Boston with an increase in 1990, 1991, and 1992 enrollment.

Entrance Requirements: Accredited high school graduation with rank in upper half of graduating class; completion of 16 units including 4 English, 3 mathematics (including Algebra II), 3 foreign language, 2 lab science, and 2 social science; SAT or ACT and interview required; TOEFL minimum score of 500 for international students required; early decision, advanced placement, early admission, rolling admission, and delayed admission plans available; $30 application fee.

Costs Per Year: $10,966 tuition; $5,528 room and board.

Collegiate Environment: The campus is comprised of nine buildings located on 16 acres in the heart of Boston. Emmanuel offers an all-women's academic program with a coed campus environment. In addition, the residence halls are open 12 months of the year so that students can participate in internships and other programs during academic breaks. The library contains 124,000 volumes, 600 periodicals, 1,370 microforms, and 3,300 audiovisual materials. Living accomodations are available for 400 women. 70% of the freshman class returns for the sophomore year. 22% of the freshman class ranked in the top fifth of the high school class. Approximately 78% of those who apply for admission are accepted. Financial aid is available and 74% of students receive some form of financial aid.

Community Environment: See Boston University.

ENDICOTT COLLEGE *(C-14)*
376 Hale Street
Beverly, Massachusetts 01915
Tel: (508) 927-0585; (800) 325-1114; Fax: (508) 927-0084

Description: The private, nonsectarian four- and two-year coeducational college offers programs in liberal and professional arts. It is accredited by the New England Association of Schools and Colleges. It is professionally accredited by respective institutions. The school operates on the 4-1-4 system. Enrollment is 800 full-time students. A faculty of 46 full-time and 38 part-time gives a faculty-student ratio of 1-11.

Entrance Requirements: Accredited high school graduation; completion of 16 units including 4 English, 1 mathematics, 1 science, 1 history; SAT or ACT recommended; early decision, delayed admission, advanced placement available; rolling admission; $25 application fee.

Costs Per Year: $11,455 tuition and fees; $6,130 room and board.

Collegiate Environment: The campus is located in the oceanfront estate section of Beverly, 20 miles from Boston on the North Shore of Massachusetts Bay opposite Marblehead. The 30 college buildings include a library of 52,000 volumes and living accommodations for 650 men and women. Classes begin in September. 86% of applicants are accepted. 75% of the previous freshman class returned to the campus for their second year of studies. There are many scholarships available and 86% of the current student body receives some form of financial aid.

Community Environment: See Montserrat College of Art.

EPISCOPAL DIVINITY SCHOOL *(D-13)*
99 Brattle Street
Cambridge, Massachusetts 02138
Tel: (617) 868-3450

Description: Episcopal Divinity School was incorporated in 1974 as the result of a merger between the Philadelphia Divinity School, founded in 1857, and the Episcopal Theological School, founded in 1867. A cooperative relationship with Harvard was given official structure in 1914 when the theological school became affiliated with the university. Students in each institution may take up to one-half their courses in the other without payment of fees, and students in each have free use of the libraries and museums of the other. Reciprocal arrangements of a similar kind exist with the Boston Theological Institute, an ecumenical assoc

Entrance Requirements: Admission is open to individuals with an A.B. degree from an accredited institution, or its equivalent, who wish to do theological study and reflection that is traditional, contemporary and innovative.

Costs Per Year: $8,000 tuition; $3,295 board and room; $1,070 per year health and student fees.

Collegiate Environment: The school is located about five minutes walk from Harvard University and Harvard Square. The center of Boston is reached within eight minutes by subway from Harvard Square. The school provides living accommodations for both single students and families, and contains a library of 250,000 volumes which is jointly operated with the Weston School of Theology. The close relationship with Harvard University allows students the use of Harvard athletic facilities and gives them opportunity to hear speakers, lecturers, and preachers making appearances at the university.

Community Environment: See Harvard University

FISHER COLLEGE *(D-13)*
118 Beacon Street
Boston, Massachusetts 02116
Tel: (617) 236-8800; (800) 446-1226; Fax: (617) 236-8858

Description: This private 2 year college for women offers a liberal arts program and career program leading to an Associate Degree. The college was founded in 1903 and was known as the Winter Hill Business College. It was approved as a junior college by the Board of Collegiate Authority of the Commonwealth of Massachusetts in 1952 and is accredited by the New England Association of Colleges and Schools. The college operates on the semester system. Enrollment includes 400 women. A faculty of 17 gives a faculty student ratio of 1-20.

Entrance Requirements: Accredited high school graduation; interview strongly recommended; completion of 16 units including 4 English, 1 mathematics, 1 science, and 1 social science; rolling admission, early decision, early admission, advanced placement plans available. $25 application fee.

Costs Per Year: $10,500 tuition; $6,300 board and room; $800 student fees; additional expenses average $600.

Collegiate Environment: The campus is located in the Back Bay region of Boston. The 10 college buildings include a library of 28,000 volumes and dormitory facilities for 246 women. Approximately 84% of students applying for admission are accepted including midyear students, and 60% return for the sophomore year. Financial aid is available on the basis of need and 70% of the current student body receive some form of financial aid. Half of 40 scholarships available are for freshman.

Community Environment: See Boston University

FITCHBURG STATE COLLEGE   *(C-9)*
160 Pearl Street
Fitchburg, Massachusetts 01420
Tel: (508) 345-2151; Fax: (508) 665-3534

Description: The state college was established as a Normal School in 1894 and became a state teachers college in 1933 and a state college in 1962. It operates on the semester system with two summer terms. Enrollment is 6,122 with a faculty of 400 giving a student-faculty ratio of 15:1. The college is accredited by the New England Association of Schools and Colleges. Professional accreditations include the National League for Nursing and the Council for Standards in Human Service Education.

Entrance Requirements: Accredited high school graduation; 16 units completed including 4 English, 3 mathematics, 2 laboratory science, 2 foreign language, 2 social studies, and 3 electives; SAT required; high school transcript and/or college transcript, $10 application fee for in-state residents, $40 application fee for out-of-state applicants.

Costs Per Year: $1,408 tuition; $5,542 out-of-state tuition; $3,830 room and board; $1,826 student fees.

Collegiate Environment: The college is comprised of 22 buildings located on ninety-two acres and includes a library of 207,455 volumes, 1,424 periodicals, 356,302 microforms and 3,528 audiovisual materials. Dormitory facilities house 550 men and 900 women. 70% of students applying for admission are accepted. Classes begin in September and midyear students are accepted. Approximately 60% of the recent student body graduated in the top half of their high school class, 25% in the top quarter, and 6% in the highest tenth. Scholarships are available, including 39 for freshmen, and 55% of students received some form of financial aid.

Community Environment: College is in an urban setting 55 miles from Boston.

FRAMINGHAM STATE COLLEGE   *(E-11)*
Framingham, Massachusetts 01701
Tel: (508) 620-1220; Admissions: (508) 626-4500; Fax: (508) 626-4592

Description: The four-year public college was established in 1839. Since its founding, Framingham State College has grown to become a multi-purpose career oriented institution of higher education with a strong liberal arts background. It is accredited by the New England Association of Schools and Colleges. The College offers Bachelor of Science and Bachelor of Arts degrees in 28 undergraduate programs and 19 Masters degree programs. The College operates on the semester system and offers two summer sessions. Enrollment includes 5,151 undergraduates and graduate students. A faculty of 220 gives a faculty-student ratio of 1-15 in the day division.

Entrance Requirements: Accredited high school graduation including completion of 16 specified academic units including 4 English, 3 mathematics, 2 foreign language, 2 laboratory science, 2 social science, and 3 electives; SAT required; early admission, rolling admission, delayed admission, midyear admission and advanced placement program available; $10 application fee, $25 for out-of-state residents.

Costs Per Year: $3,314 tuition and fees; $7,448 out-of-state tuition and fees; $3,594 room and board.

Collegiate Environment: The suburban campus of 73 acres is located 20 miles west of Boston. The 18 college buildings include a library of 171,000 volumes and residence hall facilities for 1,500 students. Approximately 68% of the students applying for admission are accepted including midyear students and those from various geographical locations. The average scores of the entering freshman class were SAT 430 verbal, 470 math. Financial aid is available for students with demonstrated financial need and 57% of the current student body receives some form of financial aid.

Community Environment: Area is located 20 miles west of Boston and has transportation facilities. Part-time job opportunities are available for students. This diversified community offers many opportunities in the areas of high technology, retailing, and manufacturing, as well as being a major residential center.

FRANKLIN INSTITUTE OF BOSTON   *(D-13)*
41 Berkeley Street
Boston, Massachusetts 02116
Tel: (617) 423-4630; Fax: (617) 482-3706

Description: This technical college offers one-year programs leading to a certificate and two-year programs leading to the Associate in Engineering degree. The school operates on the semester system and is accredited by the New England Association Schools and Colleges. Recently the institute enrolled 300 students. A faculty of 35 full-time and 5 part-time gives a faculty-student ratio of 1-10.

Entrance Requirements: Accredited high school graduation or equivalent; completion of 16 units including 4 English, 2-3 mathematics, and 1 science; rolling admission plan available; $30 application fee.

Costs Per Year: $8,340 tuition; $6,500 room and board; $75-200 student fees.

Collegiate Environment: The institute is comprised of two buildings located on one acre and includes a library of 8,000 volumes. Approximately 80% of students applying for admission are accepted. Classes begin in September and 65% of the previous entering class returned to the institute for the second year of studies. Dormitory facilities for men and women are available at Boston University. Scholarships are available and 85% of students receive some form of financial aid.

Community Environment: See Boston University.

GORDON COLLEGE   *(C-14)*
255 Grapevine Road
Wenham, Massachusetts 01984
Tel: (508) 927-2300; (800) 343-1379; Admissions: (508) 927-2300 x4217; Fax: (508) 524-3704

Description: The private college traces its history to 1889 when a small group of Christian men organized the Boston Bible and Missionary Training School. Today the college is a four-year nondenominational, Christian liberal arts college. It is accredited by the New England Association of Schools and Colleges and operates on the semester system. A limited teacher education summer program, at the Masters degree level is available. The college enrolls 438 men and 740 women. A faculty of 103 gives a faculty-student ratio of 1-14.

Entrance Requirements: Accredited high school graduation; completion of 15 units including 4 English, 2 mathematics, 2 science, 2 social science; 4 foreign language; SAT or ACT required; early admission, early decision, rolling admission, delayed admission, midyear admission and advanced placement plans available; $40 application fee.

Costs Per Year: $13,380 tuition; $4,400 room and board; $570 student fees.

Collegiate Environment: The campus of 700 acres is located on historic Cape Ann, 26 miles northeast of Boston. The 22 college buildings include a library of 309,508 titles and microforms and 6,515 recordings. Dormitory facilities accommodate 389 men and 650 women. Christian behavior and chapel attendance are required of all students. Approximately 75% of students applying for admission are accepted. The average scores of the entering freshman class were SAT 492 verbal, 524 math. Scholarships are available and 72% of the current student body receives some form of financial aid. Classes begin in August and January. 77% of a previous freshman class returned to the campus for their sophomore year. The college awarded 261 Bachelor degrees in 1993-1994.

Community Environment: Suburban area of Boston. Numerous opportunities for part-time employment plus all of the recreational, cultural, shopping, education, and medical facilities located in Boston.

GORDON-CONWELL THEOLOGICAL SEMINARY   *(B-14)*
130 Essex Street
South Hamilton, Massachusetts 01982
Tel: (508) 468-7111

Description: Private coeducational graduate school was established in 1969 by the merger of Gordon Divinity School and Conwell School of Theology. The seminary welcomes students of all denominations. The semester system is used and three summer sessions are offered. Enrollment is 556 full-time students. A faculty of 30 full-time and 64 part-time gives a faculty-student ratio of 1-13. GTS is a member of a consortium of nine seminaries in metropolitan Boston, and is accredited by the Association of Theological Schools of the United States and Canada.

Entrance Requirements: Bachelor degree; $25 application fee; rolling admission plan.

Costs Per Year: $7,092 tuition; $3,030 room and board.

Collegiate Environment: The campus occupies 118 acres with numerous buildings including a new library complex, dormitory space for 109 men and 25 women, housing for 211 married students, two large lecture theatres, and a full-size gymnasium. The library contains 180,000 volumes, 1,039 periodicals, 6,600 microforms, and 2,918 audiovisual materials. Financial aid is available.

Community Environment: See Gordon College.

GREENFIELD COMMUNITY COLLEGE   *(C-4)*
One College Drive
Greenfield, Massachusetts 01301
Tel: (413) 774-3131

Description: The public community college first opened its doors in 1962 to 125 day students. The college operates on the semester system with two summer sessions and is accredited by the New England Association of Schools and Colleges. It is professionally accredited by the National League for Nursing. Enrollment recently was 1,108 full-time, 643 part-time and 666 evening students. A faculty of 65 full-time, 47 part-time and 25 evening gives a ratio of 1-18.

Entrance Requirements: Open enrollment; non high school graduates considered; early admission, advanced placement and rolling admission plans available; $10 application fee, $35 for non-residents.

Costs Per Year: $950 tuition; $3,990 non-resident tuition; $600 student fees.

Collegiate Environment: The college is located on 92 acres in Greenfield Meadows. The building is terraced on a hillside and has five levels in the core area which houses executive offices, the College Library with 53,789 volumes, Computer Center, Media Center, TV Studio, College Store and Cafeteria. The north and south academic wings contain six faculty-student modules which serve as gathering and focal points for College activities. The present construction was built to accomodate 1500-2000 students. Plans for future construction include physical education facilities and an auditorium. Approximately 95% of students applying for admission are accepted including midyear students. Financial aid is available and 50% of students receive some form of financial aid. 6,220 scholarships are available.

Community Environment: The world's largest producer of taps and dies, Greenfield is a center for winter sports, and hunting and fishing in season. This is a combined rural and suburban area with bus service and limited rail service available. Climate is temperate. Recreational facilities include excellent ski area, 13 movie theatres, and all water sports on Connecticut River. Limited part-time employment for students. County fair held annually in September; Winter Carnival in February; Spring Farmers' Market.

HAMPSHIRE COLLEGE   *(D-5)*
West Street
Amherst, Massachusetts 01002
Tel: (413) 549-4600; Admissions: (413) 582-5471; Fax: (413) 582-5631

Description: The independent, coeducational, liberal arts college was founded and established by the administrators and trustees of Amherst, Mount Holyoke, Smith College and the University of Massachusetts. The first class of 250 students was enrolled in the fall of 1970. The college is accredited by the New England Association of Schools and Colleges. Curriculum is arranged on the basis of 4 schools of inquiry: humanities and arts, communication and cognitive science, natural science, and social science, rather than traditional departmental structure. The examination system consists of student-designed independent projects that are supervised by a faculty member. Hampshire is part of a five-college consortium that gives students access to the courses and resources of Amherst, Mount Holyoke, Smith and the University of Massachusetts. By making campus life a continuation of the classroom, the college hopes to enlist the aid of the students in shaping the college's program. There are foreign studies programs available. The college operates on the 4-1-4 system. Enrollment is 1,100 students. A faculty of 100 gives a faculty-student ratio of 1-11.

Entrance Requirements: Completion of college preparatory program recommended; early admission, early decision, midyear admission, transfer, and visiting plans available; Feb. 1 application deadline; $40 application fee.

Costs Per Year: $20,655 tuition; $5,475 room and board; $690 student fees.

Collegiate Environment: Located on an 800-acre campus, the college has been built with the library at the core and the classrooms, residences and dining areas surrounding it. Living facilities are organized into small communities called Houses, each with 250-300 students. Each house is independent and self-governing. The library contains 110,000 volumes, 800 periodicals, 400 microforms, 29,000 audiovisual materials. Approximately 65% of students applying for admission are accepted. Financial assistance is available for economically disadvantaged students. 59% of the students receive some form of financial aid.

Community Environment: See Amherst College.

HARVARD UNIVERSITY   *(D-13)*
Office of Admissions and Financial Aid
Byerly Hall, 8 Garden St.
Cambridge, Massachusetts 02138
Tel: (617) 495-1551

Description: Harvard University, which celebrated its 350th anniversary in 1986, is the oldest institution of higher learning in the United States. Founded in 1636, the private, nonsectarian university has grown from 12 students with a single Master to an enrollment of some 18,000 degree candidates. The university is coeducational in all its programs. Undergraduate women are admitted to Radcliffe College and, through their enrollment in Radcliffe, are also enrolled in Harvard College; all of the ten graduate and professional schools offer equal access to men and women. The university operates on a semester system. The Harvard Summer School provides approximately 250 courses attended by about 5,000 students of all ages each summer. ROTC courses are offered at the Massachusetts Institute of Technology and are open to Harvard and Radcliffe students by cross-registration. Enrollment in the fall of 1993 was 18,626. The Faculty of Arts and Sciences, which is responsible for both undergraduate and graduate instruction, numbers 668 men and women; the university as a whole has approximately 2,278 faculty members. Harvard University is accredited by the New England Association of Schools and Colleges and by respective professional and educational associations.

Entrance Requirements: SAT I or ACT and SAT II subject tests required; admission is competitive and selective; a strong high school record is typical of the successful applicant; recommended secondary school courses, taken at the Honors or Advanced Placement level where possible, include: 4 years English, 4 mathematics, 3 years laboratory science, 3 years history, 3 or more of at least 1 foreign language; early action, deferred admission and advanced placement programs are available; $60 application fee; applications for Harvard and Radcliffe are considered entirely without reference to the applicant's ability to pay for the cost of a Harvard education.

Costs Per Year: Costs for Harvard and Radcliffe: $17,851 tuition; $6,410 room and board.

Collegiate Environment: At the heart of the Harvard undergraduate's experience is the House Plan, which, in effect, places students in 13 small colleges, of which all but one are residential. Each House is a self-contained coeducational community of approximately 350 to 500 students and faculty members, administered by a resident Master and a Senior Tutor. Harvard's academic resources are world renowned. Its faculty has produced 33 Nobel Laureates and 30 Pulitzer Prize winners. Its library, the oldest in the United States and the largest university library in the world, houses more than 12 million volumes. The university maintains four museums of natural history and three art museums. 250 official student organizations offer extracurricular activities that appeal to a variety of student interests. 4,000 undergraduates participate in intramural athletics, and many others play on varsity teams. More than two-thirds of the students receive some form of financial aid, including scholarships, grants, loans, and work-study funds.

Community Environment: Settled in 1630, Cambridge has been the home of such famous writers as Henry Wadsworth Longfellow, James Russell Lowell, and Oliver Wendell Holmes. It is also the birthplace in Massachusetts of high technology industry. With a population of about 93,000 concentrated in 6.25 square miles, Cambridge today is the sixth largest city in the state. A vital university town, Cambridge is also a city of long-established neighborhoods with strong ethnic roots and traditions. Just across the Charles River and connected by an efficient transit system, Boston offers historical landmarks, professional sports, cosmopolitan shopping, world-famous hospitals and outstanding cultural opportunities.

HEBREW COLLEGE *(E-13)*
43 Hawes Street
Brookline, Massachusetts 02146
Tel: (617) 232-8710; Fax: (617) 734-9769

Description: The private college was established in 1921 and offers courses in Judaic studies. The college operates on the semester system with one summer term and is accredited by the New England Association of Schools and Colleges. There are 98 students and 20 faculty members, giving a faculty-student ratio of 1-5.

Entrance Requirements: Accredited high school graduation; non-high school graduates considered; early decision, midyear admission and rolling admission plans available.

Costs Per Year: $6,360 ($265/credit) tuition; $90 fees.

Collegiate Environment: The college is comprised of two buildings and contains a library of 100,000 volumes. 90% of those applying for admission are accepted, including midyear students. Financial aid is available for economically handicapped students. Cross-registration with 5 nearby universities is available.

Community Environment: Although Brookline is sizeable in itself, it is suburban to Boston. John F. Kennedy, 35th president of the United States, was born here. Metropolitan area has public libraries, Antique Auto Museum, hospitals, and excellent shopping facilities. Transportation provided with two rapid transit lines and bus service. Municipal golf course, indoor municipal swimming pool, extensive parks and outdoor and indoor recreation programs are available.

HELLENIC COLLEGE *(E-13)*
50 Goddard Avenue
Brookline, Massachusetts 02146
Tel: (617) 731-3500 X 260; Fax: (617) 738-9169

Description: The private, coeducational college is the outgrowth of the Greek Orthodox Theological School established in Connecticut in 1937. It is accredited by the New England Association of Schools and Colleges. The college is composed of an undergraduate School of Arts and Sciences and a graduate School of Theology. It operates on the semester system and offers summer sessions. Enrollment is 190 students and the faculty-student ratio is 1-6.

Entrance Requirements: High school graduation; completion of 11 units including 2 English; ACT or SAT accepted applicants to School

of Theology must have Bachelor of Arts degree or equivalent; GRE required; $35 application fee.

Costs Per Year: $7,060 tuition; $5,200 room and board; student fees and additional expenses vary.

Collegiate Environment: The 52 acre campus is located in Brookline, Massachusetts, a suburb of Boston, located ten minutes from downtown. A full range of facilities are available to all students, such as the Cotsidas-Tonnas library, the Skouras Classroom Building, the Pappas Gymnasium, the Maliotis Cultural Center, and on-campus bookstore. Extra-curricular activities also play a large role in campus life. Approximately 75% of students applying for admission are accepted. The college welcomes a geographically diverse student body. Academic and need-based scholarships are available for students.

Community Environment: See Hebrew College

HOLYOKE COMMUNITY COLLEGE *(F-4)*
303 Homestead Avenue
Holyoke, Massachusetts 01040
Tel: (413) 538-7000

Description: The public junior college was established in 1946 and is accredited by the New England Association of Schools and Colleges. It offers courses in vocational-technical and academic areas for part time, terminal, and transfer students. The college operates on the semester system and offers one summer term. Enrollment includes 3,300 full-time and 2,700 part-time students. A faculty of 245 gives a faculty-student ratio of 1-21.

Entrance Requirements: Open enrollment policy; completion of 16 units including 4 English, 3 mathematics, 2 foreign language, 1 science, 1 social science recommended for transfer students; early decision, early admission, rolling admission, midyear admission, and advanced placement plans available; $10 resident application fee, $35 nonresident application fee.

Costs Per Year: $2,890 state resident tuition; $6,800 nonresident tuition; $145 student fees; $250 average additional expenses.

Collegiate Environment: Located in suburban Holyoke, the college operates in a $40 million facility opened in 1974. The library contains 64,320 volumes, 360 periodicals and 3,240 recordings. Semesters begin in September and January and midyear students are accepted. Financial aid is available for economically disadvantaged students.

Community Environment: Holyoke is located 87 miles west of Boston on the shores of the Connecticut River and was the first planned industrial center in the country. Industries include the production of fine writing paper and various mills. The game of volleyball, first known as minonette, was invented here in 1895. The city has historical points of interest, museums, three movie theatres, public beaches and marinas, a community concert series featuring nationally known artists, and Mt. Tom Ski area. Westover Air Force Base is five miles from town. Part-time employment is available.

LABOURE COLLEGE *(E-13)*
2120 Dorchester Avenue
Boston, Massachusetts 02124
Tel: (617) 296-8300

Description: A private, coeducational two-year college founded in 1971 and operated under the auspices of the Daughters of Charity in St. Vincent de Paul. It is fully accredited by the New England Association of Schools and Colleges. Grants the Associate in Science degree in nursing and allied health fields. The college enrolls 700 students. A faculty of 63 members gives a faculty-student ratio of 1-11.

Entrance Requirements: High school graduation or equivalent; $25 application fee; early decision plan available.

Costs Per Year: $7,560 tuition; $2,200 room; $105 miscellaneous.

Collegiate Environment: Located in the Dorchester section of Boston, the college has a library of 9,750 volumes. There are dormitory facilities for 35 women. Fifty percent of those applying are admitted. Financial assistance is available.

Community Environment: See Boston University

LASELL COLLEGE (D-12)
1844 Commonwealth Avenue
Newton, Massachusetts 02166
Tel: (617) 243-2225; Fax: (617) 243-2326

Description: Founded in 1851, this private, residential, two- and four-year college for women offers degrees in both liberal arts and career specific programs. The college is accredited by the New England Association of Schools and Colleges. It operates on the semester system. Enrollment includes 519 full-time and 96 part-time undergraduate students. A faculty of 36 full-time and 86 part-time gives a faculty-student ratio of 1-9.

Entrance Requirements: Approved high school graduation or equivalent; high school transcript; letter of recommendation; rolling admission and midyear admission plans available; $25 application fee.

Costs Per Year: $12,150 tuition; $6,300 room and board; $550 student fees.

Collegiate Environment: The 50-acre campus is located in the village of Auburndale, a part of the suburban city of Newton. The 45 college buildings include a library of 50,000 volumes, 350 periodicals and 4,000 audiovisual materials. Residence halls accomodate 415 women. Other facilities include two child study centers, travel agency, bed & breakfast, advertising agency and a fashion retail training center. Internships, study abroad and exchange programs highlight all academic programs. 83% of applicants accepted. Scholarships are available and 88% of the students receive some form of financial aid. Semesters begin in September and January.

Community Environment: See Boston University.

LESLEY COLLEGE (D-13)
29 Everett Street
Cambridge, Massachusetts 02138-2790
Tel: (617) 868-9600

Description: Lesley College is an accredited, private, independent college composed of three units: the Undergraduate School; the Graduate School; and the School of Management. The Undergraduate School programs lead to the degree of Bachelor of Science in Education, Human Services, Liberal Studies, and Management Studies for women. The Graduate School's offerings include Bachelor, Master, Certificate of Advanced Graduate Study and Doctoral level programs for both men and women. Students prepare for careers in the areas of education and special education, counseling psychology, arts and human development, international studies, management, and outreach and alternative education. Programs in Management offer Master and Bachelor degrees for men and women with current experience in business, industry or other organizational settings. Enrollment is 6,024 students. There are 135 full-time and 450 part-time faculty members. The undergraduate faculty-student ratio is 1-14.

Entrance Requirements: Accredited high school graduation; completion of 15 units including 4 English, 2 mathematics, 1 American history, and 1 science; SAT or ACT required; Master's degree program requires Bachelor's degree and satisfactory GPA; Doctoral degree programs require Master's degree; $35 application fee.

Costs Per Year: $12,900 tuition; $6,075 room and board; $120 student fees; $325 per credit hour graduate school tuition.

Collegiate Environment: The college is comprised of 36 buildings located on a five-acre campus five minutes from Harvard Square. The college library contains 75,000 volumes. Housing facilities are provided for 450 students. The college is an equal educational opportunity institution and welcomes a geographically diverse and multicultural student body. Midyear students are admitted. Approximately 25% of the Undergraduate School student body graduated in the top quarter of the high school class. Scholarships and financial aid are available. Minority scholarships are also available. 60% of the recent freshman class received some form of financial assistance. Classes begin in September and January.

Community Environment: Lesley College is located in Cambridge, Massachusetts, the center of one of the greatest concentrations of higher education in the world. In addition to being the "largest college town in the world," Boston-Cambridge is a cultural center of distinction with the Boston Symphony, many museums, theaters, lectures, shows, and sports attractions. In addition to its Cambridge location,

Lesley College offers selected programs at outreach sites throughout New England, the nation, and the world.

MASSACHUSETTS BAY COMMUNITY COLLEGE (D-13)
50 Oakland Street
Wellesley Hills, Massachusetts 02181
Tel: (617) 237-0165; Admissions: (617) 237-0165; Fax: (617) 239-1047

Description: The coeducational community college was founded in 1961. It is operated by the Massachusetts Higher Education Coordination Council and grants Associate degrees in Arts, Science and Applied Science, as well as certificates. The college operates on the semester system and provides two summer terms and an evening division. An overseas program is available. It is accredited by the New England Association of Schools and Colleges. Professional accreditations include the Council for Accreditation of Allied Health Education Programs, the Joint Review Committee on Education in Radiologic Technology, the National League for Nursing, the National Automotive Technician Education Foundation, and isapproved by the National Court Reporters Association. The college offers courses in academic, technical, and semi-professional areas for full-time, part-time, career, and transfer programs. Enrollment includes 2,383 full-time and 2,650 part-time students. A faculty of 97 full-time and 194 part-time gives a faculty-student ratio of 1-21.

Entrance Requirements: Approved high school graduation or GED certificate; $35 application fee for out-of-state applicants. Rolling admission, early decision and early admission plans available.

Costs Per Year: $1,200 tuition; $4,440 out-of-state tuition; $1,290 student fees.

Collegiate Environment: The college operates two campuses. The Wellesley Hills campus consists of two buildings located on 84 acres. The Framingham Campus consists of one building located near downtown Framingham. Classes begin in September and January. There is an open admissions policy. Scholarships are available and 54% of the student body receives some form of financial aid. No living accommodations are provided by the college. The library contains 43,644 volumes, 372 periodicals, 10,564 microforms and 7,500 AV software.

Community Environment: A suburban institution 12 miles west of Boston. See Wellesley College.

MASSACHUSETTS COLLEGE OF ART (D-13)
621 Huntington Avenue
Boston, Massachusetts 02115
Tel: (617) 232-1555; Fax: (617) 566-4034

Description: The state-supported art school is accredited by the New England Association of Schools and Colleges and is a member of the National Association of Schools of Art and Design. The semester system is employed by the school. Three summer sessions and Foreign Summer Study programs are offered. The college was established as the Massachusetts Normal Art School in 1873 and was granted authorization to confer the Bachelor of Fine Arts degree in 1950. Master of Fine Arts and Master of Science in Art Education Programs are offered. Cooperative education programs in Graphic & Industrial Design give students the opportunity to be placed in full-time jobs for 20 weeks. The college operates on the semester system and offers three summer sessions. Enrollment includes 1,173 full-time and 106 part-time undergraduates and 88 graduate students. A faculty of 66 full-time and 20 part-time gives a faculty-student ratio of 1-14.

Entrance Requirements: Art portfolio, academic records, SAT scores and statement of purpose required. Emphasis in application review is placed on the portfolio. High school graduation or G.E.D. required. Completion of 16 units including 4 English, 3 mathematics, 2 science, 2 foreign language, 2 social studies, and 3 electives; rolling admission, deferred admission, early decision, midyear admission, and advanced placement plans available. $10 application fee for in-state residents, $40. application fee for out-of-state applicants, $50. application fee for graduate program.

Costs Per Year: $1,463 tuition; $6,422 out-of-state tuition; $2,520 student fees, room and board $5,839 (mandatory 19 meal plan).

Collegiate Environment: The college is located in seven buildings in the Fenway/Back Bay section of Boston. Renovations to the campus and have resulted in expanded studio space and spacious state-of-the-art facilities in all departments. The library contains 95,000 volumes, 400 periodicals, 65,000 microforms, 1,100 tapes/ recordings, 500 films and 2,365 videotapes, 100,000 slides; 2,830 College archives: bound periodical volumes. Smith Hall is a 116-bed coeducational dormitory specifically planned for art students. Also, Baker Hall is a co-ed dormitory for 136 students. Priority is given to freshman-Massachusetts residents. 59% of the freshmen applicants meet the requirments and are accepted. 58% of students receive financial aid.

Community Environment: See Boston University.

MASSACHUSETTS COLLEGE OF PHARMACY AND ALLIED HEALTH SCIENCES   *(D-13)*
179 Longwood Avenue
Boston, Massachusetts 02115
Tel: (617) 732-2850

Description: A private, independent college organized in 1823 and accredited by the New England Association of Schools and Colleges and by the American Council on Pharmaceutical Education. The undergraduate curriculum leads to the degree of Bachelor of Science in Pharmacy, Bachelor of Science in Chemistry, Bachelor of Science in Nursing, Bachelor of Science in Health Psychology, and Associate in Science in Nuclear Medical Technology and in Radiation Therapy Technology. The graduate curricula leads to the degrees of Master of Science, Doctor of Philosophy and Doctor of Pharmacy. The college operates on the quarter system, with two summer terms and enrolled 941 students recently. A faculty of 63 full-time. 18 part-time gives a faculty-student ratio of 1-14.

Entrance Requirements: Accredited high school graduation; completion of 16 units including 4 English, 3 mathematics, 1 social studies, 2 science; SAT or ACT required; $25 application fee; early admission, early decision, delayed admission, rolling admission, and advanced placement plans available.

Costs Per Year: $9,936 tuition and fees; $6,255 room and board, $100 fees

Collegiate Environment: The college has a library of 55,200 volumes, 700 periodicals, and 31,050 microforms. Students are admitted in September, November, are available and about 65% of students receive March. Scholarships and financial aid. Dormitory space is provided for students who pay their deposit by May 1.

Community Environment: See Boston University.

MASSACHUSETTS INSTITUTE OF TECHNOLOGY   *(D-13)*
77 Massachusetts Avenue
Cambridge, Massachusetts 02139
Tel: (617) 253-1000; Admissions: (617) 258-5515; Fax: (617) 258-8304

Description: This science-based university was established in 1861 and has developed into one of the most outstanding educational institutions in the country. It is a private, independent, endowed university organized into five Schools and one college. They include the School of Architecture and Planning, School of Engineering, School of Humanities and Social Science, Sloan School of Management, the School of Science, and the Whitaker College of Health Sciences, Technology and Management. There is an enrollment of 4,389 students. A faculty of 938 full-time and 16 part-time gives a faculty-student ratio of 1-9. The Institute is accredited by the New England Association of Schools and Colleges and by respective professional and scientific organizations. M.I.T. operates on the 4-1-4 system with one summer term and offers optional Army, Navy, and Air Force and Marine Corps ROTC programs. Engineering Internship Programs are available. Other special programs include Undergraduate Research Opportunities Program and Alternative Freshman Programs.

Entrance Requirements: Accredited high school graduation is not required; completion of 14 units including 4 English, 4 mathematics, 3 science, 1 foreign language and 2 social studies; recommended SAT or ACT and three Achievement Tests, mathematics, English or history, and science required; GRE required for some graduate programs; $50 application fee; early action; delayed admission, and advanced placement plans available; admission is limited and highly competitive.

Costs Per Year: $21,000 tuition; $6,150 room and board; $2,450 books and personal expenses.

Collegiate Environment: The Institute is located on a well-equipped residential campus of 142 acres fronting the Charles River in Cambridge, opposite Boston. There are 162 buildings on the campus including a library system of 2,365,695 volumes, 21,259 serials, 2,601,521 microforms, and 539,846 audiovisual materials and on-campus living accommodations for 2,775 undergraduates, 1,047 single graduate students and 4016 graduate student families. Fraternities and sororities house nearly 1,275 undergraduates. Some of the research facilities include the Francis Bitter National Magnet Laboratory; the Center for International Studies; the Energy Laboratory; the Center for Materials Science and Engineering; the Center for Space Research; the Center for Cancer Research; the programs in Science, Technology, and Society: the Harvard-MIT Division of Health Sciences and Technology; Joint Harvard-MIT Center for Urban Studies; the the Laboratory of Nuclear Science; the Lincoln Laboratory, for research and development in advanced electronics application to national defense and space exploration; the Laboratory for Computer Science, devoted to research in the computer and information sciences; the Operations Research Center; the Research Laboratory of Electronics; the Spectroscopy Laboratory and the Whitehead Institute. A wide variety of special programs of study and research is available to undergraduate students through several alternative freshman programs, the Undergraduate Research Opportunities Program, and the Engineering Internship Program. Freshman year at MIT is on a Pass/No credit basis. Graduate students may pursue courses of study in all five schools and the Whitaker College, in many interdisciplinary programs and in the Harvard-MIT Division of Health Sciences and Technology and the MIT-Woods Hole Oceanographic Institution Joint Programs in Oceanography and Oceanographic Engineering. Semesters begin in September and only transfer students are accepted at midyear. 30% of applicants are accepted.

Community Environment: See Harvard University.

MASSACHUSETTS MARITIME ACADEMY   *(I-15)*
101 Academy Drive
Buzzards Bay, Massachusetts 02532
Tel: (508) 830-5032; (800) 544-4311; Fax: (508) 830-5077

Description: Founded in 1891, the Massachusetts Maritime Academy is the oldest continuously operating maritime training institution in the country. During its century of existence, the Academy has supplied officers to the maritime industry and to the armed forces. Its graduates have advanced to positions of leadership in many areas. Four 4-year curricula programs are offered, one leading to a degree in Marine Transportation and a U.S. Coast Guard license as third mate, the other leading to a degree in Marine Engineering and a U.S. Coast Guard license as third engineer. A third major in Facilities and Plant Engineering leads to a Stationary 2nd Engineers license after one year of experience in the industry. The fourth major is in Marine Safety and Environmental Protection. This major is a joint program with Woods Hole Oceanographic Institute that leads to a Bachelor of Science degree. Additional concentrations beyond major tracking at Massachusetts Maritime Academy are available in Mechanical Engineering, Business Management and Marine Fisheries to provide the cadet with a broadened career-enhancing potential. The program is organized into two semesters on campus and one sea term. Sea training cruises on a training vessel and commercial vessels prepare the graduates to function effectively as officers aboard ships of the U.S. Navy and Merchant Fleet. Students are required to make 3 cruises of approximately 8 weeks each during their four years at the Academy. They visit 8 to 12 foreign countries. Graduates have had great success in nonmaritime professions including business management, power-plant operations, industrial and mechanical engineering. Enrollment is 750 men and 46 women. A faculty of 55 gives a faculty-student ratio of 1-15. The school is accredited by the New England Association of Schools and Colleges.

Entrance Requirements: Must be of good moral character; physical examination required; accredited high school graduation; completion of 16 college-preparatory units including 4 English, 3 mathematics, 3 science, 2 foreign language, 2 social science, 1 geometry, and 5 electives including English, foreign language, natural science, mathematics, social sciences, or computer science; SAT required; early admission, early decision, rolling admission, delayed admission, and advanced placement available; $10 application fee for state residents, $40 application fee for out-of-state residents.

Costs Per Year: $1,500 MA, CT, RI residents tuition; $2,300 VT, NH; $6,500 other states; $3,800 room and board; $650 student fees.

Collegiate Environment: The academy is located in the village of Buzzards Bay, Bourne, in the southeastern area of the state, on a peninsula adjacent to the Cape Cod Canal. About 60% of those accepted matriculate. The average SAT scores of recent freshmen were 463V, 503M. Classes begin in September. The library contains 42,000 volumes, 415 periodicals, 817 microforms, and 1,500 pamphlets. Dormitory space is provided for 850 cadets.

Community Environment: Bourne is the second largest town on Cape Cod and has a New England climate. It is located 60 miles from Boston, and bus service and air service from Hyannis are available. The Trading Post, located here, is a replica of the trading post built in 1627. Bourne Scenic Park is a good area for picnics and camping. Boating, fishing, swimming and golf are available for recreation in this resort community.

MASSASOIT COMMUNITY COLLEGE   *(G-14)*
One Massasoit Blvd.
Brockton, Massachusetts 02402
Tel: (508) 588-9100

Description: This comprehensive community college was established in 1966 and is under the auspices of the Massachusetts Board of Regents. It offers two-year transfer, general, and career programs all leading to an Associate in Arts degree or an Associate in Science degree. It also offers evening and summer courses for both regular students and adults pursuing part-time education. The college is accredited by the New England Association of Schools and Colleges. The Blue Hills Regional Technical Institute merged with Massasoit in September 1985. The college operates on the semester system and offers two summer sessions. Enrollment includes 4,262 full-time and 3,482 part-time students. A faculty of 166 full-time and 90 part-time provides a faculty-student ratio of 1-25.

Entrance Requirements: Accredited high school graduation or GED; no application fee; rolling admission plan available.

Costs Per Year: $2,490 tuition; $5,640 out-of-state; $372 student fees.

Collegiate Environment: The main campus is located on 100 acres and is comprised of ten buildings. An additional campus is now located in Canton, MA. The library contains 65,000 volumes, 300 periodicals and 17,000 microforms. Approximately 90% of students applying for admission meet the requirements and are accepted including midyear students. Over 70% of the previous entering class returned to the college for the second year. Financial aid is available for economically disadvantaged students, and 40% of students receive some form of financial aid.

Community Environment: Brockton is located 20 miles south of downtown Boston and the center of the second fastest growing area of the State. The college service area encompasses one million people in 51 cities and towns south of Boston and includes the city of Quincy.

MERRIMACK COLLEGE   *(B-13)*
Turnpike Road (Route 114)
North Andover, Massachusetts 01845
Tel: (508) 837-5100; Admissions: (508) 837-5100; Fax: (508) 837-5222

Description: Merrimack College was founded in 1947 by the Augustinian Fathers and is composed of three main divisions: Liberal Arts, Business and Science, and Engineering. The college operates on the semester system, offers two summer sessions and is accredited by the New England Association of Schools and Colleges and many professional accrediting associations. Cooperative Education programs are available in Business, Computer Science, Civil and Electrical Engineering and the Liberal Arts. Recent enrollment included 1,000 men and 1,000 women full-time and 450 men and 600 women part-time. An undergraduate faculty of 135 full-time and 29 part-time offers a faculty-student ratio of 1-14 and an average class size of 18.

Entrance Requirements: Accredited high school graduation with rank in upper 40% of graduating class; completion of 16 college-preparatory units including 4 English, 3 mathematics (4 for science and

engineering students), 1 science (3 for science and engineering students), and 2 social science; $35 application fee; SAT required; early decision, advanced placement, early admission, rolling admission, and delayed admission plans available.

Costs Per Year: $12,500 tuition; $6,400 room and board.

Collegiate Environment: The College is located on 220 acres in the towns of Andover and North Andover. It is comprised of 18 buildings that include 2 traditional residence halls, 2 apartment-style complexes, and 14 townhouse units all of which accomodate 1,178 students. About 75% of students applying for admission meet the requirements and are accepted, including midyear students. 70% of students receive financial aid. The library contains more than 120,000 volumes, 900 pamphlets, 900 periodicals, 5,700 microforms and 3,500 audiovisual materials, plus a T.V. studio and college channel.

Community Environment: North Andover is suburban to Lawrence and approximately 25 miles north of Boston in the northeastern part of state. The city has rail and bus service. Advantages of neighboring Boston and Lawrence are easily accessible.

MONTSERRAT COLLEGE OF ART   *(C-14)*
23 Essex Street
P.O. Box 26
Beverly, Massachusetts 01915
Tel: (508) 922-8222; (800) 836-0487; Admissions: (508) 921-2350; Fax: (508) 922-4268

Description: Montserrat College of Art is a professional college of art and design that offers both a Bachelor of Fine Arts Degree and a four-year Diploma. Areas of studio concentration at Montserrat are painting and drawing, illustration, graphic design, printmaking, photography and sculpture. In addition, provisional teachers certification is available. Montserrat is accredited by the National Association of Schools of Art and Design and the New England Association of Schools and Colleges. Total day enrollment is 300 students. The faculty-student ratio is 1-12, which allows for a close bond to be developed between faculty and students.

Entrance Requirements: High school graduate; admission based on portfolio, educational record, and interview; early decision, early admission, deferred admission, midyear admission, rolling admission, and advanced placement plans available; $30 application fee.

Costs Per Year: $8,960 tuition; $545 health and insurance fee; $250 student fees; $2,700 estimated housing; $450 materials kit.

Collegiate Environment: Montserrat College of Art is has two facilities located in downtown Beverly, Massachusetts. Most juniors and seniors have private studio spaces, while freshmen and sophomores have convenient access to general classroom studios. Evenings find many students using the Montserrat facility for a pleasant mixture of serious studio work and social interaction. The Montserrat library has more than ten thousand volumes and one of the most comprehensive art libraries on the north shore of Boston. The Montserrat Gallery hosts exhibitions of contemporary works of art by artists with regional and national recognition. There are also two student and alumni galleries. The Montserrat Student Life Office places students in college apartments; all within walking distance to the college, Beverly beaches, and the commuter train to Boston. Four students are placed per apartment; two per bedroom. Each apartment has a kitchen, living room and a bath.

Community Environment: Just 30 minutes north of Boston, Beverly is a residential city with a population of 52,000. The historic rocky coast of the north shore of Boston offers a contemplative setting with its harborside parks and beaches, access to the nearby fishing and yachting harbors of Gloucester, Marblehead and Rockport, and to the historic city of Salem, immediately adjacent to Beverly. The environment of the north shore is offset by the accessibility to a large metropolitan city with galleries, museums, cultural events and nightlife.

MOUNT HOLYOKE COLLEGE   *(E-5)*
College Street
South Hadley, Massachusetts 01075
Tel: (413) 538-8200; Admissions: (413) 538-2023; Fax: (413) 538-2409

Description: An independent, liberal arts college for women, Mount Holyoke is accredited by the New England Association of Schools and Colleges. The college is set within the intellectually vibrant Five College community formed by three other private colleges (Amherst, Hampshire, and Smith) and a major research institution, the University of Massachusetts. Students enrolled at any one of the five colleges regularly take courses and use the facilities at the other four without extra charge. Seminars are offered at every level, including the freshman level. More than half the classes at Mount Holyoke have less than fifteen students, and one-third of those have less than ten. Junior Year Abroad, exchange programs with other colleges, and extensive internship opportunities are available. Enrollment includes 1,869 full-time and 39 part-time undergraduate, and 17 graduate students. A faculty of 181 full-time and 32 part-time gives a faculty-student ratio of 1-9.

Entrance Requirements: A high school program providing a good preparation for Mount Holyoke includes 4 years of English, either 4 years of one foreign language or a combination of 3 years of one language and 2 years of another, and 3 years each of mathematics, history, and laboratory sciences; SAT or ACT and 3 Achievement Tests, one of which should be English Composition, are required; the College's Frances Perkins program is available for women beyond the traditional undergraduate age (18-22) who wish to initiate, continue, or enrich their undergraduate education; early decision, early entrance, deferred entrance, and advanced placement admission plans are available; application deadlines: Feb. 1, Nov. 15 early decision 1, Jan. 15 early decision 2; $40 application fee.

Costs Per Year: $19,300 tuition; $5,700 room and board; $135 student fees.

Collegiate Environment: The 800-acre residential campus includes several new facilities: the Language Learning Center, Blanchard Campus Center, Kendall Hall Sports Complex, plus an Equestrian Center and 18-hole championship golf course. Cited as the largest and best-equipped chemistry facility at any undergraduate institution is Carr Laboratory. Williston Memorial Library's holdings number 623,336 volumes, 1,811 periodicals, and 15,121 microform titles. Renovation of the library and construction of a Center for Science and Technology was completed in 1992. Nineteen residence halls of 65 to 130 students house over 97% of the student body. All four classes are mixed in each hall, and housing is guaranteed for all four years. 65% of applicants meet criteria and are offered admission. 44% of first-year students entering in 1994 graduated in the top tenth of their high school class. The middle 50% range of enrolled freshmen scores is SAT 500-640 verbal, 520-640 math. Financial aid is need-based. Students are fully funded to the extent of demonstrated need, and 67% of the student body receives some form of financial aid.

Community Environment: Across from campus in South Hadley Center is the Village Commons, a vital new shopping complex. Movie theaters, a restaurant, an ice cream shop, a pub, a video rental shop, clothing stores, offices, and apartments all attract people from across the Five College area. South Hadley is approximately 1 1/2 hours from Boston and 3 hours from New York by car. Bradley International Airport, 40 minutes by car, serves Hartford and Springfield. Springfield, 12 miles away, is accessible by Amtrak. Buses run from Boston, Hartford, and Springfield to the campus gates.

MOUNT IDA COLLEGE *(D-12)*
777 Dedham Street
Newton Centre, Massachusetts 02159
Tel: (617) 928-4500

Description: This private, coeducational junior college is a non-profit, nonsectarian institution. It operates on the semester system. The college is authorized to grant the Associate in Arts and Associate in Science degrees in 34 different programs. The College also offers a Bachelor Degree in 7 areas. The college is accredited by the New England Association of Schools and Colleges, the American Dental Association and the American Veterinary Medical Association.

Entrance Requirements: Accredited high school graduation; completion of college preparatory program; $25 application fee; rolling admission available.

Costs Per Year: $9,305; $6,545 room and board; $130 student fees.

Collegiate Environment: The college is located on 85 acres and is comprised of 18 buildings that include a library of 75,000 volumes and 2,740 microforms and living accommodations for 830 students. Approximately 80% of students applying for admission are accepted, including midyear students and those from various geographical back-

grounds. Almost 30% of the recent student body graduated in the top half of the high school class and 10% were in the top quarter. Financial aid is available and 64% of the students receive some form of financial aid. 65% of the previous freshman class returned to the college for the second year of studies.

Community Environment: See Boston University.

MOUNT WACHUSETT COMMUNITY COLLEGE *(C-8)*
444 Green Street
Gardner, Massachusetts 01440
Tel: (508) 632-6600; (800) 222-6922; Admissions: (508) 632-6600 x110

Description: The public junior college was founded in 1963 by the Massachusetts Board of Regional Community Colleges. The college operates on the semester system with two summer sessions and is accredited by the New England Association of Schools and Colleges and the National League for Nursing. An enrollment of 1,800 full-time with a faculty of 100 full-time gives a faculty-student ratio of 1-18.

Entrance Requirements: Accredited high school graduation or equivalent; completion of 16 units including 4 English, 2 math, $10 application fee; rolling admission and early admission plans available.

Costs Per Year: $1,575 tuition and fees; $3,795 out-of-state.

Collegiate Environment: College facilities include a library of 51,000 volumes. Approximately 90% of students applying for admission meet the requirements and are accepted including midyear students. Financial aid is available and 70% of the students receive some form of financial aid.

Community Environment: City has airport and bus service. Community services include three libraries, many churches of most denominations, the Henry Heywood Memorial Hospital, and a downtown shopping center. Recreational facilities are swimming pool, golf course, lakes, bowling and theatre. Excellent opportunities for part-time employment.

NEW ENGLAND COLLEGE OF OPTOMETRY *(D-13)*
424 Beacon Street
Boston, Massachusetts 02115
Tel: (617) 366-2030; (800) 824-5527; Admissions: (617) 236-6204; Fax: (617) 424-9202

Description: The private college of optometry was established in 1894 as the Klein School of Optics, and later became the Massachusetts College Of Optometry. The college is authorized by the Board of Collegiate Authority of the Commonwealth of Massachusetts to confer the degrees of Bachelor of Science in Optometry, Doctor of Optometry, Doctor of Ocular Science, and Doctor of Humane Letters. It is accredited by the Council of Optometric Education of the American Optometric Association. The four-year college employs the quarter system. Enrollment is 410 students. A faculty of 60 gives a faculty-student ratio of 1-7.

Entrance Requirements: Minimum 2.50 GPA and completion of 90 semester hours credit from accredited college; SAT or ACT and entrance exam required; rolling admission plan; two letters of recommendation required; $50 application fee.

Costs Per Year: $18,849 tuition; $70 student fee.

Collegiate Environment: The college occupies two buildings but does not maintain dormitories. Library contains 8,760 volumes and 214 different periodicals. About 33% of the students applying for admission are accepted. A twenty-four month program for students holding a degree in a science or in math is available. Scholarships are available and 81% of the students receive some form of financial aid.

Community Environment: See Boston University

NEW ENGLAND CONSERVATORY OF MUSIC *(D-13)*
290 Huntington Avenue
Boston, Massachusetts 02115
Tel: (617) 262-1120; Admissions: (617) 262-1120 X 430; Fax: (617) 262-0500

Description: The private conservatory of music is accredited by the New England Association of Schools and Colleges and is a charter member of the National Association of Schools of Music. It is composed of an Undergraduate and a Graduate Division and operates on the semester system. The Undergraduate Division offers a diploma as well as a four-year program leading to the Bachelor of Music degree in performance (26 instruments & voice), jazz studies, jazz composition, Third Stream performance, theoretical studies, music history, early music performance, music education and composition. The Graduate Division offers the Master of Music degree in performance (26 instruments & voice), vocal accompaniment, vocal pedagogy, early music perfomance, jazz studies, jazz composition, Third Stream performance, choral, orchestral, or wind ensemble conducting, music education, composition, theoretical studies, music history and musicology, and the Artist Diploma, a nonacademic award for extraordinary achievement in performance. The conservatory also offers a DMA in selected majors. The conservatory operates on the semester system and offers one summer session. Enrollment includes 381 undergraduates and 380 graduate students. A full-time faculty of 185 gives a ratio of 1-5.

Entrance Requirements: Accredited high school graduation or equivalent; SAT or ACT required; audition required. Advanced placement plan available. $75 application fee.

Costs Per Year: $16,200 tuition; $7,650 board and room; $1,000 student fees and health insurance.

Collegiate Environment: The conservatory is comprised of three buildings which are located across the street from the home of the Boston Symphony Orchestra. The conservatory library contains 80,000 volumes and dormitory facilities are provided for 150 students. All freshmen are required to reside in campus housing. Classes being in September and a limited number of applications are accepted at midyear. 50% of applicants are accepted. Scholarships are available and 85% of the students receive some form of financial aid. The conservatory welcomes a geographically diverse student body.

Community Environment: See Boston University

NEW ENGLAND SCHOOL OF LAW   *(D-13)*
156 Stuart Street
Boston, Massachusetts 02116
Tel: (617) 451-0010; Admissions: (617) 422-7210; Fax: (617) 422-7200

Description: The private law school was established in 1908 and was formerly known as the Portia Law School. It operates on the semester system and is accredited by the American Bar Association. The school also provides an evening division and grants the Juris Doctor degree to its graduates. It enrolls 615 men and 468 women. A faculty of 37 full-time and 52 part-time members gives a faculty-student ratio of 1-25.

Entrance Requirements: Completion of four years academic college work from an accredited institution; Law School Admission test required; $50 application fee.

Costs Per Year: $11,760 tuition; $150 annual fee; $585 health fees

Collegiate Environment: The school is located in one main building which includes a library of 220,000 volumes and 500 periodicals. Approximately one-third of the students applying for admission meet the requirements and one-third of these are accepted. The school accepts students from various geographical locations but will not admit midyear students.

Community Environment: See Boston University

NEWBURY COLLEGE   *(E-13)*
129 Fisher Avenue
Brookline, Massachusetts 02146
Tel: (617) 730-7000; (800) 639-2879; Admissions: (617) 730-7006; Fax: (617) 731-9618

Description: This privately supported, coeducational college offers the Associate in Applied Science in 25 majors within 7 departments of Business Administration, Communications and Media, Culinary Arts, Fashion and Design, Hospitality Management, Health Professions and Legal Studies. It is accredited by the New England Association of Schools and Colleges and several professional associations. It operates on the semester system and offers one summer term. Enrollment is 936 full-time, 67 part-time and 4,500 evening students. A fac-

ulty of 48 full-time and 278 part-time gives a faculty-student ratio of 1-17.

Entrance Requirements: High school diploma or GED; $30 application fee; rolling admission plan available.

Costs Per Year: $9,980 tuition; $5,990 room and board; $450 student fees.

Collegiate Environment: The library contains 18,000 volumes and 750 periodicals. Scholarships are available and 55% of the students receive some form of financial aid. 80% of those applying are accepted, including students at midyear. 28% of the freshman class graduated in the top half of the high school class and 80% of the freshmen return for the second year. Dormitory facilities accomodate 370 men and women.

Community Environment: See Hebrew College.

Branch Campuses: Newbury College's day program is located in Brookline, MA, a residential suburb 3.5 miles from historic Boston. The college has 13 branch campuses located in eastern Massachusetts. The branch campuses from Lowell to New Bedford serve the Division of Continuing Education evening and weekend students.

NICHOLS COLLEGE   *(G-8)*
Dudley, Massachusetts 01570
Tel: (508) 943-2055; (800) 470-3379; Fax: (508) 943-9885

Description: The institution is a private nonsectarian college of business administration and liberal arts. It is accredited by the New England Association of Schools and Colleges. The college began as an all-male institution, but became coeducational in 1972. Enrollment includes 751 full-time and 619 part-time evening undergraduates and 398 graduate students. A faculty of 35 full-time and 14 part-time gives a faculty-student ratio of 1-24.

Entrance Requirements: High school graduation with completion of 16 units including 4 English, 3 mathematics, 2 science, and 2 social science; non-high school graduates with high school equivalency diplomas may be admitted; GMAT required for graduate programs; early admission, early decision, rolling admission, midyear admission and advanced placement plans available. $25 application fee.

Costs Per Year: $9,744 tuition; $5,624 room and board; $100 student fees; $2,165 Freshman Computer Plan (one-time fee only).

Collegiate Environment: The college occupies 42 buildings located on 200 acres of land. The college library contains 65,000 volumes, 450 periodicals, 4,200 microforms and 2,500 recordings. Dormitory facilities are provided for 592 students. 83% of the students applying for admission meet the requirements and are accepted. Approximately 86% of the previous freshman class returned to the college for the sophomore year. About 52% of the recent student body graduated in the top half of the high school class and 18% in the top quarter. 680 scholarships are offered, including 383 academic and 297 need based grants. 73% of the undergraduates receive some form of financial aid.

Community Environment: The college is located in rural area 15 miles south of Worcester. Community has Catholic and Protestant churches, two libraries, Grange, and shopping center. Some part-time work available for students. Recreational facilities for boating, tennis, basketball, volleyball, swimming, fishing, and other sports.

NORTH ADAMS STATE COLLEGE   *(B-2)*
Church Street
North Adams, Massachusetts 01247
Tel: (413) 662-5000; (800) 292-6632; Admissions: (413) 662-5400; Fax: (413) 662-5179

Description: This state college was established in 1894 and was known as the State Normal School until 1932. In 1960 the name of the institution was changed to its present one and the college was authorized to grant the Bachelor and Master of Arts degrees in addition to its Bachelor of Science in Education degree. The college is accredited by the New England Association of Schools and Colleges. It operates on the semester system and offers two summer sessions. Enrollment is 1,600 students. A faculty of 97 gives a faculty-student ratio of 1-17.

Entrance Requirements: Accredited high school graduation with rank in upper 50% of graduating class; SAT or ACT required; early decision, rolling admission, delayed admission, midyear admission and advanced placement plans available; $10 application fee.

Costs Per Year: $3,440 in-state tuition; $7,300 out-of-state; $4,000 room and board.

Collegiate Environment: The 25-acre campus is located in a pleasant area in a residential section of the city, about one-half mile from the business center. The ten college buildings include a library of 141,000 volumes, 775 periodicals, 200,000 microforms and 8,000 recordings. Dormitory facilities for 515 men and 515 women are provided. The college welcomes a geographically diverse student body and accepts 65% of the students applying for admission. Classes begin in September and students are accepted at midyear. The average SAT scores of recent freshmen were 437 verbal, 480 math. Financial aid is available for economically disadvantaged students. The college awarded 400 Bachelor and 22 Master degrees to a recent graduating class.

Community Environment: In the northwestern corner of state, this Berkshire town produces a diversity of products including machinery, and electronic equipment. The area has cool summers and dry winters and heavy snowfalls. Bus lines are accessible. A hospital, Sterling and Francine Clark Art Institute, and numerous civic and service organizations are found here. There are 6 major ski areas within 25 miles and Mohawk and Taconic Trails. Part-time employment is seasonal for students. The city has an annual Fall Festival.

NORTH SHORE COMMUNITY COLLEGE   *(C-14)*
1 Ferncroft Road
Danvers, Massachusetts 01923
Tel: (508) 762-4000; Admissions: (508) 962-4042; Fax: (508) 762-4021

Description: The public junior college was founded in 1965, as the ninth college of the Commonwealth of Massachusetts Regional College System, to serve the education and community service needs of the area north of Boston. It offers programs that lead to the Associate in Arts and Associate in Science degrees for terminal and transfer students. It also offers a variety of programs for adults and college graduates as well as counseling and advisory services for all students. The school operates on the semester system and offers two summer terms. The college is accredited by the New England Association of Schools and Colleges, the American Physical Therapy Association, and the National League for Nursing. A Cooperative Education program and overseas programs are available. Enrollment is 1,894 full-time, 1,666 part-time, and 4,177 evening students. A faculty of 122 full-time and 226 part-time gives a faculty-student ratio of 1-34.

Entrance Requirements: Accredited high school graduation or equivalent; open enrollment, early admission, midyear admission and rolling admission plans available.

Costs Per Year: $2,490 ($83/credit) in-state tuition; $2,495 out-of-state tuition.

Collegiate Environment: The college has campuses in Danvers, Beverly, and Lynn, MA. It includes a library of 65,000 volumes and 400 periodicals. Approximately 90% of students applying for admission are accepted. Scholarships are available and 65% of the current students receive some form of financial aid. Approximately 60% of the previous freshman class returned to the college for the second year.

Community Environment: See Montserrat College of Art.

NORTHEASTERN UNIVERSITY   *(D-13)*
360 Huntington Avenue
Boston, Massachusetts 02115
Tel: (617) 437-2000

Description: Coeducational and nonsectarian, Northeastern University is a comprehensive private university. Founded in 1898, it is an internationally known university and world leader in cooperative education, a program in which students alternate periods of traditional college study with periods of paid, professional employment. It is accredited by the New England Association of Schools and Colleges and by respective professional and educational organizations. The University operates on the quarter system and offers one-summer session. Participation in undergraduate cooperative education program involves 6,300 students, 2,010 employers at 2,310 locations, 27 states

and 25 countries. On average, undergraduate students earn more than $8,750 per year. Northeastern University's School of Law is unique in offering cooperative education to law students. "Co-op" is also offered in the Business Administration and Professional Accounting programs. The university offers overseas opportunities to study in Dublin, Ireland, Belfast, Northern Ireland, Belgium, England, and Moscow. Semester-long field study expeditions throughout the world are available to students through the College of Arts and Sciences in affiliation with the School for Field Studies. Army, Navy, and Air Force ROTC programs are available. Special services are available to students with disabilities, including orientation, preregistration, counseling, special parking, general assistance (liaison with instructors and staff), sign language and oral interpreting, note taking, audio loops, provision of taped and Braille textbooks and materials, readers, tactile maps, adaptive physical education and Physical therapy.

Entrance Requirements: High school diploma or equivalency; 17 units completed, including 4 English, 4 Mathematics, 3 Science, 2 Foreign Language, 3 Social Studies, and 2 History. SAT required (ACT accepted as substitute); Application fee $30; Admissions Plans: rolling admission, early admission, delayed admission. College participates in CEEB Advanced Placement program.

Costs Per Year: $10,890 tuition; $6,780 room and board; $599 student fees. Freshmen: $3,830 per quarter, College of Business Administration, College of Engineering, College of Computer Science, and School of Engineering Technology; $3,630 per quarter, College of Arts and Sciences, Bouve' College of Pharmacy and Health Sciences, College of Human Development Professions, College of Criminal Justice, College of Nursing, College of Pharmacy and Allied Health Professions, and Alternative Freshman-Year Program; $2,235 room and board per quarter; $23 (per quarter) fees; $525 health service fee (annual), $25 infirmary fee (per quarter, for boarders); $200 (per quarter) books and supplies; $200 International student fees.

Collegiate Environment: Undergraduate housing is available for 1,735 men and 1,328 women. The Library's holdings number 690,000 bound volumes, 1,647,000 microforms, 7,900 serial titles, 14,000 audio and video items, and 156,000 government documents. 74% of applicants are accepted. Financial aid is available. There were 6,621 undergraduates who received $17,976,202 in scholarships/grants. Freshmen received 1,536 packages, and 55% of all undergraduates receive financial aid.

Community Environment: Students at Northeastern University have access to many cultural, educational, historical, and recreational offerings of the city. Some of Boston's cultural opportunities found near the main campus include the Museum of Fine Arts, Symphony Hall, and the Boston Public Library. The University is adjacent to the Fenway, a spacious park that includes a beautiful rose garden and paths.

NORTHERN ESSEX COMMUNITY COLLEGE   *(A-13)*
100 Elliot Street
Haverhill, Massachusetts 01830
Tel: (508) 374-3900; (800) 222-3000; Admissions: (508) 374-3600; Fax: (508) 374-3729

Description: This two-year college was established under the control of the Board of Regional Community Colleges of the Commonwealth of Massachusetts in 1960. It is accredited by the New England Association of Schools and Colleges and by several prfessional accrediting organizations. It offers general and university-parallel education in the liberal arts and vocational-technical programs for part-time, terminal, and transfer students. The opportunity to study and live overseas is available to qualified students. The school operates on the semester system and offers two summer sessions. Enrollment includes 2,580 full-time and 3,794 part-time credit students, and 1,984 non-credit students. A faculty of 125 full time and 113 part time with 150 in the evening gives a faculty-student ratio of 1-26. Air Force ROTC is offered with the University of Lowell.

Entrance Requirements: Accredited high school graduation or equivalent; completion of 16 college-preparatory units; after acceptance applicants are required to take an assessment test; rolling admission, early admission, early decision, midyear admission, and advanced placement plans available.

Costs Per Year: State resident: $1,200 ($40 per credit) tuition, $1,080 ($36 per credit) fees; NE region resident: $1,800 ($60 per credit) tuition, $1,140 ($38 per credit) fees; Nonresident & foreign:

$5,640 ($188 per credit) tuition, $1,080 ($36 per credit) fees; $360 ($12 per credit) or $180 ($6 per credit) surcharges; $300 mandatory health insurance.

Collegiate Environment: Campus facilities include a library of 57,654 hardbound volumes, 441 periodical subscriptions, 227 microforms, and 4,00 sound recordings. There are no dormitory facilities on campus. 79% of applicants are accepted. Scholarships are available and 60 % of students receive some form of financial assistance.

Community Environment: See Bradford College.

PINE MANOR COLLEGE *(D-12)*
400 Heath Street
Chestnut Hill, Massachusetts 02167
Tel: (617) 731-7104; (800) 762-1357; Fax: (617) 731-7199

Description: This private four-year liberal arts college for women is a nonprofit residential institution. Pine Manor offers the M.Ed., B.A., A.A., and A.S. degrees. It operates on the semester system and offers two summer sessions. Enrollment is 400 full-time and 50 part-time students. A faculty of 24 full-time and 44 part-time gives a faculty-student ratio of 1-12. The college is accredited by the New England Association of Schools and Colleges.

Entrance Requirements: Accredited high school graduation with rank in upper half of graduating class; completion of 16 units including 4 English and the following recommed units: 2 foreign language, 2 science, 2 mathematics, 2 social science and 4 electives; SAT or ACT required; early decision, advanced placement, rolling admission and midyear admission plans available. $40 application fee.

Costs Per Year: $15,650 tuition; $6,660 room and board; $700 student fees.

Collegiate Environment: The college is situated on 79 acres in the Chestnut Hill section of the town of Brookline, Massachusetts, which is just west of Boston. The 31 college buildings include a library of 77,000 volumes, 380 periodicals and 4,000 microforms. Dormitory facilities house 410 women. Freshmen and sophomores must live on campus. About 90% of students applying for admission are accepted. About 75% of the previous freshman class returned to the college for the second year of studies. The college has an overseas program. The student may spend a year or semester in Paris, or a year or semester in London, Spain or Italy. A semester at sea program is also available. Financial aid is available. 43% of students receive financial aid.

Community Environment: See Boston University.

QUINCY COLLEGE *(E-13)*
34 Coddington Street
Quincy, Massachusetts 02169
Tel: (617) 984-1700; Fax: (617) 984-1789

Description: This public college is a two-year community college. It has been authorized to grant degrees by the Board of Collegiate Authority of the Massachusetts Department of Education and is fully accredited by the New England Association of Schools and Colleges, the National League for Nursing, and the Committee on Allied Health Education and Accreditation. The school operates on the semester system, offering courses in vocational-technical and academic areas as well as a transfer-oriented program for part time and full time students in day, evening and summer programs; there are two summer terms. Enrollment is 1,545 full-time and 719 part-time students, with 1,692 students in the evening programs. There is a faculty of 44 full-time and 25 part-time employed in the day programs, giving a faculty-student ratio of 1-21.

Entrance Requirements: Accredited high school graduation or GED; open enrollment; $15 application fee; early admission, early decision, midyear admission, rolling admission and advanced placement plans available.

Costs Per Year: $1,920 tuition; $85 student fees.

Collegiate Environment: Approximately 83% of students applying for admission are accepted, including midyear students. Financial aid is available through government programs, institutional scholarships, work study programs and loans, and is awarded on the basis of need. 60% of students received financial aid recently. The library contains 30,000 volumes plus numerous audiovisual materials. Approximately 60% of the student body transfers to 4-year institutions.

Community Environment: An important business and industrial city today, Quincy has given the nation some of its most important patriots. Quincy was the birthplace of two presidents, John Adams and his son, John Quincy Adams. This South Shore suburb is located about seven miles from downtown Boston, a 15-minute ride by public transportation. There is easy access to all Boston facilities.

QUINSIGAMOND COMMUNITY COLLEGE *(E-9)*
670 West Boylston Street
Worcester, Massachusetts 01606
Tel: (508) 853-2300; Admissions: (508) 854-4262; Fax: (508) 852-6943

Description: This community college was established in 1963 by the Massachusetts Board of Regional Community Colleges. It offers courses in vocational-technical and academic areas for part-time, terminal, and transfer programs. It operates on the semester system and offers three summer terms. The college is accredited by the New England Association of Schools and Colleges and numerous professional accrediting associations. Enrollment includes 1,725 full-time and 2,733 part-time students. A faculty of 95 full-time, 90 part-time, and 116 evening gives a faculty-student ratio of 1-15.

Entrance Requirements: Accredited high school graduation or equivalent; $10 application fee; early admission plan available.

Costs Per Year: $1,050 tuition; $3,990 out-of-state; $1,000 students fees.

Collegiate Environment: The college moved into its newly completed quarters in 1964. It consists of four buildings located on eight acres and contains a library of 56,094 volumes, 319 periodicals, 4,928 microforms and 1,422 audiovisual materials. About 80% of students applying for admission meet the requirements and 73% of these are accepted. Financial aid is available for economically handicapped students. 42% of students receive some form of financial aid recently.

Community Environment: See Clark University.

REGIS COLLEGE *(E-12)*
235 Wellesley Street
Weston, Massachusetts 02193
Tel: (617) 893-1820; (800) 456-1820; Admissions: (800) 456-1820; Fax: (617) 899-2364

Description: The private college provides a liberal arts and sciences education for women. It was founded in 1927 and is sponsored by the Congregation of the Sisters of Saint Joseph of Boston. It is affiliated with the Catholic University of America and is accredited by the New England Association of Schools and Colleges and the Council on Social Work Education. The college operates on the 2-semester system and offers two summer sessions. Enrollment is 628 women full-time and 534 women part-time. A faculty of 54 full-time and 68 part-time gives a faculty-student ratio of 1-10. The college grants credit to students who are admitted to establish overseas programs conducted by other American colleges.

Entrance Requirements: Accredited high school graduation with rank in upper 50% of graduating class; completion of 16 college-preparatory units including 4 English, 3 mathematics, 1 laboratory science, 2 foreign language, 2 social studies, and 4 electives; $30 application fee; SAT required; rolling admission and delayed admission programs available; admission is competitive.

Costs Per Year: $12,700 tuition; $5,800 room and board; $400 books and supplies.

Collegiate Environment: The college includes 14 buildings and is located on the property of the former Morrison Estate, comprising 168 acres of beautifully wooded land. Residence facilities are provided for 440 women and the college library contains 141,290 volumes, 762 periodicals, and 28,735 microforms and sound recordings. The college welcomes a geographically diverse student body and 85% of students applying for admission are accepted. Classes begin in September and midyear students are admitted. Financial aid is available for economically handicapped students. There are a total of 451 scholarships, 117 of which are for first year students.

Community Environment: Regis College is in a suburban community located approximately 12 miles west of Boston. Community services, cultural and recreational facilities are located in Boston.

SAINT HYACINTH COLLEGE AND SEMINARY   *(F-5)*
66 School Street
Granby, Massachusetts 01033
Tel: (413) 467-7191; Fax: (413) 467-9609

Description: This Catholic college and seminary for men is conducted by the Order of Friars Minor Conventual. It operates on the semester system. Women are accepted in the Lay Ministry and A.A. Religious Studies Program (evening). The college is accredited by the New England Association of Schools and Colleges. Enrollment is 13 full-time, 16 part-time, and 27 evening students. A faculty of 9 full-time and 7 part-time gives a faculty-student ratio of 1-7.

Entrance Requirements: Accredited high school graduation; completion of 16 college-preparatory units including 4 English, 2 mathematics, 2 modern language, 1 science, and 2 social science; SAT or ACT required; early decision, rolling admission, midyear admission and advanced placement plans available; $25 application fee.

Costs Per Year: $3,600 tuition; $4,500 room and board; $185 student fees.

Collegiate Environment: The institution is comprised of five buildings located on 600 acres, and includes a library of 52,000 volumes and 157 periodicals, and dormitory facilities for 55 men. The college welcomes a geographically diverse student body and 85% of students applying for admission are accepted. Classes begin in September and midyear students are admitted provisionally.

Community Environment: Suburban community located six miles northeast of Holyoke. Bus service is available. City has public library and shopping center. Recreational facilities include a gymnasium, lake-cottage, and tennis courts.

SAINT JOHN'S SEMINARY COLLEGE OF LIBERAL ARTS
(D-13)
197 Foster Street
Brighton, Massachusetts 02135
Tel: (617) 254-2610

Description: This Roman Catholic seminary is the only diocesan seminary in New England offering a four-year program preparatory to priesthood. The college is accredited by the New England Association of Schools and Colleges. It grants the Bachelor of Arts degree in its College of Liberal Arts. It operates on the semester system and enrolls 101 men. This enrollment figure contains students from all of the suffragan dioceses of the New England province as well as six other dioceses. A faculty of 11 full-time and 14 part-time members gives a faculty-student ratio of 1-2.

Entrance Requirements: Accredited high school graduation with rank in upper fifty percent of high school class; completion of 11 college-preparatory units including 4 English, 3 mathematics, 2 foreign language, 2 social science; seminary test, SAT required; personal interview and three letters of recommendation from 2 priests required; Early decision and rolling admission.

Costs Per Year: $6,000 for tuition which also includes room and board; $50 student fees.

Collegiate Environment: The college of Liberal Arts provides dormitory facilities for 120 men and the libraries contain over 129,000 volumes. Financial assistance is available and about 50% of the students receive aid. 60% percent of the applicants is accepted.

Community Environment: See Boston University.

SALEM STATE COLLEGE   *(C-14)*
352 Lafayette Street
Salem, Massachusetts 01970
Tel: (508) 741-6200

Description: Salem State College, established in 1854, is a multi-purpose educational institution that offers a wide variety of both professional and liberal arts programs. The college is accredited by the New England Association of Schools and Colleges, the National Council for Accreditation of Teacher Education, Social Work and Nursing and several other professional accrediting associations. It operates on the semester system and offers two summer sessions. Enrollment is 5,450 full-time students. A faculty of 292 full-time and 28 part-time gives a faculty-student ratio of 1-20. Noted for its strengths in Business Administration, Nursing, Theatre, Social Work, Geogra-

phy, Sciences and Education, the college provides each student with a diverse selection of courses in an effort to meet their educational needs. An overseas program is available.

Entrance Requirements: Accredited high school graduation or its equivalent; completion of 16 units including 4 English, 3 mathematics, 2 foreign language, 2 social science, and 2 science; SAT scores; $10 application fee for state residents, $40 application fee for out-of-state applicants; early decision, early admission, rolling admissions, midyear admission, and advanced placement plans available; portfolio required of art majors.

Costs Per Year: $1,408 tuition; $5,542 out-of-state tuition; $3,789 room and board; $1,790 student fees.

Collegiate Environment: The college is situated on 62 acres one quarter of a mile from the ocean with 17 buildings that include a modern library of 330,493 volumes, 1,401 periodicals, and 300,100 microforms; a new sports complex; modern classrooms; and dormitories that house approximately 1,000 students. New and transfer students are accepted in September and January. The Financial Aid Office provides need-based financial aid, including loans, work and scholarships or grants. 60% of students currently receive aid. 60% of applicants are accepted.

Community Environment: Salem State College is located in Salem, Massachusetts. Salem was founded in 1626, and is one of the oldest cities in the country. It was one of the most active seaports in the New World, and was the capital of the Massachusetts Bay Colony until 1630. Salem was the site of the witchcraft trials in which the accusations of group of children and women caused 19 people to be hanged and one pressed to death. Many handsome old houses reminiscent of the days when sea captains and China merchants grew rich from importing are still to be seen. Marblehead harbor, one of the yatching capitals of the world, is only three miles away. The city is located approximately 14 miles north of Boston, is suburban in nature and has good bus and train service.

SCHOOL OF THE MUSEUM OF FINE ARTS   *(D-13)*
230 The Fenway
Boston, Massachusetts 02115
Tel: (617) 267-1218; (800) 643-6078; Fax: (617) 424-6271

Description: This private art school awards a diploma to those who successfully complete its professional program, and also offers degree programs in affiliation with Tufts University. The school operates on the semester system and offers three summer sessions. It is accredited by the National Association of Schools of Art and Design and offers Bachleor and Masters degrees. Enrollment is 612 full-time, 93 part-time, and 835 evening students. A faculty of 56 full-time and 70 part-time gives a faculty-student ratio of 1-10. There are 57 graduate students.

Entrance Requirements: Accredited high school graduation; transcripts from secondary school and any post-secondary school attended; $30 application fee; art portfolio of original work required; early admission, early decision, rolling admission and delayed admission plans available.

Costs Per Year: $13,980 tuition; $390 miscellaneous.

Collegiate Environment: The school is located in one main building and contains a library of 12,000 volumes, 90 periodicals, 225 pamphlets, and 50,000 slides. It has no dormitory facilities under its jurisdiction but housing facilities are available in the immediate area. Financial aid is available for economically handicapped students and 60% of the students receive some form of aid. 73% of the applicants meet the requirements and are accepted.

Community Environment: See Boston University.

SIMMONS COLLEGE   *(D-13)*
300 The Fenway
Boston, Massachusetts 02115
Tel: (617) 521-2000; (800) 345-8468; Fax: (617) 521-3190

Description: The private, nonsectarian college for women was chartered in 1899. It accepts men into its graduate programs only. The college operates on the semester system with two summer terms and is accredited by the New England Association of Schools and Colleges. Recent undergraduate enrollment was 1,160 women full-time, 150 part-time; graduate students include 2,212 men and women. An undergraduate faculty of 106 full-time equivalent gives a faculty-student ratio of 1-10.

Entrance Requirements: Accredited high school graduation or equivalent; completion of college-preparatory courses; SAT or ACT plus three Achievement Tests required; advanced placement, early admission, early decision, midyear admission and delayed admission plans available. $35 application fee.

Costs Per Year: $16,960 tuition; $7,228 room and board; $536 student fees.

Collegiate Environment: The undergraduate college consists of two campuses. The Fenway Campus is the site of the academic program, and the Brookline Avenue Campus serves as the residential center. They are situated one block apart and are within easy walking distance of each other. Dormitory facilities for 800 women are available, and the college library contains 260,000 volumes. Honors and nee-based scholarships are available and 69% of the undergraduates receive some form of financial aid.

Community Environment: Simmons College is next door to the Isabella Stewart Gardner Museum and two blocks away from the Museum of Fine Arts. Other nearby attractions are Fenway Park, the Charles River, Beacon Hill, Back Bay, Cambridge and the North End. Complete inter-city transportation is available.

SIMON'S ROCK COLLEGE OF BARD   *(F-1)*
Alford Road
Great Barrington, Massachusetts 01230
Tel: (413) 528-0771; (800) 235-7186; Admissions: (413) 528-7312;
Fax: (413) 528-7334

Description: The residential coeducational, academic institution opened in 1966 and is accredited by the New England Association of Schools and Colleges. The college offers two- and four-year liberal arts programs leading to the Associate and Bachelor degrees to students who have completed the 10th or 11th grade. It operates on the semester system and offers one summer session. Enrollment includes 155 men and 150 women. A faculty of 39 full-time and 8 part-time gives a faculty-student ratio of 1-9.

Entrance Requirements: Completion of tenth grade; PSAT or SAT required; June 15 application deadline; early admission and midyear admission plans available; $25 application fee.

Costs Per Year: $16,900 tuition; $5,620 board and room; $2,000 student fees.

Collegiate Environment: The campus is located on 270 acres and contains 15 buildings which include both single sex and coed dormitory facilities for 300 and a library of 55,000 volumes, 330 periodicals, and 1,130 audiovisual materials. Approximately 60% of those applying for admission are accepted. Classes begin in September and midyear students are accepted. Financial aid is available and 71% of the student body receives some form of aid. 85% of the freshman class returned for their second year.

Community Environment: A wooded suburban community with many scenic areas. The area has resorts and is the shopping center of the Southern Berkshires. Two miles east is Butternut Basin Ski area which has excellent facilities for winter sports. Seasonal part-time employment is available for students.

SMITH COLLEGE   *(E-4)*
Northampton, Massachusetts 01063
Tel: (413) 584-2700; Fax: (413) 585-2527

Description: The private, nonsectarian college for women was established in 1875 and is accredited by the New England Association of Schools and Colleges. Smith is a member of a College Cooperative with Amherst College, Hampshire College, Mount Holyoke College, and the University of Massachusetts, whereby the institutions combine their academic activities in selected areas for the purpose of extending and enriching their collective educational resources. In addition, a student in good standing with the necessary qualifications at any of the institutions may take a course, without additional cost, at any of the other institutions if the course is appropriate to the educational plan of the student. The college grants the Bachelor, Master's and Doctoral degrees. The college also offers a Junior Year Abroad in France, Switzerland, Germany, and Italy, and students may participate in many other programs such as those in Spain, India, republics of the

former Soviet Union, England, Rome, Japan, and China with which the college has formal affiliation. The college operates on the 4-1-4 calendar system. Enrollment includes 2,452 full-time and 85 part-time undergraduates and 97 graduates students. A faculty of 252 full-time and 24 part-time gives a faculty-student ratio of 1-10.

Entrance Requirements: High school graduation or equivalent with high academic and personal promise; completion of 16 units including 4 English, 3 mathematics, 3 foreign language, 2 science, 2 history, 2 social science; SAT and three Achievement Tests required or ACT; early decision, early admission, deferred admission and advanced placement programs available; rolling admission for transfer students only; admission is competitive; application fee $45; personal interview is strongly recommended.

Costs Per Year: $18,820 tuition; $6,390 room and board; $163 student fees.

Collegiate Environment: The college is located on 125 acres and includes 100 buildings. Dormitory facilities are available for 2,348 women. The library contains 1,108,536 volumes, 3,213 periodicals, 51,105 records and tapes, and 62,238 microforms. Approximately 52% of the students applying for admission are accepted. 90% of the freshmen return to the college for their sophomore year. Almost all of the recent student body graduated in the top quarter of the high school class and 51% of those for whom rank was given ranked in the top tenth. The middle 50% range of scores for the entering freshman class were SAT 540-640 verbal, 550-650 math, ACT 26-29 composite. Scholarships are available and 52% of the students receive some form of financial aid.

Community Environment: Settled in 1654, Northampton was an isolated frontier village for its first 150 years. Today there is a population of 30,000. Part-time work is available for students. Located in the western-central part of state about 18 miles north of Springfield, the area is easily accessible to good recreational sites. The city has a community hospital, theatres, art galleries, parks, and several hotels and motels.

SPRINGFIELD COLLEGE   *(G-5)*
263 Alden Street
Springfield, Massachusetts 01109
Tel: (413) 748-3136; (800) 343-1257; Fax: (413) 748-3694

Description: Established in 1885, the college was known as The International YMCA Training School. The college operates on the semester system and also offers two summer terms. It is accredited by the New England Association of Schools and Colleges. The college grants a Baccalaureate, Master and Doctoral degree. The college has exchange programs with a variety of countries and is a member of AIFS. Recently, the college enrolled 972 men, 959 women full-time, 40 men, 39 women part-time, and 233 graduate students. A faculty of 151 full-time, 103 part-time gives a student-faculty ratio of 1-12.

Entrance Requirements: Accredited high school graduation; completion of 16 units including 4 English, 3 mathematics, 2 science, 2 lang., 2 social science; SAT required; rolling admission, delayed admission and advanced placement programs available; $30 application fee.

Costs Per Year: $11,870 tuition and fees; $5,400 room and board.

Collegiate Environment: The college is located on 164 acres. The school's 29 buildings include a library of 150,000 volumes, 846 periodicals, 260,000 microforms, and 4,000 audiovisual materials. Dormitory facilities accommodate all students. About 82% of students applying for admission meet the requirements and are accepted. The college welcomes students from various geographical locations and nearly all students accepted for entrance are highly motivated to follow careers of human service upon graduation. Classes begin in September and freshmen students are eligible for admission for either Fall or Spring semester Approximately 70% of the recent student body graduated in the top half of the high school class, 26% in the top third. Financial aid is available for qualified students in need.

Community Environment: Established as a trading post in 1636, Springfield is located on the Connecticut River in Southwestern part of the state. City is noted today for its diversified industries including the manufacture of firearms, plastics, chemicals, radio equipment, tires, paper, and electrical equipment. Ample part-time job opportunities available. Several movie theatres, municipal auditorium, drive-ins, summer theatre, two municipal golf courses, 150 parks, civic center, and playgrounds, swimming, skating, quadrangle of museums, public libraries, provide excellent recreational and cultural opportunities. Easy access to commercial, bus and rail service.

SPRINGFIELD TECHNICAL COMMUNITY COLLEGE
(G-5)
One Armory Square
Springfield, Massachusetts 01105
Tel: (413) 781-7822

Description: This state-governed community college offers courses in vocational-technical areas for part-time and terminal programs. The school operates on the semester system and offers two summer terms. It is accredited by the New England Association of Schools and Colleges, and by several professional associations including the American Dental Association, the American Physical Therapy Association, the National League for Nursing, and the Committee on Allied Health Education and Accreditation. Enrollment is 2,701 full-time, 1,109 part-time and 2,396 evening division students. A faculty of 177 full-time, 57 part-time and 180 evening division gives a faculty-student ratio of 1-18.

Entrance Requirements: Accredited high school graduation or equivalent; completion of 16 units; SAT required for specified Health programs: nursing, P.T.A., radiography, dental hygiene, medical lab technician, nuclear medicine, and radiation therapy; $10 application fee for state residents; $35 application fee for out-of-state residents; rolling admission and advanced placement plans available.

Costs Per Year: $1,050 tuition; $4,872 out-of-state; $878 student fees; additional mandatory insurance fee.

Collegiate Environment: The college is located on 55 acres and contains 27 buildings that include a library of 58,060 volumes, 18,849 pamphlets, 462 periodicals, 171 microforms and 3,624 audiovisual materials. Approximately 82% of students applying for admission are accepted, and midyear students are admitted for certain programs. Classes begin in September and January. 43% of the students receive some form of financial aid.

Community Environment: See Springfield College.

STONEHILL COLLEGE   *(G-13)*
320 Washington Street
North Easton, Massachusetts 02357
Tel: (508) 238-1081; Admissions: (508) 230-1373; Fax: (508) 230-3732

Description: This private Roman Catholic College of Arts and Sciences was established by the Congregation of the Holy Cross in 1948. It operates on the semester system and offers two summer terms. It is accredited by the New England Association of Schools and Colleges, the National Council for Accreditation of Teacher Education, and the Association of University Programs in Health Administration. A Foreign Studies Program is available as well as International Internships in Brussels, Dublin, London, Madrid, Montreal, and Paris. A student exchange program between Stonehill College and Yaroslavl State University in the Soviet Union, a Stonehill-Quebec Exchange, domestic academic internships, and field study for course credit are also available. 3-1 or 4-1 Medical Technology programs are also offered. Recent Day Division enrollment included 835 men, 1,080 women full-time; 16 men and 12 women part-time. A Day Division faculty of 116 full-time and 68 part-time gives a student-faculty ratio of 17-1. Stonehill also has an Evening College offering degree programs on a full- and part-time basis. Recent Evening Division enrollment included 11 men, 22 women full-time; 264 men and 612 women part-time. The Evening Division faculty comprises 84 part-time faculty members.

Entrance Requirements: Freshman: Accredited high school graduation; completion of 16 academic units including 4 English, 2 Mathematics (1 Algebra, 1 Geometry), 2 Foreign Language (single language), 1 Science, 1 History, and 6 electives (no more than 3 may be in Business subjects); SAT or ACT, high school record (including class rank and test information), essay, and guidance counselor recommendation required. Transfer: Accredited high school graduation; official high school record; official transcripts and catalogs from all colleges/universities attended; a financial aid transcript; SAT or ACT required. TOEFL reqiored of foreign applicants. Advanced place-

ment, early admission, midyear admission, and delayed admission plans available. Application fee $40.

Costs Per Year: $12,170 tuition; $6,172 room and board.

Collegiate Environment: The campus of 375 acres is located 20 miles south of Boston. The college buildings include a library of 151,971 volumes, 1,097 periodical subscriptions, 250,151 microforms, and 2,878 sound recordings. Dormitory and townhouse facilities for 1,500 students. Approximately 64% of students applying for admission are accepted. The college welcomes a geographically diverse student body and 82% of a recent freshman class returned to the campus for the sophomore year. About 95% of entering freshmen graduated in the top half of the high school class; 65% in the top quarter. The average scores of the entering freshman class were SAT 480 verbal, 530 math. Academic and honors scholarships, cultural diversity scholarships, restricted endowment scholarships and academic grants are available. 84% of the students receive some form of financial aid.

Community Environment: College is in Easton, adjoining Brockton and 20 miles south of Boston. Transportation available to Brockton, and Boston subway system. Cultural, recreational and community services quite accessible.

SUFFOLK UNIVERSITY   *(D-13)*
8 Ashburton Place
Boston, Massachusetts 02108-2770
Tel: (617) 573-8460; (800) 678-3365; Fax: (617) 742-4291

Description: This private university was founded in 1906 when the Suffolk Law School was established. In 1937, the Law School and the College of Liberal Arts, Journalism, and Business Administration were incorporated by the action of the Massachusetts Legislature. The university is accredited by the New England Association of Schools and Colleges, and by the American Bar Association, the Association of American Law Schools and the American Association of Collegiate Schools of Business. It operates on the semster system and offers two summer sessions. Enrollment includes 2,395 full-time and 2,105 part-time undergraduates and 1,007 day and 675 evening students. A faculty of 200 full-time and 147 part-time gives a faculty-student ratio of 1-14.

Entrance Requirements: Accredited high school graduation with rank in upper 60% of graduating class; completion of 16 units including 4 English, 3 mathematics, 2 natural science with laboratory, 2 social science including 1 American history, 2 foreign language, and 3 electives; SAT required; 3 CEEB achievement tests optional; GRE required for graduate school; early decision, advanced placement, early admission, rolling admission, midyear admission and delayed admission plans available; $30 application fee.

Costs Per Year: $11,300 tuition; $150 student fees.

Collegiate Environment: The university is comprised of ten buildings and includes a law library of 173,249 volumes/periodicals, and 104,624 microforms. The graduate and undergraduate library consists of 105,000 volumes, 1,330 periodicals, and 167,000 microform units. As an urban university, Suffolk has a degree of commuting students, yet provides dormitory and other housing options for resident students. 80% of students applying for admission are accepted. The average SAT scores of recent freshmen were 450 verbal and 450 math. Scholarships are available and more than 73% of the students receive some form of financial aid. The university offers a celebrated retention program, consisting of intensive academic counseling and academic support services for its students.

Community Environment: Suffolk University is located in the heart of Boston, a city rich in history and culture. In addition to being an international center for high-technology, finance, architecture, and medicine, Boston boasts over 50 of the finest colleges and universities in the nation. Founded in 1630, ten years after the Pilgrims landed at Plymouth, Boston is the capital of the Commonwealth of Massachusetts and is the largest city in New England. The city of Boston has a population of over 600,000 people whose heritage is drawn worldwide. There is always something to do in Boston. The Freedom Trail brings you to 16 landmarks significant to our nation's history, including Faneuil Hall, the Old North Church, Paul Revere's house, Old Ironsides and the Bunker Hill Monument. Hidden throughout Boston are treasures such as the Isabella Stewart Gardner Museum and the African Meeting House, which is the oldest black church building still standing in this country. In Boston, entertainment takes on many different forms. You can attend the Boston Ballet, the Boston Symphony Orchestra, and the theatre, as well as comedy clubs and clubs featuring many different types of music. In addition, Boston offers some of the finest shopping and dining facilities in the country. Boston is also the home of four championship sports teams -- the Boston Bruins, the Boston Celtics, the Boston Red Sox, and the New England Patriots. Transportation is one of Boston's greatest assets. Boston is accessible by public transportation, commuter rail, bus service, air service, and taxi service. Due to its size, Boston is also an excellent walking city. At the hub of the transportation system is Suffolk University, on the edge of Beacon Hill, a maze of brick sidewalks and cobblestone streets, 18th and 19th century townhouses and mansions. The area was settled by the Boston Brahmins and is still one of the most desirable addresses.

TUFTS UNIVERSITY   (D-13)
Medford, Massachusetts 02155
Tel: (617) 627-3170; Fax: (617) 627-3860

Description: Founded in 1852 as a private, liberal arts college, Tufts has grown into a small modern university. The undergraduate colleges include a College of Liberal Arts for men and women and the College of Engineering. The graduate schools include the Graduate School of Arts and Sciences, the Fletcher School of Law and Diplomacy, the School of Medicine, the School of Dental Medicine, the School of Veterinary Medicine, the School of Nutrition, the Sackler School of Biomedical Sciences, and the Gordon Institute of Engineering Management. The university operates on the semester system and offers two summer sessions. It is accredited by the New England Association of Schools and Colleges. Army, Navy and Air Force ROTC programs are available through MIT. Tufts offers programs in London, Paris, Madrid, Tubingen, Germany, and Moscow. It has a consortium program in Lenningrad, and Engineering programs in Lyon, France and Sussex, England. Selected summer programs are offered in Talloires, France. Special programs offered include a 5-year Engineering-Liberal Arts, 5-year BA/BM with the New England Conservatory of Music, 5-year BA/BFA with the Museum School of Fine Arts and 5-year BA/MA or BS/MS Programs. Enrollment includes 4,550 undergraduates. A faculty of 330 full-time and 236 part-time gives a faculty-student ratio of 1-13.

Entrance Requirements: All candidates are evaluated individually on the basis of credentials submitted; most successful applicants have graduated from secondary school in the top 10% of their class and show high intellectual achievement and potential; recommended completion of 16 units including 4 English, 3 mathematics, 2 science, and 2 social science; SAT I and 3 SAT II subject tests required (1 English and 2 others of the student's choice). ACT accepted in place of SAT I and SAT II, for engineering, this choice should be mathematics and either chemistry or physics; $50 application fee; early admission, early decision, delayed admission with special permission, and advanced placement plans available.

Costs Per Year: $19,701 tuition; $5,968 room and board; $503 student fees.

Collegiate Environment: The university contains 150 buildings that include a library system of 803,000 volumes, 4,793 periodicals, 967,000 microforms, and 22,000 audiovisual materials. Living accommodations for 3,550 students are provided. Approximately 45% of students applying for admission are accepted. The university welcomes a geographically diverse student body and will accept midyear transfer students. About 91% of a recent student body graduated in the top quarter of the high school class and 99% of a recent freshman class returned to the university for the sophomore year. The middle 50% ranges of scores for the entering freshmen class SAT 540-630 verbal, 620-700 math. Financial aid is based on need and almost 40% of the undergraduate student body received some form of financial aid. The university sponsors programs abroad in France, Germany, England, Russia and Spain. Campus life is supported by over 140 student organizations, 33 intercollegiate sports for men and women, and very active drama, music and dance activities. A number of combined programs are available.

Community Environment: This is a residential suburb of Boston, located approximately five miles northwest of the city. One of the oldest settlements in the Commonwealth and in the United States, Medford was founded in 1630 and has many historical points of interest. Beautiful Mystic Lakes are located on northwest border of the city, and further recreational opportunities are provided by the Middlesex Fells,

a mountainous reservation of approximately 4,000 acres. Part-time employment is available in Boston.

UNIVERSITY OF MASSACHUSETTS - AMHERST CAMPUS (D-5)
Amherst, Massachusetts 01003
Tel: (413) 545-0222; Fax: (413) 545-4312

Description: Incorporated as Massachusetts Agricultural College in 1863, the state university opened to a handful of students in 1867 and has grown steadily. Current enrollment is 19,005 full-time students and 6,133 graduate students. A faculty of 1,174 full-time and 116 part-time gives a faculty-student ratio of 1-17. The University is composed of the Stockbridge School of Agriculture; the colleges of Humanities and Fine Arts, Natural Sciences and Mathematics, Social and Behaviorial Sciences; Engineering and Food and Natural Resources; and the schools of Education, Public Health and Health Sciences, Nursing, and Management. The University operates on the semester system with two summer terms and a one month winter term. Army and Air Force ROTC are available. Cooperative Education programs are available. There are also over 60 international exchanges with approximately 30 countries. It is accredited by the New England Association of Schools and Colleges and various professional organizations.

Entrance Requirements: Accredited high school graduation; completion of 16 college-preparatory units including 4 English, 3 mathematics, 2 foreign language, 2 science, and 2 social science; SAT required; rolling admission, deferred admission and advanced placement available.

Costs Per Year: $5,467 tuition and fees; $11,813 out-of-state; $4,028 room and board; $20 application fee; $35 out-of-state application fee.

Collegiate Environment: The Amherst Campus of the University consists of approximately 1,405 acres of land and 150 buildings. These structures include classroom and laboratory facilities and residence halls as well as a library system including 2,647,378 volumes, 15,312 periodical titles, 623,150 documents in a separate government documents collection, and 2,062,096 microforms. Living accomodations are provided for 5,405 men and 5,154 women, with 329 off-campus college housing units occupied. Approximately 78% of students applying for admission meet the requirements and are accepted. Almost 29% of the 1994 entering students graduated in the top fifth of their high school class and 76% were in the top half; average SAT scores for middle 50% of class are 420-530V, 480-610M. Various special curricula and programs are available, including an honors program, the unique majors of Social Thought & Political Economy, and Bachelor's Degree with Individualized concentration, interdisciplinary majors, exchange and study abroad. The University is also a member of the Five College Consortium with Amherst, Mount Holyoke, Hampshire and Smith Colleges, allowing students access to courses and facilities at these other institutions.

Community Environment: See Amherst College.

UNIVERSITY OF MASSACHUSETTS - BOSTON   (D-13)
Harbor Campus
Boston, Massachusetts 02125
Tel: (617) 287-6000; Admissions: (617) 287-6100; Fax: (617) 265-7173

Description: To augment the Commonwealth of Massachusetts facilities at the university level, the University of Massachusetts at Boston was opened in 1965. It is accredited by the New England Association of Schools and Colleges and the National League for Nursing. It offers educational programs comparable in quality to those available in Amherst. The coeducational university operates on the semester system and offers two summer terms. Enrollment includes 12,500 full-time and 2,700 part-time undergraduates and 3,500 graduate students. A faculty of 400 full-time and 270 part-time gives an overall faculty-student ratio of 1-16.

Entrance Requirements: Accredited high school graduation with rank in upper quarter of graduating class; completion of 16 college-preparatory units including 4 English, 3 mathematics, 2 foreign language, 2 science, 2 social science, and 3 college preparatory electives; SAT required; early decision and advanced placement plans available; $20 application fee for state residents, $35 application fee for out-of-state applicants.

Costs Per Year: $2,154 tuition; $4,284 out-of-state; $737 student fees.

Collegiate Environment: The university is comprised of six buildings, including a library of 500,000 volumes and 2,000 periodicals. Approximately 60% of students applying for admission are accepted including midyear students. An area exchange program with other universities is offered. Financial aid is available for economically handicapped students, and 70% of students receive some form of financial aid.

Community Environment: See Boston University.

UNIVERSITY OF MASSACHUSETTS - DARTMOUTH
(J-13)
285 Old Westport Road
North Dartmouth, Massachusetts 02747
Tel: (508) 999-8000; Fax: (508) 999-8775

Description: This publicly supported, coeducational institution of higher learning is composed of undergraduate colleges in arts and science, business and industry, engineering, nursing, and visual and performing arts as well as a school of graduate studies. It operates on the semester system and provides two summer terms and an evening school. The Southeastern Massachusetts Technological Institute was created in 1960 by the General Court of the Commonwealth of Massachusetts and is accredited by the New England Association of Schools and Colleges. The present name was adopted in 1969 and university status was granted. Enrollment is 4,781 full-time and 505 part-time undergraduates, and 464 graduate students. A faculty of 319 full time, 95 part time, and 108 evening gives an undergraduate faculty-student ratio of 1-16.

Entrance Requirements: Accredited high school graduation with rank in upper half of graduating class; completion of 12 units including 4 English, 2 mathematics, 2 social science, 2 natural (laboratory) science, 2 foreign language; SAT required; GRE required for graduate programs; advanced placement, early admission, early decision, deferred admission, midyear admission, and rolling admission plans available; $20 resident application fee, $40 out-of-state application fee.

Costs Per Year: $1,836 tuition; $6,919 out-of-state; $4,850 room and board; $1,989 student fees.

Collegiate Environment: The university is located on 730 acres and includes a library of 415,658 volumes, 2,755 periodicals, 43,505 microforms, and 8,991 audiovisual materials. Dormitory facilities are available for 2,100 students. Approximately 71% of students applying for admission are accepted, including students at midyear. The average scores of enrolled freshmen were SAT 914 combined. Financial aid is available for economically disadvantaged students and 42% of the students receive some form of aid. Of 25 scholarships, 20 are available for freshmen.

Community Environment: North Dartmouth is located near the larger city of New Bedford, MA. This city, on Buzzard's Bay, was once the greatest whaling port in the world. Fishing fleet and allied industries contribute one-fifth of New Bedford's income. The city is also known for the manufacture of fine textile goods, plastics, tire fabrics, boats, golf balls, cut glass and other products. Part-time job opportunities are available for students. The area is easily accessible by train, bus, and airlines. The city has a library and whaling museum. Major community services are located in the immediate area.

UNIVERSITY OF MASSACHUSETTS - LOWELL   *(B-11)*
1 University Avenue
Lowell, Massachusetts 01854
Tel: (508) 934-4000

Description: In 1975 Lowell State College and Lowell Technological Institute merged into one university. The university is fully accredited by the New England Association of Schools and Colleges. It operates on the semester system, and offers two summer terms. Graduate school is both full and part-time day. Recent enrollment included 5,976 men, 3,627 women full-time, 2,464 men, and 1,166 women. A faculty of 463 full-time and 390 part-time gives an overall faculty-student ratio of 1-16.

Entrance Requirements: High school graduation or equivalent; completion of 16 academic units; SAT required; Audition required for

music. GRE required for graduate programs; advanced placement, delayed admission and rolling admission plans available; $10 application fee for state residents; $25 out-of-state application fee.

Costs Per Year: $4,513 tuition; $9,424 out-of-state tuition; $4,173 room and board.

Collegiate Environment: The college is located 25 miles northwest of Boston and is situated on a 100-acre campus. It has a library of 395,000 volumes and dormitory facilities for 2,400 students and off campus apartments for 140 undergraduates. Special facilities include a $5.5 million nuclear science center. Financial aid is available for economically disadvantaged students and 40% of the current students receive some form of aid. Classes begin in September and midyear students are accepted.

Community Environment: in the metropolitan area, the cotton and woolen plants once caused city to be known as "the spindle city." Today, textile manufacture has been de-emphasized and industry is diversified with electronics paramount. Lowell is the home of the only federal Urban National Park. Part-time employment available for students. Commercial air, rail, and bus service is easily accessible. Community has public library, churches of all denominations, YMCA, YWCA, art gallery, and hospitals. All sports facilities are available as well as beaches, theatres, and famous ski area within a short distance.

WELLESLEY COLLEGE   *(E-12)*
106 Central Street
Wellesley, Massachusetts 02181
Tel: (617) 283-2270; Fax: (617) 283-3678

Description: This private liberal arts college for women was established in 1870. It is accredited by the New England Association of Schools and Colleges. The college sponsors programs in France, West Germany, and Spain. Students may study in other countries by applying to other colleges' programs. Special programs include an interdisciplinary program for first year students, Twelve College Exchange, Peace Studies Program, Technology Studies Program and cross-registration with MIT, Brandeis, Babson, Spellman, and Mills. It operates on the semester system. Enrollment includes 2,271 full-time and 177 part-time students. A faculty of 237 full-time and 95 part-time gives a faculty-student ratio of 1-10.

Entrance Requirements: Accredited high school graduation with high academic performance; completion of 4 units of English, 3-4 mathematics, 4 foreign language, 3 science, 4 social science; evidence that applicant has taken the most challenging program available at her high school; SAT and three Achievement Tests required; personal interview strongly recommended; early decision, advanced placement, early admission, early evaluation, and delayed admission plans available; $45 application fee.

Costs Per Year: $16,690 tuition; $5,885 room and board; $325 student fees.

Collegiate Environment: The campus of more than 500 acres is situated 12 miles west of Boston. The 87 college buildings include dormitory facilities for 2,096 women and a library of 844,012 volumes, 2,824 periodicals, 194,556 microforms, and 14,214 audiovisual materials. The college welcomes a geographically diverse student body and 49% of the students applying for admission are accepted. Classes begin in September; freshmen are not admitted at midyear. Financial aid is available based on economic need. 52% of the students receives some form of financial aid.

Community Environment: The campus is located in a suburb of Boston 15 miles from the heart of the city. Railroad and bus transportation is available. Community services, and cultural and recreational facilities are found in adjacent Boston.

WENTWORTH INSTITUTE OF TECHNOLOGY   *(D-13)*
550 Huntington Avenue
Boston, Massachusetts 02115
Tel: (617) 442-9010

Description: This private college was founded in 1904 for the purpose of furnishing education in the mechanical arts. The college is accredited by the New England Association of Schools and Colleges. It is professionally accredited by the Foundation for Interior Design Education Research and the National Architecture Accrediting Board. The college grants the Bachelor degree. It operates on the semester system and offers one summer session. Enrollment includes 2,800 students. A faculty of 120 full-time and 97 part-time members creates a student-faculty ratio of 1-14.

Entrance Requirements: Accredited high school graduation with rank in upper 60% of graduating class; completion of 15 units including 4 English, 3 mathematics, 1 science; entrance examinations or SAT recommended; advanced placement plan and rolling admission available. $30 application fee.

Costs Per Year: $9,850 tuition; $6,050 board and room.

Collegiate Environment: The institute contains 15 buildings which include a library of 80,000 volumes and dormitory facilities for 700 students. Approximately 79% of students applying for admission are accepted. About 50% of the recent student body graduated in the top half of the high school class, 20% in the top quarter, and 10% in the highest tenth. Classes begin in September and 75% of the previous freshman class returned to the institute for the second year of studies. A variety of scholarships are available and 62% of the students receive some form of financial aid.

Community Environment: See Boston University

WESTERN NEW ENGLAND COLLEGE   *(G-5)*
1215 Wilbraham Road
Springfield, Massachusetts 01119-2688
Tel: (413) 782-3111; (800) 325-1122; Admissions: (413) 782-1321;
Fax: (413) 782-1777

Description: In 1919, Northeastern University established a Springfield Division, which in 1951 became Western New England College. It is a private, nonsectarian institution that seeks to combine liberal with professional education. The undergraduate college is organized into the School of Engineering, the School of Business, and the School of Arts & Sciences. The College is accredited by the New England Association of Schools and Colleges; the School of Law is accredited by the American Bar Association. Curricula leading to the degrees of Bachelor of Science in Electrical, Industrial, and Mechanical Engineering are accredited by the Engineering Accreditation Commission of the Accreditation Board for Engineering and Technology. The Bachelor of Social Work degree program is accredited by the Council on Social Work Education. Army and Air Force ROTC programs are available. A 3-2 Pre-Pharmacy program with Massachusetts College of Pharmacy and Allied Health Sciences is available. The college operates ont eh semester system and offers two summer sessions. Undergraduate enrollment is 1,673 full-time and 1,050 part-time students. A faculty of 102 full-time and 142 part-time gives a faculty-student ratio of 1-17. In the Law School, an enrollment of 486 full-time students and a full-time faculty of 25 gives a ratio of 1-19.

Entrance Requirements: Undergraduate: accredited high school graduation; completion of 4 units of English, 2-4 mathematics, 1-4 laboratory science, and 1 U.S. history; SAT or ACT required; $30 application fee; rolling admission plan available. Graduate: bachelor's degree from an accredited college or university; $35 application fee; GMAT, GRE or LSAT required.

Costs Per Year: Undergraduate: $9,510 tuition; $5,740 room and board; $800 fees. Graduate: $262/credit hour tuition; $7/credit hour fees. Law: $13,890 full-time tuition; $10,416 part-time tuition; $510 full-time fees; $228 part-time fees.

Collegiate Environment: The College campus of 131 acres is located in a residential section of Springfield. Classes are centered in four buildings that provide almost 70 classrooms and laboratories. Many of the faculty offices are in these buildings as well as modern computer facilities that are available to all students. The D'Amour Library contains approximately 118,139 volumes, 440 periodicals, 253 microforms, 2,092 tapes, records, and compact discs. The D. J. St. Germain Campus Center houses two dining halls, a snack bar, student lounges, conference rooms and the bookstore. Residence facilities ranging from traditional to apartment-style are provided for approximately 1,157 students. The Healthful Living Center, a physical education and recreation complex, will open in fall 1993. It offers modern exercise and fitness equipment, racquetball and squash courts, swimming pool, running and jogging track, and a field house with seating for 2,000. The S. Prestley Blake Law Center consists of two connected buildings and contains a three-story library, tiered lecture halls, classrooms, offices, lounges, and a moot courtoom. The law library offers a collection of approximately 172,726, 4,066 periodicals, 1,152 titles on microform, 1,335 records, tapes and compact discs, and

1,200 audiovisual materials. The College provides a program of financial assistance through scholarships, grants, loans, and part-time employment. Approximately 80% of undergraduate applicants, 94% of graduate applicants and 46% of the Law School applicants are accepted.

Community Environment: The College is located in a residential section of Springfield, Massachusetts, about three miles from the city's downtown area. Because Springfield is a city of 152,000 people, there are a variety of social, cultural, and athletic activities from which to choose. Some of the city's special features are Stage West, a nationally recognized theater group with a 42-week season; the Springfield Symphony; the Quadrangle, a complex of museums; the Basketball Hall of Fame; the Springfield Falcons hockey team; the Eastern States Exposition fairgrounds; and all the activities, shows, and concerts are held in the Springfield Civic Center. Public transportation is available to locations throughout the greater Springfield area. The College is also a member of the Cooperating Colleges of Greater Springfield, a group of 8 private and public colleges in the immediate area.

WESTFIELD STATE COLLEGE   *(F-4)*
Western Avenue
Westfield, Massachusetts 01086
Tel: (413) 568-3311; (800) 322-8401; Fax: (413) 562-3613

Description: The state college is the oldest coeducational teacher-training institution in the United States, having been established in 1838. Today the college offers liberal arts, professional service preparation, and teacher preparation programs and is accredited by the New England Association of Schools and Colleges and the National Council for the Accreditation of Teacher Education. It operates on the semester system and offers two summer sessions. The college has an overseas exchange program and offers an Army ROTC program. Enrollment includes 3,171 full-time, 1,522 part-time, 1,614 evening students and 675 graduate students. A faculty of 166 full-time, 208 part-time and a faculty-student ratio of 1-18.

Entrance Requirements: High school graduation or equivalent; completion of 16 units; SAT required; advanced placement and rolling admission plans available; $10 application fee for in state residents, $40 application fee for out of state residents.

Costs Per Year: $1,408 tuition; $5,244 out-of-state tuition; $4,115 room and board; $1,785 student fees.

Collegiate Environment: The college is comprised of 19 buildings located on 227 acres and includes a library of 160,000 volumes, 1,100 periodicals, and 443,000 microforms. Dormitory facilities house 800 men and 1,200 women. Approximately 60% of students applying for admission are accepted including midyear students and those from various geographical locations. Financial aid is available. Recently the college awarded 948 Bachelor and 122 Master degrees.

Community Environment: Founded in 1669, city is located in southwestern part of state approximately nine miles northwest of Springfield. This is an industrial city manufacturing paper, machinery, and toys. Part-time employment is available for students. Several historical sites are found in the immediate area, including Grandmother's Garden, a municipally owned garden of old-fashioned flowers and herbs. Nearby Stanley Park offers 85 acres of floral gardens, arboretum, concerts, 96-foot high Carillon, covered bridge, old mill, blacksmith shop, and multicolored fountain. Adjacent cities offer many community services.

WESTON SCHOOL OF THEOLOGY   *(D-13)*
3 Phillips Place
Cambridge, Massachusetts 02138
Tel: (617) 492-1960; Fax: (617) 492-5833

Description: The privately supported, coeducational seminary prepares students for ministry in the Catholic Church. Sponsored by the Jesuit Order, the school is accredited by the Association of Theology Schools. It operates on the semester system. Enrollment includes 173 full-time 42 part-time students. A full-time faculty provides a faculty-student ratio of 1-10.

Entrance Requirements: A Bachelor's degree or equivalent from an accredited college is required for acceptance. The GRE or MAT is also required. Application fee is $40.

Costs Per Year: Tuition $8,000.

Collegiate Environment: The seminary's facilities include a library of 250,000 volumes and 800 periodicals. Some financial aid is provided by the school.

Community Environment: See Harvard University

WHEATON COLLEGE   *(G-12)*
East Main Street
Norton, Massachusetts 02766
Tel: (508) 285-8251; (800) 394-6003; Fax: (508) 285-8271

Description: The private four-year coeducational liberal arts college admitted its first coeducational class in September, 1988. It is accredited by the New England Association of Schools and Colleges and the American Chemical Society. The college offers dual degree programs with Dartmouth College and George Washington University in Engineering, and the Univeristy of Rochester in Business; and the Andover-Newton Theological School in Religion, and Emerson College in Communications. Junior year abroad is available to students with at least a B average. The college operates on the semester system. Enrollment includes 1,299 full-time and 32 part-time students. A faculty of 91 full-time and 29 part-time gives a faculty-student ratio of 1:13.

Entrance Requirements: Accredited high school graduation; completion of 17 units with recommended courses of 4 English, 3-4 foreign language, 3-4 mathematics, 3 social studies, 2 science; SAT or ACT and Achievement Tests are optional; early decision; early action; early admission plans available; $50 application fee.

Costs Per Year: $18,460 tuition; $5,970 room and board; $120 student fees.

Collegiate Environment: The 385-acre campus is located in Norton, 45 minutes from Boston and 25 minutes from Providence. It contains more than 50 buildings including a library of 317,000 volumes, 1,300 periodicals, 40,000 microforms titles, and 6,700 sound recordings. Dormitory facilities for 1,254 students are provided. Approximately 77% of students applying for admission meet the requirements and are accepted. The college welcomes a geographically diverse student body and 84% of the previous freshman class returned to the campus for the sophomore year. Eighty-four percent of the current student body graduated in the top half of the high school class. The median SAT scores of the current freshmen were 530 verbal and 550 math. Financial aid is available and 60% of the students receive some form of financial aid. The college granted 313 Bachelor degrees to its graduating class.

Community Environment: Town located in southeastern Massachusetts 35 miles from Boston, and 20 miles from Providence, Rhode Island. Access to railroad and college bus transportation. Community service facilities, recreational and cultural pursuits available in neighboring cities.

WHEELOCK COLLEGE   *(D-13)*
200 The Riverway
Boston, Massachusetts 02215
Tel: (617) 734-5200; Admissions: (617) 734-5200 x206; Fax: (617) 566-4453

Description: This private liberal arts college is accredited by the New England Association of Schools and Colleges. Founded in 1888 with a one-year training program for kindergarten teachers, the college was authorized by the Commonwealth of Massachusetts to award a Master's degree in Education in 1952. The college offers its students professional preparation in Education and Human Services combined with a strong liberal arts education. Students may study early childhood education, special education, elementary education, child life or social work. The college offers field work in the majors during all years of undergraduate or graduate study. It operates on the semester system. Enrollment includes 737 full-time and 30 part-time undergraduates and 521 graduate students. A faculty of 71 full-time and 111 part-time provides a faculty-student ratio of 1-15.

Entrance Requirements: Accredited high school graduation; 16 units including 4 English, 3 mathematics, 1 laboratory science, and 2 social science; SAT or ACT required; personal interview required; early decision, deferred admission, midyear admission, rolling admission, and advanced placement plans available. Feb.15 application deadline; $30 application fee.

Costs Per Year: $13,472 tuition; $5,528 room and board; subject to increase.

Collegiate Environment: The campus is located in Boston and borders a spacious and scenic park. The 11 college buildings include a library of 88,451 volumes, 655 periodicals, 305,300 microforms and 2,300 sound recordings and dormitory facilities for 522 students. The college welcomes a geographically diverse student body and will accept students at midyear. 78% of applicants are accepted. The average scores of the entering freshman class was SAT 430 verbal, 425 math. Scholarships are available and 76% of students receive financial aid.

Community Environment: See Boston University

WILLIAMS COLLEGE   *(B-1)*
Williamstown, Massachusetts 01267
Tel: (413) 597-3131

Description: This independent, privately endowed, liberal arts college was established in 1793. It operates on the 4-1-4 system and is accredited by the New England Association of Schools and Colleges. Enrollment includes 1,962 full-time, 26 part-time, and 57 graduate students. A faculty of 229 full-time and 29 part-time gives a faculty-student ratio of 1-11.

Entrance Requirements: High school graduation; recommended college-preparatory courses including 4 English, 4 mathematics, 3 foreign language, 2 science, and 2 social science; SAT or ACT plus 3 Achievement tests required; personal interview recommended; $50 application fee; early admission, early decision, delayed admission and advanced placement plans available; admission is competitive.

Costs Per Year: $19,629 tuition; $5,790 room and board; $141 student fees.

Collegiate Environment: The college is comprised of 98 buildings located on 450 acres and includes a library of 732,320 volumes, 2,651 periodicals, 387,530 microforms, 401 CD-ROMs, and 17,048 audio-visual materials. Dormitory facilities for 1,871 students are provided. Approximately 26.5% of students applying for admission are accepted. The college welcomes a geographically diverse student body and new students are admitted only for the semester beginning in September. The middle 50% range of recent freshmen scores were SAT Verbal 590-710, SAT Math 650-740. Financial aid is available and 50% of the students receive some form of aid. The college granted 498 Bachelor degrees and 40 Master degrees to the graduating class.

Community Environment: This pleasant colonial town was named for its founder, Col. Ephraim Williams. It is located in the Berkshire Mountains within easy commuting distance of Albany, Boston, and New York. Heavy tourist trade is found here, and the area is known as "Village Beautiful." Excellent facilities are available for skiing, horseback riding, hunting in season, fishing, hiking, bowling and golf. The city has an art museum and its own symphony orchestra. The Tanglewood Music Festival is held nearby annually.

WOODS HOLE OCEANOGRAPHIC INSTITUTION   *(K-15)*
Woods Hole Rd.
Woods Hole, Massachusetts 02543
Tel: (508) 457-2000; Fax: (508) 457-2188

Description: The private institution, founded in 1930 to encourage the study of oceanography, is engaged primarily in basic research. With a staff of over 200 scientists and engineers, and a total personnel of 1,000, the institution carries out research programs within the disciplines of biology, chemistry, geology and geophysics, applied ocean physics and engineering, physical oceanography, and marine policy. Since 1968, the institution has conducted a formal education program offering graduate degrees both jointly with the Massachusetts Institute of Technology in Oceanography - Oceanographic Engineering and independently. There are 154 students pursuing graduate studies. In addition, the Institution offers limited summer student fellowships to advanced undergraduate and beginning graduate students, a summer study program in Geophysical Fluid Dynamics, for advanced graduate students, and 18 month postdoctoral fellowships in ocean study. A Marine Policy postdoctoral program supports interdisciplinary research by marine and social scientists on problems generated by man's increasing use of the sea.

Entrance Requirements: Baccalaureate degree in basic science, engineering or math; application; GRE required; 3 letters of recommendation and a personal statement of scientific interest required; $50 application fee for graduate school only.

Costs Per Year: $26,800 12 month's tuition; $15,600 living expenses.

Collegiate Environment: The institution now occupies two campuses totalling approximately 200 acres. In the village of Woods Hole there are three large laboratories and about a dozen smaller structures plus a large shorefront marine facility. The institution runs a research fleet consisting of three ocean-going vessels plus a smaller vessel, which supports research in local waters. It also operates a 3-person, deep-diving submersible designed specifically for oceanic research. On the Quissett Campus, two miles away, are three primary laboratory-office buildings, the main administrative offices and several smaller buildings. The marine science library, a part of the neighboring Marine Biological Laboratory, contains 160,000 volumes, 250,000 pamphlets and 5,000 periodicals. Living facilities accommodate 50 students.

Community Environment: A small village, in the southwest corner of Cape Cod, Woods Hole is a world center for marine science, sharing the village with the Marine Biological Laboratory, National Marine Fisheries Service (NOAA), a branch of the U.S. Geological Survey, and Sea Education Association. Woods Hole is also the connecting port for ferries going to the island of Martha's Vineyard. State highways run into Boston and all points off Cape Cod, and major transportation facilities are found in Boston. The Woods Hole area has public libraries, churches of most denominations, a hospital, cinemas, sports and art centers and summer theatres, as well as local theatre productions throughout the year.

WORCESTER POLYTECHNIC INSTITUTE   *(E-9)*
100 Institute Road
Worcester, Massachusetts 01609
Tel: (508) 831-5000

Description: Founded in 1865 as a free institute of industrial science, the private institute still serves the basic purpose of its founder by preparing students for careers in engineering or science and management. It is accredited by the New England Association of Schools and Colleges, the Accreditation Board for Engineering and Technology, the American Chemical Society, and the Computer Sciences Accreditation Board. The institute operates on a calendar system of 4 seven-week terms per year and 1 summer term. Enrollment includes 2,781 full-time and 71 part-time undergraduates and 942 graduate students. A faculty of 203 full-time and 56 part-time gives a faculty-student ratio of 1-12. All students at this school participate in a project-oriented program of study. An optional co-op program provides an opportunity for students to alternate time in the classroom with extended periods of paid, career related employment in industry or in private and government agencies. In addition, undergraduate exchanges are available with technical universities in England, Ireland, Scotland, Switzerland, and Sweden, along with WPI staffed project centers in London and Washington. Army, Air Force, and Navy ROTC programs are available.

Entrance Requirements: Accredited high school graduation with rank in the upper 10-15 percent of graduating class; completion of college-preparatory units including 4 English, 4 mathematics, and 2 lab science; SAT and 3 Achievement Tests (Mathematics Level 1 or 2, English Composition, and a science) or ACT required; early decision, early admission, midyear admission, delayed admission and advanced placement plans available; $40 application fee.

Costs Per Year: $16,060 tuition; $5,370 room and board; $170 student fees, $1,260 average additional expenses.

Collegiate Environment: The 62-acre campus is situated about a mile from downtown Worcester. The institute buildings include a library of 300,000 volumes, 1,420 periodicals and 785,000 technical reports and 5,800 videotapes. Fifty percent of students live on campus (freshman housing is guaranteed). The institute welcomes a geographically diverse student body and accepts 76% of students applying for admission. Although most students enter in September, it is possible to matriculate any of the 5 terms. Financial aid is available and is based strictly on need. 86% of the students receive some form of financial aid. The Institute awarded 539 Bachelor, 199 Master degrees, and 12 Doctorates to the graduating class of 1992.

Community Environment: See Clark University

WORCESTER STATE COLLEGE   *(E-9)*
486 Chandler Street
Worcester, Massachusetts 01602
Tel: (508) 793-8000

Description: The state college was founded in 1874. Today, it offers undergraduate courses leading to the Bachelor of Arts or Bachelor of Science degree, as well as Bachelor of Science in Education, and graduate courses leading to a Master of Education or Master Master of Science in Biology dgree and MS in Speech Pathology and Audiology. The college operates on the semester system with two summer terms and is accredited by the New England Association of Colleges and Schools and by the National Council for the Accreditation of Teacher Education as well as the National League for Nursing and the American Medical Association (Nuclear Medicine Technology) Recent enrollment was 4,221 students. A faculty of 232 gives a faculty-student ratio of 1-18 in the day time division.

Entrance Requirements: Accredited high school graduation; SAT required, minimum 350V, 350M; GRE required for graduate programs; $10 application fee; early decision, rolling admission and advanced placement plans available.

Costs Per Year: $2,900 tuition; $5,900 out-of-state tuition; $3,600 room and board; $160 student fees.

Collegiate Environment: The college is located on 55 acres and includes 6 buildings. The library contains 148,278 volumes, 662 periodicals, 2,290 microforms and 2,426 sound recordings. Dormitories provide housing for 500 students. Approximately 60% of students applying for admission meet the requirements and are accepted. Classes begin in September and students may be admitted at midyear. Financial aid is available and 40% of the students receives aid.

Community Environment: See Clark University

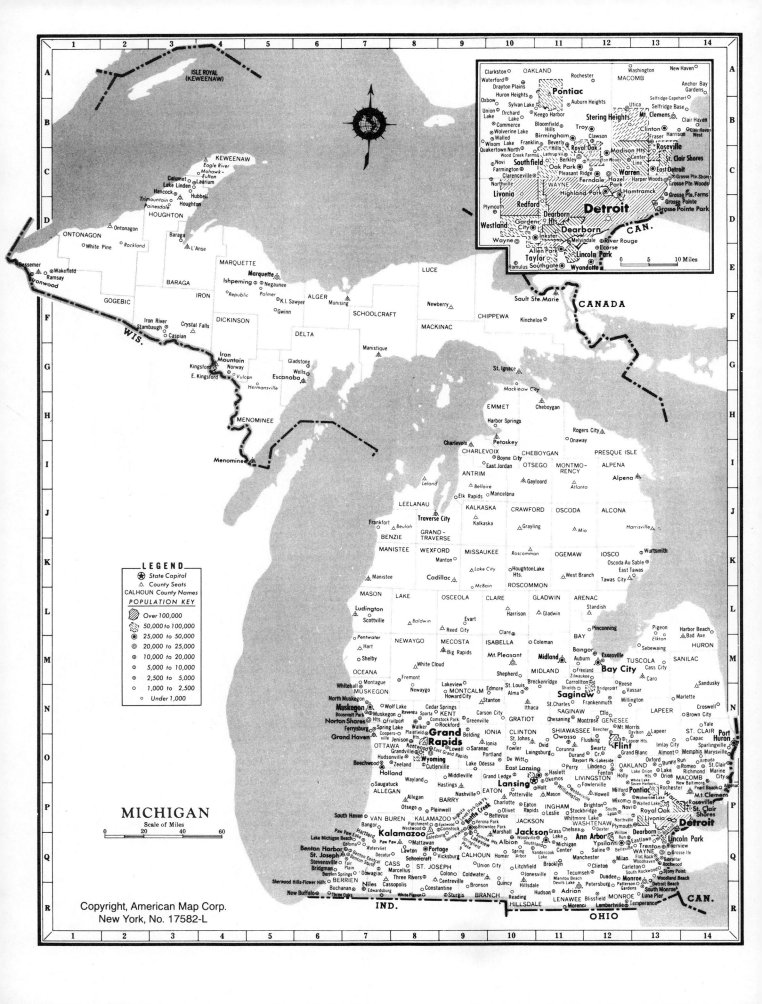

MICHIGAN
Scale of Miles
0   20   40   60

Copyright, American Map Corp.
New York, No. 17582-L

LEGEND
⭐ State Capital
△ County Seats
CALHOUN County Names
POPULATION KEY
▨ Over 100,000
▨ 50,000 to 100,000
◉ 25,000 to 50,000
⊕ 20,000 to 25,000
⊕ 10,000 to 20,000
⊙ 5,000 to 10,000
⊙ 2,500 to 5,000
○ 1,000 to 2,500
○ Under 1,000

MICHIGAN

ADRIAN COLLEGE   *(R-12)*
110 S. Madison Street
Adrian, Michigan 49221
Tel: (517) 265-5161; (800) 877-2246; Fax: (517) 264-3331

Description: The institution is a residential liberal arts college related to the United Methodist Church. It evolved from a theological institute founded by the Wesleyan Methodist denomination at Leoni, Michigan, in 1845. The college is fully accredited by the North Central Association of Colleges and Schools. It operates on the semester system with May and Summer terms. The college grants the Associate and Baccalaureat degrees. Enrollment is 968 full-time and 91 part-time students. A faculty of 69 full-time and 30 part-time gives a faculty-student ratio of 1-15. The college offers an Army ROTC program in cooperation with the University of Michigan.

Entrance Requirements: Accredited high school graduation with minimum C+ average in academic courses grades 9-12 and rank in top 50% of class; completion of 15 units including 3 English and 2 mathematics; and remaining 10 units in any combination of laboratory science, foreign language or social studies; SAT 800 or higher, ACT composite 20 or higher required; delayed admission, rolling admission and advanced placement programs available; $15 application fee.

Costs Per Year: $11,250 tuition; $3,750 room and board.

Collegiate Environment: The college is located in the county seat of Lenawee County in the southeastern area of the state. The campus consists of 100 acres on the city's west side, which is largely residential. The 32 major college buildings include a library of 136,000 volumes and dormitory facilities for 1,144 students. Social sororities and fraternities provide additional housing for 100 students and there are numerous other student organizations on the campus. The Merrillat Sport and Fitness Center opened in January 1990. 82% of the students applying for admission are accepted. Financial aid is available, which ranges from $2,000 per year to 80% of tuition, and 84% of the students receive some form of financial aid.

Community Environment: Adrian is 35 miles southwest of Ann Arbor and 35 miles northwest of Toledo, Ohio, located in the center of a large industrial, agricultural and recreational area. Leading manufactured products include aircraft, automobile and refrigerator parts, paper, wood cabinetry, plastics, tools, and chemicals. Part-time job opportunities are available for students. Water sports and fishing are easily accessible with many lakes within a 25-mile radius.

ALBION COLLEGE   *(Q-10)*
Albion, Michigan 49224
Tel: (517) 629-1000; (800) 858-6770; Fax: (517) 629-0509

Description: Albion college, chartered in 1835, is a four-year liberal arts institution that is privately supported and related to the United Methodist Church. It is accredited by the North Central Association of Colleges and Schools. The college grants the Bachelor of Arts and the Bachelor of Fine Arts degrees. It operates on the early semester system and offers one summer session. Enrollment includes 1,674 full-time and 27 part-time students. A faculty of 110 full-time and 15 part-time gives a faculty-student raio of 1-13.

Entrance Requirements: Accredited high school graduation; completion of 15 units; SAT or ACT required; early admission, early decision, rolling admission, midyear admission and advanced placement plans available; $20 application fee.

Costs Per Year: $14,770 tuition; $4,826 room and board; $140 student activity fee.

Collegiate Environment: The 225-acre campus is located in the south-central area of Michigan. The 30 college buildings include a library of 306,000 books and nonprint items, 10,000 pamphlets, 920 periodicals, 19,400 microforms, and 2,860 recordings. Living accom-

modations are provided for 1,600 students. There are social fraternities and sororities as well as numerous other student organizations located at the campus. 98% of the students live and board within the college residence system. Financial aid is available based on demonstrated need, and 50% of the students receive assistance. Merit scholarships, $1,000-$15,000 per year, are also available. About 88% of the applicants are accepted, including midyear students. The middle 50% range of scores of enrolled freshmen is SAT 980-1220 combined, ACT 22-28 composite. The Community Scholars Program allows community residents to attend classes at a greatly reduced rate. Generally, 2-4 students take advantage of this program each semester by taking one course.

Community Environment: Located one and one-half hours west of Detroit and three hours east of Chicago, the city of Albion combines small town life, a strong industrial base, and the amenities of a college town to form a unique community for its citizens. Albion boasts a rich history of educational and industrial accomplishment and prides itself on its ethnic and cultural diversity. Part-time employment is available. The area is served by Greyhound Bus and Amtrak and has a library, hospital, parks, and several civic and service organizations. Facilities are provided for tennis, golf, skating, and water sports.

ALMA COLLEGE   *(N-10)*
614 W. Superior Street
Alma, Michigan 48801-1599
Tel: (517) 463-7139; (800) 321-2562; Fax: (517) 463-7057

Description: The private, residential, liberal arts college was founded by Presbyterians in Michigan in 1886. It is accredited by the North Central Association of Colleges and Schools. The college has grown from an original student body of approximately 100 to an academic community of 1,350 men and women. A faculty of 73 full-time and 30 part-time gives an overall faculty-student ratio of approximately 1-14. The colege operates on the 4-4-1 system and offers one summer session. Cooperative plans are available with the University of Michigan and with Michigan Technological University for engineering students. A 3-2 program for occupational therapy is provided at Washington University.

Entrance Requirements: Accredited high school graduation with B average in academic subjects, completion of 16 units including 4 units English, 3 mathematics, 3 science, 3 social science; entering freshmen should have an ACT composite of 22 (equivalent to SAT scores of 500V and 500M); early admission, rolling admission, early decision and advanced placement plans available; $20 application fee.

Costs Per Year: $12,572 tuition; $4,552 board and room; $115 student activity fee; additional expenses average $1,000.

Collegiate Environment: The college is comprised of 22 buildings located on 85 acres and includes a library of 185,300 titles, 1,125 periodicals, 22,400 microforms and 2,500 audiovisual materials. Students who are not married or living at home must live in college residences which accommodate 1,198 students. Approximately 84% of all students applying for admission are accepted. Financial aid is available and more than 90% of the current students receive financial aid. The college sponsors international study programs in France, Germany, Spain, Mexico and Scotland. Terms of Alma's 4-4-1 calendar begin in September, January, and April.

Community Environment: City is located in a rural area in the center of Michigan's lower peninsula. Major industries include petroleum refining and manufacturing of automotive parts, plastic extrusions, drainage and metal products. Some part-time work available for students. Area has access to rail service and airport. Alma has its own public library, hospital and motels. Recreation facilities include golf, Community Center, swimming pool, parks and the Pine River for boating and fishing. Alma College is within two hours of Michigan's beaches and ski resorts.

ALPENA COMMUNITY COLLEGE   *(I-13)*
666 Johnson St.
Alpena, Michigan 49707
Tel: (517) 356-9021; Admissions: (517) 356-9021; Fax: (517) 356-0980

Description: The publicly supported junior college opened in 1952. The college grants Associate degrees and offers programs in business administration, dentistry, engineering, law, medicine, nursing, public accounting, and teaching. It is accredited by the North Central Association of Colleges and Schools. The school operates on the semester system and offers one summer session. Enrollment includes 371 men and 536 women full-time, and 381 men and 654 women part-time. A faculty of 44 full-time and 80 part-time provides a faculty-student ratio of 1-20.

Entrance Requirements: Open enrollment policy; high school graduation; required for applicants under 18 years of age; rolling admission and midyear admission plans available.

Costs Per Year: $1,490 in-district tuition; $2,150 out-of-district tuition; $2,810 out-of-state tuition.

Collegiate Environment: The 650-acre campus is located on the banks of Lake Besser. The buildings include a library of 25,000 volumes, 225 periodicals, and 3,500 microforms. Classes begin in September and January. Approximately 100% of students applying for admission are accepted. 60 scholarships are available and 60% of the students receive some form of financial aid.

Community Environment: Located on Thunder Bay 94 miles south of the Straits of Mackinac and 235 miles north of Detroit, Alpena is the largest port on northern Lake Huron. Industries include a cement plant, paper mill and shale quarry. Part-time employment is available for students. Mean annual temperature is 42.2 degrees. Alpena is well known for fine fishing, hunting, and winter sports. Airlines and bus service are accessible. Area has a hospital, several churches, a museum, and a planetarium. There are over 240,000 acres of public land within a one-hour drive and five city parks within the city limits. Recreation facilities include golf, sailboat racing, tennis, theater, drive-ins, and skating.

ANDREWS UNIVERSITY   *(Q-7)*
Berrien Springs, Michigan 49104
Tel: (616) 471-3203; (800) 253-2874; Fax: (616) 471-6001

Description: The college dates back to 1874 when the Seventh-day Adventist denomination founded Battle Creek College. In 1959, the college, the theological seminary and the graduate school were united under the name Andrews University. The College of Arts and Sciences and the College of Technology offer pre-professional and terminal curricula and are accredited by the North Central Association of Colleges and Schools. An academic cooperative plan with the University of Michigan and Walla Walla College is available for engineering students. The following degrees are awarded: Associate, Bachelor, Master, Professional and Doctorate. It operates on the quarter system and offers one summer session. Enrollment includes 2,952 students. A faculty of 219 full-time and 30 part-time gives a faculty-student ratio of 1-13.

Entrance Requirements: Approved high school graduation or equivalent; minimum of 13 units including English, mathematics, foreign language, science, social science; ACT required; GRE required for graduate school; non-high school graduates may be admitted as special students; advanced placement, rolling admission and delayed admission plans available; $30 application fee.

Costs Per Year: $10,495 tuition; $3,990 board and room; $135 student fees.

Collegiate Environment: The 1,650-acre campus is near the banks of the St. Joseph River. The 36 buildings include a library of 481,533 volumes. Living accommodations for 624 men, 600 women, and 500 families are provided. Admissions to the university is free of discrimination on the grounds of race, color or national origin. All unmarried students under 22 years of age are required to live in the residence halls. Classes begin in September, January, March and June. 62 % of applicants are accepted. 300 scholarships are offered, including 75 for

freshmen. The university is part of a Seventh Day Adventist organization which provides opportunities for students to study the French, German and Spanish languages abroad.

Community Environment: Small town located in the southwest part of the state. Area is accessible by bus service. Some part-time employment is available.

AQUINAS COLLEGE   *(O-8)*
1607 Robinson Rd. S.E.
Grand Rapids, Michigan 49506
Tel: (616) 459-8281; (800) 678-9593; Fax: (616) 459-2563

Description: This Roman Catholic liberal arts college was founded by the Dominican Sisters of Marywood in 1886. It began to operate as a four-year college in 1940 and confers the Bachelor, Master and Associate degrees. It is accredited by the North Central Association of Colleges and Schools. Enrollment is 2,574 students. A faculty of 82 full-time and 87 part-time gives a faculty-student ratio of 1-15. The college operates on the semester system and offers one summer term. Standard preprofessional programs in dentistry, law, medicine, social work, and engineering are available. Special programs include a semester in Ireland for the study of Irish history, literature, and culture.

Entrance Requirements: Approved high school graduation with minimum 2.5 GPA, SAT or ACT required; early admission, early decision, rolling admission, delayed admission, and advanced placement plans available; $25 application fee.

Costs Per Year: $11,208 tuition; $4,124 room and board.

Collegiate Environment: The campus consists of 107 acres and has been cited as the most beautiful campus in Michigan. The buildings include a library housing 105,000 volumes, 930 periodicals, 95,000 microforms and 4,150 recordings. Residence hall facilities accommodate 220 men and 335 women. About 90% of students applying for admission are accepted. Financial aid is available.

Community Environment: Grand Rapids is an urban setting. The greater Grand Rapids area has a population of 640,000, and is one of the fastest growing areas in the nation. It is the commercial, medical and cultural center of west Michigan.

BAKER COLLEGE OF FLINT   *(O-12)*
G-1050 W. Bristol Road
Flint, Michigan 48507
Tel: (810) 766-4000

Description: The private business school was established in 1911. Formerly Baker Business University, then Baker Junior College of Business, the present name was adopted in 1986. It is accredited by the North Central Association of Colleges and Schools. It operates on the quarter system and offers one summer session. Enrollment includes 2,607 full-time, 1,436 part-time undergraduates and 80 graduate students. A faculty of 38 full-time and 120 part-time gives an undergraduate faculty-student ration of 1:25.

Entrance Requirements: High school graduation; open enrollment policy; Rolling admission, early admission, early decision, midyear admission, and advanced placement plans available; $20 application fee.

Costs Per Year: State-resident tuition $5,760; $1,650 room. Additional expenses average $200.

Collegiate Environment: 98% of the students applying for admission are accepted. 80 scholarships are offered. Housing facilities are available for 200 students. The library contains 29,950 titles, 177 periodicals and 30,000 microforms. Classes begin in September, January, April and June. 80% receive financial aid.

Community Environment: See GMI Engineering and Management Institute.

Branch Campuses: 1020 S. Washington St., Owosso, MI 48867; 123 E. Apple Ave., Muskegon, MI 49442; 1500 University Dr., Auburn Hills, MI 48326; 3403 Lapeer Rd., Port Huron, MI 48060; 34950 Little Mack Ave., Clinton Township, MI 48035; 9600 E. 13th St., Cadillac, MI 49601; 234 S. Mechanic St., Jackson, MI 49201; 6667 Main St., Cass City, MI 48726.

BAKER COLLEGE OF MUSKEGON (N-7)
123 Apple Avenue
Muskegon, Michigan 49442
Tel: (616) 726-4904

Description: The private, coeducational, four-year business college was founded in 1888 and was first known as the Ferris Business College. The present name was taken and degree granting authority was obtained from the State in 1965. It is accredited by the North Central Association of Colleges and Schools. The college recently enrolled 267 men and 761 women full-time and 195 men and 518 women part-time, attending day and evening classes on the quarter system. There is a faculty of 60. The college grants Certificates, Associates and Bachelor degrees. One summer term is offered.

Entrance Requirements: Open enrollment policy; high school graduation or equivalent; non-high school graduates may be admitted with special permission; $20 application fee; early admission, delayed admission, rolling admission and advanced placement plans available.

Costs Per Year: $3,840 tuition; $2,100 room and board

Collegiate Environment: The one-acre campus has 4 buildings and a library of 18,556 volumes, 100 pamphlets and 249 periodicals. Dormitory space is available for 30 men and 220 women. Midyear students are admitted; classes begin in September, January, March, and June. About 100% of the applicants are accepted. Financial assistance is available.

Community Environment: See Muskegon Community College

BAY DE NOC COMMUNITY COLLEGE (G-6)
2001 N. Lincoln Road
Escanaba, Michigan 49829
Tel: (906) 786-5802; (800) 221-2001; Admissions: (906) 786-5802 x148; Fax: (906) 786-8515

Description: The publicly-supported, two-year college is recognized by the state and is controlled by municipal government. The college, which opened in 1963, operates on the semester system and offers two summer terms. Both day and evening courses are available. The academic structure of the college consists of five divisions: Applied Health, Arts and Letters, Business and Applied Technology, Physical Science, and Social Science. Enrollment includes 1,388 full-time and part-time students. The college awards the Certificate and the Associate degree. A faculty of 42 full-time and 58 part-time gives a faculty-student ratio of 1-28. The college is fully accredited by the North Central Association of Colleges and Schools.

Entrance Requirements: Open enrollment policy; accredited high school graduation; early admission, rolling admission available.

Costs Per Year: $960 tuition for county residents; $1,320 tuition for state residents; $2,100 tuition for out-of-state residents; $1,213 room, $16 student fees; additional expenses average $400.

Collegiate Environment: The campus of 150 acres is located on the shores of Little Bay de Noc. Midyear students are accepted and classes begin in August and January. The policy has been adopted of accepting students age sixty or older on a tuition free basis. Financial aid is available. Of the 56 scholarships offered, 44 are for freshmen and 60% of the student body receive some form of financial aid. The library contains 30,000 volumes, 5,000 pamphlets, 2,283 periodicals, and 200 recordings. Dormitory space is provided for 100 students. All of the applicants are accepted. The average high school standing of the current freshman class, top 60%; 20% in the top quarter, 40% in the second quarter, 20% in the third quarter, 20% in the bottom quarter. Approximately 60% of the previous freshman class returned to the campus for their second year.

Community Environment: An industrial city, Escanaba has an excellent deepwater harbor and mammouth ore docks from which about six million tons of iron ore are shipped annually. Local manufactures include truck cranes, paper, welding machines and lumber products. Part-time employment is available for students. City services include a library, hospital, and major transportation facilities. Recreation includes swimming, boating, golf, tennis, fishing and winter sports.

CALVIN COLLEGE (O-8)
3201 Burton S. E.
Grand Rapids, Michigan 49546
Tel: (616) 957-6000; (800) 688-0122; Admissions: (616) 957-6106; Fax: (616) 957-8551

Description: The four-year liberal arts institution is a college of the Christian Reformed Church. It is accredited by the North Central Association of Colleges and Schools. Founded in 1876, the former two-year college expanded to a four-year program and awarded its first Bachelor of Arts degree in 1921. The college admits students of any race or national or ethnic origin, and invites application from any student interested in the Christian atmosphere and curriculum. The college operates on the 4-1-4 system and offers three summer sessions. Enrollment includes 3,570 full-time and 272 part-time undergraduates, and 184 graduate students. A faculty of 228 full-time and 54 part-time gives an overall faculty-student ratio of approximately 1-16.

Entrance Requirements: High school graduation; completion of 15 academic units including 3 English, 2 mathematics (Algebra and Geometry required), 2 science, and 2 foreign language; SAT or ACT accepted; rolling admission, delayed admission, and advanced placement plans available; $25 application fee.

Costs Per Year: $8,630 tuition; $3,520 room and board; $350 books and supplies.

Collegiate Environment: Located in a suburban setting formerly known as Knollcrest, the modern campus boasts an award-winning Science Building and observatory, complete physical education facilities including a 25-yard swimming pool, television studio, art gallery and a new 1,000-seat chapel. Buildings include dormitory facilities for 2,800 students and a library housing 625,000 volumes. About 94% of students applying for admission meet the requirements and are accepted, including midyear students. The average scores of entering freshmen were SAT 390 verbal, 420 math; ACT 20 composite. Financial assistance is available and about 88% of the students receive some type of aid. Of 1,300 scholarships offered, 500 are available for freshmen. About 90% of the previous freshman class returned to the campus for the sophomore year.

Community Environment: The city of Grand Rapids provides a growing cultural base for the area's six colleges. It has a lively interest in the arts, as evidenced by an active symphony orchestra, civic theatre, ballet association, and art museum. For students desiring off-campus living arrangements, many houses and apartments are available, and the large number of stores and restaurants provide part-time employment opportunities.

CALVIN THEOLOGICAL SEMINARY (O-8)
3233 Burton St. S. E.
Grand Rapids, Michigan 49506
Tel: (616) 957-6034; (800) 388-6034; Fax: (616) 957-8621

Description: The seminary was founded in 1876 as the theological school of the Christian Reformed Church. Calvin College and Seminary are incorporated under one name. They are, however, distinct institutions each having its own faculty and academic life. The primary objective is preparation for the ministry. It is accredited by the Association of Theological Schools and operates on the quarter system with 3 summer sessions. The seminary grants the Master of Divinity, Master of Arts in Educational Ministry, Master of Arts in Mission and Church Growth, Master of Arts in Theological Studies, Master of Theology, and Doctor of Philosophy degrees. Enrollment includes 196 men and 46 women. A faculty of 22 full-time and 3 part-time gives an overall faculty-student ratio of 1-10.

Entrance Requirements: Bachelor of Arts degree or its equivalent; rolling admission, delayed admission plans available. $25 application fee.

Costs Per Year: $3,456-$5,184 tuition, $7,000 room and board.

Collegiate Environment: The seminary occupies the Centennial Memorial Seminary Building situated on the Knollcrest campus. The library contains 500,000 volumes. Classes begin in September; midyear students are accepted. Research courses are available for graduate students who desire concentrated study on a particular subject of interest. Numerous scholarships are offered.

Community Environment: See Calvin College.

CENTER FOR CREATIVE STUDIES - COLLEGE OF ART AND DESIGN   *(P-14)*
245 E. Kirby
Detroit, Michigan 48202
Tel: (313) 872-3118; (800) 952-2787; Fax: (313) 872-8377

Description: The private art school was established in 1926, an outgrowth of the long-established Society of Arts and Crafts. It is accredited by the North Central Association of Colleges and Schools and by the National Association Schools of Art & Design. It operates on the semester system and offers one summer session. Recent enrollment was 303 men and 207 women full-time, and 188 men and 137 women part-time. A faculty of 46 full-time and 116 part-time gives a faculty-student ratio of 1-10. The school may grant the diploma after completion of the four-year full-time program, and is authorized under the laws of the State of Michigan to grant a degree of Bachelor of Fine Arts.

Entrance Requirements: High school graduation or equivalent; a 2.5 average required for diploma programs; SAT or ACT required; non-high school graduates accepted for summer session and evening classes only; rolling admission, midyear admission, and advanced placement plans available; $35 application fee; portfolio for presentation at interview required.

Costs Per Year: $11,760 tuition; $5,500 room and board; $130 student fees; $2,800 miscellaneous.

Collegiate Environment: The ten and one-half-acre campus is located in the area of the Detroit Cultural Center and its five buildings include dormitory housing for 180 students and a library of 23,000 volumes, 78 periodicals and 50,000 slides. Freshman classes begin in September and January. 73% of students applying for admission are accepted, including midyear students. 76% of the students receive financial aid. The school awarded 133 Bachelor's degrees recently.

Community Environment: See Wayne State University.

CENTRAL MICHIGAN UNIVERSITY   *(M-10)*
104 Warriner
Mount Pleasant, Michigan 48859
Tel: (517) 774-3076; Fax: (517) 774-7267

Description: The university, founded in 1892, is governed by a Board of Trustees appointed by the Governor of the State. Academically, the university consists of the College of Arts and Sciences, the College of Business Asministration, and the College of Education, Health and Human Services. In addition, graduate offerings and an extended degree program are available. The institution is accredited by the North Central Association of Colleges and Schools. An optional Army ROTC program is offered. Programs lead to the Certificate, Bachelor degree, Master degree and Doctorate. The university operates on the semester system and offers two summer sessions of six weeks. Enrollment includes 6,937 men and 9,189 women. A faculty of 676 full-time and 157 part-time gives an overall faculty-student ratio of 1-20.

Entrance Requirements: High school graduation with rank in top 50% of class; completion of 16 units including 4 English, 4 math, 4 science, 4 social studies; high school equivalency diploma accepted; ACT recommended; early admission, rolling admission, midyear admission, and advanced placement plans available. $25 application fee.

Costs Per Year: $2,837 tuition; $7,112 nonresident; $3,900 room and board; $110 student fees, $1,650 miscellaneous.

Collegiate Environment: In addition to the main campus of 854 acres, the university owns 176 acres of original forest which is being developed for laboratory use in forestry and 45 acres at Beaver Island Biological Station for off-campus instruction. There are 91 buildings including a student activity center. The library contains 847,899 volumes. There are living accommodations for 5,510 single students and 384 units of family housing. Over 200 student organizations are located on the campus and social life is made more attractive by the existence of fraternities and sororities. Approximately 82% of students applying for admission meet the requirements and are accepted. Students are admitted at midyear as well as in the fall, and come from various geographical locations. 2,734 scholarships are offered, and 67% of the current student body receives financial assistance.

Community Environment: Located in the approximate center of the state, Mount Pleasant is the largest city in the county. Average temperature is 45.6 degrees; rainfall, 26.14; snowfall, 45.7 inches. The area has a hospital, auditoriums, theatres, motels, a public stadium, and its own airport. Ten lakes and a ski range nearby offer excellent recreational facilities. An Indian reservation is located four miles east of the city.

CHARLES STEWART MOTT COMMUNITY COLLEGE   *(O-12)*
1401 E. Court St.
Flint, Michigan 48503
Tel: (810) 762-0200

Description: Formerly Genessee Community College, this public, two-year college was founded in 1923 providing liberal arts, occupational, and community service programs. It is accredited by the North Central Association of Colleges and Schools. Enrollment includes 9,965 students full-time and part-time. A faculty of 403 gives overall faculty-student ratio of approxmiately 1:24. The semester system is used and two summer sessions and an 8-week minisemester are offered.

Entrance Requirements: Open enrollment policy; high school graduation or equivalent; non-high school graduates over 19 years of age admitted; ACT or entrance exam required; early admission, early decision, rolling admission, and advanced placement plans available.

Costs Per Year: $1,300 tuition, $1,796 out-of-district; $2,385 out-of-state resident.

Collegiate Environment: In addition to the 7 buildings used by the college, the adjacent college and cultural center includes a planetarium, theatre, art center, library, museum, and auditorium. No housing is provided for out-of-town students. The library contains 86,647 volumes, 5,422 pamphlets and 1,300 recordings. Over 130 scholarships are offered and 100 of these are available for freshmen. Approximately 95% of students applying for admission meet the requirements; almost all of these are accepted. Students may be admitted at midyear; classes begin in September and January.

Community Environment: See GMI Engineering and Management Institute

CLEARY COLLEGE   *(Q-12)*
2170 Washtenaw Road
Ypsilanti, Michigan 48197
Tel: (313) 483-4400

Description: The private business college offers courses of study in secretarial sciences, data processing, accounting, and management. Founded in 1883, the college had its beginning as a School of Penmanship. It was incorporated under the laws of the state as a business college in 1891 and was accredited by the Accrediting Commission for Business Schools in 1968 and accredited by the NCA, March, 1988. Current enrollment includes 189 men, 268 women full-time, 187 men, and 304 women part-time. The faculty consists of 18 full-time and 66 part-time. The quarter system is employed. One summer term is offered. Programs of study lead to the Diploma, Associate, and Bachelor degree in Business Administration.

Entrance Requirements: High school graduation or equivalent; open enrollment policy: $25 application fee; early admission, early decision, rolling admission, delayed admission and advanced placement plans available. Located in Ypsilanti and Howell, Michigan.

Costs Per Year: $125 per credit hour; $25 registration fee; $30 learning resources and technology fee.

Collegiate Environment: The college is housed in a new building on the western outskirts of Ypsilanti. The athletic activities of the college are confined mainly to basketball, softball, swimming and bowling. Social functions occur throughout the college year. A limited number of scholarships and loans are available and about 41% of the students receive aid. Of 130 scholarships offered, all are available to freshmen. The library contains 9,256 volumes, 200 annual business reports of corporations, and 692 periodicals. 100% of the applicants are accepted, including midyear students.

Community Environment: See Eastern Michigan University

CONCORDIA COLLEGE   *(Q-12)*
4090 Geddes Rd.
Ann Arbor, Michigan 48105
Tel: (313) 995-7300; (800) 253-0680; Admissions: (313) 995-7311;
Fax: (313) 995-4610

Description: Concordia College is a four-year coeducational institution accredited by the North Central Association of Colleges and Schools. It was founded in 1962 by the Lutheran Church-Missouri Synod to meet the need of training prospective church workers. The college offers a liberal arts curriculum and grants the Associate and Bachelor degrees. It operates on the semester system. Enrollment includes 523 full-time and 65 part-time students. A faculty of 62 gives a faculty-student ratio of 1-10.

Entrance Requirements: High school graduation ranking in upper 50% of graduating class; completion of 15 units including 3 English, 1 mathematics, 1 science, 1 social science; ACT required; rolling admission and advanced placement plans available.

Costs Per Year: $10,250 tuition; $4,560 room and board; $180 student fees; $1,000 miscellaneous.

Collegiate Environment: Concordia College provides students with a pastoral setting along the Huron River. The college buildings reach north from the river to encompass 234 acres where apple orchards and artesian springs are found. The heart of the campus is dominated by the pyramidal Chapel of the Holy Trinity. The library contains sophisticated microfilm facilities, and its holdings of over 100,000 titles include print, film and video media. 14 quads provide housing for a maximum of 224 men and 224 women. The college offers varsity sports opportunities for both men and women. Approximately 75% of applicants are accepted from diverse geographical locations. Financial aid is available and 90% of students receive some form of financial assistance. An average of 80% of freshmen return for their sophomore year.

Community Environment: See University of Michigan

CRANBROOK ACADEMY OF ART   *(B-11)*
1221 N. Woodward Avenue
Bloomfield Hills, Michigan 48013
Tel: (810) 645-3300; Admissions: (810) 645-3329; Fax: (810) 646-0046

Description: The private, coeducational, fine arts institution is a graduate school. The academy began informally with a group of artists and craftsmen assembled in 1927 by Mr. and Mrs. George G. Booth, founders of the Cranbrook Educational Community. The program for professional artists was expanded in 1942 when the academy was chartered by the State of Michigan as an institution of higher learning with the privilege of granting degrees. It was accredited in 1960 by the North Central Association of Colleges and Schools. Recent enrollment included 142 students. The academy operates on the semester system. A faculty of 9 provides a faculty-student ratio of 1-15. Programs of study lead to the Master of Fine Arts and Master of Architecture degrees.

Entrance Requirements: Prior baccalaureate degree; portfolio reflective of advanced ability in the visuals arts. $30 application fee; Feb. 1 application deadline.

Costs Per Year: $14,600 tuition; $4,950 board and room.

Collegiate Environment: The academy's group of exceptionally well-equipped buildings includes a library of 25,000 volumes and living accommodations for 80 men and women. Students come from various geographical locations. Classes begin in September and January. This highly selective institution accepts 25% of applicants. 70% receive financial assistance.

Community Environment: Beautiful residential suburb 15 miles from Detroit.

DAVENPORT COLLEGE   *(O-8)*
415 E. Fulton
Grand Rapids, Michigan 49503
Tel: (616) 451-3511; (800) 632-9569; Admissions: (616) 732-1200;
Fax: (616) 732-1144

Description: The private, coeducational business school is fully accredited by the North Central Association of Colleges and Secondary Schools. This college's history dates back to 1866. Programs include a collegiate business course of study, which leads to a diploma, an Associate, and a Bachelor of Science degree. The college operates on the quarter system and offers one summer term. Enrollment is 4,500 students. A faculty of 34 full-time and 137 part-time gives an overall faculty-student ratio of approximately 1-20.

Entrance Requirements: Open enrollment policy, high school graduation or equivalent; non-high school graduates may be admitted as special students; early admission, rolling admission, midyear admission, and advanced placement plans available; $20 application fee.

Costs Per Year: $7,380 tuition; $2,025 room; $30 student fees; $675 books.

Collegiate Environment: The 8-acre campus is located on the edge of the newly designed cultural area of downtown Grand Rapids. The library contains 34,000 volumes, and dormitories accommodate 42 men and 142 women. All applicants are accepted. Students come from various geographical locations. Approximately 250 scholarships are offered for freshmen; 84% of the students receive financial aid.

Community Environment: See Calvin College.

DELTA COLLEGE   *(M-11)*
University Center, Michigan 48710
Tel: (517) 686-9000; Admissions: (517) 686-9092; Fax: (517) 686-8736

Description: The publicly supported community college was opened in 1961. It is accredited by the North Central Association of Colleges and Schools. Voters of Bay, Saginaw, and Midland Counties formed a community college district for the purpose of establishing the new institution to carry on the educational opportunities previously offered at Bay City Junior College. Programs of study lead to a Certificate or an Associate degree. The college operates on the trimester system and offers one summer session. Enrollment includes 3,486 full-time and 6,960 part-time students. A faculty of 215 full-time and 792 part-time gives a faculty-student ratio of 1-10.

Entrance Requirements: Open enrollment policy; non-high school graduates accepted; advanced placement, early admission, early decision, rolling admission, delayed admission and midyear admission plans available.

Costs Per Year: $1,515 district resident tuition; $1,970 state resident tuition; $2,750 nonresident tuition.

Collegiate Environment: The 640-acre campus is located in the approximate center of the triangle formed by Bay City, Midland, and Saginaw. The campus includes a library of 98,100 volumes and numerous pamphlets, periodicals, microforms and audiovisual materials. Dormitory facilites are not available. 378 scholarships are available.

Community Environment: University Center encompasses the tri-county area of Bay, Midland and Saginaw counties. The area has good shopping, commuter bus service and very active churches. Saginaw Arts Council promotes and encourages the area's cultural and educational organizations. There are excellent part-time employment opportunities for students. Summer and winter sports resort areas are located nearby. Some areas are highly industrialized.

DETROIT COLLEGE OF BUSINESS   *(Q-13)*
4801 Oakman Blvd.
Dearborn, Michigan 48126
Tel: (313) 581-4400; Fax: (313) 581-1926

Description: The private, four-year, senior business college was founded in 1962. It is accredited by the North Central Association of Colleges and Schools. Students may attend day or evening classes at the college, which operates on the quarter system. One summer term is offered in evening college and two summer terms are offered in day college. The college grants the Associate and Bachelor degrees. Enrollment includes 2,916 full-time, 2,194 part-time students, and 2,092 evening students. A faculty of 43 full-time and 273 part-time provides an overall faculty-student ratio of 1-23.

Entrance Requirements: Open enrollment policy; high school graduation or equivalent required; completion of 3 units of English and 1 mathematics; $20 application fee; rolling admission, delayed admission and advanced placement plans available.

Costs Per Year: $4,860 tuition; additional expenses average $800.

THE COLLEGE BLUE BOOK

Collegiate Environment: The 13-acre campus of the college is conveniently located at the corner of Michigan Avenue and Oakman Boulevard. Administrative Offices, student center, automat, and classrooms are in one building; ample parking space is provided. The new library, which was opened in 1987, contains 18,160 volumes, 360 periodicals and approximately 518 audio-visual materials. Approximately 99% of students applying for admission are accepted. Students are admitted at midyear. Of 90 scholarships offered, 22 are available for freshman, and about 63% of the students receive financial assistance. About 50% of the previous freshman class return to the campus for their sophomore year. The college awarded 19 Certificates, 186 Associate degrees, and 185 Bachelor degrees.

Community Environment: See Henry Ford Community College

Branch Campuses: Warren, MI; Flint, MI

DETROIT COLLEGE OF LAW AT MICHIGAN STATE UNIVERSITY *(P-14)*
130 E. Elizabeth
Detroit, Michigan 48201
Tel: (313) 226-0100

Description: The Detroit College of Law was established in 1891, making it the oldest law school in the Detroit Metropolitan area. The College is a nonprofit, coeducational institution devoted exclusively to professional education in law. DCL was fully accredited by the American Bar Association in 1941 and has been a member of the American Association of Law Schools since 1946. Current enrollment is 670 with a faculty of 29. Courses are offered in both day and evening divisions beginning in the Fall (August).

Entrance Requirements: Only those applicants having a bachelor's degree from an accredited college or university with a respectable grade point average and a suitable score on the Law School Admissions Test (LSAT) will be considered for admission to Detroit College of Law. $50 application fee.

Costs Per Year: $13,000 day program; $9,750 evening program.

Collegiate Environment: The law school owns and maintains its own facilities which were designed specifically for the study of law and the training of advocates. The complex has been continually modernized to meet the needs of the student body. IBM computers are available to students for instructional, tutorial, research and word processing purposes; computer use is an integral part of legal education at the Detroit College of Law. The College houses a large, moot court room where both trial and appellate advocacy may be demonstrated before a jury or multi-judge bench. The Dean's office and the faculty offices and library are located on the fourth floor. Overall, the physical plant is a large legal laboratory and training ground of a specialized design and arrangement to fulfill the needs of every student.

Community Environment: Effective Fall 1995 Michigan State University has agreed to form an alliance with Detroit College of Law. The admissions office can answer questions regarding this transition. Call (313) 226-0169.

EASTERN MICHIGAN UNIVERSITY *(Q-12)*
Ypsilanti, Michigan 48197
Tel: (313) 487-3060; (800) 468-6368; Fax: (313) 487-1484

Description: The state university is accredited by the North Central Association of Colleges and Schools. It consists of 5 colleges: Arts & Sciences, Business, Education, Health and Human Services, and Technology, and also includes the Graduate School. Undergraduate enrollment includes 12,144 full-time and 6,224 part-time students. Graduate students number 4,953. A faculty of 702 full-time and 440 part-time gives an overall student-faculty ratio of 20:1. The university operates on a semester system with one spring and one summer term comprising the equivalent of one semester. Special programs include: Labor Studies, Arts Management, Radio-Television-Film, Music Therapy, Historical Preservaiton, Language, and International Trade. Optional Army, Navy and Air Force ROTC programs are offered. Founded by the State Legislature in 1849, granted university status in 1959, it offers a nationally recognized College of Education, an accredited College of Business and an expanding College of Technology. EMU offers 180 undergraduate and 70 graduate programs of study on campus. The continuing Education Division provides off-campus courses at 45 centers and the World College coordinates international programs.

Entrance Requirements: Completion and submission of Application for Admission, high school transcript or results of G.E.D., and SAT or ACT results. For applicants over 21, ACT/SAT not required. Transfer students must have a minimum cumulative GPA of 2.0 in transferrable courses and must submit official transcripts from all educational institutions previously attended; early admission, midyear admission, rolling admission and advanced placement plans available. $20 application fee.

Costs Per Year: $2,610 tuition; $6,750 out-of-state tuition; $4,148 room and board; $400 student fees.

Collegiate Environment: The main campus is located on 275 acres on the north side of Ypsilanti near the Huron River. An additional 182 acres west of the central campus contain Rynearson football stadium and Oestrike baseball stadium, intercollegiate and intramural athletic facilities, a field laboratory and married student apartments. Campus and local buses connect the two sites. The Olds student recreation center, an intramural facility, which includes an olympic-sized swimming pool, racquetball courts, exercise and weight rooms, and a jogging track, is conveniently located mid-campus. The 18-hole championship Huron Golf Club and the privately owned Radisson on the Lake Hotel are located in Ypsilanti Township, south of I-94. Residence halls accomodate 4,000 students, on campus apartments house 350 students, and family housing accomodates 449 families. The university library contains 828,097 volumes. Approximately 72% of students applying for undergraduate admission are accepted. 3,232 scholarships are available, including 312 athletic and 60% of the student body receives some form of financial aid. The fall 1994 freshman class had average SAT scores of 426 verbal and 484 math and a composite ACT of 21.

Community Environment: Named for the Greek general of the 1820's Demetrius Ypsilanti, the community became a city in 1858. Ypsilanti is located in southeastern Michigan, approximately 40 miles west of Detroit and 7 miles from Ann Arbor. In addition to the extensive cultural opportunities at Eastern, the resources of the University of Michigan are 15 minutes away and downtown Detroit is a 45 minute drive. Regular bus service is available. Ypsilanti has an impressive historic district and hosts a Heritage Festival annually in late August.

FERRIS STATE UNIVERSITY *(M-9)*
901 South State Street
Big Rapids, Michigan 49307
Tel: (616) 592-2000; (800) 433-7747; Admissions: (616) 592-2100; Fax: (616) 592-2978

Description: Ferris State University was founded in 1884 as a private institution by Woodbridge N. Ferris and became affiliated with the state of Michigan in 1950. It was named Ferris State College in 1963 and re-named Ferris State University in 1987 by the Michigan Legislature. Ferris is accredited by the North Central Association of Colleges and Schools and by several professional and educational organizations. It operates on the semester system and offers one summer term. The University has earned a national reputation of academic excellence in business, health, technical and professional career-oriented education programming. Enrollment includes 8,286 full-time and 1,972 part-time students. A faculty of 501 provides a faculty-student ratio of 1-16.

Entrance Requirements: High school graduation or equivalent; open enrollment policy; non-high school graduates may be admitted on specialized examination; ACT required; early admission, early decision, delayed admission, rolling admission and advanced placement plans available. $20 application fee.

Costs Per Year: $3,412 tuition; $6,911 out-of-state tuition; $4,171 board and room.

Collegiate Environment: The 600 acre campus is on the Muskegon River in an area which provides some of the best hunting, fishing, and recreation in the state. The library contains more than 200,000 books, a sizeable collection of periodicals (in print and on microfilm) and Michigan and U.S. government documents and legal materials. An Individualized Learning Center with audio-visual materials and equipment is part of the Instructional Resource Center. Living accommodations available for 3,680 men, 2,531 women and 354 married students. Freshman students may not bring a motor vehicle to the campus. Approximately 75% of students applying for admission are accepted. Students may enroll each term and classes begin in August,

January and May. 1,466 scholarships are available, 266 athletic. 70% receive financial aid.

Community Environment: Home for Ferris is Big Rapids, a city of approximately 15,000 residents. The county seat of Mecosta County, Big Rapids is at the junction of U.S. 131 and M-20, 54 miles north of Michigan's second-largest city, Grand Rapids, and within approximately 200 miles of Detroit and Chicago. As one might guess from its name, Big Rapids' primary natural feature is a river, the Muskegon, whose wooded banks wind through town and form the eastern border of the Ferris campus. The former logging community is located in the heart of an extensive recreation area of which Mecosta County, with its 101 lakes and four county parks is a significant part. The city is served by a daily newspaper, one AM and two FM radio stations, a cable television system, a movie theater, roller skating and ice skating rinks, 18-hole college golf course, community pool, diverse commercial districts, four banks, three motels, Clarion Hotel and Conference center, bus lines, a taxi service, 24 churches, a 74-bed hospital, and a community library holding nearly 50,000 volumes.

GLEN OAKS COMMUNITY COLLEGE (Q-8)
62249 Shimmel Road
Centreville, Michigan 49032
Tel: (616) 467-9945; Fax: (616) 467-4114

Description: The independent, public, community college was established when, in the pioneering tradition of their forefathers, the progressive citizens of St. Joseph County, in April of 1965, sought and received approval from the State of Michigan to organize a community college for their county. On June 14, 1965, the voters of St. Joseph County authorized the establishment of Glen Oaks Community College by electing a Board of Trustees and approving a charter millage for its operation and support. Glen Oaks Community College opened its doors in the fall of 1967. It is accredited by the North Central Association of Colleges and Schools. The college offers primarily vocational, technical programs and grants the Associate degree. It operates on the semester system and offers one summer session. Enrollment includes 379 full-time and 1,143 part-time students. A faculty of 29 full-time and 85 part-time gives a faculty-student ratio of 1-16.

Entrance Requirements: Open enrollment policy; high school graduation; non-high school graduates may be admitted on special conditions; early admission, rolling admission, delayed admission plans available.

Costs Per Year: $1,302 tuition; $1,488 out-of-district tuition; $1,953 out of state.

Collegiate Environment: The 350-acre campus is in south central Michigan. The College is located about thirty miles south of Kalamazoo, Michigan, and forty-five miles from South Bend and Angola, Indiana. Western Michigan University, Kalamazoo College, Tri-State University and The University of Notre Dame are thus within easy driving distances for advanced educational opportunities for the residents of St. Joseph County. The library contains 37,121 volumes, 303 periodicals, 182 microforms and 1,174 recordings. Almost all of the students applying for admission meet the requirements and are accepted. Classes begin in September and January.

Community Environment: Glen Oaks is located in the center of St. Joseph County, almost equidistant between Three Rivers and Sturgis, the county's two largest cities. Nestled in the hills of Sherman Township, it overlooks a county population of approximately 60,000 people. The area is primarily agricultural, with heavy-to-light industry focused in Strugis and Three Rivers. Located midway between Chicago and Detroit on the "Chicago Trail," it has the potential for vast economic and population growth. The area also abounds in lakes and rolling hills, affording many opportunities for a variety of recreational activities throughout the year. The citizens are fortunate to be served by modern medical facilities and by well-supported public educational facilities. An energetic civic outreach program provides support for the educational, cultural, civil and economic community and assures its growth and progress.

GMI ENGINEERING AND MANAGEMENT INSTITUTE
(O-12)
1700 W. Third Ave.
Flint, Michigan 48502
Tel: (313) 762-7865; (800) 955-4464

Description: The private institute is a college of engineering and management operating on a five-year cooperative plan in which students alternate between periods of academic study on the campus in Flint and related work experience in 400 sponsoring organizations internationally. It is accredited by the North Central Association of Colleges and Schools and the Accreditation Board for Engineering and Technology. Enrollment is 2,367 undergraduate students. A faculty of 130 provides a faculty-student ratio of 1:13. The institute does not discriminate by reason of an individual's race, color, sex, creed, age or national origin.

Entrance Requirements: High school graduation with rank in upper 20% of graduating class; completion of 16 units including 3 English, 3.5 mathematics, 2 science; ACT or SAT required; early decision, deferred admission, and advanced placement plans are available.

Costs Per Year: $10,150 tuition; $2,980 room and board; $90 student fees; additional expenses vary.

Collegiate Environment: The 45-acre campus is located on the Flint River. The Academic Building is devoted to laboratories that have special facilities such as automotive and instrumentation laser, radio isotope, heat transfer, electricity and electronics, human factors, polymer processing, process development robotics and computer laboratories. The library contains more than 62,000 volumes and 877 periodicals. All freshmen are required to live in the residence halls, which accommodate 530 students. 19 fraternities and sororities provide housing for an additional 500 students. Freshmen co-op students earn approximately $8,000 gross per year in their work periods. Approximately 30% of students applying for admission are accepted including midyear students. Middle 50% range for SAT is 450-570V, 580-690M; ACT composite range is 25-29. Approximately 95% of the freshmen class returned for the sophomore year. The institute recently awarded 14 Certificates and 540 Bachelor degrees to the graduating class. About 10% of last year's senior class continued on to graduate school full-time.

Community Environment: A pioneer in the early days of the automobile industry, Flint is now second only to Detroit. Commercial transportation is provided by rail, air, and bus lines. The metropolitan area has good community services including hospitals, churches and excellent shopping. Recreational facilities are available for golf, skiing, bowling, swimming, most major sports, theatres, drive-ins, and more.

GOGEBIC COMMUNITY COLLEGE (E-1)
Greenbush & Jackson Streets
Ironwood, Michigan 49938
Tel: (906) 932-4231; (800) 682-5910; Fax: (906) 932-0868

Description: The public, two-year college was established as Ironwood Junior College in 1932. Later, in recognition of the support of Gogebic County, the present name was adopted. It offers general academic and vocational-technical programs. The school operates on the semester system and offers two summer sessions. It is accredited by the North Central Association of Colleges and Schools and the National League of Nursing. Enrollment includes 677 full-time and 675 part-time students. A faculty of 40 full-time and 57 part-time gives a faculty-student ratio of 1-17.

Entrance Requirements: Open enrollment policy; accredited high school graduation or equivalent required for degree programs; applicants not meeting all requirements may be admitted as special students; ACT or SAT recommended; $5 application fee; rolling admission plan available.

Costs Per Year: $992 tuition; $1,395 nonresident tuition; $1,230 room; miscellaneous $110.

Collegiate Environment: The college is located in Ironwood on scenic Mt. Zion. The campus includes an Academic Building and a Voc-Tech Building, and a Business Education Center is being planned. The library contains 24,000 titles and 236 periodicals. Housing is provided for 24 men and 24 women. 90% of those applying for admission are accepted. About 60% of the students receive some form of financial aid. Classes begin in late August and January; midyear students are accepted.

Community Environment: On the Michigan-Wisconsin border, in the heart of the Midwest ski area, Ironwood is the trading center and lumbering headquarters of the Gogebic Range. The area has refreshing summers and snowy invigorating winters. The city has a library, churches, a hospital, and passenger transportation via air and bus lines. The community has two theatres, hunting, boating, fishing, and excellent skiing for recreation. There are some housing facilities and part-time job opportunities.

GRAND RAPIDS BAPTIST COLLEGE   *(O-8)*
1001 E. Beltline N.E.
Grand Rapids, Michigan 49505-5897
Tel: (616) 949-5300

Description: The institution is a four-year Christian liberal arts college. It is approved by the General Association of Regular Baptist Churches. The college is accredited by the North Central Association of Colleges and Schools. Enrollment is approximately 311 men and 371 women full-time and 49 men and 96 women part-time. A faculty of 37 full-time and 32 part-time gives an overall faculty-student ratio of approximately 1-11. The semester system is used and one summer session is offered.

Entrance Requirements: High school graduation with rank in upper 50% of graduating class; ACT required; early admission, rolling admission, delayed admission, and advanced placement plans available; $25 application fee.

Costs Per Year: $5,550 tuition; $3,738 room and board; $370 student fees.

Collegiate Environment: The college occupies a beautiful 132-acre campus located 4 miles from downtown Grand Rapids. Miller Library contains 93,111 volumes, 650 periodicals, 29 microfilm titles, and 3,503 nonprint materials. Housing is available for 550 students. Approximately 93% of students applying for admission are accepted. About 67% of the previous freshman class returns for the sophomore year. Students are admitted at midyear; the college seeks a geographically diverse student body. Financial aid is available and about 85% of the students receive financial assistance.

Community Environment: Conservative Christian Liberal Arts on a suburban residential campus.

GRAND RAPIDS COMMUNITY COLLEGE   *(O-8)*
143 Bostwick Street, N.E.
Grand Rapids, Michigan 49503
Tel: (616) 771-4000; Admissions: (616) 771-4100; Fax: (616) 771-3884

Description: The public, two-year college was established in 1914 by the Board of Education upon the recommendation of the University of Michigan. It is accredited by the North Central Association of Colleges and Schools. Students may attend day or evening classes. Classes are offered week days, weekends and off-campus at various locations. Enrollment totals 14,700 students with a faculty of 532. The semester system is used and two summer sessions are offered. An academic cooperative plan with Western Michigan University is available for engineering & technology and manufacturing students.

Entrance Requirements: Open enrollment policy; accredited high school graduation diploma, or GED equivalent required for degree programs; ACT composite score of 16 or college assessment process (asset testing); midyear admission and rolling admission plans available; $20 application fee.

Costs Per Year: $1,264 city-resident tuition; $1,840 state-resident tuition; $2,225 out-of-state tuition.

Collegiate Environment: The college occupies an 11-building complex which is located in the center of the city. The library contains 52,000 volumes and 524 periodicals. Midyear students are accepted and classes begin in late August and January. Financial aid is available to those who qualify. 33% receive aid. All of the students applying for admission are accepted.

Community Environment: See Calvin College

GRAND VALLEY STATE UNIVERSITY   *(O-8)*
College Landing
Allendale, Michigan 49401
Tel: (616) 895-6611; (800) 748-0246; Fax: (616) 895-2000

Description: The university was established in 1960 by the State of Michigan. It is a state-supported, self-governing college that awards the Bachelor of Arts, Science, Business Administration, Fine Arts,

Music, Music Education, Nursing and Social Work degrees, and the Master of Business Administration, Master of Public Administration, Taxation, Nursing, Social Work, Health Sciences, Master of Education degrees and an MS in Physical Therapy. The university is accredited by the North Central Association of Colleges and Schools. It operates on the early semester system and offers two summer sessions. Enrollment is 8,664 full-time and 4,889 part-time students which includes 2,580 graduate students. A faculty of 407 full-time and 312 part-time gives an overall faculty-student ratio of approximately 1-21.

Entrance Requirements: High school graduation; completion of 20 academic units, including 4 English, 3 mathematics, 3 social science, 3 science, and 7 academic electives; ACT and entrance exam required; advanced placement, midyear admission and rolling admission plans available; $20 application fee.

Costs Per Year: $2,702 tuition; $6,288 out-of-state; $4,060 room and board; $1,000 miscellaneous.

Collegiate Environment: The college is located on an 876-acre campus 12 miles west of Grand Rapids. The 38 buildings include residence halls and apartments that accommodate 1,700 students. The library system contains 450,000 volumes and numerous pamphlets, periodicals and microforms. Approximately 75% of students applying for admission are accepted, including midyear students and those from various geographical locations. The average score of the entering freshman class was ACT 23.2 composite. The school offers 1,350 scholarships including 80 athletic and 485 for freshmen. 70% of the students receive financial aid. Approximately 81% of the previous freshman class returns to the campus for the sophomore year. 30% of the senior class continues on to graduate school.

Community Environment: This is a rural community that has Protestant and Catholic churches and a small library. Many part-time job opportunities are available for students. Allendale has facilities for bowling, water sports, and winter sports. The area features an annual winter carnival and spring arts festival.

GREAT LAKES CHRISTIAN COLLEGE   *(P-11)*
6211 W. Willow Highway
Lansing, Michigan 48917-1299
Tel: (517) 321-0242; Fax: (517) 321-5902

Description: Located in Lansing, near the geographical and population centers of the Great Lakes States, the college produces servant-leaders for churches of the region. The Bible is the center of the curriculum, but students also take a core of general studies courses. Central to its purpose is training for vocational ministries in the church. Other vocational courses are available in business, education, and other areas through cooperative programs with nearby colleges and universities. The American Association of Bible Colleges accredits the college. The college operates on the semester system. A small student body of approximately 189 full-time and 13 part-time provides a personalized learning environment. A faculty of 8 full-time and 10 part-time gives a faculty-student ratio of 1-11.

Entrance Requirements: High school graduation or GED; ACT required; open enrollment; midyear admission and rolling admission plans available; $30 application fee.

Costs Per Year: $3,800 tuition; $2,800 room and board.

Collegiate Environment: The college planned and developed the campus which opened in 1972 on a 50-acre site in the capital city's suburbs. The wide-open campus has plenty of space for future growth and has excellent access to major transportation routes and facilities in the area. The library houses 30,000 volumes. Housing accommodates 85 women and 80 men. Apartments are available on campus for 18 married students, with plenty of other housing available in the area. Scholarships and state and federal financial aid are available. 90% of students receive aid. 98% of applicants for admission are accepted.

Community Environment: See Lansing Community College

HENRY FORD COMMUNITY COLLEGE   *(Q-13)*
5101 Evergreen Rd.
Dearborn, Michigan 48128
Tel: (313) 271-2750

Description: The public two-year college was founded in 1938 and was called Fordson Junior College. The present name was adopted in

1952 and shortly thereafter the Ford Motor Company gave 75 acres of land on the former Henry Ford estate for use by the Community College. Programs in technical, general, liberal arts, and preprofessional training are offered. The school is accredited by the North Central Association of Colleges and Schools. Students may attend day, evening, or weekend classes. The semester system is used and one summer session is offered. The college awards the Associate degree. Enrollment is 16,286 day and evening students. There are 904 faculty members providing a faculty-student ratio of 1:18.

Entrance Requirements: Accredited high school graduation or equivalent; open enrollment policy; ACT recommended; non-high school graduates admitted in some circumstances; early admission, early decision, delayed admission, rolling admission plans available.

Costs Per Year: $1,271 Dearborn resident; $1,829 non-residents; $25 student fees.

Collegiate Environment: 8 buildings are completed on this campus. The Fred K. Eshleman Memorial Library contains 73,009 volumes and numerous pamphlets, periodicals, microforms and recordings. Financial aid is available. Almost all applicants are accepted, and students are permitted to enroll at midyear.

Community Environment: Dearborn's boundaries have been extended to join those of Detroit, and it is difficult to discern where one city ends and the other begins. Dearborn is a distinct entity with history, government and industries of its own. The area is called the city with no slums. There are limited job opportunities within the immediate area, though Detroit offers good part-time employment. Camp Dearborn 35 miles northwest offers 6 lakes, a trout stream, picnic groves, a 1/2 mile beach, and camping facilities. Community services include two general hospitals, five public libraries, and limited access to all major forms of public transportation. The city has outstanding public recreation facilities.

HIGHLAND PARK COMMUNITY COLLEGE   *(C-12)*
Glendale at Third
Highland Park, Michigan 48203
Tel: (313) 252-0475

Description: The public, two-year junior college was established in 1918 and is accredited by the North Central Association of Colleges and Schools. Transfer, career, and continuing education programs are offered by the school. The college operates on a semester system with one summer term. Recent enrollment included 721 students. A faculty of 112 gives a faculty-student ratio of 1-21. The college grants the Certificate and Associate degrees.

Entrance Requirements: Open enrollment policy; accredited high school graduation or equivalent required for degree programs; $10 application fee; rolling admission plan available.

Costs Per Year: $1,050 tuition; $1,300 out-of-district tuition; $1,600 out-of-state tuition.

Collegiate Environment: The library contains 18,000 volumes, 2,000 pamphlets, 150 periodicals, 2,183 microforms, 1,055 recordings and audio-visual equipment to enable students to listen to lectures for makeup and review purposes. All students applying for admission are accepted, including midyear students. Classes begin in September and January. Financial assistance is available.

Community Environment: Located in the heart of metropolitan Detroit --"a city within a city." Average January temperature is 26.2 degrees, with July temperatures averaging 71.3. Area has all the major community services, and cultural and recreational facilities are easily accessible.

HILLSDALE COLLEGE   *(R-10)*
33 E. College Street
Hillsdale, Michigan 49242
Tel: (517) 437-7341; Admissions: (517) 437-7341 x2327; Fax: (517) 437-0190

Description: The private, liberal arts college was founded in 1844 under the name of Michigan Central College. Hillsdale is one of very few colleges that does not accept federal assistance. Its four-year curriculum leads to the degree of Bachelor of Arts or Bachelor of Science. It is accredited by the North Central Association of Colleges and Schools. The college operates on the semester system and offers two summer sessions. Enrollment is 1,160 full-time and 52 part-time

students. A faculty of 82 full-time and 33 part-time gives a faculty-student ratio of 1-12. Special programs include a semester in Washington D.C. with experience in congressional offices or the E.R.I. National Journalism Center. Study abroad is offered in Spain, France, Germany, and England.

Entrance Requirements: Accredited high school graduation with rank in top 50% of class; completion of 18 units, including 4 English, 3 mathematics, 2 science, 2 social science, and 2 foreign language; non-high school graduates accepted; early admission, rolling admission, and advanced placement plans available; June 15 application deadline; $15 application fee.

Costs Per Year: $11,090 tuition; $4,700 room and board; $210 student fees; $750 miscellaneous.

Collegiate Environment: The 250-acre campus is 100 miles from Detroit. Dormitory facilities are available for 300 men and 350 women with additional fraternity and sorority housing for 300 students. The library contains 200,000 volumes. The Richardson Heritage room of the Michael Alex Moggey Library is a new special collections library for first editions. Current holdings include a 1787 edition of the Federalist Papers and the first illustrated Bible printed in America with Apocrypha. 78% of students applying for admission are accepted. Students may enroll at midyear. About 90% of the previous freshman class returned to this campus for the sophomore year. Of 500 scholarships offered, 200 are available for freshmen and approximately 75% of students receive financial aid.

Community Environment: This is a county seat located in the south central part of the lower peninsula. In an agricultural region, Hillsdale is a resort and industrial community, manufacturing automobile parts and accessories and tool and die products. The area has bus service and a municipal airport.

HOPE COLLEGE   *(O-7)*
Holland, Michigan 49423
Tel: (616) 395-7000; (800) 968-7850; Fax: (616) 395-7130

Description: This privately supported, four-year, liberal arts undergraduate college is respected as an institution that balances academic excellence with a deep concern for those qualities and values which give purpose and significance to life. A sense of community embraces both residential life and academic experiences and provides numerous opportunities for cultural, physical and spiritual development. A dynamic approach to the liberal arts as preparation for life and vocation is an essential element in Hope's educational process. The historic Christian faith, with an emphasis on freedom, openness and creativity, provides the context within which Hope College operates. Hope College has an independent Board of Trustees and is affiliated with the Reformed Church in America. The institute is fully accredited by the North Central Association of Colleges and Schools. Phi Beta Kappa has chartered a chapter on campus. The college offers the B. Music degree in music history, education, theory or applied music; it also offers the B.A. or B.S. degrees with a variety of majors in more than 30 fields, including the B.S. in Nursing. The preprofessional courses of study include the areas of medicine, dentistry, law, education, engineering, medical technology, ministry and social work. A 3-2 engineering program is available in conjunction with the University of Michigan, Rensselaer Polytechnic Institute, Case Western Reserve, Washington University (St. Louis) and the University of Southern California, upon completion of which students earn 2 Bachelor's or a Bachelor's and Master's degree. The teacher education program provides courses for certification in elementary, secondary and special education. Off-campus studies include Philadelphia Urban Semester, Washington Semester, New York Arts program and extensive overseas programs. Independent study and field experience are also offered. The college operates on the semester system and offers three summer sessions. Enrollment includes 1,127 men and 1,481 women full-time, and 81 men and 136 women part-time. A faculty of 179 full-time and 76 part-time gives a faculty-student ratio of 1-13.

Entrance Requirements: Accredited high school graduation or equivalent with rank in top 50% of class and completion of a solid college preparatory course load including English, mathematics, foreign language, science, and social science; either SAT or ACT acceptable; applicants not meeting all requirements will be considered; advanced placement and rolling admission plans available; $25 application fee.

Costs Per Year: $12,275 tuition; $4,431 room and board; $84 student fees.

Collegiate Environment: The 45-acre campus is approximately 160 miles north of Chicago and 180 miles west of Detroit. Coed and single-sex dormitories, apartments, and college-owned houses accommodate 2,056 students. Approximately 20% of the students belong to Greek organizations. The new Van Wylen Library contains 300,000 bound volumes, 1,494 periodicals, 178,924 titles on microform, 11,400 records, tapes, and CDs, 14 CD-ROMs, and 18,000 ultrafiche of the Library of American Civilization (LAC). Over the past 15 years, the college has committed tremendous resources to building or renovating the following: the library, art center and gallery, the computer center, student union, theaters, academic/classroom buildings, residence halls, apartments, the science center, physical education center, athletic fields, and conference center. Many Christian activities broaden the range of student involvement. The college maintains active intramural and intercollegiate sports programs. Financial assistance is available and 598 students receive need-based aid. 85% receive some form of financial aid. 89% of the applicants are accepted.

Community Environment: Settled by the Dutch in 1847, the city still has many of the characteristics of a Dutch town. This is the tulip center of America, and millions of these flowers bloom in the parks and residential sections during May. Located on Lake Macatawa and Lake Michigan, the area offers many opportunities for water and other outdoor sports activities. Holland is surrounded by a large fruit-growing and farming area, and is also an industrial and resort town. The city has bus service, two airports, a public library, several churches, a hospital and several parks. The Greater Holland area has a population of approximately 75,000; it is a very friendly, safe and clean community.

JACKSON COMMUNITY COLLEGE   *(Q-11)*
2111 Emmons Road
Jackson, Michigan 49201
Tel: (517) 787-0800; Fax: (517) 789-1631

Description: The county community college offers 27 one-year and two-year occupational programs in its Vocational/Technical division, as well as a Transfer General Studies program. It is accredited by the North Central Association of Colleges and Schools. The college grants the Associate degree. It operates on the semester system and offers one spring session. Enrollment includes 1,348 full-time and 5,051 part-time students. A faculty of 109 full-time and 350 part-time provides an overall faculty-student ratio of 1-16.

Entrance Requirements: Open enrollment policy; Jackson County residents have first priority; non-high school graduates may be considered; SAT or ACT; ASSET; early admission, rolling admission, midyear admission and advanced placement plans are available.

Costs Per Year: $1,372 district tuition; $1,627 out-of-district; $1,927 out-of-state; various course fees.

Collegiate Environment: The college is located on a 480-acre campus with ten buildings, including a library of 50,000 volumes. Classes begin in September and January. 125 scholarships and special financial aid are available. 53% of students receive some form of financial aid. Almost all of the applicants are accepted.

Community Environment: The college is located seven miles south of Jackson, an important industrial city that manufactures mainly automobile and airplane parts and supplies. Major highways provide access to Chicago and Detroit. The county has numerous lakes, golf courses and parks. Cultural activities include a symphony orchestra, music, and dance and theater groups. Also located in the area are the Illuminated Cascades, the Ella Sharp Museum and the Michigan Space and Science Center.

KALAMAZOO COLLEGE   *(Q-9)*
1200 Academy St.
Kalamazoo, Michigan 49006-3295
Tel: (616) 337-7166; (800) 253-3602; Fax: (616) 337-7390

Description: This private liberal arts college offers a program of on-campus academic offerings and off-campus foreign study, career development, independent study, and research projects. The college was founded in 1833 through the determination of a Baptist missionary and a Michigan pioneer. It became Kalamazoo College in 1855 and was granted the power to confer degrees. The college is accredited by

the North Central Association of Colleges and Schools. It is one of 12 colleges comprising the Great Lake College Association. It operates on the quarter system. Enrollment includes 535 men and 706 women. A faculty of 91 full-time and 17 part-time provides a faculty-student ratio of 1-12. Special programs include individualized projects off-campus for seniors, and an extensive overseas program at foreign study centers in France, Germany, Spain, Equador, Sierre Leone, Senegal China, Mexico, and Kenya. An academic cooperative plan is maintained with the University of Michigan, Washington University, and Georgia Tech for engineering students. The college grants the Bachelor degree.

Entrance Requirements: Accredited high school graduation with B or higher g.p.a.; recommended completion of college-preparatory course of 16 units including 4 English, 3 mathematics, 2 science, 2 foreign language, 2 social studies; SAT or ACT required; students not meeting all requirements admitted under certain circumstances; rolling admission, delayed admission and advanced placement plans available; accepts international baccalaureate.

Costs Per Year: $16,194 tuition; $5,094 room and board.

Collegiate Environment: The campus contains 29 buildings on 50 acres in the residential area of Kalamazoo. Upjohn Library houses 309,111 volumes of print and audio visual material, 1,338 periodicals, and a rare book collection of 2,500 volumes. The Light Fine Arts Building houses the Dalton and Dungeon Theatres, a recital hall, photography labs, practice rooms, a music library which houses 3,500 musical recordings and 7,500 scores, an art gallery and studio art facilities. Six permanent residence halls accommodate 841 students. All students who are not living with their parents must live in college-approved housing. The college lists 900 placements for career internships around the country. The Foreign Study Program provides the opportunity to study abroad and involves almost 85% of the students. The Senior Individualized Project is designed to give each senior an opportunity to carry on a research or study project, free from direct faculty supervision. Students maintain radio station WJMD. The athletic program is an integral part of the college activities and the school is a member of the National Collegiate Athletic Association. Special programs on campus include the Small Business Institute, Stryker Center for Educational and Management Studies, summer athletic camps, Music Center (Suzuki instruction), Academically Talented Youth Program, and a special program for gifted and talented middle school and high school students (ATYP). Over 200 scholarships are available ranging from $1,500 to $15,000. 80% of the students receive financial assistance. About 93% of the applicants are accepted, including midyear students. The average high school standing of the 1994 freshman class placed 81% in the top quarter of their high school class. Nearly 85% of the previous freshman class return to this campus for their sophomore year. About 80% of the graduating class enters graduate or professional schools within five years of graduation.

Community Environment: Kalamazoo is a college-centered community, 130 miles from Detroit and Chicago. The airport serves nine major airlines. Locally, many companies, hospitals and local governments make internships available to students.

KALAMAZOO VALLEY COMMUNITY COLLEGE   *(Q-9)*
6767 West O Ave
Kalamazoo, Michigan 49009
Tel: (616) 372-5000

Description: This publicly supported college opened for its first class in September 1968, and has received full accreditation from the North Central Association of Colleges and Schools. Enrollment is 11,000 students. The semester system is used and three summer sessions are offered. The college grants the Certificate and the Associate degree.

Entrance Requirements: Open enrollment policy; accredited high school graduation or equivalent required for degree programs; applicants not meeting all requirements may be admitted as special students; early admission, early decision, rolling admission, delayed admission and advanced placement plans available.

Costs Per Year: $1,116 tuition; $2,077 out-of-district tuition; $3,038 out-of-state, based on 30 credit hours.

Collegiate Environment: A purchase of 187 acres of rolling farmland in Texas Township was made for the permanent campus of the college. A large, modern facility has been constructed that provides adequately for current needs. The library contains 75,279 volumes and 504 microforms. Financial assistance is available. All students applying for admission are accepted, including midyear students. There is no on-campus housing but students can arrange to stay at Western Michigan University.

Community Environment: See Western Michigan University.

KELLOGG COMMUNITY COLLEGE   *(Q-9)*
450 North Ave.
Battle Creek, Michigan 49017
Tel: (616) 965-3931; (800) 955-4522; Fax: (616) 965-8850

Description: The public, two-year college was founded in 1956. Enrollment is 1,787 full-time, 5,384 part-time, and 2,713 evening students. A faculty of 108 full-time and 160 part-time gives an overall faculty-student ratio of approximately 1-18. The college operates on the semester system and offers two summer terms. It is accredited by the North Central Association of Colleges and Schools and offers arts, science and applied science programs leading to Associate degrees.

Entrance Requirements: High school graduation or equivalent; open enrollment policy; advanced placement, early admission, early decision, and rolling admission plans available.

Costs Per Year: $1,080 county-resident tuition; $1,800 state-resident; $2,790 out-of-state.

Collegiate Environment: Classes begin in August and January. All students applying for admission are accepted, including students at midyear. The library houses 80,000 volumes, 1,000 periodicals, and 8,250 media items. Financial aid is available. Of 125 scholarships offered, many are available for freshmen. 60% of students receive financial aid.

Community Environment: This city may arouse nostalgia for college students, since this is where they mailed their boxtops in former years to receive secret codegraph rings, super spy kits, and more. This is the home of cereal manufacturers. Other manufacturers produce packaging machines and auto parts. Commercial passenger facilities include bus, rail, and air. Some part-time employment is available for students. The city has good recreational areas for picnicking, golf, camping, tobogganing and skiing. All are easily accesible. The American Amateur Baseball Series is held here annually.

KENDALL COLLEGE OF ART AND DESIGN   *(O-8)*
1111 Division Ave. North
Grand Rapids, Michigan 49503-3194
Tel: (616) 451-2787; (800) 676-2787; Fax: (616) 451-9867

Description: The school is a private, nonprofit, professional art and design college that was incorporated in 1928 as the David Wolcott Kendall Memorial School. The enrollment is 384 full-time and 190 part-time students. A faculty of 34 full-time gives a faculty-student ratio of 1-12. The school operates on the semester system and offers two summer sessions. The school grants a 4-year Bachelor of Fine Arts Degree in six different majors.

Entrance Requirements: Open enrollment policy; high school graduation or equivalent with GPA 2.25; students must submit a short statement of purpose that delineates the prospective student's artistic interests and career goals and specifies how the college may assist the student; SAT or ACT required; $35 application fee.

Costs Per Year: $9,990 tuition; additional supplies average $1,600.

Collegiate Environment: Approximately 68% of students applying for admission meet the requirements and are accepted. Students are admitted at midyear; the student body represents a diverse geographical distribution. The school library contains 15,725 volumes, 100 periodicals and 35,000 slides. 26 scholarships are available. 69% of students receive some form of financial aid.

Community Environment: See Calvin College.

KIRTLAND COMMUNITY COLLEGE   *(K-10)*
10775 N. St. Helen Road
Roscommon, Michigan 48653
Tel: (517) 275-5121; Admissions: (517) 275-5121 x284; Fax: (517) 275-8210

Description: This public, two-year college opened in 1968 and offers transfer, career, and continuing education programs. It operates on the semester system and offers one summer accelerated semester. Enrollment of 462 men and 890 women includes 630 full-time and 719 part-time students. A faculty of 39 full-time and 56 part-time provides an overall faculty-student ratio of approximately 1-14. The college is fully accredited by the North Central Association of Colleges and Schools and grants the Certificate and the Associate degree.

Entrance Requirements: Open enrollment policy; accredited high school graduation or equivalent required for degree programs; non-high school graduates are admitted for some courses; early admission, rolling admission and advanced placement plans available.

Costs Per Year: $1,496 state-resident tuition; $2,576 out-of-state tuition; $120 student fees; $2,000 miscellaneous.

Collegiate Environment: The 180-acre campus has 9 buildings including a library of 37,500 volumes, 735 records and tapes, 250 periodicals and 54 microfilms. Financial assistance is available and 74% of the students receive aid. All applicants applying for admission are accepted including midyear students. Approximately 53% of the previous freshman class returned for the sophomore year. The college awarded 102 Certificates and 175 Associate degrees to the 1989-90 graduating class.

Community Environment: The college is located in the heart of Michigan's four-season vacationland amidst excellent hunting, fishing, swimming, boating, skiing and snowmobiling lands and lakes. Interstate Route I-75 provides the most direct means of approach to within twelve miles of the campus, which is located at the juncture of Roscommon, Ogemaw, Oscoda and Crawford counties on County Road F-97. The college also operates its aircraft maintenance technology program at a college-owned instruction hangar facility located at the Grayling Airport in Grayling, Michigan.

LAKE MICHIGAN COMMUNITY COLLEGE   *(Q-7)*
2755 E. Napier Avenue
Benton Harbor, Michigan 49022-1899
Tel: (616) 927-3571; (800) 252-4562; Fax: (616) 927-6656

Description: The public, two-year college was organized in 1946 as the Junior College of Benton Harbor. The present name was adopted in 1963 after it became county affiliated. Transfer, career, and continuing education programs are offered by the school. It operates on the semester system and offers 2 summer terms. Enrollment is 369 men and 588 women full-time and 1,109 men and 1,750 women part-time. A faculty of 72 full-time and 200 part-time provides an overall faculty-student ratio of approximately 1-18. The college is accredited by the North Central Association of Colleges and Schools and grants the Certificate and Associate degree.

Entrance Requirements: Open enrollment policy; high school graduation; non-high school graduates may attend on part-time basis; early admission, early decision, rolling admission, delayed admission, and advanced placement plans available.

Costs Per Year: $1,050 county tuition; $1,350 state resident; $1,650 nonresident; $180 fees.

Collegiate Environment: The college campus is situated on 260 acres and includes a library housing 95,000 volumes, 286 periodicals and 7,000 recordings. Approximately 98% of the students applying for admission are accepted, including midyear students. Of the 200 scholarships offered, 75 are for freshmen. 40% of the freshman class returns for the sophomore year.

Community Environment: Lake Michigan College is located in Benton Harbor, Michigan, within a population center of approximately 70,000 people. Lying 90 miles northeast of Chicago, the Twin Cities of Benton Harbor and St. Joseph are located on opposite sides of the St. Joseph River, which empties into Lake Michigan. Both cities have beautiful lakeshore beaches that attract thousands of tourists yearly. There are over 170 industrial firms in the immediate area and the largest cash-to-grower fruit market in the United States. The community occupies an area approximately 600 feet above sea level. Because the Twin Cities are adjacent to Lake Michigan, boating, fishing, and swimming are major recreational interests. Major cities and universities are within easy commuting distance; hence, citizens of this community have a variety of cultural activities at their disposal.

Branch Campuses: Niles, South Campus, 111 Spruce St., (616) 684-5850; Berrien Springs, Berrian Springs High School, (616) 471-

2593; Three Oaks, River Valley High School, (616) 756-9541; South Haven, L.C. Mohr High School, (616) 637-0510; Lawrence, Van Buren Vocational/Technical Center, (616) 674-8001.

LAKE SUPERIOR STATE UNIVERSITY   *(F-11)*
Saulte Ste. Marie, Michigan 49783
Tel: (906) 632-6841; (800) 682-4800

Description: This University was established in 1946. It is accredited by the North Central Association of Colleges and Secondary Schools and grants the Certificate, Associate and Bachelor degrees and Master in Business Administration degree. It operates on the semester system and offers one summer session. Enrollment is 2,517 full-time and 640 part-time undergraduates and 144 graduate students. A faculty of 114 gives a faculty-student ratio of 1-19.

Entrance Requirements: High school graduation with 2.0 or better GPA in academic subjects only; ACT required; rolling admission and advanced placement plans available; $20 application fee for undergraduates; $25 application fee for graduates.

Costs Per Year: $3,312 tuition; $6,456 out-of-state; $4,228 room and board; $400-$600 books.

Collegiate Environment: This 120-acre campus has modern academic facilities and an extensive sports complex. The campus has housing facilities for 1,088 students. The library contains 197,821 titles, 775 periodicals, 139,128 microforms, and 2,672 audiovisual materials. Approximately 82% of students applying for admission are accepted. Students may be admitted at midyear. About 75% of the students receive financial assistance.

Community Environment: Sault Ste. Marie, population 14,500, is located at the northern end of Interstate highway 75 in Michigan's Eastern Peninsula. A favorite spot for vacationers, the area offers scenic beauty and recreational opportunities for all seasons. The University is situated on top of a hill overlooking the St. Mary's River and the famous "Soo" Locks that make it possible for ships up to 1,100 feet long to pass between Lake Superior and Lake Huron. Across the river is Sault Ste. Marie, Ontario, population 83,000.

LANSING COMMUNITY COLLEGE   *(P-11)*
422 N. Washington Square P.O. Box 40010
Lansing, Michigan 48901
Tel: (517) 483-1200

Description: The public, liberal arts college is accredited by the North Central Association of Colleges and Schools. The college grants the Associate degree and one year certificate. An Army and Air Force ROTC program is available. The college provides two-year occupationally oriented programs in health careers, business, technology, telcommunication and the arts. The college operates on the semester system and offers one summer session. The enrollment includes 4,062 full-time and 13,090 part-time students. A faculty of 198 full-time and 800 part-time gives a faculty-student ratio of 1-21.

Entrance Requirements: Open enrollment policy; high school graduation or equivalent; non-high school graduates admitted for some courses; early admission, early decision, rolling admission, midyear admission and advanced placement plans available; $10 application fee.

Costs Per Year: $1,050 tuition; $1,590 out-of-district tuition; $2,130 out-of-state tuition; $2,175 International; $15 student fees.

Collegiate Environment: The 14-acre campus has 10 buildings, including a library of over 115,000 volumes. 99% of applicants are accepted. 105 scholarships are available including 45 for freshmen. Approximately 25% of the students receive some form of financial aid.

Community Environment: Named capital of the state in 1847, Lansing is well-known for its automotive industries. Over two-thirds of its products are gas engines, automobile parts, drop forgings and castings. The State Historical Museum is located here. Area has 10 golf courses, several theatres, bowling, and many churches. Excellent part-time employment is available for students.

LAWRENCE TECHNOLOGICAL UNIVERSITY   *(C-11)*
21000 W. Ten Mile Road
Southfield, Michigan 48075
Tel: (810) 402-4000; (800) 225-5588; Admissions: (810) 204-3160; Fax: (810) 204-3727

Description: This college was founded in 1932 as a college of engineering. In 1955 the college moved from Highland Park to the 85-acre campus in Southfield, a suburb of Detroit. The university is accredited by the North Central Association of Colleges and Schools and professionally by respective accrediting organizations. At the Bachelor degree level, it has colleges of architecture & design, engineering, business and industrial management, and arts and science. The College of Arts and Science has Bachelor of Science programs in chemistry, mathematics, math/computer science, humanities and physics. There are four Associate degree programs in Engineering technologies offered through the College of Engineering. Associate degrees in Information Systems and Chemical Technology are also offered through the Colleges of Management and Arts & Science, respectively. It operates on the semester system and offers three summer sessions. Students may attend day or evening classes. Enrollment includes 1,561 full-time and 2,245 part-time undergraduates, and 353 graduate students. A faculty of 107 full-time and 185 part-time provides a faculty-student ratio of 1-26.

Entrance Requirements: High school graduation with rank in upper 60% of graduating class; completion of 20 units, distribution requirements differ depending on program; advanced placement, early admission, early decision, rolling admission and midyear admission plans available; $30 application fee.

Costs Per Year: $7,830 average tuition.

Collegiate Environment: 7 buildings are located on a campus overlooking the Rouge River. The library contains 70,000 volumes, 1,000 periodicals, and 23,000 microforms. About 78% of students applying for admission meet the requirements and are accepted. A geographically diverse student body is desired. Both merit-based and need-based financial assistance is available. 60 scholarships are offered and 65% of the undergraduates receive some form of financial aid. Day classes begin in September, December, and March. Evening classes begin in August and January. Graduate classes follow a day calendar. Housing accomodates 402 students.

Community Environment: The city is a northern suburb of Detroit, with excellent full-time and part-time employment opportunties for students. Good recreational facilities are nearby. Southfield has excellent shopping areas and a Civic Center that includes a 166-acre park. Transportation and other facilities of Detroit are easily accessible.

MACOMB COMMUNITY COLLEGE   *(P-13)*
14500 Twelve Mile Road
Warren, Michigan 48093
Tel: (313) 445-7000

Description: The two-year public institution was created by the citizens of Macomb County; first classes were held in 1954. The South Campus has been in operation since September, 1965, and offers transfer programs in arts, science and general studies, and career programs in business, Allied Health, Public Service, and industrial technology leading to the Associate degree. The college operates on the semester system and offers one summer session. Enrollment includes 25,355 students. A faculty of 305 full-time and 518 part-time gives a faculty-student ratio of 1:32. The college is accredited by the Michigan Commission on College Accreditation and received full accreditation by the North Central Association of Colleges and Schools in 1970.

Entrance Requirements: Open enrollment policy; accredited high school graduation or equivalent required for degree programs; applicants not meeting all requirements may be admitted as special students. Early admission, rolling admission, delayed admission and advanced placement plans available. $10 application fee.

Costs Per Year: $1,504 county resident tuition; $2,279 nonresident tuition.

Collegiate Environment: The college maintains 3 campuses: the 159-acre South Campus consists of 17 buildings including a library housing 120,000 volumes; the 227-acre Center Campus consists of 12 buildings. All those who apply for admission are accepted. Classes begin in August and January, and midyear students are admitted. Special financial assistance is available for economically handicapped students.

Community Environment: Community has many libraries, churches of various denominations, hospitals, and excellent shopping facilities. Some part-time work is available for students. City has major recreational facilities.

MADONNA UNIVERSITY *(P-13)*
36600 Schoolcraft Road
Livonia, Michigan 48150
Tel: (313) 591-5000; Admissions: (313) 591-5052; Fax: (313) 591-0156

Description: This private, coeducational liberal arts university is conducted by the Felician Sisters of the Roman Catholic Church and was incorporated as a senior college in 1947. The school consists of five divisions: Humanities; Science and Technology; Nursing; Business and Computer Information Systems; and Social Sciences. It is accredited by the North Central Association of Colleges and Schools. The college operates on the semester system and awards the Associate, Bachelor and Master degrees. Enrollment includes 1,367 full-time and 2,389 part-time undergraduate and 399 graduate students. A faculty of 111 full-time and 190 part-time gives an overall faculty-student ratio of 1:18.

Entrance Requirements: High school graduation or equivalent completion of 16 units for Nursing program, including 1 each of algebra, biology and chemistry, and ACT; early admission, early decision, rolling admission, midyear admission, and advanced placement plans available. $25 application fee.

Costs Per Year: $5,400 tuition; $4,000 room and board; additional expenses average $2,521.

Collegiate Environment: The university is housed in residence and academic buildings located in this Detroit suburb. The school's dormitory capacity accommodates 154 men and women in separate housing areas. The library houses 112,976 volumes. Approximately 77% of students applying for admission meet the requirements and are accepted. Students may enroll at midyear, and the college accepts students from various geographical sections of the country. The middle 50% range of scores for the entering freshman class were ACT 18-22 composite. Financial aid is available, and of the 200 scholarships offered, 35 are for freshmen. About 25% of the students receive some form of financial aid.

Community Environment: See Schoolcraft College

MARYGROVE COLLEGE *(P-14)*
8425 West McNichols Road
Detroit, Michigan 48221
Tel: (313) 862-5200; Fax: (313) 864-6670

Description: This Roman Catholic institution is a coeducational liberal arts and graduate school. The college began in 1846 with the establishment of St. Mary Academy in Monroe, Michigan, by the Congregation of the Sisters, Servants of the Immaculate Heart of Mary. In 1927 the name became Marygrove College and the move was made to Detroit. It is accredited by the North Central Association of Colleges and Schools and is approved by the American Association of Universities. The college grants the Associate, Baccalaureate, Master of Education, Master of Arts in Administration, and Master of Arts in Pastoral Ministry degrees. It operates on the semester system and offers one summer session. Enrollment includes 1,218 full-time and 539 part-time undergraduates, and 128 graduate students. A faculty of 59 full-time and 13 part-time provides a faculty-student ratio of 1-13.

Entrance Requirements: Accredited high school graduation with B average and rank in upper 25% of graduating class; completion of 16 units including 4 English, 2 mathematics, 1 science, 2 foreign languages, 2 social studies; ACT or SAT or GRE required; early admission, early decision, rolling admission, midyear admission and advanced placement programs available; application fee $15.

Costs Per Year: $8,094 tuition; $3,956 room and board; miscellaneous $100.

Collegiate Environment: The 68-acre campus is located 6 miles from the center of the city. There are 10 buildings and the library contains 185,000 volumes, 825 periodicals, 15,500 microforms, and 7000 recordings. The coed dormitory capacity is 145 students. 52% of applicants are accepted. Scholarships are available and 93% of students receive some form of financial aid.

Community Environment: Located 15 minutes from downtown Detroit, Marygrove offers considerable cultural and social opportunities. Theater, symphony, ballet, opera, and the nationally famous Detroit Institute of Arts are within easy commuting distance. Shopping centers, art galleries, sports arenas, and recreation centers are nearby.

MICHIGAN CHRISTIAN COLLEGE *(P-13)*
800 West Avon Road
Rochester Hills, Michigan 48307
Tel: (810) 651-5800; (800) 521-6010; Admissions: (810) 650-6017; Fax: (810) 650-6060

Description: This private, coeducational college was founded and is supported by the Church of Christ. It is accredited by the North Central Association of Colleges and Schools. The college operates on the semester system and offers one summer session. Enrollment is non-sectarian. Enrollment includes 194 men and 217 women full and part-time. A faculty of 23 full-time and 15 part-time gives a faculty-student ratio of 1:13. The college grants the Associate in Arts or Science degree, the Bachelor of Religious Education and the Bachelor of Business Administration.

Entrance Requirements: High school graduation or equivalent; ACT required; early admission, early decision, advanced placement, delayed admission, midyear admission and rolling admission plans available. $25 application fee.

Costs Per Year: $5,420 tuition; $3,332 room and board.

Collegiate Environment: The college encourages social activities of a wholesome nature. Each student is required to attend daily chapel and to enroll in a Bible or other approved course each quarter. The 83-acre campus is near Detroit. It contains eleven buildings, with a library of 51,952 volumes and dormitory facilities for 290 students. 90% of the students receive financial aid. About 80% of the applicants are accepted, including midyear students.

Community Environment: See Oakland University

MICHIGAN STATE UNIVERSITY *(O-11)*
East Lansing, Michigan 48824-1046
Tel: (517) 355-8332; Fax: (517) 353-1647

Description: The state university is accredited by the North Central Association of Colleges and Schools and by respective professional and educational organizations. The university grants the Bachelor degree, Master degree, Specialist degree, Doctorate Degree and professional degrees in Medicine, Osteopathy and Veterinary Medicine. Optional Army and Air Force ROTC programs are offered. It operates on the semester system with two summer sessions. Enrollment includes 26,914 full-time, 4,142 part-time undergraduate students, and 9,198 graduate students.

Entrance Requirements: Accredited high school graduation with completion of 16 units including 4 English, 3 mathematics, 3 social science, 2 science required, and 2 foreign language units recommended; SAT or ACT required; GRE required for some graduate programs; early decision, rolling admission, and advanced placement plans available. July 30 undergraduate application deadline; $30 application fee.

Costs Per Year: $4,102 tuition; $10,658 out-of-state tuition; $3,764 room and board; $524 student fees.

Collegiate Environment: The 2,010-acre campus has a familiar landmark in Beaumont Tower, which stands on the site of the first building where agriculture was taught as a science on a university campus. There are over 400 buildings on the campus. The Wharton Center for the Performing Arts, completed in 1982, is a cultural center for the campus and the area, constructed at the cost of 20.1 million dollars. On South Campus one finds the world's most powerful superconducting cyclotron, the medical complex, and sophisticated scientific research laboratories. Athletic facilities include the Jack Breslin Student Events Center, Gymnasium and Fieldhouse which seats 15,500 for basketball, concerts and other activities, the Spartan Stadium with a seating capacity of 76,000, and two intramural sports buildings, one of which has Olympic outdoor and indoor pools. The Kellogg Center for Continuing Education is one of the largest and finest-equipped conference centers in the nation. The university libraries contain 3,904,095 volumes, 28,007 periodical subscriptions, 4,883,791 microform units, and over 26,000 audiovisual materials. There are living accommodations for 16,189 single undergraduates and 858 graduate students. There are furnished apartments for married students and for faculty and staff, and coeducational residence halls are available. The university recognizes 31 national fraternity chapters and 18 sororities, most of which maintain houses for members in East Lansing. Approximately 80% of undergraduate students applying for admission meet the requirements and are accepted, including midyear students. The university has a program of financial aid offering loans, and part-time work. 45% of undergraduate students receive some form of financial assistance.

Community Environment: Located in a metropolitan area adjacent to Lansing, the state capital of Michigan. City has four hospitals, churches of all denominations, 24 movie theaters, and good shopping facilities within the immediate area.

MICHIGAN TECHNOLOGICAL UNIVERSITY   *(C-3)*
1400 Townsend Drive
Houghton, Michigan 49931-1295
Tel: (906) 487-2335; Fax: (906) 487-3343

Description: The state university was founded in 1885 as a mining college. It is accredited by the North Central Association of Colleges and Schools and by respective professional accrediting organizations. The university has steadily expanded its facilities and programs, especially in engineering and sciences, but including liberal arts and business administration. The university grants the Associate, Baccaluareate, Masters and Doctoral degrees and secondary teaching certification in the sciences. Optional Army and Air Force ROTC programs are offered. The university operates on the quarter system and offers three summer sessions. Enrollment includes 6,006 full-time and 454 part-time undergraduates and 684 graduate students. A faculty of 360 full-time and 40 part-time gives a faculty-student ratio of 1-15.

Entrance Requirements: Accredited high school graduation or equivalent rank in the upper half of the high school graduating class; completion of 15 units including 3 English, 2 mathematics, and 1 science; additional units required for various courses; rolling admission, delayed admission, midyear admission and advanced placement programs available; $30 application fee; Aug. 1 application deadline.

Costs Per Year: $3,510 tuition; $8,127 nonresident; $3,978 room and board; $126 student fees; $900 miscellaneous.

Collegiate Environment: The main campus is located 550 miles northwest of Detroit and 425 miles north of Chicago. It extends about a mile along the shores of Portage Lake. Some of the deepest copper mines are but a short distance from the campus as are thousands of acres of forest lands. The university owns approximately 4,000 acres of land including the main campus, the Ford Forestry Center at Alberta, and various experimental forest tracts. The main campus consists of 160 acres on which 61 buildings are located. Housing facilities accommodate 2,800 single students and 351 families. The library contains 785,936 volumes, 5,046 periodicals, 415,801 microforms and 3,000 audiovisual materials. 71% of the students receive financial aid. The university offers 1,718 scholarships, which include 162 athletic and 679 for freshmen. Approximately 92% of the applicants are accepted. Average SAT scores are 506V and 623M. Classes begin in September, November, March and June, and students are admitted at the beginning of each quarter. Approximately 85% of last year's freshman class returned for the second year of study.

Community Environment: Located in a rural area, the city is in the heart of the colorful Copper Country of Michigan's upper peninsula. Transportation is available via passenger air and bus service. Excellent water and winter sports are available. The community has a public library, churches for all major religions, a hospital, and opportunities for a variety of recreational and cultural activities. Part-time employment is available.

MONROE COUNTY COMMUNITY COLLEGE   *(R-13)*
1555 South Raisinville Road
Monroe, Michigan 48161
Tel: (313) 242-7300; Fax: (313) 242-9711

Description: The school is a public community college supported by the State and by Monroe County. It was established in 1964. It is a member of the American Association of Community and Junior Colleges and of the Council of North Central Community Colleges and is accredited by the North Central Association of Colleges and Schools. It operates on the semester system and offers one summer term. Enrollment includes 1,118 full-time and 2,805 part-time students. A faculty of 54 full-time and 147 part-time gives a faculty-student ratio of 1-25.

Entrance Requirements: Open enrollment policy; high school graduation or equivalent; admission is granted to non-high school graduates in special circumstances; ACT required for Nursing program. No application fee; rolling admission, midyear admission, early decision and early admission plans available.

Costs Per Year: $888 district resident tuition; $1,416 out-of-district; $1,584 out-of-state; $20/semester registration fee.

Collegiate Environment: The college is located at the west end of Lake Erie on a 150-acre campus and contains 5 buildings. The library is the focal point of the campus and contains 47,352 volumes, 321 periodicals, 146 microforms, 6,196 audiovisual materials, and 6 CD-ROMs. Dialog on-line bibliographic services are available. Financial aid is available. 99% of the applicants are accepted. Classes begin in September, January, May, and June.

Community Environment: The third oldest community in the state, Monroe was founded in 1780 by the French. This early settlement, called Frenchtown, was the scene of the River Raisin Massacre in 1813. The only Michigan port on Lake Erie, Monroe includes among its industries large nurseries, paper mills, a limestone quarry, recreation, and a branch automotive factory. It is a suburban city with a community airport and bus lines easily accessible. There are many civic, fraternal and veteran's organizations in this area. Community has a library, YMCA, museum, hospital, theater, 3 golf courses, many public parks and 4 shopping centers.

MONTCALM COMMUNITY COLLEGE   *(N-9)*
2800 College Drive
Sidney, Michigan 48885
Tel: (517) 328-2111; Fax: (517) 328-2950

Description: The public community college was established in 1965. The first classes were held in the Fall of 1967. Transfer, career, and continuing education programs are offered by the school and lead to a Certificate or an Associate degree. The college is accredited by the North Central Association of Colleges and Schools. It operates on the semester system and offers one summer session. Enrollment includes 582 full-time and 1,436 part-time students. A faculty of 27 full-time and 63 part-time provides a factulty student ratio of 1-18.

Entrance Requirements: Open enrollment policy; accredited high school graduation or equivalent; rolling admissions; No application fee.

Costs Per Year: $1,170 district tuition; $1,770 out-of-district tuition; $2,160 out-of-state tuition; $24 student fees; additional expenses average $250.

Collegiate Environment: The 140-acre campus has 5 buildings which include a library of 25,000 volumes and 200 periodicals. Financial assistance is available and of the 41 scholarships offered, 19 are available for freshmen. Approximately 68% of the current student body receives some form of financial assistance.

Community Environment: Located in a rural area. Air transportation accessible within a one-hour drive. There are 104 lakes in the county providing excellent recreational facilities. Some part-time employment is available for students. Neighboring city has theatres, libraries and hospitals.

MUSKEGON COMMUNITY COLLEGE   *(N-7)*
221 S. Quarterline Road
Muskegon, Michigan 49441
Tel: (616) 773-9131; Admissions: (616) 777-0364; Fax: (616) 777-0334

Description: The public, coeducational, junior college was established in 1926 by the Muskegon Board of Education. The present name has been used since 1963, when the college was placed on a county-wide basis. Transfer, career, and continuing education programs lead to an Associate degree. The school is accredited by the North Central Association of Colleges and Schools. It operates on the semester system and offers two summer sessions and one spring session. Enrollment is 4,720 students. A faculty of 200 gives a faculty-student ratio of 1-23.

Entrance Requirements: Open enrollment policy; accredited high school graduation or equivalent; early admission, early decision, mid-year admission, advanced placement, rolling admission plans available.

Costs Per Year: $1,209 tuition; $1751 out-of-district; $2,216 out-of-state.

Collegiate Environment: The Academic Complex, Gymnasium, and Vocational-Technical department are located on a beautiful 111-acre campus. The library contains 47,547 volumes, 400 microforms and 350 periodicals. A special program for the culturally disadvantaged enables low-mark students to successfully attend the school. All applicants are accepted. Scholarships are available and 60% of students receive some form of financial aid.

Community Environment: Formerly known as the Lumber Queen of the World, cutting 800 million board feet of lumber in 1888, Muskegon is the largest city on the east bank of Lake Michigan. Today it is an important lake port and a manufacturing and resort center. Numerous industries produce automotive parts, foundry products, paper, oil, chemicals and recreational equipment. Area has an international airport and a seaway-depth port. There are art galleries, museums, and historical sites located within the immediate vicinity. The nearby Muskegon River offers excellent fishing, boating, and canoeing.

NORTH CENTRAL MICHIGAN COLLEGE (H-10)
1515 Howard Street
Petoskey, Michigan 49770
Tel: (616) 348-6600; Admissions: (616) 348-6605; Fax: (616) 348-6672

Description: The coeducational community college is a public institution supported by the state and Emmet County. It was established in 1958 and offers two years of liberal arts curriculum, occupational programs in the technical and vocational fields, and general education for the needs of any individual who desires to obtain further education. It is accredited by the North Central Association of Colleges and Schools. The college awards the Certificate and the Associate degree. Evening classes are offered and a cooperative 3 plus 1 program with Lake Superior State University is available. The college operates on the semester system and offers one summer session. Enrollment includes 615 full-time and 1,471 part-time students. A faculty of 30 full-time and 61 part-time gives a faculty-student ratio of 1-22.

Entrance Requirements: Open enrollment policy; high school graduation or equivalent; non-high school graduates admitted to certain programs; ACT recommended; rolling admission plan available.

Costs Per Year: $1,320 district-resident tuition; $1,710 out-of-district; $2,100 out-of-state; $3,450 room and board; $36 student fees; additional expenses average $300

Collegiate Environment: The campus has 8 buildings, the first of which opened in September, 1963. Dormitory space is available for 76 men and 76 women. A Student Center, with seating for about 325 persons, is provided on the campus. The library contains 75,000 volumes and 700 periodicals. All applicants are accepted, and students may be admitted at midyear. Financial aid is available.

Community Environment: A resort and health center, the city is located on Little Traverse Bay. Within a 30-minute drive are 6 major ski resorts. Other recreational facilities include water sports on Lake Michigan, summer concerts, golf, tennis, bowling, and movies. The area has good transportation provided by air and bus service. There is some part-time employment available for students. Community services include a library, many churches, 2 hospitals, and a clinic.

NORTHERN MICHIGAN UNIVERSITY (E-5)
Marquette, Michigan 49855
Tel: (906) 227-2650; (800) 689-9797; Fax: (906) 227-2204

Description: This state university is accredited by the North Central Association of Colleges and Schools and by various professional organizations. It was established in 1899 as a teacher-training institution. In the 1960's it developed into a diversified midsized univeristy with more than 150 four-year programs and limited graduate offerings. The curriculum, through its major, minor, and liberal studies requirements, ensures that students receive an education that not only

provides them with the skills and knowledge required for a career and for advanced study in a professional discipline, but also gives them a strong foundation in the arts, humanities, and sciences. The school operates on the semester system with a one-month intercession following the winter semester and offers two summer sessions. Enrollment includes 5,809 full-time, 1,456 part-time, undergraduate, and 633 graduate students. A faculty of 302 full-time and 64 part-time gives a faculty-student ratio of 1-23. Army ROTC is available.

Entrance Requirements: High school graduation with emphasis placed on GPA, class rank and test scores; completed units including 4 English, 4 mathematics, 3 science, 2 foreign language, and 3 social science; minimum ACT 19 required; non-high school graduates may be admitted with satisfactory GED score; midyear admission, rolling admission, and advanced placement plans available; $25 application fee.

Costs Per Year: $2,836 state resident tuition; $5,242 nonresident tuition; $3,900 room and board; $900-$1,500 average additional expenses.

Collegiate Environment: The 320-acre campus contains 50 buildings including the library system containing 511,404 volumes, 2,477 periodicals, and 574,698 microforms, and housing accommodations for 2,000 students. Single freshmen and sophomores not living at home are required to live in university residence halls, with certain exceptions. There are 2 social sororities and 5 fraternities on campus. The university has its own television and radio stations. Average freshmen scores were ACT 20.6. A geographically diverse student body is sought and approximately 85% of applicants are accepted, including midyear and transfer students. About 2,220 scholarships are offered in addition to loans, grants, and work-study employment programs. Special financial aid is available for economically disadvantaged students, and 71% of freshmen receive some form of financial assistance.

Community Environment: Located on Lake Superior, Marquette is a day's driving distance from Chicago, Minneapolis, Duluth and Milwaukee. It is an important service and distribution center.

NORTHWESTERN MICHIGAN COLLEGE (J-8)
1701 East Front Street
Traverse City, Michigan 49684
Tel: (616) 922-0650; (800) 748-0566; Admissions: (616) 922-1054; Fax: (616) 722-1570

Description: This public two-year college was Michigan's first community college. Established in 1951, it is accredited by the North Central Association of Colleges and Schools and offers a liberal arts and science program as well as several technical and vocationally-oriented programs. The programs offered lead to the degrees of Associate of Arts, Associate of Applied Science or to the Certificate of Achievement. Available programs are classified as transfer, career or continuing education. The college operates on the semester system and offers seven summer sessions. Enrollment includes 2,100 full-time and 2,294 part-time students. A faculty of 103 full-time and 126 part-time gives a faculty-student ratio of 1-20.

Entrance Requirements: Open enrollment policy for district residents; high school graduation or equivalent; application fee $15; rolling admission, early decision and advanced placement plans available.

Costs Per Year: $1,700 tuition for county residents; $2,732 state resident tuition; $3,052 out-of-state tuition; $3,900 room and board; miscellaneous $900.

Collegiate Environment: The 90-acre campus of the college has 7 buildings. Mark and Helen Osterlin Library was opened in 1961 and contains 35,500 titles, 436 periodicals, 48,000 microforms and 1,925 audiovisual materials. A science building and residence hall were constructed in 1963. The school has residence hall space for 392 single students and 36 apartments. The college requires all unmarried students under 21 who do not live with their parents to reside in college residence halls. Various scholarships, awards and loans are available to students and financial assistance is offered to students with serious physical disabilities. About 40% of the students receive some form of financial aid. The college has a strong student activities intramural and sports club program that provides students with an opportunity for total involvement. Classes begin in August, January and June, and midyear students are accepted. 90% of the applicants for admission are accepted.

Community Environment: The Grand Traverse region is the center of Michigan's cherry-growing belt, with Traverse City marketing more cherries than any other city in the country. This is also an important all-year resort area. Located on Grand Traverse Bay, the temperature averages about 70 degrees in summer. Rail, bus and air transportation are easily accessible. City has many churches, 2 hospitals, 2 libraries, 2 museums, and other major community services. Recreational activities include golf, hunting, tennis, swimmming, water skiing, fishing. bowling, skiing, skating and all winter sports. Concerts and travel lectures are given here, and the National Cherry Festival is held here annually.

Branch Campuses: Northwestern Michigan College-Cadillac, 202 South Chestnut Street, Michigan, 49601, (616) 775-8611

NORTHWOOD UNIVERSITY   *(M-11)*
3225 Cook Road
Midland, Michigan 48640
Tel: (517) 832-4273; (800) 457-7878; Fax: (517) 837-4104

Description: This private, coeducational university was founded in 1959 and is accredited by the North Central Association of Colleges and Schools. It operates on the trimester system with 3 summer terms. Founded on traditional values, Northwood offers undergraduate and graduate degrees in 17 management disciplines. It has a free enterprise, global perspective and an appreciation of the business/arts relationship. Enrollment includes 1,700 undergraduates and 130 graduate students. A faculty of 33 full-time and 24 part-time gives a faculty-student ratio of 1-32. The university also has campuses in Florida, Michigan and Texas.

Entrance Requirements: High school graduation with C average or better; ACT or SAT required; early admission, midyear admission, rolling admission and advanced placement plans available. $15 application fee.

Costs Per Year: $9,450 tuition; $4,385 room and board; $215 student fees.

Collegiate Environment: The main campus and administrative offices for the university are located on a 268-acre campus at Midland, which opened in the fall of 1962. Buildings include the Vada and Alden Dow Commons, and several residence halls with capacity for 480 men and 459 women. The library contains 43,000 volumes. Approximately 95% of students applying for admission are accepted. Students may be admitted at midyear. Scholarships are available and about 70% of the current student body receives some form of financial assistance. Classes begin in September, December, March, and June. About 85% of the previous freshmen return for the sophomore year.

Community Environment: Midland is the county seat of Midland County. The city is noted for the beauty of its residential sections and for the County Courthouse, which has several unusual exterior murals. Located in Central Michigan, the area has major community services and cultural and recreational facilities. (See also Delta College.)

OAKLAND COMMUNITY COLLEGE - AUBURN HILLS
CAMPUS   *(B-11)*
2900 Featherstone Road
Auburn Hills, Michigan 48326
Tel: (810) 340-6500; Admissions: (810) 340-6572; Fax: (810) 340-6507

Description: This public junior college is a multi-campus, two-year institution of higher learning that provides academic, technical, and continuing education opportunities for both youth and adults. The college district was established in 1964 and opening enrollment took place in September, 1965, with 3,860 students. Recent enrollment at all four campus was 29,000 students. Enrollment at Auburn Hills is 8,410 students. The college operates on the semester system and offers two summer terms. The college is accredited by the North Central Association of Colleges and Schools and grants an Associate degree.

Entrance Requirements: Open enrollment policy; accredited high school graduation or equivalent; completion of 16 units required; non-high school graduates 18 years or older may be admitted; students are required to take cognitive style tests upon acceptance to school.

Costs Per Year: $1,380 ($46/credit) tuition; $2,340 ($78/credit) out-of-district tuition; $3,270 ($109/credit) out-of-state tuition.

Collegiate Environment: The Auburn Hills Campus is a 257-acre site. Recently completed facilities include a General Assembly Building, a Science Building, a Central Service Facility, a Student Union, which provides space for a cafeteria, a student lounge, and offices for student organizations.

Community Environment: Oakland County is composed of both rural and urban towns and has all types of public transportation. Average temperature in winter is 20 degrees, with 70 degrees in summer. The average precipitation is 30 inches. There are good summer and winter sports facilities within the immediate area, with more than 400 lakes nearby. Extensive health services are to be found here.

OAKLAND COMMUNITY COLLEGE - HIGHLAND LAKES
CAMPUS   *(B-10)*
7350 Cooley Lake Road
Union Lake, Michigan 48387
Tel: (810) 360-3000; Admissions: (810) 360-3067; Fax: (810) 360-3203

Description: This public two-year college is one of 4 branches of the Oakland Community College. Recent enrollment at all four campuses was 29,000 students. Enrollment at Highland Lakes is 5,285 students. The college is accredited by the North Central Association of Colleges and Schools and grants an Associate degree. An extensive career program in several fields of Allied Health is offered as well as programs in Aviation Flight Technology, Early Childhood Development and Publication Production Technology. The college operates on the semester system and offers two summer sessions.

Entrance Requirements: Open enrollment policy; accredited high school graduation or equivalent; completion of 16 units required; non-high school graduates 18 years of older may be admitted; students are required to take the cognitive style tests upon acceptance to school.

Costs Per Year: $1,380 ($46/credit) tuition; $2,340 ($78/credit) out-of-district tuition; $3,270 ($109/credit) out-of-state tuition.

Collegiate Environment: This campus is situated on a 160-acre site which overlooks 5 lakes. The campus is 15 miles southwest of Pontiac, and the architecture of the buildings is reminiscent of an Ivy League Campus. The college is situated on the grounds of a former county hospital, and includes several new buildings for science, physical education and a library.

Community Environment: See Oakland Community College - Auburn Hills Campus.

OAKLAND COMMUNITY COLLEGE - ORCHARD RIDGE
CAMPUS   *(C-10)*
27055 Orchard Lake Road
Farmington Hills, Michigan 48334
Tel: (810) 471-7500; Admissions: (810) 471-4628; Fax: (810) 471-7544

Description: This public two-year college is one of 5 branches of the Oakland Community College. It operates on the semester system with 1 spring and 1 summer term. The college is accredited by the North Central Association of Colleges and Schools and grants Associate degreesand one-year Certificates. It oalso offers college parallel courses that are transferable to four-year institutions. Enrollment includes 2,600 students at the Orchard Ridge Campus. A faculty of 100 full-time and 150 part-time provides a faculty-student ratio of 1-26.

Entrance Requirements: Open admissions policy; accredited high school graduation or equivalent; completion of 16 units required; no application fee; students are required to take the Asset Assesment test upon acceptance; early admission, midyear admission, rolling admission and advanced placement plans available.

Costs Per Year: $1,380 ($46/credit) tuition; $2,340 ($78/credit) out-of-district; $3,270 ($109/credit) out-of-state.

Collegiate Environment: The campus is a $30,000,000 complex on a 147-acre site that includes 11 buildings. Its first students were accepted in September 1967, and since it has opened the enrollment has increased eight-fold. The library contains 60,000 titles, 3,000 periodicals, 10,000 microforms and 5,000 audiovisual materials.

Community Environment: See Oakland Community College - Auburn Hills Campus.

OAKLAND COMMUNITY COLLEGE - ROYAL OAK CAMPUS *(C-10)*
739 South Washington
Royal Oak, Michigan 48067
Tel: (810) 544-4990; Fax: (810) 544-4955

Description: This public two-year college is one of 5 branches of the Oakland Community College. It was opened in 1971. The college operates on the semester system and offers 2 summer terms. The college offers both day and evening programs. A full range of college programs is offered in liberal arts and business. There are also fine arts and cultural programs, and courses in Business Information Systems, Ceramics and Art, and Photography. The school is accredited by the North Central Association of Colleges and Schools. Enrollment at Royal Oak is 8,305 students. The faculty includes 290 full-time and 498 part-time members.

Entrance Requirements: Open enrollment policy; accredited high school graduation or equivalent; non-high school graduates 18 years or older may be admitted; students are required to take ASSET upon acceptance to school.

Costs Per Year: $1,380 ($46/credit) district resident tuition; $2,340 ($78/credit) out-of-district; $3,270 ($109/credit) out-of-state.

Collegiate Environment: The Royal Oak Campus, located in the central business district of Royal Oak, represents the College's Community/Cultural Arts Center of the southeast quadrant of the county. The campus consists of four buildings enclosed by a center mall, totalling 164,000 square feet. A parking structure for 590 cars is available. Campus facilities include classrooms, a Learning Resource Center, dance rooms, and offices.

Community Environment: See Oakland Community College - Auburn Hills Campus.

OAKLAND UNIVERSITY *(P-13)*
Corner of Walton and Squirrel Road
Rochester, Michigan 48309-4401
Tel: (313) 370-3360; (800) 625-8648

Description: The public, liberal arts college is accredited by the North Central Association of Colleges and Schools. The academic structure of the university consists of the College of Arts and Sciences, the School of Business Administration, the School of Engineering and Computer Science, the School of Nursing, the School of Human and Educational Services, and the School of Health Sciences. Non-credit courses are given by the Division of Continuing Education. The university awards the Bachelor, Master, and Doctoral degrees. It operates on the semester system and offers two summer sessions. Enrollment includes 6,973 full-time and 6,192 part-time undergraduate, and 2,612 graduate students. A faculty of 363 full-time and 260 part-time gives a faculty-student ratio of 1-22.

Entrance Requirements: Accredited high school graduation with rank in upper half of graduating class; completion of 16 college-preparatory units including 4 English, 3 mathematics, 3 social science, 3 science, 1 foreign language; SAT or ACT recommended; early admission, rolling admission, and advanced placement plans available; $25 application fee.

Costs Per Year: $3,976 state resident tuition; $8,773 nonresident tuition; $4,030 room and board; $200 fees.

Collegiate Environment: The 1,500-acre campus has 21 buildings. All library collections and services are centralized in Kresge Library. It presently contains 593,868 volumes, 2,400 periodicals, 850,000 microforms, 7,000 records and 4,400 audio cassettes. There are 6 residence halls with space for 1,700 students. About 69% of students applying for admission meet the requirements and are accepted. Midyear students are admitted. Financial aid is available.

Community Environment: This is a suburban community with access to nearby Detroit via Interstate 75, and Michigan Highway 59. The immediate area has a hospital, shopping facilities, Oakland Technology Park, and several churches. Recreation is extensive both on and off campus. On campus cultural opportunities include Meadow Brook Theater, Meadow Brook Music Festival, Meadow Brook Art Gallery, and the Oakland University Center for Performing Arts. In addition, roller rinks, bowling centers, golf courses, Silverdome, the Palace (Home of NBA Champions Detroit Pistons), theatres, and the local Avon Players offer recreational and cultural activities off campus. There is seasonal part-time employment for students. Special events held annually include Meadowbrook Music Festival in summer and the Christmas Parade; the biannual Arts and Apples Festival is in September.

OLIVET COLLEGE *(P-10)*
Main Street
Olivet, Michigan 49076
Tel: (616) 749-7635; (800) 456-7189; Fax: (616) 749-7170

Description: The private four-year college was founded as part of the Congregational missionary effort in higher education. It is affiliated with the United Church of Christ. The college offers a modern, comprehensive liberal arts program. The student spends 2 years in the All-College Curriculum, sharing a common course of study. At the beginning of the junior year, the student enters the advanced curriculum, which has 3 fields of study: humanities and arts, natural sciences, and social studies. He or she is expected to concentrate his major work in one field. The school aims to provide the opportunity for concentrated study which will lead to mastery of that particular field and a Bachelor degree. The college is accredited by the North Central Association of Colleges and Schools and employs the semester system. Recent enrollment included 730 full-time and 60 part-time students. A faculty of 42 full-time and 60 part-time gives an overall faculty-student ratio of 1-14.

Entrance Requirements: Accredited high school graduation with rank in upper half of graduating class. Min. 2.6 GPA; SAT or ACT required GRE required; for graduate programs; application fee $10; rolling admission available.

Costs Per Year: $11,580 tuition; $3,860 room and board

Collegiate Environment: The college campus is about 30 miles south of Lansing. The college and the city of Olivet are one well-knit community, each an asset to the other. Freedom and growth in religious thought and action are a major concern at Olivet College. A variety of religious faiths is found among the faculty and students. The social life of the campus centers in the residence halls; students are required to reside in the residence halls and take their meals in the dining hall. Housing is available for 450 students. The library contains 93,000 volumes, numerous periodicals, microforms and sound recordings. The college is a member of the Michigan Intercollegiate Athletic Association and provides opportunity for competition with other colleges in football, basketball, baseball, tennis, golf, track and wrestling. It seeks to avoid confining the athletic program solely to those who excell in sports and offers a full program of intramural athletics for those who are not gifted with exceptional skill. Approximately 93% of students applying for admission are accepted. Students are admitted at midyear as well as in the fall. Financial aid is available; 98% of students receive some form of assistance. Almost 80% of the previous freshman class return to the campus for their second year.

Community Environment: The city is located 15 miles northeast of Battle Creek.

REFORMED BIBLE COLLEGE *(O-8)*
3333 E. Beltline Ave., N.E.
Grand Rapids, Michigan 94505
Tel: (616) 363-2050

Description: The coeducational Bible school was founded in 1940 by interested members of the Christian Reformed Church of North America. Its purpose is to prepare individuals for Christian service. The college is accredited by the North Central Association of Colleges and Schools and grants Associate and Bachelor degrees. Students not seeking a degree may enroll for as many semesters as desired. The semester system is employed with one summer session. Recent enrollment includes 78 men and 58 women full-time and 13 men and 15 women part-time. The faculty consists of 14 full-time and 3 part-time instructors. The college is an Accredited Member of the American Association of Bible Colleges. It is a member of the Associated Schools of the American Institute of Holy Land Studies in Jerusalem, Israel. An orientation in missions is held each summer in Mexico for students desiring experience in Christian missionary service.

Entrance Requirements: High school graduation or equivalent; non-high school graduates may be considered for admission; pastor's recommendation and health certificate required; $10 application fee;

early decision, rolling admission, delayed admission and advanced placement plans available.

Costs Per Year: $6,450 tuition; $3,350 board and room; $75 student fees.

Collegiate Environment: Approximately 95% of students applying for admission are accepted. Classes begin in September; students are also admitted at midyear. About 70% of the students receive some form of financial assistance. Scholarships are available for freshmen as well as upperclassmen. The library contains 29,698 volumes and dormitories provide housing for 64 men and 64 women. Approximately 70% of the previous freshman class returns to the campus for their second year. The college maintains a Student Assistance Fund for worthy students who want to prepare for service in evangelism and missions.

Community Environment: See Calvin College

SACRED HEART MAJOR SEMINARY   *(P-14)*
2701 Chicago Blvd.
Detroit, Michigan 48206
Tel: (313) 883-8500; Admissions: (313) 883-8500; Fax: (313) 868-6440

Description: The four-year liberal arts college is accredited by the North Central Association of Colleges and Schools. It was established in 1919 by the Most Reverend Michael J. Gallagher, D.D., Bishop of the Diocese of Detroit. Its primary function is to provide for the education and formation of priesthood candidates. SHMS also facilitates the professional preparation for lay persons aspiring to diverse ministries and leadership roles within the Church. It is accredited by the North Central Association of Colleges and Schools. It operates on the early semester system. Enrollment includes 26 full-time and 123 part-time students. There are 15 full-time and 12 part-time faculty members.

Entrance Requirements: Open enrollment policy; high school graduation or equivalent; SAT required; recommendation of pastor; early admission, delayed admission, rolling admission and advanced placement plans available.

Costs Per Year: $4,125 tuition per year; $60 application and registration fee; $4,100 room and board; $175 per credit hour.

Collegiate Environment: The seminary has a 20-acre campus located within 5 miles of downtown Detroit. The library contains 60,000 volumes, and dormitory capacity is 200 men. All ministerial applicants are reviewed through a pre-formation program as well as through the Formation Program. Students applying for admission who meet the requirements are accepted. Students may be admitted at midyear and classes begin in September and January. Financial aid is available; approximately 60% of the current student body receive some type of financial assistance.

Community Environment: At the turn of the 20th century, Detroit was a quiet, tree-shaded community brewing beer and producing comfortable carriages and comforting stoves. The serenity was broken by Henry Ford's creation, a vehicle "propelled by power generated from within itself." Today it is the greatest automobile-manufacturing city in the world. It is also rapidly becoming a steel center and a leader in the manufacturing of pharmaceuticals, office equipment, rubber products, salt, television components, synthetic resins and paints, meat products, marine engines, and more than half the garden seed used throughout the country. Annual mean temperature is 49.3 degrees, and annual rainfall is 31.03 inches. Definitely an industrial city, Detroit has a civic center complex on the riverfront, an excellent park system, and numerous museums and art galleries.

SAGINAW VALLEY STATE UNIVERSITY   *(M-11)*
7400 Bay Road
University Center, Michigan 48710
Tel: (517) 790-4200; (800) 968-9500; Fax: (517) 790-0180

Description: The state-supported comprehensive college opened for classes in the fall of 1963. SVSU has 5 academic colleges: Arts and Behavioral Sciences, Business and Management, Education, Nursing and Allied Health Sciences, and Science, Engineering and Technology. The college is accredited by the North Central Association of Colleges and Schools, American Chemical Society, American Society of Clinical Pathologists, American Medical Association and National League of Nursing. Curriculum choices range from technical preparation to liberal arts and professional degrees. Classes are offered on a trimester basis with a summer semester divided into four varied-length sessions. Recent enrollment includes 1,611 men and 2,101 women full-time and 1,189 men and 2,165 women part-time. A faculty of 175 full-time and 202 part-time gives an average class size of 24. The college grants a Bachelor and Master degree.

Entrance Requirements: Accredited high school graduation with 2.5 (on 4.0 scale) GPA in academic subjects preferred. Applicants whose GPA is less that 2.5 are required to submit senior year grades; an interview may also be required. Completion of 16 college preparatory units minimum; recommended 4 English, 4 math, 3 science, 3 language, 2 social studies; ACT or SAT required. Special admission plans available including early admission, early decision, rolling admission and advanced placement.

Costs Per Year: $3,103 tuition; $4,526 out-of-state tuition; $3,100 board and room

Collegiate Environment: SVSU has a physical plant valued at $79,343,500 which includes 6 classroom/office buildings, a cafeteria/student activities center, gymnasium, theater, bookstore, administrative units, children's center and dormitory facilities for 242 men and 242 women. The library houses 179,113 volumes and numerous periodicals, pamphlets and sound recordings. Approximately 75% of students applying for admission are accepted including midyear students. Army ROTC available. Financial aid is available; approximately 54% of the students receive some form of assistance. About 77% of the current student body graduated in the top half of their high school class. The average ACT scores of the present freshman class was 21. The school awarded 723 Bachelor degrees and 189 Master degree to its graduating class. Faculty members at SVSU possess a depth of educational experience obtained at more than 200 colleges and universities around the world. International exchange and guest professors and students bring the added dimension of other cultures to the campus.

Community Environment: The college has a 782-acre campus located 3 miles south of I-75 on M-84. Combined with this rural atmosphere are urban advantages available in neighboring Saginaw, Bay City and Midland, where tri-county populations total 410,000.

SAINT CLAIR COUNTY COMMUNITY COLLEGE   *(O-14)*
323 Erie Street
Port Huron, Michigan 48061-5015
Tel: (313) 984-3881

Description: The coeducational community college was established by a vote of the people in June, 1967, which transformed the former Port Huron Junior College to a county-wide community college. It is accredited by the North Central Association of Colleges and Schools. provides a two-year academic program for students who plan to transfer to institutions of higher learning, vocational programs, and continuing education to meet the needs of the community. Recent enrollment is 538 men and 807 women full-time, and 1,092 men and 1,638 women part-time attending classes on the semester system with 2 summer terms. A faculty of 97 full-time and 117 part-time gives a faculty-student ratio of approximately 1-19.

Entrance Requirements: Open enrollment policy; accredited high school graduation or equivalent; applicants not meeting all requirements may be accepted as special students; ACT recommended; early admission, early decision, rolling admission and advanced placement plans available.

Costs Per Year: $1,178 tuition; $1,860 out-of-district tuition; $2,573 out-of-state tuition; $50 student fees.

Collegiate Environment: The 21-acre campus has 7 buildings, including a library which contains 49,000 volumes, 500 periodicals, 380 microforms and 1,900 audiovisual materials. The college does not have dormitories. Financial aid is available and approximately 50% of the current student body receives some form of assistance. 150 scholarships are offered.

Community Environment: On 2 great waterways, Lake Huron and the St. Clair River, Port Huron holds an important place in maritime commerce. Linked by international bridge with its twin city, Sarnia, Canada, it is the metropolis of the St. Clair River manufacturing district which extends for 30 miles south of the city. The area has many fine beaches, camping and fishing sites, and boating facilities within the immediate area. Community facilities include municipal auditorium and arena, public library, small museum, YMCA, many churches, and 2 hospitals. Part-time employment is available for students. Mean winter temperature is 22.4 degrees; summer, 69.3 degrees; average rainfall is 29.07 inches. The Blue Water Festival in conjunction with Port Huron to Mackinac Sailboat Race is held annually.

SAINT MARY'S COLLEGE   (B-10)
3535 Indian Trail
Orchard Lake, Michigan 48324
Tel: (810) 682-1885; Admissions: (810) 683-0508; Fax: (810) 683-0402

Description: The private, coeducational, liberal arts college was at one time exclusively a seminary, but now has a dual program for regular college students and those interested in the Roman Catholic priesthood as a career. The college is fully accredited by the North Central Association of Colleges and Schools. It operates on the semester system and offers one summer session. The 14 majors offered include communication arts, biology, business, English, philosophy, Polish Studies, radiologic technology, theology, religious education, and social science. Recent enrollment included 157 men and 250 women. A faculty of 15 full-time and 22 part-time gives an overall faculty-student ratio of 1-13. The college awards the Certificate and the Associate and Bachelor degrees.

Entrance Requirements: Accredited high school graduation with rank in top 50% of class; recommended completion of 13 units including 4 English, 2 mathematics, 1 foreign language, 2 science, 4 social science; ACT required; early admission, early decision, rolling admission plans available.

Costs Per Year: $5,760 tuition; $3,800 room and board; $50 student fees.

Collegiate Environment: College includes a Polish Cultural Center and a museum containing outstanding Polish works of art. The library contains 75,000 volumes, numerous periodicals, microforms and sound recordings. Dormitory space is available for 100 men and 100 women; Financial aid is available and 30 scholarships are offered. Approximately 90% of students applying for admission are accepted, including midyear students. Approximately 85% of the previous freshman class return to the campus for their second year. About 45% of the senior class continue on to graduate school.

Community Environment: Orchard Lake is situated 4 miles southwest of Pontiac. This suburban residential area is known for its beauty. Commercial transportation is available. Community facilities include churches, a library, an art gallery, a medical center and a beautiful shopping center. 3 lakes in the area provide fishing, boating and other water sports.

SCHOOLCRAFT COLLEGE   (P-13)
18600 Haggerty Road
Livonia, Michigan 48152
Tel: (313) 462-4400

Description: The public, tax-supported community college offers transfer, career, and continuing education programs leading to a Certificate or an Associate degree. The college is accredited by the North Central Association of Colleges and Schools. It operates on the semester system and offers two summer sessions. Enrollment includes 4,224 men and 5,833 women. A faculty of 130 full-time and 170 part-time gives an overall faculty-student ratio of 1-22.

Entrance Requirements: Open enrollment policy; high school graduation with 22 total units; non-high school graduates are eligible for admission as special students; application fee $10; early admission early decision, rolling admission and advanced placement plans available.

Costs Per Year: $1,200 district-resident tuition; $1,800 out-of-district resident tuition; $2,450 out-of-state tuition; $20 registration fee.

Collegiate Environment: This 183-acre campus features 4 main classroom buildings. In addition to the Liberal Arts and Physical Education buildings, the Forum is a general instruction facility with classrooms, laboratories and faculty offices. The Applied Sciences building is the largest building on campus and houses facilities for technical, business and health careers education. The library holdings

include 64,650 hardbound volumes. Financial aid is available. 30% of students receive some form of financial assistance.

Community Environment: This is a suburban area located 20 miles west of Detroit and convenient to airports. In this region of 124 square miles live an estimated 260,000 people. Good part-time employment opportunities are available for students.

SIENA HEIGHTS COLLEGE   (R-12)
1247 E. Siena Heights Drive
Adrian, Michigan 49221
Tel: (517) 263-0731; (800) 521-0009; Fax: (517) 265-3380

Description: The four-year liberal arts college is affiliated with the Roman Catholic Church and is an independent coeducational college sponsored by the Sisters of St. Dominic. Originally known as St. Joseph College, the school was built and incorporated in 1919. It is accredited by the North Central Association of Colleges and Schools and offers programs leading to Associate, Bachelor, and Master degrees. The college operates on the semester system and offers one summer session. Recently the college enrolled 305 men and 528 women full-time and 231 men and 480 women part-time. A faculty of 130 gives a faculty-student ratio of 1-15.

Entrance Requirements: Accredited high school graduation or equivalent; SAT or ACT required; early admission, early decision, rolling admission, midyear admission and advanced placement plans available. $15 application fee.

Costs Per Year: $9,610 tuition, $4,110 room and board.

Collegiate Environment: The 140-acre campus is located in southeast Michigan about 60 miles from Detroit. It is comprised of 11 buildings, which include an art building, a chapel, a performing arts building, an athletic center for athletic recreation and other special events, and residence halls housing 440 students. The library contains 140,000 volumes, 545 bound periodicals and numerous microforms and audio-visual materials. Students may enroll at midyear; a geographically diverse student body is desired. Financial assistance is available, and 85% of the current student body receives aid.

Community Environment: See Adrian College

SOUTHWESTERN MICHIGAN COMMUNITY COLLEGE   (Q-7)
Cherry Grove Road
Dowagiac, Michigan 49047
Tel: (616) 782-5113; (800) 456-8675; Fax: (616) 782-8414

Description: The two-year state college was established in 1964 by a vote of the citizens of Cass County, and the first classes were held in the fall of 1966. The purposes of the college are to provide the two-year program in liberal arts and preprofessional fields for transfer students, career training, and general education. The college is accredited by the North Central Association of Colleges and Schools. It operates on the semester system and offers two summer terms. Enrollment includes 999 full-time and 1,666 part-time students. A faculty of 47 full-time and 115 part-time provides a faculty-student ratio of 1:17. The college awards a Certificate and an Associate degree.

Entrance Requirements: Open enrollment policy; high school graduation or equivalent; non-high school graduates may be accepted as special students; ACT or SAT required; early admission, early decision, rolling admission, delayed admission, midyear admission, and advanced placement plans available. There is no application fee.

Costs Per Year: $1,395 district resident tuition $1,643 state resident tuition; $2,015 out-of-state tuition; $124 student fees.

Collegiate Environment: The site of the college is a 240-acre tract in LaGrange Township. The library contains 33,000 volumes, 235 periodicals, 25,600 microforms, 1,200 audiovisual materials. Financial aid is available and 55% of the student body receives some form of assistance. 100% of applicants are accepted, including midyear students.

Community Environment: Located near many lakes, Dowagiac is a summer resort center. Local industries produce condensers and evaporators, flour, mobile homes, aluminum castings, molded plastics products, springs and television cabinets. The area is generally flat terrain and is located 25 miles from South Bend, Indiana. January temperatures average 24.2 degrees, with July at 73.6 degrees. The city has rail and bus accessibility. Part-time employment is available for students.

Excellent summer and winter recreation can be found in the immediate area.

Branch Campuses: Niles Area Campus in Niles, Michigan. The 16.2 acre campus is located at the intersection of U.S. 12, and M-60 and is housed in a 24,000 square foot facility. With eighteen classrooms, three computer labs, and a science laboratory, the Niles Area Campus offers easy accessibility to students in Berrien County and the South Bend area.

SPRING ARBOR COLLEGE   *(Q-10)*
106 East Main Street
Spring Arbor, Michigan 49283
Tel: (517) 750-1200; (800) 968-0011; Fax: (517) 750-1604

Description: The four-year liberal arts college was founded in 1873 by the Free Methodist Church. The private, coeducational college seeks to serve the evangelical Christian community. It is accredited by the North Central Association of Colleges and Schools for an academic program culminating in the Bachelor of Arts degree. It operates on the 4-1-4 calendar system and offers two summer terms. Enrollment includes 343 men and 507 women. A faculty of 83 full-time and 26 part-time gives a faculty-student ratio of 1-17. The college offers accelerated, degree-completion programs for working adults at several locations across the state of Michigan. The programs are designed for working adults who have earned 60 semester credits of college work and are 25 years of age or older.

Entrance Requirements: High school graduation with cumulative GPA of 2.60; ACT required, a minimum score 20; some applicants may be admitted without all requirements; early admission, rolling admission, advanced placement, midyear admission plans available. $15 application fee.

Costs Per Year: $10,000 tuition; $3,850 room and board; miscellaneous $1,610, $106 fees.

Collegiate Environment: A variety of student activities provide balance to the rigorous academic climate. These include soccer, basketball, tennis, baseball, golf, track, volleyball, and touch football. Organizations encourage development of religious, athletic, dramatic and musical interests. The library contains 86,145 volumes, 1,409 periodicals, 280 microforms, and 4,057 records, tapes, and compact discs. Housing facilities are available for 483 students. Approximately 89% of students applying for admission meet the requirements and are accepted. 61% of students receive financial aid.

Community Environment: See Jackson Community College

SUOMI COLLEGE   *(C-3)*
Qunicy Street
Hancock, Michigan 49930
Tel: (906) 487-7274; (800) 682-7604; Fax: (906) 487-7383

Description: The private two-year college was founded in 1896 by the Finnish Evangelical Lutheran Church of America and recently with the Evangelical Lutheran Church in America. It began as an academy; the junior college was established in 1923. Since 1963 the school has been affiliated with the Lutheran Church in America. Although many Lutheran students attend the school, more than half of the students are of other faiths. The college is accredited by the North Central Association of Colleges and Schools. It awards the Associate in Arts, Science, Applied Science, and a General Studies degree. It operates on the semester system and offers one summer session. Enrollment is 530 full-time and 57 part-time. This includes 217 men and 370 women. A faculty of 23 full-time and 32 part-time gives a faculty-student ratio of 1-14.

Entrance Requirements: Accredited high school graduation or equivalent; liberal enrollment policy; personal interview may be required; $20 application fee; early admission, early decision, advanced placement, rolling admission and midyear admission plans available.

Costs Per Year: $9,500 tuition; $3,700 room and board.

Collegiate Environment: The campus is located on the Keweenaw Peninsula of Northern Michigan in an area commonly known as the Copper Country. Facilities include classrooms, laboratory, chapel, gymnasium, and the library of 31,323 volumes, 298 periodicals, and 15,000 audiovisual items. Dormitories and residence accomodate 400 students. Students are urged to participate in the religious life on the campus. Financial aid is available. About 92% of the students receive

some form of financial aid. Approximately 97% of students applying for admission are accepted, including midyear students.

Community Environment: The beautiful Keeweenaw Peninsula has annual snowfalls averaging more than 13 feet, making the area around the college ideal for winter sports. The campus is located near downtown Hancock, a city that sprang up amid the region's copper mining industry. Hancock is within a day's drive of Detroit, Chicago, Milwaukee, Duluth and Minneapolis. The city has good recreational facilities encompassing fishing, camping, skiing, hunting, golfing, hockey, basketball and 4 theaters. The cold water and clean beaches of Lake Superior abound. The "Copper Country" is noted for historical remnants of the now-defunct copper industry. The area is renowned for its autumn when the expansive forests are ablaze with color. Limited numbers of off-campus jobs are available. All major civic, fraternal and service organizations, as well as extensive medical services and 2 hospitals, are easily accessible.

THOMAS M. COOLEY LAW SCHOOL   *(P-10)*
217 South Capitol Avenue
P.O. Box 13038
Lansing, Michigan 48901
Tel: (517) 371-5140

Description: The Thomas M. Cooley Law School is a fully accredited independent, graduate, professional college of law. It was founded in 1972 by a group of judges, lawyers, and businessmen, led by former Michigan Supreme Court Chief Justice Thomas Brennan. The school's unique year-round, reduced class load curriculum permits those who work, or choose to work, to receive first-rate instruction morning, afternoon, or evening, and graduate in three years or less. Enrollment includes 87 full-time and 1,625 part-time students. A faculty of 51 full-time and 100 part-time gives a faculty-student ratio of 1-12.

Entrance Requirements: Cooley uses an index comprised of cumulative undergraduate GPA times 15 plus LSAT score to determine eligibility. Applicants are accepted on a first come, first served basis; $100 application fee.

Costs Per Year: $13,350 tuition.

Collegiate Environment: The main school building is a massive, air conditioned, seven-story, steel and concrete structure that provides more than 80,000 square feet of space. Facilities include a courtroom, student lounge, and auditorium. The library houses 271,000 volumes and has been designated a federal government document depository library. Elevator service is available to all floors and access for the handicapped is provided. A 70,000-square-foot library was recently completed.

Community Environment: Thomas Cooley Law School is located across the street from the Michigan State Capitol, and a few blocks from the State Supreme Court, the State Law Library, and the State Bar Building. It is five miles from Michigan State University, whose library is available to Cooley students.

UNIVERSITY OF DETROIT MERCY   *(P-14)*
4001 W. McNichols Rd.
Detroit, Michigan 48221
Tel: (313) 927-1000; (800) 635-5020; Admissions: (313) 993-1245

Description: The university is a Catholic institution conducted by the Jesuit Fathers and the Sisters of Mercy. Founded in 1877, it was reorganized in 1911 and was then incorporated under the title University of Detroit. It consolidated with Mercy College of Detroit in 1991. The university is accredited by the North Central Association of Colleges and Schools. Academically, the university comprises the degree-granting Colleges of Liberal Arts, Engineering and Science, Education and Human Services, Business Administration, College of Health Sciences, and the Schools of Architecture, Dentistry and Law. It operates on the semester system and offers two summer sessions. Enrollment includes 1,693 men and 1,844 women attending full-time, and 1,386 men and 2,538 women attending part-time. A faculty of 292 full-time and 220 part-time gives a faculty-student ratio of 1-14.

Entrance Requirements: High school graduation with rank in upper half of graduating class; completion of 16 units including 4 English, 3 mathematics, 2 science, and 3 social science; ACT or SAT required; individual schools have special requirements; advanced placement, early admission, early decision, delayed admission, and rolling admission plans available; $25 application fee.

Costs Per Year: $11,130 average tuition; $2,070 room; $2,030 board; $60 student fees.

Collegiate Environment: The university has two campuses in the northwest residential section of Detroit. The McNichols campus houses the traditional students and the outer Drive campus is geared for the nontraditional student. A total of 39 buildings include several libraries with a collection of 784,696 volumes, 4,940 periodicals, 735,630 microforms and 23,657 films, slides and recordings. Dormitories accomodate 975 students. Students may be admitted at midyear and are from various geographical locations. 80% of applicants are accepted. Scholarships are available. 60% of students receive some form of financial aid. Classes begin in September and January. The university has campuses for Dental and Law schools in downtown Detroit.

Community Environment: See Wayne State University.

UNIVERSITY OF MICHIGAN   (-12)
1220 Student Activity Building
515 East Jefferson
Ann Arbor, Michigan 48109-1316
Tel: (313) 764-1817; Admissions: (313) 764-7433; Fax: (313) 936-0740

Description: The state university was established in 1817 by an Act of the Legislature fostered by a group of public-spirited men in Detroit. The present name has been used since 1821 and the original campus was formed at Ann Arbor on a 40-acre parcel of land, a gift to the university. It is accredited by the North Central Association of Colleges and Schools and by the respective professional and educational associations. The university operates on the trimester system and offers one summer session. It consists of the following colleges: Colleges of Architecture and Urban Planning, Engineering, Literature, Science and Arts, and Pharmacy, and Schools of Art, Business Administration, Dentistry, Education, Law, Library Science, Medicine, Music, Natural Resources, Nursing, Public Health, Social Work, and the Horace H. Rackham School of Graduate Studies. Branch campuses are located at Dearborn and Flint, Michigan; several extension courses are available at various locations throughout the state. Enrollment includes 18,221 men, 14,819 women full-time and 1,912 men and 1,591 women part-time. A faculty of 2,626 gives an overall faculty-student ratio of 1:14. The university grants Baccalaureate, Specialist, First Professional and Graduate degrees. The university offers study abroad programs of semester, year and summer length to France, England, Scotland, Florence, Italy, India, Jamaica, Seville, Spain, and Sweden. In Italy, India and Jamaica study is with a program set up by the university itself. In other countries, students study at universities of the region for Univeristy of Michigan credit. An example of the extensive courses offered is Florence, Italy which offers History of Art, Physics, English Literature, Architecture and the Italian Language. The university offers optional Army, Navy, and Air Force ROTC programs.

Entrance Requirements: Admission is dependent upon a high probability of success in the chosen school or college and the availability of places. Students are strongly encouraged to submit their applications early in the fall of their senior year.

Costs Per Year: $5,550 tuition; $16,776 out-of-state tuition; $4,898 room and board; tuition fees vary depending on the school attended; additional expenses average $1,400. Out-of-state tuition is subject to change any time by the regents of the University.

Collegiate Environment: The 2,608-acre campus encompasses 200 major buildings. Residence Halls accomodate 10,000 students. 30 national undergraduate fraternities and 17 undergraduate sororities house an additional 2,000 students. The university has several museums on campus. The library system contains nearly 6,450,000 volumes. 40% of the students receive financial assistance; about 60% of applicants are accepted, including midyear students. The university offers many excellent extra curricular activities which include the world famous Michigan marching band, a drama society, musical theatre especially for sophomores, and a dance company.

Community Environment: Predominantly a college community, Ann Arbor also serves as a center for scientific and industrial research and development. Products manufactured in the area include precision instruments, automotive parts, ball bearings, computer components and machine tools. Part-time employment is available for students. Average summer temperature is 79 degrees; winter, 27.8 degrees; average rainfall is 30.7 inches. Average snowfall is 35.3 inches. City has excellent transportation facilities including rail, bus, air service, and expressways out of Detroit. Area offers many cultural and recreational advantages usually found only in a large metropolis. For instance, the Ann Arbor Musical Society provides classical concerts of major world orchestras, chamber music groups and soloists. The Ann Arbor May Festival is an additional musical attraction each year.

UNIVERSITY OF MICHIGAN - DEARBORN CAMPUS
(Q-13)
4901 Evergreen Road
Dearborn, Michigan 48128
Tel: (313) 593-5000

Description: One of 3 University of Michigan campuses operating under the Board of Regents, the University of Michigan-Dearborn is fully accredited by the North Central Association of Colleges and Schools. The campus was founded in 1959 as a senior-level institution offering only junior, senior and graduate level courses. Since 1971, UM-D has offered full four-year degree programs and expanded its graduate offerings. Degree programs are offered in humanities, social sciences, behavioral sciences, natural sciences, engineering, education, business administration and interdisciplinary studies. Master degrees are offered in engineering, education, business administration and public administration. The school operates on the trimester system with 2 summer sessions. Overall enrollment is 8,185, representing a wide range of students from the engineer seeking to update skills to the traditional 18-year-old freshman.

Entrance Requirements: High school graduation with a minimum 3.0 GPA; completion of 15 units including 4 English, 3 mathematics, 2 foreign languages, 2 science, and 3 social science; minimum SAT composite scores of 1050 or ACT composite score of 22 preferred; class rank is considered; transfer students require a minimum 2.5 GPA; $30 application fee; early admission, early decision, rolling admission, delayed admission and advanced placement plans available.

Costs Per Year: $3,390 undergraduate resident; $3,856 graduate resident; $50 registration fee; $9,954 undergraduate nonresident; $12,154 graduate nonresident; $100 out-of-state registration fee.

Collegiate Environment: The Dearborn Campus has 210 acres located on the former Fair Lane estate of Henry Ford. 70 acres have been set aside as a nature center, which is used by students, faculty and the community as a research and tour center. In addition to academic buildings, the campus includes the Student Activities Building, the University Mall complex housing classrooms, offices, food services, student services and a bookstore, the Fieldhouse/Ice Arena Sports Center, and the University Library, which has a collection of 284,494 volumes, 1,657 periodicals, 375,036 microforms and other media and also contains audiovisual laboratories and a language lab. The campus also houses a television and production studio. Students are admitted at midyear; a geographically diverse student body is sought. Financial aid is available.

Community Environment: The university is situated in the middle of a rapidly expanding industrial, residential and social area. Nearby is the Ford Motor Company World Headquarters Complex, the Fairlane Town Center, the Hyatt Regency Hotel and several new apartment and townhouse complexes. Within one hour's driving distance are the cultural opportunities available in Ann Arbor, Meadow Brook Theatre in Rochester, the Michigan Opera Theatre and the Fisher Theatre of Detroit and the various social and cultural events in the city of Dearborn.

UNIVERSITY OF MICHIGAN - FLINT CAMPUS   *(O-12)*
303 E. Kearsley
Flint, Michigan 48502-2186
Tel: (313) 762-3300

Description: This regional college is one of the 3 campuses of the University of Michigan. The main campus is in Ann Arbor, and another campus is located in Dearborn. Primary attention is centered on the undergraduate, who may be enrolled in one of the 50 concentration programs in liberal arts and sciences, business administration or teacher education programs leading to a Bachelor degree. There are also four Master's programs. The college is accredited by the North

Central Association of Colleges and Schools. The semester system is used with 2 summer terms. Recent Enrollment includes 1,201 men and 1,650 women full-time and 1,384 men and 2,070 women part-time. The faculty includes 157 full-time and 50 part-time which gives a student-faculty ratio of 30:1.

Entrance Requirements: Accredited high school graduation or equivalent; 2.7 or higher academic grade point average; completion of 15 units including 4 English, 3 mathematics, 2 science, 2 social science; SAT or ACT required; application fee $30; early admission, early decision, delayed admission, rolling admission and advanced placement plans available.

Costs Per Year: $2,240 tuition; $7,500 out-of-state tuition.

Collegiate Environment: Flint college life centers around a new urban riverfront campus which includes a University Center and Physical Education/Recreation Building as well as classroom buildings. The library's collection contains 160,000 volumes and numerous pamphlets, periodicals, microforms and sound recordings. Students have access to recreational facilities and participate in intramural athletics. Approximately 84% of students applying for admission meet the requirements and almost all of these are accepted. Special financial aid, loans and work-study programs are available, and approximately one-third of the current student body receives financial assistance.

Community Environment: See GMI Engineering and Management Institute

WALSH COLLEGE OF ACCOUNTANCY AND BUSINESS ADMINISTRATION   *(P-13)*
3838 Livernois Road
P.O. Box 7006
Troy, Michigan 48083
Tel: (810) 689-8282; Admissions: (810) 689-8282 X 215; Fax: (810) 524-2520

Description: The private, non-profit coeducational senior college was founded in 1922 under the name of Walsh Institute of Accountancy. The present name was adopted in 1968. The college is accredited by the North Central Association of Colleges and Schools. It grants the Baccalaureate degree in accountancy and business administration. It also awards Master's degrees. The college is an upper division school, offering only junior and senior years of the programs. It operates on the semester system and offers one summer session. Enrollment includes 345 full-time and 3,570 part-tiem undergraduates and 1,908 graduate students. A faculty of 15 full-time and 150 part-time gives an overall faculty-student ratio of 1-21.

Entrance Requirements: Undergraduate: Associate in Arts degree or 60 semester credit hours including 30 SCH in Liberal Arts, at an accredited institution with a minimum grade of C; Graduate: Bachelor degree and business prerequisites; G.P.A. of 2.75 or better; open admission, rolling admission plans available. $25 application fee.

Costs Per Year: Undergraduate: $5,280 ($165/cr) tuition; Graduate: $4,725 ($225/cr).

Collegiate Environment: Located on a 20-acre campus in Southeastern Michigan. Facilities include 2 microcomputer labs, instructional centers, library and a student lounge. Classes begin in September, January, and May. Approximately 90% of the undergraduate applicants are accepted. Financial aid is available and employment opportunities are offered. About 21% of the students receive aid. The special library containing mostly information in accountancy and law includes 16,000 titles, 20,000 microforms, 475 periodicals, and 100 audiovisual materials.

Community Environment: The college is located in the city of Troy, just north of Detroit. Troy has a population of 75,025 and serves as headquarters for many businesses.

WASHTENAW COMMUNITY COLLEGE   *(Q-12)*
4800 East Huron River Drive
Ann Arbor, Michigan 48106
Tel: (313) 973-3543; Fax: (313) 677-5414

Description: In 1965, voters approved establishment of a publicly supported, countywide junior college that would offer a variety of technical, industrial and semiprofessional courses as well as fully-developed college-transfer and general education curricula. The first classes were held in the fall of 1966. The college is accredited by the North Central Association of Colleges and Schools. It awards Certificates and the Associate degree. The college operates on the semester system and offers two summer terms. Enrollment includes 2,349 full-time and 8,492 part-time students. A faculty of 182 full-time and 320 part-time gives a faculty-student ratio of 1-20.

Entrance Requirements: High school graduation or equivalent or non-high school graduates 18 years of age or older; open enrollment policy; rolling admission, and advanced placement plans available; $15 application fee.

Costs Per Year: $1,296 district resident tuition; $1,896 out-of-district tuition; $2,436 nonresident tuition.

Collegiate Environment: The college is situated on a tract of land between Ann Arbor and Ypsilanti. The library contains 68,166 volumes. All district students applying for admission are accepted. Special financial aid is available for economically disadvantaged students. Of 233 scholarships, 60 are for freshmen.

Community Environment: See University of Michigan.

WAYNE COUNTY COMMUNITY COLLEGE   *(P-14)*
801 West Fort
Detroit, Michigan 48226
Tel: (313) 832-5500

Description: The public, coeducational community college, founded in 1969, operates on the semester system with one summer session. The college offers career training, transfer programs and general service programs leading to an Associate of Arts or Science degree. The college is fully accredited by the North Central Association of Colleges and Schools. Recent enrollment includes 4,938 students. A faculty of 185 full-time and 734 part-time gives a faculty-student ratio of 1-17.

Entrance Requirements: Open enrollment policy; entrance exam required; no application fee required; applicant must be high school graduate or at least 18 years of age.

Costs Per Year: $900 tuition; $1,350 out-of-district tuition; $1,800 out-of-state tuition; $24 student fees; additional expenses average $100.

Collegiate Environment: Located in metropolitan Detroit, the college has some facilities of its own, and classes also meet in existing buildings around the county. The library contains 32,515 volumes, 300 pamphlets, 438 periodicals and 3,318 microforms. In addition, library privileges have been granted to the college from most of the neighboring schools and colleges. Financial assistance and part-time work are available. All of the applicants are accepted, including mid-year students.

Community Environment: See Wayne State University

WAYNE STATE UNIVERSITY   *(P-14)*
Detroit, Michigan 48202
Tel: (313) 577-2424; Admissions: (313) 577-3577; Fax: (313) 577-3200

Description: The state university offers opportunities for liberal education and professional training in its undergraduate and graduate programs. It is accredited by the North Central Association of Colleges and Schools and by professional and educational organizations. The university maintains a cooperative relationship with interested business, civic, cultural, educational, industrial and social agencies. The university awards the Certificate and Bachelor, Specialist, Master, Professional and Doctorate degrees. The university employs the semester system and offers two summer sessions. Enrollment is 6,983 men and 8,282 women full-time and 7,590 men and 10,051 women part-time. A faculty of 1,617 full-time and 1,078 part-time gives an overall faculty-student ratio of 1-11.

Entrance Requirements: Accredited high school graduation with a 2.75 GPA; minimum SAT score of 450 verbal and 400 math required; rolling admission, midyear admission and advanced placement plans available; $20 application fee.

Costs Per Year: $3,442 tuition; $7,534 nonresident tuition; $2,848 room.

Collegiate Environment: The university has 27 social and professional fraternities and sororities. The design of the buildings and campus allow for easy movement of persons in wheelchairs or who are otherwise restricted in mobility. The library contains 2.8 million volumes and numerous pamphlets, periodicals and microforms. 77% of the applicants are accepted, including midyear students. Freshman classes begin in September and January.

Community Environment: At the turn of the 20th Century, Detroit was a quiet, tree-shaded community brewing beer and producing comfortable carriages and comforting stoves. The serenity was broken by Henry Ford's creation, a vehicle "propelled by power generated from within itself." Today, it is the greatest automobile-manufacturing city in the world. It is also rapidly becoming a steel center and a leader in the manufacturing of pharmaceuticals, office equipment, rubber products, salt, television components, synthetic resins and paints, meat products, marine engines and more than half the garden seed used throughout the country. Annual mean temperature is 49.3 degrees, and annual rainfall is 31.03 inches. Definitely an industrial city, Detroit has a civic center complex on the riverfront, an excellent park system and numerous museums and art galleries.

WEST SHORE COMMUNITY COLLEGE   *(L-7)*
300 N. Stiles Rd.
Scottville, Michigan 49454
Tel: (616) 845-6211; Fax: (616) 845-0207

Description: The coeducational community college is supported by the college district, the state, and tuition. It is accredited by the North Central Association of Colleges and Schools. First operated on a part-time basis, it expanded to full-time in September 1969. It offers 2 years of lower-division study parallel to the first 2 years of a four-year college in general education; two-year career programs and some one-year certificate programs are available. The school operates on the semester system and offers one summer session. Enrollment includes 1,487 students with a full-time faculty of 26. The faculty-student ratio is 1-57.

Entrance Requirements: Open enrollment policy; high school graduation or equivalent; non-high school graduates admitted for non-degree programs; rolling admission, early decision, advanced placement, early admission, and midyear plans available; $10 application fee

Costs Per Year: $960 district resident tuition; $1,500 state resident tuition; $1,950 nonresident tuition; $25 student fees.

Collegiate Environment: The 375-acre campus is located in a beautiful wooded setting and includes 5 buildings. The college library contains 12,000 volumes and 227 periodicals. All applicants are accepted, including midyear students. 51% of students receive financial aid.

Community Environment: Scottville is a rural city located 80 miles northwest of Grand Rapids. Agriculture is the main economic feature of the city with a Stokley canning factory second. Recreation is provided by local Riverside Park, with camping, boating and fishing. In addition, duck and small game hunting is available in the surrounding area. Community services include a library, and five churches. Bus, rail and air transportation are easily accessible.

WESTERN MICHIGAN UNIVERSITY   *(Q-9)*
Kalamazoo, Michigan 49008
Tel: (616) 387-1000; Admissions: (616) 387-2000; Fax: (616) 387-2096

Description: The state university is accredited by the North Central Association of Colleges and Schools. The university is organized into the Colleges of Engineering and Applied Sciences, Fine Arts, Business, Education, Continuing Education, Arts and Sciences, Health and Human Services, and the Graduate College. The Honors College offers to students of exceptional ability maximum opportunity for independent study, research, and self direction. An optional Army ROTC program is also available. The university operates on the semester system and offers two summer sessions. Total enrollment is 25,673 students, consisting of 19,499 undergraduates and 6,174 graduate students. Of the undergraduates, 15,390 are full-time and 4,109 are part-time. Of the graduate students, 1,170 are full-time and 5,004 are part-time. A faculty of 775 full-time and 401 part-time which gives an overall faculty-student ratio of 1-18.

Entrance Requirements: Accredited high school graduation or equivalent; average high school GPA 3.2; high school units including 4 English, 3 math (including intermediate algebra), 3 history and so-

cial science, and 2 biological or physical science; non-high school graduates may be admitted by examination; non-degree candidates may be admitted as special students; ACT required; GRE required for graduate students; rolling admission and advanced placement plans available; application fee $25.

Costs Per Year: $3,160 state-resident tuition and fees; $7,391 out-of-state; $4,097 room and board.

Collegiate Environment: The university's location is midway between Chicago and Detroit. The East Campus consists of 70 acres, of which 15 acres are devoted to physical education and recreation. The West Campus of more than 400 acres is the location of current and anticipated university expansion. The Dwight W. Waldo Library can be found here as well as the Kanley Memorial Chapel, the University Student Center, 3 theatres, the nationally renowned Miller Auditorium and many other major buildings. Dormitory housing accomodations are provided for 5,733 students. On-campus apartments accomodate 702 students. Scholarships, loans, grants and student employment are available. Closed-circuit television is a medium of transmission used for courses and is used in several performance skills courses to permit students to observe themselves by means of videotape recordings. Approximately 72% of students applying for admission meet the requirements and are accepted, including midyear students. The library contains 3,205,619 volumes. About 80% of the previous freshmen returned for the sophomore year.

Community Environment: At one time a gathering place of the Potawatomies, the city received its name from the Indian word meaning "place where the water boils." Today the city is an important paper-manufacturing center with an annual production of over three million tons. The city is also prominent in the manufacture of pharmaceutical drugs. Part-time work is available for students. The largest city in southwest Michigan, Kalamazoo has many parks and picnic areas, 9 golf courses, ski areas, sandy beaches and good hunting in season. Community service is provided by several churches, 2 hospitals, and shopping malls. The municipal library, art center, civic players, and symphony orchestra provide cultural outlets.

WESTERN THEOLOGICAL SEMINARY   *(O-7)*
86 East 12th Street
Holland, Michigan 49423
Tel: (616) 392-8555; (800) 392-8554; Admissions: (616) 392-8555; Fax: (616) 392-7717

Description: The three-year coeducational seminary is accredited by the Association of Theological Schools in the United States and Canada and is affiliated with the Reformed Church in America. Academic programs lead to the Master of Divinity, Master of Religious Education, Master of Theology and Doctor of Ministry degrees. The seminary operates on the quarter system and offers one summer session. Enrollment is 139 students. The full-time faculty of 15 supplemented by adjunct faculty, gives a faculty-student ratio of 1-10.

Entrance Requirements: Bachelor degree from accredited college with liberal arts background; entrance exam required; endorsement from local church consistory; letter from pastor required; midyear admission, rolling admission plans available. $30 application fee.

Costs Per Year: $5,400 tuition; $3,105-$4,500 room; $85 student fees.

Collegiate Environment: The 3-acre campus consists of a colonial style classroom and office complex, a 6-story library/theological research center, and student housing. 95% of the applicants are accepted. Students may be admitted at midyear. Financial aid is available; approximately 45% of a recent entering class received some form of assistance.

Community Environment: See Hope College

WILLIAM TYNDALE COLLEGE   *(P-14)*
35700 West Twelve Mile Road
Farmington Hills, Michigan 48331
Tel: (313) 553-7200

Description: William Tyndale College is a four-year degree-granting college of biblical, vocational and general studies. There are 13 majors in a variety of fields leading to the Associate or Bachelor degree. The college is accredited by the NCA. The college is approved by the State of Michigan to grant the Associate of Arts, Bachelor of

Arts, Bachelor of Religious Education, Bachelor of Music and Bachelor of Theology degrees. The college offers majors in Bible, business, cross cultural studies, psychology, interdisciplinary, music, pastoral studies, theology, and youth studies. It operates on the semester system and offers one summer session. Enrollment is 471 students. A faculty of 40 gives an overall faculty-student ratio of approximately 1-14.

Entrance Requirements: High school graduation or equivalent with rank in upper half of graduating class; ACT or SAT required; applicants not meeting all requirements may be admitted on probationary status; early admission, early decision, delayed admission, midyear admission, advanced placement and rolling admission plans available; $25 application fee.

Costs Per Year: $5,517 tuition (based on $178 per credit hour); $2,575 room; $1,050 student fees.

Collegiate Environment: William Tyndale College is located on a beautiful 28-acre campus in Farmington Hills, Michigan, and is easily accessible from major expressways. Campus facilities include the College Library, which houses 56,200 titles, 300 periodicals, 2,109 microforms, and 5,217 audiovisual materials. The Living Center provides a dormitory for 60 resident students. Students are required to sign a statement regarding standard of conduct. Approximately 95% of students applying for admission meet the requirements and are accepted. Students may be admitted at midyear and are accepted from various geographical locations. Financial aid is available. Classes begin in August and January. About 52% of last year's senior class continued on to graduate school.

Community Environment: Farmington Hills is a growing suburban community in Oakland County, Michigan. The campus is within a short drive of lakes and parks, museums and sport centers, evangelical churches and Christian Organizations, the Detroit river front, and the border to Canada. This mix of rural, urban, suburban and international communities near the campus provides an assortment of off-campus activities for students.

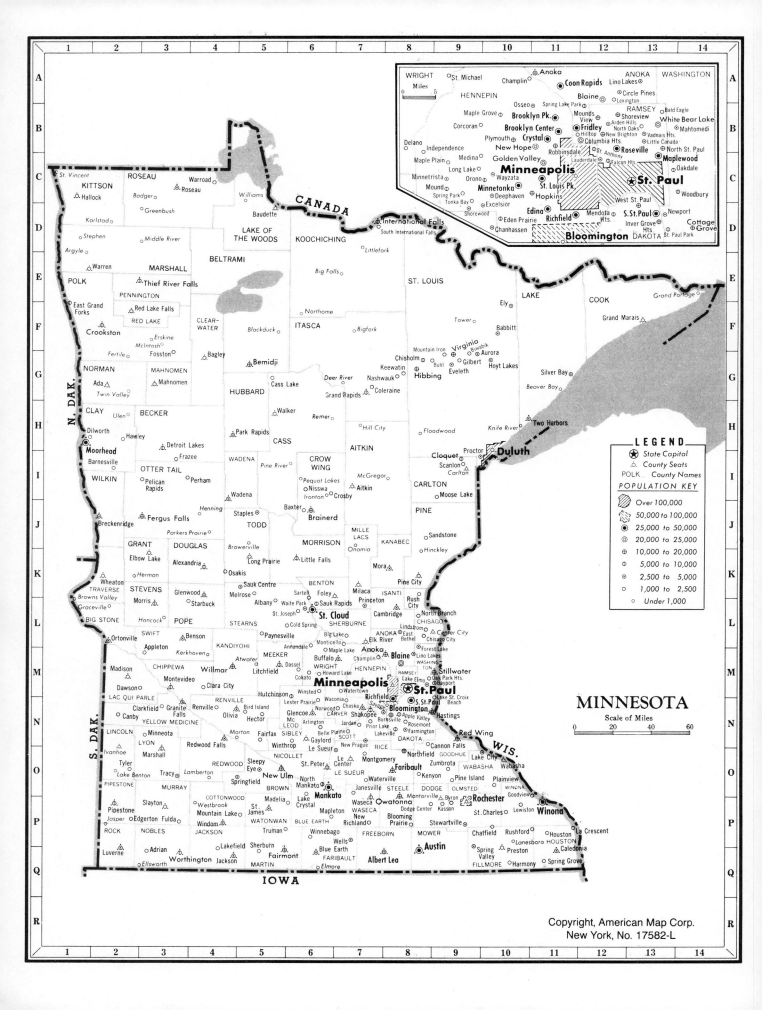

MINNESOTA

Scale of Miles

0   20   40   60

LEGEND

★ State Capital
⊛ County Seats
POLK County Names

POPULATION KEY

▨ Over 100,000
▧ 50,000 to 100,000
⊚ 25,000 to 50,000
◉ 20,000 to 25,000
⊕ 10,000 to 20,000
⊙ 5,000 to 10,000
⊛ 2,500 to 5,000
○ 1,000 to 2,500
· Under 1,000

MINNESOTA

ANOKA-RAMSEY COMMUNITY COLLEGE *(A-11)*
11200 Mississippi Blvd. N. W.
Coon Rapids, Minnesota 55433
Tel: (612) 427-2600; Admissions: (612) 422-3421; Fax: (612) 422-3341

Description: Anoka-Ramsey is a publicly supported community college established in 1965. Enrollment includes 1,895 full-time and 2,811 part-time students. A faculty of 104 full-time and 64 part-time gives a faculty-student ratio of 1-22. The college operates on the quarter system with 2 summer terms and offers transfer programs, general education programs, occupational programs, and adult education and community service programs. It also offers a two-year program leading to an A.S. nursing degree. The school is fully accredited by the North Central Association of Colleges and Schools. The Cambridge Community College Campus Branch is located on Highway 95, west of Cambridge, MN. With an enrollment of 1,100 students, Cambridge offers a wide range of general education courses and several joint programs with Pine Technical College in Pine City, MN.

Entrance Requirements: Open enrollment; high school graduation or equivalent. Rolling admission, advanced placement; early admission, early decision available. $15 application fee.

Costs Per Year: $2,007 tuition; $3,963 nonresident.

Collegiate Environment: The college is located on 85 acres and contains 9 buildings which include a library of 29,850 volumes. 99% of students applying for admission are accepted, and 32% return for the second year. Financial aid is available and 23% of the current student body receive some form of financial aid. The college awarded 475 Associate degrees to the graduating class.

Community Environment: A suburban area with a temperate climate, Coon Rapids (population 53,000) enjoys all the recreational, social and cultural advantages of the Twin Cities. All forms of commercial transportation are available. Community facilities include churches, a public library and a community hospital nearby.

AUGSBURG COLLEGE *(M-8)*
2211 Riverside Avenue
Minneapolis, Minnesota 55454
Tel: (612) 330-1001; (800) 788-5678; Fax: (612) 330-1649

Description: This institution is a liberal arts college of The Evangelical Lutheran Church in America. It operates on the 4-1-4 semester calendar system with 2 summer terms. The college is accredited by the North Central Association of Colleges and Schools. The college offers courses leading to a Bachelor of Arts degree in 42 major fields of study. It offers preparation for the state teaching certificate, band, chorus, choir, orchestra and, intercollegiate and intramural athletics. It maintains off-campus programs in Cooperative Education and Global Community and Urban Affairs. Enrollment is 1,392 full-time and 120 part-time students in the Day Program, and 169 graduate students. There are 1,172 students in the weekend program. A faculty of 129 full-time and 156 part-time provides an undergraduate faculty-student ratio of 1-14. Army and Navy ROTC programs are available.

Entrance Requirements: High school graduation or equivalent; high school units must include 4 English, 3 math, 3 social studies, 2 foreign language and 2 humanities; SAT, ACT, or PSAT required; non-high school graduates considered; early admission, early decision, rolling admission, delayed admission, midyear admission, advanced placement plans available; $20 application fee.

Costs Per Year: $11,902 tuition; $4,371 room and board; $114 student fees.

Collegiate Environment: The college is located on 22 acres near the Minneapolis Loop and the University of Minnesota. The 14 major college buildings include a library of 160,000 volumes, periodicals subscriptions, microforms and audiovisual materials. Dormitories provide housing for 833 men and women and 22 married students. About 80% of students applying for admission are accepted, including mid-year students and those from other geographical locations. Scholarships are available and 90% of the student body receives some form of financial assistance. Augsburg also offers an adult program. The Augsburg College weekend program is a fully accredited bachelors program designed for working adults.

Community Environment: Augsburg's campus is located in the heart of the Twin Cities, surrounding Murphy Square, the first of 155 parks in the "City of Lakes." The University of Minnesota West Bank campus and two of the city's largest hospitals, Fairview and St. Mary's, are adjacent to the campus. Downtown Minneapolis and St. Paul are minutes west and east via Interstate 94 which forms the southern border of the campus, or on bus routes that also connect with the suburbs.

AUSTIN COMMUNITY COLLEGE *(Q-8)*
1600 Eighth Avenue, NW
Austin, Minnesota 55912
Tel: (507) 433-0505; (800) 747-8941; Admissions: (507) 433-0517; Fax: (507) 433-0515

Description: The publicly supported two-year college is operated by the State of Minnesota through the authority of the Minnesota Community College System. It provides instruction in liberal arts, pre-professional training, nursing, general education and adult education. Accredited by the North Central Association of Colleges and Schools and the National League for Nursing, the college grants the Associate degree. It offers cooperative education program (alternating work and class periods) in certain subjects. The college operates on the quarter system with 2 summer terms. Enrollment 1,400 students. A faculty of 58 gives a faculty-student ratio of 1-19.

Entrance Requirements: Open enrollment policy; high school graduation or equivalent; non-high school graduates considered; early admission, ealry decision, rolling admission and midyear admission plans available; $15 application fee.

Costs Per Year: $1,800 tuition; $3,600 nonresident tuition

Collegiate Environment: The college was established in 1940, and moved to its present $3,000,000 campus in 1966. This campus is a complex of 5 interconnected units including the most modern facilities available and a library of 28,000 volumes, 210 periodicals, 4,000 microforms and 1,000 audiovisual materials and equipment. Almost all of the students applying for admission are accepted, including mid-year students. 70% of the students receive some form of financial aid. Classes begin in September, December, and March.

Community Environment: A rural area, Austin (population 23,000) is the location of one of the largest meatpackers in the country, the George A. Hormel Co.

BEMIDJI STATE UNIVERSITY *(G-5)*
1500 Birchmont Drive NE
Bemidji, Minnesota 56601-2699
Tel: (218) 755-2040

Description: This publicly supported university was first established as a normal school and opened in 1919. Today it offers a variety of programs leading to the Bachelor of Science, Bachelor of Arts, and Bachelor of Fine Arts degrees. It also offers the Master of Arts degree and teacher education programs that lead to the Master of Science in Education. The university is accredited by the North Central Association of Colleges and Schools. It operates on the quarter system and offers 2 summer sessions. Enrollment includes 3,670 full-time and 1,126 part-time undergraduates and 328 graduate students. In ad-

391

dition, there are 202 students in evening programs. A faculty of 217 full-time and 11 part-time gives a faculty-student ratio of 1-21. Extensive music, intercollegiate, intramural and internship programs, the Oxford/Cambridge Exchange Program called Eurospring, and European Tours are available. The university offers on-campus help for the educationally disadvantaged through the Educational Development Center. An external studies program leading to 4-year degrees in certain fields is available. Bemidji State University also offers several degree programs through the Arrowhead University Center, which is located on Minnesota's Mesabi Iron Range. The center currently serves approximately 300 students. It offers degree programs in accounting, business administration, elementary education, applied psychology, and also grants a Master's degree in education.

Entrance Requirements: Rank in top 50% of high school graduating class or ACT composite of at least 21; 2.0 GPA for transfer students; delayed admission, advanced placement, early admission, early decision, and rolling admission plans available; $15 application fee.

Costs Per Year: $2,242 tuition; $4,867 out-of-state; $2,798 room and board; $398 student fees.

Collegiate Environment: The college is located on an 89-acre campus and is landscaped to take advantage of its setting along the west shore of Lake Bemidji, one of Minnesota's beautiful lakes near the headwaters of the Mississippi River. Dormitory facilities are provided for 1,622 students and are 100% coeducational. The library contains 184,613 volumes and periodicals. Approximately 75% of students applying for admission are accepted, including midyear students and those from various geographical locations. Financial aid is available, and 75% of the students receive some form of aid.

Community Environment: A regional home for outdoor sports and cultural arts activities, Bemidji (population 12,000) lies in Minnesota North Country on the shores of Lake Bemidji. This area is noted for its scenic forests and lakes that are enjoyed by recreational enthusiasts during all seasons. From excellent fishing in the summer to cross-country and downhill skiing in the winter, residents and visitors alike have found Bemidji to be a community that satisfies a great diversity of interests.

Branch Campuses: Arrowhead University Center, 1515 E. 25th St., Hibbing, MN 55746, (800) 369-4970.

BETHANY LUTHERAN COLLEGE   *(O-6)*
734 Marsh Street
Mankato, Minnesota 56001
Tel: (507) 386-5300; Fax: (507) 386-5376

Description: This privately supported liberal arts junior college was founded in 1911 as a Lutheran academy for girls and became a coeducational college of the Evangelical Lutheran Synod in 1927. The college is accredited by the North Central Association of Colleges and Schools. It operates on the early semester system. Enrollment includes 350 full-time and 20 part-time students. A faculty of 19 full-time and 23 part-time gives a faculty-student ratio of 1-14. Religious subjects and chapel attendance are expected. The college offers chorus, choir, and intercollegiate and intramural athletics.

Entrance Requirements: High school graduation or equivalent; completion of 16 units; rolling admission, early admission, early decision, delayed admission, midyear admission, and advanced placement plans available; ACT or SAT required; $20 application fee.

Costs Per Year: $7,600 tuition; $3,254 room and board.

Collegiate Environment: The college is comprised of 12 buildings that include a library of 30,000 volumes, 225 periodicals, 100 microforms, and 450 recordings, and dormitory facilities for 350 men and women. All students not living at home are required to live in college dormitories. Approximately 95% of students applying for admission are accepted, including midyear students and those from various geographical locations. 80% of the previous freshman class returns to the college for the second year. Classes begin in August and January. Financial aid is available for economically disadvantaged students and 90% of the current student body receives some form of financial assistance. The college awarded 13 Certificates and 94 Associate degrees to the recent graduating class.

Community Environment: See Mankato State University.

BETHEL COLLEGE   *(M-8)*
3900 Bethel Drive
Saint Paul, Minnesota 55112
Tel: (612) 638-6242; (800) 255-8706; Admissions: (612) 638-6242;
Fax: (612) 638-6001

Description: The privately supported college was founded in 1871 and is owned and operated by the Baptist General Conference of America. It is accredited by the North Central Association of Colleges and Schools and by numerous professional accrediting institutions. It is a member of the Association of Theological Schools in the United States and Canada. It is composed of a standard, four-year liberal arts college and a graduate theological seminary. The college operates on the 4-1-4 semester system and offers two summer sessions. Undergraduate work requires religion courses. Extensive music and athletic programs are available. Enrollment includes 729 men and 1,149 women. A faculty of 111 full-time and 79 part-time gives a faculty-student ratio of 1-15.

Entrance Requirements: Accredited high school graduation or equivalent with rank in upper half of graduating class; SAT, ACT or PSAT required. Minimum test scores required: SAT Verbal 400, Math 400; ACT 21; PSAT Verbal 40, Math 40; early admission, rolling admission, midyear admission, and advanced placement plans available; $20 application fee.

Costs Per Year: $12,260 tuition; $4,460 room and board.

Collegiate Environment: The college and seminary are located on 231 acres in a pleasant residential area midway between the business districts of St. Paul and Minneapolis. The 30 buildings includes a college library of 129,000 titles, 630 periodicals, 2,500 microforms, and 3,500 audiovisual materials. College dormitory facilities accommodate 80% of the student population. Approximately 81% of the students applying for admission are accepted, including midyear students, and 82% return to the college for the sophomore year. Financial aid is available. 88% of the students receive some form of aid.

Community Environment: St. Paul (population 310,000), the capital of Minnesota, is a major transportation and industrial center of the midwest. Saint Paul's facilities are numerous and excellent. The recreational facilities are also exceptional: 5 public golf courses as well as numerous private ones, 30 lakes within 30 minutes excellent for swimming boating, canoeing, and fishing in the summer. As part of the Twin Cities (including Minneapolis) the college has easy access to outstanding recreational and cultural activities.

BRAINERD COMMUNITY COLLEGE   *(J-6)*
College Drive
Brainerd, Minnesota 56401
Tel: (218) 828-2525

Description: The publicly supported community college was established in 1938 as part of the Brainerd Public School System. It became a part of the state system in 1964 and became part of a 3-college region called Clearwater Community College Region in 1983. The college operates on the quarter system with 2 summer sessions. It enrolls between 1,200 and 1,600 students per quarter. Degrees offered are: Associate in Arts; Associate in Science, Nursing: Associate in Science, Child Development; and Associate in Applied Science. The Associate in Applied Science Degrees are offered jointly with three Minnesota Technical Institutes. The college is fully accredited by the North Central Association of Colleges and Schools. Enrollment includes 1,007 full-time and 849 part-time students. There are 46 full-time faculty and 51 part-time faculty, giving a faculty-student ratio of 1-19.

Entrance Requirements: Open enrollment; a person with neither a diploma nor a GED certificate may be admitted to take courses provided that her/his class has graduated and if, at the discretion of the college, that person shows promise of being a successful college student.

Costs Per Year: $1,688 tuition; $3,375 out-of-state.

Collegiate Environment: The college is located on an 82-acre campus in southwest Brainerd. College complex consists of 4 interconnected buildings that include a classroom building, library and media center, a physical education building, a fine arts building, and a college center and student lounge. Also included on campus are athletic fields, tennis courts and parking facilities. The library contains 24,000 volumes, 1,500 pamphlets, 89 periodical titles, 10,500 microforms,

2,250 audiovisual materials, and 7,801 recordings. Approximately 98% of the students applying for admission are accepted, including midyear students and those from various geographical locations. Scholarships are awarded each spring for the following academic year. 95-100 scholarships are available. 75% of students receive some form of financial aid.

Community Environment: One of the state's best developed vacation areas, Brainerd (population 12,000) is on the Mississippi River near the center of the state. The town is the supply point for resorts along 464 lakes within a 25-mile radius of the town. There are opportunities for varied types of sports activities such as fishing, golfing, skiing, snowmobiling and water sports. Other activities include summer theatre, yacht club regatta, antique shows and concerts. Shopping areas, churches, a public library, a hospital and a YMCA are available. Transportation is provided by bus, railway and airlines.

CARLETON COLLEGE   *(O-8)*
Northfield, Minnesota 55057
Tel: (507) 663-4000; (800) 995-2275; Fax: (507) 663-4204

Description: The privately supported, nondenominational college was established by the General Conference of the Congregational Churches of Minnesota in 1866. Today the college offers a liberal education leading to the Bachelor of Arts degree. It operates on the 3-3 calendar system. Enrollment includes 885 men and 870 women full-time and 20 part-time students. A faculty of 150 full-time and 14 part-time gives a faculty-student ratio of 1-11. The college is accredited by the North Central Association of Colleges and Schools and offers preparation for the State teaching certificate. It also offers overseas programs for more than 300 students per year in 30 countries, urban study, a term in Washington D.C., geology field study programs, and 3.2 cooperative programs for engineering or nursing students. Choir, orchestra and extensive intercollegiate and intramural athletic programs are available.

Entrance Requirements: High school graduation or equivalent; completion of 4 English, 3 mathematics, 2 foreign language, 3 social studies, and 2 science strongly recommended; SAT or ACT required, three Achievement Tests recommended; early decision, early admission, deferred admission, and advanced placement programs available; non-high school graduates considered under certain circumstances; $30 application fee.

Costs Per Year: $19,166 tuition; $3,957 room and board; $1,100 average additional expenses.

Collegiate Environment: The 90-acre main campus, which includes the Lyman Lakes, has a library, 9 residence halls, laboratories, classrooms and other facilities. The library contains 502,770 volumes. Dormitory facilities accommodate 1,570 students. Adjacent to the campus are an arboretum and the College Farm totalling over 900 acres, which are college-owned. Approximately 56% of the students applying for admission are accepted and 94% of the previous freshman class returns to the college for the sophomore year. The college welcomes a geographically diverse student body. All freshmen must begin classes in September. Average high school standing of the freshman class: 93% in the top quarter; Financial aid is available and more than 70% of the current student body receives some form of financial aid.

Community Environment: Northfield (population 14,500), a two-college town, located 40 miles south of Minneapolis and St. Paul, is the home of several major industries that contribute to the prosperity of the community. Part-time employment is limited. Good shopping facilities, library, churches, a hospital and an arts guild are a part of the community. Regularly scheduled bus service to Minneapolis-St. Paul is available. A Carleton - St. Olaf bus also makes round trips daily to the Twin Cities. The Defeat of Jesse James Days in September is a special annual event.

COLLEGE OF ASSOCIATED ARTS   *(M-8)*
344 Summit Avenue
St. Paul, Minnesota 55102
Tel: (612) 224-3416; Admissions: (612) 224-3416; Fax: (612) 224-8854

Description: Founded in 1924, the College of Associated Arts is a private, four-year college of art and design, located in the historic residential Summit Hill area of St. Paul, Minnesota. The college offers

Bachelor of Fine Arts degrees in three major areas: Communication Design, Illustration, and Fine Arts (painting, drawing, sculpture, printmaking, and photography). It operates on the semester system. With an enrollment of 210 students and a faculty of 38, the college blends a rigorous curriculum and individualized attention allowing students to realize their full creative and intellectual potential in a challenging yet supportive educational environment. The college is accreited by ACCSCT and is a candidate for accreditation with the North Central Association of Colleges and Schools.

Entrance Requirements: Accredited high school graduation or GED scores; high school transcripts required; application form; personal essay; art portfolio; on-campus interview; transfer students must also provide college transcripts; early admission, delayed admission, midyear admission, rolling admission, and advanced placement plans available; $25 application fee.

Costs Per Year: $8,100 tuition; $1,600 books and art supplies

Collegiate Environment: The College is located in St. Paul's beautiful, historical Cathedral Hill neighborhood. The school is housed in a Tudor Gothic mansion built in 1918 that overlooks the Mississippi River Valley which provides an attractive atmosphere for artistic study and creativity. The library houses 2,000 volumes and 10,000 slides and multimedia materials. Although the college does not provide on-campus housing, it assists students in planning their living arrangements. Financial aid is available and over 86% of the students receive some form of assistance.

Community Environment: See the University of Minnesota - Twin Cities.

COLLEGE OF SAINT BENEDICT   *(L-6)*
37 South College Avenue
St. Joseph, Minnesota 56374-2099
Tel: (612) 363-5308; (800) 544-1489; Admissions: (612) 363-5308; Fax: (612) 363-5010

Description: The privately supported Roman Catholic liberal arts college for women is engaged in a full-time, cooperative academic partnership with nearby St. John's University for men, Collegeville, Minnesota. It is accredited by the North Central Association of Colleges and Schools and operates on the 4-1-4 calendar system. The college welcomes and encourages the enrollment of qualified students of all religious faiths and enrolls 1,756 full-time and 88 part-time women. A faculty of 130 full-time and 28 part-time provides a student-faculty ratio of 13:1. College-sponsored semesters are offered in China, France, Spain, England, Ireland, Austria, and Greece-Rome. A year long exchange is available with Sophia University in Tokyo, Japan. The college offers preparation for State teaching certificate. Army ROTC is available as an elective.

Entrance Requirements: Approved high school graduation or equivalent; minimum cumulative high school GPA 2.8 (4.0 scale); minimum high school rank 60%; completion of 4 units of English, 3 mathematics, 2 foreign languages, 1 science; minimum ACT 20 composite, or minimum SAT 420 verbal, 470 math required; rolling admission, early admission, midyear admission and advanced placement. $25 application fee.

Costs Per Year: $12,951 tuition; $4,340 board and room; $135 student fees.

Collegiate Environment: The college is located on a 700-acre wooded campus, 75 miles from the Twin Cities of Minneapolis and St. Paul. St. John's University, a Benedictine college for men, is 4 miles away. The college library, which is a joint library with St. John's University, contains 509,000 volumes, 2,100 periodicals, 131,000 microforms and 13,300 audio-visual materials. Dormitory facilities are provided for 1,441 women. The college welcomes a geographically diverse student body and will accept midyear students. 89% of applicants are accepted. The average scores of the entering freshman class were SAT 480 verbal, 540 math, ACT 24 composite. Scholarships are available and 85% of students receive financial aid.

Community Environment: St. Joseph is located 7 miles west of St. Cloud. Amtrack serves the area. Greyhound bus line and limo services are available to Minneapolis International Airport.

COLLEGE OF SAINT CATHERINE   *(M-8)*
2004 Randolph Avenue
St. Paul, Minnesota 55105
Tel: (612) 690-6505

Description: Founded in 1905 by the Sisters at St. Joseph of Car-ondelet, the privately supported Roman Catholic liberal arts college is accredited by the North Central Association of Colleges and Schools. It offers four-year undergraduate programs in a variety of fields, a Master of Arts in Theology, Master of Social Work, Master of Arts in Nursing, Master of Arts in Occupational Therapy, Master of Arts in Library and Informational Sciences, Master of Physical Therapy and a Master of Arts in Organizational Leadership. Enrollment is 1,746 full-time and 607 part-time undergraduates, and 407 graduate students. A faculty of 124 full-time and 128 part-time gives a faculty-student ratio of 1-14. Study abroad programs are available during January as well as throughout the academic year. As a member of the Associated Colleges of the Twin Cities (ACTC), a consortium of five private colleges, the College of St. Catherine offers its students the possibility of registering for courses at the other colleges. Academic cooperative programs are also available with Washington University in St. Louis and with the University of Minnesota for engineering students. The college operates on a semester system and offers 3 summer terms. In 1986, the college acquired St. Mary's Junior College, now the St. Mary's Campus of the College of St. Catherine. St. Mary's offers associate degrees and certificate programs in health and human services with an enrollment of approximately 1,000 students.

Entrance Requirements: Accredited high school graduation or equivalent with rank in upper half of graduating class; recommended completion of the following college preparatory units: 4 English, 3 math, 2-3 science, 2 foreign language, and 2 academic electives; SAT, ACT or PSAT required; $20 application fee.

Costs Per Year: $12,224 tuition, $4,282 average room and board, $220 student activity fee, $450 approximate books.

Collegiate Environment: The campus covers an area of more than 110 acres in a residential section midway between St. Paul and Minneapolis. Library holdings include 231,453 volumes. Residence halls accommodate 739 women. 32 student clubs offer something for everyone including volunteer service, recreational, academic and cultural organizations. 7 intercollegiate athletic teams and various intramural sports are available. St. Catherine's and other nearby colleges and universities cosponsor several major social events each year. The College welcomes a geographically diverse student body and will accept midyear students. 87% of the students applying for admission are accepted. Average scores of the freshmen class: SAT 970 combined; ACT 23 composite. Financial aid is available and approximately 74% of the current student body receives some form of financial assistance.

Community Environment: St. Catherine's is only minutes away from downtown Minneapolis or St. Paul, and the cultural and entertainment advantages of a large metropolitan area, such as the nationally respected Guthrie Theatre, Art and Science Museums, Professional and Amateur Sports facilities, and concert halls. For recreation, the area's 900 lakes, cross country and downhill ski trails, and jogging paths along the Mississippi River and area parks provide fun and relaxation all year long.

COLLEGE OF SAINT CATHERINE - SAINT MARY'S CAMPUS   *(M-8)*
2500 S. Sixth Street
Minneapolis, Minnesota 55454
Tel: (612) 690-7800; (800) 945-4599; Fax: (612) 690-7849

Description: The privately supported junior college was established in 1964 and became part of the College of St. Catherine. It operates on the 4-1-4 system and offers a summer session. It awards the Associate of Applied Science degree and the Certificate in health and human services. The college is accredited by the North Central Association of Colleges and Schools. Enrollment includes 254 full-time and 933 part-time undergraduate students. A faculty of 75 full-time and 50 part-time gives an undergraduate faculty-student ratio of 1-8. There are also 85 graduate students.

Entrance Requirements: Accredited high school graduation or equivalent; some programs have special requirements; rolling admission and delayed admission plans available; $20 application fee.

Costs Per Year: $8,970 tuition; $2,500 approximate room and board; $600 average additional expenses.

Collegiate Environment: The college consists of 2 buildings, including a library of 25,000 volumes and dormitory facilities for 100 women and men. Most program classes begin in September, although some have other entry times. Approximately 78% of the students applying for admission are accepted. Financial aid is available and 76% of the current student body receives some form of financial assistance.

Community Environment: See University of Minnesota - Twin Cities.

COLLEGE OF SAINT SCHOLASTICA   *(I-10)*
1200 Kenwood Avenue
Duluth, Minnesota 55811
Tel: (218) 723-6000; (800) 447-5444; Admissions: (218) 723-6046; Fax: (218) 723-6290

Description: A privately supported liberal arts college operated by an Independent Board of Trustees affiliated with the Benedictine sisters of Duluth. It accepts all qualified students without prejudice to race or creed. The college operates on the quarter system and offers 2 summer terms. It is accredited by the North Central Association of Colleges and Schools and by other professional and educational organizations. Offers preparation for State teaching certificate. Enrollment includes 1,309 full-time, 279 part-time undergraduates, and 59 full-time and 202 part-time graduate students. A faculty of 124 full-time and 43 part-time gives a faculty-student ratio of 1-11. Offers chorus, touring group of abbey minstrels, intercollegiate baseball, ice hockey, men's and women's soccer, volleyball, cross country, basketball and intramural athletics. Exchange programs are available with University of Minnesota at Duluth and University of Wisconsin, Superior.

Entrance Requirements: Accredited high school graduation or equivalent; SAT, PSAT or ACT required; GRE required for graduate programs; early admission, rolling admission, delayed admission, midyear admission and advanced placement programs available; $25 application fee.

Costs Per Year: $12,459 tuition; $3,807 room and board; $75 health service student fees; additional expenses average $1,500.

Collegiate Environment: The college covers 160 acres and is located about 10 minutes from the center of the city. The college buildings include a library of 122,000 volumes and 800 periodical subscriptions, and dormitory facilities for 680 students. Approximately 88% of students applying for admission are accepted. The college welcomes a geographically diverse student body and will accept midyear students. About 80% of the previous freshman class returns to the college for the sophomore year. Financial aid is available and approximately 90% of the current student body receives some form of financial assistance. Quarters begin in September, December, and March. The college awarded 361 Bachelor degrees and 57 Master of Arts and five Master of Education degrees during the current academic year, and approximately 19% of the senior class continued on to graduate school.

Community Environment: See University of Minnesota - Duluth.

CONCORDIA COLLEGE   *(H-1)*
901 S. Eighth Street
Moorhead, Minnesota 56562
Tel: (218) 299-3004; Fax: (218) 299-3947

Description: The privately supported liberal arts college is sponsored by the Evangelical Lutheran Church in America. It is accredited by the North Central Association of Colleges and Schools. The college operates on the semester system and offers two summer sessions. Enrollment includes 2,876 full-time and 94 part-time undergraduate students. A faculty of 200 full-time and 82 part-time gives a faculty-student ratio of 1-15. Offers extensive music programs as well as intercollegiate and intramural athletics. Offers cooperative education program (alternating work and class periods) in all departments. Special programs include May Seminars Overseas to Europe, Asia and Africa (4 weeks for credit), Junior Year in Europe, Washington Semester, student exchange program, urban seminar and the Institute of German Studies. Religious subjects required. Army and Air Force ROTC programs available.

Entrance Requirements: Accredited high school graduation with rank in upper half of class; non-high school graduates considered; SAT or ACT required; early admission, rolling admission, delayed admission, and advanced placement plans available; $20 application fee.

Costs Per Year: $10,620 tuition; $3,280 room and board; $100 student fees; additional expenses average $1,250.

Collegiate Environment: The college is located on 120 acres and contains 38 buildings, including a library whose holdings include 261,503 bound volumes, 1,485 periodicals, and 34,432 microforms. Dormitory facilities for 719 men and 1,089 women are available. Approximately 88% of the students applying for admission are accepted, including midyear students, and 79% of the previous freshman class returns to the college for the sophomore year. The average socres of the entering freshman class were SAT 490 verbal, 535 math; ACT 24 composite. Scholarships are available and 86% of the current student body receives some form of financial assistance. Semesters begin in August and January, and 2 six-week summer sessions begin in May.

Community Environment: See Moorhead State University.

CONCORDIA COLLEGE   *(M-8)*
275 North Syndicate Street
Saint Paul, Minnesota 55104
Tel: (612) 641-8278; (800) 333-4705; Fax: (612) 659-0207

Description: This privately supported liberal arts and teachers college is one of 12 colleges and seminaries affiliated with the Lutheran Church-Missouri Synod. It is accredited by the North Central Association of Colleges and Schools. Founded in 1893 with a three-year classical and normal preparatory course, the first Bachelor of Arts degree was granted in 1964. The Concordia School for Adult Learning is a 15-month major degree completion program with once-a-week class sessions. It also offers a program for educationally disadvantaged freshmen and sophomores. The college operates on the quarter system and offers two summer sessions. Enrollment includes 1,077 full-time, 189 part-time undergraduate, and 9 graduate students. A faculty of 71 full-time and 60 part-time gives an undergraduate faculty-student ratio of 1-15. Air Force, Army, and Navy ROTC are available at nearby colleges.

Entrance Requirements: Accredited high school graduation or equivalent with rank in upper 50% of graduating class; completion of 16 units including 4 English, 2 mathematics, 2 science, 2 social science, 1 fine arts, and 1 health/physical education; SAT or minimum ACT 18 required; early admission, early decision, deferred admission, rolling admission, midyear admission, and advanced placement plans available; Aug. 15 application deadline; $15 application fee.

Costs Per Year: $10,500 tuition; $3,750 room and board.

Collegiate Environment: The library contains 114,000 volumes, 450 periodicals, and 10,368 microforms. Dormitories provide accommodations for 450 students. The school offers band, choir, orchestra, drama, and extensive intercollegiate and intramural athletics. Approximately 95% of applicants are accepted, including midyear students. Financial aid is available, and 82% of students receive some form of financial assistance.

Community Environment: See University of Minnesota - Twin Cities.

CROWN COLLEGE   *(M-8)*
6425 County Road 30
St. Bonifacius, Minnesota 55375-9001
Tel: (612) 446-4100; (800) 682-7696; Fax: (612) 446-4149

Description: This privately supported Christian college is the midwestern regional college of the Christian and Missionary Alliance. The college, chartered by the Minnesota Department of Education as a degree-granting institution, is accredited by the American Association of Bible Colleges and the North Central Association of Colleges and Schools. It operates on the semester system and offers two summer sessions. Enrollment includes 474 full-time and 146 part-time students. A faculty of 25 full-time and 35 part-time gives a faculty-student ratio of 1-14. The college grants Bachelor and Associate degrees, and one-year Bible and Christian Education certificates. Music programs and intercollegiate and intramural athletics are available.

Entrance Requirements: High school graduation or equivalent; ACT preferred, SAT accepted; early admission, advanced placement, rolling admission, early decision, and delayed admission plans available; $35 application fee.

Costs Per Year: $7,650 tuition; $1,850 room and $1,850 board; $425 student fees; $600 average additional expenses.

Collegiate Environment: The college is situated on a beautiful 193-acre campus 23 miles west of metropolitan Minneapolis. The college library contains 98,000 titles, 500 periodicals, 74,000 microforms, and 3,400 audiovisual materials. A residence hall provides housing for 176 men, 238 women and 58 married students. The college is interdenominational in character and the student body is composed of approximately 11 different denominations. The college will accept midyear students and about 79% of students completing the application process are accepted. 56% of the previous freshman class returns to the college for the sophomore year. The average score of the freshman class is ACT 20 composite. Scholarships are available and 93% of the current student body receives some form of financial assistance. Approximately 33% of the senior class continues on to graduate school.

Community Environment: The college is located in a small community 23 miles west of Minneapolis.

FERGUS FALLS COMMUNITY COLLEGE   *(J-2)*
1414 College Way
Fergus Falls, Minnesota 56537
Tel: (218) 739-7500; Fax: (218) 739-7475

Description: The publicly supported community college was established in 1960 and is accredited by the North Central Association of Colleges and Schools. It offers courses in adult education, employment preparation, and pre-baccalaureate and pre-professional programs. Offers a cooperative education program (alternating work and class periods) in business and human services; music programs and intercollegiate and intramural athletics are available. It operates on the quarter system. Enrollment includes 782 full-time and 655 part-time students. A faculty of 32 full-time and 60 part-time gives a faculty-student ratio of 1-16.

Entrance Requirements: High school graduation or equivalent; open enrollment policy; non-high school graduates considered; ACT minimum score 19 required for out-of-state applicants; rolling admission and midyear admission plans available; $15 application fee.

Costs Per Year: $2,055 tuition; $4,011 out-of-state tuition; $4,254 room and board; $1,107 books and transportation.

Collegiate Environment: The college moved to its new 146-acre campus in 1968 and has a library collection of 27,000 volumes, 475 periodicals, and 1,378 sound recordings. 100% of those applying for admission are accepted including midyear students. Counseling and guidance services are provided. Financial aid is available for economically disadvantaged students. 72% of students receive some form of financial aid.

Community Environment: One of the largest dairy products and poultry shipping points in the northwest, Fergus Falls (population 12,443) also has the largest cooperative creamery in this region. Trains and buses are convenient for transportation. There are 1,000 lakes in the area which are within a 10 minute drive to an hour's drive. A fine park system, public golf course, municipal swimming beach, trap-shooting facilities, tennis courts, archery range, ice skating rinks, skiing facilities and rope tows provide the recreational activities. The hunting and fishing opportunities are unsurpassed.

GUSTAVUS ADOLPHUS COLLEGE   *(O-6)*
St. Peter, Minnesota 56082
Tel: (507) 933-8000; (800) 487-8288; Fax: (507) 933-6270

Description: Gustavus Adolphus College is a selective, private, residential, 4-year, liberal arts college affiliated with the Lutheran Church in America. Its mission is to provide an education of recognized excellence that combines rigor and innovation, integrates the development of values with intellectual growth, and makes apparent the connectedness of academic disciplines. Gustavus is accredited by the North Central Association of Colleges and Schools. It operates on the 4-1-4 semester system and offers 1 summer term. It enrolls students from virtually every state and many foreign countries. Enrollment is 2,334 full-time and 38 part-time students. A faculty of 164 full-time and 51 part-time gives a faculty-student ratio of 1-13. The College offers a multitude of intercollegiate and intramural athletics; overseas study programs to complement the 7 modern foreign languages; 40 majors including preprofessional programs, teaching certification, and nursing; internships; and excellent placement opportunities.

Entrance Requirements: High school graduation or GED equivalent; completion of 13 total units, comprised of 3 units of English, 3 mathematics, 2 science, 2 foreign languages, and 3 social studies; SAT or ACT required; early admission, rolling admission, early decision, delayed admission and advanced placement plans available; non-high school graduates considered; $25 application fee.

Costs Per Year: $14,125 tuition and fees; $3,600 room and board.

Collegiate Environment: The college is located on 246 acres in St. Peter, 65 miles southwest from the Minneapolis-St. Paul area. The college buildings include a library of 230,000 volumes, 1,300 periodicals, and 32,000 microforms, and dormitory facilities for 900 men and 1,000 women. The college welcomes a geographically diverse student body and will accept midyear students. Financial aid is available and 70% of the current student body receives financial aid. Approximately 80% of the students applying for admission are accepted and 92% return for the sophomore year. Approximately 35% of Gustavus graduates continue their studies at the graduate level.

Community Environment: A city located 68 miles south of Minneapolis with the usual community facilities. Bus transportation is convenient.

HAMLINE UNIVERSITY   *(M-8)*
1536 Hewitt Avenue
St. Paul, Minnesota 55104
Tel: (612) 641-2207; (800) 753-9753; Fax: (612) 641-2458

Description: This privately supported university has a College of Liberal Arts, a Law School, and a Graduate School. It was founded in 1854. The university operates on a 4-1-4 calendar and offers 2 summer sessions. It is accredited by the North Central Association of Colleges and Schools and by the American Chemical Society, National Association of Schools of Music, and National Council for Accreditation of Teacher Education, the American Bar Association, and the Association of American Law Schools. Many affiliations abroad provide a variety of overseas programs. Extensive science, language, theater, art and music programs are offered; intercollegiate and intramural athletics are available. Undergraduate enrollment is 663 men and 853 women. There are 1,300 graduate students. An undergraduate faculty of 93 full-time and 39 part-time gives a faculty-student ratio of 1-12 in the College of Liberal Arts.

Entrance Requirements: Accredited high school graduation or equivalent with rank in upper one-third of graduating class; recommended completion of 16 units including 4 English, 3 mathematics, 3 science, 2 foreign language, 2 social science, and 2 history; SAT or ACT required; non-high school graduates and unaccredited high school graduates may be admitted upon examination; early admission, rolling admission, midyear admission, and advanced placement programs available; $25 application fee.

Costs Per Year: $13,252 tuition; $4,193 room and board; $160 student fees.

Collegiate Environment: The campus of the university, occupying 44 acres, is located in a residential district miniutes away from downtown Minneapolis and downtown St. Paul. The 18 college buildings include a library of 310,000 volumes, 3,650 periodicals and 157,700 microform titles. Living accommodations for 900 students are available. Fraternities furnish additional space for 28 men. Sororities furnish space for 19 women. The university welcomes a geographically diverse student body and will accept midyear transfer students. 75% of applicants are accepted. Financial aid is available. 75% of students receive some form of financial aid. Extensive course exchange exists with the Associated Colleges of the Twin Cities.

HIBBING COMMUNITY COLLEGE   *(G-8)*
1515 East 25th
Hibbing, Minnesota 55746
Tel: (218) 262-6700; Fax: (218) 262-6717

Description: The publicly supported community college was established in 1916 as part of the public school system of Hibbing, and became a part of the Minnesota State System of Junior Colleges under the control of the State Junior College Board in 1964. It offers courses in vocational-technical and academic areas for part-time, terminal, and transfer programs. The college operates on the quarter system and offers one summer session. Enrollment is 237 men and 341 women full-time, and 595 part-time students. A faculty of 25 full-time and 23 part-time gives a faculty-student ratio of 1-24. The school is accredited by the North Central Association of Colleges and Schools. It offers band, choir, and intercollegiate and intramural athletics.

Entrance Requirements: High school graduation; open enrollment policy; completion of 12 units including 3 English, 2 mathematics, 2 science or 2 foreign language, and 2 social science; non-high school graduates may be admitted based upon college entrance tests; rolling admission plan available; $15 application fee.

Costs Per Year: $1,850 tuition; $3,700 out-of-state.

Collegiate Environment: The campus is located on 65 acres on the eastern outskirts of Hibbing. The 6 college buildings include a library of 20,000 volumes, 1,849 periodicals, 2,243 microforms and 826 recordings. The college welcomes a geographically diverse student body and accepts 98% of students applying for admission. Quarters begin in September, December, and March, and midyear students are accepted. Financial aid is available. Approximately 65% of students receive finanical aid.

Community Environment: Hibbing (population 21,000) is the largest of the Mesabi Range towns where there are many open pits for mining ore. Located 70 miles from Duluth, plants in the area mine taconite, an ore-bearing rock that yields a rich iron ore concentrate when processed. The community facilities include a library, churches of major denominations, a hospital, 3 clinics, and shopping areas. Some part-time employment is available. Recreational activities include bowling, hunting, skiing, snowmobiling, fishing, tennis, water sports and curling. Points of interest are the Hibbing-Chisholm Pit Crossing Route and the Hull-Rust-Mahoning Mine. The Last Chance International Curling Bonspeil and the Winter Carnival are annual events.

INVER HILLS COMMUNITY COLLEGE   *(D-13)*
2500 East 80th Street
Inver Grove Heights, Minnesota 55076
Tel: (612) 450-8500; Admissions: (612) 450-8503; Fax: (612) 450-8679

Description: This publicly supported junior college is accredited by the North Central Association of Colleges and Schools. It offers university-transfer, vocational, and general programs. Cooperative education program (alternating work and class periods) in business is available. The college grants the Associate degree. It operates on the quarter system and offers two summer sessions. Enrollment includes 1,676 full-time and 4,161 part-time students. A faculty of 90 full-time and 120 part-time gives a faculty-student ratio of 1-28. Air Force ROTC is available.

Entrance Requirements: Open enrollment policy; high school graduation or equivalent; early admission, early decision, midyear admission, rolling admission, and advanced placement plans available; $15 application fee.

Costs Per Year: $1,878 state resident tuition; $3,712 nonresident tuition; room rates vary.

Community Environment: See Bethel College and Seminary.

ITASCA COMMUNITY COLLEGE   *(G-7)*
1851 East Highway 169
Grand Rapids, Minnesota 55744
Tel: (218) 327-4464; (800) 996-6442; Fax: (218) 327-4350

Description: This publicly supported community college was established in 1922. Enrollment includes 825 full-time and 400 part-time students. A faculty of 45 full-time and 30 part-time gives a faculty-student ratio of 1-18. The college offers Cooperative Education program (alternating work and class periods) in occupational areas. Intercollegiate and intramural athletics are available. The college has transfer-recognition status from the Minnesota State University System and the University of Minnesota. Also, professional programs have been designed to offer transfer credit with advanced standing at the university and other four-year institutions. Vocational certificate programs are approved by the Vocational Division of the State Department of Education. The school operates on the quarter system and also a summer term. It is fully accredited by the North Central Association of Colleges and Schools.

Entrance Requirements: Open enrollment; non-high school graduates considered; early admission, early decision, delayed admission, and rolling admission plans available; $15 application fee.

Costs Per Year: $2,064 ($43 per credit) resident tuition; $4,128 ($86 per credit) nonresident; $1 per credit technology fee.

Collegiate Environment: The college campus is located on a site formerly occupied by the University of Minnesota North Central School of Agriculture and Experiment Station. Existing buildings have been renovated and new construction has provided a modern community college campus. The library contains over 20,000 volumes, 200 periodicals, 1,000 microforms and 500 audiovisual materials. Quarters begin in September, December and March. 100% of students applying for admission are accepted including midyear students. 70% of the current student body receives some form of financial aid.

Community Environment: A rural community beautifully situated on the Mississippi River and 5 lakes, Grand Rapids (population 8,000) is the county seat of Itasca County, a bustling community with a strong tourist trade. Over 1,000 lakes in the county provide the facilities for all water sports; fishing, hunting, bowling and golf are some of the other recreational activities available. Quadna Mt. ski resort is nearby. Part-time employment opportunities are good.

LAKEWOOD STATE COMMUNITY COLLEGE   *(B-13)*
3401 Century Avenue North
White Bear Lake, Minnesota 55110
Tel: (612) 779-3200; Admissions: (612) 779-3300; Fax: (612) 773-1746

Description: The publicly supported community college is one of several community colleges operated by the Minnesota Junior College Board. It offers courses in vocational-technical and academic areas for part-time, terminal, and transfer programs. Is accredited by the North Central Association of Colleges and Schools. Grants Associate degree; offers Cooperative Education program (alternating work and class periods). The college operates on the quarter system with 2 summer terms. Enrollment includes 2,500 full-time and 3,000 part-time students. Faculty includes 85 full-time and 95 part-time members, giving a faculty-student ratio of 1-30.

Entrance Requirements: Open enrollment policy; college will accept any high school graduate, non-high school graduates with GED certification and adults 21 years of age or over.

Costs Per Year: $1,879 per quarter; $3,758 nonresident.

Collegiate Environment: All students applying for admission are accepted. Grant work, and loans are available, and all students are encouraged to apply. 40% of students receive some form of financial aid.

Community Environment: White Bear Lake (population 24,000), 9 miles north of St. Paul, is on the edge of the county's largest lake, White Bear. The city is noted for its winter fishing contest, a part of St. Paul's Winter Carnival, and for summer sports.

LUTHER SEMINARY   *(M-8)*
2481 Como Avenue
St. Paul, Minnesota 55108
Tel: (612) 641-3456; (800) 588-4373; Admissions: (612) 641-3521

Description: The seminary, through a series of mergers covering more than a half century, represents the consolidation into one seminary of what at one time were six separate institutions. It is accredited by the North Central Association of Colleges and Schools and the Association of Theological Schools. The seminary offers the Master of Divinity, Master of Arts, Master of Arts in Religious Education, Master of Theology, Master of Sacred Music, Master in Islamic Studies, Doctor of Theology, and Doctor of Ministry. Enrollment includes 656 full-time and 155 part-time students. A faculty of 60 full-time and 20 part-time gives a faculty-student ratio of 1-8.

Entrance Requirements: Varies with program of the student; $30 application fee.

Costs Per Year: $4,350 tuition; $4,200 room and board.

Collegiate Environment: More than 40 acres of rolling and wooded land host the campus. Bockman Hall and Guillixson Hall are situated in the upper part of the campus. Bockman Hall serves as a dormitory for women and men students and contains some classrooms, offices for student government and the student newspaper, an informal study and forum area, and faculty offices. Gullixson Hall houses the library which contains 230,000 volumes, 800 periodicals, 2,300 microforms and 6,000 audiovisual materials. Unifying the campus is the Olson Campus Center. Northwestern Hall houses most of the administrative offices, classrooms, an auditorium, faculty offices, and a chapel. Stub Hall houses single men and women. Burntvedt Court and Sandgren Apartments provide 152 apartments for married couples and students with families.

Community Environment: The seminary is located in the heart of the "Twin Cities," Minneapolis and St. Paul. The cities and their suburbs, a metropolitan area with a population more than 2 million people, constitute the cultural and economic gateway to the Northwest, and are the center of the most Lutheran section of North America. The Twin Cities abound in cultural advantages of every sort for students. Great art galleries, theaters for the performing arts, notable musical organizations, both choral and instrumental, parks, lakes, and professional sports enrich the life of those living there. A small-town atmosphere prevails in the immediate area of the seminary know as St. Anthony Park, one of the Twin Cities most pleasant residential neighborhoods. A variety of goods and services is available within easy walking distance. Situated between the two metropolitan campuses of the University of Minnesota, the seminary is neighbor to a dozen other colleges and professional schools.

LUTHERAN CENTER FOR CHRISTIAN LEARNING   *(J-2)*
815 Vernon Avenue West
Fergus Falls, Minnesota 56537-2699
Tel: (218) 739-3375; Fax: (218) 739-3372

Description: This privately supported Bible college was founded by the Church of the Lutheran Brethren of America in 1903. The college awards a Certificate of Biblical Studies for a one-year program focusing on Biblical studies and introduction to world views. It prepares students to live in a pluristic society in the light of the Christian faith. Originally located in North Dakota, the college moved to Minnesota in 1935, and is located on a campus with the Lutheran Brethren Seminary and Hillcrest Lutheran Academy. It operates on the semester system. Enrollment is 13 full-time and 2 part-time students. A faculty of 2 full-time and 2 part-time gives a faculty-student ratio of 1-4.

Entrance Requirements: Open enrollment policy; high school diploma required, early admission, early decision, rolling admission, and delayed admission plans available.

Costs Per Year: $2,850 tuition; $2,450 room and board; $500 student fees.

Collegiate Environment: The 16-acre campus is located on the southwest side of the city. The buildings include a library of 14,500 volumes, 750 pamphlets, 200 periodicals, 75 microforms and 1,000 recordings. Dormitory facilities are available for 23 men and 22 women. 90% of the students applying for admission are accepted, including midyear students and those from various geographical locations. Some scholarships are available, and the school has a work-study program.

Community Environment: See Fergus Falls Community College.

MACALESTER COLLEGE   *(M-8)*
1600 Grand Avenue
St. Paul, Minnesota 55105
Tel: (612) 696-6357; (800) 231-7974; Fax: (612) 696-6724

Description: This privately supported liberal arts college is related to the United Presbyterian Church, U.S.A. It was chartered in 1874 as a college for men only. It became coeducational 8 years later with its first class entering in 1885. The college operates on a 4-1-4 semester system. Enrollment includes 1,712 full-time and 84 part-time students. A faculty of 131 full-time and 61 part-time gives a faculty-student ratio of 1-11. It is accredited by the North Central Association of

Colleges and Schools. Preparation for State teaching certificate is available. Academic cooperative programs are available with Washington University (St. Louis) and the University of Minnesota for students studying engineering, Washington University for students studying architecture or occupational therapy, and with Rush Medical College for students interested in nursing. Special programs include participation in the Associated Colleges of the Twin Cities Consortium. The college offers 40 exchange opportunities with overseas universities; more than 50% of students participate before graduation. There is a wide variety of internship programs.

Entrance Requirements: Accredited high school graduation; completion of 16 academic units: 4 English, 3 mathematics, 3 science, 3 social science, and 3 foreign language; SAT or ACT required; early admission, delayed admission, and early decision programs available; advanced placement through CEEB; $40 application fee.

Costs Per Year: $16,585 tuition; $4,975 room and board; $101 student fees.

Collegiate Environment: The 55-acre campus is located in Macalester Park, a residential section nearly equidistant from the downtown areas of St. Paul and Minneapolis. The 26 college buildings include a new $10 million library housing 351,871 volumes, 1,449 periodicals, 58,050 microforms, and 8,995 sound recordings. There are dormitory facilities for 1,141 students. The college welcomes students from various geographical locations. Approximately 58% of students applying for admission are accepted. The middle 50% ranges of scores of enrolled freshmen were: SAT 550-660V, 560-690M; ACT composite 27-30. Financial aid is available for students with demonstrated need. Approximately 70% of students receive financial aid.

Community Environment: The Twin Cities, Minneapolis and St. Paul, with their suburbs, comprise a metropolitan area with a population 2.5 million people. The area is the cultural and economic gateway to the northwest and it abounds in cultural advantages of every sort for students. Great art galleries, theaters for the performing arts, notable choral and instrumental musical organizations, parks, lakes, and professional sports enrich community life .

MANKATO STATE UNIVERSITY   *(O-6)*
MSU 55, Box 8400
Mankato, Minnesota 56002-8400
Tel: (507) 389-1822; (800) 722-0544

Description: The publicly supported state university is a multipurpose institution which provides programs of general education and of specialization for professional and vocational goals. It is accredited by the North Central Assoiation of Colleges and Schools and operates on the quarter system with two summer sessions. The university is composed of the Colleges of Arts and Humanities, Business, Allied Health & Nursing, Education Science, Engineering & Technology, Social and Behavioral Sciences, and Graduate Studies. Recent enrollment included 5,382 men and 5,829 women full-time and 825 men and 967 women part-time. A faculty of 522 full-time and 180 part-time gives a faculty-student ratio of 1-21. Grants Associate, Bachelor, Master and Specialist degrees.

Entrance Requirements: Accredited high school graduation; SAT or ACT required; GRE required for most graduate programs; rolling admission, midyear admission, early admission, early decision and advanced placement plans available; $15 application fee.

Costs Per Year: $2,582 tuition, $5,200 nonresident, $2,768 room and board.

Collegiate Environment: The campus of the college occupies 380 acres. The 16 university buildings include a library with 1,000,000 volumes, 2,512 periodicals/newspapers, and 20,000 audiovisual materials. Dormitory facilities are provided for 3,000 students. There are several social fraternities and sororities on the campus, as well as numerous other student organizations. The college welcomes students from all geographical locations and will accept midyear students. Approximately 87% of students applying for admission are accepted. 65% of the current student body receives some form of financial aid. Approximately 75% of the previous freshman class return to the college for the sophomore year.

Community Environment: Mankato (population 45,000), on a great bend in the Minnesota River, is the trade and distributing center for agricultural southwestern Minnesota. Bus and air service is available. Community facilities include a number of churches, hospitals, and the

usual civic and service organizations. About 30 lakes within a 25-mile area provide facilities for all water sports and fishing; other activities include golf, hunting and skiing. Points of interest are the Blue Earth County Historical Society Museum, Minneopa State Park and Sibley Park.

MARTIN LUTHER COLLEGE   *(O-5)*
1995 Luther Court
New Ulm, Minnesota 56073
Tel: (507) 354-8221; Fax: (507) 354-8225

Description: This privately supported teachers college is supported by the member congregations of the Wisconsin Evangelical Lutheran Synod. This new college was formed by the amalgamation of Northwestern College and Dr. Martin Luther College. The college is accredited by the North Central Association of Colleges and Schools. The school seeks to give a solid liberal arts and theological language training base to its future pastors, who will attend Wisconsin Luthern Seminary in Mequon, WI. The teacher training offers early childhood, elementary, and secondary education tracks to the future teachers of WELS schools.

Entrance Requirements: High school graduation or equivalent; 18 on ACT; 2.0 in a college prep course of high school studies; $25 application fee.

Costs Per Year: $3,610 tuition; $2,010 room and board; $425 average fees; additional expenses average $2,000.

Collegiate Environment: The 50-acre campus is located about 100 miles southwest of the Twin Cities. The 13 college buildings include a library of 150,000 volumes, 54,000 pamphlets, other bound periodicals, microforms and audiovisual materials. Dormitory facilities available. Classes begin in August and January and midyear students are accepted. Financial aid is available and 85% of the current student body receives financial assistance.

Community Environment: New Ulm (population 14,700), a rural area 100 miles from Minneapolis and St. Paul, is a city where German immigrants carefully planned wide streets and numerous park areas in such a way that it has not been necessary to change the original plan. Part-time employment opportunities are good. Historical points of interest include the Brown County Historical Museum, Hermann's Monument, and Glockenspiel.

MESABI COMMUNITY COLLEGE   *(G-9)*
1001 Chestnut Street West
Virginia, Minnesota 55792
Tel: (218) 749-7700; (800) 657-3860; Admissions: (218) 749-0315; Fax: (218) 749-7782

Description: The publicly supported liberal arts junior college was established by the Minnesota Junior College Board in 1966. Their action merged the Eveleth Junior College and the Virginia Junior College into a single institution. The college is accredited by the North Central Association of Colleges and Schools. It operates on the quarter system and offers two summer sessions. Enrollment includes 611 full-time and 298 part-time students. A faculty of 58 full-time gives a faculty-student ratio of 1-22. Offers freshman program for the educationally disadvantaged and band, chorus, choir and intercollegiate and intramural athletics.

Entrance Requirements: Open enrollment; ACT suggested; CAPP placement exam required; non-high school graduates may be admitted by special permission; early decision, rolling admission, midyear admission and advanced placement plans available; $15 application fee.

Costs Per Year: $1,833.75 tuition; $3,667.50 out-of-state residents.

Collegiate Environment: The college is located on 40 acres. The library contains 27,400 volumes. The school offers programs in liberal education, vocational education and semi-professional training for part-time, terminal and transfer students. All students applying for admission are accepted. 53% of the previous freshman class return to the college for a second year of studies. Average high school standing of the freshman class: 29% in the top 20% of high school class, 67% in the middle 60%, and 4% in the lower 20%. The average score of the entering freshman class was ACT 21 composite. Scholarships are available and 50% of students receive some form of financial aid.

Community Environment: The hub of Minnesota Arrowhead country and Taconite capital of the world, Virginia offers ready access to countless waterways and forestlands, including Voyageurs National Park and the Boundary Waters Canoe Area. The Giants Ridge Ski Area features excellent alpine and cross country skiing. The city also has 2 municipal parks, 2 lakes and an 18-hole golf course. Part-time employment is available.

METROPOLITAN STATE UNIVERSITY   *(M-8)*
700 E. Seventh Street
St. Paul, Minnesota 55106-5000
Tel: (612) 772-7600

Description: Founded in 1971, the publicly supported school is accredited by the North Central Association of Colleges and Schools. The institution is part of the Minnesota State University System. It operates on the quarter system with mostly evening courses, and offers one summer session. The school offers a bachelor and masters degree. Enrollment is 1,083 full-time and 4,109 part-time undergraduates, and 318 graduate students. A faculty of 75 full-time and 500 part-time gives a faculty-student ratio of 1-12.

Entrance Requirements: $15 application fee.

Costs Per Year: $2,320 tuition; $4,933 out-of-state.

Collegiate Environment: The institution is located in St. Paul, convenient to cultural organizations and activities of the twin cities of Minneapolis and St. Paul.

Community Environment: See Bethel College and Seminary.

MINNEAPOLIS COLLEGE OF ART AND DESIGN   *(M-8)*
2501 Stevens Avenue South
Minneapolis, Minnesota 55404
Tel: (612) 874-3700; (800) 874-6223; Fax: (612) 874-3704

Description: This privately supported four-year visual arts college is accredited by the North Central Association of Colleges and Schools and professionally by the National Association of Schools of Art and Design. The college confers the Bachelor of Fine Arts degree, with majors in Fine Arts, Design and Media Arts (photo, film, and video). Areas of concentration available within the Design major are Environmental Design, Product Design and Visual Communication Design. Within the Fine Arts major, coursework is available in drawing, painting, sculpture and printmaking. The college operates on the semester system and offers one summer session. Enrollment includes 419 full-time and 95 part-time undergraduates and 29 graduate students. A faculty of 38 full-time and 17 part-time provides a faculty-student ratio of 1-12.

Entrance Requirements: Accredited high school graduation or equivalent; rolling admission available; advanced placement based on portfolio review; $35 application fee.

Costs Per Year: $12,880 tuition; $3,500 room and board; $64 student fees.

Collegiate Environment: Founded in 1886, the School of Art is located in south Minneapolis adjacent to the Minneapolis Institute of Arts and convenient to both downtown and suburban areas. A college library houses approximately 50,000 volumes, 100,000 slides and over 100 periodicals relating to art and design. 77% of students applying for admission are accepted. Students are housed in college-owned apartments. Students come from various geographical locations. 31 scholarships are available and 72% of students receive some form of financial aid.

Community Environment: See University of Minnesota - Twin Cities.

MINNEAPOLIS COMMUNITY COLLEGE   *(M-8)*
1501 Hennepin Avenue So.
Minneapolis, Minnesota 55403
Tel: (612) 341-7000; Fax: (612) 341-7075

Description: The publicly supported community college was established in 1965. It operates on the quarter system with 2 summer sessions, and offers courses in vocational and academic areas for part-time, terminal and transfer students. The college is accredited by the North Central Association of Colleges and Schools. Enrollment includes 2,191 full-time and 2,307 part-time students. A faculty of 98 full-time and 127 part-time provides a faculty-student ratio of 1-22. The college grants the Associate degree.

Entrance Requirements: Open enrollment policy; non-high school graduates accepted; advanced placement, early admission, delayed admission and rolling admissions plans available; $15 application fee.

Costs Per Year: $1,878.75 state-resident tuition; $3,712.50 nonresident.

Collegiate Environment: The college is located on 4 acres and is comprised of 5 buildings, including a library of 39,000 volumes, 390 periodicals and 400 audiovisual materials. The college is adjacent to an Area Voc-Tech School whose facilities are available to all students. Classes begin in September and midyear students are accepted.

Community Environment: Minneapolis Community College's beautiful campus borders a city park and is within walking distance of cultural centers (Guthrie Theatre, Walker Art Center) and downtown Minneapolis.

MINNESOTA BIBLE COLLEGE   *(P-9)*
920 Mayowood Road S.W.
Rochester, Minnesota 55902-2275
Tel: (507) 288-4563; (800) 456-7651; Fax: (507) 288-9046

Description: This privately supported Bible College was established in 1913 under the auspices of the Churches of Christ/Christian Churches. It is chartered by the State of Minnesota as a nonprofit theological college, with the privilege of awarding appropriate degrees and certificates. It operates on the quarter system. The college is accredited by the American Association of Bible Colleges and offers degree program majors in Preaching Ministry, Bible and Theology, and Christian Education. Degree minors are available in Christian Education, Music, Youth Ministry, Counseling, and Missions. Cooperative degree programs include Nursing, Secretarial and Elementary Education. Athletics include the intercollegiate sports of men's and women's basketball, men's and women's volleyball, golf, tennis, baseball, and an intramural sports program. Enrollment includes 60 men and 47 women full-time, and 6 men and 7 women part-time. A faculty of 8 full-time and 7 part-time gives a faculty-student ratio of 1-12.

Entrance Requirements: High school graduation is normally required; under certain circumstances a GED is acceptable; ACT or SAT required; $30 application fee.

Costs Per Year: $4,704 tuition; $1,635 room; $400 incidentals.

Collegiate Environment: Minnesota Bible College is located on 40 acres and is comprised of 6 buildings, including a library of 30,000 volumes. Living accommodations are provided for 63 men, 54 women, and 12 families. The college is open to all sincere applicants regardless of denominational preferences. 90%-95% of applicants are usually accepted. Classes begin in September; students are accepted at the beginning of each quarter if the application process is completed and approved. Financial aid is available through federal and state programs, and 85% of the current student body receives some form of financial assistance.

Community Environment: See Rochester Community College.

MINNESOTA SCHOOL OF PROFESSIONAL PSYCHOLOGY
(M-8)
3103 East 80th Street, Suite 290
Minneapolis, Minnesota 55425
Tel: (612) 858-8800; (800) 473-7684; Fax: (612) 858-8515

Description: The privately supported graduate school is fully accredited by the North Central Association of Colleges and Schools. It operates on a trimester system with one summer session. The school was established in 1987 to provide a setting in which extensive training could be pursued in the area of professional psychology. The Minnesota School of Professional Psychology is a unit of the American Schools of Professional Psychology with professional schools in Arlington, VA; Atlanta, GA; Chicago, IL; Honolulu, HI; and Rolling Meadows, IL. It does not promote any one clinical psychological orientation. Currently, it offers psychoanalytic, client-centered, experiential, family systems, integrative-eclectic, behavioral, neuropsychological, and group approaches to intervention. The schools grants a Doctorate degree. Enrollment includes 278 students. A core faculty of 40 provides a faculty student ratio of 1-7.

Entrance Requirements: Graduation from an accredited institution with a baccalaureate or more advanced degree.

Costs Per Year: $13,540 tuition per year; approximately $300-$500 fees.

Collegiate Environment: A coeducational professional school located in a spacious midrise office building, the college has a great diversity of students, ranging from recent college graduates to change-of-career students. The school maintains a curriculum support library, containing current textbooks, diagnostic testing materials, reference texts and commonly used journals. This library is supplmented by the University of Minnesota Library system. Financial aid is available.

Community Environment: The school is located in Southeast Minneapolis, surrounded by walking trails, parks, and the Minnesota River. The school is accessible from the main interstate highways and parking is available.

MOORHEAD STATE UNIVERSITY   (H-1)
9th Avenue and 11th Street South
Moorhead, Minnesota 56563
Tel: (218) 236-2161; (800) 593-7246; Admissions: (218) 236-2161; Fax: (218) 236-2168

Description: Established in 1885 as a Normal School, the publicly supported liberal arts and teachers college graduated the first 10 students from its two-year program in 1890. In 1921 it attained four-year status as Moorhead State Teachers College, in 1957 it became Moorhead State College, and in 1975, M.S.U. Today, the university offers its students a full liberal arts curriculum leading to the Bachelor, Master and specialist degrees while retaining the Associate degree programs, with undergraduate programs that include 70 major fields and 15 areas of pre-professional study. The university operates on the quarter system. 2 summer terms are also offered. The school is accredited by the North Central Association of Colleges and Schools and by respective professional organizations. It offers preparation for the State teaching certificate and internship programs (alternating work and class periods) in all subject areas. MSU belongs to a cooperative arrangement with Concordia College (Moorhead) and North Dakota State University (Fargo) through which students may take courses at the other colleges with paying any additional tuition or fees. Extensive music programs and intercollegiate and intramural athletics are available. Undergraduate enrollment includes 2,339 men and 3,447 women full-time, and 341 men and 898 women part-time. There are 127 graduate students. A faculty of 331 full-time and 68 part-time gives a faculty-student ratio of 1-18. An academic cooperative plan with North Dakota State University gives a preliminary 2-year course in engineering, agriculture, home economics, pharmacy and architecture. There is an overseas program with the Center for Medieval and Renaissance studies in Oxford, England, and study abroad opportunities in Akita, Japan. Army and Air Force ROTC available.

Entrance Requirements: Accredited high school graduation or equivalent with rank in upper 50% of graduating class; ACT, PSAT or SAT required; GRE required for graduate school; rolling admission, delayed admission, early admission, midyear admission and advanced placement plans available; $15 application fee.

Costs Per Year: $2,647 tuition; $5,273 tuition for out-of state residents; $2,814 room and board; additional expenses range from $1,500.

Collegiate Environment: The university occupies a 104-acre campus that includes 28 buildings. More than three-fourths of the buildings have been constructed since 1967. They include a library of 347,026 volumes, 1,451 periodical titles and 602,742 microforms. There are dormitory facilities for 2,200 men and women. Several social fraternities and sororities are located at the college and house a number of students. The college welcomes a geographically diverse student body and will accept midyear students. Financial aid is available and 79% of the current student body receive some form of financial assistance. Freshman and Community College transfer scholarships are available.

Community Environment: In the Red River Valley, adjoining Fargo, North Dakota, Moorhead (population 150,000) is 1 hour from the Minnesota Lake region and 170 miles from Canada. Agricultural products are sugar beets, potatoes, onions wheat, soybeans, and corn. Industries are a large creamery and a refinery of the American Crystal Sugar Co; other products of local industries are farm equipment, commercial rock pickers, fiberglass boats and snowmobiles. Part-time employment is available for students. All forms of commercial transportation are accessible.

NORMANDALE COMMUNITY COLLEGE   (N-8)
9700 France Avenue South
Bloomington, Minnesota 55431
Tel: (612) 832-6320

Description: Normandale Community College is a two-year institution of higher learning that provides transfer, technical and continuing education programs. The college was founded in 1968 and is one of eighteen state-supported community colleges operating under the Minnesota Community College Board. It is accredited by the North Central Association of Colleges and Schools. The college operates on the quarter system and offers 2 summer terms. Enrollment is 3,611 full-time and 4,560 part-time students. A faculty of 179 full-time and 49 part-time gives a faculty-student ratio of 1-37. The college grants the Associate degree.

Entrance Requirements: High school graduation; GED accepted; open enrollment; early admission, rolling admission and advanced placement plans available; $15 application fee.

Costs Per Year: $1,856 state resident tuition, $3,712 tuition for out-of-state residents.

Collegiate Environment: The campus is located on a beautiful 90-acre site and contains 7 buildings that include a library of 70,000 volumes, 400 microforms, 300 periodicals and 1300 audiovisual materials. The college welcomes a geographically diverse student body and will accept midyear students. Financial aid is available and 60% of the students receive aid.

Community Environment: The college is located in Bloomington, a suburb of 85,000 people located 10 miles south of Minneapolis and 7 miles west of the Minneapolis/St. Paul Airport.

NORTH CENTRAL BIBLE COLLEGE   (M-8)
910 Elliot Avenue S.
Minneapolis, Minnesota 55404
Tel: (612) 343-4480; (800) 289-6222; Fax: (612) 343-4778

Description: This privately supported Bible college enrolled its first students in 1930, under the name of North Central Bible Institute, and offered a three-year program with a general Bible curriculum. It became a four-year institution in 1955 and adopted its present name in 1957. It is accredited by the North Central Association of Colleges and Schools. The college is owned and supported by the Assemblies of God churches in the ten-state north-central region of the United States. The college grants one-year Bible Certificates, Diplomas, and Associate and Bachelor degrees. It operates on the semester system, with one four-week general session and three two-week summer sessions. Enrollment includes 439 men and 430 women full-time, 87 men and 99 women part-time. A faculty of 37 full-time and 27 part-time gives a faculty-student ratio of 1-18. Air Force and Army ROTC programs available.

Entrance Requirements: Accredited high school graduation; ACT required; midyear admission, rolling admission, and advanced placement plans available.

Costs Per Year: $5,280 tuition; $3,220 room and board; $670 student fees.

Collegiate Environment: The Bible college is located across the street from Elliot Park, which provides an outdoor recreation spot for the students. The college buildings include a library of 68,000 volumes, in addition to periodical subcriptions, microforms, and audiovisual materials. Residence halls accommodate 644 students. The college requires all students to attend chapel services. Band, chorus, choir, and sports are available. Over 90% of applicants are accepted from diverse geographical locations, including midyear students. Scholarships are available and 90% of students receive some form of financial assistance.

Community Environment: See University of Minnesota - Twin Cities.

NORTH HENNEPIN COMMUNITY COLLEGE   (M-8)
7411 85th Avenue North
Brooklyn Park, Minnesota 55445
Tel: (612) 424-0702

Description: This publicly supported state community college opened in 1966 and is one of 20 such colleges operating under the Minnesota Community College Board. It is accredited by the North Central Association of Colleges and Schools. It is a two-year institution of higher learning that provides transfer, vocational-technical and continuing education opportunities. The Associate degree is granted. It operates on the quarter system and offers two summer sessions. Enrollment includes 2,200 full-time and 4,000 part-time students. A faculty of 175 gives a faculty-student ratio of 1-28.

Entrance Requirements: Open enrollment; non-high school graduates considered; rolling admission; no application fee.

Costs Per Year: $1,878.75 ($41.75/credit) resident tuition; $3,667.50 ($81.50/credit) nonresident.

Collegiate Environment: The college is located on a 40-acre campus that opened in the fall of 1969. The 8 buildings include a library of 38,000 volumes. Approximately 99% of the students applying for admission are accepted, including midyear students and those from various geographical locations. Scholarships are available and 33% of students receive financial aid.

Community Environment: See University of Minnesota - Twin Cities.

NORTHLAND COMMUNITY COLLEGE   *(E-2)*
Highway 1 East
Thief River Falls, Minnesota 56701
Tel: (218) 681-2181; Fax: (218) 681-6405

Description: The publicly supported community college was established by the 1965 Minnesota Legislature and operates under the Minnesota State Community College Board. It offers programs including courses for transfer to four-year colleges and universities, general education courses and semi-professional training in some areas. The college operates on the quarter system and offers one summer session. Enrollment is 425 full-time and 379 part-time students. A faculty of 26 full-time and 7 part-time gives a faculty-student ratio of 1-23. Offers a cooperative education program (alternating work and class periods) in business, human services and law enforcement. The college is fully accredited by the North Central Association of Colleges and Schools. It is professionally accredited by the National League of Nursing.

Entrance Requirements: High school graduation or equivalent; open enrollment; non-high school graduates considered; early admission, early decision, rolling admission and delayed admission plans available; $15 application fee.

Costs Per Year: $1,850 tuition; $3,700 out-of-state; additional expenses average $500.

Collegiate Environment: The college began operation on the present campus in the fall quarter of 1969 and serves chiefly northwestern Minnesota communities within a 60-mile radius. The library contains 12,000 volumes and 250 microforms and periodicals. Midyear students are accepted, as are those from other geographical locations. Financial aid is available and 75% of the current student body receives some form of assistance.

Community Environment: Thief River Falls (population 9,000) is in northwest Minnesota. The facilities for outdoor recreation are numerous. Commercial transportation is available. The community provides a complete downtown shopping center, a public library, hospitals and an employment office.

NORTHWESTERN COLLEGE   *(B-12)*
3003 North Snelling Avenue
St. Paul, Minnesota 55113
Tel: (612) 631-5100

Description: This is a privately supported Christian college of the Bible, arts and sciences, and vocational education. Enrollment includes 1,300 full-time students. A faculty of 60 full-time and 51 part-time gives a faulty-student ratio of 1-16. The college is fully accredited by the North Central Association of Colleges and Schools. It operates on the quarter system and offers 2 summer sessions. It grants Certificates, Associate and Bachelor Degrees. Religious subjects and chapel attendance are required. A satellite radio station network that provides a noncommercial Christian ministry to the area is available, and has 10 stations in 6 midwestern cities.

Entrance Requirements: Modified open enrollment policy; ACT or SAT and PSAT required; non-high school graduates considered; early admission, early decision, rolling admission, delayed admission and advanced placement plans available; $15 application fee.

Costs Per Year: $9,825 tuition; $2,745 room and board.

Collegiate Environment: In 1970 the school purchased a campus previously used as a seminary. Its 99 acres contain 7 major buildings. Student residence buildings are located on campus and house 800 men and women. The library contains 78,500 volumes, 550 periodicals, 51,300 microforms, and 6,750 audiovisual materials. Approximately 98% of the students applying for admission are accepted including midyear students. 73% of the freshmen return for the sophomore year. Financial aid is available and 85% of students receive some form of assistance.

Community Environment: See Bethel College and Seminary.

NORTHWESTERN COLLEGE OF CHIROPRACTIC   *(M-8)*
2501 W. 84th Street
Bloomington, Minnesota 55431
Tel: (612) 888-4777; (800) 888-4777; Fax: (612) 888-6713

Description: The privately supported chiropractic college was established in 1941. It is a member of the Council on Chiropractic Education and is approved by the Minnesota State Board of Chiropractic Examiners. The college offers the Doctor of Chiropractic degree to students who have completed 10 trimesters. A Bachelor of Science degree program in Human Biology is available to those admitted to the Doctor of Chiropractic program. The college operates on the trimester system and offers one summer session. Enrollment includes 597 full-time and 26 part-time students. A faculty of 43 full-time and 21 part-time gives a faculty-student ratio of 1-10.

Entrance Requirements: Completion of 2 years of liberal arts or junior college including 1 year each of biology, organic and inorganic chemistry and physics, psychology and humanities, and 2 semesters of English or communication skills; rolling admission policy; $50 application fee.

Costs Per Year: $8,950 tuition; $600 student fees; $700 average additional expenses.

Collegiate Environment: The main campus is located in Bloomington, a suburb of Minneapolis-St. Paul. The main building and campus contain student classrooms, facilities, and a library of 10,989 volumes as well as microforms, videos, and audio holdings. There are 5 outpatient clinics, including 1 in Minneapolis, 1 in Robbinsdale, 1 in St. Paul, 1 in Bloomington, and 1 in Burnsville. Approximately 53% of students applying for admission are accepted, including students from various geographical locations. 95% of the previous entering class returned to the college for a second year of studies. Financial aid is available and approximately 95% of the current student body receives some form of financial assistance.

Community Environment: See University of Minnesota - Twin Cities.

RAINY RIVER COMMUNITY COLLEGE   *(D-7)*
Highway 11-71
International Falls, Minnesota 56649
Tel: (218) 285-7722; (800) 456-3996; Fax: (218) 285-2239

Description: The publicly supported state community college first opened its doors in September 1967. It is accredited by the North Central Association of Colleges and Schools. It is a two-year institution of higher learning that provides transfer, general and professional, technical-vocational, and continuing education programs. The college operates on the quarter system and offers one summer session. Enrollment includes 388 full-time and 397 part-time students. A faculty of 25 full-time and 18 part-time gives a faculty-student ratio of 1-14. Offers intercollegiate basketball, ice hockey, women's basketball and volleyball.

Entrance Requirements: Open enrollment; non-high school graduates considered; early admission, rolling admission, midyear admission and advanced placement plans available; $15 application fee.

Costs Per Year: $1,882 ($41.75/credit) state-resident tuition: $3,763 ($82.50/credit) nonresidents; additional expenses average $400.

Collegiate Environment: The 7-building complex reflects the north woods with open-beamed ceilings and vaulted roofs. Facilities include a theatre, an area for art exhibits, a student commons with food service and a gymnasium. Both on-campus housing and housing within the community are available. The library contains 15,500 titles, 150 periodicals, 350 microforms and 550 audiovisual materials. Special programs include services for Native Americans with off-campus courses and workshops on the reservation.

Community Environment: Located on the Rainy River, which is the Minnesota-Ontario border. International Falls (population 8,000) is the supply point for an immense wilderness region famous for hunting, fishing and canoe trips. It is also an important port of entry from Ontario vacation country. Community facilities include complete church representation, good medical services, downtown and mall shopping areas, and numerous service organizations. Because of the great influx of summer tourists, many part-time jobs are available. Millions of acres are in the wilderness, which is close to International Falls. Rainy Lake, the biggest tourist attraction in the area, is 3 miles from town and features year-round good fishing. Other sports are swimming, water skiing, camping, hunting, boating and winter sports.

ROCHESTER COMMUNITY COLLEGE *(P-9)*
851 30th Avenue Southeast
Rochester, Minnesota 55904
Tel: (507) 285-7210

Description: This publicly supported community college, which is the oldest state community college in Minnesota, was organized in 1915 and became a charter member of the American Association of Junior Colleges in 1920. In addition to the regular curriculum, it offers music programs and intercollegiate and intramural athletics. It operates on the quarter system with 2 summer terms and is accredited by the North Central Association of Colleges and Schools. Enrollment includes 2,154 full-time and 1,788 part-time students. A faculty of 92 full-time and 133 part-time provides a faculty-student ratio of 1-20. The college offers a diversified curriculum that includes many courses of study designed for those who plan to attend college for only 1 or 2 years, and also prepares students to attend a four-year college or university.

Entrance Requirements: High school graduation or equivalent; nonresidents must rank in upper 60% of class; open enrollment policy; non-high school graduates considered; rolling admission and advanced placement plans available; $15 application fee.

Costs Per Year: $1,800 state-resident tuition; $3,600 out-of-state.

Collegiate Environment: The 160-acre campus contains parking facilities, athletic fields, and a building complex housing classrooms, laboratories, offices, student common, book store, food service facilities and a library of 62,000 volumes, 600 periodicals, 10,959 microforms and 1,500 recordings. The college welcomes students from various geographical locations and will accept midyear students. Financial aid is available.

Community Environment: The Mayo Clinic, founded by Drs. William and Charles Mayo, has made Rochester (population 73,000) world famous. The transient population is estimated at 8,000 to 10,000 at any given time. Visitors are estimated at 550,000 anually. All forms of commerical transportation are available. Community cultural facilities include the Rochester Symphony Orchestra, Rochester Municipal Band, Oratorio Society, summer open-air concerts, Carillon concerts 3 times a week, and a civic theater with a full-time director.

SAINT CLOUD STATE UNIVERSITY *(L-6)*
4th Avenue and 7th Street
115 Administrative Services SCSU
St. Cloud, Minnesota 56301
Tel: (612) 255-2247; (800) 369-4260

Description: The publicly supported liberal arts and professional university is accredited by the North Central Association of Colleges and Schools. Founded in 1869 as the Third State Normal School, St. Cloud has developed from a single-purpose teacher preparation institution into a comprehensive university offering 100 majors and programs. Students may choose from Bachelor of Arts or Science Degrees in addition to Master and specialist Degree programs. The school operates on the quarter system with 2 summer sessions. Enroll-

ment includes 11,071 full-time and 2,189 part-time undergraduates and 1,413 graduate students. A faculty of 628 full-time and 124 part-time gives a faculty-student ratio of 1-22.

Entrance Requirements: Accredited high school graduation or equivalent; rank in upper half of class or composite score of 25 on ACT; early admission, early decision, midyear admission, rolling admission, and advanced placement plans available; $15 application fee.

Costs Per Year: $2,512 tuition; $4,867 out-of-state residents; $2,769 room.

Collegiate Environment: The university is located on 350 acres and contains 29 buildings, including a library of 2,209,971 volumes and 1,919 periodicals. There are dormitory facilities for 3,100 students. Approximately 83% of students applying for admission are accepted including midyear students. Merit and talent scholarships are available. 80% of students receive some form of financial aid.

Community Environment: The city is on Interstate 94, about halfway between Minneapolis-St. Paul and scenic northern Minnesota. St. Cloud students have ready access both to the cultural and entertainment activities of the Twin Cities and to the recreational attractions of Minnesota's lakes and forests.

SAINT JOHN'S UNIVERSITY *(L-5)*
Collegeville, Minnesota 56321
Tel: (612) 363-2196; (800) 245-6467; Admissions: (612) 363-2196;
Fax: (612) 363-2504

Description: Saint John's University is a private, Benedictine, liberal arts college for men, a school of divinity, a graduate school in theological studies, and an institute for advanced ecumenical studies. The liberal arts college participates in a cooperative program with the College of Saint Benedict, a nearby women's college of 1,844 students. The cooperative arrangement between Saint John's and Saint Benedict's allows students to pursue programs of study offered by either campus. Although the University is a Catholic institution, many different beliefs, personal and professional, can be found among the faculty and students. Saint John's is accredited by the North Central Association of Colleges and Schools and professionally by the National Council for the Accreditation for Teacher Education Council on Social Work Education, National League of Nursing, American Chemical Society, and Association of Theological Schools. The University offers an Army ROTC program, preparation for the State teaching certification, internship programs, and extensive overseas programs in Austria, England, France, Greece, Spain, Italy, Ireland, and Japan, China as well as a Middle East Archeological and Bible Study program in Jerusalem. Many clubs and organizations, and intercollegiate and intramural athletics are available. Saint John's operates on the 4-1-4 calendar system. Enrollment includes 1,820 full-time and 120 part-time undergraduates and 82 graduate students. A faculty of 135 full-time and 39 part-time gives a faculty-student ratio of 1-13.

Entrance Requirements: Accredited high school graduation or equivalent; completion of 17 units including 4 English, 3 mathematics, 2 science, 2 social studies, 2 foreign language, and 4 electives; cumulative high school GPA of 2.8 or higher; high school rank of 60% or higher; ACT composite of 20 or higher; SAT 420 verbal, 470 math, or higher; early admission, midyear admission, rolling admission and advanced placement plans available; $25 application fee.

Costs Per Year: $12,951 tuition, $4,224 board and room, $135 student fees.

Collegiate Environment: The library houses 509,000 volumes, 2,100 periodicals, 131,000 microforms and 13,300 recordings. There are residence halls and apartments for 1,314 men. Approximately 83% of the students applying for admission are accepted, including midyear students and those from various geographical locations. Scholarships are available and 75% of the undergraduates receive some form of aid.

Community Environment: Collegeville is in central Minnesota about 90 miles northwest of Minneapolis and Saint Paul and 15 miles from St. Cloud; the university enjoys the advantages of a rural location within convenient distance of cities. The campus covers 2,400 acres of woodlands and has three lakes with facilities for biking, cross-country skiing, fishing, canoeing and hiking. Many part-time jobs are available. Buses and trains provide frequent service to St. Cloud, St. John's and St. Benedict's. The student population in the 15-mile radius is over 21,000. Many opportunities for dining, shopping and entertainment are available. Health services are available at the University. Marcel Breuer designed the New Abbey and University Church, Library, Science Center and new residence halls. Earth sheltered and other new apartments for students have recently been constructed.

SAINT MARY'S COLLEGE OF MINNESOTA *(P-11)*
Winona, Minnesota 55987
Tel: (507) 457-1700; (800) 635-5987; Fax: (507) 457-1633

Description: This privately supported Catholic, coeducational, four-year, liberal arts college was established in 1912 and is sponsored by the Christian Brothers. The college is accredited by the North Central Association of Colleges and Schools. It awards the Bachelor of Arts, Master of Arts, and Master of Science degrees. Chorus, jazz band, theatre, internships, religious activities, volunteer services, foreign study, fraternities and sororities, and intercollegiate and intramural athletics are available; preparation for the State teaching certificate is also offered. Master's degree programs are year-round in Minneapolis, Rochester and Winona. The college operates on the semester system. Enrollment includes 1,270 full-time undergraduate and 6,269 graduate students. A faculty of 72 full-time and 26 part-time members provides a faculty-student ratio of 1-17.

Entrance Requirements: Accredited high school graduation or equivalent; completion of 16 academic units; SAT or ACT required, ACT preferred; early admission, rolling admission, early decision, advanced placement plans; $25 application fee.

Costs Per Year: $9,630 tuition; $3,150 room and board; $100 student fees.

Collegiate Environment: The college is located on 400 acres high on a plateau, almost surrounded by wooded bluffs, and overlooking the Mississippi River Valley. The 23 buildings include a library of 150,000 volumes, 800 periodicals, 100 microforms and 17,200 audio-visual materials. Residence halls and village apartments are available for 528 men and 577 women. There are also a new theater and recital hall, an ice arena, and a science addition. Approximately 85% of students applying are accepted. The college welcomes a geographically diverse student body.

Community Environment: See Winona State University.

Branch Campuses: Graduate School centers are located in Minneapolis and Rochester. These facilities include computer labs, library, classrooms, offices and study lounges.

SAINT OLAF COLLEGE *(O-8)*
Northfield, Minnesota 55057
Tel: (507) 646-2222; (800) 800-3025; Admissions: (507) 646-3025; Fax: (507) 646-3832

Description: The privately supported liberal arts college was established in 1874 and is affiliated with the Evangelical Lutheran Church in America. It is open to all qualified students and enrolls approximately 1,231 men and 1,727 women. A faculty of 276 full-time and 109 part-time gives a faculty-student ratio of 1-12. The college operates on the 4-1-4 semester system and provides 2 summer terms. Its paracollege is a small experimental unit in which innovation in education and new patterns of both learning and teaching are tested. St. Olaf is accredited by the North Central Association of Colleges and Schools and professional accrediting organizations. It offers preparation for the State teaching certificate. Overseas programs are available and 50% to 70% of the students go abroad. A special tutoring program for all students is available. Religion and foreign language required. Extensive music programs, intercollegiate and intramural athletics are offered.

Entrance Requirements: Accredited high school graduation with rank in upper 25%; completion of 15 total units including 3 English, 2 mathematics, and 2 science. 11 of the 15 units must be academic subjects such as history, foreign language, journalism, etc.; SAT, PSAT or ACT required; special admission plans: early decision, rolling admission, delayed admission, advanced placement; non-high school graduates considered; Feb. 1 application deadline, Nov. 15 for early decision; $25 application fee.

Costs Per Year: $14,350, $3,750 room & board, additional expenses average $1,100.

Collegiate Environment: The 300-acre campus is located 35 miles south of Minneapolis and St. Paul. The 30 college buildings include

library of 435,735 volumes and dormitory facilities for 2,667 students. Approximately 77% of the students applying for admission are accepted. The college welcomes a geographically diverse student body and will accept midyear students. The middle 50% of enrolled freshmen scores were SAT 520-560 math, 460-590 verbal, and ACT 23-28 composite. 90% of the previous freshman class return to the college for the sophomore year. Financial aid is available for economically disadvantaged students and 64% of the current student body receive some form of aid.

Community Environment: See Carleton College.

SOUTHWEST STATE UNIVERSITY *(O-3)*
Marshall, Minnesota 56258
Tel: (507) 537-6286; (800) 642-0684; Fax: (507) 537-7154

Description: The publicly supported, state university was established in 1963 as a four-year college offering liberal arts and technical programs in the arts, sciences and engineering technology. It is accredited by the North Central Association of Colleges and Schools. Its programs now include education, humanities, social science, science, business, and adult and continuing education courses. It offers a cooperative education program (alternating work and class periods) in hotel-restaurant management. Band, choir, orchestra, and extensive intercollegiate and intramural athletics are available. Preparation for the State teaching certificate is offered. The university operates on the quarter system and offers two summer sessions. Enrollment includes 1,124 men and 1,209 women full-time and 409 part-time students. A faculty of 128 full-time and 37 part-time gives a faculty-student ratio of 1-19.

Entrance Requirements: High school graduation with rank in upper 50% of graduating class; minimum ACT 21, or SAT 900 combined required; midyear admission, rolling admission and advanced placement plans available; $15 application fee.

Costs Per Year: $2,241 state resident tuition; $4,867 nonresident tuition; $1082 board; $1,695 room; $385 student fees.

Collegiate Environment: The university's 216-acre campus has 23 buildings. Interconnected buildings, ramps, elevators and modified living and study areas are conducive to the pursuit of a complete education by the handicapped. Twenty-seven residence halls, which provide housing for 1,200 students, promote an integrated approach to living and learning. The library contains 164,868 volumes, 778 periodicals, 74,198 microforms and 9,528 records and tapes. There are 274 scholarships, 170 for freshmen, available and 86% of the current student body receives some form of financial assistance.

Community Environment: Marshall (population 11,900) is in the heart of rural, southwestern Minnesota. Air service, bus service and major highways make it accessible to parks, Minneapolis-St. Paul, Duluth and Sioux Falls, S.D. Marshall is a "college town" with restaurants, a shopping mall, churches, 3 movie theaters and a modern downtown area. It is also an expanding commercial center with a large industrial park and is the headquarters for several national agribusinesses and related firms. Marshall has a new, multimillion dollar hospital and health care facility. 5 city parks, a county park and 2 state parks are within a short drive. The community and university combine to offer concerts, theater and art/craft exhibits. Part-time job opportunities are available for students.

UNITED THEOLOGICAL SEMINARY OF THE TWIN CITIES *(B-12)*
3000 Fifth Street, N.W.
New Brighton, Minnesota 55112
Tel: (612) 633-4311

Description: This privately supported graduate seminary opened in 1962 and was the first expression of the institutional merger in the newly-formed United Church of Christ, combining the former Mission House Theological Seminary of Wisconsin and the Yankton School of Theology of South Dakota. The seminary is a fully accredited member of the American Association of Theological Schools and the North Central Association of Colleges and Schools. It grants Master of Divinity, Master of Arts in Theology, Worship and the Arts, and Doctor of Ministry. It operates on the 4-1-4 system with one summer session. Annual enrollment includes 330 students. The faculty consists of 14 full-time and 11 part-time members.

Entrance Requirements: Bachelor's degree from recognized college or university; Theological School Inventory required; rolling admission plan; $30 application fee.

Costs Per Year: $5,400 tuition; room rates vary.

Collegiate Environment: The seminary is comprised of 4 buildings located on 10.3 acres. The library contains 73,000 volumes, and living accommodations are available for 30 students and commuters. Approximately 97% of students applying for admission are accepted, including midyear students and those from various geographical locations.

Community Environment: A suburban community of the Twin Cities, New Brighton (population 23,600), enjoys all the cultural, social and recreational facilities of St. Paul and Minneapolis. Community facilities are excellent and opportunities for part-time employment are good. See also University of Minnesota.

UNIVERSITY OF MINNESOTA - CROOKSTON   *(F-2)*
Crookston, Minnesota 56716
Tel: (218) 281-6510; (800) 232-6466; Admissions: (218) 281-8569;
Fax: (218) 281-8050

Description: This publicly supported college branch of the University of Minnesota was established in 1966 and is accredited by the North Central Association of Colleges and Schools. It operates on the quarter system with 2 summer sessions. The college offers a two-year college program leading to the Associate degree in programs of business, agriculture, home economics, and hotel, restaurant, and institutional management. A general education program is also offered to supplement technical courses and to provide a balanced educational background. Bachelor degrees offered in Agriculture and Business. Enrollment is 850 full-time and 755 part-time students. A faculty of 44 full-time and 41 part-time gives a faculty-student ratio of 1-18. The college offers band, chorus, choir and intercollegiate and intramural athletics. An internship program (alternating work and class periods) is required for all degree programs. Freshman programs for the educationally disadvantaged are available.

Entrance Requirements: High school graduation or equivalent; open enrollment; non-high school graduates considered; early admission, delayed admission, advanced placement, early decision, and rolling admission plans available; $25 application fee.

Costs Per Year: $2,750 tuition; $8,100 out-of-state; $3,450 room and board; $210 student fees, $750 technology access fee.

Collegiate Environment: The college is located on 97 acres and contains 25 buildings that include dormitory facilities for 200 men and 200 women. The library contains 27,000 volumes. All of the students applying for admission who meet the requirements are accepted, including midyear students and those from various geographical locations. 62% of the freshman class returns for the second year. 200 scholarships are available, including 110 for freshmen and 85% of the current student body receives some form of financial assistance.

Community Environment: Crookston (population 8,300) is the county seat of Polk County, one of the largest rural counties in the state. It is an agricultural processing center for the Red River Valley that produces wheat, barley, and sugar beets. Trains and buses are convenient for transportation. Recreational activities include swimming, camping, roller skating, ice skating, golf and bowling. The Old Crossing Treaty State Historic Park and the Polk County Pioneer Museum are some of the points of interest.

UNIVERSITY OF MINNESOTA - DULUTH   *(I-10)*
10 University Drive
Duluth, Minnesota 55812
Tel: (218) 726-7500; (800) 232-1339; Fax: (218) 726-6144

Description: The Duluth campus of the publicly supported University of Minnesota was established in 1947 and is accredited by the North Central Association of Colleges and Schools and by respective professional associations. The college offers liberal arts, fine arts, education, human service, business, science, and engineering programs as well as remedial programs. Intercollegiate and intramural athletics are available. Academic cooperative programs are available with the college of St. Scholastica and the University of Wisconsin - Superior. Study in England for one year with the University of Birmingham and study in France or Sweden for Spring semester quarter are available.

The university operates on the quarter system and offers two summer sessions. Enrollment is 7,497 students. A faculty of 430 gives a faculty-student ratio of 1-17. Air Force and Army ROTC programs are available.

Entrance Requirements: Students with rank in top 35% of high school class accepted; ACT required; non-high school graduates considered; GRE required for graduate school; rolling admission, midyear, and advanced placement plans available; $25 application fee.

Costs Per Year: $2,995 state resident tuition; $8,828 nonresident tuition; $3,474 room and board; $750 average additional expenses; $310 student fees.

Collegiate Environment: The campus is located on 247 acres and includes a library of 457,000 volumes, 2,700 periodicals, 6,710 microforms and 10,000 audiovisual materials. There are living facilities for 1,356 men and 1,417 women. Approximately 75% of students applying for admission are accepted, including midyear students. Financial aid is available and 72% of the current student body receives some form of financial aid.

Community Environment: On picturesque slopes, Duluth (population 90,000) commands splendid views of the St. Louis River, the harbor and Lake Superior. The city is headquarters for the Superior National Forest, which is the largest in the nation.

UNIVERSITY OF MINNESOTA - MORRIS   *(L-3)*
Morris, Minnesota 56267
Tel: (612) 589-2211; (800) 992-8863; Admissions: (612) 589-6035;
Fax: (612) 589-1673

Description: The Morris Campus of the University of Minnesota was established in 1959 and is accredited by the North Central Association of Colleges and Schools. It offers preparation for the State teaching certificate. The school conducts a liberal arts program and grants the Baccalaureate degree. Various overseas programs are available including summer in Mexico and winter quarter in Germany; intercollegiate and intramural athletics are also offered. The university operates on the quarter system and offers two summer sessions. Enrollment includes 1,896 full-time and 28 part-time students. A faculty of 128 full-time and 14 part-time gives a faculty-student ratio of 1-15.

Entrance Requirements: High school graduation; 4 years of English, 3 mathematics, 3 science, 2 second language, 2 social studies; ACT required; applicants not meeting all requirements may be considered with recommendations of high school officials; early decision and regular decision: $25 application fee.

Costs Per Year: $3,498 tuition; $10,335 tuition for out-of-state residents; $3,246 board and room; $308 student fees; additional expenses average $1,500. Freshman Academic Scholarships to anyone in top 10% of high school class.

Collegiate Environment: The Morris Campus contains 26 buildings and provides coeducational dormitory facilities for 1,005 students. Library holdings include 160,000 volumes. Approximately 49% of students applying for admission are accepted. The university welcomes students from various geographical locations. 90% of the previous freshman class return to campus for a second year. Average high school standing of the 1994 freshman class, 82% in the top quarter of class; 52% in the top 10%; the median scores of the freshman class were ACT 27 composite. The college awarded 296 Bachelor degrees during the academic year and 28% of the senior class continue on to graduate school.

Community Environment: Morris (population 5,800), a rural area, has excellent pheasant and duck hunting, and all water sports may be enjoyed. Community facilities include a library, churches, hospital and clinic, and parks. Part-time and full-time employment is available.

UNIVERSITY OF MINNESOTA - TWIN CITIES   *(M-8)*
240 Williamson Hall
231 Pillsbury Drive S.E.
Minneapolis, Minnesota 55455-0213
Tel: (612) 625-2008; (800) 752-1000; Fax: (612) 626-1693

Description: This publicly supported state university began as a preparatory school and was chartered in 1851, seven years before the Territory of Minnesota became a state. It is accredited by the North Central Association of Colleges and Schools and by respective professional and educational organizations. The university offers programs on 4 campuses. Most of the graduate and undergraduate colleges and schools, as well as the university's central administration, are on the Twin Cities campus in Minneapolis-St. Paul. Other campuses are located at Duluth, Morris, and Crookston. Each campus has an Office of Admissions and Records. Programs are offered in the following subject areas: architecture, art, business, chemistry, dentistry, dental assisting, dental hygiene, engineering (aerospace, agricultural, chemical, civil, electrical, sanitary, geological, mechanical, metallurgical mining, and geological), forestry, home economics, hospital administration, journalism, landscape architecture, law, medicine, medical technology, occupational therapy, physical therapy, music, nursing, pharmacy, psychology, public health, social work, speech pathology and audiology, teacher education and veterinary medicine. Study abroad programs are also available. The university operates on the quarter system and offers two summer sessions. Enrollment includes 16,457 full-time and 6,781 part-time undergraduate, and 11,820 graduate students. A faculty of 3,244 full-time and 1,104 part-time gives a faculty-student ratio of 1-15. Army, Navy, and Air Force ROTC programs are available.

Entrance Requirements: Freshmen: high school graduation or equivalent; requirements vary with college and program; admission based on high school rank percentile and aptitude test scores; some programs require ACT. Transfer students: requirements vary with college and program; most require 39 credits from accredited college or university and 2.00 GPA. Graduate students: Bachelor degree from accredited college; requirements vary with program; most require GRE. Early admission, early decision, midyear admission and advancement placement plans available; registration dates vary with program; application fees: $25 undergraduate, $30 graduate school.

Costs Per Year: Undergraduate: $3,395 state resident tuition; $9,191 nonresident tuition. Graduate: $3,783 state resident tuition; $8,262 nonresident tuition. $3,774 room and board; $418 student fees.

Collegiate Environment: The university's system of libraries contain 4,908,982 bound volumes, 43,478 periodicals, 3,936,564 microforms, and 471,402 records and tapes, and is one of the 10 largest university research library systems in the United States. Dormitories on the Minneapolis Campus provide for men and women and accommodate 4,500 students. Additional housing for 1,200 students is provided by numerous fraternities and sororities as well as housing for married students. 56% of applicants are accepted. The average scores of the enrolled freshman class were SAT verbal 482, math 556 and ACT 23 composite.

Community Environment: In a large metropolitan area, Minneapolis is one of the "Twin Cities." It is the manufacturing, wholesaling, retailing, financial and educational center of a large agricultural region. The city has become a major electronics manufacturing center; industries include Honeywell, Inc., 3M, and Control Data Corp. The Minnesota Orchestra, Minneapolis Institute of Arts, Tyrone Guthrie Theatre, University Art Gallery, Northrop Auditorium, and the Walker Art Center provide many cultural activities for the city. Numerous part-time jobs are available both on and off campus. 22 lakes within the Minneapolis Park System offer fishing, swimming, canoeing and sailing in summer, and iceboating, skating and cross-country skiing in winter. The Minnesota Twins baseball team, the Minnesota Vikings football team and the Minnesota Timberwolves basketball team play their games in the Metrodome Stadium and Target Center.

UNIVERSITY OF SAINT THOMAS   *(M-8)*
2115 Summit Avenue
St. Paul, Minnesota 55105
Tel: (612) 962-6150; (800) 328-6819; Fax: (612) 962-6160

Description: The University of St. Thomas, founded in 1885, is a Catholic, independent, liberal arts, diocesan university that emphasizes values-centered, career-oriented education. It is Minnesota's largest independent university and enrolls almost an equal number of men and women among its 4,916 undergraduates. St. Thomas offers the bachelor of arts degree in 54 majors plus a Bachelor of Science degree; graduation requires coursework in English, fine arts, history, social science, science and mathematics, philosophy, foreign language, theology, and physical education. The university also enrolls 5,245 graduate students, 49% of whom are women, in its 25 master's programs. It offers doctoral programs in psychology, education, ministry and is home to graduate and undergraduate seminaries. St. Thomas is accredited by the North Central Association of Colleges and Schools, the National Council for the Accreditation of Teacher

Education, and the Council of Social Work Education. Its chemistry program is approved by the American Chemical Society. St. Thomas is on a 4-1-4 system with spring and fall semesters, a four-week January Term, and summer sessions. Air Force and Army ROTC is offered. The university employs 340 full-time and 264 part-time faculty and a staff of 893. The faculty-student ratio is about 1-17.

Entrance Requirements: Automatic admission requires that students graduate from the top 40% of their high school class and have an ACT score of 20 or better or a combined SAT score of 860 or better; rolling admission plan; $20 application fee.

Costs Per Year: $13,056 tuition; $4,364 room and board; $50 fees.

Collegiate Environment: St. Thomas's principal 78-acre campus is located in a quiet residential neighborhood that borders the Mississippi River. The park-like campus, situated midway between the downtowns of Minneapolis and St. Paul, includes a new student center and library among its 34 buildings. The main library houses about 235,000 volumes; a theological library contains 78,000; and an eight-library consortium provides computerized access to more than 1 million additional volumes. St. Thomas has extensive athletic facilities; 12 men's and 10 women's varsity teams; and many intramural sports. Also offered: internships; study abroad; honors programs; volunteer and community service opportunities; more than 70 clubs, sororities and fraternities; voice groups and instrumental ensembles; and the opportunity to take full-credit classes at four nearby private colleges. Approximately 90% of applicants to undergraduate programs are accepted. The university welcomes domestic and international students of all ages and from a broad range of religious, financial and racial backgrounds.

Community Environment: See Bethel College and Seminary.

VERMILION COMMUNITY COLLEGE   *(F-10)*
1900 East Camp Street
Ely, Minnesota 55731
Tel: (218) 365-3256

Description: Established in 1922, Vermilion evolved from a small junior college under control of the local school district to a modern community college under supervision of the Minnesota Community College Board. Vermilion became part of the five-campus Arrowhead Community College administrative unit in 1982. It is accredited by the North Central Association of Colleges and Schools. Offering the first 2 years of almost any common four-year degree program as well as several technical and vocational degree programs, Vermilion has successfully transferred students to four-year colleges and provided essential job skills in several areas for over 60 years. it operates on the quarter system and offers two summer sessions. Enrollment includes 720 full-time and 300 part-timr students. A faculty of 25 full-time and 16 part-time gives a faculty-student ratio of about 1-18, which assures each student relatively small classes and individual attention. Intercollegiate and intramural athletics, chorus, drama, and many special interest clubs are available.

Entrance Requirements: Graduates of an accredited high school; graduates of a non-accredited high school who have met entrance requirements based upon college entrance tests; non-high school graduates who have passed the GED exam; other non-high school graduates under special conditions. Graduates from Wisconsin, North Dakota and South Dakota are admitted under the same conditions as Minnesota residents (see above qualifications). Residents from other states must either achieve a standard score of 19 or above on the ACT test or rank in the upper two-thirds of their high school class. $15 application fee.

Costs Per Year: $2,007 tuition; $3,960 tuition for out-of-state students; $3,280 room and board; additional expenses average $300.

Collegiate Environment: The college's modern facilities include laboratories, classrooms, a gymnasium, a student career, a cafeteria, a library, a theatre and a unique historical museum, the Vermilion Interpretive Center. Dormitory facilities are available for 301 students and a list of college-approved rooms is available. The college welcomes a geographically diverse student body and will accept midyear applicants. Financial aid is available, and 94% of the full-time students receive some sort of assistance. Organized competitive sports include football, basketball, baseball and track for men, and volleyball, basketball, softball and track for women. Intramural and informal sports activities include football, volleyball, floor hockey, basketball, softball, karate, golf and tennis. College credit classes are available in several outdoor education activities including rock climbing, backpacking, ice climbing, cross-country skiing, winter camping and canoe camping. In addition, many college students participate in the annual Wilderness Run 16-mile race and the Wilderness Trek cross-country ski race.

Community Environment: Located on the edge of the Boundary Waters Canoe Area, Vermilion offers its students one of the most beautiful wilderness areas in America for a college setting. The town of Ely, with a population of about 5,000, provides nearby shopping facilities, churches, golf courses, tennis courts, restaurants and an excellent hospital. Limited part-time work is available in the community. The area provides exceptional opportunities for camping, canoeing, fishing, hunting, snowmobiling, cross-country skiing, down-hill skiing and ski jumping at the nearby Hidden Valley Ski Area, and even dog sledding.

WILLIAM MITCHELL COLLEGE OF LAW   *(M-8)*
875 Summit Avenue
St. Paul, Minnesota 55105
Tel: (612) 227-9171; Fax: (612) 290-6414

Description: The college of law was incorporated under the laws of the State of Minnesota in 1900. Its present name was adopted in 1956, upon the merger of the St. Paul College of Law and the Minneapolis-Minnesota College of Law. It operates on the semester system and is the only law school in the area that offers both a day and evening program. The college is approved by the American Bar Association and by the Minnesota Supreme Court. It is also approved for training by the United States Veterans Administration Enrollment is 625 full-time and 510 part-time students. A faculty of 35 full-time and 64 adjunct gives a faculty-student ratio of 1-12. Grants Juris Doctor degree, and the L.L.M. degree in Taxation.

Entrance Requirements: Bachelors degree from an accredited college or university; LSAT and LSDAS required; rolling admission plan available; $35 application fee.

Costs Per Year: $11,970 tuition day program; $8,685 evening program; books average $400 per year.

Collegiate Environment: The College of Law is located in a modern building that is equidistant from downtown St. Paul and downtown Minneapolis. The building contains classrooms; courtrooms; and a library of 200,000 titles, periodicals, microforms and audiovisual materials. There are also offices, seminar rooms, a student lounge and a bookstore. Classes begin in August. 97% of the first-year class returns for the second year. Financial aid is available.

Community Environment: See Bethel College and Seminary.

WILLMAR COMMUNITY COLLEGE   *(M-4)*
Box 797
Willmar, Minnesota 56201
Tel: (612) 231-5102; Fax: (612) 231-6602

Description: The publicly supported community college operates under the Minnesota Community College Board. It is accredited by the North Central Association of Colleges and Schools. It provides preprofessional education for students planning further college work, exploratory programs to assist students in determining their vocation, technical curricula designed to produce technical personnel with a background of both technical and general education, and various adult educational programs. The college operates on the quarter system with 2 summer sessions. Enrollment includes 894 full-time and 447 part-time students. A faculty of 42 full-time and 39 part-time gives a faculty-student ratio of 1-22. Offers extensive music programs, intercollegiate and intramural athletics, a cooperative education program (alternating work and class periods) in law enforcement, social services technology, computer science, chemical dependency counseling and a variety of other fields, and a freshman program for the educationally disadvantaged.

Entrance Requirements: High school graduation or equivalent with completion of 9 units; open enrollment; ACT recommended; non-high school graduates considered; rolling admission plan available; $15 application fee.

Costs Per Year: $2,000 tuition; $4,000 out-of-state; $2,500 room and board.

Collegiate Environment: This campus, completed in 1975, is located adjacent to the area vocational-technical school overlooking Foot Lake, northwest of the city of Willmar. The library contains 25,000 volumes, 2,081 pamphlets, 32 periodicals, 50 microforms and 30 sound recordings. There is housing for 600 students. All of the students applying for admission who meet the requirements are accepted, including midyear students, and 65% of the freshman class returns to the college for a second year of studies. Financial aid is available. 87% of students receive some form of financial aid.

Community Environment: Willmar (population 22,000) is the largest city within a 60-mile radius, and is an important shipping point for grain and livestock. The division headquarters of the Burlington Northern Railway and a large turkey-processing plant are located here. Other products manufactured are plastics, furniture, sheet metal, concrete, clothing, machinery, cookies and dairy products. The many lakes in the area provide good fishing and recreation. The college is located in prime hunting country. Willmar is the fastest-growing city in the state of Minnesota. It offers a semirural setting with cultural opportunities. Part-time employment is available.

WINONA STATE UNIVERSITY   *(P-11)*
Johnson and Sanborn
Winona, Minnesota 55987
Tel: (507) 457-5100; Admissions: (507) 457-5100; Fax: (507) 457-5586

Description: The publicly assisted institution, including liberal arts and teacher education programs, traces its history to the establishment of the State Normal School at Winona in 1858. It was the first state institution of its kind west of the Mississippi and was authorized to grant the Bachelor's degree in 1921. Today the university offers Associate, Bachelor, Master and Specialist degrees. The university operates on the quarter system and enrolls approximately 6,000 full-time and 1,000 part-time students. The university also offers 2 summer terms and is accredited by the North Central Association of Colleges and Schools. Overseas program features student (and sometimes faculty) exchange with Oslo Teachers College, Norway, and other countries (such as Denmark, England, Japan, and China). A faculty of 300 full-time and 25 part-time gives a faculty-student ratio of 1-20. Offers extensive music program, dramatic productions and intercollegiate and intramural athletics. Army ROTC is available as an elective.

Entrance Requirements: Accredited high school graduation or equivalent with rank in upper half of graduating class; completion of 16 units including 4 English, 3 mathematics, 3 science, 3 social science, 2 foreign language, and 1 humanities or fine arts; ACT or SAT required; GRE or GMAT required for graduate school; early admission, rolling admission, delayed admission, midyear admission, and advanced placement plans available; April 1 application deadline; $15 application fee.

Costs Per Year: $2,400 tuition; $5,600 out-of-state; $3,000 room and board; $400 student fees.

Collegiate Environment: The college is situated on a 16-square-block plot of land with the majority of buildings constructed since 1960. These include a library of 215,000 volumes and 703,000 microforms, and dormitory facilities for 1,800 students. 61% of applicants are accepted. The average scores of the entering freshman class were SAT 460 verbal, 490 math, and ACT 22 composite. Scholarships are available and 72% of the students receive some form of financial aid.

Community Environment: Winona (population 30,000) is a small city in southeastern Minnesota, in a sector known as Hiawatha Valley. Limestone from the quarries here is comparable to much of Italy's finest travertine. Winona is headquarters for the Upper Mississippi River Wildlife and Fish Refuge. Trains and buses provide commercial transportation. Community facilities include many churches, a public library, a hospital, hotels and motels. Part-time employment is available. Recreational activities include fishing, golf, swimming, hunting, boating, skiing and tobogganing.

Branch Campuses: Rochester, Minnesota.

WORTHINGTON COMMUNITY COLLEGE   *(Q-3)*
1450 College Way
Worthington, Minnesota 56187
Tel: (507) 372-2107; (800) 657-3966; Admissions: (507) 372-2107; Fax: (507) 372-5801

Description: The publicly supported community college is a two-year institution of higher learning that provides transfer, technical and continuing education opportunities. It was established in 1936 and is a member of the American Association of Junior Colleges. It is accredited by the North Central Association of Colleges and Schools. Two years of work at the college are recognized in full at the University of Minnesota and the State Universities. The college operates on the quarter system and offers two summer sessions. Enrollment includes 900 fulll-time students. A faculty of 35 full-time and 25 part-time provides a faculty-student ratio of 1:19. Extensive music programs and intercollegiate and intramural athletics are available. Minnesota state institutions have reciprocity agreements with North Dakota, South Dakota, Wisconsin, and five counties in Iowa, which permits in-state tuition for residents of these areas.

Entrance Requirements: High school graduation or equivalent; ACT recommended; open enrollment for state residents; special admission plans include early admission, early decision, rolling admission and advanced placement; $15 application fee.

Costs Per Year: $37.50 per credit for state residents; $75 per credit for out-of-state students.

Collegiate Environment: The college is located on 80 acres with 4 buildings which include a library of 27,000 volumes, 176 periodicals, 1,257 microforms and 1,241 recordings. Housing is available for 96 students. Almost all students applying for admission are accepted, including midyear students. Quarters begin in September, December, and March. Financial assistance is available. There are 156 scholarships. 65% of students receive some form of financial aid.

Community Environment: Located in southwest Minnesota, Worthington provides excellent hunting for pheasant, duck, geese, deer and rabbits. Other recreational activities include water sports, fishing, golf, tennis and baseball. Many civic and service organizations are represented in the community. The city provides a library, many churches, and a hospital. Part-time jobs are available.

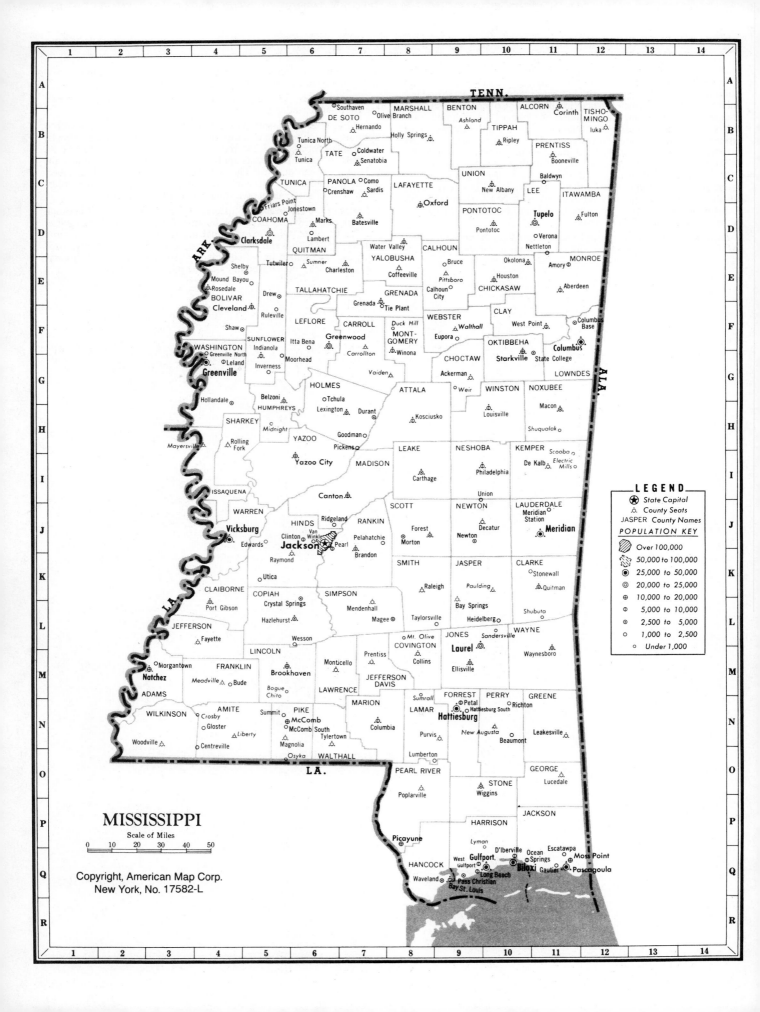

MISSISSIPPI

ALCORN STATE UNIVERSITY *(L-4)*
P.O. Box 300
Lorman, Mississippi 39096
Tel: (601) 877-6147; Admissions: (601) 877-6147; Fax: (601) 877-6347

Description: The publicly supported, coeducational state university is the oldest university of its kind in the United States, and had its beginning in 1830 as Oakland College for the education of white male students. It was sold to the state after the Civil War and was renamed in 1871. It is accredited by the Southern Association of Colleges and Schools. Today the college is composed of 7 schools of instruction which include Arts and Sciences, Education and Psychology, Agriculture and Applied Sciences, Business, Graduate Division, General College and Nursing. The college operates on the semester system and offers two summer terms. Enrollment includes 2,403 full-time and 339 part-time undergraduates and 187 graduate students. A faculty of 151 full-time and 19 part-time gives a faculty-student ratio of 1-18.

Entrance Requirements: Accredited high school graduation or GED equivalent; completion of 13.5 units, including 4 English, 3 mathematics, 3 biological scisnce, 2.5 social science, 1 elective; ACT or SAT required; early decision, early admission, midyear admission and rolling admission plans available; mature applicants not meeting all requirements may be admitted as special students.

Costs Per Year: $2,389 state-resident tuition; $4,537 non-resident $2,159 room and board.

Collegiate Environment: The college is a wholesome educational community comprising 1,756 acres of which 300 acres make up the campus and athletic fields, and 1,456 acres are devoted to agriculture. The college buildings include a library of 168,058 volumes and living accommodations are provided for 955 men and 1,060 women. 50% of all applicants accepted. Scholarships are available and 89% of students receive some form of financial aid. Semesters begin in August and January and the summer terms begin in June and July.

Community Environment: This rural community has a population of less than 2,500. Multidenominational churches serve the area. It is an ideal place for hiking, camping and other outdoor recreational activities. The university is located in Claiborne County, seven miles west of Lorman, seventeen miles southwest of Poet Gibson, and forty-five miles south of Vicksburg.

BELHAVEN COLLEGE *(J-6)*
1500 Peachtree Street
Jackson, Mississippi 39202
Tel: (601) 968-5940; (800) 960-5940; Admissions: (601) 968-5940; Fax: (601) 968-9998

Description: Belhaven College is a private, coeducational college of liberal arts and sciences is affiliated with the Presbyterian Church. It is accredited by the Southern Association of Colleges and Schools and operates on the semester system with two summer sessions. Enrollment includes 687 full-time and 422 part-time students. A faculty of 35 full-time and 45 part-time gives a faculty-student ratio of 1-17.

Entrance Requirements: Accredited high school graduation; completion of 15 units including 4 English, 2 mathematics, 1 science, 1 social science; score of 20 over on ACT or SAT score of 350 verbal, 350 math required; rolling admission, early decision, early admission, delayed admission, midyear admission and advanced placement plans available; $15 application fee.

Costs Per Year: $7,490 tuition, $2,900 room and board; $130 student fees; additional expenses average $750.

Collegiate Environment: The college is located on a 42-acre site near the heart of Jackson, the capital and largest city in Mississippi. The 14 college buildings include a library of 60,000 volumes and dormitory facilities for 410 men and women. All students are required to attend chapel once a week. Approximately 90% of students applying for admission are accepted, including midyear students. Scholarships are available and 45% of the current student body receives some form of financial assistance.

Community Environment: See Jackson State University.

BLUE MOUNTAIN COLLEGE *(B-10)*
P.O. Box 338
Blue Mountain, Mississippi 38610
Tel: (601) 685-4771

Description: This privately supported women's college is owned and operated by the Mississippi Baptist Convention, and is accredited by the Southern Association of Colleges and Schools. A liberal arts school, the semester system is employed with 2 summer sessions. The enrollment includes 218 women full-time, 102 women part-time, and 44 men who as ministers are admitted into a special program. A faculty of 36 gives a faculty-student ratio of 1-11.

Entrance Requirements: Accredited high school graduation or equivalent; non-high school graduates considered; early admission, advanced placement, rolling admission plans available; $10 application fee.

Costs Per Year: $3,248 tuition; $2,030 room and board; $310 student fees.

Collegiate Environment: Located in the "Berkshire Hills" of the South, Blue Mountain College is in the northern part of Mississippi. The library contains 53,799 volumes and 215 periodicals. Housing includes accommodations for up to 238 women. Students attend chapel services on campus. Approximately 99% of all applicants are accepted, including midyear students. There are 150 scholarships available and 30 are reserved for freshmen.

Community Environment: A rural community, Blue Mountain has a warm and pleasant climate with an average temperature of 68 degrees. Blue Mountain is about 70 miles from Memphis. Recreational facilities include a swimming pool, golf course, athletic field, physical education center, tennis courts, skating rink, student center and 2 auditoriums for productions.

COAHOMA JUNIOR COLLEGE *(D-5)*
Clarksdale, Mississippi 38614
Tel: (601) 627-2571; (800) 844-1222; Admissions: (601) 627-2501x205; Fax: (800) 844-1222

Description: The publicly supported, coeducational community college was established in 1949 and was the first educational institution for Black students to be included in Mississippi's system of public junior colleges. It provides opportunities in general education, business education, industrial arts, and teacher education. It also provides vocational-technical instruction in various community services. The college operates on the semester system and is accredited by the Southern Association of Colleges and Schools. It has an enrollment of 970 students. A faculty of 62 full-time and 26 part-time gives a faculty-student ratio of 1:10

Entrance Requirements: Accredited high school graduation; completion of 17 units; non-accredited high school graduates must take placement examinations.

Costs Per Year: $40 per credit hour, $1,692 room and board, $210 additional fees.

Collegiate Environment: The college is located on 41 acres and contains 15 buildings which include a library of 11,400 volumes and dormitory facilities for 200 men and 120 women. Approximately 90%

of students applying for admission are accepted, including midyear students. Financial assistance is available.

Community Environment: Clarksdale, an important distributing outlet in an agricultural region, is a prime example of the state's "Balance Agriculture with Industry" program. The city gins large amounts of cotton and manufactures conveyor equipment, corrugated boxes, farm machinery, tire tubes, agricultural chemicals and fertilizers, builder's hardware, electronic equipment and furniture. The Greyhound Bus line serves the city. The area has a public library, hospital, churches of all major denominations and movie theatres.

COPIAH-LINCOLN JUNIOR COLLEGE   (L-6)
P.O. Box 371
Wesson, Mississippi 39191
Tel: (601) 643-5101

Description: This publicly supported, coeducational community college was established in 1928. The college operates on the semester system with 3 summer terms and is accredited by the Southern Association of Colleges and Schools. It offers courses in vocational-technical and academic areas for terminal and transfer programs. Enrollment includes 1,250 full-time and 275 part-time students. A faculty of 104 provides a faculty-student ratio of 1-16.

Entrance Requirements: High school graduation or equivalent; open enrollment policy; completion of 15 units, including 3 English and 1 math; non-high school graduates considered; early admission plan available.

Costs Per Year: $1,000 state-resident tuition; $2,200 out-of-state; $1,760 room and board.

Collegiate Environment: The physical plant consists of 19 buildings in addition to 2 apartment buildings, 13 residences and the farm buildings. The college library contains 30,000 volumes and 216 periodicals. Dormitories provide living accommodations for 300 men and 220 women. 98% of the students applying for admission who meet the requirements are accepted, including midyear students. Financial aid is available for economically handicapped students. Of 150 scholarships offered, 85 are available to freshmen.

Community Environment: Wesson is located on U.S. Highway 51, approximately 150 miles north of New Orleans. The climate is pleasant. Transportation is provided by the Illinois Central railroad. Some part-time employment is available for students.

DELTA STATE UNIVERSITY   (F-5)
Cleveland, Mississippi 38733
Tel: (601) 846-3000

Description: The publicly supported, coeducational college was created as Delta State Teachers College in 1924. The school changed its name to Delta State College in 1955 with the addition of Baccalaureate degrees in the sciences, the arts and music. In 1965, graduate work for teachers in several fields of concentration was offered leading to the Master degree. The university adopted its present name in 1974, and offered a Doctorate of Education in Professional Studies for the first time in 1981. The university is accredited by the Southern Association of Colleges and Schools. It operates on the semester system and offers 2 summer terms. Recent enrollment included 1,249 men, 1,659 women full-time, 268 men, and 455 women part-time. A faculty of 173 full-time and 52 part-time gives a faculty-student ratio of 1-18.

Entrance Requirements: Accredited high school graduation or GED; completion of 13.5 units including 4 English, 3 mathematics, 3 science, 2.5 social science; 1 elective in math, science or language; non-high school graduates considered; early admission plan available.

Costs Per Year: $2,194 state-resident tuition; $3,174 out-of-state tuition; $1,770 room and board.

Collegiate Environment: The campus of the university consists of 263 acres adjoining the western corporate limits of Cleveland. The university buildings include a library of 265,000 books, 1,634 periodicals and 685,000 microforms. 84% of the students applying for admission are accepted, including midyear students. Several social fraternities and sororities are located on the campus as well as numerous other student organizations. University housing accommodates 680 men, 827 women and 76 married students. Financial aid and

scholarships are available, and 90% of the current student body receives some form of assistance.

Community Environment: Located midway between Memphis, Tennessee and Vicksburg, Mississippi, the city has a public library, several churches representing the major denominations, and a hospital. Bus lines are accessible to the area and a regional airport is located 30 miles from campus in Greenville. Recreation is provided in the community through a local Little Theatre, movies, swimming pools, 4 municipal parks, a nine-hole golf course, bowling, and fishing and hunting in the nearby lake region. Average living facilities are provided by a hotel, motel, several apartments, rooming houses and dormitories. The city has over 35 civic, fraternal and business organizations. Some part-time employment is available for students.

EAST CENTRAL COMMUNITY COLLEGE   (J-9)
Decatur, Mississippi 39327
Tel: (601) 635-2111; Fax: (601) 635-2150

Description: The publicly supported, coeducational junior college was founded in 1928. The college operates on the semester system and offers 2 summer terms. It is accredited by the Southern Association of Colleges and Schools. The college provides programs in liberal arts, business, computers, secretarial training and vocational-technical programs. Enrollment is 1,049 full-time and 432 part-time students. A faculty of 56 full-time and 31 part-time provides a faculty-student ratio of 1-21.

Entrance Requirements: Open enrollment policy; completion of 17 units; ACT required; high school graduate or GED.

Costs Per Year: $1,000 state resident, $2,830 out-of-state; $1,830 room and board.

Collegiate Environment: The campus is comprised of 199 acres and contains 30 buildings that include a library of 23,247 volumes and living accommodations for 236 men 200 women, and 20 families.

Community Environment: Located in a rural area with a healthful atmosphere, Decatur has 2 churches and very active civic, fraternal and veteran's organizations. Hunting in the local area, fishing and swimming provide recreation for the city.

EAST MISSISSIPPI COMMUNITY COLLEGE   (I-11)
Scooba, Mississippi 39358
Tel: (601) 476-8442; Admissions: (601) 476-8442; Fax: (601) 476-8822

Description: The publicly-supported, coeducational community college was established in 1927 and is accredited by the Southern Association of Colleges and Schools. It provides academic and preprofessional programs as well as vocational courses of a terminal nature. The college operates on the semester system and offers 1 summer session. The faculty includes 39 full-time and 20 part-time members. Enrollment is approximately 550, giving a faculty-student ratio of 1:14.

Entrance Requirements: Open enrollment policy; non-high school graduates considered.

Costs Per Year: Tuition $1,000; $2,000 out-of-state; $1,850 room and board; $100 student fees; additional expenses average $90.

Collegiate Environment: The college buildings contain a library of 18,145 volumes and living accommodations are provided for 220 men and 90 women. Average score for the freshman class, ACT 18. Financial aid is available for economically handicapped students and many scholarships are offered. Approximately 60% of the current student body receives some form of financial assistance.

Community Environment: Scooba is located in the east central part of Mississippi, 35 miles north of Meridian. The area is accessible by railroad and U.S. Highway 45. There are excellent bus, train and air facilities in nearby Meridian.

Branch Campuses: Golden Triangle Campus, P.O. Box 100, Mayhew, MS, 39753, (601) 243-1923

HINDS COMMUNITY COLLEGE   (K-6)
Raymond, Mississippi 39154
Tel: (601) 857-5261; (800) 446-3722; Admissions: (601) 857-3212; Fax: (601) 857-3539

Description: The publicly supported community college is an outgrowth of the Hinds County Agricultural High School, which opened its doors in 1917. Today the college offers courses in vocational-technical and academic areas for part-time, terminal and transfer programs. It is accredited by the Southern Association of Colleges and Schools. The college operates on the semester system and offers two summer sessions. Enrollment includes 11,665 students. A faculty of 486 provides a faculty-student ratio of 1-24.

Entrance Requirements: Open enrollment policy; accredited high school graduation or GED; completion of 17 units; entrance exam required; rolling admission, midyear admission and advanced placement plans available.

Costs Per Year: $1,020 district-resident tuition; $1,020 out-of-district; $3,226 out-of-state; $1,600 room and board.

Collegiate Environment: The 145-acre campus is located a short distance from Raymond Lake. The 66 college buildings contain a library of 140,430 volumes and dormitory facilities for 582 men and 788 women. Approximately 98% of students applying for admission are accepted, including midyear students. 181 scholarships are available, including 65 athletic, and 56% of the students receive some form of financial aid.

Community Environment: Raymond is a suburban area 15 miles east of Jackson. The community has a regional library and a general hospital 8 miles east. There are several churches of various denominations in the immediate area. Local clubs include Lions, Business & Professional Women, and the Jaycees. Hinds Community College has a part-time employment agreement with a local industry.

HOLMES COMMUNITY COLLEGE   *(H-7)*
Hill Street
P.O. Box 369
Goodman, Mississippi 39079
Tel: (601) 472-2312; Fax: (601) 472-9852

Description: The publicly supported, coeducational junior college provides a two-year college program designed for both transfer to senior colleges and terminal programs for both academic and vocational work. The college operates on the semester system and is accredited by the Southern Association of Colleges and Schools. Enrollment includes 2,200 students with a faculty of 105 full-time and 20 part-time members.

Entrance Requirements: Accredited high school graduation or GED for students over 21 years of age; completion of 17 units including at least 9 of the following 10: 4 English, 2 mathematics, 2 social sciences, 2 natural sciences required for placement; minimum ACT 14.

Costs Per Year: $1000 tuition; $2004 tuition for out-of-state students; $1,400 room and board.

Collegiate Environment: The campus consists of 227 acres located on the highest peak in the area of about 25 square miles. The 27 college buildings contain a library of 37,000 volumes and living accommodations for 225 men and 244 women. Approximately 98% of students applying for admission are accepted including midyear students. Financial aid is available for economically handicapped students.

Community Environment: Located in a rural area, there is bus service to Goodman. The climate is mild and humid. Railroad service is available in nearby Durant, Mississippi. Several churches of various denominations are located here. Many cultural, recreational and community services available in Jackson, the State Capital, 48 miles away. There is some work available for students requiring financial assistance.

ITAWAMBA JUNIOR COLLEGE   *(D-11)*
Fulton, Mississippi 38843
Tel: (601) 862-3101

Description: The publicly supported, coeducational, community junior college was established in 1948 and offers courses in vocational-technical and academic areas for part-time, terminal and transfer students. The college operates on the semester system with 2 summer terms and is accredited by the Southern Association of Colleges and Schools. Enrollment includes 848 men, 1,113 women full-time, 538 men, and 738 women part-time. A faculty of 130 full-time and 32 part-time members provides a faculty-student ratio of 1:20.

Entrance Requirements: Open enrollment policy; accredited high school graduation or GED equivalency; completion of 15 units; ACT required; early admission, early decision, delayed admission, and advanced placement plans available.

Costs Per Year: $750 tuition, $1,590 for out-of-state residents; $1,710 room and board.

Collegiate Environment: The college campus consists of 150 acres. The school is housed in 47 buildings which include a library of 35,000 volumes and dormitory facilities for 212 men and 165 women. All students applying for admission who meet the requirements are accepted, including midyear students. Approximately 60% of the previous freshman class returned to the college for the second year of studies. Financial aid is available for economically handicapped students, and 70% of the current student body receive form of aid.

Community Environment: Fulton is a rural community in northeast Mississippi. The climate is moderate to warm. The area is accessible to bus and rail lines and has several churches of various denominations. Recreation is provided by local theatres, boating water skiing, fishing, and golf. Community services include the County Health Department, a hospital, and fine shopping facilities. There are many active civic and fraternal organizations within the immediate area.

JACKSON COLLEGE OF MINISTRIES   *(D-11)*
1555 Beasley Rd.
Jackson, Mississippi 39206
Tel: (601) 981-1611

Description: The Bible college was established in 1945 by the United Pentecostal Church. It operates on the semester basis. Enrollment is 170 with approximately equal numbers of men and women. A faculty of 10 full-time, 16 part-time gives a faculty-student ratio of 1-16. The purpose of the institute is to train students as pastors, musicians, evangelists, teachers and missionaries. It grants a Bachelor's Degree in 5 areas: Missions, Theology, Christian Education, Music and Religious Studies.

Entrance Requirements: High school education or equivalent; entrance examinations required; early decision plan available; $20 application fee.

Costs Per Year: $1,500 tuition; $2,340 room and board; $350 student fees.

Collegiate Environment: The Bible college is situated on 26 acres located in the heart of Mississippi. The 19 buildings include a library of 5,000 volumes and living accommodations for 150 men, 150 women. The institute welcomes students from all geographical locations and will admit students at midyear. 90% of the students applying for admission are accepted. Scholarships are available.

Community Environment: See Jackson State University.

JACKSON STATE UNIVERSITY   *(J-6)*
1400 Lynch Street
Jackson, Mississippi 39217
Tel: (601) 968-2100; (800) 682-5390; Fax: (601) 973-3445

Description: The publicly supported, coeducational college is accredited by the Southern Association of Colleges and Schools. The college was operated as a private church school for 53 years by the American Baptist Home Mission Society and was founded at Natchez in 1877. It was moved to its present location in 1882 and became a teachers college of the State of Mississippi in 1940. The program of liberal arts and a division of graduate studies was organized in 1953. The college grants the Bachelor and Masters degrees. Army ROTC is available as an elective. The college operates on the semester system and offers one summer session. Enrollment includes 5,003 full-time and 1,221 part-time undergraduates and 975 graduate students. A faculty of 326 full-time and 68 part-time gives a faculty-student ratio of 1-17.

Entrance Requirements: Accredited high school graduation or GED; minimum C average and completion of 16 units including 4 English, 3 math, 3 laboratory science, 1 foreign language, 3.5 social studies, 2 advanced electives, and 1/2 computer applications; ACT required; GRE; early admission, early decision, rolling admission, delayed admission, and advanced placement plans available.

Costs Per Year: $2,380 tuition; $4,614 tuition for out-of-state students; $975 board and room.

Collegiate Environment: The campus is located on 120 acres and contains 39 buildings which include a library of 342,739 volumes and living accommodations for 732 men and 1,442 women. The college welcomes a geographically diverse student body representing 42 states and 33 countries and will accept midyear students. 1,256 scholarships, including 250 athletic are available. 94% of students receive some form of financial aid.

Community Environment: On the Pearl River, Jackson is the capital and largest city of Mississippi. It was first established as a trading post by the French. In the early days, many Virginians and Carolinians passed through here as they followed the Old Natchez Trace to the Southwest. The area enjoys year-round pleasant weather. Being a major city, there are good facilities for rail and air transportation. Community associations sponsoring cultural pursuits include Jackson Music Association, Little Theatre, Municipal Art Gallery and Symphony Orchestra. Local services are supplied by 5 hospitals, libraries and many churches. Recreation facilities include 12 parks, 4 municipal swimming pools, a zoo, golf courses, tennis courts, and fishing and hunting nearby.

JONES COUNTY JUNIOR COLLEGE   *(M-9)*
Ellisville, Mississippi 39437
Tel: (601) 477-4025

Description: The publicly supported, coeducational junior college is one of the largest in Mississippi in regard to both enrollment and district served. It was established in 1911 and is accredited by the Southern Association of Colleges and Schools. The college offers academic programs as well as vocational-technical programs. The school operates on the semester system and offers 2 summer terms. Enrollment is 4,400 students. A faculty of 140 provides a faculty-student ratio of 1-25.

Entrance Requirements: Open enrollment policy; accredited high school graduation or equivalent; completion of 17 units; ACT required; early decision, early admission, delayed admission, advanced placement and rolling admission plans available.

Costs Per Year: $792 district- and county-resident tuition and fees; $2,192 out-of-state tuition and fees; $2,532 room and board.

Collegiate Environment: The campus consists of 360 acres of land adjoining the southwestern section of Ellisville. The college buildings include a library of approximately 45,000 volumes and living accommodations for 465 students. Financial aid is available, and 85% of the current student body receives some form of aid.

Community Environment: The city is located 7 miles from Laurel. The climate is mild. Churches, libraries and museums all contribute to the pleasant living of the area. Transportation is provided by railroad and airways, and the town is easily accessible by highway. Fishing, hunting and golf are the major recreational pastimes. There are some part-time job opportunities for students.

MARY HOLMES COLLEGE   *(F-11)*
P.O. Drawer 1257
West Point, Mississippi 39773
Tel: (601) 494-6820; (800) 634-2749; Fax: (601) 494-1881

Description: The privately supported, coeducational, junior college is a liberal arts college that has already begun a new concept in education for people in the southeastern United States. It was founded in 1892 and is affiliated with the Program Agency of the Presbyterian Church U.S.A. The college operates on the semester system. Enrollment includes 500 students with a faculty-student ratio of 1-20.

Entrance Requirements: Accredited high school graduation or equivalent; completion of 15 units including 4 English, 2 mathematics, 2 science, 2 social science. All students are required to take a placement exam; early decision and rolling admission plans available.

Costs Per Year: $7,900 tuition; $3,890 room and board.

Collegiate Environment: The college is located on 190 acres outside the city limits of West Point. The college buildings include a library of 26,000 volumes and dormitory facilities for 554 students. The college has plans to launch a massive building program on the 200 acres adjacent to the present campus and new courses and programs have already been initiated. A new learning resources center houses the Business and Computer Science Department and Humanities. The new facility has ten rooms and is fiber optic equipped. Approximately

80% of students applying for admission are accepted. The college welcomes students from various geographical locations and will accept midyear students. Financial aid is available for economically disadvantaged students. 90% of students recive some form of aid.

Community Environment: Located in northeast Mississippi, West Point is a manufacturing community with dairy products, boilers, garments, toys, playground equipment, boats and institutional table linens being the principal commodities. Also located here are a large meat packing plant and one of the state's largest hatcheries. Some part-time employment is available for students.

MERIDIAN COMMUNITY COLLEGE   *(J-11)*
9100 Highway 19 North
Meridian, Mississippi 39307
Tel: (601) 483-8241; Fax: (601) 484-8607

Description: This publicly supported, coeducational community college offers transfer, occupational and continuing education programs for both youth and adults. It was established in 1937 and is accredited by the Southern Association of Colleges and Schools. It operates on the semester system and offers 2 summer sessions. Enrollment includes 3,081 full-time and part-time students. A faculty of 215 provides a faculty-student ratio of 1-18.

Entrance Requirements: High school graduation or equivalent; open enrollment policy; early admission, early decision, midyear admission, rolling admission, and advanced placement plans available.

Costs Per Year: $960 tuition; $2,000 nonresident.

Collegiate Environment: The college is located on 62 acres and contains 7 buildings that include a library of 42,446 volumes, 700 periodical titles, 250,000 microforms and 7,000 recordings. 84 rooms are available to accommodate students. All students applying for admission who meet the requirements are accepted, including midyear students. 60% of the student receive some form of financial aid.

Community Environment: Neither destruction by fire during the Civil War, a riot in 1871, a yellow fever epidemic in 1878, nor a cyclone in 1906 could keep Meridian down. It survived these disasters to become the state's leading industrial city. In an area providing abundant raw agricultural and industrial materials, local industries produce wood products, clothing, clay pipes, metal windows, asphalt roofing, fabricated steel and dairy and meat products. The region also produces timber, corn, cotton and cattle. Passenger air, rail and bus service is available. The city has private hospitals. Cultural activities include Little Theatre, Symphony Orchestra, Meridian Chorale and Art Association. The economic base is evenly divided between agriculture, industry and military payrolls.

MILLSAPS COLLEGE   *(J-6)*
1700 North State St.
Jackson, Mississippi 39210
Tel: (601) 974-1000; (800) 352-1050; Fax: (601) 974-1059

Description: The privately supported, coeducational, liberal arts college was founded in 1890 and is supported by the United Methodist Church. It is accredited by the Southern Associaito of Colleges and Schools and operates on the semester system with two summer sessions. Current enrollment includes 1,333. A faculty of 94 gives a faculty-student ratio of 1:14. Academic cooperative programs for engineering students are available with Columbia, Georgia Tech, Washington University in St. Louis, Auburn and Vanderbilt. A junior year abroad is available. Additional off-campus study programs include the British Studies at Oxford, Washington Semester, London and Munich summer program, semester abroad in Central Europe and several others.

Entrance Requirements: Accredited high school graduation or equivalent with rank in upper half of graduating class; completion of 16 units including a minimum total of 12 in English, math, science, social science and a foreign language; ACT or SAT required; non-high school graduates considered; early admission, delayed admission, rolling admission, advanced placement plans available; $25 application fee.

Costs Per Year: $10,080 tuition; $3,980 room and board, $200 student fees.

Collegiate Environment: The campus covers nearly 100 acres in the center of a beautiful residential section and on one of the highest points in the city. The 16 college buildings includes a library of 265,073 volumes and 730 periodicals. Dormitories provide living accommodations for 325 men and 426 women. There are several social fraternities and sororities located on the campus as well as numerous other student organizations. Fraternities provide housing for 65 men. The college welcomes a geographically diverse student body and will accept midyear students. Approximately 87% of students applying for admission are accepted. Financial aid is available and 67% of the student body receives some form of assistance.

Community Environment: See Jackson State University.

MISSISSIPPI COLLEGE   (J-6)
P.O. Box 4203
Clinton, Mississippi 39058
Tel: (601) 925-3000; (800) 738-1236; Admissions: (601) 925-3240; Fax: (601) 925-3804

Description: The privately supported, coeducational college is one of the oldest and largest Baptist colleges in the United States. Chartered by the State Legislature in 1826, it is the oldest institution of higher learning in Mississippi. The liberal arts and comprehensive college is owned and operated by the Mississippi Baptist Convention and is accredited by the Southern Association of Colleges and Schools. It employs the semester system and offers 2 summer terms. Enrollment includes 2,500 full-time and 1,100 part-time students. A faculty of 140 full-time and 75 part-time gives a faculty-student ratio of 1-18. An academic cooperative plan is available with the University of Mississippi.

Entrance Requirements: Accredited high school graduation or equivalent; score of 18 or over on ACT required; GRE required for graduate programs; LSAT and LSDAS required for Law; non-high school graduates considered; rolling admission, midyear admission plans available; $25 application fee.

Costs Per Year: $6,000 tuition; $3,250 board and room; $350 student fees; additional expenses average $600.

Collegiate Environment: The 180-acre campus is located about 5 miles west of Jackson, the capital city. The 31 college buildings contain a general library of 240,000 titles, 900 periodicals, 15,704 microforms and 9,013 audiovisual materials. Living accommodations for 570 men, 482 women and 30 married students is available. Chapel services are held 2 days a week for all undergraduate students. Approximately 73% of students applying for admission are accepted, including midyear students. Scholarships are available and 75% of the current student body receive financial aid.

Community Environment: This is a suburban community located adjacent to Jackson's city limits. The climate is warm. The area has a new shopping center, and rapid expansion of businesses and residential areas is anticipated. Clinton has excellent highways, air and rail connections.

MISSISSIPPI DELTA COMMUNITY COLLEGE   (G-5)
Moorhead, Mississippi 38761
Tel: (601) 246-5554; Fax: (601) 246-8627

Description: This publicly supported, coeducational community college is supported by Delta Counties. It was founded in connection with the Agricultural High School early in 1926 and was fully accredited by the Southern Association of Colleges and Schools in 1930. The college operates on the semester system and offers three summer sessions. Enrollment includes 2,029 full-time and 682 part-time students. A faculty of 109 provides a faculty-student ratio of 1-17.

Entrance Requirements: Open enrollment policy; accredited high school graduation or equivalent with completion of 17 units; Enhanced ACT 16 or over required; rolling admission plan available.

Costs Per Year: $770 resident tuition; $1,870 out-of-state; $1,450 room and board.

Collegiate Environment: The community college is located near the geographical center of the Mississippi Delta. The more than 20 college buildings include a library of 30,000 volumes, 250 periodicals, 1,300 microforms and 15,000 audiovisual materials. There are dormitory facilities for 258 men and 250 women. All students applying for admission are accepted including midyear students. Financial aid is available.

Community Environment: This is a rural area with bus and air transportation 8 miles distant. The immediate area supports a clinic and small stores. There is some part-time employment for men over 18. Better employment opportunities for students are available in the neighboring community. The city has a theater, swimming pool and tennis courts. 5 local lakes provide hunting and fishing within the area.

MISSISSIPPI GULF COAST COMMUNITY COLLEGE
(P-10)
P.O. Box 67
Perkinston, Mississippi 39573
Tel: (601) 928-5211

Description: The publicly-supported, coeducational community college was established in 1911. It is accredited by the Southern Assosciaition of Colleges and Schools. The college has 3 branch campuses located at Perkinston, Gautier and Gulfport. It operates on the semester system with 2 summer sessions. Enrollment is 13,812 and a faculty of 419 provides a teacher-student ratio of 1-33.

Entrance Requirements: Open enrollment policy; accredited high school graduation or equivalent with completion of 16 units; ACT required; early admission, early decision, rolling admission and advanced placement plans available.

Costs Per Year: $660 tuition fee; $1,560 out-of-state students; $355 board and $170 room; $10 activity fee.

Collegiate Environment: Mississippi Gulf Coast Junior College serves a four-county district in Southeast Mississippi. The multi-campus college consists of the Jackson County Campus in Gautier, the Jefferson Davis Campus in Gulfport, and the Perkinston Campus located in Perkinston. The campuses offer essentially the same basic academic instructional programs. The Perkinston campus owns 642 acres of land, 30 acres of which make up the main campus, with the remainder devoted to dairying and pasture, tree farming and feed production. The campus buildings are conveniently located and include a library of 127,068 volumes and dormitory facilities for 710 men and women. The college will accept midyear students as well as those from various geographical locations. Financial aid is available, and 50% of the current student body receive some form of financial assistance.

Community Environment: The city lies 25 miles north of Gulfport. Area is reached by Interstate 10 and Highway 49. Air service is available.

MISSISSIPPI STATE UNIVERSITY   (G-11)
P.O. Box 5268
Mississippi State, Mississippi 39762
Tel: (601) 325-2224; Fax: (601) 325-1846

Description: The Agricultural and Mechanical College of the State of Mississippi was established in 1878 as a land-grant institution under the provisions of the Morrill Act. Today, Mississippi State University is composed of Colleges in agriculture and home economics, arts and sciences, business and industry, education, engineering, and veterinary medicine. It also has schools in accountancy, architecture, forest resources, and graduate studies as well as summer school and a continuing education department. It is accredited by the Southern Association of Colleges and Schools and by respective professional and educational organizations. The university operates on the semester system with two summer sessions and also offers Army and Air Force ROTC programs. Enrollment includes 11,189 full-time and 2,193 part-time students. A faculty of 761 full-time and 99 part-time gives an undergraduate faculty-student ratio of 1-17. Correspondent credit is allowed: continuing education, cooperative education, and overseas programs are available.

Entrance Requirements: Accredited high school graduation or equivalent; completion of 15 units; score of 18 or over on ACT required; Bachelor's degree from accredited institution and GRE or GMAT required for graduate programs; early admission, early decision, rolling admission and advanced placement plans available.

Costs Per Year: $2,561 tuition; $5,021 out-of-state tuition; $3,000 room and board; $654 student fees.

Collegiate Environment: The grounds of the university comprise about 4,000 acres including farms, pastures, and woodlands, of the

Experiment Station. The campus proper includes more than 700 acres of land largely covered with shade trees. The many university buildings include a library of 849,983 volumes, 6,993 periodicals, 2,064,672 microforms and 9,230 records and tapes. Eight residence halls for women, eight halls for men, and three apartment complexes provide on-campus housing for 2,457 men, 2,222 women and 268 families. Nineteen social fraternities and 11 national sororities have established chapters at the university. Fraternities and sororities provide additional on-campus housing for 363 men and 280 women. Approximately 80% of students applying for admission are accepted, including midyear students. Financial aid is available for economically disadvantaged students. There are 5,289 scholarships offered.

Community Environment: Mississippi State University is situated adjacent to Starkville, a city with a population of 18,458 located in the east-central part of the state. (The county population is approximately 38,375.) Starkville is part of the Golden Triangle Area, a cluster of three communities that includes Starkville, West Point and Columbus. Airlines, railroads, and a bus line serve the community. The city has several churches, a hospital, and a public library. All cultural and recreational advantages of Starkville are available to the university. Outdoor activities abound in the area. The 50,000-acre Noxubee Wildlife Refuge, the Tenn-Tom Waterway, and Mississippi State's nationally recognized golf course are within a 20-minute drive from campus. The university is 30 miles from the Alabama line and 130 miles from the Tennessee border.

MISSISSIPPI UNIVERSITY FOR WOMEN   *(F-12)*
Columbus, Mississippi 39701
Tel: (601) 329-7106; Admissions: (601) 329-7106; Fax: (601) 329-7297

Description: Mississippi University for Women was the first state-supported institution of higher learning to be established in the United States for the education exclusively of women. In 1982, male students were admitted for the first time. The college offers a liberal education with sufficient opportunities in specialized education to prepare students to serve with professional competence in various careers. It operates on the semester system with two summer sessions. Enrollment includes 1,725 full-time and 991 part-time and 750 evening program undergraduates and 304 graduate students. A faculty of 127 full-time and 53 part-time gives a faculty-student ratio of 1:17. The college is accredited by the Southern Association of Colleges and Schools, the National Council for Accreditation of Teacher Education, the National Association of Schools of Music, the National League for Nursing, and the American Speech and Hearing Association. Correspondent credit is allowed; continuing education courses and cooperative education programs are available. Air Force and Army ROTC programs are available.

Entrance Requirements: Accredited high school graduation or equivalent; completion of 13.5 units including 4 English, 3 mathematics, 2.5 social studies; score of 18 or over on ACT required, higher score required for nursing programs; GRE required for graduate programs; mature applicant not meeting all entrance requirements may be admitted as special students; advanced placement, delayed admission, early admission, early decision, rolling admission, and midyear admission plans available.

Costs Per Year: $2,239 state resident tuition and fees; $4,199 nonresident tuition and fees; $2,217 room and board.

Collegiate Environment: The campus of the college is comprised of nearly 110 acres lying within the residential area of Columbus. The college buildings include a library of 233,403 volumes and dormitory facilities for 639 women and men. The college welcomes students from all geographical locations and will accept midyear students. 83% of applicants are accepted. 1,073 scholarships are available and 89% of the students receive some form of financial aid.

Community Environment: Located in the northeastern section of the state, Columbus is on the Tombigbee River near the place where Hernando de Soto crossed on his westward expedition in 1540. The town is graced with more than 100 antebellum homes. The climate is moderate but has 4 definite seasons. The area does have a trading and industrial center. There are excellent air, bus and highway facilities. Local recreation includes YMCA, hunting, skiing, boating, fishing, movies and shopping. Part-time work is available for students.

MISSISSIPPI VALLEY STATE UNIVERSITY   *(F-6)*
P.O. Box 61
Itta Bena, Mississippi 38941
Tel: (601) 254-9041

Description: This state university is accredited by the Southern Association of Colleges and Schools. It was established in 1946 by the Legislature of the State of Mississippi, and was known as the Mississippi Vocational College until 1964. It was created to train teachers for rural and elementary schools and to provide vocational training for black students. The university operates on the semester system and offers one summer session. Enrollment includes 1,965 full-time, 217 part-time undergraduate, and 13 graduate students. A faculty of 112 full-time and 24 part-time gives a faculty-student ratio of 1-21. Air Force and Army ROTC programs are available.

Entrance Requirements: Accredited high school graduation or equivalent; completion of 16 units including 4 English, 3 mathematics, 3 science, 2 1/2 social science, and 1 elective; minimum ACT 15 required; rolling admission and midyear admission plans available.

Costs Per Year: $2,164 state resident tuition; $4,124 nonresident tuition; $2,025 room and board; $100 student fees.

Collegiate Environment: The college is located on 450 acres and includes a library of 122,749 volumes and dormitory facilities for 1,914 students. Financial aid is available for economically disadvantaged students. 96% of students receive some form of financial aid.

Community Environment: This is a rural community with a wet, temperate climate. Bus service provides transportation for the city and adjacent areas. Community services within the immediate area include churches of major denominations and a clinic. Shopping facilities are available within the surrounding communities. There is no part-time employment available for students.

NORTHEAST MISSISSIPPI COMMUNITY COLLEGE
(B-11)
Cunningham Blvd.
Booneville, Mississippi 38829
Tel: (601) 728-7751

Description: The district-governed community college, founded in 1948, operates on the semester system with 2 summer terms and is accredited by the Southern Association of Colleges and Schools. The college offers courses in vocational, preprofessional, and academic areas for both youth and adults in part-time, terminal and transfer programs. Enrollment includes 4,984 men and women full and part-time. A faculty of 120 full-time, 5 part-time gives a faculty-student ratio of 1-19.

Entrance Requirements: Accredited high school graduation or equivalent; open enrollment policy; completion of 16 units including 4 English, 2 mathematics, 2 science, 2 social science; early admission, early decision, delayed admission, advanced placement and rolling admission plans available.

Costs Per Year: $770 tuition for state residents; $1,580 out-of-state residents; $5,724 room and board, $200 student fees.

Collegiate Environment: The college buildings include a library of 29,311 volumes and 3,164 periodicals. Dormitory facilities are available for 320 men and 328 women. About 99% of students applying for admission meet the requirements and are accepted, including midyear students. The community college provides a comprehensive student aid program of work scholarships, loans, grants and scholarships to assist needy students in meeting college expenses, and approximately 70% of the current student body receive some form of financial aid.

Community Environment: The city is located in the northeast corner of Mississippi, 100 miles southeast of Memphis, Tennessee. It has a warm and pleasant climate.

NORTHWEST MISSISSIPPI COMMUNITY COLLEGE
(C-7)
510 N. Panola Street
Senatobia, Mississippi 38668
Tel: (601) 562-3200

Description: The public junior college was established in 1927 and was accredited by the Mississippi Junior College Accrediting Association in 1928 and by the Southern Association of Colleges and Secondary Schools in 1953. Except for the credits in some technical courses, freshman and sophomore credits earned at the junior college may be transferred to any other college or university and applied toward an academic degree. The college operates on a semester system and offers 2 summer terms. Enrollment is 4,000 students. A faculty of 150 gives a faculty-student ratio of 1-27.

Entrance Requirements: Accredited high school graduation or equivalent; transcripts; completion of 15 units including 3 English; ACT or SAT required; rolling admission, midyear admission and advanced placement plans available.

Costs Per Year: $1,000 tuition; $2,000 nonresident; $1,380 room and board; $377 student fees.

Collegiate Environment: The 90-acre campus is located about 37 miles south of Memphis and 62 miles north of Grenada. The library has 23,584 volumes. Four residence halls for women and three for men provide housing for more than 900 students on the Senatobia campus. Approximately 95% of students applying for admission are accepted. About 43% of the recent students graduated in the top half of their high school class, and 20% ranked in the top quarter. 100 scholarships are offered, including 70 athletic. 50% of the current student body receives some form of financial aid. Semesters begin in September and January, and the first summer session begins in June.

Community Environment: Senatobia is the seat of Tate County, lying 40 miles south of Memphis, Tennessee. The area is served by Illinois Central Railroad. The city itself is located off Interstate Highway 55. Nearby is Arkabutla Reservoir and Dam, a well-known recreation facility.

Branch Campuses: NWCC/DeSoto Center/Southhaven, 8700 Northwest Dr., Southhaven, MS 38671, (601) 342-1570; NWCC/DeSoto Center/Olive Branch, 8750 Deerfield Dr., Olive Branch, MS 38654, (601) 895-7600; NWCC/Lafayette-Yalobusha Technical Center, 1310 Belk Dr., Oxford, MS 38655, (601) 236-2023; NWCC/Benton-Marshall Center, Rt. 2 Box 42AA, Ashland, MS 38603, (601) 224-3108.

PEARL RIVER COMMUNITY COLLEGE   (O-8)
Station A
Poplarville, Mississippi 39470
Tel: (601) 795-6801; Admissions: (601) 795-6801 x1214; Fax: (601) 795-1129

Description: The public community college is among the oldest schools of its kind in the South and the pioneer junior college in the state. It was organized as Pearl River County Agricultural High School in 1909 and college work was added in 1921. It offers transfer, general education and terminal programs as well as guidance and community services. The school operates on the early semester system and also offers 2 summer terms. It is accredited by the Southern Association of Colleges and Schools. Enrollment includes 1,944 full-time and 783 part-time students. A faculty of 136 gives a faculty-student ratio of 1-20.

Entrance Requirements: Accredited high school graduation or equivalent; open enrollment policy; completion of 17 units; midyear admission and rolling admission plans available.

Costs Per Year: $920 district/state-resident tuition; $1,826 out-of-state; $1,540 room and board.

Collegiate Environment: The 350-acre campus is located about 40 miles south of Hattiesburg, Mississippi, and 75 miles north of New Orleans, Louisiana. The 22 college buildings include a library of 39,000 volumes, 800 pamphlets, 340 periodicals and 110 sound recordings, and living accommodations for 250 men and 250 women. Almost all students applying for admission are accepted. Scholarships are available and 85% of the students receive some form of financial aid.

Community Environment: Poplarville is located in the southern portion of the state and has a temperate climate. New Orleans may be reached 70 miles southwest via Interstate Highway 59. Poplarville has its own hospital.

RUST COLLEGE   (B-8)
1A Rust Avenue
Holly Springs, Mississippi 38635
Tel: (601) 252-8000; Fax: (601) 252-6107

Description: The private liberal arts college is operated under the auspices of the United Methodist Church with headquarters in Nashville, Tennessee. It confers the degrees of Bachelor of Arts and Bachelor of Science, and is incorporated in Mississippi and governed by a Board of Trustees. The college is accredited by the Mississippi State Department of Education, by the University Senate of the United Methodist Church, and by the Southern Association of Colleges and Schools. The college operates on the semester system and offers one summer term. Enrollment includes 1,055 students. A faculty of 56 full-time and 10 part-time gives a faculty-student ratio of 1-18.

Entrance Requirements: Accredited high school graduation or equivalent with rank in upper 30% of graduating class; completion of 19 units including 4 English, 3 mathematics, 3 science, 3 social science, 6 electives; ACT or SAT required; early admission, early decision, midyear admission and advanced placement plans available. $10 application fee.

Costs Per Year: $4,625 tuition; $2,175 room and board; $552 student fees.

Collegiate Environment: The college is comprised of 26 buildings located on 125 acres, which includes a library of 113,152 volumes and 366 periodicals and dormitory facilities for 372 men and 489 women. The college welcomes students from various geographical locations and will accept midyear students. About 42% of students applying for admission meet the requirements and are accepted. High school graduates with a C average are accepted. 85% of the previous freshman class return to the college for the sophomore year. Scholarships are available and 70% of the full-time students receive some form of financial aid.

Community Environment: A typical antebellum town, Holly Springs grew up during the great cotton boom before the Civil War. The fine old mansions and churches of the town reflect the prosperity of the cotton era. There are shopping areas in nearby Memphis. No part-time employment is available for students.

SOUTHEASTERN BAPTIST COLLEGE   (L-9)
4229 Highway 15 North
Laurel, Mississippi 39440
Tel: (601) 426-6364

Description: This is a private Bible College. It was established in 1948. The school operates on the semester system and offers a summer term. Enrollment includes 36 full-time, 65 part-time, and 65 evening students. A faculty of 8 full-time and 7 part-time gives a faculty-student ratio of 1-7. Correspondent credit is allowed; continuing education courses are available and credit is allowed for certain courses by prior examination.

Entrance Requirements: Accredited high school graduation or equivalent; open enrollment policy; completion of 15 units including 3 English, 1 mathematics, 1 science; early admission, early decision, delayed admission, advanced placement and rolling admission plans available. $15 application fee.

Costs Per Year: $2,040 tuition; $1,800 room and board; $180 student fees.

Collegiate Environment: The college is located on 20 acres with 6 buildings, including a library of 23,304 volumes and dormitory facilities for 114 students. 99% of the students applying for admission are accepted including midyear students. Financial aid is available for economically disadvantaged students.

Community Environment: Laurel's growth from a small village in 1900 to its present metropolitan size has been due to its pine forests and oil development. Lumber represents an important industry, but other firms manufacture clothing, machines, doors, furniture, agricultural implements, distribution transformers, oil well drilling equipment, walk-in refrigerators, condiments and janitorial supplies. There is a complete recreation program in the city, and it is close to resorts and state parks. Railroad, bus and air transportation is available in the immediate area. Laurel is considered the medical center of the surrounding area.

SOUTHWEST MISSISSIPPI JUNIOR COLLEGE   (N-5)
Summit, Mississippi 39666
Tel: (601) 276-2001

Description: The district-governed junior college, founded in 1918 as a small agricultural high school, became a junior college in 1929. It operates on the semester system with 1 summer term and is accredited by the Southern Association of Colleges and Schools. It offers academic, preprofessional and vocational programs for both youth and adults. Enrollment is approximately 1,626 students.

Entrance Requirements: Accredited high school graduation or equivalent; completion of 15 units including 3 English, 2 mathematics, 2 science, 2 social science.

Costs Per Year: $650 tuition; $1,650 additional tuition for out-of-state students; $1,450 board and room.

Collegiate Environment: The college consists of 25 buildings located on 500 acres which include a library of 30,000 volumes and living accomodations for 184 men, 200 women and 6 families. The college welcomes students from various geographical locations and will accept midyear students. Almost all of the students applying for admission are accepted. Approximately 70% of the recent student body graduated in the top half of their high school class, 30% in the top quarter. Almost 70% of the previous freshman class return to the campus for the second year.

Community Environment: Summit is a suburban area near McComb, Mississippi. The city is served by bus and rail. Health services, a library, and churches, are to be found in the neighboring city. There are shopping facilities in the immediate area. Some part-time employment is available. Recreation in the area includes boating, fishing and camping.

TOUGALOO COLLEGE   *(J-6)*
County Line Road
Tougaloo, Mississippi 39174
Tel: (601) 956-4941

Description: The private, historically Black, liberal arts college was founded in 1869 and is affiliated with the United Christian Church and the Christian Church (Disciples of Christ). It is accredited by the Southern Association of Colleges and Schools. The college operates on the semester system and offers majors leading to the Bachelor of Arts and the Bachelor of Science degrees. The college has a cooperative program with Brown University, a term program with American University, and early identification programs with Brown and Boston University medical schools. Enrollment includes 362 men and 769 women with a faculty of 60 full-time and 27 part-time members. Army ROTC is offered.

Entrance Requirements: Accredited high school graduation or equivalent; completion of 16 units including 3 English, 2 mathematics, 2 science, 2 social science; 2 years of natural science and 2 years of language are recommended; non-high school graduates over 18 years of age may be admitted by examination; rolling admission, early decision, early admission and advanced placement plans available.

Costs Per Year: $4,610 tuition; $1,840 board and room; $480 student fees.

Collegiate Environment: The college is located on a former plantation of 500 acres, on the city line of Jackson. The 17 college buildings include a library of 91,251 titles, 400 periodicals, 3,074 audiovisual materials, and 4,799 microforms. The college welcomes students from various geographical locations and will accept midyear students. Financial aid is available for those who meet the requirements.

Community Environment: See Jackson State University.

UNIVERSITY OF MISSISSIPPI   *(C-8)*
University, Mississippi 38677
Tel: (601) 232-7226; Fax: (601) 232-5869

Description: The state-supported university initiated its first year of operation in 1848. The Oxford Main Campus includes: College of Liberal Arts; Schools of Business Administration, Education, Engineering, Pharmacy, Law, Graduate and Accountacny. It also provides a university extension center as well as Army, Navy and Air Force ROTC programs. The University of Mississippi Medical Center located in Jackson, Mississippi, includes: Schools of Medicine, Nursing, Dentistry, and Health Related Professions. The University is accredited by the Southern Association of Colleges and Schools and by respective educational and professional organizations. The university operates on the semester system with 2 summer terms and enroll-

ment of 10,075 students. A full-time faculty of 453 gives a faculty-student ratio of 1-22.

Entrance Requirements: Rolling admissions plan. Apply as early as 1 year, but not later than 20 days prior to registration. Provisional admission at end of 7th semester (1st half senior year) with minimum composite score of 18 on ACT or 840 SAT. By high school graduation must have completed at least 13 1/2 units including 4 in English, 3 in math (algebra I, geometry, algebra II or above), 3 in science (choose from biology, advanced biology, chemistry, advanced chemistry, physics, advanced physics), 2 1/2 units social studies (must include U.S. History and American Government) and 1 unit of required elective that may be chosen from a foreign language or from mathematics above algebra II or from a science course listed above. Early admission with 15 approved units and a 25 composite ACT (1,120 SAT). Transfer students who meet above requirements may transfer at any time with a 2.0 GPA. Those who fail to meet the above requirements must have 24 semester hours of 2.0 work at an regionally accredited college That transfer work must include 6 hours English composition, 3 hours college algebra or higher, 6 semester hours of laboratory science and 9 additional transferrable electives. CLEP and AP credit acceptable as well as limited military experience/coursework based upon the ACE Military Guide. Tutoring available. Developmental and study skills services offered.

Costs Per Year: $2,546 tuition; $5,366 tuition out-of-state students; $1,560 room.

Collegiate Environment: The campus of the university comprises more than 1 square mile and is noted for its natural park-like beauty. The university buildings include a library of 750,000 volumes. Living accommodations for 4,300 single students and 640 married students. Fraternities and sororities provide housing for an additional 1,000 men and women. The Cultural Center includes Rowan Oak, home of William Faulkner; the Kate Skipwith Teaching Museum and the National Centers for Physical Acoustics and the Technological Development of Natural Products. The Center for the Study of Southern Culture provides teaching, study and research related to the American South. The university welcomes students from all geographical locations. 90% of students applying for admission who meet the requirements are accepted, including midyear students, and 58% of the current student body receives some form of financial assistance. About 78% of the previous freshman class returned to the campus for the sophomore year.

Community Environment: University is a part of Oxford. Located in a cotton, corn and cattle region, Oxford is the seat of Lafayette County. Annual average temperature is 80 degrees in July and 40 degrees in January, with average rainfall 54.55 inches. Total snowfall yearly averages 1.2 inches. Bus service and shuttle service from Memphis Airport are available to the city. Area has 3 recreational parks, swimming pools, movie theatres, bowling and golf facilities. Oxford is near Holly Springs National Forest which encompasses over 90,000 acres and numerous lakes. The lakes provide excellent hunting, swimming, boating and vacation facilities.

UNIVERSITY OF MISSISSIPPI - MEDICAL CENTER   *(J-6)*
2500 North State Street
Jackson, Mississippi 39216
Tel: (601) 984-1000; Fax: (601) 984-1079

Description: The University of Mississippi Medical Center unites the interrelated activities of education in the health sciences on one metropolitan campus. Its programs include training for physicians, dentists, nurses, and allied members of the health team, graduate study in the basic medical sciences, and the delivery of medical care in the teaching hospitals and clinics. All programs and services are available to every qualified person regardless of race, color, sex, creed, national origin, age, veteran status, marital status or disability. The Medical Center was established in 1955 and both the quarter and semester systems are employed. The schools of the medical center are accredited by the Southern Association of Schools and Colleges and by appropriate professional and educational organizations. Enrollment is 1,541 full-time and 90 part-time students. A faculty of 550 gives a faculty-student ratio of 1-3.

Entrance Requirements: Requirements differ for all programs.

Costs Per Year: $6,600 state-resident tuition in medicine, and $4,400 dentistry; $12,600 nonresident in medicine and $10,400 in dentistry; fees and tuitions for other schools vary according to the program; $1,996 undergraduate state-resident fee; $2,459 undergraduate nonresident fee.

Collegiate Environment: The Medical Center occupies a 158-acre tract of University-owned land in the heart of Jackson. The original Center has grown to a major health sciences center in just 3 decades. In addition to academic, research and patient care areas, other campus facilities include student apartments and a women's residence that provide housing for 227 students. The library contains more than 142,220 volumes, and subscribes to 2,234 periodicals. The Mississippi Methodist Rehabilitation Center and the McBryde Rehabilitation Center for the Blind adjoin the Medical Center; the Veterans Administration Medical Center is also on the Medical Center campus. A new dental school and major classroom addition opened in 1977; a clinical sciences expansion of the medical school was occupied in 1978; and a new library/learning resources center and a new acute services wing were completed in 1982. A laboratory research center opened in 1993.

Community Environment: See Jackson State University.

UNIVERSITY OF SOUTHERN MISSISSIPPI *(N-9)*
Box 5166
Hattiesburg, Mississippi 39406
Tel: (601) 266-5000; Admissions: (601) 266-5000; Fax: (601) 266-5148

Description: Since its opening in 1912 as the Mississippi Normal College, this institution has existed under 4 names. In 1924 the name was changed to State Teachers College and in 1940, it became Mississippi Southern College. The present name was adopted in 1962 and today the university is composed of the College of The Arts, the College of Business Administration, the College of Education and Psychology, the College of Health and Human Sciences, the College of Liberal Arts, the College of Science and Technology, the Honors College, the Division of Lifelong Learning. The university also provides an Army and Air Force ROTC program and is accredited by the Southern Association of Colleges and Schools. It operates on the semester system with 1 summer session. Enrollment includes 9,579 full-time and 2,008 part-time undergraduates and 2,131 graduate students. A faculty of 577 provides a faculty-student ratio of 1-20. Correspondent credit is allowed; continuing education courses are offered as well as cooperative education programs.

Entrance Requirements: Accredited high school graduation or equivalent; completion of 15.5 units including 4 English, 3 math, 3 science, 3 social science and 2 elective; score of 18 or over on ACT or 720 combined SAT required; GRE required for graduate programs; applicants not seeking degrees may be admitted as special students; early admission, rolling admission, midyear admission and advanced placement plans available; $25 application fee for international students.

Costs Per Year: $2,400 tuition; $4,400 out-of-state; $1,200 room and board.

Collegiate Environment: There are more than 170 permanent buildings on the campus, including a library of 1,500,000 volumes and 500 periodicals. Dormitory accommodations are available for 3,370 students. 15 social fraternities and 12 social sororities are located at the campus as well as numerous other student organizations. 73% of students applying for admission meet the requirements and are accepted. Scholarships are available and 75% of the undergraduates receive some form of financial aid.

Community Environment: Primarily a thriving industrial city, Hattiesburg produces chemicals, clothing, concrete and corrugated containers, and has food processing plants, lumber mills and an oil refinery. The city is also a well-rounded community with a splendid balance among agriculture, commerce and industry. There are a public library and 2 hospitals located within the city limits. Each year, the Hattiesburg Concert Association brings concerts, symphonies and choral groups to the city. A full-time recreation department is operated, and both indoor and outdoor programs continue year-round. Passenger bus, rail and air service is accessible. There is good hunting and fishing in the general area.

Branch Campuses: Gulf Coast Campus, Long Beach, MS; University Campus, Jackson, MS.

WESLEY COLLEGE *(K-7)*
P. O. Box 70
Florence, Mississippi 39073
Tel: (601) 845-2265; (800) 748-9972; Fax: (601) 845-2266

Description: The privately supported coeducational Bible and liberal arts college is affiliated with the Congregational Methodist Church. It is accredited by the American Association of Bible Colleges. Continuing education courses are offered. It operates on the semester system. Enrollment includes 57 men and 27 women. A faculty of 8 full-time and 9 part-time gives a faculty-student ratio of 1:6.

Entrance Requirements: Accredited high school graduation or equivalent; open enrollment policy; minimum score of ACT 17 or SAT 350V, 350M required; early decision, rolling admission, early admission, delayed admission and advanced placement plans available. $20 applications fee.

Costs Per Year: $1,800 tuition; $2,250 room and board; $200 student fees.

Collegiate Environment: The college has a library of 23,290 volumes and 84 current periodicals. Dormitory facilities are provided for 40 men and 40 women, and 13 mobile homes are provided for married couples. Financial assistance is available for economically handicapped students. The college accepts midyear students.

Community Environment: Small, rural community located not too far from Jackson, Mississippi's capital city.

WILLIAM CAREY COLLEGE *(N-9)*
Tuscan Avenue
Hattiesburg, Mississippi 39401
Tel: (601) 582-5051; (800) 962-5991; Fax: (601) 582-6454

Description: The private college was established in 1906 and is affiliated with the Southern Baptist Convention. It operated as a women's college until 1953 when it became coeducational. The college is accredited by the Southern Association of Colleges and Schools. It operates on the trimester system and offers two summer sessions. Enrollment includes 1,885 full-time and 408 part-time undergraduate students, and 254 graduate students. A faculty of 91 full-time and 74 part-time gives a faculty-student ratio of 1-16. Continuing education courses are offered; credit is allowed for certain courses by prior examination.

Entrance Requirements: Accredited high school graduation; completion of 16 units; ACT minimum 15 recommended (higher ACT score recommended for various majors); SAT may be substituted; applicants who rank in lower half of graduating class will be considered in relation to test scores; $10 application fee; early admission, advanced placement, delayed admission, early decision and rolling admission plans available.

Costs Per Year: $5,340 tuition; $2,235-$2,460 room and board.

Collegiate Environment: The college is composed of 3 campuses. The parent campus of 64 wooded acres is located in Hattiesburg, where over 1,039 resident and commuter students enjoy full academic, social, residential and administrative facilities. A second campus exists in New Orleans where the Carey School of Nursing is affiliated with Southern Baptist Hospital. A third campus on the Mississippi Gulf Coast at Gulfport was opened in 1976. Approximately 570 students study on the Gulf Coast campus in facilities geared primarily for commuters. A graduate program enrolls over 212 involves students studying in Hattiesburg and Gulfport as well as in other strategic temporary locations. The library holdings include 136,625 volumes. Dormitory facilities are provided on the Hattiesburg and Gulfport campuses. About 90% of the applicants meet the requirements and are accepted, including midyear students. Financial aid is available. There are 130 scholarships offered.

Community Environment: See University of Southern Mississippi.

Branch Campuses: Gulfport, MS; New Orleans, LA.

WOOD JUNIOR COLLEGE *(F-9)*
P.O. Box 289
Mathiston, Mississippi 39752
Tel: (601) 263-8128; Admissions: (601) 263-5352; Fax: (601) 263-4964

Description: The private liberal arts college is related to the Methodist Church through its Board of Global Ministries. It was established in 1886 and is accredited by the Southern Association of Colleges and Schools. It is a member of the University Senate of the Methodist Church. The college operates on a calendar system of 10 three and a half week terms with summer sessions. Enrollment is 1,060 students. A faculty of 75 gives a faculty-student ratio of 1-20. Credit is allowed for certain courses by prior examination.

Entrance Requirements: Accredited high school graduation or equivalent; completion of 15 units including 4 English, 3 mathematics, 1 foreign language, 3 science, 2 social science; ACT required for placement; early decision and advanced placement plans available; $15 application fee.

Costs Per Year: $3,000 tuition; $2,200 board and room.

Collegiate Environment: The college is comprised of 28 buildings located on 400 acres and includes a library of 32,000 volumes and living accommodations for 86 men and 96 women. Almost all students applying for admission, including midyear students, are accepted. Students of other religious faiths are welcome as well as those from other geographical locations. 345 scholarships are available and 80% of the current student body receives some form of financial aid.

Community Environment: Mathiston is a small rural town with accessible bus and air transportation and a population of 700. The city has 2 private hospitals, 2 shopping centers, theaters, and claims fine fishing available nearby.

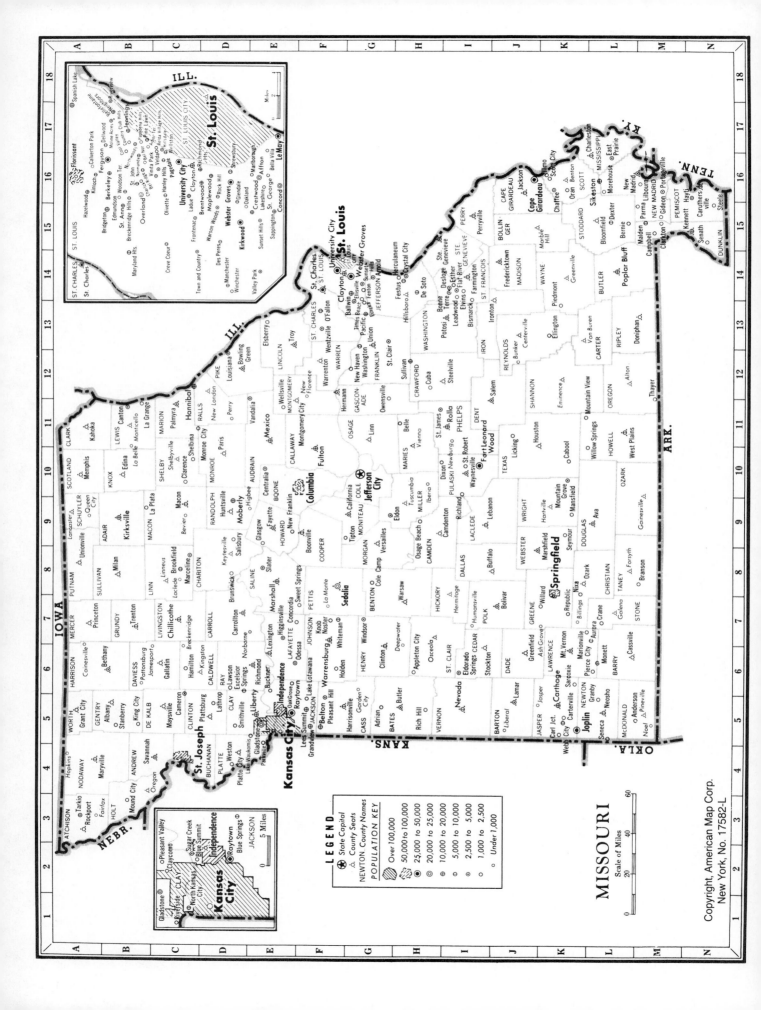

MISSOURI

Scale of Miles

LEGEND

⊛ State Capital
◉ County Seats
NEWTON. County Names

POPULATION KEY
- Over 100,000
- 50,000 to 100,000
- 25,000 to 50,000
- 20,000 to 25,000
- 10,000 to 20,000
- 5,000 to 10,000
- 2,500 to 5,000
- 1,000 to 2,500
- Under 1,000

MISSOURI

ASSEMBLIES OF GOD THEOLOGICAL SEMINARY *(K-8)*
1445 Boonville Avenue
Springfield, Missouri 65802
Tel: (417) 862-3344; (800) 467-2487; Fax: (417) 862-3214

Description: This private, professional graduate school is supported by the General Council of the Assemblies of God and was officially opened in September 1973. It is accredited by The Association of Theological Schools in the United States and Canada and The North Central Association of Colleges and Schools. It is approved by the Department of Justice, Immigration and Naturalization Service for the training of foreign students. It has also been approved for veteran's training and been authorized to grant scholastic degrees by the appropriate agencies of the State of Missouri. Enrollment includes 372 students (79% men, 21% women). A faculty of 14 full-time and 5 part-time gives a faculty-student ratio of 1-13. The seminary offers a Master of Arts in Theological Studies, Counseling, Missiology, Christian Education, Christian Ministries, and a Master of Divinity. It operates on a 4-4-1-1 semester system and offers three summer sessions.

Entrance Requirements: Baccalaureate degree or equivalent from an acceptable four-year college; basic courses in psychology, philosophy and social science; 2.5 GPA at undergraduate level required; rolling admission; $35 application fee.

Costs Per Year: $4,800 tuition.

Collegiate Environment: The library contains 68,981 hard bound volumes, 500 periodicals, 58,825 microforms and 3,593 audiovisual materials. The seminary participates in Southwest Missouri Academic Libraries Cooperative, A/G Library Consortium, the and Southwest Missouri Library Network, which makes 1.5 million volumes available to students. Financial aid is available.

Community Environment: See Southwest Missouri State University.

AVILA COLLEGE *(E-5)*
11901 Wornall Road
Kansas City, Missouri 64145
Tel: (816) 942-8400; Fax: (816) 942-3362

Description: The privately supported, Roman Catholic liberal arts college was established in 1916 by the Sisters of St. Joseph of Carondelet and operated as a two-year college until 1940, when it became a four-year liberal arts college. In the fall of 1969, the college became coeducational. It is accredited by the North Central Association of Colleges and Schools. Professional accreditations include the Committee on Allied Health Education and Accreditation, the Council on Social Work Education, and the National League for Nursing. 36 undergraduate and 3 graduate areas of study are offered. The college operates on the semester system and offers two summer sessions. Enrollment includes 678 full-time and 490 part-time undergraduate, and 226 graduate students. A faculty of 60 full-time and 75 part-time gives a faculty-student ratio of 13:1.

Entrance Requirements: Accredited high school graduation or equivalent with GPA of 2.5; recommended completion of 16 units including 4 English, 3 mathematics, 2-4 foreign language, 2-3 science, 2 social science; ACT 19 or SAT verbal 450, math 450 required; early admission and rolling admission plans available; no application fee prior to June 30, $20 thereafter.

Costs Per Year: $9,600 tuition; $4,200 room and board; $100 student fees.

Collegiate Environment: The college is comprised of nine buildings located on 50 acres. Dormitories accommodate 230 students. The college library contains nearly 80,000 volumes and 550 periodicals. 80% of the students applying for admission are accepted. The college welcomes students from other geographical locations and will accept midyear students. 87% of the previous freshman class returned to the

college for the sophomore year. Financial aid is available and 85% of the full-time student body receive some form of financial assistance.

Community Environment: See University of Missouri-Kansas City.

BAPTIST BIBLE COLLEGE *(K-8)*
628 E. Kearney
Springfield, Missouri 65803
Tel: (417) 869-9811

Description: This privately supported Baptist Bible college was established in 1950. The Bible college operates on the semester system and offers five summer terms. It provides instruction in four areas, including missions, music, secretarial teaching, and preaching. It is accredited by the American Association of Bible Colleges, and grants the Certificate and Bachelor degrees. Enrollment includes 759 full-time and 89 part-time students. A faculty of 28 full-time and 16 part-time members provides a faculty-student ratio of 1-23.

Entrance Requirements: High school graduation or equivalent; must possess genuine calling to service of Christian Church; early admission, early decision, rolling admission and delayed admission plans available; Baptist Bible Fellowship Pastor's Recommendation.

Costs Per Year: $1,888-$2,152 tuition; $2,812 room and board; $200 student fees; additional expenses.

Collegiate Environment: The college is located on 35 acres and contains 16 buildings that include a library of 64,241 volumes and living accommodations for 378 men, 414 women, and 162 families. Approximately 95% of students applying for admission are accepted, including midyear students. The college grants a Certificate for 3 years study and the Bachelor degree for 4 years study. Nearly 83% of the previous freshman class returned to the college for a second year of studies.

Community Environment: See Southwest Missouri State University.

CALVARY BIBLE COLLEGE *(E-5)*
Kansas City, Missouri 64147-1341
Tel: (816) 322-0110; (800) 326-3960; Admissions: (816) 322-3960; Fax: (816) 331-4474

Description: The privately supported, independent Bible college is accredited by the Accrediting Association of Bible Colleges and operates on the 4-4-1 semester system with one summer session. It enrolls approximately 125 men and 122 women. A faculty of 8 full-time and 17 part-time gives a faculty-student ratio 1-10. Calvary offers choir, inter-collegiate and intra-mural athletics. The college grants the Associate and Bachelor degree.

Entrance Requirements: Accredited high school graduation or equivalent; ACT or SAT required. Special admission plans: early decision, midyear admission, rolling admission, advanced placement. Character references required. $25 application fee.

Costs Per Year: $3,960 tuition; $2,830 room and board, $170 student fees.

Collegiate Environment: The Bible college occupies 55 acres located in the metropolitan area of Kansas City. The ten college buildings include a library of 57,000 volumes and dormitory facilities for 252 men and 252 women. Students from other geographical locations are welcome as well as midyear students. Financial aid is available and 62% of the current student body receives some form of assistance.

Community Environment: See University of Missouri - Kansas City

CENTRAL BIBLE COLLEGE   (K-8)
3000 N. Grant Street
Springfield, Missouri 65803
Tel: (417) 833-2551; (800) 358-3092; Fax: (417) 833-5141

Description: The Bible college was established in 1922 by the General Council of the Assemblies of God. It is accredited by the American Association of Bible Colleges. The school grants the Diploma and Associate and Bachelor degrees. It operates on the semester system and offers three summer sessions. Enrollment includes 921 full-time and 70 part-time students. A faculty of 36 full-time and 20 part-time provides a faculty-student ratio of 1-24.

Entrance Requirements: Accredited high school graduation or equivalent; ACT and entrance exam required; non-high school graduates may be admitted with GED certification; must possess genuine calling to service of Christian Church; early admission, early decision, rolling admission, midyear admission and advanced placement plans available; $75 application fee.

Costs Per Year: $3,900 tuition; $2,930 room and board; $300 student fees.

Collegiate Environment: The Bible college occupies 108 acres that are located near the summit of the Ozark Mountains plateau. Living accommodations are available for 310 men, 250 women, and 85 married students. The library contains more than 115,000 books, periodicals, and microforms as well as a song file and visual aid file. 93% of applicants are accepted. 60 scholarships are available and 75% of the current students receive some form of financial aid. Nearly 60% of the previous freshman class returned to the Bible college for the second year of studies.

Community Environment: See Southwest Missouri State University.

CENTRAL METHODIST COLLEGE   (E-9)
411 CMC Square
Fayette, Missouri 65248
Tel: (816) 248-3391

Description: The private liberal arts college was established in 1854 and in 1939 was the one educational institution of the Methodist Church in Missouri. The college operates on the semester system and offers a summer session. It is accredited by the North Central Association of Colleges and Schools. Professional accreditations include the National Association of Schools of Music, the National Council for the Accreditation of Teacher Education, the Missouri Department of Elementary and Secondary Education, the University Senate in the United Methodist Church, the Missouri State Board of Nursing, and the National Association of Intercollegiate Athletics. The college grants the Associate and Bachelor degrees. Enrollment includes 962 full-time and 169 part-time students. A faculty of 73 full-time and provides a faculty-student ratio of 1-15.

Entrance Requirements: Accredited high school graduation or equivalent with rank in upper 40% of graduating class; completion of 16 units including 4 English, 3 mathematics, 2 science, 2 social studies, and 2 humanities; ACT required; applicants not meeting all requirements may be considered for admission with successful completion of examinations; early admission, rolling admission, and midyear admission programs available; $10 application fee.

Costs Per Year: $9,160 tuition; $3,600 room and board; $270 student fees.

Collegiate Environment: The college is located at Fayette, midway between Kansas City and St. Louis, Missouri. The college buildings include a library of 89,945 titles, 257 periodicals, 51,480 microforms and 3,000 audiovisual materials. There are living accommodations for 800 students and 32 married students. 95% of the applicants are accepted. Classes begin in September and January and midyear students are accepted. Scholarships are available and 95% of students receive some form of financial aid.

Community Environment: Fayette (population 3,520) is the county seat of Howard County and is in an area that is noted for the production of purebred cattle. Both Kansas City and St. Louis are about a two-hour drive away. The cultural facilities of both large cities are available and add charm to the community.

Branch Campuses: Mineral Area College, Flat River, MO.

CENTRAL MISSOURI STATE UNIVERSITY   (F-7)
223 Humphreys
Warrensburg, Missouri 64093
Tel: (816) 543-4111; Admissions: (816) 543-4677; Fax: (816) 543-8517

Description: This publicly supported state university was founded as the second State Normal School for the Second Normal District in 1871. It was accredited as a four-year teachers college in 1915 and adopted its present name in 1972. It is accredited by the North Central Association of Colleges and Schools. The university offers 150 academic areas of study, a cooperative arrangement in engineering with several institutions, a freshman program for the educationally disadvantaged, and intramural and intercollegiate athletics. The university operates on the semester system and offers three summer sessions. Enrollment includes 9,350 undergraduate and 1,455 graduate students; 5,046 are men, 5,759 are female. A faculty of 443 full-time and 80 part-time gives an overall faculty-student ratio of 1-18. An Army ROTC program is available.

Entrance Requirements: High school graduation with rank in upper 2/3 of class; ACT required for entering freshmen and used for academic advisement purposes; early admission, early decision, rolling admission, midyear admission, and advanced placement plans available.

Costs Per Year: $2,310 ($77 per credit hour) state resident tuition; $4,620 ($154 per credit hour) nonresident tuition; $3,288 room and board.

Collegiate Environment: The university owns a total of 1,050 acres of land which includes an airport, a recreational park, and the College Farm. The 70 university buildings include a library of over 805,263 titles, 2,842 periodicals and 1,229,137 microforms. Living accommodations are available for 4,308 men and women, and 205 families. Several social fraternities and sororities are located on the campus, as well as numerous other student organizations. 87% of applicants are accepted from diverse geographical locations as well as midyear students. Financial aid is available, and 60% of the current student body receives some form of assistance. 8.6% of the recent senior class continued on to graduate school.

Community Environment: Located 50 miles southeast of Kansas City, Warrensburg (population 15,000) is one of the oldest cities in the western prairie area. The Pacific Railroad, which was completed as far as Warrensburg in 1864, was important to the town's growth. The town is close to fine fishing and hunting. Trains and buses are convenient. Part-time employment is available. Some private homes are available for housing.

COLLEGE OF THE OZARKS   (M-8)
Point Lookout, Missouri 65726
Tel: (417) 334-6411; (800) 222-0525

Description: College of the Ozarks is a private, four-year liberal arts college founded in 1906 for the purpose of providing "the advantages of a Christian education for the youth of both sexes, especially those found worthy but who are without sufficient means to procure such training." It is accredited by the North Central Association of Colleges and Schools. Each full-time student works at one of 80 campus jobs or industries to pay in part for his or her cost of education. The remaining portion of each student's expenses is made up through scholarships provided by gifts and contributions from donors who believe in and support the programs and policies of the college. While the college has evolved through secondary and junior college stages to the present liberal arts institution, the fundamental aims and objectives have remained the same: five-fold mission of academic, vocational, spiritual, patriotic, and cultural growth. The college also maintains an exchange program with Christelijke Hogeschool Noord-Nederland, a Christian college in Leeuwarden, Netherlands. The college operates on the semester system. Enrollment includes 1,264 full-time and 263 part-time students. A faculty of 97 full-time and 26 part-time gives a faculty-student ratio of 1-15.

Entrance Requirements: Accredited high school graduation or GED certificate; admission is on a comparative basis, taking into consideration courses taken, grades earned, test scores, rank in class and financial need; ACT or SAT required; early admission, early decision, midyear admission, rolling admission, and advanced placement plans available.

Costs Per Year: No tuition for full-time students living on campus, instead, each student is required to work 15 hours weekly during sessions and two 40-hour work weeks; $85 per semester hour part-time students; $1,900 room and board per year, students may apply for a summer work program in which they work 40 hours a week for twelve weeks to pay for their room and board; $100 activity fee per year.

Collegiate Environment: The campus has about 960 acres; adjacent lands include 1,200 acres of range land for cattle and farm land for crops. The library contains 90,000 volumes and dormitory facilities are available for 1,031 students. 15% of applicants are accepted.

Community Environment: Point Lookout is a rural area near Branson, 38 miles south of Springfield (see Southwest Missouri State University). Bus service is available and air travel is a little more than 60 minutes away. Shopping areas, a library, and churches of major denominations are part of the community. A great deal of part-time employment is available especially during the April-October tourist season. All recreational facilities are available in the summer resort area.

COLUMBIA COLLEGE   *(F-10)*
1001 Rogers
Columbia, Missouri 65216
Tel: (314) 875-7352; (800) 231-2391 x7352; Admissions: (314) 875-7352

Description: The privately supported college was established in 1851 by Christian Church (Disciples of Christ) as the first college for women west of the Mississippi River to be chartered by a State Legislature. The college is a coeducational comprehensive institution offering career oriented academic programs, strongly centered in the liberal arts, and is accredited by the North Central Association of Colleges and Schools. The school operates on the semester system with one summer session. Enrollment includes 656 full-time, 161 part-time and 1,148 evening students. A faculty of 47 full-time and 22 part-time gives a faculty-student ratio of 1-15.

Entrance Requirements: Accredited high school graduation or equivalent; completion of 15 units; ACT required; early admission, early decision, rolling admission, deferred admission and advanced placement plans available; application fee $25.

Costs Per Year: $8,546 tuition; $3,830 room and board.

Collegiate Environment: The college is located in Columbia, halfway between St. Louis and Kansas City. The college buildings contain a library of 70,000 volumes and dormitory facilities for 325 students. 88% of students applying for admission are accepted. The college welcomes students from other geographical locations and will accept midyear students. Financial aid is available for students and 60% of the student body receives some form of financial assistance.

Community Environment: See University of Missouri - Columbia

CONCEPTION SEMINARY COLLEGE   *(B-4)*
P.O. Box 502
Conception, Missouri 64433-0502
Tel: (816) 944-2218; Fax: (816) 944-2800

Description: The privately supported Roman Catholic seminary college for men was established in 1883 by the Benedictine Monks of Conception Abbey. Enrollment is limited to candidates preparing for the priesthood, both religious and diocesan, and 88 men are enrolled. There are 28 faculty members, which gives a faculty-student ratio of 1-3. The seminary operates on the semester system and is accredited by the North Central Association of Colleges and Schools. The school features a liberal arts curriculum.

Entrance Requirements: Accredited high school graduation or equivalent with "C" average and rank in upper 70% of graduating class; completion of 16 units; early decision, rolling admission, delayed admission and advanced placement programs available. Two recommendations and Sacramental certificates.

Costs Per Year: $6,212 tuition; $2,974 room and board; $130 student fees.

Collegiate Environment: The buildings of the seminary are located on a 30-acre campus which is part of a 720-acre tract belonging to Conception Abbey. This land contains the farm and monastic workshops of the Abbey whose production serves the material needs of both the Abbey and the seminary. Dormitory facilities are provided for 150 men and the library contains 91,383 volumes. 90% of those who apply are accepted. The seminary welcomes students from all geographical locations and will accept midyear transfer students. Scholarships are available and 100% of the student body receives financial aid.

Community Environment: Conception is located in northwest Missouri, 85 miles north of Kansas City. The Abbey contains a collection of rare manuscripts dating back to the 10th century. See also Missouri Western College for information about St. Joseph, the nearest large city.

CONCORDIA SEMINARY   *(F-14)*
801 DeMun Avenue
St. Louis, Missouri 63105
Tel: (314) 721-5934

Description: This privately supported graduate seminary is owned and operated by the Lutheran Church-Missouri Synod. It was founded in 1839 and is accredited by the Association of Theological Schools and by the North Central Association of Colleges and Schools. The seminary provides a program to train parish ministers, chaplains, and mission workers. It operates on the quarter system and offers two summer terms. Enrollment is 410 students in the seminary and 105 students in the graduate school. A faculty of 34 gives a faculty-student ratio of 1-13. Religious subjects are required. The seminary's school of graduate studies awards the Master of Arts, Master of Sacred Theology and Doctor of Theology.

Entrance Requirements: Bachelor's degree or equivalent; minimum C average and background of preseminary studies; GRE and entrance exam required; applicants not in doctrinal fellowship may enroll in the school of graduate studies; students preparing themselves for the ministry of the Lutheran Church-Missouri Synod must request a special set of application blanks from the Office of Admissions and Ministerial Recruitment; $40 application fee.

Costs Per Year: $5,040 tuition and fees; $3,015 room and board; $800 books and supplies; $1,200 personal expenses.

Collegiate Environment: The seminary occupies a beautiful 72-acre campus in the suburban Clayton area of St. Louis. Living accomodations are available for 190 men and 110 familes. The library contains 205,000 volumes. The seminary granted 110 Master of Divinity, 4 Master of Arts, 6 Master in Sacred Theology, and 4 Doctor of Theology degrees to its most recent class. Financial aid is available.

Community Environment: See Washington University.

COTTEY COLLEGE   *(I-5)*
1000 W. Austin
Nevada, Missouri 64772
Tel: (417) 667-8181; Fax: (417) 667-8103

Description: The privately supported, liberal arts junior college for women is accredited by the North Central Association of Colleges and Schools. The music department is also accredited by the National Association of Schools of Music. The College was founded in 1884 and given to the P.E.O. Sisterhood, a philanthropic educational organization in 1927. Cottey is the only college in the nation owned and supported by women for women. The college grants the Associate of Arts and Associate of Science degrees. It offers extensive music and intramural athletic programs. The school operates on the semester system. Enrollment includes 361 full-time and 9 part-time students. A faculty of 34 full-time and 6 part-time gives a faculty-student ratio of 1-11.

Entrance Requirements: Accredited high school graduation with rank in upper half of graduating class; high school equivalency diploma accepted; SAT or ACT required; rolling admission, advanced placement, early admission and midyear admission plans available; $20 application fee.

Costs Per Year: $6,500 includes tuition, music and laboratory fees, and health services; $3,400 for room and board; $100 student activity fee.

Collegiate Environment: The campus encompasses 53 acres and consists of 13 buildings which includes a library of 41,500 volumes and housing for 370 women. The college admits women regardless of race, creed, or national origin and welcomes students from diverse geographical locations as well as mid-year and transfer students. About 82% of students applying for admission are accepted. Financial assistance is available, and 94% of the current student body receives some form of financial aid.

Community Environment: Located 100 miles south of Kansas City, 60 miles north of Joplin, and 90 miles north of Springfield, Nevada has a population of 10,000 and is the county seat of Vernon County. Although historically an agricultural community, Nevada has a diverse economic base. The Jefferson Bus Lines connect Nevada to the International Airport in Kansas City and the municipal airport in Joplin. The community facilities include 27 churches, a number of civic, fraternal, and veteran's organizations, a municipal hospital, and a community center. Part-time employment for students is available. Recreational activities are hunting, fishing, golf, and bowling. The Chamber of Commerce holds a number of special events during the year.

COVENANT THEOLOGICAL SEMINARY   *(F-14)*
12330 Conway Road
St. Louis, Missouri 63141
Tel: (314) 434-4044; (800) 264-8064; Admissions: (314) 434-4044;
Fax: (314) 434-4819

Description: This privately supported graduate seminary is the official seminary of the Presbyterian Church in America. It is accredited by the North Central Association of Colleges and Schools and the Association of Theological Schools. Its purpose is the preparation of qualified candidates for the gospel ministry at home and on foreign mission fields. The seminary enrolls 722 students and welcomes those from other religious denominations. Enrollment includes 406 full-time, 166 full-time extension, 50 part-time and 100 evening graduate students. A faculty of 14 full-time and 11 part-time provides a faculty-student ratio of 1-16. The school grants the Master and Doctorate degrees. It employs the 4-1-4 semester system with three summer sessions.

Entrance Requirements: Bachelor's degree or equivalent; recommended liberal arts curriculum to include English, philosophy, Bible, history, foreign language, natural science, and social science; delayed admission and rolling admission plans available; $25 application fee.

Costs Per Year: $5,632 tuition; $1,740 room; $80 student fees; $450 approximate additional expenses.

Collegiate Environment: The seminary is located on 21 acres with 14 buildings that include a library of 57,000 volumes and dormitory facilities for 60 students. On-campus apartments for married students with children are available. 80% of applicants are accepted. About 70% of the previous entering class returned to the seminary for the second year of studies. Financial aid is available. Semesters begin in August and January.

Community Environment: See Washington University.

CROWDER COLLEGE   *(L-5)*
601 La Clede
Neosho, Missouri 64850
Tel: (417) 451-3223; Fax: (417) 451-4280

Description: The publicly supported two-year comprehensive community college serves the Junior College District of Newton and McDonald Counties. Established in 1964 and accredited by the North Central Association of Colleges and Schools, it offers programs in transfer, general, career, and continuing education. It operates on the early semester system with 3 summer sessions and enrolls 516 men, 468 women full-time, 356 men, and 555 women part-time. The faculty consists of 65 full-time and 80 part-time members. The school offers band, choir, intercollegiate baseball, basketball, golf, wrestling and cooperative education programs (alternating work and class periods) in business and construction technology.

Entrance Requirements: Open enrollment policy; accredited high school graduation or equivalent; Missouri College Testing required; applicants may substitute ACT or SAT; early admission, midyear admission, rolling admission, and advanced placement plans available. $25 application fee.

Costs Per Year: $990 district resident; $1,340 out-of-district resident; $2,090 out-of-state resident; $2,500 room and board; $550 approximate additional expenses.

Collegiate Environment: The college is located in the heart of an extensive educational and industrial complex on the site of the former military installation, Camp Crowder. The 600-acre campus includes a library of 35,000 volumes and living accommodations for 141 men, and 101 women. All students who meet the requirements are accepted, including midyear students. Financial aid is available, and 80% of the current student body receives some form of aid. 60% of last year's freshman class returned for sophomore year.

Community Environment: Neosho (population 10,000) is the birthplace of Thomas Hart Benton, 18 miles from Joplin. All forms of commercial transportation are available. Churches of most of the major denominations, two libraries, a museum, two hospitals and numerous civic and fraternal organizations are represented. Part time jobs are available in Neosho and the two county districts. Neosho provides the area with a full time recreation director and planned activities for the community. The Government Fish Hatchery is nearby.

CULVER-STOCKTON COLLEGE   *(B-11)*
College Hill - Henderson Hall
Canton, Missouri 63435
Tel: (314) 288-5221; (800) 537-1883; Fax: (314) 288-3984

Description: The privately supported college was founded originally as Christian University in 1853. The college is associated with the Christian Church (Disciples of Christ) and provides a broad liberal arts education supplemented by preprofessional and vocational preparation. The college is accredited by the North Central Association of Colleges and Schools. It operates on the semester system and offers one summer session. Enrollment is 936 full-time and 121 part-time students. It has a faculty of 55 full-time and 18 part-time, giving a faculty-student ratio of 1-16. The school offers study abroad through the Freedom Studies Program. The college also offers preparation for several State teacher certifications.

Entrance Requirements: Accredited high school graduation or equivalent with "C" average; top 50% of high school class required for admission; ACT or SAT required; rolling admission, midyear admission and advanced placement plans available.

Costs Per Year: $8,000 tuition; $3,700 room and board; $400 books; $1,700 approximate additional expenses.

Collegiate Environment: The college is located in the town of Canton, 20 miles north of Quincy, Illinois, and 30 miles south of Keokuk, Iowa. The 17 college buildings include a library of 135,924 volumes, 566 periodicals, 4,936 microforms and 4,165 audiovisual materials. Residence halls for 602 students are available. The college welcomes students from other geographical locations and will accept midyear students.

Community Environment: Canton (population 2,623) is situated on the Mississippi River, and is the site of the U.S. Lock and Dam No. 20, which is one of the series of navigation dams built between Minneapolis and St. Louis. Libraries, museums, many churches, and good shopping facilities all provide service to the community. Part-time employment is available. A state park is nearby for recreational and outdoor play. The college homecoming is a community affair.

DEVRY INSTITUTE OF TECHNOLOGY   *(E-5)*
11224 Holmes Road
Kansas City, Missouri 64131
Tel: (816) 941-0430; (800) 821-3766; Admissions: (816) 941-2810;
Fax: (816) 941-0896

Description: The school is a private coeducational college offering programs in Electronic Engineering Technology, Accounting, Computer Information Systems, and Business Operations. Programs are developed and updated regularly with input form business and industry leaders. The Kansas City campus was established in 1931 and is accredited by the Commission on Institutions of Higher Education of the North Central Association of Colleges and Schools. It operates on the semester system, has one summer session, and grants associate and bachelor's degrees. Enrollment includes 1,211 men and 277 women full-time, and 314 men and 124 women part-time. A faculty of 62 full-time and 9 part-time gives a faculty-student ratio of 1-29.

Entrance Requirements: High school diploma or GED certification; minimum of 17 years of age; must pass DeVry entrance examination or submit acceptable ACT/SAT/WPCT scores; accepts foreign students who meet requirements. Rolling admission and advanced placement available. $25 appplication fee.

Costs Per Year: $6,335 tuition.

Collegiate Environment: The present campus provides excellent accomodations for students and is easily accessible to shops, restaurants, and other business establishments. Academic, cultural, and recreational clubs are all found on campus, such as the Photo Club and the Volleyball Club. Library holdings include 8,574 volumes, 124 periodicals, and 96 microfilms. 93% of applicants are accepted. Financial aid is available and 82% of the students receive some form of financial assistance.

Community Environment: Kansas City offers its citizens and visitors a progressive and growing assortment of residential and retail developments, cultural and recreational centers, and business enterprises. The city unfolds among the hills above the Missouri River with beauty. It is said that it has more boulevards than any city except Paris, more parks than any city of its size anywhere, and more fountains than any city in the world except Rome. Cultural and entertainment highlights include the Starlight Theater, the Nelson Art Gallery, Swope Park and Zoo, and the Crown Center. Kansas City also has teams in every major sports league.

DRURY COLLEGE   *(K-8)*
900 North Benton Avenue
Springfield, Missouri 65802
Tel: (417) 873-7205; (800) 922-2274; Fax: (417) 873-7529

Description: The privately supported liberal arts college was founded by Congregationalists in 1873 and was first called Springfield College. The School of Religion, established and maintained by the Disciples of Christ, has provided for the teaching of religion and philosophy since 1909, and functions as a regular department of the college. The college, now affiliated with the United Church of Christ (Congregational), and the Christian Church (Disciples of Christ), is accredited by the North Central Association of Colleges and Schools and by the National Council for Accreditation of Teacher Education and other professional associations. It operates on the semester system and offers two summer sessions. Enrollment includes 1,110 full-time and 38 part-time students in the traditional undergraduate day school program, 1,211 evening students, and 181 graduate students. A faculty of 87 full-time and 32 part-time gives an undergraduate faculty-student ratio of 1-14. There is a faculty of 195 part-time for the graduate and evening programs. The college offers extensive music programs, intercollegiate and intramural athletics and overseas programs in England. The school also offers preparation for State teaching certificates.

Entrance Requirements: Accredited high school graduation or equivalent with C average; SAT or ACT required; special admissions plans include rolling admission, delayed admission, and advanced placement; application fee $20.

Costs Per Year: $8,730 tuition; $3,500 room and board; $272 student fees.

Collegiate Environment: The college is located on 60 acres and contains 20 buildings that include a libraray of 160,000 volumes and dormitory facilities for 193 men and 290 women. Fraternity housing is available for 100 men. There are four national social fraternities and four national sororities located on the campus as well as numerous other student organizations. 90% of those who apply are accepted. The college welcomes students from other geographical locations and will accept midyear students. Financial aid is available, and 86% of the student body receives financial aid and/or scholarships.

Community Environment: See Southwest Missouri State University.

EAST CENTRAL COLLEGE   *(G-13)*
Highway 50 and Prarie Dell Road
Union, Missouri 63084
Tel: (314) 583-5193; Admissions: (314) 583-5195 x2222; Fax: (314) 583-1897

Description: The publicly supported junior college is fully accredited by the North Central Association of Colleges and Schools. It offers liberal arts transfer, vocational, developmental, and general education programs. The school operates on the semester system and offers 4 summer sessions. Enrollment includes 1,254 full-time and 1,717 part-time undergraduate and 342 graduate students. A faculty of 68 full-time and 50 part-time gives an undergraduate faculty-student ratio of approximately 1-25. Pre-college and freshman programs for the educationally disadvantaged are available. The college grants a Certificate or Associate degree.

Entrance Requirements: High school graduation or equivalent; open enrollment; East Central College Placement Test required; ACT may be required for some programs; early admission and rolling admission plans available.

Costs Per Year: $1,224 district-resident tuition; $1,700 out-of-district state residents; $2,618 out-of-state residents.

Collegiate Environment: First facilities on the 114-acre campus were completed in 1972. The library contains 20,100 volumes and 300 periodicals. No on-campus housing is available. All applicants are accepted, including midyear students. Financial assistance is available and 40% of the student body receives financial aid.

Community Environment: Union (population 6,000) is the county seat of Franklin County, and is located 40 miles west of St. Louis; see Washington University for information about St. Louis.

EDEN THEOLOGICAL SEMINARY   *(G-14)*
475 East Lockwood Avenue
Webster Groves, Missouri 63119
Tel: (314) 961-3627; (800) 969-3627; Admissions: (314) 961-3627 x336; Fax: (314) 961-9063

Description: The privately supported graduate seminary is an ecumenical school of theology of the United Church of Christ open to students of all communions. It was founded in 1850 by the Evangelical Society of the West and continues in its purpose of the preparation of men and women for Christian ministries. The present student body includes graduates of more than 100 colleges, universities, and seminaries. Students may transfer to and from other seminaries recognized by the North Central Association of Colleges and Schools, and Association of Theological Schools both of which Eden Seminary is an accredited member. It operates on the 4-1-4 calendar system. Enrollment includes 125 men and 74 women. A faculty of 16 gives a faculty-student ratio of 1-12. The school grants Master of Theological Studies, Master of Divinity, Doctor of Ministry degrees.

Entrance Requirements: Bachelor's degree or equivalent from an accredited college or university; rolling admission plan available; $25 application fee.

Costs Per Year: $160 per credit hour tuition; $1,680 room; $80 student fees.

Collegiate Environment: The seminary occupies a 22-acre campus on the main street of suburban Webster Groves. The 12 seminary buildings include a library of 218,000 volumes and 56 living accommodations for single men, and women and 52 families. The seminary welcomes students from other geographical locations and will accept midyear students. Approximately 70% of students applying for admission are accepted. 85% of the previous entering class returned to the seminary for the second year of studies. Scholarships are available and 85% of the students receive some form of financial aid.

Community Environment: See Washington University.

EVANGEL COLLEGE   *(K-8)*
1111 North Glenstone Avenue
Springfield, Missouri 65802
Tel: (417) 865-2811; (800) 382-6435; Fax: (417) 865-9599

Description: The privately supported college of arts and sciences is owned and operated by the General Council of the Assemblies of God Church and endorsed by its Department of Education. It is also accredited by the North Central Association of Colleges and Schools and other professional accrediting bodies. The college operates on the semester system and offers two summer terms. U.S. Army ROTC is available in cooperation with Southwest Missouri State University. Enrollment includes 1,474 full-time and 90 part-time students. A faculty of 122 gives faculty-student ratio of 1-18.

Entrance Requirements: Accredited high school graduation or equivalent with minimum average of "C" and completion of academic units including 3 English, 2 mathematics, 1 science, 2 social science; ACT or SAT required; graduation in top 60% of high school class; early admission, early decision, midyear admission, rolling admission and delayed admission plans available; $25 application fee.

Costs Per Year: $7,120 tuition; $3,240 room and board; $180 student fees.

Collegiate Environment: The college is located on a 80-acre campus in the heart of the scenic Ozarks. The northwest edge of the campus borders on an attractive city park. The college buildings contain a library of 113,000 volumes and living accommodations for 636 men, 824 women, and 36 families. The college welcomes students from other geographical locations. Scholarships are available and 90% of the students receive some form of aid.

Community Environment: See Southwest Missouri State University

FONTBONNE COLLEGE   *(F-14)*
6800 Wydown Boulevard
St. Louis, Missouri 63105
Tel: (314) 862-3456; Fax: (341) 889-1451

Description: Fontbonne is an independent coeducational college under the sponsorship of the Sisters of St. Joseph of Carondelet. Established in 1917, the college is accredited and approved by the North Central Association of Colleges and Schools, NCATE, the Missouri State Department of Public Instruction, the Council on the Education of the Deaf, the American Home Economics Association, and the National Association of the Schools of Music. It operates on the semester system and offers one summer term. Enrollment includes 1,163 undergraduates and 518 graduate students. A faculty of 124 gives a faculty-student ratio of 1-14. The college has an optional Cooperative Education Program that enables students to gain a maximum of 18 hours of academic credit for one year (3 semesters) of work experience in their major field of study. The college offers intercollegiate sports programs including men's basketball, baseball, soccer and golf. The women's teams compete in volleyball, basketball, golf and softball.

Entrance Requirements: Accredited high school graduation or equivalent with rank in upper 50% of graduating class; completion of 16 units; SAT or ACT required; early admission, rolling admission, delayed admission, and advanced placement plans available; $20 application fee.

Costs Per Year: $9,040 tuition; $4,200 room and board.

Collegiate Environment: The college is located on 13 acres in Clayton, one of the finest residential suburbs of St. Louis, Missouri. The eight college buildings include a library of 90,000 volumes and dormitory facilities for 217 students. The college welcomes a geographically diverse student body and will accept midyear students. 84% of students applying for admission meet the requirements and are accepted. 310 scholarships are available and 65% of the student body receives some form of financial aid.

Community Environment: See Washington University.

HANNIBAL-LAGRANGE COLLEGE   *(C-12)*
Palmyra Road
Hannibal, Missouri 63401
Tel: (314) 221-3675; (800) 454-1119; Admissions: (314) 221-3113; Fax: (314) 221-6594

Description: The liberal arts college, formerly junior college, is owned and supported by the Southern Baptist Convention. Founded in 1858 as La Grange College, La Grange, Missouri, the college was moved down river to Hannibal in 1928 after citizens of the town raised money for its operations. The college is accredited by the North Central Association of Colleges and Schools. Programs of study lead to the Associate and Bachelor degrees. It operates on the semester system and offers two summer sessions. Enrollment includes 854 students. A faculty of 50 gives a faculty-student ratio of 1-17. The college offers band, chorus, choir, inter-collegiate basketball, intra-mural athletics. Religion subjects and chapel attendance are required.

Entrance Requirements: High school graduation of equivalent; ACT required; special admission plans include early admission, early decision, rolling admission, early admission, advanced placement; application fee $15.

Costs Per Year: $6,050 tuition; $2,510 room and board; $260 student fees.

Collegiate Environment: The 110-acre campus overlooks the Mississippi and lies just within the city limits of the northwest portion of Hannibal. The 12 college buildings include a library of 25,000 volumes and dormitory facilities for 112 men, 121 women and 22 families. 95% of those who apply are accepted, including midyear students. Financial aid is available, and 75% of the current student body receives some form of financial assistance.

Community Environment: The boyhood home of Mark Twain, Hannibal (population 18,698) is located on the west bank of the Mississippi River, 120 miles north of St. Louis. Buses and trains are the principal forms of transportation. A municipal airport serves the area. Numerous civic and service organizations, public library, YMCA, churches and a civic music association are a part of the community. Some of the sports available include swimming, bowling, and fishing.

HARRIS-STOWE STATE COLLEGE   *(F-14)*
3026 Laclede Avenue
St. Louis, Missouri 63103
Tel: (314) 533-3366

Description: The college commenced as a teacher education institution in 1857. It was the first such public institution west of the Mississippi River. In 1954, Harris Teachers College merged with Stowe Teachers College as a major step in the integration of the Public Schools of St. Louis. Later in the early 1970's the college added Stowe to its name and became Harris-Stowe College. In 1979 the college became the newest member of the State system of public higher education and changed its name to Harris-Stowe State College. The mission of the college, as mandated by the State Legislature, is threefold: to continue to provide a high quality teacher education program for the production of Early Childhood, Elementary School, and Middle School/Junior High School teachers; to provide a program of urban education designed to produce well-trained urban education specialists; and to provide a variety of community services including information and cultural opportunities for the public at large. The college operates on the semester system with three summer terms and enrolls approximately 1,800 students. A faculty of 112 gives a faculty-student ratio of 1-15. The college is accredited by the North Central Association of Colleges and Schools and by the National Council for the Accreditation of Teacher Education.

Entrance Requirements: Accredited high school graduate or equivalent with completion of 20 units including a total of 11 from English, math and social studies areas, plus 1 unit of laboratory science; delayed admission, early decision, rolling admission and advanced placement is available.

Costs Per Year: $1,400 tuition; $2,800 out-of-state resident tuition; $45 student fees. The college includes fully-equipped biological and physical science laboratories and a library containing 70,000 volumes. There is no student housing. The college accepts 84% of the students who apply, including midyear students. Financial aid is available.

Community Environment: See Washington University

JEFFERSON COLLEGE   *(H-14)*
1000 Viking Drive
Hillsboro, Missouri 63050
Tel: (314) 789-3951

Description: This publicly supported junior college is the only community college in the Junior College District of Jefferson County. It offers academic, vocational-technical, and general education programs in both day and evening divisions. The school was established in 1963. It operates on the semester system and offers two summer terms. The college is accredited by the North Central Association of Colleges and Schools. Enrollment is 1,842 full-time and 2,120 students. A faculty of 87 full-time and 111 part-time gives a faculty-student ratio of 1-20. The school offers a cooperative education program (alternating work and class periods) in business subjects and a pre-college program for the educationally disadvantaged. The college awards a Certificate or Associate degree. Preliminary preparation for State teaching certificate is available.

Entrance Requirements: Open enrollment policy for district residents; accredited high school graduation or equivalent, out-of-district applicants must rank in upper two-thirds of graduating class; ACT or entrance exam required; early admission, midyear admission, and rolling admission plans available; $15 application fee.

Costs Per Year: $960 tuition for city and district residents; $1,320 state resident; $1,680 out-of-state.

Collegiate Environment: College facilities include a library of over 56,862 volumes, 210 periodicals, 25 microforms, and 4,270 audiovisual materials. 95% of those who apply are accepted, including midyear students. Financial aid is available, and 35% of the current student body receives some form of assistance.

Community Environment: Hillsboro (population 1,508) is a rural community with a temperate climate. It is located within a 30-minute drive of metropolitan St. Louis. The town is situated near several small lakes, which are excellent for fishing and boating. Hillsboro is the headquarters for the county health unit. The community facilities include civic clubs, a shopping center, churches of major denominations, and a college library. The recreational, social and cultural facilities of St. Louis are accessible. Opportunities for part-time employment are good. See also Washington University for information on St. Louis.

KANSAS CITY ART INSTITUTE (E-5)
4415 Warwick Boulevard
Kansas City, Missouri 64111
Tel: (816) 561-4852

Description: The privately supported college was first organized as a sketch club in 1885 and was chartered in 1887 as the Fine Arts Institute. It adopted its present name in 1920 and the charter was revised by the State of Missouri in 1947 to confer professional degrees in art at the college level. The College is accredited by the National Association of Schools of Art and Design and by the North Central Association of Colleges and Schools. It operates on the early semester system and also offers two summer terms. Enrollment includes 533 full-time and 26 part-time students. A faculty of 47 full-time and 28 part-time gives a faculty-student ratio of 1-10. Offers internships (alternating work and class periods) in design and photography course. Offers Independent Study Abroad and Junior Year Abroad programs; belongs to a consortium which allows students to study at the member institutions in their junior year.

Entrance Requirements: Accredited high school graduation or equivalent; portfolio needed. Special admission plans available: early admission, early decision, rolling admission, delayed admission, advanced placement, $25 application fee.

Costs Per Year: $14,786 tuition and fees, $4,340 room and board.

Collegiate Environment: The Institute is located on the edge of a residential area adjacent to the Nelson Atkins Museum of Art and the Kemper Museum of Contemporary Art. The college buildings are on a beautifully landscaped 15-acre campus and include a library of 34,700 volumes and Living Center facilities for 150 students. Sixty-two percent of the applicants are accepted. The institute accepts students from other states and foreign countries Financial aid is available.

Community Environment: See University of Missouri - Kansas City

KEMPER MILITARY SCHOOL AND COLLEGE (F-9)
701 Third Street
Boonville, Missouri 65233
Tel: (816) 882-5623; (800) 530-5600; Fax: (816) 882-3332

Description: The privately supported military school and junior college for men and women was established in 1844. It operates on the semester system offering 1 summer session and is accredited by the North Central Association of Colleges and Schools. The institution offers high school grades 7-12 as well as junior college, and grants Associate in Arts degree to its college students. The institution enrolls approximately 150 students. There are 28 faculty members, giving faculty-student ratio of 1-15.

Entrance Requirements: High school graduation; open enrollment policy; completion of 18 units including 4 English, 1 mathematics, 1 science, 3 social science; early admission, early decision, rolling admission, advanced placement and delayed admission plans available; SAT or ACT required for commissioning programs only; application fee $50.

Costs Per Year: $7,600 tuition; $2,600 board and room; $1,850 student fees.

Collegiate Environment: Kemper is located on the edge of the city limits of the City of Boonville, on the south bank of the Missouri River. The campus is comprised of 100 acres and contains 12 buildings which include a library of nearly 20,000 volumes and dormitory facilities. A complete Army ROTC program is offered. Kemper is rated "an Honor Military School with Distinction." 90% of the applicants are accepted, including midyear students. Financial aid is available and 50% of the current student body receives some form of aid.

Community Environment: Boonville (population 7,514) is near the center of the State between St. Louis and Kansas City. It is one of the oldest towns in the state. The community supports many churches, a public library, hospital, and motels. The Greyhound bus provides transportation. There are excellent recreation facilities in the nearby Lake of the Ozarks. Some points of interest are the Boonslick State Park and the Harley Park.

KENRICK-GLENNON SEMINARY (F-14)
5200 Glennon Drive
St. Louis, Missouri 63119
Tel: (314) 644-0266; Admissions: (314) 644-0266; Fax: (314) 644-3079

Description: This privately supported Roman Catholic theological seminary for male graduate students was founded in 1818. It was legally incorporated under the laws of the State of Missouri in 1869. Archbishop Peter Richard Kenrick moved the seminary to St. Louis and gave it the name Kenrick Seminary. Kenrick Seminary merged with Cardinal Glennon College in June 1987 to become Kenrick-Glennon Seminary. The school is accredited by the North Central Association of Colleges and Schools and by the Association of Theological Schools. It operates on the semester system. Enrollment is 54 students. A faculty of 22 gives a faculty-student ratio of 1-3.

Entrance Requirements: Only students with a Bachelor's degree from college who have adequate preparation in Latin, Greek, and philosophy are admitted to the courses in theology; GRE required; sponsorship by Bishop of Diocese or by a religious community required. Midyear admission available.

Costs Per Year: $7,730 tuition; $3,526 room and board; $100 student fees.

Collegiate Environment: The seminary is located in the Village of Shrewsbury near the southwest city limits of St. Louis. The main building includes the chapel, library, auditorium, gymnasium, classrooms, and living quarters for 150 students. The library has a collection of over 80,000 volumes.

Community Environment: See Washington University.

KIRKSVILLE COLLEGE OF OSTEOPATHIC MEDICINE
(B-9)
800 W. Jefferson
Kirksville, Missouri 63501
Tel: (816) 626-2237; Fax: (816) 626-2815

Description: The privately supported osteopathic college is incorporated under the laws of the State of Missouri as a nonprofit institution. It was established in 1892 and is accredited by the American Osteopathic Association and the North Central Association of Colleges and Schools. The college operates on the quarter system and offers one summer session. Enrollment includes 410 men and 147 women, all full-time students. A faculty of 92 full-time, 45 part-time, and 33 volunteers provide a faculty student ratio of 1-5.

Entrance Requirements: Completion of 90 semester hours from accredited college or university; Medical College Admission Test required; rolling admission, application fee $50.

Costs Per Year: $21,300 tuition; $9,100 room and board.

Collegiate Environment: The main college buildings include eleven structures used for instructional and clinical purposes. Clinical rotations are completed in ten training regional sites. The college library contains 74,039 volumes, 852 periodicals, 4,377 audiovisual materials. Living accommodations are provided for 44 students. The college welcomes students from all geographical locations but midyear students are not accepted. Financial aid is available. The college is highly selective and only 8% of applicants are accepted.

Community Environment: See Northeast Missouri State University

LINCOLN UNIVERSITY (G-10)
820 Chestnut Street
Jefferson City, Missouri 65102-0029
Tel: (314) 681-5000; (800) 521-5052; Admissions: (314) 681-5022;
Fax: (314) 681-5566

Description: This publicly supported liberal arts and professional state university was founded as Lincoln Institute in 1866. College work was added by 1877, and in 1879 the college became a state institution. The university operates on the semester system and offers one summer session. It is accredited by the North Central Association of Colleges and Schools and professionally by the National Association of Schools of Music and the National Council for the Accreditation of Teacher Education. Army ROTC is available. The school grants Associate, Bachelor's, and Masters degrees. Enrollment includes 1,949 full-time, 1,563 part-time, and 363 graduate students. A faculty of 149 full-time and 69 part-time provides a faculty-student ratio of 1-20.

Entrance Requirements: Accredited high school graduation or GED equivalent; 22 total units; open enrollment for state residents; out-of-state applicants must have cumulative GPA of 2.0 or better; SAT or ACT required; $17 application fee.

Costs Per Year: $1,896 state-resident tuition; $3,792 out-of-state; $2,728 room and board; $20 student fees.

Collegiate Environment: The University's main campus is comprised of 34 buildings on 136.17 acres of landscaped slopes and flatlands overlooking the capital city of Missouri. Three farms of 732.45 acres make up another aspect of the University's grounds. Three student residences that accomodate 560 students, a student union center, a library of more than 196,000 volumes, a science and mathematics building, a fine arts center, a physical education and athletics center, a technology building, and a data processing center are among the main campus buildings. Approximately 98% of the students applying for admission are accepted. 770 scholarships are available, and 54% of students receive some form of financial aid.

Community Environment: Jefferson City, the capital of Missouri, is midway between St. Louis and Kansas City on the heights overlooking the Missouri River. The city is the headquarters of many state associations. It is the natural trading center and distributing point for central Missouri. Industries include printing and publishing, and clothing shops. Commercial transportation is convenient. Riverside Park, Memorial Park, and Lake of the Ozarks are all available for fishing, boating, hunting, and swimming. Some of the historical points of interest are the Cole County Historical Society Museum, Jefferson City National Cemetery, and the State Museum.

LINDENWOOD COLLEGE (F-14)
209 South Kingshighway
St. Charles, Missouri 63301
Tel: (314) 949-2000; Admissions: (314) 949-4949/4933; Fax: (314) 949-4910

Description: The privately supported liberal arts college was founded in 1827. The college is accredited by the North Central Association of Colleges and Schoools and the National Council for Accreditation of Teacher Education, and a member of the American Assembly of Collegiate Schools of Business. The college serves over 2,825 students pursuing B.A. and selected graduate degrees. Over 45 majors are offered in traditional liberal arts areas as well as specialized programs in Theatre, Business Administration, and Mass Communications. The college grants the Bachelor and Masters degrees. it operates on the trimester calendar system and offers three summer sessions. Enrollment includes 2,238 full-time and 172 part-time undergraduates and 905 graduate students. A faculty of 109 full-time provides a faculty-student ratio of 1-17.

Entrance Requirements: Accredited high school graduation or equivalent with "C to A" average; completion of 16 academic units, including 4 English, 3 math, 2 science, and 2 language; ACT or SAT required; rolling admission, delayed admission, midyear admission, and advanced placement plans available; $25 application fee.

Costs Per Year: $8,400 tuition; $4,400 room and board; $80 student fees.

Collegiate Environment: The 185-acre campus is located in a suburban environment 20 miles northwest of downtown St. Louis. Dormitory facilities are available for 1,100 men and women. The library contains 144,000 volumes and numerous periodicals, microforms and audiovisual materials. Students are welcome from other geographical locations and midyear students are accepted. Numerous scholarships are available, and 87% of the students receive some form of financial aid.

Community Environment: St. Charles was one of the first settlements on the Missouri River. It is located 20 miles from St. Louis. An airport is located ten miles away. Community facilities include restaurants, shopping, churches, hospital, hotels, motels, and recreation centers. Swimming, boating, and skating are some of the recreational activities found in St. Charles County.

Branch Campuses: Westport Campus, St. Louis

LOGAN COLLEGE OF CHIROPRACTIC (F-14)
Box 1065
1851 Schoettler Road
Chesterfield, Missouri 63006-1065
Tel: (314) 227-2100; (800) 782-3344; Fax: (314) 227-9338

Description: The privately supported chiropractic graduate college was established in 1935. The professional education program is based on the belief that students of chiropractic should be liberally educated in addition to being competently trained in basic sciences and chiropractic skills. The school is accredited by the Chiropractic Council of Education, and awards the degree of Doctor of Chiropractic, and the Bachelor's Degree of Human Biology. The B.S. degree is accredited by the North Central Association of College and Schools. The college operates on the trimester system and offers one summer session. Enrollment includes 801 full-time students. A faculty of 72 full-time gives a faculty-student ratio of 1-12.

Entrance Requirements: Completion of two years (60 semester hours) of preprofessional liberal arts college education which includes specific course and grade requirements; rolling admission plan available; application fee $35 for D.C.; $15 for B.S.

Costs Per Year: $4,205 tuition per trimester ($8,410 per academic year).

Collegiate Environment: The college is located on a 103-acre campus, 30 acres of which are natural woodlands. In addition to modern and well-equipped classroom facilities, the school offers an out-patient clinic for student practice and seven additional public outpatient clinics in the St. Louis metropolitan area. The library contains more than 12,000 volumes. A new Science and Research building containing laboratories for basic science, chiropractic, and research opened in 1988. 60% of those who apply are accepted. The college welcomes a geographically diverse student body and midyear students are admitted. Financial aid is available, and 80% of the current student body receives some form of financial assistance. 95% of the previous freshman class returns to the college for the second year of studies.

Community Environment: See Washington University.

LONGVIEW COMMUNITY COLLEGE (F-5)
500 Longview Road
Lee's Summit, Missouri 64081
Tel: (816) 672-2000; Admissions: (816) 672-2247; Fax: (816) 672-2025

Description: The publicly supported community college provides liberal arts transfer and vocational programs. It is a college of the Metropolitan (Kansas City) Junior College District, and is accredited by the North Central Association of Colleges and Schools. It grants the Associate degree. Offers band, chorus, inter-collegiate and intramural athletics; Cooperative Education program (alternating work and class periods) available in business, secretarial, automotive, drafting, agri-business. Pre-college programs for the educationally disadvantaged are available. The college operates on the semester system and offers one summer session. Enrollment includes 2,400 full-time and 5,900 part-time and 4,585 evening students. A faculty of 100 full-time and 300 part-time gives a faculty-student ratio of 1-22.

Entrance Requirements: High school graduation or equivalent; open enrollment; under certain circumstances non-HS graduates accepted; early admission, rolling admission, midyear admission and advanced placement plans available; placement tests required of all degree seeking students.

Costs Per Year: $1,350 ($45/credit) resident tuition, $2,250 ($75/credit) nonresident tuition.

Collegiate Environment: Occupies 146 acres of suburban area south of Kansas City; library contains 42,000 volumes. All applicants who meet the requirements are accepted. 62 scholarships are available, including 54 for freshmen. 22% of students receive some form of financial aid.

Community Environment: See University of Missouri - Kansas City

MAPLE WOODS COMMUNITY COLLEGE *(E-5)*
2601 North East Barry Road
Kansas City, Missouri 64156
Tel: (816) 436-6500

Description: The publicly supported community college is a branch campus of the Metropolitan Community College District. It is accredited by the North Central Association of Colleges and Schools. The college provides liberal arts, transfer, and vocational programs. The college offers a cooperative education program (alternating work and class periods) in business mid-management and secretarial studies, pre-college programs for the educationally disadvantaged, and a 2-year pre-engineering course granting the A.A. degree with a transfer to University of Missouri for 2 additional years for the B.S. degree. It operates on the semester system and offers one summer session. Enrollment includes 1,430 full-time and 3,325 part-time students. A faculty of 125 gives a faculty-student ratio of 1-38.

Entrance Requirements: High school graduation or equivalent; open enrollment; under certain circumstances non-high school graduates accepted; rolling admission and advanced placement plans available.

Costs Per Year: $1,290 ($43 per credit hour) district resident tuition; $2,130 ($71 per credit hour) state resident tuition; $3,060 ($102 per credit hour) nonresident tuition; $3,570 ($114 per credit hour) foreign tuition.

Collegiate Environment: The campus is located fifteen miles north of Kansas City in the midst of the largest stand of hard or sugar maples west of the Appalachian mountains. The newly built campus includes a library of 30,000 volumes. Almost all applicants are accepted including midyear students. Financial aid is available.

Community Environment: See University of Missouri - Kansas City

MARYVILLE UNIVERSITY OF SAINT LOUIS *(F-14)*
13550 Conway Road
St. Louis, Missouri 63141-7299
Tel: (314) 529-9350; (800) 627-9855; Fax: (314) 542-9085

Description: The privately supported, independent, coeducational, liberal arts, career-oriented, and teaching university is accredited by the North Central Association of Colleges and Schools. It was founded in 1872 by the Religious of the Sacred Heart. The academic curriculum and programs are based on a semester calendar with a summer session. The University offers undergraduate programs leading to the Bachelor of Arts, Bachelor of Science, and Bachelor of Fine Arts. At the graduate level, Maryville offers a Master of Business Administration degree and a Master of Arts degree in Educational Processes. Special programs include a transitional program for high school seniors, an interior design apprenticeship with professional designers, a hospital internship, and an actuarial program that prepares students for four of ten professional examinations for actuaries. There are also opportunities for many internships, cooperative education programs, continuing and corporate education programs. The University offers one of the nation's few weekend programs in nursing. Weekend College with sites at South County, Southwest, and St. Charles, enables students to attend classes on alternate weekends to earn a bachelor's degree. Army ROTC is available through Washington University. Enrollment includes 1,271 full-time, 1,588 part-time undergraduates and 566 graduate students. A faculty of 85 full-time and 191 part-time gives a faculty-student ratio of 1-14.

Entrance Requirements: Accredited high school graduation; completion of 22 units, including 4 English, 3 mathematics, 2 science, 2-3 social science and 3 electives from above list; ACT or SAT required; minimum scores: ACT 20 composite, SAT 800 combined; GMAT required for graduate studies; application form; transcripts; certain pro-

grams require letter of recommendation and interview; art portfolio for BFA or BA art; audition for music therapy program; high school achievement is single most important decision factor; early admission, early decision, rolling admission, delayed admission and advanced placement plans available; $20 application fee.

Costs Per Year: $9,250 tuition; $4,550 room and board; $500 books and supplies.

Collegiate Environment: The suburban campus is located on 130 acres. The university has a 144,680-volume library, with extensive holdings of 330,879 microforms, 42,000 government documents, CD-ROMs, audiovisual materials and 790 serials; laboratories for the natural sciences, physical therapy, nursing, and computers; art gallery; art studios; an audiovisual center; observatory; and outdoor trails for ecological studies. Two residence halls house 368 students. Athletic facilities include three outdoor tennis courts, intercollegiate soccer and softball fields, a lighted baseball complex, and a handsome multipurpose gymnasium which includes a new, state-of-the-art fitness center. MU is a member of NCAA Division II and the Saint Louis Intercollegiate Athletic Conference. MU fields women's teams in basketball, cross-country, soccer, softball, tennis, and volleyball and men's teams in baseball, basketball, cross-country, golf, soccer, and tennis. There are more than 30 clubs and an active student government association, through which students participate in sponsoring a wide range of social, cultural, ethnic, religious, community service, and intellectual events. 75% of applicants are accepted. Financial aid is available in the form of employment, loans, and grants. Merit scholarships are also available. 48% of students receive some form of financial aid. 70% of full-time students received a financial aid package averaging $3,514.

Community Environment: The campus is located at Highway 40/I-64 and Woods Mill Road, 2 miles west of I-270 in West St. Louis County. The campus is nestled on 130 acres of rolling hills, with wooded areas, creeks, and two lakes. It is within 30 minutes of downtown St. Louis and its international airport. The university maintains a close association with its near neighbors at the Maryville Centre, a unique educational, corporate, cultural, and residential complex. Within easy driving distance of the campus are many of the social, cultural, athletic, and entertainment facilities of the metropolitan area including, the St. Louis Art museum; St. Louis Symphony Orchestra; Missouri Botanical Garden; Municipal Opera; ballet, opera, and rock performances; world-renowned zoo; touring, repertory, and dinner theaters; professional baseball, hockey, and football; large park systems; and many movie theaters; St. Louis Science Center; Museum of Science and Natural History; and dozens of restaurants.

MIDWESTERN BAPTIST THEOLOGICAL SEMINARY
(E-5)
5001 North Oak Street Trafficway
Kansas City, Missouri 64118
Tel: (816) 453-4600

Description: This privately supported graduate seminary was established in 1958 by the Southern Baptist Convention. It operates on the quarter system and offers summer and January sessions. It is accredited by the North Central Association of Colleges and Schools and the Association of Theological Schools. The basic degrees offered by the seminary are the Master of Divinity, Master of Church Music, and Master of Religious Education. Diplomas in Theology, Church Music and Religious Education are also offered. Enrollment is 610 students. A faculty of 69 gives a faculty-student ratio of 1-9.

Entrance Requirements: Bachelor's degree or equivalent from accredited college or university; diploma programs require minimum entrance age of 30 years but Bachelor's degree not required; $15 application fee.

Costs Per Year: $1,000 matriculation fee; $1,140 room.

Collegiate Environment: The seminary is located on 200 acres, ten minutes from downtown Kansas City. The library contains 101,000 titles, 437 periodicals, 501 microforms and 1,560 audiovisual materials. Living accommodations are provided for 32 men, 16 women and 143 families. Limited financial aid is available.

Community Environment: See University of Missouri - Kansas City.

MINERAL AREA COLLEGE (I-14)
Park Hills, Missouri 63601
Tel: (314) 431-4593

Description: The publicly supported, district-governed junior college replaced the former Flat River Junior College, which was established in 1922. The college operates on the semester system and offers one summer term. It is accredited by the North Central Association of Colleges and Schools. Enrollment is 1,166 full-time and 1,422 part-time students. A faculty of 59 full-time and 121 part-time gives a faculty-student ratio of 1-20. The school offers band, chorus, choir, and intercollegiate athletics.

Entrance Requirements: Open enrollment for state residents; non-high school graduates admitted; SAT or ACT required; early admission, early decision, midyear admission, rolling admission, and advanced placement plans available.

Costs Per Year: $1,050 district resident; $1,500 out-of-district; $1,500 out-of-state.

Collegiate Environment: Almost all students applying for admission that meet the requirements are accepted, including midyear students and those from other geographical locations. The library contains 27,962 volumes. Financial aid is available, and 45% of the current student body receives some form of assistance. The college offers programs in vocational-technical and academic areas as well as general education and community service adult education.

Community Environment: Park Hills (population 10,000) is located in east-central Missouri, 60 miles south of St. Louis. Kentucky, Illinois and Arkansas are not too distant. The Union Pacific Railroad serves the area. District facilities include most denominations of churches, four newspapers, four radio station and parks. Outdoor activities are hunting and fishing, tennis, golf.

MISSOURI BAPTIST COLLEGE (F-14)
12542 Conway Road
St. Louis, Missouri 63141
Tel: (314) 434-1115

Description: The privately supported liberal arts college is affiliated with the Missouri Baptist Convention and offers the Bachelor degree, Associate of Science and preparation for the State teaching certificate. The school operates on the semester system and offers two summer sessions. Enrollment includes 529 full-time and 869 part-time students. A faculty of 40 full-time and 40 part-time gives an overall faculty-student ratio of approximately 1-18; 55% of the faculty have earned doctorate degrees. Religion subjects and chapel attendance required. The school is accredited by the North Central Association of Colleges and Schools.

Entrance Requirements: Accredited high school graduation or equivalent; completion of 16 units including 4 English, 2 mathematics, 2 science, 2 social studies, 1 foreign language, ACT or SAT; early decision, rolling admission, delayed admission and advanced placement plans available; $25 application fee.

Costs Per Year: $7,170 tuition; $3,540 room and board; student fees $185.

Collegiate Environment: The campus is located on 65 acres and contains five buildings which include a library of 110,215 titles, 150 periodicals, and 27,404 microforms. Residence hall will accommodate 144 students. Semesters begin in September and January. 80% of the applicants are accepted, and students are admitted at midyear as well as in September. Financial assistance is available. 75% of the student body receives some form of financial aid.

Community Environment: See Washington University

MISSOURI SOUTHERN STATE COLLEGE (K-5)
Newman & Duquesne Roads
Joplin, Missouri 64801
Tel: (417) 625-9300; (800) 606-6772; Fax: (417) 625-3121

Description: This publicly supported liberal arts and teachers college offers studies that lead to a Bachelor's degree in a number of major areas in the liberal arts, teacher education, and business administration. The college offers liberal arts and preprofessional transfer programs, terminal programs in technical education, and certificate programs. Both divisions are accredited by the North Central Associa-

tion of Colleges and Schools. Enrollment is 3,557 full-time and 1,777 part-time students. A faculty of 196 full-time and 87 part-time gives a faculty-student ratio of 1-24.

Entrance Requirements: Accredited high school graduation or equivalent; non-high school graduates with GED; ACT required; early admission, advanced placement, and delayed admission plans available; $15 application fee.

Costs Per Year: $1,536 state-resident tuition; $3,072 out-of-state; $2,948 room and board; $90 student fees.

Collegiate Environment: The college is located in southwest Missouri, 11 miles from the Kansas state line. The 334-acre campus has dormitory space for 300 men and 300 women. The library contains nearly 191,000 titles, 1,268 periodicals, and 479,858 microforms. Almost all of those who apply are accepted, including midyear students. Financial aid is available, and 78% of the current student body receives some form of assistance.

Community Environment: Located in southwest Missouri at the northern gateway of the Ozark Resort area, Joplin (population 46,000) is surrounded by numerous springfed fishing streams in scenic hill country. The city has many manufacturing and wholesale firms as well as industry involving the mining and processing of zinc ore. All forms of commercial transportation are available. Part-time employment is available. Over 100 churches, 14 elementary schools, 1 junior high school, 1 high school, 2 four-year colleges, 3 hospitals, and airport and taxicab service are available.

MISSOURI VALLEY COLLEGE (E-8)
500 E. College
Marshall, Missouri 65340
Tel: (816) 886-6924; Fax: (816) 886-9818

Description: The privately supported liberal arts college was chartered in 1888. It is accredited by the North Central Association of Colleges and Schools and professionally by the American Chemical Society, American Psychological Association, Council on Social Work Education. It operates on the 4-1-4 system and offers three summer sessions. Enrollment includes 1,206 students. A faculty of 60 gives a faculty-student ratio of 1-20.

Entrance Requirements: Accredited high school graduation or equivalent with "C" average and rank in upper 75% completion of 16 units including 4 English and 2 mathematics; SAT or ACT required; non-high school graduates admitted on examination; nondegree applicants may be admitted as special students; early admission, early decision, rolling admission, delayed admission and advanced placement programs available; $10 application fee.

Costs Per Year: $9,000 tuition; $5,000 room and board; $1,000 estimated additional expenses.

Collegiate Environment: The 80-acre campus is located 80 miles east of Kansas City. Classroom activity centers in Baity Hall, the oldest structure on the campus. Murrell Memorial Library has more than 85,000 volumes. Student housing facilities accommodate 266 men and 250 women. Fraternities house an additional 162 men. Sororities house an additional 70 women. Apartments accommodate 247 students. There is a new Burns Athletic Complex. 67% of those who apply are accepted, including students from various geographical locations. Classes begin in September and January and midyear students are accepted. Substantial financial aid is available, and 95% of the current student body receives some form of assistance.

Community Environment: Marshall (population 13,000) is located 80 miles east of Kansas City with bus transportation available. The Indian Foothills Park, at the eastern city limits, provides tennis courts, ball fields, swimming, fishing, and picnicking facilities and a golf course. Other facilities include a bowling alley, skating rink, and a philharmonic symphony.

MISSOURI WESTERN STATE COLLEGE (C-4)
4525 Downs Drive
St. Joseph, Missouri 64507
Tel: (816) 271-4200

Description: The state-supported liberal arts and teachers college evolved from the St. Joseph Junior College, organized in 1915. It is accredited by the North Central Association of Colleges and Schools. The college grants the Associate and Bachelor degrees. It operates on the semester system and offers one summer session. Enrollment is 3,663 full-time and 1,430 part-time students. A faculty of 162 full-time and 134 part-time gives an overall faculty-student ratio of 1-19.

Entrance Requirements: Accredited high school graduation or equivalent with completion of 20 units; ACT required for placement purposes only; students not meeting all requirements may be admitted as special students; early admission and midyear admission plans are available; $15 application fee.

Costs Per Year: $2,126 state-resident tuition; $4,028 out-of-state; $2,444 room and board; $10 student fees.

Collegiate Environment: All applicants who meet the requirements are accepted, including midyear students and those from various geographical locations. The library contains 169,700 volumes. Coeducational dormitories can accommodate 1,050 students. Scholarships are available, and 80% of the students receive some form of financial aid. About half of the previous freshman class returned to the campus for their second year.

Community Environment: Once a great river port, St. Joseph (population 80,000) is today one of the great livestock and grain markets of the central west and the trading center of a large agricultural area. The community facilities include a number of churches, hospitals, libraries, museum, and a Civic Music Association. Some of the recreational activities are swimming, ice skating, and tennis. Points of interest are the Albrecht Gallery, Jesse James House, Krug Park, Patee House, Pony Express Stables Museum, and St. Joseph Museum.

MOBERLY AREA COMMUNITY COLLEGE   (D-9)
College & Rollins Streets
Moberly, Missouri 65270
Tel: (816) 263-4110; (800) 622-2070; Admissions: (816) 263-4110 X 270; Fax: (816) 263-6448

Description: This publicly supported community college was founded in 1927. It is accredited by the North Central Association of Colleges and Schools. Transfer, career, and continuing education programs are offered. Enrollment is 1,050 full-time and 800 part-time students. A faculty of 34 full-time and 61 part-time gives an overall faculty-student ratio of 1-20. The semester system is employed and 2 summer sessions offered. The college offers cooperative education programs (alternating work and class periods) in business, mechanics, and health occupations. Special occupational programs for the educationally disadvantaged are available. The school has an academic cooperative plan in pre-engineering with University of Missouri, providing the first 2 years of study toward the B.S. degree.

Entrance Requirements: High school graduation or equivalent; open enrollment policy.

Costs Per Year: $1,824 ($57/cr) resident tuition; $3,424 ($107/cr) nonresident.

Collegiate Environment: The library contains 20,400 volumes. Dormitory facilities accommodate 42 students. All applicants are accepted. 420 scholarships are available including 145 merit and 24 athletic. 70% of the students receives some form of financial aid. Over 80% of a previous freshman class returned to the school for the second year.

Community Environment: Moberly (population 13,000) is the county seat of Randolph County, in central Missouri. The town is served by two major railroads and the Omar Bradley Airport. Community facilities include churches of all denominations, a regional hospital, and Little Dixie Regional Library. A moderately large shopping district is available. Student employment is available in retail, restaurants, filling stations, and warehouses. Housing may be found in hotels, motels, and rooming houses. Outdoor activities are golf, boating, fishing, hunting, baseball, and tennis.

NAZARENE THEOLOGICAL SEMINARY   (E-5)
1700 East Meyer Boulevard
Kansas City, Missouri 64131
Tel: (816) 333-6254; (800) 831-3011; Fax: (816) 333-6271

Description: The privately supported seminary is a graduate institution of the Church of the Nazarene whose purpose is to prepare students for various phases of the Christian ministry. The facilities are available for training students of other denominations who are in sympathy with the standards of the Church of the Nazarene. It is an ac-

credited member of the Association of Theological Schools. It operates on the 4-1-4 semester system and offers one summer session. Enrollment is 223 full-time and 81 part-time students. A faculty of 18 full-time and 7 part-time gives a faculty-student ratio of 1-16. The school offers overseas seminars and cross-registration with 3 other Kansas City seminaries.

Entrance Requirements: B.A. degree or equivalent from an accredited or approved college or university; rolling admission; $20 application fee.

Costs Per Year: $3,700 tuition; $103 student fees.

Collegiate Environment: About 99% of students applying for admission meet the requirements and are accepted, including those from various geographical locations. The library contains 105,000 volumes. Financial aid is available, and 30% of the students receive some form of assistance. 90% of last year's first-year class returned for their second year of studies.

Community Environment: See University of Missouri - Kansas City.

NORTH CENTRAL MISSOURI COLLEGE   (B-7)
1301 Main Street
Trenton, Missouri 64683
Tel: (816) 359-3948; (800) 880-6180; Admissions: (800) 880-6180; Fax: (816) 359-2211

Description: The publicly supported, district governed community college offers liberal arts courses and a variety of occupational-technical programs. Cooperative Education programs are available in farm management, agri-business, technology, business management, and fashion merchandising. It operates on the semester plan and 2 summer terms are offered. Enrollment is 1,100 students. A faculty of 25 full-time and 34 part-time gives a faculty-student ratio of 1-25.

Entrance Requirements: High school graduation or equivalent, or 18 years of age; open enrollment policy; rolling admission plan available.

Costs Per Year: $1,155 tuition for in-district residents; $1,725 tuition state residents; $2,595 nonresidents; $2,170 room and board.

Collegiate Environment: The college campus includes 5 classroom buildings, a student center, writing lab, computer center, and library which houses 19,669 volumes including 17,763 titles, 131 periodicals, 2,275 microforms, and 1,669 audiovisual materials. Dormitory facilities accomodate 80 students. The college accepts 99% of those who apply, including midyear students. Financial aid is available. 300 scholarships are offered, all available to freshmen. About 50% of the previous freshman class returned to the college for the second year. The college recently granted 36 Certificates and 137 Associate degrees.

Community Environment: A rural location in central north Missouri, Trenton (population 6,700) has 11 churches, libraries, a hospital, and numerous civic, fraternal, and veteran's organizations. Several lakes are nearby offering excellent fishing, swimming, and boating. City parks also provide facilities for recreation. Part-time employment is available.

NORTHEAST MISSOURI STATE UNIVERSITY   (B-9)
East Normal Street
Kirksville, Missouri 63501
Tel: (816) 785-4000; (800) 892-7792; Admissions: (816) 785-4114; Fax: (816) 785-7456

Description: Northeast Missouri State University has served as a leader in education since its founding in 1867. It is accredited by the North Central Association of Colleges and Schools. Specific programs are accredited by respective professional institutions. The oldest institution of higher learning in Missouri's original state college system, Northeast now serves as Missouri's statewide public liberal arts and sciences university. The University has received national recognition for its Value-Added Model of Assessment, designed to ensure educational accountability and academic degrees of integrity. Northeast offers Bachelor of Arts, Bachelor of Fine Arts, Bachelor of Music, Bachelor of Science, and Bachelor of Science in Nursing degrees in academic divisions: Business and Accountancy; Fine Arts; Health and Exercise Science; Language and Literature; Mathematics and Computer Science; Nursing; Science; and Social Science. Northeast offers a 5-year teacher education program leading to the

B.A./B.S. and Master of Arts in Education degree. The Department of Communication Disorders offers programs of study leading to B.S., B.A., and M.A. degrees. Students may participate in Army ROTC through the division of Military Science. The university operates on the semester system and offers two summer sessions. Enrollment includes 2,512 male and 3,273 female full-time undergraduates and 124 male and 152 female part-time undergraduates, and 256 graduate students. A faculty of 334 full-time and 56 part-time gives a faculty-student ratio of 1-16.

Entrance Requirements: Admission is based upon high school performance (class rank, grade point average, and curriculum), test scores (ACT or SAT) and special ability, talent or achievement, and features an early admission policy for high-ability students; deferred admission, midyear admission, and advanced placement plans available.

Costs Per Year: Tuition $2,704 in-state; $4,856 out-of-state; room and board $3,416.

Collegiate Environment: Northeast's 140 acre campus consists of 39 buildings, including a library of 383,419 titles, 1,943 periodicals, more than 1,290,000 microforms and 52,624 audiovisual materials. Faculty/student interaction is encouraged through small groups known as "communities of learning." Students may participate in two honors programs -- a general program in the arts and sciences and a departmental program in most areas of study. Extensive undergraduate research opportunities are available. The university has a primarily residential campus; 2,855 students live in on-campus residence halls and student apartments. 76% of applicants meet criteria and are accepted. Financial aid is available and 80% of students receive some form of aid.

Community Environment: Kirksville, Missouri is located in the northeastern part of the state, a 3 to 4-hour drive from Kansas City, St. Louis, and Des Moines, Iowa, and 80 miles west of historic Hannibal, Missouri, and Qunicy, Illinois. The town is served by a direct Amtrak connection from Chicago and Quincy, IL. A municipal airport provides daily flights to and from Kansas City. Kirksville offers an environment for serious study in a community where higher education is the focal point. Besides University students, the community is home to 17,000 townspeople and nearly 500 medical students at the Kirksville College of Osteopathic Medicine.

NORTHWEST MISSOURI STATE UNIVERSITY   *(A-4)*
Maryville, Missouri 64468
Tel: (816) 562-1562; (800) 633-1175; Fax: (816) 562-1900

Description: The publicly supported liberal arts and teachers university was established in 1905. It is accredited by the North Central Association of Colleges and Schools and by several respective professional accrediting organizations. It functioned as a Normal School until 1919 when, by an Act of the Fiftieth General Assembly, it became the Northwest Missouri State Teachers College with the privilege of granting Bachelor's degrees. In 1945 it became Northwest Missouri State College, and in Aug., 1972 became Northwest Missouri State University. The primary objective is education and training of superior teachers for the elementary and secondary schools of Missouri, and to provide the necessary preprofessional and prevocational education for students who desire to enter other professions or vocations. The university grants Bachelor and Master degrees. Cooperative programs with engineering schools in the midwest are available. Enrollment includes 4,755 full-time and 413 part-time undergraduates and 833 graduate students. A faculty of 225 gives a student-faculty ratio of 1-22.

Entrance Requirements: Accredited high school graduation or equivalent; graduation in upper 66% in state and 50% of out-of-state high school class; graduates of unaccredited high schools are given credit toward entrance to college work; adults may establish eligibility through psychological and aptitude tests; early admission, early decision, midyear admission and rolling admission plans available; applicants for admission evaluated by high school marks, rank in high school class, standardized test scores.

Costs Per Year: $2,280 tuition state residents; $3,975 out-of-state residents; $3,330 room and board.

Collegiate Environment: The 325-acre campus has 17 buildings which include the new B.D. Owens Library with over 252,226 volumes, 1,159 seat Mary Linn Performing Arts Center and living accommodations for 1,450 men and 1,550 women. 87% of those who

apply are accepted, and students are admitted at midyear as well as in September. 1,964 scholarships are available including 1,866 for freshmen and about 80% of current student body receives some form of assistance.

Community Environment: Maryville (population 10,000) is a rural area in northwest Missouri. Dormitories, fraternity houses, and private homes provide housing. Community facilities include a library, 13 churches, a hospital, and several civic, national, and international branches of clubs and organizations are represented. Train and bus transportation is available. 90 miles from Kansas City, 45 from St. Joseph, 110 from Omaha and 125 from Des Moines.

OZARK BIBLE COLLEGE   *(K-5)*
1111 North Main
Joplin, Missouri 64801
Tel: (417) 624-2518; (800) 299-4622; Fax: (417) 624-0900

Description: The privately suported theological school offers four- and five-year degrees that prepare men and women for ministerial and specialized church vocations. Supported by the New Testament Christian Churches, it operates on the semester system. Enrollment includes 495 full-time and 79 part-time students. A faculty of 19 full-time and 13 part-time gives a faculty-student ratio of 1-18. In addition to academic subjects, the school offers music, intercollegiate and intramural athletic programs. An elementary education degree is also offered on a cooperative basis with Missouri Southern State College.

Entrance Requirements: Open enrollment policy; approved high school graduation or equivalent; completion of 15 units including the following: 3 English, 2 mathematics, 1 history, 2 science; applicants not meeting the requirements will be considered as special students; early admission, early decision and midyear admission plans available; application fee $30.

Costs Per Year: $3,040 tuition; $2,980 room and board; additional expenses average $908.

Collegiate Environment: Almost all students who apply to the school are accepted, including midyear students and those from various geographical locations. Students are expected to attend religious meetings and to be involved in Christian service. Unmarried students not living with parents are required to live in the dormitories, which accomodate 300 men and 300 women. The college library contains 50,000 volumes. 85% of the students receive some form of financial aid.

Community Environment: See Missouri Southern State College.

PARK COLLEGE   *(E-5)*
8700 River Park Drive
Parkville, Missouri 64152
Tel: (816) 741-2000; (800) 745-7275; Fax: (816) 746-6423

Description: The privately supported liberal arts college is affiliated with the Reorganized Church of Jesus Christ of Latter Day Saints. It was established in 1875 and the charter states that the principles of the college shall be nonsectarian. It is accredited by the North Central Association of Colleges and Schools. The college grants the Associate and Bachelor degrees. Weekend and Evening College Division programs are offered which allow working adults degree completion opportunity. Army ROTC is available. Enrollment includes 800 full-time and 200 part-time and 400 evening and weekend program undergraduates. A faculty of 50 full-time and 50 part-time gives a faculty-student ratio of 1-13.

Entrance Requirements: Accredited high school graduation or equivalent; moderately selective enrollment policy; SAT or ACT required, minimum scores SAT 400V, 400M, or ACT 20; rolling admission, early admission, delayed admission and advanced placement plans available; $25 application fee.

Costs Per Year: $3,990 tuition ($133/credit hour); $4,000 room and board.

Collegiate Environment: The 800-acre campus is situated high on a bluff of the Missouri River. The 21 buildings include an underground library of 120,000 volumes and dormitories to accommodate 176 men and 222 women. Approximately 90% of students applying for admission meet the requirements and all of these are accepted. Students are admitted at midyear as well as in September. Students are welcomed from all parts of the nation. Financial aid is available, and 90% of the current student body receives some form of assistance. 30% of last year's senior class continued on to graduate school.

Community Environment: See University of Missouri - Kansas City.

Branch Campuses: Metro Park, Park College Downtown, 934 Wyandotte Street, Kansas City, MO 64106, (816) 842-6182; Park College Independence, 2200 S. 291 Highway, Independence, MO 64057, (816) 252-9065.

PENN VALLEY COMMUNITY COLLEGE (E-5)
3201 Southwest Trafficway
Kansas City, Missouri 64111
Tel: (816) 932-7610

Description: The publicly supported community college provides liberal arts transfer and vocational programs and is a branch campus of the Metropolitan (Kansas City) Community College District. It is accredited by the North Central Association of Colleges and Schools, and professionally by the National League for Nursing (for nursing), and American Medical Association (for medical record librarian, medical technology, physical therapy). Enrollment includes 1,400 full-time and 3,600 part-time and 2,300 evening students. A faculty of 125 full-time and 275 part-time provides a faculty-student ratio of 1-20. Offers instrumental and vocal music groups, inter-collegiate basketball and golf, intra-mural athletics. Offers Cooperative Education program (alternating work and class periods) in business, secretarial, early childhood education. Offers pre-college programs for the educationally disadvantaged; 2-year pre-engineering course granting the AS degree with a transfer to Univ. of Mo. for 2 additional years for the BS degree.

Entrance Requirements: High school graduation or equivalent; open enrollment; under certain circumstances non-HS graduates accepted; rolling admission, midyear admission and advanced placement plans available.

Costs Per Year: $1,395 ($45/credit) district resident tution; $2,325 ($75/credit) out-of-district.

Collegiate Environment: The college is located on a 130-acre campus near Penn Valley Park. The library contains 73,000 volumes. All applicants who meet the requirements are accepted. Financial assistance is available.

Community Environment: See University of Missouri - Kansas City

ROCKHURST COLLEGE (E-5)
1100 Rockhurst Road
Kansas City, Missouri 64110
Tel: (816) 926-4100; (800) 842-6776; Fax: (816) 926-4100

Description: Founded in 1910 and directed by members of the Society of Jesus and affiliated with the Catholic Church, Rockhurst is a privately supported liberal arts college for men and women. The first freshman class was admitted in 1917. It is accredited by the North Central Association of Colleges and Schools and the National League for Nursing and grants the Bachelor degree through the College of Arts and Sciences, the College of Nursing and the School of Management; a Master's degree of Business Administration and a Master of Science in Physical Therapy and Occupational Therapy are also available. Army ROTC is available. The college operates on the semester system and offers two 5-week and one 8-week summer sessions. Undergraduate enrollment includes 564 men, 692 women full-time and 193 men, 487 women part-time. There are 722 graduate students. Theology and Philosophy are required. A faculty of 132 full-time and 85 part-time, gives a faculty-student ratio of 1:11.

Entrance Requirements: Accredited high school graduation or equivalent with completion of 16 units recommended; ACT preferred with a minimum of 20 and SAT accepted with a minimum of 400V, 400M; early admission, early decision, delayed admission, midyear admission, rolling admission and advanced placement plans available; $20 application fee.

Costs Per Year: $9,450 tuition; $4,000 room and board.

Collegiate Environment: The college is one of a cluster of leading educational and cultural institutions within walking distance of the heart of the city. The buildings include the three-story library containing 103,676 bound volumes, 704 current periodicals, 112,261 microforms and 2,446 audiovisual materials. Dormitory facilities for 245

men and 345 women. 87% of students applying for admission meets the requirements and are accepted. The college offers a special program including Study Abroad, available in Rome with Loyola University, in Spain and France with Marquette University, in London (England) with Richmond University, and in Mexico with Rockhurst. There are 100 endowed scholarships and 81% of those applying were eligible for some form of assistance.

Community Environment: See University of Missouri - Kansas City

SAINT LOUIS CHRISTIAN COLLEGE (A-16)
1360 Grandview Drive
Florissant, Missouri 63033
Tel: (314) 837-6777; (800) 887-7522; Admissions: (800) 887-7522; Fax: (314) 837-8291

Description: Founded in 1956, this coeducational Bible college is affiliated with the Christian churches and the churches of Christ. It is accredited by the American Association of Bible Colleges and is approved by various U.S. Government agencies. The school operates on an early semester system and prepares students for careers as ministers, evangelists, missionaries and teachers. Enrollment recently was 143 with a faculty of 12 full-time and 7 part-time members. The faculty-student ratio is 1-10. Special programs include evening classes, off-campus extensions, one-year Christian Service Certificates, credit for correspondence courses and credit in some courses prior examinations. The college also offers a degree completion program for adults called "Adults in Ministry" (AIM). Upon completion of the program, the student would graduate with a Bachelor degree in Christian Ministry. Sixty hours of previous college work is a prerequisite to the program. The school awards the Bachelor degree.

Entrance Requirements: Open enrollment policy with high school graduation or GED; the school gives its own entrance tests; early admission, early decision, rolling admission and advanced placement plans available; $30 application fee.

Costs Per Year: $3,540 tuition per semester, $3,660 room & board, $310 fees.

Collegiate Environment: Ninety-seven percent of applicants are admitted. 50% of the students receive financial aid. The library houses 47,000 volumes, Housing is available for 100 men and 100 women with 30 units for married students.

Community Environment: Population 65,908. Located some 17 miles northwest of St. Louis in the midst of a suburban setting.

SAINT LOUIS COLLEGE OF PHARMACY (F-14)
4588 Parkview Place
St. Louis, Missouri 63110
Tel: (314) 367-8700; (800) 278-5267; Admissions: (314) 367-8700 x264; Fax: (314) 367-2784

Description: The privately supported pharmacy college was established in 1864. The college offers the five-year Bachelor of Science degree in Pharmacy and the six-year Pharmacy Doctorate degree. It is accredited by the North Central Association of Colleges and Schools and by the American Council on Pharmaceutical Education. The college operates on the semester system and offers two summer sessions. Enrollment includes 317 men and 524 women full-time. A faculty of 63 full-time and 46 part-time gives a faculty-student ratio of 1-13. In addition to academic subjects, the college offers student council, PRIDE student ambassadors, band, chorus, intercollegiate men's basketball, women's volleyball, and intramural basketball and volleyball.

Entrance Requirements: Accredited high school graduation or equivalent with rank in upper 50% of graduating class; completion of 18 units including 4 English, 3 mathematics, 2 science; ACT required; rolling admission.

Costs Per Year: $9,650 per year, years 1-5; $10,950 year 6; $4,350 room and board, $150 student fees; $500 estimated additional expenses.

Collegiate Environment: The college building is situated in the medical and hospital center of the city, one block east of Forest Park. It contains a library of 35,553 volumes, and laboratories, classrooms, offices, and student lounge. The residence hall provides housing and dining accommodations for 132 men and women; 4 fraternities and 2 sororities provide additional housing for 12 men and 6 women. 80%

Community Environment: University students come from across the nation and the world and are active in numerous community services and volunteer efforts in the greater St. Louis area. Educating students with a social conscience and a commitment to helping others is an integral part of learning at Saint Louis University.

SAINT PAUL SCHOOL OF THEOLOGY   *(E-5)*
5123 Truman Road
Kansas City, Missouri 64127
Tel: (816) 483-9600

Description: The privately supported United Methodist graduate school began operations in 1959. It is accredited by the North Central Association of Colleges and Schools and the Association of Theological Schools. Saint Paul offers two graduate, professional degrees: The Master of Divinity Degree (a three year program with specilizations available in Religious Education, Gerontology, and Parish Development). The Doctor of Ministry Degree (an advanced professional degree for ministry, built upon the Master of Divinity work, and a method of personalized learning that is flexible and academically rigiorous). The seminary operates on a 4-1-4 semester system and a series of 1 week summer sessions. Enrollment is approximately 166 students. A faculty of 33 gives a faculty-student ratio of 1-5.

Entrance Requirements: Bachelor's degree or equivalent from an accredited college or university with minimum grade average of 2.75 on a 4.0 scale; applicants not meeting requirements may be admitted on probation; $25 application fee. For more information, contact the Office of Admissions.

Costs Per Year: $6,900 tuition; $64-$392 per month housing; $75 student fees. Financial aid available.

Collegiate Environment: The seminary life involves the whole person, addressing academic, professional, spiritual and personal development for ministry. The curriculum involves interdisciplinary team teaching and core structures which seek to integrate theory and practice. The library contains over 70,000 volumes, 340 current periodicals. Housing is available from double-occupancy to dormitory rooms to two-bedroom apartments.

Community Environment: See University of Missouri - Kansas City

SOUTHEAST MISSOURI STATE UNIVERSITY   *(J-16)*
1 University Plaza
Cape Girardeau, Missouri 63701
Tel: (314) 651-2250; Fax: (314) 651-2759

Description: The publicly supported university was established in 1873 as the Missouri Normal School. Throughout its history the university has followed the policy of offering a liberal education in the arts and sciences as a necessary foundation for career and professional training. It is the only senior college in southeast Missouri. It is accredited by the North Central Association of Colleges and Schools and professionally by the National Council for the Accreditation of Teacher Education, American Chemical Society, Council on Social Work Education, American Speech - Language - Hearing Association, American Dietetic Association, National Association of Schools of Music, and National League for Nursing. The university grants Associate, Bachelor, Master and Specialist degrees, and offers preparation for the state teaching certificate. Air Force and Army ROTC programs are available. It operates on the semester system and offers two summer terms. Enrollment includes 8,100 full-time and 2,300 part-time students. A faculty of 407 full-time and 60 part-time gives a faculty-student ratio of 1-18.

Entrance Requirements: Accredited high school graduation with 16 units or equivalent and an ACT score of 21 or above; non-high school graduates accepted with certain provisions; out-of-state high school graduates admitted on same basis as in-state students; early admission, early decision, rolling admission, midyear admission and advanced placement plans available; $20 application fee.

Costs Per Year: $2,625 fees for Missouri resident; $4,845 out-of-state fees; $3,700 room & board; estimated additional expenses $1,000.

Collegiate Environment: The college is located in Cape Girardeau, a growing city of over 35,000 inhabitants and a place of genuine historic interest. The 200-acre campus has 42 buildings including a library containing 500,000 volumes, and residence halls accomodate

1,400 men and 1,650 women. 75% of those who apply are admitted, including midyear students. 500 scholarships are offered including 300 for freshmen, and 60% of the undergraduates receive some form of financial aid. 65% of last year's freshman class returned for sophomore year.

Community Environment: Cape Girardeau (population 35,800) was founded in 1793 as an Indian trading post. It is now a progressive industrial city. Commercial transportation is convenient; other community facilities include many churches, hospitals, shopping areas and a library. Part time employment is available.

SOUTHWEST BAPTIST UNIVERSITY   *(J-7)*
1600 S. Springfield
Bolivar, Missouri 65613
Tel: (417) 326-5281; (800) 526-5859; Admissions: (417) 326-1810;
Fax: (417) 326-1514

Description: The privately supported liberal arts college was organized in 1878. The early history of the university is a record of sacrificial giving and extraordinary efforts by Baptists of Southwest Missouri and their friends. It is accredited by the North Central Association of Colleges and Schools and affiliated with the Southern Baptist Church. The school employs the 4-1-4 system with two summer sessions, and offers preparation for State teaching certificates. Religion subjects and chapel attendance are required. Army ROTC is available. Enrollment includes 1,741 full-time and 1,045 part-time undergraduates, and 416 graduate students. A faculty of 101 full-time and 107 part-time gives an undergraduate faculty-student ratio of 1-15.

Entrance Requirements: Accredited high school graduation or equivalent; open enrollment; under certain circumstances non-high school graduates may be accepted. ACT required, SAT may be substituted; special admission plans include early admission, early action, deferred entrance, and midyear admission; application fee $25.

Costs Per Year: $7,070 tuition; $2,5000 room and board; $152 student fees; $75 enrollment deposit.

Collegiate Environment: The older campus is located four blocks southwest of the public square in Bolivar, 28 miles north of Springfield. The new campus is one block south of the older campus. The 38 buildings on the 123-acre campus include living accommodations for 1,160. The library system contains 200,000 volumes, periodicals, microforms and audiovisual materials. 60% of those who apply are accepted, including midyear students. Financial assistance is available, and 90% of the current student body receives aid.

Community Environment: The county seat of Polk County, Bolivar (population 5,500) is in the midst of a recreational area and is the center of a developing lake region. Continental Trailways bus maintains passenger schedules to Springfield and Kansas City from Bolivar. A community concert association, allied with Columbia Artists Management of New York, brings quality musical attractions to Bolivar each season. The Southwest Regional Library which serves three counties is located here.

SOUTHWEST MISSOURI STATE UNIVERSITY   *(K-8)*
3201 West 16th Street
Springfield, Missouri 65301-2199
Tel: (417) 836-5517; (800) 492-7900; Fax: (417) 836-6334

Description: The publicly supported university established in 1905 as a teacher training college, is now one of the major universities of the Midwest. During the past four years, the university has experienced a significant increase in enrollment, and now has 12,283 full-time and 3,294 part-time students. It also has a faculty of 669 full time and 170 part time. As a comprehensive institution, SMSU offers more than 140 programs of study in six colleges: Arts and Letters, Business Administration, Education and Psychology, Health and Applied Sciences, Humanities, and Social Sciences. It uses the semester system with one summer session. U.S. Army ROTC is available.

Entrance Requirements: Accredited high school graduation or equivalent and a minimum composite ACT score of 17. Students outside the southwest Missouri district must also rank in the top two-thirds of their graduating class or have a minimum ACT composite score of 19. A $15 nonrefundable application fee is required.

Costs Per Year: $2,0758 tuition for Missouri resident; $5,308 out-of-state tuition; $3,180 room and board.

Collegiate Environment: The 152-acre campus has more than 50 buildings. The library contains over 584,000 volumes, 4,000 periodicals and 135 newspapers. There are 844,000 units in microform and state-of-the-art technology to assist students with library needs. Student housing is available for 4,000 students and a new residence hall is available. 18 fraternities and sororities provide additional housing for 450 students. Financial aid is available. The Family Financial Statement is the preferred application. The university recently awarded 1,920 Bachelor, 239 Master degrees and 27 Specialists degrees. 54% of the current student body graduated in the top half of their high school class, over 40% rank in the top quarter. The average ACT composite score of a recent Freshman class was 21.5.

Community Environment: Springfield (population 140,000) is Missouri's third largest city and is within one hour's drive from many of the popular resort and vacation areas of the southwest Missouri Ozark region. Springfield has become a major health care center for the region and is home to several major businesses and industries including Bass Pro Shops, General Electric, Zenith, Kraft, and Associated Wholesale Grocers.

Branch Campuses: West Plains, Missouri. Research Campus at Mountain Grove, Missouri.

STATE FAIR COMMUNITY COLLEGE   *(F-8)*
3201 West 16th Street
Sedalia, Missouri 65301-2199
Tel: (816) 530-5800; Fax: (816) 530-5820

Description: This publicly supported community college was founded in 1966. The school operates on the semester system with one summer term and offers liberal arts, transfer, vocational, and technical programs. It is accredited by the North Central Association of Colleges and Schools. Enrollment is 2,700 students. A faculty of 54 full-time and 75 part-time gives a faculty-student ratio of 1-23.

Entrance Requirements: Open enrollment policy; high school graduation or GED; ACT required for placement purposes; early admission, early decision, rolling admission, midyear admission and advanced placement plans available.

Costs Per Year: $1,050 tuition; $1,650 out-of-district; $3,210 out-of-state; $300 average additional expenses.

Collegiate Environment: The college is located immediately west of the Missouri State Fair Grounds on a 128-acre site. The Yeater Learning Center, opened in 1976, contains classrooms, offices, and the Learning Resources Center and Media Center. It is the first permanent building constructed according to master plans for the campus. In 1978 the Vocational-Technical Center opened, with classrooms for vocational programs, including the Area Vocational School. The library contains 39,000 hardbound volumes. All applicants meeting the requirements are accepted, including midyear students. Financial aid is available, and 42% of the current student body receives some form of assistance.

Community Environment: Sedalia (population 20,000) is a rural community, and is the home of the Missouri State Fair. It is also an industrial area that produces truck bodies, brooms, mops, wheels, toolboxes, restaurant equipment, and fans. All forms of commercial transportation are available. Good shopping facilities, many churches, and various service clubs are a part of the community's facilities. Some part-time employment opportunities are available. Parks provide opportunities for recreation.

STEPHENS COLLEGE   *(F-10)*
Box 2121
Columbia, Missouri 65215
Tel: (314) 876-7207; (800) 876-7207; Fax: (314) 876-7237

Description: This privately supported liberal arts college for women, the second oldest in the country, began in 1833 when Lucy Wales founded the Columbia Female Academy, later known as Stephens College. It is accredited by the North Central Association of Colleges and Schools. The College commits itself to the discovery and development of the potential of each student as an individual and as a member of society, and seeks to address the changing needs, roles, and aspirations of women. It has a cooperative plan with several

universities in animal science and engineering, and offers preparation for the state teaching certificate. Stephens sponsors seminars and tours in Europe, Japan, China, Africa, Mexico, and French-speaking Canada as course extensions. A half-year tutorial in Oxford, England and a year abroad in Cambridge, England are also available. The college operates on the semester system and offers one summer session. Enrollment includes 677 full-time and 368 part-time students. The faculty consists of 68 full-time and 27 part-time members, giving a faculty-student ratio of 1-10.

Entrance Requirements: High school graduation or equivalent with C average and 12 academic units; individual assessment of applications covering the high school attended, recommendations, academic record including class rank, subjects studied, GPA, proficiency in English, and SAT or ACT test scores; rolling admission, midyear admission, early decision and advanced placement plans available; $25 application fee.

Costs Per Year: $13,900 tuition; $5,200 room and board.

Collegiate Environment: The spacious 244-acre campus has 50 buildings located in the heart of Columbia and adjacent to the University of Missouri. The college is proud of its distinctive chapel, acknowledged to be one of the most beautiful buildings of its kind in the United States. The Hugh Stephens Resources Library, containing 126,814 bound volumes, 9,623 rolls of microfilm, 463 periodicals, 14 newspapers, and 4,825 records/tapes, is the central facility of the James Madison Wood Quadrangle. A television studio, science center, the Warehouse Theatre, and Johnson Plant Laboratory are additional facilities. Seven residence halls accommodate 775 students. The Stephens House Plan for living-learning began in 1960. Under this unique plan, 60 selected students and 4 faculty members relate the living and learning aspects of the college environment. The Honors Program encourages students of unusual ability to undertake honors work during their first years at the college. The college accepts 89% of those who apply, including midyear students, and welcomes students from 43 states and 5 countries. Financial aid is available, and 65% of the current student body receives some form of assistance. 75% of last year's freshman class returned for sophomore year.

Community Environment: Stephens College is located in Columbia, Missouri. Situated between Kansas City and St. Louis, Columbia is the cultural, medical, and business center of mid-Missouri. Often called "College Town, USA", Columbia is also the home of Columbia College and the University of Missouri. Stephens students have easy access to Columbia's shopping, dining, and entertainment offerings.

THREE RIVERS COMMUNITY COLLEGE   *(L-14)*
2080 Three Rivers Boulevard
Poplar Bluff, Missouri 63901
Tel: (314) 686-4101

Description: This publicly supported community college enrolls 1,108 full-time and 954 part-time students. A faculty of 110 gives a faculty-student ratio of 1-19. The school is fully accredited by the Commission of Institutions of Higher Education of the North Central Association of Colleges and Schools. Cooperative education programs (alternating work and class periods) are available in business management, construction and design, agribusiness, and office administrative systems. A freshman program for the educationally disadvantaged is also available. The school was established in 1966 and operates on the semester system with two summer terms. It offers college-parallel, preprofessional, vocational-technical, and adult continuing education programs.

Entrance Requirements: Accredited high school graduation or equivalent; ACT or ASSET required; open enrollment policy; early admission and advanced placement plans available; $10 application fee.

Costs Per Year: $660 district-resident tuition; $960 state resident; $1,620 out-of-state; $200 student fees.

Collegiate Environment: The college moved to a new 70-acre campus in the fall of 1979. The library contains nearly 35,000 volumes and 300 periodicals. 95% of students applying for admission are accepted, including midyear students and students from various geographical locations. Approximately 265 scholarships are offered, and 80% of students receive some form of financial assistance. 46% of the previous freshman class returned to the college for the second year of studies. The college recently awarded 22 Certificates and 130 Associate degrees, and 78 Associate of Applied Sciences degrees.

Community Environment: Poplar Bluff (population 25,000), is a metropolitan area in southeast Missouri where the climate is temperate and living is pleasant. Two general private hospitals and one veteran hospital, many churches, a library and numerous civic organizations are represented and active. Part-time jobs are available. Many natural streams and lakes within driving distance of the city provide excellent facilities for all outdoor sports.

UNIVERSITY OF HEALTH SCIENCES *(E-5)*
2105 Independence Boulevard
Kansas City, Missouri 64124-2395
Tel: (816) 283-2000; (800) 234-4847; Admissions: (816) 238-2350; Fax: (816) 283-2303

Description: The University of Health Sciences-College of Osteopathic Medicine (UHS-COM) is one of the oldest osteopathic colleges in the country. It is a privately supported, four-year medical school that awards the doctor of osteopathic degree. More than 5,700 physicians have graduated from UHS-COM since it was founded in 1916. The mission of UHS-COM is to prepare men and women to be exceptionally competent osteopathic physicians with a predominance of graduates engaged in providing primary care. The college is accredited by the Bureau of Professional Education of the American Osteopathic Association (AOA). UHS-COM is also approved by the Board of Education of the State of Missouri as an educational institution offering education and training to veterans. School enrollment is 180 per class, with an approximate total student enrollment of 640. UHS-COM faculty consists of approximately 30 full-time professors, 50 clinical lecturers, and 110 adjunct professors. UHS-COM enrolls students for a full year. First and second year curriculum is operated on a four-term system. Third and fourth year clinical services are continuous without terms or recesses.

Entrance Requirements: Applicants to UHS-COM should have a baccalaureate degree, or commendable completion of at least three-fourths (90 semester hours or 135 term credit hours) of the required credits for a baccalaureate degree, from a regionally accredited college or university. The baccalaureate degree is preferred and preference is given to those candidates who will have earned the degree prior to matriculation in a medical school program. In addition, completion of the following college courses, including laboratory work is required: 12 semester hrs. biology, 8 semester hrs. general chemistry, 8 semester hrs. organic chemistry (4 semester hrs. of this can be biochemistry), 8 semester hrs. physics, and 6 semester hrs. English composition and literature. Applicants are strongly advised to provide evidence of a solid foundation and to demonstrate proficiency in the biological and physical sciences. They are expected to have studied comparative vertebrate anatomy, genetics, bacteriology, and mathematics. Further they are encouraged to have taken courses in sociology, philosophy, and psychology. Applicants are also required to have taken the Medical College Admissions Test (MCAT). The supplemental application fee is $35.

Costs Per Year: Tuition, fees, and expenses for 1995-1996 include a $500 acceptance fee and $500 matriculation fee, both credited toward the first year tuition; a $19,740 tuition fee, which includes parking, library privileges, and laboratory supplies; a $50 activities fee; approximately $1,300 for a microscope; $795 for books the first year; $770 for instruments the first year. Tuition and book fees are subject to change annually.

Collegiate Environment: The UHS-COM campus is located approximately one mile northeast of downtown Kansas City, Missouri, in a neighborhood with rich historical significance and a strong present-day commitment to revitalization. Facilities include the recently renovated Alumni Hall, which is home to the new state-of-the-art academic resource center for students; the university library, containing more than 60,000 volumes and subscribing to more than 160 periodical and 80 serial titles; classrooms; the Administration Building; Peach Hall; Johnston HAll; Memorial Building; nd the UHS Osteopathic Medical Center. Construction of a 96,000 square-foot Educational Pavilion is currently underway at UHS-COM. Begun in 1994, the new building will house basic science labs, a 225-seat theatre-style classroom, faculty offices, a campus cafeteria, a two-story library, PO&P clinical rooms, a sports medicine center, and a research wing. The $9 million project will be completed in 1996. The college is selective, with approximately 8% of applicants being accepted. Students who are in good standing at another accredited college of Osteopathic Medicine may apply for a transfer, provided they meet the

requirements for admission and have satisfactorily completed equivalent courses to those offered by UHS-COM. Financial aid is available, with 87% of the current student body receiving some form of aid.

Community Environment: See University of Missouri - Kansas City

UNIVERSITY OF MISSOURI - COLUMBIA *(F-10)*
219 Jesse Hall
Columbia, Missouri 65211
Tel: (314) 882-2456; (800) 225-6075; Fax: (314) 882-7887

Description: The University of Missouri-Columbia is a public, coeducational institution organized into 18 schools and colleges. Accredited by the North Central Association of Colleges and Schools it offers more than 250 degree programs supplemented by more than 80 undergraduate emphasis areas. It is among the top 15 universities in the nation with the most Fulbright Scholars. MU ranks near the top of the nation's public universities in the number of National Merit and Achievement Scholars enrolled. The University has the world's first journalism school, the first teacher education program west of the Mississippi, and one of the nation's first electrical engineering departments. MU's Honor college offers a small-college atmosphere with individual attention, support, and opportunities found at a research university. Programs to assure high-ability freshmen admission to law, medical, and veterinary medicine schools as well as The Learning Center to provide free small-group tutoring for students in many general classes. The University also offers a major intercollegiate athletics program. The school operates on the semester system offering one 8-week and two 4-week summer sessions. Enrollment includes 14,727 full-time, 1,712 part-time undergraduate, and 4,584 graduate students. A faculty of 1,512 full-time and 47 part-time gives a faculty-student ratio of 1-19. Air Force, Army, and Navy ROTC programs are available.

Entrance Requirements: Admission is selective and is based on a combination of high school rank, ACT test scores, and high school course work; 15 high school units required including 4 English, 3 mathematics 2 social science, 2 science, 1-2 foreign language, 1 fine art, 3 additional electives; certified high school transcript; ACT; deferred admission, midyear admission, rolling admission, and advanced placement plans available; May 1 freshman admission deadline; March 1 financial aid consideration deadline; $25 application fee.

Costs Per Year: $3,525 state resident tuition and fees; $9,707 nonresident tuition and fees; $3,700 room and board.

Collegiate Environment: The 1,340-acre campus includes the largest research library in Missouri. It contains 2.6 million volumes, more than 22,000 magazines and journal subscriptions, and an on-line card catalog. Student housing, totaling 5,157, consists of coeducational and single-sex residence halls, fraternities, sororities, and family accommodations. The University is the only public university in Missouri with a chapter of Phi Beta Kappa, and has 404 student organizations. Athletic facilities on campus are available fo swimming, basketball, football, tennis, raquetball, handball, softball, soccer, and golf. The average ACT composite score of the 1994 freshman class was 25, and most freshmen rank in the top 20% of their high school class. 90% of applicants are offered admission. 64% of undergraduates received some form of financial aid.

Community Environment: Columbia, Missouri, was the second most liveable city in the United States according to Money magazine in 1992. Columbia has excellent educational opportunities and quality of life. Situated midway between St. Louis and Kansas City, the city offers, hotels, motels, and numerous educational and medical facilities. All forms of public transportation are available. The Lake of the Ozarks recreation area is within a 2-hour drive and provides opportunities for many outdoor sports.

UNIVERSITY OF MISSOURI - KANSAS CITY *(E-5)*
4825 Troost Avenue
Kansas City, Missouri 64110
Tel: (816) 235-1000; Admissions: (816) 235-1111; Fax: (816) 235-1717

Description: This Kansas City campus of the publicly supported University of Missouri has been one of the 4 campuses of the University of Missouri system since 1963. The institution was formerly the privately endowed University of Kansas City, founded in 1929. It is accredited by the North Central Association of Colleges and Schools and by respective professional and educational organizations in the following subject areas: business, chemistry, dentistry, dental hygiene, engineering, law, medical technology, medicine, music, pharmacy, psychology, public administration, and teacher education. Preparation for State teaching certificate is available. The Schools of Dentistry and of Medicine offer a combined program with the College of Arts and Sciences that enables students to earn an undergraduate degree and an M.D. or D.D.S. degree in the course of 6 years. The university operates on the semester calendar system and offers one summer session. The total enrollment is 4,469 men and 5,493 women. Enrollment includes 5,319 undergraduates, 3,445 graduate students and 1,198 graduate professionals. The undergraduate enrollment is comprised of 1,595 men and 1,811 women full-time and 886 men and 1,027 women part-time. A faculty of 529 full-time and 273 part-time gives an overall faculty-student ratio of 1-13.

Entrance Requirements: Accredited high school graduation or equivalent; ACT required; admission on basis of combination class rank and test scores; early admission, early decision, midyear admission, rolling admission and advanced placement plans available.

Costs Per Year: $3,800 state-resident fee; $10,422 out-of-state tuition and fees; $3,690 room and board.

Collegiate Environment: The University of Missouri-Kansas City has 3 campus sites, which include such facilities as an outstanding art gallery; a new Medical School, a School of Dentistry, and various other health-related facilities; and a library system containing over 942,116 volumes and 8,764 periodicals. Dormitories accommodate 316 students. 448 scholarships are available, including 228 for freshmen. 82% of the current student body receives some form of assistance.

Community Environment: One of the country's largest railroad centers, Kansas City is also a great manufacturing city and an important distributing point located at the confluence of the Kansas and Missouri Rivers. All forms of commercial transportation are convenient. Extensive cultural activities are available. Recreational facilities are numerous. Swope Park is one the largest municipal playgrounds in the country that contains 1,705 acres, two golf courses, tennis courts, picnic grounds, a zoo, swimming pool and a lagoon for boating. Kansas City is the home of the Chiefs of the National Football League and Royals baseball team of the American League. The Country Club district in the southern part of the city has gained international attention as a model for city planning. Each home in this district is planned to harmonize with its surroundings, and careful selection of European art objects beautify street corners.

UNIVERSITY OF MISSOURI - ROLLA   *(I-11)*
102 Parker
Rolla, Missouri 65401
Tel: (314) 341-4114; (800) 522-0938; Admissions: (314) 341-4904

Description: The Rolla campus of the publicly supported University of Missouri was founded in 1870 as the University of Missouri School of Mines and Metallurgy. Recent enrollment numbered 3,281 men and 1,064 women. The undergraduate student body is composed predominantly of engineering and science majors, but a growing number of students are enrolling in its Liberal Arts degree programs. The university is accredited by the North Central Association of Colleges and Schools and professionally by the Accreditation Board for Engineering and Technology (for aerospace, ceramic, chemical, civil, electrical, engineering management, geological, mechanical, metallurgical and materials, mining, petroleum, and nuclear engineering), and the computer Science Accreditation commission. Enrollment includes 3,830 full-time and 515 part-time undergraduates and 697 graduate students. A faculty of 358 full-time and 95 part-time gives a faculty-student ratio of 1-14.

Entrance Requirements: Accredited high school graduation or equivalent, completion of 15 units including 4 English, 4 mathematics, 2 science, 2 social science; ACT, SAT required; GRE required for some disciplines; nondegree candidates 21 years of age admitted on examination; early admission, early decision, rolling admission, delayed admission, midyear admission and advanced placement plans available.

Costs Per Year: $3,954 fees for Missouri residents; $10,136 out-of-state tuition; $3,735 average room and board.

Collegiate Environment: University facilities include a library of 450,619 volumes and housing for 1,350 students. 94% of the applicants are accepted. 2,125 scholarships are available and 67% of students receive some form of financial aid.

Community Environment: Rolla, population 15,000, is one of the most scenic sections of the Ozarks, where excellent fishing and hunting are available. Situated in the center of Missouri, on Interstate 44, planes provide transportation. A number of churches of most denominations, a hospital, clinics, a library and civic organizations are all a part of the community services. Lake and river recreation available, caves to explore, tennis courts, baseball diamonds, golf courses, and bowling alleys provide recreation. Part time employment for students is available. Rolla originally was an Ozarks farm trade center. After the establishment of the university campus, several large and important federal and state government agencies located here. Today the community is unusual in its concentration of about 1,000 professional engineers, geologists, cartographers, mathematicians, and technicians who are employed by these offices.

UNIVERSITY OF MISSOURI - SAINT LOUIS   *(F-14)*
8001 Natural Bridge Road
St. Louis, Missouri 63121
Tel: (314) 553-5451

Description: The St. Louis campus of the publicly supported University of Missouri is the newest of the four branches. It was established in 1963 as a two-year residence center and advanced to senior college status in 1965. It is accredited by the North Central Association of Colleges and Schools and professionally by the American Association of Collegiate Schools of Business, American Chemical Society, National Council for Accreditation of Teacher Education and many others. The school features liberal arts and teacher education with preparation for State teaching certificate. Enrollment includes 5,078 full-time, 4,325 part-time undergraduates and 2,650 graduate students. A full-time faculty of 410 and part-time faculty of 245 gives an overall faculty-student ratio of 1-14. The college operates on the semester system and offers two summer terms.The college offers a cooperative education program (alternating work and class periods) in business administration, and pre-college and freshman programs for the educationally disadvantaged. U.S. Army and Air Force ROTC are optional.

Entrance Requirements: Accredited high school graduation or equivalent with C average; completion of 15 units including 4 English, 3 mathematics, 2 science, 2 social science, 1 fine art, and 3 additional credits, 2 of them foreign language, recommended; non-high school graduates 18 years and older may qualify by examination; out-of-state candidates must rank in upper half of graduating class; ACT or SAT required; GRE required for graduate school; rolling admission, midyear admission, and advanced placement plans available.

Costs Per Year: $2,424 state-resident tuition; $7,224 out-of-state tuition.

Collegiate Environment: The 172-acre campus is developing rapidly. Three fully equipped buildings house classrooms, laboratories, offices, and library facilities. There are administration, office buildings and a physics annex. Dormitory housing is available for 360 students. The library contains 571,363 titles, 3,000 periodicals, 1,497,563 microforms. Students may enroll at midyear and are accepted from various geographical locations. Financial aid is available, and 38% of the current student body receives some form of assistance.

Community Environment: See Washington University.

WASHINGTON UNIVERSITY   *(F-14)*
One Brookings Drive
Campus Box 1089
St. Louis, Missouri 63130
Tel: (314) 935-6000; (800) 638-0700; Fax: (314) 935-4290

Description: This private, independent university is accredited by the North Central Association of Colleges and Schools and by numerous professional accrediting organizations. It was established in 1853 under the name of Eliot Seminary. Later, as the educational program developed, the present name was adopted. Today the university is composed of 9 accredited schools in Architecture, Arts and Sciences, Business and Public Administration, Continuing Education, Engineering, Fine Arts, Law, Medicine, and Social Work. It operates on the semester system and offers three summer sessions. Enrollment includes 4,930 full-time, 1,152 part-time undergraduate, 5,087 graduate, and 1,486 evening students. A faculty of 1,966 full-time and 1,496 part-time gives an undergraduate faculty-student ratio of 1-6. Air Force and Army ROTC is available.

Entrance Requirements: Accredited high school graduation or equivalent; recommended completion of 16 academic units including 4 English, 3-4 mathematics, 2 foreign language, 3-4 science, and 2-3 social science; SAT or ACT required; GRE required for graduate school; early admission, early decision, deferred admission, midyear admission and advanced placement plans available; Jan. 1 early decision application deadline, Jan. 15 for regular admission; $50 application fee.

Costs Per Year: $18,350 tuition; $5,775 room and board; $184 student fees.

Collegiate Environment: The University is comprised of 50 buildings located on 169 acres. All schools except medicine are located on the main campus. The libraries contain 3.05 million titles, 19,000 periodicals, 2.5 million microforms and 31,400 records, tapes, and CDs. Dormitory facilities are provided for 3,000 students. Eleven national fraternities have houses located on or near the campus. Sororities have no houses on or off the campus, but maintain chapter rooms in the Women's Building. 65% of applicants are accepted. Financial aid is available, and 45% of students receive some form of financial assistance.

Community Environment: St. Louis, with its metropolitan population of 2.5 million, offers countless opportunities for undergraduates to explore. It is one of the great industrial centers of the nation and its second largest inland port, as well as a leading world market. The city is home to the Gateway Arch, St. Louis Symphony Orchestra, Missouri Botanical Gardens, Busch Memorial Stadium, Lambert-St. Louis International Airport, and a variety of impressive museums, theaters and historic sites. Forest Park, one of the country's largest municipal parks, boasts art, history, and science museums, a zoo, as well as an outdoor theater offering light opera during the summer. The cost of living in the St. Louis area is relatively low. In addition to the urban attractions, there are many leisure and recreational activities available, including bicycling, hiking, horseback riding, fishing, and sailing to name a few.

WEBSTER UNIVERSITY *(G-14)*
470 East Lockwood Blvd.
St. Louis, Missouri 63119-3194
Tel: (314) 968-6900; (800) 753-6765; Admissions: (314) 968-6991; Fax: (314) 968-7115

Description: The privately supported independent liberal arts university was established in 1915 and is accredited by the North Central Association of Colleges and Schools, the National Association of Schools of Music and the National League of Nursing. The university operates on the semester system and also offers one summer session. The university enrolls 10,335 students worldwide. The undergraduate college on the St. Louis campus enrolls 1,633 full-time, 1,285 part-time undergraduates and 1,935 graduate students. A faculty of 114 full-time and 300 part-time gives an undergraduate faculty-student ratio of 1-13. The university offers preparation for State teaching certificates; independent study, inter-institutional registration; practicums and/or internships; and an accelerated BA/MA program. The university offers a variety of study abroad opportunities at its European campuses in Geneva, Switzerland; Vienna, Austria; Leiden, The Netherlands; and London, England.

Entrance Requirements: Accredited high school graduation or equivalent is required. Recommended admission requirements include rank in upper 50% of graduating class; the completion of a college preparatory program (16 units); autobiographical statement; one or more letters of recommendation; SAT or ACT score results; rolling admission, early admission, deferred admission, midyear admission and advanced placement plans are available; priority deadline for fall applications is April 1; $25 application fee.

Costs Per Year: $9,700 tuition; $4,500 room and board.

Collegiate Environment: The university is located on a 47 acre campus and includes a library of 222,000 volumes and dormitory facilities for 310 students. 75% of those who apply are accepted, including midyear students and students from various geographical locations.

The average high school standing of the current freshmen was 47% in top quarter of class and 80% in top half of class. The average scores of the entering freshman class were SAT 486 verbal, 513 math, and ACT 23 composite. Financial aid is available, and 59% of the student body receives some form of assistance.

Community Environment: A suburban area 10 miles from St. Louis, Webster Groves (population 27,455) has the convenience of all major forms of transportation. The shopping facilities here are excellent, numerous civic and service organizations are active. Webster Groves also enjoys the recreational and cultural advantages of St. Louis. Other facilities include a library, and churches of major denominations. Some part-time employment is available.

WENTWORTH MILITARY ACADEMY AND JUNIOR COLLEGE *(E-6)*
1800 Washington Avenue
Lexington, Missouri 64067
Tel: (816) 259-2221; (800) 962-1880; Fax: (816) 259-2677

Description: The privately supported military academy comprises a four-year high school and a two-year junior college for men and women. Although the two divisions maintain a very close relationship, they are entirely separate and distinct units. The academy was established in 1880 and the junior college was organized in 1923. It is accredited by the North Central Association of Colleges and Schools. Recently the academy enrolled 300 students. A faculty of 48 gives a faculty-student ratio of 1-9. The school operates on the semester system and offers one summer term. Army ROTC program is compulsory. The school offers liberal arts and professional transfer programs. Music programs, and intercollegiate and intramural athletics are also offered in addition to academic subjects.

Entrance Requirements: Open enrollment policy; high school graduation or equivalent; SAT or ACT required; early admission, early decision, rolling admission, delayed admission, midyear admission and advanced placement plans available; application deadline for fall semester is August 15; $50 application fee.

Costs Per Year: $14,750 tuition, room and board, and required fees and uniforms.

Collegiate Environment: The academy has a campus comprising 137 acres that includes its own country club and golf course. There are 13 modern buildings, a library of 20,000 volumes and dormitory facilities for 310 students. Approximately 75% of students applying for admission are accepted, including midyear students. 10 scholarships, including five for freshmen are available. About 85% of the previous freshman class returned to the academy for a second year.

Community Environment: On the bank of the Missouri River, Lexington (population 5,388) is 40 miles east of Kansas City. All forms of commercial transportation are available. Community facilities include a regional hospital, churches of all denominations, a library, and numerous civic and fraternal organizations. Outdoor activities are golf, fishing, boating, and swimming. Several historic points of interest are the Anderson House, Civil War Battle of Lexington State Park, and the Madonna of the Train Monument.

WESTMINSTER COLLEGE *(F-10)*
7th and Westminster Avenue
Fulton, Missouri 65251
Tel: (314) 642-3361

Description: The privately supported coeducational liberal arts college was founded as Fulton College in 1851 and adopted its present name in 1853. The college operates on the semester system and offers 1 summer session. It is accredited by the North Central Association of Colleges and Schools. Enrollment includes 675 full-time undergraduate students. A full-time faculty of 62 gives a faculty-student ratio of 1-13. The college offers an overseas program with the Institute of European Studies in England, France, Germany, Austria, and Spain. Domestic programs include Washington Semester, United Nations Semester, cooperative program with William Woods University, and with Mid-Missouri Associated Colleges, 3-2 engineering program with Washington University, (Westminster grants B.A., Washington B.S.). Optional U.S. Army ROTC and preparation for State teaching certificate are available.

Entrance Requirements: Accredited high school graduation or equivalent with rank in upper 50% of graduating class; completion of

12 academic units; SAT or ACT required; under certain circumstances non-high school graduates may be accepted; special admission plans include early admission, rolling admission, delayed admission, advanced placement; applications for the fall semester should be submitted by March 15. $25 application fee.

Costs Per Year: $11,150 tuition; $4,250 board and room; $200 student fees; additional expenses average $1,200.

Collegiate Environment: The college consists of 23 buildings located on 55 acres, and includes dormitory facilities for 240 men and 180 women; 6 fraternities provide additional housing for 200 men. The Westminster library and the library of nearby William Woods University are completely cross-indexed and both collections are available to students on both campuses. Combined, these libraries contain over 150,000 volumes. 80% of the students who apply are accepted. The college welcomes a geographically diverse student body and will accept midyear students. Financial aid is available, and 75% of the current student body receives some form of assistance. About 88% of the previous freshman class returned to the college for the sophomore year.

Community Environment: See William Woods University.

WILLIAM JEWELL COLLEGE *(E-5)*
500 College Hill
Liberty, Missouri 64068
Tel: (816) 781-7700

Description: The privately supported liberal arts college was established in 1849 and is supported by the Baptist Convention. It is accredited by the North Central Association of Colleges and Schools. It operates on the semester system and offers one summer session. Enrollment includes 1,323 full-time and 71 part-time students. A faculty of 95 full-time and 51 part-time gives a faculty-student ratio of 1-14. Offers extensive programs in music, inter-collegiate and intra-mural athletics; preparation for State teaching certificate. Religion subjects required. Academic 3-2 cooperative programs in engineering with Columbia University, Washington University, The University of Missouri at Columbia, and the University of Missouri at Rolla; in forestry with Duke University. The Oxbridge Alternative is a program of tutorial and examination through which a small number of intellectually distinguished students may pursue their area of concentration. It is an American adaptation of the great English universities, Oxford and Cambridge. Numerous foreign study program provide opportunities for students to study anywhere in western Europe.

Entrance Requirements: Accredited high school graduation or equivalent with "C" average and rank in upper half of graduating class; completion of 4 units of English, 3 mathematics, 2 science, 2 foreign language; ACT or SAT required. Special admission plans: early admission, early decision, rolling admission, midyear admission, advanced placement. $25 application fee.

Costs Per Year: $10,580 tuition, $2,970 board and room.

Collegiate Environment: The college is located on a 140-acre campus in the northeastern corporate limits of Liberty. The college buildings include a library of 218,500 volumes and living accommodations for 628 men, 514 women, and 35 families. Sixty percent of the applicants are accepted, including students from other geographical locations and midyear students. Financial aid is available, and 85% of the current student body receives some form of assistance.

Community Environment: A suburban community, Liberty is 13 miles northwest of Kansas City and enjoys all the cultural and recreational advantages of Kansas City. Several points of interest are The city of Kansas City provides a place for the William Jewell Fine Arts Series to perform opportunities such as the Ballet Company of Missouri, The Kansas City Symphony and The Nelson Museum of Art are also available. Kansas City provides professional football and baseball teams. There are lakes, a zoo and many parks and recreation sites close to campus as well. The Foundations program provides a wealth of general knowledge through a core of interdisciplinary courses using the central theme of Humanities, the Social Sciences and Mathematical and Natural Science.

WILLIAM WOODS UNIVERSITY *(F-10)*
200 West 12th Street
Fulton, Missouri 65251
Tel: (314) 642-2251; (800) 995-3159; Fax: (314) 592-1146

Description: The private, applied liberal arts college for women was established in 1870 and has been accredited since 1919 by the North Central Association of Colleges and Schools. William Woods offers more than 38 major degree programs, a unique offering of dual degree programs, and foreign study semesters. The cooperative program with five colleges and universities within a 30-mile radius allows students to enroll in various courses on other campuses. Internships are incorporated into most degree programs, giving students valuable experience in their major area of study. All faculty members hold advanced degrees, there are no teaching assistants. Summer study program with trips to New York City, Los Angeles, England, Greece, and elswhere, is available. The academic calendar offers a two semester program with optional two summer terms. Enrollment includes 683 full-time and 119 part-time undergraduate, and 90 graduate students. A faculty of 46 full-time and 30 part-time gives a faculty-student ratio of 1-13.

Entrance Requirements: Accredited high school graduation or equivalent with rank in upper half of graduating class; completion of 16 units; SAT or ACT required; early admission, rolling admission, midyear admission, and advanced placement plans available; $25 application fee.

Costs Per Year: $11,300 tuition; $4,700 room and board.

Collegiate Environment: The scenic campus is located on 160 acres with two lakes. The 46 buildings include 13 residence halls that accomodate 800 students, a student center, dining hall, extensive equestrian facilities and a sports complex. The William Woods and Westminster libraries are cross-indexed and available to students on both campuses. The libraries house 146,899 volumes. A geographically diverse student body hails from 45 states and several foreign countries. 90% of applicants are accepted. Extracurricular activities include choral music, student publications, theater productions, intra-mural and intercollegiate athletics, four national sororities, and more than 40 clubs and organizations. Academic, leadership, and departmental scholarships are available. 92% of students receive some form of financial aid.

Community Environment: The wooded Missouri landscape provides a scenic setting for residents of the area. Colleges, state educational and health facilities and professional industries are primary employers. Part-time employment is available. The regional area provides major medical centers, churches, libraries, restaurants, and recreational and entertainment facilities.

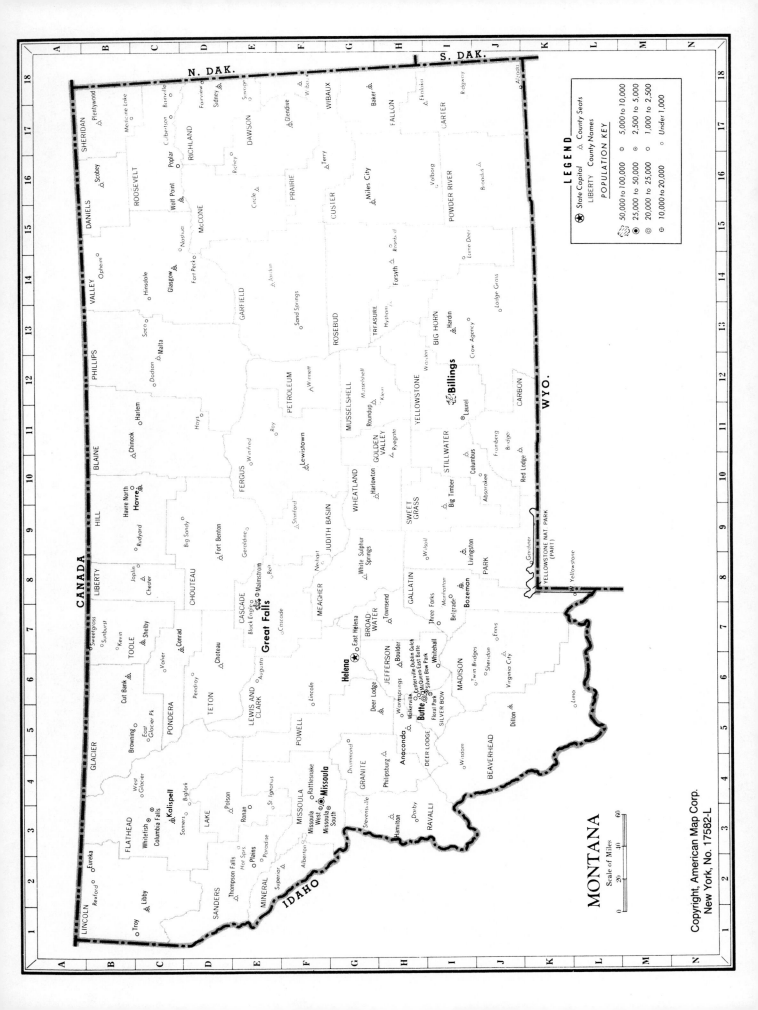

MONTANA

Scale of Miles

Copyright, American Map Corp.
New York, No. 17582-L

LEGEND

⊛ State Capital   ⊙ County Seats

LIBERTY   County Names

POPULATION KEY

MONTANA

CARROLL COLLEGE   *(G-6)*
N. Benton Avenue
Helena, Montana 59625
Tel: (406) 447-4384; (800) 992-3648; Fax: (406) 447-4533

Description: The four-year, independent college is accredited by the Northwest Association of Schools and Colleges, American Library Association of Independent Colleges and Schools, Council on Social Work Education, National Council for Accreditation of Teacher Education and the National League for Nursing. The basic purpose of the college is to teach people how to think, how to earn a living, how to live, and how to understand and appreciate other human beings. The college was founded in 1909 and is conducted under the immediate supervision of the Roman Catholic Bishop of Helena. It operates on the semester system and offers two summer sessions. Enrollment includes 1,150 full-time and 288 part-time students. A faculty of 70 full-time and 40 part-time gives a faculty-student ratio of 1-13. The college grants a Baccalaureate degree and offers continuing education and a cooperative education program.

Entrance Requirements: Accredited high school graduation with rank in upper 60% of graduating class; ACT or SAT required; application fee $25; early admission, early decision, rolling admission, delayed admission and advanced placement plans available.

Costs Per Year: $8,650 tuition; $3,810 room and board; $290 student fees; $1,440 personal expenses.

Collegiate Environment: The site for the college's 64-acre campus had previously been contemplated for the State Capitol, and accordingly got its name, Capitol Hill. Among the 11 buildings is a library of 94,000 volumes, 562 periodicals, and 25,000 microforms. The astronomical observatory houses a 12-inch reflecting telescope of the Newtonian type. A seismograph station is operated in cooperation with the United States Coast Guard and Geodetic Survey. There is dormitory capacity of 400 men and 400 women on campus. The college is primarily a residence school, and students who reside outside the city of Helena must live in the dormitories. Financial aid is available for economically handicapped students and 83% of the current student body receives some form of assistance. 92% of students applying for admission who meet the requirements are accepted. Classes begin in September, January and June, and midyear students are accepted. Almost 70% of a previous freshman class returned to the campus for their second year. The school recently awarded 205 Bachelor degrees and 5 Associate degrees.

Community Environment: Capital of Montana since 1875, Helena is the seat of many state and federal agencies. However, it owes its existence to humbler circumstances. In 1864, "The Georgians," four weary and discouraged southern prospectors, stumbled down a gulch which, after a brief inspection, they decided to prospect. Grimly they dubbed it "Last Chance Gulch," only to find gold in what is now the main street of Helena. More than $200 million in gold has since been taken from this and surrounding mines. Recreation in the local area includes hunting, fishing, boating, hiking, skiing and other winter sports. The city has a symphony orchestra, an historical library and holds art exhibits. Various civic, fraternal and veteran's organizations are active within the town.

COLLEGE OF GREAT FALLS   *(E-7)*
1301 20th Street, So.
Great Falls, Montana 59405
Tel: (406) 761-8210; (800) 856-9544; Admissions: (406) 791-5200; Fax: (406) 791-5395

Description: This independent, liberal arts, Catholic college is conducted by the Sisters of Providence and is open to qualified men and women of every race and creed. Academic programs are offered by two colleges with six schools and the College of Graduate Studies and Outreach Studies (Telecom), the College of Arts and Sciences, and the College of Professional Studies. The college operates on the semester system and offers three summer sessions. It is accredited by the Northwest Association of Schools and Colleges. Enrollment includes 287 men and 495 women full-time, and 180 men and 397 women part-time. Of these, 1,241 are undergraduates. A faculty of 42 full-time and 97 part-time provides an undergraduate faculty-student ratio of 1-15.

Entrance Requirements: Accredited high school graduation or equivalent; open enrollment policy; completion of 16 units including 4 English, 2 math, 1 lab science, 1.5 social studies, and 1 physical education; SAT or ACT recommended; early admission, early decision, and rolling admission plans available; $25 application fee.

Costs Per Year: $4,650 tuition; $990 room; $150 student fees.

Collegiate Environment: The 41-acre campus of the college is ten minutes from the heart of the city. Providence Tower, the major campus landmark, serves as the college bell tower and as a memorial of the first 100 years of service by the Sisters of Charity of Providence to Montana. A library contains 102,052 volumes. Apartment housing accomodates 98 students. Financial aid is available for economically disadvantaged students, and 77% of the current student body receives some assistance. 99% of those who apply for admission are accepted, including midyear students.

Community Environment: Montana's second largest city, Great Falls is an industrial, financial, wholesale and distributing center. Major agricultural pursuits in the area are livestock farming and wood production. Known as the city "between the parks," Great Falls is almost equidistant to Yellowstone and Glacier National Parks. The winters are moderate. Summer evenings are cool. The area is served by air, rail, and bus lines. Local attractions include dude and guest ranches, fishing, hunting, and skiing. Some employment opportunities are available in the area.

DAWSON COMMUNITY COLLEGE   *(F-17)*
300 College Drive
Glendive, Montana 59330
Tel: (406) 365-3396; (800) 821-8320; Admissions: (406) 365-3396; Fax: (406) 365-8132

Description: Dawson Community College, one of the three units in Montana's Community College System, was founded in 1940. It is a multipurpose, two-year college that offers numerous Associate of Art and Associate of Applied Science degrees as well as one-year programs in various vocational fields. Dawson Community College serves an 11-county area in Montana. It operates on the semester system and offers one summer session. Enrollment is 401 full-time and 194 part-time students. A faculty of 21 full-time and 48 part-time gives a faculty-student ratio of 1-15. Dawson is accredited by the Northwest Association of Schools and Colleges.

Entrance Requirements: Accredited high school graduation or GED; non-high school graduates 18 years or older may be admitted as special students; rolling admission and midyear admission plans; $30 application fee.

Costs Per Year: $840 tuition; $1,442 out-of-district; $3,493 out-of-state; $1,215 room; $504 student fees.

Collegiate Environment: The Dawson Community College campus is 350 acres on the southern edge of the city near the entrance to Makoshika State Park, a badlands and fossil-hunting area. On campus are classrooms, student center, a library of 20,000 titles, a gym, office building, student apartments and a new classroom/vocational technical building. Residence halls accommodate 92 students. Scholarships are available and 58% of the students receive some form of financial aid.

Community Environment: Dawson is located in Glendive, the county seat of Dawson County. It is a transportation, agricultural and energy resource center located on the Yellowstone River on I-94. The city has a library, Frontier Gateway Museum, several churches, a hospital, and most major civic, fraternal and veteran's organizations within the immediate area. Recreation facilities include indoor and outdoor theaters, good hunting, limited boating and fishing, golf, and other outdoor sports. Some part-time work is available for students.

FLATHEAD VALLEY COMMUNITY COLLEGE   *(C-3)*
777 Grandview Drive
Kalispell, Montana 59901
Tel: (406) 756-3822; Admissions: (406) 756-3846; Fax: (406) 756-3965

Description: The public, community college opened its doors in 1967 to enroll about 600 students. It operates on the semester system and offers one summer session. The school is fully accredited by the Montana State Board of Education and by the Northwest Association of Schools and Colleges. Enrollment is 807 full-time and 807 part-time students. A faculty of 35 full-time and 74 part-time gives a faculty-student ratio of 1-18.

Entrance Requirements: High school graduation or equivalent; open enrollment policy; rolling admission plan available.

Costs Per Year: $1,008 county-resident tuition; $1,540 state resident; $2,716 out-of-state; $3,825 room; $1,575 board; $475 student fees.

Collegiate Environment: The college has a brand new 4-building campus. The library has a collection of 13,000 volumes and 123 periodicals. Scholarships are available. All of the applicants are accepted. The campus is located 3 miles north of Kalispell city center. 270 scholarships are available including 98 for freshmen.

Community Environment: Kalispell is in the beautiful Flathead Valley, a region noted for the production of seed potatoes, wheat, cattle, Christmas trees, plywood, lumber and sweet cherries. The city is circled by dense forests, lakes, and mountains, with more than 2,000 miles of good fishing streams. Transportation for the area is provided by air, rail, and bus lines. There are 28 churches, one library, a hospital and a medical center. Convenient shopping is easily accessible. Although Kalispell is a resort area, the local industries include plywood production, camper and camp trailer manufacturing, log-skidding machinery, and chemical and concrete products. Part-time employment is available for students.

MILES COMMUNITY COLLEGE   *(G-16)*
2715 Dickinson
Miles City, Montana 59301
Tel: (406) 232-3031; (800) 541-9281; Fax: (406) 232-5705

Description: The public, two-year, community college offers transfer, career, and continuing education programs. The school was established in 1939 in accordance with a law passed by the Legislative Assembly of the State of Montana. The college is accredited by the Northwest Association of Schools and Colleges. It operates on the semester system and offers one summer session. Enrollment includes 160 men and 275 women full-time and 59 men and 174 women part-time. A faculty of 35 full-time and 37 part-time provides a teacher-student ratio of 1-14.

Entrance Requirements: Open enrollment policy; high school graduation or equivalent; non-graduates considered; early admission, early decision, rolling admission, midyear admission and advanced placement plans available. $30 application fee.

Costs Per Year: $784 district-resident tuition; $1,442 out-of-district tuition; $3,388 out-of-state tuition; $3,020 room and board; $504 student fees.

Collegiate Environment: 5 buildings serve the college, including the Vocational-Technical building, the library-classroom building and a recreation center and dormitory. The library contains 17,311 volumes. Financial aid is available, and 93% of the current student body receives some form of assistance. Of the 190 scholarships offered, 120 are for freshmen. All of the applicants are accepted.

Community Environment: Vast livestock ranches around Miles City raise more than one-fourth of the cattle and sheep produced in Montana. Wheat is the primary crop grown in the dryland area. The city itself is a pleasant residential town with a mean annual temperature of 44.4 degrees, and an average rainfall of 13.79 inches. Local area is served by airlines and bus lines. The community has 17 churches, tennis courts, two theaters, bowling alley, golf course, radio and TV station and various civic and fraternal organizations. Local hotels and motels provide student housing. There are limited part-time work opportunities for students.

MONTANA STATE UNIVERSITY   *(I-8)*
Bozeman, Montana 59717-0218
Tel: (406) 994-2452

Description: Montana State University is accredited by the Northwest Association of Schools and Colleges. It is the largest of six institutions that make up the Montana University System. It was established as an agricultural college in 1893. Today, Montana State University is a multipurpose university with programs in the liberal arts, professional areas, agriculture, engineering, and the basic sciences. It is a comprehensive university, with widely diversified academic offerings that lead to bachelor's degrees in 46 different areas of study covering about 125 possible majors, master's degrees in 38 areas, and doctorates in 15 areas. Voluntary Army and Air Force ROTC programs are available. It operates on the semster system and offers one summer session. Enrollment includes 8,672 full-time and 1,124 part-time undergraduate and 1,166 graduate students. A faculty of 507 full-time and 140 part-time gives a faculty-student ratio of 1-19.

Entrance Requirements: Accredited high school graduation or equivalent; 4 years English, 3 math, 3 social studies, 2 lab science, 2 language or computer, visual or vocational studies and rank in upper half of graduating class required; non-high school graduates tentatively accepted; SAT score 920 or ACT 22 composite score or 2.5 GPA required; GRE required for graduate programs; early admission, early decision, delayed admission, rolling admission, midyear admission and advanced placement plans available; application fee $30.

Costs Per Year: $2,224 tuition and fees; $6,284 out-of-state; $3,098-4,308 W.U.E. students; $3,224 room and board.

Collegiate Environment: The 1,170-acre campus is nestled in the Rocky Mountains range and in wilderness areas. The library contains 501,052 volumes, 5,078 periodicals and 1,333,061 microforms. The college has housing accommodations for 3,168 single students and families. 79% of applicants are accepted. 1,254 scholarships are available, including 293 athletic. 66% of the students receive some form of financial aid.

Community Environment: At the heart of the Gallatin Valley, known for its scenic beauty, the city is headquarters for Gallatin National Forest. The Bridger Bowl Ski Area, 18 miles northwest, and Big Sky, Inc. 50 miles south offer skiing from mid-November to mid-March. Immediately south of Bozeman, Highway 191 follows Gallatin River through the forest to Yellowstone National Park 90 miles away. The area has good public transportation including bus, and air service. Community services include many churches, two libraries, one hospital, and many hotels and motels. Various service clubs, veteran's clubs, and many fraternal organizations are represented within the immediate area. Recreation other than skiing is provided by local picnic areas, swimming pools, five parks, tennis courts, dude ranches, golf courses, hunting, boating, and fishing. Bozeman is known for its year-round outdoor recreational opportunities.

MONTANA STATE UNIVERSITY - BILLINGS   *(I-12)*
1500 North 30th Street
Billings, Montana 59101-0298
Tel: (406) 657-2011; Admissions: (406) 657-2158; Fax: (406) 657-2302

Description: Montana State University-Billings, formerly Eastern Montana College, was founded in 1927 to serve the educational needs of the community and the large rural eastern region of Montana. It is now the third largest institution of higher education in the six unit Montana University System. A metropolitan commuter university, it is comprised of four colleges: Arts and Sciences, Business, Education and Human Services, and Technology. Liberal arts programs serve as the foundation for, and are integrated with its professional and technical programs. It is fully accredited by the Northwest Association of Schools and Colleges, the National Council for the Accreditation of

Teacher Education, the National Association of Schools of Music, the National Association of Schools of Art and Design, and the Council on Rehabilitation Education. The college operates on the semester system and offers two summer sessions. Enrollment includes 2,737 full-time and 1,106 part-time undergraduate students and 398 graduate students. A faculty of 146 full-time and 45 part-time gives an undergraduate faculty-student ratio of 1-20.

Entrance Requirements: Montana graduates of accredited high school or G.E.D.; non-Montana residents must be graduates of an accredited high school and rank in the upper half of their class; ACT or SAT test required; early admission, rolling admission, delayed admission and CLEP plans available; $30 application fee.

Costs Per Year: $2,172 state-resident tuition; $5,896 out-of-state; $3,000-$5,000 room and board.

Collegiate Environment: The 96-acre campus is located just beneath the picturesque Rimrocks, which majestically overlook the city of Billings. There are 15 buildings; the Physical Education Building is notable for its 4,000-seat basketball arena and its official collegiate-size swimming pool. The library contains 145,000 titles and 660,000 microforms. Living accommodations are provided for 428 men and women. Financial aid is available for economically handicapped students, and 60% of the current student body receives some form of assistance. Freshman classes begin in September, January, March and June, and midyear students are accepted. 98% of the applicants are accepted.

Community Environment: Billings is an expanding city located in the Yellowstone River Valley between rugged mountains and sweeping plains. The city is the largest in Montana, and has a population of approximately 80,000 people living in the metropolitan area. The "Magic City" is a transportation, medical, agricultural, wholesale, and retail trade center. It is served by several major airlines, bus lines, a major railroad and excellent interstate highways. Community services in Billings include many churches representing most denominations, a city library, several museums, art galleries and two hospitals. Recreational sites are numerous and include opportunities for fishing, hunting, boating, bowling, golf, skiing, hiking, theater going, and concerts. Local YMCA, YWCA and various civic and fraternal organizations are quite active in the area.

MONTANA STATE UNIVERSITY - NORTHERN (C-10)
Havre, Montana 59501
Tel: (406) 265-3700; (800) 662-6132; Admissions: (406) 265-3704; Fax: (406) 265-3777

Description: This four-year, state university is composed of five major programmatic divisions: Teacher Education, Business, Nursing, Applied Technologies, and the Arts and Sciences. The institution is accredited by the Northwest Association of Schools and Colleges. A core of general education courses, distributed throughout the humanities, social sciences, mathematics, science, and technology provides the primary focus on the interaction between arts, science, and technology. Then, in all academic areas, each student gains "real world", practical work experience through internships. Programs of study lead to Associate and Bachelor degrees. Masters degrees are offered in Education. The university operates on the semester system and offers two summer sessions. Enrollment includes 1,428 full-time and 422 part-time students. A faculty of 76 provides a faculty-student ratio of 1-18.

Entrance Requirements: Accredited high school graduation or equivalent; freshmen must meet Montana College preparatory and admissions standards requirements; ACT or SAT required; GRE required for graduate programs; non-high school graduates may be admitted by examination; candidates over 21 years of age admitted as special students; $30 application fee; rolling admission, delayed admission, early admission available.

Costs Per Year: $2,135.40 resident tuition; $5,859.40 nonresident; $3,480 room and board.

Collegiate Environment: The university is one of the six units of the Montana University System. It serves a large segment of the state from North Dakota to Idaho, and three Canadian provinces. The main campus, located on 105 acres, consists of 30 buildings and adjoins the city of Havre. Residence halls accomodate 300 men, 200 women, and 50 families. The library holds 115,000 volumes and numerous periodical subscriptions. Campus activities include intramural athletics, an outdoor activities and recreation program (OAR), theater, and student

government. The college offers scholarships, grants, loans, and employment opportunities for students who need financial help. Approximately 70% of the current student body receives some form of assistance. Of the 148 scholarships offered, 44 are for freshmen. 95% of the students applying for admission meet the requirements and are accepted. Midyear students are admitted. There are no fraternities or sororities.

Community Environment: Havre is the transportation hub of the Northern Great Plains country -- America's agricultural heartland. Montana's panoramic Big Sky meets a horizon of rolling foothills and abundant lakes and reservoirs. The community is easily accessible from all directions by highway, daily Amtrak service and a commuter airline with links to major international airports. Rugged environments such as Glacier National Park, the Cypress Hills of Canada, the Bears Paw Mountains and the Little Rockies, are only a few hours away. Lakes less than an hour from campus provide great fishing, boating and waterskiing. Picnicking, camping, abundant wildlife, cool fishing streams, and winter and summer sports facilities offer excitemnet for outdoor enthusiasts.

Branch Campuses: Montana State University-Northern in Great Falls: 1211 Northwest Bypass, Great Falls, 59404, (406) 761-0417

MONTANA TECH OF THE UNIVERSITY OF MONTANA
(H-6)
1300 West Park Street
Butte, Montana 59701-8997
Tel: (406) 496-4178; Fax: (406) 496-4710

Description: The public, engineering college prepares students for professional service in engineering science, environmental science, mining, metallurgy, mineral processing, geology, petroleum fields, and geophysics, all main branches of the mineral industry. Fully accredited by the Northwest Association of Schools and Colleges, the college also holds membership in the American Society for Engineering Education and many other similar groups. The Division of Technology was established in 1994 through the affiliation of the former Butte Vocational Technical School, and offers 13 occupational specific programs. See Branch Campus, below. Undergraduate enrollment includes 1,382 full-time and 408 part-time students. There are 110 graduate students. A faculty of 88 and 27 part-time gives an undergraduate faculty-student ratio of 1-16. The college operates on the semester system and offers two summer sessions. It grants the Associate, Baccalaureate and Master's degrees.

Entrance Requirements: High school graduation with completion of 14 units: 4 English, 3 math, 2 lab science, 3 social studies and 2 foreign language, computer science, visual or performing arts, or vocational education; minimum ACT 22 or SAT combined 920; transfer students: transcripts and 2.0 college average; early admission, advanced placement, early decision, delayed admission, and rolling admission programs available; application deadline July 1; application fee $30.

Costs Per Year: $2,013 tuition; $6,073 out-of-state; $3,360 room and board.

Collegiate Environment: The 36-acre campus is situated on a high terrace at the foot of Big Butte. Buildings include the World Museum of Mining; a new library containing 48,972 bound volumes, 124,961 documents, 300,441 microforms, and 300 sound recordings; Student Union building and the Health, Physical Education and Recreation building. Residence hall has space available for 200 students. There are also 36 two-bedroom and 24 three-bedroom apartments for married or single students. Approximately 95% of students applying meet the requirements and are accepted. Students may be admitted at midyear. Financial aid is available for economically disadvantaged students. 67% of students receive some form of aid. Freshman classes begin in August and January.

Community Environment: Known as the "richest hill on earth," Butte has the reputation of being the world's greatest mining city. Mine workings consist of more than 10,000 miles of underground excavation. They produce a substantial percentage of the total amount of copper mined in the United States and a quantity of zinc ore. The Butte mining district is on the edge of one of the broad, faulted valleys characteristic of western Montana. During the more than 100 years of its active existence, this district has yielded manganese, copper, zinc, silver, lead, gold, and minor amounts of other metals. Three mountain ranges surround the city from the Continental Divide. The

MONTANA   THE COLLEGE BLUE BOOK

area is served by two transcontinental railroads, airlines, and bus lines. Butte community service facilities include many churches, two hospitals, five radio stations, and two TV stations. The city has a wholesale and retail shopping center. Many civic, fraternal, and professional organizations meet regularly in the immediate area. Recreation in the forms of skiing, hiking, fishing, hunting, boating, and golf are within minutes of the city.

Branch Campuses: Ms. Danetta Lee, Admissions Officer & Registrar, Division of Technology, 25 Basin Creek Road, Butte, MT, 59701, (406) 494-2910.

ROCKY MOUNTAIN COLLEGE   *(I-12)*
1511 Poly Drive
Billings, Montana 59102
Tel: (406) 657-1000

Description: The private, four-year, liberal arts college is affiliated with the United Presbyterian Church of the U.S.A., the United Church of Christ, and the United Methodist Church. It is fully accredited by the Northwest Association of Schools and Colleges, the National Association of Schools of Music and the National Council for Accreditation of Teacher Education. The college was founded in 1878. It operates on the semester system and offers two summer sessions. Enrollment includes 750 full-time and 50 part-time stuedents. A faculty of 47 full-time and 18 part-time gives a faculty-student ratio of 1-14. An Army ROTC program is available.

Entrance Requirements: Accredited high school graduation with a minimum GPA of 2.0; completion of 16 units including 4 English, 2 each in 3 of the following: foreign language, mathematics, social sciences, and 1 unit of U.S. History or Government; ACT or SAT required; candidates not meeting all requirements will be given consideration; students taking non-degree courses may be registered as special students; application fee $15; delayed admission, rolling admission and advanced placement plans available.

Costs Per Year: $9,736 tuition; $3,600 room and board; $30 student fees.

Collegiate Environment: The college is located in the residental area of Billings. The 65-acre campus has 14 buildings. The Paul M. Adams Memorial Library contains over 80,000 volumes. Dormitories accommodate 190 men and 165 women. Approximately 90% of students applying for admission meet the requirements and are accepted. Financial assistance is available. 72% of students receive some form of financial aid.

Community Environment: See Eastern Montana College.

UNIVERSITY OF MONTANA   *(F-40)*
Missoula, Montana 59801
Tel: (406) 243-6266; (800) 462-8636; Fax: (406) 243-4087

Description: The state university operates on the early semester system and offers two summer terms. The university was chartered in 1893 and is accredited by the Northwest Association of Schools and Colleges. Bachelor's, Master's, Doctor of Education, and Doctor of Philosophy degrees are offered. Two or four-year ROTC programs are offered by career Army personnel. Enrollment is 11,067 men and women. A faculty of 460 full-time and 140 part-time provides a faculty-student ratio of 1-19.

Entrance Requirements: Prospective students must satisfy the college-prep requirements, which include 4 years of English, 3 mathematics, 3 social studies, 2 laboratory science, and 2 foreign language or computer science or visual and performing arts or vocational education units; applicants must be in the top half of their graduating class or have a 2.5 GPA or score a 22 composite on ACT (920 on SAT); ACT or SAT required; $20 application fee $20; rolling admission; early admission and advance placement plans available; application deadline is July 1.

Costs Per Year: $2,011 tuition; $6,011 out-of-state; $3,600 room and board.

Collegiate Environment: The main university campus stretches over 117 acres. Just south of the campus is a 154-acre site with 394 married student housing units and a nine-hole golf course. The University Biological Station is located at Big Fork where the university controls 160 acres, including two islands, and has permission to carry on investigation on Wild Horse Island, an area of approximately 2,000 acres. The library contains 800,000 volumes, 4,900 periodicals and 367,000 microforms. Financial assistance is available, and numerous scholarships are offered; 70% of the current student body receives some form of financial aid. Dormitory capacity is 2,200 men and women. Thirteen national fraternities and sororities maintain their own residences and provide housing for an additional 700 students. Approximately 68% of students applying for admission are accepted.

Community Environment: Missoula's location at the mouth of Hellgate Canyon has helped the town economically. Abundant game and fish are available in the vicinity. Packhorse trips for big game hunting may be made into the South Fork of the Flathead and the Glacier Creek district. Located on the western slope of the Continental Divide, the winters are relatively mild and summers are bright and cool. This is a small metropolis with three libraries, several churches, local civic organizations, and health services. Transportation is provided by air and bus lines. Local recreation encompasses fishing, hunting, summer boating in nearby lakes, local golf courses, excellent skiing in season and nearby National Parks. There are part-time job opportunities for students.

WESTERN MONTANA COLLEGE   *(J-5)*
710 South Atlantic Street
Dillon, Montana 59725
Tel: (406) 683-7331; (800) 962-6668; Admissions: (406) 683-7331; Fax: (406) 683-7493

Description: The four-year, state college is one of the six units of the Montana University System. It is accredited by the Northwest Association of Schools and Colleges. It grants the degree of Bachelor of Science in Elementary Education, Secondary Education, Business; Bachelor of Liberal Arts; Master of Science in Education; and Associates degrees and pre-professional curricula in a variety of areas. The college operates on the semester system and offers one summer session. Enrollment includes 958 full-time and 192 part-time undergraduate students. The faculty of 116 full-time and 50 part-time gives a faculty-student ratio of 1-25.

Entrance Requirements: Accredited high school graduation or equivalent; out-of-state candidates must rank in upper half of high school graduating class; ACT or SAT required; non-high school graduates may be admitted as special students; application fee $20; early admission, midyear admission, rolling admission and advanced placement plans available; $30 application fee.

Costs Per Year: $1,720 tuition; $5,360 out-of-state tuition; $3,674 board and room, $250 books; $20 room fee.

Collegiate Environment: The 31-acre campus has living accommodations for 250 men, 250 women and 20 families. The library contains 60,000 volumes, 500 periodicals, 19,500 microforms and 500 audiovisual materials. Almost all of students applying for admission are accepted. 260 scholarships are available and 64% of the students receive some form of financial aid.

Community Environment: Dillon, the home of Western Montana College, is a town of 6,000 located west of Yellowstone National Park in the mountainous southwestern corner of Montana. Dillon's location in the bend of the Continental Divide offers protection from severe storms. Winters are historically mild and summers are pleasant with cool nights. Dillon provides a wholesome, small-town environment for the College. Community concerts and other programs serve the cultural needs of the community. Also available are churches of various denominations, a city library, golf course, park, hospital, and social and fraternal organizations. The surrounding area offers many recreational opportunities for the outdoor enthusiast including skiing, hiking, backpacking, fishing, hunting and canoeing.

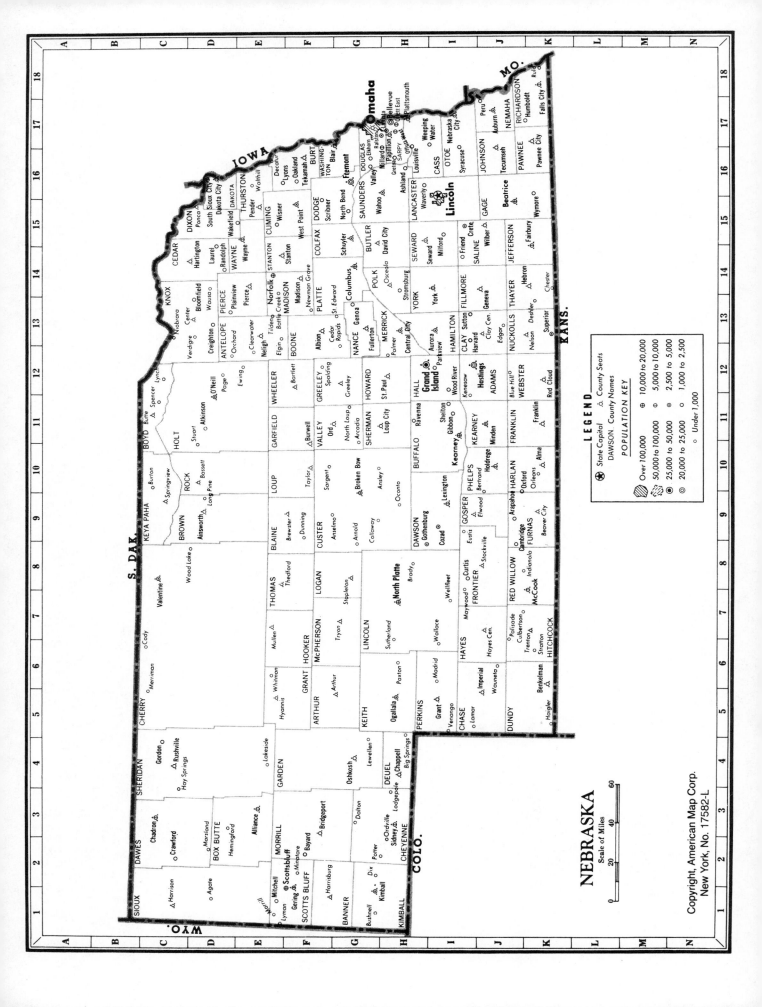

NEBRASKA

Scale of Miles

0   20   40   60

Copyright, American Map Corp.
New York, No. 17582-L

LEGEND

⊛ State Capital   ⚬ County Seats

DAWSON County Names

POPULATION KEY

⊕ 10,000 to 20,000
⊙ 5,000 to 10,000
⊘ 2,500 to 5,000
○ 1,000 to 2,500
○ Under 1,000

⬙ Over 100,000
▨ 50,000 to 100,000
◉ 25,000 to 50,000
◎ 20,000 to 25,000

NEBRASKA

BELLEVUE UNIVERSITY   *(H-17)*
Galvin Road at Harvell Drive
Bellevue, Nebraska 68005
Tel: (402) 291-8100; (800) 756-7920; Admissions: (402) 293-3766;
Fax: (402) 293-3730

Description: The private, nonprofit, four-year, liberal arts university offers both day and night classes. The day school is organized on the semester system and the night school operates on the trimester system with two summer sessions offered. Enrollment includes 2,042 undergraduate and graduate students. There are 35 full-time and 18 part-time faculty members. The univesity is accredited by the North Central Association of Colleges and Schools and grants the Bachelor and Master degrees. Air Force and Army ROTC programs are available.

Entrance Requirements: High school graduation or equivalent; SAT or ACT required for recent high shcool graduates; early admission, early decision, rolling admission and advanced placement plans available; $10 application fee.

Costs Per Year: $3,150 tuition; $50 student fees.

Collegiate Environment: The 97-acre campus is situated in the city of Bellevue. The college's location is convenient for both the civilian and the military student. The college is comprised of 9 buildings, including a library of 100,000 volumes, 285 periodicals and 800 recordings. Approximately 96% of the students applying for admission are accepted. Students are admitted midyear. Financial aid is available for economically disadvantaged students.

Community Environment: The oldest continuous settlement in Nebraska, Bellevue is located on the bluffs of the Missouri River, just south of Omaha and adjoining Offutt Air Force Base, the headquarters of the Strategic Air Command. The Fontenelle Forest Nature Center between Bellevue and the Missouri River contains displays of regional habitats.

Branch Campuses: Grand Island, NE; West Omaha, NE.

CENTRAL COMMUNITY COLLEGE - GRAND ISLAND CAMPUS   *(H-12)*
3134 W. Highway 34
P.O. Box 4903
Grand Island, Nebraska 68802-4903
Tel: (308) 384-5220; (800) 652-9177; Fax: (308) 389-6399

Description: The district-governed, vocational-technical school was established in 1976 and is one of three campuses serving the Central Community College area. It has an enrollment of 3,639 on-campus and 6,019 off-campus students. Of the on-campus students, 529 are full-time and 3,110 are part-time. A faculty of 39 full-time and 33 part-time gives a faculty-student ratio of 1-15. The school is accredited by the North Central Association of Colleges and Schools and grants the Certificate, Diploma and Associate Applied Science and Academic Transfer degrees. The semester system is used, and one summer session is offered.

Entrance Requirements: Open enrollment policy; ASSET or ACT; early admission, midyear admission, rolling admission, delayed admission and advanced placement plans available.

Costs Per Year: $1,008 state-resident tuition; $1,512 out-of-state; $72-$108 student fees.

Collegiate Environment: The school is located on 79 acres and is comprised of three buildings. Students may enroll any day the college is in session. The college is located near the intersection of highways 281 and 34 at the southwest corner of Grand Island, the 65-acre campus houses classrooms, a library of 1,200 volumes, laboratories, a cafeteria, student center, study areas, seminar and meeting rooms, and a child care center that provides day care service for the children of stu-

dents while they are in class. 16 vocational-technical programs and general education courses are offered. 70% of students receive some form of financial aid.

Community Environment: Grand Island is located in Central Nebraska and is a leading agricultural center for retailing and industry. Due to agricutural production, industry has quickly expanded, with a resulting rapid population growth. The population is currently 40,000. There are many recreational opportunities available to residents and visitors, including swimming, golfing, horse racing, bowling, hunting, and a variety of health-related activities. A large museum complex is located at Grand Island and reflects the Old West tradition. More than 40 churches, two hospitals, a children's zoo and a major library are available.

CENTRAL COMMUNITY COLLEGE - HASTINGS CAMPUS
(I-12)
P.O. Box 1024
Hastings, Nebraska 68901
Tel: (402) 463-9811; (800) 742-7872; Fax: (402) 463-9201

Description: The district-governed, vocational technical community college was established in 1966 and is one of the three campuses serving the Central Community College area. The school is accredited by the North Central Association of Colleges and Schools and grants the Certificate, Diploma, Associate of Applied Science, Associate of Arts and Associate of Science degrees. The school operates on the semester system and offers one summer session. Enrollment includes 3,8921 men and 3,676 women. A faculty of 67 full-time and 82 part-time provides a faculty-student ratio of 1-24.

Entrance Requirements: Open enrollment policy; non-high school graduates admitted; early admission, early decision, rolling admission, delayed admission and advanced placement plans available.

Costs Per Year: $1,075 estimated state-resident tuition (at $33.60/credit); $1,629 estimated out-of-state tuition (at $50.90/credit); $58/week room and board.

Collegiate Environment: The school is located on 60 acres and is comprised of 19 buildings, which include dormitory facilities for 238 students. Students may enroll any day the college is in session. Financial aid is available.

Community Environment: See Hastings College.

Branch Campuses: Grand Island Campus, P.O. Box 4903, Grand Island, NE 68802; Platte Campus, P.O. Box 1027, Columbus, NE 68601.

CENTRAL COMMUNITY COLLEGE - PLATTE CAMPUS
(G-14)
Box 1027
Columbus, Nebraska 68602-1027
Tel: (402) 564-7132; (800) 642-1083; Fax: (402) 564-7132

Description: The district-governed community college, one of three campuses serving the Central Technical Community College area, opened in the fall of 1968. It operates on the early semester system with one summer term. Enrollment includes 476 full-time and 2,800 part-time students. A faculty of 38 full-time and 40 part-time gives a faculty-student ratio of 1-23. The college is accredited by the North Central Association of Colleges and Schools and grants a Certificate, a Diploma and Associate in Arts and Associate in Science degrees.

Entrance Requirements: Open enrollment policy; rolling admission and advanced placement plans available.

Costs Per Year: $1,080 tuition; $1,620 out-of-state; $1,850 room and board.

Collegiate Environment: The 90-acre tract, upon which the campus is constructed rests on the crest of the north bluffs of the Platte River Valley three and one-half miles northwest of the city of Columbus. The library contains 35,000 volumes, 174 periodicals, 718 microforms and 770 audiovisual materials. Almost all of the applicants are accepted, including midyear students and students from various geographical locations. 32% of the current student body receives financial assistance; of 165 scholarships offered, 110 were available to freshmen.

Community Environment: Columbus was originally an agricultural area, but in the late 1940s, as the town was dying from the loss of young people to the larger cities, a concerted effort was begun to introduce industry to the community. This effort has been very successful, and to date the area has more industrial workers per capita than any other city in the midwest. Appleton Electric recently opened a plant in Columbus. The added industry has increased the population more than 65% in the past 10 years. Products range from agricultural equipment to medical equipment. Commercial transportation is available. Pawnee Park offers swimming, tennis, picnic grounds, and athletic fields. Lake North offers swimming, water skiing, and boating. Lake Babcok offers fishing and boating, plus free camp grounds equipped with electrical outlets and tables. Columbus is 85 miles from Omaha and 80 miles from Lincoln. The community facilities include 22 churches and one library.

COLLEGE OF SAINT MARY   *(G-17)*
1901 South 72nd Street
Omaha, Nebraska 68124
Tel: (402) 399-2400; (800) 926-5534; Fax: (402) 399-2341

Description: The private, four-year, Roman Catholic college for women was established in 1923 by the Religious Sisters of Mercy. The college is accredited by the North Central Association of Colleges and Schools, the Association of Independent Colleges and Schools and the National League for Nursing. It awards Associate and Bachelor degrees. Air Force and Army ROTC programs are available. The college operates on the semester system and offers one summer term. Enrollment includes 498 full-time and 67- part-time undergraduate students. A faculty of 130 full-time gives a faculty-student ratio of 1-12.

Entrance Requirements: Accredited high school graduation or equivalent with rank in upper half of graduating class; completion of 16 units including 4 English, 2 mathematics, 2 science, and 2 social science; ACT with a score of 19 required; early admission, early decision, midyear admission, rolling admission and advanced placement plans available. $20 application fee.

Costs Per Year: $8,400 tuition; $3,320 room and board; $280 student fees.

Collegiate Environment: The 26-acre campus is located in western Omaha near a suburban area of shopping centers, restaurants and recreation facilities. The 8 college buildings include dormitory facilities for 300 women and a library containing 74,500 volumes. Approximately 78% of students applying for admission meet the requirements and are accepted. The college welcomes students from diverse geographical locations, and accepts students at midyear. 674 scholarships are available and 84% of the current student body receives some form of financial assistance. The college granted 68 Associate degrees and 87 Bachelor degrees to the recent graduating class.

Community Environment: See Creighton University.

CONCORDIA COLLEGE   *(H-15)*
800 N. Columbia
Seward, Nebraska 68434
Tel: (402) 643-3651; (800) 535-5494; Admissions: (402) 643-7233; Fax: (402) 643-4073

Description: The private college is one of 10 colleges and 2 seminaries owned and operated by the Lutheran Church-Missouri Synod. The present school was founded in 1894 as a preparatory school and became a four-year teacher's college by 1939. It is accredited by the North Central Association of Colleges and Schools and the National Council for Accreditation of Teacher Education. Enrollment includes 1,014 men and women. A faculty of 71 full-time and 37 part-time gives a faculty-student ratio of 1-14. The semester system is used and three summer sessions are offered.

Entrance Requirements: Accredited high school graduation or equivalent; completion of 16 units; ACT or SAT required; early admission, rolling admission, advanced placement plans available; non-high school graduates may be admitted under certain circumstances.

Costs Per Year: $9,200 tuition; $3,370 room and board; additional expenses average $450 (books).

Collegiate Environment: The 120-acre campus is located 25 miles northwest of Lincoln, Nebraska, and 80 miles southwest of Omaha, Nebraska. The college buildings contain a library of 180,000 volumes and numerous pamphlets, periodicals, microforms, and recordings. Dormitory facilities for 450 men and 550 women are available. The college welcomes a geographically diverse student body and will accept midyear students. Approximately 84% of students applying for admission are accepted. 97% of the current student body receives financial aid.

Community Environment: Seward is located near Lincoln where all forms of commercial transportation are available. The community facilities include churches of most denominations, a hospital, and various civic and service organizations. Outdoor sports include fishing, golf, swimming, bowling, and skating.

CREIGHTON UNIVERSITY   *(G-17)*
California St. at 24th
Omaha, Nebraska 68178
Tel: (402) 280-2703; Fax: (402) 280-2685

Description: Founded in 1878, Creighton is a coeducational, independent university operated by the Jesuits. Creighton has a faculty and student body made up of individuals of many races and faiths from every geographical region of the United States and numerous foreign nations. It is one of the most diverse educational institutions of its size in the country. In addition to the College of Arts and Sciences, the university has a College of Business Administration, University College, Schools of Dentistry, Medicine, Law, Nursing, Pharmacy and Allied Health professions and a graduate school that offers Master's and Doctor's degrees. Creighton is accredited by the North Central Association of Colleges and Schools and the university's various schools and colleges are accredited by their respective professional standardizing agencies. Enrollment includes 4,094 undergraduates and 2,005 graduate and professional students. A faculty of 609 full-time and 625 part-time gives an undergraduate faculty-student ratio of 1-14. The university operates on the early semester system and offers 3 summer terms. ROTC/Army and Air Force programs are available.

Entrance Requirements: Accredited high school graduation or equivalent with rank in upper half of graduating class; completion of 16 units, including 4 English and 3 mathematics; composite score of 20 or over on ACT is highly recommended; rolling admission and advanced placement plans available; $30 application fee.

Costs Per Year: $10,964 tuition; $4,372 room and board; $650 student fees & estimated book expenses.

Collegiate Environment: Creighton's 85-acre campus is located on the northwest edge of downtown Omaha, Nebraska. The university's planned campus of more than 28 square blocks is near, yet apart from, the city's urban center. Three examples of the university's extension and growth in the last decade are: the student center, the artificial turf athletic fields, and the Lied Center for the Fine and Performing Arts. Three libraries contain a total of 690,721 volumes and a large collection of audiovisual materials and microforms. Campus residences accommodate approximately 1,800 students. The university participates in a variety of financial aid programs, and 81% of the student body receives some form of financial assistance. Midyear students are accepted.

Community Environment: Urban Omaha is in a period of rapid renewal through publicly and privately supported programs. The city is a major insurance center of the nation along with industries such as railroads, telecommunications, creative enterprises and health care institutions, though it is better known as a center for food processing because of its location in the area known as the "bread basket of America." Metropolitan Omaha has a population of over 650,000 and serves as a communication and cultural center for the Plains States. Cultural attractions include the Omaha Symphony Orchestra, the Omaha Ballet and Opera Company, the Omaha Community Playhouse, and the Joslyn Art Museum.

DANA COLLEGE *(G-17)*
2848 College Drive
Blair, Nebraska 68008-9905
Tel: (402) 426-7200; (800) 444-3262; Fax: (402) 426-7386

Description: This private college is one of 29 colleges of the Evangelical Lutheran Church in America, established in 1884. The college is accredited by the North Central Association of Colleges and Schools, the National Council for the Accreditation of Teacher Education and the Council on Social Work Education. Founded by Danish Lutheran immigrants, Dana College continues to celebrate its heritage with cultural festivals, study in Danish language, and overseas study opportunitites in Denmark. The college grants the Bachelor of Arts degree. It operates on a 4-1-4 calendar system and offers three terms yearly for weekend college and a sumemr session. Enrollment is 293 men and 357 women. A faculty of 39 full-time and 31 part-time gives a faculty-student ratio of 1-13.

Entrance Requirements: Accredited high school graduation or equivalent with preferred rank in upper half of class and minimum 2.0 grade point average; ACT or SAT required, with preferred ACT minimum score of 19 or SAT combined score of 860; applicants not meeting all entrance requirements may be considered on an individual basis; $15 application fee; early admission, rolling admission and advanced placement plans available.

Costs Per Year: $9,130 tuition; $3,322 room and board; $450 student fees.

Collegiate Environment: The 150-acre campus is located in the city of Blair, 20 miles north of the city of Omaha, Nebraska. The 16 college buildings include a library of 171,000 volumes and living accommodations for 295 men, 295 women, and 24 families. Approximately 93% of students applying for admission meet the requirements and are accepted, including midyear students and students from various geographical locations. Financial aid is available for economically qualifying students, and 95% of the current student body receives some form of aid. The college awarded 100 Bachelor degrees to a recent graduating class.

Community Environment: Blair is a suburban community located in a large farming area. Small industries contribute to the economic stability of the community. The college provides transportation to Omaha's train, bus and airport facilities. The Omaha Municipal Airport is within 25 minutes from Blair. Community facilities include 11 churches, a public library, community theatre, hospital and clinics as well as many civic, fraternal and veterans' organizations. Student employment opportunities are good. The DeSoto National Wildlife Refuge is 3 miles from Blair, the Missouri River near Blair provides boating, hunting, and fishing opportunities, and the city facilities offer golf, swimming, tennis, and hiking.

DOANE COLLEGE *(I-15)*
1014 Boswell
Crete, Nebraska 68333
Tel: (402) 826-8222; (800) 333-6263; Fax: (402) 826-8600

Description: The private, independent, liberal arts college was established in 1872 by members of the Congregational Church and is affiliated with the United Church of Christ. It is accredited by the North Central Association of Colleges and Schools and by the National Council for Accreditation of Teacher Education. An academic cooperative plan is available with Columbia and Washington Universities in St. Louis for engineering students and with Duke University for students studying foresty and environment management. Programs of study lead to the Bachelor and Master degrees. Two graduate programs and continuing education programs are offered at the Lincoln campus. The college operates on the 4-1-4 system. Enrollment includes 859 full-time and 26 part-time undergraduate, and 409 graduate students. A faculty of 57 full-time and 39 part-time gives a faculty-student ratio of 1-13. Army and Air Force ROTC programs available.

Entrance Requirements: Accredited high school graduation or equivalent; satisfactory completion of a secondary school program that would prepare the student to study will be considered by the admissions committee; SAT or ACT required; non-high school graduates (GED) considered for admission under certain circumstances; early admission, early decision, advanced placement, rolling admission and midyear admission plans available; $15 application fee.

Costs Per Year: $98,5720 tuition; $3,000 room and board; $250 general fees; $1,000 average additional expenses

Collegiate Environment: The 300-acre campus is located approximately 25 miles southwest of Lincoln, Nebraska. The 19 college buildings include a library of 198,009 volumes. Dormitories accommodate 700 students. There are 9 social fraternities and sororities on the campus as well as numerous other student organizations. The Career Development Office offers counseling and placement to students. 89% of students applying for admission are accepted. Financial aid is available, and 93% of the current student body receives some form of financial assistance. 39% of the senior class continued on to graduate school.

Community Environment: Crete, a community of 5,000 persons, is located 25 miles southwest of Lincoln. The community includes nine churches of different denominations, a hospital, library, and numerous civic, fraternal and veterans' organizations. Recreation includes bowling, fishing, hunting, golf, and numerous other activities.

Branch Campuses: Lincoln, NE

GRACE COLLEGE OF THE BIBLE *(G-17)*
9th & William
Omaha, Nebraska 68108
Tel: (402) 449-2800; (800) 383-1422; Admissions: (402) 449-2831; Fax: (402) 341-9587

Description: The private, Bible college was established in 1943 and is accredited by the North Central Association of Colleges and Schools and professionally by the Accrediting Association of Bible Colleges. Programs are available which combine a major in Bible with pastoral ministries, missions, Christian education, church music, radio communications, counseling and various kinds of technical training. The Christian education offerings include programs in Christian camping and elementary teacher education. The college grants the Bachelor degree. It operates on the semester system and offers one summer session. Enrollment includes 414 students. A faculty of 22 gives a faculty-student ratio of 1-18.

Entrance Requirements: High school graduation or equivalent with rank in upper half of graduating class; ACT required; mature non-high school graduates may be admitted as special students; early admission, early decision, midyear admission and advanced placement plans available; $25 application fee.

Costs Per Year: $4,950 tuition; $2,850 board and room; $325 student fees.

Collegiate Environment: The college is comprised of 27 buildings which are located on 7.6 acres. The library contains over 50,000 volumes, and living accommodations are provided for 190 men and 230 women. Approximately 75% of the students applying for admission are accepted including midyear students. Financial assistance is available for economically handicapped students.

Community Environment: See Creighton University

HASTINGS COLLEGE *(I-12)*
7th & Turner Avenue
Hastings, Nebraska 68901-0269
Tel: (402) 463-2402; (800) 532-7642; Admissions: (402) 461-7316; Fax: (402) 463-3002

Description: The private, four-year, college of liberal arts was established in 1882 and is affiliated with the United Presbyterian Church in the U.S.A. The college is accredited by the North Central Association of Colleges and Schools and grants the Bachelor degree. It operates on the 4-1-4 system and offers one summer session. Enrollment includes 910 full-time and 44 part-time undergraduates, and 16 graduate students. A faculty of 68 full-time and 28 part-time gives an undergraduate faculty-student ratio of 1-13.

Entrance Requirements: Accredited high school graduation or equivalent with completion of 11 units and rank in upper half of graduating class; units must include 4 English, 2 mathematics, 2 social science, 1 science, and 2 foreign language; SAT or ACT required; early decision, advanced placement, and early admission plans available; non-high school graduates considered under certain circumstances; $20 application fee.

Costs Per Year: $9,376 tuition; $3,010 room and board; $180 student fees; additional expenses average $600.

Collegiate Environment: The 80-acre campus is located in south central Nebraska, 150 miles west of Omaha and 385 miles east of Denver, Colorado. The 17 college buildings include a library of 110,450 volumes, and dormitory facilities for 555 men and women. Students from various geographical locations are accepted, as are midyear students. Approximately 93% of students applying for admission are accepted, and 70% of the previous freshman class returned for their sophomore year. Of 444 scholarships offered, 266 are available for freshmen, and 98% of the current student body receive financial aid.

Community Environment: Located in the south central section of the state, Hastings is in the heart of an important irrigated agricultural and stock-raising area. All commercial transportation is available. Part-time jobs are available for students. Community facilities include a library, churches of all denominations and numerous fraternal organizations. Prospect Park contains the Aquacourt an ultra-modern swimming pool, fishing and skiing. A municipal pool is in Libs Park. Lake Hastings, one mile north, offers water sports and fishing. Points of interest are the Fisher Rainbow Fountain and the Hastings Museum, which includes the J.M. McDonald Planetarium.

MCCOOK COMMUNITY COLLEGE   *(K-8)*
1205 East Third Street
McCook, Nebraska 69001
Tel: (308) 345-6303; (800) 658-4348; Fax: (308) 345-3305

Description: The public, community college, established in 1926, is the oldest community college in Nebraska, and is accredited by the North Central Association of Colleges and Schools. It offers college and university-parallel courses as well as vocational-occupational programs for adults. The college operates on the semester system with one summer term. Enrollment includes 720 students. A faculty of 29 gives a faculty-student ratio of 1-25.

Entrance Requirements: Accredited high school graduation or equivalent; open enrollment policy; SAT or ACT required; early admission, early decision, rolling admission, midyear admission, delayed admission and advanced placement plans available; $10 application fee.

Costs Per Year: $900 tuition; $1,035 out-of-state tuition; $2,604 room and board; $65 student fees.

Collegiate Environment: The college is located on 20 acres about 250 miles from Omaha, Nebraska, and an equal distance from Denver, Colorado. The 8 college buildings include a library of nearly 25,000 volumes and dormitory facilities for 140 men and women. Almost all students applying for admission are accepted, including midyear students. 247 scholarships, including 205 for freshmen, are available. 87% of the current student body receives some form of financial aid. Five Certificates and 76 Associate degrees were awarded to a recent graduating class.

Community Environment: McCook is in southwest Nebraska, the distributing center for the Republican River Valley, where the pheasant hunting is good. More than 200 thousand acres in the valley are under irrigation through a U.S. Bureau of Reclamation project. This is one of the state's largest livestock markets. This city was named for General Alexander McDowell McCook, one of the "fighting McCooks" of Civil War fame. Planes and trains are the commercial transportation available. Reservoirs of the Reclamation project offer facilities for fishing, boating and camping.

METROPOLITAN COMMUNITY COLLEGE   *(G-17)*
Box 3777
Omaha, Nebraska 68103
Tel: (402) 449-8300; (800) 228-9553; Admissions: (402) 449-8418; Fax: (402) 449-8334

Description: Chartered in 1974, Metropolitan is a multi-campus institution designed to serve the needs of the people in Dodge, Douglas, Sarpy and Washington Counties of Nebraska. Presently consisting of three campuses within the Omaha metropolitan area, the College began admitting its first students during the summer of 1974. A comprehensive community college, it is accredited by the North Central Association of Colleges and Schools. There is a program for hearing impaired students. The college operates on the quarter system and offers three summer sessions. Enrollment is 10,686 students. A faculty of 549 gives a faculty-student ratio of 1-20.

Entrance Requirements: High school graduation or GED; open enrollment; rolling admission and advanced placement plans available; students are admitted at midyear.

Costs Per Year: $1,035 resident; $2,070 nonresident.

Collegiate Environment: An Instructional Resource Center is located on each campus of the College. The total holdings are 43,278 hard bound volumes, 790 periodicals, 3,232 microforms and 208 audiovisual materials. Scholarships are available; currently 27% of the students receive financial aid. Student housing is not available on campus.

Community Environment: See Creighton University

Branch Campuses: Fort Omaha Campus, 5300 North 30th Street, Omaha, NE; South Omaha Campus, Northwest of 27th Q Street, Omaha, NE; Elkhorn Valley Campus, Highway 6 and 31 West Dodge Road, Omaha, NE.

MID-PLAINS COMMUNITY COLLEGE   *(H-7)*
416 N. Jeffers
North Platte, Nebraska 69101
Tel: (308) 534-9265

Description: Mid-Plains Community College was formed in 1974 by the merger of Mid-Plains Vocational Technical College and North Platte Community College. It is a public, two-year institution which grants Certificates, Diplomas and Associate degrees and is Accredited by the North Central Association of Colleges and Schools. It operates on the semester system with one summer session and enrolls 700 students. A faculty of 134 gives a faculty-student ratio of approximately 1-17.

Entrance Requirements: Accredited high school graduation or equivalent; open enrollment policy; entrance exams required; early admission, early decision, rolling admission, midyear admission, and advanced placement plans available; application fee $20.

Costs Per Year: $960 tuition; $1,104 out-of-state tuition; $40 student fees.

Collegiate Environment: Almost all applicants applying for admission are accepted, including midyear students. The library contains over 20,000 hard bound volumes, periodicals and pamphlets. Financial aid is available to economically handicapped students.

Community Environment: A rural and agricultural community, North Platte is a railroad division point with extensive railroad shops. Important crops raised are sugar beets, wheat and alfalfa. Maloney Reservoir, six miles south of North Platte, offers boating, fishing and hunting. Community facilities include many churches, a new hospital, shopping areas, a community playhouse, civic music association and numerous social and service organizations. Part-time employment opportunities are good.

MIDLAND LUTHERAN COLLEGE   *(G-16)*
900 N. Clarkson
Fremont, Nebraska 68025
Tel: (402) 721-5480; (800) 642-8382; Admissions: (402) 721-5480 x6501; Fax: (402) 727-6225

Description: The private, liberal arts college was established in 1883 and is supported by the Evangelical Lutheran Church in America. It is accredited by the North Central Association of Colleges and Schools, and the National League for Nursing. The college offers a special program for the culturally disadvantaged. It grants the Associate and Bachelor degrees. It operates on the 4-1-4 system and offers three summer sessions. Enrollment includes 907 full-time and 111 part-time students. A faculty of 55 full-time and 16 part-time gives a faculty-student ratio of 1-15.

Entrance Requirements: Accredited high school graduation or equivalent; completion of 15 units including 3 English and 2 mathematics; minimum ACT 15 required; under certain circumstances non-high school graduates are considered; early admission, midyear admission, and rolling admission plans available; $20 application fee.

Costs Per Year: $10,990 tuition; $3,060 room and board; $900 average additional expenses.

Collegiate Environment: The 27-acre campus is comprised of 18 buildings including a library containing 105,850 volumes and numerous pamphlets, periodicals, microforms, and recordings. Dormitory facilities accommodate 250 men and 300 women. 90% of students applying for admission are accepted. The college welcomes a geographically diverse student body and will accept midyear students. Financial assistance is available and 93% of the current student body receives financial aid. The college offers a special program for the culturally disadvantaged. The college awarded 7 Associate and 172 Bachelor degrees to the 1994 graduating class.

Community Environment: Situated near the Platte River, Fremont, the trading center of a dairying and livestock area, is located 35 miles northwest of Omaha and 51 miles north of Lincoln, Nebraska. Fremont is also recognized as the hybrid seed corn center of the state. Some of the products of industry are poultry, butter, flour, soybeans, and animal food. Some nationally known manufacturers such as Campbell Soup, Fel-Tex Ammonia, Magnus Metal, and Hormel Meats have plants in the area. Part-time employment is available. Boating, fishing and hunting are some of the outdoor sports available.

NEBRASKA CHRISTIAN COLLEGE   *(E-14)*
1800 Syracuse
Norfolk, Nebraska 68701
Tel: (402) 371-5960; Fax: (402) 371-5967

Description: The private Bible college is affiliated with the Church of Christ and was established in 1945. It is accredited by the Accrediting Association of Bible Colleges. The primary purpose of the college is to train ministers, missionaries and religious leaders as well as encouraging the establishment of new evangelistic churches. A two-year General Studies is offered for students who plan to continue their education at other colleges and universities to pursue careers in education, business, industry, public service and other professions. The programs all lead to a Bachelor or an Associate degree. Enrollment is 139 students. A faculty of 10 gives a faculty-student ratio of 1-14.

Entrance Requirements: High school graduation or equivalent; applicants not meeting all requirements may be admitted, but not for credit; application fee $10; SAT or ACT required; early decision and rolling admission plans available.

Costs Per Year: $3,680 tuition; $2,620 room and board; $290 student fees.

Collegiate Environment: Living accommodations are available for 50 men, 64 women, and 40 families. The library contains 25,000 volumes and numerous pamphlets, periodicals and sound recordings. Financial aid and a number of scholarships are available. 95% of the students receive some form of aid.

Community Environment: Primarily a rural community, Norfolk depends very heavily on agriculture and the raising of beef as its primary industries. The livestock business is valued at almost a $40 million industry. Community facilities include a public library, 20 churches representing 16 denominations, a YMCA and civic organizations such as Rotary, Kiwanis and the Lions Club. Part-time employment is available. Lewis and Clark Lake and other facilities provide swimming, boating, fishing and golf. The Norfolk Historical Museum exhibits a collection of local historical relics.

NEBRASKA COLLEGE OF TECHNICAL AGRICULTURE
(I-8)
404 East 7th
Curtis, Nebraska 69025
Tel: (308) 367-4124; (800) 328-7847; Fax: (308) 367-5203

Description: Founded in 1965, the public, state-supported technological college has an enrollment of 200 and a faculty of 20, with a faculty-student ratio of 1-10. Operating on the semester system with one summer session, the college awards the Associate of Applied Science degree and is accredited by the North Central Association of Colleges and Schools and the American Veterinary Medical Association.

Entrance Requirements: High school graduation or equivalent, open enrollment policy; early decision and rolling admission; $10 application fee; special admission requirements for Veterinary Technology.

Costs Per Year: $1,528 tuition; $3,096 out-of-state; $2,680 room and board; $135 student fees.

Collegiate Environment: The university occupies a 78-acre campus that adjoins the town of Curtis, Nebraska, on the northeast, plus a 392-acre farm that serves as a field laboratory. There are dormitory

facilities for 160 students. The library houses 4,500 volumes. 74% of the student body receives financial aid.

Community Environment: The city of Curtis is located on Nebraska Highway 23, 6 miles east of U.S. Hwy 83, 40 miles south of North Platte, NE, and Interstate 80. Curtis has a population of 1,000. It is not served by public transportation. It has 8 churches, summer swimming pool, hunting and fishing with 5 lakes within a 50 mile radius. Curtis is a rural community with a farm and ranch economy.

NEBRASKA WESLEYAN UNIVERSITY   *(I-15)*
5000 St. Paul Ave
Lincoln, Nebraska 68504-2794
Tel: (402) 466-2371; (800) 541-3818; Fax: (402) 465-2179

Description: The private institution is a four-year liberal arts college. It was created in 1887 as the result of the merging of three small Methodist colleges then in existence. Although a university by charter, the institution adopted the liberal arts concept in 1940. It operates on the semester system and offers three summer terms. It is accredited by the North Central Association of Colleges and Schools. Enrollment is 1,386 full-time and 224 part-time students. A faculty of 89 full-time and 69 part-time gives a faculty-student ratio of 1-13. The college grants the Baccalaureate degree.

Entrance Requirements: Accredited high school graduation or equivalent with rank in upper half of graduating class; SAT or ACT required; application fee $20; advanced placement, delayed admission, early admission, early decision and rolling admission plans available.

Costs Per Year: $9,540 tuition; $3,320 room and board; $321 student fees.

Collegiate Environment: The 50-acre campus is located in suburban northeast Lincoln. 18 buildings are included in the complex. The library contains 174,553 volumes, and dormitory facilities are available for 550 students. Fraternity and sorority houses, located within a block of the campus, provide housing for an additional 264 students. Students from other geographical locations are accepted. Approximately 66% of students applying for admission meet the requirements and are accepted. About 86% of the recent freshman class graduated in the top half of their high school class. 80% of the previous freshman class returned to the campus for their sophomore year. Financial aid is available for economically handicapped students, and 90% of the current student body receives some form of assistance.

Community Environment: The capital, Lincoln, is in southeastern Nebraska in a vast agricultural section where irrigation is an important factor. Many insurance firms have their home offices here. Part-time jobs are available. Major forms of transportation are available. Pershing Municipal Auditorium is used for conventions, concerts and athletic activities. Recreational facilities and sporting events are numerous. Some of the points of interest are the Pershing Memorial Auditorium, the Firstier Bank at 12th and N. Streets, National Bank of Commerce, Antelope Park, Fairview, a home occupied by the William Jennings Bryan family for 15 years, Pioneer Park, Sheldon Memorial Art Gallery, the University of Nebraska State Museum, and Haymarket District.

NORTHEAST COMMUNITY COLLEGE   *(E-14)*
P.O. Box 469
801 East Benjamin Avenue
Norfolk, Nebraska 68702
Tel: (402) 644-0460; (800) 348-9033; Fax: (402) 644-0650

Description: The comprehensive, community college was established in 1973 through a merger of the previous Northeastern Nebraska Technical College and Northeastern Nebraska College. It is accredited by the North Central Association of Colleges and Schools. The community college offers a two-year program either for immediate job entry or as preparation for further study at a four-year college or university. It operates on the semester system and offers two summer seesions. Enrollment is 1,985 men and 1,627 women. A faculty of 76 full-time and 48 part-time gives a faculty-student ratio of 1-18.

Entrance Requirements: Accredited high school graduation or equivalent; open enrollment policy; rolling admission plan available.

Costs Per Year: $1,088 tuition; $1,258 out-of-state; $1,044 room; $68 student fees; $400 books

Collegiate Environment: The college is comprised of 10 buildings, which include a library of 31,000 volumes and housing facilities for 204 students. All applicants are accepted, including students from other geographical locations and midyear students. Scholarships are available, including 33 athletic. 80% of the current student body receives some form of assistance.

Community Environment: See Nebraska Christian College.

PERU STATE COLLEGE   *(J-17)*
P.O. Box 10
Peru, Nebraska 68421
Tel: (402) 872-3815

Description: The state college is accredited by the North Central Association of Colleges and Schools and by the National Council for Accreditation of Teacher Education. It was established in 1867 and is Nebraska's oldest institution of higher education. The college operates on the semester system and also offers two summer terms. The college awards one-year Certificates, Associate and Bachelor degrees. The college recently enrolled 1,564 students and had a faculty of 70. ROTC/Army program available.

Entrance Requirements: Accredited high school graduation or equivalent; completion of 16 units; open enrollment policy; ACT or SAT required; application fee $10; early admission, early decision, delayed admission, rolling admission and advanced placement plans available.

Costs Per Year: $1,500 tuition; $2,700 tuition for out-of-state students; $1,360 room and board; $200 student fees.

Collegiate Environment: The college is located on 103 acres and contains 32 buildings, which include a library of 100,000 volumes, 800 periodical subscriptions, 9,158 microforms and numerous sound recordings and other miscellaneous materials. Dormitory space is available for 626 students in a variety of living arrangements. There is also space for 24 families of married students. The college welcomes students from other geographical locations and will accept midyear students both new and transfers. Almost all students applying for admission meet the requirements. Financial aid is available for the needy student.

Community Environment: Peru is situated in southeast Nebraska on bluffs overlooking the Missouri River in an agricultural region. Corn, wheat, apples and many other crops are raised in the area. The town is 65 miles from Omaha and 75 miles from Lincoln.

SOUTHEAST COMMUNITY COLLEGE - BEATRICE   *(J-15)*
RR #2, Box 35A
Beatrice, Nebraska 68310
Tel: (402) 228-3468

Description: Formerly the Fairbury Junior College, the Southeast Community College - Beatrice was established in 1976. The Fairbury campus was closed in 1986 and was merged with the Beatrice campus to form the Southeast Community College - Beatrice campus. Accredited by the North Central Association of Colleges and Schools, the college is composed of 5 departments which include Academic Transfer, Agriculture, Business, Humanities and Social Sciences, and Licensed Practical Nursing. Enrollment includes 1,050 students composed of 630 women and 420 men. The college awards the Associate of Arts, Associate of Applied Science, and Associate of Science Degrees, diploma and certificate. The faculty is composed of 51 full-time personnel. The faculty-student ratio is approximately 1-20.

Entrance Requirements: Accredited high school graduation or GED equivalent; SAT or ACT recommended, ASSET test required of all first time college students; rolling admission, midyear admission, early decision and delayed admission plans available.

Costs Per Year: $1,057 tuition; $1,283 out-of-state tuition; $916 room; $60 student fees.

Collegiate Environment: The college is comprised of classroom buildings, residential units, student center, administration building, agriculture classrooms, livestock buildings, feed building, and other facilities located on 640 acres. The library contains 10,850 volumes. Residential units accommodate 150 students. 98% of the applicants are accepted. Financial aid is available.

Community Environment: A rural community in southeastern Nebraska, Beatrice is the county seat for Gage County. Community fa-

cilities include numerous churches, hospitals, shopping centers and all the major civic, fraternal, and veteran's organizations. The YMCA and city parks provide the facilities for swimming, basketball, aerobic and weight training, tennis, and other sports activities. Student employment is good.

Branch Campuses: Beatrice is one of three campuses of the Southeast Community College District. The Milford and Lincoln campuses comprise the area. The Lincoln campus houses the area office.

SOUTHEAST COMMUNITY COLLEGE - LINCOLN   *(I-15)*
8800 O St.
Lincoln, Nebraska 68520
Tel: (402) 471-3333; (800) 642-4075; Admissions: (402) 437-2600; Fax: (402) 437-2404

Description: This two-year college is a publicly supported institution which is accredited by the North Central Association of Colleges and Schools and the National League for Nursing. Programs of study are primarily vocational-technical and academic transfer. It grants a Diploma, Certificate, and the Associate degree. The college operates on the quarter system and offers one summer session. Enrollment includes 1,700 full-time, 3,000 part-time students. A faculty of 115 full-time and 450 part-time gives a faculty-student ratio of 1-15.

Entrance Requirements: Accredited high school graduation or equivalent; open enrollment policy; early admission, early decision, rolling admission, midyear admission and advanced placement plans available; no application fee.

Costs Per Year: $1,750 state resident tuition; $2,050 nonresident tuition; $48 student fees.

Collegiate Environment: The college library contains 20,000 volumes. 99% of students applying for admission are accepted, including midyear students. Financial aid is available for economically disadvantaged students, and approximately 75% of the current student body receives some form of assistance.

Community Environment: See Nebraska Wesleyan University

Branch Campuses: Milford, NE; Beatrice, NE

SOUTHEAST COMMUNITY COLLEGE - MILFORD   *(I-15)*
P.O. Box D, RFD 2
Milford, Nebraska 68405
Tel: (402) 761-2131; (800) 933-7223; Admissions: (402) 761-2131 x243; Fax: (402) 761-2324

Description: The publicly supported, coeducational school is accredited by the North Central Association of Colleges and Schools. The primary objective of the school is to prepare students for vocational and technical occupations. The school grants an Associate of Applied Science degree. It operates on the quarter system and offers one summer session. Enrollment includes 925 students. A faculty of 82 gives a faculty-student ratio of 1-11.

Entrance Requirements: Open enrollment policy; high school graduation or equivalent required; applicants 16 years of age are admitted if not enrolled in a secondary school; ASSET or ACT required; rolling admission and advanced placement plans available; $10 application fee.

Costs Per Year: $1,598 (4 quarters) resident tuition; $1,938 (4 quarters) nonresident tuition; $2,488 (4 quarters) room and board; $48 student fees.

Collegiate Environment: The modern college serves its students with excellent laboratory facilities equipped with current industrial equipment and teaches the latest technical knowledge. The library contain 10,000 volumes. 4 dormitories provide accommodations for 342 men, women and married students. Housing is also available in the community. Scholarships are available based on scholastic ability and need. Student loans, work-study and grants are available for students with financial need, and 60% of students receive some form of financial aid.

Community Environment: The school is located in the town of Milford, which is located west of Lincoln on I-80, with a population of about 2,100.

Branch Campuses: Beatrice Campus, Beatrice, NE; and Lincoln Campus, Lincloln, NE.

UNION COLLEGE   *(I-15)*
3800 South 48th Street
Lincoln, Nebraska 68506
Tel: (402) 488-2331; (800) 228-4600; Admissions: (402) 486-2504;
Fax: (402) 486-2895

Description: The private college was founded in 1891 by the Seventh-day Adventist denomination. It is accredited by the North Central Association of Colleges and Schools, the National Council for the Accreditation of Teacher Education, the National Association of Schools of Music, and the National League for Nursing. It awards the Associate and Bachelor degrees. The college operates on the semester system and offers four summer sessions. Enrollment includes 500 full-time and 70 part-time students. A faculty of 44 full-time and 9 part-time provides a faculty-student ratio of 1:10.

Entrance Requirements: Accredited high school graduation or equivalent; open enrollment policy; completion of 18 units, including 3 English, 1 mathematics, 1 laboratory science, 1 social science; ACT required; applicants not meeting all entrance requirements may be admitted on conditional or probational status; early admission, midyear admission, and rolling admission plans available.

Costs Per Year: $9,198 tuition; $2,900 room and board; $550 books.

Collegiate Environment: The campus is comprised of about 22 acres, located in a quiet suburb of the city. The college buildings include a library of 137,472 volumes. Living accommodations are provided for 362 students. 70% of the students who apply for admission are accepted. The college welcomes students from various geographical locations and will accept midyear students. Financial aid is available for economically disadvantaged students. 570 scholarships, 125 for freshmen, are available. 70% of the current students receive some form of financial assistance. Approximately 58% of the previous freshman class returned to the campus for their sophomore year.

Community Environment: See Nebraska Wesleyan University

UNIVERSITY OF NEBRASKA - KEARNEY   *(I-11)*
Kearney, Nebraska 68849-0605
Tel: (308) 865-8441; (800) 445-3434; Admissions: (308) 865-8987;
Fax: (308) 865-8987

Description: The college was founded by the State Legislature of Nebraska in 1903 and the first classes were held during the summer of 1905 in Kearney public school facilities. In July of 1991, the college became a part of the state university system. The university is accredited by the North Central Association of Colleges and Schools and by the National League for Nursing. It operates on the semester system and offers two summer sessions. Enrollment includes 5,580 full-time and 2,004 part-time students. A faculty of 310 full-time and 93 part-time gives a faculty-student ratio of 1-20. It grants the Bachelor, Master and Specialist degrees. Several national and international exchange programs are available.

Entrance Requirements: High school graduation or equivalent with completion of 15 units; ACT score of 20 or above and/or class rank in the upper half; non-high school graduates considered in certain circumstances; GRE required for graduate school; early admission, early decision, delayed admission, advanced placement and rolling admission plans available; $25 application fee.

Costs Per Year: $1,720 tuition; $2,770 nonresident tuition; $2,830 room and board; $145 student fees; additional expenses average $700.

Collegiate Environment: The campus is located on 235 acres at the western edge of Kearney. The 32 college buildings include a library of 186,289 volumes and 463,000 microforms. Living facilities accommodate 673 men, 1,245 women, and 214 married students. The college welcomes a geographically diverse student body and will accept midyear students. Approximately 90% of the students applying for admission are accepted. 80% of the current student body receives financial aid.

Community Environment: Kearney was established at the junction of the Burlington and Union Pacific Railroads on the north bank of the Platte River. Trains, buses and air transport serve the area. A hospital, churches of most denominations and good shopping facilities provide service and comfort to the community. Baseball, golf and swimming are a few of the outdoor activities.

UNIVERSITY OF NEBRASKA - LINCOLN   *(I-15)*
14th and R Streets
Lincoln, Nebraska 68588-0415
Tel: (402) 472-7211; Admissions: (402) 472-2023

Description: The Nebraska State Legislature established the university in 1869, under the terms of the federal Morrill or "Land-Grant" Act. The university opened its doors in 1871 with an initial enrollment of 20 college students and 110 pupils in a preparatory school, which the university operated for several years. Today the university is accredited by the North Central Association of Colleges and Schools and by many respective professional and educational organizations. It is composed of 9 undergraduate colleges, the graduate course and the college of law. The colleges are Agriculture Sciences and Natural Resources, Human Resources and Family Sciences, Arts and Sciences, Business Administration, Engineering and Technology, Architecture, Fine and Performing Arts, Teachers and Journalism, and Mass Communication. Most of the colleges are located on the 239-acre city campus in Lincoln. The colleges of Agriculture Sciences and Natural Resources, Human Resources and Family Sciences. The College of Law are located on the 330-acre east campus in Lincoln. The university operates on the semester system and offers terms of various lengths during the summer. It also provides Army, Navy, and Air Force ROTC programs. The University offers an extensive exchange program in several European, Asian and Latin American countries and cooperative programs with the other universities. Enrollment includes 16,058 full-time and 2,473 part-time undergraduate and 5,154 graduate students. A faculty of 1,265 full-time and 256 part-time gives an overall faculty-student ratio of 1-13. The university awards undergraduate and graduate level degrees.

Entrance Requirements: Admission as an undergraduate freshman requires SAT or ACT; graduation from an accredited high school with completion of selected courses in language arts, mathematics, science and social science; graduates of accredited high schools who have not taken or successfully completed the required selected courses can still be considered if the high school graduate is in the top half of his or her high school class or the high school graduate presents a composite Enhanced ACT score of 20 or above, or a combined score of 850 or above on the SAT; high school graduates who do not meet either of the above requirements may be considered on a conditional basis; early admission, rolling admission, midyear admission and advanced placement plans available. $25 application fee.

Costs Per Year: $2,415 tuition and fees; $5,955 out-of-state; $3,145 room and board.

Collegiate Environment: The university includes an agricultural field laboratory at Mead, Nebraska, and agricultural experiment stations in other areas of the state. The 244 university buildings located on the city and east campuses include libraries whose holdings number 2,278,154 volumes and 20,000 active periodicals, and include links to nationwide databases. Living accommodations are provided for 4,200 men and women, and 62 families. Additional housing is available for 2,000 students through 28 national social fraternities and 16 national social sororities located at the university. Approximately 94% of the students applying for admission are accepted, including midyear students. 3,235 scholarships are offered including 405 athletic. 71% of the undergraduates receive aid.

Community Environment: See Nebraska Wesleyan University.

UNIVERSITY OF NEBRASKA - MEDICAL CENTER   *(G-17)*
42nd and Dewey Avenue
Omaha, Nebraska 68105
Tel: (402) 559-4200

Description: The Legislative Act of 1869 provided for the formation of the University of Nebraska at Lincoln and included provision for a College of Medicine. In 1883, the University of Nebraska - College of Medicine was established at Lincoln. The Omaha Medical College, incorporated in 1881, became a part of the University of Nebraska in 1902. The merger resulted in a program in which the first two years of the four-year medical course were given in Lincoln and the last two years in Omaha. Since 1913, the entire four-year medical degree course has been given in Omaha. The University of Nebraska School of Nursing was established within the College of Medicine as a three-year diploma program in 1917. In 1968 the University system was reorganized to include the University of Nebraska - Lincoln, the University of Nebraska - Omaha and the University of Nebraska

Medical Center. The Medical Center includes the College of Medicine and its School of Allied Health Professions, the College of Dentistry, located at Lincoln, the College of Nursing, the College of Pharmacy, and Graduate Studies. The College of Medicine is a member of the Association of American Medical Colleges and is approved by the Council of Medical Education and Hospitals of The American Medical Association. The College of Nursing is accredited by the National League for Nursing. The College of Pharmacy is accredited by the American Council on Pharmaceutical Education and the College of Dentistry is accredited by the American Dental Association. All programs operate on the Center's combined enrollment semester system. The enrollment includes 1,005 men and 1,322 women full-time and 77 men, 374 women part-time. A faculty of 678 full-time and 141 part-time gives an approximate faculty-student ratio of 1-4.

Entrance Requirements: College of Medicine: Minimum of 90 semester hours of college work from an accredited college or university, including 16 chemistry, 12 biology, 8 physics, 12 humanities, English composition, calculus or statistics; Medical College Admission Test required; Bachelor's degree recommended. College of Denistry: 6 English, 16 chemistry, physics, 8 biology. Dental Admission Test required. College of Nursing: Accredited high school graduation or GED; completion of college units including 3 English, 4 human anatomy, 3 sociology, 3 psychology, 3 growth and development, 3-5 chemistry; SAT or ACT recommended. College of Pharmacy: Minimum of 60 semester hours of college work from accredited college or university; minimum C average, including 4 mathematics, 6 English composition, 8 general chemistry, 8 general biology or equivalent, 8 organic chemistry, 8 physics; Pharmacy College Admission Test recommended. Admission plans vary with individual college; advanced placement program available; application fee for all colleges: $25 for all applicants.

Costs Per Year: Per semester quotes. College of Medicine: $4,945 resident tuition, $9,225 out-of-state; College of Nursing: $1,185 resident tuition, $2,796 out-of-state; College of Pharmacy: $2,152 resident tuition, $5,185 out-of-state; College of Dentistry: $3,339 resident tuition, $7,728 out-of-state.

Collegiate Environment: The resources of the Medical Center include not only the classrooms and laboratories of the 5 colleges, but also numerous clinical facilities, including the University Hospital and Clinic, the Meyer Children's Rehabilitation Institute and the Eugene C. Eppley Institute for Research in Cancer. The Medical Center also has affiliation agreements with the Veterans' Administration Hospital and with 4 private hospitals in Omaha, and similar agreements are in effect with numerous hospitals throughout the state. The school library contains nearly 191,000 volumes and numerous pamphlets, periodicals and audiovisual materials. 41% of students applying for admission are accepted. Students are not admitted at midyear. Financial aid is available, and 70% of the current student body receives some form of financial assistance.

Community Environment: See Creighton University.

UNIVERSITY OF NEBRASKA - OMAHA   *(G-17)*
60th & Dodge St.
Omaha, Nebraska 68182
Tel: (402) 554-2393; (800) 858-8648; Fax: (402) 554-3472

Description: Formerly the Municipal University of Omaha, an institution founded in 1908, this university came under the direction of the University of Nebraska Board of Regents in 1968. The University of Nebraska - Omaha has 9 colleges, including the College of Arts and Sciences, the College of Education, the College of Business Administration, the College of Engineering and Technology, the College of Continuing Studies, the College of Home Economics, the College of Fine Arts, the College of Public Affairs and Community Service, and the Graduate College. Each conducts day and evening classes and operates on the semester system, with five summer terms. The university is fully accredited by the North Central Association of Colleges and Schools, the National Council for Accreditation of Teacher Education, the American Association of Collegiate Schools of Business, and various other professional organizations. Air Force and Army ROTC programs are available. Enrollment is 17,045 full-time and part-time students. A faculty of 690 gives a faculty-student ratio of 1-30.

Entrance Requirements: Accredited high school graduation or equivalent; completion of 4 units of English, 2 math, 2 science, and 2 social science; ACT or SAT required; GRE for graduate school; mini-

mum ACT 20; early admission, rolling admission and advanced placement plans available; $10 application fee for residents, $25 for nonresidents.

Costs Per Year: $1,568 tuition (based on 30 credit hours per year); $4,560 out-of-state; $117 student fees.

Collegiate Environment: The university is located on an 88-acre site and includes a library of 641,000 volumes, 4,317 periodical subscriptions, and 1,258,000 microforms. Approximately 92% of students applying for admission are accepted, including midyear students. Financial aid is available for economically handicapped students.

Community Environment: See Creighton University.

WAYNE STATE COLLEGE   *(E-15)*
200 East 10th Street
Wayne, Nebraska 68787
Tel: (402) 375-7000; (800) 228-9972; Admissions: (402) 375-7234; Fax: (402) 375-7204

Description: This state college, established in 1910, is accredited by the North Central Association of Colleges and Schools and by the National Council for Accreditation of Teacher Education for the preparation of elementary and secondary teachers. The Education Specialist degree is the highest degree offered. An overseas program with Denmark is available. The college operates on the semester system and offers three summer sessions. Enrollment includes 2,926 full-time and 989 part-time students. A faculty of 119 full-time and 100 part-time gives a faculty-student ratio of 1-18.

Entrance Requirements: Accredited high school graduation or equivalent with completion of 16 units; SAT or ACT required; open enrollment policy for state residents; out-of-state applicants considered on an individual basis; GRE required for graduate programs; early admission, early decision, rolling admission, midyear admission, and advanced placement plans available; $10 application fee.

Costs Per Year: $1,500 state resident tuition; $2,700 nonresident tuition; $2,660 room and board; $264 student fees.

Collegiate Environment: The 127-acre campus includes 20 large modern buildings in addition to athletic fields and a beautiful outdoor amphitheater. Dormitory facilities are available for 1,600 students. Fraternities and sororities provide additional housing. Some new facilities on campus are an Intramural/Recreational complex of approximately 50,340 square feet, an addition to the existing Carlson Natatorium with a renovation of 9,000 square feet in the existing building. The new addition and the renovated building houses a multipurpose floor to be used for basketball, tennis, running, badminton, volleyball, handball/racquetball, weight lifting, dance/aerobics, and gymnastics/wrestling. The library contains 170,000 volumes, 1,000 periodicals, 6,900 microforms and 4,300 audiovisual materials. Almost all those applying for admission are accepted, including in-state midyear students. 753 scholarships are offered, 188 of which are available to freshmen. 75% of students receive some form of financial aid.

Community Environment: Located 45 miles southwest of Sioux City, Iowa, Wayne is the county seat. Bus transportation and chartered air service are available. Dormitories, motels, and rooming houses provide housing for students. Community facilities include churches of most denominations and a hospital. Hunting, swimming and golf are some of the outdoor activities available.

WESTERN NEBRASKA COMMUNITY COLLEGE   *(F-2)*
1601 E. Street NE
Scottsbluff, Nebraska 69361
Tel: (308) 635-3606

Description: The public, two-year institution is accredited by the North Central Association of Colleges and Schools and professionally by the National League for Nursing. Established in 1926 and offered a one-year program of university parallel courses. Today the college offers basic education necessary for students who plan to continue in other institutions of learning, training for vocational and semi-professional positions and opportunities for continuing education for adults. The school operates on the semester system and offers one summer term. Enrollment includes 800 full-time and 1,550 part-time students. A faculty of 108 gives a faculty-student ratio of 1-18.

Entrance Requirements: Accredited high school graduation or equivalent; open enrollment policy; ACT suggested; rolling admission, midyear admission and advanced placement plans available.

Costs Per Year: $1,100 tuition; $1,200 out-of-state; $2,410 room and board.

Collegiate Environment: The location of the new college campus, completed in 1969, is northeast of the city of Scottsbluff. Dormitory space is available for 108 students. 95% of applicants are accepted, including midyear students, and the college welcomes students from various geographical locations. 250 scholarships are offered and 75% of the students receive some form of financial aid.

Community Environment: In the valley of the North Platte River, Scottsbluff is an agriculture center. It is also called the Capital of America's Valley of the Nile. This is the location of the largest continuous area of irrigated land in the country. Recreational activities include hunting, fishing, golf, swimming and winter sports nearby.

YORK COLLEGE   *(I-14)*
York, Nebraska 68467
Tel: (402) 363-5600; (800) 950-9675; Admissions: (402) 363-5627; Fax: (402) 363-5623

Description: The private, four-year college was founded in 1890 by the United Brethren Church and has been under the operation of the Churches of Christ since 1956. It operates on the semester system and is accredited by the North Central Association of Colleges and Schools. Enrollment is 467 full-time and 35 part-time students. A faculty of 35 full-time and 4 part-time gives a faculty-student ratio of 1-14. The college awards an Associate degree in Arts and Science as well as Bachelor's degrees in Bible, Religious Education, Business Management, Administration, Accounting, and Education.

Entrance Requirements: Accredited high school graduation or equivalent; open enrollment policy; ACT or SAT required; early admission, early decision, rolling admission and advanced placement plans available; $20 application fee.

Costs Per Year: $4,950 tuition; $2,685 room and board.

Collegiate Environment: The college is located on a 15-acre campus and includes a library of 39,656 volumes and dormitory facilities for 150 men and 174 women. 90% of the students applying for admission are accepted, including midyear students and students from various geographical locations. Financial aid is available for economically handicapped students, and 92% of the current student body receives some form of aid. Every student carrying 12 or more hours is required to take one course in Bible each semester, and daily chapel attendance is required of all students and faculty members.

Community Environment: York is located about 50 miles from Lincoln, where all forms of commercial transportation are available. Various civic and service organizations are active here as well as churches of many denominations. Recreational facilities include parks, playgrounds, a swimming pool, baseball park, basketball courts, and a community center.

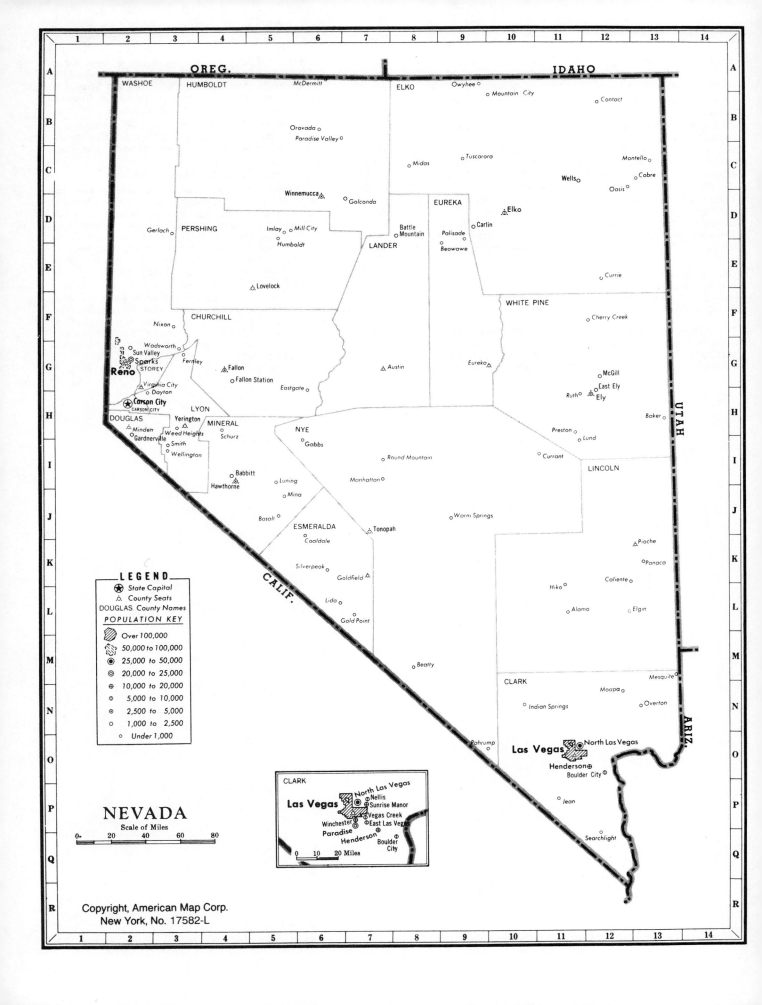

NEVADA

Scale of Miles

0   20   40   60   80

LEGEND

★ State Capital
⌂ County Seats
DOUGLAS County Names

POPULATION KEY

Over 100,000
50,000 to 100,000
25,000 to 50,000
20,000 to 25,000
10,000 to 20,000
5,000 to 10,000
2,500 to 5,000
1,000 to 2,500
Under 1,000

OREG.   IDAHO

WASHOE   HUMBOLDT   McDermitt   ELKO   Owyhee   Mountain City   Contact

Orovada   Paradise Valley   Tuscarora   Montello

Midas   Wells   Cobre   Oasis

Winnemucca   Golconda   EUREKA   Elko   Carlin

PERSHING   Gerlach   Imlay   Mill City   Battle Mountain   Palisade   Currie   WHITE PINE

Humboldt   LANDER   Beowawe   Cherry Creek

Lovelock

CHURCHILL   Nixon   Wadsworth   Eureka   McGill

Sun Valley   Fernley   Fallon   Austin   Ruth   East Ely   Ely

Sparks   STOREY   Fallon Station   Baker

Reno   Virginia City   Dayton   Eastgate   Preston   Lund

Carson City   LYON   CARSON CITY

DOUGLAS   Yerington   MINERAL   NYE   Currant   LINCOLN

Minden   Weed Heights   Schurz   Gabbs   Round Mountain

Gardnerville   Smith   Babbitt   Luning   Manhattan

Wellington   Hawthorne   Mina   Warm Springs

Basalt   ESMERALDA   Tonopah   Pioche

Coaldale   Panaca

Silverpeak   Goldfield   Hiko   Caliente

Lida   Alamo   Elgin

Gold Point

Beatty   CLARK   Mesquite

Moapa   Overton

Indian Springs

Pahrump   Las Vegas   North Las Vegas

Henderson

Boulder City

Jean

Searchlight

CALIF.   UTAH   ARIZ.

CLARK (inset)

Las Vegas   North Las Vegas   Nellis   Sunrise Manor   Vegas Creek

Winchester   East Las Vegas

Paradise   Henderson   Boulder City

0   10   20 Miles

NEVADA

COMMUNITY COLLEGE OF SOUTHERN NEVADA *(O-11)*
3200 East Cheyenne
Las Vegas, Nevada 89030
Tel: (702) 651-4000; Admissions: (702) 651-4060; Fax: (702) 643-1474

Description: The publicly supported, community college is accredited by the Northwest Association of Schools and Colleges. It grants the Associate degree in vocational technical and university parallel programs. It operates on the semester system and offers two summer sessions. Enrollment includes 2,211 full-time and 14,507 part-time students. A faculty of 250 full-time and 675 part-time gives a faculty-student ratio of 1-22.

Entrance Requirements: High school graduation; open admission, early admission, early decision, midyear admission and rolling admission plans available. $5 application fee.

Costs Per Year: $930 tuition; $3,000 nonresident tuition.

Collegiate Environment: The library contains 40,000 volumes, 1,000 pamphlets and 600 periodicals.

Community Environment: See University of Nevada - Las Vegas

Branch Campuses: Henderson Camputs, 700 College Drive, Henderson, NV 89015, (702) 564-7484; West Charleston Campus, 6375 W. Charleston Blvd., Las Vegas, NV 89102, (702) 877-1133.

NORTHERN NEVADA COMMUNITY COLLEGE *(D-10)*
901 Elm Street
Elko, Nevada 89801
Tel: (702) 738-8493; Admissions: (702) 753-2102; Fax: (702) 753-2311

Description: The state supported, community college was founded in 1967. It is accredited by the Northwest Association of Schools and Colleges. Programs of studey are career oriented and lead to the certificate or Associate degree. The college employs the semester system and offers one summer session. Enrollment includes 360 full-time and 2,640 part-time students. A faculty of 30 full-time, 260 part-time gives a student-faculty ratio of 21-1.

Entrance Requirements: Open door policy. Accredited high school graduation; early admission, early decision, rolling admission, midyear admission and advanced placement plans available. $5 application fee.

Costs Per Year: $915 tuition; nonresidents pay $3,000 plus 30.50/credit in fees.

Collegiate Environment: Students are welcomed from all parts of the nation. Freshman classes start in August and January. Financial aid is available for economically disadvantaged students. Approximately 50% of the freshman returned for their sophomore year. The library contains 25,000 volumes, 285 periodicals, 14,285 AV titles.

Community Environment: An Indian word meaning "white Woman," Elko is the trading and transportation center for Elko County. Ranching and gold mining are the primary businesses of the area. Elko is in the heart of the nation's finest hunting and fishing and is surrounded by many historic landmarks, old ghost towns and mining camps. Commercial transportation is available. Recreation facilities include Wildhorse Reservoir, Zunino's Reservoir, Ruby Marshes, Wilson Reservoir along with many streams for fishing and boating, Elko City Park for swimming and other activities. Deer, Chuckar and Antelope abound in this area for hunting.

SIERRA NEVADA COLLEGE - LAKE TAHOE *(-2)*
P.O. Box 4269
Incline Village, Nevada 89450
Tel: (702) 831-1314; (800) 332-8666; Fax: (702) 831-1347

Description: The privately supported, liberal arts college is fully accredited by the Northwest Association of Schools and Colleges. It operates on the 4-1-4 system and offers one summer term. Enrollment is approximately 300 full-time, and 500 part-time and evening students. A faculty of 83 gives a faculty-student ratio of 1-12.

Entrance Requirements: High school graduation or equivalent; ACT or SAT recommended; early decision, rolling admission, and midyear admission plans available; $35 application fee.

Costs Per Year: $9,000 tuition; $500 student fees; $4,600-$5,000 room and board.

Collegiate Environment: The college is located near the shore of legendary Lake Tahoe. Modular homes and condominiums provide housing for students. The library contains 18,000 volumes. 90% of those applying for admission are accepted. 60 scholarships are available, including 20 for freshmen. 65% of the students receive some form of financial aid.

Community Environment: Incline Village, at 6,200 ft., is a mountain community, but metropolitan Reno is located only 35 miles from the college. The area offers excellent facilities for summer and winter sports.

TRUCKEE MEADOWS COMMUNITY COLLEGE *(G-2)*
7000 Dandini Boulevard
Reno, Nevada 89512
Tel: (702) 673-7040; Fax: (702) 673-7028

Description: This publicly supported, community college is accredited by the Northwest Association of Schools and Colleges and is a member of the University and Community College System of Nevada. It offers Certificates and Associate degrees in occupational programs, and Associate degrees for students seeking to transfer to a four-year college. It operates on the semester system and offers two summer sessions. Enrollment includes 1,514 full-time and 7,312 part-time students.

Entrance Requirements: High school graduate or equivalent; open enrollment policy.

Costs Per Year: $915 ($30.50 per credit) resident tuition; $2,415 ($1,500 additional) out-of-state residents.

Collegiate Environment: Campus facilities include the Library and Learning Resource Center, the Career Development Center, and a bookstore. The college does not maintain a list of housing facilities but students may apply for space in the residence halls at the University of Nevada - Reno.

Community Environment: Reno/Sparks, cities of approximately 240,000, are bounded on the west by the majestic Sierra Nevada, and on the east by the rolling basin and range province. The climate is cool and dry, and is marked by the full pageant of the seasons. A mixture of metropolitan and quietly provincial, the area is noted on the one hand for its fashionable hotels and tourist attractions, and on the other for its beautiful parks, which line the Truckee River, and its modern residential areas. Recreational activities abound, both in Reno and its environs; within a one-hour drive of the campus are the Lake Tahoe resort area in the high Sierra and the unique prehistoric desert sea, Pyramid Lake. The adjoining Sierra is also the site of a number of nationally famed ski areas, including Squaw Valley, site of the 1960 Winter Olympics. Other scenic attractions include Virginia City, setting for one of the West's richest mining bonanzas, and Genoa, the state's first pioneer settlement.

UNIVERSITY OF NEVADA - LAS VEGAS *(O-11)*

4505 S. Maryland Parkway
Las Vegas, Nevada 89154
Tel: (702) 895-3011; (800) 334-8658; Admissions: (702) 895-3443;
Fax: (702) 895-1118

Description: The University of Nevada, Las Vegas is a coeducational facility opened in 1957. The university is accredited by the Northwest Association of Schools and Colleges. UNLV has a renown hotel administration college and programs in accounting, engineering, architecture, computer science, theatre, music, dance and education. The University of Nevada - Las Vegas is a state assisted school which offers 65 different undergraduate degree programs. The graduate college offers 60 advanced degree programs and is the largest in the state. The university grants Bachelor, Masters, and Doctorate degrees and maintains an excellent honors program. Enrollment includes 20,237 students. A faculty of 626 full-time and 418 part-time gives a faculty-student ratio of 1-25. 82% of the faculty hold Doctorate degrees.

Entrance Requirements: Nevada residents not meeting all requirements, including those with a high school equivalency diploma, may be admitted by special applications; early admission, early decision, rolling admission, midyear admission, advanced placement and delayed admission programs available; $40 application fee.

Costs Per Year: $1,830 state-resident tuition; $6,730 out-of-state tuition; $5,300 room and board.

Collegiate Environment: The 335-acre campus in Paradise Valley has 44 buildings. In the last 10 years the university has added a new engineering complex, a center for the performing arts, a physical education complex, a concert hall, a life sciences building, a physics building, a new classroom complex, a student services complex, a business and hotel college building and the Thomas and Mack Arena for concerts and sports events. Recently, the new super computer center for Environmental Studies has been completed. The university plays an increasingly important scientific role in one of the nation's major nuclear and space research centers. The Southwestern Radiological Health Laboratories are located here. It is the only such research facility on a college campus anywhere in the world. The James R. Dickinson Library houses the university's collection of 1,200,000 volumes, 6,200 periodicals, 710,000 microforms and 68,000 AV materials. 80% of applicants are accepted. The average scores for the entering freshman class were SAT 433 verbal, 472 math and ACT 20.4 composite. The university awards about 1,000 scholarships each year.

Community Environment: Situated in southeast Nevada, Las Vegas is a great vacation and convention center located near Boulder City and the mountains. Las Vegas is listed as one of the fastest growing cities in the United States. Community facilities include churches of most denominations, hospitals and clinics, and good shopping centers. The hotels feature some of the best entertainers in America. Nearby Mount Charlston provides expert ski runs and other snow sports facilities.

UNIVERSITY OF NEVADA - RENO *(G-2)*

Ninth and Center Sts.
Reno, Nevada 89557-0002
Tel: (702) 784-4636

Description: Established in 1864, the university actually started in 1874 in Elko as one of the rare preparatory higher schools in the intermountain region. In 1886 the university was moved to Reno, near the center of the state's population. It is accredited by the Northwest Association of Schools and Colleges. The university operates on the semester system and offers two summer terms. The university grants Bachelor, Master and Doctorate degrees. 60 correspondent credits allowed; continuing education courses offered; overseas programs available; ROTC Army program offered. Enrollment includes 6,3224 full-time and 2,411 part-time undergraduates and 3,011 graduate students. The faculty consists of 517 full-time and 67 part-time members.

Entrance Requirements: Accredited high school graduation; 13 1/2 units including 4 English, 3 mathematics, 3 social studies, 3 natural sciences, 1/2 computer literacy; ACT preferred but SAT accepted; Nevada residents not meeting all requirements may be admitted on probation; GPA 2.0-2.29; GRE required for graduate programs; GMAT business graduates with GRE for Economics; early decision, rolling admission, midyear admission, early admission and advanced placement plans available. $20 application fee.

Costs Per Year: $1,740 tuition for residents; $6,490 out-of-state tuition; $4,635 room and board.

Collegiate Environment: The 200-acre campus is located on rolling hills north of Reno's main business district. The library system contains 795,000 volumes, 5,100 periodicals, 3,500,000 microforms. Special facilities include the vacuum physics laboratory, the foreign language laboratory, and the Charles and Henriette Fleischmann Planetarium. There are living accommodations for 1,020 single students and 40 families, and 400 fraternity and sorority accommodations. Financial aid is available. The university recently granted 1,031 Bachelor degrees, 279 Master degrees and 34 Doctorates, and 52 Professional degrees.

Community Environment: When Reno was laid out as a townsite in 1868, it was named in honor of Major General Jesse L. Reno, who died in the Battle of the South Mountain during the Civil War. Reno is situated on the Truckee River near the base of the Sierra Nevada and has a cool, dry climate. Mining, livestock raising, lumber products, agriculture and tourism are the important industries of the area. Part-time employment is available. The city has a number of parks with facilities for swimming, tennis and picnicking; within a 25 to 90 minute drive from Reno, winter sports are available at a number of major resorts. Annual events are the rodeo, float parade and a winter carnival.

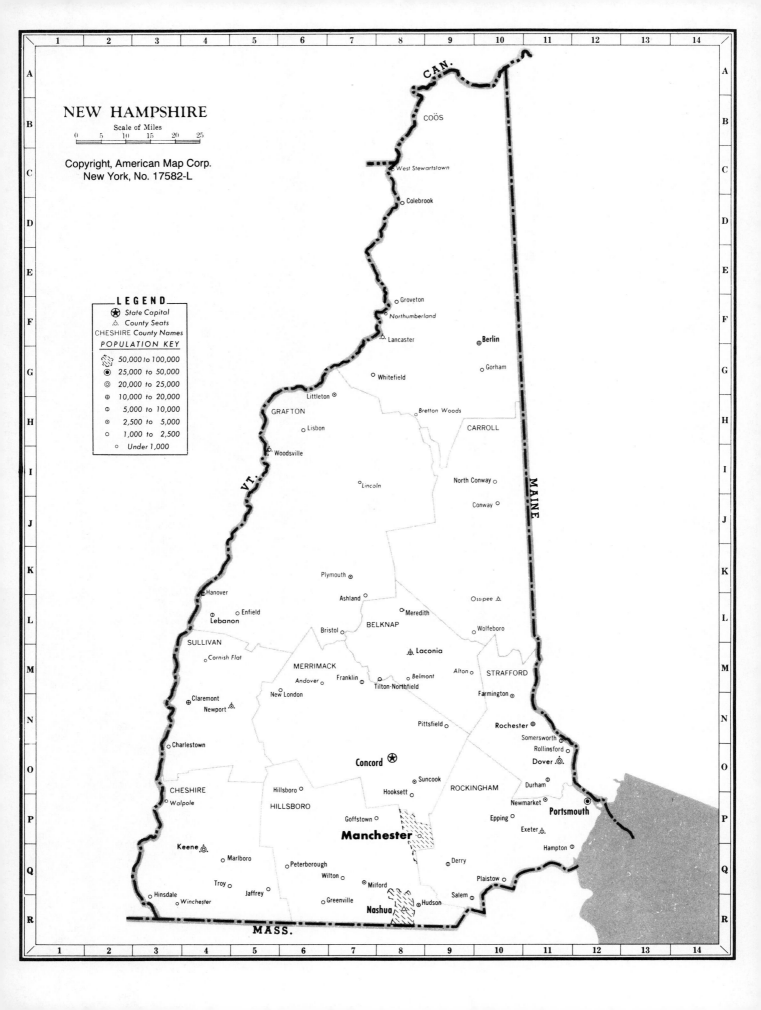

NEW HAMPSHIRE

Scale of Miles

0   5   10   15   20   25

Copyright, American Map Corp.
New York, No. 17582-L

CAN.

COÖS

West Stewartstown

Colebrook

Groveton

Northumberland

Lancaster

Berlin

Gorham

Whitefield

Littleton

GRAFTON

Lisbon

Bretton Woods

CARROLL

VT.

Woodsville

Lincoln

North Conway

Conway

MAINE

LEGEND

⯐ State Capital
⯐ County Seats
CHESHIRE County Names

POPULATION KEY

⬡ 50,000 to 100,000
◉ 25,000 to 50,000
◎ 20,000 to 25,000
⊕ 10,000 to 20,000
⬙ 5,000 to 10,000
⊙ 2,500 to 5,000
○ 1,000 to 2,500
○ Under 1,000

Plymouth

Ashland

Meredith

Ossipee

Hanover

Enfield

Lebanon

Bristol

BELKNAP

Wolfeboro

SULLIVAN

Cornish Flat

MERRIMACK

Andover

Franklin

Belmont

Tilton-Northfield

Laconia

Alton

STRAFFORD

New London

Claremont

Newport

Farmington

Pittsfield

Rochester

Somersworth

Rollinsford

Charlestown

Dover

CHESHIRE

Hillsboro

Concord

Suncook

ROCKINGHAM

Durham

Walpole

HILLSBORO

Hooksett

Newmarket

Epping

Portsmouth

Goffstown

Manchester

Exeter

Keene

Marlboro

Peterborough

Wilton

Derry

Plaistow

Hampton

Troy

Jaffrey

Greenville

Milford

Hudson

Salem

Hinsdale

Winchester

Nashua

MASS.

NEW HAMPSHIRE

CASTLE COLLEGE   (Q-9)
Searles Road
Windham, New Hampshire 03087
Tel: (603) 893-6111; Fax: (603) 898-0547

Description: This private, nonprofit, coeducational, business college was established in 1963 by the Sisters of Mercy. It is accredited by the New England Association of Colleges and Schools. The collge grants an Associate Degree in Business Science and Human Service. It also offers a 9-month Certificate program in Office Technology, Word Processing, Accounting, and Executive Administrative Assistant. Enrollment is 230 full-time, 40 part-time, and 111 evening students. A faculty of 7 full-time and 24 part-time gives a faculty-student ratio of 1-17.

Entrance Requirements: High school graduation or equivalent; students with C average or better accepted; personal interview required; early decision, early admission, deferred admission, rolling admission, midyear admission, and advanced placement plans available; $25 application fee.

Costs Per Year: $4,700 tuition; $2,800 Human Service tuition; $150 student fees.

Collegiate Environment: The campus encompasses about 140 landscaped and wooded acres. The castle, a replica of an old castle in Oxen, England, originally had 25 rooms. In 1969 additional classrooms, a library, lounge, and an auditorium were made available in the school wing of the Motherhouse of The Sisters of Mercy. The library holdings include 6,564 hardbound volumes. 80% of applicants are accepted. Five scholarships which total $3,000 are available. 86% of students receive some form of financial assistance.

Community Environment: See Rivier College.

COLBY-SAWYER COLLEGE   (M-5)
100 Main Street
New London, New Hampshire 03257
Tel: (603) 526-3000; (800) 272-1015; Admissions: (603) 526-3700;
Fax: (603) 526-2135

Description: The private college was founded in 1837. It is accredited by the New England Association of Schools and Colleges. Programs of study lead to the Bachelor degree and teacher certification. The college operates on the semester system. Enrollment includes 648 full-time and 27 part-time students. A faculty of 38 full-time and 31 part-time gives a faculty-student ratio of 1-14.

Entrance Requirements: The college recommends that prospective students present at least 15 units of college preparatory work. The usual program should include 4 years of English, 3 mathematics, 2 foreign language, 2 or more social studies, and 1 in a laboratory science. It is strongly recommended that prospective students take laboratory courses in biology and chemistry and 3 years of college preparatory mathematics. Students may select additional subjects based on their individual interests and future educational objectives. Students whose academic preparation does not follow this pattern are not precluded from applying, but they must be able to present evidence of their ability to handle college studies successfully. Deferred admission, midyear admission, rolling admission and advanced placement plans available; $40 application fee.

Costs Per Year: $14,720 tuition plus fees; $5,640 room and board; additional expenses average $1,700.

Collegiate Environment: The 26 buildings on this 80-acre campus house approximately 85% of the students in the 10 dormitories. The library contains 70,000 volumes. 85% of applicants meet criteria and are accepted. Approximately 86% of the previous freshman class returned for their sophomore year. The average scores of enrolled freshmen were SAT 416 verbal, 446 math. Financial aid is available and

63% of the current student body receives some form of financial assistance.

Community Environment: Located in the highlands of west central New Hampshire, New London enjoys a very agreeable climate and is a summer and winter tourist haven. Lake Sunapee is west of New London and King Ridge Ski Area is five minutes away. There are excellent stores and specialty shops along with hotels, inns and lodges that are found in a resort area. Recreation includes winter skiing and seasonal fishing in lakes and streams.

DANIEL WEBSTER COLLEGE   (R-8)
20 Univeristy Drive
Nashua, New Hampshire 03063-1699
Tel: (603) 577-6600; Fax: (603) 557-6001

Description: The private, coeducational, specialized college opened in 1965. Founded as the New England Aeronautical Institute, the name was officially changed to Daniel Webster College in June 1978. The college is accredited by the New England Association of Colleges and Schools. It offers four-year Bachelor Degree programs and two-year Associate in Aviation Management, Air Traffic Control, Business, Flight Operations, the Computer Sciences and Engineering. Private License through multi-engine rating is available. The college operates on the semester system. Enrollment is 474 full-time students. A faculty of 24 full-time gives an overall faculty-student ratio of 1-10.

Entrance Requirements: Accredited high school graduation or equivalent; completion of 16 units, including 4 English, 3 mathematics, 2 science , and 2 social studies; SAT or ACT required for B.S. programs; early decision, early admission, rolling admission, midyear admission and advanced placement plans available; $30 application fee.

Costs Per Year: $12,300 tuition; $4,920 room and board; $120 student fees.

Collegiate Environment: The college is located on a 50-acre campus adjacent to the Nashua Municipal Airport. The 11 buildings include dormitory space for 318 men and women and a library collection of over 25,000 volumes. Approximately 80% of students applying for admission are accepted. Scholarships are available and 82% of the students receive some form of financial aid.

Community Environment: See Rivier College.

DARTMOUTH COLLEGE   (L-4)
Hanover, New Hampshire 03755
Tel: (603) 646-2875; Fax: (603) 646-1216

Description: Founded in 1769, Dartmouth College is the nation's ninth oldest college. A private, four-year liberal arts institution, Dartmouth is a member of the Ivy League and has been a coeducational institution since 1972. Undergraduate education in the liberal arts is the primary focus of the institution and its 4,275 students. The associated professional schools (Dartmouth Medical School, Amos Tuck School of Business Administration, and Thayer School of Engineering) offer graduate-level education. Close interaction between students and faculty (12-1 ratio) and dedication of the faculty to teaching and research are hallmarks of the undergraduate college. The college operates on the quarter system and offers one summer session. Extensive off-campus and overseas programs offered.

Entrance Requirements: Admission is highly competitive. Entering classes of 1,050 students are selected from more than 8,000 candidates. The vast majority of applicants present scholastic and personal records that suggest that they can successfully complete the academic work of the College and add significantly to the quality of campus life. Evidence of intellectual capacity, motivation, and personal integrity are of primary importance in the process of selecting members of a Dartmouth class. Talent, accomplishment, and significant involvement in nonacademic areas also make a difference in the evaluation of applicants. Although there are no inflexible subject requirements for admission, each candidate is urged to undertake the strongest program of preparation available at his or her secondary school. All applicants are required to take three Achievement Tests and either SAT or ACT. All tests must be taken no later than January of the senior year in high school. Early decision (Nov. 10 application deadline), delayed admission, and advanced placement plans available. Application deadline is January 1; $60 application fee.

Costs Per Year: $19,545 tuition; $5,865 room and board.

Collegiate Environment: New students are enrolled only in the fall. Under the "Dartmouth Plan," the College operates on a year-round enrollment system and classes begin in September, January, March, and June. Students are required to be on campus during the freshman and senior year, plus the summer term between sophomore and junior year. Otherwise students structure their own enrollment plan and have the opportunity for extensive domestic and foreign study programs. Nearly all students live in over 40 residence halls on the 265-acre campus and participate in more than 150 student organizations and activities. Major facilities include the Baker Memorial Library (the nation's largest undergraduate, open stack library), the Hopkin's Center for the Creative and Performing Arts, and the Kiewit Computation Center-the hub of the most accessible computer network in any undergraduate college in the nation.

Community Environment: The northern New England surroundings and the small town pleasantness of Hanover are very much a part of undergraduate life. Located in the central western part of New Hampshire, Hanover is bordered by the Connecticut River dividing New Hampshire and Vermont. The rural location provides unsurpassed facilities and opportunities for all forms of outdoor recreation. Hanover provides convenient student shopping facilities, and is easily accessible to all major transportation centers in New England and New York by interstate highway, bus and commuter airline service. Boston, two hours away by car, is the nearest large metropolitan area.

FRANKLIN PIERCE COLLEGE   *(R-5)*
College Road P.O. Box 60
Rindge, New Hampshire 03461-0060
Tel: (603) 899-4050; (800) 437-0048; Fax: (603) 899-6448

Description: This private, coeducational, liberal arts college was founded in 1962. The college is accredited by the New England Association of Schools and Colleges. It is nonsectarian and offers a program leading to the Bachelor's degree. It operates on the semester system and offers three summer sessions. Enrollment is 1,126 full-time and 38 part-time students. A faculty of 105 provides a faculty-student ratio of 1-14.

Entrance Requirements: Accredited high school graduation; completion of 16 units including 4 English, 2 mathematics, 2 science, 2 social science; ACT or SAT required; advanced placement, rolling admission, midyear admission and early admission programs available.

Costs Per Year: $13,935 tuition; $4,900 room and board; $160 student fees.

Collegiate Environment: Main campus facilities include a 75,000-volume library and residential facilities for 600 men and 550 women. There are also 6 off-campus locations attended by 2,000 continuing education students. About 85% of the students applying for admission are accepted, and students may enroll at midyear. The college welcomes a geographically diverse student body. Financial assistance is available. 78% of the students receive financial aid.

Community Environment: Rindge is a rural community with a temperate climate. Cathedral of the Pines, an outdoor international shrine for people of all faiths, is located here. Numerous lakes in the area provide facilities for boating and fishing. There is limtied part-time work for students off campus.

HESSER COLLEGE   *(P-8)*
3 Sundial Drive
Manchester, New Hampshire 03103
Tel: (603) 668-6660; (800) 526-9231; Fax: (603) 666-4722

Description: The publicly supported, coeducational, business college was founded in 1900 and operates on the semester system. It is accredited by the New England Association of Schools and Colleges and is empowered by the State to grant the Associate in Business Science degree. Enrollment is 1,565 full-time, 500 part-time, and 1,000 evening students. A faculty of 143 full-time and 50 part-time gives a faculty-student ratio of 1-25.

Entrance Requirements: High school graduation or equivalent; $10 application fee; rolling admission, delayed admission, early decision and advanced placement plans available.

Costs Per Year: $6,180 tuition; $3,900 room and board; $300 student fees.

Collegiate Environment: The campus is located one block from Elm Street, the main street of Manchester. Dormitories are provided for 420 men and women. Financial assistance is provided for economically handicapped students and 80% of the current freshman class received some aid. The library contains 30,000 volumes, 90 pamphlets and 142 periodicals. 97% of the applicants are accepted. About 60% of the freshmen graduated in the top half of their high school class, and 20% were in the top quarter. 85% of the freshmen returned to the college for their second year.

Community Environment: See Saint Anselm College.

KEENE STATE COLLEGE   *(Q-4)*
229 Main Street
Keene, New Hampshire 03431
Tel: (603) 352-1909; (800) 833-4800; Admissions: (603) 358-2276; Fax: (603) 358-2257

Description: The four-year, multipurpose, liberal arts college is a member of the University system of New Hampshire. It is accredited by the New England Association of Schools and Colleges. Authority has been granted to award the degrees of Associate in Arts, Associate in Science, Bachelor of Arts, Bachelor of Science, and Bachelor of Music. Masters degrees are offered in Human Services and Education. Day, evening and weekend classes are offered. The college operates on the semester system with two summer sessions. Enrollment includes 3,419 full-time and 411 part-time undergraduate, and 101 graduate students. There are 929 students in the continuing education program. A faculty of 172 full-time and 171 part-time gives a faculty-student ratio of 1-19. Army and Air Force ROTC programs are available through the University of New Hampshire.

Entrance Requirements: Accredited high school graduation or equivalent; completion of 4 units English, 3 mathematics, 2 science, and 2 social science; SAT or ACT required; midyear admission, rolling admission, and advanced placement plans available; application fees: $25 state resident, $35 nonresident.

Costs Per Year: $2,620 state resident tuition; $7,870 nonresident tuition; $4,156 room and board; $756 student fees.

Collegiate Environment: The college is located in the city of Keene. The Student Union and Pondside Residence Hall are the newest buildings on campus which also includes the Thorne Art Gallery. The Mason Library collection includes 267,589 bound volumes, 1,008 periodical subscriptions, and 622,662 titles on microform. Living accommodations are available for 1,990 men and women. Housing for married students is available. Approximately 80% of students applying for admission are accepted. The average score of the admitted freshman class was SAT 872 combined. Financial aid is available and about 65% of a recent freshman class received some form of assistance.

Community Environment: Keene, population 22,000, is located in the southwest corner of New Hampshire, 90 miles from Boston. All forms of commercial transportation are available. Keene is a city of diversified industry with metal and machine industries the most important. There are a number of churches, a community hospital and library serving the area. One of the most popular resorts in the state, Keene has many lakes and ponds within a 20-mile radius as well as golf courses and facilities for winter sports. A number of covered bridges may be seen on side roads off State Highway 10 between Keene and Winchester.

MCINTOSH JUNIOR COLLEGE   *(O-11)*
23 Cataract Avenue
Dover, New Hampshire 03820
Tel: (603) 742-3518; Admissions: (603) 742-1234; Fax: (603) 742-7292

Description: The private, coeducational, business school was founded in 1896 and is accredited by the New England Association of Schools and Colleges. Enrollment includes 700 full-time, and 350 part-time students. A faculty of 15 full-time and 10 part-time gives a faculty-student ratio of 1-25.

Entrance Requirements: Open enrollment policy; midyear admission and rolling admission plans; $15 application fee.

Costs Per Year: $4,195 tuition and fees.

Collegiate Environment: All high school graduates applying for admission are accepted, including midyear students and 80% of the previous freshman class returned to the campus for their second year. The library contains 5,440 volumes and 28 periodicals. Dormitories can accommodate 3,700 students.

Community Environment: The oldest permanent settlement in New Hampshire, Dover was founded in 1623 by fishermen and traders. Primarily a manufacturing center, industries produce electrical and electronic equipment, shoes, machinery and sporting goods. Part-time jobs are available. Trains and buses are convenient; airlines service nearby Portsmouth, and Dover does enjoy all the cultural and recreational advantages of that city.

NEW ENGLAND COLLEGE   *(O-6)*
Henniker, New Hampshire 03242
Tel: (603) 428-2223; (800) 521-7642; Fax: (603) 428-7230

Description: This private, coeducational, liberal arts college is accredited by the New England Association of Schools. The school maintains a fully accredited four-year campus at Arundel, Sussex, England. The college operates on the semester system and offers two summer sessions. Enrollment at both campuses includes 690 full-time, 18 part-time, and 237 evening students. A faculty of 48 full-time and 12 part-time gives a faculty-student ratio of 1-15.

Entrance Requirements: Accredited high school graduation or equivalent; SAT or ACT optional; nondegree candidates may be admitted as special students; early admission, deferred admission, midyear admission, and rolling admission plans available; $30 application fee.

Costs Per Year: $13,325 tuition; $5,335 room and board.

Collegiate Environment: The College considers the village of Henniker as its campus. Approximately 30 buildings that represent a mix of modern facilities and restored New England-style structures of up to 150 years old are utilized by the College. A covered bridge over the Contoocook River connects the dormitories with 26 acres of athletic fields. The Danforth Library houses approximately 101,000 volumes and has access to more than 5 million volumes in other libraries throughout New Hampshire. In October 1994, the college opened the $2.5 million Simon Student Center. This facility houses an indoor-outdoor cafe, pub, gameroom, offices, conference rooms, bookstore, and "great hall" for entertainment. The Arundel, England, campus facilities include an 18th century manor house, classrooms, administrative offices, dormitory space housing 165 students, a dining room, snack bar/pub, library, auditorium, theatre, outdoor swimming pool, tennis courts and playing fields. Students attend Arundel both as permanent full-time students and as visiting students from the Henniker, N.H. campus. Average class size is less than 13, providing students with an excellent opportunity for interaction with faculty.

Community Environment: The American campus is situated in an area abounding in natural beauty. Henniker, a village of 3,200, is located on the Contoocook River in a mountainous area of New Hampshire 85 miles from Boston and 15 miles from Concord, the capital. The campus facilities are located throughout Henniker allowing students easy walking access to stores and restaurants. Alpine skiing is provided by the College at Pat's Peak two miles from Henniker. Other outdoor recreational facilities abound in the surrounding area. The campus in Great Britain is located one mile from Arundel, a small, charming town in which a medieval church and the magnificent castle and park of the Duke of Norfolk are carefully preserved. Arundel is 55 miles south of London, lying on the picturesque coastal plain between South Downs and the English Channel. Low-cost rail service provides students easy access to London and all of Great Britain.

Branch Campuses: New England College, Arundel, Sussex, BN1 80DA, Sussex, England.

NEW HAMPSHIRE COLLEGE   *(P-8)*
2500 North River Road
Manchester, New Hampshire 03104
Tel: (603) 668-2211; (800) 642-4968; Admissions: (603) 645-9611; Fax: (603) 645-9693

Description: The private, four-year college is accredited by the New England Association of Schools and Colleges. The college grants the Associate, Bachelor, and Master degrees. The college operates on the semester system and offers two summer sessions. The college has continuing education centers in Concord, Laconia, Nashua, Portsmouth and Salem, NH, and Brunswick, ME. An overseas program in London is available. Army and Air Force ROTC programs are available through the University of New Hampshire. Enrollment includes 1,048 full-time and 3,000 part-time undergraduates and 1,784 graduate students. A faculty of 70 gives a faculty-student ratio of 1-18.

Entrance Requirements: High school graduation; SAT required; personal essay; recommendations, (at least one from guidance counselor) non-degree candidates may be admitted as special students; early action, rolling admission, CLEP and advanced placement plans available.

Costs Per Year: $11,142 tuition; $4,884 room and board; $200-$500 average additional expenses.

Collegiate Environment: The college is located on the Manchester, Hookset line just 3 miles from downtown Manchester. The college library contains 85,430 volumes, 962 periodical titles, and 232,818 corporation and periodical backfile holdings in microformat. It is a federal and state government depository and houses a complete audio-visual facility with a closed circuit TV system. On-campus resident facilities house 824 students. Approximately 80% of students applying for admission are accepted, including at midyear, and 72% of the previous freshman class returned to the campus for the second year. Nearly 32% of the current students graduated in the top half of their high school class, and 15% ranked in the top quarter. 75% of the current student body receive some form of financial aid.

Community Environment: Combining the tradition of the past with the sophistciation of the future, Manchester has everything to be expected in a city with a population of more than 100,000. It offers a thriving business environment as well as numerous cultural facilities. The city is also within an hour of Boston and many ski resorts and beaches that provide opportunities for jobs and recreation.

Branch Campuses: The North campus is 4.7 miles from the South campus on Daniel Webster Highway, Route 3. Located on 500 wooded acres, this campus is comprised of faculty, administrative offices, classrooms, and dining facilities. Alumni Hall houses the Graduate School of Business. The Community Economic Development program, the American Language and Cultural Center, and the Culinary Institute are quartered in New Hampshire Hall.

NEW HAMPSHIRE TECHNICAL COLLEGE - CLAREMONT   *(N-4)*
One College Dr.
Claremont, New Hampshire 03743
Tel: (603) 542-7744; (800) 837-0658; Fax: (603) 543-1844

Description: The coeducational state technical college was founded in 1967. Recent enrollment was 492 students. A faculty of 48 gives a faculty-student ratio of 1-9. It operates on the semester system. It is accredited by the New England Association of Schools and Colleges, the American Physical Therapy Association and the Committee on Allied Health Education and Accreditation.

Entrance Requirements: High school graduation or equivalent; completion of 16 units including 4 English and 1 mathematics; ASSET placement exam; average or above-average academic performance; early decision, rolling admission, delayed admission and advanced placement plans available; $10 application fee.

Costs Per Year: $2,296 state-resident tuition; $3,444 New England regional resident; $5,408 nonresident; $80 student fees.

Collegiate Environment: 70% of students applying for admission meet the requirements and are accepted. Financial aid is available and about 80% of a recent freshman class received some form of assistance. Approximately 50% of the current students graduated in the top half of their high school class; 5% in the top quarter. The 140-acre campus has 1 building. The library contains 11,000 titles, 95 periodicals, 600 microforms and 300 audiovisual materials.

Community Environment: Located 60 miles northwest of Manchester, Claremont is adjacent to excellent ski facilities. Buses and trains serve the area. Three public parks with recreation and camping facilities, outdoor and indoor swimming pools and a community center and recreation building are nearby. There are 200 retail establishments and 100 professional offices in Claremont, as well as three shopping centers. The community includes a number of churches and two libraries.

NEW HAMPSHIRE TECHNICAL COLLEGE - LACONIA
(M-8)
Route 106, Prescott Hill
Laconia, New Hampshire 03246
Tel: (603) 524-3207; Fax: (603) 524-8084

Description: The state technical college was founded in 1967 and is accredited by the New England Association of Schools and Colleges. With the exception of graphics and automotive technology programs, which operate on a quarter system, the college operates on the semester system and offers two summer sessions. Business courses are offered during the summer. Some courses are offered on a cooperative basis with General Motors. Enrollment includes 365 full-time, 175 part-time, and 490 evening students. A faculty of 30 full-time and 9 part-time gives a faculty-student ratio of 1-13.

Entrance Requirements: High school graduation or GED; completion of 16 units; ASSET placement exam; early decision, early admission, deferred admission, and rolling admission plans available.

Costs Per Year: $2,296 resident tuition; $3,444 New England regional resident; $5,408 nonresident; $75 student fees; additional expenses average $700.

Collegiate Environment: About 85% of students applying for admission are accepted, including midyear students, and 70% return for the second year. Dormitory housing is not available on campus but is an option at a sister college 25 miles away. Financial aid is available and 85% of the current student body receives some form of assistance. The library contains 10,000 volumes, 3,500 pamphlets and 95 periodicals. The college awarded 125 Associate degrees to the graduating class.

Community Environment: Laconia is a city of approximately 16,000 people that possesses a varied number of civic and social organizations, hospital and a number of churches. It is a year-round resort including a number of lakes for all water sports a county-operated ski area. Local employment opportunities are more than sufficient to meet the needs of the college students.

NEW HAMPSHIRE TECHNICAL COLLEGE -
MANCHESTER   *(P-8)*
1066 Front Street
Manchester, New Hampshire 03102-8518
Tel: (603) 668-6706; Admissions: (603) 668-6706 X 208; Fax: (603) 668-5354

Description: The state technical, coeducational college was founded 1945. It is accredited by the New England Association of Schools and Colleges. Programs of study are primarily vocational-technical and lead to the Associate degree. The college operates on the semester system and offers one summer session. Enrollment includes 800 full-time and 700 part-time students. A faculty of 47 gives a faculty-student ratio of 1-19.

Entrance Requirements: High school graduation or equivalent; rolling admission, delayed admission and advanced placement plans available.

Costs Per Year: $2,440 tuition; $5,500 out-of-state tuition; $3,660 NERSP; $60 student fees.

Collegiate Environment: The college has 1 building on 57 acres. Financial aid is available. The college welcomes a geographically diverse student body and about 80% of the recent freshman class returned to the campus for their second year. The library contains

15,000 volumes, 110 periodicals, 500 microforms and 590 audio visual materials.

Community Environment: See Saint Anselm College.

NEW HAMPSHIRE TECHNICAL COLLEGE - NASHUA
(R-8)
505 Amherst Street
Nashua, New Hampshire 03061-2052
Tel: (603) 882-6923; Fax: (603) 882-8690

Description: The state technical college was founded in 1970 and has been granted accreditation by the New England Association of Schools and Colleges. Enrollment is 551 students. A faculty of 38 full-time and 35 part-time gives a faculty-student ratio of 1-15. The college operates on the semester system. It grants the Associate degree and also provides certificate and diploma programs.

Entrance Requirements: High school graduation or equivalent; completion of 16 units including 4 English, 2 mathematics, 1 science, and 2 social studies; non-high school graduates considered; rolling admission, advanced placement and delayed admission plans available.

Costs Per Year: $2,296 in-state; $3,444 New England regional, $5,408 out-of-state; $40 student fees; $300 average additional expenses.

Collegiate Environment: 70% of those who apply for admission are accepted. Approximately 70% of the students return for their second year. The library contains more than 10,000 volumes and numerous periodicals, microforms and audiovisual materials, and access to Internet. Financial aid is available and 70% of students receive some form of financial assistance.

Community Environment: See Rivier College.

NEW HAMPSHIRE TECHNICAL COLLEGE - STRATHAM
(P-12)
227 Portsmouth Avenue
Stratham, New Hampshire 03885-2297
Tel: (603) 772-1194; (800) 522-1194; Fax: (603) 772-1198

Description: The state technical college was founded in 1945. The college is fully accredited by the New England Association of Schools and Colleges. Programs of study lead to the Associate degree. Courses are also offered at Portsmouth High School and Pease Education and Training Center. It operates on the semester system and offers one summer session. Enrollment includes 248 full-time and 683 part-time students. A faculty of 31 full-time and 30 part-time gives a faculty-student ratio of 1-14.

Entrance Requirements: Open enrollment policy; high school graduation or equivalent; entrance exam (ASSET) required; early admission, early decision, midyear admission, rolling admission, and advanced placement plans available.

Costs Per Year: $2,075 state resident tuition; $3,113 NERSP tuition; $4,923 nonresident tuition; $45 student fees.

Collegiate Environment: The college is located five miles inland from the New Hampshire coast. The library contains 9,100 volumes. Approximately 80% of applicants are accepted. Financial aid is available and 65% of students receive some form of financial assistance.

Community Environment: Within a short drive of southern Maine and northern Massachusetts, the area is rich in heritage, as evidenced by its white churches and town greens, but its high-tech industries also reflect the future. Local economic development centers on the emerging Pease International Tradeport, the college is a partner in the Pease Education and Training Center. Surrounding communities provide medical centers and active civic and service organizations. The nearby historic city of Portsmouth, founded in 1623, offers cinemas, small clubs, the Portsmouth Music Hall, and boutique and mall shopping. There are year-round recreational opportunities including skiing, hiking, scenic drives, and boating. NH's White Mountains and dozens of lakes are an hour and a half away.

NEW HAMPSHIRE TECHNICAL INSTITUTE   *(O-8)*
Fan Road
Concord, New Hampshire 03301
Tel: (603) 225-1800; (800) 247-0179; Admissions: (603) 225-1865;
Fax: (603) 225-1895

Description: The state, coeducational, technical school is accredited by the New England Association of Schools and Colleges. Programs of study lead to Certificates and the Associate degree in primarily occupational areas. The Institute operates on the semester system and offers two summer sessions. Enrollment includes 1,748 students. A faculty of 82 gives a faculty-student ratio of 1-21.

Entrance Requirements: High school graduation or equivalent; college entrance examinations required for some programs; rolling admission plan available.

Costs Per Year: $2,296 state resident tuition; $5,408 nonresident tuition; $3,809 room and board; $66 student fees.

Collegiate Environment: The capital city location of the Institute provides students with opportunities for a wide variety of educational, cultural and recreational activities. Dormitories are available for 400 students, and all students not living with their parents are required to live in approved housing. There are 13 buildings on the 225-acre campus and the Institute library contains 35,000 volumes. About 70% of students applying for admission meet the requirements and 35% of these are accepted. Financial aid is available.

Community Environment: Bisected by the Merrimack River, Concord is the capital of New Hampshire, and is an economic and political center of the state. Concord is a key city on the interstate highway system. Community facilities include three libraries, numerous churches, a YMCA, hospitals and good shopping. Job opportunities are good.

NOTRE DAME COLLEGE   *(P-8)*
2321 Elm Street
Manchester, New Hampshire 03104
Tel: (603) 669-4298; Admissions: (603) 669-4298 X 163; Fax: (603) 644-8316

Description: The private, liberal arts college was founded by the Sisters of Holy Cross of the Roman Catholic Church and is accredited by the New England Association of Schools and Colleges. The four-year college operates the semesters system and offers two summer terms. Enrollment includes 440 full-time and 140 part-time and 120 evening program undergraduates and 520 graduate students. A faculty of 48 full-time and 70 part-time gives a faculty-student ratio of 1-12.

Entrance Requirements: Accredited high school graduation with rank in upper half of graduating class; completion of 16 units including 4 English, 2 mathematics, 2 science, 2 foreign language, 2 social studies; GRE required for graduate program; early admission, early decision, delayed admission, rolling admission, advanced placement and early decision plans available; $25 application fee.

Costs Per Year: $9,990 tuition; $4,900 room and board.

Collegiate Environment: There are 18 buildings on the campus including the library containing 51,000 volumes, 800 periodicals, 1,450 microforms and 1,700 sound recordings. Dormitory facilities accommodate 200 students. The college accepts students of all denominations, 80% of students applying for admission are accepted including midyear students, and 65% of the freshman class returned for their sophomore year. The average scores of the entering freshman class were SAT 438 verbal, 448 math. 125 scholarships are available including 35 for freshmen. 90% of the undergraduates receive some form of financial aid.

Community Environment: See Saint Anselm College.

PLYMOUTH STATE COLLEGE   *(K-7)*
Summer Street
Plymouth, New Hampshire 03264
Tel: (603) 535-2237; (800) 842-6900; Fax: (603) 535-2714

Description: The state college, part of the University System of New Hampshire, was founded in 1871. It was one of the first teachers colleges in New England to gain accreditation and is now a member of the New England Association of Schools and Colleges. Enrollment totals 4,000 with a faculty of 200. The semester system is used and two summer terms are offered. Major divisions include Liberal Arts, Science, Business and Teacher Education.

Entrance Requirements: Accredited high school graduation or equivalent; ACT or SAT required; midyear admission, rolling admission; $25 application fee in-state; out-of-state $30; non high school graduates considered with GED.

Costs Per Year: $2,590 tuition; $7,870 out-of-state tuition; $3,770 room and board; $792 student fees; additional expenses average $300.

Collegiate Environment: Lamson Library contains 225,000 volumes, 6,699 pamphlets, 75,000 periodicals, 250,000 microforms and 5,000 recordings. Student housing includes facilities for 30 families, dormitory capacity for 875 men and 875 women, 5 coed residence halls and 60 student apartments. The college welcomes a geographically diverse student body and students may enroll at midyear. Financial aid is available. Approximately 75% of the current student body receive financial assistance. About 70% of the students applying for admission are accepted.

Community Environment: Plymouth is in a popular resort region, near the center of the state at the southern end of the White Mountains, near Franconia Notch. Community facilities include a number of churches, a hospital, library, good shopping and various civic organizations. Part-time jobs are available. Loon Mountain, Tenny Mountain, Cannon Mountain and Waterville Valley ski areas are nearby for skiing. Other recreational activities are hiking, fishing, boating and hunting.

RIVIER COLLEGE   *(R-8)*
420 S. Main Street
Nashua, New Hampshire 03060
Tel: (603) 888-1311; (800) 447-4843 x7; Admissions: (603) 888-1311 x8507; Fax: (603) 888-6447

Description: As a liberal arts college, Rivier was established in 1933 by the Sisters of the Presentation of Mary of the Roman Catholic Church. It is accredited by the New England Association of Schools and Colleges and the National League of Nursing, and is approved by the American Bar Association. The enrollment totals approximately 2,800 students. The school is organized into the School of Undergraduate Studies (day, 552 students; evening, 748 students); Rivier College-St. Joseph School of Nursing (443 students); and the School of Graduate Studies, (921 students). A faculty of 66 full-time and 124 part-time gives a faculty-student ratio of 1-14. The semester system is used, plus two six-week summer sessions. The college belongs to the 13-college New Hampshire College and University Council, through which academic exchange programs are available. Air Force ROTC is available through the University of Lowell.

Entrance Requirements: Candidates for admission must have completed a minimum of 16 units in an accredited high school as follows: 4 English, 2 Social Sciences, 1 lab science, 2 mathematics (including algebra), and 2 modern foreign languages; the remaining five credits may be made up from any subjects in an accrediting high school curriculum; SAT or ACT required, SAT preferred; GED accepted in lieu of high school diploma; GRE, GMAT, and MAT required for specific graduate programs; $25 application fee; rolling admissions, early action, and deferred admission (up to one year) midyear admission plans available.

Costs Per Year: $11,010 tuition; $5,250 room and board; $400 student fees.

Collegiate Environment: The attractive 44-acre campus has 30 buildings and residence space for 300 students. Regina Library has a collection of 128,473 volumes, 752 periodicals, and 161 microfrom titles. Approximately 75% of students who apply are accepted. Tkhe middle 50% ranges of entering freshmen scores were SAT 360-510 verbal, 370-510 math. 73% of the previous freshman class returned for the sophomore year. 85% of students receive financial aid through scholarships, grants, loans and college workstudy.

Community Environment: Nashua is the second largest city in New Hampshire. It is conveniently located within an hour's drive of Boston, the White Mountains, and the seacoast, and is home to a large technology industry. Buses provide ample transportation to shopping malls, libraries, banking facilities, and many other services within just a few miles of the campus.

SAINT ANSELM COLLEGE   *(P-8)*
100 Saint Anselm Drive
Manchester, New Hampshire 03102
Tel: (603) 641-7000; Admissions: (603) 641-7500; Fax: (603) 641-7550

Description: The four-year, liberal arts college was founded in 1889 by the Order of St. Benedict. It is accredited by the New England Association of Schools and Colleges, the American Chemical Society and the National League for Nursing. Full-time enrollment for the academic year is 819 men and 1,021 women. There are also 105 part-time students. A faculty of 112 full-time and 49 part-time gives a faculty-student ratio of 1-16. The semester system is used and three summer sessions are offered. Overseas and ROTC/Army and Air Force programs are available.

Entrance Requirements: High school graduation, completion of 16 units including 4 English, 3 mathematics, 3 laboratory science, 2 foreign language, 2 social studies; non-high school graduates considered; $25 application fee; SAT required; early admission, early decision, advanced placement, rolling admission and delayed admission plans available.

Costs Per Year: $13,720 tuition; $5,550 room and board.

Collegiate Environment: The college is located 50 miles north of Boston. Its 460-acre campus with rolling woods and up-to-date resources and facilities contains 37 buildings. The Dana Center, home of the Humanities Program, is an elegant performing arts center with a 700-seat theater and auditorium. The Poisson Computer Science Center gives students and faculty virtually unlimited access to computer time. Davison Hall is a new 700-seat dining facility. The John Maurus Carr Center is an extensive athletic facility reserved for nonvarsity and intramural athletics and recreation. There is also a gymnasium for intercollegiate sports and numerous athletic fields. The Geisel Library reopened after a six-million-dollar expansion and reconstruction. It contains 200,000 volumes, 1,350 periodicals, 16,346 microform items and 7,472 audiovisual materials, and has comprehensive computer networking capabilities. The Abbey Church is the religious center of the college. Residence halls accommodate about 1,250 students. Approximately 75% of the current student body receives some form of financial aid, and about 1,050 scholarships are available.

Community Environment: On the banks of Merrimack River, Manchester is the largest city in the state. The city is a retail, industrial, distribution and financial center. About 250 concerns in Manchester produce textiles, shoes and a variety of other articles. All means of commercial transportation are available. Community facilities include 54 churches, 8 hospitals, a public library, hotels and motels. The recreational activities are numerous. They include golf, swimming, bowling, tennis, roller skating, fishing, sailing, skiing, ice skating, and tobagganing. Points of interest are the Currier Gallery of Art, Manchester Historic Association and the Old Blodgett Canal.

UNIVERSITY OF NEW HAMPSHIRE   *(O-11)*
Durham, New Hampshire 03824
Tel: (603) 862-1360; Fax: (603) 862-0077

Description: The state university was founded in 1866. The school began as the New Hampshire College of Agriculture and the Mechanic Arts, as part of Dartmouth College. In 1893 it moved to its present site and in 1923 it was chartered as the University of New Hampshire. It is accredited by the New England Association of Schools and Colleges, and by respective professional and educational organizations. The university divisions include the College of Liberal Arts; College of Life Sciences and Agriculture; College of Engineering and Physical Sciences; Whittemore School of Business and Economics; School of Health and Human Services; Thompson School of Applied Science; Division of Continuing Education; Graduate School; and the University of New Hampshire at Manchester. Army and Air Force ROTC are available as electives. The semester system is used and four summer sessions are offered. Enrollment includes 10,238 full-time and 658 part-time undergraduate students. In addition, there are 1,622 graduate students. A faculty of 641 full-time

members and 215 part-time members provides an undergraduate faculty student ratio of 1-18.

Entrance Requirements: Most successful candidates for admission have completed a secondary school program that includes at least 4 years of English, 4 or more years of college-preparatory mathematics, 4 years of science, and 3 years of study in a single foreign language or more than 1 year of study in each of two different languages; most successful candidates rank within the top 28% of their secondary school graduating classes and have SAT scores of at least 1040 combined; however, there are no "cut-off" ratings for either SAT or class standing; SAT required; out-of-state admission is limited and selective; early notification (nonbinding), advanced placement and honors program available; $25 application fee for residents; $45 for nonresidents.

Costs Per Year: $3,670 state-resident tuition; $11,990 out-of-state; $4,038 room and board; $889 compulsory fees.

Collegiate Environment: The campus in Durham is 200 acres in size and is surrounded by nearly 4,000 acres of fields, farms and woodlands owned by the University. There are 95 buildings, and 36 residence halls that provide living accommodations for 5,887 students. The university library contains more than 1,001,356 volumes, 6,500 periodicals, 11,348 records, tapes, and CDs, and a 615,706 microfilm titles. The school operates an educational television station. Among the specialized research facilities are the Earth, Ocean, and Space Center; the Center for Business and Economic Research; the Center for Health Promotion and Research; and the Institute for Policy and Social Science Research. The University Financial Aid Office assists promising students who are unable to meet educational expenses entirely from their own or family resources. 64% of the student body receives one or more forms of financial aid. A limited number of scholarships are available exclusively for freshmen.

Community Environment: Situated in southeastern New Hampshire, Durham is a quiet college town that was founded in 1635. The cultural and recreational advantages of Portland to the north and nearby Boston to the south are enjoyed by this community. A point of historical interest is the Old Sullivan Homestead of Revolutionary War fame. The University is 10 miles from the Atlantic coastline and historic Portsmouth, which is the home of Strawbery Banke, a restored maritime community dating from 1695.

WHITE PINES COLLEGE   *(P-9)*
40 Chester Street
Chester, New Hampshire 03036
Tel: (603) 887-4401

Description: The private, two-year college offers programs of study in liberal arts. The college was founded in 1965 and is fully accredited by the New England Association of Schools and Colleges. Enrollment is 74 full-time and 4 part-time students. A faculty of 19 gives a faculty-student ratio of 1-6. The college operates on the semester system.

Entrance Requirements: High school graduation or equivalent with completion of 4 units of English, 2 math, 1 science, and 1 social studies; applicants not meeting all requirements will be considered; SAT or ACT recommended; rolling admission, early decision, early admission, delayed admission and advanced placement plans available; $20 application fee.

Costs Per Year: $6,800 tuition; $3,800 room and board; $220 student fees; $800 average additional expenses.

Collegiate Environment: The school is about one hour's drive from Boston. The 83-acre campus contains 6 buildings. The Lane and Powers Buildings provide classrooms, a laboratory, offices, cafeteria, bookstore, and a library containing 28,000 volumes, 103 periodicals, and 600 recordings. Dormitories provide living accomodations for 50 students. Approximately 93% of those who apply for admission are accepted. 85% of the previous freshman class returned to the campus for the second year. Financial aid is available, and 80% of the students receive some form of financial aid.

Community Environment: Chester is a small town in close proximity to larger towns and cities such as Derry, Manchester and Boston.

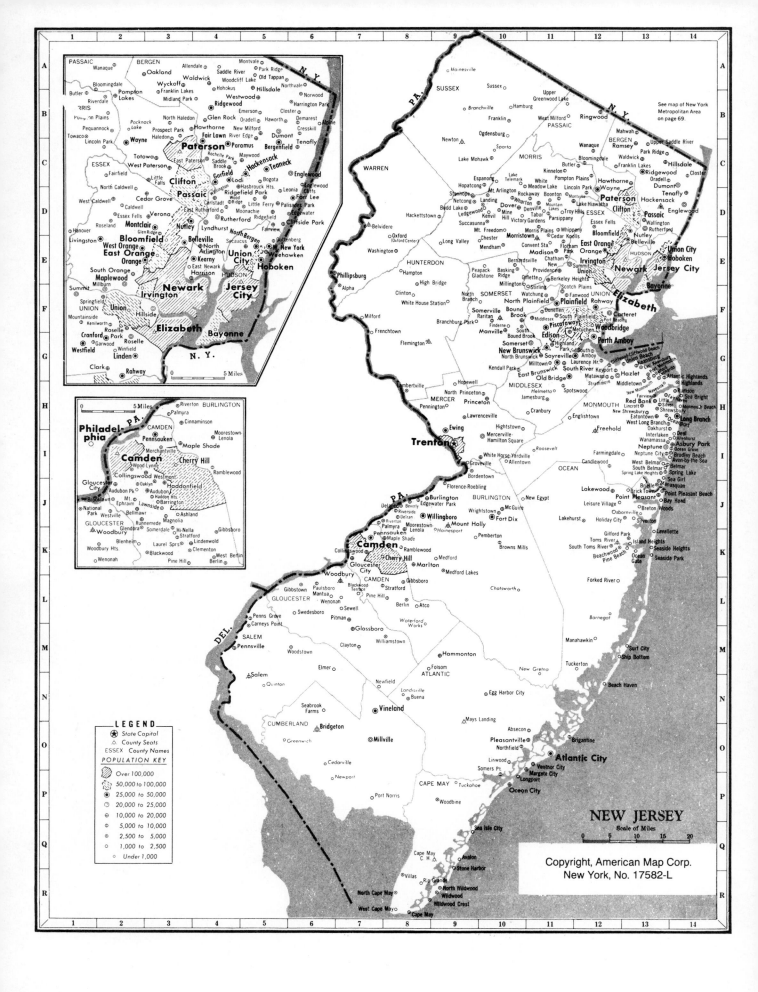

NEW JERSEY

Scale of Miles

Copyright, American Map Corp.
New York, No. 17582-L

See map of New York
Metropolitan Area
on page 69.

LEGEND
- ★ State Capital
- ⌂ County Seats
- ESSEX County Names

POPULATION KEY
- Over 100,000
- 50,000 to 100,000
- 25,000 to 50,000
- 20,000 to 25,000
- 10,000 to 20,000
- 5,000 to 10,000
- 2,500 to 5,000
- 1,000 to 2,500
- Under 1,000

NEW JERSEY

ASSUMPTION COLLEGE FOR SISTERS *(E-10)*
Mallinckrodt Convent
Hilltop Road
Mendham, New Jersey 07945
Tel: (201) 543-6528; Fax: (201) 543-9459

Description: Privately supported, liberal arts, junior college for women only. Established in 1953 generally for the education of members of religious communities, but more specifically as a Sister-Formation institution for the members of the Roman Catholic Sisters of Christian Charity. The college is accredited by the Middle States Association of Colleges and Schools and grants the Associate degree. It operates on the semester system and offers one summer session. Enrollment is 12 full-time and 20 part-time undergraduate, and 5 graduate students. A faculty of 8 full-time and 13 part-time gives a faculty-student ratio of 1-3.

Entrance Requirements: Must be a member (probationary or permanent) of a Catholic sisterhood; recommendations by applicant's pastor; personal interviews; accredited high school graduation; completion of 16 units including 4 English, 2 mathematics, 2 foreign language, 1 laboratory science, 2 social science; and 5 electives; SAT required.

Costs Per Year: $1,200 tuition.

Collegiate Environment: The college is located on 112 acres and contains a library of approximately 23,618 volumes. Classes begin in September; midyear students are accepted under special circumstances.

Community Environment: Mendham, (population 3,729) is in a suburban area with churches, civic and service organizations, and good shopping facilities. It is convenient to all commercial traffic. The climate is temperate and parks provide recreation with many water sports available.

ATLANTIC COMMUNITY COLLEGE *(N-9)*
Mays Landing, New Jersey 08330
Tel: (609) 343-4900; (800) 645-2433; Admissions: (609) 343-5000; Fax: (609) 343-4917

Description: Publicly supported, coeducational, community college jointly sponsored by the people of Atlantic County and the State of New Jersey. It is accredited by the Middle States Association of Colleges and Schools. It offers courses in vocational/technical and academic areas for part-time, terminal and transfer programs, as well as community service programs. Programs of study lead to the Associate degree. The college has facilities in Atlantic City and Cape May County. It is the world's first public institution to sponsor a casino dealer and slot-machine school. The college operates on the semester system and offers four summer sessions. Enrollment includes 1,582 full-time students. A faculty of 90 gives a faculty-student ratio of 1-20.

Entrance Requirements: Open enrollment policy; high school graduation or equivalent; entrance exam required; non-high school graduates considered; rolling admission, early admission and advanced placement plans available; residents of Atlantic County and Cape May are given preference; $20 application fee.

Costs Per Year: $1,436 county resident tuition; $2,872 state resident tuition; $5,744 out-of-state residents.

Collegiate Environment: The college is located on 537 acres and contains 9 buildings which include a library of 75,000 volumes, 400 periodical titles and 92 microforms. All students who meet the entrance requirements are accepted. 54 scholarships are available. 65% of students receive some form of financial aid.

Community Environment: Population 8,000. Mays Landing is the county seat of Atlantic County, 18 miles from Atlantic City.

BERGEN COMMUNITY COLLEGE *(C-4)*
400 Paramus Road
Paramus, New Jersey 07652
Tel: (201) 447-7100

Description: The publicly supported, coeducational, community college opened in 1968. It operates on the semester system with two summer terms and is accredited by the Middle States Association of Colleges and Schools. Enrollment includes 12,511 students. A faculty of 245 full-time and 337 part-time gives a faculty-student ratio of 1-22. Programs of study lead to the Certificate and Associate degree.

Entrance Requirements: High school graduation or equivalent; open enrollment policy, except for programs in Allied Health, Nursing and Dental Hygiene; non-high school graduates considered; early decision, midyear admission and rolling admission plans available; $20 application fee.

Costs Per Year: $1,588 county-resident tuition; $3,177.60 out-of-county; $5,736 out-of-state; $206.40 general fees.

Collegiate Environment: The college occupies 5 buildings on its new 167-acre site. The library contains 108,098 volumes, 655 periodical titles, 15,128 microforms and 19,269 audiovisual materials. Approximately 99% of students applying for admission are accepted including midyear students, and semesters begin in September and January. About 71% of previous freshmen returned for their second year.

Community Environment: Near Paterson, population 144,824. Alexander Hamilton, selecting the area for a city, foresaw the potential waterpower of the 70-foot waterfalls on the Passaic River. Paterson is now primarily a mill town, producing silk, rayon, synthetic fabric, and wood and textile dyes. Commercial transportation is available and Newark Airport is nearby. The community facilities include 95 churches representing a number of denominations, a library, and a museum. Part-time work is available. Recreational facilities include 4 golf courses and a stadium.

BETH MEDRASH GOVOHA *(J-12)*
Lakewood, New Jersey 08701
Tel: (908) 367-1060

Description: Privately supported, theological school for men. The school operates on the semester system and offers degrees in religious studies only, namely the Bachelor of Rabbinical and Talmudic Studies, and the Master of Talmudic Studies. Enrollment is 1,565 full-time and 147 part-time students. A faculty of 78 full-time and 8 part-time gives a faculty-student ratio of 1-20.

Entrance Requirements: High school graduation; entrance examinations required; rolling admission and delayed admission plans available.

Costs Per Year: $2,900 tuition; $4,025 room and board.

Collegiate Environment: The institution occupies 10 buildings located on 9 acres, and contains a library of 40,000 volumes and dormitory facilities for 535 are available. Approximately 75% of students applying for admission meet the requirements and are accepted. Students from other geographical locations are accepted as well as midyear students. Financial aid is available for economically handicapped students and 70% of the students receive some form of aid. Classes begin in October and April. About 90% of the previous senior class continued on to graduate school.

Community Environment: See Georgian Court College.

BLOOMFIELD COLLEGE   *(E-3)*
1 Park Place
Bloomfield, New Jersey 07003
Tel: (201) 748-9000; (800) 848-4555; Admissions: (201) 748-9000
x230; Fax: (201) 743-3998

Description: Bloomfield College is a private, four-year, coeducational institution founded in 1868 and affiliated with the Presbyterian Church, USA. It is accredited by the Middle States Association of Colleges and Schools and the National League of Nursing. The college grants the Bachelor of Arts and Bachelor of Science degrees. Army ROTC is available through Seton Hall. It operates on the semester system and offers three summer sessions. Enrollment includes 1,371 full-time and 803 part-time and 873 evening program students. A faculty of 52 full-time and 160 part-time gives a faculty-student ratio of 1-17.

Entrance Requirements: High school graduation with rank in top 60%; completion of 16 units including 4 English, 3 mathematics, 3 science, and 2 social science; SAT or ACT required; early admission, deferred admission, early decision, midyear admission, rolling admission and advanced placement plans available; $20 application fee.

Costs Per Year: $8,700 tuition; room and board $4,500; $250 fees; $2,100 on-campus expenses.

Collegiate Environment: There are 26 buildings on 11 acres of college campus. The library contains 62,500 volumes, 375 periodicals and audiovisual materials. Students are welcomed from other geographical locations and midyear students are accepted. Financial aid is available. About 85% of the current student body receive financial assistance. The college provides a special program for academically underprepared students. Classes begin in September and January.

Community Environment: Located between Newark and Montclair, Bloomfield, population 55,000, is a suburban, residential city. Excellent shopping facilities, libraries, churches, numerous civic and service organizations and hospitals are a part of the community. Part-time employment is available. Commercial transportation is convenient.

BROOKDALE COMMUNITY COLLEGE   *(H-13)*
Newman Springs Road
Lincroft, New Jersey 07738
Tel: (908) 842-1900; Admissions: (908) 224-2933

Description: Publicly supported, coeducational, community college was established in September 1969. It is accredited by the Middle States Association of Colleges and Schools. It is professionally accredited by the National League for Nursing. The college provides college parallel and career programs. It grants the Associaite degree. Air Force and Army ROTC programs are available at the college. It operates on the semester system and offers three summer sessions. Enrollment includes 13,000 full-time and 8,500 part-time students. A faculty of 209 full-time and 389 part-time gives a faculty-student ratio of 1-22.

Entrance Requirements: Open enrollment policy; non-high school graduates considered; $25 application fee.

Costs Per Year: $1,710 in-county tuition; $3,420 tuition for out-of-county; $6,840 tuition for out-of-state.

Collegiate Environment: The college occupies 6 buildings located on 225 acres. No dormitory facilities are provided. Midyear students are accepted and a special program for the culturally disadvantaged is offered. The library contains 128,115 volumes. 99% of applicants are accepted and Monmouth County residents are given priority. 48% of the previous freshman class returned for their sophomore year.

Community Environment: Bounded by Sandy Hook Bay and the Navesink River, the Lincroft countryside area is located along the eastern shore of central New Jersey. The area abounds in orchards and horse farms. Community facilities include a library, churches of various faiths, above-average shopping facilities and many civic and service organizations. Railroads and buses furnish public transportation. Recreational facilities are very good including 7 miles of seashore for bay fishing, swimming and water sports.

BURLINGTON COUNTY COLLEGE   *(K-9)*
Pemberton-Browns Mills Road
Pemberton, New Jersey 08068
Tel: (609) 894-9311; Admissions: (609) 894-9311 x246

Description: BCC is a publicly supported, two-year coeducational community college which opened in 1969. The college is accredited by the Commission on Higher Education of the Middle States Association of Colleges and Schools. Certain academic programs are also accredited by professional bodies. BCC offers Associate of Arts, Associate of Science and Associate of Applied Science degrees. It operates on the semester system and offers two summer sessions. Enrollment includes 6,900 students. There are 70 faculty members. Army ROTC is available.

Entrance Requirements: Open enrollment policy; non-high school graduates considered; early admission, early decision, midyear admission, rolling admission and advanced placement plans available; $15 application fee.

Costs Per Year: $1,250 resident tuition; $2,760 out-of-state tuition.

Collegiate Environment: A new campus was completed in the fall of 1970. The library contains 70,000 volumes, 600 periodicals, 42,070 microforms and 15,000 recordings. All applicants accepted and 75% of the freshman class return for their second year. Average high school standing of the freshman class, top 50%; 20% in the top quarter, 30% in the second quarter, 40% in the third quarter, 10% in the bottom quarter; financial aid is available; scholarships are available for freshman and 30% of the current students receive some form of financial assistance.

Community Environment: The main campus is located in a rural setting where the principal agricultural pursuit is the raising of berries. Bus transportation is available. The campus is located 35 minutes from Center City Philadelphia and 90 minutes from New York City. Fort Dix and McGuire Air Force Base are nearby. Burlington County, the largest of New Jersey's 21 counties, has numerous churches and synagogues and excellent health care and recreational facilities.

CALDWELL COLLEGE   *(D-2)*
9 Ryerson Avenue
Caldwell, New Jersey 07006
Tel: (201) 228-4424; Admissions: (201) 228-4424; Fax: (201) 228-2897

Description: The privately supported, Roman Catholic, liberal arts college was founded in 1939 by the Sisters of St. Dominic. It is accredited by the Middle States Association of Colleges and Schools. The college grants an Associate degree for an educational media specialist, the B.A. degree in 12 liberal arts majors; the B.S. degree in business administration, business education, medical technlogy, and computer information systems; the B.F.A. degree in Art; a Master degree in curriculum and instruction, and Certification in early childhood, elementary, and secondary education, and for school nurse. The college operates on the semester system and offers two summer sessions. Enrollment includes 722 full-time, 877 part-time undergraduate, and 89 graduate students. A faculty of 55 full-time and 58 part-time gives an undergraduate faculty-student ratio of 1-12. Army ROTC available.

Entrance Requirements: Accredited high school graduation with rank in upper 40% of graduating class; completion of 16 units, including 4 English, 2 mathematics, 2 foreign language, 2 science, 2 social science; minimum SAT Verbal 443, Math 487 required; early admission, early decision, midyear admission, rolling admission, and advanced placement plans available; $25 application fee.

Costs Per Year: $8,900 tuition; $4,900 room and board.

Collegiate Environment: The campus is a 100-acre site of rolling lawns and wooded areas on one of the highest points of northern New Jersey. The college library contains 107,134 volumes, 480 periodicals, and 6,980 recordings. Dormitory facilities are available for 250 students. Well-equipped laboratories are available for the sciences, languages and reading. The art department contains studios for work in various media and a gallery featuring professional and student work. A curriculum laboratory in the education department has texts for all subjects K-12, visual aids, films and other resources. A video studio allows hands-on experience in working with 3 color-TV cameras, a special-effects generator and related production equipment.

Community Environment: The birthplace of President Grover Cleveland, Caldwell is situated in Western Essex County with bus lines serving the area, and New York City only 20 miles away. Community services include a number of churches, a public library, hospitals and various civic organizations. The Grover Cleveland County Park, golf courses and tennis courts provide facilities for recreation. Skiing and ice skating are available during the winter season.

CAMDEN COUNTY COLLEGE   *(K-3)*
Box 200
Blackwood, New Jersey 08012
Tel: (609) 227-7200

Description: Publicly supported, coeducational, community college established in 1967. Enrollment includes approximately 4,055 full-time and 7,959 part-time students with a faculty of 344. The college operates on the semester basis with three summer sessions and is accredited by the Middle States Association of Colleges and Schools. Programs of study lead to the Certificate and Associate degree.

Entrance Requirements: Open enrollment policy; non-high school graduates admitted; entrance exam required; rolling admission, early admission and early decision plans available; $15 application fee.

Costs Per Year: $800 county resident tuition; $860 out-of county tuition; $860 nonresident tuition; $64 student fees.

Collegiate Environment: The 14 college buildings are located on 324 acres. The library contains 71,340 volumes, 652 periodicals, 15,8000 microforms and 15,493 AV materials. All students applying for admission are accepted, including midyear students. Approximately 70% of the previous freshman class returned to the campus for their second year of studies. The college provides an evening program as well as a special program for the culturally disadvantaged. 22 scholarships are offered, and 19% of the current student body receive aid. About 60% of the graduating class continued on to a four-year college.

Community Environment: Blackwood is located in Gloucester Township (population 30,461), near Camden City. See Rutgers University, College of Arts and Sciences, Camden, for information on Camden.

CENTENARY COLLEGE   *(D-9)*
400 Jefferson Street
Hackettstown, New Jersey 07840
Tel: (201) 852-1400; (800) 236-8679; Admissions: (908) 852-4696; Fax: (908) 852-3454

Description: A privately supported college for men and women established in 1867, Centenary is accredited by the Middle States Association of Colleges and Schools. Programs of study lead to the Associate and Bachelor degrees. The college operates on the semester system and offers two summer sessions. Enrollment includes 425 full-time and 563 part-time students. A faculty of 33 full-time and 53 part-time provides a faculty-student ratio of 1-13.

Entrance Requirements: High school graduation or equivalent; 12 units including 4 English, 3 mathematics, 3 science, and 2 social science; minimum SAT combined score of 700 or minimum ACT composite score of 20; rolling admission, delayed admission, midyear admission and advanced placement plans available; $25 application fee.

Costs Per Year: $11,400 tuition; $5,400 room and board; $190 student fees.

Collegiate Environment: The campus is composed of 42 landscaped acres, has a 65-acre equestrian center, and contains 21 buildings that include dormitory facilities for 480 students. The library contains 68,000 volumes. Approximately 76% of students applying for admission are accepted and 75% of the freshmen return for their sophomore year. Students are welcome from other geographical locations and midyear students are accepted. Average high school standing of the freshman class was in the top 50%; 25% were in the top quarter, 50% ranked in the second quarter, 20% ranked in the third quarter, and 5% were in the bottom quarter. Financial aid is available and 80% of the current student body receives some form of aid.

Community Environment: Population 16,000, Hackettstown is a suburban and residential community. The area industry has not destroyed the natural surroundings. Students have easy access to New

York City by bus and train (approximately 45 minutes to Port Authority). The ski resorts of the Pocono Mountains are only 30 minutes via Route 80 West. State parks maintained by New Jersey are within minutes of the campus. Shops and stores in Hackettstown cater to the college students as well as area residents.

COLLEGE OF SAINT ELIZABETH   *(E-11)*
2 Convent Road
Morristown, New Jersey 07960-6989
Tel: (201) 292-6351; (800) 210-7900; Fax: (201) 292-6777

Description: Privately supported, liberal arts, women's college conducted by the Sisters of Charity of Saint Elizabeth. It was one of the first Roman Catholic colleges for women to be established in the United States and is accredited by the Middle States Association of Colleges and Schools. The college grants the Bachelor and Master degrees. Special programs include Acceleration Program, Leadership Program, and Weekend College. The semester system is used with three summer sessions offered. Enrollment recently included 511 full-time and 961 part-time undergraduate and 127 graduate students. A faculty of 49 full-time and 84 part-time gives a faculty-student ratio of 1-10.

Entrance Requirements: Accredited high school graduation with rank in upper 50% of class; completion of 16 units including 3 English, 3 mathematics, 3 lab. science, 1 social science, and 7 academic electives; SAT (minimum: verbal 400, math 400) and Math Achievement Test (for Math Majors or if Calculus will be taken) required; early admission, midyear admission, early decision, rolling admission and advanced placement plans available; $35 application fee.

Costs Per Year: $10,900 tuition; $5,250 room and board; $350 student fees; $550 average additional expenses.

Collegiate Environment: The 200-acre campus is located within the New York metropolitan area. Buildings include the library, housing 187,653 volumes, 721 periodicals, 34,264 microforms and 2,655 audiovisual materials, and dormitory space for 350 women. 77% of full-time undergraduates receive some kind of financial aid. Approximately 78% of the applicants are accepted, including midyear students, and 85% of the previous freshmen returned for their sophomore year. Average high school standing of the freshmen class were as follows: top fifth - 34%, 2/5 20%, 3/5 20%, other 26%. About 16% of the graduating class continued on to graduate school.

Community Environment: Situated in northern New Jersey, two miles east of Morristown (population 16,839), the college is near enough to New York to enjoy the educational, cultural and social advantages of that city. All forms of commercial transportation are convenient.

COUNTY COLLEGE OF MORRIS   *(D-10)*
214 Center Grove Road
Randolph, New Jersey 07869
Tel: (201) 328-5000; Fax: (201) 328-1282

Description: Publicly supported, coeducational, two-year college is accredited by the Middle States Association of Colleges and Schools and was established in 1965. Enrollment includes 4,329 students full-time and 5,298 part-time. A faculty of 195 full-time and 358 part-time provides a faculty-student ratio of 1-19. The college offers university-parallel programs, specialized career programs leading to the Associate degree, and 1 year certificate programs. The semester system is employed and three summer sessions are offered.

Entrance Requirements: Open enrollment policy; accredited high school graduation or equivalent; rolling admission and advanced placement plans available; $25 application fee.

Costs Per Year: $1,956.80 ($61.15/credit) in-county tuition; $3,913.60 ($122.30/credit) out-of-county; $5,376 ($168/credit) out-of-state; $150 fees.

Collegiate Environment: The college is comprised of 9 buildings located on 218 acres which include a library of 125,000 volumes, 850 periodicals, 100,000 microforms, 1,543 government documents and 5,223 non-prints. 99% of students applying for admission are accepted including midyear students. Approximately 15% of the freshman class graduated in the top 30% of their high school class; 18% in the second quarter, 30% in the third quarter, 37% in the bottom quarter; About 65% of the previous freshman returned for their sophomore year. Of the 135 scholarships offered including 110 for freshman. 19% of the students receive some form of financial aid. About 65% of the graduates continued on to a senior college.

Community Environment: Randolph Township (population 18,000) is near Morristown, which has a population of 16,839. A suburban area 27 miles west of New York City, Morristown was the winter encampment of General Washington's army during the winter of 1777 and 1779-80. Many historical events took place in Morristown. The sites have been restored and are incorporated in the Morristown National Historical Park. Commercial transportation is available. Part-time employment opportunities are good. Excellent shopping facilities; recreational facilities include all water sports.

CUMBERLAND COUNTY COLLEGE   *(N-7)*
College Drive
Vineland, New Jersey 08360
Tel: (609) 691-8600; Fax: (609) 691-6157

Description: This publicly supported, coeducational, community college is sponsored by Cumberland County and the New Jersey Department of Higher Education. It is accredited by the Middle States Association of Colleges and Schools, the National League of Nursing, and the American Bar Association. The college offers transfer and career programs leading to the Associate in Arts, Associate in Science or Associate in Applied Science degrees and cerificate programs in various fields of study. It operates on the semester system and offers two summer sessions. Enrollment is 1,250 full-time and 1,500 part-time students. A faculty of 80 full-time and 40 part-time provides a faculty-student ratio of 1-23.

Entrance Requirements: High school graduation or equivalent; open enrollment policy; non-high school graduates considered, rolling admission, midyear admission and advanced placement plans available; $15 application fee.

Costs Per Year: $1,500 county resident tuition; $3,000 out-of-county; $6,000 out-of-state; $90 student fees.

Collegiate Environment: New Jersey's first community college to open on its own campus, Cumberland is located in both Millville and Vineland. Six buildings serve the instructional and administrative needs of the college, including a student activity center and a library that contains nearly 100,000 volumes, 215 periodicals, 4,134 microfilm reels featuring 70 titles, and extensive holdings of audiovisual programmed materials. The college offers soccer, archery, basketball, field hockey, baseball, fencing and a number of other sports for physical development. A new Fine and Performing Arts Center to serve the cultural enrichment needs of the campus and the community opened in 1994.

Community Environment: Cumberland County's population lies mainly in the tri-city area of Vineland, Bridgeton and Millville. Industries include glass production, clothing manufacturing, and food processing and canning. Most church denominations are represented, and a hospital, shopping facilities and numerous service and civic groups all contribute to the general well-being of the Cumberland area. Golf, tennis and water sports are the main recreational activities in the county.

DEVRY TECHNICAL INSTITUTE   *(F-12)*
479 Green Street
Woodbridge, New Jersey 07095
Tel: (908) 634-3460; (800) 333-3879; Admissions: (908) 634-9510;
Fax: (908) 634-9445

Description: For more than 60 years, DeVry has provided distinctive curricula that unites education, technology, and business. Programs are developed and updated regularly with direct input from business and industry leaders. The Woodbridge campus was established in 1969 and is accredited by the

North Central Association of Colleges and Schools. It operates on the semester system, has one summer session, and grants associate and bachelor's degrees. Enrollment includes 1,228 men and 245 women full-time, and 609 men and 98 women part-time. A faculty of 44 full-time and 37 part-time gives a faculty-student ratio of 1-35.

Entrance Requirements: High school diploma or GED certification; minimum of 17 years of age; must pass DeVry entrance exam or sub-

mit acceptable ACT/SAT/WPCT scores; accepts foreign students if requirements are met as outlined in catalog; $25 application fee.

Costs Per Year: $6,335 tuition.

Collegiate Environment: The two-story building is flexible, attractive, and furnished with movable partitions to adapt to changing classroom needs. The campus is equipped with a library of 14,709 titles, 201 periodicals, and 128 microforms, and an attractive student commons with a student canteen. DeVry is accessible to all major transportation artieries to the city. 90% of applicants are accepted. Scholarships are available and 71% of the students receive financial aid.

Community Environment: Since 1964, when Woodbridge received the All-American City Award, it has continued its growth and distinction, embodied in the Woodbridge Center, a large shopping and office center with professional offices and nationally known department stores. Not far away, the New Jersey seacoast stretches 125 miles from Sandy Hook to Cape May, providing excellent facilities for swimming and fishing.

DREW UNIVERSITY   *(E-11)*
36 Madison Avenue
Madison, New Jersey 07940
Tel: (201) 408-3000

Description: This privately supported, coeducational university was established in 1867 by the Methodist Episcopal Church and was known as Drew Theological Seminary until 1928, when its present name was adopted. Today the university is comprised of a college of liberal arts, a theological school, and a graduate school. It operates on the semester system with an optional January term. It is accredited by the Middle States Association of Colleges and Schools, the American Chemical Society and the Association of Theological Schools in the United States and Canada. Undergraduate enrollment includes 517 men and 727 women full-time, 66 part-time students, and 818 students in the graduate division. A faculty of 96 full-time and 80 part-time provides an undergraduate faculty-student ratio of 1-11. Programs of study lead to the Bachelor, Master, and Doctorate degrees. Cooperative programs lead to certification in education at the college of St. Elizabeth; 3/4 BA/MD degree at the University of medicine and Dentistry in New Jersey; degrees in forestry at Duke; and degrees in engineering at Washington University of St. Louis and Stevens Institute of Technology. The university also offers the United Nations Semester, the Brussels semester on the European Community, the London Semester, the Semester in Chile, the Drewin West Africa program, the New York Semester on Contemporary Art, and the Washington Semester. Army ROTC is available through Seton Hall University.

Entrance Requirements: Accredited high school graduation or equivalent; rank in upper third of graduating class; completion of 16 units, including 4 English, 3 math, 2 foreign language, 2 lab science, and 2 history/social studies; SAT or ACT required; early admission, early decision, delayed admission and advanced placement plans available; $35 application fee.

Costs Per Year: $17,568 tuition; $5,094 room and board; $470 student fees.

Collegiate Environment: The 186-acre campus, an hour by train from the heart of New York City, includes a forest preserve and arboretum. The 56 univeristy buildings include a library of 421,330 volumes, 2,060 periodicals, 282,187 microforms and more than 385,056 government documents. Living accomodations include 1,167 residence hall rooms and 125 apartments for married students. The college welcomes applications from students of all racial and national origins and religious persuasions. Approximately 75% of undergraduate students applying for admission are accepted. Financial aid is available and 65% of the current student body receives some form of aid.

Community Environment: Madison (population approximately 15,040) is a suburban community in historical surroundings. Bordering a rural area that features numerous equestrian horse farms and a 6,000-acre national wildlife preserve, Madison is on a commuter rail line, just 27 miles from Times Square. Some part-time employment is available.

ESSEX COUNTY COLLEGE   *(E-13)*
303 University Avenue
Newark, New Jersey 07102
Tel: (201) 877-3100

Description: This publicly supported, coeducational, junior college was established in 1966 and has been accredited fully by the Middle States Association of Colleges and Schools. It operates on the early semester system with two summer terms. Enrollment includes 4,269 full-time and 4,204 part-time students. A faculty of 153 full-time and 150 part-time gives a faculty-student ratio of 1-28. The college provides special studies programs to enable students to fulfill enrollment requirements, offers diploma and certificate programs as well as vocational and college-transfer programs and grants the Associate degree.

Entrance Requirements: Open enrollment policy; non-high school graduates admitted; early admission, rolling admission delayed admission and advanced placement plans available; $10 application fee.

Costs Per Year: $1,320 tuition; $2,640 out-of-county; $3,960 out-of-state.

Collegiate Environment: The college has two locations in Newark and West Caldwell. The main campus is located in downtown Newark. The library contains 60,000 volumes, 500 pamphlets, 600 periodicals, 6,000 microforms and 800 recordings. All students applying for admission are accepted, including midyear students, and 65% return for their second year. About 50% of the recent student body graduated in the top half of the high school class, 25% in the top quarter, and 10% in the highest tenth. Financial aid is available and 40% of the current student body receives some form of aid.

Community Environment: See New Jersey Institute of Technology.

FAIRLEIGH DICKINSON UNIVERSITY   *(C-5)*
1000 River Road
Teaneck, New Jersey 07666
Tel: (800) 338-8803; Fax: (201) 692-7319

Description: Privately supported, coeducational university offers programs on the undergraduate and graduate levels. Fairleigh Dickinson has two main New Jersey campuses located in Teaneck, Hackensack and Florham Park/Madison, and an overseas campus in Wroxton, England. It is accredited by the Middle States Association of Colleges and Schools. It operates on the semester system and offers three summer sessions. Undergraduate enrollment includes 2,541 full-time and 1,397 part-time students. Graduate enrollment is 3,718. A faculty of 262 full-time and 318 part-time gives a faculty-student ratio of 1-11.

Entrance Requirements: Accredited high school graduation or equivalent; completion of 17 units including 4 English, 3 mathematics, 2 laboratory science, 2 history, 2 foreign language; additional mathematics and science required for some majors; SAT or ACT required; early decision, advanced placement, early admission, rolling admission, midyear admission and delayed admission programs available; $35 application fee.

Costs Per Year: $11,610 tuition; $5,550 room and board; $760 resident student comprehensive fees; books average $607.

Collegiate Environment: TEANECK CAMPUS: The 115-acre campus stretches along the banks of the Hackensack River is the home of the University College of Arts, Sciences, and Professional Studies and the Samuel J Silberman College of Business Administration, providing complete undergraduate and graduate education in business, sciences, and the liberal arts. Academic buildings, the library, the athletic center and the student commons all line the river's edge. Residence halls provide accommodations for 577 students. FLORHAM-MADISON CAMPUS: The 178-acre suburban campus is 35 miles from New York City. The main buildings in the Georgian style are part of the Vanderbilt Twombly estate, built in the 1890s by architect Stanford White with grounds and gardens designed by Frederick Law Olmsted. The campus provides complete undergraduate and graduate education in the Samuel J Silberman College of Business Administration and the Maxwell Becton College of Arts and Sciences. The residence halls accommodate 775 students and include traditional-style halls plus "The Village" with suite-style buildings. The new 82,000 square feet center, opening in the fall of 1995, provides students with a state-of-the-art facility. The libraries on the New Jersey campuses are electronically linked and contain 432,239 bound volumes; 267,407 titles on microform; 2,536 periodical subscriptions; 8,866 re-

cord/tapes/cds; 48 CD-ROMS; 3 online bibliographic services. WROXTON COLLEGE: The British campus of the University is situated in the ancestral home of Lord North at Wroxton Abbey in Oxfordshire. Originally constructed in 1215, Wroxton Abbey now houses the College's classrooms, library, fully modernized student lodging facilities and a gymnasium. A resident British faculty and visiting British scholars offer undergraduate and graduate courses in English therter, literature, fine arts, social sciences, education and business. Academic offerings are supplemented by extensive tours with some classes at the Shakespeare centers in Stratford-upon-Avon.

Community Environment: Teaneck and Hackensack are suburban communities appoximately six miles from the George Washington Bridge providing easy access to New York City. Madison and Florham Park are suburban communities 35 miles from New York City, in the heart of New Jersey's most vibrant area of corporate expansion. All four communities offer convenient public transportation, churches, hospitals and shopping. The British campus, Wroxton College is in the Cotswold Hills, lying near Banbury, between Stratford-upon-Avon and Oxford. London is 75 miles away and there is regular train service from Banbury.

Branch Campuses: Teaneck Campus, 1000 River Road, Teaneck, NJ 07666, tel: (201) 692-9170; Florham Park-Madison Campus, 285 Madison Avenue, Madison, NJ 07940, tel: (201) 593-8900.

FAIRLEIGH DICKINSON UNIVERSITY - EDWARD WILLIAMS COLLEGE   *(D-13)*
150 Kotte Place
Hackensack, New Jersey 07601
Tel: (201) 692-2675; (800) 338-8803; Fax: (201) 692-7319

Description: A privately supported, coeducational, junior college established in 1964 as an affiliate of Fairleigh Dickinson University. It is accredited by the Middle States Association of Colleges and Schools. One of the major objectives is to improve the academic performance of students not initially eligible for admission to the baccalaureate programs of the university. Enrollment includes 602 full-time and 253 part-time students. The faculty consists of 26 full-time and 32 part-time members. The college offers a university-parallel program leading to the Associate degree. It operates on the semester basis.

Entrance Requirements: Accredited high school graduation; completion of 15 units, including 4 English, 2 mathematics, 3 history, 3 science, 2 foreign language, 2 social science; SAT or ACT required; non-high school graduates considered; rolling admission, delayed admission and advanced placement plans available; $35 application fee.

Costs Per Year: $10,836 tuition; $5,550 room and board; $760 comprehensive fees.

Collegiate Environment: On the Teaneck/Hackensack campus of Fairleigh Dickinson University, the college occupies 1 main building which is located on 10 acres. Approximately 74% of students applying for admission are accepted. Financial aid is available and scholarships are offered. The students share the Fairleigh Dickinson library, athletic, food and dormitory facilities. The library holdings include 432,239 bound volumes, 267,407 titles on microform, 2,536 periodical subscriptions, 8,866 records, tapes, and CDs, 48 CD-ROMS, 3 online bibliographic services.

Community Environment: Originally named New Barbados, the name was changed in 1921 to Hackensack, an Indian name. The community provides churches, representing most denominations, a hospital and a large shopping area. Some part-time employment is available. Civic and service organizations are active in the area.

FELICIAN COLLEGE   *(C-4)*
262 South Main Street
Lodi, New Jersey 07644
Tel: (201) 778-1190; Admissions: (201) 778-1029; Fax: (201) 778-4111

Description: A privately supported, coeducational liberal arts college founded by the Felician Sisters of the Lodi, New Jersey Province. It began as Immaculate Conception Normal School but was incorporated as Immaculate Conception Junior College in 1942. In June 1967, it was authorized to offer a four-year program under its new name, Felician College. The college is fully accredited by the Middle States Association of Colleges and Schools, National League of Nursing, American Library Association, Association of Independent Colleges and Schools and the National Accrediting Agency for Clinical Laboratory Sciences. Programs of study lead to the Associate and Bachelor degrees. The college operates on the semester system and offers two summer sessions. Enrollment includes 458 full-time and 610 part-time students. A faculty of 44 full-time and 53 part-time gives a faculty-student ratio of 1-15.

Entrance Requirements: Accredited high school graduation with rank in upper 40% or equivalency diploma; completion of 16 units including 4 English, 2-3 mathematics, 2 foreign language, 2-3 science, 2-3 social science; SAT or ACT required; rolling admission, delayed admission and advanced placement plans available; non-high school graduates considered; $25 application fee.

Costs Per Year: $8,550 tuition; $230 fees; $500 books and miscellaneous expenses.

Collegiate Environment: The 27-acre campus has undergone numerous changes since its founding. The library, which contains 114,075 volumes, 700 periodicals, 25,403 microforms and 15,000 audiovisual materials, is situated on the edge of the Saddle River that winds through the campus. Approximately 67% of students applying for admission are accepted including midyear students. Average high school standing of the recent freshman class: 38% in the top quarter; 31% in the second quarter; 23% in the third quarter; 8% in the bottom quarter. 50 scholarships are available and 75% of the current students receive financial aid.

Community Environment: Felician College, which is located in Bergen County, is about five miles from Hackensack and close enough to enjoy the cultural advantages of New York City.

GEORGIAN COURT COLLEGE   *(J-12)*
900 Lakewood Avenue
Lakewood, New Jersey 08701-2697
Tel: (908) 364-2200 x760; (800) 458-8422; Admissions: (908) 367-4440; Fax: (908) 367-3920

Description: This privately supported, Roman Catholic, women's college founded in 1908, and is accredited by the Middle States Association of Colleges and Schools. It offers liberal arts programs in the humanities, the natural sciences, and the social sciences. In additon, Georgian Court offers professional programs in education, business, and social work. The college organization includes a coeducational graduate shcool and a coeducational evening division. Courses of study lead to the Bachelor or Master degrees. The college operates on the semester system and offers four summer sessions. Total enrollment includes 1,034 full-time and 197 part-time undergraduates, 696 graduate, and 612 evening students. A faculty of 89 full-time and 100 part-time provides a faculty-student ratio of 1-13.

Entrance Requirements: Accredited high school graduation; completion of 16 units including 4 English, 2 mathematics, 2 foreign language, 1 laboratory science, 1 social science, 6 electives; minimum SAT 750 combined; upper half class rank; early admission, early decision, midyear admission, rolling admission, and advanced placement plans available; $30 application fee.

Costs Per Year: $9,750 tuition; $4,150 room and board; $160 student fees.

Collegiate Environment: Georgian Court College is located on the former George Jay Gould estate, a National Historic Landmark and member of the National Register of Historic Places. Situated in a quiet residential section of Lakewood, New Jersey, the 152-acre lakeside campus blends 17 modern and historic buildings with vast areas of manicured lawns, gardens, statuary and open areas to provide an atmosphere suitable to study, relaxation and recreation for over 2,500 students. The college is located in the central part of New Jersey and is convenient to the Route 9 corridor, Garden State Parkway, and Interstate 195. New York City, Philadelphia, and Atlantic City are each less than one and one-half hours from the college. The famous New Jersey beaches are less than one-half hour from the campus. The residence hallls house 308 women students; the student rooms have computer network access as well as telephone and cable TV. The library contains 151,840 volumes, 979 periodical titles, and 276,471 microform titles. Approximately 96% of students applying for admission are accepted. The average score of the entering freshman class was SAT 886.6 combined. Approximately 80% of a typical freshman class return for their second year. Scholarships are available and 55% of the student body receives some form of financial assistance.

Community Environment: Lakewood, population 47,000, is located in one of the fastest growing areas of the State of New Jersey. The area offers convenient access to the Garden State Arts Center and the famous Six Flags Great Adventure Amusement Park. Located nearby are the Naval Air Engineering Center, a sport parachuting center, shopping centers and the recreational facilities of several beach resorts. Lakewood offers the services of a public library, hospital, churches of major denominations and numerous major civic and service organizations.

GLOUCESTER COUNTY COLLEGE   *(L-7)*
RR 4, Box 203
Sewell, New Jersey 08080
Tel: (609) 468 5000; Fax: (609) 468-8498

Description: Publicly supported, coeducational, community college founded in 1968 and operated by Gloucester County and the State of New Jersey. It is accredited by the Middle States Association of Colleges and Schools. The college offers transfer, career, and certificate programs leading to the Associate degree. It operates on the semester system and offers two summer sessions. Enrollment includes 2,232 full-time and 3,060 part-time students. A faculty of 68 full-time, 122 part-time gives a faculty-student ratio of 1-28.

Entrance Requirements: Accredited high school graduation or equivalency certificate. ACT or SAT required Nursing/Allied Health only; New Jersey Basic Skills Placement Test; midyear admission and rolling admission plans available; $10 application fee; non-high school graduates considered.

Costs Per Year: $1,500 county resident tuition; $1,530 out-of-county tuition; $6,000 out-of-state tuition; $180 student fees.

Collegiate Environment: The college campus is situated on a 270-acre site in Deptford Township. Approximately 99% of students applying for admission are accepted. About 25% of the students receive some form of financial assistance.

Community Environment: See Rutgers, the State University of New Jersey - Camden College of Arts and Sciences.

HUDSON COUNTY COMMUNITY COLLEGE   *(E-13)*
901 Bergen Avenue
Jersey City, New Jersey 07306
Tel: (201) 714-2127

Description: The publicly supported community college is located in the heart of Jersey City and is within view of the New York City skyline. Accredited by the Middle States Association of Colleges and Schools, the school is noted for its multicultural student body and staff. It offers Associate degree and one-year certificates. It operates on the semester system and offers two summer sessions. One summer session is for all students and the other is for Educational Opportunity Fund students. Enrollment is 3,214 students. A faculty of 174 gives a faculty-student ratio of 1-19. Hudson County Community College defines itself as a contract college in that it enters into contractual agreements with other accredited institutions of higher education for certain facilities and resources while maintaining educational centers throughout Hudson County. The college has contractual relationships with Saint Peter's College and Jersey City State College.

Entrance Requirements: High school graduate or equivalent, or student at least 18 years old; open enrollment; advanced placement, early admission, open admission, and rolling admission plans available; $10 application fee.

Costs Per Year: $1,385.50 tuition; $2,513.50 nonresident; $3,641.50 out-of-state.

Collegiate Environment: The college is located in the heart of Jersey City within view of the New York City skyline. Classes are held at off-campus centers in Jersey City (Journal Square), Hoboken, North Hudson, and other communities. About 90% of the students receive financial aid.

Community Environment: See Jersey City State College.

IMMACULATE CONCEPTION SEMINARY   *(C-13)*
400 S. Orange Avenue
South Orange, New Jersey 07079
Tel: (201) 761-9575

Description: Immaculate Conception Seminary School of Theology offers programs in the theological and pastoral studies which lead to ordination and/or the attainment of graduate degrees, namely the Master of Divinity in Pastoral Ministry, the Master of Arts in Pastoral Ministry, the Master of Arts in Theology and the Master of Public Administration in Church Management. The Seminary seeks to serve candidates for the ordained priesthood and also those men and women, lay and religious, who are legitimately sharing various ministerial roles within the Body of Christ.

Entrance Requirements: A Bachelor of Arts degree in Humanities or its equivalent from an accredited college or university. For some degree programs, a specific amount of philosophy and religious studies are required.

Costs Per Year: $4,224 tuition; $1,925 room and board.

Collegiate Environment: Immaculate Conception Seminary was completed in 1984. It provides quarters for 100 seminarians and 15 faculty members. It also houses Immaculate Conception Seminary Library and the Seminary Dining Hall. Adjacent to Lewis Hall is the School of Theology building with four classrooms. The newly renovated Alumni Hall (built in 1881) has been incorporated into the Seminary complex. Its upper floor houses the Seminary Chapel of Christ the Good Shepherd and its lower floor contains the Seminary School of Theology administrative offices.

Community Environment: The Seminary is located on the main campus of Seton Hall University, which is on 58 acres in the Village of South Orange, (population approximately 17,000), 14 miles from New York City, a short trip by bus, train, or car and the cultural events and entertainment of one of the world's greatest cities. All types of recreational activities are found within a radius of 100 miles in shore and mountain resort areas and state parks in New Jersey, Pennsylvania and New York. The nearby city of Newark, along with its suburbs, provides a training ground for ministerial candidates, offering opportunities for field experience in varied pastoral settings.

INSTITUTE FOR ADVANCED STUDY   *(H-10)*
Olden Lane
Princeton, New Jersey 08540
Tel: (609) 734-8000

Description: Privately supported, coeducational, post-graduate level center for scholarships and research, the Institute was founded in 1930 by a gift of Mr. Louis Bamberger and his sister, Mrs. Felix Fuld. The Institute began with the appointment of professors eminent in pure mathematics and mathematical physics, in fields of archaeological and historical study, and in economics. At present, the Institute consists of four Schools; a School of Mathematics, a School of Natural Sciences, a School of Historical Studies and a School of Social Science. Enrollment at any one time numbers about 180 members. There is no formal curriculum, no scheduled courses of instruction, no laboratories are maintained. The academic year is divided into two terms: from September to December, and from January to April. An active faculty of 22 gives a faculty-member ratio of approximately 1-7.

Entrance Requirements: The Institute admits only those who have already taken the highest degree in their field. Admission to Membership is by vote of the appropriate faculty. Application deadlines vary according to school but are in the preceding year.

Costs Per Year: Fellowships are generally for the academic year and occasionally for one term. Stipend varies according to school.

Collegiate Environment: The Institute occupies an 800-acre site on the outskirts of Princeton. Buildings house libraries, dining hall, offices, and seminar and lecture rooms. A housing project is operated for temporary Members, and transportation is provided between its buildings, the town of Princeton, and Princeton University, with which it enjoys close academic and intellectual relations. About one-half of the members are supported by grants-in-aid, and the other half are supported by the members' own institutions, by the United States and foreign governments, and by private foundations.

Community Environment: See Princeton University

JERSEY CITY STATE COLLEGE   *(E-13)*
2039 Kennedy Boulevard
Jersey City, New Jersey 07305
Tel: (201) 200-2000; (800) 441-5272; Admissions: (201) 200-3234; Fax: (201) 200-2044

Description: Publicly supported, coeducational, liberal arts and teachers college which opened its doors in the fall of 1929, is one of the few colleges in the nation to have a laboratory school for the physically handicapped on its campus. It is accredited by the Middle States Association of Colleges and Schools, National Association of Schools of Music, National Association of Schools of Art and Design, National Council for Accreditation of Teacher Education, and National League for Nursing. The college operates on the semester system and offers two summer sessions. Enrollment includes 1,647 men and 2,133 women full-time and 875 men and 1,285 women part-time undergraduates and 1,275 graduate students. A faculty of 232 full-time and 13 part-time gives a faculty-student ratio of 1-18. The college grants the Bachelor of Arts degree in 24 liberal arts areas and the Master of Arts degree in 12 education areas. A Sixth Year program (Professional Diploma) is available in School Psychology.

Entrance Requirements: Approved high school graduation or equivalent; completion of 4 units of English, 3 mathematics, 2 laboratory science, 2 social science, and 5 academic electives; SAT or ACT required; GRE required for graduate programs; rolling admission, delayed admission and advanced placement plans available; $20 application fee.

Costs Per Year: $3,030 state resident tuition and fees; $4,252 non-resident tuition and fees; $4,800 room and board.

Collegiate Environment: The 17 acre campus is located about two miles south of Journal Square, the center of Jersey City. The college library contains 315,000 volumes, 1,500 periodicals and 185,000 microforms. The college dormitory provides a supervised residence for 270 men and women. Approximately 50% of students applying for admission are accepted including midyear students and 85% of the previous freshman class returned to this school for their second year. The average scores for the entering freshmen class were SAT 402 verbal, 435 math. 25 scholarships, including 20 for freshmen and 5 for transfer students, are available. 40% of the current student body receives some form of financial assistance.

Community Environment: The second largest city in the state, Jersey City, population 260,545, is opposite New York City across the Hudson River, linked by the Holland Tunnel. A great manufacturing center, Jersey City is the home of approximately 600 industrial plants. It is a world water shipping point and the terminus of some of the nation's largest railroad and many transcontinental motor freight lines. Jersey City has all the conveniences of major transportation. Recreational facilities are numerous.

KEAN COLLEGE OF NEW JERSEY   *(E-12)*
Morris Avenue
Union, New Jersey 07083
Tel: (908) 527-2000

Description: A publicly supported, coeducational, liberal arts and sciences, pre-professional and teacher preparation college founded in 1855. Accredited by the Middle States Association of Colleges and Schools, it grants degrees of Bachelor of Arts, Bachelor of Science, Bachelor of Social Work, Master of Public Administration, Master of Science and Master of Arts. Undergraduate enrollment includes 4,423 men and 2,382 women full-time, 2,588 men and 1,394 women part-time. Graduate enrollment totalled 420 men and 1,614 women. Academic calendar includes regular fall and spring semesters, January mid-year studies period and one summer term. Faculty numbers 329 full-time and 470 part-time members. Academic cooperative plans available with College of Medicine and Dentistry of New Jersey, Seton Hall University, Union College, and Union County Technical Institute. ROTC/Army and Air Force programs available.

Entrance Requirements: Graduation from accredited high school or equivalent; completion of 16 college preparatory units 4 English, 2 social science, 2 laboratory science, 2 mathematics, 2 foreign language, 4 other units; better than average achievement as measured by high school class rank; SAT or ACT; early admission, early decision, rolling admission, and advanced placement plans available; College Level Examination Program (CLEP) is offered; $20 application fee.

Costs Per Year: $2,634 undergraduate tuition; $3,458 out-of-state tuition; $3,690 room and board; additional expenses $500.

Collegiate Environment: The campus is a wooded tract of 120 acres. Its 27 buildings include Thompson Library, containing over 248,000 bound volumes, 1,200 periodical subscriptions, 900 recordings, and 600 motion pictures, and the Theatre for the Performing

Arts. Residential apartment facilities are available for 1,225 students. 27 Greek letter social groups are chartered. Students during junior or senior year may be elected to one or more honor societies, either in specific majors or broader area of school or College. The Music Department schedules a major concert series and the Theater Guild stages three full productions each academic year. Several lecture series bring outstanding speakers to campus throughout the year. The Fine Arts building houses a gallery where faculty and student work, as well as work of major artists from the metropolitan area, is displayed. About 45% of all full-time students receive financial aid administered by the College with State and College scholarships, federal and state loans available. Approximately 40% of students applying for freshman admission are accepted, including midyear; 77% return for their sophomore year. Average high school standing of a recent freshman class: 24% in top fifth, 38% in second fifth, 26% in third fifth, 11% in fourth fifth, 1% in bottom fifth. Students with limited academic preparation may apply for admission through Exceptional Educational Opportunities Program (EEO). Intensive support services provided in order to facilitate movement by EEO students into mainstream of college life. Average SAT scores: 466V, 423M. About 22% of senior class continued on to graduate school.

Community Environment: The township of Union, population 53,400, and its proximity to major automobile, bus, rail, and air transportation networks makes access to the College excellent. This provides continuous cultural, intellectual and social interchange between the cities and the College. Community facilities include library, numerous churches, hospitals and clinics, major civic and service organizations. A recreation center provides facilities for special activities.

MERCER COUNTY COMMUNITY COLLEGE　　(L-9)
P.O. Box B
1200 Old Trenton Road
Trenton, New Jersey 08690
Tel: (609) 586-4800; (800) 392-6222; Admissions: (609) 586-0505; Fax: (609) 586-6944

Description: The publicly supported, coeducational, two-year, community college was founded in 1966 with transfer, career, and continuing education programs offered leading to Associate degrees in Arts, Science and Applied Science. The college is accredited by the Middle States Association of Colleges and Schools. It operates on the semester system and offers four summer terms. Enrollment in the fall was 2,686 full-time and 5,796 part-time students. A faculty of 119 full-time and 215 part-time gives a faculty-student ratio of 1-25.

Entrance Requirements: Open door policy; rolling admission and midyear admission available. $15 application fee.

Costs Per Year: $1,650 ($55/cr) estimated county resident tuition; $2,910 ($97/cr) state resident; $4,860 ($162/cr) state resident.

Collegiate Environment: The campus consists of 292 acres adjacent to Mercer County Park, six and one-half miles north of Trenton, near Princeton and Hightstown. West Windsor Campus is composed of an Administration Building, College Center, Library, Physical Education Center, Lecture Hall and Communications Center, plus a 360-seat theater. In addition, there are 5 academic (classroom) buildings. An urban campus, the James Kerney Center, in downtown Trenton was dedicated in 1976 and recently was expanded. 84% of the student body is from Mercer County and 16% from other counties or states.

Community Environment: See Rider College.

MIDDLESEX COUNTY COLLEGE　　(G-11)
Mill Road
Edison, New Jersey 08817
Tel: (908) 906-2510; Fax: (908) 906-4686

Description: This publicly supported, coeducational, county college opened its doors for the first time in September, 1966. Enrollment includes 12,000 men and women attending classes on the semester system with three summer sessions. A faculty of 214 full-time and 350 part-time gives a faculty-student ratio of 1-18. The college grants the Associate degree and Certificate of completion. U.S. Army ROTC is available through nearby Rutgers University for qualified male students. The college offers college-transfer and vocational programs and is accredited by the Middle States Association of Colleges and Schools.

Entrance Requirements: High school graduation or equivalent; for selected health technology programs an admission exam is required; rolling admission and advanced placement plans available; $25 application fee.

Costs Per Year: $66.50 per credit county resident tuition; $133 per credit out-of-county resident tuition.

Collegiate Environment: The 160-acre campus has 158 buildings including a library containing 65,826 volumes, 1,200 microforms and 750 periodicals. Financial aid is available and 80% of the current student body receives some form of financial assistance. Nearly one-half of the current student body graduated in the top half of their high school class, with 20% in the top quarter. Approximately 75% of the applicants are accepted, including midyear students. About 55% of the previous freshman class returned to this school for their second year.

Community Environment: Edison (population, 67,120) is located in a major metropolitan area, and is both a residential and industrial city with train and bus service available. Community facilities include a library, churches of all denominations, several hospitals, museums and various civic and service organizations. Edison offers fine shopping facilities. Part-time jobs are available. Parks and the Raritan River provide for boating and swimming, etc.

MONMOUTH COLLEGE　　(H-13)
Cedar Avenue
West Long Branch, New Jersey 07764
Tel: (908) 571-3400

Description: An independent, coeducational college founded in 1933, Monmouth offers baccalaureate and masters' programs in liberal arts, sciences and certain professional programs. The college is accredited by the Middle States Association of Colleges and Schools and operates on the early semester system with five summer terms. Enrollment includes 2,757 men and women full-time and part-time. The faculty consists of 147 full-time and 141 part-time members. The college grants the Associate, Bachelor and Master degrees. There is also an integrated Bachelor of Science and Master of Business Administration program under which it is possible to complete the B.S in four years and the MBA in one additional year.

Entrance Requirements: Accredited high school graduation with rank in upper 50% of graduating class; completion of 16 units including 4 English, 2 mathematics or 2 foreign language, 2 science, 2 social science; SAT (min. 400V, 400M) or ACT required; GRE required for graduate school; non-high school graduates considered with G.E.D.; early admission, advanced placement, March 1 application deadline and early decision plans available; $30 application fee.

Costs Per Year: $5,355 tuition; $3,000 room and board; $225 student fees.

Collegiate Environment: The 125-acre campus has 29 buildings. The main building is Woodrow Wilson Hall. It contains classrooms, laboratories, offices and a theater/auditorium. The library contains 225,000 volumes, 1,700 periodicals, 171,000 microforms and audio-visual materials. Dormitories are available for 425 men and 500 women. Approximately 76% of students applying for admission are accepted. Students are admitted at midyear as well as in the fall and are welcomed from all parts of the nation. Financial aid is available and about 65% of the current full-time student body receives some form of assistance; of 634 scholarships offered, 145 are available for freshmen. Average high school standing of the recent freshman class, top 40%; 27% in the top quarter; 24% in the second quarter; 32% in the third quarter; average scores, SAT 443V, 482M. Classes begin in September and January. The college awarded 35 Associate, 625 Bachelor, and 225 Master degrees during the past academic year.

Community Environment: West Long Branch, population 7,500, just inland of shore point resorts, is located between Long Branch and Asbury Park. Bus and train transportation is available. Employment opportunities are excellent.

MONTCLAIR STATE UNIVERSITY　　(D-3)
Upper Montclair, New Jersey 07043
Tel: (201) 655-4211; (800) 624-7780; Fax: (201) 655-5455

Description: This publicly supported, coeducational college provides liberal arts and professional studies for more than 13,000 students in 73 undergraduate and graduate programs. Founded in 1908 as a normal school, it became a State Teachers College in 1927 and was empowered to give masters degrees in 1932. The present name was taken in 1958 and in 1966 the liberal arts programs were instituted. Additional professional programs for business, industry, and social services have been added since that time. Enrollment is 6,123 full-time, 3,055 part-time and 3,497 graduate students. A faculty of 419 full-time and 350 part-time gives a faculty-student ratio of 1-15. The college is composed of five schools: Business Administration, Fine and Performing Arts, Humanities and Social Sciences, Mathematical and Natural Sciences, and Professional Studies. The college is accredited by the Middle States Association of Colleges and Schools. In addition, the National Council for the Accreditation of Teacher Education has granted the college accreditation for the preparation of secondary school teachers and selected school services personnel.

Entrance Requirements: Accredited high school graduation or high school equivalency certificate; completion of 16 units including 4 English, 3 mathematics, 2 foreign language, 2 laboratory science, and 2 social science; SAT required; rolling admission and advanced placement programs available; educationally disadvantaged applicants are considered through E.O.F.

Costs Per Year: $3,000 tuition; $4,248 out-of-state; $4,834 room and board; $700 estimated books.

Collegiate Environment: The 185-acre campus has 40 buildings. The Harry A. Sprague Library contains 288,527 volumes, 3,397 periodicals, and 1,030,039 microforms. 5 dormitories and an apartment complex accommodate 2,100 students. About 41% of the students applying for the freshman class were accepted. Approximately 80% of the freshman class returned as sophomores. High school standing of the freshmen class: 48% in top fifth; 42% in the second fifth. Average SAT scores: 472V, 538M.

Community Environment: Population about 40,000, the township of Montclair is a residential suburb about 14 miles west of New York City and about six miles northwest of Newark. Residents can commute to Manhattan by bus or railroad. An art museum, theater groups, music societies, and a library are provided by the community as well as two hospitals, several shopping areas and numerous active civic and social organizations.

NEW BRUNSWICK THEOLOGICAL SEMINARY   *(G-11)*
17 Seminary Place
New Brunswick, New Jersey 08901
Tel: (908) 247-5241; (800) 445-6287; Fax: (908) 249-5412

Description: This privately supported, three-year, theological seminary founded in 1784, had as its first professor the minister of the Collegiate Church in New York City. Today it continues to be an important institution of the Reformed Church in America although many denominations are represented within its faculty and student body. It is accredited by the Association of Theological Schools in the United States and Canada. The seminary operates on the 4-1-4 system and grants the Master of Divinity and M.A. in Theology. An evening program on campus and at St. John's University in Jamaica, Queens, New York, allows students to earn the M.Div. in four years of evening study. Enrollment includes 24 men and 22 women full-time and 78 men and 20 women part-time. Students may cross register at Rutgers and Princeton Seminary. An overseas program is available every other year in the Netherlands during summer session.

Entrance Requirements: Bachelor's degree from accredited college; college GPA of 2.5; rolling admission plan available; $25 application fee.

Costs Per Year: $6,400 tuition; $110 student fees.

Collegiate Environment: The campus occupies a dozen buildings scattered over an 8-acre tract overlooking the campus of Rutgers University. Housing facilities for 59 students are available on campus. The library contains 150,000 volumes and 295 periodicals. In a recent academic year, 100% of the students received financial assistance, including grants from student aid funds, scholarships and student loans. Approximately 90% of students applying for admission are accepted including midyear students. Students may begin studies in September and January. Approximately 95% of the previous entering class returned to this campus for the second year.

Community Environment: See Rutgers, The State University of New Jersey.

NEW JERSEY INSTITUTE OF TECHNOLOGY   *(E-13)*
323 Martin Luther King Jr. Blvd.
Newark, New Jersey 07102
Tel: (201) 596-3000; (800) 222-6548; Admissions: (201) 596-3300; Fax: (201) 802-1854

Description: Publicly supported, coeducational, research university formally named Newark College of Engineering. The university was founded in 1881 as the Newark Technical School and changed to its present name in 1975. In addition to the day and evening Undergraduate Division, the school has a Graduate Division, and the Divison of Continuing Education. The school is divided into five colleges: School of Architecture, Newark College of Engineering, College of Science and Liberal Arts, the School of Industrial Management, and the Albert Dorman Honors College. An interdisciplinary program "Science, Technology and Society" is offered for students who want an understanding of the role of technology in society, but who do not plan to pursue an engineering, management, architectural, or applied sciences degree. The program includes cross registration with Rutgers-Newark, University of Medicine and Dentistry of New Jersey, and Essex County College. It is accredited by the Middle States Association of Colleges and Schools, the Accreditation Board for Engineering and Technology and National Architecture Accrediting Board and Computing Sciences Accreditation Board. Enrollment includes 3,263 men and 769 women full-time and 2,748 men and 724 women part-time. A faculty of 329 full-time and 194 part-time gives an undergraduate faculty-student ratio of 1-14. The college operates on the semester system and offers two summer sessions. Air Force ROTC is available. The college grants the Bachelor, Master, and Doctorate degrees.

Entrance Requirements: Accredited high school graduation or equivalent; completion of 16 units, including 3-4 units of math (depending on the degree program) with trigonometry and 2 lab sciences; SAT and Math Achievement Level I, II, or II C required for all students; nondegree candidates may be admitted as special students; non-high school graduates considered; early decision, rolling admission, and advanced placement plans available; $25 application fee.

Costs Per Year: $4,188 tuition; $8,532 out-of-state tuition; $5,376 room and board; $792 student fees; additional expenses average $700.

Collegiate Environment: The 40-acre campus has 24 buildings. Over the last ten years, the institute's $118 million expansion program has resulted in new construction and enhancements for research, instruction, housing and recreation. Examples are: Class 10 cleanroom, the Advanced Technology Center for Hazardous Substance Management Research, the Information Technologies Building, a third residence hall, a major addition to the gymnasium, the Microelectronics center, and the Central Avenue building which houses the library. The library contains 204,471 volumes, 1,271 periodicals and 4,735 microform titles. Students also have library privileges at Rutgers Newark Library and the Newark Public Library. CD-ROMs and on-line services are also available. Approximately 67% of students applying for admission are accepted including midyear and 80% of the previous freshman class returned to this campus for their sophomore year. About 95% of the freshman class graduated in the top three fifths of their high school class, 5% in the fourth-fifth, 0% in the fifth fifth. Financial aid is available and scholarships are offered. The college awarded 658 Bachelor, 737 Master and 29 Doctorate degrees during the recent academic year. Approximately 10% of the senior class continued on to graduate school.

Community Environment: Newark is the largest metropolis of New Jersey and contains some of the state's greatest cultural institutions: the Newark Museum, the Newark Public Library, and Symphony Hall. Construction has begun on the 12.5 acre New Jersey Center for the Performing Arts. Part-time employment opportunities are good.

OCEAN COUNTY COLLEGE   *(K-12)*
College Drive
Toms River, New Jersey 08753
Tel: (201) 255-4000

Description: This publicly supported, coeducational, junior college opened in the fall of 1966 and was created out of a community-felt need to provide facilities for higher education within commuting distance of all county residents. It is accredited by the Middle States Association of Colleges and Schools. It provides university-parallel and occupational programs and an evening program. The college grants the Associate degree. The college operates on the semester system and offers three summer terms. Enrollment includes 8,162 men and women. The faculty numbers 127 full-time and 248 part-time, giving a faculty-student ratio of 1-32.

Entrance Requirements: Open enrollment policy, New Jersey Basic Skills Test; non-high school graduates over 18 years of age may be admitted; early admission, midyear admission, rolling admission and advanced placement plans available; $15 application fee.

Costs Per Year: $1,700 county-resident tuition; $400 student fees.

Collegiate Environment: Located in the geographical center of Ocean County, the college is within 40 minutes commuting distance for all Ocean County residents. The focal point of the 275-acre campus is a pedestrian mall 900 feet in length. At one end of the mall is the Learning Resources Center, which houses 74,215 volumes, 32,000 government documents, 446 periodicals, and over 3,500 media materials. All students applying for admission are accepted, including midyear students. The college has an outstanding interdisciplinary Basic Studies Program and a successful Honors Program. Nursing and Business Administration are strong programs. 66% of the freshmen return for their second year. Financial assistance is available. The college awarded 666 Associate degrees to the recent graduating class.

Community Environment: A principality in Dover Township, Toms River is the business, vacation, financial, and industrial hub of Ocean County. The city is located four miles inland from the New Jersey shoreline where buses and trains are convenient. An airport is within 20 miles. Community facilities include churches of the major denominations, hospitals, libraries, and civic and service organizations. Recreational activities offered are swimming, picnicking, hiking, camping and canoeing. Some part-time work is available.

PASSAIC COUNTY COMMUNITY COLLEGE *(D-13)*
1 College Boulevard
Paterson, New Jersey 07505-1179
Tel: (201) 684-6868; Fax: (201) 684-6778

Description: A publicly supported, coeducational, community college offering university-parallel and occupational programs. Fully accredited by the Middle States Association of Colleges and Schools, the Committee on Allied Health Education and Accreditation and the National League for Nursing. It operates on the semester system and offers two summer sessions. Enrollment includes 1,025 full-time and 2,750 part-time students. A faculty of 65 full-time and 150 part-time gives a faculty-student ratio of 1-18. Army ROTC program is available.

Entrance Requirements: Entrance examination required for selected programs; placement examinations required for all students; open enrollment; rolling admission, midyear admission and advanced placement plans available; $15 application fee.

Costs Per Year: $1,428 tuition; $2,856 nonresident; additional student fees.

Collegiate Environment: Located in downtown Paterson, population 137,970, the College is apporoximately a 30-minute drive to midtown Manhattan. The College is comprised of 3 buildings. One houses classrooms, the Learning Resource Center, (containing 52,000 titles), and the cafeteria, run by students enrolled in the College's Food Service Program. Another is devoted to the business and computer science courses and labs. The third contains Administrative Data Processing, the Gym, an auditorium, and classrooms and offices. Transfer and midyear students are accepted. The student body is diverse in both ethnic and cultural backgrounds, and skills and abilities possessed by the individual students. The College is proud of its successful allied health, business, English as a second language, and liberal arts programs; and its articulation (placement) agreements with four-year colleges throughout the state. 76 scholarships are available and 50% of students receive some form of financial aid.

Community Environment: See Bergen Community College.

Branch Campuses: Extension centers in Pompton Lakes, West Milford, Wayne, and Clifton.

PRINCETON THEOLOGICAL SEMINARY *(H-10)*
Mercer Street
Princeton, New Jersey 08540
Tel: (609) 921-8300; (800) 622-6767

Description: This privately supported, graduate-level, theological school is affiliated with the Presbyterian Church (U.S.A.). It is accredited by the Middle States Association of Colleges and Schools by the Association of Theological Schools in the U.S. and Canada. The seminary operates on the semester system with one summer session and grants the Master and Doctorate degrees. An arrangement of reciprocity exists with Princeton University and with New Brunswick Theological Seminary with regard to class attendance without additional tuition costs, and use of libraries. Enrollment includes approximately 792 men and women. A faculty of 74 provides a faculty-student ratio of 1-11.

Entrance Requirements: Bachelor degree from accredited college or university; letter of evaluation from student's church; interview when possible; $35 application fee.

Costs Per Year: $6,250 tuition; $3,900 room and board; $715 student fees.

Collegiate Environment: The seminary welcomes a geographically diverse student body and admits midyear students. Living accommodations are available for 300 single students and 210 families. The library system contains over 450,000 volumes. Financial aid is available, and 86% of the current student body recieves some form of assistance.

Community Environment: See Princeton University.

PRINCETON UNIVERSITY *(H-10)*
Princeton, New Jersey 08540
Tel: (609) 258-3000

Description: Privately supported, coeducational university had its beginning as the College of New Jersey when John Hamilton, in 1746, issued its charter. The original trustees of the college were leaders in the evangelical wing of the Presbyterian Church. In common with other American Universities, Princeton had grown with the country, and it became evident that enrollment limits had been reached; expansion was not possible without sacrifice to quality. In 1923 a policy of limited enrollment and a new system of selective admissions was established so that henceforth the University would seek intensive rather than extensive growth. The academic program was enlarged and enriched, and the physical resources of the University were expanded. The University is accredited by the Middle States Association of Colleges and Schools. Princeton's Honor System was established by the undergraduates in 1893, and has been in effect without interruption since that time. Enrollment includes 4,525 undergraduate and 1,796 graduate students on the semester system. The faculty consists of 719 full-time and 161 part-time members. Composition of Princeton University: Undergraduate College, Graduate School, School of Architecture, School of Engineering and Applied Science and the Woodrow Wilson School of Public and International Affairs. Through cooperative and reciprocal arrangements students at Princeton University may from time to time benefit from the faculties and facilities of the Institute for Advanced Study and Princeton Theological Seminary.

Entrance Requirements: Recommended completion of 16 units including 4 English, 4 mathematics, 4 of one foreign language, 2 laboratory science, 2 social science; SAT and three Achievement tests required; non-high school graduates considered; early admission and delayed admission plans available; $40 application fee; admission is highly selective.

Costs Per Year: $17,750 tuition, $5,577 room and board.

Collegiate Environment: The university campus consists of eight adjoining tracts of land with a total area of about 2,325 acres. The library contains about 3,856,638 volumes, 36,290 periodical titles and 500,000 microforms. Almost all undergraduates live on the campus, and housing facilities are available for 2,744 men, 1,612 women and 10 families. Financial aid, in the form of scholarships, tuition loans, and employment opportunities, are awarded on the basis of need and 43% of the current student body receive financial assistance. Approximately 16% of students applying for admission are accepted. Average SAT scores, 643V, 696M. About 40% of the senior class continued on to graduate school.

Community Environment: Numerous historical events have taken place at Princeton since the time of its founding in 1746. The first state legislature met here in 1776, as well as in 1873; the Continental Congress Sessions were held here. Princeton is 50 miles southwest of

New York City and 45 miles northeast of Philadelphia. All forms of commercial transportation are available. Community facilities are excellent, housing is available for students. The James Forrestal Campus which adjoins Princeton University's campus is an integral part of the University's advanced training and research in the basic and engineering sciences. The largest single project at Forrestal is the Plasma Physics Laboratory, a long range effort to develop a controlled thermo-nuclear reactor which would provide an infinite energy source. Many of the facilities of the Department of Aerospace and Mechanical Sciences for the Aerospace Propulsion Sciences and the Gas Dynamics Laboratories are here. Rockingham, five miles north is also known as the Berrien Mansion which was used as General Washington's headquarters during 1783. His "Farewell Address to the Armies" was delivered here.

RAMAPO COLLEGE OF NEW JERSEY   (B-13)
505 Ramapo Valley Road
Mahwah, New Jersey 07430
Tel: (201) 529-7600; Fax: (201) 529-7508

Description: The publicly supported, coeducational, liberal arts college is accredited by the Middle States Association of Colleges and Schools. It is one of the newest state colleges of New Jersey, which opened in September 1971 on a wooded 300-acre campus at the foot of the Ramapo Mountains in northern New Jersey. The college is organized into smaller schools within the larger institution, in order to offer individualized programs to meet individual interests, and to develop a partnership between faculty and students in the learning process. The following Schools are used, each with its own faculty and its own students: American and International Studies, Contemporary Arts, Social Science and Human Services, Administration and Business, and Theoretical and Applied Science. The college grants the Bachelor of Arts, Bachelor of Science, Bachelor of Social Work, Nursing, and Master of Arts degrees. It operates on the semester system and offers one summer session. Enrollment included 1,296 men and 1,368 women full-time and 902 men and 1,108 women part-time. A faculty of 138 full-time gives a faculty-student ratio of 1-15.

Entrance Requirements: High school graduation with rank in upper third; completion of 16 units including 4 English, 3 mathematics, 2 social studies, and 2 laboratory science; SAT minimum 450V and 450M recommended; non-high school graduates considered; rolling admission, delayed admission and advanced placement plans available; $35 application fee.

Costs Per Year: $2,579 tuition; $3,870 out-of-state; $5,104 room and board; $774 student fees; $1,000 average additional expenses.

Collegiate Environment: On an entirely new campus, the library contains 160,000 volumes, and student housing accommodates 1,100 men and women. Darlington County Park, which adjoins the campus, offers two lakes for swimming and a third for boating. Sports facilities, skiing, nature trails and picnic areas exist at nearby Campgaw Mountain. Scholarships are available, and 44% of the current student body receives some form of financial assistance. Approximately 46% of students applying for admission are accepted and 75% of the freshmen return for their sophomore year. Average high school standing of the freshman class, top 35%; 21% in the top fifth; 39% in the second fifth; 34% in the third fifth; 6% in the bottom fifth; average scores, SAT 460V, 520M. The college awarded 756 Bachelor degrees to the recent graduating class.

Community Environment: Mahwah, population 12,000, is a suburban community near the foothills of the Ramapo Mountains on the New York-New Jersey border.

RARITAN VALLEY COMMUNITY COLLEGE   (F-10)
P.O. Box 3300
Somerville, New Jersey 08876
Tel: (908) 526-1200; Admissions: (908) 218-8861; Fax: (908) 231-8811

Description: This publicly supported, coeducational, two-year college opened in 1968 with an educational plan projected to meet the needs of the county residents. There are two semesters and three summer sessions. The college is accredited by Middle States Association of Colleges and Schools and by the National League for Nursing. The college offers university transfer, pre professional, and technical programs leading to the Associate degree. It operates on the semester sys-

tem and offers three summer sessions. Enrollment includes 1,813 full-time and 3,851 part-time students. A faculty of 91 full-time and 192 part-time gives a faculty-student ratio of 1-20.

Entrance Requirements: High school graduation or equivalent; open admission; $25 application fee.

Costs Per Year: $1,800 tuition; $3,600 out-of-county tuition; $7,200 out-of-state tuition; $270 student fees.

Collegiate Environment: The campus is located on 240 acres in Branchburg Township just west of Somerville. The campus includes 4 classroom buildings with labs, 2 lecture halls, a college center, a gymnasium facility with olympic swimming pool, a library, a 1,000 seat theatre and an arts building. The library contains 80,683 volumes, 422 different periodicals, 13,340 microforms, and 22,170 audiovisual materials. Almost all qualified applicants are accepted; students may enroll at midyear as well as in the fall. Financial aid is available.

Community Environment: Somerville is the county seat for Somerset County. It is a suburban community located ten miles west of Plainfield and ten miles northwest of New Brunswick.

RICHARD STOCKTON COLLEGE OF NEW JERSEY   (O-11)
Pomona, New Jersey 08240
Tel: (609) 652-1776; Admissions: (609) 652-4261; Fax: (609) 652-4958

Description: The publicly supported, coeducational, liberal arts college, opened for classes in September 1971. The school emphasizes interdisciplinary studies, heavy student involvement in the affairs of the College, and personally designed curricula. Fully accredited by the Middle States Association of Colleges and Schools, the college grants the Bachelor degree. It also has articulation agreements with numerous schools for seven-year programs leading to first professional degrees in dentistry, medicine, and veterinary medicine. It operates on the semester system and offers two summer sessions. Enrollment includes 4,411 full-time and 1,290 part-time students. 186 full-time and 119 part-time faculty members provide a faculty-student ratio of 1-19.

Entrance Requirements: High school graduation with rank in upper 25% of class or equivalency certificate; 16 units college-preparatory subjects; SAT required; early admission, early decision, rolling admission and advanced placement plans available; $35 application fee.

Costs Per Year: $2,992 tuition; $3,744 out-of-state; $4,174 room and board; $800 average additional expenses.

Collegiate Environment: The campus is located on a 1,600-acre site that is part and parcel of the south Jersey pine barrens. Apartments and dormitories are available to accommodate 1,862 students. The library contains 236,945 volumes, 1,500 periodicals, 150,000 films, records, filmstrips, audio and video tapes, and slides. In addition, Stockton's library serves as a depository for more than 280,000 government documents. Approximately 43% of freshman applicants and 57% of transfer applicants are accepted, including midyear students. Average high school standing of the freshman class, top 25%; average SAT scores, 491V and 563M. About 65% of the current student body receives some form of financial aid.

Community Environment: Pomona is located about 12 miles northwest of Atlantic City in an undeveloped forest area.

RIDER UNIVERSITY   (I-9)
2083 Lawrenceville Road
Lawrenceville, New Jersey 08648
Tel: (609) 896-5042; (800) 257-9026; Fax: (609) 895-6645

Description: Privately supported, coeducational, multipurpose university was founded in 1865 as the Trenton Business College. It grew and developed in the city of Trenton until 1956 when it purchased 340 acres of rolling farmland and began building a modern carefully designed campus. New facilities enabled the university to expand its curricula in the arts and sciences as well as in the fields of education and business administration. Accredited by the Middle States Association of Colleges and Schools, the university is now composed of five schools: Business Administration, Education and Human Services, Liberal Arts and Science, School for Continuing Studies, and Westminster Choir College - The School of Music of Rider University, which was formed as the result of a recent merger with the Westminster Choir College. The College of Business Administration and the

College of Education and Human Services have graduate divisions. Enrollment includes 2,927 full-time and 1,361 part-time undergraduates and 1,253 graduate students. A faculty of 239 full-time and 60 part-time gives a faculty-student ratio of 1-15. The college operates on the semester system and offers limited summer sessions. Army and Air Force ROTC are available.

Entrance Requirements: Accredited high school graduation; completion of 16 units including 4 English; SAT or ACT required; non-high school graduates with GED considered; early admission, rolling admission, and advanced placement plans available; $35 application fee.

Costs Per Year: $13,800 tuition; $5,637 room and board; $1,040 average additional expenses; $200 student fees.

Collegiate Environment: Located in an attractive residential neighborhood of Lawrenceville, New Jersey, Rider is surrounded by stately, well-maintained homes and businesses, providing a convenient and comfortable setting for students and visitors alike. Lawrenceville is 5 miles south of Princeton, 3 miles north of Trenton, 60 miles south of New York City and 30 miles north of Philadelphia. The 340-acre campus has 34 buildings with dormitory capacity for 2,263 students. Fraternities and sororities provide additional housing for 400 students. The library contains 353,000 volumes, 5,000 pamphlets, 1,500 periodicals, 16,000 microfilms and 248,000 microfiche units. Approximately 70% of students applying for admission are accepted including midyear students and 90% of the freshman class return for the sophomore year. Approximately 25% of the freshman class graduated in the top quarter of the high school class; 45% in the second quarter; 15% in the third quarter; average SAT scores were 435V, 496M. 71% of the current students receive some form of financial aid.

Community Environment: The capital of the state, Trenton's slogan is "Trenton Makes-the World Takes" and more than 400 industries support this claim. Products include pottery, wire, rope, rubber and cigars. Situated midway between New York City and Philadelphia, all forms of commercial transportation are available. Along with the usual community facilities, Trenton supports a symphony orchestra and provides community concerts. There are many part-time job opportunities in the New York to Philadelphia corridor. The mountains and seashore are a short distance, providing excellent recreational facilities. Some of the numerous points of interest are the Friends Meetinghouse, New Jersey State Museum, Old Barracks, Trent House and Washington Crossing State Park.

Branch Campuses: Westminster Choir College - The School of Music of Rider College is located at Hamilton Avenue at Walnut Lane, Princeton, NJ 08540, (800) 962-4647.

ROWAN COLLEGE OF NEW JERSEY (M-7)
Glassboro, New Jersey 08028
Tel: (609) 256-4000; (800) 447-1165; Admissions: (609) 256-4200

Description: The publicly supported, coeducational, liberal arts college is accredited by the Middle States Association of Colleges and Schools, American Chemical Society, American Dietetic Association, National Association of Schools of Music and the National Council for Accreditation of Teacher Education. The college operates on the semester system with two summer terms. Enrollment includes 5,218 full-time and 2,262 part-time undergraduates and 1,456 graduate students. Beginning as a two-year normal school in 1923, it now offers the degree of Bachelor of Arts in 18 areas of teacher preparation and 15 areas of liberal arts; Bachelor of Science in 5 areas; the Master of Arts degree is offered in 24 areas, mostly teaching fields; the MBA is also awarded.

Entrance Requirements: Approved high school graduation with rank in upper 50%; completion of 16 academic units including 4 English, 3 mathematics, 2 laboratory science, 2 social science, 5 electives; SAT or ACT required; GED certificate considered; rolling admission, early admission, delayed admission, midyear admission, and advanced placement plans available. $35 application fee.

Costs Per Year: $3,095 tuition; $5,109 out-of-state tuition; $4,830 room and board; additional expenses average $800.

Collegiate Environment: The 175-acre campus is 20 miles southeast of Philadelphia. Of the 22 buildings on the campus, Hollybush, an 1819 mansion, is the only one not built for college purposes. The Jerohn J. Savitz Library is the largest in southern New Jersey and at

present contains 358,242 volumes, 430,000 audiovisual materials, 15,038 manuscripts and Archives, over 2,000 subscriptions, and in excess of 50,000 microforms. There are living accommodations for 2,250 students in 6 dormitories and 3 apartment complexes on campus. Accommodations are also available for approximately 3,000 additional students in adjacent town houses and garden apartment complexes. First and second year students are primarily housed in the dormitories. One dorm has been set aside for upperclasspersons interested in extended quiet hours and academic programming. Approximately 41% of applicants are accepted including midyear students, and 75% of the previous freshman class returned to this campus for their sophomore year. Average high school standing of the freshman class, top 20%; 55% in the top quarter, 30% in second quarter, 5% in the bottom half. The average scores of the entering freshman class were SAT 493 verbal, 542 math. About 55% of the current student body receive some form of financial aid. The college awarded 1,897 Bachelor and 423 Master degrees to a recent graduating class. Approximately 35% of the senior class continued on to graduate school.

Community Environment: Glassboro was established in 1775 when a German widow and her seven sons organized Stanger & Co., the first successful glass factory in North America. Hollybush, a mansion of a glass manufacturer, which formed part of the original campus, was the site of a summit conference between President Lyndon Johnson and Russian Premier Alexie Kosygin in 1967. Glassboro is near enough to large cities that all forms of commercial transportation are available. Philadelphia Airport is 35 minutes away. Part-time employment is available. Nearby lakes and beaches provide recreational facilities.

RUTGERS, THE STATE UNIVERSITY OF NEW JERSEY
(G-11)
New Brunswick, New Jersey 08903
Tel: (908) 932-1766

Description: Publicly supported, coeducational university. The institution consists of 11 day-time undergraduate colleges located on campuses in Camden, Newark, and New Brunswick. Rutgers College, Douglass College, Livingston College, Cook College, Mason Gross School of the Arts, the College of Engineering, the College of Pharmacy and the upper division School of Business are located in New Brunswick. The Mason Gross School of the Arts and the College of Pharmacy offer graduate programs in addition to undergraduate programs. All are coeducational except for Douglass which enrolls only women. The other daytime undergraduate colleges are Camden College of Arts and Sciences, Newark College of Arts and Sciences, and the College of Nursing, located in Newark. The School of Business-Camden offers both undergraduate and graduate degrees. University College-Camden and University College-Newark offer part-time evening classes for adults. University College-New Brunswick provides part-time study for adult students. Advanced degrees in the arts and sciences are awarded by the Graduate School-New Brunswick in over 65 programs. New Brunswick is also home to the School of Information Communication, and Library Studies, the Graduate School of Applied and Professional Psychology, Education, the School of Social Work and the Edward J. Bloustein School of Planning and Public Policy. In Newark there is the Graduate School-Newark (arts and sciences), the School of Social Work, the Graduate School of Management, the School of Criminal Justice, and the School of Law-Newark. In Camden are the Graduate School-Camden, the School of Social Work, and the School of Law-Camden. The University is accredited by the Middle States Association of Colleges and Schools and by respective professional organizations in the following areas: teacher education, engineering (ceramic, agricultural, mechanical, industrial, electrical, civil engineering), music, pharmacy, business, chemistry, nursing, social work, landscape architecture, law, librarianship, psychology, physician's assistant, public health, theatre arts, medical technology, city and regional planning. Undergraduate enrollment includes 16,310 men and 18,126 women; 5,761 students attend evening classes. Graduate enrollment is 13,261.

Entrance Requirements: Accredited high school graduation: completion of 16 units including 4 English, 3 mathematics (4 for Engineering), 2 science (at Newark, Camden, Rutgers, Douglass, Cook and Livingston), 2 foreign language (at Camden, Douglass, Newark, Rutgers, Livingston, anf for Pharmacy), chemistry and physics for Engineering, and chemistry and biology for Pharmacy and Nursing; SAT or ACT required (except those who have been out of high school two or more years and transfers with 12 credits); applicants not meeting all requirements apply by examination; admission is selective; early admission, deferred admission, midyear admission (some colleges) and advanced placement plans available; the application fee is $50 for three colleges applied to with a single application.

Costs Per Year: See individual schools.

Collegiate Environment: Each campus of Rutgers, The State University houses its own excellent library. Students may use any library in the system, which contains 2,788,052 volumes, 2,296,836 monographs, 611,970 bound periodicals, 2,509,521 government documents and 3,662,034 microform items. In addition, the university's collection of archives, rare books, and manuscripts total more than 2.4 million items. Campus residence facilities accommodate 15,025 men and women and 384 families. Fraternities and sororities house an additional 700 students. Residence facilities are on the New Brunswick area college campuses at Cook, Douglass, Livingston and Rutgers and at the Camden College of Arts and Sciences; housing is also available at Newark College of Arts & Sciences and the College of Nursing (Newark). A network of buses connects the New Brunswick colleges and facilitates cross registration and wide participation in activities. Intercollegiate sports programs are in: baseball, basketball, crew, cross country, diving, fencing, field hockey, football, lightweight crew, golf, gymnastics, lacrosse, soccer, softball, swimming, tennis, track (indoor and outdoor), volleyball, wrestling. Approximately 55% of the entering students receive financial assistance either offered or administered by the university.

Community Environment: New Brunswick is an important manufacturing center on the Raritan River, 33 miles southwest of New York City. Commercial transportation is available; the Newark International Airport is 30 minutes away. Community facilities include libraries, churches of most denominations, YMCA, YWCA, hospitals, hotels, motels, and various fraternal, civic, and veterans organizations. The New Jersey seashore and parks provide recreational areas for fishing, boating, camping, swimming, and skiing. There are golf courses in the area. There are many part-time job opportunities.

RUTGERS, THE STATE UNIVERSITY OF NEW JERSEY - CAMDEN COLLEGE OF ARTS AND SCIENCES   *(K-7)*
Camden, New Jersey 08102
Tel: (609) 225-6104

Description: The Camden College of Arts and Sciences was established in 1927 and became a part of Rutgers University in 1950. Located in the city of Camden, the college serves students primarily from southern New Jersey. Special programs such as independent study and study abroad (in Britain, Costa Rica, France, Germany, Israel, Italy, Kenya, Mexico, Portugal, and Spain) are offered. A BA/MD 8-year program in conjunction with the University of Medicine and Dentistry of New Jersey is also available. Enrollment includes 2,420 students. A faculty of 133 full-time provides a faculty student ratio of 1-15.

Entrance Requirements: Accredited high school graduation: completion of 16 units including 4 English, 3 mathematics, 2 science, 2 foreign language; SAT or ACT required (except those out of high school two or more years and transfers with 12 credits); admission by examination; early admission, deferred admission, midyear admission, and advanced placement plans available; $50 application fee.

Costs Per Year: $3,640 state resident tuition; $7,410 nonresident tuition; $4,748 romm and board; $849 fees.

Collegiate Environment: Each campus of Rutgers, The State University, houses its own excellent library. Students may use any library in the system (see main entry for details). Most of the students commute daily. Limited residence facilities are available at the Camden College of Arts and Sciences. Many of the activities of the college are geared to a metropolitan environment. Intercollegiate sports programs are in: baseball, basketball, crew, cross country, diving, fencing, field hockey, football, lighweight crew, golf, gymnastics, lacrosse, soccer, softball, swimming, tennis, track (indoor and outdoor), volleyball, and wrestling. Approximately 55% of the entering students receive financial assistance either offered or administered by the university.

Community Environment: Population 84,910, Camden, on the Delaware River, is located directly opposite Philadelphia. The college is accessible by bus, car, or the PATCO high-speed line. The Camden campus is not isolated from, but is a part of, an active industrial and cultural community where a wealth of educational and vocational op-

portunities exist. Among the larger plants in this industrial area are Martin Marietta and the Campbell Soup corporate headquarters. Several large shopping malls are within easy driving distance of the city, and community facilities include many churches, YMCA, YWCA, and numerous civic and service organizations.

RUTGERS, THE STATE UNIVERSITY OF NEW JERSEY - COLLEGE OF ENGINEERING   *(G-11)*
New Brunswick, New Jersey 08903
Tel: (908) 932-1766

Description: A coeducational professional college founded in 1864, the College of Engineering offers a four-year program leading to the Bachelor of Science in eight fields, as well as five-year programs conducted jointly with liberal arts colleges of the University. These five-year programs lead to the Bachelor of Science degree from the College of Engineering and the Bachelor of Arts from the cooperating liberal arts college. A five-year Bioresource Engineering program is offered in cooperation with Cook College. Students may take their first two years at Camden College of Arts and Sciences or Newark College of Arts and Science. Study abroad in Britain, Costa Rica, France, Germany, Israel, Italy, Kenya, Mexico, Portugal, and Spain. Enrollment includes 82% men, 18% women for a total of 2,260 students. A faculty of 132 full-time gives a faculty-student ratio of 1-11.

Entrance Requirements: Accredited high school graduation: completion of 16 units including 4 English, 4 mathematics (2 foreign language required of 5-year engineering students who affiliate with Douglass College, Rutgers College, Livingston College, Newark College of Arts and Sciences, and Camden College of Arts and Sciences), 2 science (chemistry and physics); SAT or ACT required (except those out of high school 2 or more years and transfers with 12 credits); admission by examination; admission is competitive; early admission, deferred admission, midyear admission (for transfers only), and advanced placement plans available; $50 application fee.

Costs Per Year: $4,040 state resident tuition; $8,221 nonresident tuition; $4,748 room and board; $971-$1,045 per year fees.

Collegiate Environment: The college of Engineering occupies a modern complex on the Busch Campus. Each campus of Rutgers, The State University, houses its own excellent library. Students may use any library in the system (see main entry for details). Engineering students affiliate with Douglass, Livingston, Rutgers, or Cook College (Bioresource Engineering students only) for housing and student life facilities and services. Housing is guaranteed for all freshmen and sophomores. A network of free buses connects the New Brunswick colleges and facilitates cross registration and wide participation in activities. Intercollegiate sports programs are in: baseball, basketball, crew, cross country, diving, fencing, field hockey, football, lightweight crew, golf, gymnastics, lacrosse, soccer, softball, swimming, tennis, track (indoor and outdoor), volleyball, and wrestling. Approximately 55% of the entering students receive financial assistance either offered or administered by the university.

Community Environment: New Brunswick is an important manufacturing center on the Raritan River, 33 miles southwest of New York City. Commercial transportation is available; the Newark International Airport is 30 minutes away. Community facilities include libraries, churches of most denominations, YMCA, YWCA, hospitals, hotels, motels, and various fraternal, civic, and veterans organizations. The New Jersey seashore and parks provide recreational areas for fishing, boating, camping, swimming, and skiing. There are golf courses in the area. There are many part-time job opportunities.

RUTGERS, THE STATE UNIVERSITY OF NEW JERSEY - COLLEGE OF NURSING   *(E-13)*
Newark, New Jersey 07102
Tel: (201) 648-5205

Description: Founded in 1956, the College of Nursing is a professional school which offers a Bachelor of Science curriculum in nursing. The College of Nursing offers the Doctor of Philosophy degree in Nursing and the Master of Science degree, both awarded through the Graduate School-Newark. A four-year program, as well as a baccalaureate program for registered nurses is available. Clinical experience is obtained in various hospitals and health agencies in northern New Jersey. The program is offered also to a limited number of students at the

New Brunswick Campus. Enrollment includes 372 men and women. A faculty of 40 full-time gives a faculty-student ratio of 1-10.

Entrance Requirements: Accredited high school graduation: completion of 16 units including 4 English, 3 mathematics (4 recommended), 2 laboratory science (biology, chemistry); SAT or ACT required (except those out of high school two or more years and transfers with 12 credits); early admission, deferred admission and advanced placement plans available; $50 application fee.

Costs Per Year: $3,640 state resident tuition; $7,410 nonresident tuition; $4,748 room and board; $799 fees in Newark, $971-$1,006 fees in New Brunswick.

Collegiate Environment: Each campus of Rutgers, The State University, houses its own excellent library. Students may use any library in the system. (see main entry for details). Modern apartments are available for nursing students on the 33-acre Newark campus. Intercollegiate sports programs are in: baseball, basketball, crew, cross country, diving, fencing, field hockey, football, lightweight crew, golf, gymnastics, lacrosse, soccer, softball, swimming, tennis, track (indoor and outdoor), volleyball, and wrestling. Approximately 55% of the entering students receive financial assistance either offered or administered by the university.

Community Environment: Newark, with a population of 275,221, is the largest city in New Jersey and the center of a large higher education complex, serving as home to Essex County College, the New Jersey Institute of Technology, the University of Medicine and Dentistry of New Jersey, Seton Hall School of Law, and the Newark Campus of Rutgers University. Community facilities offer a wide range of cultural, recreational, and social activities in the city and easy access to the resources of New York City.

RUTGERS, THE STATE UNIVERSITY OF NEW JERSEY - COLLEGE OF PHARMACY   *(G-11)*
New Brunswick, New Jersey 08903
Tel: (908) 932-1766

Description: A coeducational professional college, the College of Pharmacy was founded in 1892 and incorporated into Rutgers University in 1927. It offers a five-year program. Students may also choose to spend their first two years at the Camden College of Arts and Sciences or the Newark College of Arts and Sciences. Study abroad in Britain, Costa Rica, France, Germany, Israel, Italy, Kenya, Mexico, Portugal, and Spain. Enrollment includes 889 students. A faculty of 59 full-time gives a faculty-student ratio of 1-14.

Entrance Requirements: Accredited high school graduation: completion of 16 units including 4 English, 3 mathematics (4 recommended), 2 foreign language, 2 laboratory science (chemistry, biology, physics recommended); admission by examination; SAT or ACT required (except those out of high school 2 or more years and transfers with 12 credits); admission is competitive; early admission, deferred admission and advanced placement plans available; $50 application fee.

Costs Per Year: $4,040 state resident tuition; $8,221 nonresident tuition; $4,748 room and board; $971-$1,045 fees.

Collegiate Environment: The college is housed in a modern building on the Busch Campus, adjacent to the University of Medicine and Dentistry of New Jersey and the Library of Science and Medicine. Each campus of Rutgers, The State University, houses its own excellent library. Students may use any library in the system (see main entry for details). Housing is guaranteed for all freshmen and sophomores. A network of free buses connects the New Brunswick colleges and facilitates cross registration and wide participation in activities. Intercollegiate sports programs are in: baseball, basketball, crew, cross country, diving, fencing, field hockey, football, lightweight crew, golf, gymnastics, lacrosse, soccer, softball, swimming, tennis, track (indoor and outdoor), volleyball, and wrestling. Approximately 55% of the entering students receive financial assistance either offered or administrated by the university.

Community Environment: New Brunswick is an important manufacturing center on the Raritan River, 33 miles southwest of New York City. Commercial transportation is available; the Newark International Airport is 30 minutes away. Community facilities include libraries, churches of most denominations, YMCA, YWCA, hospitals, hotels, motels, and various fraternal, civic, and veterans organizations. The New Jersey seashore and parks provide recreational areas for

fishing, boating, camping, swimming, and skiing. There are golf courses in the area. There are many part-time job opportunities.

RUTGERS, THE STATE UNIVERSITY OF NEW JERSEY - COOK COLLEGE   *(G-11)*
New Brunswick, New Jersey 08903
Tel: (908) 932-1766

Description: Cook is a coeducational residential college with major emphasis in environmental studies, agriculture, marine sciences, life sciences, and biotechnology. Established in 1864, it provides many programs formerly offered by the College of Agriculture and Environmental Sciences of Rutgers, as well as a number in other science-related fields. A cooperative education program is available. An 8-year BA/MD program is available in conjunction with the University of Medicine and Dentistry of New Jersey. Study abroad in Britain, Costa Rica, France, Germany, Israel, Italy, Kenya, Mexico, Portugal, and Spain. Enrollment includes 3,010 students of which 52% are men and 48% are women. A faculty of 97 full-time gives a faculty-student ratio of 1-16.

Entrance Requirements: Accredited high school graduation: completion of 16 units including 4 English, 3 mathematics (4 recommended), 2 science; SAT or ACT required (except those out of high school 2 or more years and transfers with 12 credits); admission by examination; admission is selective; early admission, deferred admission, midyear admission (for transfer students), and advanced placement plans available; $50 application fee.

Costs Per Year: $4,040 state resident tuition; $8,221 nonresident tuition; $4,748 room and board; $992 fees.

Collegiate Environment: The campus is adjacent to Douglass College with which it shares many facilities and classes. Each campus of Rutgers, The State University, houses its own excellent library. Students may use any library in the system (see main entry for details). Freshmen live in traditional dormitories and most upper classmen live in campus apartments. Housing is guaranteed to all freshmen and sophomores. A network of free buses connects the New Brunswick colleges and facilitates cross registration and wide participation in activities. Intercollegiate sports programs are in: baseball, basketball, crew, cross country, diving, fencing, field hockey, football, lightweight crew, golf, gymnastics, lacrosse, soccer, softball, swimming, tennis, track (indoor and outdoor), volleyball, and wrestling. Approximately 55% of the entering students receive financial assistance either offered or administered by the university.

Community Environment: New Brunswick is an important manufacturing center on the Raritan River, 33 miles southwest of New York City. Commercial transportation is available; the Newark International Airport is 30 minutes away. Community facilities include libraries, churches of most denominations, YMCA, YWCA, hospitals, hotels, motels, and various fraternal, civic, and veterans organizations. The New Jersey seashore and parks provide recreational areas for fishing, boating, camping, swimming, and skiing. There are golf courses in the area. There are many part-time job opportunities.

RUTGERS, THE STATE UNIVERSITY OF NEW JERSEY - DOUGLASS COLLEGE   *(G-11)*
New Brunswick, New Jersey 08903
Tel: (908) 932-1766

Description: Douglass, the women's college of Rutgers University, was established in 1918 as New Jersey College for women and is now the largest women's college in the United States. It stresses the value of liberal arts and recognizes a special responsibility with regard to the role of women in higher education and society. Douglass College, Livingston College, Rutgers College and University College-New Brunswick are served by the Faculty of Arts and Sciences. French, Spanish, Italian, Russian, and German language houses are available on campus, as are an African and Afro-American House, a Puerto Rican House, and the Bunting-Cobb Mathematics and Science Hall for women who are interested in and are majoring in mathematics or the sciences. An 8-year BA/MD program is available in conjunction with the University of Medicine and Dentistry of New Jersey. Study abroad in Britain, Costa Rica, France, Germany, Israel, Italy, Kenya, Mexico, Portugal, and Spain. Enrollment includes 2,986 students.

Entrance Requirements: Accredited high school graduation: completion of 16 units including 4 English, 3 mathematics (4 recommended), 2 science, 2 foreign language; SAT or ACT required (except those out of high school 2 or more years and transfer with 12 credits); admission by examination; admission is selective; early admission, deferred admission, midyear admission (for transfer students), and advanced placement plans available; $50 application fee.

Costs Per Year: $3,640 state resident tuition; $7,410 nonresident tuition; $4,748 room and board, $971 fees.

Collegiate Environment: Located approximately one mile from the Rutgers College campus, the Douglass College Campus is adjacent to Cook College. Each campus of Rutgers, The State University, houses its own excellent library. Students may use any library in the system (see main entry for details). Residence facilities consist of small houses, residence halls, and apartments, all arranged in campus groups where students serve as house chairwomen. Housing is guaranteed to all first-year students and sophomores. Women may join any of the sororities at the University. A network of free buses connects the New Brunswick colleges and facilitates cross registration and wide participation in activities. Intercollegiate sports programs are in: baseball, basketball, crew, cross country, diving, fencing, field hockey, football, lightweight crew, golf, gymnastics, lacrosse, soccer, softball, swimming, tennis, track (indoor and outdoor), volleyball, and wrestling. Approximately 55% of the entering students receive financial assistance either offered or administered by the university.

Community Environment: New Brunswick is an important manufacturing center on the Raritan River, 33 miles southwest of New York City. Commercial transportation is available; the Newark International Airport is 30 minutes away. Community facilities include libraries, churches of most denominations, YMCA, YWCA, hospitals, hotels, motels, and various fraternal, civic, and veterans organizations. The New Jersey seashore and parks provide recreational areas for fishing, boating, camping, swimming, and skiing. There are golf courses in the area. There are many part-time job opportunities.

RUTGERS, THE STATE UNIVERSITY OF NEW JERSEY - LIVINGSTON COLLEGE   *(G-11)*
New Brunswick, New Jersey 08903
Tel: (908) 932-1766

Description: Livingston is a coeducational, liberal arts college which opened in 1969. It is committed not only to seeking out students who meet traditional measures of excellence but is also interested in selecting those who demonstrate academic potential in other ways. Douglass College, Livingston College, Rutgers College, University College-New Brunswick are served by the Faculty of Arts and Sciences. Field work, independent study, and internships are vital parts of many programs. An 8-year BA/MD programs is available in conjunction with the University of Medicine and Dentistry of New Jersey. Study abroad in Britain, Costa Rica, France, Germany, Israel, Italy, Kenya, Mexico, Portugal, and Spain. Enrollment includes 3,273, 59% men and 41% women.

Entrance Requirements: Accredited high school graduation: completion of 16 units including 4 English, 3 mathematics, (4 recommended), 2 years of one foreign language, 2 years of science; SAT or ACT required (except for those out of high school two or more years and transfers with 12 credits); admission by examination; admission is selective; early admission, deferred admission, midyear admission (for transfer students), and advanced placement plans available; $50 application fee.

Costs Per Year: $3,640 state resident tuition; $7,410 nonresident tuition; $4,748 room and board; $1,045 fees.

Collegiate Environment: Livingston is located on the Livingston Campus across the Raritan River from New Brunswick. Each campus of Rutgers, The State University, houses its own excellent library. Students may use any library in the system (see main entry for details). The modern campus includes 2 residential quadrangles and 2 high-rise dormitories. Housing is guaranteed for all freshmen and sophomores. A network of free buses connects the New Brunswick colleges and facilitates cross registration and wide participation in activities. Intercollegiate sports programs are in: baseball, basketball, crew, cross country, diving, fencing, field hockey, football, lightweight crew, golf, gymnastics, lacrosse, soccer, softball, swimming, tennis, track (indoor and outdoor), volleyball, and wrestling. Approximately 55% of the entering students receive financial assistance either offered or administered by the university.

Community Environment: New Brunswick is an important manufacturing center on the Raritan River, 33 miles southwest of New York City. Commercial transportation is available; the Newark International Airport is 30 minutes away. Community facilities include libraries, churches of most denominations, YMCA, YWCA, hospitals, hotels, motels, and various fraternal, civic, and veterans organizations. The New Jersey seashore and parks provide recreational areas for fishing, boating, camping, swimming, and skiing. There are golf courses in the area. There are many part-time job opportunities.

RUTGERS, THE STATE UNIVERSITY OF NEW JERSEY - MASON GROSS SCHOOL OF THE ARTS   *(G-11)*
New Brunswick, New Jersey 08903
Tel: (908) 932-1766

Description: Founded in 1976, Mason Gross School of the Arts is the newest undergraduate unit of the State University. A coeducational, professional college, it offers the Bachelor of Fine Arts degree in Visual Arts, Theater Arts and Dance, and the Bachelor of Music degree at the undergraduate level. Overseas program throughout Europe and in Mexico. Enrollment includes 410 students with a faculty of 77.

Entrance Requirements: Accredited high school graduation: completion of 16 academic units including 4 English, 3 mathematics (4 recommended), 2 years of 1 foreign language also recommended; SAT or ACT required (except those out of high school 2 or more years and transfers with 12 credits); portfolio, audition, and, in some cases, interview required; admission by examination; admission is selective; early admission, deferred admission and advanced placement plans available; midyear admission to selected majors for transfer students if space is available; $50 application fee.

Costs Per Year: $3,640 state resident tuition; $7,410 nonresident tuition; $4,748 room and board; $971-$1,045 fees.

Collegiate Environment: The students affiliate with Cook, Douglass, Livingston, or Rutgers Colleges for housing and student life facilities and services. Each campus of Rutgers, The State University, houses its own excellent library. Students may use any library in the system (see main entry for details). Housing is guaranteed for all freshmen and sophomores. A network of free buses connects the New Brunswick colleges and facilitates cross registration and wide participation in activities. Intercollegiate sports programs are in: baseball, basketball, crew, cross country, diving, fencing, field hockey, football, lightweight crew, golf, gymnastics, lacrosse, soccer, softball, swimming, tennis, track (indoor and outdoor), volleyball, and wrestling. Approximately 55% of the entering students receive financial assistance either offered or administered by the university.

Community Environment: New Brunswick is an important manufacturing center on the Raritan River, 33 miles southwest of New York City. Commercial transportation is available; the Newark International Airport is 30 minutes away. Community facilities include libraries, churches of most denominations, YMCA, YWCA, hospitals, hotels, motels, and various fraternal, civic, and veteran organizations. The New Jersey seashore and parks provide recreational areas for fishing, boating, camping, swimming, and skiing. There are golf courses in the area. There are many part-time job opportunities.

RUTGERS, THE STATE UNIVERSITY OF NEW JERSEY - NEWARK COLLEGE OF THE ARTS AND SCIENCES   *(E-13)*
Newark, New Jersey 07102
Tel: (201) 648-5205

Description: The Newark College of Arts and Sciences was founded in 1930 and incorporated into Rutgers University in 1946. A coeducational college which serves primarily commuting students from northern New Jersey, it offers over 40 majors in the arts and sciences, as well as professional and preprofessional programs. An 8-year BA/MD program is available in conjunction with the University of Medicine and Dentistry of New Jersey. Study abroad in Britain, Costa Rica, France, Germany, Israel, Italy, Kenya, Mexico, Portugal, and Spain. Enrollment is 3,724. A faculty of 189 full-time, which also serves University College-Newark, gives a faculty-student ratio of 1:14.

Entrance Requirements: Accredited high school graduation: completion of 16 units including 4 English, 3 mathematics (4 recommended), 2 science, 2 foreign language; SAT or ACT required (except those out of high school two or more years and transfers with

12 credits); admission by examination; early admission, deferred admission, midyear admission, and advanced placement plans available; $50 application fee.

Costs Per Year: $3,640 state resident tuition; $7,410 nonresident tuition; $4,748 room and board; $816 fees.

Collegiate Environment: Each campus of Rutgers, The State University, houses its own excellent library. Students may use any library in the system (see main entry for details). Housing and dining facilities are available. Intercollegiate sports programs are in: baseball, basketball, crew, cross country, diving, fencing, field hockey, football, lightweight crew, golf, gymnastics, lacrosse, soccer, softball, swimming, tennis, track (indoor and outdoor), volleyball, and wrestling. Approximately 55% of the entering students receive financial assistance either offered or administered by the university.

Community Environment: Newark, with a population of 275,221, is the largest city in New Jersey and the center of a large higher education complex, serving as home to Essex County College, the New Jersey Institute of Technology, the University of Medicine and Dentistry of New Jersey, Seton Hall School of Law, and the Newark Campus of Rutgers University. Community facilities offer a wide range of cultural, recreational and social activities and easy access to the resources of New York City.

RUTGERS, THE STATE UNIVERSITY OF NEW JERSEY - RUTGERS COLLEGE   *(G-11)*
New Brunswick, New Jersey 08903
Tel: (908) 932-1766

Description: Rutgers College was founded in 1766 as Queen's College, a residential college for men. It became coeducational in 1972. Douglass College, Livingston College, Rutgers College, and University College-New Brunswick are served by the Faculty of Arts and Sciences. Special programs such as independent study, study abroad (in Britain, Costa Rica, France, Germany, Israel, Italy, Kenya, Mexico, Portugal, and Spain), and a student exchange program with other colleges and universities in the country are offered. An 8-year BA/MD program is available in conjunction with the University of Medicine and Dentistry of New Jersey. The largest unit of the State University, Rutgers College enrollment is 8,908, with 50% men and 50% women.

Entrance Requirements: Accredited high school graduation; completion of 16 units including 4 English, 3 mathematics (4 recommended), 2 science, 2 foreign language; SAT or ACT required (except those who have been out of high school two or more years and transfers with 12 credits); admission by examination; admission is selective; early admission, deferred admission, midyear admission (for transfers only), and advanced placement plans available; $50 application fee.

Costs Per Year: $3,640 state resident tuition; $7,410 nonresident tuition; $4,748 room and board; $1,006 fees.

Collegiate Environment: Each campus of Rutgers, The State University, houses its own excellent library. Students may use any library in the system (see main entry for details). Residence facilities consist of traditional residence halls and new suite-style housing, as well as campus apartments. Housing is guaranteed to all freshmen and sophomores. Coeducational and single-sex accommodations are available, as are nine dorms for freshmen only. A network of free buses connects the New Brunswick colleges and facilitates cross registration and wide participation in activities. Intercollegiate sports programs are in: baseball, basketball, crew, cross country, diving, fencing, field hockey, football, lightweight crew, golf, gymnastics, lacrosse, soccer, softball, swimming, tennis, track (indoor and outdoor), volleyball, and wrestling. Approximately 55% of entering students receive financial assistance either offered or administered by the university.

Community Environment: New Brunswick is an important manufacturing center on the Raritan River, 33 miles southwest of New York City. Commercial transportation is available; the Newark International Airport is 30 minutes away. Community facilities include libraries, churches of most denominations, YMCA, YWCA, hospitals, hotels, motels, and various fraternal, civic, and veterans organizations. The New Jersey seashore and parks provide recreational areas for fishing, boating, camping, swimming, and skiing. There are golf courses in the area. There are many part-time job opportunities.

RUTGERS, THE STATE UNIVERSITY OF NEW JERSEY - UNIVERSITY COLLEGE, CAMDEN   *(K-7)*
Camden, New Jersey 08102
Tel: (609) 225-6104

Description: University College-Camden, an undergraduate evening college, is oriented toward serving part-time adult students. It offers Bachelor's degree programs in arts, sciences, humanities, and professional studies. An 8-year BA/MD program is available in conjunction with the University of Medicine and Dentistry of New Jersey. Most students are candidates for the bachelor's degree, but students may take courses without establishing degree candidacy. Daytime courses are required to complete some major requirements. Enrollment includes 764 men and women. A faculty of 133 full-time which also serves Camden College of Arts and Sciences gives a faculty-student ratio of 1-15.

Entrance Requirements: Requirements for entrance are flexible with stress placed on experience, motivation, and other personal qualities; high school graduation is required with completion of 16 units to include 4 English, 3 mathematics, 2 foreign language; SAT or ACT required (except those out of high school 2 or more years and transfers with 12 credits); residency requires 30 of the last 42 credits be taken at University College; advanced placement, midyear admission, and rolling admission plans available; $50 application fee.

Costs Per Year: $118 per credit hour state resident tuition; $240 per credit hour nonresident tuition; $100 per semester fees.

Collegiate Environment: Each campus of Rutgers, The State University, houses its own excellent library. Students may use any library in the system (see main entry for details). Most students are employed full-time and the majority enter as transfers, although some students are recent high school graduates. Limited residence facilities are at the Camden College of Arts and Sciences. Approximately 55% of the entering students receive financial assistance either offered or administered by the university.

Community Environment: Camden, with a population of 84,910, lies on the Delaware River directly opposite Philadelphia. The college is accessible by bus, car, or the PATCO high-speed line. The Camden Campus is not isolated from, but is part of, an active industrial and cultural community where a wealth of educational and vocational opportunities exist. Among the larger plants in this industrial area are Martin Marietta and the Campbell Soup Company corporate headquarters. Several large shopping malls are within easy driving distance of the city, and community facilities include many churches, YMCA, YWCA, and numerous civic and service organizations.

RUTGERS, THE STATE UNIVERSITY OF NEW JERSEY - UNIVERSITY COLLEGE, NEW BRUNSWICK   *(G-11)*
New Brunswick, New Jersey 08903
Tel: (908) 932-7276

Description: University College, New Brunswick, primarily serves adult part-time students. It offers Bachelor's degree programs in the liberal arts and professional studies. An 8-year BA/MD program is available in conjunction with the University of Medicine and Dentistry of New Jersey. Most students are candidates for the bachelor's degree, but students may take courses without establishing degree candidacy. Douglass College, Livingston College, Rutgers College, and University College-New Brunswick are served by the Faculty of Arts and Sciences. Enrollment includes 3,132 men and women.

Entrance Requirements: High school graduation is required with completion of 16 units to include 4 English, 3 mathematics, 2 foreign language; admission by examination; SAT or ACT required (except those out of school 2 or more years and transfers with 12 credits); residency requires 30 of the last 42 credits be taken at University College; rolling admission, midyear admission, and advanced placement plans available; $50 application fee.

Costs Per Year: $118 per credit hour state resident tuition; $240 per credit hour nonresident tuition; $87 per semester fees.

Collegiate Environment: Each campus of Rutgers, The State University, houses its own excellent library. Students may use any library in the system (see main entry for details). Most students are employed full-time and the majority enter as transfers, although some students enter as high school graduates. Residence facilities are on the New Brunswick area college campuses at Cook, Douglass, Livingston, and Rutgers. A network of buses connects the New Brunswick colleges and facilitates cross registration and wide participation in activities. Approximately 55% of the entering students receive financial assistance either offered or administered by the university.

Community Environment: New Brunswick is an important manufacturing center on the Raritan River, 33 miles southwest of New York City. Commercial transportation is available; the Newark International Airport is 30 minutes away. Community facilities include libraries, churches of most denominations, YMCA, YWCA, hospitals, hotels, motels, and various fraternal, civic, and veterans organizations. The New Jersey seashore and parks provide recreational areas for fishing, boating, camping, swimming, and skiing. There are golf courses in the area. There are many part-time job opportunities.

RUTGERS, THE STATE UNIVERSITY OF NEW JERSEY - UNIVERSITY COLLEGE, NEWARK   *(E-13)*
Newark, New Jersey 07102
Tel: (201) 648-5205

Description: University College, Newark, an undergraduate evening college is oriented toward part-time adult students. It offers Bachelor's degree programs in arts, sciences, humanities, and professional studies. An 8-year BA/MD program is available in conjunction with the University of Medicine and Dentistry of New Jersey. Most students are candidates for the bachelor's degree, but students may take courses without establishing degree candidacy. Enrollment includes 1,865 men and women. A faculty of 189 also serves Newark College of Arts and Sciences.

Entrance Requirements: Requirements for entrance are flexible with stress placed on experience, motivation, and other personal qualities; University College has a full faith and credit policy for graduates of New Jersey two-year colleges; High school graduation is required with completion of 16 units to include 4 English, 3 mathematics, 2 foreign language; SAT or ACT required (except those out of high school 2 or more years and transfers with 12 credits); residency requires 30 of the last 42 credits be taken at University College; rolling admission, deferred admission, midyear admission, and advanced placement plans available; $50 application fee.

Costs Per Year: $118 per credit hour state resident tuition; $240 per credit hour nonresident tuition; $93 per semester fees.

Collegiate Environment: Each campus of Rutgers, The State University, houses its own excellent library. Students may use any library in the system (see main entry for details). Most students are employed full-time and the majority enter as transfers, although some students enter as recent high school graduates. Housing is available at Newark College of Arts and Sciences. Approximately 55% of the entering students receive financial assistance either offered or administered by the university.

Community Environment: Newark, with a population of 275,221, is the largest city in New Jersey and the center of a large higher education complex, serving as home to Essex County College, the New Jersey Institute of Technology, the University of Medicine and Dentistry of New Jersey, Seton Hall School of Law, and the Newark Campus of Rutgers University. Community facilities offer a wide range of cultural, recreational, and social activities and easy access to the resources of New York City.

SAINT PETER'S COLLEGE   *(E-13)*
2641 Kennedy Boulevard
Jersey City, New Jersey 07306-5944
Tel: (201) 915-9000; Admissions: (201) 915-9213; Fax: (201) 432-5860

Description: Chartered in 1872, Saint Peter's College is a coeducational, liberal arts college in the Jesuit tradition. It is accredited by the Middle States Association of Colleges and Schools. Although career-oriented the College's 34 academic programs are firmly grounded in the liberal arts and all students must complete a core curriculum requirement. Majors are offered in business, the humanities, the natural and social sciences. Enrollment includes 2,107 full-time and 1,038 part-time undergraduates and 402 graduate students. These figures include 1,240 students in evening programs. A faculty of 111 full-time and 235 part-time gives an undergraduate faculty-student ratio of 1-14. The college operates on the semester system and offers three summer sessions. The evening school operates on the trimester calendar system. True to the Jesuit tradition of academic excellence

and personal care, Saint Peter's places great emphasis on each student's personal, intellectual and career development. Small classes, a caring faculty and numerous support services combine to create an academic atmosphere that is conducive to growth, learning and creativity. Our Career Development and Cooperative Education offices are open to all students regardless of class year. Personal counseling is provided by staff professionals in the Counseling Center. The Campus Ministry Office offers spiritual programs and retreats. Peer tutoring is available in all subjects through CALL (Center for the Advancement of Language and Learning). Saint Peter's offers baccalaureate, associate and graduate degree programs. Special educational opportunities include a four-year honors program, foreign study, cooperative education and Washington Center internships and Army ROTC.

Entrance Requirements: High school graduation; completion of 16 units including 4 English, 3 mathematics, 2 foreign language, 2 science (min. 1 lab.), 2 history and 3 additional units in any of the subjects listed here; SAT required; non-high school graduates considered; rolling admission, delayed admission, early decision, early admission and advanced placement programs available; $30 application fee.

Costs Per Year: $11,456 ($358/credit) tuition; $295 student fees; $5,620 room and board.

Collegiate Environment: Saint Peter's is a friendly campus consisting of 9 acres and 23 buildings where students, faculty and administrators are part of a caring community. Approximately 50 clubs and organizations provide students with a variety of extracurricular activities. Students are strongly encouraged to become involved in student activities which include the student senate; service, social and academic clubs; and student publications such as the newspaper, yearbook and literary magazine. Saint Peter's participates in intercollegiate athletics at the NCAA Division I level in 14 sports and in football with the IAA. A member of MAAC conference, the College is probably best known for its men's and women's basketball teams, but also sponsors teams in baseball, softball, volleyball, tennis, track and cross-country, swimming, soccer, bowling, and golf. The Athletic Department also hosts an extensive intramurals program. Each year the Special Programs Office develops an interesting and varied calendar of special events. Students are actively involved in programming in the residence facility and other areas. Diversity enhances the learning environment at Saint Peter's. Approximately 40% of Saint Peter's full-time students are members of minority groups; 5% are international students. Students come from 10 states and 13 foreign countries. About 80% are from New Jersey. While Saint Peter's is a Catholic college, it is not narrowly sectarian and approximately 20% of the students are non-Catholic. Approximately 79% of students applying are accepted including midyear students. The middle 50% range of enrolled freshmen scores were SAT 300-420 verbal, 340-480 math. The library contains more than 324,921 volumes, 1,455 periodicals, 636 microforms and 5,169 audiovisual materials. Residence halls accomodate 468 students. Financial aid is available.

Community Environment: See Jersey City State College.

Branch Campuses: Englewood Cliffs Campus, Hudson Terrace, Englewood Cliffs, NJ 07632; (201) 568-7730, Katherine M. Restaino, Ph.D., Dean.

SETON HALL UNIVERSITY   *(E-2)*
400 South Orange Avenue
South Orange, New Jersey 07079
Tel: (201) 761-9000; (800) 843-4255; Admissions: (201) 761-9332; Fax: (201) 761-9452

Description: This privately supported, coeducational university was founded in 1856 and is under the auspices of the Roman Catholic Archdiocese of Newark. It now consists of the College of Arts and Sciences, the Stillman School of Business, the School of Education and Human Services, the College of Nursing, the School of Law, the Graduate School of Medicine And the Immaculate Conception Seminary. It is accredited by the Middle States Association of Colleges and Schools, and grants the Bachelor, Master, and Doctorate degrees. U.S. Army and Air Force ROTC programs are available. The university operates on the semester system and offers two summer sessions. Undergraduate enrollment includes approximately 4,207 full-time, 972 part-time, and 3,221 graduate students. A faculty of 372 full-time and 380 part-time gives an undergraduate faculty-student ratio of 1-8.

Entrance Requirements: High school graduation with rank in upper 40% of class; completion of 16 units including 4 English, 3 mathematics, 1 science, 2 foreign language, 2 social science, and 4 approved electives; SAT or ACT required; nursing candidates require biology and chemistry; deferred admission, rolling admission, deferred admission, midyear admission, and advanced placement plans available; Bachelor degree and Law SAT required by Law School; March 1 priority application date; $25 application fee.

Costs Per Year: $12,000 tuition; $6,258 room and board; $550 student fees; $600 average additional expenses.

Collegiate Environment: The university's location on 58 acres in the Village of South Orange provides students with the advantages of a quiet suburb as well as proximity to New York City, which is 16 miles away. Residence hall facilities accommodate 2,000 men and women. The several libraries contain 430,000 volumes, 2,200 periodicals, and 24,300 microforms. Approximately 76% of students applying for admission are accepted, including midyear students. 80% of the previous freshman class returned to this campus for the sophomore year. Financial aid is available and 74% of the current student body receives financial assistance. An extensive co-op and internship program is available.

Community Environment: A suburban area west of Newark, South Orange enjoys the cultural and recreational advantages of New York City and Newark. Mass transportation is available. Community facilities include a public library, two hospitals in nearby Livingston and Summit, and Catholic, Methodist, Episcopal and Presbyterian churches. The Oranges complex (including Orange and the South, East, and West Oranges) has a population of 170,000.

STEVENS INSTITUTE OF TECHNOLOGY   *(E-13)*
Castle Point on Hudson
Hoboken, New Jersey 07030
Tel: (201) 216-5194; (800) 458-5323; Admissions: (201) 216-5194; Fax: (201) 216-8348

Description: Privately supported, coeducational college of engineering founded in 1870 by Edwin Stevens, the institute offers programs at the undergraduate and graduate level. It is accredited by the Middle States Association of Colleges and Schools and grants the Bachelor, Master and Doctorate degrees. Departments of instruction include Engineering, Management and Engineering Management, Science, Computer Science and Humanities. Air Force and Army ROTC programs are available. The institute operates on the semester system and offers two summer sessions. Enrollment includes 1,213 undergraduates and 2,000 graduate students. A faculty of 144 full-time and 100 part-time gives a faculty-student ratio of 1-9.

Entrance Requirements: Accredited high school graduation; completion of 4 units English, 4 mathematics, 3 science, 2 foreign language; SAT required; early admission, rolling admission, delayed admission, early decision and advanced placement plans available; personal interview required; $35 application fee.

Costs Per Year: $17,500 tuition; $6,156 room and board; $150 student fees; additional expenses average $500.

Collegiate Environment: The institute is located on the Hudson River. The library contains 110,000 volumes, 1,000 periodicals, 611 microforms and 70 recordings. Most undergraduates live on the 55-acre campus. Students are drawn from wide sections of the United States and from foreign lands. There are six college residence halls including the Married Students Apartment Building. Facilities are available for 780 men, 240 women and 72 families. Approximately 71% of students applying for admission are accepted, and 80% of the previous freshman class returned to this school for their second year. 75% of the current student body receive financial aid. Almost all of the senior class continued on to graduate school on a part-time basis, with 15% on a full-time basis.

Community Environment: Hoboken, is a seaport, railroad terminal and industrial center, just one mile square and easily accessible to Manhattan. Recently it has become a residential center for young professionals. Many new shops, restaurants and clubs have opened in the past few years. The recreational and cultural advantages of New York are convenient for Hoboken. There are many job opportunities.

THOMAS EDISON STATE COLLEGE   *(I-9)*
101 West State Street
Trenton, New Jersey 08608-1176
Tel: (609) 984-1100; Admissions: (609) 984-1150; Fax: (609) 984-8447

Description: This publicly supported coeducational college for adult students was founded in 1972 and is accredited by the Middle States Association of Colleges and Schools. The school operates on the continuous term plan and grants an associate and baccalaureate degree. The current enrollment is 8,619 students.

Entrance Requirements: Open enrollment; rolling admission and advanced placement plans available; CLEP accepted.

Costs Per Year: $440 annual enrollment fee; $780 annual enrollment fee for out-of-state residents; additional fees for other services.

Collegiate Environment: All students are accepted, including transfer students. Scholarships are available and 1% of the students receive financial assistance. All degree work is done "at a distance." There are no residency requirements.

Community Environment: See Rider College.

TRENTON STATE COLLEGE   *(I-9)*
Hillwood Lakes CN 4700
Trenton, New Jersey 08650-4700
Tel: (609) 771-2131; (800) 624-0967; Fax: (609) 771-3067

Description: Publicly supported, coeducational, professional, and liberal arts college established in 1855. It is accredited by the Middle States Association of Colleges and Schools, the National Council for Accreditation of Teacher Education, and various other professional organizations. The college offers a wide range of programs through its five schools: Arts and Sciences, Business, Education, Nursing, and Technology. Teacher certification is available in all appropriate arts and sciences programs. The college grants the Bachelor's and Master's degrees. It operates on the semester system and offers one six-week summer session. Enrollment includes 5,205 full-time, 779 part-time undergraduates, and 997 graduate students. A faculty of 309 full-time and 280 part-time gives an undergraduate faculty-student ratio of 1-10. Army and Air Force ROTC programs are available.

Entrance Requirements: Accredited high school graduation or high school equivalency certificate; completion of 16 units including 4 English, 2 mathematics, 3 laboratory science, 2 social science; SAT or ACT required; GRE required for graduate studies; early admission, deferred admission, advanced placement, midyear admission, and early decision plans available. March 1 application deadline; $50 application fee.

Costs Per Year: $4,012 tuition; $6,287 out-of-state tuition; $5,411 room and board.

Collegiate Environment: The campus is located on 250 acres in the Hillwood Lakes district of suburban Ewing Township within 60 miles of New York City and 30 miles of Philadelphia. Buildings include residence halls for 2,700 students and a library system of approximately 500,000 volumes and 1,600 periodicals. A student center houses the college newspaper and radio station as well as lounges, a commercial bank, snack bar, college store, and game room. Holman Hall features a permanent art gallery, and all five Schools of the college are equipped with computer centers. Approximately 44% of students applying are accepted including midyear students and 94% of the previous freshman class returned to the campus for their sophomore year. The average scores of the entering freshman class were SAT 525 verbal, 599 math. Financial aid and scholarships are available and 54% of the current student body receive financial assistance. Academic and minority scholarships are awarded to outstanding students. The college awarded 1,369 Bachelor's and 298 Master's degrees during the academic year.

Community Environment: See Rider College.

UNION COUNTY COLLEGE   *(G-2)*
1033 Springfield Avenue
Cranford, New Jersey 07016
Tel: (908) 709-7500

Description: Publicly supported, coeducational, junior college founded in 1933. The college offers programs in Liberal Arts, Liberal

Arts/Education, Liberal Arts/Early Childhood Education, Liberal Arts/Urban Studies, Biology, Biology/Environmental Science, Physical Science, Engineering, Engineering/Environmental Science, Engineering Management, Business, Business/Public Administration, Business/Pre-Medical Records Administration, and Criminal Justice and is accredited by the Middle States Association of Colleges and Schools. Certificate programs in Basic Skills and Intensive English Language Learning are also offered. The semester system is used and two summer sessions are offered. The college grants the Associate degree. Enrollment includes approximately 9,590 men and women. The faculty has 169 full-time and 225 part-time members. There are 4 urban campuses: Cranford, NJ; Plainfield, NJ; Scotch Plains, NJ; and the Urban Educational Center in Elizabeth, NJ.

Entrance Requirements: Open enrollment policy for Union County residents; accredited high school graduation, GED accepted; completion of 16 units including 4 English, 2 mathematics, 2 foreign language, 1 science, 2 social science; SAT required; non-high school graduates considered; rolling admission, early admission and early decision plans are available; $15 application fee.

Costs Per Year: $1,254 resident tuition; $5,016 tuition nonresident; $269 general student fee; additional expenses average $150.

Collegiate Environment: The 48-acre campus in Cranford is accessible to a wide area of north central New Jersey. There are 7 buildings on the Cranford Campus: The Kenneth Campbell MacKay Library houses 105,500 volumes, 626 periodicals, 10,009 microforms, and 1,010 audiovisual materials; the Nomahegan, the Science, and Humanities buildings with lecture, seminar, and class rooms, laboratories, and faculty offices; the Campus Center with a theater, gymnasium, and other facilities for student activities; the James R. MacDonald Hall which contains the administrative offices; the William Miller Sperry Observatory which houses 24-inch reflector and 10-inch refractor telescopes, a lecture room, and an astronomy library. Approximately 95% of the applicants are accepted, including midyear students. There are 171 scholarships awarded and 85 of these are available for freshman. 17% of the current student body receives some form of financial assistance. The college awarded 708 Associate degrees to the graduating class. About 46% of the graduates continued on to a four-year college.

Community Environment: A suburban area, 10 miles southwest of Newark, Cranford enjoys all the cultural and recreational advantages of nearby New York. Major forms of commercial transportation are available.

Branch Campuses: Cranford; Scotch Plains; Elizabeth; Plainfield.

UNIVERSITY OF MEDICINE AND DENTISTRY OF NEW JERSEY *(E-13)*
30 Bergen Street
Newark, New Jersey 07107
Tel: (201) 456-4300

Description: This publicly supported, coeducational, health-sciences University incorporated in 1954 as the Seton Hall College of Medicine and Dentistry, but became a state school in 1965. The first class of candidates for the M.D. degree was graduated in 1960. The university operates on the semester system and is comprised of 3 Medical schools, a school of Dentistry, Graduate School of Biomedical Sciences, and the School of Health Related Professions. Enrollment is 704. The total number of faculty members is 1,700.

Entrance Requirements: Bachelor of Arts or Bachelor of Science degree is the preferred requirement for the Colleges of Medicine; the minimum requirement is completion of 90 semester hours of credit from accredited college or university; Medical College Admission Test required. Course requirements: Chemistry 16 hours, biology 12, physics 8, English 6; recommend calculus, statistics, foreign language. For College of Dentistry: Bachelor degree or three years preferred; 2 years of college required; must have 6 hours English, 8 biology, 8 physics, 8 inorganic chemistry, 4 organic chemistry; Dental Aptitude test required; GRE required; $10 application fee.

Costs Per Year: $11,053 per year tuition; $14,505 per year out-of-state tuition.

Collegiate Environment: In September, 1969, the college relocated to a new building which is part of a $200 million facility in Newark. Library contains over 124,000 volumes. Approximately 25% of students applying for admission meet the requirements and only 15% of

these are accepted. Financial aid is available and 50% of the current student body receives some form of assistance. Freshman classes begin in September.

Community Environment: See Rutgers, the State University of New Jersey - Newark College of the Arts and Sciences.

WESTMINSTER CHOIR COLLEGE OF RIDER UNIVERSITY *(H-10)*
Hamilton at Walnut
Princeton, New Jersey 08540
Tel: (609) 921-7144; (800) 962-4647; Fax: (609) 921-8829

Description: This private, professional, coeducational college of music was founded in 1926, and offers a curriculum leading to the Bachelor of Music, Bachelor of Arts, and Master of Music degrees. The college began as the outgrowth of a choir started by John Finley Williamson in the Westminster Presbyterian Church of Dayton, Ohio in 1920. It maintains its status today as an interdenominational, interracial, and international college of music. It is accredited by the Middle States Association of Colleges and Schools and by The National Association of Schools of Music. The semester system is used with one summer term. Enrollment is 209 full-time and 33 part-time undergraduate students. There are also 77 full-time and 24 part-time graduate students. A faculty of 75 provides a faculty-student ratio of 1-7. An academic cooperative plan is available with Princeton University.

Entrance Requirements: Accredited high school graduation or equivalent; SAT or ACT required; ability to demonstrate some facility in singing or in playing piano or organ and pronounced musical aptitude in respect to pitch and rhythmic sense; entrance exam and auditions in person or by tapes required; early decision, early admission, rolling admission, advanced placement and delayed admission plans available; $30 application fee for undergraduate students.

Costs Per Year: $12,200 tuition; $5,250 room and board.

Collegiate Environment: The 23-acre campus is centrally located in historic Princeton. The hub of the campus is the Quadrangle, which is surrounded by the four original buildings of the college. The library contains 56,260 volumes, 175 current periodicals, 414 microforms and 8,000 recordings. The choral library contains multiple copies of over 5,000 choral titles, totaling over 250,000 pieces of music. Dormitory facilities accommodate 230 students. Financial aid is available and 85% of the current student body receives some form of assistance. Approximately 61% of students applying for admission are accepted including midyear students. 82% of the previous freshman class returned to the campus for the second year. Average high school standing of the freshman class was in the top 50%; average SAT scores were 450V, 450M. The college awarded 31 Bachelor and 37 Master degrees to the graduating class.

Community Environment: See Princeton University.

WILLIAM PATERSON COLLEGE OF NEW JERSEY *(D-12)*
300 Pompton Road
Wayne, New Jersey 07470
Tel: (201) 595-2000; Fax: (201) 595-3593

Description: This publicly supported, coeducational, liberal arts institution is accredited by the Middle States Association of Colleges and Schools. It offers the Bachelor of Arts, Bachelor of Fine Arts, Bachelor of Music and Bachelor of Science degrees and the Masters of Arts, Master of Business Administration, Master of Education and Master of Science degrees in 32 undergraduate and 16 graduate programs. The four schools which comprise the College are: Arts and Communication, Education; Humanities, Management, and Social Science; and Science and Health. Founded in 1855 as a city normal school, it was called Paterson State College. The College changed to its present name in 1970. It operates on the semester system and offers two summer sessions. Enrollment includes 5,883 full-time, 2,287 part-time, and 1,499 graduate students. There is a faculty of 309 full-time and 19 part-time and adjunct members.

Entrance Requirements: Accredited high school graduation; completion of 16 units including 4 English, 3 mathematics, 2 lab science, 2 social science; high school class rank equal to or greater than the 65th percentile and a combined SAT score of 936; each applicant is individually evaluated with extracurricular and community activities also considered; rolling admission, early admission, early decision, midyear admission, and advanced placement plans available; $35 application fee.

Costs Per Year: $3,000 tuition; $2,952 out-of-state tuition; $4,850 room and board; additional expenses average $325-$560.

Collegiate Environment: A $100 million physical plant on 250 wooded acres with 25 major facilities, including a science complex, performing and visual arts centers, state-of-the art communications center with radio/color television studios, indoor sports arena which functions as a health spa, outdoor light-equipped athletic stadium and multifunctional student center. The Sarah Byrd Askew Library seats 686 and has a collection of 312,000 volumes of books, cassettes, films, videos and microcomputer software, 1,400 subscriptions and 886,000 microforms. Residence Halls house 1,813 men and women (coed). Approximately 42% of the students applying for admission are accepted including midyear students. Financial aid is available and approximately 53% of the current student body receive some form of assistance.

Community Environment: Population 50,000, Wayne is a suburban community located in the center of Passaic County's Wayne Township. The college lies twenty miles west of New York City and is easily accessed by all major New Jersey arteries and nearby Newark Airport. Community facilities include excellent shopping, hospitals, churches of all denominations and numerous clubs and organizations. The college is within an hour's commute of New York city, the Jersey Shore, the Delaware Water Gap and the Vernon Valley/Great Gorge ski slopes all of which offer facilities for recreation.

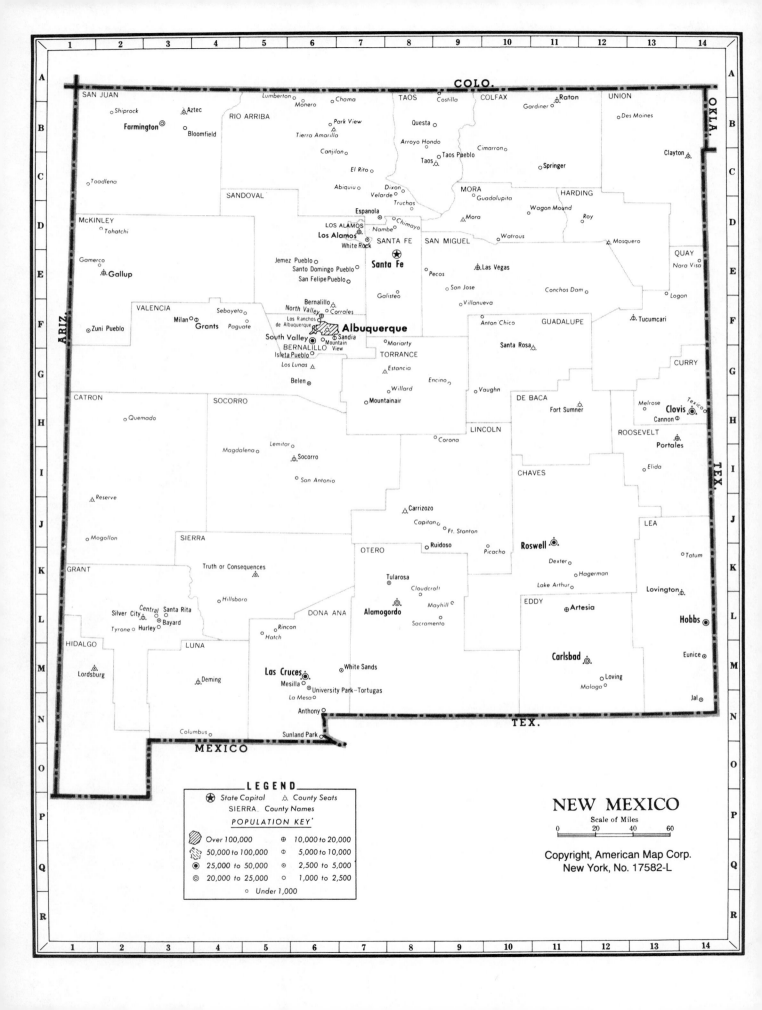

NEW MEXICO

Scale of Miles

0   20   40   60

Copyright, American Map Corp.
New York, No. 17582-L

LEGEND

⊛ State Capital   ⊙ County Seats
SIERRA   County Names

POPULATION KEY

Over 100,000   ⊕ 10,000 to 20,000
50,000 to 100,000   ⊕ 5,000 to 10,000
⊙ 25,000 to 50,000   ⊙ 2,500 to 5,000
⊚ 20,000 to 25,000   ○ 1,000 to 2,500
                    ○ Under 1,000

NEW MEXICO

CLOVIS COMMUNITY COLLEGE *(H-14)*
417 Schepps Boulevard
Clovis, New Mexico 88101
Tel: (505) 769-2811

Description: The two-year, state supported, community college was established in 1961 as a branch of Eastern New Mexico University. It became an independent community college in Sept., 1990, and is accredited by the North Central Association of Colleges and Schools. The semester system is used with one summer term. Recently the college enrolled 3,230 students; a faculty of 138 gives a faculty-student ratio of 1-24.

Entrance Requirements: High school graduation; early admission, rolling admission, advanced placement and early decision plans available.

Costs Per Year: $520 tuition; $1,528 nonresident tuition.

Collegiate Environment: The college has a library containing 1,800 volumes. Virtually all students applying for admission are accepted; students are accepted at midyear.

COLLEGE OF SANTA FE *(E-8)*
1600 St. Michaels Drive
Santa Fe, New Mexico 87501
Tel: (505) 473-6131; (800) 456-2673; Admissions: (505) 473-6133;
Fax: (505) 473-6127

Description: Originally chartered in 1874 as the "College of the Christian Brothers of New Mexico," the College of Santa Fe opened at its present site in 1947. It is accredited by the North Central Association of Colleges and Schools. Although the Christian Brothers, a Catholic order dedicated to education, no longer comprise the majority of the faculty, the philosophy of caring, personalized teaching remains strong. A belief in the importance of the liberal arts to a well-rounded education is also inherent in all CSF programs, from visual and performing arts to business and science. Students of all ages with a variety of racial, religious, geographical, and cultural backgrounds are represented. The college grants the Associate, Bachelor, Master of Education, and Master of Business Administration degrees. The traditional academic year includes two semesters and two summer terms. CSF also offers 9-week evening terms and weekend seminar classes in Santa Fe and at the college's branch in Albuquerque. Enrollment includes 1,433 full-time and 46 part-time undergraduate and 120 graduate students. A faculty of 57 full-time and 66 part-time gives a faculty-student ratio of 1-12.

Entrance Requirements: High school graduation or equivalent; completion of 21 secondary units required, including 4 English, 2 lab science, 2 history, and 2 math; non-high school graduates with GED considered; early admission, early decision, midyear admission, rolling admission, delayed admission and advanced placement plans available; $25 application fee.

Costs Per Year: $11,138 tuition; $4,138 room and board; $258 student fees.

Collegiate Environment: The 98-acre campus has 51 buildings including a modern performing arts center, science building, fine art gallery, fitness center and computer center. The library contains 150,000 volumes, 10,000 microforms, 364 periodicals and a special Southwest collection. The dormitories can house up to 186 men and 186 women, and contain an honors floor, a post office, snack bar and television rooms. The middle 50% range of scores for entering freshmen were ACT 17-23 composite, SAT 950-1150 combined. Of 240 scholarships offered each year, freshmen are eligible for 85. About 75% of the current student body receives financial aid.

Community Environment: Santa Fe, the oldest state capital in the United States, is one of the country's top art markets and cultural cen-

ters. According to Conde Nast Traveler magazine, Santa Fe is one of the top tourist destinations in the world. The charm of narrow, winding streets and fascinating architecture, combined with such exciting annual events as the Indian Market and Fiestas, make Santa Fe a fun place to visit and a great place in which to live and study. Outdoors, Santa Fe has an ideal four-season climate. Recreation includes world-class skiing, white water rafting on the Rio Grande, biking, and hiking. Any time of the year, Sante Fe's sunsets are notoriously beautiful.

COLLEGE OF THE SOUTHWEST *(L-14)*
6610 Lovington Highway
Hobbs, New Mexico 88240
Tel: (505) 392-6561; (800) 530-4400; Admissions: (505) 392-6561;
Fax: (505) 392-6006

Description: College is the Southwest is an independent, private, four-year college accredited by the North Central Association of Colleges and Schools. The four-year, arts and sciences college was first organized by a small group of Baptist laymen and was formerly known as Hobbs Baptist College. The college aims to serve the people of the Permian Basin and surrounding area by providing an overall program reflecting community interests. It grants the Bachelor degree. The college operates on the semester system and offers two summer sessions. Enrollment includes 279 full-time and 157 part-time students. There are 17 full-time and 30 part-time faculty members.

Entrance Requirements: High school graduation or equivalent from an accredited high school; college transfer from an accredited college or university; traditional enrollment policy; nonhigh school graduates accepted on basis of GED; ACT or SAT scores required; 2.0 high school or college G.P.A. is required for unconditional entrance. Student must maintain 2.0 G.P.A. for continued unconditional status; rolling admissions and midyear admission plans available; June 1 application deadline; $20 application fee.

Costs Per Year: $3,900 tuition including fees; $2,500 room.

Collegiate Environment: The college campus is located on a 162-acre site five miles north of Hobbs. 8 major buildings are located on the campus and include the J.L. Burke Administration Building, Scarborough Memorial Library, J.F. Maddox Student Center, Mabee Southwest Heritage Center, Mabee Physical Fitness Center, Science Building, Bob and Adele Daniels Hall and Jane Adams Hall. The library holds over 60,859 volumes. Heritage Center is an auditorium facilty for theatrical productions. Freshmen classes begin in September, January, June and July. Approximately 91% of students applying for admission are accepted. Campus-based college funded and campus-based federal and state funded financial aid is available. College work-study programs are available. 75% of the student body receive some form of financial aid.

Community Environment: See New Mexico Junior College.

EASTERN NEW MEXICO UNIVERSITY - PORTALES CAMPUS *(H-13)*
Portales, New Mexico 88130
Tel: (505) 562-2178; (800) 367-3668; Fax: (505) 562-2566

Description: The state university opened its doors to students in 1934. It operated as a two-year college until 1940, when the third and fourth years of college were added to the program. It is accredited by the North Central Association of Colleges and Schools, the American Chemical Society, the National Association of Schools of Music and the National Council for Accreditation of Teacher Education. The university grants the Associate, Bachelor, and Master degrees. It operates on the early semester system and offers three summer sessions. A branch campus at Roswell opened in 1957. Enrollment is 2,690 full-time and 512 part-time undergraduate students, and 557 graduate students. A faculty of 224 gives a faculty-student ratio of 1-20.

Entrance Requirements: High school graduation; ACT or SAT required; non-high school graduates at least 19 years of age may be admitted by examination; early admission, rolling admssion, and advanced placement plans available. $15 application fee.

Costs Per Year: $1,521 tuition; $5,589 out-of-state; $2,811 room and board; $500 student fees.

Collegiate Environment: The 400-acre campus is on the extreme eastern side of the state. The 32 buildings include a highly functional, modern library containing 420,000 volumes. The university operates a preschool, and the child development and psychology classes utilize this for observation purposes. There are living accommodations for 750 men and 745 women. An optional Army ROTC program is offered, and there is a special summer program for incoming freshmen who wish special assistance in preparing for a successful college career. About 95% of students applying for admission meet the requirements and are accepted. The average scores for the entering freshmen class were ACT 21 composite, SAT 860 combined. About 75% of the current student body graduated in the top half of the high school class, 35% in the top quarter, and 15% in the highest tenth. Nearly 60% of the previous freshman class returned to this campus for the second year. 85% of the undergraduates receive some form of financial aid.

Community Environment: Portales is a central eastern agricultural community with varied crops including peanuts, cotton, wheat, and grain sorghums. The area is provided transportation by railroad and highways. Some part-time job opportunities are available for students.

EASTERN NEW MEXICO UNIVERSITY - ROSWELL CAMPUS   *(J-11)*
Box 6000
Roswell, New Mexico 88202-6000
Tel: (505) 624-7000; Fax: (505) 624-7119

Description: This two-year, state supported, junior college was established in 1957 as a branch of Eastern New Mexico University. It is accredited by the North Central Association of Colleges and Schools. It grants the Associate degree. It operates on the semester system and offers one summer term. Enrollment is 2,609 students. A faculty of 58 full-time and 157 part-time gives a faculty-student ratio of 1-22.

Entrance Requirements: High school graduation; 15-16 units completed; early admission and rolling admission plans available.

Costs Per Year: $588 tuition; $1,668 out-of-state; $1,990 room and board.

Collegiate Environment: The 241-acre campus with approximately 40 buildings has a library that contains 24,651 volumes. Dormitories accommodate 145 students. 95% of students applying for admission meet the requirements and are accepted, including students at midyear. Financial aid is available.

Community Environment: See New Mexico Military Institute.

NEW MEXICO HIGHLANDS UNIVERSITY   *(E-9)*
Las Vegas, New Mexico 87701
Tel: (505) 425-7511; (800) 338-6648; Admissions: (505) 454-3593; Fax: (505) 454-3511

Description: The state university was established in 1893 and is accredited by the North Central Association of Colleges and Schools and the Council on Social Work Education. It offers undergraduate and graduate work in liberal arts, science and engineering, professional fields and teacher training. Highlands offers a friendly, intimate, academic environment for a student body that reflects the cultural diversity of the region. It operates on the semester system and offers one summer session. Enrollment includes 25,000 students. A faculty of 108 gives a faculty-student ratio of 1-26.

Entrance Requirements: High school graduation or equivalent; completion of 15 units including 4 English and 2 social studies; 2.0 GPA or GED; SAT or ACT required; students not meeting all requirements may be admitted; early admission, early decision, advanced placement, delayed admission and rolling admission plans available; $15 application fee.

Costs Per Year: $1,464 tuition; $5,652 out-of-state; $2,600 room and board.

Collegiate Environment: The 270-acre campus has 38 buildings. Donnelly Library contains 250,000 volumes, 2,000 pamphlets, 1,200 periodicals, 400,000 microforms and 525 sound recordings. There are living accommodations for 572 men, 498 women, and 89 married students. About 95% of students applying for admission meet the requirements and are accepted. More than 85% of the current students receive some form of financial assistance. Midyear students are accepted, and the college welcomes a geographically diverse student body.

Community Environment: Las Vegas has grown considerably since its days as a Mormon outpost on the Santa Fe Trail. The city is in the foothills of the Sangre de Cristo Mountains and produces lumber, dairy and wool products. The area has a stimulating, dry climate with winters that are bracing but sunny. Recreational facilities nearby include hunting, fishing and skiing. Some part-time employment is available for students.

NEW MEXICO INSTITUTE OF MINING AND TECHNOLOGY   *(I-6)*
Campus Station
Socorro, New Mexico 87801
Tel: (505) 835-5424; (800) 428-8324; Fax: (505) 835-5958

Description: This state school, founded in 1889, has 4 divisions: the College, the State Bureau of Mines and Mineral Resources, the Petroleum Recovery Research Center and the Research and Development Division. It is accredited by the North Central Association of Colleges and Schools, American Chemical Society and the Accreditation Board for Engineering and Technology. It operates on the semester system and offers one summer session. Enrollment is 1,033 men and 613 women. There are 976 full-time and 423 part-time undergraduates, and 256 graduate students. A faculty of 101 full-time, 5 part-time and 19 in the Continuing Education programs gives a faculty-student ratio of 1-13.

Entrance Requirements: Accredited high school graduation; completion of 15 units including 4 English, 3 mathematics, 2 science with labs, and 3 social science; ACT required; GRE required for graduate school; non-degree candidates may be admitted as special students; students not meeting all requirements may be granted provisional admission; early admission, early decision, midyear admission, rolling admission, delayed admission and advanced placement plans available; $15 application fee.

Costs Per Year: $1,302 tuition; $5,376 out-of-state; $3,214 room and board; $556 student fees; $1,100 average additional expenses.

Collegiate Environment: The 320-acre campus has 27 major instructional buildings. The Langmuir Laboratory in the nearby Magdalena Mountains provides facilities for research on thunderstorms and other atmospheric phenomena. The National Radio Astronomy Observatory manages the VLA, an array of telescopes located 60 miles west of Socorro. The offices for the observatory are located on campus.The library contains 242,500 volumes, most of which are pertinent to the fields of physical science, math, engineering, and natural resources. Living accommodations for 514 single students and 36 families are provided. Opportunities for part-time employment on the Tech campus are excellent. About 522 scholarships are awarded each year on the basis of high scholastic achievement, 191 of which are for freshmen. About 88% of the current enrollment receives some form of financial assistance. Over 65% of the previous freshman class returned to this campus for the second year. Average ACT score of the freshman class was 25.5. About 25% of the senior class continued on to graduate school.

Community Environment: Located 75 miles south of Albuquerque, Socorro (Spanish meaning "help") is in the valley of the Rio Grande. Socorro is the county seat of Socorro County and relies primarily on a service economy and serves a trade territory encompassing both Socorro and Catron Counties. The town draws trade and population from those who work at Stallion Site, on the northern end of the White Sands Missile Range; and at the Very Large Array (VLA), the largest radio telescope complex in the world. The VLA is located on the San Augustin Plains, about 50 miles west of Socorro. The Tech campus provides facilities for golf, tennis and swimming. The surrounding area provides mountain biking, hiking and fishing. The town also supports an improving public school system, a general hospital and 14 churches.

NEW MEXICO JUNIOR COLLEGE *(L-14)*
5317 Lovington Highway
Hobbs, New Mexico 88240
Tel: (505) 392-4510; (800) 657-6260; Fax: (505) 592-2526

Description: The publicly supported, two-year, junior college was founded in 1965. It is accredited by the North Central Association of Colleges and Schools. It operates on the early semester system and offers two 5-week summer sessions. Transfer, career and continuing education programs are available. Enrollment is 1,186 full-time and 1,643 part-time students. A faculty of 59 full-time and 51 part-time gives a faculty-student ratio of 1-26.

Entrance Requirements: Open enrollment policy; non-high school graduates 19 years of age may be admitted on probationary basis; early admission, early decision, delayed admission, midyear admission and rolling admission plans available.

Costs Per Year: $456 tuition district resident; $720 out-of-district; $840 out-of-state; $30 student fees.

Collegiate Environment: The 50-acre campus is located 4 miles north of Hobbs, on State Highway 18. There are 14 buildings including the library, which contains 110,100 volumes, 250 periodicals, 170,000 microforms and 23,000 audiovisual materials. Dormitory facilities accomodate 200 students. Almost all of the students applying for admission are accepted. Financial aid is available, and 23% of the current student body receives some form of assistance.

Community Environment: A tent city sprang up in this once little-known ranchland corner of New Mexico when oil was discovered in 1927. The settlement soon became the terminal point for oil companies, producing 90% of the state's petroleum. Farmlands in the surrounding area are irrigated by artesian wells and produce alfalfa, cotton and grain sorghums. The city has an airport and bus service for transportation. Community facilities include churches representing major denominations, a library, a hospital and various civic and fraternal organizations. Recreational areas within reasonable distance provide hunting, fishing, golf, boating and other water sports. Part-time employment is available for students.

NEW MEXICO MILITARY INSTITUTE *(J-11)*
101 W. College Blvd.
Roswell, New Mexico 88201
Tel: (505) 624-8050; (800) 421-5376; Fax: (505) 624-8058

Description: The Institute, which includes a college-preparatory high school and two-year junior college, was founded in 1891. Junior college status was acquired in 1915. It is accredited by the North Central Association of Colleges and Schools. Academic offerings are grouped into 6 divisions: Natural Science and Mathematics; Humanities; Social Sciences and Business Administration; Health, Physical Education and Recreation; Student Assistance; and Military Science. The department of Military Science stands outside the 6 divisions and is staffed by people assigned by the Department of the Army. It offers a unique two-year commissioning program. The institute operates on the semester system. Enrollment includes 500 full-time students. A faculty of 65 provides a faculty-student ratio of 1-8.

Entrance Requirements: High school graduation or equivalent; completion of 23 units including 4 English (1 English composition and speech), 3 math, 2 science, 2 foreign languages, and 3 social science; ACT required; rolling admission, early decision, delayed admission and advanced placement plans available; $60 application fee.

Costs Per Year: $700 tuition; $2,400 nonresident; $2,500 room and board; $750 student fees; $1,700 average additional expenses.

Collegiate Environment: The institute is located in the broad upland valley of the Pecos River. The main campus is about 40 acres, adjoined by larger tracts of land. The Corps of Cadets live in Hagerman Barracks and Saunders Barracks, meals are served in Bates Hall. The Toles Center, a new library facility, contains a computerized card catalog system, 68,000 volumes, 275 periodicals, microforms and photography laboratories. Dormitory facilities are available for 500 men and women. There are 5 buildings to serve the recreational needs of cadets. One of our newest facilities, the Godfrey Center, contains an Olympic-size swimming pool with sunning decks, 4 regulation basketball courts, 4 indoor racquetball courts, Nautilus equipment, Universal exercise machines and free-weight room and 12 tennis courts. NMMI also has an eighteen-hole golf course and rodeo and equestrian facilities. A controlled study atmosphere is offered in which all cadets must be in their rooms or in the library studying for two and one-half hours a night, five nights a week. 74% of the previous freshman class returned to this school for their second year. Minimum scores, ACT 17, SAT 700. About 70% of the current student body receives financial aid. 97% of the graduates go on to obtain their bachelor's degree.

Community Environment: With a population of approximately 40,000, Roswell, a Pecos Valley City, noted for its fine climate, is the distributing and supply point for a great agricultural, stockraising and oil producing territory. The summer mean temperature is 77.5 degrees, and the winter mean temperature is 41.2 degrees. The area is reached by bus, rail and air lines. Community services include several churches, a public library, a community museum and art center, a community concert association and 2 hospitals. A local park offers a swimming pool, tennis courts and golf courses.

NEW MEXICO STATE UNIVERSITY - ALAMOGORDO BRANCH *(L-8)*
North Science Drive, P.O. Box 477
Alamogordo, New Mexico 88310
Tel: (505) 434-3723

Description: The two-year, state school started classes in 1958. Enrollment includes approximately 2,007 students with a faculty of 41 full-time and 83 part-time members. The school is a branch of New Mexico State University and is accredited by the North Central Association of Colleges and Schools. The branch is not a junior college, but a lower division of the university providing freshman and sophomore class instruction of the same quality and kind as are given on the parent campus. On completion of 66 hours of work in a specified program, the student is eligible to receive the Associate degree. Students may complete the last two years of a Baccalaureate degree program at the Las Cruces campus. The semester system is employed, with two summer sessions.

Entrance Requirements: Accredited high school graduation or equivalent with completion of 15 units; open enrollment policy; early admission, early decision, rolling admissions and advanced placement plans available; $10 application fee.

Costs Per Year: $1,708 resident tuition; $4,238 nonresident; $854 fees.

Collegiate Environment: Until 1965, all classes were conducted in the evening using the facilities of the Alamogordo High School; temporary classrooms became available and were occupied for daytime use; finally construction was begun on the first phase of a new 560-acre campus in July of 1967. The average student age is 20 and the student population draws from recent high school graduates, local residents and Holloman Air Force Base Personnel. The library contains 35,000 volumes. Scholarships are available as well as loans, grants and college work-study. Almost all those who apply for admission are accepted.

Community Environment: Alamogordo is a rural-urban community with a temperate climate. The city may be reached by Highways 70 and 54, by Greyhound Bus Lines, or by airline to El Paso, Texas, which is 90 miles from Alamogordo. Community services include a public library, churches of Protestant, Catholic, and Jewish faiths, a city hospital and an Air Force Hospital at nearby Holloman Air Force Base. Service clubs such as the Veteran's, Rotary, Lions and Kiwanis are active in the immediate area. Some forms of recreation to be found here are bear hunting, elk hunting, mountain sports and winter outdoor recreation.

NEW MEXICO STATE UNIVERSITY - CARLSBAD BRANCH *(L-11)*
1500 University Drive
Carlsbad, New Mexico 88220
Tel: (505) 885-8831; Admissions: (505) 887-7533; Fax: (505) 885-4951

Description: The two-year, state school is a branch of the New Mexico State University, offering the first two years of university work to students in their home environment. It was established in 1950 and is accredited by the North Central Association of Colleges and Schools. An Associate degree is conferred after completion of 66 credit hours, and students may complete the last two years of a Baccalaureate degree program at the Las Cruces campus. The university operates on the semester system and offers two summer sessions.

Enrollment includes 480 full-time and 712 part-time undergraduates. A faculty of 26 full-time and 43 part-time gives a faculty-student ratio of 1-25.

Entrance Requirements: Accredited high school graduation or equivalent; open enrollment policy; candidates not meeting requirements may be admitted by permission of Director of Admissions; delayed admission, early admission, rolling admission, midyear admission and advanced placement plans available; $10 application fee.

Costs Per Year: $744 in-district tuition; $864 out-of-district tuition; $1,968 out-of-state tuition.

Collegiate Environment: The school moved to its own, newly completed campus in spring 1979. The library contains 21,948 volumes. Residence hall facilities are not available. 95% of applicants are accepted. There are 127 scholarships offered in a variety of categories as well as college work-study and various grant and loan programs. 35% of the students receive some form of financial aid.

Community Environment: Carlsbad profits from its neighboring rich oil and gas fields and potash mines - the largest in the country. Its summer rodeo and proximity to Carlsbad Caverns National Park support a fine tourist trade. A dam on the Pecos River has produced an excellent municipal beach with free swimming, boating and other water sports. This is a suburban area with a warm, dry climate. Transportation is provided by air and bus lines. Local community services include a library, museum, churches of all major denominations, one hospital and shopping facilities. There are 2 theatres and active civic and fraternal organizations in town. Part-time employment is available for students.

NEW MEXICO STATE UNIVERSITY - DONA ANA BRANCH COMMUNITY COLLEGE   *(M-6)*
Box 30001, Dept. 3DA
Las Cruces, New Mexico 88003
Tel: (505) 527-7500; (800) 903-7503; Admissions: (505) 527-7532; Fax: (505) 527-7515

Description: Dona Ana County was designated in 1965 as an appropriate area for a vocational-technical school on the basis of a feasibility study conducted by New Mexico State University and the State Department of Education; the Dona Ana Branch Community College of the New Mexico State University became an official entity in July 1973 and began classes that September. It is a state supported, two-year, vocational-technical school operating on the semester system with two summer sessions and is accredited by the North Central Association of Colleges and Schools. Enrollment includes 354 men, 267 women full-time, 1,224 men, 1,445 women part-time, a faculty of 52 full-time, 67 part-time provides a teacher-student ratio 1-24.

Entrance Requirements: High school graduation or GED; ACT and entrance exam required; open enrollment policy; early admission, early decision and advanced placement plans available; students are admitted at midyear; $15 application fee.

Costs Per Year: $576 tuition; $1,800 nonresident tuition; $2,386 room and board; $15 student fees.

Collegiate Environment: Classes are scheduled in existing facilities of both the University and local public schools; some programs are held at other locations, depending on the type of space and equipment needed for instruction. Dona Ana students have access to the New Mexico State University library system. Dormitory facilities are also provided by that university. Scholarships are available; 49% of the student body receives financial aid.

Community Environment: See New Mexico State University - Las Cruces

NEW MEXICO STATE UNIVERSITY - GRANTS BRANCH
(F-4)
1500 3rd Street
Grants, New Mexico 87020
Tel: (505) 287-7981; Fax: (505) 287-7992

Description: The two-year, state school is a branch of the New Mexico State University. It was established in 1968 to offer lower division work of the university to students in their home environment. The school operates on the semester system and is accredited by the North Central Association of Colleges and Schools. Enrollment is 221

full-time and 360 part-time students. A faculty of 13 full-time and 60 part-time provides a faculty-student ratio of 1-13.

Entrance Requirements: Accredited high school graduation; completion of 12 units including 4 English, 3 math, 2 science, 1 foreign language; non-high school graduates may be admitted with satisfactory completion of GED; nondegree candidates may be admitted by permission of Director of Admissions; advanced placement, early admission and rolling admissions plans available. $15 application fee.

Costs Per Year: $600 tuition; $1,824 nonresidents.

Collegiate Environment: The school library contains 28,553 volumes and numerous pamphlets, periodicals, microforms and sound recordings. There are no dormitories provided on campus. Almost all applicants are accepted, including midyear students. Financial assistance is available. 40% of students receive financial aid. The school grants an Associate degree and permits free movement of the students to all of the branch campuses. Students may complete the last two years of a Baccalaureate program at the Las Cruces campus.

Community Environment: Originally a small farming community, Grants expanded with the discovery of uranium. Now, the community is attracting private industry as well as building on its recreational opportunities and a newly dedicated national monument-El Malpais National Park. There is some limited part-time work available for students. Shopping facilities and transportation are available.

NEW MEXICO STATE UNIVERSITY - LAS CRUCES   *(M-6)*
Box 30001, NMSU
Las Cruces, New Mexico 88003
Tel: (505) 646-0111; Admissions: (505) 646-3121; Fax: (505) 646-6330

Description: New Mexico State University was founded in 1888 and was established as the land-grant university in 1889. NMSU is accredited by the North Central Association of Colleges and Secondary Schools. The university offers 77 areas of undergraduate study in 6 undergraduate colleges. The Graduate School offers 50 areas of study on the Master's level, 4 areas at the Specialist in Education level, and 20 on the Doctoral level. The school operates on the semester system and offers two summer sessions. Approximately 23,500 students attend NMSU. About 20,000 are enrolled at the Las Cruces complex, including 15,643 (7,847 men and 7,796 women) on the main campus and 3,768 on the Dona An Branch Campus. The remainder are enrolled at branch campuses in Alamogordo, Carlsbad, and Grants. Regular faculty members on the main campus number 678. The student/faculty ratio is 19-1. Army and Air Force ROTC programs are available on the main campus.

Entrance Requirements: Accredited high school graduation or equivalent with a C average or better; completion of 10 units: 4 English, 3 mathematics, 2 science, and 1 foreign language or fine arts; SAT or ACT required, ACT score of 19; non-high school graduates over 21 may be admitted with satisfactory GED completion; nondegree candidates may be admitted by permission of the Director of Admissions; $15 application fee; early admission, rolling admission, delayed admission and advanced placement plans available.

Costs Per Year: $2,088 tuition and fees; $6,966 out-of-state tuition; $3,210 room and board.

Collegiate Environment: Living accommodations provided by NMSU include 2,840 dorm rooms, 688 apartment units, and 460 family units. The library contains 929,494 volumes, 6,846 periodicals, and 1,269,869 microforms. Approximately 75% of students applying for admissions meet the requirements and are accepted. Scholarships were given to 3,526 students. The mean ACT of the current freshmen class was 21.8. Of the total freshmen class, 76% returned to this campus for their second year.

Community Environment: Las Cruces is located approximately 40 miles from the Mexican border in Dona Ana County. The city is easily reached by car, Greyhound buslines or by airlines at the El Paso International Airport. Public transportation serves the campus.

SAINT JOHN'S COLLEGE   *(E-8)*
Santa Fe, New Mexico 87501
Tel: (505) 982-3691; (800) 331-5232; Fax: (505) 989-9269

Description: The college is accredited by the North Central Association of Colleges and Schools. It has an enrollment of 411 undergraduate and 77 graduate students with a faculty of 64. St. John's College offers an almost all-required (two electives are offered) interdisciplinary program based on the Great Books of the Western intellectual heritage, which stresses connections between different branches of knowledge. The academic program is structured around seminars on major works of literature, philosophy, theology, psychology, political science, economics, and history. The work of the seminar is supported by tutorials in mathematics, language, music, and by laboratory science. Original texts are read in all classes. All classes are small discussion classes that range in size from 10 to 21 students. Student progress is monitored closely once each semester in student-teacher meetings. Final examinations are oral and individual. The college has a sister campus in Annapolis, Maryland. Students may choose to attend either or both campuses during their four years at St. John's College.

Entrance Requirements: Accredited high school graduation with rank in upper 30% of graduating class; completion of 12 units, including 4 English, 3 mathematics, 2 foreign language, 2 science, and 2 social studies; no entrance exams required of U.S. citizens; foreign students must submit TOEFL and SAT verbal scores; early admission, midyear admission, and delayed admission plans available; non-high school graduates considered.

Costs Per Year: $17,430 tuition; $5,720 room and board; $200 student fees.

Collegiate Environment: The campus of 250 acres is in the southeast corner of the city of Santa Fe. 13 buildings have been constructed, including dormitories for 370 men and women. The library collection has 52,000 volumes and 190 periodicals. The athletic program is confined to outdoor activities. There are tennis courts, and a playing field for soccer, volleyball, softball and many other activities. The Santa Fe ski basin is in operation from November to May. Approximately 86% of students applying for admission are accepted. The college serves a geographically diverse student body, and midyear students are accepted. Financial aid is available. 65% of the current student body receives financial assistance.

Community Environment: Sante Fe is the capital of New Mexico and is the oldest seat of government in the United States. Ancient narrow streets lined with buildings of distinctive architecture, tile-roofed adobe homes with shady patios, and Indian and Spanish shops create a charming atmosphere. Summer temperatures vary from 57 to 85 degrees, and winter temperatures range from 10 to 50 degrees. The city has more than 100 service clubs and organizations. The surrounding area provides many scenic routes and trails.

SAN JUAN COLLEGE   *(B-3)*
4601 College Boulevard
Farmington, New Mexico 87401
Tel: (505) 326-3311; (800) 232-6327; Admissions: (505) 599-0320;
Fax: (505) 599-0385

Description: This two-year, comprehensive, community college offers transfer-related and occupational credit programs as well as continuing education non-credit programs. The school is accredited by the North Central Association of Colleges and Schools. The school grants an Associate degree upon completion of 62 credit hours. Students may complete the last two years of a Baccalaureate degree program at any four-year accredited educational institution. The college operates on the semester system and offers one summer session. Enrollment includes 1,464 full-time and 2,790 part-time students. A faculty of 61 full-time and 168 part-time gives a faculty-student ratio of 1-16.

Entrance Requirements: Accredited high school graduation or satisfactory completion of GED; open enrollment policy; early admission, rolling admission and advanced placement plans available; non-degree candidates may be admitted by special permission; $10 application fee.

Costs Per Year: $360 tuition; $600 non-resident tuition.

Collegiate Environment: The school has a 41,166 volume library. There are no dormitories provided on campus. There are 365 scholarships available, including 102 for freshmen and 63% of the current student body receives some form of financial assistance. All applicants are accepted.

Community Environment: At the junction of the San Juan, Las Animas and La Plata Rivers, Farmington is a producer of gas and oil.

This is the starting point for two large natural gas pipelines, one leading to Los Angeles, San Diego and San Francisco, the other to the Pacific Northwest. Irrigated lands surrounding the general locale produce farm crops and grazing for livestock. The region is also noted for apple and peach raising. Some part-time employment is available for students.

UNIVERSITY OF NEW MEXICO - ALBUQUERQUE
CAMPUS   *(F-6)*
Albuquerque, New Mexico 87131
Tel: (505) 277-2446

Description: The state university is composed of nine undergraduate colleges, as well as the Graduate School, the Anderson School of Management, and the School of Law and the School of Medicine. It is accredited by the North Central Association of Colleges and Schools. The university operates three branches in Gallup, Los Alamos and Valencia as well as residence centers in Santa Fe and Los Alamos. It operates on the semester system and offers one summer session. Enrollment includes 14,524 full-time and 9,820 part-time students. A faculty of 837 provides a faculty-student ratio of 1:29.

Entrance Requirements: Accredited high school graduation with minimum C average; completion of 13 units; ACT or SAT required; nondegree candidates must be 21 years of age or have been graduated from high school, or its equivalent and been out of high school for at least one year; early decision, early admission, midyear admission, rolling admission and advanced placement plans available. $15 application fee.

Costs Per Year: $1,884 tuition; $7,115 out-of-state tuition; $3,520 room and board; $75 student fees.

Collegiate Environment: The 600-acre campus has 120 buildings. The Zimmerman Library building is frequently cited as the best example of the modified pueblo style of Southwestern architecture and is unique to this campus. Collections include 1,949,583 volumes, 16,169 periodicals, 1,199,643 microforms and 36,966 sound recordings. Military training is offered in optional Air Force, Navy and Army ROTC programs. Living accommodations are available for 1,134 men, 1,030 women and 200 families. Approximately 91% of students applying for admission met the requirements and were accepted. Financial aid is available.

Community Environment: New Mexico's largest city, Albuquerque has seen moderate to rapid growth in the past 30 years. The influx of people due to activities at Kirtland Air Force Base and at Sandia has changed the character of the city from a health and tourist resort to a bustling urban community that is a choice site for conventions. Rapid growth is occurring on the city's west side. The greater Albuquerque metropolitan area population now exceeds 1/2 million people. Though the city is growing it still benefits from the lovely mountain and desert settings nearby. Albuquerque has a temperate climate. The city is served by railroad, bus, and air lines. There are good health facilities, churches, libraries, and a zoo. Recreational facilities include swimming pools, golf, parks, and playgrounds, many theatres, several radio stations, and four TV stations. The area has active civic, fraternal and veteran's organizations. Part-time employment is available for students.

UNIVERSITY OF NEW MEXICO - GALLUP BRANCH   *(E-2)*
200 College Drive
Gallup, New Mexico 87301
Tel: (505) 722-7221

Description: This branch of the University of New Mexico was founded in 1968 as a residence credit extension center where students from McKinley County could take lower division courses in University programs and then transfer to the main campus in Albuquerque to complete the Baccalaureate programs. In 1974, University of New Mexico, Gallup Branch added certificate and applied science degrees until the total number of Associates & Certificates has reached today's high of 44. The semester system is used. The school is accredited by the North Central Association of Colleges and Schools. Enrollment is approximately 2,090 students with a faculty of 117.

Entrance Requirements: Degree candidates must have accredited high school graduation with minimum C average; completion of 13 units; ACT required; nondegree candidates must be 18 years of age or must have been graduated from high school; $15 application fee;

early admission, rolling admission and advanced placement plans available.

Costs Per Year: $552 tuition; $1,500 nonresident tuition.

Collegiate Environment: UNM-Gallup is situated on 76 acres of pine wooded hills and its 6.1 million dollar facility includes satellite TV, a snack bar, and game room for student use. UNM-G has also established an off-campus location in Zuni, NM. 100% of students applying for admission are accepted. For varying programs midyear students may be enrolled. Financial aid is available. Freshman classes begin in August and January. The library holds 28,000 volumes.

Community Environment: In a valley bordered by fantastic red cliffs, Gallup is a center for Southwest Indian trading. The Navajo Indian Reservation, northwest of the city, contains many well-preserved prehistoric ruins. The Zuni tribe practice their ancient traditions in their pueblo, 39 miles south. Part-time employment for students is limited. Transportaion is provided by bus line.

UNIVERSITY OF NEW MEXICO - LOS ALAMOS
GRADUATE CENTER   *(D-7)*
4000 University Drive
Los Alamos, New Mexico 87544
Tel: (505) 662-5919

Description: The Center is an off-campus graduate center of the University of New Mexico. It is accredited by the North Central Association of Colleges and Schools. Through this center, the University of New Mexico and the Los Alamos National Laboratory, operated by the University of California, cooperate in the advanced training of graduate students specializing in science and engineering. Under these arrangements it is possible for a properly qualified doctoral candidate to carry on research for a dissertation at the Los Alamos National Laboratory for a period of twelve months. It operates on the semester system and offers two summer sessions. Enrollment is 225 graduate students. A faculty of 25 gives a faculty-student ratio of 1-9. Some lower division, undergraduate courses are offered primarily in response to local demand, and a list of the courses offered in a particular semester should be obtained from the Center Director.

Entrance Requirements: Graduate: $1,295 ($86.35/credit) resident tuition; $4,580.25 ($305/credit) nonresident.

Costs Per Year: $69/credit hour for residents; $245/credit hour non-residents.

Collegiate Environment: Some classes are conducted in afternoon and evening sessions. Adjunct faculty are from the staff of the Los Alamos National Laboratory and the University of New Mexico. Approximately 30 courses per semester are televised live from the Albuquerque Campus to Los Alamos; in return, courses are transmitted back to the ITV network from the Graduate Center.

Community Environment: Because of its remote location on the Pajarito Plateau, the Los Alamos Boys Ranch School was selected by the Federal Government in 1942 as a site for secret research. It is today still an isolated community with a high educational level. Many residents work at Los Alamos National Laboratory.

WESTERN NEW MEXICO UNIVERSITY   *(L-2)*
1000 College Avenue
Silver City, New Mexico 88061
Tel: (505) 538-6106; (800) 222-9668 all US; Admissions: (800) 872-9668 in NM; Fax: (505) 538-6155

Description: Western New Mexico is a state university accredited by the North Central Association of Colleges and Schools. In 1893 an appropriation was made to erect a building for a normal school. The first classes were held in 1894, and the first building was dedicated in 1896. The school has grown into a multi-purpose university with programs in arts and sciences, teacher education, business administration, and provides preprofessional programs, one- and two-year terminal programs and graduate education. The university operates on the semester system and offers two summer sessions. Enrollment includes 1,850 full-time and 750 part-time students. A faculty of 90 full-time and 50 part-time gives a faculty-student ratio of 1-19.

Entrance Requirements: High school graduation or equivalent; recommended completion of 9 units including 3 English, 2 mathematics, 2 science, 2 social science; ACT required; candidates not meeting all requirements may be admitted on conditional basis; nondegree candidates over 21 may be admitted as special students; early admission, early decision, midyear admission, rolling admission and advanced placement plans available; $10 application fee.

Costs Per Year: $1,450 state resident tuition; $4,384 nonresident tuition; $1,990 room and board.

Collegiate Environment: The 84-acre campus has 25 buildings including the library containing 404,000 volumes, 1,000 periodicals, 280,000 microforms and numerous audiovisual materials. Living accommodations are available for 325 men, 228 women and 64 families. 95% of applicants are accepted. Of 220 sholarships, 84 are competitively available to freshmen, and 92% of the student body receives some form of financial aid.

Community Environment: Once an Apache Indian campsite and later a booming gold, silver, and zinc mining town, Silver City is a trading center for the cattle ranching and copper-mining area today. The city, located in the foothills of the mountains, has various active civic, fraternal, and veteran's organizations, and is served by commuter airline. Recreational activities include football, hunting, fishing, camping, and picnicking.

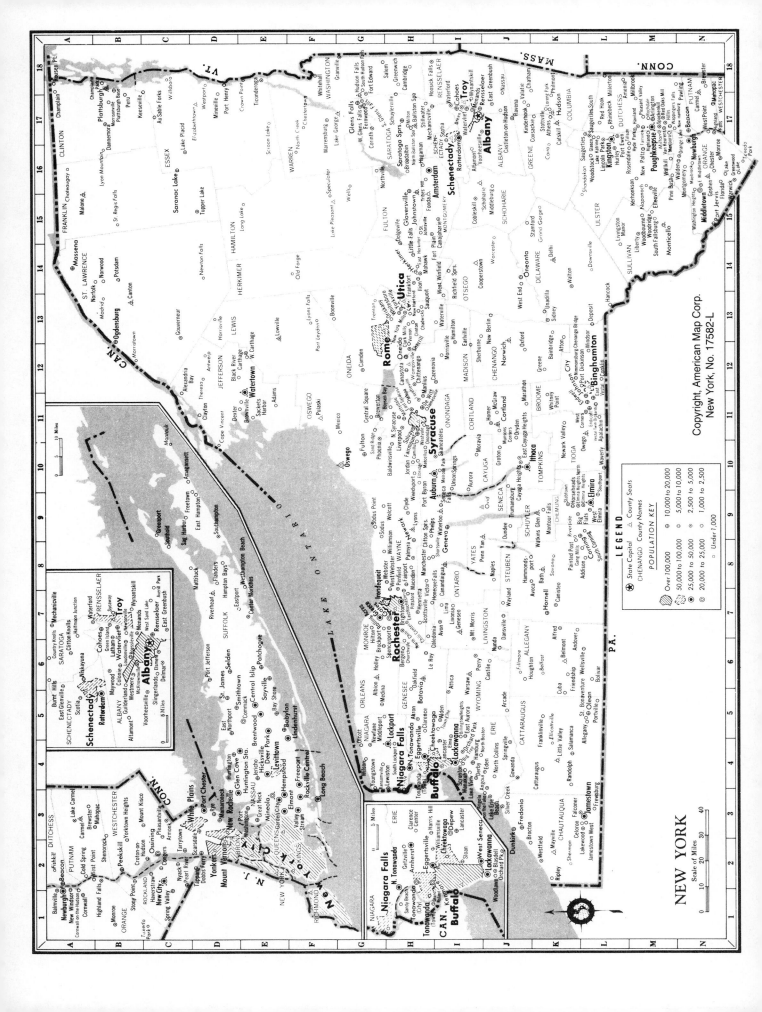

NEW YORK

NEW YORK

ADELPHI UNIVERSITY (E-3)
South Avenue
Garden City, New York 11530
Tel: (516) 877-3000; (800) 233-5744; Fax: (516) 877-3039

Description: The privately supported, coeducational university was founded in Brooklyn and chartered by the State of New York in 1896 as Adelphi College. The university was the first degree-granting liberal arts institution of higher education on Long Island. It is accredited by the Middle States Association of Colleges and Schools. Divisions of the university include the College of Arts and Sciences; School of Business Administration; School of Banking; Marion A. Buckley School of Nursing; School of Social Work; Graduate School of Arts and Sciences; School of Education; Gordon F. Derner Institute of Advanced Psychological Studies; and University College. The College of Arts and Sciences offers degrees in over 25 areas of study. The university grants undergraduate and graduate-level degrees. It operates on teh semester system and offers two summer sessions. Undergraduate class enrollment includes 1,213 men and 2,622 women. A faculty of 254 full-time and 434 part-time gives a faculty-student ratio of 1-13.

Entrance Requirements: Approved high school graduation with rank preferably in upper third of graduating class; completion of 16 units including 4 English, 3 mathematics, 2-3 foreign language, 3 science, and 4 social science; SAT or ACT required; TOEFL required for foreign students; GRE required for some graduate programs; GMAT required for graduate business programs; $35 application fee; early admission, deferred admission, rolling admission and advanced placement plans available; suggested filing date for application is March 1st for freshmen, July 1st for transfers.

Costs Per Year: $12,900 tuition and fees; $6,000 room and board.

Collegiate Environment: The university is set within a beautifully landscaped campus of 75 acres in the residential community of Garden City. 5 buildings accommodate approximately 628 men and women in dormitories; 144 students live in off-campus apartments owned by Adelphi University. The library, designed by Richard J. Neutra, was opened in 1963 and contains 478,462 volumes, 695,995 microforms, 14,134 audiovisual materials and 3,475 periodical subscriptions. Financial assistance is made available to eligible students through scholarships, financial grants-in-aid, student loans and work programs. The university grants to qualified entering students scholarships that range from $1,000 to $12,000. Approximately 84% of students applying for freshman admission are accepted. The average scores of entering freshmen were SAT 460 verbal, 510 math. Students are welcomed from all parts of the nation and midyear students are accepted.

Community Environment: Garden City, Long Island, was one of the first planned residential communities in the country. The settlement was established around the Cathedral of the Incarnation. The climate is temperate. Located near New York City, the area has good transportation connections with the adjoining metropolis. A library, churches of major denominations, and hospitals nearby all serve the city. There is some part-time employment in the immediate area. The locale has good shopping facilities and active civic, fraternal, and veteran's organizations.

ALBANY COLLEGE OF PHARMACY (I-17)
106 New Scotland Avenue
Albany, New York 12208
Tel: (518) 445-7221; Fax: (518) 445-7202

Description: The privately supported, coeducational college was founded in 1881. It is a college of Union University and operates on the semester system with two summer sessions. Graduates may become general practitioners in pharmacies located anywhere in the United States since they are eligible for State Board examination in any state. Degrees offered are the Bachelor of Science in Pharmacy and Doctor of Pharmacy. The college is a member of the American Association of Colleges of Pharmacy and is accredited by the American Council on Pharmaceutical Education and the Middle States Association of Colleges and Schools. Enrollment includes 250 men and 412 women. A faculty of 35 full-time and 100 part-time gives a faculty-student ratio of 1-19.

Entrance Requirements: Accredited high school graduation with rank in upper 50% of graduating class; completion of 17 units including 4 English, 4 mathematics, 3 science; SAT or ACT required; $25 application fee for freshmen, $35 for transfer students; rolling admission, early admission, and advanced placement plans available.

Costs Per Year: Tuition $9,000; room $2,800; books $600; personal expenses $700.

Collegiate Environment: The school building has 7 large laboratories, a library containing 40,000 volumes, gymnasium, pharmaceutical museum, and cafeteria. Dormitory facilities accomodate 100 students. A number of scholarships are awarded annually. About 85% of the students receive financial aid. About 71% of the applicants are accepted. 96% of the freshmen graduated in the top half of their high school class, 81% in the top quarter. The average scores of the entering freshmen were SAT 458 verbal, 564 math. 85% of the freshmen return to this campus for the second year.

Community Environment: See State University of New York at Albany.

ALBANY LAW SCHOOL OF UNION UNIVERSITY (I-17)
80 New Scotland Avenue
Albany, New York 12208
Tel: (518) 445-2311; Admissions: (518) 445-2326

Description: Albany Law School, founded in 1851, is one of the nation's oldest law schools. This midsize Law School is part of Union University, which includes Union College, Albany Medical College, and Albany College of Pharmacy. Albany, the capital of New York State, is an exceptional laboratory for the study of law. Clinical Legal Studies also provides opportunities for upperclassmen to work and study for credit. Students may choose to participate in the AIDS Law Clinic, Disabilities Law Clinic, Family Violence Litigation Clinic, the Litigation Clinic, or the Placement Clinic. The law school offers a four-year combined MBA/JD program with Union College, College of St. Rose and Rensselaer Polytechnic Institute and a JD/MPA with State University of New York at Albany. Enrollment is 807 full-time students. A faculty of 42 gives a faculty-student ratio of 1-19.

Entrance Requirements: Applicants for admission as candidates for the degree of Juris Doctor must hold, or have completed the requirements for, a baccalaureate or higher degree granted by a regionally-accredited institution, containing at least 45 semester hours in the liberal arts and sciences. Applicants without a baccalaureate degree are admitted only with exceptional academic credentials. In such a case, the applicant must have successfully completed a minimum of 90 semester hours in a regionly-accredited institution. Application deadline March 15; $50 application fee.

Costs Per Year: $17,150 tuition; $105 fees.

Collegiate Environment: Merit and diversity scholarships established by the Board of Trustees are available annually to entering students. The Law School building is situated on a tract of 6 acres. Schaffer Law Library was opened in 1986 and houses the computer center. The library contains more than 450,000 volumes. A coed residence hall is shared with Albany Medical College. Entering students are admitted only in September. 40% of applicants meet criteria and are accepted. Financial aid is available and 85% of students receive some form of aid.

Community Environment: Albany is a superb location for the study of law. Its unique value stems from its position since 1797 as the seat of New York government. Located here are the agencies of state government, the Legislature, executive offices, the state's highest court, the Court of Appeals and federal courts. The Capital District is also the home of 17 colleges and universities. An historic city, Albany was settled in 1624. It is comfortably-sized with a population of approximately 100,000 set in a metropolitan community of more than 800,000. Albany is located approximately 150 miles from New York City, 160 miles from Boston and 220 miles from Montreal. It is easily accessible from the New York State Thruway and has an excellent public transportation system.

ALBANY MEDICAL COLLEGE   *(I-17)*
47 New Scotland Avenue
Albany, New York 12208
Tel: (518) 262-5521

Description: Founded in 1839, the Albany Medical College is one of the oldest medical schools in the country. The college is coeducational, nondenominational, and privately supported. It is accredited by the Middle States Association of Colleges and Schools, the American Medical Association, and the Association of American Medical Colleges. The college buildings and those of the 674-bed Albany Medical Center Hospital are physically joined in one large complex that comprises Albany Medical Center. The hospital is both a community hospital for people of the immediate area and a tertiary diagnostic and treatment center for over two million residents of eastern New York and western New England. Degrees granted are M.D., M.S., Ph.D. The academic year is divided into two semesters. Medical school enrollment is 277 men and 258 women. A faculty of 493 full-time and 47 part-time provides training for both medical and graduate students.

Entrance Requirements: Bachelors degree or minimum of 3 years of study at an accredited college; completion of 1 year each (including laboratory work) of general biology or zoology, organic chemistry, inorganic chemistry and general physics; proficiency in oral and written English; Medical College Admission Test (MCAT); applications may be obtained by contacting the Association of American Medical Colleges (AMCAS); $70 application fee.

Costs Per Year: Medical School: $24,074 state resident tuition; $25,346 nonresident tuition

Collegiate Environment: Albany Medical College is a prominent part of the Albany Medical Center complex and is located in the heart of the Capital District. The Center serves a population of two million people, including adjacent areas in Western Massachusetts, southern Vermont and the Adirondack Region. Close neighbors of the Albany Medical College are the Law and Pharmacy Schools, the Veterans Administration Medical Center and the Capital District Psychiatric Center. Albany is the capital of New York State. Together with Schenectady and Troy it forms the Tri-City area with a combined population in excess of 800,000. The college library holdings include 123,328 volumes and journals, and 3,040 multi-media materials. Admission to the college is not restricted to New York state residents. The college attempts to assist all students in every feasible manner through the awarding of scholarship and loan assistance as well as through guidance in employment. Recently the college awarded 157 professional degrees including 124 Medical Doctorates, 8 Doctor of Philosophy and 25 Master of Science degrees.

Community Environment: Culturally, the area offers a wide choice of events, places and attractions. Saratoga, Tanglewood, the Empire State Plaza, the Albany Symphony and the Lake George Opera provide premiere exposure to music and dance. Community orchestras, players groups, preservation societies and art groups offer individuals an opportunity to pursue their own interests and lifestyles. There are horse races at Saratoga, battlefield monuments at Schuylerville, museums in Albany, and reminders of early American heritage throughout the region. Lakes, mountains, and rivers offer outdoors lovers unparalleled opportunities to fish, swim, camp, ski, sail, hike, drive, canoe, or just enjoy the beauties of nature.

ALFRED UNIVERSITY   *(K-7)*
26 North Main Street
Alfred, New York 14802
Tel: (607) 871-2111; (800) 541-9229; Admissions: (607) 871-2115;
Fax: (607) 871-2198

Description: Alfred University, founded in 1836 and chartered as a university in 1857, is the oldest coeducational institution in New York State, and among the oldest in the nation. It is accredited by the Middle State Association of Colleges and Secondary Schools. Courses for preparation toward teacher certification in New York State are available. The University includes the privately endowed College of Liberal Arts and Sciences, the College of Business, the College of Engineering and Professional Studies (Electrical and Mechanical Engineering), and the Graduate School; as well as the publicly funded New York State College of Ceramics (School of Ceramic Engineering and Science and the School of Art & Design). It operates on the semester system and offers two summer sessions. Enrollment includes 1,864 full-time and 111 part-time undergraduates and 388 graduate students. A faculty of 160 full-time and 33 part-time gives an undergraduate faculty-student ratio of 1-12. 86% of faculty hold Ph.D. or highest degree in their field.

Entrance Requirements: Each college has different entrance requirements; however, the following are common to all: high school graduation; completion of 16 academic units, including 4 English, 2-3 mathematics, 1-2 laboratory science, 3-4 social science; remaining credits are usually earned in a foreign language or in any of the above areas; art candidates are admitted based on their portfoloio; SAT or ACT required; $25 application fee; early admission, early decision, deferred admission, and advanced placement plans available. Deadline for application: Feb. 15th; Dec. 1st for early decision.

Costs Per Year: Tuition private sector: $16,548; NYS College of Ceramics: in-state $6,204, nonresident $8,876; room and board $5,406; fees $424.

Collegiate Environment: The 232-acre hillside campus has 54 buildings. The 2 libraries, Herrick Memorial and the Scholes Library of Ceramics, have combined holdings of 285,260 volumes, 97,901 documents, 77,000 bound periodicals and journals, 1,546 current periodical subscriptions, 150,000 slides, and 53,262 audiovisual materials. 23 residence halls offer living accommodations for 1,330 students. Most students live in coed residence halls and apartments on campus. Some upper division students live in off-campus apartments, or in fraternity and sorority houses within walking distance of campus. Alfred University has outdoor athletic fields, 7 tennis courts, and several basketball courts. McLane Physical Education Center has 2 regulation size basketball courts, a swimming pool, a fully equipped fitness center, 2 saunas, 4 handball and squash courts, 4 badminton and volleyball courts. Supplementing these facilities are an indoor track and basketball court in the adjacent Davis Gym. The Central Computer Center consists of a VAX 1785, a VAX 8530, and several VAX station systems. The cluster supports academic and research computing for batch, time sharing, and networking under the VAX/UMS operating system. There are more than 320 terminals and mircrocomputers for general use. The central facility is operational 24 hours a day, 7 days a week, free of charge. The university also provides specialized laboratory equipment and facilities, including an observatory with 8 principal telescopes; as well as professionally equipped art studios. Army ROTC is available. 70% of the student body receives some form of financial aid. On average, 70% of aid is awarded in the form of academic scholarships or grants, which do not have to be repaid. Scholarship aid ranged from $830 to $16,353; the average total aid package was about $9,200. Outright grants, loans and campus jobs are also available. Middle 50% of entering freshmen have SAT scores of 470-580V and 530-650M, which place them in the upper ranks of college students nationwide. 44% of the freshman class ranks in the top 10% of their graduating class.

Community Environment: Alfred is a small residential community situated among the foothills of the Allegheny Mountains near the Finger Lakes Region of New York. It is served by air service in nearby cities (Rochester/Elmira), and also bus service. It is the home of the Davis Memorial Carillon, which contains the oldest carillon bells in the western hemisphere. Outdoor activities including hiking, white water rafting, downhill and cross-country skiing, and horseback riding are located a short distance from campus. Numerous groups sponsor appearances by visiting professors, speakers, and artists. Student groups sponsor a number of popular entertainers and rock and folk concerts. Both a current movie series and a classics series provide weekly films. The Fosdick Nelson Gallery shows exhibits of sculpture, glass, ceramics, paintings, lithographs and photographs. Additionally, student theatre and dance productions, as well as performances by musical ensembles, are scheduled throughout the year.

BANK STREET COLLEGE OF EDUCATION   (E-2)
610 West 112th Street
New York, New York 10025
Tel: (212) 875-4404; Fax: (212) 875-4745

Description: This privately supported, coeducational graduate education college was founded in 1916 and is accredited by the Middle States Association of Colleges and Schools. It has developed as an experimental action center for the improvement of education. The college operates a school for children. Realizing that teachers, principals, supervisors, and parents are key people in improving education, the college has for several years been conducting programs designed to assist in creating change in the system. Graduate programs are designed to meet both the needs of liberal arts graduates who are prospective teachers and the needs of experienced teachers and professionals in related fields. A Master of Science degree is offered in teacher education, special education, supervision and administration, infancy education, bilingual education, museum education and computers in education. A Master of Education degree is offered in special education and in supervision and administration. It operates on the semester system and offers two summer sessions. Enrollment includes 296 full-time and 607 part-time students. A faculty of 24 full-time and 64 part-time gives a faculty-student ratio of 1-10.

Entrance Requirements: Bachelor degree from accredited college; $50 application fee; application deadline March 15; personal interview required.

Costs Per Year: $19,110 ($455/credit) plus fee for M.S. in Ed.

Collegiate Environment: The college has one building. A library containing 65,061 volumes serves all learners associated with the college: the school children, adolescents, graduate students, staff members, and parents. 48% of students receive some form of financial aid.

Community Environment: See Columbia University.

BARD COLLEGE   (L-17)
Annandale-on-Hudson, New York 12504-5000
Tel: (914) 758-7472; Fax: (914) 758-5208

Description: The privately supported, coeducational liberal arts college was founded in 1860. Originally chartered as a college of the Episcopal Church, today it enrolls students of all races and faiths. It is accredited by the Middle States Association of Colleges and Schools. The college operates on a 4-1-4 calendar system. Undergraduate full-time enrollment is 501 men and 522 women. There are 45 part-time and 145 graduate students. A faculty of 92 full-time and 43 part-time gives a faculty-student ratio of 1-10. The Bachelor of Arts degree is offered in 4 areas: Languages and Literature; Natural Sciences and Mathematics; Social Studies; and the Arts. Each of these areas constitutes a division of the college. Graduate programs are offered in Environmental Studies; Fine Arts; Curatorial Studies; and Decorative Arts. The program emphasizes intimate contact between student and teacher; a wide variety of seminars, conferences, and tutorials are offered; in consultation with faculty advisors, students have an unusual degree of freedom in shaping their own courses of studies.

Entrance Requirements: High school graduation or equivalent; completion of 16 units college-preparatory work with 4 years of English, 4 math, 4 science, 4 social sciences, and 4 foreign language recommended; early admission, early decision, midyear admission, immediate decision, and advanced placement plans available.

Costs Per Year: $19,264 tuition; $6,206 room and board; $696 student fees.

Collegiate Environment: The college has a beautiful and extensive 1,000-acre campus. Among the more than 75 buildings are the chapel, a gift of Mr. John Bard, and the Hoffman/Kellogg Library and the 1993 Stevenson addition, which contain 260,000 volumes, 745 periodicals, 8,502 microforms, and 4,000 audiovisual materials. The college has recently added a large classroom building and main auditorium, a gymnasium/swimming pool complex, and a major science wing addition. It also includes an Art Institute, a Drama/Theatre Building, a museum of late twentieth-century art, the Jerome Levy Economics Institute, the Center for Curatorial Studies, the graduate school of decorative arts located in New York City, and the Ecology Field Station. Thirty-two residence halls provide housing for 822 men and women. Financial assistance is available and about 69% of students receive some form of financial assistance. 49% of students applying for admission meet the requirements and are accepted. The college awarded 240 Bachelor degrees to recent graduating class.

Community Environment: The town is situated on the Hudson River in eastern New York. The area is accessible via Metro North and Amtrak Railroad nearby, the Taconic State Parkway, or the New York Thruway, using Exit 19 and the Kingston-Rhinecliff Bridge.

BARNARD COLLEGE   (E-2)
3009 Broadway
New York, New York 10027-6598
Tel: (212) 854-2014

Description: This privately supported, liberal arts women's college is affiliated with Columbia University and accredited by the Middle States Association of Colleges and Schools. Columbia's tenth president, Frederic A. P. Barnard first proposed that women should pursue degree studies at the university. He obtained cooperation to establish an affiliated, but independent, college for women. In 1889 the first class of Barnard College met, and 9 years later the college moved to its present site in Morningside Heights. Barnard's commitment to the liberal arts and sciences is reflected in its curriculum and the depth of scholarship expected from its students, who may view the resources of New York City as an extension of the campus. The college grants the Baccalaureate degree. Barnard is governed by its own trustees, president, faculty and dean. It's affiliation with Columbia allows student cross-registration, faculty teaching throughout the university's graduate schools, and permits students to share most resources, facilities, and extra-curricular activities. The college offers programs for the educationally disadvantaged and these students may be admitted through recommendations and high school records. The recent enrollment included 2,200 women. A faculty of 162 full-time and 121 part-time members gives a faculty-student ratio of 12-1.

Entrance Requirements: Approved high school graduation or equivalent; recommended completion of 4 units English, 3 mathematics, 4 foreign language, 2 science, 1 social science; SAT I and three SAT II subject tests or ACT required. Minimum age of 15 accepted; early admission, early decision, delayed admission, midyear admission, and advanced placement plans available. Deadline for applications is Jan. 15 freshmen. $45 application fee.

Costs Per Year: $16,854 tuition; $7,316 room and board.

Collegiate Environment: The campus occupies 4 acres of land across the street from Columbia. There are 9 buildings which include dormitories for 1,900 students. Adele Lehman Hall, a 5-story building, contains the Wollman Library with a 170,000 volume collection, and several classrooms. The library also contains 750 periodicals, 13,000 microforms and numerous audiovisual materials. Students may also use the facilities of the Columbia University libraries with 6 million volumes. 49% of the applicants are accepted. The student population is cosmopolitan in nature. 19% of the students have families within commuting distance; the others come from nearly every state in the Union and some 40 foreign countries. All represent diversity in background and training. The average scores of the entering freshman class were SAT 610 verbal, 620 math. Freshman classes begin in September but in special cases students may be admitted for January entrance. 95% of the freshman class returned for their second year. As far as possible, the college helps qualified students who have financial need.

Community Environment: See New York University.

BERNARD M. BARUCH COLLEGE OF THE CITY UNIVERSITY OF NEW YORK   (E-2)
17 Lexington Avenue
New York, New York 10010
Tel: (212) 802-2300

Description: Baruch College is the third largest among the 18 public institutions that form The City University of New York (CUNY). It is accredited by the Middle States Association of Colleges and

Schools. Undergraduate and graduate programs in business are accredited by the American Assembly of Collegiate Schools of Business. Baruch is the only college within The City University of New York that offers the Bachelor of Business Administration and the only one that enables students to pursue a Master of Business Administration and Doctor of Philosophy in business subjects. The school of Liberal and Sciences offers 15 majors leading to the Bachelor of Arts and two majors leading to the Bachelor of Science in Education. Students can also create ad hoc majors in such areas as Black and Hispanic studies, Romance languages, and premedical studies. In addition, Baruch offers opportunities to combine liberal arts and business studies in areas such as arts administration and management of musical enterprises. The School of Public Affairs, Baruch College's newest school, is initially offering graduate programs leading to the Master of Science in Education in Educational Administration and Supervision, and the Executive Master of Science in Industrial and Labor Relations. Enrollment includes 8,247 full-time, 4,328 part-time undergraduates, and 2,489 graduate students. A faculty of 455 full-time and 376 part-time gives a faculty-student ratio of 1:18. Baruch is fully accredited by the Middle States Association of Colleges and Schools. The College is also the only public institution in New York City to have all its undergraduate and graduate programs in business accredited by the American Assembly of Collegiate Schools of Business.

Entrance Requirements: To be considered for regular admission to Baruch, a student must have at least 80% high school average in academic subjects, or a minimum combined score of 900 on the Scholastic Assessment Test (SAT), or a total GED score of 300 or higher. Students who rank at or above the 66th percentile of their graduating class at the time of application will also be considered. The college recommentds a strong foundation of academic courses in high school, including 4 years of English, 4 years of social studies, 3 years of mathematics, 2 years of a foreign language, 2 years of lab science, and 1 year of performing or visual arts. Math courses have proved to be especially important. Students who have completed such a program with the highest possible grades have the greatest chance for success at Baruch. Midyear admission and advanced placement plans available; Jan. 16 application deadline for September admission. $35 freshmen application fee, $40 transfer student application fee.

Costs Per Year: $2,450 tuition for New York State students; $5,050 out-of-state tuition; fee $114.

Collegiate Environment: The first building of Baruch's new north campus on East 25th Street recently. This completely renovated 1890s classic houses a new library seating 1,500, the Computing and Technology Center (which includes and entire floor of computer labs), student and administrative offices, and a multimedia center. Students and faculty access to the college's holdings of 270,000 volumes, 1.6 million units of microform and 2,100 serials, as well as the 4.5 million volumes in the CUNY library system. The 3-station Information Technology Center has several information services on-line, including the DIALOG, Dow Jones News/Retrieval, and LEXIS/NEXIS services. The Sidney Mishkin Gallery mounts notable exhibitions of photographs, drawings, prints, and paintings. The Jean Cocteau Repertory theatre group, the Alexander String Quartet, and the Milt Hinton Jazz Workshop are in residence at the College. Athletic and recreational facilities are also available. 63% of applicants are accepted. Academic excellence is rewarded with scholarships to entering freshmen. The Abraham Rosenberg Scholarship offers $16,000 and in most cases covers the cost of tuition, books and additional expenses. Students must have minimum combined SAT scores of 1300 and a grade point average in academic subjects of 90 higher to be considered. The Baruch Scholarships, including the Isabelle and William Brunman Scholarship, the Joseph Drown Scholarship, and the Paul Odess Scholarship, offer $12,000 to approximately 50 entering freshmen annually. Students with combined SAT scores of 1100 or above and a minimum high school average in academic subjects of 87 may apply. 69% of students some form of financial aid.

Community Environment: See New York University.

BRONX COMMUNITY COLLEGE OF THE CITY UNIVERSITY OF NEW YORK   *(E-2)*
University Avenue and West 181st Street
Bronx, New York 10453
Tel: (718) 220-6450

Description: The publicly supported coeducational two-year college was founded in 1957 after a decade of effort by civic-minded citizens in Bronx County. It is accredited by the Middle States Association of Colleges and Schools. Enrollment includes 5,800 full-time and 2,200 part-time students. The college operates on the semester system with one summer session. The faculty consists of 200 full-time and 120 members.

Entrance Requirements: High school graduation or New York State Equivalency Diploma; open enrollment policy; degree candidates must take admissions and placement tests; $30 application fee; rolling admission and early admission plan available.

Costs Per Year: $2,100 tuition; $2,676 nonresidents; $56 student fees.

Collegiate Environment: Bronx Community College moved all of its operations to the site of the former NYU uptown campus at University Avenue and West 181 Street beginning with the Fall 1973 semester. The campus encompasses more than 50 acres on a bluff overlooking the Harlem River. Bronx Community College students have the same facilities that have served the university and graduate school so well. There are modern classrooms, lecture halls and laboratories; student center, cafeteria and lounges; shaded walks and a grassy mall; athletic fields, tennis courts, and a swimming pool; and advanced media and library facilities. The Hall of Fame, a national landmark, is open to the public. The Library's book collection includes 93,478 volumes, 485 periodicals and 53,281 audiovisual materials. 99% of the applicants are accepted and about 80% of the freshman return to this campus for the second year.

Community Environment: See Fordham University.

BROOKLYN COLLEGE OF THE CITY UNIVERSITY OF NEW YORK   *(F-2)*
1602 James Hall
Brooklyn, New York 11210
Tel: (718) 951-5000

Description: Brooklyn College was established in 1930 as the first coeducational liberal arts college in the City of New York. For its first 7 years, the college was housed in rented quarters in the borough's downtown business area. In 1935 ground was broken on a permanent site that provided a spacious campus in the residential Midwood section of Brooklyn. Since then, Brooklyn College--a unit of the City University of New York--has distinguished itself as one of the nation's leading public institutions of higher education. The college's Core Curriculum--10 required courses that provide a solid foundation in the liberal arts--has been praised by educators throughout the country. The college offers more than 125 majors and programs in the humanities, sciences, performing arts, social sciences, education, and pre-professional and professional studies. It is accredited by the Middle States Association Colleges and Schools, the Association of American Universities, the American Association of University Women, The National Council for Accreditation of Teacher Education, and other professional organizations. The college operates on the semester system with one summer session. Its main divisions are the College of Liberal Arts and Sciences, the School of General Studies, the Graduate division, and the Division of Adult and Community Education. Enrollment includes 7,767 full-time and 3,287 part-time undergraduates, 4,526 evening program undergraduates, and 282 graduate students. A faculty of 540 full-time and 311 part-time gives a faculty-student ratio of 1-19.

Entrance Requirements: Either graduation from an accredited secondary school or GED. It is recommended that applicants have a least 4 academic units English, 4 social studies, 3 of one foreign language, 3 mathematics, and 1 science. A minimum GPA of 80% is preferred and, if taken, a combined SAT score of 900, or a secondary school class standing in the top third. Advanced placement, early admission, midyear admission, rolling admission plans are available. Mar. 15 fall, and Nov. 1 spring application deadlines; $35 freshman application fee, $40 transfer student application fee.

Costs Per Year: $2,450 tuition for New York residents; $5,050 tuition for nonresidents; $160 student fees.

Collegiate Environment: The college occupies a 26-acre campus of broad lawns, tree-lined lanes, and red-brick Georgian-style buildings presided over by LaGuardia Hall, with its belltower topped by a white and gold cupola. The campus is located in the residential Midwood section of Brooklyn. The modern library holdings include 1,174,043 volumes, 3,833 periodicals; 16,095 audiovisual materials as well as special collections. The Brooklyn College Television Center is one of the most sophisticated teaching and production facilities of its kind in the country, and it is the only college television production facility in the New York metropolitan area that has the most advanced version of the Chyron 4200 computer graphics and animation generator. The 300-work station Computer Center, with microcomputers and terminals, is one of the largest data-processing facility in the City University system and the U.S. 60% of all applicants are accepted. Scholarships are available and 68% of the student body receives some type of financial aid.

Community Environment: The population of the Borough of Brooklyn (Kings County) is 2.2 million; that of New York City, 7.7 million. This populous county on the western end of Long Island was colonized in 1636 by the Dutch, who named it "Brueckelen." Under British domination from 1644 to 1776, the village of Brooklyn encompassed the present downtown section; the rest of the county consisted of villages that were later united as the City of Brooklyn. It was annexed by New York City in 1898, and it remains the most populous of the city's borough's. If it were still independent, Brooklyn would be the fourth largest city in the nation. Its downtown business district is experiencing a cultural and financial renaissance. There are 2,000 acres of parks and playgrounds within the area and it enjoys the educational, cultural, and recreational facilities of Greater New York City.

BROOKLYN LAW SCHOOL   *(F-2)*
250 Joralemon Street
Brooklyn, New York 11201
Tel: (718) 625-2200

Description: The privately-supported, coeducational law school was founded in 1901 as a nonprofit, educational institution under a charter granted by the Board of Regents of the State of New York. It is fully approved by the American Bar Association and the Association of American Law Schools. The school grants the Juris Doctorate degree. In conjunction with other universities in New York City, it sponsors 6 interdisciplinary programs leading to joint degrees of Juris Doctor and master in: Public Administration, Urban Planning, Law and Political Science, Planning and Lae, Business Administration, and Library and Information Science. The school operates on the semester system and offers one summer session. Enrollment includes 999 full-time and 458 part-time students of which 42% are women and 15% are minorities. A faculty of 62 full-time and 56 part-time gives a faculty-student ratio of 1-21.

Entrance Requirements: Minimum age of 18 years; first year class is admitted only in the Fall; Bachelor degree from approved college or university; letters of recommendation are recommended; LSAT required; subscription to the Law School Data Assembly Service (LSDAS); suggested application filing period is Oct. 1 & Feb. 1; $50 application fee.

Costs Per Year: $17,700 full-time tuition; $13,300 part-time tuition; including fees.

Collegiate Environment: The school's principal academic facilities are housed in two interconnected buildings, a 10 story tower, opened in 1968, and a new 11 story addition. Included are the library, student center, dining hall, seminar classrooms, conference and reception center, and faculty and student offices. The One Boerum Place building, across the street, houses clinical law offices, and administrative and student organization offices. The Henry L. Ughetta Memorial Library has one of the largest collections of legal materials in New York City. It houses over 439,000 volumes, microforms, computer programs, and cassettes, and over 1,000 periodical subscriptions to legal and law related journals. The library is an official depository for the U.S. Government Printing Office. The school owns six residence halls, offering affordable housing for a limited number of students. 32% of applicants for full-time, and 34% of applicants for part-time were accepted. The median LSAT was 159. The school offers a broad program of financial assistance including scholarships, grants, loans, and work study. About 45% of students receive financial assistance.

Community Environment: The Law School intersects the Brooklyn Heights Historic District, the oldest historic district in New York City, the Brooklyn Civic Center, and Downtown Brooklyn. Brooklyn Heights is an attractive and quaint area reminiscent of turn of the century New York. The Civic Center is comprised of the New York State Supreme and Family Courts; King's County District Attorney's Office; Borough Hall, offices of the Borough President; U.S. District

Court; U.S. Attorney's Office for the Eastern District of New York; State Appellate Division Court; City Civil and Criminal Courts; the Legal Aid Society; and numerous city, state, and federal government agency offices as well as many small law firms. A borough of New York City, Brooklyn, is across the East River from Manhattan. All the hotels, museums, restaurants, entertainments, shopping, and tourist attractions for which New York is famous are easily accessible by subway, bridges, and tunnels.

BRYANT AND STRATTON BUSINESS INSTITUTE   *(I-4)*
1028 Main Street
Buffalo, New York 14202
Tel: (716) 884-9120

Description: The privately-supported, coeducational business school was founded in 1854. In 1900, the school was registered with the newly organized New York State Board of Regents. It is accredited by the Accrediting Commission for Business Schools and awards an Associate degree or a Diploma upon completion of program. A student body of 630 and a faculty of 122 gives a faculty-student ratio of 1-14. The school year is divided into quarter terms and continues year round. The institute has 2 affiliated schools: Bryant and Stratton in Rochester, New York and Powelson Business Institute in Syracuse, New York.

Entrance Requirements: High school graduation or equivalency diploma; $25 application fee.

Costs Per Year: $4,992 tuition.

Collegiate Environment: The school is located in a residential section of Buffalo and occupies a complex of buildings on Main Street and a large two-story building on North Street. Various forms of financial assistance are available.

Community Environment: See Canisius College.

BRYANT AND STRATTON BUSINESS INSTITUTE - ALBANY   *(I-17)*
1259 Central Avenue
Albany, New York 12210
Tel: (518) 437-1802; Admissions: (518) 437-1802; Fax: (518) 437-1048

Description: Founded in 1854, the privately supported, coeducational business college is accredited by the Accrediting Commission of the Association of Independent Colleges and Schools and the New Yok State Education Department. The college has a professional, career oriented atmosphere with an emphasis on workplace knowledge required by employers. It offers one- and two-year programs leading to the Associate in Occupational Studies degree. It operates on the quarter system and offers one summer session. Enrollment includes 317 full-time and 32 part-time students. A faculty of 6 full-time and 30 part-time gives a faculty-student ratio of 1-15.

Entrance Requirements: Graduation from recognized high school, or GED; personal recommendations of guidance counselor and 2 others; academic achievement which would indicate reasonable chance of success in business curriculum; rolling admission plan available; $25 application fee.

Costs Per Year: $6,192 tuition.

Collegiate Environment: The library contains 1,450 volumes and 37 periodicals. About 97% of applicants are accepted. Financial aid is available, and 86% of students receive some form of financial assistance. The college placement department assists in finding part-time jobs for students as well as jobs for graduates.

Community Environment: The Albany campus is strategically located in the town of Colonie which affords easy access to downtown Albany, Schenectady, the New York State Thruway, and the Northway.

CANISIUS COLLEGE   *(I-4)*
2001 Main Street
Buffalo, New York 14208
Tel: (716) 888-2200; (800) 843-1517; Fax: (716) 888-2377

Description: The privately supported, coeducational, liberal arts college was founded in 1870 by German Jesuits. Founded as a liberal arts college, it now includes a Graduate Division, a School of Business Administration, a school of Education, and an Evening Division of Continuing Studies, in addition to the College of Arts and Sciences. The college is accredited by the Middle States Association of Colleges and Schools. It operates on the semester system with 3 summer terms. Enrollment includes 1,598 men and 1,329 women full-time, 189 men and 207 women part-time and 600 men and 866 women graduate students. A faculty of 200 full-time and 173 part-time gives a faculty-student ratio of 1-17. Degrees granted include an A.A., B.A., B.S., M.B.A., M.P.A., M.B.A.P.A., and M.S. in education.

Entrance Requirements: High school graduation or equivalent with rank in upper 60% of graduating class; completion of 16 H.S. units; SAT or ACT; GRE required for graduate programs; rolling admission, early admission, deferred admission, midyear admission, advanced placement plans available. $30 application fee.

Costs Per Year: $11,650 tuition; $5,500 room and board; $326 student fees.

Collegiate Environment: The campus of 25 acres is located close to the hub of the city but convenient to the suburban areas as well. The 16 college buildings include a library of 288,999 volumes, 1,183 periodicals, and more than 514,078 microforms and 4,388 audiovisual materials. There are housing facilities for 929 students. A Physical Education Complex contains 3 full basketball courts, 2 raquetball/handball courts, an Olympic-size swimming pool, a boxing and wrestling room, a fencing and ballet room, and a golf driving and archery room. The College recently completed a $5 million lighted, outdoor, astroturf, all-weather athletic field designed to accommodate 5 intercollegiate sports, including baseball, softball, soccer, lacrosse, and football. The college offers Army ROTC programs and special programs for the academically and financially disadvantaged students (C.O.P.E.). Qualified applicants are welcome and can be admitted at midyear. Financial aid is available and 81% of the students receive some form of aid, each package curently averaging $10,243. About 83% of the applicants are accepted. 61% of the current freshmen graduated in the top 40% of their high school class. The average SAT scores of the freshmen class were 453 verbal and 519 math.

Community Environment: The Buffalo metropolitan area of 1.2 million people offers varied cultural, athletic, and entertainment facilities. Among them are the world-famous Albright-Knox Art Gallery, renowned for its modern and contemporary collection; the Buffalo Philharmonic Orchestra, ranked in the top ten orchestras in North America, which makes its home in the acoustically excellent Kleinhans Music Hall; the Studio Arena, which offers legitimate theater; and the Buffalo Zoo, one of the leading zoos in the United States. For sports fans, there are the Buffalo Bills football team, the Buffalo Sabres hockey team, and the Buffalo Bisons baseball team. Artpark, Niagara Falls, the ski areas of western New York, and many attractions in Canada are within easy driving distance of the College. The central location of the College also provides many opportunities for students interested in community service, internships, and employment.

CAZENOVIA COLLEGE　*(I-12)*
Sullivan Street
Cazenovia, New York 13035
Tel: (315) 655-8005 x269; (800) 654-3210; Fax: (315) 655-2190

Description: The privately supported, 4-year coeducational college offers both 2- and 4-year degrees. There are 21 Associate Degree majors available. A Bachelor of Professional Studies in Retail Management, a Bachelor of Science in Applied Arts and Sciences, and a Bachelor of Fine Arts are offered. The school is accredited by the Middle States Association of Colleges and Schools. The college operates on a 12-week, 12-week, 6-week system and offers one summer session. Enrollment includes 877 full-time and 36 part-time students. A faculty of 45 full-time and 43 part-time gives a faculty-student ratio of 1-16.

Entrance Requirements: High school graduation or equivalent with rank in upper 60% of graduating class; completion of 18 1/2 units including 4 English, 2 math, 2 science, and 4 social studies; SAT or ACT not required; personal interview recommended; $25 application fee; early admission, rolling admission and delayed admission plans available.

Costs Per Year: $9,806 tuition; $5,060 room and board; $500 student fees.

Collegiate Environment: The campus is located 20 miles southeast of Syracuse, New York. The 12 college buildings include a library of 54,778 volumes, 484 periodicals, and 246 microforms, and dormitory facilities for 985. The Edwards Physical Education Center includes a 25-meter swimming pool, racquetball courts, weight room, and jacuzzi. Approximately 70% of students applying for admission are accepted. The college welcomes a geographically diverse student body and will accept midyear students. More than 70% of the previous freshman class returned to the college for the second year of studies. Financial aid is available. 91% of the student body receives financial aid, and scholarships are offered in all academic programs and all intercollegiate sports.

Community Environment: Cazenovia is a rural community of Syracuse with a population of 5,000. The climate is temperate with 4 definite seasons. The area is provided transportation via railroad, buses, and local highways. Cazenovia has a local library, churches of many denominations, motels and cabins, and various civic, fraternal and veteran's organizations. Nearby mountains provide good recreational facilities for boating, fishing, swimming, skating, and skiing.

Branch Campuses: Degree classes are offered in Corning, Syracuse, and Dryden, NY.

CITY COLLEGE OF THE CITY UNIVERSITY OF NEW YORK　*(E-2)*
Convent Avenue at 138th Street
New York, New York 10031
Tel: (212) 650-6977; Fax: (212) 650-6417

Description: City College is the oldest college in the City University system. The college is located on historic St. Nicholas Heights, within walking distance of the IRT and IND subways. Founded in 1847 by Townsend Harris, the first American minister to Japan, it is accredited by the Middle States Association of Colleges and Schools. City College is the only college in the CUNY system with a complex of professional schools. The college is composed of a College of Liberal Arts and Science, which is divided into divisions of humanities, science and social science, and 4 professional schools: the Schools of Architecture and Environmental Studies; Education; Engineering; and Nursing. The college operates on the semester system and offers one summer session. Enrollment includes 8,841 full-time and 3,219 part-time undergraduates and 3,132 graduate students. A faculty of 1,069 full-time and 609 part-time gives a faculty-student ratio of 1-15.

Entrance Requirements: Applicants who wish to be considered for admission to City College as freshman must meet one of the following criteria: have an academic average of 80 or better, graduate in the top third of their current senior class, have a combined SAT score of 900 or better, or have a GED score of 300 or higher. International applicants must also have a score of 500 or higher on the TOEFL exam in addition to the general admissions requirements. Qualified high school juniors may apply for early admission. Students with special education needs may qualify for admission to the SEEK (Search for Education, Elevation, Knowledge) program. Transfer students who wish to be considered for undergraduate status must file an Advance Standing Application. Please contact the college for additional information regarding admission as a transfer student. Application fee $350. Early admission and advanced placement plans available.

Costs Per Year: $2,450 resident; $5,050 nonresident.

Collegiate Environment: New facilities add a modern tone to the original Gothic style architecture on the 35-acre campus. The 14-story Robert E. Marshak Building houses over 200 teaching and research laboratories, a planetarium, a weather station, an electron microscope, laser facilities, and a science and engineering library. The School of Engineering, located in Steinman Hall, has over 40 research laboratories. Aaron Davis Hall contains a 750-seat proscenium theatre, a 200-seat experimental theatre, and a 75-seat studio workshop for rehearsals. Opened in 1984, the North Academic Center contains classrooms, laboratories, seminar halls, and a media center. In computer labs, 450 pc's, 75 terminals and 300 unix work stations for student use. The Morris Raphael Cohen Library in the North Academic Center houses over 1.1 million volumes, 3,664 periodicals, 669,160 microforms and 19,994 audiovisual materials and has one of the largest collections of any of the units in the City University. 71% of the students receive financial aid and 79% of all applicants are admitted.

Community Environment: The City College campus occupies 35 acres in Manhattan along Convent Avenue from 131st to 141st Streets in the area known as St. Nicholas Heights. The surrounding neighborhoods are predominately residential, although there are commercial shopping areas west of the campus along Broadway and south towards 125th Street.

CITY UNIVERSITY OF NEW YORK - ADMINISTRATION
(E-2)
101 West 31th Street
New York, New York 10001-3503
Tel: (212) 947-6000; Admissions: (212) 947-4800; Fax: (212) 244-2197

Description: The City University of New York encompasses seventeen undergraduate colleges, a graduate school, a law school, a medical school and an affiliated school of medicine. It is the largest municipal university system in the United States. Its colleges are spread throughout the five boroughs of New York City: ten 4-year (senior) colleges - Baruch, Brooklyn, City, Hunter, John Jay, Lehman, Medgar Evers, Queens, The College of Staten Island and York; six community colleges - Borough of Manhattan, Bronx, Hostos, Kingsborough, LaGuardia, and Queensborough; one technical college - New York City Technical; The Graduate School and University Center, The City University School of Law at Queens College, The City University of New York Medical School and the affiliated Mount Sinai School of Medicine. The undergraduate colleges offer over 250 associate and bachelor degree programs in the areas of liberal arts and sciences; business; health and allied sciences; public affairs and community and social services; engineering, architecture and related technologies. Prospective students are encouraged to call the Office of Admission Services for detailed information and application procedures: 101 West 31st St., New York, NY 10001, (212) 947-4800.

Entrance Requirements: The City University system has an open admission policy. Anyone with a high school diploma or GED is eligible for admission to a two-year college. Entrance to a senior college requires at least an 80 academic high school average. Certain programs at both senior and community colleges are selective, however. To advance beyond the sophomore year, students must pass Freshman Skills Assessment tests in reading, writing and mathematics. There is full articulation between two- and four-year CUNY colleges. Anyone with an associate degree is guaranteed transfer to a CUNY four-year, senior college. $35 application fee for freshmen, $40 for transfer.

Costs Per Year: Tuition $2,450, $5,050 nonresident; $90 fees.

Collegiate Environment: Few people, even native New Yorkers, appreciate the richness of tradition, charm, and character available on the campuses of The City University of New York. The range of atmospheres and academic specialities can provide an ideal situation for all types of students. The 21 colleges encompass campuses with trees and fields, remarkable combinations of classical architecture and state-of-the-art facilities, traditional settings complete with belltower and lilyponds, and a professional complex in the heart of New York.

Community Environment: The colleges of The City University of New York are located in the five boroughs of New York City. Transportation (subway and bus) services are easily accessible to each campus. Cultural and sports facilities abound. Government agencies and private industries provide diverse employment opportunities.

CITY UNIVERSITY OF NEW YORK - GRADUATE CENTER
(E-2)
33 West 42 Street
New York, New York 10036
Tel: (212) 642-1600

Description: The publicly supported, coeducational graduate division of the City University of New York is fully accredited by the Middle States Association of Colleges and Schools. The prime responsibility of the Graduate School and University Center is the offering of City University of New York's doctoral programs. The unit is essentially a consortium of institutions within City University, combining resources from various campuses to provide quality doctoral and research programs, a select number of master's programs, and a center for cooperation in university-wide undergraduate programs. The 1,600-member faculty primarily consists of scholars on the faculties of the City University senior colleges and the Graduate Center, and also includes researchers from various specialized New York City

cultural institutions. Doctoral programs in the social sciences, the humanities, mathematics and education, several non-laboratory science courses, and the administration of all City University Ph.D. programs are conducted at this location. Doctoral research work in the science areas is located on several of the City University senior college campuses and at the University's Mount Sinai School of Medicine; Some areas - business, engineering, and social welfare - are offered at a particular senior college. Recently approximately 3,800 students were enrolled in 32 doctoral programs. Programs leading to the Master of Arts in classics, comparative literature, Germanic languages and literatures, Liberal Studies, linguistics, philosophy, and political science are also given at the Graduate Center. The Graduate School and University Center also include an Office of Urban Policy and Programs; an Office of Research and University Programs which administers the CUNY Baccalaureate Program; and a number of special continuing education courses. Also located at the Graduate Center are 13 research centers and a number of institutes for advanced studies in such areas as Education, Theater Arts, European Studies, Human Environments, Jewish Studies, Speech and Hearing Sciences, Women and Society, and Musical Iconography.

Entrance Requirements: Bachelor's degree from an accredited institution whose requirements for the particular degree are equivalent to those of the City University; completion of prerequisites specified in a particular program; promise of ability to carry on research; approval by the admissions committee in the field of specialization; $35 application fee; GRE required for all programs.

Costs Per Year: $580-$3,350 tuition; $1,280-$5,850 nonresident tuition. Costs vary according to level of study. $39 student fees.

Collegiate Environment: The Graduate Center is housed in a 17-story building located in the heart of Manhattan and across the street from the vast research collection of the New York Public Library. The Graduate Center Library collection consists of over 229,000 volumes, 442,000 microfiche, 18,000 microfilm reels, 197,000 art slides and over 1,600 journals. Students may use the facilities of any of the 18 major libraries and several smaller ones operated by the City University; combined holdings of these libraries are more than 5,850,000 volumes and 30,000 periodical titles. Financial assistance is available for economically handicapped students in the form of scholarships, traineeships, fellowships and teaching assistantships.

Community Environment: See New York University.

CLARKSON UNIVERSITY   *(B-14)*
Potsdam, New York 13676
Tel: (315) 268-6479; (800) 527-6577; Fax: (315) 268-7647

Description: Clarkson is an independent, coeducational university that is organized into 6 major units: the School of Engineering, the School of Management, the School of Science, the Department of Engineering and Management (an interdisciplinary program that combines Engineering and Business), the Faculty of Liberal Studies and the Graduate School. Undergraduate programs lead to the degrees of Bachelor of Science and Bachelor of Professional Studies. A Cooperative Education Program is offered to students in all academic areas. The Graduate School offers programs leading to the degrees of Master of Science, Master of Business Administration and Doctor of Philosophy. The university also maintains a Division of Research and offers Army and Air Force ROTC programs. Clarkson is fully accredited by the Middle States Association of Colleges and Schools, the American Assembly of Collegiate Schools of Business and the Accreditation Board for Engineering and Technology. It operates on the semester system and offers two summer sessions. Enrollment includes 2,185 undergraduate and 335 graduate students. A faculty of 174 gives an undergraduate faculty-student ratio of 1-16.

Entrance Requirements: Accredited high school graduation with superior scholastic achievement; completion of 16 units including 4 English, 3-4 mathematics, and 2-3 science; SAT or ACT required; GRE required for Graduate School; $25 application fee; early decision, early admission, delayed admission, advanced placement and transfer admission plans available.

Costs Per Year: $15,960 tuition; $5,580 room and board; $323 student fees.

Collegiate Environment: The 650-acre campus is located in the St. Lawrence River Valley of northern New York. The 30 university buildings include the Center for Advanced Materials Processing, which is a new engineering and science facility; an Educational Resource Center featuring a library of 350,000 titles and microforms and 1,200 periodicals; a computer center with state-of-the-art computers to provide campus-wide academic, research and administrative services and access to national and international networks; the Cheel Campus Center, a new student center that includes a 3,000-seat arena area; and an indoor recreational center with facilities for swimming, racquetball courts, track, tennis courts, and other individual exercising rooms. Dormitory facilities accommodate 2,395 single students. Fraternities and sororities provide housing for an additional 450 men and 150 women. The university welcomes a geographically diverse student body. Midyear students are accepted. Average scores for a recent freshman class were SAT 520 verbal, 630 math. Financial aid is available, and 85%-90% of the students receive aid. Additionally, Clarkson is part of a four-college consortium that includes Clarkson, Potsdam College of Arts and Sciences, St. Lawrence University and Canton College of Technology. More than 700 students cross-register for courses each year, and over 1 million volumes of combined library holdings are readily available.

Community Environment: This is a primarily rural community with a population of 11,500. Bus and air lines serve the area. Local community services include a libray, a museum, a hospital, churches of major denominations, and several civic, fraternal, and veterans' organizations. There are part-time jobs available at the campus and with businesses in the area. Recreational activities include bowling, golfing, swimming, skiing, fishing, and theater. An annual Ice Carnival is held in February.

COLGATE ROCHESTER DIVINITY SCHOOL   *(H-7)*
1100, Goodman Street
Rochester, New York 14620
Tel: (716) 271-1320; (800) 843-6569; Fax: (716) 271-8013

Description: Privately supported, coeducational, graduate theological seminary. Colgate Rochester Divinity School, established in 1817, and Bexley Hall, founded in 1824, united their educational forces in 1968-69 and were joined by Crozer Theological Seminary in 1970. Together with the University of Rochester, with which Colgate Rochester is affiliated, and St. Bernard's Institute, students study together with their Protestant and Catholic counterparts in class and library. The combined divinity schools form the nucleus of an ecumenical center for theological studies. Accredited by the American Association of Theological Schools, it operates on the semester basis. Degrees granted include Master of Divinity, Master of Arts in Theology, Master of Arts in Pastoral Music, and Doctor of Ministry.

Entrance Requirements: Graduation from an accredited college with minimum 2.5 GPA; maturity of character and purpose; good physical health; competence essential to carrying on seminary work at a satisfactory level; $25 application fee; five personal references, letter of church support, and personal statement required.

Costs Per Year: $6,248 tuition; $3,230 room and board.

Collegiate Environment: The campus is at the southern edge of Rochester on 24 acres of green and rolling hillside. The 8 buildings of Gothic architecture contain a library of 270,000 volumes. Living accommodations are available for 32 men, 29 women, and 43 families. The divinity school welcomes a geographically diverse student body and will accept midyear students. Approximately 85% of students applying for admission are accepted. Almost all of the previous entering class returned to the school for the second year of studies. Financial aid is available for students who demonstrate need and 80% of the M.A. and M.Div. candidates receive some form of aid. Semesters begin in September and January.

Community Environment: See University of Rochester.

COLGATE UNIVERSITY   *(I-13)*
Hamilton, New York 13346
Tel: (315) 824-1000; Admissions: (315) 824-7401; Fax: (315) 824-7544

Description: This privately supported coeducational liberal arts college was founded in 1819 when the Baptist Education Society was incorporated by the State of New York, and the institution that was to become Colgate University came officially into being. Originally, the institution admitted only students preparing for the ministry. In 1928, the theological seminary merged with its Rochester counterpart to form the Colgate Rochester Divinity School, and Colgate became, as

it has been since, an independent college of the liberal arts. The university operates on the semester system. It is accredited by the Middle States Association of Colleges and Schools and professionally by the American Chemical Society. It is primarily an undergraduate college offering the B.A. degree, but has a small select graduate program leading to the Master of Arts degree. As a liberal arts college, Colgate emphasizes the growth of the intellect rather than the development of expertise in a specific skill. Enrollment includes 2,740 full-time and 35 part-time undergraduates and 20 graduate students. A faculty of 200 full-time and 73 part-time gives a faculty-student ratio of 1-10.

Entrance Requirements: Accredited high school graduation with rank in upper 20% of high school class; completion of 16 units including 4 English, 3 mathematics, 3 foreign language; 1 science, and 1 social science; SAT I and SAT II (Writing and two other subject tests) or ACT or SAT II (writing, mathematics and three other subject tests) required; GRE required for graduate programs; $50 application fee; early admission, early decision, delayed admission and advanced placement plans available.

Costs Per Year: $19,510 tuition; $5,565 room and board; $145 student fees.

Collegiate Environment: The 1,400-acre campus includes 24 university buildings as well as an observatory, the Dana Arts Center, an athletic center, playing fields, tennis courts, a golf course, and a 2,300-foot ski run and 4 ski trails. The library contains 472,757 volumes, 2,542 periodicals, 318,118 microforms and newspapers. Student housing, including dormitories, fraternities and sororities, accommodates 1,100 men and 708 women. Admission is highly selective and approximately 14% of students applying for admission can be enrolled. Approximately 84% of the current freshman class graduated in the top fifth of the high school class, and 60% ranked in the highest tenth. The middle 50% ranges of scores for the entering freshman class were SAT 550-650 verbal, 610-710 math; ACT 27-31 composite. Financial aid is available and 68% of the students receive some form of financial aid.

Community Environment: Hamilton (population 2,500) lies 30 miles south of Utica and 38 miles southeast of Syracuse, New York. Bus and airline connections are to be found in the neighboring cities. The climate is moderate. Part-time employment is available for students. The village has a library, a small museum, a movie theater, hospital, and numerous civic, fraternal and veterans' organizations. Local recreational facilities include hunting, fishing, boating, skiing, and golf.

COLLEGE OF AERONAUTICS   *(E-3)*
La Guardia Airport Station
Flushing, New York 11371
Tel: (718) 429-6600

Description: The privately supported, coeducational, technological college chartered by the University of the State of New York offers education in engineering technology. It is devoted to the education of men and women for careers in aviation, aerospace, electronics, and related industries. It is accredited by the Middle States Association of Colleges and Schools and the Accreditation Board for Engineering and Technology. The school operates on the trimester system with 2 summer sessions and enrolls 1,292 men and women. The faculty has 65 full-time and 15 part-time members. Degrees granted: Bachelor of Technology Degree, Associate in Applied Science, and Associate in Occupational Studies. Graduates of the aircraft maintenance technology course and the airframe and power plant technology course are qualified to write the examination for the Federal Aviation Administration Airframe and Powerplant Certificate.

Entrance Requirements: High school graduation with rank in upper 75% of graduating class; completion of 18 units including 4 English, 3 mathematics, 2 science, 4 social science; students not meeting all requirements may enroll in pre-technical program; SAT required for B.T. program; advanced placement, early admission, rolling admission, delayed admission and advanced placement programs available. $25 application fee.

Costs Per Year: $7,000 tuition.

Collegiate Environment: The college is housed in specially designed quarters at LaGuardia Airport. Laboratories provide the study-work situation best suited to the requirements of the particular area. The library collection of 54,000 volumes, 107,302 microforms, 400 periodicals, 824 audiovisual materials. 25,000 special reports and technical data provides information regarding the latest findings of the research and development efforts of the aviation and aerospace industries. An athletic field is available for extracurricular and sports activities. Midyear students are accepted and freshman classes begin in September, January, June and July. Financial aid is available and 80% receive some sort of financial aid. 95% of applicants accepted.

Community Environment: See Queens College of the City University of New York.

COLLEGE OF INSURANCE *(E-2)*
101 Murray Street
New York, New York 10007
Tel: (212) 962-4111; (800) 356-5146; Fax: (212) 732-5669

Description: The privately supported, coeducational college was created in 1962 when the Board of Regents of the State of New York allowed the Insurance Society of New York to establish and maintain its own college. It offers Associate, Bachelor, and Master degrees in several areas of insurance and related business studies. Both the BA and the BS programs are offered under a cooperative education degree program in the day division; the AOS, BA, BA/MBA joint degree program, and MBA are offered in the evening division. Also offered are a Diploma in Risk and Insurance, 10 professional certificate programs, home study courses, management programs, and special short courses and technical seminars. The college is accredited by the Middle States Association of Colleges and Schools. It operates on the semester system and offers two summer sessions. Enrollment is 139 full-time and 629 part-time students. There are also 189 graduate students and 2,338 evening students. A faculty of 93 gives a faculty-student ratio of 1-12.

Entrance Requirements: High school graduation with rank in upper half of graduating class; completion of 19 units including 4 English and at least 3 mathematics; for BA degree: SAT 450V and 450M, ACT 24; for BS degree: SAT 500V and 500M, ACT 24; $30 application fee; early decision, delayed admission, rolling admission, and advanced placement plans available.

Costs Per Year: $11,120 tuition for degree programs; tuition varies for other types of programs; $7,231 average room and board; $360 student fees.

Collegiate Environment: The college is located in the heart of New York's insurance and financial district, and its classrooms, library, and administrative offices are convenient to public transit facilities. The library contains 95,426 books, 400 periodicals, and pamphlets, and is recognized internationally as the largest and most comprehensive insurance library in the world. The college provides housing. Approximately 60% of students applying for admission are accepted, including midyear students. 48% of the students receive some form of financial aid.

Community Environment: See New York University.

COLLEGE OF MOUNT SAINT VINCENT *(E-2)*
6301 Riverdale Avenue
Riverdale, New York 10471
Tel: (718) 405-3200; (800) 665-2678; Admissions: (718) 405-3267; Fax: (718) 549-7945

Description: Privately supported coeducational liberal arts college was founded as an academy for women in 1847 by the Sisters of Charity of New York. The college is accredited by the Middle States Association of Colleges and Schools. It operates on the semester calendar system with January and May intersessions and 2 summer sessions. Programs of study lead to the Bachelor degree. Air Force and Army ROTC programs are available as electives. Also available is cross-registration with Manhattan College through a cooperative program. Internships, faculty-approved programs are available to juniors and seniors. Enrollment includes 776 full-time and 449 part-time undergraduates and 218 graduate students. A faculty of 69 full-time and 56 part-time gives a faculty-student ratio of 1-12.

Entrance Requirements: Accredited high school graduation or equivalent; completion of 16 units, including 4 English, 2 mathematics, 2 foreign language, 1 science, 2 social science. Special requirements: nursing and science majors: 3 units science, 3 units math; math majors: 3 units math; SAT or ACT required; rolling admission, early admission, early decision, diferred admission, midyear admission and advanced placement plans available; $25 application fee; personal interview suggested.

Costs Per Year: $11,790 tuition; $5,770 board and room; $790 fees.

Collegiate Environment: The 70-acre campus is conveniently located just within New York City limits in the residential area of Riverdale, Bronx. The 10 college buildings include a library, gymnasium, and 4 dormitory facilities for 570 men and women. The library houses 151,308 volumes, 628 periodicals, 16,335 microforms and 5,042 audiovisuals. The gymnasium contains a 60-foot swimming pool, a dance studio, a squash court, and is adjacent to tennis courts. Students from other geographical locations are welcome. No requirement for religious instruction. Approximately 77% of students applying for admission are accepted including mid-year students, and 94% of the previous freshman class return to the college for the sophomore year. Scholarshops are available and 88% of the students receive some form of financial aid.

Community Environment: See Fordham University.

COLLEGE OF NEW ROCHELLE *(D-3)*
29 Castle Place
New Rochelle, New York 10805
Tel: (914) 632-5300; Fax: (914) 654-5554

Description: Independent liberal arts with a Catholic tradition. Founded by the Ursuline Order as a college for women in 1904. A coeducational School of Nursing was established in 1976. The college operates on the semester basis with 2 summer terms and is accredited by the Middle States Association of Colleges and Schools. Undergraduate degrees offered: BA, BS, BFA, BS in Nursing. Enrollment in the undergraduate Schools of Arts and Sciences and Nursing recently included 674 full-time and 315 part-time undergraduates and 1,394 graduate students. The faculty of 55 full-time and 74 part-time gives a faculty-student ratio of 1-11. Cross registration with Iona College. Member of the Westchester Educational Social Work Consortium. The School of New Resources and the Graduate School are distinct from the 2 undergraduate schools. The School of New Resources offers an undergraduate baccalaureate degree program for the older students; the Graduate School provides professional study in Art, Communication Arts, Education, Psychology, and Nursing.

Entrance Requirements: Completed application form and $20 fee; high school transcript SAT/ACT; counselor recommendation is recommended. It is suggested that students have a "B" average and rank in the top half of their class completion of 15 academic units including 4 Eng., 3 math., 3 science, 3 social studies. Early admission, early decision, rolling admission, delayed admission, advanced placement plans available. Applications fee $20.

Costs Per Year: $12,200 tuition; $5,000 room and board; additional expenses average $400.

Collegiate Environment: The College of New Rochelle campus is an 18-acre suburban site in the city of New Rochelle in Westchester County, adjacent to Long Island Sound, near the shopping and theatre districts of lower Westchester, and a half hour from New York City. The 20 major buildings on campus include a 184,961 volume library with 1,417 periodicals, 276 microforms and 4,500 audiovisual materials, 4 dormitories which house 499 students, a dining hall complex, a sports building, 2 science buildings, and 3 main office and classroom buildings. Four residence halls can accommodate 499 women. There are 427 residents currently. A special facility attracting off-campus visitors is the Castle Gallery, located in the historic Leland Castle. Approximately 66% of applicants are accepted. The college welcomes a geiographically diverse student body and will accept midyear students. The average scores of the entering freshman class were SAT 405 verbal, 416 math; ACT 18 composite. 207 scholarships are available and 80% of the students receive some form of financial aid.

Community Environment: See Iona College.

COLLEGE OF SAINT ROSE *(I-17)*
432 Western Avenue
Albany, New York 12203
Tel: (518) 454-5111

Description: Privately supported, coeducational liberal arts college was established by the Sisters of St. Joseph of Carondelet in 1920. It now is nonsectarian in operation and is accredited by the Middle

States Association of Colleges and Schools. It operates on the semester system with 2 summer terms and programs of study lead to the Bachelor and Master degrees. Enrollment recently included 3,700 undergraduates. A faculty of 113 full-time and 100 part-time provides a faculty-student ratio of 1-15. Saint Rose belongs to the Hudson-Mohawk Association of Colleges and Universities, a 15-member cooperative which shares programs and resources, and whose students may exchange courses for credit.

Entrance Requirements: High school graduation with rank in upper 50% of graudating class; completion of 16 units; SAT or ACT, required minimum scores SAT combines 900 or ACT 20; non-high school graduates considered; early admission, early decision, delayed admission, rolling admission, advanced placement plans available; $25 application fee.

Costs Per Year: $8,420 tuition; $4,700 board and room; $110 student fees; additional expenses average $800.

Collegiate Environment: The college is located on 22 acres within 15 minutes driving distance of the state capital. The 45 college buildings include a library of 161,890 volumes, 1,012 periodicals, 88,000 microforms and recordings. Dormitory facilities are available for 600 students. The college welcomes a geographically diverse student body and will accept mid-year students. Approximately 70% of students applying for admission are accepted. Financial aid is available and approximately 85% of the current students receive some form of financial aid.

Community Environment: See State University of New York at Albany.

COLLEGE OF STATEN ISLAND OF THE CITY UNIVERSITY OF NEW YORK   *(F-1)*
2800 Victory Boulevard
Staten Island, New York 10314
Tel: (718) 982-2000; Admissions: (718) 982-2010; Fax: (718) 982-2404

Description: Publicly supported, coeducational college, this unit of the City University of New York is accredited by the Middle States Association of Colleges and Schools. The school was established in 1976 through the merger of Staten Island Community College and Richmond College. The enrollment recently was 6,574 full-time and 5,938 part-time students. Twosemesters are offered with 4 summer terms. A faculty of 743 gives a faculty-student ratio of 1-19. Programs of study lead to the Associate, Bachelor, and Master's degrees.

Entrance Requirements: Although The College of Staten Island accepts all New York State residents who have a high school diploma or GED and meet the university's health standards, applicants must have a high school average of 80 or rank in the upper one-third of their high school class to be eligible for admission to the 4-year programs. Applicants with lower averages or class ranks are eligible for admission to the 2-year programs. Accredited high school graduation or GED; open enrollment policy for state residents; delayed admission; rolling admission and advanced placement plans available; $25 application fee.

Costs Per Year: $2,200 tuition for residents of New York State; $4,800 non-resident tuition.

Collegiate Environment: Completed in 1994, the 204-acre campus provides an advanced educational environment and is the largest site for a college in New York City. Set in a park-like landscape, the campus is centrally located in the Island. Fourteen renovated neo-Georgian bulidings serve as classrooms and offices. The academic buildings are designed to house approximately 200 modern laboratories and classrooms. In this attractive learning environment, classrooms and academic offices are located in buildings that form the North and South Academic Quadrangles, connected by the Alumni Walk. The library and Campus Center serve as focal points for connecting walkways as well as for the Academic Quadrangles. The Center for the Arts faces the great lawn, a vast setting used for public ceremonies. The administration buildings also face the great lawn. The Sports and Recreation Center together with the athletic fields are located near the main entrance to the campus at 2800 Victory Boulevard.

Community Environment: The college is located in New York City, population 7,322,564, and the Bouough of Staten Island, population 378,977 The college is served by an extensive public transportation

system that makes readily available all of the cultural, recreational, and educational facilities of the country's largest urban area. The immediate area has public parks, bathing beaches, lakes, playgrounds, swimming pools, golf, tennis, boating, horseback riding, bowling, and theaters. Part-time employment is available for students.

COLUMBIA UNIVERSITY   *(E-2)*
212 Hamilton Hall
New York, New York 10027
Tel: (212) 854-2521; Fax: (212) 854-1209

Description: This privately supported university is acredited by the Middle States Association of Colleges and Schools. Columbia College and the School of Engineering and Applied Science (SEAS) are the two principal undergraduate divisions of the university. The university operates on the semester system and offers two summer sessions. Columbia College enrollment is 3,518 students (52% male, 48% female). 521 faculty members in Arts and Sciences provide a faculty-student ratio of 1-7 for Columbia College. The average class size is 25 students. SEAS enrollment is 996 students (81% male, 19% female). An SEAS faculty of 93 gives a faculty-student ratio of 1-5 in junior and senior years. Total university enrollment is 19,635 students. In addition to the undergraduate divisions, the graduate professional schools of the university are: School of Architecture, Planning and Preservation; Arts; Graduate School of Arts and Sciences; Business; Dental and Oral Surgery; Engineering and Applied Science (graduate level); International and Public Affairs; Journalism; Law; Medicine; Nursing; Public Health; Social Work; and Teachers College.

Entrance Requirements: Accredited high school graduation required for undergraduate programs; recommended college-preparatory courses include 4 English, 3-4 mathematics, 3-4 foreign language, 3-4 social sciences, and 3-4 laboratory science; SAT or ACT and 3 Achievement Tests required; Columbia College requires English Composition Achievement Test (with or without essay), and any other two; SEAS requires: English Composition (with or without essay), Math Level I or II, and Physics or Chemistry; high school transcript, written evaluation from school official, midyear report of student's first-term senior year work if possible, and two teacher recommendations required; interview and campus visit strongly recommended; entrance requirements for graduate programs vary in individual schools; GRE required for most graduate programs; early admission, early decision, delayed admission and advanced placement plans available. $45 application fee if postmarked before December 1; $60 application fee after December 1 and for transfers.

Costs Per Year: $18,624 tuition; tuition varies according to individual schools; $6,664 approximate room and board; $589 student fees; $800 estimated books and supplies.

Collegiate Environment: Columbia's physical plant of more than 75 buildings, laboratories, clinics and observatories, plus a small fleet of research ships, stretches into several suburban locations in New York State, Connecticut, and New Jersey. Almost all of the major facilities are concentrated in New York City, in and near the campus on Morningside Heights, and at a second site 50 blocks to the north, where the Columbia-Presbyterian Medical Center is located. The university library holdings include more than 6,000,000 volumes, 4,000,000 microforms, 26,000,000 manuscript items in 2,500 separate collections, maps and recordings, and 59,000 continuing serial subscriptions. Several types of accomodations are available in Columbia's residence halls, including single rooms, double rooms, suites, and apartment-style housing. The campus facilities for art, theater and film include the Kathryn Bache Miller Theatre, Schapiro Theatre Center, and Wallach Art Gallery. The Marcellus Hartley Dodge Physical Fitness Center, located on the main campus, contains extensive facilities and equipment for physical training. The Baker Field athletic complex contains Columbia's outdoor facilities, including Wien Stadium, which seat 17,000 for football; a 4,000-seat soccer stadium; a 300-seat baseball field; and an 8-lane all-weather track. 25% of freshmen who applied to Columbia College were accepted and 45% of these enrolled. Of the matriculating students, 76% graduated in the top tenth of their class, and 92% ranked in the top fifth. The middle 50% of the entering class had SAT ranges of 570-680V, 610-720M. 48% of freshman applicants to SEAS were accepted; of those matriculating, 70% graduated in the top tenth of their high school class, and 94% ranked in the top fifth. The middle 50% of the entering SEAS class had SAT ranges of 500-620V, 670-750M. More than 60% of Columbia College students and 65% of SEAS students receive some form of financial assistance.

Community Environment: Columbia's own neighborhood, Morningside Heights, is a remarkable community. It is home not only to Columbia students but also to more than half of Columbia's faculty members. A very academically oriented community, it contains a number of other educational and charitable institutions in addition to Columbia: Barnard College, Manhattan School of Music, Jewish Theological Seminary, Union Theological Seminary, Bank Street College of Education, St. Luke's-Roosevelt Hospital and many churches, including Riverside Church and the Cathedral of St. John the Divine, headquarters of the Episcopal Diocese of New York and the world's largest Gothic cathedral. Neighborhood merchants cater to student tastes, hours and budgets, and within a five-minute walk of Columbia's campus are located restaurants of many ethnic distinctions.

CONCORDIA COLLEGE   *(D-2)*
171 White Plains Road
Bronxville, New York 10708
Tel: (914) 337-9300

Description: Founded in 1881 as a Lutheran Academy, Concordia became a junior college in 1935, coeducational in 1939, and a four-year liberal arts college in 1972, retaining several of its two-year programs as well. The college is chartered by the Regents of the University of the State of New York and is accredited by the Middle States Association of Colleges and Schools. The college's Christian commitment is apparent in its orientation of learning and life to the principles of the Christian faith. The college operates semester calendar and makes frequent use of the vast resources of New York City. Enrollment includes 451 full-time men and women. The faculty includes 43 full-time and 25 part-time members. Concordia offers B.A. programs in Behavioral Sciences, Biology, Business, Education, Environmental Science, History, Interdisciplinary Studies, Math, Music, Religious Studies and Social Work as well as A.A. programs in Pretheology, Pre-deaconess, Business Administration, General Liberal Arts, Business and Medical Secretarial fields.

Entrance Requirements: Accredited high school graduation or equivalency; completion of 16 units including 4 English, 2 mathematics, 2 foreign language recommended, 1 science, 2 social science; ACT or SAT accepted; $15 application fee; early admission, early decision, rolling admission, delayed admission and advanced placement plans available.

Costs Per Year: $9,370 tuition; $4,330 board and room.

Collegiate Environment: The 30-acre campus is located about 15 miles north of the center of New York City. The 12 college buildings include a library of 40,000 volumes, 250 periodicals, 23,650 microforms and 3,150 other holdings such as films and recordings. Dormitory facilities are provided for 323 students. Students from other geographical locations are accepted as well as midyear students. Approximately 80% of students applying for admission are accepted. More than 60% of the recent freshman class graduated in the top half of their high school class, 35% in the top quarter, and 30% in the top third. Average SAT scores of the current freshman were 450 verbal. Financial assistance is available and about 82% of the students receive aid.

Community Environment: Concordia College's attractive campus is set in the small, affluent village of Bronxville, in suburban Westchester County. The village has imposing mansions and winding lanes, and it offers exceptional employment opportunities, shopping and entertainment services, and a very special setting for the college years. The village is just 28 minutes by commuter train from New York City, with its limitless cultural, educational, and recreational experiences.

COOPER UNION   *(E-2)*
41 Cooper Square
New York, New York 10003
Tel: (212) 353-4120; Fax: (212) 353-4343

Description: This privately endowed, coeducational, independent college offers tuition-free professional courses leading to certificates in art and to degrees in architecture, fine arts, graphic design, and engineering. It was established in 1859 and is accredited by the Middle

States Association Of Colleges and Schools. It operates on the semester basis. Enrollment includes 602 men and 331 women full-time, 14 men and 13 women part-time, and 104 graduate students. The faculty includes 59 full-time and 105 part-time members.

Entrance Requirements: Accredited high school graduation; completion of 16 units or equivalent required for all degree candidates; college entrance examinations and SAT I or ACT required; math and physics or chemistry SAT II required for engineering students; delayed admission, early decision and advanced placement plans available; hometest and portfolio required for art students; hometest required for Architecture students; $35 application fee.

Costs Per Year: $400 per year student fee; no tuition fees but students must furnish their own textbooks and supplies.

Collegiate Environment: Admission is highly selective; only 14% of applicants are accepted. All students receive a full-time scholarship. The school facilities include a library of 98,000 volumes.

Community Environment: See New York University.

CORNELL UNIVERSITY   *(J-10)*
410 Thurston Avenue
Ithaca, New York 14853-2488
Tel: (607) 255-2000

Description: The privately-supported, coeducational university was founded in 1865 and offered 3 programs of study to the first freshman class in 1868. These 3 segments have grown into an academic complex of 13 undergraduate and graduate schools and colleges. 4 of the colleges are operated by Cornell University under the general supervision of the New York State University Trustees. All colleges and schools are full-fledged components of the university and operate on the semester basis. They are as follows: Colleges of Architecture, Art, and Planning; Arts and Sciences; Engineering; Agriculture and Life Sciences; Human Ecology; Veterinary Medicine; N.Y.S. School of Industrial and Labor Relations; Schools of Law; Hotel Administration; Medical College (N.Y.C.); Cornell Graduate School, Graduate School of Management, and Graduate School of Medical Sciences (N.Y.C.). The university offers 3 summer terms as well as Army, Navy, and Air Force ROTC programs. The university is accredited by the Middle States Association of Colleges and Schools and by respective professional organizations.

Entrance Requirements: Accredited high school graduation and completion of 16 college-preparatory units; these must include 4 English, 3-4 math, laboratory science and social studies; ACT or SAT and up to 3 Achievement Tests required; GRE required for graduate programs; admission is competitive; $60 application fee; early admission, early decision, delayed admission and advanced placement plans available.

Costs Per Year: $17,276 tuition; $7,056 tuition and fees for New York State residents in statutory colleges; $13,306 tuition for nonresidents in statutory colleges; $5,676 room and board.

Collegiate Environment: The university's activities are mainly centered in Ithaca, New York, on a campus comprising more than 90 instructional buildings on about 740 acres. It has a medical college and graduate school of medical sciences in New York City. It operates the New York State Agricultural Experiment Station in Geneva, New York, and the Ionospheric Observatory in Puerto Rico. There are 5,468,870 volumes, 61,956 periodicals, and 5 million microforms in Cornell University's libraries; about 130,000 volumes are added each year. Living accommodations are available for 6,555 students and 331 families. Cornell students come from every state in the Union and from more than 100 foreign countries. Approximately 96% of the recent freshman graduated in the top quarter of their high school class and 80% in the highest tenth. 30% of students applying for admission are accepted. Financial aid is available for economically disadvantaged students and 70% of the recent undergraduates receive some form of aid.

Community Environment: Population 28,000. Located at the southern tip of Cayuga Lake, the city encompasses scenic, deep gorges through which flow Six Mile, Fall and Cascadilla Creeks. Ithaca is in the heart of central New York's Finger Lakes region. Good transportation is provided by bus and airlines, as well as state highways. Ithaca has 3 hospitals, various fraternal, civic and veteran's organizations, and over 30 churches representative of most major denominations. Part-time employment is available for students. Recreational facilities within the vicinity include YMCA, theatres, 3 state parks, indoor ice rink, fishing, boating, swimming, hunting, horseback riding, bowling, a pistol range, archery, museums, golf courses, and 14 public parks.

D'YOUVILLE COLLEGE   (I-4)
320 Porter Avenue
Buffalo, New York 14201
Tel: (716) 881-7600; (800) 777-3921; Fax: (716) 881-7790

Description: The privately and publicly supported, coeducational liberal arts college was founded in 1908 by the Grey Nuns of the Sacred Heart. It became the first women's college of western New York and second in foundation among Catholic women's colleges in New York State. It is accredited by the Middle States Association of Colleges and Schools. Professional programs are accredited by the American Physical Therapy Association, Committee on Allied Health Education and Accreditation, and the National League for Nursing. Enrollment includes 1,167 full-time and 259 part-time undergraduates and 399 graduate students. A faculty of 81 full-time and 47 part-time gives an undergraduate faculty-student ratio of 1-14. The college operates on the semester system and offers 3 summer terms.

Entrance Requirements: High school graduation with rank in upper half of graduating class; completion of 16 units; minimum SAT 400V, 400M or composite ACT 18 required; $20 application fee; early decision, early admission, rolling admission, delayed admission and advanced placement plans available.

Costs Per Year: $9,240 tuition; $4,470 room and board; 180 student fees.

Collegiate Environment: The 9-acre campus is ideally located on the historic West Side of Buffalo. Among the 7 buildings are the Administration Building, which houses classrooms, offices, conference rooms, and the Sacred Heart Chapel; fine arts studios, and an auditorium. The 140,000-volume library is open 80 hours a week. The library also contains 857 periodicals and 26,160 microforms. The College Center includes dining facilities. Approximately 69% of students applying for admission meet the requirements and are accepted. The college welcomes a geographically diverse student body. It has initiated a program for disadvantaged students that allows great flexibility in meeting admission requirements. Merit-based scholarships and other financial aid are available. About 90% of a recent student body received some form of assistance. Approximately 60% of the current freshmen graduated in the top half of their high school class, 20% in the top quarter, and 30% in the third quarter. Nearly 75% of the previous freshman class returned for the sophomore year. The average SAT scores of the current freshmen are 441V, 505M.

Community Environment: See Canisius College.

DAEMEN COLLEGE   (H-4)
4380 Main Street
Amherst, New York 14226
Tel: (716) 839-8225; (800) 462-7652; Fax: (716) 839-8516

Description: This privately supported, coeducational liberal art college opened in 1947. It is accredited by the Middle States Association of Colleges and Schools and professionally by the Council on Social Work Education, the National Accrediting Agency for Clinical Laboratory Sciences, the New York State Board of Accountancy, the American Physical Therapy Association, and the National League for Nursing. The college operates on the semester system and offers three summer sessions. Enrollment includes 1,288 full-time, 567 part-time undergraduates and 35 graduate students. A faculty of 75 full-time and 70 part-time gives an undergraduate faculty-student ratio of 1-13. Programs of study lead to Bachelor and Master degrees. Army ROTC is available.

Entrance Requirements: Approved high school graduation; completion of 18 units including 4 English; required math and science units vary by degree program; SAT or ACT required; advanced placement, early admission, delayed admission, early decision and rolling admission are available; $25 application fee.

Costs Per Year: $8,800 tuition; $4,600 room and board.

Collegiate Environment: The college is located in a northern suburb of Buffalo on a 39-acre campus. The college buildings include a library of 135,000 volumes and dormitory facilities for 175 men and 375 women. The college welcomes a geographically diverse student body and will accept midyear students. Financial aid is available for financially needy students and 92% of the current student body receives some form of aid.

DOMINICAN COLLEGE   (C-2)
470 Western Highway
Orangeburg, New York 10962
Tel: (914) 359-7800

Description: The privately supported, coeducational liberal arts college enrolls 463 men and 1,080 women. It operates on the semester basis with 2 summer sessions and a winter session. The college is accredited by the Board of Regents of the University of the State of New York and the Middle States Association of Colleges and Schools. Professional accreditations include the Council on Social Work Education, the National League for Nursing and the Occupational Therapy Committee on Allied Health Education as well as an accreditation by the American Medical Association. Dominican College has entered into a program of cooperation with Rockland Community College and St. Thomas Aquinas College, honoring each other's credits and exchanging library privileges. Grants B.A., B.S. in Education, B.S. in Nursing, B.S. in Business Administration, Social Work and Occupational Therapy. Army ROTC is also offered.

Entrance Requirements: Accredited high school graduation; completion of 16 units including 4 English, 2 mathematics, 2 foreign language, 2 science, 2 social science; SAT required; early decision, early admission, rolling admission, delayed admission and advanced placement plans available; personal interview recommended.

Costs Per Year: $7,140 tuition; $5,300 room and board; $290 student fees.

Collegiate Environment: The college is located in Rockland County, N.Y., 17 miles north of New York City. Approximately 75% of students applying for admission are accepted. Classes begin in September and January and midyear students are accepted. Library contains 95,000 volumes, 680 periodicals and 1,200 microforms. Financial aid is available and 45% of the student body receives some type of financial aid.

Community Environment: Orangeburg, population 53,533, is located in southeast New York, located 3 miles southwest of Nyack on the northern border of New Jersey. The area may be reached by the New York State Thruway, Exit 12, or Palisades Parkway, Exit 6E.

DOWLING COLLEGE   (E-6)
Idle Hour Boulevard
Oakdale, New York 11769
Tel: (516) 244-3030; (800) 369-5464; Admissions: (516) 369-5464; Fax: (516) 563-3927

Description: The privately-supported, coeducational liberal arts college was founded in 1959. Originally a branch of Adelphi University, it became independent in 1968. Now the college holds a charter from the University of the State of New York, and is fully accredited by the Middle States Association of Colleges and Schools. The college grants the M.S. in Education, M.B.A., B.A., B.S., and B.B.A. Also available are teacher education courses at graduate level (in cooperation with Adelphi University) and Doctoral programs in cooperation with New York University. Dowling features a B.S. in Aeronautics program, providing liberal arts subjects as well as preparation for careers in corporate aviation, air transport, and airways management. Flight and ground instruction lead to pilot's license, commercial pilot's license, and special ratings. Enrollment includes 5,362 full-time and part-time undergraduate students. A faculty of 105 full-time and 383 part-time gives a faculty-student ratio of 1-18.

Entrance Requirements: High school graduation with rank in upper one-half of graduating class; completion of 16 units including 4 English, 3 mathematics, 2 foreign language, 3 science, 3 social science. The most important criterion for entrance to this school is quality high school achievement in a college preparatory program; SAT required; personal interview; $20 application fee.

Costs Per Year: $9,660 tuition; $2,900 room; $570 fees.

Collegiate Environment: The college has a 43-acre campus located on the former William K. Vanderbilt estate in Oakdale, about 50 miles east of New York City. The library contains 161,014 volumes,

775 periodicals and 13,700 government documents. The residence hall accommodates 375 students and offers apartment-like living for those students who prefer to cook their own meals. 60% of applicants are accepted and 64% of the freshman class return for the second year. Scholarships are available and 78% of the undergraduates of financial aid.

Community Environment: Population 3,000. Oakdale is a suburban community west of Sayville with temperate climate. The area is served by the Long Island Railroad, and a main bus route to Patchogue and Freeport. There are 3 hospitals within 20 miles and a college health service. Adjoining cities furnish community services as well as recreational and cultural opportunities. Some part-time employment is available for students.

ELMIRA COLLEGE   *(L-9)*
Park Place
Elmira, New York 14901
Tel: (607) 735-1724; (800) 935-6472; Fax: (607) 735-1745

Description: The private coeducational college offers liberal arts and preprofessional undergraduate programs leading to the degrees of Bachelor of Arts and Bachelor of Science. A graduate study program is offered leading to the degree of Master of Science in Education. The college is accredited by the Middle States Association of Colleges and Secondary Schools with professional accreditation by the National League for Nursing. Formerly a college for women, it became coeducational in 1969. Enrollment includes 471 men and 650 women. A faculty of 66 gives a faculty-student ratio of 1-17. 2 summer sessions are combined with inter-term workshops. There are 2 12-week terms and 1 6-week term from about April 15 to June 1. The 6-week term at the end of the school year permits students to pursue field projects in connection with their academic studies and to engage in innovative forms of study-travel abroad, notably to the Bahamas. Elmira is a member of the College Center of the Finger Lakes, an educational consortium. Air Force and Army ROTC are available through Cornell University.

Entrance Requirements: High school graduation; selective admission is based on class rank, academic performance, essay and recommendations; an interview is strongly recommended; SAT or ACT required; transfer admission is based on previous college study; $40 application fee; early decision (deadline January 15), regular admission plan is on a rolling basis, early admission, delayed admission and advanced placement plans available.

Costs Per Year: $16,300 tuition; $5,380 room and board; $400 student fees.

Collegiate Environment: The main campus facilities include 28 major buildings on 40 acres of land in a residential section of the city. Residence hall capacity is 1,025. The Campus Center serves as the focal point for cocurricular, dining, and social activities. The Gannett-Tripp Library contains a collection of more than 377,000 volumes, 851 periodicals, 385,000 titles microfiche, and other materials. Students have the opportunity of spending their junior year at a selected foreign university. An excellent academic record and proficiency in the language of the country must be attained to qualify for the program. Under the Washington Semester Program, qualified students spend a semester studying at the School of Government and Public Administration of the American University in Washington, D.C. The Drew Semester on the United Nations is another special feature of the Elmira College program. Financial assistance is available and 70% of the students receive aid. 600 scholarships are offered. About 72% of the applicants are accepted. 78% of the current freshman class graduated in the top half of the high school class, and 52% were in the top quarter. Approximately 90% of the freshmen return to this campus for the second year.

Community Environment: Founded as a commercial and transportation center, Elmira (population 35,000) dominates the south-central region of New York State and nearby Pennsylvania as the trade, industrial, financial, and transportation hub of the southern Finger Lakes region. A large portion of Chemung County still remains rural in activity and atmosphere. Light industrial activity remains as the economic base for the county. The Elmira-Corning Airport handles flights daily for U.S. Air and other carriers. In addition, commuter service is available throuth these airlines. 3 interstate bus lines, Short Line, Trailways, and Greyhound fan out in all directions. Routes 13, 14, and 17 provide major connections to Elmira from adjacent cities.

Elmira is served by 4 AM radio stations, 3 FM stations, 3 television stations, 1 daily and 1 weekly newspaper. Cable television provides TV service from New York City, Binghamton, and Syracuse. There are 2 hospitals, approximately 60 churches, a public library, good shopping centers, and more than 200 fraternal, service, and social organizations. Recreational facilities include parks, playgrounds, golf, swimming, bowling, tennis, horseback riding, picnic areas, fishing, skiing nearby, ice skating, and theaters. Located within walking distance from campus is the Samuel Clemens Performing Arts Center.

FIVE TOWNS COLLEGE   *(E-3)*
305 N. Service Road
Dix Hills, New York 11746
Tel: (516) 424-7000; Fax: (516) 424-7006

Description: Privately supported, coeducational junior college opened in 1972. Offers the Bachelor of Music (B.M.) degree, Bachelor of Professional Studies (B.P.S.) degree, as well as Associate degrees in music, business, secretarial science and liberal arts. Enrollment includes 696 full-time and 36 part-time students. A faculty of 29 full-time and 43 part-time gives a faculty-student ratio of 1-17. The semester system is used and 1 summer session is offered.

Entrance Requirements: High school graduation or equivalent; completion of 18 units including 4 English, 3 math, and 3 social studies; $25 application fee; early admission, rolling admission, delayed admission, and advanced placement plans available.

Costs Per Year: $7,400 tuition.

Collegiate Environment: The college is located in a semiresidential area of Dix Hills. The campus library contains 24,509 titles, 375 periodicals, 45 microforms and 4,005 audiovisual materials. Financial aid is available, and 75% of the current student body receives some form of assistance.

Community Environment: See Adelphi University.

FORDHAM UNIVERSITY   *(E-2)*
East Fordham Road
Bronx, New York 10458
Tel: (718) 817-4000; (800) 367-3426; Fax: (718) 367-9404

Description: Fordham is a privately supported, independent Jesuit coeducational university. For more than 150 years, Fordham University has offered instruction in the liberal arts and select professional areas on both the undergraduate and graduate levels. Founded under Catholic auspices, the institute has benefited from the services of the Jesuits, but it is governed by a Board of Trustees serving under the New York State Board of Regents. It is accredited by the Middle States Association of Colleges and Schools and by respective professional organizations. Colleges of Fordham University: Fordham College; College of Business Administration; School of General Studies; College at Lincoln Center; Graduate School of Arts and Sciences; Graduate Schools of Education, Social Service, Law, Business Administration, and Religion and Religious Education. Programs of special interest include: Honors Programs; Student Exchange Programs; 3-2 Cooperative Engineering; 3-3 Law School; Internship for College Credit; Values Program; Public Administration; Medieval Studies; Double Major, and Study Abroad. It operates on the semester system and offers two summer sessions. Recent undergraduate enrollment included 2,470 men and 3,270 women full-time and part-time. Undergraduates are taught by 354 full-time faculty, 97% of whom hold earned doctorates. The faculty-student ratio is 1-17. There are 8,683 students in the graduate programs. The graduate faculty is 124 full-time and 237 part-time.

Entrance Requirements: Accredited high school graduation with rank in upper two-fifths of graduating class; completion of college-preparatory course with 18 units including 4 English, 3-4 mathematics, 1-2 science, 2 social science, 2 foreign language, and 6 electives; SAT or ACT required; early decision, delayed admission and advanced placement plans available; $50 application fee.

Costs Per Year: $13,925 tuition; $6,900 room and board; $300 student fees.

Collegiate Environment: The picturesque Rose Hill Campus is adjacent to the N.Y. Botanical Gardens and Bronx Zoological Park. There are 40 buildings on this campus. The Lincoln Center campus of 7 acres contains facilities for the School of Law, an undergraduate Liberal Arts College, Graduate School of Education, Graduate School of Social Service and the Graduate School of Business Administration. Fordham's other facilities include the Graduate Center at Tarrytown, New York, and the Louis Calder Conservation and Ecology Study Center at Armonk, New York. Residence halls on the Rose Hill campus can accommodate 2,508 men and women. Approximately 68% of students applying for admission meet the requirements and are accepted. About 92% of the previous freshman class returns for the sophomore year. Over 90% of the current student body graduated in the top half of the high school class, 58% in the top quarter, and 32% in the highest tenth. The average SAT scores of the current freshmen were 520 verbal, 549 math. The combined libraries contain 1,553,549 volumes, 9,968 periodicals, 1,850,575 microforms and 495 audiovisual materials. Financial assistance is available and 90% of the student body receives some form of aid. More than 60% of the students receive scholarships or grants. The university awarded 1,150 Bachelor degrees, 1,050 Master degrees, 439 Professional degrees and 114 Doctorates to a recent graduating class.

Community Environment: The Rose Hill campus is located in the the Bronx, which is 1 of the 5 boroughs of New York City and has a population of 1,425,000. It is the hub of a densely populated area including New Jersey, Westchester County, Upper New York City, Queens, Brooklyn, and Manhattan. The campus is located in a residential area adjacent to the New York Botanical Gardens and the Bronx Zoological Park. The area has good transportation facilities. There are churches of all denominations, 4 city hospitals, and excellent shopping centers within the immediate area. There are various civic, fraternal, and veterans' organizations represented. Job opportunities for students are good. All the recreational, cultural, and community services of a large metropolis are to be found there. The Lincoln Center Campus is located in mid-Manhattan in the heart of New York City, adjacent to Lincoln Center for the Performing Arts and very near the concert halls, theaters, libraries, and museums that contribute enormously to the life of the city. New York City may justly be described as an educational center, business capital, cultural center, and communications hub of international importance.

GENERAL THEOLOGICAL SEMINARY (E-2)
175 Ninth Avenue
New York, New York 10011
Tel: (212) 243-5150

Description: The privately supported, coeducational graduate theological seminary was established in 1817 and was the first institution in the Anglican Communion devoted exclusively to theological education. Instruction is offered for 4 degrees: Master of Arts, Master of Divinity, Master of Sacred Theology and Doctor of Theology. The 4-1-4 system is employed. Recent enrollment was 116 men and women. The faculty consists of 15 full-time and 5 part-time members.

Entrance Requirements: A regular student in the Master of Divinity program must be a communicant of the Protestant Episcopal Church, or a church in communion with it, must hold a Bachelor's degree from an accredited college, and will normally have been accepted by his/her Bishop as a candidate for Holy Orders. In certain circumstances special students may be admitted. Men and women properly qualified will be admitted in the Master of Arts program or as advanced degree students. Entrance exam and GRE required, early admission, early decision, rolling admission and delayed admission plans available. $35 application fee.

Costs Per Year: $8,500 tuition; $6,340 room and board; $345 fees.

Collegiate Environment: Chelsea Square is the site of the seminary. The buildings include the chapel, library, administrative offices, classrooms, and housing for faculty and students. Living accommodations for 150 are available. St. Mark's Library is a fine, modern building, completed in 1961 and enlarged in 1967, The book collection contains over 210,000 volumes with a concentration in the main theological disciplines. The gymnasium in Hoffman Hall is fitted for volleyball, basketball, and badminton and a game room provides equipment for pool. There is a tennis court in the Seminary Close. Financial assistance is available and 85% of students receive aid.

Community Environment: See New York University.

HAMILTON COLLEGE (H-13)
Clinton, New York 13323
Tel: (315) 859-4421; (800) 843-2655; Fax: (315) 859-5547

Description: The privately supported liberal arts college was chartered in 1812. Formerly a men's college, Hamilton combined with Kirkland College, a small liberal arts college for women, in 1978 and is now coeducational. Enrollment is limited by the trustees so that the college can continue to stress the quality of its education, its tradition for intellectual distinction and its concern with the individual student. Although the college is not affiliated with any religious denomination, it places great importance on the personal integrity of its students who govern themselves under a long-established honor system. The college is accredited by the Middle States Association of Colleges and Secondary Schools and professionally by The American Chemical Society. Enrollment includes 1,710 students. A faculty of 165 full-time and 27 part-time provides a faculty-student ratio of 1-10. The college grants a Bachelor of Arts degree and operates on the early semester system. A cooperative engineering education program is available with Columbia, University of Rochester, and Rensselaer Polytechnic Institute.

Entrance Requirements: High school graduation with rank in upper 20% of graduating class; the college recommends 16 units including 4 English, 3 mathematics, 3 of one foreign language, 2 science, 2 social science; early admission, early decision, delayed admission and advanced placement plans available. $50 application fee.

Costs Per Year: $17,650 tuition; $4,750 room and board.

Collegiate Environment: The college is located near the center of New York State, 9 miles from the city of Utica and 1 mile from the village of Clinton. The campus is a wooded park of about 1,200 acres. The college consists of 40 buildings. Dormitory buildings and apartment units supply accommodations for 1,445 students. The library, considered a laboratory of the liberal arts, contains 477,000 volumes, 1,600 periodicals, and 354,000 microforms and 20,000 audiovisual materials. Approximately 48% of students applying for admission are accepted. Financial assistance is available and 60% of the students receive aid.

Community Environment: Population of Clinton is 2,200; of Utica, 75,600. Clinton is a suburban community 10 miles southwest of Utica. The climate is temperate. The area is accessible via bus service; US Air; and railroad lines to and from Utica. Nearby Kirkland has a town library, 5 churches, an art center, a Chamber of Commerce, and several civic, fraternal and veteran's organizations. Hockey, skiing, camping and ice skating are popular sports in the immediate area.

HARTWICK COLLEGE (J-14)
Oneonta, New York 13820
Tel: (607) 431-4150; (800) 828-2200; Fax: (607) 431-4154

Description: Chartered by the state in 1928, with its roots in Hartwick Seminary that was founded in 1797, Hartwick College is a small, independent, coeducational liberal arts college. It grants Bachelor of Arts and Bachelor of Science degrees. Hartwick is accredited by the Middle States Association of Colleges and Schools, and is a member of the Hudson Mohawk Association of Colleges and Universities. It offers thirty traditional liberal arts majors, pre-law and pre-med programs, nursing, engineering, music, and museum studies. Enrollment includes 1,465 full-time and 59 part-time students. A faculty of 139 gives a faculty-student ratio of 1-13. The college operates on the 4-1-4 system, including a four-week January term when all students are required to explore new ideas on and off campus. Hartwick has an innovative curriculum rooted in the classic liberal arts, but steeped in the context of the global community in an information age. Curriculum XXI is organized around five major ideas and characteristics of the future for which Hartwick feels students should be prepared: continuity, interdependence, science and technology, critical thinking, and effective communication. The college offers an independent study program in which students work with a faculty committee to determine and pursue special courses of study. An array of off-campus programs, directed study, and internships are available.

Entrance Requirements: High school graduation; required completion of 15 units including 4 English, 3 mathematics, 2 foreign language, 3 science, and 4 social science; SAT or ACT required; personal interview strongly recommended; early decision and advanced placement programs are available; $35 application fee.

Costs Per Year: $17,480 tuition; $4,780 room and board; $100 student fees.

Collegiate Environment: Hartwick's 375-acre main campus is located 60 miles north of Binghamton and 65 miles west of Albany,

NY. Approximately 1,100 students are housed on campus in an array of traditional dorms, suites, or townhouses. The college has a state-of-the-art facility for art and music departments. In September 1992 a 40,000-square-foot building was opened that features classrooms, offices, and computer and audiovisual centers. The library contains more than 250,000 volumes and has an on-line card catalog and search technology. The campus is fully wired with video and computer networks. There is an observatory, and the Museums at Hartwick are a regional attraction. Approximately 78% of applicants are accepted. Financial aid is available, and 66% of the students receive some form of financial assistance. The 914-acre Pine Lake Environmental campus is the site of study and research by students and faculty in the college's environmental studies, biology, and anthropology fields. Students may opt to live in cabins at Pine Lake, 8 miles from the main campus.

Community Environment: Oneonta, population 14,000, is large enough to support industries and two colleges, and serves as a regional commerce center. Cooperstwon is 20 miles away and attracts many people annually who discover Oneonta (home of the National Soccer Hall of Fame) and its restaurants, motels, bed and breakfasts, and who use its local parks and facilities for swimming, golf, fishing, skiing and boating. Public transportation is available in town. Oneonta is on Interstate 80, a freeway that connects Albany, New York, and central-eastern Pennsylvania.

HEBREW UNION COLLEGE, JEWISH INSTITUTE OF RELIGION *(E-2)*
1 West 4th Street
New York, New York 10012
Tel: (212) 674-5300

Description: Privately-supported, coeducational religious college. In 1873, Rabbi Isaac Mayer Wise organized the Union of American Hebrew Congregations whose primary purpose was the creation and maintenance of a rabbinic school for American Reform Judaism. Then in 1875 he founded the Hebrew Union College. The 4 campuses of the college-institute are located at Cincinnati, New York, Los Angeles, and Jerusalem. The New York branch includes the graduate Rabbinic School and the undergraduate Schools of Education and of Sacred Music. The college is accredited by the Middle States Association of Colleges and Schools. The enrollment is 129 men and women. The normal Rabbinic Program for college graduates is a five-year-year course. During the five-year program the student may attain a Bachelor of Science or Hebrew Letters degree, Master of Arts or Hebrew Letters degree and a Bachelor or Master degree in Sacred Music. There is a one-year program in Israel for Rabbinic students. The semester system is used.

Entrance Requirements: High school graduation. Graduate Record Examination, Aptitude Test, psychiatric and Admissions Committee interviews, psychological testing required; $25 application fee; rolling admission plan available.

Costs Per Year: $7,000 tuition; $65 student fee.

Collegiate Environment: The school is located near Lincoln Center in a five-story building containing administrative offices, classrooms, a chapel, an auditorium, a social hall, and a library which contains 110,000 volumes. A number of courses are given at the South Orange, New Jersey and Rockville Center, New York extension centers. The school has no dormitory facilities. Financial assistance is available for economically handicapped students; 25% receive financial aid.

Community Environment: See New York University.

HERBERT H. LEHMAN COLLEGE OF THE CITY UNIVERSITY OF NEW YORK *(E-2)*
Bedford Park Blvd West
Bronx, New York 10468
Tel: (212) 960-8131; Fax: (212) 960-8935

Description: The publicly supported, coeducational liberal arts college was founded in 1931 and until 1968 was a branch of Hunter College. It operates on the semester system and offers 1 summer term. The college is accredited by the Middle States Association of Colleges and Schools and is a unit of the City University of New York. Recent enrollment numbered 2,862 men and 6,636 women. A faculty of 440 gives a faculty-student ratio of 1-13. Degrees granted include B.A., B.S., B.F.A., B.A., M.A., M.S., M.F.A.; doctoral programs are

available through the City University of New York. The divisions of the college are Humanities, Natural and Social Sciences, Nursing and Professional Studies.

Entrance Requirements: High school graduation; 80% high school average or rank in top 1/3 of class or combined score on SAT of 1000 or ACT composite of 20. GRE or GMAT required for some graduate school programs; $35 application fee for freshmen, $40 for transfers; early admission, early decision, rolling admission, delayed admission and advanced placement plans available.

Costs Per Year: Undergraduate: $2,450 ($100 per credit part-time) resident; $5,050 ($202 per credit part-time) nonresident; $114 student fees; Graduate: $3,350 resident, $5,850 nonresident; $130 student fees.

Collegiate Environment: The 37-acre campus has 12 buildings in addition to a new Athletic and Physical Education Complex, a Student Life Building, an Art Building and gallery, and a Performing Arts Center, which includes a 2,300-seat Concert hall, a computerized library, and a renovated Music Building that houses theatres and a recital hall. The library contains more than 500,000 volumes. Financial aid is available, and 80% of students receive aid.

Community Environment: See Fordham University.

HILBERT COLLEGE *(I-4)*
5200 South Park Avenue
Hamburg, New York 14075
Tel: (716) 649-7900

Description: The independent, private, coeducational four-year college offers two-year college programs leading to the degrees of Associate in Arts, Associate in Science and Associate in Applied Science; and four-year programs leading to a Bachelor of Science or a Bachelor of Arts in five majors. It operates on the semester system and offers 1 summer term. Enrollment is 500 full-time and 309 part-time students. A faculty of 55 full-time and 26 part-time gives a faculty-student ratio of 1-18. Hilbert is accredited by the Middle States Association of Colleges and Schools and professionally by the American Bar Association. It is charted by the Regents of the University of the State of New York.

Entrance Requirements: Approved high school graduation with rank in upper half of high school class; completion of 16 units including 4 English, 1 mathematics, 1 science, and 3 social science; SAT required; $20 application fee; early admission, rolling admission, delayed admission and advanced placement plans available.

Costs Per Year: $6,500 tuition; $4,400 room and board; $350 student fees.

Collegiate Environment: The 40-acre campus is located approximately 12 miles south of Buffalo. The new campus includes the academic building, the library, the central utility facility, the recreation center, the student center, and a residence hall for 110 men and women. The library contains 43,083 volumes, 217 periodicals, and 1,180 microforms. The college welcomes a geographically diverse student body and will accept midyear students. 94% of students applying for admission are accepted. Financial aid is available and scholarships are offered. About 76% of the students receive aid. Of the 54 scholarships offered, 20 are for freshmen.

Community Environment: Hamburg, population 10,000, is a suburban area adjacent to Buffalo. Within the immediate vicinity there are 18 churches, a theater, shopping center, and major civic, fraternal, and veteran's organizations. Some part-time employment is available for students in the immediate area. The Buffalo Raceway and annual Erie County Fair are here. Rich Stadium, home of the Buffalo Bills, is 5 minutes away and area ski resorts are nearby. All the cultural, community service, and recreational facilities of Buffalo are easily accessible.

HOBART AND WILLIAM SMITH COLLEGES *(I-9)*
Geneva, New York 14456
Tel: (315) 789-5500; (800) 852-2256 Hobart; Admissions: (315) 781-3622 Hobart; Fax: (315) 781-3914

Description: These privately supported, coordinate, liberal arts colleges are accredited by the Middle States Association of Colleges and Schools, the Regents of the University of the State of New York, and professionally by the American Chemical Society. They are also members of the Rochester Area Colleges Consortium. Hobart College, for men, was founded in 1822 and is the oldest college in western New York State. William Smith College, for women, was founded as a coordinate institution in 1908. Since 1941, classes have been held in common and facilities are shared by students of both colleges. The colleges offer a liberal education in the arts and sciences and grant the Baccalaureate degree. They operate on the trimester system. Combined enrollment includes 1,808 full-time and 5 part-time students. A combined faculty of 142 full-time and 31 part-time gives a faculty-student ratio of 1-13.

Entrance Requirements: High school graduation or equivalent with rank in upper 50% of graduating class; completion of 18 college-preparatory units including 4 English, 3 mathematics, 2 foreign language, 2 laboratory science, and 2 social science; SAT or ACT required; early admission, early decision, deferred admission, midyear admission and advanced placement plans available; Nov. 15 and Jan 1 early decision deadline, Feb. 15 regular decision deadline; $40 application fee.

Costs Per Year: $19,029 (trimester) tuition; $5,841 room and board; $431 student fees.

Collegiate Environment: The original campus of 15 acres, now more than 200 acres, overlooks Lake Seneca and is located in one of the most beautiful residential sections in the area. The college buildings include a library containing 312,000 volumes, 1,809 periodicals, 42,000 microforms, and audiovisual materials, and living accommodations for 1,412 students. A 83,000 sq. ft. Sports and Recreation Center serves the needs of the entire campus. The colleges welcome students from diverse geographical locations. Average freshmen scores were SAT 1050-1150 combined. Admission to the colleges is highly selective with approximately 73% of applicants accepted. Of the 1,029 scholarships offered, 328 are for freshmen, and 62% of students receive some form of financial assistance. 92% of freshmen return for their sophomore year.

Community Environment: Geneva, population 15,000, is on Seneca Lake, the largest of the Finger Lakes. It is the center of a rich agricultural and nursery region with a number of diversified industries adding to the city's economy. There are several churches of major denominations, a public library, historical museum, YMCA, and many service and fraternal organizations within the town. Some private homes cater to students wishing to live off campus. Seneca lake offers excellent facilities for fishing, boating, and other water sports. Some part-time employment is available.

HOFSTRA UNIVERSITY   *(E-3)*
1000 Fulton Ave.
Hempstead, New York 11550
Tel: (516) 463-6700; (800) 463-7872; Fax: (516) 560-7660

Description: The privately supported, coeducational liberal arts university was established in 1935 and is accredited by the Middle States Association of Colleges and Schools. Undergraduate enrollment is 6,395 full-time, 1,267 part-time, and 3,733 evening students. There are 3,868 graduate students. A faculty of 446 full-time and 537 part-time gives a faculty-student ratio of 1-16. The university consists of the Hofstra College of Liberal Arts and Sciences, the School of Business, the School of Education, New College of Hofstra, University College for Continuing Education, University Without Walls, Alumni College, Division of Continuing Education and a School of Law. The university operates on the 4-1-4 calendar system and offers two summer sessions. It welcomes qualified students without regard to race, creed, color, national origin, or physical handicap. Army ROTC and overseas summer programs are available.

Entrance Requirements: Accredited high school graduation with SAT score combined 1000 or ACT 23; rank in upper 33% of high school class; completion of 16 units including minimum of 4 English, 2 mathematics, 2 foreign language, 3 social science, 1 laboratory science; GRE, GMAT or LSAT are required for graduate school, and 4 electives; early admission, early decision, midyear admission, rolling admission, delayed admission and advanced placement plans available. $25 application fee.

Costs Per Year: $11,060 tuition; $5,920 room and board; $650 student fees.

Collegiate Environment: The 238-acre Hofstra University campus is a "living museum." Designated a national arboretum in 1985, a collection of trees from around the world also enable the grounds to serve as an outdoor study center. The university is also an accredited museum, and outdoor sculpture gardens complement the landscaping and more than 105 Georgian-style academic buildings. Residence halls provide living accommodations for 2,000 men and 2,100 women. Recreational resources include one of the best college physical fitness centers in the Metropolitan area, an indoor Olympic-size swimming pool, an entertainment complex, and a recreational facility. The campus is connected by the Unispan, an elevated walkway across Hempstead Turnpike. Recent additions to the campus include state of the art language labs and broadcast facilities, Sbarro's Pizzeria, and Kiosks that provide campus, course, and student information. In addition, the expanded sports stadium will allow additional sporting and concert events. The library contains 1,385,900 volumes, 5,400 periodicals, 1,000,000 microforms, and 19 CD-ROM Databases. The University also has four public access computer labs, three of which are staffed by trained assistants and a fourth which is not staffed, but is open 24 hours a day. In addition, there are special interest labs for communication, fine arts, and computer science. These labs are equipped with Power PC's, Quadra Macintosh computers, and Silicon Graphics 3D graphics workstations. Last year, approximately 77% of students applying for admission were accepted. The average scores of the entering freshman class were SAT 1010 combined. 3,287 scholarships are available, including 732 for freshmen and 244 athletic. Last year, 64% of students received financial aid.

Community Environment: Population 39,500. A residential community and retail shopping center, Hempstead is particularly interesting for its 3 historic churches. A suburban area, it is situated 25 miles east of New York City. The immediate vicinity has a public library, the Nassau Coliseum, shopping mall, YMCA, YWCA, a hospital, churches and synogogues major denominations. There are theaters, water sports, and several civic, fraternal and veterans organizations in the city. Kennedy and La Guardia airports are within 30 minutes of the campus.

HOSTOS COMMUNITY COLLEGE OF THE CITY UNIVERSITY OF NEW YORK   *(E-2)*
500 Grand Concourse
Bronx, New York 10451
Tel: (718) 518-4444; Admissions: (718) 518-6622; Fax: (718) 518-6643

Description: Publicly-supported, coeducational junior college established in 1968 and a member of the City University of New York. It is accredited by the Middle States Association of Colleges and Schools. Named for a famed Puerto Rican educator, Eugenio Maria de Hostos, the college is committed to serving the educational needs of the South Bronx community. Recent enrollment included 3,282 full-time and 742 part-time students. It employs a unique instructional approach to higher education, in which two languages, Spanish and English, are used as the medium of instruction. It is based on the premise that student growth and development are best met when they are provided with the opportunity to learn in their first language and continue to develop mastery of it as they learn to develop skills in a second language. Hostos Community College offers Associate in Arts (A.A.) and Associate in Science (A.S.) degree programs which prepare a student to transfer (with junior-year status) to a senior college upon graduation from Hostos. In addition, the college offers Associate in Applied Sciences (A.A.S.) degree programs which prepare students for specific careers; a Certificate in Word Processing is also offered. In the health sciences, requirements for certification and licensure impose additional restrictions on the time required to complete the program. The semester system is used with one summer session.

Entrance Requirements: Open enrollment policy; advanced placement, rolling admission plans available; $35 application fee for freshmen, $40 for transfer students.

Costs Per Year: New York City resident full-time $2,100, part-time $85 a credit; nonresident full-time $2,676; part-time $104 a credit; student fees $4.

Collegiate Environment: The college campus is located on the Grand Concourse and 149th Street. The library houses over 40,000 volumes, 1,000 pamphlets, 400 periodicals and 3,000 recordings. Pre-admissions counseling and job placement assistance are available throughout the year.

Community Environment: See Fordham University.

HOUGHTON COLLEGE   (J-6)
Houghton, New York 14744
Tel: (716) 567-9353; (800) 777-2556; Fax: (716) 567-9522

Description: The privately supported, coeducational liberal arts college is chartered by the Board of Regents of the University of the State of New York and is accredited by the Middle States Association of Colleges and Schools. The National Association of Schools of Music accredits the music education program. The college was established in 1883 by the Lockport Conference of the Wesleyan Methodist Church of America. The college operates on the semester system and offers three summer terms. Enrollment is 1,332 full-time and 30 part-time students. A faculty of 75 full-time and 25 part-time gives a faculty-student ratio of 1-15. The degrees granted include an Associate in Applied Science (Christian Worker's course in Bible and related studies), A.A., B.A., B.S., and B.Music. Army ROTC is available.

Entrance Requirements: High school graduation or equivalent with rank in upper 50% of high school class; completion of 16 units including 4 English, 2 math, 2 science, 2 foreign language, and 3 social science; $20 application fee; early admission, rolling admission, delayed admission and advanced placement plans available.

Costs Per Year: $10,565 tuition; $3,710 room and board; $325 student fees.

Collegiate Environment: The college is located in western New York, about 65 miles southeast of Buffalo and 60 miles south of Rochester. The 12 college buildings include a library of 220,000 volumes, 638 periodicals, 5,551 microforms and 3,422 sound recordings, and dormitory facilities for 800 men and women. The Library now uses the Virginia Tech Library System (V.T.L.S.), which puts the entire card catalog system on computer. Terminals are located throughout the library for student use. Although sponsored by the Wesleyan Church of America, the student body is represented by more than 40 denominational groups. The college welcomes students from other geographical locations and will accept midyear students. Approximately 81% of students applying for admission are accepted. More than 90% of the recent freshmen graduated in the top half of their high school class, 59% in the top quarter, and 30% in the highest tenth. The average SAT scores of the current freshmen are 507V, 540M. Houghton College also operates a suburban branch campus in West Seneca (Buffalo) New York. This campus serves as the focal point for internships in business and psychology as well as student teaching. Financial aid is available, and 91% of the students receive aid. Of the 750 scholarships offered, 300 are for freshmen.

Community Environment: Houghton is a small rural community in southwestern New York, just south of Letchworth State Park. Nearby state park makes available good fishing, hunting, and skiing in season. The college also has its own ski slopes with rope-tow, an initiatives rope course, an equestrian riding program and miles of cross-country ski trails.

HUNTER COLLEGE OF THE CITY UNIVERSITY OF NEW YORK   (E-2)
695 Park Avenue
New York, New York 10021
Tel: (212) 722-4000

Description: This publicly supported, coeducational liberal arts college is a unit of the City University of New York. It was established in 1870 as a teacher training institution for young women and became coeducational in 1964. Hunter College has three separte campuses in New York. The college operates on the semester system with 1 summer term. It is accredited by the Middle States Association of Colleges and Schools. Enrollment includes 9,755 full-time and 9,907 part-time undergraduates and 4,728 graduate students. A faculty of 674 full-time and 547 part-time provides a faculty-student ratio of 1-18.

Entrance Requirements: High school graduation or equivalent; 80% grade average or rank in top one-third of class; completion of 10 academic units; rolling admission, early admission and advanced placement plans available; $35 undergraduate and graduate application fee, $40 for transfer students.

Costs Per Year: $2,450 state-resident tuition; $3,350 graduate tuition; $3,200 room.

Collegiate Environment: The college is located in the heart of New York City and is accessible from anywhere in the five boroughs. The library contains over 725,000 volumes and is rapidly growing. Living accomodations are available for 539 students. Approximately 80% of all students applying for admission are accepted. 75% of the current student body receive some form of financial aid. Scholarships based on academic achievements are available. The college offers a special program for the culturally disadvantaged enabling low-mark students to attend. About 50% of the current freshmen graduated in the top quarter of their high school class.

Community Environment: See New York University.

IONA COLLEGE   (D-3)
715 North Avenue
New Rochelle, New York 10801
Tel: (914) 633-2000; (800) 231-4662

Description: The privately supported, coeducational, liberal arts collegeis accredited by the Middle States Association of Colleges and Schools. It was founded in 1940 by the Congregation of Christian Brothers. The college was the first degree-granting liberal arts college for men in Westchester County. The private college is open to qualified students of all denominations. The college grants the Associate, Bachelor, and Master degrees and offers permanent certification for secondary school teaching. Divisions of the colleges include the School of Arts and Sciences; the School of Business Administration; Division of General Studies; and the Center for Pastoral Counseling (leads to M.S. Education degree for clergy and laypersons). Study abroad programs are available. The college provides a special program for the culturally disadvantaged. It operates on the 4-1-4 system and offers three summer sessions. Enrollment includes 2,783 full-time, 142 part-time undergraduate, 1,571 graduate, and 1,734 evening students. A faculty of 185 full-time and 240 part-time gives a faculty-student ratio of 1-16.

Entrance Requirements: Accredited high school graduation with rank in upper 50% of graduating class; completion of 16 units including 4 English, 3 mathematics, 2 foreign language, 1 natural science, 1 American history, and 2 social science; SAT or ACT required; early decision, early admission, deferred admission, rolling admission, midyear admission, and advanced placement plans available; $25 application fee.

Costs Per Year: $11,000 tuition; $6,200 room and board; $150 fees.

Collegiate Environment: The 44-acre campus is situated in the Beechmont Area of New Rochelle. The 12 college buildings include a library containing 249,000 volumes, 1,670 periodicals, 26,000 microforms and 8,427 audiovisual materials. Limited dormitory space for 600 students is available, additional accommodations are available in the neighborhood. Approximately 75% of applicants are accepted, including midyear students. About 88% of students receive some form of financial aid, and 78% of freshmen return to the campus for their sophomore year.

Community Environment: Population 75,400. An attractive residential suburb is 35 minutes from the center of Manhattan. Located on Long Island Sound, New Rochelle was settled by the Huguenots in 1688. Many houses date from the days of Dutch and English occupancy. Easy access to New York City is provided by rail and bus lines. There are many churches, a YMCA, hospital, public library, and various fraternal, civic, and veteran's organizations. Recreation in the area is provided by 8 miles of Long Island Sound frontage, inland lakes, and public parks as well as facilities for golf, tennis, canoeing, fishing, skating, and hockey. Part-time employment is available.

Branch Campuses: Rockland Branch Campus, Orangeburg, NY; Manhattan Campus, NYC, NY.

ITHACA COLLEGE   (J-10)
Ithaca, New York 14850
Tel: (607) 274-3124; (800) 429-4274; Admissions: (607) 274-3124; Fax: (607) 274-1900

Description: The privately-supported coeducational college is accredited by the Middle States Association of Colleges and Secondary Schools and by other professional and educational organizations. The college is composed of the School of Humanities and Sciences; School of Music; School of Health Sciences and Human Performance; School of Business, School of Communications, and a Division of

Graduate Studies and Continuing Education. The college offers a total of 105 different Bachelor's and Master's Level degrees. It operates on the semester system and offers two summer sessions. Enrollment includes 5,283 full-time, 167 part-time, and 238 graduate students. A faculty of 458 full-time and 92 part-time provides a faculty-student ratio of 1-12.

Entrance Requirements: Accredited high school graduation; completion of 17 units (preferred) including 4 English, 4 mathematics, 3 foreign language, 3 science, 3 social science; SAT or ACT are required; early admission, early decision, rolling admission, midyear admission and advanced placement plans available. $40 application fee.

Costs Per Year: $14,424 tuition; $6,192 room and board.

Collegiate Environment: The college occupies an entirely new campus on a beautiful 600-acre site overlooking Cayunga Lake, Cornell University, and the city of Ithaca. The 60 modern college buildings contain a library of 500,000 volumes, and dormitory facilities for 3,820 students. Students from other geographical locations are accepted. 74% of students applying for admission are accepted. Financial aid is available and 64% of students receive aid.

Community Environment: See Cornell University.

JEWISH THEOLOGICAL SEMINARY OF AMERICA   *(E-2)*
3080 Broadway
New York, New York 10027
Tel: (212) 678-8832

Description: The Jewish Theological Seminary is the academic and spiritual center of the Conservative Movement in Judaism. It was established in 1886 and has grown from a single rabbinical training school to a university comprised of 4 degree granting schools at the New York campus: the Albert A. List College of Jewish Studies, the Graduate School, the Rabbinical School, and the Cantors Institute Seminary College of Jewish Music. It grants Bachelor, Master, Rabbi, Diploma of Hazzan and Doctor degrees. It operates on a semester basis and offers 2 summer sessions. It is accredited by the Middle States Association of Colleges and Secondary Schools. Recently, the seminary awarded 50 Bachelor, 35 Master, 37 Rabbi, 4 Diploma of Hazzan, and 13 Doctoral degrees. Recent enrollment included 243 men and 252 women. A faculty of 99 gives a faculty-student ratio of 1-5. The University of Judaism is a branch of the seminary located in Los Angeles.

Entrance Requirements: List College of Jewish Studies is an undergraduate liberal arts college whose admission is open to men and women 16 years of age or older who have completed high school. It has joint programs with Columbia University and Barnard College. The Graduate School is open to qualified students irrespective of age, race, sex, religion or national origin. Applicants must have a baccalaureate degree from an accredited college or university to enter the master's program and for the doctoral level programs, a bachelor's degree from an accredited college or university as well as an M.A. in Judaica are required. In addition, candidates for admission must meet the academic standards of the Graduate School. The Rabbinical School's program of graduate studies leads to the degree of Master of Arts in rabbinics and then to ordination. It is open to any Jew who holds an undergraduate degree from an accredited college or university and who meets the entrance requirements established by the Committee on Admissions. Candidates are expected to display devotion to Jewish tradition in their personal lives and intellectual pursuits. Cantors Institute applicants are college graduates, who are members of the Jewish faith and loyal adherents of its observances. They must also possess an adequate Jewish background including knowledge of Hebrew, Bible, Jewish history, the prayer book, and customs of the synagogue. They should be musical and possess good voices. Their musical knowledge should include the rudiments of music as well as some ear training, sight singing and instrumental instruction. Applicants for admission to the Seminary College of Jewish Music must possess a bachelor's degree from an accredited college or university. Entrance examinations in Judaica and music are required.

Costs Per Year: Undergraduate tuition $6,850 per year; fees $250; graduate tuition $365/credit; $250 fees; Rabbinical School tuition $9,730 per year; fees $250; Cantor's Institute tuition $9,730; fees $250.

Collegiate Environment: The seminary's buildings were constructed in 1929-30 on a 1-acre campus in the Morningside Heights area of New York City. A library opened in 1984. The seminary is located among a distinguished group of academic and ecclesiastical institutions that include Columbia University, Union Theological Seminary and other outstanding institutions.

Community Environment: See Columbia University.

JOHN JAY COLLEGE OF CRIMINAL JUSTICE OF THE CITY UNIVERSITY OF NEW YORK   *(E-2)*
445 West 59th Street
New York, New York 10019
Tel: (212) 237-8000

Description: The publicly supported, coeducational college of criminal justice, fire science, public administration, forensic psychology and forensic science is a unit of the City University of New York. It operates on a semester system and offers one summer session. It is accredited by the Middle States Association of Colleges and Schools. Enrollment is 6,972 full-time and 2,306 part-time undergraduates and 759 graduate students. A faculty of 325 gives a faculty-student ratio of 1:18. The educational program of the college is designed to foster the professionalization of police and other law enforcement officers, to institute study and research leading to improvement of the criminal justice system, and to prepare civilian students for public service careers.

Entrance Requirements: High school graduation or equivalent; open enrollment policy for Associate degree program; graduation in top 50% of high school class or or 800 combined SAT score; 75 average required for Bachelor degree programs; GRE required for graduate programs; early admission, rolling admission, delayed admission, advanced placement plans available; $35 application fee for freshmen, $40 application fee for transfers.

Costs Per Year: $2,450 tuition for New York State residents; $5,050 for nonresidents; $110 student fees.

Collegiate Environment: The college is located in the center of New York City, near Lincoln Center. The library contains 250,000 volumes. 80% of the students receive some form of financial assistance.

Community Environment: See New York University.

JUILLIARD SCHOOL   *(E-2)*
60 Lincoln Center Plaza
New York, New York 10023-6590
Tel: (212) 799-5000; Fax: (212) 724-0263

Description: The privately supported coeducational school was established in 1905, and the school of graduate studies was established in 1924. Both the Institute of Musical Art and the Juilliard Graduate School were amalgamated into a single school in 1946. Today the school offers education and professional training in drama, dance, opera and music. The Juilliard Board of Directors accepted the invitation by Lincoln Center to join the New York Philharmonic, Metropolitan Opera, New York City Opera, New York City Ballet, Music Theater, Repertory Theater, and the Library and Museum of Performing Arts as constituents of the New Lincoln Center for the Performing Arts, and began instruction in its current home in October, 1969. The school is accredited by the Middle States Association of Colleges and Schools. It operates on the semester system and no summer sessions are offered. Enrollment is 756 students. A faculty of 220 gives a faculty-student ratio of 1-3. Degrees granted include Bachelor of Music, Bachelor of Fine Arts, Advanced Certificate in Music, and Master of and Doctor of Musical Arts.

Entrance Requirements: High school graduation or equivalent; personal auditions required; admission is based mainly on the results of a competitive performance audition in the major study; $75 application fee.

Costs Per Year: $12,200 tuition; $6,300 room and board; $600 general fees.

Collegiate Environment: The Juilliard School at Lincoln Center is a school for the exceptional performer. Gifted young students and older students will receive the intensive training needed to become professional artists. Opportunities for advanced study and practice are provided for students with special aptitudes indicating distinguished careers as performing artists. Students from all geographical locations are accepted. Classes begin in September and midyear students are not accepted. An intensive English course is offered to foreign students during the summer. Juilliard opened its first residence hall at Lincoln Center in 1990 and accommodates 375 students. 30% of applicants are accepted. Scholarships are offered. 90% of the student body receives some form of financial aid.

Community Environment: See New York University.

KEUKA COLLEGE   *(J-8)*
Keuka Park, New York 14478
Tel: (315) 536-4411; (800) 335-3852; Admissions: (315) 536-5254;
Fax: (315) 536-5386

Description: Founded in 1890 on the shores of Keuka Lake, the jewel of New York's Finger Lakes, Keuka enrolls 815 full-time and 90 part-time students in more than 20 major fields of study. A faculty of 47 full-time and 29 part-time gives a faculty-student ratio of 1-15. It is a member of the consortium of Rochester Area Colleges. Keuka operates on the 4-1-4 calendar system and offers one summer session. Army ROTC is offered.

Entrance Requirements: High school graduation; recommended completion of 16 academic credits, including 3 English, 3 mathematics, 3 social science, and 2 language; SAT or ACT required; early decision, early admission, rolling admission, delayed admission, miyear admission and advanced placement programs available; personal interview recommended; $25 application fee.

Costs Per Year: $9,850 tuition and fees; $4,550 room and board.

Collegiate Environment: The college is located on 173 acres in the picturesque Finger Lakes region of New York State. Residence halls accomodate 520 students. The college library contains 94,434 volumes and 380 periodicals. A mandatory off-campus experience, called Field Period enables each student to put his or her academic knowledge to work in a "real world" setting. 80% of applicants are accepted. The average scores of the entering freshman class were SAT 945 combined, ACT 22 composite. Approximately 95% of the student population receives some form of financial aid.

Community Environment: The college is located on the western shore of Keuka Lake near Penn Yan (population 6,500). This pleasant rural setting is accessible by major roadways. The area provides boating, fishing, water sports, hunting, and winter sports.

KINGSBOROUGH COMMUNITY COLLEGE OF THE CITY UNIVERSITY OF NEW YORK   *(F-2)*
Manhattan Beach
Brooklyn, New York 11235
Tel: (718) 368-5000

Description: Publicly-supported, coeducational two-year college enrolls 14,000 full-time and part-time students. It offers programs in liberal arts, the sciences, business, health and social service leading to the Associate in Arts, Associate in Applied Science, and the Associate in Science degrees. The college operates on a 12-6-12-6 calendar system; a 6-week module is offered following each 12-week term. The school is accredited by the Middle States Association of Colleges and School and The National League for Nursing. A faculty of 209 full-time and 464 part-time provides an overall faculty-student ratio of 1-15.

Entrance Requirements: Accredited high school graduation or equivalent; open enrollment policy for city residents; $30 application fee for out-of-state applicants.

Costs Per Year: $1,450 tuition for New York residents; $2,025 tuition for nonresidents; $50 general fees.

Collegiate Environment: Kingsborough Community College is located on a beautiful 67-acre site at the eastern end of Manhattan Beach. Enclosed on 3 sides by the waters of Sheepshead Bay, Jamaica Bay, and the Atlantic Ocean, the college's ultra-modern campus is composed of a continuous series of interconnected buildings. Outstanding features include: library, media and computer centers; lecture halls and learning resource center; science technology and visual arts building, cafeteria, lounge, study, counseling and faculty offices; Olympic-size indoor swimming pool. Students may enroll at midyear as well as in the fall. Financial aid is available, and 82% of the current student body receives some form of assistance.

Community Environment: See Brooklyn College of the City University of New York.

LABORATORY INSTITUTE OF MERCHANDISING   *(E-2)*
12 East 53rd Street
New York, New York 10022
Tel: (212) 752-1530

Description: Privately-supported two/four year college which offers an Associate and Bachelor degree in Professional Studies in Fashion Merchandising with options in Fashion Marketing, Visual Merchandising, and Retail Management. It is accredited by the Middle States Association of Colleges and Schools. LIM operates on the 4-1-4 system and offers one summer session. The institute enrolls 172 full-time and 2 part-time students. A faculty of 46 gives a faculty-student ratio of 1-8.

Entrance Requirements: Official transcripts from all high school and colleges attended; SAT or ACT; Upper Division applicants must submit 2 letters of recommendation; All foreign students are required to submit TOEFL scores; personal interviews; $35 application fee; midyear admission and rolling admission plans available.

Costs Per Year: $9,800 tuition; $150 general fees.

Collegiate Environment: LIM is located in an elegant, gothic style townhouse, just off Fifth Avenue. Facilities include a learning center, a student lounge, computer center, and library. The library holdings include 8,750 bound volumes, 317 microfilm, 122 periodical subscriptions, and 107 records and tapes. There are 24 scholarships offered. Federal and state financial aid is available and 85% of students receive some form of financial aid. Over 85% of the students hold part-time jobs. A six week Work Project is required of all freshmen and sophomores, providing students with first-hand experience in the business of fashion. An added benefit is the opportunity for the student to earn money while learning, offsetting a percentage of the tuition costs. Seniors are required to successfully complete a 13 credit/full semester Work Coop. There is no college-owned housing, but LIM recommends a privately owned dormatory style, residence facility, along with an approved housing list. 90% of those with completed applications are accepted and 80% of the freshman return for the second year.

Community Environment: LIM's location right in the center of the greatest fashion city, New York, gives its students the best of all possible worlds. Within a block of the school are internationally known department stores, French and Italian designers' boutiques, retailing establishments of every kind, with goods imported from every continent of the world. Only a few blocks away is the heart of the garment district, Seventh Avenue. Merchandising creativity originates here and finds its way into the shopping centers of America, Europe, and the Orient.

LAGUARDIA COMMUNITY COLLEGE OF THE CITY UNIVERSITY OF NEW YORK   *(E-2)*
31-10 Thompson Avenue
Long Island City, New York 11101
Tel: (718) 482-7200

Description: The publicly-supported, coeducational junior college is accredited by the Middle States Association of Colleges and Schools. Opened in 1971, the college is the only member of the City University of New York to offer a Cooperative Education program, which is mandatory for all full-time students. Its purpose is to enhance the student's growth concerning personal responsibility and maturity by providing alternate learning situations in an off-campus, nonclassroom setting. Each internship is 13 weeks in length, and there are 3 academic credits are granted for each completed work internship. LaGuardia grants the A.A., A.S., and A.A.S. degrees. Operates on a modified semester system, with 13 weeks in each and offers one summer session. Enrollment includes 6,799 full-time and 4,124 part-time students. There are 230 full-time faculty.

Entrance Requirements: Open enrollment policy; graduation from an accredited high school or GED. $40 application fee.

Costs Per Year: New York City residents $2,100 tuition; nonresidents $2,676; $104-$182 student fees.

Collegiate Environment: Housed in a renovated building in Long Island City, the college is convenient to all transportation and is located in the Borough of Queens. Library contains 78,360 volumes, 751 periodicals and 3,760 audiovisual materials. Nursing scholarships are available and 35% of all students receive some form of financial aid.

Community Environment: See Queens College of the City University of New York.

LE MOYNE COLLEGE *(H-11)*
Syracuse, New York 13214-1399
Tel: (315) 445-4100; (800) 333-4733; Admissions: (315) 445-4300; Fax: (315) 445-4540

Description: The privately supported, coeducational, Catholic liberal arts college was founded in 1946 and is conducted by the Jesuit Society. It is accredited by the Middle States Association of Colleges and Schools and operates on the semester system with 2 summer terms. Degrees granted include B.S. in Pure Science, B.A., B.S. in Science, Arts or Business and a Masters in Business Administration. Enrollment includes 1,867 full-time and 523 part-time undergraduates and 367 graduate students. A faculty of 129 full-time and 87 part-time gives a faculty-student ratio of 1-12.

Entrance Requirements: High school graduation with rank in upper one-half of graduating class; completion of 16 units including 4 English, 3 mathematics, 1 science, 2 social science; SAT or ACT required. Early decision, rolling admission and advanced placement programs available. $25 application fee.

Costs Per Year: $11,040 tuition; $4,840 room and board; $320 student fees.

Collegiate Environment: There are 29 modern buildings on the 161-acre Le Moyne Campus. The college library includes an active collection of 210,191 books and bound periodicals. All out-of-town students are expected to live on campus. Dormitory accommodations are available for 1,350 men and women. 79% of applicants are accepted. The middle 50% ranges of scores for enrolled freshmen were SAT 420-520 verbal, 470-590 math; ACT 20-27 composite, 21-25 English. 90% of the current student body graduated in the top half of their high school class, 55% were in the top quarter, and 23% were in the highest tenth. About 92% of the previous freshman class return to the campus for their sophomore year. Scholarships are available to 79% of undergraduates. 95% of undergraduates receive some form of financial aid.

Community Environment: See Syracuse University.

LONG ISLAND UNIVERSITY - ARNOLD AND MARIE SCHWARTZ COLLEGE OF PHARMACY AND HEALTH *(F-2)*
75 Dekalb Avenue
Brooklyn, New York 11201
Tel: (718) 403-1060

Description: Privately supported, coeducational pharmacy college was chartered by the State Legislature in 1886 and continued to operate independently until 1929 when it was merged with Long Island University. Until 1977, it was known as the Brooklyn College of Pharmacy. Grants Bachelor of Science in Pharmacy in a five-year curriculum consisting of basic physical and biological sciences, humanities, social sciences and professional pharmacy coursework; Master of Science with Specializations in Biomedical Communications, Cosmetic Science, Drug Information and Communication, Hospital Pharmacy Administration, Industrial Pharmacy, Pharmaceutical and Health Care Marketing Administration, Pharmacology/Toxicology and Pharmacotherapeutics, Drug Regulatory Affairs. The college is accredited by the Middle States Association of Colleges and Secondary Schools and the American Council on Pharmaceutical Education. The semester system is used and 2 summer sessions are offered. A recent enrollment included 413 men and 459 women. The college celebrated its 100th anniversary in 1986 and has educated over 20,000 undergraduate and graduate students, many of whom have attained prominence in pharmacy and the health sciences.

Entrance Requirements: High school graduation or equivalent; completion of 16 units including 4 English, 2 science, 3 social studies and 3 mathematics; SAT required; $30 application fee; early decision, rolling admission, advanced placement plans available.

Costs Per Year: $6,000 tuition; $4,190 room and board; $100 student fees.

Collegiate Environment: The college is located on Long Island University's Brooklyn Campus and housed in a modern laboratory and classroom complex specifically designed for its curriculum. Spe-

cial facilities include the Aerosol Studies Center, Cosmetic Studies Center, Center for Toxicology and Environmental Health, Retail Drug Institute and Drug Information Center. Other academic components include the Research and Instructional Parenteral Laboratory and the Arnold & Marie Schwartz Clinical Instruction and Research Unit, which provide clinical and research experiences for students in nearby Brooklyn Hospital. Housing is provided for approximately 500 students in the campus residence facility. Financial aid is available and about 80% of the student body receives some form of assistance. A Pharmaceutical Study Center houses the college's closed-circuit television system and an extensive collection of audio-visual hardware and curriculum-related software. The Brooklyn Campus Library Learning Center also provides a variety of instructional resources.

Community Environment: See Long Island University, Brooklyn Campus.

LONG ISLAND UNIVERSITY, BROOKLYN CAMPUS *(F-2)*
University Plaza
Brooklyn, New York 11201
Tel: (718) 488-1011; Fax: (718) 797-2399

Description: Privately supported, coeducational university. The Brooklyn Campus is the original unit of the university which was founded in 1926. Although at its inception the university consisted of this one Brooklyn Campus, it was the aim of the founders to build a system of colleges spanning the length of Long Island, hence the name Long Island University. The Brooklyn Campus consists of the Richard L. Conolly College for Liberal Arts, the School of Business Administration, and the Arnold and Marie Schwartz College of Pharmacy and Health Sciences. The University is accredited by the Middle States Association of Colleges and Schools and grants the Associate, Bachelor, Master and Doctorate degrees. It operates on the semester system and offers two summer terms. Enrollment includes 5,384 full-time and 895 part-time students. A full-time faculty of 203 provides a faculty-student ratio of 1-30. There are also 1,727 graduate students on campus.

Entrance Requirements: Approved high school graduation or equivalent; completion of 16 units including 4 English, 2 mathematics, 3 science, 2 language and 3 social science; entrance exam required; GRE required for graduate programs; rolling admission, early decision, advanced placement programs are available; $30 application fee.

Costs Per Year: $7,500; $4,500 room and board; $150 student fees.

Collegiate Environment: The Brooklyn Campus, founded in 1926, has 8 buildings and is strictly urban in character and appearance. Residence facilities include dormitory accomodations for 280 men and women and furnished apartments for 200 upperclassmen and graduate students. The Library-Learning Center houses 341,000 volumes, 26,000 pamphlets, 40,000 periodicals, 70,000 microforms and 10,700 recordings. The Disabled Students organization attempts to coordinate and centralize the school's resources to meet the special needs of students with a physical disability. About 70% of the students applying for admission are accepted including midyear students, and 88% return for the sophomore year. Financial aid is available.

Community Environment: The campus in in downtown Brooklyn, at Flatbush and DeKalb Avenues, within easy distance of the Brooklyn Academy of Music, Prospect Park, the Brooklyn Museum, and midtown Manhattan.

LONG ISLAND UNIVERSITY, C.W. POST CAMPUS *(A-7)*
720 Northern Boulevard
Brookville, New York 11548-1300
Tel: (516) 299-0200; (800) 548-7526; Fax: (516) 299-2137

Description: This privately supported, coeducational liberal arts college of Long Island University was founded in 1954. The beautiful C.W. Post Campus was named in memory of the man who created the business now known as General Foods Corporation. The university is accredited by the Middle States Association of Colleges and Schools and grants the Associate, Bachelor, Master, Doctorate in Clinical Psychology, and professional degrees. The Campus contains the C.W. Post College of Arts and Sciences, the School of the Arts, College of Management, Schools of Education and the Palmer Graduate Library School. Air Force and Army ROTC are available through a consortium agreement. It operates on the semester system and offers three summer sessions. Enrollment includes 1,542 men and 1,915 female full-time undergraduates and 336 men and 667 women part-time. In addition, there are 3,459 graduate students. A faculty of 296 full-time and 654 part-time gives an undergraduate faculty-student ratio of 1-11.

Entrance Requirements: Accredited high school graduation with rank in upper one-half of graduating class; completion of 16 units including 4 English, 2 mathematics, 2 science, 2 foreign language, and 3 social studies; SAT 900 combined (with 450V) minimum; ACT 20; early admission, early decision, rolling admission, delayed admission, midyear admission, and advanced placement programs available; $30 application fee.

Costs Per Year: $11,730 tuition; $5,580 room and board; $800 average student expenses.

Collegiate Environment: The former home of Marjorie Merriweather Post is the site of this campus. Located in the village of Brookville, it was one of the most beautiful estates in America. The 305 acres contain 48 buildings including a library and living accommodations for 1,765 students. The library collection includes 2,297,679 volumes. Approximately 78% of students applying for admission are accepted, including midyear students. Scholarships and financial aid are available. 75% of the students receive some form of financial aid. The college has a Junior Year Abroad program, offered in conjunction with the Institute of European Studies. The Honors Program provides talented students with an academic environment designed to help them achieve their greatest potential. The Center for Adult Studies provides opportunity for the undergraduate student age 25 and over whose daily schedule prevents specific scheduling of courses.

Community Environment: The village of Brookville has a population of 26,000. A city bus (N20) makes pickups on campus and drops off at Long Island Railroad. The campus has the Tilles Performing Arts Center, a 2,000-seat auditorium that is the largest on Long Island, where major cultural events are held.

LONG ISLAND UNIVERSITY, SOUTHAMPTON CAMPUS (D-9)
Montauk Highway
Southampton, New York 11968
Tel: (516) 287-1273; (800) 548-7526; Fax: (516) 283-4081

Description: Privately supported, coeducational liberal arts college, the newest unit of the Long Island University, offers programs leading to the Bachelor degree and two Master's degrees. It was established in 1963 and is accredited by the Middle States Association of Colleges and Schools. The semester system is used, with 3 summer terms and 1 winter term. As a part of the learning process, the university involves students in self-government and in deliberations about the policies of the college, such as curricular change. B.A., B.S., B.F.A., Master's of Professional Studies in Gerontology and two Master of Science in Education programs are offered. Enrollment includes 1,059 full-time and 153 part-time students. A faculty of 72 full-time and 47 part-time provides a faculty-student ratio of 1-17.

Entrance Requirements: High school graduation or equivalent; completion of 4 units of English, 2 math, 1 science, 2 foreign language, and 3 social studies; counselor recommendation considered; SAT or ACT required; non-high school graduates considered; early admission, early decision, rolling admission, delayed admission, and advanced placement plans available; $30 application fee.

Costs Per Year: $10,850 tuition; $5,480 room and board; $450 books and supplies; additional fees.

Collegiate Environment: The college occupies a 110-acre campus in the gently sloping Shinnecock Hills. It includes among its 37 buildings a library, a marine station, and dormitory facilities for 785. The library contains 150,000 volumes, 625 periodicals, 8,300 microforms and 14,500 audiovisual materials. Approximately 75% of the students applying for admission are accepted, including midyear students, and 85% of the previous freshmen return to this campus for their sophomore year. Average high school standing of a recent freshman class was in the top 40%; 45% ranked in the top quarter; 30% ranked in the second quarter; 18% were in the third quarter; 7% were in the bottom quarter; average scores: SAT 465V, 487M. Financial aid is available, and 80% of the current student body receives some form of financial assistance.

Community Environment: Population 4,904. Southampton is an exclusive summer resort village with palatial residences located on Long Island. Transportation is provided by airlines, buses, and good highways. The immediate locale has a memorial library, historical museum, several churches, good shopping facilities, a hospital and 2 medical centers. Ample part-time employment is available for students. Recreational facilities include theaters, boating, fishing, and sports. Situated one-third of the way out on eastern Long Island's south fork, Southampton is an amalgram of elm trees, fertile farm fields, fishing and shell fishing, tourists, boating, beaches and the Atlantic Ocean. The Hamptons are a prime vacation spot for people from New York City (some 90 miles west), and is easily accessable via car, train, or jitney bus.

MANHATTAN COLLEGE (E-2)
Manhattan College Parkway
Riverdale, New York 10471
Tel: (718) 920-0100; (800) 622-9235; Fax: (718) 548-1008

Description: Privately supported, independent college was founded in 1853 by members of St. John Baptist de la Salle's teaching congregation, the Brothers of the Christian Schools (Christian Brothers). The college is accredited by the Middle States Association of Colleges and Schools and grants the Associate, Bachelor and Master degrees. It operates on the semester system and offers 3 summer sessions and a January intersession. The college is comprised of the Schools of Arts and Sciences, Business, Engineering, Education and Human Services and the Graduate Division. Academic cooperative plans and Air Force ROTC are available. Enrollment is 3,500 students. A faculty of 192 full-time and 84 part-time gives a faculty student ratio of 1-14.

Entrance Requirements: Accredited high school graduation; completion of 16 units including 4 English, 3 mathematics, 2 foreign language, 2 science, 3 social science; SAT or ACT accepted; non-high school graduates considered; early admission, early decision, rolling admission, delayed admission, advanced placement plans available; $25 application fee.

Costs Per Year: $12,370 tuition; $6,800 board and room; additional expenses average $600.

Collegiate Environment: The 47-acre campus is situated along Manhattan College Parkway in the Riverdale section of New York City. There are living accommodations for 1,500 men and women. The Cardinal Hayes Library contains 280,000 volumes, 42,140 bound periodical volumes, 89,321 microforms and 3,450 recordings. There are over 40 scientific and engineering laboratories at the college. Scholarships are available and 85% of students receive some form of financial aid.

Community Environment: See Fordham University.

MANHATTAN COMMUNITY COLLEGE OF THE CITY UNIVERSITY OF NEW YORK (E-2)
199 Chambers St.
New York, New York 10007
Tel: (212) 346-8100; Admissions: (212) 346-8100; Fax: (212) 346-8110

Description: The publicly supported, coeducational two-year college is sponsored by the City University of New York. Classes began in 1964 with courses offered in business career programs and in the liberal arts. A business transfer program was added in 1966, career programs in health services started in 1967, and transfer programs in social service and urban planning were included in 1968. The college is accredited by the Middle States Association of Colleges and Schools. A Cooperative Education plan is available, allowing both work and schooling at the same time. Degrees granted include Associate in Arts and Associate in Applied Science. The college operates on the semester system and offers one summer term. Enrollment includes 16,462 students. A faculty of 933 gives a faculty-student ratio of 1-19.

Entrance Requirements: High school graduation or equivalent; high school records or GED test scores must indicate potential for college work; open enrollment for city residents; $35 application fee for freshmen, $40 for transfers.

Costs Per Year: $2,100 tuition for N.Y. City residents; $2,676 tuition for N.Y. State residents and nonresidents; $80 student fees.

Collegiate Environment: The college is in a new facility in the heart of Manhattan's commercial, industrial, and business center. Library contains over 57,000 volumes.

Community Environment: See New York University.

MANHATTAN SCHOOL OF MUSIC   *(E-2)*
120 Claremont Avenue
New York, New York 10027
Tel: (212) 749-2802; Admissions: (212) 749-2802 X 2; Fax: (212) 749-5471

Description: Privately supported, coeducational college of music established in 1917-18. It is accredited by the Middle States Association of Colleges and Schools and grants the Bachelor of Music, Master of Music degrees and Doctor of Musical Arts. The semester system is used and 2 summer sessions are offered. Recently, 921 students were enrolled. The faculty included 230 full-time and 20 part-time, giving a faculty-student ratio of 1-11.

Entrance Requirements: Accredited high school graduation or equivalent; audition required; non-high school graduates considered; advanced placement plan available; $85 application fee.

Costs Per Year: $12,500 tuition; $530 student fees.

Collegiate Environment: The school houses studios and administration offices. The library contains 20,000 volumes, 55,000 musical scores, 20,000 recordings and a record room. Living accommodations are available at the school. 38% of applicants are accepted receive some form of financial assistance. Scholarships are available and 50% of students receive some form of financial aid.

Community Environment: See Columbia University.

MANHATTANVILLE COLLEGE   *(C-3)*
2900 Purchase Street
Purchase, New York 10577
Tel: (914) 694-2200; Fax: (914) 694-1732

Description: Privately supported liberal arts college is accredited by the Middle States Association of Colleges and Schools. The college has its origins in the Academy of the Sacred Heart, founded in 1841. The semester system is used and 2 summer sessions are offered. Enrollment is 540 women and 360 men full-time, and 184 part-time students. A faculty of 173 gives a faculty-student ratio of 1-10.

Entrance Requirements: Selective admissions based on high school record, class standing and SAT or ACT scores; SAT or ACT required; alternate application procedure is available allowing for submission of examples of academic work and scores of English and Math Achievement Tests; early admission, early decision, deferred admission, advanced placement, and common application plans available; $30 application fee.

Costs Per Year: $13,125 tuition; $5,250-$6,200 room and board; $260 student fees.

Collegiate Environment: The 100-acre campus is 25 miles northeast of New York City. Dormitories are provided for 900 men and women. At the center of academic life is the Manhattanville Library. The collection is housed on 6 levels of open stacks and includes 250,000 volumes, 1,600 periodicals and 6,200 microforms. Manhattanville's Portfolio System requires students to choose a major field of study set within a diversified liberal arts curriculum. The Portfolio System emphasizes working closely with a faculty advisor to gain personal and academic growth within the context of a global perspective. The financial aid program makes available grants, job opportunities, and loans. 75% of last year's entering class received some form of financial assistance. About 77% of students applying for admission are accepted, including midyear students, and 90% of the previous freshman class return to this school for the second year. The college awards approximately 250 Bachelor and 125 Master degrees each year.

Community Environment: Located approximately 25 miles from New York City, Purchase enjoys the cultural, civic, educational, and recreational facilities of its neighbor. There are railroad connections at nearby White Plains and Rye. Job opportunities are available within the immediate area.

MANNES COLLEGE OF MUSIC   *(E-2)*
150 W. 85th St.
New York, New York 10024
Tel: (212) 580-0210; (800) 292-3040; Fax: (212) 580-1738

Description: Privately supported, coeducational college of music established in 1916 and authorized to award the Bachelor of Science, the Bachelor of Music, the Master of Music degrees and the honorary degree of Doctor of Music. In 1989, the school became one of seven divisions of The New School for Social Research. It also grants the four-year Diploma, and a Professional Studies Diploma. The semester system is used and one summer session is offered. Enrollment is 130 full-time and 1 part-time undergraduates, and 138 graduate students. There are 180 faculty members. The faculty-student ratio is 1:8.

Entrance Requirements: High school graduation; completion of 16 units including 4 English, 2 mathematics, 2 foreign language, and 1 science; entrance examinations and audition required; SAT or ACT accepted but not essential; midyear admission, rolling admission, and advanced placement plans available; $60 application fee.

Costs Per Year: $12,750 tuition.

Collegiate Environment: The college occupies a 6-story building on a quiet residential street. Extensive technical equipment includes a music and academic library containing 28,000 volumes and 6,000 recordings, a concert hall noted for its excellent acoustics, spacious studios with 1 or more grand pianos, and many orchestral instruments. Financial aid is available. There is a strong sense of community among the students.

Community Environment: See New York University.

MARIA COLLEGE   *(I-17)*
700 New Scotland Avenue
Albany, New York 12208
Tel: (518) 438-3111; Fax: (518) 438-7170

Description: Privately supported, coeducational, two-year college was established in 1958. It is accredited by the Middle States Association of Colleges and Schools and professionally by the American Physical Therapy Association, the American Occupational Therapy Association, and the National League for Nursing. The college offers transfer and career programs. The college grants the Associate degree. It operates on the semester system and offers two summer sessions. Enrollment includes 54 men and 220 women full-time, and 88 men and 518 women part-time. The faculty-student ratio is 1:12.

Entrance Requirements: Accredited high school graduation; completion of 16 units including 4 English, 2 math, 2 science, 3 social studies; SAT minimum 350 verbal, 350 math; personal interview required; early admission, midyear admission, rolling admission, and advanced placement plans are available. The physical therapy program has specific application deadline dates. $20 application fee.

Costs Per Year: $4,900 tuition; $50 student fees.

Collegiate Environment: The 9-acre campus is in the heart of the city of Albany. The building program was completed in 1966. The 2 main buildings provide classrooms, a tiered science lecture hall and 3 science laboratories and workrooms, and the audiovisual room. A bookstore and cafeteria are also included. About 65% of the current student body receive some form of financial assistance. Approximately 80%-90% of students applying for admission are accepted. The library contains 49,000 volumes and 250 periodicals. Recently, the college added a multimedia center.

Community Environment: See State University of New York at Albany.

MARIST COLLEGE   *(M-17)*
290 North Road
Poughkeepsie, New York 12601
Tel: (914) 575-3000

Description: Privately-supported, coeducational, liberal arts college accredited by the Middle States Association of Colleges and Schools. It grants the Bachelor and Master degrees. The college operates on the semester system and offers three summer sessions. Enrollment includes 3,150 full-time and 606 part-time undergraduate, and 580 graduate students. A faculty of 158 full-time and 149 adjunct gives a faculty-student ratio of 1-15.

Entrance Requirements: Accredited high school graduation; completion of 16 units including 4 English, 3 mathematics, 2 science, 3 social science, and 2 American History; SAT or ACT required; non-degree candidates may be accepted by permission; early decision, early admission, midyear admission, and advanced placement programs available; Mar. 1 preferred application deadline; $30 application fee.

Costs Per Year: $11,400 tuition; $6,200 room and board; $280 student fees.

Collegiate Environment: The 120-acre campus is located on the banks of the Hudson River, one mile north of Poughkeepsie, N.Y. The 29 buildings include the Lowell Thomas Communications Center, the Margaret and Charles Dyson Center, the Marist Computer Center, the College Library which contains 180,000 volumes, and the James J. McCann Recreation Center. 70% of Marist's students live in college housing which includes a garden apartment complex, 33 townhouse apartments for upperclassmen, and 7 residence halls offering computer terminal rooms. 68% of the students applying for admission meet the requirements and are accepted. 81% of the current freshman class graduated in the top half of their high school class, 68% were in the top two fifths, 29% were in the top fifth. The middle 50% range of scores for entering freshmen were SAT 930-1090 combined. Scholarships and financial aid are available. 70% of students receive some form of financial assistance. Over 92% of the previous freshman class returned to the college for their sophomore year.

Community Environment: See Vassar College.

MARYMOUNT COLLEGE *(C-2)*
100 Marymount Avenue
Tarrytown, New York 10591
Tel: (914) 631-3200; (800) 724-4312; Admissions: (914) 332-8295; Fax: (914) 332-4956

Description: Privately-supported liberal arts college for women founded 1907 by the Religious of the Sacred Heart of Mary. The college is accredited by the Middle States Association of Colleges and Schools and grants the Bachelor degree. It operates on teh semester system and offers one summer session. Enroment includes 1,162 students. A faculty of 57 full-time and 70 part-time gives a faculty-student ratio of 1-12. Now governed by a predominantly lay Board of Trustees, representing various faiths and professions, the college encourages enrollment of students from all over the world.

Entrance Requirements: Accredited high school graduation; completion of 16 units recommended; including 4 English, 3 mathematics, 3 foreign language, 3 science, 3 social science; SAT or ACT required; Achievement tests recommended; early admission, rolling admission, delayed admission, credit granted for

advanced placement courses; $30 application fee.

Costs Per Year: $12,110 per year tuition, $6,750 room and board; $390 student fees.

Collegiate Environment: The 25-acre campus lies in a suburban setting overlooking the Hudson River and the 2 Tarrytown lakes. There are 11 buildings including 5 residence halls, sports building with olympic-size swimming pool and modern library. Housing is available for 650 students. The college is nonsectarian, and there are churches of other denominations within walking distance of the campus. About 70% of students applying for admission are accepted. A Community Leadership program is aimed specifically toward disadvantaged students in New York State. These students are given tutorial help in English; during the summer, an intensive course of study skills, reading skills, and grammar is required of all participants. On completion of this summer program, students are accepted into the freshman class. Approximately 60% of student body receives some form of financial assistance; a variety of merit scholarships are available. About 80-85% of the previous freshman class return to this school for their second year. The library contains over 117,400 volumes.

Community Environment: Population 11,115. Located on the east bank of the Hudson River, Tarrytown is joined on the south by Irvington and on the north by North Tarrytown. These 3 communities form the well-known Sleepy Hollow country, made famous by Washington Irving in "The Legend of Sleepy Hollow." The city is approximately 45 minutes from New York City and transportation is provided by rail and bus lines. The community services include a hospital, public library, and active civic and fraternal organizations. Considerable part-time employment is available to students.

MARYMOUNT MANHATTAN COLLEGE *(E-2)*
221 East 71st Street
New York, New York 10021
Tel: (212) 517-0400; (800) 627-9668 X 68; Fax: (212) 517-0413

Description: Marymount Manhattan is a small, independent, 4-year liberal arts college providing education to students from the greater metropolitan area of New York City. It is accredited by the Middle States Association of Colleges and Schools and professionally by the American Speech and Hearing Association. In addition to serving the full-time student, the college provides a full range of services and courses for the student who works or has family responsibilities and can attend college only part-time. The college offers flexible scheduling with courses available day, evening and weekends. The college operates on the 4-1-4 calendar system and offers one summer session. Enrollment includes 1,110 full-time and 948 part-time students. A faculty of 49 full-time and 151 part-time gives a faculty-student ratio of 1-18. Special programs include cooperative programs with Mannes College of Music and the Laboratory Institute of Merchandising; cooperative B.F.A. program with New York School of Interior Design; Community Leadership Program; Women in Management Honors Seminar; Academic Year Abroad Program and Honor Societies.

Entrance Requirements: Accredited high school graduation with top 20% completion of 20 units including 4 English, 3 mathematics, 3 foreign language, 3 science, 3 social science; SAT or ACT accepted; non-high school graduates considered; rolling admission, early decision, delayed admission, early admission; midyear admission and advanced placement programs available; $30 application fee.

Costs Per Year: $11,200 tuition; $5,200 room and board; additional expenses average $125.

Collegiate Environment: Marymount Manhattan College is centrally located in Manhattan at 221 East 71 Street between Second and Third Avenues. All of New York City's midtown area is easily accessible from the college. An academic facility opened in 1974 houses specialized laboratories for experimental psychology, sociology, and education; a Communication and Learning Center designed for the diagnosis and remediation of speech, hearing and learning disorders; a modern 250-seat theatre; a library-learning center and media center which contain 100,535 volumes; 855 periodicals, 13,400 microforms and 1,208 audio-visual materials and includes a multi-media center and writing center; a College Skills Laboratory designed to strengthen basic skills in reading and writing. The college provides off-campus housing for 250 students in a community-style apartment dwelling in the vicinity. The Director of Residence lives in the apartment building and acts as a liaison between students and the apartment management. Information is also available for students who wish to live in non-college sponsored housing. The majority of the students commute to the college. Approximately 85% of students applying for admission are accepted, including midyear students, and 73% of the previous freshman class return to this campus for their sophomore year. SAT or ACT and interview strongly recommended for admission. College enrolls an increasing number of transfer students each year. Recognition given to various types of nontraditional credit, including Advanced Placement, College Level Examination Program (CLEP), New York State College Proficiency Examination (CPE), and Life Experience. The college awarded 292 bachelor degrees recently and approximately 32% of the senior class continued on to graduate school. Approximately 40% of the students at the college attend on a part-time basis because of job or family commitments that limit their time. These include women in all aspects of business, and paraprofessionals in many fields. 70 scholarships are available and 85% of students receive some form of financial aid.

Community Environment: See New York University.

MATER DEI COLLEGE *(B-13)*
Riverside Drive
Ogdensburg, New York 13669
Tel: (315) 393-5930; (800) 724-4080

Description: A privately supported Roman Catholic, two-year junior college with career-oriented programs leading to the Associate Degree. Enrollment is 427 full-time and 63 part-time students. A faculty of 25 full-time and 30 part-time gives a faculty-student ratio of 1-13.

Entrance Requirements: High school graduation or GED accepted; ACT or SAT recommended; early admission, early decision, rolling admission, midyear admission, delayed admission, and advanced placement plans available; $25 application fee; deadline for applications is August 15.

Costs Per Year: $5,700 tuition; $3,870 room and board; $325 student fees.

Collegiate Environment: Located on the St. Lawrence River, just over 2 hours from Syracuse and an hour and a half from Ottawa, there are many winter sports available. A modern, well-equipped library houses 60,226 titles, 280 periodicals, 67 microforms and 502 audiovisual materials. Financial aid is available and 85% of the students receive aid. 95% of applicants are accepted.

MEDAILLE COLLEGE   *(I-4)*
18 Agassiz Circle
Buffalo, New York 14214
Tel: (716) 884-3281; (800) 292-1582; Admissions: (716) 884-3281; Fax: (716) 884-0291

Description: Independent, coeducational nonsectarian, career-oriented Liberal Arts College is accredited by the Middle States Association of Colleges and Schools. The college operates on the semester system with one summer term. The college was founded in 1875. Programs of study lead to the Bachelor and Associate degrees. Recent enrollment included 392 men, 557 women full-time, and 54 men and 141 women part-time. There are 165 faculty members providing a faculty-student ratio of 1-17.

Entrance Requirements: High school graduation; total of 18 academic units including 3 English; 2 math; 2 science; 2 social studies, early admission, rolling admission, delayed admission and advanced placement plans available; personal interview required; $25 application fee.

Costs Per Year: $9,360 tuition; $4,400 room and board.

Collegiate Environment: The school is located in central Buffalo on the edge of Delaware Park. The library contains 45,267 volumes, 311 periodicals, 3,500 microforms and 5,000 audiovisual materials. A new campus center provides a dining hall, student lounges, gymnasium, game room, weight room and student development offices. There are also a learning services center, radio station, photography and computer labs, a recreation center, and a science building. Dormitory housing is provided for an unspecified number of students. Approximately 60% of students applying for admission are accepted. Financial aid is available.

Community Environment: See Canisius College.

MEDGAR EVERS COLLEGE OF THE CITY UNIVERSITY OF NEW YORK   *(F-2)*
1650 Carroll Street
Brooklyn, New York 11225
Tel: (718) 270-4900

Description: Publicly supported, coeducational college of professional studies. It is fully accredited by the Middle States Association of Colleges and Schools and operates on the semester system. Founded by the Board of Education of the City of New York upon request from the Bedford-Stuyvesant area of Brooklyn, Medgar Evers College is a community college of the City University of New York which grants the Associate and Bachelor degrees. It was opened in 1971 on the following mandate: (1) that the college be a four-year college from its inception; (2) that the college be experimental; that it develop new and better methods of selecting, organizing, and teaching course material, and pioneer innovations which would enhance the education of its students; (3) that the college emphasize professional studies such as teaching, social work, public administration, and business; (4) that the college be responsive to and serve the educational and social needs of Central Brooklyn; (5) that the community should have a major voice in selection of the site and of its name. Enrollment includes 3,826 full-time and part-time students. A faculty of 323 provides a faculty-student ratio of 1:12.

Entrance Requirements: Accredited high school graduation or equivalent. Open enrollment policy for residents of New York City. $30 application fee. Rolling admission plan available.

Costs Per Year: $2,100 New York resident tuition; $2,676 nonresident tuition; $77 student fees.

Collegiate Environment: The college is housed temporarily in the building formerly used by Brooklyn Preparatory High School until its own campus can be built in Central Brooklyn. facilities include a 77,000 volume library.

Community Environment: See Brooklyn College of the City University of New York.

MERCY COLLEGE   *(D-2)*
555 Broadway
Dobbs Ferry, New York 10522
Tel: (914) 693-7600; (800) 637-2969; Admissions: (914) 693-7600; Fax: (914) 693-9455

Description: Privately-supported, coeducational liberal arts college founded in 1950 to train young women for the Religious Sisters of Mercy. In 1968 the college became an independent, coeducational, nonsectarian school offering both undergraduate and graduate degrees. It is accredited by the Middle States Association of Colleges and Schools and professionally by the National League for Nursing and the Council for Social Work Education. Programs are offered in the Liberal Arts and Sciences, fine arts and professional studies offering courses in general education with a concentration in a major area of study. The college confers the Associate, the Bachelor of Arts, Bachelor of Science, Bachelor of Fine Arts , and the Master of Science degrees. The semester system and offers three summer terms and a January Intersession. The college enrolls 1,800 men, 2,400 women full-time and 1,000 men and 1,288 women part-time. A faculty of 155 full-time and 500 part-time members provides a faculty-student ratio of 1:11.

Entrance Requirements: High school graduation with completion of 16 units, including 4 English, 2 mathematics, 2 foreign language, 2 science, 2 social science recommended. SAT recommended, non-high school graduates considered; early admission, rolling admission, midyear admission, early decision, advanced placement programs available; $35 application fee.

Costs Per Year: $6,600 tuition; $5,000 room and board.

Collegiate Environment: The college is located in Westchester County and draws its students from a wide area by reason of excellent dormitories and transportation facilities. The library contains 283,991 volumes, 1,254 periodicals and an expanding audiovisual collection. All students applying for admission are accepted including midyear and 62% of the previous freshman class return to the campus for their sophomore year. Average high school standing of a recent freshman class, top 80%; 5% in the top quarter; 10% in the second quarter; 70% in the third quarter; 45% in the bottom quarter; The average scores of the entering freshman class were SAT 350 verbal, 380 math. $300,000 in scholarships are available and 78% of the current student body receive some form of financial assistance.

Community Environment: Population 10,353. Primarily a residential community, Dobbs Ferry is located near Yonkers and is 15 miles from New York City.

Branch Campuses: Dobb's Ferry, Yorktown, Peekskill, White Plains, Yonkers and the Bronx.

MOLLOY COLLEGE   *(F-3)*
1000 Hempstead Avenue
Rockville Centre, New York 11570
Tel: (516) 678-5000; (800) 229-1020; Admissions: (516) 678-5000 X 240

Description: Independent, religiously affiliated, coeducational liberal arts college was established in 1955 by the Sisters of St. Dominic. It is accredited by the Middle States Association of Colleges and Schools and grants Associate and Bachelor degrees. The college operates on the 4-1-4 calendar system and offers two summer sessions. Enrollment is 1,358 full-time and 672 part-time undergraduates, and 109 graduate students. A faculty of 127 full-time and 134 part-time gives a faculty-student ratio of 1-14.

Entrance Requirements: Accredited high school graduation or equivalent with rank in upper half of graduating class; completion of 16 units, including 4 English, 2 mathematics, 2 foreign language, 2 science, and 3 social science; SAT required; non-high school graduates considered; rolling admission, early admission, early decision, delayed admission, midyear admission, and advanced placement plans available; $25 application fee.

Costs Per Year: $9,300 tuition; $500 student fees; $800 books.

Collegiate Environment: The college is comprised of 5 buildings located on 25 acres. The library contains 120,070 volumes, 1,045 periodicals, 5,700 microforms and 5,200 visual materials. The college is easily reached from all parts of Long Island, Queens, Manhattan, and Brooklyn. Approximately 76% of students applying for admission are accepted, including midyear students, and 88% of the previous freshman class return to the college for the sophomore year. The average scores of the entering freshman class were SAT 414 verbal, 473 math. 252 scholarships are available, including 10 athletic and 86% of the students receive some form of financial aid. The college awarded 21 AA degrees, 173 BA degrees, 255 BS degrees, and 23 MS degrees during the recent academic year. 19% of the senior class continued on to graduate school.

Community Environment: Rockville Centre (population 35,000) is a suburb of New York City on Long Island. Good transportation facilities make all the cultural, recreational, civic services, and employment opportunities of New York easily accessible. Within the immediate area there are a public library, churches of major denominations, and a hospital. Some part-time work is available within the local vicinity.

MOUNT SAINT MARY COLLEGE (A-1)

300 Powell Avenue
Newburgh, New York 12550
Tel: (914) 561-0800; (800) 558-0942; Admissions: (914) 569-3248; Fax: (914) 562-6762

Description: Privately-supported, coeducational liberal arts college, accredited by the Middle States Association of Colleges and Schools. The college was established in 1954 by the Sisters of the Order of St. Dominic of Newburgh. The faculty, composed of religious and laymen of both Christian and non-Christian beliefs, offers courses leading to Bachelor and Masters degrees. The college operates on the 4-1-4 system and offers two summer sessions. Undergraduate enrollment includes 492 men, 1,076 women full-time, and 200 men and 237 women part-time. A faculty of 70 full-time and 107 part-time gives a faculty-student ratio of 1-14. Graduate enrollment includes 255 students. Students may take classes at two extensions: one at the United States Military Academy at West Point; the other at Orange County Community College in Middletown, New York.

Entrance Requirements: Accredited high school graduation with rank in upper 60% of graduating class; completion of 17 units including 4 English, 2 mathematics, 2 foreign language, 1 science, 3 social science; SAT or ACT accepted; non-high school graduates considered; rolling admission, early admission, delayed admission, advanced placement plans available; $20 application fee.

Costs Per Year: $8,130 tuition; $5,000 room and board.

Collegiate Environment: The 36-acre campus overlooks the Hudson River and is located 12 miles north of the United States Military Academy at West Point. The 14 college buildings contain a library and dormitory facilities for 780 men and women. The library houses 116,113 volumes, 800 pamphlets, 1,129 periodical titles, 547,861 microforms, and 7,307 items in the media center. Students from other geographical locations are accepted, as are midyear students. Approximately 73% of students applying for admission are accepted. Almost 50% of the recent student body graduated in the top quarter of their high school class and 20% in the highest tenth. Financial aid is available for economically handicapped students and 78% of the freshman class receive some form of aid. Army ROTC is offered

Community Environment: Mount Saint Mary College is located in the historic Hudson Valley Region, at the foothills of the Catskill Mountains, 60 miles north of New York City. Cultural, historical, and outdoor activities abound.

MOUNT SINAI SCHOOL OF MEDICINE (E-2)

One Gustave L. Levy Place
Box 1002
New York, New York 10029
Tel: (212) 241-6696; Admissions: (212) 241-6696

Description: Private coeducational medical school established in 1963 and granted a provisional charter by the Board of Regents of the University of the State of New York, authorizing the school to grant the M.D. degree and to offer graduate instruction leading to the M.S. and Ph.D. degrees. In 1967, the school became affiliated with the City University of New York, but the school remains financially autonomous and self-supporting under its own Board of Trustees. Its charter was made absolute by the Board of Regents in 1968, and the school admitted a first-year class of 36 and a third-year class of 23 medical students in September, 1968. Enrollment includes 518 full-time students. The faculty consists of 1,000 full-time and 250 part-time instructors.

Entrance Requirements: Minimum 3 years of undergraduate work in an accredited college or university; completion of 1 year each of inorganic chemistry, organic chemistry, biology, college-level mathematics, English, physics; Medical College Admission Test required; those without an undergraduate degree must give evidence of exceptionally high scholastic achievement, intellectual capacity, and motivation in order to be admitted; personal interview required; $75 application fee.

Costs Per Year: $21,000 tuition; $7,950 room and board.

Collegiate Environment: The Mount Sinai Medical Center comprises 22 buildings on a campus occupying a super-block area on Fifth Avenue opposite Central Park in upper Manhattan. The complex includes the 1,300-bed Mount Sinai Hospital, the Medical School's Basic Sciences Laboratories, the Berg Institute of Research, the Atran Laboratory, 7 patient pavillions and various other facilities providing support services and administrative functions. Also in the Medical Center, and associated with the School of Medicine, are the Graduate School of Biological Sciences and the Page and William Black Post Graduate School of Medicine. The Annenberg Building, a 31-story structure and the main facility of the School of Medicine, contains modern laboratories, a library, an amphitheatre, animal care facilities, faculty offices, and lounge and dining areas for students and faculty. Affiliated hospitals that provide additional teaching resources include the New York City Hospital Center at Elmhurst, Englewood Hospital, Queens Hospital Center, Staten Island University Hospital, the Veterans Administration Hospital in the Bronx, North General Hospital, and the Jewish Home and Hospital for the Aged.

Community Environment: See New York University.

NAZARETH COLLEGE OF ROCHESTER (H-7)

4245 East Avenue
Rochester, New York 14618
Tel: (716) 586-2525; (800) 462-3944; Fax: (716) 586-2431

Description: Founded in 1924, this independent, coeducational liberal arts college admits qualified students regardless of race, creed or physical handicap. It is accredited by the Middle States Association of Colleges and Schools. The college includes an undergraduate, continuing education and graduate division. Air Force ROTC is available through Rensselaer Polytechnic Institute. It grants the Bachelor and Master degrees. It operates on the semester system and offers two summer sessions. Enrollment includes 1,316 full-time and 449 part-time undergraduates and 958 graduate students. A faculty of 109 full-time and 63 part-time gives a faculty-student ratio of 1-14.

Entrance Requirements: Approved high school graduation, completion of 17 units including 4 English, 3 math, 3 science, 4 social studies, and 3 foreign language; SAT minimum 500M, 500V or ACT 20 required; early decision, early admission, delayed admission, midyear admission and advanced placement plans available; Mar. 1 application deadline, Dec. 1 early decision application deadline; $30 application fee.

Costs Per Year: $11,450 tuition; $5,150 room and board; $200 fees.

Collegiate Environment: The college is located within the residential suburb of Pittsford, 7 miles from the center of the city of Rochester, in western New York. The 14 college buildings contain a library of more than 257,736 volumes, 1,615 periodicals, 303,758 microforms, and 11,494 records, CD's and tapes, and 10 CD-ROMs. Dormitory facilities are available for 825 men and women. Students from other geographical locations are accepted as well as midyear students. Approximately 81% of students applying for admission are accepted. Financial aid is available and 85% of the students receive aid. The college is a member of the Rochester Area College Consortium, which allows students to take up to two courses per semester at any of the cooperative institutions.

Community Environment: See University of Rochester.

NEW SCHOOL FOR SOCIAL RESEARCH, EUGENE LANG COLLEGE *(E-2)*
65 West 11th Street
New York, New York 10111
Tel: (212) 229-5665; Fax: (212) 229-5355

Description: The New School for Social Research is a private university located in the Greenwich Village section of New York City. It is accrdited by the Middle States Association of Colleges and Schools. Founded in 1919 by such notable scholars as John Dewey, Charles Beard and Thorstein Veblen, the New School today includes 6 academic divisions: the Adult Division; Eugene Lang College, the Graduate Faculty of Political and Social Science; the Graduate School of Management and Urban Policy (with entry-level and mid-career programs leading to the MA and MPS degrees); Parsons School of Design, which grants the AAS, BFA, BBA, and BA/BFA with Eugene Lang College as well as MA and MFA degrees; and the Mannes College of Music. University enrollment totals 6,400; Eugene Lang College enrollment is 363. A faculty of 59 gives a faculty-student ratio of 1-9. The school operates on the semester system and 5 broad areas of concentration within which students map out individual paths. They include Writing, Literature and the Arts (including Drama); Cultural Studies; Urban Studies; Mind, Nature, and Values (including Psychology, Philosophy, and Religion); and Social and Historical (including Economics, Anthropology, and Sociology).

Entrance Requirements: Eugene Lang College requires 16 units of rigorous college-prep work (or its equivalent); the Committee on Admissions encourages applications from students of varying backgrounds who combine inquisitiveness and seriousness of purpose with the ability to participate fully in a distinctive and challenging academic program; candidates for admission must submit the college application(s), $30 fee, high school transcript (and college transcript(s) if applying as transfers); teacher evaluation (2 if applying as Early Entrant); counselor recommendation, 2,500-word essays, and have an admissions interview; early admission, early decision, deferred admission, and advanced placement plans available.

Costs Per Year: $14,710 full-time tuition; $8,760 room and board.

Collegiate Environment: The university sponsors numerous lectures, film series, panel discussions and readings every week. The College sponsors an extensive cultural program, "Lang in the City," which opens up the worlds of theater, opera and dance to students at little or no additional charge. Students produce a literary magazine and a newspaper. There are several special interest groups that meet on a regular basis, and a student union whose purpose is to reflect and promote the interests of the student body. Students use the vast resources of the university and their Greenwich Village campus for additional social/recreational/cultural activities. A sense of mutual respectfullness dominates relationships among students and between faculty and students. Opportunities for career-related internships in professions such as law, communications, social services, media, politics, museums, education, and the arts abound. Library resources include the Raymond Fogelman and Adam and Sophie Gimbel Libraries (New School); the Cooper Union for the Advancement of Science and Art Library (Cooper Union) and the Elmer Bobst Library (New York University) for a total of more than 3 million volumes available.

Community Environment: ELC is located in historic Greenwich Village, which is characterized by tree-lined streets, brownstones, cafes, bookstores, and galleries.

NEW YORK CITY TECHNICAL COLLEGE OF THE CITY UNIVERSITY OF NEW YORK *(F-2)*
300 Jay Street
Brooklyn, New York 11201
Tel: (718) 260-5000

Description: Founded in 1947, this publicly supported, coeducational technical college of the City University of New York is accredited by the Middle States Association of Colleges and Schools. It offers more than 35 associate degree and six baccalaureate degree programs. The university divisions are Commerce, Liberal Arts and Sciences, Health and Natural Sciences, and Technology. It provides day and evening degree programs and Weekend College which combine general and technical education as well as nondegree courses in the evening. It operates on the semester basis and offers one summer session. Enrollment is 11,000 men and women. A faculty of 640 gives a faculty-student ratio of 1-20.

Entrance Requirements: High school graduation or equivalent; completion of appropriate college-preparatory courses for individual degree programs; placement tests required. Rolling admission and advanced placement plans available. Application fee $35.

Costs Per Year: $1,250 tuition for residents of New York City; $4,050 tuition for out-of-state residents; $76-$182 student fees.

Collegiate Environment: The college is located on 3 acres in the heart of Brooklyn's new Civic Center and is easily accessible by public transportation. The 8 college buildings include a library of 160,000 volumes and 700 periodicals. There are over seventy active clubs on campus reflecting the students' diverse ethnic backgrounds, career goals and interests. Classes begin in September and January and midyear students are accepted. 85% of the students receive financial aid.

Community Environment: See Brooklyn College of the City University of New York.

NEW YORK COLLEGE OF PODIATRIC MEDICINE *(E-2)*
53 East 124th Street
New York, New York 10035
Tel: (212) 410-8000; (800) 526-6966; Fax: (212) 369-4608

Description: The New York College of Podiatric Medicine (NYCPM), the first and largest college of podiatric medicine established in 1911, is an independent, nonprofit institution located in New York City. It shares its Manhattan location with the Foot Clinics of New York, the largest foot-care center in the world. It is accredited by the Middle States Association of Colleges and Schools. The Doctor of Podiatric Medicine degree is awarded. After an intensive two-year program of basic science training identical to that of an allopathic institution, students enter an extensive two-year program of clinical training. The curriculum is arranged so that courses in anatomy and physiology, bacteriology, biochemistry, biomechanics, histology, neurology, pathology, and pharmacology move from the study of normal structure and function in the human body to an admixture of basic and clinical science training. The clinical opportunities in the Foot Clinics of New York are unsurpassed in regard to the number of patients seen and the variety of podiatric treatment given. Annually 60,000 patients receive podiatric care in the seven clinical divisions (Podiatric Medicine, Surgery, General Podiatry, Orthopedics, Pediatrics, Rediology, and Sports Medicine). First-year students are introduced to the clinics through observation of patients and their treatment. Second-year students are assigned to the general clinics, where they become familiar with the diagnosis and treatment of various podiatric lesions. The third year is a blend of clinical experience and instruction, and the student begins to learn the treatment of human pathologies. The fourth year is primarily a clinical learning experience, with advanced seminars and a large array of clinical externship opportunities. There are 468 students with a faculty of 73.

Entrance Requirements: Minimum 3 years of college work at an accredited college or university; completion of at least 6 semester hours in English, and 8 each in physics, biology or zoology, general chemistry, and organic chemistry; MCAT required; admission preference will be given applicants with baccalaureate degrees; $50 application fee. Rolling admission plan.

Costs Per Year: $19,040 tuition; $1,045 student and lab fees.

Collegiate Environment: A 5-story building, completely fireproof, erected in 1927 and augmented in 1935, houses the work of the college. Ample space is provided for all the didactic, clinic and laboratory teaching, with the most modern equipment available. A closed-circuit television camera and monitors for demonstration purposes have recently been installed. The institution has begun construction of a 2-story facility which will house the Foot Clinics of New York and provide lecture rooms and laboratories. The library contains 12,902 volumes, 300 periodicals and 125 microforms. The school year begins in September. Approximately 70% of the applicants are accepted. Many scholarships are available and 90% of students receive some form of aid. An apartment is available to house students.

Community Environment: As a truly international city, New York plays host to activities that support every possible interst: music, from classical to the intricate alternative scene; clubs; Broadway and off-Broadway productions; museums beyond number; the green Adirondack Mountains and the beautiful beaches of Long Island and New Jersey, both only a short ride away. Every major professional sport is represented, many by two teams.

NEW YORK INSTITUTE OF TECHNOLOGY *(E-2)*
1855 Broadway
New York, New York 10023
Tel: (212) 399-8300

Description: Privately supported coeducational technical college has three campuses. The Metropolitan Center is located in New York City; Old Westbury and Central Islip Campuses are on Long Island. It is accredited by the Middle States Association of Colleges and Schools and operates on the semester basis with three summer terms. The institute offers programs leading to the Bachelor of Science, the Bachelor of Technology, the Bachelor of Fine Arts, and the Associate in Applied Science degrees. The new Division of Business and Management grants the Master of Business Administration with a major in management. The institute is united in a federation with Nova University of Fort Lauderdale for an interchange of academic activity. There is a Cooperative Education program available whereby students alternate a semester's attendance at classes with a full-time job in industry. The college enrolls 700 men, 500 women full-time and 250 men and 250 women part-time. A faculty of 40 full-time and 50 part-time members provides a faculty-student ratio of 17:1.

Entrance Requirements: Accredited high school graduation or equivalent with rank in upper 75% of graduating class; completion of 16 units including 4 English, 2 mathematics, 2 science, 2 social science; SAT required; early decision plan available; $15 application fee.

Costs Per Year: $8,140 tuition.

Collegiate Environment: The institute's Metropolitan Center is located near Lincoln Center in Manhattan. Space for additional classrooms and laboratores is provided in the new air-conditioned Alcoa Building, just 2 blocks from the major Metropolitan Center facilities. The Old Westbury campus comprises several estates which include 12 buildings on approximately 600 acres. The libraries contain over 80,000 volumes and students attending either campus have access to the libraries at both colleges. Semesters begin in September and January, and midyear students are accepted.

Community Environment: See New York University.

Branch Campuses: Old Westbury, Campus, Northern Boulevard, Old Westbury, NY 11568 (516) 686-7516; Central Islip Campus, 211 Carlton Avenue, Central Islip, NY 11722 (516) 348-3000.

NEW YORK INSTITUTE OF TECHNOLOGY - OLD WESTBURY *(E-3)*
Old Westbury, New York 11568
Tel: (516) 686-7516; (800) 345-6948; Fax: (516) 686-7520

Description: NYIT is a private, multi-campus institution. Founded in 1955, it is accredited by the Middle States Association of Colleges and Schools. It is coeducational and has programs at the associate, bachelor's, and master's levels. As part of NYIT, the New York College of Osteopathic Medicine also awards the Doctor of Osteopathic Medicine. Through NYIT's distance learning division, the American Open University of NYIT, students can study at home through correspondence or computer conferencing. Programs are designed to provide students with marketable skills and/or the qualifications for graduate school. Air Force ROTC is available. The institute operates on the semester system and offers two summer sessions. Enrollment includes 4,280 full-time and 1,865 part-time undergraduates and 2,349 graduate students. A faculty of 253 full-time and 562 part-time provides a faculty-student ratio of 1-18.

Entrance Requirements: Total high school units 16: 4 English, 2 math, 1 lab science, 2 social studies, 7 electives. SAT or ACT required and GRE for graduate school. High school graduates with a C

average accepted. Open enrollment; early admission, early decision, midyear admission, rolling admission and advanced placement plans available; $30 application fee.

Costs Per Year: $8,340 tuition; $900 student fees; $5,500 room and board.

Collegiate Environment: The campus spreads over 700 mostly wooded acres. Most students commute to campus where they can participate in a variety of extracurricular activities and sports. The library contains 192,830 titles, 2,822 periodicals, 542,719 microforms, and 45,556 audiovisual materials. Student housing is available for 400 men and 400 women. Special programs include correspondence courses, continuing education courses, life experience credits, and credit for certain courses by prior examination. A Cooperative Education program is available in Engineering, Technology, and Business. Summer programs are offered in Archaeological Studies (France) and Architecture (Italy or Spain). 78% of applicants are accepted. Scholarships are available.

Community Environment: In Old Westbury, NYIT is largely self-contained. There are many stores and restaurants nearby and the college provides some health care services to members of the surrounding community. Free concerts and other cultural events are also open to members of the neighboring community. Students who want to visit Manhattan theaters, museums, or sports events can take the train from nearby stations or drive.

Branch Campuses: 1855 Broadway, New York, NY 10023, and Central Islip NY 11722.

NEW YORK LAW SCHOOL *(E-2)*
57 Worth Street
New York, New York 10013-2690
Tel: (212) 431-2888

Description: Founded in 1891, The New York Law School is a private institution committed to educating students to become competent lawyers capable of assuming positions of responsibility in society. It is fully approved by the Association of American Law Schools and the American Bar Association. It operates on the semester basis system and offers a summer term. Degree granted is Juris Doctor. Enrollment is 908 full-time and 484 part-time candidates for the J.D. degree. The faculty consists of 52 full-time and 99 part-time members.

Entrance Requirements: Bachelor degree from accredited college or university; LSAT required; $50 application fee.

Costs Per Year: $17,600 tuition for day session; $13,200 evening and part-time.

Collegiate Environment: The law school consists of 4 buildings. The school's Law Library houses a collection of approximately 398,000 volumes. The library has a large collection of microforms as well as access to major metropolitan research libraries through its membership in the METRO cooperative network system. A major focus of library development recently has been in the area of technological innovation. WESTLAW and LEXIS, as well as numerous other legal and nonlegal databases, are available to students for research projects. In addition, the law school also has a Communications Law Library, which is a specialized collection of materials related to the Communications Media Center. It includes more than 4,000 volumes on media-related law, including scholarly journals, trade publications, FCC releases, communications law research tools, and studies. The New York Law School is located in close proximity to the Federal, State and City courts. Dormitory housing is available. Classes begin at the end of August.

Community Environment: Wall Street, City Hall, Foley Square, World Trade Center.

NEW YORK MEDICAL COLLEGE *(E-2)*
Sunshine Cottage
Valhalla, New York 10595
Tel: (914) 993-4507

Description: This privately supported, coeducational college is a nonprofit, nonsectarian institution that provides graduate training in the medical sciences. It was chartered in 1860 by the New York State Legislature. In 1972 the college opened a new Medical College building in Westchester, New York. Degrees granted: Doctor of Medicine, Doctor of Philosophy in the basic sciences, Master of Science in the basic sciences, and Master of Public Health. Thirty-three advanced degree programs are offered. The school enrolls 760 medical school students and 800 graduate school students. There are 1,100 full-time and 1,600 part-time faculty members. Medical students take clerkships and rotations in hospitals ranging from large urban medical centers to small suburban hospitals and technologically advanced regional tertiary care facilities. The Graduate School of Health Sciences offers programs at three locations: Valhalla and Suffern, N.Y. and in Danbury, Connecticut.

Entrance Requirements: Bachelor degree from accredited college or university; completion of 2 semesters each of inorganic and general chemistry, organic chemistry including aliphatic and aromatic compounds, physics, general biology including zoology, and English composition; MCAT, GRE, TOEFL required; $60 application fee for Medical School, $35 application fee for the Graduate School of Health Science, or Graduate School of Basic Medical Science.

Costs Per Year: $22,400 tuition.

Community Environment: See New York University.

NEW YORK STATE COLLEGE OF VETERINARY MEDICINE AT CORNELL UNIVERSITY   *(J-10)*
Ithaca, New York 14853
Tel: (607) 253-3700; Fax: (607) 253-3708

Description: Publicly supported, coeducational veterinary college was established by an Act of the State Legislature in 1894. It is a statutory college of the State University of New York and is accredited by the Middle States Association of Colleges and Schools and the American Veterinary Medical Association. The enrollment is approximately 320 Doctor of Veterinary Medicine candidates and 109 graduate students attending classes on the semester system. Clinical facilities for both large and small animals are located adjacent to the research and preclinical teaching facilities. The clinical facilities include the hospitals, the ambulatory (out-patient) service, and speciallty services. The research facilities on the campus are mainly centered in the 9-level research tower which contains over 80 laboratories, conference rooms, and animal care facilities. Poultry disease research is done on the campus at Cornell University in conjunction with the diagnostic and teaching laboratory, and at the research laboratory on Snyder Hill. Regional laboratories for poultry disease diagnosis are also maintained at the college. Six laboratories located in dairy areas of New York State conduct work on mastitis control programs under the Department of Large Animal Medicine, Obstetrics, and Surgery. The laboratory at Ithaca also helps with teaching and field research as well as diagnosis. The James A. Baker Institute for Animal Health includes 14 laboratories where diseases of dogs and virus research is conducted. A clinical nutrition program was established in 1972 for teaching and research and in 1974 the Cornell Feline Research laboratory was formed. Several tracts of land with laboratories are maintained for research on internal parasites of sheep, reproductive diseases of dairy cattle, and radiation biology studies. There are computing facilities on-campus as well as the Muenscher Poisonous Plants Garden. Also on-campus is a Diagnostic Laboratory. The Equine Research Park located adjacent to the Cornell campus awards M.S., Ph.D. and D.V.M. degrees.

Entrance Requirements: For DVM program completion of at least 3 years of study in an accredited college or university including 6 semester hours English, 6 physics, 6 biology or zoology, 16 chemistry including organic chemistry, 4 biochemistry, and 3 microbiology; all sciences except biochemistry must include laboratory instruction; GRE required; all prerequisites other than biochemistry and microbiology are expected to be completed at the time of application; application for M.S. and Ph.D., degree programs is through the Cornell Graduate School; D.V.M. application is directly to the College of Veterinary Medicine.

Costs Per Year: $12,100 resident tuition; $15,900 nonresidents; $6,000 room and board; additional expenses average $3,560.

Collegiate Environment: The College of Veterinary Medicine is located at the eastern edge of Cornell's main campus. The existing complex totals nearly 280 thousand net square feet. The main College campus is spread over nearly 20 acres and includes paddocks and exercise lots for animals. Off-campus facilities for research on infectious, parasitic, and metabolic disease include: 1) the Snyder Hill campus, situated approximately three miles south of the main campus, which is the site for the James A. Baker Institute for Animal Health,

as well as other research, animal holding and isolation facilities; 2) the Equine Research Park located about two miles north of the main campus, which includes a harness track, brood mare barn, pastures, laboratory facilities, and a farrier shop; and 3) the Equine Drug Testing Facility, located about five miles north of the main campus. In addition to local off-campus facilities, regional laboratories for the study of mastitis, duck and poultry diseases, and on-site equine drug testing are in operation throughout the State. An $82-million building program increases the College's physical plant by approximately 280,000 square feet. This project, including some renovation of existing facilities, provides two new teaching centers, major improvements to the library, a new teaching hospital (small and large animal clinics), and new research laboratories and associated support space for three basic science departments. The new Veterinary Education Center became available for use in 1993. The hospital, associated offices, and laboratories are expected to be occupied in 1995. The Veterinary College library contains more than 92,000 volumes and 1,300 periodical titles and 35,000 audiovisual units; the Cornell University Library, over 5,000,000 volumes. Living accommodations are available for all students. 80 students are accepted annually to the D.V.M. program.

Community Environment: See Cornell University.

NEW YORK UNIVERSITY   *(E-2)*
22 Washington Square North
New York, New York 10011
Tel: (212) 998-4500; Fax: (212) 995-4902

Description: Privately supported, coeducational university was founded in 1831. The University includes 7 undergraduate/colleges: College of Arts and Science; Stern School of Business; Tisch School of the Arts; School of Education; School of Social Work; Gallatin School for Individualized Study, School of Continuing Education. There are also the Robert E. Wagner Graduate School of Public Service, Graduate School of Arts and Science and graduate programs in the School of Business, Education and the Arts, and Social Work and three professional schools: The College of Dentistry, The School of Law; and the School of Medicine. In addition, there are the Institute of Fine Arts and Courant Institute of Mathematical Sciences. Further, the University maintains research activities in nearly all the above and notably at The Institute of Environmental Medicine at a 1,000 acre site in Sterling Forest, near Tuxedo, N.Y. International interests are broadened by the Deutches Haus, La Maison Francaise, The Alexander Onassis Center for Hellenic Studies, Glucksman Ireland House and the Casa Italiana. Overseas programs are conducted in more than 20 countries with a Junior year abroad program in both Paris and Madrid. The University operates on the semester basis; extensive summer and evening courses are also provided. The University is a member of the Association of American Universities and is accredited by the Middle States Association of Colleges and Schools and numerous professional agencies and boards. Enrollment recently numbered 49,307 which includes 12,778 full-time and 3,174 part-time undergraduates, 15,467 graduate students and 17,888 professional and continuing eduation students. The faculty-student ratio is 1-13. All levels of academic degrees are granted: Associate, Certificate, Bachelor, Master, Professional, Doctor, by the various schools and colleges of the University.

Entrance Requirements: High school graduation or equivalent; completion of 16 units; SAT or ACT; early decision plan, early admission, deferred admission, midyear admission and advanced placement credit available; requirements vary among the schools and colleges and admission is selective; $45 application fee.

Costs Per Year: $19,748 tuition and fees; $7,552 room and board.

Collegiate Environment: The chief center for undergraduate and graduate study is at Washington Square in Greenwich Village. University residence halls accommodate 4,500 undergraduate men and women. The library system consists of 8 distinct libraries which contain over 3,000,000 volumes. The university is open without restriction to qualified students of all religions and national or racial origins. Approximately 50% of students applying for admission are accepted, including midyear students. Although the university is large, its individual units are small enough to insure intimate instruction and advisement for every student. Average size of classes is less than 30. students. Need based and merit based scholarships, grants, loans and work study programs are available to qualified applicants. 92% of freshmen receive some form of financial aid.

Community Environment: New York City, the largest city in the nation, is also its business, entertainment, and artistic capital. This teeming city is considered the greatest center of higher education in the country, and claims the largest library outside the Library of Congress. Its intellectual and cultural opportunities are limitless and virtually impossible to duplicate elsewhere. Broadway, one of the great theatre districts of the world, Lincoln Center for the Performing Arts, more than 60 museums, and many historic sites dating from the pre-Revolutionary period are among New York's cultural attractions. More than one-sixth of the city is park land, offering facilities for many sports and activities in beautifully planned areas such as Central Park and Riverside Park. The financial district, with famous Wall Street, houses the complex mechanism of banking and security markets. A vast system of subways, roadways and buses span the areas of New York's 5 boroughs, connecting richly diverse communities and people from virtually all walks of life. Points of interest on Manhattan island include: the United Nations complex, Rockefeller Center, the "tremendous city within a city," skyscrapers like the renowned Empire State Building, and the towers of the World Trade Center. New York City, with a population of over 7 million and limitless activity, provides a unique campus.

NIAGARA UNIVERSITY   *(H-4)*
Niagara University, New York 14109
Tel: (716) 286-8700; (800) 462-2111; Fax: (716) 286-8733

Description: Founded in 1856 by the Vincentian Community, Niagara University is an independent, private, coeducational university. The University offers broadly based curriculums which provide students with a holistic education that prepares them for professional careers or continuing education. There are six academic divisions: the College of Arts and Sciences; College of Business Administration; College of Nursing; College of Education; the Institute of Travel, Hotel, Restaurant Administration and the Division of General Academic Studies. The University is accredited by the Middle States Association of Colleges and Schools and grants the Associate, Bachelor, and Master degrees. Niagara University operates on the semester basis and offers 3 summer terms. Enrollment includes 1,960 full-time and 315 part-time undergraduate and 587 graduate students. A faculty of 113 full-time and 132 part-time gives a faculty-student ratio of 1-16. The university offers several academic opportunities such as the honors program, study abroad, internships, and cooperative education programs. Army ROTC is also available as an elective.

Entrance Requirements: Accredited high school graduation or GED with rank in upper half of graduating class; completion of 16 academic units including 4 English, 2 mathematics, 2 foreign language, 2 science, 2 social science; composition of units may vary by major; SAT or ACT required; advanced placement, delayed admission, rolling admission, early decision and early admission plans available; $25 application fee.

Costs Per Year: $10,320 tuition; $4,840 room and board; $420 general fee.

Collegiate Environment: The 160-acre campus is situated along the top of the picturesque Monteagle Ridge of the Niagara River Gorge about 3 miles from the famous falls. The 27 university buildings include a library of 288,986 volumes, 1,353 periodicals and 12,635 microforms, and dormitory facilities for 1,319 men and women. Approximately 85% of students applying for admission are accepted, including midyear students. Financial aid is available and 95% of those who apply for aid receive financial assistance. The average package is over $9,500.

Community Environment: Population 61,000. The city is located near the Niagara Falls. It is joined by bridges with Niagara Falls, Ontario. There are railroads, bus lines, and an airport serving the area. Community services include 2 hospitals, libraries, and shopping centers. Local recreational facilities include movie theatres, boating, fishing, golf, tennis, bowling, baseball, and swimming. Nearby metropolitan areas include Buffalo, New York and Toronto, Canada. These cities provide students with the opportunity to enjoy other cultural, social, and sports activities. Professional sports include football, ice hockey, lacrosse, and soccer.

NYACK COLLEGE   *(C-2)*
South Boulevard
Nyack, New York 10960
Tel: (914) 358-1710; (800) 336-9225; Fax: (914) 358-3047

Description: Privately supported, coeducational professional and liberal arts college is affiliated with the Christian and Missionary Alliance. It is accredited by the Middle States Association of Colleges and Schools. Efforts of representatives of several church denominations established a college to train home and foreign missionaries and evangelists. A preprofessional curriculum was developed with majors in the liberal arts and religious, music and teaching professions. The Associate and Baccalaureate degrees are awarded. It operates on the semester system and offers two summer sessions. Enrollment includes 524 full-time and 30 part-time students. A faculty of 40 gives a faculty-student ratio of 1-13.

Entrance Requirements: High school graduation with rank in upper 50% of graduating class; completion of 16 units; minimum SAT 850 combined or ACT required; rolling admission, early admission, midyear admission and advanced placement plans available; $15 application fee. Evidence of a definite Christian conversion, qualities of excellent character evidenced by minimum of 1 year's consistent Christian experience.

Costs Per Year: $8,400 tuition; $3,930 room and board; $205 student fees; additional expenses average $605.

Collegiate Environment: The 65-acre campus is 25 miles north of New York City. The 32 buildings include a library of 80,000 volumes and living accommodations for 300 men, 300 women and 18 families. Approximately 75% of students applying for admission are accepted, including midyear students.

Community Environment: Population 16,659. Located about 20 miles from New York City, Nyack is on the west bank of the Hudson River where it widens out to lake proportions. Early Dutch settlers called it the Tappan Zee. It has a local hospital, library, YMCA, and churches of all major denominations. The area has motels, hotels and shopping centers. Recreational facilities include 2 bowling alleys, swimming pools, tennis, field sports, boating, lakes, ice skating, hunting, and fishing. There is ample part-time employment available for students.

PACE UNIVERSITY   *(E-2)*
1 Pace Plaza
New York, New York 10038
Tel: (212) 346-1200; Admissions: (212) 346-1323

Description: Founded in 1906, Pace University is a comprehensive, independent, urban and suburban institution of higher education which offers a wide range of academic and professional programs at the graduate and undergraduate levels in 6 colleges and schools: Dyson College of Arts and Sciences, Lubin School of Business, School of Computer Science and Information Systems, School of Law, School of Education, School of Law, and Lienhard School of Nursing. The university is chartered by the Regents of the State of New York and is accredited by the Middle States Association of Colleges and Schools. It grants the Associate, Bachelors, Masters, Juris Doctor, and Doctorate degrees. The semester system is used and 2 summer sessions are offered. Total enrollment is 2,293 men, 3,579 women full-time and 1,446 men, 2,578 women part-time with 4,681 graduate students. The faculty includes 445 full-time and 567 part-time members.

Entrance Requirements: High school graduation or equivalent with rank in upper 50%; completion of 16 units including 4 English, 2 math, 2 social science, and 2 science; SAT, ACT or GRE required; early admission, rolling admission, midyear admission; $30 application fee.

Costs Per Year: $11,100 tuition; $5,000 room and board; $300 miscellaneous.

Collegiate Environment: The New York City campus is a three acre urban campus; the Pleasantvelle campus is a 200 acre suburban campus in Westchester County. Campus libraries contain 838,827 volumes, 3,983 periodicals and 716,348 microforms. Dormitory facilities provide housing for 1,923 students (396 in New York City and 1,527 in Pleasantville. Approximately 56% of students applying for admission are accepted. Financial aid is available with approximately 80% of students receiving some form of it.

Community Environment: The New York City campus is just a short walk from Wall Street and the South Street Seaport. Lincoln Center, the theater district, the Metropolitan Museum, and other world-famous centers of the arts are just a few minutes away by subway or cab. The Pleasantville/Briarcliff campus is in a rural setting in Westchester County, with access to twenty-three international corporate headquarters and excellent shopping nearby. The campus offers an environmental center, riding stables, and a variety of recreational facilities.

Branch Campuses: Pace has 2 campuses from which students may choose to study: the New York City campus or the Pleasantville/Briarcliff campus.

PARSONS SCHOOL OF DESIGN   *(E-2)*
66 Fifth Avenue
New York, New York 10011
Tel: (212) 229-8910; (800) 252-0852; Admissions: (212) 229-8910; Fax: (212) 229-8975

Description: Privately supported, coeducational art school evolved from a school of painting founded in 1896, and incorporated in 1902 as the New York School of Art. It is accredited by the the Middle States Association of Colleges and Schools, and professionally by the National Association of Schools of Art and Design. The institute offers a four-year Bachelor of Fine Arts course in the following departments: Fashion Design, Illustration, Environmental Design, Photography, and Interior Design. A BBA degree is offering Design Marketing. MFA Programs are offered in Painting, Sculpture and Printmaking; AAS degrees are awarded through the part-time evening division. The MA is offered in the History of Decorative Arts and in Architecture Design and Criticism. A Master of Architecture program began in the Fall of 1990. In the summer of 1970 Parsons became affiliated with the New School for Social Research; this brought to Parsons resources that are unobtainable to most independent schools of art and design. Degree candidates are now able to choose among a vast range of courses in the humanities and social sciences. The school operates on the semester system and offers two summer sessions. Enrollment includes 1,800 full-time and 6,000 part-time students. A faculty-students. A faculty of 350 gives a faculty-student ratio of 1-18.

Entrance Requirements: Applicants must submit high school transcripts (and college where applicable), SAT or ACT scores, a portfolio of 12-20 examples of art work, a four-part home exam; applicants living within 200 miles of NYC are required to attend an interview; Parsons observes rolling admission, but a strict deadline exists for students seeking financial aid consideration; $30 application fee.

Costs Per Year: $16,070 tuition; $150 student fees; $8,200 room and board; additional expenses average $1,400.

Collegiate Environment: The design school is located in New York City in order to make use of the unique resources available only at the center of the professional designer's world. In addition to field trips to the studios, shops, and workrooms of leading designers, classwork is carried on within the world-famous collections of the various art museums, the Museum of Natural History, and the Botanical Gardens. The library contains 35,000 volumes and numerous periodicals and 25,000 slides. Parson's maintains three residence halls housing a total of 500 students. The school offers career services to assist students and alumni.

Community Environment: See New York University.

PAUL SMITH'S COLLEGE   *(C-16)*
Paul Smiths, New York 12970
Tel: (518) 327-6227; (800) 421-2605; Fax: (518) 327-3030

Description: This private, coeducational two-year college was chartered in 1937. It is accredited by the Middle States Association of Colleges and Schools. It offers Associate degree programs in career-oriented and liberal arts fields. Internships and externships are required for most majors. The college operates on the semester system and offers one summer session. Enrollment includes 574 men and 248 women. A faculty of 67 full-time and 15 part-time gives a faculty-student ratio of 1-15.

Entrance Requirements: High school graduation or GED; completion of 16 units including 4 English, 2-3 mathematics, 2-3 science, SAT or ACT optional; rolling admission, deferred admission, midyear

admission, and advanced placement plans available; personal interview recommended; $25 application fee.

Costs Per Year: $10,380 tuition; $4,500 average room and board; $300-$600 student fees; $400 average additional expenses.

Collegiate Environment: The campus is located on Lower St. Regis Lake in the midst of 13,100 acres of forests, lakes, and streams. There are 25 buildings within the campus area and on-campus housing is guaranteed. The Hotel Saranac in the village of Saranac Lake is owned and operated by the college, providing hands-on training for the Hotel and Restaurant Management, Tourism and Travel, Culinary Arts, Baking, and Business Administration programs. The area is rich with natural recreational facilities for both winter and summer activities. The college library is centrally located and contains 52,000 volumes, 500 periodicals, 270 microforms and 350 audiovisual materials. Students may be admitted for either the fall or spring semester. 90% of the applicants are accepted. 80% of students receive some form of financial aid.

Community Environment: Paul Smith's is located in the Adirondack Mountains of northeast New York near Saranac Lake and Lake Placid, the site of the 1980 Winter Olympics. The area is served by air and by bus. Saranac Lake General is an excellent hospital serving the Tri-Lakes area. The region is both a summer and winter resort area with excellent skiing, fishing, boating, swimming, and hunting.

POLYTECHNIC UNIVERSITY   *(F-2)*
333 Jay Street
Brooklyn, New York 11201
Tel: (718) 260-3100; (800) 765-9832; Fax: (718) 260-3136

Description: This privately supported, coeducational liberal arts and science-engineering institution is located in the Borough Hall area of Brooklyn and in Farmingdale, Long Island. Known previously as the Polytechnic Institute of New York, it is accredited by the Middle States Association of Colleges and Schools. The school offers four-year undergraduate programs that lead to baccalaureate degrees in 4 science and 10 engineering specialties, as well as in humanities, social science and information management. It also confers Master's degrees in 37 science, engineering, and management categories and Doctorates in 19 fields. In 1975, the Westchester Graduate Center at White Plains was opened, and in 1987 it moved to its current location in Hawthorne, NY. The Westchester center offers only graduate programs, and serves scientists, engineers, and managers who are employed in the high-tech companies of the lower Hudson Valley, southern Connecticut, and northern New Jersey. The school operates on the semester system and offers 2 summer terms. Evening classes are available for students who work in the daytime. Optional Air Force and Army ROTC programs are available. Enrollment is 3,399 students. A faculty of 195 gives an overall faculty-student ratio of 1-17.

Entrance Requirements: Approved high school graduation with rank in upper half of graduation class; completion of 4 units English, 4 mathematics, 4 science, and 2 social science; SAT or ACT required; early decision, delayed admission, rolling admission, early admission, midyear admission and advanced placement plans available; $40 application fee.

Costs Per Year: $16,200 tuition; $4,700 room and board; $3,000 average additional expenses.

Collegiate Environment: The 5 buildings of the Brooklyn campus include 65 classrooms, 83 laboratories, and the new state-of-the-art Dibner Library, which focuses on information retrieval in the sciences and technology, and holds more than 273,000 volumes and 1,200 periodicals. Residence halls accomodate 60 students in Brooklyn. The Long Island Campus is located on 25 acres of land and consists of 6 buildings. Two 50-person residence halls accomodate 100 students in Farmingdale. Researchers at both campuses are engaged in high technology, state-of-the-art projects in such areas as telecommunications, digital systems, microprocessing, imaging sciences and microwave research. 65% of applicants are accepted. The average scores of the entering freshman class were SAT 440 verbal, 640 math. Financial aid is made available to students through employment, loans, and scholarships and cooperative education. About 90% of the current student body receive some form of financial assistance. The university awards many scholarships each year.

Community Environment: See Brooklyn College of the City University of New York.

PRATT INSTITUTE   *(F-2)*
200 Willoughby Avenue
Brooklyn, New York 11205
Tel: (718) 636-3600; (800) 331-0834; Admissions: (718) 636-3669;
Fax: (718) 636-3670

Description: Pratt Institute has been educating artists, designers and architects since its founding in 1887. This privately supported, coeducational college is accredited by the Middle States Association of Colleges and Schools. It offers specialized professional training within a framework of the liberal arts. Baccalaureate programs are normally 4 years in length, although the architecture curriculum requires five years. The institute is composed of the following divisions: Schools of Architecture, Art and Design, Liberal Arts and Sciences, Engineering, Graduate School of Library and Information Science, and Phoenix School of Design. The 4-1-4 calendar system is used, and 2 summer terms are offered. Enrollment includes 1,550 full-time and 180 part-time undergraduates and 1,249 graduate students. A faculty of 112 full-time and 478 part-time gives a faculty-student ratio of 1-9.

Entrance Requirements: High school graduation, including a minimum of 16 units. Specific course requirements vary depending on program. SAT or ACT required of all freshman applicants. A portfolio review is required of all applicants. Special requirements apply to some transfer students. $30 application fee; early admission, early decision, rolling admission, midyear admission and advanced placement plans available. $35 application fee.

Costs Per Year: $14,814 tuition; $7,266 room and board; $400 student fees.

Collegiate Environment: Pratt's main campus is located in the Clinton Hill section of Brooklyn on a 25-acre tree-lined campus with 23 buildings and is located 25 minutes from Manhattan. Pratt also has a Manhattan site located in the landmark Puck building in SoHo. Campus housing is guaranteed for all students. The institute's library holdings include 208,174 volumes. Approximately 60% of students applying for admission are accepted. Students come from 47 states and 70 countries. Financial aid is available and approximately 80% of the students receive some form of financial aid.

Community Environment: See Brooklyn College of the City University of New York.

QUEENS COLLEGE OF THE CITY UNIVERSITY OF NEW YORK   *(E-2)*
65-30 Kissena Boulevard
Flushing, New York 11001
Tel: (718) 520-7000

Description: Publicly supported, coeducational liberal arts college is part of the City University of New York. The baccalaureate program is offered in the day session and in the School of General Studies, and in certain areas the college offers a preprofessional or professional curriculum. Graduate programs are provided which lead to the Master of Arts, the Master of Fine Arts, Master of Library Science, and the Master of Science in Education degrees. The college is accredited by the Middle States Association of Colleges and Schools. Enrollment recently included 14,489 men and women full-time and part-time. The semester system is used and 2 summer terms are offered. The faculty consists of 633 full-time and 648 part-time members. An academic cooperative plan is available for engineering students.

Entrance Requirements: Open enrollment policy for New York City residents; advanced placement, delayed admission, rolling admission, early admission plans available; non-high school graduates considered; $30 application fee.

Costs Per Year: $1,250 tuition N.Y. City residents; nonresident tuition $4,050; $100-$182 student fees.

Collegiate Environment: The Paul Klapper Library has a carefully selected collection of 550,000 volumes, 11,000 microforms, and 5,300 periodicals. The College Union is a $4.5 million social, cultural, and recreational center. No residence facilities are available. A Special Studies and Honors program is available. Average high school standing of the freshman class, top 33%. About 80% of the previous freshman class return for the sophomore year. The college awarded 93 Professional Certificates, 3,861 Bachelor, and 1,323 Master degrees to the recent graduating class.

Community Environment: The county of Queens was organized in 1683 and included the towns of Flushing, Jamaica, Newton, and Hempstead. Its western section became a part of New York City as the Borough of Queens in 1898. This is a completely metropolitan area with all the community services, transportation, recreational, and cultural facilities found in a large metropolitan area.

QUEENSBOROUGH COMMUNITY COLLEGE OF THE CITY UNIVERSITY OF NEW YORK   *(E-3)*
222-05 56th Avenue
Bayside, New York 11364
Tel: (718) 631-6262; Admissions: (718) 631-6236

Description: Publicly supported, coeducational junior college was established by action of the Board of Higher Education and approved by the State University of New York in 1958. As a unit of the City University of New York, it is accredited by the Middle States Association of Colleges and Schools. The semester system is used and 1 summer term is offered; the evening program was initiated in 1964. The recent enrollment was 11,747 men and women. A faculty of 300 gives a faculty-student ratio of 1-39. The college offers liberal arts and sciences and career programs in business, health sciences, and the technologies leading to the Associate degree. There are also adult education programs.

Entrance Requirements: Accredited high school graduation or New York State GED; open admissions; midyear admissions; $35 application fee; rolling admission plan available.

Costs Per Year: $2,100 tuition; $2,676 tuition for nonresidents. $99.70 mandatory fees.

Collegiate Environment: The 35-acre campus has 8 buildings. The college library was organized in 1960 and now contains 127,441 volumes. All applicants are accepted. 82% of the current enrollment receives financial aid.

Community Environment: See Queens College of the City University of New York.

RABBINICAL SEMINARY OF AMERICA   *(E-3)*
92-15 69th Avenue
Forest Hills, New York 11375
Tel: (718) 268-4700

Description: Privately supported Jewish Orthodox seminary for men founded in 1933 and incorporated under the laws of the state of New York. It provides a broad program of study leading to ordination of the highest degree; Yoreh Yoreh Yodin Yodin. On the undergraduate level the work consists of 4 years of study in broad foundational courses designed to provide the students with demonstrable competence in the disciplines associated with rabbinic authority. The seminary is accredited by the Union of Orthodox Rabbis, the Rabbinical Council of America, and the Rabbinical Alliance of America as well as the AARTS. During a recent school year 140 undergraduate and 70 graduate men attended classes on the semester system.

Entrance Requirements: High school graduation with rank in upper half of graduating class; completion of 16 units including 4 English, 2 mathematics, 4 foreign language, 2 science, 2 social science. Entrance examination in Bible, Talmud, Hebrew and Aramaic are required and candidates must be versed in and have thorough understanding of Pentateuch and the commentary of Rashi. Knowledge of the Former Prophets and ability to sight read texts from the Latter Prophets is also necessary; non-high school graduates considered; personal interview required; early admission, early decision, rolling admission, delayed admission, advanced placement plans available; $25 application fee.

Costs Per Year: Tuition $4,000; room and board $2,000.

Collegiate Environment: The 3-acre campus has 4 buildings. There are 2 libraries with a combined total of 16,000 volumes. Dormitories are available for 90 men. The seminary has traditionally maintained that its offerings be available to all young men regardless of their financial situation. Contributions for scholarships, gifts, memorials, and bequests are normally provided through the Rabbinical Seminary Fund. Of 120 scholarships offered, 20 are available for freshmen. Approximately 60% of students applying for admission are accepted and 95% of the previous freshman class return to the seminary for their second year. 24% of the students receive financial aid.

Community Environment: See Queens College of the City University of New York.

Branch Campuses: Located in Jerusalem, Israel.

RENSSELAER POLYTECHNIC INSTITUTE   *(I-17)*
8th Street
Troy, New York 12180
Tel: (518) 276-6000; (800) 448-6562; Fax: (518) 276-4072

Description: The privately supported, coeducational technological university is accredited by the Middle States Association of Colleges and Schools. The Institute consists of the following schools: Architecture, Engineering, Humanities and Social Sciences, Management, Science, and the Graduate School. Special programs include a 6-year biomedical program, a 6-year management law program, a 6-year biodental program, a 6-year podiatric program, a 5-year MBA program, and an accelerated 4-year Master in engineering. There is a Cooperative Education program available whereby selected students may alternate some semesters of school with employment in their chosen fields and participate in academic cooperative plans with 14 other institutions. A study-abroad program in 6 different countries and undergraduate research opportunities are also available. The institute grants the Bachelor, Master and Doctorate degrees. The semester system is used and two summer sessions are offered. Enrollment includes 4,292 full-time and 18 part-time undergraduate, and 2,211 graduate students. A faculty of 348 full-time and 70 part-time gives a faculty-student ratio of 1-12. Optional Air Force, Army, and Navy ROTC programs available.

Entrance Requirements: High school graduation with rank in upper 20% of graduating class; completion of 16 units including 4 English, 4 mathematics, 2 science, 3 social science; SAT or ACT required; SAT II subject tests recommended; TOEFL required for foreign applicants; portfolio required for architecture; GRE required for graduate school; GMAT required for MBA program; Jan. 15 application deadline; early admission, early decision, deferred admission, midyear admission, and advanced placement plans available; $35 application fee.

Costs Per Year: $17,995 tuition; $6,155 room and board; $570 student fees; additional expenses average $1,265.

Collegiate Environment: The 260-acre landscaped campus lies east of the main business section of Troy on a plateau overlooking the city and the Hudson River. Facilities include classroom buildings, laboratories, dining halls, a student union, a football field, a gymnasium, and the 430,000-volume library containing 3,875 periodicals, and 588,000 microforms. Residence halls are available for 2,740 men, women and families. Fraternity and sorority houses accommodate additional students. The field house and student apartments are in the section of campus known as Rensselaerwyck. The middle 50% of scores for accepted freshmen were SAT Verbal 470-590, Math 600-710. Approximately 80% of those who apply are accepted including midyear students. Financial aid is offered to students after consideration of their academic qualifications, personal qualities and need for assistance. There are more than 3,031 scholarships available and better than 86% of the current student body receives some form of financial assistance. 87% of the freshmen will return to the institute for their sophomore year and about 30% of the senior class will continue on to graduate school.

Community Environment: Troy, a city of 63,000, located at the head of navigation on the Hudson River, is an important industrial city and the eastern terminus of the New York State Barge Canal. Albany and Schenectady are both within 15 miles of the city. Troy, served by air, bus and rail lines, churches of major denominations, synagogues, 3 hospitals, civic, fraternal, and veteran's organizations, and the advantages of neighboring communities, is a pleasant city. There are numerous opportunities for part-time student employment.

ROBERTS WESLEYAN COLLEGE   *(H-7)*
2301 Westside Drive
Rochester, New York 14624-1997
Tel: (716) 594-6000; (800) 777-4792; Admissions: (716) 594-6400; Fax: (716) 594-6371

Description: Privately supported, coeducational, church-related college of liberal arts and sciences. The institution is devoted to Christian culture and learning. It is accredited by the Middle States Association of Colleges and Schools and grants the Bachelor degree, one A.S. de-

gree, and two graduate degrees, M.Ed. and M.S.W. The semester system is used, and two summer sessions are offered. Enrollment includes 981 full-time and 117 part-time undergraduates and 83 graduate students. A faculty of 51 full-time and 56 part-time gives a faculty-student ratio of 1-15. Programs include engineering, medical technology, pre-law, pre-medicine, pre-pharmacy, and pre-dental. Air Force and Army ROTC programs are available.

Entrance Requirements: Approved high school graduation; completion of 12 units including 4 English, 2 mathematics, 1 science, 3 social science; SAT or ACT accepted; early decision, early admission, rolling admission, delayed admission, midyear admission and advanced placement plans available; $25 application fee.

Costs Per Year: $10,022 tuition; $3,546 room and board; $204 student fees; additional expenses average $520.

Collegiate Environment: The 75-acre campus is located about 8 miles southwest of the city of Rochester. The 17 buildings are set on a semicircular ridge and within the semicircle a level tract furnishes an athletic field. The library contains 99,857 volumes, 680 periodicals, 52,048 microforms and 3,051 audiovisual materials. Living accommodations are available for 209 men and 403 women with apartments for 31 married students. Financial aid is available. Approximately 90% of students applying for admission are accepted. The average scores of the entering freshman class were SAT 469 verbal, 529 math, ACT 21 composite. Chapel services are held two times weekly and regular attendance is required. 770 scholarships, including 305 for freshmen, are available and 90% of students receive some form of financial aid.

Community Environment: North Chili is a suburb of Rochester, New York. A municipal airport and bus service and railroad provide transportation to Rochester which has all major transportation facilities, as well as community services, public library, museums, art gallery, and hospitals. Part-time employment is available for students. Local recreational facilities include skiing, skating, tennis, swimming and golf. See also University of Rochester.

ROCHESTER INSTITUTE OF TECHNOLOGY   *(H-7)*
60 Lomb Drive
Rochester, New York 14623-5604
Tel: (716) 475-6631; Fax: (716) 475-5476

Description: Privately supported, coeducational, professional and technological institute offers specialized courses of study in professional and technical areas. It is composed of the Colleges of Applied Science and Technology; the School of Engineering Technology; the School of Computer Science; the School of Food, Hotel, and Travel Management; Business; Engineering; Imaging Arts and Sciences (School of Art and Design, School of Photographic Arts and Sciences; School for American Crafts, and School of Printing Management and Sciences); Liberal Arts, Science, Continuing Education, and the National Technical Institute for the Deaf. It operates on the quarter system and summer sessions are offered. Enrollment is 8,069 full-time and 2,964 part-time students. A faculty of 640 full-time and 447 part-time gives a faculty-student ratio of 1-13 for full-time students. The institution is accredited by the Middle States Association of Colleges and Schools as well as many professional accrediting associations. The Certificate, Diploma, Associate, Bachelor, Master, and Doctorate degrees are awarded. RIT admits qualified men and women of any race, color, national or ethnic origin, religion, and marital status; it does not discriminate on the basis of handicap in the recruitment of admission of students, or in the operation of any of its programs or activities, as specified by federal laws and regulations.

Entrance Requirements: Graduation from high school (high school equivalency diplomas will be considered); high school grades that give evidence of the capacity to complete college work successfully; satisfactory scores on entrance examinations (SAT or ACT); and the presentation of proper credit for any prerequisite courses indicated in the current undergraduate catalog; GMAT or GRE required for graduate programs; single notification for freshmen, rolling admission for transfers, early admission, early decision, delayed admission, and advanced placement plans available; $35 application fee.

Costs Per Year: $12,525 tuition; $5,286 room and board; $195 student fees; additional expenses vary by program.

Collegiate Environment: Founded in 1829, RIT has always had a strong orientation toward professional or technological career training. Many graduates move directly into the occupations for which their RIT education has prepared them. The institute has a modern, 1,300-acre campus in a suburban location located approximately 5 miles from downtown Rochester. Cars are permitted, and many students commute from nearby areas. Single freshman not living with relatives are required to live in the institute residence halls, or in fraternity or sorority houses. 3,600 students live on campus in the residence halls. There are 959 apartments on campus that house approximately 2,500 upperclass students. A complete program of intercollegiate and intramural sports is offered, as well as complementary activities for those with special interests. An indoor ice arena is used for intercollegiate hockey and recreational skating and houses the Genesee Valley Figure Skating Club. Army, Navy and Air Force ROTC programs are available. Cooperative education, which provides alternating quarters of school with employment experience, is available in many of the academic programs. The academic year begins in September and midyear students are accepted. Approximately 79% of students applying for admission are accepted and 84% return for the sophomore year. Middle 50% scores for freshman class are: SAT, 430-540V, 510-630M; ACT, 22-28. Financial aid is available. About 65% of the current student body receives some form of financial assistance. The Wallace Memorial Library is a true multimedia learning center. It is especially strong in the areas of the arts, education of the deaf, photography, and printing. Associated with the library is the Media Design Center, which provides audiovisual support for academic programs, and the Institute Television Center.

Community Environment: The Greater Rochester area - the city and its immediate suburbs - has a population of about 713,000. Per capital income is among the highest for metropolitan areas in the nation. The area's many internationally known industries employ a high proportion of scientists, technologists and skilled workers. Rochester is the world center of photography, the largest producer of optical goods in the United States, and among the leaders in graphic arts and reproduction and in production of electronic equipment and precision instruments. Rochester's industries have always been closely associated with RIT's programs and progress to the mutual benefit of all.

ROCKEFELLER UNIVERSITY *(E-2)*
York Avenue and 66th Street
New York, New York 10021
Tel: (212) 327-8086; Fax: (212) 327-8505

Description: This privately supported graduate school and research center offers opportunities for graduate study to a limited number of outstanding young men and women who wish to prepare for careers of research and teaching in biology, chemistry, physics and behavioral sciences. Enrollment includes 98 Ph.D candidates and 33 M.D.-Ph.D candidates. Most students spend 5 years to complete the requirements for the degree. A faculty of 142 provides a faculty-student ratio of 1-1. Founded by John D. Rockefeller in 1901 and known as the Rockefeller Institute for Medical Research, it became affiliated with the State University of New York in the late 1950s, graduating its first class in 1959. In 1965 the name was changed to The Rockefeller University. The faculties of The Rockefeller University and Cornell University Medical College (N.Y.C.) and its graduate division collaborate in offering a tri-institutional program of advanced study and research in Biology and Medicine. This rigorous program lasts normally 6 or 7 years and awards 2 degrees: Doctor of Medicine by Cornell University and Ph.D. by Rockefeller University, Cornell Graduate school of Medical Sciences, or Sloan-Kettering Institute.

Entrance Requirements: Contact university. Jan. 15 suggested application deadline; $50 application fee.

Costs Per Year: No tuition; Ph.D. students receive $17,700 per annum.

Collegiate Environment: The university buildings are located on a beautifully landscaped campus of 15 acres overlooking the East River in the city of New York. 14 modern buildings provide facilities for research, teaching, and the social life of faculty, students, staff, and visiting scientists. Some of them have been built within the last 20 years; the others have recently been renovated and newly equipped. The graduate students residences provide housing for all single and married students. Some recreational and athletic facilities are also provided on campus. Welch Hall houses a library of more than 184,000 volumes, including an unusually fine collection of scientific periodicals. The university operates on a 12-month basis and is not an aggregate of departments dealing with specialized fields of science. It is

composed of large and small laboratories that pursue the interests in biomedical sciences and physics of the laboratory head.

RUSSELL SAGE COLLEGE *(I-17)*
45 Ferry Street
Troy, New York 12180
Tel: (518) 270-2000; (800) 999-3772; Admissions: (518) 270-2217; Fax: (518) 270-6880

Description: Privately supported liberal arts college for women was founded in 1916, but traces its origin to a female seminary which was established in 1814. It is accredited by the Middle States Association of Colleges and Schools. Russell Sage College is one of the Sage Colleges, a federation which also includes Sage Junior College of Albany, Sage Evening College, and Sage Graduate School. Its programs are primarily in the liberal arts but provide opportunity for concentration in professional areas, and lead to the Bachelor and the Master degrees. ROTC Army, Navy, and Air Force programs are available through a cross-town agreement with Rensselaer Polytechnical Institute. Enrollment includes 1,030 full-time and 140 part-time undergraduates, 1,200 graduate students in the Sage Graduate School, and 800 students in the Sage Evening College. A faculty of 125 full-time and 45 part-time gives a faculty-student ratio of 1-12.

Entrance Requirements: SAT or ACT; GMAT or GRE for graduate students; TOEFL for international students; completion of 16 units in an approved four-year secondary school. Academic ability is given higher consideration than the distribution of credits, although an applicant should include among the 16 units 4 English, 2 foreign language, 3 social science, 3 science, and 3 mathematics. Students interested in physical therapy should also have physics. Experience in hospitals, nursing homes, and/or clinics is also required for applicants for the physical therapy program. SAT or ACT is required. Early admission, early decision, midyear admission, rolling admission, delayed admission and advanced placement plans available. $20 application fee.

Costs Per Year: $12,350 tuition; $5,240 room and board; student fees $270.

Collegiate Environment: Buildings on 10 acres contain a library of 270,000 volumes and residence halls for 750 women. Independent study is encouraged and honors programs are available. Honorary organizations include Phi Kappa Phi, Beta Beta Beta (biology), Omicron Delta Epsilon (economics), Phi Alpha Theta (history), Psi Chi (psychology), and Psi Omega (drama). There is an extensive campus employment program enabling students to become involved in various aspects of campus life and to know many members of the Sage community. Extracurricular activities include the newspaper, drama and dance production groups, intercollegiate sports, choral groups, language clubs, student government, religious groups, and professional and honorary societies. Social activities are numerous, with over a dozen colleges in the tri-cities area. There is a professionally staffed infirmary on campus, as well as a psychiatrist and a psychologist available for consultation. The college accepts 80% of those who apply for admission. The middle 50% range of enrolled freshmen scores were SAT 950-1125 combined. Full-tuition and partial-tuition scholarships are available and over 70% of the students receive some form of financial assistance. The average amount of aid is $10,000.

Community Environment: See Rensselaer Polytechnic Institute.

SAGE JUNIOR COLLEGE OF ALBANY *(I-17)*
140 New Scotland Avenue
Albany, New York 12208
Tel: (518) 445-1730; (800) 999-9522; Admissions: (518) 445-1730; Fax: (518) 436-0539

Description: Sage Junior College of Albany (SJCA) is a privately supported two-year college for men and women. Founded in 1957, SJCA is accredited by the Middle States Association of Colleges and Schools. Programs range from liberal arts programs to career-oriented majors. All lead to associate degrees. Many SJCA graduates transfer on to four year institutions, while others immediately begin their careers after their SJCA graduation. Students from more than 8 states and 10 countries attend SJCA. It operates on the 4-1-4 calendar system and offers two summer sessions. With a student body of 750, a 12-1 student-faculty ratio allows close interaction in the learning environment. Sage JCA is one of the Sage Colleges. The others are Russell Sage, a four-year women's college, Sage Evening College, offering Associate and Bachelor degrees, and Sage Graduate School.

Costs Per Year: $7,480 tuition; $5,840 room and board; $200 student fees.

Collegiate Environment: A campus of 15 acres includes a coed residence facility, a library of 125,000 volumes, an academic computing center, a gymnasium, an art gallery, art studios, and a campus center. Phi Theta Kappa is an honor society recognizing academic excellence. There is a campus employment program for students. Extracurricular activities include intramural and intercollegiate sports, two student publications, student government, art clubs, and a Black and Latin Student Alliance. Social activities are numerous, with over a dozen colleges in the capital area.

Community Environment: See State University of New York at Albany.

SAINT BERNARD'S INSTITUTE   (H-7)
1100 S. Goodman Street
Rochester, New York 14620
Tel: (716) 271-1320; Fax: (716) 271-1152

Description: St. Bernard's Institute is a privately supported graduate school of theology that provides, in an ecumenical context, theological education, professional training, and spiritual development to students preparing for pastoral ministry primarily within the Roman Catholic tradition. Both the M.Div. and the M.A. degrees are offered; both are accredited by New York State and by the Association of Theological Schools. From its foundation in 1893, St. Bernard's has been committed to the education of candidates for ministry in Roman Catholic Church. St. Bernard's is dedicated to the preparation of candidates for the permanent diaconate, the preparation of men and women for professional pastoral ministry within the Church, the continuing professional development of those involved in pastoral ministry and the offering of educational opportunities to qualified individuals who wish to deepen their knowledge of theology and ministry. The Institute carries out its purpose by helping students: develop their potential as individuals who are part of the human family; deepen and grow in their spirtual development within the context of the Christiam community and today's world; gain a knowledge of the Christian faith; and gain experiential knowledge of theology and ministry by means of various pastoral experiences programmed into their education. It operates on a semester basis with 2 summer sessions. Enrollment includes 44 men and 36 women full-time, and 7 men and 30 women part-time on an audit basis from several Faith Traditions. A faculty of 11 gives a faculty-student ratio of 1-10.

Entrance Requirements: B.A. or B.S. degree; 18 credit hours college theology/philosophy.

Costs Per Year: $4,560 M.A. tuition; $6,080 M.Div.; $40 student fees.

Collegiate Environment: St. Bernard's Institute exists in a one-campus covenant of affiliation with Colgate Rochester Divinity School/Bexley Hall/Crozer Theological Seminary. This ecumenical setting (more than 20 denominations represented) encourages continuing dialog and cooperation among the many faith traditions. Cross-registration is available with curriculum guidelines to all students. Chapel, dormitory, dining, meeting and classroom facilities are shared with the Divinity School. The merged libraries house a collection of more than 330,000 volumes. St. Bernard's students are primarily lay, and nearly half are women. 40% of the faculty is lay, and about one-third are women.

Community Environment: See University of Rochester.

SAINT BONAVENTURE UNIVERSITY   (L-5)
PO Box D
St. Bonaventure, New York 14778-2284
Tel: (716) 375-2400; (800) 462-5050; Fax: (716) 375-2005

Description: Privately supported, coeducational university was founded by the Franciscan Friars, Province of the Most Holy Name Order of Friars Minor. It is composed of the School of Arts and Sciences, School of Business Administration, School of Education, School of Graduate Studies, and School of Franciscan Studies. The university operates on the semester system and offers two summer sessions. Enrollment includes 1,750 full-time, 125 part-time, and 675

graduate students. A faculty of 125 provides a faculty-student ratio of 1-17. The school was founded in 1858 and is accredited by the Middle States Association of Colleges and Schools. The university grants the Bachelor and Master degrees. Army ROTC training is available.

Entrance Requirements: High school graduation or equivalent; completion of 16 units including 4 English, 3 mathematics, 3 science, 4 social science and 2 language; SAT required; GRE or GMAT required for graduate programs; early decision, rolling admission, and advanced placement plans available; $30 application fee.

Costs Per Year: $10,456 tuition and fees; $4,927 room and board; $395 student fees.

Collegiate Environment: The university is located between Allegany and Olean, New York. It is comprised of 23 buildings located on 600 acres and contains a library of 253,000 volumes, 55,807 bound periodicals, and 670,000 microforms, plus 2,300 rare books and 200 incunabula (15th century). There are living accommodations for 1,800 men and women. The university seeks a geographically diverse student body and will accept mid-year students. Approximately 85% of students applying for admission are accepted. Financial aid is available and 80% of the student body received aid based on academic achievement and financial need. Recently the university awarded 509 Bachelor and 67 Master degrees.

Community Environment: Allegany (population 2,050) is a rural community located in southwest New York a short distance from Allegany State Park. The area is accessible by bus and the Southern Tier Expressway. Climate is temperate with 4 definite seasons. Allegany has 1 library, several churches of different denominations. Various civic and fraternal organizations are active here. Part-time work for students is available. The area has an annual Winter Carnival and ski resorts close by. Olean (population 19,169) is a manufacturing and regional commercial center where part-time employment is available for students. Transportation is provided by bus or airlines. Nearby "Enchanted Mountains" resort area provides hunting, fishing, skiing, and other sports. The city has 2 hospitals, 3 radio stations, and most of the major service clubs found in larger cities.

SAINT FRANCIS COLLEGE   (F-2)
180 Remsen Street
Brooklyn, New York 11201
Tel: (718) 522-2300

Description: St. Francis College is an independent, coeducational liberal arts college, accredited by the Regents of the University of the State of New York and the Middle States Association of Colleges and Schools. For over a hundred years, the college has offered quality higher education that reflects a willingness to adapt to a constantly changing society. St. Francis offers a variety of majors and programs leading to the Associate or Bachelor's degree, which prepare students for graduate study or work in the career fields they have chosen. Enrollment includes 1,800 students. A faculty of 54 full-time and 55 part-time provides a faculty-student ratio of 1-22.

Entrance Requirements: Recommendation of high school principal or guidance counselor; personal interview; 16 high school units, including 4 English, 2 math, 1 science, 3 social studies, and 6 electives; SAT or CEEB; rolling admission, early admission, and advanced placement programs available; CLEP credits accepted; $20 application fee.

Costs Per Year: $6,000 tuition; $200 student fee.

Collegiate Environment: Most students come from the greater New York metropolitan area, but St. Francis also boasts a sizeable foreign student population. An informal atmosphere in the classroom encourages supportive interaction among faculty and students. St. Francis is a closely-knit community where people care about each other's goals and accomplishments. The college has a full range or extracurricular activities, publications, clubs, fraternities, sororities and athletic teams. The campus consists of 5 interconnected buildings. Science and computer laboratories and equipment are up-to-date. The library underwent an extensive renovation and expansion and houses over 154,496 volumes. The facilities for physical education, recreation and dining are modern and comfortable. Scholarships are available and 80% of full-time students receive some form of aid. Army and Air Force ROTC programs are available.

Community Environment: St. Francis is located in Brooklyn Heights, a National Historic District and one of New York City's most desirable neighborhoods for living, working or attending school. Borough Hall and the Supreme Court building, art galleries and other cultural institutions, restaurants and shops are all nearby.

SAINT JOHN FISHER COLLEGE *(H-7)*
3690 East Avenue
Rochester, New York 14618
Tel: (716) 385-8064; (800) 444-4640; Fax: (716) 385-8129

Description: This independent, liberal arts college in the Catholic tradition was founded in 1948 by the congregation of St. Basil. In 1968, ownership and control of the college were assumed by an independent Board of Trustees which includes men and women of all major faiths who are leaders in the professional, business, and academic communities. It is an accredited member of the Middle States Association of Colleges and Schools and grants the Bachelor degree. Previously all male, it became coeducational in 1971. The college operates on the semester system and offers three summer sessions. Enrollment includes 1,517 full-time and 579 part-time undergraduates and 305 graduate students. A faculty of 106 full-time and 80 part-time gives an undergraduate faculty-student ratio of 1-11. Fisher's 27 academic degrees are complemented by extensive internship opportunities in almost every major, and such special opportunities as the 5-year Bachelors/Masters programs at Fisher, resulting in an MBA and Bachelor in Management or International Studies, or Accounting. A Washington semester and junior year abroad are also offered. The college's educational opportunities are further expanded through cooperative programs with other colleges. These cooperative programs include the 3/2 bachelors-masters program in Public Policy Analysis with University of Rochester, cooperative Environmental Science and Forestry programs with SUNY ESF, a 3/4 doctorate degree program with Pennsylvania College of Optometry, and cooperative engineering degree programs through Clarkson and Columbia Universities, Manhattan College and Universities of Buffalo and Detroit. As a member of the Rochester Area Consortium of Colleges, Fisher's students may take courses at any of 13 other colleges.

Entrance Requirements: High school graduation or equivalent; completion of 16 academic units including 4 English, 3 math, 2 science, 2 language, and 4 social studies; SAT or ACT accepted; early admission, early decision, rolling admission, delayed admission, and advanced placement programs available; $25 application fee.

Costs Per Year: $10,570 tuition; $5,600 room and board; $395 student fees.

Collegiate Environment: The 125-acre campus is located in the suburban Pittsford area of Rochester. The 13 college buildings include a library of 180,000 titles, 1,046 periodical titles, 44,000 microforms and 25,000 audiovisual materials. Dormitory facilities provide for 850 men and women. Students from diverse geographical locations are accepted, and students are admitted in the fall and spring. Approximately 76% of students applying for admission are accepted. The average scores of the entering freshman class were SAT 457 verbal, 517 math, ACT 23 composite. Merit scholarships for full-tuition, Trustees for half- to full-tuition, Presidents for $1,000 to half-tuition, and Cultural Diversity for half- to full-tuition are available scholarships. 88% of the student body receives some type of financial aid. About 14% of the senior class continues on to graduate school.

Community Environment: Fisher is located in a residential neighborhood just 12 miles from Rochester, the third largest city in New York. The campus has its own identity, but its location provides accessibility to businesses and other institutions providing internships, as well as cultural and recreational activities. See also University of Rochester.

SAINT JOHN'S UNIVERSITY *(E-3)*
8000 Utopia Parkway
Jamaica, New York 11439
Tel: (718) 990-6161; Admissions: (718) 990-6114

Description: Privately-supported, coeducational university is a Catholic institution of higher learning founded in 1870 and sponsored by the Congregation of the Mission (Vincentian Fathers). The colleges and schools of the university offer courses at the Jamaica Campus in Queens as well as on the Staten Island Campus. It is accredited by the Middle States Association of Colleges and Schools, and grants the Professional Diploma, Associate, Bachelor, Master, Professional

and Doctorate degrees. Divisions of the university are: College of Liberal Arts and Sciences, Graduate School of Arts and Sciences, School of Education and Human Services (undergraduate division), School of Education of Human Services (graduate division), College of Business Administration (undergraduate and graduate divisions), College of Pharmacy and Allied Health Professions (undergraduate and graduate divisions) St. Vincent's College, and Notre Dame College. An academic cooperative plan with Polytechnic University is available for engineering and with Niagara University for nursing. The university operates on the semester system and offers 2 summer sessions. Enrollment includes 11,785 full-time and 1,752 part-time undergraduates and 4,568 graduate students. The faculty has 618 full-time and 340 part-time members. Army ROTC is available as an elective.

Entrance Requirements: Accredited high school graduation or equivalent; completion of 16 units, including 4 English, 2 mathematics, 2 foreign language, 1 science, 1 social science; SAT required, GRE required for certain graduate programs; advanced placement; early admission, early decision, rolling admission, delayed admission plans available; $20 application fee.

Costs Per Year: $9,400 tuition; $380 fees.

Collegiate Environment: The principal administrative offices of the university are at the Jamaica Campus, which at the present time comprises 12 buildings. The university libraries contain 1.5 million volumes, 348,673 microforms and 43,271 audiovisual materials. Although there are no dormitory facilities available, students can find suitable living accommodations in the vicinity of both campuses. Approximately 70% of students applying for admission are accepted, including midyear students, and 93% of the freshman class return for the sophomore year. Average scores of the entering freshman class, SAT 450V, 481M. 80% of the students receive some form of financial assistance.

Community Environment: Population of Queens: 1,973,000; of New York City: 8,000000. This is a metropolitan area in New York City, Borough of Queens. The climate is temperate. Excellent transportation facilities include John F. Kennedy and LaGuardia Airports, railway, subway, and bus lines. Jamaica has public libraries, YMCA, hospitals, churches of all major denominations, as well as all the recreational, cultural, and community services of New York City. Part-time employment is available for students. Excellent shopping facilities are located within the immediate area.

Branch Campuses: Staten Island Campus.

SAINT JOSEPH'S COLLEGE *(F-2)*
245 Clinton Avenue
Brooklyn, New York 11205
Tel: (718) 636-6868

Description: Private, independent, coeducational college of liberal arts and sciences, established in 1916. The College of Arts and Sciences, designed for traditional college-age students, operates on the semester system, with one summer session. Enrollment includes 1,189 men and women. Faculty includes 119 instructors. The faculty-student ratio is 1:12. The Division of General Studies, designed for professional working adults, has a more flexible schedule of classes including evenings, weekends and 6-week terms. The college is accredited by the Middle States Association of Colleges and Schools, and grants B.A. and B.S. degrees. The college also has a branch campus in Patchogue, New York.

Entrance Requirements: Freshmen, Arts and Sciences: graduation from an accredited high school. Completion of 16 units, including 4 English, 3 mathematics, 2 foreign language, 2 science and 4 social science. Students planning to major in mathematics, business administration or accounting should have 4 years of mathematics. 4 years of science is recommended for proposed biology or chemistry majors. SAT required. GED holders considered. Rolling admission, early admission, delayed admission and advanced placement plans available. $25 application fee. General Studies: more liberal entrance requirements. Please call for more details.

Costs Per Year: $7,495 tuition; $322 student fee.

Collegiate Environment: St. Joseph's is located in one of the nation's most diverse academic and cultural communities. The college campus consists of 5 buildings, including the Dillon Child Study Center, a laboratory preschool used for observation and student teaching by Child Study students. The library contains over 117,403 volumes, 435 periodical subscriptions. In the College of Arts and Sciences, 53% of students applying for admission are accepted, and approximately 82% of the previous freshman class return for the sophomore year. Average high school standing of most recent freshman class, 85%; 22% in the top quintile, 21% in the second quintile. The average scores of the entering freshman class were SAT 457 verbal and 470 math. Financial aid is available to qualified students from both divisions of the college, and includes awards based on academic merit and/or need. 85% of the current student body receives some form of financial assistance.

Community Environment: See Brooklyn College of the City University of New York.

SAINT JOSEPH'S COLLEGE - PATCHOGUE CAMPUS
(E-6)
155 Roe Boulevard
Patchogue, New York 11772
Tel: (516) 447-3200; Admissions: (516) 447-3219; Fax: (516) 447-1734

Description: The cooeducational privately supported liberal arts college is accredited by the Middle States Association of College and Schools and was founded in 1916. It grants the bachelor's degree in 14 areas of study. It operates on the semester system and offers three summer sessions. Enrollment includes 1,392 full-time and 911 part-time students. A faculty of 56 full-time and 121 part-time gives a faculty-student ratio of 1-12.

Entrance Requirements: High school graduation or equivelant with 16 total units: 4 English, 2 mathematics, 1 laboratory science, 2 foreign language, 1 social studies and 6 electives. SAT or ACT required with minimum 500 verbal, 460 math, or ACT 18. Midyear admission available; early admission, rolling admission, delayed admission and advanced placement programs available.

Costs Per Year: Tuition $7,715; student fees $332; application fee $25.

Collegiate Environment: This Suffolk campus occupies the site formerly known as Seton Hall High School. The building has been significantly modified and adapted for collegiate use. A new library on campus holdings include 74,361 volumes and subscriptions to over 488 periodicals, 247 microforms and 1,541 audiovisual materials. The campus also features the Clare Rose Repertory Theatre, athletic fields, two champion-size tennis courts, and parking for 800 cars. 79% of the applicants are accepted. 65 scholarships are available and 55% of the students receives some form of financial aid. Army and Air Force ROTC available.

Community Environment: Located on the scenic South Shore of Long Island, the 28 acre Patchogue Campus is easily accessible to its students from Nassau and Suffolk counties. It is situated on the western rim of the Great Patchogue Lake.

SAINT JOSEPH'S SEMINARY   *(D-2)*
Dunwoodie Street
Yonkers, New York 10704
Tel: (914) 968-6200; Fax: (914) 968-7912

Description: Privately supported, graduate-level, Roman Catholic seminary operating under the sponsorship and control of the Archdiocese of New York. The seminary is accredited by the Middle States Association of Colleges and Schools. In 1970, St. Joseph's Seminary became a Theologate. Its purpose is the preparation of candidates for the Roman Catholic priesthood. Special courses are offered in the Spanish and Italian languages and in the cultural backgrounds of minority groups to help students understand and be prepared to work with these groups. One student is selected each year to pursue his theological studies at North America College in Rome. It operates on a semester system. The enrollment is 68 students and there are 19 full-time and 16 part-time faculty.

Entrance Requirements: Candidates must have completed an accredited college or university; personal interview required.

Costs Per Year: $2,500 tuition, room and board; $6,300 nonresident tuition, room and board.

Collegiate Environment: The seminary extends for 43 acres atop Valentine Hill. Its 4 main buildings include a library of 69,907 volumes, and over 1,000 recordings. Living accommodations are available for 210 men. Classes begin in September and midyear students are not accepted. The Archdiocese of New York has a special office for vocations.

Community Environment: See New York University.

SAINT THOMAS AQUINAS COLLEGE   *(D-2)*
125 Route 340
Sparkill, New York 10976
Tel: (914) 359-9500; (800) 999-7822; Admissions: (914) 359-8136; Fax: (914) 359-8136

Description: Independent, coeducational, liberal arts college was established in 1952. Previously for women, the college became coeducational in 1969. The college is accredited by the Middle States Association of Colleges and Schools and the Board of Regents of the State University of New York. 75 full-time and 55 part-time members. Programs of study lead to the Bachelor of Arts, Bachelor of Science and Bachelor of Science in Education, Master of Business Administration, Master of Science in Education, Associate in Arts, and Associate in Science. It operates on the 4-1-4 calendar system and offers three summer sessions. Enrollment includes 1,395 full-time and 906 part-time undergradutates and 150 graduate students. A faculty of 75 full-time and 55 part-time provides a faculty-student ratio of 1-17.

Entrance Requirements: Accredited high school graduation or equivalent; completion of 16 units including 4 English, 2 mathematics, 2 foreign language, 2 science, 1 social science; SAT or ACT required; early admission, rolling admission, midyear admission, and advanced placement programs available; $25 application fee.

Costs Per Year: $8,800 tuition; $5,700 room and board.

Collegiate Environment: The 41-acre campus is located at Sparkill, Rockland County, New York, approximately 15 miles north of the George Washington Bridge, and adjacent to Bergen County, New Jersey. The 8 college buildings contain a library of 100,000 volumes and dormitory facilities are provided for 450 men and women. Approximately 77% of students applying for admission are accepted. 75% of the students receive some form of financial aid and there are approximately 65 scholarships available.

Community Environment: This area is noted for its natural beauty and is rich in Revolutionary War historical sites. The surrounding area includes Edward Hooper's birthplace, the Sneden's Landing art colony, Nyack's Antiques Center and the old Piermont steamboat pier. Major highways connect Rockland County to New York City and its countless cultural and educational opportunities. Students may avail themselves of frequent visits to museums, theatres, art galleries and libraries in New York City as well as in Rockland, Bergen and Westchester Counties.

SAINT VLADIMIR'S ORTHODOX THEOLOGICAL SEMINARY   *(D-3)*
575 Scarsdale Road
Crestwood, New York 10707
Tel: (914) 961-8313; Fax: (914) 961-4507

Description: This privately supported, graduate level theological seminary was established in 1938 by the Russian Orthodox Greek Catholic Church of North America (now Orthodox Church in America). It now serves most of the other Orthodox institutions in America as well. Its purpose is the preparation of candidates for the priesthood in the Orthodox Church, for missionary work, teaching, or other forms of service in the church. Nonorthodox students may also be admitted to the seminary and receive academic credit for their work. The seminary operates on the semester system and enrolls 61 full-time and 31 part-time men and women. It is chartered and approved by the Board of Regents of the University of the State of New York and is a member of the Association of Theological Schools. A faculty of 18 provides a faculty-student ratio of 1-5.

Entrance Requirements: B.A. degree or equivalent from accredited college or university for the M.Div. degree program; graduation from approved theological school with B.D. or equivalent required for post-graduate program; $35 application fee.

Costs Per Year: $3,200 tuition; $2,700 board and room; $50 student fees.

Collegiate Environment: The seminary is located on 7 acres in beautiful Westchester County. The 3 seminary buildings contain a library of over 35,000 volumes and dormitory facilities for 100 men and women. Approximately 75% of students applying for admission are accepted. Classes begin in September and midyear students are not usually accepted. About 35% of the recent student body graduated in the top half of their high school class, 25% in top quarter and 10% in the highest tenth. Financial aid is available for economically handicapped students and 40 scholarships are offered.

SARAH LAWRENCE COLLEGE *(D-2)*
1 Mead Way
Bronxville, New York 10708
Tel: (914) 395-2510; (800) 888-2858; Admissions: (914) 395-2510;
Fax: (914) 395-2668

Description: This privately supported, coeducational liberal arts college was established in 1926. It is accredited by the Middle States Association of Colleges and Schools. Previously for women only, Sarah Lawrence College became coeducational in 1968. In 1962, a grant from the Carnegie Corporation enabled the college to establish a Center for Continuing Education, permitting women out of college several years to return to the pursuit of a degree. Programs of study lead to the Bachelor and Master degrees. It operates on the semester system. Enrollment includes 975 full-time and 81 part-time undergraduates and 250 graduate students. A faculty of 165 full-time and 62 part-time gives an undergraduate faculty-student ratio of 1-6.

Entrance Requirements: Accredited high school graduation; completion of 16 college-preparatory units including 4 English, 3 math, 3 science, 3 language, 2 social studies; SAT or any 3 SAT II tests or ACT required; $45 application fee; early admission, early decision, advanced placement and delayed admission plans available.

Costs Per Year: $19,300 tuition; $6,694 room and board; $394 student activity fee.

Collegiate Environment: The college is situated 15 miles north of New York City in southern Westchester County. The college library contains 200,000 volumes, 1,000 periodicals, 20,000 pamphlets and 3,000 microforms. Dormitory facilities provide housing for 900 students. The college conducts a junior year program in Paris, Florence, Oxford, London, and Moscow. The college welcomes a geographically diverse student body and will accept midyear students. Approximately 50% of those who apply for admission are accepted. Financial aid is available and 52% of the student body receives some form of financial aid.

Community Environment: Population 8,000. Bronxville is a residential community located in suburban Westchester County. Excellent connections with surrounding areas and good transportation make New York City easily accessible. The immediate area has churches, a library, and diversified local recreational programs throughout the year.

SCHOOL OF VISUAL ARTS *(E-2)*
209 East 23rd Street
New York, New York 10010-3994
Tel: (212) 592-2000; (800) 436-4204; Admissions: (212) 592-2100;
Fax: (212) 725-3584

Description: The privately supported, coeducational college, founded in 1947, is fully accreditated by the Middle States Association of Colleges and Schools. It operates on the semester system and offers one summer session. It grants Bachelor and Masters degrees. Special programs include continuing education courses and summer workshops in Greece and Spain. Enrollment includes 1,640 men, 1,134 women full-time and 1,081 men, 1,357 women part-time with a faculty of 58 men, 29 women full-time and 347 men, 187 women part-time. The faculty-student ratio is 1-13.

Entrance Requirements: High school diploma or GED required. SAT or ACT. Freshmen and transfer students admitted at midyear. Early decision and rolling admission plans. $30 application fee.

Costs Per Year: $12,000 tuition; $4,700 room; $370 student fees.

Collegiate Environment: The library contains 64,585 and 260 periodicals. Facilities include a visual arts museum and student galleries as well as a gallery in SoHo. Dormitories accommodate 416 students.

69% of applicants are accepted. $2,300,000 is available for scholarships and 70% of the students receive financial aid.

Community Environment: Located in Manhattan, population 1,487,536 (see also New York University). Students can take advantage of the theater, museums, and all the diverse cultural activities that are offered. The school is located in the Gramercy section close to Gramercy Park. It is near Bernard M. Baruch College of the City University of New York and the Pierpont Morgan Library, noted for its old master drawings and prints and medieval and Renaissance illuminated manuscripts.

SIENA COLLEGE *(B-6)*
575 Louden Road
Loudonville, New York 12211-1462
Tel: (518) 783-2300; (800) 457-4362; Admissions: (518) 783-2423;
Fax: (518) 783-4293

Description: This independent, four-year, coeducational, liberal arts college with a self-perpetuating Board of Trustees was founded by the Franciscan Friars in 1937. Previously an all-male school, Siena became coeducational in 1969. The college is registered by the Board of Regents of the University of the State of New York and is accredited by the Middle States Association of Colleges and Schools. The college is a member of the Hudson-Mohawk Consortium enabling students to register for courses offered at other institutions in the Association. Programs of study lead to the Bachelor degree. It operates on the semester system and offers two summer sessions. Enrollment includes 2,628 full-time and 796 part-time students. A faculty of 167 full-time and 96 part-time provides a faculty-student ratio of 1-16. Army ROTC program is available.

Entrance Requirements: High school graduation or equivalent; completion of a college-preparatory program including 4 English, 3-4 math, 3-4 science, 4 social science, and 2-3 foreign language; SAT or ACT required; early decision, early admission, midyear admission, and advanced placement plans available; $40 application fee.

Costs Per Year: $10,800 tuition; $5,100 room and board; $310 student fees.

Collegiate Environment: The college is located in Loudonville, the first suburban village north of Albany. The library contains 251,080 volumes, 1,654 periodicals, 30,008 microforms and 4,084 audiovisual materials. Dormitory facilities are available for 1,882 students. Approximately 75% of students applying for admission are accepted. Students from diverse geographical locations are accepted as well as midyear students. About 93% of the recent student body graduated in the top half of their high school class, 57% in the top quarter, and 19% in the highest tenth. The middle 50% range of entering freshman scores was SAT 910-1120 combined, ACT 23.3 composite. Financial aid is available for economically disadvantaged students. 89% of the freshman class, and 72% of all students receive some form of aid. More than 88% of the previous freshman class returned to the college for their sophomore year.

Community Environment: Population 11,000, Loudonville is a suburban community of Albany easily reached by bus, railroad, all major airlines, and interstate highways. The community provides a local church, hospital, and shopping facilities. Part-time employment is available for students. The Saratoga Performing Arts Center and Lake George are nearby.

SKIDMORE COLLEGE *(H-17)*
North Broadway
Saratoga Springs, New York 12866
Tel: (518) 584-5000

Description: Privately supported, coeducational liberal arts college founded in 1903 and chartered in 1922. Enrollment recently included 889 men and 1,254 women full-time and part-time. The school is accredited by the Middle States Association of Colleges and Schools and grants the Bachelor degree. The semester calendar system is used and 2 summer sessions are offered with a full summer schedule of special programs. The faculty has 182 full-time and 15 part-time members.

Entrance Requirements: High school graduation; completion of 15 units with a recommended 4 English, 3 mathematics, 3 foreign language, 2 lab. science, 3 social studies; SAT required, ACT may be substituted; 3 Achievement tests recommended. Non-high school graduates considered; early admission, deferred admission, early decision and advanced placement; $40 application fee.

Costs Per Year: $16,650 tuition; $5,550 room and board; $213 student fees.

Collegiate Environment: The Lucy Scribner Library at present holds a collection of 377,181 volumes, 1,601 periodicals, 158,887 microfilms, phonographs, slides and photograph collection. Dormitory facilities accomodate 1,700 students. Approximately 50% of students applying for admission are accepted, including midyear applicants. Army, Navy and Air Force ROTC available. Tutorial students admitted through the Higher Education Opportunity Program are given tutorial assistance, summer remedial work and the option of a reduced course load. 92% of the previous freshman class return to this campus for their sophomore year. Financial aid is available and 25% of the current student body receives some form of institutional financial assistance. 47% receive some form of aid. The college awarded 523 Bachelor degrees recently, and 35% of the senior class continued on to graduate school.

Community Environment: This resort is famous for the beauty of its setting, the reputed health-giving properties of its water and the gaiety of its summer life. It is also gaining popularity as a winter sport center with downhill and cross-country skiing available nearby. The area has rail, bus, and airline service. Activities to be found within the area include Saratoga Performing Arts Center (summer home of the New York Ballet, Philadelphia Orchestra, and the Acting Company), thoroughbred racing, night harness racing, Yaddo Artist's Colony, Congress Park, Newport Jazz Festival, Petrified Sea Gardens, State Tree Nursery, Grant's Cottage on Mount McGregor, and the Saratoga Historical Museum in the Canfield Casino. Saratoga has churches representing the major denominations. Part-time employment is available.

ST. LAWRENCE UNIVERSITY   *(B-13)*
Park Street
Canton, New York 13617
Tel: (315) 379-5261; (800) 285-1856

Description: Privately supported, coeducational university was chartered by the Legislature of the State of New York in 1856, and has been nondenominational and coeducational from its founding. It is accredited by the Middle States Association of Colleges and Schools and grants the Bachelor and Master degrees. It operates on the semester system and offers two summer sessions. Academic cooperative plans are available for engineering students. St. Lawrence is dedicated to providing its graduates with a liberal education with an international and environmental perspective. Enrollment includes 1,923 full-time and 42 part-time undergraduates and 80 graduate students. A faculty of 152 full-time and 28 part-time gives a faculty-student ratio of 1-12.

Entrance Requirements: High school graduation with rank in upper 20%. Admission is highly competitive; SAT or ACT required; 2 additional Achievement tests strongly recommended; GRE required for graduate program; non-high school graduates considered; early admission, delayed admission, early decision, midyear admission, advanced placement plans available; Feb. 15 application deadline; $40 application fee.

Costs Per Year: $18,720 tuition; $5,730 room and board; $120 student fees.

Collegiate Environment: The university is situated at Canton in the valley of the St. Lawrence River. The 35 buildings include a library of 438,360 titles, 2177 periodicals, and 380,000 microforms. Dormitories provide living accommodations for 1,348 students, and fraternities and sororities house another 400 students. Students from other geographical locations are accepted as are midyear students. Approximately 66% of students applying for admission are accepted and 90% of the previous freshman class return to the university for the sophomore year. Financial aid and scholarships are available. 67% of students receive some form of financial aid. The university routinely surveys its graduating class to determine the quality of student "outcomes" in terms of career placement and graduate school enrollment, believing that the outcomes reflect the quality of the liberal arts education, e.g. the ability to communicate well, to analyze well, to research, and to work in collaboration with others. For several years the "placement" rate has been over 90%. For the class of 1993, 71.4% were employed full-time and 24.2% were attending graduate school.

Community Environment: Population 7,000. This is a rural agricultural area near the St. Lawrence River. Canton is located near the Northern Adirondacks only minutes away from resort regions. The area has 4 definite seasons and an invigorating climate. The community has many fraternal, civic and veteran's organizations. Part-time employment for students is limited. There are many outdoor facilities within the immediate area for hunting, fishing, boating and skiing.

STATE UNIVERSITY OF NEW YORK AT ALBANY   *(I-17)*
1400 Washington Avenue
Albany, New York 12222
Tel: (518) 442-5435

Description: Publicly supported, coeducational university is the oldest of 4 university centers of the State University of New York. It offers undergraduate and graduate education in a wide variety of fields from the freshman year through to doctoral degrees. Founded in 1844, the university is accredited by the Middle States Association of Colleges and Schools. It operates on the semester system and offers several summer sessions. An Honors Program is available. Enrollment includes 10,103 full-time and 1,243 part-time students with 5,270 graduate students. A faculty of 645 full-time and 232 part-time gives a faculty-student ratio of 1-17. The university is composed of the College of Arts and Sciences, the School of Business, Rockefeller College whose constituents are the School of Criminal Justice, the School of Social Welfare, the School of Business. School of Informational Science and Policy and the Graduate School of Public Affairs and the School of Public Health Science.

Entrance Requirements: Accredited high school graduation; completion of 18 units including 4 English, 3-4 mathematics, 3 foreign language, 3 social science; SAT or ACT required; early admission, early decision, rolling admission, midyear admission, and advanced placement available; $25 application fee.

Costs Per Year: $2,650 tuition; $6,550 out-of-state tuition; $4,543 room and board; $233 student fees.

Collegiate Environment: The 473-acre campus is located at the junction of the Northway and the Thruway. The 54 buildings include housing for 5,800 men and women, and a library containing over 1.8 million volumes. Heart of the academic group is the Lecture Hall Center. Rooms seating 60-300 students are equipped with the latest visual communications devices, connected to the nearby Instructional Resources unit. A new 5,000 seat Recreation and Convocation Center recently opened. Shuttle buses connect the uptown campus with university buildings and commercial areas in town. The Financial Aid Office serves all students of the university in the planning of their educational financing.

Community Environment: Population 100,000. Capital of the state, Albany is built along the edge of a plateau that extends northwest to the Mohawk Valley. Since the deepening of the Hudson River for 30 miles, the city has become an important inland port. Chartered in 1686 with Peter Schuyler as its first mayor, Albany is the oldest city in the United States still operating under its original charter. Albany has recently been named an "All America City" in the national competition of cities. Sometimes called the "Crossroads of the Northeast," the area is served by airlines, railroad, and excellent highways. Community services include libraries, churches, hospitals, easily accessible shopping areas, and numerous civic, fraternal, and veteran's organizations. Part-time employment is available. Recreational facilities include movie theatres, local symphony orchestra, civic theatre, civic center, choral groups, golf courses, tennis courts, horseback riding, swimming, fishing, and skating and skiing in the winter.

STATE UNIVERSITY OF NEW YORK AT BINGHAMTON   *(L-12)*
Vestal Parkway East
P.O. Box 6001
Binghamton, New York 13902-6001
Tel: (607) 777-2000; Admissions: (607) 777-2171

Description: Publicly supported, coeducational university is among the most selective public universities in the country and part of the State University of New York. The university is accredited by the Middle States Association of Colleges and Schools. Binghamton offers programs leading to the Bachelor, Master and Doctorate degrees. Divisions of the university: Harpur College of Arts and Science;

Decker School of Nursing (undergraduate and graduate); School of Management (undergraduate and graduate); School of Education and Human Development (undergraduate and graduate); Thomas J. Watson School of Engineering, Applied Science and Technology (graduate and undergraduate). It operates on the semester system and offers three summer sessions. Enrollment includes 4,317 male and 4,997 female undergraduate students. A faculty of 498 full-time and 212 part-time gives an undergraduate faculty-student ratio of 1-19. Overseas programs are available in Graz, Austria; London, England; Tangier, Morocco; Leipzig, Germany; and Aarhus, Denmark.

Entrance Requirements: High school graduation or equivalent, completion of 4 units of English, 2-3 math, 2 science, 3 foreign language or 2 units each of 2 foreign languages, 2 social studies; SAT or ACT required; early admission, early decision, delayed admission, rolling admission, midyear admission, and advanced placement plans available; $25 application fee.

Costs Per Year: $2,650 tuition; $6,550 out-of-state tuition; $4,598 room and board; $349 student fees.

Collegiate Environment: The 606-acre campus is located in the town of Vestal, 1 mile west of Binghamton. Spacious modern laboratory and computer facilities are used in teaching and research for all science and mathematics, and are complemented by a greenhouse with 4 climate zones. The Fine Arts building contains the 600-seat Watters Theater, smaller concert halls, studio art facilities including a sculpture foundry, and a 3,500 square foot University Art Gallery and area devoted to music and theater rehearsal and instruction. The adjacent Anderson Center for the Arts, dedicated in 1986, includes a 450-seat music recital hall and 1200-seat theater that can accommodate an additional 2,800 viewers outdoors. The library contains 1,500,000 volumes, 1,340,000 microforms, and subscribes to 9,500 periodicals and scholarly journals, 495,000 maps and government documents, and 81,000 phono discs and CD's. The campus has 2 gymnasiums and extensive outdoor athletic facilities. Varied residences house 5,375 men and women. Recently the university awarded 2,247 Bachelor, 597 Master and 72 Doctorate degrees. Financial aid is available and 65% of the student body receives some form of financial aid. 42% of freshmen applicants are accepted to the University.

Community Environment: Population of Broome metropolitan area is approximately 252,000. At the junction of the Susquehanna and Chenango Rivers, Binghamton is the center of a dense concentration of high technology industries. This is a wholesale and shopping center for the surrounding area. Transportation is provided by bus and air lines. Community services include metropolitan hospitals, complete library services, many churches, a music association and workshop, a museum, and outstanding professional performing arts groups. Employment is available for students. Recreational facilities within the area include golf courses, bowling centers, ice skating rinks, boating, swimming and fishing, theaters, parks, and skiing.

STATE UNIVERSITY OF NEW YORK AT BUFFALO   (I-4)
3435 Main Street
Buffalo, New York 14214
Tel: (716) 645-6900; Fax: (716) 645-6498

Description: Publicly supported, coeducational university was founded in 1846 as the University of Buffalo and is today the largest single unit and most comprehensive graduate center of the State University. It is accreditedby the Middle States Association of Colleges and Schools and grants the Bachelor, Specialist, Master, Professional and Doctorate degrees. The university operates on the semester system and offers three summer sessions. The university is divided as follows: Division of Undergraduate Studies, Division of Graduate Studies, Millard Fillmore College (Evening and Adult Education), and the faculties/schools of Architecture and Planning, Arts and Letters, Social Sciences, Natural Science and Mathematics, Engineering and Applied Sciences, Graduate School of Education, Information and Library Studies, Law, Management, Social Work, Dental Work, Dental Medicine, Health Related Professions, Medicine and Biomedical Sciences, Nursing, Pharmacy. Army ROTC is available. Enrollment includes 18,375 full-time, 6,568 part-time undergraduates, and 8,532 graduate students. A faculty of 1,292 full-time and 655 part-time provides an undergraduate faculty-student ratio of 1-20.

Entrance Requirements: High school graduation; 17 units recommended including 4 English, 3 foreign language, 3 mathematics, 4 social studies or history, and 3 laboratory science; SAT or ACT

required; early admission, midyear admission, and advanced placement plans available; Jan. 5 application deadline; $25 application fee.

Costs Per Year: $2,650 tuition; $6,550 out-of-state tuition; $5,050 room and board; $450 student fees.

Collegiate Environment: Academic facilities are currently divided between 2 campuses. The South Campus is located on the northeast edge of the city of Buffalo. The North Campus is located on a 1,200-acre site in the town of Amherst. This campus provides the core facilities for the university in a totally integrated academic complex. Transformation of the Main Street Campus into a health science center has newly been completed. Dormitory capacity is 5,500 students. The library contains 2.7 million volumes. Approximately 55% of the applicants are admitted. Financial aid is available and 65% of students receive aid.

Community Environment: Situated halfway between New York and Chicago, Western New York is midwestern in its outgoing friendliness, eastern in pace. The second largest metropolitan area in New York State, the Region is home to more than one million individuals who enjoy a blend of city and countryside. Amherst, the home of UB's North Campus, is a prosperous and secure community of about 125,000, the fastest growing in the Region. Buffalo has a first rate philharmonic orchestra, one of the most dazzling modern act performances mingle to create a lively atmosphere. Also nearby are Niagara Falls and Toronto. Major sports teams have homes here in Buffalo and the ski slopes are minutes away.

STATE UNIVERSITY OF NEW YORK AT NEW PALTZ
(M-16)
75 South Manheim Boulevard
New Paltz, New York 12561-2499
Tel: (914) 257-2121; Admissions: (914) 257-3200; Fax: (914) 257-3209

Description: Publicly supported, coeducational university of liberal arts and sciences, established in 1828 and part of the State University of New York. It is accredited by the Middle States Association of Colleges and Schools and grants the Bachelor and Master degrees. There are over 104 fields of study for undergraduates within 4 academic divisions: College of Arts and Sciences, School of Education, School of Fine and Performing Arts, and School of Engineering and Business Administration. The university provides upper division undergraduate and graduate instruction at Orange Community College and Rockland Community College. It operates on the semester system and offers two summer sessions. Undergraduate enrollment includes 2,029 men, 2,824 women full-time and 447 men and 915 women part-time. A faculty of 304 full-time and 296 part-time provides an undergraduate faculty-student ratio of 1-20.

Entrance Requirements: 7 different degrees in over 104 areas of study. Freshmen applicants should have taken a strong college preparatory program, including work in English, social studies, mathematics, lab science and foreign language. Either the SAT or ACT is required. Senior mid-year grades and recommendations are often requested. Portfolio required for art studio and art education; audition for music, music therapy, and theatre arts. Transfer applications must possess a minimum of a 2.5 GPA in all previous college work for consideration for admission. Early admission, early decision, delayed admission, midyear admission, rolling admission, and advanced placemnet plans available; May 1 application deadline; application fee $25.

Costs Per Year: $2,650 tuition; $6,550 out-of-state tuition; $4,630 board and room; $351 student fees; additional expenses average $1,000.

Collegiate Environment: New Paltz is located in the mid-Hudson region of the state, about 95 miles north of New York City and 65 miles south of Albany. The 216-acre campus contains over 45 buildings including a library of 410,000 volumes, 1,800 periodicals, and 1,200,000 microforms. Residence hallls accomodate 2,240 men and women. Approximately 42% of the students applying for admission are accepted, including midyear students. 65 scholarships are available and 65% of students receive some form of financial aid.

Community Environment: Population of New Paltz is 8,500. Small village in semi-rural setting in mid-Hudson region. Noted for historical and recreational attractions, region is also noted for its strength in high technology related industries. New Paltz is easily accessible via the NYS Thruway (I-87), exit 18.

STATE UNIVERSITY OF NEW YORK AT STONY BROOK
(D-6)
Stony Brook, New York 11794
Tel: (516) 689-6000; (800) 873-7869; Admissions: (516) 632-6868;
Fax: (516) 632-9027

Description: Publicly supported, coeducational university is 1 of 4 university centers of the State University of New York. It is accredited by the Middle States Association of Colleges and Schools, and grants the Bachelor, Master, D.D.S., M.D., Advanced Certificates and Doctorate degrees. The semester system is used and 2 summer terms are offered. All freshmen enter either the College of Arts and Sciences or the College of Engineering and Applied Sciences. Upper division students may enter the School of Nursing, the School of Allied Health Professions, the School of Social Welfare, or the W. Averell Harriman School for Management and Policy. Graduate work may be pursued in Biological Sciences, Arts and Humanities, Behavioral Sciences, Liberal Studies, Engineering Sciences, Environmental Sciences, Health Sciences, Mathematical Sciences, Physical Sciences and Social Sciences. Enrollment includes 9,974 full-time and 1,335 part-time undergraduates and 6,312 graduate students. A faculty of 1,295 full-time and 322 part-time gives an overall faculty-student ratio of 1-17.

Entrance Requirements: High school graduation or equivalent; completion of 3 math, 3 language, 3 science and 4 English units; SAT or ACT required; non-high school graduates considered; GRE required for graduate school; early admission, early decision, midyear admission, rolling admission, delayed admission and advanced placement plans available; $25 application fee.

Costs Per Year: $2,650 tuition; $6,550 out-of-state; $4,942 room and board; $342 student fees.

Collegiate Environment: The 1,117-acre campus has 110 buildings, including the University Hospital. Stony Brook is located in a region of woods and hills and small historic villages on the north shore of Long Island. 25 residence hall buildings and 14 graduate and married student apartments afford living quarters for 7,432 students. The Frank Melville, Jr., Memorial Library contains 1,900,000 volumes, 2.9 million microforms and audiovisual materials. The Computing Center and the Educational Communications Center provide new methods and materials for instruction. Special programs include the Science and Technology Entry Program, the Collegiate Science and Technology Entry Program and the Pre-Freshman Engineering Program. The university gives opportunities to young people of backgrounds with severe financial or cultural problems, many of whom would not ordinarily qualify for admission. 55% of applicants are accepted. 75% of the student body receives financial aid. The university recently awarded 2,101 Bachelor, 1,146 Master, 270 Doctorate, and 128 first professional (MD and DDS) degrees and 82 advanced certificates.

Community Environment: Population 29,000 in the area. Stony Brook is a suburban area on Long Island. The proximity of New York City makes all cultural, recreational, and civic activities easily accessible. Part-time employment is available for students. The immediate vicinity has libraries, churches of major denominations, synagogues, a medical center, and good shopping centers.

STATE UNIVERSITY OF NEW YORK, ADIRONDACK COMMUNITY COLLEGE   *(G-17)*
Queensbury, New York 12804
Tel: (518) 793-4491; Fax: (518) 745-1433

Description: The publicly supported, coeducational junior college opened in 1961. It employs the semester system with 3 summer terms and is accredited by the Middle States Association of Colleges and Universities. Recent enrollment included 750 men and 900 women full-time, and 550 men and 1,300 women part-time. A full-time faculty of 97 with a part-time staff of 119 gives a faculty-student ratio of 1-17.

Entrance Requirements: SAT and ACT accepted but not required; high school graduation or equivalent required for degree programs; early admission, early decision, rolling admission, midyear admission and advanced placement plans available; application deadline August 15; $25 application fee.

Costs Per Year: $1,900 tuition; $3,800 out-of-state; $150 student fees; $4,500 room and board.

Collegiate Environment: The 141-acre campus of the college, consisting of 8 buildings, is located just north of Glens Falls. The library contains 50,000 volumes, 500 periodicals, 200 microforms and 1,900 audiovisual materials. Financial aid is available and 50% of the students receive financial assistance. Freshman classes begin in September and January, and midyear students are accepted. 98% of students applying for admission are accepted.

Community Environment: The Glens Falls area is part of the Township of Queensbury. It is located on the east side of the Hudson River approximately midway between New York City and Montreal, Canada. Bus, rail, and air lines are easily accessible. Nearby lakes and state parks make the area an ideal recreation locale. The area has many churches, and most civic, fraternal and veteran's organizations. Apartments, privately owned dormitories, and motels are available for student housing. Part-time employment is available for students. Population of the area is approximately 50,000.

STATE UNIVERSITY OF NEW YORK, BROOME COMMUNITY COLLEGE   *(L-12)*
Upper Front Street
Box 1017
Binghamton, New York 13902
Tel: (607) 771-5000

Description: The publicly supported, coeducational community college is supervised by the State University of New York and sponsored by the County of Broome. It is accredited by the Middle States Association of Colleges and Schools. It has programs designed to prepare graduates both for immediate employment and for transfer to four-year colleges and universities. The college grants the Associate degree. The college operates on the semester system offers three summer sessions. Enrollment includes 3,565 full-time and 2,421 part-time students in those courses for which credit is offered. A faculty of 159 full-time and 221 part-time provides a faculty-student ratio of 1-16.

Entrance Requirements: High school graduation or equivalent; open enrollment policy; completion of college-preparatory courses recommended; early admission, rolling admission, midyear admission and advanced placement plans available; $10 application fee.

Costs Per Year: $1,890 tuition; $3,780 tuition for out-of-state residents; $110 student activity fees.

Collegiate Environment: The 12 college buildings are located on a 120-acre campus, 3 miles north of Binghamton. In addition to classrooms and laboratories, the campus has its own cafeteria, a library of 81,059 volumes, a gymnasium and athletic field, and a Little Theatre. The college has become an integral part of the community since it was started in 1946. Most of the college's curricula are designed to help fill the economic needs of the county. 94% of those who apply for admission are accepted. Financial aid is available and 55% of the student body receives some form of financial aid.

Community Environment: The community is an industrial and agricultural area in New York State's Southern Tier. It is in the approximate center of the state, measuring from east to west, and its southern extremity touches the Pennsylvania state line. Binghamton is the principal city in Broome County, but it is only a part of the community known as the Triple Cities. Endicott and Johnson City, along with Vestal and other suburbs, help to make the community much larger in population and geography than the city of Binghamton. Binghamton has a population of approximately 55,000 yet the Triple Cities area embraces over 225,000 people. Diversified industry in the community includes such firms as IBM, General Electric, Singer Company (formerly Link), Anitec Image, New York State Electric and Gas Corporation, Endicott Johnson, and Savin.

STATE UNIVERSITY OF NEW YORK, CAYUGA COUNTY COMMUNITY COLLEGE   *(I-10)*
Franklin Street
Auburn, New York 13021
Tel: (315) 255-1743; Fax: (315) 255-2050

Description: The publicly supported, coeducational two-year college is sponsored by the Cayuga County Legislature and is an associated unit of the State University of New York. 3 types of educational programs are offered: transfer, career, and special. Enrollment is 1,283 full-time and 654 part-time students. A faculty of 54 full-time and 113 part-time gives a faculty-student ratio of 1-21. The school operates on the semester system and offers two summer sessions. It is accredited by the Middle States Association of Colleges and Schools. Degrees granted include A.A., A.S, and A.A.S.

Entrance Requirements: Accredited high school graduation; completion of 16 units; ACT or SAT accepted; early admission, early decision, advanced placement, rolling admission and delayed admission plans available.

Costs Per Year: $2,050 tuition; $4,100 out-of-state.

Collegiate Environment: The 40-acre campus has 4 large buildings and has recently been expanded and updated through a $6.5 million capital construction project. The 73,899-volume library is unusually well stocked with research and recreational material together with a large number of domestic and foreign periodicals. A well-balanced program of classroom studies, athletic and physical education activities, lecture series and the performing arts plus club and other extra-curricular activities offer numerous opportunities for the achievement of a classical and economically useful collegiate education. Financial aid is available on the basis of need.

Community Environment: Population 35,000. Located in the Finger Lakes area on Owasco Lake, Auburn is a manufacturing city in one of the state's richest agricultural regions. Among the city's diversified products are plastics, spark plugs, cordage, diesel engines, shoes, carpets and rugs. Part-time employment is available for students. Auburn has 1 hospital, a YMCA, a library, and a local museum. Recreation in the area is provided by water sports, yachting, fishing, swimming, an amusement park, extension beach, 5 golf courses, tennis courts, ball park, hunting, and skiing and skating in the winter. Various civic, fraternal and veteran's organizations are represented here.

STATE UNIVERSITY OF NEW YORK, CLINTON COMMUNITY COLLEGE *(B-18)*
Plattsburgh, New York 12901
Tel: (518) 561-4200; Admissions: (518) 561-4170; Fax: (518) 561-8621

Description: This publicly supported, coeducational community college is 1 of 30 locally sponsored two-year colleges in New York State. It is accredited by the Middle States Assocaiton of Colleges and Schools. The college opened its doors in September 1969 on a 100-acre campus, once the Hotel Champlain, overlooking Lake Champlain in Plattsburgh, New York. The college grants the Associate degree. It operates on the semester system and offers two summer sessions. Enrollment includes 1,200 full-time and 1,000 part-time students. A faculty of 120 provides a faculty-student ratio of 1-17.

Entrance Requirements: High school graduation or GED; open enrollment, rolling admission, midyear admission, delayed admission and advanced placement plans available; $25 application fee.

Costs Per Year: $1,875 state-resident tuition; $3,750 out-of-state; $109.60 student fees.

Collegiate Environment: The campus overlooks Lake Champlain and is about 4 miles from the city of Plattsburgh. The library contains about 45,000 volumes, 500 periodicals and 3,500 microforms. Financial aid is available. All of the applicants are accepted and 80% of freshmen return to this campus for their second year.

Community Environment: Population 20,300. Located on Lake Champlain, Plattsburgh is a metropolitan area. The climate is temperate with cold, snowy winters. The locale supports good shopping facilities, 1 hospital, a library, YMCA, churches of all denominations and historic homes. Lake Champlain provides excellent recreational facilities. Winter and summer sports are plentiful. Some part-time employment is available for students.

STATE UNIVERSITY OF NEW YORK, COLLEGE AT BROCKPORT *(G-6)*
Brockport, New York 14420-2915
Tel: (716) 395-2751; Fax: (716) 395-5397

Description: Publicly supported, coeducational college of arts and science, dates from 1836 when it was established by the Baptist Church as an institute to train teachers and ministers. In 1866 title to the college was transferred to the State of New York and the Brockport State Normal School came into existence. The State University of New York was created in 1948 and the teacher's college be-

came 1 of the 11 teacher education units of the university. It is accredited by the Middle States Association of Colleges and Schools and grants the Bachelor and Master degrees. The college is structured academically into 3 schools: Arts and Performance, Letters and Sciences, and Professions. A new Weekend College program started in Autumn, 1994. Additional features include the adult program of Adult and Continuing Education. The college operates on the semester system and offers four summer sessions. Enrollment includes 5,858 full-time, 1,371 part-time, and 1,919 graduate students. A faculty of 298 full-time and 225 part-time provides a faculty-student ratio of 1-21.

Entrance Requirements: Accredited high school graduation; completion of 17 units including 4 English, 2 mathematics, 2 science, 4 social science; ACT or SAT accepted; GRE required for graduate school; non-high school graduates with GED considered; early admission, rolling admission, delayed admission, advanced placement plans available; $25 application fee.

Costs Per Year: $2,650 tuition; $6,550 out-of-state tuition; $4,540 board and room; $315 student fees.

Collegiate Environment: The 591-acre campus has 60 buildings in Brockport, which is in the greater Rochester metropolitan area. Drake Memorial Library houses 530,000 volumes, 87,193 periodicals, 1.8 million microforms and 40,000 audiovisual materials. Residence halls can accommodate 2,540 students with apartments for 250 married students. The Rakov Center houses most student services including admissions, financial aid, academic advisement, registration and records, student employment, career planning and placement, veterans affairs, Cooperative Education, services for disabled students, international education, adult and continuing education and the educational opportunity program. A modern complex of physical education, athletic and recreational facilities, the Donald M. Tower Fine Arts Center, Seymour College Union, and classroom and residence halls are set along the College Mall, surrounded by gently rolling, open or wooded land. Approximately 50% of the students applying for admission are accepted, including mid-year students. 177 scholarships are available and 78% of the current student body receive some form of financial assistance. Army ROTC is available.

Community Environment: Brockport, a village of some 9,800 residents, is 16 miles west of Rochester and 60 miles east of Buffalo. It lies along the banks of the old Erie Canal within a 15-minute drive from Lake Ontario to the north and the Thruway to the south.

STATE UNIVERSITY OF NEW YORK, COLLEGE AT BUFFALO *(I-4)*
1300 Elmwood Avenue
Buffalo, New York 14222
Tel: (716) 878-4000; Fax: (716) 878-3039

Description: Buffalo State is the largest arts and science college in the SUNY system. The college pursues a broad spectrum of goals, including education in the arts and science, career preparation, continuing education for the nontraditional student, service to the community and teacher education. It is the only SUNY college located in a major metropolitan area. Army ROTC is offered off-campus at Canisius College. Enrollment includes 7,661 full-time, 2,051 part-time, 726 evening, and 1,816 graduate students. A faculty of 434 full-time and 146 part-time provides a faculty student ratio of 1-22.

Entrance Requirements: Rolling admissions plan. For fall acceptance, apply as early as October of previous year, but not later than August of year of enrollment. Applicants for admission to the freshman class must provide official high school transcripts showing all courses completed and grades earned. Satisfactory results of a state high school equivalency diploma program are also acceptable. Candidates for admission must also provide results of the Scholastic Assessment Test (SAT) or the American College Testing Program (ACT). High school preparation should be broad and balanced with study in the areas of social science, English, natural science, mathematics, and foreign language. Admission decisions are based on a variety of factors, including high school grades, rank in class, strength of program, scores on standardized examinations, i.e. SAT or ACT, and high school recommendations. The highest standardized test results are used when multiple score reports are received.

Costs Per Year: $2,650 tuition; $6,550 out-of-state tuition; $4,240 room and board; $240 student fees.

Collegiate Environment: 34 buildings on a 115 acre campus. Library holds 442,753 bound volumes, 3,194 periodical subscriptions and 695,744 microform items. Student housing capacity: 2,100. Financial aid available: Pell grants, SEOG, state grants, academic merit scholarships, Perkins loans (NDSL), PLUS, Stafford Loans (GSL), and Supplemental Loans for Students (SLS). 80% of the students receive some form of financial aid.

Community Environment: The Buffalo State College campus is located in the city of Buffalo, served by air, bus and rail. Metropolitan Buffalo, with a population of about 1 million, has manufacturing firms and research companies, as well as many government offices and cultural institutions of note. The Albright-Knox Art Gallery and the Erie County Historical Society Museum, both located in Delaware Park, are a short walk from campus. Downtown Buffalo, a ten-minute ride from campus, boasts a rejuvenated waterfront, the Theater District, restaurants and cafes. The city is also home to professional teams in the NFL, NHL and triple-A baseball.

STATE UNIVERSITY OF NEW YORK, COLLEGE AT CORTLAND   *(J-11)*
Graham Avenue
P.O. Box 2000
Cortland, New York 13045
Tel: (607) 753-4712

Description: Publicly supported, coeducational college of arts and science, founded in 1868. The college is a unit of the State University of New York. It is accredited by the Middle States Association of Colleges and Schools. The college offers undergraduate degree programs in 47 fields of study in 2 major divisions: Arts and Sciences and Professional Studies. The college grants the Bachelor and Master degrees. It operates on the semester system and offers two summer sessions. Air Force ROTC is available. Enrollment includes 2,211 men, 2,997 women full-time and 166 men and 229 women part-time. A faculty of 243 full-time and 216 part-time gives a faculty-student ratio of 1-20.

Entrance Requirements: High school graduation or equivalent; completion of rigourous college-preparatory program; GRE required for some graduate programs; early admission, early decision, midyear admission, delayed admission, and advanced placement plans available; Feb. 1 application deadline, Mar. 15 transfers, Dec. 1 spring; $25 application fee.

Costs Per Year: $2,650 tuition; $6,500 out-of-state tuition; $6,350 room and board.

Collegiate Environment: The 191-acre campus is located at the geographical center of the State of New York. The residential complex of 35 acres contains 14 buildings with accommodations for about 3,000 students (40% of men, 60% of women live in coed dormitories separated either by wing or by floor; 40% of men, 40% of women are in off-campus housing). There are 7 fraternities and 4 sororities on campus and these house an additional 99 students. The academic area comprises a 40-acre quadrangle containing 8 major buildings. College Memorial Library currently contains a collection of 350,000 volumes, 1,515 periodicals, 533,060 microforms and 9,527 audiovisual materials. Physical education area includes Olympic-sized pool; a major gymnasium divisible into three full sized gyms; ice arena; gymnastic arena; fully equipped athletic training facility, 24 tennis courts, 2 baseball diamonds, a 440-yard track, football and lacrosse stadium, softball diamonds, squash and handball courts. Dowd Fine Arts Center contains a 476 seat air conditioned theater with flexible apron stage, laboratory theater; art gallery, sculpture court; art studios; sound proofed individual instrumental and vocal practice rooms. Many forms of financial aid are offered through the Financial Aid Office and application should be made there. 80% of students receive some form of financial aid. 50% of those applying are accepted and 81% of freshmen return for the sophomore year. Mean scores of entereing freshmen were: SAT 971 combined, ACT 23 composite.

Community Environment: Population 30,000. Cortland is located in the geographical center of New York State. It is accessible by bus or automobile. The city has a library, churches of all denominations, YMCA, YWCA, a hospital, motels, and the major civic, fraternal and veteran organizations. Recreational facilities include golf, swimming pool, movie theatres, bowling centers, 4 city parks and 3 nearby ski areas. Boating and fishing is available in nearby lakes. Cortland has a civic concert series.

STATE UNIVERSITY OF NEW YORK, COLLEGE AT FREDONIA   *(J-3)*
Central Avenue
Fredonia, New York 14063
Tel: (716) 673-3251; (800) 252-1212; Fax: (716) 673-3249

Description: This publicly supported, coeducational college of arts and sciences was founded in 1826. The sole purpose of the college until 1961 was to prepare elementary and music teachers. When the State University of New York was established in 1948, Fredonia became 1 of 13 colleges of Arts and Sciences within the university. It continues the teacher-preparatory and professional curricula. It is accredited by the Middle States Association of Colleges and Schools, and grants the Bachelor and Master degrees. Undergraduate programs offered are arts and sciences, teacher-preparation and professional curricula. Overseas programs of study are also available. The college operates on the semester system and offers two summer sessions. Enrollment includes 4,180 full-time and 356 part-time undergraduates, and 356 graduate students. A faculty of 241 full-time and 91 part-time gives an undergraduate faculty-student ratio of 1-20.

Entrance Requirements: Accredited high school graduation with rank in upper 50% or equivalent; completion of 16 units including 4 English, 3-4 math, 3-4 sciences, and 4 social studies; minimum SAT 425V, 425M or minimum ACT 18 required; non-high school graduates considered; early admission, delayed admission, midyear admission, rolling admission, and advanced placement plans available; Apr. 15 application deadline; $25 application fee.

Costs Per Year: $2,650 tuition; $6,550 out-of-state; $4,400 room and board; $359 student fees.

Collegiate Environment: Fredonia is near the shore of Lake Erie, 45 miles from Buffalo. The 245-acre campus has 21 buildings with dormitory capacity to accomodate 2,621 students. Library holdings include 381,677 bound volumes, 1,897 periodicals, 946,114 microforms, and 16,720 audiovisual materials. Approximately 54% of students applying for admission are accepted, including midyear students. Average high school standing of the recent freshman class: 39% in the top quintile; 41% in the second quintile. The average SAT score was 1032 for men and 987 for women. Financial aid is available and 70% of the student body receives some type of financial aid. Scholarships average $200-$2,650. Army ROTC is available through cross enrollment at St. Bernard or Canisius.

Community Environment: opulation 10,326. Predominantly an agricultural community in the midst of a grape belt, Fredonia has one of the first units of the Women's Christian Temperance Union, organized in 1873. Today it is the home of several wineries. The city is located in western New York, about 45 miles south of Buffalo. The average annual temperature is 48.4 degrees with an average rainfall of 36.6 inches. The area has several churches of various denominations, a hospital, good shopping facilities, and civic, fraternal and veteran's organizations nearby. Some part-time employment is available for students. Local recreation includes golfing, boating, The village of Fredonia has a population of 11,000 and is located 45 miles south of Buffalo near Lake Erie. The village has preserved its traditional small-town atmosphere. Tree-lined streets lead to a spcaious downtown common surrounded by outstanding examples of nineteenth-century village architecturee. Fredonia is essentially residential in nature. It is surrounded by orchards and vineyards that lead south to the Allegheny foothills. To the north lie the city of Dunkirk and Lake Erie. Summer and winter recreation facilities abound. The college also benefits from its relative proximity to the cities of Buffalo, Niagara Falls, and Toronto.

STATE UNIVERSITY OF NEW YORK, COLLEGE AT OLD WESTBURY   *(E-3)*
Old Westbury, New York 11568
Tel: (516) 876-3000; Admissions: (516) 876-3073; Fax: (516) 876-3307

Description: The State University of New York College at Old Westbury is one of the youngest four year colleges in the state system. Opened in 1968, the college moved to its current site in 1971. The college, known for its arts and sciences programs, offers 36 majors ranging from accounting to visual arts, and grants the Bachelor of Arts and the Bachelor of Science degrees. The most popular courses of study are Business and Management, Accounting, Computer Sciences, and Teacher Education. The academic programs of the College are registered by the New York State Department of Education and accredited by the Middle States Association of Colleges and Schools. The college operates on the semester system and offers three summer sessions. Enrollment consists of 1,315 full-time males, 1,716 full-time females, 483 part-time males and 667 part-time female students. There are 133 full-time and 2 part-time faculty members giving a student-faculty ratio of 24:1. Study abroad programs are offered in Bath, England; Manchester, England; Jamaica, West Indies, Spain, Korea and China.

Entrance Requirements: High school graduation or equivalent and minimum average of 80. No entrance exams are required; however, if submitted, minimum scores of SAT 400V, 400M and ACT 19 are recommended. Early decision, deferred admission, midyear admission and advanced placement plans available; Mar. 15 applicaiton deadline; $25 application fee.

Costs Per Year: Tuition $2,650 for state resident, $6,550 nonresident; student fees $278; room and board $4,872.

Collegiate Environment: 797 of the school's 4,226 students reside on campus, the environment is quite active. The students of Old Westbury have formed nearly 50 clubs and organizations, including an A.M. radio station. There are also 9 fraternities and two sororities with chapters on campus. The intramural and intercollegiate athletic programs can make a difference in campus life. In all, there are 14 intramural activities, and 4 N.C.A.A. Division III sports teams. The library contains 243,511 volumes, 10,137 periodicals, 393,968 microforms, and 8,000 audiovisual materials.

Community Environment: Old Westbury is located in Nassau County, Long Island. Just twenty-two miles from New York's Midtown Manhattan, and fifteen miles from Jones Beach, the area offers students the best of both worlds. Located within ten minutes drive are two major shopping malls, movie theaters, banks, and restaurants. The area is also complete with public and private businesses vital for gaining internships.

STATE UNIVERSITY OF NEW YORK, COLLEGE AT ONEONTA   *(J-14)*
Oneonta, New York 13820
Tel: (607) 431-2524

Description: Publicly supported, coeducational liberal arts and teacher education college was established in 1889 as a state normal school. When the State University of New York was formed it included the Oneonta State Teachers College and expanded its program to include graduate work in education and the preparation of teachers in home economics. In 1962 the college became a multipurpose institution with the introduction of traditional liberal arts majors for students not interested in teaching careers. The college is accredited by the Middle States Association of Colleges and Schools and grants the Bachelor and Master degrees. It operates on the semester system and offers two summer sessions. Enrollment includes 4,831 full-time and 488 part-time undergraduates and 510 graduate students. A faculty of 272 full-time and 60 part-time gives an undergraduate faculty-student ratio of 1-19.

Entrance Requirements: High school graduation or equivalent; completion of 16 units, including 4 English, 3 social studies, total of 8 in math, science and foreign language; ACT or SAT required; GRE required for graduate programs; advanced placement, early admission and delayed admission available; $25 application fee.

Costs Per Year: $2,650 tuition; $6,550 out-of-state tuition; $5,328 room and board.

Collegiate Environment: The 218-acre main campus, built since 1949, consists of 35 buildings overlooking the city of Oneonta and the Susquehanna Valley. 3 miles from the campus is a 200-acre camp owned and operated by the Organization of Ancillary Services. In Cooperstown, along Otsego Lake's shore, the college has 362 acres of woodland, pond and shoreline, which serve as an aquatic and terrestrial ecological research area. 16 residence halls accomodate 3,155 students. A number of fraternities and sororities also exist on campus. Other facilities include science buildings, classroom facilities, administration building, fine arts center, health center, instructional resources center, athletic fields, physical education building, student union and a library housing 529,000 bound volumes and 760,000 microforms. The college accepts approximately 70% of applicants. The middle 50% range of scores of entering freshmen were SAT 380-470

verbal, 430-530 math, ACT 19-23 composite. Financial assistance is available. 80% of students receive some form of financial aid.

Community Environment: The college is located in one of New York State's most beautiful and historic areas, midway between Albany and Binghamton and 175 miles northwest of New York City. Oneonta, a city of 15,000, is primarily a college, residential and shopping area with the campus a short walk from downtown. It is served by 2 major bus lines with 5 daily buses to New York City. Major airlines are available in Albany and Binghamton. Rail service is available in Utica. The college, nearby Hartwick College, and the community all combine to present a wide range of cultural activities for students.

STATE UNIVERSITY OF NEW YORK, COLLEGE AT OSWEGO   *(G-10)*
211 Culkin Hall
Oswego, New York 13126
Tel: (315) 341-2250

Description: This publicly supported, coeducational college of arts and sciences was founded as the Oswego Normal School in 1861. It was one of the charter members when the State University was established in 1948. It is accredited by the Middle States Association of Colleges and Schools and grants Bachelor and Master degrees. Students select from 46 programs in various liberal arts and career-oriented areas. Many of the career-orinted programs are offered within the School of Education or the School of Business. The university operates on the semester system and offers four summer sessions. Enrollment includes 6,727 full-time, 884 part-time, and 831 graduate students. A faculty of 429 gives an undergraduate faculty-student ratio of 1-21.

Entrance Requirements: Accredited high school graduation or equivalent; high school average and a college-preparatory curriculum stressed, early admission, early decision, delayed admission, and advanced placement plans available; $25 application fee.

Costs Per Year: $2,650 tuition; $6,550 out-of-state; $4,800 room and board; $310 college fees.

Collegiate Environment: The 696-acre campus occupies more than one mile of Lake Ontario shoreline near the western city limits of Oswego. An extensive building program has resulted in superior academic and living facilities for the students. The 40 buildings include living accommodations for 1,784 men and 2,160 women. The library contains 405,000 volumes, 1,906 periodicals, 1.5 million microforms and 56,000 audiovisual materials. Approximately 55% of the students applying for admission are accepted, including midyear students, and 87% return for their sophomore year. Average high school standing of a recent freshman class: 60% in the top quarter; 38% in the second quarter; 2% in the third quarter. Average scores for entering freshmen were: SAT 480V, 550M; ACT 24. Financial aid is available and 70% of the current student body receive some form of financial assistance. Recreational facilities include the ice rink and indoor track at Romney Fieldhouse, various playing fields, tennis courts and a track.

Community Environment: Population 21,000. Oswego manufactures aluminum and paper products. It is located on the southeastern shore of Lake Ontario and has a temperate climate. A library, YMCA, museum, hospital, and many civic, fraternal and patriotic organizations are found within the city limits. Transportation is provided by rail and excellent highways. There are dormitories, fraternity and sorority houses, hotels, motels and rooming houses for student housing. Part-time employment is available for students. Recreation includes include swimming, boating, fishing, golf courses, and a winter sports area.

STATE UNIVERSITY OF NEW YORK, COLLEGE AT POTSDAM   *(B-14)*
44 Pierreport Avenue
Potsdam, New York 13676-2296
Tel: (315) 267-2180; Fax: (315) 267-2163

Description: Publicly supported coeducational college of arts and science is one of the colleges within the State University of New York. The school was founded in 1816 as the St. Lawrence Academy. It became a teacher's college in 1942 and in 1948 became a campus of the State University of New York. The college was authorized to grant Master degrees in 1947 and became a college of arts and sciences in 1962. The Crane Institute of Music was the first school of music in the United States to prepare music educators for teaching in public schools and was incorporated as a major department of the college in 1926. It is accredited by the Middle States Association of Colleges and Schools and grants the Bachelor and Master degrees. The college operates on the semester system and offers two five-week and one two-week summer sessions. Enrollment includes 3,428 full-time and 270 part-time undergraduates and 592 graduate students. A faculty of 215 full-time and 60 part-time gives an undergraduate faculty-student ratio of 1-21. Army and Air Force ROTC programs are available as an elective through cross-registration at Clarkson University.

Entrance Requirements: Accredited high school graduation or equivalent with rank in upper 40%; completion of 16 units; SAT or ACT required; personal interview recommended for all and audition for music candidates required; early admission, delayed admission, midyear admission, rolling admission, and advanced placement plans available; $25 application fee.

Costs Per Year: $2,650 tuition; $6,550 out-of-state; $4,570 room and board; $311 college fees.

Collegiate Environment: The 240-acre campus is located in northern New York's St. Lawrence Valley. The 31 college buildings include a library of 393,819 volumes, 1,584 periodicals, and 333,000 microforms. There are dormitory facilities for 2,500 students. Fraternities and sororities house an additional 175 students. 71% of applicants meet the entrance criteria and are accepted. 82% of the freshman class returns for the sophomore year. 350 scholarships are available and 77% of students receive some form of financial aid.

Community Environment: See Clarkson University.

STATE UNIVERSITY OF NEW YORK, COLLEGE OF AGRICULTURE AND LIFE SCIENCES AT CORNELL   *(J-10)*
195 Roberts Hall
Ithaca, New York 14853
Tel: (607) 255-2036

Description: The College of Agriculture and Life Science at Cornell is a state supported college functioning as part of a privately endowed, land-grant university, unique in its combination of the tradition of the Ivy League and the spirit of the great state university. The range of academic programs is also unique for a college of agriculture with programs ranging from biochemistry to crops to communication to conservation. One of 4 statutory colleges at Cornell which benefit from being part of a major research university, including a national center for biotechnology. It is accredited by the Middle States Association of Colleges and Schools. It operates on the semester system and offers one summer session. Enrollment at the college is 3,100 full-time undergraduates and graduate students. The faculty consists of 433 full-time and 20 part-time members. The college grants Bachelor of Science degrees and various Master and Doctoral degrees of Science. Army, Navy, and Air Force ROTC programs are available. Joint programs are available with other colleges of Cornell University.

Entrance Requirements: Completion of 16 high school academic units including 4 English; 3 mathematics, with 2 science required, biology and chemistry (or physics) with a third course recommended, prospective science majors should complete a minimum of 3 science courses; satisfactory SAT or ACT; New York State residents should include scores on Regents examinations; early admission, early decision, midyear admission, rolling admission, delayed admission, advanced placement plans available; $60 application fee.

Costs Per Year: $7,806 tuition; $14,966 out-of-state tuition; $6,148 room and board.

Collegiate Environment: On the portion of the Cornell campus devoted principally to the College of Agriculture, there are 14 buildings containing classrooms, auditoriums, a library, bioclimatic laboratories, 16 greenhouses, a judging pavilion, and a numerous special laboratories and barns. The college library contains over 575,000 volumes. It is the location of the primary computer center. There are 3 others in instructional buildings. The university library has 5,000,000 volumes. The college uses about 11,000 acres of land for its research program and for instructional purposes. Cornell University provides living accommodations for men and women and total housing for about 420 families. Need-based scholarships are available to students in the College of Agriculture in addition to standard university need-based assistance. Application should be made on the Cornell Univer-

sity Financial Aid Form. Admission to the four-year course is generally only in the fall term except for transfer students who may also enter in the spring term (except for the Landscape Architecture major).

Community Environment: See Cornell University.

STATE UNIVERSITY OF NEW YORK, COLLEGE OF AGRICULTURE AND TECHNOLOGY AT COBLESKILL
(I-15)
Cobleskill, New York 12043
Tel: (518) 234-5525

Description: The publicly supported, coeducational college was chartered in 1911 and officially began its program in 1916 as the Schoharie State School of Agriculture. It became part of the State University of New York in 1948, offering two-year programs leading to the A.A.S., A.S. and A.O.S. degrees as well as a number of one-year certificate programs and the four-year Bachelor of Technology in Agriculture degree. The college is accredited by the Middle State Association of Colleges and Schools. Divisions of the college include Agriculture and Natural Resources, Business, Early Childhood, Food Service Administration and Liberal Arts and Sciences. The Liberal Arts and Sciences Division offers degree programs in the humanities, social sciences, physical sciences and science technologies. The school operates on the semester system. Enrollment is 1,405 men and 1,380 women. A faculty of 137 full-time and 9 part-time gives a faculty-student ratio of 1-19.

Entrance Requirements: Accredited high school graduation or equivalent; SAT or ACT required for some programs; $25 application fee; early admission, rolling admission, delayed admission, midyear admission, and advanced placement programs available.

Costs Per Year: $2,650 tuition; $6,550 out-of-state; $4,470 room and board; $350 student fees; $500 expenses.

Collegiate Environment: The campus is located in Schoharie County on the western edge of the village of Cobleskill. The campus and college farm consist of about 500 acres. The 40 buildings include dormitories for 1,782 men and women. The Jared Van Wagenen Library contains 88,000 volumes, 958 periodicals, 438 microforms and 5,088 audiovisual materials. Outdoor recreation facilities include 12 tennis courts, a baseball diamond, 2 basketball courts, 4 handball courts, an archery range, softball fields, a soccer field, a running track, swimming pool, and ski slopes. Classes begin in late August. Financial aid is available. Approximately 62% of the applicants are accepted. 72% receive some sort of financial aid.

Community Environment: Population 5,000. Cobleskill is a rural village at the junction of Routes 7 and 145, 1 hour's drive from Albany. The city is accessible via bus lines. Community services include a hospital, a library, and various civic, fraternal and veteran's organizations. Recreational facilities include bowling, golf, tennis, hunting, fishing, roller skating, skiing, swimming, and theater. An annual county fair is held here. Nearby caverns are scenic wonders in the area.

STATE UNIVERSITY OF NEW YORK, COLLEGE OF AGRICULTURE AND TECHNOLOGY AT MORRISVILLE
(I-12)
Morrisville, New York 13408
Tel: (315) 684-6046; (800) 258-0111; Fax: (315) 684-6116

Description: This publicly supported, coeducational two-year college was founded as an Agricultural School in 1908. In 1948 the New York State Agricultural and Technical Institute at Morrisville became part of the State University of New York, and took its present name during the 1964-65 academic year. It awards the Associate in Applied Science, Associate in Arts, Associate in Science degree, Associate of Occupational Studies, and Certificates. The college houses 4 schools: Agriculture and Natural Resources Conservation; Business, Hospitality and Nursing; Liberal Arts; and Mathematics, Science and Engineering Technology. It operates on the semester system and offers one limited summer session. The college is accredited by the Middle States Association of Colleges and Schools. Enrollment includes 2,624 full-time and 527 part-time students. A faculty of 124 and 70 part-time gives a faculty-student ratio of 1-16.

Entrance Requirements: Accredited high school graduation; recommendation of high school principal or counselor; $25 application fee; rolling admission and advanced placement plans available.

Costs Per Year: $2,650 tuition; $6,550 nonresident; $4,790 room and board; $250 student fees.

Collegiate Environment: Morrisville is situated almost at the geographical center of the state. The campus of 185 acres includes residence halls with a capacity of 1,915 students. The library's book collection of over 100,000 volumes contains the best available current and historical material in the technologies as well as in the arts and sciences. Financial assistance is available. 89% of the applicants are accepted and 75% of the freshmen return to this campus for the second year.

Community Environment: Population 1,500. Morrisville is located 11 miles east of Cazenovia and 28 miles east of Syracuse. The area is served by bus line. Catholic, Community (Presbyterian), and Faith Baptist churches, and several civic, fraternal and veteran's organizations are represented here. Local recreation includes camping, hiking, fishing, and skiing. Shopping facilities and part-time employment for students are limited in the immediate area.

STATE UNIVERSITY OF NEW YORK, COLLEGE OF ARTS AND SCIENCE AT GENESEO   *(I-7)*
Geneseo, New York 14454
Tel: (716) 245-5571; Fax: (716) 245-5005

Description: This publicly supported coeducational college of arts and sciences was established in 1867 and became one of the units of the State University of New York in 1948. The college is accredited by the Middle States Association of Colleges and Schools and grants the Bachelor and Master degrees. It operates on the semester system and offers three summer sessions. Enrollment includes 4,956 undergraduate students. A faculty of 237 full-time and 86 part-time gives a faculty-student ratio of 1-20. Extensive overseas programs are available as well as an academic cooperative program with 9 other colleges for engineering. A School of Business has been established and a 3-2 MBA program is available at SUNY Buffalo, Pace, RIT and Syracuse. A 3-2 program is available with the SUNY College of Environmental Science and Forestry at Syracuse. Enrollment includes 5,226 full-time and 131 part-time undergraduates and 397 graduate students. A facutly of 251 full-time and 73 part-time gives a faculty-student ratio of 1-18.

Entrance Requirements: High school graduation or equivalent with rank in upper 50%; recommended completion of 15 units including 4 English, 4 mathematics, 4 science, 4 foreign language, and 4 social studies; SAT or ACT required; GRE required for graduate programs; non-high school graduates considered; delayed admission, early admission, early decision, midyear admission, rolling admission and advanced placement plans available; $25 application fee.

Costs Per Year: $2,650 tuition; $6,550 out-of-state; $4,170 room and board; $225 student fees; $700 average additional expenses.

Collegiate Environment: Located in the heart of the famed Genesee Valley, the college is 30 miles from Rochester. There are 38 buildings on the 220-acre campus. The Wadsworth Auditorium seats 1,000 persons; the library system contains 1,359,370 volumes and periodicals and 914,308 microforms. There are dormitories for 3,100 men and women. Approximately 48% of the students applying for admission are accepted, including midyear students, and 92% return for the sophomore year. Average high school standing of a recent freshman class: 85% in the top fifth; 39% in the second quarter. The average scores of the entering freshman class were SAT 533 verbal, 603 math, and ACT 26 composite. Financial aid is available and 65% of the current student body receives some form of financial assistance.

Community Environment: Population 7,000. Located in the Genesee country, famed for the charm of its scenery and the fertility of its farms, Geneseo, a National Landmark Village, is located 30 miles south of Rochester. Letchworth State Park nearby offers many recreational facilities. Genesee Expressway Rt. 390 makes the area easily accessible.

STATE UNIVERSITY OF NEW YORK, COLLEGE OF ARTS AND SCIENCE AT PLATTSBURGH   *(B-18)*
Plattsburgh, New York 12901
Tel: (518) 564-2000; Admissions: (518) 564-2040; Fax: (518) 564-2045

Description: Publicly-supported, coeducational college of arts and science, 1 of 13 colleges of Arts and Science in the network comprising the State University of New York. The college is accredited by the Middle States Association of Colleges and Schools and grants Bachelor and Master degrees. Major programs of study are Accounting, Computer Science, Biological and Physical Sciences, Business, Communication, Education, Environmental Science, Nursing and Psychology. Special Studies and overseas academic programs are available, sponsored by the faculty or organized in cooperation with other State University colleges. A faculty of 258 full-time and 109 part-time gives a faculty-student ratio of 1-20.

Entrance Requirements: Accredited high school graduation or equivalent with rank in upper 50%; completion of academic program including 4 units of English, 5 math and science combined, 3 social studies, foreign language preferred; SAT or ACT scores required, no pre-established minimum score; Transfer applicants considered; delayed admission, early decision, early admission, midyear admission, rolling admission and advanced placement plans available; interview and campus visit recommended; $25 application fee.

Costs Per Year: $2,650 tuition; $6,550 nonresident, $4,326 board and room; $309 student fees.

Collegiate Environment: The college campus consists of 35 buildings on 150 acres on the west shore of Lake Champlain. There are dormitory facilities for 2,631 men and women. The library contains 356,930 bound volumes, 1,455 periodical subscriptions and 828,220 microforms. The Outdoor Education Center is Twin Valleys, 38 miles south of the main campus, is a 700-acre track of Adirondack woodlands with brooks, meadows, and a 3-acre pond. Approximately 65% of the students applying for admission are accepted. Average high school GPA of the recent freshman class was 85. Theaverage scores of the entering freshman class were SAT 460 verbal, 520 math, ACT 22 composite. 80% of students receive some form of financial assistance.

Community Environment: The campus is adjacent to a residential section of the city of Plattsburgh, a community of approximately 22,000 people. Plattsburgh is located in the northeast corner of the state on the western shore of Lake Champlain, near the Adirondack Mountains. The campus is within 1 hour's drive of Lake Placid, Burlington, VT, and Montreal, Canada.

STATE UNIVERSITY OF NEW YORK, COLLEGE OF CERAMICS AT ALFRED UNIVERSITY   *(K-7)*
Alfred, New York 14802
Tel: (607) 871-2111; (800) 541-9229; Admissions: (607) 871-2115; Fax: (607) 871-2198

Description: Established in 1900 for the purpose of advancing the art and science of ceramics, the college is an integral part of Alfred University and a statutory unit of the State University of New York. The School of Ceramic Engineering and Sciences offers B.S. degrees in Ceramic Engineering, Ceramic Engineering Science, and Glass Science. A large graduate program awards M.S. and Ph.D. degrees. The School of Art and Design offers B.F.A. and M.F.A. degrees with undergraduate concentrations in Ceramics, Graphic Design, Glass, Media/Video, Painting, Photography, Printmaking, Sculpture, Wood Design, and Art Education. The program leading to the B.S. in Glass Science was initiated in 1932, the first Master's degree in Design was conferred in 1932, the first M.S. in 1933, and the first Ph.D. degree in 1958. Enrollment in the College of Ceramics includes 661 full-time and 25 part-time undergraduates and 101 graduate students. Total Alfred University undergraduate enrollment was 1,975 in fall 1994. A faculty of 52 gives an undergraduate faculty-student ratio of 1-16. The semester system is used and limited summer sessions are offered. The college is accredited by the Middle States Association of Colleges and Schools and the Accreditation Board for Engineering and Technology.

Entrance Requirements: High school graduation; recommended completion of 16 units including 4 English, 2 (art)-3 (engineering) mathematics, 1 (art)-2 (engineering) science, and 3 social studies;

portfolio (art); early decision, advanced placement, early admission, and delayed admission plans available; $25 application fee; application deadline Feb. 15th.

Costs Per Year: $6,204 tuition; $8,876 out-of-state; $5,406 room and board; $424 fees.

Collegiate Environment: There are 54 buildings on the Alfred University campus, 6 of which are used primarily by the College of Ceramics. All freshmen and sophomores and most upperclassmen live in Alfred University residence halls which accomodate 1,330 students. Meals are served in two campus dining halls. Students take most of their courses in the College of Ceramics, fulfilling general requirements by taking classes in the other colleges of the university. Ceramics and glass sciences are materials sciences, requiring understanding of basic chemistry, physics and math as a basis for the study of ceramics. Examples of engineered ceramics are the insulating tile on the space shuttles; computer chips; glass "wire" (fiber optic wave guides) for improved telephone communication; and silicon carbide engine parts. The specialized analytical facilities include a computer interfaced X-ray diffraction laboratory that is among the 10 most powerful in the world, and surface analysis equipment that can determine the composition of a material down to one part in a million. In the processing facilities, students prepare experimental ceramic materials and test their thermal and electrical properties. Laboratories and computer facilities are accessible 16 hours a day. Cooperative work experiences and study abroad are included in the undergraduate program. The middle 50% of accepted freshmen have SAT scores of 480-570V, 510-650M; 84% are in the top third of their high school class. The School of Art and Design has outstanding studio facilities that students may use 7 days a week. Distinguishing features of the art school include a flexible curriculum that includes a strong Freshman Foundation program, diverse studio selection in sophomore and junior years, and intense studio involvement in the senior year, capped by a senior show. Study abroad programs are available. The Scholes Library of Ceramics, which recently moved into a newly dedicated building, is the largest ceramics library in the world; it contains 57,026 books, 32,021 bound periodicals, and 130,000 slides. Extensive financial aid is available, and approximately 60% of the student body receives some type of assistance.

Community Environment: See Alfred University.

STATE UNIVERSITY OF NEW YORK, COLLEGE OF ENVIRONMENTAL SCIENCE AND FORESTRY   *(I-10)*
Bray Hall, Room 106
1 Forestry Drive
Syracuse, New York 13210-2779
Tel: (315) 470-6600; (800) 777-7373; Fax: (315) 470-6933

Description: A publicly supported, coeducational college of the State University of New York, that offers degrees at the Associate, Bachelor, Master, and Doctorate levels, all of which focus on a variety of issues relating to our environment. It is accredited by the Middle States Association of Colleges and Schools. The college offers seven programs that are available to the freshman and transfer applicant: Chemistry, Environmental and Forest Biology, Forest Engineering, Paper Science and Engineering, Forestry (Resources Management), Landscape Architecture and a Dual Option that is a nine semester sequence combining the Biology and Forestry programs. Two additional programs are available to transfer students only -- Environmental Studies and Wood Products Engineering. An Associate of Applied Science Degree in Forest Technology is available for transfer students who have completed one year of college. The college also supports special advising programs for students who want to pursue professional careers in Science Education (7-12 in Biology or Chemistry), Medicine, Veterinary Medicine, Dentistry, Law or the Peace Corp. The college operates on the semester system with a limited eight-week summer session at the Cranberry Lake Campus, for students of Environmental and Forest Biology. Enrollment includes 1,200 full-time undergraduates and 600 graduate students. A faculty of 133 full-time and 8 part-time gives an undergraduate faculty-student ratio of 1-13.

Entrance Requirements: Freshman applicants are required to have substantive high school backgrounds including four years each of college prepatory science and mathematics. (Chemistry is required). Transfer applicants are encouraged to consult the college catalogue since the requirements vary by curriculum. Applicants applying for the Associate degree must have two semesters of college to be consid-

ered. Bachelor degree applicants are encouraged to have four semester of college prior to transfer. Approximately 20% of the freshman applicant pool is offered admission, and 60% of of the transfer pool is similarly accepted. Jan. 1 freshman, May 1 transfer application deadlines; $25 application fee.

Costs Per Year: $2,650 state-resident tuition; $6,550 nonresident; $5,920 room and board; $287 student fees.

Collegiate Environment: The campus is situated adjacent to Syracuse University and offers many collaborative programs. The college library contains 190,250 volumes, 1,700 periodicals and 91,000 microforms, and students also have access to Syracuse University's 2-million-volume library. Housing is provided thorugh Syracuse University. 20% of freshman applicants and 60% of transfer applicants meet entrance criteria and are accepted. The middle 50% range of entering students' scores are: SAT 1060-1210 composite. 750 scholarships and financial aid are available. 85% of the students receive some form of financial aid.

Community Environment: See Syracuse University.

Branch Campuses: The college operates a system of branch campuses comprised of approximately 25,000 acres. Among the largest of these are: The Newcomb Campus, home of the Adirondack Interpretive Center; the Wanakena Campus, site of the NY State Ranger School; the Cranberry Lake Campus, location of the eight-week summer field program for students in Environmental and Forest Biology; and the Tully Campus, site of the Genetic Field Station and the Heiberg Memorial Forest.

STATE UNIVERSITY OF NEW YORK, COLLEGE OF HUMAN ECOLOGY AT CORNELL UNIVERSITY   *(J-10)*
Ithaca, New York 14850
Tel: (607) 255-2216

Description: Publicly supported, coeducational specialized college; 1 of several professional colleges of the State University of New York. It is accredited by the Middle States Association of Colleges and Schools. There are 6 departments in the college: (1) Human Service Studies, (2) Consumer Economics and Housing, (3) Design and Environmental Analysis, (4) Human Development and Family Studies, (5) Textiles and Apparel and (6) the Division of Nutritional Sciences. There are also 2 independent majors, (1) Public Policy Analysis, and (2) Biology and Society. It operates on the semester system and offers two summer sessions. The college grants the Bachelor of Science degree. Master and Doctor degrees are available through Cornell University.

Entrance Requirements: Completion of 16 units, including 4 English, 3 mathematics, 3 biology, chemistry or physics; SAT or ACT required; delayed admission, advanced placement, early admission plans available; $60 application fee.

Costs Per Year: $7,806 tuition; $14,966 out-of-state; $6,238 room and board.

Collegiate Environment: The State Colleges of Agriculture and Life Sciences, and Human Ecology are served by the Albert R. Mann Library of about 425,000 volumes. This is supplemented by the other libraries of Cornell University, which hold a total of over 5 million volumes. Comfortable, well-furnished dormitories and dining rooms for undergraduate men and women are provided at the university. Students are eligible to compete for certain scholarships that are open to undergraduates in any college of Cornell University. Approximately 30% of applicants are accepted. 48% of students receive some form of financial aid. Army, Navy and Air Force ROTC available.

Community Environment: See Cornell University.

STATE UNIVERSITY OF NEW YORK, COLLEGE OF OPTOMETRY   *(E-2)*
100 East 24th Street
New York, New York 10010
Tel: (212) 780-5100; (800) 291-3937; Admissions: (212) 780-5100; Fax: (212) 780-5094

Description: This publicly supported, coeducational, professional college was founded in 1971 and is part of the State University of New York. It is fully accredited by the Middle States Association of Colleges and Schools and by the Council on Optometric Education of the American Optometric Association. It operates on the quarter system. Enrollment is 266 students. A faculty of 49 full-time anf 100 part-time gives a faculty-student ratio of 1-6.

Entrance Requirements: 3-4 years of college required; OAT required for Doctor of Optometry program; $75 application fee.

Costs Per Year: $8,572 state resident tuition; $17,221 nonresident tuition; $120.50 student fees.

Collegiate Environment: College facilities include a library of 20,000 volumes. Housing is available. Financial assistance is available. 85% of students receive some form of financial assistance.

Community Environment: See New York University.

STATE UNIVERSITY OF NEW YORK, COLLEGE OF TECHNOLOGY AT ALFRED   *(K-7)*
Alfred, New York 14802-1196
Tel: (607) 587-4215; (800) 425-3733; Admissions: (607) 587-4215; Fax: (607) 587-4209

Description: The publicly supported coeducational college began as a State School of Agriculture in 1908. It was removed from the jurisdiction of the State Education Department in 1948 and was incorporated into the State University of New York. It is accredited by the Middle States Association of Colleges and Schools. The college operates on the semester system and offers two summer sessions. Enrollment includes 3,518 students. A faculty of 176 gives a faculty-student ratio of 1-18.

Entrance Requirements: Approved high school graduation including 16 units; SAT or ACT recommended; requirements of individual curricula vary; non-high school graduates may be admitted as special students through the Office of Continuing Education; $25 application fee; rolling admission and advanced placement plans available.

Costs Per Year: $2,650 resident tuition; $6,550 out-of-state tuition; $4,490 room and board; $320 student fees.

Collegiate Environment: The college is located in Alfred, New York, a small community with a population of about 2,000 and a student population of over 5,000, including Alfred University. It is about 75 miles south of Rochester, New York, close to the Pennsylvania border. All dormitories are coed and have a capacity of 2,348; the library system contains 59,950 bound volumes, 673 periodicals, 478 microform titles, and 1,538 records, tapes, and CD's. Scholarships, loans, and grants are available; 85% of the students receive some form of financial aid.

Community Environment: See Alfred University.

Branch Campuses: School of Vocational Technologies, Wellsville, NY, 14895, (607) 587-3105.

STATE UNIVERSITY OF NEW YORK, COLLEGE OF TECHNOLOGY AT CANTON   *(B-13)*
Canton, New York 13617
Tel: (315) 386-7123; (800) 388-7123; Fax: (315) 386-7930

Description: SUNY Canton was authorized by the Legislature in 1906 and is the first public, postsecondary two-year college in New York State. Since its founding, the college has educated students for employment as technicians, skilled workers, and practitioners in technical, agricultural, business and public service, and allied health fields. The college also offers university parallel transfer programs that lead to baccalaureate degrees. SUNY Canton is situated on a 555-acre campus on the banks of the Grasse River in the village of Canton. A 425-acre demonstration farm is removed from the main campus but supplements the educational program and public service commitments of the college. The college is fully accredited by the Middle State Association of Colleges and Schools. In addition, professional accreditation has been accorded to specialized curricula by the following accrediting agencies: National League of Nursing, American Board of Funeral Service Education, American Board for Engineering Technology, American Veterinary Medical Association, the Committe on Allied Health Education Accreditation, and the National Accrediting Agency for Clinical Labratory Science. There are 79 curricular offerings leading to the Associate degree in the fields of Business and Public Service, Engineering, and Liberal Arts. There are also 5 one-year certificate programs: 4 in Engineering and 1 in Liberal Arts. Enrollment is 2,278 students. A faculty of 115 gives a faculty-student ratio of 1-20.

Entrance Requirements: Graduation from approved secondary school or New York State Equivalency Diploma; ACT as a placement test; applicants must meet the specific requirements (including physical requirements) established by the faculty for each specialized curriculum; rolling admission, early decision, early admission, delayed admission and advanced placement plans available; curricula are limited to space and availability; candidates are encouraged to apply early; $25 application fee.

Costs Per Year: $2,650 tuition; $6,550 out-of-state; $4,657 room and board; $380 student fees.

Collegiate Environment: The college is a member of the Associated Colleges of the St. Lawrence Valley Consortium. 4 colleges within an 11-mile distance supplement and complement each other. Cross-registration for courses, shared faculty and faculty exchange, cooperative social and cultural programming, and common usage of libraries and audiovisual resources are some of the benefits resulting from this consortial arrangement. Through the Student Cooperative Alliance, the students are totally responsible for the planning, budgeting, and coordination of all activities and athletics. There are 7 intercollegiate sports for men and women. The Canton Northmen have been NJCAA ice hockey champions 12 times since the championship tournament was started. Approximately 60% of the graduates go directly to work following graduation. Placement cannot be promised but over 90% of those seeking employment have been hired despite the economic conditions of recent years. 40% of the graduates transfer to upper division study leading to baccalaureate degrees. Dormitories provide housing for 1,100 students. There are 3 sororities and 3 fraternities. The balance of the 2,204-member student body commutes.

Community Environment: Canton is a small village with a population of 5,000, 120 miles southwest of Montreal and 135 miles northeast of Syracuse. The St. Lawrence River and the city of Ogdensburg are 20 miles away. The foothills of the Adirondack Mountains begin 20 miles to the east, and it is 90 miles to Lake Placid, the site of the 1980 Olympis Winter Games.

STATE UNIVERSITY OF NEW YORK, COLLEGE OF TECHNOLOGY AT DELHI   *(K-14)*
Delhi, New York 13753
Tel: (607) 746-4000; (800) 963-3544; Admissions: (607) 746-4550; Fax: (607) 746-4104

Description: The publicly-supported, coeducational two-year college was established in 1913. It is accredited by the Middle States Association of Colleges and Schools. The college is one of New York State's pioneers in two-year higher education. A unit of the State University of New York since 1948, the college grants the degrees of Associate in Applied Science, Associate in Science, Associate in Arts and Associate in Occupational Studies. Certificates are granted in vocational programs. Educational priority and development are placed on polytechnic education with support of a broad general education component. Special programmatic emphasis is placed on the fields of Agriculture and Life Sciences, Engineering Technologies; selected Business, Marketing, Hotel-Restaurant-Food Service, and Secretarial Science. Certificate Vocational programs are offered in selected occupational clusters such as the Construction Trades and Individual Studies. The college operates on the semester system and offers two summer sessions. Enrollment includes 2,279 students. A faculty of 110 full-time and 41 part-time gives a faculty-student ratio of 1-19.

Entrance Requirements: High school graduation or equivalent; satisfactory completion of prerequisite course requirements programs for respective divisions of the college; rolling admission, early admission, midyear admission and advanced placement plans available. $25 application fee.

Costs Per Year: $2,650 tuition; $6,550 out-of-state tuition; $4,560 room and board; $295 student fees.

Collegiate Environment: The college is located on a spacious 333-acre campus overlooking the village of Delhi. A 750-acre Valley Campus Agricultural and Recreation complex complements the main campus. There are 19 major buildings including dormitories for 1,498 people. The library contains 58,939 volumes and 564 periodicals. The Student Center houses a gymnasium, theater, and Student Union. A new recreation complex houses racquetball courts, saunas and an indoor swimming pool. 76% of applicants are accepted. 65 scholarships are offered, including 45 for freshmen. 42% of the student body receives some type of financial aid.

Community Environment: Population 3,500. Delhi is located on the Western edge of the Catskill Mountain Park, a scenic rural region 135 miles northwest of New York City. The climate is temperate with 4 seasons. Within the immediate area there are a hospital, a public library, 9 churches, and a nine-hole golf course. The locale is ideal for outdoor recreation activities of almost every description. The city has major civic, fraternal and veteran's organizations.

STATE UNIVERSITY OF NEW YORK, COLLEGE OF TECHNOLOGY AT FARMINGDALE   *(E-4)*
Melville Road
Farmingdale, New York 11735
Tel: (516) 420-2000

Description: The publicly supported, coeducational four-year polytechnic college was founded by the State Legislature in 1912 and became a unit of the State University of New York in 1948. It is accredited by the Middle States Association of Colleges and Schools. It offers programs for high school graduates who wish to prepare for careers in engineering business and health, as well as programs in the social services and liberal arts. The College offers Associate level degrees as well as Bachelor of Technology degrees in seven upper division programs. It operates on the semester system and offers two summer terms. Enrollment is 3,479 full-time and 3,238 part-time students. A faculty of 237 full-time and 180 part-time provides a faculty-student ratio of 1-19.

Entrance Requirements: High school graduation or equivalent; individual programs have their own specific admissions requirements; $25 application fee; early admission, early decision, advanced placement and rolling admission plans available.

Costs Per Year: $2,650 state-resident tuition; $6,550 out-of-state; $5,315 room and board; $566 student fees.

Collegiate Environment: The college campus of approximately 400 acres is situated just north of the village of Farmingdale. There are 26 buildings including a library of 128,000 volumes, 850 periodicals, and 258 titles on microform. Dormitories provide housing for 700 students. 45% of applicants are accepted. Financial aid is available.

Community Environment: Population 8,000. Farmingdale is located approximately 30 miles from New York City, east of Levittown, on the Nassau-Suffolk border. The area has temperate climate. Community services include a public library, mobile hospitals, and nearby restaurants. Dormitories, private homes and rooms for rent provide student housing. There are part-time job opportunities for students. All the cultural, recreational, and community service facilities of New York City are easily accessible.

STATE UNIVERSITY OF NEW YORK, COLUMBIA-GREENE COMMUNITY COLLEGE   *(K-17)*
P.O. Box 1000
Hudson, New York 12534
Tel: (518) 828-4181; Admissions: (518) 828-4181; Fax: (518) 828-8543

Description: This two-year coeducational community college is publicly supported. It is accredited by the Middle States Association of Colleges and Schools. The college grants the Associate degree. It operates on the semester system and offers two summer sessions. Enrollment includes 1,700 students. A faculty of 45 members gives a faculty-student ratio of 1-38.

Entrance Requirements: Open enrollment for previous June graduates of Columbia and Greene Counties. Placement exams sometimes required of applicants. Rolling admissions, early admission and advanced placement plans available.

Costs Per Year: $1,900 for state residents; $3,800 for out-of-state residents; $50 student activity fee.

Collegiate Environment: 90% of students are from in-state, 100% commute, 15% have minority backgrounds. Student activities include student government, a variety of clubs, radio, drama. Athletics offered include baseball, basketball, soccer, bowling, and softball. Library holdings include 33,000 volumes. Scholarships are available and 85% of students receive some form of financial aid. Approximately 40% of the graduates enter four-year programs.

Community Environment: Campus is located on 420 acres on the east bank of the Hudson River and just 3 miles from Hudson, a town of approximately 10,000. The setting is rural and just minutes from the Catskills, and only 30 miles from Albany and 90 miles from New York City. A train station is found in Hudson. There is limited part-time employment available on campus and in the surrounding communities.

STATE UNIVERSITY OF NEW YORK, COMMUNITY COLLEGE OF THE FINGER LAKES   *(I-8)*
Lincoln Hill Road
Canandaigua, New York 14424
Tel: (716) 394-3500

Description: This publicly supported coeducational community college was established in 1965 as a unit of the State University of New York, under the sponsorship of Ontario County. The school is accredited by the Middle States Association of Colleges and Schools. It is authorized to grant the Associate in Arts degree, in the study areas of humanities and human services, social science, American studies, or fine arts; (music, art, theatre), the Associate in Science degree, in the study areas of business administration, mathematics, science, agriculture, environmental science and forestry, engineering science, or computer science; and the Associate in Applied Science degree, with a major in accounting, business administration, secretarial science, retailing, data processing, criminal justice, natural resources conservation, graphic arts, nursing, ornamental horticulture, mechanical technology, travel & tourism, hotel and resort management, administrative assistant, and word processing. The college operates two extension centers in the communities of Geneva (15 miles east) and Newark (23 miles northeast). The college operates on the 4-1-4 system and offers four summer sessions. Enrollment includes 1,050 men and 1,131 women full-time and 690 men and 1,204 women part-time. 240 full- and part-time faculty result in a teacher-student ratio of 1-18.

Entrance Requirements: Approved high school graduation or equivalent; completion of 4 units of English, 1 math, 1 science, 4 social studies; open admission, early admission, midyear admission, rolling admission and advanced placement plans available; $25 application fee.

Costs Per Year: $2,000 resident tuition; $4,000 out-of-state tuition; $130 student fees.

Collegiate Environment: The library contains 70,000 volumes, 450 periodicals, 276 microforms, and 2,730 audiovisual materials. There are no dormitory accommodations for resident students; however, privately owned housing information is available in the community through the college. About 85% of students receive some form of financial assistance. 97% of the applicants are accepted.

Community Environment: The Community College of the Finger Lakes is located on the east side of Canandaigua Lake (population 11,500). The city stands on the site of the Seneca Indian Village "Kan-an-dar-que," which means the chosen spot. One of the most beautiful of the Finger Lakes, Canandaigua Lake is 17 miles long and averages about a mile in width. This is a resort area with excellent skiing in winter. Canandaigua is a rural community which has good transportation connections with the surrounding area. The city has a good business district and 3 shopping plazas, medical facilities, 1 library, and several churches.

STATE UNIVERSITY OF NEW YORK, CORNING COMMUNITY COLLEGE   *(K-9)*
Spencer Hill Road
Corning, New York 14830
Tel: (607) 962-9011; (800) 358-7171; Fax: (607) 962-9456

Description: The publicly supported, coeducational community college was founded in 1956 and is the twelfth of the 38 community colleges supervised by the State University of New York. The college is accredited by the Middle States Association of Colleges and Schools. It offers transfer and occupational programs days and evenings. It operates on the semester system and offers three summer sessions. Enrollment during a recent academic year was 3,481 men and women full-time and part-time. A faculty of 111 full-time and 86 part-time gives a faculty-student ratio of 1-18. The college grants an Associate in Occupational Studies, Associate in Arts or Science, Associate in Applied Science or a Certificate.

Entrance Requirements: Accredited high school graduation or equivalent; completion of 4 units of English, 1 math, 1 science, and 3 social studies; open enrollment policy; rolling admission, midyear admission, and advanced placement plans available; $25 application fee.

Costs Per Year: $2,100 tuition; $4,200 out-of-state; $180 general fees.

Collegiate Environment: The college is located on 178 acres 2 miles south of the city of Corning. The 7 college buildings include a library of 77,500 volumes, 488 periodicals, 8,510 microforms and 11,623 audiovisual materials. There are no dormitories provided on campus. Financial aid is available for qualified students. About 99% of the applicants are accepted, and students may enroll at midyear as well as in the fall.

Community Environment: Population 16,500. This is an urban area with temperate climate. Corning is accessible via U.S. Route 15, and State Routes 17 and 414. The city has a public library, the Corning Museum of Glass, 8 churches, and 1 hospital. Some part-time work is available. There are active civic, fraternal and veteran's organizations in the immediate area.

STATE UNIVERSITY OF NEW YORK, DUTCHESS COMMUNITY COLLEGE *(M-17)*
Pendell Road
Poughkeepsie, New York 12601
Tel: (914) 471-4500 x 1000; Fax: (914) 471-4518

Description: The publicly supported, coeducational junior college was founded in 1957. It is accredited by the Middle States Association of Colleges and Schools. The college grants the Associate degree. It operates on the semester system and offers three summer sessions. Enrollment includes 1,495 men and 1,545 women full-time and 1,381 men and 2,322 women part-time and noncredit students. There are 136 full-time faculty members.

Entrance Requirements: Approved high school graduation or equivalency diploma; open enrollment policy; $25 application fee; early admission, early decision, rolling admission, delayed admission and advanced placement plans available.

Costs Per Year: $1,850 tuition; $3,700 out-of-state tuition; $113 student fees.

Collegiate Environment: The 72-acre campus is situated northeast of the City of Poughkeepsie. There are 7 buildings including the New Center for Business and Industry as well as a 3-story, air-conditioned library. The book collection now exceeds 99,217 volumes, 453 periodicals and 19,385 microfilms. Financial assistance is available through a system of scholarships, grants-in-aid, part-time employment, loans, and financial counseling; 50% of students receive some aid.

Community Environment: See Vassar College.

STATE UNIVERSITY OF NEW YORK, EMPIRE STATE COLLEGE *(H-17)*
2 Union Avenue
Saratoga Springs, New York 12866
Tel: (518) 587-2100

Description: The publicly supported, coeducational liberal arts college of the State University of New York was founded in 1971. it si accredited by the Middle States Association of Colleges and Schools. This college is non-residential and offers monthly admission to programs leading to the AA, AS, BA, BS, BPS, and MA degrees. Unique aspects of the college include independent study with faculty members on a one-to-one basis and the ability to pursue an education at times and locations convenient for people with career and family responsibilities. Academic work is organized through study plans, or learning contracts, developed by the student and a faculty member. These contracts describe activities, goals, resources, methods, evaluation process and credit to be earned by the student upon successful completion of plan. The college has no main campus; at present there are Regional Centers in Albany, Rochester, New York City, Old Westbury, Buffalo, Hartsdale and Syracuse, with 40 locations throughout New York State. Students may enroll at any time throughout the year (except August) since the program operates on a year-round basis. Recent enrollment was 6,900 men and women. There are 113 full-time faculty members and 225 part-time, giving a faculty-student ratio of 1-23.

Entrance Requirements: High school graduation or equivalent required; open enrollment policy; early admission, early decision, rolling admission and midyear admission plans available.

Costs Per Year: $2,650 state-resident tuition, $6,550 out-of-state, $37 student fees.

Collegiate Environment: The Coordinating Center (administrative offices) is located in Saratoga Springs. The college's Centers/Units are located in rural and urban communities across New York State. The size of the student body varies among the Centers. 98% of the applicants are accepted. Financial aid is available and 50% of students receive some form of aid.

Community Environment: See Skidmore College.

STATE UNIVERSITY OF NEW YORK, ERIE COMMUNITY COLLEGE *(H-2)*
6205 Main Street
Williamsville, New York 14221-7095
Tel: (716) 851-1588; Fax: (716) 851-1129

Description: This publicly supported, three-campus, coeducational junior college system is 1 of the 29 junior colleges of the State University of New York. The North Campus was established in 1946 as the New York State Institute of Applied Arts and Sciences. It was later called Erie County Technical Institute, and the present name was taken in 1969. The City Campus was added in 1971, and the South Campus joined the system in 1974. It is accredited by the Middle States Association of Colleges and Schools. Professional accreditations include the Commission on Dental Education of the American Dental Association (for Dental Hygiene), the American Occupational Therapy Association (for Occupational Therapy Assistant), the Accreditation Board for Engineering and Technology (for Engineering Technology), the National Accrediting Agency for Clinical Laboratory Sciences, the Committee on Allied Health Education and Accreditation, the National League of Nursing, the American Association of Medical Assistants and the Commission on Opticianry Associations. The college grants the A.A., A.S., A.A.S. degrees, and the AOS diploma. It operates on the semester system and offers 2 summer sessions. Enrollment includes 7,940 full-time and 5,853 part-time students.

Entrance Requirements: High school graduation or GED; completion of application; personal interview may be required; no application fee.

Costs Per Year: $2,100 tuition; $4,200 out-of-state; $78 student fees.

Collegiate Environment: The 3 campuses are located in the northern (Williamsville), city (Buffalo) and southern (Orchard Park) areas of Erie County. The city campus moved to a new location in the recently refurbished historical landmark Post Office Building in January 1982. The college serves approximately 14,000 students with its day and evening part-time and full-time offerings. Financial aid is available.

Community Environment: See Canisius College.

STATE UNIVERSITY OF NEW YORK, FASHION INSTITUTE OF TECHNOLOGY *(E-2)*
Seventh Avenue at 27 Street
New York, New York 10001-5992
Tel: (212) 760-7675; (800) 608-6348

Description: This publicly supported, coeducational college of art and design, business and technology was founded in 1944 in answer to the needs of the fashion and related industries for professionally trained men and women. It operates on the semester system and offers one winter and two summer sessions. The college is accredited by the Middle States Association of Colleges and Schools, the National Association of Schools of Art and Design, and the Foundation for Interior Design Education Research, and is empowered to award the Associate in Applied Science, Bachelor of Fine Arts, Bachelor of Science and Master of Arts degrees. It is one of the specialized colleges under the program of the State University of New York. Recent enrollment included 5,059 full-time and 7,584 part-time undergraduates and 65 graduate students. A faculty of 181 full-time and 750 part-time gives an undergraduate faculty-student ratio of 1-14.

Entrance Requirements: High school graduation or equivalent with rank in upper half of class; appropriate high school preparation for desired programs varies; interested students should refer to the Fashion Institute of Technology catalog; personal artwork evaluation required for Art and Design applicants; rolling admission, midyear admission, and advanced placement plans available; Jan. 15 and Oct. 15 application deadlines; $25 application fee.

Costs Per Year: Associate degree: $2,100 city or state resident, $5,050 out-of-state; Baccalaureate degree: $2,585 city or state resident, $6,000 out-of-state; room and board, $4,880; student fees $210.

Collegiate Environment: The college occupies a $115 million campus in midtown Manhattan, where the worlds of fashion, art design, communications, and manufacturing converge. The Library/Media Services department has over 120,000 volumes, 531 periodicals, 44,000 slides, 249 16-mm films, and 1,521 videocassettes. Special collection files and portfolios contain the contributions of leaders in fashion design, textile science, apparel manufacturing, fashion merchandising, and interior design. Included in the same building is The Museum at F.I.T., where a student or designer is offered a 3-dimensional dictionary of design through an unparalleled collection of apparel and textiles. The museum also presents major exhibitions and special programs of mutual interest to the students, faculty, and the community. F.I.T.'s facilities include 2 gymnasiums, an 800-seat auditorium, and an amphitheatre that seats approximately 350. The 3 dormitories (all coed) have the capacity for 1,300 students. Financial assistance is available and 64% of the students receive some kind of aid. About 45% of the applicants are accepted and 80% of the current freshmen return to this campus for the second year. The college awarded 1,538 Associate degrees, 519 B.F.A. and 442 B.S. degrees to the graduating class.

Community Environment: The campus of the Fashion Institute of Technology leaves behind the rolling green lawns and weathered stones of the traditional college campus in favor of the challenges and excitement of unique New York. Fashion is one of New York's biggest businesses, and F.I.T. sits squarely in the middle of it all. Students use the city as a huge working laboratory, and the college maintains a vital dialogue with the industry. Students are encouraged to participate in the cultural activities of New York, where opera, dance, theater, the art world, and the communications media are readily accessible. The Office of Special Programs works full-time to facilitate student access to the professional activities of the "fashion capital of the world" by arranging field trips and inviting prominent guest speakers to the college. F.I.T. education, career direction, technical skills, and humanistic studies are combined, taking full advantage of New York's special offerings.

STATE UNIVERSITY OF NEW YORK, FULTON-MONTGOMERY COMMUNITY COLLEGE *(H-15)*
Route 67
Johnstown, New York 12095
Tel: (518) 762-4651

Description: The publicly supported, coeducational community college is supported by state and county funds and is part of the State University of New York. It is accredited by the Middle States Association of Colleges and Schools. The current enrollment is 950 men and 1,070 women. A faculty of 107 gives a faculty-student ratio of 1-20. Degrees granted include A.A., A.S., A.A.S., A.O.S. and the Certificate.

Entrance Requirements: Accredited high school graduation or equivalent open enrollment; early admission, rolling admission, early decision, advanced placement, delayed admission plans; $25 application fee.

Costs Per Year: $1,650 tuition; $3,700 out-of-state tuition; $210 student fees.

Collegiate Environment: The 194-acre campus is midway between Amsterdam and Johnstown. There are 5 buildings. The library building contains 54,000 volumes and subscribes to over 320 periodicals, indexes, and newspapers in English and other languages. The college participates in a variety of scholarships, loans and grant programs in addition to providing for part-time student employment, both on-and off-campus. Approximately 75% of the students receive some form of financial assistance. 90% of those who apply for admission are accepted. Dormitory style housing is available adjacent to the campus.

Community Environment: Population of the counties 100,000. Johnstown was founded about 1759 by Sir William Johnson, Superintendent of Indian Affairs for Northern Colonies, who lived there

until his death. The region is identified with the glove and leather industries. The area is provided transportation by buses and a small craft airport. Local community services include libraries, churches of various denominations, 2 museums, hospitals and a county health office. Most civic, fraternal, and veteran's organizations are represented within the community. There is some part-time employment available for students. Local recreational facilities include skiing, boating, fishing hunting, camping, golfing, parks, and nearby lakes.

STATE UNIVERSITY OF NEW YORK, GENESEE COMMUNITY COLLEGE *(H-6)*
One College Road
Batavia, New York 14020
Tel: (716) 343-0055; Fax: (716) 343-0068

Description: The publicly supported, coeducational junior college was established in 1966 and is a unit of the State University of New York. The semester system is used and 2 summer terms are offered each year. The college is accredited by the Middle States Association of Colleges and Schools. Degrees granted: A.A., A.S., A.A.S., and the Certificate. The college operates four campus centers in Lakeville, Albion, Warsaw and Arcade. Enrollment is 2,513 full-time and 2,081 part-time students. A faculty of 83 full-time and 62 part-time gives a faculty-student ratio of 1-17.

Entrance Requirements: Approved high school graduation or New York State High School Equivalency Diploma; appropriate high school preparation for desired programs as listed in the college catalog; satisfactory score on New York State Regents Scholarship Examination or State University Admissions Examination; early decision, early admission, midyear admission, rolling admission and advanced placement plans available.

Costs Per Year: $1,950 tuition; $2,150 out-of-state; $300 student fees.

Collegiate Environment: The college occupies a 250-acre permanent campus on a site northeast of the city of Batavia. The campus provides modern buildings and outdoor recreation and athletic areas. The library holdings include 73,000 volumes. While the college does not provide housing to students, private facilities are adjacent to campus. Financial aid is available for economically disadvantaged students and 90% of the students receive some form of assistance.

Community Environment: Population 18,200. Founded in 1802 by Joseph Ellicott, Batavia is located 30 miles from both Buffalo and Rochester, NY.

STATE UNIVERSITY OF NEW YORK, HEALTH SCIENCE CENTER AT BROOKLYN *(F-2)*
450 Clarkson Avenue, Box 60
Brooklyn, New York 11203
Tel: (718) 270-2446; Fax: (718) 270-7592

Description: Publicly supported, coeducational medical college had its origin in 1860 as the Teaching Division of the Long Island College Hospital. It merged with the State University of New York in 1950, thus becoming the first unit of the new Downstate Medical Center. The center consists of 4 professional schools: School of Graduate Studies, Colleges of Health Related Professions, Medicine, Nursing, and the 350-bed State University Hospital. It is accredited by the Middle States Association of Colleges and Schools. Degrees granted: B.S., M.D., D.M. Sc., Ph.D., and the combination M.D.-Ph.D. degree. Enrollment includes 1,260 full-time and 410 part-time students. Faculty consists of 638 paid members and 1,757 voluntary staff.

Entrance Requirements: College of Medicine: Minimum of 3 years of study (90 semester credits) at an approved college of arts and sciences; courses taken should be in the liberal arts curriculum and accredited toward a Bachelor degree; specific course requirements are; 1 year each in English, biology, general physics, inorganic chemistry, and organic chemistry, one year of college mathematics and an advanced scientific subject recommended; admission test of the Association of American Medical Colleges required; application should be made through the American Medical College Application Service no later than December 15 of the year prior to the year for which the applicant is applying; $60 application fee. College of Nursing: minimum of 60 semester credits granted by an approved college; specific course requirements are 2 semesters or a minimum of 6 semester credit hours each in anatomy and physiology (with lab), sociological science, psychological science, and English, one semester of chemistry (with lab) and 4 semesters or a minimum of 12 semester credits in humanities; applicants must have a cumulative grade point index of at least 2.5 on a 4.0 scale; applicants presenting a cumulative grade point index of 3.0 are given preference; Nelson Denny Reading Test required; application fee $25; Feb. 1 application deadline. College of Health Related Professions: Minimum of 60 semester credits granted by an approved college; other requirements and deadlines vary by program. Programs offered: Diagnostic Medical Imaging, Health Information Management, Nurse Midwifery, Occupational Therapy, Physician Assistant, and Physical Therapy. School of Graduate Studies: applicant must have a Bachelor degree from an approved college, or equivalent education, and must take the GRE, including 1 of the achievement tests. Individual graduate programs may have particular course requirements.

Collegiate Environment: The Medical Center is located in the Flatbush section of Brooklyn across the street from Kings County Hospital Center. The library occupies the rear wing of the Basic Sciences Building. Its collection of 250,000 volumes represents the third largest medical school library in the country. There are 2 residence halls with a total capacity of 400 students.

Community Environment: See Brooklyn College of the City University of New York.

STATE UNIVERSITY OF NEW YORK, HEALTH SCIENCE CENTER AT SYRACUSE (H-11)
155 Elizabeth Blackwell Street
Syracuse, New York 13210
Tel: (315) 464-4570

Description: Publicly-supported coeducational Health Science Center includes a College of Medicine, College of Graduate Studies, College of Nursing and College of Health Related Professions. Residency internship and continuing education programs for the practicing physician are also conducted. The SUNY Health Science Center became part of the State University of New York in 1950. It is accredited by the Middle States Association of Colleges and Schools and grants the Associate, Bachelor, Master and Doctorate (Ph.D., M.D.) degrees. It operates on the semester system and offers one summer term. The College of Health Related Professions and the College of Graduate Studies are also on a semester system calendar. Enrollment includes 1,038 students. The faculty-student ratio is 1-6.

Entrance Requirements: College of Health Related Professions: Associate degree programs are offered in Extracorporeal Technology, Respiratory Care, Radiologic Technology and Radiation Therapy Technology. Cytotechnology, Physical Therapy, and Medical Technology and Respiratory Care are upper division baccalaureate programs requiring 60 or more college credits before entrance. Course requirements for admission vary by program. SAT and ACT are not required. GRE is required for master degree programs. College of Graduate Studies includes M.S. and Ph.D. programs in Anatomy and Cell Biology, Biochemistry and Molecular Biology, Microbiology and Immunology, Pharmacology Physiology, Neurosciences and Cellard Molecular Biology. An. M.S. program in Medical Technology is also available. Each department has different prerequisites for admission. The minimum requirement is a bachelor's degree or its equivalent. All applicants must present knowledge of physics, chemistry (inorganic and organic) and biology. College of Medicine: 90 semester hours (3 years) of acceptable, undergraduate credit; MCAT. The following courses are required: chemistry, including laboratory (inorganic 6-8 semester hours, organic 6-8 semester hours): biology or zoology including laboratory (6-8 semester hours); physics including laboratory (6-8 semester hours); English (6-8 semester hours).

Costs Per Year: $2,650-$8,450 tuition; $6,550-$17,100 out-of-state; $200 student fees.

Collegiate Environment: Facilities for in instruction and research are in Silverman and Weiskotten Halls. The latter contains the 136,000-volume library and the SUNY Biomedical Communication Network. Clinical instruction is in the 350-bed State University Hospital and the local hospital affiliates with an approximate total of 3,275 beds. Loans are available to all members of all classes and schools at the Health Science Center and scholarships are offered on a limited basis. Recently the university awarded 27 Associate, 69 Bachelor, 18 Master, 149 Doctor of Medicine and 4 Doctor of Philosophy degrees.

Community Environment: See Syracuse University.

STATE UNIVERSITY OF NEW YORK, HEALTH SCIENCES CENTER AT STONY BROOK (D-6)
Stony Brook, New York 11794
Tel: (516) 689-6000

Description: The Health Sciences Center is a major division of the State University of New York at Stony Brook, located on the north shore of Long Island, 60 miles east of New York City. It is the fourth and newest health center in the SUNY system. Established in 1969, the Center now consists of five schools: the Schools of Allied Health Professions, Dental Medicine, Medicine, Nursing, and Social Welfare. In addition, a full range of professional, technical and laboratory resources is available to the center, providing academic support services for students and faculty. The Health Sciences Center has also established a partnership with four Long Island Hospitals, referred to as clinical campuses, where students receive their essential patient care experience "in the field." In addition, the five schools have affiliation agreements with over 80 other hospitals and health agencies in the Long Island area. The University Hospital, a central teaching facility for all the educational programs of the Health Sciences Center, opened in February 1980. University Hospital includes surgical suites, laboratories, emergency and ambulatory care units capable of handling up to 300,000 vists per year, and ancillary facilities. When fully operational, nearly half of the 540-bed hospital will be dedicated to intensive and specialty care. Recent enrollment at the Health Sciences Center included 4,988 men, 4779 women full-time, and 494 men and 739 women part-time. The faculty consists of 1,284 full-time and 293 part-time instructors.

Entrance Requirements: Upper division students must have 57 college credits; GRE is required for the Graduate Nursing and Graduate Allied Health programs. Application deadlines vary with program.

Costs Per Year: $2,650 resident tuition; $6,550 nonresident tuition; $4,400 room and board, $138 student fees.

Collegiate Environment: The Stony Brook Campus of SUNY, which includes the Health Sciences Center, has grown to encompass 98 buildings on 1,000 acres. The Center library contains 188,683 volumes. Financial aid in the form of Federal and State loans, scholarships and/or employment is received by 82% of the student body.

Community Environment: See State University of New York at Stony Brook.

STATE UNIVERSITY OF NEW YORK, HERKIMER COUNTY COMMUNITY COLLEGE (H-14)
Reservoir Road
Herkimer, New York 13350
Tel: (315) 866-0300; (800) 947-4432; Fax: (315) 866-7253

Description: The publicly supported, coeducational junior college is a unit of the State University of New York. It was established in 1966 and is accredited by the Middle States Association of Colleges and Schools. The college offers an A.A. in General Studies program for mature students that allows earning credits through proficiency exams, independent study and correspondence courses. Enrollment is 1,981 students. A faculty of 125 gives a faculty-student ratio of 1-23. The semester system is used, with 4 summer sessions. There are 2 mini-sessions of 3 hours per day for 15 days, 1 in January and 1 in June, in which the students may earn credits.

Entrance Requirements: Accredited high school graduation, or New York State High School Equivalency Diploma; open enrollment policy; appropriate high school preparation for desired programs as listed in college catalog; satisfactory score on New York State Regents Scholarship Examination or State University Admissions Examination; no application fee; early admission and advanced placement plans available.

Costs Per Year: $1,900 tuition; $4,750 out-of-state tuition; $160 student fees.

Collegiate Environment: Architecturally accessible to the handicapped, the campus was constructed in 1971. There are seven modern buildings: classroom-administration, Johnson Hall, physical education, library, Robert McLaughlin College Center, technology center, and child care center. Facilities include an all-weather track, a 50-acre nature center, and a computerized nautilus room. The library houses a natural history museum, an archeology museum, and an art gallery. There is also a mobile production unit that produces programs for HCTV, through Paragon Cable.

Community Environment: Population 9,000. Located 15 miles east of Utica. Good transportation, shopping, and medical facilities are found within the area. There are 3 libraries, 6 churches, and several civic and service organizations within the town. Local recreational facilities include fishing, boating, swimming, parks, and skiing and skating.

STATE UNIVERSITY OF NEW YORK, HUDSON VALLEY COMMUNITY COLLEGE   *(I-17)*
Troy, New York 12180
Tel: (518) 283-1100; Fax: (518) 270-1576

Description: The publicly supported, coeducational junior college was established in 1953 and is one of the locally sponsored, two-year community colleges of the State University of New York. It is accredited by the Middle States Association of Colleges and Schools. The college grants Associate of Arts, Associate of Science, Associate of Applied Science, and Associate of Occupational Studies degrees. It operates on the semester system and offers six summer sessions. Enrollment is 5,718 full-time and 4,368 part-time students. A faculty of 268 gives a faculty-student ratio of 1-30.

Entrance Requirements: High school graduation or equivalent; Regents Scholarship Examination or State University Admissions Examination required; early decision, early admission, midyear admission, rolling admission, and advanced placement plans available; $25 application fee.

Costs Per Year: $1,710 tuition; approximately $3,520 tuition for out-of-state students; $210 student fees.

Collegiate Environment: The modern 130-acre campus of the college is located at the southern edge of the city of Troy. There are 12 college buildings and the Marvin Learning Resources Center contains a library of 121,328 volumes. 84% of applicants are accepted. Financial assistance is available for economically disadvantaged students. 60% of students receive some form of financial aid. No dormitories are provided on campus.

Community Environment: See Rensselaer Polytechnic Institute.

STATE UNIVERSITY OF NEW YORK, INSTITUTE OF TECHNOLOGY AT UTICA-ROME   *(H-13)*
P.O. Box 3050
Utica, New York 13504-3050
Tel: (315) 792-7500; Fax: (315) 792-7837

Description: The public, technical and professional college was established in 1966 as an upper-division coeducational institution. The Institute of Technology is accredited by the Middle States Association of Schools and Colleges, while specific professional accreditation is maintained by the Nursing (National League of Nursing), Engineering Technology (Accrediting Board for Engineering Technology), and Medical Record Administration (American Medical Record Association) programs. The institute grants the Bachelor and Master's degrees. It operates on the semester system and offers three summer sessions. Enrollment includes 1,425 full-time and 1,100 part-time undergraduates and 300 graduate students. A faculty of 90 full-time and 69 part-time gives a faculty-student ratio of 1-19.

Entrance Requirements: Entering students must have completed 56 semester hours of previous college course work, while the great majority possess associate degrees; two-year grade point requirements vary by program; rolling admission and midyear admission plans available. $25 application fee.

Costs Per Year: $2,650 tuition; $6,550 out-of-state; $5,020 room and board; $225 fees.

Collegiate Environment: The College's academic facilities are located on its new Marcy Campus just north of the city of Utica, and are easily accessible by municipal bus service. The campus consists of three building complexes, academic and student services, townhouse-style residence halls accommodating 415 students, and a facilities building. Kunsela Hall, named for the College's first president, contains the library, administrative offices, and classrooms and laboratories for Telecommunications, Electrical Engineering Technology, and Computer Science Departments. A second academic complex,

Donovan Hall, houses additional classrooms, faculty offices, and laboratory facilities for all other curricula, including business, industrial engineering technology, mechanical engineering technology, health services management, nursing, and arts and sciences. A comprehensive student center contains gymnasium, swimming pool, recreational facilities, cafeteria, bookstore, student service offices, and meeting rooms for clubs, special activities, and student government. In addition to on-campus housing, the college operates an off-campus housing office that assists students in apartment-mate matching and location of privately owned apartments in the Utica area. The academic year begins in September, and January admission is also available. Scholarships are available. 10% of incoming junior transfer students receive college sponsored merit scholarships. Approximately 80% of the student body receives financial aid. The library houses 135,000 volumes and 360,000 microforms.

Community Environment: The city of Utica (population 70,000) is situated in the geographic center of New York State, approximately 220 miles from New York City and 190 miles from Buffalo on the New York Thruway. An urban center for this area of New York State, Utica has a variety of entertainment, recreational, cultural, and educational opportunities. Serviced by bus routes, Amtrak, and airlines, the city is easily reached from areas throughout the eastern United States.

STATE UNIVERSITY OF NEW YORK, JAMESTOWN COMMUNITY COLLEGE   *(L-3)*
525 Falconer Street
Jamestown, New York 14701
Tel: (716) 665-5220; (800) 388-8557; Fax: (716) 665-3498

Description: The publicly supported, coeducational community college is sponsored by the city of Jamestown and governed by a Board of Trustees. It was established in 1950 and provides two-year programs of post-high school education emphasizing Liberal Arts in both the transfer and career degree areas. By authority of the Board of Regents of the State of New York, the college awards the degrees of Associate in Arts, Associate in Science, and Associate in Applied Science. Enrollment is 4,100 students. A faculty of 228 gives a faculty-student ratio of 1-20. The college operates on the semester system and offers 2 summer sessions. It is accredited by the Middle States Association of Colleges and Schools and the National League for Nursing.

Entrance Requirements: Graduation from approved high school or equivalent; open enrollment policy; requirements vary slightly according to program of study; non-high school graduates over 18 years of age who show ability and incentive are admitted; midyear admission, rolling admission and advanced placement plans available; $25 application fee.

Costs Per Year: $2,080 state-resident tuition; $4,160 nonresident; $250 student fees.

Collegiate Environment: The campus includes an arts and science center that houses the sciences, mathematics, computer science and humanities programs. The Forum building houses the nursing program, student tutoring center, an art gallery, theater in the round and other classrooms. The Collegiate Center houses the Visual and Performing Arts Department. The institution has expanded to more than 5,000 day and evening students who attend classes at a modern, multimillion-dollar campus. A Library-learning Center, Social Sciences, and Business Building is adjacent to the Collegiate Center. The library contains 64,000 volumes, 5,000 pamphlets, 609 periodicals, 1,662 microforms, and 2,502 sound recordings. No dormitories are provided on campus. Financial assistance is available; 80% of students receive financial aid. 99% of students applying for admission are accepted. 40% of the students graduated in the top half of their high school class, 20% in the top quarter and 30% in the third quarter. Almost 60% of freshmen return to this campus for the second year. 80% of students receive some form of financial aid.

Community Environment: Population 40,000. An industrial center at the southern end of Chautauqua Lake, Jamestown produces wood and metal products. The surrounding area is devoted to dairying and poultry raising. There are rail and bus lines easily accessible. The local community has churches, 1 hospital, a library, YMCA, YWCA, and various civic and service organizations, all immediately available. Recreational facilities include fishing, boating, golf courses and 4 local ski runs. A civic music and drama program series is held during the winter each year.

STATE UNIVERSITY OF NEW YORK, JEFFERSON COMMUNITY COLLEGE   (E-12)
Outer Coffeen St.
Watertown, New York 13601
Tel: (315) 786-2200; Admissions: (315) 786-2277; Fax: (315) 786-0158

Description: The publicly supported, coeducational junior college was established in 1961 and provides both university-parallel and career programs. It is sponsored by Jefferson County and supervised by the State University of New York. It is accredited by the Middle States Association of Colleges and Schools. The college operates on the semester system and offers two summer sessions. Enrollment includes 1,809 women and 1,282 men. A faculty of 74 full-time and 116 part-time provides a faculty-student ratio of 1-16.

Entrance Requirements: Accredited high school graduation or equivalent; open enrollment policy; early admission, early decision, rolling admission and advanced placement plans available. $25 application fee.

Costs Per Year: $1,608 tuition for New York State residents; $3,216 tuition for out-of-state students; $210 student fees.

Collegiate Environment: The college is located on 97 acres and the first phase of construction was completed in 1965 with an administration building and 2 classroom buildings. The second phase was completed in 1968 and included a student center and a library. Outdoor athletic facilities were completed in 1980. A new 58,000 square foot instruction building opened. Child care is available on campus for pre-school age children. A major addition to one of the classroom buildings was completed in 1986. The library contains 51,215 volumes, 346 periodicals, and 4,772 microforms. About 80% of applicants are accepted and 70% of the freshmen return to this campus for the second year. Scholarships are available and 60% of the students receive some form of financial aid.

Community Environment: Population 29,429. Water for Watertown's many industries is furnished by the Black River, which falls 112 feet over dams within the city. The area is served by airlines, railroad, local and interstate bus lines. A library, several church denominations, a museum, YMCA, YWCA and several civic, fraternal, and veteran's organizations are represented here. There are ample job opportunities for students in the area. Local recreational facilities include theatres, houseboating, motorboating, skiing, golf, swimming, riding, bowling, ice skating, hunting, and fishing. Fort Drum is nearby.

STATE UNIVERSITY OF NEW YORK, MARITIME COLLEGE AT FORT SCHUYLER   (E-3)
Throgs Neck, New York 10465
Tel: (718) 409-7200

Description: Publicly supported, 4-year coed college established in 1874. First 4-year college of the State University of New York to award engineering degrees. Cadets prepare for the civilian license as an officer for the Merchant Marine while earning bachelor degrees in engineering, science, marine environmental sciences or business. Navy, Marine & Coast Guard and Air Force ROTC is available. Cadets operate college ship EMPIRE STATE VI on 2-month training cruises to Europe each summer gaining practical and leadership experience. Enrollment includes 649 men and 101 women with a faculty of 40 full-time and 16 part-time. Students from 23 states and 18 foreign countries are enrolled. Women and members of ethnic minorities are encouraged to enroll.

Entrance Requirements: High School graduation or equivalent completion of 16 units including 4 English, 3 mathematics, 3 science, 4 Soc. Sci.; SAT or ACT required; minimum scores SAT 500V, 550M, ACT 23; early admission, delayed admission, advanced placement plans available; $25 application fee.

Costs Per Year: $2,650 tuition; $6,550 out-of-state tuition; $4,800 room and board.

Collegiate Environment: Originally constructed to protect New York City from attack by water from Long Island Sound, Fort Schuyler was leased to the State of New York by the Federal Government in 1934 as a permanent shore-based home of the Maritime College. The ship is berthed at Fort Schuyler during the academic year. During the summer months the cadets sail to European foreign ports of call on the training ship Empire State VI. A 600-foot pier and water front basin is used for mooring the training ship, the racing sloops and the recreational sailing craft of the college. There are ample facilities for intercollegiate and intramural athletics, and a gymnasium and swimming pool as well as other specialized areas are provided. Dormitory capacity is 900. The library contains 70,651 volumes. Cadets at the college have the option of participating in NROTC or AFROTC or the Merchant Marine Reserve program. Coast Guard or National Oceanic & Atmospheric Commissions are also available after graduation. The Navy teaches Naval Science courses and grants inactive Naval Reserve Commissions to those graduates meeting all qualifications. Approximately 62% of the students applying for admission are accepted. The college seeks a geographically diverse student body; midyear students are not admitted. Financial aid is available and 75% of the student body rceives aid.

Community Environment: The College is located on the Throgs Neck Peninsula, a small waterfront community within New York City.

STATE UNIVERSITY OF NEW YORK, MOHAWK VALLEY COMMUNITY COLLEGE   (H-13)
1101 Sherman Drive
Utica, New York 13501
Tel: (315) 792-5400; (800) 733-6822; Fax: (315) 792-5666

Description: Publicly supported, coeducational affiliated unit of the State University of New York. It is accredited by the Middle States Association of Colleges and Schools and professionally by respective accrediting institutions. It offers one-year and two-year collegiate programs that prepare students for technical and semiprofessional careers in business, industry, health care, criminal justice, or further college study. The college grants the Associate degree. It operates on the semester system and offers one summer term. Enrollment is 3,940 full-time and 3,000 part-time students. A faculty of 167 full-time and 213 part-time gives a faculty-student ratio of 1-18.

Entrance Requirements: Approved high school graduation or equivalent; open enrollment policy; completion of appropriate college-preparatory courses; placement testing is required for all new full and part-time matriculated students; rolling admission, early decision, early admission, midyear admission, advanced placement plans available; $25 application fee.

Costs Per Year: $2,100 tuition; $4,200 nonresidents; $3,700-$4,000 room and board; $100 student fees; additional expenses average $300-$1,000.

Collegiate Environment: The community college campus is located on an 80-acre site in southeast Utica. It is composed of an Academic building, Library/Administration Building, Gymnasium, College Center and 4 Residence Halls. A branch campus with 3 buildings exists in Rome, N.Y. The library contains 76,492 volumes, 731 peridocials, 3,905 microforms and 2,925 audiovisual materials; dormitory facilities are available for 360 students. Classes begin in September and new students are admitted at midyear as well as in the fall.

Community Environment: Population 75,000. Utica, a city of diversified industry, is noted for the production of computers, heating and ventilating equipment, cutlery, fishing equipment, paper products, clothing, hand-pneumatic and electric tools, generators, airplane parts, and electronics. Utica is also home to several major insurance corporations and is a major airline reservation and maintenance center.

Branch Campuses: 1101 Floyd Avenue, Rome, NY

STATE UNIVERSITY OF NEW YORK, MONROE COMMUNITY COLLEGE   (H-7)
1000 East Henrietta Road
Rochester, New York 14623
Tel: (716) 292-2000; Admissions: (716) 292-2000 x7700; Fax: (716) 292-3860

Description: This publicly supported, coeducational junior college is accredited by the Middle States Association of Colleges and Schools. The college operates under the supervision of the State University of New York and grants the Associate degree and the Certificate. The semester system is used and 5 summer sessions are offered. Enrollment includes 7,366 full-time and 6,365 part-time students. A faculty of 298 full-time and 401 part-time gives a faculty-student ratio of 1-19.

Entrance Requirements: Open enrollment policy; non-high school graduates considered; early admission, midyear admission, rolling admission, and advanced placement plans available; $20 application fee.

Costs Per Year: $2,100 tuition; $4,200 out-of-state; $102 student fees.

Collegiate Environment: The Brighton campus is located on a 318-acre site, 3 1/2 miles from downtown Rochester, and consists of 12 buildings. The LeRoy V. Good Library houses a collection of 100,000 volumes, 1,000 periodical subscriptions, and a collection of music CD's, cassettes, and records. The Communications Buildings houses a theater with seating for 550 people. The physical education center includes a large gymnasium, 5 raquetball courts, and swimming pool. Outdoor facilities consist of eight lighted tennis courts, baseball field, field hockey area, quarter mile track, lacrosse field, soccer field, a 2.7 mile cross-country course, an obstacle course and fitness and nature trails. Approximately 86% of students applying for admission are accepted, including midyear students, and 53% of freshmen return for the second year. Financial aid is available and 70% of students receive some form of financial assistance. In addition to its regular academic program, the college engages in a number of community service programs, and also offers evening sessions. The college awarded 94 Certificates and 1,711 Associate degrees during a recent academic year.

Community Environment: See University of Rochester.

STATE UNIVERSITY OF NEW YORK, NASSAU COMMUNITY COLLEGE *(E-3)*
1 Education Drive
Tower 2nd Fl.
Garden City, New York 11530
Tel: (516) 572-7500; Admissions: (516) 572-7345

Description: Publicly supported, coeducational junior college established in 1959 and accredited by the Middle States Association of Colleges and Schools. As part of the State University of New York, it is authorized to award the Associate degree. The college operates on the early semester basis and offers three summer sessions and an evening division. Enrollment includes approximately 5,413 men and 5,628 women full-time and 4,510 men and 6,404 women part-time. A faculty of 1,411 gives a faculty-student ratio of 1-20.

Entrance Requirements: High school graduation or GED; completion of appropriate college-preparatory courses for degree programs; open enrollment policy; $20 application fee. Rolling admission, and advanced placement plans available.

Costs Per Year: $2,120 resident tuition; $4,240 nonresident tuition; $100 student fees.

Collegiate Environment: The college is located near the center of Nassau County, Long Island. The campus itself is divided into 2 sections. The East Campus is a newly-constructed multilevel megastructure containing 2 office-classroom-laboratory wings, a library of 183,160 volumes, 1,027 periodicals, 546 microforms and 13,826 audiovisual materials; a 12-story administrative tower, and a physical education complex including swimming and diving pools, gymnasium, field house, saunas, and specialized wrestling, dancing, gymnastics rooms. The West Campus includes the quadrangle, classrooms and laboratories, student center and student center offices, galleries, and recital halls for music, art, and theatre activities. 83% of the students applying for admission are accepted. Financial aid is available. In 1995, the college awarded 34 Certificates and 3,479 Associate degrees.

Community Environment: See Adelphi University.

STATE UNIVERSITY OF NEW YORK, NIAGARA COUNTY COMMUNITY COLLEGE *(H-4)*
3111 Saunders Settlement Road
Sanborn, New York 14132
Tel: (716) 731-3271

Description: Publicly supported, coeducational community college established in 1962 and under the supervision of the State University of New York. It operates on the semester basis with 2 summer terms and enrolls approximately 4,228 students. It is accredited by the Middle States Association of Colleges and Schools and grants the Associate degree. The faculty numbered 323 full-time and part-time

recently. The college offers liberal arts and career programs and has academic cooperative plans with Morrisville Ag. & Tech., Wanakena Campus, Alfred Ag. & Tech., E.S.F. School of Forestry, and Simmons School of Mortuary Science, and has dual admissions with SUNY Baffalo.

Entrance Requirements: Open enrollment policy; non-high school graduates considered; rolling admission, early admission, delayed admission and early decision plans are available.

Costs Per Year: $1,410 tuition; $2,820 tuition for out-of-state residents; $60 student activity fee.

Collegiate Environment: The library contains 58,290 volumes, 357 periodicals and 13,280 audiovisual materials. Approximately 95% of students applying for admission are accepted including midyear students. Financial aid is available. About 33% of the graduating class continue on to four-year colleges.

Community Environment: See Niagara University.

STATE UNIVERSITY OF NEW YORK, NORTH COUNTRY COMMUNITY COLLEGE *(C-16)*
20 Winona Avenue
Saranac Lake, New York 12983
Tel: (518) 891-2915; (800) 541-1021

Description: Publicly-supported, coeducational junior college established in 1968 and under the supervision of the State University of New York. The college is a Recognized Candidate for Accreditation of the Middle States Association of Colleges and Schools and grants the Associate degree. The college operates two branch campuses: Malone and Ticonderoga. The semester system is used and two summer sessions are offered. Enrollment includes 952 full-time and 455 part-time students. A faculty of 50 gives a faculty-student ratio of 1-17.

Entrance Requirements: Open enrollment policy; non-high school graduates admitted; rolling admission, early admission, advanced placement, early decision, delayed admission and midyear admission plans available.

Costs Per Year: $2,100 tuition; $4,200 out-of-state tuition; $135 student fees; additional expenses average $700.

Collegiate Environment: The college is located in a former hospital building. The library contains 50,000 volumes and 800 periodicals. Approximately 98% of students applying for admission are accepted, including midyear students, and 70% return for the second year. Financial aid is available. About 80% of the graduating class continue on to a four-year college.

Community Environment: Population 5,500. Located approximately 9 miles from Lake Placid, Saranac Lake is one of the top winter resort areas in the Adirondack Mountains. Trains, airlines, and major highways provide easy access to Quebec and Ontario, Canada, as well as to New York City and the New England states. In the immediate locale are 9 churches, 3 libraries, a medical center and medical research center. A state school for the retarded is located here. Seasonal part-time employment opportunities are available for students. Summer recreational facilities within the area include hunting, fishing, and most water sports.

STATE UNIVERSITY OF NEW YORK, ONONDAGA COMMUNITY COLLEGE *(H-11)*
Route 173, Onondaga Hill
Syracuse, New York 13215
Tel: (315) 469-7741; Admissions: (315) 469-2201

Description: This publicly supported, coeducational community college was established in 1962 and is a unit of the State University of New York. It awards the Associate degree. The college operates on the semester system and offers three summer sessions, two day sessions and one evening. Enrollment includes approximately 8,390 students. A faculty of 437 gives a faculty-student ratio of 1-15.

Entrance Requirements: Approved high school graduation or High School Equivalency Diploma; appropriate high school preparation for desired programs as listed in the college catalogue; midyear admission, rolling admission plans available; $25 application fee.

Costs Per Year: $2,030 tuition; $4,060 out-of-district; $6,090 out-of-state; $96 student fee.

Collegiate Environment: The campus is located on 181 acres overlooking the city of Syracuse. The 6 new brick buildings are of contemporary design. The college completed its move to the new site in 1973. The library collection contains 90,000 volumes. 82% of applicants are accepted. Scholarships are available and 55% of the students receive some form of financial aid.

Community Environment: See Syracuse University.

STATE UNIVERSITY OF NEW YORK, ORANGE COUNTY COMMUNITY COLLEGE *(N-16)*
115 South Street
Middletown, New York 10940
Tel: (914) 314-4030; Fax: (914) 342-8662

Description: Publicly-supported, coeducational community college was established in 1950 by authority of the State University of New York and sponsored by the County of Orange. It is accredited by the Middle States Association of Colleges and Schools. The school operates on the semester system with 2 summer terms. Enrollment includes 2,580 full-time and 3,140 part-time students. A faculty of 152 full-time and 149 part-time gives a faculty-student ratio of 1-18.

Entrance Requirements: Approved high school graduation; or New York State High School Equivalency Diploma; open admission, early admission, early decision, rolling admission, midyear admission and advanced placement plans are available; $20 application fee.

Costs Per Year: $1,800 tuition; $3,600 out-of state.

Collegiate Environment: Orange County Community College is located on a beautifully landscaped campus, 14 buildings are located on a 37 acre campus. Laboratories include 7 in biology, 4 each in chemistry and physics, 3 in medical laboratory technology, and 2 each in electrical technology and architectural drafting. Dental hygiene, electron microscopy, nursing, criminal justice, instrumentation and computation are all taught in specially-equipped laboratories. Art, music, and typewriting each have 3 appropriate rooms. A foreign language laboratory, an office machines room, a geology lab, a greenhouse, and a data processing center round out the instructional facilities. The Physical Education Building contains 4 handball courts, a wrestling room, swimming pool, main gymnasium (seating capacity 3,000), a rifle range and an exercise room. Adjacent to the PE building are a quarter-mile all-weather track, soccer and baseball fields and tennis courts. The OCCC Library was designed to house 100,000 volumes; it now contains 97,911 books and 515 periodical titles plus microfilms, and can comfortably accommodate 700 readers. The college is primarily a school for commuting students, so there are no dormitories. Financial aid is available and 30% of students receive some form of financial aid. Freshman classes begin in September. A new OCCC Extension Center was opened in the historical School in Newburgh, NY. Designed to better serve the higher education needs of Eastern Orange County, the Center currently offers over 80 credit day and evening classes to 718 students.

Community Environment: Population 22,607. In an agricultural and dairying setting, Middletown is the site of the annual Orange County Fair. It is located 60 miles north of New York City and is accessible by the N.Y. State Thruway, Route 17, I-84, and by rail and bus. Work-study employment is available for students through the job placement office.

STATE UNIVERSITY OF NEW YORK, PURCHASE COLLEGE *(D-3)*
735 Anderson Hill Road
Purchase, New York 10577
Tel: (914) 251-6300; Fax: (914) 251-6314

Description: This publicly supported, coeducational liberal arts college, one of several such colleges of the State University of New York, began a regular schedule in September 1971. The college is fully accredited by the Middle States Association of Colleges and Schools. A College of Letters and Science offers the B.A. and B.S. degree, and a B.F.A. degree is offered by a professional School of the Arts. MFA degrees are offered in Theater Design/Technology, Visual Arts, and Music. Enrollment is 2,444 full-time and 1,478 part-time students. A faculty of 298 gives a faculty-student ratio of 1-18. Classes are small in size. The semester system is used with 1 summer session.

Entrance Requirements: High school graduation or equivalent; completion of 16 academic units. SAT or ACT recommended; advanced placement, rolling admission, and early admission plans available; an audition or portfolio is required for admission to the School of the Arts; $25 application fee.

Costs Per Year: $2,650 tuition; $6,550 out-of-state; $4,350 approximate room and board; $220 student fees.

Collegiate Environment: In an atmosphere of informality and flexibility, the faculty encourages students in serious academic and artistic pursuits. The library contains 243,000 volumes, 1,560 periodicals, 100,000 government documents and 73,100 slides that were carefully selected for the Schools of Letters and Science, and the Arts. 3 residence halls provide living accommodations for 1,700 students. 42% of applicants are accepted. 70% of the students receive financial aid.

Community Environment: Purchase is a small community within the town of Harrison, some 30 miles north of New York City. From this country setting, students have access to the resources of the city, as well as those of nearby communities. Apart from its new, contemporary buildings, the 500-acre campus consists of grassy fields and wooded areas. The campus is highlighted by the Neuberger Museum and the Performing Center for the Arts.

STATE UNIVERSITY OF NEW YORK, ROCKLAND COMMUNITY COLLEGE *(C-1)*
145 College Road
Suffern, New York 10901-3699
Tel: (914) 356-4650; Fax: (914) 574-4499

Description: Publicly supported, coeducational junior college dedicated to education in the arts and sciences and to career education, and designed to function as an educational and cultural center for all citizens of its community. The college functions under the program of the State University of New York and is sponsored by the Rockland County Legislature. It was established in 1959 and is accredited by the Middle States Association of Colleges and Schools. It operates on the semester system and offers 6 summer sessions. Programs of study lead to the Associate degree. Enrollment is 8,150 students. A faculty of 193 full-time and 558 part-time gives a faculty-student ratio of 1-25.

Entrance Requirements: High school diploma not required; early admission, advanced placement, rolling admission, and delayed admission plans are available; $20 application fee.

Costs Per Year: $1,950 state-resident tuition; $3,900 out-of-state; $75 student activity fee.

Collegiate Environment: The community college is located on an attractive rural setting 5 miles east of Suffern, New York, and 35 miles north of New York City. The academic building contains classrooms, seminar rooms, art studios, lecture rooms, laboratories, student lounges, and faculty offices. The library contains 136,112 volumes, 519 periodicals, 10,306 microforms and 430 records and tapes. All applicants are accepted. 42% of the student body receives financial aid.

Community Environment: Population 11,000. Suffern is located 35 miles from New York City, west of Spring Valley, and is accessible via Highway Routes 17 (New Jersey), 59 and 202. There is bus and railroad service. It has churches of major denominations, a hospital, and Rotary, Lions, Kiwanis, and YMCA groups.

STATE UNIVERSITY OF NEW YORK, SCHENECTADY COUNTY COMMUNITY COLLEGE *(I-17)*
78 Washington Avenue
Schenectady, New York 12305
Tel: (518) 346-6211; Admissions: (518) 346-6211 X 170; Fax: (518) 346-0379

Description: Publicly-supported, coeducational community college, member of the State University of New York, beginning classes in September, 1969. Accredited by the Middle States Association of Colleges and Schools, the college grants the Certificate and Associate degree. Enrollment includes 1,768 full-time and 1,956 part-time students. The College operates on the semester system and offer two summer sessions.

Entrance Requirements: Open admission policy; non-high school graduates considered; early admission, early decision, delayed admission plans available.

Costs Per Year: $1,840 tuition; $103 student fees.

Collegiate Environment: The college is situated on the western edge of the city of Schenectady on a 50-acre campus that overlooks the Mohawk River. The Van Curler hotel was purchased in 1968 and has been completely remodeled as a modern, well-equipped college, with bright, air-conditioned classrooms, laboratories, and special purpose rooms. Accommodations for informal activities include a student forum, community room and a cafeteria. The library contains 61,384 volumes, 438 periodicals, 11,078 microforms and 11,058 recordings. 90% of applicants are accepted and 51% return for the second year. 25 scholarships are available and 70% of students receive some form of financial aid.

Community Environment: See Union College.

STATE UNIVERSITY OF NEW YORK, SCHOOL OF INDUSTRIAL AND LABOR RELATIONS AT CORNELL
(J-10)
Cornell University - ILR
Ithaca, New York 14851-0952
Tel: (607) 255-2221

Description: Publicly-supported, coeducational specialized college was authorized in 1944 by the New York State Legislature as the first institution in the country to offer professional training at the undergraduate and graduate levels in the field of industrial and labor relations. The object of the statutory college is to improve industrial and labor conditions through the provision of instruction and research, and the dissemination of information in all aspects of industrial and labor, and relations affecting employers and employees. The college is accredited by the Middle States Association of Colleges and Schools. It operates on the semester system and offers two summer sessions. Recent enrollment was 340 men and 300 women. A faculty of 65 gives a faculty-student ratio of 1-12. The college grants these Cornell degrees: Bachelor of Science, Master of Industrial and Labor Relations, Master of Science, and the Doctorate.

Entrance Requirements: Completion of 16 high school units including 4 English, 3 mathematics, 2 science, and 3 social studies; SAT or ACT and 2 Achievement Tests required; early admission, early decision, midyear admission, delayed admission and advanced placement plans available; Jan. 1 freshmen, Mar. 15 transfer student application deadline.

Costs Per Year: $7,806 tuition; $14,966 out-of-state tuition; $6,238 board and room; $465 supplies.

Collegiate Environment: Throughout the year the school conducts noncredit educational programs on campus for practitioners in the field of industrial and labor relations. Conferences, workshops, and seminars are conducted and the school has a keen and continuing interest in the development of leadership in the various key institutions of our urban-industrial society. The I.L.R. library contains 180,000 volumes and over 200,000 pamphlets plus over 20,000 feet of linear manuscripts in the Labor Management Documentation Center. The Cornell University library contains over 5,000,000 volumes.

Community Environment: See Cornell University.

STATE UNIVERSITY OF NEW YORK, SUFFOLK COUNTY COMMUNITY COLLEGE *(D-6)*
533 College Road
Selden, New York 11784
Tel: (516) 451-4022; Fax: (516) 451-4015

Description: Publicly supported, coeducational junior college founded in 1959 and established by the authority of the State University of New York and legally sponsored by the County of Suffolk. It is accredited by the Middle States Association of Colleges and Schools. Programs of study are career-oriented or university parallel and lead to the Associate degree. It operates on the semester system and offers three summer sessions. Enrollment includes 9,165 full-time and 13,030 part-time students. A faculty of 350 full-time and 702 part-time gives a faculty-student ratio of 1-12.

Entrance Requirements: Approved high school graduation or equivalent; open enrollment policy; completion of appropriate college-pre-

paratory units; ACT required; midyear admission, rolling admission and advanced placement plans available; Jan. 1 application deadline for health programs; $25 application fee.

Costs Per Year: $1,850 tuition for state residents; $3,700 tuition for out-of-state residents; $75 college fee.

Collegiate Environment: The community college is located on its own permanent 130-acre campus, approximately 60 miles east of New York City. The 8 college buildings contain a library of 172,473 volumes. Many local and community organizations provide specific scholarships, and students in good standing at the college are eligible for New York State Scholar Incentive Awards. 67% of students receive some form of financial aid. All programs are approved for the training of veterans under the various Public Laws.

Community Environment: Population 11,467, Selden is a suburban community served by the Long Island Railroad, as well as a bus line, and airlines serve nearby MacArthur Airport. Climate is temperate with a mean temperature of 35 degrees in winter and 75 degrees in the summer. Selden has churches representing all the major denominations, 3 hospitals, and several civic, fraternal and veteran's organizations within the immediate area. Local recreational facilities include swimming, fishing, boating, and other water sports on Great South Bay, Long Island Sound, as well as horseback riding, golf, tennis, and dancing. Some part-time employment is available for students.

Branch Campuses: Eastern Campus, Speonk-Riverhead Rd., Riverhead, NY 11901, tel. (516) 548-2500; Western Campus, Crooked Hill Rd., Brentwood, NY 11717, tel. (516) 434-6750.

STATE UNIVERSITY OF NEW YORK, SULLIVAN COUNTY COMMUNITY COLLEGE *(M-15)*
Box 4002
Loch Sheldrake, New York 12759
Tel: (914) 434-5750; (800) 577-5243; Fax: (914) 434-4806

Description: This publically supported, coeducational community college, nestled in the Catskill Mountain resort region, Sullivan County Community College is a campus of the State University of New York. It is accredited by the Middle States Association of Colleges and Schools. The college offers 34 career-oriented and university parallel majors. Programs of study lead to the Associate degree. The opportunity to study abroad at the Sullivan campus in Toyama, Japan is availble. Enrollment includes 1,200 full-time and 650 part-time students. A faculty of 80 full-time and 30 part-time gives a faculty-student ratio of 1-18.

Entrance Requirements: Open admissions; accredited high school graduation or equivalent; rolling admission, midyear admission and advanced placement plans available; $25 application fee.

Costs Per Year: $2,156 tuition and fees; $4,056 out-of-state; $4,700 room and board.

Collegiate Environment: Located on 405-acres of rolling hillside, Sullivan County Community College's main academic building houses computer, travel and tourism, word processing and science laboratories. The Hospitality complex features bakeries, production kitchens and multipurpose dining room. Additional features include a New York State-licensed Child Development Center, a library of more than 62,000 volumes, classrooms, a 275 seat theater, and administrative offices. The Student Union provides areas for television, recreation and conferences for students. College approved housing with 24 hour security and supervision is available adjacent to the campus.

Community Environment: This rural region is located within a two hour drive from New York City, Albany, NY and Binghamton, NY in the Catskill resort region. Population of South Fallsburg, of which Loch Sheldrake is a hamlet, is 11,000. It is a rural community with a temperate climate. Transportation is provided by bus. The community has churches and synagogues, shopping facilities, and civic, fraternal and veteran's organizations. Recreation includes skiing, golf, tennis, swimming, boating, fishing, movies and hiking. The many restaurants, hotels and convention centers provide part-time employment for students.

STATE UNIVERSITY OF NEW YORK, TOMPKINS/CORTLAND COMMUNITY COLLEGE *(J-10)*
170 North Street, P.O. Box 139
Dryden, New York 13053-1039
Tel: (607) 844-8211

Description: This community college offers associate degree and certificate programs in a variety of career fields, and it also offers the AA and AS degree in Liberal Arts and Business for individuals who would like to transfer to a baccalaureate program. The college uses the semester system. The 3 summer sessions, beginning in May and ending in August, also allow individuals to complete a full-time schedule. The college was founded in 1968 and moved to its unusual 1-building campus on a hill overlooking Dryden in 1974. The 225-acre wooded campus includes a pond and nature trails, yet receives frequent bus service from neighboring Ithaca, New York. Enrollment includes 1,437 full-time and 1,338 part-time students with a faculty of 161. The faculty-student ratio is approximately 1-19. Because of their commitment to teaching, faculty are readily available for student assistance and support.

Entrance Requirements: Non-high school graduates accepted; open enrollment policy; ACT or SAT required for nursing students only. $18 application fee for full-time students; early admission, rolling admission, and advanced plans available.

Costs Per Year: $1,650 tuition for state residents; $3,700 for out-of-state residents; $115 student fee.

Collegiate Environment: The campus is approximately 14 miles from Ithaca, New York, home of Cornell University and Ithaca College, and it is approximately 10 miles from Cortland, New York. Bus service is available from the Ithaca area. Students may live in Dryden, in Ithaca, or in Cortland. The college has achieved excellent placement results for graduates of its business and technical programs. Admission to all programs except nursing is open. The upstate New York area is known for its winter sports, including both cross-country and downhill skiing. Tompkins Cortland is just a few miles from a major downhill skiing complex. A wide variety of musical and cultural events are available year-round. During warmer months, water sports are readily available at nearby Cayuga Lake.

Community Environment: Dryden is located 15 miles north of Ithaca in the Finger Lakes area. Limited part-time employment is available within the immediate vicinity. The city has several churches and a library. Nearby Ithaca has bus and air service. The climate is temperate.

STATE UNIVERSITY OF NEW YORK, ULSTER COUNTY COMMUNITY COLLEGE   *(L-17)*
Stone Ridge, New York 12484
Tel: (914) 687-5022; (800) 724-0833

Description: The publicly supported, coeducational community college was established in 1962 by authority of the State University of New York. It is accredited by the Middle States Association of Colleges and Schools. It awards degrees in the Associate in Arts, Associate in Science. The college awards associate degrees, has diploma and certificate programs, and offers specialized courses to respond to community interest. The college operates on a semester system and offers summer sessions. Enrollment includes 1,570 full-time and 1,200 part-time students. A faculty of 75 full-time and 117 part-time gives a faculty-student ratio of 1-18.

Entrance Requirements: Approved high school graduation or equivalent; open enrollment policy; college placement exams required; rolling admission, early decision, and early admission plans available. $25 application fee.

Costs Per Year: $2,000 tuition and fees for New York residents; $4,000 tuition and fees for nonresidents.

Collegiate Environment: The college occupies its own 165-acre campus in the general geographic and population center of Ulster County. The 9 college buildings include a library of 74,362 volumes 600 periodicals, 7,500 microforms and 3,000 audiovisual materials. Semesters begin in September and January and the summer session begins in June. 80% of applicants are accepted. Financial aid is available. 85% of the students receive some form of financial aid.

Community Environment: Stone Ridge is located 90 miles north of New York City on the west side of the Hudson River near the Catskill Mountains. While the county is rural there are several population centers and the city of Kingston with a population of 25,000 is considered a suburban community. There are public transportation services, although students find it more convenient to have their own cars or participate in a car pool. There are many area motels and private homes for housing students. Skiing, hiking and camping are major re-

creational activities. There are also nearby lakes, rivers and streams for a variety of water sports. Additional recreational activities are available through a performing arts center, movie theatres and other colleges in the Mid-Hudson area. Some part-time employment is available for students.

STATE UNIVERSITY OF NEW YORK, WESTCHESTER COMMUNITY COLLEGE   *(C-3)*
75 Grasslands Road
Valhalla, New York 10595-1698
Tel: (914) 785-6735; Fax: (914) 785-6540

Description: The publicly supported, coeducational community college was established in 1946 and is a member institution of the State University of New York. It is sponsored by Westchester County and is accredited by the Middle States Association of Colleges and Schools. The college operates on the semester system and 4 summer sessions are offered. A faculty of 536 provides a faculty-student ratio of 1-20. It offers specialized technical programs and courses of study in the liberal arts and sciences. Degrees granted: A.S., A.A., and A.A.S. Enrollment includes 11,800 students. A faculty of 536 provides a faculty-student ratio of 1-22.

Entrance Requirements: Approved high school graduation or equivalent; open enrollment policy; advanced placement, rolling admission, early decision, early admission and midyear admission plans available; $25 application fee.

Costs Per Year: $2,016 state-resident tuition per year; $5,040 out-of-state residents; $117 student fees.

Collegiate Environment: The 218-acre campus occupies a scenic hilltop site near Valhalla, northwest of White Plains. The college buildings contain a library of 87,100 volumes and seating space for 1,000 students; the campus was formerly a part of the Hartford Estate and a number of the original buildings are in use for college purposes. Financial assistance is available for students who qualify. 30% of students receive some form of financial aid.

Community Environment: Population 12,000. Valhalla is a suburban community located approximately 3 miles from the city of White Plains. There is bus service, a county airport, a railroad and major highways in neighboring Westchester. The community has a public library and 3 churches. Many cultural, recreational, and community services are found in White Plains. Part-time employment is available for students.

SYRACUSE UNIVERSITY   *(H-11)*
Syracuse, New York 13244
Tel: (315) 443-3611

Description: Syracuse University, founded in 1870, is an independent, privately endowed university with an international reputation. It is accredited by the Middle States Association of Colleges and Schools. There are eleven undergraduate colleges at Syracuse: Architecture, Arts & Sciences, Education, Engineering and Computer Science, Human Development, Information Studies, Management, Nursing, Public Communications, Social Work, and Visual and Performing Arts. Students come from all over the United States and from more than 100 foreign countries. Programs available include dual enrollment (including a dual-enrollment program with the State University of New York College of Environmental Science and Forestry), selected studies, and an honors program. An interdisciplinary concentration is available in gerontology and may be taken as part of a major program in another discipline. Through the University's Division of International Programs Abroad, students may study in England, France, Hong Kong, Italy, Spain and Zimbabwe. The University operates on a two-semester calendar with two six-week summer sessions. Students generally take five 3-credit-hour courses each semester. A minimum of 120 credit hours is required for graduation. Enrollment includes 10,014 full-time and 119 part-time undergraduate, and 4,417 graduate students. A faculty of 868 full-time and 814 part-time provides an undergraduate faculty-student ratio of 1-10. ROTC is available.

Entrance Requirements: High school graduation; completion of 20 units including 4 English, 3 math, 3 science, 2 foreign language, and 3 social studies; required subjects vary with individual schools and colleges; SAT or ACT required; early admission, early decision and deferred admission plans available; application deadlines: Feb. 1, Nov. 1 early decision; $40 application fee.

Costs Per Year: $15,150 tuition; $6,870 room and board; $358 student fees.

Collegiate Environment: The 200-acre campus features a main grassy quandrangle surrounded by academic buildings, with residential facilities nearby. The campus sits on a hill overlooking the downtown area of Syracuse. 6,594 undergraduate students live in University housing, which includes modern dormitories, apartments, and fraternity and sorority houses. Social life is centered on the campus, and there are innumerable recreational, athletic, and academic activities. The 50,000 seat Carrier Dome is the site of concerts, athletic events, and commencement. The academic buildings at Syracuse University span the century, with fifteen listed in the National Register of Historic Places and others representative of some of the most modern and technologically sophisticated architecture in the country. The Ernest Stevenson Bird Library houses more than 2,780,000 volumes, 15,650 periodicals, 3.3 million titles on microfilm, 2,000 CD-ROM disks, rare books, and archives. The University has computer facilities with laboratories and a fiber optics network that links main frame computers to hundreds of on-campus terminals. The Newhouse Communications Center has some of the finest facilities available for journalism and telecommunications. Existing facilities that have been completely renovated include those for the arts and sciences, architecture, human development, and education. In fall 1989, a new center for science and technology was completed. New facilities for the visual arts and Flanagan Gymnasium opened in the fall of 1990. Dedicated in 1994, the high-tech Melvin A. Eggers Hall offers superior facilities for several social science programs. 67% of applicants are accepted and offered admission. The middle 50% range of enrolled freshmen scores are SAT 460-570 verbal, 530-650 math. Scholarships are available and 70% of students receive some form of aid.

Community Environment: The city of Syracuse (metropolitan area population of 500,000) is the business, educational, and cultural hub of central New York. The city offers professional theater, symphony, opera, and visiting artists and performers. Highlights of the downtown area are the Everson Museum of Art, designed by I.M. Pei, the impressive Civic Center, and the popular Carousel Center shopping Mall. Central New York offers lakes, parks, mountains, and outstanding recreational opportunities. Syracuse is serviced by most major airlines, Amtrak, and Greyhound. Hancock International Airport is only a few miles from downtown and the University, and is served by taxis. The famous Finger Lakes region, offering excellent summer and winter activities, is easily accessible. Diversified industry includes electronics, electrical equipment, electrical machinery, pottery, and candles. Chemicals, drugs, steel, gears, fabricated metals, shoes, and automobile accessories are also manufactured here. Part-time employment opportunities are available for students. A transportation network includes bus lines, airlines, and excellent highways and thruways. Parking is excellent in the downtown shopping and theatrical districts. There are 35 theaters, over 100 churches of various denominations, 5 radio stations, 3 hospitals, 5 TV stations, and 173 parks located within the city.

TEACHERS COLLEGE, COLUMBIA UNIVERSITY *(E-2)*
525 West 120th Street
New York, New York 10027
Tel: (212) 678-3000; Admissions: (212) 678-3710; Fax: (212) 678-4171

Description: The privately supported, coeducational, graduate professional school of education was founded in 1887 and has always been closely associated with Columbia University. It became formaly affiliated with the university in 1898 and all degrees are granted through the university. Teachers College is a separate corporate organization, including a Board of Trustees which has general control of the college and full responsibility for financial support. It is accredited by the Middle States Association of Colleges and Schools. Divisions of the college include Philosophy, Social Sciences, and Education; Psychology and Education; Educational Institutions and Programs; Instruction; Health Services, Sciences, and Education. The school operates on the semester system and offers two summer sessions. Enrollment includes approximately 4,500 full-time and part-time students with a faculty of 130.

Entrance Requirements: Bachelor degree or equivalent; GRE for some programs; rolling admission plan available; $50 application fee.

Costs Per Year: $12,480 ($520/credit) tuition; $6,500 room; $200 fees.

Collegiate Environment: The main group of 10 Teachers College buildings is situated on Morningside Heights, adjoining the main university campus. The library contains over 550,000 volumes and living accommodations are available for 150 men, 300 women, and 150 families. Scholarships and other forms of financial aid are available.

Community Environment: See Columbia University.

TOURO COLLEGE *(E-2)*
844 6th Avenue
New York, New York 10036
Tel: (212) 463-0400

Description: Founded in 1971, Touro College is accredited by the Middle States Association of Colleges and Schools. The privately supported coeducational college operates on the semester system with one summer session. Recent enrollment was 6,469 students with a faculty of 232 full-time and 368 part-time. The school has an overseas program with participating institutions in Israel.

Entrance Requirements: High school graduate or equivalent with 16 units including 4 English, 2 mathematics, 2 laboratory science, 2 foreign language and 2 social science. SAT or ACT required. Application fee $25.

Costs Per Year: $6,800 tuition; $230 student fees; $4,600 room.

Collegiate Environment: Located in midtown New York City, the school is within walking distance of the New York Public Library and rail and bus commuter lines from New York, New Jersey, and Connecticut. Housing is available for 120 students. The college library contains over 150,000 titles. Financial aid is available and approximately 85% of the students receive some form of financial support.

Community Environment: See New York University

TROCAIRE COLLEGE *(I-4)*
110 Red Jacket Parkway
Buffalo, New York 14220
Tel: (716) 826-1200; Admissions: (716) 826-0543; Fax: (716) 826-4704

Description: Trocaire College is a private two-year coeducational, liberal arts college established in 1958 by the Buffalo Regional Community of the Sisters of Mercy. Trocaire has been granted full accreditation by the Middle States Association of Colleges and Schools. Certain programs are professionally accredited by the Committee on Allied Health Education and Accreditation and the National League for Nursing. It is chartered by the Board of Regents of the State of New York and confers the degrees of Associate in Arts, Associate in Science and Associate in Applied Science. Associate level programs include Administrative Assistant, Business Administration, Legal and Medical Office Technology, Early Childhood Education, Liberal Arts, Medical Assistant, Hotel Management, Medical Laboratory Technology, Nursing, Radiologic Technology, Health Information Technology and Surgical Technology. One-year certificates are also available in Office Technology and Surgical Technology, and Diagnostic Medical Sonography. Enrollment is 141 men and 964 women. A faculty of 40 full-time and 63 part-time gives an approximate faculty-student ratio of 1-13.

Entrance Requirements: Approved high school graduation or equivalent; completion of 16 units; SAT or ACT required; $15 application fee; personal interview recommended; school administered assessment test; early admission, early decision, rolling admission and advanced placement plans available.

Costs Per Year: $5,550 tuition; $200-$400 misc.

Collegiate Environment: The college is located in a residential area of South Buffalo and is about a 20-minute distance from the downtown area. Catherine Hall contains the administrative offices, a library of 20,981 volumes and 194 periodicals, 52 microforms and 3,468 audiovisual materials, classrooms, a bookstore, a student lounge, and an auditorium. Marian Hall contains faculty offices, a chapel, academic learning Center, Student Services, cafeteria, classrooms, and laboratories. Approximately 60% of students applying for admission are accepted including midyear students. About 50% of the recent student body graduated in the top half of their high school class, 20% in the top quarter. Close to 74% of freshmen return to the college for a second year of studies. Average scores for freshman class were SAT 347V, 352M. Recently the college awarded 6 certificates and 286 Associate degrees. 85% of the student body receives some form of financial aid.

Community Environment: Trocaire is located in the residential area of South Buffalo, adjacent to Mercy Hospital and Cazenovia Park. It is in a quiet corner of the city, but readily accessible to students; 3 bus lines serve the campus. It is also within convenient distance of the New York State Thruway and the Buffalo Skyway.

UNION COLLEGE   *(I-17)*
Union Street
Schenectady, New York 12188
Tel: (518) 370-6112

Description: Founded in 1795, Union College is an independent, primarily undergraduate, residential college for men and women. It is accredited by the Middle States Association of Colleges and Schools, the American Chemical Society and the Accreditation Board for Engineering and Technology. The college offers programs in the humanities, the sciences, the social sciences, and engineering and computer science. Air Force, Army, and Navy ROTC programs are available. Union has 3 10-week terms plus a summer session. Enrollment includes 1,994 undergraduates and 110 graduate students. The faculty includes 170 full-time and 24 part-time members.

Entrance Requirements: 4 factors are considered for admission: record in secondary school, including rank in class and quality of courses taken (normally, 16 units are required, including 4 English, 2 foreign language, 2-3 math and science); recommendations of the secondary school; personal qualities and extracurricular record; and Scores from 3 CEEB Achievement Tests; or ACT scores. Early decision, early admission, midyear admission and advanced placement are available. Application fee $35.

Costs Per Year: $18,732 tuition; $4,747 room and board; $190 fees.

Collegiate Environment: The 100-acre campus, located in a residential section of Schenectady, is the first architecturally-planned campus in America (1812-1814). Its 50 buildings include Schaffer Library (462,200 volumes, subscriptions to 2,200 journals), a science and engineering center, a computer center, humanities and social science classroom buildings, and housing for about 1,513 students. Union participates in cross-registration with nearby colleges and universities; offers its own Terms Abroad programs in 14 countries; has exchange programs with universities in Scotland, England, Switzerland, Germany, Japan, and China; offers accelerated joint degree programs with Albany Law School and Albany Medical College; and has a variety of internships, including a term in Washington, D.C. There are more than 60 student activities and an extensive intercollegiate, intramural, and recreational sports program. The faculty-student ratio is 1-13; the mean ACT score for the last freshman class was 28 and about 40% of the graduating class go directly on to graduate and professional school. The college's financial aid program is more than $11 million a year, and 40% of the students receive scholarship help from the college; 55% of all students receive aid of some form.

Community Environment: Union is located in Schenectady, a small city of 65,000 settled by the Dutch in 1661. The city is part of a metropolitan area of more than 800,000 people, including the New York State capital of Albany. Boston and New York are 3 hours away, Montreal 4; also nearby are the Adirondack and Catskill Mountains of New York, and the Berkshires of Massachusetts, and the Green Mountains of Vermont.

UNION THEOLOGICAL SEMINARY   *(E-2)*
3041 Broadway at 120th Street
New York, New York 10027
Tel: (212) 662-7100; Admissions: (212) 280-1317; Fax: (212) 280-1416

Description: Privately-supported, coeducational, graduate-level, theological seminary for training men and women for every type of Christian ministry. It is accredited by the Middle States Association of Colleges and Schools and the Association of Theological Schools. While the seminary is basically a Protestant institution, it welcomes Roman Catholic and Eastern Orthodox students. The seminary also has relationships with neighboring institutions such as Columbia University, Barnard, Teachers College, the Jewish Theological Seminary,

Fordham University, City University Graduate Center, the Riverside Church, and the National Council of Churches. Auburn Theological Seminary, a Presbyterian seminary, became associated with Union Theological Seminary in 1939. Under a reciprocal agreement with Columbia University, the seminary cooperates in offering M.A. and Ph.D. degrees in religion. Since the seminary is a graduate institution, its students may take graduate courses in the university. Degrees granted include the Master of Divinity, Master of Arts in Education and Theological Studies (includes Master of Arts and joint Master of Divinity/Master of Science in Social Work with Columbia U.), Master of Sacred Theology, Master of Philosophy, Doctor of Philosophy, and in cooperation with Columbia University, Master of Arts, Master of Philosophy, Doctor of Philosophy, and Doctor of Education. The seminary operates on the semester system. Enrollment includes 171 full-time and 112 part-time students. A faculty of 25 full-time and 25 part-time gives a faculty-student ratio of 1-8.

Entrance Requirements: Bachelor degree from an accredited college or university for S.T.M., M.Div. or equivalent; for Ph.D., 2 years of graduate theological study and GRE; application deadlines: Jan.6 for Doctoral program, Feb. 15 for Masters program; $50 application fee.

Costs Per Year: $10,900 tuition for M.Div., M.A. E.T.S., S.T.M.; $15,800 tuition for M.A. and Ph.D..

Collegiate Environment: The present main buildings on Morningside Heights were completed in 1910 and constitute a rectangle enclosing 2 city blocks with a beautifully landscaped and secluded inner quadrangle. The seminary library is unsurpassed among the theological collections of this country, and contains more than 700,000 volumes, including bound periodicals, and 50,000 microforms. Financial aid is available. The seminary granted 87 Master degrees and 5 Doctorates to a recent graduating class.

Community Environment: See Columbia University.

UNITED STATES MERCHANT MARINE ACADEMY   *(E-3)*
Kings Point, New York 11024
Tel: (516) 773-5000; (800) 732-6267; Admissions: (516) 773-5391; Fax: (516) 773-5390

Description: This publicly-supported, technological coeducational college was established in 1943 and is maintained by the Department of Transportation, under the direction of the Maritime Administration and is 1 of America's 5 service schools. It is accredited by the Middle States Association of Colleges and Schools, and professionally by the Accreditation Board for Engineering and Technology. Although the academy is under the jurisdiction of the Federal Government, its graduates are trained to serve on privately-owned ships of United States registry. The combination of technical courses and exposure to the humanities leads, upon graduation, to the Bachelor of Science degree, a commission as an Ensign in the Naval Reserve, and a license as either Third Mate or Third Assistant Engineer or both for Dual midshipmen. It operates on the four-quarter system. Enrollment includes 980 full-time students. A faculty of 74 full-time gives a faculty-student ratio of 1-11.

Entrance Requirements: United States citizenship, between 17 and 25 years of age, good moral character; accredited high school graduation with rank in upper 20% of graduating class; completion of 15 high school units including 3 English, 3 mathematics, 1 science; candidates for admission must be nominated by a member of the Congress of the United States or other nominating authorities; early admission and early decision plans available; March 1 application deadline.

Costs Per Year: $4,464 deposit against government allowance prior to reporting, mailed by June 30, required for Plebe expenses; each Midshipman is provided a government allowance and there are no tuition or room and board charges.

Collegiate Environment: The academy is situated on 80 acres on the north shore of Long Island. The 48 buildings contain a library of 232,576 volumes, 985 periodicals, and 161,576 microforms, and dormitory facilities for 750. Approximately 45% of students applying for admission are accepted. Classes begin in July and midyear students are not accepted. About 75% of freshmen graduated in the top quarter of their high school class, 34% in the top tenth. Average scores of freshmen were SAT Verbal 545, Math 592.

Community Environment: Population 5,614, Kings Point is located approximately 20 miles from New York City. Community services include recreation, and the cultural advantages of New York City are all readily accessible.

UNITED STATES MILITARY ACADEMY *(N-17)*
West Point, New York 10996
Tel: (914) 938-4041; Admissions: (914) 938-4041; Fax: (914) 938-3021

Description: A publicly supported, professional college for men and women. Known to most Americans as West Point, the academy established in 1802 is under the general direction and supervision of the Department of the Army. The academy prepares selected young men and women for service to their country as professional officers of the United States Army. The academic curriculum, which leads to the degree of Bachelor of Science, contains the essential elements of a math, science and engineering program. More than 30 academic programs are available, including 19 optional majors. The academy operates on the semester system and recently enrolled 4,100 men and women. It is accredited by the Middle States Association of Colleges and Schools. A faculty of 491 gives a faculty-student ratio of 1-8.

Entrance Requirements: United States citizenship, between 17 and 22 years of age, on 1 July of year entering, unmarried, with no legal responsibility to support a child or children, physically fit, and good moral character; accredited high school graduation; completion of 16 units including 4 English, 4 mathematics, 2 science, 2 foreign language, 1 social science is highly recommended; SAT or ACT required; official nomination by Member of Congress or other nominating authority required; early decision, rolling admission and advanced placement plans available.

Costs Per Year: All U.S. Military Academy cadets are members of the United States Army and receive an annual salary of more than $6,700.00. Room and board, medical and dental care are provided by the U.S. Army. A $1,800.00 deposit is required upon admission in order to pay for uniforms, texts, personal computer, and other similar initial issues.

Collegiate Environment: The military reservation at West Point consists of 18,000 acres. The academy buildings include a library of 600,000 volumes, 2,400 periodicals, and dormitory facilities are available for all 4,100 men and women. Current army regulations authorize and encourage army officers to continue their education in a wide variety of fields. Postgraduate schooling in various colleges and universities throughout the United States provides a fine opportunity to the officer who desires to obtain a Masters or Doctor degree. Nearly all graduates go on to graduate school after their initial six-year military service obligation. Entering classes begin in July. Approximately 9-11% of the applicants are accepted and 85-90% of the freshmen return for the second year of studies. Almost 95% of the current freshmen graduated in the top half of their high school class, 85% in the top quarter. The average SAT scores of the freshmen were 565 verbal and 647 math.

Community Environment: Population 1,500, West Point is the oldest, continuously occupied military post in the country, and is about 50 miles north from New York City overlooking the Hudson River. West Point maintains some of the finest academic facilities and equipment in the world. The Computer Center has a network of several large computers, offering one of the most advanced time-sharing systems in any American college or university. Participation in athletic and extracurricular activities is stressed. In addition to superior athletic facilities, an eighteen-hole golf course and a ski slope for instructional and recreational skiing are located on the Academy grounds. Post residents are the officers, enlisted men and women, and civilians assigned to the Military Adcademy as staff and faculty, their families, and the Corps of Cadets.

UNIVERSITY OF ROCHESTER *(H-7)*
Wilson Boulevard
Rochester, New York 14627
Tel: (716) 275-2121; Admissions: (716) 275-3221; Fax: (716) 461-4595

Description: Founded in 1850, Rochester is now one of the leading private universities in the Northeast, 1 of 58 members of the prestigious Association of American Universities and 1 of 9 members of

the University Athletic Association, made up of institutions with similar academic and athletic philosophies. Undergraduates may choose among courses in 7 colleges and professional schools: College of Arts and Science, William E. Simon Graduate School of Business Administration, Graduate School of Education and Human Development, College of Engineering and Applied Science, Eastman School of Music, School of Medicine and Dentistry, School of Nursing. The university operates on the semester system and offers six summer sessions. Enrollment includes 7,280 full-time and 1,052 part-time undergraduates and 3,114 graduate students. A faculty of 1,233 gives an undergraduate faculty-student ratio of 1-12.

Entrance Requirements: High school graduation customary; completion of 16 units recommended including 4 English; 3-4 math, at least 2 science, at least 2 language, 4 social studies; SAT or ACT tests required; early admission, early decision, delayed admission and advanced placement available; recommended application deadline Jan. 15; $50 application fee.

Costs Per Year: $17,840 tuition; $6,583 room and board; $420 fees.

Collegiate Environment: Placed in a bend in the Genesee River, the 100-acre River Campus with its rosy-brick architecture is home to most undergraduates who live in a variety of residence halls, fraternity houses, and "special interest" housing. Most of the original academic and residential buildings, dating from 1930, have been recently renovated. Among the newest structures are the I.M. Pei-designed Wilson Commons, recently designated by The New York Times as 1 of the 10 best student unions in the country, and the multipurpose Zornow Sports Center opened in 1982. Rochester's personal scale and the diversity of its colleges and professional schools permit both attention to the individual and unusual flexibility in planning undergraduate programs tailored to individual needs and interests. Most classes are small, and students work closely with a stimulating faculty of internationally renowned scholars who engage both in advanced research and in teaching at the undergraduate level. Courses are challenging, but there's a weekly break on Wednesday afternoons, left free for special events and individual pursuits. Special opportunities include the "Take Five' program allowing selected undergraduates to take a fifth year tuition-free; residential courses; a freshman-year "Ventures" program of integrated courses; and the eight-year REMS (Rochester Early Medical Scholars) program through which selected entering freshmen can be guaranteed admission to the University's Medical School upon completion of their Undergraduate Studies. Students participate in more than 90 student organizations (including FM and AM radio stations), 22 varsity teams, more than 30 intramural and club sports, 18 fraternities, 10 sororities, and an active calendar of films, concerts, drama, lectures, and special events (including the annual Yellow Jacket Day and Dandelion Day festivals.) The library contains 2,843,283 volumes; 16,000 periodicals, 3.4 million microforms and 59,213 audiovisual materials. Navy ROTC nearby. 62% of applicants are accepted and 89% of the students receive financial aid.

Community Environment: With Lake Ontario on its northern border and the scenic Finger Lakes on the south, the Rochester community of about one million people is located in an attractive setting. It offers a wide range of cultural and recreational opportunities-from concerts by the Rochester Philharmonic Orchestra and Eastman School ensembles, performances by resident professional theater companies, and an unusual concentration of first-class museums (including the University's own Memorial Art Gallery), to professional baseball and ice hockey and nearby opportunities for recreational canoeing, sculling, ice-skating, and skiing. A recently published Rand McNally "Places Rated Almanac" listed Rochester ninth nationally among its "best all-around metropolitan areas."

UTICA COLLEGE OF SYRACUSE UNIVERSITY *(H-13)*
1600 Burrstone Road
Utica, New York 13502-4892
Tel: (800) 782-8884; Admissions: (315) 792-3006; Fax: (315) 792-3292

Description: The privately supported, coeducational, liberal arts and professional college is a member of Syracuse University's family of undergraduate and professional colleges. The college offers majors leading to the Bachelor of Arts or Bachelor of Science degree and students receive their degrees from Syracuse University. The college operates on the semester basis with multiple summer sessions and is accredited by the Middle States Association of Colleges and Schools.

Enrollment includes 1,600 students in the day program and evening programs. A faculty of 111 provides a faculty-student ratio of 1-15.

Entrance Requirements: Accredited high school graduation or equivalent; recommended 16 units of college-preparatory courses of 4 English, 3 mathematics, 3 science, 2 language, and 3 social studies; rolling admission plan, except for occupational therapy, physical therapy, and academic merit scholarship applicants, which have an application deadline of February 15; SAT or ACT results are not required except for applicants for physical therapy, occupational therapy. or academic merit scholarships; early admission, early decision, and advanced placement plans available. $25 application fee.

Costs Per Year: $12,680 tuition; $4,924 room and board; $90 fees.

Collegiate Environment: The college is located in Utica, approximately 50 miles from the Syracuse University campus. The library contains more than 159,849 volumes. A strong student government, several social fraternities and sororities, speech activities, Division III sports, an FM radio station, chorus, and publications are some of the activities found on campus. Dormitory space is available for 950 men and women. Presidential and Dean's merit scholarships are available. 90% of students receive some form of financial aid. About 65% of the applicants are accepted.

Community Environment: Utica is an area rich in the history of the Iroquis Confederacy, the French and Indian Wars, the American Revolution, the great migration to the Midwest and the western expansion of American commerce via the Erie Canal. Historic treasures in the area include the Oriskany Battlefield, Revolutionary Fort Stanwix (restored as a national monument) in Rome, and the homes of Revolutionary War heros General Nicholas Herkimer and Major General Friedrich Wilhelm Baron von Steuben. Within an hour's drive of Utica are Johnson Hall, home of Sir Wiiliam Johnson, colonial superintendent of Indian Affairs, in Johnstown; the Mansion House of the Oneida Community in Oneida; and Cooperstown, birthplace of James Fenimore Cooper, site of the Baseball Museum and Hall of Fame, the Farmer's Museum, and the headquarters of the New York State Historical Association. Utica's cultural assets include Munson-Williams-Proctor Institute and School of Art, one of the finest small art institutions in the country; the Oneida Historical Society; the Utica Civic Symphony; the Broadway Theatre League; the Players Theater Company; the Great Artists Concert series; the Utica Public Library and the Oneida County Junior Museum. These are greatly enhanced by the libraries, art galleries and cultural programs of the colleges in the area. The Utica area abounds in outdoor recreational resources. The city's park system includes the Val Bialas municipal ski slopes and ice skating rink just a mile from campus, an outstanding small zoo, 3 large public swimming pools, an 18-hole public golf course, public tennis courts, picnic grounds, and an abundance of public athletic fields. Excellent golfing, swimming, boating, fishing, hiking, and camping facilities surround the city. Nearby lakes include Otsego at Cooperstown, Oneida at Verona, Delta north of Rome, and the famous Fulton Chain of Lakes in the Adirondacks at Old Forge. Fine ski facilities near Utica include Snow Ridge at Turin, and Woods Valley near Rome.

VASSAR COLLEGE   *(M-17)*
Box 77
Poughkeepsie, New York 12601
Tel: (914) 437-7000; Admissions: (914) 437-7300; Fax: (914) 437-7063

Description: This privately supported, coeducational liberal arts college opened in 1865 as the first college for women with the equipment and resources commensurate with high educational standards of men's colleges of the time. Vassar became coeducational in 1969. Vassar awards the B.A., M.A., and M.S. degrees, by way of concentration in a traditional program or discipline, the independent program, multi-disciplinary or interdepartmental programs. It also offers special programs such as Junior Year Abroad and other foreign study, 12-College Exchange, internships and field work. The college does not discriminate on the basis of race, color, religion, sex, sexual orientation, national or ethnic origin, or handicap. The college operates on a semester basis and is accredited by the Middle States Association of Colleges and Schools. The recent enrollment included 1,383 women and 836 men. The faculty numbers 240.

Entrance Requirements: High school graduation or equivalent with high academic achievement; completion of 16 units of college prepa-

ratory courses including 4 English (including literature and continuous practice in writing), 3-4 mathematics 3-4 foreign language, 2-3 laboratory science, 1 history; SAT and 3 Achievement Tests, or ACT required; early admission, delayed admission, early decision, and advanced placement programs available; admission is selective and competitive; $60 application fee; interview recommended.

Costs Per Year: $19,940 tuition; $6,150 board and room; $480 fees.

Collegiate Environment: The college is located on the outskirts of the city of Poughkeepsie, Dutchess County, New York. The college buildings include a library of 750,000 volumes, residence facilities for 1,000 men and 1,250 women, and a teaching art center. Most undergraduate students are required to live in residence at the college. Scholarships are available and 57% of students receive some form of aid. About 45% of the applicants are accepted. 82% of current freshmen graduated in the top fifth of their high school class.

Community Environment: Area population 85,000. Originally settled by the Dutch, Poughkeepsie was the capital of New York from 1778 to 1783. Situated on a plateau above the Hudson River, the Poughkeepsie area offers facilities for culture and entertainment as well as parks, recreational areas, and places of historic interest such as the Franklin D. Roosevelt National Historic Site in Hyde Park, and the Vanderbilt Mansion. Industries within the area include IBM and the Fairchild Corporation Community services include a library, churches, YMCA, YWCA, art galleries, the Mid-Hudson Civic Center (with ice-skating rink) the Bardavon 1869 Opera House, and the Jewish Community Center among others. New York City, about 75 miles to the south, is easily accessible by car, train, bus, and air.

VILLA MARIA COLLEGE OF BUFFALO   *(I-4)*
240 Pine Ridge Road
Buffalo, New York 14225
Tel: (716) 896-0700; Fax: (716) 896-0705

Description: The privately supported, coeducational two-year college was established in 1960 and is administered by the Felician Sisters. Primarily serving the Western New York area, certificate and degree programs are offered day and evening. Each program functions within a framework of the arts and sciences and incorporates cooperative education internships. Student services are provided for both traditional and nontraditional students including a Learning Support Center, Adult Learner's Group, and an on-campus Child Care Center. The school operates on a semester system and offers three summer sessions. Off-campus housing can be arranged. The college enrolled 65 men and 192 women full-time and 8 men and 107 women part-time during the recent academic year. A faculty of 18 full-time and 25 part-time gives a faculty-student ratio of 1-11. The college is accredited by the Middle States Association of Colleges and Schools and the Foundation for Interior Design Education Research.

Entrance Requirements: Accredited high school graduation or equivalent $25 application fee; early decision, rolling admission, and advanced placement plans available. All students are required to participate in the Villa Maria College Asessment and Advisement Program (VMCAAP).

Costs Per Year: $6,000 tuition; $180 student fees.

Collegiate Environment: The 9.6-acre campus is located in a suburban atmosphere of the town of Cheektowaga on the eastern boundary of Buffalo. The college consists of a complex of 4 adjoining buildings; the Main Building, Library Building, Music Building and Auditorium Building. 73% of students applying for admission are accepted, including midyear students. The library contains 46,406 volumes, 270 periodicals and 7,878 audiovisual materials. Financial aid is available and 75% of students receive aid. The college awarded 4 Certificates and 94 Associate degrees to its recent graduating class.

Community Environment: See Canisius College.

WADHAMS HALL SEMINARY COLLEGE   *(B-13)*
RD 4, Box 80
Riverside Drive
Ogdensburg, New York 13669
Tel: (315) 393-4231; Fax: (315) 393-4249

Description: This privately supported, four-year liberal arts seminary-college is operated by the Roman Catholic Diocese of Ogdensburg. It proposes to prepare and educate men for the priesthood and for the diaconate in the Roman Catholic Church; also to prepare and educate students for other ministries in the Roman Catholic Church. The seminary was founded in 1924 by the Diocese of Ogdensburg. It is accredited by the Middle States Association of Colleges and Schools. Degree granted is the B.A., with a major in philosophy or double major in philosophy and religious studies. It operates on the semester system. Enrollment is 25 full-time and 10 part-time students. A faculty of 15 full-time and 5 part-time gives a faculty-student ratio of 1-2.

Entrance Requirements: Accredited high school graduation; completion of 18 units, including 4 English, 2 language, 3 mathematics and/or science, 3 social science, and 2 foreign language; ACT 19 or minimum SAT score of 400V and 400M required; personal interview; students from other dioceses must apply; $15 application fee; rolling admission, early admission and advanced placement plans available.

Costs Per Year: $4,000 tuition; $3,890 room and board; $95 student fees.

Collegiate Environment: The seminary is located on 208 acres and contains a library of 92,000 volumes, 782 periodicals, 2,041 microforms and 4,533 audiovisual materials, and dormitory facilities for 100 men. Financial aid is available and approximately 75% of students receive some form of aid. Approximately 90% of students applying for admission are accepted, including midyear students. About 80% of the previous freshman class returns to the seminary for the second year of studies. Semesters begin in August and January.

WAGNER COLLEGE   *(F-1)*
631 Howard Ave.
Staten Island, New York 10301
Tel: (718) 390-3411; (800) 221-1010; Fax: (718) 390-3105

Description: This private, coed college offers liberal arts and pre-professional programs. It was established in 1883, and is historically related to the Lutheran Church in America. The college operates on a semester basis and also offers summer sessions. It is accredited by the Middle States Association of Colleges and Schools. Enrollment includes 1,410 full-time and 120 part-time undergraduates and 300 graduate students. A faculty of 76 full-time and 109 part-time gives an undergraduate faculty-student ratio of 1-12.

Entrance Requirements: High school graduation with rank in upper half of graduating class; completion of 18 college-preparatory units including 4 English, 3 mathematics, 2 foreign language, 2 science, 3 social science, and 4 electives; SAT required, GRE required for graduate programs; $40 application fee; early admission, early decision, rolling admission, delayed admission, midyear admission, and advanced placement programs available.

Costs Per Year: $13,500 tuition; $5,800 room and board.

Collegiate Environment: Wagner's wooded, country-like campus on suburban Staten Island, just 30 minutes from the heart of New York City, offers unique advantages. The college has a friendly, small-town atmosphere, yet Manhattan, with all of its resources for coursework and jobs, is nearby. The range of studies includes 34 majors and more than 700 courses. The library has 300,000 volumes, 1,000 periodicals and 15,000 microforms. The college has National Collegiate Athletic Division I standing in 11 sports and Division IAA standing in Football. 80% of recent freshmen graduated in the top half of their high school class; 30% in the top quarter. Average SAT scores of freshmen were 470V and 520M. About 65% of applications are accepted, and 78% of freshmen return to the campus for the second year. 70% of students receive financial aid. Army and Air Force ROTC are available.

Community Environment: See College of Staten Island of the City University of New York.

WEBB INSTITUTE OF NAVAL ARCHITECTURE   *(D-3)*
Crescent Beach Road
Glen Cove, New York 11542
Tel: (516) 671-2213

Description: The privately supported, technological, coeducational college is registered by the New York State Board of Regents as an approved college of Naval Architecture and Marine Engineering. Its curriculum is accredited by the Accrediting Board for Engineering and Technology (for naval architecture, and marine engineering), and

by the Middle States Association of Colleges and Schools. The institute was established in 1889 and is the oldest school of its kind in the United States. The founder, William H. Webb, was the foremost shipbuilder of New York City during the period when a majority of the most important shipbuilders were located there. He endowed the school, and this endowment has been extensively increased, providing funds that enable the institution to be largely self-sustaining. It has continued Mr. Webb's policy of free tuition. The institute grants a B.S. in Naval Architecture and Marine Engineering. It operates on the semester system. Enrollment includes 75 full-time students. A faculty of 14 full-time gives a faculty-student ratio of 1-5.

Entrance Requirements: United States citizenship, unmarried, usually between the ages of 16 and 24 years of age, good health and character; accredited high school graduation with high rank in graduating class; completion of 16 units including 4 English, 4 mathematics, 1 physics, 1 chemistry, 1 foreign language, and 2 social science; SAT and 3 achievement tests required; admission is competitive and selective, based upon an investigation of the applicant's entire record of scholastic and personal performance and characteristics; early admission and early decision plans available; $25 application fee.

Costs Per Year: No tuition; $5,500 room and board.

Collegiate Environment: The campus of the institute covers 26 acres, fronting directly on Long Island Sound. The property was once a private estate and its 14 buildings contain a library of 49,294 volumes, 1,148 pamphlets, 250 periodicals, 1,664 microforms, and 1,167 audiovisual materials. Dormitory facilities provide for 87 students. One of the unique features of the institute is the winter work term when each student is required to engage in 8 weeks of practical work in a shipyard, aboard ship in the engine room, in a design office, or in other course-related industries. Average freshmen scores were SAT Verbal 615, Math 715. Students from various geographical locations are accepted and 30% of applicants are accepted. Classes begin in August and no midyear students are accepted. 27% of students receive some form of financial assistance. Approximately 90% of freshmen return to the institute for their second year.

Community Environment: Population 40,000, Glen Cove lies 22 miles from New York City on Long Island's historic North Shore. The Long Island Railroad furnishes commuter service to New York City. The area has excellent boating, swimming, horseback riding, and fishing facilities. Part-time employment is available.

WELLS COLLEGE   *(I-10)*
Aurora, New York 13026
Tel: (315) 364-3264; (800) 952-9355; Fax: (315) 364-3362

Description: The privately supported liberal arts college for women was founded in 1868. It is accredited by the Middle States Association of Colleges and Schools. The college grants the Bachelor of Arts degree. It operates on the semester system. The college enrolled 425 women in the recent academic year. A faculty of 48 full-time and 11 part-time provides a faculty-student ratio of 1-8.

Entrance Requirements: Strong secondary preparation; transcript completion of 16 units including 4 English, 3 mathematics, 3 foreign language, 3 laboratory science, 3 history; SAT or ACT; 2 teacher recommendations and interview strongly recommended; early admission, early decision, delayed admission, midyear admission and advanced placement plans available; $40 application fee.

Costs Per Year: $14,900 tuition; $5,550 room and board; $300 fees. Four-year guaranteed tution.

Collegiate Environment: The 360-acre campus overlooks Cayuga Lake in New York State's Finger Lakes Region. The academic buildings are at the south end of the village of Aurora, but many of the college-owned faculty homes and apartments extend a mile to the north along the village's main street. Dormitory facilities are provided for 500 women and the college library contains 242,437 volumes, 640 periodicals, 10,434 microforms and 840 audiovisual materials. Approximately 74% of students applying for admission are accepted. About 79% of the recent freshmen graduated in the top quarter of their high school class, and 40% in the highest tenth. Almost 85% of freshmen return to campus for the sophomore year. The middle 50% range of scores of the entering freshman class was SAT 1000-1199. Financial aid is available for economically disadvantaged students and 80% of students receive aid. The college awarded 100 Bachelor degrees to its recent graduating class.

Community Environment: Population 1,075, Aurora is in the Finger Lakes region on Cayuga Lake. The immediate area has a small library, churches, dormitories for student housing, and a college infirmary. There is a hospital in Auburn 16 miles away and in Ithaca, 25 miles away.

YESHIVA UNIVERSITY   *(E-2)*
500 West 185th Street
New York, New York 10033-3299
Tel: (212) 960-5400

Description: This privately supported university is America's oldest and largest university under Jewish auspices. It provides undergraduate, graduate and professional studies in the arts and sciences and Jewish learning. It has evolved from an elementary day school offering instruction in Jewish and general studies, founded in 1886, and from a theological seminary which was organized 10 years later. Today the university is composed of 4 teaching centers located in Manhattan and the Bronx. All undergraduates enroll in a dual program: liberal arts/sciences/business and Jewish studies. Men attend the Main Center, in Manhattan's Washington Heights--Yeshiva College (Arts & Sciences) or Sy Syms School of Business. Women attend the Midtown Center, in Manhattan's Murray Hill section, 245 Lexington Avenue--Stern College for Women (Arts & Sciences) or Sy Syms School of Business. Also at the Main Center are 3 graduate schools (coeducational): Wurzweiler School of Social Work, Bernard Revel Graduate School, and Harry Fischel School for Higher Jewish Studies, and--for men undergraduates--Isaac Breuer College of Hebraic Studies, James Striar School of General Jewish studies, and Yeshiva Program/Mazer School of Talmudic Studies. Also at the Midtown Center is a graduate school (coeducational): David J. Azrieli Graduate Institute of Jewish Education and Administration. The Brookdale Center, in downtown Manhattan, 55 Fifth Avenue, is the home of the Benjamin N. Cardozo School of Law. The Bronx Center, in the Westchester Heights section, Eastchester Road and Morris Park Avenue, is the site of the Albert Einstein College of Medicine, the Sue Golding Graduate Division of Medical Sciences, and Ferkauf Graduate School of Psychology. The university is chartered by the State of New York, and accredited by the Middle States Association of Colleges and Schools and various professional agencies. It operates on the semester basis. In addition to its extensive teaching programs, the university maintains community and national service and outreach projects, conducts research programs, issues publications, and is the home of the Yeshiva University Museum. Recent enrollment numbered 1,054 men and 894 women.

Entrance Requirements: High school graduation or GED; completion of 16 units including 4 English, 2 mathematics, 2 foreign language, 2 science, 2 social science; SAT required for undergraduate programs; entrance examinations and GRE required for most other schools and divisions; $25 application fee; early admission, delayed admission and advanced placement plans available.

Costs Per Year: $11,500 tuition for undergraduate liberal arts program; $3,950 board and room; $320 student fees.

Collegiate Environment: The university is comprised of 33 buildings located on 26 acres. The Main and Midtown Centers have dormitory accommodations for a total of 820 men and 548 women; main, midtown, and Bronx Centers also have dining facilities. The libraries contain over 874,000 volumes, 7,790 periodicals and 693,000 microforms. Approximately 76% of students applying for admission are accepted. Classes begin in late August; midyear students are accepted on an individual basis. 80% of the previous freshman class return to the university for the sophomore year. Financial aid is available for economically handicapped students and 75% of students receive some form of aid.

Community Environment: See New York University.

YORK COLLEGE OF THE CITY UNIVERSITY OF NEW YORK   *(E-3)*
94-20 Guy R. Brewer Boulevard
Jamaica, New York 11451
Tel: (718) 262-2165

Description: The publicly supported, coeducational liberal arts college was founded in 1967 and is accredited by the Middle States Association of Colleges and Schools. York offers the Bachelor of Arts and Bachelor of Science degrees, providing a broad baccalaureate curriculum with emphasis on liberal arts and the areas of business and health. It operates on the semester system with 1 summer term. Enrollment is 7,000 students. A faculty of 160 gives a faculty-student ratio of 1-18.

Entrance Requirements: Open enrollment; accredited high school graduation or GED; placement examination; $35 application fee; early admission, rolling admission and advanced placement programs available.

Costs Per Year: $2,450 state-resident tuition; $5,050 out-of-state; $84 student fees.

Collegiate Environment: The library contains 145,258 volumes, 1,242 periodicals, 115,000 microforms and 4,000 cassettes. Financial aid is available and 80% of the students receive aid.

Community Environment: See the City University of New York.

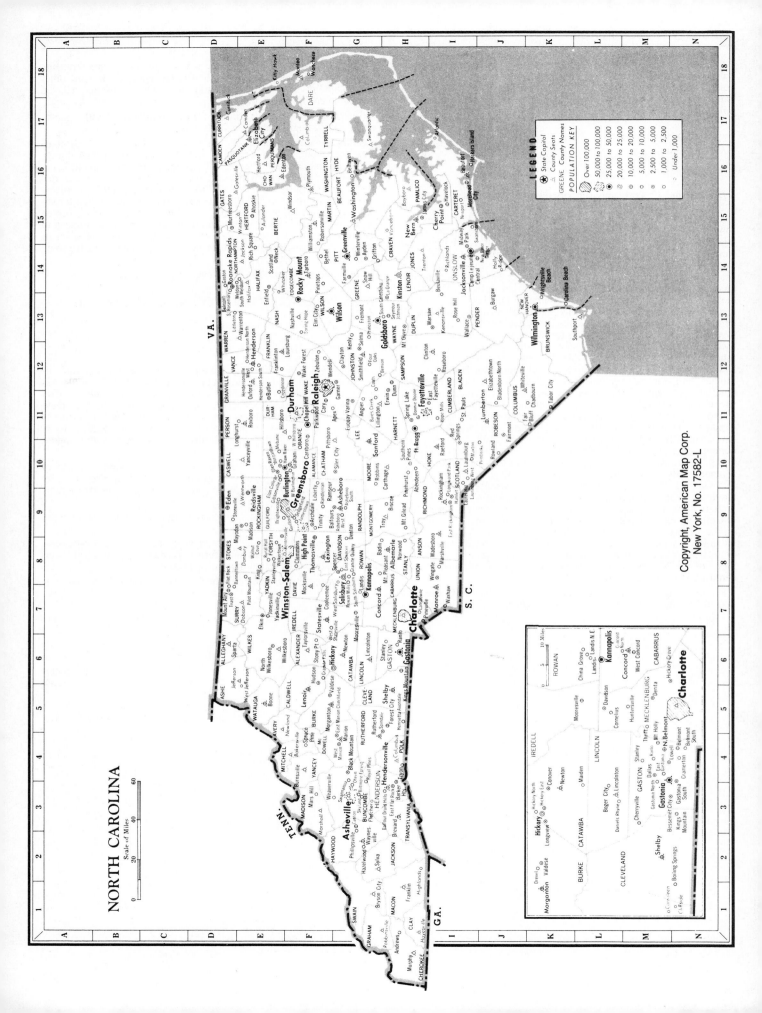

NORTH CAROLINA

Scale of Miles

NORTH CAROLINA

ALAMANCE COMMUNITY COLLEGE   (E-10)
P.O. Box 8000
Jimmy Kerr Road
Graham, North Carolina 27253
Tel: (919) 578-2002; Fax: (919) 578-1987

Description: This public community college was established in 1959 and is a member institution of the Department of Community Colleges of North Carolina. It operates on a four-quarter basis and is accredited by the Southern Association of Colleges and Schools. The school now has a college transfer option. Recent enrollment was 3,600 students. A total faculty of 85 full-time and 70 part-time gave a faculty-student ratio of 1-23.

Entrance Requirements: Open enrollment policy; high school graduation or equivalent; admission placement testing; rolling admission plan.

Costs Per Year: $742 tuition; $6,020 out-of-state; $12 student fees.

Collegiate Environment: The college is located on 48 acres and contains a library of 30,000 titles and 169 periodicals. Almost all students applying for admission are accepted. Students from other geographical locations are accepted as well as midyear students.

Community Environment: The industrialized economy of Alamance County depends primarily upon textiles, hosiery, electronics, metal cutting and fabricating, packaging and plastics. The bulk of the industries are located here. Planes and buses serve the area. A library, museum, YMCA, hospitals and various civic and service organizations are a part of the community. Some part-time employment is available for students. Recreational facilities include a supervised city recreational program, and many lakes are available for winter sports and outdoor living.

ANSON COMMUNITY COLLEGE   (I-8)
P.O. Box 126
Polkton, North Carolina 28135
Tel: (704) 272-7635; (800) 766-0319

Description: Anson Community College was established in 1962 by action of the State Department of Public Instruction and is a unit of the Department of Community Colleges of North Carolina. It is accredited by the Southern Association of Colleges and Schools. The 28 quality curriculum programs are offered in a coed environment at an affordable cost. Full-time tuition and fees for an academic quarter are only $200. While the cost is low, quality and excellence prevails; the faculty are highly qualified and provide outstanding academic support in the classroom. The college operates on the quarter system and offers one summer session. Enrollment is 1,247 students. A faculty of 57 gives a faculty-student ratio of 1-22.

Entrance Requirements: High school graduation or equivalent; open enrollment policy; entrance examinations required; applicants 18 years or older may be admitted; midyear admission and rolling admission plans.

Costs Per Year: $600 ($200/quarter) resident tuition and fees; $6,360 ($2,120/quarter) nonresident.

Collegiate Environment: The college is located in a rural setting and has one main campus on 97 acres. The faculty and staff are warm and friendly and are concerned with helping the student develop his/her total self. The Student Government Association provides a number of social, cultural and educational activities throughout each year. Modern classrooms, labs and shops are used to provide excellence in education. There is one library (Learning Resource Center) that houses approximately 19,000 volumes. Financial aid and scholarships are available to deserving students. 29% of students receive some form of financial aid.

Community Environment: The college is located in the geographic center of the Carolinas and Southeast. It's location is equidistant from the Appalachian and Blue Ridge Mountains and the Grand Strand area of the Atlantic; and is situated halfway between Washington, D.C. and Atlanta, Georgia. The average annual temperature is 61 degrees; the coldest month is January (42.5 degrees), the warmest month is July (78.9 degrees). Annual rainfall is 49".

APPALACHIAN STATE UNIVERSITY   (E-5)
Boone, North Carolina 28608
Tel: (704) 262-2120; Fax: (704) 262-3296

Description: The state university is part of the system of public higher education of the State of North Carolina. It is accredited by the Southern Association of Colleges and Schools and by several professional accreditation associations. It evolved from Watauga Academy, founded in 1899, and has grown steadily through its transformations as Appalachian State Normal School in 1925 to Appalachian State Teachers' College in 1929 to Appalachian State University in 1967 and a part of the consolidated University of North Carolina in 1971. Today the university is comprised of the General College, College of Arts and Sciences, College of Business, College of Fine and Applied Arts, College of Education, College of Continuing Education, School of Music and the Graduate School. It operates on the semester systems and offers two summer sessions. Enrollment includes 10,000 full-time and 812 part-time undergraduates and 1,058 graduate students. A faculty of 554 full-time and 176 part-time gives a faculty-student ratio of 1-16. There is an institutionally sponsored study abroad program in England, France, Germany, Mexico, Spain, and Italy. Army ROTC is available.

Entrance Requirements: Accredited high school graduation or equivalent; completion of at least 4 English, 3 mathematics (Algebra 1 & 2, Geometry), 3 science, 1 laboratory science and 2 social studies; satisfactory combination of scores on the SAT or ACT and high school class rank (or cumulative grade point average); satisfactory health record; $25 application fee.

Costs Per Year: $1,684 state-resident tuition and fees; $8,492 out-of-state; $2,370 standard room and board.

Collegiate Environment: The university's 250-acre campus is located on the crest of the Blue Ridge Mountains at an elevation of 3,333 feet above sea level. In addition, the university has developed the new 180-acre West campus that includes the Center for Continuing Education, the Art and Speech Center, College of Business, Farthing Auditorium and the new music building. Almost all of the 48 buildings on the central campus are new or have been recently renovated. They contain a library of 629,576 titles, 8,000 periodical titles, 830,000 microforms and 220,500 audiovisual materials, and dormitory facilities for 4,800 students. Fraternities and sororities can house 48 men and 252 women. Students from other geographical locations are accepted as well as midyear students. Approximately 47% of students applying for admission meet the requirements and are accepted. Almost 85% of the recent freshmen graduated in the top half of the high school class and 50% ranked in the top fifth. Nearly 85% of the previous freshman class returned to the campus for the sophomore year. 1,952 scholarships are available. Financial aid is available for economically disadvantaged students and 43% of the students receive aid. The average SAT scores of the current freshmen were 475 verbal, 519 math.

Community Environment: Located in Boone, North Carolina, Appalachian State University is in the middle of one of the most popular year-round recreation areas in the East. The campus is only a few miles from several major ski resorts, and Pisgah National Forest and the Appalachian Trail are easily accessible from Boone. Grandfather Mountain and "Tweetsie" railroad are famous tourist attractions. "Horn in the West" is a historical drama portraying with music and dance the story of Daniel Boone and the struggle to establish freedom in the southern Appalachian Highlands. This is performed in an outdoor amphitheater in a lovely mountain setting during July and August. The climate in the area is temperate. The average summer temperature rarely climbs above 80 degrees, and when it does a brief, refeshing shower usually cools things off. Fall brings clear, brisk and color-splashed days and cool evenings. Winter means picturesque snowfalls and fireside nights. Besides skiing, the area offers ample opportunities for other outdoor recreation, including river canoeing, hiking and camping. Three highways, U.S. 421, reaching from the Great Lakes to the North Carolina coast, and U.S. 321 and 221, all come through Boone, providing easy travel in all directions. The scenic Blue Ridge Parkway is only six miles from campus. The area, both urban and rural, is rich in contrasts between a growing university town and traditional southern Appalachian folkways. The university offers a wide variety of cultural events throughout the academic year, ranging from symphony orchestras to blue-grass concerts and from student talent shows to Broadway plays.

ASHEVILLE-BUNCOMBE TECHNICAL COMMUNITY COLLEGE   (G-3)
340 Victoria Road
Asheville, North Carolina 28801
Tel: (704) 254-1921

Description: The College was established in 1959 and is a member of the North Carolina State Department of Community Colleges. It operates on the quarter basis with one summer term and recently enrolled 3,476 men and women. The College is accredited by the Southern Association of Colleges and Schools.

Entrance Requirements: Open door policy; high school graduation or 18 years of age or older with completion of at least 8 units of high school work including 4 English, 2 Mathematics, and 2 Science; good physical health; admission and placement tests required. Early admission, early decision, rolling admission plans available.

Costs Per Year: $420 resident tuition; $3,924 nonresident tuition; $22 student fees.

Collegiate Environment: The College is located in seventeen modern buildings on a 126-acre campus. The mission of the College is to prepare students for employment, continuing education, and to help develop responsible attitudes necessary in modern society. The buildings contain large, well-lighted classrooms, laboratories, and shops which are fully equipped with modern test and production-type machines. Formal transfer agreements exist with area senior institutions. Students from other geographical locations are accepted, except in medical and dental programs. Financial assistance is available. 25% of students receive some form of financial aid. Programs begin once per year in September; however, general education requirements can be started prior to September.

Community Environment: See University of North Carolina - Asheville.

BARTON COLLEGE   (F-13)
College Station
Wilson, North Carolina 27893
Tel: (919) 399-6300; (800) 345-4973; Fax: (919) 237-1620

Description: The private, four-year, liberal arts college is church-related, but is nonsectarian in its policies and administration. It was established in 1902 and is a member of the Board of Higher Education of Christian Churches (Disciples of Christ). It operates on the semester system and offers two summer terms. It is accredited by the Southern Association of Colleges and Schools, the National League for Nursing, the Council on Education of the Deaf, National Council for the Accreditation of Teacher Education, North Carolina State Department for Public Instruction, North Carolina Board of Nursing, Committee on Allied Health Education, Accreditation of the American Medical Association, and Council on Social Work Education (candidacy status). Enrollment includes 1,026 full-time and 439 part-time students. A faculty of 78 full-time and 12 part-time gives a faculty-student ratio of 1-14. The college offers a special program entitled "Teacher Education for the Deaf and Hard of Hearing". A cooperative education program is available in every major at the school. A semester abroad program is currently being implemented.

Entrance Requirements: Accredited high school graduation or equivalent; preferred completion of 18 units, minimum of 12 academic units including 4 English, 3 mathematics, 2 science, 3 social science, 2 foreign language (encouraged) and 4 electives; SAT or ACT required; $20 application fee; advanced placement, rolling admission, early admission, and delayed admission plans available.

Costs Per Year: $7,795 tuition; $3,600 room and board; $600 student fees.

Collegiate Environment: The college is located in the northern section of Wilson. There are 14 main buildings as well as outdoor athletic facilities. Residence hall facilities are available for 714 men and women. The library contains 169,993 volumes, 560 periodicals and 4,962 microforms and sound recordings. Students from other geographical locations are accepted as well as midyear students. Approximately 80% of students applying for admission are accepted. Financial aid is available for economically disadvantaged students and 90% of the students receive aid.

Community Environment: Bus and train transportation are available. Community facilities include churches of all denominations, a hospital, library, shopping centers, numerous civic and service organizations, a drama theater, and other agricultural facilities. Part-time jobs are available. Recreational parks with swimming pools, golf courses, and a large stadium are located here.

BEAUFORT COUNTY COMMUNITY COLLEGE   (G-15)
P.O. Box 1069
Washington, North Carolina 27889
Tel: (919) 946-6194; Fax: (919) 946-0271

Description: The public, coeducational community college was chartered in 1967 to serve the needs of Beaufort, Hyde, Tyrrell and Washington counties and the surrounding area. It is a constituent of the North Carolina Department of Community Colleges. It is accredited by the Southern Association of Colleges and Schools. A Cooperative Education program is available in Automotive Technology, Agricultural Mechanics Service Technology, Electronics Engineering Technology and Electrical Engineering Technology. Enrollment includes 623 full-time, and 599 part-time and 285 evening students. A faculty of 47 full-time and 8 part-time gives a faculty-student ratio of 1-27.

Entrance Requirements: High school graduation or equivalent: open enrollment policy; placement test required, rolling admission, early admission, early decision, midyear admission, rolling admission, and advanced placement plans available; no application fee.

Costs Per Year: $556.50 tuition; $4,515 out-of-state; $18 student fees.

Collegiate Environment: The college is located on a 67-acre campus six miles east of Washington on Highway 264. The campus includes six buildings. The library contains 25,003 volumes, 1,000 pamphlets, 210 periodicals, 15,674 microforms, and 3,743 audiovisual materials. All applicants are accepted. Scholarships are available and 30 % of students receive some form of financial aid.

Community Environment: Washington is located on the Pamlico River, which affords excellent fishing, boating and water skiing. North Carolina's finest beach areas are only a short distance away. Year-round golf courses and tennis courts are also easily accessible.

BELMONT ABBEY COLLEGE   (N-4)
Belmont, North Carolina 28012
Tel: (704) 825-6665; (800) 523-2355

Description: Founded in 1876 and operated by monks of the Order of St. Benedict, the private college is one of the oldest Catholic institutions in the South. It operates on the semester basis. It is accredited by the Southern Association of Colleges and Schools. Enrollment was 1,038 students recently. A faculty of 53 full-time and 35 part-time gives a faculty-student ratio of 1-17. The college is a member of a consortium that includes 10 colleges in the Charlotte area.

Entrance Requirements: Accredited high school graduation or equivalent; completion of 16 units including 4 English, 3 mathematics, 2 foreign language, 2 science, and 2 social science; SAT or ACT required; $25 application fee; early admission, early decision, rolling admission, delayed admission and advanced placement plans available.

Costs Per Year: $7,664 tuition; $4,070 room and board, $190 student fees; $200 freshman fees.

Collegiate Environment: The 20 college buildings are located on a 650-acre campus. The college is located only 10 miles west of Charlotte and eight miles east of Gastonia. The college library contains a total of 150,000 volumes, pamphlets, periodicals, microforms and sound recordings. Dormitory facilities are provided for 246 men and 288 women. Approximately 85% of students applying for admission are accepted, including midyear students. About 70% of the previous freshman class returned to the college for the sophomore year. Financial aid is available for economically handicapped students and 80% of the students receive aid. Current freshman attained average SAT scores of 428V and 460M. The academic year begins in August.

Community Environment: In the southern Piedmont section of the state, Belmont is a growing textile center. Commercial transportation is available. The community facilities include churches of all denominations, hospitals and health services, a library, YMCA, and shopping centers. Numerous civic and service organizations are active. Hunting and fishing are popular sports in the area as well as all water sports, enjoyed at Lake Wylie. The Belmont Abbey, located here, was the first cathedral abbey in the United States, and is listed in the National Register of Historical Places.

BENNETT COLLEGE   *(F-9)*
900 East Washington Street
Greensboro, North Carolina 27410
Tel: (910) 273-4431; (800) 338-2366; Admissions: (910) 370-8620/8624; Fax: (910) 378-0531

Description: The private college for women was founded in 1873 as a coeducational institution. It was founded through the inspiration of a newly emancipated slave and supported by the Freedmen's Aid and Southern Education Society of the Methodist Episcopal Church. It was reorganized in 1926 as a college for women. The college is accredited by the Southern Association of Colleges and Schools and is a member of the University Senate of the Methodist Church. Bennett offers a variety of enrichment programs which enhance the curriculum. Cooperative Education allows students to alternate classroom study with paid work experience for a semester or more. Special Studies program focuses attention on the underachiever. Bennett holds membership in the Piedmont Independent College Association (PICA) of North Carolina, a program of class exchange for member schools in the area. The college operates on the semester system. Enrollment includes 640 full-time and 15 part-time students. A faculty of 55 full-time and 6 part-time gives a faculty-student ratio of 1-11.

Entrance Requirements: Accredited high school graduation with rank in upper half of graduating class; completion of 16 units including 4 English, 2 mathematics, 1 science, 1 social science, 2 foreign language; SAT or ACT required; early admission, deferred admission, rolling admission and midyear admission available; $20 application fee.

Costs Per Year: $5,600 tuition; $3,095 board and room; $1,030 student fees.

Collegiate Environment: The college is comprised of 34 buildings located on 55 acres and contains a library of 97,000 volumes and dormitory facilities for 608 women. Approximately 70% of students applying for admission are accepted. Students from other geographical locations are accepted as well as midyear students. About 50% of the recent student body graduated in the top half of the high school class, 40% in the top quarter, and 25% in the highest tenth. Almost 75% of the previous freshman class returned to the campus for the sophomore year. Scholarships are available and 85% of the students receive some form of financial aid.

Community Environment: See Greensboro College.

BLADEN COMMUNITY COLLEGE   *(J-12)*
P.O. Box 266
Dublin, North Carolina 28332
Tel: (910) 862-2164; Admissions: (910) 862-2164; Fax: (910) 862-3484

Description: The state-supported community college was established in 1967 and is fully accredited by the Southern Association of Schools and Colleges. It operates on the quarter system and offers two summer sessions. The college offers college transfer, vocational and technical programs and is a member of the American Association of Junior Colleges. Enrollment includes 375 full-time, 250 part-time and 240 evening students. A faculty of 26 full-time and 20 part-time gibves a faculty-student ratio of 1-19.

Entrance Requirements: Open door policy; high school graduation or 16 years of age or older; 16 high school units should include 4 English, 2 mathematics, 2 social science, 1 science; aptitude test required for placement; early decision, rolling admission, midyear admission and delayed admission plans available; no application fee.

Costs Per Year: $556.50 tuition; $4,515 nonresident; $28 student fees.

Collegiate Environment: The college occupies a permanent campus in the Dublin area. The library holdings include 17,000 volumes, 100 periodicals, 1,000 microforms, 1,000 audiovisual materials. There are no dormitory facilities. 95% of applicants are accepted. Students from other geographical areas are accepted. 26 scholarships are available and 35% of students receive some form of financial aid. Classes begin in September. The college awarded 75 diplomas to a graduating class.

Community Environment: Dublin is located 30 miles south of Fayetteville. The principal business is agriculture. Community facilities include 15 churches of various denominations and a public library. Bladen Arts Council frequently sponsors cultural activities in the campus's 1,000-seat auditorium. A golf course, parks, state forest and several lakes provide facilities for excellent fishing and water sports.

BREVARD COLLEGE   *(H-3)*
Brevard, North Carolina 28712
Tel: (704) 884-8300; Fax: (704) 884-3790

Description: The independent, residential junior college is specifically designed for students pursuing a 4-year college degree, offering both bachelor and associate degrees. It was founded in 1853 and is accredited by the Southern Association of Colleges and Schools. It operates on the semester system with one summer term and offers a semester in Austria. Enrollment includes 687 full-time and 42 part-time students. A faculty of 56 full-time and 34 part-time members gives a faculty-student ratio of 1-14.

Entrance Requirements: Accredited high school graduation or equivalent; rank in upper 50% of graduating class; completion of 4 units of English, 2 math, 1 science, 2 social studies; SAT or ACT required; $20 application fee; early admission, early decision, rolling decision, delayed admission, and advanced placement plans available.

Costs Per Year: $6,800 county-resident tuition; $8,050 nonresident; $3,750 room and board; $625 student fees.

Collegiate Environment: The 140-acre campus is situated in the heart of the Blue Ridge Mountains at the entrance to the Pisgah National Forest. The 26 college buildings contain a library of 49,000 volumes, periodicals, microforms, audiovisual materials, and computers. Dormitory facilties are provided for 650 men and women. Approximately 80% of students applying for admission are accepted. Students from other geographical locations are accepted as well as midyear students. 70% of the freshmen returned for the second year. Financial aid is available for all students demonstrating financial need or academic merit.

Community Environment: Brevard, known as the "Land of Waterfalls" is 33 miles southwest of Asheville, NC. The area is the location of the Carl Sandburg home, the Thomas Wolfe Home, and the Brevard Music Center. This popular summer resort is at the entrance of Pisgah National Forest. Community facilities include churches of most major denominations, hospital and many civic and service organizations. Part-time employment is available on and off campus. Recreational activities include camping, biking, backpacking, canoeing, snowskiing, kyacking, and mountain climbing.

CALDWELL COMMUNITY COLLEGE AND TECHNICAL INSTITUTE   *(F-5)*
1000 Hickory Boulevard
Hudson, North Carolina 28638
Tel: (704) 726-2200; Admissions: (704) 726-2230; Fax: (704) 726-2216

Description: The state-supported community college was established in 1964. It is accredited by the Southern Association of Colleges and Schools. Programs of study are primarily vocational-technical. The college grants the Associate degree and diplomas. It operates on the quarter system and offers four summer sessions. Enrollment is 2,938 students. A faculty of 66 full-time and 137 part-time gives a faculty-student ratio of 1-15.

Entrance Requirements: Open door policy; high school graduation or minimum age of 18 years with 20 high school units; Placement tests required.

Costs Per Year: $556.50 tuition; $4,515 tuition for out-of-state students; $21 student fees.

Collegiate Environment: The institute is located on a 78-acre tract of land in Hudson, near the population centers of Lenoir, Granite Falls, and Hickory. The seven institute buildings contain a library of 26,000 volumes. Students from other geographical locations are accepted as well as midyear students. There are no dormitory facilities. Scholarships are availabvle and 30% of the students receive some form of financial aid.

Community Environment: Since more wood furniture is manufactured here than any other place in the South, Lenoir is known as "furniture land." Numerous parks and two recreation centers provide the facilities for relaxation. A number of churches are represented in the community.

CAMPBELL UNIVERSITY   *(H-11)*
Buies Creek, North Carolina 27506
Tel: (800) 334-4111; Fax: (910) 893-1288

Description: This private liberal arts university was founded in 1887 and is supported by the Southern Baptist Convention. The college operates on the semester basis with two summer terms and is accredited by the Southern Association of Colleges and Schools. It is accredited by the American Bar Association and the American Council on Pharmaceutical Education. Army ROTC is available. Recent enrollment includes 5,494 full-time, and 586 part-time undergraduates and 1,005 graduate students. A faculty of 159 full-time and 190 part-time gives a faculty-student ratio of 1-18.

Entrance Requirements: Accredited high school graduation or equivalent; rank in upper 50% of graduating class; completion of 13 units, including 4 English, 3 mathematics, 2 foreign language, 2 science, 2 social science; SAT or ACT required; GMAT or MAT required for graduate school; $15 processing fee; early admission, early decision, delayed admission, rolling admission and advanced placement plans available; $100 application fee credited to account.

Costs Per Year: $8,430 tuition and fees; $3,180 room and board.

Collegiate Environment: The college is located on 850 acres and is comprised of 30 buildings, including a library of 181,170 volumes, 995 periodicals and over 740,311 reels of microfilm. Dormitory facilities are provided for 737 men and 786 women. Students from other geographical locations are accepted as well as midyear students. Approximately 73% of students applying for admission are accepted. Almost 84% of the previous freshman class returned to the college for the sophomore year. Financial assistance is available. There are 569 endowed scholarships over and above the academic scholarship program. 84% of students receive financial aid.

Community Environment: Located 30 miles south of Raleigh where the climate is mild, and 30 miles north of Fayetteville, the community is served by Baptist and United Methodist churches, a community civic club and a full-time campus infirmary. There is a hospital seven miles away. Part-time employment for students is available.

CAPE FEAR COMMUNITY COLLEGE   *(K-13)*
411 N. Front Street
Wilmington, North Carolina 28401
Tel: (919) 251-5100

Description: The state-supported community college was established in 1959. It operates on the four-quarter system, has 1 summer term, and is accredited by the Southern Association of Colleges and Schools. Enrollment includes 1,500 full-time and 1,453 part-time students. A faculty of 60 full-time and 34 part-time gives a faculty-student ratio of 1-31. The Institute offers a high school equivalency program.

Entrance Requirements: Open door policy; School-College ability test required; rolling admission plan available. There is no application fee.

Costs Per Year: $420 tuition; $3,924 for out-of-state students.

Collegiate Environment: The institute is comprised of three buildings located on nine acres. Classes begin in September and midyear students are accepted. Approximately 70% of the previous entering class returned to the institute for a second year of studies. The Institute's library contains 36,000 volumes, 600 periodicals, 7,000 microforms and 500 audiovisual materials. Financial assistance is available for economically handicapped students. About 98% of the applicants are accepted. 90% of the current freshman graduated in the upper half of their high school class, 20% in the top quarter and 30% in the third quarter.

Community Environment: See University of North Carolina - Wilmington.

CARTERET COMMUNITY COLLEGE   *(I-16)*
3505 Arendell St.
Morehead City, North Carolina 28557
Tel: (919) 247-4142

Description: This school was founded in 1963 and operated as a unit of the Wayne Community College until 1968. It is now administered directly under the State Board of Community Colleges as an independent institution of the North Carolina Department of Community Colleges, a statewide system of 58 institutions. It is accredited by the Southern Association of Colleges and Schools and the Committee on Allied Health Education and Accreditation. It grants the Associate degree. It operates on the quarter system and offers one summer session. Enrollment is approximately 1,600 students. A faculty of 31 full-time, 43 part-time gives a faculty-student ratio of 1-14.

Entrance Requirements: High school graduation or equivalent; open enrollment policy; completion of 12 units including 4 English, 2 mathematics, 2 science, and 2 social science; placement examinations required.

Costs Per Year: $545 tuition; $4,515 out-of-state; $12 student fees.

Collegiate Environment: The school is located in facilities completed in December 1972, less than one mile from the center of town on the banks of scenic Bogue Sound. Classes begin in September and midyear students are accepted. The library contains 16,700 volumes, 225 periodicals, 125 microforms, and 606 audiovisual materials. Financial assistance is available for economically handicapped students, and 20% of the students receive aid.

Community Environment: Morehead City is one of the most popular coastal resorts in the state. The $4 million Port Terminal with its 2,600-foot pier affords excellent facilities for oceangoing vessels. Fishing, particularly for menhaden, is an important industry. The Atlantic Beach across Bogue Sound is an excellent 24-mile beach. Recreational facilities are numerous for all kinds of ocean fishing, and for hunting wild ducks and geese.

CATAWBA COLLEGE   *(G-8)*
2300 West Innes Street
Salisbury, North Carolina 28144
Tel: (704) 637-4402; (800) 228-2922; Fax: (704) 637-4444

Description: This private, coeducational, liberal arts college was founded in Newton in 1851 by the German Reformed Church. The college moved to its present location in Salisbury in 1925 and is now affiliated with the United Church of Christ. It endeavors to attract students of good ability and character, and derives strength from Judeo-Christian values. It seeks to sustain a dynamic community of scholars and staff as active co-participants in scholarship and service. The college grants the Bachelor of Arts and Master of Education degrees. The College also serves the public through educational outreach and volunteer service programs for the world community. The college offers academic cooperative programs in forestry with Duke University, and in medical technology and physician's assistant with Bowman Gray School of Medicine of Wake Forest University. The College is accredited by the Southern Association of Colleges and Schools. It opreates on the semester system and offers 2 summer sessions. Enrollment includes 969 full-time and 47 part-time undergraduate students, and 15 graduate students. A faculty of 66 full-time and 19 part-time members give an undergraduate faculty-student ratio of 1-15.

Entrance Requirements: Accredited high school graduation with rank in upper 50% of graduating class; completion of 16 units including 4 English, 2 science, 2 social science and 2 mathematics; SAT with minimum scores of 400V, 400M, or ACT required; early admission, rolling admission, delayed admission and advanced placement plans available; $25 application fee.

Costs Per Year: $9,270; $4,100 room and board.

Collegiate Environment: The college is located on a 210-acre campus in the Piedmont section of North Carolina. The 32 college buildings contain a library of 178,000 volumes, 1,000 pamphlets, 1,150 periodicals, 24,000 microforms and 6,100 sound recordings. Dormitory facilities are provided for 696 students. 82% of applicants are accepted. Students from other geographical locations are accepted as well as midyear students. 70% of the previous freshman class returned to the campus for the sophomore year. 70% of the current freshmen graduated in the top half of the high school class, 41% in the top quarter and 11% in the third quarter. The average SAT scores of the freshmen were 450V, 450M. Financial aid, including merit-based awards, is available.

Community Environment: Salisbury was founded in 1753 and during the year 1781 the city served, at different times, as headquarters for both Cornwallis and Greene, British and patriot generals. Community facilities include numerous churches, a public library, hospitals, and various civic and service organizations. Recreational activities include golf, swimming, fishing, and other sports. Part-time employment is available.

CATAWBA VALLEY COMMUNITY COLLEGE   *(F-6)*
2250 Highway 70 SE
Hickory, North Carolina 28602
Tel: (704) 327-7000

Description: This state-supported community college was established in 1959. It operates on the quarter basis, has 1 summer session, and offers vocational and technical programs. Cooperative education programs are available in all areas except pre-liberal arts. Recent enrollment included approximately 685 men and 772 women full-time and 870 men and 1,348 women part-time. A faculty of 70 full-time and 100 part-time gives a faculty-student ratio of 1-16. The college is accredited by the Southern Association of Colleges and Schools, the Accreditation Board for Engineering and Technology, and the Committee on Allied Health Education and Accreditation.

Entrance Requirements: Open door policy; 16 high school units recommended; rolling admission and advanced placement plans available; no application fee.

Costs Per Year: $742 tuition; $6,020 out-of-state; $24 activity fee.

Collegiate Environment: The campus covers fifty acres of land about four miles east of Hickory. The library contains 32,256 volumes, 185 periodicals, 1,192 microforms, and 3,222 sound recordings. Financial assistance is available for economically handicapped students and 8% of the students receive aid. 95% of the applicants are accepted, including midyear students. About 83% of the freshmen returned to the school for the second year of studies.

Community Environment: See Lenoir Rhyne College.

CENTRAL CAROLINA COMMUNITY COLLEGE   *(G-10)*
1105 Kelly Drive
Sanford, North Carolina 27330
Tel: (919) 775-5401

Description: The public college was established in 1961 and is supervised by the Department of Community Colleges, North Carolina State Board of Education. It operates on the quarter basis with three summer terms. The college is fully accredited by the Southern Association of Colleges and Schools. The college provides programs for vocational-technical education, preparation for employment, education for high school equivalency requirements, and general education for the community. Enrollment includes 3,122 students. A faculty of 189 gives a faculty-student ratio of 1-16.

Entrance Requirements: Open door policy; high school graduation or 18 years of age or older; completion of 18 units including 4 English, 2 mathematics, 2 social studies, 2 science; admissions examination; early decision, midyear admission, early admission, and rolling admission plans available.

Costs Per Year: $742 tuition; $6,020 out-of-state; $28 student fees.

Collegiate Environment: Over 99,000 square feet of classroom, shop, and laboratory space is located on a 32-acre site. Ample equipment, a library of 36,450 volumes, 267 periodicals and 1,043 audiovisual materials and an efficient staff provide training in a variety of programs. Classes begin in September and midyear students are accepted in some programs. About 98% of the applicants are accepted. 50% of students receive some form of financial aid.

Community Environment: Sanford, known as the brick capital of the nation, is nearly the exact center of North Carolina with all forms of commercial transportation available. Over 50 manufacturing and processing firms are located here. Modern shopping facilities and the new privately owned hospital serve the community. Recreational opportunities are unparalleled at nearby Cape Fear and the resort areas of Pinehurst and Southern Pines.

CENTRAL PIEDMONT COMMUNITY COLLEGE   *(H-7)*
P.O. Box 35009
Charlotte, North Carolina 28235
Tel: (704) 342-6719

Description: This publicly supported college was established as part of the statewide community college system in 1963. The first program offered involved curricula in career education. The first liberal arts curricula for college transfer were offered in 1964. Fully accredited by the Southern Association of Colleges and Schools, the college is also accredited by the Accreditation Board for Engineering and Technology, the American Dental Association and the American Physical Therapy Association. The college operates on the quarter system and offers two summer sessions. Recent full-time enrollment was 2,015 men and 2,076 women. Part-time enrollment was 5,026 men and 7,325 women. A faculty of 1,215 gives a student-faculty ratio of 1-14.

Entrance Requirements: Open door policy; high school graduation or equivalent required for degree programs; rolling admission available; no application fee.

Costs Per Year: $483 tuition; $4,575 out-of-state; $15 student fees.

Collegiate Environment: The campus is situated in downtown Charlotte and is convenient to public transportation facilities. The campus of 33 acres includes a complex containing a library of 76,039 volumes, 8,344 pamphlets, 433 periodicals, 29,979 microforms and 2,004 sound recordings, in addition to 123 classrooms, 59 modern laboratories and specialized shop areas. The college is organized into three instructional divisions that include the Transfer Division, the Trade and Technical Division, and the Adult Continuing Education Division. Financial assistance is available for economically handicapped students.

Community Environment: See Queens College.

CHOWAN COLLEGE   *(D-15)*
Pine Drive
Murfreesboro, North Carolina 27855
Tel: (919) 398-4101; (800) 488-4101; Fax: (919) 398-1190

Description: Chowan is a four-year private college related to the North Carolina Baptist State Convention and the second oldest, founded in 1848, of North Carolina's six Baptist colleges. It is accredited by the Southern Association of Colleges and Schools and the Association of Indepentdent Colleges and Schools. It operates on the semester system and offers one summer term. Enrollment is 459 men and 354 women. A faculty of 58 full-time and 8 part-time provides a faculty-student ratio of 1-14.

Entrance Requirements: High school graduation or equivalent; completion of 18 units including 4 English, 2 mathematics, 1 science, 2 social science and 6 electives; advanced placement, rolling admission, early decision, and early admission and midyear admission plans available. $20 application fee.

Costs Per Year: $9,200 tuition; $3,660 room and board.

Collegiate Environment: The main campus and athletic fields are a part of a tract of 360 acres of land. The college buildings include a library of 92,000 volumes, 702 periodicals, 23,575 microforms and 500 sound recordings. Dormitory facilities are available for 500 men, 500 women. All students under 23 years of age must live on campus. Students from other geographical locations are accepted as are midyear students. Approximately 70% of students applying for admission are accepted. Scholarships are available and 80% of the students receive some form of aid.

Community Environment: In the northeastern section of North Carolina, Murfreesboro is the location of several historical sites. Community facilities include several churches. A hospital and commercial transportation are available in nearby towns. Hunting, fishing, boating, and water skiing are some of the recreational activities.

CLEVELAND COMMUNITY COLLEGE *(H-5)*
137 S. Post Road
Shelby, North Carolina 28150
Tel: (704) 484-4000; Admissions: (704) 484-4081; Fax: (704) 484-4036

Description: The public College is one of the institutions in the Department of Community Colleges of North Carolina. It operates on the four-quarter system and offers two summer sessions. It is accredited by the Southern Association of Colleges and Schools. Enrollment is 1,740 students. A faculty of 41 full-time and 52 part-time gives a faculty-student ratio of 1-18.

Entrance Requirements: Open enrollment policy; high school graduation or equivalent; minimum 18 years of age; rolling admission, early admission, and advanced placement plans available.

Costs Per Year: $583 tuition; $4,542 out-of-state; $32 student fees.

Collegiate Environment: The college is located on 43 acres of land. The library contains 26,482 volumes, 205 periodicals, and 4,868 sound recordings. 98% of students applying for admission are accepted. Classes begin in September and midyear students are accepted. About 70% of the previous entering class returned to the campus for a second year of studies. Financial aid is available and 15% of the students receive some form of assistance.

Community Environment: Shelby is the county seat for Cleveland County and is a diversified manufacturing area. The principal businesses are mercantile, textiles, and machine parts. The community facilities include 35 churches. A complete city park and a large lake provide the area with recreation facilities.

COASTAL CAROLINA COMMUNITY COLLEGE *(I-14)*
444 Western Blvd
Jacksonville, North Carolina 28546-6877
Tel: (919) 938-6250

Description: The public community college was established in 1964. It is accredited by the Southern Association of Colleges and Schools. It operates on the quarter system and offers two summer sessions. Courses offered range from 9 to 21 months in length and lead to a diploma or the Associate degree. A limited number of classes are available at the Marine Corps Base, Camp Lejeune and Marine Corps Air Station, New River. Enrollment is 1,860 full-time and 1,730 part-time students. A faculty of 110 full-time and 45 part-time gives a faculty-student ratio of 1-23.

Entrance Requirements: High school graduation or equivalent; open enrollment policy; completion of 18 units including 4 English, 2 mathematics, 2 science, and 2 social science; midyear admission and rolling admission plans available.

Costs Per Year: $556.50 tuition; $4,515 out-of-state; $21 student fees.

Collegiate Environment: The institute is located on 65 acres and contains ten buildings. Students from other geographical locations are accepted as well as midyear students. All students applying for admission are accepted. The library contains 38,000 volumes, 250 periodicals, 200 microforms, 3,500 sound recordings, 1,500 videotapes, and 1,500 16mm films. 279 scholarships are available, including 186 for freshmen. 25% of the students receive some form of financial aid. The college awarded 112 Diplomas and 295 Associate degrees to a recent graduating class.

Community Environment: The principal business of Jacksonville are marine-related industries, military support services, and wood products. Railroads serve the area. Thirty churches of various faiths, one library and numerous historical sites are within the community. Hunting and fishing are excellent, and there are also parks are in the area for other recreational activities.

COLLEGE OF THE ALBEMARLE *(E-17)*
P.O. Box 2327
Elizabeth City, North Carolina 27906-2327
Tel: (919) 335-0821; Fax: (919) 335-0211

Description: College of The Albemarle was the first college in the state chartered under the Community College Act, 1957. It is an accredited member of the North Carolina State Board of Community Colleges, and the Southern Association of Colleges and Schools. It offers college-transfer programs, vocational-technical programs, and adult education and community service programs. It operates on a four-quarter system and offers three summer sessions. Enrollment is 975 full-time and 1,063 part-time students. A faculty of 55 full-time and 62 part-time gives a faculty-student ratio of 1-18.

Entrance Requirements: High school graduation or equivalent; open enrollment policy; placement exam required; recommended completion of 20 units, 4 English, 3 mathematics, 3 science, 2 social science, and 7 electives; advanced placement plans available.

Costs Per Year: $556.50 tuition; $4,515 nonresident; $28 activity fee.

Collegiate Environment: The college occupies a new campus with four buildings, including a learning center and a fine arts center. The library contains 49,912 volumes, 250 periodicals, 6,000 microfiche and 4,500 audiovisual materials. Almost all students applying for admission are accepted, including midyear students. Financial aid is available for economically handicapped students and approximately one-third of the students receive aid. 150 private scholarships are available for qualified recipients, 148 of which are for freshmen.

Community Environment: Elizabeth City is the home of a variety of manufacturing firms and serves as a shipping center for a large agricultural area producing corn, soybeans, potatoes, small grains, cabbage and other vegetables. All forms of commercial transportation are available. The Pasquotant River and nearby waterways provide for water sports, and deep sea and surf fishing on the Atlantic Ocean 40 miles away. The Dismal Swamp is a paradise for hunters, fishermen and naturalists. Big and small game include black bears, deer, foxes and many small mammals. Some of the historic points of interest are the Shiloh Baptist Church, the Old Brick House, Hall Creek Church, Winslow and Bayfield Home, the site of Culpepper's Rebellion in 1677-the first open rebellion against the king. Kitty Hawk, site of the Wright brothers' first powered flight, and Manteo, location of the first attempted English Colony, are nearby.

Branch Campuses: Dare County campus is located in historic Manteo, North Carolina, on the beautiful outer banks coast. Enrollment at the Dare campus is 118 full-time and 323 part-time.

CRAVEN COMMUNITY COLLEGE *(H-15)*
P.O. Box 885
New Bern, North Carolina 28560
Tel: (919) 638-4131; Fax: (919) 638-4232

Description: The public institute began operation in 1965 as a branch of Lenoir County Community College. It became an independent institution by 1967 and offers a variety of programs in technical-vocational, general, and community service fields. It operates on the four-quarter system and offers two summer sessions. It is accredited by the Southern Association of Colleges and Schools. Enrollment is 1,016 full-time and 1,266 part-time students. A faculty of 62 full-time and 170 part-time gives a faculty-student ratio of 1-10.

Entrance Requirements: High school graduation or equivalent for most programs; at least one year of high school education or equivalent required for some one-year vocational programs; entrance examination; open enrollment policy; rolling admission plan available.

Costs Per Year: $477 tuition; $3,870 out-of-state; $27 student fees; based on 12 quarter hours/quarter for 3 quarters.

Collegiate Environment: The college is operating in permanent facilities. Classes begin in September and midyear students are accepted for most programs. Students from other geographical locations are accepted. The library contains 27,409 volumes, 290 periodicals, 41,282 microforms and 2,753 sound recordings. Financial assistance is available for economically disadvantaged students and 40% of the students receive aid. 99% of the applicants are accepted. 70% of the current freshman graduated in the top half of the high school class, 20% in the top quarter and 20% in the third quarter.

Community Environment: New Bern, one of the oldest towns in the state, is interesting for its old buildings and many historical sites and markers. The first Provincial Congresses met here in 1774 and 1775. Some points of interest are the Christ Church, Federal Building, First Presbyterian Church and the Tryon Palace Restoration.

DAVIDSON COLLEGE *(L-5)*
P.O. Box 1737
Davidson, North Carolina 28036
Tel: (704) 892-2000; (800) 768-0380; Fax: (704) 892-2016

Description: This private liberal arts college is a highly selective institution of higher learning established by the Presbyterians of North Carolina in 1837. It is accredited by the Southern Association of Colleges and Schools. The college offers a junior year Foreign Study Plan in Wurzburg, Germany, and Montpellier, France, as well as one-semester programs in England, Greece, India, Italy, Mexico, and Spain. It operates on the semester system. Enrollment includes 854 men, 755 women full-time, and 5 part-time students. A faculty of 130 full-time and 10 part-time gives a faculty-student ratio of 1-11. Army ROTC is offered.

Entrance Requirements: High school graduation; completion of 16 units including 4 English, 3-4 mathematics, 2 foreign language, 2 history, and 2-4 science; SAT or ACT required; early decision, early admission, deferred admission, and advanced placement plans available; $45 application fee.

Costs Per Year: $16,850 tuition; $5,070 room and board; $614 student fees.

Collegiate Environment: The 496-acre campus of the college contains a library of 407,402 volumes, 2,672 periodicals and 376,064 microforms and government documents. Dormitory facilities are available for 1,461 students. Other students live off-campus in town. The college welcomes students from diverse geographical locations and approximately 36% of applicants are accepted. Financial aid is available, and about 60% of students receive some form of financial assistance.

Community Environment: The town of Davidson has grown around Davidson College. The cultural, social and religious life of the community revolves around the college. Davidson is twenty minutes north of Charlotte, NC, and offers students the advantages of that city's services, amenities, and recreational opportunities.

DAVIDSON COUNTY COMMUNITY COLLEGE *(F-8)*
P.O. Box 1287
Lexington, North Carolina 27293
Tel: (704) 249-8186; (800) 501-3222; Fax: (704) 249-0379

Description: The public community college is a two-year institution under the administration of the North Carolina Department of Community Colleges. It offers a two-year college transfer curriculum, general adult continuing education courses, and technical-vocational programs. It operates on a four-quarter system with 2 summer terms. It is accredited by the Southern Association of Colleges and Schools. Enrollment is 1,120 full-time and 1,163 part-time students. A faculty of 66 full-time and 83 part-time gives a faculty-student ratio of 1-22.

Entrance Requirements: Open enrollment policy; minimum age of 18 years with evidence of ability to benefit from enrollment; placement test required; rolling admission and advanced placement plans available.

Costs Per Year: $557 tuition; $4,515 out-of-state; $9 student fees.

Collegiate Environment: The beautiful, wooded, 84-acre campus, valued at more than twelve million dollars, is located halfway between Lexington and Thomasville on Rt. 29/70. Among its buildings are the Grady Edward Love Learning Resources Center, the Dr. Edgar Holton Reich Nursing Center, the Doak and Agnes Finch Building, the Multi-Purpose Building, the William Taylor Sinclair Building, the Felix Otis Gee Building, the Public Safety Services Building, the Classroom and Administrative Building, and the Student Center. The library contains 51,035 volumes, 1,600 pamphlets, 291 periodicals, 11,529 microforms and 3,423 sound recordings. About 99% of the applicants are accepted. Midyear students are accepted and 66% of the previous entering class returned to this campus for the second year of studies. Financial aid is available for eligible students and there are many scholarships available.

Community Environment: Lexington is a suburban community located approximately 25 miles south of Greensboro, N.C. Industry here includes furniture, textiles, apparel, electronics, and food processing. Bus and train transportation are available. A YMCA, churches of all major denominations, a library, hospital, and numerous civic and service organizations serve the community. There are job opportunities for students. High Rock Lake about 12 miles south of Lexington offers boating, fishing, swimming and picnicking.

DUKE UNIVERSITY *(F-11)*
Durham, North Carolina 27706
Tel: (919) 684-3214; Fax: (919) 681-8941

Description: Duke University was founded in 1838 in Randolph County, North Carolina, as Union Academy. It was reorganized in 1859 as Trinity College, a small liberal arts college. In 1892 it moved to Durham and in 1924, under terms of The Duke Endowment, Trinity College became Duke University. It is accredited by the Southern Association of Colleges and Schools and professionally by respective accrediting organizations. Today the University is comprised of two undergraduate schools: Trinity College of Arts and Sciences and the School of Engineering; and a number of graduate and professional schools including the Graduate School, Divinity School, School of Forestry and Environmental Studies, School of Medicine, School of Law, School of Nursing, and the Fuqua School of Business. The University operates on the semester system and offers two summer sessions. Enrollment includes 6,085 full-time and 59 part-time undergraduates and 5,208 graduate students. A faculty of 1,661 gives a faculty-student ratio of 1-11. The University offers Army, Navy and Air Force ROTC programs.

Entrance Requirements: Completion of 15 college preparatory units (4 years of English; at least 3 of mathematics, natural science, and a foreign language; and 2 years of social studies); SAT and 3 Achievement Tests or ACT are required for admission; early decision plan, delayed admission, and advanced placement program available. Baccalaureate degree (or the equivalent) from an accredited institution and GRE required for Graduate School. $50 application fee.

Costs Per Year: $19,500 tuition-Trinity College; $6,320 room and board; $495 fees. Tuition varies for graduate schools and departments.

Collegiate Environment: Undergraduates admitted as first-year students are guaranteed four years of on-campus housing. The University provides classrooms and housing for undergraduates on both East and West Campuses, and some housing on North Campus and in the Central Campus Apartments. Living units provide the focus for much of the social activity on campus, and dormitories differ in nature, providing a variety of residence styles for all students. Some housing is available for graduate students in the Central Campus Apartments and Town House Apartments. Normal housing capacity accommodates 6,340 students. Library holdings include 4,338,000 volumes. 33% of applicants are accepted. Students come from all 50 states and about 80 foreign countries. Approximately 90% of the recent undergraduate student body graduated in the top 10% of their secondary school classes. The admissions process is "need blind," and Duke is committed to meeting 100% of the demonstrated need of each admitted student. A limited number of merit scholarships are also available.

Community Environment: Durham, North Carolina, a city of about 200,000 people, is approximately 250 miles south of Washington, D.C. Durham and nearby Raleigh and Chapel Hill constitute the three points of what is known as the Research Triangle, one of the nation's foremost centers for research-oriented industries and government, research, and regulatory agencies. Two major interstates and the Raleigh-Durham International Airport (a 20-minute drive from campus) make Durham easily accessible from almost anywhere in the United States. Nationally known hospitals and clinics, including the Duke University Medical Center, make Durham a center for medicine. Other community facilities include numerous churches, museums, parks, shopping areas, an arts center, and major civic and service organizations. Both beaches and mountains are within a three-hour drive.

Branch Campuses: The Duke University Marine Laboratory, located on a small island near the coastal town of Beaufort, North Carolina, offers undergraduates the opportunity to study biochemistry, ecology, developmental biology, geology, oceanography, physiology, and systemics in a marine setting. Facilities at the Marine Laboratory include dormitories, a dining hall, laboratories, classrooms, a library, and a 135-foot research vessel.

DURHAM TECHNICAL COMMUNITY COLLEGE   *(F-11)*
1637 Lawson Street
Durham, North Carolina 27703
Tel: (919) 598-9222; Admissions: (919) 598-9224

Description: The public community college was established in 1961. It is fully accredited by the Southern Association of Colleges and Schools and by the North Carolina State Department of Community Colleges. The College grants the Associate degree and diplomas. It operates on the quarter system and offers one summer session. Enrollment includes 1,443 full-time and 3,416 part-time students. A faculty of 113 full-time and 297 part-time gives a faculty-student ratio of 1-12.

Entrance Requirements: High school graduation and completion of 16 college-preparatory units required for college-parallel programs; open enrollment policy; placement examinations required; rolling admission and midyear admission plans available.

Costs Per Year: $556.50 ($185.50/quarter) resident tuition; $4,515 ($1,505/quarter) nonresident.

Collegiate Environment: The college is located on 60 acres and is comprised of 7 buildings which contain a library of 33,024 volumes. Approximately 95% of students applying for admission are accepted, including midyear students. Students from other geographical locations are accepted and 70% of the previous freshman class return to this campus for their second year. 50% of the students receive some form of financial aid.

Community Environment: See Duke University.

EAST CAROLINA UNIVERSITY   *(G-14)*
East Fifth Street
Greenville, North Carolina 27858-4553
Tel: (919) 328-6640; Fax: (919) 328-6945

Description: The state university is accredited by the Southern Association of Colleges and Schools and respective professional and educational institutions. It was founded in 1907 as a two-year teacher training institution. By 1920 it offered a four-year teacher education curriculum and was authorized to award the Master of Arts degree in 1929. By 1960 the college had become the state's third largest institution of higher learning and the General Assembly of North Carolina voted to elevate the college to the status of university in 1967. Today it is comprised of the College of Arts and Sciences, School of Allied Health, School of Art, School of Social Work, School of Business, School of Education, School of Human Environmental Sciences, School of Medicine, School of Music, School of Nursing, School of Technology, Graduate School, General College, Division of Continuing Education, Library Services, Health Science Library, Center for Leadership Development, International Studies Program, Honors Program, Gerontology Program, Cooperative Education, and Institute for Coastal and Marine Resources. It operates on the semester system and offers two summer sessions as well as Air Force and Army ROTC programs. Recent enrollment included 7,692 men and 9,988 women. A faculty of 1,188 gives a faculty-student ratio of 1-15.

Entrance Requirements: Minimum age of 16 by date of intended registration. Accredited high school graduation; completion of 20 units including 4 English, 3 mathematics, 3 science, 2 social science, 2 foreign language (recommended); 6 electives, SAT or ACT required. GRE or GMAT required for graduate programs. TOEFL or foreign students; satisfactory health certificate; early admission, early dicision, midyear admission, rolling admission, advanced placement and credit, and placement testing available, $35 application fee.

Costs Per Year: $764 tuition; $7,248 out-of-state students; $3,250 room and board; $793 student fees.

Collegiate Environment: The campus of the university, originally extending a few blocks along one of the main streets of Greenville and containing only six buildings, now encompasses approximately 450 acres on which are located over 90 structures devoted to classrooms, housing, and supporting activities. The library contains 996,312 volumes, 7,664 current serial subscriptions, and 277,086 microforms. Fraternities provide housing for 189 men, sororities for 165 women. Dormitories house 5,812 students and have extensive adapta-

tions to accommodate handicapped students. Numerous social fraternities and sororities are located at the campus as well as other student organizations. Students from various geographical locations are accepted as well as midyear students. 70% of applicants were accepted. About 93% of the current freshman graduated in the top half of high school class. Approximately 77% of the previous freshman class returned to the university for the sophomore year. The average SAT scores of the current freshman were 426 verbal and 474 math. Financial aid is available for economically disadvantaged students and about 41% of the students receive aid.

Community Environment: Greenville is one of the largest bright-leaf tobacco markets in the world; also, an agricultural market and wholesale trading center. The climate is mild, the mean annual temperature being 61 degrees. There are churches of all major denominations, a major hospital, a community art center, one library, and various civic and service organizations in the community. Employment opportunities are good. A United States Information Agency's Voice of America transmitting station is nearby.

EDGECOMBE COMMUNITY COLLEGE   *(F-14)*
2009 West Wilson St.
Tarboro, North Carolina 27886
Tel: (919) 823-5166

Description: This public technical college was established in 1968. It operates on the four-quarter system and offers one summer session. Enrollment includes 1,822 full-time and 1,150 part-time and 539 evening students. A faculty of 75 full-time and 120 part-time gives a faculty-student ratio of 1-15. The College is a member of the North Carolina Department of Community Colleges and is fully accredited by the Southern Association of Colleges and Schools, American Medical Association and the National League for Nursing.

Entrance Requirements: Open enrollment policy; completion of 16 units, including 4 English, 1 math, 1 science, and 1 social science; rolling admission, non-graduates must be 18 years or older.

Costs Per Year: $556.50 tuition; $4,533 out-of-state tuition; $18 fees.

Collegiate Environment: The college is comprised of 6 buildings and two campuses located on 90 acres. The library contains 47,000 volumes, 330 periodicals, 500 microforms, and 3,200 audiovisual materials. About 90% of students applying for admission are accepted, including midyear students, and 65% return for the second year. 420 scholarships are available, including 185 for freshmen. 65% of the students receive some form of financial aid. The academic year begins in September.

Community Environment: See North Carolina Wesleyan College.

ELIZABETH CITY STATE UNIVERSITY   *(E-17)*
1704 Weeksville Rd.
Elizabeth City, North Carolina 27909
Tel: (919) 335-3305

Description: The state university was established in 1891 as a normal school and became a four-year institution in 1937. It operates on the semester system and recently enrolled 2,019 students. It also offers 1 summer term and is accredited by the Southern Association of Colleges and Schools. Offers a cooperative education plan, Army ROTC program, a general studies division and continuing education and independent study.

Entrance Requirements: Accredited high school graduation or equivalent; completion of 16 units including 4 English, 3 mathematics, 3 science, 2 social science; SAT, ACT required $15 application fee.

Costs Per Year: $1,360 tuition; $6,378 tuition for out-of-state students, (fees are included with tuition); $3,272 board and room.

Collegiate Environment: The campus comprises 160 acres and contains a library of 116,647 volumes and dormitory facilities for 1,000 students. Eight national fraternities and sororities have chapters on the campus as well as several other social groups. Students from other geographical locations are accepted and more than 51% of students applying for admission are accepted. Classes begin in September and midyear students are accepted. Financial aid is available for economically handicapped students and 90% of the recent freshman class received some form of aid.

Community Environment: See College of the Albemarle.

ELON COLLEGE   *(E-10)*
2700 Campus Box
Elon College, North Carolina 27244
Tel: (919) 584-2370; (800) 334-8448; Fax: (919) 538-3986

Description: The private liberal arts college was established in 1889 and affiliated with the United Church of Christ. It is accredited by the Southern Association of Colleges and Schools. It operates on the 4-1-4 system and offers one five-week undergraduate summer session and two graduate summer sessions. An Army ROTC program is available. Enrollment includes 3,115 full-time and 201 part-time undergraduates and 180 graduate students. A faculty of 140 full-time and 78 part-time gives an undergraduate faculty-student ratio of 1-17.

Entrance Requirements: High school graduation or equivalent; completion of 16 units including 4 English, 3 mathematics, 2 science, 2 foreign language, and 2 social science; SAT or ACT required; $25 application fee; early decision, advanced placement, rolling admission, and deferred admission plans available.

Costs Per Year: $9,100 tuition; $3,883 room and board; $150 student fees.

Collegiate Environment: The 330-acre campus is located four miles west of Burlington, 17 miles east of Greensboro, and 60 miles west of Raleigh. The college buildings include a library of approximately 185,915 volumes, dormitory facilities for 800 men and 1,060 women, and apartments for 190. Elon's student body consists of representatives from 38 states and 20 countries. Approximately 70% of students applying for admission are accepted. About 80% of the previous freshman class returned to the campus for the sophomore year. Financial aid is available for economically disadvantaged students and 58% of the students receive some form of financial assistance. Numerous loans, grants, and scholarships are available. The average SAT scores of the freshmen were 444V and 495M.

Community Environment: See Alamance Community College.

FAYETTEVILLE STATE UNIVERSITY   *(H-11)*
1200 Murchison Road
Fayetteville, North Carolina 28301-4298
Tel: (919) 486-1141

Description: Fayetteville State University, a "constituent institution" of the University of North Carolina since 1972, is accredited by the Southern Association of Colleges and Schools. It operates on the semester system and offers two summer sessions. Enrollment is 4,109 full-time and and part-time students with a faculty of 200. Air Force ROTC is available.

Entrance Requirements: A total of 16 high school units is required; ACT or SAT required; rolling admission plan available; $20 application fee.

Costs Per Year: $1,400 tuition; $7,884 out-of-state; $2,550 room and board.

Collegiate Environment: The college is comprised of 41 buildings located on 156 acres. The library houses over 174,971 volumes and dormitory facilities are provided for 388 men and 588 women. Students from other geographical locations are admitted as well as midyear students. There are scholarships offered annually and approximately 80% of the students receive some form of aid. A new $8.5 million library provides stack space for over 350,000 volumes.

Community Environment: The "All-America City" of Fayetteville is located in Cumberland County with a metropolitan population of 285,299. It is near three of the most heavily traveled North-South Highways: US 301, US 401 and I-95. Fayetteville is the home of Pope Air Force Base and Fort Bragg, one of America's largest and most important military installations. It is the fourth largest urban population center in the state and one of the ten fastest growing counties in the southern states. Agriculture has contributed significantly to the area's economic growth and development.

FAYETTEVILLE TECHNICAL COMMUNITY COLLEGE   *(H-11)*
2201 Hull Road
P.O. Box 35236
Fayetteville, North Carolina 28303-0236
Tel: (910) 678-8473; Fax: (910) 678-8407

Description: The public technical college began in 1961 as the Fayetteville Area Industrial Education Center. It was placed under the administration of the newly created Department of Community Colleges in 1963. It is accredited by the Southern Association of Colleges and Schools and by several professional accrediting institutions. The college operates on a quarter system and offers two summer sessions. Enrollment is 3,504 full-time and 3,903 part-time students. A faculty of 198 full-time and 207 part-time gives a faculty-student ratio of 1-12. A Cooperative Education program is available.

Entrance Requirements: Open door policy; high school graduation or equivalent; some curricula have additional admission requirements; ACT, ASSET required for degree, diploma and most certificate programs; early decision, delayed admission, midyear admission and rolling admission plans available.

Costs Per Year: $556.50 state-resident tuition; $4,515 out-of-state; $12 student fees; $600 approximate additional expense for books, equipment, tools, etc.

Collegiate Environment: The college is located on a 111-acre campus. The campus is comprised of 25 buildings and contains a library of 53,525 volumes, 340 periodicals, 4,643 microforms, and 2,353 audiovisual materials. Entry into many of the programs is available on a quarterly basis. Financial aid is available for students who qualify according to federal guidelines.

Community Environment: See Fayetteville State University.

FORSYTH TECHNICAL COMMUNITY COLLEGE   *(E-8)*
2100 Silas Creek Parkway
Winston-Salem, North Carolina 27103
Tel: (919) 723-0371 x253; Fax: (910) 761-2399

Description: The technical institute was founded in 1960 and became a member institution of the Department of Community Colleges of North Carolina in 1963. It is accredited by the Southern Association of Colleges and Schools. Programs are professionally accredited by the Accreditation Board for Engineering and Technology and the Committee on Allied Health Education and Accreditation. The college grants the Associate degree. It operates on the quarter system. Enrollment inlcudes 4,947 full-time and 3,263 part-time students. A faculty of 225 full-time and 210 part-time gives a faculty-student ratio of 1-20.

Entrance Requirements: Open door policy; high school graduation or equivalent required for degree programs; non-high school graduates 18 years or older may be admitted to other programs; S.A.T. with minimum score of 350 verbal and 350 math, or ACT required; completion of 19 units including 4 English, 2 Mathematics, 1 Science, 2 Social Science recommended; rolling admission, early decision, and early admission plans available.

Costs Per Year: $225 tuition; $2,106 for out-of-state students; $6 student fees.

Collegiate Environment: The 6 institute buildings are located on 20 acres and contain a library of 36,941 volumes, 334 periodicals, 54 microforms and 3,869 audio visual materials. Approximately 95% of students applying for admission are accepted, including midyear students. Classes begin in August and 59% of the previous entering class returned to the institute for a second year of studies. About 50% of the current freshman graduated in the top half of their high school class, 15% in the top quarter and 35% in the third quarter. Financial assistance is available. 30% of students receive some form of financial aid.

Community Environment: See Wake Forest University.

GARDNER-WEBB COLLEGE   *(N-1)*
P.O. Box 912
Boiling Springs, North Carolina 28017
Tel: (704) 434-2361

Description: The private, coeducational college is supported by the Baptist State Convention of North Carolina. It is accredited by the

Southern Association of Colleges and Schools. The college began as a high school in 1905 and has offered a two-year program leading to the Associate in Arts degree since 1948. The college now offers Bachelors programs and a Master of Arts program in Education. The college operates on the semester basis and offers two summer sessions. Enrollment includes 2,330 undergraduate and graduate students. It recently enrolled 723 men and 791 women full-time and 105 men and 314 women part-time. It also offers two summer terms. There is a cooperating plan in medical technology with Bowman School of Medicine and Charlotte Memorial Hospital.

Entrance Requirements: Accredited high school graduation or equivalent; completion of 16 college-preparatory units; including 4 English, 3 mathematics, 2 foreign language, 1 science, 2 social science; SAT required; early admission, rolling admission, midyear admission and advanced placement programs available. $20 application fee.

Costs Per Year: $8,180 tuition; $4,270 board and room.

Collegiate Environment: Approximately 200 acres of land and 30 buildings comprise the physical equipment of the college. The library contains over 150,000 volumes. Dormitories can accommodate 1,000 students. Approximately 79% of students applying for admission are accepted. Students from other geographical locations are admitted as well as midyear students. The average test scores of entering freshmen were SAT 445 verbal, 420 math, and ACT 21 composite. There are 696 scholarships offered and 323 are available to freshman. 66% of the students receive some form of aid. Recently the college awarded 15 Associate and 262 Bachelor degrees.

Community Environment: Boiling Springs is located within the noted thermal belt; bus transportation is within five miles; three major railroad lines are within 10 miles; nearest airport is Charlotte, N.C., 50 miles. The community has access to the indoor swimming pool at the college, observatory, theatre, football stadium, gymnasium and the many cultural arts and entertainment programs at the college. Shopping facilities are good, other community facilities include United Methodist and Baptist churches, and in nearby Shelby, churches of most major denominations, plus numerous civic and service organizations. Part-time employment opportunities are good.

GASTON COLLEGE *(H-6)*
201 Hwy. 321 South
Dallas, North Carolina 28034
Tel: (704) 922-6200; Fax: (704) 922-6440

Description: The public junior college was established in 1963 and is one of the institutions in the department of Community Colleges of North Carolina. It is comprised of an Engineering Technologies Division; Liberal Arts (College-parallel) Division; Business, Computer Science & Public Service Division; Allied Health Division; Trade & Industrial Division; and Continuing Education Division. The enrollment is 1,943 full-time and 2,104 part-time with a faculty of 101 full-time and 206 part-time, giving a faculty-student ratio of 1-15. The college operates on the quarter system and is accredited by the Southern Association of Colleges and Schools. There are two summer sessions.

Entrance Requirements: High school graduation or equivalent required for degree programs; open enrollment policy; ACT or ASSET required for placement; rolling admission and midyear admissions plans available.

Costs Per Year: $555 tuition; $4,515 out-of-state students; $30 student fees.

Collegiate Environment: The college is located on 165 acres and is comprised of ten buildings which include a library of 44,898 volumes, 250 periodicals, 9,113 microforms and 3,362 sound recordings. Students from other geographical locations are admitted as well as midyear students. Ninety-nine percent of the applicants are accepted. Financial aid is available and 72% of the students receive some form of financial aid.

Community Environment: The 140 textile plants of Gaston County, 59 of which are in Gastonia, manufacture more than 80 percent of the fine combed cotton yarn made in the United States. Gastonia is an important industrial city of the South. Railroads serve the area with the Charlotte Airport 15 miles away. Community facilities include numerous churches, hospitals, a public library, and a number of civic and service organizations. Rankin Lake is the city's natural reservoir.

Adjoining it is a public park that provides a museum and planetarium as well as facilities for golfing, swimming, boating, fishing, and tennis. The Atlantic Coast is within a five-hour drive.

Branch Campuses: 1 Timken Drive, Lincolnton, NC 28092

GREENSBORO COLLEGE *(F-9)*
815 West Market Street
Greensboro, North Carolina 27401-1875
Tel: (919) 272-7102; (800) 346-8226; Fax: (919) 271-6634

Description: This educational institution is a private coeducational senior college affiliated with the Methodist Church. It was originally chartered in 1838. It employs the semester system. The college also offers two summer terms and is accredited by the Southern Association of Colleges and Schools. Greensboro College participates in two consortia with neighboring colleges and universities, thus expanding educational opportunities for students while maintaining a small college personal atmosphere. Enrollment includes 756 full-time and 216 part-time students. The faculty consists of 45 full-time and 34 part-time members. The faculty-student ratio is 1-14.

Entrance Requirements: Accredited high school graduation or equivalent; completion of 16 units including 4 English, 2 mathematics, 1 science, 1 history, and 10 additional units from social sciences, natural sciences or foreign languages, etc. SAT or ACT required; early admission, early decision, rolling admission, delayed admission and advanced placement plans available. $20 application fee.

Costs Per Year: $7,200 tuition; $3,500 board and room.

Collegiate Environment: The college occupies a campus of 30 acres near the heart of the city. Its 16 buildings include a library of 90,000 volumes, 322 periodicals, 2,000 microforms, and 1,760 audiovisual materials. Dormitory facilities are available for 521 men and women. Approximately 75% of students applying for admission are accepted. About 74% of the previous freshman class returned to this campus for the sophomore year. Financial aid is available for economically disadvantaged students and academic scholarships are offered. 85% of students receive financial aid.

Community Environment: Greensboro was named for General Nathanael Greene, hero of the Battle of Guilford Courthouse. Textiles are the predominant industry along with the manufacture of cigarettes. The War Memorial Auditorium and Coliseum provides one of the state's finest facilities for conventions, exhibitions, sports events, and shows. Recreation facilities include golf courses, swimming pools, and tennis courts. Part-time employment is available. Points of interest are the Greensboro Historical Museum and on the site of O. Henry's birthplace.

GUILFORD COLLEGE *(F-9)*
5800 West Friendly Avenue
Greensboro, North Carolina 27410
Tel: (910) 316-2000; (800) 992-7759; Admissions: (910) 316-2100; Fax: (919) 316-2954

Description: Guilford College is a private liberal arts institution founded in 1837 by the Society of Friends (Quakers). It is the third oldest coeducational college in the nation and the first in the south. The College accredited by the Southern Association of Colleges and Schools and is a member of the Greater Greensboro Consortium. It operates on the semester system and offers two summer sessions. The current enrollment is 546 men and 641 women full-time residential, and 427 continuing education students. A faculty of 89 full-time and 35 part-time provides a faculty-student ratio of 1-14. Honors courses are offered for exceptionally talented and motivated students. Study in foreign countries is encouraged through Semester Abroad programs in London; Paris; Brandenburg, Italy; Munich, Germany; Ghana; Guadalajara, Mexico; China and a 2-semester program in Japan. The college offers the baccalaureate degree in 28 academic disciplines including one interdisciplinary major, Humanistic Studies and five cooperative preprofessional programs and nine concentrations. The Center for Continuing Education offers a complete range of day and evening programs for nontraditional students (adults 23 and over). Dual degree programs are available in forestry and environmental science (Duke University); medical technology and physician assistant at Bowman Gray School of Medicine at Wake Forest University; and engineering (Georgia Institute of Technology).

Entrance Requirements: High school graduation with completion of at least 18 academic units; rank generally in the upper third of graduating class; SAT scores generally averaging 1,070; ACT also accepted; $25 application fee; early admission, early decision, advanced placement, deadline admission, and delayed admission plans available; credit may be awarded through the College Level Examination Program.

Costs Per Year: $13,400 tuition; $5,160 room and board; $210 student activity fee.

Collegiate Environment: Guilford College is a suburban campus situated on 300 beautiful wooded acres about five miles west of the center of Greensboro. Listed on the National Register of Historic Places by the U.S. Department of the Interior, Guilford has more than 25 Georgian-style buildings that house the academic, administrative, extracurricular, and residential facilities of the college. College facilities include residence hall accommodations for 950 students. The recently renovated Hege Library contains 255,000 volumes and a seven-room art gallery. Furthermore, students have access to an additional 2,000,000 volumes at five other area colleges with 16 miles. The physical education center houses a swimming pool, playing courts, weight rooms, and racquetball courts. The Bauman Telecommunicaitons Center and the College's central computer system is linked to all campus buildings, including residence halls, by fiber optic hookups. Seminars and lecture series, interest and service clubs, an active Community Senate (student government), an extensive program of intramural intercollegiate athletics for both men and women, and a wide range of cultural opportunities provide numerous enrichment activities. Guilford students are also active in the surrounding community, volunteering more than 40,000 hours in community service each year. 80% of applicants are accepted. Financial aid is available; 52 percent of current students receives some form form of assistance. Between 80-100 academic scholarships ranging from $2,000 to full tuition, room and board are available each year. Merit scholarships include Guilford College, Guilford College Honors, Guildford College Presidential, Bonner, Frank Fellow, and Quaker Leadership. Approximately 77% of the freshmen class returned for the sophomore year.

Community Environment: See Greensboro College.

GUILFORD TECHNICAL COMMUNITY COLLEGE *(F-9)*
P.O. Box 309
Jamestown, North Carolina 27282
Tel: (910) 334-4822; Admissions: (910) 334-4822 x5350; Fax: (910) 819-2022

Description: The technical community college was originally established as the Guilford Industrial Education Center in 1958. It was elevated to the technical degree status and was granted authority to award the Associate in Applied Science degree in 1965. In 1983 the college gained community college status and now awards the Associate in Arts and Associate in Science degrees. It offers a Cooperative Education Program in Automotive Technology and similar programs in several areas. It operates on the quarter system and offers one summer session. Enrollment is 3,157 full-time and 4,454 part-time students. A faculty of 170 full-time and 549 part-time gives a faculty-student ratio of 1-15. The college is accredited by the Southern Association of Colleges and Schools, the American Dental Association and the Accrediting Board for Engineering and Technology.

Entrance Requirements: Open door policy; high school graduation or minimum age of 18 years; placement tests required; no application fee.

Costs Per Year: $556.50 tuition; $4,515 out-of-state; $27.75 student fees.

Collegiate Environment: The main campus in Jamestown is comprised of 11 buildings and is located on 85 acres. All students applying for admission are accepted, including midyear students. Approximately 40% of the previous entering class returned to the college for a second year of studies. The Learning Resource Center holding include 64,246 volumes, 465 periodicals, 4,411 microforms, and 8,490 audiovisual materials. 250 scholarships are available, and 25% of students receive some form of financial aid.

Community Environment: Jamestown neighbors High Point and Greensboro. Primary businesses in Guilford County are textiles, furniture, and numerous other manufacturing concerns. Commercial trans-

portation, one railroad, seven airlines, and recreational facilities are convenient in High Point and Greensboro.

Branch Campuses: High Point Campus: 901 S. Main St., High Point, NC 27260. Greensboro Campus: 501 W. Washington St, Greensboro, NC 27401; 400 W. Whittington St., Greensboro, NC 27405; Small Business Assistance Center, 2207 Yanceyville St., Greensboro, NC 27403.

HALIFAX COMMUNITY COLLEGE *(-14)*
P.O. Drawer 809
Weldon, North Carolina 27890
Tel: (919) 536-2551; Admissions: (919) 536-7220; Fax: (919) 536-4144

Description: The community college is one of the newer institutions, authorized in 1967, of the Department of Community Colleges of North Carolina. It operates on the four-quarter system and recently enrolled 1,360 students. A faculty of 100 full-time, 60 part time gives a ratio of 1-20.

Entrance Requirements: High school graduation or equivalent or minimum age of 18 years.

Costs Per Year: $742 tuition; $6,060 tuition for out-of-state students; $21.75 student fees.

Collegiate Environment: The institute is comprised of three buildings and is located on 13 acres. Students from other geographical locations are accepted as well as midyear students. Financial aid is available for economically handicapped students. The library has 27,000 titles, 214 periodicals, 504 microforms, 15,000 audio visual materials.

Community Environment: Located in the northeastern section of North Carolina, Weldon is in a good agricultural area where the main industries are in textiles and paper goods. Community facilities include churches, a library, historical sites, shopping centers, and medical facilities nearby. There are three convenient lakes, with miles of shoreline, known as the Rockfish Capital of the world.

HAYWOOD COMMUNITY COLLEGE *(G-2)*
Freedlander Drive
Clyde, North Carolina 28721
Tel: (704) 627-2821

Description: This community college was established in 1965 and is a member institution of the Department of Community Colleges of North Carolina. The college is accredited by the Southern Association of Colleges and Schools and the Society of American Foresters. It operates on the quarter system and offers one summer session. Enrollment includes 719 full-time and 536 part-time students. A faculty of 63 full-time and 27 part-time gives a faculty-student ratio of 1-16. The college offers two types of programs: the two-year technical program leading to the Associate in Applied Science degree and the one-year vocational program leading to a diploma. The college is accredited by the Southern Association of Colleges and Schools and the Society of American Foresters.

Entrance Requirements: Open door policy; high school graduation required for Associate degree and recommended for all others; local test or SAT required for entering freshmen; no application fee.

Costs Per Year: $557 resident tuition; $4,515 out-of-state; $20 student fees.

Collegiate Environment: Haywood Community College is located on 80 wooded acres in Clyde, NC. The present campus, occupied in 1972, consists of modern, spacious buildings that are situated on beautifully landscaped grounds. The class contains students from 17 different states and 46 different counties. The library includes 26,611 titles, 288 periodicals, 135 microforms, and 707 audiovisual materials.

Community Environment: Haywood is a growing county of 47,000 people with an ever-expanding economy. Fine roads serve the county and new and expanding industry is experiencing a rapid increase. Agriculture is diversifing, and vegetable growing and truck farming share the market with cattle, corn, and tobacco. New and expanding tourist and recreational facilities are being developed. The county's proximity to the Great Smoky Mountains National Park and the world-famous Lake Junaluska Methodist Assembly Grounds make the area a natural tourist attraction. A large ski resort and the nearby lakes and forests have earned the area the distinction of being a winter and summer playground.

HIGH POINT UNIVERSITY   *(F-9)*
University Station, Montlieu Avenue
High Point, North Carolina 27262-3598
Tel: (910) 841-9000; (800) 345-6993; Admissions: (910) 841-9216;
Fax: (910) 841-9216

Description: The private university traces its beginning to the founding of Yadkin College in 1856 by the Methodist Protestant Church in North Carolina. The school is now affiliated with the United Mehodist Church. It is fully accredited by the Southern Association of Colleges and Schools and grants the Bachelor degree. There is a cooperating plan in forestry with Duke University. Junior Year Abroad with Westminster College, England and Leeds University, England are available. Other study programs are available through universities in Germany, France, and Spain. The university operates on the semester system and offers two summer terms. Full-time undergraduate enrollment includes 839 men and 1,220 women. There are 383 part-time undergraduates and 42 graduate students. A faculty of 102 full-time and 16 part-time provides a faculty-student ratio of 1-16.

Entrance Requirements: Accredited high school graduation with rank in upper half of graduating class; completion of 16 units including 4 English, 3 mathematics, 2 foreign language, 2 science, 3 social science, 2 electives; SAT or ACT required; early admission, rolling admisson, delayed admission, midyear admission and advanced placement plans available. There is a $20 application fee.

Costs Per Year: $8,230 tuition; $4,470 board and room; $820 student fees.

Collegiate Environment: The campus is located in the Piedmont section of North Carolina, 15 miles from Greensboro and halfway between the Atlantic Ocean to the east and the Blue Ridge Mountains to the west. The college buildings contain a library of 140,000 volumes, 1,141 periodicals, and 511 microforms. Dormitory facilities for 856 men and women are available. Approximately 83% of students applying for admission are accepted. Students from other geographical locations are admitted as well as midyear students. The middle 50% range of scores of the entering freshman class was SAT 790-1010 combined. Financial aid is available for students demonstrating need. There are 1,136 scholarships, of which 255 are for freshmen. 64% of the students receive some form of financial aid.

Community Environment: The city's name arose from the fact that the community was the highest point, on the original survey, for the old North Carolina Railroad between Goldsboro and Charlotte. Numerous diversified industries, including many furniture manufacturing plants and hosiery mills, are in High Point, the wood furniture manufacturing and hosiery production capital of the world. Parks, golf courses, and a lake provide the facilities for recreation.

ISOTHERMAL COMMUNITY COLLEGE   *(H-4)*
P.O. Box 804
Spindale, North Carolina 28160
Tel: (704) 286-3636; Admissions: (704) 286-3636 x251; Fax: (704) 286-8109

Description: The public junior college was authorized by the 1963 General Assembly as a member institution of the Department of Community Colleges of North Carolina. It is accredited by the Southern Association of Colleges and Schools. It operates on the quarter system and offers two summer terms. It provides two years of transferable college credit courses, two years of technical education, vocational education, and an adult program of community services. Enrollment is 1,603 students. A faculty of 91 gives a faculty-student ratio of 1-17.

Entrance Requirements: High school graduation or equivalent required for degree programs; college placement examinations required; early admission, early decision, delayed admission plans available.

Costs Per Year: $742; $6,020 out-of-state tuition; $28 student fees.

Collegiate Environment: The new campus is located between the towns of Forest City and Spindale, North Carolina. The modern buildings contain a library of 52,169 volumes, 269 periodicals, 15,087 microforms, and 3,556 audiovisual materials. All students applying for admission are accepted, including midyear students. Approximately

70% of the previous entering class returned to the college for the second year. Financial aid is available for economically handicapped students. A satellite campus is located in Tryon.

Community Environment: Spindale is located 20 miles from Shelby, 28 miles from Hendersonville, and 35 miles from Asheville.

JAMES SPRUNT COMMUNITY COLLEGE   *(I-13)*
P.O. Box 398
Kenansville, North Carolina 28349
Tel: (910) 296-2400; Fax: (910) 296-1222

Description: The community college was founded in 1964, was designated a unit of the Department of Community Colleges of North Carolina and is directed by a local board of trustees. It is accredited by the Southern Association of Colleges and Schools. It provides specialized occupational education for youth and adults in its area. The college operates on a four-quarter system and offers one summer session. Enrollment is 575 full-time and 425 part-time students. A faculty of 47 full-time and 38 part-time gives a faculty-student ratio of 1-14.

Entrance Requirements: Open door policy; general placement tests required; midyear admission, rolling admission and advanced placement plans available.

Costs Per Year: $556.50 tuition; $4,515 out-of-state; $24 student activity fees.

Collegiate Environment: The college contains five buildings and is located on 52 acres. All students applying for admission are accepted, including midyear students. The library contains about 22,000 volumes, 190 periodicals, 1,385 microforms, and 1,696 audiovisual materials. Approximately 40% of the recent student body graduated in the top half of the high school class, 10% in the top quarter, and 20% in the highest tenth. The average scores of the entering freshmen were SAT 480 verbal, 440 math. The college awarded 37 diplomas, 129 Associate degrees and 149 Certificates to the recent graduating class.

Community Environment: Located 40 miles from the principal city of Goldsboro and 4 miles from Interstate 40, Kenansville is a rural community with three churches, a library, and good shopping areas for this size community. The primary businesses of the area are farming, textiles, poultry, and swine production. Good fishing and hunting are available in the area.

JOHN WESLEY COLLEGE   *(F-9)*
2314 N. Centennial
High Point, North Carolina 27260
Tel: (910) 889-2262; Fax: (910) 889-2261

Description: The interdenominational Bible college was established in 1932. Today it is a four-year college. It is accredited by the American Association of Bible Colleges. It trains students as missionaries, pastors, evangelists, and for other fields of Christian service. The college operates on the semester system and offers one summer session. Enrollment is 102 full-time and 28 part-time students. A faculty of 7 full-time and 8 part-time provides a faculty-student ratio of 1-9.

Entrance Requirements: High school graduation or equivalent; $25 application fee; open enrollment policy; early decision, advanced placement, early admission, midyear admission and rolling admission plans available; $25 application fee.

Costs Per Year: $4,234 tuition; $1,400 room; $300 student fees.

Collegiate Environment: The college is located on a beautiful 24-acre wooded, park-like area in the northeast section of High Point. A 2-story building houses administrative offices, classrooms, chapel, library and student lounge. Dormitories house 32 men and women. The college library contains 35,000 volumes and 112 periodicals. The college welcomes a geographically diverse student body. 98% of the applicants are accepted. Scholarships are available and 59% of students receive some form of financial aid.

Community Environment: See High Point University.

JOHNSON C. SMITH UNIVERSITY   *(H-7)*
100 Beatties Ford Road
Charlotte, North Carolina 28216
Tel: (704) 378-1000; (800) 782-7303; Admissions: (704) 378-1010; Fax: (704) 378-1242

Description: Johnson C. Smith University, established in 1867, is a small coeducational university under private control. The general purpose of the university is to provide an environment in which men and women may realize as fully as possible their individual potential for intellectual, social, spiritual, emotional and physical growth and well being. The university operates on the semester system and offers one summer session. Enrollment includes 567 men and 846 women full-time with a total of 1,413 students. A faculty of 79 full-time and 25 part-time gives a faculty-student ratio of 1-17.

Entrance Requirements: Accredited high school graduation; completion of 16 units including 4 English, 2 mathematics, 2 social science, 1 science; and 7 units in electives; SAT required; $20 application fee; early admission, and rolling admission plans available.

Costs Per Year: $6,049 tuition; $2,578 board and room; $594 student fees.

Collegiate Environment: The 100-acre campus is located in the western part of the City of Charlotte. The 46 college buildings contain a library of 100,000 volumes and housing facilities for 1,142 students. Almost 63% of students applying for admission are accepted, including midyear students. Financial aid is available. 96% of the students receive some form of financial aid.

Community Environment: Charlotte, the largest city of the Carolinas, with a population of more than 340,000, is a commercial and cultural center of the South. The city has tall buildings, huge warehouses, and numerous factories, but the residential sections are intensively gardened and beautifully landscaped. The area is rich in historical landmarks. Charlotte offers all the cultural and recreational facilities of any large city, including sports events, excellent shopping and dining facilites, rock and classical music, concerts, theater, art, and exceptional gardens. The area is served by Southern Railway and five major airlines. Major highways provide easy access to nearby beach and mountains.

KING'S COLLEGE   *(H-7)*
322 Lamar Avenue
Charlotte, North Carolina 28204
Tel: (704) 372-0266

Description: The private business school was established in 1901 and offers programs leading to certificates, and diplomas. It operates on a specified program starting dates (July, September, February) and enrolls 347 students with a faculty of 15 full-time and 6 part-time. It is accredited as a business school by the Accrediting Commission for Business Schools.

Entrance Requirements: High school graduation or equivalent; rank in upper 75% of graduating class; completion of 16 units including 4 English; advanced placement plan available.

Costs Per Year: $6,820 tuition; $3,300 board and room.

Collegiate Environment: The site of the campus is a beautiful wooded area just one mile east of the downtown business district. The modern college buildings contain a library of 2,000 volumes and dormitory facilities for 200 women. Approximately 90% of students applying for admission are accepted. Students from other geographical locations are accepted as well as midyear students. About 58% of the recent student body graduated in the top half of the high school class, 24% in the top quarter, and 8% in the highest tenth. Financial aid and a few scholarships are available.

Community Environment: See Queens College.

LEES-McRAE COLLEGE   *(E-5)*
P.O. Box 128
Faculty Street
Banner Elk, North Carolina 28604
Tel: (704) 898-5241; (800) 280-4LMC; Admissions: (704) 898-8723; Fax: (704) 898-8814

Description: The private four-year college was established in 1900 and is supported by the Mid-Atlantic and the Western Carolina Presbytery of the Presbyterian Church (U.S.A.) The college operates on the semester system and offers two summer terms. It is accredited by the Southern Association of Colleges and Schools. Enrollment recently was 540 men and 290 women. A faculty of 35 full-time and 15 part-time gives a faculty-student ratio of 1-15. The college offers the

baccalaureate degree, college transfer programs, and business and education courses.

Entrance Requirements: Accredited high school graduation or equivalent; completion of 16 units including 4 English, 2 algebra, 2 science, and 2 social science; SAT with minimum combined score of 920on recentered SAT, or ACT with minimum score of 19 recommended; $15 application fee; early admission and rolling admission plans available.

Costs Per Year: $8,032 tuition; $3,276 room and board; $967 general fees.

Collegiate Environment: The 400-acre campus is situated 4,000 feet above sea level in the Blue Ridge Mountains of western North Carolina. The facilities of Beech Mountain and Sugar Mountain Ski Resorts are used by the college physical education department for skiing lessons. The 39 college buildings include a library of 86,000 volumes, 415 periodicals, 5,291 microforms, and 3,289 audiovisual materials. Dormitory facilities are available for 421 men and 265 women. The college welcomes a geographically diverse student body and will accept midyear students. About 60% of the recent freshman class returned to the campus for the second year of studies. Financial aid is available for economically handicapped students and 82% of the students receive aid.

Community Environment: Banner Elk is in the Blue Ridge Mountains of Western North Carolina, 100 miles from Charlotte and 83 miles northeast of Asheville. Elk River is nearby for trout fishing, and during the winter there is sufficient snow for outdoor winter sports.

LENOIR COMMUNITY COLLEGE   *(H-14)*
P.O. Box 188
Kinston, North Carolina 28501
Tel: (919) 527-6223

Description: The public junior college was established in 1958 and became a community college of North Carolina in 1964. Today the college offers transfer, occupational, continuing and community service educational opportunities to the people of the area. It operates on the quarter system with 2 summer terms. It also offers two summer sessions and is accredited by the Southern Association of Colleges and Schools. A faculty of 178 provides a faculty-student ratio of 1-12.

Entrance Requirements: Open enrollment policy; high school graduation or equivalent for transfer or technical programs; non-high school graduates over 18 years of age (or under 18 with permission) may be admitted to vocational and other programs; placement test battery required. Early admission, early decision, delayed admission, rolling admission and advanced placement available.

Costs Per Year: $348 tuition; $2,971 tuition required for out-of-state students; $27 student fees.

Collegiate Environment: The college is located on an 86-acre campus approximately two miles east of Kinston. The nine college buildings include a library of 52,000 volumes, 367 periodicals and 6,500 microforms. Students from other geographical locations are accepted as are midyear students. Financial aid is available for economically handicapped students.

Community Environment: Kinston is an important bright-leaf tobacco market as well as a grain and livestock producing region. Commercial transportation is convenient. The community facilities include a library with branches, churches representing 25 denominations, a museum, little theatre, arts council, hospitals, good shopping areas, and various civic and service organizations. Good part-time employment opportunities are available for students. Parks, swimming pools, and golf courses provide the recreational facilities for the community.

LENOIR RHYNE COLLEGE   *(F-6)*
Box 7227
Hickory, North Carolina 28603
Tel: (704) 328-7300; (800) 277-5721; Admissions: (704) 328-7300; Fax: (704) 328-7378

Description: The private, coeducational, liberal arts college was established in 1891 and is owned and operated by the North Carolina Synod of the Lutheran Church in America. It provides programs in the fields of liberal arts; business; music; nursing; teacher training in the primary, grammar grades, and high school fields, and pre-professional courses. It operates on the semester system and offers two summer terms. The college is accredited by the Southern Association of Colleges and Schools and by the National League for Nursing and the National Council for Accreditation of Teacher Education. Enrollment includes 1,130 full-time and 288 part-time undergraduate students and 9 graduate students. A faculty of 92 gives an undergraduate faculty-student ratio of 1-12.

Entrance Requirements: Accredited high school graduation with rank in upper half of graduating class; completion of 4 units of English, 3 mathematics, 1 science, 1 social science; and 2 foreign language; SAT or ACT required; GRE required for graduate program; early admission, rolling admission, delayed admission and advanced placement plans available; $25 application fee.

Costs Per Year: $10,100 tuition; $4,000 room and board; $500 student fees.

Collegiate Environment: The college is comprised of 20 buildings on 100 acres and includes a library of 137,000 volumes, 927 periodicals and 360,000 items of nonprint media. Dormitory facilities are provided for 390 men and 436 women. The college welcomes a geographically diverse student body and will accept midyear students. 88% of applicants were accepted. Financial aid is available for economically disadvantaged students. 60% of students receive financial aid. Semesters begin in August and January.

Community Environment: Hickory, located in the western Piedmont section, is best known as one of North Carolina's major furniture manufacturing cities. Textile works are here as well as hosiery and knitting mills. All forms of commercial transportation are available. The community facilities include hospitals, numerous churches, a museum of art, a city library, and various civic and service organizations. Nearby, Lake Hickory offers many recreational opportunities such as boating, fishing, and swimming.

LIVINGSTONE COLLEGE   *(G-8)*
701 West Monroe Street
Salisbury, North Carolina 28144
Tel: (704) 638-5500; (800) 835-3435; Admissions: (704) 638-5502; Fax: (704) 638-5636

Description: The private college was founded in 1879 and is largely supported by the African Methodist Episcopal Zion Church, but its academic operations are entirely nonsectarian. It is accredited by the Southern Association of Colleges and Schools. The college is comprised of the College of Liberal Arts, which offers regular college courses leading to the degrees of Bachelor of Arts and Bachelor of Science, and the Hood Theological Seminary, which offers professional training for the ministry with courses leading to the degrees of Bachelor of Theology and Master of Divinity. It operates on the semester system and offers two summer sessions. Enrollment includes 839 students. The faculty numbers 48 full-time and 20 part-time members.

Entrance Requirements: Approved high school graduation with rank in upper 60% of graduating class; completion of 20 units including 4 English, 2 mathematics, 2 social science, 2 science, 2 foreign language; SAT or ACT required; early decision, rolling admission, midyear admission and advanced placement plans available; $15 application fee.

Costs Per Year: $4,700 tuition; $2,000 board and room; $800 student fees.

Collegiate Environment: The 272-acre campus is located in Salisbury, the county seat of Rowan County. The 21 college buildings contain a library of 61,501 volumes, 495 periodicals, 10,914 microforms and 1,983 sound recordings. Residence halls accomodate 720 students. 85% of students applying for admission are accepted and 76% of the previous freshman class return for the sophomore year. Students from other geographical locations are accepted as well as midyear students. Approximately 50% of the recent freshman graduated in the top half of the high school class, 20% in the top quarter, and 30% in the third quarter. Scholarships are available and 90% of the students receive some form of financial aid. Semesters begin in August and January.

Community Environment: See Catawba College.

LOUISBURG COLLEGE   *(E-12)*
501 N. Main Street
Louisburg, North Carolina 27549
Tel: (919) 496-2521; Fax: (919) 496-1788

Description: The college, a United Methodist institution, is the oldest chartered denominational junior college in the nation and the oldest two-year college in the South. It traces its history to the founding of Franklin Academy in 1787. The college is accredited by the Southern Association of Colleges and Schools and by the University Senate of the United Methodist Church. It offers programs in business and liberal arts and grants the Associate degree. It operates on the semester system and offers one summer term. Enrollment is 299 men and 238 women full-time, and 98 students part-time. A faculty of 37 full-time and 5 part-time gives a faculty-student ratio of 1-13.

Entrance Requirements: Accredited high school graduation or equivalent; completion of 16 units including 4 English, 2 mathematics, 1 science, 2 social science; SAT or ACT required; TOEFL for foreign students; $15 application fee; midyear admission and rolling admission plans available.

Costs Per Year: $6,400 tuition; $3,651 room and board; $449 student fees.

Collegiate Environment: The 75-acre campus is situated on the highest points of land in the town and commands a fine view of the surrounding country and the valley of the Tar River. The 22 college buildings contain a library of 64,000 volumes and dormitory facilities for 306 men and 323 women. The college welcomes a geographically diverse student body and will accept midyear students. Approximately 85% of students applying for admission are accepted. Financial aid is available for economically disadvantaged students and 80% of students receive some form of financial aid. The college awards certificates and associate degrees. Semesters begin in August and January and the summer sessions begin in July.

Community Environment: Louisburg, a county seat, is 30 miles from Raleigh, the state capital, where all forms of transportation are available. A hospital, churches, good shopping facilities, and various civic and social organizations are found in the community. There are some part-time job opportunities.

MARS HILL COLLEGE   *(F-3)*
Mars Hill, North Carolina 28754
Tel: (704) 689-1201; (800) 543-1514; Fax: (704) 689-1478

Description: This private liberal arts college was founded in 1856 and is the oldest educational institution on its original site in western North Carolina. It was the first school founded by Baptists in the state west of the Blue Ridge Mountains. It operates on the semester system and also offers two summer terms. It is accredited by the Southern Association of Colleges and Schools, the National Association of Schools of Music and the Council on Social Work Education. The college enrolled 1,082 full-time and 250 part-time students recently. A faculty 80 full-time, 57 part-time gives a faculty-student ratio of 1-13.

Entrance Requirements: Accredited high school graduation with a 2.0 average; completion of 18 units including 4 English, 3 mathematics, 2 science, and 2 social science; SAT or ACT required; $15 application fee; early admission, early decision and rolling admission plans available.

Costs Per Year: $7,450 tuition; $3,550 room and board; $550 student fees.

Collegiate Environment: The 180-acre campus is located in the Mountains of western North Carolina at an elevation of 2,330 feet. The 54 college buildings contain a library of 91,000 titles, 475 periodicals, and dormitory and apartment facilities for 4 men, 4 women. The college welcomes a geographically diverse student body and will accept midyear students. Approximately 84% of students applying for admission are accepted. 285 scholarships are available and 80% of the students receive some form of financial aid. Semesters begin in August and January and the summer term begins in June.

Community Environment: Mars Hill is located 17 miles north of Asheville and 10 miles from Marshall. Plane and bus transportation are available. Community facilities include a medical center and convenient shopping.

MARTIN COMMUNITY COLLEGE *(F-15)*
Kehukee Park Road
Williamston, North Carolina 27892
Tel: (919) 792-1521; Admissions: (919) 792-1521; Fax: (919) 792-4425

Description: Martin Community College was initially established in 1968 as a technical institute and was granted community college status on July 1, 1976. This college is fully accredited by the Southern Association of Colleges and Schools and the North Carolina State Board of Education. It operates on the quarter system and offers one summer session. Vocational, technical, general education and college transfer programs are available. The college awards the Associate degree and vocational diploma. Enrollment includes 404 full-time and 361 part-time students. A faculty of 25 full-time and 27 part-time gives a faculty-student ratio of 1-16.

Entrance Requirements: Open door policy; high school diploma or equivalent; 20 units including 4 English, 3 mathematics, 2 science, 2 social studies, and 8 electives; placement tests; transcripts from high school and any post-secondary schools attended are required; rolling admissions and advanced placement plans available.

Costs Per Year: $556.50 state-resident tuition; $4,515 nonresident; $18 student fees.

Collegiate Environment: The college is located on a 65-acre tract and is comprised of four buildings equipped with a modern library, classrooms, shops, and laboratory facilities. The library contains more than 27,250 titles, 205 periodicals, 1,001 microforms, and 1,785 audiovisual materials. Scholarships and financial aid are available to eligible students. 50% of the students receive some form of financial aid.

Community Environment: The college is located in the center of a prosperous agricultural area. Recreational facilities include tennis courts, parks, and several ball fields. This area is also ideal for hunting, fishing, and camping.

MAYLAND COMMUNITY COLLEGE *(F-4)*
P.O. Box 547
Spruce Pine, North Carolina 28777
Tel: (704) 765-7351; Admissions: (704) 765-7351 x224; Fax: (704) 765-0728

Description: A publicly supported technological institute. It is fully accredited by the Southern Association of Colleges and Schools. The college operates on the quarter system and offers one summer session. Programs of study are primarily vocational and lead to the Associate degree. MCC operates two learning centers in Burnsville and Newland, NC. Enrollment includes 358 full-time and 439 part-time students. Faculty numbers 30 full-time and 40 part-time members.

Entrance Requirements: High school graduation or equivalent; placement examination required; Rolling admission and advanced placement plans available.

Costs Per Year: $477 tuition; $3,477 nonresident tuition; $18 student fees.

Collegiate Environment: The institute library contains 21,331 volumes. All those applying are admitted and 75% returns for the second year of study. 85 scholarships are available and 55% of students receive some form of financial aid.

Community Environment: Mayland Community College is located in the Blue Ridge Mountains of Western North Carolina. The Main Campus is located on Highway 19E, two miles east of Spruce Pine.

MCDOWELL TECHNICAL COMMUNITY COLLEGE *(G-4)*
Route 1
Box 170
Marion, North Carolina 28752
Tel: (704) 652-6021

Description: The public technical college was established in 1965. It provides programs in technical, business, vocational-trade, adult education, cultural, and avocational courses. It operates on a four-quarter system and offers two summer sessions. Enrollment is 857 full-time students. A faculty of 30 full-time, 14 part-time gives a faculty-student ratio of 1-20. The college is accredited by the Southern Association of Colleges and Schools.

Entrance Requirements: Open enrollment policy; high school graduation or minimum age of 18 years; selected requirements must be met for specific programs; placement and aptitude test required; rolling admission plan in most programs; applicants must submit application and transcripts, arrange to take placement and aptitude test and have a personal interview.

Costs Per Year: $420 tuition; $3,924 out-of-state; $25 student fees.

Collegiate Environment: The College is located on 31 acres and is comprised of 5 buildings. The library houses 18,900 volumes, 156 periodicals, 21,316 audiovisual materials and 1,636 microforms. Classes begin in late September; however, students may enter some curriculums at the beginning of any quarter. Approximately 95% of applicants are accepted. Financial aid is available and 35% of students received some form of aid.

Community Environment: Located in the foothills of the Blue Ridge Mountains, Marion enjoys a temperate climate. Trains, buses, and airlines provide the commercial transportation. To serve the people of this community, there are 96 churches and medical facilities. 26 major industries are located here, furnishing part-time job opportunities for students. Outdoor recreational facilities include the Blue Ridge Parkway, Mt Mitchell State Park, Lake James and Lake Tahoma.

MEREDITH COLLEGE *(F-12)*
3800 Hillsborough Street
Raleigh, North Carolina 27607-5298
Tel: (919) 829-8581; (800) 637-3348; Fax: (919) 829-2828

Description: The private liberal arts college for women was founded by the North Carolina Baptist State Convention and was first opened to students in 1899. The college operates on the semester system and also offers three summer terms. It is accredited by the Southern Association of Colleges and Schools, and by the National Association of Schools of Music, the Council on Social Work Education, the National Council for Accreditation of Teacher Education, the North Carolina Department of Public Instruction, and the Foundation for Interior Design Education Research (FIDER). There is an American Dietetic Association Approved Plan V Program. Cooperative education programs and internships are available for students in all departments. A 10-week summer study program in England and Italy is available. A semester in Florence, Italy is available for art majors. Also available are terms at l'Universite Catholique de l'Ouest in Angers, France for students of French, at the Universitas Nebrissensis in Madrid, Spain for Spanish students, exchange opportunities with two universities in Hull, England and at Obirin University in Tokyo, Japan, and a program in Chinese language and culture in the People's Republic of China. A London seminar in British history and politics and a UN semester are offered through Drew University. There is a semester in Washington at American University available, and an agreement with Marymount College in New York. Every year Meredith sponsors some short-term study travel options that may or may not include study for credit. Enrollment includes 1,686 full-time, 486 part-time, and 164 graduate students. A faculty of 103 full-time and 110 part-time gives an undergraduate faculty-student ratio of 1-17. The college is a member of a six-college Raleigh consortium affording the students use of all of the libraries and other facilities.

Entrance Requirements: High school graduation with a minimum of 16 units in grades 9-12, with a total of at least 13 academic units including 4 English, 3 Math through Algebra II, 1 Foreign Language. Must rank in top half of class; SAT or ACT scores required; recommendations including one from a school official. Early decision, rolling admission available; $25 application fee.

Costs Per Year: $6,720 tuition; $3,250 board and room.

Collegiate Environment: The 225-acre campus is located in the capital city of North Carolina. The college library contains 153,509 titles, 778 periodicals, 73,201 microfiche, and 9,739 records. Dormitory facilities are provided for 1,218 women. Approximately 85% of students applying for admission are accepted. The college welcomes a geographically diverse student body and will accept midyear students. Approximately 63% of the recent freshman graduated in the top quarter of the high school class. About 79% of the previous freshman class returned to this campus for the sophomore year. Financial aid is available for students demonstrating financial need and about 42% of the students receive aid. Competitive scholarships which recognize superior academic, artistic, interior design, and musical ability are available.

Community Environment: Meredith is located at the western edge of Raleigh, NC, the state capital and home of five other colleges and universities. Served by air, bus and rail. The campus is easily accessible from I-40, bordered by US1 and Wade Avenue, with the front entrance facing Hillsborough Street. Raleigh is a part of the Research Triangle Area, which includes Durham and Chapel Hill, NC. It is a cultural center with the N.C. Museums of Art, History and Natural Science, the North Carolina Symphony, and numerous theaters. Meredith itself is a center for many cultural events including the Fletcher School of the Performing Arts, and the National Opera Company.

METHODIST COLLEGE   *(H-11)*
5400 Ramsey Street
Fayetteville, North Carolina 28311
Tel: (910) 630-7027; (800) 488-7110; Admissions: (910) 630-7027;
Fax: (910) 630-2123

Description: This private institution was established as a coeducational, senior college of liberal arts operated under the auspices of the North Carolina Conference of the Methodist Church. It admitted its first freshman class in the fall of 1960. The college is accredited by the Southern Association of Colleges and Schools. It is also accredited by the University Senate of the Methodist General Board of Education for the undergraduate training of ministers and Christian education workers. There is a cooperating plan in engineering with Georiga Tech, North Carolina State University. Air Force and Army ROTC programs are available. It operates on the early semester system and offers three summer sessions. Enrollment includes 1,250 full-time, 394 part-time and 348 evening students. A faculty of 79 full-time and 49 part-time gives a faculty-student ratio of 1-14.

Entrance Requirements: Accredited high school graduation or equivalent; rank in upper 50% of graduating class; completion of 16 units including 4 English, 2 mathematics, 2 science, 2 history, 6 electives; SAT or ACT required; advanced placement, midyear admission and rolling admission plans available. $25 application fee.

Costs Per Year: $10,000 tuition; $4,000 room and board.

Collegiate Environment: The 600-acre campus primarily in undeveloped woodland and including Cape Fear River frontage, is located in Fayetteville, North Carolina (a 1986 All-American city); part of the Carolina Sandhills region in the heart of golfing country and two hours from the coast. Part of the campus is given over to a nature trail, and a fitness trail encircles the campus. The college is comprised of 18 modern and beautiful buildings. The Davis Memorial Library houses over 82,010 volumes and 13,293 nonbook materials, a music listening room with over 2,740 sound recordings, 1 micro materials area of 9,620 microforms with self-service microform readers and printers, a computer center with 3 microcomputers and printers, and a periodicals reading room with over 539 periodicals and newspapers. Also available are special copying services, study rooms, typewriters, and interlibrary loan services. Living accommodations include six residence halls that house 720 men and women. The college welcomes a geographically diverse student body and will accept midyear students. Approximately 68% of students applying for admission are accepted. The average scores of entering freshmen were SAT 420 verbal, 490 math. Financial aid is available based on academic excellence and need and the college participates in all available federal and state financial aid programs. 85% of the students receive some form of aid. Fall semester begins in August and applications should be submitted at the completion of junior year or early in the fall of the senior year of high school.

Community Environment: Fayetteville, a community of 60,000, is accessible by air, rail, and highway. Its economy is based on agriculture, manufacturing and processing, distribution, and the government. The community has an art guild, theater, art museum, symphony, and brass band. There are 53 public and private golf courses within an hour's drive of the city. Popular sports include golf, tennis, archery, boating and skating. There are 2 hospitals, and a public library with over 7 branches.

MITCHELL COMMUNITY COLLEGE   *(F-7)*
500 West Broad Street
Statesville, North Carolina 28677
Tel: (704) 878-3200; Fax: (704) 878-0872

Description: The state-supported community college, one of the oldest colleges in North Carolina, began operating as a women's college in 1856. It became coeducational in 1932 and was accredited by the Southern Association of Colleges and Schools in 1955. The college operates on the quarter system and offers one summer session. Enrollment includes 717 full-time and 836 part-time students. A faculty of 47 full-time and 43 gives a faculty-student ratio of 1-20.

Entrance Requirements: Accredited high school graduation or equivalent except in some vocational programs where high school diploma is not required; completion of 21 units; open enrollment admission policy; entrance exam required; midyear admission and advanced placement plans available.

Costs Per Year: $742 tuition; $6,020 nonresident tuition; fees $33.60.

Collegiate Environment: The college is comprised of 13 buildings and the main campus is located on six acres at the foothills of the Blue Ridge Mountains. It contains a library of 40,000 volumes and 6,000 microforms. All students applying for admission are accepted. Students from other geographical locations are accepted as are midyear students. More than 75% of the previous freshman class returned to this campus for the second year of studies. 216 scholarships are available and 25% of the students receive some form of financial aid.

Community Environment: On a plateau, surrounded by the foothills of the Blue Ridge Mountains, Statesville is in the heart of the Piedmont area. Industrial products and textiles, metal, and furniture are produced there. This is also a large milk-producing area. All forms of commercial transportation are available. There are churches of all denominations along with the various civic and service organizations. Excellent part-time job opportunities are available.

MONTGOMERY COMMUNITY COLLEGE   *(H-9)*
Old Biscoe Road
P.O. Drawer 787
Troy, North Carolina 27371
Tel: (910) 576-6222; (800) 839-6222; Fax: (910) 576-2176

Description: The public coeducational community college was established in 1967, opened in 1968, and is a member of such colleges operated by the North Carolina Board of Community Colleges under the direction of the Department of Community Colleges in Raleigh, and is administered by a local Board of Trustees. It is accredited by the Southern Association for Colleges and Schools. Programs of study are college transfer and vocationally oriented, and lead to the Associate degree. It operates on the quarter system and offers one summer term. Enrollment includes 548 students. A faculty of 60 gives a faculty-student ratio of 1-22.

Entrance Requirements: Open door policy; high school graduation or minimum age of 18 years; placement tests required; early decision, early admission, midyear admission, rolling admission available.

Costs Per Year: $742 tuition; $6,020 tuition for out-of-state students; $24 student fees.

Collegiate Environment: The institute is located on 143 acres and is comprised of one main campus which contains a library of 13,000 volumes. Approximately 95% of students applying for admission are accepted, including midyear students. Financial aid is available for economically handicapped disadvantaged and scholarships are offered.

Community Environment: Troy is located 50 miles from Greensboro where the main industries are lumber and textiles. The Pee Dee River is 12 miles away providing facilities for water skiing, fishing, and boating. Train transportation is available with air travel convenient to Greensboro and Charlotte.

MONTREAT-ANDERSON COLLEGE   *(G-4)*
Montreat, North Carolina 28757
Tel: (704) 669-8011; (800) 622-6968; Admissions: (704) 669-8011 X 3101; Fax: (704) 669-9554

Description: Montreat-Anderson College is a private, four-year Christian liberal arts college, established by members of the Presbyterian Church in 1916. It is accredited by the Southern Association of Colleges and Schools. It grants Bachelor of Arts and Bachelor of Science degrees. Enrollment includes 301 full-time and 23 part-time students.

Entrance Requirements: High school graduation or equivalent; ACT or SAT; early admission, early decision, delayed admission, midyear admission, rolling admission and advanced placement plans available. $15 application fee.

Costs Per Year: $8,438 tuition; $3,372 board and room; $100 fees.

Collegiate Environment: The 13-acre campus is located in the heart of the Blue Ridge Mountains. The college buildings include a library of 53,000 volumes, and dormitory facilities are provided for 209 men and 231 women. Approximately 85% of students applying for admission are accepted. The college offers an Academic Enrichment with tutors for students that are academically weak. 60 scholarships are available including 25 for freshmen and 90% of the students receive some form of financial aid.

Community Environment: A conference center of the Presbyterian Church; during the school year, the grounds and a portion of the buildings are used by Montreat-Anderson College. Situated in the Blue Ridge Mountains, 17 miles from Asheville, Montreat's recreational facilities include the Pisgah National Forest. Other activities include golf, tennis, baseball and basketball. The Assembly Inn, a resort hotel, is here.

MOUNT OLIVE COLLEGE   *(H-13)*
634 Henderson Street
Mount Olive, North Carolina 28365
Tel: (919) 658-2502; (800) 653-0854; Admissions: (919) 658-7164;
Fax: (919) 658-7180

Description: This private institution is a four-year college of arts and sciences that also offers two years of business education for both transfer and terminal students. It is accredited by the Southern Association of Colleges and Schools. From its beginning in 1951, the college has been sponsored by the North Carolina Convention of Original Free Will Baptists. It has a Cooperative Education Program available in all departments. It operates on the semester basis and has 2 summer sessions. Enrollment includes 423 full-time and 451 part-time students. A faculty of 35 full-time and 25 part-time gives a faculty-student ratio of 1-12.

Entrance Requirements: Accredited high school graduation or equivalent; rank in upper 50% of graduation class; SAT required; C or better average; 10 academic units including 4 English, 3 mathematics, and 3 science; early admission, early decision, midyear admission, rolling and advanced placement plans available; $20 application fee.

Costs Per Year: $7,825 tuition; $3,050 room and board; $80 activity fee.

Collegiate Environment: The 110-acre campus is located 15 miles south of Goldsboro and 60 miles southeast of Raleigh. The 12 modern buildings contain a library of over 57,000 volumes, and dormitory facilities are provided for 316 students. Apartments are available for 32 men and 32 women. Approximately 94% of students applying for admission are accepted. The college welcomes a geographically diverse student body. About 75% of the recent student body graduated in the top 6% of the high school class and 60% of the previous freshman class returned to this campus for the second year of studies. Financial aid is available for economically disadvantaged students, and numerous scholarships are offered; 90% of students receive some form of aid. Semesters begin in August and January, and midyear students are accepted.

Community Environment: Mount Olive is about 15 miles from the county seat, Goldsboro. Buses provide commercial transportation. Numerous civic and service organizations, hospitals in separate towns 15 miles away, churches, and a library contribute to the community. The coast is a one-hour drive for swimming and fresh water fishing; other activities are tennis, softball, and golfing.

NASH COMMUNITY COLLEGE   *(F-13)*
P.O. Box 7488
Rocky Mount, North Carolina 27801-0488
Tel: (919) 443-4011; Fax: (919) 443-0828

Description: This public technical institute was established in 1967 and is a unit of the Department of Community Colleges of North Carolina. It offers vocational-technical education, general adult education, as well as a college transfer program. The college operates on the four-quarter system. Enrollment includes 687 full-time and 1,193 part-time students. A faculty of 46 full-time and 60 part-time gives a faculty-student ratio of 1-18. The college has full Accreditation from the Southern Association of Colleges and Schools.

Entrance Requirements: Open door policy; high school graduation or equivalent required for degree programs with units to include 3 mathematics; minimum age of 18 years for other programs; Assessment and Placement Test for Community College students or minimum SAT score of 800 (400V, 400M) required; midyear admission and rolling admission.

Costs Per Year: $770 tuition; $6,048 out-of-state; $24 student fees.

Collegiate Environment: The college moved into a new facility west of Rocky Mount in the Fall of 1975. All students applying for admission are accepted, except in the Allied Health Science and Physical Therapy assistant programs, including midyear students. Financial aid is available for economically disadvantaged students. 20% of students received financial aid recently. The library contains 33,000 volumes, 120 periodicals and 1,458 microforms.

Community Environment: See North Carolina Wesleyan College.

NORTH CAROLINA AGRICULTURAL AND TECHNICAL STATE UNIVERSITY   *(F-9)*
1601 East Market Street
Greensboro, North Carolina 27411
Tel: (910) 334-7500; (800) 443-8964; Admissions: (910) 334-7946;
Fax: (910) 334-7013

Description: The state university was established as an agricultural and technical college by the General Assembly of North Carolina in 1891. Today the university is comprised of more than 40 departments in six schools and two colleges. It is fully accredited by the Southern Association of Colleges and Schools. Programs of study are accredited by numerous professional and educational organizations. The university operates on the semester system and offers two summer sessions. Air Force and Army ROTC programs are also offered. Enrollment includes 6,244 full-time and 810 part-time undergraduates and 996 graduate students. A faculty of 430 full-time and 77 part-time gives an undergraudate faculty-student ratio of 1-16. The school awards Bachelor, Master, and Doctorate degrees.

Entrance Requirements: High school graduation with rank in upper half of graduating class; completion of 16 units including 4 English, 2 mathematics, 2 sicence, 2 social science, 2 foreign language and 4 electives; college entrance examinations and SAT or ACT required; application deadlines are June 1 for fall and Dec 1 for spring; $25 application fee.

Costs Per Year: $764 tuition; $7,248 tuition required for out-of-state students; $3,120 room and board.

Collegiate Environment: The 181-acre main campus is located nine blocks from the heart of metropolitan Greensboro. The 104 university buildings contain a library of 211,895 titles, 1,939 periodicals, 612,156 microforms, and 4,580 audiovisual materials. Dormitory facilities accomodate 2,986 students. Approximately 57% of students applying for admission are accepted, including midyear students. Scholarships and financial aid are available for economically disadvantaged students and 62% of the students receive some form of aid. Semesters begin in August and January.

Community Environment: See Greensboro College.

NORTH CAROLINA CENTRAL UNIVERSITY   *(F-11)*
1902 Fayetteville Street
Durham, North Carolina 27707
Tel: (919) 560-6100

Description: The state-supported liberal arts college was chartered in 1909 as a private institution. It became a State Normal School in 1923 and was admitted to membership in the Southern Association of Colleges and Schools in 1957. It has also been approved by the Association of American Universities and the National Council for the Accreditation of Teacher Education. The college operates on the semester basis with two summer terms, and recently enrolled 1,396 men and 2,133 women full-time and 329 men and 479 women part-time. The faculty consists of 251 full-time and 125 part-time members.

Entrance Requirements: High school graduation; completion of 20 units including 4 English, 3 mathematics, 2 foreign language, 2 science, 3 social science; SAT required; rolling admission and advanced placement plans available.

Costs Per Year: $1,325 tuition; $6,997 tuition for out-of-state students; $2,915 room and board;

Collegiate Environment: The college's 38 buildings of modern brick construction are located on a 72-acre campus. The college library contains 302,845 volumes and 2,484 periodicals and dormitory facilities are provided for 1,000 men and 2,200 women. The college welcomes a geographically diverse student body and will accept midyear students. Approximately 70% of students applying for admission are accepted. Classes begin in September and 450 scholarships are offered annually.

Community Environment: See Duke University.

NORTH CAROLINA SCHOOL OF THE ARTS   *(E-8)*
200 Waughtown Street
Winston-Salem, North Carolina 27117-2189
Tel: (910) 770-3391; Fax: (910) 770-3370

Description: The school was the first state-supported arts school of its kind when it opened in 1965. It is accredited by the Southern Association of Colleges and Schools. Students are admitted by audition to the professional training programs in dance, design and production, drama, filmmaking, music, and visual arts and are taught by a faculty of working professionals with distinguished careers in the performing and allied arts. The School offers a BFA, BM, MFA, MM, and an arts diploma. A summer program of study and performance abroad in England, Germany, Italy, and Switzerland. It operates on the trimester system and offers one summer session. Enrollment includes 900 students. A faculty of 117 provides a faculty-student ratio of 1-7.

Entrance Requirements: High school graduation or equivalent; completion of 20 units including 4 English, 3 mathematics, 3 science, 3 social science; open enrollment policy; entrance audition required; SAT required; advanced placement, deferred admission, and rolling admission plans available; $35 application fee.

Costs Per Year: $1,233 state resident tuition; $8,640 nonresident tuition; $3,606 room and board; $766 student fees.

Collegiate Environment: The school is located on a 57-acre campus just south of the Old Salem restoration area in Winston-Salem. The 7 buildings include a library of 89,685 titles and 30,950 sound recordings. Dormitories accommodate 600 men and women. Other buildings include dance studios, music practice and teaching studios, a 1,300 seat theater for music and dance productions, four smaller performance areas (including a 200 seat black box and a 450 seat procenium thrust theater), and a student union/cafeteria. Approximately 32% of applicants are accepted, including midyear students. The average scores of freshmen are SAT Verbal 523, Math 502. Financial assistance is available for students with demonstrated financial need. 65% of freshmen return return for their sophomore year.

Community Environment: See Wake Forest University.

NORTH CAROLINA STATE UNIVERSITY - RALEIGH
(F-12)
Raleigh, North Carolina 27695
Tel: (515) 737-2434; Fax: (919) 515-5039

Description: The state university was founded in 1887 as a land-grant institution. It is accredited by the Southern Association of Colleges and Schools and its individual schools and departments are accredited by various associations in their respective fields. It began operations as the North Carolina College of Agriculture and Mechanic Arts in 1889 with 45 students. Since its founding, the institution's research, extension, and academic programs have expanded rapidly, now requiring the services of more than 1,000 professional staff members, nine undergraduate colleges and schools, the graduate school, 17 branch agricultural experiment stations, and extension agents for each of the state's 100 counties. Operating on the semester system and offering two summer terms, the university is a part of the University of North Carolina System. Army, Navy and Air Force ROTC programs are available. Cooperating plans with University of Georgia, Duke University, Oklahoma State University and other institutions. Enrollment includes 18,616 full-time and 8,961 part-time undergraduates and 5,023 graduate students. A faculty of 1,789 a faculty-student ratio of 1-14.

Entrance Requirements: Accredited high school graduation or equivalent; completion of 20 units including 4 English, 3 mathematics, 3 science, 2 social science; 2 foreign language; SAT or ACT required, GRE required for graduate programs; out-of-state applicants must meet higher standards; early admission, midyear admission, rolling admission and advanced placement plans available. $45 application fee.

Costs Per Year: $1,584 tuition and fees; $9,110 tuition and fees for out-of-state students; $3,540 room and board; $600 books, supplies and student fees.

Collegiate Environment: Located in Raleigh, the state's capital, North Carolina State University's main campus encompasses 623 acres and is valued at more than $200,000,000. Adjoining the main campus are several of its experimental farms and woodlands, a 1,000-acre Centennial campus and Carter Finley Stadium. In addition to its holdings in the Raleigh area, extensive agricultural and other types of research facilities are scattered throughout the state. The 140 university buildings contain library facilities which house more than 2,350,000 volumes, 18,401 serials, 3,168,471 microforms, and 118,653 audiovisual materials. Living accommodations are provided for 8,000 students. Each of the 34 social fraternities and sororities chartered by the university maintains a chapter house. 53% of students applying for admission are accepted, including midyear students. The average scors of entering freshmen were SAT 494 verbal, 578 math. The average high school grade point average range was 3.0 to 3.7. More than 90% of the previous freshman class returned to the campus for the sophomore year. 3,700 scholarships are available and 46% of students receive some form of financial assistance.

Community Environment: See Meredith College.

NORTH CAROLINA WESLEYAN COLLEGE   *(F-13)*
3400 N. Wesleyan Boulevard
Rocky Mount, North Carolina 27804
Tel: (919) 985-5100; Fax: (919) 977-3701

Description: North Carolina Wesleyan College, situated on a private and picturesque campus of 200 acres, provides students from twenty-two states and nine countries with the personal attention of a small campus. The college is accredited by the Southern Association of Colleges and Schools. Programs of study lead to the Bachelor degree and courses are offered at extension sites in Raleigh, New Bern, and Goldsboro. The college operates on the semester system and offers two summer sessions. Enrollment includes 730 students. A faculty of 55 full-time and 22 part-time provides a faculty-student ratio of 1-13.

Entrance Requirements: Accredited high school graduation or equivalent; completion of 16 units including 4 English, 2 math, 2 science, and 2 social science; SAT or ACT required; two letters of recommendation are advised; deferred admission, midyear admission, rolling admission, and advanced placement programs available. $25 application fee.

Costs Per Year: $8,600 tuition; $4,500 board and room; $550 student fees.

Collegiate Environment: The college is comprised of 13 buildings located on 200 acres. The library contains 75,000 volumes, 275 pamphlets, 565 periodicals, 12,416 microforms and 7,500 sound recordings. Dormitory facilities are provided for 220 men and 220 women. Approximately 80% of students applying for admission are accepted. Students from other geographical locations are accepted as well as midyear students. Financial aid is available for economically disadvantaged students and 80% of the students receive aid. The average composite SAT score of the current freshmen class is 800. Students are encouraged to act on their interests through involvement in such clubs and organizations as the Outdoor Club, Computer Club, sororities, fraternities, honorary socities, and educational clubs. Club Dramatica, Wesleyan Singers, Gospel Choir, Jazz Band, Brass Ensemble, Pep Band and the N. E. W. Wind Ensemble attract students interested in the performing arts. Aspiring jounalists are encouraged to explore the field by working on the student newspaper, yearboook, or with the campus radio station. North Carolina Wesleyan is a NCAA Division III school offering various intercollegiate athletics.

Community Environment: The Wesleyan campus, located in Rocky Mount, North Carolina is located three miles from Interstate 95 in the coastal plain region of the state. It is a progressive industrial and agricultural community, but still maintains its historic heritage. Rocky

Mount has a population of 50,000 with many recreational (3 hours to the beach or mountains) and health services in the area. Nash General and Community Hospital are only 10 minutes from campus.

PEACE COLLEGE   *(F-12)*
15 E. Peace St.
Raleigh, North Carolina 27604
Tel: (800) 732-2347; Fax: (919) 508-2326

Description: A liberal arts and sciences college for women, Peace College was established in 1857 and is affiliated with the Presbyterian Church, USA. It operates on the semester session. It is fully accredited by the Southern Association of Colleges and Schools to award the Associate degree and is a candidate for accreditation to award the Baccalaureate degree. It is also a member of the American Association of Junior Colleges. A 3-week study abroad program in England during the summer is available. It operates on the semester system and offers a writing institute program in the summer. Enrollment includes 399 full-time and 14 part-time students. A faculty of 26 full-time and 17 part-time gives a faculty-student ratio of 1-8.

Entrance Requirements: High school graduation with rank in upper half of graduating class; completion of 16 units including 4 English, 3 mathematics, 1-2 foreign language, 2-3 science, 2 social science; SAT required; ACT accepted; $25 application fee; early admission, rolling admission, midyear admission, advanced placement and delayed admission plans available.

Costs Per Year: $5,260 tuition and student fees; $4,850 room and board.

Collegiate Environment: The college is located in a fifteen-acre grove of native oaks. The eight college buildings contain a library of 42,000 volumes and dormitory facilities for 450 women. Students from other geographical locations are accepted as well as midyear students. Approximately 75% of students applying for admission are accepted and 90% of the previous freshman class returned to the campus for the second year of studies. The average scores of the entering freshman class were SAT 429 verbal, 454 math. Financial aid and scholarships are available for qualifying students. 62% of the students received financial assistance. Semesters begin in August and January.

Community Environment: See Meredith College.

PEMBROKE STATE UNIVERSITY   *(J-10)*
College Road
Pembroke, North Carolina 28372
Tel: (910) 521-6000; (800) 822-2185 in NC; Admissions: (910) 521-6262; Fax: (910) 521-6497

Description: The university, located in southeastern North Carolina, was established in 1887 by the North Carolina State Legislature as a normal school for the Indians of Robeson County. It is accredited by the Southern Association of Colleges and Schools. Professional accreditations include the National Association of Schools of Music and the National Council for the Accreditation of Teacher Education. The college provides a four-year liberal arts education and grants the Bachelor and Master degrees. The college operates on the semester system and offers two summer sessions. Enrollment includes 2,132 full-time and 542 part-time undergraduate, and 343 graduate students. A faculty of 146 full-time and 47 part-time gives a faculty-student ratio of 1-16.

Entrance Requirements: High school graduation; completion of 16 units including 4 English, 3 mathematics, 2 social studies, 2 language, 3 science; minimum SAT verbal 400, math 400 required; early admission, early decision, midyear admission, rolling admission, and advanced placement plans available; $25 application fee.

Costs Per Year: $1,142 state resident tuition and fees; $6,874 non-resident tuition and fees; $2,760 room and board; $1,300 miscellaneous expenses.

Collegiate Environment: The university is located in the city of the same name, situated 30 miles south of Fayetteville. Facilities include a 108-acre campus with modern on-campus housing for 434 men and 400 women. The library contains 231,000 volumes and 25,468 microforms. There are 287 scholarships available. 47% of students receive some form of financial aid.

Community Environment: Pembroke is located 30 miles southeast of Fayetteville and west of Lumberton. A national bus line, railway and major highways facilitate transportation. There is an airport in nearby Fayetteville.

PFEIFFER COLLEGE   *(G-8)*
Misenheimer, North Carolina 28109
Tel: (704) 463-1360; (800) 338-2060; Fax: (704) 463-1363

Description: The private liberal arts college can trace its beginnings to a small mountain school founded in 1885. It became a junior college in 1928 and a senior college in 1954. It is sponsored by the Western North Carolina Conference of the United Methodist Church. It operates on the semester basis. It also offers two summer terms and is accredited by the Southern Association of Colleges and Schools. Recent enrollment included 405 men and 425 women. The faculty consists of 47 full-time and 25 part-time.

Entrance Requirements: High school graduation or equivalent; completion of 16 units including 4 English, 2 mathematics, 1 science, 2 social science; early admission, rolling admission, midyear admission, and advanced placement plans available. $25 application fee.

Costs Per Year: $8,400 tuition; $3,500 board and room.

Collegiate Environment: The 300-acre campus is located in the rolling Piedmont area of North Carolina, approximately 12 miles from Albemarle and 38 miles from Charlotte. The college library contains 110,000 volumes, 380 periodicals. Living accommodations are provided for 382 men and 318 women and 24 families. Students from other geographical locations are accepted as are midyear students. Approximately 88% of students applying for admission are accepted, and 70% of the previous freshmen class return for the sophomore year. About 55% of the recent freshmen graduated in the top half of the high school class, 26% in the top quarter, and 29% in the third quarter. 90% of students receive some form of financial aid. 228 scholarships are offered, including 30 athletic and 60 for freshmen. Semesters begin in August and January.

Community Environment: The setting for Misenheimer is a rural area with moderate mild climate. Commercial transportation is available at nearby Salisbury, and airlines at Charlotte. Recreational activities include swimming, boating, hunting and camping.

PIEDMONT BIBLE COLLEGE   *(E-8)*
716 Franklin Street
Winston-Salem, North Carolina 27101
Tel: (919) 725-8345; Fax: (910) 725-5522

Description: The private Baptist Bible College was established in 1945 and is accredited by the American Association of Bible Colleges and the Transitional Association of Colleges and Schools. It operates on the semester system and offers three summer terms. Enrollment includes 254 full-time and 34 part-time undergraduates and 25 graduate students. A faculty of 13 full-time and 13 part-time gives a faculty-student ratio of 1-14.

Entrance Requirements: High school graduation or GED equivalent; open enrollment policy; completion of 10 units with recommended courses of 4 English, 2 science, 3 mathematics, 2 social science, 2 foreign language, and 1 biology; ACT and placement examinations required; early decision, early admission, midyear admission, rolling admission and advanced placement plans available; $30 application fee.

Costs Per Year: $4,090 tuition; $2,750 room and board; $300 student fees.

Collegiate Environment: The college occupies more than 4 city blocks within less than one mile of the business section of Winston-Salem. The college library contains 47,787 volumes and 200 periodicals, and living accomodations are provided for 200 men and women. 95% of the students applying for admission are accepted, including midyear students. 13 scholarships are available, including three for freshmen. Approximately 63% of the previous freshman class returned to the campus for the sophomore year.

Community Environment: See Wake Forest University.

PITT COMMUNITY COLLEGE (G-14)
Highway 11 South
P.O. Drawer 7007
Greenville, North Carolina 27835-7007
Tel: (919) 321-4200; Admissions: (919) 321-4245; Fax: (919) 321-4401

Description: Formerly know as Pitt Technical Institution, the school is under the administration of the North Carolina Department of Community Colleges. It is accredited by the Southern Association of Colleges and Schools. Programs of study are primarily voactional-technical. It operates on the quarter system. Enrollment includes 2,322 full-time and 2,351 part-time students. A faculty of 121 full-time and 117 part-time gives a faculty-student ratio of 1-19.

Entrance Requirements: High school graduation or equivalent required for degree programs; open enrollment policy; completion of 16 units including 4 English, 2 math, 2 science, 2 social studies; entrance examinations required for placement.

Costs Per Year: $742 tuition; $6,020 out-of-state tuition; $24 student fees.

Collegiate Environment: The 75-acre campus is located between Greenville and Winterville. There is approximately 142,000 square feet of usable space designed to house a technical and vocational trade school. The library contains 32,000 volumes, 354 periodicals, and 3,882 audiovisual materials. 270 scholarships are available and 23% of the students receive some form of financial aid. All students applying for admission are accepted, including midyear students. 50% of the previous entering class returned to the campus for a second year of studies.

Community Environment: See East Carolina University.

QUEENS COLLEGE (H-7)
1900 Selwyn Avenue
Charlotte, North Carolina 28274
Tel: (704) 337-2212; (800) 849-0202; Fax: (704) 337-2403

Description: Founded in 1857, Queens College is a four-year, private, coeducational, liberal arts college, affiliated with the Presbyterian Church, USA. It now includes the degree-granting New College with evening and Saturday classes and graduate programs. Queens operates on the semester system and offers one summer session. Air Force and Army ROTC are available through Charlotte Consortium. It is accredited by the Southern Association of Colleges and Schools. Recent enrollment numbered 1,602, including 169 men and 625 women in the traditional College of Arts and Sciences and 808 men and women in the New College and Graduate School. A faculty of 73 full-time and 42 part-time provides a faculty-student ratio of 1-12. Queens has a three-week international study tour for all students. This trip is taken during May, and the cost is paid for by the college.

Entrance Requirements: High school graduation or equivalent; completion of 16 units including 4 English, 3 math, 1 laboratory science, 2 foreign language, and 2 social studies; $25 application fee; early admission, rolling admission, and advanced placement plans available.

Costs Per Year: $11,020 tuition; $4,970 room and board.

Collegiate Environment: The college is located on a 25-acre wooded campus in the Myers Park residential area of Charlotte. The college buildings include a library of 115,000 titles and 590 periodicals. Dormitory facilities house 600 students. Students from other geographical locations are accepted as well as midyear students. Approximately 80% of students applying for admission are accepted. 92% of the recent freshmen graduated in the top half of the high school class; 59% in the top quintile. More than 93% of the previous freshman class returned to this campus for the sophomore year. The middle 50% range of scores for the entering freshman class were SAT 430-540 verbal and 460-580 math, and ACT 20-26 combined. Financial aid and scholarships are available; 85% of the students receive some form of financial aid.

Community Environment: Queens is located in Charlotte, the largest city in the Carolinas (population 475,000). It is one of the major centers for banking, health care and communications in the Southeast. All forms of commercial transportation are available. Charlotte's Douglas International Airport is the third busiest in the Southeast. A wide variety of performing arts, theater, opera, ballet, and road shows is available through the city's new performing arts center, Spirit Square, the Charlotte Coliseum, Ovens Auditorium and the Charlotte Little Theater. A hands-on science and technology museum, Discovery Place, opened in 1981. Charlotte's Mint Museum is recognized as one of the best in the South. Recreational facilities are numerous, including water sports on Lake Norman and Lake Wylie; the city has a professional basketball team and an NFL frachise, and many area colleges and universities sports tournaments are held in Charlotte. For outdoor recreation, the city is halfway between the Carolinas beaches to the east and the Smokey and Pisgah Mountains and ski areas to the west.

RANDOLPH COMMUNITY COLLEGE (G-9)
P.O. Box 1009
629 Industrial Park Avenue
Asheboro, North Carolina 27204-1009
Tel: (910) 629-1471; Fax: (910) 629-4695

Description: Randolph Community College is a comprehensive community college which is accredited by the Southern Association of Colleges and Schools. It offers the first two years of college through the Extension Division of the University of North Carolia at Greensboro, as well as technical (two-year) and vocational (one-year) programs designed for immediate employment, adult high school, adult basic education, and a variety of continuing education courses for adults who seek to upgrade job skills or who seek personal improvement. Randolph Community College offers specialized Associate degree programs in Interior Design, Photography, Photofinishing, and Commercial Graphics. The college grants certificates and Associate degrees. It operates on the quarter system and offers one summer session. Enrollment includes 702 full-time and 775 part-time students. A faculty of 45 full-time and 25 part-time gives a faculty-student ratio of 1-23.

Entrance Requirements: Open door admissions policy; some restrictions on admissions to specific programs, but restrictions are flexible; high school graduation or equivalent required.

Costs Per Year: $556.50 state-resident tuition; $4,515 out-of-state.

Collegiate Environment: Randolph Community College campus includes five major buildings plus a design center. The original building, constructed in 1962 with additions in 1968 and 1972 is now known as the Administration and Education Building. In addition to a centralized administrative service, this building contains many classrooms, labs, and shops. A Vocational-Technical Building containing approximately 30,000 square feet, provides an automotive body shop, a building trades shop, and electrical electronics labs. A Student Services Center of 18,000 square feet houses a student lounge, the campus bookstore, food services, and office facilities for guidance counseling, career center, information center, admissions, registration, Veteran's benefits and financial aid. The latest addition is the Business Education Center containing 11,800 square feet and housing all business courses, typing and computer labs. The Design Center currently houses both Commercial Graphics and Interior Design. The Learning Resources Center contains 30,000 titles, 240 periodicals, 3,500 microforms, and 5,000 audiovisual materials. The 25-acre campus is south of the business district of Asheboro. Students from other geographical locations are accepted as well as midyear students. 100% of students applying for admission are accepted and 75% of the previous entering class returned to the college for the second year of studies. 26% of the students receive financial aid. The newly constructed facilities at the Archdale campus include a 7,600-square-foot primary classroom building and a 3,000-square-foot metal building that houses two general-purpose shop areas. The new campus is located at 110 Park Drive, adjacent to the city of Archdale's Creekside Park. The main building houses five classrooms, a reception/office area, and a student break area.

Community Environment: Asheboro is the county seat of Randolph County and the home of the North Carolina State Zoo, and is located near the geographical center of the state. This town had grown steadily with the surrounding area, mainly agricultural. Community facilities include numerous churches, a library, and convenient shopping centers. Several lakes nearby provide facilities for hunting, fishing, boating and water skiing.

RICHMOND COMMUNITY COLLEGE   (I-9)
P.O. Box 1189
Hamlet, North Carolina 28345
Tel: (910) 582-7000; Admissions: (910) 582-7120; Fax: (910) 582-7028

Description: The public technical college was established in 1964 by the North Carolina Department of Community Colleges. It operates on the quarter system and offers one summer session. It is accredited by the Southern Association of Colleges and Schools. Enrollment includes 1,044 men and women. A faculty of 100 gives a faculty-student ratio of 1:10.

Entrance Requirements: Open door policy; high school graduation or equivalent required for degree programs; placement tests required; early decision and rolling admission plans available.

Costs Per Year: $420 tuition; $3,924 tuition for out-of-state students; $28 student fees.

Collegiate Environment: The 159-acre campus is located one mile west of Hamlet. Facilities are housed in 4 buildings with a total of 115,000 square feet. Students from other geographical locations are accepted as well as midyear students. About 99% of the students applying for admission are accepted. The library contains 27,000 volumes, 4,000 pamphlets, 200 periodicals and 2,750 audiovisual materials.

Community Environment: Located 75 miles southeast of Charlotte, Hamlet is a town with a friendly atmosphere. Its primary businesses are manufacturing and textiles. Train and bus transportation is available. Community facilities include churches of various faiths, a library, shopping areas and good medical facilities. Recreational activities include swimming, boating, tennis, and fishing.

ROANOKE-CHOWAN COMMUNITY COLLEGE   (E-15)
Rt. 2, Box 46A
Ahoskie, North Carolina 27910
Tel: (919) 332-5921

Description: The public technical college was the first unit in the state set up by direct contract with the State Board of Education, which enables it to operate directly under the control of the Department of Community Colleges. The institute enrolls 810 full-time and part-time students. It operates on a four-quarter basis. A faculty of 32 full-time, 16 part-time gives a faculty-student ratio of 1-15. The institute is fully accredited by the Southern Association of Colleges and Schools.

Entrance Requirements: High school graduation or equivalent required for most; placement tests required; completion of 18 units including 4 English, 2 mathematics, 2 science, 2 social science recommended; open enrollment policy for nondegree programs; rolling admission, advanced placement plans available.

Costs Per Year: $360 tuition; $3,360 tuition for out-of-state students; $34 student fees.

Collegiate Environment: The college is comprised of eight buildings and is located on 39 acres. Students from other geographical locations are accepted as well as midyear students. The library contains 24,765 volumes, 227 periodicals, and numerous audiovisual materials.

Community Environment: See Chowan College.

ROBESON COMMUNITY COLLEGE   (I-11)
P.O. Box 1420
Lumberton, North Carolina 28358
Tel: (910) 738-7101; Admissions: (910) 738-7101; Fax: (910) 671-4143

Description: The public technical college was established in 1964 and is a unit of the Department of Community Colleges. It operates on quarter system and offers one summer session. The college is fully accredited by the Southern Association of Colleges and Schools. The college grants the Associate degree. Enrollment includes 1,400 full-time and 350 part-time and 495 evening students. A faculty of 93 full-time and 43 part-time gives a faculty-student ratio of 1-18.

Entrance Requirements: Any high school graduate, or any non-high school graduate 18 years of age or older who is able to profit from further formal education may be admitted; placement tests required.

Costs Per Year: $2,100 tuition; $5,160 tuition for out-of-state students.

Collegiate Environment: The technical college is located approximately one mile northeast of Lumberton and twelve miles south of St. Pauls. The six institute buildings contain special equipment for all shops, laboratories, and classrooms that provide opportunities for using modern tools and machines. The library contains 35,286 volumes, 186 periodicals and numerous microforms and audiovisual materials. All students applying for admission are accepted. Students from other geographical locations are accepted as are midyear students.

Community Environment: Located in a rural setting in Robeson County, this community is a short distance from Lumberton, the county seat, and has access to all the advantages of that city. Commercial transportation is available. Lumberton is also one of the major tobacco markets; other industries are here along with a number of churches and a library.

ROCKINGHAM COMMUNITY COLLEGE   (E-9)
Wentworth, North Carolina 27375
Tel: (919) 342-4261; Fax: (919) 349-9986

Description: The public community college began operation in September of 1966. It provides college-parallel, vocational-technical, and continuing education programs. Cooperative education programs are available in several subjects. It operates on the quarter system and offers three summer terms. It is accredited by the Southern Association of Colleges and Schools. Enrollment is 1,060 full-time and 1,003 part-time students. A faculty of 52 full-time and 47 part-time gives a faculty-student ratio of 1-21.

Entrance Requirements: Open enrollment policy; high school graduation or equivalent required for degree programs; entrance exam required; rolling admission and advanced placement plans available.

Costs Per Year: $477 tuition; $3,870 out-of-state; $27 student fees.

Collegiate Environment: The college is comprised of 11 buildings and is located on 257 acres. The trilevel library houses more than 35,000 volumes in general, scientific, and occupational fields. All students applying for admission are accepted, including midyear students. Financial assistance is available for economically disadvantaged and academically talented traditional and nontraditional students.

Community Environment: Located near Reidsville and Eden in Rockingham County.

ROWAN-CABARRUS COMMUNITY COLLEGE   (G-8)
Box 1595
Salisbury Blvd. at I-85
Salisbury, North Carolina 28145-1595
Tel: (704) 637-0760

Description: This public, coeducational technical college was established in 1963 and is a unit of the Department of Community Colleges of North Carolina. It is accredited by the Southern Association of Colleges and Schools. The college offers two-year occupational degree programs, one-year diploma programs, certificate programs, and adult education courses. The college operates on the quarter system and offers one summer session. Enrollment includes 1,189 full-time and 2,234 part-time students. A faculty of 76 full-time and 55 part-time gives a faculty-student ratio of 1-26.

Entrance Requirements: High school graduation or equivalent; open enrollment policy; minimum 18 years of age; placement tests required; rolling admission and advanced placement plans available.

Costs Per Year: $577 state resident tuition and fees; $4,515 nonresident tuition and fees.

Collegiate Environment: RCCC is a multi-campus institution. A 102-acre campus is located at the intersection of Jake Alexander Boulevard and Interstate 85 in Salisbury, North Carolina. Its five buildings include a library of 22,907 hardbound volumes, 313 periodicals, and 9,266 audiovisual materials. In Cabarrus County, the college is located at Highway 73 and Interstate 85. Scholarships are available and 20% of students receive some form of financial assistance.

Community Environment: See Catawba College.

SAINT ANDREW'S PRESBYTERIAN COLLEGE   *(I-10)*
1700 Dogwood Mile
Laurinburg, North Carolina 28352
Tel: (910) 276-5555; (800) 763-0198; Fax: (910) 277-5020

Description: This private, four-year, liberal arts college was established by the Synod of North Carolina, Presbyterian Church in the United States. It is accredited by the Southern Association of Colleges and Schools. It operates on a 4-1-4 term system and offers one summer session. Enrollment is 748 students. A faculty of 41 full-time and 16 part-time gives a faculty-student ratio of 1-15.

Entrance Requirements: Accredited high school graduation; SAT or ACT required; $25 application fee; early admission, early decision, rolling admission, delayed admission and advanced placement plans available.

Costs Per Year: $10,895 tuition; $4,810 room and board.

Collegiate Environment: The contemporary style campus is situated on 600 acres of rolling land, most of which lies in the city limits. The 20 college buildings include a library of 106,382 volumes, 20,000 microforms and 2,967 sound recordings, and dormitory facilities for 350 men and 350 women. Students from other geographical locations are accepted as well as midyear students. Approximately 75% of students applying for admission are accepted. Almost 80% of the previous freshman class returned to this campus for the sophomore year. The average SAT score of the current freshman class was 921 composite. Financial assistance is available for students, and 85% of the students receive aid. The college awarded 144 Bachelor degrees to the recent graduating class.

Community Environment: Laurinburg is located at the southern edge of the peach belt and the sandhills resort region. Railroad transportation is available. Community facilities include a public library, 33 Protestant churches, 1 Catholic church, 1 hospital, and numerous civic and service organizations. Tennis courts and lakes provide the facilities for recreation on campus.

SAINT AUGUSTINE'S COLLEGE   *(F-12)*
1315 Oakwood Avenue
Raleigh, North Carolina 27611
Tel: (919) 516-4200; (800) 948-1126; Admissions: (919) 866-4811; Fax: (919) 834-6473

Description: The private liberal arts college was founded in 1867 by the Freeman's Commission of the Protestant Episcopal Church and members of the Episcopal Diocese of North Carolina. It is accredited by the Southern Association of Colleges and Schools. Recently, there were 1,852 students enrolled and a faculty of 94 full-time and 198 part-time members. The college operates on the semester system and offers one summer session.

Entrance Requirements: High school graduation with rank in upper half of graduating class; completion of 18 units including 4 English, 3 mathematics, 2 science, 2 social science; SAT required; $25 application fee.

Costs Per Year: $5,000 tuition; $1,800 board and room; $800 student fees.

Collegiate Environment: The college is comprised of 27 buildings on 110 acres. The college library contains 128,900 volumes, and dormitory facilities are provided for 580 men and 815 women. Approximately 80% of students applying for admission are accepted, including midyear students. Financial aid is available for economically handicapped students and 85% of freshmen receive some form of aid.

Community Environment: St. Augustine's College is situated on 110 acres of land in the northeast section of the capital city of Raleigh, North Carolina. Also located in Raleigh are North Carolina State University, Shaw University, Meredith, Peace and St. Mary's Colleges. The Research Triangle Park is located nearby. There are numerous cultural, social, educational professional, religious and recreational activities in the area.

SAINT MARY'S COLLEGE   *(F-12)*
900 Hillsborough Street
Raleigh, North Carolina 27603-1689
Tel: (919) 839-4100

Description: The private college for women is affiliated with the Episcopal Church. It was founded in 1842 and achieved its present status of combined high school and college in 1900. The college is accredited by the Southern Association of Colleges and Schools. It is a member of the six-college Raleigh consortium. It operates on the semester system and offers two summer sessions. Enrollment is 412 students. A faculty of 45 full-time gives a faculty-student ratio of 1-14.

Entrance Requirements: High school graduation with rank in upper half of graduating class; completion of 16 units including 4 English, 3 mathematics, 2 foreign language, 2 science, and 2 social science; SAT minimum 400V and 400M, or ACT; rolling admission, early admission, midyear admissions, and advanced placement plans available. $25 application fee.

Costs Per Year: $7,025 tuition, $6,070 room and board, $100 student fees.

Collegiate Environment: The 21 college buildings contain a library of 39,240 titles, 279 periodicals, and microforms. Dormitory facilities are available for 370 women. The college welcomes a geographically diverse student body and will accept midyear students. About 60% of the recent freshmen graduated in the top half of the high school class, 20% in the top quarter and 30% in the third quarter. 50 scholarships are available and 47% of students receive some form of financial aid.

Community Environment: See Meredith College.

SALEM COLLEGE   *(E-8)*
Winston-Salem, North Carolina 27108
Tel: (919) 721-2621; (800) 327-2536; Fax: (919) 724-7102

Description: This private liberal arts college for women was the first educational institution established in North Carolina. It was founded in 1772 by the Moravians, a Pre-Reformation Protestant denomination. It is accredited by the Souther Association of Colleges and Schools and the National Association of Schools of Music. The college grants the Bachelor degree. Special programs include a Washington Semester, study abroad, and a 3/2 engineering program with Duke and Vanderbilt. The college operates on the 4-1-4 calendar system and offers two summer sessions. The college enrolls 571 women full-time and 222 women part-time. A faculty of 48 full-time and 17 part-time gives a faculty-student ratio of 1-10.

Entrance Requirements: High school graduation; completion of 16 units including 4 English, 3 mathematics, 2 foreign language, 3 science, and 2 history; SAT or ACT required; early admission, rolling admission, midyear admission and advanced placement plans available; $25 application fee.

Costs Per Year: $10,950 tuition; $6,750 room and board; $185 student fees.

Collegiate Environment: The 57-acre campus is located in the heart of Old Salem, the original settlement founded in 1766, from which has developed Winston-Salem, a city on the Piedmont Plateau of North Carolina. The 21 college buildings include a library of 85,000 volumes, 540 periodicals, 35 microforms and 8,650 audiovisual materials; 750,000 titles are available through an automated library system (PALS) that links five private area colleges. Dormitory facilities are provided for 490 women. Students from other geographical locations are accepted as well as midyear students. 79% of applicants are accepted. Financial assistance is available for economically handicapped students and 60% of students receive aid.

Community Environment: See Wake Forest University.

SAMPSON COMMUNITY COLLEGE   *(I-12)*
P.O. Box 318
Clinton, North Carolina 28328
Tel: (910) 592-8081; Admissions: (910) 592-8084; Fax: (910) 592-8048

Description: The publicly supported, coeducational technical college is a unit of the North Carolina Department of Community Colleges and was established in 1965. It offers programs leading to the high school Diploma, Certificate and Associate degrees. Cooperative education programs are available in several areas. The college is accredited by the Southern Association of Colleges and Schools. It operates on the quarter system and offers one summer session. Enrollment includes 147 men and 374 women full-time and 160 men and 405 women part-time. A faculty of 47 full-time and 52 part-time gives a faculty-student ratio of 1-20.

Entrance Requirements: Open enrollment policy; aptitude tests required; non-high school graduates considered; rolling admission, early admission, early decision plan available. No application fee.

Costs Per Year: $600 tuition; $4,500 nonresident tuition; $34 activity fee; additional expenses average $1,200.

Collegiate Environment: The college is located in four modern buildings two miles west of Clinton. The library contains 22,819 volumes, 700 pamphlets, 128 periodicals, 2,300 microforms and 4,617 audiovisual materials. Approximately 100% of students applying for admission are accepted, including midyear students and 50% return for the second year. Financial aid is available and 40% of the current student body receives some form of financial assistance.

Community Environment: The county seat of Sampson County, Clinton is in the coastal plain section of the state. Community facilities have grown as Clinton has grown in population. A complete shopping center is located here, along with churches representing most denominations. A county hospital and numerous civic and service organizations serve the community. 28 industrial firms are based here. Job opportunities are available. Recreational activities include golf, hunting, fishing, and swimming.

SANDHILLS COMMUNITY COLLEGE   (H-10)
2200 Airport Road
Pinehurst, North Carolina 28374
Tel: (919) 692-6185; (800) 338-3944; Fax: (919) 692-2756

Description: The publicly supported, coeducational college was created as a result of legislation passed by the 1963 General Assembly of North Carolina. It is accredited by the Southern Association of Colleges and Schools. It is professionally accredited by the Committee on Allied Health Education and Accreditation, and the National League for Nursing. The college operates on the four-quarter system with 6 summer sessions. Enrollment includes 1,548 full-time and 823 part-time students. A faculty of 110 full-time and 40 part-time gives a faculty-student ratio of 1-18.

Entrance Requirements: Open enrollment policy; high school graduation or equivalent required for all programs; rolling admission plan available.

Costs Per Year: $577.50 tuition; $4,536 nonresidents; $21 student activity fee.

Collegiate Environment: The 230-acre campus is located near Southern Pines, Aberdeen, and Pinehurst. The 10 college buildings include a library of 68,000 volumes. All students applying for admission are accepted, although certain occupational programs have entry criteria. Financial aid is available. 40% of students receive some form of financial aid.

Community Environment: A small town environment, established originally as a health resort, it is now a resort area. Southern Pines is famous for its dry and mild climate. Pinehurst is noted for its golfing and tourism as well as for major horse stables. Area facilities include three libraries, a museum, churches of all denominations, and various civic and service organizations. Recreational activities include golf, tennis, horseback riding, hunting, and fishing. Special events of the season include a steeplechase in April.

SHAW UNIVERSITY   (F-12)
118 E. South Street
Raleigh, North Carolina 27611
Tel: (919) 546-8200; Admissions: (919) 546-8275; Fax: (919) 546-8301

Description: The privately supported, coeducational university was founded in 1865 by Henry Martin Tupper. In 1965, Shaw inaugurated one of the first comprehensive programs in the nation designed to remedy academic deficiencies and enable students of promise but with limited achievement to qualify for regular college study toward the Bachelor degree. The university is accredited by the Southern Association of Colleges and Schools. It operates on the semester system and offers one summer term. Enrollment includes 2,258 full-time and 174 part-time students. A faculty of 101 full-time and 221 part-time members gives a faculty-student ratio of 1-13.

Entrance Requirements: High school graduation or equivalent; completion of 18 units including 3 nglish, 2 mathematics, 2 science, 2 social studies, and 9 electives; SAT and ACT not required but recommended; early admission and rolling admission plans availabvle; $25 application fee.

Costs Per Year: $5,266 tuition; $3,476 board and room.

Collegiate Environment: Located immmediatedly adjacent to downtown Raleigh, the 15-acre campus is being quickly transformed into an urban educational center. The 20 university buildings contain a library of 129,000 titles and dormitory facilities for 817 men and women. The university provides a solid liberal arts education which allows students to progress at their own pace. The university welcomes a geographically diverse student body and will accept midyear students. Approximately 80% of students applying for admission are accepted. About 60% of the previous entering class returned to this campus for the second year of studies. Scholarships are available and 90% the students receive some form of financial aid.

Community Environment: See Meredith College.

SOUTHEASTERN BAPTIST THEOLOGICAL SEMINARY
(F-12)
P.O. Box 1889
Wake Forest, North Carolina 27588-1889
Tel: (919) 556-3101; (800) 334-7709

Description: Southeastern Baptist Theological Seminary is an agency of the Southern Baptist Convention and is accredited by the Association of Theological Schools in the United States and Canada, and the Southern Association of Colleges and Schools. The seminary opened in 1951 and its facilities are offered on an equal basis to students of all denominations. It is a graduate seminary which offers a Masters of Divinity, Masters of Theology, and Doctorate of Ministry. The seminary operates on the semester basis and also offers two summer terms. A recent enrollment included 38 men and 16 women. Faculty numbers 31 full-time, 4 part-time.

Entrance Requirements: Bachelors degree required. GRE or MAT required for the Doctorate of Ministry program. Admission requirements are very precise for each major, so students should contact school. $10 application fee.

Costs Per Year: $1,000 matriculation for students who are recommended by the Southern Baptist Convention; $2,000 for other students; $100 student service fee; $1,305 room only; $205-$275 per month married student apartment.

Collegiate Environment: The 450-acre campus is located 15 miles north of Raleigh, the capital of the state, and 22 miles east of Durham. The 150+ seminary buildings include a library of 250,000 volumes and living accommodations for 158 men, 86 women, and 213 families. Students from all geographical locations are accepted as well as midyear students.

Community Environment: Wake Forest is located 15 miles north of Raleigh and 22 miles east of Durham on US 1 and NC 98. The seminary is only 25 miles from the Raleigh-Durham Airport. 12 churches, a hospital, a public library, and numerous civic and service organizations are found within the community. A full-time recreational program, supervised by a recreational director, swimming pools, lighted athletic fields, tennis courts, racquetball courts, weight rooms, and two golf courses provide the recreational facilities.

SOUTHEASTERN COMMUNITY COLLEGE   (K-11)
P.O. Box 151
Whiteville, North Carolina 28472
Tel: (919) 642-7141

Description: The publicly supported, coeducational college opened in 1964 and is a member institution of the Department of Community Colleges of North Carolina. It operates on the quarter system with two summer sessions and is accredited by the Southern Association of Colleges and Schools. Enrollment includes 1,562 men and women. A faculty of 95 gives a faculty-student ratio of 1:16. The college offers college transfer programs, technical-vocational programs, adult educational programs, and community service programs leading to the Certificate, Diploma, and Associate degree.

Entrance Requirements: Open door policy; high school graduation or equivalent required for credit courses; completion of 18 units including 4 English, 2 mathematics, 2 sciences, 2 social studies; college placement tests required; rolling admission plan; early decision plan available.

Costs Per Year: $420 tuition; $3,924 tuition for out-of-state students; $9.50 student fees.

Collegiate Environment: The college occupies 106-acre campus. The modern campus contains 8 buildings which include a library of 46,000 volumes, 7,000 pamphlets, 200 periodicals, 74,650 microforms and 6,093 recordings. All students applying for admission that meet the requirements are accepted, and 50% of the previous entering class returned to the campus for the second year of studies. Midyear students are accepted except for nursing and selected vocational programs. Financial aid is available and 43% of the current student body receive some form of financial assistance.

Community Environment: A rural community with the mean annual temperature of 64 degrees. Bus transportation is convenient, and there is plane service at Wilmington and Fayetteville. Shopping facilities, 14 churches representing a number of denominations, and a hospital are part of the community. Opportunities for part-time employment are limited. Nearby lake and beaches, golf course, swimming pools, and tennis courts provide the recreational facilities.

SOUTHWESTERN COMMUNITY COLLEGE   *(G-2)*
275 Webster Road
Sylva, North Carolina 28779
Tel: (704) 586-4091

Description: The publicly supported community college was founded in 1964 as an area educational institution within the Department of Community Colleges of North Carolina. Jackson, Swain, and Macon Counties make up the primary service area of this institution. It operates on a four-quarter basis and is accredited by the Southern Association of Colleges and Schools. A Cooperative Education Program is available in all technical subjects. Enrollment is approximately 1,400 students. A faculty of 45 full-time and 120 part-time gives a faculty-student ratio of 1-20.

Entrance Requirements: Open enrollment policy; completion of 16 units; non-high school graduates considered; placement examinations required; rolling admission, early admission, early decision, delayed admission, and advanced placement plans available.

Costs Per Year: $742 tuition; $6,020 out-of-state; $32 student fees.

Collegiate Environment: The college is comprised of six buildings on 55 acres and contains a library of 22,000 volumes, 205 periodicals, and 1,579 microforms. Classes begin in September, and midyear students are accepted. Financial aid is available and 60% of the current students receive some form of financial assistance.

Community Environment: Sylva is a small mountain town with friendly people and an abundance of recreational opportunities. The primary business is tourism and a few small industries. Commercial transportation is not available. Community facilities include 20 churches of various faiths, three libraries, medical and shopping facilities, and a number of historical sites. The Great Smoky Mountains National Park provides facilities for camping, hiking, fishing, hunting, swimming, and water skiing.

SURRY COMMUNITY COLLEGE   *(E-7)*
P.O. Box 304
Dobson, North Carolina 27017
Tel: (910) 386-8121; Admissions: (910) 386-8121 x204; Fax: (910) 386-8951

Description: The publicly supported, coeducational, community junior college is operated under the direction of the North Carolina Department of Community Colleges and is accredited by the State Department of Education and the Southern Association of Colleges and Schools. It operates on a quarter basis and offers two summer sessions. Enrollment includes 1,800 full-time and 600 part-time students. A faculty of 82 full-time and 15 part-time gives a faculty-student ratio of of 1-22.

Entrance Requirements: Open door policy; high school graduation; early decision, rolling admission, midyear admission, and advanced placement plans available; No application fee.

Costs Per Year: $477 state resident tuition; $3,870 nonresident tuition; $18 student fees.

Collegiate Environment: The 96-acre campus is situated less than 1 mile south of Dobson. The campus includes seven major structures including a science-technical building, a shop building, a learning resources building and a library containing 30,000 volumes. Financial aid is available for economically disadvantaged students.

Community Environment: A rural community with temperate climate, Dobson is the county seat. Community facilities include a library, United Methodist and Baptist churches, a hospital within 11 miles, some shopping, and several civic and service organizations. There are job opportunities in textile factories and with a poultry processing plant.

TRI-COUNTY COMMUNITY COLLEGE   *(H-1)*
Box 40
Murphy, North Carolina 28906
Tel: (704) 837-6810; Fax: (704) 837-3266

Description: This publicly supported, coeducational community college was established in 1964. The college is accredited by the Southern Association of Colleges and Schools. It operates on the quarter system and offers one summer sesson. Enrollment is 305 full-time and 654 part-time students. A faculty of 19 full-time and 31 part-time gives a faculty-student ratio of 1-17. Technological, academic and vocational programs are offered in day and evening classes.

Entrance Requirements: Open enrollment policy; high school graduation with completion of 16 units; entrance examination; early decision, rolling admission, and advanced placement plans available.

Costs Per Year: $547 tuition; $4,515 out-of-state; $13 student fees.

Collegiate Environment: The college is comprised of ten buildings that contain a library of 20,325 books, 294 periodicals, 1,584 microforms and 1,854 audiovisual materials. All of those applying are accepted. Classes begin in September and midyear students are accepted. Financial aid is available.

Community Environment: Located in a valley in the central part of Cherokee County, Murphy has available bus and train transportation; Andrews Airport is 11 miles away. Community facilities include seven church denominations, two hospitals, and a fully equipped clinic. Mountains, streams, lakes, and forests make Murphy a sports lover's paradise. Parks, playgrounds, and other recreational facilities are available, including a new complex that offers swimming pools, an 18-hole golf course, and horseback riding.

UNIVERSITY OF NORTH CAROLINA - ASHEVILLE   *(G-3)*
One University Heights
Asheville, North Carolina 28804
Tel: (704) 251-6600; (800) 531-9842; Admissions: (704) 251-6480; Fax: (704) 251-6841

Description: The University of North Carolina at Asheville is accredited by the Southern Association of Colleges and Schools. It is the state's liberal arts university devoted to undergraduate education. Noted for its strong humanities-based general education and undergraduate research programs, UNC-Asheville features the close student-faculty teaching and learning relationships and leadership opportunities afforded by its small college environment. UNC-Asheville operates on the semester system and offers three summer sessions. International programs include summer in Oxford and Cambridge, England, China, and Equador. Enrollment includes 2,133 full-time and 1,022 part-time undergraduates and 41 graduate students. A faculty of 146 full-time and 102 part-time gives a faculty-student ratio of 1-14.

Entrance Requirements: Accredited high school graduation; rank in upper half of graduating class; completion of 16 college preparatory courses including 4 English, 3 mathematics, 3 science, 2 social science, 3 history, and 3 electives; early admission, rolling admission, midyear admission and advanced placement plans available. $25 application fee.

Costs Per Year: $628 tuition; $6,360 out-of-state; $3,467 room and board; $960 student fees.

Collegiate Environment: The UNCA campus occupies 265 acres. The 24 college buildings contain a library of 273,618 volumes, 2,106 periodicals, and 282,340 microforms. Dormitory facilities house 440 men and 474 women students. The college welcomes a geographically diverse student body. 60% of applicants are accepted. 80% of the previous freshman class return to the campus for the sophomore year. Approximately 98% of the recent freshman class graduated in the top half of the high school class; 68% ranked in the top quarter, and 31% were in the top tenth. The middle 50% raqnges of scores for the entering freshman class were SAT 440-550 verbal, 500-600 math. Financial aid and merit scholarships are available. 1,902 scholarships are offered, including 145 athletic. 34% of the students receive some form of financial aid.

Community Environment: Located in the Blue Ridge Mountains, with the Great Smoky Mountains National Park near by, Asheville is one of the most famous mountain resorts in the East. The city of 60,000 is the largest in western North Carolina, having a number of diversified enterprises fine restaurants, and extensive shopping areas. The city is served by air, bus, and the interstate highway system. Community facilities include art galleries, theater, concert hall, hospitals, YMCA, YWCA, libraries, symphony, and a number of civic and service organizations. Some of the many points of interest are the Biltmore House and Gardens, the Grove Park Inn, the Blue Ridge Parkway, Stuart Nye Silver Shop, the Thomas Wolfe Memorial, and the Carl Sandburg Memorial, National Forests, hiking, biking, and canoeing.

UNIVERSITY OF NORTH CAROLINA - CHAPEL HILL
(F-11)
Monogram Club Bldg. CB#2200 UNC-Chapel H
Chapel Hill, North Carolina 27599-2200
Tel: (919) 966-3621

Description: The University of North Carolina at Chapel Hill was the first state university to open its doors and the nation's only public university to award degrees to students in the 18th century. Authorized by the North Carolina Constitution in 1776, the university was chartered in 1789. The cornerstone for the first state university building in the United States, Old East (still a residence hall), was laid Oct. 12, 1793. Now part of the 16-campus University of North Carolina, the Chapel Hill campus has earned a worldwide reputation for vital teaching, cutting-edge research, and distinguished public service. Among the nation's most comprehensive institutions, UNCCH belongs to the select group of 58 research campuses forming the Association of American Universities. It also is accredited by the Southern Association of Colleges and Schools and respective educational and professional organizations. The university is comprised of the College of Arts and Sciences, General College (first two years), Graduate School, Kenan-Flagler Business School, School of Education, School of Journalism and Mass Communication, School of Law, School of Information and Library Science, and School of Social Work. The Division of Health Affairs includes the School of Dentistry, School of Medicine, School of Nursing, School of Pharmacy, School of Public Health, the widely acclaimed statewide Area Health Education Centers (AHEC) Program, and UNC Hospitals, a teaching facility. The university operates on the semester system and offers two summer sessions. Army, Navy and Air Force ROTC programs are available. Enrollment includes 15,895 undergraduates, and 8,568 graduate and professional students. The faculty consists of 2,328 full-time and 191 part-time members.

Entrance Requirements: Accredited high school graduation or equivalent; completion of 16 units including 4 English, 3 mathematics (2 algebra and 1 geometry or a higher level math course for which algebra II is a prerequisite), 2 years of the same foreign language, 3 science with at least one laboratory, 2 social science (one must be U.S. History), and 2 academic electives; SAT or ACT required; $55 application fee; applicants for admission to graduate programs or to one of the professional schools should apply directly to the dean or admissions officer of the school in which admission is sought. All other applications are submitted to the Graduate School Admissions Office.

Costs Per Year: $1,296 tuition and fees; $7,880 out-of-state; additional tuition required for some professional schools; $3,950 room and board; $450 books; $450 additional nonresident student fees; $1,060 personal expenses.

Collegiate Environment: It is necessary that the Office of Admissions give priority in admissions to applicants in accordance with the quality of their records. 39% of applicants were accepted. The average scores of the entering freshman class were SAT 529 verbal, 599 math. Approximately 93% of the recent freshmen graduated in the top fifth of the high school class, and 76% ranked in the highest tenth. Scholarships are available and 39% of the students receive some form of financial aid. The university provides living accommodations for 6,700 students and 306 units for families. 28 national fraternities and 15 national sororities have active chapters at the university. These accommodate 3,000 undergraduates. The university library, containing over 4,154,897 volumes, 38,000 periodicals, 3,700,000 microforms and 101,000 sound recordings, ranks among the 25 largest academic libraries in the United States.

Community Environment: A suburban community with temperate climate, Chapel Hill is the home of the oldest state university in the country. Commercial transportation is available. Libraries, the Morehead Planetarium, numerous churches of every denomination, a museum, hospital, good shopping facilities, parks, and numerous civic and social clubs are a part of the community. There are job opportunities on campus. Recreational activities include small game hunting, fishing and boating.

UNIVERSITY OF NORTH CAROLINA - CHARLOTTE   *(H-7)*
University City Blvd.
Charlotte, North Carolina 28223
Tel: (704) 547-2213

Description: The state university came into being as the result of legislation ratified by the 1965 General Assembly, making Charlotte College the fourth campus of the University of North Carolina. However, the university can trace its lineage back to 1946 with establishment of Charlotte Center of the University of North Carolina to provide instruction for returning World War II veterans. Today the University's academic structure is organized by six colleges that include Architecture, Business Administration, Engineering, Arts and Sciences, Education and Allied Professions, and Nursing. It is authorized to award the Bachelor's, Master's and Doctoral degrees and is fully accredited by the Southern Association of Colleges and Schools and by several professional accrediting institutions. Cooperative education programs are available in many fields. There is an International Student Exchange Program with schools in Africa, Asia, Australia, Canada, Europe, and Latin America. Special programs include Internships, Honors Program, Exchange Program Interdisciplinary Study Program, and Consortium Program. Army and Air Force ROTC programs are offered. It operates on the semester system with two 5-week summer terms and overlapping three- and eight-week terms. Undergraduate enrollment is 9,758 full-time and 3,214 part-time students; graduate enrollment is 2,541. A faculty of 640 full-time and 261 part-time gives a faculty-student ratio of 1-16.

Entrance Requirements: Accredited high school graduation; completion of 16 units, including 4 units English, 3 mathematics, 2 social studies (including 1 U.S. history), 3 natural science (including biological science and physical science), 2 units in 1 foreign language, and 2 electives; SAT or ACT required; early admission, delayed admission, advanced placement, and college-level examination programs are available; $25 application fee.

Costs Per Year: $764 tuition; $7,248 tuition for out-of-state students; $695 student fees; $3,260 board and room.

Collegiate Environment: The campus is located on a 1,000-acre tract of rolling wooded hills, streams and ponds in a rapidly developing area on the northeast side of Charlotte. Part of this development stems from the adjacent University Hospital and University Research Park which includes such organizations as IBM, AT&T, The Wall Street Journal and a number of technological research firms. Affiliated with both the University Research Park and UNCC is a developing new town known as University Place with office space, residential areas, a conference center, a shopping area, recreational areas, and green space. The 75 university buildings contain a library of 577,386 titles, 5,039 periodicals, 1,033,499 microforms, and 39,000 audiovisual materials. Dormitory facilities house 1,696 men and 1,865 women. Up to 18% of the undergraduate students admitted during a semester may come from out of the state. Over 73% of freshman students applying for admission are accepted, including midyear students. 87% of new transfers are accepted. The average scores of the entering freshman class were SAT 437 verbal, 495 math. Financial aid and scholarships are available.

Community Environment: See Queens College.

UNIVERSITY OF NORTH CAROLINA - GREENSBORO
(F-9)
1000 Spring Garden Street
Greensboro, North Carolina 27412
Tel: (910) 334-5000; Admissions: (910) 334-5243; Fax: (910) 334-3009

Description: The state university was established in 1891 and was known as the State Normal and Industrial College. It later became the North Carolina College for Women and from 1932 was the Woman's College of the University of North Carolina. Its present name was adopted in 1963 and it became coeducational in 1964. It is composed of the College of Arts and Sciences; School of Education; Graduate School; School of Human Environmental Sciences; School of Music; Bryan School of Business and Economics; School of Health, Physical Education, Recreation, and Dance; and School of Nursing. It is accredited by the Southern Association of Colleges and Schools and by respective educational and professional organizations. The university operates on a semester system and offers two summer sessions. All majors may have cooperative education program arrangements which vary from program to program and from student to student. Overseas programs are available by arrangement with other institutions and locally in Spain. Army and Air Force ROTC are available via consortium with A.&T.S.U. Enrollment includes 6,256 full-time and 3,081 part-time undergraduate, and 2,827 graduate students. A faculty of 613 full-time and 111 part-time members gives an undergraduate faculty-student ratio of 1-15.

Entrance Requirements: Accredited high school graduation or equivalent; completion of 15 units including 4 English, 3 mathematics, 2 foreign language, 3 science including at least 1 unit in life or biological science, at least 1 unit in physical science, at least 1 laboratory course, 2 social science including 1 unit in U.S. history, 1 unit in history, economics, sociology or civics, 1 elective; SAT or ACT required, GRE or GMAT or MAT required for graduate programs; $35 application fee; early decision, rolling admission and advanced placement program available.

Costs Per Year: $846 tuition; $7,888 tuition for out-of-state students; $3,550 board and room; $881 required fees.

Collegiate Environment: The main university campus is about one mile west of the central business district of Greensboro. It consists of 175 acres of developed and wooded land, including a new Physical Activity Complex. The 85 buildings include a library of 552,803 book titles, 786,711 book volumes, 798,771 microforms, 6,918 periodicals, and 36,214 audiovisual materials. Dormitory facilities are available for 3,664 students. Approximately 71% of students applying for admission are accepted, including midyear students. Average SAT scores were 461V, 499M. Financial aid is available for economically disadvantaged students. 431 scholarships were offered in the fall and 43% of undergraduate students receive some form of financial aid.

Community Environment: See Greensboro College.

UNIVERSITY OF NORTH CAROLINA - WILMINGTON
(K-13)
601 South College Road
Wilmington, North Carolina 28403-3297
Tel: (919) 395-3000; Admissions: (910) 395-3243; Fax: (919) 395-3038

Description: The liberal arts college opened as a county educational institution in 1947. By an Act of the General Assembly of 1963, it became a senior college with a four-year curriculum, authorized to offer the Bachelor's degree. The college is accredited by the Southern Association of Colleges and Schools and the North Carolina Association of Colleges and Universities. It operates on the semester system and offers two summer sessions. In 1969, Wilmington College became the fifth campus of the University of North Carolina. Enrollment includes 3,379 men and 4,778 women. A faculty of 462 full-time and 85 part-time gives a faculty-student ratio of 1-16.

Entrance Requirements: Accredited high school graduation or equivalent; minimum C average in 20 units including 4 English, 3 mathematics, 2 foreign language, 3 science, 2 social science, 1 U.S. History, and 5 electives; SAT with minimum score of 400 verbal and 400 math required; GRE required for graduate programs; non-high school graduates 21 years of age or older may be admitted with GED and satisfactory scores on entrance examinations; applicants not meeting all entrance requirements with evidence of ability to perform satisfactorily in college will be considered on an individual basis; $25 non-refundable application fee; rolling admissions and advanced placement plans available.

Costs Per Year: $1,528 tuition; $7,248 tuition for out-of-state students; $3,660-$4,300 room and board; $719 student fees; $1,200 additional expenses.

Collegiate Environment: The college is located on a 661-acre campus approximately four miles east of Wilmington in the southeastern part of the state. The city is situated on the east bank of the Cape Fear River and is about 15 miles from Carolina Beach and five miles from Wrightsville Beach. Co-ed dormitory facilities are provided for 1,586 students. In addition, female only dorms house 341 students. Boarding students find numerous rooms available and conveniently located with respect to the campus. Students from other geographical locations are accepted both semesters. Approximately 54% of students applying for admission are accepted. 61% are accepted in graduate school. Financial aid is available and 823 scholarships are offered. 53% of students receive some form of financial aid. A limited number of internships and cooperative education opportunities are available in Computer Science, Chemistry, Physical Science and Interdisciplinary Science. The library contains 396,102 volumes, 5,024 periodicals, 662,330 microforms and 25,340 audiovisual items.

Community Environment: Wilmington is North Carolina's principal deep-water port, and is near some of the most popular ocean beach resorts in the state. Leading industries include paper products, boilers, textiles, lumber, and petroleum products. Wilmington leads the South Atlantic ports in the handling of creosoted products, molasses, woodpulp, and petroleum products. All forms of commercial transportation are available. Some of the points of interest are the Brunswick Town and Fort Fisher State Historic Site, Greenfield Gardens, Orton Plantation, and the U.S.S. North Carolina Battleship Memorial. Annual events are the Azalea Festival, and Riverfest.

WAKE FOREST UNIVERSITY   *(E-8)*
P.O. Box 7305
Winston-Salem, North Carolina 27109
Tel: (919) 759-5201; Fax: (919) 759-6074

Description: This private institution was founded by the Baptist State Convention of North Carolina in 1834. Until 1894, the institution operated exclusively as a college of liberal arts. In 1942 the college became coeducational and its present name was adopted in 1967. Today the university is comprised of two Undergraduate Schools: the College of Arts and Sciences and the School of Business, the Graduate School of Management, School of Law, School of Medicine, and the Graduate School of Arts and Sciences. It is accredited by the Southern Association of Colleges and Schools and respective professional accrediting institutions. Overseas programs include cooperative programs with the University of Dijon, France; University of Salamanca, Spain; Residential Centers in London and Venice; Exchange Scholarships at Free University of Berlin and University of Andes in Bogota, Columbia. Other programs are available in Beijing, China, Freiburg, Germany, and Vienna, Austria. The university operates on a modified semester system and offers two summer terms as well as Army ROTC programs. Enrollment is 5,084 full-time and 540 part-time students. For undergraduates the faculty-student ratio is 1-13. Undergraduate, graduate, and professional faculty number 923 full-time, 584 part-time.

Entrance Requirements: Accredited high school graduation or equivalent; completion of 16 units including 4 English, 3 mathematics, 2 foreign language, 2 social science, 1 science, and 4 college preparatory electives; SAT required, CEEB Achievement Test in English, Mathematics, and other are recommended, but not required; GRE required for graduate programs; early admission, delayed admission, early decision program and advanced placement program available; $25 application fee.

Costs Per Year: $9,700 tuition; $3,550 room and board.

Collegiate Environment: Situated on beautifully landscaped hills, the 470-acre campus is one of the most attractive in the South. The 45 buildings are of modified Georgian architecture, constructed of Old Virginia brick and trimmed in granite and limestone. The Fine Arts Center, of sculptured architecture, was completed in 1976, housing the facilities of the Art, Theatre and Music programs. The several libraries of the university contain 1,188,534 volumes, 18,830 periodicals, and 993,382 microfilms. Living accommodations are provided for 2,900 students. Housing is available for 59 married students. Over half the students are from out-of-state. Midyear students are accepted. 44% of applicants are accepted. Almost 96% of the previous freshman class returned to the campus for the sophomore year. About 87% of the recent student body graduated in the top 20% of the high school class and 70% in the highest tenth. Financial aid is available for those with a demonstrated need. There are 496 scholarships, of which 142 are for freshmen. 25% of the current students receive some form of financial aid.

Community Environment: Wake Forest is located in Piedmont North Carolina, an hour from the Blue Ridge mountains, in the northwestern suburb of Winston-Salem, a city of 150,000 dating from the 1700s. Wake Forest shares a close working relationship with Salem College, Winston-Salem State University, and the North Carolina School of the Arts. Winston-Salem is a city of colleges, business, recreation, and the arts. The numerous points of interest include Reynolda House and Gardens, Old Salem, Wachovia Museum, Southeastern Center of Contemporary Art, Museum of Early Southern Decorative Arts, Nature Science Museum, Tanglewood Estates Park, two annual craft fairs and numerous craft and art galleries.

WAKE TECHNICAL COMMUNITY COLLEGE   *(F-12)*
9101 Fayetteville Rd.
Raleigh, North Carolina 27603
Tel: (919) 772-7500; Admissions: (919) 662-3465

Description: The publicly supported, coeducational technical school was established in 1963 as Wake Technical Institute. The college is accredited by the Southern Association of Colleges and Schools. It grants the Associate degree. The college operates on the quarter system and offers one summer session; classes are conducted on a 12-month basis. Enrollment includes 2,652 full-time and 4,688 part-time students. A faculty of 341 full-time and 169 part-time gives a faculty-student ratio of 1-20.

Entrance Requirements: Open enrollment policy; high school graduation or equivalent required for degree programs; college entrance examinations required; rolling admission and midyear admission plans available.

Costs Per Year: $742 ($185/quarter) tuition; $6,020 ($1,505/quarter) out-of-state; $12 student fees.

Collegiate Environment: The college is comprised of eight buildings, which include a library of 39,820 titles, 415 periodicals and 644 microforms. All students applying for admission are accepted, including at midyear, and about 52% of the previous entering class returned to the college for the second year of studies. Financial aid is available. 30% of the current student body receives some form of financial assistance. The college awarded 321 certificates and 363 Associate degrees.

Community Environment: See Meredith College.

WARREN WILSON COLLEGE   *(G-4)*
P.O. Box 9000
Asheville, North Carolina 28815
Tel: (704) 298-3325; (800) 934-3536; Fax: (704) 298-1440

Description: This privately supported liberal arts college had its origin in 1894 and was established by the United Presbyterian Church through its board of national missions. It is accredited by the Southern Association of Colleges and Schools. Academic cooperative plans are available with Washington University, Appalachian State University, Duke University and Friends World College. The college operates on the modular 2-2-2-2 system. Enrollment is 523 students. A faculty of 47 gives a faculty-student ratio of 1-15.

Entrance Requirements: Accredited high school graduation with rank in upper 40% of graduating class; SAT or ACT accepted; GED score of 250 acceptable; early admission, early decision, midyear admission, and advanced placement plans available; No application fee.

Costs Per Year: $10,700 tuition; all students work 15 hours per week for room and board.

Collegiate Environment: The college is located on a 1,100-acre tract of land in the Swannanoa Valley. The elevation of the campus proper is 2,200 feet. The 55 college buildings include a library of 100,000 volumes, 457 periodical titles, 21,000 microforms and 4,150 record-

ings. There are dormitory facilities for 210 men and 217 women. The college welcomes a geographical diverse student body and will accept midyear students. Approximately 68% of applicants are accepted. Financial aid is available for students with demonstrated need and 100% of the current student body receives some form of aid. 80% of freshmen return for their sophomore year.

Community Environment: Situated in the Swannanoa Valley among the Blue Ridge Mountains of western North Carolina, the campus is ten miles east of Asheville. Inhabitants enjoy all the conveniences of the smaller local community, and all the advantages of the nearby city.

WAYNE COMMUNITY COLLEGE   *(G-13)*
Caller Box 8002
Goldsboro, North Carolina 27833-8002
Tel: (919) 735-5151; Fax: (919) 736-3204

Description: The publicly supported, coeducational junior college was established in 1957 and is an institution of North Carolina Department of Community Colleges. It operates on the quarter system with one summer session and is accredited by the Southern Association of Colleges and Schools. Liberal arts, technical and vocational programs are offered leading to the Diploma and Associate degree. The college offers a variety of courses at Seymour Johnson Air Force Base. These courses may be attended by active duty, dependent, and civilian personnel. Offerings typically include college transfer courses, occupational courses and special interest continuing education courses. Active duty and dependents of active duty personnel stationed in North Carolina are eligible for in-state tuition rates. Recent enrollment included 1,071 men and 1,736 women. A faculty of 98 full-time and 49 part-time gives a faculty-student ratio of 1-20.

Entrance Requirements: High school graduation or equivalent; open enrollment policy; placement tests required; non high school graduates considered; rolling admission plans available.

Costs Per Year: $583.50 tuition; $4,542 nonresident tuition; $27 student fees.

Collegiate Environment: The college occupies a site of approximately 125 acres on which there are 7 buildings. These buildings contain more than 287,000 square feet of classrooms and offices and are equipped with the best teaching facilities available for the programs that are offered. The library contains 38,481 volumes, 347 periodicals, and 2,607 recordings. 95% of students applying for admission are accepted including midyear students. Financial aid is available for economically disadvantaged students. 20% of students receive financial aid.

Community Environment: 50% of the state's bright-leaf tobacco is produced within a radius of 60 miles of Goldsboro. The soil and climate also make livestock production and farming important. All forms of commercial transportation are available. Churches of all denominations, a hospital, and medical clinic are a part of the city's facilities. Job opportunities are plentiful. Recreational facilities are good for all outdoor sports.

WESTERN CAROLINA UNIVERSITY   *(H-2)*
Cullowhee, North Carolina 28723
Tel: (704) 227-7211; Admissions: (704) 227-7317; Fax: (704) 227-7319

Description: The state university was founded in 1889 as a semi-public school. In 1905 it became a normal and industrial school and was designated a senior college in 1929. In 1951, a program for the Master of Arts in Education degree was added and status as a regional university was established in 1967. In 1972 Western Carolina University became a constituent institution of the University of North Carolina. The university is accredited by the Southern Association of Colleges and Schools. It operates on the semester system and offers two summer sessions. Enrollment includes 5,194 full-time and 581 part-time undergraduates and 606 graduate students. A faculty of 331 full-time and 164 part-time gives a faculty-student ratio of 1-17.

Entrance Requirements: Careful consideration is given to academic records, rank in class and SAT or ACT scores. Recommendations are optional. Graduates of unaccredited high schools must pass an entrance exam; GED accepted. SAT required for freshman applicants. Non-high school graduates considered. Rolling admission, early admission, early decision, midyear admission and advanced placement plans available, $25 application fee.

Costs Per Year: $1,643 tuition; $7,839 tuition for out-of-state students; $5,068 board and room.

Collegiate Environment: The university is located in the valley between the Blue Ridge and Smoky Mountains, 6 miles south of Sylva. The 229-acre campus contains 71 university buildings. Living accommodations are provided for 2,879 men and women and 67 families. The university library houses 420,933 volumes, 2,119 periodicals, 1,124,547 microforms and 2,304 audiovisual materials. Students from other geographical locations are accepted, as are midyear students. The mean SAT scores of entering freshmen were 410 verbal, 457 math. Financial aid is available for economically disadvantaged students. Approximately 50% of students receive some form of financial aid.

Community Environment: Cullowhee is in an area containing several of the most scenic drives in western North Carolina. It is a rural area with bus transportation available. Asheville is nearby and provides an airport for air transportation. Student employment is available in clerical and cafeteria positions. Recreational activities include boating, fishing, water sports, mountain climbing and nature trails. Main shopping facilities are in Asheville.

WESTERN PIEDMONT COMMUNITY COLLEGE (F-5)
1001 Burkemont Ave.
Morganton, North Carolina 28655
Tel: (704) 438-6051; Fax: (704) 438-6015

Description: Western Piedmont Community College was chartered on April 2, 1964, as a member of the North Carolina Community College System and offered the first curriculum classes in the fall of 1966. As a public two-year college with an open-door admission policy, Western Piedmont's mission is to provide a comprehensive educational program that includes short-term vocational training, and associate degrees in technical and college transfer areas. Accredited by the Southern Association of Colleges and Schools, Western Piedmont offers more than 60 degrees and diplomas in Art, Allied Health, Business, Criminal Justice, Engineering, Natural Sciences, and Social Sciences. More than 80% of the students live in Burke County. All students commute to classes. With an average age of 29, most students work and enroll part-time. Daytime and evening curriculum classes are offered each academic quarter and summer by 48 full-time and 50 part-time faculty. Approximately 960 full-time and 1,690 part-time curriculum students enroll in the fall quarter.

Entrance Requirements: With an open-door admission policy, Western Piedmont Community College students are placed in appropriate courses of study based upon career interest, placement testing, and educational record. However, special admission requirements are attached to certain programs. Within these restrictions, any person, whether a high school graduate or nongraduate, who is able to profit from formal education, will be served by the college. Open admission, rolling admission, midyear admission plans available for selected programs.

Costs Per Year: $556 tuition; $4,515 tuition for out-of-state students; $18 student activity fee.

Collegiate Environment: The main campus of Western Piedmont Community College is located on more than 130 acres of rolling hills with eight instructional buildings, lake, greenhouse, nature trails and fit trek. All building are accessible to the handicapped with additional services provided by specially trained counselors. A new Learning Resources Center has been constructed to house the 30,000-volume library and audiovisual services. Shops and laboratories are equipped with current technologies and classroom instruction is directed toward the individual needs of students. Faculty advisors assist students in achieving their career goals. Counselors and other Student Services staff provide a broad range of support, including financial aid information and career planning. A variety of clubs and intramural activities are available.

Community Environment: Western Piedmont Community College, in Morganton (population 15,000), is situated in the Appalachian foothills of western North Carolina near the Catawba River. Burke County (population 76,000) was established in 1777 and named in honor of the third governor of North Carolina, Thomas Burke. Manufacturing is diversified and includes furniture, textiles, electronics, and assembly plants. The major employer is the State of North Caro-

lina with services at Broughton Hospital, Western Carolina Center, Western Correctional Center, and the North Carolina School for the Deaf. Burke County is located in the fastest growing region of the state but as yet maintains its rural values.

WILKES COMMUNITY COLLEGE (E-6)
P.O. Box 120
Wilkesboro, North Carolina 28697
Tel: (910) 838-6135; Admissions: (910) 838-6141; Fax: (910) 838-6277

Description: The publicly supported, coeducational community college was established in 1965 under the direction of the Department of Community Colleges of North Carolina. It operates on the quarter basis with one summer session and is accredited by the Southern Association of Colleges and Schools. Enrollment was approximately 1,950 men and women. A faculty of 57 full-time, 51 part-time gives a faculty-student ratio of 1-18.

Entrance Requirements: Open door policy; accredited high school graduation or equivalent; completion of 20 units including 4 English, 2 mathematics, 2 science, 2 social studies, and health/P.E.; non high school graduates admitted to some vocational programs; early admission, advanced placement and rolling admission plans.

Costs Per Year: $556 tuition; $4,515 nonresident tuition; $26 student fees.

Collegiate Environment: The 140-acre campus contains eight buildings with more than 200,000 square feet of classrooms, labs, shops and offices which afford the students the best teaching environment available. All of the students applying for admission are accepted, including midyear students. Financial aid is available for economically handicapped students and scholarships are offered. The college library houses 51,440 volumes, 174 periodicals, 24,635 microforms and 7,100 audiovisual materials.

Community Environment: Located 50 miles from Winston-Salem, Wilkesboro is the county seat of Wilkes County. The Kerr Scott Dam and Reservoir provides facilities for boating, fishing, water skiing and swimming. The Blue Ridge Mountains around the Boone area provides winter time sports such as skiing and ice skating. Community facilities include churches of various faiths, shopping areas and adequate medical facilities.

Branch Campuses: There are branch campuses in Ashe and Alleghany Counties.

WILSON TECHNICAL COMMUNITY COLLEGE (F-13)
902 Herring Avenue
Wilson, North Carolina 27893
Tel: (919) 291-1195; Fax: (919) 243-7148

Description: Established in early 1958 as Wilson County Technical Institute by authority of the State Board of Education, it was designed to serve the needs of Wilson County and northeastern North Carolina. It is accredited by the Southern Association of Colleges and Schools. Cooperative education programs are available in Business Administration, Business Computer Programming, Accounting and Electrical Installation. The college provides technological and vocational programs leading to diplomas and Associate degrees. It operates on the quarter system and offers one summer term. Enrollment includes 615 full-time and 692 part-time students. A faculty of 46 full-time and 30 part-time gives a faculty-student ratio of 1-18. The college is accredited by the Southern Association of Colleges and Schools.

Entrance Requirements: Open door policy; high school graduation or equivalent required for degree programs; placement tests required; non-high school graduates admitted; rolling admission plan; early decision, delayed admission and advanced placement plans available. No application fee.

Costs Per Year: $556.50 tuition; $4,515 nonresident tuition; $21 student fees.

Collegiate Environment: The institute is comprised of ten buildings located on 30 acres. The library houses 27,000 volumes, 345 periodicals, 5,000 microforms and recordings. About 60% of the previous entering class returned to this campus for the second year of studies. 58 scholarships are offered. 48% of the students receive some form of financial aid.

Community Environment: The campus is located in Wilson, NC, a community of 37,000. Raleigh, the capital, is 45 miles west of Wilson.

WINGATE COLLEGE　*(I-8)*
Wingate, North Carolina 28174
Tel: (704) 233-8000; (800) 755-5550; Fax: (704) 233-8014

Description: The privately supported senior college was established in 1896 as a private high school, became a junior college in 1923 and a senior college in 1977. While the school is sponsored by the Baptist State Convention of North Carolina, students of all denominations are welcome to attend. The college operates on the semester system and offers two summer terms. Programs of study lead to the Associate degree and Baccalaureate degree. It is accredited by the Southern Association of Colleges and Schools, the National League for Nursing, National Association of Schools of Music, and the American Association of Medical Assistants. Enrollment includes 1,500 full-time and 155 part-time undergraduate and 50 graduate students. A faculty of 80 full-time and 21 part-time gives a faculty-student ratio of 1-16. A 10-day travel/study abroad program is available to all students.

Entrance Requirements: Accredited high school graduation; SAT or ACT required; rolling admission, early admission, midyear admission and advanced placement plans available; $20 application fee.

Costs Per Year: $7,820 tuition; $3,400 room and board; $340 student fees.

Collegiate Environment: The 330-acre campus is in the heart of the Piedmont Carolinas with the scenic Appalachian Mountains to the northwest and the Atlantic Coast with its many beaches to the east. The 36 college buildings include 8 classroom buildings, 2 computer labs, 2 performance halls, and a library of 110,000 volumes 750 periodicals, and 18,000 microforms. 11 residence halls provide living accommodations for 625 men and 625 women. There is a sports and recreation center, an outdoor recreation center, a 17-acre lake, an administration building, and a student activities center. The college welcomes a geographically diverse student body and will accept midyear students. 80% of applicants are admitted. Financial aid is available for qualifying students. 352 scholarships are available. More than $5.5 million in scholarships and awards is granted annually. 80% of the current student body receives some form of financial assistance.

Community Environment: Wingate is located in the central Piedmont section of the Carolinas. Bus transportation is available and airlines are available in nearby Charlotte. There are churches of all denominations, a hospital two miles away, and several civic and service organizations. Recreational activities include swimming, boating, fishing, and many other sports.

WINSTON-SALEM BIBLE COLLEGE　*(E-8)*
4117 Northampton Drive
Winston-Salem, North Carolina 27105
Tel: (919) 744-0900; Admissions: (919) 744-0900; Fax: (919) 744-0901

Description: The Bible college was established by the Church of Christ in 1950. It is a nondenominational school dedicated to the training of minority ministers. The college operates on the semester basis with one summer session. The Bible college recently enrolled 55 students and had a faculty of 5 full-time and 3 part-time.

Entrance Requirements: High school graduation or equivalent required for degree programs; entrance examination required. $20 application fee.

Costs Per Year: $1,200 tuition; $675 room; $70 student fees.

Collegiate Environment: The Bible college is located on twenty-seven acres in the East Winston Section of the city. The five college buildings contain a library of 12,000 volumes and living accommodations for 32 single and 4 married students. Students from other geographical locations are accepted as well as midyear students. 90% of applicants are accepted.

Community Environment: See Wake Forest University.

WINSTON-SALEM STATE UNIVERSITY　*(E-8)*
1601 Martin Luther King Boulevard
Winston-Salem, North Carolina 27110
Tel: (919) 750-2070; Fax: (919) 750-3210

Description: This college is a state-supported, liberal arts institution offering Bachelor of Arts and Science degrees in 31 areas including nursing, education, computer science, and business administration. The college was chartered as the Slater Industrial and State Normal School in 1897. It became a teachers college in 1925 and was the first Negro institution in the United States to grant degrees for teaching in the elementary grades. It is accredited by the Southern Association of Colleges and Schools, several professional accrediting institutions, and operates on the semester basis with two summer sessions. Army ROTC is available. Enrollment includes 2,069 full-time and 748 part-time students. A faculty of 146 full-time and 43 part-time gives a faculty-student ratio of 1-17.

Entrance Requirements: Accredited high school graduation; completion of 12 units including 4 English, 3 mathematics, 1 laboratory science and 2 other science, and 2 social science, SAT with minimum scores of 380V, 380M or ACT with minimum score of 16 required; early decision, rolling admission, and advanced placement programs available; $20 application fee.

Costs Per Year: $1,256 tuition and student fees; $6,360 approximate for out-of-state students; $3,048 room and board.

Collegiate Environment: The campus is comprised of 58 acres. The 27 college buildings contain a library of 160,000 volumes and 1,500 periodicals. Dormitory facilities are provided for 1,110 students. The college welcomes a geographically diverse student body and will accept midyear students. 80% of applicants are accepted. The college provides an Enrichment Center that offers opportunities to those who are interested in spending time in self-directed learning.

Community Environment: See Wake Forest University.

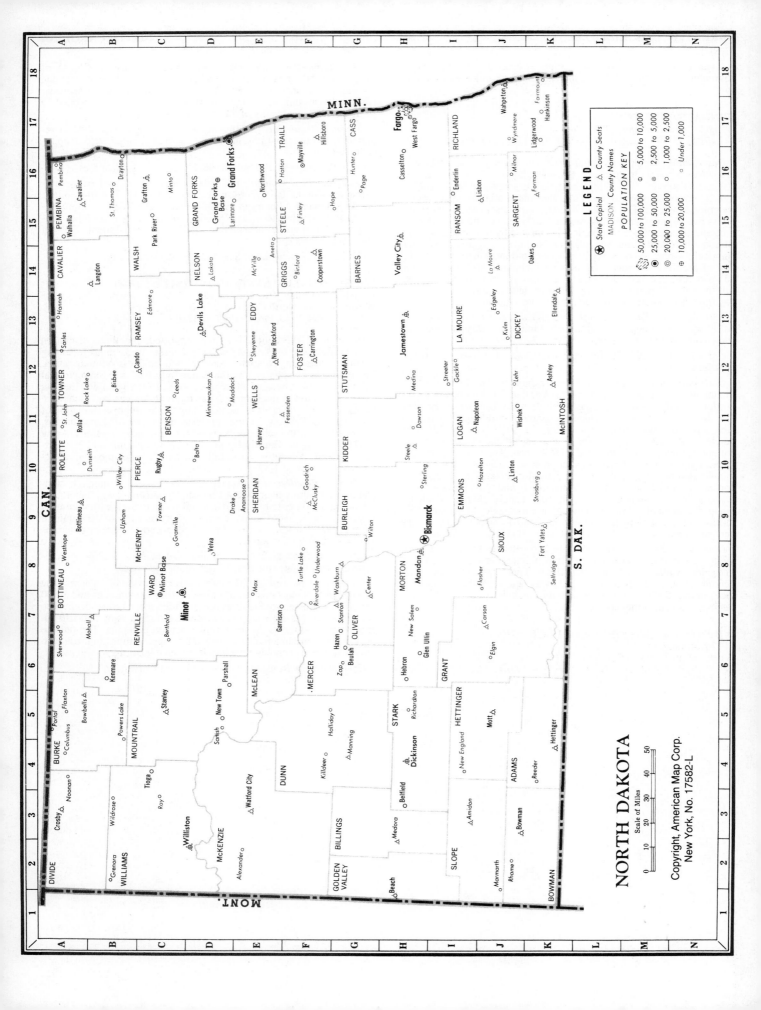

NORTH DAKOTA

Scale of Miles

0 10 20 30 40 50

Copyright, American Map Corp.
New York, No. 17582-L

LEGEND

✪ State Capital   ⌂ County Seats
MADISON County Names

POPULATION KEY

⬡ 50,000 to 100,000   ⊕ 5,000 to 10,000
◉ 25,000 to 50,000   ⊙ 2,500 to 5,000
◎ 20,000 to 25,000   ○ 1,000 to 2,500
⊕ 10,000 to 20,000   ○ Under 1,000

MINN.

CAN.

MONT.

S. DAK.

NORTH DAKOTA

BISMARCK STATE COLLEGE   *(H-9)*
1500 Edwards Avenue
Bismarck, North Dakota 58501
Tel: (701) 224-5400

Description: Established in 1939, this comprehensive community college became a part of the North Dakota state system of higher education in 1984. Its name was changed from Bismarck Junior College in 1987 to reflect its state affiliation. It is accredited by the North Central Association of Colleges and Schools. Transfer programs are offered in about 40 areas, and vocational education programs in 15 areas. Cooperative education programs are available in many areas. In addition, the college offers noncredit classes, workshops and seminars, and continuing education programs. Intramural and intercollegiate athletics, music and drama programs, a student newspaper and specialized clubs are among the activities available to students. It operates on the semester system with an 8-week summer session. Enrollment includes 1,667 full-time and 682 part-time students. A faculty of 90 full-time and 40 part-time gives a faculty-student ratio of 1-18.

Entrance Requirements: High school graduation or equivalent; open enrollment policy; rolling admission and midyear admission plans available; $25 application fee.

Costs Per Year: $1,452 state-resident tuition; $3,876 nonresidents; $1,900 room and board; $144 student fees.

Collegiate Environment: Eight buildings on the 100-acre hilltop campus include two classroom and administration buildings, a library and classroom building, a physical education and classroom building, a student union, two dormitories for 208 students, and an 8-unit apartment building for married students. The library contains 37,000 volumes and seats 200 students. Almost all who apply for admission are accepted; students may enroll midyear as well as in the fall. Financial aid is available and approximately 62% receive assistance. About 30% of the students are 25 years or older.

Community Environment: Bismarck, North Dakota's capital city, is the second largest city with a population of 50,000. Because of its central location, modern shopping centers and Civic Center, the city hosts many state and national conventions. Bismarck is considered the cultural, business and educational center of western and central North Dakota. It is also the medical center for the region with two modern medical centers and clinics. Bismarck has a large city library, a State Historical Library, and numerous libraries related to state and federal offices; a city orchestra, civic chorus, and amateur drama club; and many churches representing various denominations. The city has many parks and recreation areas, a city zoo, three golf courses, and clubs for a variety of recreational activities. The Missouri River and nearby Lake Sakakawea offer boating, fishing and other water sports. Bismarck has transportation service from several major air carriers, commuter airlines, and bus lines. Interstate 94 and U.S. Highway 83 meet in Bismarck. The city has a pleasant summer climate and moderate to severe winters.

DICKINSON STATE UNIVERSITY   *(H-4)*
Dickinson, North Dakota 58601
Tel: (701) 227-2175; (800) 279-4295; Admissions: (800) 279-4295; Fax: (701) 227-2006

Description: The publicly supported institution was established as a college of education in 1918. It is accredited by the North Central Association of Colleges and Schools and professionally by the National Council for Accreditation of Teacher Education and the National League for Nursing. The university offers correspondence courses, extensive music, and intercollegiate and intramural athletic programs. It grants Associate, Bachelor of Arts, and Bachelor of Science degrees. The university operates on the semester system and offers one summer session. Enrollment includes 1,340 full-time and 251 part-

time students. A faculty of 75 full-time and 15 part-time gives a faculty-student ratio of 1-17.

Entrance Requirements: Accredited high school graduation; completion of 17 units including 4 English, 3 mathematics, 3 science, 3 social science; non high school graduates may be admitted as special students, GED tests required; ACT or SAT required; minimum ACT 18 composite or SAT 700 combined, may be required for nonresidents; upper 50% rank of high school class for nonresidents; open enrollment for state residents; early admission, early decision, midyear admission, rolling admission, and advanced placement plans available; $25 application fee.

Costs Per Year: $1,856 state resident tuition; $4,662 nonresident tuition; $2,150 room and board.

Collegiate Environment: There are 16 buildings on the 85-acre campus. Stoxen Library has a collection of 85,500 volumes, 200 periodical subscriptions, 10,270 microforms, and 1,200 audiovisual materials. Housing facilities exist on campus for 225 men, 225 women, and 48 families. The college welcomes a geographically diverse student body and approximately 98% of the students applying for admission are accepted, including midyear students. There are 300 scholarships, 100 of them for freshmen. About 82% of students receive some form of financial assistance.

Community Environment: Dickinson (population 16,500) is approximately 95 miles fron the state capital of Bismarck and is a shipping point for lignite coal, oil, grain, dairy products, meat products, and livestock. Nearby Patterson Lake and Recreational Area and Theodore Roosevelt National Park provide ample opportunities for outdoor sports and activities.

JAMESTOWN COLLEGE   *(H-13)*
Jamestown, North Dakota 58401
Tel: (701) 252-3467; (800) 336-2554; Fax: (701) 253-4318

Description: Jamestown College was chartered in 1884 by the Presbyterian Church (U.S.A.) and is the oldest privately supported liberal arts college in North Dakota. Enrollment is 1,014 full-time and 70 part-time students. A faculty of 52 full-time and 70 part-time gives a faculty-student ratio of 1-18. The college is accredited by the North Central Association of Colleges and Schools and The National League for Nursing. It operates on the semester system and offers one summer session. The college grants the Bachelor of Arts degree.

Entrance Requirements: High school graduation or GED equivalency; ACT or SAT recommended; rolling admission, advanced placement, delayed admission, early admission, and early decision plans available; $20 application fee.

Costs Per Year: $7,970 tuition; $3,080 room and board.

Collegiate Environment: The location of the college is equidistant between Fargo and Bismarck. The 107-acre campus has 17 buildings including the 89,873-volume library and dormitories for 350 men and 350 women. Approximately 90% of students applying for admission are accepted. Students.are admitted at midyear, and the college welcomes a geographically diverse student body. About 80% of the current freshman class graduated in the top half of the high school class, 50% in the top quarter. 72% of the previous freshman class returned to this school for the second year. There are 800 scholarships awarded. Financial aid is available, and more than 98% of the students receive scholarships and grants.

Community Environment: In the valley of the James River, Jamestown (population 16,800) was originally the site of Fort Seward, which was established in 1872. Jamestown is located in southeastern North Dakota and is provided transportation by bus lines, air, and major highways. The community has churches, one hospital, a library, two radio stations, and two shopping centers. Parks in the general area provide outdoor recreation facilities. There are several active civic, fraternal, and veteran's organizations in Jamestown.

MAYVILLE STATE UNIVERSITY   *(F-16)*
Mayville, North Dakota 58257
Tel: (701) 786-2301; (800) 437-4104; Admissions: (701) 786-4873;
Fax: (701) 786-4748

Description: Mayville State University was established in 1889. Having begun as a State College of Education, it was authorized to grant the Bachelor of Science in Education and Associate degree programs in 1925. Today the university offers a Bachelor of Science degree in Education, Bachelor of Arts, Bachelor of Science in Computer Information Systems, Bachelor of Science in General Studies, and the Associate of Arts. A variety of preprofessional programs are also available, including Pre-Veterinary Medicine, Pre-Med, Pre-Law, and Pre-Physical Therapy. A strong Business Division was established in recent years so that the university now offers teacher education, liberal arts, business, and computing. Mayville State is accredited by the North Central Association of Colleges and Schools and the National Council for Accreditation of Teacher Education. The university operates on the semester system and offers a five-week summer session. Limited correspondence study is offered. Cooperative education programs (alternating work and class periods) are also offered in Business and Education. Other offerings include clubs, organizations, and intercollegiate and intramural athletics for men and women. Enrollment is approximately 675 students. A faculty of 52 provides a faculty-student ratio of 1-15.

Entrance Requirements: Accredited high school graduation or equivalent; college-preparatory units including 4 English, 3 mathematics, 3 science, and 3 social science; SAT or ACT required; early decision, rolling admission and advanced placement plans available; $25 application fee.

Costs Per Year: $1,680 state resident tuition; $1,932 Minnesota residents; $4,486 out-of-state; $2,572 room and board; $240 student fees; additional expenses average $600.

Collegiate Environment: Mayville is located in Traill County, in east-central North Dakota. The campus covers 60 acres and has 17 buildings. Adjoining the campus is a 12-acre athletic field with a baseball field, tennis courts, football stadium, track, and practice field. There are residence halls to accommodate approximately 200 men and 244 women, and there are apartments for 15 families. The Trailer Court has water and sewer service for eleven trailers. The 83,000-volume library collection is housed in the Llenora Quanbeck Library. Transfer students with a grade point average of 2.0 are admissible each term, and 75% of the students are eligible and receive financial aid.

Community Environment: Mayville and its twin community, Portland, have a combined population of 4,000 in this rural farming area between Grand Forks and Fargo, North Dakota. The local community offers a city library, many churches, a modern hospital, medical clinic, and dental and optometry offices. A modern business district is also present with air transportation available at airports in Grand Forks and Fargo. A small airport is also located in the community. Housing off campus is abundant, with many choices of apartments, duplexes, and single-family dwellings. Recreational facilities are available for camping, hiking, fishing, golf, skiing, swimming, and horseshoes; a theatre and parks are also available.

MINOT STATE UNIVERSITY   *(C-7)*
500 University Avenue N.W.
Minot, North Dakota 58702-5002
Tel: (701) 857-3350; Fax: (701) 839-6933

Description: The publicly supported state university is accredited by the North Central Association of Colleges and Schools, the American Speech-Language-Hearing Association (for speech pathology), Council on Social Work Education, National Association of Schools of Music, National League for Nursing, and the National Council for Accreditation of Teacher Education. The college offers professional education for teachers in elementary and secondary schools; liberal arts education; general and preprofessional education, a college of business, and a graduate school. It also offers extensive music programs, intercollegiate and intramural athletics and correspondence courses. The university operates on the semester system and offers

one summer session. Enrollment includes 3,150 full-time and 643 part-time students. A faculty of 180 full-time and 53 part-time gives a faculty-student ratio of 1-19.

Entrance Requirements: Open enrollment; high school graduation; completion of 17 units including 4 English, 3 mathematics, 3 science, and 3 social science; GRE required for graduate school; early admission, early decision, rolling admission, delayed admission, and advanced placement plans available; $25 application fee.

Costs Per Year: $1,780 tuition; $4,753 out-of-state; $2,225 students from bordering states or provinces; $752 room, board is optional; additional expenses average $600.

Collegiate Environment: The midsize campus offers opportunities for all kinds of outdoor sports; Old Main is the main classroom building. In it are located several divisions, departments, and classrooms, the 1,300-seat auditorium, and rooms for music practice and rehearsals. Construction is presently underway on a new $7-million library that will house a collection of over 250,000 volumes and 1,500 periodical subscriptions. Students will also have access to other state libraries via an on-line information network. Two hundred scholarships are available and 65% of the students receive financial aid. Residence halls house 30% of the student population. Midyear students are accepted.

Community Environment: Minot (population 35,000) began as a tent town of the Great Northern Railroad and now contains the electronic freight classification Gavin Yard. It grew so rapidly that it was called the "Magic City." Today it is a trade center for an area including part of Canada and Montana, as well as northern North Dakota. The town lies within the eastern boundaries of oil-rich Williston Basin and is surrounded by a number of lignite strip mines. The area has good highways, railroad, bus, and airlines. Part-time job opportunities are available for students. Minot has many churches and active civic and fraternal organizations.

NORTH DAKOTA STATE COLLEGE OF SCIENCE   *(J-18)*
800 N. 6th Street
Wahpeton, North Dakota 58075
Tel: (701) 671-1130; (800) 342-4325; Admissions: (701) 671-2201;
Fax: (701) 671-2145

Description: The publicly supported two-year college began operation in 1903. It is accredited by the North Central Association of Colleges and Schools and professionally by numerous professional accreditng organizations. A variety of curriculae are offered in areas of liberal arts, allied health, technologies, business and computer information systems. The college operates in such a way that it is possible for students to take courses from different curriculum areas at the same time. The semester system is used and a summer term is offered, with courses of varying starting and stopping times. Enrollment is 2,149 full-time and 280 part-time students. A faculty of 130 full-time and 20 part-time gives a faculty-student ratio of 1-17.

Entrance Requirements: High school graduation or equivalent; open enrollment; ACT or SAT required; the ACT is required for some majors; non-high school graduates may be admitted as special students. Rolling admission, delayed admission, early decision, early admission, midyear admission and advanced placement plans available; application fee $25.

Costs Per Year: $1,552 tuition; $4,144 out-of-state tuition; $2,320 board and room; $149 student fees; adjacent states to ND tuition $1,940; additional expenses average $2,000.

Collegiate Environment: The college is located in the southeastern corner of North Dakota. There is student housing for 1,085 men, 417 women, 134 families. The library has a collection of 78,227 volumes including what is probably the best collection of technical manuals and reference books for trade and technical areas in the region. The library also has 968 periodicals, 709 microforms, and 3,610 audiovisual materials. 94% of all applicants accepted. Of the 258 scholarships offered, 124 are available for freshmen, and 70% of the students receive some form of financial aid.

Community Environment: Wahpeton (population 9,300) is located at the origin of the Red River in southeastern North Dakota. The city is served by a bus line, and U.S. Highway 75, Interstates 29 and 94 and State Highways 13 & 81.

NORTH DAKOTA STATE UNIVERSITY (H-17)
University Station
Fargo, North Dakota 58105
Tel: (701) 231-8643; (800) 488-6378; Fax: (701) 231-1014

Description: The publicly supported state university was established as North Dakota's land grant institution in 1890. The school has three basic functions: resident education, research, and extension. Research is an integral part of the work in each of the eight colleges. Every department and office of the university is concerned with the extension of its services to the entire state through information programs, off-campus courses, summer school programs, special short courses, and activities of the Institute of Regional Studies. Programs include liberal arts, technological, teacher education, and professional programs; preparation for State teaching certificate is offered. Accredited by the North Central Association of Colleges and Schools and professionally by National Architectural Accrediting Board, Acredatation Board for Engineering and Technology (for agricultural, architectural, civil, electrical, industrial, mechanical engineering), National League for Nursing, National Association of Schools of Music, American Home Economics Association, American Council on Pharmaceutical Education, National Council for the Accreditation of Teacher Education and Computing Sciences Accreditation Board and several other accrediting associations. Army and Air Force ROTC are available. Other educational programs include Tri-College University, The Scholars Program, Interdisciplinary Studies, and Cooperative Education programs in several areas. Enrollment includes 9,700 full-time and 1,727 part-time undergraduate students, and 1,250 graduate students. A faculty of 500 full-time and 65 part-time gives an undergraduate faculty-student ratio of 1-20.

Entrance Requirements: High school graduation or equivalent; completion of 17 units including 4 English, 3 mathematics, 3 science, and 3 social studies; ACT or SAT required. GRE or GMAT required for graduate school; special admission plans: early admission, early decision, advanced placement, and rolling admission; $25 application fee.

Costs Per Year: $2,110 tuition; $5,634 out-of-state tuition; $2,744 room and board; $200 student fees. Tuition reduction for Minnesota, S.D., Montana, Manitoba, and Saskatchewan.

Collegiate Environment: The university provides housing for 3,251 single students and 367 families; fraternities and sororities house an additional 335 men and women. All entering students under age 19 not residing in the homes of their parents or guardians are required to live in university residence halls during that academic year. The library contains 463,239 volumes, 102,256 periodicals, 139,737 microform items, and 56,505 audiovisual materials. 75% of the applicants are accepted. Scholarships are available and 60% of the students receive some form of financial aid.

Community Environment: North Dakota's largest city, Fargo is the largest distribution point between Minneapolis and Spokane. The metropolitan area has over a hundred manufacturing plants producing agricultural machinery, feeds, fertilizers, foodstuffs, and dairy products. In addition, the community contains the largest medical complex between Minneapolis and the West Coast. There are part-time employment opportunities for students. Recreation facilities in the city's 765-acre park system include three golf courses, a winter sports building, and four swimming pools. The Fargo Dome, a major indoor athletic, concert, and trade show facility, opened in December 1992.

NORTH DAKOTA STATE UNIVERSITY - BOTTINEAU
(A-9)
First and Simrall Boulevard
Bottineau, North Dakota 58318
Tel: (701) 228-5487; (800) 542-6866; Fax: (701) 228-5499

Description: The publicly supported junior state college was officially opened in 1907. It offers the first two years of nearly any four-year curriculum and 19 one- and two-year vocational courses in the areas of business, forestry, agriculture, water quality, wildlife, parks & recreation, and horticulture. The school is accredited by the North Central Association of Colleges and Schools. The university operates on the semester system. Enrollment includes 339 students. A faculty of 20 gives a faculty-student ratio of 1-16.

Entrance Requirements: High school graduation with copy of high school transcript; ACT required for placement; GED accepted; adults not meeting all requirements may be admitted by special arrangement; open enrollment for state residents; early admission, early decision, rolling admission, and delayed admission plans available; $25 application fee.

Costs Per Year: $1,742 in-state tuition; $2,130 residents of SD, MT, MN, Manitoba, and Saskatchewan; $4,334 nonresidents; $2,258 room and board.

Collegiate Environment: The 35-acre campus is located on the northern edge of the city, at the base of the Turtle Mountains, the finest natural recreational area in North Dakota. Five buildings are used for instructional purposes and three other buildings provide housing for 193 men and 100 women. The library holdings number 32,000 volumes, with access to 2,500,000 volumes through its computer network. All students not living at home are required to live in the residence halls. Approximately 95% of students applying for admission meet the requirements and are accepted. The college welcomes a geographically diverse student body. Scholarships are available and 75% of the students receive financial aid.

Community Environment: Botineau (population 3,000), at the base of the Turtle Mountains, was named for Pierre Bottineau, frontier scout and guide for the Issac I. Stevens northern railway survey in 1853. The city is surrounded by excellent hunting and fishing country. Bottineau is located approximately 80 miles northeast of Minot on Highway 5. The area has eight churches representing different denominations, a hospital and clinic, hotels and motels, and various civic, fraternal and veteran's organizations.

TRINITY BIBLE COLLEGE (K-14)
50 South 6th Street
Ellendale, North Dakota 58436
Tel: (701) 349-3621; (800) 523-1603; Fax: (701) 349-5443

Description: Founded in 1948, Trinity is a privately supported bible college affiliated with the Assemblies of God. It is accredited by the American Association of Bible Colleges and the North Central Association of Colleges and Schools. It is coeducational and offers a Bachelor of Arts in Biblical Studies (with double majors in Ministry, Missions, and Elementary Education; and minors in Pastoral Studies, Missions, Christian Education, Youth Ministry, Music Ministry, Drama Ministry, Pre-Counseling, and Business), Associate of Arts degrees in Bible, Business or General Studies, and a Coaching Certificate. The college operates on the semester system and offers one summer session. Enrollment includes 355 full-time and 15 part-time students. A faculty of 18 full-time and 9 part-time gives a faculty-student ratio of 1-18.

Entrance Requirements: High school graduate or equivalent; SAT or ACT accepted, ACT preferred; rolling admission and advanced placement plans available; $25 application fee.

Costs Per Year: $4,672 tuition; $3,084 room and board; $700 student fees.

Collegiate Environment: The campus is located in the rural community of Ellendale. There are dormitories for 332 students and an additional 51 units (houses, trailers, duplexes) for married students. The library contains 78,000 volumes, 338 periodicals, and 2,806 audiovisual materials. 97% of applicants are accepted. 36 scholarships are available and 94% of the students receive some form of financial assistance.

Community Environment: Ellendale is a rural community (population 1,967) just north of the South Dakota border and 62 miles south of Jamestown on U.S. Highway 281.

UNIVERSITY OF MARY (H-9)
7500 University Drive
Bismarck, North Dakota 58501
Tel: (701) 255-7500; (800) 288-6279; Fax: (701) 255-7687

Description: The privately supported, Roman Catholic liberal arts university was incorporated as a degree-granting institution in 1959. The North Dakota Board of Nursing has approved the nursing program, and the North Dakota Department of Public Instruction has approved the college program for the Certification of Elementary and Secondary Teachers. The university is committed to providing a strong liberal arts base, supporting and complementing professional and preprofessional preparation in the service areas of nursing, teaching, social work, and medical technology and masters programs in nursing, education and management. The 4-4-1 plan is used and two summer terms are offered. Undergraduate enrollment is 538 men and 863 women full-time, 92 men and 207 women part-time. A faculty of 59 full-time and 41 part-time gives a faculty-student ratio of 1-18. There are 151 graduate students. Band, choir, jazz, women's volleyball, football, wrestling, women's softball, basketball, and intramural athletics are some of the extracurricular activities available. An overseas study program is available. The university is accredited by the North Central Association of Colleges and Schools and professionally by the National League for Nursing and the Council on Social Work Education. It grants the Associate and Bachelor degrees. There is a freshman program for the educationally disadvantaged.

Entrance Requirements: High school graduation with C average or equivalent with rank in the upper half of graduating class; completion of 16 units including 4 English, 2 mathematics, 2 science, 3 social science; non-high school graduates considered ACT or SAT required; rolling admission, delayed admission programs available; application fee $15; deadline for fall applications is August 1.

Costs Per Year: $6,190 tuition; $2,570 room and board; $150 student fees.

Collegiate Environment: The 60-acre campus is seven miles south of Bismarck. Ten new buildings on the hills overlook the Missouri River and the Western buttes. Residence halls accommodate 300 men and 300 women. In 1992, a new 123-student residence hall opened with a 2,400-square-foot fitness room. The new performing arts building contains a rehearsal hall, chapel, language laboratory, art gallery, and classrooms. The campus consists additionally of science laboratories, classrooms, a student center, chapel, and the 50,000-volume library. The library also has 6,000 bound periodicals, and 7,000 audiovisual materials. Approximately 65% of students applying for admission are accepted. Financial aid is available. 83% of students receive assistance.

Community Environment: Bismarck, North Dakota's capital city, is the second largest city with a population of 48,000. Because of its central location, modern shopping centers and Civic Center, the city hosts many state and national conventions. Bismarck is considered the cultural, business and educational center of western and central North Dakota. It is also the medical center for the region with two modern medical centers and clinics. Bismarck has a large city library, a State Historical Library, and numerous libraries related to state and federal offices; a city orchestra, civic chorus, and amateur drama club; and many churches representing various denominations. The city has many parks and recreation areas, a city zoo, three golf courses, and clubs for a variety of recreational activities. The Missouri River and nearby Lake Sakakawea offer boating, fishing and other water sports. Bismarck has transportation service from several major air carriers, commuter airlines, and bus lines. Interstate 94 and U.S. Highway 83 meet in Bismarck. The city has a pleasant summer climate and moderate to severe winters.

UNIVERSITY OF NORTH DAKOTA - GRAND FORKS
(D-17)
University Station
Grand Forks, North Dakota 58202
Tel: (701) 777-3821; Fax: (701) 777-2696

Description: The university is a publicly supported liberal arts institution founded in 1883. In addition to a Graduate School and a Division of Continuing Education, the university is composed of the Center for Aerospace Sciences, Center for Teaching and Learning, School of Law, School of Medicine, and the Colleges of Arts and Sciences, Engineering, Nursing, Business and Public Administration, and Human Resources Development. The university grants Bachelor, Specialist, Master, Professional, and Doctorate degrees. It offers music programs and intercollegiate athletics, preparation for State teaching certificate, correspondence courses, remedial education for American Indians, pre-college and freshman programs for the educationally disadvantaged. Army ROTC is available. Cooperative education programs are available in several subjects. The university operates on the early semester system and offers 3 summer sessions. Enrollment includes 8,123 full-time and 1,410 part-time undergraduate students, and 1,917 graduate and professional students. A faculty of 602 full-time and 150 part-time gives an undergraduate faculty-student ratio of 1-16.

Entrance Requirements: Accredited high school graduation or GED; 4 units English, 3 math, 3 science (2 lab science), and 3 social science; ACT or SAT required; GRE required for most graduate programs; early decision, rolling admission, early admission, midyear admission, and advanced placement plans available; $25 application fee.

Costs Per Year: $2,428 tuition; $5,952 out-of-state; $2,703 room and board; $312 student fees, included in tuition.

Collegiate Environment: The 570-acre campus has 240 buildings. Student living facilities include dormitories for 3,367 students, fraternities and sororities for 660 students, and housing for 870 families. The Chester Fritz Library contains 1.2 million volumes, 7,724 periodicals, 2 million microforms, and 169,924 audiovisual materials. Special financial aid is available for economically disadvantaged students through scholarships and regular federal aid programs. There are 2,630 scholarships, and 50% of the students receive some form of financial aid. 80% of students applying for admission are accepted.

Community Environment: In the rich farmlands of the Red River Valley, Grand Forks is a center for the processing of agricultural products. Important crops in the area are wheat, flax, oats, potatoes, malting barley, and sugar beets. The city is 90 miles from the Canadian border and has an invigorating climate. Grand Forks has a library, YMCA, YWCA, two hospitals, and major civic and fraternal organizations. Part-time employment is available for students. Transportation in the area is provided by rail, bus, and air lines. Dormitories, apartments, and private homes provide student housing.

UNIVERSITY OF NORTH DAKOTA - LAKE REGION
(D-13)
Devils Lake, North Dakota 58301
Tel: (701) 662-8683

Description: The publicly supported liberal arts and vocational community college was established in 1941 and became a part of the state system of higher education in 1984. A Community College Foundation was formed to promote the college and provide scholarships. The college is fully accredited by the North Central Association of Colleges and Schools. Cooperative education programs are available in marketing, agriculture, computer science, and secretarial studies. It operates on the semester system and offers one five-week summer session. Enrollment is 369 full-time and 264 part-time students. The faculty consists of 26 full-time and 20 part-time members.

Entrance Requirements: High school graduation or equivalent; open enrollment policy; ACT or SAT required. Rolling admission, delayed admission, advanced placement plans available. $20 application fee.

Costs Per Year: $1,552 state-resident tuition; $4,144 out-of-state; $1,674 reciprocity, SD, MT, SASK, MTB, MN; $2,310 board and room; $98 student fees.

Collegiate Environment: Classes were first held on the 70-acre campus in 1966. The campus contains classrooms, computer and science labs; a new state-of-the-art 45,000 volume library; gymnasium; dormitories for 175 students, 7 family apartments; residence dining hall; and student union. Financial aid and scholarships are available and 80% of the students receive financial aid.

Community Environment: A center of scenic, historical and recreational attractions, Devils Lake (population 7,782) was named for the largest natural body of water in the state. There are scenic drives, a golf course, a skiway, and camping and recreation facilities at nearby Shelvers Grove, Roosevelt Park, and Lakewood Park. The area is noted for its abundance of ducks and geese. The city has churches of various denominations, hospitals and clinics, a library, six motels, and various civic, fraternal and veteran's organizations. Local recreational facilities include a theatre, baseball, golf, football, bowling alley, swimming pools, hockey, skating, curling, skiing, parks, and playgrounds. Some part-time employment is available.

UNIVERSITY OF NORTH DAKOTA - WILLISTON   *(D-2)*
Box 1326
Williston, North Dakota 58802-1326
Tel: (701) 774-4200; Admissions: (701) 774-4210; Fax: (701) 774-4211

Description: UND-Williston has served its community for over 30 years. Students of all ages attend classes in the preprofessional and occupational curriculums. Modern computers and facilities combined with an excellent faculty-student ratio make UND-Williston accessible in many ways. It is accredited by the North Central Association of Colleges and Schools. The university operates on the early semester system and has limited summer offerings. Enrollment includes 650 full-time and 164 part-time students. A faculty of 34 full-time and 18 part-time gives a faculty-student ratio of 1-16.

Entrance Requirements: High school graduation or equivalent; ACT required; open admssions; rolling admission plan available; $25 application fee.

Costs Per Year: $1,658 state-resident tuition and fees; $4,082 non-resident; $1,600 room and board.

Collegiate Environment: College facilities include a library collection of 14,000 volumes; students also may use the 410,000-volume library at the main campus (Grand Forks). Dormitories accommodate 156 single and 34 married students. 95% of the students applying for admission meet the requirements and are accepted. 235 scholarships are available, including 200 for freshmen. 70% of students receive some form of financial aid.

Community Environment: Midway between two dams, Fort Peck in Montana and Garrison in North Dakota, Williston has been a railroad and distributing center since its earliest days. In the farming and stock-raising region of the oil-rich Williston Basin, the city has more than 1,000 producing wells within its trade territory. This is a rural community with temperate climate. The area is served by bus, rail, and air lines. Good U.S. Highways intersect the city. Community services include 24 churches representing 18 denominations, a public library, museum, community concert association, one modern hospital, and clinics. There are also various civic, fraternal, and veteran's organizations here. Local recreation includes theaters, a drive-in, golf clubs, bowling alley, tennis courts, baseball stadium, several softball complexes, and excellent fishing in Garrison Reservoir and the Missouri River.

VALLEY CITY STATE UNIVERSITY *(H-15)*
Valley City, North Dakota 58072
Tel: (701) 845-7101; (800) 532-8641; Fax: (701) 845-7245

Description: The publicly supported college of liberal arts and teacher education was founded in 1890. The college is accredited by the North Central Association of Colleges and Schools and the National Council for Accreditation of Teacher Education. Programs offered are the four-year degree curriculum in liberal arts leading to the Bachelor of Arts degree, the four-year degree curriculum for teaching and supervising in elementary, junior high, and senior high school fields which leads to a Bachelor of Science degree, and a junior college curriculum providing preparation for students who plan to transfer to professional colleges or other collegiate institutions. The college offers extensive music programs, intercollegiate and intramural athletics, and preparation for State teaching certificate. It operates on the semester system and offers one summer session. Enrollment includes 792 full-time and 194 part-time students. A faculty of 54 full-time and 14 part-time gives a faculty-student ratio of 1-15.

Entrance Requirements: Accredited high school graduation or equivalent; ACT or SAT required; open enrollment for state residents, out-of-state applicants must rank in upper half of graduating class; early admission, midyear admission, rolling admission, delayed admission, and advanced placement plans available; $25 application fee.

Costs Per Year: $1,889 tuition; $4,695 out-of-state tuition; $2,660 room and board; $2,000 miscellaneous expenses.

Collegiate Environment: The campus of the college consists of 94 acres of beautiful wooded parkland. Although it lies within three blocks of the heart of the city, the college is separated from it by the Sheyenne River. The 34 buildings are situated at the foot of a high tree-covered bluff. The Allen Memorial Library contains 85,877 volumes. Residence halls accommodate 511 students. Almost all those who apply for admission are accepted. The college welcomes a geographically diverse student body. 415 scholarships are available and 81% of the current students receive some form of financial assistance.

Community Environment: Valley City, in the Sheyenne River Valley, is the home of the North Dakota Winter Show, a statewide agricultural fair held in the first week in March. The area is served by buses, railroad, and Interstate Highways 94, 10, and 52.

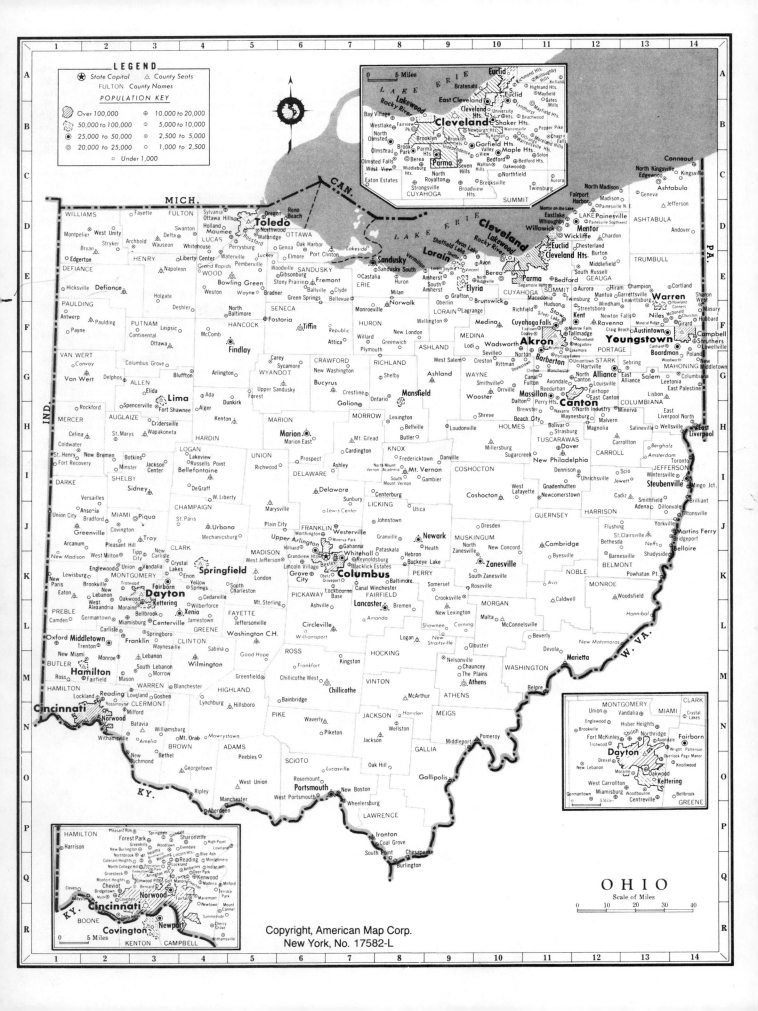

OHIO

Scale of Miles

OHIO

AIR FORCE INSTITUTE OF TECHNOLOGY *(K-3)*
AFIT-RRE
2950 P Street, Bldg. 125
Wright-Patterson AFB, Ohio 45433-7765
Tel: (513) 255-6231; Fax: (513) 255-2791

Description: The original idea of a graduate, aeronautical school within the Army was proposed in 1919. Shortly after the creation of the Air Corps in 1926, the Air Corps Engineering School became operational. When the Air Force became an autonomous unit in the military establishment, the institute took its present name and Wright Field, with its extensive research and development facilities, was combined with Patterson Field, center of Air Force supply and permanent activities, to form Wright-Patterson Air Force Base. Today, the Air Force Institute of Technology is divided into the School of Engineering, the School of Logistics and Acquisitions, and the School of Civil Engineering and Services, which grant graduate degrees. It is accredited by the North Central Association of Colleges and Schools. Enrollment is 877 with a faculty of 251. It operates on the quarter system and offers one summer session.

Entrance Requirements: Applicants must be commissioned Air Force officers in the grade of colonel or below, Army or Navy officers, or DOD civilians with a completed undergraduate degree, a GPA of 3.0 or higher, and GRE or GMAT score, depending on program.

Costs Per Year: None for active duty Air Force officers; $8,700 per year for Army, Navy and DOD civilians.

Collegiate Environment: The library contains a comprehensive collection of materials in the field of engineering and management. It includes 96,600 volumes, 106,500 pamphlets, 1,300 periodicals, and 984,250 microforms. There are 1,800 government-maintained quarters at the Air Force Base.

Community Environment: See Wright State University.

ANTIOCH COLLEGE *(K-4)*
Livermore St.
Yellow Springs, Ohio 45387
Tel: (513) 767-6400; (800) 543-9436; Admissions: (800) 543-9436; Fax: (513) 767-6473

Description: The private coeducational college of liberal arts and sciences is nonsectarian and offers the Bachelor of Arts and Bachelor of Science degrees. Horace Mann was the first president of the college, which, in 1920, adopted the cooperative, or study-plus-work plan which is now used at over a thousand colleges and universities. The primary mission of Antioch College is to empower students: the academic curriculum provides students with a broad liberal education that challenges their values and perspectives as well as increasing their knowledge, ability to question, and general intellectual consciousness about themselves and the society in which they live; the cooperative education program provides life and work experiences which develop independence, confidence, and self-motivation; and the community structure offers significant responsibility for the social, cultural, financial, and policy issues that govern college life. The college operates on the quarter system. Enrollment is 650 full-time students. A faculty of 69 full-time and 23 part-time gives a faculty-student ratio of 1-10. The university is accredited by the North Central Association of Colleges and Schools.

Entrance Requirements: High school graduation with rank in upper 40% of graduating class; completion of 16 units: 4 English, 3 mathematics, 2 science, 2 foreign language, and the remainder in art, music, dramatics or social science. SAT or ACT recommended; early admission, early decision, midyear admission, delayed admission, advanced placement plans available; applications for fall term must be submitted by Feb. 15.; $25 application fee.

Costs Per Year: $16,880 tuition and fees; $3,336 board and room.

Collegiate Environment: The college is located 18 miles east of Dayton in southwestern Ohio. The main campus, with 44 buildings, covers a hundred acres and borders Glen Helen, the college's 1,000-acre nature preserve. Because Antioch College believes that the most effective learning environment focuses on three aspects: the co-op experience, the liberal arts experience, and the community experience, students find that all three of these elements play an important role in living on campus. Residence halls accomodate 600 students. During off-campus periods the student may have different kinds of work and many new personal associations with a variety of employing organizations, thus he tests the relevance of his academic learning in real world situations. 70% of the students receive financial aid. The Antioch Education Abroad program is based on the same pattern of general education as that of the home campus program: the interplay of study, work, and living, for regular credit toward a degree. Programs are available in most areas of the world. Antioch has long sought students from diverse segments of our society, particularly young people from minority groups. The library has 273,000 hard bound volumes, 1,060 periodicals, and 46,000 microforms. A majority of the seniors continue on to graduate school.

Community Environment: Yellow Springs, Ohio, is a magnet for creative thinkers and doers. The residents are socially concerned, politically active, and intensely interested in the arts. Ingenious shops, natural food stores, unusual restaurants, and an array of art galleries line the village streets. Bookstores can be found with specialties ranging from science fiction to feminist literature. Local craft shops display items of clay, silver, wood, stained glass, unusual weavings, original clothing, oils, and essences. The Little Art Theatre offers top foreign and American arts films in three-day runs. A 1,000 Nature Preserve, Glen Helen, adjacent to campus, provides a maze of stone cliffs, waterfalls, forests, streams, wooded trails, and old bridges. It offers opportunities for hiking, horseback riding, cross-country skiing, canoeing, rock-climbing, rapelling and solitude.

ART ACADEMY OF CINCINNATI *(N-2)*
1125 Saint Gregory Street
Cincinnati, Ohio 45202
Tel: (513) 721-5205; (800) 323-5692; Admissions: (513) 721-5205; Fax: (513) 562-8778

Description: The Art Academy of Cincinnati was dedicated in the present location and under its current name in 1887. However, the school's existence predates the dedication by 20 years. The Academy is a private, degree-granting professional art school. It is one of four museum schools in the United States. The Academy is accredited by the National Association of Schools of Art and Design, of which it is a charter member, and by the Commission on Institutions of Higher Education of the North Central Association of Colleges and Schools. The Bachelor of Fine Arts Degree is awarded with majors in Fine Art, Communication Design and Art History. An Associate degree is awarded in the major area of Communication Design. Approximately 200 students are enrolled. A faculty of 16 gives a faculty-student ratio is 1-10.

Entrance Requirements: Accredited high school graduation or equivalent; interview and submission of portfolio of recent art work (20 items minimum); rolling admission, $25 application fee.

Costs Per Year: $8,990 tuition; $1,200 average supplies.

Collegiate Environment: The Academy is housed in two buildings, one attached to the Cincinnati Art Museum; the other is a short walk away, and contains studio-classrooms, a student lounge and gallery and small studios for individual projects. Curriculum includes Drawing, Painting, Sculpture, Printmaking, Illustration, Graphic Design, Photography, Photo Design, Art History and Liberal Studies. The facilities of the museum include 100 exhibition rooms and galleries; and a library of 50,000 volumes, 120 periodicals, 200 pamphlets and articles, and a variety of modern visual aids. Students must maintain a 2.0 grade point average. 95% of the current student body receives some form of financial aid. Approximately 90% of the previous freshman class return for the second year. Approximately 72% of applicants are accepted.

Community Environment: The Art Academy is located in Eden Park, a metropolitan park of 184 acres that also contains the Cincinnati Historical Society. Mirror Lake, the Krohm Conservatory, two dramatic theaters, one outdoor theater and the Ohio River overlook the area.

ASHLAND UNIVERSITY   *(G-9)*
College Avenue
Ashland, Ohio 44805
Tel: (419) 289-5052; (800) 882-1548; Admissions: (419) 289-5052;
Fax: (419) 289-5353

Description: This privately supported, coeducational, liberal arts college was founded in 1878 by members of the German Baptist Brethren Church. It is accredited by the North Central Association of Colleges and Schools, American Association of Colleges, Ohio College Association and A.A.U.W. Enrollment includes 1,823 full-time, 89 part-time and 2,124 graduate students. A faculty of 179 full-time and 6 part-time gives a faculty-student ratio of 1-16. The semester system is used with two summer terms and a 3-week minimester. The college grants the degrees of Associate, Bachelor, and Master. In 1930, Ashland Theological Seminary was made a graduate school of Ashland College.

Entrance Requirements: High school graduation with rank in upper half of graduating class; completion of 16 units including 4 English, 2 mathematics, 2 foreign language, 2 science, and 1 social science; SAT or ACT required; $15 application fee; early admission, rolling admission, delayed admission, and advanced placement plans available.

Costs Per Year: $11,431 tuition; $4,684 room and board; $290 student fees.

Collegiate Environment: The college occupies a beautiful site in a fine residential section of Ashland. The main campus of 80 acres is adjacent to athletic fields located to the south on 16 acres of recently acquired land. The seminary is located on the properties of the late industrialists John C. Myers and Mr. & Mrs. T.W. Miller on Center Street. The library contains 187,400 hard bound volumes, 11,411 pamphlets, 22,472 periodicals, 80,000 microforms, and 5,516 sound recordings. Living accommodations are available for 688 men and 731 women. 95% of the students receive financial assistance. Approximately 80% of students applying for admission are accepted including midyear students, and 80% of the freshmen returned to this college for the second year of studies. Average high school standings of the current freshmen: 32% top fifth, 30% 2nd fifth, 19% 3rd fifth, 16% fourth fifth, and 3% fifth fifth. The average composite ACT is 20.5.

Community Environment: Five rubber manufacturers in Ashland produce most of the world's toy balloons; other industries produce spray equipment, hydraulic cylinders, and clothing. Bus transportation is available; Mansfield Airport, and Cleveland Airport furnish air transportation. Recreational facilities within the city are good; the Mohican State Park nearby provides additional facilities for fishing and camping.

ATHENAEUM OF OHIO   *(N-2)*
6616 Beechmont Avenue
Cincinnati, Ohio 45230
Tel: (513) 231-2223; Fax: (513) 231-3254

Description: The Athenaeum of Ohio is an accredited center for education and formation providing programs of preparation for and development in ministry within the Roman Catholic tradition. The Athenaeum of Ohio consists of three divisions: Mount St. Mary's Seminary of the West, the Lay Pastoral Ministry Program and the Special Studies Division. The Athenaeum of Ohio grants a certificate in Lay Ministry, and Masters of Divinity, Master of Arts in Religion, Theology, Biblical Studies, and Pastoral Counseling. The main campus for this graduate school is located in Mount Washington. Enrollment includes 86 full-time and 14 part-time graduate students and 57

students in the lay ministry program. A faculty of 21 full-time and 35 part-time gives a faculty-student ratio of 1-5. It operates on the quarter system. The school is accredited by the North Central Association of Colleges and Schools, and the Association of Theological Schools in the United States and Canada.

Entrance Requirements: Open enrollment. Entrance requirements vary depending upon the particular degree; early decision, rolling admission and advanced placement plans available. $25 application fee.

Costs Per Year: $8,100 tuition; $4,500 room and board.

Collegiate Environment: The graduate school and seminary in suburban Mt. Washington occupies a campus of 75 acres. The total library facilities of The Athenaeum of Ohio include 71,899 hard-bound volumes, 400 pamphlets, 386 periodical subscriptions, 1,124 microform titles, and 3,400 records and tapes. Dormitory facilities are available for 180 students.

Community Environment: See University of Cincinnati.

BALDWIN-WALLACE COLLEGE   *(E-10)*
275 Eastland Road
Berea, Ohio 44017
Tel: (216) 826-2222; Fax: (216) 826-2329

Description: Baldwin University and German Wallace College were united as Baldwin-Wallace College in 1913. The privately supported, coeducational, liberal arts college is affiliated with the United Methodist Church and is accredited by the North Central Association of Colleges and Schools. Enrollment includes 2,686 full-time, 1,419 part-time, and 611 graduates.

A faculty of 156 full-time and 99 part-time gives a faculty-student ratio of 1-14. The college operates on the quarter system and offers two five-week summer sessions. Air Force ROTC program is available. A wide variety of internships are offered, through which the student can work and receive college credit. An overseas program is available.

Entrance Requirements: Accredited high school graduation class; completion of 4 units English, 3 mathematics, 2 foreign language, 3 science, 3 social science; SAT or ACT required; delayed admission, rolling admission, and advanced placement plans available; $15 application fee.

Costs Per Year: $12,270 tuition & fees; $4,635 room and board.

Collegiate Environment: The 52-acre campus is a short distance from the Ohio Turnpike and the progressive cultural area of downtown Cleveland. Buildings include dormitories for 1,555 men and women. The library contains 230,000 volumes, 950 periodicals, 102,865 microforms, and 18,300 audiovisual materials. The college has its own radio station, and there are 5 national fraternities on campus and 6 national sororities. Housing is available for 1,700 students. Intercollegiate competition is conducted in 13 varsity sports: softball, volleyball, football, soccer, basketball, track, baseball, wrestling, cross country, tennis, swimming & diving, and golf. There is also an extensive intramural program. Approximately 75% of students applying for admission meet the requirements and are accepted. All financial aid is based upon need and 66% of the students receive aid. 90% of the current student body graduated in the top 3/5 of the high school class, and 56% were in the top quarter. The average scores of the freshmen were SAT 463V, 528M; ACT 23. About 85% of the previous freshman class returned to this campus for the sophomore year. An MBA and MAE program are offered.

Community Environment: Berea, with its tree-lined streets and picturesque homes, is an ideal college town, yet it is only 20 minutes from the heart of Cleveland, home to many fortune 500 companies and recreational and cultural opportunities.

BELMONT TECHNICAL COLLEGE   *(J-13)*
120 Fox-Shannon Place
St. Clairsville, Ohio 43950
Tel: (614) 695-9500; (800) 423-1188; Fax: (614) 695-2247

Description: This publicly supported technical college was opened in 1970 and is accredited by the North Central Association of Colleges and Schools. The college awards Certificates and Associate degrees. It operates on the quarter system and offers one summer. Enrollment includes 1,087 full-time and 602 part-time students. A faculty of 37 full-time and 96 part-time gives a faculty-student ratio of 1-21.

Entrance Requirements: Open enrollment policy; high school graduation or equivalent; ASSET required;non high school graduates considered; rolling admission, midyear admission and advanced placement plans available; $20 application fee.

Costs Per Year: $1,584 tuition; $2,088 nonresident tuition; additional expenses average $600.

Collegiate Environment: The library contains 4,889 volumes, 229 periodicals, 584 microforms, and 1,312 audiovisual materials. All applicants are accepted, including midyear students. There are no dormitories provided on campus. 75% of students receive financial aid.

Community Environment: Belmont Technical College is located in a rural area of Belmont County, Ohio, just 10 miles west of Wheeling, WV. The college has recently expanded its physical size and has added an auditorium. The college is active in the community and exposes students to a variety of activities, including the fine arts.

BOWLING GREEN STATE UNIVERSITY *(E-5)*
Bowling Green, Ohio 43403
Tel: (419) 372-2531

Description: The state-supported university is accredited by the North Central Association of Colleges ans Schools and professionally by respective accrediting organizations. Six undergraduate colleges offer degree programs: Arts and Sciences, Business Administration, Education and Allied Professions, Health and Human Services, Musical Arts, and Technology. The university grants the Bachelor, Masters' and Doctoral degrees. Air Force and Army ROTC are available. The university operates on the early semester system and offers three summer sessions. Enrollment is 13,424 full-time and 2,371 part-time undergraduates, and 2,703 graduate students. A faculty of 673 full-time and 193 part-time gives a faculty-student ratio of 1-21.

Entrance Requirements: Accredited high school graduation or equivalent; completion of 16 units including 4 English, 3 mathematics, 2 foreign language, 3 science, 3 social science, and 1 performing arts; ACT or SAT required; GRE required for graduate programs; early admission, rolling admission, and advanced placement programs available; $30 application fee.

Costs Per Year: $3,730 state-resident tuition; $8,112 nonresident fee; $3,352 room and board; $550 average books and academic supplies.

Collegiate Environment: The university is situated on a 1,338-acre campus, 23 miles south of Toledo and 15 miles south of the Ohio Turnpike. There are 113 buildings, including residence halls for men and women and a library system containing 1,800,000 volumes; 1,772,683 microforms; 617,118 records; tapes, and CDs; and 5,427 periodical subscriptions. All high school graduates are eligible for admission consideration. However, due to limited academic and residence hall facilities, all are not eligible to enroll for the fall semester. Some students are required to begin their program during the summer term. Various forms of financial aid are available and 55% of the students receive aid. Of the scholarships offered, many are for freshmen. About 75% of the applicants are accepted and 78% of the freshmen returned to this campus for their sophomore year. Average high school standing of the current freshman class: 13% in the top 10%, 41% in the top quarter, 41% in the second quarter; average composite ACT was 22.

Community Environment: Bowling Green, the county seat of Wood County, is located 23 miles south of Toledo. Community facilities in this metropolitan area include libraries, many churches, a hospital, shopping areas, and major civic and service organizations. Lake Erie and the Maumee River provide facilities for recreation.

CAPITAL UNIVERSITY *(K-6)*
2199 East Main Street
Columbus, Ohio 43209
Tel: (614) 236-6101; (800) 289-6289; Fax: (614) 236-6820

Description: Founded in 1830, Capital is the oldest university in central Ohio. The university is accredited by the North Central Association of Colleges and Schools and respective professional organizations. It operates on the early semester system and offers two summer sessions. Army ROTC training is available on campus. The Bachelor

of Arts, Fine Arts, General Studies, Social Work, Bachelor of Science in Nursing, and Master of Science in Nursing are awarded. The Conservatory of Music awards the Bachelor of Music. The Juris Doctor, Master of Laws in Taxation and Master in Taxation are offered by the law school. The Graduate School of Administration grants the Master in Business Administration degree. Undergraduate enrollment includes 1,621 full-time and 48 part-time students. An undergraduate daytime faculty of 113 full-time and 67 part-time provides a faculty-student ratio of 1-15.

Entrance Requirements: Completion of a minimum of 16 academic units including 4 English, 3 mathematics, 3 science, 3 social studies, 2 foreign language and 1 fine arts; SAT or ACT and counselor evaluation; Conservatory applicants must audition; rolling admission, early admission, deferred admission and advanced placement available; $15 application fee.

Costs Per Year: $13,050 tuition; $4,000 room and board.

Collegiate Environment: There are two campuses. The main campus is located just four miles from downtown Columbus in suburban Bexley. The Law School is in downtown Columbus. The main library has 180,000 bound volumes, 893 periodicals, 116,644 microforms, 13,600 audiovisual materials, and 1,400 CD-ROMs. There are residence hall facilities for 985 students. Classes start in August and January. 76% of applicants are accepted. 95% of the current student body receives some form of financial assistance and there are special financial aid resources for economically disdavantaged students. 20% of the graduating class continues to graduate school. More than 95% of the graduates are employed or in graduate programs within four months of graduation.

Community Environment: See Ohio State University - Columbus Campus.

CASE WESTERN RESERVE UNIVERSITY *(E-11)*
10900 Euclid Avenue
Cleveland, Ohio 44106
Tel: (216) 368-4450; Fax: (216) 368-5111

Description: This private nonsectarian university was formed by the federation in 1967 of Western Reserve University (established 1826) and Case Institute of Technology (established 1880). It is accredited by the North Central Association of Colleges and Schools and by many professional accrediting organizations. The university has seven professional schools, a College of Arts and Sciences, and a School of Graduate Studies. CWRU offers the B.S. degree in fields of engineering, science, mathematics, management, education, nursing and the health sciences, and the B.A. in the fields of arts, humanities, social sciences, natural sciences and mathematics. Special programs include Undergraduate Scholars Program (for students designing individualized programs of study), Integrated Graduate Studies, allowing students to begin work on a graduate degree in senior year, and 3-2 programs in engineering and nutrition with a number of liberal arts colleges. CWRU offers the following special programs: Preprofessional Scholars Programs in Dentistry, Law, Medicine, Nursing, Management, and Social Work carrying a conditional guarantee of admission to professional school for a small number of highly qualified entering freshmen; a Six-Year Dental Program; Early Admission program with the School of Law; Integrated Professional Studies in Management; Junior Year Abroad; Washington Semester for history and political science majors; Joint Program in Music with the Cleveland Institute of Music; Joint Program in Art Education with the Cleveland Institute of Art, and the Minority Engineers Industrial Opportunity Program. Cooperative education programs are available in accounting, engineering, management, math and science. The university operates on the semester system and offers one summer session. Enrollment includes 3,107 full-time and 551 part-time undergraduate, and 3,401 full time and 2,510 part-time graduate students. A faculty of 1,850 full-time and 25 part-time gives a faculty-student ratio of 1-8. Air Force and Army ROTC programs are available.

Entrance Requirements: The undergraduate colleges require 16 units of full credit high school work in solid academic subjects including 4 years of English, 3 years of mathematics (4 for science and engineering majors), and 1-2 years of laboratory science (chemistry and physics for engineering applicants); SAT or ACT required; three CEEB Achievement tests strongly recommended for students who submit the SAT (English Composition and two others; for engineering applicants, recommend Math I or II, and chemistry or physics);

early admission, early decision, delayed admission, midyear admission, and advanced placement plans available; no application fee.

Costs Per Year: $16,300 tuition; $4,940 room and board; $130 student fees.

Collegiate Environment: Approximately 75% of the undergraduates live on campus with 1,793 in residence halls and 521 in fraternities and sororities. All but one of the dormitories are coed, some with suites of six single rooms and some with double rooms. 17 fraternities and 5 sororities are available. Extracurricular activities include intercollegiate sports for men and women, intramural sports, music groups, student newspapers, and over 100 special interest organizations. The libraries of the university contain 1,871,260 volumes and 13,819 periodical subscriptions. Other facilities include a computer center, many instructional and research laboratories, two observatories and a 272 acre biological field station. A fiber-optic network connects every residence hall room with offices, labs, and libraries across campus. Approximately 81% of those who apply for admission are accepted. The middle 50% range of scores for the current freshman class were ACT 27-31 composite, SAT 526-650 verbal, 620-730 math. Financial aid is available, and 81% of current students receive some form of assistance. More than 250 merit scholarships ranging from $750 to full tuition are awarded each year to freshmen.

Community Environment: The university is located on the eastern edge of Cleveland in University Circle, a 500-acre area of parks, gardens, museums, schools, hospitals, churches and human service institutions. The Cleveland Museum of Art and the Cleveland Orchestra are within walking distance, and downtown Cleveland, offering restaurants, music, theatre, and professional sports, is only ten minutes away by RTA rapid transit. Students also have easy access to many facilities provided by the city of Cleveland and the outlying areas. Among these are Cleveland's well-known "Emerald Necklace" of parks, and Blossom Music Center, the summer home of the Cleveland Orchestra. CWRU also owns a 400-acre farm in Hunting Valley, about 10 miles east of the campus, that is open to students. Recreational facilities include a picnic area, fishing ponds, hiking and ski trails, and buildings for social events.

CEDARVILLE COLLEGE   *(K-4)*
Box 601
Cedarville, Ohio 45314
Tel: (513) 766-2211; Admissions: (513) 766-7700; Fax: (513) 766-2760

Description: The privately supported coeducational college is approved by the General Association of Regular Baptist Churches. It is accredited by the North Central Association of Colleges and Schools and operates on the quarter system with two summer terms. The college grants five degrees: Bachelor of Arts, Bachelor of Science (Nursing), Bachelor of Music Education, Bachelor of Science in Engineering, and the Associate of Arts. Elementary and high school teacher training is available with full approval granted by the Ohio State Board of Education in June, 1968. Enrollment includes 2,305 full-time and 73 part-time students. The faculty consists of 130 full-time and 40 part-time members which provides a faculty-student ratio of 1-18. Army and Air Force ROTC programs are available. Study abroad includes Germany, Spain, France, England, and the Holy Land.

Entrance Requirements: High school graduation with rank in upper half of graduating class; completion of 15 units including 4 English, 3 mathematics, 3 science, 2 foreign language, 3 social science; SAT or ACT required; $30 application fee; early admission, delayed admission, rolling admission and advanced placement plans available.

Costs Per Year: $7,344 tuition; board and room $4,410; additional expenses average $126.

Collegiate Environment: The 110-acre campus is located in the rural community of Cedarville, easy driving distance from Columbus, Dayton, and Cincinnati. The library contains 120,454 volumes, 1,030 periodicals, 21,452 microforms, and 10,493 audiovisual materials. Dormitory facilities available for 838 men and 1,000 women. Students 25 years of age or younger must live in dormitories. Married students must provide their own living quarters. Students and faculty meet together each day for worship and fellowship in a chapel service, and every student is required to attend. Applicants to the college must give evidence of having been born again and of having lived a consistent Christian life as indicated by his or her personal testimony

and pastor's recommendation. 73% of applicants are accepted. Use of cars by the students is permitted only when required grade point averages are maintained. Financial assistance is available. 79% of students receive financial aid.

Community Environment: Cedarville is a rural community 20 miles east of Dayton with plane, train and bus transportation available. Libraries, churches of major denominations, and some of the various civic and service organizations serve the community. Opportunities for part-time employment are available. The John Bryan State Park, nearby, provides facilities for fishing and camping. The valley of the Little Miami River is a scenic part of this park; the foot trail which winds along the Little Miami River was once the old Cincinnati-Pittsburgh stage road.

CENTRAL OHIO TECHNICAL COLLEGE   *(J-8)*
University Drive
Newark, Ohio 43055
Tel: (614) 366-1351; (800) 963-9275; Admissions: (614) 366-9222; Fax: (614) 366-5047

Description: The state-assisted, two year, technical college is fully accredited by the North Central Association of Colleges and Schools, the American Physical Therapy Association, Committee on Allied Health Education and Accreditation of the American Medical Association, and the National League for Nursing. The college awards an Associate degree in applied science and applied business. A cooperative education program is available in business and engineering. Off-campus coursework is offered in Mt. Vernon and Coshoctos. The quarter system is employed and two summer sessions are offered. Enrollment includes 223 men and 550 women full-time and 289 men and 650 women part-time. A faculty of 48 full-time and 96 part-time gives a faculty-student ratio of 1-12.

Entrance Requirements: Open enrollment policy; high school graduation or equivalent; Placement tests required; early decision, early admission, rolling admission, midyear admission and delayed admission plans available; $15 application fee.

Costs Per Year: $2,178 state resident tuition; $3,114 out-of-state tuition; $55 student fees.

Collegiate Environment: The library contains over 42,000 volumes, over 500 periodicals, 7,285 microforms and 3,000 recordings. No dormitories are provided on campus. Financial assistance is available and 60% of students receive some form of financial aid, including midyear students.

Community Environment: See Denison University.

CENTRAL STATE UNIVERSITY   *(L-4)*
Wilberforce, Ohio 45384
Tel: (513) 376-6478; Fax: (513) 376-6648

Description: The coeducational university is a general multipurpose, publicly supported institution of higher education, offering bachelor degree programs. Enrollment is 2,634 full-time and 627 part-time students. A faculty of 127 full-time and 20 part-time gives a faculty-student ratio of 1-21. The quarter system is used and one eight-week summer term is offered. The university is accredited by the North Central Association of Colleges and Schools. The university is a member of the Dayton-Miami Valley Consortium.

Entrance Requirements: Accredited high school graduation or equivalent; open enrollment policy for Ohio residents; out-of-state students must have minimum C average; completion of 4 English, 3 math, 3 science, 2 foreign language, and 2 social studies; ACT required; early admission, advanced placements, early decision and rolling admission plans available; application fee $15.

Costs Per Year: $2,679 state-resident tuition; $5,895 nonresidents; $4,293 room and board.

Collegiate Environment: The university is located 18 miles east of Dayton. The 60-acre campus has 42 buildings and provides living accommodations for 787 men and 842 women. The library contains 155,643 volumes, 890 periodicals, 555,443 microforms, and 400 tapes. 85% of the applicants are accepted. Financial aid is available. Approximately 40% of the senior class continues on to graduate school.

Community Environment: A college community, Wilberforce was named after William Wilberforce, the English philanthropist who fought for the abolition of slave trade. The community is known as a noted African-American cultural center. Part-time employment opportunities are available for students.

CINCINNATI BIBLE COLLEGE (N-2)
2700 Glenway Avenue
P.O. Box 04320
Cincinnati, Ohio 45204
Tel: (513) 244-8100; Fax: (513) 244-8141

Description: The Cincinnati Bible College and Seminary came into being in 1924 as a result of the consolidation of two colleges organized the previous year: McGarvey Bible College of Louisville, Kentucky, and Cincinnati Bible Institute of Cincinnati. The mission of the seminary is to equip and empower effective Christian leaders with insight, skills and vision. CBC offers three four-year degrees: the Bachelor of Arts, the Bachelor of Music, the Bachelor of Science, and two-year Associate of Science. It is administratively affiliated with Cincinnati Bible Seminary. It operates on the semester system and offers one winter session and two summer sessions. Enrollment is 519 full-time and 106 part-time undergraduates, and 285 graduate students. A faculty of 21 full-time and 22 part-time gives a faculty-student ratio of 1-20. The school is a member of the Ohio College Association and the Greater Cincinnati Consortium of Colleges and Universities. It is also an accredited member of the American Association of Bible Colleges ad the North Central Association of Colleges and Schools.

Entrance Requirements: Accredited high school graduation or equivalent; open enrollment policy; ACT required; $35 application fee; rolling admission, early decision, and delayed admission plans available.

Costs Per Year: $3,872 tuition; $3,124 room and board.

Collegiate Environment: The campus is located on the highest hill in the skyline of western Cincinnati. There are eight buildings on the 40-acre campus. Dormitories accommodate 484 students and 22 families and the library collection numbers 86,883 volumes, 721 periodicals, 34,000 microforms, and 10,949 audiovisual materials. 40% of the current students receive some form of financial aid. The seminary receives a number of gifts each year to its scholarship fund and it also has a limited endowment for student aid in the form of grants. 100% of the applicants are accepted.

Community Environment: See University of Cincinnati.

CINCINNATI COLLEGE OF MORTUARY SCIENCE (N-2)
3860 Pacific Avenue
Cincinnati, Ohio 45207
Tel: (513) 745-3631

Description: The private college was founded in 1882 as the Clarke School of Embalming. In 1966 the college established a cooperative relationship with the University of Cincinnati in order to offer general college studies in addition to the purely professional subjects, and at that time adopted its present name. The college discontinued its programs with U.C. in favor of new programs with Edgecliff College. At the same time, Edgecliff announced that it would offer Associate and Baccalaureate degree programs in mortuary science, in conjunction with CCMS. In September of 1979 CCMS moved onto the campus of Edgecliff College. In 1980, Edgecliff was purchased by Xavier University. In 1987, all programs were moved to Xavier's main campus, where CCMS remains as an independent college. In 1980, CCMS was authorized by the Ohio Board of Regents to offer its own Associate of Applied Science Degree to those who qualify. This option was added to the regular 12-month Diploma Programs. In 1986, CCMS began to offer the Bachelor of Mortuary Science degree. CCMS is accredited by the North Central Association of Colleges and Schools, and by the American Board of Funeral Service Education. The college operates on the quarter system and offers one summer session. Enrollment includes 125 students. A faculty of 9 gives a faculty-student ratio of 1-14.

Entrance Requirements: Accredited high school graduation or equivalent, preferably with C or better average; 16 units including 3 English, 1 mathematics, 2 laboratory science, 2 social science, and 8 electives; applicants desiring to practice in states requiring one or two years of college prior to mortuary training must conform with individ-

ual state requirement; rolling admission plan available; $25 application fee.

Costs Per Year: $6,350 tuition; $4,000 room and board; $100 student fees.

Collegiate Environment: The college building, Cohen Center, is located in the campus of Xavier University, giving students full access to facilities and campus life at Xavier. The mortuary college library contains 6,000 volumes, 200 periodicals and 100 audiovisual items. Limited dormitory space is available for students. Most students live in apartments or funeral homes in Cincinnati and northern Kentucky. For additional information regarding individual state licensing requirements, candidates should request the assistance of the State Board involved. Scholarships and financial aid programs are available. About 95% of the applicants are accepted. 60% of students receive financial aid.

Community Environment: See University of Cincinnati.

CINCINNATI STATE TECHNICAL AND COMMUNITY COLLEGE (N-2)
3520 Central Parkway
Cincinnati, Ohio 45223
Tel: (513) 861-7700; Fax: (513) 569-1562

Description: The college was established in 1966 by the Cincinnati Board of Education as a two-year technical institute called the Cincinnati Cooperative School of Technology. In 1968, the Ohio Board of Regents established a Technical Institute District and approved the Cincinnati Cooperative School of Technology as the nucleus serving this district. In December 1969, the college became independent from the Cincinnati Board of Education, being governed by its own Board of Trustees and its own charter. The coeducational college grants certificates and two-year associate degrees. It operates on a five-term system including one summer session. Enrollment includes 2,246 full-time and 3,316 part-time students. A faculty of 139 full-time and 178 part-time gives a faculty-student ratio of 1-35. The college is fully accredited by the North Central Association of Colleges and Schools.

Entrance Requirements: Graduation from accredited high school or equivalency diploma; open enrollment policy; placement tests required; rolling admission, early decision, and advanced placement plans available; $10 admission fee on first invoice.

Costs Per Year: $2,500 tuition; $5,000 nonresident tuition; $200 student fees.

Collegiate Environment: The college is located in the heart of Cincinnati. The library contains 18,000 volumes, 365 pamphlets, 438 periodicals and 50,653 microforms. The college offers the newest instructional gear available for those programs requiring it. 40% of the current students receive financial aid. All facilities are housed in one building. Men's and women's basketball and intramural sports are available.

Community Environment: See University of Cincinnati.

CIRCLEVILLE BIBLE COLLEGE (L-7)
1476 Lancaster Pike
Circleville, Ohio 43113
Tel: (614) 474-8896; Admissions: (614) 477-7701; Fax: (614) 477-7755

Description: The coeducational Bible college produces a major portion of the persons entering the ministry, both home and foreign, of The Churches of Christ in Christian Union. Founded in 1948, the college is dedicated to fulfilling the mandate of 1947 to provide an adequate training center for persons preparing for Christian Service. The college is a member of the American Association of Bible Colleges. The college grants a Diploma and a Bachelors degree. The college operates on the semester system and offers one summer session. Enrollment is 217 students. A faculty of 13 full-time and 8 part-time gives a faculty-student ratio of 1-10.

Entrance Requirements: High school graduation with rank in upper half of graduating class; ACT with minimum score of 15, or SAT required; rolling admission and midyear admission plans available; $15 application fee.

Costs Per Year: $3,500 tuition; $3,500 board and room; $500 student fees; additional expenses average $361.

Collegiate Environment: The college is situated on a beautiful 40 acre campus just east of Circleville. Eight modern buildings provide excellent facilities for the 200 students enrolled. The library contains 22,200 titles, 135 periodical subscriptions, 1,425 microforms, and 216 audiovisual materials. Intercollegiate sports began in 1980. Financial assistance is available for economically disadvantaged students. 95% of students receive financial aid. About 30% of the senior class continue on to graduate school.

Community Environment: Circleville is situated in the central part of the state, 23 miles south of Columbus. A shopping center and a number of civic and service organizations serve the community. The annual Circleville Pumpkin Show features a 350-pound pumpkin pie, five feet in diameter, attracting over 500,000 visitors from throughout the world.

CLARK STATE COMMUNITY COLLEGE *(K-4)*
P.O. Box 570
Springfield, Ohio 45501
Tel: (513) 325-0691; Fax: (513) 328-3853

Description: The state-supported institution was founded in 1962. It operates under the jurisdiction of both the Ohio Board of Regents and the State Department of Education. The name changed in 1988 to Clark State Community College. The institute has as its objective the training of technicians to support professionals in the fields of business, agriculture, engineering and engineering technologies, and health and human services. The college's Arts and Sciences Division also provides the first two years of a B.A. degree through its Associate of Arts and Associates of Science degree programs. The quarter system is used and 3 summer terms are offered. The college is accredited by the North Central Association of Colleges and Schools. It is also a member of the Southwestern Ohio Council for Higher Education. Enrollment includes 1,049 full-time and 1,777 part-time students. A faculty of 58 full-time and 131 part-time gives a faculty-student ratio of 1-18.

Entrance Requirements: Accredited high school graduation or equivalent; entrance exam required; open enrollment policy; application fee $15; early admission, midyear admission and rolling admission plans available.

Costs Per Year: $1,761 state-resident tuition and fees; $3,291 out-of-state; $585 books and supplies.

Collegiate Environment: The college is located on 60 acres on the southern perimeter of Springfield. There are four buildings used as classrooms, offices and laboratories. The library contains 32,000 volumes and 350 periodicals. The institute does not have housing facilities, but students who do not commute live in private homes or apartments. There is a Placement Service to aid students who want help in finding employment and to assist graduates who wish to improve their positions. The college also operates a downtown campus in Springfield's business district, 1 1/2 miles north of its main campus. About 99% of students applying for admission meet the requirements and are accepted. Financial assistance is available for economically disadvantaged students.

Community Environment: See Wittenberg University.

CLEVELAND INSTITUTE OF ART *(E-11)*
11141 East Boulevard
Cleveland, Ohio 44106
Tel: (216) 421-7400; (800) 223-6500; Fax: (216) 421-7438

Description: This private art school has been in operation since 1882. The institute is accredited by the North Central Association of Colleges and Schools. The basic program is a series of courses required of each degree candidate during his/her first two years of study. Required subjects include studio courses in drawing, painting and design, along with English, history, art history and literature. The three-year advanced program of concentrated studio courses and selected academic studies culminates in the Bachelor of Fine Arts degree. 15 major subjects are available, including an art education major offered jointly with Case Western Reserve University. The institute operates on the semester system and offers one summer session. Enrollment includes 238 men and 191 women full-time, 19 men and 47 women part-time, plus 220 students in the evening division. A faculty of 29 full-time and 48 part-time and an additional 14 in the evening program gives a faculty-student ratio of 1-10.

Entrance Requirements: Approved high school graduation or equivalent; completion of 15 units including 4 English, 4 mathematics, 2 science, 2 social science, and 3 art; portfolio of 12-20 original works required; ACT and/or SAT required; personal interview required of all candidates living within 500 miles of Cleveland; early admission, early decision, midyear admission, delayed admission, rolling admission and advanced placement plans available; $30 application fee.

Costs Per Year: $11,400 tuition; $4,770 room and board; $300 student fees; $800 average additional expenses.

Collegiate Environment: The art school has its own $3,000,000 buildings in University Circle in a 488-acre setting. Students and faculty alike are justly proud of this unique structure with its many studios, classrooms, galleries, and auditorium. The institute participates in the loan program of the National Defense Education Act of 1958. Students who can demonstrate financial need and good academic standing are eligible to apply for assistance. Of the 45 scholarships available, 21 are for freshmen. 80% of students receive some form of financial aid. The dormitories of Case Western Reserve University, one and one-half blocks away, are available to 100 freshmen of the Art Institute. The library consists of over 38,000 volumes, 60,000 mounted pictures and photographs for reference, 20,000 microforms, 1,000 sound recordings, 200 current periodicals and 50,000 slides. About 60% of students applying for admission are accepted, including midyear students. The average scores of the entering freshman class were SAT 461 verbal, 474 math.

Community Environment: See Case Western Reserve University.

CLEVELAND INSTITUTE OF MUSIC *(E-11)*
11021 East Boulevard
Cleveland, Ohio 44106
Tel: (216) 795-3107; (800) 791-5000; Admissions: (216) 795-3107; Fax: (216) 795-1530

Description: The private conservatory was founded in 1920 and is a charter member of the National Association of Schools of Music. It is accredited by the North Central Association of Colleges and Schools. The undergraduate school offers the Bachelor of Music degree and the Diploma course. The graduate school offers the Master and Doctor of Musical Arts degree as well as the Artist Diploma and Professional Studies Certificate. A summer session of six weeks is open to preparatory, special, and conservatory students. The Institute cooperates in a Joint Program at both the graduate and undergraduate levels with adjacent Case Western Reserve University. It operates on the semster calendar system. Enrollment includes 335 full-time and 16 part-time students. A faculty of 107 provides a faculty-student ratio of 1-3.

Entrance Requirements: Accredited high school graduation or equivalent; completion of 16 units including 4 English, 3 mathematics, 3 foreign language, 3 science, 3 social science; candidates for performance course must pass entrance audition in their major area; candidates not meeting all requirements may be admitted but deficiencies must be made up during the first year of study; application fee $50. Advanced placement available.

Costs Per Year: $14,756 tuition; $4,800 room and board.

Collegiate Environment: The Institute is located in University Circle, a unique educational and cultural center in the Cleveland metropolitan area. The Circle comprises over 30 institutions including The Cleveland Orchestra, and constitutes one of the largest cultural complexes in the world. It affords opportunity for study in many fields and creates in its 488 acres one of the most beautiful areas in the city. Dormitory facilities for 100 students are available on campus, adjacent to CIM. The library contains 47,000 volumes, 153 periodicals, 850 microforms, and 13,000 recordings. 45% of applicants are accepted. Scholarships are available and 88% of the students receive some form of financial aid. About 95% of the previous freshman class returned to school for their second year.

Community Environment: See Case Western Reserve University.

CLEVELAND STATE UNIVERSITY *(E-11)*
1983 East 24th Street
Cleveland, Ohio 44115
Tel: (216) 687-2000; Admissions: (216) 687-3754; Fax: (216) 687-9210

Description: The state university was created by the action of the General Assembly of the State of Ohio in 1964. CSU consists of seven colleges: the College of Arts and Sciences, the James J. Nance College of Business Administration, the College of Education, Fenn College of Engineering, the Maxine Goodman Levin College of Urban Affairs, the College of Graduate Studies, and the Cleveland-Marshall College of Law. These seven colleges offer 57 major programs leading to baccalaureate degrees, 3 advanced degrees in law, 28 master's degrees, 2 post-master's Educational Specialist programs, and 7 doctoral degrees. There are day and evening divisions. The university is accredited by the North Central Association of Colleges and Schools and by respective professional organizations. The school uses the quarter system with three summer terms offered. The undergraduate enrollment is approximately 12,716 students and the graduate enrollment is 5,483. The faculty has 561 full-time members. The university grants Bachelors degrees, Masters, Post-Masters and Doctorate degrees and the Juris Doctor in the Law School.

Entrance Requirements: High school graduation with rank in upper half of graduating class; completion of 15 1/2 units including 4 English, 3 mathematics, 3 science, 3 social science, 2 foreign languages and 1/2 fine arts; SAT or ACT required; application fee $25; early decision, rolling admission, delayed admission, and advanced placement plans available.

Costs Per Year: $2,976 tuition; $5,952 out-of-state tuition; $3,835 board and room.

Collegiate Environment: The university has 33 buildings on the 72-acre campus. To obtain more space until new buildings are ready, they have been buying and leasing facilities in the immediate area. Meanwhile, the development plan, which includes new Music-Communication and Convocation Center buildings, is well under way. The library contains 750,000 volumes, 4,000 periodicals, 600,000 microforms, and 19,000 sound recordings. Numerous scholarships are available. Dormitories are available for 600 students. Approximately 99% of students applying for admission are accepted, including mid-year students. The average high school standing of the current freshman class 40% in the top quarter, 30% in the second quarter, 25% in the third quarter; average SAT scores, 420V and 450M or a composite ACT of 17.

Community Environment: See Case Western Reserve University.

CLEVELAND-MARSHALL COLLEGE OF LAW   *(E-11)*
1801 Euclid Avenue
Cleveland, Ohio 44115
Tel: (216) 687-2344

Description: The Cleveland-Marshall College of Law of Cleveland State University is the largest Law School in the State of Ohio with an enrollment of approximately 1,000 students in the Juris Doctor program. A faculty of 39 full-time and 31 part-time gives a ratio of 1-18. Originally established as an independent degree granting institution in 1897, the Law College merged with Cleveland State University in 1969. It is fully accredited by the North Central Association of Colleges and Schools. It is fully approved by the American Bar Association, accredited by the Association of American Law Schools, and a charter member of the League of Ohio Law Schools. Instruction is offered in both day and evening programs for full-time and part-time students.

Entrance Requirements: Applicants for the Juris Doctor degree must have been awarded a baccalaureate degree by a college or university approved by a regional accrediting agency and have taken the LSAT. Transcripts of all previous college or university records must be submitted through the Law School Data Assembly Service (LSDAS). Many students are admitted primarily upon the basis of an index combining grades and LSAT scores. Since strict numerical indicators are not infallible, however, some students are admitted on the basis of factors other than numerical index. Such admission, through an educational effort known as the Legal Career Opportunities Program, follows a full consideration of all relevant information provided by the applicant to the Law College Committee on Admissions. Application fee $35.

Costs Per Year: $2,088 state-resident tuition; $4,176 nonresident tuition.

Collegiate Environment: In September 1977 the College of Law moved into a new multimillion dollar law center located on the university's modern urban campus in downtown Cleveland. Law li-

brary contains 260,000 volumes, 3,113 periodicals, 526,716 microforms, and 689 audiovisual materials. Financial assistance is available, and approximately 40% of the current students receive some form of aid.

Community Environment: See Case Western Reserve University.

COLLEGE OF MOUNT SAINT JOSEPH   *(N-2)*
5701 Delhi Road
Cincinnati, Ohio 45233-1672
Tel: (513) 244-4531; (800) 654-9314; Fax: (513) 244-4601

Description: This college was founded in 1920 by the Sisters of Charity. Nearly 40 majors are offered in four-year programs, 13 in two-year programs, and 4 in certificate programs. The college is accredited by the North Central Association of Colleges and Schools and respective professional accrediting associations. The school operates on the semester system with 4 summer sessions. The Bachelor of Arts, Bachelor of Fine Arts, Bachelor of Science, Bachelor of Science in Nursing, and the Associate in Arts and Science degrees are awarded. Also awarded is the Master of Arts in Education and Pastoral Family Studies. Cooperative education programs are available all areas. Study abroad is available. Enrollment is 1,703 women and 630 men. Graduate enrollment is 175 students. There are also 1,267 students in the Continuing Education program. A faculty of 83 full-time and 111 part-time gives a faculty-student ratio of 1-15.

Entrance Requirements: High school graduation with rank in upper 3/5 of graduating class; 2.25 GPA; completion of 13 core credits including 4 English, 2 mathematics (including algebra and geometry), 2 science, 2 social science, 1 fine art, and 2 foreign language or 2 additional in above areas; minimum composite SAT of 960 (480V, 480M) or ACT 19 composite; students who meet at least 3 of the 4 listed conditions will be offered admission; students who meet 2 of the 4 conditions will be reviewed by committee; rolling admission plan available; $25 application fee.

Costs Per Year: $9,800 tuition; $4,430 room and board for semi-private room and 21-meal plan (other options available); $400 books.

Collegiate Environment: The 75-acre campus has nine buildings. The Mater Dei Chapel seats about 800 and the interior design and decoration is the work of the faculty and graduates of the art department of the college. There is a library of 90,000 titles, 734 periodicals, and 8,127 audiovisual items. There are 500 rooms available for students in Seton Hall, a seven-story U-shaped structure. Approximately 73% of students applying for admission are accepted, including mid-year students. The college welcomes a geographically diverse student body. 85% of the students receive financial aid. The middle 50% range of test scores of enrolled students are: Act 19-25 composite, SAT 400-510V, 440-560M. The high school standing of the freshman class is in the top two-fifths: 38% in the top fifth and 33% in the second fifth. About 10% of the senior class continue on to graduate school.

Community Environment: Located in a western suburb of Cincinnati, Mount St. Joseph enjoys the cultural and recreational facilities of that city.

COLLEGE OF WOOSTER   *(G-10)*
Wooster, Ohio 44691
Tel: (216) 263-2000

Description: College of liberal arts and sciences granting three Baccalaureate degrees: Bachelor of Arts, Bachelor of Music, Bachelor of Music Education. Founded in 1866, affiliated with the United Presbyterian Church, accredited by the North Central Association of Colleges and Schools, the American Chemical Society, and the National Association of Schools of Music. Enrollment of 1,637 men and women and a faculty of 147 full-time and 24 part-time. Semester system and one summer session. Special programs include one of only four required Independent Study programs in the United States; required Freshman Seminar; interdisciplinary sophomore seminars; extensive overseas program; domestic programs including urban studies, fine arts, government, business internships, and pre-professional cooperative plans in architecture, communicative disorders, dentistry, economics, engineering, forestry and environmental studies, law, mathematics, nursing, physics, and social work. Teacher certification for elementary and secondary. Study abroad is available to China, the Soviet Union, Great Britain, Germany and other countries.

Entrance Requirements: High school graduation or equivalent; rank in upper one-third of graduating class; completion of 16 units including 4 English, 3 mathematics, 2 foreign language, 3 science, 3 social science; SAT or ACT required; early admission, delayed admission, advanced placement plans available; $25 nonrefundable application fee.

Costs Per Year: $14,380 tuition, $2,518 room and board.

Collegiate Environment: The college accepts 81% of those who apply for admission and permits both freshmen and transfer students to enroll in August and January. College facilities include a library of 665,947 titles, 207,322 microfilms, 6,646 audiovisual materials, and 1,632 periodical subscriptions. The 320-acre campus includes recently renovated geology and math/physics/computer science buildings, and a new Music Center. On-campus residence halls house 95% of the student body, available for 900 men and 800 women. 300 students involved with social service agencies in Wooster City area; leadership opportunities in student organizations and groups; intercollegiate athletics in the North Coast Athletic Conference which includes 21 varsity programs for men and women. Financial aid available, 55% of current students receive some form of assistance.

Community Environment: City of Wooster population of 22,000, county seat of Wayne County, and leading agricultural region in the United States. In Ohio, Wayne County ranks first in cash receipts from dairy products, cattle and calves, and first in production of hay and oats. The Ohio Agricultural Research and Development Center is second largest in the United States. Companies in the city include Rubbermaid Incorporated, Wooster Brush Company, Regal Ware, the Gerstenslager Company, Bell and Howell, Frito-Lay, and others. Other educational institutions include OSU's Agricultural Technical Institute, and the Wayne General and Technical College. City has been designated Tree City, U.S.A. Students given access to Cleveland, Columbus, Pittsburgh, Cincinnati, and Akron.

COLUMBUS COLLEGE OF ART AND DESIGN *(K-6)*
107 N. Ninth Street
Columbus, Ohio 43215
Tel: (614) 224-9101

Description: The private college was established in 1879 and is incorporated under the laws of the State of Ohio. It is composed of the professional day school, the evening school, and the Saturday school, which is for young people from elementary through high school. The college is affiliated with the Columbus Museum of Art and awards a Bachelor of Fine Arts to its graduates. The college is accredited by the North Central Association of Colleges and Schools. It is a member of the National Association of Schools of Art and Design, operates on the early semester system and offers one summer session. Enrollment includes 1,232 full-time and 494 part-time and 494 part-time students. A faculty of 67 full-time and 63 part-time gives a faculty-student ratio of 1-13.

Entrance Requirements: High school graduation with is required; must submit a portfolio of samples of student's work; rolling admission, and midyear admission plans available. $25 application fee.

Costs Per Year: $9,700 tuition; $5,400 room and board; $340 student fees; additional expenses average $850.

Collegiate Environment: The college is located on four acres near the center of metropolitan Columbus adjacent to the Columbus Museum of Art. The 35,000 volume library also contains 238 periodicals and 45,111 slides. Dormitory capacity at the school is 250 students. 63% of students applying for admission are accepted. 133 freshman scholarships are available. 80% of the students receive aid. About 70% of the previous freshman class return to this school for their second year.

Community Environment: See Ohio State University - Columbus Campus.

COLUMBUS STATE COMMUNITY COLLEGE *(K-6)*
550 East Spring Street
Columbus, Ohio 43216
Tel: (614) 227-2400

Description: The state-supported coeducational technical institute was founded in 1963 to satisfy the needs of industry in central Ohio for adequately trained technicians. The Institute was chartered by the Ohio Board of Regents in 1967 and is fully accredited by the North Central Association of Colleges and Schools. Total enrollment is 12,168 students. Faculty is 176 full-time and 403 part-time and gives a student-faculty ratio of 15-1. The quarter system is used for both day and evening classes. Degrees granted are the Associate in Applied Science and the Associate in Applied Business.

Entrance Requirements: High school graduation or equivalent; completion of 17 academic units, placement exam required; interviews required; early admission, early decision and rolling admission plans available.

Costs Per Year: $1,908 state-resident tuition; $4,140 out-of-state.

Collegiate Environment: Some financial aid is available and the counseling office will aid students in finding part-time employment. Library contains 16,000 volumes, 700 pamphlets, 50 periodicals, 80 microforms, and 1,770 recordings. Students are permitted to enroll at midyear as well as in fall.

Community Environment: See Ohio State University - Columbus Campus.

CUYAHOGA COMMUNITY COLLEGE - DISTRICT *(E-11)*
700 Carnegie Avenue
Cleveland, Ohio 44115
Tel: (216) 987-4000

Description: Cuyahoga Community College (CCC) is the oldest and largest community college in Ohio, and the largest in Greater Cleveland. Since its opening in 1963, Cuyahoga Community College has expanded to three modern campuses; Metropolitan campus (downtown), Eastern campus (Warrensville Twp.), and Western campus (Parma). The expansion also includes the new Unified Technologies Center (Metro campus), one of the largest technology training facilities in the country. The college is accredited by the North Central Association of Colleges and Schools and is approved by the Ohio Board of Regents. The quarter system is used and two summer terms are offered. The college grants the Associate degree in three curriculum areas: arts and science, technical and career areas, labor studies. In addition to the traditional college curriculum which is transferable to four-year colleges or universities, CCC also offers programs that lead to certificates of proficiency and awards of study, as well as continuing education courses designed to increase the opportunity for development of skills, personal and professional growth. Enrollment during the recent year was approximately 25,000 students. A faculty of 338 full-time and 951 part-time gives a faculty-student ratio of approximately 1:24.

Entrance Requirements: Open admissions policy; open to all high school graduates as well as non-high school graduates, 18 years of age or older. ACT/SAT scores are useful in planning a course of study, but not required for admission. For admission, submit a completed Application for Admission form, a $10 application fee, all transcripts (high school and college), and request that scores for college admission tests (if one has been taken), be sent to the campus of your choice.

Costs Per Year: Cuyahoga County residents' tuition is $988.75; other Ohio residents $1,302.75; out-of-state residents $2,562.75. Student fees total $10.00. Students may be charged supplementary course and incidental fees due to the nature of certain courses.

Collegiate Environment: Having served the community from a two-story brick building in downtown Cleveland for its first six years, Cuyahoga Community College opened its Metropolitan campus in the fall of 1969. This 10-building modern complex was the college's first permanent campus. It is also the location of the Unified Technologies Center (UTC), which was designed to effectively introduce new technology to the marketplace. The Eastern campus opened its permanent 3-level facility in the fall of 1981, after a ten-year residence in temporary facilities. Its mall design displays modern classrooms, a computer center, auditorium and other aesthetic structures. Western campus opened in 1966 in an old Veterans' hospital. In 1975, the facilities were replaced with a 6-building, interconnected structure that includes a three-story galleria and a glass-roofed mall. Library holdings, by campus are as follows: Volumes - 49,064 (Metropolitan), 27,190 (Eastern), 41,394 (Western); Periodical subscriptions - 258 (Metropolitan), 151 (Eastern), 284 (Western); Audiovisual materials-Number of titles - 2,168 (Metropolitan), 2,042 (Eastern), 1,610 (Western); Units of microform - 10,228 (Metropolitan), 5,594 (Eastern), 32,875 (Western). Cuyahoga Community College is designed primarily to serve residents of Cuyahoga County, and therefore does not provide housing for its students. Financial aid, consisting of scholarships, grants, loans and part-time employment is designed to supplement students' own resources. No student who is interested in CCC should hesitate to apply to the college due to lack of financial resources. Applicants are accepted at the start of any quarter.

Community Environment: See Case Western Reserve University.

CUYAHOGA COMMUNITY COLLEGE - EASTERN CAMPUS *(E-11)*
4250 Richmond Rd.
Highland Hills, Ohio 44122
Tel: (216) 987-2014; Admissions: (216) 987-2024; Fax: (216) 987-2214

Description: Ohio's first public community college is a two-year post secondary educational and training institution serving greater Cleveland and environs. Chartered by the State of Ohio in 1962, CCC (or Tri-C) is accredited by the North Central Association of Colleges and Schools. Eastern Campus is the convenient focal point of 6,000 credit and continuing education students in the expanding and diversifying eastern segment of the northeast Ohio area. An open door policy is facilitated by having 3 11-week quarters and both 8-week and 5-1/2 week summer sessions. The Arts and Sciences (University Parallel) program provides the first two years of a traditional college curriculum, allowing transfer to four-year colleges and universities. Over 40 career degree and certificate programs are offered. Enrollment is 1,654 full-time and 3,957 part-time students. The faculty consists of 59 full-time and 175 part-time, for a faculty-student ratio of 1-22.

Entrance Requirements: Open door policy; high school graduation, or G.E.D. required for degree courses; non-high school graduates 19 years of age or older may be admitted for certain courses; rolling admission plan available.

Costs Per Year: $1,552 county resident tuition; $2,059 state resident; $4,118 nonresident; additional expenses average $750.

Collegiate Environment: Recent completed renovations of the campus' original facility (now called East I) houses comprehensive theatre, music, and arts programs. The Division of Continuing and Professional Education reaches out to 24 off-campus sites in the community. An expanding library contains over 40,000 titles. Financial aid is available (currently 48% of students receive aid) in the form of economic assistance and over 185 scholarships. Dual admissions programs with Kent State, Dyke College, and Cleveland State Universities are in operation.

Community Environment: See Case Western Reserve University.

CUYAHOGA COMMUNITY COLLEGE - WESTERN CAMPUS *(C-9)*
11000 W. Pleasant Valley Rd.
Parma, Ohio 44130
Tel: (216) 987-5150; Admissions: (216) 987-5150; Fax: (216) 987-5071

Description: The first branch of Ohio's first public community college opened in 1966. Offerings at Tri-C Western include the Arts and Sciences curriculum, and concentrations in a variety of career-oriented technological and business areas. Dual admissions programs are in operation with Cleveland State University, Kent State University and Dyke College. A full range of credit and noncredit courses are available that reflect the community's special needs and interests. The college is accredited by the North Central Association of Colleges and Schools and several respective professional accreditation associations. The enrollment recently was 1,697 men and 2,403 women full-time and 3,352 men and 5,871 women part-time. Faculty number 155 full-time and 381 part-time, giving a faculty student ratio of 1-22. Two summer terms are offered along with the quarter calendar of instruction. Cooperative education programs are available in several areas. The automotive service educational program is a combined degree program with General Motors.

Entrance Requirements: Open door policy; high school graduation required for degree candidates; nonhigh school graduates 18 years of age or over may be admitted for certain courses; midyear admission, rolling admission and advanced placement available; $10 application fee.

Costs Per Year: $1,552 ($34.50 per credit) county resident; $2,059 ($45.75 per credit) state resident; $4,118 ($91.50 per credit) out-of-state; $750 average additional expenses.

Collegiate Environment: The 200-acre campus is located on the site of the former Crile Veterans Administration Hospital in Parma. The acreage and 60 buildings were assigned to the college by the federal government for a nominal transfer fee early in 1966. The focal point is the Galleria, the area where three major traffic corridors converge. The library, cafeteria, bookstore, theatre and Learning Center are located nearby. Scholarships are available and 32% of students receive financial aid.

Community Environment: A suburb of Cleveland, Parma Heights enjoys the recreational, cultural and social advantages of the large city. Major transportation facilities are available in Cleveland. Recreational facilities include water sports on Lake Erie.

DEFIANCE COLLEGE *(E-2)*
701 North Clinton Street
Defiance, Ohio 43512
Tel: (419) 784-4010; Fax: (419) 784-0426

Description: The 150-acre campus is a one hour drive from the airports in Toledo and Ft. Wayne, Indiana, and 30 miles from the Ohio Turnpike. Founded in 1850, the first classes were held at this private four-year liberal arts college in 1886, and its affiliation with the United Church of Christ dates back to 1957. The college operates on the semester system and offers two summer sessions. It is accredited by the North Central Association of Colleges and Schools, Council on Social Work Education and the Ohio State Department of Education. Enrollment includes 885 undergraduate and 40 graduate students. A faculty of 60 full-time and 15 part-time gives faculty-student ratio of 1-13. The college offers Bachelor of Arts, Bachelor of Science and Master of Education Degrees. A cooperative education program is available to all degree-seeking students.

Entrance Requirements: Recommended completion of 15 units, including 4 English, 3 mathematics, 3 science, 3 social science, and 2 foreign language; SAT with minimum combined score of 900, or ACT with composite score of at least 18; high school transcript (GPA, class rank); interviews recommended; each application is reviewed when it is completed, and the applicant receives word from the admissions committee within one week; early admission, early decision, rolling admission, delayed admission, and advanced placement available; application fee $25.

Costs Per Year: $10,850 tuition and fees; $3,750 room and board.

Collegiate Environment: The college's 150-acre campus is located in a residential area, a short walk from the center of the city. The buildings include the new Pilgrim Library, which houses a collection of 100,000 volumes, 520 subscriptions of periodicals, a 6,725-unit microfilm library, and 6,365 audiovisual materials. The Carma J. Rowe Science Hall opened in 1987 and the McMaster Fitness Center opened in 1988. A new $2.6 million athletic center and stadium was recently completed, including an 8 lane all-weather track. The campus also includes seven other academic buildings, two large and five small residence halls, three fraternity houses, gymnasium, and fields. Housing is provided for 600 students. Students are accepted for enrollment for Fall and Spring and the college welcomes a geographically diverse student body. Approximately 75% of those who apply for admission are accepted. Financial aid is available, and 87% of the current students receive some form of assistance. Freshman students are allowed to have cars on the campus. The college offers a wide range of student activities and organizations. Organizations presently active include: Honor Societies, sororities and fraternities, chamber singers, theatre productions, intramurals, student religious groups, and the athletic teams (men's: football, basketball, baseball, track, golf, cross country soccer, and tennis; women's: volleyball, basketball, cross country, track, softball, soccer, and tennis).

Community Environment: Defiance College is located in Defiance Ohio, site of Fort Defiance, and birthplace of the Indian Chief Pontiac. Today, Defiance is a community of over 18,000 persons and one of the fastest growing areas in Northwest Ohio. Highly diversified industry and some of the richest farmland in the nation contribute to the areas prosperity. A major shopping mall is 2 blocks north of the campus.

DENISON UNIVERSITY *(J-8)*
Box H
Granville, Ohio 43023
Tel: (614) 587-6276; (800) 336-4766; Fax: (614) 587-6417

Description: Denison University, an indeprndent, coeducational, residential, liberal arts college was founded in 1831 as the Granville Literary and Theological Institution by the Ohio Baptist Education Society, an organization of laymen. In 1856 the present name was adopted, but the institution has remained an undergraduate college. It is accredited by the North Central Association of Colleges and Schools. The college grants the Bachelor of Arts, Science, and Fine Arts degrees. It operates on the semester system and offers an optional May term. Full-time enrollment is 820 men and 897 women. A faculty of 161 gives a faculty-student ratio of 1-11.

Entrance Requirements: Accredited high school graduation; completion of 16 units including 4 English, 3 mathematics, 3 foreign language, 3 science, and 3 social science; SAT or ACT required; early admission, early decision, delayed admission, midyear admission and advanced placement credit plans available. $35 application fee.

Costs Per Year: $14,900 tuition; $4,220 room and board; $740 student fees; $1,100 average books and personal expenses.

Collegiate Environment: Granville is 27 miles east of the state capital, Columbus. The 1,100-acre campus is on a horseshoe-shaped, wooded ridge with the major academic buildings at the center. The science complex includes the recently completed F.W. Olin Science Hall. At the east end are residence halls accommodating 988 students, a dining hall, and the college hospital. To the west are quarters for 665 men and women, a dining hall, and eight fraternity houses that accomodate 335 men. Extensive athletic and recreation fields and the newly opened 81,418 square foot Mitchell Recreation and Athletics Center are in the valley directly north of the ridge. To the south are the buildings used for the Fine Arts and five sorority chapter lodges. The library system has a collection of 315,243 volumes and 285,251 periodicals, 16,000 sound recordings and 2,500 video cassettes. The college is a member of the Great Lakes Colleges Association. The 250-acre Biological Reserve is a facility for instruction and research in the environmental sciences. 84% of applicants are accepted. About 85% of the freshmen returned for the sophomore year. The average high school standing of the current freshman class was 53% in the top fifth, 28% in the second fifth, and 11% in the third fifth. The middle ranges scores for the entering freshman class were SAT 460-570 verbal, 520-630 math, and ACT 25-29 composite. More than 15% of the senior class continued on to graduate school. Over 1,000 freshmen scholarships are available and 41% of the current students receive some form of assistance.

Community Environment: Of interest are the many beautiful homes in Granville. The town was founded by settlers from the Massachusetts town of the same name in 1805.

DEVRY INSTITUTE OF TECHNOLOGY *(K-6)*
1350 Alum Creek Drive
Columbus, Ohio 43209-2705
Tel: (614) 253-7291; (800) 426-3909; Admissions: (614) 263-1525; Fax: (614) 252-4108

Description: The Columbus campus of this proprietary, coeducational school was established in 1952 and is accredited by the North Central Association of Colleges and Schools. Programs are developed and updated regularly with direct input from business and industry leaders. It operates on the semester system, has 1 summer session, and grants associate and bachelor degrees. Enrollment includes 1,644 men and 429 women full-time, 452 men and 141 women part-time. A faculty of 60 full-time and 18 part-time gives a faculty-student ratio of 1-39. Army ROTC is available.

Entrance Requirements: High school diploma or GED certification; minimum 17 years of age; must pass DeVry entrance examination or submit acceptable ACT/SAT/WPCT scores; foreign students accepted if qualified. Rolling admission, advanced placement plans available. $25 application fee.

Costs Per Year: Tuition $6,335.

Collegiate Environment: In 1973, the institute more than doubled in size by adding a 52,000 square foot structure to the original building. A sunken commons area at the center of the building is the focus of the campus. Dining areas, a student lounge, and meeting rooms for

clubs encourage extracurricular activities. DeVry has a full intramural sports program. The library has over 16,360 bound volumes, 158 periodicals, and 148 microfilms. 91% of applicants are accepted. Scholarships are available and 83% of the students recieve financial aid.

Community Environment: Columbus is the 20th largest city in the U.S. but retains its small town atmosphere. Colombus is a blend of leisurely living, educational centers, business, industry, and culture. It is also a world center of scientific and technological research and data dissemination. Places of interest include the Center of Science and Industry, the State Capitol area, and the Gallery of Fine Arts.

DYKE COLLEGE *(E-11)*
112 Prospect Avenue
Cleveland, Ohio 44115
Tel: (216) 696-9000; Fax: (216) 696-6430

Description: This private coeducational college offers mainly academic majors in business and business-related fields of study. The Bachelor degree consists of two years of general education coupled with a strong, application-oriented concentration of the student's preference in a business-related field. Cooperative work experience includes work-study and intership options. Students may earn an Associate in Science degree or an Associate in Arts degree in several business and business-related majors. Academic programs include arts and sciences, business administration, extended learning, paralegal, secretarial science, developmental education, and continuing education. The college offers an Accelerated Management Degree program for working adults who hold an Associate degree or its equivalent and who wih to complete a Bachelor's degree in management in less than 2 years and as few as 60 weeks. Course work is offered at three academic sites: Wickliffe, OH; Brecksville, OH; and Lorain County, OH. The college is accredited by the North Central Association of Colleges and Schools. It offers classroom instruction year-round during days, evenings and Saturdays, as well as an External Degree Program. Enrollment is 723 full-time and 703 part-time students. A faculty of 100 provides a faculty-student ratio of 1-14.

Entrance Requirements: High school graduation or recognized equivalent; ACT or SAT or placement test required; personal interview recommended; early admission, early decision, rolling admission, delayed admission and advanced placement plans available; $25 application fee.

Costs Per Year: $5,200 full-time tuition; $185 per credit hour part-time; $50 student fees.

Collegiate Environment: The college is located in the center of cultural and business activity in the downtown section of Cleveland. The Cleveland Public Library that contains more than two million volumes and a 25-acre cultural mall are within one block of the college. In addition to its classroom facilities, the college maintains a bookstore, student center, and a library of 14,000 volumes. Approximately 85% of the applicants are accepted. Financial aid is available, and half of the current students receive some form of assistance. Most students live within commuting distance of the college. The college occupied new facilities in 1985 located directly off Public Square, the center of downtown Cleveland.

Community Environment: See Case Western Reserve University.

EDISON STATE COMMUNITY COLLEGE *(J-3)*
1973 Edison Drive
Piqua, Ohio 45331
Tel: (513) 778-8600

Description: Chartered in 1973, Edison State Community College is a two-year, public coeducational, state-supported college centrally located in the Darke, Miami and Shelby County area. Edison State offers courses of instruction in the arts and sciences, technical education and adult and continuing education. Many students pursue Associate of Arts, Associate of Applied Science or Associate of Applied Business degrees while others are enrolled in university parallel (transfer) programs. Still other students pursue Certificate programs or individual interest courses. The college offers evening classes as well as the day session, and 3,297 students are enrolled in these programs. Enrollment includes 1,003 full-time and 2,294 part-time students. A faculty of 40 full-time and 145 part-time provides a faculty-student ratio of 1-19 for day classes. The academic year at Edison State is organized around the semester system with two summer terms. Additionally, continuing education (noncredit) courses begin throughout the year. Edison State College is fully accredited by the North Central Association of Colleges and Schools and the National League for Nursing.

Entrance Requirements: Open enrollment; high school graduation or GED; ACT required; rolling admission, early admission, early decision, delayed admission, and advanced placement plans available; $15 application fee.

Costs Per Year: $1,845 state-resident tuition, $3,420 nonresident; $200 student fees.

Collegiate Environment: Edison State Community College moved to its $5.5 million building on its 130-acre campus in September 1976. The rapidly growing library contains 32,000 volumes, 365 periodical subscriptions, 86,000 microforms and 1,137 audiovisual materials. Approximately 40% of Edison State's students receive some form of financial aid. All applicants are accepted. Most Edison State students are employed at least part-time.

Community Environment: Located in Piqua, Ohio, Edison State Community College serves the Darke, Miami and Shelby County area of west-central Ohio. The region, made up of small-sized and medium-sized towns, has an excellent balance among agricultural, industrial and residential areas.

Branch Campuses: Limited offerings are available at the Darke County Center.

FRANCISCAN UNIVERSITY OF STEUBENVILLE (I-14)
Franciscan Way
Steubenville, Ohio 43952
Tel: (614) 283-6226; (800) 783-6220; Fax: (614) 283-6472

Description: The coeducational Catholic liberal arts college is operated by the Franciscan Friars of the Third Order Regular. The first classes were held in 1946 when 197 full-time students were enrolled. The college operates on the semester system and offers three summer sessions. Enrollment is 1,305 full-time, 233 part-time, and 370 graduate students. A faculty of 95 full-time and 44 part-time gives an undergraduate faculty-student ratio of 1-12. The college is accredited by the North Central Association of Colleges and Schools and the National League for Nursing. The college offers three Baccalaureate degrees: the Bachelor of Arts, the Bachelor of Science, and the Bachelor of Science in Nursing; it also awards Associate, M.A., M.B.A., and M.S. degrees. An Austrian campus allows the students the opportunity to fulfill sophomore year core study requirements overseas. It also permits students to study in Europe and travel during the two 10-day beaks or on long weekends, which run from noon on Thursaday to noon on Monday.

Entrance Requirements: High school graduation or equivalent; rank in top 50% of class; completion of 15 academic units including 4 English, 3 mathematics, 3 social science, and 2 science; minimum SAT score of 425V and 425M or ACT of 19 required; GRE and GMAT required for some graduate programs; early admission, early decision, delayed admission, advanced placement and rolling admission plans available; June 30 application deadline; $20 application fee.

Costs Per Year: $9,650 tuition; $4,400 room and board; $260 student fees; $850 Austrian Study Abroad fee; $700 Nursing fee; $500 average additional expenses.

Collegiate Environment: The 100-acre campus is located on a high plateau at the northernmost edge of the city of Steubenville. The Holy Spirit Monastery looks down on the green Ohio Valley, 1,000 feet below. Within its walls live the Franciscan Friars who serve the college. There are four residence halls on this east side of the campus. The intellectual life of the college revolves around the West Campus where the John Paul II Library is located, which houses more than 205,000 volumes, 2,500 recordings, 10,000 microforms, and bound copies of approximately 32,700 periodicals. Total dormitory capacity is 330 men and 460 women. An evening degree program is offered. Over 82% of students receive financial assistance. 76% of applicants are accepted, including midyear students.

Community Environment: The county seat of Jefferson County, Steubenville is a city in eastern Ohio situated on the Ohio River. An unlimited supply of both deep-mine and strip coal is available in the Steubenville district. Because of the coal and the Ohio River, more steam electricity is generated within a 40-mile radius of the city than

in any other area in the world. Steel, iron, and paper are some of the products of industries here.

FRANKLIN UNIVERSITY (K-6)
201 South Grant Avenue
Columbus, Ohio 43215
Tel: (614) 341-6237; Fax: (614) 221-7723

Description: The private university offers programs of higher education in the College of Business and Technology and the College of Arts and Sciences. The university offers day, evening and weekend courses. It operates on the trimester system. Programs of study lead to the degrees of Associate and Bachelor of Science and the Bachelor of Science in Nursing. Majors are offered in the areas of business, accounting, marketing, finance, human resources management, computer science, electronics and mechanical engineering technology, applied communication, and employee assistance counseling. The university holds membership in the Ohio College Association. The university is accredited by the North Central Association of Colleges and Schools. It is also accredited by the Accreditation Board for Engineering and Technology, and the National League for Nursing. Army ROTC is available on campus. Air Force ROTC is available off campus. An overseas program of study is available at Richmond College in London and at other AIFS locations. Enrollment includes 1,144 full-time and 2,708 part-time students. A faculty of 46 full-time and 150 adjunct gives a faculty-student ratio of 1-20.

Entrance Requirements: High school graduation or equivalent; no entrance exam required; non-high school graduates may be admitted as special students; open admission policy; application fee $25; rolling admission, early admission, deferred admission and advance placement plans available.

Costs Per Year: $4,352 tuition; $45 student fees; additional expenses average $200.

Collegiate Environment: The university is a downtown facility with 5 buildings. The library contains 83,458 bound volumes, 1,120 periodicals, 143,735 microforms and 639 recordings. Financial assistance is available and 60% of the students receive aid. There are 250 scholarships offered, 65 for freshmen. About 99% of students applying for admission are accepted, including midyear students.

Community Environment: See Ohio State University - Columbus Campus.

GOD'S BIBLE SCHOOL AND COLLEGE (N-2)
1810 Young St.
Cincinnati, Ohio 45210
Tel: (513) 721-7944; (800) 486-4637; Fax: (513) 721-3971

Description: The Bible college was founded in 1900 for the purpose of training Christian workers for service at home and abroad. The school's religious affiliation is interdenominational and Wesleyan-Arminian in doctrinal teachings. The semester system is used and one summer session is offered. Enrollment is 164 men and women full-time and 30 part-time. A faculty of 23 full-time and part-time gives a faculty-student ratio of 1-9. The institute offers a variety of courses of study, including those given through its Bible college divisions and high school, and a correspondence course for those desiring to study at home. The college grants a certificate, and B.A. and B.R.E. degrees.

Entrance Requirements: Approved high school graduation or equivalent; completion of 17 units including 3 English, 2 mathematics, 2 science, and 2 social science; early admission and early decision plans available; application fee $50.

Costs Per Year: $2,820 tuition; $2,050 room and board; $150 student fees.

Collegiate Environment: The college is located on Mount Auburn in Cincinnati. Very strict dress regulations and rules of conduct are observed. Attendance at chapel services is required. About 91% of students applying for admission are accepted. Approximately 80% of the current students receive some form of financial assistance. The school maintains a work-study program that is set up to benefit the economically and culturally disadvantaged youth of Wesleyan-Arminian doctrinal persuasion. These include youths from the Appalachian region, and normally include black and, occasionally, Native American youths. The library has 24,500 volumes, 210 periodicals,

202 microforms and 1,437 audiovisual materials. There is housing for 302 men and women.

Community Environment: See University of Cincinnati.

HEBREW UNION COLLEGE-JEWISH INSTITUTE OF RELIGION *(N-2)*
3101 Clifton Avenue
Cincinnati, Ohio 45220
Tel: (513) 221-1875; Admissions: (513) 221-1875 x213; Fax: (513) 221-0321

Description: Hebrew Union College was founded in 1875 in Cincinnati, the first institution of Jewish higher learning in America. It is accredited by the North Central Association of Colleges and Schools. The college was founded by Rabbi Isaac Mayer Wise, the architect of American Reform Judaism, who had established the Union of American Hebrew Congregations two years earlier for the primary purpose of supporting a seminary to train rabbis for the Reform Movement. In 1922, Rabbi Stephen S. Wise established the Jewish Institute of Religion in New York. The similar orientation of the two schools led to their merger in 1950. A third center was opened in Los Angeles in 1954 to serve the growing Jewish community on the West Coast. A fourth branch was established in Jerusalem, Israel, in 1963. From modest beginnings, Hebrew Union College-Jewish Institute of Religion has developed into an institution providing a wide variety of academic programs. The institute in Cincinnati operates on the semester system. It's enrollment is 131 graduate students. A faculty of 30 provides a faculty-student ratio of 1-4.

Entrance Requirements: College graduates in upper 10% of graduating class; application fee $70; GRE required; rolling admission, delayed admission plans available; aptitude and psychological tests and interview necessary.

Costs Per Year: $8,000 tuition.

Collegiate Environment: The Cincinnati campus, situated adjacent to the University of Cincinnati, comprises twenty acres of land and nine buildings. These include the Classroom Building, which also houses the S.H. and Helen R. Scheuer Chapel and the College Store of textbooks and heirloom quality Judaica; the Sisterhood Dormitory, containing faculty and student dining rooms and various social rooms; the New Dormitory; the Klau Library; the Dalsheimer Rare Book Building; the American Jewish Archives; the National Administration Building; Mayerson Hall, which houses the Skirball Museum Cincinnati Branch, the HUC-UC Center for the Study of Ethics and Contemporary Moral Problems, the Starkoff Institute of Ethics; and the Freiberg Gymnasium. The Klau Library is one of the most extensive Jewish libraries in the world. It contains approximately 330,000 volumes, among them 150 incunabula, and over 2,000 manuscript codices and many thousands of pages of archival documents. Special collections include Jewish Americana, music, an outstanding Spinoza collection, and extensive microforms. It also houses the American Jewish Periodical Center, which preserves American Jewish periodicals and newspapers on microfilm. More than 875 titles, with over 12,000,000 pages, are available in the Center. The American Jewish Archives is a major center of study, research and publication in the field of American Jewish history. The Archives collects and catalogues material, both published and manuscript, reflecting the life and history of American Jewry. It now has approximately 8,000,000 pages of documents. Two million of these are from the archives of the World Jewish Congress. This collection makes the Archives the central research institution on the Holocaust in the United States. Scholars from various parts of the world participate in the doctoral and postdoctoral fellowship programs of the American Jewish Archives in the field of Jewish history of the Americas. The Center for the Study of Ethics and Contemporary Moral Problems, a joint project of the Hebrew Union College-Jewish Institute of Religion and the University of Cincinnati, is a national resource cneter for the exploration of critical, ethical, and moral issues. The Center's activities include lectures taught by visiting faculty and faculty from the College-Institute and the University of Cincinnati. Housing is available for 30 students. 90% of the students receive financial aid.

Community Environment: See University of Cincinnati.

HEIDELBERG COLLEGE *(F-6)*
310 E. Market Street
Tiffin, Ohio 44883
Tel: (419) 448-2000; (800) 434-3352; Admissions: (419) 448-2330; Fax: (419) 448-2124

Description: The coeducational college was founded in the year 1850 and confers the Baccalaureate, Master of Arts and Master of Buisiness Administration degrees. It is accredited by the North Central Association of Colleges and Schools and by several respective professional accrediting associations. The early semester system is used and two summer terms are offered. The private school is affiliated with the United Church of Christ. It sponsors the American Junior Year Program and the Heidelberg Semester at the University of Heidelberg, Germany. The college has cooperative programs with several institutions including Ohio State (agriculture), Duke University (forestry), Case Western Reserve (nursing, engineering, and medical technology), and a medical technology program in cooperation with Mansfield General Hospital and Toledo Hospital. Enrollment recently was 1310 students full- and part-time and a faculty of 62 full-time and 46 part-time.

Entrance Requirements: Accredited high school graduation; completion of 14 units including 4 English, 3 mathematics, 2 science, 3 social science, 2 foreign language; SAT or ACT required; early decision, advanced placement, delayed admission, rolling admission and early admission programs available; application fee $20.

Costs Per Year: $14,606 tuition; $4,674 board and room; $100 students fees; additional expenses average $700.

Collegiate Environment: Heidelberg's Total Student Development Program attempts to integrate each student's social, cultural, and religious values with his or her academic program, activities, and career goals. About 97% of students applying for admission are accepted, including midyear students. Beeghly Library contains 157,224 titles, 746 periodical subscriptions, 6,000 microfilms and 5,000 audiovisual materials. Residence hall space is available for 850 students. Financial assistance is available and about 97% of the students receive aid. Of the 437 scholarships offered, 162 are for freshmen. The high school standing of the current freshmen class, 18% in the first quintile, 36% in the second quintile; average SAT scores, 401V and 450M and a composite ACT of 21. About 20% of the senior class continued on to graduate school.

Community Environment: The 110-acre campus is located in Tiffin, Ohio, at the intersection of U.S. route 224 and Ohio Route 53, 50 miles southeast of Toledo and 92 miles west of Cleveland. Bus transportation is available from Tiffin: Amtrack stops in Toledo, Lima and Crestline. Churches, civic, service and social service agencies, and private enterprises offer many opportunities for volunteer and class-related experiences. Places of worship are available on campus and in the immediate community for Protestants and Catholics, and within 23 miles for Jewish students.

Branch Campuses: An accelerated degree program is offered in Maumee, Ohio for students who have completed at least 39 semester hours of college level work. General education undergraduate courses and graduate education courses are offered at the branch campus in Sapporo, Japan.

HIRAM COLLEGE *(E-12)*
Box 96
Hiram, Ohio 44234
Tel: (216) 569-5169; (800) 362-5280; Fax: (216) 569-5944

Description: This private liberal arts college was founded in 1850 by the Christian Church (Disciples of Christ). It is accredited by the North Central Association of Colleges and Schools. Its principle aim is to encourage scholarship and citizenship, and it is known for its high academic standards and innovation in education. The college has a chapter of Phi Beta Kappa. A modified semester system is used. Each semester is divided into a 12 week term and a 3 week term. Enrollment is 847 students. A faculty of 81 full-time gives a faculty-student ratio of 1-12. The college grants the Bachelor of Arts degree.

Entrance Requirements: Completion of 16 units in secondary school; SAT or ACT required; early admission, rolling admission, delayed admission and advanced placement plans available; $25 application fee.

Costs Per Year: $14,065 tuition; $4,560 room and board; $430 student fees.

Collegiate Environment: Located in one of America's principal industrial regions, the college combines the advantages of a rural location with access to the libraries, churches, and cultural resources of the metropolitan centers of Cleveland, Akron, and Youngstown, all of which are about 35 miles from Hiram. The college is situated on a campus of 125 acres, and includes a recreation area with excellent facilities for football, soccer, track and field, and baseball. Living accommodations are available for 800 students. The library contains more than 170,698 volumes, 939 periodicals, 80,829 microforms and 7,200 sound recordings. Special programs offered are the Departmental Honors Program and the Extra-Mural Program for off-campus study. Financial assistance is available. About 80% of the applicants are accepted, including midyear students.

Community Environment: Located in a dairy and orchard growing area, Hiram is a rural community with numerous buildings in the Western Reserve style. This area has long been famous for the production of maple syrup. Bus and train transportation is available. Nearby lakes provide the facilities for boating, swimming, and fishing. Job opportunities are available mainly at the college.

HOCKING COLLEGE   *(M-9)*
3301 Hocking Parkway
Nelsonville, Ohio 45764
Tel: (614) 753-3591; (800) 282-4163; Admissions: (614) 753-3591; Fax: (614) 753-1452

Description: State-supported technical college was founded in 1968 and is accredited by the North Central Association of Colleges and Schools. Its programs are professionally accredited by the Accreditation Board for Engineering and Technology, American Dietetic Association, and the Committee on Allied Health Education and Accreditation. Programs of study are career oriented and lead to the Associate degree. The college operates on the quarter system and offers two summer sessions. Enrollment includes 3,381 full-time and 2,614 part-time students. A faculty of 156 full-time and 101 part-time gives a faculty-student ratio of 1-23.

Entrance Requirements: Open enrollment policy; high school graduation or equivalent; $15 application fee; non-high school graduates considered and advanced placement plan available.

Costs Per Year: $1,920 state-resident tuition; $3,840 nonresident tuition; room and board $3,500; additional expenses average $500.

Collegiate Environment: The 1,400-acre campus has 18 buildings; facilities include privately owned dormitories for 326 men and women and a library of 26,956 volumes, and 300 periodical subscriptions. Freshman students are accepted in September, December, and March. All applicants are accepted. Financial assistance is available and about 60% of the students receive aid. About 12% of the graduates continued on to a four-year school.

Community Environment: Nelsonville is a small community on the Hocking River. It is easily accessible from all points north and south Ohio via US route 33. It is 65 miles from Columbus and is serviced by Greyhound bus lines.

JEFFERSON TECHNICAL COLLEGE   *(I-14)*
4000 Sunset Blvd.
Steubenville, Ohio 43952
Tel: (614) 264-5591; Fax: (614) 264-1338

Description: The state-supported technical college was chartered by the Ohio Board of Regents in 1967. The first classes began in 1968 with 320 students. The college is accredited by the North Central Association of Colleges and Schools. It grants certificates and Associate degrees. It operates on the quarter system and offers three summer sessions. Enrollment includes 755 full-time and 773 part-time students. A faculty of 46 full-time and 60 part-time gives a faculty-student ratio of 1-16.

Entrance Requirements: Open enrollment policy; any high school graduate will be accepted; rolling admission, early admission, and midyear admission plans available; ACT required for entry in some programs; $15 application fee.

Costs Per Year: $1,665 county-resident tuition; $1,800 state-resident; $2,340 out-of-state; $50 student fees; additional expenses average $300.

Collegiate Environment: The college is located on an 83-acre tract and includes a modern structure housing laboratories, classrooms, a student lounge, a library and administrative offices. The library contains 20,420 volumes, 200 periodicals, 3,000 microforms and 2,301 sound recordings. Some financial aid is available. All of the applicants are accepted and approximately 40% return after the first year. The average ACT score of the students is 16.3.

Community Environment: See Franciscan University of Steubenville.

JOHN CARROLL UNIVERSITY   *(E-11)*
20700 North Park Blvd.
University Heights, Ohio 44118
Tel: (216) 397-1886; Admissions: (216) 397-4294; Fax: (216) 397-4256

Description: The private, coeducational, liberal arts university was founded in 1886 by members of the Society of Jesus. This Roman Catholic order first named the school St. Ignatius College. In 1923 the present name was adopted in honor of the first Catholic archbishop of the United States. The university uses the semester system and offers three summer terms. It is accredited by the North Central Association of Colleges and Schools. Enrollment is 3,469 students. A faculty of 213 full-time and 134 part-time gives a faculty-student ratio of 1-15. The university grants Bachelor and Master degrees. Army ROTC program offered.

Entrance Requirements: High school graduation or equivalent; rank in upper half of graduating class; completion of 16 units including 4 English, 3 mathematics, 2 science and 2 social science, 2 language; 3 academic electives; application fee $25; GRE required for graduate programs; early admission, rolling admission, delayed admission and advanced placement plans available.

Costs Per Year: $12,390 tuition; $5,550 room and board; no fees.

Collegiate Environment: The 60-acre campus is located on the east side of the city of Cleveland in the residential suburb of University Heights. The modern library contains 549,618 volumes, 1,457 periodicals, 170,000 microforms and 7,966 recordings. Student housing is available for 2,100 men and women. There are 1,250 scholarships offered; approximately 700 are designated for freshmen. About 95% of the student body receives financial aid. Approximately 80% of the applicants are accepted, including midyear students. The average SAT scores of the current freshman class were 512V and 566M or a composite ACT of 23.

Community Environment: See Case Western Reserve University.

KENT STATE UNIVERSITY   *(F-12)*
Kent, Ohio 44242
Tel: (216) 672-2444

Description: The state-supported university and its seven regional campuses span Northeastern Ohio from Lake Erie to the Ohio River. Within easy reach of Akron, Canton, Cleveland, Pittsburgh, and Youngstown, the Kent campus provides baccalaureate, masters, and doctoral study opportunities and research facilities in a spacious, residential setting. The regional campuses, while providing students with a more intimate opportunity for their first two years of college, also serve specific local needs with associate degree programs in more than 18 technical and business fields and community services. Drawing from across the state, nation and around the world, Kent State currently has 16,620 full-time and 2,825 part-time students comprising 14,645 undergraduates and 4,800 graduate students at the Kent campus. There are 8,318 students at the regional campuses in Ashtabula, East Liverpool and Salem and in Geauga, Stark, Trumbull and Tuscarawas counties. Accredited by the North Central Association of Colleges and Schools, the university operates on semester system with three summer sessions. It is also accredited by several respective professional accrediting institutions. There are 716 full-time and 583 part-time faculty members in the six undergraduate colleges and schools and the two graduate schools and graduate college, providing learning opportunities in more than 170 acres of undergraduate study. The faculty-student ratio is 1-21. Established in 1973, the Northeastern Ohio Universities College of Medicine is a consortium of the University of Akron, Kent State University and Youngstown University. N.E.O.U.C.O.M. is fully accredited by the Liason Committee on Medical Education of the American Medical Association. The college was established to provide new opportunities in medical education by preparing well qualified physicians during a six year program oriented to the practice of medicine at the community level. Kent offers many programs in conjunction with other colleges and universities, allowing students several travel options as a part of their course of study.

Entrance Requirements: Students can increase their chances for Fall Semester admission by achieving a 2.5 high school g.p.a., completing the 16 college-preparatory units including a recommended 4 units of English, 3 mathematics, 3 science, 3 social studies, 2 foreign language and 1 art (or a 3rd year of foreign language) and achieving a minimum ACT score of 21 or SAT combined score of 870. Foreign students should apply for admission at least six months before they wish to begin class. TOEFL test is required. Transfer applicants must present a minimum collegiate cumulative g.p.a. of 2.00. Several areas of study employ additional selective admission criteria. 80% of freshman applicants were accepted. 70% of enrolled freshmen receive financial aid. Admission plans include early admission, rolling admission, and advanced placement. Application fee is $25. Freshman application deadline for Fall is March 15.

Costs Per Year: $3,927 resident tuition; $7,854 nonresident tuition; $3,666 room and board; student fees are included in tuition.

Collegiate Environment: Buildings on the Kent campus number 100 with 30 residence halls capable of housing 6,350 students. The residence hall system emphasizes a living, learning community to create a total environment where students and staff share in intellectual and personal development. Students are required to live in residence halls until they achieve junior academic standing. Kent State University has the largest open stack library building in the nation, housing more than 2.1 million volumes, 8,000 periodicals, 1.3 million microforms, and 22,727 audiovisual materials. The University encompases a total of 2,272 acres of land including a 287-acre airport, an 18-hole golf course, a stadium with seating for more than 30,000 people, and several nature and wildlife preserves. The Honors College is a non-degree granting college that draws upon the pedagogical, research, and logistical support of the entire University community. It provides opportunities for students and faculty to develop and implement unique learning experiences. It is the largest source of academic scholarships. 65% of students receive some form of financial aid. Air Force and Army ROTC are available.

Community Environment: Kent, a city of some 30,000, is situated on the banks of the Cuyahoga River, in Portage County, 11 miles east of Akron, 33 miles south of Cleveland, 40 miles west of Youngstown and 28 miles north of Canton. The community provides students with many places to shop and entertain themselves and places of worship for most major denominations. Recreational activities include fishing, boating, skiing, swimming, and golf. The campus also offers many recreational games. The university is located near two major jetports, Cleveland Hopkins International and Akron-Canton.

Branch Campuses: Ashtabula Campus, 3325 West 13th Street, Ashtabula, OH 44004; East Liverpool Campus, 400 East 4th Street, East Liverpool, OH 43920; Geauga Campus, 14111 Claridon-Troy Road, Burton, OH 44021; Salem Campus, 2491 State Route 45 South, Salem, OH 44460; Tuscarawas Campus, University Drive N.E., New Philadelphia, OH 44663; Stark Campus, 6000 Frank Avenue N.W., Canton, OH 44720.

KENT STATE UNIVERSITY - ASHTABULA CAMPUS   *(C-13)*
3325 West 13th Street
Ashtabula, Ohio 44004
Tel: (216) 964-3322

Description: This campus of the state university was established in 1958 and is accredited by the North Central Association of Colleges and Schools. Enrollment is 1,100 students. A faculty of 35 full-time and 30 part-time gives a faculty-student ratio of 1-17. The semester system is used and two summer sessions are offered. Two-year Associate degree programs are offered.

Entrance Requirements: High school graduation or equivalent; open enrollment policy; completion of 16 units including 4 English, 3 mathematics, 3 science, 3 social science, 3 foreign language; ACT required; nondegree candidates may be admitted under certain circum-

stances; $25 application fee; rolling admission, midyear admission, early decision, early admission, and advanced placement plans available.

Costs Per Year: $2,885 tuition; $6,811 out-of-state; $550 average additional expenses.

Collegiate Environment: The library contains 54,750 volumes, 230 periodical subscriptions, 5,633 microforms and 1,295 audiovisual materials. All students applying for admission are accepted, including midyear students. The campus consists of three buildings: a multipurpose classroom, technology building and the library. About 60% of the previous freshman class returned to this campus for the sophomore year. Financial aid is available, and 70% of students receive some form of aid.

Community Environment: This growing industrial city is on Lake Erie at the mouth of the Ashtabula River. Two municipal parks on Lake Erie have excellent facilities for swimming, boating, and fishing.

KENT STATE UNIVERSITY - EAST LIVERPOOL CAMPUS
(H-14)
400 East 4th Street
East Liverpool, Ohio 43920
Tel: (216) 385-3805; Fax: (216) 385-3757

Description: The state-supported campus of Kent State University is a two-year college that opened in 1965. It is accredited by the North Central Association of Colleges and Schools and the National League for Nursing. Two-year Associate degree programs are offered in arts, applied science, applied business and nursing. It operates on the semester system and offers three summer sessions. Enrollment is 518 full-time and 347 part-time students. A faculty of 25 full-time and 35 part-time gives a faculty-student ratio of 1-14.

Entrance Requirements: High school graduation; open enrollment policy; completion of 16 units including 4 English, 3 mathematics, 3 science, 3 social science, 1 art and 2 foreign language, or 3 foreign language; SAT or ACT required; entrance examination required, non-degree candidates may be admitted under some conditions; application fee $25; early admission, rolling admission, delayed admission, and advanced placement plans available.

Costs Per Year: $2,882 state-resident tuition; $6,811 out-of-state; additional expenses average $400.

Collegiate Environment: There are two buildings on the four-acre campus. About 60% of the students receive some form of financial assistance. All of the applicants are accepted. The library contains 31,000 volumes and 110 periodical subscriptions. Midyear students are accepted.

Community Environment: East Liverpool is in one of the most scenic sections of the upper Ohio Valley and is a leading pottery center producing semivitreous porcelain ware. Train and bus transportation is available and a local airport is available for private planes. Community facilities include numerous churches, representing 18 denominations, and a library. Thompson park provides facilities for all outdoor sports including winter sports; Beaver Creek provides facilities for camping, fishing, and picnicking.

KENT STATE UNIVERSITY - GEAUGA CAMPUS   *(D-12)*
14111 Claridon-Troy Road
Burton, Ohio 44021
Tel: (216) 834-4187; Admissions: (216) 834-4187; Fax: (216) 834-8846

Description: This regional campus of the state-supported university was established in 1964 and is accredited by the North Central Association of Colleges and Schools and by several respective professional accrediting institutions. The semester system is used and three summer sessions are offered. Two-year Associate degree programs are offered in general studies, applied business and applied science. Students may also complete the first two years of more than 170 baccalaureate degree programs. The coeducational center enrolls 573 students. A faculty of 42 gives a faculty-student ratio of 1-13.

Entrance Requirements: High school graduation or equivalent; open enrollment policy; completion of 16 units including 4 English, 3 Mathematics, 3 Science, 2 Foreign Language, 3 Social Science, 1 Fine Arts; SAT or ACT required; non-degree candidates admitted under special circumstances; early decision, rolling admission, early admission, delayed admission, midyear admission and advanced placement plans available. $25 application fee.

Costs Per Year: $2,885 full-time, $131.25/cr part-time, resident; $3,616 full-time, $163.50/cr part-time nonresident

Collegiate Environment: The campus offers both day and evening classes. The library contains 12,500 volumes and 85 periodical subscriptions. All applicants are accepted, including midyear students. Limited financial aid is available, and 24% of students receive financial aid.

Community Environment: Burton located 30 miles from Cleveland, is primarily a residential area with a few small businesses. Planes and trains are within 18 miles. Community facilities include shopping facilities, churches, and civic and service organizations. Ski resort is nearby for all winter sports.

KENT STATE UNIVERSITY - SALEM CAMPUS   *(G-13)*
2491 State Route 45 South
Salem, Ohio 44460
Tel: (216) 332-0361; Fax: (216) 332-9256

Description: The coeducational college is a regional campus of the state-supported Kent State University. It was opened in 1962 and is accredited by the North Central Association of Colleges and Schools. Associate degree programs are offered in arts, applied science, technology, and applied business. It operates on the semester system and offers three summer sessions. Enrollment includes 511 full-time and 469 part-time students. A faculty of 37 full-time and 34 part-time gives a faculty-student ratio of 1-14.

Entrance Requirements: High school graduation or equivalent with 16 units recommended, including 4 English, 3 mathematics, 3 science, 3 social science, 1 art and 2 foreign language or 3 foreign language; open enrollment policy; ACT or SAT required; nondegree candidates may be considered for admission under special circumstances; application fee $25; rolling admission, early decision, midyear admission, and early admission plan available.

Costs Per Year: $2,884 tuition; $6,811 out-of-state tuition.

Collegiate Environment: The one school building contains gymnasium, classrooms, laboratories, and a library which includes 18,531 volumes, and 152 periodicals, 2,624 microforms, and 613 audiovisual materials. All students applying for admission are accepted including midyear students. Financial aid is available and 60% of students receive some form of financial aid. Army and Air Force ROTC programs are available.

Community Environment: Known as the "Quaker City" because of its founders, Salem is one of the most productive dairy and fruit growing sections of Ohio. Salem is an area of thriving manufacturing and commercial establishments were full- and part-time employment is available. Centennial Park offers varied recreational facilities.

KENT STATE UNIVERSITY - STARK CAMPUS   *(G-11)*
6000 Frank Avenue, N.W.
Canton, Ohio 44720
Tel: (216) 499-9600

Description: The state-supported campus is currently the largest regional campus of Kent State University. It was established in 1964. It is accredited by the North Central Association of Colleges and Schools. Total enrollment during the school year was 2,401. The semester system is used and three summer terms are offered. The faculty consists of 55 full-time and 61 part-time members. The school awards the Associate degree.

Entrance Requirements: High school graduation; open enrollment policy; completion of 16 units; ACT required; nondegree candidates are considered for admittance under special circumstances; application fee $25; early admission, rolling admission, and advanced placement plans available.

Costs Per Year: $1,443 state-resident tuition; $3,241 nonresident tuition; additional expenses average $1,000.

Collegiate Environment: The campus has four buildings on 227 acres. The library contains 82,000 volumes and 411 periodicals. All of the applicants are accepted, including midyear students. Financial assistance is available.

Community Environment: Jackson Township's growth in recent years is due in great part to Belden Village Mall. The regional shopping center offers a total of 64 stores, including three major department stores, and 53 acres of a wide range of shopping, dining and entertainment options. The township also encompasses three industrial parks within its boundaries. The Timken Research Center, the Hoover Company, and Babcock and Wilcox are just a few of the companies represented in these industrial parks. Community facilities include 13 churches of various faiths. Jackson contains 3 lakes around which are three country clubs, four golf courses, two skating rinks, two bowling alleys, and five theatres.

KENT STATE UNIVERSITY - TRUMBULL CAMPUS   *(F-13)*
4314 Mahoning Avenue N.W.
Warren, Ohio 44483
Tel: (216) 847-0571; Fax: (216) 847-6172

Description: The state-supported school is one of seven branches of Kent State University. It is accredited by the North Central Association of Colleges and Schools. Enrollment is 1,083 full-time and 1,019 part-time students. A faculty of 50 full-time and 50 part-time gives a faculty-student ratio of 1-17. This branch offers Associate degrees. The semester system is used and three summer terms are offered.

Entrance Requirements: High school graduation; open enrollment policy; completion of 16 units including 4 English, 3 mathematics, 3 science, 2-3 language, 3 social studies; nondegree candidates are considered for admittance under special circumstances; application fee $25; early admission, rolling admission, and advanced placement plans available.

Costs Per Year: $2,885 tuition; $6,811 out-of-state tuition; additional expenses average $750.

Collegiate Environment: The campus presently consists of 4 buildings. The library contains 66,201 volumes, 776 periodicals and 35,923 microforms. All applicants are accepted including midyear students. Scholarships are available and 50% of the students receive financial aid.

Community Environment: Located in the northeastern part of Ohio, the New England influences brought here by early settlers are still strongly felt. Warren, an industrial city, is in the great Mahoning Valley steel district and also has an active electrical and automotive parts industry. Shopping facilities here are good. Mosquito State Park, located 10 miles north, provides facilities for fishing, boating, swimming and camping. Points of interest are the John Stark Edwards House and the Nelson and Kennedy Ledges State Park.

KENT STATE UNIVERSITY - TUSCARAWAS CAMPUS
(I-11)
University Drive N.E.
New Philadelphia, Ohio 44663
Tel: (216) 339-3391

Description: This state-supported school was established in 1962 and is one of seven branches of Kent State University. It is accredited by the North Central Association of Colleges and Schools. Additional accreditations held are the National League for Nursing and the Accreditation Board for Engineering and Technology for the Mechanical and Electrical/Electronic Engineering Technology programs. The branch awards an Associate degree. It operates on the semester system and offers one summer session. Enrollment includes 645 full-time, 601 part-time, and approximately 620 evening students. The faculty of 33 full-time and 50 part-time gives a faculty-student ratio of 1-16..

Entrance Requirements: High school graduation or equivalent; open enrollment policy; completion of 16 units including 4 English, 3 mathematics, 3 science, 3 foreign language, or 2 foreign language and 1 fine arts, and 3 social studies recommended; ACT 21 recommended; nondegree candidates are considered for admittance under special circumstances; $25 application fee; early admission, early decision, midyear admission, rolling admission and advanced placement plans available.

Costs Per Year: $2,885.40 tuition; $6,811 out-of-state tuition and fees; $500 average additional expenses.

Collegiate Environment: The school has one building on 168 acres. Freshman students are accepted throughout the year. The library contains 49,447 volumes, 370 periodical subscriptions, 1,447 microforms, and 20,000 audiovisual materials. About 67% of the students receive financial aid. 99% of the applicants are accepted, including midyear students. Approximately 55% of the freshman class returns for the sophomore year.

Community Environment: New Philadelphia is the headquarters for the Muskingum Conservancy District, an 18-county project that provides fine recreational facilities along its 14 lakes. Medical and hospital facilities, a number of churches, and shopping facilities are part of the community services. Part-time employment is available.

KENYON COLLEGE   *(I-8)*
Gambier, Ohio 43022
Tel: (614) 427-5776; (800) 848-2468; Fax: (614) 427-2634

Description: This coeducational liberal arts institution was originally chartered in 1824 by the Protestant Episcopal Church and continues to maintain relations with that Church. Kenyon was Ohio's first private college. It is accredited by the North Central Association of Colleges and Schools and grants a Bachelor degree. It offers a summer writing institute. It operates on the semester system. Enrollment is 1,510 students. A faculty of 122 full-time and 32 part-time gives faculty-student ratio of 1-11. There are also 15 music instructors and 8 coaches who provide some instruction.

Entrance Requirements: High school graduation with rank in top 40% of class; completion of 15 units (although 20 are preferred) including 4 English, 4 mathematics, 3-4 foreign language, 2-3 science, and 2 social science; SAT or ACT required; early decision, delayed admission and advanced placement plans available.

Costs Per Year: $19,240 tuition; $3,690 room and board; $560 student fees; $700 average additional expenses.

Collegiate Environment: The 800-acre campus in Gambier is located in central Ohio. The library contains 411,479 volumes, 1,200 periodicals, 35,469 microforms, and 2,500 sound recordings. All students live in college-owned dormitories and apartments; most married students live off-campus. Services in the College Chapel are open to all students. Worship services for 3 major faiths are held regularly on campus. About 65% of students applying for admission are accepted. The average scores of the entering freshman class were SAT 580 verbal, 600 math and ACT 27 composite. 500 scholarships are available and 40% of students receive some form of financial aid. Special programs include the Foreign Study program available through the Great Lakes Colleges Association, the Kenyon-Exeter Program, American Studies, Asian Studies, gender studies, international studies, and the Integrated Program in Humane Studies.

Community Environment: Located in a hamlet 50 miles northeast of Columbus, just east of Mount Vernon, Gambier is a village of pre-Civil War days. Many buildings of that era still remain.

KETTERING COLLEGE OF MEDICAL ARTS   *(L-3)*
3737 Southern Blvd.
Kettering, Ohio 45429
Tel: (513) 296-7228; (800) 433-5262; Fax: (513) 296-4238

Description: This two-year, educational division of the Kettering Medical Center was established in 1967. It is accredited by the North Central Association of Colleges and Schools. The junior college is affiliated with the General Conference of Seventh-day Adventists. Its two-year program leads to the Associate in Science degree. The college operates on the early semester calendar system and offers two summer sessions. Enrollment includes 299 full-time and 320 part-time undergraduates and 176 graduate students. A faculty of 54 full-time and 4 part-time gives a faculty-student ratio of 1-10.

Entrance Requirements: High school graduation; composite ACT score on college-bound norms of 19 required; candidates 21 years of age or over may be admitted with satisfactory scores on GED tests; early decision, rolling admission, midyear admission and advanced placement plans available; $25 application fee.

Costs Per Year: $4,008 tuition; $3,766 room and board; $116 student fees; $300 average additional expenses.

Collegiate Environment: The college campus in the city of Kettering is a few miles from downtown Dayton. The educational building contains classrooms, laboratories, a 67,666 volume library, gymnasium, assembly hall, dormitory accommodation for 39 men and 112 women. The 481-bed Charles F. Kettering Memorial Hospital was opened in 1964 and serves as a clinical teaching facility for the students. The third major facility on the campus is the Cox Institute, a medical research center. Sycamore Hospital, a 120-bed satellite seven miles away, is an integral part of the Kettering Medical Center and serves as an additional clinical facility. The college accepts approximately 85% of those who apply for admission. Scholarships are available and 50% of students receive some form of financial aid.

Community Environment: The city is surrounded by rolling, wooded hills and is a suburb of Dayton. The recreational, educational, and cultural advantages of Dayton are enjoyed by the citizens of Kettering also. Kettering is the home of the world's largest supply of electronic components. Community facilities include 37 churches of many denominations and many shopping centers and plazas. Nine golf courses are in the area.

LAKE ERIE COLLEGE   *(D-12)*
391 West Washington Street
Painesville, Ohio 44077
Tel: (216) 352-3361; (800) 533-4996; Admissions: (216) 639-7879; Fax: (213) 352-3533

Description: An independent coeducational four-year liberal arts and residential college founded in 1856, Lake Erie College is designed for men and women who seek academic excellence, small classes, individual attention and flexible programming. It is accredited by the North Central Association of Colleges and Schools. It offers traditional liberal arts and career-oriented programs including pre-professional programs such as Equestrian studies and Business Administration. 22 majors are offered. In its innovative approach, Lake Erie College is able to extend its focus to include local, regional, and international study experiences. It grants the Bachelor of Arts, Bachelor of Fine Arts, Bachelor of Science, Master of Business Administration and Master of Education degrees. It operates on the semester system and offers one summer sessions. Enrollment includes 350 full-time undergraduates and 160 graduate students. A faculty of 36 full-time and 30 part-time gives a faculty-student ratio of 1:12.

Entrance Requirements: Lake Erie College: completion of 16 units including 4 English, 2 mathematics, 2 science, 2 foreign language, and 4 social science; SAT or ACT required; 2.75 GPA required; early admission, midyear admission, rolling admission, advanced placement and delayed admission programs available; $20 application fee.

Costs Per Year: $10,560 tuition; $4,378 room and board; student fees per term vary.

Collegiate Environment: Lake Erie College is located 28 miles east of Cleveland. The main campus occupies approximately 57 acres in the heart of the city's residential district. The college's 300-acre Morley Farm is located approximately 5 miles from the main campus. It houses the George Humphrey Equestrian Center including a large indoor riding arena and stable facilities. Lake Erie College students are housed in 4 dormitories that provide accommodations for 300 students. The library contains 100,000 volumes, 350 periodicals and 4,163 microforms. Classes are coeducational. Approximately 80% of Lake Erie College students applying for admission are accepted, including midyear students. Financial assistance is available, and 80% of the current students receive some form of aid.

Community Environment: Painesville is a city of 30,000 residents located 30 miles east of Cleveland and 3 miles from Lake Erie. The surrounding area boasts numerous fine commercial nurseries, the home of President Garfield, maple sugar industries, and the Holden Arboretum. Lake Erie College sponsors an ongoing series of cultural activities at the B. K. Smith Fine Arts Gallery and the C. K. Rickel Theater on the Lake Erie campus. Other community facilities include a variety of churches, the YMCA, and Morley Library, as well as various civic and service organizations.

LAKELAND COMMUNITY COLLEGE   *(D-12)*
Mentor, Ohio 44060
Tel: (216) 953-7000; (800) 589-8520; Fax: (216) 975-4330

Description: The public junior college opened in September 1967. Enrollment is 9,174. A faculty of 107 full-time, 320 part-time gives a ratio of 1-21. It operates on the quarter system and two summer terms are offered. The transfer program emphasizes the Arts and Sciences for the first two years of a conventional college curriculum and the technical program prepares students for employment at paraprofessional levels. The college is accredited by the North Central Association of Colleges and Schools. It is also accredited by the American Dental Institution and the National League for Nursing.

Entrance Requirements: Open enrollment policy; high school graduation; ACT required for some programs; non-high school graduates may be admitted; $15 application fee.

Costs Per Year: $1,800 county-resident tuition; $2,000 state-resident tuition; $4,200 out-of-state tuition.

Collegiate Environment: The college occupies several modern buildings on a 400-acre campus. The library contains 74,864 volumes, 382 periodicals, 12,474 microforms, and 758 audiovisual materials. All applicants accepted including midyear students. Scholarships are available and 40% of students receive some form of financial aid.

Community Environment: Lakeland is a comprehensive community college located in attractive Lake County, Ohio, in the northeastern portion of the state along Lake Erie, 20 miles east of Cleveland. The land area amounts to 231 square miles with a total population of 212,800. The county itself consists of two distinctly different areas: a densely populated western end with approximately 68% of the population and a sparsely populated eastern end. The college and surrounding community offer exceptional opportunity for personal and professional growth.

LIMA TECHNICAL COLLEGE   *(G-3)*
4240 Campus Drive
Lima, Ohio 45804
Tel: (419) 221-1112; Fax: (419) 221-0450

Description: This state-supported, coeducational, community college was established in 1971 to provide technical education to the Lima area community. The college shares a campus with the Ohio State University-Lima. It operates on the quarter system and offers two summer sessions. The college offers transfer, technical and general education programs that lead to the Associate degree. It is accredited by the North Central Association of Colleges and Schools. Enrollment is 1,496 full-time and 1,254 part-time students. A faculty of 80 full-time and 60 part-time gives a faculty-student ratio of 1-20.

Entrance Requirements: Open enrollment policy; high school graduation or equivalent; non-high school graduates considered; $10 application fee; early admission, delayed admission, rolling admission and advanced placement plans available.

Costs Per Year: $1,998 tuition; $4,896 out-of-state.

Collegiate Environment: The five buildings on campus include a library of 45,000 volumes, 3,000 pamphlets, 470 periodicals, 5,000 microforms and 1,900 recordings. Financial assistance is available and about 50% of the students receive financial aid. All applicants are accepted, including midyear students.

Community Environment: See Ohio Northern University.

LORAIN COUNTY COMMUNITY COLLEGE   *(E-9)*
1005 North Abbe Rd.
Elyria, Ohio 44035
Tel: (216) 365-4191; (800) 995-5222; Admissions: (216) 365-4191 X 4032; Fax: (216) 365-6519

Description: The publicly supported junior college was established in 1963 to provide higher education to residents of Greater Lorain County. It is accredited by the North Central Association of Colleges and Schools, and by professional accrediting institutions. Transfer, career, and continuing education programs are offered. The school grants Associate degrees in Arts, Science, Applied Business, Applied Science, Individualized Studies, and Technical Studies; Certificate of Proficiency and Certificate of Completion. It operates on the quarter system and offers two summer sessions. Enrollment includes 2,414 full-time and 4,883 part-time students. A faculty of 110 full-time and 250 part-time gives a faculty-student ration of 1-8.

Entrance Requirements: Open enrollment policy: high school graduation or equivalent; ACT or SAT used for counseling purposes. Non-degree and part-time candidates may be admitted on unclassified status; early admission, early decision, rolling admission, delayed admission, midyear admission and advanced placement plans available. $10 application fee.

Costs Per Year: $2,070 county-resident tuition; $2,520 out-of-county tuition; $5,265 out-of-state tuition; $112.50 student fees.

Collegiate Environment: The $55 million campus on Abbe Road consists of 12 buildings on 480 acres. The library collection numbers 110,000 volumes, 722 periodical subscriptions, and 10,751 microforms. Financial assistance is available; 36% of students recently received financial aid. All of the applicants are accepted, including midyear students. The average ACT composite score of the current freshman class was 19.

Community Environment: Situated in the far northeast corner of the city of Elyria and 26 miles west of Cleveland, the campus is just four miles from downtown Elyria, a city of over 57,500 and the county seat; eight miles to the north lies Lorain, an industrial community on Lake Erie at the mouth of the Black River; its harbor is one of the best on the Great Lakes. One of Ford Motor Co.'s largest assembly plants is located here with Lake Shore Development. Community facilities include churches representing all denominations, YMCA, YWCA, six hospitals, and all leading civic and service organizations. Boating, fishing, swimming, golf, and tennis are some of the outdoor sports. Job opportunities are excellent. Lakeview Park is noted for its extensive rose garden and colorfully lighted fountain. Cascade Park is a favorite recreation area and is located in the city of Elyria. A rapidly expanding network of major state and interstate highways, including the nearby Ohio Turnpike, makes the college easily reached by automobile.

LOURDES COLLEGE   *(D-4)*
6832 Convent Blvd.
Sylvania, Ohio 43560
Tel: (419) 885-3211; (800) 878-3210; Fax: (419) 882-3987

Description: The four-year liberal arts college was founded in 1958 and is conducted by the Sisters of St. Francis. It is accredited by the North Central Association of Colleges and Schools and other professional accrediting institutions, and operates on the semester system. Enrollment is 482 full-time and 1,184 part-time students. A faculty of 66 full-time and 67 part-time gives a faculty-student ratio of 1-13.

Entrance Requirements: Accredited high school graduation; C average; completion of 12 units of college prep work including 4 English, and 3 math (Alg I, Alg II, Geo); ACT or SAT required; $20 application fee; early admission, early decision, rolling admission, delayed admission plans available.

Costs Per Year: $237 per credit; students who take more than 15 credit hours receive 1 semester hour free.

Collegiate Environment: The college is located ten miles west of Toledo. The 89-acre campus serves several educational and community service facilities conducted by the sisters of St. Francis. Other facilities include: the Franciscan Center (a cultural arts building), the St. Francis education center (an elementary school), the Chiara Center retreat facility, and the Lourdes College Child Development Laboratory School. The main college building is comprised of three connected halls: Mother Adelaide Hall, Lourdes Hall, and St. Claire Hall. In Addition the Franciscan Center allows LC students to use its gym and exercise room, as well as the 900-seat auditorium. Financial assistance is available in the form of grants, loans and a limited number of scholarships. Applications for admission are accepted on a continuing basis. Affiliations exist with St. Vincent's Hospital School of Nursing in Toledo, Providence Hospital School of Nursing in Sandusky, and the Professional Skills Institute of Toledo. Lourdes College is also a participant in the Post-Secondary Option Program for eligible high school juniors anf seniors.

Community Environment: Sylvania is a suburban area with a temperate climate; plane and bus transportation is available. Job opportunities are good for students. Community facilities include a public library, adequate hospital services, churches, numerous major civic and service organizations, and shopping facilities.

MALONE COLLEGE   *(G-12)*
515 25th St. N.W.
Canton, Ohio 44709
Tel: (216) 471-8100; (800) 521-1146; Admissions: (216) 471-8145; Fax: (216) 454-6977

Description: The private four-year liberal arts college was founded in 1892. The semester system is used and three summer sessions are offered. Enrollment is 2,005 students. A faculty of 74 gives a faculty-student ratio of approximately 1-16. The college awards the Bachelor of Arts degree and is accredited by the North Central Association of Colleges and Schools. The college is affiliated with the Evangelical Friends Church - Eastern Region.

Entrance Requirements: High school graduation with grade point average of 2.5 or above; ACT composite of 20 or above; completion of 16 units including 4 English, 3 mathematics, 3 science, 2 foreign language, and 3 social science; nondegree candidates may be admitted as special students; midyear admission, advanced placement and rolling admission plans available; $20 application fee.

Costs Per Year: $10,200 tuition; $4,020 room and board; $145 student fees; additional expenses average $800.

Collegiate Environment: The 78-acre campus has 13 buildings including the library and dormitories that house 904 men and women. The library contains 130,068 volumes, 170,858 microforms and 4,842 sound recordings. The college participates in intercollegiate football, basketball, track, baseball, tennis, soccer and several other sports. The twice-weekly chapel service is part of the educational program and all students are required to attend. The college seeks a geographically diverse student body and welcomes applications from prospective part-time students. 89% of students applying for admission meet the requirements and are accepted. Scholarships are available and 92% of the students receive some form of financial aid.

Community Environment: Canton is an industrial, residential, and cultural city of 110,000. The city is the home of the Pro Football Hall of Fame, and birthplace of former president William McKinley. A beautiful Cultural Center for the Arts and an extensive park system enhances the city's beauty and provides many cultural and educational opportunites for the students.

MARIETTA COLLEGE   (M-11)
Fifth St.
Marietta, Ohio 45750
Tel: (614) 373-4643; (800) 331-7896; Fax: (614) 376-8888

Description: The private liberal arts college is accredited by the North Central Association of Colleges and Schools, and by the Accreditation Board for Engineering and Technology and the American Chemical Society. It operates on the semester system and offers three summer sessions. The college grants the degrees of Bachelor of Arts, Bachelor of Science, Bachelor of Science in Petroleum Engineering, and Bachelor of Fine Arts. It also offers professional degrees in Education. Enrollment is 1,087 full-time and 170 part-time undergraduates and 62 graduate students. A faculty of 85 full-time and 40 part-time gives an overall faculty-student ratio of 1-13.

Entrance Requirements: High school graduation with rank in upper 40% of graduating class; completion of 15 units including 4 English, 3 mathematics, 3 science, 3 social science, and 2 foreign language; SAT or ACT required; early admission, midyear admission, rolling admission, delayed admission and advanced placement plans are available; $25 application fee.

Costs Per Year: $13,850 tuition; $3,920 room and board; $500 average additional expenses.

Collegiate Environment: The 120-acre campus has 40 buildings. The Dawes Memorial Library perpetuates the name of a distinguished family with a long record of devotion and service to the college. The library collection numbers 278,600 volumes, 935 periodical subscriptions, 28,384 microforms, and 6,179 sound recordings. There are 7 fraternities and 4 sororities that house 106 men and 66 women in addition to the college residence halls, which accommodate 432 men and 314 women. The college reserves the right to require all students, except commuting students living at home, to live in college housing. Special programs offered are the Honors Program, Junior Year Abroad program, and the Binary Curricula, a cooperative study program with five institutions that enables qualified Marietta students to earn two degrees - one from Marietta College, where they spend three years, and one from the cooperative institution, where they usually spend two years and a summer. These binary programs are in engineering, forestry, nursing, natural resources. 62% of students applying for admission are accepted including midyear students. The middle 50% ranges of scores for entering freshmen were ACT 21-27 composite, SAT 950-1150 combined. Approximately 80% of the freshman class returns for the sophomore year. About 20% of the senior class continues on to graduate school. Academic and fine arts scholarships

are available an 92% of the undergraduates receive some form of financial aid.

Community Environment: Marietta, the center of an area rich in gas, coal, lime and limestone, clays, and timbers, is in the Ohio Valley industrial and chemical area. Commercial transportation is available. Part-time employment opportunities are available.

MEDICAL COLLEGE OF OHIO   (D-5)
P.O. Box 10008
Toledo, Ohio 43699
Tel: (419) 381-4229

Description: The state-supported college is accredited by the Liaison Committee on Medical Education, and awards a professional degree. The college offers a standard curriculum over a four-year period and students are accepted for the entering class beginning Sept. 1st only. There are approximately 560 students enrolled in the four years.

Entrance Requirements: Three years of college; MCAT required; $30 application fee. Bachelor's Degree highly recommended.

Costs Per Year: $7,000 state resident tuition; $10,000 nonresident tuition; $200 student fees.

Collegiate Environment: The college has approximately 90% of the student body from Ohio. The Medical College does not have campus housing. Off-campus housing is readily available within walking distance of the campus. The library contains 62,193 volumes and 2,500 periodicals. The Medical College of Ohio also offers M.D./Ph.D., Ph.D., M.S.N., and M.S.B.S. degrees. Financial Aid available. Minorities encouraged to apply.

Community Environment: See University of Toledo.

METHODIST THEOLOGICAL SCHOOL IN OHIO   (I-6)
3081 Columbus Pike
Delaware, Ohio 43015-0931
Tel: (614) 363-1146; (800) 333-6876; Fax: (614) 362-3135

Description: The General Conference of the Methodist Church in session in Minnesota in 1956 authorized the establishment of two new theological schools, one of which was to be located in Ohio. The first class was admitted in the fall of 1960. The institute is approved by the University Senate of the Methodist Church and the Association of Theological Schools and North Central Association of Colleges and Schools. It has a cooperative educational relationship with Ohio State University, Trinity Lutheran Seminary, and Pontifical College Josephium. Field education, required of students in programs for the Master of Divinity and for the Christian Education degree, learn and grow while serving as Pastors or staff members of churches or other agencies. A Latin American Culture Seminar in Mexico and internship in England are available. The graduate school confers the Master of Divinity Degree, the Master of Theological Studies, the Master of Arts in Christian Education, the Master of Arts in Liturgical Arts, the Master of Arts in Alcoholism and Drug Abuse Ministries, and the Doctor of Ministry Degrees. The school operates on the quarter system and offers one summer session, from May through August of 15 classes. Enrollment is approximately 240 students. A faculty of 18 full-time and 21 part-time gives a faculty-student ratio of 1-13.

Entrance Requirements: B.A. or equivalent degree from an accredited college or university with 2.5 GPA or better; $35 application fee.

Costs Per Year: $7,920 tuition; $2,595 room and board.

Collegiate Environment: The school is located three miles south of Delaware and 20 miles north of Columbus. The 70-acre campus of rolling wooded land overlooks the Olentangy River. There is dormitory space for 70 students. The library contains over 113,000 volumes, and 360 periodicals. The program of financial assistance has been designed with a single end in mind. Its purpose is to release students for participation in the kinds of experience, academic and practical, that will enable them most fully to develop their potential for faithful ministry in the church. Therefore, financial assistance is granted on the basis of academic performance and financial need. Of students who applied for aid from the school, 95% received it. This represents 95% of the student body.

Community Environment: See Ohio Wesleyan University.

MIAMI UNIVERSITY   *(L-1)*
East High Street
Oxford, Ohio 45056
Tel: (513) 529-1809; Admissions: (513) 529-2531; Fax: (513) 529-1550

Description: The state supported university opened its doors to students for collegiate instruction in 1809. It is accredited by the North Central Association of Colleges and Schools. It is also accredited by the American Assembly of Collegiate Schools of Business. In addition to the undergraduate program, the university offers the Master's degree in more than 65 areas of graduate study. A Specialist in Education degree is awarded for a year of professional study beyond the Master's level in the field of educational psychology. The Doctor of Philosophy degree is awarded ten departments and the Doctor of Education in one. The university operates on the semester system and offers two summer terms. Enrollment includes 6,551 men and 7,699 women full-time, and 606 men and 1,026 women part-time. A faculty of 767 full-time and 215 part-time gives a faculty-student ratio of 1-17. Navy and Air Force ROTC programs are offered on two-year or four-year contracts.

Entrance Requirements: Accredited high school graduation; completion of 17 units of preparatory study, including 4 English, 3 mathematics, 3 science, 2 foreign language, 3 social science, 1 fine arts; ACT or SAT required; GRE required for graduate studies; admission is based on rank in class and test scores; early decision, midyear admission, and advanced placement plans available; $30 nonrefundable application fee.

Costs Per Year: $4,612 state resident tuition; $9,728 nonresident tuition; $3,960 room and board; $2,000 average additional expenses.

Collegiate Environment: The college is located about 35 miles from Cincinnati and 46 miles from Dayton. The campus consists of more than 1,900 acres with 150 buildings. The King Library, Peabody Library and five departmental libraries contain 1,500,000 cataloged volumes and bound documents, 11,850 periodical subscriptions, 2,400,000 microforms and 185,000 recordings. Freshmen are required to live in university housing unless they live at home. Housing facilities in 38 residence halls accommodate 6,946 single students and 108 families. Fraternities provide housing for an additional 1,500 men. The middle 50% of scores for the accepted freshmen were a Act 24-28 composite or SAT Verbal 470-570, Math 550-640. Approximately 72% of applicants are accepted. The university awards about 1,100 scholarships each year, 275 for freshmen, on the basis of academic performance, leadership, creativity and ambition. About 49% of the students receive aid. Approximately 92% of the previous freshman class returned to the school for their sophomore year.

Community Environment: A college town with many beautiful old homes, Oxford, the location of Miami University, is where Professor McGuffey compiled the first of his readers. Recreational facilities provide for tennis, bowling, and golf, and the Hueston Woods State Park for boating, swimming, and picnicking.

Branch Campuses: Hamilton Campus, 1601 Peck Blvd., Hamilton, OH 45011; Middletown Campus, 4200 East University Blvd., Middletown, OH 45042

MIAMI UNIVERSITY - HAMILTON CAMPUS   *(M-2)*
1601 Peck Blvd
Hamilton, Ohio 45011
Tel: (513) 863-8833; Fax: (513) 863-1655

Description: The regional campus of Miami University was established in 1968 and is accredited by the North Central Association of Colleges and Schools. It offers a variety of certificates, associate degree programs, and the beginning course work for most four-year degrees. Advanced and graduate credit courses are offered in the late afternoon and evening for part-time students. The commuter campus was created to provide educational opportunities for large numbers of students who could not easily reach the Oxford Campus. The school operates on the semester system and offers three summer sessions. Enrollment is 840 full-time and 1,389 part-time students. The faculty-student ratio is 1-27. Navy and Air Force ROTC programs are available. All of the degrees are granted at the main campus in Oxford.

Entrance Requirements: Open admission campus for entering freshmen; all students who have graduated from an accredited hight school or who have a GED can be admitted; completion of 16 college prepa-

ratory units; ACT or SAT required; $25 application fee, no admission deadline.

Costs Per Year: $3,014 state-resident tuition; $8,130 out-of-state; $500 average additional expenses.

Collegiate Environment: The campus occupies 76 acres on the east bank of the Great Miami River, in southern Butler county, just south of the Hamilton business section. Currently, the campus consists of four buildings. The library contains 65,000 volumes and 375 periodical subscriptions, and 1,300 audiovisual items. 98% of the applicants are accepted. Financial assistance is available and 42% of the current students receive aid. About 98% of the applicants are accepted. Approximately 64% of the students attend on a part-time basis and the average age is 26.

Community Environment: The town of Hamilton is easily accessible from most of northern and western Hamilton County via several state and interstate routes. Employment opportunities are good in this area.

MIAMI UNIVERSITY - MIDDLETOWN CAMPUS   *(L-2)*
4200 E. University Boulevard
Middletown, Ohio 45042-3497
Tel: (513) 424-4444; Fax: (513) 424-4632

Description: The regional campus of Miami University was established in 1966 and offers two years of lower division work as well as Associate degree programs. Advanced and graduate credit courses are offered in the late afternoon and evening for part-time students. It operates on the semester system and offers three evening summer sessions. Enrollment is 3,014 students. A faculty of 55 gives a faculty-student ratio of 1-25. The college is accredited by the North Central Association of Colleges and Schools. Navy and Air Force ROTC programs are available on the main campus in Oxford, Ohio.

Entrance Requirements: Open enrollment policy; high school graduation required; completion of 17 college preparatory units including 4 English, 3 mathematics, 3 science, 3 social science, 2 foreign language; ACT or SAT required; ACT or SAT not required if applicant has been out of high school more than 5 years; $25 application fee; rolling admission, advanced placement, and midyear admission plans available.

Costs Per Year: $2,748 state-resident tuition; $252 student fees; additional expenses average $600.

Collegiate Environment: The 140-acre campus consists of seven buildings including the library which contains 95,700 volumes, 493 periodicals and 35,400 microforms. About 99% of the applicants are accepted, including midyear students. Financial aid is available, and 30% of the current student body receive some form of assistance.

Community Environment: See Miami University.

MIAMI-JACOBS JUNIOR COLLEGE OF BUSINESS   *(K-3)*
400 East Second Street
Dayton, Ohio 45401
Tel: (513) 461-5174; Fax: (513) 461-5774

Description: The Miami Commercial School and the Jacobs Business College merged in 1916 and became the Miami-Jacobs College of Business. It is accredited by the Accrediting Council for Independent Colleges and Schools. The quarter system is used and one summer term is offered. Current enrollment was 30 men and 282 women full-time and 5 men and 69 women part-time. A faculty of 7 full-time and 33 part-time gives a faculty-student ratio of 1-10.

Entrance Requirements: High school graduation or equivalent; applicants not meeting requirements may be enrolled as special students; early admission, early decision, rolling admission, delayed admission, advanced placement plans available; $25 application fee.

Costs Per Year: $4,000 tuition; $300 student fees; $500 average additional expenses.

Collegiate Environment: The college is located in the downtown section of the thriving industrial and business center of Dayton. The library contains 5,000 volumes and 65 periodical subscriptions. In addition to the regular daytime classes, an evening school program is offered throughout the year. Special Saturday morning business classes are also available. Approximately two-thirds of the student body hold part-time or full-time employment and 80% of the current students receive some form of financial assistance. About 90% of students applying for admission are accepted including midyear students.

Community Environment: See Wright State University.

MOUNT UNION COLLEGE   *(G-12)*
1972 Clark
Alliance, Ohio 44601
Tel: (216) 821-5320; (800) 994-6682; Fax: (216) 821-0425

Description: This liberal arts college was founded in 1846. It is affiliated with the United Methodist Church and is accredited by the North Central Association of Colleges and Schools. A cooperative education program is available in several majors. The college grants the Bachelor of Arts or Bachelor of Science, and Bachelor of Music or Bachelor of Music Education degrees. An overseas program is available. The college operates on the semester system and offers two summer sessions. Enrollment is 1,450 full-time and 67 part-time students. A faculty of 81 full-time and 15 part-time provides a faculty-student ratio of 1-15. Army and Air Force ROTC are available.

Entrance Requirements: Accredited high school graduation with rank in upper half of graduating class; recommended completion of 15 units including 4 English, 3 mathematics, 2 foreign language, 3 science, and 3 social science; SAT or ACT required; early admission for local applicants, advanced placement, delayed admission, and rolling admission plans available; $20 application fee.

Costs Per Year: $12,950 tuition; $3,530 room and board; $700 student fees.

Collegiate Environment: There are 40 buildings on the 75-acre campus. Freshmen must reside in residence halls except for married students and those living at home with parents or with relatives; upper class members in good standing may reside off campus. Accommodations on campus are available for 650 men and 650 women. There are four chapters of national fraternities that house an additional 120 men. The library system contains 215,397 volumes, 2,000 pamphlets, 925 periodicals, 29,523 microforms, and 1,000 recordings. Erected and furnished at a cost of over $1 million, the library building is the gift of friends and graduates of the college. The college welcomes a geographically diverse student body. About 82% of students applying for admission are accepted including midyear students. Financial assistance is available and 80% of students receive aid. 300 scholarships are offered, 100 of which are available for freshmen.

Community Environment: Alliance is located within a circle of large cities, Cleveland, Akron, and Pittsburgh. Heavy steel equipment and forgings are the products of industry. Commercial transportation is available. Recreational activities include swimming, golfing, fishing, boating and tennis. The Carnation Festival is an annual event. Part-time employment is available.

MOUNT VERNON NAZARENE COLLEGE   *(I-8)*
800 Martinsburg Road
Mount Vernon, Ohio 43050
Tel: (614) 397-1244

Description: The coeducational college of arts and sciences is the official college of the East Central education zone of the Church of the Nazarene. The college was founded in 1964, with classes beginning in 1968, and is accredited by the North Central Association of Colleges and Schools. A 4-1-4 calendar system is used and two summer sessions are offered. The enrollment included 458 men and 559 women full-time and 49 men and 35 women part-time. The faculty of 51 full-time and 33 part-time gives a faculty-student ratio of 1-19.

Entrance Requirements: High school graduation or equivalent; completion of 15 units including 3 English, 2 mathematics, 1 science, 2 language, 2 social science; ACT required; early decision, rolling admission, delayed admission, midyear admission and advanced placement plans available; $20 application fee.

Costs Per Year: $8,200 tuition; $3,676 room and board; $390 student fees; additional expenses average $800.

Collegiate Environment: The campus consists of 210 acres and includes a library of 94,875 volumes, 504 periodicals, 3,834 microforms, 2,253 audiovisual materials and dormitories accommodate 790 students. Full-time single students not living at home must live on campus. About 95% of students applying for admission are accepted. The college welcomes a geographically diverse student body and ac-

cepts midyear students. Financial assistance is available and about 90% of the students receive aid.

Community Environment: The campus is located on the edge of Mt. Vernon, Ohio, a city of 16,000 people. Mt. Vernon, called Ohio's colonial city, provides a friendly home town atmosphere, while located 45 minutes from 3 major cities, including Columbus, Ohio.

MUSKINGUM AREA TECHNICAL INSTITUTE   *(K-10)*
1555 Newark Rd.
Zanesville, Ohio 43701
Tel: (614) 454-2501

Description: The two-year state-supported institute was established in 1969 and is accredited by the North Central Association of Colleges and Schools. Recent enrollment was 2,701 students and there were 48 full-time and 95 part-time faculty. The quarter system is used and two summer sessions are offered. The school offers technology programs leading to an Associate degree.

Entrance Requirements: State requirements for a high school diploma; ACT required; $20 application fee; open enrollment policy; rolling admission, advanced placement, early admission plans available.

Costs Per Year: $2,640 state resident tuition and fees; $4,260 nonresident tuition and fees; $20 student fees; additional expenses average $600.

Collegiate Environment: The college features include coeducational dormitories accommodating 29 men and 74 women. There is an on-campus Student Union, a campus cafeteria and air-conditioned buildings with well equipped laboratories. The library contains 14,000 volumes, 2,000 pamphlets, 240 periodicals, and 1,780 recordings. All applicants are accepted. Financial aid is available.

Community Environment: Settled in 1799, Zanesville was the capital from 1810 to 1812. Today the population has reached 33,045. Architect Cass Gilbert and novelists Zane Grey and Charles D. Stewart were born here. Eight miles south of Zanesville is one of the largest steam electric plants in the country.

MUSKINGUM COLLEGE   *(K-10)*
New Concord, Ohio 43762
Tel: (614) 826-8137; (800) 752-6082; Fax: (614) 826-8404

Description: The private, nonprofit college was established in 1837. It is affiliated with the United Presbyterian Church in the U.S.A. and seeks to help its students become more truly and intelligently Christian. It is accredited by the North Central Association of Colleges and Schools. The college grants the Bachelor degree. Special programs include a Washington semester, United Nations semester, an affiliate program with the Art Institutes, academic cooperative plans with Southwest General Hospital for medical technology students, and with Case Western Reserve University for a 3-2 year engineering program, overseas exchange programs, and a junior year abroad. It operates on the semester system and offers one summer session. Enrollment includes 1,113 full-time and 75 part-time undergraduate, and 56 graduate students. A faculty of 76 full-time and 27 part-time gives a faculty-student ratio of 1-15.

Entrance Requirements: High school graduation or equivalent; completion of 15 units, preferably 4 English, 3 mathematics, 2 foreign language, 2 science, 2 social science; SAT or ACT required; advanced placement, early admission, rolling admission, and delayed admission plans available; $20 application fee.

Costs Per Year: $13,240 tuition; $3,914 room and board; $700 student fees.

Collegiate Environment: The 215-acre campus is located 70 miles east of Columbus. 15 major buildings include residence halls that accommodate 1,000 students. The library contains 222,039 volumes, 700 periodical titles, 164,501 microforms and 5,589 audiovisual materials. Financial assistance is available and about 80% of the students receive aid. Academic scholarships are available, many for freshmen. 112 of 304 enrolling students received scholarships. About 83% of students applying for admission are accepted, including midyear students. About 89% of the freshmen ranked in the top two-fifths of their high school class. Average freshman scores were SAT verbal 445, math 491 and ACT 22 composite. About 77% of the previous freshman class returned to this campus for their sophomore year. 15% of the senior class continued on to graduate school.

Community Environment: New Concord is the boyhood home of John H. Glenn, Jr., the first American astronaut to orbit the earth. Also of interest is the log cabin birthplace of William Rainey Harper, first president of the University of Chicago and an alumnus of Muskingum College. Recreational activities include golf, boating, fishing, hunting, and skating.

NORTH CENTRAL TECHNICAL COLLEGE   *(G-8)*
2441 Kenwood Circle
P. O. Box 698
Mansfield, Ohio 44901
Tel: (419) 755-4800

Description: The state-assisted technical college operates on the quarter system and offers one summer session. The college is accredited by the North Central Association of Colleges and Schools. Enrollment includes 1,241 full-time and 1,621 part-time students. Many courses are also available during evening and weekend hours. A faculty of 77 full-time and 105 part-time members provides an overall faculty-student ratio of 1-16. The college offers programs leading to a Certificate or an Associate degree.

Entrance Requirements: Open enrollment policy; high school graduation; GED acceptable; ACT, ASSET and entrance exam required; $35 application fee; early admission and rolling admission plans available; special admission requirements in Health and Public Service programs.

Costs Per Year: $2,200 state-resident tuition; $4,171 nonresident; $189 student fees; $600 average additional expenses.

Collegiate Environment: The Learning Resources Center contains 126,125 volumes, 466 periodicals, 2,500 microforms and 15,000 audiovisual materials. A complete Physical Activity Center is available as well as a bookstore, cafeteria, student lounge and game room. All applicants are accepted, including midyear students. The average age of the students is 28.

NORTHWEST STATE COMMUNITY COLLEGE   *(D-3)*
22-600 State Route 34
Archbold, Ohio 43502
Tel: (419) 267-5511; Fax: (419) 267-3688

Description: The college was established in 1969 to provide training to residents of Defiance, Fulton, Henry, Paulding, and William counties. It operates on the quarter system and offers four summer sessions. It grants an Associate degree and is fully accredited by the North Central Association of Colleges and Schools. Enrollment includes 127 men and 375 women full-time and 504 men and 826 women part-time. A faculty of 38 full-time and 45 part-time gives a faculty-student ratio of 1-24.

Entrance Requirements: High school graduation or equivalent; open enrollment policy; non-high school graduates considered; advanced placement offered; ASSET required for placement purposes; $10 application fee; early admission, midyear admission and rolling admission plans available.

Costs Per Year: $2,022 tuition; $3,780 out-of-state; $600 average additional expenses.

Collegiate Environment: The college is located on a 78-acre campus near the intersection of State Routes 66 and 34, six miles south of Archbold. The facilities include classrooms, a library, 15 laboratories, and a data processing center. No living accommodations are available but the student service office aids students in making living arrangements. The library contains 17,208 volumes, 2,000 pamphlets, 285 periodicals, 58 microforms and 2,141 recordings. Financial assistance is available and 48% of the students receive aid. All applicants are accepted, and students may enroll at the beginning of any semester. 10% of the graduates continue on to a four-year college.

Community Environment: The campus is in rural setting with a small town six miles to the north. The major metropolitan area of Toledo is 50 miles northeast, with easy access by major highways.

NOTRE DAME COLLEGE   *(E-11)*
4545 College Rd.
South Euclid, Ohio 44121
Tel: (216) 381-1680

Description: Founded in 1922 by the Sisters of Notre Dame of Cleveland, Ohio, Notre Dame College of Ohio is a Catholic, liberal arts college. It is one of only 84 remaining institutions of higher education dedicated to women's education in the United States. It is accredited by the North Central Association of Colleges and Schools. The college confers the Bachelor of Arts, Bachelor of Science, and Associate of Arts degrees. It operates on the semester system and offers one summer session. The college also has a branch campus in Toledo, Ohio, which was fully approved by the Ohio College Association in 1950. Enrollment at Notre Dame College of Ohio is 333 full-time and 309 part-time undergraduates, and 46 graduate students. A faculty of 36 full-time and 48 part-time gives a faculty-student ratio of 1-10.

Entrance Requirements: High school graduation or equivalent with rank in upper half of graduating class; completion of 15 units including 4 English, 2 mathematics, 2 foreign language, 1 science, and 2 social science; minimum SAT scores of 400V, 400M or ACT of 15 required; rolling admission plan available; $20 application fee.

Costs Per Year: $8,064 tuition; $3,860 room and board

Collegiate Environment: he college is just minutes from University Circle, hub of many educational centers. Severance Hall, the home of the world-famous Cleveland Symphony Orchestra, and the Cleveland Museum of Art are nearby. Lovely landscaped walkways, a small Notre Dame woods, playing fields, and tennis courts offer the student a variety of outdoor activity. The library contains 89,952 holdings. Residence halls provide living accommodations for 240 women. Daily Mass is offered for the convenience of both commuting and resident students. About 82% of students applying for admission meet the requirements and are accepted, including midyear A wooded 53-acre provides the setting for the college. The Administration building, of English Tudor Gothic architecture, houses most of the classrooms and offices, science laboratories, the Garvin Computer Center, the Miday Media Center and the Little Theater. In 1987, it was designated a national historic site by the U.S. Department of the Interior. The Clara Fritzsche Library has a media center, which has carrels for use of audiovisual materials and offers a wide range of production services. The library also has capacity for 100,000 volumes and receives more than 300 periodicals. Business students also have access to the business reference section and an extensive collection of annual reports. The Joseph H. Keller houses an NCAA-size swimming pool and a gymnasium for physical education classes and intercollegiate competitions. Other buildings include student residence halls that accomodate 240 women, and Connelly Center, which houses the cafeteria, student center, and lounge. Daily mass is offered for the convenience of both commuting and resident students. About 70% of applicants meet the requirements and are accepted, including midyear students. Scolarships are available and 69% of all undergraduates receive some form of financial aid.

Community Environment: Notre Dame College is located in South Euclid, Ohio, a suburb less than 30 minutes east of downtown Cleveland, an historical city that is growing, changing, and rebuilding. Notre Dame College is 15 minutes away from University Circle, a one-square-mile complex that contains an unusual blend of cultural, educational, medical, religious, and social service institutions. The Cleveland Museum of Art, the Museum of Natural History, the Cleveland Institute of Art and the Institute of Music are open year-round. Also located in University Circle is Severence Hall, where the world-famous Cleveland Orchestra performs. The Cleveland Play House, the oldest repertory company in the nation, operates three theaters in a major new theater complex located near University Circle. Downtown is home to Playhouse Square, a cluster of three elaborate old motion picture palaces that have been meticulously restored and house the Cleveland Ballet, the Cleveland Opera Company, and the Great Lakes Theater Festival. next door, touring Broadway casts perform at the Hanna Theater. For recreation, Cleveland has the beauty of the north coast and the waters of Lake Erie. The Metro Parks system is Cleveland's Emerald Necklace, and provides 84 miles of park drives, picnic areas, ponds, and hiking and biking trails. The college campus is located within walking distance of the Euclid Creek Reservation. There are also three area ski resorts located within a short driving distance of the city. Cleveland hosts a variety of professional sports teams. Top-name music groups also perform in the area.

OBERLIN COLLEGE   *(E-9)*
153 West Lorain Street
Oberlin, Ohio 44074
Tel: (216) 775-8411

Description: Oberlin College was founded in 1833 and was the nation's first coeducational college as well as an early leader in the education of blacks. It is accredited by the North Central Association of Colleges and Schools and by respective professional organizations. The private, liberal arts college comprises two divisions. The College of Arts and Sciences offers a four-year undergraduate program leading to the Bachelor of Arts degree. The Conservatory of Music offers undergraduates a four-year course of professional and academic studies that leads to a degree of Bachelor of Music. The conservatory also offers a limited program in Music Education, Teaching, Historical Performance, Conducting and Opera Theater leading to a degree of Master of Music. A five-year double-degree program leads to bachelor's degrees in both the college and the conservatory. The college operates on the 4-1-4 calendar system. Enrollment includes 2,685 full-time and 59 part-time undergraduates and 17 graduate students. A faculty of 241 gives an overall faculty-student ratio of approximately 1-12.

Entrance Requirements: Admission is selective; high school graduation with rank in top 10% of class recommended; completion of 15-18 academic units required (preferably 4 English, 3 foreign language, 4 mathematics, 3-4 laboratory science, and 3-4 social science,); SAT or ACT required; 3 CEEB achievement tests recommended; candidates to the Conservatory of Music must be sufficiently advanced in some field of music to make it a specialty or major; audition required; early admission, early decision, deferred admission, and advanced placement plans available; $45 application fee.

Costs Per Year: $19,670 tuition; $5,820 room and board; $144 student fees.

Collegiate Environment: Many of the campus buildings were designed by renowned American architects (Cass Gilbert, Minoru Yamasaki, Robert Venturi) in a variety of styles. Facilities include the finest college art museum in the country; the fully equipped Philips Physical Education Center; and excellent facilities for theater and music performance. The library system contains 1 million volumes, 4,500 periodicals, 170,000 microforms, and 27,500 audiovisual materials. Dormitories house 71% of the students; 5% live in cooperative houses. Oberlin offers nearly 1,000 courses and over 21 study-abroad programs. The college is a member of the North Coast Athletic Conference (NCAA Div. III). Oberlin has aid-blind admissions and and 55% of students received financial aid. 1,867 scholarships are available. 60% of the freshmen graduated in the top 10% of their high-school class. 67% of applicants are admitted. The average scores for the entering freshmen class were SAT 1250 combined, ACT 29 composite. More Oberlin graduates later earn Ph.D.s than do graduates of any other predominantly undergraduate institution.

Community Environment: Oberlin College is located 35 miles southwest of Cleveland in a small town.

OHIO COLLEGE OF PODIATRIC MEDICINE   *(E-11)*
10515 Carnegie Avenue
Cleveland, Ohio 44106
Tel: (216) 231-3300; (800) 238-7903; Admissions: (216) 231-3300 X 374; Fax: (216) 231-1005

Description: The private college was founded in 1916 following the passage of the Platt-Ellis Bill regulating the limited branches of medicine and recognizing Podiatry as an essential branch of the health care professions. The college is maintained in conformity with the laws, rules, and regulations of the Ohio State Medical Board, the Council of Podiatric Medical Education and the North Central Association of Schools and Colleges. The four year course of study leads to the Doctor of Podiatric Medicine degree. A full-time graduate placement office assists students in securing post-graduate, residency programs. The school operates on the semester system and upperclass students are responsible for completing a summer clinic rotation. Total student enrollment is 469 and there is a faculty of 22 full-time and 29 part-time members.

Entrance Requirements: Minimum of 90 semester hours or 135 quarter hours of accredited undergraduate studies. 97% of accepted applicants are college graduates. Course work should include biology, chemistry, organic chemistry, physics, and English, in addition to humanities and liberal arts. A minimum of two letters of recommendation are also required. Application is made through American Association of Colleges of Podiatric Medicine Application Service (AACPMAS). MCAT is required; Rolling admission.

Costs Per Year: $16,500 tuition; $576 fees.

Collegiate Environment: The college is located in the heart of Cleveland's University Circle. OCPM houses laboratories, classrooms, a library, the Cleveland Foot and Ankle Clinic, and the Carnegie Surgery Center. The library holdings number 14,000 volumes and 1,200 periodicals, a large collection of audiovisual materials and a biomedical communications center. The college welcomes applicants from all areas of the country. Scholarships available and 95% of the students receive some form of financial aid.

Community Environment: See Case Western Reserve University.

OHIO DOMINICAN COLLEGE   *(K-6)*
1216 Sunbury Rd.
Columbus, Ohio 43219
Tel: (614) 251-4500; (800) 955-6446; Fax: (614) 252-0776

Description: The Catholic liberal arts college was formerly the College of St. Mary of the Springs. Founded in 1911, it is accredited by the North Central Association of Colleges and Schools. In addition to the regular day session, continuing education classes in evening school and weekend college programs leading to a degree are available. Enrollment includes 440 men and 688 women full-time, and 163 men and 422 women part-time. A faculty of 54 full-time and 46 part-time gives an overall faculty-student ratio of 1-16. The semester system is used. One summer session plus a pre-session and post-session are available. The college offers Associate of Science and Art degrees, as well as four-year courses leading to the degrees of Bachelor of Arts, Bachelor of Science, and Bachelor of Science in Education. Army, Navy and Air Force ROTC training is available off campus on an elective basis. Arrangements for study abroad may be made on an individual basis.

Entrance Requirements: Accredited high school graduation with rank in upper half of graduating class; completion of 16 units recommended including 4 English, 3 mathematics, 3 foreign language, 3 science, and 3 social science; SAT or ACT required; advanced placement, rolling admission, and midyear admission plans available.

Costs Per Year: $8,490 tuition; $4,450 board and room; $1,500 average additional expenses.

Collegiate Environment: The college's 46-acre campus is situated in a quiet, residential area approximately four miles from the heart of Columbus. The library collection, containing 154,000 volumes, 550 periodicals, and 5,595 microforms, is housed in a new three-story building with a complete Audiovisual Center. Residence halls accommodate 350 students. Approximately 86% of students applying for admission meet the requirements and are accepted. Students may also be accepted at midyear. The college welcomes a geographically diverse student body and accepts students of all faiths. Freshman classes begin in September and January. Of 200 scholarships recently awarded, 64 were given to freshmen. All students with 3.0 or better grade point average are automatically considered for scholarships.

Community Environment: See Ohio State University - Columbus Campus.

OHIO NORTHERN UNIVERSITY   *(G-4)*
525 S. Main Street
Ada, Ohio 45810
Tel: (419) 772-2260

Description: The university, established in 1871, consists of five colleges. The institution currently offers academic programs and professional preparation in the Colleges of Arts and Sciences, Business Administration, Engineering, Pharmacy, and Law. The institution is accredited by the North Central Association of Secondary Schools and Colleges with the professional colleges holding accreditation by their respective professional organizations. The quarter system is used for the undergraduate colleges, while the semester system is used for the college of Law. Three summer terms are also offered. Army and Air Force ROTC are available. Enrollment includes 2,792 full-time and 80 part-time undergraduates. A faculty of 178 full-time and 65 part-time gives a faculty-student ratio of 1-13.

Entrance Requirements: Completion of 16 academic units including 4 in English with requirements by colleges as follows: College of Business Administration and Arts and Sciences - 2 mathematics (1 algebra and 1 plane geometry), 6 social studies or natural sciences; College of Engineering - 4 mathematics (2 algebra, 1 plane geometry and at least 1/2 in trigonometry), 2 science (1 physics and 1 chemistry preferably); College of Pharmacy - 3 mathematics (2 algebra and 1 plane geometry), 3 science (including biology and chemistry); minimum SAT score of 950 combined or a composite ACT of 20 and graduation in the upper half of graduating class recommended; $30 nonrefundable application fee; early decision, advanced placement, early admission, rolling admission, midyear admission, admission plans available.

Costs Per Year: $15,990 tuition; $4,080 room and board.

Collegiate Environment: The 280-acre campus is located in northwestern Ohio. The 29 campus buildings include the Heterick Memorial Library, containing 321,157 volumes equivalent which includes 407,928 bound volumes, 93,403 government documents, 135,785 microfilm items equal to 27,157 volume equivalents, 4,689 recordings as well as 2,193 other audio-visual items. Single undergraduate students must live in residence halls or fraternity/sorority houses. Residence hall accomodate 1,500 students. Eight of the chartered national fraternities and four national sororities have houses either on campus or in the village with living accomodations for most of their members. Commuters or students living with relatives are exempted from residence requirements. Approximately 75% of students applying for admission are accepted, including midyear students. About 90% of students receive financial aid. Average high school standing of a recent freshmen class: 39% in upper 10%, 65% in upper 25%, 90% in upper 50%. The average ACT composite of freshmen class is 24. 82% of freshmen class returned for second year.

Community Environment: Ada, a community of nearly 5,000 persons is located 15 miles east of Lima and 22 miles south of Findlay, and only 8 miles from I-75. Health services are provided by the university. Some of the usual civic and service organizations are active.

OHIO STATE UNIVERSITY - AGRICULTURAL TECHNICAL INSTITUTE   (G-10)
1328 Dover Road
Wooster, Ohio 44691
Tel: (216) 264-3911; (800) 647-8283; Fax: (216) 264-7634

Description: This coeducational institute is a college within the Ohio State University College of Agriculture. It offers 2-year technical training for the occupational needs of the students, and grants the Associate Degree. The college is one of two institutions of its type in the United States that is devoted solely to programs in the agricultural technologies. It operates on the quarter system and offers 2 summer sessions. It is accredited by the North Central Association of Colleges and Schools. Enrollment includes 548 men and 192 women. A faculty of 41 full-time and 19 part-time gives a faculty-student ratio of 1-12.

Entrance Requirements: High school graduation or equivalent; recommended completion of 15 units including 4 English, 3 mathematics, 2 science, and 2 social science; ACT or SAT used for placement; conference strongly advised; $30 application fee; open admission for all quarters and rolling admission.

Costs Per Year: $3,125 tuition; $9,664 out-of-state; $2,211 room.

Collegiate Environment: The technical library contains 16,913 volumes, 560 periodicals, and 26,166 microforms. Apartments are available on campus for 181 students. Other off-campus facilities are nearby in the community. Need-based financial assistance is available, and a percentage of the students receive some form of aid. Approximately 96% of the applicants are accepted, including midyear students. Average high school standing of the current freshman class: 18% in the top quarter, 30% in the second quarter, and 37% in the third quarter.

Community Environment: City of Wooster (population of 22,000), county seat of Wayne County, is a leading agricultural region in the United States. In Ohio, Wayne County ranks first in cash receipts from dairy products, cattle and calves, and first in production of hay and oats. The Ohio Agricultural Research and Development Center is the second largest in the United States. Companies in the city include Rubbermaid Incorporated, Wooster Brush Company, Regal Ware, the Gerstenslager Company, Bell and Howell, Frito-Lay, and others. Other educational institutions include OSU's Agricultural Technical Institute, the Wayne General and Technical College, and the College of Wooster. The city has been designated Tree City, U.S.A. Students have access to Cleveland, Columbus, Pittsburgh, Cincinnati, and Akron.

OHIO STATE UNIVERSITY - COLUMBUS CAMPUS   (K-6)
1800 Cannon Drive
Columbus, Ohio 43210-1200
Tel: (614) 292-3980; Admissions: (614) 292-3980

Description: The state-supported university began in 1870 as the Ohio Agricultural and Mechanical College. The school is accredited by the North Central Association of Colleges and Schools and by several professional accrediting institutions. The university includes 19 colleges and a graduate school. There are nine schools within the colleges. The university is the major center for graduate and professional education in Ohio. There are 219 undergraduate majors leading to a Bachelor's degree, 125 programs leading to a Master's degree, and 94 to a doctorate. Air Force, Army, and Navy ROTC is available. The university operates on the quarter system and offers three summer sessions: one of 10 weeks and two of 5 weeks. Enrollment includes 39,511 full-time and 10,031 part-time undergraduates and 10,734 graduate students. A faculty of 2,977 full-time and 858 part-time gives an undergraduate faculty-student ratio of 1-14.

Entrance Requirements: Competitive selective admission for summer, autumn, and winter quarters for freshmen; required units, 4 English, 3 years of mathematics, 2 science, 2 social science, 2 foreign language, 1 visual or performing arts, and 1 from any of the previous categories; in addition, 1 more unit each in mathematics, science, and foreign language is recommended. ACT or SAT required for placement purposes; English and math placement tests required; advanced placement, early admission, rolling admission plans available; $30 nonrefundable application fee.

Costs Per Year: $3,087 tuition; $9,315 nonresident tuition; $4,484 board and room; books $500; acceptance fee $50.

Collegiate Environment: The campus has 380 buildings on 3,317 acres, including a 500-acre airport, and two 18-hole golf courses. University Libraries include the Main Library and 33 departmental libraries with a total of 4,693,081 volumes, 32,381 periodicals, 3.5 million microforms, and 32,962 sound recordings. There are 24 residence halls with housing for 9,100 undergraduate students. In addition to a unified honors program for the Colleges of the Arts and Sciences, each undergraduate college has its honors program for academically talented students. The ROTC program offers courses in Military, Naval, and Air Science on a voluntary basis. Cooperative programs are available in several areas. There are many study abroad programs. Approximately 91% of freshmen students applying for admission meet the requirements and are accepted, including midyear students. About 65% of students receive financial aid. The middle 50% range of freshmen scores is ACT 20-26 composite. About 83% of the previous freshman class returned for the sophomore year.

Community Environment: The capital of Ohio, Columbus, is a spacious city and the largest of the world's cities named in honor of Christopher Columbus. Columbus is one of the fastest growing metropolitan areas in the United States. It is primarily a service-industry community, although there is some light manufacturing. Museums, theaters, art galleries, a symphony orchestra, and professional sports teams are a part of the city.

OHIO STATE UNIVERSITY - LIMA CAMPUS   (G-3)
4240 Campus Drive
Lima, Ohio 45804
Tel: (419) 221-1641

Description: The coeducational, regional campus of Ohio State University was established in 1960. It offers the first years of undergraduate study in most fields offered by the university, an Associate of Arts degree, and baccalaureate degree programs in elementary education and psychology. The university operates on the quarter system and offers two summer sessions. The school is accredited by the

North Central Association of Colleges and Schools. Enrollment includes 860 full-time and 372 part-time undergraduates and 148 graduate students. A faculty of 55 full-time and 34 part-time gives an undergraduate faculty-student ratio of 1-14.

Entrance Requirements: Open enrollment policy; high school graduation or equivalent; completion of 15 units including 4 English, 3 math, 2 science, 2 foreign language recommended, 2 social studies; 1 visual or performing arts; and 1 additional unit from any of the above; ACT required; non-high school graduates considered if passed GED; early admission, midyear admission, early decision, rolling admission, delayed admission, and advanced placement plans available; $30 application fee.

Costs Per Year: $3,125 state-resident tuition; $9,664 out-of-state.

Collegiate Environment: The campus comprises 565 acres and includes a library containing 78,476 volumes, 5,500 pamphlets, 533 periodicals, and 13,477 microforms. Financial assistance is available and 45% of the students receive aid. 95% of applicants are accepted, including midyear students.

Community Environment: See Ohio Northern University.

OHIO STATE UNIVERSITY - MANSFIELD CAMPUS   *(G-8)*
1680 University Drive
Mansfield, Ohio 44906
Tel: (419) 755-4011; Admissions: (419) 755-4226; Fax: (419) 755-4241

Description: The coeducational, regional campus of Ohio State University was established in 1958 and offers the first 2 years of undergraduate study in most fields available at the Columbus campus, an Associate of Arts degree, and a baccalaureate degree program in elementary education. The school is accredited by the North Central Association of Colleges and Schools. It operates on the quarter system and offers two summer sessions. Enrollment includes 862 full-time and 642 part-time undergraduates and 230 graduate students. A faculty of 40 full-time and 45 part-time gives an undergraduate faculty-student ratio of 1-23.

Entrance Requirements: Open enrollment policy; high school graduation or equivalent; completion of 4 units English, 3 math, 2 science, 2 foreign language, 2 social science, 1 visual or performing arts, 1 additional unit in any of the above; early admission, early decision, rolling admission, and advanced placement plans available; $30 application fee.

Costs Per Year: $3,125 state-resident tuition; $9,664 out-of-state tuition.

Collegiate Environment: The campus is situated on 600 acres. The library contains 44,377 volumes and 421 periodicals. Financial aid is available in the form of various scholarships, grants, loans, and work study programs. 65% of students receive some form of financial aid. Any Ohio resident who is a high school graduate (or equivalent) of an accredited high school will be admitted. 91% of freshmen applicants are accepted. The majority of students reside in the area surrounding Mansfield.

Community Environment: The financial and commercial center of north central Ohio, Mansfield is located halfway between Columbus and Cleveland, about 60 miles north of Columbus. Major employers include General Motors, Sprint United Telephone, and Mansfield General Hospital. With a metropolitan population of 130,000, the community offers numerous recreational, cultural and educational opportunities.

OHIO STATE UNIVERSITY - MARION CAMPUS   *(H-6)*
1465 Mt. Vernon Ave.
Marion, Ohio 43302
Tel: (614) 389-2361; Admissions: (614) 389-6786; Fax: (614) 389-6786

Description: This coeducational, regional campus of Ohio State University was established in 1957. It offers the first 2 years of undergraduate study in most fields available at the Columbus Campus, an Associate of Arts degree, and a baccalaureate and masters degree program in elementary education. The school is accredited by the North Central Association of Colleges and Schools. It operates on the quarter system and offers two summer sessions. Enrollment includes 1,209

students. A faculty of 32 full-time and 54 part-time gives an overall faculty-student ratio of 1-14.

Entrance Requirements: Open enrollment policy; high school graduation or equivalent; completion of 4 units of English, 3 math, 2 science, 2 foreign language, 2 social studies 1 visual or performing arts, and 1 additional unit in any of the above; any state resident who is a high school graduate (or equivalent) of an accredited high school will be admitted; early admission, early decision, midyear admission, rolling admission, and advanced placement plans available; $30 application fee.

Costs Per Year: $3,125 tuition; $9,664 out-of-state.

Collegiate Environment: The 180-acre campus includes the library containing 36,344 volumes, 374 periodicals, 2,837 microforms and 3,478 recordings. The majority of students reside in the Central Ohio region. Apartment housing is available for students who desire to live near campus. Meal plans are available. 96% of students applying are accepted. Financial aid is available in the form of various scholarships, grants, loans, and work-study programs. In addition to intercollegiate sports, an extensive intramural sports program is available to men and women.

Community Environment: Marion is located about 40 miles north of Columbus and is centrally situated in Marion County.

OHIO STATE UNIVERSITY - NEWARK CAMPUS   *(J-8)*
University Drive
Newark, Ohio 43055
Tel: (614) 366-3321; Fax: (614) 366-5047

Description: The coeducational, regional campus of Ohio State University was established in 1957. It offers the first 2 years of undergraduate study in most fields offered at the Columbus Campus, an Associate of Arts degree, and a master's degree program in elementary education. It is accredited by the North Central Association of Colleges and Schools. The school operates on the quarter system and offers two summer sessions. Enrollment is 611 men and 949 women, of which 80 are graduate students. A faculty of 48 full-time and 52 part-time gives an undergraduate faculty-student ratio of 1-17.

Entrance Requirements: Open enrollment policy; high school graduation or equivalent; completion of 4 units of English, 3 math, 2 science, 2 foreign language, 2 social studies, and 1 art; ACT or SAT required for course placement and counseling purposes; $30 application fee; rolling admission, midyear admission, and advanced placement plans available.

Costs Per Year: $3,125 tuition; $9,664 out-of-state; $55 student fees.

Collegiate Environment: The school is situated on a 150-acre campus. The library contains 48,580 volumes and 320 periodicals. Financial aid is available. All Ohio-resident freshmen applicants who meet the requirements are accepted, including midyear students.

Community Environment: See Denison University.

OHIO UNIVERSITY   *(M-9)*
120 Chubb Hall
Athens, Ohio 45701-2979
Tel: (614) 593-4100; Fax: (614) 593-0560

Description: Founded in 1804, Ohio University was the first institution of higher learning established in the state. Ohio University is a state-assisted, coeducational institution. Enrollment is 15,029 full-time and 920 part-time undergraduate students. There are 2,906 graduate students. A faculty of 832 full-time and 144 part-time gives an undergraduate faculty-student ratio of 1-18. Approximately 12% of the student body comes from out of state, including every state in the nation and about 100 foreign countires. The university offers 300 undergraduate programs of study, master's degrees in about 60 fields, 20 doctoral programs, and a D.O. degree through the College of Osteopathic Medicine. Qualified freshmen may enroll directly in a degree program, or may enter University College if they are undecided about a major. The university operates on a quarter system with two five-week summer terms. Cooperative education programs are available in Engineering and Computer Science. Many study abroad programs are available. Although freshman and transfer applicants are accepted for all quarters, they are encouraged to apply for fall. Requirements for all graduate programs are under the jurisdiction of the individual academic department; the Office of Graduate Student Services administers all requirements. The university's Honors Tutorial College offers a unique opportunity for highly qualified and motivated students to study on a one-to-one basis with professors from their chosen major area.

Entrance Requirements: Admission and housing are assigned to the best-qualified applicants; admission is based upon high school performance (class rank, grade-point average, and curriculum), aptitude test scores (ACT and/or SAT), and diversity, special ability, talent, or achievement; early decision, early admission, midyear admission, rolling admission, and advanced placement plans available; $25 application fee; application deadline March 1.

Costs Per Year: $3,552 tuition; $7,629 out-of-state; $4,095 room and board.

Collegiate Environment: The campus is a historical one, characterized by red-brick walkways and Georgian architecture. The College Green is the location of most classroom and administrative buildings, including Cutler Hall, which was built in 1816 and is registered as a National Historic Landmark. Three other "greens"--East, West, and South--include the university's residence hall system that can accommodate approximately 7,000 students. Married student housing can accommodate about 250 families. Although it is a major, state-assisted institution, Ohio University has the look and feel of a small, private college. The campus is compact, and all academic and extracurricular activities are within easy walking distance of the residence halls. 73% of applicants meet admissions criteria and are accepted. Most freshmen rank in the top 30% of their graduating high school class. The middle 50% ranges of scores for the entering class were: ACT 21-26 composite, SAT 880-1100 combined. 3,589 merit-based scholarships were awarded recently. 65% of students receive some form of financial aid.

Community Environment: Athens, home of Ohio University, is a traditional college town with a nonstudent population of approximately 21,000. The city is located about 75 miles southeast of Columbus, the state capital, in the foothills of the Appalachian mountains and on the banks of the Hocking River. Several state parks and thousands of acres of national forest are within easy driving distance, and provide ample facilities for swimming, hiking, camping, fishing, and picnicking.

Branch Campuses: Regional campuses are located in Chillicothe, Ironton, Lancaster, St. Clarisville, and Zanesville, Ohio.

OHIO WESLEYAN UNIVERSITY   *(I-6)*
Sandusky Street
Delaware, Ohio 43015
Tel: (614) 369-4431; (800) 922-8953; Admissions: (614) 368-3020; Fax: (614) 368-3314

Description: The liberal arts university was founded in 1842 and is affiliated with the United Methodist Church. It is accredited by the North Central Association of Colleges and Schools and operates on the semester system with one summer term. Enrollment includes 828 men, 859 women full-time, and 15 men and 30 women part-time. A faculty of 130 full-time and 57 part-time gives a ratio of 1-13.

Entrance Requirements: Accredited high school graduation with rank in upper 30% of graduating class; completion of 16 units including 4 English, 3 mathematics, 3 foreign language, 3 science, 3 social science; SAT or ACT required; non-degree candidates may be admitted as special students; $35 application fee; early admission, early decision, delayed admission, and advanced placement plans available; March 1 application deadline.

Costs Per Year: $16,732 tuition; room and board $5,650.

Collegiate Environment: The 200-acre campus is located 20 miles north of Columbus. The 55 buildings include the 440,000 volume library and living accommodations for 900 men and 900 women. Several off-campus programs are offered including programs in Paris (France), and Salamanca (Spain), the Oakridge Science Semester, New York Arts Program, Newberry Library Semester Program, and the Philadelphia Urban Semester, of the Great Lakes College Association. The university participates in the study-abroad and critical language programs of the Great Lakes Colleges Association which are the European Urban Semester, programs in Africa and India, the Latin American Program in Bogota (Columbia), the Far Eastern Program in Tokyo (Japan), and Hong King (China), the British Program in Aber-

deen (Scotland), and the Critical Language Programs which are available at other institutions of the Great Lakes Colleges Association. Financial aid is available and 80% of students receive aid (including both merit and need-based awards). 80% of those who apply for admission are accepted.

Community Environment: Delaware, a city of 20,000 and county seat of Delaware County, is a 25-minute drive from Columbus, with convenient access by air, highway or bus. The Delaware State Parks provide facilities for fishing, boating, camping, and swimming. An annual event is the Little Brown Jug, which is the largest pacing event in the United States. About half the faculty live within a ten minute walk of student halls and houses, in the architecturally historic northwest section of the city. Ohio Wesleyan is a national school; students are from 45 states and 44 countries. About 50% are from the midwest and 30% are from the east.

OTTERBEIN COLLEGE   *(J-7)*
West College Ave.
Westerville, Ohio 43081
Tel: (614) 823-1500; (800) 488-8144; Fax: (614) 898-1200

Description: Founded in 1847, the college offers a comprehensive liberal arts education in the Christian tradition. The school is affiliated with the United Methodist Church, and is accredited by the North Central Association of Colleges and Schools and by respective professional organizations. Special programs include Semester at Sea, foreign study programs in Spain and France, and the Washington Semester Plan. Internships are available in many departments. The college operates on the quarter system and offers one summer session. Enrollment includes 1,650 full-time, 949 part-time undergraduate, and 111 graduate students. A faculty of 132 full-time and 29 part-time gives an undergraduate faculty-student ratio of 1-13. Air Force, Army, and Navy ROTC programs available.

Entrance Requirements: High school graduation with rank in upper 50% of graduating class; completion of 16 units including 4 English, 3 mathematics, 3 science, 2 foreign language, and 2 social science; minimum SAT Verbal 430, Math 430, or ACT 20 composite required; deferred admission, rolling admission, midyear admission, and advanced placement plans available; April 20 application deadline; $15 application fee.

Costs Per Year: $13,611 tuition; $4,569 room and board.

Collegiate Environment: The 140-acre campus has 25 buildings. Towers Hall is the central landmark of the campus and contains classrooms, faculty offices, and the Clements Memorial Carillon. The Courtright Memorial Library houses a collection of 200,000 volumes, 900 periodical subscriptions, 112,138 titles on microfilm, and 10,000 records and tapes. Several residence halls provide housing for 780 students. Sororities and fraternities house an additional 124 students. The college welomes students from diverse geographical locations, and about 75% of applicants are accepted, including midyear students. A campus radio and TV station are operated by students under the supervision of the Department of Speech. The college offers a full scholarship program for freshmen and upperclassmen, and about 95% of students receive some form of financial aid.

Community Environment: Westerville was settled by Connecticut, New York and Virginia families and Quakers from Pennsylvania in 1813. The community, seven miles north of Columbus, has excellent city and college libraries, many churches, a modern medical center, and various civic and service organizations. A site of interest is the Hanby House. Hoover Reservoir is located about four miles east, and offers facilities for picnicking, fishing, and boating. Part-time employment is available.

OWENS COMMUNITY COLLEGE   *(D-5)*
P.O. Box 10000
30335 Oregon Road
Toledo, Ohio 43699
Tel: (419) 666-3282; (800) 466-9367; Admissions: (419) 661-7777

Description: The state-supported, coeducational, college was chartered by the Ohio Board of Regents in 1967. It is accredited by the North Central Association of Colleges and Schools and operates on the semester system and offers one summer session. The college offers technical, and continuing education programs which lead to the Associate degree. The college has 2 campuses, one in Toledo and one in Findlay, Ohio. Recent enrollment was approximately 1,094 men, 1,640 women, 3,319 men and 2,630 women part-time. A faculty of 117 full-time and 412 part-time gives a faculty-student ratio of 1-30. The enrollment at the Findlay branch is 1,572.

Entrance Requirements: Open enrollment policy; high school graduation or equivalent; non-high school graduates may be considered; ACT preferred, required only for health program applicants. No application fee; rolling admission and midyear admission plans available.

Costs Per Year: $1,788 tuition; $3,336 out-of-state tuition; $40 student fees.

Collegiate Environment: There are nine buildings on the 100-acre campus including the library which contains 45,000 volumes, 800 periodicals, 400 microforms and 4,000 AV materials. Financial assistance is available and about 40% of the students receive aid. All applicants are accepted, including midyear students. The average high school standing of the recent freshman class was 15% in the top quarter, 43% in the second quarter; 30% in the third quarter, 20% in the bottom quarter; average ACT composite score, 17. About 60% of the previous freshman class returned for the second year of studies.

Community Environment: See University of Toledo.

Branch Campuses: Findlay Campus, 300 Davis St., Findlay, OH 44840, (800) 346-3529.

PAYNE THEOLOGICAL SEMINARY   (L-4)
1230 Wilberforce-Clifton Road
Wilberforce, Ohio 45384
Tel: (513) 376-2946

Description: The graduate school of theology was established in 1844 and is supported by the African Methodist Episcopal Church. It is concerned with the training of men and women for the Christian ministry. The seminary has an interracial, interdenominational faculty and student body. Special programs are constantly being developed to meet the needs of minority groups. It operates on the semester system. Enrollment of 46 students with a faculty of 6 gives a faculty-student ratio of 1-8.

Entrance Requirements: Bachelor's degree based on four years of work in a college or university approved by a regional accrediting agency. Graduates of unaccredited American schools may be admitted only on probation. Entrance exams required; $10 application fee.

Costs Per Year: $3,000 tuition; $1,980 room.

Collegiate Environment: The seminary is situated on 10 acres of beautiful wooded land. The four seminary buildings include a library of 31,000 volumes, the administration building, and living quarters for 48 students. Cooperation among the three schools of the academic community, Central State University, Wilberforce University, and Payne Seminary greatly increases the facilities of the seminary. Cross-registration is permitted with the United Theological Seminary in Dayton. Every attempt is made to provide scholarship aid to those who qualify for admission and who have genuine economic need. 95% of the students receive some form of financial assistance.

Community Environment: See Central State University.

PONTIFICAL COLLEGE JOSEPHINUM   (J-6)
7625 N. High St.
Columbus, Ohio 43085
Tel: (614) 885-5585

Description: This Catholic men's seminary owes its existence to the vision of Monsignor Joseph Jessing and to the generosity of American Catholics, particularly those of German origin and descent. The first students were admitted to classes in 1888. The main objective of the seminary college is to prepare students for the priesthood. The school is fully accredited by the North Central Association of Colleges and Schools. Enrollment is 120 students. A faculty of 25 full-time and 22 part-time gives an overall faculty-student ratio of approximately 1-4. The semester system is used in the College of Liberal Arts and the quarter system is used in the School of Theology. The seminary grants the Bachelor and Master degrees.

Entrance Requirements: Open enrollment policy; high school graduation or equivalent; completion of 16 academic units including 4 English and 2 mathematics, ACT or SAT required; GRE required for graduate school; $25 undergraduate application fee; $35 graduate application fee; rolling admission, early decision and advanced placement plans available.

Costs Per Year: $5,512 tuition; $3,780 room and board; $5,841 graduate tuition.

Collegiate Environment: The 120-acre campus is located two miles north of Worthington. The main building is a large, four-story building that houses the administration offices, chapel, auditorium, lecture rooms, dormitories, and 106 private rooms. The A.T. Wehrle Memorial Library houses 110,000 volumes and 500 periodicals. There are dormitory accommodations for 224 men. Approximately 85% of students applying for admission meet the requirements and are accepted. The college welcomes a geographically diverse student body. Approximately 95% of last year's senior class continued on to graduate school.

Community Environment: See Ohio State University - Columbus Campus.

SAINT MARY SEMINARY   (D-11)
28700 Euclid Ave.
Wickliffe, Ohio 44092-2585
Tel: (216) 943-7600; Fax: (216) 943-7577

Description: As its primary mission this Catholic seminary prepares students for ordination to the priesthood. As its secondary mission Saint Mary Seminary places at the use of other students who qualify the resources of its library, faculty and facilities. The founding of the seminary was very nearly coincident with the founding of the Diocese of Cleveland. Ground for the present seminary was broken in 1924. Since 1954 Saint Mary Seminary has been exclusively a graduate theologate. It offers the M.Div. and the M.A. degrees. It is accredited by the Association of Theological Schools and the Commission on Institutions of Higher Education of the North Central Association of Colleges and Schools. It operates on the quarter system and offers one summer session each June. Recent enrollment was 39 students. There is a faculty of 13 full-time and 11 part-time members.

Entrance Requirements: For the M.Div. degree a Bachelor of Arts degree or equivalent from an institution accredited by a regional association; candidates for ordination must be sponsored by a bishop, church or religious superior. GRE required. For the M.A. degree a Bachelor of Arts degree or its equivalent from an institution accredited by a regional accrediting association.

Costs Per Year: $5,690 tuition, $7,600 room and board. $225 student fees. Special arrangements are made for students for the priesthood of the Diocese of Cleveland.

Collegiate Environment: The Center for Pastoral Leadership, where Saint Mary Seminary is housed, is located in Wickliffe, Ohio, fourteen miles from the center of Cleveland at the western extremity of Lake County. Access to several major interstates makes the seminary centrally located. The main building has rooms for about 90 students and the library holdings include 50,000 bound volumes, 365 periodicals, and 917 microforms. Dormitory facilities are available for 90 students. Approximately 80% of students applying for admission are accepted. About 90% of the previous first-year class returned to this school for their second year.

Community Environment: See Case Western Reserve University.

SHAWNEE STATE UNIVERSITY   (O-7)
940 Second Street
Portsmouth, Ohio 45662
Tel: (614) 355-2221; (800) 959-2778

Description: Shawnee State Community College was created in 1977 as a two year college offering associate degrees in occupational programs and liberal arts transfer programs. The University now offers both associate degrees and several baccalaureate programs. There are also courses leading to certification in Elementary Education. It is fully accredited by the North Central Association of Colleges and Schools. Enrollment is 3,200 students. The faculty-student ratio is 1-15.

Entrance Requirements: High school graduate or equivelant. Open enrollment. ACT or SAT for advisement and placement. Recommended high school units: 4 English, 3 math, 3 social science, 3 science, 2 foriegn language, 1 visual or performing arts; rolling admission, midyear admission and advanced placement; $30 application fee.

Costs Per Year: $2,262 tuition for state resident; $4,128 tuition for out-of-state students; $3,800 room and board; $393 per quarter student fees.

Collegiate Environment: Shawnee State's 50-acre campus is situated between the Ohio River and downtown Portsmouth, Ohio, providing both the beauty and inspiration of nature and the convenience of town life. The library houses 100,000 books and 600 periodical subscriptions and offers the latest in high technology information gathering equipment. Fully furnished 3-level townhomes provide 120 students with on-campus housing. Students participate in intramural sports and in intercollegiate basketball for men and women, men's golf and soccer, and women's softball, volleyball, and tennis. Financial aid is available in the form of scholarships, grants, loans, and work-study.

Community Environment: A quaint city of 23,000 residents, Portsmouth is Scioto County's largest retail center and a popular tourist area as well. Its Bonneyfiddle area, with its old-world charm, is a treasure trove for antique buffs, and the winding Ohio River offers opportunities for boating, waterskiing, and fishing.

SINCLAIR COMMUNITY COLLEGE   (K-3)
444 W. Third St.
Dayton, Ohio 45402
Tel: (513) 226-3000; Fax: (513) 449-5192

Description: This school began in 1887 with one room set aside for an evening school in the Dayton YMCA. In 1965 the Montgomery County Community College District was created and the board of trustees acquired 18 acres of downtown urban renewal land for a new campus. Continuing education, transfer courses and semi-professional and technical programs are offered. The college is authorized to grant Associate degrees in Arts and Science. It is accredited by the North Central Association of Colleges and Schools and by various professional organizations. Army ROTC is available. The college operates on the quarter system and offers four summer sessions. Total enrollment includes 20,075 full-time and part-time students. A faculty of 396 full-time and 534 part-time gives a faculty-student ratio of 1-22.

Entrance Requirements: Open enrollment policy; high school graduation or equivalent; placement tests required; non-high school graduates may be admitted as special students; $10 application fee; early admission, rolling admission and advanced placement plans available.

Costs Per Year: $1,395 tuition; $2,115 out-of-county; $3,420 out-of-state.

Collegiate Environment: Sinclair Community College is an urban campus located on over 50 acres in Dayton, Ohio. The library has a collection of 125,861 volumes, 654 periodicals, 200 microforms and 3,268 recordings. The college offers 110 scholarships with 55 available for freshmen. About 40% of the students receive financial aid. All applicants are accepted, including midyear students.

Community Environment: See Wright State University.

SOUTHERN OHIO COLLEGE   (N-2)
1055 Laidlaw Ave.
Cincinnati, Ohio 45237
Tel: (513) 242-3791

Description: The private junior college of business founded in 1927 is part of a national network of colleges and schools owned by the Career Com Corporation of Harrisburg, Pa. The main campus and the other Southern Ohio College junior college branches are regionally accredited by the North Central Association and by the Association of Independent Colleges and Schools. It is empowered to grant associate degrees, diplomas and certificates. The enrollment at the main campus is 410 students. The main campus faculty numbers 11 full-time and 25 part-time.

Entrance Requirements: High school graduation or equivalent; open enrollment policy; non-high school graduates may be admitted as special students; $100 application fee; entrance examinations required.

Costs Per Year: $4,140 tuition, $140 fees.

Collegiate Environment: The main campus is located in an urban area. The suburban branch campuses provide convenient access and

service to a large number of people. The main campus library contains over 8,000 volumes. A lifetime placement service is available to all graduates. The Cincinnati area junior college branches are located in Ft. Mitchell, Kentucky, and Fairfield, Ohio. Another junior college branch is located in Akron, Ohio.

Community Environment: See University of Cincinnati.

SOUTHERN STATE COMMUNITY COLLEGE   (N-5)
200 Hobart Dr.
Hillsboro, Ohio 45133
Tel: (513) 393-3431; Fax: (513) 393-9370

Description: This state-supported school is a two-year college that offers the Associate degree in Arts, Associate degree in Science, Associate of Technical Studies, Associate of Applied Business and Associate of Applied Sciences. It is accredited by the North Central Association of Colleges and Schools. The school was founded in 1975. It operates on a quarter system and offers three summer sessions. Enrollment includes 857 full-time and 703 part-time students. There are 47 full-time and 76 part-time members. The faculty-student ratio is 1-16.

Entrance Requirements: High school graduation, GED; non-high school graduates over 21 years of age admitted; open enrollment policy; early admission, early decision, rolling admission and advanced placement plans; $15 application fee.

Costs Per Year: $2,574 state-resident tuition; $4,739 nonresidents.

Collegiate Environment: Almost all applicants are admitted. 70% of the students receive financial aid. The library consists of 28,150 hardbound volumes, pamphlets and periodicals and 1,430 audiovisual materials. Noncredit courses are available for those who wish to strengthen their academic skills.

Community Environment: Primarily a rural setting with small towns and villages, Hillsboro is approximately 40 miles east of Cincinnati.

STARK TECHNICAL COLLEGE   (G-12)
6200 Frank Avenue N.W.
Canton, Ohio 44720
Tel: (216) 494-6170

Description: This state-supported, coeducational, two-year technical college began in 1960 with the establishment of the Canton Area Technical School under the jurisdiction of the Canton City Board of Education. It met in the local high school. Due to the growing needs of the community for higher education, the Ohio Board of Regents took over the jurisdiction of the school and in 1972 the present name was adopted. It is accredited by the North Central Association of Colleges and Schools and by other professional accrediting institutions. It operates on the quarter system and offers three summer sessions. Cooperative Education programs are available in the business division and engineering division. Enrollment is 4,565 students. A faculty of 99 full-time and 82 part-time gives a faculty-student ratio of 1-22.

Entrance Requirements: Open enrollment policy; high school graduation or equivalent; non-high school graduates may be considered; SAT or ACT required; early admission, early decision, and rolling admission plans available; $35 application fee.

Costs Per Year: $2,250 state-resident tuition; $3,120 out-of-state; $180 student fees.

Collegiate Environment: The college, at present, meets in one building that contains the classrooms, offices and library. The library contains 60,000 books, periodicals and microforms. Financial assistance is available and 25% of the students receive aid. All applicants are accepted, including midyear students.

Community Environment: See Walsh College.

TEMPLE BAPTIST COLLEGE   (N-2)
11965 Kenn Road
Cincinnati, Ohio 45240
Tel: (513) 851-3800

Description: The privately supported coeducational college began classes in 1972 and is affiliated with the Baptist Church. It operates on the quarter system and offers one summer session. A recent nrollment included 30 men and 15 women full-time, and 20 men and 10 women part-time. The college grants Baccalaureate, Master's and Doctoral degrees.

Entrance Requirements: Open enrollment policy; high school graduation or equivalent; non-high school graduates may be considered; ACT required; $35 application fee; early admission, early decision, rolling admission, delayed admission, and advanced placement plans available.

Costs Per Year: $2,370 tuition; $40 student fees; $300 average additional expenses.

Collegiate Environment: The college shares its quarters with the Temple Baptist Church in a new building in the center of town. The rapidly growing library contains 16,000 volumes.

Community Environment: See University of Cincinnati.

TERRA COMMUNITY COLLEGE   (E-6)
2830 Napoleon Road
Fremont, Ohio 43420-9670
Tel: (419) 334-8400; (800) 334-3886

Description: Formerly Vanguard Technical Institute, the state-supported two-year technical school was founded in 1968 and is fully accredited by the North Central Association of Colleges and Schools. It operates on the quarter system and offers one summer session. Enrollment includes 1,128 full-time and 1,463 part-time students. A faculty of 50 full-time and 100 part-time gives a faculty-student ratio of 1-17.

Entrance Requirements: High school graduation or equivalent; open enrollment policy; non-high school graduates are accepted under special circumstances; ACT recommended; $15 nonrefundable application fee; early admission, early decision, delayed admission, rolling admission, and advanced placement plans available.

Costs Per Year: $2,004 tuition; $4,860 out-of-state tuition; additional expenses average $600.

Collegiate Environment: The original 20-acre campus has three buildings including a library housing 19,816 volumes, 1,000 pamphlets, 367 periodicals, 41,924 microforms and 3,074 audiovisual materials. A new 103-acre campus, with 3 recently completed buildings, will be of the site of all future expansion. Plans include a Student Activities Center and Engineering Building. All of the students applying for admission are accepted. The college welcomes a geographically diverse student body and accepts midyear students. Financial aid is available, and 75% of the current students receive some form of assistance. Average score for the freshman class was ACT 17.5. Approximately 60% of last year's freshman class returned for the sophomore year. About 20% of the graduates continued on to a four-year school.

Community Environment: Fremont is an industrial city and an agricultural center on the Sandusky River. Major commercial transportation is available. Community facilities include three libraries, two hospitals, shopping facilities, and several of the major civic and service organizations. Part-time employment opportunities are good. Nearby Lake Erie provides facilities for water sports. The County Fair is an annual event.

TIFFIN UNIVERSITY   (F-6)
155 Miami Street
Tiffin, Ohio 44883
Tel: (419) 447-6442; (800) 968-6446; Fax: (419) 447-9605

Description: Tiffin University is accredited by the North Central Association of Colleges and Schools. This private university grants the Associate, Bachelor's and Master's degrees. Cooperative education programs are available in accounting and hotel-restaurant management. A study abroad program is available to Regents College in London. The university operates on the semester system and offers two sumer sessions. Enrollment includes 674 full-time and 349 part-time undergraduates and 67 graduate students. A faculty of 30 full-time and 51 part-time gives a faculty-student ratio of 1-19.

Entrance Requirements: Liberal enrollment policy; high school graduation or equivalent; recommended completion of 16 units including 4 units English, 2 mathematics, 2 science; and 2 social science; SAT or ACT required for recent high school graduates; early admission, early decision, delayed admission, midyear admission, advanced placement and rolling admission plans available; $20 application fee.

Costs Per Year: $8,000 tuition; $3,900 room and board; $750 average additional expenses.

Collegiate Environment: The college is 50 miles southeast of Toledo. There are 16 buildings on the two-acre campus. The library contains 17,191 volumes, 110 periodical subscriptions, 25,950 microforms, and 623 audiovisual materials. OCLC (On-line Computer Library Catalog) and Dialog (on-line bibliographic service) are available. Dormitory facilities accommodate 366 students, and an additional 28 students live in fraternity and sorority houses. The college welcomes a geographically diverse student body. About 90% of students applying for admission are accepted, including midyear students. Scholarships are available and 78% of the students receive financial aid.

Community Environment: See Heidelberg College.

TRINITY LUTHERAN SEMINARY   (K-6)
2199 East Main Street
Columbus, Ohio 43209
Tel: (614) 235-4136; Admissions: (614) 235-4136; Fax: (614) 238-0263

Description: The graduate institution is dedicated to preparing men and women for the wide and varied demands of the modern ministry, particularly in the Evangelical Lutheran Church in America. The seminary is fully accredited by the Association of Theological Schools and the North Central Association of Colleges and Schools. Completion of the four-year program results in the conferring of the Master of Divinity degree. A two-year program provides a Master of Theological Studies for lay ministry. The seminary was founded in 1830 by the Evangelical Lutheran Joint Synod of Ohio and Other States. A consolidation in 1978 combined Lutheran Theological Seminary with Hamma School of Theology. Cooperative programs are available with nearby theological schools, the Methodist Theological School in Ohio and the Pontifical College Josephinum. Students may elect courses at any of these schools. A Master of Sacred Theology and a post-graduate program is available. The school operates on the quarter system and offers one summer session. Enrollment is 240 full-time students. A full-time faculty of 25 gives a faculty-student ratio of 1-10.

Entrance Requirements: B.A. degree or its equivalent from an accredited college or university; $25 application fee; rolling admission plan available.

Costs Per Year: $4,576 tuition for non-ELCA students; $3,500 for ELCA students; $882 room; $193 student fees.

Collegiate Environment: The seminary is located in Bexley, a pleasant suburb of Columbus. The library contains 100,000 volumes, more than 600 periodicals and 3,000 audiovisual units, and dormitories are available for 114 single students and 36 families. The devotional life of the students centers around daily morning chapel. Many service opportunities are provided through requests for students to conduct services of worship, part-time chaplaincies in hospitals and prisons in the Columbus area, volunteer work and work-study at other institutions. Financial aid is available. The seminary welcomes a geographically diverse student body.

Community Environment: See Ohio State University - Columbus Campus.

UNITED THEOLOGICAL SEMINARY   (K-3)
1810 Harvard Blvd.
Dayton, Ohio 45406-4599
Tel: (513) 278-5817; (800) 322-5817; Fax: (513) 278-1218

Description: The seminary is a graduate professional school affiliated with the United Methodist Church. It is an accredited member of the Association of Theological Schools and the North Central Association of Schools and Colleges. Persons of all religious affiliations are welcomed. The purpose of the seminary is to educate persons for Christian ministry. The seminary was founded in 1871 and took its present name as the result of the union of the Bonebrake Theological Seminary and the Evangelical School of Theology in 1954. Enrollment is 575 students. A faculty of 25 full-time and 33 part-time gives a faculty-student ratio of 1-10. The 4-1-4 system is used and one summer session and one intensive term in August are offered.

Entrance Requirements: A.B. degree or equivalent based on four years of study in a college approved by a regional accrediting agency;

OHIO

graduates of unaccredited colleges may be admitted in harmony with ATS standards; rolling admission plan available; $25 application fee.

Costs Per Year: $6,600 tuition.

Collegiate Environment: The seminary is located in the northwest area of Dayton. The 35-acre campus is a wooded and landscaped area in the heart of a residential section. Buildings include a library of 131,000 volumes and 500 periodical subscriptions, the administration building, chapel, and two dormitory-apartment buildings accommodating 100 students. About 50% of the students receive some form of financial assistance. About 85% of applicants are accepted, including midyear students.

Community Environment: See Wright State University.

UNIVERSITY OF AKRON   *(F-11)*
302 Buchtel Commons
Akron, Ohio 44325-2001
Tel: (216) 972-7100; (800) 655-4884; Fax: (216) 972-7022

Description: This state university traces its origin to 1870 with the establishment of Buchtel College by the Ohio Universalist Convention. In 1913 the college was turned over to the citizens of the City of Akron to become the nucleus of the nonsectarian Municipal University of Akron. The following year the name was changed to the University of Akron and in 1967 the transition was made from municipal to state institution. The comprehensive urban university is accredited by the North Central Association of Colleges and and Schools. Day and evening classes are offered on the semester system, and two summer terms are offered. Nine degree-granting colleges offer two-year Associate degree programs, four-year Baccalaureate degree programs, and Master's degree programs, as well as programs of study leading to the Doctorate degree. Army and Air Force ROTC programs are offered. Undergraduate enrollment includes 6,011 men and 6,296 women full-time, and 4,276 men and 5,210 women part-time. A faculty of 729 full-time and 963 part-time gives an undergraduate and graduate faculty-student ratio of 1-23. In a consortium with neighboring educational institutions, the university established in 1973 the Northeastern Ohio Universities College of Medicine to prepare well-qualified physicians oriented to the practice of primary care and family medicine at the community level.

Entrance Requirements: In Fall 1994 The University of Akron (UA) implemented a conditional/unconditional admissions policy for entering freshmen. Students graduating from high school beginning in 1994 were affected by this permanent change in policy. UA supports the minimum core curriculum for college preparation in Ohio. College prep curriculum is defined by the following sequence of courses: English 4 units, mathematics 3 units, natural science 3 units, social science 3 units, foreign language 2 units. Business, computer science, engineering, and natural science majors should take a fourth year high school mathematics. Natural science and engineering majors shold complete biology, chemistry, physics, and a fourth year of science if available. Nursing majors should complete additional credits in mathematics and science. Most students at UA begin their college careers in University College, where they enroll in courses to meet the General Education requirements and courses which are prerequisite to their majors. Students are admitted unconditionally to University College or to the Community and Technical College if their credentials are below the requirements for direct admission. All undecided students are admitted to the University College. Students will be considered for conditional admissions if they have less than a 2.3 grade point average or lower than a 16 ACT/650 SAT score, or if they are deficient in completing the core curriculum. Students who are admitted to UA with conditions will participate in the P.L.U.S. (Prescribed Learning for Undergraduate Success) program which will aid in making a positive transition to college while addressing any academic deficiencies. To be admitted directly to a specific academic program, students must exemplify outstanding college preparation through completion of the core curriculum. Other criteria which are considered include high shcool grade point average, test scores, and class rank. After an initial meeting with a professionsl academic adviser, students will be advised by a faculty member in their college. A $25 application fee is required.

Costs Per Year: $3,192.32 tuition; $7,954.82 out-of-state; $4,062 room and board.

Collegiate Environment: The campus in Akron, just south of the Ohio Turnpike, is a short traveling distance from Interstates 71, 76,

77, and 271. A complex of 76 modern buildings is situated on a 170-acre campus centrally located in the city, but set apart from the downtown area. The university strives for a symbiotic relationship with the urban community for its own vitality as a responsible social institution. Residence halls accommodate 945 men and 915 women. The Bierce Library holdings include 1,114,010 volumes and numerous periodicals, microforms and audiovisual materials. A Performing Arts Center containing Guzzeta Hall and the world-famous E.J. Thomas Performing Arts Hall provide a cultural link between the university and the community. The Institute for Polymer Science is known throughout the world and the Center for Urban Studies serves local, regional, and state needs in meeting urban problems. In support of viable academic programs, the university offers a Learning Resources Center, a Computer Assisted Instruction Program, Developmental Programs, a Computer Center, an American History Research Center, a Center for Peace, a Center for Urban Studies, a Center for International Studies, a Center for Afro-American Studies, a Black Cultural Center, an Educational Research and Development Center, a Center for Economic Education, a Speech and Hearing Center, an Institute for Lifespan Development and Gerontology, and an Institute for Civic Education. A center for Information Services operates the Informational Retrieval Project of the Division of Rubber Chemistry, American Chemical Society. University athletic facilities include a 35,000-seat Rubber Bowl with an AstroTurf gridiron. A privately endowed Ecumenical Campus Ministry is located within the university campus district for the convenience of students and the community. Financial aid is available.

Community Environment: The city is a merchandising center and a vital distribution gateway between the industrial East and the Midwest. The Portage Lakes district south of the city provides facilities for boating, swimming, fishing and ice skating. A number of parks provide additional facilities for skiing and other outdoor activities. A short distance to the north, are the New Gateway Complex, Jacobs Field -- home of the Cleveland Indians, Gund Arena, of the Cleveland Cavaliers, and the Rock 'n Roll Hall of Fame. To the South are Thurman Munson Stadium and The Pro-Football Hall of Fame. Local points of interest are the Akron Art Museum, Blossom Music Center, Goodyear Aircraft Hanger, Perkins Mansion and the Stan Hywet Hall. Special events are the American Golf Classic and the World Series of Golf, both held at the Firestone Country Club, and the All-American Soap Box Derby.

UNIVERSITY OF AKRON - WAYNE COLLEGE   *(G-10)*
1901 Smucker Road
Orrville, Ohio 44667-9758
Tel: (216) 683-2010; (800) 221-8308; Admissions: (216) 684-8900; Fax: (216) 684-8989

Description: Wayne College is the regional campus of The University of Akron. Opened in 1972, Wayne College is fully accredited by the North Central Association of Colleges and Schools and is authorized by the state of Ohio through the Ohio State Board of Regents to offer general education courses, including baccalaureate preparation, which can lead to the Associate of Arts or Associate of Science degree, and technical education programs, resulting in the Associate of Applied Business, Associate of Applied Science, or Associate of Technical Studies degree. Specific majors include business management technology, environmental health and safety technology, microprocessor service technology, office administration, and social services technology. Day, evening, and weekend courses are offered on a semester calendar, and during two summer terms. Wayne College enrolls a total of 1,639 students and employs 150 full- and part-time faculty members.

Entrance Requirements: Graduation from an accredited high school. Unconditional/conditional admission policy for students enrolling within two years of high school graduation, beginning spring semester 1994. Unconditional admission requires minimum high school grade point average, test scores, class rank, and completion of a college preparatory program to include: 4 units of English, 3 units of mathematics, 3 units of natural science, 3 units of social science, and 2 units of foreign language. Additional units in some areas may be necessary depending on major. Conditional admission will require one or more prescriptive activities. Open enrollment for Ohio residents; early decision, rolling admission, early admission, delayed admission, and advanced placement plans available; $25 application fee.

Costs Per Year: $2,830.84 state-resident tuition; $7,342 out-of-state tuition; $84.78 general fee; $500.00 average additional expenses, including books.

Collegiate Environment: Located in the heart of Wayne County, Wayne College sits on a 163-acre site in the northeast corner of Orrville. Instructional and administrative activities are housed in a single modern facility. There are no dormitories on campus. The college library contains 20,000 volumes, 400 current periodicals, and numerous vertical files. The library is also a part of the OhioLINK university and research libraries computer network. The campus includes an arboretum, nature trails, and a marshlands area. Wayne College is a smoke-free facility. Financial assistance is available to qualifies applicants. Veterans assistance is available.

Community Environment: Orrville is a thriving community with a diversified business and industry base, best known for being the home of The J. M. Smucker Company. Located 30 miles southwest of Akron and The University of Akron campus, and 50 miles south of Cleveland, the city of Orrville has a population of 7,800. Residents of this area have relatively easy access to metropolitan amenities while maintaining a more relaxed suburban atmosphere. The community park provides many recreational facilities and the Rehm Performing Arts Pavilion is the setting for many musical and cultural events. There are also 26 churches of various denominations, a community library, and a 38 bed hospital.

UNIVERSITY OF CINCINNATI   *(N-2)*
Clifton Avenue
Cincinnati, Ohio 45221
Tel: (513) 556-6000; (800) 827-8728; Admissions: (513) 556-1100;
Fax: (513) 556-1105

Description: The coeducational university is a state institution, accredited by the North Central Association of Colleges and Schools and by respective professional organizations. The university grants Associate, Baccalaureate, Master, Doctoral, and Specialist degrees within its many colleges and divisions. The university operates on the quarter calendar and the normal undergraduate program is designed to be completed in four academic years. Three summer sessions are offered. Army and Air Force ROTC training is offered. Cooperative education programs are available in many areas. Study abroad is also available. Undergraduate enrollment at the main campus (Baccalaureate Colleges) includes 5,808 men and 5,355 women full-time and 1,117 men and 951 women. There are 5,242 graduate students. A fauclty of 967 gives a faculty-student ratio of 1-19.

Entrance Requirements: High School graduation with rank in upper half of graduating class; completion of 16 units, 4 English, 3 mathematics, 2 foreign language, 2 sci., 2 soc. sci.; SAT or ACT required; GRE required for graduate studies; application fee $30; rolling admission and advanced placement plans available.

Costs Per Year: $3,732 state-resident tuition; $9,405 out-of-state tuition; $4,698 board and room; $498 student fees; additional expenses for books average $480.

Collegiate Environment: The university library system contains 1,900,000 volumes, 19,650 periodicals, and 2,600,000 microforms. It ranks as one of the major research libraries of the country. Living accommodations are available for about 2,748 students. Approximately 85% of first-time freshman applicants meet the requirements and are accepted. 65% of students receive some form of financial aid.

Community Environment: Called by Longfellow, "The Queen City of the West," Cincinnati was founded in 1788 and was named Losantiville. The following year the name was changed to Cincinnati, after the Society of Cincinnati. The city is the third largest in Ohio and is situated on a series of plateaus above the Ohio River surrounded by hills. The altitude varies from 435 to 938 feet. Some of the industries located here are Proctor & Gamble Co., General Electric Co., Ford Motor Co., and the Kroger Co. The Cincinnati Convention-Exposition Center provides facilities for meetings as well as 95,000 square feet of exhibition space. Cultural facilities include the Cincinnati Symphony Orchestra, Art Academy of Cincinnati, and the University of Cincinnati College Conservatory of Music; Cincinnati is famous as a center of music and art. Recreational facilities are numerous. Among the points of interest are the Carew Tower Observatory, Cincinnati Art Museum, Cincinnati Museum of Natural History, King's Island which is a recreational facility, Hebrew Union College

Museum, Mount Airy Forest, St. Peter in Chains Cathedral, Stowe House, and Taft Museum.

Branch Campuses: Clermont College, College Drive, Batavia, OH 45103; Raymond Walters College, 9555 Plainfield Road, Cincinnati, OH 45236

UNIVERSITY OF CINCINNATI - CLERMONT COLLEGE
(N-3)
College Drive
Batavia, Ohio 45103
Tel: (513) 732-5200; Fax: (513) 732-5303

Description: Clermont General and Technical College is a two-year, associate degree granting college of the University of Cincinnati, founded in 1972. It is fully accredited by the North Central Association of Colleges and Schools and operates under the authority of the Ohio Board of Regents. The college offers degree programs in both transfer and technical curricula. The college operates on a quarter system and offers a 10-week summer session, featuring two 5-week half quarters and a full 10-week calendar. Enrollment includes 925 full-time and 993 part-time students. A faculty of 31 full-time and 107 part-time gives a faculty-student ratio of 1-14.

Entrance Requirements: As an open-access institution, Clermont College will accept any graduate of an accredited high school or preparatory school or by presenting General Educational Developmental Test scores that meet the standards established for the High School Equivalency Certificate by the State of Ohio; rolling admission plan is available; credit by examination; advanced placement program; SAT or ACT recommended for matriculating students under 21 years of age; open enrollment; midyear admission, rolling admission and advanced placement plans available; non-high school graduates may attend as nonmatriculants.

Costs Per Year: $2,961 state resident; $7,245 out-of-state; $80 student fees.

Collegiate Environment: Located on 67-acre site, the Clermont College campus incorporates both instructional and administrative activities under one roof. The College Library has 20,849 titles, 182 periodicals, 11,034 microforms and 767 audio-visual materials. No college housing is available. Financial Aid is available to those students demonstrating need. Priority deadline for financial aid is March 1. Counseling Services and Developmental Programs are available to all students. A number of student groups and activities provide a collegial balance. The college is located approximately 25 miles from the parent institution, the University of Cincinnati.

Community Environment: Batavia, the Clermont County seat, is central to the entire county. Clermont County is recognized as the fastest growing county in Ohio. The completion of the Interstate Highway System and belt-freeway have made the Cincinnati metropolitan and Northern Kentucky areas easily accessible.

UNIVERSITY OF CINCINNATI - RAYMOND WALTERS COLLEGE   *(N-2)*
9555 Plainfield Road
Cincinnati, Ohio 45236
Tel: (513) 745-5600; Admissions: (513) 745-5700; Fax: (513) 745-5768

Description: The college is a 2-year campus of the University of Cincinnati, founded in 1967, that offers career, transfer, and general education programs. It is accredited by the North Central Association of Colleges and Schools and the National League for Nursing. The quarter system is employed and three summer sessions are offered. Army and Air Force ROTC are available. Cooperative Education Programs are available in Office Administration, Computer Programming and Computer Support Services. Enrollment includes 2,179 full-time and 1,800 part-time students. A faculty of 108 full-time and 152 part-time gives a faculty-student ratio of 1-20.

Entrance Requirements: Open enrollment policy; high school graduation or equivalent; non-high school graduates may be considered; $25 application fee; ACT or SAT suggested and entrance exam required; early admission, early decision, rolling admission, and advanced placement plans available.

Costs Per Year: $3,372 Ohio resident tuition; $7,533 out-of-state tuition; $80 student fees.

Collegiate Environment: The college is located in Blue Ash, a suburb of Cincinnati. There are no dormitories provided on campus. Students can use the university library as well as all of the other facilities offered. The college library contains 50,000 volumes, 400 periodicals, 1,500 microforms, and 2,500 audiovisual materials. All of the applicants are accepted, including midyear students. About 50% of the previous freshman class returned for the second year of studies. Scholarships are available and 33% of the students receive some form of financial aid.

Community Environment: See University of Cincinnati.

UNIVERSITY OF DAYTON   *(K-3)*
300 College Park
Dayton, Ohio 45469-1630
Tel: (513) 229-4411; (800) 837-7433; Admissions: (513) 299-3717;
Fax: (513) 229-4545

Description: This private, coeducational Catholic university was founded more than a century ago by the Catholic teaching order, the Marianists, whose educational philosophy is to encourage and challenge each student while recognizing one's talent and developing one's potential. The university is accredited by the North Central Association of Colleges and Schools and by several professional accrediting institutions. Components of the university structure include the College of Arts and Sciences, the School of Business Administration, the School of Education, the School of Engineering, and the Division of Engineering Technology. The university grants the Bachelors, Masters, Doctoral, and first professional degrees upon completion of programs of study. Army ROTC training is available. Air Force ROTC is available through Wright State University. The university is a member the Dayton-Miami Valley Consortium. It operates on the trimester systema and offers two summer terms. Enrollment includes 5,840 full-time and 595 part-time undergraduates and 3,315 graduate and 450 graduate Law students. A faculty of 419 full-time and 394 part-time gives a faculty-student ratio of 1-14.

Entrance Requirements: High school graduation or equivalent; completion of 4 units of English, 3 mathematics, 2 social science, 2 science, 2 years of a single foreign language; SAT or ACT required; GRE required for graduate programs; early admission, delayed admission, midyear admission, rolling admission and advanced placement plans available; nonrefundable application fee $25.

Costs Per Year: $11,380 tuition; $4,220 board and room; $535 student fees.

Collegiate Environment: The residential campus is located on a 110-acre hilltop at the southern edge of Dayton. Resources of the university include advanced reearch facilities. The Roesch Library is the university's main library and contains over 1.1 million bound volumes, pamphlets, and 4,900 periodicals. Other qualities include small class sizes, undergraduate emphasis, and student-centered faculty and staff. Total housing capacity is 5,045 students. The Chapel of the Immaculate Conception is the focal point of religious life on the campus. 85% of students applying for admission are accepted, including midyear students. The average scores of the entering freshman class were SAT 502 verbal, 576 math, ACT 25 composite. Over 3,000 scholarships, including 100 athletic were offered in 1994. 85% of students receive financial aid. Campus life includes NCAA Division I intercollegiate athletics.

Community Environment: See Wright State University.

UNIVERSITY OF FINDLAY   *(F-5)*
1000 North Main Street
Findlay, Ohio 45840
Tel: (419) 424-4540; (800) 548-0932; Fax: (419) 424-4822

Description: The liberl arts university is affiliated with the Churches of God General Conference and was founded in 1882. It is accredited by the North Central Association of Colleges and Schools. The semester is used and three summer terms are offered. The college confers the Bachelor of Arts degree. Army and Air Force ROTC programs are available on a cooperative basis with B.G.S.U. Enrollment is 2,020 full-time and 1,652 part-time students. A faculty of 117 and 127 part-time gives a faculty-student ratio of 1:15

Entrance Requirements: Accredited high school graduation with rank in upper half of graduating class; completion of 17 units including 4 English, 3 mathematics, 2-3 science; and 3 social science, mini-

mum SAT score of 390V and 400M or composite ACT of 18 recommended; early admission, rolling admission, delayed admission, and advanced placement plans available; no application fee.

Costs Per Year: $12,500 tuition; $5,210 room and board; $72 student fees; $800 average additional expenses.

Collegiate Environment: The college is located in northwestern Ohio, within 150 miles of Dayton, Columbus, and Detroit. The campus has academic, social, and residence facilities, including 2 farms. Fraternities and sororities maintain houses that accommodate 63 students. The library system contains 120,000 volumes and 750 monthly periodicals. Approximately 84% of students applying for admission are accepted, including midyear students. Financial aid is available and 85% of the students receive some form of assistance.

Community Environment: Findlay is located in the northwestern part of Ohio, which is both a rich agricultural and manufacturing region. Excellent internship and employment opportunities are available. Recreational activities include swimming, golf, boating, and fishing.

UNIVERSITY OF RIO GRANDE   *(O-8)*
Rio Grande, Ohio 45674
Tel: (614) 245-5351; (800) 288-2746; Admissions: (614) 245-7208;
Fax: (614) 245-7260

Description: The University of Rio Grande is a two- and four-year independent college that offers a wide range of programs and degrees. It is accredited by the North Central Association of Colleges and Schools and the National League for Nursing. Enrollment is 1,820 full-time and 340 part-time undergraduates and 113 graduate students and 60 evening students. A faculty of 90 full-time and 36 part-time gives an overall faculty-student ratio of 1-18. The college awards the Associate and the Bachelor degrees. The quarter system is used and two summer terms are offered. An Army ROTC program is available.

Entrance Requirements: Open enrollment policy; high school graduation with completion of 17 units including 4 English, 2 mathematics, 3 science, and 4 social science; ACT required; students not meeting all requirements may be admitted as special students for up to 12 credit hours; early admission, rolling admission, midyear admission, and advanced placement plans available; $15 application fee.

Costs Per Year: $2,256 county-resident tuition; $2,592 state-resident; $6,552 out-of-state; $4,068 room and board; $225 institutional fees; $600 average additional expenses.

Collegiate Environment: The 170-acre campus has 19 buildings. Davis Library is a modern air-conditioned structure which opened in the fall of 1965 and now contains 72,500 volumes, 4,000 pamphlets, 600 periodicals, 11,000 microforms and 1,200 recordings. The Paul R. Lyne Physical Education Center includes an Olympic-size swimming pool, two full-size basketball courts, a gymnastic area, wrestling rooms, handball court, badminton and volleyball areas, and seminar rooms. There are dormitories for 655 students. Approximately 95% of students applying for admission meet the requirements and are accepted, including midyear students. Scholarships are available and 82% of students receive financial aid.

Community Environment: A rural community, Rio Grande is located 90 miles southeast of Columbus and 90 miles north of Charleston, W.Va. Civic and service organizations and church groups are very active. Shopping facilities are available; Holzer Medical Center and Holzer Clinic are nearby. Opportunities are good for part-time employment. Recreational activities are golf, tennis, basketball, swimming, hiking, and skiing.

UNIVERSITY OF TOLEDO   *(D-5)*
2081 W. Bancroft
Toledo, Ohio 43606-3398
Tel: (419) 537-2696; Fax: (419) 537-4504

Description: This state-supported university has a full-time enrollment of 15,972 and a part-time enrollment of 7,135. A faculty of 1,377 gives a faculty-student ratio of approximately 1-19. An additional 3,379 students are enrolled in graduate programs. The university is accredited by the North Central Association of Colleges and Schools and by respective professional and educational organizations. The university has eight colleges that confer degrees: Arts and Sciences, Business Administration, Education, Engineering, Law, Pharmacy, University College, and the University Community and Technical College, which offers two-year Associate degrees. Through the Graduate School, programs leading to the Master's degree are offered by the Colleges of Arts and Sciences, Business Administration, Education, Pharmacy, and Engineering. Doctoral programs are offered in varied fields. The university operates on the quarter system and offers 3 summer terms. Army ROTC is available on campus and Air Force ROTC is available with Bowling Green State University. Cooperative education programs are available in all majors. Qualified students in Chemistry and Biology may study abroad in Salford, England.

Entrance Requirements: Open enrollment for state residents; high school graduation or equivalent; completion of 12-16 units, depending on course of study, including a minimum 4 English, 3 mathematics, 2 foreign language (College of Arts and Sciences), 3 science, and 3 social science; SAT or ACT required (ACT required for scholarships); GRE required for graduate school; non-resident students should have SAT composite score of 900 or ACT composite 21; early decision, rolling admission, and advanced placement plans available; $30 application fee.

Costs Per Year: $3,398 state-resident tuition; $8,146 nonresident; $3,718 average room and board; $700 average additional expenses.

Collegiate Environment: The university encompasses 487 acres on five campuses throughout the city of Toledo. The main campus has 57 buildings. An area known as Scott Park is the site of the University's Community and Technical College campus. During recent years the university has experienced rapid growth in its enrollment and facilities. Facilities recently completed include a $17 million Student Recreation Center, on-campus Greek Housing, which houses sixteen of the fraternities and sororities, and major renovations to UT's football stadium, the Glass Bowl. Major additions to the campus include a $10 million classroom and office building for the College of Engineering, a $10 million Center for the Visual Arts building on the grounds of the world-renowned Toledo Museum of Art, and an Honors Academic Centre/housing complex. UT's Carlson Library contains 1,525,595 million volumes, 7,698 periodicals, and 1,446,240 million audiovisual materials and microfilms. Residence halls provide living accommodations for 730 men and 1,002 women. Nearly 2,700 students live within convenient walking distance from Bancroft (main) campus. Approximately 95% of the applicants meet the requirements and are accepted, including midyear students. UT annually awards more than 350 freshman scholarships that range in value from $100 to $5,000 per year. Full, four-year scholarships covering all costs of tuition, fees, room, and board are offered to National Merit, National Achievement, and National Hispanic Finalists. Each year four entering freshmen are selected as Presidential Scholars. The Presidential Scholarship covers all costs of tuition, fees, room, board, and books for four years of undergraduate study at UT. 50% of students receive financial aid.

Community Environment: Toledo's importance as a port stems from its location at the mouth of the Maumee River. It is the busiest freshwater port in the world. It ranks second on the Great Lakes, and ninth in the nation in tonnage handled.

URBANA UNIVERSITY   *(J-4)*
579 College Way
Urbana, Ohio 43078
Tel: (513) 484-1356; Fax: (513) 484-1322

Description: Founded in 1850, the liberal arts college has progressed from the junior college ranks to become a four-year degree granting institution of higher learning. The university is accredited by the North Central Association of Colleges and Schools and other professional accrediting institutions. It operates on the semester system and offers two summer sessions. Enrollment is 776 full-time and 224 part-time students. A faculty of 36 full-time and 39 part-time gives a faculty-student ratio of 1-16. Air Force ROTC is available through cross-registration with Wright State University.

Entrance Requirements: High school graduation or equivalent; including 4 English, 2 mathematics, 2 science, 2 social studies; ACT or SAT required; rolling admission, early admission, early decision, and midyear admission plans available. $15 application fee.

Costs Per Year: $8,976 comprehensive tuition fee; $4,350 room and board; $508 student fees including health insurance.

Collegiate Environment: Urbana College was founded by Colonel John James and other followers of Emanuel Swedenborg, the Swedish philosopher-scientist-theologian. Degrees offered include the Bachelor of Science, Bachelor of Arts, and Associate of Arts in business, social science and liberal studies. The primary academic areas are Humanities, Science, Business, Social Service, and Education. Self-designed majors, independent study, and off-campus field experiences present a variety of options for students. The campus lies in the southwest corner of Urbana and combines the charm of the past with the freshness of the present. The library contains over 70,676 volumes. Residence halls accommodate 265 students. A number of scholarships are awarded annually by the Scholarship and Financial Aid Committee. 84% of students applying for admission meet the requirements and are accepted. 95% of students receive financial aid.

Community Environment: Urbana is the county seat of Champaign county and has a population in excess of 12,000 residents. The community has become well known regionally for the restoration of the historic downtown business district. The Urbana community provides a modern small-town environment with easy access to major metropolitan areas. Urbana is located just 15 minutes from downtown Springfield and 45 minutes from Dayton and Columbus.

Branch Campuses: Classes are taught at three off-campus site locations in Bellefontaine, Columbus and Dayton. The Columbus and Dayton programs offer bachelor's degrees in business administration whereas the Bellefontaine site offers a community education program.

URSULINE COLLEGE   *(B-11)*
2550 Lander Rd.
Pepper Pike, Ohio 44124
Tel: (216) 449-4200

Description: Ursuline College was founded in 1871 by the Ursuline Nuns of Cleveland and was the first chartered women's college in Ohio. Enrollment is 616 full-time and 732 part-time students. The college has a faculty of 141. The college is accredited by the National League for Nursing, the National League for Nursing Council of Baccalaureate and Higher Degree Programs, the North Central Association of Colleges and Schools, the State of Ohio Board of Nursing Education and Nurse Registration, and the State of Ohio Department of Education. Ursuline operates on the semester system and also offers courses during the summer.

Entrance Requirements: High school graduation or equivalent; completion of 15 units including 4 English, 2 mathematics, 2 foreign language, 2 science, and 2 history; SAT or ACT required; non-high school graduates considered; advanced placement, early decision, rolling admission, delayed admission plans available; $15 application fee.

Costs Per Year: Tuition $7,632; room and board (double occupancy) $4,960.

Collegiate Environment: The college is one-half hour driving time from downtown Cleveland. The Pepper Pike campus of 115 acres has nine buildings: the Mullen Academic Building, Dauby Science Center, the Florence O'Donnell Wasmer Art Gallery, the Fritzsche Center, the Ralph M. Besse Library, the Matthew J. O'Brien Campus Center, the St. Mark Center, Gladys Murphy Residence Hall and Grace Residence Hall. Approximately 82% of students applying for admission meet the requirements and are accepted. Freshman students are admitted in September and January, and the college welcomes a geographically diverse student body. Financial assistance is available.

Community Environment: See Case Western Reserve University.

WALSH UNIVERSITY   *(G-12)*
2020 Easton St. N.W.
North Canton, Ohio 44720
Tel: (216) 499-7090; (800) 362-9846; Fax: (216) 490-7165

Description: This Catholic college was granted affiliation as a four-year college by the Catholic University of America in the 1960-61 school year. It is a member of the Ohio College Association and is accredited by the North Central Association of Colleges and Schools. Special objectives of the liberal arts institute are to prepare elementary and secondary school teachers, nurses and business personnel; candidates for medical, dental, and law schools; and students for graduate schools. At its origin, the school was a commuter college for men. It became coeducational in the summer of 1966. The university operates on the semester system and offers three summer sessions. Enrollment is 822 full-time and 728 part-time undergraduate students. There are

242 graduate students. A faculty of 72 full-time and 55 part-time gives an overall faculty-student ratio of approximately 1-23.

Entrance Requirements: High school graduation or equivalent; rank in upper half of graduating class; completion of 16 units including 4 English, 3 mathematics, 3 science, 2 foreign language, 1 fine or performing art, and 3 social science; SAT or ACT required; early admission, advanced placement, early decision, rolling admission, and midyear admission plans available; $15 application fee.

Costs Per Year: $9,392.50 ($289/cr) undergraduate tuition; $4,100 room; $325 ($10/cr) student fees; $203 per credit graduate tuition.

Collegiate Environment: The site of the college is a 58-acre piece of land that offers excellent possibilities for future development. There are 8 buildings including the library, which contains 110,000 volumes, 620 periodicals, 2,782 microforms, and 578 recordings. Dormitories accommodate 350 students. Approximately 81% of students applying for admission meet the requirements and are accepted. Students are admitted at midyear as well as in September. The college welcomes a geographically diverse student body. Scholarships are available to students with a 3.0 GPA and higher, and 95% of the students receive financial assistance.

Community Environment: Situated in northeastern Ohio, 56 miles southeast of Cleveland, Canton is an industrial city. The city was the home of President McKinley. Products of industry are brick, roller bearings, housewares, rubber gloves, alloy and electric furnace steel, Hoover vacuum cleaners, bank vaults, and papier mache products. All forms of commercial transportation are available. Community facilities include a good library, art museum, churches, YMCA, YWCA, a little theater, a symphony orchestra, other cultural groups, and excellent hospitals. Canton's park system extends five miles along West Creek. Canton is the home the National Pro Football Hall of Fame.

WILBERFORCE UNIVERSITY   (L-4)
Wilberforce, Ohio 45384
Tel: (513) 376-2911; (800) 367-8568; Admissions: (513) 376-7321; Fax: (513) 376-2627

Description: Founded in 1856, the university has been under the auspices of the African Methodist Episcopal Church since 1863. It is a liberal arts college and is accredited by the North Central Association of Colleges and Schools. Students of all races, creeds, and national origins are welcome. Wilberforce is the only predominantly black 4-year college with a mandatory cooperative education program. Two successful work semesters are required for graduation. The school has Dual Degree Programs in Engineering and Computer Science with the University of Dayton. Air Force and Army ROTC programs are available. The university opreates on the semester system. Enrollment includes 856 students. A faculty of 55 full-time and 16 part-time gives a faculty-student ratio of 1-12.

Entrance Requirements: High school graduation with rank in upper two-thirds of graduating class; 2.0 GPA; completion of 12-15 units including 4 English, 2-3 mathematics; 2-3 social studies, 2-3 science; ACT or SAT required; early decision plan and midyear admission plans available; $20 application fee.

Costs Per Year: $6,670 tuition; $3,720 room and board, $340 fees.

Collegiate Environment: The 125-acre campus is in rural, Southern Ohio. Activities and student associations are shared by Antioch College, Cedarville College, Wilmington College, Sinclair Community College, Central State and Wright State Universities as well as the University of Dayton. There are dormitory facilities for 705 men and women, as well as a 24-unit apartment complex fraternity and sorority houses which accommodate an additional 76 students. The Learning Resources Center contains a library of 60,000 volumes, 240 reading stations, workshops and classrooms, four learning laboratories and an educational materials area. Financial aid is available and 95% of students receive some form of assistance. Approximately 90% of students applying for admission meet the requirements and are accepted. 60% of the previous freshman class returned to this campus for their sophomore year. Approximately 15% of last year's senior class continued on to graduate school.

Community Environment: Located in rural village of Wilberforce with a history of significant activity in the underground railroad of pre-Civil War days. The city of Xenia, Ohio is nearby with a population of 25,000 and is a good shopping center. It provides a resource

for field study, cultural and recreational activities plus the close urban centers of Dayton, Springfield, Columbus and Cincinnati.

WILMINGTON COLLEGE   (G-4)
College Street
Wilmington, Ohio 45177
Tel: (513) 382-6661; (800) 341-9318

Description: The four-year liberal arts college was founded in 1870 by the Religious Society of Friends, and awards the Bachelor of Arts and Bachelor of Science degrees. It is accredited by the North Central Association of Colleges and Schools. It operates on the early semester system and offers one summer session. An academic cooperative plan with the University of Chicago is available for social science students. Enrollment includes 874 full-time, 132 part-time, and 98 evening students. A faculty of 65 provides a factulty student ratio of 1-15.

Entrance Requirements: High school graduation or equivalent; completion of 16 units including 4 English, 2 mathematics, 2 science, 2 social science; SAT or ACT required; early decision, midyear admission, and rolling admission plans available. $15 application fee.

Costs Per Year: $10,230 tuition; $4,110 room and board; $180 student fees; additional expenses average $550.

Collegiate Environment: The campus has developed along simple and well-defined lines. The central mall is bounded on the north by the 35-bell carillon which rings class hours, and on the south by the gymnasium and playing fields. The library contains over 115,000 volumes, subscriptions, microforms and recordings. Residence buildings accommodate 261 men and 255 women students. Scholarships are available and 90% of the students receive financial aid. Thomas R. Kelly Religious Center is the religious life center for all faiths represented among students and faculty. Under the Junior Year Abroad Program students are encouraged to spend the junior year studying in another country. Credit earned in Vienna, Austria; Reims, France; and Cuernavaca, Mexico is readily transferable to Wilmington College.

Community Environment: In a rich agricultural area in southern Ohio, the town of Wilmington provides a friendly and safe environment with easy access to Cincinnati, Dayton, and Columbus. Wilmington's manufacturing plants produce steel drill bits, automobile parts, compression valves, and is the home of one of the oldest bridge companies in the world, and is a hub for Airborne Express. Job opportunities are good. A wildlife conservation farm nearby offers facilities for picnicking, trapshooting, and fishing. Lakes provide facilities for sailing and other water sports.

WINEBRENNER THEOLOGICAL SEMINARY   (F-5)
701 E. Melrose Ave.
P.O. Box 478
Findlay, Ohio 45839
Tel: (419) 422-4824; Fax: (419) 424-3433

Description: The seminary is a graduate professional school maintained by The Churches of God, General Conference. The school was opened in 1942. It is a member of the Association of Theological Schools and is accredited by the Commission on Institutions of Higher Education of the North Central Association of Colleges and Schools. In addition to granting Master degrees, the seminary offers a 3-year diploma program and an off-campus certificate program. Enrollment includes 36 full-time and 48 part-time students. A faculty of 6 full-time and 8 part-time gives a faculty-student ratio of 1-6. The semester system is used. The seminary sponsors a Summer Seminar for ministers and lay persons as well as a yearly continuing education lecture series for pastors.

Entrance Requirements: Bachelor of Arts Degree or equivalent from an approved college; high school graduation required for admission to diploma program; rolling admission plan available; $25 application fee.

Costs Per Year: $5,510 tuition; $24 student fees; $500 average additional expenses (books).

Collegiate Environment: The 15-acre campus has five buildings. The library contains 38,055 volumes and 158 periodicals. Over 50% of those who apply for admission are accepted. Dormitory facilities are eight 2-bedroom apartments. All students are eligible for financial assistance based on demonstrated need; about 35% of students receive financial aid.

Community Environment: See University of Findlay.

WITTENBERG UNIVERSITY *(K-4)*
P.O. Box 720
Springfield, Ohio 45501
Tel: (513) 327-6314; (800) 677-7558; Fax: (513) 327-6340

Description: The private liberal arts institute was founded in 1845. It is affiliated with the Evangelical Lutheran Church in America and is accredited by the North Central Association of Colleges and Schools and by respective professional and educational organizations. The university operates on the semester system and offers two summer sessions. Enrollment included 930 men and 1,181 women full-time and 37 men and 65 women part-time. A faculty of 155 full-time and 25 part-time gives a faculty-student ratio of 1-14. There are academic cooperative plans available with Case Western Reserve, Columbia, Georgia Institute of Technology, Washington University, Duke University as well as extensive overseas programs. There is a 30 hour community services requirement in sophomore year. Army and Air Force ROTC are available through the consortium of schools. The university offers extensive overseas programs.

Entrance Requirements: High school graduation completion of 16 units including 4 English, 3 math, 3 science, 3 social studies, 3 foreign language; SAT or ACT required; early admission, early decision, delayed admission, midyear admission, rolling admission and advanced placement plans available. $40 application fee.

Costs Per Year: $16,854 tuition; $4,536 board and room; $842 student fees; additional expenses average $1,000-$1,200.

Collegiate Environment: The university is located 45 miles west of Columbus. The beautiful campus of 71 acres has 31 buildings. The Thomas Library has a collection of over 350,000 volumes, 1,500 periodicals, 55,000 microforms and 40,000 audiovisual materials. There are 15 academic buildings, a chapel and 9 residence halls to accommodate 2,200 men and women. Fraternities and sororities house an additional 450 students. Apartments are available for 450 students. 85% of students applying for admission meet the requirements and are accepted. The university welcomes a geographically diverse student body. The average high school standing of the current freshman class, 66% in the top fifth; 26% in the second fifth; 8% in the third fifth. The average scores of the entering freshman class were SAT 526 verbal, 576 math, and ACT 24 composite. 1400 scholarships are offered, including 428 for freshmen. 65% of the students receive some form of financial aid. Nearly 87% of the previous freshman class returned to the campus for their second year. About 22% of last year's senior class continued on to graduate school, 75% at a later point in time.

Community Environment: Springfield is located 25 miles northeast of Dayton with all forms of commercial transportation available. Community facilities include churches and synagouges of all denominations, two hospitals, libraries, museum, a new $15 million Springfield Performing Arts Center, a symphony orchestra, and two theatre groups. Recreational activities include tennis and golf. Job opportunities are available.

WRIGHT STATE UNIVERSITY *(K-3)*
Colonel Glenn Highway
Dayton, Ohio 45435
Tel: (513) 873-2211; (800) 247-1770

Description: Wright State University, founded in 1964 and granted full university status in 1967, is a fully accredited, independent state university The university serves nearly 17,000 students in approximately 100 undergraduate programs and 38 graduate and professional degree programs. Enrollment includes 10,833 full-time and 5,990 part-time undergraduates, 3,995 graduate students, and 2,227 evening students. A faculty of 680 full-time and 320 part-time gives a faculty-student ratio of 1-20. Air Force and Army ROTC programs are available. Cooperative education programs are available in several areas. Exchange programs with universities in Japan, China, and Brazil are available during the summer quarter.

Entrance Requirements: Open enrollment policy; high school graduation or equivalent with completion of 16 units of academic studies to include 4 units of English, 3 mathematics (including algebra I and II), 3 social science (including 2 history), 3 natural science, 2 same foreign language, and 1 visual or performing arts; ACT or SAT re-

quired; nonmatriculating students may be admitted on part-time basis; early admission, delayed admission, rolling admission, and advanced placement plans available; $30 application fee.

Costs Per Year: $3,234 tuition; $6,468 out-of-state; $4,140 room and board.

Collegiate Environment: Most students commute from Dayton and surrounding communities, but about 2,000 live in one of the seven residential communities on or adjacent to the campus. The University Library offers extensive resources with over 520,429 bound volumes, 1,183,117 microforms, 306,625 government documents, and 4,103 periodical subscriptions. The library features one of the most extensive collections of Wright brothers' material and collections on local and regional history. 98% of applicants are accepted. The average scores of the freshman class were SAT 410 verbal, 452 math, ACT 20 composite. 345 scholarships are available. 50% of the students receive some form of financial aid.

Community Environment: Located in the Miami Valley at the junction of the Miami, Stillwater, and Mad Rivers in southwestern Ohio, Dayton is the state's fourth largest metropolitan area. Within a twenty-five mile radius, there is a population of over one million. The city lies fifty-four miles north of Cincinnati and seventy-two miles west of Columbus. Dayton International Airport, serviced by most major airlines, offers convenient access to almost any place in the Continental United States and abroad. The river corridor provides twenty-six scenic miles for walking, jogging, or cycling. Aullwood Gardens and Aullwood Farm, the Museum of Natural History, and Cox Arboretum present nature education activities. Dayton also supports the arts, including a philharmonic orchestra, a ballet company, several art galleries and museums, and theater events for adults and children. The Opera Association presents fine productions with top stars on the bill each year.

Branch Campuses: Lake Campus, Celina, OH.

XAVIER UNIVERSITY *(N-2)*
3800 Victory Parkway
Cincinnati, Ohio 45207-5311
Tel: (513) 745-3301; (800) 344-4698; Fax: (513) 745-4319

Description: The Catholic university of the Jesuit tradition was founded in 1831. It is accredited by the North Central Association of Colleges and Schools and numerous professional accrediting organizations. The university consists of the College of Arts and Sciences, the College of Business Administration, and the College of Social Sciences. The Center for Adult and Part-Time Students is available for students taking evening and weekend classes and nondegree students. The university operates on the semester system and offers two summer session. Undergraduate enrollment includes 2,873 full-time and 1,054 part-time students. Graduate enrollment is 2,253 students. A faculty of 437 provides an undergraduate faculty-student ratio of 1-16.

Entrance Requirements: Accredited high school graduation with rank in upper 50% of graduating class; completion of 4 units English, 2 mathematics, 2 foreign language, 2 science, and 2 social science; SAT or ACT required; rolling admission, early admission, advanced placement plans available; $25 nonrefundable application fee.

Costs Per Year: $12,270 tuition; $5,190 room and board.

Collegiate Environment: The main campus has 100 acres. University libraries contain 307,454 volumes and 1,557 periodicals. Housing is provided on campus for 1,400 men and women. The Department of Military Science is adequately equipped for the conduct of both field work and classroom instruction. The Army ROTC unit offers a wide variety of specialities. About 85% of students receive some form of financial assistance.

Community Environment: The University is located in a residential area of Cincinnati. See University of Cincinnati.

YOUNGSTOWN STATE UNIVERSITY *(F-14)*
410 Wick Avenue
Youngstown, Ohio 44555
Tel: (216) 742-3150; (800) 336-9978; Fax: (216) 742-1408

Description: Youngstown State University was founded in 1908 and was sponsored by the Young Men's Christian Association as the School of Law of the Youngstown Association School. Over the years the name was changed to the Youngstown Institute of Technology, Youngstown College, the Youngstown University and finally, in 1967, to Youngstown State University, marking its state affiliation. YSU offers complete curriculums in the liberal arts and in many technical and professional fields. The university, accredited by the North Central Association of Colleges and Schools, awards six Master degrees in 53 fields, nine Baccalaureate degrees in 111 fields, and four Associate degrees in 21 fields. YSU is a member of a consortium formed by three universities to operate the Northeastern Ohio Universities College of Medicine. It operates on the quarter system and offers two summer sessions. An academic cooperative plan with Duke University is available for forestry students. An Army ROTC program is offered under a cross-enrollment agreement with the University of Akron. Enrollment includes 9,646 full-time and 4,333 part-time students comprising 12,833 undergraduates and 1,146 graduate students. A faculty of 461 full-time and 426 part-time provides a faculty student ratio of 1-20.

Entrance Requirements: Open enrollment for Ohio residents; high school graduation rank in the upper 2/3 of graduating class for non-residentsor have an ACT composite score of 17 or higher; or have a combined SAT score of 700 or higher. Those who have been out of school for two or more years and who are not pursuing a restricted program are exempt from this requirement. GRE, MAT, or GMAT required for graduate school; non-high school graduates will be considered for admission with satisfactory GED scores; early admission, delayed admission, advanced placement and rolling admission plans available; $25 application fee.

Costs Per Year: $2,910 tuition; $5,430 out-of-state tuition; $3,750 board and room; $570 books & supplies; additional expenses average $1,665.

Collegiate Environment: 28 major buildings are in use on the campus. Many of its 28 major buildings have been constructed during the past 10 years; others have been renovated and enlarged. Campus improvement is a continuing project. The University currently operates 4 residence halls. Kilcawley House, located in the center of campus was opened in 1965 and recently refurbished. Students like its convenient location and its spacious study and recreational facilities. Lyden House, located on the north side of campus, opened in 1990. Students like its oversized rooms and the overall beauty of the facility. Wick and Weller Houses provide small group living on campus. These facilities are available to upperclass students only. The library contains 831,586 volumes, and 842,626 microforms. About 65% of the students receive some form of financial aid. Approximately 81% of the students applying for admission meet the requirements and are accepted, including midyear students. Of the current freshman class, 27% were in the top fifth of their class, 23% were in the second fifth, 22% in the third fifth, and 18% in the fourth fifth; average composite ACT score was 19.4%.

Community Environment: The Youngstown area is a vibrant community, rich in heritage, natural and man-made resources, industry and business, and skilled responsible citizens. It is successfully undergoing a change from basic steelmaking to many diversified industries and businesses. Youngstown is located in bustling Northeast Ohio, five miles from the Pennsylvania line, equidistant between New York and Chicago, and 65 miles from both Pittsburg and the Ohio River and the ports and beaches of Lake Erie. A network of interstate highways and Youngstown Airport have made it a major transportation center. Residents enjoy the areas lakes, fields, and forest, plus unusual 2,400-acre Mill Creek Park near the heart of the city. There are more than 350 churches, numerous fine teaching hospitals, a community playhouse, symphony orchestra, an outstanding public library system, excellent schools and many other cultural attractions, including the internationally famous Butler Institute of American Arts.

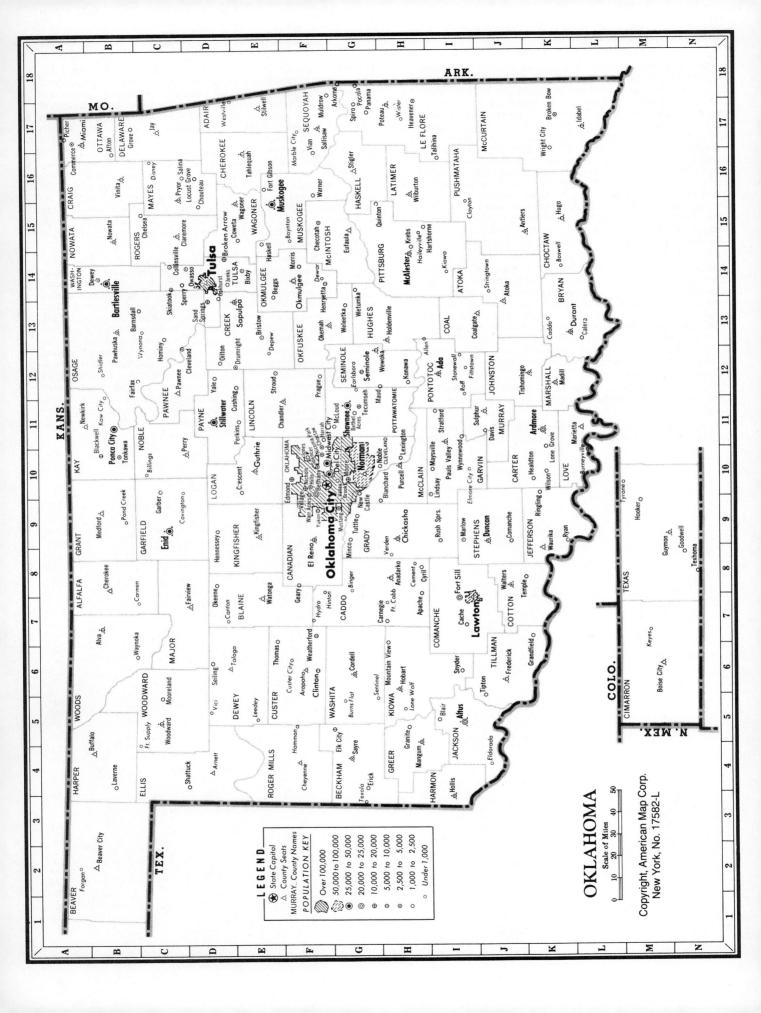

OKLAHOMA

Scale of Miles

0 10 20 30 40 50

Copyright, American Map Corp.
New York, No. 17582-L

LEGEND

State Capital
County Seats
MURRAY.. County Names
POPULATION KEY
Over 100,000
50,000 to 100,000
25,000 to 50,000
20,000 to 25,000
10,000 to 20,000
5,000 to 10,000
2,500 to 5,000
1,000 to 2,500
Under 1,000

OKLAHOMA

BACONE COLLEGE (E-15)
2299 Old Bacone Road
Muskogee, Oklahoma 74403
Tel: (918) 683-4581

Description: The private junior college was founded in 1880 and is the oldest institution of higher education in the State of Oklahoma. It is affiliated with the American Baptist Convention and is a nonprofit, nondenominational college for students of all racial, religious, and socio-economic backgrounds. Bacone serves both Indian and non-Indian students and is accredited by the North Central Association of Colleges and Secondary Schools. Enrollment includes 287 men and 372 women full-time and 16 men and 20 women part-time. The faculty has 22 full-time and 13 part-time members. The semester system is used and one summer session is offered. The college grants the Associate and the Associate in Nursing degrees.

Entrance Requirements: Open enrollment policy; high school graduation or over 19 years of age; ACT or SAT required; early decision, early admission, rolling admission, midyear admission; $10 application fee.

Costs Per Year: $2,520 tuition; $2,800 room and board; $16 student fees; additional expenses average $350.

Collegiate Environment: The college is located in the northeast section of Muskogee, Oklahoma, the hub of the oldest historical area in Oklahoma. Dormitory facilities accommodate 150 men and 200 women. The library contains 23,000 volumes, 205 periodicals, 390 microforms and 400 recordings. Most students applying for admission are accepted, including midyear students. Approximately 80% of the previous entering class returned to this campus for the second year of studies. The college offers 197 scholarships and 92% of the current student body receives financial aid.

Community Environment: Bacone is a suburban community reached by highway. The city consists of the campus of the college. One mile distant is Muskogee, a town of 60,000. All the cultural, recreational, and community services are located in Muskogee.

BARTLESVILLE WESLEYAN COLLEGE (B-14)
2201 Silver Lake Road
Bartlesville, Oklahoma 74006
Tel: (800) 468-6292; Fax: (918) 335-6229

Description: The private college is a result of the merging of Western Pilgrim College, El Monte, California, Central Pilgrim College, Bartlesville, Oklahoma, and Miltonvale Wesleyan College, Miltonvale, Kansas. It is fully accredited by the North Central Association of Colleges and Schools and is affiliated with the Wesleyan Church. Programs of study lead to the Associate and Bachelor degrees. The college operates on the semester system and offers two summer sessions. Enrollment includes 202 men and 302 women. A faculty of 35 full-time and 31 part-time gives a faculty-student ratio of 1-14.

Entrance Requirements: Open enrollment policy; graduation from an accredited high school or equivalent; ACT required; rolling admission; $25 application fee.

Costs Per Year: $7,000 tuition; $3,400 room and board.

Collegiate Environment: The 27-acre campus is located on a knoll overlooking the City of Bartlesville, 50 miles north of Tulsa. The 22 college buildings include a library of 125,000 volumes and 375 periodicals. There are living accommodations for 124 men and 138 women. The college welcomes a geographically diverse student body and will accept midyear students. 98% of all applicants are accepted. Of the 250 scholarships offered, 100 are for freshmen. About 88% of the students receive financial aid.

Community Environment: A major oil and gas-producing company is located in Bartlesville. The first oil well of commercial importance drilled in Oklahoma is in Johnstone Park, which adjoins the city limits. This area has a temperate climate and an average annual temperature of 59.9 degrees. Bartlesville, with a population of 40,000, has a public library, a museum, art center, YMCA, YWCA, many churches of major denominations, two hospitals, and almost 100 civic, fraternal and veteran's organizations. Local recreation includes two theaters, bowling, fishing, hunting, softball, golf, swimming, waterskiing, concerts, and Little Theatre Guild.

CAMERON UNIVERSITY (I-7)
2800 West Gore Boulevard
Lawton, Oklahoma 73505
Tel: (405) 581-2230; Fax: (405) 581-5514

Description: The state college began as a state school of agriculture in 1908. Junior college work was added in 1927 and the function of the college was changed to a four-year, degree-granting institution in 1966. The first Baccalaureate degrees were awarded in the spring of 1970. The college operates on the semester system and offers a summer session. Army ROTC programs are available. Enrollment includes 3,929 full-time and 2,008 part-time undergraduates and 333 graduate students. A faculty of 213 full-time and 14 part-time gives an undergraduate faculty-student ratio of 1-24. The school is fully accredited by the North Central Association of Colleges and Schools and by several professional accrediting institutions. It grants the Associate, Bachelor, and Masters degrees.

Entrance Requirements: Accredited high school graduation or equivalent; rank in upper 50% of graduating class; ACT required; non-high school graduates considered; rolling admission and advanced placement plans available; $15 application fee.

Costs Per Year: $1,691 tuition; $4,122 out-of-state; $2,300 board and room; $35 student fees.

Collegiate Environment: The college library contains 228,815 volumes, 2,021 periodicals, 122,104 microforms, and 5,125 audiovisual items. Dormitory facilities are provided for 300 men and 300 women. Semesters begin in August and January and the summer term begins in June. 97% of applicants are accepted. Financial aid is available and 60% of the current student body receives financial assistance. Of $120,000 available for scholarships, 25% is available for freshmen.

Community Environment: Lawton is a metropolitan area that enjoys a dry, temperate climate. The city is served by two airlines, two railroads for freight, bus service, and a turnpike. Community services include a public library, museum, churches of most denominations, two general and one public health hospital, major civic and fraternal organizations, and good shopping facilities. Part-time employment is available for students. Local recreational facilities include camping, water sports, theaters, and bowling.

CARL ALBERT STATE COLLEGE (H-13)
1507 S. McKenna
Poteau, Oklahoma 74953
Tel: (918) 647-1200; Admissions: (918) 647-1300; Fax: (918) 647-1269

Description: The public community college serves the citizens of LeFlore County and the surrounding areas. It was established in 1934 and offers a two-year program in liberal arts and general education. The college is accredited by the North Central Association of Colleges and Schools. It operates on the semester basis and also offers a summer term. Enrollment is 1,687 and a faculty of 83 provides a faculty-student ratio of 1-20.

Entrance Requirements: High school graduation or equivalent; ACT required; adult non-high school graduates, degree, may be admitted; early admission, early decision, rolling admission, midyear admission, and advanced placement plans available.

Costs Per Year: $1,034.10 state-resident tuition; $1,740 out-of-state tuition.

Collegiate Environment: Almost all students applying for admission are accepted, including midyear students. Semesters begin in September and January. The college library has a collection of 23,000 volumes, 260 periodicals, 8,090 microforms and 1,535 audiovisuals. Dormitory housing is available for 74 students.

Community Environment: Poteau is located in central eastern Oklahoma in the Cavanal Mountain area. This is the county seat and may be reached by bus lines. Nearby Ouachita National Forest offers excellent recreational facilities.

CONNORS STATE COLLEGE   *(F-16)*
Warner, Oklahoma 74469
Tel: (918) 463-2931; Admissions: (918) 463-6241; Fax: (918) 463-2233

Description: The public junior college was established in 1908 and is accredited by the North Central Association of Colleges and Schools. Recent enrollment was 550 men and 1,083 women full-time and 246 men and 538 women part-time. The faculty includes 55 full-time and 67 part-time giving a faculty-student ratio of 1-28. The semester system is used and one summer session is offered. The college grants the Associate degree, and Certificates.

Entrance Requirements: Open enrollment policy; ACT required with a minimum score of 19 on each section to qualify for higher level courses. Oklahoma non-high school graduates 21 years of age or older may be admitted with provisional status; rolling admission.

Costs Per Year: $1,050 tuition; $2,760 nonresident tuition; $2,054 room and board. $40 fees.

Collegiate Environment: The college is located 20 miles southeast of Muskogee and 70 miles from Tulsa, and includes 960 acres for agricultural purposes; 716 acres for preservation of wildlife habitat; a 35-acre campus; ten major buildings serving student needs; dormitory facilities for 150 men and 150 women, 11 faculty residences; three farm buildings; a modern water plant; a lake; and a library containing 60,000 volumes, 2,500 pamphlets, 180 periodicals, 750 microforms and 794 recordings. Approximately 100% of students applying for admission are accepted, including midyear students. Scholarships are available and 63% of the students receive some form of financial aid.

Community Environment: Warner is a rural community with mild winters and warm to hot summers. The area is provided transportation by bus lines, and U.S. Highways 64 and 266. There are several churches of various denominations, and civic and service clubs within the city. Recreational facilities within the area include theatres, restaurants, and nearby lakes. Within driving distance, there is the Five Civilized Tribes Museum.

EAST CENTRAL UNIVERSITY   *(I-12)*
Ada, Oklahoma 74820-6899
Tel: (405) 332-8000

Description: The state college was established in 1909 as one of three regional state normal schools founded that year in the eastern half of the state, which had been Indian Territory only two years before. It was authorized to increase its college programs to four years of education in 1919 and expanded its programs to include degree curricula in arts and sciences as well as education in 1939. Enrollment is 4,474 students. A faculty of 200 gives a faculty-student ratio of 1-25. The semester system is used and one summer session is offered. The college is accredited by the North Central Association of Colleges and Schools and grants the Certificate, Bachelor and Master degrees. Army ROTC is available as an elective.

Entrance Requirements: Accredited high school graduation or equivalent; ACT minimum 18 required; non-high school graduates may be admitted on a provisional basis; early decision, rolling admission and early admission plans are available.

Costs Per Year: $1,200 tuition; $3,210 nonresident; $1,988 room and books; $30 student fees; $250 books.

Collegiate Environment: The college owns 130 acres of land and is located in Ada, the geographic center of the East Central State College District. The college library contains over 203,301 volumes, 1,525 periodicals, 293,094 microforms and 5,274 audiovisual materials. Living accommodations are provided for 551 men, 526 women, and 95 families. 95% of the students applying for admission were accepted, including midyear students. The college awards 604 scholarships of which 210 are available for freshmen and 75% of the current student body receives financial aid. Approximately 25% of the senior class continued on to graduate school.

Community Environment: Ada is the site of large cement and glass factories and meat-packing plants, and a feed-milling machinery company. Oil and natural gas are produced in the area. The climate is temperate with mild winters. The average temperature is 64 degrees. Ada is served by freight lines, an airport, and three railroad lines. Community services include hospitals, several clinics, 30 churches, and many active civic and fraternal organizations. Local recreational facilities include parks, swimming pools, picnic areas, hiking, golf, fishing, hunting, waterskiing, and tennis. An annual county fair and rodeo is held.

EASTERN OKLAHOMA STATE COLLEGE   *(H-16)*
Wilburton, Oklahoma 74578
Tel: (918) 465-2361; Fax: (918) 465-2431

Description: Eastern Oklahoma State College operates on the semester basis and offers one summer session. Current enrollment is 2,290 students. A faculty of 55 full-time gives a faculty-student ratio of 1-40. The college is accredited by the North Central Association of Colleges and Schools and grants Certificates and the Associate degree.

Entrance Requirements: Open enrollment policy; ACT required; completion of 11 units required; rolling admission plan available; $25 application fee.

Costs Per Year: $945 tuition; $2,250 out-of-state; $2,000 room and board; $60 student fees.

Collegiate Environment: The college is located in the heart of the beautiful valley between the San Bois and Winding Stair Mountain Ranges. The 41 college buildings contain a library of 46,720 volumes; there are living accommodations for 347 students. 97% of the students applying for admission are accepted, including midyear students. Financial aid is available, and 80% of the students receive some form of aid. The school offers 436 scholarships.

Community Environment: Wilburton is a small community located in the San Bois Mountains. The area is served by commercial bus lines, U.S. Route 270 and State Highway 2. A small municipal airport is located here, but commercial airlines are approximately 30 miles distant. Good recreational facilities for outdoor sports include nearby Robber's Cave State Park, and Kiamichi National Forest. The nearest large cities are Muskogee and Fort Smith, Arkansas.

HILLSDALE FREE WILL BAPTIST COLLEGE   *(G-10)*
P.O. Box 7208
Moore, Oklahoma 73153-1208
Tel: (405) 794-6661

Description: Formerly Oklahoma Bible College, the private Christian college is authorized by the Oklahoma State Regents for Higher Education. It offers an Associate of Arts degree and a Bachelor of Arts degree in Theology. It was established in 1959 and is supported by the Free Will Baptist denomination. The college operates on the semester system and offers a fall and spring minimester and one summer session. Enrollment includes 142 full-time and 61 part-time students. A faculty of 14 full-time and 17 part-time gives a faculty-student ratio of 1-12.

Entrance Requirements: Open enrollment policy; high school graduation with recommended completion of 16 units including 4 English, 3 mathematics, 2 laboratory science, and 2 history; non-high school graduates may be admitted by test of ability to benefit; ACT required; early admission, early decision, rolling admission, delayed admission, midyear admission and advanced placement plans available; $20 application fee.

Costs Per Year: $3,150 tuition; $3,350 room and board; $340 student fees.

Collegiate Environment: Located on a 39-acre campus approximately three miles south of Moore, the college contains nine buildings, including the administration building with classroom areas; a library of 17,081 volumes, 163 periodicals, 109 microforms, and 400 audiovisual materials; administrative offices; a dining hall; a chapel; and dormitory facilities for 62 men, 60 women, and 32 married students. Approximately 90% of the students applying for admission are accepted. The school offers 32 scholarships including 25 for freshmen. 75% of the current student body receives financial aid.

Community Environment: Listed recently in the National Homebuilder's Magazine as the fastest growing city in the United States, Moore is a young town. Community transportation is provided by bus and rail. Will Rogers International Airport is 10 minutes away. The city has many churches, a library, and health facilities. Nearby Lake Draper offers water skiing and fishing. There are many businesses in town, and part-time employment is available for students.

LANGSTON UNIVERSITY   *(E-10)*
P.O. Box 728
Langston, Oklahoma 73050
Tel: (405) 466-2231; Admissions: (405) 466-3231; Fax: (405) 466-3381

Description: This coeducational state university was established as the Colored Agricultural and Normal University in 1897. Its present name was officially adopted in 1941 and since 1954, it has been open to qualified students of all races. The university is accredited by the North Central Association of Colleges and Schools as well as by several professional accrediting institutions. It grants the Associate, Bachelor and Master's degrees. The university operates on the semester system and offers one summer session. Enrollment includes 3,500 undergraduates (60% female, 40% male) full-time and 50 graduate students. A faculty of 100 full-time and 50 part-time gives a faculty-student ratio of 1-24.

Entrance Requirements: High school graduation or equivalent; completion of 16 units including 4 English, 3 mathematics, 2 science and 2 history; ACT required; non-high school graduates may be admitted on a provisional basis with satisfactory score on ACT; rolling admission and midyear admission plans.

Costs Per Year: Undergraduate: $1,252-$1,277 ($40.39-$41.20/cr) resident; $3,383-$3,632 ($109.14-$117.17/cr) nonresident; Graduate: $1,675 ($54.04/cr); $4,420 ($142.58/cr) nonresident; $899 ($29/cr) student fees; $1,290 room and board.

Collegiate Environment: The university is comprised of ten buildings located on a 40-acre campus. The library contains 238,000 volumes, 1,732 periodical titles, and 15,000 U.S. government documents. Living accommodations are provided for 458 men, 362 women, and 50 families. Four national social fraternities and four national sororities maintain chapters at the campus. The Melvin B. Tolson Black Heritage Center focuses on African history and on the Afro-American experience in the United States and in humanities and arts since 1900. The center houses approximately 15,000 volumes including books, audio visuals, rare collection on microfilm or microfiche, and more than 80 black newspapers and journals. The instructional program is augmented with a Class D, 10-watt raio station, a video taping studio, talk-back TV classroom and an Olympic-size indoor swimming pool. The unversity is acclaimed for its research projects in the soils, grains, and water of Oklamoma. The American Institute of Goat Research gives an added dimension to the cooperative research program. The university offers NAIA inter-collegiate competition for men in basketball, football and track and for women in basketball and track. The intramural-Recreational Sports Program provides opportunities for participation in basketball, football, soccer, softball, tennis, volleyball and swimming. Cocurricular activities are available through twenty-three departmental clubs, six national honor societies, one national service and four national social fraternities, four national social sororities, five musical organizations and six publications. The university welcomes a geographically diverse student body and will accept midyear students. All students applying for admission are accepted. 3 academic scholarships are available for first-time freshmen. Other financial aid is also available. Semesters begin in August and January and the summer term begins in June.

Community Environment: Langston is a small rural community located 40 miles northeast of Oklahoma City and 90 miles west of Tulsa, OK.

MID-AMERICA BIBLE COLLEGE   *(F-10)*
3500 S.W. 119th St.
Oklahoma City, Oklahoma 73170
Tel: (405) 691-3800; Fax: (405) 692-3165

Description: The privately supported, coeducational Bible college is an undergraduate institution of the Church of God, whose primary purpose is to provide courses of study as preparation for persons called to serve in various aspects of the work of the Church and especially the Christian ministry. It is accredited by the American Association of Bible Colleges and by the North Central Association of Colleges and Schools. The college operates on the semester system and offers two summer sessions. Enrollment includes 375 full-time and 74 part-time students. A faculty of 15 full-time and 21 part-time gives a faculty-student ratio of 1-24. The college grants the Associate and Bachelor degrees.

Entrance Requirements: High school graduation or equivalent; non-high school graduates may be admitted as special students; ACT or SAT required; early admission, early decision, midyear admission and advanced placement plans available; $25 application fee.

Costs Per Year: $3,900 tuition; $3,236 room and board; $250 student fees; $300 books.

Collegiate Environment: The campus consists of 65 acres in southwest Oklahoma City. There are six dormitories, student commons, library, student services, classroom buildings with chapel and business and administration buildings. Residence halls accomodate 260 students. The library holdings include 40,700 volumes and numerous microforms and additional materials. The college awards an average of 44 bachelor degrees each year. 86% of students receive some form of financial aid.

Community Environment: See Oklahoma City University.

MURRAY STATE COLLEGE   *(K-12)*
1100 S. Murray
Tishomingo, Oklahoma 73460
Tel: (405) 371-2371; Fax: (405) 371-9844

Description: The state junior college was established in 1908 and is under the control of the Board of Regents for Murray State College and under the supervision of the State Regents for Higher Education. It operates on the semester system and offers one summer session. Enrollment is 952 full-time and 715 part-time students. A faculty of 44 full-time and 32 part-time gives a faculty-student ratio of 1-22. The school is accredited by the North Central Association of Colleges and Schools, the American Veterinary Medical Association, and the National League for Nursing. The college grants the Associate degree.

Entrance Requirements: Open enrollment policy; ACT required; non-high school graduates admitted on a provisional basis with satisfactory scores on ACT or GED; early admission and rolling admission plans available.

Costs Per Year: $1,512 tuition; $2,028 out-of-state; $2,218 room and board; $180 student fees.

Collegiate Environment: The 30-acre campus is located at Tishomingo, Oklahoma, the county seat of Johnston County, and originally founded as the capital of the Chickasaw Nation. The campus is adjacent to Lake Texoma, one of the largest artificial lakes in the world. The 16 college buildings contain a library of 20,000 volumes, 250 periodicals, 25 microforms, and 2,500 recordings, and living accommodations for 150 men and 156 women. Students from other geographical locations are accepted as well as midyear students. Approximately 100% of students applying for admission are accepted. Financial aid is available for economically disadvantaged students.

Community Environment: Historically noted as the original capital of the Chickasaw Nation, Tishomingo is situated on the banks of Lake Texoma within a wildlife refuge. This is a rural area with a temperate climate. The city is served by five highways. Tishomingo has six churches, a hospital, and major civic, fraternal and veteran's organizations. Local recreational facilities include water sports, hunting, fishing, and hiking.

NORTHEASTERN OKLAHOMA AGRICULTURAL AND MECHANICAL JUNIOR COLLEGE   *(A-17)*
200 I Street NE
Miami, Oklahoma 74354
Tel: (918) 542-8441; (800) 234-4727; Fax: (918) 542-9759

Description: The state junior college began as the Miami School of Mines in 1919. It became a junior college in 1925 and was placed under the Board of Regents for Agricultural and Mechanical Colleges in 1943. It is fully accredited by the North Central Association of Colleges and Schools and grants the Associate degree. The college enrolls 2,805 students. A faculty of 125 gives a faculty-student ratio of 1-23. The college operates on the semester system and offers a summer term.

Entrance Requirements: Open enrollment policy; ACT required; non-high school graduates admitted on a probationary basis; rolling admission, delayed admission, and advanced placement plans available.

Costs Per Year: $1,085 ($35/cr) resident tuition; $2,852 ($92/cr) nonresident; $2,100 room and board; $14 student fees.

Collegiate Environment: The attractively landscaped main campus of the college covers approximately 70 acres. The 25 college buildings include living accommodations for 700 men, 500 women, and 52 families. The library contains 50,000 volumes, 4,000 periodicals, 4,000 microforms and 1,027 recordings. Students from other geographical locations are accepted as well as midyear students. Approximately 95% of students applying for admission are accepted. Of 800 scholarships offered, 600 are available for freshmen, and 60% of the current student body receives some form of financial aid.

Community Environment: Miami is headquarters for the Grand Lake recreation area. Items produced by the city's manufacturers include automotive parts, tires and tubes, clothing, food products and boats and accessories. Part-time employment is available. The climate is temperate. There are dormitories and housing units on campus. Good health services are available.

NORTHEASTERN STATE UNIVERSITY   *(E-16)*
Tahlequah, Oklahoma 74464
Tel: (918) 456-5511; (800) 722-9614; Fax: (918) 458-2193

Description: The state university had its beginning in 1846 when the Cherokee National Council passed an Act providing for the establishment of the National Male Seminary and the National Female Seminary. In 1909, the State Legislature of Oklahoma provided for the purchase of the Female Seminary and for the creation of a State Normal School. It later became a state teachers college and became a member institution of the Oklahoma State System of Higher Education in 1941. The university is accredited by the North Central Association of Colleges and Schools and grants the Bachelor and Master degree. In August 1974 the school's name was changed to Northeastern State University. It operates on the semester basis and also provides a summer session. Enrollment includes 7,499 students. The faculty consists of 279 full-time and 73 part-time members. The faculty-student ratio is 1-26. Army ROTC is available as an elective.

Entrance Requirements: Oklahoma residents with accredited high school graduation and one of the following requirements: minimum B average in four years of high school work; rank in upper 1/2 of graduating class; or score of 20 or over on ACT; out-of-state accredited high school graduates must rank in upper half of graduating class or score 20 or over on ACT. Oklahoma non-high school graduates 21 years of age or over may be admitted on a provisional basis with satisfactory scores on ACT. GRE required for graduate programs; early admission, early decision, rolling admission plan available.

Costs Per Year: $1,406 state-resident tuition; $3,469 nonresident tuition; $2,392 room and board, $25 fees.

Collegiate Environment: The state university is located in northeastern Oklahoma in Tahlequah, a small city of unique spirit which lies cradled in the scenic foothills of the Ozarks. Surrounded by several of Oklahoma's most beautiful lakes, the city provides year-round recreational facilities such as hunting, fishing, and other water sports. The university buildings include a library of 176,000 titles, 290,554 microforms, 2,320 periodicals and 4,015 audiovisual materials. Living accommodations are available for 1,750 students. 88% of the applicants are accepted, and students may enroll at midyear as well as in

fall. Financial aid is available, and 84% of the student body receives some form of assistance.

Community Environment: In a region of lakes within the foothills of the Ozark Mountains, Tahlequah is the former capital city of the Cherokee Indian Nation. There are many historic sites and artifacts in the area. The city is accessible by five highways and two bus lines. Community services includes several churches of various denominations, two hospitals, two libraries, and a museum. Rooms and apartments provide student housing. There are various civic and fraternal organizations within the city. Limited part-time employment is available for students. Local recreational facilities include boating, fishing, hunting, water skiing, and swimming.

NORTHERN OKLAHOMA COLLEGE   *(B-10)*
1220 East Grand
Tonkawa, Oklahoma 74653
Tel: (405) 628-6200; Admissions: (405) 628-6220; Fax: (405) 628-6209

Description: The state junior college was established as the university preparatory school in 1902. The college department was added in 1920 and the present name was adopted in 1965. Enrollment is 2,240 students. The faculty numbers 43 full-time and 62 part-time. The school operates on the semester system and one summer session is offered. The college is accredited by the North Central Association of Colleges and Schools and grants the Certificate and Associate degree.

Entrance Requirements: Open enrollment policy; ACT required; Oklahoma nonhigh school graduates 18 years or older may enroll on a provisional basis; rolling admission plan.

Costs Per Year: $1,140 tuition; $2,760 nonresident tuition; $2,120 room and board.

Collegiate Environment: The campus of the college consists of 58 acres of land adjoining the City of Tonkawa on the east. The city is beautifully situated between the Salt Fork and Chikaski Rivers, about 90 miles north of Oklahoma City. The 16 college buildings contain a library of over 30,000 volumes and dormitory facilities for 206 men and 204 women. Approximately 95% of students applying for admission are accepted. The college welcomes a geographically diverse student body and will accept midyear students. Financial aid is available for economically handicapped students. Semesters begin in late August and January and the summer session begins in June. The college has an outstanding competitive sports program for women and men. A well rounded intramurals program is also available.

Community Environment: Tonkawa is located 14 miles west of Ponca City and enjoys a mild climate. The city has a public library, churches representing 10 denominations, a nearby hospital, a Chamber of Commerce and other civic, fraternal and veteran's organizations. Housing for students is provided by dormitories and one hotel. There are limited job opportunities for students. Fishing in nearby rivers is considered excellent sport.

NORTHWESTERN OKLAHOMA STATE UNIVERSITY   *(B-7)*
Alva, Oklahoma 73717
Tel: (405) 327-1700; (800) 299-6978; Fax: (405) 327-1881

Description: The state college, which was started as a normal school in 1897, was increased to a four-year teacher college in 1919. It was further expanded to include degrees in liberal arts as well as education in 1939. Beginning with the summer term of 1954, a fifth-year program of teacher education leading to the degree of Master of Education was instituted at this college. The college is fully accredited by the North Central Association of Colleges and Schools and the National Council for Accreditation for Teacher Education. It grants the Bachelor and Master's degrees. The college operates on the semester system and offers one summer session. Enrollment includes 539 men and 630 women full-time and 275 men and 415 women part-time. Of these, undergraduates constitute 1,113 full-time and 485 part-time students. Graduate enrollment includes 56 full-time and 205 part-time. A faculty of 81 full-time and 32 part-time gives a faculty-student ratio of 1-21.

Entrance Requirements: High school graduation with rank in upper 50%, a cumulative GPA of 2.7, or ACT score of 19 or better, ACT required; non-high school graduates 18 years of age or older may be admitted on a provisional basis with satisfactory scores on ACT or

GED; rolling admission, midyear admission and advanced placement plans available.

Costs Per Year: $1,556 tuition; $3,756 nonresident tuition; $1,956 room and board; $30 student fees.

Collegiate Environment: The state university is located on a 71-acre campus near the south edge of the City, Alva. The 23 college buildings include a library of 225,000 volumes including government documents, 1,411 periodicals, 650,000 microforms, and 2,000 recordings. The University owns a 160-acre farm with a farm headquarters building. Dormitory facilities are available for 404 men and women. 97% of freshmen applicants are accepted. The average score of the entering freshman class is ACT 20.5 composite. Semesters begin in August and January and the summer session begins in June. Numerous scholarships are available and 80% of undergraduates receive some form of financial aid.

Community Environment: Alva is located in northwestern Oklahoma. The average mean temperature is 59.1 degrees. Rainfall averages 16 inches annually. Local public services include a hospital, many churches, five motels, and active civic and fraternal groups. One park, picnic areas, lighted baseball fields, playgrounds, a movie theatre, golf course, municipal swimming pool, tennis courts, fishing, and hunting are all easily accessible. Little Sahara State Park and Alabaster Caverns are located approximately 25 miles distant.

OKLAHOMA BAPTIST UNIVERSITY *(G-11)*
500 West University
Shawnee, Oklahoma 74801
Tel: (405) 275-2850; (800) 654-3285

Description: Founded in 1910, and supported by the Baptist General Convention of Oklahoma, this private university is accredited by the North Central Association of Colleges and Schools. The university is comprised of two colleges: the College of Arts & Sciences and the Warren M. Angell College of Fine Arts; and three schools: the Paul Dickinson School of Business, the Joe L. Ingram School of Christian Service, and the School of Nursing. An academic exchange program is available with St. Gregory's College and with Seinen Gakuin University in Japan. It grants the Bachelor degree. The university operates on the semester system and offers two summer sessions. Enrollment includes 764 men and 974 women full-time and 309 men and 393 women part-time. There are 28 graduate students. A faculty of 14 full-time and 46 part-time gives a faculty-student ratio of 1-14.

Entrance Requirements: Accredited high school graduation or equivalent; rank in upper half of graduating class; completion 4 English, 3 mathematics, 3 science, 3 foreign language, 3 social science recommended; minimum ACT 20 required (SAT 720 may be substituted); applicants not meeting all entrance requirements may be admitted on probation; rolling admission and advanced placement plans available; $25 application fee.

Costs Per Year: $5,920 tuition; $3,140 room and board

Collegiate Environment: The university owns approximately 180 acres of land two miles north of the business center of Shawnee. The 25 university buildings include a library of 200,000 volumes, 742 periodicals, and 7,200 recordings. Living accommodations are provided for 1,268 men and women. Students from other geographical locations are accepted as well as midyear students. Approximately 95% of students applying for admission are accepted. Average high school standing of the freshman class: 29% were in the top 10%, 27% in the top 11%-25%, 26% in the 26%-50%.; average ACT 23.8 composite. Financial aid is available for economically disadvantaged students; 85% of the current student body receives financial aid. Almost 80% of the previous freshman class returned to the university for their sophomore year.

Community Environment: On the North Canadian River, Shawnee is in a rich agricultural and oil-producing area. The altitude of the city is 1,080 feet above sea level and the average temperature is 62.3 degrees. It is located near the geographical center of the state approximately 40 miles by interstate highway from Oklahoma City. The area is accessible via bus lines and a municipal airport. There are churches of most denominations and a YMCA in town. Local recreational facilities provide for golf, fishing, tennis, boating, hunting, bowling, and roller skating as well as picnic grounds, three swimming pools, parks, theatres, museums, and one drive-in. Events include horse shows and rodeo. There are various civic, fraternal and veterans' organizations here.

OKLAHOMA CHRISTIAN UNIVERSITY OF SCIENCE AND ARTS *(F-10)*
Box 11000
2501 E. Memorial Road
Oklahoma City, Oklahoma 73136-1100
Tel: (405) 425-5000; (800) 877-5010; Admissions: (405) 425-5055; Fax: (405) 425-5208

Description: Four year private university founded in 1950. Fully accredited by the North Central Association of Colleges and Schools. Over 70 options are available for undergraduate majors. A Masters degree in ministry is also offered. It operates on the trimester calendar and offers three summer sessions. Enrollment includes 1,419 full-time, 144 part-time undergraduates and 28 graduate students. A faculty of 84 full-time and 50 part-time provides a faculty-student ratio of 1-14. An International Studies Program includes: Vienna, Austria; Ibaraki, Japan; and Latin America. Air Force and Army ROTC programs are available through cross-town agreements with OU and UCO.

Entrance Requirements: Completion of 15 units; SAT or ACT scores required; early admission, midyear admission, rolling admission, advanced placement plans available; $25 application fee.

Costs Per Year: $6,400 tuition; $3,280 room and board; $140 student fees.

Collegiate Environment: The university is located on a 200-acre campus in northeast Oklahoma City. The 24 college buildings include a library of over 125,000 volumes. Dormitory facilities accommodate 638 men and 680 women and 87 married students. Financial aid is available and 80% receive some form of aid. Trimesters begin in August, January, and April. Activities include student government, radio, TV, student newspaper, yearbook, choral groups, concert band, jazz and pep band, theater, social service clubs, intramurals, and a well-equipped health center. The 1,650 students come from 44 states and 32 countries.

Community Environment: The university is in the northeast quadrant near I-35 in Oklahoma City which has a metropolitan population of 958,000. It is close to the smaller suburban community of Edmond, population 55,000. Many cultural, entertainment, and job opportunities are readily available. Most of the major airlines serve Will Rogers World Airport. I-40 and I-35 intersect in Oklahoma City.

OKLAHOMA CITY COMMUNITY COLLEGE *(F-10)*
7777 South May Avenue
Oklahoma City, Oklahoma 73159
Tel: (405) 682-1611

Description: This publicly supported community college was established in 1972 and is fully accredited by the North Central Association of Colleges and Schools, as well as the Oklahoma State Regents for Higher Education. The college operates on the semester system and offers one summer session. A full range of associate degree programs are offered, along with many degree and certificate programs that are designed to prepare students for immediate employment or to enhance current skills. Enrollment includes 3,533 full-time and 7,652 part-time students. A faculty of 105 full-time and 362 part-time gives a faculty-student ratio of 1:24.

Entrance Requirements: Open enrollment. High school graduation required for those 18 or younger.

Costs Per Year: $779.10 tuition, $318 fees, resident; $1,685.40 tuition, $2,782.50 fees, nonresident.

Collegiate Environment: The college's seven interconnected buildings are situated on a 143-acre campus located in the rapidly growing southwest quadrant of Oklahoma City. The Library contains 109,410 books, 410 periodicals, 60,000 microforms, and 14,000 audiovisual materials. Financial aid is available and 40% of the students receive some form. A wide variety of student activities is offered.

Community Environment: Oklahoma City was born on April 22, 1889, when the population jumped from zero to 10,000 as a result of a unique land run. The city is currently one of the largest municipalities in the nation, covering a total of 621 square miles. The more than 970,000 residents enjoy temperatures ranging from the mid-80's in

July to the mid-30's in January. The community is served by all major forms of transportation. Entertainment, cultural and sport-related activities are numerous.

OKLAHOMA CITY UNIVERSITY *(F-10)*
2501 N. Blackwelder
Oklahoma City, Oklahoma 73106
Tel: (405) 521-5000; (800) 633-7242 x1; Fax: (405) 521-5916

Description: The private university was established as Epworth University by the Methodist Episcopal Church and the Methodist Episcopal Church, South, in cooperation with the Chamber of Commerce of Oklahoma City. The first meetings were held in 1901 and classes began in the fall of 1904. Since the merger of the three main branches of Methodism, the university has been owned and controlled by the Methodist Church. Today it is comprised of the College of Arts and Sciences, the School of Music and Performing Arts, the School of Management and Business Sciences, the School of Law, the School of Nursing, and the School of Religion. The university operates on the semester basis and also provides two summer terms. It is accredited by the North Central Association of Colleges and Schools, the American Bar Association, National Association of Schools of Music, and the National League for Nursing. Air Force and Army ROTC are available. Study abroad is available in England and Asian countries. Enrollment includes 1,719 full-time and 518 part-time undergraduates and 1,695 graduates and 639 first professionals (Law). A faculty of 160 full-time and 172 part-time gives a faculty-student ratio of 1-20.

Entrance Requirements: Accredited high school graduation; recommended courses of 4 English, 3 mathematics, 2 foreign language, 2 laboratory science, 3 social science; SAT combined score of 900, or composite ACT of 20 required; early admission, rolling admission, delayed admission, midyear admission and advanced placement plans available; $20 application fee.

Costs Per Year: $7,050 tuition; $3,420 room and board; $155 student fees.

Collegiate Environment: The university occupies a campus of 64 acres in the northwest section of Oklahoma City. The 24 university buildings include a library and a Law Library. Combined, these libraries hold 292,651 volumes, 4,180 periodicals, 577,525 microforms, 11,594 audiovisual materials, and 230,966 government publications. Living accommodations are provided for 462 students. Students from other geographical locations are accepted as well as midyear students. Approximately 74% of students applying for admission are accepted. Almost 69% of the previous freshman class returned to this campus for the sophomore year. Average high school standing of the freshman class, top 50%; 46% in the top quarter. Financial aid is available for economically disadvantaged students. $3,756,834 in scholarships is available. Presently, 77% of the students receive financial aid. The average scores of the current freshman class were SAT 1030 combined; ACT 23 composite. The university provides special programs for outstanding students in cooperation with the American University in Washington, D.C., with Drew University in Madison, New Jersey, as well as study at Harlaxton College in Grantham, England, at Hawaii Loa College, and in Asian nations.

Community Environment: Oklahoma City is the capital of the state. A leading wholesale and distributing point for the state, the city ranks as one of the eight primary livestock markets in the country. There are many manufacturing concerns including packing plants, flour mills, printing and publishing houses, electronic firms and machine works. Two of the world's largest high gravity oil fields are within the city and surrounding area. The community is served by all major forms of transportation. Part-time employment is available. Good fishing, hunting, and water sports are easily accessible at nearby Lakes Hefner, Overholser, and Stanley Draper.

OKLAHOMA PANHANDLE STATE UNIVERSITY *(H-8)*
Box 430
Goodwell, Oklahoma 73939
Tel: (405) 349-2611; Admissions: (405) 349-2611 X 374; Fax: (405) 349-2302

Description: The state college was established in 1909 and is accredited by the North Central Association of Colleges and Schools. It operates on the semester system and offers one summer session. Enrollment is 895 full-time and 266 part-time students. A faculty of 52

full-time and 31 part-time gives a faculty-student ratio of 1-16. The College grants Associate and Baccalaureate degrees.

Entrance Requirements: 20 high school units including 4 Englich, 3 mathematics, 2 science, and 2 social science. ACT required; early admission, early decision, midyear admission, and advanced placement plans available.

Costs Per Year: $1,132.50 tuition; $3,060 out-of-state; $1,800 room and board; $216 student fees; $90 book rental.

Collegiate Environment: The college is comprised of 28 buildings and is located on 40 acres. The library contains 93,623 volumes, 520 periodicals and 7,463 microforms and 5,928 audiovisual materials. Living accommodations are provided for 550 students and 160 families. Students from other geographical locations are accepted as well as midyear students. 98% of applicants are accepted. Scholarships are available. 33% of the students receive some form of financial aid.

Community Environment: Goodwell is located in the center of the Oklahoma Panhandle in Texas County. The climate is cool and arid. The area is served by railroad, bus line, and Highway 54. Goodwell has three churches, and various civic, fraternal and veteran's organizations.

OKLAHOMA STATE UNIVERSITY *(D-1)*
104 Whitehurst
Stillwater, Oklahoma 74078-0103
Tel: (405) 744-5000; (800) 852-1255; Admissions: (405) 744-6858; Fax: (405) 744-5285

Description: The state university was founded in 1890 and is governed by the Board of Regents for Oklahoma State University and the Oklahoma Agricultural and Mechanical Colleges. The university is organized into the Division of Agriculture, the College of Arts and Sciences, the College of Business Administration, the College of Education, the College of Engineering, Architecture and Technology, the Division of Home Economics, the College of Veterinary Medicine and the Graduate College. It is accredited by the North Central Association of Colleges and Schools and by respective educational and professional organizations. The university operates on the semester basis and also offers four three to eight-week summer sessions. Army and Air Force ROTC programs are available. The university also provides an Honors Program for the academically superior student. Enrollment includes 7,848 men and 6,434 women full-time and 2,274 men and 2,005 women part-time. A faculty of 809 full-time and 59 part-time gives a faculty-student ratio of 1-24.

Entrance Requirements: Accredited high school graduation with rank in upper half of graduating class; completion of 11 units including 4 English, 3 mathematics, 2 science, 2 history (1 must be American history); minimum scores of ACT 21 composite or SAT 990 combined; early admission, early decision, advanced placement, and rolling admission plans available. $15 application fee for all undergraduate applicants.

Costs Per Year: $1,892 tuition; $5,339 nonresident tuition; $3,360 room and board, $385 fees.

Collegiate Environment: The university property includes the main campus of 840 acres at Stillwater, the university farms totaling 2,245 acres which immediately adjoin the campus on the west and on the north, and 19 experiment stations located throughout the state. The present valuation of the university property including 337 major buildings is about $706,000,000. Branches of the university are located at Okmulgee, Oklahoma City, Tulsa and Kyoto, Japan. The university library contains 1,700,000 titles, 16,130 periodicals and 2,800,000 microforms and 4,456 audiovisual films. Living accommodations are provided for 2,468 men, 2,597 women and 713 families. Approximately 85% of students applying for admission were accepted, including midyear students. 60% receive financial aid; of the approximately 6,000 scholarships offered, over 2,000 are available for freshman. About 76% of the freshmen returned to school for the sophomore year.

Community Environment: Stillwater is located in north central Oklahoma. The climate is mild with an average annual temperature of 59.8 degrees and average rainfall of 33.3 inches. The city is accessible by Highways 51 and 177, and nearby U.S. Highways 64 and Interstate 35. There are bus lines to the city. Stillwater has several churches of major denominations, a hospital, two clinics, and a health center. Local recreational facilities include 15 parks, two golf courses, fishing, camping, picnicking, hiking, hunting, boating, waterskiing, theatres, and a drive-in. Rooming houses, apartments and private homes provide housing for students. There is part-time employment available.

OKLAHOMA STATE UNIVERSITY - OKLAHOMA CITY
(F-10)
900 N. Portland
Oklahoma City, Oklahoma 73107
Tel: (405) 947-4421; Fax: (405) 945-3277

Description: The Oklahoma State University at Oklahoma City is a branch campus of Oklahoma State University and is accredited by the North Central Association of Colleges and Schools. It began operations in the fall of 1961. It operates on the semester basis and also provides a summer term. Enrollment is approximately 4,367 students. A faculty of 51 full-time and 155 part-time gives a faculty-student ratio of 1-18. The college awards an Associate of Applied Science degree.

Entrance Requirements: Accredited high school graduation; completion of 18 units including 4 English, 3 mathematics, 2 science and 2 social science; ACT required; non-high school graduates admitted on a provisional basis with satisfactory scores on ACT; $15 nonresident application fee; early admission, early decision, and advanced placement plans available.

Costs Per Year: $1,100 tuition; $3,800 out-of-state; $220 student fees.

Collegiate Environment: The college occupied a new campus of 14 buildings on 80 acres in the summer of 1970. The new Engineering Technology Building has a down-link satellite facility. Its present library contains over 12,000 volumes, 220 pamphlets, 248 periodicals, 160 microforms and 800 sound recordings. Approximately 99% of students applying for admission were accepted including midyear students. Financial aid is available and 35% of the current student body receives some form of assistance. The average ACT composite score of the current freshman class was 17. 60% of the freshmen graduated in the upper half of their high school class, 20% in the third quarter and 20% in the bottom quarter. Semesters begin in August and January.

Community Environment: See Oklahoma City University.

OKLAHOMA STATE UNIVERSITY COLLEGE OF OSTEOPATHIC MEDICINE *(D-14)*
1111 West 17 Street
Tulsa, Oklahoma 74107-1898
Tel: (918) 582-1972; (800) 677-1972; Admissions: (918) 561-8469;
Fax: (918) 561-8412

Description: This state supported institution founded in 1972 offers a coeducational, professional study program leading to the degree of Doctor of Osteopathic Medicine. The college meets the accreditation standards set by the American Osteopathic Association. It operates on the semester system. An enrollment of 350 students and a faculty of 41 full-time and 159 part-time provides a teacher-student ratio of 1-8.

Entrance Requirements: Completion of at least 3 years of study at an accredited college or university with not less than 75% of the prescribed requirements for a baccalaureate degree; no grade below C in English, biology, general chemistry, organic chemistry, and physics; science grade point average of at least 2.75 on a 4.0 scale and overall grade point average of 3.0; Medical College Admission Test score of 7 required; $25 application fee.

Costs Per Year: $6,566 tuition for state residents; $16,226 tuition for out-of-state residents; $700 student fees.

Collegiate Environment: The College is located on a 16-acre site and consists of three buildings containing classrooms, basic and clinical science teaching laboratories, faculty and administrative offices, research areas, and an innovative Learning Resources Center. The library holdings include 44,500 volumes. The facilities of affiliated hospitals throughout the state are used for clinical practice during the student's third and fourth year. There is also experience in physicians' offices, primary care clinics and other community health centers throughout Oklahoma. 10% of applicants are accepted. 95% of students receive some form of financial aid.

Community Environment: See Oral Roberts University.

ORAL ROBERTS UNIVERSITY *(D-14)*
7777 South Lewis
Tulsa, Oklahoma 74171
Tel: (918) 495-6518; (800) 678-8876; Fax: (918) 495-6033

Description: Privately supported, coeducational liberal arts institution was established in 1963 by the Trustees of Oral Roberts Evangelistic Association. Operates on a semester basis. Stated purpose is: "In its commitment to the historic Christian faith, to assist the student in his quest for knowledge of his relationship to God, man, and the universe." Enrollment recently included 3,641 undergraduate students. A faculty of 281 full-time and 109 part-time gives a faculty-student ratio of 1-13. The university undergraduate and Master's degree programs have received accreditation from the North Central Association of Colleges and Schools and several professional accrediting institutions. The school grants four Baccalaureate degrees and Master's degrees in Business (M.B.A.), Theology (M.A. and M.Div.); ORU also offers a Doctor of Ministry degree. Army ROTC is available through another institution.

Entrance Requirements: High school graduation or equivalent with rank in upper 45% of graduating class; completion of 16 units including 4 English, 2 mathematics, 2 foreign language, 2 science, 2 social science; SAT or ACT required; GRE required for graduate program; early decision, early admission, rolling admission, and delayed admission plans available; $35 application fee.

Costs Per Year: $5,825 undergraduate tuition, $155-$180/semester hour for most graduate programs; $13,500/year School of Medicine tuition; $3,495 room and board; $150 student fees.

Collegiate Environment: The campus consists of 500 acres of scenic, rolling land within the city limits of Tulsa. The 21 campus buildings contain a library of 285,000 volumes, 21,012 microforms, and 1,975 periodical titles. Living accommodations are provided for 3,462 students. All students are required to attend semiweekly chapel and to go to the church of their choice on Sunday. Students from other geographical locations are accepted as are midyear students. 60% of applicants were accepted recently. Nearly 85% of the previous freshman class returned to this campus for the second year of studies. Average high school standing of the freshman class, top 40%; 70% in the top quarter; 20% in the second quarter. The average score of the entering freshman class was SAT 1005 combined. Scholarships are available and 87% of the student body received some form of financial aid.

Community Environment: Tulsa is located in northeast Oklahoma. The area has four distinct seasons, and is served by major airlines, bus lines, and U.S. highways. Tulsa is located on the fringe of the southwest's greatest inland vacation and recreation areas. Nearby lakes provide fishing, golf, boating, hunting, and other outdoor sports. Community services include many churches, an Opera Association, Philbrook and Gilcrease Museums, and major health and civic organizations.

PHILLIPS UNIVERSITY *(C-9)*
100 S. University Ave
Enid, Oklahoma 73701-6439
Tel: (405) 237-4433; (800) 238-1185; Admissions: (405) 548-2203;
Fax: (405) 237-1607

Description: This private university opened in 1907 and was known as the Oklahoma Christian University until 1913 when its present name was adopted. It is accredited by the North Central Association of Colleges and Schools. It is an institution of Christian higher education, operating with its own Board of Trustees in full cooperation with the Christian Churches (Disciples of Christ) and receives primary support from the states of Arkansas, Colorado, Kansas, Oklahoma, and Wyoming. The university is comprised of one undergraduate college and a division of graduate studies. An exchange program with the People's College in Sweden and a semester in Washington, D.C., are offered to qualified students. It operates on the semester system and offers three summer sessions. Enrollment includes 595 full-time, 99 part-time, and 102 graduate students. A faculty of 43 full-time and 24 part-time gives a faculty-student ratio of 1-13.

Entrance Requirements: Accredited high school graduation or equivalent; rank in upper 50% of graduating class; ACT or SAT required; minimum scores, ACT 18 and SAT 750 combined; completion of units including 4 English, 3 mathematics, 2 social sciences, and 2 natural sciences; early admission, rolling admission, delayed admission, and advanced placement plans available; $20 application fee.

Costs Per Year: $6,000 tuition; $3,904 room and board; $400 student fees.

Collegiate Environment: The university is comprised of 25 buildings and is located on 135 acres. The undergraduate library contains over 179,748 volumes. Dormitory familities are provided for 380 men, women and married students. The university welcomes a geographically diverse student body and will accept midyear students. Approximately 75% of students applying for admission are accepted. Financial aid is available and 87% of the current student body receives some form of financial assistance.

Community Environment: Although some sources hold that the town's name came from Tennyson's "Idylls of the King," more colorful stories credit the naming of Enid to a playful bunch of Old Chisholm Trail Cattle drovers who turned the "Dine" sign on the local cook tent upside-down. The principal crop of the area is wheat, which is handled in Enid's large flour mills and huge grain elevators that have a combined storage capacity of nearly 69 million bushels. Also economically important are the raising of beef cattle and the production and refining of oil. The area is served by three railroads, four highways, and airlines. Community facilities include a library, hospital, hotels and motels. Local recreational facilities include golf courses, swimming pools, tennis courts, theaters, softball, basketball, bowling, and a skating rink; nearby state parks have fishing and boating. Part-time employment is available.

REDLANDS COMMUNITY COLLEGE *(F-9)*
Box 370
1300 South Country Club Road
El Reno, Oklahoma 73036
Tel: (405) 262-2552

Description: The district-governed junior college was established in 1938. It operates on the semester system and offers one summer session. Enrollment includes 841 men and 1,067 women, registered as 915 full-time and 993 part-time students. A faculty of 85 gives a faculty-student ratio of 1-18. It is fully accredited by the Oklahoma State Regents for Higher Education, by the North Central Association of Colleges and Schools, and the National League for Nursing. The college grants the Associate degree.

Entrance Requirements: Accredited high school graduation or equivalent; open enrollment policy; ACT required; nonaccredited high school graduates and non-high school graduates 21 years of age or older may be admitted on a provisional basis with satisfactory scores on ACT; rolling admission available.

Costs Per Year: $735 tuition; $2,325 nonresident tuition; $225 student fees.

Collegiate Environment: Open admissions. Students from other geographical locations are accepted, as are midyear students. Scholarships are available. 47% of the students receive financial aid. The college library contains 20,276 volumes, 256 periodicals, 33,295 microforms, and 17,750 audiovisual materials.

Community Environment: El Reno is located on the south bank of the North Canadian River. The average annual temperature is 60 degrees. The city is served by bus lines, railroad, and an airport. Nearby lakes offer waterskiing, fishing, and boating. El Reno has many community service facilities including a hospital, hotel and many motels, a library, and various civic, service, and fraternal organizations. Part-time job opportunities are good. Local recreational facilities include two movie theatres, drive-ins, parks, tennis, golf, and a municipal swimming pool.

ROGERS STATE COLLEGE *(C-15)*
College Hill Drive
Claremore, Oklahoma 74017
Tel: (918) 341-7510; Admissions: (918) 341-7542; Fax: (918) 341-3811

Description: This state-supported junior college was established in 1909 as the Eastern University Preparatory School. It is fully accredited by the North Central Association of Colleges and Schools. It operates on the semester system and offers one summer session. Enrollment recently included approximately 670 men and 797 women

full-time, and 654 men and 1,237 women part-time. A faculty of 52 full-time and 69 part-time gives a faculty-student ratio of 1-29.

Entrance Requirements: Open enrollment policy; ACT required; non-high school graduates considered for admission in certain circumstances; early decision, delayed admission, early admission, midyear admission, rolling admission, and advanced placement plans available. No application fee.

Costs Per Year: $1,824 tuition; $2,672 nonresident; $2,800 room and board; $30 student fees.

Collegiate Environment: The 36 school buildings are located on 602 acres. The library contains more than 24,800 volumes, 2,000 pamphlets, 175 periodicals, 2,300 microforms and 1,700 audiovisual materials. Dormitory facilities accommodate 165 men and 165 women. All of the students applying for admission are accepted. Financial assistance is available for economically disadvantaged students. 50% of students receive some form of financial aid. Students from other geographical locations are accepted as well as midyear students. Semesters begin in August and January.

Community Environment: Known as a health and tourism center, Claremore has several artesian mineral wells with properties regarded as beneficial in the treatment of rheumatism, arthritis, and skin ailments. The city is the site of the U.S. Indian Hospital, the Claremore Health Center, the Claremore Veteran's Center, the Will Rogers Tomb & Memorial, the J. M. Davis Gun Museum, the Oklahoma Military Academy Memorial, the Lynn Riggs Memorial, and the Jefferson Memorial. Nearby Lake Claremore and Lake Oologah offer fishing, boating, and picnicking. The climate is temperate with an average temperature of 62 degrees. The city has bus transportation. An annual Indian pow-wow, round-up and rodeo is held. Limited part-time employment is available.

ROSE STATE COLLEGE *(F-10)*
6420 S.E. 15th
Midwest City, Oklahoma 73110-2799
Tel: (405) 733-7673; Admissions: (405) 733-7312; Fax: (405) 736-7312

Description: The publicly supported coeducational college was established in 1970. The college has been granted full accreditation by the North Central Association of Colleges and Schools and Oklahoma State Regents for Higher Education. It is also accredited by the American Bar Association, and the American Medical Association. Programs of study lead to the Associate degree. The college operates on the semester system and offers three summer sessions. Enrollment includes 2,900 full-time and 6,183 part-time students. A faculty of 137 full-time and 334 part-time gives a faculty-student ratio of 1-19.

Entrance Requirements: Open enrollment policy; completion of 11 units including 4 English, 3 math, 2 social science, and 2 science; non high school graduates admitted provisionally; ACT required. Mature persons not candidates for a degree may receive admission as special or unclassified students; early admission, early decision, rolling admission, deferred admission, midyear admission and advanced placement plans available. No application deadline; $15 application fee.

Costs Per Year: $623.28 resident tuition; $1,971.60 nonresident; $180 student fees.

Collegiate Environment: The college occupies new modern buildings including a library containing over 80,000 volumes. Dormitory housing is not available. 100% of those applying for admission are accepted. The college offers local, state, and federal scholarships, grants, and loans, and 33% of the students receive some form of financial aid.

Community Environment: See Oklahoma City University.

SAINT GREGORY'S COLLEGE *(G-11)*
1900 West MacArthur Drive
Shawnee, Oklahoma 74801
Tel: (405) 273-9870

Description: The private junior college was established in 1915 by the Benedictine Fathers of Sacred Heart Abbey, the earliest permanent Roman Catholic mission in what is now the state of Oklahoma. The college is affiliated with the Catholic University of America and is accredited by the North Central Association of Colleges and Schools. The college offers a two-year program of arts and sciences leading to academic degrees. It grants the Associate degree and operates on the semester system. Enrollment includes 202 full-time and 66 part-time students. A faculty of 6 full time and 27 part-time gives a student ratio of 1-17.

Entrance Requirements: High school graduation; completion of 13 units recommended with courses of 4 English, 3 mathematics, 2 foreign language, 2 science, 2 social science; ACT required; non-high school graduates considered; application fee $25; early admission, early decision, midyear admission, rolling admission, and advanced placement plans available.

Costs Per Year: $4,870 tuition; $510 student fees.

Collegiate Environment: The 160-acre campus is located within the city limits of the City of Shawnee, about four miles from the central business district. The ten college buildings include a library of 53,781 volumes, 4,796 periodicals, 1,356 microforms, 25 recordings and dormitory facilities for 310 men and women. The college welcomes a geographically diverse student body and will accept midyear students. Approximately 98% of students applying for admission are accepted. 155 scholarships are offered, including 80 for freshmen. 67% of the students receive some form of financial aid. Semesters begin in August and January.

Community Environment: See Oklahoma Baptist University

SEMINOLE JUNIOR COLLEGE   *(G-12)*
2701 State Street
Seminole, Oklahoma 74868
Tel: (405) 382-9950; Admissions: (405) 382-9230; Fax: (405) 382-3122

Description: The public junior college was organized in 1931 in order to provide opportunities for higher education to the graduates of high schools of Seminole and surrounding territory. The college is accredited by the North Central Association of Colleges and Schools. It awards the Associate degree. The college operates on the semester system and offers one summer session. Enrollment includes 993 full-time and 605 part-time students. A faculty of 42 full-time and 40 part-time gives a faculty-student ratio of 1-19.

Entrance Requirements: High school graduation; open enrollment policy; non-high school graduates considered; ACT required; rolling admission, midyear admission plans available.

Costs Per Year: $1,071 tuition; $2,869 out-of-state tuition; $1,880 room and board.

Collegiate Environment: The junior college has modern and well-equipped science laboratories and contains a library of 28,000 volumes. All of students applying for admission are accepted. Financial aid is available.

Community Environment: Seminole is an urban community enjoying temperate climate. Local transportation services include railroad, bus, and airlines. The city has a public library, 30 churches of various denominations, a hospital, and three clinics. Some part-time employment is available for students. Recreational facilities in Seminole include a theater, a drive-in, bowling, and water sports. The major civic, fraternal and veteran's organizations are active within the immediate community. There are several historic sites located nearby.

SOUTHEASTERN OKLAHOMA STATE UNIVERSITY
(K-13)
Durant, Oklahoma 74701-0609
Tel: (405) 924-0121; Admissions: (405) 924-0121 X2264

Description: The state college was established in 1909 by authority of an Act passed by the Legislature of the State of Oklahoma. It is accredited by the North Central Association of Colleges and Schools and by the National Council for Accreditation of Teacher Education. The college operates on the semester basis and offers one summer session. Enrollment includes 1,430 men and 1,620 women full-time and 362 men and 692 women part-time. The faculty has 156 full-time and 49 part-time members. The college grants a Bachelor and a Master degree.

Entrance Requirements: For admittance to Southeastern, in-state and out-of-state graduates of accredited high schools must: have 20 high school units, 11 of which are required (English, 4 units; Lab Science, 2 units; Math, 3 units; and History, 2 units), participate in the American College Testing Program or a similar acceptable battery of

tests, and meet the following criteria: score of 19 or higher on ACT, or rank in the top 50% of their graduating class and have a minimum high school GPA of 2.7. Certain mature persons not candidates for a degree may receive admission as special or unclassified students; early admission, early decision, rolling admission and advanced placement plans available.

Costs Per Year: $1,224 in-state tuition and fees; $3,395 for out-of-state students; $2,619 room and board; $307 student fees.

Collegiate Environment: The 110-acre campus is located in Durant, within ten minutes drive of beautiful Lake Texoma. The ten college buildings contain a library of 167,580 volumes and living accommodations for 600 students. Approximately 98% of students applying for admission are accepted. Students from other geographical locations are accepted as well as midyear students. About 50% of the previous freshman class returned to this campus for the sophomore year. About 50% of the recent student body graduated in the top half of the high school class; 20% in the top quarter. Financial aid is available for economically handicapped students and of the 1,533 scholarships offered. 50% were for freshmen. The average ACT composite score of the current freshman class was 19. Semesters begin in August and January.

Community Environment: Durant is a rural community served by railroad and bus lines. The community has one hospital, Bryan County Health Center, a recreation center, and active civic, fraternal, and veteran's organizations. There are libraries, churches, and motels. Local recreational facilities include hunting, boating, fishing, golf and other sports.

SOUTHERN NAZARENE UNIVERSITY   *(F-10)*
6729 N.W. 39th Expressway
Bethany, Oklahoma 73008
Tel: (405) 789-6400; (800) 648-9899; Admissions: (405) 491-6324; Fax: (405) 491-6381

Description: The private, four-year university, founded in 1899, is the second oldest independent institution in the state of Oklahoma, the recognized college for the South Central Educational Zone of the Church of Nazarene. This territory includes the states of Oklahoma, Arkansas, Texas, and Louisiana, with a student body representing 36 other states and 28 foreign countries. It is accredited by the North Central Association of Colleges and Schools, the National Council for Accreditation of Teacher Education, the National League for Nursing, and the American Association of Colleges for Teacher Education. The university operates on the semester system, offers a summer session, and two miniterms in January and May. Enrollment includes 559 men and 664 women full-time and 95 men and 173 women part-time. The faculty consists of 69 full-time and 26 part-time members. SNU offers academic cooperative programs with the University of Oklahoma Medical Center for students majoring in medical technology and Central State University for students interested in the U.S. Army ROTC program; there are three programs sponsored by the Christian College Coalition, as well as the American Studies Program in Washington, D.C., a semester internship in Hollywood, California, and the Latin American Studies Program in Costa Rica. Programs of study lead to the Certificate, Associate of Arts, Bachelor and Master degrees.

Entrance Requirements: Open enrollment policy; ACT minimum 18 required or minimum SAT combined score of 700 required; early admission, rolling admission, delayed admission, advanced placement plans available; $25 application fee.

Costs Per Year: $6,780 tuition; $3,810 room and board; $348 student fees.

Collegiate Environment: The university occupies a campus of 40 acres located in the center of Bethany, a suburb of Oklahoma City. The campus consists of 20 major facilities, the newest being a $3.2 million dollar 58,000 sq. ft. University Commons, completed in 1988, and the R.T. Williams Learning Resource Center which contains 106,745 volumes, 156,223 titles on microfilm, 2,857 recordings, and 607 regular periodicals. In addition, the resource center is connected to the Dialog On-Line Bibliographic Database, providing access to 10 million volumes nationwide; and home for the R.T. Williams Holiness Collection, Hayslip Bible Collection, and Hymnology Collection. Living facilities accommodate 706 students. Approximately 96% of students applying for admission are accepted, including midyear students. Students from other religious denominations are admitted with attendance at chapel services required of all undergraduate students. Average scores of a recent freshman class, ACT 21. Financial aid is available on both need and non-need basis, with 350 scholarships offered, 150 awarded to freshman. 84% of the current student body receive some financial assistance. The average financial package is over $4,600 per year.

Community Environment: Bethany is a metropolitan community in central Oklahoma. The climate is mild. Located on U.S. Highway 66, eight miles from Will Rogers Airport, the city also has train service. The community provides adequate motels for student housing. Unusual job opportunities are available for students. Community services include active churches, a Chamber of Commerce, and nearby health centers and hospitals.

SOUTHWESTERN COLLEGE OF CHRISTIAN MINISTRIES
(F-10)
P.O. Box 340
Oklahoma City, Oklahoma 73008
Tel: (405) 789-7661

Description: The private junior college of Christian Ministry was established in 1946 and is sponsored by the Pentecostal Holiness Church. In 1973 the college became accredited by the North Central Association of Colleges and Schools. It operates on the semester system and also offers two summer sessions. Enrollment includes 125 men and women with a faculty of 33. The college awards an Associate degree.

Entrance Requirements: High school graduation; open enrollment policy; ACT required; non-high school graduates admitted on a provisional basis with satisfactory scores on ACT or GED; rolling admission plan available.

Costs Per Year: $3,270 tuition; $2,450 room and board; $42 student fees.

Collegiate Environment: The college is located in the rapidly growing northwest area of Oklahoma City. The campus is composed of 26 acres of choice property only a few moments from numerous shopping and employment opportunities. The college buildings contain a library of 30,000 volumes and dormitory facilities for 80 men and 138 women. Students from other geographical locations are accepted as well as midyear students. Financial aid is available. Semesters begin in August and January.

Community Environment: See Oklahoma City University

SOUTHWESTERN OKLAHOMA STATE UNIVERSITY
(F-7)
100 Campus Drive
Weatherford, Oklahoma 73096
Tel: (405) 772-6611; Fax: (405) 774-3795

Description: The state college was established by an Act of the Oklahoma Territorial Legislature in 1901 as the Southwestern Normal School, authorized to offer two years of training for public school teachers. Two additional years of college work were added in 1920. The college is authorized to offer curricula in teacher education, health sciences, business, and the arts and sciences. It is accredited by the North Central Association of Colleges and Schools. Enrollment is 1,749 men and 2,141 women full-time, and 365 men and 698 women part-time. A faculty of 214 full-time and 10 part-time gives a faculty-student ratio of 1-19. The school operates on the semester system and offers a summer session. It grants undergraduate and graduate-level degrees.

Entrance Requirements: Accredited high school graduation with 20 units including 4 English, 3 math, 2 laboratory science, and 2 history; rank in upper 50% of graduating class; score of 19 or over on ACT; non-high school graduates considered; rolling admission and early admission plans.

Costs Per Year: $1,312 tuition and fees; $3,341 out-of-state; $1,860 room and board.

Collegiate Environment: The college is located in Weatherford, 70 miles west of Oklahoma City. The college buildings contain a library of 995,038 volumes, 242,406 bound volumes, 751,114 microform volumes and 1,518 periodicals, and living accommodations for 724 men and 823 women. Approximately 98% of students applying for admission are accepted, including midyear students. Financial aid is available for economically handicapped students. Of 758 scholarships offered, 268 are available to freshmen. 48% of the student body presently receives financial aid. The college provides a special program for the culturally disadvantaged that enables low-mark students to attend. Semesters begin in August and January.

Community Environment: Weatherford is located 70 miles west of Oklahoma City. The area is served by bus and a local airport. There are 20 churches, as well as recreational areas and a municipal hospital within the city. There are various civic, fraternal, and veteran's organizations within the community. Limited part-time employment is available for students.

SOUTHWESTERN OKLAHOMA STATE UNIVERSITY AT SAYRE   *(G-4)*
409 East Mississippi
Sayre, Oklahoma 73662
Tel: (405) 928-5533; Admissions: (405) 928-5533; Fax: (405) 928-5533

Description: The public junior college was established in 1938 and serves Beckham, Roger Mills, and Washita Counties as well as adjoining areas in Texas and Oklahoma. Originally, the college emphasized its transfer program, but since 1950 it has placed equal emphasis on such other programs as terminal and adult education. The college operates on the semester basis and enrolls 625 men and women. A faculty of 23 gives a faculty-student ratio of 1-27. The college is accredited by the North Central Association of Colleges and Schools and grants an Associate degree.

Entrance Requirements: High school graduation or equivalent; open enrollment policy; completion of 15 units including English, 1 mathematics, 1 social studies; ACT required; non-high school graduates 18 years or older may be admitted; early admission, rolling admission plans.

Costs Per Year: $1,547.20 ($48.35/cr) resident tuition.

Collegiate Environment: The 45-acre campus is located at Sayre, one of the older towns in southwestern Oklahoma. The four college buildings include a library of 10,000 volumes. All students applying for admission are accepted, including midyear students. Scholarships are available and 75% of the students receive some form of financial aid.

Community Environment: Sayre is a small community noted for its fine registered quarter horses and rich oil and gas fields. The area is served by railway and bus lines. Nearest airport is a two-hour drive away. Sayre has churches, motels, and various civic, fraternal, and veteran's organizations. Part-time employment is available. Recreational facilities in the area include many fishing lakes within a 15-minute drive, a 20-acre park, and a swimming pool.

TULSA JUNIOR COLLEGE - METRO CAMPUS   *(D-14)*
909 South Boston
Tulsa, Oklahoma 74119
Tel: (918) 587-6561

Description: Tulsa Junior College opened in 1970, and is accredited by the North Central Association of Colleges and Schools. It offers the associate degree in a wide variety of courses for students planning to go on to a four-year program, and also offers one- and two-year technical and occupational programs. Tulsa Junior College is the largest junior college in Oklahoma, and has three campuses in operation. Ninety percent of the students come from Tulsa county. The enrollment for all three campuses is approximately 22,000, with 9,000 at the Metro Campus. The semester system is used and one summer term is offered.

Entrance Requirements: Open enrollment; high school graduation or equivalent; high school units required: 4 English, 3 math, 2 laboratory science, and 2 history; adult non-high school graduates may be eligible for admission.

Costs Per Year: $31 per semester hour; $84 per semester hour non-residents.

Collegiate Environment: Tulsa Junior College has 3 Campuses. A large variety of intramural sporting events, drama, music, and other activities is available. Facilities and services include a Learning Resources Center, Career Center, Student Activities Center, various labs, and a Student Activities Program, which are available on all 3 campuses. There is no on-campus housing.

Branch Campuses: Northeast Campus, 3727 E Apache, Tulsa, OK 74115, (918) 631-7000; Southeast Campus, 10300 E 81 St. S, Tulsa, OK, 74133, (918) 631-7000.

UNIVERSITY OF CENTRAL OKLAHOMA *(F-10)*
Edmond, Oklahoma 73060
Tel: (405) 341-2980; Fax: (405) 341-4964

Description: The state university is the oldest state educational institution in Oklahoma and was established as the Territorial Normal School in 1890. It is fully accredited by the North Central Association of Colleges and the National Council for the Accreditation of Teacher Education, the National League for Nursing, and the American Board of Funeral Service Education. The university operates on the early semester system and offers a summer term. The university grants the Certificate, Bachelor and Master degrees. Enrollment includes 8,978 full-time, 7,061 part-time undergraduates, 8,689 evening, and 3,663 graduate students. A faculty of 395 full-time and 300 part-time gives a faculty student ratio of 1-23.

Entrance Requirements: All Oklahoma residents with accredited high school diploma and one of the following requirements: 2.7 GPA in four years of high school work; completion of 11 units including 4 English, 3 mathematics, 2 laboratory science, 2 history; rank in upper 50% of graduating class; score of 19 or over on ACT. Non-high school graduates 18 years of age or older may be admitted on a provisional basis. Early decision and midyear admission availble; $15 application fee.

Costs Per Year: $1,213 tuition; $3,274 nonresident; $2,311 room and board; $285 student fees.

Collegiate Environment: The 200-acre campus is located 12 miles from the state capital and 12 miles from the state's largest city. The 39 college buildings contain a library of 466,293 volumes and living accommodations for 1,157 students.

80% of applicants are accepted. A total of 1,489 scholarships are offered. Financial aid is available and 33% receive assistance.

Community Environment: Edmond is a suburban city 12 miles north of Oklahoma City. All modes of transportation are available to the community. Edmond has churches of most denominations, a movie theatre, numerous parks, a swimming pool, and shopping centers. Part-time employment is plentiful.

UNIVERSITY OF OKLAHOMA *(G-10)*
660 Parrington Oval
Norman, Oklahoma 73019
Tel: (405) 325-0311

Description: The university was established in 1890 by the Oklahoma Territorial Legislature. It is accredited by the North Central Association of Colleges and Schools. The university now has 20 colleges offering 160 undergraduate degree programs; 124 master's gegree programs; doctoral programs in 79 fields; professional degrees in four areas, and 20 dual professional/master's programs. The university also maintains exchange agreements with 50 foreign universities on five continents. Norman campus enrollment includes 6,908 men, 5,650 women full-time, 1,333 men, and 1,197 women part-time for a total of 14,980 undergraduate students. Full-time students comprise 75 percent of the total undergraduate and graduate enrollment. More than 1,200 undergraduates are active participants in the OU Honors Program, and OU is ranked third nationally among all public universities in the number of freshman National Merit Scholars. A Norman campus faculty of 835 full-time and 155 part-time provides a faculty-student ratio of approximately 1-20.

Entrance Requirements: Accredited high school graduation with composite score of 21 or over on ACT, or average grade of B (3.0 or above on a 4.0 scale) in four years of high school study, or rank in upper half of graduating class; or a combined verbal and math score of 950 on the SAT. Oklahoma non-high school graduates admissible on a provisional basis with satisfactory scores on ACT; application fee $25 for non-residents; early admission, early decision, delayed admission, rolling admission and advanced placement plans are available.

Costs Per Year: $1,918 tuition and fees; $5,365 out-of-state; $3,526 room and board.

Collegiate Environment: The University of Oklahoma has campuses in Norman, Oklahoma City and Tulsa comprising more than 3,200 acres and 338 buildings. The university libraries include 2,484,094 volumes, 3,394,894 titles on microform and 17,400 current periodicals. Living accommodations are provided in residence halls for 1,971 men and 1,611 women, and 921 apartment units are maintained for married, upper-division and graduate students. Fraternities and sororities house an additional 1,600 men and women. Need-based and merit-based financial aid is available. Of 19,294 scholarships awarded, 3,288 are for freshmen. 62% of students on the Norman campus and 60 percent of Health Sciences Center students receive some form of financial aid.

Community Environment: Norman is a mid-sized city in central Oklahoma with award-winning public schools; cultural offerings, such as theaters and museums; and recreational facilities, including parks, golf courses and nearby Lake Thunderbird. The community is served by major highways, bus lines, and Will Rogers World Airport, located 18 miles north in Oklahoma City. The university operates Max Westheimer Airpark, a general aviation, reliever category airport in Norman. Community services also include churches, hospitals and a public library.

UNIVERSITY OF OKLAHOMA - HEALTH SCIENCES CENTER *(F-10)*
1000 Stanton L. Young Boulevard
Oklahoma City, Oklahoma 73190
Tel: (405) 271-4000

Description: The university medical school was established at Norman, Oklahoma, in 1900 and merged with the Epworth Medical College in Oklahoma City in 1910. In 1928, the first building of the present complex was completed and the basic science departments were then transferred from the Norman campus to the present Health Sciences Center campus. The College of Nursing was organized in 1911 and was granted authority to award baccalaureate degrees in 1957. The College of Health was established in 1967, was divided into the College of Allied Health and the College of Dentistry, and admitted its initial class in August 1971. The College of Pharmacy transferred from the Norman campus to the HSC campus in 1976. A branch of the College of Medicine has been established in Tulsa, and third and fourth-year medical students may transfer (in limited numbers) to that campus for completion of clinical requirements. Graduate degrees are offered in the medical sciences, public health, nursing, pharmacy, audiology, speech pathology, physical therapy, orthodontics, periodontics, prosthondontics on the Oklahoma City HSC campus. A total enrollment of 2,799 and a faculty of 841 gives a faculty-student ratio of 1:4.

Entrance Requirements: Entrance requirements vary with program. At the undergraduate level a minimum of 60 to 64 semester hours from an accredited institution is required. For dentistry a minimum of 60 hours is required for application and 90 semester hours are the minimum for medicine. Many applicants to both professional programs possess baccalaureate degrees. A baccalaureate degree is required for entry into all graduate programs. Professional school applications (dentistry & medicine) are via national application services, AADSAS and AMCAS. The professional test of the American Dental Association (ADAAT) and the American Medical College Association (AMCAT) are required respectively. The GRE is required for graduate admissions in most programs. $25 application fee.

Costs Per Year: $1,465 undergraduate resident; $4,627 nonresident; $1,882 graduate resident; $5,749 nonresident; medical, dental and pharmaceutical programs vary.

Collegiate Environment: Four major hospitals are located on campus and several other large hospitals are available for clinical experience in Oklahoma City, Tulsa and other locations within the state. A limited number of third and fourth-year medical students may complete their degree requirements at these locations. No university housing is available at the HSC or in Tulsa and none is currently projected. Housing is obtainable in private facilities near the campus and throughout the city. The campus is a modern complex, branching mainly East and South from the original structure at the corner of N.E. 13th and N. Phillips in Oklahoma City. It has a number of new structures including laboratories, clinical facilities, classroom buildings, hospitals, institutes, a major research foundation and associated organizations. A new Library and Learning Resources Center has opened recently. Financial aid is available and some 200 scholarships are granted. The center library houses over 200,080 volumes and the library resources of the Norman campus are available on call.

Community Environment: See Oklahoma City University.

UNIVERSITY OF SCIENCE AND ARTS OF OKLAHOMA
(H-9)
17th & Grand
Chickasha, Oklahoma 73018
Tel: (405) 224-3140; Fax: (405) 521-6244

Description: The first Oklahoma Legislature established this college in 1908 as the Industrial Institute and College. It operated as the Oklahoma College for women from 1916 to 1965, when it became coeducational. It is accredited by the North Central Association of Colleges and Schools, the National Association of Schools of Music, and the National Council for Accreditation of Teacher Education. It offers a Baccalaureate degree. Enrollment is 437 men and 786 women full-time and 157 men and 307 women part-time. A faculty of 53 full-time and 21 part-time provides an overall faculty-student ratio of approximately 1-23. It operates on a trimester system and offers a summer session.

Entrance Requirements: High school graduation or equivalent; rank in upper half of graduating class; ACT or SAT required, scores average 19 on ACT or 870 on SAT; completion of 20 units including 4 English, 3 mathematics, 2 science, 2 social studies; early admission, early decision, rolling admission, and advanced placement plans available; non-high school graduates may be admitted on a provisional basis with satisfactory scores on ACT.

Costs Per Year: $1,440-$1,770 tuition; $3,510-$3,750 out-of-state; $1,900 room and board.

Collegiate Environment: The 75-acre campus is located in the southwest residential section of Chickasha, approximately 50 miles southwest of Oklahoma City. The 15 college buildings include a library of 90,000 volumes, 1,200 periodicals, 6,000 microforms, and 3,483 audiovisual materials. The college provides dormitory facilities for 135 men and 148 women. Approximately 83% of students applying for admission are accepted, including midyear students. About 50% of the previous freshman class returned to this campus for the sophomore year. Average high school standing of the 1994 freshman class was top 55%; 25% in the top quarter; 13% in the second quarter; 4% in the third quarter; average score of ACT was 20. 63% of the students receive financial aid. 130 scholarships are offered. Trimesters begin in August, January, and April.

Community Environment: Chickasha is a suburban area southwest of Oklahoma City. Located in the fertile Washita River Valley, the city lies within one of the largest gas fields in the world. The community has rail, bus and airline service. Community services include Catholic and Protestant churches, a hospital, a public library, and major civic, fraternal and veteran's organizations. Local recreational facilities include theatres and several good lakes within a few miles for boating, fishing and water sports. Some part-time employment is available for students.

UNIVERSITY OF TULSA   *(D-14)*
600 South College Ave.
Tulsa, Oklahoma 74104
Tel: (918) 631-2307; (800) 331-3050; Admissions: (918) 631-2307/2274; Fax: (918) 631-3172

Description: Henry Kendall College, forerunner of the university, was founded at Muskogee, Indian Territory, in 1894, by the Presbyterian Board of Home Missions. The college moved to its permanent campus in 1907 and its present name was adopted in 1920 with the addition of a Fine Arts College. Today the university is composed of the College of Business Administration, College of Arts and Sciences, College of Law, College of Engineering and Applied Sciences, and the Graduate School. The university is accredited by the North Central Association of Colleges and Schools, and its colleges and professional schools are accredited by respective professional and educational organizations. The university operates on the semester basis and offers two summer terms. A Washington, D.C. internship program is available. Numerous study abroad programs are available. Enrollment includes 1,302 men, 1,460 women full-time, 159 men, 241 women part-time, and 1,411 graduate students. A faculty of 331 full-time and 114 part-time gives a faculty-student ratio of 1-12. The university awards undergraduate and graduate level degrees.

Entrance Requirements: High school graduation; completion of 15 college-preparatory units including 4 English, 3 mathematics, 3 science, 3 social science, 2 foreign language are recommended as a minimum; additional units may be required for individual colleges; SAT or ACT required; early admission, rolling admission, delayed admission, midyear admission and advanced placement plans available; $25 application fee.

Costs Per Year: $11,750 tuition; $4,160 room and board.

Collegiate Environment: The university is located on 140 acres. The university libraries contain 2,011,145 volumes and 4,300 periodicals, and 1.8 million audiovisual materials. Housing facilities are provided for 727 men and 499 women, and housing provided by seven national fraternities and seven national sororities accommodates another 200 men and 212 women. Apartments accommodate 150 families and 38 students are in an honor house. The university welcomes a geographically diverse student body and will accept midyear students to meet its commitment to making quality private higher education accessible to all qualified students. 86% of all applicants are accepted. The average SAT scores of the freshman class were 525 verbal and 576 math; Average ACT composite score of 24.3. More than 70% of the students receive some form of financial aid, including grants, loans, scholarships and work-study.

Community Environment: The climate is temperate. The average year-round high temperature is 71 degrees. The population is 750,000 in the metropolitan area. The city features a professional opera company, a national ballet company, a symphony orchestra, museums, art galleries, community theatres, parks, minor league teams in hockey and baseball and recreation and shopping facilities. Public bus transportation is available.

WESTERN OKLAHOMA STATE COLLEGE   *(I-5)*
2801 N. Main Street
Altus, Oklahoma 73521
Tel: (405) 477-2000

Description: Formerly Altus Junior College, the public junior college was founded in 1926 and is Oklahoma's oldest municipal junior college. The college is accredited fully by the North Central Association of Colleges and Schools. Programs of study lead to the Certificate and Associate degree. Adult evening classes are offered. The college operates on the semester system and offers one summer session. Enrollment includes 698 full-time and 1,005 part-time students. A faculty of 88 gives a faculty-student ratio of 1-20.

Entrance Requirements: Accredited high school graduation; units should include 4 English, 3 mathematics, 2 social science, and 2 science; ACT required; non-high school graduates 18 years of age or older may be admitted; early admission, early decision, rolling admission, midyear admission and delayed admission plans available; no application fee.

Costs Per Year: $780 tuition; $1,680 nonresident; $180 student fees.

Collegiate Environment: The college is located on 142-acre site. Facilities include three modern buildings with a library housing approximately 40,000 volumes, 229 periodicals, 46,000 microforms and 1,211 audiovisual materials. Approximately 100% of students applying for admission are accepted, including midyear students. About 60% of the recent student body graduated in the top half of the high school class, 40% in the top quarter, and 15% in the highest tenth. Over 55% of the previous freshman class returned to this campus for the sophomore year. 370 scholarships are available, including 175 for freshmen.

Community Environment: Altus is an urban community served by bus, railroad, and major interstate highways. The climate is temperate. The community has one hospital, a public library, many churches, and recreational facilities.

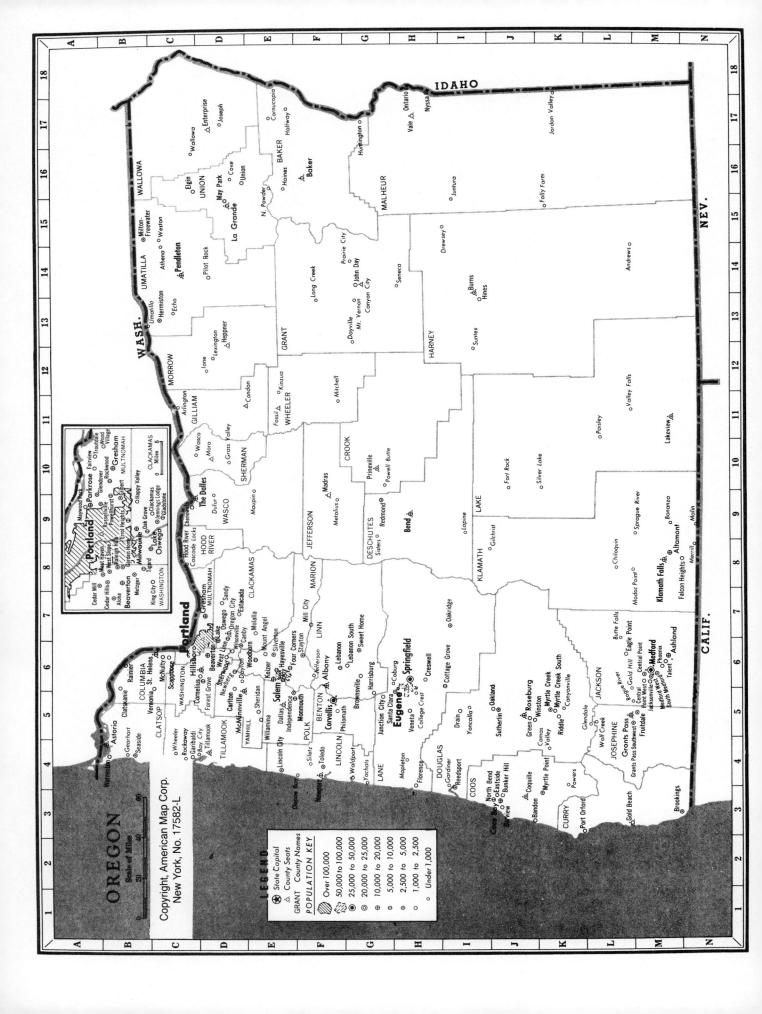

OREGON
Scale of Miles

Copyright, American Map Corp.
New York, No. 17582-L

LEGEND
⊛ State Capital
⚲ County Seats
GRANT County Names
POPULATION KEY
⬨ Over 100,000
⬨ 50,000 to 100,000
◉ 25,000 to 50,000
◉ 20,000 to 25,000
⊕ 10,000 to 20,000
⊕ 5,000 to 10,000
○ 2,500 to 5,000
○ 1,000 to 2,500
○ Under 1,000

IDAHO

WASH.

NEV.

CALIF.

OREGON

CASCADE COLLEGE (D-6)

9101 East Burnside
Portland, Oregon 97216
Tel: (503) 255-7060; (800) 550-7678; Admissions: (503) 257-1218;
Fax: (503) 257-1222

Description: The private coeducational college was established in 1956 and is maintained and supported by members of the Church of Christ. The college has been granted full accreditation by the Northwest Association of Schools and Colleges. The college offers a liberal arts and Bible program. It operates on the semester system. Enrollment is 247 full-time and 32 part-time students. A faculty of 20 full-time and 25 part-time gives a faculty-student ratio of 1:11.

Entrance Requirements: Accredited high school graduation or GED equivalent; 4 units of English, 2 mathematics, 2 science, and 2 social studies; ACT or SAT required; non-high school graduates 18 years or older may be admitted as special students; early admission, midyear admission, and rolling admission available; $25 application fee.

Costs Per Year: $6,400 tuition; $3,200 room and board; $200 student fees.

Collegiate Environment: 67% of applicants are accepted including mid-year students. Financial aid is available and 96% of the students receive aid. The college library contains 35,000 volumes, 245 periodicals, 26,500 microforms and 1,000 audiovisual materials.

Community Environment: See Portland State University.

CENTRAL OREGON COMMUNITY COLLEGE (H-9)

2600 N.W. College Way
Bend, Oregon 97701
Tel: (503) 383-7500; (800) 422-3041; Fax: (503) 383-7503

Description: The public community college is the oldest community college in Oregon, founded in 1949 as a part of the Oregon State General Extension Division. The college is accredited by the Northwest Association of Schools and Colleges. It serves a district consisting of Crook, Deschutes, and Jefferson Counties, the northern portions of Klamath and Lake County, and that portion of the Warm Springs Indian reservation lying within Wasco County. The quarter system is used and one summer session is offered. The enrollment includes 1,433 full-time and 1,705 part-time students. A faculty of 84 full-time and 120 part-time gives a faculty-student ratio of 1-15.

Entrance Requirements: Open enrollment policy; high school graduation or equivalent required for degree program; early admission, rolling admission, early decision, and advanced placement plans available.

Costs Per Year: $1,510 district resident tuition; $1,958 state resident tuition; $4,658 nonresident tuition; $3,750 room and board.

Collegiate Environment: The 193-acre main campus sits on the western slope of Awbrey Butte, two miles west of Bend, Oregon. The main campus consists of 17 buildings and includes a modern gymnasium, activity field, tennis courts, a large student union, 102-student coeducational residence hall and six major classroom buildings. The library of 36,438 volumes, 370 periodicals, 32,617 microforms, and 1,308 audiovisual materials serves both the campus and the community. 55% of the students receive some form of financial aid.

Community Environment: Bend is an extremely scenic town of some 27,000 people located at the foothills of the Oregon's Cascade Mountain range. The college serves a 10,000-square-mile district that includes part of Central Oregon's high desert country east of Bend. The area's primary industries are lumber and tourism. Bus lines connect Bend with other parts of the state. Two airlines serve the nearby town of Redmond, 14 miles distant, with jet air transport. Bend is 157 miles from Portland and 120 miles from Eugene, Oregon. Community facilities include a public library, churches of major denominations, a new hospital, three major shopping malls and many service and civic organizations. Bend is known nationally for its recreational environment. Bordering the 1.6 million-acre Deschutes National Forest, the town affords excellent hunting, fishing, hiking and camping opportunities. The full-facility Mt. Bachelor Ski Area, which is normally open from November through June, is 22 minutes from the college campus. Rain is rare in the area. Bend receives an average snowfall of three feet per year, although the mountainous areas receive considerably more.

CHEMEKETA COMMUNITY COLLEGE (E-6)

4000 Lancaster Drive N.E.
P.O. Box 14007
Salem, Oregon 97309
Tel: (503) 399-5000; Fax: (503) 399-3918

Description: In 1955, the community college was established as a post-high school institution to meet the increasing technical and vocational needs of Marion, Polk, and parts of Linn Counties. The college is accredited by the Northwest Association of Schools and Colleges, the American Dental Association, and the National League for Nursing. The college operates on the quarter system and offers one summer session. Cooperative education programs are available for all vocational programs. Air Force and Army ROTC prgrams are available as an elective. Enrollment includes 1,262 men and 1,416 women full-time and 6,047 men and 8,508 women part-time. A faculty of 251 full-time and 443 part-time provides a faculty-student ratio of 1-18.

Entrance Requirements: Open door policy; minimum age is 16 years; high school graduation or equivalent required for some programs; rolling admission plan; entrance examinations required for some programs.

Costs Per Year: $1,152 tuition; $4,320 out-of-state; $5,040 international.

Collegiate Environment: The college is located on a 72-acre campus. Since 1955, programs have been added and expanded to cover many of the technologies, business, and health occupations. The library contains 57,715 volumes, 750 periodicals, 147 microforms, 5,140 recordings, and 9 CD-ROMs. There are no dormitories provided. 99% of applicants are accepted. 50% of the students receive some form of financial assistance. Midyear students are accepted.

Community Environment: See Willamette University.

CLACKAMAS COMMUNITY COLLEGE (D-7)

19600 S. Molalla Ave.
Oregon City, Oregon 97045
Tel: (503) 657-8400; Admissions: (503) 657-6958; Fax: (503) 650-6654

Description: This public community college was established in 1966 and serves all of Clackamas County except the Lake Oswego and Sandy High School Districts. It provides business, occupational, and professional assistant programs; a college transfer program; a general education program; guidance and counseling services; and community services. The college is accredited by the Northwest Association of Secondary and Higher Schools and operates on the quarter system with three summer terms. Enrollment is 3,174 full-time and 10,200 part-time students. A faculty of 144 full-time and 383 part-time gives an overall faculty-student ratio of 1-25.

Entrance Requirements: Open enrollment policy; non-high school graduates 18 years of age or older may be admitted as special students; applicants to vocational programs will be considered on the basis of results of special entrance and placement tests; early admission, early decision, rolling admission, and advanced placement plans available.

Costs Per Year: $1,344 resident tuition for 3 terms; $4,704 nonresident.

Collegiate Environment: The college occupies 158 acres located about one-half mile from the southeast corner of Oregon City. The 8 buildings and 2 off-campus sites contain a computer room and a library of 52,684 volumes, 285 periodicals, 324 microform titles and 3,392 recordings. All students applying for admission are accepted, including midyear students. More than half of the previous freshman class returned to this campus for the second year of studies. Financial aid is available and 43% of the current student body receives financial assistance.

Community Environment: Oregon City was the capital of the Old Oregon Territory, founded in 1829. The city is on the bank of the Willamette River where there are 40-foot falls that provide waterpower for the production of paper, batteries, lumber and electric power. A municipal free elevator lifts pedestrians 90 feet up the steep face of a cliff to a residential business district. An observation deck at the top overlooks the downtown area and the falls. The Holly Knoll Museum is 7 miles southeast where antique furniture and harness and horsedrawn vehicles may be seen. The John McLoughlin House National Historic Site was built in 1846.

CLATSOP COMMUNITY COLLEGE   *(D-7)*
1653 Jerome
Astoria, Oregon 97103
Tel: (503) 325-0910

Description: This public two-year college was established in 1958 and in 1965 became the first public Oregon Community College to be fully accredited by the Northwest Association of Schools and Colleges. It offers programs in liberal arts and sciences, general studies, vocational-technical, and adult education. The college operates on the quarter system and provides one summer term. Enrollment is 450 full-time and 2,200 part-time students. A faculty of 164 gives a faculty-student ratio of 1-13.

Entrance Requirements: Open admissions; high school graduation not required; ASSET placement examinations may be required.

Costs Per Year: $1,080 tuition; $3,600 nonresident; $2,830 room and board.

Collegiate Environment: The 40-acre campus is located in Astoria, the county seat of Clatsop County. The city is a sheltered harbor on the Columbia River in the oldest historical section of Oregon. The four college buildings include a library of approximately 36,500 volumes. 100% of students applying for admission are accepted, including midyear students. Financial aid is available and 70% of the current student body receives some form of assistance.

Community Environment: Located on the Columbia River, about 10 miles from its mouth, Astoria is known principally for its salmon and tuna industries. Astoria's history dates from the winter of 1805 when the Lewis and Clark expedition camped at Fort Clatsop. Many plants here are in the fish canning, curing, and freezing business. At the larger docks, ocean liners load for world ports. Commercial transportation is available. There are a number of churches, a city-owned library, museums, hospitals, and many of the major civic and service organizations in the community. The opportunities are good for part-time employment. Recreational facilities are numerous; lakes, streams, rivers, and the ocean for fishing, swimming, boating, picnicking and digging for clams. During the fishing season, August 1 to September 10, more than 15,000 large fish are taken from the Columbia River near Astoria. Some of the points of interest are the Astoria Column, 125 feet high, which illustrates incidents in the early history of the region, Clatsop County Historical Museum, the Columbia River Maritime Museum, and Fort Astoria. The Astoria Regatta is an annual event.

CONCORDIA UNIVERSITY   *(D-6)*
2811 NE Holman Street
Portland, Oregon 97211
Tel: (503) 288-9371; (800) 321-9371; Admissions: (503) 280-8501;
Fax: (503) 280-8531

Description: The private institution began operation as a four-year academy in 1905, and the junior college department for men was added in 1950. The college became coeducational in 1954. In 1980, the first Baccalaureate degrees were granted. The college is owned and maintained by the Lutheran Church-Missouri Synod. It is accredited by the Northwest Association of Schools and Colleges and operates on the quarter system. Enrollment is 865 full-time and 230 part-time students. A faculty of 49 full-time and 40 part-time gives a faculty-student ratio of 1-20.

Entrance Requirements: Accredited high school graduation or equivalent; minimum 2.50 average GPA; recommended completion of 21 units including 4 English, 3 mathematics, 3 science, and 3 social science; SAT, ACT or WPCT required; rolling admission, advanced placement, and delayed admission plans available.

Costs Per Year: $10,500 tuition; $3,500 room and board.

Collegiate Environment: The college occupies an attractive, 13-acre campus in northeast Portland. The eleven college buildings include a library of 53,000 volumes and four dormitory facilities for 200 students. Approximately 70% of students applying for admission are accepted, including midyear students. Financial aid is available, and about 88% of the students receive aid.

Community Environment: Portland lies along both sides of the Willamette River at its juncture with the Columbia River, where there is a splendid port deep enough for the largest ships to dock. Portland has a beautiful background of snow-capped mountain peaks to the north and east, and because of the Japanese Current, enjoys a mild and equable climate. The Columbia River Highway is a beautiful drive, particularly through the Columbia River Gorge with cliffs 2,000 feet high. The city is one of the country's leading wheat-exporting cities, as well as a wool center. Its livestock market is the largest on the northwest coast. The Columbia and Willamette Rivers nearby offer year-round water sports, the ocean beach is also nearby, and skiing is available at nearby Mount Hood. Part-time employment and commercial transportation are available. Some of the points of interest are the Hoyt Arboretum, Portland Art Museum, National Sanctuary of Our Sorrowful Mother, Oregon Museum of Science and Industry, Crystal Spring Rhododendron Garden, Washington Park Zoo, Japanese Gardens, World Forestry Center, and Washington Park Rose Test Gardens.

EASTERN OREGON STATE COLLEGE   *(D-15)*
8th and K Avenue
La Grande, Oregon 97850-2899
Tel: (503) 962-3672; (800) 452-8639; Admissions: (503) 962-3393;
Fax: (503) 962-3849

Description: The state college was established as a normal school and opened in 1929. In 1964, the State Board of Higher Education restated institutional allocations and described the college as a regional liberal arts college with emphasis on teacher education. It is accredited by the Northwest Association of Schools and Colleges and the National Council for Accreditation of Teacher Education. The college operates on the quarter system and offers two summer terms. A National Guard Officer Leadership Detachment Program is available. ROTC is no longer available. Cooperative education opportunities are available in all disciplines. Study abroad is available to Denmark, Korea, France, Japan, Germany, and China. Enrollment includes 1,421 full-time, 492 part-time undergraduates and 10 graduate students. A faculty of 117 full-time and 30 part-time gives an undergraduate faculty-student ratio of 1-14.

Entrance Requirements: Accredited high school graduation or equivalent; completion of 14 units including 4 English, 3 mathematics, 2 science, 3 social studies, 2 electives; high school GPA minimum 2.5 on 4.0 scale; application form, official transcripts and $50 application fee; SAT or ACT required; if GPA is 2.5-2.99, applicant must provide "portfolio" including 300-500 word typewritten essay on educational goals, 2 letters of recommendation (one from teacher or counselor or administrator if candidate is under age 21), and other evidence of academic and community achievements; applicants who have not met standards may be considered for special admission; all portfolios must be submitted 30 days prior to the beginning of the desired term of entry; international students must submit TOEFL scores of minimum: 500 for undergraduates, 550 for graduates; rolling admission, early admission, early decision, and advanced placement plans available.

Costs Per Year: $2,766 tuition; $3,600 room and board.

Collegiate Environment: The 121-acre campus with 15 college buildings is located in the Grande Ronde Valley with the scenic Wallowa Mountains to the east and the Blue Mountains to the west. The library contains 120,481 bound volumes, 961 periodicals, 7,786 titles on microforms and 6,008 recordings. Dormitory facilities provide accommodations for 451 students and 17 families. Students from other geographical locations are admitted, as well as midyear students. 95% of applicants are accepted. Financial aid is available for economically disadvantaged students. 70% of students receive some form of financial aid.

Community Environment: The city of La Grande has a population of about 12,000 and is located in the Grande Ronde Valley with the scenic Wallowa Mountains to the east and the Blue Mountains to the west.

Branch Campuses: Branch Campuses: Hermiston; Pendleton; Ontario; Baker.

EUGENE BIBLE COLLEGE   *(H-5)*
2155 Bailey Hill Road
Eugene, Oregon 97405
Tel: (503) 485-1780; (800) 322-2638; Fax: (503) 343-5801

Description: The Bible college was established in 1925 and is the national college of the Open Bible Standard Churches, Inc. It is a member of the Evangelical Teacher's Training Association, and National Association of Evangelicals. It has full membership with the American Association of Bible Colleges. The college operates on the quarter system. Full-time enrollment includes 130 men and 82 women. A full-time faculty of 14 provides a faculty-student ratio of 1-14.

Entrance Requirements: Open enrollment policy; SAT or ACT and entrance exam required; non-high school graduates considered; early decision, midyear admission plans available; $30 application fee.

Costs Per Year: $4,017 tuition; $2,766 room and board; $549 student fees.

Collegiate Environment: The Bible college provides dormitory facilities for 108 students. Its library contains more than 32,000 volumes. Dormitories house 48 men and 60 women. Approximately 95% of students applying for admission are accepted including midyear students. 80% of the students receive financial aid. A limited number of scholarships are available.

Community Environment: See University of Oregon.

GEORGE FOX COLLEGE   *(D-6)*
Newberg, Oregon 97132
Tel: (503) 538-8383; Fax: (503) 538-7234

Description: This private liberal arts college was established by the Northwest Yearly meeting of Friends in 1891. It was known as Pacific College until 1949. The college operates on the 4-1-1 system and is accredited by the Northwest Association of Schools and Colleges. Enrollment includes 1,042 full-time, 42 part-time, 215 evening and 182 graduate students. A faculty of 70 full-time and 63 part-time gives a faculty-student ratio of 1-15.

Entrance Requirements: Accredited high school graduation or equivalent; completion of 13 units recommended, including 4 English, 2 mathematics, 2 foreign language, 2 science, 2 social science, and 1 physical education; SAT or ACT required; applicants who do not meet all requirements for admissions may be admitted on a provisional basis; $20 application fee; early admission, rolling admission, and advanced placement plans available.

Costs Per Year: $11,600 tuition; $3,890 room and board; $150 student fees.

Collegiate Environment: The college has 20 buildings located on 60 acres. Financial aid is available for needy students. About 71% of applicants are accepted. About 90% of the students receive financial aid and 350 scholarships are offered. The library contains 90,000 volumes, numerous phamphlets, 1,100 periodical subscriptions, 400 microforms and 1,800 audiovisual items. Residential space is provided for 564 men, women and families.

Community Environment: Located 24 miles southwest of Portland, Newberg has a number of churches, the Newberg Community Hospital, and various civic and service organizations. Part-time employment is available. Commercial transportation is available.

LANE COMMUNITY COLLEGE   *(H-6)*
4000 E. 30th Avenue
Eugene, Oregon 97405
Tel: (503) 747-4501

Description: The public community college was established in 1964 and serves a district of 5,000 square miles, which includes Lane County and small portions of Linn, Benton, and Douglas Counties. The college employs the quarter system and offers three summer terms. Total enrollment is 9,600 students. The faculty numbers 282 full-time. The faculty-student ratio for full-time students is 1-31. The college is accredited by the Northwest Association of Schools and Colleges.

Entrance Requirements: Open enrollment policy; non-high school graduates admitted; delayed admission, early admission, early decision, rolling admission, and advanced placement plans available.

Costs Per Year: $1,380 tuition; $4,830 out-of-state.

Collegiate Environment: The college is comprised of 17 buildings, located on 292 acres. Almost all students applying for admission are accepted, including midyear students. The college library contains 62,805 volumes, 50,000 pamphlets, 496 periodicals, 66,207 microforms and 2,955 audiovisual items. The college offers 35 scholarships.

Community Environment: See University of Oregon.

LEWIS AND CLARK COLLEGE   *(D-6)*
0615 SW Palatine Hill Road
Box 32
Portland, Oregon 97219
Tel: (503) 768-7040; (800) 444-4111; Fax: (503) 768-7055

Description: The private liberal arts college was established in 1867. It is accredited by the Northwest Association of Schools and Colleges and the National Association of Schools of Music. The college operates on the semester system and offers two summer sessions. 15 study abroad programs are available. Enrollment includes 1,758 full-time and 39 part-time undergraduate students. A faculty of 116 full-time and 20 part-time gives an undergraduate faculty-student ratio of 1-14. There are also 1,437 graduate students.

Entrance Requirements: High school graduation with units including 4 English, 3-4 mathematics, 2 laboratory science, 2 foreign language, 3 social science and 1 fine arts recommended; SAT or ACT required, except for Portfolio Path applicants; early decision, early notifications, delayed admission and advanced placement and I.B. credit accepted; $40 application fee.

Costs Per Year: $16,640 tuition; $5,070 room and board; student fees $180.

Collegiate Environment: The campus occupies a country estate of 130 acres, which contains 40 college buildings. The libraries house 276,800 volumes, 3,430 periodicals, 247,000 microforms and 12,500 records, tapes, and compact discs. Residence hall facilities provide housing for 939 students. The college welcomes a geographically diverse student body and will accept midyear students. Approximately 77% of students applying for admission are accepted and 76% of the previous freshman class returned to this campus for the sophomore year. The average high school standing of the current freshman class, top 20%; 65% were in the top quarter and 26% in the second quarter. Financial aid is available based on need and about 65% of first-year students receive aid. The college provides overseas study programs, and over 50% of the graduates study abroad or somewhere off campus.

Community Environment: See Portland State University.

LINFIELD COLLEGE   *(D-5)*
McMinnville, Oregon 97128
Tel: (503) 434-2200; (800) 640-2287; Admissions: (503) 434-2213; Fax: (503) 434-2472

Description: This private liberal arts college was established in 1849 and is accredited by the Northwest Association of Schools and Colleges, the National Association of Schools of Music, and the National League for Nursing. It operates on the 4-1-4 calendar system and offers two summer sessions. Enrollment includes 1,555 full-time and 58 part-time undergraduates and 21 graduate students. A faculty of 121 full-time and 12 part-time gives a faculty-student ratio of 1-12. Academic cooperative plans are available for students majoring in engineering and medical technology. Language majors must spend a year abroad where the language is spoken. Six study centers for the semester abroad program for non language majors are located in Nottingham, England; Paris, France; San Jose, Costa Rica; Yokohama, Japan and Seoul, South Korea. Degree programs offered through the Division of Continuing Education may be completed on a part-time basis at nine sites in Oregon and Southwest Washington.

Entrance Requirements: High school graduation with rank in upper 50% of graduating class; SAT or ACT required; early decision and delayed admission plans available; $30 application fee. Feb. 15 application deadline.

Costs Per Year: $13,380 tuition; $4,210 room and board; $900 average additional expenses.

Collegiate Environment: The 100-acre campus is situated in the beautiful Willamette Valley, about 24 miles northwest of Salem and 45 miles south of Portland. The 34 college buildings contain a library of 135,000 titles, 1,074 periodical subscriptions, 140,166 microfilms, and 6,149 audiovisual materials. Residence hall facilities house 341 men and 449 women. Fraternities provide housing for 90 men. Students from other geographical locations are admitted. 70% of applicants are accepted. The average scores of the entering freshman class were SAT 479 verbal, 558 math, ACT 25 composite. Approximately 565 scholarships are available, including 205 for freshmen. 84% of the current student body receives financial aid. 73% of the freshman class returned for the sophomore year.

Community Environment: The campus is located in a rural area where agricultural products such as turkeys, walnuts, hazelnuts, grains, fruit, grapes, beans, and strawberries are abundant. Industries in town produce electronic products, steel, and food products. Part-time employment opportunities are available. Community facilities include 36 churches, one hospital, and major civic and service organizations. The Yamhill County Fair, the Turkey-Rama, and the international Pinot Noir Festival are annual events.

LINN-BENTON COMMUNITY COLLEGE   *(F-6)*
6500 Pacific Boulevard SW
Albany, Oregon 97321
Tel: (503) 967-6105

Description: This public community college offered its first classes in 1967. It is accredited by the Northwest Association of Schools and Colleges, the American Dental Association, and the National League for Nursing. The college operates on the quarter system and offers one summer term. Army, Air Force, Navy, and Marine Corps ROTC are available. Enrollment includes 2,112 full-time and 3,625 part-time students. There are also 6,119 non-credit students. There is a faculty of 169 full-time and 500 part-time members.

Entrance Requirements: High school graduation or 18 years of age or older; open enrollment policy; placement test required; early admission, early decision, midyear admission, rolling admission, and advanced placement plans available; $20 application fee.

Costs Per Year: $1,440 resident tuition; $5,355 out-of-state.

Collegiate Environment: All students applying for admission are accepted including midyear students. Library holdings number 38,435 bound volumes, 398 periodicals, 225 microforms, 1,973 audio materials and 1,200 videos. Scholarships are available and 60% of the full-time students receive some form of financial aid.

Community Environment: Noted for its rare metals industries, Albany is also in the fertile Willamette Valley, a rich timber area; the valley is one of the leading producers of rye grass seed and mint. The rare metals industries produce tantalum, tungsten, zirconium, hafnium, columbium, and molybdenum. Other manufactured products are plywood lumber, furniture, and mill machinery. The average rainfall is 39.7 inches. Community facilities include a number of churches, a YMCA, Boys Club, a hospital, and many clinics, excellent shopping areas, and a number of civic and service organizations. Part-time jobs are available. Recreational activities are swimming, tennis, and other sports. The World's Champion Timber Carnival in July draws loggers from all over to compete in log rolling, tree topping, axe throwing, and other events.

MARYLHURST COLLEGE   *(D-7)*
Marylhurst, Oregon 97036
Tel: (503) 636-8141; (800) 634-9982; Fax: (503) 636-9526

Description: Founded in 1893 as a Catholic women's college, Marylhurst reorganized in 1974 as an independent coeducational liberal arts college dedicated to making innovative post secondary education accessible to a great diversity of students. Flexibility in scheduling and delivery of academic services makes a college education available to working adults and distance learners as well as day-time students. Marylhurst offers both degree and non-degree programs designed to meet the learning needs of students motivated toward professional and personal excellence. Programs leading to a Bachelor of Arts degree include majors in Art, Communication, Humanities, Human Studies, Interdisciplinary Studies, Music, Religious Studies, Science-Mathematics, and Social Science. Also offered are a Bachelor of Fine Arts degree in Art, a Bachelor of Music degree, and a Bachelor of Science degree in Management. At the graduate level, a Master of Science degree in Management, a Master of Business Administration, a Master of Arts degree in Art Therapy, and a Master of Arts degree in Interdisciplinary Studies are offered. Marylhurst is regionally accredited by the Northwest Association of Schools and Colleges and is approved by the Oregon Office of Educational Policy and Planning. Marylhurst is professionally accredited by the National Association of Schools of Music. Enrollment includes 1,961 students. A faculty of 124 provides a faculty-student ratio of 1:15.

Entrance Requirements: High school graduation; SAT or ACT recommended; open enrollment; rolling admission, and advanced placement plans available; $81 application fee.

Costs Per Year: $8,505 tuition; $45 student fees.

Collegiate Environment: Marylhurst College, animated by its Catholic and liberal arts heritage dating to 1893, emphasizes the uniqueness and dignity of each person, and is committed to the examination of values, as well as to quality academic and professional instruction. The College seeks to aid students in advancing their goals for responsible participation in a rapidly changing world by pursuing, and encouraging its students to pursue, the ideals of competence, leadership and service. Study at Marylhurst is enhanced by small class size and individualized attention. Many faculty members come to the classroom directly from the working world and therefore bring with them a wealth of practical as well as theoretical knowledge. Students and faculty learn with and from each other on a 65 acre wooded campus minutes from downtown Portland. Shoen Library serves both students and Marylhurst residents. All applicants accepted. Its collection includes 100,000 volumes, 400 periodicals, 2,511 microforms, and 9,400 audiovisual materials. 60% receive financial aid.

Community Environment: See Portland State University.

MOUNT ANGEL SEMINARY   *(E-6)*
St. Benedict, Oregon 97373
Tel: (503) 845-3951

Description: The seminary was established in 1887 and is conducted by the Benedictine Monks of Mount Angel Abbey. It is an independent seminary devoted to the training of candidates for the Roman Catholic Priesthood. It is composed of a College of Liberal Arts, and a School of Theology and is accredited by the Northwest Association of Schools and Colleges. Enrollment recently was 114 including part-time students. A faculty of 9 full-time and 12 part-time gives an over all faculty-student ratio of 5:1. The semester system is used with two summer sessions offered.

Entrance Requirements: High school graduation or GED; SAT score of 440V, 450M, TOFEL 500. Early admission, early decision, rolling admission, delayed admission and advanced placement plans available.

Costs Per Year: $3,200 tuition; $2,800 room and board; $415 student fees.

Collegiate Environment: College facilities include dormitory facilities for 110 men and a library of 115,000 volumes. 80% of the applicants is accepted, and students may enroll at midyear as well as in the fall. Financial aid is available, and approximately 25% of the current student body receives some form of assistance.

Community Environment: Located in northwest Oregon, 40 miles from Mt. Hood. Community facilities include a number of churches, public library, hospitals, and a number of the civic and service organizations. Part-time employment is available. Hunting, fishing, and winter sports may all be enjoyed in the area. Other activities are tennis, swimming, bowling, and golf.

MOUNT HOOD COMMUNITY COLLEGE   *(D-7)*
26000 S.E. Stark Street
Gresham, Oregon 97030
Tel: (503) 667-6422

Description: This public community college opened in 1966 with 850 students enrolled. It operates on the quarter system with two summer sessions. The college is accredited by the Northwest Association of Schools and Colleges. Enrollment includes 3,413 full-time, 9,530 part-time, and 4,520 evening students. A faculty of 166 full-time and 277 part-time provides a faculty-student ratio of 1-24.

Entrance Requirements: High school graduation or GED equivalent; open enrollment policy; non-high school graduates 18 years of age and older may be admitted; early admission, early decision and rolling admission plans available.

Costs Per Year: $1,170 tuition; $96 per credit hour tuition out-of-state.

Collegiate Environment: The campus is comprised of 215 acres, and contains a library of 100,000 volumes and 500 microforms.

Community Environment: This suburban area has bus transportation available, and the Troutdale Airport is three miles away. Mt. Hood and the Columbia River are nearby providing facilities for many water sports including fishing and skiing. A YWCA, 40 churches, good shopping facilities, and various civic and service organizations serve the community. Part-time work opportunities are available. The Strawberry Festival and Mt. Hood Festival of Jazz are special annual events.

MULTNOMAH BIBLE COLLEGE AND BIBLICAL SEMINARY   *(D-6)*
8435 N.E. Glisan St.
Portland, Oregon 97220
Tel: (503) 255-0332

Description: The private Bible school was established in 1936, and is accredited by the Accrediting Association of Bible Colleges. It also holds membership in the Associated Schools of the Institute of Holy Land Studies, which makes available to graduates, and certain qualified seniors, a unique opportunity for studying in the Holy Land. The school operates on the early semester system and offers one summer session. Enrollment includes 331 men and 189 women full-time, and 76 men and 46 women part-time. A faculty of 34 full-time and 11 part-time gives a faculty-student ratio of 1-14.

Entrance Requirements: High school graduation or equivalent with 2.0 GPA; SAT required; applicants should be affiliated with a church; rolling admission plan available; Nov. 15 and July 15 application deadlines; $30 application fee.

Costs Per Year: $6,700 tuition; $3,260 room and board.

Collegiate Environment: The Bible school is located on a 17-acre campus in the residential area of the east part of Portland. The 17 school buildings include a library of 57,013 volumes and 550 periodicals. Dormitory facilities number 350 units. Semesters begin in August and January. Approximately 93% of the students applying for admission are accepted, including midyear students. Financial aid is available for ecomically disadvantaged students. 70% of the current student body receives some form of financial assistance.

Community Environment: See Portland State University.

NATIONAL COLLEGE OF NATUROPATHIC MEDICINE *(D-7)*
11231 SE Market street
Portland, Oregon 97216
Tel: (503) 255-4860

Description: Established in 1956, this four-year graduate institution grants a Doctor of Naturopathic Medicine (N.D.) degree that prepares students for the general practice of naturopathic medicine, a profession founded on the principle of restoring and maintaining health by emphasizing nature's inherent capacity to heal. The course of study includes two years of standard medical sciences and two additional years of clinical training in diagnosis and naturopathic therapeutics, including the traditions of herbal, oriental, homeopathic and other natural medicines as well as clinical nutrition, physiotherapy, and counseling. The curriculum is designed to meet the education requirements for licensure in those states and provinces that license naturopathic physicians. The quarter system is used. Two courses, organic chemistry and physics, are offered during the summer. Enrollment is 170 men and women. A faculty of 44 full-time and part-time gives a faculty-student ratio of 1-4. The school is accredited by the Council on Naturopathic Medical Education.

Entrance Requirements: Three years of course work from an accredited college or university with specific area requirements; Bachelors degree recommended; rolling admission, some early decisions, and transfer credit available; deadline for submission of applications for the fall term is April 30; $60 application fee, $100 outside of the U.S.

Costs Per Year: $10,098 tuition; $1,000 student fees and books.

Collegiate Environment: The campus is located on seven acres of Oregon greenery in a quiet neighborhood in southeast Portland. Academic facilities include classrooms, labs, bookstore, and a library with one of the largest collections of books on natural medicine in the country, 7,000 volumes and 800 audiovisual materials. Sharing the campus with the school is the Portland Naturopathic Clinic that, with 12,000 patients visits per year and a staff of eight supervising naturopathic physicians, provides a rich practical learning environment for students. In addition, there is a state-licensed laboratory, a large natural products dispensary, X-ray, physiotherapy, and hydrotherapy facilities. Financial aid is available and 65% of the students receive some form of assistance.

Community Environment: There is a small, close family environment at the school in the student body. This atmosphere is set in the larger context of the city of Portland, which has a fairly concentrated downtown with a much larger residential and suburban area. Portland is unique in that it affords a great deal of cultural opportunity with financial affordability.

NORTHWEST CHRISTIAN COLLEGE   *(H-5)*
828 East 11th Avenue
Eugene, Oregon 97401
Tel: (503) 343-1641; (800) 888-1641; Fax: (503) 343-9159

Description: The private college traces its beginnings to the establishment of the Eugene Divinity School in 1895. It is sponsored and supported by the Christian Church (Disciples of Christ) and Christian Churches (Churches of Christ). The college is accredited by the Northwest Association of Schools and Colleges. The college operates a degree completion program through centers in Roseburg, Medford, and Grant's Pass. It operates on the quarter system. Enrollment includes 122 men and 128 women full-time and 48 men and 79 women part-time students. A faculty of 11 full-time and 14 part-time gives a faculty-student ratio of 1-16.

Entrance Requirements: High school graduation or equivalent; non-high school graduates considered; recommended 16 college-preparatory units including 4 English, 2 mathematics, 2 foreign language, 1 science, 2 social science; SAT required; early decision, delayed admission, midyear admission, rolling admissions and advanced placement plans available. $25 application fee.

Costs Per Year: $8,550 tuition; $3,870 room and board; $215 student fees; additional expenses average $150.

Collegiate Environment: The campus is adjacent to the western boundary of the University of Oregon. The 10 college buildings contain a library of 60,000 volumes, 230 periodicals, 551 microforms, 4,576 recordings. Dormitory facilities are provided for 117 students and 12 married students. The college welcomes a geographically diverse student body and will accept midyear students. Approximately 96% of the students applying for admission are accepted. The average scores of the entering freshman class were SAT 425 verbal, 452 math. Academic and need based scholarships are available, ranging from $600 to $4,800. Additional financial aid in the forms of loans and grants are awarded and 83% of the current student body receives financial aid. About 53% of the freshman class returned to the college for the sophomore year.

Community Environment: See University of Oregon.

OREGON HEALTH SCIENCES UNIVERSITY   *(D-6)*
3181 S.W. Sam Jackson Park Road
Portland, Oregon 97201
Tel: (503) 494-7800; Fax: (503) 494-4629

Description: The Oregon Health Sciences University is devoted to
education and research in the health sciences and to patient care. The
university is accredited by the Northwest Association of Colleges and
Schools, the American Dental Association, American Dietetic Association, and several other professional accrediting institutions. The
Schools of Dentistry, Medicine and Nursing, previously affiliated
with the University of Oregon, were combined in 1974 to form the
Oregon Health Sciences University. The programs enrolling the most
students are medicine and medical technology, dentistry and dental
hygiene, and nursing. Two new programs include Radiation Therapy
Technology, and the Physician Assistant program, each requiring two
years of college preparation. Each program also requires coursework
at an accredited college or university before entrance. The minimum
college preparation required of applicants is: two years for nursing,
two years for dental hygiene, and not less than two years for dentistry,
and three years medical technology and medicine. Full-time undergraduate enrollment included 65 men and 369 women and the graduate enrollment consisted of 1,148 students with a full-time faculty of
465 and 244 part-time.

Entrance Requirements: Vary with each program. $40 undergradu-
ate application fee. $75 graduate application fee.

Costs Per Year: Undergraduate: $4,500 ($1,500/quarter) resident
tuition, $10,500 ($3,500/quarter) nonresident; Graduate and Professional: $9,000 ($3,000/quarter) resident; $18,000 ($6,000/quarter)
nonresident.

Collegiate Environment: The Oregon Health Science University is
located on a 116-acre tract in Sam Jackson Park overlooking the city
of Portland, away from the congested area but within one and one-
half miles of the business district. It contains the University Hospital
and clinics, the crippled children's division, the library and auditorium the Medical Research Laboratories Building, and the Student
Activities Building. The library's holdings number 63,603 volumes,
2,500 periodicals, 200 microforms, and 700 audiovisual materials.
The residence hall houses 109 students from the Medical, Nursing,
and Dental Schools. Many apartments and boarding houses are located close to the campus. The Medical School Farm on 180 acres
southwest of Portland, was purchased in 1961 to house and breed animals for teaching and investigative programs. Headquarters for the
Portland Center for Hearing and Speech have been constructed adjacent to the Crippled Children's Division Building. The Doernbecher
Memorial Hospital for Children is part of University Hospital, and the
Veterans Administration Medical Center is located nearby. Newest
building on the campus is the Institute for Advanced Biomedical Research.

Community Environment: See Portland State University.

OREGON INSTITUTE OF TECHNOLOGY   *(M-8)*
3201 Campus Drive
Klamath Falls, Oregon 97601-8801
Tel: (503) 882-6321; (800) 343-6653; Fax: (503) 885-1115

Description: Oregon Tech is the only institute of technology in the
Oregon State System of Higher Education (OSSHE). It is accredited
by the Northwest Association of Schools and Colleges and by respected professional organizations. Bachelor degrees are offered in
technological programs and Associate degrees are offered in the liberal arts college transfer program. Instructional programs are offered
through the School of Health and the Arts and Sciences, and the
School of the Engineering and Industrial Technologies. Oregon Tech
maintains an upper-division satellite campus in Portland. The institute
operates on the quarter system and offers one summer session. Enrollment includes 1,408 men and 1,070 women. A faculty of 119 full-
time and 52 part-time members gives a faculty-student ratio of 1-16.

Entrance Requirements: Accredited high school graduation or GED
certification: 14 units including 4 English, 3 mathematics, 2 science, 3
social studies, and 2 other college-preparatory courses; minimum 2.5
GPA in all high school subjects; SAT or ACT required; non-high
school graduates considered; rolling admission and advanced placement plans available; $50 application fee.

Costs Per Year: $3,150 tuition; $9,336 nonresident; $3,804 room
and board.

Collegiate Environment: Located on a 173 acre site at the northern
edge of Klamath Falls, the campus overlooks Upper Klamath Lake
with its mountain background. Natural hot water wells, adequate to
heat all campus buildings, are located on the campus. The 10 institute
buildings include a library of 97,000 volumes, 2,000 periodicals, and
40,027 microforms, and living accommodations are available for 550
men and women. Approximately 90% of students applying for admission are accepted. Financial assistance is available, and 70% of students receive aid.

Community Environment: Klamath Falls is located nearly equidistant from Portland, OR, San Francisco, CA, and Reno, NV. Bus, train
and air transportation is available. A local phenomenon is a stratum of
hot water underlying certain sections of the city, which is used to heat
homes and offices. Numerous lakes are in Klamath County, including
Crater Lake National Park. Outdoor recreation of all sorts is readily
available and enjoyed year-round.

Branch Campuses: The Portland Metro Center of Oregon Tech offers upper-division technology programs in Electronics Engineering
Technology, Manufacturing Engineering Technology, and Industrial
Management. Selected courses are also offered in response to the industrial community and the Office of Extended Studies.

OREGON STATE UNIVERSITY   *(F-5)*
Corvallis, Oregon 97331
Tel: (503) 737-0123; Admissions: (503) 737-4411; Fax: (503)
737-2482

Description: The state university started as an academy incorporated as Corvallis College in 1858. It was designated the Agricultural
College of the State of Oregon in 1868 and the first baccalaureate degrees were awarded in 1870. Today the university is comprised of the
College of Agricultural Sciences, College of Business, School of Education, College of Engineering, College of Forestry, College of Health
and Human Performance, College of Home Economics and Education, College of Liberal Arts, College of Science, College of Pharmacy, College of Oceanic and Atmospheric Sciences, College of
Veterinary Medicine and the Graduate School. Enrollment includes
12,571 full-time and 1,752 part-time undergraduates and 3,102 graduate students. Army, Navy, Air Force, and Marine Corps ROTC programs are also offered. A total faculty of 1,414 gives a faculty-student
ratio of 1-10. The quarter system is used and three summer sessions
are offered. The university is accredited by the Northwest Association
of Schools and Colleges and by respective educational and professional organizations.

Entrance Requirements: High school graduation or equivalent; 14
units of required courses; a minimum 3.0 GPA in all high school subjects; SAT or ACT accepted; advanced placement available; $50 ap-
plication fee, early application encouraged.

Costs Per Year: $3,048 tuition; $9,096 nonresident tuition; $3,842
board and room.

Collegiate Environment: The 400-acre main campus is located in
the heart of the Willamette Valley between the Cascade Mountains on
the east and the Coast Range on the west, 82 miles south of Portland.
The university provides living accommodations for 5,496 men and
women and 124 families. Fraternities and sororities provide additional
living accommodations for 1,450 men and 710 women and off-campus housing is also available. The university library contains
1,275,473 volumes, 19,130 periodicals, and 1,939,973 microforms.
Approximately 69% of the students applying for admission are accepted including midyear students. 79% of the freshman class returned for the sophomore year. The average SAT scores of the current
freshman class, 443V and 522M. 600 scholarships are offered and
70% of the students receive aid.

Community Environment: Corvallis is situated in the Willamette
Valley which is noted for crops and dairy goods. Plane, rail and bus
transportation are available. Community facilities include churches of
major denominations, a hospital, library, shopping areas, and the
major civic, fraternal and veteran's organizations. Part-time employment opportunities are fair. Willamette River is nearby for fishing and
boating, and the Pacific Coast is a 50-mile drive.

PACIFIC NORTHWEST COLLEGE OF ART *(D-6)*
1219 S.W. Park Ave.
Portland, Oregon 97205
Tel: (503) 226-4391; Admissions: (503) 226-0462; Fax: (503) 226-4842

Description: The college is affiliated with the Portland Art Museum and the Northwest Film Center. It is accredited by the Northwest Association of Schools and Colleges and the National Association of Schools of Art and Design. The faculty is drawn from the practicing professional artists of the community and from throughout the nation. PNCA offers a four-year Bachelor of Fine Arts degree program in Drawing, Painting, Graphics Design, Illustration, Ceramics, Sculpture, Printmaking, and Photography. Reed College and the Pacific Northwest College of Art offer a five-year course, which leads to a B.A. degree from Reed College and a B.F.A. degree from the College of Art. In this course approximately two and one-half years study are taken at each institution. The school operates on the semester system. Enrollment is 237 full-time and 32 part-time students. A faculty of 18 full-time and 23 part-time gives a faculty-student ratio of 1-10.

Entrance Requirements: High school graduate or GED; SAT or ACT recommended; art portfolio; letters of recommendation; deferred admission, midyear admission and rolling admission; $30 application fee.

Costs Per Year: $8,836 tuition; $4,500 room and board (estimated, not provided); $500 student fees; $900 art supplies (estimated).

Collegiate Environment: .PNCA is housed in a 5-story building of art studios attached to the north side of the Portland Art Museum and also has an annex one block away that houses the College's Design Arts department. The College is located in the downtown section of Portland, Oregon, on a park-like setting that includes the Performing Arts Center, Historical Society and Museum and Portland State University. Library contains 25,000 books, 80 periodicals and 75,000 slides. Approximately 90% of students applying for admission are offered enrollment. 80% of all students receive financial aid. Semesters begin in September and January.

Community Environment: See Portland State University.

PACIFIC UNIVERSITY *(D-6)*
2043 College
Forest Grove, Oregon 97116
Tel: (503) 357-6151; (800) 677-6712; Fax: (503) 359-2242

Description: The private university began as an orphan school in 1842 established by independent missionaries. The Territorial Legislature granted a charter in 1849 and the first Baccalaureate degree was awarded in 1863. Today the university is comprised of the College of Arts and Sciences, the College of Optometry, the School of Professional Psychology, the School of Physical Therapy, the School of Occupational Therapy and the School of Education. It is accredited by the Northwest Association of Schools and Colleges and other professional accrediting institutions. The university operates on a semester 4-1-4 calendar system and offers three summer sessions. Army ROTC is available. Semester or full academic year abroad programs are available. Internships are available for all undergraduate majors. Enrollment includes 1,638 full-time and 201 part-time students. A faculty of 128 full-time and 48 part-time gives a faculty-student ratio of 1-14.

Entrance Requirements: Accredited high school graduation or equivalent; SAT or ACT required; Recommended 4 English, 3 mathematics, 2 science, 2 foreign language, 4 social studies. Rolling admission, midyear admission, and advanced placement plans available. $30 application fee.

Costs Per Year: $14,920 tuition; $16,916 Optometry; $13,332 Physical Therapy; $13,706 Occupational Therapy; $14,715 Psychology; $12,300 Education; $4,100 room and board; $220 student fees.

Collegiate Environment: The campus consists of 57 acres in the heart of Forest Grove. The 22 university buildings include a library of 220,000 volumes, 1,216 periodicals, 112,000 U.S. Government documents, microforms and audiovisual materials. Living accommodations are available for 710 men and women. Students come from a variety of geographic locations, and admits midyear students. Approximately 84% of students applying for admission are accepted and almost all of the recent student body graduated in the top half of high school class. The average scores of the entering freshman class were SAT 471 verbal, 535 math, ACT 24 composite. 80% of the student body receives financial aid. 600 merit scholarships are available.

Community Environment: Located 30 miles west of Portland, Forest Grove (population 12,000) is the home of Pacific University, the first school to be chartered in the Oregon Territory. Part-time employment is available. Community facilities include 15 churches, 2 libraries, a hospital, and various civic and service organizations. Bus transportation is available. The Pacific Coast beaches are an hour's drive and skiing on Mt. Hood is two hours away.

PORTLAND COMMUNITY COLLEGE *(D-6)*
P.O. Box 19000
Portland, Oregon 97280-0990
Tel: (503) 977-4519; Fax: (503) 977-4947

Description: Portland Community College offers vocational-technical, liberal arts and general studies, adult education, and community education programs. The college operates on the quarter system with one summer session. It is accredited by the Northwest Association of Schools and Colleges. Enrollment includes 7,073 full-time and 16,085 part-time students. A faculty of 353 full-time and 767 part-time gives a faculty-student ratio of 1:34.

Entrance Requirements: Open enrollment policy; high school graduation, personal interview, and placement examination recommended for students.

Costs Per Year: $1,485 resident tuition; $4,725 tuition for nonresidents.

Collegiate Environment: The principal campus is located on 120 acres overlooking the Tualatin Valley and provides space for many of the career-technical programs and about half of the general studies and liberal arts programs. There are three additional campuses, offering over 500 separate courses. All students applying for admission are accepted, including midyear students. The library contains 113,400 volumes, 815 periodicals, 90,000 microforms and 4,223 audiovisual aids. Financial assistance is available and about 41% of the current students receive aid.

Community Environment: See Portland State University.

PORTLAND STATE UNIVERSITY *(D-6)*
P.O. Box 751
Portland, Oregon 97207-0751
Tel: (503) 725-3511; (800) 547-8887; Fax: (503) 725-5525

Description: Portland State University became a degree-granting institution in 1955. It is accredited by the Northwest Association of Schools and Colleges. It was founded in 1946, when Vanport Extension Center was established by the State Board of Higher Education to help assimilate the overflow of student-veterans following World War II. Today the university is comprised of the College of Liberal Arts and Sciences, School of Business Administration, School of Education, Graduate School of Social Work, School of Urban and Public Affairs, School of Engineering and Applied Science, School of Fine and Performing Arts, School of Extended Studies, Center for Population Research and Census, Center for Urban Studies, International Trade Institute, Center for Black Studies, Cartographic Center, Center for Economic Education, Center for Public Health Studies, Center for Sociological Research, Center for Urban Research in Education, Institute for Psychological Study of Living Systems, Middle East Studies Center, North Pacific Applied Research Center, Political Research Bureau, Psychological Clinic, Research & Training Center to Improve Services for Seriously Emotionally Handicapped Children and Their Families, Speech & Hearing Clinic, Transportation Studies Center, and the Center for Software Quality Research. The university operates on the quarter system and offers summer session courses of varying lengths. Enrollment includes 14,426 undergraduates and graduate students recently. A faculty of 482 full-time and 154 part-time provides a faculty-student ratio of 1-19. The university grants Bachelor's, Master's and Doctorate degrees.

Entrance Requirements: Accredited high school graduation or GED certification; minimum 2.5 GPA on all high school grades; SAT or ACT required, minimum score SAT 890 combined or ACT 20 composite if GPA requirements not met; subject requirements: English 4 years, math 3 years, science 2 years, social studies 3 years, and other college-prep 2 years; early admission, rolling admission, delayed admission, and advanced placement available; $50 application fee.

Costs Per Year: $3,060 tuition; $9,108 out-of-state.

Collegiate Environment: The 36-acre campus is situated only a few blocks from the core of downtown Portland. Housing is available through College Housing NW, a nonprofit student housing corporation that operates accommodations on or near campus. The university library contains 900,000 volumes, 11,193 periodicals, 1,137,168 microforms, and 90,078 audiovisual materials. Approximately 86% of the first-time freshmen applying for admission are accepted. Scholarships are available and 66% of students receive some form of financial aid.

Community Environment: Portland lies along both sides of the Willamette River at its juncture with the Columbia River, where there is a splendid port deep enough for the largest ships to dock. Portland has a beautiful background of snow-capped mountain peaks to the north and east, and because of the Japanese Current, enjoys a mild and equable climate. The Columbia River Highway is a beautiful drive, particularly through the Columbia River Gorge with cliffs 2,000 feet high. The Columbia and Willamette Rivers nearby offer year-round water sports, the ocean beach is also nearby, and skiing is available at nearby Mount Hood. Part-time employment and commercial transportation are available. Some of the points of interest are the Hoyt Arboretum, Oregon Art Institute, Oregon Historical Center, Oregon Museum of Science and Industry, Crystal Spring Rhododendron Garden, Washington Park Zoo, Japanese Gardens, World Forestry Center, and the Washington Park Rose Test Gardens.

REED COLLEGE   *(D-6)*
3203 S.E. Woodstock Blvd.
Portland, Oregon 97202
Tel: (503) 777-7511; (800) 547-4750; Fax: (503) 777-7553

Description: The private, independent college of liberal arts and sciences was founded in 1909. It is accredited by the Northwest Association of Schools and Colleges and certain departmental programs have additional accrediting by appropriate professional agencies. The college operates on the semester system and grants a Bachelor in Liberal Arts & Sciences, and a Masters degree in Liberal Studies. A variety of study abroad programs are available. Current enrollment includes 1,199 full-time and 31 part-time students. A faculty of 81 full time and 36 part time gives a faculty student ratio of 1-11. Army ROTC is available through Portland State University.

Entrance Requirements: High school graduation or equivalent; completion of college-preparatory courses including 4 English, 3-4 mathematics, 2 lab science, 2 foreign language and 2 social science recommended; SAT or ACT required; three achievement tests strongly recommended; application fee $40; early admission, advanced placement, early decision, midyear admission, and delayed admission plans available.

Costs Per Year: $19,100 tuition; $5,230 room and board; $150 student fees; additional expenses average $900-$1,200.

Collegiate Environment: The 100-acre campus is located on the edge of Eastmoreland, an attractive residential area, five miles from the center of Portland. The 39 college buildings include a library of 330,000 volumes, 1,500 periodicals, and 37,300 microforms. On-campus housing facilities include both residence halls and apartments, which can accommodate up to 627 students. Approximately 63% of students applying for admission are accepted, including midyear students. Nearly 90% of the previous freshman class returned to this campus for the sophomore year. The average high school standing of the recent freshman class was 73% of entering freshmen in the top 20% with average SAT scores 612V and 635M. Financial aid is available for students who demonstrate financial need, and almost half of the freshmen class received financial assistance from the College. Of the 579 grants offered, 119 were for freshmen. The College granted 213 Bachelor degrees and 4 Masters degrees to its recent graduating class. The majority of the senior class continued on to graduate school.

Community Environment: See Portland State University.

ROGUE COMMUNITY COLLEGE   *(L-5)*
3345 Redwood Highway
Grants Pass, Oregon 97527
Tel: (503) 479-3500; Admissions: (503) 471-3500; Fax: (503) 471-3588

Description: The publicly supported community college offers programs in liberal arts as well as technology. The quarter system is employed and one summer session is offered. The college is accredited by the Northwest Association of Schools and Colleges. Enrollment includes 1,220full-time and 1,437 part-time students. A faculty of 65 full-time and 225 part-time gives a faculty-student ratio of 1:10.

Entrance Requirements: Open enrollment policy; non-high school graduates considered; ASSET or placement exams; early admission and advanced placement plans available.

Costs Per Year: $1,224 district resident tuition; $1,440 state resident tuition; $2,988 out-of-state tuition.

Collegiate Environment: The library contains 33,000 volumes, 200 periodicals and 200 recordings. All of the applicants are accepted, including midyear students. 70% of the students receive financial aid.

Community Environment: See Southern Oregon State College.

SOUTHERN OREGON STATE COLLEGE   *(M-6)*
1250 Siskiyou Blvd.
Ashland, Oregon 97520
Tel: (503) 552-6411

Description: The publicly supported college, founded in 1926, is a comprehensive college under the governance of the Oregon State Board of Higher Education. It operates on the quarter basis and also offers a summer term. The enrollment is 4,500 undergraduate and graduate students. A faculty of 250 full-time and 100 part-time gives a faculty-student ratio of 1-19. An additional 1,200 students, both on and off campus, are also served through continuing education and and various non-credit classes during evening hours. The college holds accreditation from the Northwest Association of Schools and Colleges. The National Commission for Accreditation of Teacher Education, the National Association of Schools of Music, the American Chemical Society and the National League for Nursing. Opportunities for study abroad are available in Mexico, Japan, China, France, Germany, Hungary, Ecuador, England, Denmark, Mexico Korea. The college participates in a National Student Exchange with 75 other colleges at in-state tuition rates.

Entrance Requirements: Standard high school graduation or equivalent; minimum 2.75 or above in all high school subjects taken toward graduation; or a combined score of 900 on SAT or a composite ACT of 21; satisfactory completion of required 14 units of college preparatory work in the areas of 4 English, 3 mathematics, 2 science, 3 social studies. Early admission, early decision, rolling admission, delayed admission and advanced placement plans available; application fee $50.

Costs Per Year: $2,930 tuition; $8,415 out-of-state students; $3,800 board and room.

Collegiate Environment: The college campus occupies nearly 175 acres within a short distance of the center of Ashland. The 20 college buildings include a library of 270,000 volumes, 2,150 periodicals 725,000 microforms. Dormitory facilities are provided for 600 men and 600 women. Approximately 80% of students applying for admission are accepted, including midyear students. 63% of the previous freshman class returned to this campus for their sophomore year. Financial aid is available for economically disadvantaged students. About 60% of the current student body receives aid.

Community Environment: The college is located in Ashland, a town of 17,000 people, is nestled at the base of the Sikiyou Mountains in the Rogue Valley of Oregon. The college and community are a focus of cultural activity and have gained national recognition through the Oregon Shakespearean festival and associated legitimate theatres, annually drawing over 300,000 patrons. The town is surrounded by natural forests, mountain lakes and rivers spectacular for outdoor sports and ecological studies. For the skier, it's only 30 minutes from campus to the 7,000 foot Mt. Ashland Ski Resort.

SOUTHWESTERN OREGON COMMUNITY COLLEGE   *(J-3)*
1988 Newmark
Coos Bay, Oregon 97420
Tel: (503) 888-2525

Description: Publicly supported community college established in 1961. The quarter system is used and one summer session is offered.

The college is accredited by the Northwest Association of Schools and Colleges. All lower-divisions, transfer courses applicable to a Baccalaureate degree are accepted by the Oregon State System of Higher Education. Day and evening classes are available. Enrollment includes 921 full-time and 3,649 part-time students. A faculty of 83 full-time and 175 part-time gives a faculty-student ratio of 1:18.

Entrance Requirements: Accredited high school graduation or equivalent required for degree program; open enrollment policy; non-high school graduates 18 years of age or older are eligible for admission; placement examinations required. Early admission, rolling admission, advanced placement programs available; $13 application fee.

Costs Per Year: $1,188 tuition in-state; $3,564 out-of-state, $115 per credit for international students.

Collegiate Environment: The college is situated on a 125-acre campus, bordering the Empire Lakes in the Empire District of Coos Bay. Classes are held in 15 permanent buildings. A student center is situated on campus. The library contains 53,585 titles, 477 periodicals, 2,580 microforms, and 8,855 audio-visual materials. Additional construction is planned to remodel the learning resources center and to enlarge the physical education facilities. Almost all applicants are accepted. Financial assistance is available.

Community Environment: Coos Bay is an important seaport and trading center as well as one of the world's largest lumber export points. Opportunities for part-time employment are good. Community facilities include a library, hospital, churches representing many major denominations, and civic and service organizations. Coos Bay and adjacent North Bend are the shopping centers for southwestern Oregon. The Golden and Silver Falls State Park is 24 miles away, offering facilities for picnicking, camping and fishing as does Millicoma-Myrtle Grove State Park and Shore Acres State Park.

TREASURE VALLEY COMMUNITY COLLEGE (H-18)
650 College Boulevard
Ontario, Oregon 97914
Tel: (503) 889-6493

Description: The district-governed community college was established in 1962. It is accredited by the Northwest Association of Schools and Colleges. The college operates on the quarter system and offers one summer term. Enrollment includes approximately 2,500 students. A faculty of 54 members provides a faculty-student ratio of 1:37. The college offers lower division college courses, occupational programs and adult basic education courses all leading to an Associate degree as well as certificate programs.

Entrance Requirements: Open enrollment policy; entrance exam required; high school graduation or equivalent required for some programs; early admission, early decision, rolling admission, delayed admission and advanced placement plans available.

Costs Per Year: $1,485 tuition; $2,205 out-of-state tuition; $3,000 room and board.

Collegiate Environment: The college library contains 28,000 volumes. Dormitory facilities are provided for 150 men and 50 women. All freshman students carrying 10 or more hours not residing with family are generally required to live in college approved housing. All of the students applying for admission are accepted. The college welcomes a geographically diverse student body and will accept midyear students. Financial aid is available, and over 70% of the current student body receives some form of assistance.

Community Environment: Ontario, one mile from the Oregon-Idaho state line, lies in an agricultural area that produces potatoes, onions, sugar beets, corn, and hay. All forms of commercial transportation are available. Community facilities include the Malheur County Library, a hospital, and several civic and service organizations. Job opportunities are available. Mule, deer, and antelope hunting on the vast rangeland, and fishing in Owyhee Lake and the Malheur and Snake Rivers attract the sportsman. Semiprecious stones may be found in Malheur County. Skiing may be enjoyed at nearby ski resorts.

UMPQUA COMMUNITY COLLEGE (J-5)
P.O. Box 967
Roseburg, Oregon 97470
Tel: (503) 440-4600; Fax: (503) 440-4612

Description: The public two-year college was established by a vote of the people of Greater Douglas County in 1964. It is accredited by the Northwest Association of Schools and Colleges. The college operates on the quarter system and also offers 1 summer term. Enrollment includes 900 full-time and 4,643 part-time students. There is faculty of 70 full-time, 105 part-time giving a faculty-student ratio of 1-30.

Entrance Requirements: Open enrollment policy; accredited high school graduation or GED certification required for college transfer program. Midyear admission plan available.

Costs Per Year: $1,300 state-resident tuition; $3,822 out-of-state.

Collegiate Environment: The 98-acre campus is located approximately five miles north of Roseburg on the north bank of the North Umpqua River. The 13 college buildings include a library of 65,000 volumes, 465 periodicals and 5,879 audiovisual materials. Almost all of the applicants are accepted. including midyear students. 102 scholarships offered, including 85 for freshmen. About 60% of the students receive some form of financial aid.

Community Environment: Roseburg is the county seat of Douglas County, one of the largest lumber centers in the country. Roseburg is also a noted sheep producing point. The town is the headquarters for the Umpqua National Forest, where good salmon and trout fishing may be enjoyed. Hunting is permitted in season for deer, elk, bear, and cougar in the Umpqua National Forest.

UNIVERSITY OF OREGON (H-5)
240 Oregon Hall
Eugene, Oregon 97403
Tel: (503) 346-3201

Description: This state university was established by an act of the Oregon Legislature in 1872, but did not open its doors to students until 1876. The first university courses were limited almost entirely to classical and literary subjects and the first class was graduated in 1878. Today the university is composed of The College of Arts and Sciences, School of Architecture and Allied Arts, College of Business Administration, School of Education, School of Journalism, School of Law, School of Music, The Graduate School and the College of Human Development and Performance. The university is accredited by the Northwest Association of Schools and Colleges and its programs are accredited by respective educational and professional organizations. The university operates on the quarter system and offers two summer sessions. An Army ROTC program is available. Enrollment includes 14,203 full-time and 2,478 part-time students. A faculty of 890 gives a faculty-student ratio of 1-19.

Entrance Requirements: Standard or accredited high school graduation; minimum 3.0 GPA in all high school subjects; or a GPA combined with a satisfactory score on SAT; SAT or ACT required of all entering undergraduate students; early decision, rolling admission, competitive admission, and advanced placement programs available; $50 application fee.

Costs Per Year: $3,227 tuition; $10,770 out-of-state; $3,727 room and board.

Collegiate Environment: The main campus of the university is located in Eugene, 109 miles south of Portland at the head of Willamette Valley. The university contains 91 buildings located on 185 acres. Living accommodations are provided for 3,121 students and 995 families. Fraternities and sororities provide additional living accommodations for 600 men and 700 women under university supervision. The university libraries contain over 2 million volumes, 21,000 periodicals, 1.7 million microforms, 2,760,000 manuscripts, 997,000 pamphlets and other materials. Approximately 75% of students applying for admission are accepted including midyear students. The middle 50% SAT score ranges of enrolled freshmen are 440-570V, 470-600M. Financial assistance is available for economically disadvantaged students. 55% of students receive financial aid.

Community Environment: Eugene, the center of a vast recreational area, is an important lumbering center. Bicycles are a major form of student transportation. Airline, bus and train transportation are available. Eugene's facilities include more than 80 churches, a large public library, a YMCA, YWCA, three hospitals, and a number of motels. Eugene is 60 miles east of the Pacific Ocean and 60 miles west of the Cascade Mountains. The Willamette National Forest nearby provides fine hunting and fishing opportunities; skiing is enjoyed at the Hoodoo Ski Bowl and Willamette Pass Ski area.

UNIVERSITY OF PORTLAND   *(D-6)*
5000 N. Willamette Blvd.
Portland, Oregon 97203-5798
Tel: (503) 283-7147; (800) 227-4568; Admissions: (503) 283-7147;
Fax: (503) 283-7399

Description: The University of Portland is an independently governed, Catholic university founded in 1901 by a society of priests and brothers from the Congregation of Holy Cross. Today, an independent Board of Regents governs the University. The University operates on the semester system and offers one summer session. Accredited by the Northwest Association of Schools and Colleges, the University offers an undergraduate and graduate curriculum of arts, sciences, and humanities. The university also offers a School of Education and nationally accredited professional programs in Business, Engineering, and Nursing. Enrollment is 1,146 men and 1,454 women. This includes 2,161 undergraduate, 437 graduate students, and 2 auditors. A faculty of 138 full-time and 71 part-time gives an undergraduate faculty-student ratio of 1-17. Air Force and Army ROTC programs are offered.

Entrance Requirements: Accredited high school graduation or equivalent; overall quality of high school preparation is considered; SAT or ACT required; GRE required for graduate programs; completion of 12 units recommended including 4 English, 3-4 mathematics, 2-4 science, 3-4 social science or history, and 2-4 foreign language; $30 application fee; rolling admission, delayed admission and advanced placement plans available.

Costs Per Year: $12,040 tuition; $4,100 room and board; $180 student fees.

Collegiate Environment: Located on a scenic bluff overlooking the Willamette river and the city of Portland, the campus is nestled within a residential neighborhood. Twenty-nine buildings are located on the 92-acre campus, including a 350,000-volume library, and two coeducational and three single-sex residence halls that house 1,054 students. 905 undergraduates live on campus. Undergraduates may choose from 38 academic majors and 24 minors. Students also have the opportunity to study in Salzburg, Austria, during their sophomore year. Summer programs are available in Tokyo and London. Approximately 80% of the students receive some form of financial aid. The average high school GPA is 3.47.

Community Environment: See Portland State University.

WARNER PACIFIC COLLEGE   *(D-6)*
2219 S.E. 68th Avenue
Portland, Oregon 97215
Tel: (503) 775-4366; (800) 582-7885; Admissions: (503) 788-7495;
Fax: (503) 775-8853

Description: This private institution is a Christian liberal arts college, affiliated with the Church of God, whose general offices are located in Anderson, Indiana. It is accredited by the Northwest Association Schools and Colleges. It was founded in 1937, in Spokane, Washington, and was known as Pacific Bible College. It moved to its present location in 1940 and adopted its present name in 1959. The college operates on the semester system and offers one summer session. Enrollment includes 194 men and 344 women full-time and 71 men and 83 women part-time. A faculty of 40 full-time and 5 part-time gives a faculty-student ratio of 1-15.

Entrance Requirements: Accredited high school graduation or equivalent; completion of 4 units of English, 2 mathematics, 2 science, 3 social science and 1 health and physical education; SAT with combined score of 750 or composite ACT score of 18 required; personal interviews recommended; two recommendations required; early admission, midyear admission, rolling admission and advanced placement plans available. $25 application fee.

Costs Per Year: $8,940 tuition; $4,200 room and board; $161 student fees; $1,200 average additional expenses.

Collegiate Environment: The campus is beautifully situated on the southern slope of Mount Tabor. It joins the spacious Mount Tabor Park, which offers recreational facilities to students enrolled at the college. The college buildings include a library of 60,000 volumes, 4000 pamphlets, 500 periodicals, 1500 microforms, and 2000 audiovisual materials. Dormitory facilities house 124 men, 152 women and 32 families. The college welcomes a geographically diverse student body and will accept midyear students. Approximately 80% of students applying for admission are accepted, with an additional 5%

given provisional acceptance; a special counseling program is available for these students. 75% of the freshmen returned for the sophomore year. 75% of the current students receive aid. There are numerous competitive, merit, and need-based scholarships offered.

Community Environment: See Portland State University.

WESTERN BAPTIST COLLEGE   *(E-6)*
5000 Deer Park Drive, S.E.
Salem, Oregon 97301
Tel: (503) 581-8600; (800) 845-3005; Fax: (503) 585-4316

Description: The privately supported coeducational Bible and liberal arts college operating on the semester system is accredited by the Northwest Association of Schools and Colleges and the American Association of Bible Colleges. The college is endorsed by the General Association of Regular Baptist Churches. Enrollment includes 457 men and women full-time and 122 part-time students. A faculty of 29 full-time and 28 part-time gives a faculty-student ratio of 1-10. An Army ROTC program is available.

Entrance Requirements: All candidates for admission must provide satisfactory evidence of a definite Christian conversion. A candidate's Christian character must be established by active church membership, by a recommendation from his pastor, and by recommendation from other Christians in his community. All applicants are required to be graduates of high school with a C average considered as minimum. SAT, minimum score 400V, 400M, or ACT, minimum score 18, required; housing is provided by the college; application fee $25; rolling admission, midyear admission, and advanced placement plans available.

Costs Per Year: Tuition $9,800; room and board $4,260; student fees $230.

Collegiate Environment: The college is located in Salem, Oregon. Training includes preparation for the fields of business administration, psychology, teaching and ministry-related vocations. The library contains 64,114 volumes, 5,606 bound periodicals, 2,850 unbound periodicals, 1,205 microforms, and 2,935 audiovisual materials. Dormitory space is provided for 131 men and 161 women. All single students under the age of 21 are required to live in college halls. 98% of those who apply for admission are accepted, including midyear students. Financial aid is available and 95% of the current student body receives assistance.

Community Environment: See Willamette University.

WESTERN CONSERVATIVE BAPTIST SEMINARY   *(D-6)*
5511 S.E. Hawthorne Boulevard
Portland, Oregon 97215
Tel: (503) 233-8561; (800) 547-4546

Description: The graduate theological seminary formally opened its doors in 1927. In 1951 the seminary was reorganized with new articles of incorporation that conformed to the changed situation of the seminary subsequent to its separation from the Oregon Baptist Convention. At this time, the word "conservative" was inserted in the corporate name to clarify and emphasize its definite alignment with the Conservative Baptist Movement. The seminary operates on the semester system with two regular terms and a summer term and offers a Master of Arts, Divinity, Theology, Christian Leadership, Doctorate of Ministry, and Missiology. Specializations include Theology, Biblical Studies, Pastoral Ministry, Counseling Ministry, Music Ministry, Educational Ministry, Chaplaincy Ministry, and Intercultural Ministry. The Seminary is accredited by the Northwest Association of Schools and Colleges and an associate member of the Association of Theological Schools. and presently enrolls a total of 300 students. A faculty of 24 full-time and 3 part-time gives a faculty-student ratio of 1-15.

Entrance Requirements: Baccalaureate degree in liberal arts from a recognized college or university; application fee $25; rolling admission and delayed admission plans available; recommendation of pastor required.

Costs Per Year: $4,610 tuition; books and fees average $380.

Collegiate Environment: The seminary is located on a five and one-fourth acre campus in a residential Portland neighborhood. The seminary library contains 85,000 volumes, 8,000 periodicals, 13,000 microforms and 10,500 recordings. The seminary welcomes a geographically diverse student body and will accept midyear students. Approximately 90% of students applying for admission are accepted. About 85% of the previous entering class returned to the seminary for the second year of studies. Financial assistance is available for economically disadvantaged students and 23% of the students receive aid. The seminary has an academic corporative plan with the Institute of Holy Land Studies.

Community Environment: See Portland State University.

WESTERN EVANGELICAL SEMINARY *(D-6)*
12753 SW 68th Avenue
Tigard, Oregon 97223
Tel: (503) 639-0559; (800) 493-4937; Admissions: (503) 598-4309; Fax: (503) 598-4338

Description: Established in 1945, the seminary is accredited by the Northwest Association of Schools and Colleges and the Association of Theological Schools. WES provides programs of academics, theory, and practice designed to equip students for professional and lay ministry in the church and in a variety of clinical and cross-cultural settings. WES grants the Master of Divinity and Master of Arts degrees with programs of study in Counseling Psychology, Marriage and Family Therapy, Christian Education, and Theological Studies. It operates on the quarter system and offers three summer sessions. Enrollment includes 82 full-time and 131 part-time students. A faculty of 12 full-time and 11 part-time gives a faculty-student ratio of 1-9.

Entrance Requirements: Bachelor of Arts degree or equivalent from accredited college or university; cumulative GPA of 2.7 or above; applicant whose cumulative GPA is less than 2.7 may be granted probationary student status; rolling admissions; $25 application fee.

Costs Per Year: $7,680 tuition.

Collegiate Environment: The WES campus is located five miles south of downtown Portland. The library contains more than 65,000 volumes. Need-based financial aid is available.

Community Environment: See Portland State University.

WESTERN OREGON STATE COLLEGE *(E-5)*
345 North Monmouth Avenue
Monmouth, Oregon 97361
Tel: (503) 838-8000

Description: The state institution is a liberal arts college with special emphasis on the preparation of elementary and secondary teachers and research in teacher education. The college also offers strong programs in Business, Computer Science, Corrections, Law Enforcement, Psychology, and many more. The college is accredited by the Northwest Association of Schools and Colleges and operates on the quarter system with one summer session. An Army and Air Force ROTC program is available. Study abroad programs are available. Recent enrollment included 1,571 men and 2,365 women. A faculty of 312 gives a faculty-student ratio of 1:14.

Entrance Requirements: Standard high school graduation or GED certification; 14 units including 4 English, 3 mathematics, 2 science, 3 social Studies, 2 electives; non high school graduates may be considered; SAT or ACT required. Out-of-state graduates must have 2.75 GPA average or above in all high school subjects; $35 application fee; rolling admission, delayed admission and advanced placement plans available.

Costs Per Year: $827 per quarter resident tuition; $1,994 per quarter out-of-state residents; $3,355 room and board.

Collegiate Environment: The 134-acre campus is located in the mid-Willamette Valley, 15 miles from Salem, 61 miles from Portland and 60 miles from the Oregon Coast. The 34 college buildings contain a library of 186,000 volumes, 1,682 periodicals, 368,166 microforms, 857 recordings and there are living accommodations for 1,150 students. Approximately 87% of students applying for admission are accepted including midyear students. More than 65% of the previous freshman class returned to this campus for the sophomore year. Financial aid is available for economically disadvantaged students. About 50% of the current student body receives aid.

Community Environment: Monmouth is located in the Willamette Valley. Its main industries are agriculture and logging. Apartments are available for students. Some part-time employment is available.

WESTERN STATES CHIROPRACTIC COLLEGE *(D-6)*
2900 N.E. 132nd Avenue
Portland, Oregon 97230
Tel: (503) 251-5734; (800) 641-5641; Fax: (503) 251-5723

Description: The private, chiropractic college was founded in 1904. It operates on the quarter system and offers 1 summer session. Enrollment includes 286 men and 113 women. Full-time faculty numbers 41, part-time 8. The college is accredited by the Council on Chiropractic Education and by the Northwest Association of Schools and Colleges and grants a Doctor of Chiropractic Degree and a Bachelor degree in Human Biology.

Entrance Requirements: Two years of basic pre-med. Candidates should contact the Admissions office for information on the specific courses required for entry. Rolling admission, midyear admission. Application fee $50.

Costs Per Year: $11,955 tuition and $420 fees; estimated expenses: $549 books and supplies, $6,462 room and board (not provided on campus), $3,669 personal, $705 travel.

Collegiate Environment: The college is located in suburb of Portland. The 22-acre campus contains 9 buildings and much open space. A major freeway system and bus system serve the area. Facilities consist of administrative offices, classrooms, laboratories, student lounges, a library of 12,000 volumes, 450 periodicals, 2,540 sound recordings, and 3,000 microforms. The college welcomes a geographically diverse student body. Approximately 60% of students applying for admission are accepted. Financial aid is available for economically disadvantaged students. 90% of students receive financial aid.

Community Environment: See Portland State University.

WILLAMETTE UNIVERSITY *(E-6)*
900 State Street
Salem, Oregon 97301
Tel: (503) 370-6300

Description: This private institution is an independent university of residential character offering undergraduate instruction in the liberal arts, sciences, and professional work in the College of Law and Atkinson Graduate School of Management. The university was founded in 1842 by missionaries of the Methodist Church. It is accredited by the Northwest Association of Schools and Colleges, the National Association of Schools of Music, and by the American Bar Association. It operates on the early semester system. Enrollment is 2,519 full-time and 180 part-time undergraduate students. An undergraduate faculty of 144 full-time and 77 part-time provides a faculty-student ratio of 1-14.

Entrance Requirements: Accredited high school graduation or equivalent; rank in upper third of graduating class; completion of 16 college-preparatory courses including 4 English, 3 mathematics, 3 foreign language, 3 science, and 3 social science; SAT; early admission, early decision, deferred admission, midyear admission and advanced placement plans available; $35 application fee.

Costs Per Year: $16,400 tuition; $4,800 room and board; $90 student fees; $400 books.

Collegiate Environment: The 72-acre campus is located directly across the street from the Capitol. Nearly all state agencies are in Salem, offering students the advantage of outstanding internship opportunities. The 42 university buildings include the new Mark O. Hatfield Library with 241,344 volumes, the law and music libraries, and residence facilities for 1,245 students. Students from other geographical locations are accepted, as well as midyear students. Approximately 78% of students applying for admission are accepted. The median scores of the entering freshman class were SAT 520 verbal, 590 math, ACT 26 composite. The median scores for first-year graduate and professional students were GMAT 540, LSAT 156. 912 scholarships are available and 77% of students receive some form of financial aid. Semesters begin in September and January.

Community Environment: Salem, the capital city, has a population of 110,000. All forms of commercial transportation are available. Recreational activities include tennis, fishing, swimming, boating, riding, and hiking. Ski area facilities are nearby. Part-time employment is available. Points of interest are the Bush Park, a large city park planted with rare trees and shrubs, Salem Art Center, Mission Mill Museum and the Oregon State Capitol.

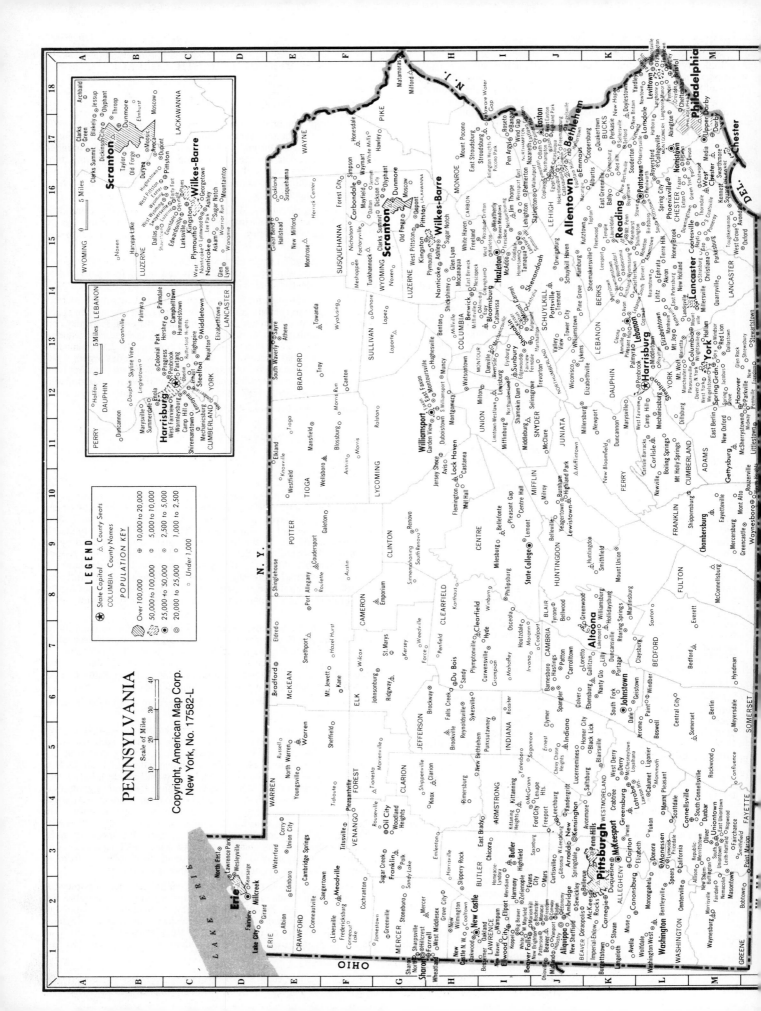

PENNSYLVANIA

ACADEMY OF THE NEW CHURCH COLLEGE *(M-17)*
Box 717 ANCC
Bryn Athyn, Pennsylvania 19009
Tel: (215) 938-2543; Fax: (215) 938-2658

Description: A privately supported, coeducational liberal arts college and seminary. The Theological School educates men for the ministry of the General Church of the New Jerusalem; its regular course of study covers three years and leads to the degree of Master of Divinity. The College offers three associate in arts degrees and three bachelor's degrees. The academy is accredited by the Middle States Association of Colleges and Schools. College enrollment is 110 students attending classes for three 12-week terms. A faculty of 24 full-time and 17 part-time gives a faculty-student ratio of 1-6.

Entrance Requirements: High school graduation; 16 high school units required; SAT or ACT required for placement; recommendation by minister of the General Church required; rolling admission plan available.

Costs Per Year: $3,792 tuition; $3,729 room and board; $648 student fees.

Collegiate Environment: The 130-acre campus has 11 buildings, including the 105,000-volume library and dormitories for 50 men and 50 women. Most students applying for admission are accepted. Special financial aid is available.

Community Environment: Population of Philadelphia is 1,950,098. Bryn Athyn is a suburban community accessible by bus and railroad. The mean winter temperature is 35 degrees, and the mean summer temperature is 85 degrees. Annual rainfall reaches 42 inches. This is a suburb of Philadelphia, and all the cultural, recreational, and civic advantages of the bigger city are easily available. See also Temple University for information of Philadelphia.

ALBRIGHT COLLEGE *(K-15)*
P.O. Box 15234
Reading, Pennsylvania 19612-5234
Tel: (215) 921-7512; (800) 252-1856; Fax: (610) 921-7530

Description: This privately supported, coeducational liberal arts college traces its origin from 1856, when Union Seminary was founded by the Central Pennsylvania Conference of the Evangelical Association of New Berlin, Pennsylvania. In 1928, it consolidated with Schuylkill, under the name of Albright College of the Evangelical Church (later Evangelical United Brethren, and as of 1968 United Methodist Church), in Reading, at its present location. The college is open to all qualified students without distinction of race or creed. Enrollment includes 940 students. A faculty of 69 gives a faculty-student ratio of 1-12. The college operates on the 4-1-4 system and offers evening and two summer sessions. It is accredited by the Middle States Association of Colleges and Secondary Schools, and several professional accrediting institutions. A popular advisory program called Alpha provides academic guidance and personal direction for first-year students who are undecided about their major. Programs for Secondary and Elementary School State teacher certification are offered. A five-year cooperative engineering program with Penn State and University of Pennsylvania grants two degrees. A five-year program is also available in Forestry with Duke University and University of Michigan that grants the B.S. and M. Forestry or Environmental Management. The Albright International Study program allows students to arrange either a semester or a year abroad in a dozen foreign countries. Army ROTC is available through neighboring colleges.

Entrance Requirements: High school graduation with rank in upper 30% and average above B-; completion of 15 units including 4 English, 2 mathematics, 2 foreign language, 2 science, and 2 social science; SAT or ACT required; 3 Achievement Tests accepted for placement consideration; non-high school graduates considered; early

decision, rolling admission, delayed admission, and early admission programs available; Feb 15 application deadline, Nov 15 for early action; $25 application fee.

Costs Per Year: $15,595 tuition; $4,400 room and board; $200 student fees; $650 average additional expenses.

Collegiate Environment: The 110-acre campus is located at the base of Mount Penn at the edge of one of the residential sections of Reading. The 30 college buildings contain a library of 170,000 volumes, 960 periodicals, 8,300 microforms, and 600 recordings, and dormitory facilities for 530 men and 630 women. The college welcomes a geographically diverse student body. Approximately 85% of students applying for admission are accepted, including midyear, and 96% of the previous freshman class returned to this campus for the sophomore year. Average high school standing of a recent freshman class: 56% in top fifth and 90% in top two-fifths. Middle 50% ranges of SAT scores were 900-1090 combined. Financial aid is available for students with demonstrated financial need. 92% of the current student body receives some form of financial assistance. 50 merit scholarships are available for freshmen. The College awarded 352 Bachelor degrees to a recent graduating class, and 51% of the senior class continued on to graduate school.

Community Environment: Thomas and Richard Penn, sons of William Penn, founded Reading in 1748 and named it for their ancestral home in England. This region was among the first in America to produce iron, and for nearly a century it maintained its supremacy in that line. Located in the eastern foothills of the Appalachian Mountains, the area has a temperate climate with four definite seasons. The community is served by airlines and several bus companies. Reading has many churches representing major denominations, three hospitals, a library with several branches, a symphony orchestra, and a cultural program series. Local recreation includes a museum and art gallery, a park with facilities for picnicking, theaters, raquetball and tennis facilities and bowling. Part-time employment is available. Also available is an extensive internship program throughout the community that incorporates business, industry, medical centers, hospitals, social and psychological agencies and communications systems. There are outreach programs such as United Way and MS that are available to the community through on-campus service groups.

ALLEGHENY COLLEGE *(-2)*
Box 40
Meadville, Pennsylvania 16335
Tel: (814) 332-3100; (800) 521-5293; Admissions: (814) 332-4351; Fax: (814) 337-0988

Description: This privately supported, coeducational liberal arts and sciences college was established in 1815 and has been affiliated with the United Methodist Church since 1833. It is accredited by the Middle States Association of Colleges and Schools and grants the Bachelor's degree. The college divides the academic year into two semesters of 15 weeks each; a small summer school is also available. Enrollment is 905 men and 949 women. A faculty of 156 full-time and 42 part-time gives a faculty-student ratio of 1-11. Special programs include pre-health professions and pre-law, as well as academic cooperative plans in engineering with Columbia, Duke, University of Pittsburgh, Washington University, and Case Western Reserve University; in Forestry with Duke and University of Michigan; and in Nursing and many Allied Health fields with Case Western Reserve University, University of Rochester, and Thomas Jefferson University.

Entrance Requirements: High school graduation required; completion of 4 units of English, 3 math, 3 science, 3 social studies, and 2 foreign language recommended; SAT or ACT required; essay; early admission, deferred entrance, early decision, and advanced placement programs available; admission is very competitive; $30 application fee.

Costs Per Year: $18,020 tuition and fees; $4,550 room and board; $830 average additional expenses.

Collegiate Environment: The college is located on a 254-acre campus adjacent to the residential section of Meadville, a small city in northwestern Pennsylvania. The 32 major college buildings include a library of 599,000 volumes, 1,200 periodical subscriptions, and 187,000 government documents. Housing facilities are provided for 1,365 men and women. Students from all geographical locations are accepted, as are midyear students. About 73% of students applying for admission are accepted and 86% of the freshmen return for the sophomore year. Average high school standing of the freshman class: 73% in the top 20%; 92% in top two-fifths, and 99% in top three-fifths. Mid-50% ranges of SAT scores are 460-570V, 530-640M. Financial aid is available for needy students and 77% of the current students receive it. The educational philosophy emphasizes the individuality of each student and the value of close communication with members of the faculty in establishing the most appropriate academic plan. The flexibility of the academic program permits the fulfillment of personalized objectives and needs while still ensuring the proper diversification of course experiences. Independent study, interdepartmental study, student-designed majors, and other options contribute to this end. Numerous study-abroad and domestic off-campus programs are offered.

Community Environment: Population 14,000. Meadville is the seat of Crawford County, a rich agricultural and active vacation area. The community lies on the western Appalachian slope. The area is served by plane, bus and interstate highways. There are many churches, a public library, active arts organizations, and a large medical center within the community. Local recreational facilities include five movie screens, a professional theater, parks, lakes, and picnic groves. Recreational activities include a major summer jazz festival, fishing, boating, hunting, swimming, golf and tennis. Most civic, fraternal and veteran's organizations are represented here. Part-time employment is available.

ALLENTOWN COLLEGE OF ST. FRANCIS DE SALES (K-17)
2755 Station Avenue
Center Valley, Pennsylvania 18034-9568
Tel: (215) 282-4443; (800) 228-5114

Description: This privately supported, coeducational Roman Catholic liberal arts college opened in 1965 and is conducted by the Oblate Fathers of St. Francis de Sales. It operates on the semester system and offers a three-week January term and three eight-week summer sessions. The college is accredited by the Middle States Association of Colleges and Secondary Schools and the National League for Nursing. Enrollment includes 1,007 full-time, 107 part-time, 765 evening students, and 408 graduate students. A faculty of 69 full-time and 29 part-time provides a faculty-student ratio of 1-14. Special programs include cross registration as a member of the Lehigh Association of Independent Colleges. The college grants the Bachelor degree. Army ROTC is available as an elective. Internships are available for all majors. Study abroad is available in French, Spanish, and German-speaking countries.

Entrance Requirements: High school graduation; completion of 16 units including 4 English, 3 mathematics, 2 laboratory science, 3 social science, 2 foreign language and 2 electives; SAT or ACT required; nonhigh school graduates considered; early admission, rolling admission, midyear admission, deferred admission, and advanced placement programs available; admission is competitive; $30 application fee.

Costs Per Year: $9,690 tuition; $4,815 room and board; $60 student fees; $700 average additional expenses.

Collegiate Environment: The college is located on a 300-acre campus and has 15 buildings. The new Trexler Library contains 147,000 volumes, 800 periodicals, 4,256 microforms, and 5,195 recordings. Residence halls provide accomodations for 721 students. The college welcomes a geographically diverse student body and will accept midyear students. Approximately 77% of students applying for admission are accepted and 80% of the previous freshman class returned to this campus for the sophomore year. The middle 50% range of scores for entering freshmen is SAT is 820-1070 combined. Financial aid is

available and 90% of the current students receive some form of financial assistance.

Community Environment: Center Valley is a rural area that enjoys a temperate climate. The area is accessible by railroad, airlines and bus (Route 309). The nearby towns of Allentown (population 110,000) and Bethlehem (population 73,000) have libraries and hospitals.

ALVERNIA COLLEGE (K-15)
400 Saint Bernardine
Reading, Pennsylvania 19607
Tel: (610) 796-8200; Admissions: (610) 796-8220; Fax: (610) 796-8336

Description: This privately supported, Roman Catholic liberal arts college is sponsored by the Bernardine Sisters of the Third Order of St. Francis. Alvernia achieved college status in 1961. It is accredited by the Middle States Association of Colleges and Schools and several professional accrediting organizations. The college grants the Associate and Bachelor degrees. It operates on the semester system and offers two summer terms. Enrollment includes 794 full-time and 202 part-time, and 253 evening students. A faculty of 59 full-time and 51 part-time gives a faculty-student ratio of 1-14.

Entrance Requirements: Accredited high school graduation; completion of 16 units including 4 English, 2 mathematics, 2 foreign language, 2 science, 2 social science, and 4 electives; minimum ACT 18 or SAT Verbal 400, Math 400 required; early admission, deferred admission, midyear admission, rolling admission, and advanced placement plans available; $25 application fee.

Costs Per Year: $9,600 tuition; $4,300 room and board; $350 student fees.

Collegiate Environment: The college is situated on a 85-acre campus overlooking Angelica Lake. The eight college buildings include a library housing 95,000 volumes, 795 periodicals, 1,441 microforms, and 20,600 audiovisual materials, and dormitory facilities for 250 students. Approximately 85% of applicants are accepted, including midyear students. Financial aid is available and 85% of students receive some form of financial assistance. 90% of freshmen return for their sophomore year.

Community Environment: See Albright College.

BAPTIST BIBLE COLLEGE OF PENNSYLVANIA (G-16)
538 Venard Road
Clarks Summit, Pennsylvania 18411
Tel: (717) 586-2400; (800) 451-7664; Admissions: (717) 586-2400; Fax: (717) 586-1753

Description: Privately supported, coeducational Bible college founded in 1932, offering a liberal arts curriculum to prepare young men and women for Christian service. It specializes in training pastors, missionaries, Christian education workers, Christian school teachers, counselors, secretaries, and church musicians. The college is affiliated with the General Association of Regular Baptist Churches and is accredited by the Association of Bible Colleges and the Middle States Association of Colleges and Schools. It grants the one-year Certificate, Associate, three-year Diploma, Bachelor, and Master of Science in Education degrees. It operates on the semester system and offers two summer sessions. Enrollment includes 495 full-time and 67 part-time undergraduate, and 16 graduate students. A faculty of 43 full-time provides a faculty-student ratio of 1-24.

Entrance Requirements: Approved high school graduation or equivalent; SAT or ACT required; early admission, advanced placement, delayed admission, early decision, rolling admission plans available; $20 application fee.

Costs Per Year: $6,120 tuition; $4,070 room and board; $566 student fees; additional expenses average $500.

Collegiate Environment: The 145-acre campus is located in a residential suburb that is a part of the greater Scranton metropolis. The 15 buildings contain a library of 78,745 volumes, 472 periodicals, 3,307 microforms, 14,334 audiovisual materials and dormitory facilities for 484 students. Approximately 98% of students applying for admission are accepted, including midyear students. About 65% of the previous freshman class returned to the campus for the sophomore year. Financial aid is available and 80% of the current student body receives some form of assistance. The college awarded 12 Certificates, 16 Associate, 85 Bachelor and 4 Masters degrees to a recent graduating class.

Community Environment: Clarks Summit is a suburb of Scranton, just six miles away.

BEAVER COLLEGE   (M-17)
450 Southeastern Road
Glenside, Pennsylvania 19038
Tel: (215) 572-2900

Description: Privately supported coeducational liberal arts and science college established in 1852. Originally under the auspices of the Methodist Episcopal Church, it is now one of the Church-related colleges of the Presbyterian Church (U.S.A.), but is independently controlled and ecumenical in spirit. The college is accredited by the Middle States Association of Colleges and Schools and several professional accrediting institutions and grants the Associate, Bachelor and Master degree. The college follows a two semester calendar and offers two six-week summer sessions. Undergraduate enrollment includes 2,269 students. A faculty of 67 full-time and 100 part-time, gives a ratio of 1-13. Students are encouraged to explore career fields before graduation by engaging in internships, cooperative education, and student-faculty research and writing. Special programs include several foreign study programs, a Washington Semester in conjunction with American University, and a Philadelphia Semester. The Beaver Evening College was established in 1978. Evening courses in business administration and computer science are offered leading to the Associate and/or Bachelor of Science Degrees in Business Administration, Personnel/Human Resource Administration, Computer Science and Communications. Majors are available in Accounting, Finance, Marketing, and Management.

Entrance Requirements: High school graduation with rank in upper 40% of class; emphasis on high school achievement including the type of program followed, grades and class rank earned. 16 units, including 4 English, 3 Mathematics, 1 Laboratory Science, 2 Foreign Language, 3 Social Studies, and electives. SAT or ACT required; counselor and teacher recommendations are required; interviews are encouraged; non high school graduates considered; early admission, rolling admission, delayed admission, early decision, advanced placement programs available; transfer admission; $25 application fee.

Costs Per Year: $11,520 tuition; $4,600 room & board.

Collegiate Environment: The 55-acre campus is located on a large country estate in Glenside, approximately 20 minutes by train from historic Philadelphia. The 14 college buildings contain a library of 120,596 volumes, 2,000 pamphlets, 672 periodicals, 94,139 titles on microfilm, 2,065 audiovisual materials and dormitory facilities for 522 students. The college welcomes a geographically diverse student body and will accept midyear students. Financial aid is available for economically disadvantaged students and 63% of the current student body receive financial assistance. Parent loans and monthly payment plans help other families meet college costs. Students must submit FAF, federal income tax and Beaver Aid Application forms for consideration. Presidential Scholarships and Achievement Awards are given to a limited number of students each year. The Rev. Dr. Martin Luther King, Jr. Scholarship is awarded to qualified minority applicants. To assist students interested in foreign study, the college established the Center for Education Abroad. Approximately 1,500 students from 200 Colleges throughout the USA study at colleges and universities in London, England, Ireland, Austria, and Greece.

Community Environment: Population 18,000. Glenside is a suburb of Philadelphia served by railroad, buses, and major highways. There are many churches in the immediate area as well as various civic and fraternal organizations. Local recreational facilities include golf courses, ice rinks, three parks, and a swimming pool. See also Temple University for information of Philadelphia.

BLOOMSBURG UNIVERSITY OF PENNSYLVANIA   (I-13)
Main and Penn Streets
Bloomsburg, Pennsylvania 17815
Tel: (717) 389-4316

Description: Publicly-supported, coeducational liberal arts and teachers college which began as an academy in 1839 and remained a private institution until 1916, when it was purchased by the Commonwealth of Pennsylvania. The transition from Normal School to State Teachers College was begun in 1927 when authority to confer the Bachelor of Science degree in education was granted. In 1969, it became a state college and authorization to offer courses leading to the Master of Education degree was given in the same year. By 1962, the college was granted approval to offer courses leading to the Bachelor of Arts degree in the natural sciences, social sciences, and the humanities. The college is accredited by the Middle States Association of Colleges and School, by the National Council for the Accreditation of Teacher-Education and by several other professional accrediting institutions. It operates on the semester system with seven summer terms offered. The college enrolls 2,371 men and 3,645 women full-time and 404 men and 1,044 women part-time. A faculty of 367 full-time and 33 part-time gives a faculty-student ratio of 1-19. An Army ROTC program is available in cooperation with Bucknell, Air Force, ROTC in cooperation with Wilkes College. An International Education Program is available.

Entrance Requirements: Approved high school graduation or equivalent; rank in top 40% of graduating class; completion of 16 units including 4 English, 3 Mathematics, 2 Foreign Language, 4 Social Studies, 2 Sciences, and 1 Physical Science recommended; SAT with minimum scores of 450V and 450M required; early admission, rolling admission, delayed admission, advanced placement plans available; $25 application fee.

Costs Per Year: $3,086 tuition; $7,844 tuition for out-of-state students; $2,948 board and room; $170 student fees.

Collegiate Environment: The state college campus is comprised of 170 acres and overlooks the town of Bloomsburg and the picturesque Susquehanna River. The 31 college buildings include a library of 317,706 volumes, 1,693 periodicals, 1,591,228 microforms, 5,994 recordings. Dormitory facilities for 744 men, 1,250 women and 248 coed. Six university owned apartment buildings are available for 380 upper division students. Approximately 38% of students applying for admission are accepted, including midyear students, and 84% of the previous freshman class returned to this campus for the sophomore year. Average high school standing of the freshman class, top 25%; 55% in the top quarter; 40% in the second quarter; 5% in the third quarter. Financial aid is available for economically handicapped students, 80% of the current student body receive some form of financial assistance.

Community Environment: Population 11,500. Bloomsburg is located 40 miles southeast of Williamsport. Average winter temperature is 31 degrees; with a summer mean temperature of 70 degrees. The area is served by railroad, bus, and airlines. The community has one hotel, four motels, several churches of various denominations, a public library, and a hospital. There are numerous civic, fraternal and veteran's organizations in the area. Part-time employment is available.

BRYN MAWR COLLEGE   (M-17)
Bryn Mawr, Pennsylvania 19010
Tel: (610) 526-5000

Description: Privately-supported, liberal arts college for women founded by members of the Society of Friends and opened in 1885 as the first college for women with undergraduate instruction for the Bachelor degree and graduate instruction, which includes men students, for the Master and Doctorate degrees in many departments. By the terms of its charter the college offers instruction in the liberal arts and sciences on both undergraduate and graduate level. Its resources as a small residential college are augmented by its participation with Haverford College and Swarthmore College in a plan which coordinates the facilities of the three institutions while preserving the individual qualities and autonomy of each. The college operates on the semester system and is accredited by the Middle States Association of Colleges and Secondary Schools. Enrollment inlcudes 1,150 full-time and 90 part-time undergraduates and 540 graduate students. A faculty of 150 full-time and 60 part-time gives a faculty-student ratio of 1-9.

Entrance Requirements: Accredited high school graduation; completion of 16 units including 4 English, 3 math, 1 science, 3 foreign language and 1 social science; SAT I, SAT II and three Achievement Tests required; GRE required for graduate programs; early decision, early admission, delayed admission and advanced placement program available; admission is selective; $40 application fee.

Costs Per Year: $19,250 tuition; $7,085 room and board.

Collegiate Environment: The 135-acre campus is located approximately 11 miles west of Philadelphia and nine east of Paoli. The college buildings contain a library of 850,000 volumes and dormitory facilities for 1,180 undergraduates. Students from other geographical locations are accepted. Approximately 50% of students applying for admission are accepted. Almost all of the recent student body graduated in the top quarter of the high school class and 75% in the highest tenth. Financial aid is available for economically disadvantaged students and numerous scholarships are available. Over 48% of undergraduates received some form of financial aid.

Community Environment: Population 5,737. Bryn Mawr is a suburban area 11 miles from Philadelphia. The immediate area has two clinics and a hospital, a public library, and churches of major denominations. Nearby Philadelphia offers all the facilities of a large city. Part-time employment opportunities are limited. See also University of Pennsylvania for information of Philadelphia.

BUCKNELL UNIVERSITY   *(I-12)*
Lewisburg, Pennsylvania 17837
Tel: (717) 524-1101; Fax: (717) 524-3760

Description: Privately supported, coeducational university, devoted to study in the liberal arts and sciences, management, and engineering. Founded in 1846, the university is accredited by the Middle States Association of Colleges and Schools and by several professional accrediting organizations. The university grants the Bachelor and Master degrees. Special programs include engineering combination B.A.-B.S. in a 5-year program and B.S.-M.S. programs in several departments. Study abroad programs include a semester abroad in England or France, and a year abroad program in Europe or Japan. It operates on the semester system and offers one summer session. Enrollment includes 3,317 full-time and 53 part-time undergraduate, and 227 graduate students. A faculty of 245 full-time and 19 part-time gives an undergraduate faculty-student ratio of 1-13. Army ROTC is available as an elective.

Entrance Requirements: Approved high school graduation or equivalent; non-high school graduates considered; completion of 16 units including 4 English, 4 math, 2 science, 2 foreign language, and 4 social science; SAT or ACT required; GRE required for graduate studies; early admission, early decision, midyear admission, and advanced placement plans available; Jan. 1 application deadline; $45 application fee.

Costs Per Year: $19,360 tuition; $4,925 room and board; $110 student fees.

Collegiate Environment: A major portion of the 300-acre campus and most of the academic buildings are situated on College Hill, about 100 feet above the Susquehanna River. Most of the 65 university buildings follow the Tidewater colonial style of architecture. The library contains 565,000 hardbound volumes, 2,600 periodical subscriptions, 40,000 periodicals, 111,000 microforms and 3,100 audiovisual materials. Dormitories accommodate 2,800 students. Twelve Greek-letter fraternities, accommodating 800 men, have houses on or near the campus, and each of the eight sororities has a suite in Hunt Hall. The students' broadcasting station, WVBU-FM, a member of the College Radio Corporation, has its own studio, and broadcasts daily programs throughout the collegiate year. The university participates in 24 intercollegiate sports and has an extensive program of intramural athletics. The university welcomes a geographically diverse student body, and a limited number of midyear students are accepted. Approximately 58% of students applying for admission are accepted. Financial aid is available, and 60% of the current student body receives some form of financial assistance. 94% of the previous freshman class returned to this campus for their sophomore year, and approximately 31% of the senior class continued on to graduate school.

Community Environment: Lewisburg, population 8,100, is the county seat and the commercial center of a prosperous farming area. Some industries in the city produce textiles, furniture, business forms, and electronic materials. Some part-time employment is available.

BUCKS COUNTY COMMUNITY COLLEGE   *(L-18)*
Swamp Road
Newtown, Pennsylvania 18940
Tel: (215) 968-8100; Fax: (215) 968-8100

Description: Publicly supported, coeducational junior college founded in 1964 and accredited by the Middle States Association of

Colleges and Schools. It operates on the semester system and also provides evening and three summer sessions. Enrollment is 11,300 students. A faculty of 203 full-time and 186 part-time gives a faculty-student ratio of 1-33. The college grants the Associate degree.

Entrance Requirements: Open enrollment policy; non-high school graduates considered; ACT or SAT recommended for placement but not required; early admission, rolling admission and advanced placement plans available; $30 application fee.

Costs Per Year: $1,650 county resident tuition; $3,300 out-of-county; $4,950 out-of-state; $40 student fees.

Collegiate Environment: The college is located on the former Tyler Estate on the outskirts of Newtown. All resident students applying for admission are accepted, including midyear students, and 49% of the previous freshman class returned to this campus for the second year of studies. 50 scholarships are available including 25 for freshmen and 30% of the current student body receives financial assistance. The library contains 135,000 volumes, 6,500 pamphlets, 720 periodicals, 150,000 microforms and 9,600 recordings.

Community Environment: Population 4,238. Newtown is a suburb of Philadelphia located approximately 20 miles from the heart of the downtown area. See also Temple University.

BUTLER COUNTY COMMUNITY COLLEGE   *(I-3)*
College Drive, Oak Hills
Butler, Pennsylvania 16001
Tel: (412) 287-8711; Fax: (412) 285-6047

Description: This publicly supported, coeducational community college was founded by the authority of the Pennsylvania State Board of Education in 1965 and opened in 1966. It is accredited by the Middle States Association of Colleges and Schools. The college grants Certificates and the Associate degree. The college operates on the semester system and offers three summer terms. Enrollment includes 1,560 full-time and 1,594 part-time students. A faculty of 65 full-time and 150 part-time gives a faculty-student ratio of 1-19.

Entrance Requirements: High school graduation or equivalent; open enrollment policy; college-administered tests required for placement; non-high school graduates considered; early admission, early decision, midyear admission, rolling admission, and advanced placement plans available; $10 application fee.

Costs Per Year: $1,500 district resident tuition; $3,000 out-of-district resident tuition; $4,500 nonresident tuition; $300 average additional expenses.

Collegiate Environment: The 288-acre campus is situated on the former Oak Hills golf course two miles south of Butler. The 12 college buildings include a library of 62,000 volumes, 355 periodicals, and 8,500 microforms. All applicants are accepted, including midyear students. Students from diverse geographical locations are accepted. Of 125 scholarships available, 50 are for freshmen. Financial aid is available and about 65% of students receive some form of assistance. 73% of freshmen return for their sophomore year.

Community Environment: In a region rich in coal, oil, natural gas and limestone, Butler's industries produce steel, pullman cars, cement, oil, glass, and metal products. The climate is temperate, and the average annual temperature is 50.6 degrees. The community has access to rail and air, and services include hospitals, churches, a library, YMCA, and YWCA. Local recreation includes boating, swimming, skiing, tennis, parks, and movie theaters. Part-time employment is available.

CABRINI COLLEGE   *(M-17)*
King of Prussia Road
Radnor, Pennsylvania 19087
Tel: (610) 902-8100; (800) 848-1003; Admissions: (610) 902-8552; Fax: (610) 902-8309

Description: Privately supported, Roman Catholic liberal arts coeducational college, established in 1957 by the Missionary Sisters of the Sacred Heart. It is accredited by the Middle States Association. The college initiated a new core curriculum based on the college's mission of developing a liberally educated person who understands social responsibility, possesses moral values and has a commitment to society. Students must demonstrate competency in the areas of computers, math, English, and a foreign language. They must also enroll in courses in broad areas designed to help an understanding of society, the world, social and political institutions, imagination and creativity and contemporary issues. Freshmen will take a seminar course on self-understanding, and juniors will enroll in a seminar course addressing the Common Good. There are cooperative programs in medical technology with Eastern College and eight hospitals in PA and NJ. The college grants Bachelors and Masters degrees. It operates on the semester system and offers two summer sessions. Enrollment includes 1,027 full-time and 49 part-time and 509 evening undergraduates and 428 graduate students. A faculty of 43 full-time and 105 part-time gives a faculty-student ratio of 1-13.

Entrance Requirements: Accredited high school graduation with rank in upper 50%; completion of 21 units including 4 English, 3 mathematics, 3 science, 3 social studies, 2 foreign language, 2-6 electives; SAT with minimum score of 450V, 450M, or ACT required; G.E.D. accepted; early admission, rolling admission, programs available; $25 application fee.

Costs Per Year: $10,518 tuition; $6,250 board and room; $480 student fees.

Collegiate Environment: The college is located on the 110 acres of the former Dorrance Estate in Radnor, Pennsylvania. The eight college buildings contain a library of 101,897 volumes, 2,250 pamphlets, 367 periodicals, 1,834 microforms, 625 audiovisuals. Dormitory facilities are provided for 368 women, 116 men. The college welcomes a geographically diverse student body and will accept midyear students. Approximately 78% of students applying for admission are accepted and 85% of the previous freshman class returned to this campus for the sophomore year. The average scores of enrolled freshmen were SAT 455 verbal, 468 math. 145 scholarships ar available and 77% of the current students receive some form of financial assistance.

Community Environment: See Villanova University.

CALIFORNIA UNIVERSITY OF PENNSYLVANIA   *(L-3)*
Third Street
California, Pennsylvania 15419
Tel: (412) 938-4000

Description: Publicly supported, coeducational teachers liberal arts and science and technology University established and maintained to help provide the schools of Pennsylvania with well-trained, competent teachers as well as to provide a liberal education for those not planning to teach. It is accredited by the Middle States Association of Colleges and Secondary Schools. Special programs are assigned to each state University by the Department of Public Instruction; California has been assigned industrial arts, special education, elementary education, secondary education, arts and sciences, and speech. Students may elect to specialize in any of these areas of their subdivisions. In order that additional study opportunities might be available the college sponsors Summer Tours which make available low-cost, travel-study trips for interested persons. The university grants Associate Bachelor, Specialist and Master degrees. It operates on the semester system with two summer sessions and provides evening programs in several other departments. Enrollment includes 4,502 full-time and 710 part-time undergraduates and 1,003 graduate students. A faculty of 310 full-time and 35 part-time gives a faculty-stuent ratio of 1-20.

Entrance Requirements: Accredited high school graduation; units should include 4 English, 2 mathematics, 4 social science, 1 science; selective enrollment policy; SAT or ACT required; advanced placement, delayed admission, early admission, midyear admission, early decision and rolling admission programs available; $25 application fee.

Costs Per Year: $3,902 tuition; $8,660 tuition for out-of-state students; $3,730 room and board; $328 student activity fee; additional expenses average $300.

Collegiate Environment: The 65-acre campus is located at California, a community situated on Monongahela River, 35 miles south of Pittsburgh. The 34 college buildings contain a library of 338,863 volumes, 12,000 pamphlets, 1,200 periodicals, 668,024 microforms, recordings and dormitory facilities for 1,450 men and women. Fraternities and sororities provide housing for 300 men and 300 women. Approximately 85% of students applying for admission were accepted, including midyear students. Almost 85% of the previous freshman class returned to this campus for the sophomore year. Average high school standing of the recent freshman class, top 40%; 30% in the top quarter, 40% in the second quarter, 20% in the third quarter.

The average scores of entering freshmen were SAT 470 verbal, and 430 math. Financial aid is available for economically disadvantaged students and 72% of the current students receive some form of aid.

Community Environment: Population 6,635. California is located 35 miles south of Pittsburgh on the Monogahela River. This is a coal mining region of the Appalachian Foothills. Some part-time employment is available.

CARLOW COLLEGE   *(K-2)*
3333 Fifth Avenue
Pittsburgh, Pennsylvania 15213
Tel: (412) 578-6000; (800) 333-2275; Fax: (412) 578-6019

Description: This privately supported liberal arts college was established in 1929 and formerly known as Mount Mercy College. It is accredited by the Middle States Association of Colleges and Secondary Schools and grants BA, BS, BSN, and M.Ed. degrees. The college operates on the semester system and offers four summer terms for four different programs. Enrollment is 983 full-time and 1,136 part-time undergraduates, and 55 graduate students. A faculty of 61 full-time and 128 part-time gives a faculty-student ratio of 1-14.

Entrance Requirements: High school graduation with rank in upper 2/5 of graduating class; completion of 18 units including 4 English, 3 mathematics, 3 natural science, 4 arts or humanities, and 4 electives; SAT or ACT required; early decision, rolling admission, delayed admission, early admission, and advanced placement plans available; $20 application fee.

Costs Per Year: $9,826 tuition; $4,434 room and board; $306 fees; $1,250 average additional expenses.

Collegiate Environment: Approximately 81% of students applying for admission are accepted, including students at midyear. Financial aid is available for economically handicapped students. 203 scholarships are offered, 52 of which are for freshmen. Athletic scholarships include basketball, cross country running, and volleyball. The college gymnasium includes a weight room, pool, and dance room. Semesters begin in September and January. The college has open cross-registration with 9 neighboring colleges and universities, whereby students may participate in certain courses and facilities at the member institutions. The library holdings include 75,036 titles.

Community Environment: See University of Pittsburgh, Pittsburgh Campus.

CARNEGIE MELLON UNIVERSITY   *(K-2)*
5000 Forbes Avenue
Pittsburgh, Pennsylvania 15213
Tel: (412) 268-2082; Fax: (412) 268-7838

Description: Carnegie Mellon, a privately supported, coeducational university is accredited by the Middle States Association of Colleges and Schools, and professionally by several accrediting institutions. The university is comprised of the College of Fine Arts, Mellon College of Science, Carnegie Institute of Technology, College of Humanities and Social Sciences, the Heinz School of Policy and Management, the Graduate School of Industrial Administration, and the School of Computer Science. The university grants the Bachelor, Master, and Doctoral degrees. Air Force, Army, and Navy ROTC programs are available. Study abroad is available to France and Japan. The university operates on the semester system and offers two summer sessions. Enrollment is 4,340 full-time and 97 part-time undergraduates and 2,704 graduate students. A faculty of 549 full-time and 200 part-time provides a faculty-student ratio of 1-6.

Entrance Requirements: High school graduation; completion of 16 college preparatory units; SAT or ACT and three Achievement Tests required; required units and Achievement Tests vary with each college; non-high school graduates considered; early admission, delayed admission, early decision, and advanced placement programs available; $40 application fee; personal interview strongly recommended.

Costs Per Year: $17,900 tuition; $6,170 room and board; $100 student fees.

Collegiate Environment: The university is located 5 miles from the heart of Pittsburgh. Its 100-acre campus is ideally situated between the leafy seclusion of Schenley Park and the city's distinguished cultural-research center, Oakland. In addition to the main campus, the university operates a radiation chemistry laboratory at Bushy Run.

The 28 university buildings contain a library of 852,241 volumes, 4,300 periodicals, and 544,000 microforms; a computer center; approximately 400 research and teaching laboratories; a theater; and living accommodations for 3,233 students. There are 14 social fraternities and 5 social sororities, all chapters of national organizations, on the campus. Each fraternity has its own residence including dining facilities and housing for 432 men. Sorority students, along with other students, live in the Margaret Morrison Apartments. The university welcomes a geographically diverse student body. Limited midyear students are accepted. 59% of students applying for admission are accepted. About 93% of the recent student body graduated in the top half of the high school class, 77% in the top quarter, and 49% in the highest tenth. About 92% of the previous freshman class returned to this campus for the second year of studies. Scholarships are available and 65% of the current student body receives some form of financial assistance. The Carnegie Mellon Action Project was begun in 1968 to provide an opportunity to students whose race and/or economic circumstances have traditionally excluded them from entering college and to prove that persons of differing cultural backgrounds can, without losing this difference, successfully pursue the same education goals.

Community Environment: See University of Pittsburgh, Pittsburgh Campus.

CEDAR CREST COLLEGE   *(J-16)*
100 College Drive
Allentown, Pennsylvania 18104-6169
Tel: (610) 437-4471; Admissions: (610) 740-3780

Description: This privately supported liberal arts college for women was founded in 1867 and is affiliated with the United Church of Christ. It is accredited by the Middle States Association of Colleges and Schools, and by several professional accrediting institutions. It welcomes students of different cultural, national, racial, and religious backgrounds on the basis of their ability to do college work. The college operates on the semester system and offers four summer sessions. Enrollment includes 661 full-time and 681 part-time students. A faculty of 64 full-time and 77 part-time provides a faculty-student ratio of 1-12. The college grants the Bachelor degree. It offers more than 30 academic programs including nursing, nuclear medicine, genetic engineering, education, legal assistant certification, and business administration. Army ROTC program is available.

Entrance Requirements: High school graduation or equivalent; completion of 16 units including 4 English, 3 mathematics, 2 foreign language, 2 laboratory science, and 3 social science; SAT or ACT; interview required for all applicants who live within 500 miles of campus; early admission, rolling admission, and advanced placement plans available; $30 application fee.

Costs Per Year: $14,340 tuition; $5,290 room and board; $850 average additional expenses.

Collegiate Environment: The college is located on 84 acres in the Lehigh Valley of eastern Pennsylvania, within 55 miles of Philadelphia and 90 miles of New York City. The 14 college buildings include a library of 313,975 volumes, 1,652 periodical subscriptions, 120,180 microforms, and 3,341 audio titles. Dormitory facilities are available for 482 women. The college welcomes a geographically diverse student body and will accept midyear students. Average high school standing of the freshman class: 75% in the top 2/5ths. The middle 50% ranges of enrolled freshmen verbal are SAT 420-520, 430-550 math. Financial aid is available and 83% of the current student body receives some form of financial assistance. There are $7,000 in merit scholarships available to freshmen. The college awarded 167 Bachelor degrees to a recent graduating class and 14% of the senior class continued on to graduate school.

Community Environment: See Muhlenberg College.

CENTRAL PENNSYLVANIA BUSINESS SCHOOL   *(L-12)*
College Hill Road
Summerdale, Pennsylvania 17093-0309
Tel: (717) 732-0702

Description: Privately supported, coeducational business school founded in 1922. The school is accredited by the Middle States Association of Colleges and Schools, American Bar Association (Legal Assistant), Committee on Allied Health Education in cooperation with the American Medical Association and the American Association of Medical Assistants, the Association of Physical Therapist Assistants, and the National Court Reporters Association (Court Reporting), and grants the Associate degree. The college operates on the trimester system and offers one summer session. Enrollment includes 650 full-time students. A faculty of 40 provides a faculty-student ratio of 1-17.

Entrance Requirements: Open enrollment policy; non-high school graduates considered; rolling admission, delayed admission, early admission, early decision, advanced placement plans available; no application fee.

Costs Per Year: $5,390 tuition; $2,390 room; $325.00 student fees; additional expenses average $1,350.

Collegiate Environment: The school occupies 20 wooded acres 5 miles west of Harrisburg. The buildings include housing accommodations for 490 students and a library containing 9,500 titles, 100 pamphlets, 95 periodicals and 160 tape recordings. Approximately 90% of students applying for admission are accepted, including midyear students and 60% return for the second year. Financial assistance is available and about 80% of the current students receive aid.

Community Environment: See Harrisburg Area Community College.

CHATHAM COLLEGE   *(K-2)*
Woodland Road
Pittsburgh, Pennsylvania 15232
Tel: (412) 365-1100; Fax: (412) 365-1294

Description: Privately supported liberal arts college for women, founded as a degree-granting institution in 1869 as the Pennsylvania Female College. The college is accredited by the Middle States Association of Colleges and Schools and the Americal Chemical Society. It operates on the 4-1-4 semester basis and offers 1 summer session. Chatham students may cross-register without payment of additional fees in one course for credit each term at any of nine nearby institutions: Carlow College, Carnegie-Mellon University, LaRoche College, Pittsburgh Theological Seminary, Point Park College, Robert Morris College, and the University of Pittsburgh. Also available are Washington Semester programs. Chatham sponsors several Study Abroad Programs for Juniors during the Interim. The Internship Program, supervised cooperatively by the Chatham faculty and on-site employers, enables students to gain first-hand experience in a wide variety of Pittsburgh agencies, businesses, and professional organizations. Enrollment includes 389 full-time and 117 part-time students. A faculty of 41 full-time and 35 part-time provides a faculty-student ratio of 1-9.

Entrance Requirements: High school graduation; completion of college preparatory units including 4 English, 3 mathematics, 3 social science, 3 physical science (2 laboratory science) and 2 foreign language; SAT scores; GED accepted; rolling admission; early admission, delayed admission, advanced placement programs available; personal interview recommended; $25 application fee.

Costs Per Year: Tuition $13,550; room and board $5,440; $350 student activity fee; additional expenses average $400.

Collegiate Environment: The 50-acre campus is located in a particularly beautiful residential section of Pittsburgh, within a 20-minute drive from the downtown area. The 41 college buildings contain a library of 100,000 volumes, 560 periodicals, microforms, and audiovisual materials; a computer center providing a computer-student ratio of 1-10; and living accommodations for 450 students. Approximately 66% of students applying for admission are accepted. Financial aid is available for economically disadvantaged students and 86% of the current student body receives financial assistance. The Chatham student body is diverse, and the College seeks to enroll students with a wide range of interests and talents from a variety of cultural, geographic, racial, religious, and socioeconomic backgrounds.

Community Environment: See University of Pittsburgh, Pittsburgh Campus.

CHESTNUT HILL COLLEGE   *(M-17)*
Germantown and Northwestern Avenues
Philadelphia, Pennsylvania 19118
Tel: (215) 248-7000; (800) 248-0052; Fax: (215) 248-7056

Entrance Requirements: High school graduation or equivalent; early admission, early decision, midyear admission, rolling admission and advanced placement plans available; $25 application fee.

Costs Per Year: $5,085 tuition; $115 student fees; $3,200 room and board; $750 average additional expenses.

Collegiate Environment: The library contains 1,200 titles and 1,700 periodicals. About 90% of the applicants are accepted, including mid-year students. 75% of the freshmen returned for the second year. One scholarship is available and 56% of the current student body receives financial aid.

Community Environment: See Lafayette College.

CLARION UNIVERSITY OF PENNSYLVANIA   (H-4)
Clarion, Pennsylvania 16214
Tel: (814) 226-2000; (800) 672-7171; Admissions: (814) 226-2306;
Fax: (814) 226-2030

Description: Publicly supported, coeducational liberal arts Professive and teachers university established in 1867 and officially maintained for the education and preparation of teachers for the public schools of Pennsylvania and for education in the arts and sciences and business administration communication, computer science and nursing. Preprofessional preparation and a cooperative pre-engineering program is offered. It is accredited by the Middle States Association of Colleges and Schools and grants the Associate, Bachelor and Master degree. The semester system is used and two summer sessions are offered. There are 5,324 men and women full-time and 1,277 part-time students. Faculty numbers 350, giving a faculty-student ratio of 1-19.

Entrance Requirements: High school graduation; SAT or ACT required, Achievement Tests required for some programs; early admission, early decision, rolling admission, delayed admission, advanced placement plans available; $25 application fee; personal interview required.

Costs Per Year: $3,221 tuition; $8,114 tuition for out-of-state students; $2,924 board and room; $806 student fees; $550 books and personal expenses.

Collegiate Environment: The main campus of the state college occupies a tract of 99 acres. The Memorial Athletic Field provides a recreational area of 29 acres for athletic events. The state college also operates an off-campus center located in Oil City, Pennsylvania, called the Venango Campus. The Clarion Campus contains 34 buildings which include a library of 370,000 volumes, 1,704 periodicals, 800,000 microforms, 15,000 audiovisual items, and dormitory facilities for 2,100 students. Financial aid is available for economically disadvantaged students; 75% of the current students receive some form of aid.

Community Environment: Clarion is in a rural area located near Cook Forest State Park and Allegheny National Forest. The area offers excellent hunting and fishing. The city has a public library, historical museum, nine churches, a hospital, and good shopping facilities. Two airports with commercial commuter and charter service are located within easy driving distance.

Branch Campuses: Venango Campus, 1801 West First Street, Oil City, PA, 16301.

CLARION UNIVERSITY OF PENNSYLVANIA, VENANGO CAMPUS   (G-3)
1801 West First Street
Oil City, Pennsylvania 16301
Tel: (814) 676-6591; Fax: (814) 676-1348

Description: Clarion University is a publicly supported, coeducational liberal arts and teachers college. Clarion's Venango Campus was established in 1961 and is a tribute to the civil spirit of the Oil City-Franklin area, which supported and financed the venture. Staffed with full-time faculty members of Clarion University, the branch campus offers students a convenient, inexpensive opportunity for two years of their college education. Courses offered at the branch campus are identical with those offered on the main campus. Enrollment includes 318 full-time and 267 part-time students. A resident faculty of 32 gives a faculty-student ratio of 1-20. See also Clarion Campus for further information.

Entrance Requirements: High school graduation with rank in upper half of graduating class; completion of college-preparatory units: 4 English, 2 math, 2 science, and 4 social science; SAT or ACT required; Achievement Tests optional for certain programs; early admission, early decision, rolling admission, delayed admission and advanced placement plans available; $25 application fee.

Costs Per Year: $3,086 tuition; $7,844 nonresident; $782 student fees.

Collegiate Environment: The branch campus is located on a 62-acre wooded area overlooking the Allegheny River. The classroom building contains classrooms, laboratories, and college offices. The Charles L. Suhr Library, opened in July 1976, has 20,000 volumes, 6,254 pamphlets, 201 current periodical subscriptions, 3,001 microforms, 341 recordings and 3,000 art slides. In January 1976, the Robert W. Rhoades Center was opened. This center houses student recreational rooms, a bookstore, snack bar, gymnasium, and auditorium. Semesters begin in August and January.

Community Environment: Population 15,033. Oil City is a progressive community located in northwestern Pennsylvania. There are many churches of various denominations, a library, a community playhouse, and a civic opera association within the immediate area. Local recreational facilities include tennis, bowling, skating, swimming, hunting, and fishing. Nearby forest and mountains offer climbing, hiking, and camping. There are several industries here, the primary one being oil refining. Oil City has accessible medical and shopping facilities. Some part-time employment is available.

COLLEGE MISERICORDIA   (B-15)
Lake Street
Dallas, Pennsylvania 18612
Tel: (717) 674-6461

Description: This is a privately supported, coeducational, liberal arts based college. The first college to be established in Luzerne County, it opened its doors in 1924. The college is conducted by the Sisters of Mercy of the Union in the United States of America, under the auspices of the Roman Catholic Church. It is accredited by the Middle States Association of Colleges and Schools and grants the Bachelor degree, plus 4 graduate programs. The college operates on the semester system and offers three summer sessions. Enrollment includes 962 full-time and 482 part-time students and a faculty of 77 full-time and 61 part-time members.

Entrance Requirements: High school graduation or equivalent; completion of 16 units; special programs require 2 or 3 units of a laboratory science; SAT or ACT required; early decision, early admission, delayed admission, rolling admission and advanced placement programs available; $15 application fee.

Costs Per Year: $9,050; $4,870 board and room; $450 student fees.

Collegiate Environment: The college is located in the beautiful Back Mountain area of Wyoming Valley, between Dallas and Harvey's Lake, nine miles from Wilkes-Barre. The 15 college buildings contain a library of 90,000 books, 763 periodicals, 3,700 microforms are available and 11,445 audiovisual materials. Dormitory facilities for 550 women and men. Approximately 80% of students applying for admission are accepted including midyear students. Financial aid is available for economically handicapped students and approximately 88% of the current students receive aid. The college regularly sponsors concerts, dances, lectures and plays. Campus Ministry, the newspaper and yearbook, a variety of special interest clubs, drama and music groups, and intercollegiate and intramural sports provide many opportunities for social and personal development. Intercollegiate sports for women includes volleyball, field hockey, basketball, softball and soccer; for men, basketball, baseball, soccer and golf.

Community Environment: The community of Dallas surrounding College Misericordia has a suburban atmosphere. It is located just nine miles from the city of Wilkes-Barre. The area provides shopping centers, a mall, cinemas, sporting events and a variety of cultural activities. Also nearby are Pennsylvania's largest natural lake, two state parks, the ski resorts of the Poconos, and five other colleges. New York and Philadelphia are within a three-hour drive. Public transportation is available to and from the campus.

COMMUNITY COLLEGE OF ALLEGHENY COUNTY, ALLEGHENY CAMPUS *(K-2)*

808 Ridge Avenue
Pittsburgh, Pennsylvania 15212
Tel: (412) 237-2525; Admissions: (412) 237-2511; Fax: (412) 237-4678

Description: Publicly-supported, coeducational junior college, part of a program of higher education approved by the Pennsylvania State Board of Education, sponsored by Allegheny County, and governed by an appointed Board of Trustees representing the citizens of the community. There are four campuses and a variety of centers. The Allegheny Campus in Pittsburgh; the Boyce Campus in Monroeville; the South Campus in West Mifflin; and North Campus in North Hills. Each in the system is academically autonomous. All offer university-transfer programs, technical and semiprofessional career programs, adult education, summer, and evening programs. All operate on the semester system and offer three summer sessions. All campuses are accredited by the Middle States Association of Colleges and Schools. Classes began on the Allegheny Campus in the fall of 1966. Enrollment includes 6,163 full-time and part-time students. A faculty of 503 gives a faculty-student ratio of 1-18. Programs of study lead to the Associate in Arts Science, and Applied Science and there are also certificate programs in various occupational areas.

Entrance Requirements: High school graduation or equivalent; open enrollment policy; early admission, advanced placement and rolling admission plans available. Placement tests are required in English, reading and mathematics.

Costs Per Year: $1,488 Allegheny County resident tuition; $2,976 out-of-district; $4,464 foreign and out-of-state tuition.

Collegiate Environment: The 14-acre campus is located on the north side of Pittsburgh. The present campus consists of six buildings and contains a library of over 76,000 volumes, 478 periodical titles as well as microfilm and record collections. Beginning students are accepted for Fall and Spring semester and for summer sessions. Honors scholarships are available. 60% of the current student body receives some form of aid.

Community Environment: See University of Pittsburgh, Pittsburgh Campus.

COMMUNITY COLLEGE OF ALLEGHENY COUNTY, BOYCE CAMPUS *(K-2)*

595 Beatty Road
Monroeville, Pennsylvania 15146
Tel: (412) 325-1327

Description: The publicly supported, coeducational junior college is part of a program of higher education approved by the Pennsylvania State Board of Education, sponsored by Allegheny County, and governed by an appointed Board of Trustees representing the citizens of the community. There are four campuses at present: the Allegheny Campus in Pittsburgh; the Boyce Campus in Monroeville; the South Campus in West Mifflin and North Campus in North Hills. Each in the system is academically autonomous. All offer university-transfer programs, technical and semiprofessional career programs, adult education, summer and evening programs. All operate on the semester system with two summer sessions. All campuses are accredited by the Middle States Association of Colleges and Schools. Enrollment includes 4,800 students. A faculty of 90 full-time, 110 part-time gives a ratio of 1-24. Programs of study lead to the Associate degree.

Entrance Requirements: Open enrollment policy; early admission, advanced placement and rolling admission plans available. GED and/or High School diploma

Costs Per Year: $1,272 Allegheny County resident tuition; $2,544 out-of-district tuition, without a junior college; $3,816 out-of-state tuition.

Collegiate Environment: The college is currently occupying one building on 112 acres. The library contains 15,000 volumes, 500 pamphlets, 450 periodicals, 880 microforms and 3,320 audiovisual materials. All students applying for admission are accepted, including midyear students. Financial aid is available.

Community Environment: Population 33,500. Monroeville is a suburban area near Pittsburg. It is a center of industrial research. The climate is moderate with an annual temperature range from below zero to 80 degrees. The community is served by bus, turnpike, railroad, and the Pittsburgh airport approximately 45 minutes away. There are 22 churches of various denominations, a YMCA, YWCA, and hospital within the immediate area. Recreation facilities include golf courses, parks, drive-ins and theaters, and swimming pools. Good shopping centers are nearby. Part-time employment is available. Accessible to disabled; shuttle buses; student clubs/organizations; cooperative education options, TV studio, various high technology laboratories.

COMMUNITY COLLEGE OF ALLEGHENY COUNTY, CENTER NORTH *(K-2)*

1130 Perry Highway
Pittsburgh, Pennsylvania 15237
Tel: (412) 366-7000

Description: Publicly supported, coeducational community college, part of a program of higher education approved by the Pennsylvania State Board of Education, sponsored by Allegheny County, and governed by an appointed Board of Trustees representing the citizens of the community. There are four campuses at present: the Allegheny Campus in Pittsburgh; the Boyce Campus in Monroeville; the South Campus in West Mifflin; and Center-North in North Hills section of Pittsburgh. Each in the system is academically autonomous. All offer university transfer programs, technical and semiprofessional career programs, adult education, summer, and evening programs. All operate on the semester system with one summer sessions. All campuses are accredited by the Middle States Association of Colleges and Schools. College Center-North opened in 1972. Enrollment is 3,068 men and women. A faculty of 170 gives a faculty-student ratio of 1-15. Programs of study lead to the Associate degree.

Entrance Requirements: High school graduation or GED; open enrollment; rolling admission, early admission and advanced placement plans available.

Costs Per Year: $1,770 resident tuition; $3,540 out-of-district; $5,310 out-of-state tuition; student fees average $107-$321.

Collegiate Environment: Classroom facilities are available at the Pines Plaza location and at additional locations throughout the North Hills area. The library houses 20,000 hardbound volumes and 5984 audiovisual materials.

Community Environment: See University of Pittsburgh, Pittsburgh Campus.

COMMUNITY COLLEGE OF ALLEGHENY COUNTY, SOUTH CAMPUS *(K-2)*

1750 Clairton Road
West Mifflin, Pennsylvania 15122
Tel: (412) 469-1100

Description: Publicly-supported, coeducational community college; part of a program of higher education approved by the Pennsylvania State Board of Education, sponsored by Allegheny County, and governed by an appointed Board of Trustees representing the citizens of the community. There are four campuses at present: the Allegheny Campus in Pittsburgh; the Boyce Campus in Monroeville; the South Campus in West Mifflin; and College-Center North in North Hills. Each in the system is academically autonomous. All offer university-transfer programs, technical and semiprofessional career programs, adult education, summer and evening programs. All operate on the semester system. All campuses are accredited by the Middle States Association of Colleges and Schools. South Campus opened in 1967 with 425 students, and now enrolls approximately 5,100 students. A faculty of 225 gives a faculty-student ratio of 1-22. Programs of study lead to Certificates and the Associate degree.

Entrance Requirements: High school graduation or equivalent; open enrollment policy; early admission, advanced placement and rolling admission plans available.

Costs Per Year: $1,272 Allegheny County resident tuition; $2,544 out-of-district, $3,816 foreign and out-of-state tuition; $50 student activity fee.

Collegiate Environment: South Campus, located on a beautiful 200-acre site in West Mifflin, blends its ultra-modern educational facility with the natural surroundings to create a perfect balance with the environment. The six-story structure has 86 classrooms, faculty, and administrative offices, laboratories, and audiovisual center, library, theatre, lecture halls, and a student dining area. The newest building on campus is a solar-heated greenhouse. The library has over 48,000 volumes, 500 periodicals, 2000 microforms and 17,000 sound recordings. Almost all students applying for admission are accepted, and students may enroll at midyear. Financial aid is available and nearly 60% of the current student body receives some form of assistance.

Community Environment: See University of Pittsburgh, Pittsburgh Campus.

COMMUNITY COLLEGE OF BEAVER COUNTY   (J-2)
College Drive
Monaca, Pennsylvania 15061
Tel: (412) 775-8561; Fax: (412) 774-8995

Description: Publicly supported, coeducational community college established in 1966 and approved by the Pennsylvania Department of Public Instruction and the Bureau of Community Colleges. It is fully accredited by the Middle States Association of Colleges and Schools. The college operates on the semester system and offers three summer sessions and evening sessions. The college grants the Associate degree. Enrollment includes 1,383 full-time and 1,252 part-time students. A faculty of 60 full-time and 100 part-time gives a faculty-student ratio of 1-19.

Entrance Requirements: Open enrollment policy for all adults; high school graduation or equivalent required for degree and diploma programs; entrance exam required; ACT required for allied health majors only; early decision, midyear admission, rolling admision and advanced placement plans available; $20 application fee.

Costs Per Year: $1,760 Beaver district-resident tuition; $3,670 out-of-district; $5,780 out-of-state.

Collegiate Environment: The college is located on 100 acres and includes a library of more than 63,000 volumes, 300 periodicals, and 1,100 microforms. All students applying for admission who meet the requirements are accepted, including midyear students. Financial aid is available and 67% of the current students receive some form of assistance.

Community Environment: Beaver County covers 436 square miles of rolling hills and valleys in southwestern Pennsylvania. Money magazine recently rated Beaver County fourth in the United States in livability. Professional sporting events, world-renowned museums, and numerous cultural events are within commuting distance in nearby Pittsburgh.

COMMUNITY COLLEGE OF PHILADELPHIA   (M-17)
1700 Spring Garden St.
Philadelphia, Pennsylvania 19130
Tel: (215) 751-8000

Description: A publicly supported, coeducational community college that was officially created in 1964. The college operates on the semester basis and also offers two summer terms. The college is accredited by the Middle States Association of Colleges and Schools and its programs in allied health areas are accredited by pertinent professional societies. The college grants an Associate degree and a Certificate. There is a continuing education program for adults. Enrollment includes 15,150 men and women full-time and part-time.

Entrance Requirements: Open enrollment policy; accredited high school graduation or GED certification for degree programs; pre-entrance standardized testing required for applicants to nursing program. Preference given to Philadelphia residents; rolling admission plan available; $20 application fee.

Costs Per Year: $1,650 tuition; $3,300 tuition for out-of-district students; $4,950 tuition for out-of-state students; $40 student fees; additional expenses average $450.

Collegiate Environment: The college occupies a newly constructed 14 acre campus in Center City Philadelphia. A library containing 85,370 volumes, 436 periodicals, and extensive collection of microforms, pamphlets, and recordings, a student lounge area with offices for student activities, and a foods service area and bookstore. Financial assistance is available for economically handicapped students. Approximately 95% of the applicants are accepted, including midyear students.

Community Environment: See Temple University.

CURTIS INSTITUTE OF MUSIC   (M-17)
1726 Locust Street
Philadelphia, Pennsylvania 19103
Tel: (215) 893-5252

Description: The private institute of music was founded in 1924. The school is operated under a charter granted by the Commonwealth of Pennsylvania and is approved by the State Council of Education for the granting of degrees and the National Association of Schools of Music. Enrollment is 155 men and women and the faculty has 82 full-time members. The institute operates on the semester system and grants the Diploma, Bachelor and Master of Music (Opera) degrees and Master of Music (Accompanying).

Entrance Requirements: High school graduation or equivalent; students are accepted only after an audition or the examination of original compositions submitted; early admission, advanced placement plans available; $65 audition fee, $40 application fee.

Costs Per Year: Students are accepted on the scholarship basis exclusively, and pay no tuition fees, however an annual registration fee of $350 is required; average expenses $7,500 for living accommodations.

Collegiate Environment: The auditorium, Curtis Hall, provides facilities for faculty and student recitals, organ teaching and practice, school gatherings, and commencement exercises. Designated practice studios are provided at the institute. The library of 36,750 volumes consists mainly of solo, chamber and orchestra music for performance and study as well as authoritative editions of the standard repertoire, a small collection of books and periodicals, and 4,000 recordings. The school has no dormitories; living accommodations and expenses are the responsibility of the student. About 10% of the applicants are accepted and 99% of the freshman returned for the sophomore year.

Community Environment: See Temple University.

DELAWARE COUNTY COMMUNITY COLLEGE   (M-17)
901 South Media Line Road
Media, Pennsylvania 19063-1094
Tel: (610) 359-5050; Admissions: (610) 359-5050; Fax: (610) 359-5343

Description: This publicly supported, coeducational community college was organized under the Pennsylvania Community College Act of 1963. It is accredited by the Middle States Association of Colleges and Schools. While the college receives substantial state support, it is managed and governed by its own Board of Trustees, chosen by local sponsoring public school districts. The college opened in 1967 with over 300 students enrolled in college and university parallel, occupational, and developmental programs. The college grants Certificates and the Associate degree. In addition, the Life Experience Assessment Program and the CLEP examinations may lead to the granting of college credits. The college operates on the semester system and offers two summer sessions. Enrollment includes 3,670 full-time and 6,599 part-time students. A faculty of 132 full-time and 354 part-time gives a faculty-student ratio of 1-21.

Entrance Requirements: Open enrollment policy; high school diploma, GED or equivalent life experience required; early admission, rolling admission, midyear admission and advanced placement plans available; $20 application fee.

Costs Per Year: $1,550 sponsoring local school districts resident tuition; $3,400 state resident tuition; $4,850 nonresident tuition.

Collegiate Environment: The college has its main campus in Marple Township located on 122 acres. The library contains 59,250 volumes, 6,000 pamphlets, 480 periodicals, 35,870 microforms, and 2,230 recordings. All students applying for admission are accepted, including midyear students. Need-based financial assistance and a limited number of non-need-based scholarships are available. About 42% of the current students receive aid. 58% of the previous freshman class returned to the campus for their second year.

Community Environment: Maple Township, population 23,123, is in central Delaware County. The city is located 20 miles from Philadelphia with all its cultural, educational, and recreational opportunities.

DELAWARE VALLEY COLLEGE   (K-17)
700 East Butler Avenue
Doylestown, Pennsylvania 18901
Tel: (215) 345-1500; (800) 233-5825; Fax: (215) 230-2968

Description: This privately supported coeducational professional college was established in 1896. It became a junior college in 1946 and was accredited by the State Council of Education as a senior college in 1948. Today, the college offers its students, selected without regard for race, creed, or economic status, a scientific education in specialized fields of agriculture, biology, chemistry, and in business administration. It operates on the semester system and also provides evening and two summer sessions. The college is accredited by the Middle States Association of Colleges and Schools and the American Chemical Society. It grants the Bachelor degree and an Associate degree in Equine Science. Enrollment includes 790 men and 560 women full-time, 40 men and 30 women part-time, and 500 men and 500 women in the evening division. A faculty of 80 full-time, 2 part-time and 32 evening provides a faculty-student ratio of 1-16.

Entrance Requirements: Approved high school graduation or equivalent; completion of 15 units including 3 English, 2 mathematics, (Algebra I and Algebra II), 2 science (Biology and Chemistry), and 2 social science; SAT or ACT accepted; midyear admission, rolling admission, early admission, and advanced placement plans available; $35 application fee.

Costs Per Year: $12,500 tuition; $5,000 room and board; $500 fees.

Collegiate Environment: The college is located in Bucks County, Pennsylvania, in one of the richest and most colorful agricultural sections in the United States. The college property consists of more than 750 acres of fertile land, with a campus of 37 acres of landscaped lawns containing two football fields, a baseball field, soccer field, field hockey field, tennis courts, and recreation areas. The 74 college buildings contain dormitory facilities for 640 men and 310 women, and a library housing 72,000 titles, 612 periodicals, 17,000 microforms and 1,000 audiovisual materials. Approximately 76% of students applying for admission are accepted. About 74% of the previous freshman class returned to this campus for the sophomore year. Average high school standing of the freshman class: 34% in the top quarter; 34% in the second quarter; 30% in the third quarter; 1% in the bottom quarter. The average scores for the entering freshman class were SAT 454 verbal, 475 math. 1,000 scholarships are available including 350 for freshmen. 82% of the current students receive some form of financial aid.

Community Environment: Population 25,000. Founded in 1745, Doylestown is in one of the finest farming sections of the state, Bucks County. The city is located 30 miles north of Philadelphia, and is reached by railroad, bus lines, and good highways. There are several churches, a hospital, public library, and historical society in the town. Part-time employment is available. Local recreational facilities include theaters, a swimming pool, bowling lanes, and a radio station. There are more than 50 civic, fraternal and veteran's organizations.

DICKINSON COLLEGE   (L-11)
Carlisle, Pennsylvania 17013
Tel: (717) 243-5121; Admissions: (717) 245-1231; Fax: (717) 245-1442

Description: Dickinson, founded in 1773, is a privately supported, coeducational liberal arts college and, by its charter, an independent institution. A self-perpetuating board of trustees governs it, although an historical relationship with the United Methodist Church continues. The college is accredited by the Middle States Association of Colleges and Schools. There is a required freshman seminar program, a career advising network that parallels the the academic advising system, and an accelerated three-year program. Special programs include a laboratory/workshop approach to the natural and mathematical sciences; off-campus internships; self-developed majors; interdisciplinary majors in American studies, Policy and Management studies, Environmental studies, International studies, Judaic studies, Russian and Soviet area studies, and East Asian studies; and a 3-2 engineering programs in cooperation with three other institutions. A wide range of opportunities for study abroad including Bologna, Toulouse, Bremen, Malaga, Nagoya, Norwich, Moscow, Beijing, Yaounde (Cameroon). It grants the B.A. and B.S. degrees. The college operates on the semester system and offers two summer sessions. Enrollment includes 1,805 full-time and 70 part-time students. A faculty of 153 full-time

and 31 part-time gives a faculty-student ratio of 1-10. Army ROTC is available.

Entrance Requirements: Approved high school graduation or equivalent; completion of 16 units including 4 English, 3 foreign language, 3 science, 3 mathematics, and 2 social science; SAT or ACT; admission highly competitive; early decision, early admission, deferred admission, midyear admission, and advanced placement plans available; $35 application fee.

Costs Per Year: $19,600 tuition; $5,270 room and board; $150 student fees; $1,595 average additional expenses.

Collegiate Environment: The 53 college buildings include a library of 409,266 volumes, 151,125 government documents, 1,707 periodicals, 161,374 microforms, and 10,689 audiovisual materials. Residence halls accommodate 1,700 students. The college welcomes students fron diverse geographical locations. Between half and two-thirds of applicants are accepted. Financial aid is available for economically disadvantaged students, and about 999 grants in aid are awarded with 334 for freshmen. Over 63% of students receive some form of financial aid. 94% of freshmen return for their sophomore year, and an estimated 35% of the senior class continued on to graduate school.

Community Environment: Carlisle, population 20,000, is in the Cumberland Valley located at the western edge of Harrisburg, the state capital. It is 3 miles from I-76 and I-81, and within 2-3 hours of Baltimore, Washington and Philadelphia. Founded in 1751, it was the focus of the Scotch-Irish colonists who settled in Pennsylvania in the pre-revolutionary period. Several historic figures made their homes in Carlisle during the revolutionary period. Numerous buildings of Colonial and Federal architecture, many of native limestone, have been restored in the historic district of Carlisle. The eastern most ranges of the Appalachian Mountains are within a few miles of the downtown area, and the Appalachian Trail passes within five miles. Four state parks provide opportunities for hiking, fishing, hunting, and water and winter sports. The Carlisle Hospital, a variety of theatres, restaurants, and chuches, three amusement parks, and public golf courses are within easy reach.

DICKINSON SCHOOL OF LAW   (L-11)
150 South College Street
Carlisle, Pennsylvania 17013
Tel: (717) 243-4611

Description: The Dickinson School of Law, founded in 1834, was the first school in Pennsylvania to grant a law degree and is the oldest independent law school in the United States. A private, free-standing, complete, and modern law school of moderate size, Dickinson is approved by and fully accredited by the American Bar Association and the New York State Board of Regents and is a member of the Association of American Law Schools. The school offers more than 100 courses in the full-time, three-year program of studies leading to the Juris Doctor degree. Also offered is a Master of Comparative Law (M.C.L.) degree program for foreign lawyers. Known for training skilled trial lawyers, The Dickinson School of Law has received the Emil Gumpert Award for Excellence in the Teaching of Trial Advocacy. The school has won national championships recently in appellate moot court and trial advocacy competitions as well as regional competitions in Trial Moot Court and International Law Moot Court. Student teams participate in as many as nine moot court events each year. Students also receive instruction in client counseling, interviewing, negotiation, and mediation, and they operate a neighborhood dispute settlement program. Clinic programs allow students to develop additional skills for understanding people and their problems. Clinical education at Dickinson includes the Family Law and Disability Law clinics on campus, clinics for prison inmates at two state correctional facilities, administrative law clinics with seven state government agencies in Harrisburg, and clinics in legal services offices. There are opportunities for summer study abroad with annual Summer Seminars in Vienna, Austria; Strasbourg, France; and Florence, Italy. It operates on the semester system. Enrollment includes 530 students with a faculty of of 28 full-time and 30 part-time.

Entrance Requirements: A baccalaureate degree or an equivalent from an approved college or university and LSAT are required; $50 application fee.

Costs Per Year: $13,300 tuition; $6,100 room and board; $100 student fees.

Collegiate Environment: Facilities include classrooms, office space, and dormitory housing for 69 men and women. The 350,000-volume library also includes a videotape collection used in courses in trial advocacy, counseling and negotiation; computerized legal instruction programs; Lexis and Westlaw computer research terminals; and a computer laboratory with IBM personal computers. The Dickinson School of Law campus adjoins that of Dickinson College, a separate undergraduate school that affords law students access to its library, food service and cultural activities. Financial aid is available for qualifying students. Students are admitted to begin their studies in the Fall semester, which begins in late August.

Community Environment: Carlisle, an historic town of 20,000 residents, lies 18 miles west of Harrisburg, the state capital. The school's close proximity to Harrisburg allows opportunities for part-time work in state government agencies and private law firms during the school year and in the summer. Nearly 70% of second and third-year students find part-time, law-related jobs in the Carlisle-Harrisburg area. Housing in Carlisle and in surrounding communities is both readily available and affordable.

DREXEL UNIVERSITY   (M-17)
Philadelphia, Pennsylvania 19104-9984
Tel: (215) 895-2400; (800) 237-3935; Fax: (215) 895-5939

Description: Privately supported, coeducational university, founded in 1891, consists of 5 educational units including the Colleges of Business and Administration, Engineering, Arts and Sciences, Information Studies The university is accredited by the Middle States Association of Colleges and Schools. Programs of study are accredited by their respective accrediting institutions. Enrollment includes 11,927 students with a faculty of 426. The university operates on the quarter system and offers one summer session. Army, Navy and Air Force ROTC programs are available. A Cooperative Education plan is available whereby students may elect to alternate terms of school with work in applicable industry of business. Grants Bachelor, Master, and Doctor of Philosophy degrees.

Entrance Requirements: Accredited high school graduation; completion of college preparatory course with rank in upper 40% of class and 4 units of English, 2 science, 3-4 math. Applicants for Engineering and Science programs must complete trigonometry in math progression. SAT required for all applicants. Three achievement tests required for all Engineering and Science curriculae. GRE required for graduate programs; personal interview recommended; early admission, rolling admission, early decision, delayed admission, advanced placement programs available. Transfer students welcomed; $35 application fee.

Costs Per Year: $12,300 tuition; $5,000 room and board; $700 student fees; additional expenses average $2,500 per year.

Collegiate Environment: The campus of the university is located in Philadelphia's University City, within a few minutes of central Philadelphia. The buildings include dormitory facilities for 1,800 men and women, and fraternities and sororities house an additional 460 men and women. The library contains 500,000 titles, 4,200 periodical titles, 572,000 microforms, and 32,300 audiovisual materials. Approximately 80% of students applying for admission are accepted. Classes begin in September but transfer students are accepted at midyear. Average high school standing of a recent freshman class: 45% in the top fifth; 31% in the second fifth; 17% in the third fifth. More than 80% of the previous freshman class return to this campus for the sophomore year. Financial aid is available for economically handicapped students. 10% of the seniors continue on to graduate school immediately upon graduation.

Community Environment: Drexel's 37-acre campus in West Philadelphia consists of 70 buildings. An 18-acre athletic field is located 10 blocks west of the campus. The campus is located in University City, a section that is undergoing major development as a center of education, research and industry. Pleasant residential neighborhoods are also nearby. Drexel is close to public transportation, the Schuykill Expressway (I-76), and Amtrak's 30th Street station, which offers rail service to Philadelphia International Airport.

DUBOIS BUSINESS COLLEGE   (H-6)
One Beaver Drive
DuBois, Pennsylvania 15801
Tel: (814) 371-6920; (800) 692-6213; Fax: (814) 371-3974

Description: The privately supported, coeducational business school operates on the quarter system. The college is accredited by the Accrediting Commission of the Association of Independent Colleges and Schools. Enrollment is 250 students. A faculty of 12 fulltime gives a faculty-student ratio of 1-15.

Entrance Requirements: High school graduation or equivalent; open enrollment policy; $25 application fee; early decision, early admission, rolling admission, and advanced placement plans available.

Costs Per Year: $4,950 tuition; $1,800 room and board; $600 student fees.

Collegiate Environment: The school's library contains 1,500 volumes. Apartments are provided on campus. Financial aid is available for 75% of the students.

Community Environment: See Penn State University, DuBois Campus.

DUQUESNE UNIVERSITY   (K-2)
600 Forbes Avenue
Pittsburgh, Pennsylvania 15282
Tel: (412) 396-6049; (800) 456-0590; Admissions: (412) 396-6220; Fax: (412) 396-5779

Description: Privately supported, coeducational university is affiliated with the Roman Catholic Church. In 1878, the Fathers of the Congregation of the Holy Ghost and of the Immaculate Heart of Mary established a college of arts and letters which was incorporated in 1882 as the Pittsburgh Catholic College of the Holy Ghost with authority to grant degrees in the arts and sciences. In 1911, the College and University Council of the Commonwealth of Pennsylvania approved the amendment in favor of the corporate title, Duquesne University and extended the charter to university status. The university is comprised of the College and Graduate School of Liberal Arts, Bayer School of Natural and Environmental Sciences, School of Business Administration, School of Education, School of Law, School of Music, School of Nursing, School of Health Sciences, School of Pharmacy, and Division of Continuing Education. It is accredited by the Middle States Association of Colleges and Schools and operates on the semester system with two summer sessions offered. Army and Air Force ROTC programs available. The university enrolls 1,942 men and 2,508 women full-time and 389 men and 543 women part-time on the undergraduate level. The faculty consists of 353 full-time and 351 part-time members. Degrees granted: Bachelor, Professional, Master, and Doctor.

Entrance Requirements: Admission to Duquesne University is based on such data as high school transcripts, rank in class, College Board examinations, counselor recommendations, grade predictors, and interviews. Interviews are recommended but not required. Transfer students in good academic standing are admitted with advanced standing for the fall and spring semesters and for all summer sessions. High school graduation with rank in upper 50% of graduating class; completion of 16 units including 4 English; required courses vary within individual schools; SAT or ACT required; open admission for veterans; rolling admission, delayed admission, advanced placement plans available; $45 application fee.

Costs Per Year: $11,107 tuition; $5,418 board and room; $780 health and services fee.

Collegiate Environment: The university is comprised of 24 buildings and is located on 39 acres. It contains a library of 732,915 volumes, 8,746 periodicals, and 421,136 microforms. Dormitory facilities house 2,500 students. It accepts midyear students. Approximately 59% of students applying for admission are accepted and 91% of the previous freshman class returned to this campus for the sophomore year. Average high school standing of the freshmen class, 44% in the top quintile; 26% in the second quintile; 15% in the third quintile; 4% in the fourth quintile; mid 50% score ranges, SAT 420-560V, 480-600M. Financial aid is available for economically disadvantaged students and 78% of the current student body receive some form of financial assistance.

Community Environment: See University of Pittsburgh, Pittsburgh Campus.

EAST STROUDSBURG UNIVERSITY OF PENNSYLVANIA
(I-17)
East Stroudsburg, Pennsylvania 18301
Tel: (717) 424-3542; Admissions: (717) 424-3542; Fax: (717) 424-3777

Description: Publicly supported, coeducational liberal arts and teachers college opened as a private normal school in 1893. It came under state control in 1920 and was raised to the status of a teachers college in 1926. Graduate programs were introduced in 1962, and curriculum in liberal arts was inaugurated in 1963. It is accredited by the Middle States Association of Colleges and Schools, National Council for the Accreditation of Teacher Education, the American Chemical Society, The National League for Nursing and grants the Bachelor and Master degrees. The college operates on the semester system and offers three summer sessions. Enrollment includes 3,871 full-time and 813 part-time undergraduates and 900 graduate students. The faculty consists of 257 full-time and 8 part-time members.

Entrance Requirements: Approved high school graduation with rank in upper 40% of graduating class; SAT required; March 1 notification for fall freshmen applicants, advanced placement, $25 application fee.

Costs Per Year: $3,086 tuition; $7,844 out-of-state tuition; $3,456 board and room, $758 student fees.

Collegiate Environment: The 183-acre campus is located in the foothills of the Pocono Mountains. The library contains over 411,000 volumes, 2,100 periodicals, 1,600,000 microforms. Dormitory facilities accommodate 928 men and 1,072 women. Approximately 50% of students applying for admission are accepted and 85% of the freshman return for the sophomore year. The college seeks a geographically diverse student body. Average high school standing of the freshman class, top 30%; 28% in the top quarter; 44% in the second quarter; 23% in the third quarter. The average scores of the entering freshman class were SAT 400 verbal, 499 math. About 25% of the seniors continue on to graduate school.

Community Environment: Population 7,894. East Stroudsburg is an urban area with temperate climate. The community is served by bus lines and Routes 611, 80 and 191. The community has a public library, YMCA, a hospital, good shopping facilities, and churches of major denominations. Part-time employment opportunities are excellent. The area offers good recreational facilities with nearby resorts.

EASTERN BAPTIST THEOLOGICAL SEMINARY *(M-17)*
6 Lancaster Avenue
Philadelphia, Pennsylvania 19096
Tel: (215) 896-5000; Fax: (215) 649-3834

Description: This privately supported, coeducational, graduate theological seminary was founded in 1925. It is affiliated with the American Baptist Churches U.S.A., but admission to the seminary is open to all qualified persons of all evangelical denominations. It is accredited by the Middle States Association of Colleges and Schools the Association of Theological Schools and is affiliated with the Association for Clinical and Pastoral Education. The Seminary is approved for Veterans education under the provisions of the Veterans Administration. It operates on the 4-1-4 system and offers one summer session. Enrollment is 376 students. There are 16 full-time and 33 part-time faculty members. The seminary is also affiliated with Eastern College (formerly Eastern Baptist College).

Entrance Requirements: Baccalaureate degree from a recognized college or university; aptitude and personality tests required.

Costs Per Year: $5,830 tuition; $2,020 room; $30 student fees; $250 average additional expenses.

Collegiate Environment: The seminary is comprised of three buildings located on seven acres. It contains a library of 84,000 volumes, 3,900 pamphlets, 540 periodicals, 560 microforms, and 850 recordings, and living accommodations for 44 men, 16 women, and 32 families. Financial aid is available for economically handicapped students. The seminary awarded 44 Master degrees and 43 Doctor of Ministry degrees to the 1990 graduating class.

Community Environment: See Temple University.

EASTERN COLLEGE *(M-17)*
10 Fairview Drive
St. Davids, Pennsylvania 19087-3696
Tel: (610) 341-5967; Admissions: (610) 341-5967; Fax: (610) 341-1723

Description: Privately supported, affiliated with the American Baptist Churches. Coeducational liberal arts college, founded in 1932 as a department of Eastern Baptist Theological Seminary. It became an independent institution in 1952 and was accredited by the Middle States Association of Colleges and Schools in 1954. Both the faculty and student body come from many denominational backgrounds, and from many states and foreign countries. The college is evangelical and conservative in character. The college operates on the semester plan with an additional three summer sessions. Academic cooperative plans with various hospitals are available for medical technology majors. Enrollment includes 1,136 full-time and 400 part-time and 529 graduate students. A faculty of 55 full-time and 151 part-time provides a faculty-student ratio of 1-12.

Entrance Requirements: High school graduation or equivalent; rank in upper half of graduating class; college preparatory program required; SAT or ACT required; early decision, advanced placement, early admission, delayed admission, rolling admission programs available; $25 application fee.

Costs Per Year: $11,190 tuition; $4,800 room and board; $1,300 average additional expenses.

Collegiate Environment: The 100-acre campus occupies lands that formerly belonged to five private estates. It is located in a residential area on Philadelphia's Main Line, 30 minutes away from the downtown area. The college buildings contain dormitory facilities for 550 men and women. The library houses 116,875 volumes, 798 periodicals, 156,609 microforms and 2,466 audiovisual materials. Approximately 78% of students applying for admission are accepted, and about 70% of the freshmen return for their sophomore year. Scholarships are available and 80% of the students receive some form of financial aid. About 8% of the graduating students continue on to graduate school.

Community Environment: See Villanova University.

EDINBORO UNIVERSITY OF PENNSYLVANIA *(E-2)*
Edinboro, Pennsylvania 16444
Tel: (814) 732-2761; (800) 626-2203; Admissions: (814) 732-2761; Fax: (814) 732-2420

Description: Publicly supported, coeducational college offering arts and sciences and teacher education. It is accredited by the Middle States Association of Colleges and Schools and several professional accrediting. Chartered in 1856, the state college is the oldest Pennsylvania training institution west of the Allegheny Mountains, and the second oldest such school in the state. It became a four-year college in 1926, began undergraduate programs of teacher education in 1927, and inaugurated curriculum in arts and sciences in 1952. The university operates on the semester system and offers two summer sessions. It grants the Associate, Bachelor and Master degrees. Army ROTC is available. Enrollment includes 6,371 full-time and 1,113 part-time undergraduates and 637 graduate students. A faculty of 403 full-time and 22 part-time gives a faculty-student ratio of 1-18.

Entrance Requirements: Approved high school graduation or equivalent; SAT or ACT required; early admission, deferred admission, midyear admission, rolling admission, and advanced placement plans available; $25 application fee.

Costs Per Year: $3,086 resident tuition; $7,844 out-of-state; $3,650 room and board; $599 student fees.

Collegiate Environment: The campus is located adjacent to the Borough of Edinboro. To the north lies Lake Erie, about 20 miles away. The college occupies 585 acres. The college buildings include a library of 417,930 volumes, 1,982 periodicals, and 1.2 million microforms. Dormitory facilities are provided for 2,600 men and women. Approximately 76% of students applying for admission are accepted, including midyear students. More than 72% of the previous freshman class returned to this campus for the sophomore year. 620 scholarships and financial aid are available for economically disadvantaged students and 80% of the current student body receives some form of financial assistance. The university awarded 1,556 degrees recently.

Community Environment: Population 7,725, Edinboro lies approximately 18 miles south of Erie, Pennsylvania. The community has several churches that represent various denominations. Bus and highway transportation is available. Local recreational facilities include hunting, boating, swimming, fishing, golf, and skiing. Edinboro Lake, which is one mile from the campus, has three beaches.

Branch Campuses: Porreco Extension Center.

ELIZABETHTOWN COLLEGE   *(L-13)*
One Alpha Drive
Elizabethtown, Pennsylvania 17022-2298
Tel: (717) 361-1400; Fax: (717) 361-1365

Description: This private, comprehensive, coeducational college is accredited by the Middle States Association of Colleges and Schools. Founded in 1899 by members of the Church of the Brethern, it continues its tradition of education for service, through its blend of arts and professional studies with new majors in Philosophy and International Business. Programs of study lead to the Bachelor of Arts or Bachelor of Science degree. It operates on the semester system and offers one seven-week summer session. The college offers study abroad in Europe, Asia, and South America through the Brethern Colleges Abroad program and the American University. Elizabethtown College offers accredited college level courses through the University Center at Harrisburg. Late afternoon, evening, and Saturday classes are available at the Center. Enrollment is 1,553 full-time and 265 part-time students. A faculty of 106 full-time and 45 part-time gives a faculty-student ratio of 1-14.

Entrance Requirements: High school graduation with rank in top quarter of graduating class; completion of 18 college-preparatory courses including 4 English, 3 mathematics, 2 lab science, 2 foreign language, 2 social studies, and 5 academic electives; SAT and/or ACT required; personal interview and campus visit recommended; two letters of recommendation; official high school transcript; personal essay required; early admission, rolling admission and advanced placement plans available; $20 application fee.

Costs Per Year: $14,190 tuition; $4,400 room and board; $400 fees.

Collegiate Environment: The 170-acre campus is located in a residential community 9 miles south of Hershey in Lancaster County, within easy reach of the metropolitan centers of Philadelphia, Baltimore, and Washington, DC. The college buildings contain a library of 158,357 volumes, over 1,100 periodical subscriptions, 652 titles on microform, and 10,254 recordings, tapes, and CDs. Dormitory facilities accommodate 1,300 men and women. The college welcomes a geographically diverse student body and will accept midyear students. Approximately 76% of students applying for admission are accepted and 85% of the previous freshman class returned to this campus for the sophomore year. The middle 50% range of freshmen scores was SAT 950-1120 combined. Recently, the college awarded $9.9 million in grants and scholarships. In addition, students received nearly $6.9 million from federal, state, and private sources. 86% of the current student body receives some form of financial assistance.

Community Environment: Population 10,000. Located in Lancaster County, Elizabethtown enjoys the advantages of the neighboring communities' facilities. This suburb has a library, several churches, and major fraternal and civic organizations within the immediate locale. Some part-time employment is available.

EVANGELICAL SCHOOL OF THEOLOGY   *(K-14)*
121 South College Street
Myerstown, Pennsylvania 17067
Tel: (717) 866-5775; (800) 532-5775; Fax: (717) 866-4667

Description: Privately supported, graduate-level school of theology established in 1953 and affiliated with the Evangelical Congregational Church. It operates on the 4-1-4 system with one summer session. Enrollment is 120 students. The school is open to all qualified students, regardless of race or denominational affiliations. Grants Master of Divinity degree and Master of Arts in Religion. A faculty of 10 provides a faculty-student ratio of 1-12. The school is accredited by the Middle State Association of Colleges and Schools, and the Association of Theological Schools in the United States and Canada.

Entrance Requirements: Baccalaureate degree from accredited college or university required for all programs; GRE or MAT required; $25 application fee; rolling admission plan.

Costs Per Year: $3,960 tuition; $1,000 room; $15 student fees.

Collegiate Environment: The ten-acre campus is located about seven miles east of Lebanon and 32 miles east of Harrisburg, the capital of Pennsylvania. The school buildings include a library of 57,000 volumes, 300 periodicals, and 20 microforms, and dormitory facilities for 20 men, 6 women, and 12 married students. Approximately 90% of students applying for admission are accepted including midyear students.

Community Environment: Myerstown is located 20 miles north of Lancaster and 30 miles from Harrisburg, the state capital.

FRANKLIN AND MARSHALL COLLEGE   *(M-14)*
College Avenue, P.O. Box 3003
Lancaster, Pennsylvania 17604-3003
Tel: (717) 291-3951; Fax: (717) 291-4389

Description: Privately-supported, coeducational liberal arts college. Franklin College, seventeenth oldest college in the nation, was established in 1787. In 1853, it was joined by Marshall College which had been established in 1836 at Mercersburg, Pennsylvania. From a historical relationship to the United Church of Christ the college has developed into an independent, free-standing institution and welcomes students and faculty members of all faiths. The college is accredited by the Middle States Association of Colleges and Schools. The Bachelor of Arts degree is offered with majors in 29 programs. The college offers strong preparation in pre-professional curriculums especially in business, law and medicine. Army ROTC is available through nearby Millersville University. It operates on the semester system and offers two summer sessions. Enrollment includes 1,794 full-time and 40 part-time students. A faculty of 149 full-time and 20 part-time gives a faculty-student ratio of 1-11.

Entrance Requirements: Accredited high school graduation with rank in upper 25%; completion of 16 units with recommended courses of 4 English, 4 mathematics, 3 foreign language, 3 laboratory science, 3 social science; SAT or ACT and SAT II (Writing) required; standardized tests are optional for students in the top 10% of their class who instead submit two graded writing samples; early decision, early admission, delayed admission, candidate reply date-May 1; advanced placement programs available; $40 application fee.

Costs Per Year: $24,940 comprehensive fee.

Collegiate Environment: The 52-acre main campus and nearby 54 acre Baker Memorial campus are located in the northwestern section of Lancaster, Pennsylvania, about 60 miles west of Philadelphia. The 32 college buildings include two libraries with holdings of 366,000 volumes, 1,692 periodicals and 258,000 microform items; and dormitory facilities for 1,320 men and women. The Steinman College Center Building, designed by Minoru Yamasaki, provides major facilities for non-academic activities and programs. Students from 40 states and 37 nations matriculated recently. Approximately 66% of students applying for admission are accepted. About 50% of a recent freshman class graduated in the top 10% of the high school class; the middle 50% range of scores for entering freshmen: SAT 510-620 verbal, 560-670 math. Financial aid is available based on demonstrated need. 45% of the current students receive some form of financial assistance from the public and private sources.

Community Environment: Metropolitan area of 300,000; vital, historic city. See Lancaster Theological Seminary.

GANNON UNIVERSITY   *(D-2)*
1 University Square
Erie, Pennsylvania 16541
Tel: (814) 871-7240; (800) 426-6668; Fax: (814) 459-0996

Description: Privately supported, coeducational liberal arts university established in 1925 under the auspices of the Roman Catholic Church. It operates on the semester system and provides 2 summer sessions as well as afternoon and evening sessions. Enrollment is 2,758 full-time, 1,626 part-time undergraduate and 749 graduate students. A faculty of 203 full-time and 128 part-time gives a ratio of 1-12. The college is accredited by the Middle States Association of Colleges and Schools and professional accrediting institutions, and grants the Bachelor and Master degree. Army ROTC is available. Academic cooperative plans are available with Mercyhurst College and for students majoring in elementary education.

Entrance Requirements: High school graduation with rank in upper 60%; completion of 16 units including 4 English, 3 mathematics, 2 laboratory science, 3 social science, 2 foreign language; SAT minimum 425V, 425M required; GRE required for graduate programs; non-high school graduates considered; rolling admission, advanced placement programs available; $25 application fee.

Costs Per Year: $9,120 tuition; $3,780 board and room.

Collegiate Environment: The college is located on 9 acres in the City of Erie. Its 36 buildings contain a library of 200,000 volumes, 1,200 periodicals, 85,000 microforms and 800 recordings. Dormitory facilities accommodate 1,094 students, fraternities house 101 men, sororities house 50 women. Students from other geographical locations are accepted as well as midyear students. Approximately 77% of students applying for admission are accepted and 74% return for the sophomore year. Financial aid is available for economically disadvantaged students. 86% of students receive financial aid.

Community Environment: Pennsylvania's third largest city and its only port on the Great Lakes, Erie is a city of widely diversified industry and commerce. Tremendous traffic in ships carrying heavy cargoes of lumber, coal, petroleum, grain, iron ore, and fish is carried on here. Part-time employment opportunities are excellent. The area is served by railroad, air, and bus lines. The community has many churches representing the major denominations, numerous civic and fraternal organizations, and community health clinics and hospitals. Local recreational facilities include theatres, drive-ins, golf courses, many city parks, fishing, boating, yacht regattas, ice fishing, and skating.

GENEVA COLLEGE   (I-1)
College Avenue
Beaver Falls, Pennsylvania 15010
Tel: (412) 846-5100; (800) 847-8255; Fax: (412) 847-5017

Description: This privately supported, coeducational liberal arts college was established in 1848 by the Reformed Presbyterian Church of North America, and governed by a Board of Corporators elected by that church. The college operates on the semester system and offers two summer sessions. It is accredited by the Middle States Association of Colleges and Schools and grants the Associate and Bachelor degree. Enrollment is 1,334 full-time and 226 part-time undergraduate students. There are 118 graduate students. A faculty of 53 full-time and 54 part-time gives a faculty-student ratio of 1-18.

Entrance Requirements: Accredited high school graduation or equivalent; rank in upper 60% of graduating class; completion of 16 units including 4 English, 2 mathematics, 2 foreign language, 1 science, and 3 social science; early admission, delayed admission, rolling admission, and advanced placement plans available; $15 application fee.

Costs Per Year: $10,000 tuition; $4,400 room and board; $84 student fees.

Collegiate Environment: The 52-acre campus is situated on College Hill overlooking the Beaver River. The city of Beaver Falls is approximately 30 miles northwest of Pittsburgh, in the Beaver Valley. The 41 college buildings include a library of 151,481 volumes, 751 periodicals, 80,434 microforms, and 22,229 audiovisual materials. Dormitory facilities are provided for 380 men and 378 women. Approximately 86% of students applying for admission are accepted, including midyear students. 73% of the previous freshman class returned to this campus for the sophomore year. Financial aid is available for economically handicapped students and minority students. Approximately 93% of the current student body receives some form of financial aid.

Community Environment: Rich in natural resources and historical heritage, Beaver County supports commercial and industrial growth as well as a thriving agribusiness enterprise. 18,000 acres of park lands, excellent health care facilities, and numerous churches of various denominations help to meet needs of residents. Public transportation is accessible and proximity to Pittsburgh makes cultural and professional sports events available year-round. Part-time employment is available.

GETTYSBURG COLLEGE   (M-11)
Gettysburg, Pennsylvania 17325
Tel: (717) 337-6000; (800) 431-0803; Admissions: (717) 337-6100; Fax: (717) 337-6145

Description: Privately-supported coeducational liberal arts college established in 1832 and was the first Lutheran College in America. The college is accredited by the Middle States Association of Colleges and Schools and grants the Bachelor degree. The college operates on the early semester system. Enrollment includes 1,065 men and 1,043 women. A faculty of 150 full-time gives a faculty-student ratio of 1-12. A summer school program is available in cooperation with Central Pennsylvania Consortium of Dickinson, Franklin and Marshall and Gettysburg. Teacher Certification Program offered. Academic cooperative plans are available with Rensselaer Polytechnic Institute, Washington University, Penn State and Duke University. Army ROTC is available.

Entrance Requirements: High school graduation or equivalent; rank in upper 25%; SAT or ACT required; non-high school graduates considered; early decision plan, advanced placement, early admission, delayed admission programs available; $35 application fee.

Costs Per Year: $20,834 tuition; $4,522 board and room; additional expenses average $900.

Collegiate Environment: The college is comprised of 43 buildings located on 200 acres. It contains a library of 340,000 volumes, 70,000 periodicals, 38,000 microforms and 59,100 audiovisual materials. Dormitory facilities accommodate 1,600 students and fraternities house 650 men. There are 12 social fraternities and 7 social sororities located on or near the campus. Students from other geographical locations are accepted as well as midyear students. Approximately 65% of students applying for admission are accepted and 90% of the previous freshman class returned to this campus for the sophomore year. About 68% of the current freshman class graduated in the top fifth of the high school class; 29% of the second fifth; 3% in the third fifth. The average scores of the entering freshmen class were SAT verbal, 582 math. Financial aid is available and 51% of the current student body receive some form of financial assistance.

Community Environment: Population of Gettysburg 9,000. Here, one of the most important battles of the Civil War was fought. Today, Adams County surrounding Gettysburg has 20,000 acres of apple orchards. There are many historical sites within the surrounding area. Gettysburg is served by railroad, bus lines, and an airport. There are several churches, 13 museums, a library, two radio stations, YWCA, and a youth center to serve the community. Recreational facilities include horseback riding, two state parks nearby, three movie theatres, 2 ski resorts, The Appalachian trail, and a summer theatre. Part-time employment is available.

GRATZ COLLEGE   (M-17)
Old York Road & Melrose Avenue
Melrose Park, Pennsylvania 19027
Tel: (215) 329-3363

Description: Privately supported, coeducational, nondenominationally affiliated college of Jewish Studies, established in 1895. The College is accredited by the Middle States Association of Colleges and Schools. It operates on the semester system and offers two summer sessions. Enrollment includes 36 full-time and 184 part-time undergraduates and 142 graduate students. A faculty of 8 full-time and 28 part-time gives a faculty-student ratio of 1-12. The college offers courses leading to Bachelor of Arts in Jewish Studies, as well as the following graduate degrees: Master of Arts in Jewish Education, Master of Arts in Jewish Music, Master of Arts in Jewish Studies and Master of Arts in Jewish Liberal Studies. Joint graduate programs in Jewish Communal Service with the University of Pennsylvania's School of Social Work, Judaica Librarianship with Drexel University and Special Needs Education with LaSalle University have been established.

Entrance Requirements: Open enrollment policy for undergraduate programs; rolling admission, early admission, early decision, delayed admission and advanced placement plans available.

Costs Per Year: $5,920 undergraduate tuition; $7,440 graduate tuition.

Collegiate Environment: The College, situated on a suburban 28-acre campus, welcomes a geographically, religiously and racially diverse student body and will accept midyear students. The Tuttleman Library contains more than 100,000 items including 75,000 volumes, 150 periodicals and 25,500 music and audiovisual items. The College is housed in a modern building that is accessible to the handicapped, and it is adjacent to several other major communal institutions, as well as near other major colleges and universities (Temple University, La-Salle University, University of Pennsylvania, and Beaver College). A warm, friendly and helpful atmosphere prevails.

Community Environment: All the amenities of Greater Philadelphia's cultural and academic environment (museums, concert halls, colleges and universities, etc.) are available and accessible to Gratz's multifaceted student body by either private or public transportation. A large, diverse and well-organized Jewish community enables those interested in an active Jewish communal life to thrive.

GROVE CITY COLLEGE   *(H-2)*
Grove City, Pennsylvania 16127
Tel: (412) 458-2100

Description: This privately supported, coeducational liberal arts college was founded in 1876 and is affiliated with the United Presbyterian Church U.S.A. It is fully accredited by the Middle States Association of Colleges and Schools. By the authority of the Pennsylvania Department of Public Instruction it has the right to recommend candidates for elementary and secondary school certification. It grants the Bachelor degree. The college operates on the semester system and offers a May intersession. Enrollment includes 1,138 men full-time, 1,114 women full-time, and 17 men, 11 women part-time. A faculty of 108 full-time and 37 part-time gives a faculty-student ratio of 1-20.

Entrance Requirements: Approved high school graduation; completion of 18 units including 4 English, 3 mathematics, 2 science, 3 foreign language, and 4 social science; Nov. 15 early decision application deadline, Feb. 15 regular application deadline; early admission, early decision, midyear admission, and advanced placement plans available; $25 application fee.

Costs Per Year: $5,224 tuition; $3,048 room and board; $500 average additional expenses.

Collegiate Environment: The original location of the school, now commonly called the lower campus, was in the heart of the town of Grove City. The buildings of the lower campus include the Robert E. Thorn Field for football and track, tennis courts, Phillips Field House, and Carnegie Hall. All other buildings are located on the beautiful 150-acre hillside campus across Wolf Creek from the town. The 27 college buildings include a library of 169,000 volumes, 1,200 periodicals, and 244,000 microforms, and dormitory facilities for 983 men and 965 women. Students from other geographical locations are accepted as well as midyear students. Approximately 46% of students applying for admission are accepted. Average scores of entering freshmen were SAT Verbal 539, Math 606. Financial aid is available. 87% of freshmen returned for their sophomore year.

Community Environment: Population 8,000, Grove City is an urban community that produces compressors, gas and diesel engines, soldering equipment and linemen's supplies. Bituminous coal mining is very important to the area. The city has one new hospital, several churches, a library, YMCA, and various civic and fraternal organizations. Local recreation includes a theater, hunting, fishing, golf, football, baseball, swimming, tennis, basketball, bowling, boating, and ice and roller skating.

GWYNEDD-MERCY COLLEGE   *(M-17)*
Sumneytown Pike
Gwynedd Valley, Pennsylvania 19437
Tel: (215) 641-5510; (800) DIA-LGMC; Fax: (215) 641-5556

Description: Privately supported college of arts and sciences established in 1948 and sponsored by the Sisters of Mercy. It is accredited by the Middle States Association of Colleges and Schools, the National League for Nursing, and the American Medical Association, the Committee on Allied Health Education and Accreditation. The college operates on the semester system and offers two summer terms. Enrollment is 135 men and 577 full-time, and 231 men and 1,075 women part-time. These figures include a graduate enrollment of 178 students. A faculty of 94 full-time and 82 part-time gives a faculty-student ratio of 1-11. The college grants the Associate and Bachelor degrees as well as programs leading toward Teacher Certification in

both elementary and secondary education, early childhood, special education and athletic training preparation. Army ROTC is available through the University of Pennsylvania.

Entrance Requirements: High school graduation with rank in upper 40%; completion of 16 units including 4 English, 3 mathematics, 2 foreign language, 3 science, and 2 social science; SAT or ACT required; non-high school graduates with GED considered; early admission, early decision, rolling admission, delayed admission, and advanced placement plans available; $25 application fee.

Costs Per Year: $11,450 tuition; $12,300 Nursing & Allied Health; $5,800 room and board; additional expenses average $500.

Collegiate Environment: Combining the quiet atmosphere of the country with easy access to Philadelphia, the college is located in a beautiful section of Montgomery County, between Ambler and North Wales. The 15 college buildings include a library of 93,600 volumes, 766 periodicals, 79 microform titles, and 5,494 recordings; a student union building; and dormitory facilities for 188 students. Students from other geographical locations are accepted as well as midyear transfer students. Approximately 60% of students applying for admission are accepted and 91% of the previous freshman class returned to this campus for the sophomore year. Average high school standing of the recent freshman class, top 30%; 68% in top third, 87% in top half; average SAT scores 450V, 490M. Financial aid is available for economically disadvantaged students and 82% of the current student body receives some form of financial assistance. The college awarded 153 Associate and 218 Bachelor degrees during a recent academic year.

Community Environment: Gwynedd Valley is a suburban location. The community is located 20 miles from Center City, Philadelphia, which has cultural, recreational, and community service opportunities. The immediate locale has churches, recreational facilities, shopping malls, movies and restaurants.

HARCUM JUNIOR COLLEGE   *(M-17)*
Morris and Montgomery Avenues
Bryn Mawr, Pennsylvania 19010
Tel: (215) 525-4100

Description: Privately supported, two-year independent college for women established in 1915. It operates on the semester system with two summer terms and enrolls 750 women. The college is accredited by the Middle States Association of Colleges and Schools. A faculty of 35 full-time and 38 part-time gives a faculty-student ratio of 1-19. The college offers university-parallel and occupational courses and grants the Associate degree.

Entrance Requirements: Accredited high school graduation; letter of recommendation, requirements vary according to course to be studied; early admission, rolling admission, delayed admission, and advanced placement plans available; $15 application fee.

Costs Per Year: $6,550 tuition; $4,300 room and board; $440 student fees.

Collegiate Environment: The college's main campus is located in Bryn Mawr, twelve miles from central Philadelphia and in the heart of the Main Line suburbs. The college buildings include a library of 37,000 volumes, 250 periodicals, and 150 recordings. Dormitory facilities are provided for 500 women. Students from other geographical locations are accepted as well as midyear students. Approximately 90% of the students applying for admission are accepted and 80% of the freshman class returned to this campus for the second year. Financial aid is available and 72% of the current student body receives financial assistance.

Community Environment: See Bryn Mawr College.

HARRISBURG AREA COMMUNITY COLLEGE   *(L-12)*
One HACC Drive
Harrisburg, Pennsylvania 17110-2999
Tel: (717) 780-2400; (800) 222-4222; Admissions: (717) 780-2410; Fax: (717) 231-7674

Description: Publicly-supported, coeducational community college began its first year of classes in 1964. The college was the first public community college in Pennsylvania. It is accredited by the Middle States Association of Colleges and Schools and various professional accrediting organizations. It operates on the semester system and offers four summer sessions. Enrollment includes 3,851 full-time and 7,056 part-time students. A faculty of 270 full-time and 30 part-time gives a faculty-student ratio 1-35. The college grants the Associate degree, Diplomas, and Certificates.

Entrance Requirements: The college is an open admission institution. Non-high school graduates may be admitted as "non-degree" students. Students seeking admission to degree programs must have a high school diploma. ACT required of applicants to Allied Health Programs. $25 application fee.

Costs Per Year: $1,657 resident tuition; $3,315 tuition for residents of nonsponsoring districts; $4,792 tuition for out-of-state students.

Collegiate Environment: The college occupies a 157-acre campus in Wildwood Park, deeded to the college by the City of Harrisburg. The library contains over 73,000 volumes and is a member of a 7 college consortium making over 3 million volumes available to students. The physical plant consists of 9 buildings worth $21,000,000 all constructed since 1967. The college runs both a day and evening division for its commuter students. There are no dormitories. Semesters begin in August and January.

Community Environment: Population 68,061. On the Susquehanna River, Harrisburg lies between mountains which rise abruptly to the north and west and rolling hills which slope to the south and east. Extensive coal and iron mines in the vicinity furnish raw materials for the city's large steel plants. Part-time employment opportunities are good. Harrisburg is a metropolitan area served by airlines, railroad, and bus lines. The community has state and public libraries, a State Museum, several hospitals, and major civic, fraternal and veteran's organizations. Shopping facilities are excellent. Local recreational opportunities include theatres, summer theatres, parks, golf, professional hockey, and water sports.

Branch Campuses: Lancaster Campus, 1008 New Holland Avenue, Lancaster, PA 17601, (717) 293-5000; Lebanon Campus, 735 Cumberland Street, Lebanon, PA 17042, (717) 270-6330; Gettysburg Center, 22 Liberty Street, Gettysburg, PA, 17325, (717) 337-3855.

HAVERFORD COLLEGE (M-17)
370 Lancaster Avenue
Haverford, Pennsylvania 19041-1392
Tel: (610) 896-1000; Admissions: (610) 896-1350; Fax: (610) 896-1338

Description: Privately supported, independent coeducational liberal arts college was founded in 1833 as the first college established by members of the Society of Friends in the United States. The college operates on the semester basis and enrolls 567 men and 542 women. It is accredited by the Middle States Association of Colleges and Schools and grants the Bachelor degree. 48 international study programs in 33 countries are available. A faculty of 97 full-time and 14 part-time provides a faculty-student ratio of 1-11.

Entrance Requirements: High school graduation; 4 English, 3 mathematics, 3 foreign language, 1 science, 1 social science; SAT I and 3 SAT II tests, including the Writing Test are required; non-high school graduates with GED considered; early decision, delayed admission, and advanced placement programs available; $45 application fee.

Costs Per Year: $19,884 tuition; $6,550 room and board; $191 student fees.

Collegiate Environment: The 216-acre campus is located in the Main Line suburbs ten miles west of Philadelphia. The 40 major college buildings include a library of 400,000 volumes, and 1,265 periodicals. Dormitory facilities accommodate 1,065 students. The college welcomes a geographically diverse student body. Approximately 39% of students applying for admission are accepted. About 96% of the recent freshman class graduated in the top fifth of the high school class. The middle 50% ranges of scores for entering freshmen were SAT 570-670 verbal, 630-720 math. Semesters begin in September. Financial aid is available and 35% of the current students receive some form of financial assistance from the college. The college awarded 273 Bachelor degrees to a recent graduating class and 25% continued on to graduate school immediately.

Community Environment: The school has cooperative arrangements with several colleges and universities (see Bryn Mawr College, Swarthmore College, University of Pennsylvania). Located near many colleges and universities in metropolitan Philadelphia area.

HOLY FAMILY COLLEGE (M-17)
Grant and Frankford Avenues
Philadelphia, Pennsylvania 19114
Tel: (215) 637-7700; Admissions: (215) 637-3050

Description: Privately supported liberal arts college accredited by the Middle States Association of Colleges and Schools and the National League for Nursing. The college was established in 1954 by the Sisters of the Holy Family of Nazareth under the auspices of the Roman Catholic Church. Programs of study emphasize the liberal arts, education and career preparation. The College grants the Associate, Bachelor's, and Master's degrees. It operates on the semester system and offers two summer terms. Enrollment is 1,128 full-time and 1,207 part-time undergraduate students, and 280 graduate students. A faculty of 85 full-time and 156 part-time gives a faculty-student ratio of 1-12.

Entrance Requirements: Approved high school graduation with a B or better average; completion of 16 units including 4 English, 2 mathematics, 2 foreign language, 2 science, and 2 social science; SAT minimum 400V, 400M required; early admission, early decision, delayed admission, rolling admission, advanced placement programs available; $25 application fee.

Costs Per Year: $8,800 tuition; $200 student fees.

Collegiate Environment: The 46-acre campus is located in the suburban residential section of Torresdale, near the extreme northeastern boundary of Philadelphia. The seven college buildings include a library of 106,709 volumes, 596 periodicals, 7,054 microforms, and 2,483 audiovisual materials. Approximately 58% of students applying for admission are accepted including midyear, and 70% of the previous freshman class returned to this campus for the sophomore year. The average scores of the entering freshmen class were SAT 424 verbal and 454 math. Scholarships are available, including 50 for freshmen. 89% of the students receive some form of financial aid.

Community Environment: See Temple University.

IMMACULATA COLLEGE (M-16)
Immaculata, Pennsylvania 19345
Tel: (215) 647-4400, x3015; Fax: (215) 251-1668

Description: Privately supported, liberal arts college for women established in 1920 by the Sisters, Servants of the Immaculate Heart of Mary, under the auspices of the Roman Catholic Church. It is accredited by the Middle States Association of Colleges and Schools, and grants the Bachelor, Master, and Doctoral degrees. The college operates on the semester basis and offers three summer sessions. Enrollment includes 500 full-time, 1,100 part-time, and 830 evening undergraduate students and 538 graduate students. (Of the evening students, 181 are men.) A faculty of 65 full-time and 95 part-time gives a faculty-student ratio of 1-10.

Entrance Requirements: Accredited high school graduation with rank in upper 50%; completion of 16 units including 4 English, 2 mathematics, 2 foreign language, 2 science, and 2 social science; high school equivalency certificate considered; SAT required; early admission, midyear admission, rolling admission, delayed admission, and advanced placement programs available; $25 application fee.

Costs Per Year: $10,000 tuition; $5,454 room and board; $180 student fees; additional expenses average $1,500.

Collegiate Environment: The 390-acre campus is situated on a hilltop overlooking the beautiful Chester Valley, about 20 miles west of Philadelphia, on the Main Line. The 12 college buildings contain a library of 110,000 volumes, 729 periodicals, 20 microforms, 4,356 records, tapes and compact discs; and dormitory facilities for 500 women. The college welcomes a geographically diverse student body and will accept midyear students. Over 70% of students applying for admission are accepted and 76% of the freshman class return for the sophomore year. Average high school standing of a recent freshman class, 35% in the top quarter, 47% in the second quarter; 13% in the third quarter; 5% in the bottom quarter; average scores, SAT 460V, 470M. Financial aid is available and 78% of the current students receive some form of financial assistance. Of the 325 scholarships offered, 19 are for freshmen. The college awarded 190 Bachelor degrees to a recent graduating class. 12% of the senior class continued on to graduate school.

Community Environment: Immaculata is a suburban area with a temperate climate. An airport, railroad, and bus lines serve the area. The school is located in Chester County, twenty miles west of Philadelphia, at the junction of routes 30 and 352. The community has a public library, churches of major denominations, two hospitals, and a large shopping center. There are active civic and fraternal organizations within the area. See also Temple University for information about Philadelphia.

INDIANA UNIVERSITY OF PENNSYLVANIA *(J-5)*
Indiana, Pennsylvania 15705
Tel: (412) 357-2230

Description: Publicly supported, coeducational university which began as a normal school in the ninth district at Indiana, PA, in 1875. In 1920, control and ownership passed to the Commonwealth of Pennsylvania. It operated as a state college until 1965, when it was re-designated as a university and given the right to expand its curricular offerings and to grant degrees at the doctoral level as well as in a number of additional areas at the master's level. Today, it is a multi-purpose institution composed of six colleges: Fine Arts, Education, Social Sciences and Humanities; Natural Sciences and Math, Business, and Health Sciences and Human Ecology; and two schools: Continuing Education and Graduate School. There are also branch campuses in Kittanning and Punxsutawney. It is accredited by the Middle States Association of Colleges and Schools and operates on the semester basis with two summer sessions. Enrollment includes 5,006 men and 6,228 women full-time, 484 men, 526 women part-time, and 1,570 graduate students. A faculty of 730 full-time and 80 part-time gives a faculty-student ratio of 1-18. The university provides Army ROTC programs and grants the Associate, Bachelor, Master and Doctorate degrees.

Entrance Requirements: High school diploma or equivalent; SAT or ACT required; GRE required for graduate school; early decision, early admission, delayed admission, and advanced placement plans available; $20 application fee.

Costs Per Year: $3,086 tuition; $7,844 nonresident tuition; $3,058 board and room;

$639 student fees.

Collegiate Environment: Located in Indiana Borough, Indiana County Seat, in the foothills of the Alleghenies at an elevation of about 1,300 feet, the 162-acre campus is ideally situated. The 60 university buildings contain a library of 600,000 volumes, 95,000 bound periodicals, 4,500 periodical subscriptions, 1,700,000 microforms, and dormitory facilities for 1,720 men and 2,580 women. The University Lodge plays an important part in the recreational and instructional life of the university. Owned by students and faculty, this 270 acres of wooded hillside, with its rustic lodge, picnic shelters, rope ski tow, toboggan run, and nature and hiking trails, not only offer opportunities for classes to study nature and conservation but also is in demand for picnics, meetings, and winter sports. Several social fraternities and sororities are located at the campus as well as numerous other student organizations. Approximately 49% of students applying for admission are accepted including midyear and 82% return for the sophomore year. 86% of freshmen class rank in top 2/5 of their graduating class; average ranges of scores, SAT 420-520V and 480-570M. Financial aid is available and 85% of the current students receive some form of financial assistance.

Community Environment: Population 35,000. Indiana is known as the "Christmas Tree Capital of the World" and is the birthplace of actor Jimmy Stewart. The town is located 50 miles northeast of Pittsburgh in the foothills of the beautiful Allegheny Mountains. Indiana has churches of all denominations, a library, a recreation center, a hospital, and various civic, fraternal and veteran's organizations. Local recreational facilities include golf courses, theatres, swimming pool, ice skating rink, tennis, baseball fields, a grandstand and an outdoor stage. Some part-time employment is available.

JUNIATA COLLEGE *(K-8)*
1700 Moore Street
Huntingdon, Pennsylvania 16652
Tel: (814) 643-4310; (800) 526-1970; Fax: (814) 643-9657

Description: Privately supported, coeducational, liberal arts college founded in 1876. It is accredited by the Middle States Association of

Colleges and Schools. The college offers a number of programs providing a semester or year of study abroad. In addition, many departments offer U.S. or international internships. It grants the Bachelor of Arts and Bachelor of Science degrees. The college operates with two 14-and-a-half-week semesters and offers variable summer sessions. Enrollment includes 514 men and 556 women full-time and 10 men and 32 women part-time. A faculty of 76 full-time and 30 part-time gives a faculty-student ratio of 1-13.

Entrance Requirements: Approved high school graduation or GED with completion of 16 college preparatory units, 4 English, 2 foreign language, mathematics, social science, and laboratory science; SAT or ACT, SAT preferred; admissions interview strongly recommended; early decision; rolling admission, midyear admission, early admission, and advanced placement plans available; Mar. 1 application deadline; $30 application fee.

Costs Per Year: $14,850 tuition; $4,460 room and board.

Collegiate Environment: The 100-acre campus is located in the high west end of Huntingdon. The 31 college buildings (15 of which have been built since 1960) include a library of 208,000 volumes, over 950 periodicals, microform titles, and audiovisual materials. There is access to 15 million volumes through a college cooperative with a computerized card catalogue. Dormitory facilities (both traditional and coed) house 1,100 students; currently 48% are men. Students from other geographical locations are accepted as well as midyear students. Approximately 72% of students applying for admission are accepted. Average test scores of the current freshman were SAT verbal 508, math 556. Financial aid is available and of 750 scholarships offered, 250 are for freshmen. About 80% of the current student body receives some form of financial assistance. The college awarded 230 Bachelor degrees recently. 96% of the freshman class return ed for their sophomore year and 32% of the senior class continued on to graduate school.

Community Environment: Huntingdon, population 8,500, on the Juniata River, is in one of the most scenic sections of the state. It was founded on the site of an Indian Village called Standing Stone. The city is the county seat and lies approximately 30 miles east of Altoona. The area is served by railroad. Penn State (32 miles away) offers cultural and social activities. Nearby state parks, forests, and the Raystown Lake recreation area provide excellent camping, fishing, canoeing, hunting, swimming, and boating opportunities. In winter ski slopes are less than 40 miles away.

KEYSTONE JUNIOR COLLEGE *(F-15)*
P.O. Box 50
LaPlume, Pennsylvania 18440-0200
Tel: (800) 824-2764

Description: Privately supported, coeducational, residential junior college that opened as an academy in 1868. It became a junior college in 1934 and was accredited by the Middle States Association of Colleges and Schools in 1936. The college operates on the semester system and offers 2 summer terms. Enrollment includes 700 full-time and 300 part-time students. A faculty of 44 full-time and 44 part-time gives a faculty-student ratio of 1-13. The college provides university-parallel and occupational programs and grants the Associate degree.

Entrance Requirements: Approved high school graduation with rank in upper 75% of graduating class; completion of 16 units including 4 English, 2 mathematics, 2 science, 2 social science; SAT or ACT required; non-high school graduates considered; early admission, early decision, rolling admission, delayed admission, advanced placement programs available; $25 application fee.

Costs Per Year: $8,060 tuition; $5,240 room and board; $926 student fees.

Collegiate Environment: The campus, covering 260 acres, is 15 miles northwest of Scranton, at the southeastern gateway to the Endless Mountains Region of northeastern Pennsylvania. The 31 college buildings contain a library of 37,854 volumes, 252 periodicals, 27 microforms, 3,042 audiovisual materials and dormitory facilities for 517 students. Students from other geographical locations are accepted as well as midyear students. Approximately 85% of students applying for admission are accepted and 70% of the previous freshman class returned to this campus for the second year of studies. Financial aid is available and 80% of the current student body receives some form of financial assistance.

Community Environment: Population of Scranton is 103,564. The city is provided transportation by bus and air. Air facilities are located near Scranton. This is a semi-rural community with many churches and synagogues close at hand. There are service clubs active locally. Five modern hospitals are easily accessible. Local recreation includes movies, museum, art gallery, professional sports, lakes, streams, ski slopes, hunting, and fishing areas. Stores are adequate in the area.

KING'S COLLEGE   *(H-15)*
133 N. River Street
Wilkes-Barre, Pennsylvania 18711
Tel: (717) 826-5858; (800) 955-5777; Fax: (717) 825-9049

Description: Privately supported, coeducational, Roman Catholic liberal arts college is conducted by the Congregation of Holy Cross. It is accredited by the Middle States Association of Colleges and Schools and grants the Master's, Bachelor's and Associate degrees. The college operates on a semester system and offers two summer terms. Enrollment includes 1,771 full-time and 541 part-time undergraduates and 44 graduate students. A faculty of 97 full-time and 65 part-time gives an undergraduate faculty-student ratio of 1-17. Academic Cooperative plans are available with neighboring colleges. Air Force and Army ROTC programs are available.

Entrance Requirements: High school graduation or GED required; completion of 15 units including 4 English, 3 math, 3 science, 2 foreign language, 3 social science; acceptance decision based upon the total academic performance of diploma students and GED scores, maturity, and motivation of GED students; SAT or ACT accepted; early admission, rolling admission, delayed admission, early decision, advanced placement plans available; liberal transfer policy with sixty (60) credit residency required by the College; $30 application fee; $100 tuition deposit required upon acceptance; students may enter in September, January, or June.

Costs Per Year: $10,910 tuition; $5,160 room and board.

Collegiate Environment: The college is approximately two hours from Philadelphia and three hours from New York City. It has a 15-acre campus facing the River Common, a Wilkes-Barre Park along the bank of the Susquehanna River. The college buildings include a library of 143,741 volumes, 750 periodicals, 418,248 microforms, and 4,219 audiovisual materials. Dormitory facilities are provided for 736 men and women. The opportunity of living off campus is available to students. Students from other geographical locations are accepted as well as midyear students. Approximately 74% of students applying for admission are accepted and 84% of the previous freshman class returned to the college for the sophomore year. Financial aid is available and 82% of the current student body receives some form of financial assistance.

Community Environment: The campus faces a beautiful riverside park and is situated within a four-block area in the downtown residential section of the city. The shopping area, only a 5-minute walk from the campus, has received acclaim for its attractive modern architecture.

KUTZTOWN UNIVERSITY OF PENNSYLVANIA   *(K-15)*
P.O. Box 730
Kutztown, Pennsylvania 19530
Tel: (215) 683-4000; Fax: (215) 683-4010

Description: Kutztown University is a multipurpose coeducational state institution of higher education offering the bachelor's and master's degrees. In cooperation with other institutions of higher education, the University offers programs of study leading to the doctoral degree. The University is accredited by the Middle States Association of Colleges and Schools, and is nationally accredited in education and nursing. The university operates on the semester system and offers two summer sessions. Combined undergraduate and graduate enrollment is 6,028 full-time and 1,763 part-time students. A faculty of 346 full-time and 54 part-time gives a faculty-student ratio of 1-19. Army ROTC is available. Air Force ROTC is available off campus.

Entrance Requirements: high school diploma or GED required; completion of 16 units including 4 English, 2 foreign language, 3 mathematics, 4 social sciences, 2 science, and 1 other; SAT or ACT (SAT preferred) required for freshmen; National League for Nursing Pre-admissions and Classification Test required of registered nursing applicants; art test required for communication design applicants; roll-

ing admission, deferred admission, and early admission plans available; $20 application fee.

Costs Per Year: $2,728 tuition; $6,122 out-of-state; $2,700 room and board; $432 resident student fees; $517 nonresident.

Collegiate Environment: The 325-acre campus is located midway between Reading and Allentown. The 42 university buildings contain a library of 401,482 volumes, microforms, and subscriptions; and a cartography lab, observatory, day care center, campus bookstore, student center, art gallery, indoor track, campus radio station, television studio, and residence hall facilities that accommodate approximately 2,850 students. Approximately 48% of students applying for admission are accepted. 79% of the freshman class return for the sophomore year. Financial aid is available, and 75% of the current student body receives some form of financial assistance.

Community Environment: Kutztown is a rural small town located on U.S. Route 222, midway between Reading and Allentown, one and a half hours from Philadelphia, and three hours from New York City. Airports are located in Allentown and Reading; bus transportation services are provided daily to Philadelphia and New York in addition to local destinations. Hospitals are located in nearby Reading and Allentown; there are also local civic organizations and churches. Area recreation includes golf, bowling, tennis, hunting, fishing, swimming, basketball, football, theatre, nature study at Hawk Mountain Sanctuary, and the Kutztown Folk Festival.

LA ROCHE COLLEGE   *(M-3)*
9000 Babcock Blvd.
Pittsburgh, Pennsylvania 15237
Tel: (412) 367-9300

Description: This private, coeducational, liberal arts college was chartered in 1963. It offers a four-year course that leads to a Bachelor degree, and a two-year course that leads to a Masters degree. It is accredited by the Middle States Association of Colleges and Secondary Schools. The Interior Design program is professionally accredited by the Foundation for Interior Design Education Research. Both the Interior and Graphic Design programs are accredited by the National Association of Schools of Arts and Design. Graduate programs are offered in Human Resource Management and Nursing. Army and Air Force ROTC are available through cooperative institutions. The college operates on the semester system and offers three summer sessions. Enrollment includes 642 full-time and 704 part-time undergraduates, and 341 graduate students. A faculty of 44 full-time and 89 part-time gives an undergraduate faculty-student ratio of 1-16.

Entrance Requirements: High school graduation or equivalent; 15-16 academic units required including 4 English, 3 math, 2 science, 2 foreign language, and 4 social studies; SAT or ACT required; early admission, rolling admission, midyear admission and advanced placement programs are available; $25 application fee.

Costs Per Year: $8,842 tuition; $4,783 room and board; fees; $600 average additional expenses.

Collegiate Environment: The spacious 100-acre campus forms one of the landmarks in the beautiful North Hills area of suburban Pittsburgh. The library contains 67,000 volumes, 676 periodicals, 219 microforms and 1,700 recordings. There are housing facilities for 304 students. The college welcomes a geographically diverse student body. Of those applying, 84% are accepted. Financial aid is available, both full-time and part-time scholarships are offered, and 80% of the full-time student body receives some form of financial aid.

Community Environment: The college is located just ten miles north of the center of Pittsburgh. The campus has an ideal combination of rural and urban life: within a five-mile radius of its own natural beauty are the recreational facilities and wooded expanse of North Park and the shops, restaurants and theaters of the McKnight Road malls.

LA SALLE UNIVERSITY   *(M-17)*
20th St. and Olney Avenue
Philadelphia, Pennsylvania 19141
Tel: (215) 951-1500; (800) 328-1910

Description: Privately supported, coeducational, Catholic liberal arts university founded in 1863 by the Christian Brothers. It is accredited by the Middle States Association of Colleges and Schools, and several professional accrediting institutions, and grants the Bachelor and Master degrees. Previously an all-male school, La Salle became coeducational in 1970. Enrollment is 2,650 full-time and 1,600 part-time undergraduates, and 1,400 graduate students. A faculty of 228 full-time and 96 part-time gives an undergraduate faculty-student ratio of 1-15. The university operates on the semester system and offers three summer sessions. Army ROTC training is available through other area institutions. Navy ROTC is available with the University of Pennsylvania. Academic cooperative plans are available with Chestnut Hill College. All majors have approved cooperative education programs.

Entrance Requirements: High school graduation or equivalent; rank in upper 60% of graduating class; completion of 16 units including 4 English, 3 mathematics, 2 foreign language, 1 natural science, 1 social science, and 5 academic electives; SAT or ACT required; advanced placement, early admission, rolling admission, and delayed admission plans available; $30 application fee.

Costs Per Year: $12,600 tuition; $5,300 room and board.

Collegiate Environment: There are 60 buildings on the 110-acre campus. The library contains 345,000 volumes and 1,650 periodical titles, 66,400 microforms, and 3,250 records. The LaSalle Union Building encloses a portion of the stadium and is probably the busiest place on campus. Residence halls accommodate 1,850 students, and apartment-housing facilities are available. The university welcomes a geographically diverse student body. Students who would like to study in Europe may take advantage of the La Salle in Europe Program, which gives students full credit for study in Fribourg, Switzerland, and Seville, Spain. An Honors Program provides challenge and stimulation to the most academically talented students. 60% of applicants are accepted. Financial aid is available. Approximately 90% of the current student body receives some form of financial assistance. Of 160 scholarships available, 45 are for freshmen.

Community Environment: See Temple University.

LACKAWANNA JUNIOR COLLEGE   *(G-16)*
901 Prospect Ave.
Scranton, Pennsylvania 18505
Tel: (717) 961-7810; (800) 458-2050; Admissions: (717) 961-7814; Fax: (717) 961-7858

Description: Privately supported, coeducational junior college established in 1894. Lackawanna is accredited by the Middle States Association of Colleges and Schools. It operates centers in Hazelton, Honesdale and Towanda. The college awards certificates and grants the Associate in Science degree in career oriented fields of study and liberal arts. It operates on the early semester system and offers two summer sessions. Enrollment includes 545 full-time and 299 part-time students. A faculty of 24 full-time and 113 part-time gives a ratio of 1-6.

Entrance Requirements: Open admssions policy; applicants with GED considered; ACT or SAT for placement, but not mandatory; applicants without test scores will take the College Assessment Test; rolling admission, midyear admission and delayed admission plans available. Admissions interview required; $20 application fee. $50 commitment deposit.

Costs Per Year: $6,368 tuition; $180 student fees; $400 books; $80 graduation fee.

Collegiate Environment: Students are accepted for both fall and spring terms. A variety of merit, athletic and other scholarships are available. 85% of the student body receives financial aid. Facilities include a library of 25,000 volumes.

Community Environment: See University of Scranton.

LAFAYETTE COLLEGE   *(J-17)*
High Street, Markle Hall
Easton, Pennsylvania 18042
Tel: (610) 250-5100; Fax: (610) 250-5355

Description: This privately supported, coeducational liberal arts college was founded in 1826 and is affiliated with the United Presbyterian Church (U.S.A.). Chartered as a men's college, it became coeducational in fall 1970. It is accredited by the Middle States Association of Colleges and Schools and offers four-year programs leading to the Bachelor degree. A number of five-year combination programs

leading to two Bachelor's degrees (A.B. and B.S.) are also offered. Students can spend all or part of their junior year abroad. An optional January Interim program exists with classes offered for credit on campus as well as overseas. The college operates on the semester system and offers three summer sessions. Army ROTC is available through Lehigh University. Enrollment is 1,104 men and 932 women full-time, and 192 part-time students. A faculty of 180 full-time and 52 part-time provides a faculty-student ratio of 1-11. 96% of the faculty hold Doctoral degrees.

Entrance Requirements: High school graduation with rank in upper 20% of graduating class; completion of 16 units including 4 English, 3 mathematics, 2 foreign language, 2 science, and 3 social science; SAT; admission is highly competitive; early admission, deferred admission, early decision, midyear admission, and advanced placement programs available; $40 application fee.

Costs Per Year: $19,546 tuition; $6,000 room and board; $75 activity fee; $1,450 books and additional expenses.

Collegiate Environment: The college overlooks the community of Easton, which is about 80 miles west of New York City. Lafayette has 58 buildings on its 110-acre campus. The David Bishop Skillman Library is the key building on the campus. This structure has a collection of 420,000 bound volumes, 1,808 periodicals, 93,913 microforms and 6,000 audiovisual materials. There are dormitory facilities for 1,939 students. Fraternities and sororities accommodate 371 students. Approximately 58% of students applying for admission are accepted. The college welcomes a geographically diverse student body and no religious restrictions are placed on students seeking admission. 96% of the previous freshman class returned to this campus for the sophomore year. Average high school standing of the recent freshman class: 35% in the top 10%, 57% in the top fifth, 99% in the top half. Median SAT ranges were 470-560V, 550-660M. Financial aid is available and 60% of the current student body receives some form of financial assistance.

Community Environment: Population 29,000. Easton is located at the confluence of the Lehigh and Delaware Rivers in the Lehigh Valley. The Lehigh Valley is served by railroad, bus lines, and a county airport. The valley has many churches, synagogues, nine hospitals, four public libraries, and a local YMCA and YWCA. Recreational facilities include softball, tennis, bowling, boating, swimming, golf, baseball, hunting, fishing, and a community concert association. There are numerous fraternal and civic organizations in the community.

LANCASTER BIBLE COLLEGE   *(M-14)*
901 Eden Road
Lancaster, Pennsylvania 17601
Tel: (717) 569-7071; (800) 544-7335; Admissions: (717) 560-8271; Fax: (717) 560-8213

Description: Privately supported, coeducational Bible college founded in 1933. It is an accredited member of the American Association of Bible Colleges. It is accredited by the Middle States Association of Colleges and Schools. It grants the Bachelor and Associate of Bible degrees. Students are trained to take their places as pastors, youth workers, musicians, missionaries, secretaries, teachers, or in computer ministries, or to go on for further training. Two one-year programs are offered in addition to the four- and two-year programs. It operates on the semester system and offers two summer sessions. Enrollment includes 197 men and 210 women full-time and 85 men and 80 women part-time. A faculty of 26 full-time and 18 part-time gives a faculty-student ratio of 1-11.

Entrance Requirements: High school graduation or equivalent; early admission, early decision, delayed admission, and rolling admission plans available; ACT required; $15 application fee.

Costs Per Year: $7,360 tuition; $3,400 room and board; $260 student fees; additional expenses average $300.

Collegiate Environment: The 100-acre campus has 16 buildings. Offices are located in the Administration Building and in Old Main. The library houses 130,977 volumes, 340 periodicals, 1,995 microform titles, and 2,620 records/tapes. Living accommodations are available for 258 dormitory students plus 8 family apartments. It is expected that all single, out-of-town students will reside on the campus. The school observes strict regulations regarding dress habits and social customs. Approximately 88% of students applying for admission are accepted. The school welcomes a geographically diverse student body and 70% of the previous freshman class returned to this school for their second year. Average high school standing of a recent freshman class: 18% in the top fifth; 37% in the top two fifths; average score, ACT 17. Financial aid is available and 80% of the current student body receives some form of financial assistance. The college awarded 43 Bachelor and 14 Associate degrees to a recent graduating class and approximately one-third of the senior class continues on to graduate school.

Community Environment: See Lancaster Theological Seminary.

LANCASTER THEOLOGICAL SEMINARY   *(M-14)*
555 West James Street
Lancaster, Pennsylvania 17603
Tel: (717) 393-0654; (800) 393-0654; Admissions: (717) 290-8741;
Fax: (717) 393-4254

Description: Privately supported, coeducational theological seminary is broadly ecumenical in both student body and faculty, but closely related to the United Church of Christ. Founded in 1825, the seminary grants the Doctorate and Master degrees. The institution is accredited by the Association of Theological Schools in the United States and Canada. The seminary operates on the semester system. Current enrollment includes 141 Master's Degree students and 35 Doctor of Ministry. A faculty of 12 full-time and 5 part-time members are employed.

Entrance Requirements: Bachelor's degree from an accredited college or university; applicants lacking a college degree may be admitted as candidates for a Certificate of Graduation. $15 application fee for Master's program, $40 application fee for Doctoral program.

Costs Per Year: $3,005 for dormitory; $4,7701 for one bedroom apartment.

Collegiate Environment: The seminary is located near the heart of the city of Lancaster, adjacent to Franklin and Marshall College. These two institutions cooperate in library acquisitions, cultural events, and athletic facilities. The seminary library contains 135,000 volumes, and 350 periodicals, 1,500 microforms, 3,500 audiovisual materials. On campus housing in apartments is available for full-time students. Commuter students have access to dormitory style housing. Financial aid is available for students who take 12 or more credit hours.

Community Environment: Located in southeastern Pennsylvania, 10 miles from the Susquehanna River, Lancaster is the trading and financial center of one of the most fertile agricultural regions of the Nation. The region is known as the home of the Amish, Mennonite, and Brethren religious sects. The community is provided transportation by railroad, bus, and airlines. Part-time employment is available in the area and rooms are available for student housing. Lancaster has a public library, many churches, a community concert association, and a symphony orchestra. Local recreational facilities include parks, tennis courts, golf courses, riding club, and excellent hunting and fishing sites.

LEBANON VALLEY COLLEGE   *(K-13)*
Annville, Pennsylvania 17003
Tel: (717) 867-6181; (800) 445-6181; Fax: (717) 867-6026

Description: This privately supported, coeducational liberal arts college is affiliated with the United Methodist Church and is accredited by the Middle States Association of Colleges and Schools. The college began operations in the building of the Annville Academy in 1866. It operates on the semester system and offers two summer sessions and an evening school. It has a cooperative relationship with the University of Pennsylvania, Duke University and Thomas Jefferson University. The college grants the Bachelor degree and the Masters in Business Administration, and offers a program for teacher certification. Enrollment is 1,058 full-time and 484 part-time undergraduates and 211 graduate students. A faculty of 69 full-time and 25 part-time gives an undergraduate faculty-student ratio of 1-14.

Entrance Requirements: High school graduation with rank in upper half of graduating class; completion of 16 units including 4 English, 2 mathematics, 2 foreign language, 1 science, and 1 social science; SAT required; non-high school graduates considered; early admission, early decision, early admission, rolling admission, delayed admission, and advanced placement programs available; $25 application fee.

Costs Per Year: $13,850 tuition; $4,755 room and board; $395 student fees.

Collegiate Environment: The 200-acre campus has 33 buildings including dormitories for 750 men and women. Approximately 78% of students applying for admission are accepted including at midyear, and the college welcomes a geographically diverse student body. About 80% of the previous freshman class returned to this campus for the sophomore year. Average high school rank of the recent freshman class was in the top 30%. Average SAT scores were 461V, 526M.

Community Environment: Population 5,000. Annville is located seven miles east of Hershey. The area has a temperate climate. The city has many churches that represent various denominations, a public library, three hospitals that are easily accessible, and major civic, fraternal, and veteran's organizations. Community recreational facilities include theaters and radio and TV stations. Community concerts are also available.

LEHIGH CARBON COMMUNITY COLLEGE   *(J-16)*
2370 Main Street
Schnecksville, Pennsylvania 18078
Tel: (215) 799-2121; Fax: (215) 799-1527

Description: The publicly supported, coeducational community college, founded in 1966, is accredited by the Middle States Association of Colleges and Schools, the National League for Nursing, and the American Physical Therapy Association. Transfer courses, general education, and vocational programs including the Ford Asset Automotive Program are offered leading to Certificates and the Associate degree. It operates on the semester system and offers two summer sessions. Enrollment includes 1,437 full-time and 2,947 part-time students. A faculty of 82 full-time and 111 part-time gives a faculty-student ratio of 1-26. Air Force ROTC is available as an elective.

Entrance Requirements: Open enrollment policy; non high school graduates over 18 years old considered; midyear admission, rolling admission, and advanced placement plans available; $25 application fee.

Costs Per Year: $1,740 district resident tuition; $3,660 state resident tuition; $5,580 nonresident tuition.

Collegiate Environment: The College is located on a 153-acre campus in the northern countryside of Lehigh County. The campus consists of four buildings: Administration, Science-Technology, Learning Resources, and Physical Education-Auditorium. The college is used by local business as a training and conference site. The library contains 43,876 volumes, 400 periodicals, and 101 microforms. Approximately 25% of the student body receives financial aid.

Community Environment: See Muhlenberg College.

LEHIGH UNIVERSITY   *(J-17)*
Bethlehem, Pennsylvania 18015
Tel: (610) 758-3000; Admissions: (610) 758-3100; Fax: (610) 758-4361

Description: Privately supported, coeducational university comprised of three undergraduate colleges: Arts & Sciences, Business and Economics, Engineering and Applied Science; and a graduate school and graduate level College of Communication. Founded in 1865, the university is accredited by the Middle States Association of Colleges and Schools. Programs of study lead to the Bachelor, Master and Doctorate degrees. The semester system is used and two summer terms are offered. Enrollment includes 2,774 men and 1,632 women in the undergraduate division and 2,041 graduate students. The faculty consists of 418 full-time and 85 part-time members. The undergraduate faculty-student ratio is 1-11. Army ROTC is available. Six-year medical program with the Medical College of Pennsylvania and a seven year dental program with the School of Dental Medicine of the University of Pennsylvania. Five-year Bachelor and MBA degrees.

Entrance Requirements: High school graduation; completion of 16 units including 4 English, 3 mathematics, 2 foreign language, 2 laboratory science, 2 social studies, and 3 electives; SAT required; ACT accepted on individual basis; early admission, delayed admission, early decision, advanced placement programs and IB available; $40 application fee.

Costs Per Year: $18,700 tuition; $5,580 room and board; books and personal spending $1,100.

Collegiate Environment: Located on a 1,600-acre wooded hillside campus on the south side of the Lehigh River, the university overlooks the city of Bethlehem. Approximately 80% of the undergraduates live on-campus in 17 dormitories, 8 sorority houses, 29 fraternity houses, 6 2-story garden apartment buildings, and special interest houses (International, Volunteer, Creative Arts, and Hillel). The Saucon Valley playing field area includes the 17,000 seat Goodman Stadium, the 6,500 seat Stabler Arena, the Field House, and the Squash Court Building. Students take part in over 100 clubs and course societies and in 34 intramural and recreational activities. The libraries contain 1,077,408 volumes, 24,000 rare books, 10,510 periodicals and serials, 1.7 million microfilm units, 57 CD-ROM databases, 17,000 audiovisual resources, and a government documents collection of more than 623,423 units. 50% of the students receive Lehigh administered financial aid available to U.S. citizens and permanent residents. Part-time employment on campus is available.

Community Environment: Population: 70,000. Bethlehem is famous for the Moravian Community, the Bach Choir, the corporate headquarters of Bethlehem Steel and Lehigh University. The historic area of Bethlehem has many 18th century buildings still in use; others are being restored by active community groups. The town contains 6 colonial and Victorian museums. The Bach Festival is held annually in May in Packer Chapel on the Lehigh campus.

LINCOLN UNIVERSITY *(N-15)*
Lincoln University, Pennsylvania 19352
Tel: (215) 932-8300

Description: State-related, coeducational liberal arts college. Founded in 1854, Lincoln University is the oldest college in the United States having as its original purpose the highest education of Negro youth. It is a nonsectarian, four-year college. It is accredited by the Middle States Association of Colleges and Schools and the American Chemical Society, and grants the Bachelor degree and a Master's degree in Human Services. The university operates on the trimester system with one summer session. Enrollment includes 508 men, 741 women full-time, 13 men, 17 women part-time and 206 graduate students. The faculty consists of 94 full-time and 37 part-time members. Army and Air Force ROTC is available with the University of Delaware. Special programs include a research program and an advanced science and engineering program.

Entrance Requirements: High school graduation or equivalent with preference to those who rank in upper 50% of graduating class; completion of 21 units including 4 English, 3 mathematics, 3 science, 2 social science; SAT required; early admission, rolling admission, early decision and advanced placement programs available; $10 application fee.

Costs Per Year: $2,800 tuition; $4,000 out-of-state tuition; $2,815 room and board; $492 state resident fees; $712 nonresident.

Collegiate Environment: The campus is part of a tract of 422 acres of farm and woodlands owned by the University. There are 24 main buildings on the campus and 21 faculty residences. Langston Hughes Memorial Library contains 167,438 volumes, 4,317 pamphlets, 752 periodicals, 196,600 microforms and 611 recordings. There are dormitories for 5 men and 7 women. A broad range of financial aid is available to those students who qualify for admission and demonstrate financial need. Financial assistance is provided through a combination of scholarships, grants-in-aid, loans, and work opportunities. The financial aid program is administered by the Financial Aid Officer under the direction of the Financial Aid Committee. About 90% of the current student body received some form of financial assistance. 60% of the students applying for admission are accepted including midyear. Approximately 78% of the current student body graduated in the top half of their high school class, 60% in the top quarter, and 22% in the highest tenth.

Community Environment: Population of Oxford 3,658. Located in open country, Lincoln University is four miles east of Oxford, and 45 miles southwest of Philadelphia. The area has temperate climate. Nearby there is a campus church, library, and a community hospital, U.S. Highway 131. Local recreational facilities include baseball, soccer, basketball, cross country, track, bowling, tennis, dance troupe, golf, wrestling, and a local drama group.

LOCK HAVEN UNIVERSITY OF PENNSYLVANIA *(H-10)*
Lock Haven, Pennsylvania 17745
Tel: (717) 893-2011

Description: This publicly supported, coeducational liberal arts and teachers college is accredited by the Middle States Association of Colleges and Schools, the National Council for the Acreditation of Teacher Education, and the National Council on Social Work Education. The university offers a four-year liberal arts curriculum, as well as programs in elementary, secondary, early childhood, special, and physical education. The college also offers a four-year curricula in mathematical computer science, management science and speech communication. Programs of study lead to the Bachelor degree. There are student exchange programs with 24 countries, and student teaching opportunities in 22 countries. There is a branch campus in Clearfield Pennsylvania which is now in its fifth year of operation with an enrollment of 319 students. The university operates on the semester system and offers two summer sessions. Enrollment includes 3,730 full-time, 336 part-time undergraduate, and 15 graduate students. A faculty of 200 full-time and 17 part-time gives a faculty-student ratio of 1-18. Army ROTC is available.

Entrance Requirements: Approved high school graduation or equivalent with rank in upper 40% of graduating class; completion of academic program; minimum SAT Verbal 460, Math 510, or ACT 24 preferred; CLEP programs available; early admission, deferred admission, rolling admission, midyear admission, and advanced placement plans available; $25 application fee.

Costs Per Year: $3,086 state resident tuition; $7,844 nonresident tuition; $3,716 room and board; $576 student fees.

Collegiate Environment: The campus overlooks the West Branch of the Susquehanna River in the residential section of Lock Haven. A large portion of the college's 135 acres is wooded. Stevenson Library holds 354,500 volumes, 1,260 periodicals, 573,286 microforms and 8,447 audiovisual materials. Seven residence halls accommodate 800 men and 800 women. Approximately 47% of applicants are accepted, including midyear students. About 1,500 grants are awarded annually and 80% of students receive some form of financial assistance.

Community Environment: Population 10,500. The town was laid out at the site of old Fort Reed, which was erected to protect the frontier settlers from the Indians. The fort was evacuated in the great runaway of 1778. Today, lumbering is a major industry and paper products are produced here. The city lies in a central mountainous region with a moderate climate. Local hunting, fishing, boating, hangliding, and skiing are considered good. Private homes provide supplemental student housing.

Branch Campuses: Clearfield, PA

LUTHERAN THEOLOGICAL SEMINARY AT GETTYSBURG *(M-11)*
Gettysburg, Pennsylvania 17325
Tel: (717) 334-6286; (800) 658-8437; Fax: (717) 334-3469

Description: The privately supported, coeducational seminary is a graduate-level school of theology which was created and is maintained by the Evangelical Lutheran Church in America. It is accredited by the Middle States Association of Colleges and Schools and the Association of Theological Schools. The school was founded in 1826. Its primary goal is the preparation of persons for ordained and lay ministries especially in the ELCA. Programs prepare men and women to serve as parish pastors, missionaries, as specialists in Christian Education, youth ministry, church music, general parish work and diaconal ministry. The seminary maintains a program of continuing education for public ministers and the laity, as well as graduate study. The 4-1-4 system with a three-week pre-session is employed and three one-week summer sessions are offered. Enrollment includes 122 men and 118 women. A faculty of 20 full-time and 9 part-time members provides a faculty-student ratio of 1-12. The Seminary grants the following degrees: M.A.-M.S., M.A.R., M.Div., and S.T.M.

Entrance Requirements: Accredited college or university graduation with Bachelor of Arts or equivalent degree.

Costs Per Year: $4,350 tuition, $4,250 ELCA member tuition.

Collegiate Environment: The college occupies 52-acres with 18 buildings. The library contains over 134,000 volumes. Housing facilities are available for men, women and married students. Scholarships are available and 75% of students receive some form of financial aid.

Community Environment: See Gettysburg College.

LUTHERAN THEOLOGICAL SEMINARY AT PHILADELPHIA   *(M-17)*
7301 Germantown Avenue
Philadelphia, Pennsylvania 19119
Tel: (215) 248-4616

Description: Privately supported coeducational theological seminary founded in 1864 to prepare Christian men and women for the public ministry and also for specialized ministries. It is accredited by the Middle States Association of Colleges and Schools, and is affiliated with the Lutheran Church in America. The seminary grants the Master, Doctorate, and Professional degrees. It operates on the 4-1-4 calendar system and offers one summer session. Enrollment inlcudes 201 men and women in first professional degree programs. A faculty of 18 full-time and 18 part-time provides a faculty-student ratio of 1-10 (FTE basis).

Entrance Requirements: Graduation from an accredited college. Rolling admission plan. $25 application fee.

Costs Per Year: $4,826 tuition; $3,990 board and room; $4,000 additional expenses average.

Collegiate Environment: The 14-acre campus has 21 buildings. The library contains 180,000 volumes, receives 597 periodicals, holds 13,250 microforms and 10,000 recordings. Housing facilities are available for 72 students and 32 families. Approximately 80% of students applying for admission are accepted and 95% of the freshman class return for the second year. Students are accepted in September and the seminary welcomes a geographically diverse student body. 65% of the current students receive some form of financial assistance. The seminary awarded 35 Professional and 2 Doctorate of Ministry, 4 Master (of Divinity and S.T.M.) degrees to the graduating class.

Community Environment: See Temple University.

LUZERNE COUNTY COMMUNITY COLLEGE   *(H-15)*
Prospect Street & Middle Road
Nanticoke, Pennsylvania 18634
Tel: (717) 829-7300; (800) 377-5222; Admissions: (717) 829-7337; Fax: (717) 821-1525

Description: This publicly supported, coeducational community college opened in 1967. It operates on the semester system and offers two summer sessions. In the College Foundation Program students are given the opportunity to prove themselves over a maximum of two semesters in a schedule of up to 12 semester hours. Students may combine these noncredit courses with some college credit courses. The program is very closely supervised and special counseling services are provided for students enrolled in this program. The college is fully accredited by the Middle States Association of Colleges and Schools. It offers university-parallel as well as occupational programs. Programs of study lead to the Associate degree. Enrollment includes 2,896 full-time and 4,241 part-time students. A faculty of 84 full-time and 200 part-time gives a faculty-student ratio of 1-20.

Entrance Requirements: Open enrollment policy; non-high school graduates considered; early admission, early decision, rolling admission, delayed admission, and advanced placement plans available; $20 application fee.

Costs Per Year: $1,590 county-resident tuition; $3,030 state resident; $4,470 nonresident; $120 student fees.

Collegiate Environment: All students applying for admission are accepted including at midyear. 60% of the previous freshman class returned to this campus for the sophomore year. Scholarships are available and 65% of the students receive financial aid. The library contains 60,000 volumes, 1,665 pamphlets, 370 periodicals, 14,987 microforms and 3,221 recordings.

LYCOMING COLLEGE   *(H-12)*
Washington Boulevard & College Place
Williamsport, Pennsylvania 17701
Tel: (717) 321-4000; (800) 345-3920; Fax: (717) 321-4337

Description: Privately supported, coeducational liberal arts and sciences college, founded in 1812 as Williamsport Academy. It is affiliated with the United Methodist Church and is accredited by the Middle States Association of Colleges and Schools. The 4-4-1 system is used and one summer term is offered. Enrollment includes 648 men, 758 women full-time and 117 part-time students. A faculty of 94 full-time and 45 part-time provides a faculty-student ratio of 1-14. Optional programs offered: Washington Semester or Washington International Semester (at American Univ.); United Nations Semester (at Drew Univ.); London Semester (at London Univ.). Engineering cooperative program with Penn State and forestry program with Duke are available. The college grants the Bachelor degree, BFA and BSN.

Entrance Requirements: Approved high school graduation; recommended completion of 16 units including 4 English, 3 mathematics, 2 foreign language, 2 science, 3 social science; SAT or ACT required; early admission, early decision, rolling admission, advanced placement programs available; $25 application fee.

Costs Per Year: $14,700 tuition; $4,400 room and board; additional expenses average $500.

Collegiate Environment: There are 19 buildings on the 32-acre campus. The Academic Center houses classrooms, laboratories, offices, planetarium, theatre, and a library containing 168,358 volumes, 951 periodicals, 11,202 microforms and 1,756 recordings. There are dormitories for 1,100 men and women. Approximately 75% of students applying for admission are accepted. Students are admitted in September and the college welcomes a geographically diverse student body. High school standing of a recent freshman class was 36% in the top quintile; 34% in the second quintile; and 21% in the third quintile. The average score of the entering freshman class were SAT 980 combined, ACT 21 composite. 78% of the freshman class return for the sophomore year. Financial aid is available and 86% of the current student body receives some form of financial assistance. The college awarded 265 Bachelor degrees to the graduating class.

Community Environment: Population 35,000. This town, in a scenic mountainous region on the west branch of the Susquehanna River, was known as a great lumber center until the 1890s. As the forests were depleted, it became a manufacturing city and now has a diversified production including steel wire rope, computer components, batteries, flashbulbs, radio tubes, power piping, chemicals, lumber and its byproducts, aircraft engines, textiles, furniture, leather, and mobile homes. The area is provided transportation by bus and air lines. The community has many churches representing various faiths. There are two hospitals, numerous health agencies, a library, a museum, and various civic, fraternal and veteran's organizations in the immediate area. Part-time employment is available. Local recreation includes boating, golf, shooting, archery ranges, picnic areas, fishing, hunting and skiing.

MANOR JUNIOR COLLEGE   *(L-17)*
Fox Chase Manor
Jenkintown, Pennsylvania 19046
Tel: (215) 885-2360

Description: Privately supported, liberal arts and career-oriented junior college for women with co-ed evening classes, established in 1959. The college is a church-related school under private control and directed by the Order of Sisters of Saint Basil the Great of the Roman Catholic Church. Manor is accredited by the Middle States Association of Colleges and Schools and grants the Associate degree. The semester system is used. Enrollment includes 366 full-time and 138 part-time students. A faculty of 13 full-time, 26 part-time provides a faculty-student ratio of 1-10.

Entrance Requirements: Completion of 16 units including 4 English, 2 mathematics, 1 foreign language, 1 science, 1 social science; SAT required; advanced placement program available; $20 application fee.

Costs Per Year: $6,276 tuition; $3,120 room and board.

Collegiate Environment: The college is located in Fox Chase Manor, 15 miles north of Philadelphia. Basileiad Library contains over 26,000 volumes, with 800 reference books, 400 periodicals, and newspapers. Students living on campus reside in Josaphat Hall, a modern dormitory which was first opened for use in 1964. The three-story building can accommodate 90 students. The college regards the religious training of the student of prime importance and all Catholic students attend the various renewal days. Approximately 77% of students applying for admission are accepted. Freshman classes begin in September and the college welcomes a geographically diverse student body. About 50% of the current student body graduated in the top half of their high school class, 31% in the top quarter, and 11% in the highest tenth. 65% of the previous freshman class returned to this campus for their sophomore year.

Community Environment: Population 10,000. Jenkintown is located approximately 20 minutes from Philadelphia by car. The community is served by train, plane, and bus lines. Tennis and swimming facilities are located nearby. The immediate locale has churches of various denominations, and a local YMCA. Part-time employment is available.

MANSFIELD UNIVERSITY OF PENNSYLVANIA   *(E-11)*
Beecher House
Mansfield, Pennsylvania 16933
Tel: (717) 662-4243

Description: Publicly supported, coeducational liberal arts established as a normal school in 1857. A modern laboratory school for the lower grades was opened on the campus in 1914. It is accredited by the Middle States Association of Colleges and Schools. Since it was first authorized to grant the Bachelor of Science degree in Education, Mansfield has expanded its curriculum to over 60 degree programs including Music, Education, Business Administration, Criminal Justice Administration, and Computer Science. The College consists of two divisions: the College of Arts and Sciences and the School of Professional Studies. The College also offers Masters Degree programs through its Office of Graduate Studies. It operates on the semester system and offers two summer sessions. Enrollment includes 3,200 students. A faculty of 200 gives a faculty-student ratio of 1-19.

Entrance Requirements: Approved high school graduation or equivalent with rank in upper 60% of graduating class; SAT or ACT required; SAT minimum 400V, 400M preferred; completion of 21 units including 4 English, 3 mathematics, 3 science, 2 foreign language, 3 social studies and 6 academic electives; early admission, rolling admission, delayed admission, and advanced placement plans available; $25 application fee.

Costs Per Year: $3,086 tuition; $7,844 out-of-state; $3,324 room and board; $530 student fees.

Collegiate Environment: The Borough of Mansfield is located in Tioga County in the heart of Pennsylvania's beautiful Northern Tier. The 175-acre campus has 30 buildings including dormitories for 1,670 students. The library building houses 197,000 volumes, 2,240 periodicals, 550,000 microforms and 14,000 audiovisual materials. Approximately 71% of students applying for admission are accepted. Midyear students are accepted and classes begin in September, January, and June. Average high school standing of the 1982 freshman class: 34% in the top fifth; 31% in the second fifth; 21% in third fifth. The average scores of the entering freshman class were SAT 440 verbal, 490 math. Financial aid is available and 80% of the current student body receives some form of financial assistance. The informal student-oriented campus community contains more than 60 clubs and organizations.

Community Environment: Population 4,114. This is a rural town located on the north-central border of Pennsylvania. Mansfield is mild in summer and often near freezing in winter. The community is served by Trailways bus lines. It is located at the intersection of U.S. Highways 6 and 15. Ski slopes, camping areas, lakes and hiking trails are all within a one-hour drive away. Other available outdoor sports are river-rafting, cross-county skiing, fishing, and hunting.

MARYWOOD COLLEGE   *(G-16)*
2300 Adams Avenue
Scranton, Pennsylvania 18509
Tel: (717) 348-6234; (800) 346-5014; Fax: (717) 348-1899

Description: Founded in 1915, Marywood is a privately supported, comprehensive, Roman Catholic college accredited by the Middle States Association of Colleges and Schools. Its programs are professionally accredited by several respective accrediting institutions. The college became coed in 1964. It is owned and operated by the Congregation of Sisters, Servants of the Immaculate Heart of Mary. The college consists of an Undergraduate School, two graduate schools (Graduate School of Arts and Sciences and the School of Social

Work), a School of Continuing Education and an Off-Campus degree program. The college grants Baccalaureate and Masters degrees. Air Force and Army ROTC programs are available. It operates on the semester system and offers two summer sessions. Enrollment includes 1,480 full-time and 368 part-time undergraduates and 1,220 graduate students. A faculty of 143 full-time and 123 part-time gives a faculty-student ratio of 1-15.

Entrance Requirements: High school graduation or equivalent; rank in upper 50%; completion of 16 units including 4 English, 2 college-prep mathematics, 1 lab science, 3 social science, and 6 units of any subject approved for graduation by an accredited high school; SAT minimum combined score of 780 (higher score required for some programs) or ACT; TOEFL or SAT for international students; early admission, rolling admission, deferred admission, delayed admission, midyear admission, early decision and advanced placement programs available; $20 application fee.

Costs Per Year: $11,040 tuition; $4,500 room and board; $350 student fees; $200 average additional expenses.

Collegiate Environment: Located on 180 acres of land in Scranton, the college welcomes a geographically diverse student body and accepts midyear students. Freshmen must live on campus. Special programs offered include Study Abroad. Other special features are the Human Services Clinic, the Language Laboratory, the Reading Clinic, Psychology/Education Research Lab, Science Multimedia Lab, Fricchione Day Care Center, Performing Arts Center, Suraci Gallery, student-run on-air radio and TV stations, and a computerized editing facility. Most programs require field experience or internships. A data and video fiber optic network links the campus, which also maintains an Internet connection. The Center for Health Sciences has four laboratories, a nursing laboratory, and three computer laboratories. In addition, a music computer laboratory and art graphics computer laboratory are available. The library contains over 202,015 volumes, 119,125 titles on microform, 6 CD-ROMs, 1,114 periodical subscriptions, 10,438 records, tapes, and CDs, and 28,374 other media formats. Dormitory facilities are provided for 2,000 women and men. The college is affiliated with the Community Medical Center in Scranton, for the purposes of providing the preclinical program of training for their student nurses. Athletic failities include an Olympic-sized pool, human performance lab, gymnasium, athletic training rooms, athletic field, tennis and racquetball courts, dance studio, game room, hockey field, picnic grounds and weight room. Intercollegiate and intramural sports are available. Need-based and merit-based scholarships and financial aid are available. 85% of eligible undergraduates receive financial aid.

Community Environment: The city of Scranton is a regional center for business, health care, social services and recreation in northeastern Pennsylvania. It is 120 miles west of New York City and 115 miles north of Philadelphia. Sports, special events, music, theater, and parks are available. The nearby Pocono Mountains region offers six major ski areas, resorts, campgrounds, snowmobiling, canoeing, whitewater rafting and various other activities. The Scranton area is home to seven other colleges and universities in addition to Marywood.

MEDICAL COLLEGE OF PENNSYLVANIA   *(M-17)*
3300 Henry Avenue
Philadelphia, Pennsylvania 19129
Tel: (215) 842-7015

Description: Privately supported, coeducational medical college founded in 1850 by a group of courageous men physicians who wanted to give women the opportunity to study medicine. Only women were accepted as candidates for the degree of Doctor of Medicine before 1971, but both men and women were accepted as graduated students, fellows, interns, and residents. The College is now fully coeducational. The Graduate Program offers Master and Doctorate Ph.D. degrees in the basic medical sciences. Enrollment includes approximately 566 students. A mixed system is used and one summer term is offered. The School of Nursing was established in 1908 and is accredited by the National League for Nursing.

Entrance Requirements: Applicants generally obtain Bachelor's degree before entering. Candidates may be admitted on completion of minimum of 90 semester hours; Medical College Admission Test required; advanced placement plan available; $20 application fee. The catalogue should be requested for requirements and other details regarding the School of Nursing.

Costs Per Year: $16,005 tuition; room and board available; additional expenses average $800.

Collegiate Environment: The hospital of the college is conducted by the Board of Corporators under the professional direction of the college faculty. A new nine-floor wing was opened in 1968 providing an additional 246 beds to make a total of 400. In addition to classrooms and laboratories set aside for the use of the School of Nursing, the lecture rooms and laboratories of the College and the clinical facilities are available. The Ann Preston Residence Hall has accommodations for 120 women. Special financial aid is available.

Community Environment: See Temple University.

MEDICAL COLLEGE OF PENNSYLVANIA AND HAHNEMANN UNIVERSITY   (M-17)
Broad and Vine Streets
Philadelphia, Pennsylvania 19102-1192
Tel: (215) 762-8288

Description: Hahnemann University has three educational components: The School of Health Sciences and Humanities, organized in 1968, The Graduate School established in 1949 and The Medical School founded in 1848. The schools are strategically situated in Center Philadelphia. All of the schools are accredited by their respective professional accrediting agencies. The institution is accredited by the Middle States Association of Colleges and Schools, the Liaison Committee on Medical Education, the American Medical Association and the National League for Nursing. Enrollment includes 1,551 full-time and part-time students with a faculty of 165.

Entrance Requirements: All schools are open to any qualified applicant regardless of race, religion, sex, age or national origin; School of Health Sciences and Humanities (SHSH) requires an approved high school degree or equivalency and ACT/SAT; other prerequisites vary by program; applicants for Baccaluareate Degree programs must have completed a minimum of 60 semester credits at an accredited college; $25 application fee; Graduate School requires an undergraduate program in preparation of chosen field of study and the Aptitude Test (Part I) of the GRE or the Miller Analogies Test; School of Medicine recommends 90 semester hours of credit as the minimum requirement predominately in the sciences; each applicant is judged on the basis of previous college record, Medical College Admission Test score, character, initiative, personality and by personal interview; Hahnemann participates in the American Medical College Application Service; $50 application fees.

Costs Per Year: $7,100 tution for School of Health Sciences and Humanities; $8,200 for Graduate School; $17,000 for Medical College.

Collegiate Environment: The School of Medicine/Graduate School building was fully occupied in 1974. It provides a modern TV studio, and piped programs provide the latest in audiovisual and self-instructional educational opportunities. A modern renovated building completed in 1976 houses the School of Health Sciences and Humanities. In 1974, the Student Towers, a modern housing facility was opened. Off-campus housing lists are available.

Community Environment: See Temple University. The university, as situated in Center City Philadelphia, provides students with immediate and close access to the city's many cultural, historical, entertainment and sports activities and facilities. Hahnemann students participate in several community activities, including food and clothing drives, and providing assistance in community health screenings.

MERCYHURST COLLEGE   (D-2)
Glenwood Hills
Erie, Pennsylvania 16546
Tel: (814) 824-2202; (800) 825-1926; Fax: (814) 824-2071

Description: This privately supported, Catholic coeducational liberal arts college offers a broad education in both the liberal arts and specialized career training. It is accredited by the Middle States Association of Colleges and Schools, the American Dietetic Association, and the Council on Social Work Education. It operates on the trimester system and offers one summer session. Enrollment is 1,999 full-time and 427 part-time undergraduates, and 98 graduate students. A faculty of 61 full-time and 53 part-time provides a faculty-student ratio of 1-16. The college grants the Bachelor degree in 33 subject areas, an Associate degree in 9 areas, Master of Science degrees in 2

areas, and offers teacher certification programs in 17 areas. Special programs include Cooperative Education in all major areas; cross registration is available with other colleges in the area. Army ROTC is available as an elective. Study abroad to England is available.

Entrance Requirements: Accredited high school graduation rank in upper 50% of graduating class; completion of 16 units including 4 English, 2 mathematics, 2 science, 2 foreign language, 4 social studies, and 2 electives; SAT or ACT required; non-high school graduates considered; early admission, early decision, rolling admission, delayed admission, and advanced placement programs available; $25 application fee.

Costs Per Year: $9,810 tuition; $4,050 room and board; $653 student fees.

Collegiate Environment: The campus is located on an 88-acre expanse overlooking Lake Erie. The campus center includes a gymnasium, fitness center, recreation center, indoor rowing tanks, sauna, and whirlpool. The Learning Resources Center and library collection numbers 140,613 volumes and numerous periodicals, microforms and recordings. Housing accommodations include 3 residence halls, 11 apartment buildings and 16 townhouses, which provide living quarters for 1,200 students. The Cadet Teacher Program offers to students interested in teaching on the elementary level the opportunity to participate in a teaching-learning experience and enables them to receive an education for less than half the cost of the regular program. Financial aid is available; various scholarships are offered, and 88% of the current student body receives some form of assistance. Approximately 68% of students applying for admission are accepted, including mid-year, and 75% of the freshmen return for the second year.

Community Environment: See Gannon University.

MESSIAH COLLEGE   (L-12)
College Avenue
Grantham, Pennsylvania 17027
Tel: (717) 691-6000; (800) 233-4220; Fax: (717) 691-6025

Description: This privately supported, coeducational liberal arts college is affiliated with the Brethren in Christ Church and was founded in 1909. It is accredited by the Middle States Association of Colleges and Schools and by respective professional accrediting institutions. Although Messiah College was founded by educators having strong denominational concerns, it has never been narrowly sectarian. Students have always been welcome without regard to religious affiliation. The college is now composed of thirteen departments offering over forty majors. These departments include Behavioral Science, Education, Engineering, Health, Physical Education, and Recreation, History and Political Science, Language, Literature, and Communications, Management, and Business, Mathematical Sciences, Music, Natural Sciences, Nursing, Religion and Philosophy, and Visual and Theatrical Arts. The semester system is used and two summer sessions are offered. Enrollment includes 833 men and 1,311 women full-time, and 69 part-time students. A faculty of 152 full-time and 75 part-time provides a faculty-student ratio of 1-15. Study abroad opportunities are available in Japan, China, England, France, Germany, Costa Rica, and Kenya. Messiah College has a Philadelphia campus at 2026 North Broad Street in cooperation with Temple University for upper-division courses; approximately 90 students reside at this campus.

Entrance Requirements: Approved high school graduation or equivalent with rank in upper half of graduating class; completion of 16 units including 4 English, 2 mathematics, 2 science, 2 foreign language, 2 social science and 4 academic electives; SAT minimum score of 450V, 450M or ACT 19 required; non-high school graduates considered; early decision, early admission, rolling admission, delayed admission, and advanced placement plans available; $20 application fee.

Costs Per Year: $9,070 tuition; $4,550 room and board; $70 student fees; $400 average additional expenses.

Collegiate Environment: There are 24 buildings on the 300-acre campus. Living accommodations are available. The library contains 200,000 volumes, 5,000 periodicals, 10,000 microforms and 3,000 recordings. The chapel is centrally located and has a seating capacity of 550. Dormitory facilities accommodate 1,050 men and 1,050 women. The college provides for a variety of activities for both men and women in the intramural and intercollegiate programs. Approximately 70% of students applying for admission are accepted including midyear students, and 85% of the previous freshman class returned to this campus for the sophomore year. Average high school standing of a recent freshman class: 64% in the top fifth; 21% in the second fifth; average scores: SAT 503V, 546M; ACT 24. 84% of students receive financial aid.

Community Environment: Population of Harrisburg 100,000. Grantham is a semirural community located 10 miles south of Harrisburg. The city may be reached via U.S. 15, bus lines, the Reading Railroad, or the Pennsylvania Turnpike. There are various civic and fraternal organizations as well as a local church in the immediate area. Part-time employment is available on campus.

MILLERSVILLE UNIVERSITY OF PENNSYLVANIA *(M-14)*
Millersville, Pennsylvania 17551
Tel: (717) 872-3011; Fax: (717) 871-2147

Description: Publicly-supported coeducational liberal arts and teachers university founded in 1855 as a normal school. It became a State Teachers College in 1927 and was empowered to grant the Bachelor of Science in Education degree. In 1959, a Master's degree program in Education, Science, Arts was added. The university was authorized to grant the Bachelor of Arts degree in 1962 and the Bachelor of Science in 1970. The present name was taken in 1983. It is accredited by the Middle States Association of Colleges and Schools and by several professional accrediting institutions. Enrollment is 2,134 men and 2,989 women full-time and 645 men and 1,496 women part-time. The semester system is used and two summer terms offered. The faculty consists of 319 full-time and 98 part-time members. Program for State Teacher Certification. There is an Honors Program. An academic cooperative plan with Penn State and the University of Pennsylvania, is available for engineering students. Cooperative Education and internships are also available in other fields. Junior Year Abroad Program to Marburg, Germany is available. Army ROTC is available.

Entrance Requirements: Approved high school graduation or equivalent with rank in upper 35% of graduating class; 13 units including 4 English, 3 Mathematics, 2 Laboratory Science, 4 Social Science; SAT or ACT required; Achievement tests required for some programs; rolling admission, advanced placement plans available; $25 application fee.

Costs Per Year: $3,086 tuition; $7,844 out-of-state tuition; $3,830 room and board; $834 student fees; $400 estimated books and supplies, $900 estimated personal expenses, $300 estimated travel expenses.

Collegiate Environment: The campus has grown to 235 acres. A library contains 486,703 volumes, 1,700 periodicals, 355,915 microforms and 43,796 audiovisual materials. Physical facilities include a health services building, dining halls, and dormitories for 966 men and 1,227 women are completed. Most recently completed facilities include a research and learning center, a student union, gymnasium, stadium, classrooms and dormitory. Financial aid is available and 70% of the current student body received some form of assistance. Approximately 48% of students applying for admission are accepted, including midyear and 85% of the previous freshman class returned to this campus for their second year. Average high school standing of the freshman class, 21% in the top 10%; 59% in the top quarter; 90% in the top half; average scores, SAT 476V, 529M. The Honors Course is available for superior students and a program for disadvantaged and low-mark students has been developed. The college awarded 1,167 Bachelor and 147 Master degrees during the recent academic year. Approximately 10% of the senior class continued on to graduate school.

Community Environment: Population 7,894. Millersville is a suburban community adjacent to Lancaster. The climate is temperate. There is air and train service, bus lines, and major highways easily accessible. The community has churches, theatres, hospitals, and shopping facilities located in Lancaster. Major civic, fraternal and veteran's organizations are represented here.

MONTGOMERY COUNTY COMMUNITY COLLEGE *(L-17)*
340 DeKalb Pike
Blue Bell, Pennsylvania 19422
Tel: (215) 641-6300; Fax: (215) 641-6681

Description: Publicly supported, coeducational junior college provides a comprehensive college education to residents of Montgomery County at a low rate of tuition and within reasonable commuting distance of every home in the County. It is accredited by the Middle States Association of Colleges and Schools and operates on the semester system with two summer sessions. Transfer programs leading to degrees of Associate in Arts or Associate in Science are offered as well as non-transfer programs leading to the Associate in Applied Science degree. Enrollment includes 2,745 full-time and 6,461 part-time students. A faculty of 147 full-time and 326 part-time provides a faculty-student ratio of 1:25.

Entrance Requirements: High school graduation or equivalent; SAT or ACT required for nursing and allied health programs; non high school graduates considered; open enrollment policy for most programs; early admission, deferred admission, midyear admission, rolling admission, and advanced placement plans available; $20 application fee; residents of county given preference for admission.

Costs Per Year: $1,800 county resident tuition; $3,600 state resident tuition; $5,400 out-of-state tuition.

Collegiate Environment: The library has 75,600 volumes, 503 periodicals, 24,000 microforms, 13,500 audiovisual materials. 99% of applicants are accepted. Midyear students are accepted and freshman classes begin in August and in January. Special financial aid is available. 23% of students receive some form of financial aid.

Community Environment: Rural community (under 2,500). Suburban campus environment. 5 miles from (north) Norristown. Some bus transportation. Approximately 45 minute commute to Philadelphia. Surrounding industries include pharmaceutical and chemical-product companies; some farming.

MOORE COLLEGE OF ART AND DESIGN *(M-17)*
20th and The Parkway
Philadelphia, Pennsylvania 19103
Tel: (215) 568-4515

Description: Privately supported art institute, America's oldest professional art college for women. It was founded in 1844 and its four-year courses in the fine and applied arts lead to the Bachelor degree. The school is accredited by the Middle States Association of Colleges and Schools. It operates on the semester system. Enrollment is approximately 450 women. A faculty of 60 gives a faculty-student ratio of 1-8.

Entrance Requirements: Accredited high school graduation or equivalent with rank in upper half of graduating class; recommended completion of 16 units including 4 English, 2 mathematics, 2 foreign language, 2 science, 2 social science, and as many secondary-school courses in art as possible; SAT and art portfolio required; early decision, early admission, deferred admission, midyear admission, and rolling admission plans available; $35 application fee.

Costs Per Year: $12,594 tuition; $4,864 room and board.

Collegiate Environment: The college is located in the center of Philadelphia's cultural mecca. The campus is composed of six units; an art college building, an auditorium, a dining hall, art galleries and residence halls. Noncommuting freshman are not required to live in the residence halls. The second-floor library has a panoramic view of Logan Square. In addition to more than 36,000 texts and specialized books, it contains extensive collections on art subjects. Total capacity in the women's dormitories is 337. Financial aid is available.

Community Environment: See Temple University.

MORAVIAN COLLEGE *(J-17)*
Main Street and Elizabeth Avenue
Bethlehem, Pennsylvania 18018
Tel: (610) 861-1300; Admissions: (610) 861-1320; Fax: (610) 861-3919

Description: This privately supported coeducational liberal arts college is the sixth oldest in the nation. The college is accredited by the Middle States Association of Colleges and Schools. The college grants the Bachelor degree in 36 major fields of study, and offers professional accreditation in chemistry, medical technology, and teacher certification in elementary, secondary, and music. Preprofessional preparation is provided for medicine, law, theology, and graduate study. Enrollment includes 1,184 full-time, 19 part-time, and 495 evening students. A faculty of 78 full-time and 45 part-time provides a faculty-student ratio of 1-14. The college operates on the semester system and offers two summer sessions. Study abroad in England and Western Europe, independent study, honors and field study programs are available. Students may cross-register with Lafayette College, Lehigh University, Muhlenberg, Cedar Crest and Allentown colleges. Army ROTC is available through Lehigh University.

Entrance Requirements: High school graduation or equivalent; rank in upper two-fifths of graduating class; completion of at least 16 units including 4 English, 3 mathematics, 2 foreign language, 2 laboratory science, and 2 social science; SAT or ACT required, but SAT preferred; early admission, early decision and advanced placement programs available; $30 application fee.

Costs Per Year: $14,990 tuition; $4,730 room and board; $180 student fees.

Collegiate Environment: Moravian is located 60 miles northeast of Philadelphia and 90 miles southwest of New York City. The college is known for its high standards, its friendliness, its rich cultural heritage, and the quality of its faculty. There is a close student-faculty contact, and there are scores of opportunities for participation in athletic, cultural, social, and service activities. Moravian's 70-acre campus includes the Center for Music and Art, in the historic Church Street area, and Media Center with TV studio. The Hall of Science, which has won national architectural honors, offers individual research laboratories and houses Moravian's Computer Center. The Center operates an Ethernet connecting Sun and Masscomp hardware through remote terminals and work stations. The Reeves Library collection numbers 230,000 volumes, 1,258 periodicals, 2,395 microforms, and 4,500 records and tapes. Cooperation with other Lehigh Valley colleges makes one million volumes readily accessible to Moravian students. Approximately 89% of Moravian's students live on campus in a variety of accommodations ranging from traditional dormitory to apartment and townhouse-style units. Approximately 75% of those who apply for admission are accepted; over 80% of the current student body graduated in the top two-fifths of the high school class. The middle 50% ranges of SAT scores were 440-540V, 480-600M. Financial aid is available, and 80% of the students received some form of financial aid.

Community Environment: See Lehigh University.

MOUNT ALOYSIUS COLLEGE   *(K-7)*
William Penn Highway
Cresson, Pennsylvania 16630
Tel: (814) 886-4131; Fax: (814) 886-5061

Description: Privately supported, coeducational Roman Catholic liberal arts college sponsored by the Religious Sisters of Mercy and founded in 1939. It is accredited by the Middle States Association of Colleges and Schools and by several professional accrediting institutions. The semester system is used and two summer sessions are offered. The college offers two divisions of study; the first prepares students to continue their studies in four-year colleges and universities, the second gives two years of study in broad, practical education. Programs of study lead to the Associate or Baccalaureate degree. Enrollment includes 1,047 full-time students, 411 part-time, and 822 evening students. A faculty of 45 full-time and 40 part-time provides a faculty-student ratio of 1-13.

Entrance Requirements: Accredited high school graduation; completion of 16 units including 4 English, 3 mathematics, 3 science, 3 social science; SAT or ACT required; non-high school graduates considered; early decision, rolling admission, plans available; $15 application fee.

Costs Per Year: $7,960 tuition; $3,670 board and room; additional expenses average $1,500.

Collegiate Environment: The college is in the heart of the Allegheny Plateau in central Pennsylvania. The 125-acre campus has nine buildings which include residence halls to accommodate 195 men and women. The library contains 50,000 volumes, 5,000 pamphlets, 245 periodical titles, 73 microforms, and 890 audiovisual materials. Freshmen do not have to reside on campus. Difference in religion or race is no obstacle to admission at the college. Approximately 45% of students applying for admission are accepted including midyear, and 88% of the previous freshman class returned to this campus for their sophomore year. Average high school standing of a recent freshman class, top 50%; 20% in the top quarter; 30% in the second quarter;

30% in the third quarter; 20% in the bottom quarter; average scores, SAT 400V, 400M. Of the 60 scholarships offered, 30 are available for freshmen. 88% of the students receive some form of financial aid.

Community Environment: Population 5,000. Cresson is a rural community with humid climate and moderately high temperatures in summer. The area is served by bus, highway, and an airport at Martinsburg 45 minutes away. The city has two Catholic, a Methodist, Presbyterian, Christian, and Missionary Alliance Churches. There are several civic, fraternal, and veteran's organizations within the area. Theatres, concerts, sport events, and other recreational facilities are located in nearby Altoona and Johnstown. There are part-time employment opportunities for students on campus.

MUHLENBERG COLLEGE   *(J-16)*
2400 W. Chew Street
Allentown, Pennsylvania 18104
Tel: (610) 821-3200; Admissions: (610) 821-3200; Fax: (610) 821-3234

Description: This privately supported, coeducational liberal arts college was founded in 1848, and has been officially affiliated with the Lutheran Church in America since 1867. The college was exclusively a men's college from its foundation until 1957. The semester system is used and three summer terms are offered. It is accredited by the Middle States Association of Colleges and Schools, the Department of Education of the Commonwealth of Pennsylvania, and the New York State Board of Regents. Recent enrollment included 799 men and 901 women full-time, 57 men and women part-time and 805 men and women in the evening college. A faculty of 129 full-time gives a faculty-student ratio of 1-13. The college grants the Bachelor degree. Special programs include cooperative plans with Columbia and Washington University for engineering students, Columbia for nursing, Duke for forestry, the University of Pennsylvania for dentistry, MCOP- Hahnemann University for medicine, and the Lehigh Valley Association of Independent Colleges, which shares faculty, library resources and cooperative cultural programs. Army ROTC is available in cooperation with Lehigh University. Study abroad programs, internships, and Washington semester also available.

Entrance Requirements: Various factors are carefully considered in each decision made by the Admissions Committee; the following credentials are of primary importance: high school graduation with rank in upper 30% of graduating class; completion of 16 units including 4 English, 2 (preferably 3) mathematics, 2 (preferably 3) foreign language, and 2 social science; class rank when available; SAT or ACT required; early decision, advanced placement, early admission, delayed admission programs available; non-high school graduates considered; $30 application fee.

Costs Per Year: $17,550 tuition; $4,720 room and board; $1,600 average additional expenses.

Collegiate Environment: There are 30 buildings on the 75-acre college campus, including dormitories for 1,370 students and a library containing 213,000 volumes, 1,483 current periodical subscriptions, 83,520 government documents, and 19,453 microforms. Fraternities house 178 men. Sororities house 57 women. Special financial aid is available and 73% of the current student body received some form of assistance. Approximately 68% of students applying for admission are accepted and 92% of the freshman class return for sophomore year. The college welcomes a geographically diverse student body. Average high school standing of a recent freshman class: 50% in the top fifth; middle 50% of entering students scored between 1019 and 1129 on the SAT I.

Community Environment: Population 110,000. Allentown is located on the Lehigh River. It is Pennsylvania's third largest industrial market. Diversified manufacturing includes machinery and tools, trucks, electrical appliances, electronic equipment, apparel, cement, and gas-generating equipment. Other industries manufacture metal products, batteries, foodstuffs, textiles, and shoes. The area has good transportation facilities including four railroad lines, air service, and bus lines. The community has many churches representing various denominations. Four hospitals, a dental hospital, a library system, a museum and an Equity theater company are located here. Local recreational facilities encompass volleyball, baseball, tennis, basketball, pools, hiking, band concerts, opera, community theatre, five radio stations, and many motion picture and drive-in theatres. Part-time employment is available for students.

NEUMANN COLLEGE   *(M-17)*
Aston, Pennsylvania 19014
Tel: (610) 459-0905; Admissions: (610) 558-5616; Fax: (610) 459-1370

Description: The privately supported, Catholic, liberal arts college opened in 1965. It is accredited by the Middle States Association of Colleges and Schools. The school operates on the semester system and offers two summer terms. It is a four-year coeducational college offering undergraduate and graduate programs in liberal arts, education, nursing and physical therapy. In addition, an advanced certificate program in Pastoral Counseling is offered in the division o continuing education. The college awards the Baccalaureate and Master degrees. Enrollment includes 1,358 undergraduate students. A faculty of 41 full-time and 45 part-time gives a faculty-student ratio of 1-16.

Entrance Requirements: Approved high school graduation or equivalent; rank in upper 60% of graduating class; completion of 16 units including 4 English, 2 mathematics, 2 foreign language, 2 science, 2 social science; SAT score of 400V, 400M required or ACT 18; $25 application fee; early admission, rolling admission, early decision, midyear admission and advanced placement available. In special adult programs SAT scores, etc. are waived.

Costs Per Year: $10,080 tuition(nursing tuition is $11,290).

Collegiate Environment: The college's four buildings form a complex on the 14-acre campus. A new theater and gymnasium is located on campus. The library has a book collection numbering 82,000 volumes as well as 700 periodicals, 40,000 microforms and 2,400 audiovisual materials. There are no dormitory facilities for resident students. 72% of students applying for admission are accepted. The average scores of the entering freshman class were SAT 467 verbal, 471 math. Scholarships are available and 88% of the students receive some form of financial assistance.

Community Environment: Population of Philadelphia 1,950,098. Aston is a suburban township serving a commuter population from the Tri-state area of Philadelphia, Wilmington and South Jersey. The city enjoys temperate climate. Local historical sites include Valley Forge National Park, Brandywine Battlefield, and many others. Nearby Philadelphia offers all the cultural, recreational, and community service facilities normally found in a metropolis. The immediate area is served by railroad and bus lines with an airport located 10 miles away. There are three hospitals and numerous shopping centers in the area. Part-time employment opportunities are good.

NORTHAMPTON COUNTY AREA COMMUNITY COLLEGE *(J-17)*
3835 Green Pond Road
Bethlehem, Pennsylvania 18017
Tel: (610) 861-5300; Admissions: (610) 861-5500

Description: The publicly supported, coeducational junior college was established in 1967. It operates on the semester system and offers two summer sessions. The school graduated its first class in June, 1969 and enrolls 2,229 full-time and 3,926 part-time students. A faculty of 87 full-time and 287 part-time gives a faculty-student ratio of 1-16. It is authorized to award the Associate in Arts degree, Associate in Science, and the Associate in Applied Science. The college is accredited by the Middle States Association of Colleges and Schools and the Council on Dental Hygiene, American Dental Association, National League for Nursing, Commission of Schools of the American Board of Funeral Service Education, Inc., and the National Accrediting Agency for Clinical Laboratory Sciences.

Entrance Requirements: All high school graduates are admitted; non-high school graduates 18 years or older will be admitted under certain circumstances; early admission, rolling admission; $20 application fee.

Costs Per Year: $1,740 ($58/credit) district resident tuition; $3,480 ($116/credit) out-of-district residents; $5,220 ($174/credit) out-of-state residents; $3,440 room and board; fees additional.

Collegiate Environment: The 165-acre campus has 15 buildings including the library whose holdings number 74,739 volumes, 448 periodicals, 61 microforms, and 2,093 records, tapes, and CDs. There are apartments for 48 students plus dormitory space for 101 students. The college welcomes a geographically diverse student body. 98% of applicants are accepted. Classes begin in August, January, and June; the

college offers many evening courses. Financial aid is available and 47% of students receive some form of assistance.

Community Environment: See Lehigh University.

PEIRCE JUNIOR COLLEGE   *(M-17)*
1420 Pine Street
Philadelphia, Pennsylvania 19102
Tel: (215) 545-6400

Description: The private, nonprofit, coeducational junior college is accredited by the Middle States Association of Colleges and Schools and is authorized by the State Board of Education to award the Associate in Arts and the Associate in Science degrees. The college was founded in 1865, and places strong emphasis on Cooperative Education available in most programs, and on hands-on experience for all students. Equipment available to students includes an extensive personal computer environment for word processing and programming. A simulated office is available to secretarial students. The college operates on the semester system and offers two summer sessions. Enrollment is 750 full-time and 450 part-time students. A faculty of 37 full-time and 32 part-time provides a faculty-student ratio of 1-20. The Continuing Education division offers evening and Saturday classes for employed adults seeking career advancement.

Entrance Requirements: Accredited high school graduation or equivalent with rank in upper 50% of graduating class; completion of 16 units including 4 English; SAT or entrance exams required; exams may be waived for transfer students; admissions interview is recommended; admission is on a rolling basis; early admission is possible for qualified high school juniors; $20 application fee.

Costs Per Year: $6,300 tuition per year; $3,200 room and board; $160 student fees.

Collegiate Environment: There are five buildings on the college campus. The library contains over 38,000 volumes, 178 periodicals and numerous microforms and audiovisual materials. The Placement Office helps students find jobs while they are attending college and provides career placement for graduates. A full array of counseling and support services are also available. Dormitory facilities are available for 40 students on-campus; 20 additional students may be housed in college rented facilities off-campus. 85% of applicants are accepted. Financial aid is available. 90% of the student body receives a variety of grants, loans, work study and scholarships. Peirce encourages geographic diversity in its student body and currently enrolls 20 international students. Despite the strong career orientation of Peirce's programs, 30% of the graduating class opt to transfer immediately to four-year schools.

Community Environment: See University of Pennsylvania.

PENN STATE UNIVERSITY   *(I-9)*
University Park, Pennsylvania 16802
Tel: (814) 865-5471

Description: This publicly supported, coeducational, state related university was chartered by the Pennsylvania Legislature in 1855 and is composed of 22 campuses throughout the state. The university is accredited by the Middle States Association of Colleges and Schools and by various professional accrediting organizations. Undergraduates may choose from 139 majors, while graduate students have 130 approved fields of study. Present at the University Park Campus and in varying numbers at the 21 branch campuses are the ten undergraduate colleges: Agricultural Sciences; Arts and Architecture; Business Administration; School of Communications; Earth and Mineral Sciences; Education; Engineering; Health and Human Development; Liberal Arts; and Science. The campuses: Allentown, Altoona, Beaver, Behrend College, Berks, Harrisburg Capital College, Delaware County, DuBois, Fayette, Hazleton, Hershey Medical Center, Great Valley Graduate Center, McKeesport, Mont Alto, New Kensington, Ogontz, Schuylkill, Shenango, Wilkes-Barre, Worthington-Scranton, York, and University Park. The colleges of Agricultural Sciences, Education, and Health and Human Development have been designated as being responsible for teacher preparation, and accordingly offer Bachelor degree programs leading directly to Certificates to teach the subjects offered most in elementary and secondary schools. The Milton S. Hershey Medical Center offers the M.D. degree, the M.S. and the Ph.D. The Honors Program and Foreign Studies Program are open to qualifying students. The continuing education program at most campuses offers class instruction, correspondence instruction, and informal instruction throughout the state. Degrees granted include the Associate, Bachelor, Master and Doctorate. The school operates on the early semester system and offers three summer sessions. Enrollment at University Park includes 19,034 men and 14,620 women full-time, and 2,447 men and 2,193 women part-time. A faculty of 2,628 full-time and 381 part-time gives a faculty-student ratio of 1-18. Air Force, Army, and Navy ROTC programs available.

Entrance Requirements: Accredited high school graduation or GED; admission requirements vary throughout the university system; applicants are selected from those who have demonstrated by secondary school records and SAT scores that they are adequately prepared for this university; ACT scores may be submitted; highest qualified are offered admission first, following in descending order; when openings at one location of the university are filled, qualified applicants will be notified of campuses where openings still exist; minimum 15 high school units, varying depending on the college desired, liberal arts: 4 English, 3 mathematics, 3 arts/humanities/social science, 3 science, 2 foreign language; rolling admission, midyear admission, and advanced placement plans available; Nov. 30 deadline for priority consideration; $35 application fee.

Costs Per Year: $4,966 state resident undergraduate tuition; $10,654 nonresident undergraduate tuition; $3,920 room and board; $2,906 average additional expenses; $70 required computer fee.

Collegiate Environment: The library collection is housed in the Fred Lewis Pattee Library Building and includes 2,540,921 volumes, 27,634 periodicals, 2.0 million microforms, and 59,346 audiovisual materials. There are seven branch libraries and statewide the library system contains nearly 3.6 million volumes. There are 375 principal buildings on the University Park Campus. There are living accommodations on the University Park Campus for 12,744 students. Fifteen varsity athletic teams for men and fourteen athletic teams for women, along with a well-rounded intramural program, offer opportunities to train for sports, recreation, and physical fitness. Average scores of freshmen were SAT Verbal 507, Math 592. 54% of applicants are accepted. 72% of students receive some form of financial assistance. Regular, part-time, and odd jobs are available on most of the Penn State campuses and in the communities in which these campuses are located.

Community Environment: Population 37,500, University Park is located in the Allegheny Mountains. In a suburban area with temperate climate, there is a university airport and bus lines. The community has many churches, a public library, a hospital, shopping facilities, and many major civic and fraternal organizations. State parks surround the area and provide water sports, skiing, hunting, and fishing. Part-time job opportunities are available.

PENN STATE UNIVERSITY, ALLENTOWN CAMPUS   (J-16)
Academic Building
Fogelsville, Pennsylvania 18051
Tel: (215) 285-5035; Fax: (215) 285-5220

Description: This publicly supported, coeducational campus of the Pennsylvania State University is accredited by the Middle States Association of Colleges and Schools. It offers two-year Associate degree programs and the first two years of most Penn State Baccalaureate degree programs. It operates on the early semester system and offers two summer sessions. Enrollment includes 426 full-time, 185 part-time undergraduate, and 41 graduate students. A faculty of 22 full-time and 39 part-time gives a faculty-student ratio of 1-21. Air Force and Army ROTC are available. See also information in University Park Campus description.

Entrance Requirements: Accredited high school graduation or GED; admission requirements vary throughout the university system; applicants selected from those who have demonstrated by secondary school records and SAT scores that they are adequately prepared for this university; ACT scores may be submitted; highest qualified are admitted first, following in descending order; when openings at one location of the university are filled, qualified applicants will be notified of campuses where openings still exist; minimum 15 high school units, varying depending on the college desired, liberal arts: 4 English, 3 mathematics, 3 arts/humanities/social science, 3 science, 2 foreign language; rolling admission, midyear admission, and advanced placement plans available; $35 application fee.

Costs Per Year: $4,808 state resident tuition; $7,404 nonresident tuition; $70 computer fee.

Collegiate Environment: The Commonwealth Campus Library contains 33,351 volumes, 171 periodicals, and 3,076 microforms. There are no dormitories on campus. Average freshmen scores were SAT Verbal 423 and Math 485. 89% of applicants are accepted. Financial aid is available, and 49% of students receive some form of financial assistance.

Community Environment: See Muhlenberg College.

PENN STATE UNIVERSITY, ALTOONA CAMPUS   (K-7)
3000 Ivyside Park
Altoona, Pennsylvania 16603
Tel: (814) 949-5446

Description: This publicly supported, coeducational campus of the Pennsylvania State University is accredited by the Middle States Association of Colleges and Schools. It offers two-year Associate degree programs and the first two years of most Penn State Baccalaureate programs. It operates on the early semester system and offers two summer sessions. Enrollment includes 2,079 full-time, 389 part-time undergraduate, and 26 graduate students. A faculty of 77 full-time and 64 part-time gives a faculty-student ratio of 1-27. See also information in University Park Campus description.

Entrance Requirements: Accredited high school graduation or GED; admission requirements vary throughout the university system; applicants selected from those who have demonstrated by secondary school records and SAT scores that they are adequately prepared for this university; highest qualified admitted first, following in descending order; when openings at one location of the university are filled, qualified applicants will be notified of campuses where openings still exist; minimum 15 high school units, varying depending on the college desired, liberal arts: 4 English, 3 mathematics, 3 arts/humanities/social science, 3 science, 2 foreign language; rolling admission, midyear admission, and advanced placement plans available; Nov. 30 deadline for priority consideration; $35 application fee.

Costs Per Year: $4,808 State resident tuition; $7,400 nonresident tuition; $3,920 room and board; $70 computer fee.

Collegiate Environment: This 105-acre campus has a 48,902-volume library and dormitory facilities for 575 students. 91% of applicants are accepted, including midyear students. Average scores of freshmen were SAT Verbal 423, Math 485. Freshman classes begin in August and January. Financial aid is available, and 72% of students receive some form of financial assistance.

Community Environment: Population 63,115. Altoona is a suburban and rural area originally founded in 1849 by the Pennsylvania Railroad as the base of operations in the pioneer work of building the first railroad over the Alleghenies. For years the town's economy depended primarily on the railroad building and repair shops. The economy is more diversified today. Part-time employment is available for students. The community has a library system, many churches, as well as two general, one veteran's and one mental hospital. Major civic, fraternal, and veteran's organizations are active within the general locale. Local recreational opportunities include theater, water sports on a large nearby lake, bowling, tennis, and other major sports. Shopping centers are accessible.

PENN STATE UNIVERSITY, BEAVER CAMPUS   (J-1)
Brodhead Road
Monaca, Pennsylvania 15061
Tel: (412) 773-3800

Description: This publicly supported, coeducational campus of the Pennsylvania State University opened in 1965 and is accredited by the Middle States Association of Colleges and Schools. It offers two-year Associate degree programs and the first two years of most Penn State Baccalaureate degree programs. It operates on the early semester system and offers one summer session. Enrollment includes 693 full-time, 146 part-time undergraduate, and 50 graduate students. A faculty of 45 full-time and 22 part-time gives a faculty-student ratio of 1-18. See also information in University Park Campus description.

Entrance Requirements: Accredited high school graduation or GED; admission requirements vary throughout the university system; applicants selected from those who have demonstrated by secondary school records and SAT scores that they are adequately prepared for this university; ACT scores may be submitted; highest qualified are admitted first, following in descending order; when openings at one location of the university are filled, qualified applicants will be notified of campuses where openings still exist; minimum 15 high school units, varying depending on the college desired, liberal arts: 4 English, 3 mathematics, 3 arts/humanities/social science, 3 science, 2 foreign language; rolling admission, midyear admission, and advanced placement plans available; $35 application fee.

Costs Per Year: $4,808 state resident tuition; $7,400 nonresident tuition; $3,920 room and board; $70 computer fee.

Collegiate Environment: There are ten buildings on the 94-acre campus including the library of 35,935 volumes, 206 periodicals, 9,356 microforms, and 5,953 recordings. Residence halls accommodate 314 students. Average freshmen scores were SAT Verbal 423, Math 480. 91% of applicants are accepted, including midyear students. The student body is predominantly local. Financial aid is available, and 59% of students receive some form of financial assistance.

Community Environment: Population 7,600, Monaca is a suburban community in Beaver County. The average summer temperature is 80 degrees, and winter temperatures vary from 50 to zero degrees. Shopping facilities and various civic and fraternal organizations exist in the community. In the area are two hospitals, municipal parks, a swimming pool, golf courses, fishing streams, and wooded hills and valleys with small game. Part-time employment is available.

PENN STATE UNIVERSITY, BERKS CAMPUS *(K-15)*
P.O. Box 7009
Reading, Pennsylvania 19610-6009
Tel: (215) 320-4864

Description: This publicly supported, coeducational campus of the Pennsylvania State University opened in 1958 and is accredited by the Middle States Association of Colleges and Schools. It offers two-year Associate degree programs and the first two years of most Penn State Baccalaureate degree programs. It operates on the early semester system and offers two summer sessions. Enrollment includes 1,267 full-time, 456 part-time undergraduates, and 95 graduate students. A faculty of 52 full-time and 66 part-time gives a faculty-student ratio of 1-25. Air Force ROTC is available. See also information in University Park Campus description.

Entrance Requirements: Accredited high school graduation or GED; admission requirements vary throughout the university system; applicants selected from those who have demonstrated by secondary school records and SAT scores that they are adequately prepared for this university; ASSET scores may be submitted; highest qualified are admitted first, following in descending order; when openings at one location of the university are filled, qualified applicants will be notified of campuses where openings still exist; minimum 15 high school units, varying depending on the college desired, liberal arts: 4 English, 3 mathematics, 3 arts/humanities/social science, 3 science, 2 foreign language; rolling admission, midyear admission, and advanced placement plans available; $35 application fee.

Costs Per Year: $4,808 state resident tuition; $7,400 nonresident tuition; $3,920 room and board; $70 computer fee.

Collegiate Environment: The campus is in Spring Township, a suburban area near Reading. The library contains 37,748 volumes. Average freshmen scores were SAT Verbal 423, Math 485. 83% of applicants are accepted, including midyear students. Financial aid is available, and 49% of students receive some from of financial assistance. Evening classes are held in order to provide continuing education for adults.

Community Environment: Population of Spring Township is 17,000, and of Reading, 79,000. The climate is temperate. The community has a public library, museum, YMCA, YWCA, and an Institute of Fine Arts. Shopping facilities, and air and rail service are nearby. Some part-time employment is available.

PENN STATE UNIVERSITY, COLLEGE OF MEDICINE, MILTON S. HERSHEY MEDICAL CENTER *(C-13)*
Hershey, Pennsylvania 17033
Tel: (717) 531-8521

Description: This publicly supported, coeducational campus of the Pennsylvania State University was founded in 1963 through a trust created by Milton S. Hershey, the founder of the Hershey Chocolate Company. It is accredited by the Middle States Association of Colleges and Schools and the Liasion Committee of the American Association of Medical Colleges and the American Medical Association. The college offers the M.D. degree, the M.S. in laboratory animal medicine, and the M.S. and Ph.D. in anatomy, biochemistry and molecular biology, cell and molecular biology, genetics, microbiology & immunology, neuroscience, pharmacology, and physiology. It operates on the semester system. Enrollment includes 560 full-time, 19 part-time undergraduate, and 579 graduate students. A faculty of 485 full-time and 40 part-time gives an undergraduate facultu-student ratio of 1-1. See also information in University Park Campus description.

Entrance Requirements: M.D. program: exceptional students with three years of undergraduate college may be considered, but completion of requirements for a Bachelor's degree is recommended; acceptable score on Medical College Admissions Test required by the spring before application is submitted; admission to graduate programs depends upon specific program requirements; $40 application fee.

Costs Per Year: M.D. Program: $15,476 state resident tuition, $22,020 nonresident tuition; Graduate Program: $5,554 state resident tuition, $11,326 nonresident tuition; $70 computer fee.

Collegiate Environment: The campus occupies 380 acres. The Medical Sciences Building and Teaching Hospital are the principal structures. The Animal Research Farm is located on the campus. The library contains 101,188 volumes and 1,824 periodicals. Financial aid is available, and 86% of students receive some form of financial assistance.

Community Environment: Population 20,000. Hershey was founded in 1903 by Milton S. Hershey. This is the home of the world-famous Hershey Bar. Limited part-time employment is available. See also Harrisburg Area Community College for information on Harrisburg, 12 miles away.

PENN STATE UNIVERSITY, DELAWARE COUNTY CAMPUS *(M-17)*
25 Yearsley Mill Road
Media, Pennsylvania 19063
Tel: (215) 892-1200

Description: This publicly supported, coeducational campus of the Pennsylvania State University opened in 1967 and is accredited by the Middle States Association of Colleges and Schools. Established in Chester, the college moved into a new campus in Media, north of Chester, in 1970. It offers two-year Associate degree programs and the first two years of most Penn Satae Baccalaureate degree programs. It operates on the early semester system and offers two summer sessions. Enrollment includes 935 full-time, 481 part-time undergraduate, and 20 graduate students. A faculty of 52 full-time and 32 part-time gives a faculty-student ratio of 1-20. Air Force and Army ROTC programs available. See also information in University Park Campus description.

Entrance Requirements: Accredited high school graduation or GED; admission requirements vary throughout the university system; applicants selected from those who have demonstrated by secondary school records and SAT scores that they are adequately prepared for this university; ACT scores may be submitted; highest qualified are admitted first, following in descending order; when openings at one location of the university are filled, qualified applicants will be notified of campuses where openings still exist; minimum 15 high school units, varying depending on the college desired, liberal arts: 4 English, 3 mathematics, 3 arts/humanities/social science, 3 science, 2 foreign language; rolling admission, midyear admission, and advanced placement plans available; $35 application fee.

Costs Per Year: $4,808 state resident tuition; $7,400 nonresident tuition; $70 computer fee.

Collegiate Environment: The 90-acre campus includes a two-story modern library containing 42,653 volumes, 233 periodicals, 4,431 microforms, and 1,707 audiovisual materials. There are also a main classroom building, and a gymnasium/student commons building with a bookstore and cafeteria. Hiking and jogging trails, tennis and basketball courts, a soccer field, and a baseball diamond complete the facilities. Average freshmen scores were SAT Verbal 423, Math 485. 82% of applicants are accepted, including midyear students. Financial aid is available, and 45% of students receive some form of financial assistance.

Community Environment: Media is a rural town located twenty miles west of Philadelphia, and is a suburb of Chester, population 56,331. Settled by the Swedes and Finns, Chester is the oldest settlement in Pennsylvania and historic sites exist throughout the area. Located on the Delaware River with a channel to the sea, it is a U.S. customs port of entry. It is also the center of an industrial area with enormous ship and turbine plants. Part-time employment is available. Excellent shopping facilities are locally available. Philadelphia is located eight miles from the heart of Chester. All the civic, cultural and recreational facilities of that city are easily accessible.

PENN STATE UNIVERSITY, DUBOIS CAMPUS   *(H-6)*
College Place
DuBois, Pennsylvania 15801
Tel: (814) 375-4700

Description: This publicly supported, coeducational campus of the Pennsylvania State University opened in 1935 and is accredited by the Middle States Association of Colleges and Schools. It offers two-year Associate degree programs and the first two years of most Penn State Baccalaureate degree programs. It operates on the early semester system and offers one summer session. Enrollment includes 671 full-time, 302 part-time undergraduate, and 21 graduate students. A faculty of 43 full-time and 19 part-time gives a faculty-student ratio of 1-17. See also information in University Park Campus description.

Entrance Requirements: Accredited high school graduation or GED; admission requirements vary throughout the university system; applicants selected from those who have demonstrated by secondary school records and SAT scores that they are adequately prepared for this university; ACT scores may be submitted; highest qualified are admitted first, following in descending order; when openings at one location of the university are filled, qualified applicants will be notified of campuses where openings still exist; minimum 15 high school units, varying depending on the college desired, liberal arts: 4 English, 3 mathematics, 3 arts/humanities/social science, 3 science, 2 foreign language; rolling admission, midyear admission, and advanced placement plans available; $35 application fee.

Costs Per Year: $4,808 state resident tuition; $7,400 nonresident tuition; $70 computer fee.

Collegiate Environment: The 25-acre campus includes a library containing 37,957 volumes, 241 periodicals, 9,306 microforms, and 616 recordings. Average freshmen scores were SAT Verbal 423, Math 485. 82% of applicants are accepted, including midyear students. Freshman classes begin in August and January. Financial aid is available, and 74% of students receive some form of financial assistance.

Community Environment: DuBois, population 10,112, is located at the entrance to the lowest pass in the Alleghenies and is near the big game region of Pennsylvania. The surrounding mountains and streams offer good hunting and fishing in season. It is serviced by good highways, busses, and a community airport. This area has a service-oriented economy, and part-time employment is available.

PENN STATE UNIVERSITY, ERIE BEHREND COLLEGE
(D-2)
Station Road
Erie, Pennsylvania 16563
Tel: (814) 898-6100

Description: The coeducational campus of the Pennsylvania State University opened in 1948 and is accredited by the Middle States Association of Colleges and Schools. Behrend offers 23 two-year Penn State Baccalaureate degree programs, the first two years of most other Penn State Baccalaureate degree programs, as well as Associate and Graduate degree programs. It operates on the early semester system and offers two summer sessions. Enrollment includes 2,386 full-time, 704 part-time undergraduate, and 149 graduate students. A faculty of 142 full-time and 80 part-time gives a faculty-student ratio of 1-17. See also information in University Park Campus description.

Entrance Requirements: Accredited high school graduation or GED; admission requirements vary throughout the university system; applicants selected from those who have demonstrated by secondary school records and SAT scores that they are adequately prepared for this university; ACT scores may be submitted; highest qualified are admitted first, following in descending order; when openings at one location of the university are filled, qualified applicants will be notified of campuses where openings still exist; minimum 15 high school units, varying depending on the college desired, liberal arts: 4 English, 3 mathematics, 3 arts/humanities/social science, 3 science, 2 foreign language; rolling admission, midyear admission, and advanced placement plans available; Nov. 30 deadline for priority consideration; $35 application fee.

Costs Per Year: $4,966 state resident tuition; $10,654 nonresident tuition; $3,920 room and board; $70 computer fee.

Collegiate Environment: The college is located in Harborcreek Township in Erie County, approximately 6 miles from downtown Erie. The 500-acre campus has a library containing 79,709 volumes, 972 periodicals, 35,460 microforms, and 1,672 recordings with access to over three million volumes in the Penn State library system. Construction of a new library began in 1991. Residence halls and apartments accommodate 1,099 students. Average freshmen scores were SAT Verbal 450, Math 521. 84% of applicants are accepted.

Community Environment: Erie is a city of 125,000 with the population of greater Erie being 300,000. Located on the shores of Lake Erie, the city is rich in cultural and recreational activities. It has a symphony orchestra, civic theater, convention center, ballet, and arts center, and facilities for boating, fishing, canoeing, golfing, skiing, ice-skating, and many other outdoor and indoor activities. There is wide variety of restaurants and shopping facilities, including a large mall. Public transportation to Erie and its environs is available from the campus every half hour. The bayfront and downtown area is currently undergoing redevelopment and is rapidly becoming revitalized.

PENN STATE UNIVERSITY, FAYETTE CAMPUS   *(M-3)*
P.O. Box 519
Uniontown, Pennsylvania 15401
Tel: (412) 430-4130

Description: This publically supported, coeducational campus of the Pennsylvania State University opened in 1965 and is accredited by the Middle States Association of Colleges and Schools. It offers two-year Associate degree programs and the first two years of most Penn State Baccalaureate degree programs. It operates on the early semester system and offers two summer sessions. Enrollment includes 631 full-time and 272 part-time students. A faculty of 47 full-time and 23 part-time gives a faculty-student ratio of 1-15. Army ROTC is available. See also information in University Park Campus description.

Entrance Requirements: Accredited high school graduation or GED; admission requirements vary throughout the university system; applicants selected from those who have demonstrated by secondary school records and SAT scores that they are adequately prepared for this university; ACT scores may be submitted; highest qualified are admitted first, following in descending order; when openings at one location of the university are filled, qualified applicants will be notified of campuses where openings still exist; minimum 15 high school units, varying depending on the college desired, liberal arts: 4 English, 3 mathematics, 3 arts/humanities/social science, 3 science, 2 foreign language; rolling admission, midyear admission, and advanced placement plans available; $35 application fee.

Costs Per Year: $4,808 state resident tuition; $7,400 nonresident tuition; $70 computer fee.

Collegiate Environment: This campus includes a library containing 42,588 volumes.

Community Environment: Population 16,282. Uniontown is an urban area accessible by bus and U.S. Route 40 and 119. The climate is temperate. The community has a public library, churches of major denominations, two theatres, one hospital, a YMCA, and civic, fraternal, and veteran's organizations. Shopping facilities are good. Local recreation includes boating, fishing, hunting, skiing, and white-water rafting at the nearby lakes, forests, mountains, and rivers. Part-time employment for students is increasing.

PENN STATE UNIVERSITY, GREAT VALLEY   *(L-17)*
30 E. Swedesford Rd.
Malvern, Pennsylvania 19355
Tel: (215) 648-3282

Description: This publicly supported coeducational graduate school of the Pennsylvania State University, founded in 1963, is accredited by the Middle States Association of Colleges and Schools. It is the nation's first permanent campus structure built in an existing corporate park, and forged a merger of higher education with business and industry. It operates on the early semester system. Enrollment includes 71 full-time, 1,123 part-time undergraduate, and 1,188 graduate students. A faculty of 18 full-time and 42 part-time gives a faculty-student ratio of 1-19. See also information in University Park Campus description.

Entrance Requirements: Accredited high school graduation or GED; admission requirements vary throughout the university system; applicants selected from those who have demonstrated by secondary school records and SAT scores that they are adequately prepared for this university; ACT scores may be submitted; highest qualified are admitted first, following in descening order; when openings at one location of the university are filled, qualified applicants will be notified of campuses where openings still exist; minimum 15 high school units, varying depending on the college desired, liberal arts: 4 English, 3 mathematics, 3 arts/humanities/social science, 3 science, 2 foreign language. Graduates: advanced Baccalaureate degree from a regionally accredited institution; collegiate junior/senior GPA of 2.5; additional requirements depending on degree; completed graduate school application, two official transcripts from each postsecondary institution attended, and any other materials required by specific programs; nondegree students may enroll for a limited number of credits before changing to degree status; rolling admission plan; $35 application fee.

Costs Per Year: $291 per graduate credit state resident; $515 per graduate credit nonresident.

Collegiate Environment: The school has a library containing 21,378 volumes and access to the main library of over three million volumes. Direct telefacsimile service provides interlibrary loans and immediate service in securing photocopies over the telephone. 87% of applicants are accepted. Financial aid is available, and 13% of students receive some form of financial assistance.

Community Environment: Malvern is conveniently located in the heart of the Route 202 high-tech corridor of Pennsylvania.

PENN STATE UNIVERSITY, HARRISBURG CAPITAL COLLEGE *(L-18)*
Route 230
Middletown, Pennsylvania 17057
Tel: (717) 948-6000

Description: This publicly supported, coeducational campus of the Pennsylvania State University is a senior college and graduate center. It is accredited by the Middle States Association of Colleges and Schools. The college operates the early semester system and offers two summer sessions. Enrollment includes 1,497 full-time, 2,131 part-time undergraduate, and 1,366 graduate students. A faculty of 139 full-time and 73 part-time gives a faculty-student ratio of 1-16. Army ROTC program available. See also information in University Park Campus description.

Entrance Requirements: Associate degree from accredited institution or 60 credits from a four-year college; TOEFL required for foreign students; GRE required for some graduate programs; midyear admission and rolling admission plans available; $35 application fee.

Costs Per Year: $4,966 state resident tuition; $10,654 nonresident tuition; $3,920 room and board; $70 computer fee.

Collegiate Environment: The library has 185,804 volumes, 1,563 periodicals, 1,056,379 microforms, and 1,971 sound recordings. Housing is available on this campus for 684 students, including families. 79% of applicants are accepted, including midyear students. Financial aid is available, and 52% of students receive some form of financial assistance.

Community Environment: Penn State Harrisburg is located eight miles from Harrisburg, the state capital and a thriving urban center. Close proximity to Harrisburg as well as Hershey, Lancaster, York and Lebanon provides diverse cultural, recreational, and employment opportunities.

PENN STATE UNIVERSITY, HAZLETON CAMPUS *(I-15)*
Highacres
Hazleton, Pennsylvania 18201
Tel: (717) 450-3162

Description: This publicly supported, coeducational campus of the Pennsylvania State University opened in 1934 and is accredited by the Middle States Association of Colleges and Schools. It offers two-year Associate degree programs and the first two years of most Penn State Baccalaureate programs. It operates on the early semester system and offers two summer sessions. Enrollment includes 1,093 full-time, 118 part-time undergraduate, and 2 graduate students. A faculty of 51 full-time and 28 part-time gives a faculty-student ratio of 1-21. Air Force and Army ROTC programs available. See also information in University Park Campus description.

Entrance Requirements: Accredited high school graduation or GED; admission requirements vary throughout the university system; applicants selected from those who have demonstrated by secondary school records and SAT scores that they are adequately prepared for this university; ACT scores may be submitted; highest qualified are admitted first, following in descending order; when openings at one location of the university are filled, qualified applicants will be notified of campuses where openings still exist; minimum 15 high school units, varying depending on the college desired, liberal arts: 4 English, 3 mathematics, 3 arts/humanities/social science, 3 science, 2 foreign language; rolling admission, midyear admission, and advanced placement plans available; $35 application fee.

Costs Per Year: $4,808 state resident tuition; $7,400 nonresident tuition; $3,920 room and board; $70 computer fee.

Collegiate Environment: There are fifteen buildings on the 75-acre campus including a library containing 74,980 volumes, and dormitories for 455 students. Average freshmen scores were SAT Verbal 423, Math 485. 90% of applicants are accepted. Financial aid is available, and 72% of students receive some form of financial assistance.

Community Environment: Located in Luzerne County, Hazleton, population 30,426, is 24 miles from Wilkes-Barre. The surrounding area has anthracite mining and agriculture. Some part-time employment is available. The city has churches of many denominations, a library, YMCA, YWCA, and a radio station.

PENN STATE UNIVERSITY, MCKEESPORT CAMPUS *(K-3)*
University Drive
McKeesport, Pennsylvania 15132
Tel: (412) 675-9010

Description: This publicly supported, coeducational campus of the Pennsylvania State University opened in 1948 and is accredited by the Middle States Association of Colleges and Schools. It offers two-year Associate degree programs and the first two years of most Penn State Baccalaureate programs. The school operates on the early semester system and offers two summer sessions. Enrollment includes 595 full-time, 242 part-time undergraduate, and 3 graduate students. A faculty of 39 full-time and 35 part-time gives a faculty-student ratio of 1-16. Army ROTC is available. See also information in University Park Campus description.

Entrance Requirements: Accredited high school graduation or GED; admission requirements vary throughout the university system; applicants selected from those who have demonstrated by secondary school records and SAT scores that they are adequately prepared for this university; ACT scores may be submitted; highest qualified are admitted first, following in descending order; when openings at one location of the university are filled, qualified applicants will be notified of campuses where openings still exist; minimum 15 high school units, varying depending on the college desired, liberal arts: 4 English, 3 mathematics, 3 arts/humanities/social science, 3 science, 2 foreign language; rolling admission, midyear admission, and advanced placement plans available; $35 application fee.

Costs Per Year: $4,808 state resident tuition; $7,400 nonresident tuition; $3,920 room and board; $70 computer fee.

Collegiate Environment: The 55-acre campus includes a library containing 35,861 volumes, 313 periodicals, 8,059 microforms, and 1,201 audiovisual materials, and dormitory facilities for 214 men and women. Average freshmen scores were SAT Verbal 423, Math 485. 88% of applicants are accepted. Financial aid is available, and 81% of students receive some form of financial assistance.

Community Environment: Population 31,000, McKeesport is a highly developed industrial city located at the junction of the Youghiogheny and Monongahela Rivers. The climate is temperate and seasonal. A suburban area approximately 15 miles from Pittsburgh, community services include a hospital, clinics, churches of various denominations, and many civic and fraternal organizations. The surrounding area has three theaters, a public library, YMCA, YWCA, and access to major sports. Part-time employment is available. See also University of Pittsburgh.

PENN STATE UNIVERSITY, MONT ALTO CAMPUS   *(M-10)*
Mont Alto, Pennsylvania 17237
Tel: (717) 749-3111

Description: This publicly supported, coeducational campus of the Pennsylvania State University opened in 1963 and is accredited by the Middle States Association of Colleges and Schools. It offers two-year Associate degree programs and the first two years of most Penn State Baccalaureate programs. It operates on the early semester system and offers two summer sessions. Enrollment includes 804 full-time, 307 part-time undergraduate, and 71 graduate students. A faculty of 45 full-time and 22 part-time gives a faculty-student ratio of 1-20. Army ROTC is available. See also information in University Park Campus description.

Entrance Requirements: Accredited high school graduation or GED; admission requirements vary throughout the university system; applicants selected from those who have demonstrated by secondary school records and SAT scores that they are adequately prepared for this university; highest qualified are admitted first, following in descending order; when openings at one location of the university are filled, qualified applicants will be notified of campuses where openings still exist; minimum 15 high school units, varying depending on the college desired, liberal arts: 4 English, 3 mathematics, 3 arts/humanities/social science, 3 science, 2 foreign language; rolling admission, midyear admission, and advanced placement plans available; $35 application fee.

Costs Per Year: $4,808 state resident tuition; $7,400 nonresident tuition; $3,920 room and board; $70 computer fee.

Collegiate Environment: The library contains 31,404 volumes. Dormitory facilities are available for 446 students. Average freshmen scores were SAT Verbal 423, Math 485. 79% of applicants are accepted, including midyear students. Financial aid is available, and 66% of students receive some form of financial assistance.

Community Environment: Population 1,532. Mont Alto is a rural community reached by highway. The climate is temperate with 39.9 inches of rainfall annually. The community has chuches of many denominations and a public playground. Hospitals and a shopping center are accessible. Nearby state parks provide for swimming, golfing, and camping. See also Gettysburg College for information on nearby Gettysburg.

PENN STATE UNIVERSITY, NEW KENSINGTON CAMPUS   *(J-3)*
3550 Seventh Street
New Kensington, Pennsylvania 15068
Tel: (412) 339-5400

Description: This publicly supported, coeducational campus of the Pennsylvania State University is accredited by the Middle States Association of Colleges and Schools. It offers two-year Associate degree programs and the first two years of most Penn State Baccalaureate programs. A building and expansion program will enable this campus to offer a much wider program of two-year undergraduate work. It operates on the early semester system and offers two summer sessions. Enrollment includes 664 full-time, 376 part-time undergraduate, and 1 graduate student. A faculty of 44 full-time and 29 part-time gives a faculty-student ratio of 1-17. See also information in University Park Campus description.

Entrance Requirements: Accredited high school graduation or GED; admission requirements vary throughout the university system; applicants selected from those who have demonstrated by secondary school records and SAT scores that they are adequately prepared for this university; ACT scores may be submitted; highest qualified are admitted first, following in descending order; when openings at one location of the university are filled, qualified applicants will be noti-

fied of campuses where openings still exist; minimum 15 high school units, varying depending on the college desired, liberal arts: 4 English, 3 mathematics, 3 arts/humanities/social science, 3 science, 2 foreign language; rolling admission, midyear admission, and advanced placement plans available; $35 application fee.

Costs Per Year: $4,808 state resident tuition; $7,400 nonresident tuition; $70 computer fee.

Collegiate Environment: The college has a 27,758-volume library and access to 3 million volumes via a computer access system. Housing is available through an apartment complex adjacent to the campus that is exclusively for students. Average freshmen scores were SAT Verbal 423, Math 485. 87% of applicants are accepted. Financial aid is available, and 64% of students receive some form of financial assistance.

Community Environment: Population 20,312. This is a rural community located 18 miles northeast of Pittsburgh and 5 miles from New Kensington. The climate is temperate. The city is serviced by railroad, turnpike, Routes 20, 56, and 366, and the Greater Pittsburgh Airport. New Kensington has a public library, YMCA, over 60 churches, a hospital, and shopping facilities. Part-time employment is limited. There are theaters, water sports, golf, camping, skiing, and major civic and fraternal organizations within the community. See also University of Pittsburgh.

PENN STATE UNIVERSITY, OGONTZ CAMPUS   *(L-17)*
1600 Woodland Road
Abington, Pennsylvania 19001
Tel: (215) 881-7300

Description: This publicly supported, coeducational campus of the Pennsylvania State University opened in 1950 and is accredited by the Middle States Association of Colleges and Schools. It offers two-year Associate degree programs and the first two years of most Penn State Baccalaureate programs. It operates on the early semester system and offers two summer sessions. Enrollment includes 1,644 full-time, 1,314 part-time undergraduate, and 50 graduate students. A faculty of 95 full-time and 85 part-time gives a faculty-student ratio of 1-21. Air Force and Army ROTC programs are available. See also information in University Park Campus description.

Entrance Requirements: Accredited high school graduation or GED; admission requirements vary throughout the university system; applicants selected from those who have demonstrated by secondary school records and SAT scores that they are adequately prepared for this university; ACT scores may be submitted; highest qualified are admitted first, following in descending order; when openings at one location of the university are filled, qualified applicants will be notified of campuses where openings still exist; minimum 15 high school units, varying depending on the college desired, liberal arts: 4 English, 3 mathematics, 3 arts/humanities/social science, 3 science, 2 foreign language; rolling admission, midyear admission, and advanced placement plans available; $35 application fee.

Costs Per Year: $4,808 state resident tuition; $7,400 nonresident tuition; $70 computer fee.

Collegiate Environment: The library contains 50,643 volumes, 362 periodicals, 6,273 microforms, and 3,680 recordings. Dormitory housing is not available. Average freshmen scores were SAT Verbal 423, Math 485. 80% of applicants are accepted. Financial aid is available and 42% of students receive some form of financial assistance.

Community Environment: Abington is a suburb of Philadelphia. All the cultural, recreational and civic services of Philadelphia are easily accessible. See also Temple University for information on Philadelphia.

PENN STATE UNIVERSITY, SCHUYLKILL CAMPUS   *(J-14)*
200 University Drive
Schuylkill Haven, Pennsylvania 17972
Tel: (717) 385-6252

Description: This publicly supported, coeducational campus of the Pennsylvania State University opened in 1934 and is accredited by the Middle States Association of Colleges and Schools. It offers two-year Associate degree programs and the first two years of most Penn State Baccalaureate degree programs. It operates on the early semester system and offers one summer session. Enrollment includes 656 full-time and 362 part-time undergraduate, and 5 graduate students. A faculty of 37 full-time and 30 part-time gives a faculty-student ratio of 1-20. Army ROTC is available. See also information in University Park Campus description.

Entrance Requirements: Accredited high school graduation or GED; admission requirements vary throughout the university system; applicants selected from those who have demonstrated by secondary school records and SAT scores that they are adequately prepared for this university; ACT scores may be submitted; highest qualified are admitted first, following in descending order; when openings at one location of the university are filled, qualified applicants will be notified of campuses where openings still exist; minimum 15 high school units, varying depending on the college desired, liberal arts: 4 English, 3 mathematics, 3 arts/humanities/social science, 3 science, 2 foreign language; rolling admission, midyear admission, and advanced placement plans available; $35 application fee.

Costs Per Year: $4,808 state resident tuition; $7,400 nonresident tuition; $3,920 room and board; $70 computer fee.

Collegiate Environment: The 70-acre campus is situated south of the borough of Schuylkill Haven, at the banks of the Schuylkill River and at the foot of Blue Mountain. Facilities include a library containing 32,076 volumes, 248 periodicals, 15,638 microforms, and 484 audiovisual materials, dormitory facilities for 176 students, a new student/community/activity center, a modern gymnasium, classrooms, laboratories (both scientific and technical), an auditorium, and a full-service cafeteria. The college offers its students a wide variety of intercollegiate and intramural athletics for both men and women. Average freshmen scores were SAT Verbal 423, Math 485. 85% of applicants are accepted, including midyear students. Financial aid is available, and 60% of students receive some form of financial assistance.

Community Environment: Schuylkill Haven is a rural community, located midway between Allentown and Harrisburg, about 90 miles from Philadelphia. See also Kutztown University.

PENN STATE UNIVERSITY, SHENANGO CAMPUS   (G-1)
147 Shenango Avenue
Sharon, Pennsylvania 16146
Tel: (412) 983-5830

Description: This publicly supported coeducational campus of the Pennsylvania State University opened in 1965 and is accredited by the Middle States Association of Colleges and Schools. It offers two-year Associate degree programs and the first two years for most Penn State Baccalaureate degree programs. The school operates on the early semester system and offers two summer sessions. Enrollment includes 587 full-time, 516 part-time undergraduate, and 46 graduate students. A faculty of 30 full-time and 47 part-time gives a faculty-student ratio of 1-22. See also information in University Park Campus description.

Entrance Requirements: Accredited high school graduation or GED; admission requirements vary throughout the university system; applicants selected from those who have demonstrated by secondary school records and SAT scores that they are adequately prepared for this university; ASSET scores may be submitted; highest qualified are admitted first, following in descending order; when openings at one location of the university are filled, qualified applicants will be notified of campuses where openings still exist; minimum 15 high school units, varying depending on the college desired, liberal arts: 4 English, 3 mathematics, 3 arts/humanities/social science, 3 science, 2 foreign language; rolling admission, midyear admission, and advanced placement plans available; $35 application fee.

Costs Per Year: $4,808 state resident tuition; $7,400 nonresident tuition; $70 computer fee.

Collegiate Environment: The campus is situated in the heart of Downtown Sharon on the Shenango River. The college library contains 25,594 volumes, 147 periodicals, 3,603 microforms, 1,850 audiovisual materials, and computer links to all 20 campus libraries. Other buildings include classrooms, modern laboratories, an auditorium, CAD/CAM and robotics facilities, and a bookstore. No on-campus dorms are provided, but private apartments and rooms are available within walking distance. Average freshmen scores were SAT Verbal 423, Math 485. 83% of applicants are accepted, including midyear students. Financial aid is available, and 64% of students receive some form of financial assistance.

Community Environment: Situated on the Shenango River, the Shenango Valley, population 22,653, represents the majority of the communities in Mercer and Lawrence Counties of Pennsylvania. Although many of these communities are rural, the area is also home to several industries that produce steel and electrical parts. Sharon is located on the Ohio border, 2 miles north of Interstate 80. The total population within a 20-mile radius is approximately 500,000.

PENN STATE UNIVERSITY, WILKES-BARRE CAMPUS
(H-15)
P.O. Box 1830
Wilkes-Barre, Pennsylvania 18627
Tel: (717) 675-9238

Description: This publicly supported, coeducational campus of the Pennsylvania State University opened in 1947 and is accredited by the Middle States Association of Colleges and Schools. It offers two-year Associate degree programs and the first two years of most Penn State Baccalaureate programs. It operates on the early semester system and offers two summer sessions. Enrollment includes 571 full-time, 198 part-time undergraduate, and 64 graduate students. A faculty of 34 full-time and 34 part-time gives a faculty-student ratio of 1-17. Air Force and Army ROTC programs available. See also information in University Park Campus description.

Entrance Requirements: Accredited high school graduation or GED; admission requirements vary throughout the university system; applicants selected from those who have demonstrated by secondary school records and SAT scores that they are adequately prepared for this university; ACT may be submitted; highest qualified are admitted first, following in descending order; when openings at one location of the university are filled, qualified applicants will be notified of campuses where openings still exist; minimum 15 high school units, varying depending on the college desired, liberal arts: 4 English, 3 mathematics, 3 arts/humanities/social science, 3 science, 2 foreign language; rolling admission, midyear admission, and advanced placement plans available; $35 application fee.

Costs Per Year: $4,808 state resident tuition; $7,400 nonresident tuition; $70 computer fee.

Collegiate Environment: The 48-acre campus has a 27,890-volume library. Dormitory housing is not available. Average freshmen scores were SAT Verbal 423, Math 485. 82% of applicants are accepted. Financial aid is available and 73% of students receive some form of financial assistance.

Community Environment: See Wilkes University.

PENN STATE UNIVERSITY, WORTHINGTON-SCRANTON CAMPUS   *(G-16)*
120 Ridge View Drive
Dunmore, Pennsylvania 18512
Tel: (717) 963-4757

Description: This publicly supported, coeducational campus of the Pennsylvania State University opened in 1968 and is accredited by the Middle States Association of Colleges and Schools. It offers two-year Associate degree programs and the first two years of most Penn State Baccalaureate programs. It operates on the early semester system and offers two summer sessions. Enrollment includes 841 full-time, 427 part-time undergraduate, and 219 graduate students. A faculty of 47 full-time and 34 part-time gives a faculty-student ratio of 1-20. Air Force and Army ROTC programs are available. See also information in University Park Campus description.

Entrance Requirements: Accredited high school graduation or GED; admission requirements vary throughout the university system; applicants selected from those who have demonstrated by secondary school records and SAT scores that they are adequately prepared for this university; ACT scores may be submitted; highest qualified are admitted first, following in descending order; when openings at one location of the university are filled, qualified applicants will be notified of campuses where openings still exist; minimum 15 high school units, varying depending on the college desired, liberal arts: 4 English, 3 mathematics, 3 arts/humanities/social science, 3 science, 2 foreign language; rolling admission, midyear admission, and advanced placement plans available; $35 application fee.

Costs Per Year: $4,808 state resident tuition; $7,400 nonresident tuition; $70 computer fee.

Collegiate Environment: The college has a 43,179-volume library. Average freshmen scores were SAT Verbal 423, Math 485. 79% of applicants are accepted. Financial aid is available, and 65% of students receive some form of financial assistance.

Community Environment: See University of Scranton.

PENN STATE UNIVERSITY, YORK CAMPUS   *(M-12)*
1031 Edgecomb Avenue
York, Pennsylvania 17403
Tel: (717) 771-4040

Description: This publicly supported, coeducational campus of the Pennsylvania State University opened in 1956 and is accredited by the Middle States Association of Colleges and Schools. It offers two-year Associate degree programs and the first two years of most Penn State Baccalaureate programs. It operates on the early semester system and offers two summer sessions. Enrollment includes 872 full-time, 996 part-time undergraduate, and 156 graduate students. A faculty of 50 full-time and 66 part-time gives a faculty-student ratio of 1-21. See also information in University Park Campus description.

Entrance Requirements: Accredited high school graduation or GED; admission requirements vary throughout the university system; applicants selected from those who have demonstrated by secondary school records and SAT scores that they are adequately prepared for this university; ACT scores may be submitted; highest qualified are admitted first, following in descending order; when openings at one location of the university are filled, qualified applicants will be notified of campuses where openings still exist; minimum 15 high school units, varying depending on the college desired, liberal arts: 4 English, 3 mathematics, 3 arts/humanities/social science, 3 science, 2 foreign language; rolling admission, midyear admission, and advanced placement plans available; $35 application fee.

Costs Per Year: $4,808 state resident tuition; $7,400 nonresident tuition; $70 computer fee.

Collegiate Environment: The 33-acre campus is located in a residential area and has a library containing 35,929 volumes, a main classroom building with a conference center, a science and technology building, and a student community center complete with a gymnasium. 89% of applicants are accepted. Average freshmen scores were SAT Verbal 423, Math 485. Financial aid is available, and 48% of students receive some form of financial assistance.

Community Environment: York is in one of the fastest growing areas in Pennsylvania. Situated at the junction of I-83 and U.S. Route 30, it is convenient to nearby attractions such as Gettysburg, Lancaster, Hershey, Philadelphia, Baltimore, and Washington DC. York itself has a rich heritage and is the site where the Continental Congress adopted the Articles of Confederation that first described the colonies as the United States of America. City parks provide recreational facilities.

PENNSYLVANIA COLLEGE OF OPTOMETRY   *(M-17)*
1200 West Godfrey Avenue
Philadelphia, Pennsylvania 19141
Tel: (215) 276-6262

Description: This privately supported, coeducational optometry college was founded in 1919 and awards the degrees of Doctor of Optometry, Bachelor of Science, Master of Science in Visual Rehabilitation, Master of Education in Education of Visually Handicapped. It is accredited by the Middle States Association of Colleges and Schools, the Council on Optometric Education and the Council on Clinical Optometric Care of the American Optometric Association. Enrollment includes 265 men and 328 women full-time in the professional/O.D. program with 70 graduate students. The faculty includes 51 full-time and 30 part-time members. The college operates on the quarter system and offers one summer session.

Entrance Requirements: Completion of minimum three years of preoptometric study in an accredited college or university to include a minimum of 90 semester or 135 quarter credits of the following courses: one year each of English, mathematics (suggest calculus), chemistry, organic chemistry, biology or zoology, and physics. Prerequisites to include at least 1 semester or two quarters of microbiology or bacteriology, psychology and statistics. The natural science course should have appropriate laboratory experience. Additional courses in anatomy, cell biology, physiology and related subjects

strongly reccommended. Basis for selection: Preprofessional college achievement, faculty recommendations, entrance examination, personal achievements and an interview.

Costs Per Year: $16,700 tuition; $3,150 room and board; $160 student fees.

Collegiate Environment: The main college building is located on a 13-acre campus in the Oak Lane residential section. The Library contains 15,821 volumes, 970 audio, 330 periodicals. Two student apartment buildings contain single apartments providing housing for 194 students. There are 18 apartments for married students. Approximately 49% of students applying for admission are accepted. Special financial aid is available and 85% of the students receive some form of college based assistance. The Eye Institute of the Pennyslvania College of Optometry, located on campus, has been in operation since 1978. This clinical facility provides expanded eye care and health services to citizens of the Philadelphia and Delaware Valley area.

Community Environment: The Pennsylvania College of Optometry is located on a 13 acre campus in Philadelphia's residential Oak Lane section, approximately one mile south of suburban Montgomery County.

PENNSYLVANIA COLLEGE OF PODIATRIC MEDICINE   *(M-17)*
Eighth and Race Streets
Philadelphia, Pennsylvania 19107
Tel: (215) 629-0300; (800) 220-3338

Description: Privately supported, coeducational professional college is one of seven colleges of podiatric medicine in the United States. It was founded in 1963 by a group of interested podiatric physicians who recognized the need for such a school in the Delaware Valley area. The college is chartered by the Commonwealth of Pennsylvania and is fully approved by the Department of Education and accredited by the Council on Podiatric Medicine Education of the American Podiatric Medical Association. The Doctor of Podiatric Medicine (D.P.M.) is offered to students completing the four-year course of instruction. There are 294 men and 150 women enrolled. Faculty number 33 full-time and 62 part-time, giving a faculty-student ratio of 1-4. There are joint D.P.M./Ph.D. degree programs with the University of Pennsylvania and Drexel University.

Entrance Requirements: Approved high school graduation and a minimum of 90 undergraduate semester hours of college work including 8 semester hours general or inorganic chemistry, 8 organic chemistry, 8 biology or zoology, 8 physics or mathematics, 6 English, MCAT required; rolling admission; Applications may be obtained by writing to the American Association of Colleges of Podiatric Medicine Application Service at, 1350 Piccard Drive, Suite 322, Rockville, MD, 20850, (800) 922-9266.

Costs Per Year: $17,375 tuition; $18,375 out-of-state tuition.

Collegiate Environment: The college is located in Philadelphia's historic downtown section. 72 apartments are available in the college complex. The library contains more than 23,000 bound volumes, as well as all major medical periodicals, 9,603 bound periodicals, 253 microforms, 982 audiovisual materials. Three other medical libraries are open to students of the college. Special facilities include the Foot and Ankle Institute, Gait Study Center, and the Video Histology Laboratory. 33% of applicants are accepted. About 90% of the students receive some form of financial assistance.

Community Environment: See Temple University.

PENNSYLVANIA COLLEGE OF TECHNOLOGY   *(H-12)*
One College Avenue
Williamsport, Pennsylvania 17701
Tel: (717) 326-3761; (800) 367-9222

Description: Formerly the Williamsport Area Community College, Pennsylvania College of Technology is a comprehensive two-year institution, an affiliate of the Pennsylvania State University (Penn State), which is accredited by the Middle States Association of Colleges and Schools. It has a national reputation for the quality and diversity of its educational programs in traditional and advanced technologies. The college grants the Associate and Bachelor degrees. Certificate and continuing education programs are also available. Enrollment includes 4,300 students. A faculty of 204 gives a faculty-student ratio of 1-18. The school operates on the semester system and offers two summer sessions.

Entrance Requirements: High school graduation or satisfactory performance on GED Test. Open enrollment policy; entrance exam required. Early admission, early decision, rolling admission, midyear admission, and advanced placement plans available. $35 application fee.

Costs Per Year: $5,800 tuition; $7,000 out-of-state tuition; $3,800 room and board; $800 books and supplies; $1,800 other expenses.

Collegiate Environment: Dormitory facilities are not provided by the college. Privately owned housing is available adjacent to the university. New facilities include a $6 million aviation center, $11 million community arts center, and a new diesel center at the Earth Science Center. Scholarships are available and 70% of students receive some form of financial aid.

Community Environment: See Lycoming College.

PHILADELPHIA COLLEGE OF BIBLE *(M-17)*
Langhorne Manor
Langhorne, Pennsylvania 19047-2990
Tel: (215) 752-5800; (800) 366-0049; Fax: (215) 752-5812

Description: The privately supported, coeducational Bible college is an interdenominational, undergraduate, four-year collegiate-level professional school, designed basically to prepare young people for Christian vocations, with courses leading to the B.S. degree in Bible. Five-year dual degree programs leading to the Bachelor's degree in Music, Teacher Education, and Social Work are also offered. The college represents a merger, in 1951, of the Bible Institute of Pennsylvania, founded in 1913, and the Philadelphia School of the Bible, founded in 1914. It is an accredited member of the American Association of Bible Colleges and of the Middle States Association of Colleges and Schools, the National Association of Schools of Music, the Council on Social Work Education, and the Association of Christian Schools International. On the state level the college is approved by the State Council on Education Commonwealth of Pennsylvania. It operates on the semester system and offers three summer terms. Enrollment includes 831 full-time and 219 part-time students. A faculty of 36 full-time and 9 part-time gives a faculty-student ratio of 1-15. The Bible College is not affiliated with any one particular denomination; there are over 60 denominations represented in the student body. Its purpose is to provide a quality college education in both the liberal arts and Biblical arts in a dynamic intellectual, and pragmatic climate. Special programs include study in Israel, Bible ministries and an extensive music program. A cooperative program with Bucks County Community College makes an Associate of Arts in Business degree possible. Air Force, Army, and Navy ROTC programs are available through nearby colleges.

Entrance Requirements: High school graduation or equivalent; recommended completion of 15 units including 4 English, 2 foreign language, 1 mathematics, 2 science, and 3 social science; SAT or ACT required; $15 application fee; early admission, early decision, and rolling admission plans available.

Costs Per Year: $7,800 tuition; $4,444 room and board; $260 student fees.

Collegiate Environment: The eight educational buildings are clustered together and contain a library of 86,000 volumes, 500 periodicals, 18,000 microforms, and 3,000 audiovisual materials. Living accommodations are provided for 372 students. Students from other geographical locations are accepted as well as midyear students. Financial aid is available for economically disadvantaged students and 87% of the students receive some form of financial assistance. There are 40 scholarships available, 15 for freshmen. Average high school standings of the current freshman class: 46% in the top fifth, 22% in the second fifth, 15% in the third fifth, 8% in the fourth fifth. About 75% of the freshmen returned to this campus for the second year.

Community Environment: The College is located on a 105-acre wooded campus in Langhorne Manor, a suburban community in Lower Bucks County, Pennsylvania.

Branch Campuses: Wisconsin Wilderness campus, Cable, WI; New Jersey campus, Liberty Corner, NJ.

PHILADELPHIA COLLEGE OF OSTEOPATHIC MEDICINE
(M-17)
4170 City Avenue
Philadelphia, Pennsylvania 19131
Tel: (215) 871-1000; (800) 999-6998; Admissions: (215) 871-6700; Fax: (215) 871-6719

Description: Privately supported, coeducational osteopathic college, founded in 1899, dates its current corporate functioning from a merger of the Osteopathic Hospital of Philadelphia and the Osteopathic Foundation of Philadelphia. It is accredited by the American Osteopathic Association and the Department of Education, Commonwealth of Pennsylvania. There are 808 students enrolled. Full-time faculty numbers 75 members. The college operates on the trimester term system and grants the Doctor of Osteopathy degree.

Entrance Requirements: Accredited high school graduation; completion of Baccalaureate degree at an accredited college of arts and sciences; completion of required college semester-hour courses of 6 English, 8 biology, 8 inorganic chemistry, 8 organic chemistry, 8 mathematics, 8 physics; Medical College Admission Tests required; $50 application fee.

Costs Per Year: $20,500 tuition; $50 student fees; microscopes required for first year students.

Collegiate Environment: Philadelphia College of Osteopathic Medicine is the largest of 16 osteopathic medical colleges in the United States. The college forms the hub of an osteopathic medical center which is comprised of Evans Hall, a seven-level classroom, library, laboratory and research building; a 250-bed hospital and an administration building. The library contains 75,000 volumes, 785 periodicals, 5,000 audiovisual materials. Since its founding PCOM has strongly emphasized community service along with the education of osteopathic physicians. Today the college operates six health care centers--five in urban Philadelphia and one rural center. These centers provide comprehensive health care to physician-poor areas and provide education in general medicine for students. The five inner-city centers, provide services for 100,000 outpatients a year. With the opening of a rural health, outreach and training center in Laporte in 1970, the college began an expanded program of rural health care delivery. This primary health care center provides students with in-service training, experience and exposure to the practice of rural medicine. 25% of applicants are accepted. Scholarships are available and 95% of students receive some form of financial aid.

Community Environment: See Temple University.

PHILADELPHIA COLLEGE OF PHARMACY AND SCIENCE
(M-17)
600 South 43rd Street
Philadelphia, Pennsylvania 19104-4495
Tel: (215) 596-8810; Fax: (215) 895-1100

Description: This privately supported, coeducational professional college was established in 1821 and was the first college of pharmacy in North America. It is accredited by the Middle States Association of Colleges and Schools. The college operates on the semester system and offers two summer sessions. Undergraduate enrollment includes 673 men and 1,108 women full-time and 4 men and 3 women part-time. A faculty of 140 full-time and 40 part-time gives a faculty-student ratio of 1-13. An Army ROTC program is available at the University of Pennsylvania.

Entrance Requirements: High school graduation or equivalent; completion of 16 units including 4 English, 3 mathematics including 2 algebra and plane geometry, 3 science including biology, chemistry and physics, 2 social science and 4 humanities; minimum: SAT verbal 400 and math 500 (Physical Therapy major SAT verbal 450, math 500) or ACT 22 required; rolling admission plan available; $25 application fee.

Costs Per Year: $11,200 tuition; $4,050 room and board; $75 student fee; $1,700 average additional expenses.

Collegiate Environment: The 15 present buildings of the college are located in the university section of Philadelphia. The college library contains 72,000 volumes, 3,000 pamphlets, 820 periodicals, 415 microforms and 1,400 audiovisuals. Dormitories are available for 650 students. Classes begin in September and midyear students are not accepted. Financial aid is available for economically disadvantaged students. 75% of students receive financial aid.

Community Environment: See University of Pennsylvania.

PHILADELPHIA COLLEGE OF TEXTILES AND SCIENCE
(M-17)
School House Lane and Henry Avenue
Philadelphia, Pennsylvania 19144
Tel: (215) 951-2800; Fax: (215) 951-2907

Description: This independent institution offering a career-oriented curriculum was founded in 1884 to educate professionals for the textile industry. Since then, the college has expanded to encompass programs in architecture, business, fashion, design and science. It is fully accredited by the Middle States Association of Colleges and Schools. The Bachelor of Science Degree is awarded for 21 different majors. Graduate degrees offered include the Master of Business Administration, Master of Textiles and the Master of Science in Computer Education. Student services include academic advising, comprehensive counseling, tutoring, health services and career planning and placement. An extensive cooperative education program is available to all undergraduates. Extracurricular activities are provided through an active student government and a wide variety of social, professional and religious clubs. The college has sixteen varsity men's and women's intercollegiate athletic teams, and offers a substantial intramural sports program. Student housing is provided. The college operates on the semester system and offers two summer sessions. Enrollment includes 1,714 full-time, 1,013 part-time undergraduates, 976 evening, and 581 graduate students. A faculty of 90 full-time and 75 part-time gives an undergraduate faculty-student ratio of 1-16.

Entrance Requirements: High school graduation or equivalent; completion of 15 unit college-preparatory program including 4 English and 3 mathematics including algebra 2; SAT or ACT required; rolling admission, and advanced placement plans available. $25 application fee.

Costs Per Year: $12,240 general tuition; $13,378 Architecture and Interior Design; $12,830 all other design majors; $12,240/year Physician Assistant first and second year students; $15,575/year Physician Assistant third and fouth year students; $2,764 residence hall, $3,970 townhouse; $2,734-$2,912 meal charges.

Collegiate Environment: The college is located on an 100-acre tree-lined campus in a quiet, residential area. The college buildings include a library of 85,000 volumes, 1,800 periodicals, 5,000 microforms and 5,740 audiovisual materials. College dormitories, apartments and townhouses accommodate 846 students. Campus news and sports information are provided by a weekly student newspaper. There are more than 40 student clubs and organizations on campus. Scholarships are available and more than 75% of the students receive financial aid. Approximately 72% of those who apply for admission are accepted, including midyear students. The average scores of entering freshmen were SAT 450 verbal, 510 math, and ACT 22 composite.

Community Environment: This suburban campus is 15 minutes from the heart of Philadelphia. See also Temple University.

PITTSBURGH THEOLOGICAL SEMINARY   *(K-2)*
616 North Highland Avenue
Pittsburgh, Pennsylvania 15206
Tel: (412) 362-5610

Description: The privately-supported, coeducational theological seminary was created in 1959 by the consolidation of the Pittsburgh-Xenia Theological Seminary (United Presbyterian Church of North America) and Western Theological Seminary (Presbyterian Church U.S.A.). The Seminary has adopted a wide range of degree options planned to meet individual varying vocational intentions of students and diverse needs of the Church's ministry. There are ten degree programs: Master of Arts (M.A.) and Master of Divinity (M.Div.); Master of Divinity/Master of Social Work (M.Div./M.S.W.), Master of Divinity/Master of Business Admin. (M.Div./M.B.A.), Master of Divinity/Master of Health Admin. (M.Div./M.H.A. or M.P.H.) and the Master of Divinity/Master of Library Science (M.Div./M.L.S.), offered jointly with the University of Pittsburgh; the Master of Divinity/Juris Doctor (M.Div./J.D.) and the Master of Arts (Religious Education) Church Music (MA/MA) offered in conjunction with Duquesne University; and the Master of Science in Public Management and Policy (M.Div./M.S.) offered in conjunction with Carnegie

Mellon University; Doctor of Ministry (D.Min.); and the Doctor of Philosophy (Ph.D.), which is offered in cooperation with the University of Pittsburgh. The Seminary is affiliated with the Pittsburgh Council on Higher Education (PCHE), the American Schools of Oriental Research, and the Arsenal Family and Children's Center. It operates on a quarter system, with no summer sessions, and is accredited by the Middle States Association of Colleges and Secondary Schools, and the Association of Theological Schools in the United States and Canada. There are 343 students enrolled with a faculty of 20 full-time and 13 part-time professors.

Entrance Requirements: Baccalaureate degree from an accredited college or university; $25 application fee; 500-1000 word statement describing motives for entering the ministry; results of mental capacity and psychological tests may be required.

Costs Per Year: $5,292 tuition; $3,195 board and room; $24 student fee.

Collegiate Environment: The seminary is located in the heart of the metropolitan center and contains new modern buildings of American Colonial Design. The seminary library contains over 220,000 volumes and living accommodations both dormitories and apartments are available on campus. The seminary welcomes a geographically diverse student body and accepts 70% of students applying for admission.

Community Environment: See University of Pittsburgh, Pittsburgh Campus.

POINT PARK COLLEGE   *(K-2)*
201 Wood Street
Pittsburgh, Pennsylvania 15222
Tel: (412) 392-3430; (800) 321-0129; Fax: (412) 391-1980

Description: The privately supported, coeducational college was established in 1960 and is accredited by the Middle States Association of Colleges and Schools. The college operates on the semester system and also provides evening and 3 summer sessions. Enrollment includes 1,071 full-time, 1,246 part-time undergraduate, and 80 graduate students. A faculty of 77 full-time and 142 part-time gives a faculty student ratio of 1-14.

Entrance Requirements: Completion of 16 units including 4 English, 2 mathematics, 2 laboratory science, 4 social science; SAT or ACT required; non high school graduates with GED considered; early admission, rolling admission, midyear admission, and advanced placement plans available; $20 undergraduate application fee, $30 graduate application fee.

Costs Per Year: $9,700 tuition; $4,830 room and board; $50 activity fee; $300 college fee.

Collegiate Environment: College facilites include a library of 127,294 volumes and 600 periodicals, and housing accommodations for 465 students with single, double, triple, and married student options. Approximately 82% of those who apply for admission are accepted, including midyear students. 82% of students receive financial aid.

Community Environment: The college is centrally located in the city of Pittsburgh, population 365,000. See also University of Pittsburgh, Pittsburgh Campus.

READING AREA COMMUNITY COLLEGE   *(K-15)*
10 South Second Street
P.O. Box 1706
Reading, Pennsylvania 19603
Tel: (610) 372-4721; (800) 626-1665; Fax: (610) 375-8255

Description: This publicly supported community college was founded in 1971 and is accredited by the Middle States Association of Colleges and Schools. It operates on the trimester system and has two summer sessions. The college is coeducational and offers programs in over forty areas of study, leading to an associate degree. Enrollment includes 1,733 full-time and 1,500 part-time students. A faculty of 59 full-time and 190 part-time gives a faculty-student ratio of 1-20.

Entrance Requirements: High school graduate or equivalent; open enrollment; early admission, rolling admission plans available.

Costs Per Year: $1,710 tuition; $3,420 out-of-district; $5,070 out-of-state; $60 student fees for district residents, $120 for all others.

Collegiate Environment: The campus is located in Reading and has a very diverse student population. There are a variety of student activities and sports, including basketball, cross-country, soccer, and volleyball at the varsity level. The library has 25,541 volumes, 284 periodicals, and 6,500 microforms.

Community Environment: Reading is located about 60 miles north of Philadelphia (see Albright College) and approximately 2 1/2 hours by bus or car to New York City.

REFORMED PRESBYTERIAN THEOLOGICAL SEMINARY
(K-2)
7418 Penn Avenue
Pittsburgh, Pennsylvania 15208-2594
Tel: (412) 731-8690

Description: The privately supported graduate theological seminary grants the Master of Divinity. Since its founding in 1810, the seminary has been under the direct control of the Synod of the Reformed Presbyterian Church of North America. It operates on the quarter system and offers one summer session. Enrollment includes 30 men full-time and 49 men and 11 women part-time. A faculty of 6 full-time and 2 part-time gives a faculty-student ratio of 1-8.

Entrance Requirements: Bachelor's degree or its equivalent from a college or university recognized by the United States Office of Education; minimum of one year of Greek recommended; psychological testing required; rolling admission and midyear admission plans available; letter of recommendation from church official required. $15 application fee.

Costs Per Year: $4,200 tuition; $3,600 room and board; $300 student fees.

Collegiate Environment: The seminary occupies the former Durbin Horne Estate, located near the eastern edge of the city. It contains a library of 40,000 volumes, 215 periodicals, 63 microforms and 824 audiovisual materials. There are dormitory facilities for 16 men. 90% of applicants are accepted. Scholarships are available and 25% of the current student body received aid. The Seminary awarded 8 Professional degrees to a recent graduating class.

Community Environment: See University of Pittsburgh, Pittsburgh Campus.

ROBERT MORRIS COLLEGE   *(K-2)*
Narrows Run Road
Coraopolis, Pennsylvania 15108
Tel: (412) 262-8200; (800) 762-0097; Fax: (412) 262-8619

Description: The privately supported, coeducational four-year college was founded in 1921. The college is accredited by the Middle States Association of Colleges and Schools. The College awards the Associates degree in Liberal Arts, Business, Administration/Administrative Services, the Bachelor of Science degree in Business Administration, Bachelor of Arts in English Communication, English Education, and Communication Education at the secondary level, the M.B.A., and the M.S. degree in Business Administration, Business Education and Taxation. The undergraduate school operates on the semester system, the graduate school on the term system, and the college provides evening and summer sessions. Enrollment includes 2,643 full-time, 1,739 part-time undergraduate, and 964 graduate students. A faculty of 134 full-time and 158 part-time gives a faculty-student ratio of 1-21. Air Force and Army ROTC programs are available off campus.

Entrance Requirements: High school graduation or equivalent; SAT or ACT required; early admission, midyear admission, rolling admission, and advanced placement plans available; $20 application fee.

Costs Per Year: $6,540 tuition; $4,326 room and board; $330 student fees.

Collegiate Environment: The 230-acre suburban campus is situated in the western part of the metropolitan area of Pittsburgh and includes a classroom cluster; a library of 122,645 bound volumes, 874 periodicals, 10,655 media pieces, and 290,763 microform items; computer centers at both locations; dormitory facilities for 911 students; a dining service building; a physical education building with an outdoor pool; a student union building with bowling and recreation room; and Sewall Center, a multiuse facility. The Pittsburgh Center features a college atmosphere in a business setting for 2,500 students. Located

in the center of the business district, facilities include an eight-story classroom building, a four-story administration complex, a library, and an academic and student services annex. Approximately 89% of freshmen applying for admission are accepted, including midyear students. Financial aid is available.

Community Environment: See University of Pittsburgh, Pittsburgh Campus.

ROSEMONT COLLEGE   *(M-17)*
Wendover Road & Montgomery Avenue
Rosemont, Pennsylvania 19010
Tel: (610) 527-0200; (800) 331-0708; Admissions: (610) 526-2966; Fax: (215) 527-0341

Description: This privately supported, Roman Catholic, liberal arts college for women was founded in 1921 by the Religious of the Society of the Holy Child Jesus. Chartered in 1921, the college is accredited by the Middle States Association of Colleges and Schools and by the National Catholic Educational Association. It operates on the semester system and offers two summer sessions. Enrollment is 500 women full-time and 150 part-time. A faculty of 42 full-time and 40 part-time gives a faculty-student ratio of 1-12. The college welcomes qualified students from all economic, social, religious, and racial groups.

Entrance Requirements: Accredited high school graduation or equivalent required with rank in upper 50% of graduating class strongly recommended; completion of 16 units including 4 English, 2 mathematics, 2 foreign language, 2 laboratory science, and 2 social science; SAT required; $35 application fee; early admission, rolling admission, delayed admission and advanced placement plans available.

Costs Per Year: $11,980 tuition; $6,100 room and board; $425 student fees; $1,400 average additional expenses.

Collegiate Environment: Located just 11 miles west of metropolitan Philadelphia, the 56 acres of scenic woodland campus provide an unusually attractive setting for the 18 college buildings. The college library contains 154,626 volumes, 525 periodicals and 23,382 microforms. Dormitory facilities accommodate 500 women for all four years. The academic resources of the college are augmented by its participation with Villanova University, Eastern College and Cabrini College in certain shared courses of study. The college welcomes a geographically diverse student body and will accept midyear students. Approximately 70% of students applying for admission are accepted. 90% of the previous freshman class returned to this campus for the second year of studies. About 60% of a recent freshman class graduated in the top half of the high school class. The average SAT scores of the current freshman were 490 verbal, 490 math. Scholarships are available. Over 60% of the current student body receives some form of financial aid.

Community Environment: See Villanova University.

SAINT FRANCIS COLLEGE   *(K-7)*
Loretto, Pennsylvania 15940
Tel: (814) 472-3100

Description: The privately supported, Catholic, coeducational liberal arts college was founded in 1847 and is sponsored by the Franciscan Friars of the Third Order Regular. It operates on the semester basis and also offers two summer terms. A recent enrollment included 1,100 students and a faculty of 80. An additional 239 are enrolled in graduate programs. The college is accredited by the Middle States Association of Colleges and Schools and grants the Associate, Bachelor and Master degrees. The college provides an honors program for the academically talented students as well as support services through the Learning Resource Center and ACT 101 (PA) Program, and Career Planning and Placement for four years.

Entrance Requirements: Approved high school graduation; completion of 16 college-preparatory units including 4 English, 2 mathematics, 1 science, 2 social science, 7 academic electives; SAT or ACT required; students can be accepted to the college at midyear; $20 application fee; early admission, rolling admission, deferred admission, advanced placement plans available. Additional high school math and science is required for those pursuing degrees in math, science, engineering or health careers.

Costs Per Year: $9,696 tuition; $4,490 room and board; student fees $688; books $420; miscellaneous $1,020.

Collegiate Environment: The college library contains 178,000 volumes, 1,300 periodicals, 100 microforms and 1,000 sound recordings. Residence halls are provided for 410 men and 420 women and 9 apartments are available. Four year guaranteed on-campus housing is available. There are four national fraternities. There are 3 national sororities. Students from other geographical locations are accepted as well as midyear students. 38% of current students are from out-of-state. Financial aid and merit-based scholarships are available. The college provides a comprehensive Division I athletic program for men and women (Division III football) and an extensive intramural program available.

Community Environment: Population 1,599. Loretto was founded in 1799 as a Catholic colony by Prince Gallitzin, a priest later disinherited by the Russian emperor because of his religion. The town was also the home of Charles Schwab, the steel magnate. The town is located in the central part of the state between Altoona and Johnstown. The climate is moderate. Railroad and airlines serve the nearby community of Johnstown and Altoona.

SAINT JOSEPH'S UNIVERSITY   *(M-17)*
5600 City Avenue
Philadelphia, Pennsylvania 19131
Tel: (610) 660-1300

Description: Privately supported, coeducational liberal arts Jesuit university that was founded in 1851 under the auspices of the Roman Catholic Church. It is accredited by the Middle States Association of Colleges and Schools. The college operates on the semester system and offers two summer sessions. Cooperative education programs are available in food marketing, chemistry, and physics. Study abroad is available to London, England; Strasbourg, France; Mexico City, Mexico; Tokyo, Japan; and Quebec. Air Force ROTC is available. Formerly an all-male college, the school became coeducational in 1970. Enrollment includes 2,490 full-time and 1,136 part-time undergraduates and 3,145 graduate students. A faculty of 156 full-time and 215 part-time gives an undergraduate faculty-student ratio of 1-16. The university grants the Certificate, Associate, Bachelor and Master's degrees.

Entrance Requirements: Approved high school graduation with rank in upper 40% of graduating class; completion of 12 college-preparatory units including 4 English, 3 mathematics, 3 modern foreign language, 2 science, and 3 social science; $30 application fee; early admission, competitive admission, rolling admission, delayed admission, and advanced placement programs available.

Costs Per Year: $12,650 tuition; $5,600 room and board; $1,000 average additional expenses.

Collegiate Environment: The college is located on 52 acres and is comprised of 51 buildings. Its library contains 317,000 volumes and 1,800 periodicals. Dormitory facilities are provided for 1,460 students. 78% of applicants are accepted. 80% of students receive financial aid. Students from other geographical locations are accepted, and there are no religious or racial requirements for admission. Semesters begin in September, and freshmen are accepted at midyear.

Community Environment: See Temple University.

SAINT VINCENT COLLEGE   *(K-4)*
Latrobe, Pennsylvania 15650
Tel: (412) 539-9761; Admissions: (412) 537-4540; Fax: (412) 537-4554

Description: Saint Vincent is a privately supported Roman Catholic liberal arts college for men and women. St. Vincent Archabbey and College was founded in 1846 and is sponsored by Catholic Benedictine Monks. It operates on the semester system and offers seven summer terms. It is accredited by the Middle States Association of Colleges and Schools. Enrollment includes 548 men and 529 women full-time, and 70 men and 90 women part-time. A faculty of 74 full-time and 32 part-time evening gives a faculty-student ratio of 1-15. The college offers a cooperative program with Seton Hill College. In addition to the regular liberal arts programs, St. Vincent sponsors a graduate professional School of Theology. The basic three-year program leads to the M.Div. degree. Air Force ROTC is available through cross enrollment at the University of Pittsburgh.

Entrance Requirements: High school graduation with rank in upper half of graduating class or GED; completion of 15 units, including 4 English, 2 mathematics, 2 foreign language, 1 laboratory science, and 3 social science; $25 application fee; early admission, early decision, rolling admission, delayed admission and advanced placement plans available.

Costs Per Year: $10,850 tuition; $3,962 room and board; $900 average additional expenses.

Collegiate Environment: The 100-acre campus is situated in the Laurel Highlands of Western Pennsylvania. The 23 college buildings include a library of 249,496 volumes, 862 periodicals, 98,601 microforms, and 3,312 audiovisual materials. Dormitory facilities are provided for 393 men and 409 women. Approximately 78% of students applying for admission are accepted, including midyear students. 84% of the previous freshman class returned to this campus for the sophomore year. The college has a special program for the educationally disadvantaged, as well as special tutoring programs. The college granted 250 Bachelor degrees to a recent graduating class. 22% of the students continued on to graduate school.

Community Environment: Population 10,813. Located at the foot of Chestnut Ridge in the Appalachian Mountains, Latrobe is an important steel center for 46 industries. The area is provided transportation by air, railroad and bus lines. There is a county airport adjacent. The community has a public library, churches and a synagogue for three major religious faiths. Good recreational facilities are located within the area. Some part-time employment is available.

SETON HILL COLLEGE   *(K-4)*
Seton Hill Drive
Greensburg, Pennsylvania 15601
Tel: (412) 838-4255

Description: Privately supported liberal arts college for women was founded in 1883 by the Sisters of Charity, under the auspices of the Roman Catholic Church, and operated as an academy for girls and a lower school for boys until rechartered in 1918. Today the college grants the following degrees: Bachelor of Arts; Bachelor of Science in Home Economics, Medical Technology, Biology and Chemistry; Bachelor of Music; and Bachelor of Fine Arts. Seton Hill is accredited by the Middle States Association of Colleges and Schools, the American Chemical Society, the National Association of Schools of Music, and the American Dietetic Association. The college operates on the semester system. Enrollment is 729 full-time and 308 part-time students. A faculty of 56 full-time and 49 part-time gives a faculty-student ratio of 1-13. The college offers a cooperative program with Saint Vincent College and a 3-2 program in Engineering with Georgia Institute of Technology, Pennsylvania State University and the University of Pittsburgh; a 2 plus 2 nursing program is offered. The college also provides several summer sessions. The Washington Semester, and United Nations Semester are offered by the college to qualified students. Men are admitted for matriculation to the School of Fine Arts. Army ROTC is available through the University of Pittsburgh.

Entrance Requirements: High school graduation; completion of 15 units including 4 English, 2 mathematics, 2 of same foreign language, 1 laboratory science, and 2 social science; SAT or ACT required; non-high school graduates may be admitted as unclassified students; $20 application fee; early decision, early admission, rolling admission, delayed admission and advanced placement plans available.

Costs Per Year: $9,712 tuition; $3,908 room and board; $100 student fees.

Collegiate Environment: Seton Hill's campus covers 200 acres. The college overlooks the city of Greensburg, county seat of Westmoreland County, and is 35 miles southeast of Pittsburgh, PA. The 20 college buildings include a library of 100,000 volumes, 530 periodical subscriptions, 4,600 microforms, and 3,600 records. Dormitory facilities will accommodate 550 students. The college welcomes qualified students of all faiths, races, and geographical locations. Approximately 80% of students applying for admission are accepted, including midyear students. Fall 1990 middle 50% freshman SAT score range was 410-510V, 420-540M. Financial aid is available and 73% of the current students receive aid. The college granted 111 Bachelor degrees in May 1990. Approximately 25% of the students continue on to graduate school.

Community Environment: Population 17,000. Located in the western Pennsylvania Laurel Highlands, the city was founded in 1787 by General Nathanael Greene. The annual mean temperature is 59.9 degrees, and the average rainfall is 50 inches. The city has many churches representing various denominations, a hospital, public library, YMCA, several civic and fraternal organizations, several shopping malls and an art museum. Local recreational facilities include a swimming pool, aerobic center, movie theaters, several major ski areas and golf courses. Part-time employment is available.

SHIPPENSBURG UNIVERSITY OF PENNSYLVANIA *(M-10)*
Shippensburg, Pennsylvania 17257
Tel: (717) 532-9121; (800) 822-8028; Fax: (717) 532-1273

Description: This state-supported, coeducational liberal arts university was founded in 1871. It operates on the semester system and offers three summer terms. The university is accredited by the Middle States Association of Colleges and Schools. Enrollment includes 5,288 men and women full-time, 289 part-time, and 1,026 graduate students. A faculty of 388 gives a faculty-student ratio of 1-19. The university grants Bachelors and Master's degrees.

Entrance Requirements: Approved high school graduation or equivalent with rank in upper 40% of graduating class; SAT required; MAT or GRE required for some programs; $20 application fee; rolling admission, early admission, delayed admission, and advanced placement plans available.

Costs Per Year: $3,086 tuition; $7,844 out-of-state; $3,504 room and board; $660 student fees; $1,000 average additional expenses.

Collegiate Environment: The university is located on a 200-acre campus adjacent to Shippensburg, 40 miles southwest of Harrisburg. The 35 university buildings include a library of 428,845 volumes, 1,758 periodicals, 1,433,831 microforms, and 13,882 audiovisual materials. Dormitory facilities are available for 999 men and 1,409 women. The fall term begins in September and students are admitted at the beginning of each semester. 57% of applicants are accepted. Financial aid is available. 67% of students receive financial aid.

Community Environment: Population 6,500. Located in south-central Pennsylvania, Shippensburg is a semirural community. The area has 32 churches of various denominations, a library, and many civic and fraternal organizations. Recreational facilities include fishing, hunting, swimming, football, baseball, parks, bowling, and a picnic pavilion. Limited part-time employment opportunities are available.

SLIPPERY ROCK UNIVERSITY OF PENNSYLVANIA *(H-2)*
Maltby Center
Slippery Rock, Pennsylvania 16057
Tel: (412) 738-2015; (800) 662-1102; Fax: (412) 738-2913

Description: Publicly supported, coeducational liberal arts and teachers university opened as a normal school in 1889. It became a four-year institution in 1926 and its present name was adopted in 1983. Today the university offers undergraduate degree programs toward the B.A. and B.S. degrees in the College of Arts and Sciences, College of Business and Information Science, College of Education, and the College of Health and Human Services. Graduate programs leading to the Master of Education, Master of Science, Master of Arts, and Master of Physical Therapy are offered also. The university is accredited by the Middle States Association of Colleges and Schools and by the National Council for the Accreditation of Teacher Education. It operates on the semester system and offers four summer sessions. Enrollment includes 5,817 full-time and 974 part-time undergraduate and 772 graduate students. A faculty of 376 full-time and 36 part-time gives an undergraduate faculty-student ratio of 1-20. The university offers studies abroad for International Education in conjunction with the Pennsylvania Consortium, and Army ROTC is available.

Entrance Requirements: High school graduation; completion of 16 college-preparatory units with recommended courses of 4 English, 3 mathematics, 2 foreign language, 3 laboratory science, 4 social science, and 1 elective; SAT or ACT required; $25 application fee; early decision, early admission, advanced placement, rolling admission and delayed admission plans available.

Costs Per Year: $3,086 tuition; $7,844 out-of-state; $3,374 room and board; $820 student fees; $500 average additional expenses.

Collegiate Environment: The university is located in the borough of Slippery Rock, which is in Butler County, Pennsylvania, on the western edge of the Allegheny Plateau at an elevation of approximately 1,300 feet above sea level. The university has a campus of over 600 acres approximately 50 miles north of Pittsburgh. Besides the 40 acres on which the present university plant of 34 buildings is located, there are extensive athletic fields and wide stretches of woodland. The library contains 485,047 volumes, 1,727 periodicals and 1,212,711 microforms, and dormitory facilities are provided for 2,700 men and women. In a cooperate program of collegiate education in the liberal arts and engineering at both Slippery Rock University and the Pennsylvania State University, a program has been established whereby the pre-engineering students may take a program in natural sciences at Slippery Rock in three years and engineering courses at Penn State in two years. Upon completion, the student will be granted two degrees: a liberal arts degree (B.A.) from Slippery Rock, and an Engineering Degree (B.S.) from Penn State. Slippery Rock is also a member of the Regional Council for International Education, which provides students an opportunity to study abroad during any year of university. The university accepts 60% of students applying for admission, including midyear students. About 95% of a recent freshman class graduated in the top 3/5ths of the high school class. The average SAT scores of the current freshmen were 415V, 461M; ACT 24. Financial aid is available for economically handicapped students, and 80% of the students receive assistance. The college granted 1,200 Bachelor and 130 Master degrees to a recent graduating class.

Community Environment: Population 5,000. Slippery Rock is located approximately an hour's drive from Pittsburgh. The climate is pleasant both in winter and in summer. There are several Protestant and Catholic churches in the community. The area has good highways and bus service. Local recreation includes hunting, fishing, boating, swimming, golf, and theatres, all easily accessible. Rooms are available in private homes. Many special interest and veteran's clubs are active in the community.

SUSQUEHANNA UNIVERSITY *(I-12)*
Selinsgrove, Pennsylvania 17870
Tel: (717) 374-0101

Description: A privately supported, coeducational, liberal arts college founded as the Missionary Institute of the Evangelical Lutheran Church in 1858. It became a pioneer in the field of coeducation by admitting women in 1873 and its present name was adopted in 1895. The university is accredited by the Middle States Association of Colleges and Schools and by the National Association of Schools of Music. It operates on the semester system and also provides one summer term. There are 1,354 students enrolled with a faculty of 110 full-time and 35 part-time members. The college offers a summer program at Oxford University in England and an academic cooperative plan with the University of Pennsylvania for engineering students. Army ROTC is available by a cross agreement through nearby Bucknell University.

Entrance Requirements: Accredited high school graduation with rank in upper half of graduating class; completion of 16 units including 4 English, 4 college-preparatory mathematics, 2 foreign languages, 3 laboratory science, 3 social science; SAT or ACT required; $25 application fee; rolling admission, early decision, deferred admission and advanced placement plans available.

Costs Per Year: $14,510 tuition; $4,200 board and room; $270 student fees; additional expenses average $1,200.

Collegiate Environment: The university is located on a 190-acre campus, approximately 50 miles north of Harrisburg. The more than 40 university buildings include a library of 145,000 volumes, 1,650 periodicals, 39,000 microforms and 7,000 sound recordings. Residential facilities are provided for 1,200 students including fraternities and sororities. Approximately 60% of students applying for admission are accepted. Financial aid is available and 88% of the current student body receive assistance.

Community Environment: Population 5,500. The beautiful Susquehanna River winds through this quiet town. Route 80 is one half hour north and the Pennsylvania Turnpike is one hour south of campus. Selinsgrove is 50 miles north of Harrisburg. Limited part-time employment is available.

SWARTHMORE COLLEGE   (M-17)
College Avenue
Swarthmore, Pennsylvania 19081
Tel: (610) 328-8000; Admissions: (610) 328-8300; Fax: (610) 328-8673

Description: This privately supported, coeducational liberal arts college was founded in 1864 by members of the Religious Society of Friends. Although it has been nonsectarian in control since the beginning of the present century, the college seeks to preserve the religious traditions out of which it grew. It is accredited by the Middle States Association of Colleges and Schools. The college operates on the semester system. Enrollment is 1,388 men and women. A faculty of 150 full-time and 20 part-time provides a faculty-student ratio of 1-9.

Entrance Requirements: Accredited high school graduation; completion of college-preparatory subjects with recommended courses in English, mathematics, foreign language, science, and social science; SAT I and 3 SAT II including writing exam required; $50 application fee; early decision, delayed admission, and advanced placement plans available.

Costs Per Year: $19,992 tuition; $6,880 room and board; $194 student fees.

Collegiate Environment: The college occupies a campus of about 300 acres of rolling, wooded land in and adjacent to the borough of Swarthmore in Delaware County, Pennsylvania. It is located in a residential suburb within half an hour's commuting distance of Philadelphia. Its location makes cooperation possible with three other nearby institutions: Bryn Mawr, and Haverford Colleges and the University of Pennsylvania. The 41 college buildings include libraries with total of 775,000 volumes, 78,000 pamphlets, 4,500 periodicals, 173,000 microforms and 14,000 sound recordings; and dormitory facilities for 1,300 men and women. The college welcomes a geographically diverse student body, and 29% of students applying for admission were accepted. Classes begin in September but transfer students may be accepted at midyear. 95% of the recent freshman class graduated in the top 1/5 of their high school class, and 82% ranked in the highest tenth. Financial aid is available to all students with need. About 43% of the students receive financial aid, including federal loan programs. Almost 95% of the freshmen return to this campus for their sophomore year.

Community Environment: Population 6,500, Swarthmore is a suburban area 11 miles from Philadelphia. The climate is temperate. There is bus and rail service to Philadelphia, New York and Washington. The immediate community has a library and churches of various denominations. There are hospitals nearby. For civic services, recreation and cultural facilities, see Philadelphia. Part-time employment is available. See also Temple University for information about Philadelphia.

TEMPLE UNIVERSITY   (M-17)
Broad Street and Montgomery Avenue
Philadelphia, Pennsylvania 19122
Tel: (215) 204-7200; Fax: (215) 204-5694

Description: The publicly supported, coeducational university was founded in 1884 and became a state-related institution in 1965. It was supported by income from endowments, yearly gifts from friends and corporations, and by annual appropriations from the Commonwealth of Pennsylvania. The university, like every major university, consists of a group of schools and colleges, each of which has one or more academic programs leading to an appropriate degree. The schools offering four-year Baccalaureate degrees include the College of Arts & Sciences, College of Engineering, Computer Sciences and Architecture, College of Education, School of Business and Management, School of Communications and Theater, College of Health, Physical Education, Recreation and Dance, School of Social Administration, Tyler School of Art, Esther Boyer College of Music, College of Allied Health Professions, School of Pharmacy, and the Department of Landscape Architecture and Horticulture. The schools offering advanced and professional degrees include the Graduate School in cooperation with the above-named colleges and schools, the School of Dentistry, the School of Law, and the School of Medicine. The Department of Landscape Archeitecture and Horticulture offers Associate degrees in both Horticulture and Landscape Design. The university operates on the early semester basis and also provides two summer terms. A senior unit of the Reserve Officer's Training Corps is maintained by the department of the Army. The university is accredited by the Middle States Association of Colleges and Secondary Schools and by respective professional and educational organizations. Total enrollment is 32,657.

Entrance Requirements: Accredited high school graduation with rank in upper 60% of graduating class; completion of 16 college-prepatory units, including a minimum of 4 English, 2 mathematics, 2 foreign language, 1 laboratory science, 1 social science. The SAT or ACT is required. Approximately 64% of students applying for admission are accepted, including midyear students. More than 75% of the previous freshman class returned to this campus for their sophomore year. About 80% of the recent student body graduated in the top half of their high school class, 60% in the top quarter, and 20% in the third quarter. The average SAT scores of the current freshman class were 460 Verbal and 504 Math. The university has a Special Recruitment and Admissions Program (SRAP) to fill the needs of high school graduates who are not likely to meet normal admission requirements; they must be highly motivated and recommended. The application fee is $30. Early admission, rolling admission, and advanced placement plans are available.

Costs Per Year: Average tuition $4,868 for Pennsylvania residents, $9,082 for out-of-state residents; $4,868 room and board.

Collegiate Environment: The academic program of Temple University is conducted on seven campuses, located in central and north Philadelphia, its nearby suburbs and in Tokyo, Japan. The Academic Center is located at a point approximating the geographic center of the Delaware Valley Region. One mile north of the Academic Center is the Health Sciences Center at Broad and Ontario Streets. The Schools of Medicine, Dentistry, Pharmacy, the College of Allied Health Professions, and the Temple University Hospital are located here. The Tyler School of Art has a 14-acre campus in Cheltenham Township just north of the Philadelphia city line. Several miles north, in Ambler, is the Ambler Campus of 186 acres. The Temple University Center City Campus is in the heart of downtown Philadelphia. The twelve university libraries house more than 2.1 million volumes, 1.6 million microforms, and have many other library materials available. Dormitory space for 3,600 men and women along with apartments adjacent to or on campus are available at the main campus. The university welcomes students from other geographical locations. The university also sponsors a summer programs in Rome, London, Dublin, Israel and Tokyo. The opportunity to study at the Temple Campus in Rome, Italy is offered to other qualified students. The university awarded 142 Associate, 3,672 Bachelor, 1,421 Doctorate, and 625 Professional degrees to its recent graduating class. Scholarships are available and approximately 70% of the students receive some form of financial assistance. The average amount of assistance is $2,500.

Community Environment: The population of the Philadelphia area is over 2,000,000. Birthplace of the Nation, Philadelphia has retained much of the charm of its colonial origins even while developing into one of the great industrial cities of the world. Distinctive colonial characteristics such as the Liberty Bell and Independence Hall blend with evidence of vast manufacturing. Narrow cobblestone streets may be found within blocks of the business district. The city has museums, churches of all denominations, YMCA, YWCA, and many libraries (including the first Free Library in the United States). All the cultural and community service facilities of a large metropolis are to be found here. Local recreation includes Fairmount Park, the largest city park in the United States, golfing, tennis, horseback riding, hunting, boating, fishing, swimming, the zoo, planetarium, theaters, major sports teams, and several collegiate sports.

THIEL COLLEGE   (G-2)
College Avenue
Greenville, Pennsylvania 16125
Tel: (412) 589-2345

Description: The privately supported, coeducational liberal arts college was founded in 1866 and is affiliated with the Lutheran Church in America. Its purpose is to afford to all students a liberal education in accordance with the Christian faith. It is accredited by the Middle States Association of Colleges and Schools. Enrollment is 416 men and 476 women full-time and 39 men and 104 women part-time. The school is on the semester system plus two summer terms. The Bachelor of Arts and Associate of Arts degrees are offered. The faculty has 61 full-time and 39 part-time members. Cooperative education programs are available in all subjects.

Entrance Requirements: High school graduation or equivalent; rank in upper 60% of graduating class; completion of 16 units including 4 English, 2 mathematics, 2 units in 1 foreign language, 2 science, 3 social science, $20 application fees; advanced placement, early decision, delayed admission, early admission, and rolling admission plans available. Personal interview is recommended.

Costs Per Year: $9,773 tuition; $4,505 board and room; $415 student fees; additional expenses average $800.

Collegiate Environment: The 135-acre campus has 38 buildings including the 125,000 volume library. The college library receives 813 periodicals annually and provides about 2,421 microforms and 4,093 recordings. Dormitories house 374 men and 504 women. Fraternities house an additional 144 students. Special financial aid is available and 90% of the current student body received some form of assistance. Midyear students are accepted and the college welcomes a geographically diverse student body. About 77% of the students applying for admission are accepted and 75% of the freshmen return for the sophomore year.

Community Environment: Local industry is devoted principally to the manufacture of steel, cars, tanks, structural steel and other steel and aluminum products. The community is served by railroad, bus lines, and airlines located at nearby Youngstown airport. Greenville has several churches, public library, hospital, a hotel and motels. Part-time employment is available. Local recreational facilities include a symphony orchestra, outdoor swimming pool. Nearby lakes provide boating, swimming, fishing, water skiing, and golf courses. There are various civic, fraternal, and veteran's organizations active in the community.

THOMAS JEFFERSON UNIVERSITY   (M-17)
11th and Walnut Sts.
Philadelphia, Pennsylvania 19107
Tel: (215) 955-6000

Description: This is a privately supported, coeducational university of health sciences. Since its founding, it was known as the Jefferson Medical College, but in 1969 Thomas Jefferson University was formed; it includes Jefferson Medical College, the College of Graduate Studies, the College of Allied Health Sciences, and Thomas Jefferson University Hospital. The college was established as a medical school in 1824 with additional space provided for an infirmary and dispensary. This was the first such clinic directly connected with a medical college anywhere in the world. It was the forerunner of the Jefferson Hospital which was opened in 1877. A nurses training school was founded in 1891 and postgraduate instruction was formalized as a college activity in 1949. The college and hospital with their ancillary services and related institutions today constitute one of America's most important medical centers. The university is accredited by the American Medical Association, National League for Nursing and the Middle States Association of Colleges and Secondary Schools. The university generally operates on the quarter system; howver, Allied Health operates on the early semester system and graduate studies operate on the semester system. Allied Health offers two summer sessions. Undergraduate enrollment, (Nursing and Allied Health) includes 622 full-time, 109 part-time and 440 evening students. The faculty-student ratio is 1-9 for the Medical School and 1-10 for Allied Health.

Entrance Requirements: The specific requirements of each branch of the University vary; contact Director of Admissions for specific school of interest; $40 application fee, Allied Health; $65 application fee, Medicine.

Costs Per Year: $20,650 Medical School; other tuitions and fees vary by program.

Collegiate Environment: The central plant consists of four large buildings joined either directly or by bridges; four other buildings are located nearby. Jefferson Alumni Hall, a structure which houses the Basic Science Departments and the Jefferson Commons, opened for college activities in the fall of 1968. A new clinical teaching hospital was opened in June 1978. The Orlowitz Residence Hall is a 20-floor apartment facility. The Barringer Residence Hall, which opened in 1976, is a 10-story, 138-apartment complex. The university library contains 130,000 books and bound journals, 1,880 current periodical subscriptions. In a cooperative effort between Jefferson Medical College and The Pennsylvania State University, selected students can earn both the Bachelor of Science and the Doctor of Medicine degrees

in six calendar years after graduating from high school. Students in this program spend the first two years on the University Park Campus and then proceed to Jefferson Medical College. A joint medical education program administered by the Delaware Institute of Medical Education and Research has been developed between Jefferson Medical College and the State of Delaware. Indiana University of Pennsylvania and Jefferson Medical College have established a cooperative Family Medicine Physician Education Program. Need-based financial aid is available.

Community Environment: See Temple University.

TYLER SCHOOL OF ART OF TEMPLE UNIVERSITY
(L-17)
Beech and Penrose Avenues
Elkins Park, Pennsylvania 19027
Tel: (215) 782-2828; Fax: (215) 782-2711

Description: Tyler is the school of art of Temple University, located on an independent campus in Elkins Park, a suburb of Philadelphia. Tyler offers both professional degrees in the visual arts, and the BFA and MFA in 8 different studio majors including Ceramics/Glass, Fibers/Fabric Design, Graphic Design, Jewelry/Metalsmithing, Painting, Photography, Printmaking and Sculpture. Since 1935 Tyler has brought together a faculty of practicing artists and craftspeople with highly motivated and talented students in an atmosphere rich with visual stimulation and influence. A summer program is available in Scotland. The school has a branch campus in Rome, Italy. Army ROTC is available. Teaching certification is also available. Current enrollment is 700 students with a faculty of 72.

Entrance Requirements: High school graduation or equivalent; completion of 16 units including 4 English, 2 mathematics, 2 language, 1 science, and 1 history; SAT with minimum combined score of 900, or ACT with minimum score of 21 required; personal art portfolio required; $30 application fee; midyear admission, rolling admission, advanced placement, and early decision plans available.

Costs Per Year: $6,140 tuition; $10,990 out-of-state; $5,282 room and board.

Collegiate Environment: Located on a fourteen-acre estate eight miles north of Temple's main campus, Tyler offers professional facilities for the painter, sculptor, designer and craftsperson. Extensive foundry facilities for casting and welding sculpture, five large well-lit studios exclusively for painters, stat cameras and a fully equipped offset printing facility enable the graphic artist to gain experience in all phases of graphic production. Tyler's metal studios offer the only fully equipped electroforming lab in the country. The campus galleries as well as the Tyler Gallery in center city exhibits a wide range of contemporary art with an international flavor. All of the studio and liberal art requirements are offered on the Elkins Park campus. The Tyler library contains more than 30,000 volumes, 100 periodicals, 1,200 microfilms and an extensive slide collection numbering over 223,000, and students have access to all of the library collection of the other colleges of the University. Dormitory facilities house 142 students. 46% of applicants are accepted.

Community Environment: See Temple University.

UNIVERSITY CENTER AT HARRISBURG   (L-12)
2986 N. Second St.
Harrisburg, Pennsylvania 17110
Tel: (717) 787-0866

Description: A privately supported, coeducational consortium. Five institutions participate in this coeducational center to provide a special source of educational competency for persons desiring to continue their higher education on a part-time, evening basis. Elizabethtown College, Lebanon Valley College, Temple University, the Pennsylvania State University, and the University of Pennsylvania are the participating institutions and all are accredited by the Middle States Association of Colleges and Schools. Founded in 1958, this center enrolls 400 men and 600 women on the semester system. Two summer terms are available. Two-year Associate degree programs are offered as well as four-year Baccalaureate programs and graduate programs leading to the Master's and several doctoral degrees. The degrees are granted by the home campus of the participating institution.

Entrance Requirements: In graduate, technical, adult education, and other such courses, the requirements are determined separately and the Office of the Director of the Center should be contacted for further information. Nondegree candidates (any adult or recent high school graduate) may be admitted as special students.

Costs Per Year: Varies with specific program.

Collegiate Environment: The school is situated on six acres. It has seven buildings including Richards Hall which houses the 4,000 volume library and book store. Freshman classes begin in September, January and June.

Community Environment: See Harrisburg Area Community College.

UNIVERSITY OF PENNSYLVANIA   *(M-17)*
1 College Hall
Philadelphia, Pennsylvania 19104-6376
Tel: (215) 898-7507

Description: The privately supported, coeducational Ivy-League university is an independent, nonsectarian institution of higher learning, founded in Philadelphia in 1740. It is privately endowed and gift-supported, though it is privileged to share in the educational appropriations of the commonwealth of Pennsylvania. It is accredited by the Middle States Association of Colleges and Schools and by respective professional and educational organizations. The university is a composite of schools. Four are devoted to undergraduate education and include the College of Arts and Sciences, Wharton School, the College of Engineering and Applied Science, and the School of Nursing. There are graduate and professional schools or divisions as follows: Graduate Faculty of Arts and Sciences, Graduate School of Education, Schools of Engineering, Wharton Graduate School, Annenberg School of Communications, School of Dental Medicine, School of Social Work, Law School, School of Veterinary Medicine, School of Medicine, Graduate School of Fine Arts, and School of Nursing - Graduate Division. The College of General Studies provides educational opportunities for those who must attend on a part-time basis. All schools are coeducational. The university grants Associate, Bachelor, Professional, Master, and Doctor degrees. Army, Air Force and Navy ROTC programs are available. Study abroad programs include a year or semester in Edinburgh, London, Madrid, Paris, Munich, Bologna, Levven, Rome, Prague, Moscow, St. Petersburg, Sri Lanka, Oaxaca, Nigeria, Tel Aviv, Tokyo, and China. The university operates on the semester system and offers two summer sessions. Enrollment is 9,493 full-time undergraduate students and 8,437 graduate students. A faculty of 2,132 full-time and 1,548 part-time gives a faculty-student ratio of 1-5.

Entrance Requirements: High school with high rank in graduating class; completion of college-preparatory program with recommended courses of 4 English, 3-4 mathematics, 3 foreign language, 3 lab science, and 3 social science; SAT or ACT and three Achievement Tests required; GRE, DAT, GMAT, MCAT, or LSAT required for graduate programs; $55 application fee; early admission, deferred admission, early decision and advanced placement program available.

Costs Per Year: $18,856 tuition and fees; $7,270 room and board.

Collegiate Environment: The university occupies a 260-acre campus in The University City section of Philadelphia, to which it moved in 1872 from its earlier location in the heart of Colonial Philadelphia. The university libraries include more than 4,209,747 books, 33,384 periodicals, and 2,824,013 microforms. The largest portion of the collection is housed in the Library Center, which includes the Van Pelt Library, opened in 1962, and the Dietrich Library, opened in the fall of 1967. Living accommodations are provided for undergraduates. New dormitories increased accommodations to 5,803 men and women and 125 families. Fraternities and sororities house an additional 620 students. 36% of applicants are accepted. The middle 50% range of scores for the entering freshman class was SAT 1200-1360 combined. All the states and more than 85 foreign countries are represented in the current student body. Classes begin in September and midyear freshmen are not accepted. Financial aid is available and based on need. 45% of students receive some form of financial aid.

Community Environment: Philadelphia is a large city with the feel of small villages; many with distinct characters. It is a center of history, culture and business, opera, symphony and ballet, museums, major sports teams and theater. The city is ideally located near both seashore and ski resorts.

UNIVERSITY OF PITTSBURGH AT BRADFORD   *(E-7)*
300 Campus Drive
Bradford, Pennsylvania 16701
Tel: (814) 362-7555; (800) 872-1787; Fax: (814) 362-7578

Description: The school is a publicly supported, coeducational regional college of the larger university. The Bradford campus opened in 1963, and offers a small college atmosphere in combination with the high academic qualities for which the university is known. It is fully accredited by the Middle States Association of Colleges and Schools and the National League for Nursing. Operating on a semester system with two summer sessions, the school awards the Bachelor and selected Associate degrees. Army ROTC is available. Enrollment includes 934 full-time and 400 part-time students. A faculty of 64 full-time and 25 part-time gives a faculty-student ratio of 1-14.

Entrance Requirements: High school graduation or GED required; SAT or ACT; high school preparation must include 15 units: 4 English, 2 math, 1 laboratory science, 1 social science, 2 history, and 4 academic electives; early admission, early decision, rolling admission, delayed admission, midyear admission, and advanced placement plans available; the school allows 60 credits by prior examination, such as CLEP; $35 application fee.

Costs Per Year: $4,962 tuition; $10,786 nonresidents; $4,030 room and board; $187 student fees.

Collegiate Environment: The 143-acre campus has an academic and a science complex as well as townhouse-style and garden apartment housing for 595 students; a sports center; and a student commons. In addition to the academic program, the school sponsors athletic, recreational, and cultural organizations and events to enhance the student's learning experiences. The Hanley Library houses 113,000 volumes, 650 periodicals, 27,000 microforms and 1,500 audiovisual aids. Of those applying, 70% are accepted. Scholarships are available for students requiring financial aid. 80% of the students receive some form of financial aid.

Community Environment: Bradford has a population of 12,000, and lies amid the Allegheny Mountains. This area is part of an expanding complex of recreational facilities. The proximity to Allegheny State Park, the Allegheny National Forest, and the Holiday Valley Resort provides opportunity for camping, hiking, fishing, and skiing. The town itself has a variety of industries, and is readily accessible by commercial transportation.

UNIVERSITY OF PITTSBURGH AT GREENSBURG   *(K-4)*
1150 Mount Pleasant Road
Greensburg, Pennsylvania 15601-5898
Tel: (412) 837-7040

Description: The state-supported, coeducational university offers courses in liberal arts, teacher education, engineering, health related professions and business, and awards the Bachelor degree in some of these areas. It is fully accredited by the Middle States Association of Colleges and Schools. The school, a regional campus of the University of Pittsburgh, provides the atmosphere of a small college while enabling its students to benefit from additional resources of the main campus. The trimester system is used and two summer sessions are offered. There is a special program to enable mature women to complete undergraduate work. Enrollment includes 1,050 full-time and 350 part-time students enrolled. A faculty is 60 full-time and 30 part-time gives a faculty-student ratio of 1-17.

Entrance Requirements: High school graduation required; completion of 15 units, including 4 English, 2 mathematics, 1 laboratory science, and 2 social studies; GED acceptable; SAT or ACT required; early admission, rolling admission, delayed admission and advanced placement (through CLEP) plans are available; $35 application fee; application deadline for fall term is August 1st.

Costs Per Year: $4,962 tuition; $10,786 out-of-state; $3,800 room and board; $366 student fees.

Collegiate Environment: The school is located on 165 acres and combines the buildings of a previously private estate with newly constructed academic and recreational facilities. A nature trail and wildlife sanctuary complement the other facilities to create a relaxed, informal atmosphere. The library has 68,000 volumes, 1,000 pamphlets, 350 periodicals, and 7,000 microforms. Dormitory facilities house 110 men and 110 women. Approximately 70% of applicants for admission are accepted and new and transfer students are accepted at midyear. The average acores of enrolled freshmen were SAT 430 verbal, 470 math. Scholarship aid is available to students demonstrating financial need. 65% of students receive some form of financial aid.

Community Environment: The Greensburg campus is located 30 miles east of Pittsburgh. Its students have easy access to the facilities of the university there as well as to cultural, recreational, and athletic opportunities within the city itself. There are many museums, churches, libraries and medical facilities in addition to 29 year-round recreational centers for swimming, golf, tennis, skiing, hunting and fishing.

UNIVERSITY OF PITTSBURGH AT JOHNSTOWN   *(K-6)*
Johnstown, Pennsylvania 15904
Tel: (814) 269-7000; (800) 765-4875; Admissions: (814) 269-7050; Fax: (814) 269-7044

Description: The publicly supported university is accredited by the Middle States Association of Colleges and Schools. It grants the bachelor's degree, and offers programs in the Arts and Sciences, the Social Sciences, the Natural Sciences, Education, Engineering, and Humanities. In addition, the school offers an associate degree in Respiratory Therapy. The college offers self-directed majors, study aborad, and a Washington semester. It operates on the semester system and offers two summer sessions. Enrollment includes 2,603 full-time and 534 part-time students. A faculty of 145 full-time and 46 part-time gives a faculty-student ratio of 1-20.

Entrance Requirements: High school graduation or GED is required; SAT or ACT required; high school preparation must include 15 units, including 4 English, 1 Laboratory Science, 2 Algebra, 2 Foreign Language, 4 History; for Engineering Program: 4 English, 2 Algebra, 1 Plane Geometry, 1/2 Trigonometry, 1 Chemistry, 1 Physics, 1 History; early admission, deferred admission, midyear admission, rolling admission and advanced placement plans available; $35 application fee.

Costs Per Year: $4,962 resident tuition, $10,786 nonresident; $4,086 room and board.

Collegiate Environment: The campus is located on 650 acres in a natural environment with two-story stone buildings. Residence halls accomodate 1,593 students. Library holdings include 132,000 bound volumes. 70% of applicants are accepted. Scholarships are available and 85% of students receive some form of financial aid.

Community Environment: Johnstown and the surrounding area are inhabited by 100,000 people. Public transportation available on campus. Arts centers, museums, sports arena nearby. Campus is located 7 miles from the city in a suburban area. Amtrak serves the city and utilizes the national historic site of the "horseshoe curve" between Johnstown and Altoona, PA.

UNIVERSITY OF PITTSBURGH, PITTSBURGH CAMPUS
(K-2)
Bruce Hall, 2nd floor
Pittsburgh, Pennsylvania 15260
Tel: (412) 624-4141

Description: Established in 1787, the University of Pittsburgh is a co-educational, nonsectarian, state-related, public research institution of the Commonwealth of Pennsylvania. Accredited by the Middle States Association of Colleges and Schools and various other specialized accrediting associations, the University offers undergraduate and graduate level certificate programs, baccalaureate, master's, doctoral, and first professional degree programs. There are 17 Pittsburgh Campus schools: Faculty of Arts and Sciences, College of Arts and Sciences, College of General Studies, University Honors College and the Schools of Education, Engineering, Law, Social Work, Library and Information Science, Dental Medicine, Nursing, Pharmacy, Medicine, Health and RehabilitationSciences, the Joseph M. Katz Graduate School of Business, the Graduate Schools of Public and International Affairs, and Public Health. In addition, there are interschool academic programs and academic programs offered through the University Center for International Studies. There are many educational opportunities for students in the health sciences schools through University-affiliated hospitals, clinics and institutes. The University operates four regional campuses in western Pennsylvania at Johnstown, Greensburg, Titusville, and Bradford. The academic calendar is comprised of three 15-week terms and two 7-1/2 week summer sessions which run con-

currently with the 15-week summer term. The Fall and Spring terms comprise the typical academic year for an undergraduate. Overseas programs include a Semester at Sea, and study abroad programs in many countries, including Asia, Latin America, and Europe. Army, Air Force, and Navy ROTC programs are available. Special programs include an Honors College, cross registration with other universities, and internships. There are 9,606 men and 9,191 women enrolled full-time and 7,531 part-time in undergraduate and graduate programs at the Pittsburgh campus. There are 3,386 full-time and part-time faculty at the Pittsburgh campus.

Entrance Requirements: All applicants to the undergraduate College of Arts and Sciences (CAS) must have completed at least 15 academic units in an accredited secondary school, including 4 English, 3 Math, 3 laboratory science, 1 social Studies and 4 academic electives. Of the 4 academic electives, it is strongly recommended that three be of a single foreign language. High school transcripts and SAT or ACT test scores are required. Admissions are on a rolling basis - there is no admissions deadline, applicants are considered for and informed of admission on a first-come, first-served basis. There is a $30 application fee. For financial aid consideration, applications should be submitted, however, no later than March 1. For housing consideration, the tuition deposit should be submitted no later than May 1. Offered early admissions, midyear admissions, advanced placement, and deferred admissions programs. Entrance requirements for undergraduate schools other than CAS vary and students are advised to contact The Office of Admissions and Financial Aid. Applicants for graduate study should contact the appropriate school directly.

Costs Per Year: Undergraduate: state-resident tuition, $4,962; non-resident, $10,786; Graduate: state-resident tuition, $6,758; non-resident, $13,780. Room and board, $4,560; undergraduate student fees, $454; graduate student   fees, $392. (Undergraduate tuition rates are for the faculty of Arts and Sciences. Rates may vary by school and program.)

Collegiate Environment: The main campus of the University is located three miles from downtown Pittsburgh, on a 132-acre site in Oakland, the medical and cultural center of Pittsburgh. The 42-story Cathedral of Learning, a Gothic skyscraper, is at the center of the campus and houses administrative offices, classrooms and the famed Nationality Rooms. The 25 library collections total 3,042,043 volumes, 2,796,902 pieces of microforms and 21,508 periodicals. The main library is the Hillman Library which houses undergraduate and research collections and has seating for 1,530 users. There is on-campus housing for 5,000 students, including women's dormitories, co-ed dormitories, and fraternity and sorority housing. There are 22 fraternities, and 14 sororities. Scholarships are available and 74% of the students receive some form of financial assistance. Activities include student government, Pitt Program Council, newspaper, radio station, choral groups, intramural and intercollegiate sports, marching band, theatre groups, international clubs, and clubs for service, religion, politics and recreation.

Community Environment: Pittsburgh is a city of hills, rivers, and bridges, traditional and contemporary lifestyles. Its attractions include concerts, folk festivals, the Pittsburgh Symphony, professional sports, museums, libraries, parks, and art galleries. The campus is located just 3 miles from downtown Pittsburgh, near the world-renowned Phipps Conservatory. The University is easily accessible by air, bus, and rail transportation.

Branch Campuses: University of Pittsburgh at Johnstown, Johnstown, PA 15904 (814) 269-7050; University of Pittsburgh at Greensburg, 1150 Mt. Pleasant Road, Greensburg, PA 15601 (412) 836-9880; University of Pittsburgh at Titusville, 504 E. Main St., Titusville, PA 16354, (814) 827-4427; University of Pittsburgh at Bradford, Campus Drive, Bradford, PA 16701 (800)-UPB-1787.

UNIVERSITY OF SCRANTON   *(G-16)*
800 Linden Street
Scranton, Pennsylvania 18510-4699
Tel: (717) 941-7540; Admissions: (717) 941-7540; Fax: (717) 941-6369

Description: The privately supported, Roman Catholic university was founded as St. Thomas College in 1888. Its university charter was received in 1938 and in 1942 it became the 24th of the 28 Jesuit Colleges and Universities in the United States. The university includes a College of Arts and Sciences, a college of Health, Education and

Human Resources, a School of Management, an evening college, (Dexter Hanley College), and a Graduate School. 24 states and 21 foreign countries are represented among the undergraduates. The university operates on the 4-1-4 system and offers two summer sessions. It is accredited by the Middle States Association of Colleges and Schools and by several respective professional accrediting institutions. Enrollment includes 1,778 men and 2,093 women full-time, and 216 men and 285 women part-time. A faculty of 236 full-time and 155 part-time gives a faculty-student ratio of 1-14. Programs of study lead to the Associate, Bachelor and Master degrees. An academic cooperative plan with the University of Detroit/Mercy and Widener University is offered to engineering students. Army and Air Force ROTC programs are available.

Entrance Requirements: High school graduation or equivalent; completion of 18 units including 4 English, 3 math, 3 science, 2 language, 3 social studies; SAT or ACT required for undergraduate studies; early admission, early decision, rolling admission, delayed admission and advanced placement plans available; $30 application fee.

Costs Per Year: $12,480 tuition; $6,074 room and board; $870 student fees; $800 average additional expenses.

Collegiate Environment: College facilities include a library of 328,000 volumes, 2,100 periodicals, 306,000 microforms and 9,400 audiovisual materials. There is housing for 1,000 men and 1,050 women. The university accepts 55% of those who apply for admission. Average SAT scores of the entering class were 503V, 556M. Approximately 80% of the students receive some form of financial aid.

Community Environment: Settled in the late eighteenth century, Scranton is the commercial and industrial center of northeast Pennsylvania. Scranton's manufactured items include textiles, clothing, electronic equipment, furniture, plastic, canvas, and metal products. Lying in the Appalachian Mountains on the Lackawana River, Scranton is 10 minutes from the Montage Ski and Recreation Area. Also of interest are the Everhart Museum of Natural History, Science, and Art, Steamtown, and McDade State Park and Coal Mine Tour.

UNIVERSITY OF THE ARTS   *(M-17)*
Broad and Pine Streets
Philadelphia, Pennsylvania 19102
Tel: (215) 875-4800; (800) 272-3790; Fax: (215) 875-5467

Description: The University of the Arts was formed in 1987 after the merger of the Philadelphia College of Art and the Philadelphia College of Performing Arts. Each college was over 100 years old at the time of the merger. The College of Art and Design is a professional community, dedicated to the visual arts, where art is the primary and central concern. Founded in 1876 to train artists to translate the technological advances of the Industrial Revolution, today it is one of the nation's leading art colleges. It operates on the semester system and offers two summer sessions. It is fully accredited by the Middle State Association of Colleges and Schools, the National Association of Schools of Art and Design, and the National Association of Schools of Music. The College of Performing Arts focuses on the areas of music, dance, and theater. Founded in 1870 to educate musicians, it has expanded in recent years to offer a demanding program of ballet, modern dance, and jazz dance, as well as acting, stage combat and musical theater programs in theater arts. In 1995 the University introduced a "Writing for Media and Performance" program. Students come from 37 states, and approximately 5% are from foreign countries. Current enrollment is 1,206 full-time and 100 part-time students. A faculty of 85 full-time and 209 part-time gives a faculty-student ratio of 1-9.

Entrance Requirements: Accredited high school graduation with four years of English. Applicants should have a strong commitment to the visual or performing arts and be interested in exposure to the liberal arts as well. SAT or ACT required for freshmen; GED accepted; TOEFL for foreign applicants required. The College of Art and Design requires a portfolio of 10-20 pieces representing drawing from life, design, and color. The portfolio may be submitted by mail (35-mm slides only). Students are advised to arrange a personal interview and may submit their portfolio at that time if they wish. The College of Performing Arts requires an audition. The College offers a number of dates for the convenience of applicants and also accepts taped auditions when necessary. Applicants to the "Writing for Media and Performance" program must submit a portfolio of written works. Early entrance and deferred entrance are possible. Transfer students may be given advanced standing. In addition to submitting a portfolio or auditioning, applicants should submit their high school transcript, test scores, one letter of recommendation, and a 100-word personal statement of purpose. The placement of transfer students is made after an evaluation of their portfolio or audition and a determination of their approved credits. All students are notified within four weeks of the receipt of all required materials. The suggested deadline for freshman applications is March 15; recommended date for transfer applications is April 1. The deadline for submitting the $200 tuition deposit is May 1.

Costs Per Year: $12,520 tuition; $3,860 room; $500 general fees.

Collegiate Environment: The College of Art and Design is housed in the historic Haviland-Strickland Building. Directly across the street is the major studio facility. The College has photo labs, printmaking and typesetting equipment, sculpture, computer lab, Heidelberg press, and ceramics workshops, and glassblowing and weaving studios. Each department has exhibition space, and the College also has a gallery for exhibitions by students, faculty members, and renowned artists and designers from around the world. Dormitories house 262 students. The library holdings number 100,992 volumes, 359 serial publications, 461 microforms, 14,984 audiovisual materials, and extensive indexed pictures and catalogs, as well as a slide library. The College of Performing Arts is housed in the Merriam Theatre Building, at 313 and 309 South Broad. The School of Music provides chamber music studios, practice rooms, a two-manual Challis harpsichord, a Moog synthesizer, "MIDI" laboratory and a complete computer laboratory. The School of Dance has light-filled studios with barres, mirrors, and resilient floors. The School of Theatre offers a 180-seat enclosed theater and a "blackbox" theater that provides flexible space for 3/4-thrust, environmental theater or theater-in-the-round. The Shubert Theatre, Drake Theater, and Wagman Hall serve all three schools for major performances.

Community Environment: The campus is located in the heart of Philadelphia's cultural community. The area has theaters, museums, galleries, music and dance facilities, restaurants of many ethnic varieties, and major department stores and shops. Philadelphia offers a broad mix of experiences. Of historical importance, the city is also known as a supporter of the arts. Urban and sophisticated, it is at the same time a series of small, close-knit neighborhoods. Fairmount Park, the largest municipal park in the world, provides facilities for boating, fishing, hiking, biking, picnicking, and relaxing.

URSINUS COLLEGE   *(L-16)*
Collegeville, Pennsylvania 19426
Tel: (610) 489-4111; Admissions: (610) 489-3200; Fax: (610) 489-0627

Description: This privately supported, coeducational liberal arts college is affiliated with the United Church of Christ and is accredited by the Middle States Association of Colleges and Schools. A Cooperative Engineering program is available as is a secondary teaching certification program. The college operates on the semester system and offers four summer sessions. Enrollment includes 539 men and 558 women full-time and 10 men and 6 women part-time. A faculty of 93 full-time and 27 part-time provides a faculty-student ratio of 1-12.

Entrance Requirements: Approved high school graduation; completion of 16 units including 4 English, 3 mathematics, 2 foreign language, 1 science, and 1 social science; SAT required; 3 CEEB achievement tests are strongly recommended; nondegree candidates may be admitted as special students; early admission, early decision, deferred admission, midyear admission and advanced placement plans available; $30 application fee.

Costs Per Year: $14,900 tuition; $5,160 room and board; $180 student fees.

Collegiate Environment: The 140-acre campus is less than an hour from central Philadelphia. Within its friendly, tree-covered campus, Ursinus offers over 60 different clubs and organizations, fraternities, sororities, student government, newspaper, and radio stations. The Myrin Library houses 185,000 volumes, 900 periodicals, 155,000 microforms, and 30,500 audiovisual materials. Students who are not living in their own homes are required to room at the college and take their meals in the college dining rooms. There are dormitories for 1,100 men and women. The middle 50% of scores for entering freshmen were SAT Verbal 460-560, Math 510-630. Special scholarships are are available for freshmen. 75% of students receive some form of financial assistance. About 92% of freshmen return for their sophomore year.

Community Environment: Collegeville is 25 miles northwest of Philadelphia. Within a one-hour drive are museums, libraries, historical sights, educational institutions, recreational facilities, and theaters. Part-time employment is available.

VALLEY FORGE CHRISTIAN COLLEGE   *(L-16)*
Charlestown Road
Phoenixville, Pennsylvania 19460
Tel: (610) 935-0450; (800) 432-8322; Fax: (610) 935-9353

Description: Privately supported, coeducational, theological school chartered in 1939 for the training of pastors, evangelists, missionaries, and Christian lay workers. The school is accredited by the American Association of Bible Colleges and is affiliated with the church of the Assemblies of God. The college operates on the semester system and offers two summer sessions. Enrollment includes 507 full-time and 10 part-time students. A faculty of 20 full-time and 12 part-time gives a faculty-student ratio of 1-17.

Entrance Requirements: Accredited high school graduation or equivalent; open enrollment policy; SAT or ACT; early admission, early decision, rolling admission, midyear admission, and advanced placement, plans available; Aug. 15 application deadline; $25 application fee.

Costs Per Year: $8,200 tuition, room and board.

Collegiate Environment: There are 77 buildings on the 80-acre campus including the 48,000 volume library and dormitories for 300 men, 300 women. The college welcomes a geographically diverse student body. Approximately 90% of students applying for admission are accepted including midyear. About 75% of the student body receive some form of financial assistance.

Community Environment: Phoenixville is a quiet residential town on the boundary of Valley Forge State Park and is approximately 40 miles from Philadelphia. The climate is temperate. The immediate area provides an abundance of shopping areas and malls, as well as religious, medical and professional services. Recreational opportunities include picnicking, fishing, swimming, boating, camping, and tennis. There are considerable job opportunities available.

VALLEY FORGE MILITARY ACADEMY AND COLLEGE
(M-17)
1001 Eagle Road
Wayne, Pennsylvania 19087-3695
Tel: (610) 989-1300; (800) 234-8362; Fax: (610) 688-1545

Description: This privately supported military, two-year transfer college offers Associate in Arts degrees in Science, Liberal Arts, Business Administration, Engineering and Criminal Justice. All eligible cadets are enrolled in Army ROTC. The Valley Forge Military Academy and College was founded in 1935 and is accredited by the Middle States Association of Colleges and Schools. It operates on the semester system. Enrollment includes 250 students. A faculty of 16 full-time and 15 part-time provides a faculty-student ratio of 1-10.

Entrance Requirements: Completion of 15 units including 4 English, 3 mathematics, 1 laboratory science and 2 social studies; SAT with minimum scores of 400V, 400M, or ACT with minimum score of 17 accepted; early decision, rolling admission, and advanced placement plans available; $25 application fee.

Costs Per Year: $10,900 tuition; $6,670 room and board and uniforms; $450 books.

Collegiate Environment: The landscaped campus is situated on the southern slope of the Radnor Hills in one of Philadelphia's most exclusive and beautiful suburbs. The library contains 66,000 volumes, 138 periodicals, 5,301 microforms, and 1,126 audiovisual materials. Dormitory facilities accommodate 250 students. Approximately 80% of students applying for admission are accepted. Financial aid is available and 52% of the current student body receives some form of financial assistance. There are 150 scholarships offered.

Community Environment: See Villanova University.

VILLANOVA UNIVERSITY   *(M-17)*
Villanova, Pennsylvania 19085
Tel: (610) 645-4000; (800) 338-7927; Fax: (610) 519-6450

Description: This privately supported, coeducational Roman Catholic university was founded in 1842 and operates under the aegis of the Order of St. Augustine, one of the oldest teaching teaching orders of the Roman Catholic Church. It is accredited by the Middle States Association of Colleges and Schools. Four-year undergraduate programs leading to the Bachelor's degree are offered in the Colleges of Liberal Arts and Sciences, Engineering, Commerce and Finance, and Nursing; graduate programs lead to the Professional, Masters, and Doctor Degrees. Academic cooperative plans with Rosemont College (including Pennsylvania Elementary School teaching certification) and Cabrini College (including Pennsylvania Special Education teaching certification) are offered along with a seven-year joint Dentistry program offered in conjunction with University of Pennsylvania, a seven-year joint optometry program offered in conjunction with the Pennsylvania College of Optometry, a six-year or seven-seven year joint Medical degree program with the Medical College of Pennsylvania, and four-year to six-year programs in Physical Therapy, Occupational Therapy, Medical Technology, Cytotechnology, Dental Hygiene, and Diagnostic Imaging with Thomas Jefferson University. The university operates on the semester system and offers three summer sessions. Enrollment includes 6,309 full-time and 579 part-time undergraduate students. A faculty of 478 full-time and 305 part-time gives a faculty-student ratio of 1-12. Graduate and first professional enrollment includes 2,190 students. Navy ROTC is available as an elective, Army ROTC is available on campus through a program with Widener University, and Air Force ROTC is available on an exchange program with St. Joseph's University.

Entrance Requirements: High school graduation completion of 16 units including 4 English, 4 mathematics, 2 foreign language, and 1-2 science; minimum SAT verbal 500, math 500 or ACT 25; CEEB Achievement tests required for College of Arts and Sciences in Foreign Language; early admission, midyear admission, early action, and advanced placement plans available; application deadlines: Dec. 15 for early action, Jan 15 for regular admission; $40 application fee.

Costs Per Year: $15,530 tuition; $6,850 room and board.

Collegiate Environment: The 240-acre campus is among the showplaces of suburban Philadelphia. There are 50 buildings including the Falvey Memorial Library containing a collection of over 642,800 volumes, 2,615 periodicals and 310,703 microforms. Residence halls accommodate 3,812 students. Freshman classes begin in September. The college welcomes a geographically diverse student body. 72% of applicants are accepted. The middle 50% range of enrolled freshmen scores is SAT 1041-1252 combined. About 76% of the current students receive financial aid. 93% of the previous freshman class returned to this campus for their sophomore year.

Community Environment: The "Main Line" is a suburban residential area located 12 miles due west of downtown Philadelphia, which includes the towns of Radnor, Rosemont, Villanova, St. Davids, Wayne, Haverford, and Merion Station. The mean temperature for the area is 54.3 degrees. The area is served by Amtrak and local commuter rail lines, regional bus lines and the Schuylkill Expressway. The total locale has more than 200 civic, social, and church groups. There are art centers, theater groups, a symphony orchestra, several museums, many libraries, two hospitals, and good shopping facilities. Local recreation includes golf courses, swimming pools, skating rinks, parks, playgrounds, and most sports.

WASHINGTON AND JEFFERSON COLLEGE   *(L-2)*
S. Lincoln Street
Washington, Pennsylvania 15301
Tel: (412) 223-6025

Description: The privately supported, coeducational liberal arts college was founded in 1781. It is accredited by the Middle States Association of Colleges and Schools and grants the Bachelor degree. The 4-1-4 calendar year and two summer terms are offered. Enrollment includes 1,100 students full-time and part-time and 204 in the evening. A faculty of 87 full-time and 20 part-time and 14 evening gives a faculty-student ratio of 1-12. An academic cooperative plan is available for students majoring in medical technology. A 3-2 engineering program is available with Case Western Reserve and the University of St.

Louis. Junior Year Abroad is available with any approved institution. Army ROTC is available through a nearby university.

Entrance Requirements: Accredited high school graduation; completion of 15 units including 3 English, 3 mathematics, 2 foreign language, 1 science, 1 social science; SAT or ACT required; 3 CEEB achievement tests if SAT is submitted; $25 application fee; early admission, early decision, delayed admission and advanced placement plans available.

Costs Per Year: $16,360 tuition; $4,005 room and board; $280 student fees; additional expenses average $600.

Collegiate Environment: The campus is the focal point for a well-planned public affairs and public events program. The library houses 195,000 volumes, 715 periodicals, 5,400 microforms, 2,950 recordings, 15,000 slides, and 3,100 musical scores. Ten national fraternities and three sororities have chapters at the college and their houses are grouped together in a fraternity quadrangle. Dormitory accommodations are available for 348 men and 318 women and rooms for 247 men are offered in the fraternities. Approximately 78% of students applying for admission are accepted. Midyear students are accepted and the college welcomes a geographically diverse student body. Financial assistance is available for economically handicapped students and 53% of the current students receive aid.

Community Environment: Population 20,000. Washington is an urban community 25 miles from Pittsburgh. Glass factories, steel mills, paper plants, and tool producers are among the manufacturers here. The climate is temperate. Bus service is available to Pittsburgh. The community has churches representing 21 denominations, one hospital, and a public library.

WAYNESBURG COLLEGE   *(M-2)*
51 W. College Street
Waynesburg, Pennsylvania 15370
Tel: (412) 852-3248; (800) 225-7393; Fax: (412) 627-6416

Description: The college is a private, independent, coeducational institution affiliated with the Presbyterian Church (U.S.A.). It is accredited by the Middle States Association of Colleges and Schools. The college grants the Associate, Bachelor's and Master's degrees. It operates on the semester system and offers two summer sessions. Enrollment includes 1,225 full-time and 56 part-time undergraduates and 38 graduate students. A faculty of 66 full-time and 47 part-time gives a faculty-student ratio of 1-16.

Entrance Requirements: Accredited high school graduation or equivalent; satisfactory GPA and class rank in high school; completion of 16 units are required including 4 English, 3 mathematics, 2 science, 2 foreign language, 2 social science, and 6 electives; SAT or ACT may be required; early admission, midyear admision, rolling admission, and advanced placement plans available; $15 application fee.

Costs Per Year: $8,840 tuition; $3,620 room and board; $220 student fees.

Collegiate Environment: Situated in the heart of Greene County, the 30-acre campus is located on a park overlooking the town. The 15 buildings include housing accommodations for 379 men and 264 women. Fraternities provide housing for an additional 50 men. The College Library now contains 100,000 volumes, 550 periodicals and 3,450 microforms, and is a depository for selected government documents. Many student activities are available. Financial aid is available and 93% of the students receive some form of assistance. Approximately 82% of students applying for admission meet the requirements and are accepted. The college awarded 225 Bachelor degrees and 17 Associate degrees to the graduating class.

Community Environment: Population 5299, Waynesburg is located 50 miles from Pittsburgh in southwestern Pennsylvania. The climate is moderate. Community service facilities include a library, several churches, a hospital, hotels, motels, and rooming houses. There is bus service available. Local recreation includes theatres, hunting, boating, fishing, golf, and movies. Many civic, fraternal and veteran's organizations are active in the community.

WEST CHESTER UNIVERSITY OF PENNSYLVANIA   *(M-16)*
University Avenue
West Chester, Pennsylvania 19383
Tel: (610) 436-1000; Admissions: (610) 436-3411; Fax: (610) 436-3411

Description: This publicly supported, coeducational, multipurpose University is comprised of five major academic divisions: the College of Arts and Sciences, the School of Business and Public Affairs, the School of Education, the School of Health Sciences, and the School of Music. Enrollment includes 5,476 women and 3,779 men undergraduates and 1,913 graduate students. A faculty of 538 full-time and 140 part-time provides a faculty-student ratio of 1-18. Sixty percent of the full-time faculty hold doctorate degrees. The University is accredited by the Middle States Association of Colleges and Schools, the American Chemical Society, the Council on Social Work Education, the National Association of Schools of Music, and the National League for Nursing.

Entrance Requirements: Approved high school graduation with rank in upper half of graduating class based on solid academic preparation; recommended minimum SAT combined score of 900; GED recipients considered; early admission, midyear admssion, modified rolling admission, delayed admission and advanced placement plans available. $25 application fee.

Costs Per Year: $2,728 state-reesident tuition; $6,122 out-of-state; $3,630 room and board; $430 student fees.

Collegiate Environment: The 275-acre campus has 34 buildings including residence halls for 3,600 students. Library holdings include 440,000 bound volumes, 688,000 titles on microform, 2,603 periodical subscriptions, and 31,000 records and tapes. Financial assistance is available to those with demonstrated need. The Speech and Hearing Clinic provides evaluation and therapy for children of the area. The National Student Exchange and a Junior Year Abroad Program are available.

Community Environment: Population 20,000. Essentially a residential and college community, West Chester is the county seat of a region rich in colonial history. Local industries include pharmaceuticals, firefighting foam, electrical appliances, air compressors, tags and labels, and refrigerated cabinets. The average January temperature is 31.5 degrees, and the average July temperature is 75 degrees. The community is provided transportation by railroad, bus lines, and an airport nearby. There are several churches, a YMCA, hospital, and public library serving the community. Local recreation includes swimming, bowling, volleyball, tennis, hunting, fishing, and golf. Civic and fraternal organizations are active within the area.

WESTMINSTER COLLEGE   *(H-1)*
Market Street
New Wilmington, Pennsylvania 16172
Tel: (412) 946-7100; (800) 942-8033; Fax: (412) 946-7171

Description: This privately supported, coeducational liberal arts college is related to the Presbyterian Church U.S.A. It operates on the 4-1-4 system and offers one summer term. The college is accredited by the Middle States Association of Colleges and Schools. Cooperative engineering programs are available with Penn State, Case Western Reserve University and Washington University (St. Louis, Mo.) that enable students to get a Bachelor degree from Westminster and an engineering degree from participating colleges. Degrees offered include the Bachelor of Arts, Bachelor of Science, Bachelor of Music, and Master of Education. Enrollment includes 1,543 full-time and 154 part-time students. A faculty of 98 full-time and 42 part-time gives a faculty-student ratio of 1-15.

Entrance Requirements: High school graduation with rank in upper half of graduating class; completion of 16 units including 4 English, 3 mathematics, 2 foreign language, 2 science, and 2 social science; SAT with minimum score of 400V, 400M or ACT composite score of 20 required; non-high school graduates considered; $20 application fee; early admission, rolling admission, delayed admission and advanced placement plans available.

Costs Per Year: $12,065 tuition; $1,635 room; $1,740 board.

Collegiate Environment: The campus extends over 300 acres. There are 20 major buildings including dormitories for 436 men and 717 women and a library collection of 219,000 volumes, 1,100 periodicals, 1,600 microforms and 2,600 audiovisual materials. Approximately 81% of students applying for admission are accepted, including at midyear. Financial aid is available and about 85% of the current students receive some form of assistance. Average high school standing of a recent freshman class: 47% in the top fifth, 33% in the second fifth, and 16% in the third fifth. 94% of the previous freshman class returned to this campus for the sophomore year. The average

SAT scores of the current freshmen are 479V, 521M. The average ACT composite score is 24. The college awarded 249 Bachelor and 24 Master degrees to the graduating class. 30% of the senior class continued on to graduate school.

Community Environment: Population 2,500. New Wilmington is a small residential area with a temperate climate. There is bus service available to Pittsburgh, and all the major transportation facilities are available. The immediate locale has a hospital, several churches, and active civic and fraternal organizations. Some part-time employment is available. There are facilities for golfing and fishing, as well as major sports.

WESTMINSTER THEOLOGICAL SEMINARY *(M-17)*
P.O. Box 27009
Philadelphia, Pennsylvania 19118
Tel: (215) 887-5511; (800) 373-0119; Fax: (215) 887-5404

Description: The privately supported coeducational graduate-level theological seminary was founded in 1929. It is accredited by the Middle States Association of Colleges and Schools and the Association of Theological Schools. Special programs include overseas research in missions and Evangelism, Holy Land Studies and cross registration with other seminaries. The seminary grants the degrees of Master of Theology, Master of Divinity, Master of Missiology, and Master of Arts in Religion, and the Doctor of Philosophy and Ministry. It operates on the 4-1-4 calendar system and offers one summer session. Enrollment includes 557 students. A full-time faculty of 42 gives a faculty-student ratio of 1-13.

Entrance Requirements: Bachelor of Arts degree or equivalent including 80 hours of liberal arts; $25 application fee; recommendation from applicant's church; personal statement showing reasons for wishing to pursue theological study; rolling admission, midyear admission and delayed admission plans available; $25 application fee.

Costs Per Year: $6,600 tuition; room and board available.

Collegiate Environment: The seminary is located near the border of Philadelphia on a 22-acre wooded campus with 8 buildings. The Montgomery Library holdings include 100,000 bound volumes, 760 periodicals, 14,000 microforms and 3,000 recordings. There are dormitories for 40 men and accommodations for 11 women. 90% of applicants are accepted. The college welcomes a geographically diverse student body. Scholarships are available and 20% of the students receive some form of finanacial aid.

Community Environment: See Temple University.

WESTMORELAND COUNTY COMMUNITY COLLEGE *(L-3)*
Youngwood, Pennsylvania 15697-1895
Tel: (412) 925-4000

Description: Publicly supported, coeducational 2-year college. Opened in 1971. Accredited by the Middle States Association of Colleges and Schools. Enrollment includes 2,923 full-time and 3,354 part-time students. A faculty of 85 full-time and 240 part-time gives a faculty-student ratio of 1-23. The college offers 30 degree, 14 diploma, and 18 certification programs. It operates on the semester system and offers 2 six-week summer sessions.

Entrance Requirements: High school graduation, GED accepted; open enrollment; placement exam; some programs have special admission prerequisites; early admission plan available; $10 application fee.

Costs Per Year: $1,290 district and county tuition; $2,580 state-resident tuition; $3,870 out-of-state; $28 student fees.

Collegiate Environment: The library contains 33,520 volumes, 417 periodicals, 26,468 government documents, 339 microforms, and 5,156 recordings. Approximately 95% of the students applying for admission are accepted. Certain programs require waiting lists based on test scores. Various student activities are available. There is a Skill Training Center and a Computer Literacy Plan providing instruction in occupational applications.

WIDENER UNIVERSITY *(M-17)*
1 University Place
Chester, Pennsylvania 19013
Tel: (610) 499-4000; Admissions: (610) 499-4126; Fax: (610) 876-9751

Description: Widener University, founded in 1821, is a private, coeducational institution composed of eight schools and colleges which offer liberal arts and sciences, professonal and pre-professional curricula. Acomprehensive teachnig institution centered in both Pennsylvania and Deleware, Widener is today a three-campus university offering 97 majors leading to the associate, baccalaureate, masters or dioctoral degrees. The university's schools include: the College of Arts and Sciences, School of Engineering, School of Management, School of Nursing, School of Law, School of Hotel and Restaurant Management, School of Human Service Professions and University College. Two semesters plus summer sessions. Evening and weekend programs are available. Current enrollment is 8,850. Widener is accredited by the Middle States Association of Colleges and Schools. Army ROTC program available.

Entrance Requirements: Accredited high school graduation with rank in upper half of graduating class; completion of 17 college-preparatory units including 4 English, 3-4 mathematics, 1-3 science, 2 foreign language, 2 social studies; SAT or ACT ; early admission, rolling admission, delayed admission, early decision and advanced placement programs available; $25 application fee,

Costs Per Year: $120,950 tuition; $5,650-$6,410 board and room; additional expenses average $500.

Collegiate Environment: The campus is located in suburban Delaware County, just 10 miles from Philadelphia. The campus contains 100 acres and 85 buildings that inclued a library of 228,600 volumes of books and periodicals inclúding microforms, audiovisual, and other nonprint media. Approximately 60% of the undergraduate students live on campus in 21 residence facilities. There are also special interest housing and fraternity/sorority houses. Students come from 28 states and 40 foreign countries.

Community Environment: See Penn State University, Delaware County Campus.

WILKES UNIVERSITY *(H-15)*
170 S. Franklin Street
Wilkes-Barre, Pennsylvania 18766
Tel: (717) 831-5000; (800) 945-5378; Admissions: (717) 831-4400; Fax: (717) 831-4904

Description: The privately supported, coeducational comprehensive university is accredited by the Middle States Association of Colleges and Schools was founded in 1933. It operates on the semester system and offers three summer sessions. Enrollment includes 1,810 full-time and 545 part-time undergraduate students. A faculty of 140 full-time and 70 part-time members gives an undergraduate faculty-student ratio of 1-12. Graduate enrollment includes 625 students. There is a guaranteed medical acceptance program with the Medical College of Philadelphia, Hahnemann Medical School and the State University of New York Health Science Center at Syracuse. Further, there are a number of 3/4 programs with other medical schools. A Docotor of Pharmacy program was initiated Fall, 1994 with its first class to graduate in the year 2000. Air Force ROTC is also available.

Entrance Requirements: High school graduation with rank in upper half of graduating class; completion of 18 units including 4 English, 3 mathematics, 3 science, 1 social studies, 5 electives; SAT or ACT required; GRE required for graduate programs, non-high school graduates considered; $30 application fee; early admission, early decision, rolling admission, delayed admission and advanced placement plans available.

Costs Per Year: $11,150 tuition; $5,300 room and board.

Collegiate Environment: The campus has 64 buildings including the Eugene S. Farley Library with its collection of 220,000 volumes, 1,080 periodicals, 700,000 microforms and 10,000 audiovisual materials. Dormitories are available for men and women. 73% of applicants are accepted. Midyear students are accepted; freshman classes begin in September and in January. Financial aid is available and 80% of the students receive some form of assistance.

Community Environment: Population 58,856. In the Wyoming Valley on the Susquehanna River, the town was named in honor of John Wilkes and Isaac Barre. Once Pennsylvania's major anthracite coal-mining region, diversified industries have grown and are now of greater importance. The city enjoys temperate climate. Wilkes-Barre may be reached by bus and air lines. The community has theatres, Choral Groups, a symphony orchestra, art exhibits, libraries, and a historical society. There are several hotels and numerous motels. Local recreation includes golf courses, hunting, fishing, skiing and lakes in the nearby mountains. There are many part-time jobs available. The area has several hospitals and various civic and fraternal organizations.

WILSON COLLEGE   *(M-10)*

1015 Philadelphia Avenue
Chambersburg, Pennsylvania 17201-1285
Tel: (717) 264-4141; (800) 421-8402; Fax: (717) 264-1578

Description: The privately supported women's college was founded in 1869 by the United Presbyterian Church in the United States. The liberal arts college operates on the 4-1-4 system and is accredited by the Middle States Association of Colleges and Schools. Enrollment is 199 women full-time and 676 part-time. A faculty of 35 full-time and 6 part-time provides a faculty-student ratio of 1-8. Academic cooperative plans are available with the University of Pennsylvania for dentistry and nursing.

Entrance Requirements: High school graduation with rank in upper 1st or 2nd quarter of high school class; include 4 English, 3 mathematics, 2 science, 2 language, 4 history or civics; SAT with minimum score of 450 verbal and 450 math, or ACT required; non-high school graduates considered; $20 application fee; early admission, early decision, rolling admission, delayed admission and advanced placement plans available.

Costs Per Year: $11,428 tuition; $5,279 room and board and Health Center; $118 student fees.

Collegiate Environment: The campus comprises 260 acres with 32 buildings. Residence halls accommodate 500 women. The library contains 163,526 volumes, 391 periodicals, 10,437 microforms and 1,444 audiovisual materials. Financial assistance is available. 82% of students receive financial aid. 79% of applicants were accepted.

Community Environment: Population 20,000. Chambersburg was occupied three times during the Civil War and burned in 1864 when it refused to pay an indemnity of $100,000. Today, this diversified manufacturing community also is considered the state's greatest apple and peach orchard section. Part-time employment is available for students both on and off campus. The city has two libraries, many churches and historic sites, and one hospital.

YORK COLLEGE OF PENNSYLVANIA   *(M-12)*

Country Club Road
York, Pennsylvania 17405-7199
Tel: (717) 846-7788

Description: The history of York College is long and varied. The College began in 1787 as York Academy, merged in 1927 with the York Collegiate Institute (which was founded in 1883), and became York Junior College in 1941 and York College of Pennsylvania in 1968. York College is accredited by the Middle States Association of Colleges and Schools. Programs are also accredited by the National League for Nursing and the National Recreation and Park Association. The College and its programs are approved by the Pennsylvania Department of Education, the Pennsylvania Board of Nurse Examiners, the American Medical Association's Committee on Allied Health Education and Accreditation, and Veterans Administration. The college offers an evening program at the Hanover Senior High School. York operates on the semester system and offers three summer sessions. Enrollment includes 3,419 full-time, 502 part-time and 1,089 evening program undergraduates, and 128 graduate students. A faculty of 130 full-time and 180 part-time gives an undergraduate faculty-student ratio of 1-17.

Entrance Requirements: Considers high school record, national test results, and personality; the Committee on Admissions endeavors to admit those students whose records indicate that they possess the qualities needed to achieve satisfactorily at the college level; the goal is to seek the student who sincerely wants to go to college, who is mature enough to understand the responsibilities, and who will work hard to live up to them; applicants should be graduates of an approved secondary school; they should present records of academic achievement showing ability to do college work along with letters of recommendation commenting on their character and out-look; the applicant's high school program should include 15 units of study as follows: 4 in English, 3 in social sciences, 3 in mathematics, and 5 in laboratory sciences and/or languages; $20 application fee; high school transcript; SAT or ACT; TOEFL (for international students); early admission, delayed admission, midyear admission, and advanced placement plans available; rolling admissions; notification date is continuous; admission is moderately selective.

Costs Per Year: $4,990 tuition; $3,560 room and board; $225 student fees.

Collegiate Environment: York College is situated on a pleasant, beautifully landscaped 80-acre campus in the suburbs of York. A stream runs through the campus and enhances the beauty of the meticulously maintained landscape. All campus facilities are of modern architectural design and include science, foreign language and computer laboratories, radio, television, and learning resource facilities. York also offers a comprehensive computerized library, a student union, a telecommunications center with satellite receive and broadcast capabilities, an athletics complex and a chapel which offers a full range of religious services. York College has a fine collection of instructional computers. The collection includes a main computer and scores of microcomputers, and there are computer facilities for the teaching of English composition. Students are welcome to bring their own personal computers to the College. 1,275 resident students have a wide choice of housing, including standard dorms; minidorms, which feature 10-student units; suites; campus-sponsored houses and apartments; and off-campus housing. The library contains 300,000 volumes, 500,000 microforms, 1,500 periodicals, 70,000 documents and 75,000 audio-visual materials. 58% of York College students receive some form of financial aid. In addition to government aid, the College offers a full-tuition Trustee Honors Scholarship for students with a top 20% class rank and SAT I recentered score of 1180, one-half tuition Presidential and Salutatorian Scholarships, and one-third tuition Dean's Scholarships are offered for any student with an SAT recentered score over 1100 (minimum 520 math, 540 verbal) and a top two-fifths high school class rank. A premedical scholars program with Hershey Medical School and York Hospital is also offerd. Other College financial aid is available. Any student interested in scholarships of financial aid should apply to the Office of Financial Aid.

Community Environment: York College is located in the heart of one of the most naturally beautiful and historically rich sections of Pennsylvania. Traveling by car, York is just four hours from New York and Pittsburgh, less than two hours from Philadelphia and Washington, DC, and an hour from Baltimore. The area has much to offer, including great local food, interesting places to visit and shop, and parks, lakes and miles of trails that afford opportunities for picnicking, hiking and skiing. On the practical side, there is a shopping center, a bank and York Hospital within walking distance of the campus. Culture is an important part of York's heritage as well. The York Symphony Orchestra, the York Little Theater, and the Strand-Capitol Performing Arts Center bring well-known performing artists to the York area. Throughout the year, numerous galleries exhibit a wide variety of artwork.

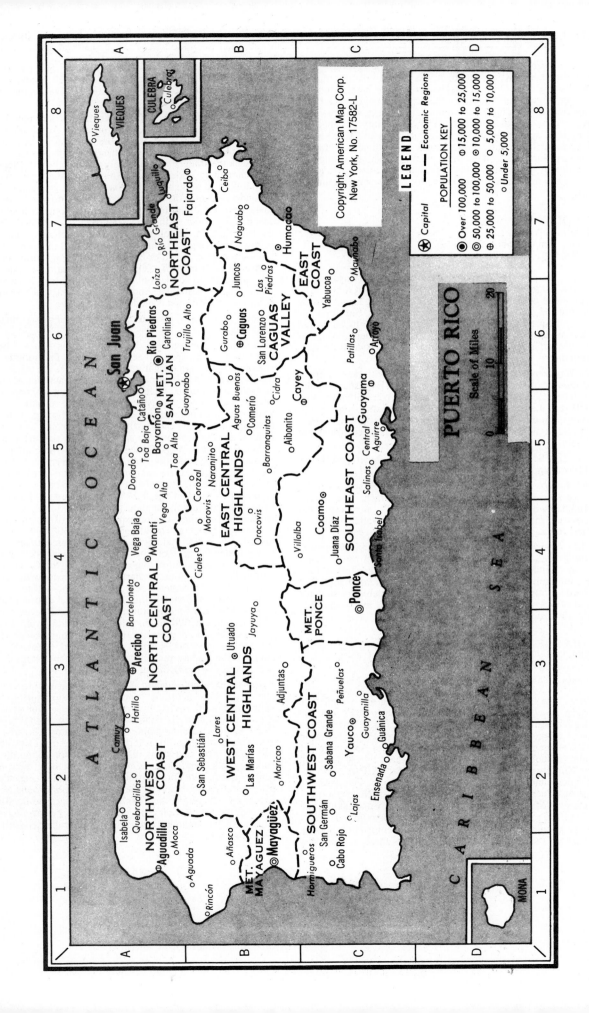

PUERTO RICO

Scale of Miles

LEGEND

--- Economic Regions

POPULATION KEY

✪ Capital

◉ Over 100,000
◎ 50,000 to 100,000   ⊕ 15,000 to 25,000
◎ 25,000 to 50,000   ⊕ 10,000 to 15,000
                        ○ 5,000 to 10,000
                        ○ Under 5,000

Copyright, American Map Corp.
New York, No. 17582-L

ATLANTIC OCEAN

CARIBBEAN SEA

MONA

VIEQUES
○ Vieques

CULEBRA
○ Culebra

San Juan
Río Piedras ◎
Bayamón ⊕ MET. SAN JUAN
Cataño ○
Toa Baja ○
Dorado ○
Carolina ○
Trujillo Alto ○
Guaynabo ○
Toa Alta ○
Vega Alta ○

NORTHEAST COAST
Luquillo ⊕
Río Grande ○
Loíza ○
Fajardo ⊕
Ceiba ○
Naguabo ○

Camuy ○
Hatillo ○
Barceloneta ○
Manatí ◎
Vega Baja ○

NORTH CENTRAL COAST
⊕ Arecibo

Quebradillas ○
Isabela ○
Moca ○
Aguada ○
Rincón ○
Aguadilla ◎
NORTHWEST COAST

Añasco ○
San Sebastián ○
Lares ○
Las Marías ○
Maricao ○

WEST CENTRAL HIGHLANDS
Utuado ◎
Adjuntas ○
Jayuya ○

EAST CENTRAL HIGHLANDS
Ciales ○
Corozal ○
Morovis ○
Naranjito ○
Orocovis ○
Barranquitas ○
Comerío ○
Aguas Buenos ○
Gurabo ○
⊕ Caguas
San Lorenzo ○
CAGUAS VALLEY
Juncos ○
Las Piedras ○

Humacao ◎
EAST COAST
Yabucoa ○
Maunabo ○

Cidra ○
Cayey ⊕
Aibonito ○
Villalba ○
Coamo ◎
Juana Díaz ○
SOUTHEAST COAST
Salinas ○
Central Aguirre ○
Guayama ⊕
Arroyo ○
Patillas ○
Santa Isabel ○

MET. PONCE
◎ Ponce

MET. MAYAGÜEZ
◎ Mayagüez
Hormigueros ○
San Germán ○
Cabo Rojo ○
Lajas ○
Sabana Grande ○
Ensenada ○
Guánica ○
Guayanilla ○
Peñuelas ○
Yauco ◎
SOUTHWEST COAST

PUERTO RICO

AMERICAN UNIVERSITY OF PUERTO RICO *(A-5)*
P.O. Box 2037
Bayamon, Puerto Rico 00621
Tel: (809) 798-2022; Admissions: (809) 740-3995; Fax: (809) 785-7377

Description: The publicly supported university was founded in 1963 and is accredited by the Middle States Association of Colleges and Schools. It is coeducational and uses the semester system with one summer session. The current student enrollment is 4,152, with 250 faculty members. The college offers an associate and a bachelor degree and has a continuing education program.

Entrance Requirements: High school graduate or equivalent; SAT required. Open enrollment. $15 application fee.

Costs Per Year: $2,500 tuition.

Collegiate Environment: The library contains 41,116 books and 784 periodicals. There is no student housing. Approximately 90% of the students receive some form of financial aid.

Community Environment: Bayamon is the principle city of the district of Bayamon. The city has a population of more than 185,000 and is approximately 25 miles from San Juan.

Branch Campuses: P.O. Box 708, Manati 00701, (809) 854-2835.

CARIBBEAN UNIVERSITY *(A-5)*
P.O. Box 493
Bayamon, Puerto Rico 00960-0493
Tel: (809) 780-0070; Fax: (809) 785-0101

Description: The privately supported university was founded in 1969 and is accredited by the Middle States Association of Colleges and Schools. The institution has grown from a junior college with a center located in Bayamon to a university with four centers including ones at Carolina, Vega Baja, and Ponce. The college grants the Associate and Bachelor degrees. It operates on the semester system and offers two summer sessions. Enrollment includes 2,998 students. A faculty of 203 full-time and 43 part-time gives a faculty-student ratio of 1-11.

Entrance Requirements: High school graduate or equivalent; completion of 15 units including 3 English, 2 mathematics, 2 laboratory science, 3 foreign language, early admission, early decision, midyear admission, 2 social studies, and 3 electives; ACT or SAT required. $15 application fee.

Costs Per Year: $3,240 tuition; $50 student fees.

Collegiate Environment: The main center is located in Bayamon and other centers are located at Carolina, Vega Baja, and Ponce. The university library contains 61,777 volumes with an additional 1,492 units of audiovisual materials. About 90% of the students applying for admission are accepted. Scholarships are available and 93% of the students receive some form of financial aid.

Community Environment: Bayamon is the principle city in the district of Bayamon. The city has a population of more than 185,000 and is approximately 25 miles from San Juan.

Branch Campuses: Carolina Campus, Carolina, PR 00630; Ponce Extension Center, Box 7733, Ponce, PR 00731; Vega Baja Campus, Vega Baja, PR 00763.

COLEGIO UNIVERSITARIO DEL ESTE *(A-6)*
P.O. Box 2010
Carolina, Puerto Rico 00983-2010
Tel: (809) 257-7373

Description: The private, junior college was founded in 1949 and was the first of its kind to be established on the island. It was char-

tered in 1950 as a nonprofit institution by the Government of Puerto Rico and was accredited by the Middle States Association of Colleges and Schools in 1959. The college has two campuses, one in Rio Piedras and one in Cupey. (A third campus established at Caguas in 1967 is now an independent institution, the Colegio Universitario del Turabo.) The total student enrollment of both campuses is 2,242 men and 3,873 women. The college operates on the semester system and offers two summer terms. A faculty of 255 provides a faculty-student ratio of 1-24.

Entrance Requirements: Accredited high school graduation with minimum C average; completion of at least 15 units of college-preparatory courses; college placement test and SAT required; early admission, early decision, rolling admission and advanced placement plans available; $15 application fee.

Costs Per Year: $3,550 tuition; $14 student fees.

Collegiate Environment: The Rio Piedras campus is easily accessible to students living in San Juan and adjacent cities and towns. The library contains 34,239 volumes. The college welcomes a geographically diverse student body and will accept midyear students. Approximately 82% of students applying for admission were accepted. Financial aid is available for economically handicapped students.

Community Environment: See University of Puerto Rico - Rio Piedras Campus.

CONSERVATORY OF MUSIC OF PUERTO RICO *(A-6)*
P.O. Box 41227 Minillas Station
Santurce, Puerto Rico 00940
Tel: (809) 751-0160

Description: The public, nonsectarian, university level institution was established in 1959 by State Law of the Commonwealth of Puerto Rico. The Conservatory of Music is coeducational and offers a music curriculum with specialization in all symphonic disciplines. It's a small institution tendering to an average enrollment of 259 students. An intermediate (preparatory) level operates to aid students for qualification to enter university level. A Special String Program for Children 6 to 12 years old is managed by the Conservatory. A Faculty of 39 music educators and instrumentalists gives an approximate teacher-student ratio of 1-10. The institution operates on the semester system without a summer session and is accredited by the Middle States Association of Colleges and Schools.

Entrance Requirements: Applicants to undergraduate programs must be high school graduates with high scholastic abilities; College Entrance Examination Board and two Institutional Achievement Tests required; admission is competitive and selective.

Costs Per Year: $150 tuition; $30 student fees.

Collegiate Environment: The Conservatory welcomes a geographically diverse student body. Admissions are accepted once a year during the month of April. Financial aid is available for economically handicapped students. The Conservatory of Music of Puerto Rico is part of the Festival Casals, Inc., an organization of which the Casals Festival annual concert series and the Puerto Rico Symphony Orchestra form part. All were founded and managed by the late world reknowned cellist Pablo Casals.

Community Environment: San Juan is a bustling capital city, well known for its historical monuments and founded over 450 years ago; Rio Piedras is the site of the main campus of the University of Puerto Rico, housing over 28,000 students.

EVANGELICAL SEMINARY OF PUERTO RICO *(A-6)*
San Juan, Puerto Rico 00925
Tel: (809) 763-6084; Fax: (809) 751-0847

Description: The seminary was established in 1919 and offers programs for the preparation of future ministers and evangelical workers. The evangelical churches that cooperate in the seminary are the Baptist Churches of Puerto Rico, Disciples of Christ, United Methodist Church, United Presbyterian Church, Lutheran Church in America, and the United Evangelical Church of Puerto Rico. The seminary is a member of the Association of Theological Schools in the United States and Canada and the Latin American Association of Bible-Theological Institutions. It is a candidate for accreditation by the Middle States Association of Colleges and Schools. The seminary operates on the semester system and offers one summer and one winter term. Enrollment is 19 full-time and 140 part-time undergraduates, and 25 graduate students. A faculty of 14 gives a faculty-student ratio of 1-10.

Entrance Requirements: Bachelor of Arts degree or equivalent from an accredited institution; satisfactory evidence of Christian character and ability to pursue graduate studies; GRE or PAEG.

Costs Per Year: $4,050 tuition; $1,500 room and board.

Collegiate Environment: The seminary is located on 5 acres, two blocks from the University of Puerto Rico. The seminary library contains 50,000 titles, and dormitory facilites are provided for 66 men and 40 women. Students from other geographical locations are accepted. Approximately 98% of students applying for admission are accepted. All of the previous entering class continued their studies at the seminary for their second year. Semesters begin in August and February.

Community Environment: See University of Puerto Rico - Rio Piedras Campus.

I.C.P.R. JUNIOR COLLEGE   *(A-6)*
Munoz Rivera Avenue 558
Hato Rey, Puerto Rico 00919
Tel: (809) 763-1010; Fax: (809) 763-7249

Description: The privately supported junior college was founded in 1946 and is accredited by the Middle States Association of Colleges and Schools. The school is coeducational and operates on the trimester system. Enrollment includes 1,300 full-time and 290 part-time students. A faculty of 46 gives a faculty-student ratio of 1-18. The college offers an associate degrees and certificates programs.

Entrance Requirements: High school graduate or equivalent; immunization certificates required if student is less than 21 years old; open enrollment; $28 application fee.

Costs Per Year: $2,700 tuition; $25 laboratory fee; $30 graduation fee.

Collegiate Environment: The campus is located in Hato Rey, approximately midway between old San Juan and Rio Piedras. The library contains 11,000 volumes, 100 periodicals, and 50 audiovisual materials. Approximately 90% of those applying for admission are accepted, including students at midyear. There are no dormitory facilities.

Community Environment: See Conservatory of Music of Puerto Rico.

Branch Campuses: Arecibo Branch Campus, Road 2, Km. 80.4, Bo. San Daniel Box 140067, Arecibo, 00614-0067, (809) 878-0524; Hato Rey Branch Campus, 558 Munoz Rivera Ave., Box 190304, Hato Rey 00919-0304, (809) 763-1010; Mayaguez Campus, McKinley, 80 West, P.O. Box 1108, Mayaguez 00681-1108.

INTER AMERICAN UNIVERSITY OF PUERTO RICO   *(A-6)*
G.P.O. Box 363255
San Juan, Puerto Rico 00936-3255
Tel: (809) 766-1912

Description: The private university was founded in 1912 as the Polytechnic Institute. The first college-level courses were introduced in 1921 and its present name was adopted in 1956. Accredited in 1944, it was the first institution outside of the continental United States to be fully accredited by the Middle States Association of Colleges and Schools. The university offers liberal arts, career and professional programs at campuses located in San German and San Juan; at a University College in Bayamon; at regional colleges in Aguadilla, Arecibo, Barranquitas, Fajardo, Guayama and Ponce; and at the School of Law in San Juan. The total student body enrollment includes 41,427 men and women. The university operates on the semester system and also offers two summer terms. A faculty of 2,107 provides a faculty-student ratio of approximately 1-18.

Entrance Requirements: Accredited high school graduation or equivalent; SAT, ACT, or Spanish achievement test required; early admission and advanced placement plans available; application fee varies according to school.

Costs Per Year: Approximately $1,050 undergraduate tuition; $1,920 tuition for graduate programs; $3,360 tuition for School of Law; $8,000 tuition School of Optometry; $1,600 room and board; $150 general fees.

Collegiate Environment: The campus at San German is located on 250 acres of rolling, wooded land. The Metropolitan Campus is located in a new building complex with modern teaching facilities at Rio Piedras. Each of the university's campuses has its own library, and the library system contains approximately 328,000 volumes. Both Spanish and English are spoken and used at the university. Housing facilities for men and women are available at the San German campus. Students are responsible for finding their housing at the other campuses. The academic year begins in August and midyear students are accepted. Scholarships, loans, and grants are available, and about 90% of the current student body receives some form of financial assistance.

Community Environment: Inter American University has campuses and colleges spread throughout Puerto Rico. Puerto Rico is a tropical island with over 3.2 million inhabitants. Its people are mainly of hispanic descent and their culture, including the use of the Spanish language, reflects their origin. The climate is ideal with temperatures ranging between 70 and 85 degrees throughout the whole year. Rainfall is moderate. Beaches provide facilities for boating, fishing and swimming.

PONTIFICAL CATHOLIC UNIVERSITY OF PUERTO RICO *(C-4)*
2250 Avenue de las Americas
Ponce, Puerto Rico 00731-6382
Tel: (809) 841-2000; Fax: (809) 840-4295

Description: The private university was established in 1948 and has been affiliated from the beginning of its history with the Catholic University of America in the United States. In 1949, it was accredited by the Council on Higher Education of Puerto Rico and in 1963 it became accredited by the Middle States Association of Colleges and Schools. The university operates on the early semester system and also provides night sessions, Saturday classes and two summer sessions. Enrollment is 9,975 full-time and 2,391 part-time students. There are also 1,162 graduate students and 934 evening students. A faculty of 456 full-time and 22 part-time gives a faculty-student ratio of 1-21.

Entrance Requirements: Accredited high school graduation; minimum C average and completion of 16 units including 4 English, 3 mathematics, 2-3 foreign language, 1 science, and 1 social science; SAT with minimum 490V, 482M and three Achievement Tests required; GRE required for some graduate programs; early admission, early decision, rolling admission and advanced placement plans available; $15 application fee.

Costs Per Year: $2,520 tuition; $2,473 room and board; $207 student fees.

Collegiate Environment: The campus occupies 120 acres of land in the city of Ponce. Campus buildings include: Spellman Hall, where the Law School, the Msgr. Torres Oliver Law Library and the College of Business Administration are located; Ferre Science Hall, which contains laboratories for Biology and Chemistry departments; and the Valdes Building, which houses the Nursing School and the bookstore. The main library, Encarnacion Valdes, has over 322,030 volumes and is located opposite the Founders Hall where most of the administrative offices are located. A series of smaller buildings are scattered throughout the campus containing dining facilities for students and faculty, meeting rooms for student activities, the Guidance Center and various offices. Dormitory facilities are provided by the university for 193 students. In addition to the main campus, the university operates educational centers in Arecibo, Guayama and Mayaguez. Students from other geographical locations are accepted as well as midyear students. Financial aid is available for economically handicapped students.

Community Environment: Ponce is a metropolitan area. Mercedita Airport furnishes transportation to Mayaguez and San Juan. Bus transportation is available to all parts of the island. Community facilities include a public library, museums, churches of major denominations, hospitals, excellent shopping facilities and a number of the major civic, fraternal and service organizations. Part-time employment opportunities are limited. Carnival celebrations and Fiesta Patronales are special annual events.

Branch Campuses: Arecibo Branch Campus, P.O. Box 495, Arecibo 00613, (809) 881-1212; Mayaguez Branch Campus, P.O. Box 1326, Mayaguez 00681, (809) 833-8478; Guayama Branch Campus, Guayama 00785, (809) 864-8550.

UNIVERSITY OF PUERTO RICO - AGUADILLA REGIONAL COLLEGE   *(A-1)*
P.O. Box 160, Ramey
Aguadilla, Puerto Rico 00604
Tel: (809) 890-2681

Description: The publicly supported, junior college is fully accredited by the Middle States Association of Colleges and Schools. Operating on the semester system, the school lately enrolled 1,585 students. A faculty of 80 established a teacher-student ratio of 1-20.

Entrance Requirements: High school graduation with completion of 12 units required, including 3 English, 2 math, 1 laboratory science, 3 foreign language, 3 social studies; SAT required; rolling admission and advanced placement plans available.

Costs Per Year: $492 tuition; $2,000 nonresident tuition; $40 student fees.

Collegiate Environment: 38% of the students applying are accepted. Freshmen are admitted at the beginning of the year only; transfer students may enroll at midyear. The college library contains 23,008 volumes. Scholarships are available.

UNIVERSITY OF PUERTO RICO - ARECIBO   *(A-3)*
Call Box 4010
Arecibo, Puerto Rico 00613
Tel: (809) 878-2830

Description: This technical college was established in 1967. It is accredited by the Middle States Association of Colleges and Schools. It operates on the semester calendar system and offers one summer session. Current enrollment includes 3,227 full-time and 610 part-time students. The faculty consists of 182 full-time and 36 part-time members, giving a teacher-student ratio of 1-20. An Army ROTC program is available.

Entrance Requirements: High school graduation; 15 units required including 3 English, 2 mathematics, 2 laboratory science, 3 Spanish, 2 social studies, and 3 electives; SAT (450 verbal, 550 math); high school graduates with a C average accepted; CEEB (English, Spanish, mathematics); $15 application fee.

Costs Per Year: $900; $2,400 foreign students; $444 student fees.

Collegiate Environment: 83% of all applicants are accepted. Scholarships are available and 87% of the students receive some form of financial aid. The library's holdings include 72,486 bound volumes, 53,910 titles, 718 periodical subscriptions, 5,963 microforms and 1,257 audiovisual materials.

Community Environment: Settled in 1556, Arecibo is the site of pre-Columbian drawings and carvings, the World's largest radar-radio telescope, and the Ron Rico rum distillery. An urban community with a tropical climate, the area offers good shopping, churches (Catholic, Episcopal, Methodist, Presbyterian), hospitals, service organizations, and a public library. Swimming, boating, and fishing are year round activities.

UNIVERSITY OF PUERTO RICO - BAYAMON TECHNOLOGICAL UNIVERSITY COLLEGE   *(A-5)*
Bayamon Gardens
Bayamon, Puerto Rico 00959
Tel: (809) 787-2885

Description: Founded in 1971, Baymon offers two-year programs in the liberal arts and the technologies. Four-year programs are available for technological and technical fields. Fully accredited by the Middle States Association of College and Schools, the college operates on the semester system and offers one summer session. Enrollment includes 3,697 students. A faculty of 203 provides a faculty-student ratio of 1-18.

Entrance Requirements: High school graduation; 12 units required: 3 English, 2 mathematics, 1 laboratory science, 3 Spanish, 3 social studies; SAT or CEEB; admissions index determined by high school GPA and CEEB scores in verbal and math aptitude tests; admissions index varies per program and is set yearly; $30 application fee.

Costs Per Year: $830 tuition and fees, $2,000 nonresident tuition; $2,950 room and board.

Collegiate Environment: 38% of applicants are accepted. A total of 2,349 students received some kind of financial aid, of which 520 were freshmen. The library has 51,704 books, 624 periodicals and 16,497 audiovisual materials.

Community Environment: Part of metropolitan San Juan, Bayamon lies six miles southwest of old San Juan.

UNIVERSITY OF PUERTO RICO - CAROLINA REGIONAL COLLEGE   *(A-6)*
P. O. Box 4800
Carolina, Puerto Rico 00984-4800
Tel: (809) 757-2000

Description: The Carolina Regional College is the only experimental College of the University of Puerto Rico located in the Metropolitan area, east of San Juan. It is a publicly supported junior college, founded in 1974. Carolina is the only unit of the University System that does not operate on a two semester basis. Its academic year consist of "cuatrimestre" (three-four months sessions). This provides the students the opportunity of completing their studies in one year and a quarter. The College offers a two-year in-transfer program towards the bachelor's degree and two-years associate degree programs in technical careers. Recently, 1,923 students were enrolled and a faculty of 128 rendered a teacher-student ratio of 1-18. It is accredited by the Middle States Association of Colleges and Schools.

Entrance Requirements: High school graduation; 15 units required, 3 English, 2 mathematics, 3 foreign language, 3 social studies; SAT (450 verbal, 550 math); GRE; high school graduates with a C average accepted; CEEB (English, Spanish, mathematics).

Costs Per Year: $717 technical tuition; $804 transfer tuition; $3,000 nonresident tuition; $177 student fees; $2,995 room and board.

Collegiate Environment: 14% of applicants accepted. Freshmen have scholarships available to them. The current library collection breaks down to 23,251 books, 222 periodicals, and 4,028 audiovisual materials.

Community Environment: Carolina, midway between San Juan and the 3848-foot El Yunque Mountain, is known for its exotic Monoloro Animal Park.

UNIVERSITY OF PUERTO RICO - CAYEY   *(C-5)*
A. R. Barcelo Avenue
Cayey, Puerto Rico 00633
Tel: (809) 738-2161

Description: Established in 1967, this branch of the University of Puerto Rico operates on the semester system and is accredited by the Middle States Association of Colleges and Schools. Cayey's enrollment is 2,780 full-time and 369 part-time students. A faculty of 188 full-time and 6 part-time provides a faculty-student ratio of 1-17. Liberal arts and teacher education are emphasized along with a special natural science program. Army ROTC program is available. Scholarships are available and 85% of the students receive some form of financial aid.

Entrance Requirements: High school graduation; 15 units are required, 3 English, 3 mathematics, 3 laboratory science, 3 Spanish, 3 social studies; SAT required; advanced placement plan available; Dec. 15 application deadline; $15 application fee.

Costs Per Year: $1,020 tuition; $2,400 nonresidents; $2,290 room and board; $80 student fees.

Collegiate Environment: The college library contains 116,528 titles, 564 periodicals and 1,473 audiovisual materials.

UNIVERSITY OF PUERTO RICO - HUMACAO UNIVERSITY COLLEGE   *(B-7)*
CUH Station
Humacao, Puerto Rico 00661
Tel: (809) 850-0000; Fax: (809) 852-4638

Description: This publicly supported, four-year university offers Bachelor and Associate degrees. It is part of the University of Puerto Rico. The school operates on the semester system and offers one summer session. It is accredited by the Middle States Association of Colleges and Schools. Enrollment is 3,260 full-time and 665 part-time students. A faculty of 235 full-time and 25 part-time gives a faculty-student ratio of 1-15. Army ROTC is available.

Entrance Requirements: High school graduation or equivalent with completion of 15 units, including 3 English, 2 math, 2 science, 2 social studies, and 3 foreign language; PEAU required; CEEB English, Spanish and mathematics achievement tests required; midyear admission and advanced placement plan available.

Costs Per Year: $510 average Associate degree program tuition; $510 Bachelor's degree program tuition; $2,400 foreign students; $474.50 student fees.

Collegiate Environment: The library contains 90,345 volumes. 61% of applicants are accepted. Financial assistance is available and 72% of the students receive some form of aid.

UNIVERSITY OF PUERTO RICO - LA MONTANA REGIONAL COLLEGE   *(B-3)*
Call Box 2500uo Hospital
Utuado, Puerto Rico 00641
Tel: (809) 894-2828

Description: The newest (1978) branch of the University of Puerto Rico system, La Montana's curricula covers the liberal arts, technical and professional studies at junior college and college levels. The semester system is employed. Enrollment is 639 students with a faculty of 53 providing a teacher-student ratio of 1-12. Accredited by the Middle States Association of Colleges and Schools.

Entrance Requirements: High school graduation; 12 units required, 3 English, 2 mathematics, 1 laboratory science, 3 Spanish, 3 social studies; SAT (450 verbal, 550 mathematics); GRE; GED and USAF high school graduates with a C average accepted; CEEB (English, Spanish, mathematics).

Costs Per Year: $500 tuition; $127 student fees.

Collegiate Environment: 43% of applicants accepted. Of 397 scholarships available, 216 are for freshmen. At present, the library contains 13,589 books, 185 periodicals, and 577 audiovisual materials.

Community Environment: Located in Puerto Rico's central mountain region, Utuado is a mountain town twenty miles south of Arecibo. Amidst the lush landscape are numerous ancient Indian caves and coffee plantations.

UNIVERSITY OF PUERTO RICO - MAYAGUEZ   *(B-1)*
Post Street
P.O. Box 5000
Mayaguez, Puerto Rico 00681
Tel: (809) 832-4040

Description: The Mayaguez Campus is one of three main campuses of the University of Puerto Rico. It was established in 1911 as the College of Agriculture and Mechanic Arts. Today, it is comprised of the College of Agriculture, College of Arts and Sciences, College of Business Administration, College of Engineering, a Technical Institute, a Division of Extension and Community Services, and the Center for Energy and Environment Research. Army and Air Force ROTC programs are provided. The university operates on the semester system and also offers one summer term. It is accredited by the Middle States Association of Colleges and Schools, the Association of Hispano-American Universities, the Accreditation Board of Engineering and Technology, American Chemical Society and the National League for Nursing. A recent enrollment included 9,932 men and women.

Entrance Requirements: Accredited high school graduation or equivalent, 30 units, minimum C average; SAT required; advanced placement plan available; application fee $15.

Costs Per Year: $590 resident tuition; $2,890 room and board; $111 student fees.

Collegiate Environment: Library holdings include 191,018 volumes, 6,975 periodicals, and 235,266 microfiche. The college accepts 80% of the students who apply for admission. Freshmen are admitted only at the beginning of the academic year; transfer students may enroll at mid-year. Financial aid is available.

Community Environment: A metropolitan area with a tropical climate, Mayaguez has bus transportation available to San Juan, a public library, museum, Catholic and Protestant churches, five hospitals, excellent shopping facilities and a number of the major civic organizations that serve the community. Part-time employment is available. Outdoor activities include all water sports.

UNIVERSITY OF PUERTO RICO - MEDICAL SCIENCES CAMPUS   *(A-6)*
G.P.O. Box 5067
San Juan, Puerto Rico 00936
Tel: (809) 758-2525

Description: The Medical Sciences Campus is accredited by the Middle States Association of Colleges and Schools and is one of the University of Puerto Rico's three main campuses. It has five schools: Medicine, Dentistry, Public Health, Allied Health professions and Pharmacy. In addition to its Bachelors, Masters and Doctoral programs, the school offers 46 postgraduate Certificates in various medical specialities and subspecialities. Enrollment includes 2,787 full-time and 463 part-time undergraduates and 1,376 graduate and first professional students. There are 404 resident students of medicine. The faculty is 587 full-time and 172 part-time.

Entrance Requirements: High school graduation with Spanish-speaking ability for undergraduate courses; graduate schools require two full years in an accredited college or university with a minimum grade point average of 2.00 to 2.75 in majors, emphasizing chemical and biological sciences; GRE; Dental Admission Test; Medical College Admission Test; Feb. 28 undergraduate application deadline; Mar. 1 graduate application deadline; Dec. 15 first professional programs deadline. $25 application fee.

Costs Per Year: $1,425 undergraduate tuition; $2,250 ($75/cr) graduate; $5,000 Medicine and Dentistry; $3,325 room and board; $2,625 instruments.

Collegiate Environment: The Medical Campus has its own library that contains 39,150 volumes, 37,473 titles, 3,500 journals, 58,362 periodicals and 1,610 audiovisual materials. 50% of applicants to undergraduate programs and 60% of applicants to graduate programs are accepted. Scholarships are not available.

Community Environment: San Juan juxtaposes the old and the new: Old San Juan and the moss-covered El Morro castle are contrasted with high-rise office buildings. Founded in 1521, San Juan is a metropolitan city with a mild climate. Museums (e.g. colonial architecture, rare books Puerto Rican art), outdoor sports (swimming, surfing, baseball, fishing, cock fighting), hospitals and excellent shopping are available to everyone. Special San Juan events include drama festivals, native carnivals, the International Theatrical Festival and the Casals Festival.

UNIVERSITY OF PUERTO RICO - PONCE TECHNOLOGICAL UNIVERSITY COLLEGE   *(C-3)*
P.O. Box 7186
Ponce, Puerto Rico 00732
Tel: (809) 844-8181

Description: A coeducational, public, junior college offering instruction in the liberal arts and technical/vocational disciplines. It is fully accredited by the Middle States Association of Colleges and Schools. Employing the semester system, Ponce enrolled 2,292 students. A faculty of 103 provides a teacher-student ratio of 1-22.

Entrance Requirements: High school graduation; 15 units required; 3 English, 2 mathematics, 3 Spanish, 2 laboratory sci., 2 electives. 3 social studies; SAT 450 verbal, 550 mathematics; high school graduates with a C average accepted; CEEB (English, Spanish, mathematics).

Costs Per Year: $450 tuition; $2,200 nonresident tuition; $72 student fees.

Collegiate Environment: 40% of applicants accepted. Available scholarships to freshmen number 289. Library figures tally up to 30,269 books, 190 periodicals and 24,040 audiovisual materials.

Community Environment: Puerto Rico's second city, Ponce is known as the "Pearl of the South." The city is known for its much photographed ancient firehouse, the Edward Stone-designed museum of art, old Spanish houses replete with rejas, the first rate El Tuque Beach and the Don Q Rum Distillery. Its Carnival ranks above San Juan's.

UNIVERSITY OF PUERTO RICO - RIO PIEDRAS CAMPUS
(A-6)
University Station, Box 23302
Rio Piedras, Puerto Rico 00931
Tel: (809) 764-0000; Admissions: (809) 764-0000 X 5653; Fax: (809) 764-3680

Description: The university has grown out of normal school for the training of public school teachers, which was opened in 1900. It was incorporated by law as the University of Puerto Rico in 1903. Today the university is comprised of three main campuses at Rio Piedras, Mayaguez and in San Juan the campus of Medical Sciences. University colleges have been established at Humacao and Cayey, and Regional Colleges at Aguadilla, Arecibo, Bayamon, Carolina and Ponce. The principal campus and the oldest is at Rio Piedras, in the metropolitan area of San Juan. It contains colleges of Business Administration, Education, General Studies, Humanities, Natural Science, Social Sciences, Architecture; schools of Law, Planning, Public Administration, and Social Work. Army and Air Force ROTC programs are provided. The university operates on the semester system and offers one summer term. Enrollment includes 15,580 undergraduates and 3,420 graduate students. A faculty of 1,294 full-time and 186 part-time gives a faculty-student ratio of 1-15. The university is accredited by the Middle States Association of Colleges and Schools and by respective professional and educational organizations; early admission, deferred admission, midyear admission and advanced plans available. $15 application fee.

Entrance Requirements: Accredited high school graduation or equivalent; minimum C average; CEEB Spanish version SAT accepted; students must have a working knowledge of Spanish and English.

Costs Per Year: $836 tuition and fees; $2,000 foreign student tuition; $2,890 room and board; U.S. residents tuition equal to home state, nonresident, public university.

Collegiate Environment: The university is comprised of 123 buildings, located on 280.58 acres. The university library contains 1,194,133 volumes, 7,698 subscriptions, 1,431,173 microforms, and 183,226 other library materials. Dormitory facilities on the Rio Piedras Campus are available for 437 men and 346 women. Approximately 60% of students applying for admission were accepted.

Scholarships are available and 62% of students receive some form of financial aid.

Community Environment: Located a few miles from San Juan, Rio Piedras has mostly sunny weather with little fluctuation during the different seasons of the year. Plane transportation available to and from the United States, South America and the Caribbean area, bus transportation around the island. There are a number of libraries, museums, art galleries, churches of different faiths and hospitals. YMCA, YWCA, and various civic organizations serve the city. Recreational facilities include the San Juan beaches for all water sports. Part-time employment is available.

UNIVERSITY OF THE SACRED HEART   *(A-6)*
P.O. Box 12383
Loiza Station
Santurce, Puerto Rico 00914
Tel: (809) 728-1515

Description: The private college was established in 1880 and is affiliated with the Roman Catholic Church. Formerly for women only, it became coeducational in 1970. It operates on the semester system and also offers two summer terms. The college is accredited by the Middle States Association of Colleges and Schools, the Committee on Allied Health Education and Accreditation, Council on Social Work Education and the National League for Nursing. There are 7,480 students enrolled. A faculty of 383 gives a faculty-student ratio of 1-20.

Entrance Requirements: Accredited high school graduation; completion of 20 units including 3 English, 3 mathematics, 3 science, 4 social science, 4 Spanish; SAT required, minimum score 450V, 450M; CEEB English achievement test required; advanced placement plan available; $15 application fee.

Costs Per Year: $2,550 tuition; $1,200 room; $160 student fees.

Collegiate Environment: The college buildings contain a library of 80,518 volumes and dormitory facilities for 156 women. Students from other geographical locations are accepted, as well as midyear students. Approximately 79% of students applying for admission are accepted. About 85% of the previous freshman class returned to this campus for their sophomore year. Financial aid is available for economically handicapped students. The college awarded 113 Associate and 240 Bachelor degrees to a recent graduating class. Semesters begin in August and January.

Community Environment: San Juan juxtaposes the old and the new: Old San Juan and the moss-covered El Morro castle are contrasted with high-rise office buildings. Founded in 1521, San Juan is a metropolitan city with a mild climate. Museums (e.g. colonial architecture, rare books Puerto Rican art), outdoor sports (swimming, surfing, baseball, fishing, cock fighting), hospitals and excellent shopping are available to everyone. Special San Juan events include drama festivals, native carnivals, the International Theatrical Festival and the Casals Festival.

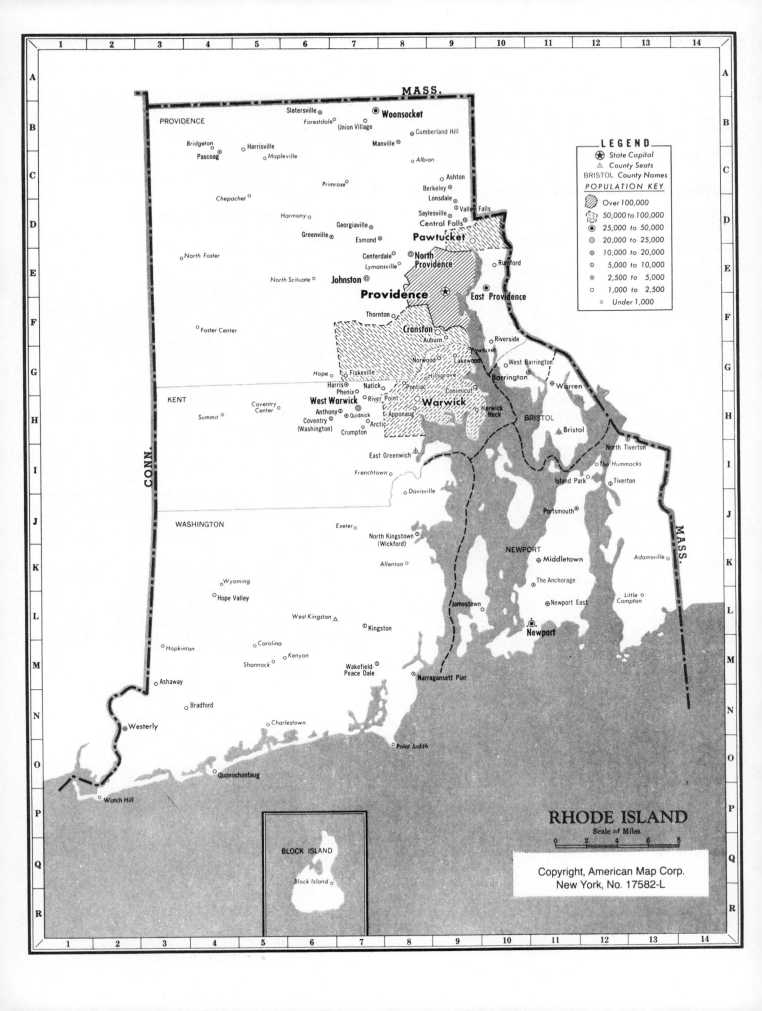

RHODE ISLAND

Scale of Miles

0   2   4   6   8

MASS.

CONN.

MASS.

PROVIDENCE

KENT

WASHINGTON

NEWPORT

BRISTOL

LEGEND
- State Capital
- County Seats
- BRISTOL County Names

POPULATION KEY
- Over 100,000
- 50,000 to 100,000
- 25,000 to 50,000
- 20,000 to 25,000
- 10,000 to 20,000
- 5,000 to 10,000
- 2,500 to 5,000
- 1,000 to 2,500
- Under 1,000

Slatersville
Forestdale
Woonsocket
Union Village
Cumberland Hill
Manville
Albion
Bridgeton
Harrisville
Pascoag
Mapleville
Ashton
Berkeley
Lonsdale
Primrose
Saylesville
Valley Falls
Chepachet
Harmony
Georgiaville
Central Falls
Greenville
Esmond
Pawtucket
North Foster
Centerdale
North
Providence
Lymansville
Rumford
North Scituate
Johnston
Providence
Foster Center
East Providence
Thornton
Cranston
Riverside
Auburn
Pawtuxet
Norwood
Lakewood
West Barrington
Hope
Fiskeville
Hillsgrove
Barrington
Warren
Harris
Natick
Pontiac
Conimicut
Phenix
River Point
Coventry
Center
West Warwick
Warwick
BRISTOL
Summit
Anthony
Quidnick
Warwick Neck
Coventry
(Washington)
Arctic
Bristol
Crompton
Apponaug
East Greenwich
North Tiverton
Frenchtown
The Hummocks
Island Park
Tiverton
Davisville
Portsmouth
Exeter
North Kingstown
(Wickford)
NEWPORT
Adamsville
Allenton
Middletown
The Anchorage
Wyoming
Little
Compton
Hope Valley
Newport East
West Kingston
Jamestown
Hopkinton
Kingston
Newport
Carolina
Kenyon
Shannock
Wakefield-
Peace Dale
Ashaway
Narragansett Pier
Bradford
Westerly
Charlestown
Point Judith
Quonochontaug
Watch Hill

BLOCK ISLAND

Block Island

Copyright, American Map Corp.
New York, No. 17582-L

RHODE ISLAND

BROWN UNIVERSITY   *(E-9)*
Box 1876
Providence, Rhode Island 02912
Tel: (401) 863-1000

Description: Brown University, founded in 1764, is the seventh oldest college in the United States and the third oldest college in New England. It is private, nonsectarian, and coeducational. Current enrollment includes 2,741 men, 2,717 women full-time, 21 men, 20 women part-time, and 772 men, 568 women graduate students. Faculty includes 531 full-time and 23 part-time members with the titles Professor, Associate Professor, Assistant Professor, Instructor and Lecturer. The student-faculty ratio is currently 9 to 1. The Graduate School offers courses leading to six degrees -- including the Ph.D., in 30 disciplines. In 1972, Brown initiated a Medical Education Program which awards Doctor of Medicine (MD) and Master of Medical Science (MMSc) degrees, there are 290 students in the Program.

Entrance Requirements: High school graduation; secondary school preparation of the following is desireable: 4 years of English, at least 3 years of college preparatory mathematics, at least 3 years of foreign language study, at least 2 years of history, including American history, at least 1 year of study in music or art, and at least 2 years of laboratory science above the freshmen-year level; SAT and at least three Achievement Tests of the College Board no later than January of the senior year; early decision, early admission and advanced placement plans available; $55 application fee.

Costs Per Year: $18,512 tuition and fees; $6,106 room and board.

Collegiate Environment: The campus consists of approximately 210 buildings occupying an area of 146 acres on the east side of Providence. All University buildings on the main campus are included within the College Hill Historic District of the National Register for Historic Places, United States Department of the Interior. The Brown University Library contains more than 4,000,000 items including bound volumes, periodicals, maps, microforms, data bases, sheet music and manuscripts. There are seven libraries within the University Library System. The John Carter Brown Library is an independent research library also on campus. The Haffenreffer Museum of Anthropology, located seventeen miles south of Providence, in Bristol, RI, consists of over 500 acres of woodland overlooking Mount Hope Bay. The museum was a gift to Brown in 1955 from the Rudolf F. Haffenreffer family and foundation. The University provides extensive, modern laboratory facilities designed for undergraduate instruction graduate instruction and reseach. The Computer Center operates the campus central computing facility, public terminal and microcomputer centers, and provides training, consulting, documentation and software support to the community. Resources available to students include Foreign Student Advising, Office of Career Planning Services, the Office of the Chaplain, Faunce House Student Center, Health Services, Psychological Services, the Sarah Doyle Women's Center and more.

Community Environment: In its early days, Providence was a shipping and ship-building town, running the Triangular Trade route with slaves, rum and molasses between Africa, the West Indies and the colonies. Providence, the second largest city in New England, is the industrial and commercial center in addition to being the capital of Rhode Island. The city is one of the largest manufacturing centers in the world and excels in several branches of the metal and rubber industries. Textile manufacturing is of first importance. Historical sites and points of interest include Cathedral of St. John, Cathedral of St. Peter and St. Paul, Gorham Manufacturing Co., Rhode Island Historical Society, Round Top Church and the State House.

BRYANT COLLEGE   *(E-9)*
1150 Douglas Pike
Smithfield, Rhode Island 02917
Tel: (401) 232-6100; (800) 622-7001; Fax: (401) 232-6741

Description: Founded in 1863, this privately supported, coeducational college is accredited by the New England Association of Schools and Colleges. The college offers Bachelor of Science and Bachelor of Arts programs in business and Bachelor of Arts programs in business-related areas at the collegiate level. The college grants Bachelor's and Master's degrees. Army ROTC is available. The college operates on the early semester calendar system and offers one winter session and one summer session. Enrollment includes 2,895 full-time and 783 part-time undergraduates and 769 graduate students. A faculty of 134 full-time gives a faculty-student ratio of 1-18.

Entrance Requirements: High school graduation, completion of 16 units, including 4 English, 2 algebra, 2 social studies, and 1 science; SAT or ACT required; GMAT or GRE required for graduate school; rolling admission, delayed admission, midyear admission and advanced placement plans available; $30 application fee.

Costs Per Year: $13,100 tuition; $6,500 room and board.

Collegiate Environment: In 1971, the college moved to its present location 12 miles from Providence and 40 miles from Boston. The campus occupies 387 acres and includes a library of 113,000 volumes, 1,300 periodicals, 233 microform subscriptions, and 18,316 other microform items. Dormitory facilities are available for 2,484 students. 81% of those who apply for admission are accepted. Of the entering freshmen class, 25% scored on the SAT at 500 or higher, math. Scholarships are available and 62% of students receive some form of financial aid.

Community Environment: The college is located in the midst of the social, cultural, and recreational center that is southern New England. Its 387-acre campus offers the best of two worlds: the security of its suburban location with easy access to the excitement of the city. The setting, the campus, and the ultramodern facilities have been designed to maximize the interaction between faculty, students and administrators. This intergrative atmosphere contributes to an individualistic approach to education and fosters an intimate relationship among all segments of the college community.

COMMUNITY COLLEGE OF RHODE ISLAND - KNIGHT CAMPUS   *(E-9)*
400 East Avenue
Warwick, Rhode Island 02886-1807
Tel: (401) 825-1000; Fax: (401) 825-2418

Description: This publicly supported, coeducational, two-year college offers programs of liberal arts education, transferable and terminal, and programs of vocational education. The college opened in 1964 and is accredited by the New England Association of Schools and Colleges. It operates on the semester system and offers two summer sessions and an evening division of continuing education programs. Enrollment includes 7,000 full-time, 9,000 part-time, and 8,000 evening students which includes students at the three main campuses and six satellite locations that offer credit and noncredit courses. There is a faculty of 310 full-time and 410 part-time.

Entrance Requirements: High school graduation or equivalent; open enrollment policy; midyear admission and rolling admission plans available; $20 application fee.

Costs Per Year: $1,700 full-time tuition; $73 per credit for students taking 11 credits or less; $55 full-time student fees; $15 part-time student fees.

Collegiate Environment: The 205-acre Knight campus is located in the western section of Warwick within 15 minutes of the center of

Providence. The Flanagan campus, opened in 1976, consists of 300 acres. The Providence campus opened its doors in September 1990. Combined facilities of the three campuses include a library of 83,144 volumes. All qualified applicants are accepted.

Community Environment: See Brown University.

Branch Campuses: Flanagan Campus, 1762 Louisquisset Pike, Lincoln, RI 02865-4585; Providence Campus, 1 Hilton St., Providence, RI 02905-2313.

JOHNSON AND WALES UNIVERSITY   *(E-9)*
Abbott Park Place
Providence, Rhode Island 02903
Tel: (401) 598-1000; (800) 353-2565; Admissions: (401) 598-4664; Fax: (401) 598-1835

Description: Privately supported college and vocational school, founded in 1914, accredited by the New England Association of Schools and Colleges. It offers Associate, Bachelor's and Masters degrees. The college operates on a trimester system with two summer sessions. Army ROTC is available as an elective at Providence College. A degree in Culinary Arts is available at a branch campus in Charleston, SC. Enrollment includes 6,202 full-time, and 1,120 part-time undergraduates and 467 graduate students. A faculty of 282 full-time and 153 part-time gives a faculty-student ratio of 1-26.

Entrance Requirements: High school graduation or equivalent; early admission, early decision, rolling admission, delayed admission and advanced placement plans available; non-high school graduates considered; no application fee.

Costs Per Year: $9,864 tuition; $4,728 room and board; $312 general fees; additional expenses average $750.

Collegiate Environment: The college is located in the heart of downtown Providence, convenient to all modes of transportation. The urban population of Providence is approximately 155,000. The facilities include a library of 600,269 volumes and 60,000 microforms. Housing facilities are available for 3,310 men and women. 81% of the students applying for admission are accepted including midyear students. Financial aid is available for needy students and 84% of the current student body receives financial assistance. Of 500 scholarships offered, 290 are available for freshmen. The college is geared for the average high school graduate.

Community Environment: See Brown University.

Branch Campuses: 1701 N.E. 127th St., North Miami, FL 33181, (305) 895-7111; 701 E. Bay St., BTC Box 1409, Charleston, SC 29403, (803) 723-4638; 2428 Almeda Ave., Suite 316/318, Norfolk, VA 23513, (804) 853-3508; 616 West Lionshead Circle, Suite 101, Vail, CO 81657

PROVIDENCE COLLEGE   *(E-9)*
Eaton Street & River Avenue
Providence, Rhode Island 02918
Tel: (401) 865-1000; Fax: (401) 865-2826

Description: Providence College is primarily a four-year college of the liberal arts and sciences with an undergraduate enrollment of 3,747 full-time and 1,498 part-time students. A faculty of 256 full-time and 47 part-time gives a faculty-student ratio of 1-14. It is conducted under the auspices of the Order of Preachers of the Province of St. Joseph, commonly known as the Dominicans. Founded in 1917 under an Act of Incorporation approved by the General Assembly of the State of Rhode Island, its charter contains the following statement: "No person shall be denied any of the privileges, honors or degrees of said college on account of the religious opinions he may entertain." It is a coeducational, privately supported, equal-opportunity institution and is duly accredited by the New England Association of Schools Colleges, the American Chemical Society and the Council on Social Work Education. Army ROTC is available as an elective. In addition to the undergraduate division, the College has a school of continuing education, a summer school of religious studies, a graduate school, and an MBA program. Overseas programs are available in Switzerland, Italy, Japan, England, and Canada.

Entrance Requirements: High school graduation or equivalent; completion of 4 units of English, 3 foreign language, 3 mathematics, 2 history, 2 science and 4 electives; SAT or ACT required; GRE required for graduate school; early admission, early decision, delayed

admission and advanced placement plans available; $30 application fee.

Costs Per Year: $12,600 tuition; $5,600 room and board; $400 student fees.

Collegiate Environment: The campus is located on 105 acres in the city of Providence. The college enjoys both the advantages of an atmosphere removed from the traffic and commerce of the metropolitan area, and easy access to the many cultural attractions of the city. There are 36 buildings on the campus; the library houses 307,655 volumes; dormitories and apartments house 2,272 students. Approximately 62% of those who apply for admission are accepted. Approximately 56% of the student body receives some form of financial aid through various federal, state and institutional programs administered by the Office of Financial Aid (application deadline February 15th). The Liberal Arts Honors Program and the Humanities Program are special programs offered at this college.

Community Environment: See Brown University.

RHODE ISLAND SCHOOL OF DESIGN   *(E-9)*
2 College Street
Providence, Rhode Island 02903
Tel: (401) 454-6300; Fax: (401) 454-6309

Description: The privately supported, coeducational college is accredited by the New England Association of Schools and Colleges. The college, founded in 1877, is a privately endowed college committed to education in all forms of art, architecture and design. The college operates on the 4-1-4 calendar system and offers three summer programs and workshops. An academic cooperative plan with Brown University is available for students interested in liberal arts courses beyond those offered at RISD. Enrollment includes 2,011 students. A faculty of 121 full-time and 172 part-time gives a faculty-student ratio of 1-12. There are also students enrolled in nondegree evening courses.

Entrance Requirements: High school graduation; SAT required for all freshman applicants; early admission and advanced placement plans available; $35 application fee.

Costs Per Year: $17,600 tuition; $6,700 room and board.

Collegiate Environment: The college maintains one of the nation's most extensive and well-equipped physical plants for the study of design. There are 32 buildings located in a three-block area of historic College Hill, with a library of 80,000 volumes, 360 bound periodicals and 125,000 slides. Dormitory facilities house 606 men and women. Approximately 33% of students applying for admission are accepted. Financial aid is available for students. For honor students, there is an excellent program of study abroad in Rome, where the college maintains headquarters in the Palazzo Cenci.

Community Environment: See Brown University.

ROGER WILLIAMS COLLEGE   *(H-11)*
Ferry Road
Bristol, Rhode Island 02809
Tel: (401) 253-1040

Description: The privately supported, coeducational college was founded in 1948. The College is an outgrowth of a branch of Northeastern University founded in 1919, which conducted an evening program in the Providence YMCA. In 1956 the college became independent. The college is accredited by the New England Association of Schools and Colleges and offers programs in liberal arts and professional studies. The semester system is used and a summer session is offered. The college occupies a waterfront campus with an enrollment of 902 men, 938 women full-time and 836 men, 731 women part-time with a faculty of 117.

Entrance Requirements: High school graduation or equivalent; ACT or SAT required; $35 application fee.

Costs Per Year: $11,920 tuition; $5,330 room and board.

Collegiate Environment: The college is located in Bristol, 18 miles from Providence. The library contains 97,000 volumes, 966 periodicals, 2,311 microforms and 7,516 audiovisual materials. Dormitory facilities accommodate 1,400 students. Approximately 80% of those that apply for admission are accepted including midyear students.

More than 75% of the previous freshman class returned to the college for their second year.

Community Environment: In its early days Bristol was a port for trading vessels, but now its harbor mainly shelters pleasure craft. Bristol is on Narragansett and Mt. Hope Bays and is connected by the Mount Hope Bridge with Aquidneck Island. Recreational facilities are excellent for all summer sports. A yacht basin is located at Barrington a few short miles away. Community facilities include quaint shopping areas and many historical sites.

SALVE REGINA UNIVERSITY *(L-11)*
100 Ochre Point Avenue
Newport, Rhode Island 02840
Tel: (401) 847-6650 x2908; (800) 321-7124; Fax: (401) 848-2823

Description: Salve Regina University, founded in the Catholic tradition, is an independent, coeducational university of arts and sciences, and is accredited by the New England Association of Schools and Colleges, Inc. The National League of Nursing accredits the Nursing Program, which is approved by the Rhode Island Board of Nurses Registration and Nursing Education. The elementary and special education programs are interstate approved and provide certification in 36 states. The Social Work Department offers a baccalaureate program accredited by the Council on Social Work Education. The Studio Art programs are accredited by the National Association of Schools of Art and Design. The university awards the associate, bachelor, master and doctoral degrees. It operates on a semester calendar system and offers two summer sessions. Enrollment is 2,200 students from 30 states and many foreign countries. A faculty of 208 gives a faculty-student ratio of 1-13.

Entrance Requirements: High school graduation with rank in upper 50% recommended; completion of 16 units including 4 English, 1 history, 2 foreign language, 3 mathematics, 2 laboratory science, and 4 electives are recommended; no more than 2 units accepted in vocational subjects; high school transcript, class rank, SAT scores, 2 letters of recommendation, 1 of which must be a character reference, and essay required; early decision, advanced placement, early admission and rolling admission plans available; non-high school graduates considered; $25 application fee; room deposit of $200 and acceptance deposit of $250 are due by May 1.

Costs Per Year: $14,650 tuition; $6,700 room and board.

Collegiate Environment: Salve Regina is located in a section of Newport, RI that has been designated by the National Register of Historic Places as the Ochre Point Historic District. The campus includes 17 historic and exceptionally significant buildings that were constructed around the turn of the century. These former "summer cottages" bordering the Atlantic Ocean on Ochre Point have been adapted to house administrative, educational, and student facilities. A student residence and a new library have been constructed to harmonize with the surrounding historic neighborhood. The library houses 107,123 volumes and advanced educational technological resources that are available to both the university and civic community. Single-sex student housing consists of 14 residence halls, most of which are restored mansions. Apartments are available for upperclass students. 850 students are housed. Athletic facilities on campus include tennis courts, outdoor track, soccer, baseball/softball fields, and a weight training room. The university offers financial aid from its own resources in addition to federal and state programs. It is based on financial need demonstrated through a Salve Regina application form, a completed financial aid form, and copies of the student's and parents' federal income tax forms. The due date is March 1.

Community Environment: Newport, RI, an island community and home of Salve Regina, was founded in 1639 and thrived as a Colonial seaport. Today, yachting and sailing regattas still fill its harbor and the Museum of Yachting displays America's Cup memorabilia. The Newport Historical Society and Newport Preservation Society support the City-by-the-Sea's bountiful historic and architectural legacy, including colonial structures, Victorian cottages, and Gilded Age mansions. The Cliff Walk and Ocean Drive provide stirring ocean vistas. The Redwood Library is the oldest library building in the United States in continuous use. The Newport Art museum exhibitions focus on the art of Newport and New England. The Newport Casino, which contains the Tennis Hall of Fame, hosts international tennis matches on its grass courts. World-acclaimed musicians perform at the Newport Music Festival. Opportunities abound for students to participate in the rich historical and cultural aspects of the community through university-sponsored work-study, volunteer, and intern programs.

UNIVERSITY OF RHODE ISLAND *(L-7)*
Kingston, Rhode Island 02881
Tel: (401) 792-9800; Fax: (401) 792-5523

Description: This publicly supported, coeducational state university was founded in 1892 as one of the land grant colleges. It is accredited by the New England Association of Schools and Colleges. The university is composed of the Colleges of Resource Development, Arts & Sciences, Business Administration, Engineering, Human Science and Services, Nursing and Pharmacy. It operates on the semester system and offers two summer sessions. Enrollment includes 9,014 full-time, 2,756 part-time undergraduate, and 3,681 graduate students. A faculty of 723 full-time and 27 part-time gives a faculty-student ratio of 1-16. Army ROTC is available as an elective.

Entrance Requirements: High school graduation; completion of 18 units including 4 English, 3 mathematics, 2 science, 2 history, 2 foreign language and other units to meet requirements of the college in which the candidate expects to earn a degree; SAT or ACT required; March 1 graduate school application deadline; early admission, early decision, midyear admission, rolling admission, and advanced placement plans available; $30 state resident application fee, $45 nonresident application fee.

Costs Per Year: $3,004 state resident tuition; $10,330 nonresident tuition; $5,410 room and board; $666 student fees.

Collegiate Environment: The university's main campus in Kingston encompasses 1,200 acres. The library houses more than 1,000,000 bound volumes. The Graduate School of Oceanography is located on the 153-acre Narragansett Bay Campus, as is the Rhode Island Atomic Reactor, and several federal laboratories devoted to the marine sciences. The 2,300-acre W. Alton Jones Campus in West Greenwich is where research and conference facilities, a Youth Science Center, and camp are located. 70% of applicants are accepted. The average scores of entering freshmen were SAT Verbal 461, Math 527. $1,500,000 in scholarships is available to freshmen and 60% of students receive some form of financial assistance.

Community Environment: The quiet village of Kingston was founded about 1700. Some of the many interesting houses here date from pre-Revolutionary days. Community facilities include churches of all faiths, a museum, art center, hospitals and numerous major civic, fraternal and veteran's organizations. Recreational activities include boating, fishing, golf, skiing, and summer theatre. International and deep-sea Yacht Races are special events. Many part-time jobs are available.

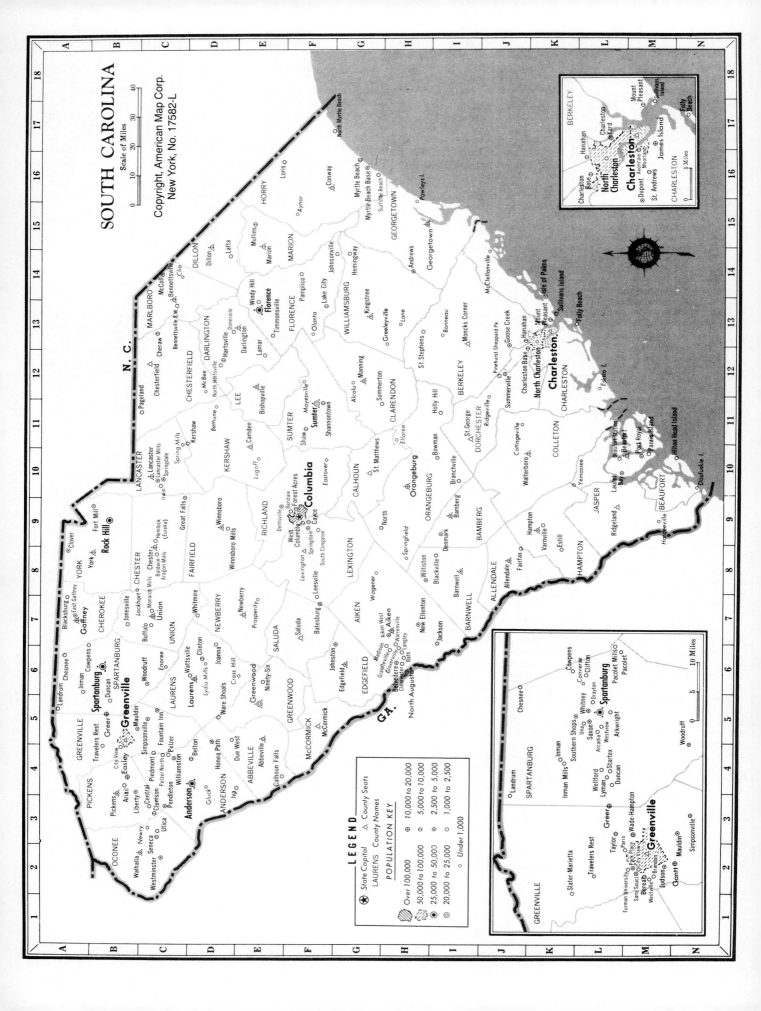

SOUTH CAROLINA

Scale of Miles

Copyright, American Map Corp.
New York, No. 17582-L

LEGEND

✪ State Capital   ⌂ County Seats

LAURENS County Names

POPULATION KEY

✪ Over 100,000	⊕ 10,000 to 20,000
⬤ 50,000 to 100,000	⊕ 5,000 to 10,000
◉ 25,000 to 50,000	⊙ 2,500 to 5,000
⊙ 20,000 to 25,000	○ 1,000 to 2,500
	○ Under 1,000

SOUTH CAROLINA

ALLEN UNIVERSITY   *(F-9)*
1530 Harden Street
Columbia, South Carolina 29204
Tel: (803) 376-5701; Admissions: (803) 376-5716; Fax: (803) 376-5709

Description: Operated since 1870 by the African Methodist Episcopal Church, the university is accredited by the Southern Association of Colleges and Schools. The educational program is organized into six divisions which encompass business and economics, education, humanities, natural sciences and mathematics, social sciences, and religion and philosophy. The school operates on the semester system and offers one summer term. It grants the Bachelor of Arts and Bachelor of Science degrees. The program is designed to make available for all students a substantial and organized curriculum in general education and to insure that each student attains depth of knowledge and breadth of understanding in a specific field of interest. An Upward-bound program is offered for disadvantaged high school juniors and seniors. Army ROTC is available. Enrollment includes 255 full-time and 4 part-time students. A faculty of 24 full-time and 16 part-time provides a faculty-student ratio of 1-8.

Entrance Requirements: High school graduation; completion of 18 units including 4 English, 2 mathematics, 1 science, 2 social science, 1 U.S. history, 1 physical education; entrance examination required; non-high school graduates considered; early admission, early decision and rolling admission plans available; $10 application fee.

Costs Per Year: $4,850 tuition; $200 student fees; $3,990 room and board.

Collegiate Environment: Located on 20 acres adjacent to the quiet and cultural section of the city known as Waverly, the university has 21 buildings all located within eight blocks of the central business district of Columbia. Residence halls accomodate 425 students. Frank Madison Reid Hall built in 1946 provides dormitory space for junior and senior students, while Coppin Hall houses freshmen and sophomores. The library contains 44,000 volumes. 95% of those who apply for admission are accepted. Financial aid is available in many forms.

Community Environment: See University of South Carolina.

ANDERSON COLLEGE   *(D-4)*
316 Boulevard
Anderson, South Carolina 29621
Tel: (803) 231-2030; (800) 542-3594; Fax: (803) 231-2033

Description: Privately supported, coeducational, senior college founded in 1911, the college is accredited by the Southern Association of Colleges and Schools as a four-year college. The college, affiliated with the Baptist Church, is an associate member of the National Association of Schools of Music. Chapel attendance is required for graduation. Associate and Bachelor degrees are granted. The school operates on the semester system and offers three summer sessions. Enrollment includes 694 full-time and 234 part-time students. A faculty of 53 gives a faculty-student ratio of 1-17. Air Force and Army ROTC programs are available.

Entrance Requirements: High school graduation or GED; completion of 18 units; SAT required, ACT may be substituted; early decision, early admission, midyear admission, rolling admission and advanced placement plans available; $20 application fee.

Costs Per Year: $8,821 tuition; $4,145 room and board.

Collegiate Environment: More than 100 oak trees grow on the campus that is landscaped in a series of rising terraces. The library contains 50,000 volumes, 200 periodicals, 150 microforms, and 1,000 sound recordings. Dormitories are arranged in two-room suites, and have a capacity of 450. While serving the immediate area, the college seeks students from diverse geographical locations. Approximately 80% of applicants are accepted, including midyear students. Scholarships are available, and approximately 95% of students receive some form of financial assistance. 74% of freshmen returned for their second year.

Community Environment: Located in the Piedmont Plateau section, Anderson enjoys moderate climate and is a busy manufacturing town with 32 textile plants and many other factories. The area is accessed by major highways, air, bus, and limited rail service. The community has a county-wide library system, churches of many denominations, hotel and motels, hospitals, shopping malls, and various civic and fraternal organizations. Local recreation includes theatres, bowling, tennis, excellent golf facilities, two large lakes, swimming, boating, fishing, hunting, and other outdoor sports. Part-time employment is available.

BENEDICT COLLEGE   *(F-9)*
208 Harden Street
Columbia, South Carolina 29204
Tel: (803) 253-5143; (800) 868-6598; Fax: (803) 253-5167

Description: Privately supported, coeducational, liberal arts college founded in 1870, the church-related school views as basic the exploration of the traditions of the Christian Faith, the heritage of the Afro-American communities, and the larger American culture. Upward Bound Program for 10th, 11th and 12th graders for preparation for college is offered. This four-year institution is accredited by the Southern Association of Colleges and Schools, and operates on the semester system with two summer terms. Enrollment is 1,209 full-time students. A faculty of 100 gives a faculty-student ratio of 1-17.

Entrance Requirements: High school graduation, completion of 20 units including 4 units of English, 3 mathematics, 2 science, 3 social science, 1 physical education or ROTC, and 7 electives; SAT or ACT required; $25 application fee; rolling admission and advanced placement plans available.

Costs Per Year: $6,196 tuition and fees; $3,294 room and board.

Collegiate Environment: Located on a 20-acre campus, the school has 20 buildings including a library with approximately 151,756 volumes. There is dormitory space available for 474 men and 756 women. South Carolina Tuition Grants, Education Opportunity Grants, College Work Study and loan funds are available to eligible students. Of students applying for a previous freshman class, 83% were admitted. A geographically diverse student body is being sought as the school seeks to attract students from beyond the immediate community. Midyear students are welcome.

Community Environment: See University of South Carolina.

BOB JONES UNIVERSITY   *(B-4)*
Wade Hampton Boulevard
Greenville, South Carolina 29614
Tel: (803) 242-5100; (800) 252-6363; Admissions: (803) 242-5100 x2050; Fax: (803) 242-5100

Description: This university is a privately controlled, coeducational, Protestant fundamentalist school recognized by the Attorney General's office and the state of South Carolina. It is composed of six schools: the College of Arts and Science, the School of Fine Arts, the School of Education, the School of Applied Studies, the School of Business Administration, and the School of Religion. It offers Associate, Bachelor, Master, and Doctor degrees. The university operates on the early semester system and offers two summer sessions. Enrollment includes 3,303 full-time, 309 part-time, and 331 graduate students. A faculty of 240 full-time and 100 part-time gives a faculty-student ratio of 1-11. The university allows credit for correspondence courses and by prior examination for previous training.

Entrance Requirements: High school graduation with rank in the top 60% of the high school class; required completion of 16 units including 3 English, 2 mathematics, 2 foreign language, 1 science, and 2 social science; ACT required; non-high school graduates considered; early decision and rolling admission plans available; $45 application fee.

Costs Per Year: $4,500 tuition; $3,660 room and board; $220 student activity fees; $500 average additional expenses.

Collegiate Environment: Located on a beautiful 200-acre tract of rolling land just within the city limits of Greenville, the school has modern buildings of cream-colored brick and Bedford limestone. There is dormitory space for 3,468 men and women. The library houses 228,000 volumes, 1,050 periodicals, 175,000 microforms and 10,500 recordings. Approximately 79% of the students applying for admission are accepted including midyear students. Average high school standing of the freshman class: 36% in the top quarter; 30% in the second quarter; 19% in the third quarter; 15% in the bottom quarter. Financial aid is available and 60% of the current student body receives some form of financial assistance.

Community Environment: See Furman University.

CENTRAL CAROLINA TECHNICAL COLLEGE   *(F-11)*
506 N. Guignard Drive
Sumter, South Carolina 29150
Tel: (803) 778-1961; (800) 221-8711; Admissions: (803) 778-6605; Fax: (803) 773-4859

Description: By an act of the Legislature of the State of South Carolina in May 1961, an extensive program of technical training was made possible through the establishment of regional technical education centers. The college was established in 1961 to provide educational opportunities in the fields of engineering technologies and industrial training, business, and health occupations. The state-controlled, coeducational college offers one-year courses awarding certificates and diplomas and two-year courses offering Associate degrees. The college is accredited by the Southern Association of Colleges and Schools, and the Accreditation Board for Engineering and Technology. It operates on the semester system and offers one summer session. Enrollment is 975 full-time and 1,248 part-time students. A faculty of 78 full-time, 103 part-time gives a faculty-student ratio of 1-20.

Entrance Requirements: Accredited high school graduation or equivalent; SAT (minimum SAT scores 375M, 375V) or ACT (minimum 17) and entrance exam required; non-high school graduates considered; early admission, early decision, advanced placement, rolling admission and delayed admission plans available; $20 application fee.

Costs Per Year: $825 county-resident tuition; $980 state-resident tuition; $1,500 out-of-state resident.

Collegiate Environment: The modern school building is located on a 28-acre campus. The library houses 20,000 volumes. There are 45 scholarships awarded, all of which are available to freshmen. 48% of students receive financial aid. All students applying for admission who meet the requirements are accepted including midyear. 53% of the previous freshman class returned for the sophomore year.

Community Environment: See Morris College.

CENTRAL WESLEYAN COLLEGE   *(C-3)*
Wesleyan Drive
Central, South Carolina 29630
Tel: (803) 639-2453; Fax: (803) 639-0826

Description: Privately supported, coeducational, liberal arts college founded in 1906 as the Wesleyan Methodist College, the institution is dedicated to offering a college education in an evangelical Christian environment. It was accredited in 1973 by the Southern Association of Colleges and Schools, and is recognized by the Attorney General's office and the State. The college is affiliated with the Wesleyan Church of America. It operates on the semester system and offers two summer sessions. Enrollment is 390 full-time students. A faculty of 48 gives a faculty-student ratio of 1-14. An academic cooperative plan in nursing is available with Clemson, with C.W.C. offering the first 2 years and Clemson offering the second 2 years and granting the B.S. Army and Air Force ROTC are available.

Entrance Requirements: High school graduation or equivalent with C or better average; rank in upper half of graduating class; completion of 16 units including 4 English, 2 science, 2 social science, and 2 mathematics; SAT minimum combined score of 740 required; ACT minimum score of 19 may be substituted; early admission, early decision, midyear admission, rolling admission and advanced placement plans available.

Costs Per Year: $8,100 tuition; $3,080 room and board; additional expenses average $500.

Collegiate Environment: Located in the Piedmont region close enough to the Blue Ridge Mountains to get the benefit of the Southern breezes, the school has 11 buildings. The library houses more than 75,000 volumes. Dormitory space is available in Childs Hall and Stuart-Bennett Hall for 184 men and 200 women. Financial assistance is available and 90% of the current student body receives financial aid. Midyear students are admitted and a geographically diverse student body is sought. Approximately 90% of the students applying for admission are accepted.

Community Environment: Central is located in the Piedmont section of South Carolina, between Atlanta, Georgia, and Charlotte, North Carolina. The community is five miles North of Clemson and is located near the metropolitan area of Greenville.

CHARLESTON SOUTHERN UNIVERSITY   *(K-13)*
P.O. Box 10087
Charleston, South Carolina 29411
Tel: (803) 863-7050; (800) 947-7474; Fax: (803) 863-7070

Description: Privately supported, coeducational, liberal arts college affiliated with the South Carolina Baptist Convention, the college is accredited by the Southern Association of Colleges and Schools and operates on the 4-1-4 system with two summer sessions. Enrollment includes 1,554 full-time, 850 part-time, and 276 graduate students. A faculty of 78 full-time and 70 part-time gives a faculty-student ratio of 1-16. The Bachelor of Arts, Bachelor of Science, MBA, Master of Education, and Master of Arts of Teaching degrees may be earned. Students holding an Associate degree in an approved field may earn a Bachelor of Technology degree. Teacher certification in secondary education fields may also be earned. Academic cooperative plans are available with Medical University of South Carolina, University of South Carolina and University of North Carolina system. Air Force ROTC is available.

Entrance Requirements: High school graduation or equivalent in upper half of class; completion of 20 units, including 4 English, 3 mathematics, 2 science, and 2 social science; SAT or ACT required, minimum SAT scores of 400V, 400M; early admission, early decision, rolling admission, delayed admission and advanced placement plans available; $25 application fee.

Costs Per Year: $8,192 tuition and fees; $3,170 room and board; additional expenses average $1,000.

Collegiate Environment: Built on 300 acres of land in Charleston County, the institution is continuing to expand its facilities. The library contains more than 190,000 volumes. Approximately 82% of the students applying for admission are accepted. Average high school standing of the freshman class is top 30%. Dormitory space is available for 350 men, 350 women and 52 couples. Full-time unmarried students under 21 who do not live at home or with close relatives are required to live in college residences. Financial aid is available.

Community Environment: See The Citadel.

CHESTERFIELD-MARLBORO TECHNICAL COLLEGE
(C-13)
P.O. Drawer 1007
Highway 9
Cheraw, South Carolina 29520
Tel: (803) 921-6900; Fax: (803) 537-6148

Description: The two-year technical vocational college was opened in 1968. The college operates on the semester system, and offers two summer sessions. Four semesters are usually needed for graduation. The college is fully accredited by Southern Association of Colleges and Schools and day and evening classes are offered. Enrollment includes 111 men, 210 women full-time, and 235 men, 472 women part-time. A faculty of 26 full-time and 44 part-time gives a student-faculty ratio of 15-1.

Entrance Requirements: High school graduation; placement examination required; $12.50 application fee; non-high school graduates considered; open enrollment policy; early admission, early decision, rolling admission and advanced placement plans available.

Costs Per Year: $800 Marlboro & Chesterfield counties; $850 out-of-county; nonresident $1,150.

Collegiate Environment: 7 buildings are located on the 59-acre campus. The library contains 19,518 volumes, 155 periodicals, 640 audiovisual and CD-ROM materials, and the collection is rapidly growing. Financial assistance is available. All students applying are accepted. The institution seeks to assist students in the immediate area.

Community Environment: Cheraw is a small community enjoying mild climate year-round. The city has a public library, a shopping center, churches of many denominations, and good medical facilities. There are several service and civic organizations active in the area.

Branch Campuses: Some classes are held off-campus in Bennettsville, Pageland, and Dillon, in South Carolina.

THE CITADEL   *(K-13)*
Citadel Station
Charleston, South Carolina 29409
Tel: (803) 953-5230; (800) 868-1842; Fax: (803) 953-7630

Description: A four-year, liberal arts, military college, the institute was founded 1842. It is accredited by the Southern Association of Colleges and Schools, the Accreditation Board for Engineering and Technology, the American Chemical Society and the National Council for Accreditation of Teacher Education. The college operates on the semester system with two summer terms. It is state supported and has an ROTC program for Army, Air Force, Navy and Marine Corps. The school furnished several outstanding officers in the Civil War and today is still proud of its men who leave to become commissioned officers. The college grants the Bachelor degree in biology, business, chemistry, civil engineering, computer science, electrical engineering, English, history, modern language, physical education, psychology, mathematics, education, physics, and political science. Enrollment includes 2,000 full-time students. A faculty of 150 gives a faculty-student ratio of 1-13.

Entrance Requirements: High school graduation; at least 5 feet tall and physically qualified for ROTC; unmarried; completion of 16 units including 4 English, 3 mathematics-2 of which must be algebra, 1 history, 2 lab science, 2 foreign language, 1 social studies, 3 electives; SAT or ACT required; Math Level II Achievement Tests recommended; $25 application fee; rolling admission and advanced placement plans available.

Costs Per Year: $3,686 tuition; $7,680 nonresident; $4,074 room and board.

Collegiate Environment: The college is located on a 130-acre campus in the northwestern part of the city. The buildings are moorish architecture. Dormitory space is available for 1,960 students in the Corps of Cadets. 77% of applicants are accepted. Over 600 scholarships are avaailable and almost 70% of the freshman class receives some form of financial assistance. There are over 200,000 volumes, 1,392 periodicals and 996,000 microforms in the school library.

Community Environment: Noted for its splendid harbor, Charleston is on a peninsula formed by the Cooper and Ashley Rivers. Founded in 1680, it is the official state port and as one of America's oldest cities retains many of its 18th century historical features. Of interest are Battery and East Bay Streets, Bay Street, Meeting Street, and King Street. The community has many churches, museums, hospitals, and civic and fraternal organizations. Part-time employment is available. The semitropical weather makes outdoor activities such as golfing, swimming, water skiing, bicycle riding, fishing, crabbing, sailing and surfing enjoyable throughout the year.

CLAFLIN COLLEGE   *(H-10)*
400 Magnolia Avenue
Orangeburg, South Carolina 29115
Tel: (803) 534-2710

Description: Founded in 1869 and incorporated as Claflin University, the college is privately controlled by the Methodist Church. The liberal arts school offers Bachelor of Arts and Bachelor of Science degrees and operates on the semester system. One summer term is also offered. The college is accredited by the Southern Association of Colleges and Schools. There are four major divisions encompassing education, humanities, natural science and mathematics, and social science. It allows 12 credits by prior examination for previous training and experience. Army ROTC is available. Recent enrollment included 340 men, 527 women full-time, and 13 men and 20 women part-time. A faculty of 54 full-time and 7 part-time gives a faculty-student ratio of 1-14.

Entrance Requirements: High school graduation or equivalent; completion of 16 units including 4 English, 1 mathematics, 1 laboratory science, 1 social studies; SAT or ACT required; non high school graduates considered; early admission plan available; $5 application fee.

Costs Per Year: $4,230 tuition; $2,280 room and board; $85 fee for freshman and transfer students.

Collegiate Environment: One of the 16 buildings located on the campus is the Bowen Library which houses 135,530 volumes. The T. Willard Lewis Memorial Chapel will seat 750 and has a spacious stage equipped for dramatics. Almost centrally located in Orangeburg, the campus consists of 25 acres and has dormitory space for 221 men and 322 women. 81% of students applying in the previous year were admitted; for their second year, 92% returned to campus. About 20% of the students graduated in the top quarter of their high school class, and 50% in the top half. Financial assistance is available for financially handicapped students and 96% of the current enrollment receives financial aid.

Community Environment: See South Carolina State College.

CLEMSON UNIVERSITY   *(C-3)*
Clemson, South Carolina 29634-5124
Tel: (803) 656-2287; Fax: (803) 656-0622

Description: Publicly supported, coeducational, state university founded in 1889, the university operates on the early semester system with two summer terms and other special summer programs. The Colleges of Agricultural Sciences, Engineering, Forest and Recreation Resources, Architecture, Education, Commerce and Industry, Nursing, Sciences, Liberal Arts and the Graduate School form a background of training for the occupations and professions in which students engage. Enrollment is 9,823 men and 7,843 women, including 12,488 full-time and 817 part-time undergraduates. A faculty of 1,405 gives a faculty-student ratio of 1-19. Academic cooperative plans in medicine with Medical University of South Carolina are available. It allows credit by examination for previous training and experience. Cooperative Education program (alternating work and class periods) available in engineering, sciences, education, liberal arts, textiles and management. The university is accredited by the Southern Association of Colleges and Schools and professionally by the National Architecture Accrediting Board, National Council for Accreditation of Teacher Education, Accreditation Board for Engineering and Technology, Society of American Foresters, National League for Nursing, and American Assembly of Collegiate Schools of Business. Army and Air Force ROTC programs are available.

Entrance Requirements: High school graduation or equivalent; SAT required and Mathematics Achievement Test recommended; early admission, midyear admission, rolling admission and advanced placement plans available; $35 application fee.

Costs Per Year: $3,086 tuition; $8,166 nonresident tuition; $3,744 average room and board; additional expenses average $2,046.

Collegiate Environment: Located on a 1,400-acre campus, the university has a library containing 1,453,368 volumes and 218,674 microforms. 70% of students applying for admission are accepted and 87% of the freshmen return for their sophomore year. Average high school standing of the freshman class; 36% are in the top 10%, 60% in top 20%, 94% in top half of their high school class; The average scores of the entering freshman class were SAT 485 verbal, 563 math. 2,200 scholarships are offered and 55% of the undergraduates receive some form of financial aid. The university awarded 2,602 Bachelor, 845 Master, and 93 Doctorate degrees during a recent academic year.

Community Environment: Clemson is located in the foothills of the Blue Ridge Mountains approximately 135 miles from Charlotte and Atlanta. The average temperatrue is 61 degrees. The area is served by U.S. Highways 76 and 123. Airline service is available nearby. Clemson has several churches of different denominations, a library, YMCA, Concert series, and Little Theatre. Hotels, apartments, rooming houses provide additional student housing. Job opportunities are available. Local recreational facilities include fishing, hunting, golf, tennis, swimming, sailing and skiing.

CLINTON JUNIOR COLLEGE   *(B-9)*
1029 Crawford Road
Rock Hill, South Carolina 29730
Tel: (803) 327-7402

Description: Founded in 1894 as Clinton Normal and Industrial Institute, it was incorporated in 1909. The private, junior college is controlled by the African Methodist Episcopal Zion Church. The school operates on the semester system and requires four semesters for graduation. It is recognized by the South Carolina Department of Education. The small college has a capacity for 200 students and grants the Associate degree in liberal arts subjects. A faculty of 12 gives a faculty-student ratio 1-17.

Entrance Requirements: High school graduation or college entrance examination.

Costs Per Year: $1,220 tuition; $1,890 room and board.

Collegiate Environment: Approximately 98% of students applying for admission are accepted, and almost 98% return for a second year. Midyear students are accepted and a geographically diverse student body is sought. Financial assistance is available in the form of scholarships, grants-in-aid, and part-time employment. Approximately 15% of the current freshman class receives financial assistance. 98% of all students receive some form of financial aid. The campus is located on a rock-ribbed plain of 20 acres. Bus service provides transportation to town for the students. Library contains 15,000 volumes, 600 pamphlets, and 68 periodicals.

Community Environment: See Winthrop College.

COASTAL CAROLINA UNIVERSITY   *(F-15)*
P.O. Box 1954
Conway, South Carolina 29526
Tel: (803) 347-3161; (800) 277-7000; Admissions: (803) 349-2026; Fax: (803) 349-2127

Description: This state supported, liberal arts college was founded in 1954 and is accredited by the Southern Association of Colleges and Schools. It offers preparation for state teaching certificate and awards the Bachelor and Masters degrees. A Bachelor of Interdisciplinary Studies Program exists to help students customize a degree program that is not formally listed in the catalogue. Credit is allowed for certain courses by prior examination, such as CLEP, and continuing education courses are offered. The university operates on the semester system and offers two summer sessions. Enrollment includes 1,513 men and 1,693 women full-time, and 337 men, 873 women part-time. A faculty of 176 full-time, 76 part-time gives a faculty-student ratio of 1-18.

Entrance Requirements: High school graduation with a C average or better, GED accepted, total 21 units required; SAT required; ACT may be substituted; early admission, early decision, rolling admission and advanced placement plans are available; $25 application fee.

Costs Per Year: $2,710 tuition; $7,000 nonresident; $2,640 room.

Collegiate Environment: The campus is located on 201 acres and consists of an Edward M. Singleton Building, Arts Center, Science Building, Kimbel Library, Wheelwright Auditorium, Bookstore/Police Building, Wall Business Building, Print/Mail Shop, Athletic Support Building, residential facilities, Continuing Admissions Building, Student Union Building, Kearns Hall Building and the Williams-Brice Building, which houses a regulation basketball gymnasium, an olympic-size swimming pool, racquetball courts, a mini-gymnasium, a dance studio, weight room, complete physical education facilities and offices. Presently, the library contains 156,797 hard bound volumes and 45,361 microforms and other media. Athletic scholarships are available in all sports and all sports have freshmen scholarships. Academic scholarships are available to all students, including fresh-

men. Approximately 46% of the student body receives financial aid. There is housing for 500 students. The college is located five miles east of Conway and nine miles west of Myrtle Beach.

Community Environment: See Horry-Georgetown Technical College.

COKER COLLEGE   *(D-12)*
Hartsville, South Carolina 29550
Tel: (803) 383-8000; Admissions: (803) 383-8050; Fax: (803) 383-8056

Description: This privately supported, small, independent, coeducational college of liberal arts deliberately limits enrollment in order to promote personalized instruction and a family-like atmosphere. An active teaching method predominates which features large round tables to facilitate discussion and interaction. The course of study leads to a Bachelor of Arts or Bachelor of Science degree in 25 fields. A Field Service program is available in any academic area. The college is accredited by the Southern Association of Colleges and Schools. It operates on the semester system and offers two summer sessions. A Summer Abroad program is available. Enrollment includes 651 full-time and 172 part-time students. A faculty of 47 full-time and 42 part-time gives a faculty-student ratio of 1-10.

Entrance Requirements: High school graduation with rank in upper 50%; SAT or ACT accepted; rolling admission, delayed admission, early admission, midyear admission and advanced placement plans available; $15 application fee.

Costs Per Year: $9,888 tuition; $4,516 room and board; $185 student fees.

Collegiate Environment: Located on 25 acres in an attractive residential section, the school is conveniently near the heart of the business district. It has a college clubhouse and dock on a nearby lake and a 28-acre botanical garden. Dormitory facilities accommodate 300 students. The library contains 75,000 volumes, 390 periodicals, 1,400 microforms and 200 audiovisual materials. 72% of applicants are accepted. 150 scholarships are available and 85% of students receive some form of financial aid.

Community Environment: Coker College is located in Hartsville, a community of approximately 20,000 people. It is located in the northeastern part of the state, 20 miles off I-95, and approximately a two-hour drive from South Carolina's beautiful beaches and mountains. The climate is temperate and mild year-round. There is a township library and many churches of various denominations. Florence airport is 24 miles away. Part-time employment is available for students. Local recreational facilities include two theaters, Lake Robinson, Prestwood Lake, golf, tennis, two city parks, and racing. There are various civic and fraternal organizations that are active within the community. Health service facilities are available.

COLLEGE OF CHARLESTON   *(K-13)*
66 George Street
Charleston, South Carolina 29424
Tel: (803) 953-5670; Admissions: (803) 953-5670; Fax: (803) 953-6322

Description: This publicly supported, coeducational, liberal arts college is accredited by the Southern Association of Colleges and Schools, the American Assembly of Collegiate Schools of Business, the American Chemical Society and the National Council for Accreditation of Teacher Education. The institution grants the Bachelor and Master degrees. The college operates on the semester system and offers four summer terms and a mini-semester in May (Maymester). Enrollment includes 2,754 men and 4,544 women full-time, and 658 men and 1,989 women part-time. This enrollment includes 7,122 full-time and 1,140 part-time undergraduates and 1,683 graduate students. A faculty of 410 full-time and 174 part-time gives a faculty-student ratio of 1-19. An academic cooperative program in medicine with local institutions provides extended library facilities as well as Bachelors degrees in Medicine and Dentistry. The Honors Program, instituted in 1967, is a course of study designed to attract superior students irrespective of their departmental majors and guide them toward a more substantial education. The International Programs Office coordinates programs for the college student wishing to study abroad as well as programs for foreign students who desire to study at the college either as degree candidates or special students for a semester, a summer, or a year. Continuing Education office offers some 120 courses each semester, in the late afternoon or evening; CLEP tests are accepted in 21 areas.

Entrance Requirements: High school graduation or equivalent; SAT required; GRE required for graduate programs; non-high school graduates considered; delayed admission, early decision, rolling admission and advanced placement plans available; $25 application fee.

Costs Per Year: $3,060 tuition; $6,120 nonresident; $3,460 room and board; $25 student fees.

Collegiate Environment: The campus is located on George Street and encompasses an 8-block area. The college in its painstaking restoration of the historic buildings on its campus, in its restoration of numerous old homes on adjacent streets, and in its construction of new buildings to complement the old, has literally rebuilt its campus on its historic foundations. There are 89 buildings including a library housing 486,670 volumes and 580,073 microforms. Dormitory facilities are available for 2,073 men and women. Approximately 67% of the students applying for admission are accepted including midyear students. Average high school standing of the freshman class: 48% in the top fifth; 34% in the second fifth; 15% in the third fifth; and 3% in the bottom two-fifths. The average scores of the entering freshman class were SAT 489 verbal, 538 math. Scholarships are available and 64% of the current student body receives some form of financial aid.

Community Environment: See The Citadel.

COLUMBIA BIBLE COLLEGE   *(F-9)*
P.O. Box 3122
Columbia, South Carolina 29230
Tel: (803) 754-4100; (800) 777-2227; Fax: (803) 786-4209

Description: Privately supported, coeducational, Evangelical Protestant Bible college. Distinctly a Bible college, not secular, the school courses are designed to hold high academic standards, and programs of study lead to the Associate, Bachelor and Master degrees. The college is accredited by the Southern Association of Colleges and Schools and the Accrediting Association of Bible Colleges. It operates on the semester system and offers three summer sessions. Enrollment includes 473 full-time and 57 part-time undergraduates and 41 graduate students. A faculty of 21 full-time and 10 part-time provides a faculty-student ratio of 1-18.

Entrance Requirements: High school graduation; GED or high school equivalency; completion of 16 units including 4 English, 2 mathematics, 1 science, 2 foreign language, and 2 history; SAT preferred or ACT accepted; non-high school graduates must attain satisfactory grade on college entrance examination; rolling admission, delayed admission and advanced placement plans available; $20 application fee.

Costs Per Year: $6,950 tuition; $150 student fees; $3,792 room and board; $500 average additional expenses.

Collegiate Environment: In 1960 the college moved to its present location, a 450-acre campus on the edge of metropolitan Columbia. Students are housed in residence halls that accommodate 486 men and women. Unmarried freshman students are required to live on campus for the first year if working for a degree. The library contains 84,361 volumes, 725 periodicals and 4,199 audiovisual materials. Approximately 88% of students applying are admitted. Midyear students are accepted. Scholarships are available and 66% of the undergraduates receive some form of aid.

Community Environment: See University of South Carolina.

COLUMBIA COLLEGE   *(F-9)*
1301 Columbia College Drive
Columbia, South Carolina 29203
Tel: (803) 786-3871; Fax: (803) 786-3674

Description: Accredited by the Southern Association of Colleges and Schools and several other councils and associations, the school, founded in 1854, is the tenth oldest college for women. The private, independent, liberal arts college is affiliated with the United Methodist Conference of South Carolina. The college grants the Bachelors and Masters degrees. It operates on the semester system and offers two summer sessions. Enrollment includes 906 full-time and 101 part-time and 173 evening program undergraduates and 49 graduate students. A faculty of 78 full-time and 26 part-time gives a faculty-student ratio of 1-14.

Entrance Requirements: High school graduation in top 50% of class; completion of 16 or more units, including 4 English, 3 mathematics, 2 science, 2 language, and 3 social science; SAT or ACT required; non-high school graduates considered; early decision, deferred admission, midyear admission, rolling admission and advanced placement plans available; personal interview recommended; $20 application fee.

Costs Per Year: $10,925 tuition; $3,975 room, board and student fees; $700 average additional expenses.

Collegiate Environment: The campus is located on 33 landscaped acres in a suburban section of Columbia. The college is proud of its new plant, which incorporates modern trends of expansion and growth. The library contains 135,000 volumes, 259 pamphlets, 670 periodicals, 10,200 microforms and 10,100 sound recordings. Dormitory space is available for 660 women. 87% of applicants are accepted. Midyear students are accepted. 350 scholarships are available and 80% of the students receive some form of financial aid. A geographically diverse student body is sought.

Community Environment: See University of South Carolina.

CONVERSE COLLEGE   *(B-6)*
580 East Main Street
Spartanburg, South Carolina 29302-0006
Tel: (803) 596-9000; (800) 766-1125; Fax: (803) 583-2563

Description: Privately supported, liberal arts institution devoted primarily to the higher education of women. The college is fully accredited by the Southern Association of Colleges and Schools and professionally by the National Association of Schools of Music. The school is nondenominational, but its emphasis is Christian. Enrollment includes 659 full-time and 68 part-time undergraduates and 433 graduate students. A faculty of 73 full-time and 14 part-time provides an undergraduate faculty-student ratio of 1-9. The 4-2-4 system is used and two summer sessions are offered. The college also offers a Junior year in France or Spain, a fall term in London, and many short-term travel programs. Army ROTC is available through a nearby institution.

Entrance Requirements: High school graduation with 16 units including 4 English, 2 foreign language, 3 mathematics, 2 science, and 1 social studies; non-high school graduates considered; SAT or ACT required; early admission, rolling admission and advanced placement plans available; $30 application fee; priority given to applications received by March 15.

Costs Per Year: $12,050 tuition; $3,700 room and board.

Collegiate Environment: The campus encompasses 70 acres with 27 buildings. The library has 200,000 volumes, 9,895 music scores, 720 periodicals, 56 microforms and 7,000 recordings. Dormitory space is available for 675 women. Approximately 75% of the students applying for admission are accepted, including midyear students. 70% of the current student body receives financial aid.

Community Environment: One of the leading textile manufacturing cities in the South, Spartanburg is also one of the largest peach shipping centers in the world. The city was named after the Spartan Regiment, which represented this community in the Revolutionary War. The community is located in the Piedmont section of South Carolina and has an average temperature of 60 degrees. Airlines, railroads, and bus lines serve the area. There are many churches representing various denominations, 3 hospitals, libraries, a YMCA Family Center, and various civic and fraternal groups serving the city. Motels, hotels, and rooming houses are available for guests. Local recreation includes football, basketball, baseball, golf, stock car racing, swimming, tennis, picnicking, water skiing, theater, and series of concerts. Part-time employment is available.

ERSKINE COLLEGE   *(D-5)*
Due West, South Carolina 29639
Tel: (803) 379-8838; (800) 241-8721; Fax: (803) 379-8759

Description: Founded in 1839, this small, liberal arts college is affiliated with the Associate Reformed Presbyterian Church. The Erskine Theological Seminary was founded in 1837, and became the School of Theology of Erskine College in 1925. The college grants the Bachelor's degree and is accredited by the Southern Association of Colleges and Schools. The School of Theology has its own dean and faculty, and is a member of the Association of Theological Schools (ATS). The college operates on the 4-1-4 calendar system and offers two summer terms. Enrollment is 551 full-time and 24 part-time undergraduates and 227 graduate students at Erskine Theological Seminary. A faculty of 47 full-time and 10 part-time gives a faculty-student ratio of 1-12.

Entrance Requirements: High school graduation; completion of 14 units of college-prep courses including 4 English and 2 mathematics; SAT required (ACT may be substituted); rolling admission, midyear admission and advanced placement plans available; $15 application fee.

Costs Per Year: $11,156 tuition; $710 student fees; $4,128 room and board.

Collegiate Environment: Two campuses comprise the college: West Campus, which was formerly Erskine College, and East Campus, which was formerly the Woman's College of Due West. McCain Library contains 282,709 volumes, including both the Erskine College and Erskine Theological Seminary collections. Dormitory space is available for 305 men and 310 women. Midyear students are accepted and a geographically diverse student body is sought. Approximately 75% of students applying for admission are accepted. There are 658 scholarships awarded, including 112 for freshmen and 83% of the current student body receives some form of financial aid.

Community Environment: Due West is a town of approximately 1,300 residents. It enjoys a temperate climate. There is easy access to Interstate Routes 26 and 85, and the cities of Anderson, Greenwood, and Greenville are nearby. The major metropolitan areas of Atlanta and Charlotte are within a 2.5-hour drive. The college arranges transportation to meet students arriving at these points by train, bus or plane. Local recreational facilities include tennis courts, a swimming pool, movies and a new physical education/athletic center.

FLORENCE-DARLINGTON TECHNICAL COLLEGE (E-13)
P.O. Box 100548
Florence, South Carolina 29501-0548
Tel: (803) 661-8324; Fax: (803) 661-8041

Description: The publicly controlled, vocational, technical institution opened its doors in September 1964 with the aim of preparing students through technical education to meet the demands of a modern industrial, business and agricultural society. It is accredited by the Southern Association of Colleges and Schools and operates on the semester system with one summer session. The college awards Associate of Science degrees and diplomas. It now offers a college transfer program of A.A. and A.S. degrees. Two full years of credit can be transferred to a four year university or college. The courses of study are in three major divisions including Art and Sciences, Health Studies, and Technological Studies. The Continuing Education Division encompasses special and supervisory developmental courses. Enrollment includes 489 men, 704 women full time, 426 men, and 1,020 women part-time. With a faculty of 89 full-time, 132 part-time, the faculty-student ratio is 1-23. ROTC is available.

Entrance Requirements: High school graduation or equivalent; non high school graduates considered; early decision, early admission, midyear admission, open admission, rolling admission and advanced placement plans available; ACT, SAT or entrance examinations required; non-refundable application fee $15.

Costs Per Year: $1,000 tuition; $1,150 out-of-county tuition; $1,376 out-of-state tuition; $10 student fee.

Collegiate Environment: The college is located on Highway 52 between Florence and Darlington. The campus is comprised of six modern buildings residing on approximately 80,000 square feet of space, located on 180 acres. Both the laboratories and the large, modern shops are equipped with the most modern test and production equipment. The library houses 31,449 volumes, 374 periodicals and 25,208 microforms. Financial aid is available and 50% of the students receive some form of assistance.

Community Environment: Cotton, tobacco, and industry support the economy of Florence. There are several diversified manufacturing companies within the area. Florence can be called an urban and a suburban community. It is located approximately 70 miles from the Atlantic Ocean resort areas. The city enjoys a temperate climate.

Community services include public library, hospitals, museums, many churches of various denominations and major civic, fraternal and veteran's organizations. Part-time employment is limited. Local recreation encompasses the Little Theatre group, movie theatres, a YMCA, and major sports including swimming, hunting, golf, and tennis.

FRANCIS MARION UNIVERSITY (E-13)
P.O. Box 100547
Florence, South Carolina 29501-0547
Tel: (803) 661-1362; Admissions: (803) 661-1231; Fax: (803) 661-1219

Description: Publicly supported, coeducational college established in 1970, offering liberal arts and sciences and a limited number of pre-professional programs. Accredited by the Southern Association of Colleges and Schools, the college grants the Bachelor and Master degrees. Day and evening classes are available, the semester system is used and two summer sessions are offered. Enrollment includes 3,117 full-time and 775 part-time undergraduates and 342 graduate students. A faculty of 168 full-time and 51 part-time gives a faculty-student ratio of 1-19. The college allows credit for correspondence courses (up to 30 semester hours) and by prior examination for previous training and experience (no limit) toward degrees and has an extensive academic cooperative program, including several engineering technologies, forestry, nursing, and geography, among others. Army ROTC program is offered.

Entrance Requirements: High school graduation or equivalent; 16 units including 4 English, 3 mathematics, 2 laboratory science, 2 foreign language, 3 social science, and 2 electives; SAT with minimum combined score of 900 for automatic acceptance, or ACT required; GRE, NTE, GMAT required for graduate schools; rolling admission, early admission, delayed admission and advanced placement plans available; $25 application fee.

Costs Per Year: $2,920 general college tuition; $5,840 nonresidents; $3,138 estimated room and board.

Collegiate Environment: The campus is located on a 309-acre tract of land. The library presently contains 300,000 bound volumes, 1,640 periodicals and 208,513 microforms. Residence halls accomodate 785 students. 75% of applicants are accepted. Financial aid is available and 486 scholarships are offered. 50% of the current student body receives some form of financial assistance.

Community Environment: See Florence-Darlington Technical College.

FURMAN UNIVERSITY (B-4)
Poinsett Highway
Greenville, South Carolina 29613
Tel: (803) 294-2034; Fax: (803) 294-3127

Description: Founded in 1826, this liberal arts college aspires to academic excellence under Christian influences. The university became independent in 1992, when its 166-year affiliation with the South Carolina Baptist Convention ended. It is accredited by the Southern Association of Colleges and Schools, the American Chemical Society, and the National Association of Schools of Music. The school operates on the 3-2-3 system and offers two summer sessions. Enrollment includes 2,288 full-time and 160 part-time undergraduate students and 215 graduate students. A faculty of 188 full-time and 10 part-time gives an undergraduate faculty-student ratio of 1-12. Academic cooperative plans are available with Auburn University, Clemson University, Duke University, Georgia Institute of Technology, North Carolina State University, and Washington University in St. Louis. An optional ROTC program is offered by the Department of the Army, and ROTC scholarships are available for all entering freshmen. Credit is allowed by prior examination. Overseas study programs in England, Germany, Spain, France, Japan, Belgium, Greece, Middle East and Africa, China, Scandinavia and Russia, Costa Rica and Galapagos Islands are available.

Entrance Requirements: Graduation from high school; completion of 20 units including 4 English, 3 mathematics, 2 science, 2 in the same foreign language, and 3 social studies; SAT or ACT required; non-high school graduates considered; early admission, early decision and advanced placement plans available; $25 application fee.

Costs Per Year: $13,440 tuition; $4,048 room and board; $134 student fees; $1,300 average additional expenses.

Collegiate Environment: The school is located on U.S. Highway 25, five miles north of Greenville. The campus occupies a 750-acre tract with many of the buildings close to a 30-acre lake. Scholarships are available and 70% of the current student body receives some form of financial assistance. The library houses 360,000 volumes, 1,550 periodicals and 2,000 microforms. Dormitory facilities are available for 750 men and 800 women. The university seeks a geographically diverse student body and a number of foreign nations are represented on campus. Approximately 76% of the students applying for admission were accepted for the 1994-95 school year.

Community Environment: An industrial city, Greenville is in an important manufacturing region with very diverse industry. It is a metropolitan community that enjoys a temperate climate. Part-time employment is available. The city is served by air, rail and bus lines. Community facilities include a performing arts center, public library, art museum, YMCA, YWCA, 5 general and 1 children's hospital, and over 400 churches that represent major denominations. Local recreation includes several community theatre groups, lakes and rivers for water sports, and most major sports, including golf and a minor league baseball team.

GREENVILLE TECHNICAL COLLEGE   (B-4)
P.O. Box 5616
Greenville, South Carolina 29606-5616
Tel: (803) 250-8000; Fax: (803) 250-8534

Description: Greenville Technical College is a publicly supported, two-year institution that began operations in September 1962. The college operates on the semester system and offers two summer sessions. It is accredited by the Southern Association of Colleges and Schools. The main divisions of the college are Engineering Technologies, Nursing, Business, Allied Health, Related Studies, Industrial Technologies, and Arts and Sciences, which prepares students for transfer. A Cooperative Education program (alternating work and class periods) is available in Business, Engineering Technologies, Industrial Technologies, Nursing, Arts & Sciences and Allied Health. Enrollment includes 3,849 full-time and 4,885 part-time students. There are also 2,171 evening students. A faculty of 238 full-time and 302 part-time gives a faculty-student ratio of 1-16 using full-time equivalent figures.

Entrance Requirements: Open enrollment; high school graduation or equivalent; SAT or ACT optional; college entrance examinations required; non-high school graduates considered; early admission and rolling admission plan available; $20 application fee.

Costs Per Year: $1,000 in-county tuition; $1,080 out-of-county; $1,600 out-of-state; $3,360 out-of-country.

Collegiate Environment: Located in the northwestern part of the state in the industrial Piedmont area, the college is situated in foothills at an altitude of 1,040 feet. The campus consists of 407 acres with modern, air-conditioned buildings. The library houses approximately 49,500 bound volumes, 658 periodical subscriptions, 1,511 microfilm and 17 CD-ROMs, which are primarily scientific and technical in nature. Midyear students are accepted. Financial aid is available. 22% of students receive some form of aid. Students are accepted each semester in many programs.

Community Environment: See Furman University.

HORRY-GEORGETOWN TECHNICAL COLLEGE   (F-16)
P.O. Box 1966
Conway, South Carolina 29526
Tel: (803) 347-3186; Admissions: (803) 349-5277; Fax: (803) 347-4207

Description: This publicly supported technical college, established in 1966, is fully accredited by the Southern Association of Colleges and Schools. It is a comprehensive commuter college with three convenient campus sites located in Conway, Myrtle Beach, and Georgetown. The college offers 49 degrees, dipomas, and certificates from Associate in Arts and Associate in Science degrees to a varied technical and business curriculum. In adition, the college has an active Continuing Education program which enrolls more than 10,000 people each year. It maintains an intensive on-site industrial training program serving 12-50 businesses and industries annually. It operates on the semester system and offers three summer sessions. Enrollment includes 2,300 full-time and part-time students. A faculty of 87 full-time and 70 part-time gives a faculty-student ratio of 1-19.

Entrance Requirements: Open admissions policy; placement test scores required for admission to curriculum programs; high school diploma with 20 units may be required for some programs; rolling admission, midyear admission, and advanced placement plans available; some programs have specific application deadlines; $15 application fee.

Costs Per Year: $1,000 resident tuition; $2,000 nonresident.

Collegiate Environment: HGTC is a comprehensive commuter college with three convenient campus sites located in Conway, Myrtle Beach, and Georgetown. Over 77,171 square feet of classrooms, laboratories, equipped with the latest in cutting edge technology, are supported by three libraries housing in excess of 45,000 volumes. Financial aid is available and 60% of students receive some form of financial aid.

Community Environment: The college in Conway is located at the center of the largest tourist/recreational environment along the Eastern Seaboard. Over 75 miles of white sand beaches, many different golf courses, restaurants, hotels, comprise the local environment. Airlines serve the area, as well as Greyhound and Trailways bus services. Highway 17 the "Kings Highway" is the major coastal route in the area, and a major interstate connector is currently under consideration. A number of major arts and entertainment centers, libraries, churches, as well as numerous fraternal and civic organizations serve the community. There are extensive part-time employment opportunities for students in the local area, especially from March through September, during the height of the tourist season.

Branch Campuses: Grand Strand Campus, 904 65th Avenue North, Myrtle Beach, SC, 29572, (803) 449-7416; Georgetown Campus, Route 6, Box 960, Georgetown, SC, 29440-9620, (803) 546-8406

LANDER UNIVERSITY   (E-5)
Greenwood, South Carolina 29649
Tel: (803) 229-8400; (800) 768-3600; Fax: (803) 229-8890

Description: Founded originally in 1872 as a Methodist college for women, this four-year university became a part of the South Carolina state system of higher education as a state-supported college in 1973, and now is coeducational. The university is accredited by the Southern Association of Colleges and Schools, and professionally by the National League for Nursing. An academic cooperative plan is available with Clemson University in Engineering Majors. Lander grants the Bachelor's and Master's degrees. Programs are offered in liberal arts, the sciences, education and nursing. The semester system is used with three summer terms. Enrollment includes 716 men, 1,329 women full-time, and 145 men, 288 women part-time undergraduates and 301 graduate students. A faculty of 126 full-time, 26 part-time gives a faculty-student ratio of 1-16.

Entrance Requirements: High school graduation or equivalent; rank in upper 50% of graduating class; recommended completion of 20 units in college prep curriculum including 4 English, 3 math, 2 lab science, 2 language, 3 social studies, 1 physical education or ROTC, and 5 electives; SAT or ACT required; non-high school graduates considered; early admission, early decision, rolling admission and midyear admission plans available; $25 application fee.

Costs Per Year: $3,340 state-resident tuition; $4,938 nonresident; $2,770-$3,170 room and board; $50 student fees.

Collegiate Environment: Located on 700 acres of campus, the school has 31 buildings. The college library houses 136,368 titles, 1,062 periodicals and 83,616 microforms. There is dormitory space available for 1,062 men and women. 90% of applicants are accepted. Midyear students are accepted. 480 scholarships of varying amounts are offered, including 135 for freshmen 57% of the students receive some form of financial aid.

Community Environment: Greenwood is an industrial city noted for its production of textiles. The city is located in west-central South Carolina. The climate is temperate and mild. Five railroads, commercial air service, buses, and major highways serve the community. Public service facilities include one hospital and various health centers, an area mental health center, churches of all denominations, a library and a YMCA. There are several motels, 3 radio stations, modern stores and various civic and fraternal organizations within the immediate area. Recreation includes several swimming pools, two recreation centers, 3 golf courses, baseball, football, tennis, basketball, and nearby Greenwood State Park, which provides water sports and picnic areas. Part-time employment is available.

LIMESTONE COLLEGE   (A-7)
1115 College Drive
Gaffney, South Carolina 29340
Tel: (803) 489-7151; (800) 795-7151; Fax: (803) 487-8706

Description: The privately supported, coeducational, liberal arts college was founded in 1845 and managed to remain open throughout the Civil War although a great deal of equipment was carried off or destroyed. The Baptist Convention of South Carolina returned the charter to the college, to a self-perpetuating board of trustees that operates the institution as an independent Christian school. The college is accredited by the Southern Association of Colleges and Schools, the National Association of State Directors of Teacher Education and Certification, and the National Association of Schools of Music. It grants the Bachelor degree. An academic cooperative plan is available with Bowman-Grey for medical technology majors. It operates on the semester system and offers three summer sessions. Enrollment includes 340 full-time, 20 part-time, and 900 evening students. A faculty of 26 full-time and 15 part-time gives a faculty-student ratio of 1-10. Army ROTC program is available.

Entrance Requirements: Graduation from high school; minimum SAT verbal 350, math 350 or ACT 17 composite required; non-high school graduates considered; early admission, early decision, midyear admission, rolling admission and advanced placement plans available; $15 application fee.

Costs Per Year: $7,600 tuition; $3,600 room and board; $800 average additional expenses.

Collegiate Environment: The campus consists of 115 acres with 23 buildings. The college library, which is a three-story building, contains 88,000 volumes, 500 periodical titles, 900 microforms and 2,028 recordings. The school year begins in late August. 75% of applicants are accepted including midyear students. 90% of current students receive some form of financial assistance.

Community Environment: Once predominantly a cotton-textile manufacturing city, Gaffney has other diversified industries today including the manufacture of clothes, gloves, rugs, and clay and concrete products. The surrounding agricultural area produces cotton, peaches, grain and livestock. The city is located on Interstate I-85. Approximately 45 miles away are 2 jet airports. The community has several churches representing many denominations, and more than 56 civic and service organizations.

LUTHERAN THEOLOGICAL SOUTHERN SEMINARY (F-9)
4201 North Main Street
Columbia, South Carolina 29203-5898
Tel: (803) 786-5150; (800) 804-5233; Fax: (803) 786-6499

Description: Accredited in 1943 by the Association of Theological Schools in the United States and Canada and by the Southern Association of Colleges and Schools, the seminary is a graduate school offering Masters and Professional degrees. In 1911, the seminary found its permanent home in the city of Columbia. Founded in 1830 and owned and operated by the Evangelical Lutheran Church in America, it is under the direction of a Board of Trustees. The seminary opened on extension center in Atlanta in 1988. The seminary operates on the semester system and offers two summer sessions. Enrollment includes 175 full-time and 25 part-time graduate students with a faculty of 25.

Entrance Requirements: College graduation; $35 application fee.

Costs Per Year: $5,000 tuition; $6,000 non-Lutheran; 2,000 room and board; $20 student fees.

Collegiate Environment: Worship services are held in the Chapel, Monday through Friday and are conducted by the students and faculty in rotation. The Lineberger Memorial Library houses 130,000 volumes, 650 periodicals and 8,000 microforms and is supported by appropriations of the Board of Trustees and from gifts by the Auxiliary and interested friends. Dormitory facilities accommodate 38 men and women and apartments and houses for 36 families. The choir serves the community through worthy church music.

Community Environment: See University of South Carolina.

MEDICAL UNIVERSITY OF SOUTH CAROLINA   (K-3)
171 Ashley Avenue
Charleston, South Carolina 29425-1020
Tel: (803) 792-3281; Admissions: (803) 792-3281; Fax: (803) 792-3764

Description: The state-supported, coeducational, Medical University of South Carolina was originally established as the Medical College of South Carolina in 1824 and is now comprised of 6 colleges on campus. Enrollment is 1,846 full-time and 432 part-time students, residents and fellows. The University employs approximately 1,038 full-time faculty and 1,238 part-time faculty (statewide). More than 1,900 teaching beds are utilized in the Charleston area, including the 573-bed Medical University Hospital. Consortium hospitals throughout the state enable the students to broaden and enrich their clinical experiences.

Entrance Requirements: Requirements vary with each college; $45 application fee.

Costs Per Year: Tuition varies with each college.

Collegiate Environment: The University is a professional institution dedicated to health education, service, and research in the field of health science. Facilities on campus include the University Hospital, the Storm Memorial Eye Institute, the Children's Hospital, the Clinical Sciences Building, the Basic Sciences/Dental Medicine Building, the Family Medicine Center, the Quadrangle, the Psychiatric Institute, and the newly constructed Hollings Oncology Center. The Health Affairs Library contains 222,649 volumes, 2,469 current journal subscriptions, 3,872 microforms and 7,027 audiovisual materials; the Learning Resources Center facilitates the use of audiovisual learning materials and offers programmed material in a variety of formats (computer-assisted instruction, video tapes, slides, audio tapes, learning simulators and programmed texts) for student use. The Colleges of Nursing, Pharmacy, and Health Related Professions accept students after two years of college. The Colleges of Dental Medicine, Graduate Studies, and Medicine each accepts students after four years of undergraduate study. About 23% of applicants are accepted. Financial aid is available. 51% of students receive some form of assistance. The campus is located in the historic peninsula city of Charleston.

Community Environment: See The Citadel.

MIDLANDS TECHNICAL COLLEGE   (F-9)
P.O. Box 2409
Columbia, South Carolina 29202
Tel: (803) 738-1400; Admissions: (803) 738-7840; Fax: (803) 738-7784

Description: Founded in 1974 by the South Carolina General Assembly, the school provides education through day and extension programs for high school graduates to upgrade and update skills. The four major areas of education covered are engineering, technology, business, industrial and allied health services. It is accredited by the Southern Association of Colleges and Schools. The college is professionally accredited by the American Dental Association for dental hygiene and the Engineers' Council on Professional Development for Engineering Technology. It grants the Associate degree. The college allows credit for up to 70 semester hours by prior examination for previous training and experience. Air Force ROTC is available as an elective. It operates on the semester system and offers two summer sessions. Enrollment includes 1,949 men and 2,383 women full-time and 1,947 men, 2,381 women part-time with a faculty of 225 full-time and 230 part-time members.

Entrance Requirements: High school graduation or equivalent; open enrollment; early admission, early decision, rolling admission, midyear admission and advanced placement plans available.

Costs Per Year: $990 tuition resident; $1,980 nonresident.

Collegiate Environment: The school is housed in modern, air-conditioned buildings. The library houses 52,000 volumes, 414 periodical titles and 1,489 microforms. Approximately 98% of students applying are accepted for admission. Midyear students are accepted but the school does not assure full academic load for other than fall entrance. 60% of a current freshman class returned to campus for their second year. Of 25 scholarships available, 18 are for freshmen. 30% of the students receive financial aid.

Community Environment: See University of South Carolina.

MORRIS COLLEGE   *(F-11)*
North Main Street
Sumter, South Carolina 29150
Tel: (803) 775-9371; Fax: (803) 773-3687

Description: The institution was founded in 1908 to provide elementary school, high school and college training for "Negro youth" but by 1946 only the college level remained. With the deletion of the word "Negro" from the charter in 1961, the college began admitting all ethnic groups. The privately supported, coeducational, liberal arts college is owned and operated by the Baptist Education and Missionary Convention of South Carolina. The school operates on the semester system and offers two summer terms. The college is accredited by the Southern Association of Colleges and Schools. Enrollment is 889, including 309 men and 567 women full-time and 13 part-time students. A faculty of 46 full-time and 17 part-time gives a faculty-student ratio of 1-17. The school allows credit by prior examination for previous training and experience (up to 12 hours) and religious subjects are required for graduation. Army ROTC program is available.

Entrance Requirements: Graduation from high school; completion of 20 units including 4 English, 3 mathematics, 2 science and 2 social science; non-high school graduates who hold a GED are considered; SAT or ACT not required; rolling admission, midyear admission and delayed admission plans available; $10 application fee.

Costs Per Year: $4,515 tuition; $2,550 room and board; $115 student fees.

Collegiate Environment: Located on a 34-acre campus, the college has 16 buildings including a new library that houses 111,630 volumes, 765 periodicals, 152,243 microforms and 3,022 audiovisual materials. There is dormitory space available on campus for 594 students. Students may live in approved housing off campus, but permission must be approved prior to entrance into college in the fall. Approximately 60% of students applying are accepted. Financial assistance is available. 100% of the students receive some form of financial aid. A geographically diverse student body is sought and midyear students are accepted.

Community Environment: Sumter was named for General Thomas Sumter, "The Gamecock of the Revolution." The community is served by two bus lines, and is 50 miles from an airport and 35 miles from rail service. The mean summer temperature is 90 degrees, and the mean winter temperature is 40 degrees. The city has many churches of various faiths, and a public library. Recreation includes the large natural parks and many lakes in the Sumter area. It is famed for its Swan Lake Iris Gardens. Sports and recreation go hand in hand with the compatible climate and natural resources found in the community. Recreation also includes 4 theaters, 1 bowling lane, a skating rink, and lighted tennis courts.

NEWBERRY COLLEGE   *(E-7)*
College Street
Newberry, South Carolina 29108
Tel: (803) 321-5127; (800) 845-4955; Fax: (803) 321-5627

Description: Chartered in 1856, the liberal arts, four-year college is privately controlled by the Evangelical Lutheran Church in America. The institution is accredited by the Southern Association of Colleges and Schools, the National Council for Accreditation of Teacher Education, and the National Association of Schools of Music, and grants the baccalaureate degree. Students who complete the requirements for the B.A. degree in elementary education also fulfill the requirements for teacher certification in South Carolina for elementary schools. The student enrollment is 650, approximately half female. A faculty of 60 gives a faculty-student ratio of 1-11. The school operates on the semester system and offers two summer terms. Academic cooperative plans are available with Duke University, Medical University of South Carolina, and Clemson University. Army ROTC is available.

Entrance Requirements: High school graduation or equivalent; SAT combined score of 700 or ACT score of 17 required; completion of 18 units including 4 English, 2 mathematics, 2 science, and 2 social studies; early admission, rolling admission, midyear admission and advanced placement plans available; $25 application fee.

Costs Per Year: $10,194 comprehensive fee; $2,600 room and board.

Collegiate Environment: Consisting of 60 acres, the college is situated on a pine-studded hillside. The architecture is a harmonious blend of traditional and modern. There are dormitory facilities available for all who apply. The college library contains 88,704 volumes, 362 periodicals, 822 microforms and 250 video tapes. There are academic and athletic scholarships offered and 90% of the current student body receives some form of financial assistance. Average high school standing of the freshman class; 40% in the top quarter; 31% in the second quarter; 19% in the third quarter; 10% in the bottom quarter. Midyear students are accepted. The college awarded 102 baccalaureate degrees to the graduating class, and 7% of the senior class continued on to graduate or professional school.

Community Environment: Newberry is located in the Piedmont region of South Carolina between Lakes Murray and Greenwood. The city enjoys mild weather. Community services include churches of many denominations, a hospital, a county library, and various civic and fraternal organizations. Local recreation includes a swimming pool, barbecue facilities, parks, theaters, fishing, boating, swimming, and camping on nearby lakes. Part-time employment is available for college students.

NORTH GREENVILLE COLLEGE   *(A-5)*
P.O. Box 1892
Tigerville, South Carolina 29688
Tel: (803) 895-1410

Description: Privately controlled by the South Carolina Southern Baptist Convention, this four-year college is accredited by the Southern Association of Colleges and Schools. It grants the Associate degree, a Bachelor's degree in Church Music and a Bachelor of Liberal Arts in Religion. It was established in 1892 as North Greenville Baptist Academy. In 1934, a group enlarged the vision of Christian education in the junior college field and the institution became North Greenville Baptist Academy and Junior College. In 1950, the charter was again amended to change the name to its present one. The Bachelor's degree programs were added in 1992. The college operates on the early semester system and offers two summer sessions. Enrollment includes 321 men and 155 women. A faculty of 25 full-time and 17 part-time gives a faculty-student ratio of 1-16.

Entrance Requirements: High school graduation or equivalent; SAT or ACT required; early decision, rolling admission, early admission and advanced placement plans available; $15 application fee.

Costs Per Year: $6,200 tuition; $3,600 room and board.

Collegiate Environment: Located within Tigerville, the college is situated in a beautiful setting. The Hester Memorial Library contains 42,762 volumes, 360 periodicals, 1,133 microforms and 4,580 audiovisual materials. Housing is available for 276 men, 180 women and 12 families. Over 80% of the students return for their second year. 95% of students receive financial aid.

Community Environment: Tigerville is a rural area adjacent to Greenville in the foothills of the Blue Ridge Mountains. The climate is temperate. There are several civic and fraternal organizations and a Baptist Church in the community. Part-time employment is available. Local recreation includes hunting, fishing, rafting, fine arts and the advantages of nearby Greenville.

ORANGEBURG-CALHOUN TECHNICAL COLLEGE   *(H-10)*
3250 St. Matthews Road, NE
Orangeburg, South Carolina 29115
Tel: (803) 536-0311; Fax: (803) 535-1388

Description: Established in 1968 by legislative charter, the college provides training for qualified students. It is accredited by the Southern Association of Colleges and Schools and the National League for Nursing. It operates on the semester system with the academic year beginning in August and offers two summer sessions. There are five main divisions including technology, business, industrial, allied health and nursing. The college provides the opportunity for additional education for all citizens of the area who wish to avail themselves of the programs offered. Credit by prior examination for previous training and experience (no limit) is allowed, and a Cooperative Education program (alternating work and class periods) is available. The college also offers special schools to train potential employees and upgrade current employee skills for new and expanding industry. Enrollment is 1,002 full-time and 762 part-time students. A faculty of 125 full-time and 30 part-time gives a faculty-student ratio of 1-15. Army ROTC is available.

Entrance Requirements: High school graduation and/or ability to pursue and successfully complete proposed course of study; SAT or ACT/ASSET required; early admission, early decision, rolling admission, delayed admission and advanced placement plans available.

Costs Per Year: $1,200 county-resident tuition; $1,350 state-resident tuition; $1,650 out-of-state tuition.

Collegiate Environment: The school has a new, modern 100-acre campus with 16 buildings to date. The library houses more than 30,000 volumes. Approximately 75% of the current student body receives some form of financial assistance. Non-high school students, as well as midyear students, are accepted. 95% of the students applying are accepted. A geographically diverse student body is sought. 81% of the previous freshman class returned for their sophomore year. Activities include student organizations, on campus events, and special off-campus events.

Community Environment: See South Carolina State College.

PIEDMONT TECHNICAL COLLEGE   (E-5)
Emerald Road
Greenwood, South Carolina 29648
Tel: (803) 223-8357

Description: Publicly supported, coeducational, two-year, technical college established in 1966, the college accepts high school graduates with the idea of providing technical training to upgrade and update proficiency and knowledge. It offers the Associate in Arts and Associate in Science degrees. The college operates on the quarter system with one summer session and is fully accredited by the Southern Association of Colleges and Schools, the Accreditation Board for Engineering and Technology and the Committee on Allied Health Education and Accreditation. Enrollment is 2,700 students. A faculty of 130 gives a faculty-student ratio of 1-20.

Entrance Requirements: High school graduation or equivalent; open enrollment; SAT with minimum combined score of 800 or ACT required; early admission early decision and rolling admission plans available; $25 application fee.

Costs Per Year: $900-$1,100 county resident tuition; $1,200 state resident tuition; $1,520 non-resident tuition.

Collegiate Environment: Located on 60 acres, the college consists of a modern, well-equipped complex of buildings. The library has over 25,000 volumes. All students applying are accepted. The college is primarily for the training of local men and women and does not seek a geographically diverse student body. There are special programs for culturally disadvantaged students enabling low-mark students to attend. Almost 47% of the current enrollment receives some form of financial assistance.

Community Environment: See Lander College.

PRESBYTERIAN COLLEGE   (D-6)
Broad Street
Clinton, South Carolina 29325
Tel: (803) 833-8230; (800) 476-7272; Fax: (803) 833-8481

Description: The college is a fully accredited institution of higher learning that offers the Bachelor of Arts and Bachelor of Science degrees. The four-year, liberal arts school is supported by Presbyterians of the Synods of Georgia, South Carolina, and Florida. The school was founded in 1880 and today maintains a selective enrollment of 1,122 students including 560 men and 562 women full-time, and 8 men, 9 women part-time. With a faculty of 75 full-time and 37 part-time, the faculty-student ratio is 1-15. Accredited by the Southern Association of Colleges and Schools, the college offers several major divisions including the humanities, business, the social sciences, mathematics, the natural sciences, and military science. The school operates on the semester system and offers two summer terms. Army ROTC is available as an elective. Correspondent credit allowed toward degree; summer, academic year, and semester study programs are available in France, England, Austria, Spain, Mexico, Japan, Wales, India, Taiwan and China; summer session in Marine Biology offered in several locations.

Entrance Requirements: High school graduation; SAT or ACT required; essay required; rolling admission, delayed admission and advanced placement plans available; $30 application fee.

Costs Per Year: $12,751 tuition; $1,983 student fees; $3,635 room and board

Collegiate Environment: Situated on an oak-shaded, 212 acre campus within the corporate limits of Clinton, the college has 26 major buildings. The library contains 140,000 volumes, 772 periodicals, 4,627 microforms and 4,000 audiovisual materials. A collection of rare books, pamphlets, pictures and manuscripts connected with the history of the state are housed here. Dormitories provide housing for 84% of students. Financial aid is available. 78% of students receive some form of financial aid.

Community Environment: Located in the Piedmont section of South Carolina, Clinton is approximately 64 miles northwest of Columbia. The annual mean January temperature is 43.6 degrees; July 79.9 degrees. The community has air and bus service and is adjacent to U.S. Highway 76, I-385; I-26. There are many churches of various denominations, a hospital, hotels and motels in town. Part-time employment is available. Local recreational facilities include tennis, golf, theatre and swimming; nearby Lake Greenwood provides boating, fishing and hunting. Various civic, fraternal and veteran's organizations are active in the community.

SOUTH CAROLINA STATE UNIVERSITY   (H-10)
300 College Street, N.E.
Orangeburg, South Carolina 29117
Tel: (803) 536-7000

Description: The Constitutional Convention of 1895 enacted provisions authorizing the Legislature to create the college by a severance of the state's interest with Claflin University. Fully accredited by the Southern Association of Colleges and Schools, the four-year, publicly controlled college offers the Bachelor and Master degrees. The college is comprised of the following schools: Arts and Sciences, Education, Home Economics, Industrial Education and Engineering Technology, Graduate Studies and Summer School. Operating on the semester system, the college offers one summer term. Enrollment includes 1,810 men, 2,343 women full-time and 134 men, 339 women part-time with a faculty of 256.

Entrance Requirements: Graduation from high school with rank in upper 50%; completion of 18 units including 4 English, 2 mathematics, 2 science, and 2 history; SAT required; early decision and advanced placement plans available; $10-$15 application fee.

Costs Per Year: $3,576 tuition; $5,696 nonresident; $1,420 room and board; $50 fees.

Collegiate Environment: Located 40 miles east of the state capital, the campus consists of 450 acres of land with 350 being used for experimental farming. The Miller F. Whittaker library contains 217,000 volumes. The college has several residence halls with capacity for 850 men, 1,177 women and 25 families. Financial aid in the form of jobs, loans, and grants is available to qualified students. Almost 97% of the current student body receives some form of financial assistance. Of the students applying for the freshman class, 78% were accepted for admission. The college has a special program for the educationally disadvantaged enabling low-mark students to attend.

Community Environment: Orangeburg is in an agricultural and dairying area. Its industries include textiles, wood products, meat packing, chemicals, and baking goods. This is a suburban community with a temperate climate. Airline service is available at nearby Columbia. Railroad and bus lines serve the immediate community. There is a public library, churches of major denominations, a hospital, and major civic and fraternal organizations. Some part-time employment is available. Local recreation includes four theatres, swimming, fishing and many sports.

SOUTHERN METHODIST COLLEGE   (H-10)
P.O. Box 1027
Orangeburg, South Carolina 29116-1027
Tel: (803) 534-7826; Admissions: (803) 534-7826; Fax: (803) 534-7827

Description: Southern Methodist College, founded in 1956, is located in Orangeburg, South Carolina. The small Bible college offers programs leading to the degree of Bachelor of Arts with a core curriculum in Bible and with minors offered in specific areas of specialization, such as Church Music, Pre-Seminary, Missions, Christian Education, Christian Couseling, Christian Ministries, Elementary Christian School Education, or Secondary Christian School Education. The minor or a double emphasis in education are designed to prepare students for teaching in Christian schools or other private schools. In the Department of Practical (Professional) Studies, Southern Methodist College offers programs leading to a one-year Certificate in Bible, an Associate of Arts in Bible and an Associate of Arts in General and Religious Education. The college operates on the early semester system and offers one summer session. Enrollment includes 16 full-time and 67 part-time students. A faculty of 7 full-time and 5 part-time gives a faculty-student ratio of 1-7.

Entrance Requirements: High school graduation or GED; rolling admission, early admission, early decision, midyear admission and rolling admission plans available. $25 application fee.

Costs Per Year: $2,000 tuition; $2,600 room and board; $110 student fees.

Collegiate Environment: The college occupies one of the most attractive sites in the city of Orangeburg, located on a beautiful 50-acre tract of rolling land. Chapel service is held regularly, and all students participate. A geographically diverse student body is sought. There is dormitory space available for 30 men and 30 women. The school library contains 15,000 volumes, 2,500 pamphlets, 56 current subscriptions to various periodicals and 250 recordings. 90% of applicants are accepted. Scholarships are available and 50% of the students receive some form of financial aid.

Community Environment: See South Carolina State College

SPARTANBURG METHODIST COLLEGE   *(B-6)*
1200 Textile Drive
Spartanburg, South Carolina 29301
Tel: (803) 587-4213; Fax: (803) 574-6919

Description: Owned and operated jointly by the South Carolina Annual Conference and the General Board of Global Ministries of the United Methodist Church, the two-year, liberal arts college provides basic education in the social sciences, natural sciences, and humanities. The basic program aims at enabling the students to transfer to a four-year college or university, but it also provides a two-year terminal program in criminal justice. Established in 1911 as the Textile Industrial Institute, the college opened its doors with one student and one teacher. Enrollment is 715 full-time and 163 part-time students. A faculty of 45 full-time and 12 part-time gives a faculty-student ratio of 1-20. The junior college is accredited by the Southern Association of Colleges and Schools and operates on the semester system with two summer sessions. Army ROTC program is available.

Entrance Requirements: High school graduation; SAT minimum 300V and 320M or ACT minimum 16 required; non-high school graduates considered; early decision, advanced placement and rolling admission plans available; $20 application fee.

Costs Per Year: $6,380 tuition; $3,850 room and board; $300 student fees.

Collegiate Environment: Situated in the heart of the Piedmont section of South Carolina, the 100-acre campus lies three miles west of the downtown area of Spartanburg. The five residence halls on campus give the college dormitory space for 258 men and 226 women. The library houses 34,600 volumes, 225 periodicals, 2,060 microforms and 1,025 audiovisual materials. A special program for culturally disadvantaged students is offered. Financial aid is available.

Community Environment: See Converse College.

SPARTANBURG TECHNICAL COLLEGE   *(B-6)*
Spartanburg, South Carolina 29303
Tel: (803) 591-3600; Admissions: (803) 591-3800; Fax: (803) 591-3642

Description: By an act of the Legislature of the State of South Carolina in May, 1961, an extensive program of technical training was made possible through the establishment of regional technical educational centers. Spartanburg opened its doors in 1962. Since then, the school has established itself in providing educational opportunities in the fields of engineering technologies and industrial training, business, arts and sciences, and health occupations. The state controlled college offers one-year courses awarding diplomas and certificates and two-year courses awarding Associate degrees. Accredited by the Southern Association of Colleges and Schools, the center operates on the semester system with one summer term offered. Enrollment includes 1,140 men and 1,435 women with a faculty of 100 full-time and 65 part-time.

Entrance Requirements: High school graduation or equivalent; ASSET required; non-high school graduates considered; open enrollment; early admission, early decision, rolling admission and delayed admission plans available; mid-year students admitted; $10 application fee.

Costs Per Year: $850 tuition; $1,700 nonresident.

Collegiate Environment: The center is located on 104 acres of land along Interstate Highway 85 South. The school library has over 28,000 volumes excluding periodicals. The extension division enrolls approximately 5,300 annually and is geared toward updating and upgrading business and technical skills in evening classes.

Community Environment: See Converse College.

TRI-COUNTY TECHNICAL COLLEGE   *(C-3)*
P.O. Box 587
Pendleton, South Carolina 29670
Tel: (803) 646-8361; Admissions: (803) 646-8361 x2200; Fax: (803) 646-8256

Description: Opened in 1962, Tri County Technical College is part of the South Carolina Technical and Comprehensive Education System. It is accredited by the Southern Association of Colleges and Schools, the Accreditation Board of Engineering and Technology, American Veterinary Medical Association, and the Committee on Allied Health Education and Accreditation. The College is composed of 5 major divisions offering one and two-year programs that award certificates, diplomas, or Associates degrees. These are the Industrial and Technical Division, Health Education Division, Business and Human Services Division, and the Arts and Sciences Division. The Arts and Sciences Division offers the Associate of Arts and the Associate of Science Degrees for students planning to transfer to four-year institutions. The college operates on the semester system and offers two summer sessions. Enrollment is 1,386 full-time and 1,776 part-time students. A faculty of 203 full-time and 250 part-time gives a faculty-student ratio of 1-26.

Entrance Requirements: Graduation from high school or equivalent; entrance examinations required; non-high school graduates considered; rolling admission, early admission, early decision, midyear admission, and advanced placement plans available; no application fee.

Costs Per Year: $950 state-resident tuition; $1,728 out-of-state.

Collegiate Environment: Located on 55 acres, the center is comprised of 8 buildings. The library contains 35,287 bound volumes, 170 periodicals, 35,944 microforms and 4,178 records and tapes. The center seeks to serve the local community and does not seek a geographically diverse student body. 324 scholarships are available and 58% of students receive some form of aid.

TRIDENT TECHNICAL COLLEGE   *(K-13)*
P.O. Box 10367
Charleston, South Carolina 29411
Tel: (803) 572-6111

Description: Trident Technical College provides comprehensive, postsecondary education at the two-year level in the areas of vocational, technical, college transfer education, developmental studies, special industrial training, manpower development, adult and continuing education, and community service. On July 1, 1973, the Berkely-Charleston Dorchester Technical Education Center and Palmer College officially merged to become Trident Technical College. The College operates on the quarter system and has an "open door" admissions policy which allows any adult, regardless of his education, socio-economic or ethnic background the opportunity to achieve the career goal of his or her choice. Enrollment includes 1,263 men, 1,754 women full-time, and 2,574 men, 3,577 women part-time with a faculty of 185 full-time and 225 part-time members.

Entrance Requirements: An applicant for any diploma program must be at least 18 years old, or be a high school graduate, or possess a high school equivalency diploma (GED); an applicant for any Associate Degree program must be a high school graduate or possess a high school equivalency diploma (GED); SAT, ACT, or College administered entrance examination required; early admission plan available; $20 application fee.

Costs Per Year: $1,080 tuition resident; $1,518 nonresident.

Collegiate Environment: The TTC Main Campus is located on Highway 52, one mile north of Aviation Avenue in North Charleston, SC. The TTC Palmer Campus is situated in downtown Charleston on Columbus Street. Extension center is located at Charleston Air Force Base. Berkeley Campus is located in Moncks Corner. College facilities included a library of 68,000 volumes and numerous periodicals, microforms and audiovisual materials. All qualified applicants are accepted and students may enroll at midyear as well as in the fall. Financial aid is available, and 65% of the current student body receives some form of assistance.

Community Environment: North Charleston is a suburb located just eight miles from downtown Charleston. The community enjoys all the cultural, recreational and civic advantages of the nearby larger community, yet retains an air of the small town. There are good shopping areas, churches, parks and theatres.

Branch Campuses: Palmer Campus, Columbus, Charleston, S.C. 29411, (803) 722-5500. Berkely Campus, Highway 17A, Moncks Corner, S.C. 29461, (803) 761-8380.

UNIVERSITY OF SOUTH CAROLINA   (F-9)
Columbia, South Carolina 29208
Tel: (803) 777-7700; (800) 868-5872; Admissions: (803) 777-7700; Fax: (803) 777-0101

Description: The university began in 1801 as South Carolina College. In pre-Civil War days it was known as one of the finest schools in the nation. After World War I, development continued and enrollment rose from 500 to 1,600 students. During World War II, a Naval ROTC unit was established which practically turned the university into a naval base. Today, Naval, Air Force and Army ROTC programs are still offered, but are optional. The university is accredited by the Southern Association of Colleges and Schools. The various colleges encompass arts and sciences, business administration, engineering, criminal justice, education, health and physical education, humanities, social sciences, journalism, librarianship, nursing, pharmacy, science and mathematics, social work and schools of law and medicine and the graduate school. It grants the Bachelor, Master and Doctorate degrees. Undergraduate enrollment includes 5,839 men and 6,571 women full-time and 1,599 men and 2,019 women part-time. Graduate and first-professional enrollment includes 4,379 full-time and 6,347 part-time students. A faculty of 1,460 gives a faculty-student ratio of 1-16. The semester system is used and two summer sessions are offered. Correspondent credit of 30 semester hours maximum are allowed and continuing education courses are offered.

Entrance Requirements: Admission based on high school record and SAT or ACT scores (SAT preferred); TOEFL required for applicants whose native language is not English; GRE required for graduate school; midyear admission, rolling admission and advanced placement plans available; non-high school graduates considered; $35 application fee.

Costs Per Year: $3,196 resident tuition; $8,074 nonresident tuition; $3,600 room and board.

Collegiate Environment: Situated downtown in Columbia, the state capital, the 242-acre campus is spacious, well maintained and close to the principal governmental and shopping areas, which makes it advantageous to the student for part-time work, shopping and conducting business affairs. The library contains 2,526,408 volumes, 20,722 periodicals, 3,777,699 microforms and 12,153 audiovisual materials, and has the largest collection of manuscripts and journals in South Carolina. There is residence hall space available for 2,711 men and 3,424 women, and apartments for 300 families. Fraternities provide housing for 350 men and sororities for 391 women. Midyear students are admitted. University regional campuses offering courses for freshmen and sophomores are located in Beaufort, Lancaster, Allendale, Sumter, and Union with residence credit given. Four-year campuses are located at Aiken, Spartanburg, and Columbia (main campus). The maximum number of credits that can be transferred to the Main Campus from a two-year campus is 76. 3,843 scholarships aer available and 50% of the students receive financial aid.

Community Environment: Originally settled on the opposite bank of Congaree River, Columbia already had several thousand residents when, in 1786, the legislature decreed it the new state capital and moved it to its present site. A great part of the city's development is due to its diversified interests as a manufacturing, trading and governmental community. Textiles, truck building, computers, lumbering, quarrying, printing and other industries are active here. The mean annual temperature is 64.4 degrees with an average rainfall of 41.58 inches. The city is served by 4 railroad lines, 4 airlines, 3 bus lines and 6 major highways. The community has many parks, two art museums, a Music Festival, Choral Society, a new Performing Arts Center and a new state museum. Local services include a public library, hospitals, hotels and over 175 churches of major denominations. Recreational facilities found in the city are theatres, a golf course, radio stations, TV stations, and nearby Lake Murray with year-round fishing, boating, picnicking, summer swimming, water skiing and hunting. Part-time employment is available.

UNIVERSITY OF SOUTH CAROLINA, AIKEN   (H-7)
171 University Parkway
Aiken, South Carolina 29801
Tel: (803) 648-6851; Admissions: (803) 641-3366

Description: This coeducational, publicly supported, state university is accredited by the Southern Association of Colleges and Schools and was founded in 1961. It grants the Associate Degree in two areas of study, and the Bachelor's Degree in fifteen areas of study. The semester system is used with two summer terms. The school has an enrollment of 616 men, 1,001 women full-time and 471 men, 889 women part-time with a faculty of 145 full-time and 100 part-time members.

Entrance Requirements: High school graduation or equivalent is required with 4 units in English, 3 mathematics, 2 laboratory science, 2 foreign language, 3 social studies, and 2 others; SAT is required with a minimum of 300V, 300M or ACT with a minimum of 14; early admission, rolling admission, delayed admission and advanced placement plans available; $25 application fee.

Costs Per Year: $2,500 state resident tuition; $6,250 nonresident tuition.

Collegiate Environment: The campus of USCA moved from Banksia, a mansion in downtown Aiken, to the present 144-acre site in 1972. Educational programs were initially housed in one large multipurpose building. A library was completed in 1975, currently housing 127,053 volumes and periodicals, and 18,951 microforms. A classroom-office building and a student activities center opened in 1977-78. Other buildings include an auxiliary services building, a fine arts center, a new science building, a science education center, and a new Business and Education building. Housing is available for 358 students. 78% of applicants are accepted. 275 scholarships are available and 47% of the students receive some form of financial aid.

Community Environment: Aiken, population c. 18,350, is the seat of Aiken County and is about 17 miles from Augusta, Georgia.

UNIVERSITY OF SOUTH CAROLINA, LANCASTER CAMPUS   (C-10)
Hubbard Drive
Lancaster, South Carolina 29721
Tel: (803) 285-7471

Description: The school is a state supported, coeducational, system campus of a large state university. It was founded in 1959, and offers programs in liberal arts, business, arts and science, nursing and criminal justice. The university grants Associate degrees. It is fully accredited by the Southern Association of Colleges and Schools. It operates on the semester system and offers two summer sessions. Enrollment includes 440 full-time and 803 part-time students. A faculty of 35 full-time and 40 part-time gives a faculty-student ratio of 1-17.

Entrance Requirements: High school graduation required; applicants must take either SAT or ACT; open enrollment policy dependent upon SAT scores; Rolling admission and advanced placement plans are available; allows 30 hours toward degrees from correspondence credit or CLEP; special admission requirements for underachievers; $35 application fee.

Costs Per Year: $1,840 resident tuition; $4,344 out-of-state tuition.

Collegiate Environment: This campus offers a broad range of extra-curricular programs and activities: athletic, literary and social. The library has 51,746 books, 490 periodicals, 314 microforms and 1,095 audiovisual aids. There is a close association with the Columbia campus of the University, so that students may benefit from activities taking place there. Of those applying, 90% are accepted. Scholarships are available, 20% of the student body receives some form of financial aid and midyear students are accepted.

UNIVERSITY OF SOUTH CAROLINA, SPARTANBURG
(B-6)
800 University Way
Spartanburg, South Carolina 29303
Tel: (803) 599-2246; Admissions: (803) 599-2246; Fax: (803) 599-2375

Description: One of four baccalaureate campuses in the University system, it opened its doors in September, 1967. It is accredited by the Southern Association of Colleges and Schools and the National League for Nursing. This regional campus of the University of South Carolina system offers bachelor's degree programs in the liberal arts, sciences, business administration, and teacher education, plus baccalaureate and associate degree programs in nursing. Additionally, the University offers masters programs in Elementary Education and Early Chilhood Development. Complementing the academic offerings are broad-based intercollegiate athletic programs and a wide spectrum of student activities and services that make the USCS experience a well-rounded one. It operates on the semester system with two summer sessions. Enrollment is 2,286 full-time and 984 part-time undergraduates and 150 graduate students. A faculty of 142 full-time and 76 part-time gives a faculty-student ratio of 1-16. Army ROTC and overseas summer programs are available.

Entrance Requirements: High school graduation or GED; SAT with minimum combined score of 700, or ACT composite score of 18 is required; rolling admission plan available; $25 application fee.

Costs Per Year: $2,500 tuition; $6,250 nonresident; $4,035 room and board.

Collegiate Environment: The first building on the campus, known as the Administration Building, is a three story brick structure that has become the symbol of the Spartanburg Campus. Located on 298 acres at the intersection of Interstate Highways 85 and 585, near the foothills of the Blue Ridge Mountains, USCS has a modern, roomy campus. The Humanities Building and Performing Arts Center, which opened for classes in the fall of 1990, features specialized areas for teaching art, music, drama, journalism and foreign languages, plus a 450-seat theater with an orchestra pit and state-of-the-art sound and lighting systems. The most recent addition is the Quality Institute, which opened in December 1992. The Quality Institute is a facilitator of Total Quality information and training to small-sized and medium-sized businesses throughout the state of South Carolina. The University has six other major facilities, an activities building, a child development center and athletic fields. The library houses 113,000 bound volumes, more than 55,787 microforms and 1,142 periodicals. Scholarships are available. 68% of those applying for admission are accepted, as are midyear students. 625 scholarships are available. 45% of students receive some form of aid.

Community Environment: Spartanburg, South Carolina, is one of the fastest-growing communities in the region, located on the thriving Interstate 85 corridor about three hours from Atlanta and an hour and a half from Charlotte, North Carolina. The Blue Ridge Mountains are less than an hour away; South Carolina's Grand Strand and historic Low Country are a four-hour drive in the other direction. The area has a growing international presence, and arts and cultural activities that would be the envy of many larger cities.

VOORHEES COLLEGE *(I-9)*
Voorhees Road
Denmark, South Carolina 29042
Tel: (803) 793-3351

Description: Elizabeth Evelyn Wright, with one teacher, fourteen pupils, a borrowed bell and two chairs, began the college in April 1897. Finally, it was decided to move the institution one and a quarter miles out of town, and in 1929, the junior college was added. Since then, 11 brick buildings and a church have been built, and the junior college was changed to its present four-year status in 1962. The college is accredited by the Southern Association of Colleges and Schools and operates on the semester system with one summer session. The private school, operated and controlled by the Protestant Episcopal Church, offers Bachelor of Arts, Bachelor of Science and Associate degrees. An Army ROTC program is available. Enrollment includes 280 men, and 436 women full-time, 13 men, and 20 women part-time, and 45 evening students. A faculty of 34 full-time and 10 part-time gives a faculty-student ratio of 1:17.

Entrance Requirements: Accredited high school graduation or equivalent with completion of 18 units and rank in class and grade point average; units should include 4 English, 4 mathematics, 2 science, 2 social science, 2 foreign language, and 4 electives; early admission, rolling admission and midyear admission plans available; $10 application fee.

Costs Per Year: Tuition $4,450; room and board $2,522, student fees $45.

Collegiate Environment: The College is located on a 350-acre site 1 1/2 miles east of Denmark. The library contains 120,000 Volumes and about 500 periodicals and seeks to serve the total community. 97% of the students currently receive financial assistance. Facilities for housing 508 students are available.

Community Environment: Denmark is a rural community located in south central South Carolina. The climate is temperate. Seaboard Airlines, Atlantic Coast Line, and Southern serve the community. There is a public library, local hospitals and several churches representing various denominations. The Lions Club, Masonic Lodge, and Woodmen of the World are active within the community. Recreation includes golf, swimming, boating, fishing and a local theatre.

WINTHROP UNIVERSITY   *(B-9)*
Oakland Avenue
Rock Hill, South Carolina 29733
Tel: (803) 323-2211; Fax: (803) 323-2137

Description: The college was founded in 1886 as a training school for teachers. The state supported institution has evolved into a selective, residential, comprehensive teaching university that offers programs leading to Bachelor, Master and Specialist degrees. The university is accredited by the Southern Association of Colleges and Schools, American Assembly of Collegiate Schools of Business, American Dietetic Association, Council on Social Work Education, Foundation of Interior Design Education Research, National Association of Schools of Art and Design, National Association of Schools of Music and the National Council for Accreditation of Teacher Education, Computing Science Accreditation Board. It operates on the semester system with two summer terms. Enrollment includes 3,507 full-time, 600 part-time, and 918 graduate students. A faculty of 297 full-time and 123 part-time gives a faculty-student ratio of 1:18. Continuing education courses offered as is ROTC/Army program.

Entrance Requirements: High school graduation or equivalent, completion of 16 units; SAT required, (ACT may be substituted); non-high school graduates considered; early admission, rolling admission, delayed admission and advanced placement plans available; $35 application fee.

Costs Per Year: $3,092 tuition; $5,492 out-of-state tuition; $3,132 room and board.

Collegiate Environment: The university's 100 acre campus features a rich blend of architecture in its 34 buildings, many of which are included in the National Register of Historic Places. In addition, a 450 acre area surrounding Winthrop Lake is dedicated to sports and recreation. Dormitories provide space for approximately 2,500 students in seven residence halls. Recreational sports and more than 100 clubs and organizations provide students the opportunity to compete in the Big South Conference of NCAA Division I. Sports include women's and men's basketball, tennis, golf, track and cross-country. women's softball and volleyball, and men's baseball and soccer. Recreational facilities include a nine hole golf course, a 6,100 seat sports coliseum, an indoor pool and training facilities. Educational resources include a library of 3,986 periodicals, 982,836 microforms and 1,739 audiovisual materials. Students are accepted in midyear. Institutionally funded aid programs are available in conjunction with athletic participation, performance talent, and academic achievement. The college also administers externally funded need based programs.

735

Community Environment: Rock Hill is a small progressive city of nearly 50,000 residents located 30 miles below Charlotte, North Carolina. The city is uniquely situated to offer the advantages of both small town living and big city amenities. Diversified industry fuels a growing local economy which produces textiles, wood, paper, concrete, plastic and chemical products. Rock Hill's facilities include the Museum of York County (featuring the world's largest collection of hooved African animals); Winthrop Galleries, host to local, national and international artists; Winthrop Coliseum, Glencairn Gardens, a six acre garden spot; and Cherry Park, a 68 acre recreation park featuring five major league baseball and softball diamonds, which attracts major tournaments from throughout the United States. Opportunities for recreation in the mild piedmont climate are plentiful. The city maintains a system of 28 parks that offer athletic fields and courts, play areas, fitness, walking and jogging trails, and amphitheaters. Lakes 20 minutes away are a convenient destination for water sports and sailing.

WOFFORD COLLEGE *(B-6)*
429 N. Church Street
Spartanburg, South Carolina 29303-3663
Tel: (803) 597-4130; Fax: (803) 597-4149

Description: This privately supported, coeducational, liberal arts college provides a general education and offers Bachelor degrees in arts and science. Students can, after completing the core or general education requirements, major in one of 22 fields. The college was founded in 1854 by a local minister of the Methodist Episcopal Church and is accredited by the Southern Association of Colleges and Schools. Enrollment is 1,062 full-time and 44 part-time students. A faculty of 67 full-time and 26 part-time gives a faculty-student ratio of 1-14. The college operates on the 4-1-4 calendar system and offers two summer sessions. The Army ROTC program on campus is one of the oldest in the state. Academic cooperative plans are available with Converse College, and with Columbia and Georgia Tech for engineering students. Wofford participates in three international studies programs: the Institute for European Studies; the American Institute for Foreign Studies; and the Council for International Educational Exchange. In recent years, students have studied in England, France, Spain, Germany, the Soviet Union, Japan and several South American countries. A Presidential International Scholar is chosen each year to undertake a year-long, all-expenses-paid tour to study a specific problem of global importance. Group travel-study is also an important part of the Interim program.

Entrance Requirements: High school graduation with rank in the top 25% of the high school graduating class; completion of 16 units including 4 English, 4 mathematics, 2 foreign language, 3 laboratory science, and 2 social studies; SAT or ACT required; early admission, midyear admission and advanced placement plans available; Feb. 1 application deadline; $25 application fee.

Costs Per Year: $13,795 tuition; $4,185 room and board.

Collegiate Environment: The college consists of 31 buildings, a stadium, and athletic facilities. The library houses 210,946 bound volumes and microforms, and 645 current periodical subscriptions. The Frank W. Olin Building opened in 1992, and contains computer-equipped faculty offices, student study and work stations, the campus media center, and model classrooms with computer, video and audio technology. The building's Micro Vax 3800/3100 computer center eventually will be the hub of a campus-wide technology network that will link almost all classrooms, offices, and residence hall rooms with computer, video, and library sources. An 80-seat teaching theater is fully equipped for film, video and other on-screen presentations. It is also the ideal space for public speaking and foreign language interpretation exercises. The departments of mathematics, computer science, finance, foreign languages and education are now located in the building. Several offices will be rotated among visiting faculty and Wofford professors who are working on revising and designing courses. 82% of applicants are accepted. The middle 50% range of scores for the entering freshman class was SAT 1000-1193 combined. The mean SAT score was 1098 combined. Of 630 scholarships offered, approximately 120 were awarded to freshmen. 74% of the current student body receives some form of financial assistance. 54% of students received need based aid only. Midyear students are accepted and 92% of the previous freshman class returned for the second year.

Community Environment: Spartanburg County (population 227,000) is a thriving, rapidly growing Sunbelt business center that is particularly well known for its international community. Wofford students live in a downtown setting near restaurants, churches of all denominations, shopping districts, a busy arts center, and four other college campuses. Memorial Auditorium, Wofford's next-door neighbor, features concerts, touring Broadway plays, and other special attractions. Several major airlines serve the convenient Greenville-Spartanburg Airport, which is only twenty miles from the campus. Interstate highways 26 and 85 intersect at Spartanburg. Charlotte, Atlanta, historic Charleston, and South Carolina's world-famous coastal resorts are all within a pleasant afternoon drive.

YORK TECHNICAL COLLEGE *(B-9)*
Rock Hill, South Carolina 29730
Tel: (803) 327-8000; (800) 327-8008; Fax: (803) 327-8059

Description: York Technical College opened in 1964 to provide facilities for updating and upgrading existing skills as well as awarding certificates, diplomas and Associate degrees in various skill areas. The publicly controlled, two-year institution offers courses under three major divisions: Industrial and Engineering Technology; Business, Computer, Arts and Science; and Health and Human Services. Courses vary in the time required for completion and certification. Programs vary in amount of time rquired for completion. York Tech operates on the semester system. It is accredited by the Southern Association of Colleges and Schools. Enrollment is 1,465 full-time and 2,171 part-time students. A faculty of 150 full-time and 100 part-time gives a faculty-student ratio of 1-16.

Entrance Requirements: High school graduation or GED; recommend completion of units in English, 2 math, and 2 science; entrance exam or SAT or ACT required; open enrollment; early decision, early admission, rolling admission and midyear admission plans available; requirements may vary with specific courses and programs.

Costs Per Year: $816 county-resident tuition; $980 state-resident; $1,632 out-of-state.

Collegiate Environment: Located on 94 acres, the college includes 12 buildings and a library that houses approximately 22,507 volumes. The buildings are modern and air-conditioned. Students are accepted at the beginning of each semester. 35 scholarships are available, including 15 for freshmen. 38% of the students receive some form of financial aid.

Community Environment: See Winthrop College.

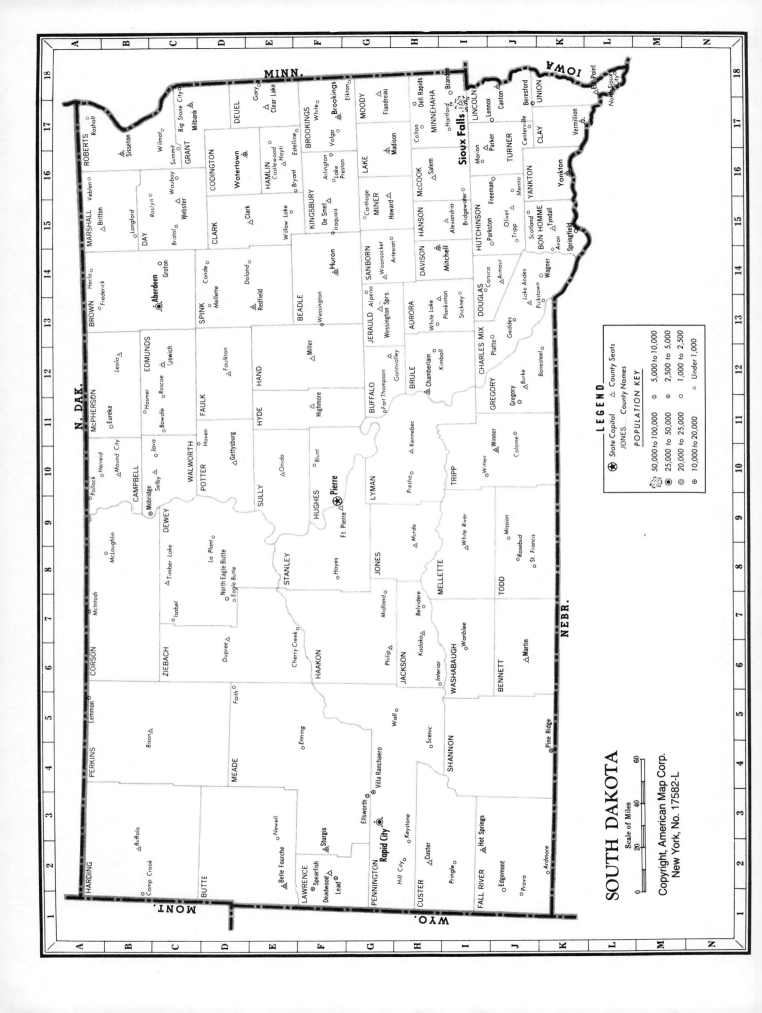

SOUTH DAKOTA

Scale of Miles

0 20 40 60

Copyright, American Map Corp.
New York, No. 17582-L

LEGEND

⊛ State Capital   ⚬ County Seats
JONES___ County Names

POPULATION KEY

⊛ 50,000 to 100,000	⊕ 5,000 to 10,000	
⊚ 25,000 to 50,000	⊙ 2,500 to 5,000	
◎ 20,000 to 25,000	⚬ 1,000 to 2,500	
⊕ 10,000 to 20,000	○ Under 1,000	

SOUTH DAKOTA

AUGUSTANA COLLEGE (I-17)
2001 South Summit Avenue
Sioux Falls, South Dakota 57197
Tel: (605) 336-5516

Description: The aim of this privately supported, American Lutheran, liberal arts college is to provide a Christian liberal education for men and women. The college is accredited by the North Central Association of Colleges and Schools, the South Dakota Department of Public Instruction as a teacher education institution, and by several other professional organizations. It is approved by the South Dakota Board of Nursing, by agencies of the American Medical Association for Medical Technology and X-Ray Technology, by the Conference of Executives of the American Schools of the Deaf. The college operates on the 4-1-4 system with three summer sessions. Continuing education courses are offered; overseas programs are offered through the Upper Midwest Association for Intercultural Education. Recent enrollment included 558 men, 934 women full-time and 135 men, 263 women part-time. A faculty of 109 full-time and 25 part-time gives a faculty-student ratio of 1:15.

Entrance Requirements: High school graduation or equivalent with C average; ACT is required, SAT is optional; rolling admission, advanced placement and delayed admission plans available; $20 application fee.

Costs Per Year: $9,800 tuition; $3,000 room and board.

Collegiate Environment: The campus is located in a quiet residential area of Sioux Falls. The 100-acre campus contains 19 buildings with a library housing 221,136 volumes. There are living accommodations for 496 men and 776 women. Special financial aid is available for economically handicapped students. Each application is considered on the basis of probable success at this college, and there is no set cut-off point in class rank or college aptitude score. Recommendations and personal interviews play an important part in determining admission, 85% of applicants accepted.

Community Environment: See Sioux Falls College.

BLACK HILLS STATE UNIVERSITY (F-2)
1200 University Avenue
Box 9502
Spearfish, South Dakota 57783
Tel: (605) 642-6343

Description: The territorial legislature provided for the establishment of a normal school at Spearfish within five years after the gold rush of 1876. The institution officially opened in 1883. The university is accredited by the North Central Association of Colleges and Schools and the National Council for the Accreditation of Teacher Education. It offers programs of preparation for the State teaching certificate, correspondence courses, business courses, junior college program, cooperative education program, extensive music program, and intercollegiate and intramural athletics. A second campus, the Black Hills State University Center at Ellsworth Air Force Base, exists to enable military personnel to pursue a college education. The university awards Certificates, and the Associate, Bachelor, and Master degrees. It operates on the semester system and offers four summer sessions. Enrollment includes 2,418 full-time, 415 part-time undergraduate, and 81 graduate students. A faculty of 108 full-time and 2 part-time gives a faculty-student ratio of 1-26. Army ROTC program is available.

Entrance Requirements: High school graduation or equivalent, with C average and rank in upper two-thirds of high school class; 13 high school units required, including 4 English, 3 mathematics, 3 lab science, 3 social science, 1/2 computer science, and 1/2 fine art; minimum ACT 20 composite or SAT 720 combined required; open admissions policy exists in the Junior College program; GRE required

for graduate school; under certain circumstances non high school graduates accepted; early admission, rolling admission, midyear admission, and advanced placement plans available; Sept. 1 application deadline; $15 application fee.

Costs Per Year: $1,411 South Dakota & Minnesota residents tuition; $2,117 WUE residents tuition; $3,437 nonresident tuition; $2,393 average room and board; $971 student fees; $500 average additional expenses.

Collegiate Environment: The college campus consists of 123 acres situated in the western part of Spearfish. There are 11 buildings on the campus, including a library that houses 200,000 volumes, 870 periodicals and 170,000 microforms. Dormitory facilities accommodate 660 students. Financial assistance is available and 80% of students receive some form of financial assistance.

Community Environment: Spearfish (population 10,000) is in a beautiful agricultural valley at the mouth of Spearfish Canyon. There are libraries, museums, churches, hospitals and a number of civic and service organizations in the community and surrounding area. Recreational activities include hunting, fishing, hiking, skiing, golf and boating. The Black Hills Passion Play is presented during the summer months in a specially constructed amphitheater. Part-time employment is available.

DAKOTA STATE UNIVERSITY (G-16)
Madison, South Dakota 57042
Tel: (605) 256-5111; (800) 952-3230; Fax: (605) 256-5020

Description: This publicly supported state university was chartered by the territorial legislature in 1881 for the purpose of teacher education. Its mission was changed by legislative decree to include the integration of computer technology in all degree programs. Enrollment includes 1,438 full-time undergraduate students. A faculty of 64 full-time and 11 part-time gives a faculty-student ratio of 1-19. The college operates on the semester system and offers three summer sessions. It is accredited by the North Central Association of Colleges and Schools, the National Council for Accreditation of Teacher Education and the Committee on Allied Health Education and Accreditation. The former name, General Beadle State College, was changed to Dakota State College on July 1, 1969, and then to Dakota State University on July 1, 1990. The college offers student teaching experience in England and has academic cooperative programs with the University of South Dakota, South Dakota State University and Northern State University giving preliminary courses in law and law enforcement. Also available are band, choir, intercollegiate and intramural athletics and Army ROTC.

Entrance Requirements: High school graduation or equivalent; rank in upper two thirds of high school class (upper half for out-of-state residents); ACT with a score of 20 or over; early decision, rolling admission, delayed admission, early admission and advanced placement plans available; $15 application fee.

Costs Per Year: $1,300 tuition; $2,550 room and board; $1,000 student fees.

Collegiate Environment: Dakota State University enhances its academic programs with the appropriate integration of computer technology. Students don't just learn about computers; they learn to apply them in their major field of study: Business, computer information systems, the sciences, mathematics, teacher education, respiratory therapy, medical records programs, English and other areas. At DSU, students have access to computers at a rate that is better than the national average. The latest hardware and software is provided in a 24-hour access facility and in the dormitories as well as computer labs throughout the campus. Also, an introductory course teaches students to use computers for word processing, data base and spreadsheet management, giving them the ability to apply these skills in coursework

739

throughout their college and professional careers. Students also have ready access to professionals in their fields of study. Financial assistance is available, and 84% of the current student body receives some form of aid.

Community Environment: Dakota State University is located in the heart of the Midwest, in Madison, South Dakota, just minutes from Interstates 29 and 90, which are major highways. Two nearby lakes provide the best in outdoor recreation. In the summer, this includes water sports, fishing and camping, followed in the fall and winter by hunting, snowmobiling, cross-country skiing and more. One of South Dakota's finest state parks provides excellent facilities for all of these activities. Cultural events are provided by a local arts association, a summer theater group and through college-sponsored events. Madison is also located just an hour away from the state's largest city, Sioux Falls.

DAKOTA WESLEYAN UNIVERSITY   *(I-15)*
1200 West University Avenue
Mitchell, South Dakota 57301-4398
Tel: (605) 995-2650; (800) 333-8506; Admissions: (605) 995-2650;
Fax: (605) 995-2699

Description: This privately supported university is a four-year college of the liberal arts and sciences, granting the degrees of Bachelor of Arts and Associate of Arts in Business, Nursing and Master of Arts in Elementary Education. The university is accredited by the North Central Association of Colleges and Schools and is affiliated with the United Methodist Church. The university is on the approved list of the Methodist University Senate and is approved as a teacher training institution by the State Department of Elementary and Secondary Education of South Dakota. It operates on the semester system with two summer sessions. Enrollment includes 526 full-time and 178 part-time students. An evening school program is offered as a community service each semester. A faculty of 32 full-time and 30 part-time gives a faculty-student ratio of 1-15. It offers the Cooperative Education program (alternating work and class periods) in education, business, psychology, sociology, recreation and social work; urban semester (sociology); practicum in rehabilitation (psychology); community recreation (physical education); nursing. Also choir and intercollegiate and intramural athletics.

Entrance Requirements: High school graduation or equivalent with 2.0 or higher GPA; ACT or SAT is required; Those who give evidence of good moral character and future promise are generally eligible for admission; rolling admission, midyear admission, and advanced placement plans available; $15 application fee.

Costs Per Year: $7,540 tuition and fees; $2,710 room and board.

Collegiate Environment: The university has an attractive 40-acre campus with 9 buildings; Layne Library houses 55,000 volumes. There is student housing for 125 men and 239 women. About 70% of the previous freshman class returned to the college for their second year. Applicants are urged to initiate admissions procedures early in the senior year of high school, and they are acted upon as soon as they are completed and received. 84% of applicants are accepted. The average score for the entering freshman class was ACT 20 composite. 500 scholarships are available and 93% of the students receive some form of financial aid.

Community Environment: Located in the James River Valley, Mitchell (population 15,000) is one of the most fertile and diversified agricultural areas in the United States. Products are corn, sorghum, small grain, cattle and hogs. Mitchell is the trading center for the surrounding counties. Community facilities include shopping areas, churches, a library, YMCA, 2 hospitals and a number of the customary civic and service organizations. Recreational activities include boating, fishing, swimming and pheasant hunting.

HURON UNIVERSITY   *(F-14)*
9th Street & Ohio Avenue, S.W.
Huron, South Dakota 57350
Tel: (605) 352-8721; (800) 942-5826

Description: With a long history of success in combined liberal arts and vocational training, the privately supported college maintains that a program of teaching the liberal arts is necessary for leadership and a full life, together with the teaching of skills. The college is accredited by the North Central Association of Colleges and Schools, the Na-

tional Council for Accreditation of Teacher Education and the National League for Nursing. The Bachelor of Arts, Bachelor of Science and Associate degrees are awarded. Huron offers preparation for the State teaching certificate. The college has freshman and upper-class programs for the educationally disadvantaged. It operates on the semester system and offers two summer sessions. Enrollment includes 518 full-time students. A faculty of 32 full-time and 16 part-time gives a faculty-student ratio of 1-14.

Entrance Requirements: High school graduation or equivalent; GED; open enrollment; ACT is recommended, SAT may be substituted; early admission, early decision, rolling admission and advanced placement plans available; no application fee.

Costs Per Year: $7,887 tuition; $3,300 room and board.

Collegiate Environment: The 15-acre college campus is located four blocks from downtown Huron and seven blocks from the State Fairground. The library houses 55,720 volumes, and the dormitory facilities will accommodate 200 students. 96% of applicants are accepted including midyear students. Academic, athletic, and need based scholarships are available. 87% of students receive some form of financial assistance.

Community Environment: Huron (population 14,300) is widely known for its excellent pheasant hunting. This is a large irrigated farming and livestock area. Industries located here include meat packing and produce. Air, bus and train transportation is available. A public library, museum, YWCA, churches of major denominations, a regional medical center, and a number of civic and service organizations serve the community. Part-time employment is available. The James River provides facilities for boating, fishing and swimming, other activities are golf, tennis and baseball. The State Fair in September and Pow Wow Day in October are special annual events.

Branch Campuses: Huron University, Landsdowne Campus, London, England; Huron University, Sioux Falls Branch, Sioux Falls, SD; Huron University, Tokyo, Japan.

MOUNT MARTY COLLEGE   *(K-16)*
1105 West 8th Street
Yankton, South Dakota 57078
Tel: (605) 668-1545; (800) 658-4552; Fax: (605) 668-1357

Description: Mount Marty is a Catholic, Benedictine, coeducational, liberal arts college founded in 1936 by the Sisters of St. Benedict of Yankton. It was named for Matin Marty, first Catholic Bishop of the Dakota Territory. The college is accredited by the North Central Association of Colleges and Schools, the National League for Nursing, the American Dietetic Association, and the National Council for the Accreditation of Teacher Education. The college offers preparation for state teaching certificates and a special selected studies program allows students to develop their own degree contracts. Undergraduate degrees include 18 majors and eight pre-professional programs. The college's size and mission combines sound knowledge with "hands-on" learning in a setting that promotes community involvement, personal values and professional ethics. Music programs are offered as well as intercollegiate and intramural athletics. A Masters Degree is offered in Anesthesia. The college operates on a 4-1-4 system and offers three summer sessions. Enrollment includes 341 men, 638 women in undergraduate programs and 39 graduate students. A faculty of 50 full-time and 24 part-time gives an undergraduate faculty-student ratio of 1-14.

Entrance Requirements: Graduation from an accredited high school with an average of "C" or better, or GED; ACT or SAT required; early admission, rolling admission, advanced placement plans available; March 1 application deadline; $10 application fee.

Costs Per Year: $7,178 tuition, $3,128 room and board, $652 student fees.

Collegiate Environment: The 80-acre campus has 6 buildings, including a 77,000 volume library. Dormitory facilities accommodate 400 students. Average ACT score of 1994 freshmen was 21.5. MMC strives to provide its students with an atmosphere and program conducive to their total personal development. Academic advisory office is designed to give assistance in course selection, registration and evaluation of academic progress. Career planning office helps students develop meaningful and satisfying career goals. Intercollegiate sports include men's basketball, baseball, track and cross-country, and women's volleyball, basketball, track and cross-country. The college offers an active intramural athletic program throughout the school year. Campus activities provide over 300 opportunities for involvement including student government, instrumental and choral music, theatre productions, student publications, honor societies, campus clubs and pastoral council. 98% of students applying for financial assistance receive awards in the forms of scholarships, grants, loans, and campus work-study.

Community Environment: Yankton is situated on the Missouri River, 60 miles northwest of Sioux City, Iowa, and 80 miles southwest of Sioux Falls, S.D. The city is located four miles downstream from Gavins Point Dam, and Lewis and Clark Lake, which create some of the best fishing, swimming, boating and picnicking areas in the midwest. The All-American city served as the first capital of Dakota Territory and is known as the Mother City of the Dakotas. Its 12,000 friendly people take a deep interest in the activities of the college.

NATIONAL COLLEGE   *(G-3)*
321 Kansas City Street
Box 1780
Rapid City, South Dakota 57709
Tel: (605) 394-4800

Description: The privately supported, senior college is accredited by the North Central Association of Colleges and Schools, the American Veterinary Medical Association, Committee on Allied Health Education and Accreditation and the American Association of Medical Assistants. It operates on the quarter system with one summer session. Enrollment includes 104 men, 216 women full-time and 16 men, 36 women part-time with a faculty of 18 full-time and 35 part-time members. The college grants Certificates, Diplomas, Associate and Bachelor degrees. Army ROTC program is available.

Entrance Requirements: High school graduation; under certain circumstances non-HS graduates considered; $25 application fee.

Costs Per Year: $6,624 tuition; $3,263 room and board.

Collegiate Environment: The college is located in a pleasant residential area on a 2-acre campus with 9 buildings, the library housing 31,841 volumes. The residence hall will accommodate approximately 270 students. Approximately 97% of those that apply for admission are accepted. Average ACT score of Freshman class: composite 16. Special financial aid is available for economically handicapped students with 90% of the recent class receiving some form of financial assistance. Individual instruction and counseling is stressed. 66% of the previous freshman class returned to the college for their second year; quarters begin September, December, March and June.

Community Environment: See South Dakota School of Mines and Technology.

Branch Campuses: 3201 S. Kiwanis Ave., Sioux Falls, SD, 57105, (605) 334-5430; 2577 N. Chelton, Colorado Springs, CO, 80909, (303) 471-4205; 1325 S. Colorado Blvd., Suite 100, Denver, CO, 80222, (303) 758-6700; 330 Lake Ave., Pueblo, CO 81004, (719) 545-8763; 600 West 39th St., Kansas City, KS, 64111, (816) 753-4554; 1380 Energy Lane, St. Paul, MN, 55108, (612) 644-1265; 1202 Pennsylvania, N.E., Albuquerque, NM, 87198, (505) 265-7517.

NORTH AMERICAN BAPTIST SEMINARY   *(I-17)*
1525 S. Grange Avenue
Sioux Falls, South Dakota 57105-1599
Tel: (605) 336-6588; (800) 440-6227; Admissions: (605) 336-6588; Fax: (605) 335-9090

Description: This graduate school of theology prepares men and women for effective practice of Christian ministry. The seminary is accredited by the North Central Association of Colleges and Schools and the Asssociation of Theological Schools in the United States and Canada. The Master of Divinity program is a three-year course normally pursued in preparation for pastoral ministry. Master of Arts programs are available with specializations in Christian Education, Bible and Theology, Christian Music, Marriage and Family Therapy, and Religious Studies. A combined Bachelor of Arts and Master of Divinity program, developed in cooperation with local Augustana and Sioux Falls colleges, allows academically superior students to complete undergraduate work in three years. The Doctor of Ministry program of professional development is offered for those already engaged in the practice of ministry. January term visiting field mis-

sion offered. It operates on the 4-1-4 semester plan and offers one summer session. Enrollment includes 173 full-time and 154 part-time students with a faculty of 15 full-time and 10 part-time members.

Entrance Requirements: The B.A. degree or its equivalent from an accredited school; midyear admission, and rolling admission plans available; $25 application fee; $100 reservation fee.

Costs Per Year: $6,500 tuition; $3,600 room and board; $10 fees.

Collegiate Environment: The seminary is a constituent member of the North Central University Center which includes Augustana and Sioux Falls colleges. Through this cooperative center the library, teaching and athletic facilities, and other resources are available to seminary students. The seminary library contains 56,500 volumes as well as archival materials relating to the history of the North American Baptist Conference. Housing is available for 83 students. Midyear students are accepted. 30 scholarships are available and financial aid is awarded in varying amounts on the basis of need.

Community Environment: See Sioux Falls College.

NORTHERN STATE UNIVERSITY   *(C-13)*
South Jay Street and 12th Avenue
Aberdeen, South Dakota 57401
Tel: (605) 622-2521

Description: Publicly supported, Northern State University was established as the Northern Normal and Industrial School in 1901. It operates on the semester system and offers 2 summer sessions. It is accredited by the North Central Association of Colleges and Schools, the National Association of Schools of Music and the National Council for the Accreditation of Teacher Education. Enrollment is 2,900 students. A faculty of 150 full-time and part time gives a faculty-student ratio of 1-19. The college granted 95 Associate, 326 Bachelor and 62 Master degrees recently. It features liberal arts, teacher education, a 2-year program and graduate school and offers correspondence courses. Half-year credit is allowed toward the MA degree in education from Mary College. Music, intercollegiate and intramural athletic programs are offered.

Entrance Requirements: High school graduation with average of C and rank in upper two-thirds of graduating class for nonresident students; ACT required; completion of 16 units including 4 English, 5 mathematics and science, 3 social science, 1/2 fine arts and 1/2 computer science; early admission, early decision, rolling admission, delayed admission and advanced placement plans available; deadline for fall term applications is August 15; $15 application fee.

Costs Per Year: $1,978 state-resident tuition; $3,500 nonresidents; $2,000 room and board; $800 average additional expenses.

Collegiate Environment: The 50-acre campus is located in the residential section of the city. The Beulah Williams Library houses 210,000 volumes and has listening facilities, a microfilm reader, and photocopy service. There are living accommodations for 400 men and 700 women. Approximately 95% of those applying for admission were accepted including midyear students. Average ACT score of the freshman class was 20. Average high school standing of the freshman class was in the top 60%; 20% ranked in top quarter and 70% were in the top half. Of the 300 scholarships available, 193 are for freshmen. There is a program for the educationally disadvantaged. 80% of the previous freshman class returned to the college for the second year. Semesters begin in September and January.

PRESENTATION COLLEGE   *(C-13)*
1500 North Main Street
Aberdeen, South Dakota 57401
Tel: (605) 229-8492; (800) 437-6060; Fax: (605) 229-8430

Description: This privately supported college is a Roman Catholic educational institution sponsored by the Presentation Sisters of the Blessed Virgin Mary. The baccalaureate and the associate degrees are awarded in both the arts and sciences. The college is accredited by the North Central Association of Colleges and Schools, South Dakota Department of Education, National League for Nursing, and the Committee on Allied Health Education and Accreditation. Baccalaureate degrees are offered in nursing, social work, business, English and communications, and radiologic technology. Associate degree programs include histologic technology, medical lab technology, radiologic technology, surgical technology, and business management. The college operates on the semester system and offers two summer sessions. Enrollment includes 292 full-time and 147 part-time students. A faculty of 28 full-time and 31 part-time gives a faculty-student ratio of 1-10. The Student Services Center provides counseling, academic and study skills services as well as tutoring. Philosophy and Theology coursework is required.

Entrance Requirements: High school graduation or equivalent; high school transcript; ACT required; SAT accepted; ASSET required; rolling admissions; $15 application fee.

Costs Per Year: $6,550 tuition; $2,480 room and board; $275 student fees; $250 average additional expenses.

Collegiate Environment: The college is located in the northwest section of Aberdeen on a 100-acre campus in an area called Presentation Heights. The library houses 36,000 volumes and is computer linked to the South Dakota Library Network with access to over 3 million titles. Living accommodations are available for 81 women and 14 men. There is a special program for the culturally disadvantaged. Scholarships are available. The college has a satellite program on the Cheyenne River Lakota Sioux Reservation to educate Native American students in Associate Degree Nursing.

Community Environment: Aberdeen is a regional retail and market center with a population of 30,000. It is served by bus lines, two major U.S. highways, and daily airline service.

SOUTH DAKOTA SCHOOL OF MINES AND TECHNOLOGY
(G-3)
501 East St. Joseph St.
Rapid City, South Dakota 57701-3995
Tel: (605) 394-2400

Description: This publicly supported, technological college is accredited by the North Central Association of Colleges and Schools and professionally accredited by the American Chemical Society and the Accreditation Board for Engineering and Technology. The primary objective is to offer educational programs in science and engineering to the young men and women of the state. As a secondary objective, the college provides a general studies two-year program to serve the needs of higher education in western South Dakota. Degrees awarded are Bachelor of Science in chemistry, computer science, geology, mathematics, physics, and engineering, with an enriched program in the humanities, and graduate programs at the Master and Doctorate levels. Chorus, orchestra, glee club, and intercollegiate and intramural athletics are available. The institution operates on the semester system with one summer session and one mini semester (3 weeks). Enrollment includes 1,678 full-time, 534 part-time undergraduate, and 237 graduate students. A faculty of 136 full-time and 39 part-time gives a faculty-student ratio of 1-17. Army ROTC is available.

Entrance Requirements: High school graduation, or equivalent with C average and rank in the upper 50% of graduating class; completion of 16 units including 4 English, 2-3 mathematics, 3 social science, 1/2 fine arts, 1/2 computer science, 2-3 science; minimum ACT 22 (23 for nonresidents) required; SAT accepted; GRE recommended for graduate school; early decision, midyear admission, rolling admission, and advanced placement plans available; mid-July deadline for Fall applications; $15 application fee.

Costs Per Year: $1,545 state resident tuition; $4,049 nonresident tuition; $2,900 room and board; $1,462 student fees; $1,000 average additional expenses.

Collegiate Environment: The 120-acre campus has 18 buildings including the library housing 627,539 volumes. Residence halls accommodate 542 students. 89% of applicants are accepted for admission. The average score of freshmen was ACT 24 composite, and 50% were in the top quarter of their high school class. 47% of students receive some form of financial assistance.

Community Environment: Rapid City, founded in 1876, two years after gold was discovered in the Black Hills, is now a trading center and tourist headquarters of the Black Hills area. All commercial transportation is available. Community facilities include many churches, museums, hospitals, a library, radio stations, three TV stations, and a number of the major civic and service organizations.

SOUTH DAKOTA STATE UNIVERSITY *(F-17)*
Box 2201
Brookings, South Dakota 57007
Tel: (605) 688-4121; (800) 952-3541; Admissions: (605) 688-4121; Fax: (605) 688-6384

Description: The publicly supported universitys operates on the semester system and offers two summer sessions. An act of the Territorial Legislature, approved in 1881, provided that an Agricultural College for the Territory of Dakota be established at Brookings. In July 1964, the name of the college was officially changed to South Dakota State University. The university is accredited by the North Central Association of Colleges and Schools; the departments of agricultural, civil, electrical, and mechanical engineering, are accredited by the Accreditation Board for Engineering and Technology. The College of Nursing is accredited by the National League for Nursing. The chemistry department is accredited by the American Chemical Society; curriculum in journalism is accredited by the American Council on Education in Journalism and Mass Communications; pharmacy is accredited by the American Council on Pharmaceutical Education. Preparation of secondary teachers at both the undergraduate and graduate level is accredited by the National Council for Accreditation of Teacher Education. The University is comprised of the Colleges of Agriculture and Biological Sciences, Arts and Sciences, Education and Counseling, Engineering, General Registration, Home Economics, Nursing, Pharmacy, and a Graduate College. Army and Air Force ROTC programs are offered. Enrollment includes 7,122 full-time and 956 part-time undergraduates and 1,062 graduate students. A faculty of 494 full-time and 17 part-time gives an overall faculty-student ratio of 1-17.

Entrance Requirements: High school graduation with a C average including 4 units English, 3 social science, 2-3 mathematics, 2-3 lab science, (if 2 units of math, then 3 of science), 1/2 computer science and 1/2 fine arts; students with one course deficiency may be admitted conditionally if high school rank is upper half or ACT composite score is 22 or above, 23 or above for nonresidents; ACT required; rolling admission available; $15 application fee.

Costs Per Year: $1,455 state-resident tuition; $3,812 nonresident; $2,140 room and board; $1,024 student fees.

Collegiate Environment: The 270-acre campus with approximately 80 buildings has a library that houses 474,903 volumes plus 600,000 government documents and 440,000 titles on microfilms. Residence hall facilities have living accommodations for 3,094 students and 88 families. 92% of applicants are accepted. 1,827 scholarships are available and 82% of the undergraduates receive some form of financial aid.

Community Environment: Brookings is located in the eastern part of the state, an agriculturally rich area with diversified farming influenced by research done at South Dakota State University. Located 55 miles from Sioux Falls, the community facilities include a library, 23 churches, an hospital, and many civic and service clubs. Recreational activities include deer and pheasant hunting, golf, and water sports at the center lake region.

UNIVERSITY OF SIOUX FALLS *(I-17)*
1101 West 22nd Street
Sioux Falls, South Dakota 57101
Tel: (605) 331-5000; (800) 888-1047; Admissions: (605) 331-6600; Fax: (605) 331-6615

Description: The University of Sioux Falls is a four-year Christian institution that is affiliated with the American Baptist Churches. It is accredited by the North Central Association of Colleges and Schools and other professional organizations. Founded in 1883, the mission of the university is to foster the academic excellence and development of mature Christian persons for service to God and humankind. It offers a demanding liberal arts education with a core of Christian Perspective, Cultural and Artistic Heritage, Natural and Human Environment, and Modes of Communication, for 30 fields of study, as well as masters programs in Reading Education and Business Administration. Special programs include an American Studies Program in Washington, D.C., and cooperative programs with a neighboring college and seminary as well as in Japan. It operates on a 4-1-4 calendar system and offers two summer sessions. Enrollment includes 586 full-time, 156 part-time undergraduate, and 83 graduate students. A faculty of 37 full-time and 30 part-time gives a faculty-student ratio of 1-15.

Entrance Requirements: High school class rank in the upper 50% of graduating class, or minimum ACT 19, or SAT 800; completion of high school units: 4 English, 3 history, 3 mathematics, 2 science, and 1 foreign language recommended; transcripts required; interview not required; early decision, early admission, rolling admission, and advanced placement plans available; $20 application fee.

Costs Per Year: $9,490 tuition; $3,260 room and board.

Collegiate Environment: Personal relationships between faculty and students promote learning and produce graduates who, over the past five years, have enjoyed a placement rating ranging from 92 to 97 percent. Library holdings include 80,000 volumes, and residence halls accommodate 375 students. Weekly chapel is offered. Special services for nontraditional students are provided, along with special programming for degree completion. Opportunities for involvement in everything from campus ministry to music to conference-winning athletic teams. 90% of applicants are accepted. 90% of students receive some form of financial assistance.

Community Environment: Sioux Falls (population 130,000) is a commercial and industrial center. Credit card corporations, banking, retailing and meat packing are the leading industries of the community. Air and bus transportation are available. Community facilities include churches of many denominations, hospitals, an art center, and excellent shopping. Recreation includes all winter sports, water sports, hunting, and fishing. Part-time employment opportunities are excellent.

UNIVERSITY OF SOUTH DAKOTA *(K-17)*
414 East Clark
Vermillion, South Dakota 57069
Tel: (605) 677-5434; Fax: (605) 677-5073

Description: USD is a public university that was founded in 1862. The College of Arts and Sciences, College of Fine Arts, School of Business, School of Education, School of Law, School of Medicine, and the Graduate School make up the units of the University. USD has been accredited through the doctoral level by the North Central Association of Colleges and Schools since 1913 and is an active member of the National Association of State Universities and Land-Grant Colleges and many other educational agencies. Individual schools and departments have received additional accreditation from their appropriate professional organizations. The University offers degrees at the Associate, Bachelor, Master, Specialist, and Doctorate levels. It operates on the semester system and offers three summer sessions. Enrollment includes 2,695 male and 3,333 female undergraduates full-time and part-time, and 1,711 graduate students. A faculty of 471 full-time and part-time gives an undergraduate faculty-student ratio of 1-17.

Entrance Requirements: High school graduation or equivalent, 2.0 or above GPA in the following course areas: 4 years of English, 3 social science, 2-3 years of mathematics (including algebra), 2-3 years of lab science (if 2 years of mathematics, then 3 of science and vice-versa), 1 semester computer science, and 1 semester fine arts; applicants could also be accepted if ranked in top 1/2 of graduating class or have in-state ACT 22 (out-of-state 23); undergraduate early admission, advanced placement and rolling admission plans available; $15 application fee.

Costs Per Year: $1,455; $3,812 nonresident; $2,492 room and board, $1,133 student fees; (tuition based on $45.45 per credit hour in-state; $119.10 per credit hour out-of-state).

Collegiate Environment: The 216-acre campus is just six blocks from the business district. The library, which opened in April 1967, is the largest and finest in the state and houses 445,215 volumes, 322,438 government documents, 519,565 microform holdings, 2,687 serial titles, and 8,443 audiovisual materials. Residence hall facilities provide housing for 2,122. Financial aid is available to all those who qualify based on an approved standardized needs analysis system. 78% of undergraduates receive some form of financial assistance. Average ACT score of the freshman class was 21.8. Midyear students are accepted.

Community Environment: Vermillion is situated on a bluff overlooking the Missouri and Vermillion Rivers and was named for the red clay on the riverbanks. There is a public library, museums, churches of a number of denominations, a hospital, and major civic and service organizations. Shopping facilities are excellent. Part-time employment opportunities are good. There are a number of recreational activities, and hunting and fishing opportunities are excellent.

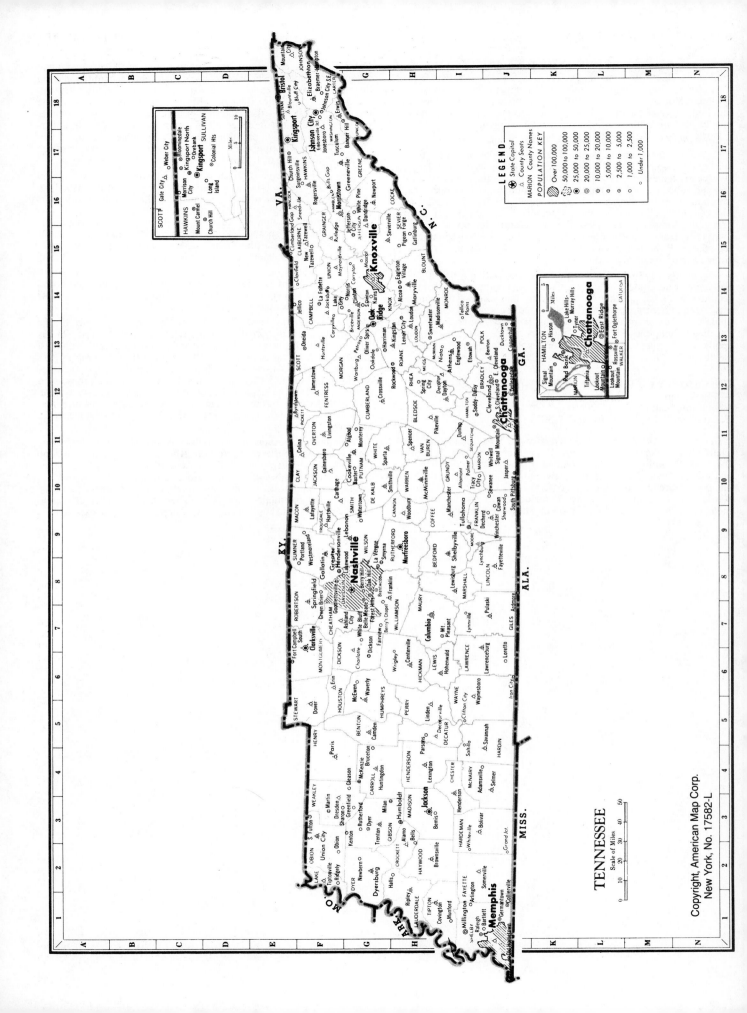

TENNESSEE

Scale of Miles

0 10 20 30 40 50

LEGEND

⊛ State Capital
⊙ County Seats
MARION County Names
POPULATION KEY
▨ Over 100,000
◉ 50,000 to 100,000
◉ 25,000 to 50,000
◎ 20,000 to 25,000
⊕ 10,000 to 20,000
⊙ 5,000 to 10,000
⊙ 2,500 to 5,000
○ 1,000 to 2,500
○ Under 1,000

TENNESSEE

AMERICAN BAPTIST COLLEGE (G-8)
1800 White's Creek Pike
Nashville, Tennessee 37207
Tel: (615) 228-7877; Admissions: (615) 262-1369; Fax: (615) 226-7855

Description: The founding of the American Baptist Theological Seminary was the result of a unique interracial venture undertaken cooperatively by the National Baptist Convention and the Southern Baptist Convention in the early years of this century. This seminary is operated jointly by the National Baptist Convention and the Southern Baptist Convention through a board of directors representing both conventions. Enrollment is 189 full-time and 10 part-time students. A faculty of 12 full-time and 8 part-time gives a faculty-student ratio of 1-10. The college is accredited by the American Association of Bible Colleges and operates on the semester system with two summer sessions.

Entrance Requirements: Open enrollment policy; completion of 16 units including 4 English, 3 mathematics, 2 foreign language, 2 social science and 2 natural science; SAT or ACT accepted; non-high school graduates considered for admission under certain circumstances; rolling admission plan available; $15 application fee.

Costs Per Year: $2,000 tuition; $1,984 board and room.

Collegiate Environment: The campus of the college occupies 53 acres on White's Creek Pike. The 15 buildings on the campus include 11 buildings that provide housing for 82 men, 2 women. The library houses 37,565 volumes, 210 periodicals and 200 recordings, including a large biblical and theological section. Over 50% of students applying for admission are accepted including midyear students. Various scholarships are available and 95% receive some form of aid.

Community Environment: See Vanderbilt University.

AQUINAS JUNIOR COLLEGE (G-8)
4210 Harding Road
Nashville, Tennessee 37205
Tel: (615) 297-7545; Fax: (615) 297-7557

Description: The college, founded in 1961, is accredited by the Southern Association of Colleges and Secondary Schools and is affiliated with the Roman Catholic Church. The college grants the Associate degree and a Bachelor's degree in Elementary Education. It operates on the semester system and offers two summer sessions. Enrollment includes 368 students. A faculty of 21 full-time and 30 part-time gives a faculty-student ratio of 1-15.

Entrance Requirements: Accredited high school graduation or equivalent; G.E.D. minimum score of 50; 2.0 (4.0 scale) high school GPA; minimum ACT 18 composite; 2.0 GPA for transfers; rolling admission; $20 application fee.

Costs Per Year: $4,200 tuition; $70 student fees; additional expenses average $1,590.

Collegiate Environment: Nashville's first Catholic College spreads over 92 acres in a residential area, with two buildings. The college provides an intellectual and cultural exchange between college and community. About 90% of the students applying for admission are accepted, including midyear students. Financial aid is available from Federal and State governments and local sources including scholarships and grants-in-aid.

Community Environment: See Vanderbilt University.

AUSTIN PEAY STATE UNIVERSITY (F-7)
College Street
Clarksville, Tennessee 37044
Tel: (615) 648-7011; (800) 844-2778; Admissions: (615) 648-7661; Fax: (615) 648-5994

Description: The publicly supported university began as Austin Peay Normal School in 1927. It is accredited by the Southern Association of Colleges and Schools. Programs of study lead to the Associate, Bachelor, Master, and Ed. S. degrees. Preprofessional curricula includes law, medicine, dentistry, physical therapy, radiologic technology, pharmacy, veterinary medicine, and forestry. The university operates on the semester system and offers two summer sessions. Enrollment includes 5,740 full-time and 2,713 undergraduates and graduate students. A faculty of 275 gives an overall faculty-student ratio of 1-20.

Entrance Requirements: ACT composite of 19 or high school GPA of 2.75; completion of 14 units including 4 English, 2 algebra, 1 advanced math, 2 natural or pysical science, 1 U.S. history, 1 social science, 2 foreign language, and 1 visual or performing art; early admission, early decision, rolling admission, midyear admission, and advanced placement plans available; $5 application fee.

Costs Per Year: $1,880 in-state tuition; $5,814 out-of-state; $2,930 room and board.

Collegiate Environment: There are 51 buildings on the 200-acre campus. The library houses 264,630 volumes, 975 periodicals, 388,074 microforms and 7,425 audiovisual forms. The dormitory facilities provide living accommodations for 533 men, 534 women and 96 families. Approximately 90% of the students applying for admission are accepted including midyear students. The average score of the entering freshman class was ACT 20.57 composite. 986 scholarships are offered, including 308 for freshman and 176 athletic. 68% of the undergraduates receive some form of financial aid. The university offers an Army Reserve Officers Training Corps program. The university awarded 112 Associate, 604 Bachelor, and 91 Master degrees to the graduating class.

Community Environment: Clarksville, an urban area, was founded in 1784 and was named for General George Rogers Clark. Bus transportation is available. Community facilities include a number of churches, a hospital, a public library, and a number of the major civic and service organizations. Some part-time employment is available. Water sports are enjoyed on the Cumberland River and nearby lakes.

BELMONT UNIVERSITY (G-8)
1900 Belmont Boulevard
Nashville, Tennessee 37212-3757
Tel: (615) 383-7001; Admissions: (615) 386-6785; Fax: (615) 386-4434

Description: This privately supported, church-related college is accredited by the Southern Association of Colleges and Schools and is affiliated with the Tennessee Baptist Convention. It is also accredited by professional accrediting institutions. Preprofessional programs are offered in dentistry, engineering, law, medicine, nursing, optometry, pharmacy, medical technology, and theology. The college grants Associate, Bachelor, and Master's degrees. Army ROTC is available through Vanderbilt University. Overseas programs are available in England, France, Spain, Russia, Germany, and China. Enrollment includes 2,300 full-time and 400 part-time undergraduate students, and 300 graduate students. A faculty of 160 full-time and 150 part-time members gives a faculty-student ratio of approximately 1-14.

Entrance Requirements: Completion of 15 units including 4 English, 2 mathematics, 2 science, 2 social studies, 2 foreign languages, 1 history, 4 electives; minimum ACT score of 20 or SAT combined score of 800 required; early decision, delayed admission, advanced placement, early admission, and rolling admission plans available; $25 application fee.

Costs Per Year: $7,100 tuition; $3,490 room and board; $200 student fees; $450 average additional expenses.

Collegiate Environment: The school's 30-acre campus is situated conveniently near the campuses of Peabody, Scarritt, and other colleges. Classes are centered in seven main buildings with the library and other facilities in close proximity. The library, completed in 1964 contains 90,000 volumes, 1,843 microforms, 7,690 periodicals, and 200 recordings; it seats 500 persons. Dormitory facilities provide living accommodations for 800 students. Approximately 80% of students applying for admission are accepted including midyear students. Financial aid is available for economically disadvantaged students, and about 75% of the current class receives some form of financial assistance. Nearly 67% of the previous freshman class returned to the college for the second year. The college awarded 229 Associate and Bachelor degrees to the graduating class. About 40% of the senior class continued on to graduate school.

Community Environment: See Vanderbilt University.

BETHEL COLLEGE   *(G-4)*
Cherry St.
McKenzie, Tennessee 38201
Tel: (901) 352-1000; (800) 441-4940; Fax: (901) 352-1008

Description: The privately-supported college, founded in 1842, is a Christian college committed to a program of liberal education that shall fit young men and women in Christian character and in academic culture for adequate living. The college is accredited by the Southern Association of Colleges and Schools and is affiliated with the Cumberland Presbyterian Church. Programs of study lead to the Bachelor degree. The college operates on the semester system and offers one summer session. Enrollment is 500 students. A faculty of 26 full-time and 19 part-time gives a faculty-student ratio of 1-14.

Entrance Requirements: High school graduation with rank in upper half of graduating class; completion of 18 units including 4 English, 2 mathematics, 1 science, and 1 social science; ACT score of 19 or SAT score of 700 required; early admission, rolling admission, delayed admission, midyear admission and advanced placement plans available; $10 application fee.

Costs Per Year: $6,750 tuition; $3,200 room and board.

Collegiate Environment: The college campus consists of approximately 100 acres within the city limits of McKenzie. The library facilities house 64,000 volumes, 123 periodicals, 780 microforms and 700 audiovisuals. Dormitory facilities provide housing for 120 men and 171 women. All unmarried students who do not commute daily from home are required to live in one of the dormitory facilities and to take their meals in the cafeteria. Any exceptions to these regulations must be approved by the Director of Student Resources. Even though this is a church-related college and it recognizes a special obligation to meet the particular needs of the Church by which it is maintained, students of all denominations are cordially welcomed. Approximately 90% of the students applying for admission are accepted including midyear students. Average high school standing of the recent freshman class was 36% in top quartile, 33% in second quartile, 21% in third quartile, and 10% in fourth quartile. The average score for the entering freshman class was ACT 19 composite. 473 scholarships are offered and 90% of the current students receive some form of financial aid. Nearly 60% of the previous freshman class returned to the college for the second year. The college awarded 60 Bachelor degrees to the graduating class. About 10% of the senior class continued on to graduate school.

Community Environment: McKenzie is situated halfway between Memphis and Nashville and is 25 miles from Kentucky Lake. Churches of all denominations, a radio station, and FM station, various civic and service organizations, are a part of the community. Nearby lakes provide excellent facilities for fishing, swimming, and hunting. There are supervised recreational programs within the town.

Branch Campuses: Bethel College teaches regular and special courses leading to the baccalaureate degree at Covington and Brownsville, TN.

BRYAN COLLEGE   *(I-12)*
Box 7000, Bryan Hill
Dayton, Tennessee 37321-7000
Tel: (615) 775-2041; (800) 277-9522; Fax: (615) 775-7330

Description: Founded in 1930, nonsectarian in character, conservative and evangelical by commitment, and interdemoninational in fellowship, the four-year Christian liberal arts institution was named after the three-time democratic candidate for the presidency of the United States, William Jennings Bryan. Shortly before his death, Mr. Bryan, who had defended the authority of the Bible in the famed Scopes trial, suggested that a Christian school be established near Dayton. Privately controlled, the college is accredited by the Southern Association of Colleges and Schools. Programs of study lead to the Bachelor degree. The college operates on the early semester calendar system and offers two summer sessions. Enrollment includes 220 men and 269 women. A faculty of 29 full-time and 16 part-time gives a faculty-student ratio of 1-15. Programs of study lead to the Bachelor degree. The college and student organizations sponsor a wide range of athletic, social, cultural, and religious activities.

Entrance Requirements: High school graduation; completion of 20 units including 4 English, 3 mathematics, 1 U.S. history, 3 science, 2 foreign language, 3 social studies; ACT with minimum composite score of 20, or SAT with minimum score of 800, required; advanced placement, early admission, rolling admission, midyear admission, delayed admission and early decision plans available; $20 application fee.

Costs Per Year: $8,900 tuition; $3,950 room and board; $600 student fees.

Collegiate Environment: Over 100 acres, located on a wooded hilltop, compose the campus proper. There are 17 buildings plus 17 apartments in Bryan Village. The Ironside Memorial Library houses over 80,472 volumes, 435 periodicals, 36,911 microforms and 3,250 audiovisual materials. A Bible and Rare Book Collection was begun in 1962. Dormitory space available on campus provides housing for 198 men and 274 women. The fall term begins in August, but midyear students are accepted. 53% of applicants are accepted, and 77% of the freshman class return to the campus for the second year. The average score of the entering freshman class was ACT 23. 90% of the current students receive some form of financial aid.

Community Environment: Dayton is located 38 miles from Chattanooga, enjoying a very desirable climate the year round. Air and bus transportation are convenient. Community facilities include some 20 churches representing Protestant and Roman Catholic faiths, a public library, a hospital, and motels. TVA lakes provide fishing and water sports. Part-time employment is available for students. The East Tennessee Strawberry Festival is held in May.

CARSON-NEWMAN COLLEGE   *(G-15)*
Russell Avenue
Jefferson City, Tennessee 37760
Tel: (615) 471-3223; (800) 678-9061; Fax: (615) 471-3502

Description: The privately supported college, founded in 1851, endeavors to provide a quality Christian education committed to preparing capable men and women for meaningful service in society. It is affiliated with the Tennessee Baptist Convention. It is accredited by the Southern Association of Colleges and Schools. The college grants the Bachelor degree and provides academic cooperative plans for medical technology and engineering students. It operates on the semester system and offers two summer sessions. Enrollment is 2,100 students. A faculty of 115 full-time and 35 part-time gives a faculty-student ratio of 1-13. An Army ROTC program is available.

Entrance Requirements: High school graduation with rank in upper 50% of graduating class; completion of 20 units including 4 English, 2 mathematics, 2 science, and 2 social science; minimum ACT 19 or minimum SAT 800 composite required; early admission, rolling admission, early decision, delayed admission and advanced placement plans available; $25 application fee.

Costs Per Year: $8,550 tuition; $3,300 room and board.

Collegiate Environment: There are 34 buildings on the 95-acre campus. The library houses 180,000 volumes, 874 periodicals, 3,029 microforms and 395 pamphlets. Dormitory facilities provide housing for 662 men, 752 women, and 64 families. About 60% of the students applying for admission are accepted including midyear students. Financial aid is available. 90% of students receive some form of financial assistance.

Community Environment: Jefferson City is located 27 miles from Knoxville, a city of approximately 400,000. Plane and bus transportation are available. Recreational activities are fishing, water skiing, swimming, and boating at Cherokee and Douglas Lakes, which are a short drive away. Skiing is available in the Great Smoky Mountains National Park. Part-time employment opportunities are available.

CHATTANOOGA STATE TECHNICAL COMMUNITY COLLEGE *(J-11)*
4501 Amnicola Hwy.
Chattanooga, Tennessee 37406
Tel: (615) 697-4400; Admissions: (615) 697-4709; Fax: (615) 697-4709

Description: This institution makes every effort to provide its students with an academic environment conducive to personal growth. The technical college is a state institution accredited by the Southern Association of Colleges and Schools. The purpose of Chattanooga State's technical and comprehensive programs is to serve the educational needs of the community. The primary goal is to offer post secondary educational experiences for citizens within the institutional service area, providing marketable job skills through career programs as well as academic preparation for transfer to four-year institutions. The college grants the Associate degree. It operates on the semester system and offers two summer sessions of varying length, from 1-10 weeks. Enrollment is 7,793 students. A faculty of 173 gives a faculty-student ratio of 1-45.

Entrance Requirements: High school graduation or equivalent (GED diploma); ACT or college placement test required. Allied health programs have additional admissions requirements. $5.00 application fee.

Costs Per Year: $1,010 tuition for residents; $4,800 nonresident tuition.

Collegiate Environment: The library houses 75,000 volumes. All students meeting admission requirements are accepted including midyear students. About 50% of the previous freshman class returned to the college for the second year. For technical programs, a strong background in math and science is recommended. There were 350 Associate degrees awarded to the graduating class.

Community Environment: Located in southeastern Tennessee on the Tennessee River, Chattanooga is an important industrial center with over 500 manufacturing plants. All forms of commercial transportation are convenient. Part-time employment is available. Recreational facilities are plentiful, Chickamauga Lake, formed by the TVA dam, provides a wonderful place for water sports, and fishing; also there are other lakes, rivers and streams, and Harrison Bay State Park and Hamilton County State Park for other activities. Chattanooga has a number of city parks, and five golf courses for activities within the city. Some points of interest are Lookout Mountain, Lookout Mountain Incline Railway, Rock City Gardens, the Ruby Falls-Lookout Mountain Caves, and the Chattanooga Choo-Choo.

CHRISTIAN BROTHERS UNIVERSITY *(J-1)*
650 East Parkway South
Memphis, Tennessee 38104
Tel: (901) 722-0205; (800) 288-7576; Fax: (901) 722-0494

Description: The college, chartered in 1871, operates on the early semester system, with two summer sessions. This private institution, an independent Catholic college, is accredited by the Southern Association of Colleges and Secondary Schools. The college is a member of the Greater Memphis Consortium, enabling students to take credit courses at any of the member institutions. The University grants the Bachelor degree and Master's Degree. Enrollment includes 1,382 full-time, 329 part-time, and 208 graduate students. A faculty of 106 full-time provides a faculty student ratio of 1-12.

Entrance Requirements: High school graduates with a minimum C average; must have a minimum total of 16 units with 3 in English; ACT required with score of 20 or over; early decision, rolling admission and advanced placement plans available; $25 application fee.

Costs Per Year: $8,390 tuition Engineers, $7,990 all other, $3,080 room and board.

Collegiate Environment: There are 15 buildings on the 60-acre campus. The library houses 90,000 volumes, 600 periodicals, 3348 microforms and 511 recordings. Dormitory facilities provide living accommodations for 335 men and women. Approximately 70% of the students applying for admission are accepted, including midyear students. There is special financial aid available for economically handicapped students. The college has a broad co-curricular activity program.

Community Environment: See Memphis State University.

CLEVELAND STATE COMMUNITY COLLEGE *(J-12)*
P.O. Box 3570
Cleveland, Tennessee 37320
Tel: (615) 472-7141; Admissions: (615) 478-6212; Fax: (615) 478-6255

Description: This publicly-supported college is dedicated to the ideal of providing educational opportunities for all who can profit from such experiences. These experiences will be in transfer, technology, para-professional, and vocational programs. The two-year college is accredited by the Southern Association of Colleges and Schools. It operates on the semester system and offers two summer sessions. Enrollment includes 3,315 students. A faculty of 81 gives a faculty-student ratio of 1-34. The college awards the Certificate and Associate degrees.

Entrance Requirements: Open enrollment policy; high school graduation or GED required; early admission, rolling admission delayed admission and advanced placement plans available; $5 application fee.

Costs Per Year: $966 tuition; $3,752 out-of-state tuition.

Collegiate Environment: The 105-acre campus is located in northwest Cleveland. The library houses about 55,083 titles, 450 pamphlets, 351 periodicals, 24,107 microforms and 5,266 recordings. 99% of the students meeting requirements for admission are accepted, including midyear students. About 62% of the previous freshman class returned to the college for the second year. Special skills courses to assist disadvantaged students are offered. Financial assistance is available; of the 198 scholarships offered, 71 are for freshmen. 48% of students receive some form of financial aid. Average ACT score of the recent freshman class, 16. The college awarded 20 Certificate and 325 Associate degrees to the graduating class.

Community Environment: Cleveland was first settled in 1837 and served as headquarters for both General Grant and General Sherman during the Civil War. The city is in the heart of the great Tennessee Valley and is the gateway to the awe inspiring Cherokee National Forest. The climate is mild-temperate, long warm summers, and short mild winters. All forms of commercial transportation are available. The community facilities include a public library, many churches representing all denominations, YMCA, a hospital, community theatre, concert series, and a number of the usual civic and service organizations. Nearby, TVA lakes offer facilities for swimming, fishing, boating, and skiing; the city facilities provide for other activities such as tennis and golf. Part-time employment is available.

COLUMBIA STATE COMMUNITY COLLEGE *(H-7)*
Hampshire Pike
P.O. Box 1315
Columbia, Tennessee 38402-1315
Tel: (615) 540-2722; Admissions: (615) 540-2545; Fax: (615) 540-2535

Description: This two-year state college was dedicated by Mrs. Lyndon B. Johnson on March 15, 1967, when it first opened. The college, operating on the semester system with one summer session, is accredited by the Southern Association of Colleges and Schools. It awards the Associate degree. A student who is planning to transfer from the college at the conclusion of two years of work to a four-year institution should secure a copy of the catalog of the institution selected for use in planning a transfer program. Enrollment is 1,608 full-time and 1,933 part-time students. A faculty of 147 gives a faculty-student ratio of 1:25.

Entrance Requirements: Open enrollment policy; high school graduation or equivalent for degree programs; ACT is required for entering students; early admission, delayed admission, advanced placement plans available; $5 application fee.

Costs Per Year: $1,006 tuition; $3,752 out-of-state tuition.

Collegiate Environment: The 104-acre campus is located four miles from downtown Columbia. The Learning Resources Center, one of six buildings, houses 57,408 print and nonprint items. Approximately 99% of the students applying for admission are accepted, including midyear students. 60 scholarships are available and 60% of students receive some form of aid. A special program for the culturally diadvantaged enabling low-mark students to attend is offered.

Community Environment: A metropolitan community with temperate climate, Columbia is the boyhood home of James K. Polk. Columbia is in Bluegrass country and is noted for its diversified industry and agriculture. Particularly notable is the phosphate industry, and the Saturn automobile plant. Outstanding recreational facilities include city parks, tennis courts, swimming pools, golf courses and many TVA lakes for swimming, boating, fishing, and skiing. Numerous civic and service organizations and excellent shopping facilities are part of the community. There are good opportunities for part-time employment. The National Tennessee Walking Horse Spring Jubilee is held each May in Maury County Park, three miles west. The Maury County Fair is an annual event.

CRICHTON COLLEGE   *(J-1)*
6655 Winchester Road
Memphis, Tennessee 38115
Tel: (901) 367-3888; (800) 524-5554/6722; Fax: (901) 367-3883

Description: Founded in 1944, the interdenominational college is accredited by the Southern Association of Colleges and Schools. The institution operates on the semester system with two summer sessions and freshman classes commencing in January and August. Enrollment is 450 full-time students. A faculty of 16 full-time and 15 part-time gives a faculty-student ratio of 1-17. The college awards Bachelors degrees.

Entrance Requirements: High school graduation or equivalent; completion of 16 units; ACT score of 18; early admission, early decision, and rolling admission and plans available; $25 application fee.

Costs Per Year: $5,232 tuition; $1,560 room; $50 student fees.

Collegiate Environment: Located on a 7-acre campus, the physical plant comprises 6 buildings. The college library houses 42,000 volumes, 259 periodicals, 600 sound recordings, and 100 videocassettes. There are 30 scholarships available with 20 of them being awarded to freshmen. Approximately 70% of the current freshman class received some form of financial assistance. There are dormitories for 15 men and 15 women. Almost 90% of students applying for admission are accepted. A diverse student body is sought, and midyear students are accepted. About 70% of the previous freshman class returned for the second year.

Community Environment: See Memphis State University.

CUMBERLAND UNIVERSITY   *(G-9)*
S. Greenwood
Lebanon, Tennessee 37087
Tel: (615) 444-2569; (800) 467-0562

Description: The coeducational college is a four-year liberal arts institution accredited by the Southern Association of Colleges and Schools. The University offers an Associate and Bachelor Degree program, as well as a Master's Degree in Education. The semester system is used and three summer sessions and an intersession are offered. Enrollment includes 747 full-time and 223 undergraduates and 43 graduate students. A faculty of 50 full-time and 25 part-time gives a faculty-student ratio of 1-18.

Entrance Requirements: Open enrollment policy; high school graduation with a minimum C average; ACT or SAT required; rolling admission, advanced placement plans available; $25 application fee.

Costs Per Year: $6,000 tuition; $3,200 board and room; $250 fees.

Collegiate Environment: The 45-acre campus in the city of Lebanon, which is 30 miles east of Nashville, is comprised of ten buildings. The library houses 48,000 volumes. There are dormitory facilities for 152 men and 124 women. Approximately 89% of the students applying for admission are accepted, including midyear students. About 50% of the student body graduated in the top half of their high school class, 25% in the upper quarter, and 10% in the top tenth. There is financial assistance available for economically disad-

vantaged students with 89% of students receiving some form of financial aid. Over 65% of the previous freshman class returned to the college for the second year.

Community Environment: Named for the Biblical Lebanon because of the tall cedars found in the area. There are TVA Lakes on three sides of the town, and the Cedars of Lebanon State Park is on the fourth side. Bus transportation is available. Nashville Airport is 25 miles away. Community facilities include three libraries, many churches of major denominations, hospitals and clinic, four major shopping areas and a number of the civic and service organizations. Recreational facilities are excellent for fishing, boating, hunting, swimming, and water skiing.

DAVID LIPSCOMB UNIVERSITY   *(G-8)*
3901 Granny White Pike
Nashville, Tennessee 37204
Tel: (615) 269-1000; (800) 333-4358; Fax: (615) 269-1804

Description: Lipscomb is a private coeducational liberal arts and sciences university that was founded in 1891. It is affiliated with the Church of Christ and is committed to providing a liberal arts education in a Christian environment. It offers the Bachelor of Arts degree in 55 fields and the Bachelor of Science degree in 42 fields, as well as a Master in Education and Religion. The university operates on the semester system and offers two summer sessions. Enrollment is 2,466 full-time and 360 part-time students who represent 42 states and 16 countries. A faculty of 177, 80% of whom hold earned doctorates, provides a faculty-student ratio of 1-17.

Entrance Requirements: Academic achievements, overall creative abilities, and extracurricular activities are considered; completion of 14 or more academic units including 4 English, 2 math, 2 natural science, 2 history, 2 same foreign language, and 2 academic electives; ACT or SAT required; interview strongly recommended; early admission plan available; $25 application fee.

Costs Per Year: $4,690 tuition; $2,680 room and board; $840 student fees.

Collegiate Environment: The 65-acre campus is located in Green Hills, one of the most desirable residential sections of Nashville. The majority of students (1,594) live on campus in 6 Georgian-style residence halls. Facilities include 30 structures nestled among towering elm and maple trees. The library houses 168,000 volumes, over 29,000 bound periodicals, 49,000 microforms, and 4,800 recordings, tapes, phonodiscs, and filmstrips. Approximately 71% of the students applying for admission are accepted including midyear students. Of those, 78% matriculated. The composite scores of the middle 50% of freshmen are: ACT 26, SAT 1060. More than 50% of the freshmen were in the top 10% of their high school class. Approximately 78% of the freshman class returns for the sophomore year. There is special financial aid available for economically handicapped students, and 75% of the current student body receives some form of financial assistance. Of the 1,500 available scholarships, 500 are offered to freshmen. About 40% of the graduates eventually continue on to graduate school.

Community Environment: Lipscomb University is a vital part of Nashville, the capital of Tennessee, and a regional and national center for education, business, and culture. A recent report listed Nashville as one of the top five cities for business opportunity in the country. Nashville was also named one of the most liveable cities in the United States. It is centrally located and easy to reach. Half the population of the United States is within 600 miles of its borders. There are 3 major interstates in addition to Nashville International Airport. Nashville abounds in history and culture. From antebellum mansions like the Hermitage, home of President Andrew Jackson, to Cheekwood Botanical Gardens, the Parthenon, and the Tennessee State Museum, Nashville offers abundant resources to strengthen and complement student education.

DYERSBURG STATE COMMUNITY COLLEGE   *(G-2)*
Lake Road
Dyersburg, Tennessee 38024
Tel: (901) 286-3200; Admissions: (901) 286-3330; Fax: (901) 286-3333

Description: This publicly supported, coeducational junior college was established in 1967. The college is accredited by the Southern

Association of Colleges and Schools. Day and evening classes are available and programs of study lead to the Associate degree. It operates on the semester system and offers two summer sessions. Enrollment includes 1,061 full-time and 1,094 part-time students. A faculty of 51 full-time and 104 part-time gives a faculty-student ratio of 1-19.

Entrance Requirements: Open enrollment policy; high school graduation or equivalent; ACT or SAT required; students not meeting all requirements may be admitted as special students; early admission, midyear admission, rolling admission, and advanced placement plans available; $5 application fee.

Costs Per Year: $1,012 state resident tuition; $3,800 nonresident tuition.

Collegiate Environment: The college is located on a naturally landscaped 100-acre campus in the northwest portion of the city known as Okeena Park. The college occupies 6 buildings. The library contains 36,000 volumes, 1,226 pamphlets, 236 periodicals, 102 microforms and 994 recordings. All of the applicants are accepted, including midyear students. The average high school standing of the recent freshman class was in the top 50%; 40% were in the top quarter, 40% were in the second quarter, and 30% ranked in the third quarter; average ACT score was 15. Financial assistance is available and of the 105 scholarships offered, 46 are available for freshmen.

EAST TENNESSEE STATE UNIVERSITY   *(F-18)*
Johnson City, Tennessee 37614
Tel: (615) 929-4213; (800) 462-3878; Fax: (615) 461-7156

Description: East Tennessee State University was founded in 1911 and is fully accredited by the Southern Association of Colleges and Schools. The instructional program is organized into the colleges of Arts and Sciences, Business, Education, Medicine, Applied Science and Technology, Nursing, Public and Allied Health, and the school of Graduate Studies. Enrollment includes 11,500 students. A faculty of 563 full-time gives a faculty-student ratio of 1-28. The university operates on the semester system and offers three summer sessions. The University grants the Certificate, Associate, Bachelor, Master, Specialist, and Doctorate degrees. An Army ROTC program is offered. The Quillen-Dishner College of Medicine was established in 1974.

Entrance Requirements: Students seeking admission as first-time freshmen must present a minimum composite ACT score of 19, a comparable SAT combined score or a minimum high school GPA of 2.3 (on 4.0 scale); high school courses must include 4 English, 3 mathematics, 1 social studies, 1 history, 2 natural science, 2 same foreign language, 1 visual or performing arts; Tennesseans who graduate from public high schools must successfully complete the Tennessee Proficiency Examination; assessment evaluation examinations to determine levels of proficiency are required for entering freshmen who present ACT composites lower than 19. $5 application fee.

Costs Per Year: $1,720 tuition; $5,554 nonresidents; $2,600 room and board; additional expenses average $600.

Collegiate Environment: The campus consists of a 366-acre main campus in Johnson City situated in an attractive mountain and lake area in the foothills of the Appalachian Mountains. Facilities for recreational and physical education activities include a baseball field; indoor and outdoor track and tennis courts; handball courts; riflery range; and one of only two indoor college football stadiums in the eastern United States. The library houses 523,956 volumes, 255,843 government documents, 1,238,610 microforms and 3,272 subscriptions. Dormitory facilities provide accommodations for 950 men, 1,369 women, and 116 families. Approximately 83% of students applying for admission are accepted. The average freshman ACT score is 21.3 composite. 52% of students receive financial aid. Approximately 740 scholarships are available. 29% of the graduates continuing on to graduate school.

Community Environment: Johnson City, Kingsport and Bristol compose the Tri-Cities area, which is Tennessee's fifth largest metropolitan area, having one million people living within a 50-mile radius. Johnson City, a progressive city with a population of approximately 50,000, is located close to the state lines of Virginia, Kentucky, West Virginia, North Carolina and South Carolina. Recreational opportunities abound and include boating and water skiing on major TVA lakes, a variety of snow skiing resorts featuring downhill and cross-country, mountain hiking trails including easy access to the Appalachian Trail, and white water rafting. Interstate highways I-40, I-81 and I-26 provide access by automobile, with Tri-Cities Regional Airport providing access by commercial airlines. All major religious denominations are represented.

EMMANUEL SCHOOL OF RELIGION   *(F-17)*
One Walker Drive
Johnson City, Tennessee 37601
Tel: (615) 926-1186; (800) 933-3771; Admissions: (615) 461-1536;
Fax: (615) 461-1556

Description: Affiliated with the Christian Churches and the Churches of Christ, this Seminary was founded in 1961. It is accredited by the Southern Association of Colleges and Schools and the Association of Theological Schools of the United States and Canada. It offers the Master of Divinity and Master of Arts in Religion degrees and Doctor of Ministry degree. Enrollment includes 109 men, 10 women full-time and 46 men, 10 women part-time with a faculty of 11 full-time and 4 part-time members. It operates on a 4-1-4 system with four summer sessions.

Entrance Requirements: Entrance examination; rolling admission; midyear admissions; application deadline is one month prior to beginning of semester; $25 admission fee.

Costs Per Year: $3,000 tuition; $180 student fees.

Collegiate Environment: The library holdings include 88,659 volumes, 733 periodicals, 12,000 microforms and 810 audiovisual materials. Dormitory facilities are not available. 95% of those applying for admission are accepted. Scholarships are available and 60% of students receive some form of aid.

Community Environment: See East Tennessee State University

FISK UNIVERSITY   *(G-8)*
17th Ave. N
Nashville, Tennessee 37203
Tel: (615) 329-8500

Description: The university was founded in 1866 and makes available its educational resources, as originally conceived, to students of all races, colors, and creeds. Fisk is accredited by the Southern Association of Colleges and Schools. It operates on the semester system. Enrollment includes 912 students. A faculty of 75 gives a faculty-student ratio of 1-12. The academic structure at Fisk is organized four three divisions: Natural Sciences and Mathematics; Social Sciences; Humanities and Fine Arts; and Business Administration. The curriculum is divided into three course groupings: the core curriculum, the student's curriculum concentration and electives. The core curriculum includes six interdisciplinary courses and a one-semester freshman orientation course. The curriculum concentration provides specialized instruction and research that lead to the Bachelor and Masters degrees.

Entrance Requirements: High school graduation with rank in the upper half of the graduating class; completion of minimum 15 units; including 4 English, 2 mathematics, 1 social science, 1 science, 2 foreign language, and 6 electives; SAT or ACT strongly recommended; early admission, early decision, rolling admission, midyear admission and advanced placement programs available; $25 application fee.

Costs Per Year: $5,445 tuition; $3,355 room and board; $50 student fees.

Collegiate Environment: The library was built to serve the reading needs of 1,800 students; there are 184,835 volumes in the stacks. Dormitory facilities house 450 men and 680 women. Approximately 65% of those applying for admission are accepted including midyear students. There are five types of financial aid for which a student may apply: University tuition scholarships, Supplemental Educational Opportunity Grants, federal Stafford Loans, federal work study and federal Pell Grant. In addition, the university offers a limited number of University Honor Scholarships based upon exceptional academic potential.

Community Environment: See Vanderbilt University.

FREE WILL BAPTIST BIBLE COLLEGE   *(G-8)*
3606 West End Ave.
Nashville, Tennessee 37205
Tel: (615) 383-1340; Fax: (615) 269-6028

Description: The college, founded in 1942, is a church-related school affiliated with the National Association of Free Will Baptists. The Bible College has the specific goal of training for more effective service for Christ, and this service is taken to include both the ministry and laity. Enrollment includes 166 men and 144 women full-time and 25 men and 19 women part-time. A faculty of 17 full-time and 11 part-time gives a faculty-student ratio of 1-11. The semester system is used and two summer sessions are offered. The college grants the Associate and the Bachelor degree and is accredited by the American Association of Bible Colleges. Air Force ROTC is available through Tennessee State University and Army ROTC is available through Vanderbilt University.

Entrance Requirements: High school graduation or equivalent; open enrollment policy; under certain circumstances non-high school graduates are considered for admission; ACT required; any student applying for admission to the college will be expected to certify that he/she is a Christian and sincerely interested in Christian education; 3 letters of reference; early decision, early admission, rolling admission, advanced placement plans and delayed admission available; $25 application fee.

Costs Per Year: $4,224 tuition; $3,068 room and board; $444 student fees.

Collegiate Environment: The college now includes twelve major buildings, five of which are of new and modern construction. The Welch Library has ample room for study areas and houses 58,463 volumes. Dormitory facilities provide living accommodations for 175 men and 200 women. Approximately 95% of students applying for admission are accepted including midyear students. Recent average ACT score was 18.8. About 8% of the senior class continued on to graduate school.

Community Environment: See Vanderbilt University.

FREED-HARDEMAN UNIVERSITY   *(I-4)*
Henderson, Tennessee 38340
Tel: (901) 989-6651; (800) 342-7837; Fax: (901) 989-6065

Description: This private, endowed, non-profit, senior, liberal arts university is accredited by the Southern Association of Colleges and Schools. It is not owned or operated by a church but is under the control of a self-perpetuating board that is a member of the Churches of Christ. The faculty and the majority of the students are members of the Churches of Christ. The college enrolls students of any religious faith or those who have no affiliation with any religion. The university grants Bachelor of Arts, Science, Social Work, and Business Administration. Cooperative education programs are available in several departments on an individual basis and a summer semester in Florence, Italy. It operates on the early semester system and offers two summer sessions. Enrollment includes 1,144 full-time and 60 part-time undergraduate, and 263 graduate students. A faculty of 87 full-time and 13 part-time gives a faculty-student ratio of 1-18.

Entrance Requirements: High school graduation or equivalent; completion of 20 units including 4 English, 2 mathematics, 2 laboratory science, 2 social studies, and 10 electives; under certain circumstances non-high school graduates with GED are considered for admission; minimum ACT 19 required; advanced placement, early admission, midyear admission, rolling admission, and delayed admission plans available.

Costs Per Year: $5,500 tuition; $3,240 room and board; $770 student fees; $800 average additional expenses.

Collegiate Environment: The campus is comprised of about 95 acres that provide space for a parking area and tennis courts. There are 25 main buildings including a library housing 133,000 volumes, 729 periodicals, 4,847 microforms and 28,945 audiovisual materials. Dormitory facilities provide living accommodations for 541 men and 692 women. Students are expected to attend church services regularly on Sunday and are also required to attend daily chapel. Approximately 66% of the students applying for admission are accepted including midyear students. There are 1,378 scholarships, 385 for freshmen, available. 85% of the current student body receives some form of financial assistance.

Community Environment: Henderson is a rural town with bus transportation and an airport within 25 miles. A metropolitan area (population 51,000) is located 15 miles away via a 4-lane highway. The community facilities include churches, good shopping facilities, and

some major civic and service organizations. The Tennessee River, Kentucky Lake, Chickasaw State Park, and Pickwick Dam provide a number of facilities for all kinds of water sports and other recreation. Some part-time employment is available.

HARDING UNIVERSITY GRADUATE SCHOOL OF RELIGION   *(J-1)*
1000 Cherry Road
Memphis, Tennessee 38117
Tel: (901) 761-1356; (800) 680-0809; Fax: (901) 761-1358

Description: This graduate school is an outgrowth of a desire to provide graduate education and training by enlarging the service of the Harding University in Searcy, Arkansas. The graduate school, affiliated with Churches of Christ, operates on a trisemester system and offers four summer sessions and one week short courses every semester. Enrollment includes 45 full-time and 137 part-time students. A faculty of 18 provides a faculty-student ratio of 1-10. The school is accredited by the Southern Association of Colleges and Schools and is a candidate for the Association of Theological Schools. It grants Masters of Arts, Masters of Arts in Religion, Master of Divinity, and Doctor of Ministry degrees.

Entrance Requirements: Bachelor degree from accredited institution; GRE required if entering from non-accredited school; a student must be of good character and standing in his community; he or she should furnish the names and addresses of four references to the Director of Admissions. A student transferring from another school must furnish a letter of honorable dismissal from that school; midyear admission, rolling admission plan available. Application fees: $30 Masters, $40 D.Min., $70 M.A. Counseling.

Costs Per Year: $4,968 (based on 12 hours per semester) tuition; $1,272 room; $6 student fees; additional expenses average $4,200.

Collegiate Environment: The school occupies a wooded and beautiful 35-acre campus. There are five buildings on the campus including a library which contains 100,000 volumes and 605 periodicals. Living accommodations for 34 students are available. Approximately 90% of the students applying for admission is accepted, including midyear students and 80% of the first year students returned for the second year. Financial aid is available for economically disadvantaged students. 80% of the current enrollment receives some form of financial assistance.

Community Environment: See Memphis State University.

HIWASSEE COLLEGE   *(I-13)*
Madisonville, Tennessee 37354
Tel: (615) 442-3283; (800) 356-2187; Fax: (615) 442-3520

Description: The two-year college, founded in 1849, is affiliated with the Methodist Church. Students may complete one of several courses of study that are designed to provide a complete unit of education in two years. Students are required to attend chapel once a week. The college operates on a semester system and offers two summer sessions. The college is accredited by the Southern Association of Colleges and Schools and grants the Certificate and the Associate degree. The enrollment is 426 students. The faculty-student ratio is 1-15.

Entrance Requirements: High school graduation, minimum C average with rank in the upper two-thirds of the graduating class; ACT required with score of 17 or above preferred or SAT.

Costs Per Year: $4,930 tuition; $3,300 room and board.

Collegiate Environment: The 50-acre campus, located two miles north of Madisonville, has a total of 19 buildings; the library was built in 1955 and contains 57,080 volumes. Dormitory facilities provide living accommodations for both men and women. There is special financial aid available for economically disadvantaged students. About 98% of applicants are accepted for admission. 80% of the students receive financial aid. Since the earliest recorded history of the college, it has maintained close ties with the church.

Community Environment: Madisonville is a rural area with community facilities that include a public library, two hospital, churches, and a number of the major civic and service organizations. Part time employment is available. Five TVA Lakes and 111 miles of trout streams are within 20 miles for all water sports. The Cherokee National Forest provides facilities for swimming, picnicking, and camping.

JACKSON STATE COMMUNITY COLLEGE *(H-3)*
2046 North Parkway
Jackson, Tennessee 38301-3797
Tel: (901) 424-3520; (800) 355-5722; Admissions: (901) 425-2644;
Fax: (901) 425-2647

Description: The two-year state college opened in 1967 and is accredited by the Tennessee Board of Education. The college is fully accredited by the Southern Association of Colleges and Schools; and is a member of the American Association of Community and Junior Colleges and the Southern Association of Junior Colleges. The college offers two general areas of study to meet the diversified needs of its students. The academic programs were designed to meet the needs of students planning on continuing toward a degree in a four-year institution. Career programs were designed basically as terminal programs. The continuing education programs were designed for those who wish to take a course for personal improvement, for vocational advancement or for personal enhancement. The college operates on the semester system and offers two summer sessions. Enrollment includes 582 men and 979 women full-time; 649 men, and 1,187 women part-time. A faculty of 80 full-time and 92 part-time gives a faculty-student ratio of 1-28.

Entrance Requirements: Open enrollment policy with stipulations; high school graduation or equivalent; completion of 14 units for degree programs. Degree-seeking students under age 21 are required to submit ACT test results. If the ACT composit score is less than 19, a placement test is required of the applicant. Degree-seeking students over age 21 with no previous collegiate work must take a placement test. $5 application fee. Early admission, early decision, rolling admission, delayed admission and advanced placement plans available.

Costs Per Year: $966 resident tuition; $3,752 nonresident tuition.

Collegiate Environment: The college is located three miles from the downtown court square, and there are seven buildings on the 104-acre campus. The library contains 60,000 volumes and numerous periodicals, microforms and audiovisual materials. 97% of those who apply for admission is accepted, and students are admitted at midyear as well as in the fall. Financial assistance is available.

Community Environment: Jackson, at one time a small cotton port, is now a trading and shipping center. All forms of commercial transportation are available. Because of direct access to major thoroughfares, Jackson is one of the fastest growing cities in Tennessee. Jackson is the trade center for a large populated area. Its facilities include hospitals, clinics, many churches, art association, and symphony orchestra. The city is known as the home and burial place of John Luther "Casey" Jones, who became a part of American folklore and the legend of early railroading. The Casey Jones Railroad Museum may be seen here.

JOHN A. GUPTON COLLEGE *(G-8)*
1616 Church Street
Nashville, Tennessee 37203
Tel: (615) 327-3927

Description: The college is a nonprofit institution dedicated to the education of men and women in the field of Mortuary Science. The school is accredited by the Southern Association of Colleges and Schools and grants the Associate degree in Mortuary Science. The college encourages its students to continue their education and work toward a Bachelor degree; the curriculum is specifically oriented to give the student the basic general education courses required in most colleges and universities. It operates on the quarter system with one summer session. Enrollment includes 40 full-time and 20 part-time students with a faculty of 12.

Entrance Requirements: High school graduation or equivalent; 16 units including 4 English, 1 mathematics, 1 science, and 1 social studies; $10 application fee.

Costs Per Year: $4,800 tuition including fees.

Collegiate Environment: The college is located directly across from Centennial Park in the University Center of Nashville. The Memorial Library contains over 4,850 volumes; students have access to the library during each school day and in the evening.

Community Environment: See Vanderbilt University

JOHNSON BIBLE COLLEGE *(G-14)*
7900 Johnson Drive
Knoxville, Tennessee 37998
Tel: (615) 573-4517; Fax: (615) 579-2336

Description: The Bible college, affiliated with the Christian Church, was founded in 1893. The purpose of the college is to educate students in specialized Christian ministries, with primary emphasis on the preaching ministry, through a program of Biblical, general and special studies. It is accredited by the American Association of Bible Colleges and the Southern Association of Colleges and Schools. The college operates on a semester system and offers one summer session. All degree programs have a Bible major. Chapel services are conducted in the chapel four days a week. Faculty members and students are expected to attend. It grants the Bachelor and Master degrees. Enrollment includes 368 full-time and 35 part-time undergraduates and 50 graduate students. A faculty of 19 full-time and 8 part-time gives a faculty-student ratio of 1-19.

Entrance Requirements: Liberal enrollment policy; completion of 16 units including 4 English; ACT required; early decision, delayed admission, midyear admission, rolling admission, advanced placement plans available; $35 application fee.

Costs Per Year: $4,000 tuition; $3,125 room and board; $475 student fees; additional expenses average $1,500.

Collegiate Environment: The campus consists of about 150 acres overlooking the French Broad River. The library, one of 26 buildings, contains 76,691 volumes, 300 periodicals, 12,500 microforms and 6,582 recordings. Dormitory facilities provide living accommodations for 204 men, 195 women, and 115 married couples or familes. Approximately 98% of the students applying for admission are accepted including midyear students and 67% of the previous freshmen returned for the second year. Financial aid is available for economically disadvantaged students with about 98% of the current student body receiving some form of financial assistance. About 5% of the senior class continued on to graduate school.

Community Environment: The college is located in the rural community of Kimberlin Heights within a 20-minute drive of Knoxville where shopping, jobs, recreation, hospitals, churches, and civic cultural, and service organizations are abundant.

KING COLLEGE *(E-18)*
1350 King College Rd.
Bristol, Tennessee 37620
Tel: (615) 968-1187; (800) 362-0014; Fax: (615) 652-4727

Description: The privately supported liberal arts college was founded in 1867 and is affiliated with the Presbyterian Church. Enrollment includes 241 men and 255 women full-time and 57 part-time students. A faculty of 42 full-time and 25 part-time gives a faculty-student ratio of 1-14. The 4-4-1 system is used and two summer sessions are offered. Academic cooperative plans with the University of Tennessee, Georgia Tech, Vanderbilt, and the University of Maryland are available for engineering students. Army ROTC is available through East Tennessee State University. Study abroad programs include Holy Land studies and Latin American studies. The college is accredited by the Southern Association of Colleges and Schools, is a member of the Christian College Coalition, and grants the Bachelor degree.

Entrance Requirements: High school graduation with rank in upper 50% of graduating class; completion of 16 units including 4 English, 3 mathematics, 2 science, 2 foreign language, and 1 social studies; minimum SAT 900 combined or ACT 22 composite required; under certain circumstances non-high school graduates are considered for admission; early admission, rolling admission, delayed admission, midyear admission and advanced placement plans available; no application fee.

Costs Per Year: $8,914 tuition; $3,250 room and board; $710 student fees.

Collegiate Environment: The college is in the foothills of the Appalachian Mountains at an altitude of about 1,800 feet. The 135-acre campus is comprised of 15 buildings; the library houses more than 97,805 volumes. 7 million titles are available through a bibliographic service. Dormitory facilities provide housing for 400 students. Approximately 86% of those students applying for admission were accepted including midyear students. There is special financial aid available for economically disadvantaged students, and 98% receive some form of financial aid.

Community Environment: The main street of Bristol is bisected by the Virginia-Tennessee State line. Industrial products include food products, textiles, electronics, pharmaceuticals, business machines, and metal products. Bristol is where Daniel Boone and many other distinguished pioneers bartered and also planned the campaign that resulted in defeat for the British at the Battle of Kings Mountain. Bus and train transportation is available, and air service is 14 miles away. Recreational activities include tennis, golf, boating, fishing, and water skiing.

KNOXVILLE COLLEGE   *(G-15)*
901 College Street
Knoxville, Tennessee 37921
Tel: (615) 524-6500; (800) 743-5669; Fax: (615) 524-6686

Description: In each of its students, the college seeks to develop the highest possible capacity for life. It also recognizes a special responsibility to well-prepared students and provides for particular aptitudes and interests and the development of intellectual alertness and initiative. The school operates on the semester system and offers two summer sessions. Enrollment is 914 students. A faculty of 63 full-time and 25 part-time gives a faculty-student ratio of 1-16. Affiliated with the United Presbyterian Church, the school is accredited by the Southern Association of Colleges and Schools. The curriculum of the college is organized within five instructional divisions: humanities, natural sciences and mathematics, social sciences, education, and music. Preprofessional curricula are available, including engineering.

Entrance Requirements: High school graduation or equivalent with rank in the top half of the graduating class; completion of 15 units including 3 English, 2 mathematics, 1 natural science, 1 social studies, and 8 electives selected from the following subjects: English, commercial subjects, foreign language, history, social studies, home economics, manual training, mathematics, music, and natural science; SAT required; advanced placement program available; $15 application fee.

Costs Per Year: $5,100 tuition; $3,600 room and board.

Collegiate Environment: The college of liberal arts and sciences, dedicated to Christian ideals, was founded in 1875. On the 39-acre campus are 21 buildings. The library houses 42,000 volumes. Dormitory facilities provide living accommodations for 700 men and 800 women. Approximately 90% of those students applying for admission are accepted including midyear students. There is a special program for the culturally disadvantaged enabling low-mark students to attend. Semesters begin in August and January. Financial assistance is available.

Community Environment: Knoxville is the business center of the East Tennessee Valley, a burley tobacco market, and a livestock center. A number of diversified manufacturing plants are situated here also. Tennessee marble is quarried in this vicinity with some of the quarries within the city limits. One of the largest plants in the world to produce finished marble is located here. Knoxville is the headquarters for the Tennessee Valley Authority. Part-time employment is available. Facilities for recreation are excellent; the Tennessee River and the TVA Lakes offer boating, swimming, fishing, and other water sports. The Great Smoky Mountains National Park provides additional facilities for hunting, camping, and riding. Several very scenic drives may be taken here; one is the famous 100-mile scenic Loop Trip, and the other is through the Great Smoky Mountains National Park on the Newfound Gap Highway. Many historic points of interest may be seen here; some of them are the Confederate Monument, Governor Blount Home, Ramsey House, and the Memorial to the 79th New York Regiment, which took part in the siege of Fort Sanders.

Branch Campuses: Morristown Campus, 517 James St., Morristown, TN 37813, (615) 637-2142.

LAMBUTH UNIVERSITY   *(H-3)*
705 Lambuth Boulevard
Jackson, Tennessee 38301
Tel: (901) 425-2500; (800) 526-2884

Description: Founded in 1843, the university is affiliated with the United Methodist Church. The four-year liberal arts school is accredited by the Southern Association of Colleges and Schools and grants the Bachelor of Arts, Bachelor of Business Administration, Bachelor of Music, and Bachelor of Science degrees. Enrollment includes 436 men, 404 women full-time and 131 men, 182 women part-time with a faculty of 75 full-time and 25 part-time members. It operates on the semester system with two summer terms as well as a May term.

Entrance Requirements: High school graduation with as many academic units as possible; ACT or SAT required; non high school graduates considered; early admission, rolling admission, delayed admission, advanced placement plans available; $10 application fee.

Costs Per Year: $4,634 tuition; $3,160 room and board; $150 student fees.

Collegiate Environment: There are 13 buildings on the 50-acre campus. Luther L. Gobbel Library is a completely modern, air-conditioned facility housing 130,000 volumes. Dormitory facilities provide living accommodations for 550 students. Approximately 61% of students applying for admission are accepted including midyear students. High school standing of the recent freshman class, 36% in the top quarter, 32% in the second quarter, 24% in the third quarter, 8% in the fourth quarter, 2% in the bottom quarter; 10% not ranked; average scores, ACT 20.3 There is special financial aid available for economically handicapped students. 63% of the previous freshman class returned to the college for the second year. Of the 758 available scholarships, 233 are available for freshmen and 75% of the current students receive financial aid. Approximately 29% of the senior class continued on to graduate school.

Community Environment: See Jackson State Community College.

LANE COLLEGE   *(H-3)*
545 Lane Avenue
Jackson, Tennessee 38301
Tel: (901) 426-7500; (800) 960-7533; Admissions: (901) 426-7532; Fax: (901) 426-7553

Description: Founded in 1882 by the Colored Methodist Episcopal Church in America, this liberal arts college is accredited by the Southern Association of Colleges and Schools, and affiliated with the Christian Methodist Episcopal Church. It operates on the semester system and offers one five-week summer session. Enrollment includes 656 full-time and 11 part-time students. A faculty of 37 full-time and 5 part-time provides a faculty-student ratio of 1-16. The college offers the Bachelor degree. Chapel attendance is encouraged of all students in accordance with plans outlined by the Dean of Chapel.

Entrance Requirements: High school graduate with 16 units or equivalent completion of 16 units including 4 English, 2 mathematics, 2 science, and 2 social science; ACT or SAT required; $10 application fee.

Costs Per Year: $4,566 tuition; $2,862 room and board; $350 student fees.

Collegiate Environment: The campus occupies 17 acres. The library building houses 85,000 volumes, and the dormitories provide living accommodations for 250 men and 400 women. There is special financial aid available for economically disadvantaged students, and 98% of students receive some form of financial assistance.

Community Environment: See Jackson State Community College.

LEE COLLEGE   *(J-12)*
North Ocoee
Cleveland, Tennessee 37311
Tel: (615) 472-2111; (800) 533-9930; Fax: (615) 478-7499

Description: The first class of twelve students opened in 1918 as part of a Bible Training School affiliated with the Church of God. In 1925, plans were initiated to expand the then junior college to a four-year college of liberal arts. The college is accredited by the Southern Association of Colleges and Schools and the respective educational agencies. The college operates on the semester system and offers 2 summer sessions. Enrollment includes 2,098 full-time and 149 part-time students. A faculty of 94 full-time and 93 part-time gives a faculty-student ratio of 1-21.

Entrance Requirements: High school graduation with C average; ACT with minimum score of 17 or SAT with minimum combined score of 745 required; advanced placement, early decision, early admission, midyear admission and rolling admission programs available; application fee $25.

Costs Per Year: $4,992 tuition; $3,420 room and board; $140 fees.

Collegiate Environment: Located on 50 acres, the campus houses 33 buildings. Religious chapel services are conducted on Tuesday, Thursday and Sunday night of each week. All students are required to attend. There is dormitory space for 500 men and 620 women. 108 scholarships are available including 42 for freshmen. 90% of the current student body receives some form of financial aid. There are 108 scholarships granted, with 42 offered to entering freshmen. The college library contains 130,000 volumes, 12,690 periodicals, 1,624 microforms and 6,410 sound recordings. Almost 83% of students applying for admission are accepted, and nearly 87% of a current freshman class returned to campus for the second year. Average high school standing of the recent freshman class, top 70%; 20% in the top quarter, 50% in the second quarter, 30% in the third quarter; average ACT score, 21. About 40% of the senior class continued on to graduate school.

Community Environment: See Cleveland State Community College.

LEMOYNE-OWEN COLLEGE   *(J-1)*
807 Walker Avenue
Memphis, Tennessee 38126
Tel: (901) 774-9090

Description: The merger of Owen and LeMoyne Colleges was voted by the trustees of the two institutions in meetings on May 24-25, 1968. LeMoyne is an accredited four-year college founded in 1862, and Owens is an accredited junior college founded in 1954 by the Tennessee Baptist Missionary and Education Convention. The privately controlled merged institution is affiliated with the United Church of Christ and the Tennessee Baptist Missionary and Education Convention and is fully accredited by the Southern Association of Colleges and Schools. Presently, the college is organized on the cooperative education plan to offer programs in the Division of Business Administration, Humanities, Natural Science, Social Science and Health, Physical Education, and Recreation, leading to a Bachelor degree. A Master of Science in Education is offered. Air Force and Army ROTC programs are available. Enrollment includes 1,200 full-time, 103 part-time, and 150 graduate students. A faculty of 75 full-time and 25 part-time provides a faculty-student ratio of 1:16.

Entrance Requirements: Open enrollment policy; high school graduation or equivalent; ACT required; early decision, rolling admission, delayed admission plans available; $25 application fee.

Costs Per Year: $4,200 tuition.

Collegiate Environment: LeMoyne-Owen College occupies a beautifully landscaped 15-acre campus at 807 Walker Avenue in South Memphis. Dormitories for men and women are available. The college library contains 90,231 volumes, 275 periodicals, 1,276 microforms and 1,916 recordings. Financial aid is available and 85% of the students receive some form of aid.

Community Environment: See Memphis State University.

LINCOLN MEMORIAL UNIVERSITY   *(E-15)*
Cumberland Gap Parkway
Harrogate, Tennessee 37752-0901
Tel: (615) 869-3611; (800) 325-2506; Admissions: (615) 869-6280

Description: Chartered by the State of Tennessee in 1897, the university is privately controlled. It is accredited by the Southern Association of Colleges and Schools and is a member of the respective education agencies. The independent, four-year College of Arts and Sciences offers specific courses in teacher preparation leading to certification for either elementary or high school teaching in the states of Tennessee, Virginia, and Kentucky. The university operates on the semester system and offers two summer terms. Enrollment includes 563 men and 1,351 women with a faculty of 73 full-time and 33 part-time members. The faculty-student ratio is 1-14.

Entrance Requirements: Liberal enrollment policy; high school graduation; ACT with minimum score of 16, or SAT required; completion of 16 units including 4 English, 3 mathematics, 2 laboratory science, 2 social studies, 1 U.S. history; advanced placement, early admission, early decision, rolling admission, midyear admission plans available. $25 application fee.

Costs Per Year: $6,070 tuition; $2,890 room and board; $120 student fees.

Collegiate Environment: The location is considered one of the most beautiful in America. There are over 1,000 acres of land comprising the campus. Farming is done on 900 acres, with 100 acres encompassing the campus proper. There are five residence halls for students, with dormitory capacity for 223 men and 270 women. The Carnegie Library houses approximately 140,000 volumes and receives nearly 700 periodicals regularly. Special collections in the library include books and historical material on the university, and books written by alumni. There is also a department of Lincolniana which contains almost 16,000 books, pamphlets, magazines, pictures, relics, and oil paintings of Abraham Lincoln. Financial aid is available and about 60% of the current student body received some form of financial assistance. Scholarships are available. Nearly 80% of students applying for admission are accepted, including midyear students. There is a special program for the culturally disadvantaged low-mark students on campus, and geographically diverse students are sought.

Community Environment: Harrogate is six miles from Middlesboro, Kentucky in Cumberland Gap, Tennessee, a rural community having an average rainfall of 51 inches annually. Recreational activities are hunting, fishing, boating, camping, golf, and hiking.

MARTIN METHODIST COLLEGE   *(J-7)*
433 W. Madison Street
Pulaski, Tennessee 38478
Tel: (615) 363-9804; (800) 467-1273; Fax: (615) 363-9818

Description: The privately supported, four-year college is affiliated with The United Methodist Church. The college opened in 1870 and is noted for its reputation of academic excellence and the exceptionally high success rates of its alumni at the senior colleges. The institution is fully accredited by the Southern Association of Colleges and Schools and respective professional organizations. The major academic divisions include: business, health and physical education, humanities, mathematics and natural sciences, and social science. The college grants the Associate and Bachelor degrees. It operates on the semester system and offers two summer sessions. Enrollment includes 468 students. A faculty of 24 gives a faculty-student ratio of 1-20.

Entrance Requirements: High school graduation; completion of 12 units including 4 English, 1 mathematics, 1 science, 1 social science; non-high school graduates considered; ACT or SAT required; early decision; early admission, rolling admission, midyear admission, and advanced placement plans available; $10 application fee.

Costs Per Year: $5,400 tuition; $2,900 room and board; $50 graduation fee; $1,000 average additional expenses.

Collegiate Environment: Located on 11 acres within the city limits of Pulaski, the campus houses 11 buildings. Martin Hall, erected in 1957, and the Johnston Center, erected in 1975, are the centers of administrative and educational activities for the school. The library contains 26,000 volumes, 400 pamphlets, 160 periodicals, 745 microforms and 190 sound recordings. Residence halls are available for 178 men and 98 women. Nearly 90% of students applying for admission are accepted including midyear students. Almost 60% of the current student body receives some form of financial assistance. Of the previous freshman class, 69% returned to campus for the second year.

Community Environment: Pulaski is located in south-central Tennessee where the climate is mild. The college is between Nashville, Tennessee, and Huntsville, Alabama. Pulaski is a small friendly town with much civic pride in the college.

MARYVILLE COLLEGE   *(H-14)*
Maryville, Tennessee 37801
Tel: (615) 982-6412; (800) 597-2687; Admissions: (615) 981-8092; Fax: (615) 981-8010

Description: The four-year liberal arts college is affiliated with the Presbyterian Church U.S.A. The institution was founded in 1819 and claims the honor of being one of the 50 oldest colleges in the United States. It is accredited by the Southern Association of Colleges and Schools and by the National Association of Schools of Music. The college grants Bachelors degrees. The school calendar divides the school year into two semesters with a 3-week January term. Two summer sessions are also offered. Study abroad programs are offered in Japan, Mexico, Korea, Wales, and Puerto Rico. Enrollment includes 709 full-time and 141 part-time students. A faculty of 50 full-time and 19 part-time gives a faculty-student ratio of 1-14.

Entrance Requirements: High school graduation with rank in top 25% of graduating class; minimum 3.0 or B average; completion of 15 units including 4 English, 2 laboratory science, 3 mathematics, 2 foreign language and 2 social studies; SAT with minimum score of 500V, 500M, or ACT with minimum score of 18 required; rolling admission; $25 application fee.

Costs Per Year: $9,430 tuition; $3,865 room and board; $150 student fees.

Collegiate Environment: About one-third of the 350-acre campus constitutes the central area on which the 24 buildings and the athletic fields are located. The remainder consists of woods containing picnic areas, a naturally formed amphitheater, and a ropes course. Residence halls provide housing for 388 men and 360 women. Financial aid is available. Lamar Memorial Library houses 105,000 volumes, and is fully automated with on-line access to library holdings across the country. 65% of students applying for admission are accepted. A geographically diverse student body is sought, and midyear students are welcome.

Community Environment: Maryville was founded in 1819 and named for Mary Blount, wife of Governor William Blount. The town is located near the entrance of the Great Smoky Mountains National Park. Bus and air transportation is available. Fishing, boating, water skiing, golfing, and hiking are favorite sports in the county. Maryville is a suburban community located 15 miles from Knoxville in a metropolitan area of half a million.

MEHARRY MEDICAL COLLEGE   *(G-8)*
1005 Dr David Todd Boulevard
Nashville, Tennessee 37208
Tel: (615) 327-6904

Description: The college was established in 1876 as the medical department of Central Tennessee College. In 1900, the college became Walden University and the medical department became known as Meharry Medical College of Walden University. In 1915, a new charter was granted by the State of Tennessee and the college began its separate corporate existence. The first graduating class consisted of one student. Enrollment was 594 students recently. The private college is fully accredited by the regional and professional agencies and the Southern Association of Colleges and Schools. The institution consists of the School of Medicine, School of Dentistry, School of Allied Health Professions, Dental Hygiene Division and the School of Graduate Studies and Research. The semester system is employed with one summer session.

Entrance Requirements: School of Medicine requires graduation from accredited high school; at least three full years of accredited college credit; three years premedical education by June of the year applicant desires to be admitted, with 8 semester hours of general biology or zoology with laboratory, 8 hours general physics with laboratory, 6 hours English composition; MCAT required. The School of Dentistry requires the DAT and two years of previous college; School of Medical Technology requires three years previous college credit; Dental Hygiene Division requires DHAT and a high school diploma; Graduate Studies Division is divided into Behavioral Science requiring GRE and four years college credit; and the Master of Medical Science requiring the MCAT, GRE, and four years previous college credits. Application fee $25; character recommendation from minister or physician who has known applicant for five years; recommendations from 2 science teachers required.

Costs Per Year: $15,330 tuition Dentistry, Medicine; $6,000 Graduate Studies; $4,000 MSPH Program.

Collegiate Environment: Located on 17 acres, the college consists of seven buildings. Only 6% of students applying for admission are accepted. The college prefers a regional student body. Scholarship and loan funds are available on campus for students.

Community Environment: See Vanderbilt University

MEMPHIS COLLEGE OF ART   *(J-1)*
Overton Park
Memphis, Tennessee 38112
Tel: (901) 726-4085; (800) 727-1088; Fax: (901) 726-9371

Description: This professional school of art was founded in 1936. The school serves as a studio that trains students in the skills and tools of the visual arts. It teaches respect for excellence and fosters critical appraisal. Liberal studies courses round out a strong program of visual arts. The college operates on the semester system and offers one summer term. The Bachelor of Fine Arts degree is awarded at the completion of eight semesters of work. Enrollment includes 250 students. A faculty of 30 gives a faculty-student ratio of 1-10. The privately controlled and operated college is accredited by the Southern Association of Colleges and Schools and by the National Association of Schools of Art and Design.

Entrance Requirements: High school graduation or equivalent; portfolio of artwork; early admission, midyear admission, rolling admission, and advanced placement plans available; $25 application fee.

Costs Per Year: $9,450 tuition; $4,000 room and board; $50 student fees.

Collegiate Environment: The college is housed in one building in a 324-acre park next to the Brooks Art Museum. Faculty committees meet at the end of each semester to interview all full-time students to discuss their programs of study, review their work, and decide if they are to progress to the following semester's work. Scholarships are available and 80% of the students receive financial aid. The library houses more than 14,000 volumes and many slides, prints, and reproductions. Approximately 85% of students applying for admission are admitted to the school. Placement services are available.

Community Environment: Memphis is a friendly city. It's large enough to support a cultural life of high quality, but small enough not to overwhelm. The cost of living is low. The school is located in midtown, near the Mississippi River.

MEMPHIS THEOLOGICAL SEMINARY   *(J-1)*
168 E. Parkway, South
Memphis, Tennessee 38104
Tel: (901) 458-8232; Fax: (901) 452-4051

Description: The church-related, coeducational religious seminary was founded in 1852 by the Cumberland Presbyterian Church and held its classes on the Bethel College campus in McKenzie. The present site was opened in Memphis in 1964 as a graduate theological seminary granting the Master of Divinity degree, the Master of Arts in Religion degree, and the Doctor of Ministry degree. It operates on the semester system and offers one summer session. The seminary is accredited by the Association of Theological Schools, the Southern Association of Colleges and Schools, and is recognized by the State of Tennessee. Enrollment is 124 full-time and 58 part-time students. A faculty of 9 full-time and 12 part-time gives a faculty-student ratio of 1-10.

Entrance Requirements: Bachelor's degree required from accredited college; rolling admission plan available; $25 application fee.

Costs Per Year: $4,560 tuition.

Collegiate Environment: The Seminary occupies a converted Italian Renaissance mansion in the city of Memphis. A library building was added to the original structure and now includes 76,000 volumes and 600 periodicals. The seminary has 6 duplex apartments. 25% of the students receive financial aid.

Community Environment: See Memphis State University.

MIDDLE TENNESSEE STATE UNIVERSITY   *(H-9)*
Murfreesboro, Tennessee 37132
Tel: (615) 898-2300; (800) 433-6878; Admissions: (615) 898-2111; Fax: (615) 898-5478

Description: This publicly controlled university is fully accredited by the Southern Association of Colleges and Schools and by respective professional institutions. The institution is comprised of the College of Basic and Applied Sciences, College of Business, College of Education, School of Liberal Arts, College of Mass Communications, and the Graduate School. The foundations of the university date back to 1911 with the establishment of the parent, Middle Tennessee Normal School. The name was changed by act of the Legislature in 1943. The Bachelor of Arts has been offered since 1947 and the Master degree and Doctorate since 1972. An Army ROTC program is offered on campus. Air Force ROTC is available through Tennessee State University, Nashville. The "Academic Common Market" is an arrangement that allows students to share unique academic programs at both undergraduate and graduate levels at southern colleges. Freshman classes begin in January, June, and August. The university operates on the early semester system and offers four summer sessions. Enrollment includes 12,091 full-time and 3,017 part-time undergraduates and 2,012 graduate students. A faculty of 677 gives an undergraduate faculty-student ratio of 1-22.

Entrance Requirements: At least 16 years of age, evidence of good moral character; minimum ACT score of 20 (out-of-state students may take SAT) required; minimum 2.8 average on first or last three years of high school work; 14 units including 4 English, 3 mathematics, 2 science, 1 global studies, 2 foreign language, 1 U.S. history, and 1 visual or performing arts; GED acceptable; $5 application fee; early admission, early decision, rolling admission, and advanced placement plans available.

Costs Per Year: $1,616 state-resident tuition; $5,550 out-of-state; $2,302 room and board; $88 student fees.

Collegiate Environment: The large and beautifully landscaped campus consists of 500 acres and 76 major buildings. The university library houses 508,612 volumes, 3,131 periodical subscriptions, 818,782 microforms and 8,526 audiovisual materials. Dormitory facilities include rooms for 5,000 students. Financial aid is available and 60% of the current student body receives aid. 75% of students applying for admission are accepted. A geographically diverse student body is sought, and midyear students are accepted.

Community Environment: Murfreesboro is a small city of about 40,000 that is 32 miles southeast of the state capital, Nashville. Capital of the state from 1819 to 1825, Murfreesboro is a city proud of its history, but one that is changing with the times. Community and area facilities include historical landmarks such as Stones River Battlefield and Old Fort Park. Facilities range from an amphitheater to tennis courts, growing industries, charming old homes, new apartment complexes, churches, numerous recreational areas including many for water sports, the Veteran's Hospital, and Opryland. Because of its geographic location in the center of the state, MTSU is easily accessible from any direction.

MILLIGAN COLLEGE *(F-18)*
Milligan, Tennessee 37682
Tel: (615) 461-8730; (800) 262-8337; Fax: (615) 461-8960

Description: This nondenominational, Christian, liberal arts college is accredited by the Southern Association of Colleges and Schools. It is supported by Christian Churches and Churches of Christ. The college was founded in 1866, then renamed in 1881 and given the motto "Christian Education - the Hope of the World." The college unites humanities, sciences, and fine arts into a Christian world view. A choice from 25 major areas of study leads to the Bachelor of Science or the Bachelor of Arts degree. Additional offerings include the Master of Education and Master of Business Administration degrees. The college operates on the early semester system and offers two summer sessions. Enrollment is 811 students. A faculty of 46 gives a faculty-student ratio of 1-14.

Entrance Requirements: High school graduation or equivalent; ACT or SAT required; recommendation from minister and school personnel required; completion of 16 units including 4 English, 3 mathematics, 1 science, 1 social science, and 2 foreign language; early admission, early decision, rolling admission, midyear admission, and advanced placement plans available; $25 application fee.

Costs Per Year: $8,800 tuition; $3,400 room and board.

Collegiate Environment: The 145-acre campus is situated on the banks of Buffalo Creek. The Administration Building occupies the site on which the original brick buildings of the college were erected. The P.H. Welshimer Memorial Library is a modern fire-proof, air-conditioned building that houses more than 110,000 volumes. Dormitories house 272 men, 336 women and 32 families. Over $1.2 million in scholarship funds is available and 90% of students receive some form of financial assistance.

Community Environment: Milligan, in northeast Tennessee, is located between the suburban areas of Johnson City and Elizabethton. It is one of the leading industrial areas of the south. Recreational facilities are excellent with five TVA lakes offering fishing, boating, and water skiing, and other activities available at federal and state parks.

MOTLOW STATE COMMUNITY COLLEGE *(I-9)*
P.O. Box 88100
Tullahoma, Tennessee 37388
Tel: (615) 393-1500; (800) 654-4877; Admissions: (615) 393-1524; Fax: (615) 393-1681

Description: The state-supported, coeducational junior college provides day and evening programs in college transfer and vocational-technical areas. The college is accredited by the Southern Association of Colleges and Schools and the National League for Nursing. It operates on the semester system with two summer sessions. The college grants an Associate degree. Enrollment includes 1,678 full-time and 1,522 part-time students. A faculty of 75 full-time and 160 part-time gives a faculty-student ratio of 1-20.

Entrance Requirements: Open enrollment policy; high school graduation, minimum ACT 16 required; non-high school graduates may be accepted for non degree courses; early admission, early decision, midyear admission, and advanced placement plans available; $5 application fee.

Costs Per Year: $1,000 state resident tuition; $3,800 nonresident tuition; $22 student fees; $350 average additional expenses.

Collegiate Environment: The college campus is located on 187 acres of wooded land about three miles west of the city limits of Tullahoma. The library includes 62,000 volumes, 362 periodicals, 444 microforms, and 678 audiovisual materials. Various forms of financial assistance are available for students requiring aid. 450 scholarships offered included 50 athletic. 64% of students receive some form of financial aid. 97% of the applicants are accepted, including midyear students.

Community Environment: Tullahoma is located in the southwest corner of Coffee County, not far from Shelbyville. See University of Tennessee - Space Institute.

NASHVILLE STATE TECHNICAL INSTITUTE *(G-8)*
120 White Bridge Road
Nashville, Tennessee 37209-4515
Tel: (615) 353-3333; Admissions: (615) 353-3215; Fax: (615) 353-3243

Description: Founded in 1970, this technical institute is coeducational and is state supported. The institute is accredited by the Southern Association of Colleges and Schools. Serving middle Tennessee, the school provides instruction to prepare adults for employment and to increase the competence of employed workers. The employment rate of graduates is 97% with 80% in related areas. Cooperative education programs are available. The institute awards Certificates and the Associate of Applied Science degree. It operates on the semester system and offers one summer session. Enrollment includes 1,407 full-time and 4,675 part-time students. A faculty of 100 full-time and 220 part-time provides a faculty-student ratio of 1-19.

Entrance Requirements: High school graduation or GED; ACT is required for students under 21; open enrollment policy; rolling admission, midyear admission, and advanced placement plans available; $5 application fee.

Costs Per Year: $966 state resident tuition, $3,752 nonresident tuition.

Collegiate Environment: The 109-acre site presently contains seven institute buildings and a vocational-technical school. The institute campus covers 60 well tended, green acres. The library houses 37,420 hardbound volumes, 445 periodicals, 155 microforms, and 2,063 audiovisual materials. All those who apply are accepted. There are 31 scholarships available for students and an estimated 30% of students receive some form of financial aid.

Community Environment: See Vanderbilt University.

NORTHEAST STATE TECHNICAL COMMUNITY COLLEGE *(E-18)*
P.O. Box 246
Blountville, Tennessee 37617
Tel: (615) 323-3191

Description: Northeast State was founded in 1966 as part of the Tennessee Board of Regents system and is accredited by the Commission on Colleges of the Southern Association of Colleges and

Schools. This state-supported college offers associate degrees and certificates in technical programs designed for students who are looking for immediate employment after graduation. University transfer programs are also available; written transfer agreements are in place with several universities. The school operates on the semester calendar with short-term offerings during the summer. Enrollment is 3,600 students on the main campus and seven off-campus sites.

Entrance Requirements: Open enrollment policy; high school diploma or GED required. ACT and other assessment used for course placement only. Early admission, joint enrollment available. Application fee $5.00.

Costs Per Year: $1,000 full-time in-state fees; $3,786 full-time non-resident fees and tuition.

Collegiate Environment: Located in the center of the Tri-Cities triangle of Bristol-Kingsport-Johnson City, approximately 15 miles from each city. The library has 30,000 volumes, including reference sources, books, CD ROM capabilities, video and audio cassettes, periodicals and newspapers, and other current multimedia resources. Average ACT score of recent freshman class was 16. Developmental studies instruction is available. Club membership is available for organizations in both technical and university transferr areas. Close cooperation with and input from local business and industry results in a job placement rate of 90% for associate degree technical graduates. Financial aid is available from local, state, and federal sources. Approximately 500 students graduate each year. The college is home to the National Center for Quality and the Quality First program, specializing in total quality management training for business, industry, service, and government organizations.

Community Environment: The Tri-Cities is located approximately halfway between Knoxville, TN, and Roanoak, VA. Chemical, defense, manufacturing, and banking industries are numerous. The medical industry is a growing part of the economy. Part-time employment is available. The northeast Tennessee area is bordered by Virginia and North Carolina and is less than a day's drive to both East Coast recreation areas and large metropolitan areas such as Atlanta, Georgia, and Washington, DC. A system of TVA lakes offer warm weather recreation and snow skiing is a short drive away in the winter. The area is also famous for the beauty of its fall colors.

PELLISSIPPI STATE TECHNICAL COMMUNITY COLLEGE (G-14)
10915 Hardin Valley Road
P.O. Box 22990
Knoxville, Tennessee 37930
Tel: (615) 694-6400; (800) 548-6925; Admissions: (615) 694-6570; Fax: (615) 539-7016

Description: Founded in 1974 as a state-supported technical institute, in 1987, State Technical Institute became Pellissippi State Technical Community College. It is accredited by the Southern Association of Colleges and Schools. As well as two-year transfer programs, Pellissippi State offers the Associate degree with programs in Engineering and Business Technologies and Continuing Education. Cooperative education programs are available in all career technical programs in Business, and Engineering. Courses are offered at various centers in Knox County. The college operates on the semester system and offers one summer term. Enrollment includes 7,869 full-time and 4,205 part-time students. A faculty of 145 full-time and 302 part-time gives a faculty-student ratio of 1-19.

Entrance Requirements: High school graduation or GED accepted; ACT required for placement purposes; open enrollment policy; early and rolling admission. $5 application fee.

Costs Per Year: $1,040 tuition, $3,826 nonresident.

Collegiate Environment: The new $46 million campus is located in the Tennessee Technology Corridor. One hundred percent of students who apply, including midyear transfers, are accepted. Of 110 scholarships offered, all are available for freshmen. 30% percent of the students are receiving financial aid. The library contains 31,600 hardbound volumes, 527 periodicals and 2,897 microforms and audiovisual units.

Community Environment: The city is a business center in the East Tennessee Valley with markets in tobacco, livestock, marble, and zinc. It is the headquarters for the Tennessee Valley Authority and there are facilities for varied water sports. The Great Smoky Mountains National Park provides additional outdoor facilities as well as many historic points of interest. The Knoxville-Oak Ridge Alcoa-Maryville area is the site of the Tennessee Technology Corridor, a rapidly growing center of technology related business, industrial, and educational development.

RHODES COLLEGE   (J-1)
2000 N. Parkway
Memphis, Tennessee 38112
Tel: (901) 726-3700; (800) 844-5659; Fax: (901) 726-3719

Description: This four-year college of liberal arts and sciences is fully accredited by the Southern Association of Colleges and Schools, and by the respective professional and educational agencies. The college was founded in 1848 when the Clarksville Academy was merged into the Masonic University of Tennessee. Various reorganizations took place until 1925, when the college was moved to its present site in Memphis, and it assumed the name of Southwestern. In 1984 the college changed its name to Rhodes College honoring the longtime former President, Peyton Nalle Rhodes. The institution is affiliated with the Presbyterian Church and offers the Bachelor of Arts and Bachelor of Science degrees. It operates on the semester system. Enrollment is 622 men and 789 women full-time, and 19 men and 39 women part-time. The faculty is 114 full-time and 35 part-time. Various overseas and summer programs in Europe are available including European Studies, a 17-week, 18-credit-hour program, British studies at Oxford, year abroad in France, Spain, or Latin America, and an exchange program with University of Tubingen, Germany and with Kansai University of Foreign Studies in Osaka, Japan. Other programs allow study in Brazil, Hungary, Poland, and Czechoslovakia. Army and Air Force ROTC are available.

Entrance Requirements: Rank in the top 50% of high school graduating class; 16 academic high school units required including 4 English, 3 mathematics, and 2 foreign language; SAT or ACT required; early decision, early admission, delayed admission, and advanced placement programs available; $35 application fee.

Costs Per Year: $15,762 tuition; $4,912 room and board.

Collegiate Environment: The library contains 232,620 volumes, 1,187 periodicals, 40,354 microform units and 7,573 records, tapes, and video cassettes. The collegiate Gothic architecture of the campus affords pleasant surroundings for residence halls with a total capacity of 1,124. Financial aid is available and 716 scholarships were awarded recently. 72% of the current student body receives some form of financial assistance. Approximately 80% of the students applying for admission were accepted and 91% returned for the second year on campus. The middlle 50% range of scores for entering freshmen were SAT 1100-1200 combined, and ACT 25-30 composite. 95% those applying are accepted into graduate/professional school.

Community Environment: See Memphis State University.

ROANE STATE COMMUNITY COLLEGE   (G-13)
Patton Lane
Harriman, Tennessee 37748
Tel: (615) 354-3000

Description: The publicly-supported, two year college was founded in 1970. It is accredited by the Southern Association of Colleges and Schools and by respective professional institutions. The college grants the Associate degree. It operates on the semester system and offers two summer sessions. Enrollment includes 818 men and 1,093 women full-time and 577 men and 1,365 women part-time. A faculty of 89 full-time and 113 part-time gives a faculty-student ratio of 1-19.

Entrance Requirements: Open enrollment policy; high school graduation or equivalent; completion of 20 units including 4 English, 3 mathematics, 2 laboratory science, 2 foreign language, 2 social studies, and 1 performing or visual arts; early admission, early decision, rolling admission, delayed admission and advanced placement plans available. $5 application fee.

Costs Per Year: $716 tuition; $3,146 out-of-state tuition; $8 student fees; additional expenses average $1,000.

Collegiate Environment: The new campus consists of 104 acres. The library contains 46,380 volumes, 546 periodicals, 8,023 microforms and 5,644 audiovisual units. Financial assistance is available. 210 scholarships are offered, 120 for freshmen. 30% of students receive some form of financial aid. 99% of the applicants are accepted, including midyear students. About 55% of the previous freshman class returned for the second year.

Community Environment: Harriman is located near the cities of Kingston and Rockwood and is easily accessible via U.S. highways.

SHELBY STATE COMMUNITY COLLEGE   *(J-1)*
P.O. Box 40568
Memphis, Tennessee 38174-0568
Tel: (901) 528-6700

Description: Shelby State Community College, founded in 1970, is one of 14 community college and six universities governed by the Board of Regents of the State University and Community College System of Tennessee. After opening in temporary quarters in the fall of 1972 to an initial enrollment of 1,059, the College has grown to a student body of 4,763. Enrollment includes 2,072 full-time and 2,691 part-time students. Faculty numbers 111 full-time and 141 part-time members, giving a faculty-student ratio of 1:19. The College is an open-admissions, state-supported institution of higher education. Academic courses are offered within the framework of up to two-year programs of study and provisions are made for awarding both certificate and associate degrees. It operates on the semester system with two summer sessions. Army and Air Force ROTC programs are available through Memphis State University.

Entrance Requirements: Regular admission as a candidate for an Associate Degree or Certificate will be granted to graduates of accredited high schools, or the equivalent, and to transfer students in good standing from the last college attended. Completeion of 14 units including 4 English, 3 mathematics, 2 science, 2 foreign language, 1 social studies, 1 U.S. History, 1 visual or performing art; $5 application fee.

Costs Per Year: Tuition and fees $846 resident, $3,270 nonresident.

Collegiate Environment: Shelby State Community College currently operates two campuses (one in midtown-Memphis and one in North Memphis), two multi-purpose learning centers, and a number of additional teaching stations throughout this area. The College and the Memphis and Shelby County Public Library and Information Center make available more than 4,000,000 volumes for student use. The library contains 46,712 volumes, 374 periodical subscriptions, 5,998 microforms, and 3,814 audiovisual materials. 44% of the students receive some form of financial aid.

Community Environment: See Memphis State University.

SOUTHERN COLLEGE OF OPTOMETRY   *(J-1)*
1245 Madison Avenue
Memphis, Tennessee 38104
Tel: (901) 722-3225; (800) 238-0180; Fax: (901) 722-3279

Description: The private, nonprofit, four-year professional school is accredited by the Commission on Colleges of the Southern Association of Colleges and Schools and by the American Optometric Association's Council on Optometric Education. The college is approved for enrollment of veterans. Founded in 1932 by Dr. J. J. Horton, the school aims to stimulate intellectual curiosity and the achievement of knowledge with which the student may develop a competent and ethical practice of optometry, and to afford graduate optometrists the opportunity of enhancing their clinical proficiency and theoretical knowledge through postgraduate study. The college operates on the quarter system with one summer session. The enrollment in the doctor of optometry program consists of 444 full-time students. A faculty of 5 full-time and 41 part-time gives a faculty-student ratio of 1-10.

Entrance Requirements: 90 semester or 135 quarter hours minimum previous college, Bachelor's degree preferred; Optometry Admissions Test required; $50 application fee.

Costs Per Year: $8,100 regional tuition; $13,100 nonresident; $118 student fees.

Collegiate Environment: Located on 15 acres of campus, the school presently consists of three building clusters, including a 12-story classroom-clinic-laboratory-office building. One floor of the building is a student center, with another designed as a library providing room for 15,385 volumes, 172 periodical subscriptions, 4,677 bound periodical journals, 529 microforms, and 1,151 audiovisual materials. The

college is situated in the midcity locale known as the Medical Center area, about three miles east of downtown. Midyear students are not accepted. Approximately 30% of students applying for admission are accepted, and more than 98% of the current freshman class returned for the second year of study. Almost 90% of the current freshman class receives some form of financial assistance.

SOUTHERN COLLEGE OF SEVENTH-DAY ADVENTISTS
(J-12)
P.O. Box 370
Collegedale, Tennessee 37315
Tel: (615) 238-2111; (800) 768-8437; Admissions: (615) 238-2844; Fax: (615) 238-3005

Description: The Christian, liberal arts college is supported by the Seventh-day Adventist Church. Fully accredited by the Southern Association of Colleges and Schools and the respective professional and educational agencies, the institution offers 39 majors and 31 minors in which students may qualify for the Baccalaureate degree, as well as various preprofessional and two-year terminal programs of a technical or vocational nature. Founded as Graysville Academy in 1892, the college moved in 1916 to its present location and became a junior college. The senior college status and present name was established in 1944. The college operates on the semester system and offers four summer terms. Enrollment includes 1,289 full-time and 363 part-time undergraduate students. A faculty of 89 full-time and 28 part-time gives a faculty-student ratio of 1-13.

Entrance Requirements: ACT required; high school graduation with 18 units including 4 English, 2 mathematics (including algebra) 2 science, 2 history, with 2 foreign language recommended; three recommendations required; early decision, early admission, midyear admission, rolling admission and advanced placement plans available; $20 application fee.

Costs Per Year: $8,888 tuition; $3,642 room and board.

Collegiate Environment: Located in a quiet, peaceful valley, the campus is 18 miles east of Chattanooga. The modern McKee Memorial Library houses approximately 100,000 volumes and 1,000 periodicals. The college seeks a geographically diverse student body. Students come from all 50 states and 35 overseas countries. The institution has campuses abroad in Germany, France, and Austria. 91% of all applicants are accepted. Unmarried students are required to reside in either Thatcher or Talge Halls with a total capacity of 1,275, unless living with parents. Chapel service and a religion course are required of all students. Scholarships are available and 87% of the students receive some form of financial aid.

Community Environment: Collegedale is located 18 miles east of Chattanooga where the recreation areas of the TVA lake system are within 10 miles. There are residence halls for the students; part-time employment opportunities are available.

STATE TECHNICAL INSTITUTE AT MEMPHIS   *(J-1)*
5983 Macon Cove
Memphis, Tennessee 38134-7693
Tel: (901) 377-4100; Admissions: (901) 383-4194; Fax: (901) 383-4473

Description: The state-supported, coeducational, two-year technical college was established by the state legislature in 1963 and graduated its first class in 1968. The institute is accredited by the Southern Association of Colleges and Schools and the Accreditation Board for Engineering and Technology. It grants an Associate of Applied Science degree. The institute operates on the semester system and offers three summer terms. Enrollment includes 11,000 students. A faculty of 546 gives a faculty-student ratio of 1:20. Cooperative education courses are available through all degree programs. Army and Air Force ROTC are offered through Memphis State University.

Entrance Requirements: Open enrollment policy; high school graduation or equivalent; ACT required for students under age 21; early admission, early decision, midyear admission and rolling admission plans available. $5 application fee.

Costs Per Year: $966 in-state tuition; $3,752 out-of-state tuition.

Collegiate Environment: The Institute occupies a multi-million dollar physical plant located in Memphis. There is no student housing available on campus. The library contains 45,380 volumes, 424 periodicals, 336 microforms, and 111 audiovisual titles. All of the applicants are accepted. 13% of students receive financial aid.

Community Environment: See Memphis State University.

TENNESSEE STATE UNIVERSITY   *(G-8)*
3500 John A. Merritt Blvd.
Nashville, Tennessee 37203
Tel: (615) 963-5101; Fax: (615) 963-5108

Description: Tennessee State University was founded in 1912. In 1922, the institution was raised to the status of a four-year teachers college and was empowered to grant the Bachelor degree. In 1941, The General Assembly authorized the State Board of Education to upgrade the education program of the college which included the establishment of graduate studies leading to the Master degree. The reorganization included establishing the Graduate School, the School of Arts and Sciences, the School of Education, and the School of Engineering. In 1958, the university was elevated to a full fledged landgrant university program. The university is accredited by the Southern Association of Colleges and Schools. The institution operates on the semester system and offers two summer terms. Enrollment includes 1,949 men and 3,091 women with a faculty of 342.

Entrance Requirements: Graduation from high school; 4 units of English; 1 unit visual and/or performing arts; 2 units of algebra; 1 unit of geometry or other advanced math; 2 units natural/physical sciences; 1 unit social sciences; 1 unit U.S. history; 2 units in one foreign language; ACT score of 19 required; early decision and midyear admission plans available; application fee $5.

Costs Per Year: $1,778 state-resident tuition; $5,712 nonresident; $2,920 room and board.

Collegiate Environment: Located in northwest Nashville, the campus, farm lands and pastures occupy 450 acres of scenic rolling grounds and fertile fields extending to the southwest banks of the Cumberland River. There are several on-campus dormitories. An Air Force ROTC program is offered. The Brown-Daniel Memorial Library is located near the center of the campus and has 342,543 volumes, 14,488 microfilms; 628,944 microfiche, pamphlets, and 70,286 periodicals. Residence halls accomodate 2,500 men and women. Scholarships are available.

Community Environment: See Vanderbilt University.

TENNESSEE TECHNOLOGICAL UNIVERSITY   *(G-11)*
Dixie Avenue
Cookeville, Tennessee 38505
Tel: (615) 372-3888; (800) 255-8881; Fax: (615) 372-6250

Description: The university was established by an act of the General Assembly in 1915 and opened its doors to students on September 14, 1916. From its beginning as a state-supported technical college, the institution has emerged as a multipurpose institution. The university is organized into seven undergraduate schools and colleges, plus a graduate school. Degrees are offered in each school and college. An Army ROTC program is offered. The university operates on the semester system and offers two summer terms. The semesters begin in January, June, and August. The school is accredited by the Southern Association of Colleges and Schools. The enrollment is 8,228 students. A faculty of 379 full-time and 120 part-time gives a faculty-student ratio of 1-18.

Entrance Requirements: High school graduation or equivalent; 14 units including 4 English, 3 mathematics (Algebra I, and II, and Geometry), 2 science, 2 foreign language (of 1 language), 1 social studies, 1 U.S. history, 1 visual or performing arts; advanced placement, early admission, early decision, rolling admission programs available; ACT required, $5 application fee.

Costs Per Year: $1,710 state resident tuition; $5,492 nonresident tuition; $2,812 room and board.

Collegiate Environment: Paved highways radiate in all directions and bus lines furnish convenient transportation from any point of Tennessee to the 200-acre campus. The Library houses 390,915 volumes, 3,828 periodicals, 131,000 government documents, 1,091,495 microforms, and 65,327 audiovisual materials. There is dormitory space available for 2,707 students. 1,371 scholarships are offered by the university and 75% of the students receive some form of financial aid.

Community Environment: Cookeville, located in middle Tennessee, is predominantly an agricultural area. Bus transportation is available. Churches of most denominations, libraries, a hospital, and various civic and service organizations serve the community. Recreational activities include swimming, softball, baseball, tennis, and golf. Center Hill Dam and Reservoir are nearby for many other sports, such as boating, water sports, fishing, and camping.

TENNESSEE TEMPLE UNIVERSITY   *(J-11)*
1815 Union Avenue
Chattanooga, Tennessee 37404
Tel: (615) 493-4100

Description: The university is divided into three divisions. The Bible and Christian Ministries Division offers majors in three fields: Bible, Missions, and Christian Education. Degrees offered are BS and BA. The Arts and Sciences Division offers majors in Business Administration (accounting, administrative management, general business administration, office administration, two-year secretarial certificate), Communications (broadcasting, pulpit communications) Educational (hearing impaired, elementary and secondary), English, History, Mathematics, Music, (General, Sacred, Christian School music), Physical Education, and Psychology. The Seminary offers work leading to the Bachelor or Master of Divinity, Master or Doctor of Religious Education, and the Master and Doctor of Theology. The private Baptist University enrolls 500 students with a faculty of 37 members. The faculty-student ratio is 1-11. It operates on the semester system with one summer term.

Entrance Requirements: High school graduation with rank in 70% of class; completion of 18 units including 3 English, 2 mathematics, 2 social science. ACT or SAT is required. The application fee is $25. Early admission, early decision, delayed admission and advanced placement plans available.

Costs Per Year: $4,250 tuition; $3,980 room and board; $250 student fees.

Collegiate Environment: There are approximately 94,031 volumes, 1038 periodicals, 2605 microform, and 1,718 recordings in the library. Dormitory space included space for 1,100 men and women. Students are required to attend all regular church services including Sunday School, Training Union, and Prayer Service, and attend the nearby Highland Park Baptist Church for a period of eight weeks before requesting permission to work in another church. Students applying for admission are accepted including midyear.

Community Environment: See Chattanooga State Technical Community College.

TENNESSEE WESLEYAN COLLEGE   *(I-13)*
P.O. Box 40
Athens, Tennessee 37371-0040
Tel: (615) 745-7504; Fax: (615) 744-9968

Description: The college was founded in 1857 and has been related to one of the branches of The Methodist Church during its entire history. Organized as a female college, the institution served as a junior college from 1925 to 1954 at which time it gained the status of a senior college. The small, private, liberal arts institution is affiliated with the United Methodist Church. It is fully accredited by the Southern Association of Colleges and Schools and the respective educational agencies. The various departments of the college include biology, business administration chemistry and physics, education, English, foreign languages, health and physical education and recreation, history and political science, mathematics, music, speech and theater, psychology and sociology, religion and philosophy. The school operates on the semester system, with three summer sessions. Enrollment includes 437 full-time and 195 part-time students. Faculty has 30 full-time and 26 part-time members, giving a faculty-student ratio of 1-12. There are summer programs in France, and Great Britain, and a year long exchange with colleges in Japan.

Entrance Requirements: High school graduation; 16 units including 4 English, 2 mathematics, 1 laboratory science, 1 social studies, 1 U.S. history; ACT or SAT required; rolling admission and advanced placement plans available. $25 application fee.

Costs Per Year: $6,100 tuition; $3,700 board & room, $100 student fees.

Collegiate Environment: The campus covers more than 40 acres and is located within two blocks of Public Square in Athens. The Merner-Pfeiffer Library contains approximately 87,417 volumes, pamphlets, 395 periodicals, 2,553 microforms and 1,808 sound recordings. There are dormitory facilities for 200 men and 300 women. All students not living with parents are required to reside in the student residence halls and eat in the school cafeteria. Financial assistance is available on campus and 77% receive some form. chapel service is held each week. 85% of students applying for admission are accepted including midyear students.

Community Environment: Athens is the county seat of McMinn County, located between Chattanooga and Knoxville. The town is an industrial community providing jobs for approximately 7,000 people and serving as a shopping center for 50,000 rural residents. Recreational activities in the beautiful mountainous area include big game hunting, fresh water fishing, rafting, kayaking, hiking, and many other sports.

TREVECCA NAZARENE COLLEGE   *(G-8)*
333 Murfreesboro Road
Nashville, Tennessee 37203
Tel: (615) 248-1320; (800) 210-4862; Fax: (615) 248-7728

Description: The four-year senior college was founded in 1901, and is today the official college of the Church of the Nazarene in the southeastern United States. The privately controlled institution is accredited by the Southern Association of Colleges and Schools. Recent enrollment was 1,358 students. Graduate enrollment is 350. A faculty of 73 full-time and 29 part-time gives a faculty-student ratio of 1-13. Offering the Bachelor of Arts or Bachelor of Science degrees, the institution has programs in nine major divisions: allied health, business administration and economics, communications studies, education and psychology, music, history and social science, physical education health and recreation, religion and philosphy, and science and mathematics. The college operates on the semester system and offers one summer term. Army, Navy, and Air Force ROTC programs are available. The school also offers a Masters of Education in Elementary Education and Curriculm, Religion and Organizational Mangement.

Entrance Requirements: High school graduation; recommended units including 4 English, 2 mathematics, 2 foreign language, 2 social science, and 1 science; non-high school graduates considered; ACT or SAT required; academic enrichment program for students with less than 15 on ACT; early admission, early decision, midyear admission, rolling admission and advanced placement plans available.

Costs Per Year: $6,656 tuition; $3,345 room and board; $380 student fees; $1,600 average additional expenses.

Collegiate Environment: Located on 80 acres, the physical plant comprises 22 buildings. The college library contains approximately 83,194 volumes, 21,945 periodicals, 17,387 microforms and 3,093 audiovisual materials. There is dormitory space available for 314 men, 345 women, and 72 families. Chapel attendance is required of all students. Financial assistance is available and about 85% of the student body receives aid. The average composite ACT score of the current freshmen was over 20. 95% of students applying for admission are accepted, including midyear students. About 67% of the previous freshmen returned for the sophomore year. The campus has a special program for culturally disadvantaged low-mark students.

Community Environment: See Vanderbilt University.

TUSCULUM COLLEGE   *(G-17)*
Box 5097, Tusculum Station
Greeneville, Tennessee 37743
Tel: (615) 636-7312; (800) 729-0256; Fax: (615) 638-7166

Description: Chartered in 1794, the four-year liberal arts college is accredited by the Southern Association of Colleges and Schools. The institution offers Bachelor of Arts, Bachelor of Science degrees, Masters in education, and Master of Arts, as well as preprofessional training in dentistry, law, and medicine. Enrollment is 1,191 full-time and 26 part-time students with a faculty of 30 full-time and 90 part-time. The college operates on the semester system and offers 1 summer session.

Entrance Requirements: High school graduation with rank in top 50% of high school class; completion of college preparatory units including 4 English, 2 mathematics, 2 science, 2 social science; ACT

with minimum score of 18, or SAT with minimum scores of 400V and 400M, required; early admission, early decision, rolling admission, delayed admission, and advanced placement plans available; no application fee.

Costs Per Year: $8,400 tuition/fees; $3,500 room and board; additional expenses average $400.

Collegiate Environment: The 140-acre campus is located five miles east of downtown Greeneville. The main buildings are constructed of brick and are built in the Georgian-Colonial architectural style. The Tate Library houses a collection of 185,000 volumes and microform texts, approximately 900 current periodical subscriptions, and 4,000 sound recordings. Financial assistance is available and 85% of the current class received some form of financial assistance. There are 120 scholarships offered, with 37 of them granted to entering freshmen. Dormitory facilities provide room for 246 men and 177 women. Unmarried students who do not live with parents or relatives must reside in college-approved residence halls. 95% of students applying for admission are accepted, including midyear students and 88% of freshmen return to campus for the second year. The average high school standing of the freshman class, 52% in the top quarter, 19% in the second quarter, 25% in the third quarter, 4% in the bottom quarter; average SAT scores, 410V, 450M or a composite ACT of 24. Approximately 15% of the senior class continued on to graduate school.

Community Environment: Greeneville is near the Andrew Johnson Wildlife Management Area where each year managed hunts are held. Greene County is the birthplace of Davy Crockett. Bus and train transportation are available. The city has a full-time recreational director who supervises a year-round program. Recreational activities are hunting, boating, fishing, golf, whitewater rafting, and cycling.

UNION UNIVERSITY   *(H-3)*
2447 Highway 45 Bypass
Jackson, Tennessee 38305
Tel: (901) 668-1818; (800) 338-6466; Fax: (901) 661-5177

Description: The Tennessee Baptist-controlled college is coeducational and liberal arts in nature. It is accredited by the Southern Association of Colleges and Schools. The university operates on the 4-1-4 system and offers two summer sessions. Enrollment includes 1,643 full-time and 287 part-time undergraduate and 110 graduate students. A faculty of 99 full-time and 47 part-time gives an undergraduate faculty-student ratio of 1-14.

Entrance Requirements: High school graduation or equivalent; ACT 20 or more; completion of 22 high school units required, including 4 English, 3 mathematics, 3 laboratory science, and 3 social science; $10 application fee; non-high school graduates considered; early admission, rolling admission, advanced placement and credit by examination plans available.

Costs Per Year: $6,350 tuition; $200 average additional expenses.

Collegiate Environment: The college is now located on its new campus of approximately 230 acres. All academic facilities are located under a multi-level roof. The library holdings are 193,146 volumes. Dormitory space is available for 347 men and 527 women. 32 apartments are available for married students, and additional dormitories are being built. 80% of applicants are accepted. 79% of the current class received some form of financial aid. Almost 21% of the student body graduated in the top 10% of the high school class, 39% in the top quarter, and 71% in the top half. Approximately 80% of students applying for admission are accepted and 84% of the freshman class returned to the campus for the second year. About 51% of the senior class continued on to graduate school or professional programs.

Community Environment: Jackson is a small town of 50,000 that is 75 miles from Memphis and 125 miles from Nashville. There are 3 other colleges located in the same town.

UNIVERSITY OF MEMPHIS   *(J-1)*
159 Administration Building
Memphis, Tennessee 38152
Tel: (901) 678-2000; (800) 669-2678; Admissions: (901) 678-2111; Fax: (901) 678-3053

Description: The largest of six four-year institutions within the State University and Community College System of Tennessee, the University of Memphis is accredited by the Southern Association of

Colleges and Schools. The university awards Bachelor's, Master's, and Doctoral degrees and first professional and educational specialist's degrees. Founded in 1912 as a teacher training school, it became Memphis State College in 1941, Memphis State University in 1957, and the University of Memphis in 1994. The university is presently comprised of ten colleges and schools: the College of Arts and Sciences, the Fogelman College of Business and Economics, the College of Communication and Fine Arts, the College of Education, the Herff College of Engineering, the Graduate School, the Cecil C. Humphreys School of Law, the School of Audiology and Speech-Language Pathology, the University College, and the School of Nursing. The Air Force, Army and Navy ROTC programs are available as electives. The university operates on the semester system with two summer terms offered. Enrollment includes 10,445 full-time and 4,642 part-time undergraduates and 4,761 graduate students. A faculty of 750 full-time and 309 part-time provides a faculty-student ratio of 1-17.

Entrance Requirements: The admission of entering freshmen is based on the transcript of a four-year course of study at an approved or accredited high school, acceptable scores on the American College Testing Program examination or Scholastic Aptitude test. (The General Educational Development test and high school equivalency diploma are accepted when applicable.) Applicants must be at least 16 years old. Application fee $5; rolling admission and advanced placement plans available. The admission of transfer students is based on the applicant's quality point average, academic standing at his former institution, and scores on the admission tests mentioned previously.

Costs Per Year: $2,042 in-state tuition; $3,934 out-of-state; $3,220 room and board additional expenses average $2,500 to $3,000.

Collegiate Environment: The University is an urban research and resource university located in a park-like setting in suburban east Memphis. The 195-acre main campus is surrounded by stately homes with beautifully landscaped grounds. The library provides one of the most electronically up-to-date information respositories within hundreds of miles. Library holdings include nearly 1 million bound volumes and more than 107,500 units of microfilm. Residence halls can accomodate 2,900 students. An active student activities council brings a number of academic apeakers and enterainment events to the campus each year. Campus recreational facilities include 31 tennis courts, four softball fields, an all-weather track, 15 racquetball courts, and indoor and outdoor Olympic-sized pools, in addition to other facilities. A number of intercollegiate sports are available at the University. 68% of applicants are accepted. The average score for the entering freshman class was ACT 22.3 composite. Most states and 80 countries are represented in the student body. 50% of the students are between the ages of 18-22 and 55% are women. Scholarships of $5 million total are offered annual and 60% of the students receive some form of financial aid.

Community Environment: Memphis, with a metropolitan area population of over one million, is one of the South's largest and most attractive cities. As a primary medical, educational, communication, distribution, and transportation center, Memphis offers a rich and full range of research opportunities and cultural experiences. The city, known worldwide for its musical heritage, has many fine restaurants, museums, and theaters, as well as one of the nation's largest urban park systems. All forms of commercial transportation are available. Oppurtunities are numerous for part-time employment. Annual events include the St. Jude Liberty Bowl Football Classic, the Memphis in May International Festival, the Great River Carnival, and the Mid-South Fair. Some of the points of interest are the Brooks Memorial Art Gallery, Chuclissa Indian Villiage and Museum, Elvis Presley's Graceland, Mud Island, Libertyland, and the Great American Pyramid.

UNIVERSITY OF TENNESSEE - CHATTANOOGA *(J-11)*
615 McCallie Avenue
Chattanooga, Tennessee 37403
Tel: (615) 755-4111; (800) 882-6627; Admissions: (615) 755-4662; Fax: (615) 755-4157

Description: Founded in 1886, the University of Chattanooga merged with the Chattanooga City College to become part of the University of Tennessee. It is accredited by the Southern Association of Colleges and Schools and by respective professional organizations. The now publicly controlled university offers four-year programs leading to the degrees of Bachelor of Arts, Bachelor of Science, Bach-

elor of Fine Arts and Bachelor of Music. There is also a division of graduate studies that grants a Masters degree. Cooperative education programs are offered in majors. The institution operates on the semester system and offers five summer sessions. Enrollment for the Chattanooga campus includes 5,263 full-time and 1,738 part-time undergraduate, and 1,280 graduate students. A faculty of 320 full-time and 208 part-time gives a faculty-student ratio of 1-18. An Army ROTC program is offered on campus.

Entrance Requirements: High school graduation with diploma; completion of 14 units including 4 English, 3 mathematics, 2 laboratory science, 2 foreign language, 1 U.S. history, 1 World or European history or World geography, and 1 fine arts; minimum ACT 16 or SAT 620; GRE required for graduate admission; early admission, early decision, and advanced placement programs available; $15 application fee.

Costs Per Year: $1,746 state resident tuition; $5,678 nonresident tuition; $4,572 room and board; $104 student fees.

Collegiate Environment: The campus, comprising 101.4 acres and 60 buildings, rises above downtown Chattanooga. The UT-C library holdings include 1,544,476 hardbound volumes as well as numerous periodical subscriptions, microforms, and audiovisual materials. There are living accommodations available for 1,334 men and women. 1,507 academic and 193 athletic scholarships are available. 70% of the students receive some form of financial assistance.

Community Environment: See Chattanooga State Technical Community College.

UNIVERSITY OF TENNESSEE - KNOXVILLE *(G-15)*
320 Student Services Building
Knoxville, Tennessee 37996-0230
Tel: (615) 974-2184; (800) 221-8657; Admissions: (615) 974-2184

Description: Founded in 1794, the university is state-controlled. The various colleges and schools are fully accredited by the Southern Association of Colleges and Schools and the respective educational and professional agencies. Both Army and Air Force ROTC are offered on campus. Cooperative education programs are offered in all engineering majors and in other major areas. The university offers programs in agriculture, architecture, business administration, communications, engineering, human ecology, arts and sciences, education, nursing, and social work. Graduate programs are offered in library and information science, and planning. Professional degrees areawarded by the College of Law and the College of Veterinary Medicine. The university operates on the semester system and offers two summer sessions. Enrollment includes 16,349 full-time and 2,993 part-time undergraduates and 6,656 graduate students. A faculty of 1,110 full-time and 45 part-time gives a faculty-student ratio of 1-17.

Entrance Requirements: High school graduation or equivalent; completion of 16 units including 4 English, 3 mathematics, (2 Algebra, 1 Geometry or Trigonometry or Advanced Math or Calculus), 2 foreign language, 2 laboratory science, 2 social studies (1 U.S. history and European or World history), and 1 visual or performing art; 2.0 high school GPA required; ACT required with minimum composite score range of 18-21 depending on GPA, or SAT required with minimum combined score range of 720-860 depending on GPA; early admission, midyear admission, rolling admission and advanced placement available; application fee $15; GRE required for graduate school.

Costs Per Year: $2,052 state resident tuition; $5,986 out-of-state tuition; $3,400 room and board.

Collegiate Environment: Five library units are available to students, faculty, and staff. The contents of the libraries include 1,914,672 volumes, 18,269 periodicals, 2,820,840 microforms, and 29,310 audio-video materials. There are various forms of financial assistance available and 50% of students receive aid. Dormitory and housing are available for 7,616 men and women, and 1,690 families. Fraternities provide additional housing for 535 men. There are 27 fraternities and 19 sororities. Approximately 73% of students applying are accepted and 79% of freshmen return to the campus for the second year of study.

Community Environment: See Knoxville College.

UNIVERSITY OF TENNESSEE - MARTIN   *(F-3)*
Martin, Tennessee 38238
Tel: (901) 587-7020

Description: The university began as the Hall-Moody Institute in 1900. The University of Tennessee established UT Junior College in 1927 after Hall-Moody closed. In 1951, the institution was made a senior college by legislative enactment. It is accredited by the Southern Association of Colleges and schools and offers bachelor and master's degrees. It operated on the semester system commencing in August with two summer terms. Enrollment includes 2,149 men, 2,572 women full-time and 256 men, 449 women part-time with a faculty of 239 full-time and 35 part-time members. Army ROTC is offered on campus.

Entrance Requirements: High school graduation with 2.6 GPA; completion of 13 units including 4 English, 3 mathematics (Algebra I and II, and one other advanced math), 1 American history, 2 units of the same foreign language, 2 natural or physical sciences, 1 Social Study in World, Modern, Ancient, or European history; ACT composite score of 19, or SAT required; GRE required for graduate studies; application fee $10; early admission, early decision, advanced placements, and concurrent admission plans available.

Costs Per Year: $1,658 state resident tuition; $3,458 out-of-state; $2,780 room and board.

Collegiate Environment: The campus at Martin is a primary campus of the university system with significant responsibility for, and concern with, undergraduate classroom teaching. Regular admission requirements: 2.6 high school GPA or a 19 ACT composite score. A geographically diverse student body is sought. There are various forms of financial assistance available to students. Of the 920 scholarships awarded, 241 of them are granted to entering freshmen. The campus is composed of 250 acres and 41 buildings, with another 650 acres used for agriculture. 65% of the students applying for admission are accepted. In the current freshman class, nearly 68% returned to campus for a second year of study. The library contains 270,000 titles, 1,600 periodicals, 306,190 miroforms and 8,240 audiovisual materials. Dormitory space is available for 1,162 men and 1,333 women and 224 families. Fraternities provide additional housing for 175 men.

Community Environment: Martin, approximately 10,000 population, is in Northwest Tennessee about 125 miles northeast of Memphis and 150 miles northwest of Nashville. All commercial transportation is available. Community facilities include a city library, a state regional library, churches, hospital, and various civic, fraternal and veteran's organizations. Boating, fishing, hunting, golf, swimming, and bowling are some of the many activities here; also nearby lakes provide other recreational activities.

UNIVERSITY OF TENNESSEE - SPACE INSTITUTE, TULLAHOMA   *(I-9)*
Tullahoma, Tennessee 37388
Tel: (615) 393-7432; Fax: (615) 393-7346

Description: The University of Tennessee Space Institute offers graduate education, research, post-doctoral study and continuing education in advanced engineering and scientific disciplines. The Space Institute is a part of the University of Tennessee, Knoxville, and makes available to its students a number of academic programs and resources of the Knoxville campus. Programs are offered leading to degrees of Master of Science and Doctor of Philosophy with majors in Aerospace Engineering, Mechanical Engineering, Engineering Science & Mechanics, Physics, and Electrical Engineering; and Master of Science degrees in Applied Mathematics, Engineering Management, Aviation Systems, Computer Science, and Chemical Engineering. Located adjacent to the Arnold Engineering Development Center, selected Institute students and faculty have opportunities through appropriate contractual arrangements to work in some of the world's most advanced research and development facilities. Subjects of current academic and research emphasis include: aerospace propulsion; aerodynamics; energy conversion; laser technology and application; environmental research, development and management; and large scale computations. It operates on the semester system and offers one summer session. Enrollment includes 100 full-time and 400 part-time students. A faculty of 50 members gives a faculty-student ratio of 1:3.

Entrance Requirements: Baccalaureate degree from an accredited institution; GRE required for some programs; $15 application fee; rolling admission plan available.

Costs Per Year: $2,398 tuition; $6,332 out-of-state tuition; $120 student fees; additional expenses average $4,000.

Collegiate Environment: The Tullahoma center has dormitory facilities for 40 students. Financial assistance is available through graduate research assistantships and fellowships. The technical library contains 19,332 volumes, 47,704 technical reports, 175 periodicals, and 189,299 microforms. About 80% of the applicants are accepted, including midyear students.

Community Environment: Located 70 miles northwest of Chattanooga, Tullahoma is the world's largest manufacturer of baseballs. Bus and train transportation are available. The area has a wonderful year-round climate with excellent facilities for recreation including two golf courses, swimming pools, and other water sports. Medical and shopping facilities are good.

UNIVERSITY OF TENNESSEE, MEMPHIS - HEALTH SCIENCE CENTER   *(J-1)*
790 Madison Avenue, Suite 119
Memphis, Tennessee 38163
Tel: (901) 448-5560; Admissions: (901) 448-5560; Fax: (901) 448-7772

Description: The Health Science Center at Memphis is one of four major campuses of the statewide University system. The Memphis campus offers programs in medicine, dentistry, graduate health sciences, nursing, and pharmacy and allied health. Founded in 1851, the institution is accredited by the Southern Association of Colleges and Schools and the respective professional agencies. The semester system is used and there is one summer session. Enrollment includes 64 men and 327 women undergraduates, 1,635 graduate students, and a faculty of 771 full-time and 190 part-time members. The university grants undergraduate and graduate level degrees.

Entrance Requirements: Previous college study required; GRE required; application fee $25; rolling admission, delayed admission, and advanced placement plans available. Requirements vary so applicants should contact the director of admissions for specific requirements in each school. No application fee for graduate school applicants.

Costs Per Year: Tuition varies in each college. Nonresidents must also pay an additional fee which varies by college. $2,820-$4,200 room, $3,600 food and supplies.

Collegiate Environment: The Center's 55-acre urban campus includes a top research hospital, a Level 1 trauma center, a major Veterans Administration facility, and half a dozen oustanding private hospitals and specialty clinics. The campus library houses over 163,700 volumes. There is dormitory space for 454 students on campus. Various forms of financial assistance are available and 80% of the student body receives financial aid.

Community Environment: See University of Memphis.

UNIVERSITY OF THE SOUTH   *(J-10)*
735 University Avenue
Sewanee, Tennessee 37383-1000
Tel: (615) 598-1238; (800) 522-2234; Fax: (615) 598-1667

Description: This formerly men's university was founded in 1857 as a Christian institution owned by 28 dioceses of the Episcopal Church. The university began admitting qualified women students to the College of Arts and Sciences in September 1969. Enrollment is purposely limited. University of the South is a unique blend of Oxford-Cambridge traditions and classical learning. Seniors take comprehensive examinations in their majors as part of graduation requirements, and students live by an Honor Code. The institution is accredited by the Southern Association of Colleges and Schools. The Bachelor of Arts and Bachelor of Science degrees are granted. Graduate degrees conferred include the Master of Divinity (M.Div.), Master of Sacred Theology, Doctor of Ministry, Master of Theological Studies and Licentiate in Theology. The university operates on the early semester system and offers one summer term. Special programs include Business, the Toyota Internship Program, Environmental Science, Pre-Law, Pre-Medical, Pre-Dental, Pre-Veterinary, study abroad, 3/2 Engineering, teacher certification and Pre-Peace Corps.

The 3/2 Engineering program utilizes the engineering schools of Columbia University, Rensselaer Polytechnic Institute, Vanderbilt University, and Washington University of St. Louis. Special educational opportunities include the St. Catherine's Island ecology program and the Oak Ridge Semester, which allows juniors to conduct research under the supervision of a scientist at Oak Ridge National Laboratories. Internships in Public Affairs and Economics are also available. Study abroad is encouraged, and opportunities include summer programs at St. John's College, Oxford University, and University of London, and a semester or year at the Institute of European Studies. To be recommended, students must have a cumulative GPA of 2.5. Enrollment includes 1,195 full-time and 18 part-time undergraduates and 85 graduates. A faculty of 108, 94% with earned Doctorates and 25 part-time gives a faculty-student ratio of 1-11.

Entrance Requirements: High school graduation; completion of 15 units including 4 English, 3-4 mathematics (algebra I, II, and geometry), 2 foreign language, 2 laboratory science, and 2 social science (1 history); SAT or ACT required; GRE required for graduate studies; 3 letters of recommendation and interview required; early admission, early decision, advanced placement, and delayed admission plans available; $40 application fee.

Costs Per Year: $15,350 tuition; $4,020 room and board; $175 student fees.

Collegiate Environment: The campus consists of more than 10,000 acres with 42 modern and traditional buildings. Housing is guaranteed for all students. Dormitories house 1,060 men and women. Fraternities house 12 men. 124 students are accommodated off campus in rental housing. French, German, and Spanish language houses are available. The university library contains 443,463 volumes, 2,628 periodicals, 194,443 microforms, and 5,789 audiovisual materials. A geographically diverse student body is sought and midyear students are accepted. 67% of students applying for admission are accepted and 98% of the freshmen returned for a second year on campus. Merit scholarships are awarded to 50 freshmen. The middle 50% ranges of scores for entering freshmen were SAT 510-610 verbal, 550-650 math, 1060-1260 combined; ACT 25-29 composite. 45% of the current class receives some form of financial assistance. All undergraduate students with documented need are aided. More than 70% of the senior class continued on to graduate school.

Community Environment: Sewanee is on a plateau area. It has an average temperature of 57 degrees and an average rainfall of 58 inches. Summer nights are cool and there is some snow in the winter. Churches, a hospital and clinic, and several civic and service organizations are a part of the community. Job opportunities are limited. Seventeen lakes in the surrounding area provide facilities for a number of sports, swimming, boating, fishing, and skating. Other activities are hunting, camping, mountain climbing, golf and tennis. There are many tourist attractions in this area.

VANDERBILT UNIVERSITY   *(G-8)*
2305 West End Avenue
Nashville, Tennessee 37203-1700
Tel: (615) 322-2561; Fax: (615) 343-7765

Description: An independent, privately-supported university which was founded in 1873 and opened its doors for classes in 1875. The university includes a liberal arts college and eight other graduate and professional schools. The degrees offered include undergraduate and graduate level as well as Juris Doctor, Doctor of Medicine, and Doctor of Divinity, Master of Business Administration, and Master of Science. The University is accredited by the Southern Association of Colleges and Schools. The university operates on the semester system and offers 3 summer terms. Army and Navy ROTC programs are offered on campus. Opportunities for foreign study include programs in France, England, Germany, Spain, Israel, China, and Japan. These programs are available in the junior or senior year. Vanderbilt offers a semester of study in Washington, D.C., and an exchange program with Howard University is available. Enrollment is 10,088 students with a faculty of 1,733 full-time giving a faculty-student ratio of 1:8 (undergraduate).

Entrance Requirements: High school graduation; completion of 15 units including 4 English, 3 mathematics, 2 foreign language, 1 social studies, and 2 science; SAT (preferred) and/or ACT required. 3 Achievement Tests required by January (except Blair School of Music which requires only 2 Achivement Tests. Early admission, early deci-

sion, delayed admission, and advanced placement programs available; application fee $50.

Costs Per Year: $18,860 tuition; $6,786 room and board; $272 required fees.

Collegiate Environment: Located on a 330-acre campus. The library houses over 2 million volumes, 16,357 periodicals, 150,064 titles on microform, 20,731 record/tapes/cds, and 1,547 CD-ROM units. There are dormitory facilities for 4,575 undergraduates. More than 90% of students live on campus. About half of all undergraduates are members of the 12 sororities and 17 fraternities which are non-residential. Over 51% of the current student body received some form of financial assistance in the current year. There are 1,400 scholarships awarded on campus. A total of 412 merit scholarships are available, each averaging $13,038. 58% of the students applying for admission were accepted. Almost 91% of the previous freshman returned to campus for the second year. Midyear transfers are accepted. Average high school standing of the freshman class: 78% in the top 10%, 94% in the top 25%, 100% in the top 50%. Average SAT scores range between 25th and 75th percentiles, between 1,120 and 1,310.

Community Environment: A metropolitan area of over half a million people. Nashville, Tennessee's capital city, is one of the South's foremost centers for banking, insurance, and publishing, a medical referral center for the region, and the home of the American music industry. Ranking high among American cities in "quality of life" surveys, it offers four-star restaurants, sprawling shopping complexes, and entertainment to suit all tastes. Entertainment and cultural opportunities are rich and varied. Sound studios in Nashville create the music of America. Contemporary bands as well as country music artists record here. Music clubs of all types abound throughout the city. The Tennessee Repertory Theatre, Community Concerts, Broadway touring companies, classical ensembles and the Nashville Symphony Orchestra, and the Circle Players perform regularly. The Tennessee Performing Arts Center continually hosts major orchestral and theatrical groups from throughout the nation. Among the attractions that bring visitors to Nashville each year are the Cheekwood Botanical Gardens and Fine Arts Center, the Cumberland Museum and Science Center, the Tennessee State Museum, Opryland, U.S.A. and Printer's Alley.

VOLUNTEER STATE COMMUNITY COLLEGE   *(F-9)*
Nashville Pike
Gallatin, Tennessee 37066
Tel: (615) 452-8600; Admissions: (615) 452-8600 X 466; Fax: (615) 230-3577

Description: This publicly supported, two-year college was established in 1970 and is accredited by the Southern Association of Colleges and Schools and by respective professional institutions. It operates on the semester system and offers two summer sessions. Enrollment includes 2,714 full-time and 3,543 students. A faculty of 114 full-time and 234 part-time gives a faculty-student ratio of 1-18.

Entrance Requirements: Open enrollment policy; high school graduation or equivalent; Completion of 14 units including 4 English, 3 mathematics, 2 laboratory science, 2 foreign language, 1 social studies, 1 visual or performing arts, and 1 U.S. history; ACT required; $5 application fee; early admission, early decision, rolling admission and advanced placement plans available.

Costs Per Year: $966 tuition; $3,762 out-of-state.

Collegiate Environment: The library contains 43,442 volumes, 319 periodicals, 150 microforms and 1,003 recordings. There are no dormitories provided on campus. All of the applicants are accepted, including midyear students. The average composite ACT score of the freshman class was 15.9. 180 scholarships are available.

Community Environment: See Vanderbilt University.

WALTERS STATE COMMUNITY COLLEGE   *(F-16)*
500 South Davy Crockett Parkway
Morristown, Tennessee 37813-6899
Tel: (615) 587-9722

Description: The state-supported community college was authorized by the 1967 General Assembly. Its doors were opened in 1970 as the sixth college of this type to open. The goal of these community colleges is to service areas of the state without access to higher education and provide a school that is not restrictive to high school graduates, but serves an entire community regardless of age. The college operates on the semester system with two summer sessions. It is accredited by the Southern Association of Colleges and Schools, the Accreditation Board for Engineering and Technology, and the National League for Nursing. A recent enrollment included 973 men and 1,522 women full-time, and 1,181 men and 1,751 women part-time. A faculty of 111 full-time and 142 part-time gives a faculty-student ratio of 1-21.

Entrance Requirements: High school graduation or equivalent; ACT or SAT scores required; open enrollment policy; early admission, rolling admission, and advanced placement plans available; application fee $5.

Costs Per Year: $900 tuition; $3,500 out-of-state; $10 student fees.

Collegiate Environment: Located on the southern edge of the city of Morristown, the campus occupies 134 acres of beautifully rolling land at the junction of several major highways, thus providing access to all parts of the state. The library contains 55,923 volumes, 350 periodicals, 490 microforms and 1,104 audiovisual materials. All applicants are accepted including midyear students. 65% of students receive financial aid.

Community Environment: The City of Morristown, centrally located in the college's 10-county service area, has become a market center for the region with the establishment of a new shopping mall as well as a growing industrial center of 113 industries. Farming remains an important part of the local economy with primary crops of light burley tobacco, corn, hay, and wheat. Known as the "City between the lakes," Morristown's area lakes provide for fishing, swimming, hunting, and picknicking. Scenic drives lead to the nearby Great Smoky Mountains, Clinch Mountain, as well as the larger urban areas to both the north and south of the college.

Branch Campuses: Greene County Center, (615) 639-6123; Knox County Extension, (615) 974-6681; Sevier County Center, (615) 453-7720; Cocke County Extension, (615) 623-6631; Claiborne County Extension, 1-(800) 225-4770; Hawkins County Extension, 1-(800) 225-4770 or 392-8044.

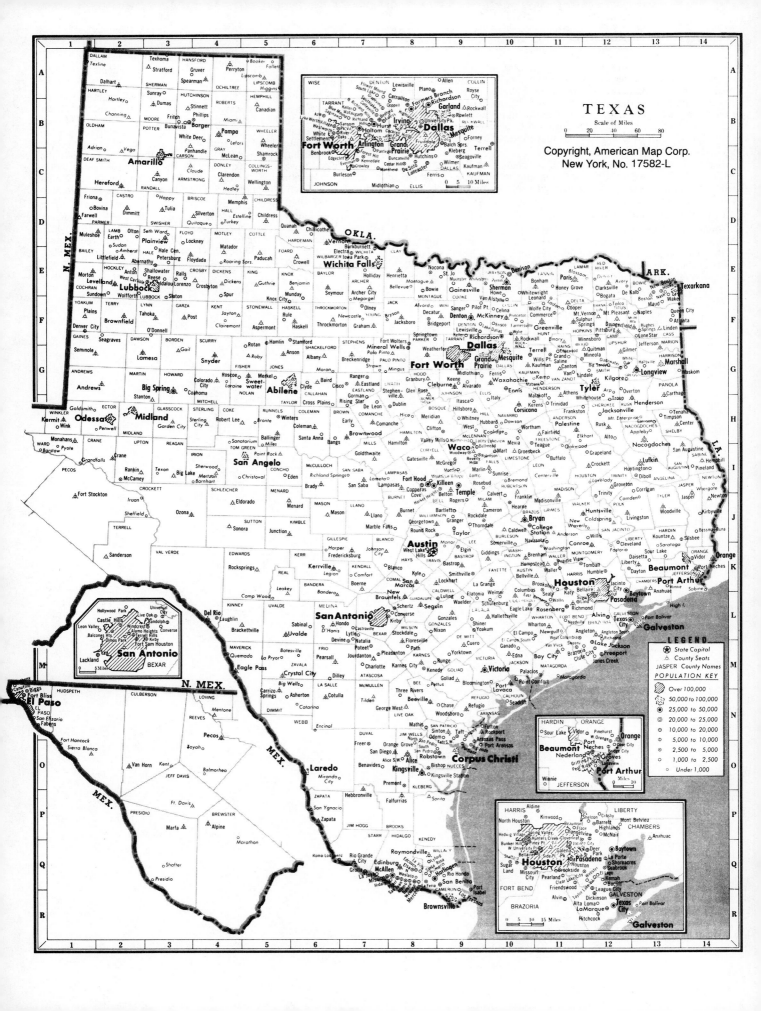

TEXAS

Scale of Miles

0   20   40   60   80

Copyright, American Map Corp.
New York, No. 17582-L

LEGEND

⊛ State Capital
☆ County Seats
JASPER County Names

POPULATION KEY

▨ Over 100,000
⊠ 50,000 to 100,000
◉ 25,000 to 50,000
⊙ 20,000 to 25,000
◎ 10,000 to 20,000
⊚ 5,000 to 10,000
○ 2,500 to 5,000
∘ 1,000 to 2,500
° Under 1,000

TEXAS

ABILENE CHRISTIAN UNIVERSITY   (G-6)
1600 Campus Court
Abilene, Texas 79699
Tel: (915) 674-2000; (800) 888-0228; Fax: (915) 674-2130

Description: Privately supported, coeducational liberal arts college was founded in 1906 for the purpose of educating students for Christian service and leadership throughout the world. The college is accredited by the Southern Association of Colleges and Schools and professionally by numerous accrediting organizations. It is affiliated with the Church of Christ. Enrollment is 4,207 and includes 3,317 full-time and 890 part-time, and 691 graduate students. Faculty includes 174 full-time and 54 part-time members, giving a faculty-student ratio of 1-18. The university operates on the semester system and offers two summer sessions. An academic cooperative plan with Hardin-Simmons University is available for Law Enforcement students and Army ROTC. The Chemistry Department has a cooperative program with Dow Chemical Company. A Nursing program is offered in cooperation with the Abilene Intercollegiate School of Nursing. A study abroad program in France, England or Spain is available. The university awards the Associate, Bachelor, Master, and Doctoral degrees. Daily chapel is required.

Entrance Requirements: Accredited high school graduation with rank in upper 75% of graduating class; completion of 4 English, 2 Mathematics, 2 Laboratory Science, 2 Social Science; ACT required with minimum score of 20; early admission, rolling admission, early decision, delayed admission, midyear admission, and advanced placement plans available; $25 application fee.

Costs Per Year: $7,410 ($247 per cr. hr.) tuition; $3,310 room and board; $300 student fees; $600 estimated additional expenses.

Collegiate Environment: The 208-acre campus has 40 buildings on a site overlooking the city from the northeast, plus a 27 acre residential park with 7 buildings. All single freshman and sophomore students under age 21, except those living with their parents, must live in college residence halls which accommodate 1,032 men and 1,225 women. Junior and senior students may live off-campus with permission of the Dean of Students. A 200-unit on-campus apartment is also available for upperclassmen. The library contains 1,023,088 volumes, 1,800 periodicals, 427,739 microforms, and 159,610 audiovisual materials. 81% of students applying for admission are accepted. Financial aid is available and 80% of the current student body receives financial assistance.

Community Environment: Population 110,000. The buffalo lured settlers to this west Texas city and the railroad encouraged them to stay. Today, this community serves the agricultural, marketing and oil interests of the area. It is the site of Dyess Air Force Base. Local manufacturing includes airplane parts, cottonseed oil products, cattle feed, valves, and bakery products. The cost of living is low. Abilene's unemployment rate and crime rate are among the lowest in the state. The climate is high and dry. Transportation to and in the city includes airlines, bus lines, taxis, and major highways. Local community services include churches representing 21 denominations, two hospitals and several clinics, West Texas Rehabilitation Center, Abilene State School for the Mentally Retarded, and various civic, fraternal and veterans' organizations. There are several art and history museums, YMCA, YWCA, community theatre, philharmonic orchestra, three TV stations, and seven radio stations. Recreational facilities include swimming, boating, fishing, water sports, golf courses, zoo, roller rink, tennis, and bowling alleys. Part-time employment is available.

Branch Campuses: The Bible Department offers courses at Bible Chairs located in the following cities: Alberquerque, NM; College Station, TX; San Antonio, TX; San Angelo, TX; and San Marcos, TX.

ALVIN COMMUNITY COLLEGE   (L-12)
3110 Mustang Road
Alvin, Texas 77511-4898
Tel: (713) 331-6111; Admissions: (713) 388-4636; Fax: (713) 388-4929

Description: Publicly supported, coeducational, two-year comprehensive Community College offering educational opportunities beyond the high school level and accredited by the Southern Association of Colleges and Schools. Provides instructional programs designed to prepare students to enter the upper division of senior colleges and universities or to make immediate entry into a career field. The college grants certificates and Associate degrees. It operates on the semester system and offers two summer sessions. Enrollment is 1,345 full-time and 2,305 part-time students. A faculty of 93 full-time and 136 part-time gives a faculty-student ratio of 1-16.

Entrance Requirements: High school graduation; GED accepted; open enrollment policy; early admission, early decision, midyear admission and advanced placement plans available.

Costs Per Year: $567 in-district tuition; $814 out-of-district; $1,480 out-of-state.

Collegiate Environment: The campus of this well-maintained, modern, community college, consists of 15 buildings situated on 113 acres. There are more than 30,000 volumes in the learning resources center. In 1988, the campus installed a comprehensive computer network. In addition to state-of-the-art instructional labs, students are encouraged to use the open microcomputer facilities for completion of homework. Local area networks and Internet are part of the current computer environment. 92% of applicants are accepted. 377 scholarships are available and 30% of the students receive some form of financial aid.

Community Environment: Population 22,000, Alvin is a suburban community located 30 minutes from Houston, Galveston, and NASA. The city is served by a private airport, railroad, bus line, and State Routes 6 and 35. There are churches of major denominations, a public library, and hospital. Public recreation includes a theatre, bowling, fishing, and boating. Major civic, fraternal, and veteran's organizations are active in Alvin.

AMARILLO COLLEGE   (C-3)
P.O. Box 447
Amarillo, Texas 79178
Tel: (806) 371-5030; Fax: (806) 371-5066

Description: The publicly supported, coeducational junior college is accredited by the Southern Association of Colleges and Schools. It was founded in 1929. The college operates on the semester system and offers two summer terms. Technical and vocational courses, freshman and sophomore transfer courses, and continuing education are available. Enrollment (degree programs only) is 6,800 students. A faculty of 280 full-time and part-time gives a faculty-student ratio of 1-23. The college grants the Certificate and the Associate degrees.

Entrance Requirements: Open enrollment policy; non-high school graduates may be admitted on the basis of written examination or satisfactory GED test score; rolling admission, midyear admission and early admission plans available.

Costs Per Year: Total yearly cost: $543 district-resident; $759 non-district state resident; $1,642 out-of-state.

Collegiate Environment: 56 acres and 27 buildings comprise the three campuses of the college. The library contains 74,828 volumes, 519 periodicals, 12,350 microforms and 6,162 recordings. The college Union is the center of social activities. It has a snack bar and private dining facilities, and game areas. There is no on-campus housing. The college offers 200 scholarships annually. 45% of the students receive some form of financial aid. About 55% of the previous freshman class returned to this campus for the sophomore year. The average scores of the entering freshman class were SAT 444 verbal, 473 math, and ACT 17.9 composite. The college awarded 113 Certificates and 505 Associate degrees during the school year.

Community Environment: Population 165,425. Situated on the high plains of the Texas Panhandle, Amarillo is the capital of the oil and gas industry. Pipelines from adjacent fields extend as far as the east coast. The average temperature ranges from 37.4 degrees in winter to 76 degrees in summer. The community is provided transportation by rail, bus, and airlines, as well as five national highways and one state highway. Amarillo has many churches representing various faiths, public libraries, museums, several hospitals, a YMCA and YWCA, and various civic, fraternal, and veteran's organizations. Part-time employment is available. Off-campus housing is plentiful.

AMBASSADOR COLLEGE   *(G-12)*
Big Sandy, Texas 75755
Tel: (903) 636-2000; Admissions: (903) 636-2190; Fax: (903) 636-2375

Description: This privately supported, coeducational, liberal arts college was founded in 1947 by the Worldwide Church of God. It is accredited by the Southern Association of Colleges and Schools. It operates on the semester system and offers one summer session. The college grants undergraduate degrees. Theology is a required study at this school. Enrollment includes 1,111 full-time and 61 part-time students. A faculty of 68 full-time and 7 part-time gives a faculty-student ratio of 1-16. The college has overseas projects in several countries.

Entrance Requirements: High school graduation with rank in upper half of class; completion of 16 units including 3 English, 2 mathematics, 1 social studies, and 1 science; rolling admission, midyear admission and advanced placement plans available; $35 application fee.

Costs Per Year: $3,150 tuition; $3,000 room and board; $500 student fees.

Collegiate Environment: The library contains 144,000 volumes, 1,500 periodicals, 37,000 microforms and 46,500 audiovisual materials. Student housing is available for 1,077 men and women. Approximately 95% of the applicants meet the requirements and 68% are accepted. All students receive financial aid.

Community Environment: The college is situated on a beautiful 347-acre campus in the heavily forested "Piney Woods" of East Texas. The college is located on U.S. Highway 80 and is just outside the community of Big Sandy. The campus is 20 miles west of Longview, 23 miles north of Tyler and 100 miles east of Dallas.

ANGELINA COLLEGE   *(I-3)*
P.O. Box 1768
Lufkin, Texas 75902
Tel: (409) 639-1301; Fax: (409) 639-4299

Description: Founded in 1968, this publicly supported coeducational junior college is accredited by the Southern Association of Colleges and Schools. It offers preparation for senior college, occupational programs, general and continuing education programs, and student personnel and guidance programs. It grants the Associate degree. It operates on the semester system and offers two summer sessions. Enrollment is 4,006 students. A faculty of 95 full-time and 90 part-time gives a faculty-student ratio of 1-21.

Entrance Requirements: Accredited high school graduation or GED required; application for admission and high school transcript required; early admission, early decision, deferred admission, midyear admission, rolling admission, open admission, and advanced placement plans available; no application fee.

Costs Per Year: $550 tuition county resident; $700 state-resident; $950 out-of-state resident; $2,600 room and board; $132 student fees.

Collegiate Environment: The 138-acre campus contains 14 buildings including the library of 41,000 volumes, 325 periodicals, 8,200 microforms and 1,700 audiovisual materials. 165 scholarships are available including 120 fro freshmen. About 40% of students receive some form of financial aid. Approximately 99% of students applying for admission are accepted.

Community Environment: Population 33,000. Lufkin derives most of its income from the lumber and paper-making indutries, two iron

foundries and one chromium corporation. This urban community is headquarters for four national forests. The climate is temperate and mild. Lufkin is served by three railroad lines, airlines, and U.S. Routes 59 and 69. The community has a public library, 20 churches, three hospitals, and many civic, fraternal, and veteran's organizations. Part-time employment opportunities are unlimited. Local recreation includes theatres, hunting, fishing, boating, nearby Rayburn Lake, baseball, and swimming pools.

Branch Campuses: College offers credit classes at seven off-campus teaching centers in East Texas, which include Crockett, San Augustine, Livingston, Jasper, Woodville, Groveton, Terral Prison Unit and Eastham Prison Unit.

ANGELO STATE UNIVERSITY   *(I-5)*
2601 W. Ave. N.
San Angelo, Texas 76904
Tel: (915) 942-2041; Fax: (915) 942-2078

Description: Publicly supported coeducational liberal arts college founded in 1928 and accredited by the Southern Association of Colleges and Schools. Enrollment includes 4,382 full-time and 1,499 part-time undergraduate students, and 395 graduate students. A faculty of 213 full-time, 31 part-time gives a faculty-student ratio of 1-25. The university operates on the early semester system and offers two summer terms. Undergraduate programs in the arts and sciences, teacher training, and business administration are offered; and pre-professional training in the fields of dentistry, engineering, law, and medicine. The college grants the Associate, Bachelor and Master degrees.

Entrance Requirements: High school graduation with rank in upper quarter of class; ACT or SAT required; GED accepted, entrance plans: early admission, early decision, and midyear admission.

Costs Per Year: $1,694 tuition state resident; $5,984 tuition out-of-state resident; $3,732 room and board.

Collegiate Environment: The 268-acre campus has 34 buildings including the library of 236,352 volumes and periodicals, 286,907 microforms, and 2,908 audiovisual materials. There are housing accommodations for 1660 men and women, and 84 families. The college welcomes a geographically diverse student body and does accept midyear students. Freshmen classes begin in September and in January. 68% of applicants are accepted. Almost 92% of a recent freshman class graduated in the top half of their high school class, with 58% in the top quarter. About 63% of a recent freshman class returned to this campus for their sophomore year. The average scores of the entering freshman class were ACT 21 composite, SAT 923 combined. 1,161 scholarships are available, including 907 academic and 250 need-based. 53% of students receive some form of financial aid. The college awarded 146 Associate, 798 Bachelor and 98 Master degrees to the graduating class.

Community Environment: Population 80,000. San Angelo is an attractive city located in the heart of West Texas ranch country. San Angelo and the surrounding area provide a readily accessible social and physical environment for cultural and recreational activities so essential to the university community. Three nearby lakes make water sports a popular attraction among students and those living in San Angelo.

ARLINGTON BAPTIST COLLEGE   *(B-7)*
3001 W. Division
Arlington, Texas 76012
Tel: (817) 461-8741

Description: Privately supported coeducational Bible college supported by the World Baptist Fellowship. The semester system is used and two summer terms are offered. Enrollment includes 133 full-time and 46 part-time students. The faculty consists of 5 full-time and 16 part-time members. The faculty-student ratio is 1-9. The college grants the Bachelor of Arts, Bachelor of Science, and Diplomas of Bible.

Entrance Requirements: High school graduation; completion of 16 units including 3 English, 2 mathematics, 2 soical science, and 1 science; under certain circumstances non-high school graduates are considered; $15 application fee.

Costs Per Year: $1,950 tuition; $1,320 room and board; $80 student fees.

Collegiate Environment: The 55-acre campus has nine buildings. The library contains 24,533 volumes, 126 periodicals, and 876 audio-visual materials and there are dormitories for 100 men and 100 women. Approximately 98% of students applying for admission meet the requirements and are accepted. Freshman are admitted in August, January and May and the college welcomes a geographically diverse student body. 34% of students receive some form of financial assistance. Over 49% of a recent freshman class returned to this campus for their sophomore year. The school awarded 33 Bachelor degrees to a recent graduating class.

Community Environment: See University of Texas at Arlington.

AUSTIN COLLEGE *(E-10)*
900 North Grand Avenue P.O. Box 1177
Sherman, Texas 75091-1177
Tel: (903) 813-2000; (800) 442-5363

Description: Privately supported, coeducational liberal arts college is affiliated with the Presbyterian Church (U.S.A.). It is accredited by the Southern Association of Colleges and Schools and the American Chemical Society. 3-2 plans are available for engineering students, both on campus and with other universities. A semester of studying in Washington, D.C., semester internships, and off-campus January term courses are offered. The college participates in the Institute for European Studies' study abroad program. It grants the Bachelor and Master degrees. The college operates on the 4-1-4 system and offers one summer session. Enrollment includes 1,049 full-time, 17 part-time undergraduate, and 57 graduate students. A faculty of 85 full-time and 15 part-time gives an undergraduate faculty-student ratio of 1-13.

Entrance Requirements: Accredited high school graduation in upper 50% of graduating class; completion of minimum 15 units recommended including 4 English, 3 mathematics, 2 foreign language, 3 science, 2 social science, 1 art; SAT or ACT required; early admission, midyear admission, rolling admission, and advanced placement plans available; Dec. 1 and Feb. 1 application deadlines, then rolling; $25 application fee.

Costs Per Year: $12,070 tuition; $4,524 room and board; $125 student fees; $1,412 average expenses.

Collegiate Environment: The 60-acre campus is located in a residential area of northeast Sherman. There are 30 buildings. Wynne Chapel is the center of religious life on the campus and all buildings are air-conditioned. Abell Library has a collection of 408,276 volumes, receives 899 periodicals, has 99,438 microforms, 700 audiovisual materials, and is a depository for U.S. Government documents. Dormitory facilities accommodate 951 students. There is also a small apartment complex which can house up to 75 students. The campus also includes a language laboratory, computer center, communication center (with extensive media capabilities), art and music studios, a modern science building with excellent physics, chemistry and biology laboratories, and extensive recreation facilities which provide for swimming, racquet ball, weight training, and tennis, as well as intercollegiate and intramural sports. Approximately 85% of applicants are accepted. 90% of students receive some form of financial aid.

Community Environment: Sherman, population 33,000, is a retail trade and industrial center located in north central Texas 60 miles north of Dallas. The climate is mild and temperate. The average annual temperature is 64 degrees. Two bus lines, and U.S. Highways 82 and 75 serve the area. Community services include a library, two hospitals, two shopping malls, and various civic and fraternal organizations. Local recreation includes three theatres, golf, bowling, skating, hunting, and on Lake Texoma with a 1,250 mile shoreline, fishing, swimming, water skiing, and boating. Part-time employment is available.

AUSTIN COMMUNITY COLLEGE *(K-8)*
5930 Middle Fiskville Road
Austin, Texas 78752
Tel: (512) 483-7504; Fax: (512) 483-7791

Description: This publicly supported coeducational community college was founded in 1972. It is accredited by the Southern Association of Colleges and Schools. It operates on the semester system and offers three summer sessions. Enrollment is 6,336 full-time and

18,850 part-time students. A faculty of 265 full-time and 1,069 part-time gives a faculty-student ratio of 1-18. The college offers an associate degree and has a continuing education program.

Entrance Requirements: High school graduate or equivalent; open enrollment, early admission and early decision plans available; CLEP accepted.

Costs Per Year: $608 tuition; $660 out-of-district; $2,300 out-of-state; $380 student fees (based on 12 hours for fall and spring semesters, and 8 hours for summer semester full-time).

Collegiate Environment: The campus is located in Austin, the capital of Texas. The library contains 88,424 volumes, 1,399 periodicals, and 192 microforms. There are no dormitory facilities. Midyear students are admitted.

Community Environment: See University of Texas at Austin.

AUSTIN PRESBYTERIAN THEOLOGICAL SEMINARY *(K-8)*
100 East 27th St.
Austin, Texas 78705
Tel: (512) 472-6736; (800) 777-6127; Fax: (512) 479-0738

Description: Privately supported, graduate-level, coeducational seminary related to the Synod of the Sun and the Presbyterian Church (U.S.A.). The seminary is accredited by the Southern Association of Colleges and Schools and by the Association of Theological Schools in the United States and Canada. The Master of Divinity program offers basic preparation for service in the ministry, while the program leading to the degree of Doctor of Ministry is designed primarily for ministers in service. The degree of Master of Arts is a two-year graduate degree and is designed for persons seeking coursework in general religious studies. There are shared courses with the Episcopal Theological Seminary of the Southwest, and the Lutheran Theological Program of the Southwest. Study abroad is during the January term to Central America, the Holy Land, or Europe. The seminary operates on the 4-1-4 system and offers one summer session. Enrollment includes 300 students with a faculty of 20, giving a faculty-student ratio of 1-9.

Entrance Requirements: Baccalaureate degree from accredited college or university; active membership in some branch of the Christian Church; 2.5 GPA; personal interview; deferred admission and rolling admission plans; $25 application fee.

Costs Per Year: $4,760 tuition; $3,032 room and board; $85 student fees.

Collegiate Environment: There are eight buildings on the 12-acre campus. The Stitt library contains 133,000 volumes. Housing accommodations are available for 28 single students and 63 families. The seminary welcomes a geographically diverse student body. About 90% of applicants meet the requirements and are accepted. Financial aid is available, and 77% of students receive some form financial aid.

Community Environment: See University of Texas at Austin.

BAYLOR COLLEGE OF DENTISTRY *(G-10)*
3302 Gaston Avenue
Dallas, Texas 75246
Tel: (214) 828-8230

Description: A private, nonprofit, nonsectarian, coeducational college of dentistry, founded in 1905. It is fully accredited by the Commission on Dental Accreditation, a specialized accrediting body recognized by the Council on Postsecondary Accreditation and the U.S. Department of Education. Enrollment includes 428 graduate and undergraduate students. There is a faculty of 106 full-time and 128 part-time. The college operates on the quarter system and offers one summer session. The college offers work leading to the degrees of Doctor of Dental Surgery, Bachelor of Science in Dental Hygiene, and graduate work leading to the degrees of Master of Science, in Dental Specialities and certain basic sciences, and postgraduate professional certificates.

Entrance Requirements: Completion of 60 or more semester hours of college-level preprofessional work with C+ average or better; completion of at least one year's work in English, physics, biology, inorganic chemistry, and organic chemistry; comparative anatomy and embryology are strongly recommended; American Dental Association Admissions Test required; $35 application fee.

Costs Per Year: $5,400 state-resident tuition; $16,200 out-of-state.

Collegiate Environment: No dormitories are available. The library has a collection of 35,000 volumes. The Caruth School of Dental Hygiene is operated by the College of Dentistry. First-year classes begin in September and 97% of the previous first year class returned to this campus for the second year. Special financial aid is available and 70% of the first-year class receives some form of assistance.

Community Environment: See Dallas Christian College.

BAYLOR COLLEGE OF MEDICINE   *(K-12)*
One Baylor Plaza
Houston, Texas 77030
Tel: (713) 798-4841

Description: Privately supported coeducational medical college was formerly named Baylor University College of Medicine. It is operated by its own Board of Trustees and is no longer a part of the Baylor University or the Baptist General Convention of Texas. The college is accredited by the Southern Association of Colleges and Schools and by the American Medical Association and the Association of American Medical Colleges Liaison Committee. Enrollment is 656 students. The faculty consists of 1,304 full-time and 117 part-time members. Grants M.D. degree; graduate work with programs leading to the Master of Science and the Doctor of Philosophy degrees are offered in various departments.

Entrance Requirements: Completion of 90 undergraduate semester hours (or equivalent number of quarter hours) at a fully accredited college or university in the United States. All candidates for admission are required to take the MCAT test in April or August of the year prior to anticipated enrollment. A baccalaureate degree and satisfactory scores on the GRE are minimum requirements for graduate school. 90 undergraduate semester hours of prescribed college work, inclusive of course requirements, is the minimum requirement for the Physician Assistant Master of Science Program. The Master of Science in Nurse Anesthesia requires a Bachelors degree and the GRE. Early decision and advanced placement plans available; $35 application fee for Medical School, $30 application fee for Graduate School. Application deadline is Nov. 1.

Costs Per Year: $6,550 resident tuition; $15,487 nonresident tuition.

Collegiate Environment: Baylor College of Medicine is in the Texas Medical Center, a complex of 40 institutions and their various divisions located on a 223 acre tract in Houston's South Main area. The Jesse H. Jones Library contain 204,000 volumes and is part of the Center. The college offers scholarships annually.

Community Environment: See University of Houston.

BAYLOR UNIVERSITY   *(I-9)*
P.O. Box 97008
Waco, Texas 76798-7008
Tel: (817) 755-1011; (800) 229-5678; Admissions: (817) 755-1811

Description: Privately supported, coeducational university consists of 6 colleges and schools located in Waco and Dallas, Texas, as follows: College of Arts and Sciences, Hankamer School of Business, School of Education, School of Law, School of Music, and School of Nursing. It has a Baptist affiliation, and its schools and departments are accredited by the Southern Association of Colleges and Schools. A program of liberal arts and professional education is offered, and as a Christian institution, the university strives to integrate the essence of the Christian faith in its whole process of education. The university grants the Bachelor, Professional, Master's and Doctorate degrees. It operates on the semester system and offers two summer terms. Enrollment includes 9,822 full-time and 551 part-time undergraduates and 1,867 graduate students. A faculty of 599 full-time and 56 part-time gives a faculty-student ratio of 1-18.

Entrance Requirements: Accredited high school graduation with rank in upper half (preferably top one-fourth) of graduating class; completion of 16 units including 4 English, 3 mathematics, 2 science, 2 units of 1 foreign language, SAT required (ACT can be substituted); early admission, rolling admission, and advanced placement available; $25 application fee.

Costs Per Year: $7,740 tuition; $4,140 room and board; $654 student fees.

Collegiate Environment: The 428-acre campus has more than 60 buildings. There are no restrictions on housing, although it is recommended that freshmen live on campus. Housing accommodations are available for 3,602 students. Those desiring campus housing must sign a nine-month contract (both fall and spring semesters). Financial aid is available and 60% of students receive some form of assistance. The libraries are priority learning resources at Baylor University and the book collections of over 1,500,000 volumes cover every phase of the college curriculum. The library regularly receives more than 9,200 journals and magazines. Most students applying are in the top quarter of their high school class and have a combined SAT score of 1,000 or above, or an ACT of 25 or above.

Community Environment: The campus adjoins the historic Brazos River in Waco, a Central Texas city of 110,000 people. The climate is temperate with a mean annual temperature of 67.4 degrees, and an average rainfall of 35 inches. Waco is reached by airlines, railroad, and bus lines. There are almost 200 churches of various faiths, public hospitals and a veteran's hospital, excellent libraries, and convenient shopping facilities in the area. Nineteen civic clubs and many fraternal organizations are active in Waco. Local recreation includes boating, swimming, fishing, picnicking, bowling, tennis, parks, a zoo, and Lake Waco. Part-time employment is available for students.

BEE COUNTY COLLEGE   *(N-8)*
3800 Charco Road
Beeville, Texas 78102
Tel: (512) 358-3130

Description: This publicly supported, coeducational junior college was founded in 1965. It is accredited by the Southern Association of Colleges and Schools, and grants the Certificate and Association degree. It offers the first two years of college degree programs, technical and vocational courses, and general continuing education. The college operates on the semester system and offers two summer sessions. Enrollment is 1,461 full-time and 1,059 part-time students. A faculty of 84 full-time and 27 part-time gives a faculty-student ratio of 1-22.

Entrance Requirements: High school graduation or equivalent; placement examination.

Costs Per Year: $328 tuition district or county resident; $520 state resident; $1,000 out-of-state resident; $2,080 room and board; $706 approximate additional expenses.

Collegiate Environment: The 100-acre campus is located one mile north of the city. There are 14 buildings on the campus including the 42,018-volume library and dormitory facilities for 80 men and 80 women. All of the students applying for admission are accepted and 40% of the freshman class returned for the sophomore year. 200 scholarships are avialable and 60% of the current student body receives financial aid. Midyear students are admitted.

Community Environment: Population 14,865. Beeville is the county seat of Bee County. The community is located 60 miles from the Gulf Coast, and 60 miles from Corpus Christi.

BLINN COLLEGE   *(K-10)*
902 College Avenue
Brenham, Texas 77833
Tel: (409) 830-4140

Description: This publicly supported, coeducational junior college was founded in 1883 as the first county district junior college in Texas. It is accredited by the Southern Association of Colleges and Schools. Enrollment is 4,982 full-time and 3,733 part-time students. A faculty of 125 full-time and 236 part-time provides an overall faculty-student ratio of 1-25. The semester system is used and two summer terms are offered. The college offers two-year transfer programs and terminal education and grants the Associate degree.

Entrance Requirements: SAT or ACT recommended; Texas Academic Skills Program Test (TASP) required; non-high school graduates 18 years of age or older may be admitted upon individual approval; rolling admission, early admission and advanced placement plans available.

Costs Per Year: $750 tuition state resident; $2,400 tuition out-of-state resident; $2,516 room and board; $600 student fees.

Collegiate Environment: The 100-acre campus is located at the intersection of the Santa Fe and the Southern Pacific Railways. There are 31 buildings including the W. L. Moody Library containing 120,000 volumes. Housing accommodations are available for 800 men and women. Approximately 98% of the students applying for admission are accepted and 50% of the freshman class returns for the sophomore year. Financial aid is available and 50% of the current student body receives financial assistance.

Community Environment: Population 10,900. Brenham is a suburban community enjoying temperate climate. The city has libraries, and churches of various denominations. Railroad, bus lines, and major highways serve the area. Part-time employment is available for students. There are motels and apartment houses available for student housing. Brenham has hospitals, and civic and fraternal organizations are active within the area. Local recreation includes theaters, hunting, fishing, golf, and sports.

BRAZOSPORT COLLEGE *(M-12)*
500 College Drive
Lake Jackson, Texas 77566
Tel: (409) 266-3000; Admissions: (409) 266-3216

Description: This publicly supported, coeducational community College opened its doors to its first class in l968. It is accredited by the Southern Association of Colleges and Schools. The College awards Certificates upon completion of vocational courses, such as Machine Tools and Office Education, and grants the Associate degree. An Adult education program is also offered. The college operates on the semester system and offers two summer sessions. Enrollment includes 837 full-time and 2,352 part-time students. A faculty of 61 full-time and 100 part-time gives a faculty-student ratio of 1-17.

Entrance Requirements: Open enrollment policy; high school graduation required for degree courses; under certain circumstances non-high school graduates are considered; early admission, early decision, rolling admission, midyear admission, and advanced placement plans available.

Costs Per Year: $4760 district resident tuition and fees; $620 county resident tuition and fees; $2,120 nonresident tuition and fees.

Collegiate Environment: The college is situated on 156 acres of beautiful, naturally landscaped land and has a unique layout in that all of its 300,000 square feet of floor space is under one roof. The library collection numbers 51,225 hardbound volumes. Freshman classes begin in September and January with midyear students accepted. Numerous scholarships are available and 26% of students receive some form of financial aid.

Community Environment: Population 25,000, Lake Jackson is located 50 miles south of Houston. Major cities in the district are Lake Jackson and Freeport (population 17,000), located on a stretch of beach on the Gulf Coast. The area is serviced by rail, four major highways, commuter planes, and good local bus service. Recreation in the area includes fishing, surfing, swimming, and other water sports in the Gulf of Mexico.

CENTRAL TEXAS COLLEGE *(I-8)*
P.O. Box 1800
Killeen, Texas 76540-9990
Tel: (817) 526-1104; (800) 792-3348; Admissions: (817) 526-1104; Fax: (817) 526-1481

Description: Publicly supported, coeducational junior college opened its doors in 1967 and on December 12th of that year received its greatest honor when the 36th president of the United States, Lyndon Baines Johnson, dedicated the college. The college is accredited by te Southern Association of Colleges and Schools and operates on the semester system with two summer terms. Enrollment includes 2,277 full-time and 6,689 part-time students. A faculty of 118 full-time and 217 part-time gives a student-faculty ratio of 1-27. The first two years of college work are offered for students planning to transfer to senior colleges or universities; vocational, technical, and general education courses are also available. Special programs include technical & vocational courses offered to military personnel in Europe and the Far East. The college grants the Certificate and the Associate degree.

Entrance Requirements: Open enrollment policy; ACT or SAT accepted; rolling admission, delayed admission, advanced placement, early admission, early decision plans available;

Costs Per Year: $700 tuition state resident; $2,100 tuition out-of-state resident; $3,400 room and board, $50 student fees.

Collegiate Environment: The college is made up of 21 buildings on 560 acres and is completely surrounded by Fort Hood and adjacent to Killeen Base, and Robert Gray Army Airfield. Residence halls accomodate 328 students. The library holdings include 74,159 volumes, 423 periodicals, 132,900 microfilms, and 667 audiovisual materials. All students applying for admission are accepted. Scholarships are available and 28% of students receive some form of financial aid. Freshman classes begin in September, January, June and July.

Community Environment: Population 135,000. Killeen is considered an outstanding recreation area with beautiful lakes and streams located nearby. The climate is temperate. All types of transportation are accessible. The community has shopping centers, medical facilities, and churches of many different faiths. Part-time employment is available.

CISCO JUNIOR COLLEGE *(G-7)*
Route 3, Box 3
Cisco, Texas 76437
Tel: (817) 442-2567

Description: This publicly supported, coeducational junior college was established in 1940 as a partially state-supported institution by farsighted citizens of Cisco; now, both the state and Eastland County provide funds. It is accredited by the Southern Association of Colleges and Schools. Two-year transfer, vocational, and continuing education programs are offered. Enrollment is 483 men and 432 women full-time, 442 men and 615 women part-time. The school operates on the semester system and offers 4 summer sessions. A faculty of 55 full-time and 43 part-time gives a faculty-student ratio of 1-20. The college grants Certificates and Associate degrees.

Entrance Requirements: Open door policy; degree candidates require approved high school graduation with completion of 15 units including 3 English, 2 mathematics, 1 science, 2 social science, and 1 foreign language; GED may substitute for 15 units; early decision, rolling admission, delayed admission and advanced placement plans available.

Costs Per Year: $258 tuition district resident; $310 tuition county resident; $450 tuition state resident; $950 room and board; $20 student fees; $200 estimated additional expenses.

Collegiate Environment: The 41-acre campus is situated on a hill one mile north of Cisco that overlooks the city. There are 15 buildings including dormitories for 270 students. The library contains 26,332 volumes. The Leon Maner Memorial Library was built during the spring of 1969. Freshmen are admitted in September, January, and in June and the college welcomes a geographically diverse student body. Financial aid is available, and 36% of students receive some form of aid.

Community Environment: Population 4,160. Cisco is a rural community that enjoys a temperate climate. The community is served by railroad, bus lines, and highways 80, 380, 183, 206 and Interstate-20. Local service facilities include a hospital, Rotary Club, Lions Club, and Veterans of Foreign Wars and Veterans of World War I. Merchants in the community provide jobs for many students. Recreation includes nearby Lake Cisco for boating, fishing, and water sports.

CLARENDON COLLEGE *(C-4)*
Box 968
Clarendon, Texas 79226
Tel: (806) 874-3571; Fax: (806) 874-3201

Description: Publicly supported, coeducational junior college established in 1898. The college is accredited by the Southern Association of Colleges and Schools and operates on the semester system with two summer terms. Course offerings include two-year Associate degree courses, vocational and continuing education. Recent enrollment included 198 men, 252 women full-time, and 180 men and 148 women part-time. A faculty of 27 full-time and 40 part-time gives a student-faculty ratio of 1-20.

Entrance Requirements: High school graduation or GED equivalency required for degree candidates. Open enrollment policy; ACT required. Early admission, early decision, rolling admission, delayed admission plans available.

Costs Per Year: $544 ($16/cr) district resident tuition; $612 ($18/cr) out-of-district; $640 ($200 + $20/cr after 11 cr) out-of-state; $210 student fees; $1,760 room & board; $400 estimated books.

Collegiate Environment: There are six buildings on the 30-acre campus occupied in 1968. Air-conditioned residence halls accommodate 220 men and women. The library contains a collection of 22,500 volumes. 100% of students applying for admission meet the requirements and are accepted. Freshman classes begin in September and January. A full service financial aid office is available to students. 75% of students receive financial aid.

Community Environment: Population 2,300. A rural community, Clarendon is the center of a ranching and farming area 54 miles southwest of Amarillo. The climate is temperate with an average temperature of 61 degrees, and rainfall average of 23 inches. The area is served by railroad, bus lines, and Highways 70 and U.S. 287. The community has many churches, a hospital and clinic, museum, and adequate shopping facilities. Local recreation includes a city park, theatres, a Youth Center, golf course, hunting and fishing, all sports, and Greenbelt Lake with a 35-mile shoreline. Part-time employment is available.

COLLEGE OF THE MAINLAND   *(L-12)*
8001 Palmer Highway
Texas City, Texas 77591
Tel: (409) 938-1211

Description: Publicly supported, coeducational junior college opened in 1967 and services five independent school districts including Texas City, La Marque, Dickinson, Hitchcock, and Santa Fe, on the mainland of Galveston County. It is accredited by the Southern Association of Colleges and Schools and grants diploma, certificate, and associate degrees. The college operates on the semester system and provides two summer terms. Enrollment includes 495 men, 631 women full-time and 993 men, 1,382 women part-time with a faculty of 83. There are approximately 4,500 students in the Continuing Education program.

Entrance Requirements: Accredited high school graduation or equivalent; $1,014 tuition for out-of-state students; student fees be substituted; open enrollment; non-high school graduates admitted upon approval of college officials; early admission, early decision, advanced placement plans available.

Costs Per Year: $578 tuition district resident; $1,068 out-of-district; $1,578 out-of-state.

Collegiate Environment: The new campus, one of the most modern in the southwest, is comprised of 10 boldly contemporary buildings: an Administration Building; College Center housing a snack bar, meeting, and recreational facilities; Fine Arts Building featuring an arena theatre, gallery, ceramics, art, and music studios; Learning Resources Center containing a 49,428 volume library, auditorium, and nonprint media department; Math and Science Building, housing modern laboratories, classrooms, and a greenhouse; Physical Education complex with a gymnasium, swimming pool, fitness rooms, whirlpools, sauna rooms, handball/racquetball courts, outdoor tennis courts, baseball field and track; Technical/Vocational Buildings, housing classrooms and completely-equipped laboratories to teach electronics, data processing, and graphic arts/printing, a cosmetology building with classrooms and a working salon; a new, Industrial Education building with classrooms and labs for welding, automotive and diesel technology. Almost all applicants are accepted. Limited financial aid is available.

Community Environment: Population 70,000 Texas City is a suburban community located approximately 40 miles from the center of Houston.

CONCORDIA UNIVERSITY AT AUSTIN   *(K-8)*
3400 Interstate 35 North
Austin, Texas 78705
Tel: (512) 452-7661; (800) 285-4252; Fax: (512) 459-8517

Description: Concordia University at Austin offers a variety of liberal arts programs within the atmosphere of a Christian community. Founded in 1926 by the Lutheran Church-Missouri Synod, it awards the Associate of Arts and Bachelor of Arts degrees, and is accredited by the Southern Association of Colleges and Schools. It operates on the early semester calendar system and offers three sessions. Enroll-

ment is 650 full-time and 150 part-time students. A faculty of 44 full-time and 20 part-time gives a faculty-student ratio of 1-12. Concordia provides small classes and individual attention to students of all religions and races. Army and Air Force ROTC are available.

Entrance Requirements: Accredited high school graduation with average of C+ (2.5) or better; strong college-preparatory program is recommended; early admission, midyear admission, rolling admission and advanced placement plans available. $25 application fee.

Costs Per Year: $7,000 tuition; $3,800 room and board; $360 student fees; $750 estimated additional expenses.

Collegiate Environment: Eleven major buildings are located on the 20-acre campus. Founders Library holdings number 70,000 volumes, 6,623 periodicals, 5,018 microforms and 2,088 audiovisual materials. Birkmann Chapel is the campus house of worship. Four residence halls provide dormitories for 125 men and 125 women. There is a central dining hall. There is a large gymnasium-activities center. A new student center was completed in 1991. A communication and fine arts center, dedicated in 1987, includes complete video production equipment and a sound stage. Approximately 60% of students applying are women. Approximately 75% of students applying for admission meet the requirements and are accepted. Freshman classes begin in September and January. 120 scholarships are available, 55 for freshmen, and 82% of a recent student body received some form of assistance. About 76% of the current student body graduated in the top half of the high school class, and 41% were in the top quarter. 77% of the previous freshman class returned to this campus for the sophomore year.

Community Environment: See University of Texas at Austin.

DALLAS BAPTIST UNIVERSITY   *(G-10)*
3000 Mountain Creek Parkway
Dallas, Texas 75211
Tel: (214) 445-5300; (800) 460-1328; Admissions: (214) 333-5360; Fax: (214) 333-5586

Description: Privately supported, coeducational liberal arts college is affiliated with the Southern Baptist Convention and is accredited by the Southern Association of Colleges and Schools. Enrollment includes 944 full-time and 1,557 part-time undergraduate students and 492 graduate students. The school operates on the 4-1-4 system and offers three summer terms. A faculty of 64 full-time and 150 part-time gives a faculty-student ratio of 1-18. The university grants BA, BS, BM, BMEd, BAAS, BABA, and BBA degrees. Graduate programs include the MBA, MA, MEd, MLA, and MEd in Counseling. The university offers accredited courses at 22 satellite campuses throughout the Dallas-Fort Worth area in conjunction with area churches, corporations, and industrial complexes.

Entrance Requirements: Accredited high school graduation with rank in upper 50% of graduating class; high school equivalency diploma accepted; ACT or SAT required; concurrent enrollment in high school, rolling admission and delayed admission plans available; $25 application fee.

Costs Per Year: $6,750 tuition; $3,413 room and board; $630 estimated additional expenses.

Collegiate Environment: The modern 285-acre campus was occupied in 1965, and has 13 buildings including dormitories for 224 men and 275 women. The library contains 175,779 volumes. Approximately 85% of students applying for admission meet the requirements and are accepted. Financial aid is available and 80% of the student body receives some form of assistance. In the recent academic year, the university awarded 576 Bachelor degrees and 136 Master degrees.

Community Environment: See Dallas Christian College.

DALLAS CHRISTIAN COLLEGE   *(G-10)*
2700 Christian Parkway
Dallas, Texas 75234
Tel: (214) 241-3371

Description: Founded in 1950, this privately supported, coeducational Bible college is affiliated with several Christian colleges in the area. The college grants the Associate and Bachelor degrees in Bible, elementary education, music and secretarial science, with a variety of church related minors available. It operates on the 4-4-4 system. Enrollment includes 114 students. A faculty of 18 gives a faculty-student ratio of 1-9.

Entrance Requirements: Accredited high school graduation; students not meeting all requirements may be admitted as special students, high school equivalency accepted; ACT required; midyear admission and rolling admission plans; Aug. 1 application deadline; $20 application fee.

Costs Per Year: $2,040 tuition; $2,500 room and board; $50 student fees.

Collegiate Environment: Five buildings are on the 22-acre campus. The library contains 60,000 volumes. There are dormitory accommodations for 80 men and 80 women. The college welcomes a geographically diverse student body. 90% of applicants meet the requirements and are accepted. Freshman classes begin in Sept.

Community Environment: A manufacturing, financial and distributing center, Dallas is a center for scientifically oriented industry in the electronics and aerospace fields and ranks high in cotton, oil and consumer goods production. The city also houses a principal banking and insurance complex. Dallas is a transportation hub for rail, bus and airlines.

DALLAS THEOLOGICAL SEMINARY   *(G-10)*
3909 Swiss Avenue
Dallas, Texas 75204
Tel: (214) 824-3094; (800) 992-0998; Fax: (214) 841-3664

Description: Privately supported Evangelical Protestant theological seminary, whose primary purpose is to train men and women for an effective Christian ministry in the exposition of the Scriptures. Founded in 1924, the graduate school is nondenominational. Enrollment includes 357 men, 25 women full-time, 491 men, 110 women part-time. A faculty of 60 gives a faculty-student ratio of 1-18. The semester system is used and five summer sessions are offered. The school is accredited by the Southern Association of Colleges and Schools, and a candidate member of the Association of Theological Schools in the United States and Canada. The seminary grants Master and Doctorate degrees.

Entrance Requirements: Baccalaureate degree or its equivalent; $20 application fee; early decision, rolling admission, and delayed admission plans available.

Costs Per Year: $4,800 tuition; $2,850 room and board; $245 student fees.

Collegiate Environment: The 16-acre campus has 20 buildings. Turpin Library is one of the most modern and efficient library buildings in the Southwest. It has a collection of 143,000 volumes, 38,400 microforms and 19,400 other items. Living accommodations are available for 110 single students and 113 couples. Approximately 75% of students applying for admission meet the requirements and are accepted. Classes begin in September and January. The seminary welcomes a geographically diverse student body. About 90% of a recent first year class returned to the seminary for the second year. The seminary awarded 227 Master and 20 Doctorate degrees to a recent graduating class.

Community Environment: See Dallas Christian College.

DEL MAR COLLEGE   *(O-9)*
Baldwin Blvd. and Ayers St.
Corpus Christi, Texas 78404
Tel: (512) 886-1248; Fax: (512) 886-1595

Description: Publicly supported, coeducational junior college offers both day and evening classes, and is coordinated by three major divisions: Arts and Sciences, Business, Occupational Education and Technology and Continuing Education. Founded in 1935, it is accredited by the Southern Association of Colleges and Schools. Enrollment is 3,865 full-time and 7,794 part-time students. A faculty of 253 full-time and 174 part-time provides a faculty-student ratio of 1-23. The semester system is used and two summer sessions are offered. The college grants the Certificate and Associate degree. Army ROTC is available.

Entrance Requirements: High school graduation or equivalent; open enrollment policy; completion of 15 units, including 3 English, 2 math, and 2 social studies; SAT or ACT required; early admission,

midyear admission, advanced placement and rolling admission plans available.

Costs Per Year: $480 district-resident tuition; $680 out-of-district; $4,080 out-of-state; $4,080 foreign students.

Collegiate Environment: The college has 40 buildings on 150 acres. The 27 buildings on the main campus include the Administration Building, the gymnasium, and the library containing 135,000 volumes, 743 periodicals, 12,078 microforms and 10,725 audiovisual materials. 13 buildings on the Technical Institute campus include a commercial foods laboratory, a 300-seat cafeteria, and an 8,000-square-foot Diesel Mechanics Building. About 99% of students applying for admission meet the requirements and are accepted. Special financial aid is available. Midyear students are accepted.

Community Environment: See Corpus Christi State University.

DEVRY INSTITUTE OF TECHNOLOGY   *(G-10)*
4801 Regent Blvd.
Irving, Texas 75063-2440
Tel: (214) 929-6777; (800) 443-3879; Admissions: (214) 929-5777; Fax: (214) 929-6778

Description: The Irving campus of this proprietary, coeducational school was established in 1952 and is accredited by the North Central Association of Colleges and Schools. Programs are developed and updated regularly with direct input from business and industry leaders. It operates on the semester system, has one summer session, and grants associate and bachelor degrees. Enrollment includes 1,141 men and 259 women full-time, and 437 men and 182 women part-time. A faculty of 64 full-time and 47 part-time gives a faculty-student ratio of 1-23.

Entrance Requirements: High school diploma or GED certification; minimum 17 years of age; must pass DeVry Entrance Examination or submit acceptable ACT/SAT/WPCT scores; accepts international students if requirements are met as outlined in catalog. All applicants who meet the requirements are accepted, including midyear students. Financial aid, loans and grants are available; Veterans Administration benefits are also available. $25 application fee.

Costs Per Year: Tuition $6,335.

Collegiate Environment: In July 1981 the campus was moved to Las Colinas, a master-planned, 4,500-acre development in Irving, the metroplex area between Dallas and Fort Worth. In October 1983, increased enrollment warranted the opening of an additional 30,000 square foot building, southeast of the main campus. All students belong to the Student Activities Organization. The library houses 7,840 volumes. 91% of applicants are accepted. Scholarships are available and 80% of the students receive some form of financial assistance.

Community Environment: In the heart of the Sunbelt, Irving serves as the regional office to many of today's leading corporations. Within the Las Colinas urban center is the 125-acre Lake Carolyn. Its canals pass between high-rise office centers and retail stores. Water taxis cruise along the shore. The climate warmly welcomes all to Irving with mild and sunny Texas blue skies. The average annual temperature is 65.7 degrees.

EAST TEXAS BAPTIST UNIVERSITY   *(G-13)*
1209 N. Grove Street
Marshall, Texas 75670
Tel: (214) 935-7963

Description: This privately supported, coeducational liberal arts university is chartered by the State of Texas and governed by the Baptist General Convention of Texas. It is accredited by the Southern Association of Colleges and Schools and the National Association of Schools of Music. Enrollment includes 1,054 full-time and 150 part-time students. A faculty of 49 full-time and 31 part-time gives a faculty-student ratio of 1-17. The semester system is used and two summer terms are offered with a January term of 4 weeks as well. Within the framework of a Christian institution, ETBU views the preparation of teachers for elementary and secondary schools as one of its primary objectives. The college grants the Bachelor and the Associate degree.

Entrance Requirements: Accredited high school graduation; completion of 16 units including 4 English, 2 mathematics, 2 science, and 2 social science; ACT required; non-high school graduates may be admitted with satisfactory scores on GED test; early decision, rolling admission and delayed admission plans available; $25 application fee.

Costs Per Year: $4,350 tuition; $2,640 room and board; $20 student fees; $400 books and supplies.

Collegiate Environment: Located on Van Zandt Hill, the college campus of 180 acres has 16 buildings. Housing accommodations are available for 659 students. The library contains 105,139 volumes, 677 periodical subscriptions, and 7,220 microforms. The college is a member of the Big State Conference and engages in intercollegiate athletics in basketball and baseball. Special financial aid is available. Nearly 80% of students received some form of assistance. 95% of students applying for admission are accepted.

Community Environment: See Wiley College.

EAST TEXAS STATE UNIVERSITY   *(F-11)*
East Texas Station
Commerce, Texas 75428
Tel: (903) 886-5081; (800) 331-3878; Admissions: (903) 886-5081;
Fax: (903) 886-5888

Description: Publicly supported, coeducational university accredited by the Southern Association of Colleges and Schools. The semester system is used and two summer terms are offered. The University is composed of Colleges of Business and Technology, Education, Arts and Sciences, and the Graduate School. The Division of Continuing Education provides extension courses, non-credit courses, and seminars. The university grants the Bachelor, Master and Doctorate degrees. Enrollment includes 5,117 undergraduate and 2,862 graduate students. The faculty includes 232 full-time and 192 part-time members. The faculty-student ratio is 1-19.

Entrance Requirements: Accredited high school graduation or equivalent; ACT with a minimum enhanced score of 20 required; SAT combined verbal and math score of 800; non-high school graduates 21 years of age may be admitted on individual approval; advanced placement, early admission, delayed admission, early decision, rolling admission plans available.

Costs Per Year: $1,140 resident tuition; $4,452 out-of-state tuition; $3,103 room and board; additional expenses average $400.

Collegiate Environment: The university owns 1,883 acres of land. The main campus consists of 140-acres. The library was completed at a cost of more than $1,000,000 and contains nearly 1 million volumes, 2,099 periodicals and 422,620 microforms. There are housing accommodations for 1,200 students. There is also housing available for married students. The university welcomes a geographically diverse student body and does accept midyear students. Approximately 75% of the students applying for admission are accepted and 75% returned for the sophomore year. Scholarships are available and 50% of the current student body receives some form of financial aid. Three graduation ceremonies are held each year.

Community Environment: Population 8,136. Commerce is located 65 miles northeast of Dallas. The city may be reached by good highways. The community has several churches, one hospital, and dormitories and apartments for students. Local recreation includes a movie theatre, boating and fishing on nearby lakes, swimming, tennis, bowling, and golf. Commerce is near enough to Dallas to enjoy its cultural, civic, and recreational opportunities. There are limited job opportunities in the immediate area.

EASTFIELD COLLEGE   *(G-10)*
3737 Motley Drive
Mesquite, Texas 75150
Tel: (214) 324-7100

Description: Publicly supported, coeducational junior college of the Dallas County Community College District opened in September 1970. It is accredited by the Southern Association of Colleges and Schools. It provides university-transfer, vocational, technical, and general educational programs leading to the Certificate and Associate degree. It operates on the semester system and offers two summer terms. Enrollment includes 1,245 men, 1,231 women full-time and 2,494 men, 3,746 women part-time with a faculty of 110 full-time and 350 part-time.

Entrance Requirements: Open door policy; accredited high school graduation or equivalent required for degree courses; advanced placement plans available.

Costs Per Year: $426 county resident tuition; $806 out-of-county; $1,610 additional expenses average $1,000.

Collegiate Environment: The college does not operate dormitories. The library contains 46,659 volumes, 456 periodicals, 4500 microforms and 3725 recordings. Scholarships are available.

Community Environment: See Dallas Christian College.

EL CENTRO COLLEGE   *(G-10)*
Main and Lamar Streets
Dallas, Texas 75202-3604
Tel: (214) 746-2311; Fax: (214) 746-2335

Description: Publicly supported, coeducational community college founded in 1966 and accredited by the Southern Association of Colleges and Schools. Transfer courses, vocational and technical training, and continuing education programs lead to the Certificate and Associate degree. El Centro is the first of seven institutions that comprise the Dallas County Community College District. It operates on the semester system and offers two summer sessions. Enrollment includes 1,069 full-time and 3,783 part-time students. A faculty of 156 full-time and 289 part-time gives a faculty-student ratio of 1-15.

Entrance Requirements: Open door policy; accredited high school graduation or equivalent required for degree courses; early admission and advanced placement plans available.

Costs Per Year: $426 county-resident tuition; $1,008 state resident; $1,610 out-of-state; $70 student fees.

Collegiate Environment: The two and a half-acre campus has one building that includes a library containing 69,458 volumes, 250 periodicals, 7,151 microforms and 5,940 audiovisual materials. The college does not operate dormitories. Special financial aid is available.

Community Environment: See Dallas Christian College.

EL PASO COMMUNITY COLLEGE   *(N-1)*
P.O. Box 20500
El Paso, Texas 79998
Tel: (915) 594-2000; Admissions: (915) 594-2150; Fax: (915) 594-2161

Description: This publicly supported, coeducational junior college grants the Associate degree. It operates on the semester system and offers two summer terms. The college is accredited by the Southern Association of Colleges and Schools. Enrollment includes 12,000 full-time and 9,000 part-time students. A faculty of 309 full-time and 676 part-time gives a faculty-student ratio of 1-21.

Entrance Requirements: High school graduation; open enrollment policy; non-high school graduates considered under certain circumstances; early admission, early decision, midyear admission, rolling admission and advanced placement plans available; $10 application fee.

Costs Per Year: $690 state-resident tuition; $132 student fees; $2,800 out-of-state tuition.

Collegiate Environment: All students who meet admission criteria are accepted. Scholarships are available and 70% of the students receive financial aid. Housing is not provided on campus. Library holdings include 78,000 volumes.

Community Environment: See University of Texas - El Paso.

Branch Campuses: Trans Mountain Campus; Rio Grande Campus; Valle Verde Campus; F. Bliss Military Base.

EPISCOPAL THEOLOGICAL SEMINARY OF THE
SOUTHWEST   *(K-8)*
606 Rathervue Place
P.O. Box 2247
Austin, Texas 78705
Tel: (512) 472-4133; Fax: (512) 472-3098

Description: Privately supported, coeducational, graduate-level Episcopal seminary, whose purpose is to serve the mission of the church by professional preparation of students for competent Christian ministry. It is accredited by the Southern Association of Colleges and Schools and the Association of Theological Schools. The seminary grants the Master's degree. The seminary operates on the semester calendar system. Enrollment includes 68 men and women. A faculty of 12 provides a faculty-student ratio of 1-6.

Entrance Requirements: Degree candidates must possess a Bachelor degree; students not meeting this requirement may be admitted as candidates for the diploma in Sacred Theology; rolling admission; $25 application fee.

Costs Per Year: $8,500 tuition; $3,000 room.

Collegiate Environment: The seminary is located in the midst of the educational institutions of Austin. Dormitory facilities are available for 20 persons. The library contains over 129,000 volumes. The seminary gladly receives men and women of all communions who are seeking more adequate preparation in Christian service. The school welcomes a geographically diverse student body and does not accept midyear students. Scholarships are available.

Community Environment: See University of Texas at Austin.

FRANK PHILLIPS COLLEGE   *(B-3)*
1301 Roosevelt
Borger, Texas 79008
Tel: (806) 274-5311

Description: Publicly supported, coeducational junior college, founded in 1948, is accredited by the Southern Association of Colleges and Schools. Transfer courses, vocational training, and continuing education programs in day and evening classes lead to the Associate degree. The college operates on the semester system and offers two summer sessions. Enrollment includes 1,142 full-time students. A faculty of 54 full-time and 26 part-time gives a faculty-student ratio of 1-14.

Entrance Requirements: Open enrollment policy; completion of 16 units including 3 English, 2 mathematics, and 2 social science; ACT or SAT accepted; graduates from nonaccredited high schools may be admitted by examination; early decision, early admission, midyear admission, rolling admission, and advanced placement plans available.

Costs Per Year: $365 county resident tuition; $425 state resident tuition; $465 nonresident tuition; $1,600 room and board; $130 student fees.

Collegiate Environment: The 60-acre campus is located in the southwest part of the city. The six buildings include a library consisting of 42,903 volumes, 4,057 microforms, and 384 audiovisual materials, and dormitories for 120 men and 80 women. All students applying for admission are accepted. Freshman classes begin in September and in February. The college offers 300 scholarships, 200 of which are for freshmen. Approximately 35% of students receive some form of financial aid. 40% of freshmen return for their sophomore year.

Community Environment: Population 14,195, one of the youngest towns in Texas, Borger was born as an oil boomtown in 1926. Today it is the center of the Panhandle gas reservoir, which produces more natural gas and allied products than any other field in the world. The community enjoys temperate climate. Air, rail, and bus service is available. Community services include a public library, churches of major denominations, a hospital, major civic, fraternal, and veteran's organizations, and shopping facilities. Local recreation includes theaters, golf, and other sports. The Oil Show, Rodeo, and Art Show are held annually. Part-time employment is available.

GALVESTON COLLEGE   *(L-13)*
4015 Avenue Q
Galveston, Texas 77550
Tel: (409) 763-6551; Fax: (409) 762-9367

Description: Publicly supported, coeducational junior college opened for its first semester of operation in September, 1967. It operates on the semester system and offers two summer sessions. Enrollment is 2,461 students. A faculty of 50 full-time and 70 part-time gives a faculty-student ratio of 1-21. Accredited by the Southern Association of Colleges and Schools, the college grants the Certificate and Associate degree.

Entrance Requirements: Open door policy; accredited high school graduation or equivalent required for degree programs; ACT required;

early admission, rolling admission, and advanced placement plans available.

Costs Per Year: $96 tuition; $311 out-of-state; $111 student fees.

Collegiate Environment: The college has 3 diverse campuses located in major business and residential areas of the community. The library collection numbers 40,007 volumes, 291 periodicals, 3,846 microforms, and 10,463 audiovisual materials. There are no dormitories. All students applying for admission are accepted, including students at midyear. Special financial aid is available, and 38% of a recent student body received some form of assistance. The college awards 70 scholarships annually.

Community Environment: Galveston is a port and recreational city. Major business activities include the tourist, maritime, and banking industries. Known as the "playground of the Southwest," Galveston has an average maximum temperature of 74.9 degrees, and an average minimum of 65.2 degrees. The climate is semitropical. The community is reached by railroad, bus lines, and airlines. There are churches of various faiths, a library, YMCA, YWCA, and medical facilities. Local recreation includes 32 miles of hard sand beaches, bathing, motoring, water sports, boating, deep-sea fishing, golf, horseback riding, a civic orchestra, Little Theatre, civic music association, and an art league. Part-time employment is abundant. Various fraternal, civic and veteran's organizations are active in the community.

GRAYSON COUNTY COLLEGE   *(E-10)*
6101 Grayson Drive
Denison, Texas 75020
Tel: (903) 465-6030

Description: This publicly supported, coeducational junior college is accredited by the Southern Association of Colleges and Schools. It was founded in 1964 and opened its doors to 1,479 students in September 1965. Enrollment includes 1,437 full-time and 2,100 part-time students. A faculty of 90 gives a faculty-student ratio of 1-17. The college grants the Associate degree. It operates on the semester system and offers two summer sessions.

Entrance Requirements: Open enrollment policy; students over 21 years of age who are not high school graduates may be admitted conditionally; ACT or SAT required; early decision and rolling admission plans available.

Costs Per Year: $660 district tuition; $780 out-of-district; $1,860 out-of-state; $1,920 room and board.

Collegiate Environment: The college has 34 buildings on 480 acres. The dormitory has facilities for 285 men and 250 women. The two-story library is in the center of the campus and contains 50,000 volumes, 5,800 periodicals, 1,429 microforms and 1,764 recordings. Over 99% of students applying for admission meet the requirements and are accepted. Midyear students are accepted. The college welcomes a geographically diverse student body. Special financial aid is available to economically handicapped students and 25% of the current student body received some form of assistance. Over 50% of the recent freshman class graduated in the top half of the high school class; 10% in the top quarter. Average scores: SAT 350V, 240M; ACT 16.7. The college awarded 489 Associate degrees recently.

Community Environment: Population 94,965. Principal industries in this manufacturing city include railroad cars, furniture, fishing lures, wigs, pickup campers, mattresses, venetian blinds, food processing and pipes. This is a metropolitan community served by railway transite and bus lines. The community has a library, over 40 churches representing most denominations, four hospitals, and various civic, fraternal and veteran's organizations. Some part-time job opportunities are available. Local recreation includes nearby lakes featuring all water sports, and three downtown theater complexes.

HARDIN-SIMMONS UNIVERSITY   *(G-6)*
2200 Hickory Street
Abilene, Texas 79698
Tel: (915) 670-1206

Description: This privately supported coeducational, liberal arts university was founded in 1891 and was originally known as Abilene Baptist College. The present name was adopted in 1934. The school has been affiliated with Baptist General Convention of Texas in 1941; since that date, the school's trustees have been elected by the convention. The university is accredited by the Southern Association of Colleges and Schools, and the National Council for Accreditation of Teacher Education. Bachelors and Masters degrees are granted. The university's organization consists of a College of Arts and Sciences, School of Business, School of Theology, School of Music, Graduate School, School of Nursing, School of Education, and Division of Continuing Education. Enrollment includes 1,423 full-time, 527 part-time, and 148 graduate students. A faculty of 101 full-time and 39 part-time gives a faculty-student ratio of 1-18. 81% of the full-time faculty have doctoral or terminal degrees. Average class size is about 17 students; the average freshman class size is about 22 students. The semester system is used, with 2 summer sessions and a May term. Intercollegiate enrollment and cooperative programs are available with Abilene Christian University and McMurry University. Army ROTC is available on campus.

Entrance Requirements: Accredited high school graduation, completion of 16 units including 3 English, 2 mathematics, and 2 social science; ACT or SAT required; minimum comospite ACT score of 19 or combined SAT score of 860 with no minimum class rank, or minimum composite ACT of 18 or combined SAT of 810 and rank in top half of high school class; students not meeting these requirements may be admitted with satisfactory GED test score or by special approval; early admission and advanced placement plans available; $25 application fee.

Costs Per Year: $6,000 tuition; $2,710 room and board; $700 books and supplies; $480 fees; $1,247 estimated personal expenses; $772 transportation expenses.

Collegiate Environment: The campus consists of 36 buildings, a 460,738-volume library, two athletic fields, rodeo grounds and stadium, dormitory accommodations for 800 students, and married students' housing for 46 families. Approximately 95% of students applying for admission are accepted. Average scores of a recent freshman class were SAT 910 composite, ACT composite 19. Average high school standing was in the top 40%; 65% were in the upper half; 18% ranked in the third quarter; and 7% were in the bottom quarter. About 78% of the current student body receives financial aid. The college welcomes a geographically diverse student body and accepts midyear students. The university awarded 193 Bachelor, 26 Master and 10 Associate degrees to a recent graduating class.

Community Environment: See Abilene Christian University.

HILL COLLEGE *(H-9)*
P.O. Box 619
Hillsboro, Texas 76645
Tel: (817) 582-2555; Fax: (817) 582-7591

Description: Publicly supported, coeducational junior college founded in 1923 and reactivated in 1962 provides three types of training; transfer courses for students planning to pursue Baccalaureate degree programs, vocational and technical education, and continuing education for adults. It is accredited by the Southern Association of Colleges and Schools and operates on the semester system with two summer terms. Recent enrollment included 964 men and 1,125 women. A faculty of 48 full-time and 42 part-time gives a faculty-student ratio of 1-20. The college grants the Certificate and Associate degree.

Entrance Requirements: Open enrollment policy; completion of 15 units including 3 English, 2 mathematics, 1 science, 2 social science; students over 21 years of age who are not high school graduates may be admitted by individual approval. Early admission, midyear admission, and rolling admission plans available.

Costs Per Year: $564 tuition; $1,108 out-of-state tuition; $2,500 room and board.

Collegiate Environment: The college is located on a 73-acre tract. There are 11 buildings. The library has a collection of 35,000 volumes. Residence halls accomodate 181 students. All students applying for admission are accepted and 80% return for the sophomore year. Scholarships are available and 50% of the current student body receives some form of financial assistance. The college awarded 40 Certificates and 150 Associate degrees to a recent graduating class.

Community Environment: Population 7,224. Located 55 miles from Fort Worth and 65 miles from Dallas, Hillsboro is a small community reached by railroad, bus service, and Interstate 35. There is a public library, two hospitals, and churches of 11 different denominations.

Local recreation includes two theatres, and 10 miles distant, Lake Whitney for all water sports. The American Legion and other service clubs are active in the area.

HOUSTON BAPTIST UNIVERSITY *(K-12)*
7502 Fondren Road
Houston, Texas 77074
Tel: (713) 995-3210; (800) 969-3210; Fax: (713) 995-3209

Description: Privately supported, coeducational liberal arts college founded in 1960 by the Baptist General Convention of Texas. It is accredited by the Southern Association of Colleges and Schools and the National League for Nursing. The university grants the Bachelor and Master degrees. It operates on the quarter system and offers two summer sessions. Enrollment is 1,220 full-time, 390 part-time undergraduate, and 521 graduate students. A faculty of 102 full-time and 35 part-time gives a faculty-student ratio of 1-13. Navy and Army ROTC programs are available through Rice University, also located in Houston.

Entrance Requirements: Accredited high school graduation; copleted units of 4 English, 4 mathematics, 3 science, 2 foreign language; unconditional admissions offered to students in 1st quarter with any score on SAT/ACT, 2nd, 3rd and 4th quarter with SAT 900/ACT 20; conditional admissions also offered; GED accepted; early admission, early decision, midyear admission, rolling admission, and advanced placement plans available; $25 application fee.

Costs Per Year: $7,920 (33 hours) tuition; $2,310 room and board; $276 student fees.

Collegiate Environment: There are 14 buildings on the 196-acre campus. The library has a collection of 128,000 volumes, 951 periodicals, 4,659 tapes and records, and 365,193 microforms. Housing accommodations are available for 100 men and 120 women. About 70% of applicants are accepted. Average scores of entering freshmen were ACT 20, SAT Verbal 460, Math 500. Of 490 scholarships offered, 175 are available for freshmen. 70% of students recieve some form of financial aid. 65% of freshmen return for their sophomore year.

Community Environment: See University of Houston.

HOUSTON COMMUNITY COLLEGE *(K-12)*
P.O. Box 7849
Houston, Texas 77270
Tel: (713) 869-5021

Description: Publicly supported community college for men and women operating on the semester system with two summer sessions. The college is accredited by the Southern Association of Colleges and Schools and awards the Certificate and the Associate degree. With a total enrollment of 37,410 full-time and part-time credit students and a faculty of 555 full-time, 1,722 part-time, the student-faculty ratio is 1-23.

Entrance Requirements: High school graduation; open enrollment policy; under certain circumstances non-high school graduates accepted; HCCS placement test required; no application fee.

Costs Per Year: $300 tuition district resident; $690 tuition out-of-district resident; $1,710 tuition out-of-state resident; $510 student fees district and state resident; $900 student fees out-of-state resident.

Collegiate Environment: The library contains 159,188 volumes, 975 periodical titles, 516 microforms, 10,593 visual materials. 100% of applicants are accepted. 55% of last year's freshman class returned for sophomore year. In a recent academic year, the college granted 631 Certificates and 735 Associate degrees.

Community Environment: See University of Houston.

HOWARD COLLEGE *(G-3)*
1001 Birdwell Lane
Big Spring, Texas 79720
Tel: (915) 264-5000; Admissions: (915) 264-5105; Fax: (915) 264-5028

Description: Founded in 1945, this publicly supported, coeducational junior college is accredited by the Southern Association of Colleges and Schools. The semester system is used and two summer terms are offered. The first two years of college work leading toward a Baccalaureate degree, technical and vocational courses, and continuing education are offered. The college grants Certificates and the Associate degree. The college operates on the semester system and offers two summer sessions. Enrollment includes 1,000 full-time and 1,600 part-time students. A faculty of 190 gives a faculty-student ratio of 1-16.

Entrance Requirements: Open enrollment policy; completion of 16 units; ACT or SAT accepted; applicant not meeting all requirements may be admitted under special circumstances; rolling admission, early decision, early admission plans available.

Costs Per Year: $474 district resident tuition; $524 out-of-district tuition; $1,024 out-of-state tuition; $2,090 room and board; $268 student fees; additional expenses average $1,200.

Collegiate Environment: There are 14 buildings on the 100-acre campus including dormitory facilities for 143 men and 96 women. The library contains 27,589 volumes. 98% of all students applying for admission are accepted. Freshman classes begin in September and January. Almost 30% of a recent freshman class graduated in the top half of the high school class; 10% in the top quarter. The average score of the entering freshman class was ACT 17 composite. 280 scholarships are available, including 168 for freshmen. 60% of the students receive some form of financial aid. Approximately 30% of a recent freshman class returned to the campus for the sophomore year. The college awarded 190 Associate degrees during a recent school year.

Community Environment: Population 26,000. Big Spring is an urban community noted for its varied industries, which include oil refining and production, petro-chemical manufacturing, one carbon black plants, two bottling plants and an ammonia plant. The climate is temperate and dry. The community is served by air, rail, and bus lines. There is a public library, YMCA, many churches of various faiths, three general and one Veteran's hospital, as well as crippled children's rehabilitation center. Part-time employment opportunities are limited. Local entertainment includes three theatres, skating rank, bowling alleys, and water sports on nearby lakes. The area has good shopping facilities and major civic, fraternal and veteran's organizations.

HOWARD PAYNE UNIVERSITY　　(H-7)
1000 Fisk
Brownwood, Texas 76801
Tel: (915) 649-8020; (800) 880-4478; Fax: (915) 649-8901

Description: Privately supported, coeducational liberal arts college founded in 1889 and affiliated with the Southern Baptist Convention. It is accredited by the Southern Association of Colleges and Schools. The semester system is used and two summer terms are offered. Enrollment includes 616 men, 601 women full-time, and 126 men and 111 women part-time. A faculty of 90 full-time and 31 part-time gives a faculty-student ratio of 1-17. The university grants the Bachelor degree.

Entrance Requirements: Accredited high school graduation with completion of 15 units including 3 English; 2 mathematics; 1 laboratory science; 2 social science; ACT or SAT required; students not meeting all requirements may be admitted conditionally; early decision, midyear admission and rolling admission plans available; $25 application fee.

Costs Per Year: $5,490 tuition; $3,494 room and board; $450 student fees; $1,250 approximate additional expenses.

Collegiate Environment: The main campus of the college contains 45 acres and part of this is a 25-acre stadium. There are housing accommodations for 467 men, 457 women. The library contains 118,000 volumes, 877 periodicals, 38,500 microform titles, 3,250 records, tapes and CD's, and 406 CD-ROMs. Freshman classes begin in August, January, June and July. About 90% of the students applying for admission are accepted, and 57% returned for the sophomore year. The average scores of the entering freshman class were ACT 21 composite and SAT 650 combined. 683 scholarships are available, including 178 for freshmen. 88% of the current student body receives financial assistance. The college awarded 121 Bachelor degrees to a recent graduating class. 37% of last year's senior class continued on to graduate school.

Community Environment: Population 20,000. Brownwood is located 26 miles from the geographic center of the state, which designates the community "deep in the heart of Texas." The annual average temperature is 66.7 degrees, with an average annual rainfall of 27.4 inches. Railroad, airlines, and bus lines serve the area. The community has many churches of various faiths, a public library, two hospitals, and various civic, fraternal and veteran's organizations. Recreation includes Lake Brownwood with fishing, hunting, boating, water skiing, bathing, and picnicking; many city parks, golf course, municipal swimming pool, tennis courts, and five ball parks.

HUSTON-TILLOTSON COLLEGE　　(K-8)
900 Chicon Street
Austin, Texas 78702
Tel: (213) 476-7421; (800) 321-7421; Fax: (512) 474-0762

Description: The privately supported, coeducational liberal arts college had its origin in two former institutions, Tillotson College and Samuel Huston College. It was founded in 1877 and is accredited by the Southern Association of Colleges and Schools. It is supported jointly by the United Church of Christ and the United Methodist Church. It grants the Bachelor degree. The college operates on the semester system and offers one summer session. Enrollment includes 506 full-time and 105 part-time students. A faculty of 38 full-time and 12 part-time gives a faculty-student ratio of 1-13.

Entrance Requirements: Accredited high school graduation with preferred rank in upper 1/3 of graduating class; completion of 18 units including 4 English, 3 mathematics, 2 science, 2 social science, and 7 electives; ACT with minimum score of 18, or SAT with minimum score of 375V and 375M required; students not meeting all requirements may be admitted by letter of recommendation and interview; early decision, midyear admission, rolling admission and advanced placement plans available. $25 application fee.

Costs Per Year: $4,816 tuition; $3,814 room and board; $728 student fees.

Collegiate Environment: The campus of the college consists of 23 acres of land in the Eastern half of Austin. There are residence halls to accommodate 196 men and 276 women. The library system contains 80,406 volumes. Approximately 50% of students applying for admission meet the requirements and are accepted. Midyear students are accepted, and the college welcomes a geographically diverse student body. Freshman classes begin in August. Financial aid is available. 87% of students receive financial aid.

Community Environment: See University of Texas at Austin.

INCARNATE WORD COLLEGE　　(L-7)
4301 Broadway
San Antonio, Texas 78209
Tel: (210) 829-6005; (800) 749-9673; Fax: (210) 829-3921

Description: Privately supported, coeducational liberal arts college established in 1881 and conducted by the Sisters of Charity of the Incarnate Word, under the auspices of the Roman Catholic Church. It is accredited by the Southern Association of Colleges and Schools and by respective accrediting institutions. The college grants the Bachelor and the Master degrees. Air Force and Army ROTC programs are available. It operates on the semester system and offers two summer sessions. Enrollment includes 1,661 full-time and 599 part-time undergraduates and 555 graduate students. A faculty of 128 full-time and 117 part-time gives a faculty-student ratio of 1-14.

Entrance Requirements: Accredited high school graduation or equivalent; rank in upper 50% of graduating class; completion of 18 college preparatory units including 4 English, 2 mathematics, 2 foreign language, 2 science, 2 social science, 6 electives; minimum ACT 20 composite required or SAT 800 combined; GRE, MAT or GMAT required for graduate programs; non-high school graduates considered under certain circumstances; early admission, early decision, rolling admission, delayed admission, midyear admission and advanced placement plans available; $20 application fee.

Costs Per Year: $9,500 tuition; $4,337 room and board.

Collegiate Environment: The college is located on a 56-acre campus of natural wooded park in the residential section of San Antonio, immediately adjacent to Brackenridge Park. The college buildings include a library of 185,678 volumes, 675 periodicals, 21,000 microforms and 33,000 audiovisual materials. Residence halls accommodate 190 men and 415 women. 75% of applicants are accepted. The middle 50% ranges of scores for the entering freshman class were SAT 450-500 verbal, 430-480 math, ACT 19-22 composite. Average high school standings of the freshmen: 87% in the top half, 13% in the third quarter. Various scholarships are available and 67% of the current student body receives some form of financial aid. The college awarded 276 Bachelor and 100 Master degrees to a recent graduating class. About 20% of the senior class continued on to graduate school.

Community Environment: See San Antonio College.

JACKSONVILLE COLLEGE   *(H-12)*
500 Pine Street
Jacksonville, Texas 75766
Tel: (903) 586-2518; (800) 256-8522; Fax: (903) 586-0742

Description: Privately supported, coeducational junior college founded by members of the Baptist Church in 1899. It functioned as a senior college until 1918, when it was reorganized on the junior college level. Jacksonville College is governed by the Baptist Missionary Association of Texas which appoints its Board of Trustees. It provides university-parallel, vocational, and general programs leading to the Certificate and Associate degree. The college is accredited by the Southern Association of Colleges and Schools. It operates on the semester system and offers two summer sessions. Enrollment is 272 full-time and 18 part-time students. A faculty of 14 full-time and 18 part-time gives a faculty-student ratio of 1-19.

Entrance Requirements: Accredited high school graduation or equivalent; ACT or SAT required; open enrollment policy; advanced placement plan available.

Costs Per Year: $2,400 tuition; $2,600 room and board; $250 student fees.

Collegiate Environment: The college is located on a 17-acre campus in the northwest section of the City of Jacksonville. The 12 college buildings include a library of 23,000 volumes, 160 periodical subscriptions, 3,000 microforms, and 1,200 audiovisual materials. There are living accommodations for 75 men and 55 women. The college welcomes a geographically diverse student body and will accept midyear students. Approximately 97% of students applying for admission are accepted. Financial aid is available and in recent years, approximately 90% of students applying for aid receive some form of scholarship, grant, or other assistance.

Community Environment: Population 12,000, Jacksonville is a small community enjoying temperate climate. The average annual rainfall is 45 inches. The community is reached by railroad, bus lines, major air service, and highways. Community service facilities include many churches, one hospital, a library, and three clinics. There is a local radio station, parks, and facilities for golf, hunting, fishing, rodeos, and swimming pools. Various civic and fraternal organizations are active in the area. Part-time employment is plentiful.

JARVIS CHRISTIAN COLLEGE   *(G-12)*
Highway 80 West
P.O. Drawer G
Hawkins, Texas 75765
Tel: (903) 769-5700; Admissions: (903) 769-5733; Fax: (903) 769-4842

Description: This privately supported, coeducational, liberal arts college, established in 1912, is affiliated with Texas Christian University and derives much of its support from the Christian (Disciples of Christ) Church. It is accredited by the Southern Association of Colleges and Schools. Programs of study lead to the Bachelor degree. The college operates on the semester system and offers one summer session. Enrollment includes 400 full-time students. A faculty of 35 gives a faculty-student ratio of 1-11. Programs of study lead to the Bachelor degree.

Entrance Requirements: Accredited high school graduation with rank in upper 50% of graduating class; completion of 16 units including 3 English, 2 mathematics, 1 science, 3 social science; college entrance examinations and ACT required; applicants not meeting all entrance requirements may be admitted on a conditional basis or as special students; midyear admission and rolling admission plans; Aug. 1, Dec. 1 application deadlines; $25 application fee.

Costs Per Year: $4,200 tuition; $3,485 room and board; $385 student fees.

Collegiate Environment: The 425-acre campus is located one mile east of Hawkins and four miles west of Big Sandy. The 57 college buildings contain a library of 80,000 volumes, a health center, and dormitory facilities for 269 men and 257 women. Students from diverse geographical locations are welcome. Approximately 95% of applicants are accepted, including midyear students. Financial aid is available for economically disadvantaged students and 95% of students receive some form of financial assistance. 69% of freshmen return for their sophomore year.

Community Environment: Hawkins is located in southwestern Wood County, population 18,589. The area enjoys moderate, temperate climate. Serviced by U.S. Highway 80 and bus lines, there are churches of many denominations, a hospital and clinic, and various civic, fraternal, and veteran's organizations. Local recreation includes camping and hunting, with rivers, creeks, springs and lakes furnishing opportunities for fishing and boating.

KILGORE COLLEGE   *(G-12)*
1100 Broadway
Kilgore, Texas 75662
Tel: (903) 984-8531; Fax: (903) 983-8600

Description: Publicly supported, coeducational junior college established in 1935 and offers preparatory courses for transfer to college and university programs, two-year occupational training programs, adult education programs, and general education programs. The college is accredited by the Southern Association of Colleges and Schools and grants the Certificate and Associate degree. It operates on the semester system and also provides two summer sessions. Enrollment includes 2,154 full-time and 2,197 part-time students. A faculty of 163 full-time and 97 part-time provides a faculty-student ratio of 1-19.

Entrance Requirements: Accredited high school graduation; ACT or Local Placement Test required; non-high school graduates over 18 years of age may be admitted conditionally.

Costs Per Year: $530 tuition city or district resident; $962 tuition state resident; $1,346 tuition out-of-state resident; $2,200 room and board; $150 estimated additional expenses.

Collegiate Environment: The total college plant includes a 25-acre campus, shared use of the St. John Memorial Stadium in Kilgore, and shared use of the 450-acre Kilgore College Demonstration Farm in nearby Overton. The college buildings contain a library of 85,000 volumes and dormitory facilities for 100 men and 500 women. Students from other geographical locations are accepted as well as midyear students. Scholarships are available and 50% of students receive some form of aid.

Community Environment: Population 10,000. Kilgore is a suburban area enjoying temperate climate and four distinct seasons. The community has over 40 churches representing various faiths, a library, and medical facilities. The area is reached by bus, railroad, airlines, and Interstate Highway 20, U.S. 259, and State 31. Part-time employment is available. Local community recreation includes a swimming pool, tennis courts, picnic areas, bowling, theatres, go-kart racing, golf, water skiing, fishing, camping, and hunting. There are dormitories and apartments available for student housing. Many civic, fraternal and veteran's organizations are active in the community.

LAMAR UNIVERSITY   *(K-14)*
4400 Martin Luther King Jr. Parkway
P.O. Box 10009
Beaumont, Texas 77710
Tel: (409) 880-7011

Description: Publicly supported, coeducational, liberal arts and technical college established in 1923 as the South Park Junior College by the South Park Independent School District. It became a four-year, state-supported institution in 1951 and graduate work in specified fields was added in 1960. The college is accredited by the Southern Association of Colleges and Schools and grants the Bachelor, Master and Doctorate degrees. It operates on the semester system and also provides two summer terms. The college is composed of the following schools: Business, Education, Engineering, Fine and Applied Arts, Liberal Arts, Sciences, Technical Arts, Graduate. A Cooperatus Education program is available whereby the student spends alternate terms at work or study. The program is offered to a limited number in the School of Engineering. Enrollment includes 2,204 men, 2,725 women full-time, 1,353 men, 1,947 women part-time with a faculty of 94 full-time and 392 part-time members.

Entrance Requirements: High school graduation. SAT and ACT required. Engineering students require M1 CEEB Achievement Test. Early admission, rolling admission and advanced placement plans available. Open enrollment policy and non-high school graduates may be considered for admission under certain circumstances.

Costs Per Year: $1,150 tuition state resident; $4,502 out-of-state resident; $4,380 room and board; $50 fees.

Collegiate Environment: The 200-acre campus is located in the center of industrial southeast Texas. The college plant includes many new and functional buildings of modern design with a library of 300,000 volumes and living accommodations for 887 men, 683 women, and 70 families. Financial aid is available.

Community Environment: Beaumont and the surrounding area form one of the largest concentrations of petroleum refineries in the nation. Top manufactures of the area include deep sea and dry-land oil-drilling equipment and oil-processing apparatus. The city is located on the Neches River approximately 20 miles north of the Gulf of Mexico. The climate is mild the year round. Airlines, railroad, and bus lines serve the community. The community has many churches representing various faiths, three libraries, YMCA, and YWCA, several hospitals, and various civic and fraternal organizations. Part-time employment is available.

LAREDO COMMUNITY COLLEGE   (O-6)
Laredo, Texas 78040
Tel: (512) 722-0521

Description: This publicly supported, coeducational junior college was created officially in 1947. It is accredited by the Southern Association of Colleges and Schools. The college offers academic and pre-professional courses, two-year general college education, occupational and technical courses, two-year business training, and accredited program in nursing, medical laboratory technology, and radiological technology, and an adult basic education program. It operates on the semester system and offers two summer terms. There are 5,944 men and women enrolled. A faculty of 212 provides a faculty-student ratio of 1-20. The college grants the Certificate and Associate degree.

Entrance Requirements: Accredited high school graduation; open enrollment policy, non-high school graduates with GED certification or 21 years of age or older may be admitted on a probationary status; ACT recommended; rolling admission plan.

Costs Per Year: $312 district-resident tuition; $936 out-of-district tuition and fees; $1,560 out-of-state tuition, $78 student fees.

Collegiate Environment: The college is located on 195 acres and is comprised of several modern buildings including a library of 124,245 volumes. Almost all students applying for admission are accepted, including midyear students. Financial aid is available.

Community Environment: Population approximately 100,000. A chief port of entry into Mexico, Laredo is separated from Nuevo Laredo, Mexico, by the Rio Grande. This is a metropolitan community located in the center of a rich cattle, oil, gas and agricultural district. It is a major import-export center. The city is reached by airlines, railroad, and bus service. The climate is temperate and dry. Laredo has a public library, churches of major denominations, two hospitals, and various civic and fraternal organizations. Shopping facilities are good. Part-time employment is available for students. Local recreation includes theaters, water sports, and most major sports.

LEE COLLEGE   (K-12)
P.O. Box 818
Baytown, Texas 77522
Tel: (713) 427-5611; Admissions: (713) 425-6393; Fax: (713) 425-6831

Description: Publicly-supported, coeducational junior college established in 1934. Operating under a comprehensive community college concept, facilities are maintained for academic, technical-vocational, and adult and continuing education programs. The college is accredited by the Southern Association of Colleges and Schools and grants the Associate degree. It operates on the semester system and offers

two summer terms. Enrollment includes 2,242 full-time and 3,386 part-time students. A faculty of 162 full-time and 65 part-time gives a faculty-student ratio 1-25.

Entrance Requirements: Open enrollment policy; accredited high school graduation or GED certificate; non-high school graduates admitted; early admission, early decision, and advanced placement available; no application fee. All students must provide measures of their reading, mathematics, and writing skills, i.e., local placement exams, SAT, ACT, or TASP scores.

Costs Per Year: $288 district resident tuition; $576 out-of-district tuition; $960 state or out-of-state residents; $112 student fees.

Collegiate Environment: The 30-acre campus is located in Baytown, one of the most rapidly developing suburban areas in the Houston metropolitan complex. The five major college buildings comprise academic facilities, a modern gymnasium with an Olympic-sized swimming pool, and a library with over 100,000 volumes. There is an extension at Huntsville, the Texas Department of Criminal Justice extension. Students from other geographical locations are accepted as well as midyear students. About 33% of the previous entering class returned to this campus for the second year of studies. 265 scholarships are available and 33% of the student body receives some form of financial aid. In the previous academic year, the college awarded 399 Associate degrees.

Community Environment: Population 60,000. Baytown is located midway between Houston and the open sea on the Houston Ship Channel. The city is a consolidation of three towns: Baytown, Goose Creek, and Pelly. There are many churches in the immediate area, and four hospitals are easily accessible.

LETOURNEAU UNIVERSITY   (G-13)
P.O. Box 7001
Longview, Texas 75607
Tel: (903) 237-2780; (800) 759-8811; Fax: (903) 237-2732

Description: Privately-supported, coeducational, liberal arts and technological college founded in 1946 as a senior college limited to technological studies and strongly emphasizing Christian principles and beliefs. In 1961 the Board of Trustees approved the expansion of the program to a four-year college with the addition of arts and sciences. The university seeks to integrate faith, learning, and living. Enrollment includes 1,879 full-time and 135 part-time undergraduate and 168 graduate students. There are also 957 evening students. A faculty of 55 full-time and 148 part-time gives an undergraduate faculty-student ratio of 1-15. The early semester system is used and two summer terms are offered. Accredited by the Southern Association of Colleges and Schools with an engineering degree accredited professionally by the Accrediting Board for Engineering and Technology, the college grants the Associate and Bachelor degrees. Cooperative education programs are available in a number of fields.

Entrance Requirements: Accredited high school graduation; minimum C average and completion of 16 units including 4 English, 2-4 mathematics, 1 science, 2 social science; ACT or SAT required; non-high school graduates over 21 years of age or veterans may be admitted as special students; the Degree Completion Program requires 60 transferable college level hours; minimum 2.0 "C" GPA; 4 years relevant work experience; 2 letters of recommendation; completion, with "C" or above, at least one 3 credit hour course in English composition; open to the Christian mission of the University; midyear admission, rolling admission, and advanced placement plans available; $20 application fee.

Costs Per Year: $9,400 tuition; $4,430 room and board; $150 student fees; $300 estimate additional expenses.

Collegiate Environment: The college occupies a 164-acre campus, the former site of the Harmon General Hospital, in Longview, Texas. The 50 college buildings contain a library of 108,500 volumes, 480 periodicals, 37,500 microforms and 2,700 audio-visual materials. Housing facilities accommodate 674 students and 49 families. Students from other geographical locations are accepted as well as midyear students. Approximately 85% of students applying for admission are accepted and 73% of the previous freshman class returned to this campus for the sophomore year. Of 325 scholarships offered, 103 are available for freshman and 75% of the current student body receives financial aid. LeTourneau now offers a degree completion program for adult students.

Community Environment: Population 70,000. Oil is the major source of economy for this community. Longview has a city library, community center, two hospitals, and a number of medical clinics. Major civic and fraternal clubs are active in the area. Longview is reached by airlines, railroad, and bus lines. Residence halls, mobile homes and apartments furnish student housing. Local recreation includes theatres, drive-ins, parks, municipal swimming pools, hunting, fishing, golf, and water skiing. Part-time employment is available.

Branch Campuses: Longview/Tyler, P.O. Box 7668, Longview, TX, 75607, (903) 237-2780; Dallas/Mid-Cities; 5710 LBJ Frwy. #150, Dallas, TX, 75240; (214) 387-9835; Houston, Three Riverway, Suite 130, Houston, TX, 77056-1909, (713) 622-1368

LON MORRIS COLLEGE   *(H-12)*
College Avenue
Jacksonville, Texas 75766
Tel: (903) 586-2471; (800) 594-2201; Admissions: (903) 589-4005;
Fax: (903) 586-8562

Description: Privately supported, coeducational liberal arts junior college founded as Alexander Institute at Kilgore, Texas, in 1873. In 1875, it was turned over to the East Texas Conference of the Methodist Episcopal Church, South, and was moved to Jacksonville in 1894. It offers the first two years of standard college work, with additional training in the fine arts, and is now owned by the Texas Conference of the United Methodist Church. It is accredited by the Southern Association of Colleges and Schools. The college grants the Associate degree. The college operates on the semester system and also provides two summer terms. Enrollment includes 180 men, 147 women full-time and 15 men, 19 women part-time. A faculty of 16 full-time and 20 part-time gives a faculty-student ratio of 1-17.

Entrance Requirements: Accredited high school graduation; ACT or SAT required; applicants over 21 years of age may be admitted by individual approval; rolling admission, early decision, early admission, midyear admission, delayed admission and advanced placement plans available; $25 application fee.

Costs Per Year: $5,900 tuition; $1,700 room; $1,990 board; $500 student fees.

Collegiate Environment: The 76-acre campus is located in Jacksonville, approximately 115 miles southeast of Dallas. The 12 college buildings contain a library of 20,000 volumes and dormitory facilities for 174 men and 172 women. Students from other geographical locations are accepted as well as midyear students. Nearly 65% of the previous freshman class returned to this campus for the sophomore year. 300 scholarships are offered, including 240 for freshmen and 95% of the students receive some form of financial aid.

Community Environment: See Jacksonville College.

LUBBOCK CHRISTIAN UNIVERSITY   *(E-3)*
5601 19th Street
Lubbock, Texas 79407
Tel: (806) 796-8800

Description: This privately supported, coeducational liberal arts college was established in 1957 by members of the Church of Christ. Accredited by the Southern Association of Colleges and Schools the college grants the Certificate, Associate and Bachelor degree. The college operates on the semester system and also offers three summer terms. Enrollment includes 881 full-time, 291 part-time and 42 graduate students. A faculty of 60 full-time and 55 part-time gives a faculty-student ratio of 1-17.

Entrance Requirements: Open enrollment policy; ACT or SAT required; applicants not meeting all entrance requirements, over 21 years of age or veterans, may be admitted with successful completion of entrance examinations; rolling admission, early decision, and advanced placement plans available; $20 application fee.

Costs Per Year: $6,050 tuition; $3,200 room and board; $400 student fees.

Collegiate Environment: The college is located on 120-acre campus and is comprised of 15 buildings. The college library contains 83,000 volumes, 500 periodicals, 1,000 microforms and 100 recordings. Living accommodations are provided for 432 men and 428 women and in apartments for 328 men and women. Approximately 95% of students applying for admission are accepted. Average ACT score is 20. Al-

most 65% of the previous freshman class returned to this campus for the second year of studies. Financial aid is available and 85% of the current student body receives financial assistance. The college awarded 5 Certificates, 5 Associate and 106 Bachelor degrees in a recent school year. 15% of last year's senior class continued on to graduate school.

Community Environment: Population 180,000. The industrial, agricultural and educational center of the South Plains of Texas, Lubbock is the third largest inland cotton market in the Nation. There are also many oil wells in the community. This metropolitan center is called "The Hub of the Plains." The climate is mild and arid. Community service facilities include over 200 churches, county libaries, hospitals, a planetarium, museum, and municipal auditorium. There are four TV stations, seven radio stations, four golf courses, movie theaters, drive-ins, hunting, water skiing, horseback riding, and many other forms of recreation available in the area. Part-time employment is available. The city is served by railroad, airlines, and a bus line.

MCLENNAN COMMUNITY COLLEGE   *(I-9)*
1400 College Drive
Waco, Texas 76708
Tel: (817) 750-3529

Description: Publicly supported, coeducational community college was established in 1965 and opened its doors in 1966. It offers college-transfer programs, terminal technical-vocational programs, adult education programs, community services and grants the Certificate and Associate degree. The college is accredited by the Southern Association of Colleges and Schools. Enrollment recently included 2,347 students full-time and 3,118 students part-time. A faculty of 167 full-time, 79 part-time gives a faculty-student ratio of 1-22. The semester system is used and two summer sessions are offered. There is also 1 nine-week evening term in the summer. Academic cooperative plan with Baylor University for ROTC is available.

Entrance Requirements: Open enrollment policy; ACT or SAT required; non-high school graduates, 18 years of age or older, may be admitted by successful completion of entrance examinations; early admission. No application fee.

Costs Per Year: $510 tuition state resident; $2,400 nonresident; $260 student fees; no application fee.

Collegiate Environment: The college has a new permanent campus, consisting of 19 buildings on a beautiful wooded 160-acre site adjacent to Cameron Park and the Bosque River. The library contains 80,241 volumes, 2,508 pamphlets, 559 periodicals, 387 microforms, and 2,850 recordings. There is no on campus housing but abundant housing facilities are available adjacent to the campus. All of the students recently applying for admission were accepted including midyear students. A total of 445 scholarships are available, 270 of them for freshmen. 47% of students received some form of financial aid recently. The College granted 132 Certificates and 328 Associate degrees in the recent academic year. Approximately 42% continued on to senior college.

Community Environment: See Baylor University.

MCMURRY UNIVERSITY   *(G-6)*
14th & Sayles
Abilene, Texas 79697
Tel: (915) 691-6226; (800) 477-0077; Admissions: (915) 691-6226;
Fax: (915) 691-6599

Description: This privately supported, coeducational liberal arts university was established in 1923 and is owned and supported by the United Methodist Church. It is accredited by the Southern Association of Colleges and Schools and grants the Bachelor and Associate degrees. The university operates on the 4-4-1 system and offers two summer terms. Enrollment includes 920 full-time and 464 part-time students. A faculty of 68 full-time and 63 part-time gives a faculty-student ratio of 1-13. United States Army ROTC is available at nearby Hardin-Simmons University.

Entrance Requirements: Accredited high school graduation; completion of 14 units including 4 English, 3 mathematics, 2 science, 3 social science, and 2 foreign language, ACT or SAT required; non-high school graduates over 21 years of age may be admitted on individual approval; early admission, rolling admission, and advanced placement plans available; $20 application fee.

Costs Per Year: $6,480 tuition; $3,452 room and board; $450 student fees.

Collegiate Environment: The university occupies a 41-acre campus and is comprised of 20 buildings. It contains a library of 141,681 volumes and living accommodations for 574 students. Students enrolled at the university may also enroll in courses at either Abilene Christian University or Hardin-Simmons University with courses counting toward degree requirements at McMurry University. Chapel services of divine worship are held each Thursday morning with attendance voluntary. The university welcomes a geographically diverse student body and will accept midyear students. Approximately 78% of students applying for admission were accepted. About 70% of the previous freshman class returned to this campus for the sophomore year. Average high school standing of the recent freshman class was in the top 88%; and 49% in the top quarter; 39% in the second quarter, and 12% in the third quarter. Average ACT score was 22. Of 249 scholarships offered, 90 are available for freshmen. More than 85% of the current students receive financial aid. The university awarded 173 Bachelor degrees to a recent graduating class. About 13% of the senior class continued on to graduate school.

Community Environment: See Abilene Christian University.

MIDLAND COLLEGE   *(H-2)*
3600 North Garfield
Midland, Texas 79705
Tel: (915) 685-4500

Description: The publicly supported community college is accredited by the Southern Association of Colleges and Schools, and was founded in 1972. The school offers university parallel education. Associate degrees are offered in the Arts and Sciences that parallel the lower division offerings of four-year colleges. Also offered are General Education programs and Occupational-Technical programs. Associate degrees in applied science, or certificates, are awarded for Occupational-Technical programs. The semester system is used with 2 summer terms.

Entrance Requirements: Accredited high school graduation or GED equivelant; non-high school graduates 18 years of age or older may be admitted without examination; open enrollment policy; early admission plan available.

Costs Per Year: $690 district-resident tuition; $738 out-of-district; $1,182 plus $25 per hour above 18 hours for out-of-state resident.

Collegiate Environment: The 115-acre campus includes a Learning Resource Center, a Physical Education Building, a Health Sciences Center, and a Fine Arts Building. Activities include intercollegiate and intramural sports, and a student senate. Financial aid and part-time employment are available. There are no dormitories on campus.

MIDWESTERN STATE UNIVERSITY   *(E-7)*
3400 Taft Boulevard
Wichita Falls, Texas 76308
Tel: (817) 689-5321; (800) 842-1922; Fax: (817) 689-4302

Description: Publicly supported coeducational university began as the Wichita Falls Junior College in 1922 and became a senior college in 1946. In 1948 it became a member of the Association of Texas Colleges and Universities, and in 1950 it was granted full accreditation by the Southern Association of Colleges and Schools. The university operates on the early semester system and also offers two summer terms. Enrollment includes 3,395 full-time and 1,939 part-time undergraduates and 485 graduate students. A faculty of 173 full-time and 78 part-time gives a faculty-student ratio of 1-22. Special programs include radiologic technology programs in cooperation with the U.S.A.F. School of Health Care Sciences at Sheppard A.F.B.

Entrance Requirements: Accredited high school graduation with rank in upper 60% of high school graduating class; score of 20 or over on ACT or 950 combined on the recentered SAT required; mid-year admission, advanced placement and credit by examination available; non-high school graduates considered for admission under certain circumstances.

Costs Per Year: $868 ($28/hr, $100 minimum) resident tuition; $5,301 ($171/hr) nonresident; $3,226 room and board; $938 student fees.

Collegiate Environment: The 165-acre campus is located in the southwestern part of Wichita Falls, Texas, the center of a rich agricultural, oil, and ranching region. The 35 university buildings contain a library of over 480,000 items including 260,546 volumes, 1,200 periodicals, government publications and microforms. Dormitory facilities accommodate 337 men and 263 women. Students from other geographical locations are accepted as well as midyear students. Approximately 96% of students applying for admission are accepted. About 93% of the previous freshman class returned to the university for the sophomore year. Average high school standing of a recent freshman class, top 50%; 20% in the top quarter; 30% in the second quarter; 40% in the third quarter; and 10% in the bottom quarter; average scores, ACT 18. Of 324 scholarships offered, over half are available for freshman and 26% of the current students receive financial aid. The college awarded 57 Associate, 727 Bachelor and 128 Master degrees to the 1994 graduating class. Approximately 11% of the senior class continued on to graduate school.

Community Environment: Population 97,000. A distributing point for both southern Oklahoma and northwestern Texas, Wichita Falls is one of the important trade centers of the Southwest. The community has a library, museum, two hospitals, a YMCA and YWCA. Various civic, fraternal and veteran's organizations serve the city. Rooms in private homes are available for student housing. Part-time employment is available. Local recreational facilities include theatres, nightclubs, bowling, skating, boating, fishing, municipal golf course, and two country club golf courses.

MOUNTAIN VIEW COLLEGE   *(G-10)*
4849 West Illinois Avenue
Dallas, Texas 75211
Tel: (214) 333-8600; Fax: (214) 333-8570

Description: Publicly supported, coeducational community college; opening in September, 1970, it was the third institution in the newly formed Dallas County Community College District. The college is accredited by the Southern Association of Colleges and Schools. The college offers university-transfer, vocational, technical, and general educational programs. Vocational, educational, recreational and cultural non-credit courses are also offered. The college grants the certificate and Associate degree. Enrollment includes 3,406 men, 2,503 women full-time and 188 men and 1,297 women part-time. A faculty of 80 full-time and 130 part-time gives a faculty-student ratio of 1-26.

Entrance Requirements: Open door policy; accredited high school graduation or equivalent required for degree courses; ACT required; non-high school graduates considered for admission under certain circumstances; rolling admission, early admission plans available.

Costs Per Year: $348 district tuition; $1,532 out-of-county tuition; $2,100 out-of-state tuition.

Collegiate Environment: The colleges of the Dallas County Community College District have no geographical boundary restrictions for enrollment at any of the campuses. Admissions requirements are all the same, and students may enroll in more than one college at the same time. The library contains over 65,000 holdings.

Community Environment: See Dallas Christian College.

NAVARRO COLLEGE   *(H-10)*
3200 W. 7th Avenue
Corsicana, Texas 75110
Tel: (903) 874-6501; (800) 628-2776 in TX; Admissions: (903) 874-6501; Fax: (903) 874-4636

Description: Publicly supported, coeducational junior college established in 1946 and accredited by the Southern Association of Colleges and Schools. It offers two-year academic, technical, and vocational programs leading to a Certificate or an Associate degree. The college established centers in two of the larger communities in the college service area: the Bi-Stone center in Mexia, and the Ellis center in Waxahachie. Operating on the semester system it also offers two summer terms. Enrollment includes 3,300 full-time and part-time students. A faculty of 78 full-time and 97 part-time gives a faculty-student ratio of 1-20.

Entrance Requirements: Open enrollment policy; ACT or SAT recommended; TASP and local placement test required; non-high school graduates, over 18 years of age, may be admitted by successful completion of GED examinations; early admission, rolling admission, early decision, and advanced placement plans available.

Costs Per Year: $1,033 ($33.33 per credit hour) state resident tuition; $1,206 ($38.89 per credit hour) nonresident tuition; $4,000 room and board; $410 student fees.

Collegiate Environment: The college is located on 117 acres and is comprised of 8 academic buildings and 16 resident halls for 550 students. The library contains 40,000 volumes and 250 periodical subscriptions. Students participate in many extra-curricular activities via student organizations and performance groups. All qualified students applying for admission are accepted. 400 scholarships are available and 50% of students receive some form of aid.

Community Environment: Navarro College is located in historic Corsicana, Texas. The economy is diversified and part-time jobs are available for students. The local climate is moderate to mild. The area is served by bus and major highways. There are several churches, a library, YMCA, and outstanding medical facilities. Residents can enjoy restaurants, shopping, and local fine arts events as well as excellent recreational facilities for boating, water skiing, fishing, golf, and hunting. Annual events include rodeo finals, bicycle races, and food destivals.

NORTH CENTRAL TEXAS COLLEGE   *(E-9)*
1525 West California
Gainesville, Texas 76240
Tel: (817) 668-7731; Fax: (817) 668-6049

Description: Publicly supported, coeducational junior college, formerly known as Gainesville College and Cooke County College, opened for students in 1924. It is accredited by the Southern Association of Colleges and Schools. Total enrollment is 1,116 full-time and 2,952 part-time students. A faculty of 70 full-time and 156 part-time gives a faculty-student ratio of 1-18. The semester system is used and two summer sessions are offered. Two-year transfer courses, vocational preparation and adult education programs are offered. The college grants the Certificate and the Associate degree.

Entrance Requirements: Approved high school graduation or equivalent required for degree program; completion of 16 units including 4 English, 2 mathematics, 2 science, and 2 social science; non-high school graduates over 18 years of age admitted under certain circumstances.

Costs Per Year: $600 tuition; $960 out-of-state; $2,940 room and board.

Collegiate Environment: There are ten buildings on the 135-acre campus. The library contains 40,185 volumes, 350 periodicals, 422 microforms and 271 audiovisual aids. There are dormitories for 52 men and 54 women. Special financial aid is available, and 20% of a recent freshman class received some form of assistance.

Community Environment: Population 13,830. Gainesville is a rural community that enjoys a temperate climate. The area is reached by bus lines. There is a public library, churches of major denominations, a local hospital, and over 80 civic, fraternal and veteran's organizations in the city. Part-time employment is limited. Local recreation includes boating, tennis, fishing, and golf.

NORTH HARRIS MONTGOMERY COMMUNITY COLLEGE DISTRICT   *(K-12)*
250 N. Sam Houston Parkway East
Houston, Texas 77060
Tel: (713) 443-5400; Fax: (713) 443-5402

Description: This publicly supported, coeducational community college is accredited by the Southern Association of Colleges and Schools. It commenced operation in 1973. The college operates on the semester system and offers two summer sessions. It grants the Certificate and the Associate degree. Enrollment includes 6,306 full-time, 12,769 part-time and 4,874 evening students. A faculty of 313 full-time and 716 part-time gives a faculty-student ratio of 1-21.

Entrance Requirements: Open enrollment policy; high school graduation; ACT required for placement purposes; under certain circumstances non-high school graduates are considered for admission; early decision, advanced placement, and rolling admission plans are available.

Costs Per Year: $640 district-resident tuition; $1,600 state-resident; $1,920 out-of-state; $700 approximate additional expenses.

Collegiate Environment: The college maintains a library of 116,593 volumes, 1,536 periodicals, 163,950 microforms and audiovisual materials. No on-campus housing is provided. 130 scholarships are available and 20% of the students receive some form of financial aid.

Community Environment: See University of Houston.

Branch Campuses: Kingwood College, 20000 Kingwood Dr., Kingwood, TX 77339, Dir.: Elizabeth Lunden, tel.: (713) 359-1600; Tomball College, 30555 Tomball Pkwy., Tomball, TX 77375, Dir.: Janice Peyton, tel.: (713) 351-3300.

NORTHWOOD UNIVERSITY   *(C-8)*
P.O. Box 58 - 1114 W. FM 1382
Cedar Hill, Texas 75104
Tel: (214) 291-1541; (800) 927-9663; Admissions: (214) 293-5400; Fax: (214) 291-3824

Description: This privately supported, coeducational, business education college is one of three campuses; the others being in Midland, Michigan, and in West Palm Beach, Florida. All branches are accredited by the North Central Association of Colleges and Schools. The purpose of the three campuses is to provide a college in which an education in management education would be teamed with a knowledge of both general and specific business skills. The Associate degree is granted in automotive marketing, business management, hotel and restaurant management, fashion merchandising, automotive aftermarket management and advertising. The Bachelors degree is offered in Business Administration, Automotive Market, Marketing, and Management. The university was established in 1966. It operates on the quarter system and also provides 3 summer terms. Enrollment includes 765 full-time students. A faculty of 9 full-time and 18 part-time gives a faculty-student ratio of 1-17.

Entrance Requirements: High school graduation; recommended completion of 16 units including 3 English, 2 mathematics, and 3 social studies; ACT or SAT required, ACT preferred; early decision and rolling admission plans available; honors admission requirements are 2 of 3: 3.25 GPA, 1050 composite SAT or 25 composite ACT, or top 10% of class.

Costs Per Year: $9,948 tuition; $4,422 room and board; $215 student fees.

Collegiate Environment: The university buildings contain a library of 35,000 volumes and living accommodations for 108 men and 56 women. The university prepares students with skills for middle management positions and also provides a continuing education program. A 10-week term in Europe, traveling and studying for 18 credits, is available. Financial aid is available. 82% of students receive financial aid. Fraternities, sororities, student government, varsity baseball and cross country, intramural sports, various organizations and off-campus activities are available.

Community Environment: Population 16,000. Cedar Hill is a suburb of Dallas, located 28 miles from Fort Worth.

OBLATE SCHOOL OF THEOLOGY   *(L-7)*
285 Oblate Drive
San Antonio, Texas 78216-6693
Tel: (210) 341-1366; Fax: (210) 341-4519

Description: Privately supported, graduate and doctoral-level school of theology of the Roman Catholic Church, under the direction of the Missionary Society of the Oblate Fathers of Texas. The school is a member of the National Catholic Education Association and is accredited by the Southern Association of Colleges and Schools, and the Association of Theological Schools. The school is a member of the United Colleges of San Antonio, a consortium for interinstitutional cooperation, and is also a member of HECSA (the Higher Education Council of San Antonio). The Doctor of Ministry (D.Min), the highest professional degree in ministry, is offered in two three-week sessions annually, with specializations in the Supervision of Ministry or Hispanic Ministry. The school offers a 4- to 5- year graduate program to equip men for the religious, social, and educational work of the Catholic priesthood and leading to the degree of Master of Divinity (M.Div.). Since nearly half of the graduates will engage in parochial ministry among the Spanish-speaking people of the Southwest and

Mexico, special attention is given to the language and the customs of these people. Besides providing for the continuing education of the clergy, the school offers the Master of Arts in Pastoral Ministry (M.A.P. Min.) to students to deepen their theological education and prepare them to serve church and community. The Master of Arts in Theology (M.A.Th.) is offered to those who want to continue for a Ph.D. or to teach at the secondary or college level. The Pre-Theology program is offered to students without the pre-requisite undergraduate religious and/or philosophy courses. The school operates on the early semester system and offers two summer sessions. Enrollment includes 29 full-time and 92 part-time students. 105 of these are graduate students. A faculty of 16 full-time and 8 part-time provides a faculty-student ratio of 1-5.

Entrance Requirements: Baccalaureate degree from an accredited college or university; minimum of 18 semester hours of credit in religious studies and/or philosophy; Miller Analogies Test (MAT); statement of goals and objectives; three references for recommendation.

Costs Per Year: $5,280 tuition ($220/semester hour); $155 student fees.

Collegiate Environment: The school is located on 25 acres and is comprised of 5 buildings. It contains a library of 36,185 volumes and 310 periodicals. A Renewal Center is under construction. The sports facilities include a swimming pool and handball alleys. The school welcomes a geographically diverse student body and will accept midyear students. Almost all students applying for admission recently were accepted. 85% of the previous entering class returned for the second year.

Community Environment: See San Antonio College.

ODESSA COLLEGE   *(H-2)*
201 West University
Odessa, Texas 79764
Tel: (915) 335-6400

Description: Publicly supported, coeducational community college was established in 1946 and is accredited by the Southern Association of Colleges and Schools. The college grants an Associate degree. It operates on the semester system and offers a mid-winter term and two summer sessions. Enrollment includes 1,911 men and 2,618 women. A faculty of 124 full-time and 114 part-time provides a faculty-student ratio of 1-19. It offers preprofessional training, terminal education, adult and vocational training, and general courses.

Entrance Requirements: Accredited high school graduation; Open admissions and enrollment policy; applicants over 18 years of age who do not meet all entrance requirements may be admitted with successful completion of proper guidance examinations. Early admission, midyear admission plans available.

Costs Per Year: $674 tuition; $794 tuition out-of-county residents; $914 tuition out-of-state residents; room and board $2,983; $50 student fees.

Collegiate Environment: The 80-acre campus is located in Odessa, the oil capital of Texas, 140 miles southwest of Lubbock. The 23 college buildings include a library of 81,440 volumes and dormitory facilities for 130 men and women. 77 are for athletes only. Financial aid is available.

Community Environment: Population of Odessa 100,000; of Midland 87,000. Odessa is one of the largest domestic oilfield supply centers in Texas. The community enjoys a mild climate. The city is reached by airlines, two bus lines, and railroad. Churches representing all denominations, two hospitals, a library, and many civic and fraternal organizations serve the area. Part-time employment is available. Local recreation includes theatres, bowling alleys, hunting, and sports.

OUR LADY OF THE LAKE UNIVERSITY OF SAN ANTONIO *(L-7)*
411 S.W. 24th Street
San Antonio, Texas 78207-4689
Tel: (210) 434-6711; (800) 436-6558; Fax: (210) 436-2314

Description: Privately supported, coeducational university established by the Congregation of the Sisters of Divine Providence in 1895. In 1923, the university became the first Roman Catholic women's college in the South to receive accreditation from the South-

ern Association of Colleges and Schools, and in 1927, the third Texas school to be approved by the American Association of Universities. The undergraduate curriculum features an individualized and competence-based degree plan, providing advanced placement, credit for life/work experience, opportunities for external competence validations, and a wide variety of alternative learning experiences. Besides the usual liberal arts fields, the university offers undergraduate professional specializations in management, media, medical technology, speech pathology, generic special education, bilingual/bicultural education, early childhood education, and social work. Master's degree programs include education, counseling psychology, business administration, English, library science, speech pathology, language and learning disabilities, social work and a doctoral program in psychology. In addition to the Fall and Spring semesters, the calendar includes two five-and-one-half week summer sessions. Enrollment includes 1,452 full-time, 1,886 part-time undergraduates, and 1,043 graduate students. A faculty of 106 full-time and 99 part-time gives a faculty-student ratio of 1-16.

Entrance Requirements: High school graduation; completion of 16 units including 4 English, 2 mathematics, 2 foreign language, 2 science, 2 social science; SAT score of 400 verbal and 380 math or a composite ACT and SAT required; applicants not meeting all entrance requirements may be admitted on a conditional basis or upon individual approval; early decision, early admission, rolling admission, delayed admission, midyear admission and advanced placement plans available; application fee $15.

Costs Per Year: $9,000 tuition; $3,500 room and board; $144 student fees; $500 estimated additional costs.

Collegiate Environment: The campus of the university is a 32 acre tract bordering Elmendorf Lake and the city-owned Elmendorf Park. The 23 university buildings include libraries containing 265,000 volumes, 872 periodicals and 130,000 microforms which include a complete ERIC collection. Dormitory facilities are available for women and men. The college welcomes a geographically diverse student body. 60% of the previous freshman class returned to this campus for the sophomore year. Approximately 70% of the recent student body graduated in the top half of the high school class, and 20% in the top quarter. Over 80% of the students receive some form of student aid. The average SAT scores of the current freshman were 401 verbal and 429 math or an average composite ACT score of 18.

Community Environment: See San Antonio College.

PANOLA JUNIOR COLLEGE   *(H-13)*
West Panola Street
Carthage, Texas 75633
Tel: (903) 693-2038; Admissions: (903) 693-2037; Fax: (903) 693-5588

Description: Publicly supported, coeducational junior college opened to its first class of students in 1948. It offers freshman and sophomore courses leading to transfer programs; preprofessional training for professional schools such as law, medicine, and engineering; terminal or vocational training; continuing education for adults. The school is accredited by the Southern Association of Colleges and Schools and grants a Certificate of Completion and an Associate degree. The semester system is used and two summer terms are offered. Enrollment includes 1,600 full-time and 735 part-time students. A faculty of 54 full-time and 19 part-time gives a faculty-student ratio of 1-22.

Entrance Requirements: Accredited high school graduation or equivalent; ACT required; open enrollment policy. Students not meeting these requirements may be admitted by examination; early admission, rolling admission, and advanced placement plans available.

Costs Per Year: $450 tuition state resident; $490 tuition out-of-state resident; $2,080 room and board; $120 student fees; $500 approximate additional expenses.

Collegiate Environment: The 35-acre campus has 12 buildings. There are dormitories for 83 men and 75 women. The library contains 30,000 volumes, 150 periodicals and 300 sound recordings. All students applying for admission who meet the requirements are accepted. The college welcomes a geographically diverse student body. Freshman classes begin in September, January, June and July. There is special financial aid available. Of a total of 100 scholarships, 75 are for freshmen. Approximately 44% of students receive some form of financial aid. 45% of the previous freshman class returned to this campus for their sophomore year. The college granted 29 Certificates and 128 Associate degrees to a recent graduating class.

Community Environment: Population 6400. Carthage is a rural community with temperate climate. The community is served by railroad, bus lines, and U.S. Route 59 and 79. The community service facilities include a public library, hospital, and churches of eight denominations. Part-time employment is somewhat limited. There are theatres, 35-mile lake shoreline for all water sports, swimming pool, golf courses, bowling alley, and several rodeos and livestock shows held annually.

PARIS JUNIOR COLLEGE   *(E-11)*
2400 Clarksville St.
Paris, Texas 75460
Tel: (903) 785-7661; (800) 232-5804; Admissions: (903) 784-9425;
Fax: (903) 784-9370

Description: Publicly supported, coeducational junior college established in 1924 as part of the public school system. It is accredited by the Southern Association of Colleges and Schools. It operates on the semester system and offers two summer terms. The college offers the first two years of a Baccalaureate program, technical-occupational training, and continuing education leading to a Certificate of Completion or an Associate degree. The enrollment includes 2,017 full-time and 800 part-time students.

Entrance Requirements: Accredited high school graduation or equivalent; open enrollment policy; non-high school graduates 18 years of age may be admitted upon examination; students over 18 years of age may be admitted on individual approval; midyear admissions, early decision and rolling admission plans available.

Costs Per Year: $630 tuition district residents; $870 tuition other Texas residents; $1,374 tuition out-of-state residents; room and board available; $170 student fees.

Collegiate Environment: The 700-acre campus includes a 238-acre bilogical field lab; a 363-seat theatre for the perfoming arts and a 110-seat recital hall; the $1.1 million Hunt Physical Education center, consisting of a gymnasium with a seating capacity of 1,500, two large classrooms including the Dragon Athletic Hall of Fame, dressing rooms, a training room, and concession area; a gymnasium and fitness center; laboratories for instruction in science, computer cosmetology; the Mike Rheudasil Learning Center houses a 54,110-volume library and the A.M. and Welma Aikin Rgional Archives. Additional holdings include 601 pamphlets, 368 periodicals, 15,025 microforms and 3,479 audiovisual materials. Outdoor athletic facilities include a one-mile jogging/fitness track at Dragon Park; four tennis courts; baseball field and soccer fields; golf driving range and archery range. Residence halls accomodate 250 students. 100% of students applying for admission meet the requirements and are accepted. Freshman classes begin in September, January, June and July. Special financial aid is available. The college offers 330 scholarships annually.

Community Environment: Population 25,000. A farming and industrial center, Paris has a modern attractiveness which is the result of planned reconstruction following a fire that swept the town in 1916. Today the local industries produce furniture, light bulb parts, clothing, and food items. Located in the heart of Red River Valley, the area has a mean annual temperature of 63.9 degrees. There are four railroad lines, two bus lines and five main highways to serve the community. An airport is approximately seven miles away. A public library, over 40 churches, two hospitals, and civic and fraternal organizations are active in the city. Local recreation includes parks, bowling, golf, theatres, and drive-ins, and nearby Pat Mayse Lake providing boating, swimming, and fishing.

PAUL QUINN COLLEGE   *(G-9)*
3837 Simpson Stuart Road
Dallas, Texas 75241
Tel: (214) 376-1000; (800) 237-2648; Admissions: (214) 302-3520;
Fax: (214) 302-3559

Description: Privately supported, coeducational, liberal arts and teachers college founded by a small group of African Methodist Episcopal circuit-riding preachers in Austin in 1872. The college operates on the semester system and offers one summer term. The college is accredited by the Southern Association of Colleges and Schools and by the Texas Education Agency. Recent enrollment included 310

men, 349 women full-time and 50 men and 79 women part-time. A faculty of 55 full-time and 6 part-time gives a ratio of 1-12. The college grants a Baccalaureate degree.

Entrance Requirements: Accredited high school graduate; completion of 15 units including 3 English, 2 mathematics, 2 social science; ACT required; students over 21 years of age not otherwise unqualified may be considered for admission by individual approval; applicants not meeting all requirements may be admitted for nondegree courses; application fee $15; early decision, rolling admission, early admission and advanced placement plans available.

Costs Per Year: $3,400 tuition; room and board $2,950; $300 approximate additional expenses.

Collegiate Environment: The 130-acre campus is located in the South Oak Cliff section about eight miles south of downtown Dallas. The college welcomes a geographically diverse student body and does accept midyear students. The college offers academic, athletic, and need based scholarships. Approximately 98% of the applicants are accepted.

Community Environment: See Dallas Christian College.

PRAIRIE VIEW A&M UNIVERSITY   *(K-11)*
Prairie View, Texas 77446
Tel: (409) 857-3311

Description: Publicly supported, coeducational teachers, liberal arts and professional college was established by enactment of the Texas State Legislature in 1876. It is accredited by the Southern Association of Colleges and Schools and operates on the semester system with two summer terms. The three separate and distinct functions of the university are to prepare and train teachers, to offer four years of liberal arts and scientific curricula, and as a Texas Land Grant College, to provide opportunities for training in agriculture, home economics, engineering, and related branches of learning. The college is a part of the Texas A. and M. University System. The college grants Bachelor and Masters degrees. U.S. Army and U.S. Navy ROTC programs are available. Enrollment includes 2,480 full-time and 458 part-time undergraduates. A faculty of 245 full-time gives a faculty-student ratio of 1-15.

Entrance Requirements: Accredited high school graduation; completion of 16 units including 4 English, 3 mathematics, 3 science, 2 social science and 4 electives. ACT/SAT required with minimum score of ACT 18 and SAT 700; any or all requirements may be met by passing entrance examinations; early admission, early decision, midyear admission plans available.

Costs Per Year: $1,540 tuition state resident; $5,690 tuition out-of-state; $3,450 room and board; $402 miscellaneous.

Collegiate Environment: The 1,400-acre campus is located in Waller County, 46 miles northwest of Houston. There are dormitory facilities for 1,791 men and 1,735 women on the campus and the library has a collection of 240,117 volumes, 1,655 periodicals, 322,614 microforms and 7,443 sound recordings. 75% of students applying for admission meet the requirements and are accepted. The college offers 108 scholarships for freshmen. 85% of the student body receive some form of financial aid. About 60% of the current student body graduated in the top half of their high school class, 20% in the top quarter. About 70% of the current freshman class returned for the sophomore year.

Community Environment: Population 3,589. Prairie View is a rural community enjoying temperate climate. The area is reached by bus lines and Route 290. There are Catholic, Baptist, and Episcopal Churches in the community. The college hospital serves the city.

RANGER COLLEGE   *(G-7)*
College Circle
Ranger, Texas 76470
Tel: (817) 647-3234; Fax: (817) 647-1656

Description: Publicly supported, coeducational junior college was founded in 1926. It is accredited by the Southern Association of Colleges and Schools. It operates on the semester system and offers two summer terms. The college offers freshman and sophomore years for students working toward a Baccalaureate degree, two-year Associate degree programs, and vocational training leading to the Associate degree and Applied Arts Diploma. Enrollment is 505 full-time and 269 part-time students. A faculty of 31 full-time and 24 part-time gives a faculty-student ratio of 1-13.

Entrance Requirements: High school graduation; completion of 15 units including 4 English, 2 mathematics, 2 social science; ACT or SAT recommended, ACT preferred; open admission, midyear students accepted; early admission, early decision and rolling admission available.

Costs Per Year: $660 tuition; $850 out-of-state; $2,400 room and board; $100 student fees.

Collegiate Environment: The 50-acre campus is located 89 miles west of Fort Worth. There are 15 buildings on the campus including dormitories for 304 men and 148 women and a library of 24,000 volumes. About 90% of students applying for admission meet the requirements and are accepted. Special financial aid is available and 80% of a recent freshman class received some form of assistance. The college awarded 300 scholarships recently. Approximately 40% of the current student body graduated in the top half of the high school class, 20% in the top quarter, and 7% in the highest tenth. 30% of the previous freshman class returned to this campus for the sophomore year.

Community Environment: Population 3,094. Ranger's name was derived from a camp of Texas Rangers, organized near here to protect settlers from marauding Indians. In 1917, oil was discovered and the community expanded. Today, there are several churches representing the major denominations. The community is reached by railroad and interstate highway. Local recreation includes fishing, swimming, boating, water skiing, a municipally owned swimming pool, hunting for deer, duck, dove, squirrel, and rabbit. Part-time employment is limited.

RICHLAND COLLEGE   *(G-10)*
12800 Abrams Road
Dallas, Texas 75243-2199
Tel: (214) 238-6101; Fax: (214) 238-6346

Description: This publicly supported, coeducational community college was established in September 1972 as the fourth institution in the newly formed Dallas County Community College District. It provides university-transfer, vocational, technical, and general educational programs, as well as community service courses. The college is accredited by the Southern Association of Colleges and Schools. The semester system is used and two summer terms are offered. Associate degree and Certificates are granted. Cooperative education programs are available in Engineering, Horticulture, Management, Accounting, and Office Careers. A study abroad program and an honors program are available. Enrollment is 11,897 full-time and part-time students. A faculty of 159 full-time and 467 part-time gives a faculty-student ratio of 1-21.

Entrance Requirements: Open door policy; accredited high school graduation or equivalent required for degree courses; SAT or ACT required or entrance exam; applications are processed until enrollment limits are reached.

Costs Per Year: $54 per credit hour tuition Dallas county resident; $150 per credit hour resident of other Texas counties; $225 per credit hour out-of-state; student fees vary.

Collegiate Environment: The colleges of the Dallas County Community College District have no geographical boundary restrictions for enrollment at any of the campuses. Admission requirements are all the same, and students may enroll in more than one college at the same time. 22 scholarships are available. 12% of students receive some form of financial aid. The library contains 80,000 volumes, 525 periodical titles, and 7,500 audiovisual materials.

SAINT EDWARD'S UNIVERSITY   *(K-8)*
3001 South Congress Avenue
Austin, Texas 78704
Tel: (512) 448-8400; Admissions: (512) 448-8500; Fax: (512) 448-8492

Description: Privately supported, coeducational, liberal arts college, whose fundamental purpose is to participate in a significant way in satisfying the educational needs of the individual and society. Founded in 1885, the Roman Catholic institute is accredited by the Southern Association of Colleges and Schools. The university had previously consisted of two coordinate colleges, Holy Cross for men

and Maryhill for women. In 1970 the two were amalgamated into one coeducational institution. The university operates on the semester system and offers four summer sessions. Enrollment includes 1,782 full-time and 868 part-time undergraduates and 479 graduate students. A faculty of 101 full-time and 133 part-time members provides a faculty-student ratio of 1-16. The school grants the Baccalaureate degree. Two masters programs, MBA and Master of Arts in Human Services are available. Air Force and Army ROTC programs are offered.

Entrance Requirements: Accredited high school graduation with rank in upper 50% of graduating class; ACT or SAT required; applicants not meeting all requirements may be admitted by individual approval; advanced placement program available. Application fee $25.

Costs Per Year: $9,950 tuition; $3,940-$4,370 room and board; $1,000 approximate additional expenses.

Collegiate Environment: The library contains approximately 150,000 volumes. Newly completed IBM classroom with 15 PS/2 Model 30 workstations. Learning Assistance Center - provides services to help students develop and use effective cognitive and affective skills for successful learning performance. Academic counseling, assistance with the enhancement of concentration, test-taking, time management skills, and tutorial support are available. Overseas study program - our affiliation with the International Student Exchange Program (ISEP) makes it possible for a student to study at any of hundreds of participating universities world-wide. Internships are either required or highly encouraged in almost all majors. There are 4 newly-renovated residence halls which accomodate 536 men and women on this beautiful campus overlooking Austin. 70% of applicants are accepted. Scholarships are available and 60% of the students receive some form of financial aid.

Community Environment: See University of Texas at Austin.

SAINT MARY'S UNIVERSITY   *(L-7)*
One Camino Santa Maria
San Antonio, Texas 78228-8503
Tel: (210) 436-3126; Fax: (210) 436-3503

Description: This privately supported, coeducational Roman Catholic university was founded in 1852 and is accredited by the Southern Association of Colleges and Schools. It is composed of the School of the Humanities and Social Sciences, the School of Business Administration, the School of Science, Engineering and Technology, the Law School and the Graduate School. It grants a Bachelor, Master, and Doctor of Jurisprudence degree. A teacher certification program is available. An Army ROTC program is voluntary. The school operates on the semester system and offers two summer terms. Enrollment is 2,188 full-time and 211 part-time undergraduates, and 1,662 graduate students. A faculty of 132 full-time and 79 part-time gives an overall faculty-student ratio of 1-14.

Entrance Requirements: Accredited high school graduation or equivalent; rank in upper 50% of graduating class; completion of 16 units including 4 English, 3 mathematics, 2 science, 2 social science, 2 foreign language, and 3 academic electives; test grades of SAT or ACT at 50th percentile; $15 application fee; rolling admission and advanced placement plans available.

Costs Per Year: $4,664 tuition; $2,135 room and board; $375 fees.

Collegiate Environment: The 135-acre campus is located in the Woodlawn Hills section of San Antonio. There are 30 permanent buildings on the campus. All out-of-town freshmen and sophomores must live in approved housing, which includes on-campus dormitories or the homes of students' relatives. Dormitory facilities are available for 550 men and 550 women. The library system contains 335,000 volumes, 1,320 periodicals, 55,000 microforms and 19,300 audiovisual materials. Approximately 77% of students applying for admission meet the requirements and are accepted. The university welcomes a geographically diverse student body and accepts midyear students. Financial aid is available and 77% of the undergraduate students received some form of assistance. Approximately 84% of the current student body graduated in the top half of the high school class; 56% ranked in the top quarter.

Community Environment: St. Mary's is located in a suburban area approximately 5 miles northwest of downtown San Antonio.

SAINT PHILIPS COLLEGE (L-7)
2111 Nevada Street
San Antonio, Texas 78203
Tel: (512) 531-3291

Description: Publicly supported, coeducational junior college opened its doors in September, 1927, to serve the immediate need of the black community of San Antonio and vicinity but dropped its all-black classification in 1955. It is accredited by the Southern Association of Colleges and Schools. There are 5,500 students attending classes. A faculty of 210 full-time, 150 part-time gives a faculty-student ratio of 1-16. The college provides programs in general and vocational-technical education, transfer courses to senior colleges or professional schools, and provides opportunities for students to remove subject or scholarship deficiencies. The college operates on the semester system and three summer sessions are offered. The college grants a Certificate and an Associate degree.

Entrance Requirements: Accredited high school graduation or equivalent; open enrollment policy; completion of 15 units including 3 English and 2 mathematics, applicants not meeting all requirements may be admitted by special approval; SAT, ACT, or entrance exam required; early admission and advanced placement plans available.

Costs Per Year: $450 state-resident tuition, $1,490 out-of-state; $104 district-resident student fees, $295 out-of-district and out-of-state; $200 estimated additional expenses.

Collegiate Environment: The 13-acre campus is located on the east side of San Antonio, two miles from the center of the city. There are eight buildings including the library, which contains 51,661 volumes, 4,129 periodicals, 14,745 microforms and 362 sound recordings. There are no dormitories. Approximately 98% of students applying for admission are accepted, including midyear students. Special financial aid is available, and 70% of the students receive some form of assistance.

Community Environment: See San Antonio College.

SAM HOUSTON STATE UNIVERSITY (J-12)
Huntsville, Texas 77341
Tel: (409) 294-1056; Admissions: (409) 294-1828

Description: Publicly supported, coeducational liberal arts and teacher training university was founded in 1879. It is accredited by the Southern Association of Colleges and Schools. The university offers undergraduate and graduate programs in the College of Arts and Sciences, Education and Applied Science, Library Science, Business and Administration and the College of Criminal Justice leading to the Bachelor, Master and Doctoral degrees. In addition, the university offers course programs required for entrance into professional schools of medicine, law, engineering, dentistry, and other professions. It operates on the semester system and offers two summer sessions. Enrollment is 9,239 full-time, 3,173 part-time undergraduate, and 1,575 graduate students. A faculty of 335 full-time and 135 part-time gives a faculty-student ratio of 1-23. Army ROTC program available.

Entrance Requirements: Accredited high school graduation, completion of 15 units including 3 English, 2 math, and 2 science; minimum ACT 21 or SAT 900 combined required; non-high school graduates may be admitted with satisfactory score on admissions test; early admission, and midyear admission plans available; $15 application fee.

Costs Per Year: $758 state resident tuition; $4,860 nonresident tuition; $2,880 room and board; $676 fees; $1,000 estimated additional expenses.

Collegiate Environment: The 1,186-acre campus has 110 buildings including the library which contains 766,350 volumes, 3,111 periodicals, and 501,762 microforms. There are housing accommodations for 1,408 men, 1,586 women and 49 families. The college welcomes a geographically diverse student body. 77% of applicants are offered admission. The university awards about 118 scholarships annually and half of these are offered to freshman students. 40% of the freshman class receive some form of financial assistance.

Community Environment: Huntsville (population 26,000) is located in the pine belt 70 miles north of Houston. This was the home of General Sam Houston, and museums commemorate his honor. The average temperatures are 51.1 degrees in winter and 82.6 degrees in summer. The community has a hospital, various fraternal, civic, and veterans's organizations, and is served by rail, bus lines, and U.S. Highway I-45. A nearby state park offers fishing, boating, swimming, and picnicking. Part-time employment is available.

SAN ANTONIO COLLEGE (L-7)
1300 San Pedro Avenue
San Antonio, Texas 78212-4299
Tel: (512) 733-2575

Description: This publicly supported, coeducational junior college was founded in 1925. Enrollment was 20,998 students recently. A faculty of 388 full-time and 466 part-time gives a faculty-student ratio of 1-24. The college operates on the semester system and two summer terms are offered. It is accredited by the Southern Association of Colleges and Schools and offers courses designed to fulfill freshman and sophomore degree requirements of senior colleges and universities, as well as vocational courses and continuing education courses that lead to a Certificate of Completion and an Associate degree in Arts, Science, Applied Science, Mortuary Science, and Nursing.

Entrance Requirements: Open door policy; degree candidates require accredited high school graduation; ACT or SAT and TASP required; no formal application required; advanced placement program available.

Costs Per Year: $525 district-resident tuition; $40 district-resident student fees; $1,535 out-of-state tuition; $180 out-of-state student fees.

Collegiate Environment: The 40-acre campus has a library collection of 225,285 volumes. There are no dormitory facilities on the campus. An evening division of the college is available for students who are unable to attend classes during the day. Special financial aid is available and 15% of a recent freshman class received some form of assistance.

Community Environment: Population 975,000. Called the cradle of Texas liberty because of its history, San Antonio is the birthplace of the rough riders and th home of the Alamo. San Antonio is a mixture of its early Spanish background and a modern metropolis. Skyscrapers exist alongside 18th-century adobe restorations. There are many historic sites to be seen in the area. The transportation to and within the city is excellent. There are local and transcontinental bus lines. More than 500 churches representing most denominations, many civic and fraternal organizations, hospitals and museums serve the community. San Antonio has a symphony orchestra and an art museum. The annual Fiesta San Jacinto, Everett Colborn World's Championship Rodeo, and Grand Opera Festival are held here. Local recreation includes 56 parks, sunken garden theater, golf courses, polo fields, baseball diamonds, tennis courts, bridle paths, picnic grounds, swimming pools, hunting, fishing, and boating. Part-time employment is available.

SAN JACINTO COLLEGE - CENTRAL CAMPUS (L-12)
8060 Spencer Highway
P.O. Box 2007
Pasadena, Texas 77501
Tel: (713) 476-1501

Description: Publicly supported, coeducational comprehensive community college is owned and operated by the San Jacinto College District. It is accredited by the Southern Association of Colleges and Schools. The semester system is used with two summer terms. Day and evening classes are available and students completing the first two years of a four-year college curriculum may transfer with junior standing to senior colleges and universities. Technical and vocational courses, adult education, and general educational programs are offered leading to a Certificate or an Associate degree. Recent enrollment included approximately 9,262 students. A faculty of 282 gives a faculty-student ratio of 1-25.

Entrance Requirements: Accredited high school graduation; non-high school graduates may be admitted upon individual approval.

Costs Per Year: $360 tuition district or state resident; $1,350 tuition out-of-state resident.

Collegiate Environment: San Jacinto College Central is a member of multicampus district. The Central Campus library contains 108,854 volumes. Freshman classes begin in September, January, June and July. There are no dormitories available on campus.

Community Environment: Population 118,000. Pasadena is a suburban community enjoying a semi-tropical climate. The city has a public library system, churches, and museums. Nearby Houston offers many cultural, recreational and community services. By automobile, the Gulf of Mexico is only 20 minutes away. The immediate community has hospitals, and many civic and fraternal organizations. Part-time employment is available.

SAN JACINTO COLLEGE - NORTH CAMPUS *(K-12)*
5800 Uvalde
Houston, Texas 77049
Tel: (713) 458-4050

Description: The state supported junior college was founded in 1961; the north campus was officially opened in 1974. The school is accredited by the Southern Associaton of Colleges and Schools. Day and evening classes are offered to prepare students for the transition from high school to a program leading to a baccalaureate degree after completion of the two year program. The college also offers occupational and technical training which may lead to a certificate or Associate degree. Adult, continuing, and general education programs are available. Enrollment was 1,061 full-time, 2,644 part-time students. A faculty of 93 full-time teachers and 106 part-time produces a student-faculty ratio of 20-1. The semester system is used with two summer sessions.

Entrance Requirements: High school graduation; GED accepted; open enrollment policy; early admission plan.

Costs Per Year: $256 tuition, district or state resident; $1,280 non-resident tuition, $78 student fees.

Collegiate Environment: 99% of students applying are accepted. Seventy nine scholarships, of which 47 are athletic, are offered. The library contains 37,000 volumes, 500 periodicals, 7,059 microforms, 1,409 audio-visual materials.

Community Environment: See University of Houston.

SCHREINER COLLEGE *(K-6)*
Highway 27 South
Kerrville, Texas 78028
Tel: (210) 896-5411; (800) 343-4919; Fax: (210) 896-3232

Description: Privately supported, coeducational college is a fully accredited member of the Southern Association of Colleges and Schools. The college opened in 1923 following a grant from Captain Charles Schreiner to the Presbyterian Church of the United States. Currently operating on a 4-1-4 calendar with one summer term, the college offers baccalaureate and associate degrees with majors in liberal arts and business disciplines. Enrollment is 483 full-time and 101 part-time students, about equally divided between women and men. A faculty of 38 full-time and 14 part-time provides a faculty-student ratio of 1-13. The curriculum encourages understanding of the incorporation of the academic aspects of life-long learning and career preparation into the whole of the Schreiner experience including the goal of harmonious development with social, cultural, spiritual, and service aspects. There is an exchange program for sophomores with Nagasaki Wesleyan College in Japan.

Entrance Requirements: Accredited high school graduation or equivalent; completion of 15 units including 4 English, 3 mathematics, 2 laboratory science, and 2 social studies; ACT or SAT required; applicants not meeting all requirements may be considered for admission by individual approval; rolling admission, midyear admission, and advanced placement plans available; $20 application fee.

Costs Per Year: $8,955 tuition; $6,140 room and board; $500 student fees and books.

Collegiate Environment: The college is located at Kerrville, the heart of the Hill Country of Texas. The 172-acre campus within walking distance of the center of town has 34 buildings including the William M. Logan Library with a collection of 75,000 volumes and 500 current periodical subscriptions. There are dormitories for 165 men and 159 women. Approximately 73% of students applying for admission meets the requirements and are accepted. Freshman classes may begin in September, January and June. 125 scholarships are available and 75% of the current student body receives some form of financial aid.

Community Environment: Population 24,000. In the rugged hill region by the Guadalupe River, Kerrville is a popular summer and winter resort area. The hill country is famous for fishing and hunting. The city is located 65 miles northwest of San Antonio and enjoys moderate climate. The community has churches of major denominations, a hospital, and various civic, fraternal, and veteran's organizations. Local recreation includes theatres, boating, fishing, water skiing, and deer and turkey hunting. Job opportunities are available.

SOUTH PLAINS COLLEGE *(E-2)*
1400 College Avenue
Levelland, Texas 79336
Tel: (806) 894-9611; Fax: (806) 894-5274

Description: Publicly supported, coeducational junior college was founded in 1957 and is accredited by the Southern Association of Colleges and Schools. It provides Associate degree programs designed to prepare individuals for semiprofessional employment or for further college study and vocational training, leading to employment or to advancement in present fields. The college grants a Certificate of Achievement and an Associate degree. The semester system is used, and two summer terms are offered. Both day and evening classes are held. A full-time enrollment of 5,137 men and women with a faculty of 270 gives a faculty-student of 1-19. There are also 5,960 part-time students and 290 part-time faculty.

Entrance Requirements: Accredited high school graduation or equivalent; open enrollment policy; early admission, early decision, delayed admission, advanced placement and rolling admission plans available.

Costs Per Year: $350 tuition; $550 out-of-district tuition; $1,150 room and board.

Collegiate Environment: The 177-acre campus is 30 miles west of Lubbock. The campus has 22 buildings including five men's dormitories and three women's, which accommodate 600 men and women. The library contains 47,000 volumes, 350 periodicals, 15,000 microforms and 50 sound recordings. Approximately 99% of students applying for admission meet the requirements and are accepted. The college welcomes a geographically diverse student body. Freshman classes begin in August, January, June and July. Financial aid is available.

Community Environment: Population 14,500. Levelland is a rural community enjoying temperate climate. The area is reached by bus lines, an airport, and Routes 114 and 385. The city has a public library, churches of major denominations, and one hospital. There are civic, fraternal and veteran's organizations active in the area. Local recreation includes theatres, rodeos, and outdoor sports. Part-time employment is available.

SOUTH TEXAS COLLEGE OF LAW *(K-12)*
1303 San Jacinto Street
Houston, Texas 77002
Tel: (713) 646-1810; Fax: (713) 659-3807

Description: South Texas College of Law is a private, nonprofit independent educational institution located in downtown Houston. Founded in 1923 by leading members of the Houston bench and bar, South Texas is one of the oldest law schools in the metropolitan area and one of the largest private law schools in the nation. The College is approved by the American Bar Association, as well as the Supreme Court of Texas and the Texas Education Agency. It also is approved for the training of veterans entitled to federal educational benefits. Enrollment includes 833 full-time and 461 part-time students. The faculty includes 56 full-time members and 40 adjunct members resulting in a faculty-student ratio of 1-22.

Entrance Requirements: Baccalaureate degree from an accredited college or university and demonstrated satisfactory performance on LSAT required; evaluation of transcripts by the Law School Data Assembly Service is required, and applicants must submit official transcripts of all undergraduate work directly to the LSDAS; beginning and transfer students are admitted on a rolling admission basis for the fall and spring terms, and early application is encouraged; $40 application fee.

Costs Per Year: $12,750 tuition; $300 student fees.

Collegiate Environment: The South Texas College of Law physical plant is among the most modern and attractive law school complexes in the country. The Jesse H. Jones Legal Center, dedicated in1984, includes the South Texas College of Law Tower, the Roy and Lillie Cullen Building and the Garland R. Walker Terrace. The Center occupies a city block in downtown Houston. The eleven-story South Texas College of Law Tower houses administrative, business, and faculty offices, three classroom floors, and the hearing rooms and chambers of the 1st and 14th Texas Courts of Appeals (intermediate appellate tribunals with both civil and criminal jurisdiction). South Texas is the only American law school to house two such appellate courts on a permanent basis. The Cullen Building houses student offices, bookstore, food services, student areas and the Green Jr. Advocacy Center. Also housed in the Cullen Building are the law library, housing 250,000 volumes, and the 240-seat Garrett-Townes Hall. All facilities are barrier free, and all programs and activities are open to handicapped individuals. 40% of applicants are accepted. Scholarships are available and 70% of the students receive some form of financial aid.

Community Environment: Houston is a city of superlatives: the fourth-largest city (population 1,630,553) in the United States; America's third-largest deep-water port; the only city in the United States ever to exceed $3 billion in building permits during a single year; home of the first air-conditioned domed stadium, the Astrodome; and home to the Texas Medical Center, the world's largest healthcare and medical-research complex. More than 167,000 students from around the world currently are enrolled in Houston schools of higher education. South Texas College of Law is located in the heart of this bustling metropolis, at the heart of Houston's downtown legal and financial district.

SOUTHERN METHODIST UNIVERSITY   (G-10)
P.O. Box 296
Dallas, Texas 75275
Tel: (214) 768-2058; (800) 323-0672

Description: Privately supported, coeducational university was founded in 1911 by and is affiliated with the United Methodist Church. It is accredited by the Southern Association of Colleges and Schools in addition to numerous professional agencies. The semester system is used and two summer sessions are offered. The university is composed of the following schools: Dedman College of Humanities and Sciences, Meadows School of the Arts, the Edwin L. Cox School of Business, School of Engineering and Applied Science, the School of Law, and the Perkins School of Theology. Enrollment includes 4,907 full-time, 340 part-time, and 3,767 graduate students with a faculty of 483 full-time and 165 part-time members. The university grants Baccalaureate, Master's, Doctoral, and professional degrees. Army and Air Force ROTC programs are available.

Entrance Requirements: Accredited high school graduation or equivalent; completion of 15 college-preparatory units including 4 English, 3 mathematics, 2 foreign language, 3 natural science, 3 social science; SAT or ACT required. Admission is selective and based upon high school record (most important), college preparatory courses, ACT and SAT I scores, and academic recommendations. Application should be made soon after the completion of junior year in high school; application fee is $40; early decision and advanced placement plans available.

Costs Per Year: $12,772 tuition; $5,073 room and board; $1,624 student fees.

Collegiate Environment: Approximately 37% of undergraduates live in university housing, with an additional 10-14% residing in university owned apartments and fraternity and sorority houses. The library system contains over 2 million volumes. Three fourths of the freshman students ranked in the top third of their high-school classes. The school welcomes a geographically diverse student body and does accept transfer students. Special financial aid is available and 70% of the student body receives some form of financial aid. Composite SAT scores of the freshman class were 960-1160; ACT scores ranged from 23-28.

Community Environment: See Dallas Christian College.

SOUTHWEST TEXAS JUNIOR COLLEGE   (L-5)
Garner Field Road
Uvalde, Texas 78801
Tel: (210) 278-4401

Description: Publicly supported, coeducational community college was founded in 1946 and is approved and accredited by the Southern Association of Colleges and Schools, the Association of Texas Colleges and Universities, and the Texas Education Agency. Fall, spring and two summer semesters are offered annually. The college offers traditional academic courses that will transfer to four-year institutions and that culminate in Associate in Arts and Associate in Science degrees. Also offered are eleven technical/vocational programs that award Associate in Applied Science degrees or technical/vocational diplomas after one or two years. Enrollment is 2,895 students.

Entrance Requirements: High school graduation or G.E.D. (high school equivalency), health form completed by the students with an immunization record completed by a public health official, A.C.T. scores, and a transcript from the last school attended. Non-high school graduates may be admitted to technical/vocational program on individual approval; midyear students accepted.

Costs Per Year: For 12 credit hours in fall and spring semesters (24 hours total), $450 residents of Real, Ovalde and Zavala counties; $570 Texas residents out-of-district; $2,010 out-of-state and foreign students. Room and board: $1,980.

Collegiate Environment: The 76-acre campus has 20 modern buildings, many recently remodeled. The Will C. Miller Memorial Library contains approximately 25,000 volumes, 300 periodicals, and 250,000 microforms. On campus housing for 192 students in co-ed dorm; 64 in women's dorm; housing placement service for off-campus housing. Work-study positions, and local, state and federal financial aid programs are administered through Director of Financial Aid; numerous local scholarships also available. Recreational opportunities include 38,000 square foot student center with game room, large screen TV, cafeteria and snack bar; fully-equipped gymnasium featuring 13 Nautilus machines, racquetball courts, basketball court, indoor swimming pool and aerobic dance rooms; National Intercollegiate Rodeo Association sanctioned rodeo team, tennis courts, and full intramural schedule. Most students applying for admission are accepted. Freshman classes begin in August, January and June, and the college welcomes a geographically diverse student body.

Community Environment: Population 15,000. Uvalde is located at the base of the Texas Hill Country 75 miles west of San Antonio and is known for its agriculture production; hunting for deer, wild turkey, quail and doves; and fishing. The climate is moderate. City services include a memorial hospital, public library, community theatre in the historic Grand Opera House, U.S. Vice-President John Nance Garner Memorial Museum, and churches of various denominations. Uvalde is reached by buslines, major highways and a private airport. Dormitories, apartments and rental houses provide student housing. Local recreation includes four screen theater complex, golf course, parks, two rivers, private clubs, various community celebrations including annual Cactus Jack Festival.

SOUTHWEST TEXAS STATE UNIVERSITY   (K-8)
San Marcos, Texas 78666
Tel: (512) 245-2364; Fax: (512) 245-8044

Description: The school is a comprehensive four-year public residential university which was chartered in 1899 as a normal school. It is accredited by the Southern Association of Colleges and Schools. It operates on the semester system with 2 summer sessions and awards bachelor's and master's degrees. Enrollment includes 13,874 full-time and 4,054 part-time students including 2,961 graduate students. A faculty of 605 full- and 310 part-time gives a faculty-student ratio of 1:22. The seven undergraduate schools are: Applied Arts and Technology; Business; Education; Fine Arts and Communication; Health Professions; Liberal Arts; and Science. Air Force and Army ROTC programs are available.

Entrance Requirements: Accredited high school graduation; SAT or ACT required. Minimum score is determined by class rank; students in top 10% guaranteed admission. 1st qtr. requirements, (SAT/ACT) 920/20; 2nd qtr., 1010/22; 3rd qtr. 1180/26; 4th qtr. 1270/29. Rolling admission and early admission available; midyear students accepted. $25 application fee.

Costs Per Year: $800 tuition state resident; $5,280 nonresident; $934 fees; $3,676 room and board.

Collegiate Environment: The 332-acre campus is located on the spring-fed San Marcos River in the Texas hill country and stretches two miles from east to west. At the heart of the campus is the Alkek

Library with 313,000 square feet and total holdings of 2,288,744 of which 966,191 are bound volumes. Approximately 25% of the students live in the 21 campus residence halls and apartment complexes. Students may choose to participate in varsity and club sports and a wide variety of physical education activities. The SWT Bobcats compete in Division I of the Southland Conference. Cultural and leadership opportunities include: 200 student organizations including student government, numerous fine arts performances and gallery showings, debate, lectures, and other entertainment. SWT welcomes students from other countries and from diverse ethnicities. 25% of the student body are minorities. The university owns and maintains an additional 5,000 acres which includes a farm, a ranch, and a university camp on the Blanco River.

Community Environment: The university is located in San Marcos, a large historic community of 30,000 on I-35 located between San Antonio, 50 miles to the south, and Austin, 30 miles to the north. Both cities are within commuting distance of San Marcos and have major airports. San Marcos has a municipal airport. The central Texas climate offers sunshine most of the year with moderate to cool winters and warm to hot summers. The area enjoys a healthy economy bolstered by clean, light industry, active tourism, and well-preserved historic districts. It is the home to churches of many denominations and various civic organizations. Local recreation includes golfing, fishing, hunting, swimming, "tubing," canoeing and other outdoor activities. Annual celebrations include Chilympiad, Sights and Sounds of Christmas, Summerfest, Cinco de Mayo, and weekly summer concerts in the park.

SOUTHWESTERN ADVENTIST COLLEGE *(G-9)*
P.O. Box 567
Keene, Texas 76059
Tel: (817) 645-3921; (800) 433-2240; Fax: (817) 556-4744

Description: Privately supported, coeducational liberal arts and teachers college was founded as Keene Academy in the year 1893 primarily for the Seventh-day Adventist young people in the State of Texas. It became a junior college in 1916 and in 1963 converted to a four-year curriculum. In April 1976, the name was changed from Southwestern Union College to Southwestern Adventist College. The college is accredited by the Southern Association of Colleges and Schools and by respective professional accrediting institutions. It operates on the semester system with three summer terms. Enrollment includes 665 full-time and 306 part-time students. A faculty of 47 full-time and 16 part-time gives a faculty-student ratio of 1-14. The college grants an Associate degree and a Bachelor degree, as well as an M.Ed. A cooperative education program is available in business. Overseas study is available at campuses in Spain, France, and Austria.

Entrance Requirements: Accredited high school graduation; open enrollment policy; SAT or ACT required; applicants not meeting all entrance requirements may be accepted provisionally; rolling admission, midyear admission, and delayed admission plans available. No application fee.

Costs Per Year: $6,984 tuition; $3,466 room and board; $80 student fees; $600 approximate additional expenses.

Collegiate Environment: The college is located at Keene, a thriving suburban community located 25 miles south of Fort Worth and 55 southwest of Dallas. The 140-acre campus contains a small lake, a picnic area, and an airstrip as well as college buildings. The library contains 126,491 volumes, 759 periodicals, 292,448 microforms and 11,490 sound recordings. Living accommodations are available for 469 men and women and 37 families. Qualified students of all economic backgrounds, classes, races, or religions are welcome. 99% of applicants are accepted. 90% of students receive some form of financial aid. About 60% of the freshmen returned for the sophomore year.

Community Environment: Population 5,019. Keene is a small community in a rural area. The climate is temperate. The city is reached by bus lines and U.S. Route 67. There is a local Seventh Day Adventist Church. A shopping center is located seven miles distant. Part-time employment is available.

SOUTHWESTERN ASSEMBLIES OF GOD COLLEGE
(G-10)
1200 Sycamore St.
Waxahachie, Texas 75165
Tel: (214) 937-4010

Description: Privately supported, coeducational Bible college is regionally accredited by the Southern Association of Colleges and Schools and professionally by the Accrediting Association of Bible Colleges. Three schools were brought together to form this private Bible college. They were Southwestern Bible School, Shield of Faith Bible School, and Southern Bible College. Founded in 1927, the college grants the Bachelor of Arts, Bachelor of Science, and Bachelor of Career Arts degrees as well as conferring a diploma upon completion of 72 hours of Bible and practical training. Enrollment is 832 full-time and 175 part-time students. A faculty of 22 full-time and 18 part time gives a faculty-student ratio of 1:29. The semester system is employed and two summer sessions are offered.

Entrance Requirements: Accredited high school graduation; open enrollment policy; ACT required; medical datamation required. Early decision, rolling admission and midyear admission available; $30 application fee.

Costs Per Year: $2,990 tuition; $3,140 room and board; $288 student fees; $120 approximate additional expenses.

Collegiate Environment: The college occupies a 70-acre plot on the north perimeter of Waxahachie. The Nelson Memorial Library was completed in 1960 and contains 111,913 volumes and 651 periodicals. The main building on the campus is a majestic four-story structure that houses the administrative offices, the college chapel, classrooms and science laboratories. Primarily a residential college, there are dormitories to house 208 men, 229 women and 20 families. Financial assistance is available and 85% of students receive some form of financial aid. 98% of applicants are accepted.

Community Environment: Population 20,000, the area is the capital of Ellis County. It is located 28 miles south of Dallas and 40 miles southeast of Fort Worth. The area can be reached by railroad, bus, and major highways. Community facilities include a medical center, a hospital and health clinic, many churches of various denominations, and several civic and fraternal organizations. Local recreation includes baseball, bowling, golf, parks, hunting, boating, and fishing. Apartments are available for students. Part-time employment is available.

SOUTHWESTERN BAPTIST THEOLOGICAL SEMINARY
(G-9)
2001 West Seminary Drive
Fort Worth, Texas 76122
Tel: (817) 923-1921; (800) 792-8701; Fax: (817) 923-1921

Description: Privately supported, coeducational, graduate-level theological seminary was an outgrowth of the theological department of Baylor University, established in 1901. In 1907, the Baptist General Convention of Texas authorized the separation of the seminary from Baylor University. Today the seminary has three Schools including Theology, Religious Education, and Church Music. It is accredited by the Southern Association of Colleges and Schools, the National Association of Schools of Music, and the Association of Theological Schools. The Seminary operates on the semester system and also offers two summer terms. Enrollment includes 4,157 students. The faculty has 96 members. The primary purpose of the Seminary is to prepare the students for the Christian ministry. The Masters degree is offered in Theology (Master of Divinity), Music, Church Music, and Religious Education. The seminary grants the Doctor of Philosophy, Doctor of Ministry, and Doctor of Musical Arts.

Entrance Requirements: Bachelor's degree from an accredited college or university; non-graduate applicants who are 30 years of age or older and are high school graduates or equivalent may apply for the diploma courses. References and church endorsement of sincere commitment to the Christian ministry required; physical examination required.

Costs Per Year: $800 matriculation fees, non-Southern Baptists fee is $1,600; $936 room and $981.80 board; $400 approximate additional expenses.

Collegiate Environment: The campus, known as Seminary Hill, consists of approximately 130 acres including seven main buildings, a plant department, a library of 785,612 volumes, an extensive music library, and living accommodations for 240 men, 171 women, and 867 families. Various forms of financial assistance are available.

Community Environment: See Texas Christian University.

SOUTHWESTERN CHRISTIAN COLLEGE (G-10)
206 Bowser Circle
Terrell, Texas 75160
Tel: (214) 524-3341

Description: Privately supported, coeducational, Christian junior college was established in 1950. It offers the first two years of college training in liberal arts and limited professional areas leading to upper division college work. The college is accredited by the Southern Association of Colleges and Schools. It is affiliated with the Church of Christ and operates on the semester system. Recent enrollment included 101 men, 82 women full-time, and 4 men and 14 women part-time. A faculty of 18 full-time and 6 part-time gives a faculty-student ratio of 1:10. The college grants an Associate degree and a Certificate of Achievement.

Entrance Requirements: Approved high school graduation; completion of 15 units including 3 English, 2 mathematics, 2 social science; open enrollment policy; non-high school graduates, over 21 years of age or veterans, may be admitted on individual approval; application fee $10. Open door policy.

Costs Per Year: $3,050 tuition; $2,208 room and board; $100 approximate additional expenses.

Collegiate Environment: The 25-acre campus is located in Terrell, 30 miles east of Dallas. The 15 college buildings contain a library of 21,000 volumes, 200 periodicals, and 658 sound recordings and living accommodations for 170 men, 134 women. Approximately 95% of students applying for admission were accepted recently; including midyear students. About 85% of the previous freshman class returned to this campus for the second year of studies. Of the 21 scholarships offered, 21 are for freshman and 85% of students receive some form of financial aid. About 60%of the freshman graduated in the upper half of their graduating class; 30% were in the top quarter.

Community Environment: Terrell is a suburban community enjoying dry, temperate climate. The city is reached by bus, railroad, and major highways. Community services include many churches representing most major denominations, hospitals, a public library, YMCA, and YWCA. There are theatres, parks, and nearby lakes for water sports. Part-time employment opportunities are limited. Various civic, fraternal and veteran's organizations are active in Terrell. Small city and all necessary items are within walking distance.

SOUTHWESTERN UNIVERSITY (J-9)
University at Maple
Georgetown, Texas 78626
Tel: (512) 863-6511; (800) 252-3166; Fax: (512) 863-5877

Description: Privately supported, coeducational, liberal arts college, whose forerunner was chartered as Rutersville College. In 1840, by action of the five Texas Methodist Conferences, a central university was planned and located at Georgetown. The institution reopened in 1873 and its present name was adopted in 1875. It is accredited by the Southern Association of Colleges and Schools and the National Association of Schools of Music. The college grants a Baccalaureate degree. The University is composed of two schools: the Brown College of Arts and Sciences, and School of Fine Arts. The university operates on the semester system and offers two summer terms. Enrollment is 567 men and 671 women. Faculty numbers 91 full-time and 52 part-time, giving a faculty-student ratio of 1-12. A study abroad program to London is available. There are a number of exchange programs to Korea, China, Japan and many other countries.

Entrance Requirements: Accredited high school or equivalent; rank in upper quarter of graduating class; recommended B average; completion of 16 units including 4 English, 4 mathematics, 3 science, 2 foreign language, 3 social science, 1 academic elective; SAT or ACT required; rolling admission with regular decision deadline of Feb. 15, delayed admission, early decision, advanced placement and early admission plans available; application fee $40.

Costs Per Year: $12,700 tuition; $4,868 room and board.

Collegiate Environment: The grounds of the university comprise more than 500 acres within and adjoining the corporate limits of Georgetown, approximately 26 miles north of Austin. The university buildings contain a library of 261,353 volumes, 1,391 periodicals, and 30,064 microforms. There are dormitory facilities for 350 men and 550 women. Fraternities house an additional 100 men. The university welcomes a geographically diverse student body. 71% of applicants are accepted. Middle 50% of entering freshmen scored 1030-1200 combined SAT, 24-28 ACT. 70% of students receive some financial aid.

Community Environment: Population 25,000. Georgetown enjoys the advantage of being a small town and at the same time is only 26 miles from the state capital, Austin. The climate is moderate, both in winter and summer. The community is reached by railroad, national bus lines, Austin's Robert Mueller Airport, and Interstate Highway 35. Located in the heart of the highland lakes region, the recreational facilities include fishing, boating, and water sports. Part-time employment is available. Student housing is available in dormitories and fraternity houses. The community has a modern hospital, clinic, and campus infirmary.

STEPHEN F. AUSTIN STATE UNIVERSITY (H-13)
Box 13051
Nacogdoches, Texas 75962
Tel: (409) 468-2504; (800) 259-9732; Fax: (409) 468-3849

Description: Publicly supported, coeducational, multipurpose university that offers, within the framework of an arts and sciences curriculum, the preparation for teaching and administrative work in public schools and colleges; specialized undergraduate and Master's degree work in virtually all other fields; professional training in business, education, fine arts, forestry and nursing; and prepartatory for dentistry and medicine, engineering, law, osteopathy, forestry, and veterinary medicine. The State University began operation in 1923 and is accredited by the Southern Association of Colleges and Schools and by several professional accrediting institutions. Composed of the Colleges of Applied Arts and Sciences, Business, Education, Fine Arts, Forestry, Liberal Arts, Sciences and Mathematics, and Graduate School, the University offers the Baccalaureate, Master's degree, and the Doctor of Forestry degree. It operates on the semester basis and also provides two summer terms. Army ROTC is available. Enrollment is 10,599 full-time and 2,122 part-time students. A faculty of 407 full-time and 260 part-time gives a faculty-student ratio of 1-21.

Entrance Requirements: Accredited high school graduation; ACT score of at least 21, or SAT score of at least 900 (1010 recentered), or rank in upper half of graduating class; non-high school graduates, 21 years of age or older or veterans, may be admitted by special permission; advanced placement, early admission, early decision and rolling admission plans available.

Costs Per Year: $900 state-resident tuition; $5,130 out-of-state; $3,768 room and board; $705 fees.

Collegiate Environment: In addition to the main 200-acre campus, the university has a college beef farm of 100 acres, a second college farm for dairying and poultry of 200 acres, an experimental forest in southwestern Nacogdoches County, and a summer forestry camp in the Sabine National Forest near Hemphill. The 72 college buildings include a library of 3,995 serial titles, 571,216 books and bound periodicals, 650,000 microforms, and 235,000 state and U.S. government documents. There are living accommodations available for 2,000 men, 2,800 women, and 200 families. Financial aid is available.

Community Environment: Population 35,000. Nacogdoches is one of the oldest settlements in Texas. This is a rural community enjoying temperate climate. There are more than 30 churches representing 15 different denominations, a library, museums, two hospitals, garden clubs, and major civic and fraternal organizations within the community. Nacogdoches is reached by railroad, bus lines, and Highways 59, 259, 7 and 21. Part-time employment is available. Local recreation includes movie theatres, several lakes for boating, swimming, and other water sports, and national forests for hiking, picnicking and hunting.

SUL ROSS STATE UNIVERSITY (P-4)
Alpine, Texas 79832
Tel: (915) 837-8032; Admissions: (915) 837-8050; Fax: (915) 837-8046

Description: Publicly supported, coeducational, liberal arts and teachers university opened as a normal school in 1920, was authorized to grant the Bachelor's degree in 1924, and offered programs for both the Bachelor's and Master's degrees in 1931. In addition to its program of training teachers for the State, the university offers preprofessional training, liberal arts education, and training in the vocational fields of business, criminal justice, industrial technology and range animal science. It is accredited by the Southern Association of Colleges and Schools and is a member of the American Council on Education. The university consists of School of Arts and Sciences, School of Professional Studies and Division of Range Animal Science, Pre-Professional Preparations, and Vocations. The college operates on the semester system and also offers two summer terms. Enrollment includes 1,548 full-time, 195 part-time, and 676 graduate students. A faculty of 88 full-time and 14 part-time gives a faculty student ratio of 1-20. An upper division and graduate center with 726 students is located in Uvalde, Texas.

Entrance Requirements: Accredited high school graduation or GED; ACT or SAT required; GRE or GMAT required for graduate programs; probational admission and advanced placement available. $50 application fee for foreign students only.

Costs Per Year: $720 full-time tuition, state resident; $4,224 tuition out-of-state resident; $3,160 room and board; $612 student fees; $540 graduate, resident tuition; $1,584 graduate, nonresident; $322 graduate fees.

Collegiate Environment: The university is located in the city of Alpine in the Big Bend area of Texas. It serves an area some 800 miles long by 400 miles wide and is the meeting ground of the Spanish and English cultures. The campus proper consists of 40 acres, and lies adjacent to a tract of 500 acres which provides facilities in range animal science. The 80 college buildings contain a library of 246,288 volumes, 1,909 periodicals, 429,345 microforms and 12,729 audiovisual materials. Residence halls accomodate 708 students and 61 families. Students from other geographical locations are accepted as well as midyear students. Financial aid is available. The Uvalde Center, an upper-level component of the university, offers junior, senior, and graduate work in selected programs in Uvalde, Del Rio, and Eagle Pass, and is headquartered on the campus of the Southwest Texas Junior College in Uvalde.

Community Environment: Population 7,000. Located between El Paso on the west and Del Rio on the east, Alpine is known for its Highland Hereford breed of cattle. The city is also the gateway to travel to Big Bend National Park, Fort Davis National Historic Sites, Davis Mountains State Park and McDonald Observatory. The climate in the area is mild. Railroad, commuter airline, and three bus lines serve the community. Local recreation includes baseball, hunting, golf course, fishing, a theatre, and Summer Theatre during July and August. There is a hospital, a library, and churches of various denominations within the city. Part-time employment is available.

TARLETON STATE UNIVERSITY   *(H-8)*
Box T-2003, Tarleton Station
Stephenville, Texas 76402
Tel: (817) 968-9000; Admissions: (817) 968-9125; Fax: (817) 968-9920

Description: This publicly supported, coeducational, liberal arts and professional college was opened in 1899 as a private, 4 year coeducational academy. Tarleton became a two year degree granting institution in 1908 and joined the Texas A&M University System in 1917. In 1959, the Texas Legislature expanded the role and scope of the institution to a four year institution. In 1973 it was renamed Tarleton State University. With more than 80 undergraduate Baccalaureate Degree for the past twenty-one years. Fully accredited by the Southern Association of Colleges and Schools, Tarleton operates in the semester system and offers two summer terms. Enrollment, equally distributed between male and female students, includes 4,689 full-time and 829 part-time undergraduates and 942 graduate students. A faculty of 231 full-time and 2 part-time gives a faculty-student ratio of 1-20.

Entrance Requirements: Affiliated high school graduation; completion of 15 units including 4 English, 3 mathematics, 2 science, 3 social science, 1.5 physical education, and .5 health; SAT with minimum composite score of 800, or ACT minimum of 19 required; early admission, early decision, rolling admission, delayed admission, and advanced placement plans available; $100 room deposit required. $20 application fee.

Costs Per Year: $900 state-resident tuition; $5,280 out-of-state; $2,800 room and board; $866 student fees.

Collegiate Environment: In addition to the 185 acre main campus, the University also has a fully operational farm and a beef production ranch. To complement the bachelor's degree program in Hydology and degree options in the Environmental Sciences, the Texas Institute for Applied Environmental Research (TIAER) is located on campus and conducts research focusing on point and non point source water pollution. The Dick Smith Library has more than 310,000 volumes and access to more than 15,000,000 volumes through a North Texas Inter-Library Loan consortium. The fully automated library system includes a comprehensive multi-media collection with video tapes, records, compact discs and audio tapes. Dormitory facilities and university apartments can accommodate 1,200 students. Student organizations exceed 100 ranging from Greek fraternities and sororities to scholarly clubs and societies. About 70% of students applying for admission were accepted recently including midyear students. 60% of the previous freshman class returned to this campus for the sophomore year. Approximately 60% of the recent student body graduated in the top half of the high school class; 30% in the top quarter. Academic, leadership, need based and minority scholarships are available. 45% of the current freshmen class receives financial aid. The college granted 884 Bachelor degrees and 173 Master degrees last year.

Community Environment: Stephenville, Texas, with a population of 15,000 is located in west central Texas, approximately 60 miles from the Ft. Worth/Dallas metroplex. With a typically mild climate average rainfall of 32 inches yearly, the region is commonly known as the Cross Timbers area, a term that refers to the many varieties of oak trees, including a heavy concentration of the live oak tree. Community services include churches of all denominations, a full-service hospital, including a new emergency wing and 24 hour care flight service, libraries and dozens of restaurants and shopping options. Railroad, bus, and a local airport are available. In addition, the Dallas/Ft. Worth International Airport is within a one and one-half hour drive.

TARRANT COUNTY JUNIOR COLLEGE   *(G-9)*
1500 Houston Street
Fort Worth, Texas 76102
Tel: (817) 336-7851; Fax: (817) 882-5295

Description: This public junior college was founded in 1965 by a vote of the citizens of Tarrant County. Quality education is the primary objective of the college, whether in university parallel curricula, occupational education, or continuing education programs. The college is multi-campus, with three, comprehensive campuses and a central administrative and continuing education center. The college awards the Associate of Arts, Associate of Applied Science degrees and a certificate of completion. It operates on a semester system with two six-week summer sessions. The college is accredited by the Southern Association of Colleges and Schools and by respective professional accrediting institutions. Recently, the college enrolled 15,114 women and 11,728 men, including 19,373 part-time and 7,469 full-time students. A faculty of 429 full-time and 524 part-time gives a faculty-student ratio of 1-22.

Entrance Requirements: Tarrant County Junior College has an "open door" admissions policy; all high school graduates are eligible for admission, as are other students through a program of individual approval or submission of satisfactory GED scores; early admission, midyear admission, rolling admission and advanced placement plans available; $10 application fee.

Costs Per Year: $512 ($16/cr) county resident tuition; $768 ($24/cr) tuition for other Texas residents, $3,840 ($120/cr) tuition for out-of-state and foreign students.

Collegiate Environment: Tarrant County Junior College consists of three campuses, all located on or near Interstate Loop 820. The South Campus has an enrollment of 10,349; the Northeast Campus, 11,906; and the Northwest Campus, 4,583. Under the open door admissions policy, 99% of those who apply are accepted. Fall semester classes begin late August or early September; 14% of students receive financial aid. There is no on-campus housing. The library has 226,168 titles, 1,455 periodicals, 725 microforms, and 11,137 audiovisual materials.

Community Environment: Tarrant County, Texas, has a population of about 1.2 million, the largest cities being Fort Worth and Arlington. It is part of the Dallas-Fort Worth Metroplex, which features two opera companies, three symphony orchestras, two ballet companies, and numerous theater groups and museums. There also is ample opportunity for sports and recreation, including major league football, basketball, and baseball.

TEMPLE JUNIOR COLLEGE   *(I-9)*
2600 South First Street
Temple, Texas 76504-7435
Tel: (817) 773-9961; Fax: (817) 773-5265

Description: This publicly supported, coeducational community college was founded in 1926 and is accredited by the Southern Association of Colleges and Schools and by respective professional associations. Since its beginning, it has offered preprofessional courses leading to degrees in medicine, law, engineering, and similar fields. Terminal courses have been offered since 1947 and the vocational-technical program was greatly expanded with the opening of the Applied Arts and Sciences Building in 1967. Adult education and the evening and summer sessions have been expanded in recent years. The college grants a Certificate of Completion and an Associate degree. The college operates on the semester system and offers two summer sessions. Enrollment includes 1,027 full-time and 1,445 part-time students. A faculty of 75 full-time and 47 part-time gives a faculty-student ratio of 1-22.

Entrance Requirements: Accredited high school graduation or GED certification; open enrollment policy; completion of 16 units including 3 English, 2 mathematics, 2 science, and 2 social science; applicants not meeting all entrance requirements may be admitted by passing admission examinations or by individual approval; early admission, midyear admission and rolling admission plans available.

Costs Per Year: $768 district-resident tuition ($24 per credit hour); $1,184 out-of-district ($37 per credit hour); $2,272 nonresident ($71 per credit hour); $2,630 room and board; $1,548 student fees, books, and miscellaneous expenses.

Collegiate Environment: The 104-acre campus is located in Temple, about 60 miles from Austin. Temple is recognized as the Hospital Center of the southwest. Scott and White Memorial Hospital and Temple Junior College cooperate in an educational program for nurses. The nine college buildings include a library of 43,340 volumes, 354 periodicals, 366 microforms and 1,124 audiovisual items. Dormitories are provided for 126 men and women. All qualified students applying for admission are accepted, including midyear students. About 50% of the previous entering class returned to this campus for the second year of studies. Financial aid is available for economically disadvantaged students. 40% of students receive some form of financial aid. The college granted 233 Certificates and 201 Associate degrees to its recent graduating class.

Community Environment: Population 45,000. Temple today is a medical center visited annually by thousands of patients. Located in central Texas, the city enjoys a temperate climate. The community has air, rail, and bus service available. Community service facilities include four excellent hospitals, many churches representing all major denominations, a library, and several hotels and motels. There are various civic, fraternal, and veteran's organizations active in the area. Local recreation includes hunting, fishing, boating, water skiing, and most water sports at nearby Lake Belton. Part-time employment is available.

TEXARKANA COLLEGE   *(E-13)*
2500 N. Robinson Road
Texarkana, Texas 75501
Tel: (903) 838-4541

Description: Publicly supported, coeducational junior college, founded in 1927 as a branch of the Texarkana, Texas, Public School System. It provides educational opportunities in academic transfer, vocational and technical training, and in continuing education leading to an Associate degree. It is approved and accredited as a two-year college by the Southern Association of Colleges and Schools. It operates on the semester system, offers 2 summer sessions and also provides evening classes. Enrollment includes 3,689 students. A faculty of 118 full-time and 56 part-time gives a faculty-student ratio of 1-20.

Entrance Requirements: Approved high school graduation or equivalent; open enrollment policy; ACT or SAT requested for all students; applicants not meeting all entrance requirements may be admitted by passing entrance examinations or by individual approval. Rolling admission plan.

Costs Per Year: $528 tuition; $848 tuition for out-of-district students; $1,150 tuition for out-of-state students.

Collegiate Environment: The 80-acre campus is located on the northwest border of the City of Texarkana, Texas, about three miles from the downtown business district. The 19 college buildings contain a library of 158,000 volumes, 810 periodicals and 1,133,915 microforms. Financial aid is available.

Community Environment: Texarkana is located on the Arkansas-Texas border which runs approximately through the center of town. A trading center, there are many railroad lines coming into the area. The community has two hospitals, motels and hotels, and various civic, fraternal and veteran's organizations. Local recreation includes golf, hunting, fishing, boating, and water skiing. Part-time employment is available.

TEXAS A & M UNIVERSITY - KINGSVILLE   *(O-8)*
Campus Box 116
Kingsville, Texas 78363
Tel: (512) 595-3907

Description: Publicly assisted, coeducational university is accredited by the Southern Association of Colleges and Schools. Founded as the South Texas State Teachers College in 1925, it became the Texas College of Arts and Industries with the addition of technological programs in 1929. The name Texas Arts and Industries University was adopted in 1967. The Sixtieth Texas Legislature authorized the adoption of the present name in 1972. Today, the university is composed of College of Agriculture and Home Economics, College of Arts and Sciences, College of Business Administration, College of Engineering, College of Education, and College of Graduate Studies. The university operates on the semester system and offers two summer sessions. Army ROTC is available. Cooperative education programs are being developed. Enrollment is 4,302 full-time and 1,048 part-time undergraduates, and 1,198 graduate students. A faculty of 337 gives a faculty-student ratio of 1-19.

Entrance Requirements: Accredited high school graduation or GED; completion of 16 units including 4 English, 3 mathematics, 2 foreign language or science, 2 1/2 social science, and 4 1/2 electives; SAT or ACT required; GRE required for graduate programs; delayed admission, rolling admission, and advanced placement available; no application fee.

Costs Per Year: $1,370 tuition; $4,802 out-of-state; $3,090 room and board.

Collegiate Environment: The university is situated in Kingsville, the county seat of Kleberg County, about 40 miles southwest of Corpus Christi. The university property consists of 1,600 acres. The campus is located on 245 acres and the additional acreage is used for agricultural purposes. The 82 college buildings contain a library of 922,204 holdings, and living accommodations for 788 men, and 648 women, and 24 families. Financial aid is available. Midyear students are accepted. 60% of students receive financial aid. About 64% of the recent entering freshmen graduated in the top half of the high school class; 33% in the top quarter. The average ACT composite score range of entering freshmen was 15-19.

Community Environment: In the coastal plains region, Kingsville is a rural location with a semitropical climate. The community has a public library, many churches of various faiths, a college health service and a county hospital. Various civic, fraternal and veteran's organizations are active in the area. Part-time employment is available. Local recreation includes fishing, hunting, bowling, and water sports.

TEXAS A&M INTERNATIONAL UNIVERSITY   *(O-6)*
1 West End Washington Street
Laredo, Texas 78040-9960
Tel: (210) 722-8001; Fax: (210) 724-9991

Description: This upper-level state-supported university was founded in 1969 and is fully accredited by the Southern Association of Colleges and Schools. The school offers Bachelor's and Masters degrees in the liberal arts and sciences, education, and business administration. The semester system is used with two summer sessions. Enrollment includes 212 men and 391 women full-time, and 430 men and 918 women part-time. There are 802 graduate students. A faculty of 93 gives a faculty-student ratio of 1-21. The University is now part of the Texas A & M University system.

Entrance Requirements: Course prerequisites required.

Costs Per Year: $840 state-resident tuition; $5,612 nonresident; $482 student fees.

Collegiate Environment: The school shares a campus with Laredo Junior College. The main campus is comprised of 196 acres and is located at the western edge of Laredo on the south portion of Fort McIntosh. University Hall houses specialized classrooms and faculty and administrative offices. The library is located in the center of the campus and houses more than 188,653 bound volumes and receives approximately 2,146 current serial subscriptions, including periodicals. While the student body is predominantly Hispanic, a sizable portion of the student population includes international students hailing from countries as diverse as Mexico, Japan, Ghana, Malaysia, France and Germany. Dormitories are available for 120 students. 11% of students receive financial aid.

Community Environment: Laredo, one of the oldest cities in the United States, is situated in the southern part of Texas on the Rio Grande River. Its sister city, Nuevo Laredo, Mexico is located immediately across the Rio Grande and has population of about 300,000. The city of Laredo, which itself has a population of over 155,000, reflects the influences of seven flags: Spain, France, Mexico, Texas, the Confederacy, the United States, and the Republic of the Rio Grande, a short-lived nation that had Laredo as its capital. Located 154 miles south of San Antonio, 143 miles west of Corpus Christi, and 147 miles north of Monterrey, Mexico, Laredo can be accessed via I-35, various state highways or through a regional airport that is serviced by Continental and American Eagle airlines.

TEXAS A&M UNIVERSITY   *(J-10)*
Office of Admissions and Records
College Station, Texas 77843
Tel: (409) 845-1031; Admissions: (409) 845-3741; Fax: (409) 847-8737

Description: State-assisted coeducational university began as a land-grant college in 1876 and is the state's oldest public institution of higher education. It is accredited by the Southern Association of Colleges and Schools and by respective professional organizations. The university operates on the semester system and offers two summer sessions. The Texas A&M University System is composed of Texas A&M University and all colleges, agencies, and services under the supervision of the System's Board of Regents, including: Texas A&M University at Galveston in Galveston, Texas; Prairie View A&M University in Prairie View, Texas; Tarleton State University in Stephenville, Texas; Texas A&M University - Corpus Christi, Texas; Texas A&M University - Kingsville, Texas; Texas A&M University, Laredo, Texas; West Texas State University in Canyon, Texas; Texas Agricultural Experiment Station; Texas Agricultural Extension Service; Texas Engineering Experiment Station; The Texas Engineering Extension Service; The Texas Forest Service; Texas Transportation Institute; and the Texas Veterinary Medical Diagnostic Laboratory. The University is comprised of the Colleges of Agriculture and Life Sciences; Architecture; Liberal Arts; Business Administration and Graduate School of Business; Education; Dwight Look College of Engineering; Veterinary Medicine; Geosciences; Medicine and Science; Office of Graduate Studies and the School of Military Sciences. Army, Navy, and Air Force ROTC programs are also provided. Undergraduate enrollment includes 17,270 men, 14,169 women full-time and 1,643 men and 1,196 women part-time. A faculty of 1,946 full-time and 385 part-time provides a faculty-student ratio of 1-20. The university offers many degrees on the undergraduate and graduate levels. Study abroad coordinates programs in 11 countries including France, Germany, Great Britain, Greece, and Mexico. Cooperative education programs are available in the Colleges of Agriculture, Architecture, Business Administration, Engineering, Geosciences, Liberal Arts, Science, and Veterinary Medicine.

Entrance Requirements: Admission to Texas A&M University and any of its sponsored programs is open to qualified individuals regardless of race, color, religion, age, sex, national origin or educationally unrelated handicaps. Freshman applicants must have graduated from an accredited high school and completed 16 units, including 4 English, 3 1/2 mathematics, 2 science, 3 social science, 2 foreign language; Texas residents who graduate in the top 10% have no minimum required SAT or ACT score. Those in the first quarter of their HS class must have SAT score of 920 combined or ACT of 24. Two Achievement Tests in English Composition and Math Level I or

II are highly recommended. Texas residents in the 2nd quarter of their high school class must have an SAT minimum composite score of 1,050, or 22 on the ACT. Those in the 3rd or 4th quarter must have 1,180 or 27 respectively. GRE or GMAT required for graduate programs. Early admission and advanced placement plans available. Notification of admission is on a rolling basis. Admission may also be granted to undergraduate students who have begun their work at other colleges or universities. An applicant may not disregard the academic record of any previous enrollment at another institution. $25 application fee.

Costs Per Year: $840 tuition; $5,130 tuition for out-of-state students; $3,412 room and board.

Collegiate Environment: The campus of Texas A&M University is in the community of College Station. This university community is located 100 miles northwest of Houston, 100 miles east of Austin, and 170 miles south of Dallas. The University buildings on the main campus include a library of 1,900,000 volumes, over 10,000 periodicals and 3,800,000 titles on microform. Living accomodations on or near campus are available for approximately 10,000 single students and 650 families. The Office of Student Life Programs, an office of the Department of Student Affairs, strives to meet the needs of 30,000 off-campus students by providing a variety of programs and services. 67% of undergraduate students receive some form of financial assistance.

Community Environment: Combined population of 120,000 in College Station and the adjacent city of Bryan in Brazos County.

TEXAS A&M UNIVERSITY - CORPUS CHRISTI   *(O-9)*
6300 Ocean Drive
Corpus Christi, Texas 78412
Tel: (512) 994-5700; (800) 482-6822; Admissions: (512) 994-2624; Fax: (512) 994-5887

Description: Publicly supported, coeducational university is accredited by the Southern Association of Colleges and Schools and is part of the Texas A&M University system. The university is composed of four constituent colleges: Arts and Humanities, Business Administration, Education, and Science and Technology. It grants the Bachelor, Master, and Doctorate degrees. The university operates on the semester system and offers two summer sessions. Enrollment includes 1,852 full-time and 1,407 part-time undergraduates and 1,892 graduate students. A faculty of 175 full-time and 138 part-time gives a faculty-student ratio of 1-14.

Entrance Requirements: High school graduateion; units should include 4 English, 3 mathematics, 2 science, 3 social science; SAT with minimum score 800 combined, or ACT with minimum score 19 composite; GMAT or GRE for graduate programs; TOEFL for those whose native language is not English; early decision and advanced placement plans available. July 1 application deadline for fall admission; $10 application fee; $30 application fee for international students.

Costs Per Year: $900 state-resident tuition; $5,130 out-of-state; $2,385 room, $688 student fees. Rates based on full-time load of 15 credit hours per semester, fall and spring.

Collegiate Environment: This 240-acre island university is surrounded by Oso Bay and Corpus Christi Bay. There are dormitory facilities for 600 students on the campus and a 350,000-volume library. Approximately 81% of students applying for freshmen admission meet the requirements and are accepted. 74% of transfer students are accepted. 265 scholarships are available, and 50% of students receive some form of financial aid.

Community Environment: Population 258,067. Legends of shipwreck treasures and the buried booty of pirates still persist in modern Corpus Christi. The city is located on the Gulf Coast on the southwestern shore of Corpus Christi Bay. The community has many churches representing several denominations, libraries, museums, a theater, civic music group, YMCA and YWCA, and five hospitals. Local recreation includes movies, symphony orchestra, hunting, fishing, boating, golfing, water skiing, and 100 miles of beach. There are various civic, fraternal and veteran's organizations active in the area.

TEXAS CHIROPRACTIC COLLEGE   (L-12)

5912 Spencer Highway
Pasadena, Texas 77505
Tel: (713) 487-1170; (800) 468-6839; Fax: (713) 487-2009

Description: Privately supported, coeducational institute began operation in 1908 at San Antonio, Texas. Ownership of the college was transferred to the Texas Chiropractic College Alumni Association in 1948, and the school was moved to its present location in 1965. The college is accredited by the Southern Association of Colleges and Schools and the Council on Chiropractic Education. It operates on the trimester system and offers one summer session. Enrollment includes 520 full-time students. A faculty of 45 gives a ratio of 1-15. The college awards the Doctor of Chiropractic degree. Pre-chiropractic studies are offered at San Jacinto College but may be taken at any accredited two or four year college.

Entrance Requirements: 2 years (60 semester hours) of college credit, including 1 year each of English and biology, 2 years of chemistry, 1 year of physics, and a semester each of general psychology and sociology with a minimum grade point average of 2.5.

Costs Per Year: $11,700 tuition; various book and lab fees.

Collegiate Environment: The college is located on 18 acres and is comprised of four buildings which contain a library of 8,000 volumes. Approximately 70% of students applying for admission are accepted. Classes begin in September, May, and January. About 90% of the previous freshman class returned to this campus for the second year of studies. There are 13 scholarships offered and one is available for freshmen. 95% of students receive financial aid. The college recently granted 105 Doctor of Chiropractic degrees.

Community Environment: See San Jacinto College - Central Campus.

TEXAS CHRISTIAN UNIVERSITY   (G-9)

2800 South University Drive
Fort Worth, Texas 76129
Tel: (817) 921-7490; (800) 828-3764; Fax: (817) 921-7333

Description: Privately supported, coeducational university began as the AddRan male and female college at Thorp Spring in 1873. It became affiliated with the Christian Churches (Disciples of Christ) of Texas in 1889 and moved to its present location Fort Worth, Texas, in 1911. Today, the University is comprised of the AddRan College of Arts and Sciences, M.J. Neeley School of Business, Brite Divinity School, School of Education, Graduate School, Harris College of Nursing, and School of Fine Arts and Communication. Army and Air Force ROTC programs are provided. The university is accredited by the Southern Association of Colleges and Schools and by respective educational and professional organizations. It operates on the semester basis and offers three summer terms. Enrollment includes 4,955 full-time and 611 part-time undergraduate students. There are 1,140 graduate students. A faculty of 336 gives an undergraduate faculty-student ratio of 1-14. The University awards undergraduate and graduate-level degrees.

Entrance Requirements: Accredited high school graduation; 17 units including 4 English, 3 mathematics, 3 science, 3 social science, 2 foreign language, 2 academic electives; ACT or SAT required; early admission, advanced placement, and delayed admission plans available; $30 application fee; application deadlines: Feb. 15, early notification Nov. 15, academic scholarships Jan. 15; students applying to graduate school or Brite Divinity School should apply directly to individual school.

Costs Per Year: $8,490 tuition; $3,320 board and room; $1,030 student fees.

Collegiate Environment: Texas Christian University combines the resources of a major teaching and research institution with the person-centered atmosphere of a small college. The university is situated on a 237-acre campus in the southwestern residential district of Fort Worth. Its 60 buildings contain libraries of more than 1.5 million volumes, periodicals and microforms and audiovisual materials. Dormitories, fraternity and sorority houses accomodate close to 3,000 men and women. 72% of applicants are accepted. Of the recent entering freshmen, more than 81% returned for their sophomore year. Approximately 58% of the student body receives some type of financial aid. The average SAT scores of the current freshman class were above the national average.

Community Environment: The University is easily accessible to a variety of recreational, educational and professional opportunities in the Fort Worth/Dallas metroplex. Major museums, parks, theatres, churches, and restaurants are within a few miles from the campus. A new business complex and residence halls were recently completed.

TEXAS COLLEGE   (G-12)

2404 N. Grand
Tyler, Texas 75702
Tel: (214) 593-8311; Fax: (903) 592-2372

Description: This privately supported, coeducational liberal arts and teachers college was organized as a liberal arts college by a group of ministers of the Colored Methodist Church in 1894. It was among the first members of the United Negro College Fund and is accredited by the Southern Association of Colleges and Schools. It operates on the semester system and offers a four-week summer session. Enrollment is 503 full-time and 40 part-time students. The faculty-student ratio is 1-15.

Entrance Requirements: Accredited high school graduation; completion of 16 units including 4 English, 2 mathematics, 2 science, and 2 social science; ACT or SAT required; applicants not meeting all entrance requirements may be admitted by examination or by individual approval.

Costs Per Year: $3,150 tuition; $2,430 room and board; $455 student fees.

Collegiate Environment: The 66-acre campus is located approximately 90 miles east of Dallas and 90 miles west of Shreveport. The 15 college buildings include a library of 90,000 volumes and dormitory facilities for 300 men and 200 women. Midyear students as well as students from other geographical locations are accepted. A complete program of financial aid is available.

Community Environment: See Tyler Junior College.

TEXAS LUTHERAN COLLEGE   (L-8)

1000 West Court Street
Seguin, Texas 78155
Tel: (210) 372-8000; (800) 771-8521; Admissions: (210) 372-8050; Fax: (210) 372-8096

Description: This privately supported, coeducational liberal arts college was established in 1891 and is owned by the Evangelical Lutheran Church of America. It maintains an educational center at Randolph Air Force Base at Universal City, Texas. The college is accredited by the Southern Association of Colleges and Schools. It operates on a 4-1-4 semester system and also offers two summer terms. Enrollment is 873 full-time and 395 part-time students. A faculty of 64 full-time and 30 part-time gives a faculty-student ratio of 1-14. The college grants the Bachelor of Arts, Bachelor of Science, and the Bachelor of Music Education degrees. A semester or year abroad program is available and Air Force ROTC is offered.

Entrance Requirements: Accredited high school graduation or equivalent; rank in upper half of graduating class; completion of 16 units including 4 English, 3 mathematics, 2 foreign language, 3 science, and 2 social science; SAT or ACT required; applicants not meeting all entrance requirements may be admitted by individual approval; advanced placement, early admission, midyear admission and rolling admission plans available; $20 application fee.

Costs Per Year: $7,900 tuition; $3,410 room and board.

Collegiate Environment: The 161-acre campus is located in the county seat of Guadalupe County, within easy driving distance of San Antonio and Austin. The 32 college buildings include a library of 143,000 volumes, 678 periodicals, 12,345 microforms and numerous audiovisual materials. There are accommodations for 451 men and 417 women. Approximately 83% of students applying for admission are accepted. Almost 70% of a recent freshman class returned to this campus for the sophomore year. Financial aid is available. 85% of students receive some financial aid.

Community Environment: Population 18,000. Seguin is a rural community enjoying temperate climate. The city is reached by Interstate 10. There is a library, a museum, churches representing 10 different denominations, and a hospital serving the community. Various job opportunities are available here. Various civic, fraternal and veteran's organizations are active in Seguin. Nearby Lake McQueeney offers water skiing.

TEXAS SOUTHERN UNIVERSITY (K-12)
3100 Cleburne
Houston, Texas 77004
Tel: (713) 527-7011

Description: Publicly supported coeducational university was established in 1947 and opened with the Graduate School, the College of Arts and Sciences, the School of Law, and the School of Industries. The School of Business developed from the College of Arts and Sciences and the School of Pharmacy was added in 1949. The university is accredited by the Southern Association of Colleges and Schools and respective educational and professional organizations. It operates on the early semester system and also offers two summer terms. U.S. Navy ROTC program and cooperating engineering program available through Rice University. The University recently enrolled 9,430 students.

Entrance Requirements: Accredited high school graduation; ACT required; early decision and rolling admission plans available, GRE required for graduate applicants. students.

Costs Per Year: $1,004 tuition; $4,316 out-of-state students; $1,660 room and board.

Collegiate Environment: The university is located on a 70-acre campus and is comprised of 41 buildings. Its library contains over 443,639 volumes, 301,146 periodicals and 3,398 microforms and dormitory facilities are provided for 680 students.

Community Environment: See University of Houston.

TEXAS SOUTHMOST COLLEGE (R-9)
80 Fort Brown
Brownsville, Texas 78520
Tel: (210) 544-8200; Fax: (210) 544-8832

Description: Publicly supported, coeducational junior college was established in 1926 and became part of the University of Texas system in 1989. It offers academic and professional courses, vocational-technical courses, adult education, and community services leading to a Certificate of Completion and an Associate degree. The college operates on the semester system and offers one summer term. It is accredited by the Southern Association of Colleges and Schools. There are 8,000 students enrolled. A faculty of 300 gives a faculty-student ratio of 1-27.

Entrance Requirements: Accredited high school graduation or GED certification; open enrollment policy; applicants not meeting entrance requirements may be admitted by individual approval.

Costs Per Year: $609 tuition; $999 nondistrict; $2,934 nonresident, $2,900 room and board.

Collegiate Environment: The campus of the college is a beautifully landscaped area of approximately 45 acres. The 30 college buildings include a library of 25,720 volumes. 100% of students applying for admission are accepted, including midyear students. The college offers a full range of basic remedial studies as well as a special program for the culturally disadvantaged. Financial aid is available and more than 50% of the current student body receives some form of assistance.

Community Environment: Population 85,000. An international seaport, airport, and railroad interchange point, Brownsville is an important port of entry on the Mexican border. It is also the oldest city in the Lower Rio Grande Valley. The city is a suburban community which has subtropical climate. There is a public library, two museums, churches of various faiths, a hospital, and major civic, fraternal and veteran's organizations. Part-time employment is seasonal with good job opportunities in the summer months. Water sports and deep sea fishing are good in the area. Charro Days Fiesta is held each year preceding Lent.

TEXAS STATE TECHNICAL INSTITUTE (I-9)
Waco Campus
Waco, Texas 76705
Tel: (817) 799-3611; (800) 792-8784; Admissions: (817) 867-2363; Fax: (817) 867-2250

Description: This publicly supported, coeducational, technological post-secondary institution was founded in 1969. It operates on the full four-quarter system and offers 1 summer term. It is accredited by the Southern Association of Colleges and Schools, and professionally accredited by the American Dental Association and the American Veterinary Medical Association. Enrollment is 2,417 full-time and 699 part-time students. A faculty of 274 gives a faculty-student ratio of 1-23. The institute awards the Certificate and the Associate degree.

Entrance Requirements: High school graduation; open enrollment policy; all entrance exams required; rolling admission, early admission, midyear admission, and advanced placement plans are available.

Costs Per Year: $840 state-resident tuition; $3,840 out-of-state; $2,040 room.

Collegiate Environment: All qualified applicants are accepted. Scholarships are available. The library contains 61,500 volumes, 660 periodicals, 500,000 microforms and 22,200 audiovisual materials. Dormitory facilities on campus house 1,271 men and women. Programs are available for the educationally disadvantaged. Scholarships are available and 71% of students receive some form of financial aid.

Community Environment: See Baylor University.

Branch Campuses: Amarillo, P.O. Box 11035, Amarillo 79111, (806) 335-2316; Harlingen, P.O. Box 2628, Harlingen 78551-2628, (512) 425-0600; Sweetwater, Route 3, Sweetwater 79556, (915) 235-8441.

TEXAS TECH UNIVERSITY (E-3)
P.O. Box 45005
Lubbock, Texas 79409-5005
Tel: (806) 742-3661; Fax: (806) 742-2007

Description: Publicly supported, coeducational university created by legislative action in 1923. It is made up of the colleges of: Agricultural Sciences and Natural Resources, Arts and Sciences, Business Administration, Education, Engineering, Human Sciences, the School of Law, and the Graduate School. Texas Tech University School of Medicine at Lubbock has been established by the Governor of Texas and the State Legislature and will be located on the campus of this university. Army and Air Force ROTC programs are provided. The University is accredited by the Southern Association of Colleges and Schools and respective educational and professional organizations. It operates on the semester system and also offers two summer terms. Undergraduate enrollment totals 19,652 including 9,315 men and 7,713 women full-time and 2,624 part-time students. A faculty of 947 gives a ratio of 1-18. The Bachelor, Master, and Doctorate degrees are granted.

Entrance Requirements: Accredited high school graduation; completion of 15 college preparatory units including 4 English, 3 mathematics, 2 science, 2 1/2 social science; 2 foreign language, 3 1/2 electives; ACT or SAT required; GRE required for graduate programs; non-high school graduates, 21 years of age or older, may be admitted conditionally; advanced placement program available. $50 application fee for international students only. $25 application fee.

Costs Per Year: $900 tuition; $5,280 tuition out-of-state students; $3,853 board and room; $967 students fees.

Collegiate Environment: With 1,839 acres in one contiguous tract, the university campus is one of the largest in America. In addition, the university operates a Research Farm near Amarillo consisting of 5,821 acres of deeded lands and holds an agricultural use permit on another 8,000 acres. The University provides many special facilities for research, such as the Computer Center, the Siesmological Observatory, and the Southwest Collection, which is a major respository for historical materials pertaining to the American Southwest. The university library totals over 1.4 million items, including books, periodicals, government documents, and other materials. It is designated as one of the two Regional Depositories for U.S. Government Documents in Texas and as depository of the Atomic Energy Commission. Dormitory facilities are provided for 3,703 men and 3,754 women.

Community Environment: See Lubbock Christian University.

Branch Campuses: The Texas Tech University Center at Junction, Texas, an educational facility consisting of 411 acres in the Texas Hill country.

TEXAS WESLEYAN UNIVERSITY   *(G-9)*
1201 Wesleyan
Fort Worth, Texas 76105
Tel: (817) 531-4422; (800) 580-8980; Fax: (817) 531-4814

Description: Privately supported, coeducational liberal arts college had its beginning in 1890 as Polytechnic College, a coeducational institution founded by the Methodist Episcopal Church. It became Texas Woman's College in 1914 but resumed coeducation in 1934, and has maintained its relationship with the United Methodist Church. It is accredited by the Southern Association of Colleges and Schools. It grants Bachelor and Master degrees. Army and Air Force ROTC programs are available at Texas Christian University. The university operates on the semester system and offers two summer terms. Enrollment is 1,238 full-time and 561 part-time undergraduates and 794 graduate students. A faculty of 102 full-time and 53 part-time gives a faculty-student ratio of 1-17.

Entrance Requirements: Accredited high school graduation or equivalent; rank in upper 50% of graduating class; completion of 17 units including 4 English, 2 mathematics, 2 social science, and 2 natural science; ACT or SAT required; graduates from unapproved high schools may be unconditionally admitted on successful completion of college examinations; applicants 21 years of age not meeting all requirements may receive conditional admission; early admission, early decision, midyear admission, rolling admission and advanced placement plans available. $20 application fee.

Costs Per Year: $6,900 tuition; $3,550 room and board; $390 student fees.

Collegiate Environment: The 74-acre campus has 25 buildings. The James and Eunice L. West Library contains approximately 239,000 volumes, 41,201 periodicals, 51,050 microforms, and 2,511 audiovisual aids. There are dormitories for 170 men and 200 women on the campus. 90% of students applying for admission meet the requirements and are accepted. About 35% of the current students graduated in the top quarter of the high school class, and 20% were in the highest tenth. 350 scholarships are available, including 70 athletic, and 80% of the students receive some form of financial aid.

Community Environment: The campus is located in Dallas/Fort Worth, the 7th largest metropolitan area in the U.S. public bus system. There are world-famous museums, cultural events, and professional football, basketball, baseball and soccer teams in the area. The economy is widely diverse.

TEXAS WOMAN'S UNIVERSITY   *(F-9)*
1322 Oakland-Clock Tower
Denton, Texas 76204
Tel: (817) 898-3000

Description: Publicly supported university for women. This multi-purpose institution was created by an act of the Texas Legislature in 1901. Its major purpose is to make the advantages and opportunities of an excellent university education available to its women students. Emphasis is placed on the importance of both liberal education and specialized or professional study. The university is accredited by th Southern Association of Colleges and Schools and by respective professional and educational organizations. The semester system is used and three summer sessions are offered. Men are admitted to the Health Sciences programs and Graduate School. Only women are admitted to the General Divisions. Recent undergraduate enrollment included 155 men, 4,670 women full-time, and 98 men and 4,713 women part-time. A faculty of 385 full-time and 153 part-time gives a ratio of 1-14. General Divisions include the College of Natural and Social Science; Education; Humanities and Fine Arts; Health, Physical Education, Recreation and Dance; Nutrition, Textiles and Human Development; and School of Library and Information Studies. The Institute of Health Sciences includes the College of Nursing, School of Health Care Services, Occupational Therapy, and Physical Therapy.

Entrance Requirements: Accredited high school graduation; completion of 15 units including 3 English, 2 mathematics, 2 science, 2 social science; ACT or SAT required; early decision; rolling admission, delayed admission, early admission and advanced placement plans available; GRE required for graduate applicants; $25 application fee for residence halls; no application fee for admission.

Costs Per Year: $1,218 tuition and fees; $4,530 out-of-state tuition and fees; $3,085 room and board.

Collegiate Environment: The 270-acre campus is 35 miles from the great Dallas-Fort Worth metropolitan center. There are 74 buildings including dormitory facilities for 2,000 students. The University Library contains over 729,251 volumes, 4,428 periodicals and 362,173 microforms. The university provides, without charge, career planning for all students and placement assistance for students who are candidates for degrees. The Institute of Health Sciences has two campuses in Dallas and one in Houston in addition to many offerings on the main campus in Denton. Its affiliations are nationwide and the TWU College of Nursing is the largest in the United States. The Speech and Hearing Clinic serves both children and adults who need remedial help. The Nursery School and Child Care Center enable those majoring in child development and family living to observe and participate in two programs. The Institute for Mental and Physical Development provides diagnosis, treatment, training, and education for children and some adults who have physically or mentally handicapping conditions.

Community Environment: Population 48,000. Denton is a farming and industrial area adjacent to the Dallas-Fort Worth metroplex. The climate is temperate. Airline service is available in Dallas and Fort Worth. The immediate community is served by three railroad lines and U.S. Interstate 35. Denton has libraries, two museums, two hospitals, and many churches representing several faiths. There are part-time job opportunities. Local recreation includes all major water sports due to 183 mile shoreline on Garza-Little Elm Lake. There are three theatres, three golf courses and excellent shopping facilities in the community.

TRINITY UNIVERSITY   *(L-7)*
715 Stadium Drive
San Antonio, Texas 78212-7200
Tel: (210) 736-7011; (800) 874-6489; Fax: (210) 736-8164

Description: Trinity University is a private, coeducational, independent university related by covenant to the Presbyterian Church, U.S.A. It is governed by a 36-member, self-perpetuating Board of Trustees. The university is accredited by the Southern Association of Colleges and Schools and is a recognized member of: The American Association of Colleges for Teacher Education, American Chemical Society, Association of American Colleges and Universities, Association of Texas Colleges, the College Board, National Council for Accreditation of Teacher Education, Presbyterian College Union, Southern University Conference, and Texas Education Agency. Undergraduate study is offered in 29 major fields in 3 divisions: Behavioral and Administrative Studies; Humanities and the Arts; and Sciences, Mathematics and Engineering; B.A., B.S., and B.M. degrees are awarded. The M.A., M.S., M.Ed., and M.A.T. degrees are offered in 5 areas of study. The university operates on the semester system with one summer session. Air Force ROTC is available through U.T.S.A. Study abroad programs are also available, as is a Washington Semester program. Enrollment includes 2,236 full-time and 243 part-time students. A faculty of 224 provides a faculty-student ratio of 1-10.

Entrance Requirements: High school graduation or equivalent; SAT or ACT required; GRE required for graduate programs; Trinity admissions takes into consideration extracurricular activities, standards set by the applicant's school, advanced placement or honors courses and leadership potential; advanced placement, credit by examination, early decision, early admission, block, midyear admission, delayed admission, and college-level examination programs available; $25 application fee; housing applications should be submitted as early as possible.

Costs Per Year: $12,900 tuition; $4,640 room and board; $144 student fees.

Collegiate Environment: Situated on a hill overlooking San Antonio, the 113-acre campus is four miles north of the skyline of the nation's tenth largest city. Facilities include complete laboratories for the natural sciences, with such sophisticated equipment as electron microscopes, a nuclear magnetic resonance spectrometer, and computer terminals. The university has an IBM 4381 computer, complete music rehearsal and performance halls, and radio and television studios. The libraries have total holdings of more than 760,600 volumes, 2,485 periodicals, 268,288 microforms, 17,852 audiovisual materials, and 191,826 government documents. Students come from 50 states and foreign countries, with 62% of the student body from Texas. The average SAT score for entering freshmen is 1205 combined, and average high school GPA is 3.5. The university awarded 507 Bachelor and 95 Master degrees to the graduating class.

Community Environment: San Antonio is a city with a population of more than one million persons. It is the 10th largest city in the United States, has a healthy economy and supports many cultural and athletic activities. Trinity University is located within a 15-minute ride of the international airport and is 5 miles from downtown.

TRINITY VALLEY COMMUNITY COLLEGE (H-11)
500 South Prairieville
Athens, Texas 75751
Tel: (903) 675-6357; Fax: (903) 675-6316

Description: Publicly supported coeducational community college founded in 1946 and accredited by the Southern Association of Colleges and Schools. Enrollment is 1,935 students. A faculty of 122 full-time and 48 part-time gives a faculty-student ratio of 1-21. The semester system is used and two summer terms are offered. The college offers two-year courses for transfer to senior colleges or universities, technical and vocational courses, and continuing education for adults and grants the Certificate and Associate degree.

Entrance Requirements: Open enrollment policy; TASP required; early admission, early decision and advanced placement plans available.

Costs Per Year: $210 county-resident tuition; $360 state resident; $960 out-of-state; $1,248 room and board; tuitions are based on average class load of 15 hours.

Collegiate Environment: The college has 25 buildings on 65 acres. There are dormitories for 190 men and 160 women, and the library contains 22,000 volumes. All students who apply for admission are accepted, and 50% return for the sophomore year. Approximately 70% of a recent freshman class received some form of financial assistance. The average ACT score of a recent freshman class was 15.

Community Environment: Population 10,680. Athens is a rural community located approximately 70 miles from Dallas. The climate is unusually mild and dry. The average high temperature is 95 degrees, and the low temperature range is 18 to 30 degrees. Annual rainfall in the area is 25 inches. Airport facilities, bus lines, and six major highways provide transportation for the city. There is a hospital, libraries, churches of various denominations, and various civic and fraternal organizations. Recreation includes theaters, drive-ins, hunting, fishing, golf, boating, tennis, parks, and swimming pools. Part-time employment is available.

TYLER JUNIOR COLLEGE (G-12)
East 5th Street
P.O. Box 9020
Tyler, Texas 75711
Tel: (903) 510-2200; Fax: (903) 510-2634

Description: Publicly supported, coeducational junior college was established in 1926 and gives priority to students residing in the Tyler Junior College District. Others are admitted if facilities are available. The school is accredited by the Southern Association of Colleges and Schools. Enrollment is 8,124 students. A faculty of 346 gives a faculty-student ratio of 1-24. The semester system is used and two summer terms are offered. The college provides transfer courses, continuing education, vocational and technical training and awards Associate degrees and Professional Certificates. It also has a cooperative education program in electronics.

Entrance Requirements: Open enrollment policy. High school graduation or satisfactory scores on the GED test; TASP (Texas Academic Skills Program); adult applicants not meeting requirements may be admitted by individual approval. Early admission, midyear admission, rolling admission, and advanced placement plans available.

Costs Per Year: $800 district tuition; $1,220 state resident tuition; $1,550 out-of-state tuition; $2,300 board and room.

Collegiate Environment: The college occupies a 73-acre campus upon which 30 modern buildings have been erected. There are dormitory facilities for 200 men and 400 women. An excellent reference library consisting of more than 84,000 volumes, 350 periodicals, 3,000 microforms, and 2,500 audiovisual materials. is housed in the learning resources center. Special financial aid is available for economically disadvantaged students. Of 378 scholarships, approximately 140 are offered to freshmen. 20% of students receive financial aid.

Community Environment: Population 80,454. Incorporated in 1846, the city was named for President John Tyler who was responsible for bringing Texas into the Union. Industry is varied with a principal production of fieldgrown rose bushes shipped throughout the United States. Located in the Pine region of East Texas, the community is reached by railroad, bus, and airlines, as well as eight major highways. The Texas Rose Festival is held each autumn. Community facilities include a symphony orchestra, a library system. There are hospitals and medical facilities readily available. Tyler is the medical center for East Texas. Local recreation includes golf courses, parks, and nearby Tyler State Park and Lake Tyler. Part-time employment is available.

UNIVERSITY OF CENTRAL TEXAS (I-8)
Box 1416
Killeen, Texas 76540-1416
Tel: (817) 526-8262; Fax: (817) 526-8403

Description: UCT is a private, nonprofit institution providing upper-level and graduate study. The university began operation in 1973. It is accredited by the Southern Association of Colleges and Schools, and is recognized by the Texas Commission on Law Enforcement Officers Standards and Education. The university operates on the semester system one summer session. Programs lead to the Bachelor's and Master's degrees. Enrollment includes 293 full-time and 565 part-time students. A faculty of 20 full-time and part-time gives a faculty-student ratio of 1:20.

Entrance Requirements: Each undergraduate student enrolling at UCT has already completed 60 semester hours at another accredited institution with a grade point average of 2.0 on a 4.0 scale. Each graduate student has earned a Bachelor's degree from an accredited institution with a 2.5 grade point average in upper-level coursework. Graduate students must submit a satisfactory graduate exam score before completion of their first 12 semester hours or second semester at UCT, whichever comes first.

Costs Per Year: $3,780 ($126/cr) undergraduate; $2,538 ($141/cr) graduate.

Collegiate Environment: The campus is shared with Central Texas College, a lower-level institution. Dormitoty and married student housing is available through the college. There is an athletic field, swimming pool, and tennis courts on campus. The library contains 200,000 titles, 1,100 periodicals, 104,451 microforms, 15 audiovisual materials, ERIC, National Criminal Justice Reference Service, and a U.S. Military Library. Tables, carrels, typing, and conference facilities are provided.

Community Environment: The campus is located in scenic Central Texas between Killeen and Copperas Cove near Fort Hood, the Largest U.S. Army base in the world. UCT is about 70 miles north of austin, and 150 miles south of Dallas and Fort Worth, and is served by an airport 7 miles from campus. A moderate climate complements hunting, fishing, and water sports around two large, nearby lakes. An active community theatre group and numerous musical activities are popular with receptive civilian and military audiences in the area.

UNIVERSITY OF DALLAS (G-10)
1845 East Northgate Drive
Irving, Texas 75062-4799
Tel: (214) 721-5000; (800) 628-6999; Fax: (214) 721-5017

Description: This private, coeducational, Roman Catholic university was founded in 1956 and is accredited by the Southern Association of Colleges and Schools. Enrollment is 1,116 undergraduate and 1,755 graduate students. A faculty of 86 provides a faculty-student ratio of 1-13. The university operates on the semester system and offers three summer sessions. Internships, to a maximum of 6 credit hours, are available in all fields. A Washington Semester program is available. The university has its own campus in Rome, Italy. 85% of students spend one semester there during sophomore year. The university grants the Bachelor, Master and Doctorate degrees.

Entrance Requirements: High school graduation or equivalent; ACT or SAT required; early admission, early action, delayed admission, and advanced placement plans available; $30 application fee.

Costs Per Year: $11,430 tuition; $4,830 room and board; $50 student fees.

Collegiate Environment: The 1,069-acre campus is located 15 minutes from downtown Dallas. There are 30 buildings including dormitories that house 800 students. The William A. Blakley Library contains 225,885 volumes and 807 periodicals. The Chapel of the Incarnation serves the religious needs of the Catholic faculty and students. Midyear students are accepted, and the college welcomes a geographically diverse student body. Special financial aid and scholarships are available for students. 82% of students receive some form of financial aid.

Community Environment: Population 150,000. Irving is a suburb of Dallas. The community enjoys a temperate climate. Transportation facilities in the community include a railroad, bus lines, excellent highways, and air lines at nearby Dallas and Fort Worth airports. The city has a public library, YMCA, many churches of various faiths, and hospital facilities. Some part-time employment is available. Local recreation includes four theaters, water sports on nearby lakes, and athletic facilities of neighboring communities. There are major civic, fraternal and veteran's organizations active in the area. The Dallas-Ft. Worth area has a population of nearly 3,000,000.

UNIVERSITY OF HOUSTON   *(K-12)*
4800 Calhoun Blvd.
Houston, Texas 77204-2161
Tel: (713) 749-2321

Description: Publicly supported, coeducational university was founded as a four-year institution in 1934. It is accredited by the Southern Association of Colleges and Schools and by several respective professional organizations. The semester system is used and four summer sessions are offered. The university is composed of the Colleges of Architecture, Humanities & Fine Arts, Natural Sciences & Mathematics, Social Sciences, Business Administration, Cullen College of Engineering, Education, Bates College of Law, Optometry, Pharmacy, and Technology, Graduate School of Social Work, and the Hilton School of Hotel and Restaurant Management. Recent undergraduate enrollment included 21,646 students, consisting of 14,888 full-time and 6,758 part-time. There are also 7,248 graduate students. Forty-two separate degrees are granted at the Bachelor, Master, and Doctor levels.

Entrance Requirements: Accredited high school graduation; high school units recommended; 4 English, 3 mathematics, 2 science, 3 social science. Minimum test scores required of the: top 10% of high school class, no minimum; 1st quarter-800 SAT or 19 EACT; 2nd quarter-900 SAT or 22 EACT; 3rd quarter-1000 SAT or 24 EACT; 4th quarter-1100 SAT or 27 EACT; SAT or ACT required; GRE required for graduate programs; rolling admission.

Costs Per Year: $840 tuition; $5,130 tuition nonresidents; $4,608 room and board; $762 student fees.

Collegiate Environment: The 557-acre main campus is accessible from all parts of the city by excellent public transportation and freeway systems. There are 85 buildings including the M.D. Anderson Memorial Library Building which contains the central University Library collections numbering 1.5 million volumes, 22,300 periodicals, 2.9 million microforms, 30,000 audiovisual (including recordings), 28,000 pamphlets and other materials. and a new rare book room. This building is topped by a 163-bell electronic carillon. It houses the Audio-Visual Center. Dormitory facilities are available for 2,263 men and women. Approximately 72% of students applying for admission are accepted. Freshman classes begin in September, January, June and July. Special financial aid is available and approximately 39% of the current student body receives some form of assistance. Army and Navy ROTC is available. The University-Industry Cooperative Education Program is a work-study plan available to undergraduate students majoring in Engineering, natural sciences, mathematics, business or technology. The Honors Program is intended for the student with strong intellectual motivation and leadership potential. Humanities and Fine Arts study abroad programs are available.

Community Environment: Population 1,630,533. Although Houston lies 50 miles inland, it is a major seaport due to the conversion of Buffalo Bayou into the Houston Ship Channel. The city was named in honor of Sam Houston, hero of the Battle of San Jacinto. The community has excellent air, bus, and railroad facilities. Many points of interest in the city include L. B. Johnson Manned Spacecraft Center, Texas Medical Center, Sam Houston Coliseum and Music Hall, Burke Barker Planetarium, Museum of Fine Arts, Contemporary Arts Museum, Zoological Gardens, and the San Jacinto Battleground and Monument, the Astrodome and Battleship U.S.S. Texas. There are over one thousand churches representing all the major denominations, excellent medical facilities, ample shopping centers, and good student housing in the area. Full- and part-time employment is available.

UNIVERSITY OF HOUSTON - CLEAR LAKE   *(K-12)*
2700 Bay Area Boulevard
Houston, Texas 77058
Tel: (713) 283-2500

Description: Publicly supported coeducational university opened for instruction in the fall of 1974. The university is an upper-level institution accepting transfer students at the junior, senior and graduate levels only. It operates on the semester system with three overlapping summer sessions and is fully accredited by the Southern Association of Colleges and Schools. The Bachelor's and the Master's degrees are offered. Enrollment is 2,313 full-time and 4,005 part-time students. A faculty of 372 gives an overall faculty-student ratio is 1-20.

Entrance Requirements: Transfer students at junior, senior and graduate levels only. An associate degree of 54 semester hours with grades of C or better; must pass all parts of the TASP Test, college algebra or higher mathematics; GRE, GMAT, or MAT required for Master degree candidates; rolling admission plan.

Costs Per Year: $576 state-resident tuition; $3,800 out-of-state; $572 student fees.

Collegiate Environment: The 487-acre campus is situated adjacent to the NASA Space Center, approximately 20 miles south of Houston. The library holds 650,000 books and microforms and 1,600 periodicals. No on-campus housing facilities are available. Scholarships are available. Programs are offered in education, public affairs, business and industrial management, accounting and finance, human sciences, humanities, science and technologies.

Community Environment: A planned community 20 miles south of Houston, and 35 miles from Galveston, Texas. Mixture of education and space related employers. Many cultural activities available, both in the Clear Lake area, and within easy access of Houston. Abundance of outdoor recreational opportunities. See also University of Houston.

UNIVERSITY OF HOUSTON - VICTORIA   *(M-10)*
2302C Red River
Victoria, Texas 77901
Tel: (512) 567-3151; Admissions: (512) 788-6222

Description: The University of Houston-Victoria is a publicly supported upper-level university serving students seeking baccalaureate and graduate degrees. The university opened in 1973. It is accredited by the Southern Association of Colleges and Schools. It operates on the semester system and offers two summer terms. Enrollment is 1,100 students. A faculty of 30 provides a faculty-student ratio of 1-37. Students transfer to UH-Victoria after completing freshman and sophomore work elsewhere, or with a minimum of 54 hours while progressing toward their 4-year degree. The school serves students returning to college as well as traditional students.

Entrance Requirements: 54 hours of college credit required, with a minimum GPA of 2.0.

Costs Per Year: Undergraduate: $868 ($28/credit) resident; $5,301 ($171/credit) nonresident; Graduate: $38/credit; there is a $100 minimum tuition charge; other fees vary by number of credit hours.

Collegiate Environment: UH-Victoria resides on the Victoria (Junior) College campus and shares its facilities. A model preschool and kindergarten serves as a laboratory for students in childhood education courses. The Small Business Institute involves business students in real-world activities with local businesses. There is no on-campus housing. The library contains 202,000 volumes, 1,800 periodicals, and 5,900 audiovisual titles. There is also a Local History Collection.

Community Environment: The campus is located in Victoria, a city of 58,000 inhabitants at the center of South Texas Crossroads in the heart of the Golden Gulf Coast. This expanding city on the banks of the Guadalupe River is more than 150 years old, and is one of the first 3 towns chartered by The Republic of Texas. The city is near the Gulf of Mexico and is a popular coastal route between Houston and Mexico. The home of many petrochemical companies, such as Dupont, Alcoa, and Union Carbide, it is surrounded by vast expanses of ranch-land.

UNIVERSITY OF MARY HARDIN - BAYLOR   *(I-9)*
P.O. Box 375 UMHB Station
Belton, Texas 76513
Tel: (817) 939-8642; (800) 727-8642; Fax: (817) 939-4535

Description: Privately supported, coeducational liberal arts college operated under the auspices of the Baptist General Convention of Texas. It was chartered in 1845 and was one of the early colleges in the southwest to be fully accredited by the Southern Association of Colleges and Schools. The college operates on the semester system and also provides two summer terms. Air Force ROTC is available. Enrollment includes 1,585 full-time and 659 part-time students. A faculty of 95 full-time and 61 part-time gives a faculty-student ratio of 1-17. The college grants the Bachelor's and Master's degrees.

Entrance Requirements: High school graduation with rank in upper half of graduating class; completion of 15 units including 3 English, 2 mathematics, and 2 social science; ACT 18 or SAT combined 700 required; applicants not meeting all entrance requirements may be admitted on probationary status; rolling admission, delayed admission and advanced placement plans available; $35 application fee.

Costs Per Year: $5,550 tuition; $3,086 room and board; $700 average additional expenses.

Collegiate Environment: The 101-acre campus is located in central Texas, a drive of about two and a half hours from Dallas and Fort Worth. The 21 college buildings contain a library of 125,000 volumes, 229 pamphlets, 830 periodicals, and 34,940 microforms, and dormitory facilities for 711 students. Students from other geographical locations are accepted as well as midyear students. Approximately 95% of students applying for admission are accepted and 80% of the previous freshman class returned to the college for the sophomore year. The average high school standing of the freshman class was in the top 50%; 30% graduated in the top quarter and 40% in the second quarter. The average ACT composite score of a recent entering class was 18. Financial aid is available; 176 scholarships were recently offered and 75% of the current student body receives financial assistance.

Community Environment: Population 12,000. Located in central Texas, Belton has a mild climate. The community is served by railroad lines, bus lines, U.S. Highway I-35 and Texas State 317. There is an airport eight miles away. Local community services include a library, museum, several churches, a hospital, and various civic, fraternal and veteran's organizations. Part-time employment is available. The city is a one-hour drive from Waco and Austin for out-of-town entertainment. Belton has a theater, a swimming pool, and nearby Lake Belton for fishing, water skiing, swimming, and speed boat races.

UNIVERSITY OF NORTH TEXAS   *(F-9)*
P.O. Box 13797
Denton, Texas 76203
Tel: (817) 565-2000; (800) 868-8211; Admissions: (817) 565-2681; Fax: (817) 565-2408

Description: Publicly supported, coeducational university began in 1890 as a private normal school. It became a state institution in 1899 and its present name was adopted in 1988. It is accredited by the Southern Association of Colleges and Schools and numerous professional agencies. Today the university consists of the College of Arts and Sciences, the Toulouse School of Graduate Studies, the College of Business Administration, The School of Community Service, the College of Education, the School of Library and Information Sciences, and the College of Music. The university grants the Bachelor, Master's and Doctorate degrees. It operates on the semester system and offers two summer terms. Cooperative education programs are available in 34 majors. Air Force ROTC is available. There is a study abroad program available for the United Kingdom, France, Germany, Spain and 32 other countries. UNT is a member of ISEP. Recent enrollment included 9,704 men, 10,796 women full-time and 2,628 men and 2,477 women part-time. A faculty of 825 full-time and 257 part-time gives a faculty-student ratio of 1-17.

Entrance Requirements: High school graduation with SAT and/or ACT requirements are as follows; Freshman Requirements Top 10%; No minimum score required, but must submit scores. Remainder of top quarter: Minimum 800 SAT or 19 ACT. 2nd quarter: Minimum 900 SAT or 21 ACT. 3rd quarter: Minimum 1000 SAT or 24 ACT. 4th quarter: Minimum 1100 SAT or 27 ACT. GRE required for graduate programs GMAT in Business; early admission, early decision, rolling admission, midyear admission and advanced placement plans available. $25 application fee.

Costs Per Year: $720 state resident tuition; $4,860 tuition out-of-state residents; $3,579 room and board; $150 student fees.

Collegiate Environment: The 425-acre campus is located in Denton, approximately 38 miles from Dallas and 36 miles from Fort Worth. The 119 university buildings contain a library of 1,206,758 volumes, 8,775 periodicals, 2,190,831 microforms, 49,357 records and tapes. There are living accommodations for 4,300 students and 50 families. The average combined SAT score of the entering freshman class was 982. Approximately 900 scholarships are available. The university seeks a geographically diverse student body and midyear students are accepted. In the academic year, the university awarded 3,574 Bachelor, 1,152 Master and 193 Doctorate degrees.

Community Environment: Denton is a community of approximately 68,350. Texas' largest and most modern airport, Dallas - Fort Worth International, is only a short drive from Denton.

UNIVERSITY OF NORTH TEXAS HEALTH SCIENCE CENTER   *(G-9)*
3500 Camp Bowie Boulevard
Fort Worth, Texas 76107-2699
Tel: (817) 735-2204; (800) 535-8266; Fax: (817) 735-2225

Description: The college opened in 1970, and is accredited by the American Osteopathic Association. The goal of the college is to change the emphasis in the education of physicians from "defensive" treatment of disease to "offensive" promotion of health. The Doctor of Osteopathy degree is offered. The college operates 6 general family clinics and 13 specialty clinics. There are 435 students. A full-time faculty of 185 gives a faculty-student ratio of 1-2.

Entrance Requirements: MCAT required and must be taken within three years of application; at least 90 semester hours at accredited college or university; baccalaureate degree strongly preferred; early decision, early admission, deferred admission, and rolling admission plans available.

Costs Per Year: $6,550; $19,650 out-of-state.

Collegiate Environment: The campus is adjacent to the Osteopathic Medical Center of Texas, the college's primary teaching hospital. The campus has 3 main buildings and includes a library, several clinics and laboratories. There is no on-campus housing.

Community Environment: Fort Worth has a population of over 400,000 and is the seat of Tarrant County. The campus is adjacent to the city's cultural district, which includes the Kimball Art Museum, the Amon Carter Museum, and the Fort Worth Museum of Science and History.

UNIVERSITY OF SAINT THOMAS   *(K-12)*
3812 Montrose Boulevard
Houston, Texas 77006
Tel: (713) 522-7911

Description: Privately supported, coeducational, Roman Catholic, liberal arts admitted its first undergraduate students in 1947. The semester system is employed and one summer term is offered. The institute is accredited by the Southern Association of Colleges and Schools. The University grants the B.A., B.M., M.Ed., MBA and Nursing degree. The School of Theology, formerly the independent St. Mary's Seminary, joined St. Thomas in 1968, and grants the Master of Divinity (M.Div.), Master of Theological Studies, and the Master of Religious Education (MRE) degrees. U.S. Navy and Army ROTC programs available through nearby Rice University. Enrollment includes 322 men, 598 women full-time, 183 men and 246 women part-time, and 764 graduate students. A faculty of 103 full-time and 70 part-time gives an overall faculty-student ratio of 1-11.

Entrance Requirements: Approved high school graduation or equivalent; rank in upper 75% of graduating class; completion of 16 units including 4 English, 2 mathematics, 2 foreign language, 1 science, 2 social science; ACT or SAT required; GRE required for graduate programs; advanced placement, delayed admission, rolling admission, early decision and early admission plans available; application fee $15, personal interview recommended; midyear students accepted.

Costs Per Year: $7,300 tuition; $3,390 room and board; $300 books and student fees.

Collegiate Environment: The 15 acre campus has 40 buildings. The library has a collection of 80,000 volumes. The Learning Resource Center has equipment for slide and film projection and audio devices for all university courses. The Language Laboratory is for oral-aural practice in modern languages. The Institute for Storm Research is another special feature of the university. There are accommodations for 100 men and 100 women in the dormitories. Approximately 80% of students applying for admission meet the requirements and are accepted. Special financial aid is available and 60% of the current student body receives some form of assistance.

Community Environment: See University of Houston.

UNIVERSITY OF TEXAS - EL PASO   *(N-1)*
500 W. University Avenue
El Paso, Texas 79968
Tel: (915) 747-5000; Admissions: (915) 747-5576

Description: Publicly supported, coeducational state university is accredited by the Southern Association Colleges and Schools. The Texas Legislature created this educational institution in 1913 as the Texas School of Mines and Metallurgy. It became a branch of the University of Texas in 1919, and in 1949, the name was changed to Texas Western College in recognition of the steady broadening and deepening of the college program. Its present name became official in 1967. The institution now offers 114 Baccalaureate and Master degrees in addition to the Doctorate in Geology, Electrical Engineering, Medical Science, Engineering and Psychology. It is comprised of the College of Liberal Arts, College of Nursing, College of Engineering, College of Business, College of Education, College of Science, and the Graduate School. Army and Air Force ROTC programs are provided. The university operates on the semester system and also offers one summer term. Enrollment includes 4,467 men, 5,435 women full-time and 3,013 men and 3,773 women part-time. A faculty of 407 full-time and 401 part-time provides a faculty-student ratio of 1-23.

Entrance Requirements: Accredited high school graduation; recommend completion of 16 units including 4 English, 3 mathematics, 2 foreign language, 3 science, 3 social science; SAT or ACT required; GRE required for graduate programs; non-high school graduates, 18 years of age or older, may be admitted by individual approval upon favorable results of GED; early admission, early decision, rolling admission, midyear admission and delayed admission plans available.

Costs Per Year: $840 tuition; $5,730 tuition for out-of-state students; $3,660 room and board.

Collegiate Environment: The university is located in the foothills of a southern spur of the Rockies just across the Rio Grande from Juarez, Mexico. The 74 University buildings include a six story library of 657,308 volumes, 7,595 periodicals, and 1,090,296 microforms. There are living accommodations for 750 students and 60 families. Athletic events are held in the 12,000 seat Special Events Center and in the 51,000-seat Sun Bowl. The Engineering-Science Complex covers 257,763 sq. ft. and the Fine Arts Complex housing art, drama, and music covers 215,121 sq. ft. Station KTEP-FM is owned by the university and staffed entirely by students. About 60% of the current students receive financial aid. The school granted 1,584 Bachelor degrees and 385 Master degrees to a recent graduating class. Approximately 87% of the students are from Texas.

Community Environment: The university is less than one mile from downtown El Paso (population 505,000). The city, which lies in westernmost tip of Texas, still shows the influence of the Spanish Conquistadores and missionaries who colonizied the land over 400 years ago. An even older heritage is present in the Pueblo Indians who make their home in nearby Ysleta. Because of the proximity to Mexico, the community is bilingual and bicultural. The international flavor of the environment is also enhanced by Ft. Bliss, which not only brings in military personnel from all over the United States but also has members of many European and Asian armed forces present. In addition to Ft. Bliss and White Sands Missle Range, there are several major civilian industries including a copper refinery, three major

oil refineries, and a smelter. Other industries include farming and dry goods manufacturing. The climate is mild and dry, with sunshine 80% of the time. Recreation activities are abundant and all land sports can be played year-round. Snow skiing; fishing; rodeos; horse, dog, and stock car racing; exploring, and small game hunting are among popular pastimes. There are several state and federal parks within driving distance. The city is served by eight major airlines, Amtrak, and two national bus lines. There are several hospitals, shopping centers, five local television stations, and the El Paso Diablos, a baseball farm club of the Milwaukee Brewers. To supplement cultural life, there is a symphony orchestra, three city run museums, and over 100 churches representing practically all religious faiths.

UNIVERSITY OF TEXAS - HEALTH SCIENCE CENTER AT HOUSTON   *(K-12)*
P.O. Box 20036
Houston, Texas 77225
Tel: (713) 792-7444; Fax: (713) 794-5701

Description: Publicly-supported coeducational institution, located in the Texas Medical Center, offering upper division, graduate, and first-professional study only. It is accredited by the Southern Association of Colleges and Schools. It employs the semester and trimester systems and offers two summer sessions. Enrollment includes 2,189 full-time and 994 part-time graduate and first-professional students. There are 865 full-time and 211 part-time faculty members.

Entrance Requirements: Varies with school.

Costs Per Year: Graduate: $1,008 state resident tuition; $6,156 non-resident tuition; $401 student fees.

Collegiate Environment: Draws upon the extensive resources of the Texas Medical Center. University operated apartments are available to students. Scholarships are available and 43% of the student body receives some form of financial assistance.

Community Environment: See University of Houston - Urban

UNIVERSITY OF TEXAS - HEALTH SCIENCE CENTER AT SAN ANTONIO   *(L-7)*
San Antonio, Texas 78284
Tel: (210) 567-7000

Description: The publicly supported, coeducational state university medical school was created in 1959 by an Act of the 56th Texas Legislature. The Center is comprised of five schools: Medical School, Dental School, School of Allied Health Sciences, Graduate School of Biomedical Sciences, and the School of Nursing. The school employs and academic year system composed of four terms and enrolls 2,456 students with a faculty of 1,165. Grants M.D., B.S., B.S.N., M.S., M.S.N., Ph.D., D.D.S. and certificates and is accredited by the Southern Association of Colleges and Schools and the American Medical Association.

Entrance Requirements: Preference is given to students with a Baccalaureate degree; however, candidates with 90 semester hour credits are evaluated closely if they are higher than average academically and possess the necessary maturity they are considered for admission. In general, applicants should have a B average or better and completion of 1 year of English, 2 biology, 1/2 mathematics (calculus), 1 physics, 1 general chemistry, and 1 organic chemistry. The Medical College Admission Test is required; application may be obtained from University of Texas Medical and Dental Application Center, 702 Colorado St., Suite 620, Austin, Texas 78701; application fee $35; advanced placement plan available; personal interview required. Entrance requirements for other degrees vary.

Costs Per Year: $5,463 tuition; $21,852 tuition for out-of-state students (medical students); $250-$350 per month average off-campus room rental fee; $20 per semester hour for undergraduate and graduate students, $122/hr for out-of-state students; dental student tuition $4,511, out-of-state $18,044; $24 microscope rental fee; $125 student fees.

Collegiate Environment: The University of Texas Health Science Center's physical plant, valued in excess of $174 million, is composed of the Medical School, Dental School, and Nursing School buildings; a multidisciplinary lecture hall; a cafeteria; a library; an auditorium; the University Plaza Building; and administration and auxiliary service structures. Construction has been continuous on the campus since the original Medical School Building was begun in 1966. The annual budget for operations exceeds $176 million. Some 3,600 faculty and staff are employed on the 100-acre campus.

Community Environment: See San Antonio College.

Branch Campuses: University of Texas - Pan American at Brownsville, 1614 Ridgley Road, Brownsville, TX 78520, (512) 542-6882.

UNIVERSITY OF TEXAS - MEDICAL BRANCH AT GALVESTON   *(L-13)*
Galveston, Texas 77555-1305
Tel: (409) 772-1215; Admissions: (409) 772-1215; Fax: (409) 772-5056

Description: Since it opened its doors in 1891, the University of Texas Medical Branch at Galveston (UTMB) has remained true to its threefold mission of providing scholarly teaching, innovative scientific investigations and state-of-the-art patient care to citizens of Texas and beyond. It is accredited by the Southern Association of Colleges and Schools, and professionally by the American Medical Association. Over its 104-year history, the Medical Branch has graduated more than 19,000 health care professionals, including more than 10,000 medical doctors, more than 5,000 nurses, more than 3,000 allied health professionals, and nearly 1,000 biomedical researchers. It operates on the semester system and offers two summer sessions. Enrollment includes 1,905 full-time and 422 part-time undergraduates and 1,355 graduate students. A faculty of 907 full-time and 57 part-time gives a faculty-student ratio of 1-3.

Entrance Requirements: Entrance requirements vary by School and program. Students are encouraged to contact the School of their choice for specific information regarding deadlines, prerequisites, entrance exams, interviews, etc. Application fees are as follows: School of Allied Health Sciences ($30 per program); School of Nursing (Undergraduate - $10); Graduate School of Biomedical Sciences ($25 for U.S. applicants per program and $50 for international applicants per program). Some programs in the School of Allied Health require the Health Occupations Admission Exam (HOAE). The Nurse Entrance Test (NET) is require the for the Generic Nursing program. The Graduate Record Exam (GRE) is required for the Graduate School. Applications for the School of Medicine may be obtained from the Medical and Dental Application Center, 702 Colorado, Suite 620, Austin, Texas 78701. The MCAT is required for the School of Medicine.

Costs Per Year: $6,550 tuition; $19,650 out-of-state tuition, for School of Medicine; $336 tuition, $2,052 out-of-state tuition for Graduate School and Medical Services Curricula; tuition varies for Postgraduate Division; $180 approximate student fees; additional fees required for books and room and board.

Collegiate Environment: Now in its second century of service, UTMB is one of the nation's major academic medical centers. Well over 2,000 students are enrolled in the degree and residency training programs administered by UTMB's four schools and two institutes: the School of Nursing, the School of Medicine, the School of Allied Health Sciences, the Graduate School of Biomedical Sciences, the Marine Biomedical Institute and the Institute for the Medical Humanities. The campus includes 73 buildings on 86 acres. Many of those buildings house renowned biomedical researchers, whose work delves into a broad range of promising topics and often has immediate application to patient care. The Medical Branch's commitment to interdisciplinary research brings basic scientists and clinicians together, resulting in better health care training through shared information. Facilities also include a major medical library, convenient bookstore and food service facilties, and state-of-the-art classrooms. The university's first dedicated student center is under construction. Numerous and varied housing opportunities are available close to campus. As Texas' only state-supported, multicategorical health referral center, UTMB offers students a wealth of practical learning opportunities through a seven-hospital complex and more than 100 on-campus outpatient clinics. The Medical Branch records tens of thousands of inpatient visits and hundreds of thosusands of outpatient visits each year. Library holdings include 248,138 bound volumes and 120,00 perodicals. Residence halls accomodate 206 students. 35% of applicants are accepted. 455 scholarships are available and 47% of students receive some form of financial aid.

Community Environment: Located on the Texas Gulf Coast, the Houston-Galveston metroplex UTMB calls home combines the amenities of one of the nation's largest urban centers with the unique ambi-

ance of island living. The Gulf of Mexico and Galveston Bay provide the area with miles of beaches, making the island the perfect setting for boating, swimming, fishing and surfing enthusiasts. Seasonal festivals and community events, including an annual Mardi Gras celebration, are an important, and popular, part of the Galveston lifestyle. The city of Galveston, with a population of appoximately 63,000, covers most of Galveston Island. The bay side of the city features a restored wharffront district known as The Strand. Dating back to the 1840's, this historic area was once known as "The Wall Street of the Southwest." Today, a variety of shops, museums, banks, art galleries, businesses and restaurants keep the district bustling. Numerous cargo vessels keep the nearby port hummming, and Galveston's Elissa, the 1887 Tall Ship for Texas, and the Texas Seaport Museum are open for tours. A few mildes west, Moody Gardens features a one-acre tropical rainforest housed in a 10-story glass pyramid, as well as a 3-D IMAX theater.

UNIVERSITY OF TEXAS - PAN AMERICAN   *(Q-8)*
1201 W. University Drive
Edinburg, Texas 78539
Tel: (810) 381-2011; Admissions: (810) 381-2201/2206

Description: Publicly supported, coeducational, liberal arts college first began operation as the Edinburg Junior College in 1927. In 1952, a full four-year program was offered. In 1965, the college became the twenty-second Texas institution of higher learning to receive state support. The college operates on the early semester system and also offers two summer terms. Accredited by the Southern Association of Colleges and Schools, the college grants Associate degree, Bachelor degree and a Master degree. Enrollment includes 3,032 men, 3,959 women full-time and 2,633 men and 3,904 women part-time. A faculty of 346 full-time and 165 part-time provides a student-faculty ratio of 35:1.

Entrance Requirements: Accredited high school graduation; completion of 16 units including 3 English, 2 mathematics, and at least two units from two of the fields of foreign language, social science, and natural science; ACT or SAT required; non-high school graduates, 21 years of age or older, may be admitted conditionally with acceptable scores on GED examinations; early admission, early decision, midyear admission and rolling admission available.

Costs Per Year: $1,182 tuition; $4,446 tuition and fees out-of-state residents; $2,200 room and board; $25 student fees.

Collegiate Environment: The college is located on 200 acres. The Pan American University contains a library of 250,000 volumes and 563,365 microforms. Dormitory facilities accomodate 197 men and 197 women. About 98% of students applying for admission were accepted. Scholarships are available and 60% of students receive some form of financial aid.

Community Environment: Population 30,000. Edinburg is located in the subtropical lower Rio Grande Valley of Texas and enjoys a mild year-round climate. The average summer maximum temperature is about 90 degrees, with winter average of 70 degrees. The community is served by bus lines and U.S. Highway 281. Edinburg has a hospital and major civic, fraternal and veteran's orgainzations. Part-time employment is available. Local recreation includes hunting, fishing, golf, and swimming in the Gulf of Mexico approximately 70 miles away.

UNIVERSITY OF TEXAS - PERMIAN BASIN   *(H-2)*
4901 E. University
Box 8422-UTPB
Odessa, Texas 79762
Tel: (915) 367-2011

Description: An upper-level and graduate division of The University of Texas System founded in 1969. It operates on the semester system with two summer terms. Recent enrollment consisted of 824 men and 1,491 women. A faculty of 74 full-time and 46 part-time gives a ratio of 1-16. Full accreditation was granted in 1975 by the Southern Association of Colleges and Schools.

Entrance Requirements: Students must complete 54 semester hours of accredited college work prior to enrollment. In special cases, a student with 48 semester hours credit may enroll, provided the lower division credit requirements are completed during the first semester of enrollment. GRE required for graduate programs, rolling admission plan.

Costs Per Year: Tuition $915; nonresident $5,820; room $1,350.

Collegiate Environment: There is a library with 348,579 volumes, 755 current periodical subscriptions, 902,247 microforms and 6,562 audiovisual materials. Financial aid is available and 41% of the student body receive aid.

UNIVERSITY OF TEXAS - SAN ANTONIO   *(L-7)*
6900 N. Loop 1604 W
San Antonio, Texas 78249
Tel: (210) 691-4011; (800) 669-0919; Admissions: (210) 691-4530

Description: This publicly supported university is accredited by the Southern Association of Colleges and Schools. It opened in the summer of 1973 to graduate students. Upper-division undergraduates were admitted for the first time in the fall of 1975 and all four years of the undergraduate program was implemented in the fall of 1976. The first Doctor of Philosophy degree program was implemented in 1992-93 in Biology. The university operates on the semester system and offers two summer sessions. Enrollment is 8,174 men and 9,405 women. (These enrollment figures include 9,098 full-time and 6,110 part-time undergraduates and 2,371 graduate students.) A faculty of 397 full-time and 298 part-time gives a student-faculty ratio of 1-25. Army and Air Force ROTC are offered.

Entrance Requirements: High school graduation or equivalent; SAT or ACT required; GMAT or GRE required for graduate programs; TOEFL required for international students; early admission, early decision, midyear admission, rolling admission, and advanced placement plans available; $20 application fee.

Costs Per Year: Undergraduate: $1,456 (full-time/12 hours) resident tuition; $4,888 nonresident tuition; Graduate: $1,644 (full-time/9 hours) resident tuition; $3,876 nonresident tuition; $5,000 room and board.

Collegiate Environment: The campus library contains 601,000 volumes (including government documents), 2,200 periodicals, 1,950,000 microforms and 5,843 audiovisual materials. 86% of applicants are accepted. Scholarships are available and approximately 61% of the students receive some form of financial aid. Recently the university awarded 1,967 Bachelor's degrees and 504 Master degrees.

Community Environment: See San Antonio College.

UNIVERSITY OF TEXAS - SOUTHWESTERN MEDICAL CENTER AT DALLAS   *(G-10)*
5323 Harry Hines Boulevard
Dallas, Texas 75235-9002
Tel: (214) 648-3111

Description: Since its formation in 1943, Southwestern Medical College has grown from a small wartime medical school into The University of Texas Health Science Center at Dallas, a multi-faceted academic institution of nationally recognized excellence in the education of physicians, medical scientists and health-care personnel. The Council on Medical Education and Hospitals of the American Medical Association and the Association of American Medical Colleges placed Southwestern Medical College on the list accredited medical schools in 1944. It is also accredited by the Southern Association of Association of Colleges and Schools. It became Southwestern Medical School of the University of Texas in 1949, and in November 1972, the name and scope of the medical school was changed with its reorganization into The University of Texas Health Science Center at Dallas (which in 1988, formally became the University of Texas Southwestern Medical Center)--comprised of Southwestern Medical School, Southwestern Graduate School of Biomedical Sciences and Southwestern Allied Health Sciences School. Southwestern Medical School has maintained a classical four-year curriculum based on departmental as well as interdisciplinary teaching. The first two years provide the student with an opportunity to develop a strong background in the basic sciences, as well as an introduction to clinical medicine. The third and fourth years offer intense clinical experiences involving the student in direct patient care. The semester system is used in the Southwestern Allied Health Sciences School and the Southwestern Graduate School of Biomedical Sciences, which award baccalaureate, master's and doctoral degrees. The University enrolls 1,458 men and women. Faculty numbers 931.

Entrance Requirements: Medical: Bachelor degree or a minimum of 3 years college work (90 semester hours) including 2 years English, 1 1/2 biology or zoology, 1 physics, 2 chemistry, 1 mathematics; Medical College Admission Test required; applicants with B average or above are preferred. Total of 20 non-residents per year admitted; application fee $50; application should be sent before 1 yr. prior to fall enrollment; form may be obtained from The University of Texas Medical/Dental Application Center, 210 W. 6th Street, B41, Austin, Texas 78701. Graduate: Bachelors degree or its equivalent from an accredited institution in the United States or proof of equivalent training at a foreign university required; satisfactory grades (generally at least an overall GPA of 3.0) in undergraduate or graduate course work. Each applicant is required to have sent to the Office of the Registrar two certified transcripts from each institution of higher learning attended; a satisfactory score on the Graduate Record Examination (GRE) Aptitude Test -- generally, admitted students will present a combined score of 1200 on the verbal and quantitative parts of the examination. Allied Health: A minimum of 60 semester hours of earned credit (exclusive of physical education and military science) is required for admission as a regular student including 6 semester hours of English, 6 of US History, 9 of humanities and social science, science credit as required by the specific program of interest; minimum overall GPA of 2.0 on a 4.0 scale -- individual programs may set a higher requirement.

Costs Per Year: Medical tuition: resident $5,400, nonresident $21,600 Tuition for allied health and graduate students: $16 per hour (minimum $100); $120 per hour for non-Texas residents.

Collegiate Environment: The Medical Center main campus is located on 60 acres three miles north of downtown Dallas. Its 16 buildings have over three million square feet of space for teaching and research. The library contains 224,732 volumes, 2,476 periodicals, 22,600 microforms and 3,089 sound recordings. More than $95 million of improvements have been completed within the past 15 years. Parkland Memorial Hospital is located on a site immediately adjacent to the Medical Center Campus and is the principal teaching hospital of Southwestern Medical School. Affiliated institutions are the Woodlawn Hospital, Baylor University Medical Center, Methodist Hospital of Dallas, St. Paul Hospital, the Children's Medical Center, Texas Scottish Rite Hospital for Crippled Children, Dallas Veterans Administration Hospital, Presbyterian Hospital of Dallas, John Peter Smith Hospital, the US Public Health Service Hospital, Timberlawn Sanitarium, Terrell State Hospital, and the Dallas Guild Guidance Clinic. Southwestern Medical Center does not furnish living quarters for its students. The Oak Lawn area has many apartment and boarding houses, but competition is keen enough to make early efforts necessary. Financial assistance is available.

Community Environment: See Dallas Christian College.

UNIVERSITY OF TEXAS - SYSTEM   *(K-8)*
601 Colorado Street
Austin, Texas 78701-2982
Tel: (512) 499-4200; Fax: (512) 499-4371

Description: The University of Texas System is governed by a 9 member Board of Regents appointed to staggered 6 year terms by the governor and is administered by the System Administration headed by Chancellor William H. Cunningham. Today the University of Texas System is comprised of 15 component institutions: The University of Texas of Arlington, The University of Texas at Austin, The University of Tesxas at Brownsville, The University of Texas at Dallas, The University of Texas at El Paso, The University of Texas-Pan American, The University of Texas of the Permian Basin, The University of Texas at San Antonio, The University of Texas at Tyler, health institutions at Dallas, Galveston, Houston, San Antonio, and Tyler, and the M. D. Anderson Cancer Center in Houston. It is accredited by the Southern Association of Colleges and Schools and by the respective professional associations. Total enrollment for the system is 152,000 students with 12,696 faculty members. See descriptions of the individual campuses for detailed information. Further information concerning officers and administration, admissions policies, fees, academic calendars, curicula, and degrees may be obtained from catalogs published by the individual institutions.

UNIVERSITY OF TEXAS - TYLER   *(G-12)*
3900 University Boulevard
Tyler, Texas 75701
Tel: (903) 566-7000; (800) 888-9537; Admissions: (903) 566-7202; Fax: (903) 566-7173

Description: The upper-level state supported school is accredited by the Southern Association of Colleges and Schools and was founded in 1971. It grants the bachelor's and master's degrees. The school is organized into four schools: School of Business Administration, School of Education and Psychology, School of Liberal Arts, and School of Sciences and Mathematics. The semester system is used with three summer terms. Enrollment includes 545 men and 970 women full-time and 845 men and 1,490 women part-time. A faculty of 140 full-time and 71 part-time gives a student-faculty ratio of 18:1.

Entrance Requirements: 54 hours from an accredited college with a minimum GPA of 2.0 on a 4.0 scale.

Costs Per Year: $840 for state students; $5,130 for nonresidents; $6,549 room and board; $782 student fees.

Collegiate Environment: The campus resides on 200 acres with a lake of its own. It is one of 3 upper-level universities in the University of Texas system. The library has holdings of 177,900 titles, 132,100 microforms, 7,121 audiovisual materials and 1,313 periodicals. There is no on-campus housing. It is situated in southeast Tyler and is bordered by three major streets. 90% of applicants are accepted. Scholarships are available and 67% of students receive some form of financial aid.

Community Environment: UTT is located in the heart of East Texas midway between Dallas and Shreveport. Known for its roses, azalea trails, and Spring Flower Show, Tyler is a progressive city of 75,000 people and is considered the educational and medical center of East Texas.

UNIVERSITY OF TEXAS AT ARLINGTON   *(B-7)*
701 S. Nedderman
P.O. Box 19120
Arlington, Texas 76019
Tel: (817) 273-3365; (800) 687-2882; Admissions: (817) 273-2225

Description: This publicly supported, comprehensive, multidiscipline, coeducational, state university is located in Arlington, Texas, in the heart of the Dallas-Fort Worth area. It is accredited by the Southern Association of Colleges and Schools and by numerous professional accrediting organizations. The institution was founded in 1895 and during early years had a number of names and missions. In 1965, it became a part of the University of Texas System. The university is organized into the following units: College of Business Administration, College of Engineering, College of Liberal Arts, College of Science, School of Architecture, School of Nursing, Graduate School of Social Work, Graduate School, Institute of Urban Studies and Center for Professional Teacher Education. Army and Air Force ROTC programs are available. Cooperative education programs are available in the College of Engineering and the College of Business Administration. A London Semester program is available. The university operates on a semester system and during the summer has both eleven-week and five-week sessions. Enrollment is 10,733 full-time and 8,193 part-time undergraduate students. There are 4,364 graduate students. A faculty of 935 gives a faculty-student ratio of 1-20. In 1993-94 the university granted 2,950 Bachelor, 1,081 Master and 85 Doctoral degrees.

Entrance Requirements: Undergraduate admission is based upon rank in high school class in relation to score on either SAT or ACT, minimum: ACT 18 or SAT 700 combined for student rank in 2nd quarter, ACT 21 or SAT 800 combined for rank in 3rd quarter, ACT 25 or SAT 1000 combined for rank in 4th quarter; 20 units required, including 4 English, 3 mathematics, 3 social science, 2 science, 2 foreign language or additional mathematics and/or science, and 6 electives; early admission, rolling admission, and provisional admission, individual approval (for applicants over 21 years of age) are available; graduate admission is based upon the applicants' previous record in addition to acceptable scores on the GRE or GMAT.

Costs Per Year: $1,374 resident tuition; $5,454 out-of-state; $4,180 room and board.

Collegiate Environment: The university is located in the heart of the Dallas-Fort Worth metropolitan area and is highly accessible. The institution is primarily regional in nature, drawing about 80% of its students from the D/FW metroplex. Because of its unique location and high accessibility to people, the university serves a broad spectrum of students ranging from the recent high school graduate to the older student who wishes to upgrade or redirect a career. Classes are held from 8 a.m. to 10 p.m. The campus encompasses 351 acres. The library has

more than 943,000 books, journals, documents, and technical reports; it subscribes to 5,770 periodicals and newspapers and maintains a collection of microfilm, microfiche, motion pictures, sound recordings, video tapes, filmstrips, and slides. Approximately 2,300 students are housed in university-owned facilities. The 200 student organizations include honorary, political, religious, special interest, professional, recreational, social, and military groups. The Financial Aid Office offers financial assistance in a variety of areas including loans and grants, scholarships, and on-campus and off-campus employment. 35% of students receive some form of financial aid.

Community Environment: Arlington has a population of about 300,000, and the metroplex has more than 3.5 million residents. The city is in close proximity to the Dallas/Fort Worth Regional Airport. There are numerous public libraries, recreational facilities, churches, theaters, and shopping centers. Arlington recently attracted 5,000,000 visitors to Wet-and-Wild, Six Flags Over Texas, and Texas Rangers Baseball. Both Dallas and Fort Worth are readily accessible.

UNIVERSITY OF TEXAS AT AUSTIN   *(K-8)*
Austin, Texas 78712
Tel: (512) 471-7601; Admissions: (512) 475-7399; Fax: (512) 475-7478

Description: The University of Texas at Austin is a publicly supported, coeducational state university. The Act of the Legislature providing for the organization of the University of Texas was passed in 1881. The Medical Branch was established at Galveston, and the Main University was located at Austin, opening in 1883. Today, the University of Texas at Austin is comprised of the School of Architecture, College of Liberal Arts, College of Business Administration, College of Education, College of Engineering, College of Fine Arts, Graduate School, Graduate School of Library and Information Science, School of Social Work, the Lyndon B. Johnson School of Public Affairs (a graduate-level school), Graduate School of Business, School of Law, College of Pharmacy, College of Communication, School of Nursing, and the College of Natural Sciences. Army, Navy, and Air Force ROTC programs are provided. Cooperative education programs are available in actuarial studies, business, chemistry/biochemistry, computer sciences, engineering, geology, and mathematics. Study abroad is also available. The University is accredited by the Southern Association of Colleges and Schools and by respective educational and professional organizations. It operates on the semester system and offers two summer sessions. Enrollment includes 29,724 full-time and 5,022 part-time undergraduates and 13,211 graduate students. A faculty of 2,161 full-time and 181 part-time gives an undergraduate faculty-student ratio of 1-20. The University grants Bachelor, Master, Law and Doctorate degrees.

Entrance Requirements: Accredited high school graduation; SAT or ACT required and is combined with high school rankning; out-of-state students must rank in top quarter of graduating class and have combined SAT score of 1100; completion of 16 units including 4 English, 3 mathematics, 2 science, 3 social science, and 2 language; GRE required for graduate programs; non-high school graduates over 21 years of age with SAT score of 1000 or ACT 28 may be admitted by individual approval; rolling decision and advanced placement plans available; $35 application fee.

Costs Per Year: $1,815 state-resident tuition and fees; $6,105 non-resident; $4,420 room and board.

Collegiate Environment: The university is located on a 300-acre campus and is comprised of 110 buildings. The General Libraries comprise the sixth largest academic library in the United States. It consists of the Perry Castaneda Library, the Undergraduate Library, the special collections, and the college, school, and departmental libraries. These various branches of the library are located in 19 campus buildings and contain more than 6,265,236 titles and 79,400 periodicals, 4,000,000 microforms, and 71,000 audiovisual materials. University housing provides living accommodations for 5,314 single students and 668 families. 69% of those who apply for admission are accepted. The median scores of enrolled freshmen were SAT 1135 combined, ACT 28 composite. Financial aid is available and 50% of students receive some form of assistance.

Community Environment: Population 495,000. Located on the Colorado River in the heart of Texas, Austin is the capital of the State. The city enjoys sunny days and blue skies. The mean temperature is 78 degrees, with a minimum of 57 degrees. Good transportation facilities including railroad, bus lines, taxicabs, private airport and major airlines, and major highways are all found here. Many community services are available such as churches, hospitals, libraries, and museums. Recreation includes parks, swimming pools, tennis courts, golf courses, athletic fields, lakes, water sports, and fishing.

UNIVERSITY OF TEXAS AT DALLAS   (G-9)
P.O. Box 830688
Richardson, Texas 75083-0688
Tel: (214) 883-2111; (800) 889-2443; Fax: (214) 883-2599

Description: A tradition of strong research programs at the University of Texas at Dallas dates to its founding in 1961 as the Graduate Research Center of the Southwest. Becoming a branch of the University of Texas system in 1969, the institution was open to upper-level undergraduates and graduates only. In fall 1990, the first freshman class was admitted. The institution is accredited by the Southern Association of Colleges and Schools. It operates on the semester system and offers two summer sessions. Enrollment includes 2,226 full-time and 2,501 part-time undergraduates and 3,760 graduate students. A faculty of 279 full-time and 128 part-time gives an overall faculty-student ratio of 1-18. Members of the local business community and employees of high-technology firms teach additional specialized classes. Minority students accounted for 21.5% of the enrollment; foreign students for 6%. The average student age is 29.5. Most students are employed, almost half are married, and many students attend part-time. An extensive schedule of night courses is offered. Nearly half of the students attend exclusively at night.

Entrance Requirements: High school units include 4 language arts (including 1 writing course), 2 same foreign language, 3.5 mathematics (including algebra I and trigonometry), 3 lab science, 3 social science, 1.5 electives, and 0.5 fine arts; 3.0 GPA required for lower-level transfer applicants; 2.5 GPA required for upper-level transfer applicants; SAT preferred, ACT accepted; TOEFL required of foreign applicants; TASP must taken during the semester nine hours that are earned at a Texas State institution of higher education and passed prior to enrollment in upper-level undergraduate courses; GRE or GMAT required for admission to graduate programs; rolling admissions, deferred admission and advanced placement plans available; $25 application fee, $75 for foreign applicants.

Costs Per Year: $720 tuition; $4,224 out-of-state; $706 student fees (based on 12 hours per semester for undergraduate courses for two semesters); graduate courses are assessed additional $30/hour residents and $40/hour nonresidents.

Collegiate Environment: The main campus of 455 acres is comprised of 13 major buildings, most built within the last 10 years. The newest building is a state-of-the-art engineering/computer science facility including 24,000 square feet of temperature/humidity/vibration/dust-controlled clean rooms. A full range of student services is provided. These include financial aid, student employment assistance, career planning and placement, health care, counseling services, student government, organizations and publications, intramural sports, evening day care, housing assistance, entertainment and instructional activities, volunteer opportunities, advisors, leadership training, study skills, test preparation, and tutoring. Financial aid, including scholarships, is available. The library contains 524,958 bound volumes, 1.5 million microfilm titles, and 2,409 periodical subscriptions. It is a depository of U.S. government and Texas state publications, maps and Educational Captioned Films for the Deaf. It houses a variety of special collections, including the Jaffe Holocaust Collection, Lundell Rare Books Library, Belsterling Botanical Library, and the History of Aviation Collection. The Geographical Information Library contains the world's largest collection of petroleum well logs. A full range of services is provided on site or through networks and consortia. Computer-assisted information services are available. Interconnection is available to Internet and NSFNet and supercomputing capabilities are available through the University of Texas System Center for High Performance Computing in Austin. The Callier Center for Communication Disorders is an internationally recognized institution that offers assessment, treatment, education and social services to the communicatively handicapped. The complex is located adjacent to The University of Texas Southwestern Medical School in the center of Dallas. Privately owned and operated on-campus apartments are available for student housing.

Community Environment: Located 18 miles north of downtown Dallas, in the suburb of Richardson, the university is accessible to the high-technology corridor of northern Dallas County and southern Collin County. Adjacent to the campus is Synergy Park, a 468-acre joint university-industry business and industrial park. Dallas and Fort Worth and the surrounding communities offer a comprehensive selection of art, entertainment, transportation, library, museum, and sports activities and facilities.

VERNON REGIONAL JUNIOR COLLEGE   (D-6)
4400 College Drive
Vernon, Texas 76384
Tel: (817) 552-6291; Fax: (817) 553-1753

Description: Publicly supported, coeducational junior college. Offers university transfer, occupational and general educational programs. Opened fall of 1972. Accredited by the Southern Association of Colleges and Schools. It operates on the semester system and offers two summer sessions. Enrollment is 1,825 students. A faculty of 50 full-time and 48 part-time gives a faculty-student ratio of 1-18.

Entrance Requirements: High school graduation, GED acceptable; open enrollment; midyear admission and rolling admission; no application fee.

Costs Per Year: $450 district tuition; $630 state tuition; $980 out-of-state tuition; $200 student fees; $1,950 room and board.

Collegiate Environment: Library holdings number 34,000 volumes, 177 periodicals, 19,450 microforms, 2,568 audiovisual materials. Cooperative education programs are available in all occupational programs. 153 scholarships are available. 38% of students receive some financial aid. Dormitories accomodate 200 students.

VICTORIA COLLEGE   (M-10)
2200 E. Red River
Victoria, Texas 77901-4494
Tel: (512) 573-3291

Description: Publicly supported, coeducational county-wide junior college was established in 1925 to provide increased educational opportunities for the people of Victoria County and the surrounding communities. It is accredited by the Southern Association of Colleges and Schools and the National League for Nursing. It provides academic courses for students planning to transfer to senior colleges and universities, general and vocational education, and continuing education for adults. The college grants the Associate degree and Certificate of General Studies. It operates on the semester system and offers two summer sessions. Enrollment includes 1,384 full-time and 2,283 part-time students. Two semesters and two summer terms are offered. A faculty of 73 full-time and 46 part-time gives a faculty-student ratio of 1-25.

Entrance Requirements: Approved high school graduation; completion of 15 units including 4 English, 2 mathematics, 1 science, 2 social science; non-high school graduates over 17 years of age may be admitted by examination and approval of the Dean. Opern admission and early admission.

Costs Per Year: $410 resident tuition; $2,400 out-of-state; $230 student fees.

Collegiate Environment: The 80-acre campus is situated in the northeast part of the city of Victoria. The Victoria College Library has a collection of 168,000 volumes, 1,940 periodicals, 184,000 microforms, and 6,900 audiovisual materials. The evening school offers the same academic courses and operates under the same standards. All students who apply for admission are accepted. About 33% of a recent freshman class received some form of financial assistance.

Community Environment: Population 50,000. After the battle of San Jacinto, the first military capital of the new republic was established here in Victoria. Today, the area is known for its cattle raising. The city is located 25 miles from the Gulf of Mexico. Local industries include chemicals, sand and gravel mining, and oil and gas production. Part-time employment is limited. The climate is mild. Victoria is reached by bus and airline connections. The community has several churches. Local recreation includes salt water fishing, boating, swimming and water skiing in the Gulf of Mexico, a municipal park and golf courses.

WAYLAND BAPTIST UNIVERSITY (D-3)
1900 W. 7th Street
Plainview, Texas 79072
Tel: (806) 296-5521; (800) 588-1928; Fax: (806) 296-4580

Description: Privately supported, coeducational liberal arts college was founded in 1908 and became part of the system of institutions supported by the Baptist General Convention of Texas in 1914. The college is accredited by the Southern Association of Colleges and Schools. Its doors were opened to qualified students of all races in 1951. It has always welcomed students from a variety of religious denominations and faiths but maintains its strongly Christian orientation. Enrollment includes 708 full-time and 153 part-time students. A faculty of 64 full-time and 18 part-time gives a faculty-student ratio of 1-13. Operating on the 4-1-4 system, with 4 four-week summer microsessions, the college awards the Bachelor of Arts, the Bachelor of Science, Bachelor of Music, Bachelor of Business Administration, Bachelor of Science in Occupational Education, two Associate and three Master's degrees.

Entrance Requirements: Accredited high school graduation with rank in upper 70% of graduating class; completion of 3 years of English, 2 mathematics, 1 science, 2 social science; ACT or SAT required; GED admitted on individual approval; advanced placement, rolling admission, early admission, delayed admission; application fee $35. GRE required for graduate programs.

Costs Per Year: $5,400 tuition; $2,888 room and board; $350 student fees; $450 books.

Collegiate Environment: The 80-acre campus is in the center of Plainview. The Van Howeling Memorial Library contains 128,432 volumes, 760 periodicals, 75,275 microforms and 22,592 AV materials. There are housing accommodations for 277 students. Approximately 99% of students applying for admission meet the requirements and are accepted. The college welcomes a geographically diverse student body and accepts midyear students. Freshman classes begin in August, January and June. Approximately 68% of the students receive some form of financial assistance.

Community Environment: Population 22,000. Plainview is an agricultural and industrial community located on the High Plains of Northwest Texas. The area is served by railroad, bus, and U.S. Highway 70 and Interstate 27; State Highways 194 and FM400. The city has many churches, a municipal airport, a memorial library, YMCA, and one hospital as well as several clinics to serve the community. Local recreation includes five swimming pools, summer baseball programs, golf courses, theatres, miniature golf, bowling facilities, and boating facilities. There are a great many civic and fraternal groups active in the area. Part-time employment is available.

WEATHERFORD COLLEGE (G-8)
308 East Park Avenue
Weatherford, Texas 76086
Tel: (817) 594-5471; Admissions: (817) 594-5471 x249; Fax: (817) 594-9435

Description: Publicly-supported, coeducational junior college. It was founded in 1869 and is presently accredited by the Southern Association of Colleges and Schools. Enrollment includes 1,100 full-time and 1,250 part-time and 600 evening students. A faculty of 55 full-time and 66 part-time provides a faculty-student ratio of 1-21. It operates on the semester system and offers two summer terms. Continuing education, transfer courses, and two-year vocational and technical programs are offered leading to an Associate degree.

Entrance Requirements: High school graduation, GED examination, or individual approval; open enrollment policy; early admission, midyear admission, rolling admission plans available.

Costs Per Year: $450 tuition in-district residents; $550 tuition out-of-district residents; $1,350 tuition out-of-state resident; tuitions are based on a 15 hour course load. $2,600 room and board.

Collegiate Environment: In 1967, the college purchased 90 acres as a site for a new campus. Construction was completed in 1968. The eight buildings include the library building containing 54,000 volumes and the Administration Building housing offices, classrooms, business administration laboratories, and the auditorium. A West Campus has been established with facilities for welding, auto mechanics, machine shop, and cosmetology. Housing is available for 192 students. All students applying for admission are accepted. Scholar-

ships are available and 25% of the current freshman class received some form of assistance.

Community Environment: Population 13,800. Watermelons are the best known product of this diversified crop and livestock market. Weatherford is reached by railroad, bus lines, and air and Interstate 20. The climate is mild with a mean average temperature of 64 degrees and an average rainfall of 31.6 inches. There is a city library, a local hospital, several churches representing the major denominations, and various civic and fraternal organizations. Part-time employment opportunities are very limited. Weatherford is the county seat of Parker County and has the Parker Plaza Shopping Center and College Park Shopping Center for the adjoining area. Local recreation includes Weatherford Lake with boating, fishing, swimming, a local picnic grounds, golf, and three public parks.

WEST TEXAS A&M UNIVERSITY (C-3)
WTAMU Box 907
Canyon, Texas 79016
Tel: (806) 656-2020; (800) 999-8268; Fax: (806) 656-2936

Description: Publicly supported, coeducational, liberal arts and teachers college is accredited by the Southern Association of Colleges and Schools. It began its first regular session in the fall of 1910; its previous name, West Texas State University, was used from 1963 to 1994. The Institution has been reorganized into a College of Agriculture, Nursing and Natural Sciences, College of Business and Technology, College of Education and Social Sciences, College of Fine Arts and Humanities. It grants Bachelor and Master degrees. It operates on the semester system and offers two summer sessions. Enrollment is 6,094 students. A faculty of 324 gives a faculty-student ratio of 1-20.

Entrance Requirements: Accredited high school graduation or equivalent; ACT or SAT required; GRE required for graduate programs; non-high school graduates may be considered for admission by individual approval; early admission, early decision, rolling admission and advanced placement plans available.

Costs Per Year: $448 state-resident tuition; $2,736 out-of-state; $1,382 room and board; $346 student fees.

Collegiate Environment: The 92-acre campus is located 17 miles south of Amarillo. The university also operates the University Farm and the Nance Ranch, which have 2,400 acres of farm and pasture land. There are eight residence halls that accommodate 1,257 women and 1,278 men. Fraternities provide housing for an additional 250 men. All single freshmen and sophomores are required to live in dormitories. The library contains a collection of more than 512,000 volumes. Since 1942 the university has maintained resident evening class instruction. There are eight men's national fraternities on campus and five women's. Approximately 80% of students applying for admission meet the requirements and are accepted. The university welcomes a geographically diverse student body and accepts midyear students. Scholarships are available and 65% of students receive some form of financial aid. Freshman classes begin in September and in January. Special financial aid is available.

Community Environment: Population 11,000. Canyon is an urban area located 17 miles from Amarillo. The climate is temperate. The community is served by railroad, bus lines and Routes 60 and 87, and I-27. Community service facilities include two libraries, a museum, churches of major denominations, and one hospital. Some part-time employment is available. Local recreation includes theatres, major sports facilities, lakes for water sports, and nearby Palo Duro State Park. The city enjoys all the cultural, recreational, and civic benefits of nearby Amarillo. Local shopping facilities are good. See also Amarillo College for information about that nearby city, whose population is 145,790.

WESTERN TEXAS COLLEGE (G-4)
6200 S. College Ave.
Snyder, Texas 79549
Tel: (915) 573-8511; Admissions: (915) 573-8511 x394; Fax: (915) 573-9321

Description: Founded in 1971, this publicly supported, coeducational junior college is accredited by the Southern Association of Colleges and Schools. It offers university-transfer, occupational and general programs. Programs of study lead to the Associate degree. The college operates on the semester system and offers one summer session. Enrollment includes 532 full-time and 668 part-time students. A faculty of 70 full-time and 10 part-time gives a faculty-student ratio of 1-16.

Entrance Requirements: High school graduation or GED; no application fee.

Costs Per Year: $450 state-resident tuition; $750 out-of-state; $990 room; $1,060 board; $136 student fees.

Collegiate Environment: Student housing is available for 112 men and 80 women. There are a total of 237 scholarships and 40% of the student body receives some financial support. The college seeks a geographically diverse student body and accepts students at midyear. The library contains 38,335 volumes, 215 periodicals, 3,339 microforms and 17,724 audiovisual aids.

Community Environment: Snyder is a small rural city, population 12,000. Agriculture and oil are important industries.

WHARTON COUNTY JUNIOR COLLEGE   *(L-11)*
911 Boling Highway
Wharton, Texas 77488
Tel: (409) 532-4560; Admissions: (409) 532-6303

Description: Publicly supported, coeducational junior college was founded in 1946 and is accredited by the Southern Association of Colleges and Schools. Enrollment includes 1,974 full-time and 1,421 part-time students. A faculty of 100 full-time and 100 part-time gives a faculty-student ratio of 1-21. The college operates on the early semester system and offers two summer terms. The college offers the first two years of baccalaureate and professional degree programs, vocational and technical training, and continuing education and grants an Associate degree.

Entrance Requirements: Accredited high school graduation or equivalent; other candidates may be admitted by individual approval with satisfactory scores on GED or ACT; early admission, midyear admission, rolling admission; $10 application fee.

Costs Per Year: $1,290 in-state tuition; $2,460 nonresident tuition; $2,100 room and board.

Collegiate Environment: The 93-acre campus of the college is located 60 miles southwest of Houston. Frankie Hall Dormitory provides housing for 80 men and Mullins Hall, completed in 1964, houses 55 women. The air-conditioned library contains about 53,333 volumes. An estimated 99% of students applying for admission meet the requirements and are accepted. Midyear students are accepted. Freshman classes begin September, January, June and July. About 50% of the current student body graduated in the top half of the high school class, 28% in the top quarter. About 42% of the previous freshman class returned to this campus for the sophomore year. Approximately 35% of the students receive some form of financial assistance.

Community Environment: Population 9,881. Situated on the banks of the Colorado River, Wharton lies 45 miles from the Gulf of Mexico. The community is served by bus lines, a municipal airport, and U.S. Highway 59. Community service facilities include a county library, hospital and clinic, several churches of various faiths, and many civic and fraternal organizations. Wharton has a theatre, municipal swimming pool, hunting, fishing, a concert series, a health club, stage plays, museum. Part-time employment is available. An annual Wharton County Youth Rodeo is held here.

WILEY COLLEGE   *(G-13)*
711 Wiley Avenue
Marshall, Texas 75670
Tel: (903) 927-3300

Description: Privately supported, coeducational, liberal arts and teachers college had a recent enrollment of approximately 543. The semester system is employed. This school was the first of the Traditional Black colleges west of the Mississippi River to be accredited by the Southern Association of Colleges and Schools. The degree of Bachelor of Science is conferred upon students majoring in the fields of biological sciences, chemistry, mathematics, elementary education, health and physical education. Students who are preparing to be secondary school teachers and administrators may qualify for a Bachelor of Science degree appropriate for secondary schools. The Bachelor of Arts degree is conferred upon those whose major is one of the following: English, social sciences, business, religion or music. Premedical,

prenursing and predental courses may be pursued. Founded and maintained by the United Methodist Church. Divisions of the College include Education and Teacher Training; Natural Sciences and Mathematics; Humanities; Social Science; Business.

Entrance Requirements: High school graduation with rank in upper 40% of graduating class; completion of 15 units including 3 English, 2 mathematics, 2 foreign language recommended, 2 science, 2 social science; SAT and college entrance examinations required; non-high school graduates may be admitted with satisfactory performance on GED test; non-degree candidates may be admitted as special students.

Costs Per Year: $3,450 tuition; $2,544 board and room; $496 general fees.

Collegiate Environment: There are 16 buildings on the 63-acre campus. Thomas Cole Library has a collection of 80,000 volumes augmented by the increasing number of government documents as an official depository for U.S. Government Publications. The dormitories have capacity for 196 men and 398 women. Courses in American Negro History are required; in an effort to promote emotional adjustment and social maturity; programs have been selected which include orientation, personal and academic counseling and guidance, corrective discipline, scholarships, part-time jobs, placement, and alumni relations. Freshman classes begin in September and in January. The college welcomes a geographically diverse student body.

Community Environment: Population 25,000. Marshall is located at the junction of Highways U.S. 59 and 80 and Interstate 20, approximately 40 miles west of Shreveport, and 150 miles east of Dallas. The climate is temperate and mild. Natural gas fields surround the city. Railroad and bus lines serve the community, and Harrison County Memorial Airport located three miles east offers airline facilities. There are many churches of various faiths, hospitals, radio stations, and public library serving the area. Skilled and unskilled employment opportunities are available. Local recreation includes camping, fishing, and hunting.

WILLIAM MARSH RICE UNIVERSITY   *(K-12)*
Office of Undergraduate Admissions-MS17
6100 Main Street
Houston, Texas 77005
Tel: (713) 527-8101

Description: This privately supported, coeducational four-year institution opened in September 1912, with an entering class of 77 students. Undergraduate enrollment is 2,604. A faculty of 462 provides a faculty-student ratio of 1-7. The school operates on the semester system and is accredited by the Southern Association of Colleges and Schools and by the Accreditation Board for Engineering and Technology. The college grants a Bachelor degree, Bachelor of Architecture, Master of Music, a Masters degree, a Professional Masters degree in seven engineering subject areas. Ph.D. Honors Programs are offered in several major fields of study, and Army and Navy ROTC programs are available. There is an exchange program with Trinity College of Cambridge University in England.

Entrance Requirements: High school graduation or equivalent; 16 units including 4 English, 3-4 mathematics, 2 foreign language, 2 science, 2 social science, and 3 additional of above or electives; SAT and 3 CEEB achievement tests required; GRE required for graduate studies; early decision, early admission, delayed admission and advanced placement programs available; admission is highly competitive and based upon application, scholastic record, test scores, teacher and counselor evaluations, and personal interview.

Costs Per Year: $8,500 tuition; $5,200 room and board; $325 student fees.

Collegiate Environment: The university campus occupies approximately 340 acres about three miles from the center of the city of Houston. There are more than 40 major buildings exclusive of Rice Stadium. Dormitories are available. The library system contains over 1.5 million volumes. Approximately 75% of students applying for admission meet the requirements but only 19% are accepted. Approximately 95% of the freshman class returned for the sophomore year. Special financial aid is available and 80% of the current student body received some form of assistance. About 75% of a recent freshmen class graduated in the highest tenth of the high school class.

Community Environment: See University of Houston.

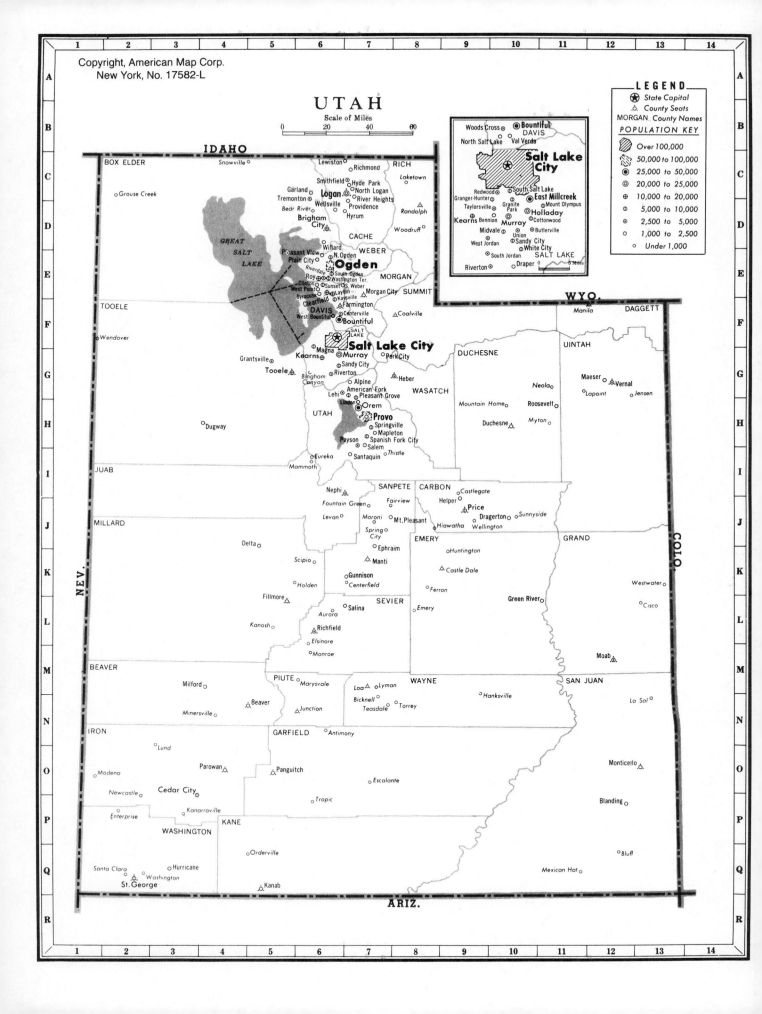

UTAH

BRIGHAM YOUNG UNIVERSITY (H-7)
Provo, Utah 84602
Tel: (801) 378-2507

Description: This private university began as an academy of the Church of Jesus Christ of Latter-Day Saints in 1875 and became a university in 1903. Today the university is comprised of colleges of biological and agricultural sciences, Management, education, family, home and social sciences, fine arts and communications, humanities, engineering sciences and technology, law, nursing, physical and mathematical sciences, physical education, religious instruction, and graduate studies. Army and Air Force ROTC programs are available. The university is accredited by the Northwest Association of Schools and Colleges and by respective educational and professional organizations. It operates on a semester system. Each semester is four months duration followed by two eight-week terms. Enrollment includes 28,213 full-time graduate and undergraduate students, 2,200 part-time graduate and undergraduate students. A faculty of 1,325 full-time and 355 part-time gives a faculty-student ratio of 1-18.

Entrance Requirements: High school graduation; recommended completion of high school units including 4 English, 3 foreign language, 2 mathematics, 2 social science, 2 biological science, and 2 physical science; ACT required; non-high school graduates, 19 years of age or over, may be admitted with successful completion of GED and ACT examinations; GRE required for graduate studies; application fee $25; early admission, early decision, rolling admission, and advanced placement plans available.

Costs Per Year: $2,450 members; $3,740 room and board (members and nonmembers); $3,675 nonmembers of sponsoring church.

Collegiate Environment: The university is comprised of 487 buildings on 634 acres. Its library contains 2,400,000 volumes, 18,000 periodicals, and 2,229,622 microforms. Living accommodations are provided for 2,250 men, 2,950 women, and 968 families. Qualified students of any race, creed, color, or national origin are accepted for admission. 73% of freshman applicants and 57% of transfer applicants are admitted. High standards of honor, integrity, and morality as well as Christian ideals in every day living are required of every student. Students may enroll at midyear. Financial aid is available for economically handicapped students. The university has semester abroad programs in Austria, France, Israel, England, Hawaii, Italy, Brazil, China, Korea, Canada, Jerusalem and Mexico.

Community Environment: Located 45 miles from Salt Lake City, Provo lies in the midst of large irrigated farming and fruit lands. Local industries also produce steel, computer software, pig iron, and foundry products. The community may be reached by air, railroad, bus lines, and Highways 6, 91, 89, 50, and Interstate 15. The community has hospitals, shopping centers, and national monuments nearby. Part-time employment is available. Local recreation include hunting, fishing, picnicking, hiking, swimming, boating, water skiing, horseback riding, golf, tennis, ice skating, bobsledding, and snow skiing.

COLLEGE OF EASTERN UTAH (J-9)
451 E. 400 N.
Price, Utah 84501
Tel: (801) 637-2120

Description: The public junior college was established in 1938 and was made a branch of the University of Utah in 1959. It was known as Carbon College until 1965, when its present name was adopted to reflect the larger geographical area that it served. It is accredited by the Northwest Association of Schools and Colleges. The college offers the first two years of most programs leading to a four-year Bachelor's degree, two years of preprofessional study, one- and two-year terminal programs, and appreciation classes to all interested citizens. It operates on the quarter basis and also provides 3 summer

terms. Enrollment includes 1,593 full-time and 1,530 part-time students. A faculty of 77 gives a faculty-student ratio of 1-41.

Entrance Requirements: High school graduation; SAT or ACT required for placement; non-high school graduates, 19 years of age or older, may be admitted into terminal trade courses.

Costs Per Year: $918 tuition; $3,717 out-of-state tuition; $2,715 board and room; $271.50 student fees.

Collegiate Environment: The college is located on 27 acres, and new modern facilities have recently been completed. The 18 college buildings contain a library of 18,000 volumes and living accommodations for men and women. Students from other geographical locations are accepted, as well as midyear students. Almost all of the students applying for admission are accepted. Financial aid is available for economically handicapped students.

Community Environment: A trade center, Price is in a large coal mining and farming district. Helium and natural gas deposits have also been found in the surrounding areas. The city is located at the base of Wasatch Mountain Range and has a temperate climate. There are churches of most denominations in the community. Several clinics, a hospital, library, and various civic and fraternal organizations serve the area. There is a prehistoric museum here showing actual dinosaurs. Part-time employment is available for students. Hotels, motels, rooming houses, and furnished apartments are available for student housing. Local recreation includes skiing, sledding, snowshoe hiking, movies, boating, water skiing, fishing, hunting, rodeos, and baseball.

DIXIE COLLEGE (Q-2)
225 S. 700 East
Saint George, Utah 84770
Tel: (801) 673-4811; Fax: (801) 673-8552

Description: Dixie is a state-supported community college under the direction of the Utah System of Higher Education. It officially began operation in 1911 and was granted full accreditation by the Northwest Association of Secondary and Higher Schools in 1936. The college operates on the quarter system and offers one summer term. College-transfer, vocational, technical, and adult education programs are offered. Enrollment is 2,203 full-time and 2,171 part-time students. A faculty of 72 full-time and 65 part-time gives a faculty-student ratio of 1-32.

Entrance Requirements: Accredited high school graduation or equivalent; 2 math and 2 English units required; ACT or Dixie College Assessment test required; non-high school graduates may be considered with satisfactory completion of GED tests; rolling admission plan available.

Costs Per Year: $1,331.64 tuition (based on $443.88 per quarter); $4,839 out-of-state (based on $1,613.04 per quarter); $2,649 room and board ($883 per quarter).

Collegiate Environment: The college is located approximately 300 miles south of Salt Lake City and 100 miles northeast of Las Vegas, NV. The city of St. George (population 38,000) is in a strategic position in relation to the scenic wonders of Zion National Park, Bryce Canyon, North Rim of the Grand Canyon, Cedar Breaks, Lake Mead, and Lake Powell. The college library contains 58,014 volumes, and dormitory facilities are provided for 288 students. Off-campus housing is available adjacent to campus to house 1,135 students. Almost all students applying for admission are accepted. Approximately 25% of the previous freshman class returned to the campus for the second year of study. Financial aid is available for economically handicapped students.

Community Environment: St. George is in Utah's Dixie area. It has semitropical temperatures during the long summer, and the climate is mild in winter. The area is noted for tourism, recreation, and national parks. The first Mormon Temple in Utah was built here. The community may be reached by bus, highway, and air from Salt Lake City or Las Vegas via Interstate 15. Most religious denominations are represented in St. George. Varied recreation in the area includes swimming, picnicking, baseball, hunting, fishing, snow and water skiing, and many nearby scenic wonders. Many job opportunities are available. Various civic and fraternal, and college culture programs serve the community.

LATTER-DAY SAINTS BUSINESS COLLEGE   (F-6)
411 East South Temple
Salt Lake City, Utah 84111-1392
Tel: (801) 363-2765; (800) 999-5767; Admissions: (801) 524-8144;
Fax: (801) 524-1900

Description: The private business college began in 1886 under the name of the Salt Lake State Academy. It became Utah's first business college, and its present name was adopted in 1888. The college is accredited by the Northwest Association of Schools and Colleges and operates on a four-quarter basis. The college offers three-month certificate courses, one-year diploma courses, and two-year associate degree courses. Enrollment totaled 850 students. Faculty number 20 full-time, 30 part-time with an average class size of 18.

Entrance Requirements: High school graduation or GED; ACT recommended for placement; $20 application fee.

Costs Per Year: LDS member $1,875 tuition; non LDS $2,355; room $1,422.

Collegiate Environment: The business college has dormitory facilities for 112 women. Approximately 98% of students applying for admission are accepted, including midyear students.

Community Environment: See University of Utah.

SALT LAKE COMMUNITY COLLEGE   (F-6)
P.O. Box 30808
4600 S. Redwood Road
Salt Lake City, Utah 84130
Tel: (801) 957-4297; Fax: (801) 957-4522

Description: This state-supported technical community college was established in 1948 and is operated under the direction of the Utah State Board of Regents. It is accredited by the Northwest Association of Schools and Colleges. It grants certiifcates, diplomas, and the Associate degree. Cooperative education programs are available. The college operates on the quarter system and offers one summer session. Enrollment is 6,540 full-time and 10,672 part-time students. A faculty of 312 full-time and 560 part-time gives a faculty-student ratio of 1-22.

Entrance Requirements: Open enrollment policy; aptitude test required for non-high school graduates; early admission (concurrent enrollment), rolling admission, early admission, midyear admission and advanced placement plans available; $20 application fee.

Costs Per Year: $1,194 tuition; $4,254 out-of-state; $252 student fees.

Collegiate Environment: The Redwood campus is located on 80 acres and is comprised of seven buildings that include a library of 54,000 volumes. All applicants are accepted. Scholarships are available and 53% of students receive some form of financial aid.

Community Environment: See University of Utah.

Branch Campuses: Redwood Road campus, 4600 S. Redwood Rd., (801) 957-4111; South City campus, 1575 S. State St., (801) 957-3353.

SNOW COLLEGE   (J-7)
150 East College Avenue
Ephraim, Utah 84627
Tel: (801) 283-4021

Description: The public junior college was founded in 1888 and is one of the oldest two-year colleges in the west. It is a residential college that prepares students for transfer to four-year colleges and universities, and offers a limited number of "job ready" one- and two-year certificates. It has been accredited continuously since 1937

by the Northwest Association of Schools and Colleges. The college operates on the quarter system and enrolls 2,100 men and women. A faculty of 85 full-time and 31 part-time gives a faculty-student ratio of 1-18.

Entrance Requirements: Accredited high school graduation or equivalent; completion of college-preparatory courses; ACT and transcript; non-high school graduates 25 years or older may be admitted without ACT; open early admission, early decision, rolling admission and advanced placement plans available.

Costs Per Year: $1,173 tuition/fees; $4,935 out-of-state; $2,800 room and board.

Collegiate Environment: The main campus is located on 40 acres situated in the center of town. The 26 college buildings include a library of 35,000 volumes and 240 periodicals; a student center; a new humanities building that houses an active performing arts program; and athletic facilities that include a swimming pool, basketball court, racquetball courts, and more. A full range of intramural sports is offered, as well as intercollegiate competition in basketball, football, baseball, softball, and volleyball. On-campus dorms house 35% of the students. Almost all students applying for admission are accepted, including midyear students. Financial aid is available for economically handicapped students.

Community Environment: Ephraim is a small, rural, college town located in central Utah. The area has a moderate climate with four definite seasons. The community is reached by rail, bus lines, and Highway 89. The city has four churches in the immediate vicinity and others in the surrounding area, a hospital 13 miles distant, and a clinic in the town. Public restaurants, motels, and limited entertainment facilities are available. Student housing and part-time employments opportunities are available in the community. Local recreation includes boating, fishing, hunting, cross-country skiing, golf, and winter sports. The county fairs and local festivities highlight the heritages of local communities.

SOUTHERN UTAH UNIVERSITY   (P-3)
351 West Center Street
Cedar City, Utah 84720
Tel: (801) 586-7740; Fax: (801) 865-8223

Description: The college is the same age as the state, having been founded by action of the first Utah State Legislature in 1897. It was created as a branch of the University of Utah and became an independent educational institution in 1965. It is accredited by the Northwest Association of Schools and Colleges. Academic departments of the university are organized into arts and letters, business and technical education, education, sciences, and continuing education. The college operates on the three-quarter basis and also provides two summer terms. The college grants a Certificate and Baccalaureate degree as well as a Masters in Business and Education. Enrollment includes 3,787 full-time and 1,239 part-time students. A faculty of 165 full-time and 41 part-time gives a faculty-student ratio of 1-22.

Entrance Requirements: Accredited high school graduation; 2 social science; non-high school graduates, 25 years of age or older, will be admitted upon satisfactory completion of GED examinations; CLEP; early admission, early decision, rolling admission, midyear admission, and advanced placement plans available. $25 application fee.

Costs Per Year: $1,308 tuition; $5,238 out-of-state tuition; $2,727 board and room & board; $390 student fees.

Collegiate Environment: The college is operated from 27 buildings on an 113-acre campus in the center of Cedar City. In addition, the college owns and operates a 1,000-acre farm in western Cedar Valley and a 3,700-acre ranch in Cedar Canyon. The college library contains 189,048 volumes, 1,215 periodicals, and 567,238 microforms. Living accommodations are provided for 161 men and 184 women. Students from other geographical locations are accepted, as well as midyear students. Approximately 97% of students applying for admission are accepted. Scholarships are available and 77% of students receive some form of financial aid.

Community Environment: Cedar City is located within minutes of the Grand Canyon, Lake Powell, Cedar Breaks National Monument, Bryce Canyon, Zion National Park and other scenic wonders. It is 2 1/2 hours from Las Vegas. Cedar City is accessible by airlines, railroad, bus lines, and major highways. The community has churches representing most denominations, a hospital, public library, and a museum. Student housing is available in the community. Various civic, fraternal, and veteran's organizations are active in the area. Local recreation includes indoor and outdoor theatres, hunting, fishing, skiing, golf, and boating. There is a shopping center in the area.

STEVENS HENAGER COLLEGE   *(E-6)*
2644 Washington Boulevard
Ogden, Utah 84401
Tel: (801) 375-5455

Description: A private junior college of business. It was established in 1891 and is accredited by the accrediting commission for Business Schools. The college employs the 10-month program for a diploma and 14 months for an Associate. Enrollment recently was 127 men and 260 women. A faculty of 26 gives a faculty-student ratio of 1:20.

Entrance Requirements: High school graduation or equivalent required for degree or diploma courses; non-high school graduates considered with satisfactory scores on GED; early decision plan and advanced placement are available.

Costs Per Year: $5,170 tuition

Collegiate Environment: The college has no dormitory facilities, but housing is available in nearby boarding houses and apartments. Approximately 95% of students applying for admission are accepted, including midyear students. More than half of the previous entering class returned to the college for the second year of studies. Financial aid is available for economically handicapped students.

Community Environment: See Weber State College.

UNIVERSITY OF UTAH   *(F-6)*
Salt Lake City, Utah 84112
Tel: (801) 581-7200; Admissions: (801) 581-7281; Fax: (801) 585-3034

Description: The University of Utah was founded in 1850 and is the oldest state university west of the Missouri River. Today, it is a comprehensive institution of higher learning, with a Graduate School, a Division of Continuing Education, a Division of International Education, that offers programs of instruction, inquiry, and research in more than 90 fields of study. Army, Navy, and Air Force ROTC programs are provided. The university is accredited by the Northwest Association of Schools and Colleges and by respective educational and professional organizations. It operates on the quarter system and offers one summer session. Enrollment includes 18,000 full-time and 4,000 part-time undergraduates and 4,000 graduate students. A faculty of 1,400 gives a faculty-student ratio of 1-25.

Entrance Requirements: Approved high school graduation including the following units: 4 English, 3 mathematics, 3 science, 1 history, 2 foreign language; ACT or SAT required; early admission, advanced placement, early decision, and midyear admission plans available. $25 application fee.

Costs Per Year: $2,400 tuition; $6,800 tuition for out-of-state students; additional tuition also required for College of Law and College of Medicine; double room $1,600, single room $1,950. Meals purchased on an individual basis. Tuition pending change.

Collegiate Environment: The university is located on a campus of 693 acres at the eastern edge of Salt Lake City, in the foothills of the Wasatch Mountains. The mountain country adjacent to the campus provides outdoor diversion through the four seasons of the year with hiking, boating, fishing, and skiing facilities a few minutes away from the campus. The 160 university buildings contain libraries housing more than 2,500,000 volumes and 560,000 microforms. Living accommodations for 2,000 men and women and 943 families are provided. University centers on campuses outside of the United States, programs of one quarter or more duration, Foreign Summer Study programs, and Travel Study are all available as an integrated part of the total program of the university. Students are accepted at midyear. 92% of undergraduate applicants are accepted. Financial aid is available for students qualifying under federal guidelines and 58% of students receive some form of financial aid.

Community Environment: The capital of the state, Salt Lake City is located at the foot of the beautiful Wasatch Mountains. The Great Salt Lake is northwest of the city, and the desert is only a few miles away to the west. The city was founded by Brigham Young and his follow-

ers, and many of the original buildings may still be seen. The city is a metropolis today enjoying excellent transportation facilities. There are five libraries, a law library, many churches of various denominations, hospitals, and clinics to serve the community. Salt Lake City is the headquarters of the Church of Jesus Christ of Latter Day Saints, and is noted for Temple Square and the Mormon Temple and Tabernacle. Some part-time employment is available. Local recreation facilities includes 23 parks, golf courses, fishing, hunting, bowling, skiing, several theatres, and outdoor sports. There are excellent shopping facilities located here. The Utah State Fair is held annually as well as the Music Festival.

UTAH STATE UNIVERSITY   *(C-7)*
University Hill
Logan, Utah 84322
Tel: (801) 797-1107; Admissions: (801) 797-1096; Fax: (801) 797-4077

Description: The state university was founded in 1888 and belongs to the family of institutions known as Land-Grant Universities, which had their origin in 1862. The university includes eight resident colleges with 54 departments, a School of Graduate Studies, extension services, and research programs. It is accredited by the Northwest Association of Schools and Colleges and by respective educational and professional organizations. Army and Air Force ROTC programs are provided. The university operates on the quarter system and offers two summer sessions. Enrollment includes 11,945 full-time and 8,426 part-time undergraduates and 2,475 graduate students. A faculty of 750 full-time gives a faculty-student ratio of 1-20.

Entrance Requirements: Approved high school graduation or equivalent; minimum C average in college-preparatory courses; high school units should include 4 English, 3 mathematics, 3 biological or physical science, 1 American history, 4 academic electives; SAT or ACT with minimum score of 19, required; non-high school graduates, over 18 years of age, may be admitted with acceptable scores on ACT; early admission, early decision, rolling admission, midyear admission and advanced placement plans available; CLEP plans are available; $35 application fee.

Costs Per Year: $2,010 tuition and fees; $6,138 out-of-state; $3,400 room and board.

Collegiate Environment: The university is located on 332 acres and is comprised of 120 buildings. Its library contains 984,000 volumes, 6,000 periodicals, 1,453,000 microforms, and 17,300 audiovisual materials. Living accommodations are provided for 988 men, 936 women, and 1,352 families. There are eight social fraternities and six social sororities located on the campus, as well as numerous other student organizations. The university welcomes a geographically diverse student body and will accept midyear students. 90% of applicants are accepted. 1,100 scholarships, including 500 for freshmen are offered. 47% of students receive some form of financial aid. Quarters begin in September, January, and March.

Community Environment: Located in the fertile Cache Valley, Logan is the headquarters for the adjacent Cache National Forest. The Cache Valley was originally an ancient lakebed 500 feet deep, and shorelines of the lake are still visible along the foothills. Today, the community has excellent transportation with airlines, railroad, and bus connections. Major highways enter the city from four directions. Dairying is an important economic feature of the community, and the city has one of the largest swiss cheese factories in the world. Some part-time employment is available. Local recreation includes hunting, fishing, skiing, and all the water sports.

UTAH VALLEY STATE COLLEGE   *(H-7)*
800 West 1200 South
Orem, Utah 84058
Tel: (801) 222-8000; Admissions: (801) 222-8464; Fax: (801) 226-5207

Description: The school was originally established as the Central Utah Vocational School in 1941. In 1967, the name was changed to Utah Technical College at Provo. It continued as UVCC from 1987 to 1993, when it began to offer a limited number of four-year programs. The college is accredited by the Northwest Association of Schools and Colleges. It offers programs in trade, industrial, and technical education; business education; general education; adult education; and occupational and educational guidance services. Cooperative education programs are available. The college operates on the semester system and offers one summer session. Enrollment includes 5,721 full-time and 5,661 part-time students. A faculty of 228 full-time and 342 part-time gives a faculty-student ratio of 1-24.

Entrance Requirements: Minimum of 18 years of age and able to profit from instruction; high school diploma or equivalent; $15 application fee.

Costs Per Year: $1,158 state resident tuition; $4,160 nonresident tuition; $262 student fees.

Collegiate Environment: The college is made up of two campuses. The 13-acre Provo site provides six programs while the 185-acre Orem campus is home to over 30 programs in facilities that were completed in 1977. A new student and activity center on the Orem Campus house student services and programs including student government and athletics. The library holdings number 58,604 volumes, 408 periodicals, and 220 audiovisual materials. No on-campus housing is available, but many apartments are located within walking distance of the college. Financial aid is available for economically eligible students. 60% of students receive some form of assistance.

Community Environment: See Brigham Young University.

WEBER STATE UNIVERSITY   *(E-6)*
3750 Harrison Blvd.
Ogden, Utah 84408-1137
Tel: (801) 626-6000; Admissions: (801) 626-8700; Fax: (801) 626-7922

Description: This state college was founded as the Weber State Academy in 1889 by the Board of Education of the Church of Jesus Christ of Latter-Day Saints. In 1933, Utah Legislature established Weber as a state junior college and placed it under the control of the State Board of Education. The addition of upper division courses began in 1959, and the college has been accredited as a four-year, degree-granting institution by the Northwest Association of Schools and Colleges since 1963. It is also accredited by professional organizations. In 1990, the name was changed to Weber State University. It offers masters degrees in Accounting and Education. The college also provides continuing or adult education programs, one-year and two-year programs for positions in semiprofessions, business, and allied health sciences; and degree programs in the fields of art, letters and science, business, education, and technology. Army, Air Force, and Navy ROTC programs are available. Study abroad, for one quarter, is available in England, Spain, Germany, and Europe. The college operates on the quarter system and offers a summer term. Enrollment includes 8,720 full-time and 5,510 part-time undergraduates and 90 graduate students. A faculty of 417 gives an undergraduate faculty-student ratio of 1-34.

Entrance Requirements: High school graduation; completion of 16 college-preparatory units; SAT or ACT required; $20 application fee; early admission, advanced placement, early decision, rolling admission, and delayed admission plans available.

Costs Per Year: $1,743 tuition; $5,514 out-of-state.

Collegiate Environment: The college has a total of 400 acres on which there are a technical building, a student union building, an allied health building, a business building, an athletic center, gymnasium, auditorium and fine arts building, library, art building, education building, social science building, natural science building, and the new Dee Events Center. The library contains 244,918 titles, 63,658 periodicals, and 530,679 microforms. The 36 college buildings also contain dormitory facilities for 363 men and 327 women. 90% of the students applying for admission are accepted, including midyear students. Financial aid is available for economically disadvantaged students. 50% of students received some form of aid.

Community Environment: Located at the confluence of the Weber and Ogden Rivers, this community is an important railroad distribution center for products directed to west coast markets. Mormon pioneers settled the community. The climate is temperate with four distinct seasons. Ogden is reached by railroad, airlines, and highways. The community has many churches representing over 30 denominations. There are two hospitals, four health centers, a library and branch, 2 major shopping malls, and various civic and fraternal organizations serving the area. There are also five TV stations and a radio station. Part-time employment is available. Local recreation includes fishing, hunting, swimming, skiing, boating, picnicking, camping, golfing, and horseback riding.

WESTMINSTER COLLEGE OF SALT LAKE CITY   *(F-6)*
1840 South 1300 East
Salt Lake City, Utah 84105
Tel: (801) 488-4200; (800) 748-4753; Fax: (801) 466-6916

Description: The private liberal arts college was established in 1875 and is affiliated with the United Presbyterian Church, United Methodist Church, and United Church of Christ. It is privately endowed and is nonsectarian in its instruction. The college is accredited by the Northwest Association of Schools and Colleges. It has four divisional areas within a liberal arts curriculum, with training for business, teaching, finance, premedical, predental and prelaw. The college operates on the semester system. Enrollment includes 965 full-time, 728 part-time undergraduate, and 95 graduate students. A faculty of 95 full-time and 113 part-time gives a faculty-student ratio of 1-17. Air Force, Army, and Navy ROTC programs are available.

Entrance Requirements: High school graduation; early decision, early admission, midyear admission, rolling admission, and advanced placement plans available; no application fee.

Costs Per Year: $8,880 tuition; $4,050 board and room; $110 student fees.

Collegiate Environment: The campus is comprised of 27 acres situated in a residential area of Salt Lake City. The 16 college buildings contain a library of 72,000 volumes and dormitory facilities for 100 men and women. Students from other geographical locations are accepted, including midyear students. Almost 85% of students applying for admission are accepted. Academic merit awards are offered and financial aid is available for applicants who demonstrate financial need. Approximately 75% of the students receive financial aid. 70% of freshmen return for their sophomore year.

Community Environment: See University of Utah.

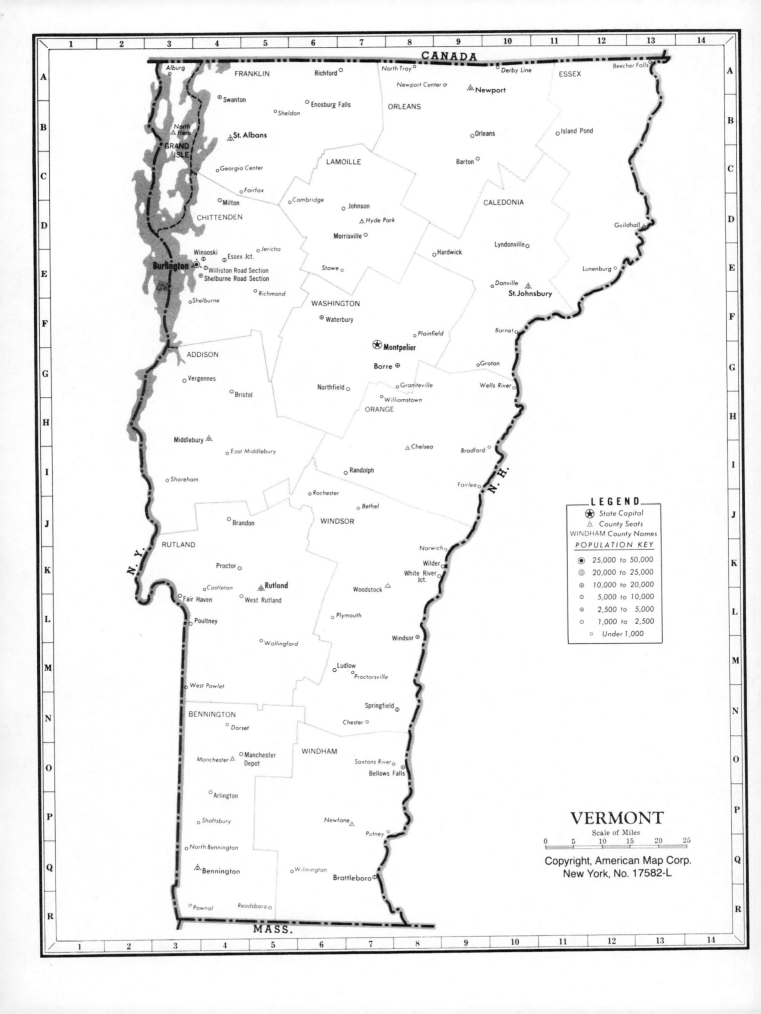

VERMONT

Scale of Miles

0 5 10 15 20 25

Copyright, American Map Corp.
New York, No. 17582-L

LEGEND

⊛ State Capital
⊙ County Seats
WINDHAM County Names

POPULATION KEY

◉ 25,000 to 50,000
◎ 20,000 to 25,000
⊕ 10,000 to 20,000
⊙ 5,000 to 10,000
⊙ 2,500 to 5,000
○ 1,000 to 2,500
○ Under 1,000

VERMONT

BENNINGTON COLLEGE   (Q-3)
Bennington, Vermont 05201
Tel: (802) 442-5401; (800) 833-6845; Fax: (802) 442-6164

Description: The private college was opened in 1932 as a nontraditional, four-year, undergraduate college for women and in 1969, the college became coeducational. It makes available to students individually planned programs of study leading to the Bachelor of Arts degree. It is accredited by the New England Association of Schools and Colleges. The college operates on semester system plus an 8-week field work term. Enrollment is 373 full-time undergraduates and 82 graduate students. A faculty of 48 full-time and 12 part-time gives a faculty-student ratio of 1-7.

Entrance Requirements: High school graduation or equivalent; 16 or more units including 4 English, 3 mathematics, 3 laboratory science, 3 foreign language, 3 social science, and 2 or more music, art; SAT or ACT required; non-high school graduates considered; early decision, early admission, and delayed admission plans available; January 15 regular decision deadline; December 1 early action deadline; Dec. 1 early decision deadline; $45 application fee.

Costs Per Year: $25,800 comprehensive.

Collegiate Environment: The 550-acre campus is located in the southwest corner of Vermont, four miles from the village of Bennington and one mile from North Bennington. The 40 college buildings contain a library of over 116,000 titles, 600 periodicals, 5,250 microforms, 23,000 slides, 818 records and tapes, and open dormitory facilities for 600 men and women. 58% of applicants are accepted. Approximately 59% of the current student body receives need-based financial aid. 79% of students receive some form of financial aid.

Community Environment: A rural section of Vermont, Bennington is in an area where sports facilities are good; the ski centers near Manchester and Wilmington are in the immediate vicinity. Community facilities include three libraries, a museum, churches, recreational center, and a number of civic and service organizations. Part-time employment is available. Other recreational activities include canoeing, boating, horseback riding, fishing and golf. Some of the historical points of interest are the Bennington Battle Monument and the Old First Church where Robert Frost is buried.

BURLINGTON COLLEGE   (E-4)
95 North Ave.
Burlington, Vermont 05401
Tel: (802) 862-9616; (800) 862-9616; Fax: (802) 658-0071

Description: Burlington College has been an integral part of the Burlington community since opening in 1972. Students and faculty live in the area, and participate in community agencies and projects. Accredited by the New England Association of Schools and Colleges, Burlington College offers a Bachelor of Arts degree and an Associate of Arts degree. The focus is on liberal arts. A low-residency independent degree program is available for students with 45 or more previous college credits. The college operates on the semester system and offers one summer session. Enrollment is 80 full-time and 140 part-time students. The faculty-student ratio is approximately 1-4.

Entrance Requirements: High school graduation or GED; open enrollment for Associate degree and some Bachelor degree programs; rolling admission; $30 application fee.

Costs Per Year: $7,800 tuition; $150 student fees.

Collegiate Environment: Geared towards adult learners who are ready to take charge of their own education, Burlington College offers small, seminar-style classes, flexible learning options, and self-designed majors, in a friendly, supportive environment. 88% of BC students receive financial aid.

Community Environment: With five other colleges in the area, Burlington offers a wealth of cultural, economic and recreational opportunities, but still offers a friendly, small-city ambience. Human-scale neighborhoods, and the college's governance structure itself, give students the chance to get involved, and make a difference.

CASTLETON STATE COLLEGE   (K-4)
Castleton, Vermont 05735
Tel: (802) 468-5611; (800) 639-8521; Admissions: (802) 468-5611 x213; Fax: (802) 468-5237

Description: Founded in 1787, Castleton State College was the first institution of high learning in Vermont, and the eighteenth in the United States. Castleton today is a small liberal arts college that offers teacher preparation and other professional programs. It is accredited by the New England Association of Schools and Colleges. It is also accredited by the National League for Nursing and the Council on Social Work Education. A semester abroad through the Experiment in International Living is available. Through the "Soundings" program, freshmen earn academic credit by attending a series of special events, which include theater, music, dance, film, debate and lectures. The college operates on the semester system and offers three summer sessions. Enrollment includes 1,543 full-time and 299 part-time undergraduates and 224 graduate students. A faculty of 90 full-time and 77 part-time gives a faculty-student ratio of 1-17.

Entrance Requirements: High school graduation or equivalent; selective policy for resident and nonresident applicants; completion of 16 units recommended including 4 English, 3 mathematics, 2 foreign language, 2 science, and 3 social science; SAT or ACT required; rolling admission, delayed admission, midyear admission and advanced placement plans available; $40 application fee.

Costs Per Year: $3,312 tuition; $7,656 out-of-state; $4,690 room and board; $720 student fee.

Collegiate Environment: The college is located in the picturesque, colonial town of Castleton, Vermont, 12 miles west of Rutland. The college library contains 115,000 titles, 850 pamphlets, 850 periodicals, 73,067 microforms, and 337 audiovisiual materials. Dormitory facilities are available for 706 students. 59% of the student body comes from Vermont. The out-of-state students come primarily from the Mid-Atlantic and New England states. Approximately 70% of the applicants are accepted. Financial aid and academic scholarships are available, and 75% of the current student body receives some form of assistance.

Community Environment: Adjacent to outstanding ski and summer resorts, the area is rural and surrounded by Vermont's beautiful lakes and mountains.

CHAMPLAIN COLLEGE   (E-4)
163 South Willard Street
P.O. Box 670
Burlington, Vermont 05402-0670
Tel: (802) 860-2727; (800) 570-5850; Fax: (802) 860-2775

Description: This private college was founded in 1878. It is accredited by the New England Association of Schools and Colleges, the Accreditation Board for Engineering and Technology, and the Committee on Allied Health Education. It also has accreditation through the Joint Review Committee on Education in Radiologic Technology. Champlain College is authorized to confer degrees of Associate in Science in 26 majors and now offers baccalaureate programs in accounting, business management, and professional studies in its two-plus-two division. The college operates on the semester system and offers 2 mini-summer terms. Enrollment includes 1,230 full-time, 605 part-time and 550 evening students. A faculty of 60 full-time and 60 part-time gives a faculty-student ratio of approximately 1-16.

Entrance Requirements: Accredited high school graduation with rank in upper 70%; GED graduates considered; SAT or ACT recommended; rolling admission, early decision, delayed admission, and advanced placement plans available; $25 application fee.

Costs Per Year: $8,195 tuition; $5,950 room and board; $100 student fees; $600 average additional expenses.

Collegiate Environment: The college is located on 26 acres in Burlington, Vermont's largest city and the educational center of the state. The 31 college buildings contain a library of 33,000 volumes, 11,000 periodicals, 7,779 microforms, 1,012 audiovisual materials, and dormitory facilities for 527 men and women. Students from other geographical locations are accepted as well as midyear students. Approximately 90% of students applying for admission are accepted and 71% of the previous freshman class returned to the college for the second year of studies. Financial aid is available and approximately 90% of the current student body receives some form of financial assistance. The average class size is 25.

Community Environment: Burlington offers the best of both worlds: the excitement of life in the city and the tranquility and recreational splendor of the northern Vermont countryside. Three blocks from the Champlain campus, the Church Street Marketplace provides an exciting collection of more than 100 shops, services, and restaurants. Within one hour's drive are five major ski resorts: Stowe, Sugarbush, Bolton Valley, Mad River Glen, and Smugglers' Notch.

COLLEGE OF SAINT JOSEPH   (K-5)
71 Clement Road
Rutland, Vermont 05701
Tel: (802) 773-5905

Description: The privately supported Catholic coeducational college offers two- and four-year programs that combine career preparation with a liberal arts core. Career programs are offered in the areas of elementary, special and early childhood education; secondary education; business, accounting management, and computer information systems; and human services (mental health, developmental disabilities). Masters of Education degrees are offered in Early Childhood, Elementary, and General Education; Reading; and Special Education. The college is accredited by the New England Association of Schools and Colleges and operates on the early semester system. Three summer sessions are offered. Enrollment is 207 full-time and 180 part-time students. A faculty of 16 full-time and 33 part-time gives a faculty-student ratio of 1-11. The college was founded by the Sisters of St. Joseph of Rutland, and now operates under the direction of an Independent Board of Trustees with active participation from the Sisters of St. Joseph.

Entrance Requirements: High school graduation or equivalent with a minimum C average; recommended completion of 16 units including 4 English, 3 math, 2 science, and 2 social science; early admission, delayed admission. early decision, rolling admission; $25 application fee; SAT submission but no required score.

Costs Per Year: $7,450 tuition; $4,420 room and board; $100 student fees.

Collegiate Environment: There are three buildings on the 99-acre campus. Resident students are housed in two on-campus dormitories that provide living accommodations for 160 students. The library houses a collection of 36,000 volumes. The education students spend a minimum of fifteen weeks in observation and directed teaching in one of the elementary schools of the Rutland County area during the senior year. Similar practica are available in the human services and business programs. Approximately 90% of students applying for admission are accepted, including midyear students. There is special financial aid available for economically disadvantaged students and scholarships are available. About 60% of the current students receive some form of financial assistance.

Community Environment: Rutland, though a small city of 30,000, is the second largest city in Vermont. All forms of commercial transportation are available. Community facilities include a number of churches, a library, museum, community concert series, a hospital, and a number of the civic and service organizations. Rutland is the headquarters for the Green Mountain National Forest. Nearby are Pico and Killington Ski areas. Recreational areas provide facilities for

boating, swimming, fishing, camping, horseback riding, hunting, cross-country and alpine skiing and mountain climbing.

GODDARD COLLEGE   (F-8)
Plainfield, Vermont 05667
Tel: (802) 454-8311; (800) 468-4888; Admissions: (802) 454-8311; Fax: (802) 454-8017

Description: This small residential college has a four-year program leading to the Bachelor of Arts degree. It is accredited by the New England Association of Schools and Colleges. There are on-campus and unique off-campus, low residency programs. Off-campus Goddard offers: Bachelor of Arts (individually designed), Master of Arts (individually designed), Master of Arts in Teacher Education, Master of Arts in Psychology and Counseling, Master of Arts in Social Ecology, Master of Arts in Expressive Arts in Education, and Master of Fine Arts in Writing. The faculty places primary emphasis on the creation of an atmosphere in which learning can and will take place, and constantly work to improve that learning atmosphere. The private institution, operating on a semester system, has an enrollment of 125 campus students and 325 off-campus graduate and undergraduate students. Goddard remains a leader in progressive education. All students design their own curricula and have the ability to work independently. Group studies, field semesters, internships, and co-op experiences can be integrated into study plans.

Entrance Requirements: High school graduation; SAT recommended; $40 application fee on-campus and off-campus undergraduates; $40 application fee graduate students.

Costs Per Year: $14,632 tuition; $4,936 room and board.

Collegiate Environment: The college's campus lies among pastures and woods on 250 acres with a total of 32 buildings. The library houses 72,000 volumes, 214 periodicals and 54,000 microforms, 937 records and 1,700 audiotapes. Dormitory facilities provide living accommodations for 185 men and 185 women. About 70% of those students applying for admission meet the admission requirements and are accepted. There is financial aid available for economically disadvantaged students. Applicants for the adult degree program should be able to show ability to work independently. The semester for regular students is about 15 weeks long. A student needing help with college expenses should ask for it when applying for admission. Admissions decisions are made without regard to financial status, and financial aid decisions are made only about persons who have been admitted. School terms begin in September and February.

Community Environment: Located in the Upper Valley of Winooski River, this rural setting has the typical beauty of northern New England surrounded by the lower ranges of the Green Mountains. Winters are cold with heavy snow for good skiing. Opportunities are few for part-time employment.

GREEN MOUNTAIN COLLEGE   (L-3)
16 College Street
Poultney, Vermont 05764
Tel: (802) 287-9313; (800) 776-6675; Fax: (802) 287-9313

Description: A private, nonsectarian, coeducational college offering four-year Bachelor Degrees in liberal studies, business management, elementary education, art, English, special education, behavioral sciences, retail management, recreation, therapeutic recreation, leisure resource facilities management. The college is accredited by the New England Association of Schools and Colleges. It operates on the semester system and offers an extensive internship program. Enrollment includes 494 full-time and 24 part-time students. A faculty of 34 full-time and 16 part-time provides a faculty-student ratio of 1-14.

Entrance Requirements: High school graduation with rank in upper 60%; SAT or ACT required; completion of 16 units including 4 English, 2 mathematics, 2 laboratory science, 2 social studies, and 6 academic electives; non-high school graduates considered; early admission, early decision, rolling admission, delayed admission, and advanced placement plans available; $20 application fee.

Costs Per Year: $12,710 tuition; $2,900 room and board.

Collegiate Environment: Inside the college entrance gates is a 155-acre campus containing 26 buildings, playing fields, and tennis courts, swimming pool (indoor), gymnasium. The library houses a collection of 68,000 volumes and 200 periodicals. Dormitory facilities provide living accommodations for 600 students. 75% of applicants are accepted. 75% of the previous freshman class returned to the college for the second year. Average high school standing of the freshman class, top 40%; 23% in the top quarter; 40% in the second quarter; 30% in the third quarter. Financial aid is available and 50% of students receive some form of financial assistance.

Community Environment: Poultney is in a small town community with a typical New England climate. Train and bus stations and airport are within 20 minutes. Lake Saint Catherine provides facilities for water sports, and other facilities in nearby areas offer winter sports. Pico and Killington Ski resorts, as well as 4 other major ski resorts.

JOHNSON STATE COLLEGE *(D-7)*
Johnson, Vermont 05656
Tel: (802) 635-2356; (800) 635-2356; Fax: (802) 635-9745

Description: The college is a four-year, coeducational residential institution founded in 1828. It operates on the semester system and offers one summer session. It is accredited by the New England Association of Schools and Colleges. The college is state supported and features teacher education and liberal arts majors. Enrollment includes 1,145 full-time and 503 part-time undergraduates and 104 graduate students. A faculty of 66 full-time and 53 part-time gives a faculty-student ratio of 1-16.

Entrance Requirements: High school graduation; completion of 16 units including 4 English, 3 college-prep math, 2 social science, and 2 science (1 must be a lab science); SAT or ACT required; rolling admission, advanced placement program available; $40 application fee.

Costs Per Year: $3,897 resident tuition; $8,241 nonresident; $4,690 room and board.

Collegiate Environment: At Johnson State College, there are over thirty majors. Business Management, Hotel Hospitality, and Education are among the most popular programs. The Education Department includes Special, Elementary, and Early Childhood Education. JSC provides many support services, including academic advising, tutoring, and career services. The library houses 84,000 volumes. Dormitory facilities accomodate 625 students. The campus has many computer laboratories equipped with a variety of word-processing materials. JSC recently opened a new athletics facility that benefits the Physical Education and Health Sciences programs. Exchange programs with Quebec and London are available. Financial aid is available and 70% of students receive some form of financial aid.

Community Environment: The 350-acre hilltop campus of Johnson State is home for more than 1,700 students. Its location in the heart of the Green Mountains places it just minutes away from some of the East's finest skiing at Stowe and Smuggler's Notch. Its modern facilities include one of the finest performing arts centers in northern New England.

LYNDON STATE COLLEGE *(E-10)*
Vail Hill
Lyndonville, Vermont 05851
Tel: (802) 626-9371; (800) 225-1998; Fax: (802) 626-9770

Description: The four-year liberal arts college is part of the Vermont State College system and is fully accredited by the New England Association of Schools and Colleges as a degree-granting institution for the preparation of teachers, and by the Vermont State Board of Education. It is also accredited by the National Recreation and Parks Association. The semester system is used and one summer session is offered. The college prepares teachers for early childhood through high school grades and offers general education in the liberal arts. Enrollment recently included 544 men, 462 women full-time and 53 men and 76 women part-time. A faculty of 62 full-time and 54 part-time provides a faculty-student ratio of 1-17. The college grants Associate and the Bachelor degrees. Air Force ROTC is available.

Entrance Requirements: High school graduation or equivalent; completion of 16 units including 4 English, 2 algebra, 1 geometry, 2 science, 2 social science, and 2 history; SAT or ACT required; rolling admission, delayed admission plans available; $40 application fee.

Costs Per Year: $3,312 tuition; $7,656 nonresident tuition; $4,690 room and board; $586 student fees.

Collegiate Environment: The campus includes in its 175 hillside acres, several athletic fields, and open and wooded areas. The library houses a collection of over 70,000 volumes, 500 periodicals, 6,000 microforms, and 1,300 audiovisual materials. Dormitory facilities available. A new physical education facility houses a swimming pool, gym, and locker rooms. Financial aid is available and 65% of the current enrollment receive some form of assistance. Approximately 78% of those applying for admission are accepted.

Community Environment: Lyndon is a rural community in the northeastern part of Vermont with community facilities that include churches of major denominations, civic and service organizations, a library, two hospitals, and good shopping areas. Opportunities for part-time employment are limited. A ski resort at Burke Mountain and other ski areas provide facilities for skiing and other winter sports.

MARLBORO COLLEGE *(Q-6)*
Marlboro, Vermont 05344
Tel: (802) 257-4333

Description: One of the smallest 4-year liberal arts colleges in the country, Marlboro College was founded in 1947. The college is accredited by the New England Association of Schools and Colleges. With only 270 students Marlboro is small enough to permit flexibility, self-government, and a dialogue among disciplines. In order to graduate, students must complete a two-year project called a Plan of Concentration, pursued under the supervision of a faculty sponsor. The plan is evaluated in an intense oral examination by an outside evaluator who is an expert in the chosen field of research. The college operates on the semester system. A faculty of 39 full-time and 7 part-time provides a faculty-student ratio of 1-6.

Entrance Requirements: High school graduation or equivalent; completion of 15 units including 4 English, 3 social studies, 3 foreign language, 3 mathematics, 2 science; SAT or ACT required; interview, autobiographical statement and writing sample required, advanced placement, early admission, early decision, early action, rolling admission and delayed admission plans available. $30 application fee.

Costs Per Year: $18,375 tuition, $5,960 room and board, $485 fees.

Collegiate Environment: The campus of 350 acres is in the Green Mountains west of Brattleboro. The 27 buildings include a library which houses a collection of 60,000 volumes. Dormitories are small, accomodating 13 to 28 students each. Most dorms are co-ed, but separate living areas are available for those who prefer single-sex housing. About 75% of the students applying for admission are accepted. Financial aid is available. The library is run on an honor system and is open to students 24 hours a day.

Community Environment: Marlboro is located on the scenic Molly Stark Trail near Hogback Mountain which offers a panoramic view and facilities for skiing. Other outdoor activities include canoeing and kayaking, cross country skiing, hiking, rock climbing, biking. 75% of the students are on the college's work/study program. The Marlboro Summer Music Festival is an annual event.

MIDDLEBURY COLLEGE *(H-4)*
Middlebury, Vermont 05753-6002
Tel: (802) 388-3711; Admissions: (802) 388-3711 X 5153; Fax: (802) 388-0258

Description: The college, founded in 1800, believes in the importance of the liberal arts and the liberal sciences. The 4-1-4 system is used and several summer sessions are offered. The college is accredited by the New England Association of Schools and Colleges. The summer language schools of English, French, German, Italian, Russian, Spanish, Chinese, Japanese, and Arabic have achieved international reputation. Enrollment in the undergraduate school includes 975 men and 975 women with a faculty of 180 full-time and 40 part-time. There are special preprofessional programs available whereby students preparing for engineering, medicine, law, veterinary medicine, allied health services, business/management, nursing, forestry/environmental studies, architecture, dual degree or dentistry may transfer at the end of the junior year to accredited professional schools, and upon receipt of the professional degree, become eligible by vote of the faculty for an A.B.

Entrance Requirements: High school graduation; SAT and three Achievement Tests, or 5 Achievement Tests, or ACT required; 16 high school credits required, including 4 English, 4 math, 3 social science, 3 science, and 4 language; advanced placement, early decision, early admission, midyear admission, and delayed admission plans available; non-high school graduates considered; $50 application fee.

Costs Per Year: $25,750 comprehensive fee.

Collegiate Environment: The campus includes 350 acres for buildings and athletic grounds. The United States Government maintains an adjacent area as part of the Green Mountain National Forest, which students use for outings and winter sports. The library houses a collection of 750,000 volumes, 2,000 periodicals, 75,000 microforms, and 20,000 recordings. Dormitory facilities provide living accommodations for 1,950 men and women. Approximately 31% of students applying for admission are accepted. The middle 50% ranges of the entering freshmen class scores were SAT 1150-1350 combined, ACT 27-30 composite. Language students may spend a complete academic year in France, Spain, Italy and Germany at facilities owned by Middlebury College, or in almost any other country through reciprocal agreement arrangements. There is a Junior Year Abroad program. 100% of those students with demonstrated need receive financial aid. The Bread Loaf School of English is a community of teachers and students devoted to the humanistic ideals of the liberal arts at the graduate level.

Community Environment: Middlebury, population 8,000, is located between Burlington and Rutland. There are many job opportunities for students on campus. Churches, libraries, and various civic and service organizations serve the community. The college's Bread Loaf Mountain is nearby and has facilities for skiing and other winter sports. Other sports include golf, skating, tennis, and horseback riding. The College owns and operates an 18-hole golf course, an alpine ski area, and 2 cross-country ski areas. Lake Champlain and Green Mountain National Forest are nearby and provide numerous facilities.

NORWICH UNIVERSITY *(G-7)*
Northfield, Vermont 05663
Tel: (800) 468-6679; Admissions: (802) 485-2001; Fax: (802) 485-2032

Description: Norwich University was founded in 1819 and is the oldest private military college in the United States. The University is accredited by the New England Association of Schools and Colleges. Professional programs are accredited by the Accreditation Board for Engineering and Technology and the National League for Nursing. Norwich University was founded as a military school and in 1972 merged with Vermont College. On the Northfield Vermont campus traditional age students live in either the Corps of Cadets or civilian lifestyle. The Vermont College campus, which is located in Montpelier, Vermont, the state capital, is dedicated to adult learners and Masters programs. The University operates on the semester system and offers two summer sessions. Over 25 academic majors are offered within the fields of liberal arts, engineering, architecture, business, the sciences and nursing. Army, Air Force and Naval ROTC are available and mandatory for students in the Corps of Cadets. Military service is not mandatory. A peace Corps Preparatory Program is also available. Norwich students participate in 20 intercollegiate sports and several club sports. Enrollment is 1,650 students. Over 200 faculty members provide a faculty-student ratio of 1-14.

Entrance Requirements: High school graduation or GED; SAT or ACT scores; early decision, rolling admission, and advanced placement plans available; $25 application fee.

Costs Per Year: $14,134 tuition and fees; $5,270 room and board; $1,000 average additional expenses.

Collegiate Environment: The military college is situated on 2,000 acres in the middle of Vermont's ski resorts area. Vermont College is located on a scenic hill overlooking the small city of Montpelier. A new 58,000-square-foot library that houses 220,000 volumes and 1,500 periodical subscriptions opened in April 1993. Dormitory facilities provide living accommodations for 1,700 men and women. About 90% of the students applying for admission are accepted. 58% of the students graduated in the top half of their high school class. Financial aid is need-based, and 85% of the students receive some form of financial aid.

Community Environment: A rural community in the central section of Vermont, Northfield is 11 miles south of Montpelier, the state capital. Train, bus and plane transportation is available. Recreational activities include skiing, hiking, bicycling, fishing, and hunting.

SAINT MICHAEL'S COLLEGE *(E-4)*
Winooski Park
Colchester, Vermont 05439
Tel: (802) 654-3000; (800) 762-8000; Fax: (802) 654-2591

Description: The four-year liberal arts and sciences college was founded in 1904 by the Society of St. Edmund. It operates on the semester system and offers two summer sessions. It is accredited by the New England Association of Schools and Colleges. A program in English for international students is offered to meet the needs of students from foreign countries. A program of study abroad during the student's junior year in college is incorporated with established programs of other colleges and universities. Preprofessional programs are offered. Air Force and Army ROTC programs are available. Enrollment includes 1,684 full-time and 31 part-time undergraduate students. A faculty of 107 full-time and 60 part-time gives a faculty-student ratio of 1-14.

Entrance Requirements: High school graduation or equivalent; completion of 16 units including 4 English, 3 mathematics, 2 foreign language, 2 social studies, 2 science and 3 electives; SAT required; GRE required for graduate study; early notification and advanced placement plans available; $35 application fee.

Costs Per Year: $13,810 tuition; $6,010 room and board; $140 student fees.

Collegiate Environment: The 400-acre campus is adjacent to Burlington. The 40 buildings include a library of approximately 180,500 volumes, 1,390 periodicals, 34,812 titles on microform, and 20,000 audiovisual materials. Dormitory facilities provide living accommodations for 1,500 students. Approximately 70% of students applying for admission are accepted, including midyear students, and 85% of the previous freshman class returned to campus for the second year. Average high school standing of the freshman class, top 30%; 49% were in the top quarter. SAT score range for the middle 50% of students was 922-1138. Financial aid is available and 62% of the current student body receives some form of financial assistance.

Community Environment: The Burlington area, Vermont's most populous, is characterized by 4 colleges and 1 university as well as by high-tech industry. Commercial transportation is available. Canada is a half-hour drive away. Facilities are nearby for skiing. Job opportunities are available, and summer work is plentiful.

SCHOOL FOR INTERNATIONAL TRAINING *(Q-7)*
444 Kipling Road
Brattleboro, Vermont 05301
Tel: (802) 257-7751; (800) 451-4465; Fax: (802) 258-3248

Description: This nonprofit undergraduate and graduate school was founded in 1964 and prepares its graduates for effective international/intercultural careers. It is accredited by the New England Association of Schools and Colleges. All programs combine on-campus study with internships, many of which are served overseas. Graduate programs lead to M.A. degrees in intercultural management and training and second language teaching. The two-year upper division bachelors program has an emphasis on global issues and leads to a degree in International Studies. The School also offers college semester and summer study abroad programs for students from other schools. A choice of 53 locations in the Third World and in traditional European cities is offered, including Tibetan Studies in Nepal, East-West relations in Berlin, Ecology in Brazil and many others. Degree student enrollment totals 250 students. A faculty of 45 gives a faculty-student ratio of 1-6. Contact the school for program dates and calendars, which vary from program to program.

Entrance Requirements: Baccalaureate degree or equivalent for graduate programs; undergraduate program requires 60 transferable semester credits or an A.A. degree; personal interview required; $35 application fee.

Costs Per Year: $11,700 undergraduate tuition; $15,000-$15,500 graduate; $709 student fees.

Collegiate Environment: Located on a hillside site 3 miles from town, the campus comprises 200 acres. The library contains 30,000 titles, 335 periodicals, 7,900 microforms and 500 recordings. There are dormitory facilities for 225 students. 50% of applicants are accepted. Financial aid is available to qualified applicants. 85% of students receive financial aid.

Community Environment: Located on the Connecticut River, surrounded by hills of the Green Mountains, Brattleboro is a year-round resort. Community facilities include churches, a library, a hospital and medical center and excellent shopping facilities. The Brattleboro Outing Club's Ski jump is one of the finest in the East. Nearby are Stratten Mountain, Maple Valley, Mount Snow, and Haystack Ski areas.

SOUTHERN VERMONT COLLEGE *(Q-3)*
Monument Road
Bennington, Vermont 05201
Tel: (802) 442-5427; Fax: (802) 442-5529

Description: Southern Vermont College was founded in 1926 as the St. Joseph Business College. Ownership was transferred to an independent Board of Trustees in 1974, and the name was changed to Southern Vermont College. The college is accredited by the New England Association of Schools and Colleges. The primary goal of the College is to provide men and women with practical educational opportunities to prepare for work and life in an increasingly complex world. Career oriented programs have been designed to give Southern Vermont College graduates management skills as well as a solid liberal arts background. The College consciously strives to remain accessible to all persons seeking educational growth by maintaining low tuition costs relative to those of other private institutions. A program at Oxford, England is available. A Learning Disabilities Program is available. Associate and Bachelor degrees are offered in a variety of career fields. It operates on the semester system and offers two summer sessions. Enrollment includes 425 full-time and 41 part-time students. A faculty of 30 full-time and 41 part-time gives a faculty-student ratio of 1-17.

Entrance Requirements: High school graduation; 3 years English, 2 years mathematics; SAT or ACT recommended; letters of recommendation; interview and essay strongly recommended; rolling admission plan; $25 application fee.

Costs Per Year: $8,940 tuition; $4,304 room and board; $200 fees.

Collegiate Environment: Located on 371 acres on Mount Anthony in Old Bennington, the campus includes eight buildings. The library houses a collection of 25,000 volumes and 287 periodicals. Dormitory facilities provide living accommodations for 250 men and women. Approximately 85% of students applying for admission are accepted. Financial aid is available and 97% of freshmen and 71% of all students receive some form of financial aid. Nearly 73% of the previous freshmen returned for their sophomore year.

Community Environment: See Bennington College.

TRINITY COLLEGE OF VERMONT *(E-4)*
Colchester Avenue
Burlington, Vermont 05401
Tel: (802) 658-0337; Fax: (802) 658-5446

Description: This four-year liberal arts college for the higher education of women is conducted by the Sisters of Mercy. Founded in 1925, the college is accredited by the New England Association of Schools and Colleges Operating on a 2-semester calendar and a flexible summer schedule, the focus of the academic program is on the individual student in order to provide all students with an educational environment. Enrollment is 1,084 women. A faculty of 70 gives a faculty-student ratio of 1-15. Programs providing professional preparation include social work, which is accredited by the Committee on Social Work Education, and teacher education, which is approved for certification by the State Board of Education in Vermont and by 30 other states.

Entrance Requirements: High school graduation with rank in upper half of class; completion of 16 units including 4 English, 2 mathematics, 2 foreign language, 1 laboratory science, 1 history and 5 electives; non-high school graduates considered; early decision, rolling admission, delayed admission, and advanced placement plans available; $25 application fee.

Costs Per Year: $9,780 tuition; $4,736 board and room; $453 student fees; $1,050 average additional expenses.

Collegiate Environment: The 17-acre campus is about 10 minutes from the center of the city of Burlington. The 13 buildings include a library containing 50,000 volumes, 800 pamphlets, 306 periodical ti-

tles, and 42,613 microforms. Dormitory facilities provide living accommodations for 290 women. Approximately 84% of the students applying for admission are accepted. Average high school standing of the recent freshman class: 25% in top fifth; 34% in second fifth, and 59% in top 40%. Average SAT scores were 420V, 450M. There is special financial aid available for economically handicapped students, and 80% of the current student body receives some form of financial assistance. 70% of the previous freshman class returned to the college for the second year.

Community Environment: Burlington is the largest city in Vermont and is an important industrial and retail trading center. Burlington is located on Lake Champlain. A number of parks, a golf course, and nearby ski areas provide the facilities for a great many activities. Burlington is also a principal port of air entry on the United States-Canada border. The annual Three Day Music Festival and the annual Champlain Shakespeare Festival are special events.

UNIVERSITY OF VERMONT *(E-4)*
South Prospect Street
Burlington, Vermont 05405
Tel: (802) 656-3480; Admissions: (802) 656-3370; Fax: (802) 656-8611

Description: Chartered in 1791, the university is one of the 20 oldest institutions of higher learning in the United States authorized to grant degrees. The university operates on the semester system and offers a summer session. It is accredited by the New England Association of Schools and Colleges and by several professional institutions. The university consists of Colleges of Arts & Sciences, Agriculture and Life Sciences, Education & Social Services and a School of Natural Resources. A Division of Health Sciences includes the College of Medicine and Schools of Nursing and Allied Health Science; the Division of Engineering, Math and Business Administration includes a college of Engineering and Mathematics and the School of Business Administration. There is a campus-wide Environmental Studies Program and a Graduate College. Cooperative education programs are available in business, agriculture and life sciences, engineering and mathematics, and in natural resources. European, Soviet, and Far East programs are available. Army ROTC at UVM and Air Force ROTC at St. Michael's College are available. Enrollment includes 7,496 full-time and 1,500 part-time undergraduates and 1,124 graduate students. A faculty of 859 full-time and 140 part-time gives a faculty-student ratio of 1-15.

Entrance Requirements: High school graduation or equivalent; rank in upper 40% of graduating class; completion of 16 units including 4 English, 3 mathematics, 2 foreign language, 2 science and 3 social studies; additional math and science for some majors; SAT required; GRE required for graduate school; rolling admission available for in-state students only; advanced placement, early admission, early decision and delayed and midyear admission plans available; $45 application fee.

Costs Per Year: $7,496 state-resident tuition; $15,516 nonresident; $4,514 room and board; $550 student fees and miscellaneous.

Collegiate Environment: The Bailey-Howe Library houses a collection of 1,028,976 volumes, 857,430 government documents, 10,159 periodicals, 1,223,000 micoform units, 191,331 cartographic materials, and 18,938 audiovisual and visual materials. Dormitory facilities provide living accommodations for 3,750 men, women, and families. Fraternities and sororities house additional men and women. About 82% of in-state students applying for admission are accepted. 71% of out-of-state applicants are accepted. The middle 50% of scores for entering freshmen were SAT 430-550 verbal and 480-610 for state residents, and 470-560 verbal and 530-640 math for nonresidents. 140 scholarships are available and approximately 56% of the current students receive some form of financial assistance. Cooperative programs at the University include the Study Abroad Program.

Community Environment: Burlington is Vermont's largest city and, while the University is a significant resource, the city has manifold cultural, recreational, and social offerings. Burlington is a tourist and business center with a rich history and significant business development.

VERMONT LAW SCHOOL *(J-7)*
South Royalton, Vermont 05068
Tel: (802) 763-8303; (800) 227-1395

Description: This private, coeducational law school is fully accredited by the New England Association of Schools and Colleges, the American Bar Association, and is a member of the Association of American Law Schools. 34 full-time and 22 part-time professors make up the faculty. Entering class size is limited to 160 students for an overall enrollment of 498 students. The faculty-student ratio is 1-16. The school operates on the semester calendar system and offers four summer sessions. It is the only law school in the State of Vermont, and its environmental law program has a national reputation.

Entrance Requirements: Bachelor's degree from an accredited institution; applicant must take the LSAT and register with the Law School Data Assembly Service; two written recommendations and a personal statement required; first-year students are admitted only at the start of the academic year; application fee $50.

Costs Per Year: $17,250 tuition; $75 student fees.

Collegiate Environment: Although faculty members are committed to rigorous training of law students, an intimate and informal learning atmosphere is characteristic of the school. Twelve buildings complete the principal school complex. The library holdings include 194,000 volumes and 1,034 periodical susbscriptions. Students come from 47 states and alumni are practicing in more than 40. 80% of the students receive financial aid.

Community Environment: The town is located northwest of White River Junction, Vermont. The area is served by bus, train and airplane service. There are opportunities for outdoor activities in the area surrounding this New England village in the upper Connecticut River Valley.

VERMONT TECHNICAL COLLEGE   *(I-7)*
P.O. Box 500
Randolph Center, Vermont 05061
Tel: (802) 728-3391; (800) 442-8821; Admissions: (802) 728-1243;
Fax: (802) 728-1390

Description: The college is a two-year technical institute offering collegiate level programs leading to an Associate degree in Applied Science, Associate degree in Engineering, and Bachelor of Science in Engineering Technology. Founded in 1866, the college is accredited by the New England Association of Schools and Colleges, and the Accreditation Board for Engineering and Technology. The Veterinary Technology Program is accredited by the American Veterinary Medical Association as a program for educating verterinary technicians. The semester system is used and 2 summer sessions are offered. Enrollment is 638 full-time and 34 part-time students. A faculty of 66 full-time and 22 part-time gives a faculty-student ratio of 1-10.

Entrance Requirements: High school graduation; completion of 16 units including 4 English, 2 mathematics, 2 science, 2 social sciences for the applied science degree; 4 English, 3 mathematics, 2 science, 2 social sciences for the engineering tech program; SAT or ACT required; $40 application fee.

Costs Per Year: $4,168 in-state tuition; $6,252 regional student; $8,336 nonresidents; $4,878 room and board; $608 student fees.

Collegiate Environment: The Hartness Library, one of eleven buildings on the campus, was built in 1967. It has a collection of 56,000 volumes and 425 periodicals. Residence halls house 488 men and 70 women. Approximately 90% of those students applying for admission are accepted. About 65% of a recent freshman class returned to college for the second year. 68% of students receive financial aid.

Community Environment: Randolph Center is a rural area, three miles from Randolph. Churches, a library, hospital, shopping facilities, and several of the civic and service organizations serve the town. Outdoor sports include golf, fishing, hunting, skiing, ice skating and tennis.

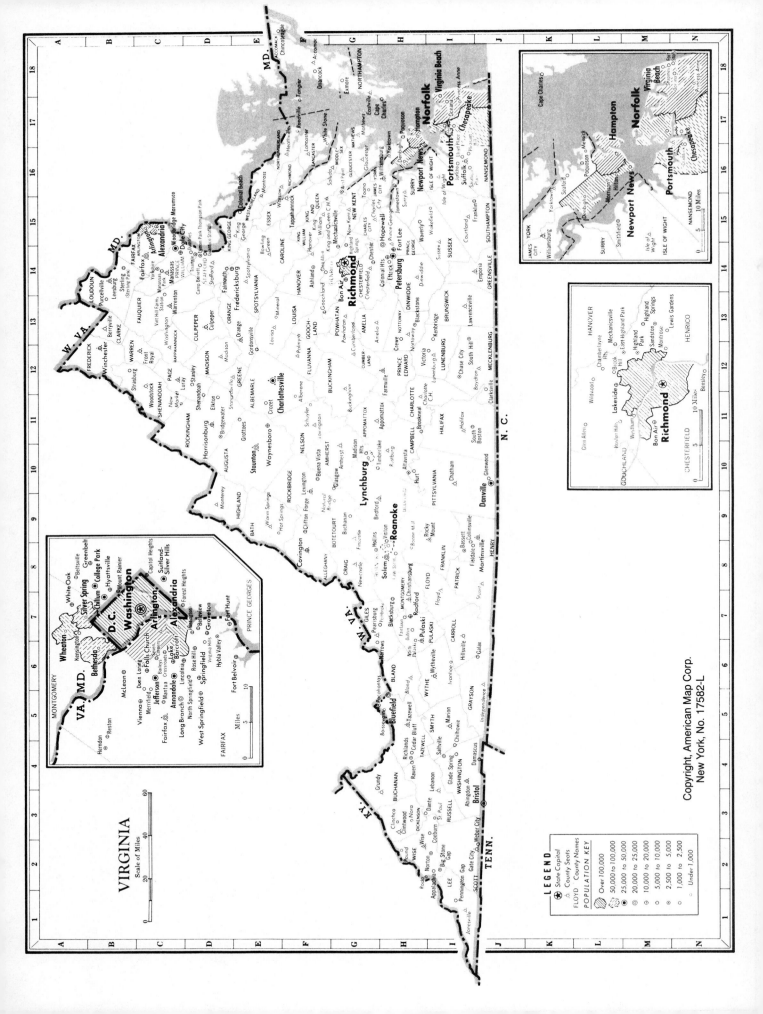

VIRGINIA

Scale of Miles

LEGEND

⊛ State Capital
⊙ County Seats
FLOYD County Names

POPULATION KEY

Over 100,000
50,000 to 100,000
25,000 to 50,000
20,000 to 25,000
10,000 to 20,000
5,000 to 10,000
2,500 to 5,000
1,000 to 2,500
Under 1,000

VIRGINIA

AMERICAN SCHOOL OF PROFESSIONAL PSYCHOLOGY
(C-15)
1400 Wilson Boulevard, Suite 110
Arlington, Virginia 22209
Tel: (703) 243-5300; (800) 572-0231; Fax: (703) 243-8973

Description: The privately supported graduate school is fully accredited by the North Central Association of Colleges and Schools. It operates on a trimester system with one summer session. The school was established in 1994 to provide a setting in which extensive training could be pursued in the area of professional psychology. It does not promote any one clinical psychological orientation. Currently, it offers psychoanalytic, client-centered, experimental family systems, integrative-eclectic, behavioral, neuropsychological, and group approaches to intervention. The school grants Masters and Doctorate (PsyD) degrees. Current enrollment is 71 students with a faculty of 8.

Entrance Requirements: Graduation from an accredited institution with a baccalaureate or more advanced degree.

Costs Per Year: $13,540 tuition; $300-$500 fees.

Collegiate Environment: A coeducational professional school, it has a diversity of students, ranging from recent college graduates to change-of-career students. The curriculum is supported by the Georgetown Medical School Library where students of the school have full privileges. Students have access to the rich library resources of the Washington, DC, area including the National Library of Medicine and the Library of Congress. Financial aid is available.

Community Environment: The school is conveniently situated to provide access to most major highways in the Washington, DC area. In close proximity to Georgetown, students may take advantage of the many diverse attractions of the DC area. Training sites are available in hospitals, clinics and agencies in DC, Maryland, and Virginia.

Branch Campuses: The school is a unit of the American Schools of Professional Psychology with professional schools in Atlanta, GA, Chicago, IL, Honolulu, HI, Minneapolis, MN, and Rolling Meadows, IL.

AVERETT COLLEGE   *(J-10)*
420 West Main Street
Danville, Virginia 24541
Tel: (804) 791-5660; (800) 283-7388

Description: Averett is a private, liberal arts coeducational college founded in 1859 and affiliated with the Virginia Baptist Association. It is accredited by the Southern Association of Colleges and Schools. All buildings are centrally located on a beautiful residential campus. Offering over 50 undergraduate majors and several masters degree programs. Averett's academic options are diverse. The college operates on the semester system and offers three mini-terms in May, June and July. The traditional undergraduate enrollment is about 750 students at the Danville campus. All classes are taught by fully qualified professors with a student/faculty ratio of 12:1. Throughout the commonwealth, 2,423 students are enrolled in Averett programs which includes the Averett Adult Curriculum for Excellence (AACE). The college grants the Associate, Bachelor, and Master degrees.

Entrance Requirements: High school graduation or GED required; completion of 15 units: 4 English, 3 math, 2 laboratory science, and 2 social studies; SAT or ACT required; GRE required for graduate studies; early admission, early decision, advanced placement, rolling admission and delayed admission plans available; $20 application fee.

Costs Per Year: $10,800 tuition; $4,150 room and board; $350 fee.

Collegiate Environment: The college is located in the residential section of Danville. Four of the major living and instructional areas are in connected buildings. They contain dormitory rooms, classrooms, labs and a student center. The library has 128,000 volumes,

3,526 pamphlets and 517 periodicals. Dormitories accomodate 200 men and 200 women. Construction is underway for a new convocation and athletic center and a new equestrian center is nearby. The Danville Regional Airport is five miles from campus. There are a wide range of social, cultural and athletic programs at the college to complement the academic programs. 85% of applicants are accepted; new students and transfers admitted at midyear. Scholarships are available and 85% of the student body receives some form of financial aid. $6,000,000 in financial aid is awarded to students each year.

Community Environment: The Wreck of the Old 97, the accident that inspired the ballad by that name, occurred in Danville in 1903. Danville was the last capital of the Confederacy; it was here that President Jefferson Davis received the news that General Lee had surrendered. The Dan River Mills, Inc., one of the largest single-unit textile mills, consumes 90 million pounds of cotton annually. Danville, population 60,000, is the second largest tobacco auction center in the nation. Lakes in the area provide facilities for all water sports; other activities are bowling, tennis, and horseback riding. Danville is home to the Atlanta Brave's rookie league baseball team, the Danville Braves.

Branch Campuses: Adult education, and graduate undergraduate programs: Fairfax County, VA; Roanoke, VA; Richmond, VA; and Lynchburg, VA.

BLUE RIDGE COMMUNITY COLLEGE   *(E-11)*
P.O. Box 80
Weyers Cave, Virginia 24486
Tel: (703) 234-9261; Fax: (703) 234-9066

Description: The two-year community college was opened in 1967. It is operated and controlled by the State of Virginia and is accredited by the Southern Association of Colleges and Schools. The institution provides opportunities for adults as well as college-age youth. It serves local industries by conducting special in-plant programs that upgrade employees' specialized skills. The occupational-technical programs are designed to meet the demand for technicians, semiprofessional workers, and skilled craftsmen. The university parallel-college transfer program includes college freshmen and sophomore courses in arts and sciences and preprofessional programs meeting standards acceptable for transfer to Baccalaureate degree programs in four-year institutions. Enrollment is 2,808 men and women full-time and part-time. A faculty of 44 full-time and 110 part-time gives a faculty-student ratio of 1-19. The college operates on the semester system and offers three summer terms.

Entrance Requirements: High school graduation or equivalent; open enrollment policy; college transfer program requires completion of 4 units of high school English, 2 math, 1 science, and 1 social studies; open admission and midyear admission plans available.

Costs Per Year: $1,131.60 tuition; $3,756 out-of-state.

Collegiate Environment: Located on 65 acres, the school has several buildings. Almost 97% of students applying for admission are accepted. Limited financial assistance is available and approximately 22% of the students receive some form of aid. The college library houses more than 50,000 volumes.

Community Environment: Weyers Cave is a rural community located near Staunton and Harrisonburg.

BLUEFIELD COLLEGE   *(H-5)*
Bluefield, Virginia 24605
Tel: (703) 326-3682; (800) 872-0175; Admissions: (703) 326-4214; Fax: (703) 326-4288

Description: This private coeducational college is affiliated with the Baptist General Association of Virginia. Opened in 1922, the institution is accredited by the Southern Association of Colleges and Schools and the Virginia State Board of Education. Enrollment is 603 full-time and 223 part-time students. A faculty of 48 full-time and 13 part-time gives a faculty-student ratio of 1-16. The college operates on the two-semester system and offers two summer sessions. Classes start in January and September. The college awards Associate and Bachelor degrees.

Entrance Requirements: High school graduation; or equivalent; completion of 16 units including 4 English, 2 mathematics, 1 science, and 1 social science; SAT or ACT required; rolling admission, delayed admission and advanced placement plans available. $15 application fee.

Costs Per Year: $7,770 tuition; $4,430 room and board.

Collegiate Environment: Situated on 85 acres, the campus has 9 buildings. The library holdings include 44,000 volumes. Housing is available for 174 men and 126 women. All students are required to take at least one course in Religion. Financial assistance is available, and 85% of the current student body receives financial aid. Approximately 89% of the applicants are accepted.

Community Environment: A suburban area in the Virginia Highlands, Bluefield is a center of diversified industry. Products of its industries are fabric dyes, mattresses, hardwood flooring, textiles, and mining equipment. All commercial transportation is available. Public libraries, churches, hospitals, and a number of the civic and service organizations are a part of the community. Some part-time employment is available. Nearby mountains provide facilities for numerous recreational activities.

BRIDGEWATER COLLEGE *(D-11)*
402 East College Street
Bridgewater, Virginia 22812
Tel: (540) 828-2501; (800) 759-8328; Fax: (540) 828-5481

Description: This small, private, coeducational, liberal arts college was founded in 1880 as Spring Creek Normal and Collegiate Institution by Daniel Christian Flory. The privately supported college is affiliated with the Church of the Brethren and is accredited by the Southern Association of Colleges and Schools. It operates on the 3-3-1-3 trimester system and offers two summer terms. The numbers refer to the number of courses a student takes in 10-10-3-10 week terms. Academic cooperative programs are available with Penn State in engineering, Duke University in forestry and environmental science, and Virginia Tech in veterinary science. Enrollment includes 950 full-time students. A faculty of 65 full-time and 13 part-time provides a faculty-student ratio of 1-15.

Entrance Requirements: High school graduation with rank in top 50% of graduating class; SAT, ACT or TOEFL required; completion of 16 units including 4 English, 2 mathematics, 2 foreign language, 2 lab science, and 2 social science; midyear admission, rolling admission, advanced placement plans available; $15 application fee.

Costs Per Year: $11,925 tuition and student fees; $4,975 room and board; additional expenses average $1,700.

Collegiate Environment: The 190-acre campus is comprised of 27 buildings. The single sex residence halls provide housing for 506 men and 525 women. The Alexander Mack Memorial Library, erected in 1962-63, contains more than 154,419 volumes, 563 periodicals, 383,000 microforms, 39,000 government documents, 6,057 audiovisuals, and is fully automated on a local area network with direct on-line internet access to libraries across the nation. The college welcomes students from a wide geographical area, including foreign students. Scholarships of up to 50% of tuition are offered and 95% of the students receive some form of financial aid.

Community Environment: Bridgewater is located in the Shenandoah Valley, seven miles south of Harrisonburg. The community facilities include churches, banks, restaurants, parks, museums, and shops. The city, its suburbs and the surrounding area offer entertainment, fine dining experiences, a shopping mall, libraries, a hospital, historic towns, civil war battlefields, the George Washington National Forest, the Massanutten Four Seasons Resort, the Shenandoah Regional Airport, various civic organizations, and events at James Madison Convocation Center.

CENTRAL VIRGINIA COMMUNITY COLLEGE *(G-10)*
3506 Ward's Road
Lynchburg, Virginia 24502
Tel: (804) 386-4567

Description: The two-year institution was established in 1967 as a member of the Virginia Community College system to provide state-supported educational facilities beyond the high school level for the cities of Lynchburg and Bedford and the counties of Amherst, Appomattox, Bedford, and Campbell. The college offers two-year transfer programs in arts and sciences and in certain preprofessional areas such as engineering, business, and teaching. Its occupational and technical programs lead to diplomas, certificates, or Associate of Applied Science degrees. Cooperative education programs are available in all areas. Enrollment is 1,011 students full-time and 2,972 students part-time. A faculty of 60 full-time and 50 part-time provides a faculty-student ratio of 1-16. The college is accredited by the Southern Association of Colleges and Schools and the Committee on Allied Health Education and Accreditation. It operates on the semester system and offers two summer sessions.

Entrance Requirements: Open enrollment policy; non-high school graduates 18 years of age or older admitted; early admission, rolling admission, and advanced placement plans available; no application fee.

Costs Per Year: $1,230 tuition; $4,260 out-of-state.

Collegiate Environment: Consisting of approximately 100 acres with a view of the Blue Ridge Mountains, the campus houses the modern college buildings. The library contains 35,000 volumes, 170 periodicals and 2,000 audiovisual materials. Financial assistance is available on campus. 12% of students receive financial aid. All of the students applying for admission are accepted, including midyear applicants.

Community Environment: See Lynchburg College.

CHRISTOPHER NEWPORT UNIVERSITY *(H-17)*
50 Shoe Lane
Newport News, Virginia 23606-2998
Tel: (804) 594-7000; (800) 333-4268; Admissions: (804) 594-7015; Fax: (804) 594-7713

Description: Established in 1960 as a branch of the College of William and Mary, America's second-oldest college, Christopher Newport University is now one of 9 state-supported comprehensive universities in Virginia's public university system. The university takes its name from Captain Christopher Newport, the English mariner who was put in command of the three ships that arrived at Jamestown in 1607. It is accredited by the Southern Association of Colleges and Schools. Organized into the colleges of Arts and Jumanitites, Business and Economics, Social Science and Professional Studies, and Science and Technology, the university focuses on excellence in teaching and scholarship. The liberal arts serve as the foundation for all degree programs. The university prepares its students to pursue lives with meaning and purpose and to become responsible and contributing members of society. It awards bachelor's and master's degrees in approximately 50 areas. It operates on the semester system and offers three summer sessions. Enrollment includes 2,893 full-time and 1,696 part-time undergraduates and 33 graduate students. A faculty of 232 full-time and 7 part-time gives a faculty-student ratio of 1-19.

Entrance Requirements: Accredited high school graduation with minimum C average; freshman applicants should have completed a college preparatory curriculum; SAT required; non-high school graduates considered; early admission, rolling admission, midyear admission and advanced placement plans are available. $25 application fee.

Costs Per Year: $3,350 tuition; $7,946 out-of-state tuition.

Collegiate Environment: Christopher Newport University has a 75-acre campus located in Newport News, VA. It opened its first residence hall in 1994 and accommodates 440 students. Its library holdings include 153,236 volumes. 93% of applicants are accepted. The average scores of the entering freshman class were SAT 480 verbal, 440 math. Scholarships are available and 37% of students receive some form of financial aid. The university is organized and instruction is provided to take into consideration the life-long learning interests and needs of a largely part-time and mobile student body. It offers programs of equivalency testing and other nontraditional means of earning college-level academic credit, and cooperates with other colleges and local agencies with diverse missions, thereby expanding its learning resources. The university offers special advising and credit programs to meet the needs of its many transfer students. Christopher Newport University is the home of the Japanese Tea House in Virginia.

Community Environment: The 75-acre campus located in Newport News, VA, is easily accessible to residents of that city, as well as to residents of Hampton, Poquoson, York County, James City/County and Williamsburg. Newport News is a world port with a good harbor on Hampton Roads at the mouth of the James River. The docks and piers of Newport News are capable of receiving the largest ships in the world. The campus is centrally located between recreational centers at Colonial Williamsburg and the Norfolk/Virginia Beach resorts.

COLLEGE OF WILLIAM AND MARY   *(H-16)*
P.O. Box 8795
Williamsburg, Virginia 23185
Tel: (804) 221-4223; Fax: (804) 221-1773

Description: The state-supported liberal arts college was chartered in 1693. It is accredited by the Southern Association of Colleges and Schools and by respective professional organizations. Enrollment is 3,567 men and 4,143 women, including 2,234 graduate students. A faculty of approximately 600 gives a faculty-student ratio of 1-13. The college operates on the semester system and offers two summer terms. Army ROTC is available. Study abroad programs are available in Australia, Canada, China, England, Germany, Italy, Spain, Scotland, Japan, and the Netherland Antilles.

Entrance Requirements: Strongest college-prep program possible with rank typically in upper tenth of class; SAT or ACT required for undergraduate admission; 3 Achievement tests recommended; GRE, MAT, GMAT or LSAT required for graduate programs; $40 undergraduate application fee; early decision, delayed admission, early admission, and advanced placement programs available.

Costs Per Year: $4,048 tuition; $11,428 out-of-state; $3,900 room and board.

Collegiate Environment: The college campus comprises about 1,200 acres of land and extends from the western edge of Colonial Williamsburg to Lake Matoaka and an extensive stretch of beautifully wooded land known as the College Woods. Within its boundaries are three sections known as the Old Campus, the Main Campus, and the New Campus. Residence halls that accommodate 1,900 men and 2,240 women are found on the Main Campus and New Campuses as are several libraries with a total collection of 1,172,814 volumes and more than 5,500 periodicals. On the New Campus is Phi Beta Kappa Memorial Hall, which contains an 805-seat theater, the Earl Gregg Sivern Library, the Muscarelle Art Museum, the Millington Hall of Life Sciences, the William Small Physical Laboratory, Adair Gymnasium, William and Mary Hall, Richard Lee Morton Hall, Rogers Hall, and several residence halls. There are chapters of 13 social fraternities on the campus and 12 national sororities, which provide housing for an additional 407 men and 160 women. Approximately 36% of students applying for admission are accepted. Midyear students are accepted, and the college welcomes a geographically diverse student body. Need-based financial aid is available, and 23% of the students receive some form of financial aid.

Community Environment: Williamsburg, the historic capital of Colonial Virginia, has been restored as nearly as possible to its 18th-century appearance. The Colonial Williamsburg project has been made possible by the generous provisions of the late John D. Rockefeller, Jr. The restored town offers excellent facilities, and the colonial shops on Merchant's Square provide historical interest. Williamsburg is a popular tourist center and has recreational activities such as fishing, boating, golf, and hunting. Major historic points of interest include William and Mary's Sir Christopher Wren Building (1695), the Bruton Parish Church, the Capitol, Governor's Palace, Peyton Randolph House, Raleigh Tavern, and the Wythe House.

COLLEGE OF WILLIAM AND MARY - RICHARD BLAND
COLLEGE   *(H-14)*
11301 Johnson Road
Petersburg, Virginia 23805
Tel: (804) 862-6225; Fax: (804) 862-6189

Description: Richard Bland College of the College of William and Mary is the only state-supported, junior college in Virginia. The college is accredited by the Southern Association of Colleges and Schools. It was established in 1960 to provide opportunities for higher education to the citizens of communities located away from the main campus of William and Mary in Williamsburg. Enrollment is 716 full-time and 308 part-time students. A faculty of 33 full-time and 15 part-time gives a faculty-students ratio of 1-21. The primary objective is to offer transfer associate degree programs in liberal arts and science. Transfer agreements have been developed with most Virginia institutions, many of which guarantee automatic acceptance of Richard Bland College graduates.

Entrance Requirements: Accredited high school graduation or GED; recommended completion of 4 units English, 3 mathematics, 2 science, history and 2 foreign language; TOEFL minimum 500 for foreign students; applications evaluated on basis of high school courses, grades, extracurricualar activities, SAT or ACT scores, and personal recommendations; $20 application fee.

Costs Per Year: $1,950 in-state tuition; $5,710 out-of-state tuition.

Collegiate Environment: 712-acre campus is located about three miles south of Petersburg. Administrative offices, classrooms, laboratories, library, student activities room, cafeteria, bookstore, lounges, and faculty offices are contained in five buildings. Physical education classes and extra-curricular activities are held in the Gymnasium, on the courts and fields on the campus, at the Petersburg Y.M.C.A. and at a local riding academy. Classroom-laboratory building was completed in 1968. The college has no dormitories, but assists students in obtaining suitable boarding accommodations. The library contains 59,829 volumes, 6,500 periodicals, 2,365 microforms and 3636 audiovisual items. Financial aid is available; of the $500,000 available last year, $250,000 was granted to freshmen. 40% of the students receive financial aid. 85% of applicants meet admission criteria and are accepted. The college welcomes a geographically diverse student body. Most students are recent high school graduates; 60% are female and 30% are ethnic or racial minorities. Average class size is 26. The faculty and staff strive to provide a personal approach to the students' educational experience, and to help each student discover and attain educational and career goals. More than 90% of the graduates transfer to four-year institutions of higher learning.

Community Environment: Located only five miles south of Petersburg, the college's 712 acres of woodland, pecan grove, lawns, and gardens provide the beauty and serenity of the country. Easily accessible from Interstates 95 and 85, the college is 25 miles south of Richmond, one and a half hours from Virginia Beach or Charlottesville, and two and a half hours from Washington, D.C.

COMMONWEALTH COLLEGE   *(I-18)*
301 Centre Pointe Drive
Virginia Beach, Virginia 23462
Tel: (804) 499-7900; (800) 735-2421; Admissions: (804) 499-7900; Fax: (804) 486-7982

Description: Commonwealth College was founded in 1952 and is accredited by the Southern Association of Colleges and Schools and the Association of Independent Colleges and Schools. It operates on the quarter system and both day and evening classes are offered. The college has degree-granting authority from the State Council of Higher Education for Virginia, to grant the A.A.S. degree in 12 majors. Recent enrollment included 380 full-time students. A faculty of 7 full-time and 28 part-time provides a faculty-student ratio of 1:11. The college has its own library and is located at the intersection of Independence Boulevard and Baxter Road in Virginia Beach. 96 credit hours are required for the A.A.S. degree programs. Transfer credits are accepted, but the student must have at least a C in those courses accepted and at least 50% of the work must be completed at the college. Commonwealth College also has two branch campuses with a total additional enrollment of 725 students.

Entrance Requirements: All applicants must take and pass the CPAt. All students must have a high school diploma or have passed the GED. The College has a rolling enrollment plan. There is a $50 application fee; advanced placement, early admission, and deferred admission plans are offered.

Costs Per Year: $6,900 tuition; $4,950 room and board.

Collegiate Environment: There is housing for 40 students. Financial aid offered includes SLS, SEOG; CWS, need-based and nonneed college scholarships and grants.

Community Environment: Commonwealth College is located at the intersection of Independence Boulevard and Baxter Road in a new 28,000 square foot facility in the heart of Virginia's largest (by population) and fastest growing city. The population is over 250,000. The campus is easily accessible either by car or mass transit. (See also Virginia Wesleyan College.)

Branch Campuses: Hampton Campus: 1120 W. Mercury Blvd, Hampton, VA 23666; Richmond Campus: 8141 Hull Street Road, Richmond, VA 23235

DABNEY S. LANCASTER COMMUNITY COLLEGE   *(F-9)*
Route 60 West
Clifton Forge, Virginia 24422
Tel: (703) 862-4246

Description: Opened in September 1964, as the Clifton Forge-Covington Division of the Virginia Polytechnic Institute, the college was expanded in 1965, 1966, and 1967. All programs are controlled by the Virginia Department of Community Colleges. The two-year college is accredited by the Southern Association of Colleges and Schools and offers programs leading to the Certificate and Associate degree. The college operates on the semester system and offers a summer program. Enrollment includes 422 full-time and 1,200 part-time students. A faculty of 38 full-time and 122 part-time provides a faculty-student ratio of 1-10.

Entrance Requirements: Open enrollment policy; completion of 4 units English, 2 math, 1 science, 2 social studies; placement examinations required; non-high school graduates 18 years of age or older admitted; rolling admission, midyear admission, delayed admission, and early admission plans available.

Costs Per Year: $1,359 tuition; $4,470 out-of-state tuition; $22.50 student fees.

Collegiate Environment: The principal college structures are five new buildings containing modern laboratories, classrooms, offices and the library housing over 47,000 volumes, 500 periodicals, 4,000 microforms and 1,155 films with access to worldwide data networks. The campus has 117 acres. All qualified students applying are accepted. 60% of the freshman class returned to campus for the second year. Approximately 31% of the current student body receives some form of financial assistance.

Community Environment: A rural community, Clifton Forge is served by limited modes of transportation. Libraries, churches of major denominations, a hospital, and various civic and service organizations are part of the community. Some part-time job opportunities are available. A state park, lakes and streams provide facilities for fishing and outdoor sports; other activities include baseball, basketball, football, tennis, canoeing, backpacking and skiing.

DANVILLE COMMUNITY COLLEGE   *(J-10)*
1008 S. Main Street
Danville, Virginia 24541
Tel: (804) 797-3553

Description: The two-year institution of higher education established under a state-wide system of community colleges serves an area within driving distance of the city of Danville, Pittsylvania County, a portion of Halifax, and the city of South Boston. The state-supported comprehensive community college was opened in 1967 and is accredited by the Southern Association of Colleges and Schools. Enrollment is 1,089 full-time, 2,989 part-time, and 1,009 evening students. A faculty of 70 full-time and 60 part-time provides a faculty-student ratio of 1-31. The college operates on the semester system and offers two summer sessions.

Entrance Requirements: Open enrollment policy; non-high school graduates 18 years of age or older admitted; rolling admission plan; advanced placement available.

Costs Per Year: $41 per credit hour tuition; $142 out-of-state.

Collegiate Environment: Located on 67 acres of campus, the college offers Associate in Arts, Associate in Science, Associate in Applied Science, diplomas, and certificate programs. The library

contains 65,800 volumes, 12,000 pamphlets, 313 periodicals, 204 microforms and 1,488 sound recordings.

Community Environment: See Averett College.

EASTERN MENNONITE UNIVERSITY   *(D-11)*
1200 Park Road
Harrisonburg, Virginia 22801
Tel: (703) 432-4118; (800) 368-2665; Fax: (703) 432-4444

Description: Eastern Mennonite University offers a liberal arts education from an Anabaptist/Mennonite Christian perspective and operates under the auspices of the Mennonite Church. The institution was established in 1917 and confers the Associate, Bachelor, and Master degrees. All students study off-campus in a cross-cultural, often overseas, setting for one semester or summer term. Enrollment includes 897 full-time and 64 part-time undergraduate, and 150 graduate students. Faculty number 67 full-time and 14 part-time giving a faculty-student ratio of 1-12.

Entrance Requirements: High school graduation; 18 or more units completed including 4 English, 3 mathematics, 2 social science, 2 science, 2 foreign language recommended, 5 or more college prepatory electives; SAT 750 combined or ACT 19 composite required; rolling admission, early admission, delayed admission, and advanced placement plans available; $15 application fee.

Costs Per Year: $9,650 tuition; $3,800 room and board.

Collegiate Environment: The campus is comprised of 90 acres. A modern Campus center sits in the center of campus. The Menno Simons Historical Library and Archives of the J.B. Smith Library are housed in the college's Hartzler Library, which contains 139,000 volumes, 1,120 periodicals, and 52,170 microforms. Dormitory facilities are available for 1,111 students. The semesters begin in late August or September, and January. Scholarships are available. 92% of students receive financial aid.

Community Environment: The college is located in the heart of Virginia's beautiful Shenandoah Valley, near a national park. See James Madison University.

EASTERN SHORE COMMUNITY COLLEGE   *(F-18)*
29300 Lankford Highway
Melfa, Virginia 23410
Tel: (804) 787-5900; Admissions: (804) 787-5913; Fax: (804) 787-5919

Description: Opened originally in September 1964 as a branch campus of the University of Virginia, it became a member of the Virginia Community College System in July 1971 as Eastern Shore Community College. It is accredited by the Southern Association of Colleges and Schools. The college is committed to serving the educational needs of the local community and assumes the responsibility through a cooperative effort with local industry, business, professions, government and public and private groups; educational opportunities are provided for adults as well as college-age youth. It operates on the semester system with one summer session. Enrollment includes 235 full-time and 456 part-time students. A faculty of 30 gives a faculty-student ratio of 1-23.

Entrance Requirements: High school graduation or GED; entrance examination; open enrollment policy; early admission, early decision, deferred admission, rolling admission, and advanced placement plans available; deadline for submission of Fall applications is three full working days prior to registration.

Costs Per Year: $1,310 state resident tuition; $4,214 nonresident tuition.

Collegiate Environment: The College occupies a 115-acre site south of Melfa on U.S. Route 13. The facilities are in an air-conditioned building that includes a learning resource center housing 20, 479 hadbound volumes, classrooms, laboratories, administrative offices, a lecture hall, occupational trades areas, and a student lounge. All applicants are accepted. Scholarships are available, and 50% of students receive some form of financial aid.

Community Environment: Located midway down the Delmarva Peninsula, which separates Cheasepeake Bay from the Atlantic Ocean, Melfa has a population of 450. The area is known for vegetables, poultry, oysters, fish, sailing, and swimming.

EMORY AND HENRY COLLEGE   *(I-4)*
Emory, Virginia 24327-0947
Tel: (703) 944-4121; (800) 848-5493; Fax: (703) 944-3935

Description: The four-year liberal arts college is affiliated with the Holston Conference of the United Methodist Church. It is accredited by the Southern Association of Colleges and Schools. The college was founded in 1836 and today is a "community for intellectual integrity, religious growth, and social development." Academic cooperative plans are available for students majoring in engineering, medical technology, and forestry. Exchange programs are available for England and Korea. Study abroad is available in France, Germany, and Spain. The college operates on the early semester system and offers one summer session. Enrollment includes 850 students. A faculty of 60 full-time and 8 part-time gives a faculty-student ratio of 1-14.

Entrance Requirements: High school graduation or equivalent; recommended rank in top 50% of high school class; completion of minimum 16 units including 4 English, 3 mathematics; 2 foreign language, 2 science, and 2 social science; SAT or ACT required; non-high school graduates considered; early decision, early admission, midyear admission, rolling admission, and advanced placement plans available; Feb. 15 deadline for priority fenancial aid application; $25 application fee.

Costs Per Year: $9,990 tuition and fees; $4,502 room and board.

Collegiate Environment: The 22 buildings of the campus are located on a 150-acre site. The library houses 250,000 volumes, 80,000 government documents, 895 periodical titles, and 4,679 microforms. Freshmen, sophomores, and juniors must live on campus. Residence halls provide housing for 320 men and 297 women. Approximately 79% of applicants are accepted. Financial aid is available and 89% of students receive some form of financial assistance.

Community Environment: Emory, in the Virginia Highlands, is approximately 20 miles north of Bristol, VA, just off exit 26 of I-81. The area is known for its scenic beauty, recreational opportunities, and abundance of talented craftspeople. In Abingdon, an historic town dating from the middle 1700's, the annual Virginia Highlands Festival brings together artists and craftspeople from throughout the eastern U.S. Just twenty minutes from the college campus is Mt. Rogers National Recreational Area, featuring numerous campgrounds, mountain streams, and miles of the Appalachian Trail.

FERRUM COLLEGE   *(I-8)*
Ferrum, Virginia 24088
Tel: (703) 365-2121; (800) 868-9797; Admissions: (703) 365-4290; Fax: (703) 365-4203

Description: The church-related college operates under the auspices of the Virginia Methodist Church and is accredited aby the Southern Association of Colleges and Schools. The college was founded in 1913 and received its charter in 1914. Enrollment is 1,052 full-time and 72 part-time students. A faculty of 74 full-time and 24 part-time gives a faculty-student ratio of 1-14. The college operates on the semester system and offers two summer sessions. The college awards the Bachelor of Arts, Bachelor of Science and Bachelor of Social Work degrees.

Entrance Requirements: Graduation from high school or equivalent; SAT or ACT required; deferred admission, midyear admission, advanced placement and rolling admission plans available; $20 application fee.

Costs Per Year: $9,400 tuition; $4,200 room and board.

Collegiate Environment: The 754-acre campus has over 70 buildings. The library contains 98,761 volumes, 571 periodicals, 5,320 microforms and 2,600 recordings. Residence halls on campus provide housing for 1,067 students. Approximately 82% of students applying for admission are accepted, including midyear students. The average score of entering freshman was SAT 820 combined. A comprehensive financial assistance program is available. 94% of the students receive some form of assistance. Academic scholarships are also available.

Community Environment: Located in the Blue Ridge Mountains of Virginia, Ferrum has an ideal environment for study and cultural enrichment. The College's proximity to the mountains and lakes enables students to enjoy outdoor activities such as hiking, camping, fishing, boating, swimming and skiing. Ferrum is 35 miles south of Roanoke, Virginia, which has excellent shopping, living, cultural and recrea-

tional facilities. Bus service and air transportation are available in Roanoke.

GEORGE MASON UNIVERSITY   *(C-14)*
4400 University Drive
Fairfax, Virginia 22030-4444
Tel: (703) 993-2100; Fax: (703) 993-2392

Description: This university operates on the semester system and offers three summer sessions. It offers bachelor, master's and doctoral degree programs. Enrollment is 13,331 undergraduates and 7,763 graduate students. A faculty of 1,007 gives a faculty-student ratio of 1-20. The institution is accredited by the Southern Association of Colleges and Schools, the American Bar Association, the Accreditation Board for Engineering and Technology, the American Assembly of Collegiate Schools of Business, and the Council on Social Work Education. The university is a member of the Council of Graduate Schools, the National Council for the Accreditation of Teacher Education, and the American Chemical Society. The nursing program is accredited by the National League of Nursing. The doctoral clinical program is accredited by the American Psychological Association. The Masters of Public Administration program is accredited by the National Association of Schools of Public Affairs and Administration. Cooperative education programs are available in any major, combined with part-time study, part-time work, or via alternate semesters full-time. Overseas programs are available and must be approved by the International Programs Director, the department of major, and the appropriate Dean. Army and Air Force ROTC are available. Two special programs, Page and BASIC, replace the first 2 years of general education requirements with an innovative, interdisciplinary collection of courses.

Entrance Requirements: Graduates of accredited high schools with 16 units are eligible; units should include 4 English, 3 mathematics, 2 laboratory science, 2 foreign language, 1 social studies, and 4 academic electives; computer science and engineering majors require an additional year of math and science; SAT and 3 achievement tests required; basis for selection: SAT scores, high school class rank and academic record; the university does not limit out-of-state enrollment; $30 application fee; Apply by February 1; applicants notified of decisions on a rolling admissions basis immediately after all records received; early admission, early decision, midyear admission, and advanced placement available.

Costs Per Year: $4,044 tuition and fees; $10,800 out-of-state tuition; $4,880 room and board.

Collegiate Environment: The 583-acre campus, located in suburban Virginia, 16 miles from Washington, DC., blends the cosmopolitan atmosphere of the capital with the rural charm of the wooded region. The campus complex includes 55 academic/administrative facilities, a performing arts center, sports complex, library and 2 student unions. The university is organized into six colleges and schools, a graduate school, a Law School and an individualized study program for mature students. The library contains 532,253 volumes, 6,858 periodicals, and 1,061,450 microforms. Other libraries in the Washington, DC, area are open to students. Garden-style apartment housing for 500 students and residence halls for 3,000 students are available. The school offers men and women's intercollegiate athletics, student government (honor committee), newspaper, yearbook, drama, chorus, orchestra, wind ensemble, jazz band, ethnic and social organizations, 27 fraternities and sororities (one chapter house) as well as a counseling center (psychological and career), health services, student employment, and career planning. 51% of applicants are accepted, including midyear students. About 40% of the full-time undergraduate students receive financial aid.

Community Environment: Fairfax is a rapidly growing residential area on the western fringes of Washington, DC. Shopping facilities, commercial transportation, recreation activities, part-time employment and moderate-to-expensive rental apartments are available nearby.

GERMANNA COMMUNITY COLLEGE   *(D-14)*
Star Route Box 57
Locust Grove, Virginia 22508
Tel: (703) 423-1333

Description: The two-year institution of higher education was established in 1966 under a state wide system of community colleges. Accredited by the Southern Association of Colleges and Schools, the college offers university-parallel, technological and occupational programs leading to the Certificate and Associate degree. 2,500 students and a faculty of 88 create a student faculty ratio of 28:1. The semester system is used and four summer sessions are offered.

Entrance Requirements: Open enrollment policy; non-high school graduates 18 years of age or older admitted; rolling admission, midyear admission, early admission, early decision, and advanced placement plans available. English and math placement tests required.

Costs Per Year: $1,111 tuition; $3,600 nonresident tuition; $200 student fees.

Collegiate Environment: The college is located approximately 18 miles west of Fredericksburg on a beautiful wooded site overlooking the Rapidan River. The library houses 25,753 volumes, 1,000 pamphlets, 160 periodicals, 1,281 microforms and all other AV material-6,040. 40% of the current student body receives financial assistance. All students applying for admission are accepted, including midyear.

Community Environment: See Mary Washington College.

HAMPDEN-SYDNEY COLLEGE *(H-12)*
Hampden-Sydney, Virginia 23943
Tel: (804) 223-6120; (800) 755-0733; Fax: (804) 223-6346

Description: Affiliated with the Presbyterian Church in the United States, the four-year liberal arts college for men has been in continuous operation since 1776 and is accredited by the Southern Association of Colleges and Schools. It operates on the early semester system and offers one summer session. The BA or BS degrees and preprofessional training are offered at the nondenominational school. The college enrolls 970 men. A faculty of 65 full-time and 30 part-time gives a faculty-student ratio of 1-13. A cooperative engineering program is available with University of Virginia and Virginia Tech.

Entrance Requirements: High school graduation or equivalent; completion of 16 units including 4 English, 3 mathematics, 2 science, 2 foreign language, and 1 social science; early admission, early decision, midyear admission and advanced placement plans available; $30 application fee.

Costs Per Year: $13,878 tuition; $4,942-$5,174 room and board; $444 activity and telecommunications fees.

Collegiate Environment: The college is located on 820 acres. The library holdings include 212,000 volumes. Residence halls and fraternities house 946 men. Scholarships are available and 74% of the students receive financial assistance. 75% of the applicants are accepted. The average scores of the entering freshman class were SAT 510 verbal, 569 math, 1079 combined; ACT 25 composite.

Community Environment: Hampden-Sydney is a rural area, with the town consisting of a post office, store, and numerous homes. Nearby Farmville provides shops and hospital facilities.

HAMPTON UNIVERSITY *(H-17)*
East Queen Street
Hampton, Virginia 23668
Tel: (804) 727-5328

Description: Founded in 1868, in the days of the Reconstruction, the school listed as assets two teachers, 15 students, little money or equipment and the faith of its principles in "learning by doing" and "education for life." Until 1923 when Indian schools became more numerous, the institute educated groups sent by the government. Today, the private, coeducational, four-year university offers programs in the Schools of Liberal Arts and Education, Business, Nursing, and Pure Applied Sciences. The School of Graduate Studies offers the M.A. and M.S degree in 7 areas, and a Ph.D. in Physics. The College of Continuing Education offers degrees in 6 areas. The university operates on the semester system and offers three summer sessions. It is accredited by the Southern Association of Colleges and Schools and by respective professional organizations. Enrollment is approximately 5,000 students. A faculty of 281 full-time and 84 part-time gives a faculty-student ratio of 1-16. A cooperative engineering program is available. In general, the student's major determines the type of 'coop.' Army and Navy ROTC programs are available.

Entrance Requirements: High school graduation with rank in upper half of graduating class; completion of 17 units including 4 English, 3 mathematics, 2 science, 2 social science and 7 academic electives; SAT minimum 400V, 400M or ACT required; GRE required for graduate school; early admission, early decision, delayed admission and advanced placement plans available; $15 application fee.

Costs Per Year: $6,500 tuition; $3,000 room and board; $210 student fees.

Collegiate Environment: The campus is comprised of 47 main buildings and 75 auxiliary structures located on 200 acres of land. There is housing provided for 980 men and 1,797 women. The library has a collection of more than 280,000 volumes, 1,260 periodicals and 250,356 microforms. 80% of the current student body received some form of financial assistance. Approximately 65% of students applying for admission are accepted. Average SAT scores of the current freshmen were 400V, 400M. The school terms begin in January and August. Midyear students are accepted.

Community Environment: Hampton is the oldest English settlement still in existence in the nation; the city was settled in 1610. Hampton is the center of the fishing industry of Virginia. All modes of transportation are available. The Syms-Eaton Academy, first free school of America, and Hampton University, of which Booker T. Washington was an alumnus, are only two of the area's important sites. St. John's Church, which survived a partial burning during the Civil War, is another historic point of interest. Its most precious relic is communion silver made in 1618. The window dedicated to Pocahontas was donated by Indian students at Hampton Institute.

HOLLINS COLLEGE *(G-8)*
Roanoke, Virginia 24020
Tel: (703) 362-6000; (800) 456-9595; Admissions: (703) 362-6401;
Fax: (703) 362-6642

Description: Hollins College was founded in 1842 as Virginia's first chartered women's college. Today it is the only women's college with graduate programs in Psychology, English, Creative Writing, Liberal Studies, and Teaching. It is also the first college in the country to offer a Master of Arts in the writing and study of children's literature. It is accredited by the Southern Association of Colleges and Schools. The professors at Hollins give priority to each student's intellectual development and personal growth. It is dedicated to providing international education and study abroad opportunities, and was one of the first colleges in the nation to establish a study-abroad program. Study and community service programs are combined on four continents with coursework in seven languages to provide students with a wide range of opportunities in international studies. 40% of Hollins students study abroad. Enrollment includes 882 undergraduates (women) and 188 graduate students (men and women). A faculty of 91 gives a faculty-student ratio of 1-9. The Baccalaureate programs include majors in the humanities, social sciences, natural sciences, mathematics, and the fine arts. The college operates on the 4-1-4 system and offers one summer session for graduate programs.

Entrance Requirements: High school graduation; completion of 16 academic units including 4 English, 3 mathematics, 3 science, 3 social science, and 3 foreign language; SAT or ACT required; Achievement Tests recommended; advanced placement, early decision, midyear admission, and early admission plans available; $25 application fee.

Costs Per Year: $13,470 tuition; $5,515 room and board.

Collegiate Environment: The 475-acre campus lies two miles north of the city limits of Roanoke. There are 35 buildings including 9 residences that house 737 women, a new athletic complex, a writing center, an art gallery and an electron-microscope facility. The library contains approximately 233,000 volumes, 886 periodicals/serials, 193,000 microforms and microfiche, 41 CD-ROMs, and 3,220 records, tapes, and CDs. 54% of the student body receives financial aid. The school year begins in September, but midyear students are accepted on a limited basis. Approximately 82% of students applying for admission are accepted and 75% of the freshmen return to campus the second year. The middle 50% ranges of entering freshmen scores were SAT 440-540 verbal, 460-550 math. Scholarships are available and 54% of students receive some form of financial aid.

Community Environment: In this suburban area, the city of Roanoke is the business, cultural, and commercial center of Southwest Virginia. Air and bus transportation are available in Roanoke. Other community facilities of Roanoke are accessible to the students. There is also a symphony, etching company, ballet, theatre company, art and science museums, and a farmers' market.

INSTITUTE OF TEXTILE TECHNOLOGY *(E-12)*
2551 Ivy Road
Charlottesville, Virginia 22903
Tel: (804) 296-5511

Description: The Institute of Textile Technology is a two-year graduate school offering the Master's degree in Textile Technology and Management. It is accredited by the Southern Association of Colleges and Schools. The Institute is private, funded by selective and competitive. The Insitute provides total financial support to each student during their two-year studies. The financial support or fellowship is awarded to all students offered admission by the Insitute's Academic Committee. Approximately 18 top-ranking stuenets are awarded a $7,500 fellowship each academic year, and each graduate receives an additional $6,500 through summer internship work. Student tuition, books, and thesis research are also funded. Current 1995 graduate enrollment is 28 (twelve women and 16 men). The faculty-student ratio is approximately 1.5 faculty to each student. Institute graduates have enjoyed 100% job placement for the 50 years of the Insitute's existence.

Entrance Requirements: Bachelor's degree required; must receive a fellowship from the Committee on Academic Studies; applicants should have a degree in science, engineering or textile technology; an excellent undergraduate scholastic record; and a demonstrated interest in textiles as a career, preferably with some experience in the textile field; early decision plan available.

Costs Per Year: See above.

Collegiate Environment: The Institute is located on a 15-acre site at Charlottesville, Virginia. The buildings and grounds are situated on a landscaped knoll with a view of the Blue Ridge Mountains. The library contains a collection of 60,000 publications. About 30% of the applicants are accepted. The Merchants Laboratory contains the laboratories of the Textile Testing Section. Another laboratory can be used for specialized testing; in addition, a well-equipped room has been reserved for student research work. Specialized equipment that must be used in air-conditioned atmosphere is used in this laboratory as well as the necessary routine testing equipment. All of the freshman return for the second year of studies.

Community Environment: See University of Virginia.

J. SARGEANT REYNOLDS COMMUNITY COLLEGE
(G-14)
P.O. Box 85622
Richmond, Virginia 23285-5622
Tel: (804) 371-3270

Description: This state-supported, coeducational community college was founded in 1972 as one of 23 colleges in the statewide system of community colleges. It offers programs in occupational-technical education, liberal arts, adult education and employment training. The school employs the semester system and offers two summer sessions. There are cooperative education programs in engineering and business. Enrollment is 7,400 students; a faculty of 320 full-time and 425 part-time gives a faculty-student ratio of 1-20. It is fully accredited by the Southern Association of Colleges and Schools.

Entrance Requirements: High school graduation or GED required; open enrollment policy; advanced placement plan available; three correspondent credits or CLEP credits may be allowed toward degrees; no application fee.

Costs Per Year: $820 tuition; $2,840 out-of-state.

Collegiate Environment: The school has two campuses at the present time: one downtown on Grace Street and another on Parnum Road. The latter is located on a 105-acre site in Henrico County. There is a diversity in the composition of the student body owing to the school's philosophy to provide education for adults as well as college-age youth. The library has 20,000 books, 3,000 pamphlets, 1,400 periodicals, 50 microforms and 100 audiovisual aids. All applicants are accepted and new and transfer students are accepted at midyear. Of the students enrolled in the school, 30% receive financial aid.

Community Environment: See University of Richmond.

Branch Campuses: Downtown Richmond; Goochland County.

JAMES MADISON UNIVERSITY *(D-11)*
Harrisonburg, Virginia 22807
Tel: (540) 568-6147

Description: Founded in 1908, the institution is accredited by the Southern Association of Colleges and Schools and by several professional organizations. Enrollment includes 10,744 undergraduates and 795 graduate students. A faculty of 520 full-time and 215 part-time gives a faculty-student ratio of 1-18. The institution operates on the early semester system and offers five summer terms, three of which are overlapping. More than 100 challenging academic programs and a variety of extracurricular programs are offered. Army ROTC and an Honors Programs are available.

Entrance Requirements: High school graduation with rank in top 50% of graduating class; challenging high school curriculum that includes English, mathematics, laboratory science, foreign language, and social science; SAT or ACT required; the competitive applicant should exhibit solid achievement in five or more academic courses each year of the four years of high school; non-high school graduates may be admitted as special students; early action admission program provides for early acceptance of superior applicants in mid-January; advanced standing offered for advanced placement; $25 application fee for undergraduate and graduate programs.

Costs Per Year: $3,900 tuition; $7,994 nonresident; $4,544 room and board; $2,000 average additional expenses.

Collegiate Environment: The university library contains 352,160 volumes, 2,312 periodicals, 1,273,176 microforms. Dormitories house 1,996 men and 2,481 women. Fraternities and sororities house another 239 men and 218 women. Approximately 53% of students applying for freshman admission are accepted, including transfer students at midyear. 92% of the freshman class returned to campus for the second year. 35% of all undergraduates receive need based financial aid and 24% receive non-need based aid.

Community Environment: Located in the geographic center of Shenandoah Valley, Harrisonburg is an attractive city of 30,000 people. The Shenandoah National Park and the George Washington National Forest are here. All forms of commercial transportation are available. Community facilities include a number of churches, a library, hospital, and various civic and service organizations. Recreational facilities are available for camping, fishing, and picnicking. A snow skiing resort is also nearby.

JOHN TYLER COMMUNITY COLLEGE *(G-14)*
13101 Jefferson Davis Highway
Chester, Virginia 23831
Tel: (804) 796-4000; (800) 552-3490; Admissions: (804) 796-4150; Fax: (804) 796-4163

Description: The college, a two-year public institution of higher education established as part of a statewide system of community colleges, was opened in 1967. It is accredited by the Southern Association of Colleges and Schools. The college offers occupational technical programs, university parallel-college transfer education, general education courses, and continuing adult education. It has an Extended Learning Institute. Army ROTC is available. The college operates on the semester system and offers one summer term. Enrollment includes 1,034 full-time and 4,848 part-time students. A faculty of 67 full-time and 186 part-time gives a faculty-student ratio of 1-24.

Entrance Requirements: Open enrollment policy; non-high school graduates 18 years of age or older admitted.

Costs Per Year: $1,399.50 tuition; $4,700 out-of-state; $20 student fees.

Collegiate Environment: Located on 62 acres, the school has four major buildings. The library houses 39,917 volumes, 156 periodicals, 41,549 microforms, and 7,480 audiovisual materials. Dormitory facilities are not furnished by the college. The school year begins in August, but midyear students are accepted. 100% of students applying for admission are accepted. 20% of the current freshman class receives some form of financial aid.

Community Environment: Located 10 miles from Richmond, the state capital, and Petersburg. See also Virginia State University and University of Richmond.

Branch Campuses: JTCC-Midlothian, 1807 Huguenot Rd., Midlothian, VA 23113.

LIBERTY UNIVERSITY (G-10)
3765 Candler's Mountain Road
Lynchburg, Virginia 24506
Tel: (804) 582-2000

Description: The university was established in 1971 under the auspices of the Thomas Road Baptist Church and operates as one of the ministries of this local church. It is fully accredited by the Southern Association of Colleges and Schools. The semester system is used with two summer sessions. One and two week modulars are offered in summer and between semesters. Programs leading to the Bachelor of Science and Bachelor of Arts degrees are offered in business, government, applied science, English and modern languages, mass communications, health and physical education, religion, education, fine arts, natural science and mathematics, and social sciences. Graduate school and graduate professional programs are offered in education, business, counseling, and religion. While striving for academic excellence, Liberty is also dedicated to training Christian young people. Enrollment includes 1,640 men and 1,710 women full-time and 134 men and 119 women part-time. A faculty of 173 full-time and 20 part-time provides a faculty-student ratio of 1-22.

Entrance Requirements: High school graduation or GED; completion of 16 units; SAT or ACT; open enrollment; early decision, rolling admission, delayed admission and advanced placement; students are admitted at midyear. The deadline for submission of applications for the Fall term is August 1; $35 application fee.

Costs Per Year: $6,350 tuition; $4,380 room and board.

Collegiate Environment: College facilities include a library of 165,300 volumes, 1,346 periodicals, 402,000 microforms and 3,900 audiovisual materials. There is student housing for 1,676 men and 1,699 women on campus. Financial aid is available. 92% of students applying for admission are accepted.

Community Environment: Lynchburg, with a population of 70,000, is in the heart of Virginia on the south bank of the historic James River, with the scenic Blue Ridge Mountains as a backdrop. The city is over 200 years old and is noted for its culture, beauty and educational advantages. It is at the crossroads of U.S. highways 29 and 460 and has adequate transportation facilities by bus, railway and air.

LONGWOOD COLLEGE (H-12)
Farmville, Virginia 23901
Tel: (804) 395-2060; (800) 281-4677; Fax: (804) 395-2635

Description: Founded in 1839, Longwood is a coeducational, state-supported college that offers 100 undergraduate majors, minors, and concentrations. It also provides a graduate program leading to the Master of Arts degree in English and Master of Science degree in Education. The college is fully accredited by the Southern Association of Colleges and Schools, the National Council for the Accreditation of Teacher Education, and the Council on Social Work Education. Enrollment includes 3,254 men and women. A faculty of 153 full-time and 52 part-time provides a faculty-student ratio of 1-14. The college operates on the early semester system and offers three summer terms. Special programs include academic cooperative plans with Hampden-Sydney College, University of Virginia, Georgia Tech, Old Dominion University, the Medical College of Virginia, and Eastern Virginia Medical School.

Entrance Requirements: High school graduation or equivalent; rank in upper 50% of high school class; completion of 16 units including 4 English, 3 mathematics, 3 science, 2 foreign language, 2 physical education and 3 social science; SAT or ACT required; rolling admission and advanced placement plans available; $25 application fee.

Costs Per Year: $8,208 tuition, room and board.

Collegiate Environment: The college is located on a 54-acre campus near the Historic Farmville Business District. Housing accomodates 2,354 students. The library contains 911,119 holdings, including 300,119 volumes, 468 microfilms, 34,000 audiovisual materials, and 2,000 periodical subscriptions. 60% of the student body receives some form of financial assistance. About 1,500 different awards of federal, state and private funds are made annually. Approximately 65% of students applying for admission are accepted. The

middle 50% range of entering freshmen scores were SAT 900-1040 combined.

Community Environment: Farmville is a small, quiet residential town. Bus transportation is available. Most major religious denominations are represented, and a community hospital is 5 blocks from campus. Nearby state parks provide swimming, boating, camping and hiking facilities.

LORD FAIRFAX COMMUNITY COLLEGE (B-12)
P.O. Box 47
Middletown, Virginia 22645
Tel: (703) 869-1120

Description: The publicly supported, two-year college was opened in 1970 as a part of the state wide system of community colleges. Accredited by the Southern Association of Colleges and Schools, the college offers university parallel, technological and occupational programs. Enrollment during the Fall semester includes 1,021 men and 2,038 women. A faculty of 37 full-time and 93 part-time gives a faculty-student ratio of 1-23. The college employs the semester system with one summer session.

Entrance Requirements: Open enrollment policy; non-high school graduates 18 years of age or older admitted; rolling admission, and advanced placement programs available.

Costs Per Year: $1,495 ($45.30/credit hour) resident tuition; $4,917 ($149/credit hour) nonresident tuition.

Collegiate Environment: The campus is situated on a 101-acre tract within the northern region of the historic Shenandoah Valley. The library contains 44,000 volumes, 300 pamphlets, 287 periodicals, 12,400 microforms and 2,996 audio and video recordings. Financial aid is available and 40% of the students receive some form of assistance.

Community Environment: The area is rural and does not offer public transportation. There is medium industry and seasonal employment in the apple industry.

LYNCHBURG COLLEGE (G-10)
Lynchburg, Virginia 24501
Tel: (804) 522-8100; (800) 426-8101; Fax: (804) 522-0653

Description: The senior nonsectarian liberal arts college is related to the Christian Church-Disciples of Christ. The institution was founded in 1903 and attained senior rating by the State Board of Education in 1916. It is accredited by the Southern Association of Colleges and Schools, the National League for Nursing, the National Council for Accreditation of Teacher Education and by the American Medical Association for premedical training. It operates on the semester system and offers four summer terms. The Bachelor and Master degree programs and preprofessional studies are offered by the college. Students may enroll in various overseas programs sponsored by other universities. A 3-2 medical technology program is available with Duke. The college participates in a college consortium. The undergraduate enrollment includes 620 men and 1,026 women. There are 421 graduate students. A faculty of 154 gives an undergraduate faculty-student ratio of 1-11.

Entrance Requirements: High school graduation; completion of 16 units including 4 English, 2 mathematics, 2 science, 2 foreign language, 3 social studies, and 3 additional from those listed; SAT or ACT and three Achievement Tests for placement required; advanced placement, early admission, early decision, delayed admission and midyear admission plans available; Feb. 15 regular admission application deadline; Nov. 15 early admission application deadline; $30 application fee.

Costs Per Year: $13,980 tuition; $4,400 room and board.

Collegiate Environment: 32 buildings, predominantly of colonial design, are grouped on the 214-acre campus. The college library contains 178,490 volumes, 367,676 microforms, 771 periodicals and 23,163 audiovisual materials. Housing facilities accomodate 1,045 men and women. 80% of applicants are accepted. Financial assistance aids approximately 70% of the students.

Community Environment: Founded in 1786, Lynchburg is rich in history. It is a modern community with diversified industry in a traditional, handsome setting. Although it has a metropolitan area population of 150,000, Lynchburg maintains intimate contact with the countryside since it is very near the Blue Ridge Mountains and is in the center of perhaps the most historic of states. Washington, D.C., is less than 4 hours away, Williamsburg approximately 3, and Richmond about 2 1/2. The area provides excellent climate, convenient shopping, and many cultural opportunities. There is an active Lynchburg Fine Arts Center, and professional musical and theatrical groups visit. Some of the 7 colleges in the area also present fine arts programs.

MARY BALDWIN COLLEGE *(E-10)*
P.O. Box 1500
Staunton, Virginia 24402
Tel: (703) 887-7000; (800) 468-2262; Admissions: (703) 887-8019;
Fax: (703) 886-6634

Description: The privately supported four-year liberal arts college for women offers the Bachelor of Arts degree. The institution was founded in 1842 by Rufus W. Bailey as Augusta Female Seminary and renamed in 1895 to honor Mary Julia Baldwin, pioneer educator and principal. The college is affiliated with the Presbyterian Church and accredited by the Southern Association of Colleges and Schools. The college operates on the 2-2-1 calendar system (2 semesters and a May term). Enrollment is 950 women. A faculty of 73 provides a faculty-student ratio of 1-11. Summer courses are available in England and Japan. A semester or a year may be spent in England, France, or Italy as part of a consortium of Virginia private colleges. Army, Air Force, and Navy ROTC programs are available. Independent study and externships are available.

Entrance Requirements: Graduation from high school or GED; rank in upper 50% of high school class; completion of 4 units of English, 2 foreign language, 2 social science, 3 mathematics, and 2 science; SAT required; early decision, early admission, rolling admission, delayed admission, midyear admission and advanced placement plans are available; non-high school graduates considered; $25 application fee.

Costs Per Year: $19,100 includes tuition, room, board, and fees.

Collegiate Environment: Thirty-eight classical buildings reflect the charm of the old South on the 54-acre campus. The college library contains 176,000 volumes, 15,500 microforms, and 800 periodicals. Residence halls accommodate 650 women. 82% of applicants are accepted. 70% of the current students receive some form of financial aid. Baldwin Scholarships and Bailey Scholarships are offered.

Community Environment: Staunton, one of the oldest cities west of the Blue Ridge Mountains, originated the city manager form of government. Annual snowfall here is 16 inches. All modes of commercial transportation are available. Community facilities include a public library, YMCA, many churches, a hospital, shopping areas, and many civic and service organizations. Recreational activities include golf, tennis, skiing, horseback riding, bowling, swimming, fishing, and hunting. Part-time opportunities for work are limited. Some of the points of interest are the birthplace of Woodrow Wilson and the Old Trinity Church.

MARY WASHINGTON COLLEGE *(D-14)*
Fredricksburg, Virginia 22401-5358
Tel: (703) 654-2000; (800) 468-5614

Description: A coeducational, state-supported college of the liberal arts and sciences offering the Bachelor of Arts and Bachelor of Science degrees. One graduate degree program is available for part-time commuting students, the Master of Arts in Liberal Studies. The college is accredited by the Southern Association of Colleges and Schools and the National Association of Schools of Music. It operates on the early semester plan and offers two summer sessions. Enrollment includes 2,983 full-time and 744 part-time undergraduates and 55 graduate students. A faculty of 168 full-time and 65 part-time provides a faculty-student ratio of 1-17. Nearly 90% of the faculty holds terminal degrees in their teaching fields.

Entrance Requirements: High school graduation or equivalent; completion of at least 16 academic units including 4 English, 4 mathematics, 3-4 science, 3-4 foreign language, and 3-4 social science, and 3 academic electives; SAT I and SAT II or ACT required; Early admission, early decision, midyear admission and advanced placement plans available. $25 application fee.

Costs Per Year: $2,026 tuition; $6,490 out-of-state tuition; $4,942 board and room; $1,180 comprehensive fees.

Collegiate Environment: Located on 176 acres, the college consists of 34 major buildings. The library houses 336,000 volumes and pamphlets, 1,630 periodicals, 205,623 microforms and 1,590 sound recordings. Housing accommodates 2,110 students. 51% of students applying for admission to the college are accepted including midyear students. The middle 50% ranges of entering freshmen scores were SAT 480-590 verbal, 520-620 math. Financial assistance aids 55% of the students.

Community Environment: Fredericksburg is located an hour south of Washington, DC and an hour north of Richmond, in one of the fastest growing regions in the state. One of the most historic cities in the country, Fredericksburg was the childhood home of George Washington and was the site of several major battles of the Civil War. Today the surrounding metropolitan population reaches upwards of 150,000 people yet still maintains the charm of a small town. The 40-block Historic District is located within easy walking distance of the campus and includes fine shopping, restaurants, movie theaters as well as historic attractions. Located on I-95, Fredericksburg offers access to both Washington and Richmond by Amtrak, Greyhound/Trailways bus lines, and transportation service to National Airport in Washington and Richmond International. Fredericksburg is on the regularly scheduled commuter rail to Washington.

MARYMOUNT UNIVERSITY *(C-15)*
2807 North Glebe Road
Arlington, Virginia 22207
Tel: (703) 284-1500; (800) 548-7638; Fax: (703) 522-0349

Description: The suburban Washington university is a coeducational liberal arts institution with a focus on career preparation. An independent university founded in 1950 and associated with the Roman Catholic Church, Marymount offers programs in the liberal and applied arts, business, education, human services, sciences, and nursing. It is accredited by the Southern Association of Colleges and Schools and several professional organizations. Undergraduate enrollment is 338 men and 1,748 women full-time, and 801 students part-time. There are 2,061 graduate students. An undergraduate faculty of 115 full-time and 218 part-time gives a faculty-student ratio of 1-14. The private institution operates on the semester system and offers 2 summer terms. Programs of study lead to the Associate, Baccalaureate and Master degrees. Army ROTC is available.

Entrance Requirements: High school graduation; completion of 16 units; recommended distribution: 4 English, 2 mathematics, 1 science, and 2 social science; SAT or ACT required; delayed admission, rolling admission, midyear admission and advanced placement plans available. $30 application fee.

Costs Per Year: $11,390 tuition; $5,280 room and board.

Collegiate Environment: Seven major buildings are housed on the 19-acre campus. Two satellite campuses have classrooms, offices, parking, and the Academic Computer Center. The college library contains 107,656 volumes, 942 current periodicals, 158,931 microforms, and 966 audiovisual materials. Dormitories house 650 men and women. The school year begins in September, but midyear students are accepted. 70% of undergraduate applicants are accepted. 254 scholarships are available, including 45 for freshmen. 84% of full-time undergraduates receive financial aid.

Community Environment: While Marymount's Campus is in a suburban setting, the cultural and educational advantages of Washington are only minutes away. The government complex, the Smithsonian Institution, the National Archives, the National Gallery of Art and the John F. Kennedy Center for the Performing Arts are only a few of the Washington resources available to students. Union Station and the National Airport are easily accessible, and the Public Metro System goes directly to campus and connects the university with the entire Washington area. Activities involve students from American University, Georgetown University, the U.S. Naval Academy, and other schools in the metropolitan area.

MOUNTAIN EMPIRE COMMUNITY COLLEGE *(I-2)*
Drawer 700
Big Stone Gap, Virginia 24251
Tel: (703) 523-2400; Admissions: (703) 523-2400 X 209; Fax: (703) 523-2400

Description: The publicly supported, coeducational community college was founded in 1972, and is accredited by the Southern Association of Colleges and Schools. The school grants and Associate degree and offers continuing education courses. It operates on the semester system and offers three summer sessions. Enrollment includes 1,200 full-time and 1,800 part-time students. A faculty of 138 gives a faculty-student ratio of 1-22.

Entrance Requirements: High school graduate or equivalent. Open enrollment. Early admission, early decision, rolling admission, delayed admission, and advanced placement.

Costs Per Year: $1,680 tuition; $5,724 tuition for out-of-state residents.

Collegiate Environment: The campus is located in rural Big Stone Gap in the Cumberland Mountains providing ample recreational facilities. 30 scholarships are available are available and 82% of the student body receives some form of financial aid.

Community Environment: Big Stone Gap is a rural community in the southwest corner of Virginia, situated in the Cumberland Mountains. It has a population of 4,847. Many state parks and recreational areas are within an easy drive of the campus. Kingsport, Tennessee is approximately 30 miles south of the campus.

NATIONAL BUSINESS COLLEGE, MAIN BRANCH   *(H-8)*
1813 East Main Street
Salem, Virginia 24153
Tel: (703) 986-1800; (800) 666-6221

Description: Opened in 1886 by J.A. Timmer, the private business college operates on the quarter system with one summer session. It offers an associate degree, a Bachelor's degree in Management and Accounting, and a one-year diploma program. The school is accredited as a Senior College of Business by the Accrediting Council for Independent Colleges and Schools. Enrollment is 1,400 students. A faculty of 109 gives a faculty-student ratio of 1-12.

Entrance Requirements: High school graduation; $20 refundable application fee.

Costs Per Year: $3,924 tuition; $2,385 room and board.

Collegiate Environment: One building in downtown Salem makes up the main branch college. The library contains 40,930 volumes. A dormitory accomodates 72 men and women at the Roanoke campus. Approximately 80% of the freshman class receives financial assistance. Almost 90% of students applying meet the requirements and are accepted.

Community Environment: See Roanoke College.

Branch Campuses: 100 Logan St, Bluefield, VA 24605; 300A Piedmont Ave., Bristol, VA 24201; 1819 Emmet St., Charlottesville, VA 22903; 734 Main St., Danville, VA 24541; 51 B Burgess Rd., Harrisonburg, VA 22801; 104 Candlewood Ct., Lynchburg, VA 24502; 10 Church St., Martinsville, VA 24114; 1813 E. Main St., Salem, VA 24153.

NEW RIVER COMMUNITY COLLEGE   *(H-7)*
P.O. Box 1127
Dublin, Virginia 24084
Tel: (703) 674-3600; Fax: (703) 674-3642

Description: Founded in 1959 as a vocational technical school, the college came into being through the foresight and determination of members of the local school boards of Montgomery and Pulaski Counties and the City of Radford. In 1969 the college became a part of the state-wide system of Community Colleges in Virginia and offers occupational technical education programs, university parallel-college transfer education, general education, continuing adult education, and specialized training programs. Enrollment includes 1,643 full-time and 1,997 part-time students. A faculty of 62 full-time and 106 part-time provides a faculty-student ratio of 1-26. The college is accredited by the Southern Association of Colleges and Schools and operates on the semester system with two summer sessions.

Entrance Requirements: Open enrollment policy; non high school graduates 18 years of age or older admitted; rolling admission, early admission, early decision and advanced placement plans are available.

Costs Per Year: $1,404 ($45.30/credit hour) tuition; $4,619 ($149/credit hour) nonresident tuition; $24 student fees.

Collegiate Environment: The three buildings located on 100 acres comprise the school. The library contains 23,299 volumes, 238 periodical titles, 25,300 microforms and 572 audiovisual materials. All students applying for admission are accepted including midyear and 40% return for the second year on campus. Financial assistance is available on campus, and 35% of the current student body received financial assistance. There are 70 scholarships available.

Community Environment: See Radford University.

NORTHERN VIRGINIA COMMUNITY COLLEGE   *(B-16)*
4001 Wakefield Chapel Road
Annandale, Virginia 22021
Tel: (703) 323-3000

Description: The college is a multi-campus two-year institution of higher education established under a statewide system of Community Colleges in Virginia serving the counties of Arlington, Fairfax, Loudoun, Prince William and the cities of Alexandria, Falls Church, Fairfax, Manassar and Manassar Park. The college consists of five campuses located at Alexandria, Loudoun, Manassas, Annandale, and Woodbridge. It is accredited by the Southern Association of Colleges and Schools and by several professional organizations. It operates on the semester system with one summer session. The college offers the following degrees or certificates for students who successfully complete approved programs: Associate in Arts, Associate in Science, and Associate in Applied Science degrees. Cooperative education courses are offered in many subjects. Enrollment is 17,372 full-time and 17,823 part-time. A full-time equivalent faculty of 774 gives a faculty-student ratio of 1-45.

Entrance Requirements: High school graduation or equivalent. No application fee.

Costs Per Year: $715 tuition; $3,564 nonresident tuition.

Collegiate Environment: Almost all of the students applying for admission are accepted including midyear students. 10% of students receive financial aid. The library contains 205,338 volumes, 47,881 periodical subscriptions, 28,625 microforms and 118,600 audio visual materials.

Community Environment: Northern Virginia Community College is a five campus college located in the suburban communities of Northern Virginia, just outside Washington, D.C. The Northern Virginia region is rapidly growing, provides excellent job opportunities and has high quality public schools and community services. Part-time job opportunities are excellent for students and graduates of the occupational and technical programs and career placements attractive. Students seeking transfer to a university to earn a Bachelor's degree can enroll in appropriate programs that parallel most university programs.

Branch Campuses: 3001 N. Beauregard St., Alexandria, VA 22311; 1000 Harry Flood Byrd Highway, Sterling, VA 22170; 6901 Sudley Road, Manassas, VA 22110; 15200 Neabsco Mills Road, Woodbridge, VA 22191; 8333 Little River Turnpike, Annandale, VA 22003.

OLD DOMINION UNIVERSITY   *(I-17)*
Hampton Boulevard
Norfolk, Virginia 23508
Tel: (804) 683-3637; (800) 348-7926; Admissions: (804) 683-3637; Fax: (804) 683-5357

Description: The university was established in 1930 as a branch of the College of William and Mary. In 1962, the university gained its independence from the College of William and Mary by state legislative action. It is accredited by the Southern Association of Colleges and Secondary Schools. The university is organized into six colleges: the College of Arts and Letters, Business and Public Administration, Engineering and Technology, Health Sciences, Sciences and the Darden College of Education. It operates on the semester system and offers seven summer sessions.

Entrance Requirements: High school graduation; completion of 16 academic subjects; minimum 2.0 GPA; SAT minimum 425V, 425M required; non-high school graduates considered; rolling admission, early admission, early decision, midyear admission and advanced placement plans available; $30 application fee.

Costs Per Year: $3,990 resident tuition; $10,350 nonresident; $4,500 room and board. Graduate: $170/cr, resident; $452/cr nonresident.

Collegiate Environment: There are 77 buildings on the 162-acre campus. There are 3 dormitories and 2 apartment complexes housing 2,260 students on the campus. Library holdings number 1,600,000 volumes. Approximately 67% of the freshmen applying for admission are accepted including midyear students and 80% of the freshmen return for the sophomore year. Average SAT score for incoming freshmen is 970; the average GPA is 2.7. Financial aid and scholarships are available and 57% of the current student body receives some form of financial assistance.

Community Environment: See Virginia Wesleyan College.

PATRICK HENRY COMMUNITY COLLEGE   *(I-9)*
P.O. Box 5311
Martinsville, Virginia 24115-5311
Tel: (703) 638-8777

Description: The state-supported two-year college opened in 1962 as a branch of the University of Virginia. In 1971 the college joined the Community College System and became one of the 23 comprehensive community colleges serving the Commonwealth of Virginia. It offers a cooperative education program. It operates on the semester system and offers two summer sessions. Enrollment is 215 men and 350 women full-time and 670 men and 1,200 women part-time. A faculty of 96 gives a faculty-student ratio of 1-25. It is accredited by the Southern Association of Colleges and Schools.

Entrance Requirements: High school graduation or equivalent; open enrollment policy; completion of 4 units of English 3 math, 1 science, 1 social science, entrance exam required; non high school graduates considered; early admission, early decision, delayed admission and advanced placement plans; No application fee.

Costs Per Year: $894 tuition; $3,564 out-of-state tuition; $3 student fees.

Collegiate Environment: The college began operation in an elementary school in Martinsville while land was purchased and construction began. The library contains 32,000 volumes, 250 pamphlets, 420 periodicals, 5200 microforms, 31,150 government documents and 292 sound recordings. All of the students applying for admission are accepted, including midyear students. Financial aid assists all eligible applicants. Approximately 25% of the student body receives financial assistance. Of 25 scholarships offered, 21 are for freshmen.

Community Environment: Martinsville is an important textile and furniture market as well as an industrial city with a wide range of products. It provides all forms of commercial transportation. Job opportunities are excellent and shopping is good. Philpott Reservoir, about 19 miles northwest of Martinsville, is a popular spot for fishing, boating, water skiing, and swimming. Other facilities within the city provide for swimming, baseball, and football.

PAUL D. CAMP COMMUNITY COLLEGE   *(I-15)*
P.O. Box 737
100 North College Drive
Franklin, Virginia 23851
Tel: (804) 569-6700; Fax: (804) 569-6795

Description: The publicly supported two-year college was established in 1971 under a statewide system of community colleges. The college serves the counties of Isle of Wight and Southampton and the cities of Franklin and Suffolk. The college operates on the semster system and offers one summer session. Programs offered include occupational-technical, college transfer, and certificate programs. Continuing education, special training, and developmental programs are also available. Enrollment is 1,600 men and women. The faculty-student ratio is 1-17. The college is accredited by the Southern Association of Colleges and Schools, and approved by the State Approving Agency for the payment of veterans' benefits.

Entrance Requirements: Open enrollment policy; high school graduates 18 years of age or older admitted; rolling admission plan available.

Costs Per Year: $1,359 tuition; $4,470 nonresident.

Collegiate Environment: All students applying for admission that meet the requirements are accepted including students at midyear.

About 40% of the freshman class return for the sophomore year. Average high school standing of the freshman class, top 50%; 10% in the top quarter, 20% in the second quarter, 20% in the third quarter; 50% in the bottom quarter. The library houses 22,000 volumes, 310 periodicals, 1,550 recordings and 772 microforms. 46% of the current student body receives financial assistance.

Community Environment: The college service area includes the counties of Isle of Wight and Southampton and the cities of Franklin and Suffolk. The college has two campuses located in Franklin and in Suffolk. The college is in a rural setting. The population of its service area is 96,000.

Branch Campuses: Suffolk Campus, 271 Kenyon Road, Suffolk, VA, 23434, phone: (804) 925-2283; fax: (804) 925-2440; Smithfield Center, 253 James Street, Smithfield, VA, 23430, phone: (804) 357-5782.

PIEDMONT VIRGINIA COMMUNITY COLLEGE   *(E-12)*
Route 6, Box 1
Charlottesville, Virginia 22901
Tel: (804) 977-3900

Description: The college is a two-year, coeducational, publicly supported school. It was founded in 1972 as part of the statewide system of community colleges. The college is accredited by the Southern Association of Colleges and Schools and by the National League for Nursing. Offering technological, business and allied health programs, as well as liberal arts, the college is primarily intended to meet the educational needs of neighboring counties. The school operates on a semester system with two summer sessions. It awards a Certificate and an Associate degree. Cooperative education programs are encouraged for all technical programs, and available for selected liberal arts transfer students. Enrollment is 800 full-time and 3,403 part-time students. A faculty of 63 full-time and 192 part-time gives a faculty-student ratio of 1-16.

Entrance Requirements: High school graduation or GED required; open enrollment; rolling admissions plans; credit may be obtained from correspondence courses and examination, such as CLEP; no application fee.

Costs Per Year: $1,312 tuition; $4,544 nonresident; $10 student fees.

Collegiate Environment: The college occupies a 120-acre site in the beautiful foothill country adjacent to Monticello. In addition to the academic program, the college provides intramural sports and recreational services. Its library has 28,000 volumes, 300 pamphlets, 246 periodicals and 122 microforms, and 5,389 audiovisual materials. 25% of students receive financial assistance.

Community Environment: Charlottesville is situated in the foothills of the Blue Ridge Mountains. The area has many old homes and estates. Albemarle County is renown for its horses, dogs and fruit orchards. Outdoor activities available include: golf, tennis, hunting, fishing and hiking. Points of interest are the Lewis and Clark Memorial, Monticello, and the University of Virginia. Commercial transportation and part-time employment are available.

PRESBYTERIAN SCHOOL OF CHRISTIAN EDUCATION
(G-14)
1205 Palmyra Avenue
Richmond, Virginia 23227
Tel: (804) 254-8041; (800) 678-7723; Fax: (804) 254-8060

Description: The privately supported church-related graduate school was founded in 1914 for the purpose of preparing men and women for service in church vocations with emphasis upon the educational work of the church. The academic year for the school is as follows: 12-week fall term, two 3-week winter terms, and a 12-week spring term. A summer program is offered which consists of a combination of at-home and two week on campus work. Enrollment includes 160 students. A faculty of 11 full-time and 2 part-time gives a faculty-student ratio of 1-13. Affiliated with the Presbyterian Church, U.S., the school is accredited by the Southern Association of Colleges and Schools and by the Association of Theological Schools of the U.S. and Canada. Union Theological Seminary in Virginia and the Baptist Theological Seminary at Richmond are located across the street from the PSCE campus. These two seminaries, in addition to the School of Theology of Virginia Union University, form a consortium with the Presbyterian School of Christian Education. Classes of each institution are open to students of the others, and there is a frequent interchange of professors among the four schools.

Entrance Requirements: Bachelor's degree or its equivalent; $35 application fee; rolling admission and midyear plans available.

Costs Per Year: $5,200 tuition for the M.A. program; $5,700 tuition for Ed.D. program; $3,615 room and board.

Collegiate Environment: The seven-acre campus is situated on two city blocks in the city of Richmond. The library is located on the campus of Union Theological Seminary, housing a collection of 239,610 volumes, 1,500 periodicals, 41,176 microforms and 40,630 media resources. Dormitory facilities provide living accommodations for 48 men and 70 women, and there are 12 apartments for married students. Institutional grants, loans and work study are available. 60% of the current student body receives financial assistance.

Community Environment: See University of Richmond.

PROTESTANT EPISCOPAL THEOLOGICAL SEMINARY IN VIRGINIA   *(C-15)*
Alexandria, Virginia 22304
Tel: (703) 370-6600

Description: A diversity of backgrounds is represented in the student body of the seminary. Affiliated with the Protestant Episcopal Church, the school was founded in 1823. It is accredited by the Association of Theological Schools in the U.S. and Canada and awards the Master in Divinity, Master in Theological Studies and Doctor of Ministry degrees. It employs the semester system. The school operates in small groups for six-week terms in fall, winter, and spring, includes short term conferences, and an eight-day summer refresher. Approximately one-third of the students are women. This graduate school enrolls approximately 83 men, 58 women full-time and 41 men and 17 women part-time. A faculty of 27 full-time and 23 part-time provides a faculty-student ratio of 1:7. The center for continuing education was begun in 1967 as a year-round advanced training school for experienced clergy of all Christian traditions. The Center for the Ministry of Teaching was established for the purpose of promoting excellence in christian education.

Entrance Requirements: Bachelor's degree; GRE required; personal interview required.

Costs Per Year: $5,100 tuition; $3,675 room and board; $60 student fees.

Collegiate Environment: The campus expresses something of the traditional spirit of the seminary in the arrangement of its buildings; the chapel and 14 other buildings including the library form a widely spaced quadrangle in the center of the campus. Circling these buildings in a great arc are a dozen or more faculty homes, easily accessible to all students. The library houses a collection of over 110,000 volumes. Dormitory facilities provide living accommodations for men and women.

Community Environment: Alexandria, in the Washington, D.C. metropolitan area, is a city in its own right and was founded in 1749. The city was named for John Alexander; during the Revolutionary period it was one of the principal colonial ports as well as a trade, social, and political center. Alexandria was also the home of "Light Horse Harry" Lee. The Old Town area provides fine shops and a very pleasant stroll into another century where the shady streets, some of which are cobblestoned, are closely flanked by 18th century houses. Some of the other historical points of interest are the Carlyle House, Gadsby's Tavern, Stabler-Leadbeater Apothecary Shop, Christ Church, Presbyterian Meetinghouse, Woodlawn, Gunston Hall, and Mount Vernon.

RADFORD UNIVERSITY   *(H-7)*
P.O. Box 5430
Radford, Virginia 24142
Tel: (703) 831-5000; (800) 890-4265; Admissions: (703) 831-5371;
Fax: (703) 831-5138

Description: This state-supported, coeducational instituion was founded in 1910 and is accredited by the Southern Association of Colleges and Schools. The curriculum has a strong international component in recognition of the need to prepare tomorrow'd workforce for the global marketplace they will encounter. A nationally recognized Honors Program and special programs like Writing Across the Curriculum and the Oral Communications Program prepare students to be lifelong learners. Radford offers more than 140 undergraduate and graduate degrees. Students from throughout the Commonwealth of Virginia, from 41 other states and from 60 foreign countries, are enrolled in six colleges: Arts and Sciences, Business and Economics, Education and Human Development, Waldron College of Nursing and Health Services, Visual and Performing Arts and the Graduate College. Faculty members are available to students not only during office hours, but for informal discussions and at extracurricular activities. All students have access to the Internet. The university awards Bachelor of Arts, Bachelor of Science, Bachelor of Fine Arts, Bachelor of Business Administration, Bachelor of Music Therapy, Master of Science, Master of Arts and educational specialists degrees. Army ROTC is available. Enrollment includes 7,679 full-time and 467 part-time undergraduates and 959 graduate students. A faculty of 406 full-time and 139 part-time provides a faculty-student ratio of 1-16.

Entrance Requirements: High School graduation with rank in the upper half of graduating class; completion of 17 units including 4 English, 2 mathematics, 2 science, 2 social studies, 1 history, and 6 electives; SAT I or ACT required; rolling admission and advanced placement plans available; $15 application fee.

Costs Per Year: $3,034 state-resident tuition and fees; $7,206 out-of-state; $4,210 room and board.

Collegiate Environment: The 175-acre campus is located in a residential section of the city of Radford, and is within walking distance of the central business district of the city. In addition to the main campus, the university foundation owns a 376-acre tract of land known as Selu Conservancy which is available for academic and recreational use. The recently expanded library houses a collection of 303,654 volumes, 3,248 periodicals, 1,265,124 microforms and 125,000 audiovisual materials. Dormitories accommodate 3,000 students. Complete athletic and recreational facilities include two gymnasiums, two indoor swimming pools, racquetball courts, playing fields, outdooor tennis courts, indoor and outdoor jogging tracks and weight rooms. Radford participates in Division I intercollegiate sports in basketball, baseball, soccer, volleyball, tennis, cross country, gymnastics, golf, lacrosse, field hockey and softball. Also featured are two modern perfomance/recital halls, two student centers, campus radio station WVRU, and a cable television channel. 85% of applicants are accepted. Scholarships are available and 55% of students receive some form of financial aid.

Community Environment: Located on the banks of the scenic New River in the foothills of the beautiful Blue Ridge Mountains, the city of Radford, Virginia (population 16,000), is 45 miles southwest of Roanoke. First settled in 1756, the city features a number of churches, a public library, hospital, and many civic and service organizations. The city is clean and the weather is moderate. Outdoor sports enthusiasts can enjoy nearby Claytor Lake, the New River, the Appalachian Trail and many other streams, lakes and trails in close proximity.

RANDOLPH-MACON COLLEGE   *(F-14)*
Ashland, Virginia 23005
Tel: (804) 752-7305; (800) 888-1762; Admissions: (804) 752-7305;
Fax: (804) 752-4707

Description: This coeducational four-year college was founded in 1830 and is historically affiliated with the Methodist Church. The purpose of Randolph-Macon education is to develop the mind and character of its students. They are challenged to communicate effectively, to think analytically and critically, to experience and appreciate the creative process, to develop qualities of leadership, and to synthesize what they know with who they are. The college operates on the 4-1-4 system, which consists of three terms: two of fourteen weeks and a one-month term in January. It offers one summer session. It is accredited by the Southern Association of Colleges and Secondary Schools, and offers Bachelor of Arts and Bachelor of Science degrees. Enrollment is 1,074 full-time and 19 part-time students. A faculty of 96 full-time and 61 part-time gives a faculty-student ratio of 1-11.

Entrance Requirements: Successful completion of secondary school course of study; completion of at least 16 units including 4 English, 3 mathematics, 2 foreign language, 2 laboratory science and 2 social science; SAT required; $30 application fee; delayed admission, early decision and advanced placement programs available.

Costs Per Year: $14,630 tuition; $3,835 room and board; $325 student activity fee; $400 estimated book cost.

Collegiate Environment: The campus and grounds contain about 100 acres amid a fine grove of oaks and maples. The new library contains 150,000 volumes and 919 periodicals. Residence halls accomodate 950 students. Fraternity and sorority houses provide additional accomodations for 100 students. The college does not offer graduate programs, but it does offer 29 undergraduate programs that prepare students for immediate employment as well as for advanced study in medicine, dentistry, law, education, and the ministry. Cooperative programs are also available in forestry, accounting and engineering. Randolph-Macon also offers a state-approved teachers education program that leads to certification for elementary and secondary teaching. The middle 50% of enrolled freshmen scores are: SAT 420-520 Verbal, 480-570 Math. 79% of the students receive financial aid.

Community Environment: Ashland is a suburban area 15 miles from Richmond, and 90 miles south of Washington DC. Community facilities include a public library, six churches, 2 medical centers, and a number of civic and service organizations. Facilities at the college provide for most sports activities. The college located here is, by date of charter, one of the oldest of the Methodist colleges in the United States.

RANDOLPH-MACON WOMAN'S COLLEGE   *(G-10)*
2500 Rivermont Avenue
Lynchburg, Virginia 24503
Tel: (804) 947-8100; (800) 745-7692; Fax: (804) 947-8138

Description: This four-year liberal arts college seeks to provide an education in accordance with the highest academic standards in the humanistic tradition. While affiliated with the Methodist Church and standing in the liberal Christian tradition, it maintains a nonsectarian, ecumenical attitude. Founded in 1891, this was the first college for women admitted to membership in the Southern Association of Colleges and Schools. The college operates on the semester system and offers one summer session. The college confers the degree of Bachelor of Arts. Students may create their own interdisciplinary major with the permission of the Dean and the department chair involved. Enrollment is 616 full-time and 60 part-time students. A faculty of 67 full-time and 20 part-time gives a faculty-student ratio of 1-9. The college provides individual counseling for any able student who is strongly motivated to extend her academic experience beyond the offerings on this campus. Qualified students are permitted to do the work of the junior year at the University of Reading, England, under approved conditions. Each year 30 students spend their junior year in the college's program at The University of Reading in England. The American School of Classical Studies at Athens provides the opportunity to study classical antiquities at first hand. The Near Eastern Archaeological Seminar, sponsored by the Institute for Mediterranean Studies, offers students three weeks of actual archaeological field experience at an ancient site, in addition to courses in archaeology of Palestine and the history of Palestine. Army ROTC is available. Internships are available.

Entrance Requirements: High school graduation or equivalent with rank in upper 30% of graduating class; completion of 16 units including 4 English, 3-4 foreign language, 3 mathematics, 2 science and 2 social studies, and 1 or 2 electives; SAT or ACT required; $25 application fee; early admission, early decision, delayed admission and advanced placement plans available.

Costs Per Year: $12,450 tuition; $5,500 room and board; $120 student fees.

Collegiate Environment: The campus of more than 100 acres is located in a residential section and extends from Rivermont Avenue to the bluffs overlooking the James River. Most of the main buildings are connected by enclosed corridors. The library contains more than 162,000 volumes, 852 periodicals, and 252 microforms. Dormitory facilities provide living accommodations for 626 women. Approximately 75% of the applicants are accepted, including midyear students. About 80% of the previous freshman class returned to the college for the second year. There is financial aid available for economically disadvantaged students, and about 84% of a recent class received some form of financial assistance. 30 academic honor scholarships are also offered, 25 of which are for freshmen; financial need is not a factor in selection. Average SAT scores for freshmen were 525V and 520M. About 30% of the senior class continued on to graduate school.

Community Environment: See Lynchburg College.

RAPPAHANNOCK COMMUNITY COLLEGE   *(F-16)*
P.O. Box 287
Glenns, Virginia 23149
Tel: (804) 758-5324

Description: This publicly-supported, two-year multicampus college opened in 1971 under the statewide system of community colleges. The Warsaw Campus is located in Warsaw, Va. Accredited by the Southern Association of Colleges and Schools, the college offers university parallel, technological and occupational programs. It operates on the semester system with one summer session. Enrollment includes 1,443 students.

Entrance Requirements: Open enrollment policy; non-high school graduates 18 years of age or older admitted; advanced placement and rolling admission plans available.

Costs Per Year: $906 tuition; $1,327 nonresident tuition.

Collegiate Environment: The campus occupies a 100-acre site. The libraries house 46,000 volumes, 1,576 pamphlets, 85 periodicals, 102 microforms and 1,900 recordings. All students applying for admission are accepted including midyear. Financial aid is available.

Community Environment: Glenns is centrally located in the Rappahannock River Tidewaters serving a 13-county region.

ROANOKE COLLEGE   *(H-8)*
221 College Lane
Salem, Virginia 24153
Tel: (504) 375-2270; (800) 388-2276; Admissions: (504) 375-2270; Fax: (504) 375-2267

Description: This independent, liberal arts college was founded in 1842. It is related to the Evangelical Lutheran Church in America, is accredited by the Southern Association of Colleges and Secondary Schools and is approved by the American Chemical Society. The college operates on the modified semester system, which offers two summer sessions and a May travel option. The college offers three degrees: Bachelor of Arts, Bachelor of Science, and the Bachelor of Business Administration. Enrollment includes 578 men, 894 women full-time and 98 men and 124 women part-time. A faculty of 100 full-time and 60 part-time members gives a faculty-student ratio of 1-14.

Entrance Requirements: High school graduation with rank in upper half of graduating class; completion of 16 units including 4 English, 3 mathematics, 2 foreign language, 2 science and 3 social science; SAT required; $30 application fee; Early admission, early decision, and advanced placement plans available.

Costs Per Year: $14,100 tuition and student fees, $4,640 room and board.

Collegiate Environment: The 68-acre campus lies in the center of the town of Salem. The library contains 171,000 volumes, periodicals, microforms and sound recordings. Dormitories house 400 men and 550 women. Housing is guaranteed for 4 years. Approximately 60% of the students applying for admission are accepted, including midyear students. Close to 80% receive financial aid. An off-campus study abroad program is available.

Community Environment: Salem is located in the heart of the Roanoke Valley between the Blue Ridge Mountains to the east, and the Allegheny Mountains to the west. Many national manufacturing companies contribute to the diversified industry of Salem. Plane and bus transportation are available. Part-time employment opportunities are excellent. The Dixie Caverns subterranean wonderland is seven miles away. State parks, the Blue Ridge Parkway & the Appalacian Trail provide outdoor activities, and facilities within the city provide for tennis, skating, and golf.

SAINT PAUL'S COLLEGE   *(I-13)*
406 Winsor Ave.
Lawrenceville, Virginia 23868
Tel: (804) 848-3111; (800) 678-7071; Fax: (804) 848-0403

Description: Founded in 1888, this private institution is accredited by the Virginia State Board of Education and by the Southern Association of Colleges and Schools. The college regards its educational task as a cooperative quest for complete Christian living. It operates on the semester system and offers two summer sessions. The college offers the degrees of Bachelor of Arts, Bachelor of Science and the

Bachelor of Science in Education. Enrollment is 654 full-time and 47 part-time students. A full-time faculty of 43 gives a faculty-student ratio of 1-16.

Entrance Requirements: High school graduation or equivalent; completion of 16 units including 4 English, 2 mathematics, 2 science, 2 social science and 6 electives, the two units in mathematics should be algebra and geometry; SAT required; $15 application fee; advanced standing program.

Costs Per Year: $4,636 tuition; $3,380 room and board.

Collegiate Environment: The 75-acre campus, with its rolling hills, is beautifully landscaped with lawns, walks, shrubbery and trees. The library, one of 11 buildings, contains 100,000 volumes and 275 periodicals. Dormitory facilities provide living accommodations for 270 men and 252 women. Approximately 85% of the students applying for admission are accepted, including midyear students.

Community Environment: Lawrenceville is an urban area with a temperate climate. Train and bus transportation are convenient. Community facilities include a public library, six churches, clinic, public health center, and a number of the civic and service organizations. Part-time employment opportunities are limited.

SHENANDOAH UNIVERSITY   *(B-12)*
1460 University Drive
Winchester, Virginia 22601
Tel: (703) 665-4581

Description: Shenandoah is a United Methodist related four-year college and conservatory (music, theater, and dance) located 70 miles west of Washington, D.C. in the historic Shenandoah Valley. Shenandoah has offered a distinguished program since 1875, and is accredited by the Southern Association of Colleges and Schools. It is also a member of the National Association of Schools of Music. The college operates on the semester system and offers two summer terms. Founded at Dayton, Virginia, Shenandoah moved to Winchester in 1960. Shenandoah offers both two year and four year programs in addition to the Master of Business Administration, Master of Music, the Master of Music Education, and Master of Education degree. Enrollment includes 1,213 full-time and 439 part-time students with 458 graduate students. A full-time faculty of 103 and part-time faculty of 114 gives a faculty student ratio of 10:1.

Entrance Requirements: High school graduation or equivalent; completion of 15 units including 4 English, 3 mathematics, 2 science, 2 foreign language, and 2 social studies; SAT with minimum scores of 425 verbal and 425 math, or ACT required; GRE required for graduate programs; non-high school graduates considered; $20 application fee, early admission, delayed admission, advanced placement and rolling admission plans available. An audition in one area of music, dance, or theatre is required for entrance to those Respective Programs.

Costs Per Year: $16,270 resident full-time undergraduate students; $11,470 full-time undergraduate commuting students.

Collegiate Environment: Twelve modern buildings on the college's 60-acre campus provide facilities for the school's many programs and activities. The 700-seat Armstrong Auditorium and Goodson Chapel/Recital Hall provide space for concerts, performances and religious services as well as practice rooms, studios and offices. Other buildings include the Howe Library, with a collection of 87,000 volumes, 650 periodicals, 9,000 recordings and 14,000 music scores; a classroom-laboratory center; health and allied health building; a student center; and five residence halls which accommodate at total of 200 men and 240 women. Approximately 80% of the students applying for admission are accepted, including midyear students. Financial aid is available for economically disadvantaged students and 90% of the students receive some form of aid.

Community Environment: Winchester, a town of 23,000, is located 70 miles from Washington, D.C. surrounded by extensive apple orchards near the northern end of the Shenandoah Valley. Winchester was founded in 1732 and played an important part in the French and Indian War and the Civil War. Bus transportation is available. Community facilities include a public library, museums, churches of major denominations, a hospital, excellent shopping areas, and a number of various civic and service organizations. Winchester is the host to the Shenandoah Apple Blossom Festival. George Washington began his career in Winchester in 1748 as surveyor to Lord Fairfax. Some of the historical points of interest are the Hollinsworth House, Sheridan's Headquarters, "Stonewall" Jackson's Headquarters, and Washington's Office.

SOUTHERN VIRGINIA COLLEGE   *(F-10)*
One College Hill Drive
Buena Vista, Virginia 24416
Tel: (703) 261-8420; (800) 229-8420; Fax: (703) 261-8451

Description: This private two-year college for women was founded in 1867. It operates on the semester system and offers one summer session. Enrollment is 247 students. A faculty of 38 gives a faculty-student ratio of 1-8. It is accredited by the Southern Association of Colleges and Schools. The Associate in Arts and Associate in Science degrees are offered. The college enjoys a collegial relationship with surrounding colleges and universities such as VMI, Sweet Briar, Mary Baldwin, JMU, Hollins, and Washington and Lee University.

Entrance Requirements: High school graduation or equivalent; recommended completion of 4 units of English, 2 math, 1 science, 2 foreign languages, and 2 social sciences, SAT or ACT required; $35 application fee; rolling admissions; students are notified of their application status within 14 working days.

Costs Per Year: $8,650 tuition; $3,950 room and board.

Collegiate Environment: The 100-acre campus and buildings are situated on a hill overlooking the town of Buena Vista. The library contains 60,000 volumes, and dormitory facilities are available for 250 women. Approximately 95% of the applicants are accepted. Financial aid is available, and 65% of the current student body receives some form of assistance.

Community Environment: The city is an urban and industrial community located in a scenic and historic area. Train and bus transportation is available. Air service is accessible through connection in Roanoke, Virginia, 45 minutes away. A public library, churches, a hospital, and some of the major civic and service organizations serve the community. Excellent riding facilities exist on campus. The surrounding Blue Ridge Mountains provide outstanding recreational opportunities.

SOUTHSIDE VIRGINIA COMMUNITY COLLEGE   *(H-12)*
Alberta, Virginia 23821
Tel: (804) 949-1000; (800) 801-6160; Admissions: (804) 949-1014; Fax: (804) 949-7863

Description: This publicly supported multicampus two-year college was established in 1970 as a part of a statewide system of community colleges. It is accredited by the Southern Association of Colleges and Schools. The college offers comprehensive, university-parallel, technological and occupational programs and grants the Associate degree. It operates on the semester system and offers two summer sessions. Enrollment includes 1,076 full-time and 2,925 part-time students. A faculty of 56 full-time and 158 part-time provides a faculty-student ratio of 1-15.

Entrance Requirements: Open enrollment policy; non-high school graduates 18 years of age or older admitted; rolling admissions, early admission, delayed admission, midyear admission and advanced placement plans available.

Costs Per Year: $1,359 tuition; $4,470 nonresident; $21 student fees.

Collegiate Environment: The Christanna campus occupies 109 acres and is located to serve the counties of Brunswick, Greensville, Nottoway, Mecklenburg, and Lunenburg, as well as the City of Emporia. The John H. Daniel Campus includes 98 acres and is located to serve the counties of Charlotte, Buckingham, Cumberland, Prince Edward, Nottoway, Lunenburg, Mecklenburg, and Halifax, along with the City of South Boston. All students applying for admission are accepted, including at midyear. The libraries house a combined total of 28,972 volumes, 266 periodicals, 18 microforms and 3,408 audiovisual materials. 23 scholarships are offered and 50% of the current curricular students receive financial assistance.

Community Environment: See Hampden-Sydney College.

SOUTHWEST VIRGINIA COMMUNITY COLLEGE *(H-4)*
P.O. Box SVCC
Richlands, Virginia 24641
Tel: (703) 964-2555; (800) 822-7822; Fax: (703) 964-7543

Description: This new college, opened in 1968, is a two-year institution of higher education established as a part of a statewide system of community colleges. The college is accredited by the Southern Association of Colleges and Schools. It operates on the semester system and offers two summer sessions. The college offers the following degrees: Associate of Arts and Sciences and Associate in Applied Science. Cooperative education programs are available in technologies areas. Enrollment includes 1,861 full-time and 2,924 part-time students. A faculty of 110 full-time and 125 part-time gives a faculty-student ratio of 1-25.

Entrance Requirements: High school graduation or equivalent, or 18 years of age; modified open enrollment policy; SAT or ACT required of transfer students; general placement tests required; early admission, early decision, rolling admission, midyear admission and advanced placement plans available.

Costs Per Year: $1,385 tuition; $4,680 nonresidents; $15 (.50/cr) student fees.

Collegiate Environment: The 100-acre site is situated at the top of a mountain overlooking the mountains and valleys of the region. The initial phase of the building program consists of four buildings, which are the Business Techincal Library complex, the Instructional-Laboratory-Administrative facility, the Mechanical-Shop area and the Police Science Building. The master plan includes the addition of several buildings. Scholarships are available and 55% of full-time students receive some form of financial aid. The library contains 35,200 volumes, 368 periodicals, 41,000 microforms and 1,800 recordings. About 98% of the applicants are accepted, including midyear students. 60% of the previous freshmen returned for the second year.

Community Environment: Richlands is a rural community in the Applachian Mountain region. Bus and plane transportation are convenient. The main industries of the area are agriculture, mining, and manufacturing.

SWEET BRIAR COLLEGE *(G-10)*
Route 29
Sweet Briar, Virginia 24595
Tel: (804) 381-6142; (800) 381-6142; Fax: (804) 381-6152

Description: This four-year residential college for women, founded in 1901, offers a liberal arts and sciences curriculum which includes programs in Management, Asian Studies, International Studies, Environmental Studies, and European Civilization, as well as a major in mathematics-computer science and dual-degree programs in engineering. It is accredited by the Southern Association of Colleges and Schools. The college operates on the 4-1-4 system. The college offers the Bachelor of Arts and Bachelor of Science degrees and sponsors overseas programs in Spain, England, Scotland, France and Germany; other programs approved by the college include the Washington Semester Program conducted by the American University in Washington, D.C., and winter term and summer internships. There is a dual degree program in Engineering with the Georgia Institute of Technology, Columbia University, or Washington University. Enrollment includes 559 full-time and 50 part-time students. A faculty of 75 full-time and 7 part-time provides the faculty-student ratio of 1:8. A four-year honors program leads to an Honors Degree.

Entrance Requirements: High school graduation with rank in upper half of class; recommended completion of 16 units including a minimum of 4 English, 3 mathematics, 2 foreign language, 2 science and 3 social science; SAT or ACT required; 3 Achievement tests recommended; early admission, early decision, delayed admission, midyear admission and advanced placement plans available; application deadlines are Feb. 15, Jan. 15 for scholarships; $25 application fee.

Costs Per Year: $14,500 tuition; $6,000 room and board; $125 student activity fee.

Collegiate Environment: The college has an unusually beautiful campus, covering 3,300 acres, which includes 18 academic buildings, meadows and woodlands, and two small lakes. The library contains a collection of over 230,000 volumes, 1,133 periodicals, 350,000 microforms, 5,363 audio-visual materials and over 85,000 Art History slides. Dormitory facilities provide living accommodations for 600 women. Approximately 80% of the students applying for admission are accepted including midyear students. Approximately 70% of the student body receives some form of financial aid. More than 55% received need-based assistance in 1994-1995. Nearly 81% of the previous freshman class returned to the college for the second year. The college offers a wide range of clubs organized around special interests, and a full cultural calendar of concerts, plays, lectures, and films. Social events often include students from neighboring colleges.

Community Environment: Sweet Briar is located on U.S. 29, 165 miles southwest of Washington, D.C., 50 miles south of Charlottesville, VA., and 100 miles west of Richmond. The nearest shopping area is in the town of Amherst, two miles north of Sweet Briar. Lynchburg, home of three other colleges, is 12 miles south of Sweet Briar. The Blue Ridge Mountains, visible a few miles to the west, offer numerous recreational possibilities, including the ski slopes at Wintergreen.

THOMAS NELSON COMMUNITY COLLEGE *(H-17)*
99 Thomas Nelson Drive,
Hampton, Virginia 23666
Tel: (804) 825-2700

Description: This two-year community college was founded in 1967 as a unit of the Virginia Community College System. It operates on the semester system and offers one ten-week summer session. Enrollment is 7,800 students. A faculty of 300 provides a faculty-student ratio of 1-26. The institution is accredited by the Southern Association of Colleges and Schools. It offers university-parallel, occupational-technical, general education and continuing adult education programs leading to an Associate degree or a Certificate.

Entrance Requirements: High school graduation or equivalent, or 18 years of age; open enrollment policy; rolling admission, early admission and early decision plans available; no application fee.

Costs Per Year: $1,100 tuition; $3,590 nonresident.

Collegiate Environment: There are 6 buildings on the 80-acre campus. Approximately 99% of the students applying for admission are accepted including midyear students. 35% of students receive financial aid. The library contains 50,000 volumes, 650 periodicals, 20,000 microforms and 10,000 audiovisual materials.

Community Environment: See Hampton University.

TIDEWATER COMMUNITY COLLEGE *(I-17)*
7000 College Drive
Portsmouth, Virginia 23703
Tel: (804) 484-2121

Description: Tidewater Community College, founded in 1968, is one of several multi-campus institutions in the state-supported Virginia Community College System. The college was established to meet the educational needs of the cities of Chesapeake, Norfolk, Portsmouth, Virginia Beach, and part of Suffolk. It is accredited by the Southern Association of Colleges and Schools. It presently operates on three permanent campuses, and at several off-campus locations. The college grants the Associate degree. It operates on the semester system and offers one summer session. Enrollment includes 18,000 full-time and part-time students. A faculty of approximately 884 gives a faculty-student ratio of 1-20.

Entrance Requirements: High school graduation or equivalent or minimum 18 years of age; advanced placement plans available. Open enrollment policy; placement exam required.

Costs Per Year: $1,683 ($51/cr) resident tuition; $5,291.55 ($160.35/cr) nonresident.

Collegiate Environment: The Portsmouth Campus, located on historic Hampton Roads about seven miles west of Portsmouth, was established on the site of a private four-year liberal arts college known as Frederick College. The Portsmouth campus encompasses approximately 680 acres of waterfront property on beautiful and historic Hampton Roads. The Virginia Beach Campus, opened in 1974, is located in the Green Run area of Virginia Beach. It opened in 1971 and continues to provide educational programs and services. Chesapeake Campus is located in the Great Bridge section of Chesapeake on the site of a former private two-year college. There are 117,462 volumes, and numerous pamphlets, periodicals, microforms and sound recordings in the libraries. Financial assistance is available.

Community Environment: A metropolitan area, Tidewater is located on the Chesapeake Bay, and has been a strategic military location in this country's conflicts because of its shipbuilding and ship repair. All forms of commercial transportation are available. Recreational activities are numerous, all water sports are enjoyed on nearby beaches. There is excellent hunting and fishing in the area also. Part-time employment opportunities are limited.

UNION THEOLOGICAL SEMINARY IN VIRGINIA   *(G-14)*
3401 Brook Road
Richmond, Virginia 23227
Tel: (804) 355-0671

Description: The seminary offers a basic three-year graduate course which is designed to give general training for the Christian ministry in all its phases but with special reference to the work of the pastorate. Founded in 1812, the seminary is affiliated with the Presbyterian Church (U.S.A.) and is an accredited member of the Southern Association of Colleges and Schools and the American Association of Theological Schools. It operates on the semester system. The school offers a program of studies leading to the degrees of Master of Divinity, Doctor of Ministry, Master of Theology, and Doctor of Philosophy. Enrollment includes 249 students. A faculty of 23 gives a faculty-student ratio of 1:8.

Entrance Requirements: Any student who is a communicant of any Christian Church, being a graduate of any accredited college, may be admitted to the seminary. No one without a college degree will be admitted. GRE is required; the seminary requires some preparation in philosophy and Greek; rolling admission and midyear admission plans available. $35 application fee.

Costs Per Year: $5,550 tuition; $4,850 room and board; $40 student fees.

Collegiate Environment: The seminary occupies a spacious and beautiful 50-acre site in Ginter Park, a residential suburb. The library contains 250,000 volumes, 1,200 periodicals and 17,000 sound recordings. Dormitory facilities provide living accommodations for 103 single students and 99 families. Financial assistance is available.

Community Environment: See University of Richmond.

UNIVERSITY OF RICHMOND   *(G-14)*
Richmond, Virginia 23173
Tel: (804) 289-8640; Fax: (804) 287-6003

Description: The university, founded in 1830, is affiliated with the Baptist General Association of Virginia. It operates on the semester system and offers three summer sessions. It is accredited by the Southern Association of Colleges and Schools and by professional accrediting institutions. Academic divisions include the School of Arts and Sciences; Richard S. Reynolds is the graduate division to the E. Claiborne Robins School of Business; the Jepson School of Leadership Studies; the T.C. Williams School of Law; the Graduate School; and University College. Undergraduate residential colleges include Richmond College for men and Westhampton College for women. Study abraod programs are coordinated through the Office of International Education; university-sponsored programs are offered to two countries during the academic year and to eleven countries during the summer. Exchange programs with eleven unviersities in five countries around the world are offered. Students can study in any other area of the world with approval. Army ROTC is available. Enrollment is approximately 2,857 full-time undergraduates, 935 evening and part-time undergraduates, and 444 men and 404 women in graduate programs. A faculty of 271 full-time and 129 part-time gives a faculty-student ratio of 1-12.

Entrance Requirements: High school graduation with very significant achievement in a strong academic program; apply the senior year of high school; completion of 16 units, including 4 English, 3 mathematics, 1 history, 1 science; and 2 years of foreign language preferred; SAT and three Achievement tests, or ACT required; the applicant is required to take three subject tests: writing, math, and a third from a different subject area, e.g. literature, history, foreign language or science; GRE required for graduate studies; early admission, early decision, deferred admission and advanced placement available; $40 application fee.

Costs Per Year: $14,500 tuition; $3,285 room and board; $14,600 MBA Program; $14,900-15,100 Law School.

Collegiate Environment: The university is located in the western suburb of Richmond on a 350-acre campus of rolling hills and woodlands and surrounding a 10-acre lake. The libraries of the university contain 857,403 volumes, 82,144 periodicals, 276,000 microforms and 6,027 other items. Dormitory facilities provide living accommodations for 2,651 students. About 55% of the applicants are accepted. The middle 50% ranges of enrolled freshmen scores were SAT 1130-1260 combined; ACT 26-29 composite. Scholarships are available and 59% of students receive financial aid.

Community Environment: Richmond, capital of the Commonwealth of Virginia, is one of the University of Richmond's most valuable assets. Steeped in history and tradition, it is a city of museums and galleries, cultural activity and sporting events. Eclectic is the best word to describe Richmond and its menu of artistic, historical and scientific pursuits. The Virginia Museum of Fine Arts houses the south's largest art collection while the Science Museum displays its collection in an old railroad station, itself an historical landmark. The Universe Planetarium adjacent to the Science Museum is the only one of its kind in the world. The Carpenter Center for the Performing Arts is home to the City's symphony orchestra and ballet company. Famous Virginia Beach and Washington, D.C., are only a few hours away.

UNIVERSITY OF VIRGINIA   *(E-12)*
P.O. Box 9017
Charlottesville, Virginia 22906
Tel: (804) 982-3200; Fax: (804) 924-3587

Description: Chartered by the General Assembly in 1819 under the sponsorship of Thomas Jefferson, the university officially opened for instruction on March 7, 1825. The major undergraduate divisions include the College of Arts and Sciences, the School of Architecture, the School of Commerce, the School of Education, the School of Engineering and Applied Science, and the School of Nursing. Graduate school and graduate professional programs leading to advanced degrees are offered in arts and sciences, architecture and planning, business administration, education, engineering and applied science, law and medicine. The university operates on the semester system and offers two summer terms. Foreign study is both sponsored by the university and coordinated through other agencies. Army, Navy, and Air Force ROTC is available. The university recently enrolled approximately 11,371 undergraduates, 4,565 graduate students, and 1,668 students in the professional schools. A faculty of 1,887 provides a faculty-student ratio of 1-11. The university is accredited by the Southern Association of Colleges and Schools and by respective professional and educational agencies.

Entrance Requirements: High school graduation; most students rank in top 10% of high school class; completion of 16 units including 4 English, 4 mathematics, 2 foreign languages, 2 science, 1 social science; SAT and 3 Achievement tests required; GRE required for graduate programs; $40 application fee; early decision and advanced placement plans available.

Costs Per Year: $3,890 tuition; $10,826 out-of-state tuition; $3,470 room and board; $500 books; $1,000 personal expenses.

Collegiate Environment: Located on 1800 acres, the university has 240 major buildings. Thomas Jefferson designed the Academical Village at the center of campus. It is comprised of the Rotonda, and Pavillions where faculty reside above and teach below. In between the Pavillions are lawn rooms where students live. The library contains 3,842,344 volumes, 29,913 periodicals, 4,871,904 microforms and 14,988 audio recordings. Financial aid helps economically disadvantaged students. 33% of students receive financial aid. On-campus dormitories house all freshmen and 35% of all other students, 2,800 men and 2,900 women. 35% of students applying for admission are accepted. Special programs for culturally disadvantaged low-mark students enable them to attend the university.

Community Environment: Charlottesville, situated in the foothills of the Blue Ridge Mountains, was the home of Thomas Jefferson and James Monroe. Numerous old homes and estates in Charlottesville and the surrounding areas, reveal Jefferson's architectural influence. All forms of commercial transportation are available. Albemarle County is known for its horses, dogs, fox hunting, and for its peach and apple orchards. The many outdoor activities include golf, tennis, hunting, fishing, and hiking. Some part-time employment is available for students. Points of interest include the Lewis and Clark Memorial,

Monticello, the home of Thomas Jefferson, Old Courthouse, and the University of Virginia-founded by Thomas Jefferson.

UNIVERSITY OF VIRGINIA - CLINCH VALLEY COLLEGE
(H-2)
College Avenue
Wise, Virginia 24293-0016
Tel: (703) 328-0100; (800) 468-3412; Admissions: (703) 328-0102; Fax: (703) 328-0251

Description: This four-year college of the University of Virginia is fully accredited by the Southern Association of Colleges and Schools. Fourteen majors are offered to fulfill the Baccalaureate requirements for professional study. A nursing program is offered for Associate degree nurses with a license. Cooperative education credit is available in all majors. The college operates on the semester system and offers two summer sessions. Enrollment includes 1,018 full-time and 180 part-time students. A faculty of 58 full-time and 32 part-time gives a faculty-student ratio of 1-22.

Entrance Requirements: High school graduation with 2.3 academic GPA; completion of 16 units including 4 English, 3 mathematics, 2 science, and 2 social science; SAT or ACT required; non-high school graduates considered; rolling admission and advanced placement plans available; $15 application fee.

Costs Per Year: $2,650 state resident tuition; $6,024 nonresident tuition; $1,600 dormitory; $1,850 apartment; $1,600 board; $250-$300 estimated books and fees.

Collegiate Environment: The college encompasses 27 buildings located on 326 acres of land. The library houses 142,000 books, 1,396 periodicals, 7,000 pamphlets, 54,800 microforms and 15,017 sound recordings. It was built to double its stack capacity as the need increases. Limited dormitory space available can accommodate 450 students. 69% of applicants are accepted. 65% of students receive some form of financial aid. About 58% of the freshmen returned for the second year of studies. About 10% of the senior class continued on to graduate school.

Community Environment: Wise is a small community in the Appalachian Mountains with includes churches of major denominations, 3 hospitals, 3 shopping centers, several restaurants, theatres, bowling, and a number of civic and service organizations. The Jefferson National Forest provides access to fishing, hunting, picnicking, and camping. Many other facilities near Wise offer outdoor activities.

VIRGINIA COMMONWEALTH UNIVERSITY   (G-14)
821 West Franklin Street
Box 2526
Richmond, Virginia 23284
Tel: (804) 828-1200; (800) 828-3678; Fax: (804) 828-1899

Description: The university was created by an act of the Virginia General Assembly during the 1968 session of the Legislature. The Richmond Professional Institute and the Medical College of Virginia were combined to become the university. It is accredited by the Southern Association of Colleges and Secondary Schools and by respective professional agencies. The Associate, Bachelor, and Master degrees are offered as well as a Professional and Doctoral degree. International studies are available. Army ROTC is available. The university operates on the semester system and offers 8 to 10 summer sessions. Enrollment includes 10,071 full-time and 4,857 part-time undergraduates and 6,595 graduate students. A faculty of 1,561 full-time and 1,045 adjunct gives a faculty-student ratio of 1-13.

Entrance Requirements: High school graduation or equivalent; completion of 23 units including 4 English, 3 mathematics, 3 science, and 3 foreign language; SAT required; non-high school graduates considered; $20 application fee; GRE required for graduate school; early admission, early decision and advanced placement plans available.

Costs Per Year: $3,914 tuition; $11,097 out-of-state; $4,192 room and board; $615 student fees.

Collegiate Environment: The university is located in a residential section of downtown Richmond. The 13-acre campus has 47 buildings. The library contains a collection of 1,083,795 titles, 8,300 journal subscriptions, and 216,000 government documents. Dormitories provide living accommodations for 3,594 students. 77% of applicants

are accepted. Scholarships are available and 60% of students receive some form of financial aid. A special program is offered for the culturally disadvantaged, enabling low-mark disadvantaged students to attend.

Community Environment: See University of Richmond.

VIRGINIA HIGHLANDS COMMUNITY COLLEGE   (I-4)
P.O. Box 828
Abingdon, Virginia 24210
Tel: (703) 628-6094

Description: The two-year college opened in 1969 with a comprehensive offering of university-parallel and occupational curricula. It operates on the semester system and offers one summer term. The curriculum program offered includes liberal arts, science, engineering, business administration and pre-teacher education as well as several terminal occupational programs in business and technical areas. Enrollment is 910 full-time and 1,028 part-time students. Faculty numbers 47 full-time and 77 part-time members, giving a faculty-student ratio of 1-17.

Entrance Requirements: High school graduation equivalent, or must be 18 years of age. No application fee.

Costs Per Year: $1,268 tuition; $4,172 tuition for nonresident students.

Collegiate Environment: The college is located on a 100 acre campus one mile west of Abingdon. The modern buildings include laboratories, shops, classrooms and a library which has 24,254 titles, 232 periodicals, 4,299 microforms, and 1,938 audiovisual materials. 98% of applicants are accepted. Financial assistance aids economically disadvantaged students. 65% of students receive financial aid. An open-door college.

Community Environment: Abingdon is known as a handicraft center as well as being the largest burley tobacco market and the largest livestock auction in Virginia. Commercial transportation is available. The Blue Ridge and Holston Mountains are nearby providing facilities for many outdoor activities.

VIRGINIA INTERMONT COLLEGE   (J-3)
1013 Moore Street
Bristol, Virginia 24201-4298
Tel: (703) 669-6101

Description: Virginia Intermont is an accredited four-year private coeducational college. The college is affiliated with the Baptist General Association of Virginia and is accredited by the Southern Association of Colleges and Schools. A cosmopolitan enrollment includes students (admitted without regard to race, creed, or national origin) from 34 states and 5 countries. The college operates on the semester system and offers 2 summer terms. Enrollment includes 432 men and 24 women full-time and 61 students part-time. A faculty of 35 full-time and 21 part-time gives a faculty-student ratio of 1-12.

Entrance Requirements: High school graduation or equivalent; completion of 15 units including 4 English, 2 mathematics, 1 science, 2 social studies, and 6 humanities or other academic electives; SAT with minimum score of 350V, 350M, or ACT required; early decision, delayed admission, rolling admission, early admission, midyear admission and advanced placement plans available; $15 application fee.

Costs Per Year: $9,500 tuition; $4,250 room and board; $100 general fee.

Collegiate Environment: There are 14 buildings on the 25-acre campus. Included on the campus are four newly constructed tennis courts, and an amphitheater with seating capacity for 1,200. The 129-acre riding center consists of 2 indoor riding rings, a 60-stall barn and open fields. The library contains a collection of 68,000 volumes, 145 periodicals, 26,701 microforms and 11,718 audiovisual materials. 4 dormitory facilities provide living accommodations for 205 students. About 87% of the applicants are accepted, including midyear students. Financial assistance aids economically disadvantaged students, and 80% of the student body receives aid. Of 150 scholarships offered, 60 are for freshmen.

Community Environment: Bristol is located in the southwest corner of Virginia, in the Holston Mountains. The Tennessee State line corresponds with the main street of Bristol, so the city operates under two types of government. Bristol is a city of diversified industry; some of the products are textiles, electronics, pharmaceuticals, business machines, and metal products. Recreational activities are fishing, boating, swimming, water skiing, and picnicking.

VIRGINIA MILITARY INSTITUTE *(F-10)*
Lexington, Virginia 24450
Tel: (703) 464-7211; (800) 767-4207; Fax: (703) 464-7746

Description: Founded in 1839, the Institute provides a twofold educational program; academic and military. The state-aided undergraduate college of liberal arts, sciences, and engineering awards a Baccalaureate degree. The college is fully accredited by the Southern Association of Colleges and Schools and the respective professional agencies. Enrollment includes 1,200 men. Operating on the semester system, the Institute offers two summer terms. A study abroad program is available. All students must A full-time faculty of 99 gives a faculty-student ratio of 1-11.

Entrance Requirements: Unmarried male; good physical condition; high school graduation with rank in top 50% of class; completion of 16 units including 4 English, 3 mathematics, 2 social studies, 2 science, and 2 foreign language; SAT or ACT required; $25 application fee; rolling admission, advanced placement and early decision plans available; early decision application deadline is November 15, notice by December 15.

Costs Per Year: $2,980 state-resident tuition; $9,020 nonresident; $3,800 room and board; $1,410 student fees.

Collegiate Environment: The College is situated on a plateau near the northern end of the city, and the buildings of Tudor-Gothic architecture stand on the perimeter of the pleateau facing the parade ground. Dormitory facilities house all cadets in the barracks, a National Historic Land and three or four cadets share each room. The Preston Library contains 261,000 volumes, 1,000 periodicals, 6,300 microforms and 3,800 recordings. 66% of the current class receives some form of financial assistance. About 75% of the applicants are accepted.

Community Environment: See Washington and Lee University.

VIRGINIA POLYTECHNIC INSTITUTE AND STATE UNIVERSITY *(H-7)*
104 Burruss Hall
Blacksburg, Virginia 24061-0202
Tel: (540) 231-6267; Fax: (540) 231-3242

Description: Opened in 1872, Virginia Tech began its first session with 43 students and one building. Today the Land-Grant university enrolls 10,960 men and 7,694 women full-time and 347 men and 228 women part-time. A full-time faculty of 1,466 gives a faculty-student ratio of 1-18. The state-supported institution is the largest university in the state of Virginia. Undergraduate courses of study lead to a Bachelor of Science or Bachelor of Arts degree; with the exception of the five-year Bachelor of Architecture, Bachelor of Landscape Architecture, and Bachelor of Fine Arts programs. The university also offers graduate work in 81 fields of study leading to the Master's degrees in art, science, education, engineering, business, agriculture, architecture, and urban and regional planning. The doctorate is offered in 74 separate fields of study. The University also offers the professional degree in Veterinary Medicine. The university operates on the semester system with two summer sessions and with the school year commencing in late August. Army, Navy, Marine, and Air Force ROTC is offered on campus. The university is fully accredited by the Southern Association of Colleges and Schools and by regional, professional, and educational agencies.

Entrance Requirements: High school graduation with rank in top half of class; completion of 18 units including 4 English, 2 algebra, 1 geometry (4 units mathematics required for science and engineering programs and recommended for business programs) 1 social science, 1 history, 2 laboratory science, 3 college prep; SAT or ACT and 2 Achievement tests required for placement; $20 application fee; early admission, early decision, delayed admission, midyear admission, and advanced placement plans available.

Costs Per Year: $3,500 tuition; $10,152 out-of-state tuition; $32,120 room and board; $487 student fees.

Collegiate Environment: Encompassing 2,600 acres, the university system has over 100 major buildings. The Carol M. Newman Library houses 1,900,000 volumes, 20,380 periodicals of general and technical interest, 5,753,876 microforms, and 15,450 audiovisual materials. Enrollment consisits of 18,654 full-time, 575 part-time, and 4,324 graduate students. Full-time faculty of 1,466 and part-time faculty of 508 gives a student-faculty ratio of 18-1. Dormitories house 3,340 men and 4,611 women. Approximately 52% of students applying for admission meet the requirements and are accepted for admission. Of 4,111 scholarships offered, about 1,225 are available to freshmen; about 57% of the present students receive some form of financial assistance.

Community Environment: Blacksburg is primarily a rural town located on a plateau between the Blue Ridge and Allegheny Mountains, 38 miles southwest of Roanoke. Nearby are the Jefferson National Forest, the Appalachian Trail, the New River, and other parks and lakes. Students are surrounded by outdoor recreation oppportunities, including hiking, horseback riding, fishing, swimming, boating, water skiing, and camping. Bus service is convenient and free with a student I.D., servicing the campus, town, and all off-campus apartments. Civic and service organizations are active and welcome student participation.

Branch Campuses: Northern Virginia Graduate Center, 2990 Telestar Court, Falls Church, VA 22041, (703) 698-6000; Roanoke Graduate Center, 117 Church Ave. SW, Roanoke, VA 24011-1905, (703) 231 3855; Hampton Roads Graduate Center, 418 Pembroke Four, Virginia Beach, VA 23462, (804) 552-1880

VIRGINIA STATE UNIVERSITY *(H-14)*
Petersburg, Virginia 23803
Tel: (804) 524-5000; Admissions: (804) 524-5902; Fax: (804) 524-5055

Description: Virginia State University, a land-grant institution founded 1882, is one of Virginia's two traditionally back institutions. It is fully accredited by the Southern Association of Colleges and Schools and professionally by respective accrediting institutions. Twenty-nine undergraduate majors are offered through its Schools of Agriculture, Science and Technology, School of Business, School of Liberal Arts and Education, and Continuing Education. The Baccalaureate degrees conferred by VSU are the Bachelor of Arts, Bachelor of Science, Bachelor of Fine Arts, Bachelor of Music, Bachelor of Individualized Studies, and Bachelor of Arts in Social Work. The School of Graduate Studies offers programs leading to the Master of Arts, Master of Science, Master of Education, Master of Interdisciplinary Studies, and the Ceritificate of Advanced Graduate Study. Army ROTC is available. The University operates on the semester system and offers two summer sessions. Enrollment includes 2,983 full-time and 334 part-time undergraduates and 690 graduate students. A faculty of 186 full-time and 71 part-time gives a faculty-student ratio of 1-21.

Entrance Requirements: High school graduation; completion of 16 units including 4 English, 2 mathematics, 2 foreign language, 2 science, 2 social science; SAT or ACT required, SAT preferred; non-high school graduates considered with G.E.D.; rolling admission, midyear admission and advanced placement plans available; $25 application fee.

Costs Per Year: $1,894 in-state tuition; $5,787 nonresident tuition; $1,307 comprehensive fee; $2,750 room; $2,095 board.

Collegiate Environment: Located on 236 acres of campus, with a 416-acre farm, the university has 50 major buildings. The library houses 180,791 titles, 1,147 current serials, 180,879 government documents and 599,627 microforms (units). Dormitories house 1,901 students. Approximately 91% of students applying for admission meet the requirements and are accepted. Scholarships are available and 85% of students receive financial aid. A geographically diverse student body is sought by the university.

Community Environment: The immediate environs of the university offer an exciting atmosphere involving a variety of interesting sites and events for leisure-time activities. The Petersburg National Battlefield and Old Blandford Church are historical landmarks that are recognized in the National Historical Register. Other popular attractions include museums, art exhibits, parks, the Petersburg Symphony, and theatrical groups. The close proximity of Virginia's capital, Richmond, 25 minutes north, enhances the "VSU experience." Colonial

Williamsburg and nearby Busch Gardens; Norfolk, home of one of America's busiest seaports; Virginia Beach, the top tourist attraction in the state; and the Blue Ridge Mountains are within easy driving distance.

VIRGINIA UNION UNIVERSITY   (G-14)
1500 North Lombardy Street
Richmond, Virginia 23220
Tel: (804) 257-5600; (800) 368-3227; Fax: (804) 257-5818

Description: The university is an accredited coeducational, liberal arts college with a graduate school of religion that resulted from the merger in 1899 of two institutions that had been established in 1865 by the American Baptist Home Mission Societies. The private university is affiliated with the American Baptist Convention and is accredited by the Southern Association of Colleges and Schools. It operates on the semester system and offers two summer terms. The Baccalaureate program is organized into the Division of Humanities, The Division of Social Science, The Division of Natural Science and Mathematics, the Division of Education and Psychology, and the School of Business. Enrollment includes 572 men, 709 women full-time, 27 men, 53 women part-time, and 150 graduate students. A faculty of 88 full-time and 34 part-time provides a faculty-student ratio of 1:14.

Entrance Requirements: High school graduation; completion of 16 units including 4 English, 3 mathematics, 2 foreign language; 2 social science, and 2 science; SAT or ACT required; early decision, rolling admission and early admission plans available; $10 application fee.

Costs Per Year: $6,646 tuition; $3,494 room and board; $372 fees.

Collegiate Environment: The 65-acre campus has a combination of older buildings of Virginia granite and more recent ones of brick and Belgian Tile. Dormitory facilities on campus house 311 men and 415 women. Approximately 92% of students receive financial aid. The package may include grants, loans, work study, and/or scholarships. The university library contains 131,087 volumes, 770 microforms, and 310 periodical subscriptions.

Community Environment: See University of Richmond.

VIRGINIA WESLEYAN COLLEGE   (I-7)
Wesleyan Drive
Norfolk, Virginia 23502
Tel: (804) 455-3208; (800) 737-8684; Fax: (804) 461-5238

Description: The private, coeducational college was chartered in 1961 and is affiliated with the Methodist Church. It is accredited by the Southern Association of Colleges and Schools. It operates on the semester system and offers two summer sessions. Enrollment is 1,170 full-time and 398 part-time students. A faculty of 73 full-time and 21 part-time gives a faculty-student ratio of 1-17. The college offers a liberal arts curriculum and grants the Bachelor of Arts degree. A study abroad program is available.

Entrance Requirements: High school graduation or equivalent; rank in upper 60% of graduating class; completion of 16 units including 4 English, 4 mathematics, 1 science, 3 social science, 3 foreign language, 1 advanced science, 1 computer science; non-high school graduates considered; SAT with minimum score of 450V and 450M required; $25 application fee; early admission, deferred admission, midyear admission, rolling admission and advanced placement plans are available.

Costs Per Year: $11,650 tuition; $5,200 room and board; $150 student fees.

Collegiate Environment: The college is set apart on a quiet, beautifully wooded 300-acre campus. The buildings include the library with 112,000 volumes, 549 periodicals, 7,898 microforms, and 100 audiovisual materials, and dormitories for 600 students. Approximately 70% of students applying for admission meet the requirements and are accepted. The college welcomes a geographically diverse student body and does accept midyear students. The average scores of the entering freshman class were SAT 439 verbal, 459 math. The average high school standing of the class was 36% in the top quarter, 46% in the second quarter, 15% in the third quarter, and 5% in the bottom quarter. Financial aid is available for economically disadvantaged students. Of 240 scholarships available, 80 are for freshmen. 72% of the students receive some form of financial assistance.

Community Environment: Tidewater, Virginia, is the cultural center of the Commonwealth. Norfolk features the Chrysler Museum, MacArthur Memorial, Scope Arena, Chrysler Hall for professional theatre, and is headquarters of the Virginia Orchestra Group, Fedlman String Quartet and the Tidewater Ballet Association. Virginia Beach, in addition to its world-famous beaches, is proud of Seashore State Park, the Little Theater, Edgar Cayce's Association for Research and Enlightment, the Virginia Beach Pops and other art groups. Within one hour's driving time are Colonial Williamsburg, Yorktown and Jamestown, several nationally known museums including the Mariners Museum, and Busch Gardens.

VIRGINIA WESTERN COMMUNITY COLLEGE   (H-18)
3095 Colonial Avenue, S.W.
Roanoke, Virginia 24015
Tel: (703) 857-7200; Admissions: (703) 857-7231; Fax: (703) 857-7544

Description: The state-supported community college was established in 1966 to serve an area within driving distance of the City of Roanoke and is a division of the Virginia Community College System. The semester system is employed with one summer term. Programs include occupational-technical education, college transfer courses, and general continuing adult education. The college is accredited by the Southern Association of Colleges and Schools and by respective professional organizations. The enrollment includes 1,670 students full-time and 4,920 students part-time. A faculty of 95 full-time and 220 part-time gives a faculty-student ratio of 1-21.

Entrance Requirements: High school graduation or equivalent; open enrollment policy. Placement test required; rolling admission and advanced placement plans available.

Costs Per Year: $898 tuition; $4,455 out-of-state tuition; $2 student fees.

Collegiate Environment: There are 12 buildings on the 70-acre campus. The library holdings include 67,129 hardbound volumes, 1,326 periodicals, 11,285 microforms, and 2,538 audiovisual materials; there are no dormitories. Approximately 20% of a recent freshman class received some form of financial assistance. The college awards 30 scholarships, 12 of them for freshmen.

Community Environment: Roanoke is a manufacturing, regional service and trading center, and a metropolitan area with all modes of transportation available. Community facilities include libraries, YMCA, YWCA, many churches, hospitals, and a number of the civic and service organizations. Part-time employment opportunities are available to certain students. Roanoke is headquarters for the Norfolk and Western Railway System and the Blue Ridge Parkway. Smith Mountain Lake is a favorite water recreation area. Carvin's Cove Lake nine and one-half miles north offers fishing, boating, and picnicking. Some of the points of interest are the Crystal Spring, Mill Mountain, and Transportation Museum.

WASHINGTON AND LEE UNIVERSITY   (F-10)
Lexington, Virginia 24450
Tel: (703) 463-8400; Fax: (703) 463-8473

Description: The private university was founded by Scotch-Irish pioneers in 1749. It is accredited by the Southern Association of Colleges and Schools and by respective professional organizations. It was empowered to grant degrees by the Virginia legislature in 1782 and adopted its present name in 1871. The University enrolled both men and women at the undergraduate level for the first time in 1985; however, women have been admitted to the graduate School of Law since 1972. The university is made up of the College of Arts and Sciences, the School of Commerce, Economics and Politics, and the School of Law. In addition to the regular degree programs, the university offers an Honors program, independent study programs, an endowed research program, preprofessional ethics programs in journalism, law, medicine and business, and Asian studies. It also offers Spring term study-abroad programs in Europe and the Far East, a junior year abroad program in Hong Kong or Tokyo, and Summer study in England and Taiwan. The school operates on a calendar system of two 12-week terms followed by a 6-week Spring term. Enrollment includes 1,619 undergraduate and 370 graduate students. An undergraduate faculty of 140 gives a faculty-student ratio of 1-11.

Entrance Requirements: High school graduation; completion of 16 units including 4 English, 3 mathematics, 2 foreign language, 1 science, 2 social science; SAT plus 3 achievement tests, one of which must be English Composition with or without an essay, or ACT required; LSAT required for Law School; early decision, delayed admission and advanced placement plans available; $40 application fee.

Costs Per Year: $13,750 tuition; $4,620 average room and board; $135 student fees.

Collegiate Environment: The 327-acre campus in Lexington is in the central part of the Great Valley of Virginia about 50 miles northeast of Roanoke. The main campus consists of approximately 50 acres with 36 buildings including housing accommodations for 850 single students. Fraternities provide housing for an additional 225 men. Washington Hall houses the administrative offices. Lee Chapel is perhaps the most famous building on the campus and is a National Historic Landmark. The University Library has a collection of 445,552 volumes, 1,464 periodicals, 721 microforms, 84,173 government documents and 281,339 manuscript items. The college seeks a geographically diverse student body and does not accept midyear students. 28% of applicants are accepted. The middle 50% range of scores for the enrolled freshman class were SAT verbal 580-650, math 620-690, ACT 28-30 composite. Of a total 457 scholarships offered, 131 are for freshman. 30% of students received financial aid. Approximately 96% of the previous freshman class returned to this campus for the sophomore year.

Community Environment: Lexington is located in the Great Valley of Virginia between the Blue Ridge and Allegheny Mountains. Two of the greatest Confederate heroes, Robert E. Lee and Thomas J. "Stonewall" Jackson, lived and are buried in Lexington, the "Shrine of the South." Bus transportation is available. Some of the points of interest are the Natural Bridge, Lee Chapel, Home of "Stonewall" Jackson, Virginia Military Institute, and Washington and Lee University. Cyrus McCormick, inventor of the reaper, lived nearby. Lexington is also the home of the Virginia Horse Center.

WYTHEVILLE COMMUNITY COLLEGE (I-6)
1000 E. Main Street
Wytheville, Virginia 24382
Tel: (703) 228-5541; Fax: (703) 228-6506

Description: The state-supported community college opened in 1963 and is a division of the Virginia Community College System. It is fully accredited by the Southern Association of Colleges and Schools and by the State Board of Education; the Associate degree curriculums have been approved by the State Council of Higher Education for Virginia. The college offers occupational-technical education, transfer courses for Baccalaureate degree programs, general continuing education, and special training programs. It operates on the semester system and offers three summer sessions. Enrollment includes 2,500 students full-time and part-time. A faculty of 49 full-time and 94 part-time gives a faculty-student ratio of 1-15.

Entrance Requirements: Open enrollment policy; high school graduation or equivalent required for degree programs; non-graduates must be 18 years of age; early admission, early decision, rolling admission, delayed admission, midyear admission and advanced placement plans available.

Costs Per Year: $1,494 tuition; $5,364 out-of-state.

Collegiate Environment: The 105-acre campus has five buildings. The library contains 25,898 volumes, 262 periodicals, 1,587 microforms and 2,091 audiovisual titles. There are no dormitories. All the applicants are accepted. Scholarships are available and 46% of students receive some form of financial aid. Freshman classes begin in August, January, and May. The college welcomes a geographically diverse student body.

Community Environment: Wytheville is located in a rich agricultural and cattle-raising area with most forms of commercial transportation available. A growing number of industries are located in the area, providing good part-time employment opportunities. Community facilities include a public library, churches, Jewish Synagogues in the neighboring towns of Bluefield and Bristol, a hospital, shopping areas, and a number of the civic and service organizations. Claytor Lake and the Jefferson National Forest provide opportunities for hunting, fishing, camping, and picnicking; other facilities within the city offer swimming and golf.

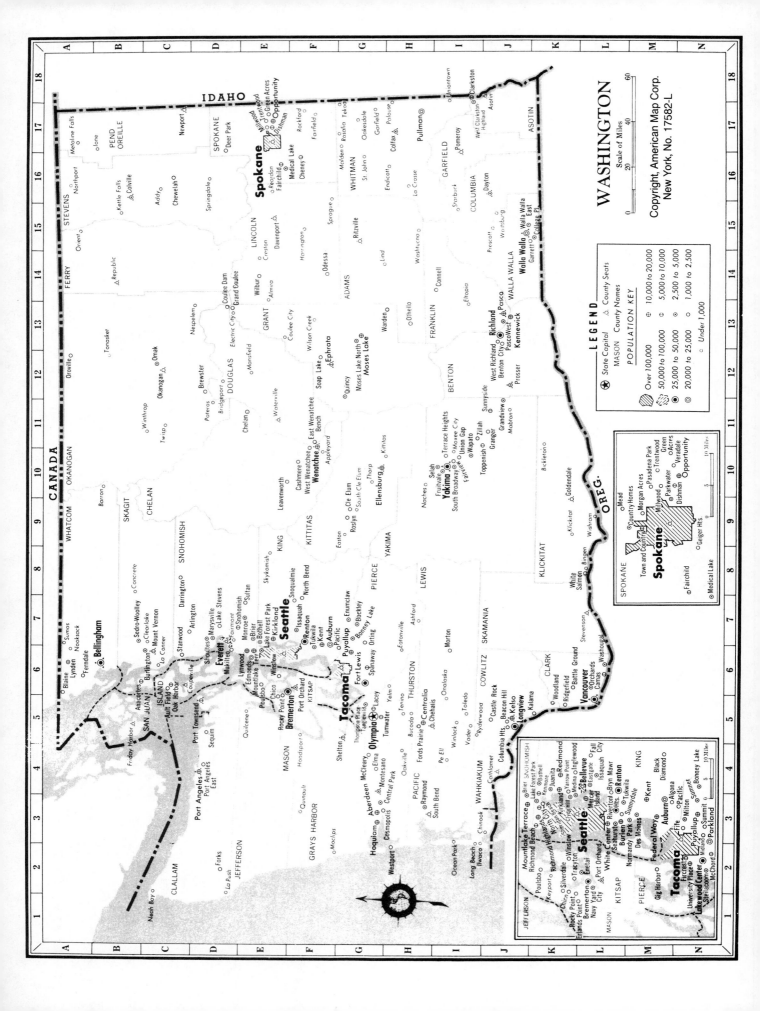

WASHINGTON

Scale of Miles

0   20   40   60

Copyright, American Map Corp.
New York, No. 17582-L

LEGEND

⊛ State Capital   ⊙ County Seats

MASON County Names

POPULATION KEY

Over 100,000   ⊕ 10,000 to 20,000
50,000 to 100,000   ⊙ 5,000 to 10,000
⊚ 25,000 to 50,000   ○ 2,500 to 5,000
◎ 20,000 to 25,000   ○ 1,000 to 2,500
                        ○ Under 1,000

WASHINGTON

BELLEVUE COMMUNITY COLLEGE   (K-4)
3000 Landerholm Circle S.E.
Bellevue, Washington 98007-8464
Tel: (206) 641-0111; Admissions: (206) 641-2222; Fax: (206) 641-2230

Description: This two-year institution is supported by the state and is accredited by the Washington State Board of Community and Technical Colleges and the Northwest Association of Schools and Colleges. The school was established in 1966. It offers college transfer courses, general vocational education, telecourses and continuing education courses leading to a certificate or an Associate degree. The college operates on the quarter system and offers one summer session. Enrollment includes 10,249 students. A faculty of 132 full-time and 508 part-time gives a faculty-student ratio of 1-26.

Entrance Requirements: Open door policy; accredited high school graduation required for degree courses; non-high school graduates may be admitted by special permission; no application fee; early admission, early decision, rolling admission and advanced placement plans available.

Costs Per Year: $1,338 tuition; $5,136 out-of-state tuition.

Collegiate Environment: This 100-acre campus has three buildings. The Library-Media Center combines library and audio-visual services. A book collection of 55,000 volumes, 455 periodicals, 41,115 microforms and 3,148 sound recordings are housed here. There are no dormitory facilities at this time. The college welcomes a geographically diverse student body as well as midyear students. Freshman classes begin in September, January, April, and June. Special financial aid is available for economically deprived students. A limited number of scholarships are available for students who meet required stipulations and 23% of the current student body receive financial assistance. Approximately 99% of students applying for admission are accepted and 53% have returned to this campus for the sophomore year.

Community Environment: Bellevue is a suburban community of Seattle and enjoys temperate climate with an average rainfall of 33.5 inches. The city has churches of most denominations, a hospital, good shopping facilities, and major civic and fraternal organizations serving the area.

BIG BEND COMMUNITY COLLEGE   (G-13)
7662 Chanute Street
Moses Lake, Washington 98837
Tel: (509) 762-5351; Admissions: (509) 762-6226; Fax: (509) 762-6243

Description: Founded in 1962, this public community college is accredited by the Northwest Association of Schools and Colleges. It operates on the quarter system and offers one summer session. Transfer, vocational and technical training, and general continuing education are available. Enrollment includes 1,100 full-time and 950 part-time students. A faculty of 47 full-time and 100 part-time gives a faculty-student ratio of 1-20. Programs of study lead to Certificates and Associate degrees.

Entrance Requirements: Open enrollment policy; accredited high school graduation or GED required for degree courses if receiving financial aid; $10 application fee.

Costs Per Year: $1,290 tuition; $5,094 out-of-state; $3,600 room and board; one year state residency prior to any quarter required for resident tuition.

Collegiate Environment: The campus is situated at the Grant County Airport, five miles north of Moses Lake. There are 22 buildings including dormitories that accommodate 140 men and women. The library has a collection of 37,000 volumes, 300 periodicals, and 3,800 audiovisual materials. The college welcomes a geographically diverse student body and accepts midyear students. Of 176 scholarships offered, 88 are available to freshmen. All students applying for admission are accepted.

Community Environment: Moses Lake is an important agricultural processing and shipping center for the Columbia Basin. This is a rural area with dry climate. The community has a library, many churches, a museum, a hospital and clinics, and modern shopping facilities. Local recreation includes lakes for fishing, swimming, boating, water skiing, and hydroplane boat races, as well as picnic areas and hunting areas for geese and pheasant. Part-time employment is available. The community has major civic, fraternal and veteran's organizations. Grant County Fair, and a rodeo and parade are held here annually.

CENTRAL WASHINGTON UNIVERSITY   (G-10)
Mitchell Hall
Ellensburg, Washington 98926
Tel: (509) 963-3001

Description: This state-supported university was established by the legislature in 1891. It is accredited by the Northwest Association of Schools and Colleges and by various professional and educational associations. It operates on the quarter system and offers three summer sessions. The university offers undergraduate programs in 101 subject areas and graduate programs in 35 subject areas. The degrees granted include Bachelor of Arts, Bachelor of Arts in Education, Bachelor of Science; Bachelor of Music; Master of Arts, Master of Education, Master of Arts for Teachers, Master of Music, Master of Fine Arts, Master of Sciences. Certificates are awarded in 18 different subject areas. The college offers a Cooperative Education Program in several areas. The enrollment includes 7,401 full-time and 762 part-time undergraduates and 305 graduate students. A faculty of 334 full-time and 117 part-time gives a faculty-student ratio of 1:22.

Entrance Requirements: High school graduation with an Admissions Index of 18 or higher. This Index is a combination of high school GPA and ACT or SAT test scores. 14.5 units including 4 English, 3 mathematics, 1 laboratory science, 2 science, 2 foreign language, 3 social science; ACT or SAT required; GRE required for graduate programs; non high school graduates considered; midyear admission, rolling admission, and advanced placement plans available; $35 application fee.

Costs Per Year: $2,256 resident tuition; $7,974 nonresident; $3,597 room and board.

Collegiate Environment: The 380-acre campus is 106 miles east of Seattle in a quiet setting at the foot of the Cascade Mountains. There are 80 buildings including a library of 500,000 volumes, 2,276 periodicals, 825,352 microforms and 20,000 audiovisual materials. There are housing accommodations for 2,468 students. Air Force and Army ROTC programs are available. The office of International Studies coordinates bilateral and consortia exchange programs with more than 100 universities in approx. 38 countries abroad. It is also a member of the National Student Exchange Program. Cooperative education programs are available in all subjects. Freshman classes begin in September, January and March. 68% of the students applying for admission are accepted. 565 scholarships are available, including 180 for freshmen and 60% of students receive some form of financial aid.

Community Environment: Ellensburg is a small university town in central Washington. The climate is mild and dry. The community has several churches, three libraries, a hospital and infirmary. Ellensburg may be reached by railroad, bus lines, and Interstate 90 and 82. Local recreation includes camping, hiking, river rafting, rodeo, snow sports, fishing, hunting, boating, skiing and golf. There are many job opportunities available at the university. Various civic and fraternal organizations are active in the community.

843

Branch Campuses: There are 4 extended university campuses available for placebound students who are of junior status. They are Lynnwood, Ft. Steilacoom, So. Seattle and Yakima. Contact office of admission for more information.

CENTRALIA COMMUNITY COLLEGE   *(H-5)*
600 West Locust Street
Centralia, Washington 98531
Tel: (206) 736-9391; Fax: (206) 753-3404

Description: This state-supported community college was founded in 1925. It is accredited by the Northwest Association of Schools and Colleges. Two-year transfer courses, vocational and technical training, and general continuing education are available. The college grants the Associate degree. It operates on the quarter system and offers one summer session. Enrollment includes 3,200 students. A faculty of 54 full-time, 37 part-time and 116 evening gives a faculty-student ratio of 1-35.

Entrance Requirements: Open enrollment policy; non-high school graduates considered; ASSET required for placement; open admission.

Costs Per Year: $1,296 tuition; $5,094 out-of-state tuition.

Collegiate Environment: The college has fourteen buildings on twelve acres of land. The college library contains 30,000 volumes, 350 periodicals, 4,000 microforms and 600 audio-visual materials. Federal and State financial aid is available. 150 scholarships are offered, including 80 for first year students. 56% of the current students receive some form of financial assistance. Approximately 99% of students applying for admission are accepted.

Community Environment: Centralia was founded by a former slave named George Washington. The community is surrounded by timberland and farmland and is designed as the "Hub City." Average winter temperature is 41.4 degrees, spring - 55 degrees, summer - 64.4 degrees, and fall - 59.2 degrees. The community is reached by railroad, bus lines, and major highways. There are several churches of various denominations, a library, hospital, and many civic, fraternal and veteran's organizations. Local recreation includes hunting, fishing, boating, skiing, parks, swimming pools, tennis, bowling, rollerskating rink, theatres and three golf courses. Part-time employment is available.

CITY UNIVERSITY   *(E-7)*
919 S.W. Grady Way
Renton, Washington 98055
Tel: (206) 637-1010; (800) 422-4898; Admissions: (206) 637-1010;
Fax: (206) 277-2437

Description: City University is an independent, decentralized, higher educational institution accredited by the Northwest Association of Schools and Colleges. Founded in 1973 as City College in Seattle, its primary purpose is to provide educational opportunity to a segment of the population not being fully served by traditional means. Undergraduate and graduate degree programs in business, management, liberal arts and education are made available to students with daytime, evening and weekend classes. The Distance Learning Center coordinates independent study programs for students worldwide, including computer-assisted Distance Learning which enables students to submit course work by personal computer. The University has 22 teaching locations in the states of Washington, Oregon, California, and in the Province of British Columbia, Germany, Austria, Denmark, Switzerland, and Slovakia. These instructional locations are suited to the university's mission, which is to make education convenient to all. Adjunct faculty is comprised of distinguished representatives from the business community, law, government, health care, civic and research organizations. The faculty has strong academic preparation and most are active professionals in their fields. The university's Office of Continuing Education and Lifelong Learning oversees the QUEST program, which provides an extensive range of instruction in outdoor, environmental and human development education. The university grants the Associate, Bachelor's, and Master's degrees. It operates on the quarter system. Undergraduate enrollment includes 127 men and 149 women full-time, and 864 and 1,137 women part-time. There are 3,160 graduate students. A faculty of 48 full-time and 1,082 part-time gives a faculty-student ratio of 1-20.

Entrance Requirements: Open enrollment policy is in effect and rolling admission is used. $50 application fee.

Costs Per Year: $7,560 undergraduate tuition, $50 student fees.

Collegiate Environment: Most students are working adults (average age early 30's) who live in the communities surrounding City University locations. Cooperative arrangements with libraries in service communities provide students with access to 18,200 volumes and periodicals germane to University curricula. Several University locations maintain extensive computer labs for student use. There are 16 scholarships offered each year. 10% of the students receive financial aid.

Community Environment: The dispersed nature of City University instructional locations allows students to enjoy the economic, civic and recreational features of their own communities. The University seeks to provide programs that help satisfy current needs and anticipate future ones in its service communities.

CLARK COLLEGE   *(L-5)*
1800 E. McLoughlin Blvd.
Vancouver, Washington 98663
Tel: (360) 694-6521; Admissions: (360) 992-2107; Fax: (360) 992-2878

Description: This school is accredited by the Northwest Association of Schools and Colleges and operates on the quarter system with one summer term. It provides freshman and sophomore years of college including a significant amount of occupational training. Founded in 1933, the college is a part of the state system of community colleges. Enrollment includes 1,755 men, 2,157 women full-time and 1,737 men and 3,047 women part-time. A faculty of 144 full-time and 384 men part-time provides a teacher-student ratio of 1-21.

Entrance Requirements: Open enrollment policy; accredited high school graduation required for degree programs; advanced placement, early admission, early decision, midyear admission and rolling admission plans available; some vocational programs have limited entry; $40 application fee for health occupation programs.

Costs Per Year: $902 tuition; $3,992 out-of-state tuition.

Collegiate Environment: This college has a 78-acre campus in the heart of Vancouver. The library has a collection of 50,000 volumes. There are no dormitories on the campus. Almost all applicants are accepted including midyear students. Financial aid is available for economically disadvantaged students. 103 scholarships are available. 50% of full-time students receive some form of financial aid.

Community Environment: The oldest city in the state, Vancouver is located at the head of the deep-water navigation of the Columbia River. This is an industrial city with job opportunities for students. The city is served by rail, bus and major highways. Local recreation includes fishing, hunting, boating, skiing, and nearby beaches.

COLUMBIA BASIN COMMUNITY COLLEGE   *(J-13)*
2600 North 20th Avenue
Pasco, Washington 99301
Tel: (509) 547-0511; Fax: (509) 546-0401

Description: This two-year community college was authorized by the State Board of Education in 1955. It is accredited by the Northwest Association of Schools and Colleges. The college provides a program of lower division college work leading toward a Baccalaureate degree, technical and vocational courses and general continuing education courses. Classes are held on the quarter system and 1 summer session is offered. Enrollment is 3,725 full-time and 3,667 part-time students. A faculty of 95 full-time and 250 part-time gives a faculty-student ratio of 1-23.

Entrance Requirements: Open door policy; accredited high school graduation required for degree courses; completion of 16 units; rolling admission and advanced placement plans available; no application fee.

Costs Per Year: $1,380 tuition, $6,000 out-of-state.

Collegiate Environment: The 156-acre Pasco campus houses seventeen permanent buildings with plans for additional buildings as funding becomes available in accordance with the long-range plan for campus expansion. The library houses 55,799 volumes, 539 periodicals, 48,072 microforms, and 4,020 audiovisual materials. CBC also maintains a Richland Center on a 2.2-acre site in the city of Richland to serve Benton County residents more conveniently. 95 scholarships are available. 21 athletic scholarships and 22 other scholarships are for freshmen. 21% of the students receive financial aid.

Community Environment: Columbia Basin College is a fully accredited two-year institution that serves district 19, which comprises all of Benton-Franklin Counties that have a combined population in excess of 143,108. This area includes McNary Dam, Ice Harbor Dam, and the world-famed Hanford project near Richland. Benton and Franklin Counties have an intensive agricultural industry, and Franklin County anticipates a continued rapid growth in irrigation farming. The general area offers students opportunities for part-time work to defray college expenses.

CORNISH COLLEGE OF THE ARTS   *(E-6)*
710 East Roy Street
Seattle, Washington 98102-4696
Tel: (206) 323-1400; (800) 726-2787; Admissions: (206) 323-1400 x205; Fax: (206) 720-1011

Description: This privately supported coeducational college was founded in 1914 and is accredited by the Northwest Association of Schools and Colleges. It operates on the semester system and offers one summer session. Enrollment is 580 students. A faculty of 131 provides a faculty-student ratio of 1-4. The college offers a Bachelor of Fine Arts degree.

Entrance Requirements: High school graduate or equivalent; life experience credits given and CLEP accepted; rolling admission and advanced placement plans available; $30 application fee; application deadline for fall semester is August 15.

Costs Per Year: $9,950 tuition; $20 student fee.

Collegiate Environment: The campus is located on 4 acres and the library has holdings of 23,887. Of those applying, 69% are accepted. 80% of the students receive financial aid. There are no dormitories.

EASTERN WASHINGTON UNIVERSITY   *(F-16)*
526 5th Street
117 Showalter Hall
Cheney, Washington 99004
Tel: (509) 359-2397; Fax: (509) 359-6153

Description: This state-supported liberal arts college was founded in 1882. It is accredited by the Northwest Association of Schools and Colleges and by respective professional accrediting institutions. As a multi-purpose institution the college provides the following programs: liberal education in the arts and sciences leading to the Baccalaureate degree, teacher education for elementary and secondary teachers, school administrators and other specialists leading to state certification and the Master of Education degree and preprofessional studies for students interested in graduate work in certain professional schools. It operates on the quarter system and offers two summer sessions. Enrollment includes 7,217 full-time and 1,146 part-time students. A faculty of 416 full-time and 145 part-time provides a faculty-student ratio of 1-16.

Entrance Requirements: Liberal admissions policy with 2.0+ GPA. Accredited high school graduation or equivalent required for degree programs; units should include 4 English, 3 mathematics, 2 laboratory science, 2 foreign language, 3 social science; SAT or ACT required; rolling admission, midyear admission, deferred admission and advanced placement available. $35 application fee.

Costs Per Year: $2,349 tuition; $7,407 out-of-state tuition; $4,170 room and board.

Collegiate Environment: This 143-acre campus is located 16 miles southwest of Spokane. The college library contains 520,605 volumes, 91,327 periodicals, and 1,189,920 microforms. Housing facilities accommodate 1,749 students. The Campus School is maintained to provide a complete laboratory experience in elementary education for college students. A Speech and Hearing Clinic is maintained, and Army ROTC training is offered. Study abroad is available to France, Mexico, Thailand, Pakistan, Japan, Korea, China, Soviet Union, Spain, and Ireland. Approximately 86% of students applying for admission are accepted. Freshman classes begin in September, January, March, and June. Financial aid is available, and 38% of a recent freshman class received some form of assistance.

Community Environment: Cheney is located 16 miles from Spokane. The community is reached by railroad, bus lines, and major highways. Spokane airport is approximately 11 miles away. The city has many churches and various civic, fraternal and veteran's organizations. Local recreation includes hunting, fishing, skiing, swimming and nearby lakes. Part-time employment is available.

EDMONDS COMMUNITY COLLEGE   *(E-6)*
20000 68th Avenue West
Lynnwood, Washington 98036
Tel: (206) 640-1372; Fax: (206) 771-3366

Description: This state-supported community college opened in the fall of 1967 and is accredited by the Northwest Association of Schools and Colleges. The school operates on the quarter system and offers technical and vocational courses, freshman and sophomore years of a Baccalaureate degree program, and general continuing education. It offers one summer session. Enrollment includes 3,711 full-time and 4,939 part-time students. A faculty of 141 full-time and 172 part-time provides a faculty-student ratio 1:28.

Entrance Requirements: Open enrollment policy; non high school graduates considered; early admission, advanced placement plans available; $12 application fee.

Costs Per Year: $1,029 tuition; $3,969 out-of-state tuition.

Collegiate Environment: Construction of the first buildings for the 100-acre permanent campus started in March 1969. Now, over 23 million dollars of construction has been completed. The college is located in southwest Snohomish County, just minutes away from Seattle. The library collection numbers 38,000 volumes. All students applying for admission are accepted. The college welcomes a geographically diverse student body and does accept midyear students. Special financial aid is available for economically deprived students and 80% of accepted freshmen with judged need receive some form of assistance. Freshman classes begin in September, January, March, and June.

Community Environment: Lynnwood overlooks the Puget Sound and the Olympic Mountains, and is connected with the Olympic Peninsula by ferry. This is a large, rapidly growing suburban community. The city has a large public marina, good shopping facilities, and good recreation areas. There is a public library, churches, and theatres. Good skiing and winter sports may be found within an hour's drive.

EVERETT COMMUNITY COLLEGE   *(D-7)*
801 Wetmore Avenue
Everett, Washington 98201
Tel: (206) 388-9100; Fax: (206) 339-9129

Description: The state-supported coed community college is accredited by the Northwest Association of Schools and Colleges and the National League of Nursing. It grants certificates and Associate degrees. Enrollment is 9,000 students. A faculty of 113 gives a faculty-student ratio of 1-24. The school operates on the quarter system and offers one summer session.

Entrance Requirements: Open enrollment policy; non-high school graduates 18 and older admitted; rolling admission, early admission, midyear admission, and delayed admission available; $10 application fee.

Costs Per Year: $1,335 tuition; $5,153 out-of-state.

Collegiate Environment: The college occupies a campus of 14 buildings on a 30-acre site adjoining the Municipal Golf Course. The college library contains 16,750 volumes, 380 periodicals, 176 microforms and 4,965 recordings. All applicants are accepted including midyear students. Financial aid is available for economically disadvantaged students. 250 scholarships are available. 30% of the current student body receives some form of assistance.

Community Environment: Located on a natural landlocked harbor at the mouth of the Snohomish River, Everett looks across the Sound at the snowy crags of the Olympic Range. The chief industries of the area are lumbering and the manufacture of airplanes. Railroad lines, bus lines, and Interstate 5 serve the community. More than 60 churches of major denominations, two hospitals, and a library are within the immediate community. Local recreation includes a civic auditorium and stadium, ballfields, tennis courts, roller rinks, bowling alleys, golf courses, outdoor theaters, hunting, fishing, and boating.

Skiing areas are a few hours away. Part-time employment is available for students.

EVERGREEN STATE COLLEGE (G-5)
Olympia, Washington 98505
Tel: (206) 866-6000; Admissions: (206) 866-6000 x6170; Fax: (206) 866-6680

Description: The state-supported arts and sciences college was created by an act of the Washington State Legislature in 1967 and admitted its first student in 1971. Undergraduates may earn a Bachelor of Arts or Bachelor of Science degree. Master's degree programs are offered in Teaching, Public Administration and Environmental Studies. Evergreen provides an innovative academic program that enables students to enroll each quarter in a single, comprehensive program rather than several separate courses. These comprehensive programs, called Coordinated Studies, bring a group of students and faculty into extended contact, allowing students and faculty to work intensively in ways that encourage intellectual growth and friendships. The study of one topic at a time from a variety of perspectives provides students with an excellent opportunity to combine the elements of an undergraduate education in a meaningful, cohesive whole. Studies at Evergreen are interdisciplinary. Students master one or more major fields of study by drawing knowledge from several different academic disciplines to develop an understanding of the relationships between the arts, humanities, and natural and social sciences. A student's academic progress is monitored through letters of evaluation written by faculty members. These letters describe in detail each student's academic activities, objectives, area or concentration, and degree of success in the attempted program. Each bachelor's degree requires the completion of 180 quarter credit hours, 60 credit hours are required for a Master's degree in Public Administration and 72 credit hours are required for a Master's in Environmental Studies. Internships are available to any upper division student, irrespective of concentration. The college is accredited by the Northwest Association of Schools and Colleges and operates on the quarter system with two summer sessions. Enrollment includes 1,412 men and 1,825 women full-time and 193 men and 243 women part-time undergraduates. There are also 277 graduate students. A faculty of 172 full-time and 25 part-time gives an undergraduate faculty-student ratio of 1:19.

Entrance Requirements: High school graduation; consideration on the basis of GPA, ACT or SAT, and diversity factors; advanced placement plans available. $35 application fee.

Costs Per Year: $2,352 tuition; $8,070 out-of-state tuition; $4,480 room and board; $32 student fee per quarter.

Collegiate Environment: At Evergreen, the individual is emphasized not only in the academic program but also in student services, housing, and governance. A classroom at Evergreen is likely to contain students whose ages range from 18 to 65 and whose life-styles range from very traditional to very individual. Students from many other states and several foreign countries have been attracted to Evergreen because of its innovative curriculum and its reasonable cost. It is a state-supported college that offers all the advantages of a small, private liberal arts college. The library has 218,000 volumes, 1,645 periodicals and 4,000 audiovisual materials. About 1,150 students live on campus in the residence halls and in the "mods," a collection of nineteen duplexes containing 2-6 bedroom apartments as well as single and double studios. Housing is close to classrooms and other campus facilities. Evergreen social life is centered in the dormitories, academic programs, student clubs, and special-interest groups. On-campus activities include dances, athletics, plays, films, visiting speakers, concerts, and other special events. The College is situated on 1,000 acres of woods and hills including 3,300 feet of waterfront (salt water) just outside the city of Olympia, Washington's capital. The campus, most of which is forested with alder, maple, and Douglas fir, has trails for walking, jogging, and bicycling, and the beach provides a perfect place for strolling, sunbathing, or marine research. 59% of all applicants accepted. 50% of the students receive financial aid.

Community Environment: Olympia is a seaport community of 37,000, located at the southernmost tip of Puget Sound. The Pacific Ocean is about an hour's drive west of the campus. The rain forests of the Olympic Peninsula lie to the northwest, and the Cascade mountain range is a few hours east of the campus. Seattle, 60 miles from campus, offers all the cultural and recreational activities typically found in a large city.

GONZAGA UNIVERSITY (E-17)
East 502 Boone Avenue
Spokane, Washington 99258-0001
Tel: (509) 328-4220; (800) 523-9712; Fax: (509) 484-2818

Description: This independent Catholic Institution is open to qualified men and women of every race and creed and was founded in 1887 by the Jesuits. One of 28 American colleges and universities under the direction of the Jesuit Fathers, Gonzaga University offers degrees in 45 fields of undergraduate study, several Master's degree programs and a Doctorate in Educational Leadership. The School of Law offers the degree of Juris Doctor. A four-year military science program is offered, and students who qualify may take the programs leading to a reserve commission in the United States Army. The school operates on the early semester system and offers two summer sessions. It is accredited by the Northwest Association of Schools and Colleges and by respective professional organizations. Enrollment includes 2,022 men and 2,100 women full-time, and 317 men and 606 women part-time. A faculty of 272 gives a faculty-student ratio of 1-15.

Entrance Requirements: Accredited high school graduation recommended; completion of 17 units, preferably 4 English, 3 mathematics, 2 foreign language, 1 science, 1 social science, and 6 electives, 4 from the above listed subjects; SAT or ACT required, non-high school graduates considered; rolling admission, delayed admission and advanced placement programs available; $30 application fee.

Costs Per Year: $12,200 tuition; $4,150 room and board; $400 student fees.

Collegiate Environment: The 39 major buildings of the college stand on an 84-acre campus beside the Spokane River. The university also maintains a retreat house for students at the Bozarth Center, a ten-acre suburban estate overlooking the Little Spokane River. There are dormitories for 1,160 men and women. The Foley Center Library houses 114,368 volumes, 231,924 current serials, 2,000 microforms, 1,849 audiovisual materials, and 14,000 machine-readable materials. The Law Library houses 61,505 volumes, 316,197 current serials, 11,793 microforms, 3,397 audiovisual materials, and 9,743 machine-readable materials. Much of campus life centers around the central Student Union Building popularly known as the COG, and the Crosby Student Center. Approximately 79% of students applying for admission meet the requirements and are accepted. The college seeks a geographically diverse student body and admits disadvantaged students. Financial aid is available; 1,200 scholarships are available to freshmen, 84 of which are athletic. 75% of students receive financial aid. The university has an overseas campus in Florence, Italy, where qualified students of junior standing may partake of the riches of European travel and residence while completing one year of the regular Gonzaga curriculum. Additional study abroad opportunities are available in England, France, Spain, and Japan. Qualified high school juniors and seniors are allowed to take courses. Limited enrollments are available for students who do not meet regular admission standards.

Community Environment: See Spokane Falls Community College.

GRAYS HARBOR COLLEGE (G-3)
1620 Edward P. Smith Drive
Aberdeen, Washington 98520
Tel: (206) 532-9020; (800) 562-4830; Admissions: (206) 538-4026; Fax: (206) 538-4299

Description: The state-supported community college is accredited by the Northwest Association of Schools and Colleges. It was founded in 1930. The quarter system is used and one summer term is offered. The four objectives are to provide students with a general education, with vocational or semiprofessional education, with two-year transfer courses, and adult education in academic, vocational, and recreational areas. Recent enrollment included 1,253 men and 1,708 women. The faculty consists of 50 full-time and 104 part-time instructors. The faculty-student ratio is 1:23. Programs of study lead to a Certificate and Associate degree.

Entrance Requirements: Open enrollment policy; non high school graduates considered; candidates for degree programs must be high school graduates or equivalent; early admission, midyear admission and advanced placement plans available.

Costs Per Year: $1,374 tuition; $5,400 out-of-state tuition; additional expenses average $750.

Collegiate Environment: There are eleven buildings on the 120-acre campus. The library opened in 1966 and now contains 43,000 volumes, 1,500 pamphlets, 366 periodicals and 1,378 recordings and audiovisual materials. The college has no dormitories. Financial aid is available for many students, and 60% of the current student body receives some form of assistance. The college awards 110 scholarships, and 80 of these are typically given to freshman students. The college awarded 136 Certificates and 186 Associate degrees during the school year.

Community Environment: Aberdeen is located in a heavily wooded area and is known chiefly for its lumbering and fishing. The area has good harbors where the fishing fleet anchors. The city has mild winters and cool summers, with up to 75 inches of rainfall per year. There is a public library, YMCA, two hospitals, and churches of the major denominations serving the community. Aberdeen may be reached by bus lines and state highways. Local recreation includes theatres, hunting and fishing in the surrounding area, golf courses, swimming pool, public parks, tennis and skiing three hours drive away. The community has civic, fraternal and veteran's organizations. Part-time employment is available.

GREEN RIVER COMMUNITY COLLEGE   *(F-6)*
12401 S.E. 320th Street
Auburn, Washington 98092-3699
Tel: (206) 833-9111; Admissions: (206) 833-9111 x248; Fax: (206) 939-5135

Description: Authorization for the establishment of this two-year college was granted by the State Board of Education in 1963, and the college opened officially in September of 1965. It is accredited by the Northwest Association of Schools and Colleges. It operates on the quarter system and offers one summer session. The college offers two-year transfer courses, vocational and technical education, and general adult education leading to the Associate degree. Enrollment includes 4,870 full-time and 3,830 part-time students. A faculty of 113 full-time and 200 part-time provides a faculty-student ratio of 1-26.

Entrance Requirements: Open enrollment policy; high school graduation required for degree programs; Assessment test required for placement purposes; rolling admission plan.

Costs Per Year: $1,296 tuition; $5,094 out-of-state; $600 average additional expenses.

Collegiate Environment: There are 22 buildings on the 168-acre campus in Auburn. The Holman Library contains 40,000 volumes, 500 periodicals and 1,300 audiovisual materials. The Performing Arts Buildings include a theater with 230 seats, music practice rooms, drama classes, and faculty offices. The Physical Education Fieldhouse has athletic facilities, classrooms, rhythm room, locker rooms, and faculty offices. Instruction in golf, swimming, skiing, and bowling is offered in facilities off campus. Financial aid is available. Approximately 25% of the students receive some form of assistance.

Community Environment: Auburn is a suburban community in the Seattle area. It is located approximately 30 miles from the heart of downtown Seattle. The climate is mild. Auburn may be reached by railroad, the Seattle airport, and major highways. One library, several churches, a museum, YMCA, general hospital, and clinics serve the community. Local recreation includes a city park, a golf club, community theater, a nearby beach and rivers, hunting for deer, bear, birds and elk, lake fishing, water sports, skiing and mountain climbing. Some part-time employment is available. Various civic and fraternal organizations are active in the community. There are good shopping facilities.

HERITAGE COLLEGE   *(J-10)*
3240 Fort Road
Toppenish, Washington 98948
Tel: (509) 865-2244; Fax: (509) 865-4469

Description: Heritage College is a four-year, independent, non-denominational, liberal arts college. Its mission is to provide quality, accessible, higher education at the undergraduate and graduate levels to a multicultural population that is educationally isolated. Heritage College, accredited by the Northwest Association of Schools and Colleges, began granting credits on July 1, 1982, and is the successor institution to Fort Wright College of the Holy Names, Spokane,

Washington, 1907-1982. The calendar consists of two semesters and one summer session. The liberal arts curriculum leads to Associate, Baccalaureate and Master degrees. Enrollment includes 708 women and 258 men; the average age is about 33 years. A faculty of 34 full-time and 145 part-time provides a faculty-student ratio of 1-16.

Entrance Requirements: Accredited high school graduation with a satisfactory academic grade point average is recommended but successful completion of the General Educational Development (GED) test is also acceptable. Recommended completion of three years of English, three years of history, one year of laboratory science, and two years of mathematics; SAT or ACT recommended. Open admission, rolling admission; no undergraduate application fee.

Costs Per Year: $4,656 tuition; $10 student activity fees.

Collegiate Environment: The small, friendly campus is located in a rural area three miles from Toppenish (7,000 population). Included in student services is a library which houses over 55,000 volumes and 195 current periodicals; personalized academic advising; tutoring services; a computer lab which is available to students during the day, evening and Saturdays; and a food service. Both day and evening courses are available; working students may obtain a degree through evening courses. Financial aid is available; approximately 95% of the full-time undergraduates receive some form of aid. The College is an approved Veterans Administration school. Heritage College awarded 55 Bachelor and 220 Master degrees last year.

Community Environment: Toppenish is located in the fertile lower Yakima Valley twenty miles south of Yakima (48,000). The Valley produces fruit, grapes, hops and includes agricultural related industries. The climate is mild and dry. Toppenish has churches representing most denominations and a hospital. Local recreation includes swimming, skiing, boating, fishing, hunting, and golf. Local events include the Toppenish Rodeo and Pow-Wow, the Cinco de Mayo celebrations, Yakima Indian Nation cultural Center events. Yakima has its own symphony, civic theatre, community concert series, and arts events.

HIGHLINE COMMUNITY COLLEGE   *(L-3)*
2400 South 240th Street
Des Moines, Washington 98198-9800
Tel: (206) 878-3710; Admissions: (206) 878-3710; Fax: (206) 870-3782

Description: The state-supported community college was founded in 1961. It is accredited by the Northwest Association of Schools and Colleges. The college has four principal objectives; to provide a broad, general education, to offer university-parallel courses equivalent to the first two years of a senior college, to provide a program of technical and vocational curricula, and to offer a program for adults. The college grants the Associate degree. It operates on the quarter system and offers one summer session. Enrollment includes 9,500 students. A faculty of 132 full-time and 300 part-time gives a faculty-student ratio of 1-34.

Entrance Requirements: Open door policy. Accredited high school graduation required for degree programs; early admission, early decision, rolling admission, and advanced placement plans available.

Costs Per Year: $1,296 tuition; $5,094 out-of-state tuition.

Collegiate Environment: The 80-acre campus has 30 buildings. No on-campus housing is available at the college but off-campus housing is available in the vicinity of the campus for those who cannot commute. The library collection numbers 60,710 volumes, 4,000 pamphlets, 500 periodicals, 3,000 microforms, and 6,000 sound recordings. The Student Center is the focus of the co-curricular program of the college. Food service is available throughout the day and evening for meals and snacks. Financial aid is available. About 25% of a recent freshman class received some form of assistance. The college offers a limited number of scholarships for athletics, performing arts, and academic achievement. Approximately 50% of the current student body graduated in the top half of the high school class, 25% in the top quarter, and 10% in the highest tenth. Over 65% of the previous freshman class returned to this campus for the sophomore year. The college awarded 850 Associate degrees to the graduating class. Cooperative programs are offered.

Community Environment: Overlooking the Puget Sound, Des Moines is a suburb of Seattle, approximately 15 miles from the heart of downtown. (See Seattle University.) The community has all the advantages of a small town, and yet is easily accessible to all the cultural, recreational, and civic opportunities of the neighboring community.

LOWER COLUMBIA COLLEGE   (J-5)
P.O. Box 3010
Longview, Washington 98632
Tel: (360) 577-2303; Admissions: (360) 577-2311; Fax: (360) 577-3400

Description: This public community college was founded in 1934 and is accredited by the Northwest Association of Schools and Colleges. The college provides two-year transfer courses leading to the Associate degree, technical and vocational education leading to an Associate Degree or a Certificate, and general continuing education for those who wish to attend college on an evening or part-time basis. One quarter of study in London is available. The college operates on the quarter system and offers one summer session. Enrollment includes 1,800 full-time and 2,200 part-time students. A faculty of 78 full-time and 80 part-time gives a faculty-student ratio of 1-26.

Entrance Requirements: Open door policy; non-high school graduates considered; early admission, rolling admission, and early decision plans available; no application fee.

Costs Per Year: $1,320 tuition; $5,118 out-of-state tuition.

Collegiate Environment: The 25-acre campus is adjacent to Longview's civic center. There are sixteen buildings including a library of 35,000 volumes, 1,000 periodicals, and 500 audiovisual materials. Many home owners and apartment dwellers in the area provide rooms or room and board for students. There are no dormitories on campus. The college welcomes a geographically diverse student body and accepts midyear students. Financial aid is available for economically disadvantaged students, and 40% of a recent class received some form of assistance. About 400 scholarships are granted annually. All students applying for admission are accepted and 75% of the previous freshman class returned to this campus for the sophomore year. The college awarded 310 Associate degrees during the school year.

Community Environment: Longview is a planned city located on the banks of the Columbia and Cowlitz Rivers. The city is 50 miles north of Portland, Oregon, and has a mild climate. There are several churches, a public library, YMCA and two hospitals accessible. Longview may be reached by five railroad lines, and an airport. Local recreation includes theatres, boating, fishing, golf, hunting, skiing, and other sports. Part-time employment is available for students. Hotels, motels, and apartments are available for student housing. The community has several large shopping centers.

NORTH SEATTLE COMMUNITY COLLEGE   (E-6)
9600 College Way North
Seattle, Washington 98133
Tel: (206) 527-3600; Admissions: (206) 527-3664; Fax: (206) 527-3606

Description: This state-supported community college opened in 1970 as part of the Seattle Community College District. The college is accredited by the Northwest Association of Schools and Colleges and the Committee on Allied Health Education and Accreditation. It offers university transfer, general education, and vocational and technical programs, and grants the Associate degree. It operates on the quarter system and offers one summer session. Enrollment is 5,017 women and 3,785 men with 63% of the students attending part-time and 37% attending full-time. A faculty of 203 gives a faculty-student ratio of 1-43.

Entrance Requirements: Open enrollment policy. Rolling admission and midyear admission plans available.

Costs Per Year: $1,278 tuition; $5,076 out-of-state tuition.

Collegiate Environment: The campus is located eight miles north of downtown Seattle and west of the Northgate Shopping Center. The library contains 38,000 volumes, 3,400 pamphlets, 406 periodicals, 585 units and 598 sound recordings. All of the applicants are accepted. 13% of the students receive financial aid. 90 scholarships are offered, including 49 for freshmen.

Community Environment: See Seattle University.

NORTHWEST COLLEGE   (E-6)
P.O. Box 579
Kirkland, Washington 98083
Tel: (206) 822-8266; (800) 669-3781; Fax: (206) 827-0148

Description: This Christian liberal arts college offers programs on the undergraduate level providing general education, training for Christian service or preparation for other professional fields of activity. The college is operated under the control of the Northwest, the Montana, the Alaska, the Southern Idaho and the Wyoming District Councils of the Assemblies of God. Founded in 1934, it is accredited by the American Association of Bible Colleges and the Northwest Association of Schools and Colleges. It is also a member of the Christian College Coalition. Enrollment includes 839 students. A faculty of 35 full-time and 25 part-time provides a faculty-student ratio of 1-19. The semester system is used. The college grants an Associate or a Baccalaureate degree.

Entrance Requirements: High school graduation; completion of 16 units including 4 English, 3 math, 2 science, 2 social science, 2 foreign language; ACT or SAT required; candidates not meeting all requirements may be admitted as special students; application fee $20; rolling admission plan; references and recommendations required.

Costs Per Year: $7,140 tuition; $3,660 room and board; $660 student fees; additional expenses average $1,000.

Collegiate Environment: The 60-acre campus is ten miles from downtown Seattle. Nineteen buildings of modern design and colorful decor include the chapel building, which houses the chapel sanctuary. The college library contains 92,000 volumes and 4,200 periodicals. There are five residence halls that accommodate 520 students. The college welcomes a geographically diverse student body, and midyear students are accepted. Special financial aid is available. 86% of students receive some form of financial aid.

Community Environment: Kirkland is a suburb of Seattle. See Seattle University.

OLYMPIC COLLEGE   (F-6)
16th and Chester
Bremerton, Washington 98310-1699
Tel: (206) 478-4504; Fax: (206) 792-2135

Description: The state-supported community college opened in 1946. It has an enrollment of 1,461 men and 1,326 women full-time and 1,762 men and 2,162 women part-time. A faculty of 99 full-time and 318 part-time gives a faculty-student ratio of 1-15. The quarter system is used and one summer term is offered. It is accredited by the Northwest Association of Schools and Colleges. Transfer courses, vocational and technical courses, community service, extension and general educational courses offering continuing education for adults are offered.

Entrance Requirements: Open enrollment policy; high school graduation or GED usually required; delayed admission, early admission, rolling admission, early decision and advanced placement plans available; no application fee.

Costs Per Year: $1,296 tuition; $5,094 out-of-state tuition.

Collegiate Environment: There are 18 buildings on the 21-acre campus. The library contains 58,024 volumes, 421 periodicals, 145 microforms and 10,049 audiovisual materials. Financial aid is available for economically disadvantaged students and 35% of the students receive financial aid. Half the 312 scholarships offered are for freshmen. All students applying for admission are accepted including midyear students.

Community Environment: Bremerton is a metropolitan community enjoying mild summer and winter temperatures. The major local industry is shipbuilding. The community has a library, churches of most denominations, a hospital, and active civic, fraternal and veteran's organizations. Local recreation includes hunting, salt water and fresh water fishing, water skiing, sailboating, and skiing in the winter. Job opportunities are available for students. Rooming and boarding houses and small apartments are available for student housing.

PACIFIC LUTHERAN UNIVERSITY   (G-6)
Park Avenue and 121 Street
Tacoma, Washington 98447
Tel: (206) 531-6900

Description: This private, coeducational university was founded in 1890 and has occupied the same location since its beginning. It is fully accredited by the Northwest Association of Schools and Colleges as a four-year institution of higher education. It is also accredited by several respective professional institutions. It operates on the 4-1-4 system and offers three summer sessions. The university is affiliated with the American Lutheran Church. Enrollment includes 1,078 men and 1,586 women full-time, and 110 men and 190 women part-time. There is a faculty of 231 full-time and 89 part-time. The university grants a Baccalaureate and a Master's degree. Academic cooperative plans with several universities are available for students majoring in engineering. All departments have cooperative education programs. Army ROTC is available.

Entrance Requirements: Accredited high school graduation with rank in upper half of graduating class; recommended completion of 16 units including 4 English, 3 mathematics, 2 foreign language, 2 science, 2 social science, SAT with minimum combined score of 800 or ACT minimum composite score of 21 recommended; GPA of 2.5; recommended evidence of community, school, church or volunteer service; GRE required for graduate programs; $35 application fee; rolling admission, delayed admission, early decision, advanced placement, and early admission plans available.

Costs Per Year: $12,677 tuition; $4,030 room and board.

Collegiate Environment: The 143-acre campus is in Parkland, an unincorporated suburb of Tacoma, seven miles south of the city and adjacent to Mt. Rainier highway. There are 28 buildings including housing accommodations for 798 men, 959 women and 40 families. Outdoor recreational facilities include a nine-hole golf course, tennis courts and athletic fields. The university operates a noncommercial FM broadcasting station (National Public Radio). The Robert Mortvedt Library is a multimedia learning center that contains 333,010 volumes, 2,110 periodicals, 54,151 microforms and 2,561 audiovisual materials. Eastvold Auditorium seats 1,238 persons and is used for concerts, special events, and plays. Approximately 80% of students applying for admission meet the requirements and are accepted including midyear students. 75% of the current enrollment receives some form of financial assistance. The college awards 1,801 scholarships, 650 of which are made available to freshmen and 150 of which are athletic scholarships. More than 80% of the previous freshman class returned for the sophomore year.

Community Environment: The third largest city in Washington, Tacoma is a shipping, industrial and distributing center located in the Puget Sound region. The city has diversified industries including electrochemicals, food and beverage processing, clothing manufacturing, iron, steel and shipyards. Tacoma is near Mt. Rainier National park and its residents enjoy easy access to ocean beaches, the many waterways of Puget Sound, and Olympic and North Cascades National Parks. The area is provided transportation by railroads, airlines, twelve bus lines and major highways. Nearby lakes and streams offer excellent fishing. The city has many parks, public library system, museums, hospitals and many civic and fraternal organizations to serve the community.

PENINSULA COLLEGE   *(D-4)*
1502 E. Lauridsen Blvd.
Port Angeles, Washington 98362
Tel: (206) 452-9277

Description: This public comprehensive community college was founded in 1961 and is accredited by the Northwest Association of Schools and Colleges. The quarter system is used and one summer term is offered. Enrollment includes 498 men, 519 women full-time and 571 men and 595 women part-time. The faculty consists of 50 full-time and 55 part-time members. The first two years of college education for those planning to transfer to a four-year college or university, vocational and technical education, and general continuing education are offered.

Entrance Requirements: High School graduation or equivalent; open enrollment policy; placement exams required; advanced placement plan available

Costs Per Year: $999 tuition; $3,939 out-of-state tuition; $2,350 room and board; $30 student fees.

Collegiate Environment: Campus buildings are designed to complement the scenic setting in the forested foothills of the Olympic Mountains. There are special facilities for art, music, journalism, speech and dramatics, including a theatre with seating for 270. The library contains 37,150 volumes, 379 periodicals 1,700 microforms and 10,970 audio-visual materials. The Student Center has a cafeteria and snack bar, areas for student relaxation and socializing, a bookstore and offices for student activities. Special financial aid is available for economically disadvantaged students.

Community Environment: Called the gateway to Olympic National Park, Port Angeles is a popular resort and tourist area located between the Olympic Mountains and Strait of Juan de Fuca. The area enjoys temperate climate with temperature ranges from 30 to 80 degrees. Average rainfall is 22.8 inches. The city may be reached by airlines and highways. There are libraries, churches representing many denominations, a YMCA, and a modern hospital. Local recreation includes theatres, parks, concerts, plays, swimming, golf, skiing, bowling, hiking, crabbing, fishing, sailing and other sports. The community has many civic organizations, a symphony orchestra, choral and theater groups.

PIERCE COLLEGE   *(G-6)*
9401 Farwest Drive, S.W.
Tacoma, Washington 98498
Tel: (206) 964-6500

Description: This college, formerly known as Fort Steilacoom Community College, was founded in 1967. The name was changed by the Board of Trustees on March 12, 1986, to better reflect the college's service district. It is accredited by the Northwest Association of Schools and Colleges. This state-supported two-year community college offers the first two years of a baccalaureate degree program, occupational education in many fields, continuing education for professional and personal development, customized training for business and industry, basic skills training, high school completion, and personal and career counseling. It operates on the quarter system with one summer session. Enrollment includes approximately 2,416 men and 2,723 women full-time and 1,593 men and 1,427 women part-time. A faculty of 164 full-time and 378 part-time gives a faculty-student ratio of 1-21.

Entrance Requirements: Open enrollment policy; rolling admission and midyear admission plans available.

Costs Per Year: $1,326 state resident tuition and fees; $5,124 nonresident tuition and fees.

Collegiate Environment: Pierce College at Fort Steilacoom is located in the suburban Lakes district of Tacoma on a 135-acre campus with a view of majestic Mount Rainier. The mall-concept campus provides year-round protection from inclement weather. The Library/Media Center houses 55,000 volumes, 360 periodicals and numerous microforms and audiovisual materials. A student center provides food service, meeting rooms, a games room, a performance lounge, and space for many student and community activities. The college also boasts athletic programs for men and women, a fine arts gallery, a performing arts theatre, indoor swimming pool and fitness center, tennis courts, and a dental clinic. Nearby are park facilities for outdoor recreation. Pierce College at Puyallup is located on the city's rapidly growing South Hill. Day and evening programs in college transfer, business, and technological programs are offered in a convenient, modern facility that serves more than 2,000 students each quarter. All Pierce College students are encouraged to participate in social and cultural events and organizations, college governance, and tenure review. A wide variety of extension programs are offered throughout greater Pierce County, at military bases and at local high schools. Financial aid and learning assistance services are available.

Community Environment: The Pierce College service district is all of Pierce County south and east of the city limits of Tacoma, an area stretching from the shores of Puget Sound on the west to Mount Rainier on the east. It includes suburban communities adjacent to Tacoma (see Tacoma Community College for a description), the rapidly growing cities of eastern Pierce County, military installations at Fort Lewis and McChord Air Force Base, and picturesque rural areas. Scenic outdoor recreation sites including Mount Rainier National Park, numerous lakes, saltwater parks, and forests are contained within the district. High-tech "clean" industires are a growing part of the area's economy, along with shipping, timber, paper, manufacturing, tourism, aerospace, agriculture, and health-related industries.

PUGET SOUND CHRISTIAN COLLEGE (E-6)
410 Fourth Ave. North
Edmonds, Washington 98020-3171
Tel: (206) 775-8686; Admissions: (206) 775-8686; Fax: (206) 775-8688

Description: This private Christian college was founded in 1950 by members of the West Seattle Christian Church. Its purpose is to conduct a nondenominational institution that prepares men and women in the various general ministries of the Gospel of Christ. Enrollment includes 78 full-time, 10 part-time and 9 evening students. A faculty of 11 gives a faculty-student ratio of 1-8. The college offers the Bachelor of Arts degree with a choice of nine second majors. All graduates receive a major in Bible. Also offered are a one-year Bible certificate and an Associate of Arts in Church Office Management. The college also offers a degree-completion program for older students who have completed two years of college.

Entrance Requirements: Accredited high school graduation or equivalent; open enrollment policy; rolling admission available; $25 application fee.

Costs Per Year: $5,097 tuition; $3,300 room and board; $285 student fees.

Collegiate Environment: College facilities include one large classroom-office building, a library building, a music building and one apartment building that provides housing for 33 students and 1 family. The library contains 31,000 volumes. Classes begin in September, January, and March. The college welcomes a geographically diverse student body. Financial aid is available for economically disadvantaged students. 90% of those who apply for admission are accepted.

Community Environment: Edmonds is a suburban community of 38,000, fifteen miles north of Seattle. The campus is 4 blocks from the shopping area and Sunset Beach on the Sound. The Olympic mountains to the west and the Cascade mountains to the northeast give the area a natural beauty that is calm and serene. It is situated on the Puget Sound and has a ferry dock for the Washington State Ferry System. Cultural and educational benefits abound in the area. There is also an ample supply of part-time jobs for students. See also Seattle University.

SAINT MARTIN'S COLLEGE (G-5)
5300 Pacific Avenue SE
Lacey, Washington 98503
Tel: (360) 438-4311; (800) 368-8803; Fax: (360) 459-4124

Description: The four-year coeducational college was founded by Benedictine educators in 1895 and is accredited by the Northwest Association of Schools and Colleges. It offers liberal arts and sciences, business, and education programs. The college awards the Associate, Bachelor's and Master's degrees. It operates on the semester system and offers one summer session. Enrollment includes 472 full-time and 414 part-time students. A faculty of 79 gives a faculty-student ratio of 1-12.

Entrance Requirements: Accredited high school graduation; completion of 16 units including 4 English, 2 mathematics, 2 science, 2 social science, 1-2 foreign language; SAT or ACT required; $25 application fee.

Costs Per Year: $11,550 tuition; $4,270 room and board; $155 student fees.

Collegiate Environment: The 380-acre campus is primarily undeveloped, forested land. The Chapel, Monastery, the 84,019-volume library, classrooms, laboratories and offices are on the hill in the south portion of the campus. Other buildings and the athletic fields are found below the hill. The residence halls can accomodate 300 students. Approximately 95% of students applying for admission meet the requirements, and 95% of these are accepted. Freshman classes begin in September and January. The college welcomes a geographically diverse student body. 8% of student body are international students. Financial aid and merit based scholarships are available. 75% of a recent freshman class received some form of assistance. About 50% of the current student body graduated in the top half of the high school class, 25% in the top quarter, and 15% in the highest tenth. Almost 61% of the previous freshman class returned for the sophomore year.

Community Environment: Lacey is a surburb of Olympia, capital of the State, and an important commercial city. Olympia is situated at the southern end of Puget Sound with low green hills surrounding it. This is a seaport town with mild climate. The average temperature is 50 degrees, with an average rainfall of 52 inches. Olympia is accessible by U.S. Highways 5 and 101, and Amtrak, Greyhound, local Olympia Transit Company, all provide transportation to the area. There are many churches representing approximately 24 religious denominations. Hospitals, YMCA and YWCA, Washington Center for the Performing Arts and libraries also serve the community. Local recreation includes 20 nearby lakes, boating, swimming, fishing, salt water sports, golf and skiing. There are several annual shows held in the community and a water carnival called "The Lakefair." Part-time employment is available.

Branch Campuses: McChord AFB and Ft. Lewis Army Base. The two branch campuses offer 10 undergraduate degrees and 1 masters degree.

SEATTLE CENTRAL COMMUNITY COLLEGE (E-6)
1701 Broadway
Seattle, Washington 98122
Tel: (206) 587-5450

Description: Opened in 1966, this state-supported junior college is an open-door educational institution organized to provide the courses needed by individuals and the community. It is accredited by the Northwest Association of Schools and Colleges and professionally by the Committee on Allied Health Education and Accreditation. The programs are grouped into three major areas: College, Occupational, and Community Service. It grants diplomas, certificates, and Associate degrees, and offers cooperative education programs in several fields. It operates on the quarter system and offers one summer term. Enrollment is 2,289 men and 3,033 women full-time and 1,701 men and 3,006 women part-time. A faculty of 114 full-time and 267 part-time gives an overall faculty-student ratio of 1-25.

Entrance Requirements: Open enrollment policy; non-high school graduates considered; early admission, rolling admission, delayed admission and advanced placement available.

Costs Per Year: $1,278 tuition; $5,322 out-of-state; $400 average additional expenses.

Collegiate Environment: One campus in the north section and one in the south section have been designed so that each will offer a comprehensive program. Freshman classes begin in September. The library contains more than 42,000 volumes, 20,000 pamphlets, 440 periodicals, 33,000 microforms, and 20,500 audiovisual materials. The college offers 220 scholarships, and about 65% of the day students receive some form of financial aid.

Community Environment: See Seattle University.

SEATTLE PACIFIC UNIVERSITY (E-6)
3307 Third Avenue West
Seattle, Washington 98119
Tel: (206) 281-2021; (800) 366-3344

Description: Founded in 1891, Seattle Pacific is a private co-educational university of the liberal arts, sciences and professional studies affiliated with the Free Methodist Church of North America. It is accredited by the Northwest Association of Schools and Colleges. Programs of study are accredited by professional accrediting institutions. The university meets the requirements of the Commission of Christian Education for the collegiate preparation of ministers and missionaries. As an evangelical Christian institution, it seeks to nurture students through a comprehensive and quality education that is both academically sound and distinctly Christian. Baccalaureate degrees are offered in 43 majors. In addition, the university awards the MA, MS, M.Ed, MBA, MAT, and MSN degrees. Master's degree programs are offered by the Schools of Business and Economics, Education, Health Sciences, Religion, and Social and Behavioral Science. The university operates on the quarter system and offers two summer sessions. Off-campus studies and international study opportunities are available throughout Europe, Latin America and Asia. Air Force and Army ROTC programs are available. Undergraduate enrollment includes 858 men and 1,504 women. A faculty of 159 full-time and 52 part-time gives an overall faculty-student ratio of 1:14.

Entrance Requirements: High school graduation or equivalent; SAT or ACT required; GRE, GMAT or Miller's Analogies required for graduate programs; non-high school graduates considered; early decision, rolling admission, advanced placement plans available; $35 application fee.

Costs Per Year: $12,669 tuition; $4,875 room and board.

Collegiate Environment: The 35-acre campus is located in the heart of Seattle. There are 37 buildings. Housing includes dormitory accommodations for 1,001 students, 229 apartment spaces, and 71 family housing units. The library contains 176,500 volumes, 1,570 periodicals, 418,800 microforms and 4,300 recordings. The "hub" of the activities is the hour chapel assembly. Participation by the entire student body gives campus life a unique unity, and attendance is required of undergraduates. Approximately 87% of students applying for admission are accepted, including midyear students. The college welcomes a geographically diverse student body. About 67% of the current student body receives some form of financial assistance. The college awards 1,110 scholarships of which 412 are available for freshmen. Average scores of the current freshman class, SAT 472V, 528M.

Community Environment: See Seattle University.

SEATTLE UNIVERSITY   *(E-6)*
12th and E. Columbia
Seattle, Washington 98122
Tel: (206) 296-6000; (800) 426-7123; Admissions: (206) 296-5800; Fax: (206) 296-5656

Description: The Roman Catholic university is operated under the sponsorship and direction of the members of the Jesuit Society. It is open to students of all races and denominations and is accredited by the Northwest Association of Schools and Colleges and by respective professional and educational organizations. The university is composed of eight major academic units: The College of Arts and Sciences, the Albers School of Business, the School pf Law, the School of Education, the School of Science and Engineering, the School of Nursing, the Graduate School and Matteo Ricci College, a three-year baccalaureate degree program. Overseas programs are available in Austria, France and Japan. The university operates on the quarter system and offers two summer sessions. Enrollment includes 2,357 full-time and 1,063 part-time undergraduate and 2,671 graduate students. A faculty of 280 full-time and 183 part-time gives an overall faculty-student ratio of 1-14. Army, Navy, and Air Force ROTC programs are available.

Entrance Requirements: Accredited high school graduation or equivalent; completion of 16 units including 3 English, 2 mathematics, 1 science, 1 history, 9 academic electives; 2 foreign language units are recommended for arts and science applicants with 7 academic electives; ACT or SAT (minimum: 850 combined) is required; students not meeting all requirements may be admitted by examination; early admission, rolling admission, delayed admission, midyear admission, early decision and advanced placement plans available; $40 application fee.

Costs Per Year: $12,825 tuition; $4,890 room and board.

Collegiate Environment: The 46-acre campus is situated on Seattle's historic First Hill. There are coed dormitory facilities for 1,100 students. The library system contains 199,685 hardbound volumes, 1,430 periodicals and 1,874 microforms. 79% of freshmen, 66% of transfer, and 56% of graduate applicants are accepted and offered admission. The average scores of the admitted freshman class were ACT 24 composite, SAT 1000 combined. Scholarships are available and 63% of the current student body receives some form of financial aid. Awards are based on both scholastic achievement and financial need. Matteo Ricci College program represents the last three years of a six-year integrated high school-college experience in which collegiate and secondary school faculties of Seattle U. and Seattle Preparatory School coordinate in curriculum planning and cooperate in instruction. Enrollment is restricted to those who begin Matteo Ricci as freshmen in high school.

Community Environment: Built upon the hills between Lake Washington and Puget Sound, Seattle is the metropolis of the Pacific Northwest. A fine protected harbor makes the city one of the world's great seaports. The community has a prosperous fishing industry, and is important for shipping of fir, red cedar and salmon. Other industries in the area include aerospace and related fields, foundries, electronics,

marine science firms and the processing of food and forest products. The summer average temperature is 63 degrees, and the winter average is 42 degrees. Mountains surround the city and 193 miles of waterfront accommodate ocean-going vessels. The community has 45 parks, art galleries, museums, year-round theater, and opera. There are churches representing all major denominations, and civic, fraternal and veteran's organizations active in the area. Part-time employment is available. Professional sport teams include the Seahawks (football), Mariners (baseball), and Sonics (basketball).

SHORELINE COMMUNITY COLLEGE   *(E-6)*
16101 Greenwood Avenue North
Seattle, Washington 98133
Tel: (206) 546-4101; Admissions: (206) 546-4621; Fax: (206) 546-5826

Description: This state-supported community college was founded in 1964 and is accredited by the Northwest Association of Schools and Colleges and the National League for Nursing. Enrollment includes 7,500 men and women. A faculty of 160 full-time and 152 part-time gives an overall faculty-student ratio of 1-24. The quarter system is employed and one summer term is offered. The college offers transfer programs, occupational courses, and general continuing education for adults. Study abroad in London is available.

Entrance Requirements: Open enrollment policy; non-high school graduates considered; rolling admission available; $10 application fee.

Costs Per Year: $1,284 tuition; $5,082 out-of-state tuition.

Collegiate Environment: The college has 25 buildings on the 82-acre campus. The library learning center contains 75,000 volumes, 700 periodicals, 7,000 microforms and 10,000 audio-visual materials. Financial aid is available for economically disadvantaged students. 11% of students receive financial aid. Freshman classes begin in September, January, March, and June. About 95% of students applying for admission are accepted.

Community Environment: See Seattle University.

SKAGIT VALLEY COLLEGE   *(C-6)*
2405 College Way
Mount Vernon, Washington 98273
Tel: (206) 428-1261

Description: This public community college offers transfer courses, vocational-technical programs and continuing education for citizens in the community who may desire further preparation in general education. It was founded in 1926 and is accredited by the Northwest Association of Schools and Colleges. Enrollment includes 1,309 men, 1,440 women full-time and 1,317 men and 2,490 women part-time. A faculty of 85 full-time and 75 part-time gives a faculty-student ratio of 1:20. The quarter system is used and one summer term is offered.

Entrance Requirements: Open enrollment policy; non-high school graduates considered; early admission, early decision, rolling admission, delayed admission and advanced placement plans available;

Costs Per Year: $999 tuition; $3,939 out-of-state tuition; additional expenses average $250.

Collegiate Environment: The 85-acre campus has ten buildings. The library seats 250 students and houses 32,000 volumes. No dormitories are available. Special financial aid is available for economically disadvantaged students and 35% receive some form of assistance. All students applying for admission are accepted.

Community Environment: Agriculture, mixed industries and tourism are the principal industries in this city located on the Skagit River. The climate here is moderate with neither cold nor hot extremes. Mount Vernon is accessible by Burlington Northern Railroad, Greyhound Bus Lines and major highways. The community has several churches, two hospitals and YMCA serving the residents. Local recreation includes hunting, fishing, skiing, golfing, boating, swimming, salt water or fresh water sports and nearby mountains and forests recreation areas. Various fraternal and civic organizations are found within the community.

Branch Campuses: Whibey Campus, Oak Harbor; South Whidbey Center, Langley; San Juan Center, Friday Harbor.

SOUTH SEATTLE COMMUNITY COLLEGE - SOUTH CAMPUS *(E-6)*
6000-16 Avenue S.W.
Seattle, Washington 98106
Tel: (206) 764-5378; Fax: (206) 764-7942

Description: Publicly supported community college was planned to function as the true community education center of urban Seattle. The college offers programs of vocational and technical education, liberal arts and community service education. The college is fully accredited by the Northwest Association of Schools and Colleges. The quarter system is used and one summer session is offered. Enrollment includes 2,670 full-time students and 3,885 part-time students. A faculty of 296 gives a faculty-student ratio of 1-22.

Entrance Requirements: Open enrollment policy; non-high school graduates admitted; advanced placement plan available.

Costs Per Year: $1,278 tuition; $5,076 nonresident tuition.

Collegiate Environment: The college is a comprehensive community college designed and operated to serve a wide variety of students with differing educational needs and objectives. The library contains 27,711 bound volumes, 14 CD-ROMs, internet, and 8,674 audiovisual materials. All students applying for admission are accepted. Financial aid is available and approximately 30% of the current student body receives some form of financial assistance.

Community Environment: See Seattle University

SPOKANE COMMUNITY COLLEGE *(E-17)*
North 2000 Greene Street-Mailstop 2150
Spokane, Washington 99207
Tel: (509) 533-7000; (800) 248-5644; Fax: (509) 533-8839

Description: In 1963 the State Board of Education authorized establishment of a two-year community college in Spokane; a college transfer program was added to the curriculum of the 47-year old Spokane Technical and Vocational School, and it became Spokane Community College. In 1967 the college was enlarged by the opening of a second campus, and in 1970 the two campuses became two separate colleges. The original school retained the name Spokane Community College, and the other campus became Spokane Falls Community College. The College is accredited by the Northwest Association of Schools and Colleges and respective professional organizations. It operates on the quarter system and offers one summer session. Enrollment is 6,733 full-time and part-time students. A faculty of 270 gives a faculty-student ratio of 1-25. Army ROTC is available. Cooperative education is available in several areas.

Entrance Requirements: High school graduation or GED; SAT, ACT, or school's own exam required; open enrollment; midyear admission, rolling admission and advanced placement plans available.

Costs Per Year: $867 tuition; $3,402 nonresident tuition; $12 student fees.

Collegiate Environment: The library houses 32,706 hardbound volumes, 511 periodicals, 11,643 microforms, and 5,348 audiovisual materials. 101 athletic scholarships are available. There is no student housing on campus. 100% of those applying for admission are accepted.

Community Environment: See Spokane Falls Community College.

SPOKANE FALLS COMMUNITY COLLEGE *(E-17)*
W. 3410 Fort George Wright Drive
Spokane, Washington 99204-5288
Tel: (509) 533-3500; Fax: (509) 533-3237

Description: The state-supported two year college is the district's primary center for liberal arts education. It is accredited by the Northwest Association of Schools and Colleges. Freshman and Sophomore level courses in the liberal arts and professional areas lead to an Associate of Arts degree. Associate in Applied Science degree programs offered are two-year courses in various occupational areas including business, broadcasting, advertising, art, human services, photography, library technology and real estate. Students finishing a three-year technical program are granted the appropriate professional diploma. The college operates on the quarter system and one summer session is offered. Army ROTC is available as an elective. Enrollment is 3,952

full-time and 1,361 part-time students. A faculty of 157 full-time and 710 part-time gives an overall faculty-student ratio of 1-39.

Entrance Requirements: Open door policy; non-high school graduates considered, early decision and midyear admission plans available; $10 application fee.

Costs Per Year: $1,267 resident tuition; $5,094 out-of-state.

Collegiate Environment: The college occupies a 113-acre campus situated at Fort Wright, above the Spokane River. The library contains 52,500 bound volumes, 673 periodicals, and 40,000 microforms. The college welcomes a geographically diverse student body and does accept midyear students. Approximately 99% of the students applying for admission are accepted and 55% of the freshmen return for the sophomore year. In addition to financial aid, the college awarded 95 scholarships and 65 of these were awarded to freshman students. The college granted 58 Certificates and 578 Associate degrees to a recent graduating class. About 40% of the students continued on to a 4-year college.

Community Environment: The second largest city in the state, Spokane has diversified natural resources including timber lands, tremendous waterpower, and mineral wealth. There are many industries in the area, and part-time work is available. The city is considered the economic and cultural capital of the region between the Rockies and the Cascades. The mean temperature is 47 degrees. Two airports, and several private fields, railroads, and bus lines serve the area. Over 200 churches of all denominations, a public library system, several hospitals, and many civic and fraternal organizations are active here. There are military establishments representing all the services within the area. The community has many fine cultural and recreational facilities as well as excellent shopping facilities.

TACOMA COMMUNITY COLLEGE *(G-6)*
5900 South 12th Street
Tacoma, Washington 98465-1971
Tel: (509) 566-5000; Fax: (506) 566-6011; Admissions: (206) 566-6001

Description: This state-supported comprehensive community college was founded in 1965 and is accredited by the Northwest Association of Schools and Colleges, and by several professional organizations. It is one of 33 colleges in the Washington State Community and Technical College System. The college offers an academic transfer curriculum, vocational and technical training and continuing education for adults. The college operates on the quarter system and offers one summer session. Enrollment includes 3,771 full-time and 4,266 part-time students. A faculty of 99 full-time and 210 part-time gives a faculty-student ratio of 1-22.

Entrance Requirements: Open enrollment policy; placement tests required; accredited high school graduation required for degree programs; rolling admission, midyear admission and advanced placement plans available.

Costs Per Year: $1,302 tuition; $5,100 nonresident tuition per year (3 quarters).

Collegiate Environment: The 150-acre campus is located on the west side of Tacoma and serves the needs of more than 200,000 residents of the Tacoma-Pierce county areas of the state. There are 30 buildings including the 70,000-volume library with 400 periodicals, 100 microforms, and 899 audiovisual materials, and the instructional resource center. No dormitories are available. Classes are also offered at various sites in the college's service area including two off-campus centers, the Big Harbor and Peninsula College Center and the Downtown Business Resource Center. Financial aid is available for economically disadvantaged students. 20% of students receive financial aid.

Community Environment: The third largest city in Washington, Tacoma is a shipping, industrial and distributing center located in the Puget Sound region. The city has diversified industries including electrochemicals, food and beverage processing, clothing manufacturing, iron, steel and shipyards. Tacoma is near Mt. Rainier National park and its residents enjoy easy access to ocean beaches, the many waterways of Puget Sound and Olympic and North Cascades National Parks. The area is provided transportation by railroads, airlines, twelve bus lines and major highways. Nearby lakes and streams offer excellent fishing. The city has many parks, a public library system, museums, hospitals and many civic and fraternal organizations to serve the community.

UNIVERSITY OF PUGET SOUND   (G-6)
1500 North Warner
Tacoma, Washington 98416
Tel: (206) 756-3211

Description: The university is a privately endowed, liberal arts school historically affiliated with the United Methodist Church. It is accredited by the Northwest Association of Schools and Colleges and by respective professional and educational organizations. Enrollment numbers 1,138 men and 1,699 women full-time and 101 men and 226 women part-time. A faculty of 210 full-time and 25 part-time gives a faculty-student ratio of 1:13. The early semester system is used and two summer terms are offered. Numerous overseas programs are available.

Entrance Requirements: High school graduation; 4 years English, 3-4 years mathematics, 3-4 years lab science, 2-3 years of a single foreign language, 3 years social studies and 1 year fine/visual/performing arts recommended; SAT or ACT required; early admission, rolling admission, delayed admission, advanced placement plans available; $35 application fee.

Costs Per Year: $16,230 tuition; $4,500 room and board; $140 student fees.

Collegiate Environment: The university occupies 37 academic Tudor structures conveniently spaced over the campus of 95 acres of attractive lawns and natural woods. The campus is located a short distance from the shores of Puget Sound and the Pacific Ocean, as well as the ski slopes of the Cascade and Olympic Mountains. There are dormitory facilities for 790 students plus space for 286 students in university-owned residences. Fraternities and sororities can house an additional 238 men and 256 women. The library system contains 363,205 volumes, 1,933 periodicals, 146,320 microforms, and 98,523 government documents. Approximately 75% of students applying for admission are accepted and 86% of the freshman class return for the sophomore year. Freshmen classes begin in late August and mid-January. The university welcomes a diverse student body. Financial aid is available for students demonstrating financial need. 75% of the current student body recieves some form of assistance. Over 1,200 scholarships are offered. The university granted 645 Bachelor and 144 Master degrees recently.

Community Environment: The third largest city in Washington, Tacoma is a shipping, industrial and distributing center located in the Puget Sound region. The city has diversified industries including electrochemicals, food and beverage processing, clothing manufacturing, iron, steel and shipyards. Tacoma is near Mt. Rainier National park and its residents enjoy easy access to ocean beaches, the many waterways of Puget Sound and Olympic and North Cascades National Parks. The area is provided transportation by railroads, airlines, bus lines, ferries, and major highways. Nearby lakes and streams offer excellent fishing. The city has a zoo, an aquarium, many parks, a public library system, museums, hospitals, and many civic and fraternal organizations to serve the community.

UNIVERSITY OF WASHINGTON   (E-6)
1400 N.E. Campus Parkway
Seattle, Washington 98195
Tel: (206) 543-2100

Description: This state-supported university was founded in 1861 on a ten-acre knoll in what is now downtown Seattle. In 1895 it was moved to its present 690-acre site on the shores of Lake Washington. The university is accredited by the Northwest Association of Schools and Colleges and by respective professional organizations. Most of the colleges, schools, and departments offer both graduate and undergraduate courses. Air Force, Army and Navy ROTC programs are available. The university operates on the quarter system and offers two summer sessions. Undergraduate enrollment is 12,180 men and 12,412 women. There are 9,062 graduate students. The teaching faculty includes 2,689 full-time and 334 part-time members.

Entrance Requirements: High school graduation or equivalent with completion of 15 units required including 4 English, 3 math, 2 science, 2 foreign language, 3 social science, 0.5 fine arts; SAT or ACT required; combined test scores and GPA that yield a competitive Ad-

missions Index; GRE required for some graduate programs; early admission, midyear admission, rolling admission, and advanced placement plans available; $35 application fee.

Costs Per Year: $2,907 tuition; $8,199 out-of-state tuition; $4,218 board and room.

Collegiate Environment: There are more than 215 buildings on the campus, including a modern, fully equipped 320-bed teaching hospital. The extensive athletic plant, playing fields and recreational areas are situated on the campus. The botanical and drug-plant gardens and a 200-acre arboretum contain thousands of varieties of trees, plants and shrubs from all over the world. The Odegaard Undergraduate Library and Suzzalo Library plus 21 branch libraries contain over 5,400,000 volumes, 56,000 periodicals as well as numerous maps, newspapers, microfilms and manuscripts. Students are free to make their own housing arrangements and accommodations on campus are available for 3,810 men and women, 566 families, and 524 apartments for single students. Twenty sororities and 28 fraternities own and operate complete living facilities near the university, housing an additional 2,900 students. As a member of the Northwest Interinstitutional Council or Study Abroad, the university has cooperated with other institutions in developing study locales in London, Avignon, Cologne and Guadalajara. In addition, the university cooperates with other American and Canadian institutions in offering an academic year abroad in various fields of study. The Departments of Military Science, Naval Science, and Aerospace Studies offer ROTC programs. Participation is elective. Scholarships are available and 38% of the students receive some form of financial aid.

Community Environment: The University is located in residential section of Seattle, a cosmopolitan city of 500,000. Set on many hills that command striking views of the surrounding water, Seattle is noted for its temperate climate, access to outdoor recreation, excellent transportation system, and generally liveable atmosphere.

WALLA WALLA COLLEGE   (K-15)
204 South College Avenue
College Place, Washington 99324-1198
Tel: (509) 527-2327; (800) 541-8900; Fax: (509) 527-2397

Description: The four-year liberal arts college was founded in 1892 and is operated by the Seventh-day Adventist Church. It is accredited by the Northwest Association of Schools and Colleges, Accreditation Board for Engineering and Technology, National Assn. of Schools of Music, Council on Soc. Work Educ. and the Dept. of Baccalaureate and Higher Degree Programs of the National League for Nursing. It operates on the quarter system and offers two summer sessions. While serving primarily the Seventh-day Adventist youth of the Pacific Northwest, the college accepts students from other states and countries who are qualified and who are willing to abide by the Christian principles enjoined on the campus. Enrollment is 1,388 full-time undergraduate students with 179 part-time and 158 graduate students. A faculty of 128 full-time and 62 part-time provides a teacher-student ratio of 1-9. Study abroad is available.

Entrance Requirements: Accredited high school graduation; completion of 16 units including 4 English, 2 mathematics, 2 science, 2 social science; students not meeting all requirements may be required to take examinations to validate their credits; ACT required; nondegree candidates may be admitted as non-matriculated students; early admission, early decision, rolling admission, delayed admission and advanced placement plans available; $30 application fees.

Costs Per Year: $11,193 tuition; $3,483 room and board; $282 student fees.

Collegiate Environment: The 28 college buildings are situated on a 55-acre campus. The college church is a large, modern, brick building. It seats 2,500 worshipers and 150 choir members. The combined libraries contain over 17,330 volumes and 1,240 periodicals. The Marine Biological Station located on Puget Sound occupies 40 acres of beach and timberland. Nursing students obtain their clinical practice at Portland Adventist Medical Center. There are housing accommodations for 475 men and 422 women. Approximately 95% of students applying for admission are accepted. The college welcomes a geographically diverse student body. Financial aid is available and 84% of the students receive some financial aid.

Community Environment: College Place is a residential community adjacent to Walla Walla. The climate is temperate. Three miles away, all major forms of transportation are available. The immediate community has four churches and two hospitals. Part-time employment opportunities are fair.

WALLA WALLA COMMUNITY COLLEGE   (J-15)
500 Tausick Way
Walla Walla, Washington 99362
Tel: (509) 522-2500; Admissions: (509) 527-4283; Fax: (509) 527-3661

Description: This state-supported community college opened its doors for the first time in September, 1967. It is accredited by the Northwest Association of Schools and Colleges and the National League for Nursing. The quarter system is used, and one summer term is offered. College transfer courses offer premajor programs and provide the first two years of academic study for most baccalaureate degrees. Vocational-technical courses provide occupational instruction that enables students to learn employable skills for technical trades and for semiprofessional employment in business and industry. A cooperative education program is available in Irrigation Technology. Continuing education offers both transfer and nontransfer college credit courses in the evening. Enrollment includes 1,787 full-time and 2,300 part-time and 800 evening students. A faculty of 106 full-time and 170 part-time gives an overall faculty-student ratio of 1-20.

Entrance Requirements: Open door policy; non-high school graduates considered; GED available on campus; early decision, early admission, rolling admission, advanced placement, and delayed admission plans available; $30 application fee.

Costs Per Year: $1,326 tuition; $5,124 out-of-state.

Collegiate Environment: There are 11 buildings on the 88-acre rural campus. Dormitory facilities are not available. The library has a collection of 38,000 volumes, 360 periodicals, 4,353 microforms and 3,911 recordings. Financial aid is available for economically disadvantaged students. 145 scholarships are available, 90 of them are athletic scholarships. 59% of the current student body receives financial aid. All students applying for admission are accepted and 50% of the freshman class returns for the sophomore year. Freshman classes begin in September, January, March and June. The College granted 93 certificates and 267 Associate degrees.

Community Environment: Walla Walla is rich agricultural area in southern Washington near the Oregon State line. The chief crop is wheat. The area has excellent highways, a commuter airline and buslines serving the community. The climate is mild. Local recreation includes hunting, boating, fishing, camping and skiing in the nearby mountains. There are churches representing most denominations, health facilities and shopping centers in the area. All major lodges and service clubs are active here. Frontier days and a rodeo are held annually in September.

Branch Campuses: Clarkston, Washington.

WASHINGTON STATE UNIVERSITY   (H-17)
Pullman, Washington 99164-1036
Tel: (509) 335-3564

Description: Since its founding in 1890, this state-supported university has been a multipurpose public institution. It consists of seven colleges and a graduate school and offers more than 125 undergraduate major fields of study. It is accredited by the Northwest Association of Schools and Colleges and by several professional institutions. Student enrollment is 16,894 full-time, and 2,420 part-time. The early start semester system is used and two summer terms are offered. A faculty of 967 full-time and 184 part-time gives an overall faculty-student ratio of 1-16. 86% of the teaching faculty holds Ph.D.s. Army, Air Force and Navy, ROTC are available as electives. Exchange programs and study abroad programs with 80 countries are offered.

Entrance Requirements: Accredited high school graduation or equivalent; admitted on Admissions Index, which is a combination of GPA and test scores; SAT or ACT required; completion of units including 4 English, 3 mathematics, 3 social science, 2 science, 2 foreign language and 1 fine, visual, or performing arts; advanced placement and rolling admission plans available; $35 application fee.

Costs Per Year: $2,908 tuition; $8,200 out-of-state; $4,050 room and board; $145 fees.

Collegiate Environment: The 2,000-acre main campus is located in the beautiful Palouse region of southeast Washington. One of the larg-

est residential universities west of the Mississippi, WSU-Pullman offers residence halls for 5,173 men and women, and apartments for 558 married students. The university provides quality academic study, including nationally ranked programs in business, broadcasting, hotel and restaurant administration, sociology and more, plus the personal attention of a university of 17,882 students. The Honors Program, one of the few all-university programs at a major university, has a reputation as one of the five strongest in the country. The library system, a member of the Association of Research Libraries, contains 1,679,500 volumes, 2,827,170 microforms, 23,386 periodicals and over 10,000 audiovisual materials. WSU also teaches nursing through the Intercollegiate Nursing Center in Spokane, hotel and restaurant administration through a center in Seattle, and professional courses in fields such as engineering and education through branch campuses in Spokane, the Tri-Cities and Vancouver. Washington's land-grant university, WSU has extension offices in all 39 counties and eight agricultural research centers around the state, and manages 5,000 acres of farmland in addition to the main campus. KWSU/Radio-Television Services, a pioneer in educational broadcasting, now serves many areas of the state. Important research centers include the Institute for Biological Chemistry, the Social and Economic Research Center, Nuclear Radiation Center, the Wood Products Researach Laboratory, an Archaeological Research Center and more. WSU leads a tristate program in veterinary medical education, and participates in a four-state program in human medical education. The university's many historical and contemporary buildings include a new Food Science and Human Nutrition Building and Food Quality Lab.

Community Environment: Pullman is located 7 miles west of the Idaho border. The summer temperature averages in the 80s and the winter temperature averages around 30 degrees. The area is accessible by airlines and bus lines. There are 30 churches, a public library, and various civic, fraternal, and veteran's organizations serving the community. Local recreation includes four parks, baseball diamonds, swimming pools, theaters, bowling alleys, a golf course, tennis courts and nearby lakes and rivers offering swimming, boating and skating.

Branch Campuses: Spokane, W. 601 First Ave., Spokane, WA 99204-0399, (509) 456-3132; Tri-Cities, 100 Sprout Rd., Richland, WA 99352, (509) 375-9250; WSU Vancouver, 1812 E. McLoughlin, Vancouver, WA 99663-3597, (206) 737-2010.

WENATCHEE VALLEY COLLEGE   (F-11)
1300 Fifth Street
Wenatchee, Washington 98801
Tel: (509) 662-1651

Description: This state-supported community college was established in 1939 to provide post-high school educational opportunities to residents of the North Central Washington area. It is accredited by the Northwest Association of Schools and Colleges. The quarter system is used and one summer term is offered. The college provides continuing education for adults, Baccalaureate programs equivalent to the first two years of senior college or university study and specialized training courses to meet vocational and technical needs of business and industry. Enrollment is 3,217 men and women full-time and part-time. A faculty of 200 provides a faculty student ratio of 1-18.

Entrance Requirements: Open door policy; non-high school graduates admitted; early admission, early decision, midyear admission, rolling admission, advanced placement plans available; no application fee.

Costs Per Year: $1,296 tuition; $5,094 nonresident; $3,519 room and board.

Collegiate Environment: The college moved to its present 47-acre campus in 1951. The library has a collection of 27,000 volumes. There is one dormitory for 70 men and women. Freshman classes begin in September, January, March, and June. There is special financial aid available for economically disadvantaged students. All students applying for admission are accepted.

Community Environment: At the confluence of the Wenatchee and Columbia Rivers, Wenatchee is the apple capital of the world. Located in the eastern foothills of the Cascade Mountains, the city has a temperate climate with four definite seasons. The average maximum temperature is 75 degrees, with an average minimum of 28 degrees. The average rainfall in the area is 9.58 inches. The community is provided transportation by bus, air lines, and major highways. There are almost 40 churches representing various denominations, a YMCA,

YWCA, library, museum and medical facilities serving the residents. Local recreation includes theaters, a drive-in, hunting, boating, fishing, golf and skiing. Part-time employment is available. There are motels, hotels and good shopping areas here. Many civic and fraternal organizations are active within the community. An annual state apple blossom festival is held here.

WESTERN WASHINGTON UNIVERSITY   (B-6)
513 High Street
Bellingham, Washington 98225-9009
Tel: (360) 650-3440; Fax: (360) 650-7369

Description: This regional university is one of 5 universities, one college, and 27 community colleges that comprise the state-supported higher educational system in Washington. It is accredited by the Northwest Association of Schools and Colleges. It was founded in 1893 and at that time was known as the State Normal School; it was first authorized to grant degrees in 1933. The college became a state college in 1961 and a university in 1977. It is a multipurpose institution offering degree programs in the arts and the sciences and professional education for teachers at both the undergraduate and graduate level. Professional degrees are offered on the graduate level and pre-professional studies are available for transfer to other universities and professional schools. Upper division programs in Human Services and Education are offered in Bellingham, Seattle, Everett, Oak Harbor and Bremerton. Admissions criteria include junior status and completion of Western's General Education requirements. The college operates on the quarter system and offers two summer sessions. Total enrollment includes 9,166 full-time and 865 part-time students. A faculty of 408 full-time and 127 part-time gives an overall faculty-student ratio of 1-21.

Entrance Requirements: High school graduation or equivalent with a 2.5 GPA; 4 units English, 3 mathematics, 2 science (1 chemistry), 2 years of 1 foreign language, 3 social studies, 1/2 fine arts, and 1/2 academic elective in one of the areas previously listed required; SAT or ACT; TOEFL for foreign students; GPA 2.0 required for transfer students; GRE required for graduate studies; midyear admission and advanced placement plans available; $35 application fee.

Costs Per Year: $2,406 tuition and fees; $8,125 out-of-state; $4,144 room and board; $1,764 average additional expenses.

Collegiate Environment: The 190-acre main campus is located in the northwest corner of the state near the Canadian border. The campus overlooks Bellingham Bay and the San Juan Islands. There are 77 buildings including university-owned residence halls for 3,877 students. The library contains 558,692 volumes, numerous pamphlets, 4,255 periodicals, 1,000,000 microforms and recordings. The average high school GPA of the freshman class was 3.37. The average scores of the entering freshman class were SAT 470 verbal, 530 math. 71% of the students applying for admission are accepted and almost 84% return for the sophomore year. There are 825 scholarships available and 61% of the students receive some form of financial aid. The 6 colleges and 1 school that comprise the university include the College of Business and Economics, the College of Fine and Performing Arts, Huxley College of Environmental Studies, the Woodring College of Education, the College of Arts and Sciences, Fairhaven College and the graduate school.

Community Environment: Bellingham overlooks Puget Sound and the San Juan Islands. The city enjoys temperate climate with a summer temperature seldom exceeding 73 degrees, and winter temperatures range from 28 to 55 degrees. There are frequently winters without snow, and the average rainfall is 34 inches. County industry includes shipbuilding; food processing; oil refining and manufacturing of aluminum, cement, plywood, paper products and alcohol. There is also a commercial fishing fleet. Part-time employment is available. Local recreation includes theaters, boating, fishing, sailing, golf, water sports, horse shows, baseball, softball, bowling, track and field, lakes and hiking trails in the surrounding area, and Mt. Baker for skiing and climbing 50 miles from campus. There are also community hospital facilities and major civic and fraternal organizations.

WHITMAN COLLEGE   (J-15)
Walla Walla, Washington 99362
Tel: (509) 527-5111; Fax: (509) 527-4967

Description: This private college was founded in 1859 in honor of a medical missionary. It is accredited by the Northwest Association of Schools and Colleges. The college provides a four-year liberal arts curriculum leading to the degree of Bachelor of Arts. There is a 3-2 Engineering Program with Duke, Columbia, and Cal-Tech; 3-2 Forestry Program with Duke; 3-3 Law Program with Columbia. The college operates on the semester system. Enrollment includes 1,295 full-time and 74 part-time students. A faculty of 93 full-time and 76 part-time provides a faculty-student ratio of 1-11. The average class size is 14. 93% of the faculty hold doctorate degrees, and most serve as academic advisors. Study abroad programs are available in 120 locations.

Entrance Requirements: Accredited high school graduation; recommended completion of 16 units including 4 English, 4 mathematics, 2 science, 2 foreign language, 2 social studies, 2 history, 2 electives; SAT or ACT required; early admission, deferred admission, midyear admission, advanced placement, and early decision programs available; $45 application fee.

Costs Per Year: $17,630 tuition; $5,160 room and board; $155 student fees.

Collegiate Environment: The 38 buildings of the 55-acre campus are located in Walla Walla, a historic community of 30,000 nestled in the foothills of the Blue Mountains of southeastern Washington. Library holdings number 254,000 volumes, 1,850 periodicals, 10,000 microforms, and audiovisual materials. Whitman is a residential college accommodating 1,050 students in its residence halls. Junior and senior men and women are permitted to live off campus. 52% of applicants are accepted. The median high school GPA of the most recent freshman class was 3.78; median SAT scores were 560V, 620M. The college welcomes a geographically diverse student body. Freshman classes begin in September and in January. 830 scholarships are available, including 251 for freshmen. 80% of students receive some form of financial aid. The college granted 310 Bachelor degrees to the recent graduating class.

Community Environment: See Walla Walla Community College.

WHITWORTH COLLEGE   (E-17)
Hawthorne Street
Spokane, Washington 99251
Tel: (509) 466-1000; (800) 533-4668; Admissions: (509) 466-3212; Fax: (509) 466-3773

Description: The Christian liberal arts college was founded in 1890. In 1914 the Presbyterian Church (U.S.A.) invited the college to move to its present location. The college continues in cooperation with the Synod of Alaska-Northwest of the church and with the Board of Christian Education of the denomination. The college is accredited by the Northwest Association of Schools and Colleges. Army ROTC is available. A semester abroad program, exchange program, and January term abroad are available. The college operates on the 4-1-4 system and offers four summer sessions. Enrollment includes 2,000 students. A faculty of 72 full-time and 65 part-time gives a faculty-student ratio of 1-16.

Entrance Requirements: Accredited high school graduation or equivalent; recommended completion of 16 units including 4 English, 3 mathematics, 3 lab science, 2 foreign language, and 2 social studies; SAT or ACT required; early admission, rolling admission, delayed admission, early decision, midyear admission and advanced placement programs available; no application fee.

Costs Per Year: $12,600 tuition; $4,550 room and board; $185 student fees; additional expenses average $1,400.

Collegiate Environment: There are 40 buildings on the 200-acre campus. A new 4 million dollar campus center was completed in June 1995. The Eric Johnston Science Center was completed in 1966 and contains classrooms and laboratories for biology, chemistry, earth science and physics. The Music and Fine Arts Center was completed in 1977 and the Seely Mudd Chapel was completed in 1979. The Harriet Cheney Cowles Memorial Library which was completed in 1992 to celebrate the college's centennial contains 221,590 volumes and 41,911 microforms. There are housing accommodations for 890 men and women. Approximately 75% of students applying for admission are accepted and 85% of the freshman class returns for the sophomore year. The college welcomes a geographically diverse student body and accepts midyear transfer students. The average scores of the entering freshman class were SAT 1048 combined, ACT 25 composite. 85% of the current student body receives financial aid.

Community Environment: See Spokane Community College.

YAKIMA VALLEY COMMUNITY COLLEGE *(I-10)*
16th Ave. & Nob Hill Blvd.
P.O. Box 1647
Yakima, Washington 98902
Tel: (509) 575-2350; Admissions: (509) 575-2373; Fax: (509) 575-2461

Description: Founded in 1928, this state-supported community college is the third oldest in Washington state and is accredited by the Northwest Association of Schools and Colleges. It provides the first two years of college work for those who plan to transfer to a four-year college or university, technical-vocational training, and general continuing education. The college offers technical degrees in 24 areas and a direct transfer degree. In cooperation with Central Washington University and Heritage College it provides a four-year Baccalaureate degree in Early Childhood Education, with CWU to provide a B.A. in Law and Justice, and with WSU Intercollegite Center for Nursing Education for a B.S. in Nursing. A foreign study program in London, England is available. It operates on the quarter system and offers one summer session. Enrollment includes 2,360 men and 3,689 women. A faculty of 374 gives an overall faculty-student ratio of 1-23.

Entrance Requirements: Open enrollment policy; ASSET required; rolling admission, midyear admission, and advanced placement plans available.

Costs Per Year: $1,425 ($475 per quarter) state resident tuition; $5,094 ($1,698 per quarter) nonresident tuition; $4,020 room and board; $650 books and supplies; $900 average additional expenses average.

Collegiate Environment: The 14-acre campus adjoins a 20-acre park, making available to the college a total of 40 acres which includes tennis courts and other recreational facilities. A student resident center can accomodate 300 men and women. The Raymond library contains 42,000 volumes and its on-line catalog and CD-ROM disks provide expanded research opportunities for students and community residents. Other college facilities include a state-of-the-art Dental Hygiene clinic. The average age of students is 29 years and 61% of students are female. The college enrolls the largest number of Hispanics and Native Americans of any community or technical college in the state. Financial aid is available for economically disadvantaged students, and 51% of a recent freshman class received some form of assistance. Approximately 150 full-tuition scholarships, over $100,000, are awarded each year. All of the students applying for admission are accepted. About 31% of the graduating class continued on to senior college.

Community Environment: Located in the fertile Yakima Valley known as the "Fruit Bowl of the Nation," the area produces cherries, peaches, pears, apples, and other small fruit. The climate is mild and dry with an average of 302 days of sun per year. The community is served by railroad, air, and main arterial highways. Local recreation includes swimming, skiing, boating, fishing, hunting and golf. Part-time employment is available for students. There are churches representing most of the religious denominations, as well as many civic and fraternal organizations serving the community. Many "western" type celebrations are held in the area. Yakima was named an "All-America City" in 1994.

Branch Campuses: Grandview Campus, 500 West Main, Grandview, WA 98930

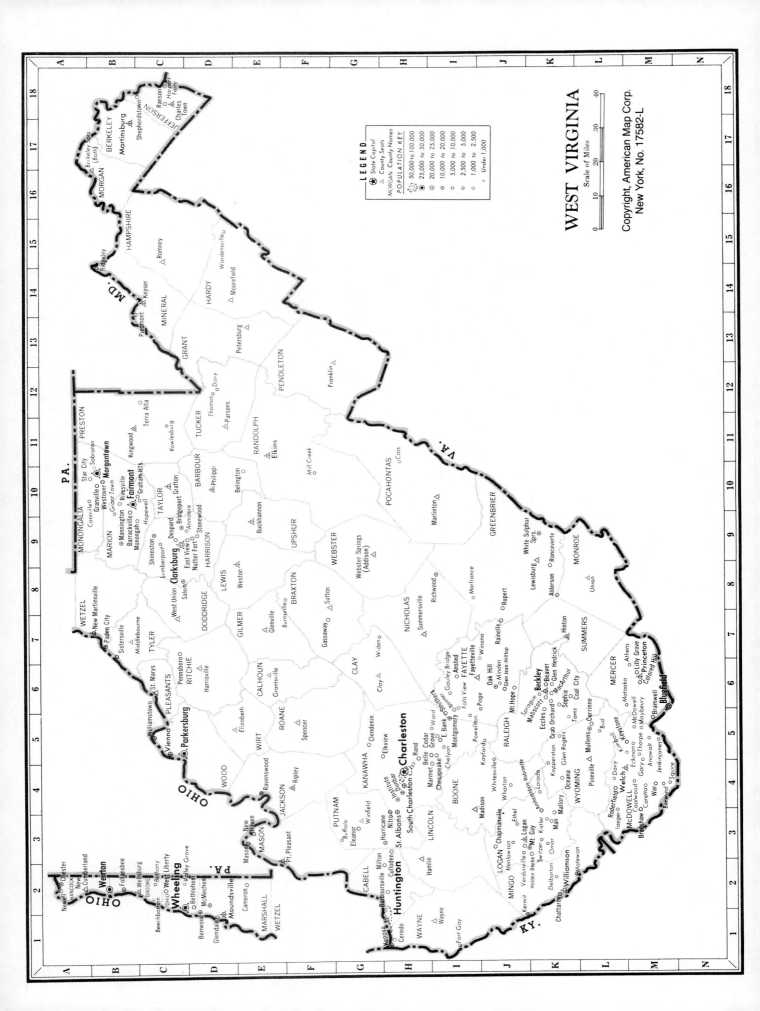

WEST VIRGINIA

Scale of Miles

LEGEND

⊛ State Capital
⚬ County Seats
MORGAN County Names

POPULATION KEY

50,000 to 100,000
25,000 to 50,000
20,000 to 25,000
10,000 to 20,000
5,000 to 10,000
2,500 to 5,000
1,000 to 2,500
Under 1,000

WEST VIRGINIA

ALDERSON-BROADDUS COLLEGE (D-10)
P.O. Box 216
Philippi, West Virginia 26416
Tel: (304) 457-1700; Fax: (304) 457-6239

Description: The privately supported, coeducational liberal arts college traces its beginning to 1871. The school was established through the union of 2 colleges that merged in 1932 and today is the only institution of higher education in West Virginia related to the American Baptist Churches/USA. It is accredited by the North Central Association of Colleges and Schools, the American Accreditation, the National League for Nursing, and the Council on social Work Education. The teacher education programs are accredited by the National Council for Accreditation of Teacher Education. The college is nonsectarian in outlook. Students are admitted without regard to color, sex, national and ethnic origin, class, or creed. The college operates on the semester system and offers two summer sessions. Enrollment is 395 men and 541 women and includes 827 full-time and 72 part-time undergraduates and 37 graduate students. A faculty of 60 full-time and 12 part-time gives a faculty-student ratio of 1-11.

Entrance Requirements: Accredited high school graduation; completion of 10 units including 3 English, 2 math, 1 science, 1 foreign language, and 3 social science; ACT or SAT required; advanced placement, early decision, rolling admission, and early admission plans available; $10 application fee.

Costs Per Year: $10,468 tuition; $3,380 room and board; $92 student fee.

Collegiate Environment: The college is located on a mountain commanding a magnificent view of the Tygarts Valley and of the Laurel Mountains, the first western ridge of the Appalachians. The campus of more than 170 acres has been attractively developed and landscaped, although a portion has been left in its natural wooded state. The 14 college buildings include a library of 110,000 volumes and living accommodations for 320 men and 500 women. The college welcomes a geographically diverse student body and accepts students at the beginning of each term. The college offers a semester abroad in Salzburg, Austria. Financial aid is available. The college awards academic scholarships and talent scholarship regardless of financial need. 95% of students receive financial aid. Special counseling services are provided for those who are undecided about their major, need academic assistance, or need advisement on career planning and placement.

Community Environment: Philippi is a rural community enjoying a moderate climate ranging from balmy summers to snowy winters. The community is reached by railroad, bus lines, and U.S. Route 250. There are churches of major denominations, a hospital, and a clinic in the area. Some part-time employment is available. There are more than 50 civic, fraternal, and veteran's organizations active in the community. Local recreation includes swimming, roller skating, bowling, theater, and major outdoor sports. Skiing and whitewater rafting are within minutes of the campus.

APPALACHIAN BIBLE COLLEGE (J-6)
P.O. Box ABC
Bradley, West Virginia 25818
Tel: (304) 877-6428; (800) 678-9222; Fax: (304) 877-6423

Description: This privately supported, coeducational Bible school was established in 1950, and was fully accredited by the American Association of Bible Colleges in 1967. It operates on the early semester system. Enrollment is 168 full-time and 60 part-time students. A faculty of 17 full-time and 3 part-time provides a faculty-student ratio of 1-13. The college is primarily concerned with preparing eligible students for various branches of the Christian ministry. Programs of

study lead to the Bachelor degree, a one-year certificate, or Associate of Arts degree.

Entrance Requirements: High school graduation or equivalent; personal reference; ACT required; advanced placement, early admission, early decision, and rolling admission plans available; $10 application fee.

Costs Per Year: $3,200 tuition; $2,600 room and board; $190 student fees; $400 average additional expenses.

Collegiate Environment: The 95-acre campus was first occupied in 1957. The 28 buildings include a library of 34,062 volumes; dormitory facilities for 101 men and 90 women; duplex housing for 24 families; and a gymnasium/conference center. All unmarried students are required to room and have meals at the college. Students from other geographical locations are accepted as are midyear students. Almost all students applying for admission are accepted, and 59.2% of the previous freshman class returns to this campus for the second year. Financial aid is available, and numerous scholarships are offered. Semesters begin in August and January.

Community Environment: Bradley is a rural community enjoying temperate climate. There is a railroad line 15 miles distant, an airline 14 miles away, buses, and Highways I-77, I-64, 19, 21, and 16 to serve the community. The city has 5 churches and a Lions Club. Within walking distance is Crossroads Mall. The community provides numerous part-time employment opportunities, and enjoys all the cultural, recreational, and medical facilities of nearby Beckley.

BETHANY COLLEGE (C-2)
Bethany, West Virginia 26032
Tel: (304) 829-7611; (800) 922-7611; Fax: (304) 829-7108

Description: This privately supported, coeducational liberal arts college was chartered under the laws of the Commonwealth of Virginia in 1840. The religious body known variously as the Christian Churches, Disciples of Christ, or Churches of Christ, have been and continue to be a significant factor in the support and encouragement of the college. The college operates on the 4-1-4 system with a January term devoted to special projects. The college is accredited by the North Central Association of Colleges and Schools and grants the Bachelor degree. Enrollment is 800 full-time and 26 part-time students. A faculty of 67 full-time and 8 part-time provides a faculty-student ratio of 1-13.

Entrance Requirements: High school graduation with rank in upper half of graduating class; completion of 15 units including 4 English; SAT or ACT required; early decision, early admission, delayed admission, rolling admission and advanced placement plans available; $20 application fee.

Costs Per Year: $14,800 tuition; $5,050 room and board.

Collegiate Environment: The college campus of approximately 1,600 acres is located in Bethany, in the northern Panhandle of West Virginia, 2 miles from Pennsylvania and 5 miles from Ohio. The college buildings contain a library of 175,000 volumes and living accommodations for 500 men and 400 women. The college grounds include about 1,300 acres of farm and timberland adjacent to the campus area that are available for use by the students. These include the Alexander Campbell Farm, the Point Breeze Farm, the Parkinson Woods, and other properties. Nature trails and picnic areas have been developed in some of these areas. Financial aid is available for economically handicapped students. Approximately 76% of those applying for admission are accepted.

Community Environment: Bethany is a small college town. The area is served by Pittsburgh's airport and bus service. Campus entertainment includes drama productions, concerts, lectures, dances, and athletic events. Nearby Pittsburgh, PA, and Wheeling, WV, offer cultural programs, professional sports events and outdoor activities. Fraternities and sororities provide extensive social programs.

BLUEFIELD STATE COLLEGE (M-6)
219 Rock Street
Bluefield, West Virginia 24701
Tel: (304) 327-4000; (800) 344-8892; Fax: (304) 325-7747

Description: The state college was established in 1895 and today provides for the fulfillment of the educational goals of qualified students in various fields of teacher education, arts and sciences, technical education, and business occupations and professions. It is accredited by the North Central Association of Colleges and Schools. It operates on the semester system and offers two summer sessions. Enrollment is 1,458 full-time and 1,151 part-time students. A faculty of 94 full-time and 86 part-time provides a faculty-student ratio of 1-18.

Entrance Requirements: Accredited high school graduation or GED; open enrollment for A.S. degree; 4 English, 2 mathematics, 2 science, 3 social studies required of B.S. degree candidates; SAT or ACT required; non-high school graduates considered; early admission, early decision, rolling admission, midyear admission and advanced placement plans available; no application fee.

Costs Per Year: $1,856 tuition; $4,498 out-of-state.

Collegiate Environment: The 45-acre campus is located in the city of Bluefield, the southernmost city in the state. The 13 college buildings include a library of 72,538 volumes, 513 periodicals, 377,955 microforms, and 24,000 audiovisual materials. 84% of applicants are accepted. Scholarships are available and 74% of the students receive some form of financial aid.

Community Environment: At the foot of the East River Mountain, high in the Appalachian chain, Bluefield is situated at the southern tip of West Virginia, bordering on the Virginia state line. The city is the commercial and industrial center for the surrounding area. The climate is temperate with a mean annual temperature of 53.7 degrees and an average rainfall of 38.52 inches. Due to a high altitude and low humidity, the city known as "Nature's Air Conditioned City." Bluefield is accessible by railroad, airlines, bus lines, and major highways. There are many churches representing most denominations, community health facilities, and major civic, fraternal, and veteran's organizations to serve the community. Local recreation includes nearby Bluestone Reservoir and lakes for fishing, swimming, and boating; municipal swimming pools, golf, a football stadium, tennis courts, softball, a band festival, and Little Theatre group.

Branch Campuses: Lewisburg, WV; Beckley, WV; Wesch, WV.

COLLEGE OF WEST VIRGINIA (K-6)
P.O. Box AG
Beckley, West Virginia 25801
Tel: (304) 253-7351; (800) 766-6067; Fax: (304) 253-0789

Description: This privately supported, coeducational four-year college was established in 1933 and is approved by the West Virginia Board of Regents. It is accredited by the North Central Association of Colleges and Schools. The college operates on the semester system and offers 2 summer terms. Programs of study lead to the Associate or Bachelor's degree. Recent enrollment includes 1,847 men and women full-time and part-time. A faculty of 132 gives a faculty-student ratio of 1-14.

Entrance Requirements: High school graduation or equivalent; non-graduates considered; open enrollment policy; early admission, early decision, rolling admission and advanced placement plans available.

Costs Per Year: $3,120 tuition and fees.

Collegiate Environment: This four-year college is located on 4 acres and is comprised of 6 buildings. Its library contains over 60,000 volumes. Approximately 99% of students applying for admission are accepted. Students from other geographical locations are accepted as well as midyear students. Financial aid is available for economically handicapped students.

Community Environment: A business and industrial community surrounded by rich agricultural lands, Beckley is the center of southern West Virginia's smokeless coal region. The climate is temperate with not too severe winters. The summers are delightful and cool. Beckley is accessible by railroad lines, airline connections at Charleston and Roanoke, and highways. The community has a public library, almost 50 churches of various denominations, several shopping centers, and medical facilities. Part-time employment is available. Local recreation includes 2 nearby lakes for swimming, boating and fishing, basketball, baseball, golf courses, and 3 movie theaters. A local play, "Honey in The Rock," a Civil War drama, is enacted here each summer. Various civic and fraternal organizations are active in the community.

CONCORD COLLEGE (L-6)
Athens, West Virginia 24712
Tel: (304) 384-3115; Admissions: (304) 384-5249

Description: Founded in 1872, Concord College is a publicly supported four-year liberal arts college and teacher education institution. It is accredited by the North Central Association of Colleges and Schools, the Council on Social Work Education, and the National Council for Accreditation of Teacher Education. It grants the Bachelor degree. The college operates on the semester system and offers two summer sessions. Enrollment includes 2,028 full-time and 773 part-time students. A faculty of 144 gives a faculty-student ratio of 1-20.

Entrance Requirements: Approved high school graduation; completion of 17 units including 4 English, 2 mathematics (algebra I and above), 2 laboratory science (biology I and above), 3 social science, and 1 health & physical education; SAT or ACT required; non high school graduates considered; early admission, early decision, midyear admission, rolling admission and advanced placement plans available; No application fee.

Costs Per Year: $2,053 state resident tuition; $4,426 nonresident tuition; $3,368 room and board; $700 average additional expenses.

Collegiate Environment: The college is located on 95 beautiful acres of rolling land, some 2,600 feet above sea level, along the Appalachian Ridge. The 20 college buildings include a library of 152,145 volumes, 525 periodical titles, 35,430 microforms, and 4,091 audiovisual materials. Dormitories provide living accommodations for 575 men, 585 women, and 96 families. Students from other geographical locations are accepted, as are midyear students. Approximately 94% of applicants are accepted. Financial aid is available for economically disadvantaged students and 68% of students receive some form of financial assistance.

Community Environment: Located in the mountains in a quiet rural area, this is an excellent atmosphere for students. The climate is moderate with cool summers. Local recreation includes good hunting and fishing. Pipestem State Park and Winterplace Ski Resort are located nearby.

DAVIS AND ELKINS COLLEGE (E-11)
100 Sycamore Street
Elkins, West Virginia 26241
Tel: (304) 636-1900; (800) 624-3157; Fax: (304) 636-8624

Description: This private, coeducational college is supported by the Presbyterian Church. The college was originally established under the auspices of Lexington and Winchester Presbyteries of the Synod of Virginia in 1904. The semester system is used with two summer terms. Academic cooperative plans are available with West Virginia University, Duke University, and the College of Environmental Science and Forestry, Syracuse, N.Y. The college is accredited by the North Central Association of Colleges and Schools. Enrollment is 707 full-time and 170 part-time students. A faculty of 52 full-time and 27 part-time gives a faculty-student ratio of 1-14. Study abroad is available to France, Austria, Spain, and Mexico.

Entrance Requirements: High school graduation; completion of 11 units including 4 English, 2 mathematics including Algebra I, 2 science including 1 laboratory course, 3 social studies, and 2 foreign language; SAT or ACT required; non-high school graduates considered; advanced placment, early admission, rolling admission, midyear admission, delayed admission plans available; $25 application fee.

Costs Per Year: $9,400 tuition; $4,450 room and board; additional student fees.

Collegiate Environment: The 170-acre campus is located 2,000 feet above sea level in the foothills of the Allegheny Mountains. The 20 college buildings include a library of 212,000 volumes. Dormitory facilities are available for 734 students. Approximately 90% of students applying for admission are accepted, including midyear students. Applicants are considered individually, and no qualified student is denied admission because of race or creed. Financial aid is available for economically disadvantaged students. 75% of students receive financial aid.

Community Environment: Elkins is located in the foothills of the Alleghenies and is the headquarters for the nearby Monongahela National Forest. The community is accessible by auto and airline. The climate is temperate. Elkins has several churches of various denominations, 1 hospital, a YMCA, and major civic and fraternal organizations. The nearby national forest offers excellent trout streams, hunting, camping, 4 modern ski resorts, and bathing beaches. An annual autumn State Forest Festival is held here. Part-time employment is limited.

FAIRMONT STATE COLLEGE   (C-10)
Locust Avenue
Fairmont, West Virginia 26554
Tel: (304) 367-4000; (800) 641-5678; Fax: (304) 366-4870

Description: Founded as a private teacher training school in 1865, the state college became a state-supported normal school in 1867. It became a teachers college in 1931, and its present name was adopted by the Legislature in 1943 when authorization was given to offer Bachelor of Arts and Bachelor of Science degrees, in addition to the Bachelor degrees in education. The college also grants the Associate degree. It is accredited by the North Central Association of Colleges and Schools. It operates on the semester system and offers 2 summer terms. Army ROTC is available. Enrollment includes 4,316 full-time and 2,039 part-time students. A faculty of 182 full-time and 235 part-time gives a faculty-student ratio of 1-18.

Entrance Requirements: Approved high school graduation; SAT or ACT required; early decision, rolling admission, delayed admission, and advanced placement plans available.

Costs Per Year: $1,800 tuition; $4,238 out-of-state; $3,300 room and board.

Collegiate Environment: The 75-acre campus is located in Fairmont, the county seat of Marion County and the center of the coal industry of northern West Virginia. The 13 college buildings include a library of 218,647 volumes, 650 periodicals, 6,669 microfilms, and recordings. There are dormitory facilities for 132 men and 316 women. The college welcomes a geographically diverse student body and will accept midyear students. Approximately 95% of students applying for admission are accepted, and 60% of the previous freshman class returns to this campus for the second year of studies. Financial aid is available for economically disadvantaged students. 65% of students receive financial aid.

Community Environment: Located in the Monongahela Valley coalfield, the city has 40 industries producing machinery, sheet aluminum, fluorescent lamps, cement, brick, and structural steel. The city is located in the northern part of the state and has a mild, temperate climate; the mean average temperature is 66 degrees. The community is served by churches of all denominations, 2 hospitals and health services, a library, and various civic, fraternal, and veteran's organizations. There is a Little Theatre, civic concert, bowling alleys, swimming pool, 3 golf courses, boating, fishing, skiing, and 3 radio stations. Dormitories, hotels, several motels, and private homes provide housing for students. Part-time job opportunities are available.

GLENVILLE STATE COLLEGE   (E-7)
Glenville, West Virginia 26351
Tel: (304) 462-7361; (800) 924-2010; Fax: (304) 462-8619

Description: Publicly supported coeducational college was founded in 1872. It became a state normal school in 1898, a state teachers college in 1930, and a state college in 1943. The college is accredited by the North Central Association of Colleges and Schools and by respective professional accrediting institutions. It operates on the semester system with 2 summer terms. Enrollment includes 802 men and 806 women full-time and 260 men and 347 women part-time. A faculty of 74 full-time and 68 part-time gives a faculty-student ratio of 1-18.

Entrance Requirements: Limited enrollment policy; completion of 18 units including 4 English, 2 mathematics, 2 science, and 3 social

studies; SAT or ACT required; non-high school graduates considered; rolling admission available.

Costs Per Year: $1,800 tuition; $5,000 out-of-state; $3,200 room and board.

Collegiate Environment: The college buildings include a library of approximately 200,000 volumes. Dormitories provide living accommodations for 436 men, 368 women and 20 families. Fraternities and sororities provide some additional housing facilities. Students from other geographical locations are accepted, as are midyear students. 98% of applicants are accepted. Financial aid is available. Of 64 scholarships available, 52 scholarships are awarded to freshmen. 80% of students receive some form of financial aid.

Community Environment: Glenville is located in the approximate geographical center of the state. Interstate 79 passes within 16 miles of the campus. Glenville has 5 churches, a modern clinic, hotel and motels, and several civic and fraternal organizations. Within the area there are facilities for hunting, fishing, golf, baseball, softball. A state park is located 6 miles away. Job opportunities are available. An annual West Virginia Folk Festival is held each year in June.

MARSHALL UNIVERSITY   (H-1)
400 Hal Greer Boulevard
Huntington, West Virginia 25755-2020
Tel: (304) 696-3160; (800) 642-3463; Fax: (304) 696-3333

Description: Marshall University was founded as Marshall Academy in 1837 and became a private college in 1858. In 1867 the Legislature passed an act creating a normal school to be established at the college. It became a teachers college in 1920 and was granted university status in 1961. The university functions through several divisions: College of Education, College of Liberal Arts, College of Science, College of Fine Arts, School of Medicine, School of Nursing, College of Business, Graduate School, and Community and Technical College. Army ROTC programs are offered in the Department of Military Science. The university is accredited by the North Central Association of Colleges and Schools and by several respective professional accrediting institutions. It operates on the semester system with 2 summer terms. An academic cooperative plan is available with Duke University for students majoring in Forestry. The university also maintains cooperative graduate degree programs in Humanistic Studies with the West Virginia College of Graduate Studies, and in Education Administration with West Virginia University. Enrollment includes 7,886 full-time and 2,417 part-time undergraduates and 2,356 graduate students. A faculty of 525 full-time and 276 part-time provides a faculty-student ratio of 1-18.

Entrance Requirements: Approved high school graduation with a 2.0 GPA or ACT composite score of 17, SAT 680 combined, or equivalent; ACT or SAT required; non-high school graduates considered; early admission, early decision, rolling admission, delayed admission and advanced placement plans available.

Costs Per Year: $3,644 metro-tuition; $1,990 state resident tuition; $5,424 out-of-state resident tuition; $4,010 room and board.

Collegiate Environment: The main campus of the university occupies 66 acres near the center of Huntington, located on the Ohio River close to the boundary of Kentucky, Ohio, and West Virginia. The 35 university buildings include a library of 422,025 volumes, 3,000 periodicals, and 186,065 microforms. Housing is available for 2,100 men and women. Approximately 95% of students applying for admission are accepted including midyear students. Financial aid is available for economically disadvantaged students.

Community Environment: Huntington is a busy river terminal and serves as the shipping point for millions of tons of coal mined annually from the great bituminous fields to the south of the city. It is also the center of a large natural gas and oil-producing area. The annual mean temperature is 56.6 degrees with an annual rainfall of 41.8 inches. The community is provided transportation by bus, train and air. There are over 140 churches of various denominations, a public library, numerous radio stations and 3 TV stations, YMCA and YWCA, and medical facilities serving the area. Local recreation includes municipal swimming pools, theatres and drive-ins, golf, tennis, bowling, boating, roller skating rinks, the Memorial Field House, and the Huntington Civic Center which attracts top entertainment. Part-time employment is available.

OHIO VALLEY COLLEGE (C-5)
College Parkway
Parkersburg, West Virginia 26101
Tel: (304) 485-7384; (800) 678-6780; Fax: (304) 485-3106

Description: The privately supported, four-year, coeducational liberal arts college was established in 1958 and is operated by members of the Church of Christ. The college is accredited by the North Central Association of Colleges and Schools. It accepts qualified students of all races and religions but full-time students are required to take a Bible course each semester. The college operates on the semester system and offers a "maymester" in lieu of a summer session. Enrollment includes 168 men, 146 women full-time, and 6 men and 4 women part-time. A faculty of 20 full-time and 4 part-time gives a faculty-student ratio of 1-15.

Entrance Requirements: Accredited high school graduation; completion of 15 units including 3 English, 1 math, 1 science, 1 social science; score of 14 or over on ACT encouraged; non high school graduates considered; early admission, early decision, midyear admission, rolling admission and advanced placement plans available; $20 application fee.

Costs Per Year: $5,400 tuition, $3,070 room and board; $230 student fees.

Collegiate Environment: The 260-acre campus is located in Parkersburg adjoining the city of Vienna. The college buildings include a library of 20,000 volumes, 2,000 periodicals, 3,873 microforms, and 4,230 audiovisual materials. There are dormitory facilities for 225 men and 142 women. Financial aid is available.

Community Environment: A city of diversified industry, Parkersburg is also the trading center and livestock market for the surrounding agricultural region. This is a metropolitan community enjoying temperate climate. The area is reached by airlines, railroad, bus lines, Interstate Route 77, and U.S. Routes 2 and 50. There are public library system, 2 hospitals, and a county health center serving the community. Part-time employment is available. Local recreation includes a civic theatre, water sports including crew racing, and flying. There are good shopping facilities. All the major civic, fraternal, and veteran's organizations are represented here.

POTOMAC STATE COLLEGE OF WEST VIRGINIA UNIVERSITY (C-14)
Fort Avenue
Keyser, West Virginia 26726
Tel: (304) 788-6800

Description: The publicly supported, coeducational junior college was established as a secondary school in 1901. It became a junior college in 1921 and was placed under the supervision of the Board of Governors of West Virginia University in 1935. The college is accredited by the North Central Association of Colleges and Schools and operates on the semester system with two summer terms. The enrollment is 579 men, 343 women full-time and 115 men and 169 women part-time. The faculty consists of 38 full-time and 35 part-time members.

Entrance Requirements: Accredited high school graduation or GED; Open enrollment; ACT or SAT required; early admission, advanced placement and rolling admission plans available.

Costs Per Year: $1,472 tuition; $4,278 out-of-state tuition; $3,150 room and board; $25 student fees.

Collegiate Environment: The main campus of 16 acres is located on Fort Hill, site of a Civil War fortification. Additional college land of about 375 acres immediately adjoins the main campus. The 35 college buildings include a library of 37,948 volumes, 2,269 pamphlets, 216 periodicals, 15,597 microforms, and 1,313 recordings. There are dormitory facilities for 200 men and 160 women. Approximately 98% of students applying for admission are accepted including midyear students. Financial aid is available for economically handicapped students. Of 116 scholarships offered, 63 are for freshmen. The college awarded 112 Associate degrees to the recent graduating class. Semesters begin in August and January.

Community Environment: During the Civil War, the country around Keyser was a frequent battleground. The community was a supply point for, alternately, the Union Army and the Confederate forces. It changed hands 14 times in 4 years of war. The climate is temperate.

There are churches of many denominations, libraries, a hospital and various civic, fraternal, and veteran's organizations serving the area. The city has good shopping facilities and is accessible by railroad, buses, and U.S. Highways 48,50 and 220. Residence Halls provide student housing. Part-time employment is available. Local recreation includes hunting, boating, fishing, golf, swimming, skiing, and tennis.

SALEM-TEIKYO UNIVERSITY (C-8)
223 West Main Street
Salem, West Virginia 26426
Tel: (304) 782-5389; (800) 283-4562 X 25; Admissions: (304) 782-5336; Fax: (304) 782-5592

Description: The privately supported, coeducational institution was established in 1888 and is a small liberal arts school with an international focus. It is accredited by the North Central Association of Colleges and Schools and operates on a modular or block calendar system with twelve 4-week-long modules offered. Enrollment includes 713 full-time and 98 part-time undergraduates and 73 graduate students. A faculty of 55 full-time and 25 part-time gives a faculty-student ratio of 1-14. Army and Air Force ROTC programs are available.

Entrance Requirements: Accredited high school graduation; 16 units required including 4 English, 2 mathematics, 2 natural science, 3 social studies, and 2 foreign language; average 3.0 high school G.P.A., SAT combined score of 1000, or ACT with composite score of 22; rolling admission, midyear admission, and advanced placement plans available; $25 application fee.

Costs Per Year: $11,103 tuition; $3,952 room and board; $200 student fees.

Collegiate Environment: The college has 2 principal campus locations in north central West Virginia. The main campus is located on 120 acres in the town of Salem. The other campus unit is located in the downtown Clarksburg area. The 20 college buildings include a library of 348,635 volumes, 655 periodical titles, 235,948 microforms, and 2,500 phonodiscs. There are dormitory facilities for 665 men and women. In addition to its regular program, the college offers a unique program leading to the Bachelor of Science degree in Equestrian Studies and Career Aviation. Approximately 80% of students applying for admission are accepted. The college welcomes a geographically diverse student body and will accept midyear students. 70% percent of the previous freshman class return to this campus for the second year of studies. Financial aid is available, and 85% of the current student body receives some form of financial assistance. The institution offers a wide array of merit scholarship awards to those who qualify on the basis of academic, athletic, or leadership achievement.

Community Environment: Salem was settled in 1790 by 40 families who had migrated from New Jersey. Today, oil and gas fields in the surrounding area are important to the economy. This is a suburban city 12 miles from Clarksburg. The climate is temperate. Within 12 miles are located 9 churches and 2 hospitals. Some part-time employment is available. Local recreation includes skiing, hiking and white water rafting. There are civic and fraternal organizations active in the area.

SHEPHERD COLLEGE (C-18)
Shepherdstown, West Virginia 25443
Tel: (304) 876-5212/5213; (800) 344-5231; Fax: (304) 876-3101

Description: A publicly supported, coeducational liberal arts institution, the college was founded in 1871. It is accredited by the North Central Association of Colleges and Schools and respective professional accrediting institutions. It operates on the early semester system and offers 2 summer terms. Cooperative education programs are available in most fields of study. Air Force ROTC is available through University of Maryland, and Army ROTC is available through Western Maryland College. Enrollment includes 1,395 men and 2,253 women. A faculty of 116 full-time and 132 part-time gives a faculty-student ratio of 1-15.

Entrance Requirements: Approved high school graduation with a grade point average of 2.5; completion of 21 units including 4 English, 3 mathematics, 3 science, 3 social science, 2 foreign language and 6 electives. ACT 21 or over, or SAT minimum combined score of 1060; early admission, early action, delayed admission, and advanced placement plans available; $25 application fee.

Costs Per Year: $2,064 tuition; $4,694 nonresident; $3,820 room and board; $1,500 average additional expenses.

Collegiate Environment: The 323-acre campus is situated on the banks of the beautiful Potomac River in historic Shepherdstown. The 31 college buildings include a library of 255,336 bound volumes, 957 periodical titles, 45,235 microforms, and 7,369 audiovisual materials. There are dormitory facilities for 1,100 men and women. The college welcomes a geographically diverse student body and will accept midyear students. Approximately 40% of students applying for admission are accepted, and 68% of the previous freshman class return to this campus for the sophomore year. Financial aid is available for economically disadvantaged students, and 39% of the current student body receives some form of financial assistance. Of 500 scholarships offered, 120 are for freshmen.

Community Environment: This is a small town of about 5,000 located near Martinsburg, Charles Town and Harpers Ferry, West Virginia, and Hagerstown, Maryland. The town was established by English and German farmers who had crossed the river from Maryland before 1730. There are many historic sites in the area. The climate is temperate and the community is reached by State Route 45. There are 10 churches, 4 libraries, and 7 hospitals nearby. Some part-time employment is available in the surrounding area. Water sports on the Potomac River are popular.

SOUTHERN WEST VIRGINIA COMMUNITY COLLEGE
(J-13)
Dempsey Branch Road
Box 2900
Mt. Gay, West Virginia 25637-2900
Tel: (304) 792-4300; Admissions: (304) 792-4318

Description: The publicly supported, coeducational multi-campus community college was established in 1971. The college is accredited by the North Central Association of Colleges and Schools and professionally by the National League for Nursing. The college operates on the semester system and offers one summer session. Enrollment includes 1,859 full-time and 1,372 part-time students. A faculty of 61 full-time and 144 part-time gives a faculty-student ratio of 1-20. Programs of study are career oriented and lead to the Associate degree. Late afternoon and evening classes facilitate scheduling for working students.

Entrance Requirements: Open enrollment policy; completion of 12 units including 4 English, 2 mathematics, 2 science, 2 social studies; non-high school graduates considered; early admission, early decision, rolling admission plans available.

Costs Per Year: $1,015 tuition; $2,900 out-of-state tuition.

Collegiate Environment: The library contains 36,345 volumes, 496 periodicals, 7,428 microforms, and 283 recordings. All students applying for admission who meet the requirements are accepted including midyear students. Dormitory facilities are not available. Financial aid is available.

Community Environment: Southern West Virginia is a rural, rugged section of "The Mountain State". The mountains in the extreme south of the state are an extension of the Cumberland Plateau. The southern mountains are cut irregularly by rivers, mostly the Ohio River and its tributaries, and river valleys ranging in elevation from 2,000 to 4,000 feet. Logan, WV is on the Guyandotte River, while Williamson borders Northeastern Kentucky. An abundance of forests, white pine, hemlock and spruce on the mountain heights, hickory, oak, black walnut and other hardwoods, make hunting an important sport. Good sport fishing is also found in the many lakes of the state.

Branch Campuses: Logan Campus, P.O. Box 2900, Mt. Gay, WV, 25637; Williamson Campus, Armory Drive, Williamson, WV, 25661; Boone County Campus, P.O. Box 398, Madison, WV, 25130; Wyoming County Campus, P.O. Box 638, Pineville, WV, 24874.

UNIVERSITY OF CHARLESTON *(H-4)*
2300 MacCorkle Avenue, S.E.
Charleston, West Virginia 25304
Tel: (304) 357-4750; (800) 995-4682; Fax: (304) 357-4715

Description: The University of Charleston is a private university founded in 1888. The University presently has 763 full-time and 648 part-time students who are majoring in 40 undergraduate degree and two graduate degree programs. The degrees are within the three divisions and two schools: The Morris Harvey Division of Arts and Sciences, The Jones-Benedum Division of Business, The Division of Health Sciences, The Carleton Varney Department of Art and Design, and the Department of Music and Fine Arts. Each undergraduate degree is in three parts: the 47 credit liberal arts core, major degree requirements, and general college electives. A minimum of 120 credits are required for a bachelor's degree. Cooperative education programs are available in many departments. There is an exchange program with Sophia University in Japan. Army ROTC is available. The University is accredited by the North Central Association of Colleges and Schools, the National League for Nursing and the National Council for Accreditation of Teacher Education. A faculty of 74 full-time and 164 part-time gives a faculty-student ratio of 1-16.

Entrance Requirements: A candidate for admission must present a transcript of work from an accredited secondary school. The record must show 16 units with grades indicating intellectual ability and promise. The units should include 3 English, 3 mathematics, 2 science, 2 foreign language, 2 social studies, 2 history, and 2 electives. ACT with minimum composite score of 18, or SAT with minimum combined score of 800, required. Early admission, early decision, delayed admission and advanced placement plans are available. Acceptance to the University is on a rolling admission basis. $20 application fee.

Costs Per Year: $8,550 tuition; $3,500 room and board.

Collegiate Environment: The University has a 40-acre riverfront campus. Facilities include two coed residence halls, a large field house with handball courts, swimming pool and sports medicine center. The library contains 100,000 volumes with 800 periodicals. 76% of the applicants are accepted with 75% of all students receiving financial aid. Both academic scholarships and athletic grants are available for both freshmen and transfer students.

Community Environment: Charleston, with a metropolitan population of 280,000, is the state capital, as well as the cultural, social, political, and economic center of West Virginia. Located in the Kanawha Valley, near the foothills of the Appalachian Mountains, it offers scenic tranquility as well as the convenience and excitement of a modern city. Downtown Charleston, just a 5-minute drive from campus, offers social and cultural opportunities that can be found only in a large city.

WEST LIBERTY STATE COLLEGE *(C-2)*
West Liberty, West Virginia 26074
Tel: (304) 336-8076; (800) 732-6204; Admissions: (306) 336-8076; Fax: (304) 336-8285

Description: The West Liberty Campus, where the college opened as an academy in 1838 following the granting of a charter by the Legislature of Virginia in 1837, is the main campus of this state college. It is accredited by the North Central Association of Colleges and Schools and operates on the semester system with three summer terms. The college offers programs in teacher education, liberal arts, fine arts, sciences, business, and preprofessional, professional and technical programs. Enrollment includes 1,012 men, 1,117 women full-time and 100 men and 152 women part-time. A faculty of 129 full-time and 14 part-time gives a faculty-student ratio of 1-18.

Entrance Requirements: Accredited high school graduation, with 2.00 G.P.A. or score of 17 or over on enhanced ACT or 680 combined SAT score required; 4 units of English, 2 math, 2 sciences, 3 social science; non-high school graduates considered; early admission, early decision, rolling admission, midyear admission and advanced placement plans available.

Costs Per Year: $1,900 tuition; $4,470 out-of-state tuition; $2,890 room and board; additional expenses average $700.

Collegiate Environment: The college owns 290 acres of ground, of which about 115 acres are used for the campus. Located 50 miles southwest of Pittsburgh and 8 miles north of Wheeling, the West Liberty campus is part of a semirural community. The college buildings include a library of 202,505 volumes, 6,000 pamphlets, 1,500 periodicals, 150,000 microforms, and 11,000 recordings. Dormitories provide living accommodations for 1,377 students and 21 families. Approximately 91% of the students applying for admission are accepted. Students from diverse geographical locations are accepted as are midyear students. Students applying to the dental hygiene course are admitted only in August of each school year. Scholarships are available and 64% of the current student body receives some form of financial aid. Approximately 15% of the senior class continues to graduate school.

Community Environment: West Liberty is located 8 miles from the city limits of Wheeling. There are 2 Protestant churches and a visiting priest for Catholic students. Famous Oglebay Park, 6 miles from the campus, is used for recreation. Job opportunities are good in the area. There are dormitories, campus health services, and an infirmary for students. Fraternities and sororities are prominent here.

WEST VIRGINIA GRADUATE COLLEGE *(H-4)*
100 Angus E. Peyton Dr.
South Charleston, West Virginia 25303-1600
Tel: (304) 746-2500; (800) 642-9842

Description: The public, state-supported graduate school was established in 1972. It is accredited by the North Central Association of Colleges and Schools. The college offers primarily evening and weekend programs for employed, part-time students. It awards the Master degree. Operating on the early semester system it offers two summer sessions. Enrollment includes 2,750 full-time and 200 part-time graduate students. A faculty of 60 full-time and 80 part-time gives a faculty-student ratio of 1-20.

Entrance Requirements: Bachelor degree; General Section of the GRE; also required is a personal statement of life and work experiences since completion of the Bachelor degree, including interests and objectives in graduate school; letter of recommendation; no application fee.

Costs Per Year: $780 state resident tuition; $2,526 nonresident tuition.

Collegiate Environment: A new and innovative model for graduate education enabling qualified faculty from other institutions to supplement the Graduate College faculty, expanding the use of existing facilities in the region served by the college, and providing the timely offering of needed new graduate programs in locations convenient to prospective students.

Community Environment: Courses offered state-wide with administrative offices in urban surroundings.

WEST VIRGINIA INSTITUTE OF TECHNOLOGY *(I-5)*
Montgomery, West Virginia 25136
Tel: (304) 442-3167; Fax: (304) 442-3097

Description: The publicly supported, coeducational state institute began in 1895 as a preparatory branch of West Virginia University. The first Bachelor of Arts degrees were conferred in 1929, and the college was formally approved for the Bachelor of Science degree in 1933. Today, the institute offers programs in engineering and related technical fields, science, business administration, printing management, secondary teacher education, and liberal studies in the arts and sciences. Cooperative education programs are available for 4 year degree programs if a 2.2 GPA is maintained. There are no cooperative education programs for Nursing, Dental Hygiene, and Teacher Education. Army ROTC is available. It is accredited by the North Central Association of Colleges and Schools and respective professional accrediting institutions. It operates on the semester system with 2 summer terms. Undergraduate enrollment includes 1,625 men and 786 women full-time and 330 men and 286 women part-time. A faculty of 146 full-time and 68 part-time gives a faculty-student ratio of 1-18.

Entrance Requirements: High school graduation or equivalent; completion of 17 academic units including 4 English, 2 mathematics, 2 laboratory science, and 3 social studies; minimum ACT composite score of 17 and ACT math score of 21 required or minimum SAT combined score of 690 and math score of 460 required; out-of-state students must rank in upper 75% of graduating class; early decision, rolling admission, early admission, delayed admission and advanced placement plans available; no application fee.

Costs Per Year: $2,120 tuition; $4,790 out-of-state tuition; $3,600 room and board.

Collegiate Environment: The 109-acre campus overlooks the city of Montgomery and the Great Kanawha River. The city is located 30 miles southeast of West Virginia's capital city of Charleston. The 18 institute buildings include a library of 153,167 volumes, more than 763 periodicals, and 398,053 microforms. Coed dormitory facilities, 5

fraternity houses, and private homes are available for student housing. Approximately 97% of students applying for admission are accepted including midyear students. Financial aid is available for economically disadvantaged students. Academic and athletic scholarships are available.

Community Environment: The community has nearby plants that include the world's largest producer of ferro alloys for steel and a steam-produced electric power plant. Montgomery may be reached by bus lines and Amtrak. There is a shopping center available.

WEST VIRGINIA NORTHERN COMMUNITY COLLEGE *(C-2)*
College Square
Wheeling, West Virginia 26003
Tel: (304) 233-5900

Description: The publicly supported comprehensive community college traces its origin to 1938 with the founding of the Wheeling Campus of West Liberty State College. In 1972 it was united with the Weirton Campus by the West Virginia Board of Regents as a dual campus community college. In 1975, a campus was established in New Martinsville, making West Virginia Northern a comprehensive Tri-Campus institution. The college is accredited by the North Central Association of Colleges and Schools, the Committee on Allied Health Education and Accreditation and the National League for Nursing. It operates on the semester system and offers two summer sessions. The college offers the Associate degree and the College Certificate. Enrollment includes 1,148 full-time and 1,773 part-time students. A faculty of 67 full-time and 91 part-time gives a faculty-student ratio of 1-19.

Entrance Requirements: Open enrollment policy; non-high school graduates admitted; SAT or ACT required if graduated or obtained GED in past 5 years, otherwise ASSET; early admission, early decision, midyear admission, rolling admission, and advanced placement plans available.

Costs Per Year: $1,416 tuition; $3,864 out-of-state; $16 student fees; expenses vary for specialized programs.

Collegiate Environment: The college has campuses in downtown Wheeling and downtown New Martinsville, and in the Weirton heights section of Weirton, West Virginia. Each campus has classrooms and modern library and laboratory facilities, as well as a student lounge and conference rooms. Combined library holdings for the 3 campuses total 35,000 volumes. Financial aid is available, including 60 scholarships. 46% of students receive some form of financial aid. All applicants are accepted, including midyear students.

Community Environment: Wheeling, one of the country's most liveable small cities, is a one-hour drive from Pittsburgh, PA, and a two-hour drive from Columbus, OH. It is in a central area of approximately 150,000 people. Many recreational and cultural facilities are available, including 1,500-acre Oglebay Park and 250-acre Wheeling Park. Excellent local recreation areas provide opportunities for camping, golf, hiking, skiing, swimming, and other such activities.

Branch Campuses: New Martinsville and Weirton.

WEST VIRGINIA STATE COLLEGE *(H-4)*
Institute, West Virginia 25112
Tel: (304) 766-3000; Fax: (304) 766-4104

Description: The publicly supported, coeducational college had its origin in 1891 as the West Virginia Colored Institute. The college is accredited by the North Central Association of Colleges and Schools. The college grants the Associate and Bachelor degrees. It operates on the semester system and offers two summer sessions. Enrollment is 4,685 students. A faculty of 128 provides a faculty-student ratio of 1-22. The college is known for its "integration in reverse" program, which successfully recruited white students. Army ROTC program is available. In 1978, the college implemented a community college component. Extension courses are offered at the historic Capital Theater in downtown Charlestown.

Entrance Requirements: Approved high school graduation or equivalent; completion of 17 units, including 4 English, 2 mathematics, 2 science, 3 social science; score of 17 or over on ACT required; non-high school graduates with GED considered; open enrollment policy for community college division; early admission, early decision, rolling admission, advanced placement, delayed admission and advanced placement plans available.

Costs Per Year: $1,988 tuition; $4,616 out-of-state; $3,200 room and board.

Collegiate Environment: The college is located in Institute, West Virginia, 8 miles west of Charleston, the capital of the state. Its campus is set in the beautiful Appalachian foothills along the Great Kanawha River. College facilities include a library of 250,000 volumes, and living accommodations for 497 single students and 45 students with families. Approximately 85% of students applying for admission are accepted. Students from other geographical locations are accepted as well as midyear students. Developmental programs exist in English and mathematics. The level campus is completely accessible to the handicapped. Scholarships are available and 45% of students receive some form of financial aid.

Community Environment: Institute is a suburb of Charleston and is reached by railroad, bus lines, feeder airlines, and a local transit system. There are churches of major denominations and community services in the easily accessible neighboring community. Part-time employment is available.

WEST VIRGINIA UNIVERSITY   *(B-10)*
P.O. Box 6009
Morgantown, West Virginia 26506-6009
Tel: (304) 293-2121; (800) 344-9881; Fax: (304) 293-3080

Description: West Virginia University, founded in 1867, is one of only 38 public universities in the United States that serve as both a land-grant and research institution. WVU is fully accredited by the North Central Association of Colleges and Schools, and 71 academic programs are accredited by 29 specialized external accrediting agencies. Enrollment includes 14,284 full-time, 1,099 part-time, and 7,017 graduate students. An instructional faculty of 1,417 full-time and part-time provides an undergraduate to faculty ratio of 1-17. The student body is composed of individuals from every county in West Virginia, 50 other states, and 77 other nations around the world.

Entrance Requirements: Freshman admission is based on high school courses taken, GPA, and ACT or SAT score. For residents, a high school GPA of 2.0 and an enhanced ACT composite score of 19 or SAT combined score of 770 is required. For nonresidents, a high school GPA of 2.25 and an enhanced ACT composite score of 20 or a SAT combined score of 820 is required. All students must have 2 units of college preparatory mathematics, 4 English, 3 social studies, and 2 laboratory science at a minimum. Many academic units, including engineering, have admission standards that exceed these minimum requirements. Special admissions regulations for these programs appear in the WVU Undergraduate Catalog.

Costs Per Year: Undergraduate: $2,128 resident tuition and mandatory fees; $6,370 nonresident; Graduate: $2,244 resident; $6,682 nonresident. Typical room and board is $4,016.

Collegiate Environment: The campus of WVU combines traditional and modern architectural styles, and 10 of the 153 campus buildings are on the National Register of Historic Places. In recent years, many of the original buildings have been restored and new buildings have been constructed. The Morgantown campus covers 541 acres. Transportation is provided by the Personal Rapid Transit System (PRT), a series of computer-directed, driverless, electric powered cars that run on a steel and concrete guideway constructed in the 1970's as a research and demonstration project funded by the U.S. Department of Transportation. The University library system consists of 1.7 million volumes, 2.2 million microforms, over 11,000 periodicals, 4 million archives, and various electronic databases. The collections are especially strong in the biological sciences, chemistry, engineering, economics, and African, Southern Appalachain, and West Virginia history. Microcomputers are available in individual departments, dormitories, libraries, and computer sites about campus.

Community Environment: West Virginia University's main campus is located in Morgantown, a city of 45,000 in the Appalachain Mountains on West Virginia's northern border adjacent to Pennsylvania. Although the state is rural and the community quiet, Greater Morgantown is within easy traveling distance, on modern interstate highways, of the metropolitan areas of Pittsburgh, which is 75 miles north, and Baltimore and Washington, both of which are 200 miles east. The community has churches of various denominations, two hospitals, a city library and various civic and fraternal organizations. Local recre-

ation is available through the city's park system which includes several municipal pools and an ice skating rink; there are golf courses, 1800 acre Cheat Lake, and nearby Cooper's Rock State Forest. Morgantown's climate has four distinct seasons. A half dozen snow skiing areas are within easy driving distance from campus, as are some of the best remaining wilderness areas in the eastern United States. Whitewater rafting is another favorite activity within the state.

Branch Campuses: Charleston Division of the WVU Health Sciences Center; Wheeling Division of the School of Medicine; Potomac State College at Keyser; WVU at Parkersburg; and 5 off-campus graduate centers at Jackson's Mill, Parkersburg, Keyser, Shepherdstown, and Wheeling.

WEST VIRGINIA UNIVERSITY AT PARKERSBURG   *(C-5)*
Route 5, Box 167-A
Parkersburg, West Virginia 26101
Tel: (304) 424-8000

Description: This publicly supported junior college was established in 1971; it offers an Associate degree and the Certificate. It is accredited by the North Central Association of Colleges and Schools and operates on the semester basis. Enrollment includes 832 men, 1,169 women full-time and 659 men and 1,319 women part-time. A faculty of 68 full-time and 119 part-time gives a student-faculty ratio of 18-1.

Entrance Requirements: High school graduate or GED required; SAT or ACT required; open enrollment policy; early admission plan.

Costs Per Year: $864 tuition; $2,880 out-of-state tuition.

Collegiate Environment: The college is housed in a modern, air-conditioned building located on a 122-acre campus near Parkersburg, West Virginia. The college library contains 35,463 volumes, 316 periodical titles, 5169 microforms, and 3354 audiovisual materials. There are 130 scholarships available.

Community Environment: See Ohio Valley College.

WEST VIRGINIA WESLEYAN COLLEGE   *(E-9)*
52 College Avenue
Buckhannon, West Virginia 26201
Tel: (304) 473-8000; (800) 722-9933; Fax: (304) 473-8108

Description: Privately supported, the coeducational liberal arts college was founded in 1890 as the West Virginia Conference Seminary. The college is affiliated with the United Methodists. It is accredited by the North Central Association of Colleges and Schools and professionally by respective accrediting organizations. The general aims and commitments of the present college are essentially the same as they were in its founding, but the campus and facilities have greatly expanded. The college grants the Bachelor and Master's degrees. Academic cooperative plans are available with the University of Pennsylvania for engineering students, with Duke University for students majoring in forestry or environmental management, and with NASA-Langley Research Center for aeronautical engineering. Study abroad is available and requires planning one year in advance with a faculty advisor. It operates on the 4-1-4 calendar system and offers 2 summer sessions. Enrollment includes 1,466 full-time and 214 part-time undergraduates and 60 graduate students. A faculty of 78 full-time and 58 part-time gives a faculty-student ratio of 1-15.

Entrance Requirements: Accredited high school graduation with rank in upper half of graduating class; completion of 16 units including 4 English, 3 mathematics, 2 laboratory science, 3 or 4 social studies; interview recommended; each prospective student is individually evaluated. ACT or SAT required; advanced placement, midyear admission and rolling admission plans available; $25 application fee.

Costs Per Year: $14,200 tuition; $3,775 room and board.

Collegiate Environment: The 80-acre campus is located in Buckhannon, near the geographical center of West Virginia. The 24 college buildings include a library of 147,154 volumes, 642 periodicals, and 6,988 microforms and 1,617 audiovisual materials. There are dormitory facilities for 1,390 men and women. The college welcomes a geographically diverse student body. 76% of students applying for admission are accepted. 90% of the current student body receive some form of financial assistance. There are 939 scholarships available, 350 for freshmen and 101 of those are athletic scholarships.

Community Environment: Buckhannon is a rural community supported by agriculture, coal, natural gas, and local industries. The climate is temperate with an average annual temperature of 53 degrees. Bus and airlines are accessible 25 miles distant at Clarksburg. The community has a public library, restaurants, hotels, churches of most denominations, 1 hospital, and a YWCA. Part-time employment is available. Buckhannon is the home of the West Virginia Strawberry Festival. Local recreation includes hunting, fishing, boating, skiing, white-water rafting, and most outdoor sports. Civic, fraternal, and veterans' organizations are active in the area.

WHEELING JESUIT COLLEGE *(C-2)*
316 Washington Avenue
Wheeling, West Virginia 26003
Tel: (304) 243-2359; (800) 624-6992; Fax: (304) 243-2243

Description: The college is a privately supported, coeducational four-year college of liberal arts and sciences. Founded in 1954, it is the newest of 28 Jesuit colleges and universities in the United States and the only Jesuit college between Philadelphia and Cleveland. It is accredited by the North Central Association of Colleges and Schools, and by respective professional accrediting organizations. The college confers Bachelor of Art, Bachelor of Science, and Bachelor of Science in Nursing (B.S.N.) degrees in 28 majors and provides a strong background in philosophy, theology, and modern languages. Pre-engineering (in association with Case Western Reserve University, School of Engineering), Industrial Engineering and other pre-professional programs as well as a five-year MBA program are offered. The college operates on the semester system and offers two summer sessions. Enrollment includes 1,440 students. A faculty of 60 full-time and 16 part-time provides a faculty-student ratio of 1-13.

Entrance Requirements: High school graduation with rank in upper half of graduating class; completion of 15 units including 4 English, 2 mathematics, 1-2 science, 2 social science, 2 foreign language recommended; minimum ACT 18 composite or SAT 850 combined, required; advanced placement, early admission, early decision, rolling admission, and midyear admission plans available; $25 application fee.

Costs Per Year: $10,500 tuition; $4,445 room and board.

Collegiate Environment: The college is located on 65 acres and is comprised of 12 buildings including the newly renovated Bishop Hodges Learning Center containing 122,000 volumes, 550 periodicals and 58,000 microforms, and equipped with a computer that serves as a major link to the public and private libraries in the Pittsburgh area. New buildings include the Chapel of Mary and Joseph, a fitness center, and newly designed laboratories. Dormitories house 600 students. 75% of the students live on campus and participate in numerous clubs, sports, dramatics and social activities. The college welcomes all qualified students regardless of race, creed, color, or national origin. Approximately 87% of students applying for admission are accepted, including midyear students. The average scores of entering freshmen were ACT 21 composite, SAT 945 combined. Financial aid is available. 80% of students receive financial aid.

Community Environment: Wheeling, one of the country's most liveable small cities, is a one-hour drive from Pittsburgh, PA and a two-hour drive from Columbus, OH. In a central area of approximately 150,000 people, many cultural and recreational facilities are available for golf, camping, hiking, skiing, and swimming, including 1,500-acre Oglebay Park and 250-acre Wheeling Park.

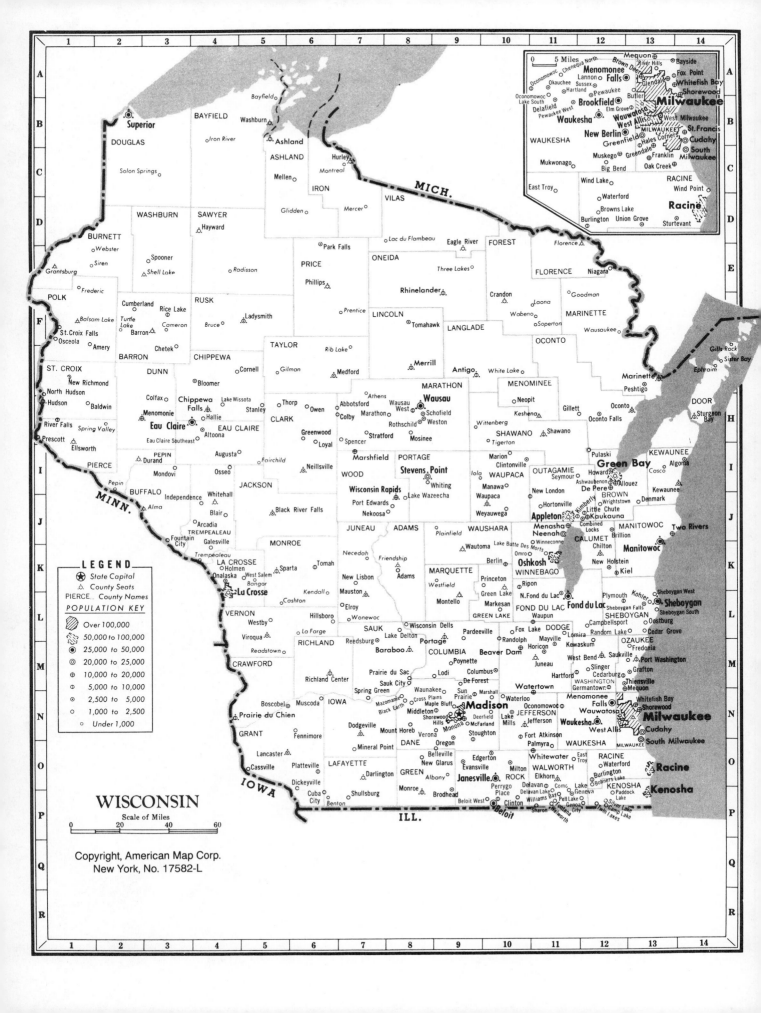

WISCONSIN

Scale of Miles

New York, No. 17582-L

WISCONSIN

ALVERNO COLLEGE   (N-13)
P.O. Box 343922
3401 South 39th Street
Milwaukee, Wisconsin 53234-3922
Tel: (414) 382-6100; (800) 933-3401; Fax: (414) 382-6354

Description: This privately supported Roman Catholic liberal arts college for women was founded in 1887 by the School Sisters of St. Francis. It is accredited by the North Central Association of Colleges and Schools, National Council for Accreditation of Teacher Education, National League for Nursing, and the National Association of Schools of Music. The college operates on the semester system and offers 1 summer term. There are required internships for all majors. Army ROTC is available through Marquette University. Music programs including vocal and instrumental music groups are offered. Enrollment includes 1,245 full-time and 1,212 part-time students. A faculty of 116 full-time and 94 part-time gives a faculty-student ratio of 1-13.

Entrance Requirements: Accredited high school graduation or equivalent with completion of 17 units, 4 English, 3 mathematics (which must include Algebra and Geometry), 3 science (laboratory science preferred), 3 social science, and 2 foreign language recommended; ACT with minimum score of 19 required; placement examinations in applied music and theory required for applicants to music programs; early admission, rolling admission, delayed admission, and advanced placement programs available; deadline for fall applications is August 1; $10 application fee.

Costs Per Year: $7,784 tuition; $3,460 room and board; $60 student fees.

Collegiate Environment: Alverno's 46-acre campus is located on the south side of Milwaukee. The 9 college buildings contain a library of 94,144 volumes, 17,400 periodicals, 215,642 microforms and 21,994 audiovisual materials. Dormitory facilities are available for 250 women. The college welcomes a geographically diverse student body and accepts midyear students. 67% of applicants are accepted. Scholarships which range from $500 to $6,000 per year and are renewable, are available and 78% of students receive some form of financial aid.

Community Environment: See Milwaukee Area Technical College.

BELOIT COLLEGE   (P-10)
700 College Street
Beloit, Wisconsin 53511
Tel: (608) 363-2000; (800) 356-0751; Admissions: (608) 363-2500; Fax: (608) 363-2075

Description: The charter of this privately supported liberal arts college was enacted into law by the Legislature of the Territory of Wisconsin in 1846. It is one of the earliest charters known providing for nonsectarian educational institution, though the college retains historic ties to the United Church of Christ. The college operates on the semester system with 1 summer session. This special summer session offers 9 weeks of foreign language instruction, including Russian, Hungarian, Spanish, Chinese, Japanese, and English as a Second Language, in addition to off-campus field work in anthropology, geology, and other areas. The college is accredited by the North Central Association of Colleges and Schools. Enrollment includes 1,053 full-time and 86 part-time undergraduates and 11 graduate students. A faculty of 86 full-time and 50 part-time (excluding part-time instrumental music instructors) gives a faculty-student ratio of 1-12. It offers vocal and instrumental music programs, theatre, poetry and public affairs events, and intercollegiate and intramural athletics. Preparation for state teaching certificate offered. Field Term and Internship programs offer 15-week terms of work, service, or research away from home and college, many for credit. The Summer Employment Program of-

fers summer job opportunities in many parts of the nation. Several overseas programs are offered, including the student-faculty exchange program with Fudan University, Shanghai, and in Indonesia and Japan, and a variety of programs in cooperation with the Associated Colleges of the Midwest. Beloit seminars are held in Hungary, France, Scotland, the Middle East, Indonesia and South America. Domestic programs include Washington semester, Archeological and Geology Field Schools. Offers 3-2 programs in cooperation with Columbia, Rensselaer, Georgia Tech, Iowa State, Michigan, Illinois, Northwestern, Purdue, Washington University (in engineering), Duke (in forestry), University of Chicago (in social work and classics), and Rush Medical Center (in health professions), 3/2 MBA with Washington University and the University of Chicago, and reserved admissions program with Medical College of Wisconsin. Beloit grants B.A., B.S., and M.A.T. degrees.

Entrance Requirements: High school graduation or equivalent with rank in upper 30% of graduating class; SAT or ACT required; recommend completion of units including 4 English, 3 mathematics, 2-3 foreign language, 3 social science, 2 laboratory science; campus interview strongly recommended; early admission, early decision, rolling admission, delayed admission and advanced placement plans available; $25 application fee.

Costs Per Year: $17,544 tuition; $3,846 board and room; $200 student fees.

Collegiate Environment: The 40-acre wooded campus is located a short walk from the central business section of the city of Beloit, Wisconsin. A 25-acre athletic field and stadium are located east of the main campus. The 45 college buildings include a newly renovated library of 235,439 volumes, 868 periodical subscriptions, 126,817 microforms and 3,168 audiovisual materials, as well as a new campus center and sports-fitness center. Residence hall facilities are provided for 418 men and 437 women. Fraternities and sororities house 107 men and 17 women respectively. 74% of the applicants are accepted. The average scores of the entering freshman class were SAT 559 verbal, 571 math, ACT 26. 681 scholarships are offered and 68% of students receive some form of financial aid.

Community Environment: Beloit (population 35,000) is located on the border of Illinois, 50 miles south of Madison, 100 miles northwest of Chicago and 75 miles southwest of Milwaukee. Direct bus service is available 16 times daily from O'Hare International Airport (90 minute trip). The manufacture of diesel engines, pumps, paper-making machinery, food products, machine tools, and shoes is of great importance to the economy of the city. The college is accessible to year-round sports and recreation areas of southern Wisconsin; recreational activities include golf, swimming, bowling, tennis, hiking, sailing, skiing, and ice skating. The community has a symphony orchestra and masterworks chorus based on campus, a civic theater, and other cultural programs. Nationally recognized anthropology and art museums are located on the campus. Various civic and service organizations are active.

BLACKHAWK TECHNICAL COLLEGE   (O-10)
6004 Prairie Road
P.O. Box 5009
Janesville, Wisconsin 53547
Tel: (608) 756-4121

Description: The school is a publicly supported, coeducational institute offering technological programs. It was originally begun as a vocational school in the early 1900's. In 1968, a statewide reorganization process was implemented to broaden technical and adult educational opportunities. The present college became a reality as a result of that endeavor. The school operates on a semester system, with one summer session. It is fully accredited by the North Central Association of Colleges and Schools, and awards Certificates, Diplomas, and

Associate degrees. Cooperative education programs are available in Nursing, Allied Health, and in some business courses. Enrollment includes 1,284 men, 1,284 women full-time and 856 men and 856 women part-time. A faculty of 96 full-time and 300 part-time members provides a teacher-student ratio of 1-8.

Entrance Requirements: High school graduation or GED is required; open enrollment; early admission, early decision, rolling admission and advanced placement; credits may be allowed from correspondence courses and prior examination, such as CLEP; $25 reservation fee.

Costs Per Year: $410 tuition for district or county resident; nonresident tuition $2,800. Subject to increase.

Collegiate Environment: At present, the school has facilities at Janesville, North Janesville and Airport. Each houses specialized instructional rooms, labs, and offices or study areas. The library has 30,000 volumes, 265 periodicals and 300 microforms. 95% of those applying are accepted, and financial aid is available to students requiring it. In addition to its academic program, the school sponsors subject related clubs and other student activities. Services are available for vocational guidance and job information.

CARDINAL STRITCH COLLEGE (N-13)
6801 North Yates Road
Milwaukee, Wisconsin 53217
Tel: (414) 352-5400; (800) 347-8820; Admissions: (414) 351-7504; Fax: (414) 351-7516

Description: This privately supported liberal arts college was chartered in 1937 as St. Clare College and was established for the Sisters of St. Francis of Assisi. It is a Catholic coeducational, independent liberal arts college with a genuine commitment to high-quality education, individualized learning and the personal development of each student. When the college was opened to lay students in 1946, its present name was adopted. In 1956, 2 graduate programs were inaugurated, one leading to a Master's degree in reading, the other in special education for teachers of the mentally retarded. In 1976, the Master of Education/Professional Development in Teaching degree was added. Besides these graduate programs, the college today offers work leading to the Baccalaureate or Associate degree in 30 major areas. The college is accredited by the North Central Association of Colleges and Schools and the National Council for Accreditation of Teacher Education and other professional organizations. It operates on the semester system and offers two summer sessions. Study abroad is available through other colleges. The college enrolls 942 men and 1,392 women full-time, 94 men and 265 women part-time, plus 636 full-time and 930 part-time graduate students. Of the full-time students, 1,610 are in the evening program and 724 are full-time day students. A faculty of 76 full-time and 100 part-time gives a faculty-student ratio of 1:16.

Entrance Requirements: High school graduation or equivalent with rank in upper half of graduating class; completion of 16 units including 4 English, 2 mathematics, 2 science, 3 social science, 1 history, 2 foreign language and 4 electives; SAT or ACT required; early admission, early decision, rolling admission, delayed admission and advanced placement programs available; application fee $20.

Costs Per Year: $8,000 tuition; $3,600 room and board.

Collegiate Environment: The 40-acre campus of the college is located in the northeastern Milwaukee suburbs of Fox Point and Glendale. The 10 college buildings include a library of 110,040 volumes, 1,142 periodicals, 82,000 microforms, and 8,000 audiovisual materials. Dormitory facilities are available for 150 men and 150 women. Students from other geographical locations are accepted as well as midyear students. 70% of applicants are accepted. Over 90% of the freshman class received some form of financial aid. About 85% of the recent freshman class graduated in the top half of their high school class.

Community Environment: See Milwaukee Area Technical College.

CARROLL COLLEGE (N-12)
100 N. East Avenue
Waukesha, Wisconsin 53186
Tel: (414) 547-1211; (800) 227-7655; Fax: (414) 524-7139

Description: Carroll College, founded in 1846, is Wisconsin's oldest undergraduate institution. Carroll maintains a covenant with the Presbyterian Church (U.S.A.), but is ecumenical and nonsectarian. The academic program leads to the granting of a bachelor's degree in over 35 fields of study. The college is accredited by the North Central Association of Colleges and Schools. It operates on the 4-1-4 semester system and offers two summer terms. Enrollment includes 1,480 full-time and 741 part-time students. A faculty of 74 full-time and 55 part-time members provides an undergraduate student-faculty ratio of 1-17. There are 58 graduate students. It offers a wind ensemble, choir, intercollegiate and club athletics and many other student organizations. Overseas study opportunities include the new Cultural Experiences Program. The college offers a cooperative engineering program with Marquette University. Carroll collaborates with Columbia College of Nursing in Milwaukee to offer a B.S.N. degree.

Entrance Requirements: High school graduation or equivalent with rank in upper half of graduating class; recommend completion of 16 units; SAT or ACT required; non-high school graduates over 21 years of age may be admitted as special students; C average in high school may be accepted if total record is satisfactory; average test scores of freshman class: ACT 23; special admission plans include early admission, rolling admission, delayed admission, advanced placement and midyear admission.

Costs Per Year: $12,740 tuition, $4,000 room and board.

Collegiate Environment: The 52-acre campus is located in a pleasant residential city on the edge of metropolitan Milwaukee. The 29 college buildings contain a library of 184,590 volumes and dormitory facilities for 347 men and 548 women. Fraternity houses accommodate 118 men. Approximately 90% of students applying for admission are accepted. The college welcomes a geographically diverse student body, and financial aid is available. 78% of the previous freshman class return to this campus for the sophomore year. 90% of all applicants accepted. 90% receive financial aid.

Community Environment: The name Waukesha comes from an Indian word meaning "by the Little Fox." today Waukesha is a city of 56,000 residents, located in one of Wisconsin's most prosperous counties. The college campus is just south of downtown. The cultural, athletic and recreational opportunities of metropolitan Milwaukee are 15 minutes from the Carroll campus.

CARTHAGE COLLEGE (P-13)
2001 Alford Drive
Kenosha, Wisconsin 53141
Tel: (414) 551-8500; (800) 351-4058; Admissions: (414) 551-6000; Fax: (414) 551-5762

Description: The privately supported liberal arts college is affiliated with the Evangelical Lutheran Church of America. The college is accredited by the North Central Association of Colleges and Schools and professionally by respective professional accrediting institutions. It offers preparation for the state teaching certificate. A 3-2 degree program in Engineering is available. Three years of liberal arts study followed by two years at Washington University, Case Western Reserve or University of Wisconsin-Madison, results in two Bachelors degrees. A similar program in Occupational Therapy with Washington University is available. An overseas program provides study abroad. Extensive vocal and instrumental music programs and intercollegiate and intramural athletics are available. Religion studies are required and chapel attendance is encouraged. The school operates on the 4-1-4 calendar and offers two summer sessions. It enrolls 666 men, 799 women full-time, and 170 men and 420 women part-time. A faculty of 88 full-time and 35 part-time gives a faculty-student ratio of 1-17.

Entrance Requirements: High school graduation or equivalent with rank in upper 50% of graduating class; completion of a minimum 16 units including 4 English, 2 mathematics, 2 science, 2 social science, 6 academic electives; C average accepted; SAT or ACT required; average standing of freshmen in top 30% of high school class; special admission plans include early admission, deferred admission, rolling admission, delayed admission and advanced placement; $25 application fee.

Costs Per Year: $13,125 tuition; $3,775 room and board.

Collegiate Environment: The college is located on a 72-acre campus that was a former city park overlooking Lake Michigan. The 12 college buildings contain a library of 207,159 volumes, 1,159 periodicals, and 15,151 microforms, and dormitory facilities for 505 men and 612 women. Students from other geographical locations are accepted as well as midyear students. Approximately 91% of students applying for admission are accepted. 94% of students receive some form of financial aid. Scholarships ranging from $500-$16,900 are available. About 69% of the previous freshman class return to this campus for the sophomore year. Nearly 72% of the recent student body graduated in the top half of the high school class, 46% in the top quarter. The college granted 258 Bachelor degrees recently.

Community Environment: See Gateway Technical College.

CHIPPEWA VALLEY TECHNICAL COLLEGE   *(H-3)*
620 West Clairemont Avenue
Eau Claire, Wisconsin 54701
Tel: (715) 833-6200

Description: This publicly supported vocational, technical and adult school, designated as the Area School for District One, initiated training programs in 1912. The college provides vocational and technical education for gainful employment. It awards vocational diplomas and Associate degrees. The college operates on the semester system with a summer term. Enrollment includes 3,800 full-time, 1,700 part-time, and 800 evening students. A faculty of 365 provides a faculty-student ratio of 1-19. A branch center is located in Chippewa Falls, Wisconsin, and Menomonie, Wisconsin. It offers intercollegiate and intramural athletics, and special programs for the educationally disadvantaged. A cooperative education program is available in health majors. The college is accredited by the North Central Association of Colleges and Schools and approved by the State Board of Vocational, Technical and Adult Education.

Entrance Requirements: High school graduation or equivalent; open enrollment; recommended completion of 4 years of high school work; aptitude tests required for some programs; early admission, early decision, rolling admission, and advanced placement plans available; $30 application fee.

Costs Per Year: $41 per credit resident; $278.80 per credit nonresident; $250 book and material fees.

Collegiate Environment: The institute is comprised of several buildings and is located on 50 acres. Its library contains over 46,000 volumes, 1,000 periodicals, 600 microforms, 2,500 audiovisual materials. Financial aid is available.

Community Environment: See University of Wisconsin - Eau Claire.

CONCORDIA UNIVERSITY WISCONSIN   *(N-13)*
12800 N. Lake Shore Drive
Mequon, Wisconsin 53092
Tel: (414) 243-5700; Fax: (414) 243-4351

Description: The privately-supported university was founded in Milwaukee in 1881 as one of 12 institutions in a system of schools owned and maintained by the Lutheran Church-Missouri Synod. The college offers college training prerequisite to the study of theology and church vocations as well as a basic liberal arts program. It is accredited by the North Central Association of Schools. The college operates on the 4-1-4 semester system and offers 2 summer terms. Enrollment is 2,136 full-time and 821 part-time students. A faculty of 97 full-time and 110 part-time provides a faculty-student ratio of 1-17.

Entrance Requirements: Accredited high school graduation or equivalent with completion of 16 academic units including 4 English, 2 mathematics, 2 science, and 2 social science; SAT, or ACT with minimum score of 18 required; 2.25 GPA accepted; rolling admission; $25 application fee.

Costs Per Year: $10,300 tuition; $3,600 room and board.

Collegiate Environment: The 155-acre campus is located on the north side of the city along Lake Michigan, easily reached from downtown Milwaukee. The college library contains 100,000 volumes, 740 periodicals, 19,000 microforms and 2,400 audiovisual materials. Dormitory facilities are provided for 620 single students. The college welcomes a geographically diverse student body and will accept midyear students. 80% of applicants are accepted. 75% of the previous entering class returns to the campus for the second year of studies. About 80% of the recent student body graduated in the top half of the

high school class, and 60% ranked in the top quarter. Financial aid is available. 88% of students receive financial aid.

Community Environment: See Milwaukee Area Technical College.

EDGEWOOD COLLEGE   *(N-9)*
855 Woodrow Street
Madison, Wisconsin 53711
Tel: (608) 257-4861; (800) 444-4861; Fax: (608) 257-1455

Description: The privately supported Roman Catholic liberal arts college at Edgewood, founded in 1927, was developed by the Dominican Sisters of Sinsinawa, Wisconsin. It is accredited by the North Central Association of Colleges and Schools. The college collaborates academically with the University of Wisconsin and with Madison General Hospital. It operates on the 4-1-4 semester system and offers a summer term. Enrollment is 896 full-time and 572 part-time undergraduates, and 425 graduate students. A faculty of 60 full-time and 74 part-time gives a faculty-student ratio of 1-17. Chorus and intramural athletics are offered. Some remedial courses are available. The college also offers preparation for State teaching certificate.

Entrance Requirements: High school graduation or equivalent; completion of 16 units including 12 from a combination of English, mathematics, foreign language, science, social science and speech; ACT required; C average required; early admission, rolling admission, and advanced placement available; $25 application fee.

Costs Per Year: $9,000 tuition; $3,800 room and board; $1,700 average additional expenses.

Collegiate Environment: Edgewood seeks a diverse student body, and accpets students at midyear. The library contains 70,464 volumes, and 85,082 microforms. There is student housing for 300 students. Financial aid is available and 80% of the students receive some form of assistance. 75% of all applicants are accepted.

Community Environment: See University of Wisconsin - Madison.

FOX VALLEY TECHNICAL COLLEGE   *(J-11)*
1825 North Bluemound Drive
Appleton, Wisconsin 54913
Tel: (414) 735-5727

Description: The publicly-supported Fox Valley Technical College, main campus in Appleton, WI with branches in Neenah, and Oshkosh are part of the same educational system which serves the five county Fox Valley Technical District. The college is accredited by the North Central Association of Colleges and Schools. The college operates on the semester system and offers one summer session. Enrollment includes approximately 2,500 men and women full-time. A faculty of 200 full-time, 28 part-time gives a faculty-student ratio of 1-24 for the day session. There is a faculty of 60 for the evening session. Offers two-year and one-year programs preparing the student to begin a career. Grants Vocational Diploma, Associate Degree.

Entrance Requirements: Open to anyone who can benefit; high school graduation required for Associate degree programs; recommend high school graduation, require aptitude examinations for diploma programs. All applicants accepted; early decision, delayed admission, advanced placement and rolling admission plans; $25 application fee.

Costs Per Year: $1,500 tuition for residents of district; $11,500 tuition for out-of-state residents.

Collegiate Environment: The Appleton branch is housed in 8 multi-purpose buildings and is located on a 140-acre campus. Its library contains over 28,000 volumes, 700 periodicals, 700 microforms and 4000 audiovisual materials. A commuter school, no student housing is available. About 35% of the previous entering class return to this campus for the second year of studies.

Community Environment: See Lawrence University.

GATEWAY TECHNICAL COLLEGE   *(P-13)*
3520 30th Avenue
Kenosha, Wisconsin 53144-1690
Tel: (414) 656-6900; (800) 353-3151; Admissions: (414) 656-6911; Fax: (414) 656-6909

Description: State legislation established publicly-supported vocational, technical, and adult education in 1911, and Kenosha Technical Institute began in 1912. Under its new name the junior college's original goals are still being met. It is accredited by the North Central Association of Colleges and Schools. Students are being trained for employment with programs offered on a part-time, full-time, day and evening basis. It also offers pre-college programs for the educationally disadvantaged. The college operates on the semester system and offers one summer session. Enrollment includes 1,800 full-time and 7,600 part-time students. A faculty of 280 full-time and 6 part-time gives a faculty-student ratio of 1:19.

Entrance Requirements: Open enrollment policy; high school graduation or equivalent desired for degree programs; ACT; early decision, midyear admission, and rolling admission plans available.

Costs Per Year: $1,546 state resident tuition; $11,410 nonresident tuition; $50 student fees.

Collegiate Environment: There are 13 buildings on 3 campuses including the aviation center. The Library-Learning Resource Center contains 39,642 volumes with 25 individual study carrels. No dormitories are available, but the office of housing services lists available housing for student use. A student lounge and cafeteria are located in the Science Building. Intercollegiate and intramural athletics are available. 100% of applicants are accepted. Special financial aid is available for economically disadvantaged students, and 50% of students receive some form of financial assistance. Approximately 30% of freshmen return to this campus for their sophomore year.

Community Environment: Located on the shore of Lake Michigan, Kenosha (population 79,000) has an excellent harbor with 83% of its shoreline providing recreation. It is surrounded by a prosperous agricultural area and is one of the chief industrial centers of the state. Both Chicago and Milwaukee are an hour away. Points of interest are the Hall of Fame, Art Museum, County Historical Society, and Petrifying Springs Park.

IMMANUEL LUTHERAN COLLEGE   *(H-3)*
501 Grover Road
Eau Claire, Wisconsin 54701-7199
Tel: (715) 836-6621

Description: This privately supported seminary and college was founded in 1959 when the need arose for a church-affiliated school. The college enrolls approximately 42 men and women each year. A faculty of 12 provides a faculty-student ratio of 1-4. The semester system is used. The college aims to prepare future leaders for the church. The general course provides a basic foundation of junior college subjects; the education course provides 4 years of preparation for the teaching ministry in the Church of the Lutheran Confession; the pretheological course provides 4 years of liberal arts, languages, and other disciplines prerequisite for entrance into the seminary department. Music and athletic programs are available.

Entrance Requirements: High school graduation; ACT or SAT required; C average accepted; rolling admission plan; application fee $25.

Costs Per Year: $3,470 tuition; $2,050 room and board, $310 student fees; additional expenses average $100.

Collegiate Environment: The college's present campus opened in September of 1963. It is about 3 miles south of the business district of Eau Claire. There are 75 acres, of which the building area is beautifully landscaped. Ingram Hall contains the 7,500-volume library, the 5,000-volume seminary library, and the dining room. North West Hall contains the administration office and a bookstore. Dormitories accommodate 60 women and 60 men. Freshman classes begin in August and midyear students are accepted.

Community Environment: See University of Wisconsin - Eau Claire.

LAKELAND COLLEGE   *(L-13)*
Box 359
Sheboygan, Wisconsin 53082-0359
Tel: (414) 565-2111; (800) 242-3347; Admissions: (414) 565-1217; Fax: (414) 565-1206

Description: This privately supported liberal arts college was founded in 1862 and is affiliated with the United Church of Christ. It is accredited by the North Central Association of Colleges and Schools. The 4-1-4 semester system is employed and 1 off-campus summer term is offered. Enrollment includes 892 full-time and 2,186 part-time undergraduates and 108 graduate students. A faculty of 54 full-time and 142 part-time gives a faculty-student ratio of 1:15. Offers band, choir, intercollegiate and intramural athletics; preparation for state teaching certificate. Offers Internship program (alternating work and class periods) in Business, Accounting, and several subject areas during the regular semester and the January term. Overseas program includes Junior Semester Abroad with a German university.

Entrance Requirements: Accredited high school graduation or equivalent with rank in upper 50% of graduating class or ACT of 19; G.P.A. of 2.0 minimum; ACT or SAT required. Rolling admission plan available; $20 application fee.

Costs Per Year: $9,825 tuition; $4,005 room and board. Additional expenses average $1,000.

Collegiate Environment: The college is situated on a 240-acre campus close to state forests and campgrounds and within 18 miles of Lake Michigan's beaches. The 16 major campus buildings are surrounded by woods and farmlands. Approximately 65% of the applicants are accepted. Students attend from all parts of the United States and several foreign countries. The largest number of students are from Wisconsin, Illinois, and Indiana. The cultural mix in the student body provides for social development and valuable educational opportunities. The library houses 68,000 books, subscribes to approximately 290 periodicals and has 21,935 microforms. Most students live on campus in one of 6 residence halls which can accommodate 240 men and 240 women. All students are encouraged to participaate in extracurricular activities including theater, choir, student government, social fraternities, sororities, and clubs. The college offers an extensive program of varsity sports for men and women. The college stresses intramural sports in addition to intercollegiate athletics. Financial aid is available, and 92% of the students receive some form of assistance. Career counseling resources are available from the career planning and placement office.

Community Environment: The college is located 12 miles northwest of Sheboygan, Wisconsin, 60 miles north of Milwaukee and 60 miles south of Green Bay. Sheboygan has a population of 50,000 and offers students off-campus opportunities for work and recreation. Sheboygan's county airport, the bus depot, and Interstate 43 offer easy access to Lakeland.

LAKESHORE TECHNICAL COLLEGE   *(L-13)*
1290 North Avenue
Cleveland, Wisconsin 53015
Tel: (414) 458-4183

Description: Enrollment at this branch of the publicly supported, two-year technical institute was 1,086 full-time, 1,664 part-time. A faculty of 142 full-time, and 560 part-time gives a faculty-student ratio of 1-13. Maintains adult learning centers, apprenticeship courses, programs for the educationally disadvantaged. It is accredited by the North Central Association of Colleges and Schools and by various professional organizations and associations. The semester system is used and 1 summer term is offered. District 11, which comprises Manitowoc and Sheboygan Counties, is organized to provide training at this campus and at Lakeshore Technical Schools at Manitowoc and at Sheboygan. The types of educational programs found in the divisions are: Associate degree programs, one- and two-year vocational diploma programs, continuing general education, apprenticeship training, adult basic education, and seminars an clinics. Cooperative education programs are available in business and marketing.

Entrance Requirements: Open enrollment policy. High school graduation or equivalent and 16 units required for degree programs. Rolling admission, advanced placement, early admission and early decision plans available. Application fee $30.

Costs Per Year: $1,392 tuition; $3,084 out-of-state residents; $4,000 room and board.

Collegiate Environment: The 20,000 volume library collection is housed in the Education Resource Center. There are 350 periodicals, 284 microforms, and 4,000 audiovisual materials. There are no dormitories, but the Student Services Office lists housing accommodations available to students who wish to live away from home. All qualified applicants are accepted. About 60% of the students in the degree programs return to this school for the second year. 70% of the students receive some financial aid.

Community Environment: See Lakeland College.

LAWRENCE UNIVERSITY (J-11)
Box 599
Appleton, Wisconsin 54912-0599
Tel: (414) 832-6500; (800) 227-0982; Fax: (414) 832-6782

Description: From its beginning in 1847, Lawrence University has been a private, coeducational college offering a broad-based education in the liberal arts and sciences and, since 1874, has been enriched and enlivened by a companion Conservatory of Music. The institution is accredited by the North Central Association of Colleges and Schools and professionally by both the American Chemical Society and the National Association of Schools of Music. Lawrence's academic year consists of 3 ten-week terms; during the year, 1,200 students are enrolled with a faculty of 125 full-time and 10 part-time, giving a faculty-student ratio of 1-11. Students enjoy extensive opportunities for independent research through honors programs, student-designed courses and majors, tutorials, and writing-for-credit. Interdisciplinary programs are available in Biomedical Ethics, Environmental Studies, Gender Studies, International Studies, Linguistics, Neuroscience, and Cognitive Science. Dual-degree programs include allied health sciences, engineering, forestry and environmental studies, and social services administration. Off-campus study options are available in Chicago, Washington, China, London, the Caribbean, Mexico or Spain, France, Italy, Germany, Japan, India, Costa Rica, the Czech Republic, Russia, Senegal, and Zimbabwe. Special on-campus services include the Career Center, the Writing Lab, the Learning Resources Center, the Health and Counseling Center, and the campus store.

Entrance Requirements: Recommended graduation from accredited secondary school with 16 academic units including 4 English, 2 foreign language, 3 math, 2 science, and 3 social studies; minimum of B average; SAT or ACT required; early admission, delayed admission, early decision and advanced placement plans available; application fee $30.

Costs Per Year: $17,163 for tuition; $4,000 room and board; $1,500 books and personal expenses.

Collegiate Environment: The main portion of Lawrence's 84-acre campus is located on the north bank of the Fox River, near Appleton's downtown shopping district. Among the 32 instructional, recreational, and administrative buildings are the Seeley G. Mudd Library, boasting over 320,000 volumes, 1,200 periodicals, approximately 247,000 government documents, and a variety of special collections; and the Alexander Gymnasium, the Recreation Center, and a new Art Center. Over 95% of the students live on campus in 7 coeducational residence halls with facilities for 437 men and 542 women and 6 fraternity houses, and 5 theme houses. Activities abound, with 23 varsity sports, 25 club and intramural sports, 75 clubs and organizations, and ample opportunities in music and theater for nonmajors. 65% of applicants are accepted. 65% of the students receive financial assistance.

Community Environment: Appleton is a thriving and dynamic small city (pop. 65,000), located in the paper-making center of the country and rated among the best communities in the United States for quality of life. The city is accessible by car, bus, and plane.

MADISON AREA TECHNICAL COLLEGE (N-9)
3550 Anderson Street
Madison, Wisconsin 53704
Tel: (608) 246-6100; (800) 322-6282; Admissions: (608) 246-6205; Fax: (608) 246-6880

Description: This publicly-supported technical, vocational, and liberal arts junior college is accredited by the North Central Association of Colleges and Schools, and professionally by the American Dental Association and the National League for Nursing. The Wisconsin Technical College System, has accredited the technical associate degree programs of the college. The Coordinating Committee for Higher Education and the Wisconsin Technical College System have approved the liberal arts curricula, and the college is authorized to offer collegiate transfer courses. The college operates on the semester system and offers one summer session. Enrollment includes 24,019 full-time and part-time students. Current enrollment is 24,019 men and

29,238 women full and part-time. A faculty of 395 full-time and 1,200 part-time gives a faculty-student ratio of 1:25. It offers pre-college programs for the educationally disadvantaged including adult basic education, and vocational-development programs. Cooperative education programs are available in agribusiness, business, data processing, and animal technology.

Entrance Requirements: Requirements vary with program choice; additional tests may be required. Rolling admission and advanced placement plans.

Costs Per Year: $2,178 ($48.40/cr) district resident; $16,049.25 ($356.65/cr) out-of-state; fees vary according to selected program.

Collegiate Environment: 3 buildings presently house the college on the 150 acres of campus located in the Madison area. The Apprentice Center on the east side of the city houses the Apprentice Facilities. The library, located on the second floor of the main building, presently contains 47,000 volumes, 6,800 pamphlets, 450 periodical titles, 1,930 microforms, and 3,000 audiovisual materials. No housing is provided for students, but a list of apartments is on file in the Office of Student Services. The college takes no other responsibility regarding housing arrangements. 98% of students applying for admission meet the requirements and are accepted. Special programs are available on campus for culturally disadvantaged students enabling them to attend.

Community Environment: Home of the state capital and the University of Wisconsin, Madison is a lovely city situated between two lakes. Four campuses are in smaller cities with growing industrial bases.

MARIAN COLLEGE OF FOND DU LAC (L-11)
45 South National Avenue
Fond du Lac, Wisconsin 54935
Tel: (414) 923-7600; (800) 262-7426; Fax: (414) 923-7154

Description: Marian College, founded in 1936, is a privately supported Catholic liberal arts college. The college is fully accredited by the North Central Association of Colleges and Schools and professionally by the National Council for Accreditation of Teacher Education, National League for Nursing, Council on Social Work Education, and other professional organizations. Marian College offers programs of study leading to baccalaureate degrees with majors in accounting, administration of justice, art, art education, biology, business administration, chemistry, communication, cytotechnology, early childhood education, elementary education, english, history, human relations, leisure management, psychology, social work, sports, mathematics, radiological technology, nursing, and a graduate program leading to a Master of Science in Qulaity Values and Leadership or a Master of Arts in Education. Individually designed majors and preprofessional programs are also offered. The college operates on the semester system and offers 2 summer terms. A business cooperative education program is required of all business students. Marian College offers completion programs for all adults in business, quality control, nursing, and radiologic technology on the Fond du Lac campus and at off-campus sites in Milwaukee, Appleton, Green Bay, Racine, Wausau, and Wisconsin. Total enrollment is 2,510, with 564 graduate students. A faculty of 72 full-time and 48 part-time gives a faculty-student ratio of 1-15.

Entrance Requirements: Applicants must present evidence of ability and potential for college work; Admissions Committee considers high school record; completion of 16 units including 3 English, 2 mathematics, 1 social science, and 1 laboratory science; ACT with minimum score of 18 or SAT with minimum scores of 420V, 420M required; early decision, early admission, delayed admission, advanced placement, and rolling admission plans available; $15 application fee.

Costs Per Year: $9,400 tuition; $3,700 room and board; $150 general fee.

Collegiate Environment: Situated 54 miles northwest of Milwaukee, the Marian College campus has 11 modern buildings. There are residence halls that accommodate 430 men and women. The college library contains 95,000 books, 2850 microfilm items, and 500 periodicals. The chapel, commons, and classroom buildings complete the complex. The school year begins in August, but students are also accepted to begin in the January semester. 82% of those who apply for admission are accepted. A variety of scholarships, ranging from $1,000-$4,500 are available. Nearly 85% of the students receive some form of financial assistance. The total placement success within 6 months after graduation is nearly 98.5%.

Community Environment: Marian College of Fond du Lac, Wisconsin (population 36,000) is located on the edge of the scenic Kettle Moraine region, the dominant glacial formation of Wisconsin. It is less than a mile from beautiful Lake Winnebago. The campus is easily reached by U.S. Highways 41, 45, and 151. There is efficient bus service from other cities and airports. Fond du Lac offers its own cultural attractions: a modern public library, churches, local community theaters, and the Civic Music Center. Students who wish to expand their cultural horizons may easily travel to the nearby cities of Green Bay, Madison or Milwaukee.

MARQUETTE UNIVERSITY (N-13)
P.O. Box 1881
Milwaukee, Wisconsin 53233-9988
Tel: (414) 288-7302; (800) 222-6544; Admissions: (414) 288-7302; Fax: (414) 288-3764

Description: The privately supported university is conducted by the members of the Roman Catholic Society of Jesus. Founded in 1881, the institution was named for Pere Jacques Marquette, a renowned French Jesuit who explored Lakes Superior and Michigan, the Mississippi River, and the Fox River Valley of Wisconsin in the Seventeenth Century. One of the largest Catholic universities in the nation, the institution operates on the semester system and offers 2 summer terms. The university is accredited by the North Central Association of Colleges and Schools and by professional organizations. The College of Arts and Sciences with its related graduate studies forms the core of the university and has the primary responsibility for the liberal arts and science education of the students. The university has a College of Business Administration; College of Communication; College of Engineering; College of Nursing; and programs in Medical Laboratory Technology, Physical Therapy, and Dental Hygiene. There are also a School of Education, School of Dentristy, Graduate School, and Law School. Army, Air Force, Navy and Marine ROTC programs are offered on campus. Undergraduate enrollment includes 3,294 men and 3,560 women full-time, and 427 men and 410 women part-time. There are 3,059 graduate students. A faculty of 569 full-time and 479 part-time gives an undergraduate faculty-student ratio of 1-15. Offers band, chorus, orchestra, and extensive intercollegiate and intramural athletic programs. It offers cooperative education programs (alternating work and class periods) in engineering. A variety of overseas study programs are available. An honors program is available. A Freshman Frontier Program for marginally admissable students and an Educational Opportunity Program for educationally disadvantaged students is also offered. Some course work in theology is required for most students.

Entrance Requirements: High school graduation or equivalent; recommend completion of 16 units including 4 English, 3 mathematics (4 units for engineering course), 2 science (specific science course requirements for health fields), 2 foreign language, 2 social science, and 3 academic electives; SAT or ACT required; TOEFL required for some; GRE required for graduate school; rolling admission (with exception of Physical Therapy, which has a December 15th application deadline), advanced placement, and CLEP available; $30 undergraduate application fee.

Costs Per Year: $11,610-$12,260 tuition, $4,930 room and board.

Collegiate Environment: Encompassing 80 acres, the university has 42 major buildings. The library system houses 1,006,238 volumes, 8,694 periodicals, and 362,178 microforms. Residence hall facilities provide housing for 3,381 men and women. 90% of those applying for admission are accepted, and students may enroll at midyear as well as in the fall. 70% of all undergraduates and 75% of all freshmen receive scholarships and grants ranging from $500-$11,610. Athletic scholarships are available. 80% of undergraduates, 96% of freshmen receive some form of aid.

Community Environment: Marquette University is located near the business and cultural center of the city of Milwaukee, which has a metropolitan-area population in excess of one million. As a result, the city's many cultural and social opportunities are easily accessible to Marquette students and faculty. Much of Milwaukee's extensive frontage on Lake Michigan is public land, offering numerous recreational assets. An active port provides a direct link to many parts of the world. A superb county park system offers public facilities for golf,

swimming and tennis, as well as musical, horticultural, and zoological activities. Ethnic groups in Milwaukee add flavor and variety, and excellent restaurants, museums, and the Performing Arts Center provide social and cultural opportunities. Marquette also prides itself on being an active participant in its urban environment. Campus Circle, a neighborhood revitalization project initiated by Marquette and other major institutions in Milwaukee in 1991, is bringing Marquette to the forefront of urban higher education by forging links with neighborhood residents, community organizations, businesses and the City of Milwaukee. The city's major expressway interchange frames the south and east borders of the University allows the campus to be reached conveniently by car and bus from all parts of the metropolitan area. Major airlines and Amtrak also serve the city.

MEDICAL COLLEGE OF WISCONSIN (N-13)
8701 Watertown Plank Road
Milwaukee, Wisconsin 53226
Tel: (414) 456-8296; Admissions: (414) 456-8246

Description: The privately supported medical college was formerly known as Marquette University School of Medicine. The school is accredited by the North Central Association of Colleges and Schools and the Liaison Committee on Medical Education of the Association of American Medical Colleges/American Medical Association. It had its origin in 1913 when a spirited group of physicians urged that two existing proprietary schools be merged and joined with Marquette University. Today, the medical school is closely affiliated with five major teaching hospitals: Clement J. Zablocki Veterans Administration Hospital, Children's Hospital of Wisconsin, Milwaukee Psychiatric Hospital, Curative Rehabilitation Center and Froedtert Memorial Lutheran Hospital. The affiliation with the Veterans Administration Hospital dates from 1946 and is one of the oldest in the country. In addition to the MD degree, the college grants MS, MA and PhD degrees. Enrollment includes 807 professional students and 137 graduate students. There are 350 faculty members.

Entrance Requirements: Minimum college prerequisite requirements for admission (expressed in years completed): biology 1, chemistry 2, physics 1, English 1, math 1. Medical College Admission Test (MCAT) required. Early decision and delayed admission plans available. Nov. 1 application deadline; $50 application fee.

Costs Per Year: $12,904 tuition resident; $22,995 nonresident.

Collegiate Environment: Students interested and qualified to obtain a Doctor of Medicine and a Doctor of Philosophy degree in a basic science may be admitted to a combined degree program. Housing is not provided on campus for the students. Medical College library contains 180,890 volumes, 89,668 periodicals, 3,210 microforms, and 494 audiovisual aids. 5.4% of applicants are accepted. 80% of students receive some form of financial aid.

Community Environment: See Marquette University.

MID-STATE TECHNICAL COLLEGE (J-8)
500 32nd Street N.
Wisconsin Rapids, Wisconsin 54494
Tel: (715) 423-5650; Admissions: (715) 422-5444; Fax: (715) 422-5440

Description: Publicly supported, two-year technological college offering vocational and technical training for youth and adults wishing to prepare for job entry, upgrade existing skills, or retrain for a different career. The college is fully accredited by the North Central Association of Colleges and Schools. It grants the Associate degree. It operates on the semester system and offers one summer session. Enrollment includes 1,196 men, 1,703 women full-time, and 1,675 men and 2,013 women part-time. A faculty of 95 full-time, 180 part-time provides a teacher-student ratio of 1-14.

Entrance Requirements: Open enrollment policy; high school graduation required for most programs; entrance exam required; rolling admission and advanced placement plans available; $10 application fee.

Costs Per Year: $1,475 resident tuition; $11,340 nonresident; $75 student fees.

Collegiate Environment: Financial assistance available. Almost all students applying for admission are accepted. Library contains 19,500 volumes, 410 periodicals, 72 microform titles, and 1,502 audiovisual materials. A total of 30 scholarships are available and 70% of students receive some form of financial aid.

Community Environment: The college serves the area which includes Mansfield (population 18,200), Stevens Point (population 23,996), and Wisconsin Rapids (population 18,587), the county seat of Wood, near the geographical center of the state of Wisconsin.

MILWAUKEE AREA TECHNICAL COLLEGE   *(N-13)*
700 West State Street
Milwaukee, Wisconsin 53233
Tel: (414) 278-6600

Description: The publicly supported college offers one- and two-year programs designed to increase the productivity of the people in the community through the delivery of high quality instruction and programs. It provides occupational programs and liberal arts courses for entry into the job market or to pursue further education, training and upgrading for advancement or technical competence in a new skill, development education for effective employment, opportunities for personal, civic, and multicultural enrichment, and programs to assist in the economic development of business and industry in the community. Associate Degrees, Diplomas and Certificates are offered through the divisions of Business and Graphic Arts, Consumer and Hospitality Services, General Education, Health, Technical and Industrial, and Telecasting, which are accredited by the North Central Association of Colleges and Schools. The college operates on the semester system with 1 summer term. Recent enrollment includes 72,755 day and evening students. A faculty of 600 full-time and 1,300 part-time gives a faculty-student ratio of 1-38. The college is committed to providing equality of educational opportunities.

Entrance Requirements: High school graduation or equivalent degree programs; ASSET required, ACT or SAT accepted; Open enrollment rolling admission, early admission, advanced placement plans and midyear admission. 3 units of high school English and 2 of social science recommended for all programs; for some technical programs 1 algebra and 1 plane geometry required; 1-2 science recommended.

Costs Per Year: $1,309 resident tuition for associate program; $8,765 nonresident tuition for associate program; $1,674 resident tuition for transfer program; $3,990 nonresident tuition for transfer program; various fees.

Collegiate Environment: The college, centrally located, can easily be reached by all public transportation lines. The library, which serves all college divisions, contains over 35,000 volumes, 360 periodicals, 500 microforms and 500 audiovisual materials. Special financial aid is available for economically handicapped students. Approximately 100% of the applicants are accepted.

Community Environment: Located on the west shore of Lake Michigan, Milwaukee (population 640,000) is the largest city in Wisconsin with all major forms of commercial transportation available. Milwaukee is the nation's brewing center, also a major grain market and manufacturing center. Products of industry are metal, machinery, food, leather, chemicals, textiles, electrical machinery, and other items. The city is headquarters of the Lake States National Forest Region. The county has a park system and many of the units contain public golf courses, tennis courts, and other recreational facilities. Milwaukee's State Fair is held each year in August.

Branch Campuses: Oak Creek, WI; Mequon, WI, and West Allis, WI.

MILWAUKEE SCHOOL OF ENGINEERING   *(N-13)*
P.O. Box 644
Milwaukee, Wisconsin 53201-0644
Tel: (414) 277-7200; (800) 332-6763; Fax: (414) 277-7475

Description: MSOE is a private engineering college founded in 1903 and currently owned by a nonprofit, nonstock corporation composed of leaders of business and industry. The college is accredited by the North Central Association of Colleges and Schools and the Accreditation Board for Engineering and Technology. The close association with industry that the college has enjoyed over its 86-year history has resulted in modern industrial quality laboratories and excellent placement of its graduates. In addition to the corporation, MSOE maintains industrial advisory committees for each of its degree programs and requires faculty to have industrial experience. MSOE also operates an Applied Technology Center to work on industrially spon-

sored research projects, thus serving industry and providing real-world experience for students while assisting the faculty in the maintenance of their professional competency. The Fluid Power Institute and Biomedical Research Institute perform similar functions for their industries. It operates on the quarter system and offers one summer session. Enrollment includes 1,703 full-time and 909 part-time undergraduate, and 415 graduate students. A faculty of 103 full-time and 100 part-time gives a faculty-student ratio of 1-18. Air Force ROTC is offered on campus, and there are agreements at nearby campuses for Navy and Army programs.

Entrance Requirements: High school graduation or equivalent with rank in top half of high school class; completion of 15 units including 2 algebra, 1 geometry, 1/2 trigonometry, 1 physics, 1 chemistry, and 4 English; ACT required, SAT may be substituted; applicants who meet the standard qualifications for admission and who desire to enter the regular freshman curriculum will be given proficiency tests to determine their exact academic standing in English, mathematics, and physical science; rolling admission and advanced placement plans available; $20 application fee.

Costs Per Year: $12,375 tuition; $3,465 room and board.

Collegiate Environment: The school is located in downtown Milwaukee. The Walter Schroeder Library, containing 45,000 volumes, also houses modern classrooms and offices. The campus is also equipped with more than 39 modern engineering laboratories that utilize the latest full-size industrial equipment, 4 computer labs, the Student Life and Campus Center, and a bookstore. Housing is available for 691 men and 85 women. 85% of applicants are accepted. The average score of freshmen was ACT 25 composite. Financial aid is available and 85% of students receive some form of assistance.

Community Environment: See Milwaukee Area Technical College.

MORAINE PARK TECHNICAL COLLEGE   *(L-11)*
235 N. National Avenue
Fond du Lac, Wisconsin 54935
Tel: (414) 922-8611; Fax: (414) 929-3421

Description: Publicly supported 2 year technical college was established in 1967 and is accredited as a public educational institution by Wisconsin Technical College System State Board. Fond du Lac has been desigated the main campus with campuses at Beaver Dam, West Bend, and other centers to serve the district. The college is accredited by the North Central Association of Colleges and Schools. Programs of study lead to the Associate degree in vocational subjects. The college operates on the semester system and offers one summer session. Enrollment includes 1,194 full-time and 4,906 part-time students. A faculty of 138 gives a faculty-student ratio of 1-44.

Entrance Requirements: High school graduation or equivalent recommended but not required; minimum age of 16 years required for diploma programs; recommended high school units of 3 English, 1 math, 1 science, 3 social studies; open enrollment for most programs, early admission, early decision, rolling admission, delayed admission, midyear admission, rolling admission, and advanced placement plans available; $25 application fee.

Costs Per Year: $1,383 district-resident tuition; $10,631 out-of-state tuition; $160 student fees.

Collegiate Environment: The college is housed in 1 main building and is located on 80 acres. Each division within the college is provided with technical equipment consistent with good instruction. The instruction is competency based with an applied focus. A student success focus is a main component at the college. Its library contains 19,500 titles, 565 periodicals, 112 microforms, and 6,100 audiovisual materials. 95% of students applying for admission are accepted. 45% receive financial aid. Students from other geographical locations are accepted as well as midyear students.

Community Environment: See Marian College of Fond du Lac.

MOUNT MARY COLLEGE   *(N-13)*
2900 Menomonee River Parkway
Milwaukee, Wisconsin 53222
Tel: (414) 259-9220; (800) 321-6265; Fax: (414) 256-1205

Description: Mount Mary is Wisconsin's oldest liberal arts college for women, chartered by the state to grant Bachelor of Arts and Bachelor of Science degrees, as well as a Master of Science degrees in Dietetics, Education and Art Therapy. It is accredited by several professional organizations. The School is conducted by the Sisters of Notre Dame and operates on the semester system with one summer term. Students may select from more than 30 major areas of study or may combine areas of concentration to tailor a major that suits personal interests. Enrollment is 967 women full-time, 433 women part-time, and 124 graduate students. A faculty of 77 full-time and 90 part-time gives a full-time faculty-student ratio of 1-10.

Entrance Requirements: High school diploma or its equivalent; completion of 15 units, including 3 English, 2 mathematics, 2 laboratory science, 4 history, science, or foreign language, and 4 electives; SAT or ACT required; admission is based on record and ACT or SAT scores; applicants should rank in upper half of graduating class, but every prospective student is given consideration; $15 application fee.

Costs Per Year: $9,750 tuition; $3,322 room and board; $800 average additional expenses.

Collegiate Environment: Mount Mary is a friendly medium-sized college, dedicated exclusively to the educational needs of women. There are 8 buildings on the 80-acre campus, and housing is available for 230 women. The architecture is English Gothic in design and attractive and collegiate in tone. The main library contains 107,695 volumes, 798 periodicals, 8,900 microforms and 4,197 audiovisual materials. Approximately 86% of students applying for admission are accepted including midyear students. About 66% of the students graduated in the top half of their high school class, 37% were in the upper quarter, and 14% ranked in the highest tenth. Financial aid is available for economically disadvantaged students. 74% of those who apply receive some form of financial assistance. Classes start in September and January.

Community Environment: Mount Mary is one of 5 private colleges located right in Milwaukee. The campus is located on the northwest side of Milwaukee, about 15 minutes from the downtown area. It is within walking distance of a shopping mall and restaurants. The city of Milwaukee boasts a major symphony, well-respected dance companies, a beautiful lakefront art museum and a fine natural history museum. 3 professional sports divide the Milwaukee seasons. Milwaukee is also the ideal site in which to explore various career interests.

MOUNT SENARIO COLLEGE   *(F-5)*
College Avenue West
Ladysmith, Wisconsin 54848
Tel: (715) 532-5511; Admissions: (715) 532-5511; Fax: (715) 532-7690

Description: Mount Senario College is an independent, four-year, nonsectarian, liberal arts college for men and women and is approved for teacher education by the Wisconsin Department of Public Instruction. It is fully accredited by the North Central Association of Colleges and Schools. It operates on the early semester system and offers two summer terms. Grants 4 four-year degrees: BA, BS, plus a two-year AA degree. Enrollment is 445 full-time students. A faculty of 32 gives a faculty-student of 1-14. Offers preparation for State teaching certificate, vocal music groups, intercollegiate basketball, football, softball, baseball, and volleyball. Offers External Degree Program, Cooperative Education Program, and Independent Study Program (students may plan individual course which allows wider field of study); a Bachelor of Science program in Public Administration, Criminal Justice, and Business is offered at 26 outreach sites throughout Wisconsin. A strong American Indian Studies Program has made the college a leading midwest institution in the education of American Indians. It is also a leader in Laotian Hmoug Education. A semester abroad in Latin America or in Scandinavia is available.

Entrance Requirements: High school graduation or equivalent with C average; completion of 16 units including 3 English, 2 mathematics, and 1 science; ACT with minimum score of 15 or SAT required; rolling admission, early admission, early decision, advanced placement, and midyear admission plans available; $10 application fee.

Costs Per Year: $8,438 tuition; $3,250 room and board; $120 student fees.

Collegiate Environment: The campus occupies 130 acres adjacent to the Flambeau River. 3 modern buildings comprise the campus's physical plant. The library contains a collection of 42,886 volumes, 106 periodicals, and 1,430 microforms. On-campus housing for 80 men and 80 women is available in the Residence Hall, a modern dormitory building overlooking the Flambeau River. 75% of applicants

are accepted, including midyear students. 93% of the students receive financial aid.

Community Environment: Ladysmith (population 4,000) is the gateway to the resort and vacation country of northwest Wisconsin. It has a diversified economy of light industry, recreation, commerce, agriculture, and education. Facilities include churches, a hospital, shopping areas, and a number of civic and service organizations. Recreational activities are bowling, golf, baseball, archery, football, basketball, skating, boating, hunting, skiing (cross country and downhill), and backpacking. Part-time jobs are available. The Mardi-Gras and County Fair are annual events. The college is 60 miles north of Eau Claire, Wisconsin, and 120 miles east of Minneapolis/St. Paul, Minnesota.

NASHOTAH HOUSE   *(A-11)*
2777 Mission Road
Nashotah, Wisconsin 53058-9793
Tel: (414) 646-3371; Fax: (414) 646-2215

Description: The privately supported graduate theological seminary of the Episcopal Church is accredited by the Association of Theological Schools. The seminary operates on a modified trimester system. Enrollment is 30 men and 2 women. A faculty of 11 gives a faculty-student ratio of 1-4. The seminary offers the Master of Divinity, Master of Sacred Theology, Master of Theological Studies, and Licentiate in Theology degrees.

Entrance Requirements: Applicant must be a postulant or candidate for Holy Orders or be authorized to attend by a Bishop of the Episcopal Church; Bachelor of Arts degree or an equivalent from an accredited college or university is required. A limited number of applicants who are not graduates of an accredited college may be admitted on probation if, after presentation of their scholastic records and other credentials, they are judged capable of pursuing the work of the seminary profitably. GRE and Miller Analogies Test required.

Costs Per Year: $8,000 tuition; $4,825 room and board.

Collegiate Environment: The 400-acre campus with 23 buildings is located near Nashotah and Delafield. The library contains a collection of more than 80,000 volumes to which acquisitions are constantly being made. Dormitory facilities provide living accommodations for 36 men, 8 women, and apartments are provided for 29 families. Financial aid is available.

Community Environment: A rural setting with all outdoor sports such as hunting, riding, fishing, skiing, and boating. Hospitals and medical centers are nearby. There is semi-structured community life centered around daily corporate worship. Day care for preschool children is available.

NICOLET AREA TECHNICAL COLLEGE   *(E-9)*
Box 518
Rhinelander, Wisconsin 54501
Tel: (715) 365-4451; (800) 544-3039; Fax: (715) 365-4445

Description: The publicly supported community college holds full institutional membership in the American Association of Community and Junior Colleges and is fully accredited by the North Central Association of Colleges and Schools. One-year vocational programs and two-year technical programs in the areas of business and distributive education, trades and industry, health and service occupations, and two-year liberal arts transfer courses are offered. It operates on the semester system and offers one summer session. Enrollment is 240 men and 350 women full-time, 327 men and 802 women part-time. A faculty of 59 full-time and 23 part-time gives a faculty-student ratio of 1-20. Offers pre-college and freshman programs for the educationally disadvantaged.

Entrance Requirements: High school graduation or equivalent; open enrollment policy; persons without a high school diploma who can benefit from a post-secondary level instructional program will be admitted upon the recommendation of the admissions office after testing; advanced placement plans available; $25 application fee.

Costs Per Year: $1,780 average resident tuition, college transfer; $1,450 resident, associate degree program; $8,200 average out-of-state.

Collegiate Environment: The campus on Lake Julia is located 1 mile south of Rhinelander. 99% of applicants are accepted. Financial aid is available for economically disadvantaged students, and about 75% of students receive some form of financial assistance. There are 50 scholarships for new and continuing students. Classes begin in August. College facilities include a 35,000-volume library with 400 periodicals, 300 microforms, and 8,000 audiovisual materials.

Community Environment: The county seat for Oneida County, Rhinelander (population 8,218) is a summer and winter resort, located in the most concentrated lake area of the Middle West. Rhinelander has one of the largest paper mills under one roof in America. All commercial transportation is available. Parks and many lakes and trout streams and rivers provide facilities for all water sports and fishing. The Logging Museum is a reproduction of a logging camp with living quarters. Also on display is a narrow gauge engine built in 1879.

Branch Campuses: Lakeland Campus - Minocqua, tel: 1-(800) 585-9304.

NORTH CENTRAL TECHNICAL INSTITUTE *(H-8)*
1000 Campus Drive
Wausau, Wisconsin 54401
Tel: (715) 675-3331; Admissions: (715) 675-3331 X 4007; Fax: (715) 675-9776

Description: The publicly supported, 2-year technological institute provides vocational, technical, and general curriculums and services which are designed to prepare persons for employment in the labor market, and to upgrade the job capabilities of employed persons who are looking for job advancement or change. The institute is one of the first vocational-technical schools to become accredited by the Commission on Higher Education, North Central Association of Colleges and Schools. It is member of the American Association of Junior Colleges. Two year Associate degree programs are offered as well as one- and two-year vocational programs. Special programs are offered for hearing and visually impaired plus for educationally disadvantaged (both pre-college and freshman). The institute operates on the early semester system. Enrollment includes 708 full-time and 2,932 part-time students. A faculty of 143 full-time and 77 part-time gives a faculty-student ratio of 1-17.

Entrance Requirements: High school graduation, or equivalent; open enrollment; students are urged to take the ACT or SAT. Rolling admission, midyear admission, early decision and advanced placement plans available. $20 application fee.

Costs Per Year: $1,475.20 ($46.10/cr) resident; $11,339.20 ($334.35/cr) nonresident; $2,700 room and board; $50 fees.

Collegiate Environment: The main campus is located at the north edge of Wausau, with branch campuses at Antigo, Medford, Wittneberg and Spencer. The library contains 30,000 volumes. Approximately 50% of the student body graduated in their top half of their high school class, 20% in the upper quarter, and 5% in the highest tenth. 55% receive some form of financial assistance. About 54% of the previous freshman class return to the school for the second year. Classes begin in August, January, with a summer session in June. More than 60% of students participate in campus clubs and organizations, with over 900 students members in clubs organized around the occupational training programs in which they are enrolled. Average student age is 27, with students enrolling in 34 career programs, or in preparation for career programs. NCTI students participate in sports through the University of Wisconsin.

Community Environment: The Wausau area (population 70,000) is one of the major industrial centers in the state. Over 70 highly diversified industries are located here, producing over 40 different products. The area is one of the nation's leading producers of cheddar cheese, and it is a major center of dairy farming in both the state and nation and a leading exporter of ginseng. The community offers many cultural and recreational programs plus an excellent public school system. The school works closely with the branch campus of the University of Wisconsin to maximize use of facilities and programs and to eliminate duplication.

NORTHEAST WISCONSIN TECHNICAL COLLEGE *(I-12)*
2740 West Mason Street
P.O. Box 19042
Green Bay, Wisconsin 54307-9042
Tel: (414) 498-5600; (800) 422-6982; Fax: (414) 498-5655

Description: A publicly supported, 2-year technological college, it is fully accredited by the North Central Association of Colleges and Schools. Professional accreditations include the American Dental Association and the Council on Medical Education of the AMA. Branch centers exist at Marinette nad Sturgeon Bay. It offers vocational programs to anyone who can profit from the training. Special pre-college and freshman programs for the educationally disadvantaged, and intramural athletics are available. The college grants the 2-year Diploma and Associate degree. It operates on the semester system and offers one summer session. Enrollment includes 1,115 men and 1,134 women full-time, 2,832 men and 4,444 women part-time. A faculty of 206 full-time gives a faculty-student ratio of 1-45.

Entrance Requirements: High school graduation or equivalent; open enrollment; ACT required for certain programs; average ACT score of 20; early decision, early admission, rolling admission, midyear admission, and advanced placement plans available; $25 application fee.

Costs Per Year: $1,567 ($46.10 per credit) district resident tuition; $12,047.90 ($354.35 per credit) nonresident tuition; $3,850 estimated living expenses.

Collegiate Environment: The school is located near the heart of the business and industrial center of Green Bay. The library contains 23,000 volumes, 650 periodicals, 3,600 microforms, and 8,900 audiovisual materials. There is no student housing. Approximately 99% of those applying for admission are accepted, including midyear students. Classes begin in August and January. About 50% of the previous freshman class returned to the college for their second year.

Community Environment: Green Bay (population 92,000), the oldest permanent settlement in Wisconsin, is in an important harbor for the Great Lakes-St. Lawrence Seaway System. Industries in the area are: shipping, cheese producing, paper, and jobbers wholesale and distribution. Points of interest are the Bay Beach Park, Heritage Hill Park, Neville Public Museum, Cotton House, Fort Howard Hospital Museum, Lambeau Stadium, National Railroad Museum, Tank Cottage, and Green Bay Packer Hall of Fame.

Branch Campuses: Marinette, Wisconsin, and Sturgeon Bay, Wisconsin.

NORTHLAND COLLEGE *(B-5)*
1411 Ellis Avenue
Ashland, Wisconsin 54806
Tel: (715) 682-1224; Admissions: (715) 682-1224; Fax: (715) 682-1258

Description: The privately supported liberal arts environmental college, founded in 1892, is affiliated with the United Church of Christ and is accredited by the North Central Association of Colleges and Schools. It is also accredited by the Wisconsin State Department of Public Instruction for the education of teachers for the elementary and secondary schools in Wisconsin. Northland students must complete a core of liberal arts courses in addition to their chosen academic major requirements. A 4-4-1 calendar, with the short (4-week) term in the spring, permits the flexibility needed to take advantage of off-campus study and field experience. The longer terms make possible more maturation within courses. The short term provides for intensive work in one subject. One summer term is also offered. The college offers the Bachelor of Arts and Bachelor of Science Degrees. Enrollment includes 737 full-time and 76 part-time students. A faculty of 42 full-time and 15 part-time gives a faculty-student ratio of 1-15. Offers vocal and instrumental music groups, intercollegiate and intramural athletics and club sports. Cooperative Education program alternates work and class periods. Short spring term offers opportunities for study in Europe or at any of 9 cooperating colleges. Offers 15 integrated majors combining liberal arts courses with those of Environmental Studies, Native American Studies or Outdoor Education/Recreation. Also offers dual degree program in forestry and engineering.

Entrance Requirements: High school graduation or equivalent, upper 1/2 of high school class; SAT or ACT recommended. Although no minimum has been established for any 1 factor, the typical entrant has entrance examination scores above the median and college preparatory subjects. Average ACT score 23. Special admission plans: early admission, early decision, rolling admission, midyear admission, advanced placement. Special Opportunity Program for applicants with less-than-average credentials.

Costs Per Year: $10,500 tuition, $3,750 board and room; $230 fees.

Collegiate Environment: The college grounds are located on the southern edge of the city; there are 15 buildings on the 76 acres. There is a collection of 77,200 volumes in the library. Dormitory facilities provide living accommodations for 460 students. Approximately 85% of those students applying for admission are accepted, including midyear students. About 77% of the students graduate in the top half of their high school class, 48% in the top quarter, and 18% in the highest tenth. Special financial aid is available for economically disadvantaged students and 95% receive some form of financial assistance.

Community Environment: Ashland (population 9,615) is located on Lake Superior near the Chequamegon National Forest.

RIPON COLLEGE   *(K-10)*
300 Seward Street
P.O. Box 248
Ripon, Wisconsin 54971
Tel: (414) 748-8102; (800) 947-4766; Fax: (414) 748-7243

Description: This is a privately supported non-denominational liberal arts college, founded in 1851. The school is accredited by the North Central Association of Colleges and Schools, and American Chemical Society. The school limits its enrollment. Promising students are chosen without regard to race, creed, or religion and from diverse economic, cultural, and social backgrounds. The college operates on the semester system. Enrolment includes 800 full-time students. A faculty of 70 full-time and 26 part-time gives a faculty-student ratio of 1-10. Ripon College provides liberal and pre-professional training in a wide range of areas through a traditional multiple course-credit system; courses carry 1 to 5 credit hours each. The academic year begins late in August and the first semester is completed before Christmas, while the second semester runs from late January to mid-May. The curriculum of the college provides for instruction in 29 different fields of study, leading to the Bachelor of Arts degree. Offers a full range of cocurricular activities including vocal and instrumental music groups, forensics, intercollegiate and intramural athletics. A variety of off-campus study programs here and abroad offer opportunities for varied experience, in-the-field training, and application of skills. Offers preparation for teaching certification. Overseas programs are available in Costa Rica, England, France, Spain, Italy, Germany, Hungary, Czech Republic, Russia, Zimbabwe, India, Japan, and China. U.S. Army ROTC available.

Entrance Requirements: High school graduation or equivalent with rank preferable in the upper 40% of the class; completion of 17 units including 4 English, 1 algebra, 1 geometry, 2 social science, 2 natural science, and 7 additional distributed among foreign language, science, and social science. SAT or ACT required. Early decision, delayed admission, advanced placement, early admission and midyear admission programs are available. Because enrollment is limited, candidates are urged to file the completed application forms before March 15 of the senior year of high school; $25 application fee.

Costs Per Year: $15,200 tuition; $4,100 room and board; $190 fees.

Collegiate Environment: The college accepts 85% of those who apply for admission, and allows students to enroll at midyear as well as in the fall. The average scores of entering freshmen were: 24 ACT coomposite, SAT 540 verbal, 565 math. Dormitory facilities are available for 1,073 men and women. The library houses a total collection of 325,000 books, documents, bound periodicals, and microforms, and 715 current periodicals. Financial aid is available, and 80% of the students receive some form of assistance.

Community Environment: Students who select Ripon seek a small-town community and enjoy the recreational opportunities of Green Lake. In east central Wisconsin, the town is a one and one-half hour drive to Madison and Milwaukee, and 3 hours from Chicago. Various community groups encourage student participation in service-oreinted activities.

SACRED HEART SCHOOL OF THEOLOGY   *(C-13)*
7335 South Highway 100
Box 429
Hales Corners, Wisconsin 53130-0429
Tel: (414) 425-8300; Admissions: (414) 425-8300 X 6983; Fax: (414) 529-6999

Description: Established as Sacred Heart Monastery in 1929, the first program of studies in theology was initiated in 1932. Originally founded for the preparation of candidates for the Sacred Heart Fathers and Brothers, the school now serves over 59 dioceses and religious communities. It is a Charter member of the Midwest Association of Theological Schools and an accredited member of the Association of Theological Schools in the United States and Canada. It offers the Master of Divinity degree and M.A. in Theology. There is an enrollment of 110 full-time and 21 part-time students. A faculty of 26 full-time and 17 part-time gives a ratio of 1-3.

Entrance Requirements: A minimum of 2 years of college background in the liberal arts and sufficient background in philosophy are required. Only those who have a first degree are awarded the Master of Divinity degree; others receive a Certificate of Graduation; $25.00 application fee.

Costs Per Year: $12,000 tuition including room & board; $500 fees.

Collegiate Environment: The graduate school is located in 1 large complex of 4 connected buildings and situated on 20 acres. Almost all students who have sponsorship by a religious community or diocese and meet the entrance requirements are accepted. 20% of students receive financial aid. The school year is divided into 2 semesters. The fall semester begins in late August and ends before Christmas. The spring semester begins in January and ends in May. The library contains over 85,000 volumes. Dormitory facilities are available for 125 students.

Community Environment: Hales Corners (population 7,771) is a suburban area near Milwaukee where the average snowfall is 30 inches and the annual rainfall is 27 inches. All major transportation facilities are available in Milwaukee. A shopping center, churches, clinic and YWCA are all part of the community. Opportunities are good for part-time employment. See also Milwaukee Area Technical College for information about Milwaukee.

SAINT NORBERT COLLEGE   *(I-12)*
De Pere, Wisconsin 54115
Tel: (414) 337-3005; (800) 236-4878; Admissions: (414) 337-3005; Fax: (414) 337-4072

Description: This private college of arts and science was established in 1898, and is sponsored by the Norbertine Fathers. It is accredited by the North Central Association of Colleges and Schools. The college operates on the semester system and offers two summer sessions. A pre-engineering program with Marquette is available: 3 years at St. Norbert, 2 years at Marquette gives a B.S. degree from both institutions. The college offers vocal, instrumental, and theatre groups, and intercollegiate, intramural athletics. Enrollment includes 848 men and 1,140 women full-time and 28 men and 43 women part-time. A faculty of 118 full-time and 38 part-time provides a faculty student ratio of 1-15.

Entrance Requirements: Accredited high school graduation with rank in upper 50% of graduating class; completion of 16 academic units: 4 English, 3 mathematics, 3 science, 2 foreign language, 2 social science, 1 history; SAT or ACT required. GED accepted; C average accepted. Special admission plans: rolling admission, deferred admission, midyear admission, and advanced placement plans available. Deadline for fall applications June 1. Application fee $25.

Costs Per Year: $12,940 tuition; $4,730 room and board; $75 student fees.

Collegiate Environment: The campus is scenically situated on the west bank of the Fox River, 5 miles south of Green Bay. The main campus covers about 35 acres of land and is surrounded on 3 sides by water. The new library-learning center contains 170,551 volumes, 852 periodicals, 24,879 microforms and 6,476 audiovisual materials. The campus includes the newly expanded Abbot Pennings Hall of Fine Arts and the recently completed Cofrin academic building, which houses the computer center. Construction on a new International Center began in 1994. Dormitory and apartment facilities as well as houses are provided for 1,385 men and women. The college welcomes a geographically diverse student body and will accept midyear students. Approximately 90% of students applying for admission are accepted. About 84% of the previous freshman class returns to this campus for the sophomore year. 83% of the student body graduated in the top half of their high school class, 60% in the top quarter, and 31% in the highest tenth. Of 1,109 scholarships available, 341 are for freshmen. Financial aid is available and 89% of the students receive some form of assistance.

Community Environment: DePere (population 15,000) is located 5 miles south of Green Bay (metropolitan population 180,000) and enjoys the cultural and recreational facilities of Green Bay. Commercial transportation is available. Part-time employment is available for students. Recreational activities include golfing, swimming, boating, skiing, tobogganing, hunting, and fishing. See also Northeast Wisconsin Technical College for information about Green Bay.

SILVER LAKE COLLEGE *(K-13)*
2406 South Alvero Road
Manitowoc, Wisconsin 54220
Tel: (414) 684-6691; (800) 236-4752 x175; Admissions: (414) 684-5955 x175; Fax: (414) 684-7082

Description: Privately supported Catholic commuter college was founded in 1935 as Holy Family College, an academy and normal school conducted by and for the Franciscan Sisters of Christian Charity until 1957. It became coeducational in 1969 and in 1972 the name was changed to Silver Lake College. Silver Lake College is nondenominational. Fully accredited by the North Central Association of Colleges and Schools and the National Council for the Accreditation of Teacher Education, National Association Schools and Music. The college operates on the semester system and offers one summer session. Enrollment includes 374 full-time and 615 part-time students. A faculty of 48 full-time and 68 part-time gives a faculty-student ratio of 1-9.

Entrance Requirements: Accredited high school graduation with completion of 16 units, including 3 English, 2 mathematics, 2 social science, and 1 science; ACT or SAT required; early admission, early decision, rolling admission, delayed admission, and advanced placement plans available; $20 application fee.

Costs Per Year: $8,950 tuition; $2,910 room and board.

Collegiate Environment: The college is comprised of 5 units: science laboratories, a computer science lab, curriculum labs for elementary and secondary education, a speech clinic, and extensive art and music and environmental science facilities. Dormitory housing is available for an unspecified number of students. The library contains 91,652 volumes. 68% of all applicants are accepted. Scholarships are available to all freshmen. 85% of the students receive some form of financial aid.

Community Environment: The communities of Manitowoc and Two Rivers were founded in 1838 and are located on the shore of Lake Michigan with convenient access to major Wisconsin cities. This industrial and tourism-based community has 37 churches, 3 modern hospitals, museums, and numerous parks and recreation areas.

UNIVERSITY OF WISCONSIN - EAU CLAIRE *(H-3)*
105 Garfield Avenue
Eau Claire, Wisconsin 54701
Tel: (715) 836-5415; Fax: (715) 836-2380

Description: The publicly supported member of the University of Wisconsin System was founded in 1916 as the Eau Claire State Normal School. Its present name was adopted when it gained university standing in 1964. Today the university is comprised of the School of Arts and Sciences, School of Business, School of Education, School of Nursing, School of Human Sciences and Services, and School of Graduate Studies. It is a member of the American Association of Colleges for Teacher Education, the American Association of State Colleges and Universities, the American Counsel on Education, the Council for International Educational Exchange and the West Central Wisconsin Consortium. The university operates on the semester system and offers one summer term. It enrolls 3,500 men and 5,213 women full-time, 519 men and 1,099 women part-time. A faculty of 743 gives a faculty-student ratio of 1-19. Offers preparation for State teaching certificate. Offers vocal and instrumental music groups, and intercollegiate and intramural athletics. Various course offerings for summer programs overseas include the Institute of Technology and Higher Studies in Monterey, Mexico, with courses in geography, Spanish, and business.

Entrance Requirements: Accredited high school graduation or equivalent with C average; completion of 17 units including 4 English, 3 math, 3 social studies, 3 science, and 4 academic electives;

ACT or SAT required; applicants not meeting all entrance requirements may be admitted on probation or admitted to the summer session; rolling admission and advanced placement plans available; $25 application fee.

Costs Per Year: $2,312 tuition; $7,100 out-of-state; $2,705 room and board.

Collegiate Environment: The 333-acre campus is located on the banks of the Chippewa River and is built on 2 levels, separated by a wooded hill. The University has numerous, well-equipped structures located on the lower campus, including the Davies University Center, Schneider Social Science Hall, the seven-story Hibbard Humanities Hall, Phillips Science Hall, Brewer Hall, the School of Nursing, 2 residence halls, Schofield Hall, which contains administrative offices, and the McIntyre Library, which houses the latest in multimedia, audiotutorial, and automated learning equipment, reading and seminar rooms, 590,453 volumes in open stacks and 206,189 government documents. The multipurpose Fine Arts Center and the Allied Health and Clinical Services Center, located at an 11-acre addition across the Chippewa River, are connected by footbridge to the main campus. The upper campus contains 7 residence halls and the modern McPhee Physical Education Center. Dormitory facilities are provided for a total of 3,600 students. Numerous social, cultural, informative and entertaining events and opportunities are available on campus throughout the year. Exchange programs are available with several countries. 82% of applicants are accepted. Financial aid is available and 88% of students receive some form of assistance.

Community Environment: Eau Claire is a cultural, commercial, educational and medical center in west-central Wisconsin. The city, which is located at the confluence of the Eau Claire and Chippewa Rivers, is served by air and bus lines. Community facilities and services include numerous hotels, motels, hospitals, churches, restaurants, shopping areas, a public library and YMCA, as well as numerous civic organizations and clubs. The city and the surrounding area abound in colorful, natural beauty and offer numerous year-round recreational activities. Local lakes and parks provide opportunities to enjoy aquatic sports, golf, skiing, skating, tennis, baseball and many other sports.

UNIVERSITY OF WISCONSIN - GREEN BAY *(I-12)*
2420 Nicolet Drive
Green Bay, Wisconsin 54311-7001
Tel: (414) 465-2111; Fax: (414) 465-2032

Description: Established by an act of the Legislature in 1965 as a degree-granting unit of the University of Wisconsin, and opening in September 1968, this publicly supported, undergraduate, liberal arts and teaching education university granted its first degrees in June 1970. It is accredited by the North Central Association of Schools and Colleges. The university offers unique interdisciplinary majors in addition to traditional majors. The interdisciplinary majors combine several disciplines to help students study along "problem-oriented" lines. The state university operates on the semester calendar and offers one summer session. Enrollment is 3,959 full-time and 1,311 part-time undergraduates, and 239 graduate students. A faculty of 194 full-time and 60 part-time gives a faculty-student ratio of 1-21. UWGB offers extensive vocal and instrumental music groups, and intercollegiate and intramural athletics. Preparation for the state teaching certificate, various overseas programs, and an Educational Opportunity Program to assist the educationally disadvantaged are included in the offerings. Studies include pre-engineering, pre-pharmacy, and other pre-professional programs.

Entrance Requirements: High school graduate or equivalent; must rank in upper half of high school graduating class; ACT required; completion of 17 units including 4 English, 3 mathematics, 3 science, 3 social science, and 2 other academic units and 2 other electives; rolling admission, midyear admission and advanced placement available; $25 application fee.

Costs Per Year: $2,285 state-resident tuition; $7,073 out-of-state; $2,800 room and board.

Collegiate Environment: The UWGB campus is on a wooded 700-acre site overlooking the bay of Green Bay. Major complexes include the College of Environmental Sciences buildings (housing laboratories, media services, computer services, classrooms, lecture hall and the campus radio station), the College of Creative Communication buildings (housing a 450-seat theater, art studios, dance studio, music practice rooms and classrooms) and the College of Community Sciences buildings (which feature a lecture hall, vivarium and computer simulation rooms). The campus is home to the new 2,000 seat Weidner Center for the Performing Arts. The eight-story library holds a collection of more than 300,000 volumes, 1,200 periodicals, 500,000 microforms, and 125,000 audiovisual materials. All academic buildings are connected underground by enclosed walkways. About 80% of students applying for admission meet the requirements and are accepted. Students are admitted for terms beginning in September, January, and June. Approximately 90% of all regular students graduated in the upper half of their high school class, with about 50% in the top quarter. Apartments on campus house 550 students. Residence halls accomodate an additional 800 students. Scholarships are available and 55% of the undergraduates receive some form of financial aid. The University Student Union, a short walk from student housing, provides a cafeteria, recreation areas, lounges and meeting rooms. The Phoenix Sports Center features a 96-foot swimming pool, gymnasium, weight training room and racquetball courts. The campus also has a nine-hole golf course, outdoor tennis courts, soccer field and the Bayshore Outing Center, which rents sailboats, canoes, snow skis and camping gear.

Community Environment: Green Bay, a trading and transportation center in Northeastern Wisconsin, is a city of approximately 90,000 inhabitants located in Wisconsin's third largest population area. The city has an outstanding new regional museum, an excellent public library system and many parks. A community symphony orchestra, community chorus and several theater groups provide cultural enrichment and added opportunities for participation and performance by qualified students. Nearby resort areas provide a variety of recreational opportunities and summer jobs for students. The university is easy to reach by air, bus or interstate highway.

UNIVERSITY OF WISCONSIN - LA CROSSE *(L-4)*
Main Hall
1725 State Street
La Crosse, Wisconsin 54601
Tel: (608) 785-8000; Admissions: (608) 785-8939; Fax: (608) 785-6695

Description: As a comprehensive university UW-La Crosse is accredited by the North Central Association of Colleges and Schools. The university is comprised of the College of Health, Physical Education and Recreation; the College of Business Administration; the College of Science and Allied Health; the College of Liberal Studies; the School of Arts and Communication; and the School of Education. The University grants the Bachelor and Master degrees. An Honors Program is offered. A Cooperative Education and Internship Program places over 400 students a year in field experiences in business and government agencies throughout the United States. Through these experiences students can earn from 1 to 15 credits and/or wages. Opportunities to study abroad are available through the office of International Education. A wide range of student support services are available for all students. The university operates on the semester system and provides four- and eight-week summer sessions. Enrollment includes 7,400 full-time and 700 part-time undergraduate, and 650 graduate students. The faculty, of which 86% hold doctorate degrees, is comprised of 360 full-time and 90 part-time giving a faculty-student ratio of 1-19. Army ROTC is available.

Entrance Requirements: Accredited high school graduation with rank in upper 35% of class with minimum ACT 21 composite or upper 60% of class with minimum ACT 23 composite; completion of 17 college-preparatory units including 4 English, 3 mathematics, 3 laboratory science, 3 social science, and 4 additional academic units; ACT required; GRE required for some graduate programs; advanced placement and rolling admission plans available; $25 application fee.

Costs Per Year: $2,400 state resident undergraduate tuition and fees; $7,160 nonresident tuition; $2,360 room and board; $1,500 average miscellaneous and living expenses.

Collegiate Environment: The 67-acre main campus is in a residential section of historic La Crosse and is less than 1 mile from downtown. Towering river bluffs, wide green areas, and 27 academic and service buildings make the campus environment a good place in which to live and learn. The buildings include 11 modern residence halls, 10 of which are coed, with a total capacity of 2,836, a student union, and a food service center. Supporting the academic programs are a library with 356,277 volumes, 2,176 periodicals, 949,312 micro-

forms, and 200 audiovisual materials, a science-math complex with a planetarium and complete audiotutorial labs, computer labs in all major academic buildings and the student union, a communications center with closed-circuit TV throughtout the campus, a campus-based FM radio station, a new fine arts center, research/laboratory vessels for river studies, and a Human Performance Laboratory in the physical education complex. 76% of those who apply for admission are accepted. Students are admitted at midyear as well as in the fall. Financial aid is available, and 50% of the students receive some form of assistance.

Community Environment: Founded in 1842 as an Indian trading post, La Crosse is situated on the east bank of the Mississippi River in southern Wisconsin. It is approximately midway between Minneapolis-St. Paul and Chicago. Noted for its exceptional natural beauty and outstanding recreational opportunities, the city is the industrial, commercial and medical center of Wisconsin's famous "Coulee Country." The city was named the "All American City" in 1965 and the nation's "Number One Small City" in 1975. The population is approximately 50,000. All commercial transportation is convenient.

UNIVERSITY OF WISCONSIN - MADISON *(N-9)*
750 University Ave.
Madison, Wisconsin 53706
Tel: (608) 262-3961

Description: The publicly supported university was founded in 1848 and operates on the semester system. It is accredited by the North Central Association of Colleges and Schools and by respective professional and educational agencies in the following subject areas: business, chemistry, engineering (agricultural, chemical, civil, electrical, engineering mechanics, industrial, mechanical, metallurgical, mining, nuclear), forestry, journalism, landscape architecture, medicine, music, nursing, occupational therapy, social work, speech pathology and audiology, teacher education, law, librarianship, medical technology, pharmacy, physical therapy, psychology. The major fields of study on campus include the College of Letters and Science, College of Engineering, College of Agriculture and Life Sciences, School of Allied Health Professions, School of Family Resources and Consumer Sciences, School of Business, School of Education, Law School, Veterinary Medicine, Medical School, School of Nursing, School of Pharmacy, Department of Air Force Aerospace Studies, Department of Military Science, and the Department of Naval Science. Army, Navy, and Air Force ROTC programs are available on campus. Enrollment includes 35,979 men and women, 7,217 part-time students, and 12,250 graduate students. A faculty of 2,418 gives a faculty-student ratio of 1:16. The university does have a program for minority/disadvantaged students who are not otherwise eligible for admission. Courses in Afro-American history are presently offered with the Department of Afro-American Area Studies.

Entrance Requirements: High school graduation rank in upper 35% (in-state) or upper 20% (out-of-state) of high school graduating class; ACT or SAT required; completion of 16 units including 4 English, 3 mathematics, 2 science, and 3 social science; 2 foreign language; early admission, rolling admission, advanced placement plans. $10 application fee.

Costs Per Year: $2,346 tuition for residents; $7,841 out-of-state tuition; $3,600 room and board.

Collegiate Environment: The beautiful, sprawling campus is located on a series of wooded hills overlooking Lake Mendota, 1 mile from the state capitol. The libraries of the campus contain 5,988,000 volumes. The library of the State Historical Society, which faces the Memorial Library on the lower campus, contains 4,800,000 volumes. There are residence halls for 6,700 students. 70% of all applicants accepted. Midyear students are accepted. Financial aid is available and 40% receive some form of assistance.

Community Environment: Founded in 1836, the city was named for James Madison, the fourth President of the United States, and is the capital of Wisconsin. Madison is the center of one of the richest dairy regions in America and has over 200 industries. The city is also important as a medical center with its 12 hospitals and its manufacturing of precision surgical instruments. Recreational facilities include 10 golf courses, 3 of which are public, tennis courts, and a number of beaches for water sports. Fishing boats are for hire. Points of interest are the Henry Vilas Park Zoo, Nevin Fish Hatchery, U.S. Forest Products Laboratory, State Historical Society Museum, and the Wisconsin State Capitol which is one of the most impressive in the United States.

UNIVERSITY OF WISCONSIN - MILWAUKEE   (N-13)
P.O. Box 413
Milwaukee, Wisconsin 53201
Tel: (414) 229-3800

Description: Established in 1956 to meet the growing need for a distinguished university in the large metropolitan area of Milwaukee, the publicly supported campus of the University of Wisconsin System is accredited by the North Central Association of Colleges and Schools and the respective educational and professional agencies in the following subject areas: business, chemistry, engineering (electrical science, energy conversion, engineering mechanics, materials science, mechanical design, structural engineering), librarianship, music, nursing, social work, speech pathology, architecture, geology, journalism, rehabilitation education and audiology, and teacher education. Encompassed within the system are the Schools of Allied Health Professions, Architecture and Urban Planning, Business Administration, Education, Fine Arts, Nursing, Social Welfare, Library Science; Colleges of Engineering and Applied Science, Letters and Science; and the Graduate School. Army ROTC is available on campus. The university operates on the semester system and offers three summer terms. Semesters begin in January and September; summer sessions are in May, June, and July. Enrollment includes 11,054 full-time and 7,190 part-time undergraduates and 4,740 students. A faculty of 852 full-time and 506 part-time gives a faculty-student ratio of 1-18. A Cooperative Education program (alternating work and class periods) is available in engineering. Study abroad to many countries is also available. Pre-college and freshman programs for the educationally disadvantaged are offered as well as band, orchestra, and intercollegiate and intramural athletics.

Entrance Requirements: Graduation from accredited high school or equivalent; rank in top 50% of high school class; completion of 17 units including 4 English, 3 mathematics, 3 science, 2 social studies, 7 academic units and 4 electives; ACT or SAT required; GRE required for some graduate programs; early decision, rolling admission, midyear admission, and advanced placement programs available; $35 application fee for graduate students; $25 application fee for undergraduates.

Costs Per Year: $2,775 resident tuition; $8,788 nonresident; $3,500 room and board; $210 student fees.

Collegiate Environment: The university campus totals 90 acres in the north shore area of Milwaukee. As an urban university, it has a multiplicity of programs located throughout the city. The intellectual center of the campus is the library, which contains approximately 2.5 million bibliographic items. Included in this is the newly acquired American Geographical Society Collection, which has 180,000 titles, 350,000 maps, 33,000 pamphlets, 5,500 atlases, 45,000 photographs and 67 rare and special globes. Although the choice of living accommodations is primarily the student's responsibility, there is dormitory space available for 1,964 students. 75% of the applicants are accepted, including midyear students. Of 562 scholarships offered, 168 are for freshmen. 47% of the students receive some form of financial aid.

Community Environment: Located on the west shore of Lake Michigan, Milwaukee (population 640,000) is the largest city in Wisconsin. All major forms of commercial transportation are available. Milwaukee is the nation's brewing center, as well as a major grain market and manufacturing center. Products of industry are metal, machinery, food, leather, chemicals, textiles, electrical machinery, and other items. The city is the headquarters of the Lake States National Forest Region. The county has a park system and many of the units contain public golf courses, tennis courts, and other recreational facilities. Milwaukee's State Fair is held each year in August.

UNIVERSITY OF WISCONSIN - OSHKOSH   (K-11)
800 Algoma Boulevard
Oshkosh, Wisconsin 54901
Tel: (414) 424-0224; (800) 624-1466; Admissions: (414) 424-0202

Description: A part of the University of Wisconsin System, UW-Oshkosh opened as the Oshkosh Normal School and enrolled its first student in 1871. The school was designated Wisconsin State Teachers College in 1925, and upon the approval of curricula in the liberal arts in 1949 became Wisconsin State College, Oshkosh. With the growth of the institution and the inauguration of several graduate programs, the college was elevated to university status in 1964. The university is comprised of the College of Business Administration, College of Education and Human Services, College of Letters and Science, College of Nursing, and the Graduate School. It is accredited by the North Central Association of Colleges and Schools. The university operates on the semester system, which includes an optional 3-week interim per semester, and offers 1 summer term. Enrollment is approximately 4,353 men and 6,214 women. A faculty of 534 gives a faculty-student ratio of 1-19. Freshman programs for the educationally disadvantaged and U.S. Army ROTC are available. Three-year pre-engineering program for transfer to UW-Madison and 2 additional years results in both B.S. and B.E. degrees. Extensive vocal and instrumental music groups, and intercollegiate and intramural athletics are available.

Entrance Requirements: Accredited high school graduation or equivalent. Rank in top 50% of graduating class or ACT composite score of at least 23; must have earned 4 credits in English (composition literature and rhetoric); 3 credits in math (algebra and/or geometry), 3 science, 3 social science (at least 1 of these in history), and 4 academic electives; school courses may not satisfy these requirements for acadmic course work; rolling admission and advanced placement plans available; $25 application fee.

Costs Per Year: $2,160 tuition; $6,970 out-of-state; $2,250 room and board.

Collegiate Environment: The university campus consists of 185 acres and 51 buildings. Its library contains over 500,000 volumes. Dormitory facilities are provided for about 4,000 men and women. There are 7 social fraternities and 6 social sororities located on the campus. The university welcomes a geographically diverse student body and will accept midyear students. About 58% of applicants are accepted. 60% of the students receive some form of financial aid.

Community Environment: Oshkosh is on the west shore of Lake Winnebago at the mouth of the Fox River. The city, an important industrial center, manufactures candles, work clothes, sashes, doors, marine motors, and boats. Oshkosh has 240 acres of public parks, 3 public beaches, and golf courses. Other activities include fishing, boating, and hunting. Winter sports include ice boating, ice skating, and ice fishing.

Branch Campuses: The UW system has 13 two-year campuses scattered throughout Wisconsin that are called UW centers. All credits earned at any of these campuses are transferable to UW-Oshkosh.

UNIVERSITY OF WISCONSIN - PARKSIDE   (P-13)
900 Wood Road, Box 2000
Kenosha, Wisconsin 53141-2000
Tel: (414) 595-2345

Description: The University of Wisconsin-Parkside is one of 13 degree-granting campuses in the distinguished University of Wisconsin System, one of the nation's largest. It is accredited by the North Central Association of Colleges and Schools and operates on the semester system with one summer session. The campus which opened in 1969, is located between the cities of Racine and Kenosha near Lake Michigan, in the larger Chicago-Milwaukee urban corridor. UW-Parkside offers undergraduate BA and BS degrees in 60 different majors, specialties, and options and certificate programs within majors, and preprofessional studies in a wide range of fields, including an accelerated three-year pre-med program and the state's only two-year certificate program in labor studies. UW-Parkside offers two graduate degree programs, one in Business Administration, the other in Applied Molecular Biology. Consortial graduate programs in Education with the University of Wisconsin-Milwaukee and the University of Wisconsin-Whitewater are also available. Current enrollment inlcudes approximately 4,688 undergraduate students, 350 graduate students, and 7,000 alumni. A faculty of 150 full-time and 150 part-time provides a faculty-student ratio of 1:14. The university grants the Master's and Bachelor's degree.

Entrance Requirements: Top 50% of high school class and 16 credits including 4 English, 2 math, 2 language, 2 science, 3 social science, and 7 academic electives for standard admission; ACT required. Early admission, early decision, delayed admission and advanced placement plans available. $10 application fee.

Costs Per Year: $1,988 tuition; $6,174 out-of-state tuition; $2,938 room and board; $20 fees.

Collegiate Environment: The campus is set on 700 acres of rolling land, much of it retained in its natural wooded and prairie state. The campus features a network of connected academic buildings whose striking architecture was carefully conceived to complement the natural beauty of the land. The academic buildings are connected by glass-walled corridors which widen within buildings into concourses containing study areas and lounges which are favorite meeting places for students and faculty. The focal point of the campus is the Wyllie Library-Learning Center. The library contains 355,000 bound volumes, 1,440 periodicals, 761,000 items in microformat, and 20,000 audiovisual items. 3 other modern and superbly equipped academic buildings - Greenquist and Molinaro Halls and the Communication Arts complex - radiate from the Library-Learning Center, as does the Campus Union, the center of student life. Apartment-style housing, opened in Fall, 1986, is just northwest of the Union. Other campus buildings are a short walk from the central academic area, including the Physical Education Center. 82% of all applicants accepted. 27% of the students receive financial aid.

Community Environment: See Gateway Technical College.

UNIVERSITY OF WISCONSIN - PLATTEVILLE   *(Q-6)*
1 University Plaza
Platteville, Wisconsin 53818
Tel: (608) 342-1125; (800) 362-5515; Fax: (608) 342-1122

Description: The origin of the present publicly supported campus of the University of Wisconsin can be traced to the Platteville Academy, which was established in 1839. In 1866, the Platteville Normal School was opened in the New Academy Building that had been donated to the State of Wisconsin. By 1951, the Wisconsin Legislature authorized the granting of liberal arts degrees and the official name of the college became Wisconsin State College - Platteville. In 1959, the two colleges in Platteville, namely, the Wisconsin State College - Platteville and the Wisconsin Institute of Technology, were merged under the name of the Wisconsin State College and Institute of Technology, Platteville, and in 1972 its present name was adopted by action of the Wisconsin Legislature. Today, the university includes the College of Business, Industry, Life Science and Agricultural, the College of Engineering, Mathematics and Science, and the College of Liberal Arts and Education, and the School of Graduate Studies. It is accredited by the North Central Association of Schools of Music, and the National Commission for the Accreditation of Teacher Education. The university operates on the semester system and also provides a summer term. An extensive cooperative education program is available in programs within each of the three colleges. The university study Abroad program has programs in England, France, Italy, Germany, Spain and Mexico. Enrollment is 4,714 full-time undergraduate student and 240 graduate students. A faculty and staff of 360 provides a faculty student ration of approximately 1-20.

Entrance Requirements: Accredited high school graduation with rank in the upper 40% of the graduating class or an ACT score of 22 composite or higher; completion of a minimum of 17; college preparatory units including 4 English (completion, literature and rhetoric), 3 mathematics (algebra 1 and 2, geometry, and higher), and 5 or more electives from the areas previously mentioned; ACT with minimum score of 22 required; $25 application fee.

Costs Per Year: $1,916 tuition; $6,704 out-of-state; $2,680 room and board; $425.50 student fees.

Collegiate Environment: The university library contains 171,948 volumes, 2,938 periodicals, and 122,351 microforms. Dormitory facilities are provided for 1,650 men and 666 women. Students from other geographical locations are accepted as well as midyear students. Approximately 75% of the students applying for admission are accepted. The average score of the entering freshman class was ACT 23 composite. About 72% of the freshman class returns to this campus for the sophomore year. Financial aid is available. More than 200 different scholarships are offered, 33 of them for freshmen. 64% of students receive financial aid.

Community Environment: Located in the heart of Wisconsin's dairyland and lead and zinc mining district, Platteville (population 9,950) was settled in 1827. Scheduled air transportation is available from Dubuque, Iowa, 20 miles away. Community facilities include a hospital, library, churches, mining museum, other historical sites, and various civic and service organizations. Recreational activities are golf, hunting, fishing, swimming, tennis, bowling, and horseback riding.

UNIVERSITY OF WISCONSIN - RIVER FALLS   *(H-1)*
Cascade Avenue
River Falls, Wisconsin 54022
Tel: (715) 425-3500; Fax: (715) 425-0676

Description: The University of Wisconsin-River Falls is a comprehensive institution with a distinctive curriculm in the liberal arts and sciences and technologies. It has a distinguished tradition of providing a core of general education classes for all students and a special commitment to life-long learning. As a public university, it has offered an affordable education to the residents of Wisconsin and the nation for over a century. Its purposes are to instill within students of all ages an appreciation of knowledge for its own sake, and to prepare them for a variety of careers. The University is organized around the Colleges of Agriculture, Arts and Sciences, Education, and the Graduate School. The Colleges provide educational choices from over 50 programs of study including most pre-professional areas. The Departments of Chemisty and Physics have recently been designated as a Center of Excellence by the University of Wisconsin System in recognition of their outstanding undergraduate instruction. The university operates on the semester system and offers two summer sessions. Enrollment includes 5,400 full-time, 525 part-time, and 480 graduate students. A faculty of 242 full-time and 7 part-time gives a faculty-student ratio of 1-24.

Entrance Requirements: Accredited high school graduation; completion of 16 college-preparatory courses including: 4 English, 2-4 mathematics, 2-4 natural science, 3-4 social science, 3 additional from the above or foreign languages, and 2 academic electives; rank in the top 40% of graduating class or ACT composite score of 22 or above; ACT required; rolling admission plan available; $25 application fee.

Costs Per Year: $2,304 tuition; $7,029 out-of-state; $2,510 room and board.

Collegiate Environment: The 250-acre campus has 22 well-equipped buildings. There is dormitory space for 2,000 students, and fraternities house an additional 40 men. The library contains 226,284 volumes, 1,315 periodicals, 464,000 microforms and audiovisual materials. Approximately 95% of students applying for admission meet the requirements and are accepted. A total of 250 scholarships are available, 140 of which are for freshmen. 60% of students receive some form of financial aid.

Community Environment: Location is an important asset to the learning environment of the university. At UW-River Falls, students are exposed to the quiet charm of a friendly community nestled in the scenic St. Croix River Valley. Balanced against that setting is the opportunity and excitement of the metropolitan area of the Twin Cities of Minneapolis and St. Paul, located 20 minutes away. This unique region offers access to internationally renowned theater and cultural resources, major league sports, and an industrial and business complex that provides opportunities for internships and cooperative education experiences as well as employment.

UNIVERSITY OF WISCONSIN - STEVENS POINT   *(I-8)*
2100 Main Street
Stevens Point, Wisconsin 54481
Tel: (715) 346-0123

Description: Originally Stevens Point Normal School, the university was authorized by an Act of the State Legislature in 1891 and began its first term in 1894. The publicity controlled multipurpose university, a branch of the University of Wisconsin, is accredited by the North Central Association of Colleges and Schools. The institution operates on the semester system and offers 1 summer term. A wide range of majors and minors in the usual academic fields is available. In addition, majors are offered in several special fields: art, business education, natural resources, home economics, medical technology, and music. The Master's degree program was implemented on an academic year basis in September, 1966. Classes are available on a Saturday and late afternoon basis as well as during the summer session. A cooperative education program is available in business and in communications. Study abroad is available to England, Germany, Poland, Spain, Australia, Far East, and Greece. Army ROTC is available. Offers preparation for State teaching certificate. Enrollment includes 7,363 full-time and 1,252 part-time undergraduate and 556 graduate students. A faculty of 371 full-time and 87 part-time provides an undergraduate faculty-student ratio of 1-19.

Entrance Requirements: Accredited high school graduation or equivalent; GED accepted. Completion of 16 college-preparatory courses including 4 English, 2 math, 2 science, and 3 social studies; ACT with minimum score of 22 required or rank in upper 50% of class; campus interview recommended. Applicants not meeting all entrance requirements may be admitted on probation to the summer session. Rolling admission, midyear admission, and advanced placement available. $10 application fee.

Costs Per Year: $2,395 state-resident tuition; $7,422 out-of-state tuition; $3,150 room and board.

Collegiate Environment: The 335-acre campus lies in the Wisconsin River Valley, and in a metropolitan area of 27,000. The 37 buildings, include Old Main for administrative offices, the University Center, the College of Natural Resources Building, the Science Building, the College of Professional Studies Building, the Collins Classroom Center, the Fine Arts Center, and the Physical Education Building. A 200-acre reserve borders the campus and a 960-acre living laboratory called Treehaven is owned and operated by the university. The library has a collection of over 351,000 volumes, plus 450,000 volumes of government documents, 2,003 periodical subscriptions, and 543,824 microforms. Dormitory facilities are available for 3,857 students. Financial aid is available and 86% of students receive financial assistance.

Community Environment: Stevens Point is located in the very center of the state on the Wisconsin and Plovers Rivers, and has been a center of travel and commerce since the days of heavy river traffic. Products of industry include lumber and millwork, furniture, woodwork, and fishing flies. The community supports a symphony orchestra and has churches, a youth center, and a year-round recreation center. Natural streams and lakes for fishing are plentiful as are facilities for summer and winter sports.

UNIVERSITY OF WISCONSIN - STOUT   *(H-2)*
Menomonie, Wisconsin 54751
Tel: (715) 232-1411; (800) 447-8688; Fax: (715) 232-1667

Description: Publicly-supported, special mission university of the University of Wisconsin System was founded in 1891. It is accredited by the North Central Association of Colleges and Schools, and professionally by the American Home Economics Association and the National Council for Accreditation of Teacher Education. It is comprised of the School of Industry and Technology, School of Home Economics, School of Liberal Studies, School of Education and Human Services, and the Graduate College. Courses are available in Scotland. It operates on the semester system and offers one summer session. Enrollment includes 6,042 full-time, 714 part-time undergraduates, and 657 graduate students. A faculty of 323 full-time and 47 part-time gives a faculty-student ratio of 1-20.

Entrance Requirements: Accredited high school graduation with rank in upper 60% of graduating class; completion of 17 units; minimum ACT 22 composite required; non high school graduates over 18 may be admitted with GED tests and by interviews conducted by the university; early admission, deferred admission, rolling admission, midyear admission, and advanced placement plans available; $10 application fee.

Costs Per Year: $1,916 state resident tuition; $6,704 nonresident tuition; $2,592 room and board; $338 student fees.

Collegiate Environment: The university has 31 buildings which are located on a 120-acre campus. Its library contains over 219,525 books, 1,527 periodicals, 982,616 microforms, and 11,370 audiovisual materials. Living accommodations are provided for 3,000 men and women. Students from other geographical locations are accepted as well as midyear students. 89% of applicants are accepted. Of 285 scholarships available, 123 are for freshmen. 65% of students receive some form of financial assistance.

Community Environment: Menomonie (population 13,349) is located on the Red Cedar River and Lake Menomin, with all commercial transportation available.

UNIVERSITY OF WISCONSIN - SUPERIOR   *(B-2)*
1800 Grand Avenue
Superior, Wisconsin 54880
Tel: (715) 392-8230

Description: Established in 1896 as a state normal school by an Act of the Legislature, the publicly supported branch of the University of Wisconsin became a state teacher's college with full collegiate rank and with the authority to grant Bachelor degrees in 1925. It is accredited by the North Central Association of Colleges and Schools. The graduate program was begun in 1950 and the university now grants the Master of Education and the Master of Science degrees. Air Force ROTC is available. The university operates on the semester system and offers one summer session. Enrollment includes 2,611 undergraduates and 300 graduate students. A faculty of 146 gives a faculty-student ratio of 1-16.

Entrance Requirements: Accredited high school graduation or equivalent with rank in upper 50% of graduating class, applicants not meeting all entrance requirements may be admitted on probation to the summer session; ACT required; early admission, early decision, midyear admission and rolling admission plans available; $25 application fee.

Costs Per Year: $2,182 tuition and fees; $2,716 room and board.

Collegiate Environment: The 230-acre campus is located in the downtown residential area within easy walking distance of churches and the main shopping district. The campus is modern with the oldest building completed in 1916. Five residence halls provide living accommodations for 700 men and women. The Jim Dan Hill library contains more than 250,000 volumes, and 250,000 microforms. 80% of all applicants are accepted. Extensive financial assistance is available, and 83% of students receive scholarships, grants, or other forms of financial aid.

Community Environment: Superior is Wisconsin's leading port of entry and is located at the head of Lake Superior at the northwest corner of the state. The largest iron ore dock, grain elevator and briquet plant in the world are here at Superior. The area is a leading summer and winter recreation resort.

UNIVERSITY OF WISCONSIN - WHITEWATER   *(O-11)*
800 West Main Street
Whitewater, Wisconsin 53190
Tel: (414) 472-1440

Description: The publicly supported campus of the University of Wisconsin is accredited by the North Central Association of Colleges and Schools. It was founded in 1868 as the Whitewater Normal School. Today it offers 50 majors through its 4 colleges: the College of Arts, Business and Economics, Education, and Letters and Sciences. It grants the Bachelor and Master's degrees and Army ROTC is available. The university operates on the early semester calendar system and offers three summer sessions. undergraduate enrollment of includes 7,724 full-time and 1,504 part-time; graduate enrollment includes 1,210 students. A faculty of 426 full-time and part-time gives an undergraduate faculty-student ratio of 1:22.

Entrance Requirements: Accredited high school graduation or equivalent with rank in upper 50% of graduating class or combined class and ACT/SAT percentile ranks of 100 or above; completion of 16 college-preparatory courses including 4 English, 2 mathematics, 2 laboratory science, 3 social studies; rolling admission, midyear admission and advanced placement plans are available, $25 application fee.

Costs Per Year: $2,400 state-resident tuition and fees; $7,400 nonresidents; $2,546 room and board.

Collegiate Environment: Composed of 385 acres, the university campus is situated in the northwestern part of Whitewater. The campus academic buildings center around an attractive mall through the middle of the campus and there is housing for 4,100 students with sororities and fraternities accommodating another 300 students. The institution library contains 352,500 volumes, 51,000 periodical volumes, over 950,907 microforms and 10,000 audiovisual materials. Over 80% of those who apply for admission are accepted. Financial aid is available and 55% of the student body receives some form of assistance.

Community Environment: UW-Whitewater is located in a city of 12,000 near the scenic beauty of the Southern Kettle Moraine State

Forest. It is a one-hour drive from Madison and Milwaukee, and a two-hour drive from Chicago. The area around Whitewater offers lakes, recreation, cross country skiing, backpacking, hiking, and other forms of outdoor activity. The campus is within walking distance of 2 shopping areas and a city park is adjacent to the campus.

UNIVERSITY OF WISCONSIN CENTERS - ADMINISTRATION   (N-9)
780 Regent Street
P.O. Box 8680
Madison, Wisconsin 53708-8680
Tel: (608) 262-1234

Description: The publicly supported University of Wisconsin Centers contain 13 branch campuses throughout the state. They are fully accredited by the North Central Association of Colleges and Schools. The various campuses of the Center System operate on the semester system and offer one summer term. Each Center campus offers a complete two-year liberal arts and preprofessional curriculum, as well as adult and continuing education courses. In this manner, the first 2 years of a university educational experience are made readily and economically available on a fully transferable system. Each center has its own administration, faculty, and staff. Enrollment totals 4,922 men and 6,038 women. The faculty consists of 430 instructors. A complete listing including addresses is given below. Offers vocal and instrumental music groups, intercollegiate and intramural athletics.

Entrance Requirements: High school graduation or equivalent; completion of 17 university preparatory units including 4 English, 2 mathematics, 3 Natural Science, 3 Social Science; ACT required; Special admission plans: early admission, early decision, advanced placement. Contact Director of Student Services at any campus.

Costs Per Year: $1,600 tuition; $5,630 out-of-state tuition; room and board cost varies; $160 student fees.

Collegiate Environment: The 13 campuses as a rule do not provide dormitory facilities since most of the students live at home while attending. However, the Marathon County, Marinette County, Richland County campuses have limited dormitory or apartment space. Financial aid is available.

Branch Campuses: UWC - Baraboo-Sauk County, 1006 Connie Road, Baraboo, Wisconsin 53913, (608) 356-8351; UWC - Barron County, 1800 College Drive, Rice Lake, Wisconsin 54868, (715) 234-8176; UWC - Fond du Lac, Campus Drive, Fond du Lac, Wisconsin 54935, (414) 929-3600; UWC - Fox Valley, 1478 Midway Road, Menasha, Wisconsin 54952, (414) 832-2620; UWC - Manitowoc County, 705 Viebahn Street, Manitowoc, Wisconsin 54220, (414) 683-4700; UWC - Marathon County, 518 South 7th Avenue, Wausau, Wisconsin 54401, (715) 845-9602; UWC - Marinette County, Bay Shore, Marinette, Wisconsin 54143, (715) 735-7477; UWC - Marshfield-Wood County, 2000 West Fifth Street, Marshfield, Wisconsin 54449, (715) 387-1147; UWC - Richland, Richland Center, Wisconsin 53581, (608) 647-6186; UWC - Rock County, 2909 Kellogg Avenue, Janesville, Wisconsin 53545, (608) 755-2811; UWC - Sheyboygan County, One University Drive, Sheboygan, Wisconsin 53081, (414) 459-3700; UWC - Washington County, 400 University Drive, West Bend, Wisconsin 53095, (414) 338-5200; UWC - Waukesha County, 1500 University Drive, Waukesha, Wisconsin 53188, (414) 521-5200.

VITERBO COLLEGE   (L-4)
815 South 9th Street
La Crosse, Wisconsin 54601
Tel: (608) 791-0420; (800) 848-3726; Fax: (608) 791-0433

Description: The privately supported coeducational Christian liberal arts college was established in 1890 by the Sisters of St. Francis of Perpetual Adoration. It is accredited by the North Central Association of Colleges and Schools, American Chemical Society, National Association of Schools of Music, American Dietetic Association, National Council for the Accreditation of Teacher Education, and the Council on Medical Education of the American Medical Association, National League for Nursing and Wisconsin State Board of Nursing. The college operates on the semester system and provides two summer terms. It enrolls 293 men and 869 women full-time, 61 men and 325 women part-time, and 155 graduate students. A faculty of 19 full-time and 84 part-time gives a faculty-student ratio of 1:12. Cooperative education

programs are available in several majors. Army ROTC is available. Offers choir, ensembles, orchestra, intercollegiate basketball, volleyball, soccer, baseball, softball and intramural sports. Preparation for State teaching certificate.

Entrance Requirements: Accredited high school graduation or equivalent with rank in upper half of graduating class; completion of 16 units including 4 English, 2 mathematics, 2 science, 2 social science; SAT or ACT required, ACT for nursing, medical records, and dietetics students. Average standing of freshmen: top 40% of high school class. Early decision, rolling admission, delayed admission, advanced placement, early admission. Application fee $15.

Costs Per Year: $9,780 tuition; $3,750 room and board; student fees $70.

Collegiate Environment: The college is located on 5 acres. Its library houses 62,437 volumes and 9,575 periodicals. Dormitory facilities are available for 135 men and 260 women. 75% of the freshmen return for the second year. Students from other geographical locations are accepted as well as midyear students. About 90% of the students receive some financial assistance and approximately 85% applying for admission are accepted.

Community Environment: See University of Wisconsin - La Crosse.

WAUKESHA COUNTY TECHNICAL INSTITUTE   (N-12)
800 Main Street
Pewaukee, Wisconsin 53072-4698
Tel: (414) 691-5200

Description: The publicly supported technical institute was established in 1923 and offers educational programs and training necessary to prepare students for entering semi-professional, technical, and vocational occupations. It also provides community service programs as well as vocational and academic counseling. WCTI is fully accredited by the North Central Association of Colleges and Schools. The institute operates on the semester system and also provides a summer term. It enrolls approximately 1,406 men and women full-time. A faculty of 110 full-time and 672 part-time gives a faculty-student ratio of 1-5. Grants the Associate degree. Offers Adult Basic Education programs for the educationally disadvantaged. Band, choir, intercollegiate and intramural athletics are available. Accredited by National League for Nursing (for technical nursing).

Entrance Requirements: High school graduation or equivalent required for degree programs; open enrollment; pre-enrollment tests required for placement and counseling. Special admission plans: early admission, rolling admission, advanced placement. There is a $20 application fee.

Costs Per Year: $38.90 per credit for residents, $268.50 per credit for nonresidents; plus miscellaneous course fees.

Collegiate Environment: The institute is presently operating in a transitional period while its new plant is being constructed on a 90-acre campus. It is currently leasing facilities in addition to its own building, to carry on its educational programs. The library contains 18,000 volumes. The institute also has a special program for minority nationality groups which offers courses in basic English, basic arithmetic, and basic reading. Semesters begin in September and January, and midyear students are accepted.

Community Environment: The name Waukesha comes from an Indian word meaning "by the Little Fox." The city (population 52,000) is known as a resort town. Manufacturers here produce gasoline and diesel engines; the city is also a cattle market. The cultural facilities of metropolitan Milwaukee are 30 to 40 minutes away.

WESTERN WISCONSIN TECHNICAL COLLEGE   (L-4)
304 N. 6th
La Crosse, Wisconsin 54602-0908
Tel: (608) 785-9585; (800) 322-9982; Fax: (608) 789-4760

Description: The publicly supported two-year technical college was founded in 1912 and was formerly known as the Coleman Technical Institute. It provides preparatory and general education courses, training in apprenticeship trades, technical-vocational programs and adult education courses. The college is accredited by the North Central Association of Colleges and Schools and the Wisconsin Technical System Board to offer two-year technical courses of study leading to Associate degrees. It also offers vocational diploma programs. It operates on the semester system and offers a summer session. Enrollment includes 827 men and 1,062 women full-time, and 986 men and 1,355 women part-time. A contracted faculty of 190 full-time and 30 part-time gives a faculty-student ratio of 1-18.

Entrance Requirements: High school graduation or equivalent required for degree programs; early admission and advanced placement plans are available.

Costs Per Year: $1,580 tuition; $11,340 nonresidents.

Collegiate Environment: The college is housed in 7 main buildings that are located on an 8-acre campus. Its library contains more than 30,000 volumes. Dormitory facilities are provided for 34 men and 76 women. All students applying for admission are accepted, including midyear students. Financial aid is available for economically disadvantaged students. 60% of students receive some form of financial aid.

Community Environment: See University of Wisconsin - La Crosse.

WISCONSIN INDIANHEAD TECHNICAL COLLEGE AT RICE LAKE   *(F-3)*
1900 College Drive
Rice Lake, Wisconsin 54868
Tel: (715) 234-7082

Description: This publicly supported vocational technological institute was established in 1942. It operates on the semester system. It is accredited by the North Central Association of Colleges and Schools. Enrollment is 920 and a faculty of 45 provide a teacher-student ratio of 1-18.

Entrance Requirements: High school graduation or GED; high school graduates with a C average are accepted; open enrollment; early admission, early decision, rolling admission and advanced placement; students are admitted at midyear; $25 application fee.

Costs Per Year: $1,475 ($46.10/cr) resident tuition; $9,864 ($308.25/cr) out-of-state tuition; $1,800 room and board; $75 student fees; $450-$750 additional expenses.

Collegiate Environment: The library houses 32,000 hard bound volumes, 3,000 pamphlets, 154 periodicals, 7,200 microforms and more than 1,000 audio-visual materials. Scholarships are available; 73% of the student body receive financial aid. There is no student housing on campus. 95% of those applying for admission are accepted.

Community Environment: Rice Lake is located in the heart of the famous Indianhead Country; waterfalls, facilities for skiing, conoeing, biking, and snowmobiling, and many state parks and one national forest are nearby.

WISCONSIN INDIANHEAD TECHNICAL COLLEGE AT SUPERIOR   *(B-2)*
600 N. 21st St.
Superior, Wisconsin 54880
Tel: (715) 394-6677; (800) 243-9482; Fax: (715) 394-3771

Description: This publicly-supported technological institute, the first Vocational and Adult School in Superior, was started in 1912. Today, the institute is comprised of the Associate Degree Division, the Vocational Division, the Apprenticeship Division, and the Continuing Education Division. It is approved and accredited by the Wisconsin State Board of Vocational, Technical and Adult Education and the North Central Association of Colleges and Schools. The Institute operates on the semester system and also provides an evening school program and a summer term that consists of six eight-week courses. Enrollment is 485 full-time and 397 part-time credit students. A faculty of 48 full-time and 32 part-time gives a faculty-student ratio of 1-18. A special program in adult basic education for the educationally disadvantaged is offered.

Entrance Requirements: High school graduation or equivalent; open enrollment; pre-admission testing and counselor interview; rolling admission, midyear admission and advanced placement plans available; $20 application fee.

Costs Per Year: $981.60 tuition; $5,914.80 out-of-state; $125 student fees; $100-$300 additional expenses.

Collegiate Environment: The institute is located on 3 acres in the northwest corner of the state on the largest natural inland harbor in the world. The physical plant includes 37 classrooms and classroom laboratories in a modern new building. Many sources of financial aid are available. Nearly 80% of the previous entering class returns to the institute for the second year of studies.

Branch Campuses: WITC-Ashland, 2100 Beaser Ave., Ashland, WI 54806, (715) 682-4591; WITC-New Richmond, 1019 S. Knowles Ave., New Richmond, WI 54017, (715) 246-6561; WITC-Rice Lake, 1900 College Drive, Rice Lake, WI 54868, (715) 234-7082.

WISCONSIN LUTHERAN SEMINARY   *(A-13)*
11831 North Seminary Drive
Mequon, Wisconsin 53092
Tel: (414) 242-7200; Fax: (414) 242-7255

Description: The privately supported men's graduate theological seminary of the Wisconsin Synod was opened in 1863 in Watertown, Wisconsin, in conjunction with the Synod's Lutheran College. In 1878, the seminary was established in Milwaukee and in 1929 at Mequon. It provides preparation for those who desire to enter the ministry of the Wisconsin Evangelical Lutheran Synod (or of churches within its confessional fellowship). The seminary operates on the quarter system and offers one summer session. Enrollment is 150 men. A faculty of 15 gives a faculty-student ratio of 1-10. Grants Master of Divinity degree.

Entrance Requirements: Bachelor of Arts degree or its equivalent; completion of college courses should include heavy emphasis on history and modern and classical languages (Greek and Hebrew); delayed admission plan; apply to the president of the seminary for application forms and further information.

Costs Per Year: $3,080 tuition; $2,390 room and board; $45 student fees.

Collegiate Environment: The seminary is located on 80 acres that contain the administration building, the refectory, dormitory facilities for 126 men, and a library of more than 40,000 volumes. Classes begin in September and midyear students are not accepted.

Community Environment: Mequon (population 16,500) is a suburban area with a temperate climate. The community enjoys the cultural and recreational advantages of Milwaukee. Part-time employment opportunities are very good. Lake Michigan, which is nearby, provides facilities for all water sports. See also the entry for the Milwaukee Area Technical College.

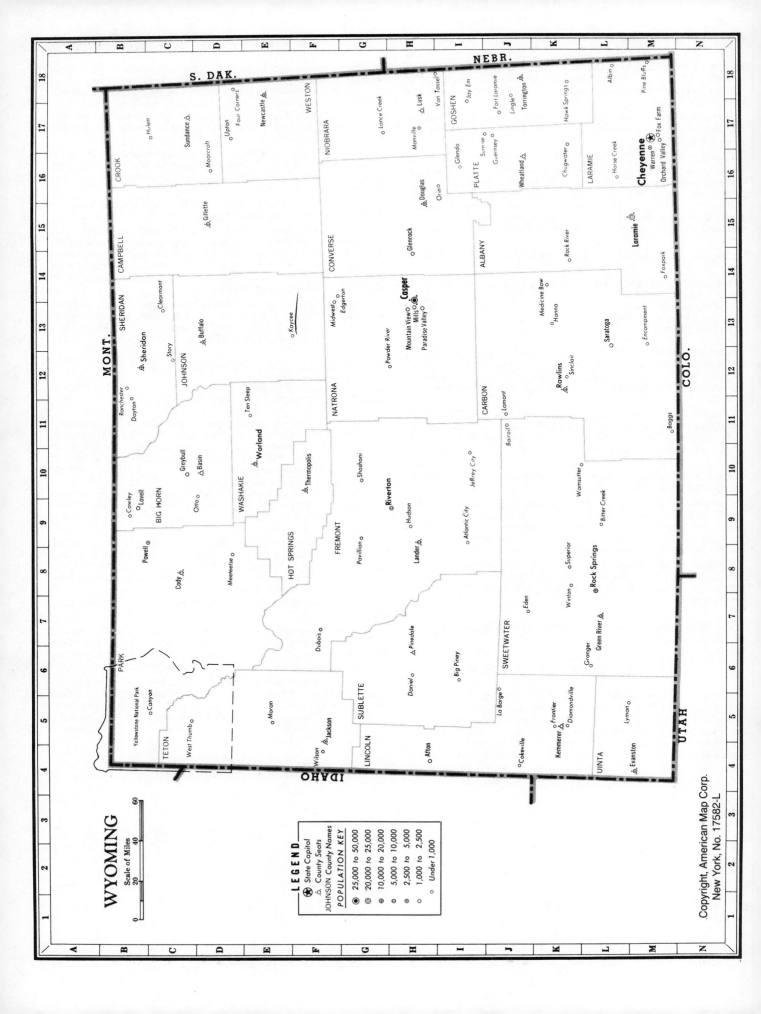

WYOMING

Scale of Miles

0 20 40 60

LEGEND

⊛ State Capital
⊙ County Seats
JOHNSON County Names

POPULATION KEY

⊚ 25,000 to 50,000
⊙ 20,000 to 25,000
⊕ 10,000 to 20,000
⊘ 5,000 to 10,000
○ 2,500 to 5,000
○ 1,000 to 2,500
○ Under 1,000

Copyright, American Map Corp.
New York, No. 17582-L

S. DAK.

NEBR.

MONT.

COLO.

UTAH

IDAHO

CROOK

CAMPBELL

SHERIDAN

JOHNSON

WESTON

NIOBRARA

CONVERSE

GOSHEN

PLATTE

LARAMIE

ALBANY

NATRONA

CARBON

BIG HORN

WASHAKIE

HOT SPRINGS

FREMONT

PARK

TETON

SUBLETTE

LINCOLN

SWEETWATER

UINTA

Cheyenne

Laramie

Casper

Hulett

Sundance

Moorcroft

Upton

Four Corners

Newcastle

Gillette

Lance Creek

Monville

Lusk

Van Tassel

Joy Em

Albin

Pine Bluffs

Fort Laramie

Lingle

Torrington

Hawk Springs

Horse Creek

Warren

Fox Farm

Orchard Valley

Glendo

Sunrise

Guernsey

Wheatland

Chugwater

Douglas

Orin

Glenrock

Rock River

Foxpark

Medicine Bow

Hanna

Saratoga

Encampment

Clearmont

Buffalo

Story

Sheridan

Ranchester

Dayton

Kaycee

Ten Sleep

Midwest

Edgerton

Powder River

Mountain View

Mills

Paradise Valley

Rawlins

Sinclair

Lamont

Baggs

Bairoil

Worland

Greybull

Basin

Otto

Cowley

Lovell

Powell

Meeteetse

Cody

Thermopolis

Shoshoni

Riverton

Hudson

Lander

Pavillion

Atlantic City

Jeffrey City

Wamsutter

Bitter Creek

Dubois

Pinedale

Big Piney

Daniel

La Barge

Eden

Winton

Superior

Rock Springs

Granger

Green River

Frontier

Kemmerer

Diamondville

Lyman

Cokeville

Evanston

Moran

Jackson

Wilson

Afton

Yellowstone National Park

Canyon

West Thumb

WYOMING

CASPER COLLEGE   (H-13)
125 College Drive
Casper, Wyoming 82601
Tel: (307) 268-2110; (800) 442-2963; Admissions: (307) 268-2110; Fax: (307) 268-2611

Description: The two-year college, founded in 1945, is accredited by the North Central Association of Colleges and Schools. The college operates on the semester system and offers one summer session. Enrollment includes 2,119 full-time and 1,798 part-time students. A faculty of 132 full-time and 60 in the evening school gives a faculty-student ratio of 1-20.

Entrance Requirements: High school graduation required; open enrollment policy for residents. High school graduation with C average or better for nonresidents; ACT recommended; non-high school graduates considered; advanced placement, delayed admission, early admission, early decision, and rolling admission plans available.

Costs Per Year: $880 tuition; $1,200 nonresident tuition; $2,330 room and board.

Collegiate Environment: The college consists of 28 buildings on the 175-acre campus; it boasts one of the finest higher educational plants and facilities of any two-year college in the Rocky Mountain region. The library was completed in June, 1967, and contains a collection of 80,000 volumes, 500 periodicals, 800 microforms and 1,200 recordings. Dormitory facilities provide living accommodations for 350 students. 95% of the applicants are accepted. Financial aid is available and 50% of students receive some form of assistance. Classes begin in June, August and January.

Community Environment: Rich in oil and uranium, Casper is Wyoming's leading industrial city. Cattle and sheep ranches in the surrounding area provide the basis for the city's wool and livestock markets. Casper is situated at the foot of Casper Mountain in the approximate geographic center of Wyoming. The climate is invigorating with 300 days of sunshine each year. The community has almost 70 churches, a hospital, library, symphony orchestra, theatre group, and community concert series. Local recreation includes a multi-purpose event center; 8 radio stations, 3 TV stations; 4 large lakes, nearby Rocky Mountains with excellent fishing and hunting, golf, swimming pools, tennis, trap shooting, bowling alleys, city and mountain parks, archery and rifle ranges, theatres, and a ski area. Several rodeos are held here each year, as well as skiing and mountain climbing events.

CENTRAL WYOMING COLLEGE   (H-9)
2660 Peck Avenue
Riverton, Wyoming 82501
Tel: (307) 856-9291; (800) 735-8418 in WY; Admissions: (307) 856-9291 x119; Fax: (307) 856-2264

Description: Founded in 1966, the two-year college is accredited by the North Central Association of Colleges and Schools. It endeavors to meet a wide range of needs and interests by offering the College Transfer Program, the Technical Education Program, and the Career Education Program. The institution maintains a close relationship with the University of Wyoming, which well serves the transfer student. Cooperative education is available in business, horsemanship, and many career and technical areas. Telecourses for credit are available on the local public broadcasting station. The college operates om the semester system and offers one summer session. Enrollment includes 706 full-time and 844 part-time students. A faculty of 50 full-time and 60 part-time provides a faculty-student ratio of 1-14.

Entrance Requirements: Open enrollment policy; high school diploma or GED required prior to graduation from college; ACT recommended; early admission, early decision, midyear admission, and rolling admission plans available.

Costs Per Year: $900 state resident tuition; $2,970 nonresident tuition; $2,338 room and board; $276 student fees.

Collegiate Environment: The 220-acre campus is located within the Wind River Indian Reservation, home of 5,000 Arapahoe and Shoshone Indians. The library contains a collection of 34,603 volumes, 348 periodical subscriptions, 146 microform subscriptions, and 2,500 audiovisual materials. Dormitory facilities accommodate 23 men, 23 women and 156 families. Special financial aid is available for economically disadvantaged students. About 68% of the current student body receives some form of financial assistance.

Community Environment: Located in the lower Wind River Basin, Riverton (population 10,000) is the center of a large farming, lumbering and livestock producing region. The area has a stimulating climate with a summer average temperature of 66 degrees and a winter average of 35 degrees. There are less than 10 inches of rainfall annually. The community is reached by bus and air lines. There are 25 churches, a modern library, 2 hospitals, 3 clinics, and good shopping available. Local recreation facilities include an olympic-size swimming pool, and provide for golf, baseball, bowling, hunting, fishing, boating, water skiing, snow skiing, rock hunting, and hiking. An Antique Museum, the Wind River Indian Reservation, and many national and state parks are of interest. Part-time employment is available for students.

Branch Campuses: Outreach centers offer credit and noncredit classes throughout west-central Wyoming.

EASTERN WYOMING COLLEGE   (J-18)
3200 West C
Torrington, Wyoming 82240
Tel: (307) 532-8200; (800) 658-3195; Fax: (307) 532-8222

Description: Publicly supported junior college is owned and operated by the Eastern Wyoming Community College District. The college is accredited by the North Central Association of Colleges and Schools and the American Veterinary Medical Association. Enrollment is 225 men and 278 women full-time and 1,521 students part-time. A full-time faculty of 43 gives a faculty-student ratio of 1-47. The college operates on the semester system.

Entrance Requirements: Open enrollment policy; high school diploma or equivalent; ACT or SAT required; rolling admission plan available; no application fee.

Costs Per Year: $624 tuition; $1,872 out-of-state; $2,400 room and board; $96 student fees.

Collegiate Environment: The college opened in the fall term of 1968 with a new campus and buildings. The 40-acre campus is located on the northwest side of Torrington. The library contains 25,000 volumes, 300 periodicals, and 1,500 microforms. Dormitory facilities accommodate 44 men and 80 women. 99% of the students applying for admission are accepted including midyear students. Financial aid is available for economically disadvantaged students. 112 scholarships are available, 40 of which are athletic. 80% of students receive financial aid. Classes begin in September and January.

Community Environment: Torrington is located in the southeastern part of the state, and is a small western town in a rural environment. The climate is invigorating.

LARAMIE COUNTY COMMUNITY COLLEGE   (M-17)
1400 East College Drive
Cheyenne, Wyoming 82007
Tel: (307) 778-5222

Description: The college was created by the voters of Laramie County on May 21, 1968, to help fill the need for academic, technical, and community service/continuing education in the county. Wyoming community colleges are approved by the University of Wyoming for transfer of academic credits. Programs are offered in the following divisions: transfer, vocational-technical, and adult continuing education. The semester system is used, and day and evening classes are offered. The college is fully accredited by the North Central Association of Colleges and Schools. Enrollment is 1,200 full-time and 3,100 part-time students. A faculty of 100 full-time and 100 part-time gives a faculty-student ratio of 1-24.

Entrance Requirements: Open enrollment policy; non-high school graduates considered; ACT recommended; $10 application fee.

Costs Per Year: $928 tuition; $2,448 out-of-state; $1,308 Western Undergraduate Exchange (WUE).

Collegiate Environment: The campus is located on a 271-acre site immediately southeast of Cheyenne. Financial aid is available, and a foundation has been established to give financial support to students attending the new community college. The library has 36,000 volumes, 410 periodicals, and 139 microforms. A total of 251 scholarships are available.

Community Environment: Founded in 1867, Cheyenne is the capital of Wyoming. It is located on a rolling plain at the foothills of the Rocky Mountains and has a population of 52,000. The town keeps the spirit of the "Wild West" with its well-known annual Cheyenne Frontier Days celebration held in July. The State Capitol, State Museum, and Cheyenne Art Center are features of the city.

NORTHWEST COLLEGE   *(C-9)*
231 West 6th Street
Powell, Wyoming 82435
Tel: (307) 754-6111; (800) 442-2946; Admissions: (307) 754-6601; Fax: (307) 754-6700

Description: This two-year college was founded in 1946 and offers a transfer program, occupational education program, community service, and adult education programs. Operating on the early semester system with 1 summer session, the college is accredited by the North Central Association of Colleges and Schools. Preprofessional programs are offered in forestry, law, medicine, nursing, optometry, and physical therapy. Enrollment includes 1,100 full-time and 750 part-time students. A faculty of 90 full-time and 60 part-time gives a faculty-student ratio of 1-12.

Entrance Requirements: High school graduation or equivalent; non-high school graduates considered; ACT or SAT required; early admission, early decision, and rolling admission plans available; $10 application fee nonresidents; $25 application fee foreign applicants.

Costs Per Year: $1,060 tuition; $2,580 out-of-state; $2,764 room and board.

Collegiate Environment: The 90-acre campus with 29 buildings is just 70 miles from Yellowstone Park and is surrounded by mountains on 3 sides. The library contains 35,000 volumes, 300 periodicals, and 975 audiovisual materials. Dormitory facilities provide living accommodations for 350 men and 350 women. Approximately 90% of students applying for admission are accepted, including midyear students, and 62% of the previous freshman class returns to the college for the second year. Average high school standing of a recent freshman class was in the top 50%; 20% were in the top quarter; and 30% ranked in the second quarter. Of the 180 available scholarships, 140 were granted to freshmen. 70% of the current student body receives financial aid. Classes begin in August and January.

Community Environment: A clean and attractive community of 6,000 people, Powell owes its growth to the development of irrigated farmlands and to the discovery of local oil and gas fields. This is basically a rural area with dry, temperate climate. The community is accessible by a bus branch line and major highways. There are a public library, several churches, a modern hospital, and major civic, fraternal and veteran's organizations to serve the area. Some part-time employment is available. Nearby areas provide good hunting, fishing, and lakes for water sports.

SHERIDAN COLLEGE   *(B-12)*
Sheridan, Wyoming 82801
Tel: (307) 674-6446; (800) 913-9139; Fax: (307) 674-7205

Description: This two-year school, founded in 1948, is a comprehensive community college that is dedicated to serving the citizens of the area. The institution provides transfer and occupational programs leading to the Associate degree and/or the Certificate. The college operates on the semester system and offers one summer session. Enrollment is 993 full-time and 1,515 part-time students. An additional 2,500 individuals participate in the college's noncredit continuing education and community service offerings. A faculty of 81 full-time and 75 part-time gives a faculty-student ratio of 1-20. Sheridan College is accredited by the North Central Association of Colleges and Schools.

Entrance Requirements: Open enrollment policy for residents; non-high school graduates considered; early admission, rolling admission, and midyear admission plans available.

Costs Per Year: $844 tuition and fees; $2,244 out-of-state; $2,600 room and board; $36 student insurance; $450 average book expenses.

Collegiate Environment: The campus consists of 19 buildings situated on 64 acres just south of the town of Sheridan and has been planned to make maximum use of the natural beauty of the setting. The building program has been geared to student growth. Additions to the original Whitney building have been made to accommodate growth in the Allied Health, Business, Fine Arts, and Student Services areas. In 1977 a new Technical Center was constructed and a 12,000 diesel area added in 1981. The Mohns Center classroom and observatory opened in 1980 and the Griffith Memorial Building opened in 1982, which houses the 54,650-volume library, instructional resources and learning skills center. A new PE Center and Science Center were opened in 1983 and new family housing was completed in 1985. Dormitory housing accomodates 160 students. The college participates in federal financial assistance programs and also qualifies for veteran's benefits. Approximately 65% of the students currently receive some form of financial assistance. A variety of student clubs are available for students to pursue professional or recreational interests.

Community Environment: The town of Sheridan is located in northeastern Wyoming at the foot of the scenic Big Horn Mountains. The Big Horns rise to 13,165 feet above Sheridan's 3,745-foot elevation and provide year-round opportunities for outdoor recreation from wilderness hiking to rock climbing, skiing, camping, hunting and fishing. With a population of about 17,000, Sheridan retains an atmosphere of small-town friendliness while offering its citizens many fine services. The YMCA, Sheridan Recreation District, and other organizations provide activities for all ages. The community also supports a number of high-quality programs for the visual and performing arts.

UNIVERSITY OF WYOMING   *(M-15)*
Box 3435
Laramie, Wyoming 82071
Tel: (307) 766-5160; (800) 342-5996; Fax: (307) 766-4042

Description: Founded in 1886, the university is a land-grant institution and is Wyoming's only four-year institution of higher learning. The institution is accredited by the North Central Association of Colleges and Schools. The various colleges encompass the fields of agriculture, arts and sciences, business, education, engineering, health sciences, and law. The university grants the Bachelor's, Master's, and Doctoral degrees and postgraduate certification. It operates on the semester system and offers one summer session. Air Force and Army ROTC are available as electives. Enrollment includes 8,942 full-time and 3,078 part-time students. A faculty of 635 full-time and 103 part-time gives an overall faculty-student ratio of 1-18.

Entrance Requirements: High school graduation or equivalent; completion of 4 units English, 3 mathematics, 3 science, and 3 cultural context required as of fall 1995; open enrollment policy for Wyoming high school graduates as freshmen; early decision, rolling admission, and advanced placement plans available; ACT or SAT must be submitted before final admission for freshmen; $30 application fee.

Costs Per Year: $1,908 tuition; $5,988 nonresident; $3,422 room and board.

Collegiate Environment: The campus, comprising 753 acres, is located a few blocks from the center of Laramie. The library contains a collection of more than 1.2 million bound volumes, 7,000 periodical titles, 1,336,188 microforms and 3,000 films. Through the CARL library computer system, students have access to library holdings of several other Rocky Mountain universities. The residence halls provide living accommodations for 2,300 men and women, and university apartments house 428 married students. Fraternities and sororities accommodate 287 men and 263 women. 5,800 scholarships are available, 1,400 of which are specifically for freshmen. 71% of the students receive some form of financial aid. The university welcomes a geographically diverse student body, and midyear students are accepted. Average score of the freshman class was 23 composite and average GPA was 3.3.

Community Environment: Named for Jacques LaRamie, an early trapper for the American Fur Company, Laramie was established in 1868. Today, the community is known as the "Gem City of the Plains." The mean annual temperature is 42 degrees. The city is accessible by airlines, Amtrak, and bus lines. 24 churches in the area represent 20 different religious denominations. A full-service hospital, library, and civic and fraternal organizations serve the community. Local recreation includes the Snowy Range ski area, 3 movie theaters, bowling alleys, golf, and nearby parks. An annual rodeo and jubilee are held in July. Hunting and fishing opportunities are excellent near Laramie.

WESTERN WYOMING COMMUNITY COLLEGE *(L-8)*
2500 College Drive
Rock Springs, Wyoming 82901
Tel: (307) 382-1600; Fax: (307) 382-1636

Description: The college was established in 1959 as a community institution to serve Sweetwater County and western Wyoming. It is accredited by the North Central Association of Colleges and Schools and by the University of Wyoming. It grants the Associate degree. It operates on the semester system. Enrollment includes 1,151 full-time and 1,646 part-time students. A faculty of 72 full-time and 115 part-time gives a faculty-student ratio of 1-18.

Entrance Requirements: Open enrollment policy; ACT or SAT recommended; non-high school graduates considered; early admission, early decision, midyear admission, rolling admission, and advanced placement plans available.

Costs Per Year: $863 tuition; $2,173 out-of-state; $2,050 room and board.

Collegiate Environment: The 380-acre campus, completed for the 1968-69 school year, consists of 6 buildings with modern facilities and equipment. The college recently completed a $63 million expansion that tripled the size of the campus. The library contains 30,000 volumes and 1,500 periodicals, and on-campus apartments accommodate 270 men and women. All students applying for admission are accepted, including midyear students, and 60% of the previous freshman class return to the college for the second year. Average high school standing of a recent freshman class, top 50%; average scores, ACT 18.9. Financial aid is available for economically disadvantaged students, and 420 scholarships are available. The college awarded 35 Certificate and 130 Associate degrees to a recent graduating class. Classes begin in August and January.

Community Environment: This is a rural area with cold, dry climate. Airlines, railroad, bus lines, and Routes 30, 1-80, and 191 make the city accessible. There are a public library, churches of major denominations, a hospital, and a mental health clinic serving the community. Local recreation includes theatres, drive-in, bowling, hunting, fishing, and hiking, and nearby attractions include Yellowstone and Grand Teton National Parks, Flaming Gorge National Recreation Area, the Wind River Mountains and the Bridger Wilderness. Some part-time work is available. Major civic and fraternal organizations are active in the community. The city has adequate shopping facilities. A county fair is held annually.

U.S. TERRITORIES

COLLEGE OF MICRONESIA - FSM
P.O. Box 159, Kolonia, Ponape Island
Federated States of Micronesia
Trust Territory, U.S. Territories 96941
Tel: (691) 320-2480; Fax: (691) 320-2479

Description: Formerly the Micronesian Teacher Education Center, the college was established in 1963 to educate elementary teachers employed by the Trust Territory of the Pacific Islands; the program was administered by the University of Hawaii in cooperation with the Trust Territory Government. In 1970 the Center was renamed the Community College of Micronesia with the Trust Territory Government taking increasing responsibility for the administration, and the University of Hawaii involvement was phased out by July 1971. When the name of the Trust Territory became the Federated States of Micronesia, the name was changed to College of Micronesia - FSM. The College is a degree granting, postsecondary institution operating on the semester system with 1 summer session; it is accredited by the Western Association of Schools and Colleges. Enrollment is 519 students with a faculty of 35 providing a teacher-student ratio of 1-15.

Entrance Requirements: High school graduation or GED; 10 high school units required including 4 English, 2 mathematics, 2 science, 2 social studies; entrance exam required; delayed admission plan available. The deadline for submission of applications for the fall term is June 15. $10 application fee.

Costs Per Year: $2,160 tuition; $3,912 room and board; $145 student fees.

Collegiate Environment: Presently located on a 2-acre interim campus in Kolonia, the college complex has grown from 5 prefabricated metal buildings to an acceptable combination of buildings and other facilities capable of supporting 500 students. The library houses 22,400 volumes, 120 periodicals, 60 microforms, 1,290 audiovisual materials, and more than 1,500 titles of U.S. Government depository. There is housing on campus for 100 men and 50 women. Each state/entity has an extension center that offers college courses. Approximately 30% of the applicants are accepted into degree programs. All students receive some form of financial aid.

Community Environment: The community served by the college is scattered throughout some 3 million square miles of ocean. Students come from the 3 political entities of Micronesia, also known as the Republic of Palau, Republic of Marshall Islands, and the Federated States of Micronesia. Students represent a diversity of cultural backgrounds and speak 1 or more of the 9 major languages or numerous dialects.

PANAMA CANAL COLLEGE
DOODS-PAN APO, U.S. Territories 34002
Tel: (507) 52-3107; Admissions: (507) 52-3107; Fax: (507) 52-1555

Description: This 2-year college, founded in 1933 as Canal Zone Junior College, provides higher education for dependents of U.S. personnel, as well as Panamanians, equal to that available in the U.S. It is accredited by the Middle States Association of Colleges and Schools. The college adopted its present name in 1979 when it became a division of the Department of Defense Dependent School System. Plans are now underway to transition the college to a private four-year American University. It offers a broad-based liberal arts program resulting in Associate in Arts and Associate in Science degrees. The college is a member of SOC and SOCAD programs. It operates on a 15-week early semester system and offers one six-week summer session and one six-week inter-semester. Five nine-week terms are offered on military installations as part of the SOCAD program. Enrollment includes 162 full-time and 1,434 part-time students with a faculty of 10 full-time.

Entrance Requirements: High school graduation or equivalent; English placement test required for foreign students; open enrollment.

Costs Per Year: $1,432 U.S. dependents tuition; $6,364 non-dependents tuition.

Collegiate Environment: Situated along the banks of the Canal under the Bridge of the Americas, the college facilities consist of the Learning Resource Center which houses 50,000 titless, 150 periodicals and 25,000 audiovisual materials, a 3-story academic building, a gymnasium, an auditorium, a weight training room, and a track and field. Limited financial assistance is available. All applicants are accepted, including midyear students.

Community Environment: The college is located on the Pacific side of the Panama Canal, within the town of La Boca.

UNIVERSITY OF THE VIRGIN ISLANDS
Charlotte Amalie
Saint Thomas, U.S. Territories 00802
Tel: (809) 693-1150

Description: Established in 1962 by the government of the Virgin Islands to meet the need for higher education in the Virgin Islands and the Caribbean; it seeks to be of service to this area in much the same capacity as state colleges and universities serve their states and regions on the mainland. Founded on the established traditions of American higher education, the University seeks to accommodate these traditions to the location and cultural background which characterize the Virgin Islands and other islands of the Caribbean. It is accredited by the Middle States Association of Colleges and Schools. It offers a four-year baccalaureate curriculum to provide students with an education for leadership in such fields as teaching, government and business; also offered are two-year occupational programs and a Master's degree programs in teacher education, business and public administration. It operates on the semester system and offers one summer session Enrollment includes 1,299 full-time, 1,564 part-time undergraduates, and 329 graduate students. A faculty of 93 full-time and 100 part-time gives an undergraduate faculty-student ratio of 1-15. Another campus is located on Saint Croix.

Entrance Requirements: High school graduation or GED; high school graduates with a C average accepted, high school units required are 4 English, and 2 math; early admission, midyear admission, rolling admission and advanced placement plans available; deadline for submission of applications for the fall term is April 15; $20 application fee.

Costs Per Year: $1,650 tuition; $4,950 nonresidents; $4,510 room and board; $105 student fees.

Collegiate Environment: The 175-acre campus currently includes the Ralph M. Paiewonsky Library that houses more than 71,000 hardbound volumes, 4 academic buildings, residence halls with accommodations for 246 students, a student center, the Classroom-Administration Building, a field house, and the Reichhold Center for the Arts. The campus includes a 9-hole golf course, beach facilities, tennis courts and playing fields. The Caribbean Research Institute, a division of the university, has environmental laboratories and facilities including a Virgin Islands Ecological Research Station at Lamshur Bay on St. John. Financial aid is available. 80% of the students receive some form of assistance.

Canadian Colleges

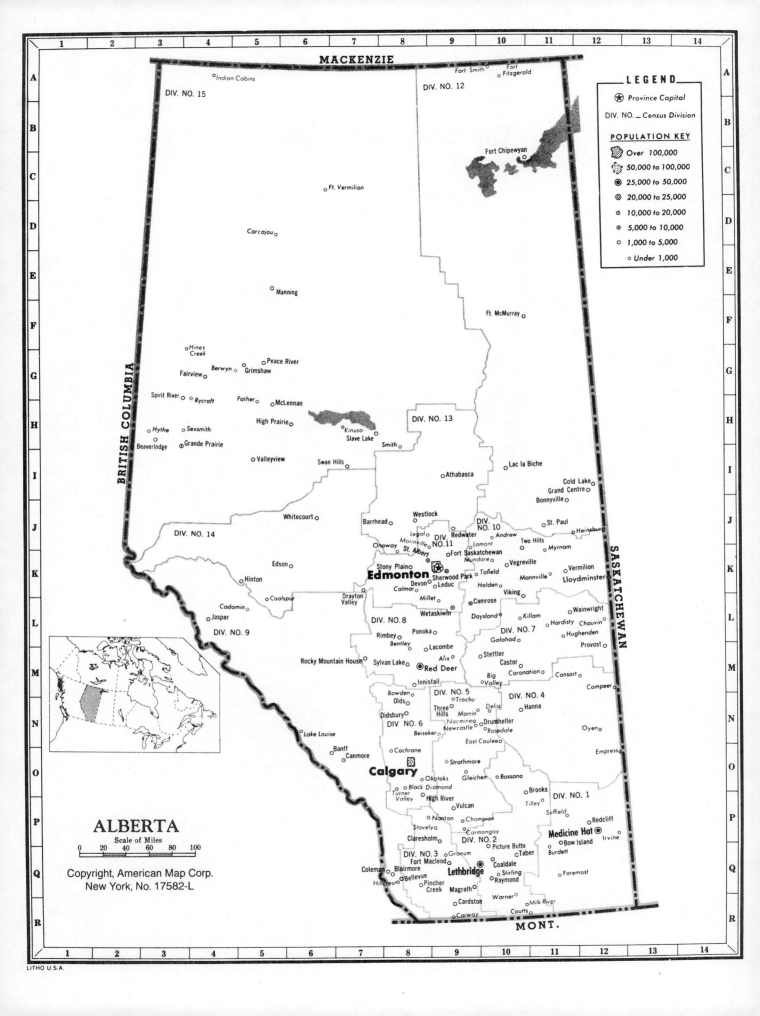

ALBERTA

MACKENZIE

DIV. NO. 15

DIV. NO. 12

Indian Cabins

Fort Smith
Fort Fitzgerald

Fort Chipewyan

Ft. Vermilion

Carcajou

Manning

Ft. McMurray

Hines Creek
Peace River
Berwyn
Fairview
Grimshaw
Spirit River
Rycroft
Falher
McLennan
High Prairie
Hythe
Sexsmith
Kinuso
Beaverlodge
Grande Prairie
Slave Lake
Smith
Valleyview
Swan Hills

DIV. NO. 13

Athabasca
Lac la Biche

Cold Lake
Grand Centre
Bonnyville

Whitecourt
Barrhead
Westlock
DIV. NO. 10
St. Paul
Legal
Redwater
Andrew
Two Hills
Heinsburg
Onoway
Morinville
DIV. NO. 11
Lamont
Myrnam
Edson
St. Albert
Fort Saskatchewan
Vegreville
Vermilion
Hinton
Stony Plain
Mundare
Lloydminster
Edmonton
Sherwood Park
Tofield
Mannville
Cadomin
Coalspur
Devon
Leduc
Holden
Calmar
Millet
Camrose
Viking
Jasper
Drayton Valley
Wetaskiwin
Daysland
Killam
Wainwright
DIV. NO. 14
DIV. NO. 8
Ponoka
DIV. NO. 7
Hardisty
Chauvin
Rimbey
Bentley
Lacombe
Galahad
Hughenden
DIV. NO. 9
Alix
Stettler
Provost
Rocky Mountain House
Sylvan Lake
Red Deer
Castor
Coronation
Consort
Innisfail
Big Valley
Compeer

Lake Louise
Bowden
Olds
DIV. NO. 5
Trochu
DIV. NO. 4
Hanna
Three Hills
Morrin
Delia
Banff
Canmore
Didsbury
Nacmine
Drumheller
Oyen
DIV. NO. 6
Beiseker
Newcastle
Rosedale
Cochrane
East Couleeo
Empress

Strathmore
Calgary
Okotoks
Gleichen
Bassano
Black Diamond
Brooks
DIV. NO. 1
Turner Valley
High River
Vulcan
Tilley
Suffield
Nanton
Champion
Redcliff
Staveloy
Carmangay
Medicine Hat
Irvine
Claresholm
DIV. NO. 2
Picture Butte
Bow Island
Burdett
DIV. NO. 3
Graum
Taber
Fort Macleod
Coaldale
Coleman
Blairmore
Lethbridge
Stirling
Hillcrest
Bellevue
Raymond
Foremost
Pincher Creek
Magrath
Warner
Milk River
Cardston
Coutts
Carway

MONT.

BRITISH COLUMBIA

SASKATCHEWAN

Scale of Miles
0 20 40 60 80 100

LEGEND
⊛ Province Capital
DIV. NO. — Census Division

POPULATION KEY
Over 100,000
50,000 to 100,000
25,000 to 50,000
20,000 to 25,000
10,000 to 20,000
5,000 to 10,000
1,000 to 5,000
Under 1,000

ALBERTA

ATHABASCA UNIVERSITY   (K-9)
P.O. Box 10,000
Athabasca, Alberta T0G 2R0
Tel: (403) 675-6168; Fax: (403) 675-6174

Description: The university was established in 1972 by Order in Council under the Statues of the Province of Alberta and gained permanent status as self-governing post-secondary degree-granting institution in 1978. It is a member of the Association of Universities and Colleges of Canada, the Association of Commonwealth Universities, and the International Council for Distance Education. It is dedicated to the removal of barriers that traditionally restrict access to and success in university-level studies, and to increasing equality of educational opportunity for all adult Canadians regardless of their geographical location and prior academic credentials. In common with all universities, it is committed to excellence in teaching, research and scholarship, and to being of service to the general public. There are 11,353 undergraduates and 180 undergraduate students enrolled with 277 faculty members. It grants degrees and university certificates at the undergraduate level and Masters and provides for transfer of credit both to and from other institutions. There is no set term system; however, in general, each 3-credit course must be completed within a 6-month period, and each 6-credit course must be completed within a 12-month period. Courses begin on the first of every month.

Entrance Requirements: Open admissions policy; students are admitted at any time; applicants must be eighteen years of age or older and a Canadian resident; $55 Canadian application fee.

Costs Per Year: $370 per 3-credit course; $520 per 6-credit course; $650 foreign student 3-credit course; $1,110 foreign student 6-credit course.

Collegiate Environment: The university's approach to learning is nontraditional, operating on the open distance learning concept. It is open to all adult students regardless of the level of formal education they have attained previously; it is a university without a residential campus, its campus being wherever its students live. The university's central campus is in Athabasca. Learning Centers are located in Edmonton, Calgary, and Fort McMurray. The university has a collection of 110,506 volumes and 1,200 periodicals. Volumes of those books are listed as supplementary reading in courses. There is no student housing.

Community Environment: The central campus is located in a small rural town (population 2,000) in the northern section of the province. Learning Centers are located in larger urban centres.

Branch Campuses: Learning Centers in Edmonton, Calgary and Fort McMurray.

AUGUSTANA UNIVERSITY COLLEGE   (L-9)
4901 46th Street
Camrose, Alberta T4V 2R3
Tel: (403) 679-1100; (800) 661-8714; Admissions: (403) 679-1132; Fax: (403) 679-1129

Description: A coeducational, undergraduate university of the Evangelical Lutheran Church in Canada, Augustana welcomes students of all faiths. Founded in 1910 by Scandinavian pioneers, it was once a high school, then a junior college, and in 1985 became the first private institution in Alberta to receive degree-granting authority. In recognition of its enhanced status, it became the province's first and only university college in 1989. Students in the three-year general degree program major in any of 20 subjects; in six of these disciplines, a four-year special degree program also is offered. Modest in size, Augustana seeks to offer an uncommon educational experience: it focuses on meeting the needs of each student; concerns itself with the student's total growth; teaches exclusively the liberal arts and sci-

ences; emphasizes effective teaching; offers a values-oriented education; and fashions a strong sense of community. It operates on the semester calendar system. Enrollment includes 922 full-time and 312 part-time students. A faculty of 60 gives a faculty-student ratio of 1-15.

Entrance Requirements: Students with matriculation standing must present five Grade 12 subjects or equivalents, including English; an average of at least 60% is required in these subjects, with no mark below 50%; August 1 is the deadline for application for the fall term; December 1 for the winter term; early admiaaion, midyear admission and rolling admission plans available; $30 application fee.

Costs Per Year: $4,834 tuition; $6,446 nonresident; $3,934-$4,434 room and board.

Collegiate Environment: A five-minute walk from downtown Camrose, the university college's 40-acre campus overlooks Golden Jubilee Park in Stoney Creek Valley. Its 15 buildings include a new campus center, and Founder's Hall, an Alberta historic site. A residential school, two-thirds of its students, 560 men and women, live on campus in seven residences. Library holdings include 82,000 volumes. Augustana fashions a strong sense of community: its members work to turn the campus into a supportive, hospitable place. Approximately 270 scholarships are available and 75% of the students receive some form of financial aid.

Community Environment: Camrose, a city of 14,000, is a service center for Alberta's Aspen Parklands. A family-oriented community, it is an education center, as well; it is home to two other postsecondary schools in addition to Augustana. It is fifty miles southeast of Edmonton, Alberta's capital, and 50 minutes from Edmonton International Airport, which is served by seven airlines. Greyhound Canada operates 19 trips a week each way between Edmonton and Camrose.

FAIRVIEW COLLEGE   (G-4)
Box 3000
Fairview, Alberta T0H 1L0
Tel: (403) 835-6600; Admissions: (403) 835-6605; Fax: (403) 835-6698

Description: The college is a maximum two-year, career oriented school offering programs in agriculture, business and trades. Operating on the semester system, the curriculum attempts to provide for individual differences. Abilities will be further developed by continued study and on-the-job training and experience. The school attracts students from the region, the province, other provinces, and other countries. Enrollment includes approximately 1,500 students annually with a faculty of 110.

Entrance Requirements: Usually high school graduation for 1- and 2-year programs; adult status considered with relevant work or life experience; admission varies for shorter programs; fall and winter intakes vary by program; rolling admission and advanced placement plans available; $20 (Canadian dollars) application fee.

Costs Per Year: $1,000 tuition; $2,000 nonresident tuition; $5,000 room and board; $102 student fees; course specific fees from $20 to $2,500 for certain courses. (All fees in Canadian dollars).

Collegiate Environment: The college offers an excellent variety of student housing ranging from single rooms and 2- and 3-bedroom apartments to family housing units. The total residential capacity is 504 students. Recreational facilities include a fully equipped gymnasium, two weight rooms, a games room, an on-campus 3-hole golf course, playing fields, a sauna, squash and racquet ball courts, a fishing/boating/skating pond, and a jogging trail. Active student leadership and participation has resulted in a variety of year-round social and recreational functions. The college also boasts excellent on-campus counselling and health services. The library houses 52,773 hardbound volumes, 363 periodicals, and 12,000 additional items. A new 300-seat concert hall attracts music, dance, and theatre.

Community Environment: This is the "Heart" of the Peace River country, the most northerly agricultural area in North America. The region boasts spectacular scenery and offers some of the best hunting, fishing, and canoeing on the continent. Ample opportunities exist in the town of Fairview for shopping, dining, and recreational activities (biking, biking trails, outdoor swimming pool, curling rink, playing fields, etc.).

LETHBRIDGE COMMUNITY COLLEGE   *(Q-9)*
Lethbridge, Alberta T1K 1L6
Tel: (403) 320-3200; Admissions: (403) 329-7235; Fax: (403) 320-1461

Description: After ten years of planning, the Lethbridge Junior College officially opened in 1957. From 1962 to 1967, increasing pressures were put on the provincial government for the establishment of a full degree-granting liberal arts university in Lethbridge. On January 1, 1967, the University of Lethbridge was established and on July 1, 1967, it absorbed the university section of the College. Left with the technical-vocational programs, the College was steadily developing into a true "community college." In 1969, the name was officially changed to Lethbridge Community College as a new provincial Colleges Act deleted the term "junior" from the name of all public colleges. Lethbridge Community College uses a semester system for 37 programs within the divisions of Business and Industry, Science and Technologies, and Continuing Studies. The College enrolls 3,000 full-time and 1,000 part-time students. A faculty of 163 provides a faculty-student ratio of 1-25. The division of Continuing Studies processes 30,000 registrations annually.

Entrance Requirements: High school graduation; open enrollment policy.

Costs Per Year: Specific information on request.

Collegiate Environment: Until 1962 the College was housed in the Lethbridge Collegiate Institute. Then, in 1962, a building was constructed on the present campus. The building has been enlarged since then to meet continually expanding programs. The main College campus offers some of Western Canada's finest training facilities. The Trades and Technologies complex was opened in 1983 and offers state-of-the-art equipment for instruction in the many trades and engineering technology programs. The College Centre, officially opened in 1985, features an expanded library, Student Services, Bookstore and administrative area. An $11.4-million Physical Education Complex was officially opened in February 1990. A $5.0-million Food Services area was scheduled for completion in January 1991. On-campus housing is available for 255.

Community Environment: Lethbridge is Alberta's third largest city (61,000) and is situated on the banks of the Oldman River, approximately 100 kilometers north of the U.S. border. The Southern Alberta is rich in agricultural and mineral resources. Special features include the Sir Alexander Galt Museum, Japanese Gardens, and several historic sites.

Branch Campuses: Thirteen additional off-campus learning centers provide instruction to residents throughout Southern Alberta. Teleconferencing and correspondence programs also spread LCC education opportunities throughout North America.

NORTHERN ALBERTA INSTITUTE OF TECHNOLOGY *(K-9)*
11762 106th Street
Edmonton, Alberta T5G 2R1
Tel: (403) 471-7411

Description: A two-year government-supported institute, the Northern Alberta Institute of Technology was established in 1962. Its primary objectives are career preparation and individual development. Preparation for a career is provided through the organized and structured presentation of theoretical and practical material through lecture, lab, CMC and other methodologies. Personal development is achieved through the informal and voluntary participation in any of the many student activities on campus. Enrollment is 7,200 full-time and 300 part-time students. Faculty numbers 800.

Entrance Requirements: Vary from a grade X to a high school diploma; primarily a high school diploma with the need for key subjects such as English, Math, Physics, Chemistry, depending on the program; advanced placement, early admission, and rolling admission plans available; ten programs have multiple intakes.

Costs Per Year: $1,100 tuition; $2,200 nonresident; $97 student fees.

Collegiate Environment: NAIT is a modern multicampus institution. Its main campus buildings are located on A 46-acre site adjacent to the Industrial Airport and close to downtown Edmonton. Included are laboratories, shops, classrooms, administrative offices and many service areas. The library houses 71,000 hardbound volumes, 528 periodicals and more than 4,000 additional materials. There are 287 scholarships available, 15 of which are for freshmen.

Community Environment: See University of Alberta.

OLDS COLLEGE   *(N-8)*
Olds, Alberta T0M 1P0
Tel: (403) 556-8281; Fax: (403) 556-4711

Description: A two-year diploma agricultural college established in 1913, Olds is administered by a board of governors and funded by Alberta Advanced Education. Programs offered at Olds emphasize the specialized nature of farm enterprises, the business aspects of farming, and the operation and maintenance of farming equipment. Transitional voacational programs are also offered. The college operates on the semester system. Enrollment includes 1,000 full-time and 30 part-time students. A faculty of 83 provides a faculty-student ratio of 1-20.

Entrance Requirements: High school graduation or GED; high school graduates with a C average accepted plus specific program requirements; open enrollment; early decision, rolling admission and advanced placment plans available.

Costs Per Year: $676 tuition; $1,242 tuition foreign students; $440/month room and board. Fees and charges are subject to change without notice.

Collegiate Environment: The 1,200-acre campus includes a well-equipped and stocked farm that meets all the needs of agricultural instruction and applied research. The library contains 36,200 volumes, 344 periodical subscriptions and more than 33,000 additional materials. There is student housing on campus for 500 men and women. 83 scholarships are available.

Community Environment: Located at the center of a very rich and productive farming area, Olds is midway between Calgary and Red Deer and within striking distance of the Canadian Rockies.

RED DEER COLLEGE   *(M-8)*
P.O. Box 5005
Red Deer, Alberta T4N 5H5
Tel: (403) 342-3300; Admissions: (403) 342-3400; Fax: (403) 340-8940

Description: Established in 1964 under provisions of the Colleges Act of the Province of Alberta, the philosophy of the College is eclectic in nature in that its objectives are to provide both general education and career training for all students. Furthermore, it is intended that the College adhere to an open-door policy of admission insofar as this is possible, and in keeping with the comprehensiveness of the definition of a two-year public institution. The college operates on the semester system andoffers two summer sessions. Enrollment includes 1,527 men and 2,815 women. A faculty of 322 provides a faculty-student ratio of 1-15.

Entrance Requirements: High school graduation; open enrollment policy; early admission, early decision, rolling admission, deferred admission, and advanced placement admission plans available. Early application is advised. $25 application fee Canadian permanent resident, $40 fee International Student.

Costs Per Year: $772.50 ($51.50/credit) Canadian citizens and permanent residents; $1,493 ($99.50/credit) international students.

Collegiate Environment: Red Deer College is situated in a rich and vibrant area of Alberta. The energy sector and agriculture industry provide the base for keeping the Red Deer area economy strong. The graduates of the career, vocational and university transfer programs are able to find employment in their chosen careers. The campus includes a 580 seat performing arts centre, a 125,000 hardbound volume library collection, athletic and fitness facilities, a child care centre, a cafeteria and student residences for 409 singles, families and the disabled, in addition to the teaching facilities. 60% of all applicants are accepted. Nearly 200 scholarships, totalling $175,000 are available, annually. The provincial and federal governments financially assist 60%-65% of the students who attend Red Deer College.

Community Environment: Red Deer is located in Central Alberta approximately equidistant from the two major cities of Alberta, Calgary and Edmonton.

UNIVERSITY OF ALBERTA   *(K-9)*
Administration Bldg., Room 120
Edmonton, Alberta T6G 2M7
Tel: (403) 492-3113; Fax: (403) 492-7172

Description: The University of Alberta is a publicly funded coeducational nondenominational institution established in 1906 at the first session of the legislature of Alberta. Classes opened in September 1908, in what is now Queen Alexandra School, with 45 students and a faculty of 5. It is a member of the Association of Commonwealth Universities and the Association of Universities and Colleges of Canada. The academic year runs from September to April with one intersession, consisting of two 6-week terms. Enrollment is 22,213 full-time and 3,194 part-time students. A full-time faculty of 1,401 provides a faculty-student ratio of 1-10.

Entrance Requirements: High school graduation; completion of college preparatory courses including a full course of English at the grade 12 level; GRE required for graduate school in selected departments only; rolling admission and advanced placement plans available; $50 application fee.

Costs Per Year: $1,610 tuition for fall session; $1,952 engineering; $2,357 medicine and dentistry; students who are not Canadian citizens or permanent residents are required to pay additional 100% of course, program, library and computing services fees; $3,215 room and board double occupancy; $256 student fees.

Collegiate Environment: The campus is situated on a 15-acre site, two miles southwest of downtown. There are 30 major buildings on site, including the University Hospital Complex, North Alberta Jubilee Auditorium, and a wide variety of associated institutes. Facilities include one of the largest academic library systems in Canada, which houses 3.4 million hardbound volumes. Undergraduate scholarships are available to all continuing students; a limited number of graduate assistantships are available within the departments offering graduate work. Seven separate complexes provide housing for approximately 4,300 students. Students are admitted in September only.

Community Environment: Edmonton is the provincial capital of Alberta, the province's largest city with a population of 760,000. It takes its name from Fort Edmonton, an early trading post of the Hudson Bay Company. The city is the center of an important farming region, and is an oil and gas exploration and manufacturing center. Major industries include pipeline construction, chemical plants, meat packing, construction, oilfield construction and servicing, and food processing. The city was the first to establish a municipal airport and has long been the Gateway to the North; it is easily accessible by air, rail, bus and car. It is also home to the Alberta Research Council and Edmonton Research Park.

UNIVERSITY OF CALGARY   *(O-8)*
2500 University Drive, N.W.
Calgary, Alberta T2N 1N4
Tel: (403) 220-5110; Admissions: (403) 220-6645; Fax: (403) 289-1253

Description: The University of Calgary had its origin in 1945 when the former Normal School became a branch of the Faculty of Education of the University of Alberta in Edmonton. A year later, the education faculty was moved to the present campus of the Southern Alberta Institute of Technology and courses in arts and sciences were offered to education students. In 1947, the first two years of a four-year Bachelor of Education program was offered and in 1951, a branch of the Faculty of Arts and Science was established in Calgary. In 1960, the University moved to its present campus in the northwest area of the city; in 1964, it gained autonomy in academic matters and in 1966 it gained full autonomy. A coeducational, nondenominational, government-supported institution, the University is a member of the Association of Universities of the British Commonwealth, the Association of Universities and Colleges of Canada, and the International Association of Universities. The university operates on the semester system and offers two summer sessions. Enrollment includes 15,904 full-time and 3,095 part-time undergraduates and 2,886 graduate students. A faculty of 1,303 full-time and 860 part-time gives a faculty student ratio of 1-10.

Entrance Requirements: High school graduation with 20 academic units required; units include 4 English, 4 mathematics, 4 social science, 4 science, 3 foreign language; SAT I with 400V, 400M minimum, and three appropriate SAT II tests (overall minimum average of 500 required on all 5 tests) required of United States applicants; GRE required for graduate school; students are admitted at midyear; deadline for submission of applications for the fall term is June 1 for most faculties (earlier for limited enrollment faculties); $60 application fee.

Costs Per Year: $2,660 tuition; $5,320 nonresident; $2,900-$4,300 room and board; $348 student fees.

Collegiate Environment: The 122-hectare campus, located in the northwest section of Calgary, has grown from two buildings in 1960 to 30 well-equipped facilities today for teaching, research, and continuing education. The University Libraries contain over 1,900,000 volumes of books, journals, documents, and other print materials, 2,600,000 microforms, more than 1,300,000 items in collections of architecture plans, maps, and air photos, and audiovisual materials. About 13,600 serials are on current subscription. Residence halls accomodate 1,150 students and there 250 student family housing units. Athletic facilities incude the continent's only covered speedskating oval, 2 hockey rinks, tennis courts, a triple gymnasium, the city's largest racquet center, an olympic-size swimming pool, a weight room, jogging tracks, and a huge, indoor climbing wall.

Community Environment: Calgary is the head office stronghold of Canada's oil, gas and sulphur industries. Increasingly, Calgary is becoming a major center for financial activities. Manufacturing, tourism, and agriculture also support the city's economy. Calgary is home to more than 738,184 people, which makes it Canada's fifth largest city. Cultural activities abound in Calgary. The city has a philharmonic orchestra, as well as theater and dance companies, museums, art galleries, libraries, and a planetarium.

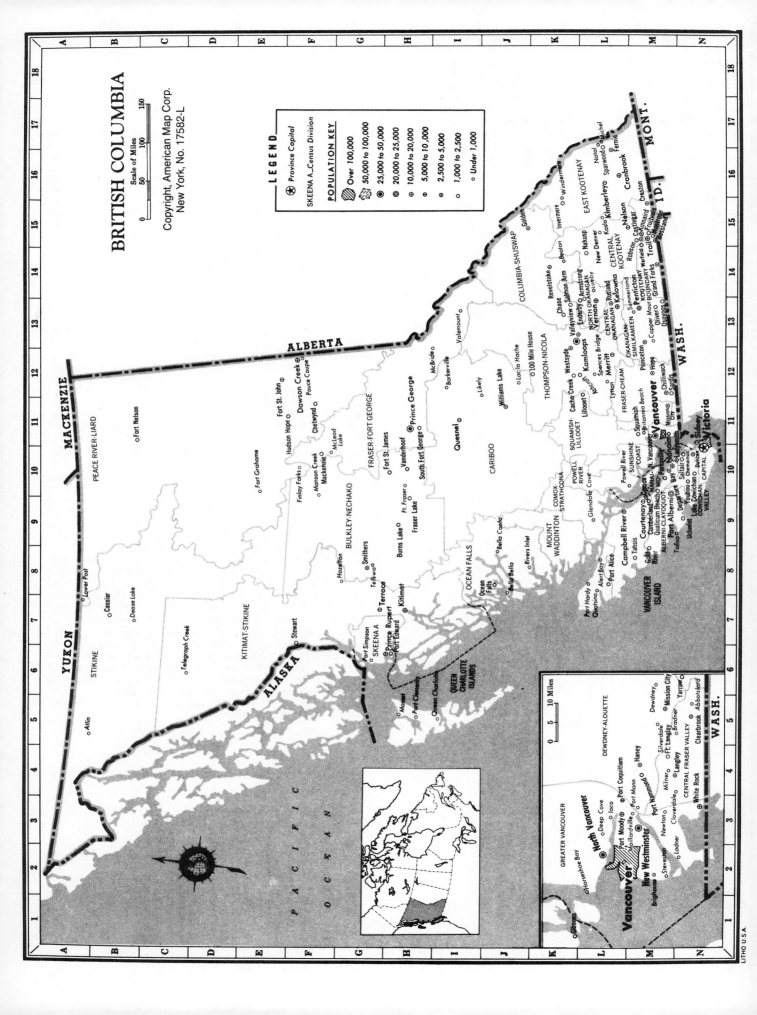

BRITISH COLUMBIA

CAPILANO COLLEGE   *(M-11)*
2055 Purcell Way
North Vancouver, British Columbia V7J 3H5
Tel: (604) 986-1911; Admissions: (604) 984-4913; Fax: (604) 984-4985

Description: A two-year liberal arts and career program college established in 1968, Capilano College has grown both in size and prestige, offering programs in academic studies (2-year university transfer) and in career/vocational (2-year diploma or 1-year certificate). The college also offers post-baccalaureate programs in Environmental Science and Asia Pacific Management. Degrees in Business, Music Therapy, and Jazz studies are offered in collaboration with the Open University. The college operates on the semester system and offers a limited summer session. Enrollment is 6,000 students. A faculty of 240 gives a faculty-student ratio of 1-25.

Entrance Requirements: High school graduation or equivalent; must include English 12 plus 3 academic courses with an average of 2.0 or better; early admission, early decision and pre-registration plans available; application deadline for fall term is May 31; $15 application fee; $100 application fee for international students.

Costs Per Year: $39.30 per credit hour residents; $220 per credit hour nonresidents; $41.25 student fees.

Collegiate Environment: The main core campus of Capilano College is located just north of the second narrows bridge in North Vancouver. This Lynnmour campus provides a unique natural forest and garden setting for over 280,000 square feet of facilities including new science, computer, and music labs and media program studios, a Learning Assistance Center, and a library that houses 80,000 hardbound volumes, 750 periodicals and more than 35,000 additional materials. Capilano College is noted for its very large and very strong academic studies (university transfer) program and for certain very successful two-year professional career programs such as Business Management, Media Resources, Outdoor Recreation, Music, and Legal. Some postdegree programs are offered, such as the Asia-Pacific Management Program and the Art Institute. There is no student housing on campus. Scholarships and other financial aid are available.

Branch Campuses: Sechelt Campus, 5627 Inlet Ave, P.O. Box 1609, Sechelt, BC V0N 3A0, (604) 885-9310; Squamish Campus, 37827 Second Ave., P.O. Box 1538, Squamish, BC V0N 3G0, (604) 892-5322.

COLLEGE OF NEW CALEDONIA   *(H-11)*
3330 22nd Avenue
Prince George, British Columbia V2N 1P8
Tel: (604) 562-2131; Fax: (604) 561-5861

Description: The College of New Caledonia is one of fourteen community colleges in British Columbia and is part of the B.C. provincial system of post-secondary education. In 1963 the Northern Interior Branch of the British Columbia School Trustees Association established a Regional College Committee which recommended the establishment of a two year community college at Prince George to serve the North Central Interior. The Council of the College of New Caledonia was formed in 1968, and agreed that the college should offer a program of academic and technical courses. The college opened on September 15, 1969, using the facilities of the Prince George Senior Secondary School. On July 9, 1971 the existing college amalgamated with the British Columbia Vocational School, and the College of New Caledonia, College, Technical and Vocational Institute was created. In September, 1971, the college reopened on the former British Columbia Vocational School site as an institution offering a variety of university transfer, technical, and vocational programs. There are now several divisions including Business and Management Studies, Health and Social Sciences, Technology Programs, University Credit, Trades

Training, regional operations and ancillary services, and planning and student records. The college operates on the semester system. Enrollment includes 2,015 full-time and 935 part-time students. The consists of 153 full-time and 150 part-time instructors.

Entrance Requirements: High school graduation; graduates with a C average accepted; early admission, early decision, midyear admission, and advanced placement plans available; May application deadline for Fall term.

Costs Per Year: $1,100 Canadian resident tuition; $6,900 nonresident tuition; $50 student fees (Canadian $)

Collegiate Environment: The present campus has expanded into over a quarter of a million square feet of permanent and temporary building space. A recently completed building program provided additions of a new gymnasium, shop space, a permanent library of 81,000 volumes, expanded laboratory facilities, classrooms, office space, and a food services facility. 43 scholarships are available and 10% of the student body receives financial aid.

Community Environment: Prince George, located approximately 500 miles north of Vancouver and approximately 110 miles west of the Province of Alberta, is the largest city in the northern part of British Columbia. The surrounding area is rich in Canadian history. A trading post at nearby Fort St. James was founded in 1806 by Simon Fraser and was the seat of administration for the vast area he named New Caledonia. The major industries are farming, lumbering, mining, and administration. Prince George is on the Fraser River and is adjacent to excellent winter sports in the nearby mountains.

DOUGLAS COLLEGE   *(M-3)*
Box 2503
New Westminster, British Columbia V3L 5B2
Tel: (604) 527-5400; Admissions: (604) 527-5518; Fax: (604) 527-5095

Description: This is a publicly supported, coeducational, liberal arts and technological community college which was founded in 1970. The college is a member of the Association of Colleges of Canada. Completion of the requirements for the two-year program results in an Associate Diploma or Associate Degree; completion of a special program of under two years results in a Certificate. Areas of concentration are in university transfer, humanities, social sciences, natural science, English, communications, music, health, human services and business. It operates on the semester system and offers one summer session. Enrollment includes 3,336 full-time and 4,715 part-time students. There are 346 full-time and 145 part-time faculty members.

Entrance Requirements: High school graduation or GED; open enrollment policy; early decision and midyear admission plans available; $25 application fee (Canadian $).

Costs Per Year: $1,340 ($670 per semester) full-time annual tuition; $34.50 student fees (Canadian $).

Collegiate Environment: There are faculty tutorials as well as career seminars provided for the student body. Full bookstore facilities are available. There is no student housing on campus. Financial aid is available.

Community Environment: The college region is composed of Burnaby, New Westminster, Coquitlam, and the Maple Ridge school districts. See Simon Fraser University.

KWANTLEN COLLEGE   *(M-3)*
12666 72nd Ave
P.O. Box 9030
Surrey, British Columbia V3W 2M8
Tel: (604) 599-2000

Description: This is a publicly supported, coeducational, liberal arts and technological junior college which was founded in 1981. The school is a member of the Association of Universities and Colleges of Canada. Completion of the requirements for the two-year program results in a Diploma; completion of a special program of under two years results in a Certificate. Areas of concentration are in university transfer, humanities, social sciences, natural science, English, communications, various career programs, and engineering technologies. It operates on the semester system and offers one summer session. Enrollment includes 4,263 full-time and 2,418 part-time students. A faculty of 193 full-time and 156 part-time members.

Entrance Requirements: High school graduation or GED; open enrollment policy; early decision and midyear admission plans available; $20 application fee (Canadian $).

Costs Per Year: $1,300 Canadian resident tuition; $6,000 nonresident tuition; (Canadian $)

Collegiate Environment: The college library contains 74,710 volumes, 454 periodicals, 1,132 microforms, and 1,808 audiovisual materials. There is no student housing on campus. Full bookstore facilities are found on all campuses. There are faculty tutorials as well as career seminars provided for the student body. 90% of applicants are accepted. Of 94 scholarships available, 36 are for freshmen. Financial aid is available.

Community Environment: The college region is composed of Langley, Delta, Surrey, and Richmond School Districts. See Simon Fraser University

MALASPINA COLLEGE   (M-10)
900 5th Street
Nanaimo, British Columbia V9R 5S5
Tel: (604) 753-3245; Fax: (604) 755-8725

Description: This four-year university college was established in 1969 pursuant to legislation enacted by the Government of the Province of British Columbia. The college, which moved to a new $12.5-million campus in 1976, is financed by the Provincial Government, and the college region comprises the school districts of Cowichan, Lake Cowichan, Nanaimo, Parksville, Qualicum and Powell River. The college serves the citizens of these five participating school districts. Students from other school districts are regularly admitted. The college offers vocational, academic, university transfer, career and technical programs designed to meet the needs of the students of all ages and from a variety of educational backgrounds. The semester system is used in academic and career programs; vocational programs are offered on a year-round basis. Enrollment is approximately 3,000. A faculty of 500 provides a faculty-student ratio of 1-6. The Community Education division offers credit and noncredit courses to approximately 15,000 people per year, including in-service professional development programs and precollege educational upgrading.

Entrance Requirements: High school graduation or GED; open enrollment; early decision, rolling admission, early admission, and advanced placement plans available; $15 application fee.

Costs Per Year: $33 per semester credit hour to a maximum of $495 per semester; $47 per credit for upper-level (3rd and 4th year) course; student activity fees are 8% of tuition.

Collegiate Environment: Facilities include a 276-seat theater and the Learning Resources Center, which houses 72,000 volumes, 1,200 microforms, and 450 periodicals. Fifty scholarships and 35 bursaries are available. 95% of those applying for admission are accepted, including students at midyear.

Community Environment: Nanaimo is situated on Vancouver Island, across the straits of Georgia from the city of Vancouver. The island is the largest on the Pacific Coast, both in North and South America. Nanaimo is the second largest community (85,000) on the island, being outranked by Victoria (250,000), the provincial capital located at the southern tip of the island. There are many excellent recreational facilities in the nearby mountains, forests, and lakes. Attractions include the Bastion and the Centennial Museum. Direct and frequent ferry service exist for Vancouver as well as rail, bus, and road connections to Victoria.

SELKIRK COLLEGE   (M-15)
301 Frank Beinder Way
Box 1200
Castlegar, British Columbia V1L 3J1
Tel: (604) 365-7292; Fax: (604) 365-3929

Description: Selkirk is a comprehensive multicampus community college that operates pursuant to the provisions of the B.C. College and Institute Act. It is committed to the provision of learning opportunities leading to employment and further education through a broad range of quality programs, courses and services. Selkirk opened with a single campus in Castlegar in 1966. Today there are several campuses throughout the college region. The Nelson Campus has been part of the college system since 1972, and the Trail Campus offers a variety of full- and part-time courses. All full-time programs operate on the semester system. Enrollment includes 1,820 full-time and 325 part-time students. A faculty of 138 full-time and 36 part-time gives a faculty-student ratio of 1-9.

Entrance Requirements: High school graduation or GED; mature student admission; open enrollment; early decision, delayed admission and advanced placement plans available; $25 application fee (Canadian $).

Costs Per Year: $1,200 ($600 per semester) for academic and technology programs; costs vary with the number of hours in a course; $150 per month for vocational programs (Canadian $).

Collegiate Environment: The library houses 72,000 hardbound volumes, 550 periodical subscriptions, a federal and B.C. Government documents collection, and a film library. The Castlegar campus has a residence hall for 100 students. Scholarships, awards and bursaries are available. A well-organized Campus Recreation office provides a variety of athletic and special events of interest to the students. An active student government sponsors a number of clubs and social events during the academic year. 70% of all applicants are accepted. Students are admitted at midyear for some programs. 40% of the students receive financial aid.

Community Environment: Located in the West Kootenay/Boundary region of southeastern British Columbia, Selkirk College campuses are less than 35 miles from the United States. The region was made famous by gold discoveries in the late 1800s, and today boasts a number of provincial and national parks, glacier-fed lakes, rugged wilderness areas, and hot springs. Located in the Selkirk Mountains, the college region is rich in mining, logging and tourist resorts. Major ski resorts are located near Rossland and Nelson.

SIMON FRASER UNIVERSITY   (M-11)
Burnaby, British Columbia V5A 1S6
Tel: (604) 291-3224

Description: The University takes its name from Simon Fraser, fur trader and explorer, who played one of the greatest roles in helping to open Canada's west. By ancestry, Simon Fraser was a member of the Fraser clan of Scotland. The University maintains this Scottish heritage with its coat of arms and with the University pipers and drummers, who wear the ancient hunting tartan of the Frasers. In September of 1965 Simon Fraser University opened its doors to 2,500 students. Today over 3,800 men, 4,626 women full-time and 2,987 and 4,518 women part-time are currently enrolled at the university. A faculty of 614 members provides a faculty-student ratio of 30:1. Simon Fraser University offers students flexibility in the timing of their studies, with 3 four-month semesters a year and evening, off-campus and correspondence courses. It offers one summer session. Special features of the more than 60 programs include tutorials, cooperative education options, directed study courses, pre-professional transfer training and innovative program areas--such as kinesiology, communication, and management and systems science.

Entrance Requirements: High school graduation; CEEB recommended for United States applicants; early admission, early entry plans available; deadline for submission of applications for the Fall term is June 1; $20 application fee; $40 for foreign students.

Costs Per Year: $2,190 resident tutiton; $6,570 tuition for international students; $1,714-$2,908 room; all fees subject to annual review.

Collegiate Environment: The W.A.C. Bennett Library houses 1.2 million hardbound volumes, 9,725 periodicals, 902,430 titles on microforms and 7,278 records and tapes. Fourteen on-campus residences accommodate up to 1,418 students. Academic Advice Centre advisors provide assistance with academic program planning, clarifying academic goals, university regulations and procedures.

Community Environment: The 1,200 acre campus is situated atop Burnaby Mountain, making Simon Fraser a striking campus with spectacular views of the coastal mountains and the cities of the Lower Mainland. The outstanding architecture has won many awards. Services on campus include day care centres, Health Services (including physicians, a psychiatrist, nurses and physiotherapists), Athletic and Recreational Services (two full gymnasia, swimming and diving pools, tennis, squash and racquetball courts, sauna, and weight rooms), a campus radio station, printshop, legal advice clinic, women's centre, bookstores and student Pub. Simon Fraser University is wheelchair accessible.

Branch Campuses: Simon Fraser University at Harbour Centre, 515 West Hastings Street, Vancouver, B.C., Canada V6B 5K3.

TRINITY WESTERN UNIVERSITY   *(M-4)*
7600 Glover Road
Langley, British Columbia V3A 6H4
Tel: (604) 888-7008; Fax: (604) 888-7548

Description: Trinity Western University began in the 1950s when members of the Evangelical Free Church saw the need for a Christian liberal arts and science college in Canada. They selected a historic 100-acre farm, which had originally been established by the Hudson's Bay Company to supply food for Fort Langley (the first capital of British Columbia), as the site of the university. Trinity Western began in 1962 as a Junior College, with 17 students. Today it is a full member of the Association of Universities and Colleges of Canada, granting BA, BBA, BSc, and BEd degrees with 26 majors and 33 minors. Preprofessional programs and cooperative education are special features. Trinity Western's graduate theological school offers MA, MDiv, MTS, and MMin degrees. It offers an MA degree in Counseling Psychology. Trinity Western operates on a semester system with two four-month semesters, as well as a three-week Interweave program in the spring. Enrollment is 1,623 full-time and 505 part-time undergraduates, and 163 graduate students. A faculty of 59 full-time and 38 part-time gives an undergraduate faculty-student ratio of 1-18. Students enjoy small classes and a "personal" approach to their education. Trinity Western is a private, Christian liberal arts university committed to the development of Christian leaders. The whole student approach to education provides an environment that challenges students to develop intellectually, socially, physically, and spiritually.

Entrance Requirements: High school graduation with English and three other grade 12 academics at C+ average; SAT 970 or ACT 22 required for U.S. students; TOEFL 570 required for foreign students; early admission and rolling admission plans available; $35 fee.

Costs Per Year: $12,254 comprehensive fee includes full-time tuition ($7,066), mandatory fees ($480), and university room and board ($4,708). Part-time tuition: $240 per semester hour.

Collegiate Environment: Residence facilities are available for 650 students. The library holds 89,666 bound volumes, 155,422 titles on microform, 587 periodical subscriptions, and 221 records and tapes. Financial aid is available, including 300 need-based scholarships (average $906 each) and 130 nonneed scholarships (average $325 each).

Community Environment: Trinity Western is set on a wooded 100-acre campus adjacent to the Trans Canada Highway No. 1, between Langley and Fort Langley. Students enjoy the solitude of a rural environment and have easy access to the beautiful urban center of Vancouver, just 45 minutes away. Public transportation is available off university lane. Services on campus include health clinic, counselling center, gymnasium, weight room, tennis courts, and book stores. Campus activities include student-run newspaper, intramurals, social clubs, music/drama groups, and student union.

UNIVERSITY OF VICTORIA   *(N-11)*
P.O. Box 1700
Victoria, British Columbia V8W 2Y2
Tel: (604) 721-7211; Admissions: (604) 721-8119; Fax: (604) 721-6225

Description: The University of Victoria is one of Canada's leading universities. A young institution, it has developed innovative programs in interdisciplinary research, professional and cooperative education, and many other areas. It operates on an academic year. The school is known for quality teaching and excellence in research. The University of Victoria, a public institution, received degree-granting status in 1963 and has seven faculties: Arts and Science, Education, Engineering, Fine Arts, Graduate Studies, Human and Social Development, and Law. In addition, the University has a number of unique or unusual programs: child and youth care, health information science, public administration and several interdisciplinary programs such as the environmental, medieval, and women's studies programs. Recently created programs at the University include a certificate program in the administration of aboriginal governments; a certificate program in technology and management; the School of Business with specializations in entrepreneurship and small business, international business, and tourism management; and the School of Earth and Ocean Sciences. The University of Victoria has one of the largest cooperative education programs in Canada, integrating academic studies with relevant work experience in 13 academic areas. Current enrollment includes 8,080 full-time, and 5,166 part-time undergraduate students and 1,937 graduate students. A faculty of 659 full-time and 298 part-time provides a faculty-student ratio of 1-12. The university offers degrees at the Bachelor's, Master's, and Doctoral levels.

Entrance Requirements: High school graduation; no entrance exams required; early admission is available; application deadline is May 15; application fee $15.

Costs Per Year: $2,130 resident tuition; $6,390 tuition for international students; $3,940 minimum room and board; $172.90 student fees.

Collegiate Environment: The 381-acre campus contains 58 buildings and provides 2.9 kilometers of on-campus cedar chip jogging trails. The University's off-campus facilities include the 20-acre Jeanne S. Simpson Field Studies Resource Centre at Cowichan Lake, and the 100-acre Dunsmuir Lodge conference facilitiy in North Saanich. The McPherson Library contains over 1.6 million volumes, over 1.7 million microforms, and about 45,000 sound recordings. The Faculty of Education's Curriculum Laboratory has a specialized collection to support student teaching requirements. The Law Library contains over 150,000 volumes. The University is home to numerous interdisciplinary centers and programs, including the Centers on Aging, Asia-Pacific Initiatives, Forest Biology, Public Sector Studies, and Sustainable Regional Development, the School of Earth and Ocean Research, the Institutes for Disputes Resolution and for Integrated Energy Systems, and an office of the Institute of Research on Public Policy. The University of Victoria has won 56 Canada West University Athletic Association titles and 24 national sports championships. It played a major role in the 1994 Commonwealth Games in Victoria, a fact which has left the school with a rich legacy of world-class facilities.

Community Environment: The university is located in the suburban Gordon Head area of Greater Victoria. It is a 10-minute drive from downtown Victoria and is easily accessible by car, bus, and bicycle. Victoria, the capital of British Columbia, boasts magnificent legislative buildings and downtown which has been developed to retain its turn-of-the-century architecture and historic landmarks. The city is a thriving center of artisitic activity, offering the exceptional Royal British Columbia Museum, several art galleries, a symphony orchestra, an opera company and several professional theatre companies. Greater Victoria has a population of 270,000. The regional economy is based on government, tourism, the University, and growing service, high technology, and clean manufacturing sectors.

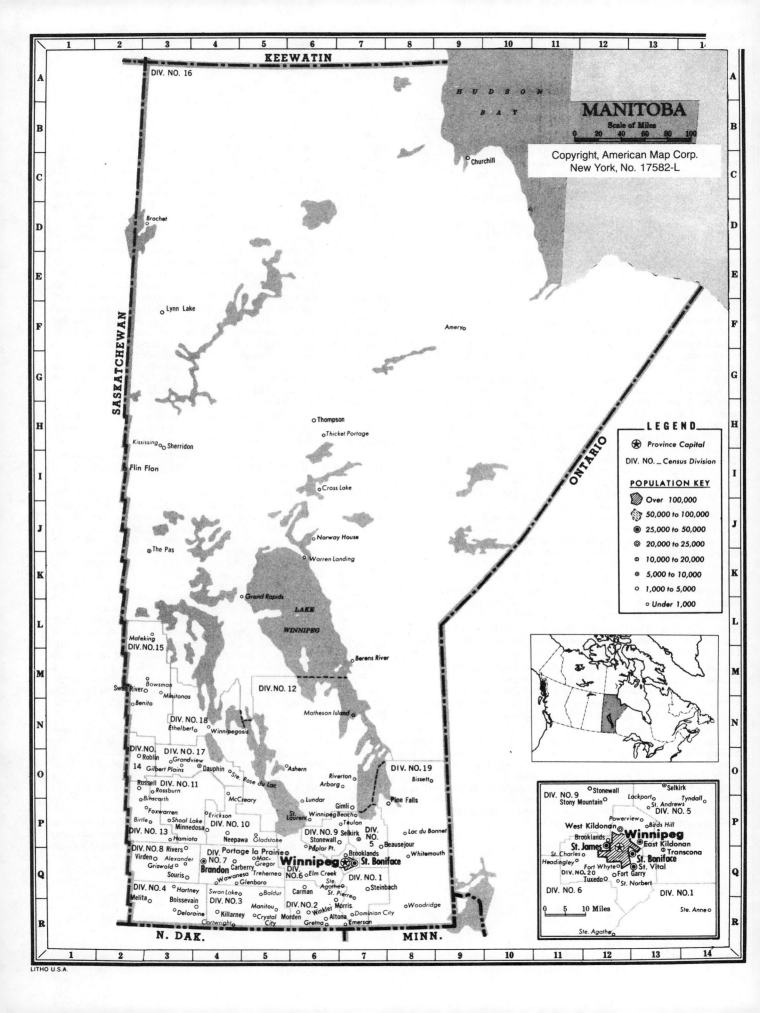

MANITOBA

BRANDON UNIVERSITY   *(Q-4)*
270 18th Street
Brandon, Manitoba R7A 6A9
(204) 726-4573

Description: A coeducational, nondenominational, government-supported university within the Province of Manitoba, Brandon University was established in 1880 by the Baptist Union of Canada and became an affiliate of McMaster University from 1910 to 1938, after which Brandon was affiliated as a nondenominational college of the University of Manitoba. Brandon University was established as an independent institution in July 1967. Operating on a year-term system with two summer sessions, it is accredited by the Association of Universities and Colleges of Canada and the Association of Commonwealth Universities. Three-year and four-year Bachelor degree programs are offered in general studies, arts and science, education, and music. The university offers a postgraduate Masters in Music as well as a Bachelor of Science in Nursing. Enrollment is 1,783 full-time and 1,521 part-time students. A faculty of 140 gives a faculty-student ratio of 1-28.

Entrance Requirements: High school graduation or GED; open enrollment; rolling admission, midyear admission and advanced placement plans available; $30 application fee.

Costs Per Year: $1,987.50 tuition; $4,400 room and board; $242 student fees.

Collegiate Environment: College facilities include student housing for 280 men and 280 women. The library, which is available to the citizens of Manitoba subject to adequate priorities being set for members of the university community, houses 358,000 bound volumes, 2,500 periodicals, and 189,000 microforms. 73% of the applicants are accepted, including students at midyear. Financial assistance is available. Of 374 scholarships offered, 90 are for freshmen; 12 of those are athletic.

Community Environment: Brandon, a city of 40,000, is located in the heart of the prairie land of Manitoba, on the Assiniboine River. The Manitoba Provincial Exhibition is held in Brandon every year. There are excellent recreational facilities in the nearby area, including camping, hunting, winter sports and fishing. Brandon is easily accessible by rail, road and air.

KEEWATIN COMMUNITY COLLEGE   *(J-3)*
7th Street and Charlebois
Box 3000
The Pas, Manitoba R9A 1M7
Tel: (204) 623-3416; Fax: (204) 623-7316

Description: A technical vocational community college, Keewatin was established in 1966. It operates under the authority of the Minister of Education of the Province of Manitoba in cooperation with the Federal Government. The majority of courses are from 5 months to 20 months duration.

Entrance Requirements: Minimum academic prerequisites as listed for each course; or equivalent standing in an approved adult education program; or equivalent standing in GED (General Education Development); or mature student status; sandardized test (CAAT) may be required only as counseling tool.

Costs Per Year: Tuition fees $75/month; room and board approximately $500/month; student fees $8 per month; for a 10-month course $750 tuition, $5,592 room and board, $80 student fees.

Collegiate Environment: The Learning Resource Center, which supplies a support service to the student population of the College, the teaching staff and the administration, is also available to the community as facilities and conditions permit. The center contains 20,000 books, 250 periodicals, and 1500 A-V materials. There is housing on campus for 164 men and 76 women. There are also apartments for 24 families. 40% of those applying for admission are accepted and 40% of the students receive financial aid.

Community Environment: The Pas is one of the few communities in the largely undeveloped area of Northern Manitoba. It is connected by rail, air and highway to Winnpeg, nearly 400 miles to the south. The town has a rich heritage as one of the early trading centers for fur trapping and each year an annual 3-day Trappers' Festival is held. The nearby area has extensive fishing and other recreational facilities and Clearwater Provincial Park is just 20 miles away. Mining and lumbering are its major industries. The Pas is at the junction of the Saskatchewan and Pasqua Rivers.

UNIVERSITY OF MANITOBA   *(Q-7)*
Winnipeg, Manitoba R3T 2N2
Tel: (204) 474-8880; Fax: (204) 269-6629

Description: Established in 1877, the University of Manitoba is Western Canada's oldest university. Today it has twenty faculties offering over 90 different undergraduate degree programs, plus graduate studies to the Masters and Doctoral levels. Professional programs include Architecture, Engineering, Medicine, Dentistry, Law and Pharmacy. There are five member or affiliate Colleges including St. Andrew's, St. Boniface, St. John's, St. Paul's and University College. Enrollment is approximately 21,000 undergraduates and 3,500 graduate students. There are 1,480 academic staff; 91% of whom have Ph.D. degrees. The faculty-student ratio is 1-16.

Entrance Requirements: High school graduation with 28 academic units; high school graduates with a C average are accepted; early admission, early decision and advanced placement plans are available; $30 (Canadian dollars) application fee for Canadians; $50 (Canadian dollars) application fee for international students.

Costs Per Year: $2,200 (Canadian dollars) Arts tuition; $2,600 (Canadian dollars) Science tuition.

Collegiate Environment: The University of Manitoba Students' Union provides coordination for student involvement in university government, the campus newspaper, cultural events, and the Sports Activity Complex. Housing for 1,160 students is available in five residences, one of which (University College) is entirely student operated. Intramural, extramural, and intercollegiate athletics include archery, ice hockey, volleyball, weightlifting, football, basketball, track, and swimming. Of particular interest is the Wilderness Program that offers to all students noncredit canoeing, hiking, and cross country skiing. The library contains 1,650,000 titles. 67% of all applicants are accepted. The second campus of the university is comprised of a complex of nine buildings located west of the Health Sciences Centre between McDermot Avenue and Bannatyne Avenue in central Winnipeg. This complex houses the medical and dental instructional units of the university. The major health science units located at this campus are the Faculty of Dentistry, the Faculty of Medicine, and the School of Dental Hygiene and Medical Rehabilitation.

Community Environment: Winnipeg, despite its small size (652,350) and big winter cold (zero to 30 degrees below Fahrenheit), offers students an extraordinary range of activities: opera, ballet, symphony orchestra, major league football and hockey, cosmopolitan restaurants, the only stone and fur trade fort still intact (Lower Fort Garry), and the 8,000-acre Oak Hammock Marsh wildlife preserve.

UNIVERSITY OF WINNIPEG   *(Q-7)*
515 Portage Avenue
Winnipeg, Manitoba R3B 2E9
Tel: (204) 786-9159

Description: The University was established July 1, 1967, by granting full university status to United College. This culminated a long record of service to the community in higher education begun over a hundred years ago with the establishment of Manitoba College by the Presbyterian Church in 1871 and of Wesley College by the Methodist Church in 1888. In 1926, following the union of the Presbyterian and Methodist Churches, Manitoba College and Wesley College were united by agreement. Each retained its separate charter and separate board of directors, but both were administered by a joint executive committee. In 1938 they were officially joined in the founding of United College. Since becoming an independent university in 1967, Winnipeg has continued to serve the city and the province by offering a full program of studies in arts and science, by maintaining the operation of its Collegiate Division, by developing various new offerings in theology, especially in continuing education and in graduate work, and by establishing in 1968, an Institute of Urban Studies. A new association was formed in time for the opening of the 1970-71 academic session whereby students of the Mennonite Brethren College of Arts could receive instruction and sit examinations at the University in a limited selection of General Arts courses, and in the 1973-74 session, a new four-year program in education was instituted jointly with the University of Manitoba. In 1976 the University entered into Joint Masters programs with the University of Manitoba in English, History, Religious Studies and in 1977 in Public Affairs. A cooperative education program is available in chemistry. In May 1986, Menno Simons College (MSC) was established as an affiliated college on the campus of the University of Winnipeg to specialize in Social and Economic Development Studies, and in Conflict Resolution Studies, thereby laying the foundation for a Canadian Center for International Development Education. Enrollment includes 7,456 students. A faculty of 247 full-time and 69 part-time provides a faculty-student ratio of 1-21.

Entrance Requirements: High school graduation; 20 high school academic units required; high school graduates with C average accepted; rolling admission and midyear admission plans available; application deadline for fall term is mid-August; $30 (Canadian dollars) application fee.

Costs Per Year:

$2,400 Arts tuition; $3,300 Science tuition; $175 student fees.

Collegiate Environment: The years from 1938 saw steady progress in the development of United College with major new buildings opening in 1951, 1959, and 1962. After attaining full university status as the University of Winnipeg, the expansion continued with a new six-story academic building. Another building was designed to rise above and integrate most of the earlier structures and provide space for an enlarged and modern library, facilities for expanding teaching departments, offices for an increasing number of faculty and a new cafeteria. An Athletic Center is the latest addition. The library houses over 530,602 hardbound volumes, 1,961 periodicals, and 102,161 microforms. No housing is provided. Of the 530 scholarships available, 176 are for freshmen and 36 are athletic. 50% of the students receive financial aid. 62% of those applying for admission are accepted, including students at midyear.

Community Environment: Winnipeg is the largest city (550,000) in Manitoba, its provincial capital, and the center of its cultural, political and social life. The city has the Winnipeg Art Gallery, Centennial Center with the Manitoba Museum of Man and Nature, Concert Hall and Theatre Center and many other cultural facilities and organizations, such as the Winnipeg Symphony and the Royal Winnipeg Ballet. Nearby Lake Winnipeg (which is larger than Lake Ontario) provides excellent recreation facilities. The city is the major east-west railroad junction and is accessible by all means of transportation. Industries include agriculture, meat packing and livestock, and manufacturing.

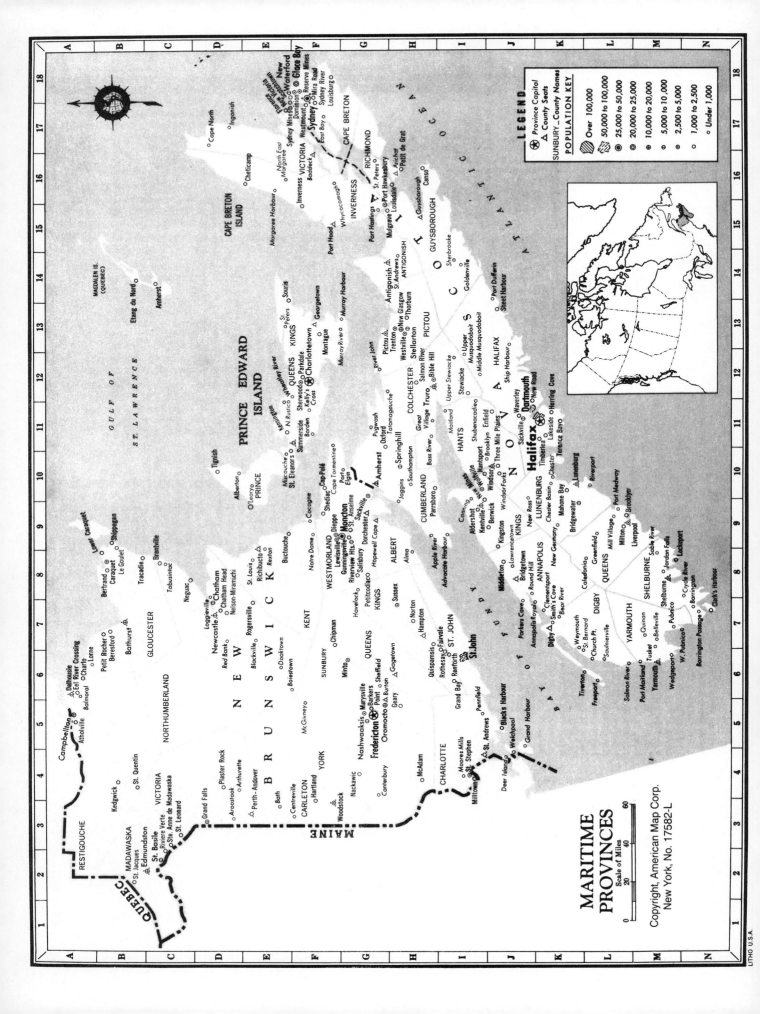

MARITIME PROVINCES

Scale of Miles

0 20 40 60

Copyright, American Map Corp.
New York, No. 17582-L

LEGEND

⊛ Province Capital
△ County Seats
SUNBURY—County Names

POPULATION KEY

⊛	Over 100,000
▨	50,000 to 100,000
◉	25,000 to 50,000
⊙	20,000 to 25,000
⊕	10,000 to 20,000
•	5,000 to 10,000
•	2,500 to 5,000
○	1,000 to 2,500
○	Under 1,000

ATLANTIC OCEAN

GULF OF ST. LAWRENCE

BAY OF FUNDY

QUEBEC

MAINE

NEW BRUNSWICK

RESTIGOUCHE
MADAWASKA
VICTORIA
GLOUCESTER
NORTHUMBERLAND
CARLETON
YORK
KENT
SUNBURY
QUEENS
WESTMORLAND
KINGS
ST. JOHN
CHARLOTTE
ALBERT

NOVA SCOTIA

CUMBERLAND
COLCHESTER
HANTS
PICTOU
ANTIGONISH
GUYSBOROUGH
INVERNESS
VICTORIA
CAPE BRETON
RICHMOND
KINGS
ANNAPOLIS
DIGBY
YARMOUTH
SHELBURNE
QUEENS
LUNENBURG
HALIFAX

PRINCE EDWARD ISLAND

PRINCE
QUEENS
KINGS

CAPE BRETON ISLAND

MAGDALEN IS. (QUEBEC)

MARITIME PROVINCES

NEW BRUNSWICK

ST. THOMAS UNIVERSITY   *(G-5)*
Fredericton, New Brunswick E3B 5G3
Tel: (506) 452-0532; Fax: (506) 450-9615

Description: St. Thomas University is a state-supported, coeducational, Roman Catholic institution of higher learning that offers undergraduate degrees in arts, education and social work. Founded in 1910 as a college, the university was awarded a provincial charter to grant degrees in 1934. It is accredited by the Association of Universities and Colleges of Canada. Enrollment includes 1,970 full-time and 300 part-time students. The faculty is 70 full-time and 65 part-time. Students and faculty share a campus with the University of New Brunswick in Fredericton, the provincial capital. St. Thomas operates on a semester system. The academic year runs from early September to late April. There are also a limited number of course offerings available in May and June.

Entrance Requirements: Successful completion of a high school college-preparatory program with a minimum average of B- required; high school record should be supported by a letter of reference and SAT test scores of 500V, 500M or better. Application deadline is July 30.

Costs Per Year: Tuition varies by program; $2,047 arts and social work tuition; $2,540 education tuition; $1,700 additional for nonresidents; $3,830 room and board, double occupancy.

Collegiate Environment: St. Thomas students enjoy the best of two worlds: the collegiality and personal attention that comes with a small, undergraduate university and all the amenities of a much larger campus. The university library, shared with the University of New Brunswick, has nearly one million volumes. Athletic facilities are among the best in Atlantic Canada. Three university residence halls on campus accomodate approximately 265 women and 200 men.

Community Environment: New Brunswick's capital city has a population of about 45,000. The university's hillside campus overlooks the downtown and the Saint John River Valley. Fredericton is home to the historic Legislative Assembly, a thriving artistic community, a professional theater troupe, one of Atlantic Canada's more impressive art galleries, tree-lined city streets and scores of elegant Victorian mansions. The city's per capita income is among the highest in the country.

UNIVERSITY OF NEW BRUNSWICK   *(G-5)*
P.O. Box 4400
Fredericton, New Brunswick E3B 5A3
Tel: (506) 453-4864; Admissions: (506) 453-4865; Fax: (506) 453-5016

Description: The University of New Brunswick is a state-supported institution that awarded its first degree in 1828. The university is coeducational, nondenominational, and is administered by a board of governors. Enrollment includes 6,945 full-time and 1,364 part-time undergraduates and 788 graduate students. A faculty of 515 full-time and 100 part-time gives a faculty-student ratio of 1-16.

Entrance Requirements: U.S. citizens must provides minimum SAT scores of 400V, 400M; high school diploma; ACT acceptable; application deadline is March 31; early admission, early decision, and rolling admission plans are available.

Costs Per Year: $2,470 tuition; $4,170 non-Canadian; $4,145 room and board; $99 student fees.

Collegiate Environment: The university has over 50 buildings on its Fredericton campus. Another campus is located in Saint John, New Brunswick. The library at the main campus contains over 920,000 volumes, and the campus includes St. Thomas University, a Catholic institution federated with UNB. 40% of those applying are admitted and the administration requires that at least half of the student's degree work be completed on campus. Housing is provided for approximately 1,450 students.

Community Environment: Fredericton, the capital of New Brunswick, has a population of 45,000. The city is located in the Saint John River Valley, about 55 miles from the city of Saint John. Local industry is oriented toward lumber, footwear, and, of course, government.

NOVA SCOTIA

ACADIA UNIVERSITY   *(I-10)*
Wolfville, Nova Scotia B0P 1X0
Tel: (902) 542-2201; Admissions: (902) 542-2201 X 1427; Fax: (902) 542-4666

Description: In 1838, the Nova Scotia Baptist Educational Society founded a liberal arts institution under the corporate name of "The Trustees, Governors, and Fellows of Queen's College." Regular instruction began in January 1839. In 1841, the Act of Incorporation was amended and the corporate name changed to Acadia College. In 1851, the power of appointing the Governors was transferred to the Baptist Convention of the Maritime Provinces, and in 1891 the Nova Scotia Legislature approved a special bill that changed the name of Acadia College to Acadia University. The University is a member of the Association of Universities and Colleges of Canada. A cooperative education program is available in computer science. The school operates on the semester system and offers two summer sessions. Enrollment is 3,700 students. A faculty of 225 provides a faculty-student ratio of 1-16.

Entrance Requirements: High school graduation with 16 academic units; SAT with minimum 500V, 500M; recommendation from school principal or guidance officer; GRE required for graduate school in some departments; advanced placement, early decision and rolling admission plans available; $25 application fee. (Canadian)

Costs Per Year: $3,205 Canadian resident tuition; $6,510 international student; $4,570 room and board; $161 student fees (Canadian funds).

Collegiate Environment: The university accepts 30% of those who apply for admission at the undergraduate level and 35% of those who apply to the graduate school. The Harold Campbell Vaughan Memorial Library is a 6-story building that was formally opened in 1965. Currently it houses 550,000 hardbound volumes. While library materials are acquired primarily for the use of Acadia students and faculty, they may be borrowed by alumni and residents of the town of Wolfville and the Annapolis Valley area as well. There is student housing for 857 men and 826 women. Approximately 15% of the student body receives financial aid.

Community Environment: Acadia University is located in the Annapolis Valley town of Wolfville, 100 kilometers northwest of Halifax. The main buildings are on a high terraced slope, facing the broad diked meadows of the Evangeline Country and the Minas Basin, the body of water in the northeastern part of the Bay of Fundy. Wolfville is a beautiful, residential town of 3,700 people, with four churches and good elementary and secondary schools.

ATLANTIC SCHOOL OF THEOLOGY   *(K-11)*
640 Francklyn Street
Halifax, Nova Scotia B3H 3B5
Tel: (902) 423-5592; Fax: (902) 492-4048

Description: An ecumenical school of theology and Christian ministry, the Atlantic School of Theology was founded in 1971 by Holy Heart Theological Institute (Roman Catholic), Pine Hill Divinity Hall (United Church of Canada), and University of King's College (Anglican Church of Canada) to provide training for Christian ministries and opportunities for theological study within the context of a community of faith. A member of the American Association of Theological Schools, the school enjoys recognized standing as a graduate school. It was formally incorporated in 1974 by an Act of the Legislature of Nova Scotia, and it has in its own right and name the power to grant degrees. The basic degrees offered are the Master of Divinity and the Master of Theological Studies. Enrollment is 69 full-time and 50 part-time students. A faculty of 16 gives a faculty-student ratio of 1-7.

Entrance Requirements: Bachelor's degree from a recognized university; under certain conditions a person lacking a Bachelor's degree, who wishes to prepare for ordination, may be admitted to the basic program leading to suitable academic recognition such as Bachelor of Theology.

Costs Per Year: $2,860 tuition; $4,425 room and board; $60 student fees; (Canadian $)

Collegiate Environment: Each college maintained its own library until 1972 when the libraries of Pine Hill and Holy Heart were brought together using the expanded facilities at Pine Hill. King's retains its own library. Main entry cards for books in the divinity library at King's and the Atlantic School are exchanged and interfiled in the catalogs for the two institutions so that resources may be shared. The library is a member of NOVANET, an online system. The volumes housed number about 70,000. Financial assistance is available through government loans, grants, and funds from the Churches for which the student is a candidate for the ministry.

Community Environment: See University of King's College.

DALHOUSIE UNIVERSITY   *(K-11)*
Halifax, Nova Scotia B3H 3J5
Tel: (902) 494-2450; Fax: (902) 494-1630

Description: Dalhousie is a public university administered by a board of governors and a senate. Enrollment 10,079 full-time and 1,619 part-time with a faculty of 800 giving a faculty-student ratio of 1:19. It operates on the semester system and offers two summer sessions. It is the largest university in Atlantic Canada, offering over 3,000 courses in 48 academic programs. The universtiy grants the Bachelor's, Master's, and Doctoral degrees. Cooperative education programs are available in mathematics, statistics, computer science, biochemistry, physics, marine biology and commerce. Exchange programs are available to students in Russian, Spanish, and French.

Entrance Requirements: High school graduation; applicants with good standing from U.S. grade 12 will be considered. SAT with minimum combined scores of 1100 is required. Academic records assessed on an individual basis. $30 application fee.

Costs Per Year: Varies according to program. Arts and Sciences tuition approximately $3,100 including student and society fees. Differential fee for international students is $2,700. Other costs may include books (approximately $500) and residence, including meals (approximately $4,700).

Collegiate Environment: Dalhousie is located on a 60-acre campus in downtown Halifax. Dormitories and residence houses on campus accommodate 1,900 students, including 112 married students. Fraternities and sororities house 20 men and 10 women. There is an art gallery, arts center, a library housing more than 1,385,000 titles, a range of computing facilities, and extensive recreation and education centers.

Community Environment: See University of King's College

MOUNT SAINT VINCENT UNIVERSITY   *(K-11)*
Halifax, Nova Scotia B3M 2J6
Tel: (902) 457-6128; Fax: (902) 443-4727

Description: Mount Saint Vincent University is concerned primarily with the education of women. It provides a strong liberal arts and science core and selected professional disciplines. It is dedicated to promoting academic excellence in an environment characterized by Catholic tradition and a high degree of personalized education. The Mount offers a Diploma and a Master degree in a variety of subjects. Cooperative Education options are available in business administration, human ecology, public relations, tourism, and hospitality management. The enrollment is 3,500. A faculty of 261 gives a faculty-student ratio of 1-16.

Entrance Requirements: High school graduation with 15 appropriate academic units one of which must be Grade 12 or enriched English and Grade 11 mathematics; high school graduates with 65% average are accepted; special consideration given to students out of school for five years; early admission and advanced placement plans available; $30 application fee (Canadian $).

Costs Per Year: $2,825 tuition (plus $356 per work team for Cooperative Education students); $4,000 room and board; $379 student fees; $2,200 foreign students fee supplement (Canadian $).

Collegiate Environment: Evaristus Hall, the main university administration building, houses classrooms, laboratories, and residence facilities for female students. Seton Academic Centre comprises classrooms, cafeteria and lounge facilities. It has a circular auditorium that can accommodate more than 1,000 people, an art gallery, various language and psychology laboratories, board rooms and faculty offices. Rosaria Centre contains a gymnasium, several multipurpose and fitness rooms, lounges, student counselling and medical services, the Centre for Continuing Education, Registrar's and Admissions offices, all student government facilities including the newspaper and yearbook offices and dining rooms. Residence facilities are for female students only, ranging from a 12-story highrise to townhouses, accommodating a total of 350 students. The E. Margaret Fulton Communications Centre houses the library consisting of more than 150,000 volumes, 960 current periodicals, newspapers and selected government documents, as well as audiovisual equipment, microfilms, tapes and recordings; computing services and Distance University Education are available via television facilities.

Community Environment: Mount Saint Vincent University is situated in Halifax, the capital of Nova Scotia. Overlooking the Bedford Basin, it offers scenic walkways and recreational facilities. Public transport and a good highway provide easy access both to the International Airport and to to the heart of Halifax, which offers cultural and intellectual opportunities, shopping, parks and entertainment.

NOVA SCOTIA AGRICULTURAL COLLEGE   *(H-12)*
Truro, Nova Scotia B2N 5E3
Tel: (902) 893-6600; Admissions: (902) 893-6722; Fax: (902) 895-5529

Description: The College was formally opened in 1905 to assume and expand the work which for several years had been carried on by the School of Horticulture in Wolfville and the School of Agriculture in Truro. It operates under authority of an act of the Legislature of Nova Scotia. During its existence, the College has had very close affiliations with the Ontario Agricultural College, University of Guelph, and Macdonald College of McGill University, where some students complete their studies. The college now offers a complete four-year Bachelor of Science degree in Agriculture Science with eight options. It also offers two years of the Bachelor of English degree program and a two-year pre-Veterinary program. Enrollment includes 800 full-time and 50 part-time undergraduates and 10 graduate students. A faculty of 87 gives a faculty-student ratio of 1-10.

Entrance Requirements: High school graduation; early admission plan available; deadline for submission of applications for the Fall term is July 1.

Costs Per Year: Estimates: $2,750 ($275/degree course) degree tuition; $1,200 ($100/technical course) technical tuition; $3,700 room and board; $200 student fees.

Collegiate Environment: The College is well equipped with buildings. Nine academic buildings and a modern farm building complex provide adequate teaching facilities for all programs offered and offices and laboratories for a large proportion of the staff of the Nova Scotia Department of Agriculture and Marketing. The library houses 21,000 hardbound volumes and 800 periodicals. Fraser House, Trueman House, and Chapman House provide living accommodations for 400 students. Scholarships are available; 57% of the student body receives financial aid. 80% of those applying for admission are accepted.

Community Environment: See Nova Scotia Teachers College

NOVA SCOTIA COLLEGE OF ART AND DESIGN   *(K-11)*
5163 Duke Street
Halifax, Nova Scotia B3J 3J6
Tel: (902) 422-7381; Fax: (902) 425-2420

Description: The history of the College goes back to 1887 and its founding as the Victoria School of Art and Design. Since that time it has experienced two changes in name. In 1925, the provincial government incorporated it as the Nova Scotia College of Art and in 1969, in recognition of the importance of design studies in the curriculum, the province gave it the present name. Also in 1969, the College instituted its degree-granting programs. Since 1974 it has been a full member of the Association of Universities and Colleges of Canada. Chartered by act of the provincial legislature of Nova Scotia, the College offers programs of study leading to the Master's degree in fine arts or art education, the Bachelor's degree in fine art, design or art education; and to the diploma in fine art or design. It also offers evening courses for adults in art and design. It operates on the semester system. Enrollment is 566 students. A faculty of 45 full-time and 43 part-time gives a faculty-student ratio of 1-13.

Entrance Requirements: Nova Scotia grade 12 or equivalent; deadline for submission of applications for the fall term is May 15th for first-year students and April 30th for advanced students; $20 application fee for MFA students.

Costs Per Year: $2,904 tuition; $4,604 non-Canadians; $3,400 room and board; $65.70 student fees; $635 health insurance.

Collegiate Environment: Since 1978 the College has occupied thirteen buildings in the Historic Properties development in the old commercial section of Halifax. The College library houses 20,000 volumes, 220 periodicals, and 100,000 photographic slides. The collection emphasizes the areas of art history of the past 100 years, contemporary art, and Canadian art. There are also extensive materials in the various craft and design areas. 55% of all applicants are accepted. 50% receive federal financial aid.

Community Environment: The College is located in Halifax, the capital city of Nova Scotia, with a metropolitan population of 300,000. Halifax is the largest city in the Atlantic region. It is the home of a number of cultural institutions including the Atlantic Symphony Orchestra, the Neptune Theatre and the Nova Scotia Museum. In addition, there are a number of active art galleries, most notably the Art Gallery of Nova Scotia and the galleries connected with the city's three universities. The Arts Center at Dalhousie University provides, during the fall and winter months, a constant round of music concerts, plays, and other performances.

ST. FRANCIS XAVIER UNIVERSITY   *(G-14)*
Antigonish, Nova Scotia B2G 1C0
Tel: (902) 863-3300; Fax: (902) 867-2329

Description: Since its beginnings as a Catholic grammar school on Cape Breton in 1823, St. Francis Xavier University has distinguished itself in academic social responsibility: in 1897 it was the first Catholic coeducational institution in North America to grant degrees to women; in 1899 it established Nova Scotia's first engineering school; and in 1959 it set up an adult education program for miners, fisherman, and farmers to help combat poverty and social unrest in Atlantic Canada that became known worldwide as the "Antigonish Movement". The Coady International Institute, a training program for students from developing countries, is based on the Antigonish Movement and named for its leader. The university maintains through its faculties of arts and science community service tradition by devising new patterns of training tailored to industrial society's technological needs without sacrificing humanist and social education. Enrollment is 3,050 students. A faculty of 175 provides a faculty-student ratio of 1-17.

Entrance Requirements: High school graduation with 16 academic units; SAT with a combined score of 900; rolling admission and delayed admission plans available.

Costs Per Year: $2,925 tuition; $4,625 nonresident; $4,285-$5,050 room and board; $123 student fees.

Collegiate Environment: The 100-acre campus is dotted with playing fields, monuments, and more than 30 brick and stone buildings. Varied athletic and recreational programs exist on both intramural and intercollegiate levels. Interdenominational services are available and the student body is represented in the University Senate by elections.

Community Environment: Pretty in its rural setting, Antigonish lies 140 miles from Halifax and each July hosts the Highland Games, a kind of Olympics of the Clans.

TECHNICAL UNIVERSITY OF NOVA SCOTIA   *(K-11)*
P. O. Box 1000
Halifax, Nova Scotia B3J 2X4
Tel: (902) 420-7500

Description: In 1906 the universities of Acadia, Dalhousie, King's College and Mount Allison met with the Halifax Board of Trade and the Mining Society of Nova Scotia to discuss the need to centralize engineering education in Nova Scotia. The solution was the establishment in 1907 of the College that is today's Technical University of Nova Scotia (TUNS). Since that time, TUNS has developed the Associated University system in which students pursue studies in the sciences and humanities at one or another of ten universities in the region for two years followed by three years (Engineering) or two years (Computer Science) at TUNS concentrating on the professional subjects. Architecture draws its students from across the country; the program is a four-year cooperative, for which the entrance qualification is not less than two successful years at another university. In 1987 TUNS had a total of twelve research and development centers additional to the research and teaching activities of the academic departments. It operates on the semester and trimester system. Enrollment is 1,476 students. A faculty of 98 gives an overall faculty-student rati of 1-15.

Entrance Requirements: High school graduates are accepted into the associated universities and into the Computer Science program; entrance to Archictecture and Engineering programs at TUNS follows a minimum of two years at another university.

Costs Per Year: $2,304 tuition; $4,654 foreign students; $4,660 room and board; $105 student fees.

Collegiate Environment: The most visible building on campus is the Sexton Student Centre comprising the gym, common room, and student/alumni offices. Athletic facilities include courts for basketball, tennis, volleyball and badminton, as well as a playing field and a weight training room. Other significant buildings include the Computer Centre, O'Brien Hall residence for 112 students, and the Architecture building, the historical edifice in which the university began its life. The library has 100,000 books, 1,200 current periodical subscriptions, 75,000 microfiche and 2,300 microfilms. Technical associations and societies are well represented on campus.

Community Environment: See Nova Scotia College of Art and Design.

UNIVERSITE SAINTE-ANNE   *(L-6)*
Pointe-de-l'Eglise, Nova Scotia B0W 1M0
Tel: (902) 769-2114; Fax: (902) 769-2930

Description: This government supported maritime university was founded in 1890. Enrollment is 116 men and 272 women full-time, and 853 part-time students. Faculty is 45 full-time and 55 part-time. There is a mature student program for those 22 years of age and over who do not meet the standard admissions requirements. The school operates on the trimester system and offers two 6-week french immersion summer sessions. The language of instruction at Universite Sainte-Anne is French.

Entrance Requirements: High school graduation; French language proficiency; $20 application fee.

Costs Per Year: $2,870 tuition; $4,570 non-Canadians; $4,875-$5,257 room and board; $106.40 student fees; $400 books; $500 miscellaneous.

Collegiate Environment: Universite Sainte-Anne, until 1971 administered by the Eudist Fathers, is now a government supported university and the only Francophone university in the province. The sizeable university library has more than 85,000 volumes, and the entire campus overlooks St. Mary's Bay in southwestern Nova Scotia. The university provides housing for 360 men and women. Approximately 75% of those applying for admission are accepted. Students without sufficient knowledge of French must enroll in an immersion program at the appropriate level.

Community Environment: Pointe-de-l'Eglise (Church Point), Nova Scotia, is a rural community of Acadian heritage situated on the shores of Saint Mary's Bay. The climate is temperate.

UNIVERSITY COLLEGE OF CAPE BRETON   *(F-18)*
P.O. Box 5300
Sydney, Nova Scotia B1P 6L2
Tel: (902) 539-5300; Fax: (902) 562-0119

Description: The University College of Cape Breton was established by an Act of the Nova Scotia Legislature on June 28, 1974. It combines into one institution the former Sydney Campus of St. Francis Xavier University (founded in 1951) and the Nova Scotia Eastern Institute of Technology (founded in 1968). It is unique because it brings together types of educational organizations that have not been joined before in Canada and that have totally different goals and traditions. The technology division offers two- and three-year diploma programs and the university division grants Bachelor degrees in Arts, Community Studies, Science, Technology (environmental), and Business Administration. Formerly situated on 2 different campus sites, both divisions of the College now share a 120-acre campus approximately 5 miles from downtown Sydney. The total enrollment is 3,241 with a faculty of 158, providing a faculty-student ratio of 1-16. The university component operates on the year term system with two summer sessions; technology programs operate on the semester system. Most technology programs are now offered as cooperative education programs. The college is a member of the Association of Universities and Colleges of Canada and the Association of Canadian Community Colleges.

Entrance Requirements: High school graduation with 15 academic units; high school graduates with a C average are accepted; early decision, rolling admission plans available; students are admitted at midyear on a part-time basis. $20 application fee.

Costs Per Year: Technology programs $2,375 tuition; arts and science programs $2,375 for residents, $4,075 for nonresidents; $117 student fees for both; single room and board $4,075.

Collegiate Environment: University College facilities include a library of 250,000 volumes and 400 periodicals. 90% of the applicants are accepted. Scholarship and bursary assistance is available and 12% of the students receive financial aid. An on-campus residence houses 154 students in single rooms.

Community Environment: Sydney is the principal city on Cape Breton Island, which is at the northeast end of Nova Scotia. The island is connected to the mainland by a causeway. Sydney is an industrial city with a self-contained steel plant. It is also a port city. There are numerous historical sites and recreational facilities. A major restoration project being undertaken on Cape Breton Island is at the Fortress of Louisbourg National Historic Park.

UNIVERSITY OF KING'S COLLEGE   *(K-11)*
6350 Coburg Road
Halifax, Nova Scotia B3H 2A1
Tel: (902) 422-1271; Admissions: (902) 422-1271; Fax: (902) 423-3357

Description: King's College is the oldest established university in Canada, having been founded in 1789 in Windsor, Nova Scotia. It was founded as an Anglican university and it still retains certain close connections with the Anglican Church. There is now, however, no requirement that students or members of the faculty be Anglican. A fire having destroyed a large part of the University's buildings in Windsor, the University in the 1920s took advantage of a grant from the Carnegie Corporation and reestablished itself in Halifax, the major city of Canada's Atlantic Provinces. A condition of the grant was that King's would become closely associated with Dalhousie University, and this association has persisted. The arrangement between the two universities is such that a joint Faculty of Arts and Social Sciences, and joint Faculty of Science are maintained, undergraduates of King's reading for the BA or BS degree of Dalhousie. King's has left its own degree-granting powers in abeyance in these areas and at present awards degrees only in journalism. It also awards the honorary degrees of DD, DCL, and DCN. It operates on the regular session system and offers, through the joint Faculties with Dalhousie University, two summer sessions. The College has at present an enrollment of approximately 700 students. The faculty numbers 37 full-time members. The faculty-student ratio is 1-15. The College provides an alternative program of studies for first-year students, the Foundation Year Programme, which seeks an integrated approach for the study of Western thought and culture. A French exchange program is offered in Aix-en-Provence, France. A Russian exchange program is available in Moscow or Leningrad.

Entrance Requirements: High School graduation; for students from the U.S.A., good standing in grade 12, with subject distribution as follows: English, plus at least two of biology, chemistry, French, German, history, Latin, mathematics or physics, plus two more classes either from the preceding list or from computer-related studies, economics, geography, geology, law, modern world problems, music, political science, sociology, or Spanish; SAT scores should be submitted; early admission and early decision plans available; $30 application fee.

Costs Per Year: $2,920 tuition; $4,400 room and board; $295 student fees; $2,700 supplement for visa students.

Collegiate Environment: King's strength at the present time lies in the valuable opportunity that it gives to students to participate fully in the life of a small academic community, with approximately one-third of the students living in residence. Because of the association with Dalhousie University, King's students also partake of the benefits of a large university with a fine library and laboratories, a complete range of facilities, and a wide variety of cultural activities. King's College occupies a site contiguous with the campus of Dalhousie University and includes residence accomodations for 250 students (both male and female) and for two deans and seven dons, the President's Lodge, a chapel, a gymnasium with swimming pool, a dining hall, a library of 92,000 volumes and 187 periodicals, a studio theater, and various other public rooms. Student Union activities are very diverse, including a dramatic society, a debating society and the Haliburton Society (the oldest literary association in Canada). 35% of the applicants are accepted.

Community Environment: King's College is situated approximately one mile from the center of the city of Halifax, the metropolitan area that has a population approaching 300,000. Halifax is Canada's major commercial and naval port on the Atlantic and is well recognized as an important educational and cultural location in the nation, being the home of six degree-granting institutions, Symphony Nova Scotia, the Neptune Theater, and a number of other small theater enterprises, as well as a number of commercial cinemas and film societies. Facilities exist for a complete range of summer and winter sports and the city is well provided with a number of fine restaurants.

PRINCE EDWARD ISLAND

UNIVERSITY OF PRINCE EDWARD ISLAND   *(F-12)*
550 University Avenue
Charlottetown, Prince Edward Island C1A 4P3
Tel: (902) 566-0439; Fax: (902) 566-0420

Description: A public liberal arts university, the University of Prince Edward Island was established by an Act of the Legislature of Prince Edward Island in April 1969. It was a merger of two institutions of higher learning, Prince of Wales College established in 1834 and St. Dunstan's University established in 1855. The University is accredited by the Association of Universities and Colleges of Canada and the Association of Commonwealth Universities. Degrees are offered in the arts, science, business administration, veterinary medicine, nursing, education and music. Diplomas are offered in Engineering (preprofessional) and Public Administration. The semester system is used with two summer sessions. Enrollment includes

2,600 full-time and 600 part-time students. A faculty of 192 provides a faculty-student ratio of 1-15.

Entrance Requirements: High school graduation with 65% average; two aptitude and three achievement tests are recommended; advanced placement available for transfer students only; April 1st is the deadline for submission of foreign applications for the fall term; $35 application fee for nursing, veterinary medicine, and 1-year B.Ed programs.

Costs Per Year: $2,600 Canadian resident tuition, $4,200 nonresidents; $4,600 room and board; $450 student fees, higher in veterinary medicine program.

Collegiate Environment: The library complex houses 475,000 hardbound volumes, 1,700 periodicals, 80,000 microforms, and 24,000 audiovisual materials. There is student housing for 450 men and women.

Community Environment: Charlottetown is the provincial capital and the largest community (approximately 30,000) on the island. It has an excellent harbor and is the center of the cultural and commercial activities of the island. Scenic attractions include Province House, St. Dunstan's Basilica, St. Peter's Anglican Cathedral, the Confederation Center and Government house.

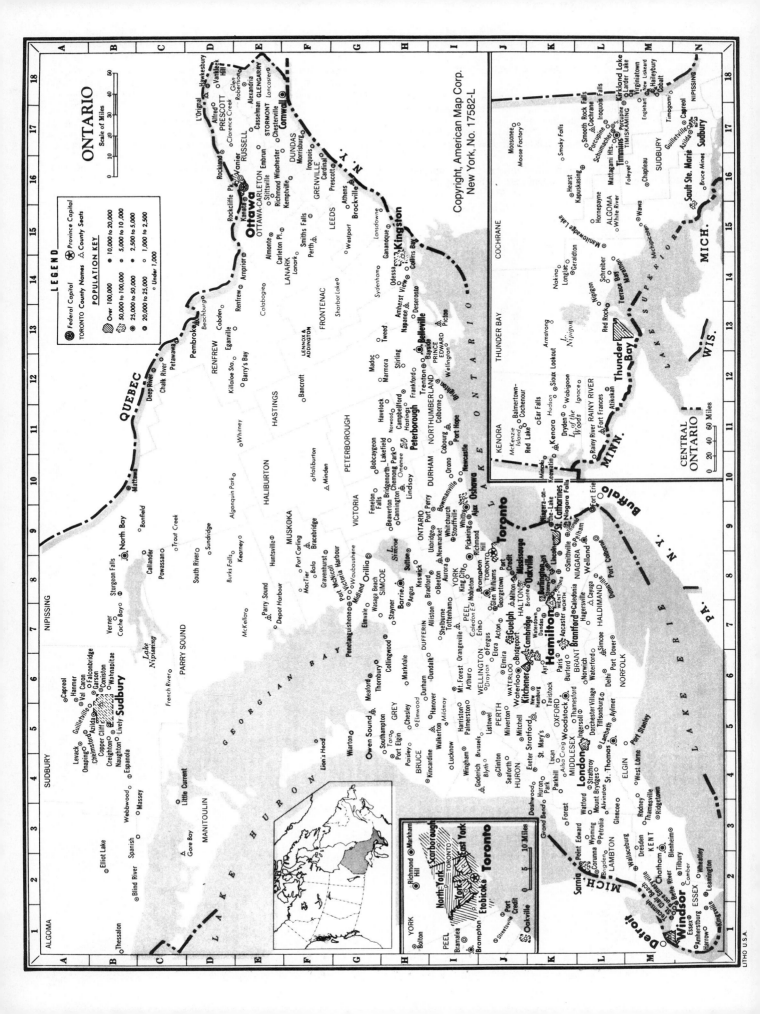

ONTARIO

BRESCIA COLLEGE   *(L-5)*
1285 Western Road
London, Ontario N6G 1H2
Tel: (519) 432-8353; Fax: (519) 697-6484

Description: Founded as Ursuline College for women in 1919 by the Ursuline Sisters and affiliated with The University of Western Ontario. In 1963, the original name was changed to Brescia College. The college operates the Home Economics department for The University of Western Ontario and is governed by that institution. Enrollment is 779 full-time and 127 part-time students. A faculty of 50 provides a faculty-student ratio of 1:18.

Entrance Requirements: High school graduation; high school students with a B average are eligible for consideration; rolling admission, early admission and delayed admission plans are available.

Costs Per Year: $2,340 tuition; $7,585-$12,085 nonresident; $4,630 room and board.

Collegiate Environment: Brescia's students share in all academic, social, athletic, and cultural activities of The University of Western Ontario. However, Brescia has its own housing for 174 students as well as library of 60,000 volumes.

Community Environment: See University of Western Ontario

CARLETON UNIVERSITY   *(E-16)*
1125 Colonel By Drive
Ottawa, Ontario K1S 5B6
Tel: (613) 788-3663; Fax: (613) 788-3847

Description: This nondenominational, publicly supported university was founded as Carleton College in 1942. It is accredited by the Associated by the Association of Universities and Colleges of Canada. It grants the Bachelor's, Master's and doctoral degrees. It offers cooperative education programs in computer science, commerce and public administration. An internship or practicum program is offered in art history, social work, journalism, geology, industrial design, and criminology. An industrial work experience program is offered in Engineering. There are exchanges in France, Scotland, Denmark, the United States, Great Britain, Germany, Spain, Hungary, Poland, Russia, China, Japan, Latin America, and Africa. Enrollment includes 16,382 full-time, and 5,386 part-time students. The faculty, including part-time instructors, numbers 750, giving a faculty-student ratio of 1:24.

Entrance Requirements: High school graduation with 16 units. Achievement tests are required: Chemistry and Physics for Engineering; 2 Physics, Chemistry, and Biology for Sciences; Mathematics for Science and Engineering. U.S. applicants must have B average and minimum SAT scores of 550V and 550M or 1100 combined. Application fee of $85 for non-Canadians, $75 for Canadians.

Costs Per Year: Tuition $2,234-$2,412, non-Canadians $7,480-$11,980; room and board $4,164.

Collegiate Environment: Carleton University is located on 62 hectares in Canada's capital. The university has 11 teaching buildings, as well as facilities housing administration and physical recreation facilities. The library contains over 2,000,000 volumes, 6,000 periodical subscriptions (14,000 total periodicals), 600,000 microforms, 15,100 audiovisual materials. The dormitories shelter 1,682 students. 70% of the applicants are accepted. Of 919 scholarships offers extended to freshmen, 280 were accepted. 34% receive financial assistance.

Community Environment: As the site of the Parliament Buildings, the National Arts Center, and many of Canada's finest museums, Ottawa is a vibrant political and cultural center that provides Carleton's students with many unique opportunities. With its impressive network of trails, pathways, and waterways, Ottawa is an ideal location for jogging, skiing, and cycling enthusiasts. Outdoor recreation ex-

tends year-round, for Carleton is located beside the historic Rideau Canal, which in the winter becomes the world's longest skating rink, and the site of Ottawa's annual winter carnival.

CENTENNIAL COLLEGE OF APPLIED ARTS AND TECHNOLOGY   *(I-3)*
Box 631 Station A
Scarborough, Ontario M1K 5E9
Tel: (416) 694-3241; Fax: (416) 694-1503

Description: Centennial is a liberal arts and technological community college established and funded by the Province of Ontario through the Ministry of Colleges and Universities. It operates on the semester system and offers one, two, and three year programs of study, as well as a wide range of continuing education opportunities. Centennial opened in 1966 as the first community college in Ontario. The total enrollment is 10,500 full-time and 50,000 part-time students. A faculty of 500 full-time gives a faculty-student ratio of 1:20.

Entrance Requirements: High school graduation; 30 Ontario grade 12 credits or the equivalent required; open enrollment; early admission, early decision, advanced placement plans available.

Costs Per Year: $1,109 tuition; $9,215 tuition for foreign students.

Collegiate Environment: Centennial has 4 major campuses: Ashtonbee, Bell Centre, Progress, and Warden Woods. There is no student housing on campus. Scholarships and bursaries are available. 30% of those applying for admission are accepted.

Community Environment: See University of Toronto.

CONESTOGA COLLEGE OF APPLIED ARTS AND TECHNOLOGY   *(J-6)*
299 Doon Valley Drive
Kitchener, Ontario N2G 4M4
Tel: (519) 748-5220; Fax: (519) 895-1097

Description: This college is one of 25 colleges of applied arts and technology established by the Province of Ontario. Students were first registered in 1967. Enrollment consists of approximately 4,500 students in full-time programs, and 33,000 evening students. A faculty of 360 gives a faculty-student ratio of 1-12. Programs are offered either on a semester or alternative basis. Semestered programs generally begin in September, with a few in the winter; non-semestered programs start on specific dates in the year. The College has a mandate to provide educational opportunities to graduates of secondary schools, adults and out-of-school youth.

Entrance Requirements: Graduation from secondary school is a requirement for admission to semestered programs; provision is made to admit mature students who do not have the academic qualifications; the general admission requirement to non-semestered programs is two years of secondary school; open enrollment; rolling admission plan available.

Costs Per Year: $1,008 tuition; $8,375 nonresident; $105 student fees; addditional fees depending on program.

Collegiate Environment: The College has campuses that serve the communities in four counties in midwestern Ontario. A residence for 230 students is located adjacent to the Doon Campus in Kitchener. Financial assistance is available to students under a loan program provided by the federal and provincial governments. 60% of students receive financial aid. 30% of those applying are admitted.

Community Environment: Kitchener-Waterloo (population 220,000) is 30 miles northwest of Hamilton (see Mohawk College of Applied Arts and Technology). The area has numerous historical and scenic attractions and a German and Mennonite (Pennsylvania Dutch) community. The four counties served by the College have strong rural and urban economics. The four-city area of Kitchener-Waterloo, Cambridge and Guelph is known as Canada's Technology Triangle, for its concentration of advanced-technology research, design and manufacturing enterprises. Some of the most productive agricultural land in the Province of Ontario is in the four counties. The Kitchener-Waterloo area is only a one-hour drive from Toronto.

Branch Campuses: Doon (Kitchener): main campus, administrative offices, recreation center, dedicated technology centers, early childhood education center; Waterloo: business, preparatory studies, early childhood education center; Guelph: technical and preparatory studies; Cambridge: preparatory studies; Stratford: preparatory studies, nursing.

CONFEDERATION COLLEGE OF APPLIED ARTS AND TECHNOLOGY   *(M-13)*
Box 398
Thunder Bay, Ontario P7C 4W1
Tel: (807) 475-6158; (800) 465-5493; Admissions: (807) 475-6130;
Fax: (807) 577-2766

Description: A public two-year college, Confederation delivers a wide range of programs from four divisions: Aborignal, Applied Arts and Business, Health Sciences and Technology, and Community Educational Programs. The college operates on teh semester system. Many programs have extensive on-the-job fieldwork and other related practical experience. Total yearly enrollment is 3,700 full-time post secondary students and 18,000 continuing education students. A faculty of 245 full-time and 300 part-time members provides a faculty-student ratio of 1-20. Confederation College has been widely recognized for its delivery of programs through the area campuses and distance education network, to communities throughout Northwestern Ontatio. The college has an Aboriginal Studies Division and delivers a variety of programs designed to meet the needs of Aboriginals. Aviation, Hospitality and Tourism are three other areas for which the college has been widely recognized. The Trades and Apprentice programs serve as an apprenticeship training center for Northwestern Ontario.

Entrance Requirements: To apply to a postsecondary program, applicatnts require an Ontario Secondary School Diploma or its equivalent. Secondary school subjects must be completed at or above the general level. Applicants lacking a high school diploma may apply as mature student if they are 19 years of age or older on or before the commencement of classes. Mature students are required to complete any prerequisite subjects and admission testing. Ontario College Application Service (OCAS) accepts applications after January 1. All aplications received by OCAS before March 1 are considered on an equal basis by Confederation College. Applicants are accepted in order in which their completed and eligible applications are received. Admission decisions (acceptance, rejection or waiting list) will be issued after May 15. Exceptions to this admissions process are oversubscribed programs. These programs use selective admissions. Selective admission requirements are outlined in the college calendar. Applicants to oversubscribed programs need to apply before March 1.

Costs Per Year: $1,109 tuition; $9,000 international student tuition; $3,600 room; $270 student fees. All figures are in Canadian dollars. Please note that these costs are approximate and vary widely with programs. For International Fees contact the International Student Services Officer at (807) 475-6626.

Collegiate Environment: The library houses 50,000 hardbound volumes and 5,750 additional titles. Sibley Hall residence houses 300 students. College offers Fitness Centre facilities, Counseling Services, Financial Assistance, Placement and Career Services, Alumni Association, College Council of Students, Student Union, Aboriginal Student Support and Learning Centre.

Community Environment: Thunder Bay has a population of 130,000 is Ontario's 11th largest city and Canada's second largest port. It is easily accessible, by roads and train, to all parts of eastern and central Ontario and to the United States. A distinctly multicultural community, Thunder Bay features a rich ethnic mosaic of cultural and recreational opportunities. The city features the finest skiing facilities including a world-class ski jump was the home of the 1995 Nordic Games, as well as an excellent aquatic sports facility and community auditorium.

Branch Campuses: The College delivers programming from its main cmapus in Thunder Bay and regional campuses located throughout Northewstern Ontario, in Dryden, Fort Frances, Geraldton, Kenora, Marathon, Atikokan, and Sioux Lookout.

FANSHAWE COLLEGE   *(L-5)*
1460 Oxford Street East
Box 4005
London, Ontario N5W 5H1
Tel: (519) 452-4100; Admissions: (519) 452-4277; Fax: (519) 452-4420

Description: A coeducational college of applied arts and technology, Fanshawe College was established in 1967 and is funded by the Province of Ontario through the Ministry of Education and Training. It has 4 campuses, a main campus in London, one in St. Thomas, one in Woodstock and one in Simcoe and courses are offered at 22 centers outside London. Operating on the trimester system with one summer session, the college offers study leading to a Certificate, awarded on completion of a program of less than two years duration, and the Diploma, awarded on completion of a program of at least two years duration. Recent enrollment included 12,500 full-time and 500 part-time students attending daytime classes and 50,000 evening students. The faculty consists of 500 members. The faculty-student ratio is 1-20. In addition to the main campus in London, there are branch campuses in St. Thomas, Woodstock and Simcoe, Ontario.

Entrance Requirements: High school graduation; TOEFL; early decision admission plan available; students are admitted at mid-year for some programs. The deadline for submission of applications for the Fall term is March 1 (for guaranteed consideration). $25 (Canadian) application fee.

Costs Per Year: $1,100 tuition; $8,300 non-Canadian tuition; $200 student fees (Canadian funds).

Collegiate Environment: The library houses 50,000 hardbound volumes, 658 current periodicals, and 1,467 reels of microfilm plus 6,500 bound periodicals. There are various forms of financial aid available to the students.

Community Environment: The city has a population of approximately 300,000 and is located on the Thames River, midway between Windsor and Toronto. Scenic attractions include the 325-acre Springbank Park, London Art Museum and Fanshawe Pioneer Village. There are excellent recreational facilities throughout the surrounding area.

GEORGIAN COLLEGE OF APPLIED ARTS AND TECHNOLOGY   *(H-8)*
1 Georgian Drive
Barrie, Ontario L4M 3X9
Tel: (705) 728-1951; Fax: (705) 722-5123

Description: Georgian is one of 23 Colleges of Applied Arts and Technology created by the Department of Education Amendment Act of 1965. Each college was established to meet the needs of its own geographic area. The area served by Georgian College encompasses the counties of Bruce, Grey, Dufferin, and Simcoe and the district municipalities of Muskoka and Parry Sound. To meet local needs, branch campuses have been established at Owen Sound to serve Grey and Bruce counties and at Orillia to serve the northern portion of Simcoe county and the districts of Muskoka and Parry Sound. These campuses offer a limited number of programs and do not offer all of the programs that are available on the main campus in Barrie. Cooperative education programs are available in all business, technology, and hospitality and tourism programs. Georgian is funded by the Province of Ontario through the Ministry of Colleges and Universities; it operates on a three-semester system. Enrollment is 5,000 full-time, 500 part-time and 20,000 evening students. There are 18,000 graduate students. There is a faculty of 300 full-time, 125 part-time, and 220 evening members.

Entrance Requirements: High school graduation; out-of-province applicants must submit evidence of equivalent standing to the Ontario Secondary School Diploma; open enrollment; rolling admission and advanced placement plans available; deadline for submission of applications for the Fall term is March 1 for oversubscribed programs, open date for all other programs.

Costs Per Year: $1,109 tuition; $9,215 foreign students. $8,000 room and board; $122 student fees.

Collegiate Environment: In 1968, the 140-acre site for the main campus was purchased and the first permanent building was erected that year. The second building housing the technological division was opened in 1969 and the third building, to accommodate additional technological facilities and the Applied Arts Division, was opened in 1970. In the fall of 1971, construction commenced on the new Central Services Building; it was formally opened in November 1973. The college library houses 29,500 hardbound volumes, 300 periodicals, 5,900 microforms, and 200 audiovisual materials. Dormitories near each campus house 252 students. 70% of the applicants are accepted including midyear students. 2,000 students or 55% of the students receive financial aid.

Community Environment: Barrie, population 50,000, is located 45 miles north of Toronto in the heart of the Simcoe area. The area is well known for its recreational facilities (hunting, skiiing, fishing, boating, camping), and Georgian Bay and Lake Simcoe are within easy reach.

KING'S COLLEGE *(L-5)*
266 Epworth Avenue
London, Ontario N6A 2M3
Tel: (519) 433-3491; (800) 265-4406; Fax: (519) 433-2227

Description: King's College is a Catholic coeducational, liberal arts university affiliated with the University of Western Ontario. Students enjoy the resources and opportunities of a world class university, and also belong to a small college community where individual attention is a priority. Enrollment is 1,750 full-time and 400 part-time students. A faculty of 100 gives a faculty-student ratio of 1:20.

Entrance Requirements: High school graduation with at least a B average accepted; early admission, early decision, and delayed admission plans available.

Costs Per Year: $2,228 Canadian citizen and permanent resident tuition; $8,403 international student tuition; $5,281 room and board; $774 student fees.

Collegiate Environment: King's College is located two blocks from the University of Western Ontario and an "interlecture" bus operates between the campuses. Besides classrooms, residences, administrative offices, lounges, and a chapel, King's campus includes a library (93,141 volumes, 580 current periodical titles, 14,955 volumes of periodicals, 1,747 microforms) and residences for 420 students.

Community Environment: See University of Western Ontario

LAURENTIAN UNIVERSITY *(B-5)*
Ramsey Lake Road
Sudbury, Ontario P3E 2C6
Tel: (705) 675-1151; Admissions: (705) 675-4843; Fax: (705) 675-4812

Description: Laurentian was founded in 1960 as a result of attempts by various church and government leaders to create in Sudbury one unified institution of higher learning for Northern Ontario. The Act establishing Laurentian provided for the inclusion of church-related universities, and in September 1960 agreements of federation were reached with the University of Sudbury, the Roman Catholic institution, and with Huntington University, sponsored by the United Church of Canada. Thorneloe University of the Anglican Church of Canada joined the federation in January 1963. Two colleges in Northern Ontario are affiliated with Laurentian: Algoma College in Sault Ste. Marie and College de Hearst in Hearst. All students in the federated universities and affiliated colleges receive their degrees from Laurentian. The University is organized on the collegiate system that groups students either on the basis of religious affiliation or for the promotion of some major common interest. Under the federating agreements, each of the church-related universities provides a college for students in Arts and Science at Laurentian. Laurentian also has its own nondenominational University College. The University is a member of the Association of Universities and Colleges of Canada. An overseas program at Universite Canadienne en France is available. It operates on an academic year term system and offers a 13-week spring term and a 6-week summer session. Enrollment includes 5,780 full-time and 2,981 part-time undergraduates and 146 full-time and

143 part-time graduate students. A faculty of 333 full-time and 124 part-time gives an overall faculty-student ratio of 1-17.

Entrance Requirements: Candidates for admission from the USA must present verification of first year standing in an accredited college or university with a minimum of 30 semester-hour credits in the subjects acceptable to Laurentian Univeristy; ordinarily, a US high school diploma will not qualify a candidate for admission; however, applicants with high standing in secondary schools participating in the Advanced Placement program may ask the Senate Committee on Admissions for special consideration; early admission plan is available.

Costs Per Year: $2,451 Canadian tuition; ($2,661 Engineering); $8,636-$13,925 visa students; $2,290-$2,735 residence fees, $700 books, $1,800 miscellaneous

Collegiate Environment: University facilities include the Horace J. Fraser Science Building, the new, 120,000-square-foot J.N. Desmarais Library with 1.5 million volumes and numerous on-line data bases, a Classroom Building, the Arts and Humanities Building, the Dining Assembly Building, the Ralph D. Parker Building, the Benjamin F. Avery Physical Education Centre, and the Alphonse Raymond School of Education Building. There is housing on campus for 1,200 students. Scholarships and loans are available for non-Canadians after completion of a full year of studies. 53% of the students receive some form of financial aid.

Community Environment: Sudbury is the largest city (population 90,000, region 160,100) in Northern Ontario. Thunder Bay is 300 miles to the West. Sudbury is 100 miles east of Sault Ste. Marie. The campus is on 750 acres of scenic countryside, surrounded by three lakes, just a 10-minute drive from the downtown area.

Branch Campuses: Complementing the main Sudbury Campus of Laurentian University are two affiliated colleges that grant Laurentian degrees in other northern centres: Algoma University College in Sault St. Marie, and Le College universitaire de Hearst (offering porgrams in French) in Hearst.

MCMASTER UNIVERSITY *(K-7)*
1280 Main Street, West
Hamilton, Ontario L8S 4L8
Tel: (905) 525-4600; Admissions: (905) 525-4600; Fax: (905) 527-1105

Description: The University is publicly supported and was established in 1887 in Toronto by Baptists. McMaster moved to Hamilton in 1930, and became nonsectarian in 1957. Programs are offered in the Faculties of Business, Engineering, Health Sciences, Humanities, Science, Social Science, and Special Arts and Science. The university operates on a year-around basis and offers two summer sessions. It is fully accredited by the Association of Universities and Colleges of Canada. Full-time enrollment is 13,187 undergraduate and graduate students. A faculty of 1,044 gives a faculty-student ratio of 1-21.

Entrance Requirements: High school graduation with prescribed academic units; United States high school graduates with an A average (80%) or one year of college level work accepted; midyear admission plan available. $75 application fee plus $50 for assessment of postsecondary transcripts.

Costs Per Year: $2,568-$2,830 tuition and fees; $8,743-$14,105 nonresident; $4,625-5,025 room and board.

Collegiate Environment: The university is located on a spacious campus in Hamilton's west end, adjacent to the Royal Botanical Gardens and on Lake Ontario's shores. Hamilton is within a one-hour drive of both Toronto and Niagara Falls. There are over 40 buildings, and the central campus is restricted to pedestrians. The University Library System holdings include 1.6 million bound volumes, 1.4 million titles on microform, 13,859 periodical subscriptions, 38,274 records,tapes,CDs, 136 CD-ROMs as well as a number of special collections including the Bertrand Russell Archives and a 30,000-volume collection of eighteenth-century British material. The new Museum of Art contains five Exhibition Galleries, a Paper Centre and an Educational Access Gallery. McMaster's permanent art collection contains 4,700 Canadian, American, Oriental and European art works with a specialized collection of over 230 German Exhibition prints. In addition, McMaster offers research facilities through CIS (Computing Center), Nuclear reactor and Van De Graaf Accelerator installation, and the areas of Gerontology Polymer Production, Flexible Manufacturing, Communications, Energy Studies, Molecular Biology and Biotechnology, among others. Dormitories accommodate 2,763 students. 70% of the places are reserved for first-year students. 1,000 scholarships are available, including 308 for freshmen.

Community Environment: Hamilton is the western point of the "Golden Triangle," Ontario's economic heartland. A major Great Lakes seaport, Hamilton's care for its past and present is reflected in the restored 36-room Regency Villa Dundurn Castle, and the 1,200-acre Coote's Paradise wildlife sanctuary. See also Mohawk College.

MOHAWK COLLEGE OF APPLIED ARTS AND TECHNOLOGY   *(K-7)*

P.O. Box 2034
Hamilton, Ontario L8N 3T2
Tel: (416) 575-1212; Fax: (416) 575-2378

Description: One of the largest of the 25 Colleges of Applied Arts and Technology in Ontario, Mohawk College presents two- and three-year diploma programs in Applied Arts and Health Care, Business, and Engineering and Health Technology. The college also provides a wide variety of Continuing Education part-time courses as well as programs in retraining and apprenticeship. Full-time post-secondary enrollment is 8,000 students, of which 48% are women. Enrollment in all other types of programs and courses gave the college a total full-time enrollment of more than 10,000. A faculty of over 600 gives a faculty-student ratio of 1-14. The college maintains 11 teaching campuses in the Hamilton, Brantford, Stoney Creek and Hagersville areas of Ontario, the three large ones being the Fennell campus in Hamilton, the Brantford campus in Brantford, and the Stoney Creek campus in Stoney Creek, Ontario. One of Mohawk's postsecondary programs is unique to Canadian community colleges: packaging management and technology.

Entrance Requirements: High school graduation with specific subject requirements; $25 application fee.

Costs Per Year: $1,008 tuition; $8,367 nonresident; $187.30 miscellaneous.

Collegiate Environment: Mohawk College is a multicampus operation including three large campus locations in Hamilton, Brantford, and Stoney Creek. Library and resource center facilities are at each of the larger campus locations as well as audiovisual facilities. Cafeteria service is available at the three large campuses. The main campus, Fennell, has a full-size gymnasium, a theater designed for the performing arts that seats 1,050 people, and a number of lecture theaters. A new addition to the college is a student center located at the Fennell campus.

Community Environment: The college serves an area of southwestern Ontario containing a population in excess of half a million people. Hamilton and Brantford are the centers of heavy industry, including Dofasco, Inc., in Hamilton, which is the largest steel company in Canada. Other communities the college serves are rural and embrace a variety of agriculture activities. The climate is tempered by Lake Ontario and the area is ideal for both summer and winter recreation. Hamilton, with a metropolitan population close to 400,000, boasts one of the finest theatrical centers in Canada: Hamilton Place. The city is approximately 45 miles from Toronto, Ontario, so the people of the region have easy access to the best of city as well as country life. Hamilton is served by rail, road and air transport, and Hamilton Bay is the site of a busy Great Lakes port for international shipping.

Branch Campuses: Fennell Campus, P.O. Box 2034, Hamilton, Ontario L8N 3T2; Brantford Campus, 441 Elgin St., Brantford, Ontario N3T 5V2; Stoney Creek Campus, 481 Barton St. E., Stoney Creek, Ontario L8G 344; Health Science Education Centre, Sanitorium Rd., Hamilton, Ontario.

NIAGARA COLLEGE OF APPLIED ARTS AND TECHNOLOGY   *(L-9)*

300 Woodlawn Road
P.O. Box 1005
Welland, Ontario L3B 5S2
Tel: (905) 735-2211; Admissions: (905) 735-2211 X 7618; Fax: (905) 735-0419

Description: Niagara College, established in 1967, is funded by the Province of Ontario through the Ministry of Education and Training. The college offers more than 50 post-secondary and post-diploma programs through its schools of business and entrepreneurship; health

and community studies; enrironment, horticulture and agribusiness; foundation studies and general education; hospitality and tourism; lifelong learning; and technology, media and design. There are main campuses in Niagara Falls, St. Catharines and Welland. The institute operates on the semester system. Enrollment includes 6,539 full-time and 14,785 part-time students. The faculty consists of 249 full-time and 1,632 part-time members.

Entrance Requirements: High school graduation; 30 high school academic units required; open enrollment; early admission and advanced placement plans available. Post-diploma programs require a two or three-year college diploma, university degree or a minimum of relevant career experience.

Costs Per Year: $1,500 (Canadian) per academic year. $5,850 ($650/month) residence fees, including mandatory seven day per week meal plan. Books and supplies are additional.

Collegiate Environment: The college offers a full range of student services, including health services, couselling, career counselling and placement, special needs office, housing office and a new student residence which accommodates 200 students, learning resource centres, campus store, a new child care centre, athletics, student adminstratice council, food services, parking, recreation facilities, student newspaper, student clubs, student radio station and transportation. The Resources Centre houses 42,000 hardbound volumes, 600 periodicals and 3,000 media items, including film, video, slide and tape sets. 60% of the student body receives financial aid.

Community Environment: The college's campuses are located in Niagara Falls, St. Catherines and Welland in the Niagara Region. Niagara Falls, the destination of more than 12-million visitors annually, has a permanent population of about 75,000. St. Catherines, known as the Garden City, is the Region;s largest municipality with 130,000 population. It houses three college campuses: Mack Nursing Education Centre, Horticultural Centre and the St. Catherines Campus all of which will be relocated to the new Glendale Site when it opens in 1997. St. Catherines is also home to the world-famous Royal Canadian Henley Regatta. Welland, the Rose City with more than 350 acres of parkland, has a multicultural population of 48,500 and is home to the Welland Campus.

QUEEN'S UNIVERSITY   *(H-14)*

Kingston, Ontario K7L 3N6
Tel: (613) 545-2218; Fax: (613) 545-6810

Description: Queen's University, founded in 1841, is a nondenominational institution granting the Bachelor's, Master's, and Doctoral degrees. It operates on the semester system with two summer sessions. Enrollment includes 13,302 students. A faculty of 1,145 members provides a faculty-student ratio of 1:15.

Entrance Requirements: High school graduation with a strong overall program and an A average; rank in class - top 10 to 15%; ACT or SAT, minimum combined score of 1100, minimum 550 verbal, 550 math; early decision plan; $85 application fee.

Costs Per Year: $2,730-$2,992 resident tuition; $8,024-13,080 international student tuition; $5,133-$5,333 room and board.

Collegiate Environment: The university is located in downtown Kingston (pop. 65,000) and has extensive facilities for physical recreation and academic training. A separate campus, also in Kingston, houses the Faculty of Education. The university library has a collection of over 1,700,000 titles. Approximately 42 percent of those applying for admission are accepted, and university housing is available for 3,357 students.

Community Environment: The Queen's campus is set on the shores of Lake Ontario at Kingston, Canada's historic "Limestone City." An easy drive from Toronto, Ottawa, Montreal, and New York State, Kingston is readily accessible and a popular stop for visitors and for performers on tour. The community of 65,000 enjoys an unhurried lifestyle, enhanced by the proximity of Queen's, the Royal Military College, and St. Lawrence College. Tempting and unusual restaurants, unique shops, and a thriving cultural and social life set Kingston apart from other cities of its size. Sports enthusiasts can take advantage of the Olympic sailing waters of Lake Ontario and the gently rolling countryside that surrounds Kingston.

REDEEMER COLLEGE   *(K-7)*
Ancaster, Ontario L9G 3N6
Tel: (905) 648-2131; (800) 263-6467; Fax: (905) 648-2139

Description: Redeemer College is an independent Christian university that has its origins in the Ontario Christian College Association which was established on November 13, 1976. On Dec 12, 1980, the association was granted a charter by the Ontario Legislature. The college is a member of the Association of the Universities and Colleges of Canada and in June 1986 became the first Canadian institution to be a member of the Christian College Coalition. It offers scripturally directed liberal arts and sciences education that explores the relation of faith, learning and living from a Reformed Christian perspective and grants a Bachelor degree. It operates on a semester system, with no summer term. Enrollment is 446 full-time and 33 part-time students. A faculty of 36 full-time and 21 part-time gives a faculty-student ratio of 1-14.

Entrance Requirements: U.S. applicants will be considered with an academic program from an accredited high school or other educational institution that is equivalent to the Ontario Secondary School Diploma, including equivalent of 6 OAC credits; satisfactory scores on ACT, SAT or PSAT required; applicants whose native language is not English must demonstrate proficiency in oral and written English by presenting a TOEFL score of at least 550; $30 application fee (Canadian $).

Costs Per Year: $6,360 Canadian tuition; $4,020 room and board; $278 student fees (Canadian $).

Collegiate Environment: All of the college's facilities, except residences, are housed under an attractive and modern interconnected building that includes: classrooms, laboratories, library, chapel auditorium, faculty offices, administration, cafeteria, bookstore, gymnasium, art gallery and music rooms. The library collection contains over 121,000 volumes. Over 363 students can be housed in 43 on-campus townhouses or apartments. There are 18 apartments for independent and married students. Redeemer College offers renewable scholarships based on academic achievement ranging from $750-$2,000 per year. In addition the Redeemer foundation also provides scholarships (academic and leadership) and forgivable loans to eligible students.

Community Environment: Redeemer College is located just inside the southwestern corner of the town of Ancaster (population 16,542), Ontario, which is adjacent to Hamilton (population 307,690), on its southwest side. It is readily accessible by road or air transportation. The nearest international airport is at Toronto, 50 miles to the northeast. Ancaster is mainly a residential community for the large Hamilton industrial base, mainly the steel industry and related secondary industries. Hamilton is well provided with modern cultural and sport facilities.

ROYAL MILITARY COLLEGE OF CANADA   *(H-15)*
Kingston, Ontario K7K 5L0
Tel: (613) 541-6000 x6302; Fax: (613) 542-3565

Description: The Royal Military College is now Canada's only military university and it prepares students for service in Canada's Air Force, Army, and Navy. It is accredited by the Council of Ontario Universities. All students, known as officer cadets, are enrolled in the Canadian Armed Forces and are subject to its code of regulations. Canadian citizenship is a mandatory entrance requirement. Cadet life at RMC is dominated by four interlocking segments: academics, military training, physical education, and second language training. Academics is the most demanding portion. Stressing a broadly based curriculum, the university offers degrees in Arts, Science and Engineering. Enrollment includes 900 full-time and 15 part-time undergraduates and 76 graduate students. A faculty of 137 full-time and 16 part-time provides an undergraduate faculty-student ratio of 1-6. All academic programs are fully accredited. RMC is a bilingual, coeducational university.

Entrance Requirements: High school graduation with academic units in English, laboratory science, and mathematics; C average high school students are not accepted; early decision plan available; medical examination and Canadian citizenship required. Applications are processed by Canadian Forces Recruiting Centres.

Costs Per Year: Regular Officer Training Plan: nil; Reserve Entry Training Plan: $1,500 tuition; $2,300 room and board; $250 student fees.

Collegiate Environment: The RMC campus is beautifully situated on Point Frederick, a small peninsula at the eastern system of Lake Ontario. Point Frederick has been a military site since 1789 and it is an historic site in its own right. Some early structures remain such as the Stone Frigate (1819) and the Martello Tower of East Frederick (1846). The inner inclosure is dominated by these and other old limestone buildings. Student activities run from noncompulsory church services to a full range of sports and nonathletic clubs. The library contains 139,000 periodicals and technical reports and 230,000 titles. Dormitory facilities accomodate 900 students.

Community Environment: Kingston is situated at the confluence of Lake Ontario and the St. Lawrence River. Since 1673 as a trading post called Fort Frontenac, it has been of Canadian commercial and geographic importance. Kingston's interest in preserving its historical flavor is exemplified in the restoration of Fort Henry, the key defense of the St. Lawrence River's southern end during the War of 1812. Kingston is very much a university town that enjoys the presence of Queen's, RMC and St. Lawrence College.

RYERSON POLYTECHNIC UNIVERSITY   *(J-9)*
350 Victoria Street
Toronto, Ontario M5B 2K3
Tel: (416) 979-5000; Admissions: (416) 979-5027; Fax: (416) 979-5221

Description: Ryerson, Canada's only polytechnic university, was founded in 1948 as a provincial institute of technology. It was awarded degree-granting authority in 1971, and gained university status in 1993. It offers 32 programs leading to degrees and 4 diploma programs. Programs are offered through the Faculties of Arts, Applied Arts, Business, Community Services, and Engineering and Applied Science. The Continuing Education division offers 62 certificate programs, 500 credit courses, and 350 personal and professional development courses. Full-time programs are offered on a semester system, fall and winter, while Continuing Education offers courses in the spring and summer as well. Current enrollment is 9,621 in full-time and 4,167 in part-time programs. Continuing Education has 42,000 registrations annually. A faculty of 570 full-time and 285 part-time provides a faculty-student ratio of approximately 1-16.

Entrance Requirements: Minimum requirement is the Ontario Secondary School Diploma (OSSD) with a minimum average of 60% in six Ontario Academic Courses (OACs) or equivalent. There are individual prerequisite courses and grades required for specific programs. Some programs consider nonacademic factors such as auditions, admission essays, interviews, portfolios, etc. Out-of-province applicants must submit evidence of equivalent standing. Some programs have advanced placement, depending on applicants' previous academic experinece. $30 application fee.

Costs Per Year: $2,567.22 for Canadian students; $8,741.22 for international students. Residence fees range from $2,320 (double room, no meal plan) to $6,218 (large single room, meal plan). All figures are in Canadian funds.

Collegiate Environment: Ryerson is continually growing and changing to meet the needs of its students. The International Living/Learning Center opened in 1993 in a former hotel and combines residence facilities for 252 students with learning opportunities. Hospitality and Tourism Management students earn credits for assisting in front desk operations and running the restaurant. Pitman Hall provides 555 residence spaces and O'Keefe House, now co-ed, provides another 33 spaces. The Rogers Communications Centre, opened in 1991, has quickly established its reputation as a leading source of undergraduate education and professional development in communications and electronic media. It is home to the Applied Computer Science, Journalism, and Radio and Television Arts program. The Recreation and Athletics Centre comprises six gyms, seven international squash courts, a fitness centre that includes an indoor running track and conditioning room, a Sports Injury Clinic, and a 25-yard pool. Library holdings include 301,158 volumes. 35% of those applying for admission are accepted. Scholarshipss are available and 37% of students receive some form of financial aid.

Community Environment: Located in the heart of downtown Toronto, Ryerson offers the vibrant cosmopolitan atmosphere of Canada's largest city. The campus is easily accessible, and most of the students use Toronto's convenient transit service. All building are within easy walking distance of each other, and some are joined by underground and overhead walkways. Most buildings at Ryerson are accessible by wheelchair; several provide special facilities that accommodate wheelchair users.

SAINT CLAIR COLLEGE OF APPLIED ARTS AND TECHNOLOGY   *(M-1)*
2000 Talbot Road West
Windsor, Ontario N9A 6S4
Tel: (519) 966-1656; (800) 265-2506; Fax: (519) 972-3811

Description: St. Clair is a community college established and funded by the Province of Ontario through the Ministry of Colleges and Universities. It is meant to be a commuter college; it is career-oriented and has numerous business, technology, applied arts and health programs designed to meet the needs of the local community. Campuses and centers are conveniently located throughout Essex and Kent Counties. Educational television and audiovisual aids, a complete library service, and recreation facilities open to the public all make St. Clair truly a community resource. St. Clair operates on the semester system for most day and evening programs (except some non-semestered continuous programs of up to 65 weeks); it offers programs of study leading to certificates (for one-year programs) and to two- and three-year diplomas. Enrollment includes 5,000 full-time day students, several hundred part-time day students and more than 30,000 evening registrants annually. There is a teaching faculty of nearly 600, and there are numerous part-time instructors.

Entrance Requirements: High school graduation or equivalent; entrance and placement test may be required; early admission plan available; $25 application fee (Canadian dollars).

Costs Per Year: $1,008 Canadian-resident tuition; $8,375 nonresidents. (Canadian dollars).

Collegiate Environment: The St. Clair Library Resource Centre that contains 70,000 volumes, and recreation facilities, including a modern indoor athletic complex with a 25-meter swimming pool, as well as outdoor facilities, are open to students and the public. Since St. Clair is a commuter college, no on-campus housing is provided. Scholarships, awards and loans are available.

Community Environment: Windsor is a major industrial city with close ties to Detroit, Michigan. Like the Motor City, Windsor is an automobile city and the three major American car manufacturers (Ford, Chrysler and General Motors) all have Canadian affiliates. Windsor (population over 200,000) also has numerous other industries and is a good inland port. The city is readily accessible to U.S. and Canadian cities. (See Wayne State University, Michigan, for additional information.)

SAULT COLLEGE OF APPLIED ARTS AND TECHNOLOGY   *(N-15)*
443 Northern Avenue
P.O. Box 60
Sault Ste. Marie, Ontario P6A 5L3
Tel: (705) 759-6700; (800) 461-2260; Fax: (705) 759-3273

Description: Sault College of Applied Arts and Technology was established in 1965. It is large enough to support meaningful student activities, yet is small enough to allow reasonable class size and personal interaction among students and faculty. Although the bulk of Sault's enrollment is from the Sault Ste. Marie area, it attracts top level instructors and a growing number of students from larger centers because of its size, location, and excellent facilities. Enrollment is 3,300 full-time, 300 part-time, and 2,700 evening students. A faculty of 200 gives a faculty-student ratio of 1-15. The College is funded by the Province of Ontario. It operates on the semester system and offers one-, two- and three-year diploma and certificate programs of study.

Entrance Requirements: Ontario Secondary School Graduation Diploma; 30 high school academic credits (or equivalent) required.

Costs Per Year: $1,060 tuition; from $2,200 for residence fees; $143 student fees; $7,785 tuition for foreign students.

Collegiate Environment: The library houses 33,000 hardbound volumes and 500 periodicals. Scholarships and bursaries are available; 65% of the student body receives financial aid. There is housing on campus for 198 students.

Community Environment: Sault Ste. Marie is midway between Toronto and Thunder Bay. Like Windsor (and Detroit) it is closely

linked to a Michigan city; in this case, Sault Ste. Maire, Michigan. (See Lake Superior State University, Michigan.) The city is a vital link in the Great Lakes water traffic through the Soo Locks and Canal. There are excellent recreation facilities.

Branch Campuses: Elliot Lake and North Shore Campus, 1 College Pl., Elliot Lake, ON P6A 3G9; North Algoma Campus, 3 Maple St., Box 1490, Wawa, ON T0S 1K0; Chapleau Campus, 34 Birch St., Box 787, Chapleau, ON P0M 1K0.

SHERIDAN COLLEGE   *(J-8)*
1430 Trafalgar Road
Oakville, Ontario L6H 2L1
Tel: (416) 845-9430 x2074; Fax: (416) 815-4062

Description: Located within the heart of south central Ontario, one of the most economically and socially dynamic areas of Canada, 7 Sheridan College Campuses serve the community of Oakville, Brampton, Missassauga and Burlington. Enrollment includes 10,500 full-time and 661 part-time post-secondary students, and approximately 65,000 continuing education students. A faculty of 414 full-time and 251 part-time provides a faculty-student ratio of 1-25. Established by the Government of Ontario in 1967 and funded by the province through the Ministry of Colleges and Universities, Sheridan was created to serve the regions of Halton and Peel and has made phenomenal progress in the past 25 years with full-time day and evening programs. Sheridan has developed several distinct and unique aspects. The Sheridan School of Crafts and Design is the only facility of its kind in the province. The three-year Animation program is taught on a scale unprecedented in North America (in 1980, Sheridan started the International Summer School of Animation.) Sheridan is a college of Applied Arts and Technology offering one, two and three year certificale and diploma programs of study. Cooperative education programs are available in arts and science, accounting, marketing, drafting, design, and engineering.

Entrance Requirements: The basic college admission requirements are the Ontario Secondary School Diploma awarded on completion of grade 12, and accumulation of 30 credits, or mature student 19 years of age. $25 application fee.

Costs Per Year: $1,008 Canadian student; $8,553 foreign student. $218 student fees.

Collegiate Environment: The college has grown from two campuses in 1967 with 400 full-time students to seven campuses and growth continues. For the current academic year, Sheridan enrolls 10,500 full-time and 661 part-time post-secondary students in 86 programs, as well as approximately 65,000 Continuing Education students. Campuses are located in Brampton, Burlington, Mississauga and Oakville. Another 65,000 are enrolled in Continuing Education Training and Leadership Development, and Skills Development. Faculty numbers 414 full-time and 251 part-time members. The College library houses more than 50,000 volumes, 430 periodicals, 17 CD-ROM subscriptions, and 30,869 audiovisual materials. There is a residence at the Credit Valley Campus for 100 men and 200 women. The college offers a number of services including, athletics and recreation, career education, career services, computer skills center, placement, counselling, student government, clubs and organizations. 39% of all applicants are accepted. 49% of the students receive financial aid.

Community Environment: Oakville (population 115,000) is midway between Toronto and Hamilton. Brampton (population 254,000) is west of Toronto. Mississauga (population 517,800) is west of Toronto.

Branch Campuses: Skills Training Centre, Davis Campus, Burlington Campus, Credit Valley Campus, Dixie Campus, Mississauga Campus, Trafalgar Road Campus.

TRENT UNIVERSITY   *(H-11)*
Peterborough, Ontario K9J 7B8
Tel: (705) 748-1215

Description: Trent is one of the youngest and smallest universities of Ontario. Its intent is not to compete in size, but rather in excellence. Formally created as an independent university with full degree granting powers by the Ontario Legislature in April 1963, the university has chosen to expand gradually in both its undergraduate and graduate programs. The university has been a member of the Association of Universities and Colleges of Canada since 1968. In its educational program and in its academic and physical structure, Trent seeks to assert the place of the individual student at the center of the University's concern. It does so principally through the implementation of two significant concepts in education: the tutorial and seminar teaching system, and the college system, both of which encourage students and faculty to work together closely. All colleges are coeducational and operate on the year system with three summer part-time sessions and a spring part-time session. Enrollment includes 3,750 full-time, 1,500 part-time undergraduate, and 150 graduate students. A faculty of 250 gives a faculty-student ratio of 1-19.

Entrance Requirements: High school graduation; 6 Ontario Academic Credits or equivalent; OAC English required; SAT required of United States applicants; 550 TOEFL score required of international students who cannot demonstrate proficiency in English; June 1 application deadline for Fall term; midyear admission plan available; $75 application fee (Canadian $).

Costs Per Year: $2,228 Canadian resident tuition; $8,403 foreign tuition; $5,297 room and board; (Canadian $)

Collegiate Environment: Trent University's 1,500-acre Nassau Campus is set in the forests, lakes, and gently rolling hills of the Kawartha Lakes. The striking design of the buildings has won international awards and acclaim, and the combination of architecture and surroundings creates a setting of startling beauty. The university's Thomas J. Bata Library, the focal point of the Nassau Campus, houses 461,328 volumes, 2,920 serial subscriptions, 216,360 microforms, and 267 motion pictures. On campus are also administrative offices, the athletic complex, science labs, and three of the five residencial colleges where student housing accommodates 1,130 men and women. 51% of applicants are accepted. There are 237 scholarships awarded, both entrance and in-course. 36% of students receive financial aid.

Community Environment: The university is situated on the banks of the Otonabee River, three miles north of Peterborough, Ontario. Two other colleges are located in residential areas of downtown Peterborough, one of Ontario's oldest and loveliest cities.

UNIVERSITY OF GUELPH *(B-5)*
Guelph, Ontario N1G 2W1
Tel: (519) 824-4120

Description: The University of Guelph is a provincially supported, coeducational, nondenominational university located in the heart of southweatern Ontario. Established in 1964, the university combined the Ontario Agricultural College, the Ontario Veterinary College, and MacDonald Institute, which began providing postsecondary education in the late 1800s. The University has since developed into an academically diverse institution rich in academic reputation and research. Guelph receives more than $60 million in research funding each year, making it the third most research-intensive university in Canada. Students at Guelph have the opportunity to combine work with their studies in one of 35 cooperative education programs. The University grants an Associate Diploma in Agriculture and a Bachelor degree in Applied Science, Arts, Environmental Science, Landscape Architecture, Science, Agriculture, Commerce, and Engineering, and a Doctor of Veterinary Medicine. Master's and Doctorate degrees are also available. It operates on a trimester system and offers two summer sessions. Enrollment includes 13,053 undergraduate, and 1,805 graduate students. A faculty of 739 gives an undergraduate faculty-student ratio of 1-20.

Entrance Requirements: Ontario students must present the Ontario Secondary School Diploma (OSSD) with six Ontario Academic Credits including specific subject requirements; a 60% overall average is required but higher averages may be required where the demand exceeds spaces available; applicants who are seeking admission from outside Canada must present academic standing equivalent to Ontario students and must satisfy in full the subject requirements as listed for Ontario applicants; early admission plan available; $75 application fee (Canadian $).

Costs Per Year: $3,342 ($1,114 per trimester) Canadian resident tuition; $11,718 ($3,906 per trimester) foreign tuition; $7,800 ($2,600 per trimester) room and board; (Canadian $)

Collegiate Environment: Classic diversity in a friendly setting is the dominant impression of the beautifully landscaped 1,200-acre campus, encompassing an attractive mixture of historical stone buildings and modern architectural trends. The University of Guelph has the

second largest residence community in Canada, housing more than 4,000 undergraduates in traditional, coed and special theme buildings. The library has a deserved reputation as one of North America's finest and has more than 2.1 million volumes and a number of outstanding special collections, on open shelves, that include theater, Scottish studies, and the George Bernard Shaw collection. The computer-based catalogue system is extremely user-friendly. Study space is available for 2,400 students. The Student Finance and Awards Office administers a variety of financial services that include scholarhips, bursaries, part-time employment, emergency loans, budget counselling and applications for the Ontario Student Assistance Program. The Counselling and Student Resource Centre provides support to students in their learning and personal development through the Disabled Students Centre, Learning Resource Centre, Career Services, International Student Advisor and Campus Ministers.

Community Environment: In the heart of southwestern Ontario, is the city of Guelph. This lively, multicultural community of 89,000 blends the sophistication of city life with the beautiful scenery of the countryside. Just a short walk from campus, students can enjoy sidewalk cafes, specialty boutiques and craft shops, and a wide variety of restaurants. An hour drive west of Toronto, Guelph is easily accessible by bus or train. It is the home of the Guelph Spring Festival (May-June) and will be the site for the Guelph Centre for the Performing Arts.

UNIVERSITY OF OTTAWA *(E-16)*
550 Cumberland Street
Ottawa, Ontario K1N 6N5
Tel: (613) 564-3928

Description: The University of Ottawa was founded in 1848 as a Roman Catholic college. Subsidies are received from the Ontario government. Classes are conducted in both French and English. This bilingual university awards Bachelor's, Master's and doctoral degrees. Enrollment includes 14,132 full-time and 6,577 part-time undergraduates and 3,587 graduate students. A faculty of 1,109 full-time and 466 part-time gives an undergraduate faculty-student ratio of 1-19.

Entrance Requirements: For U.S. students, high school graduation with a strong B average and minimum scores of SAT 500 verbal, 500 math. $75 (Canadian currency) application fee.

Costs Per Year: $2,451-$2,660 Canadian resident tuition; $8,998-$14,000 non-Canadian tuition; $1,585-$1,864 room; fees are in Canadian dollars and are approximate.

Collegiate Environment: Located in the Sandy Hill section of Ottawa along the famous Rideau Canal, the university has an extensive variety of modern and traditional buildings and facilities on 70 acres, and considerable expansion is planned over the next twenty years. The library system has more than 2,000,000 titles in its collection, including specialized collections in medicine and the sciences. Summer courses abroad are offered in Spain, England, Israel, and France.

Community Environment: Selected by Queen Victoria as the Canadian capital in 1854, Ottawa today has a population of 300,000 with a metropolitan population of close to 600,000. Since it is the seat of the Canadian government, the Parliament buildings and many other impressive public buildings are located in the city. The national performing arts center is located near Parliament, providing numerous opportunities for cultural enrichment. The university is within walking distance from the Canadian Parliament Buildings, the National Arts Center, various museums and cultural attractions.

UNIVERSITY OF SUDBURY *(B-5)*
Ramsey Lake Road
Sudbury, Ontario P3E 2C6
Tel: (705) 673-5661; Fax: (705) 673-4912

Description: The University of Sudbury was founded by the Jesuit Order in 1913 under the name Sacred Heart College of Sudbury. It is a member of the Association of Universities and Colleges of Canada. In 1914, the Ontario Legislature granted the College a charter empowering it to award university degrees. For many years, the College du Sacre-Coeur served the French community of Northern Ontario, awarding degrees in arts in affiliation first with the University of Ottawa and later with Universite Laval. In 1957, the name of the College was changed to the University of Sudbury and it began to award degrees in its own right. When Laurentian University was established in 1960, the University of Sudbury was one of the founding members of the federation and agreed to hold its degree-granting powers in abeyance except in the field of theology. It operates on the semester system and offers one summer session. Enrollment is consolidated with the figures for Laurentian University. The faculty numbers 21.

Entrance Requirements: High school graduation; United States applicants accepted with 30 semester hour credits from an accredited college or university, or excellent standing in grade 12; July 1 application deadline; early admission plan available.

Costs Per Year: $2,450 tuition; $8,636 foreign students; $2,492-$2,888 room (Canadian $).

Collegiate Environment: The University of Sudbury is situated on the Laurentian Campus on a hill overlooking Ramsey and Nepahwin Lakes. Two buildings have been erected: Canisius Hall and Lucien Matte Residence. Canisius Hall houses administration and faculty offices, classrooms, the library and chapel, and a Jesuit residence. The library contains more than 40,000 volumes covering religious studies, philosophy, native studies, and folklore, as well as 162 periodicals, most of which are related to ethics and the above mentioned four subjects.

Community Environment: See Laurentian University.

UNIVERSITY OF TORONTO   *(J-9)*
Toronto, Ontario M5S 1A1
Tel: (416) 978-2190

Description: Nine constituent colleges, 33 research institutes, and four related graduate schools (e.g. Pontifical Institute for Mediaeval Studies) comprise the University of Toronto. Founded in 1827 as King's College at York, Toronto offers courses of study at the undergraduate level in nine professional faculties and the Faculty of Arts and Science which offers over 300 programs of study. There are also six additional graduate-level faculties and four other faculties entrance to which requires completion of undergraduate study. Degrees awarded range from certificates to doctorates and diplomas. The university operates on and academic year calendar system and offers one summer session for overseas students already enrolled. Current enrollment includes 17,961 men, 19,202 women full-time, and 6,472 men and 10,266 women part-time. A faculty of 6,000 gives a faculty-student ratio of 1:9.

Entrance Requirements: The Faculty of Arts and Science will consider applicants from Grade 12 in an accredited high school who have obtained a cumulative grade point average of at least 3.0 and an average of at least 550 on two CEEB aptitude tests and three achievement tests. A minimum score of 500 is required in each test. Scarborough College and the Faculty of Music will review applications on an individual basis, taking into consideration the overall high school record and scores on the SAT and ACH tests. The Faculty of Forestry, and School of Physical and Health Education will consider applicants from Grade 12 who have obtained an average of 550 on two CEEB aptitude tests and on three appropriate CEEB achievement tests. All other divisions require First Year university standing (30 semester hours or 45 quarter hours) from accredited institutions. Excellent students with high school diplomas and two CEEB advanced placement examinations in appropriate subjects will be considered. $50 application fee.

Costs Per Year: $2,419 resident tuition; $13,699 international student tuition; $2,180-$5,810 room and board; $350-$700 student fees (Canadian $).

Collegiate Environment: The university is composed of several different locations. St. George campus is in downtown Toronto; Scarborough is 20 miles to the east; Erindale is 20 miles to the west; dentistry in the hospital district; the David Dunlop Observatory; a university survey camp; and the 20,000-acre university forest north of Toronto. Other facilities include the medical sciences building, a low-power nuclear reactor named Slowpoke, sonic boom testing at the Institute for Aerospace Studies, and a geomagnetic laboratory. Fifty libraries with more than 6,600,000 books and nearly 2,800,000 non-book items contain special collections in science and medicine, Shakespeare and W. B. Yeats, Darwin and Hobbes, Italian libretti, Spanish literature, and Canadian authors. Each college provides student housing; in total 4,114 students may be accommodated and there are 717 units set aside for married students. Financial aid is available.

Community Environment: Toronto is the financial and industrial capital of Canada as well as Provincial capital of Ontario. It is often compared to New York and, in fact, was known as "York" (after the Duke of York) until 1834. The name "Toronto" was selected and is taken from an Indian word which means "meeting place" and it has become the meeting place or crossroads for nearly all Canadian activities. Cultural attractions abound and include the Art Gallery of Ontario, the Ontario Science Center, the Marine Museum of Upper Canada, Royal Ontario Museum and the O'Keefe Center (which is home to the National Ballet of Canada, the Canadian Opera Company and scene of numerous plays). Toronto is one of two Canadian cities with baseball teams in the major leagues but more important to Canadians, it is the home of the Hockey Hall of Fame and of the Maple Leafs. The city also has many other sport and recreation facilities including the Skydome, a domed stadium. The city is one of the great inland ports of North America and is easily accessible by air, rail, bus and road. It has one of the best subway systems in the world and an excellent public bus system.

UNIVERSITY OF TORONTO, FACULTY OF EDUCATION
(J-9)
371 Bloor Street, West
Toronto, Ontario M5S 2R7
Tel: (416) 978-8833; Fax: (416) 978-6775

Description: A publicly supported, coeducational facility for the education of teachers, the Faculty traces its history to 1910. In 1972, the then College of Education was formally designated as the Faculty of Education, University of Toronto. Enrollment includes 950 men and women. A faculty of 112 gives a faculty-student ratio of 1-10. The faculty offers a one-year nonsemester program for basic teacher certification and the Bachelor of Education degree as well as winter, evening, and summer day courses for certificated teachers.

Entrance Requirements: Bachelor degree required; rolling admission plan available; $75 application fee plus $60 application service fee.

Costs Per Year: $2,709 tuition; $14,180 nonresident; $5,100 room and board; $92 student fees; $388 campus service fees.

Collegiate Environment: Facilities include a faculty library of 40,000 volumes, and university libraries totalling 7,000,000 volumes, laboratories, gymnasia, an educational media center, a theater studio, and a computer center. There is no faculty housing; however, a variety of accommodation is listed by the Housing Service, on the St. George Campus of the University of Toronto. 25% of all applicants are accepted. 82% of those accepting admission enroll. Limited financial aid is available and 14% of the students receive financial assistance.

Community Environment: Toronto is the financial and industrial capital of Canada as well as Provincial capital of Ontario. It is often compared to New York and, in fact, was known as "York" (after the Duke of York) until 1834. The name "Toronto" was selected and is taken from an Indian word that means "meeting place," and it has become the meeting place or crossroads for nearly all Canadian activities. Cultural attractions abound and include the Art Gallery of Ontario, the Ontario Science Center, the Marine Museum of Upper Canada, Royal Ontario Museum and the O'Keefe Center (which is home to the National Ballet of Canada, the Canadian Opera Company and scene of numerous plays). Toronto is one of two Canadian cities with baseball teams in the major leagues but more important to Canadians, it is the home of the Hockey Hall of Fame and of the Maple Leafs. The city also has many other sport and recreation facilities. The city is one of the great inland ports of North America and is easily accessible by air, rail, bus and road. It has one of the best subway systems in the world and an excellent public bus system.

UNIVERSITY OF WATERLOO   *(J-6)*
University Avenue
Waterloo, Ontario N2L 3G1
Tel: (519) 885-1211; Fax: (519) 746-2882

Description: Thirty-eight years ago the University of Waterloo was just an idea: co-operative education (alternate four-month academic and work terms in career fields). In 1957 Waterloo opened its doors with an engineering program, subsequently adding programs in applied health sciences, arts, sciences, mathematics, and environmental studies. Paralleling cooperative growth was the installation of traditional university instruction. About 65% of Waterloo's full-time undergraduates participate in the cooperative system. Enrollment inlcues 15,476 full-time and 7,082 part-time undergraduates and 1,690 graduate students. Faculty numbers 754 full-time and 70 part-time giving a faculty-student ratio of 1-29. The University also has schools of accountancy, architecture, optometry and urban and regional planning. Four church-related colleges (Anglican, Catholic, Mennonite, United) provide unique academic programs within the larger campus. Other Waterloo innovations are its 300-course audiotaped correspondence program, the Institute for Computer Research, and the Canadian Industrial Innovation Center. (Cooperative education available to only Canadian citizens and Landed Immigrants.) Exchange programs for overseas studies are available.

Entrance Requirements: Ontario high school graduation; US high school diploma with exceptionally high standing and advanced placement examinations in prerequisite subjects. $75 application fee for residents; $85 for nonresidents.

Costs Per Year: $2,228-$3,700 tuition resident: $7,640-$15,000 nonresident; $5,000 room & board; $230-$460 incidental fees.

Collegiate Environment: Waterloo's picturesque 900 acre campus in the city's northwest corner has two theaters, an art gallery, a 4,000 seat gymnasium, a six lane swimming pool, ice arena, and a health services building. On campus housing accommodates 3,981 students all of whom have use of lighted tennis courts, jogging trails, and playing fields. University libraries contain 3,067,380 bound volumes, 6,200 periodicals, 775,000 microforms, and 4,400 audiovisual materials. The computer center is one of North America's largest. Four museums (games, earth science/biology, optometry, Brubacher House) lend a special depth to the academic setting. 43% of the applicants are accepted. Financial aid is available. Of 1,800 scholarships offered, 640 are for freshmen. 34% of the students receive some form of financial aid.

Community Environment: Situated in mid-Ontario's bustling Kitchener-Waterloo area, the university is 50 miles west of Toronto and is easily reached by air, bus, train, and car. Kitchener is the site of the renowned nine-day Oktoberfest celebration.

UNIVERSITY OF WESTERN ONTARIO   (L-5)
Stevenson-Lawson Building
London, Ontario N6A 5B8
Tel: (519) 679-2111; Admissions: (519) 661-2100; Fax: (519) 661-3388

Description: The University of Western Ontario received its charter from the Ontario legislature in 1878. Since that time, it has grown into a prominent liberal arts university with particular emphasis on the health sciences (22 acres of floor space, a cancer research laboratory), engineering (wind tunnels), astronomy (observatories), law, theology, music, and business. It is fully accredited by the Association of Universities and Colleges of Canada, the Association of Universities of the Commonwealth, and the International Association of Universities. The nearby arts colleges, Brescia, Huron and King's, are affiliates of the university. The semester system is employed and three summer sessions are offered. Study abroad is available in Australia, Denmark, France, Germany, and Scotland. Enrollment includes 16,453 full-time and 5,022 part-time undergraduates and 2,834 graduate students. A faculty of 1,370 full-time and 400 part-time provides a faculty-student ratio of 1-17.

Entrance Requirements: High school graduation; United States students of high academic standing or one year of college accepted. June 1 application deadline; $75 application fee; $85 for out-of-country students.

Costs Per Year: $2,500 tuition; $8,270 international student tuition; $5,500 room and board.

Collegiate Environment: Student clubs abound at Western Ontario, and include debating, drama, music, politics, languages, chess, and investment. Student activities include an undergraduate student council, a student newspaper (The Gazette), and a radio station. Intramural and intercollegiate sports are essential aspects of campus life. Housing facilities accommodate 3,700 people. The D. B. Weldon Library supports instruction with 2,060,000 books, 2,700,000 microforms, and 14,841 periodicals subscriptions, 971,416 records and tapes. Located off campus is the Museum of Indian Archaeology. 47% of the applicants are accepted. Financial aid is not available for international students. 47% of the resident students receive some form of financial assistance.

Community Environment: Western Ontario's 402 acres surround the Thames River in London which is well known as the Forest City for its many acres of parkland and shady thoroughfares. The London Regional Children's Museum, a hands-on museum, Labatt's 1828 brewery, and the Ska-Nah-Doht Indian village are specific points of interest. Cosmopolitan restaurants and shopping are bountiful (London reputedly has more shopping area per capita than any place in Canada).

Branch Campuses: Three affiliated colleges: Brescia College, Huron College, King's College

UNIVERSITY OF WINDSOR   (M-1)
401 Sunset Avenue
Windsor, Ontario N9B 3P4
Tel: (519) 253-4232

Description: First named Assumption College on its founding in 1857, the University of Windsor became such during 1963. Liberal arts, professional, and teacher education are stressed at Windsor in combination with affiliated colleges: Canterbury, Holy Redeemer, and Iona. Cooperative education programs are available in human kinetics, engineering, business, Great Lakes biology and arts. There are exchange programs with the University of Nice, France, and with Wayne State University, the University of Detroit, the University of Michigan and the University of Central Florida. Enrollment includes 10,400 full-time and 5,0000 part-time undergraduate and 650 graduate students. A faculty of 600 gives an undergrduate faculty-student ratio of 1-26.

Entrance Requirements: High school graduation with 16 academic credits; high school graduates with a 2.75 GPA (B-) average normally qualify for admission; SAT with minimum 450V, 450M; GRE; early decision plan available.

Costs Per Year: $1,300-$1,400 tuition; $4,700-$7,500 nonresident; $4,900 room and board; (fees per semester).

Collegiate Environment: Windsor's campus organizations provide social, political, religious, cultural, and recreational activities. Students also involve themselves with national and local organizations, the university radio station, and intercollegiate competition. Housing capacity is 1,800, and the library contains 1,500,000 volumes, 900,000 microforms, and 8,000 periodicals.

Community Environment: The city of Windsor lies across the Detroit River from Detroit, Michigan, and its cultural, entertainment, athletic attractions. Yet by itself Windsor is an attraction as the hub of Canada's automotive industry, the City of Roses, the site of a three-story Art Gallery displaying Canadian painting and sculpture from the eighteenth century on, home of the Windsor Symphony, and host of the International Freedom Festival.

VICTORIA COLLEGE   (J-9)
73 Queen's Park Crescent East
Toronto, Ontario M5S 1K7
Tel: (416) 585-4508

Description: Victoria College is accredited by the Association of Universities and Colleges of Canada. It is one of seven colleges on the downtown campus of the University of Toronto. Victoria University was established by Royal Charter in 1836 in Cobourg, Ontario, and became a federated college of the University of Toronto in 1892. Originally a Methodist foundation, it remains affiliated with the United Church of Canada, granting degrees in theology though Emmanuel College. The original Victoria College building in the Romanesque Revival style, which opened in 1892, is surrounded by residences, dining hall and library to form a secluded space of lawn, trees and pleasing architecture. Students and teachers have been living and working together for over 100 years, striving to achieve all that is best in university education. Enrollment includes 2,500 full-time and 800 part-time students. A faculty of 85 gives a faculty-student ratio of 1-39. The university grants the Bachelor and Masters degrees. It operates on the semester system and offers one summer session.

Entrance Requirements: High School graduation; 600 average on five CEEB tests; application deadline for fall term is March 31. See University of Toronto for admission information.

Costs Per Year: $3,000 tuition; $5,700 room and board.

Collegiate Environment: A center of student life at Victoria is the E. J. Pratt Library; all students have full privileges at the University of Toronto libraries, but Victoria students also enjoy the use of first-rate library facilities in their own college. The Pratt Library, opened in 1961, contains a basic collection of books and periodicals in Arts and Science subjects, presently numbering 200,000. The college also offers a language lab, a computing centre, student centre, equipped with meeting rooms, a Cafe, a pub space, a darkroom, a music room with a grand piano, a games room with pool tables, and lounge space. There is housing on campus for 620 men and women. 125 scholarships are available including 25 for freshmen. Victoria has its own Film Society, Theatre Company, Chorus, Music Society, Photography Club and the College newspaper. The college has extensive sports programs for both and women, utilizing the college's gymnasium, tennis courts, and playing field, as well as the University of Toronto Athletic Centre.

Community Environment: See University of Toronto.

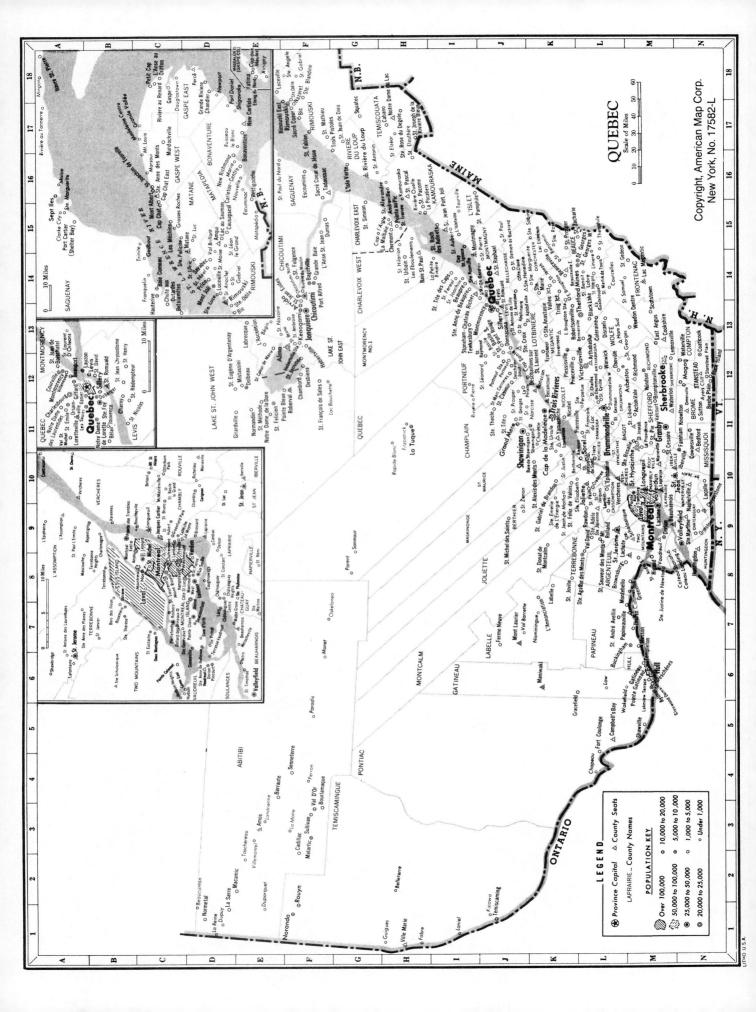

QUEBEC

Scale of Miles

Copyright, American Map Corp.
New York, No. 17582-L

LITHO U.S.A.

LEGEND

⊕ Province Capital   △ County Seats
LAPRAIRIE — County Names

POPULATION KEY

⊛ Over 100,000   ◉ 10,000 to 20,000
▨ 50,000 to 100,000   ◎ 5,000 to 10,000
◉ 25,000 to 50,000   ○ 1,000 to 5,000
◉ 20,000 to 25,000   ∘ Under 1,000

QUEBEC

BISHOP'S UNIVERSITY   *(M-12)*
Lennoxville, Quebec J1M 1Z7
Tel: (819) 822-9600; (800) 567-2792 not US; Fax: (819) 822-9661

Description: The University was founded as Bishop's College in 1843 under the sponsorship of the Right Reverend G. J. Mountain, third Anglican Bishop of Quebec, with the assistance of a group of clergy and laypeople of the Eastern Townships. Ten years later, the college received a royal charter granting it the right to confer degrees. Bishop's administration remained under the aegis of the Church of England until 1947 when the Corporation of the University was reconstituted as a nondenominational body. The university is a member of the Association of Universities and Colleges of Canada. It has integrated its academic resources into a single faculty to facilitate communication in university affairs and to provide maximum flexibility in the design of programs. The undergraduate programs lead to Bachelor degrees in arts, science, social sciences, and business administration. Master's degree programs are offered in biology, chemistry, economics, education, history, physics, and religion. Bishop's belongs to provincial exchange programs in Belgium, California, China, Denmark, England, France, Italy, New England, New Mexico, North Dakota, Sweden, and Switzerland. Enrollment includes 1,900 full-time, 600 part-time, 700 evening undergraduate, and 50 graduate students. A faculty of 104 gives a faculty-student ratio of 1-17.

Entrance Requirements: High school graduation; SAT; minimum TOEFL 550; early admission, midyear admission, rolling admission, and advanced placement plans available; $30 application fee (Canadian $).

Costs Per Year: $1,530 Canadian resident tuition; $7,300 foreign tuition; $4,300-$4,700 room and board; $800 student fees; (Canadian $).

Collegiate Environment: The John Bassett Memorial Library houses a collection of 400,000 books, 1,650 periodicals, and 350,000 microform and audiovisual titles. Facilities at the Cole Computer Center are available to undergraduates, graduates, and faculty. Student housing accommodates 520. Other facilities are the Centennial Theatre, is one of Canada's best university theaters, and the John H. Price Sports and Recreation Center. 56 scholarships are awarded to entering students. Champlain College, a provincial pre-university level institution, is situated on the campus and shares facilitites with Bishop's.

Community Environment: Bishop's University is attractively situated at Lennoxville amid the rolling hills of the eastern townships of southern Quebec. The campus occupies a 500-acre tract at the junction of the St. Francis and Massawippi Rivers, bordered on the west by the town of Lennoxville and on the east by open countryside. Several lakes and numerous ski resorts within short driving distances supplement the recreational facilities on the campus.

CHAMPLAIN REGIONAL COLLEGE   *(M-12)*
Lennoxville, Quebec J1M 2A1
Tel: (819) 564-3651; Fax: (819) 564-5171

Description: Champlain, one of the vast network of college-level institutions (CEGEPs), was established in 1971. Since that time its student population has nearly doubled in size. Enrollment is 1,060 full-time, 37 part-time and 1,200 evening students. A faculty of 80 full-time and part-time and 55 evening gives an overall faculty-student ratio of 1-15. A liberal arts and technological community college funded by the Province of Quebec, Champlain operates on the semester system with one summer session and offers two-year pre-university diploma programs and three-year paraprofessional diploma programs.

Entrance Requirements: High school graduation; open enrollment; application deadline for the fall term is March 1st; for the winter term, November 1st; $25 application fee.

Costs Per Year: No tuition for full-time students who reside in Quebec; $2 per instructional hour tuition for part-time students; $4,316 tuition for foreign students; $4,000 room and board; $150 student fees.

Collegiate Environment: Champlain students and staff have complete access to a university library on campus that houses a collection of 250,000 bound volumes and 1,500 periodicals, several special collections, and rare books in the fields of literature, history and religion. There is housing on campus for 318 students. Quebec Government loans and bursaries are available. 70% of those applying are accepted. 25% of the students receive financial aid.

Community Environment: Champlain offers its students a community environment that enables them to participate in a unique educational experience. More than one half of the student body lives in residence or within walking distance of the campus. The campus, shared with Bishop's University, is a happy combination of traditional and modern structures situated on superb grounds in the town of Lennoxville in the heart of the scenic eastern townships.

CONCORDIA UNIVERSITY   *(M-9)*
1455 de Maisonneuve Boulevard West
Montreal, Quebec H3G 1M8
Tel: (514) 848-2424; Admissions: (514) 848-2668; Fax: (514) 848-2621

Description: Concordia University was founded in 1974 with the merger of Loyola College and Sir George Williams University. It has two campuses. The Sir George Williams Campus is located in an urban setting in downtown Montreal while the Loyola Campus is located in a more traditional setting in the west end of the city. The University offers undergraduate programs in four faculties: Arts and Science, Commerce and Administration, Engineering and Computer Science, and Fine Arts. At the bachelor's level, the University offers the degrees of Bachelor of Administration, Bachelor of Arts, Bachelor of Commerce, Bachelor of Computer Science, Bachelor of Education, Bachelor of Engineering, Bachelor of Fine Arts, and Bachelor of Science. Undergraduate level cerfificates are also awarded in a growing number of areas. In addition, many cooperative education programs are available. At the graduate level a wide range of master's and doctoral programs is offered as well as a number of graduate displomas. Enrollment totals 25,078 students, consisting of 13,634 full-time, 9,183 part-time, and 2,261 other. Faculty numbers 720 full-time and 1,101 part-time.

Entrance Requirements: Applicants are required to have a better than average school record and high ranking in their graduating class. While no set pattern of courses in high school is required, all applicants are expected to have taken four units of English. Those applying for admission to Science and Engineering must include three or four units in mathematics and two in the sciences. At least three units of mathematics are recommended for admission to Commerce and Administration. $20 application fee. (Canadian dollars).

Costs Per Year: $1,842 tuition; $8,120.50 international students; $6,600-$7,200 room and board.

Collegiate Environment: Loyola campus is the university's physical education focal point with its playing fields, ice rink, and gymnasium. Loyola has student housing for 144; a 600-seat concert hall ; the George P. Vanier Library 104 laboratories. The J.W. McConnell Building on the downtown Sir George Williams campus is a cultural mall. It houses the Leonard and Bina Ellen Art Gallery, the Seve cinema, the university's main bookstore and the R. Howard Webster library. All are open to the public. The library includes 1,600,000 titles and is growing at a rate of 65,000 items annually. Several public access personal computer computers and workstations can be found on each campus, as well as an Ombuds office.

Community Environment: Concordia counts Montreal itself as an invaluable asset to the university experience. Situated on an island where the St. Lawrence and Ottawa Rivers meet, this city (with over 2,000,000 inhabitants) provides a fascinating cosmopolitan environment. Although French is the language heard most often in the shops and streets, more than a third of the population is English speaking. A wide range of ethnic groups--Chinese, Greek, Italian, Portuguese, and Vietnamese among them--also maintain their language, culture, and cuisine, as can be seen in the city's multilingual cinemas and its wide variety of restaurants, corner grocers, merchants, bakeries, and other speciality shops. As one of the oldest cities in North America, Montreal is rich in history and tradition. Yet it is also a dynamic city with an impressive array of modern buildings, boutiques, and plazas.

LAVAL UNIVERSITY *(J-13)*
Cite Universitaire, Quebec G1K 7P4
Tel: (418) 656-2131; Admissions: (418) 656-5216; Fax: (418) 656-5216

Description: The University owes its origin to the Seminary of Quebec, founded in 1663 by Francois de Montmorency Laval, the first bishop of Quebec. In December 1852 Queen Victoria signed a royal charter granting the Seminary the rights and privileges of a university. 118 years later, in December 1970, the national assembly of Quebec granted a new charter to Laval University. This charter was promulgated at the same time as the first statutes of the university on September 1, 1971. Laval concentrates teaching and research in many fields. Laval is a member of the Association of Commonwealth Universities. It operates on the trimester system with two summer sessions and offers programs of study leading to bachelor, master and doctorate degrees. Current enrollment includes 9,492 men, 11,606 women full-time, 2,950 men, 4,609 women part-time, and 6,334 graduate students. The faculty consists of 1,620 full-time and 60 part-time members provides a student-faculty ratio of 15-1. The language of instruction is French.

Entrance Requirements: Diplome d'etudes collegiales; American Students are required to have one year of college. $55 application fee (Canadian $).

Costs Per Year: $55.60 per credit; $248.60 per credit for nonresidents; $168.50 per month for room and board.

Collegiate Environment: Since 1964 the Universite Laval has gradually occupied the new Cite Universitaire, one square mile in the western outskirts of Quebec, about five miles from the old city. The library houses 2,000,000 hard bound volumes, 17,000 periodicals, 1,000,000 microforms, and 209,000 audiovisual materials. There is housing on campus for 2,300 students. Scholarships are available; 55% of the student body receives financial aid.

Community Environment: Quebec, on the St. Lawrence River, is the provincial capital and is almost completely a French-speaking city. Because of this and its very rich historic past, the city is very interesting for tourists. Attractions include the Musee du Quebec, The Champlain monument, the Citadelle, Parliament and the Grand Theatre du Quebec. There are many beautiful churches, shops, restaurants, theaters, etc.

MCGILL UNIVERSITY *(M-10)*
847 Sherbrooke Street West
Montreal, Quebec H3A 3N6
Tel: (514) 398-3910; Admissions: (514) 398-3910; Fax: (514) 398-4193

Description: This is a publicly supported, coeducational university made up of 12 faculties, 11 schools, and 3 affiliated theological colleges. It was founded in 1821 and is a member of the American Association of Collegiate Registrars and Admissions Officers and the Association of American Universities. The school has two terms of 13 weeks each and a summer session. The special French Summer School program is a six-week residential program which offers courses at graduate and undergraduate levels. There is also a center for continuing education. Concentration of studies are in the faculties of Agriculture, Arts, Education, Engineering, Dentistry, Graduate Studies and Research, Law, Management, Medicine, Music, Religious Studies and Science which include the schools of Architecture, Computer Science, Dietetics and Human Nutrition, Human Communication Disorders, Library and Information Studies, Nursing,

Occupational Health, Physical and Occupational Therapy, Social Work and Urban Planning. Bachelor's, Master's and Doctoral degrees are awarded. Recent enrollment included 15,700 full-time, 7,896 part-time, and 5,188 graduate students. There are 2,085 full-time and 1,700 part-time faculty members.

Entrance Requirements: High school graduation with B+ average or better; Grade 12 level Mathematics, Chemistry and Physics required for engineering programs, Grade 12 level Mathematics and at least 2 of Biology, Chemistry, Physics required for Science, Grade 12 Mathematics required for Management; SAT and three CEEB Achievement tests are required appropriate to program of study; GRE required for graduate school; deferred admission, midyear admission available; advanced placement test credit is given; $60 (Canadian) application fee.

Costs Per Year: $1,700 tuition; $7,460 tuition for non-Canadians; $4,560-$6,100 room and board; approximately $2,000 additional for fees and books.

Collegiate Environment: In addition to classrooms and lecture halls, the university provides research facilities, residences, gymnasium, swimming pools, winter stadium, University Center and a concert hall. The University Library system is composed of five areas - the Humanities and Social Science, Law, Life Sciences, Physical Sciences and Engineering, Undergraduate - and contains 2,347,242 books, 1,461,705 government documents, 804,556 microtexts and 618,994 other items. There is housing for 1,100 students on campus, while most occupy apartments in the "Student Ghetto." An additional 320 can be housed at Macdonald College. An off-campus housing service is available for students wishing alternate housing. McGill has an extensive program of entrance awards based on academic achievement or a combination of outstanding achievement and leadership qualities.

Community Environment: Montreal is the second largest French-speaking city in the world, second only to Paris. It is the second largest city in Canada and has a history rich in tradition and culture. The city is named after Mont Real (royal mountain). Cultural attractions include Musee des Beaux-Arts, McCord Museum at McGill University; Musee des Arts Contemporains, Place des Arts (home of the Montreal Symphony, Les Grands Ballets Canadiens and the Quebec Opera), along with many art galleries, museums, cathedrals and historic sites. Scenic attractions include Old Montreal, Mount Royal and the downtown core. There are many fine restaurants, shops and stores representing many ethnic groups. The city is the home of the Montreal Canadians hockey team, the Expos (baseball) and other professional teams. It has many recreational areas and the Laurentian Mountain region just 35 miles north of the city and the Eastern Townships provide all year outdoor facilities.

UNIVERSITE DE MONTREAL *(M-10)*
3744, rue Jean-Brillant
C.P. 6205, Succursale Centre-ville
Montreal, Quebec H3C 3T5
Tel: (514) 343-7076; Fax: (514) 343-5788

Description: The University of Montreal was established in 1878 as a branch of Laval University; in 1920, it first granted degrees as an independent institution. In 1967 it became an independent institution of the Roman Catholic Church, and is now a private university. Montreal enrolls 50,788 students. Faculty is 2,020. The language of instruction is French. The University of Montreal has two administratively affiliated schools: l'Ecole Polytechnique (school of engineering) and l'Ecole des Hautes Etudes Commerciales (school of business studies).

Entrance Requirements: Quebec Collegiate Studies diploma or equivalent.

Costs Per Year: $1,860 (Canadian dollars) Canada-resident minimum full-time tuition for 2 trimesters; $7,454 for foreign students.

Collegiate Environment: Universite de Montreal occupies a large campus on the northern side of Mount Royal Park. As a major research university, it has a large library collection, including 4,150,085 volumes and periodicals. Specialized facilities are maintained in different parts of Quebec, including a research center in the Laurentian Mountains, north of Montreal and the Astronimical Observatory at the Mont Megantic. The Faculty of Veterinary Medicine is situated at St-Hyacinthe. Approximately 50% of applicants are offered admission. Housing is available for 1,200 students.

Community Environment: See McGill University.

UNIVERSITE DU QUEBEC A MONTREAL   *(C-8)*
870, boulevard de Maisonneuve Est
Case Postale, Succursale Centre-Ville
Montreal, Quebec H3C 3P8
Tel: (514) 987-3000; Admissions: (514) 987-3132; Fax: (614) 987-8932

Description: Established December 18, 1968, by an act of the National Assembly in the Province of Quebec, the Universite du Quebec is the province's first public university. It is accredited by the Association of Universities and Colleges of Canada. It is a multi-campus institution (see addresses below) including six university centres (in Chicoutimi, in Hull, in Montreal, in Rimouski, in Trois-Rivieres and in the Abitbi-Temiscamingue region) and five specialized institutions: Ecole de technologie superieure, Ecole nationale d'administration publique, Institut national de la recherche scientifique, Institut Armand-Frappier and Tele-universite. The six constituent universities offer programmes at the undergraduate (including professional) and graduate levels in most of the fields of study (except medecine) found in major North-American universities. Programme offering in specialized institutions are as follows: the Ecole de technologie superieure offers undergraduate programmes in engineering technology; the Ecole nationale de'administration publique offers master's degree programmes in public administration and in urban analysis and management; the Institut national de la recherche scientifique offers graduate programmes in water sciences, energy, pharmacology, telecommunications and in urban analysis and management; the Institut Armand-Frappier offers graduate programmes in virology and applied microbiology; the Tele-universite is a distance learning institution offering undergraduate programmes and courses. It operates on the trimester system with one summer session and offers programmes of study leading to bachelor's, master's and doctorate degrees, as well as certificate and diploma programmes. Enrollment includes 17,500 full-time and 18,800 part-time students, and 4,200 graduate students with a faculty of 949 teachers full-time and 1,169 lecturers part-time. The faculty-student ratio is 1-34.

Entrance Requirements: Very good working knowledge of the French language is required; diploma of collegial studies or equivalent diploma (i.e. normally a completed freshman year); entrance examinations required for some programmes; students admitted at midyear. The deadline for submission of applications for the Fall term is March 1; $30 application fee.

Costs Per Year: $1,665 Canadian resident, $7,455 nonresident, $130 fees.

Collegiate Environment: The traditional university organization by faculties and schools has been replaced by a two tiered structure composed of departments and programme committees (often called modules). Departments are responsible for teaching and research in their discipline whereas students are identified to a particular programme committee from whom he receives guidance and academic counseling (admissions, course choice, degree requirements, advanced placement/standing). Libraries contain 2,091,457 volumes and other documents as well as 980,082 monographs, 11,696 periodical subscriptions, and 245,519 audiovisual materials.

Community Environment: Multi-campus university.

Branch Campuses: Universite du Quebec a Montreal, Case postale 888 Succursale A, Montreal, Quebec I3C 3P8, (514) 987-3152; Universite du Quebec, A Trois-Rivieres, Trois-Rivieres, Quebec G9A 5H7, (819) 376-5045; Universite du Quebec a Chicoutimi, 555, boulevard de l'Universite, Chicoutimi, Quebec G7H 2B1, (418) 545-5005; Universite du Quebec a Rimouski, 300, avenue des Ursulines, Rimouski, Quebec G5L 3A1, (418) 724-1432; Universite du Quebec A Hull, Case postale 1250, succursale B, Hull, Quebec J8X 3X7, (819) 595-3844, Universite du Quebec Ea Abitibi-Temiscamingue, 42, Mgr-Rheaume est, Rouyn, Quebec J9X 5E4, (819) 762-0971; Ecole Nationale d'Administration, Publique 945, rue Wolfe, Sainte-Foy, Quebec G1V 3J9, (418) 657-2485; Ecole de Technologie Superieure, 4750, rue Henri-Julien, Montreal, Quebec H2T 1R0, (514) 289-8887; Institut Armand-Frappier, 531, boulevard des Prairies, Ville de Laval, Quebec H7V 4Z3, (514) 687-5010; Institut National de la Recherche Scientifique, 2635 boulevard Hochelaga Bureau 640, Sainte-Foy, Quebec G1V 4C7, (418) 654-7518, Tele-Universite, 2635 boulevard Hochelaga 7e etage, Sainte Foy, Quebec G1V 4V9, (418) 657-2262.

VANIER COLLEGE   *(M-10)*
821 Ste-Croix Avenue
Saint-Laurent, Quebec H4L 3X9
Tel: (514) 744-7100; Fax: (514) 744-7111

Description: Vanier is located in the western part of Montreal. The College was established in 1970, and is currently the second largest English (CEGEP) College in Quebec. Enrollment is 5,400 day and 3,000 evening students. A faculty of more than 450 provides a faculty-student ratio of 1-19. The school operates on the semester system and offers 9 two-year pre-university programs and 14 three-year technology programs.

Entrance Requirements: High school graduation; certain prerequisites required for specific programs; early admission plan available; $25 application fee (subject to change).

Costs Per Year: Because Vanier is a publicly supported institution, there is no tuition charge for Canadian citizens or landed immigrants; foreign student tuition is $4,316; $115 student activity, association and registration fees.

Collegiate Environment: The College has four buildings including a sports complex; the library houses over 85,000 volumes. Approximately 75% of those applying for admission are accepted. Financial aid is available for residents of Canada, and over 90% of the students applying for such aid receive it.

Community Environment: See McGill University.

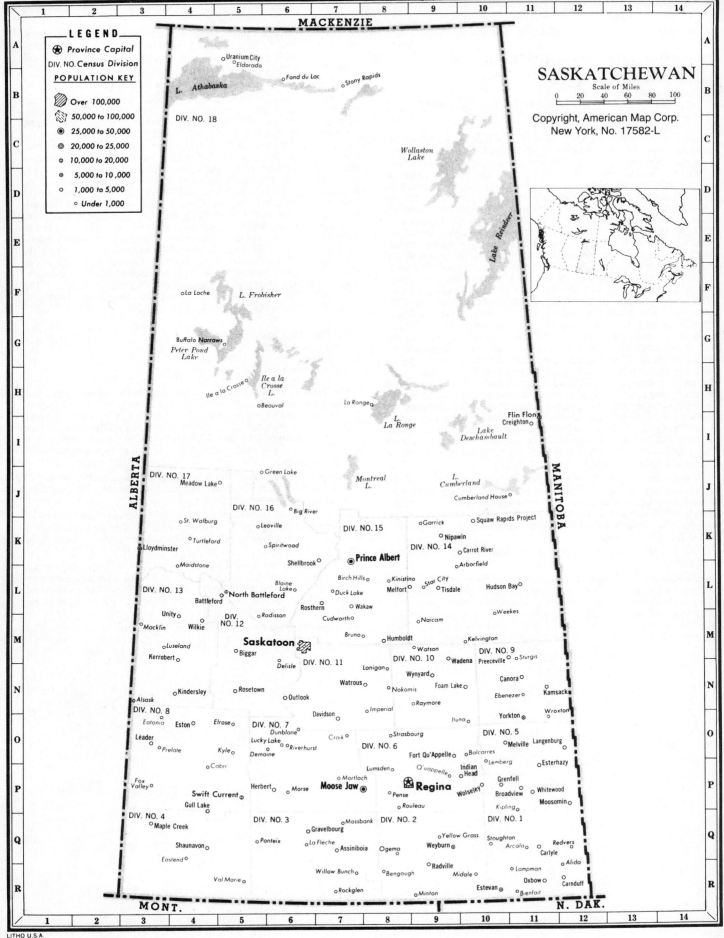

SASKATCHEWAN

SASKATCHEWAN INDIAN FEDERATED COLLEGE (P-8)
118 College West
University of Regina
Regina, Saskatchewan S4S 0A2
Tel: (306) 584-8333

Description: The Saskatchewan Indian Federated College (SIFC) is federated with the University of Regina and is fully accredited. While being academically and physically part of the university, the college hires its own faculty and staff and offers unique programs and a personalized student service department. The college operates under the mandate and control of the Indian Governments of Saskatchewan. SIFC, which serves both Indian and non-Indian students, has grown from an initial enrollment of nine students in 1976 to over 1,150 students in 1992.

Entrance Requirements: High school graduation with an average of 65%; University Entrance Program available for students who do not meet regular admission requirements; students who are at least 21 years old or who have an average of 60-64.9% may qualify; $25 application fee.

Costs Per Year: $67 per credit hour tuition.

Collegiate Environment: Saskatchewan Indian Federated College is located on the campus of the University of Regina. The university is situated just at the edge of the provincial capital on a modern campus that is part of the unique 2,300-acre Wascanna Centre Project.

Community Environment: See the University of Regina.

ST. THOMAS MORE COLLEGE (M-6)
1437 College Drive
Saskatoon, Saskatchewan S7N 0W6
Tel: (306) 966-8900

Description: St. Thomas More is a coeducational Catholic college offering Bachelor degrees in arts, fine arts, music, and science conferred by the University of Saskatchewan. Faculty is drawn from both St. Thomas and Saskatchewan. Innovative schedules exist in interdisciplinary programs (e.g. French Canadian Studies) and combined studies (one course in place of two). Enrollment is 975 full-time and 79 part-time students with a faculty of 35 giving a faculty-student ratio of 1:30.

Entrance Requirements: High school graduation with 24 academic credits; high school graduates with a C average accepted; advance placement and rolling admission plans available. $35 application fee.

Costs Per Year: $1,478 tuition; $3,286 room and board; $71.50 student fees.

Collegiate Environment: St. Thomas More College is located on the University of Saskatchewan campus. It maintains its own offices, cafeteria, an art gallery, and the Shannon Library (46,000 books with special collections in Canadian church history and Christian social sciences.)

Community Environment: See University of Saskatchewan.

UNIVERSITY OF REGINA (P-8)
Wascana Parkway
Regina, Saskatchewan S4S 0A2
Tel: (306) 585-4111; Fax: (306) 585-5203

Description: The University of Regina is, like most Canadian universities, state-supported, and was established by the provincial legislature in 1910 as Regina College. It was joined until 1974 to the University of Saskatchewan, but is now governed by a separate Board of Governors. Bachelor's, Master's, and doctoral degrees are conferred. Cooperative education programs are available in many areas. It operates on the semester system and offers one summer session. Enrollment includes 7,856 full-time, 3,483 part-time, and 917 graduate students. A faculty of 404 provides a faculty-student ratio of 1-19.

Entrance Requirements: High School graduation with an average of 65%; SAT not required.

Costs Per Year: Tuition $2,010; non-Canadian $3,316.50; room and board $3,760.

Collegiate Environment: The university is situated just at the edge of the provincial capital on a remarkable, modern campus which is part of the unique 2,300-acre Wascana Centre Project. The Project is jointly sponsored by the Government of the Province, the City of Regina, and the University, and is designed to provide an integrated plan for the development of Government and University facilities as well as for community cultural and recreational activities. The library holdings number 452,000 government publications, 659,657 periodicals, 824,000 microforms, and 107,936 other resource materials. Dormitories house 539 students.

Community Environment: Regina, population 185,000 is the capital city of Saskatchewan. Serving as a business and industrial center of the mainly agricultural province, Regina offers a wide range of cultural activities.

UNIVERSITY OF SASKATCHEWAN (M-6)
105 Administration Place
Saskatoon, Saskatchewan S7N 5A2
Tel: (306) 966-6766; Admissions: (306) 906-6718; Fax: (306) 966-6730

Description: Established in 1907, the University of Saskatchewan opened its doors in 1909. In 1911 Regina College became a campus of Saskatchewan and continued until 1974 when it was granted separate university status. Coeducational and nondenominational, the University of Saskatchewan offers comprehensive programs on both the undergraduate and graduate levels. Areas of study include agriculture, arts and science, commerce, dentistry, education, engineering, law, medicine, nursing, pharmacy, nutrition and dietetics, physical education, physical therapy, and veterinary medicine. In addition, the university conducts research in many areas including northern studies, space and atmospheric studies, and pedology. Of special note are the Indian teacher education programs and a five college affiliation. Enrollment includes 13,205 full-time and 2,762 part-time undergraduate and 1,852 graduate students. Faculty numbers 1,090 full-time members.

Entrance Requirements: Complete Saskatchewan secondary level standing (24 credits) or equivalent, with a minimum average of 65% on subjects used for admission. The subjects required vary according to the student's chosen area of study. Qualified Saskatchewan residents are given preference in admissions selection, however, places are normally available for Canadian out-of-province and international students.

Costs Per Year: $2,430-$4,253 tuition; $3,371-$3,667 room and board; $95.50 undergraduate, $148.50 graduate student fees.

Collegiate Environment: The University of Saskatchewan overlooks the South Saskatchewan River on a 755 hectare site on the edge of the city of Saskatoon. One hundred and forty-seven hectares comprise the campus and the rest are used for the University farm and experimental plots. Thirty hectares have been provided for a research park (Innovation Place). In addition to academic buildings, a linear accelerator laboratory, a library (1,490,000 volumes and over 2 million items on microform, with special collections of Pitirim Sorokin and the Adam Shortt library of Western Canadiana), a physical education centre, the Rt. Hon. John G. Diefenbaker Centre, farm buildings, facilities for administration, a bookstore, food services and student activities, a faculty club, and student residences (1,456 students) are provided on campus. Dormitories house 300 men and 271 women. There are apartments for 305 single persons and 580 married students. One federated and three affiliated colleges also have buildings on the campus. Also located on the campus are the Royal University Hospital, the Animal Resources Centre, Veterinary Infectious DiseaseOrganization, the Prairie Migratory Bird Research Centre of the Canadian Wildlife Service, the Canada Department of Agriculture Research laboratory, Canada Agriculture Health of Animals Pathology laboratory, Proteins Oils and Starches Pilot Plant, Regional Medical Centre of the Canadian Penitentiary Service, the Saskatchewan Research Council building, a Prairie Farm Rehabilitation Administration building, the Cancer Clinic, the Medical Research Institute building, and the St. Pius X Seminary. The university also has under lease a 52-hectare site on Emma Lake. The university also owns and operates three farms for research purposes primarily in the Colleges of Agriculture and Veterinary Medicine.

Community Environment: Saskatoon (population 195,597), on the banks of the South Saskatchewan River, is known as the City of Bridges with its riverfront and many parks. It is the home of the Western Development Museum featuring "Boomtown 1910", museums of Ukrainian arts and culture, the Mendel Art Gallery (Canadian, European, and Eskimo art), the Forestry Farm Park, and Saskatchewan Place (local and international sports, entertainment, and cultural events.)

Index of U.S.Colleges

Index of Canadian Colleges